Oxford Dictionary of
Quotations

Oxford Dictionary of
Quotations

SEVENTH EDITION

Edited by **Elizabeth Knowles**

OXFORD

UNIVERSITY PRESS

OXFORD

UNIVERSITY PRESS

Great Clarendon Street, Oxford OX2 6DP

Oxford University Press is a department of the University of Oxford.
It furthers the University's objective of excellence in research, scholarship,
and education by publishing worldwide in

Oxford New York

Auckland Cape Town Dar es Salaam Hong Kong Karachi
Kuala Lumpur Madrid Melbourne Mexico City Nairobi
New Delhi Shanghai Taipei Toronto

With offices in

Argentina Austria Brazil Chile Czech Republic France Greece
Guatemala Hungary Italy Japan Poland Portugal Singapore
South Korea Switzerland Thailand Turkey Ukraine Vietnam

Oxford is a registered trade mark of Oxford University Press
in the UK and in certain other countries

Published in the United States
by Oxford University Press Inc., New York

British Library Cataloguing in Publication Data

Data available

Library of Congress Cataloging in Publication Data

Data available

Designed by Jane Stevenson
Typeset by Interactive Sciences Limited, Gloucester
Printed in China
on acid-free paper by

ISBN 978–0–19–923717–3

10 9 8 7 6 5 4 3 2 1

Contents

Project team

Commissioning editor	Ben Harris
Associate editor	Susan Ratcliffe
Library research	Ralph Bates Russell Inglis
Reading programme	Carolyn Garwes Jean Harker Verity Mason
Data capture	Susanne Charlett
Proof-reading	Kim Allen Juliet Field Penny Trumble

Introduction to the Seventh Edition

This new seventh edition of the *Oxford Dictionary of Quotations* maintains and extends its established coverage of quotations in use in the English language. It is now nearly seventy years since (in 1941) the *Dictionary* was first published, and as well as reprinting the Introduction to that first edition, we have provided a separate History of the *Dictionary*. This is an appropriate acknowledgement of the earlier editions which provide the foundations of the book we have today.

Every edition of the *Oxford Dictionary of Quotations* has to be remade for its own publication year, and for 2009 Oxford's customary language monitoring of what is being quoted in print and online has ensured that there are more quotations than ever to consider for inclusion. The Oxford Corpus, a major language resource for current English, is now a significant source of quotations in use among the online community, many of which were new to the *Dictionary*. Items of this kind added to the text include 'The worth of a soul cannot be told' (the African writer and former slave Olaudah Equiano), and Jeremy Bentham's dry noting of what he called 'one of the corner stones of political science—the more strictly we are watched, the better we behave'. Schiller's adjuration, 'It is wise to disclose what cannot be concealed' is complemented by Elias Canetti's view that 'Secrecy lies at the very core of power.' We now have the succinct advice of the American writer and feminist Charlotte Perkins Gilman, 'Work first—love afterwards'; the comment of the Austrian satirist Karl Kraus that 'A journalist is stimulated by a deadline. He writes worse when he has time'; and Florence Nightingale's reflection that 'Were there none who were discontented with what they have, the world would never reach anything better.'

The *Oxford Dictionary of Quotations* needs to function as a reference resource for past as well as present. We monitor very successfully what is being quoted today, but we need also to be aware of what has been quoted in the past, in sources which are likely to be encountered in the present. Work on the current edition has included a systematic examination of Oxford World's Classics and other annotated editions of classic works, to ensure that such material is covered. Results of this programme included the maxim of Confucius for a ruler, 'If you desire what is good, the people will be good', found in Henry David Thoreau's *Walden* (1854); the view of the Phrygian Stoic philosopher

Epictetus that 'Not things, but opinions about things, trouble men', quoted by Laurence Sterne in *The Life and Opinions of Tristram Shandy* (1759–67); the judgement of the Greek physician Hippocrates that 'When two pains occur together, but not in the same place, the more violent obscures the other', which appears in Thomas Hardy's *Far From the Madding Crowd* (1874); and Joseph Addison's note on 'the old song of Chevy Chase' that 'Ben Jonson used to say he would rather have been the author of it than of all his works', quoted by Edmund Burke.

We have, of course, continued to maintain our traditional monitoring of printed and written sources, and this reading programme has once more greatly enriched our book. Items added from this source include 'To be ignorant of what occurred before you were born is to remain forever a child' (Cicero); 'We must be the change we wish to see in the world' (Mahatma Gandhi); 'I think you should only read those books which bite and sting you' (Franz Kafka); 'Life is either a daring adventure or it is nothing' (Helen Keller); and 'In this life it is not aunts that matter but the courage which one brings to them' (P. G. Wodehouse). A *New York Times* column of May 2006 by Maureen Dowd on the invasion of Iraq made ominous use of the opening words of a short story by O. Henry, 'It looked like a good thing, but wait till I tell you.' The death in 2008 of the jazz musician and broadcaster Humphrey Lyttelton prompted quotation of his advice that

> As we journey through life, discarding baggage along the way, we should keep an iron grip, to the very end, on the capacity for silliness. It preserves the soul from desiccation.

A number of quotations from different times may have the same central topic. The desire to explore the unknown is a constant element across the centuries, vividly expressed by the pioneer New Zealand aviator Jean Batten:

> Every flyer who ventures across oceans to distant lands is a potential explorer; in his or her breast burns the same fire that urged the adventurers of old to set forth in their sailing-ships for foreign lands.

Other quotations relating to travel and exploration include the reassurance of Columbus to his sponsors, Ferdinand and Isabella of Spain, that he was worth their support, since 'I can give them as much gold as they desire, if they will give me a little assistance'; the recommendation by the explorer Matthew Flinders that the name 'Australia' should be used for *Terra Australis*, since 'It is necessary … to geographical propriety that the whole body of land should be designated under one general name'; André Gide's view that 'One doesn't discover new lands without consenting to lose sight of the shore for a very long time'; and G. K. Chesterton's assessment that 'The whole object of foreign travel is not to set foot on foreign land; it is at last to set foot on one's own country as a foreign land.'

As always with quotations, there are items which are firmly lodged in the public consciousness as originating with a particular person, but which are wholly or partly apocryphal. One notable example came to light in 2007, when coverage of a total lunar eclipse included the words, attributed to the explorer Magellan while opposing the view that the earth was flat:

> I have seen the shadow of the earth on the moon and I have more faith in the shadow than the Church.

This apparent example of early scientific observation and free-thinking (possibly coupled with a readiness to believe that acceptance of the flatness of the Earth was a doctrine of the Church) is clearly well-known today. However, investigation reveals that its origins are rather more recent. It seems to go back to the 19th-century American lawyer, orator, and atheist Robert Green Ingersoll, in his lecture 'Individuality' (1873): 'I believe it was Magellan who said: "The Church says the earth is flat; but I have seen its shadow on the moon, and I have more confidence even in a shadow than the Church."'

Ingersoll's attribution can be linked with the work of a contemporary. The American Unitarian minister and writer Minot Judson Savage in his poem 'Magellan', published in *Poems of Modern Thought* (1884), wrote:

> In the moon's eclipse,
> The earth's round shadow on its face I see!
> I read God's works, which are his book indeed,
> And trust the hint that falleth from his lips
> More than all man's infallibility.

However, although it seems exceedingly likely that Magellan's free-thinking is a nineteenth-century construct, the misquotation has now probably established a continuing existence for itself.

We have the propensity to edit as we repeat, unconsciously changing the words to our own expression of the gist of what we have heard or read. The resulting 'misquotation' is much more than a simple mistake; it can represent a real form of language change, as the pithier version establishes itself in the language. Graham Greene on several occasions attributed to Tom Paine the warning: 'We must guard even our enemies against injustice' (he found the words particularly significant as he watched the rise of McCarthyism in the early 1950s). The expression itself has not been traced in Paine's writings, and it seems likely to be Greene's own paraphrase of a longer passage in Paine's *Dissertation on the First Principles of Government* (1795):

> He that would make his own liberty secure, must guard even his enemy
> from oppression; for if he violates this duty, he establishes a precedent that
> will reach to himself.

Previously it was possible to expand the book to include new material without too great a necessity on cutting back on what was already there. However, after nearly seventy years, the *Dictionary* had reached the point at which length could be a problem, since the book as a physical object needs to retain its capacity to be easy to handle. For this edition, we have accordingly looked at the usage evidence on which inclusion of existing items rests, and we have applied more stringent standards to the addition of more recent remarks which have caught the public attention.

With the help of our colleagues from the Dictionaries Department, we tested the existing text of the *Oxford Dictionary of Quotations* against the Oxford Corpus, to assess the currency of individual items. This process gave us approximately 50% of the existing book—10,000 quotations—for which the evidence was sufficiently strong for continued inclusion to be unquestioned. We needed then to look more closely at material for which less usage evidence had been found. Was the usage, though numerically lower, still sufficient to justify inclusion? And were there other circumstances which meant that although the item might not have been quoted frequently, there was a context which gave it importance? Some passages are associated by quotations with particular events or people. Other items have been quoted in classic sources which are still likely to be known and read, or have been used in letters or journals by well-known people.

There is no great modern currency for David Garrick's lines from 'A Riddle' (1762):

> Kitty, a fair but frozen maid
> Kindled a flame I still deplore.

However, in Jane Austen's *Emma* (1816), they are recalled nostalgically by Mr Woodhouse. He tells his daughter:

> Your dear mother was so clever at all those things! If I had but her memory! But I can remember nothing;—not even that particular riddle which you have heard me mention; I can only recollect the first stanza; and there are several.

He goes on to quote the stanza beginning with the lines we have.

In Thomas Otway's play *Venice Preserved* (1682), we find the assertion

> Give but an Englishman his whore and ease
> Beef and a sea-coal fire, he's yours for ever.

Otway is probably not much read or performed today, but in a letter of 22 August 1822 Lord Byron wrote to his friend Hodgson:

> If you should feel a disposition to come here, you will find 'beef and a sea-coal fire', and not ungenerous wine. Whether Otway's two other requisites for an Englishman or not, I cannot tell, but probably one of them.

Clearly Byron expected Hodgson to be familiar with Otway's lines.

Tennyson's poem 'The Palace of Art' was published in 1832. One stanza runs:

> An English home—grey twilight poured
> On dewy pasture, dewy trees,
> Softer than sleep—all things in order stored,
> A haunt of ancient Peace.

'A haunt of ancient peace' makes a couple of significant appearances. Dante Gabriel Rossetti, writing in a letter of 1871 of William Morris's home Kelmscott, said, 'This house and its surroundings are the loveliest "haunt of ancient peace" that can well be imagined.' In 1908, L. M. Montgomery's children's classic *Anne of Green Gables* featured Anne Shirley walking through her Prince Edward Island home in the evening: 'All Avonlea lay before her in a dreamlike afterlight—"a haunt of ancient peace".'

Some quotations from an earlier time have had a notable resonance. The introduction to the first canto of Sir Walter Scott's poem *Marmion* (1808) included the lines:

> Now is the stately column broke,
> The beacon-light is quenched in smoke,
> The trumpet's silver sound is still,
> The warder silent on the hill!

The occasion for these lines was the death, in office as Prime Minister, of William Pitt the Younger in 1806. Forty-four years later, the Commons assembled to pay tribute to another (former) Prime Minister, on the death following a riding accident of Sir Robert Peel. Winding up his tribute, William Ewart Gladstone said:

> I ... quote those most touching and feeling lines which were applied by one of the greatest poets of this country to the memory of a man great indeed, but yet not greater than Sir Robert Peel.

He went on to quote Scott's stanza.

In 1847, the American philosopher and poet Ralph Waldo Emerson made a speech in Manchester, England, in which he said:

> I feel in regard to this aged England ... that she sees a little better on a cloudy day, and that, in storm of battle and calamity, she has a secret vigour and a pulse like a cannon.

In May 1991, the words were quoted on a very high-profile occasion indeed, when the

Queen of England addressed the two Houses of Congress, following on the conclusion of the first Gulf War.

In Shakespeare's *Julius Caesar*, Caesar himself tells Mark Antony that

> … if my name were liable to fear
> I do not know the man I should avoid
> So soon as that spare Cassius.

At the end of the 18th century, 'that spare Cassius' was a key phrase in Abigail Adams's warning to her husband John against Alexander Hamilton. Distrusting Hamilton's machinations in the presidential election in which John Adams was an (ultimately successful) candidate, she wrote: 'Beware that spare Cassius has always occurred to me when I have seen that cock sparrow. Oh, I have read his heart in his wicked eyes.'

The name of the English poet Matthew Prior (1664–1721) may not be widely known today, and his lines

> Euphelia serves to grace my measure,
> But Chloe is my real flame

not necessarily widely quoted. However, it does occur in a passage which is still likely to be encountered. In Dorothy L. Sayers' *Busman's Honeymoon* (1937), Lord Peter Wimsey discovers that the philandering murderer has acquired from the locksmith father of one girlfriend the key to the barn in which he makes love to another of his inamoratas. As Lord Peter comments:

> There is a certain lack of the finer feelings … Euphelia serves to grace my
> measure but Chloe is my real flame, no doubt. But to get Euphelia's father
> to cut the key for Chloe is—tactless.

The continuing popularity of Dorothy L. Sayers makes it very probable that Prior's words will have some level of familiarity.

The title of Richard Dawkins' *Unweaving the Rainbow: Science, Delusion and the Appetite for Wonder* (1998) derives from a passage from Keats's poem *Lamia* (1820):

> Philosophy will clip an Angel's wings,
> Conquer all mysteries by rule and line,
> Empty the haunted air, and gnomèd mine –
> Unweave a rainbow.

One of the highlights of the dictionary has always been the extensive and detailed sourcing given for each quotation. For Shakespeare, this has included even the line number, taken from the Oxford Standard Authors edition in widespread use when the dictionary was first published. It was always recognized that line numbers for prose scenes would vary from one edition to another, but over more than sixty years scholarship has moved on, and today in some cases scene numbers, and even the words themselves, have changed. In this seventh edition the traditional wording and numbering have been retained, but where modern texts differ this has been indicated in a note.

The foregoing looks at passages whose inclusion in the *Dictionary* was justified, but obviously not everything was kept. The easiest cuts are those for quotations which were topical at the time of inclusion, but which have now faded from sight. Beyond that, we were able to remove material for which there really was no usage evidence, and which seemed to have little resonance. Typical examples, which probably represent no more than an instance of a significant author using a particular expression, include 'I do not ask too much: I beg cold comfort' from Shakespeare's *King John*, and 'Rouse the lion from his lair' from Sir Walter Scott's *The Talisman* (1825).

The more recent a remark is, the more difficult it is to predict whether or not it has lasting qualities, and at times it is necessary to make a judgement call. For example, at the time of writing (autumn 2008), coverage of the recent Republican Convention has given substantial attention to a line in the speech of the Vice-Presidential nominee, Sarah Palin: 'Do you know what they say is the difference between a hockey mom and a pitbull? Lipstick.' It seems likely, whatever the outcome of the election, that the one-liner has lodged itself in the vocabulary of political commentators, and will remain part of the story of this campaign. More frivolously, a comment from 2004 on fashion does already seem to have established a level of currency: Paris Hilton's advice, 'Dress cute wherever you go. Life is too short to blend in.' Other more recent utterances for which evidence justifies inclusion are: Bo Diddley's comment on not receiving royalties, 'I've never got paid. A dude with a pencil is worse than a cat with a machine gun'; Stephen Hawking's suggestion that 'I think computer viruses should count as life. Maybe it says something about human nature, that the only form of life we have created so far is purely destructive'; and Terry Pratchett's summing up of the news that he has a form of Alzheimer's disease, 'An embuggerance.'

By contrast, coverage of the tenth anniversary (in August 2007) of the death of Diana, Princess of Wales, featured a comment from her younger son which at the time was widely reported: 'To us, just two loving children, she was quite simply the best mother in the world.' Since that date, however, there is no further usage evidence to show that the words are being quoted. While flagging it up for watching, we have not at present put it into the *Dictionary*. We have however, as part of our online resources, established a 'bubbling under' category: material for which evidence for inclusion in the Dictionary is lacking, but whose immediate profile is such that it is possible that it will surface at a later date. Other items in this category include Pete Doherty on prison life ('A lot of gangsters and Radio Four'), Boris Johnson on the Olympics ('I say to the Chinese, and I say to the world, ping pong is coming home'), and Amy Winehouse on the debacle of her Birmingham concert ('If you're booing, you're a mug for buying a ticket').

Compilation of this new edition has, as always, drawn on the resources of Oxford Quotations Dictionaries: our published texts (and the research which supports them), and the systematic reading programmes described above, all of which have fed into our growing database of new quotations. We have as always benefited from the generosity of readers who take the trouble to write to us with questions, comments, and suggestions; support from colleagues in the Reference Department and other departments of Oxford University Press who have once more put forward quotations encountered in work and leisure; and the computing expertise of the Data Technology Group. Among those to whom we are particularly grateful we would like to thank Mark Baillie, Amira Bennison, Cat Clark, Rose Goddard, Richard Harmes, Tim Harper, Kate Fleet, James McCracken, Annie Mcdermott, Lauren Macleod, David McMullen, Rosemary March, Ken Moore, Toni Roberts, Rebecca Ross, Christine van Ruymbeke, and Fiona Stafford. Most importantly, the *Dictionary* has benefited inestimably from the meticulous and expert editing of Susan Ratcliffe, Associate Editor for Quotations, and from the wise guidance of our Commissioning Editor, Ben Harris.

It continues to be an enormous pleasure and privilege to edit the *Oxford Dictionary of Quotations*, ensuring as far as we can that the text once more records and reflects the fascinating movement of quotations in the language.

ELIZABETH KNOWLES

Oxford 2009

History of the Dictionary

The richness and diversity of the *Oxford Dictionary of Quotations* is one of its great strengths, and abiding pleasures, but the book originally proposed would have been much less expansive. In 1915 there was an initial suggestion for 'an Oxford Dictionary of Poetry Quotations (not foreign quotations)', to be based on 'Oxford texts and the N.E.D. [now the *Oxford English Dictionary*]'.

The idea was not immediately followed up, and it was not until the 1930s that the project got under way. An assessment of what was wanted, in a letter of 1931, shows an extension of the original vision of 1915, highlighting especially familiar quotations from foreign languages and 'modern quotations that have not yet got into the books'. With major sources such as the Bible and Shakespeare, they would have to limit themselves to what was 'eminently *quotable* and constantly quoted'. The Classics were a particular consideration: if the book were not to be limited to English, it would seem illiterate to give 'a mere handful of classical tags'. It would however be essential to give translations. The question of overall organization was also debated, and the principle of A–Z author organization finally agreed.

There was a strong view that 'non-English quotations must be reduced to very narrow limits' (partly, it must be said, on grounds of extent and cost). A distinction was to be drawn between what a French scholar would quote in French, and 'that rather small number of French phrases which are almost current English (or have been)'. Latin should provide the bulk of the foreign quotations, with German, Italian, and Spanish being satisfied by a handful of tags. There was doubt too about the currency of classical Greek, with the question being asked 'Isn't it a fact that Greek has disappeared from the House of Commons?'

Consideration of the collection of material came with the warning that 'Even in English we shall have to guard against things quotable, as apart from things commonly quoted.' From a practical point of view it was thought risky to have texts read by people who were devoted to them. 'They probably quote, or think they quote, those texts to an abnormal extent.' The result would be a flood of material, and preparatory work that was 'vast or uneven'.

In conclusion, then, they were looking at a dictionary of quotations which would have a primarily literary base, and which would include quotations from major writers likely to be quoted in English by the literate and cultured person. The importance of the American market was somewhat grudgingly acknowledged ('We must consider the Americans lovingly'), but in reality this was more likely to mean American authors regarded as having honorary status in English literature, rather than a true reflection of American culture.

By the end of the 1930s, the *Oxford Dictionary of Quotations* was nearing publication. One problem, however, remained. In May 1941, an appeal was made to the writer Bernard Darwin, noted for his knowledge and love of quotations, with the words 'Come over into Macedonia and help us' (Bible, Acts 16:9; Darwin had served in Macedonia during the First World War). It was explained that many months previously, in duty bound, they had asked the Vice-Chancellor, George Gordon, President of Magdalen, to write an Introduction to the *Dictionary*. According to the rueful explanation,

> With his customary charming politeness he said he would, but with his I fear equally customary press of business and, if I may be guilty of *scandalum magnum*, habit of postponement he has not delivered the goods.

The failure might have been predicted: according to the article on Gordon in the *Dictionary of National Biography*,

> It was hard to persuade him that even a lecture was fit to be printed; if he parted with the manuscript, he clung to the proof. Of anything much more than a lecture his friends learned to despair.

OUP sensibly did despair of Gordon's producing what was needed, and instead appealed to 'the sister University [to] come, as so often' to the rescue. Would Darwin write, and moreover write very quickly, the Introduction? If he would come over to Oxford as soon as possible he could be provided with a quiet room, the proofs of the book, and the factual Preface. They would 'gladly and thankfully' pay him fifteen guineas if at the end of six hours Darwin could produce an Introduction.

Darwin may have been flattered by the terms of the appeal ('You are the man … It's a great book, and we want a great Introduction'), or touched by its frankness ('We really are in a hole'). Whatever his reason, he accepted, and provided the Introduction which is reprinted here on pages xix–xxiv.

The *Dictionary* was published in October 1941, and generally extremely well received, the first printing of 20,000 being exhausted about a month after publication. For three months subsequently they struggled with wartime restrictions to get a reprint on to the market. This was 'the constantly recurring trouble with all our books nowadays'; a more individual difficulty is recorded in an exchange of correspondence with the famously litigious Lord Alfred Douglas.

Lord Alfred wrote to Humphrey Milford, Publisher to the Oxford University Press, in November 1941, to complain that he was represented in the *Dictionary* by two lines taken from his early nonsense verse. He was undecided as to whether this indicated deliberate rudeness or that the compiler was 'merely ignorant & illiterate'. The line on which the subsequent correspondence centred was 'The placid pug that paces in the park', from *The Placid Pug, and Other Rhymes*, by the Belgian Hare (London, 1906).

Milford, replying two days later, stated the general position, that the *Dictionary* was a collection of familiar quotations and not an anthology of chosen authors, good and bad, and then went on to the particular:

> I see a pug (not often, thank Heaven, in these days) and I at once think of your line and so do many other people. Therefore it naturally appears in a book of familiar quotations.

This was not an argument to appeal to Lord Alfred, and he found the letter 'singularly unconvincing'. The correspondence rumbled on, involving at one stage Lord Alfred's solicitors. It is possible to feel some sympathy for the solicitor whose instructions forced him to write,

> We are acting for Lord Alfred Douglas, who, as you must know, is one of the greatest living poets and has been so described by those best able to form an opinion and entitled to express it.

Today Lord Alfred is represented by the line

> I am the love that dare not speak its name.
> *Two Loves* (1896)

It is far from clear that he would have been happy with this sole evidence of his poetic mastery, but it is almost certainly the only line of his which today can be described as 'familiar'.

To return to the *Dictionary* as published in 1941. The book was, inevitably, Anglocentric, a feature reinforced by the arrangement of material. The quotations were organized in such separate sections as *Authors Writing in English*, *Book of Common Prayer*, *Holy Bible*, *Anonymous*, *Ballads*, *Nursery Rhymes*, *Quotations from Punch*, and *Foreign Quotations* (Latin, Greek, French, Italian, Spanish, and German have the language of origin; Russian, Norwegian, and Swedish appear only in translation). Opening the pages is rather like walking into a traditional study lined with leather-bound volumes.

The selection was pre-eminently a literary one: according to the prefatory note, 'The Compilers to the Reader', the writers most frequently quoted were Browning, Byron, Cowper, Dickens, Johnson, Kipling, Milton, Shakespeare, Shelley, Tennyson, and Wordsworth. Beyond the dominance of the canonical writers, room was also found for lesser figures. The Victorian writer Thomas Ashe (1836–89), whose poems according to the *Dictionary of National Biography* 'failed entirely to gain the ear of his generation' is represented by the plaintive line, 'Meet we no angels, Pansie?' The moderns were cautiously admitted: the single quotation from Virginia Woolf is the title of *A Room of One's Own*.

In his hastily compiled Introduction, Bernard Darwin had reflected that, 'It is difficult today not to deal in warlike metaphors', but in fact the text of the first *Dictionary* reflected little of the period leading up to the Second World War. Winston Churchill, outnumbered by his father Randolph, has a single quotation from 1906, 'It cannot in the opinion of His Majesty's Government be classified as slavery in the extreme acceptance of the word without some risk of terminological inexactitude.' George V's official last words, 'How is the Empire?' were there, but not the former Edward VIII's reference to 'the help and support of the woman I love' in his Abdication broadcast. The Prime Minister who had to deal with the Abdication Crisis, Stanley Baldwin, did not appear at all, although his warning that 'the bomber will always get through' was given in 1932. Franklin Roosevelt had a single quote: his assertion during his 1932 election campaign that, 'I pledge you—I pledge myself—to a new deal for the American people.' Neville Chamberlain was also absent: it should have been possible to record his mistaken 'I believe it is peace for our time' (returning from Munich in 1938), although the equally erroneous 'Hitler has missed the bus' of April 1940 did come too late for a book published in the autumn of 1941. There was in fact very little to indicate the coming storm, other than an item in the Addenda to German quotations, Hermann Goering's comment in a radio broadcast of 1936, 'Guns will make us powerful; butter will only make us fat.'

The novelist Norman Douglas once suggested that 'You can tell the ideals of a nation by its advertisements', and a number appeared in the *Dictionary*. Darwin's Introduction referred to what in 1941 was still a familiar advertising slogan, 'Pink pills for pale people', and the Oxford English Dictionary notes that the slogan for Kruschen salts, 'that Kruschen feeling', became a catchphrase of the 1920s to indicate a feeling of vigorous health. Health and concurrent good looks were in fact of particular concern, although some of the slogans seem to verge on the personal: for example, 'Good morning! Have you used Pears' soap?' Wright's Coal Tar soap (corrected to Pears in the 2nd edition of 1953) has the somewhat surprising statement, 'He won't be happy till he gets it.'

Popular songs included soldiers' songs from the First World War ('Pack up your troubles in your old kit bag') and earlier music-hall favourites ('We don't want to fight, but by jingo, if we do'). There were a few precursors of larger entries in later editions: Irving Berlin was included for 'Alexander's Ragtime Band' (1911), but not for 'Let's face the music and dance' (1936). The possible dangers of social life (prefiguring Flanders and Swann's 'Have some madeira, m'dear' of the 1950s) were indicated by an anonymous limerick about a young lady of Kent who,

> When men asked her to dine,
> Gave her cocktails and wine,
> She knew what it meant—but she went!

The warm reception given to the *Dictionary* ensured that a second edition would follow, and in 1949 it was agreed that the time had come to start on a revision. There was already 'an immense accumulation of suggestions' which would have to be sorted through by a committee, and there were proposals for what could be dropped, including advertising slogans and lines from comic songs. Book titles and the opening lines of hymns were tags rather than quotes, and if they went so too could the opening words of Latin prayers. It was noted however that, 'No one has successfully solved what is and is not a quotation': a question which may still be debated today.

The ensuing discussion recognized that there was a point of view which 'would like to see all frivolities go' but felt that what was genuinely popular should keep its place. While it could be said that 'the post-first war jocularities which have by now completely faded out' (i.e., what was in 1941 the most topical and ephemeral should go), the 'frivolities of the '80s and '90s' had 'stood up to time much better': an interesting distinction which most quotations editors would find valid today. There were doubts about coverage of some of the 'canonical' authors, a comment on the Jane Austen entry running, 'I am not certain that the expert … is the best person to select from his author. To him all is familiar.'

A revision committee was set up, which was to go through the *Dictionary* considering existing matter for deletion or rearrangement, and through addenda held for inclusion. It was agreed that any item receiving two votes should be included.

Between April 1949 and August 1950, the committee met 17 times. Authors and texts identified for examination were quite diverse. At the first meeting, it was agreed to to get an outside opinion on the Addison entry, to look for additional quotations from Emily Brontë, and to examine Charles I's speech on the scaffold for quotable passages. The minutes of 5 May 1949 noted both Donne's prose and *The Wind in the Willows* as possible sources. Overall the coverage was still fairly Anglocentric—Roosevelt's speeches being an exception, although it was also agreed that the 'Foreign Section' needed thorough revision. It is noticeable however that reference to these items is made in the form 'French quotations' or 'German quotations': individual authors are not given. The meeting of 8 September was a key one, as it also made a momentous decision as to the organization of the material:

> It was then decided that reference would be facilitated if all the separate sections—including Greek—were to be incorporated into the main body of the book.

In other words, the overall author organization would be maintained, while entries like Anonymous, Ballads, and The Bible, would be incorporated into the alphabetic sequence.

The index would similarly be single-sequence with the exception of Greek: this would have its own index. It was also agreed that 'every key word' should be indexed: an over-ambitious plan which in August 1950 had to be rescinded when the extent (and cost) implications became apparent.

Another plan, which was wisely abandoned, was to include a section at the end of the text for quotations which had not been successfully sourced. By 1951 it was decided that any such should be held over to the next edition, although they made a last effort to verify outstanding problems. An appeal elicited this lament from Dorothy L. Sayers:

> Oh, dear…! I never know where things come from. Nearly all are familiar, but I can't at the moment say where <u>any</u> of them come from.

The second edition of the *Oxford Dictionary of Quotations* was published in 1953, and is much more recognizably the *Dictionary* we know today. The single alphabetic sequence has already been described, and for the first time quotations were individually numbered through the page, providing the page number to quotation number (e.g. 223:11) which is still the form of reference today.

The content, however, was more reordered than substantially different. Items dropped were from the more ephemeral end of the scale: for example, 'Dr Brighton', as exemplifying Brighton's health-giving propensities, and the slogan 'Where's George? Gone to Lyonch', which reflected the popularity of Lyons' Corner Houses in the 1920s. Key material added focused on Second World War quotations, especially reflected, of course, in the enhanced entry for Winston Churchill.

1979 was to present the first substantial revision of the *Dictionary* since the original compilation, and it was at this point that particular categories of material were excluded. Nursery rhymes were cut altogether, on the assumption that they were fully covered by Iona and Peter Opie's *Oxford Dictionary of Nursery Rhymes* (first published in 1951). Songs were also excluded:

> The rule of thumb, given to the revision team and followed by the editors, has been that if the words cannot be said without the tune (*a* tune, in the case of many hymns) coming to mind, they are *not* quotations in the same sense as others.

Advertisements, slogans, catchphrases, and other items from the world of 'broadcasting and other mass-media' were similarly to be avoided.

The existing text had been considered by the revision team. Each of the core members read the whole text (ten copies of the book with interleaved blank pages for comment were prepared). Suggestions for quotations to be added were circulated on specially prepared forms with a voting box for each item: the lists were then photocopied and distributed to the whole team, with three votes being considered necessary for inclusion. The aim was to compile a collection of popular (as distinct from familiar) quotations: the editors were particularly concerned that the book should not be:

> An anthology displaying the choice and taste of one man, or even of a
> small committee of the Press such as compiled the first edition of the
> *Dictionary*.

The result of their efforts was to return the collection firmly to its mainstream and literary tradition: quotations reflecting what we would think of now as the western canon rather than current affairs. (Although this was not necessarily their own view of their endeavours: according to the introduction, one of the revisers had commented on the necessity of clearing the 'huge snowdrifts of Wordsworth'). Perhaps more than any of the other editions it is a committee book, with fewer examples of the odd or quirky. The compilation's solid worth was to sustain the *Dictionary* for another thirteen years, until the publication of the fourth edition in 1992.

The fourth edition, the last to be compiled on paper, was notable for improving the coverage of non-English authors, thinkers, and public figures, both European and American. Scientists, like a number of women writers, began to make a long-delayed appearance, and more attention was paid to current affairs. Existing material was re-evaluated and verified (songs and hymns, rightly, were allowed to 'make a welcome reappearance' as the then Editor put it), and quoted authors were given brief descriptions (for nationality and occupation) as well as dates.

This particular introduction underlines a trend that can be traced through the life of the *Dictionary*: the further we get from 1915, the clearer a particular social and cultural change becomes. In 1941, it could be assumed that the educated reader would have had a particular kind of education, following a monolithic classical curriculum (with possibly a nod to the 'Modern Side'). That is now a world away: our readers come to us from many and diverse educational and cultural backgrounds, and the notion of 'English-speaking culture' has to incorporate World English.

Another result of this, of course, was the identification of gaps which needed to be addressed. The fifth edition, of 1999, for the first time gave proper place to the sacred texts of world religions other than Christianity. This was of course appropriate to a multicultural age, but it was fascinating to see how words and phrases from such sources were already permeating the English language. More contextual information was provided: because something is familiar to one section of our readership, we could not necessarily assume that everyone will know it. We also responded to queries from readers by restoring proverbs and nursery rhymes (it has been clear from correspondence over the years that our readers expect to find this kind of material in the *Dictionary*). The 1999 edition was also the first to be compiled online, and this fed back to the presentation of material: more navigational paths were provided for our readers, including a consciously generous system of cross-referencing. These trends were developed and reinforced in the sixth edition of 2004.

In the 21st century, electronic monitoring of the language has contributed increasingly to the collection of new material: quotations likely to be encountered by the general public, on which they may well seek information. The Oxford Corpus in particular (as discussed in the Introduction to this edition) has offered access to what is being quoted online, on personal websites and blogs. The *Dictionary* itself is available electronically (through Oxford Reference Online), and we need now, while editing a printed book, to be aware of the need of the online community for an electronic resource. As we look towards the seventieth anniversary (in 2011) of the book's first publication, our challenge is to respond to the needs of that community, while maintaining the distinct identity which has ensured the loyalty of readers over the decades.

Introduction to the First Edition

By **Bernard Darwin**

Quotation brings to many people one of the intensest joys of living. If they need any encouragement they have lately received it from the most distinguished quarters. Mr Roosevelt quoted Longfellow to Mr Churchill; Mr Churchill passed the quotation on to us and subsequently quoted Clough on his own account. Thousands of listeners to that broadcast speech must have experienced the same series of emotions. When the Prime Minister said that there were some lines that he deemed appropriate we sat up rigid, waiting in mingled pleasure and apprehension. How agreeable it would be if we were acquainted with them and approved the choice! How flat and disappointing should they be unknown to us! A moment later we heard 'For though the tired waves, vainly breaking' and sank back in a pleasant agony of relief. We whispered the lines affectionately to ourselves, following the speaker, or even kept a word or two ahead of him in order to show our familiarity with the text. We were if possible more sure than ever that Mr Churchill was the man for our money. He had given his ultimate proofs by flattering our vanity. He had chosen what we knew and what, if we had thought of it, we could have quoted ourselves. This innocent vanity often helps us over the hard places in life; it gives us a warm little glow against the coldness of the world and keeps us snug and happy. It certainly does its full share in the matter of quotations. We are puffed up with pride over those that we know and, a little illogically, we think that everyone else must know them too. As to those which lie outside our line of country we say, with Jowett as pictured by some anonymous genius at Balliol, 'What I don't know isn't knowledge.' Yet here again we are illogical and unreasonable, for we allow ourselves to be annoyed by those who quote from outside our own small preserves. We accuse them in our hearts, as we do other people's children at a party, of 'showing off'. There are some departments of life in which we are ready to strike a bargain of mutual accommodation. The golfer is prepared to listen to his friend's story of missed putts, in which he takes no faintest interest, on the understanding that he may in turn impart his own heart-rending tale, and the bargain is honourably kept by both parties. The same rule does not apply to other people's quotations, which are not merely tedious but wound us in our tenderest spot. And the part played by vanity is perhaps worth pointing out because everybody, when he first plunges adventurously into this great work, ought in justice to the compilers to bear it in mind.

It is safe to say that there is no single reader who will not have a mild grievance or two, both as to what has been put in and what has been left out. In particular he will 'murmur a little sadly' over some favourite that is not there. I, for instance, have a small grievance. William Hepworth Thompson, sometime Master of Trinity, the author of many famous and mordant sayings on which I have been brought up, is represented by but a single one. Can it be, I ask myself, that this is due to the fact that an Oxford Scholar put several of the Master's sayings into his Greek exercise book but attributed them to one Talirantes? Down, base thought! I only mention this momentary and most unworthy suspicion to show other readers the sort of thing they should avoid as they would the very devil. It is not that of which any one of us is fondest that is entitled as of right to a place. As often as he feels ever so slightly aggrieved, the reader should say to himself, if need be over and over again, that this is not a private anthology, but a collection of the quotations which the public knows best. In this fact, moreover, if properly appreciated, there ought to be much comfort. 'My head' said Charles Lamb, 'has not many mansions nor spacious', and is that not true of most of us? If in this book there are a great many quotations that we do not know, there are also a great many that we do. There is that example of Clough with which I began. We may have to admit under cross-examination that we have only a rather vague acquaintance with Clough's poems, but we do know 'Say not the struggle'; and there on page so-and-so it is. Both we and the dictionary's compilers are thereupon seen to be persons of taste and discrimination.

If I may be allowed to harp a little longer on this string of vanity, it is rather amusing to imagine the varied reception given to this book by those who are quoted in it. They will consist largely of more or less illustrious shades, and we may picture them looking over one another's pale shoulders at the first copy of the dictionary to reach the asphodel. What jealousies there will be as they compare the number of pages respectively allotted to them! What indignation at finding themselves in such mixed company! Alphabetical order makes strange bedfellows. Dickens and Dibdin must get on capitally and convivially together, but what an ill-assorted couple are Mrs Humphrey Ward and the beloved Artemus of the same name! George Borrow may ask, 'Pray, who is this John Collins Bossidy?' Many readers may incidentally echo his question, and yet no man better merits his niche, for Mr Bossidy wrote the lines ending 'And the Cabots talk only to God', which have told the whole world of the blue blood of Boston. John Hookham Frere, singing of the mailed lobster clapping his broad wings, must feel his frivolity uncomfortably hushed for a moment by his next-door neighbour, Charles Frohman, on the point of going down with the *Lusitania*. And apropos of Frere, there rises before me the portentous figure of my great-great-grandfather, Erasmus Darwin. He was thought a vastly fine poet in his day and there is a family legend that he was paid a guinea a line for his too fluent verses. And yet he is deservedly forgotten, while those who parodied him in the Anti-Jacobin attain an equally well-deserved immortality. He was a formidable old gentleman, with something of the Johnson touch, but not without a sense of humour, and I do not think he will be greatly hurt.

The most famous poets must be presumed to be above these petty vanities, though it would be agreeable to think of Horace contemplating his array of columns and saying, 'I told you so—Exegi monumentum'. In any case the number of columns or pages does not constitute the only test. Another is the number of words in each line by which any particular quotation can be identified, and this gives me a chance of making my compliments to the ingenuity and fullness of the index. The searcher need never despair and should he draw blank under 'swings' he is pretty sure to find what he wants under 'roundabouts'. There is a little game to be played (one of the many fascinating games which the reader can devise for himself) by counting the number of 'key words' in each line and working out the average of fame to which any passage is entitled. Even a short time so spent shows unexpected results, likely to spread envy and malice among the shades. It might be imagined that Shakespeare would be an easy winner. It has been said that every drop of the Thames is liquid history and almost every line of certain passages of Shakespeare is solid quotation. Let us fancy that his pre-eminence is challenged, that a sweepstake is suggested, and that he agrees to be judged by 'To be or not to be'. It seems a sufficiently sound choice and is found to produce fifty-five key words in thirty-three lines. All the other poets are ready to give in at once; they cannot stand against such scoring as that and Shakespeare is about to pocket the money when up sidles Mr Alexander Pope. What, he asks, about that bitter little thing of his which he sent to Mr Addison? And he proves to be right, for in those two and twenty lines to Atticus there are fifty-two key words. I have not played this game nearly long enough to pronounce Pope the winner. Very likely Shakespeare or somebody else can produce a passage with a still higher average, but here at any rate is enough to show that it is a good game and as full of uncertainties as cricket itself.

Though the great poets may wrangle a little amongst themselves, they do not stand in need of anything that the dictionary can do for them. Very different is the case of the small ones, whose whole fame depends upon a single happy line or even a single absurd one. To them exclusion from these pages may virtually mean annihilation, while inclusion makes them only a little lower than the angels. Their anxiety must therefore be pitiful and their joy when they find themselves safe in the haven proportionately great. Sometimes that joy may be short-lived. Think of Mr Robert Montgomery, who was highly esteemed till the ruthless Macaulay fell upon him. With trembling hand he turns the pages and finds no less than four extracts from 'The Omnipresence of the Deity'. Alas! under his own letter M the traducer is waiting for him, and by a peculiar refinement of cruelty there are quoted no less than five of Lord Macaulay's criticisms on that very poem. This is a sad case; let us take a more cheerful one and still among the M's. Thomas Osbert Mordaunt has full recognition as the author of 'Sound, sound the clarion, fill the fife', after having for years had to endure the attribution of his lines to Sir Walter Scott, who in pure innocency put them at the head of a chapter. This to be sure was known already, but whoever heard the name of the author of 'We don't want to fight', the man who gave the word 'Jingo' to the world? We know that the Great McDermott sang it, but even he may not have known who wrote it, just as Miss Fotheringay did not know who wrote 'The Stranger'. Now G. W. Hunt comes into his kingdom and with him another who helped many thousands of soldiers on their way during the last war. Mr George H. Powell is fortunately still alive to enjoy the celebrity of 'Pack up your troubles in your old kit bag'. How many thousands, too, have sung 'Wrap me up in my tarpaulin jacket' without realizing that it was by Whyte Melville? To him, however, recognition is of less account. His place was already secure.

Among the utterers of famous sayings some seem to have been more fortunate than others. Lord Westbury, for instance, has always had the rather brutal credit of telling some wretched little attorney to turn the matter over 'in what you are pleased to call your mind'; but how many of us knew who first spoke of a 'blazing indiscretion' or called the parks 'the lungs of London'? We may rejoice with all these who, having for years been wronged, have come into their rights at last, but there are others with whom we can only sympathize. They must be contented with the fact that their sayings or their verses have been deemed worth recording, even though their names 'shall be lost for evermore'. The Rugby boy who called his headmaster 'a beast but a just beast' sleeps unknown, while through him Temple lives. He can only enjoy what the dynamiter Zero called 'an anonymous infernal glory'. So do the authors of many admirable limericks, though some of the best are attributed to a living divine of great distinction, who has not disclaimed such juvenile frolics. So again to those who have given us many household words from the advertisement hoardings, the beloved old jingle of 'the Pickwick, the Owl, and the Waverley pen', the alluring alliteration of 'Pink Pills for Pale People'. Let us hope that it is enough for them that they did their duty and sent the sales leaping upward.

So much for the authors without whom this book could never have been. Now for the readers and some of the happy uses to which they will put it. 'Hand me over the Burton's *Anatomy*', said Captain Shandon, 'and leave me to my abominable devices.' It was Greek and Latin quotations that he sought for his article, but fashion has changed and today it would rather be English ones. Here is one of the most obvious purposes for which the dictionary will be used. It cannot accomplish impossibilities. It will not prevent many an honest journalist from referring to 'fresh fields and pastures new' nor from describing a cup-tie as an example of 'Greek meeting Greek'. There is a fine old crusted tradition of misquoting not lightly to be broken and it might almost seem pedantry to deck these ancient friends in their true but unfamiliar colours. Misquoting may even be deemed an amiable weakness, since Dickens in one of his letters misquoted Sam Weller; but here at least is a good chance of avoiding it. There is likewise a chance of replenishing a stock grown somewhat threadbare. 'Well, you're a boss word', exclaimed Jim Pinkerton, when he lighted on 'hebdomadary' in a dictionary. 'Before you're very much older I'll have you in type as long as yourself.' So the hard-pressed writer in turning over these pages may find and note many excellent phrases against future contingencies, whether to give a pleasing touch of erudition or to save the trouble of thinking for himself. These, however, are sordid considerations, and the mind loves rather to dwell on fireside quoting-matches between two friends, each of whom thinks his own visual memory the more accurate. There are certain writers well adapted to this form of contest and among the moderns Conan Doyle must, with all respect to Mr Wodehouse, be assigned the first place. Sherlock Holmes scholars are both numerous and formidable; they set themselves and demand of others a high standard. It is one very difficult to attain since there often seems no reason why any particular remark should have been made on any particular occasion. This is especially true of Dr Watson. He was constantly saying that his practice was not very absorbing or that he had an accommodating neighbour, but when did he say which? Even the most learned might by a momentary blunder confuse 'A Case of Identity' with 'The Final Problem'. It would be dry work to plough through all the stories, even though the supreme satisfaction of being right should reward the search. Now a glance at the dictionary will dispose of an argument which would otherwise 'end only with the visit'.

It is incidentally curious and interesting to observe that two authors may each have the same power of inspiring devotion and the competitive spirit, and yet one may be, from the dictionary point of view, infinitely more quotable than the other. Hardly any prose writer, for instance, produces a more fanatical adoration than Miss Austen, and there are doubtless those who can recite pages of her with scarce a slip; but it is perhaps pages rather than sentences that they quote. Mr Bennet provides an exception, but generally speaking she is not very amenable to the treatment by scissors and paste. George Eliot, if we leave out Mrs Poyser, a professed wit and coiner of aphorisms, is in much poorer case. Another and a very different writer, Borrow, can rouse us to a frantic pitch of romantic excitement, but it is the whole scene and atmosphere that possess this magic and we cannot take atmosphere to pieces. These are but three examples of writers who do not seem to lend themselves to brief and familiar quotations. They have jewels in plenty, but these form part of a piece of elaborate ornament from which they cannot be detached without irreparable damage. The works of some writers may by contrast be said to consist of separate stones, each of which needs no setting and can sparkle on its own account. Dickens is an obvious and unique instance. Stevenson, too, has the gift of producing characters such as Prince Florizel and Alan Breck, John Silver and Michael Finsbury, whose words can stand memorable by themselves, apart from context and atmosphere. Those who share my love for Florizel will rejoice to observe that he has had some faithful friend among the compilers. As for Michael I cannot help feeling that he has been rather scurvily used, for 'The Wrong Box' is admirably suited to competition and even learned Judges of the Court of Appeal have been known, all unsuspected by their ignorant auditors, to bandy quotations from it on the Bench. Here, however, I take leave to give any indignant reader a hint. Let him not cry too loudly before he is hurt! It is true that 'nothing like a little judicious levity' is not in the main body of the dictionary, but someone awoke just in time and it is among the addenda.

To return to those friends by the fireside whom I pictured indulging in a heated quoting-match, it may be that they will presently become allies and united to use the dictionary over a crossword puzzle. It is hardly too much to say that the setters of these problems should not use a quotation unless it is to be found in the dictionary. A crossword quotation should not be too simple, but it should be such that that hypothetical personage, the reasonable man, might have heard of it. The solver demands fair play, and the setter who takes a volume of verse at haphazard, finds a word that fits, and subtitutes a blank for it, is not playing the game. There are solvers whose standard of sportsmanship is so high that they would as soon allow themselves to cheat at patience as have recourse to a book. We may admire though we cannot emulate this fine austere arrogance. It is the best fun to win unaided, but there is good fun too in ferreting out a quotation. It well repays the ardours of the chase. Moreover a setter of puzzles who oversteps honourable limits should be fought with his own weapons. He has palpably used books and this is an epoch of reprisals. Then let us use books today and hoist him with his own petard.

It is difficult today not to deal in warlike metaphors, but perhaps the truest and most perfect use of the dictionary is essentially peaceful. Reviewers are apt to say of a detective story that it is 'impossible to lay it down till the last page is reached'. It is rather for books of reference that such praise should be reserved. No others are comparable with them for the purposes of eternal browsing. They suggest all manner of lovely, lazy things, in particular the watching of a cricket match on a sunshiny day. We have only dropped in for half an hour, but the temptation to see just one more over before we go is irresistible. Evening draws on, the shadows of the fielders lengthen on the grass, nothing much is happening, a draw becomes every minute more inevitable, and still we cannot tear ourselves away. So it is with works of reference, even with the most arid, even with Bradshaw, whose vocabulary, as Sherlock Holmes remarked, is 'nervous and terse but limited.' Over the very next page of Bradshaw there may be hidden a Framlingham Admiral; adventure may always be in wait a little farther down the line. So, but a thousand times more so, is some exciting treasure-trove awaiting us over the next page of this dictionary. What it is we cannot guess, but it is for ever calling in our ears to turn over just one more. We have only taken down the book to look up one special passage, but it is likely enough that we shall never get so far. Long before we have reached the appropriate letter we shall have been waylaid by an earlier one, and shall have clean forgotten our original quest. Nor is this all, for, if our mood changes as we browse, it is so fatally, beautifully easy to change our pasture. We can play a game akin to that 'dabbing' cricket, so popular in private-school days, in which the batsman's destiny depended or was supposed to depend—for we were not always honest—on a pencil delivered with eyes tightly shut. We can close the book and open it again at random, sure of something that shall set us off again on a fresh and enchanting voyage of not too strenuous discovery. Under this enchantment I have fallen deep. I have pored over the proofs so that only by a supreme effort of will could I lay them down and embark on the impertinent task of trying to write about them. I now send them back to their home with a sense of privation and loneliness. Here seems to me a great book. Then

> Deem it not all a too presumptuous folly,

this humble tribute to Oxford from another establishment over the way.

B.D.

May 1941

How to Use the Dictionary

Quotations

Author's date of birth and death

Author name ···· **Douglas Adams** 1952–2001

Description of author, including nationality and occupation

English science fiction writer

Number of quotation on page ····

5 The Answer to the Great Question Of . . . Life, ···· Text of quotation
the Universe and Everything . . . [is] Forty-two.

Source of quotation ········ *The Hitch Hiker's Guide to the Galaxy* (1979) ch. 27

Other name by which author is known ····

Erasmus (Desiderius Erasmus) *c.*1469–1536

Dutch Christian humanist

17 *In regione caecorum rex est luscus.* ········ Original language of translated quotation
In the country of the blind the one-eyed man is king.
Adages bk. 3, century 4, no. 96; see **PROVERBS** 636:2 ···· Cross reference to related quotation

Hippocrates *c.*460–357 BC

Greek physician

Further information about the quotation ····

13 Life is short, the art long.
often quoted as 'Ars longa, vita brevis', after **SENECA**'*s* ···· Person with own entry in the dictionary
rendering in De Brevitate Vitae *sect. 1*

Author of cross-referenced quotation ····

Aphorisms sect. 1, para. 1 (translated by W. H. S. Jones); see
CHAUCER 220:21, **LONGFELLOW** 499:15, **PROVERBS** 626:35

Page on which cross-referenced quotation appears ····

Number of cross-referenced quotation on page

Harry S. Truman 1884–1972

Cross reference to quotation about this author ····

American Democratic statesman, 33rd President of the US 1945–53. On Truman: see **ROOSEVELT** 666:17; see also ···· Cross reference to quotation associated with this author
NEWSPAPER HEADLINES AND LEADERS 573:5

15 *to reporters the day after his accession to the Presidency on* ···· Information setting the quotation in context
the death of Franklin D. **ROOSEVELT**:
When they told me yesterday what had happened, I felt like the moon, the stars and all the planets had fallen on me.
on 13 April 1945

ORDER OF ENTRIES

- Entries are in alphabetical order of author.
- Authors' names are given in the form by which they are best known: usually by surname but where appropriate by forename, pseudonym, or nickname.
- Major works known by their title (such as the **Koran**) are included in the alphabetical sequence, as are some special categories of material (such as **Epitaphs**), listed on p. v.

ORDER WITHIN ENTRIES

- Within each entry, the quotations are grouped by literary form (novels, plays, poems, etc.) and within each group arranged by alphabetical order of title.
- Quotations from diaries, letters, and speeches are given in chronological order.
- The form for which the author is best known takes precedence. So for political figures, speeches appear first, and poetry quotations precede those in prose for poets.
- Undated quotations from secondary sources are arranged in alphabetical order of quotation text.
- Quotations in the special category entries are arranged alphabetically according to the first word of the quotation.
- Sub-headings have been used as a guide to the very large entries for the **Bible**, **Dickens**, and **Shakespeare**. **Anonymous** quotations are grouped by language.
- Spellings have been Anglicized and modernized except in those cases, such as **Burns** or **Chaucer**, where this would have been inappropriate.

Index

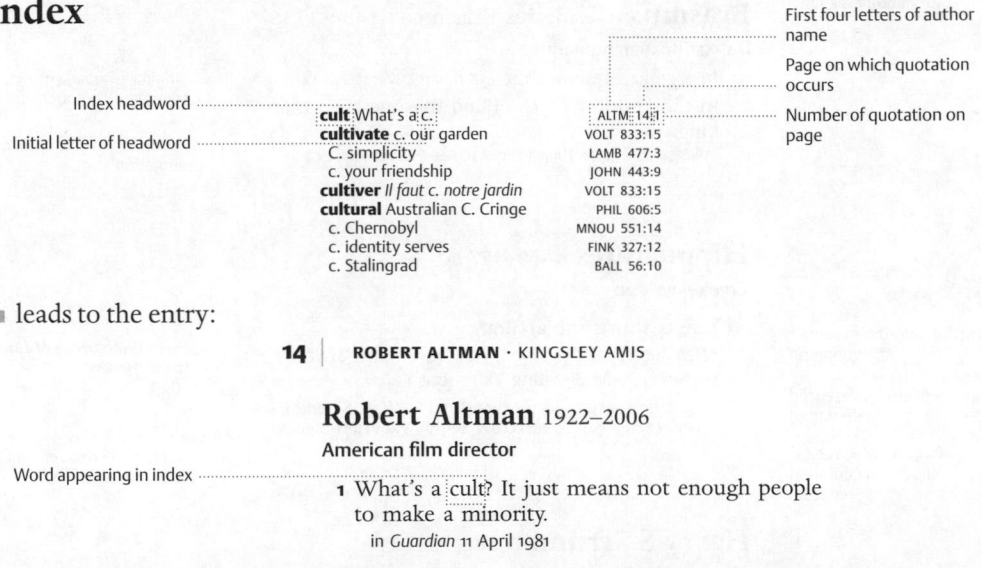

- leads to the entry:

14 | **ROBERT ALTMAN** · KINGSLEY AMIS

Robert Altman 1922–2006
American film director

Word appearing in index

1 What's a cult? It just means not enough people to make a minority.
in Guardian 11 April 1981

- Each significant word is indexed within a short line of context from the quotation.
- Both the headwords and the context lines are in strict alphabetical order.
- Singular and plural nouns (with their possessive forms) are grouped separately; for 'some old lover's ghost' see **lover**; for 'at lovers' perjuries' see **lovers**.
- Variant forms of common words (fresshe/fresh, luve/love) are grouped under a single heading: **fresh**, **love**.

Quotations

Peter Abelard 1079–1142

French scholar, theologian, and philosopher, lover of
HÉLOISE

1 *O quanta qualia sunt illa sabbata,*
Quae semper celebrat superna curia.
O what their joy and glory must be,
Those endless sabbaths the blessèd ones see!
Hymnarius Paraclitensis bk. 1, pars altera 'Hymni Diurni' no. 29
'Sabbato. Ad Vesperas' (translated by J. M. Neale, 1854)

2 *Non enim facile de his quos plurimum diligimus*
turpitudinem suspicamur.
For we do not easily expect evil of those whom
we love most.
Historia Calamitatum Mearum ch. 6

Dannie Abse 1923–

Welsh-born doctor and poet

3 Are all men in disguise except those crying?
'Encounter at a Greyhound Bus Station' (1986)

4 I know the colour rose, and it is lovely,
But not when it ripens in a tumour;
And healing greens, leaves and grass, so
springlike,
In limbs that fester are not springlike.
'Pathology of Colours' (1968)

5 So in the simple blessing of a rainbow,
In the bevelled edge of a sunlit mirror,
I have seen visible, Death's artifact
Like a soldier's ribbon on a tunic tacked.
'Pathology of Colours' (1968)

Abu Bakr 573–634

Arab ruler, first Islamic caliph

6 Give brief orders; speeches that are too long are
likely to be forgotten.
advice to his army; R. W. Maqsood *Sayings of Abu Bakr* (1989)

Accius 170–c.86 BC

Roman poet and dramatist

7 *Oderint, dum metuant.*
Let them hate, so long as they fear.
often quoted by **CALIGULA**, *according to* Suetonius Lives of
the Caesars 'Caligula' *sect. 30*
from *Atreus*, in Cicero *De Officiis* bk. 1, ch. 28

Goodman Ace 1899–1982

American humorist

8 TV—a clever contraction derived from the words
Terrible Vaudeville . . . we call it a medium
because nothing's well done.
letter to Groucho Marx, in *The Groucho Letters* (1967)

Chinua Achebe 1930–

Nigerian novelist

9 Whatever you are is never enough; you must
find a way to accept something however small
from the other to make you whole.
Anthills of the Savannah (1987) ch. 12

10 Writers don't give prescriptions. They give
headaches.
Anthills of the Savannah (1987) ch. 12

11 The world is like a Mask dancing. If you want
to see it well you do not stand in one place.
from an Igbo proverb
Arrow of God (1988) ch. 4

Dean Acheson 1893–1971

American politician, Secretary of State 1949–53

12 I will undoubtedly have to seek what is happily
known as gainful employment, which I am glad
to say does not describe holding public office.
in *Time* 22 December 1952

13 Great Britain has lost an empire and has not yet
found a role.
speech at the Military Academy, West Point, 5 December
1962, in *Vital Speeches* 1 January 1963

14 A memorandum is written not to inform the
reader but to protect the writer.
in *Wall Street Journal* 8 September 1977

Lord Acton 1834–1902

English historian and moralist

15 Liberty is not a means to a higher political end.
It is itself the highest political end.
The History of Freedom in Antiquity (1907), lecture delivered 26
February 1877

16 Power tends to corrupt and absolute power
corrupts absolutely.
letter to Bishop Mandell Creighton, 3 April 1887, in Louise
Creighton *Life and Letters of Mandell Creighton* (1904) vol. 1,
ch. 13; see **PITT** 607:10

17 Beware of too much explaining, lest we end by
too much excusing.
attributed by Acton to the Duc de Broglie, *Lectures in Modern
History* (1906), lecture delivered Cambridge, June 1895

Abigail Adams 1744–1818

American letter writer, wife of John **ADAMS** and mother of
John Quincy **ADAMS**

18 In the new code of laws which I suppose it will
be necessary for you to make I desire you would
remember the ladies, and be more generous and
favourable to them than your ancestors. Do not
put such unlimited power into the hands of the
husbands. Remember all men would be tyrants
if they could.
letter to John Adams, 31 March 1776, in Butterfield et al.
(eds.) *The Book of Abigail and John Adams* (1975); see **DEFOE**
270:18

19 It is really mortifying, sir, when a woman
possessed of a common share of understanding

considers the difference of education between the male and female sex, even in those families where education is attended to . . . Nay why should your sex wish for such a disparity in those whom they one day intend for companions and associates. Pardon me, sir, if I cannot help sometimes suspecting that this neglect arises in some measure from an ungenerous jealousy of rivals near the throne.
> letter to John Thaxter, 15 February 1778, in *Adams Family Correspondence* vol. 2 (1963)

1 These are times in which a genius would wish to live. It is not in the still calm of life, or the repose of a pacific station, that great characters are formed . . . Great necessities call out great virtues.
> letter to John Quincy Adams, 19 January 1780

2 A little of what you call frippery is very necessary towards looking like the rest of the world.
> letter to John Adams, 1 May 1780

3 Patriotism in the female sex is the most disinterested of all virtues. Excluded from honours and from offices, we cannot attach ourselves to the State or Government from having held a place of eminence . . . Yet all history and every age exhibit instances of patriotic virtue in the female sex; which considering our situation equals the most heroic of yours.
> letter to John Adams, 17 June 1782

Charles Francis Adams 1807–86
American lawyer and diplomat

4 It would be superfluous in me to point out to your lordship that this is war.
> *of the situation in the United States during the American Civil War*
> dispatch to Earl Russell, 5 September 1863, in C. F. Adams *Charles Francis Adams* (1900) ch. 17

Douglas Adams 1952–2001
English science fiction writer

5 The Answer to the Great Question Of . . . Life, the Universe and Everything . . . [is] Forty-two.
> *The Hitch Hiker's Guide to the Galaxy* (1979) ch. 27

Frank Adams *and* Will M. Hough

6 I wonder who's kissing her now.
> title of song (1909)

Franklin P. Adams 1881–1960
American journalist and humorist

7 When the political columnists say 'Every thinking man' they mean themselves, and when candidates appeal to 'Every intelligent voter' they mean everybody who is going to vote for them.
> *Nods and Becks* (1944)

8 Years ago we discovered the exact point, the dead centre of middle age. It occurs when you are too young to take up golf and too old to rush up to the net.
> *Nods and Becks* (1944)

9 Elections are won by men and women chiefly because most people vote against somebody rather than for somebody.
> *Nods and Becks* (1944); see **FIELDS** 327:10

Henry Brooks Adams 1838–1918
American historian

10 Politics, as a practice, whatever its professions, has always been the systematic organization of hatreds.
> *The Education of Henry Adams* (1907) ch. 1

11 Accident counts for much in companionship as in marriage.
> *The Education of Henry Adams* (1907) ch. 4; see **USTINOV** 823:6

12 All experience is an arch to build upon.
> *The Education of Henry Adams* (1907) ch. 6; see **TENNYSON** 800:16

13 A friend in power is a friend lost.
> *The Education of Henry Adams* (1907) ch. 7

14 Sumner's mind had reached the calm of water which receives and reflects images without absorbing them; it contained nothing but itself.
> *of Charles* **SUMNER**
> *The Education of Henry Adams* (1907) ch. 13

15 Chaos often breeds life, when order breeds habit.
> *The Education of Henry Adams* (1907) ch. 16

16 A teacher affects eternity; he can never tell where his influence stops.
> *The Education of Henry Adams* (1907) ch. 20

17 Morality is a private and costly luxury.
> *The Education of Henry Adams* (1907) ch. 22

18 Symbol or energy, the Virgin had acted as the greatest force the Western world had ever felt, and had drawn man's activities to herself more strongly than any other power, natural or supernatural, had ever done.
> *The Education of Henry Adams* (1907) ch. 25

19 No one means all he says, and yet very few say all they mean, for words are slippery and thought is viscous.
> *The Education of Henry Adams* (1907) ch. 31

John Adams 1735–1826
American Federalist statesman, 2nd President of the US 1797–1801; husband of Abigail ADAMS and father of John Quincy ADAMS

20 The law, in all vicissitudes of government . . . will preserve a steady undeviating course; it will not bend to the uncertain wishes, imaginations, and wanton tempers of men . . . On the one hand it is inexorable to the cries of the

prisoners; on the other it is deaf, deaf as an adder to the clamours of the populace.

argument in defence of the British soldiers in the Boston Massacre Trials, 4 December 1770; see **SIDNEY** 750:11

1 There is danger from all men. The only maxim of a free government ought to be to trust no man living with power to endanger the public liberty.

Notes for an Oration at Braintree (Spring 1772), in Diary and Autobiography of John Adams vol. 2 (1960)

2 A government of laws, and not of men.

in Boston Gazette (1774) no. 7, 'Novanglus' papers; later incorporated in the Massachusetts Constitution (1780); see **FORD** 337:1, **MARSHALL** 523:23

3 I agree with you that in politics the middle way is none at all.

letter to Horatio Gates, 23 March 1776, in R. J. Taylor (ed.) Papers of John Adams 3rd series (1979) vol. 4

4 You bid me burn your letters. But I must forget you first.

letter to Abigail Adams, 28 April 1776

5 Yesterday, the greatest question was decided which ever was debated in America, and a greater perhaps never was nor will be decided among men. A resolution was passed without one dissenting colony, 'that these United Colonies are, and of right ought to be, free and independent States.'

letter to Abigail Adams, 3 July 1776

6 I must study politics and war that my sons may have liberty to study mathematics and philosophy. My sons ought to study mathematics and philosophy, geography, natural history, naval architecture, navigation, commerce, and agriculture, in order to give their children a right to study painting, poetry, music, architecture, statuary, tapestry, and porcelain.

letter to Abigail Adams, 12 May 1780

7 My country has in its wisdom contrived for me the most insignificant office that ever the invention of man contrived or his imagination conceived.

of the vice-presidency

letter to Abigail Adams, 19 December 1793

8 You and I ought not to die before we have explained ourselves to each other.

letter to Thomas Jefferson, 15 July 1813, in L. J. Cappon (ed.) The Adams–Jefferson Letters (1959) vol. 2

9 The fundamental article of my political creed is that despotism, or unlimited sovereignty, or absolute power, is the same in a majority of a popular assembly, an aristocratic council, an oligarchical junto, and a single emperor.

letter to Thomas Jefferson, 13 November 1815, in P. Wilstach (ed.) Correspondence of John Adams and Thomas Jefferson (1925)

10 Liberty cannot be preserved without a general knowledge among the people, who have a right . . . and a desire to know; but besides this, they have a right, an indisputable, unalienable, indefeasible, divine right to that most dreaded and envied kind of knowledge, I mean of the characters and conduct of their rulers.

A Dissertation on the Canon and Feudal Law (1765), in M. J. Kline (ed.) Papers of John Adams vol. 1 (1977)

11 The jaws of power are always opened to devour, and her arm is always stretched out, if possible, to destroy the freedom of thinking, speaking, and writing.

A Dissertation on the Canon and Feudal Law (1765), in Charles Francis Adams (ed.) Works of John Adams (1851) vol. 3

12 The happiness of society is the end of government.

Thoughts on Government (1776)

13 Fear is the foundation of most governments.

Thoughts on Government (1776)

14 Thomas—Jefferson—still surv—

JEFFERSON *died on the same day*

last words, on 4 July 1826

John Quincy Adams 1767–1848

American statesman, 6th President of the US 1825–9; son of Abigail ADAMS and John ADAMS

15 Think of your forefathers! Think of your posterity!

Oration at Plymouth 22 December 1802; see **TACITUS** 786:22

16 *Fiat justitia, pereat coelum* [Let justice be done, though heaven fall]. My toast would be, may our country be always successful, but whether successful or otherwise, always right.

letter to John Adams, 1 August 1816, in A. Koch and W. Peden (eds.) The Selected Writings of John and John Quincy Adams (1946); see **DECATUR** 270:4, **MANSFIELD** 520:10, **MOTTOES** 563:9, **SCHURZ** 687:9, **WATSON** 841:8

17 Wherever the standard of freedom and Independence has been or shall be unfurled, there will her heart, her benedictions and her prayers be. But she [America] goes not abroad in search of monsters to destroy.

speech to House of Representatives, 4 July 1821

18 This, this is the end of earth. I am content.

last words on collapsing in the Senate, 21 February 1848 (he died two days later)

William H. Seward Eulogy of John Quincy Adams to Legislature of New York (1848)

Michael Adams

Canadian market researcher and writer

19 North of the 49th parallel we value equality; south of it, they treasure freedom.

Sex in the Snow (1997)

Samuel Adams 1722–1803

American revolutionary leader

20 What a glorious morning is this.

on hearing gunfire at Lexington, 19 April 1775; traditionally quoted as, 'What a glorious morning for America'

J. K. Hosmer Samuel Adams (1886) ch. 19

1 A nation of shopkeepers are very seldom so disinterested.

> *Oration in Philadelphia* 1 August 1776 (the authenticity of this publication is doubtful); see **NAPOLEON I** 568:9, **SMITH** 756:5

2 We cannot make events. Our business is wisely to improve them . . . Mankind are governed more by their feelings than by reason. Events which excite those feelings will produce wonderful effects.

> J. N. Rakove *The Beginnings of National Politics* (1979) ch. 5

Sarah Flower Adams 1805–48

English hymn-writer

3 Nearer, my God, to thee,
Nearer to thee!

> 'Nearer My God to Thee' in W. G. Fox *Hymns and Anthems* (1841)

Harold Adamson 1906–80

American songwriter

4 Comin' in on a wing and a pray'r.

> *words derived from the contemporary comment of a war pilot, speaking from a disabled plane to ground control*
> title of song (1943)

Jane Addams 1860–1935

American social worker

5 A conception of Democracy not merely as a sentiment which desires the well-being of all men, nor yet as a creed which believes in the essential dignity and equality of all men, but as that which affords a rule of living as well as a test of faith.

> *Democracy and Social Ethics* (1902)

6 The cure for the ills of Democracy is more Democracy.

> *Democracy and Social Ethics* (1902); see **SMITH** 756:10

7 Perhaps I may record here my protest against the efforts, so often made, to shield children and young people from all that has to do with death and sorrow . . . Young people themselves often resent this attitude on the part of their elders; they feel set aside and belittled as if they were denied the common human experiences.

> *Twenty Years at Hull House* (1910)

8 The common stock of intellectual enjoyment should not be difficult of access because of the economic position of him who would approach it.

> *Twenty Years at Hull House* (1910)

Joseph Addison 1672–1719

English poet, dramatist, and essayist; co-founder of *The Spectator*. On Addison: see **JOHNSON** 436:16, **POPE** 614:22, **TICKELL** 811:3

9 He more had pleased us, had he pleased us less.

> *of Abraham* **COWLEY**
> *An Account of the Greatest English Poets* (1694)

10 'Twas then great Marlbro's mighty soul was proved.

> *The Campaign* (1705) l. 279

11 And, pleased th' Almighty's orders to perform,
Rides in the whirlwind, and directs the storm.

> *The Campaign* (1705) l. 291; see **PAGE** 591:15

12 'Tis not in mortals to command success,
But we'll do more, Sempronius; we'll deserve it.

> *Cato* (1713) act 1, sc. 2, l. 43; see **CHURCHILL** 229:18

13 Blesses his stars and calls it luxury.

> *Cato* (1713) act 1, sc. 4, l. 70

14 'Tis pride, rank pride, and haughtiness of soul;
I think the Romans call it stoicism.

> *Cato* (1713) act 1, sc. 4, l. 82

15 The pale, unripened beauties of the north.

> *Cato* (1713) act 1, sc. 4, l. 135

16 The woman that deliberates is lost.

> *Cato* (1713) act 4, sc. 1, l. 31; see **PROVERBS** 634:21

17 Curse on his virtues! they've undone his country.
Such popular humanity is treason.

> *Cato* (1713) act 4, sc. 1, l. 205

18   What pity is it
That we can die but once to serve our country!

> *Cato* (1713) act 4, sc. 1, l. 258; see **HALE** 377:2

19 Content thyself to be obscurely good.
When vice prevails, and impious men bear sway,
The post of honour is a private station.

> *Cato* (1713) act 4, sc. 1, l. 319

20 It must be so—Plato, thou reason'st well!—
Else whence this pleasing hope, this fond desire,
This longing after immortality?
Or whence this secret dread, and inward horror,
Of falling into naught?

> *Cato* (1713) act 5, sc. 1, l. 1

21 'Tis the divinity that stirs within us,
'Tis heaven itself that points out an hereafter.

> *Cato* (1713) act 5, sc. 1, l. 7

22 Eternity! thou pleasing, dreadful thought!

> *Cato* (1713) act 5, sc. 1, l. 10

23   Let guilt or fear
Disturb man's rest; Cato knows neither of them,
Indifferent in his choice, to sleep or die.

> *Cato* (1713) act 5, sc. 1, l. 38

24 From hence, let fierce contending nations know
What dire effects from civil discord flow.

> *Cato* (1713) act 5, sc. 1, closing line

25 There is nothing more requisite in business than dispatch.

> *The Drummer* (1716) act 5, sc. 1

26 Our Grubstreet biographers . . . watch for the death of a great man, like so many undertakers, on purpose to make a penny of him.

> *The Freeholder* (1751) no. 35

27 Poetic fields encompass me around,
And still I seem to tread on classic ground.

> *Letter from Italy* (1704)

28 A painted meadow, or a purling stream.

> *Letter from Italy* (1704); see **POPE** 614:19

1 Music, the greatest good that mortals know,
And all of heaven we have below.
'A Song for St Cecilia's Day' (1694)

2 Should the whole frame of nature round him
break,
In ruin and confusion hurled,
He, unconcerned, would hear the mighty crack,
And stand secure amidst a falling world.
translation of Horace *Odes* bk. 3, no. 3; see **HORACE** 412:19,
POPE 614:16

3 A reader seldom peruses a book with pleasure
until he knows whether the writer of it be a
black man or a fair man, of a mild or choleric
disposition, married or a bachelor.
The Spectator no. 1 (1 March 1711)

4 In all thy humours, whether grave or mellow,
Thou'rt such a touchy, testy, pleasant fellow;
Hast so much wit, and mirth, and spleen about
thee,
There is no living with thee, nor without thee.
The Spectator no. 68 (18 May 1711); see **MARTIAL** 524:11

5 The old song of Chevy Chase is the favourite
ballad of the common people of England; and
Ben Jonson used to say he would rather have
been the author of it than of all his works.
The Spectator no. 70 (21 May 1711)

6 As Sir Roger is landlord to the whole
congregation, he keeps them in very good order,
and will suffer nobody to sleep in it [the church]
besides himself; for if by chance he has been
surprised into a short nap at sermon, upon
recovering out of it, he stands up, and looks
about him; and if he sees anybody else nodding,
either wakes them himself, or sends his servant
to them.
The Spectator no. 112 (9 July 1711)

7 Sir Roger told them, with the air of a man who
would not give his judgement rashly, that much
might be said on both sides.
The Spectator no. 122 (20 July 1711)

8 What sculpture is to a block of marble,
education is to a human soul.
The Spectator no. 215 (6 November 1711)

9 I have often thought, says Sir Roger, it happens
very well that Christmas should fall out in the
Middle of Winter.
The Spectator no. 269 (8 January 1712)

10 A true critic ought to dwell rather upon
excellencies than imperfections, to discover the
concealed beauties of a writer, and communicate
to the world such things as are worth their
observation.
The Spectator no. 291 (2 February 1712); see **HORACE** 409:13

11 These widows, Sir, are the most perverse
creatures in the world.
The Spectator no. 335 (25 March 1712)

12 Mirth is like a flash of lightning that breaks
through a gloom of clouds, and glitters for a

moment: cheerfulness keeps up a kind of daylight in the mind.
The Spectator no. 381 (17 May 1712)

13 The Knight in the triumph of his heart made
several reflections on the greatness of the British
Nation; as, that one Englishman could beat three
Frenchmen; that we could never be in danger of
Popery so long as we took care of our fleet; that
the Thames was the noblest river in Europe;
that London Bridge was a greater piece of work
than any of the Seven Wonders of the World;
with many other honest prejudices which
naturally cleave to the heart of a true
Englishman.
The Spectator no. 383 (20 May 1712)

14 Wide and undetermined prospects are as
pleasing to the fancy, as the speculations of
eternity or infinitude are to the understanding.
The Spectator no. 412 (23 June 1712)

15 Through all Eternity to Thee
A joyful Song I'll raise,
For oh! Eternity's too short
To utter all thy Praise.
The Spectator no. 453 (9 August 1712)

16 We have in England a particular bashfulness in
every thing that regards religion.
The Spectator no. 458 (15 August 1712)

17 The spacious firmament on high,
With all the blue ethereal sky,
And spangled heavens, a shining frame,
Their great Original proclaim.
The Spectator no. 465 (23 August 1712) 'Ode'

18 In Reason's ear they all rejoice,
And utter forth a glorious voice,
For ever singing, as they shine:
'The hand that made us is divine.'
The Spectator no. 465 (23 August 1712) 'Ode'

19 A woman seldom asks advice before she has
bought her wedding clothes.
The Spectator no. 475 (4 September 1712)

20 Our disputants put me in mind of the skuttle
fish, that when he is unable to extricate himself,
blackens all the water about him, till he
becomes invisible.
The Spectator no. 476 (5 September 1712); a 'skuttle fish' is a
cuttlefish

21 If we may believe our logicians, man is
distinguished from all other creatures by the
faculty of laughter.
The Spectator no. 494 (26 September 1712)

22 'We are always doing', says he, 'something for
Posterity, but I would fain see Posterity do
something for us.'
The Spectator no. 583 (20 August 1714)

23 There is sometimes a greater judgement shewn
in deviating from the rules of art, than in
adhering to them; and . . . there is more beauty
in the works of a great genius who is ignorant
of all the rules of art, than in the works of a

little genius, who not only knows but scrupulously observes them.
> *The Spectator* no. 592 (10 September 1714); see **POPE** 615:27

1 I remember when our whole island was shaken with an earthquake some years ago, there was an impudent mountebank who sold pills which (as he told the country people) were very good against an earthquake.
> *The Tatler* no. 240 (21 October 1710)

2 See in what peace a Christian can die.
> *dying words to his stepson Lord Warwick*
> Edward Young *Conjectures on Original Composition* (1759)

George Ade 1866–1944
American humorist and dramatist

3 After being turned down by numerous publishers, he had decided to write for posterity.
> *Fables in Slang* (1900)

4 R-E-M-O-R-S-E!
Those dry Martinis did the work for me;
Last night at twelve I felt immense,
Today I feel like thirty cents.
My eyes are bleared, my coppers hot,
I'll try to eat, but I cannot.
It is no time for mirth and laughter,
The cold, grey dawn of the morning after.
> *The Sultan of Sulu* (1903) act 2

5 'Whom are you?' he asked, for he had attended business college.
> 'The Steel Box' in *Chicago Record* 16 March 1898

Konrad Adenauer 1876–1967
German statesman, first Chancellor of the Federal Republic of Germany

6 A thick skin is a gift from God.
> in *New York Times* 30 December 1959; see **TROLLOPE** 816:19

Adi Granth *see* Sikh Scriptures

Alfred Adler 1870–1937
Austrian psychologist and psychiatrist

7 The truth is often a terrible weapon of aggression. It is possible to lie, and even to murder, for the truth.
> *The Problems of Neurosis* (1929) ch. 2

8 To be a human being means to possess a feeling of inferiority which constantly presses towards its own conquest . . . The greater the feeling of inferiority that has been experienced, the more powerful is the urge for conquest and the more violent the emotional agitation.
> Heinz and Rowens Ansbacher (eds.) *The Individual Psychology of Alfred Adler* (1956) ch. 4, sect. 3

Polly Adler 1900–62
Russian-born American brothel-keeper and writer

9 A house is not a home.
> title of book (1954)

Theodor Adorno 1903–69
German philosopher, sociologist, and musicologist

10 It is barbarous to write a poem after Auschwitz.
> attributed

☐ Advertising slogans *see* box opposite

Æ (George William Russell) 1867–1935
Irish poet and essayist

11 In ancient shadows and twilights
Where childhood had strayed,
The world's great sorrows were born
And its heroes were made.
In the lost boyhood of Judas
Christ was betrayed.
> 'Germinal' (1931)

Aeschylus *c.*525–456 BC
Greek tragedian

12 The rest, I keep silent: a great ox is treading on my tongue—but the house itself, if it got a voice, would speak very plainly.
> *Agamemnon* l. 35; see **HEANEY** 387:12

13 In our sleep, pain which cannot forget falls drop by drop upon the heart until, in our own despair, against our will, comes wisdom through the awful grace of God.
> *quoted by Robert* **KENNEDY** *on the night of the assassination of Martin Luther* **KING**
> *Agamemnon* l. 176

14 Justice inclines her scales so that wisdom comes at the price of suffering.
> *Agamemnon* l. 250

15 Hell to ships, hell to men, hell to cities.
> *of Helen (literally 'Ship-destroyer, man-destroyer, city-destroyer')*
> *Agamemnon* l. 689

16 The sea is there—and who shall quench it?—nurturing the juices which yield much purple worth its weight in silver, wholly renewable, the dye of vestments; there is a remedy for these here with the gods' help, my lord, from our reserve: the house does not know how to be poor.
> *Agamemnon* l. 958

17 And from your city do not wholly banish fear, For what man living, freed from fear, will still be just?
> *The Eumenides* l. 698

18 Let war stay abroad; it makes no difficulty in coming, for the man who will have in him a strong desire for glory. I disapprove of a bird's battling in its own home.
> *The Eumenides* l. 863

19 Countless chuckles of the waves of the sea.
> *Prometheus Bound* l. 89

continued

Advertising slogans

1 Access—your flexible friend.
Access credit card, 1981 onwards

2 An ace caff with quite a nice museum attached.
the Victoria and Albert Museum, February 1989

3 All human life is there.
the *News of the World*; used by Maurice Smelt in the late 1950s; see **JAMES** 429:18

4 All the news that's fit to print.
motto of the *New York Times*, from 1896; coined by its proprietor Adolph S. Ochs (1858–1935)

5 American Express? . . . That'll do nicely, sir.
American Express credit card, 1970s

6 And all because the lady loves Milk Tray.
Cadbury's Milk Tray chocolates, 1968 onwards

7 Australians wouldn't give a XXXX for anything else.
Castlemaine lager, 1986 onwards

8 Beanz meanz Heinz.
Heinz baked beans, c.1967; coined by Maurice Drake

9 Beauty is power.
Helena **RUBINSTEIN**'s Valaze Skin Food, 1904

10 Because I'm worth it.
advertising slogan for L'Oreal, from mid 1980s

11 Bovril . . . Prevents that sinking feeling.
Bovril, 1920; coined by H. H. Harris

12 . . . But I know a man who can.
Automobile Association, 1980s

13 Can you tell Stork from butter?
Stork margarine, from c.1956

14 Cool as a mountain stream.
Consulate menthol cigarettes, early 1960s onwards

15 A diamond is forever.
De Beers Consolidated Mines, 1940s onwards; coined by Frances Gerety; see **LOOS** 500:15

16 Does she . . . or doesn't she?
Clairol hair colouring, 1950s

17 Don't be vague, ask for Haig.
Haig whisky, c.1936

18 Don't forget the fruit gums, Mum.
Rowntree's fruit gums, 1958–61; coined by Roger Musgrave (1929–)

19 Drinka Pinta Milka Day.
National Dairy Council, 1958; coined by Bertrand Whitehead

20 Dr Williams' pink pills for pale people.
patent medicine advertisement, from 1890

21 Even your closest friends won't tell you.
Listerine mouthwash, US, in *Woman's Home Companion* November 1923

22 Every picture tells a story.
advertisement for Doan's Backache Kidney Pills (early 1900s); see **PROVERBS** 631:33

23 Exceedingly good cakes.
Mr Kipling cakes, 1967 onwards

24 Full of Eastern promise.
Fry's Turkish Delight, 1950s onwards

25 The future's bright, the future's Orange.
slogan for Orange telecom company, mid 1990s

26 Go to work on an egg.
British Egg Marketing Board, from 1957; perhaps written by Fay Weldon or Mary Gowing

27 Guinness is good for you.
reply universally given to researchers asking people why they drank Guinness
adopted by Oswald Greene, c.1929; see **ADVERTISING SLOGANS** 8:6

28 Happiness is a cigar called Hamlet.
Hamlet cigars; see **LENNON** 489:1

29 Have a break, have a Kit-Kat.
Rowntree's Kit-Kat, from c.1955

30 Heineken refreshes the parts other beers cannot reach.
Heineken lager, 1975 onwards; coined by Terry Lovelock

31 High o'er the fence leaps Sunny Jim
'Force' is the food that raises him.
advertising slogan for breakfast cereal (1903); coined by Minnie Hanff (1880–1942)

32 Horlicks guards against night starvation.
Horlicks malted milk drink, 1930s

33 If you want to get ahead, get a hat.
the Hat Council, 1965

34 I liked it so much, I bought the company!
Remington Shavers, 1980; spoken by the company's new owner Victor Kiam (1926–2001)

35 I'm only here for the beer.
Double Diamond beer, 1971 onwards; coined by Ros Levenstein

36 It beats as it sweeps as it cleans.
Hoover vacuum cleaners, devised in 1919 by Gerald Page-Wood

37 It could be you.
British national lottery, from 1994

38 It's finger lickin' good.
Kentucky fried chicken, from 1958

39 It's good to talk.
British Telecom, from 1994

40 It's tingling fresh. It's fresh as ice.
Gibbs toothpaste; the first advertising slogan heard on British television, 22 September 1955

41 I was a seven-stone weakling.
Charles Atlas body-building, originally in US

42 Keep that schoolgirl complexion.
Palmolive soap, from 1917; coined by Charles S. Pearce

43 Kills all known germs.
Domestos bleach, 1959

44 Let the train take the strain.
British Rail, 1970 onwards

continued

Advertising slogans *continued*

1 Let your fingers do the walking.
Bell System Telephone Directory Yellow Pages, 1960s

2 The man you love to hate.
billing for Erich von Stroheim in the film *The Heart of Humanity* (1918)

3 A Mars a day helps you work, rest and play.
Mars bar, c.1960 onwards

4 The mint with the hole.
Life-Savers, US, 1920; and for Rowntree's Polo mints, UK, from 1947

5 More doctors smoke Camels than any other cigarette.
Camel cigarettes, 1940s–50s

6 My Goodness, My Guinness.
Guinness stout, 1935; coined by Dicky Richards; see ADVERTISING SLOGANS 7:27

7 Naughty but nice.
fresh cream cakes for the National Dairy Council, 1980s; sometimes said to have been coined by Salman RUSHDIE when a copywriter, although the phrase itself goes back to the late 19th century; see also FILM TITLES 331:8

8 Never knowingly undersold.
motto of the John Lewis Partnership, from c.1920; coined by John Spedan Lewis (1885–1963)

9 Nice one, Cyril.
taken up by supporters of Cyril Knowles, Tottenham Hotspur footballer; the Spurs team later made a record featuring the line
Wonderloaf, 1972

10 No manager ever got fired for buying IBM.
IBM

11 Oxo gives a meal man-appeal.
Oxo beef extract, c.1960

12 Persil washes whiter—and it shows.
Persil washing powder, 1970s

13 Put a tiger in your tank.
Esso petrol, 1964

14 Say it with flowers.
Society of American Florists, 1917; coined by Patrick O'Keefe (1872–1934)

15 Sch . . . you know who.
Schweppes mineral drinks, 1960s

16 Someone, somewhere, wants a letter from you.
British Post Office, 1960s

17 Stop me and buy one.
Wall's ice cream, from spring 1922; coined by Cecil Rodd

18 Stuffing instead of potatoes?
General Foods' Stove Top Stuffing, 1974; invented by the home economist Ruth M. Siems (1931–2005)

19 Tell Sid.
privatization of British Gas, 1986

20 They come as a boon and a blessing to men,
The Pickwick, the Owl, and the Waverley pen.
advertisement by MacNiven and H. Cameron Ltd., current by 1879; see PRINCE 624:2

21 Things go better with Coke.
Coca-Cola, 1963

22 Think different.
Apple Computers, 1997

23 Top people take *The Times*.
The Times newspaper, from January 1959

24 *Vorsprung durch Technik.*
Progress through technology.
Audi motors, from 1986

25 We are the Ovaltineys,
Little [*or* Happy] girls and boys.
'We are the Ovaltineys' (song from c.1935); Ovaltine drink

26 We're number two. We try harder.
Avis car rentals

27 We won't make a drama out of a crisis.
Commercial Union insurance

28 Where's the beef?
Wendy's Hamburgers, from January 1984; coined by Cliff Freeman; see MONDALE 553:8

29 Worth a guinea a box.
Beecham's pills, from c.1859, from the chance remark of a lady purchaser

30 You press the button, we do the rest.
advertising slogan to launch Kodak camera 1888; coined by George Eastman (1854–1932)

31 You're never alone with a Strand.
Strand cigarettes, 1960; coined by John May

Aeschylus *continued*

32 I count false words the foulest plague of all.
Prometheus Bound l. 685

33 Everyone's quick to blame the alien.
The Suppliant Maidens l. 972

34 Bronze is a mirror of the face, wine of the mind.
fragment 221, in Herbert Weir Smith (tr.) *Fragments of Uncertain Plays* (1926)

35 The saying of the noble and glorious Aeschylus, who declared that his tragedies were large cuts taken from Homer's mighty dinners.
Athenaeus *Deipnosophistae*

Aesop

Greek storyteller of the 6th century BC

36 Then one day there really was a wolf, but when the boy shouted they didn't believe him.
'The Boy Who Cried Wolf'

37 Woe is me! I foolishly abandoned what I had in order to grab hold of a phantom, and thus I ended up losing both that phantom and what I had to begin with.
'The Dog, the Meat, and the Reflection'

38 Oh, you aren't even ripe yet! I don't need any sour grapes.
'The Fox and the Bunch of Grapes'

1 O raven, you do have a voice but no brains to go with it!
'The Fox and the Raven'

2 While I see many hoof-marks going in, I see none coming out.
'The Fox, the Lion, and the Footprints'; see **HORACE** 410:2

3 Pray to the gods only when you're making some effort on your own behalf, otherwise your prayers are wasted.
'Heracles and the Driver'

4 Since you rejected what was good in order to get something bad, you had better put up with it—or else something even worse might happen.
'Jupiter and the Frogs', often known as 'King Log'

5 The wolf in sheep's clothing.
title of fable

Herbert Agar 1897–1980
American poet and writer

6 The truth which makes men free is for the most part the truth which men prefer not to hear.
A Time for Greatness (1942) ch. 7; see **BIBLE** 107:30

James Agate 1877–1947
English drama critic and novelist

7 Shaw's plays are the price we pay for Shaw's prefaces.
diary, 10 March 1933

8 My mind is not a bed to be made and re-made.
diary, 9 June 1943

9 A professional is a man who can do his job when he doesn't feel like it. An amateur is a man who can't do his job when he does feel like it.
diary, 19 July 1945

Agathon b. c.445 BC
Greek tragic poet

10 Even a god cannot change the past.
literally 'The one thing which even God cannot do is to make undone what has been done'
Aristotle *Nicomachaean Ethics* bk. 6; see **BUTLER** 184:2

11 One might perhaps say that this very thing is probable, that many things happen to men that are not probable.
Aristotle *Art of Rhetoric* 1402a; see **ARISTOTLE** 27:22

Agesilaus 444–360 BC
Greek monarch, King of Sparta

12 Every honourable action has its proper time and season, or rather it is this propriety or observance which distinguishes an honourable action from its opposite.
Plutarch *Lives* 'Agesilaus'

Spiro T. Agnew 1918–96
American Republican politician

13 I didn't say I wouldn't go into ghetto areas. I've been in many of them and to some extent I would have to say this: If you've seen one city slum you've seen them all.
in *Detroit Free Press* 19 October 1968; see **BURTON** 181:13

14 In the United States today, we have more than our share of the nattering nabobs of negativism.
speech in San Diego, 11 September 1970

Agnolo di Tura b. c.1300
Sienese chronicler

15 No one wept for the dead, because everyone expected death itself.
Rerum Italicarum scriptores; M. Meiss *Painting in Florence and Siena after the Black Death* (1951)

Maria, Marchioness of Ailesbury
d. 1902
English peeress

16 My dear, my dear, you never know when any beautiful young lady may not blossom into a Duchess!
Duke of Portland *Men, Women, and Things* (1937) ch. 3; see **MITFORD** 551:8

Alfred Ainger 1837–1904
English lecturer

17 No flowers, by request.
summarizing the principle of conciseness for contributors to the Dictionary of National Biography
Supplement to the Dictionary of National Biography 1901–1911 (1912)

Arthur Campbell Ainger 1841–1919
English schoolmaster

18 God is working his purpose out as year succeeds to year;
God is working his purpose out and the time is drawing near;
Nearer and nearer draws the time, the time that shall surely be,
When the earth shall be filled with the glory of God as the waters cover the sea.
'God is working his purpose out' (1894 hymn); see **BIBLE** 92:18

Jonathan Aitken 1942–
British Conservative politician

19 If it falls to me to start a fight to cut out the cancer of bent and twisted journalism in our country with the simple sword of truth and the trusty shield of British fair play, so be it.
statement, London, 10 April 1995, in *The Times* 11 April 1995

Max Aitken *see* **Lord Beaverbrook**

Mark Akenside 1721–70
English poet and physician

1 Mind, mind alone, bear witness, earth and
   heaven!
   The living fountains in itself contains
   Of beauteous and sublime.
   The Pleasures of Imagination (1744) bk. 1, l. 481

2   Nor ever yet
   The melting rainbow's vernal-tinctured hues
   To me have shone so pleasing, as when first
   The hand of science pointed out the path
   In which the sun-beams gleaming from the west
   Fall on the wat'ry cloud.
   The Pleasures of Imagination (1744) bk. 2, l. 103

Anna Akhmatova 1889–1966
Russian poet

3 All has been looted, betrayed, sold; black death's
   wing flashed ahead.
   'All has been Looted' (1921) (translated by Dmitri Obolensky)

4 As if I were a river
   The harsh age changed my course,
   Replaced one life with another,
   Flowing in a different channel
   And I do not recognize my shores.
   'As if I were a River' (1944) (translated by Amanda Haight)

5 It was a time when only the dead smiled, happy
   in their peace.
   Requiem (1935–40) (translated by Richard McKane)

6 I'd like to name the names of all that host
   but they snatched up the list and now it's lost.
   I've woven them a garment that's prepared
   out of poor words, those that I overheard,
   and will hold fast to every word and glance
   all of my days, even in new mischance.
   Requiem (1935–40) (translated by Stanley Kunitz and Max
   Hayward)

7 In the young century's cool nursery,
   In its chequered silence, I was born.
   'Willow' (1940)

Zoë Akins 1886–1958
American poet and dramatist

8 The Greeks had a word for it.
   title of play (1930)

William Alabaster 1567–1640
English divine and Latin poet

9 Tell them, my soul, the fears that make me
   quake:
   The smouldering brimstone and the burning
   lake,
   Life feeding death, death ever life devouring,
   Torments not moved, unheard, yet still roaring,
   God lost, hell found,—ever, never begun.

Now bid me into flame from smoke to run!
   'Away, fear, with thy projects' (written 1597–8)

Alain (Émile-Auguste Chartier) 1868–1951
French poet and philosopher

10 *Rien n'est plus dangereux qu'une idée, quand on n'a
   qu'une idée.*

   Nothing is more dangerous than an idea, when
   you have only one idea.
   Propos sur la religion (1938) no. 74

Alain-Fournier (Henri Alban) 1886–1914
French novelist

11 *Mais quelqu'un est venu qui m'a enlevé à tous ces
   plaisirs d'enfant paisible. Quelqu'un a soufflé la
   bougie qui éclairait pour moi le doux visage maternel
   penché sur le repas du soir. Quelqu'un a éteint la
   lampe autour de laquelle nous étions une famille
   heureuse, à la nuit, lorsque mon père avait accroché
   les volets de bois aux portes vitrées. Et celui-là, ce fut
   Augustin Meaulnes, que les autres élèves appelèrent
   bientôt le grand Meaulnes.*

   But someone came and put an end to these mild
   and childish pleasures. Someone blew out the
   candle which illumined for me the sweet
   maternal face bent over the evening meal.
   Someone extinguished the lamp around which
   we had been a happy family group at night-time
   when my father had closed all the wooden
   shutters. And that someone was Augustin
   Meaulnes, whom in no time the other boys
   began to call le grand Meaulnes.
   Le Grand Meaulnes (1912) pt. 1, ch. 2 (translated by Frank
   Davison)

12 *Quand on a, disait-il, commis quelque lourde faute
   impardonnable, on songe parfois, au milieu d'une
   grande amertume: 'Il y a pourtant par le monde des
   gens qui me pardonneraient'. On imagine de vieilles
   gens, des grandparents pleins d'indulgence, qui sont
   persuadés à l'avance que tout ce que vous faites est
   bien fait.*

   When you've done something inexcusable, you
   try to ease your conscience by telling yourself
   that someone, somewhere would forgive you.
   You think of old people, perhaps indulgent
   grandparents, who are convinced that whatever
   you do is right.
   Le Grand Meaulnes (1912) pt. 1, ch. 14

13 *Notre aventure est finie. L'hiver de cette année est
   mort comme la tombe. Peut-être quand nous
   mourrons, peut-être la mort seule nous donnera la
   clef et la suite et la fin de cette aventure manquée.*

   Our adventure is ended. The winter of this year
   is as dead as the grave. Perhaps when we come
   to die, death will provide the meaning and the
   sequel and the ending of this unsuccessful
   adventure.
   Le Grand Meaulnes (1912) pt. 2, ch. 12

1 *Un homme qui a fait une fois un bond dans le paradis, comment pourrait-il s'accommoder ensuite de la vie de tout le monde?*

How can a man who has once strayed into Heaven ever hope to make terms with the earth!
Le Grand Meaulnes (1912) pt. 3, ch. 4

2 *C'est d'abord comme une voix tremblante qui, de très loin, ose à peine chanter sa joie . . . Cet air que je ne connais pas, c'est aussi une prière, une supplication au bonheur de ne pas être trop cruel, un salut et comme un agenouillement devant le bonheur.*

It is at first like some far-away tentative voice intimidated by an excess of joy . . . This melody, which I've never heard before, is a kind of prayer to happiness, an entreaty asking fate not to be too cruel, a salutation to happiness and at the same time a genuflexion.
Le Grand Meaulnes (1912) pt. 3, ch. 7

Edward Albee 1928–
American dramatist

3 Who's afraid of Virginia Woolf?
title of play (1962)

Prince Albert (Albert Francis Charles Augustus Emmanuel of Saxe-Coburg-Gotha) 1819–61
German-born prince, British Consort of Queen **VICTORIA** from 1840. On Albert: see **TENNYSON** 793:24, **VICTORIA** 827:7

4 The works of art, by being publicly exhibited and offered for sale, are becoming articles of trade, following as such the unreasoning laws of markets and fashion; and public and even private patronage is swayed by their tyrannical influence.
speech at the Royal Academy Dinner, 3 May 1851, in *Addresses* (1857)

Scipione Alberti

5 *I pensieri stretti ed il viso sciolto* [Secret thoughts and open countenance] will go safely over the whole world.
letter from Henry Wotton to John Milton, 13 April 1638, prefixed to *Comus* in Milton *Poems* (1645 ed.)

Mary Alcock *c.*1742–98
English poet

6 A masquerade, a murdered peer,
His throat just cut from ear to ear—
A rake turned hermit—a fond maid
Run mad, by some false loon betrayed—
These stores supply the female pen,
Which writes them o'er and o'er again,
And readers likewise may be found
To circulate them round and round.
'A Receipt for Writing a Novel' l. 65

Louisa May Alcott 1832–88
American novelist

7 'Christmas won't be Christmas without any presents,' grumbled Jo, lying on the rug.
Little Women (1868–9) ch. 1, opening words

8 I am angry nearly every day of my life . . . but I have learned not to show it; and I still hope to learn not to feel it, though it may take me another forty years to do so.
Mrs March to her daughter Jo
Little Women (1868–9) ch. 8

Alcuin *c.*735–804
English scholar and theologian

9 What has Ingeld to do with Christ?
to the monks of Lindisfarne who apparently preferred listening to Beowulf *than to the Gospels*
letter no. 124, AD 797; in E. Dümmler *Monumenta Germaniae Historica* (1895); see **TERTULLIAN** 802:13

10 *Nec audiendi qui solent dicere, Vox populi, vox Dei, quum tumultuositas vulgi semper insaniae proxima sit.*

And those people should not be listened to who keep saying the voice of the people is the voice of God, since the riotousness of the crowd is always very close to madness.
letter 164 in *Works* (1863) vol. 1; see **POPE** 617:22, **PROVERBS** 646:4, **SHERMAN** 749:7

Richard Aldington 1892–1962
English poet, novelist, and biographer

11 Patriotism is a lively sense of collective responsibility. Nationalism is a silly cock crowing on its own dunghill.
The Colonel's Daughter (1931) pt. 1, ch. 6

Brian Aldiss 1925–
English science fiction writer

12 Keep violence in the mind
Where it belongs.
Barefoot in the Head (1969) 'Charteris'

Henry Aldrich 1647–1710
English scholar; Dean of Christ Church, Oxford, from 1689

13 If all be true that I do think,
There are five reasons we should drink;
Good wine—a friend—or being dry—
Or lest we should be by and by—
Or any other reason why.
'Reasons for Drinking' (1689)

Thomas Bailey Aldrich 1836–1907
American writer

14 The fair, frail palaces,
The fading alps and archipelagoes,
And great cloud-continents of sunset-seas.
'Miracles' (1874)

'Buzz' Aldrin (Edwin Eugene Aldrin Jnr)

1930–

American astronaut; second man on the moon after Neil
ARMSTRONG

1 Beautiful! Beautiful! Magnificent desolation.
of the lunar landscape
on the first moon walk, 20 July 1969

Alexander the Great 356–323 BC

Greek monarch, King of Macedon from 336 BC. See also
DIOGENES 283:14

2 If I were not Alexander, I would be Diogenes.
Plutarch *Parallel Lives* 'Alexander' ch. 14, sect. 3

3 Is it not worthy of tears that, when the number
of worlds is infinite, we have not yet become
lords of a single one?
*when asked why he wept on hearing from Anaxarchus that
there was an infinite number of worlds*
Plutarch *Moralia* 'On Tranquillity of the Mind'; see **WATTS**
842:8

4 I am dying with the help of too many
physicians.
attributed

Alexander II ('the Liberator') 1818–81

Russian monarch, Tsar from 1855

5 Better to abolish serfdom from above than to
wait till it begins to abolish itself from below.
speech in Moscow, 30 March 1856

Cecil Frances Alexander 1818–95

Irish poet and hymn-writer

6 All things bright and beautiful,
All creatures great and small,
All things wise and wonderful,
The Lord God made them all.
'All Things Bright and Beautiful' (1848)

7 The rich man in his castle,
The poor man at his gate,
God made them, high or lowly,
And ordered their estate.
'All Things Bright and Beautiful' (1848)

8 Once in royal David's city
Stood a lowly cattle-shed,
Where a mother laid her baby
In a manger for his bed:
Mary was that mother mild,
Jesus Christ her little child.
'Once in royal David's city' (1848)

9 I bind unto myself to-day
The strong name of the Trinity,
By invocation of the same
The Three in One and One in Three.
'St Patrick's Breastplate' (1889); see **PATRICK** 599:17

10 There is a green hill far away,
Without a city wall,

Where the dear Lord was crucified,
Who died to save us all.
'There is a green hill far away' (1848)

William Alexander, Lord Stirling

c.1567–1640

Scottish poet and courtier

11 The weaker sex, to piety more prone.
'Doomsday' 5th Hour (1637)

Alfonso 'the Wise' 1221–84

Spanish monarch, King of Castile and León from 1252

12 Had I been present at the Creation, I would
have given some useful hints for the better
ordering of the universe.
on studying the Ptolemaic system
attributed

Alfred the Great AD 849–899

English monarch, King of Wessex from AD 871

13 *Đa ic đa gemunde hu sio lar Lædengeđiodes ær
đissum afeallen wæs giond Angelcynn, ond đeah
monige cuđon Englisc gewrit arædan, đa ongan ic on
gemang ođrum mislicum ond manigfealdum bisgum
đisses kynerices đa boc wendan on Englisc đe is
genemned on Læden Pastoralis, ond on Englisc
Hierdeboc, hwilum word be worde, hwilum andgit of
andgite.*
When I recalled how knowledge of Latin had
previously decayed throughout England, and yet
many could still read things written in English, I
then began, amidst the various and multifarious
afflictions of this kingdom, to translate into
English the book which in Latin is called
Pastoralis, in English 'Shepherd-book', sometimes
word for word, sometimes sense for sense.
preface to the Anglo-Saxon version of St Gregory's *Pastoral
Care* (translated by S. Keynes and M. Lapidge, 1983)

Nelson Algren 1909–81

American novelist

14 A walk on the wild side.
title of novel (1956)

15 Never play cards with a man called Doc. Never
eat at a place called Mom's. Never sleep with a
woman whose troubles are worse than your
own.
in *Newsweek* 2 July 1956

Ali ibn-Abi-Talib c.602–661

Arab ruler, fourth Islamic caliph

16 He who has a thousand friends has not a friend
to spare,
And he who has one enemy will meet him
everywhere.
A Hundred Sayings

17 Men are more like the times they live in than
they are like their fathers.
attributed

Muhammad Ali (Cassius Clay) 1942–
American boxer

1 I'm the greatest.
adopted as his catchphrase from 1962, in *Louisville Times* 16 November 1962

2 Float like a butterfly, sting like a bee.
summary of his boxing strategy (probably originated by his aide Drew 'Bundini' Brown)
G. Sullivan *Cassius Clay Story* (1964) ch. 8

3 I ain't got no quarrel with the Viet Cong.
refusing to be drafted to fight in Vietnam
at a press conference in Miami, Florida, February 1966

Abbé d'Allainval 1700–53
French dramatist

4 *L'embarras des richesses.*
The embarrassment of riches.
title of comedy (1726)

Fred Allen (John Florence Sullivan)
1894–1956
American humorist

5 Committee—a group of men who individually can do nothing but as a group decide that nothing can be done.
attributed

Lewis Allen (Abel Meeropol)
American teacher

6 Southern trees bear strange fruit,
Blood on the leaves and blood at the root,
Black bodies swinging in the Southern breeze,
Strange fruit hanging from the poplar trees.
'Strange Fruit' (1939), adapted and sung by Billie **HOLIDAY**

William Allen d. 1867, Michael Larkin d. 1867, *and* William O'Brien d. 1867
Irish nationalists

7 God save Ireland!
called out from the dock by the Manchester Martyrs
Robert Kee *The Bold Fenian Men* (1989); see **SULLIVAN** 780:5

Woody Allen (Allen Stewart Konigsberg)
1935–
American film director, writer, and actor

8 That was the most fun I ever had without laughing.
of sex
Annie Hall (1977 film, with Marshall Brickman)

9 Don't knock masturbation. It's sex with someone I love.
Annie Hall (1977 film, with Marshall Brickman)

10 Is sex dirty? Only if it's done right.
Everything You Always Wanted to Know about Sex (1972 film)

11 If it turns out that there is a God, I don't think that he's evil. But the worst that you can say about him is that basically he's an underachiever.
Love and Death (1975 film)

12 My brain? It's my second favourite organ.
Sleeper (1973 film, with Marshall Brickman)

13 A fast word about oral contraception. I asked a girl to go to bed with me and she said 'no'.
Woody Allen Volume Two (Colpix CP 488) side 4, band 6

14 It's not that I'm afraid to die. I just don't want to be there when it happens.
Death (1975)

15 If only God would give me some clear sign! Like making a large deposit in my name at a Swiss bank.
'Selections from the Allen Notebooks' in *New Yorker* 5 November 1973

16 On bisexuality: It immediately doubles your chances for a date on Saturday night.
in *New York Times* 1 December 1975

17 I don't want to achieve immortality through my work . . . I want to achieve it through not dying.
Eric Lax *Woody Allen and his Comedy* (1975) ch. 12

Svetlana Alliluyeva 1925–
Russian daughter of Joseph STALIN

18 He is gone, but his shadow still stands over all of us. It still dictates to us and we, very often, obey.
of her father, Joseph **STALIN**
Twenty Letters to a Friend (1967)

William Allingham 1824–89
Irish poet

19 Up the airy mountain,
Down the rushy glen,
We daren't go a-hunting,
For fear of little men.
'The Fairies' (1850)

St Alphonsus (Alfonso Maria de' Liguori)
1696–1787
Italian theologian, founder of the Redemptorists

20 O Mother blest, whom God bestows
On sinners and on just,
What joy, what hope thou givest those
Who in thy mercy trust!
'O Mother Blest', translated by E. Vaughan

Joseph Alsop 1910–89
American journalist

21 Gratitude, like love, is never a dependable international emotion.
in *Observer* 30 November 1952

Robert Altman 1922–2006
American film director

1 What's a cult? It just means not enough people to make a minority.
  in *Guardian* 11 April 1981

Luis Walter Alvarez 1911–88
American physicist

2 There is no democracy in physics. We can't say that some second-rate guy has as much right to opinion as Fermi.
  D. S. Greenberg *The Politics of Pure Science* (1969)

St Ambrose c.339–397
French-born bishop of Milan. On Ambrose: see **AUGUSTINE** 39:5; see also **PRAYERS** 623:8

3 *Ubi Petrus, ibi ergo ecclesia.*

  Where Peter is, there must be the Church.
  'Explanatio psalmi 40' in *Corpus Scriptorum Ecclesiasticorum Latinorum* (1919) vol. 64

4 *Cum Romanum venio, ieiuno Sabbato; cum hic sum, non ieiuno: sic etiam tu, ad quam forte ecclesiam veneris, eius morem serva, si cuiquam non vis esse scandalum nec quemquam tibi.*

  When I go to Rome, I fast on Saturday, but here [Milan] I do not. Do you also follow the custom of whatever church you attend, if you do not want to give or receive scandal.
  St Augustine: Letters vol. 1 (translated by Sister W. Parsons, 1951) 'Letter 54 to Januarius'; see **PROVERBS** 646:41

Leo Amery 1873–1955
British Conservative politician

5 For twenty years he has held a season-ticket on the line of least resistance and has gone wherever the train of events has carried him, lucidly justifying his position at whatever point he has happened to find himself.
  of Herbert **ASQUITH**
  in *Quarterly Review* July 1914

6 Speak for England.
  to Arthur Greenwood in the House of Commons, 2 September 1939; see **BOOTHBY** 151:5

7 I will quote certain other words. I do it with great reluctance, because I am speaking of those who are old friends and associates of mine, but they are words which, I think, are applicable to the present situation. This is what Cromwell said to the Long Parliament when he thought it was no longer fit to conduct the affairs of the nation: 'You have sat too long here for any good you have been doing. Depart, I say, and let us have done with you. In the name of God, go.'
  speech, House of Commons, 7 May 1940, in the debate on the invasion of Norway; see **CROMWELL** 260:14

Fisher Ames 1758–1808
American politician

8 A monarchy is a merchantman which sails well, but will sometimes strike on a rock, and go to the bottom; whilst a republic is a raft which would never sink, but then your feet are always in the water.
  attributed to Ames, speaking in the House of Representatives, 1795; quoted by R. W. Emerson in *Essays* (2nd series, 1844) no. 7, but not traced in Ames's speeches

Kingsley Amis 1922–95
English novelist and poet

9 If there's one word that sums up everything that's gone wrong since the War, it's Workshop.
  Jake's Thing (1979) ch. 14

10 His mouth had been used as a latrine by some small creature of the night, and then as its mausoleum.
  Lucky Jim (1954) ch. 6

11 Alun's life was coming to consist more and more exclusively of being told at dictation speed what he knew.
  The Old Devils (1986) ch. 7

12 Outside every fat man there was an even fatter man trying to close in.
  One Fat Englishman (1963) ch. 3; see **CONNOLLY** 248:10, **ORWELL** 586:21

13 He was of the faith chiefly in the sense that the church he currently did not attend was Catholic.
  One Fat Englishman (1963) ch. 8

14 Should poets bicycle-pump the human heart
  Or squash it flat?
  Man's love is of man's life a thing apart;
  Girls aren't like that.
  'A Bookshop Idyll' (1956); see **BYRON** 188:3

15 We men have got love well weighed up; our stuff
  Can get by without it.
  Women don't seem to think that's good enough;
  They write about it.
  'A Bookshop Idyll' (1956)

16 Women are really much nicer than men:
  No wonder we like them.
  'A Bookshop Idyll' (1956)

17 Death has got something to be said for it:
  There's no need to get out of bed for it;
  Wherever you may be,
  They bring it to you, free.
  'Delivery Guaranteed' (1979)

18 The delusion that there are thousands of young people about who are capable of benefiting from university training, but have somehow failed to find their way there, is . . . a necessary component of the expansionist case . . . More will mean worse.
  in *Encounter* July 1960

1 If you can't annoy somebody with what you write, I think there's little point in writing.
  in *Radio Times* 1 May 1971

Anacharsis
Scythian prince of the 6th century BC

2 Written laws are like spiders' webs; they will catch, it is true, the weak and poor, but would be torn in pieces by the rich and powerful.
  Plutarch *Parallel Lives* 'Solon' bk. 5, sect. 2; see **SHENSTONE** 747:20, **SWIFT** 783:21

Anatolius *c.*400–458
Alexandrian Patriarch of Constantinople

3 Fierce was the wild billow,
  Dark was the night;
  Oars laboured heavily,
  Foam glimmered white;
  Trembled the mariners,
  Peril was nigh:
  Then said the God of God,
  'Peace! it is I.'
  'Fierce was the wild billow' (translated by John Mason Neale, 1862)

Hans Christian Andersen 1805–75
Danish novelist and writer of fairy stories

4 The Emperor's new clothes.
  title of story in *Danish Fairy Legends and Tales* (1846); see **LOESSER** 498:9

5 'But the Emperor has nothing on at all!' cried a little child.
  Danish Fairy Legends and Tales (1846) 'The Emperor's New Clothes'

6 It doesn't matter about being born in a duckyard, as long as you're hatched from a swan's egg!
  Danish Fairy Legends and Tales (1846) 'The Ugly Duckling'

7 I never dreamt I should find so much happiness when I was the ugly duckling!
  Danish Fairy Legends and Tales (1846) 'The Ugly Duckling'

8 And so they could see she was a real princess, because she had felt the pea through twenty mattresses and twenty eiderdowns.
  Tales Told for Children (1835) 'The Princess and the Pea'

9 There sat the dog with eyes as big as millstones!
  Tales Told for Children (1835) 'The Tinder-box'

Maxwell Anderson 1888–1959
American dramatist

10 But it's a long, long while
  From May to December;
  And the days grow short
  When you reach September.
  'September Song' (1938 song)

Maxwell Anderson 1888–1959 *and*
Lawrence Stallings 1894–1968
American dramatists

11 What price glory?
  title of play (1924)

Robert Anderson 1917–
American dramatist

12 Tea and sympathy.
  title of play (1953)

Lancelot Andrewes 1555–1626
English preacher and writer of sermons; bishop, successively, of Chichester, Ely, and Winchester

13 What shall become of me (said Righteousness)? What use of Justice, if God will do no justice, if he spare sinners? And what use of me (saith Mercy), if he spare them not? Hard hold there was, inasmuch as, *Perii, nisi homo moriatur* (said Righteousness) I die, if he die not: And *Perii, nisi Misericordiam consequatur* (said Mercy) if he die, I die too.
  Of the Nativity (1616) Sermon 11; see **MILTON** 542:22

14 *Verbum infans*, the Word without a word, not able to speak a word . . . He, that . . . taketh the vast body of the main Sea, turns it to and fro, as a little child, and rolls it about with the swaddling bands of darkness; He, to come thus into clouts, himself!
  Of the Nativity (1618) Sermon 12; see **BIBLE** 87:10, **ELIOT** 309:24

15 It was no summer progress. A cold coming they had of it, at this time of the year; just, the worst time of the year, to take a journey, and specially a long journey, in. The ways deep, the weather sharp, the days short, the sun farthest off *in solstitio brumali*, the very dead of Winter.
  Of the Nativity (1622) Sermon 15; see **ELIOT** 310:2

Norman Angell 1872–1967
English pacifist

16 The great illusion.
  on the futility of war
  title of book (1910), first published as 'Europe's Optical Illusion' (1909)

Maya Angelou 1928–
American writer. See also **DUNBAR** 299:8

17 Children's talent to endure stems from their ignorance of alternatives.
  I Know Why The Caged Bird Sings (1969) ch.17

18 You may shoot me with your words,
  You may cut me with your eyes,
  You may kill me with your hatefulness,
  But still, like air, I'll rise.
  'Still I Rise' (1978)

Paul Anka 1941–

Canadian singer and composer

1 I've lived a life that's full, I've travelled each and ev'ry highway
And more, much more than this. I did it my way.
'My Way' (1969 song)

Anne, Princess Royal 1950–

British princess; daughter of **ELIZABETH II**

2 I don't work that way . . . The very idea that all children want to be cuddled by a complete stranger, I find completely amazing.
on her work for Save the Children
in *Daily Telegraph* 17 January 1998

Anonymous

ENGLISH

3 An abomination unto the Lord, but a very present help in time of trouble.
definition of a lie
an amalgamation of Proverbs 12.22 and Psalms 46.1, often attributed to Adlai **STEVENSON**; Bill Adler *The Stevenson Wit* (1966); see **BIBLE** 88:5, **BOOK OF COMMON PRAYER** 142:17

4 Adam
Had 'em.
on the antiquity of microbes
noted as an example of a short poem

5 All human beings are born free and equal in dignity and rights.
Universal Declaration of Human Rights (1948) article 1

6 All this buttoning and unbuttoning.
18th-century suicide note

7 Along the electric wire the message came:
He is not better—he is much the same.
parodic poem on the illness of the Prince of Wales, later King **EDWARD VII**
F. H. Gribble *Romance of the Cambridge Colleges* (1913); sometimes attributed to Alfred Austin (1835–1913), Poet Laureate

8 And they lived happily ever after.
traditional ending to a fairy story
recorded (with slight variations) from the 1850s

9 Anyone here been raped and speaks English?
shouted by a British TV reporter in a crowd of Belgian civilians waiting to be airlifted out of the Belgian Congo, c.1960
Edward Behr *Anyone Here been Raped and Speaks English?* (1981)

10 Appeal from Philip drunk to Philip sober.
paraphrase of the words of an unidentified woman alluding to Philip II of Macedon (382–336 BC), in Valerius Maximus Facta ac Dicta Memorabilia (AD c.32) bk. 6, ch. 2

11 Back and side go bare, go bare,
Both foot and hand go cold:
But belly God send thee good ale enough,
Whether it be new or old.
Gammer Gurton's Needle (1575) act 2 'Song', the play being attributed to William Stevenson (c.1530–75) and also to John Still (1543–1608), the song possibly of earlier origin

12 A beast, but a just beast.
a schoolboy's description of Dr Temple, Headmaster of Rugby School
F.E. Kitchener *Rugby Memoir of Archbishop Temple 1857–1869* (1907) ch. 3

13 The best defence against the atom bomb is not to be there when it goes off.
contributor to *British Army Journal*, in *Observer* 20 February 1949

14 Bigamy is having one husband too many. Monogamy is the same.
Erica Jong *Fear of Flying* (1973) ch. 1 (epigraph)

15 Cathedral time is five minutes later than standard time.
order of service leaflet, Christ Church Cathedral, Oxford, 1990s

16 The Christians to the lions!
saying reported by the Roman theologian **TERTULLIAN**; see **TERTULLIAN** 802:10

17 The cloud of unknowing.
title of mystical prose work (14th century)

18 Collapse of Stout Party.
supposed standard dénouement in Victorian humour
R. Pearsall *Collapse of Stout Party* (1975) introduction

19 A committee is a group of the unwilling, chosen from the unfit, to do the unnecessary.
various attributions (origin unknown)

20 A community in which power, wealth and opportunity are in the hands of the many not the few, where the rights we enjoy reflect the duties we owe . . . in which the enterprise of the market and the rigour of competition are joined with the forces of partnership and cooperation.
new Clause Four of the Labour Party constitution, passed at a special conference 29 April 1995; see **ANONYMOUS** 21:3

21 A Company for carrying on an undertaking of Great Advantage, but no one to know what it is.
The South Sea Company Prospectus (1711), in Virginia Cowles *The Great Swindle* (1963) ch. 5

22 A contingency for the space shuttle has been declared.
Mission Control in Houston indicating that contact with the space shuttle Columbia had been lost
in *Sunday Times* 2 February 2003

23 [Death is] nature's way of telling you to slow down.
American life insurance proverb, in *Newsweek* 25 April 1960

24 Do not fold, spindle or mutilate.
instruction on punched cards (found in this form in the 1950s, and in differing forms from the 1930s)

25 Earned a precarious living by taking in one another's washing.
attributed to Mark **TWAIN** by William **MORRIS**, in *The Commonweal* 6 August 1887

26 The eternal triangle.
book review title, in *Daily Chronicle* 5 December 1907

27 Every country has its own constitution; ours is absolutism moderated by assassination.
Ernst Friedrich Herbert, Count Münster, quoting 'an

intelligent Russian', in *Political Sketches of the State of Europe, 1814–1867* (1868)

1 Everyman, I will go with thee, and be thy guide,
In thy most need to go by thy side.

spoken by Knowledge

Everyman (c.1509–19) l. 522

2 Expletive deleted.

in *Submission of Recorded Presidential Conversations to the Committee on the Judiciary of the House of Representatives by President Richard M. Nixon* 30 April 1974, appendix 1

3 Exterminate . . . the treacherous English, walk over General French's contemptible little army.

allegedly a copy of Orders issued by the Kaiser **WILHELM II** *but most probably fabricated by the British*

annexe to BEF [British Expeditionary Force] Routine Orders of 24 September 1914, in Arthur Ponsonby *Falsehood in Wartime* (1928) ch. 10; see **CROMWELL** 260:18

4 Faster than a speeding bullet! . . . Look! Up in the sky! It's a bird! It's a plane! It's Superman! Yes, it's Superman! Strange visitor from another planet . . . Who can change the course of mighty rivers, bend steel with his bare hands, and who—disguised as Clark Kent, mild-mannered reporter for a great metropolitan newspaper—fights a never ending battle for truth, justice and the American way!

Superman (US radio show, 1940 onwards) preamble

5 The fault is great in man or woman
Who steals a goose from off a common;
But what can plead that man's excuse
Who steals a common from a goose?

in *The Tickler Magazine* 1 February 1821

6 Fee-fi-fo-fum
I smell the blood of an Englishman.
Be he alive or be he dead
I'll grind his bones to make my bread.

versions of this rhyme exist from the early 15th century in tales involving man-eating giants, and survive in 'Jack the Giant-Killer' and 'Jack and the Beanstalk'; see **NASHE** 568:24, **SHAKESPEARE** 716:5

Iona and Peter Opie *The Classic Fairy Tales* (1974)

7 A form of statuary which no careful father would wish his daughter, or no discerning young man his fiancée, to see.

on Jacob **EPSTEIN**'s *sculptures for the former BMA building in the Strand, London*

in *Evening Standard* 19 June 1908

8 [A] frozen flash of history.

Pulitzer Prize (1945) citation on the photograph by Joe Rosenthal (1911–2006) of US Marines raising the flag at Iwo Jima

quoted in *New York Times* 9 May 1945

9 A gentleman haranguing on the perfection of our law, and that it was equally open to the poor and the rich, was answered by another, 'So is the London Tavern'.

Tom Paine's Jests (1794) no. 23; also attributed to John Horne Tooke (1736–1812) in W. Hazlitt *The Spirit of the Age* (1825) 'Mr Horne Tooke'; see **MATHEW** 527:18

10 Good at a fight, but better at a play,
Godlike in giving, but—the devil to pay!

lines written on a cast from **SHERIDAN**'s *hand*

Thomas Moore *Memoirs of the Life of . . . Richard Brinsley Sheridan* (1825) ch. 21

11 Great Chatham with his sabre drawn
Stood waiting for Sir Richard Strachan;
Sir Richard, longing to be at 'em,
Stood waiting for the Earl of Chatham.

'At Walcheren, 1809'; attributed to Joseph Jekyll (1753–1837)

12 Have you heard? The Prime Minister has resigned and Northcliffe has sent for the King.

joke circulating in 1919, suggesting that Lord **NORTHCLIFFE**, **LLOYD GEORGE**'s *implacable enemy, would succeed him as Prime Minister*

Hamilton Fyfe *Northcliffe, an Intimate Biography* (1930) ch. 16

13 He may be one of its [the Church's] buttresses, but certainly not one of its pillars, for he is never found within it.

of John Scott, Lord Eldon (1751–1838)

H. Twiss *Public and Private Life of Eldon* (1844) vol. 3 (later attributed to Lord **MELBOURNE**)

14 He talked shop like a tenth muse.

on **GLADSTONE**'s *Budget speeches*

G. W. E. Russell *Collections and Recollections* (1898) ch. 12

15 He tickles this age that can
Call Tullia's ape a marmasyte
And Leda's goose a swan.

'Fara diddle dyno', in Thomas Weelkes *Airs or Fantastic Spirits* (1608); reprinted in N. Ault *Elizabethan Lyrics* (1925)

16 Hierusalem, my happy home
When shall I come to thee?
When shall my sorrows have an end,
Thy joys when shall I see?

'Hierusalem' (c.1600 hymn)

17 Hip young gunslinger.

New Musical Express advertisement for a journalist in 1976, answered by Julie **BURCHILL**; *the phrase was coined by the assistant editor Tony Tyler (1943–2006)*

Julie Burchill *I Knew I Was Right* (1998)

18 How different, how very different from the home life of our own dear Queen!

comment overheard at a performance of Cleopatra by Sarah Bernhardt

Irvin S. Cobb *A Laugh a Day* (1924) (probably apocryphal)

19 Icham of Irlaunde
Ant of the holy londe of irlonde
Gode sir pray ich ye
for of saynte charite,
come ant daunce wyt me,
in irlaunde.

fourteenth century

20 The idea that the PM gets integrated advice is nonsense. You could not see a more *unjoined* system. To say they have imported the White

House to No. 10—Washington to Downing Street—is absolutely right.

a senior Whitehall figure on the Blair administration, January 2000

> Peter Hennessy *The Prime Minister: the Office and its Holders since 1945* (2000)

1 I don't like the family Stein!
There is Gert, there is Ep, there is Ein.
Gert's writings are punk,
Ep's statues are junk,
Nor can anyone understand Ein.

> rhyme current in the US in the 1920s; R. Graves and A. Hodge *The Long Weekend* (1940) ch. 12

2 I feel no pain dear mother now
But oh, I am so dry!
O take me to a brewery
And leave me there to die.

> parody of 'The Collier's Dying Child'; see **FARMER** 323:15

3 If you really want to make a million . . . the quickest way is to start your own religion.

> previously attributed to L. Ron Hubbard (1911–86) in B. Corydon and L. Ron Hubbard Jr. *L. Ron Hubbard* (1987), but attribution subsequently rejected by L. Ron Hubbard Jr., who also dissociated himself from this book

4 I'm armed with more than complete steel—The justice of my quarrel.

> *Lust's Dominion* (1657) act 4, sc. 3 (attributed to **MARLOWE**, though of doubtful authorship)

5   In Affectionate Remembrance
                        of
                ENGLISH CRICKET,
            Which Died at The Oval
                        on
                29th August, 1882.
        Deeply lamented by a large circle of
        sorrowing friends and acquaintances.
                    R. I. P.
        N. B.—The body will be cremated and
            the ashes taken to Australia.

following England's defeat by the Australians

> in *Sporting Times* September 1882

6 I saw my lady weep,
And Sorrow proud to be exalted so
In those fair eyes where all perfections keep.
Her face was full of woe;
But such a woe, believe me, as wins more
    hearts,
Than Mirth can do with her enticing parts.

> lute song set by John Dowland, in *New Oxford Book of Sixteenth-Century Verse* (1991)

7 It became necessary to destroy the town to save it.

statement by unidentified US Army Major, referring to Ben Tre in Vietnam

> in Associated Press Report, *New York Times* 8 February 1968

8 It's taking your face in your hands.

*on the dangers of sitting for one's portrait to John Singer **SARGENT***

> W. Graham Robertson *Time Was* (1931) ch. 21

9 Jacques Brel is alive and well and living in Paris.

title of musical entertainment (1968–72) which triggered numerous imitations

10 June 3, Cold Harbor. I was killed.

the diary entry of a Unionist soldier, found in his pocket after the failed attack on Cold Harbor, 3 June 1864
attributed, perhaps apocryphal

11 Just when we thought it was safe to go back in the water, the sharks are circling again.

unidentified British Cabinet Minister on the forthcoming report of the European Convention

> in *Daily Telegraph* 11 June 2003 (electronic edition); see **CLARK** 233:11, **TAGLINES FOR FILMS** 788:6

12 Liberty is always unfinished business.

title of 36th Annual Report of the American Civil Liberties Union, 1 July 1955–30 June 1956

13 Like Caesar's wife, all things to all men.

impartiality, as described by a newly-elected mayor

> G. W. E. Russell *Collections and Recollections* (1898) ch. 30; see **CAESAR** 192:18

14 Little Englanders.

term applied to anti-imperialists

> in *Westminster Gazette* 1 August 1895; in *Pall Mall Gazette* 16 September 1884 the phrase 'believe in a little England' occurs

15 Lizzie Borden took an axe
And gave her mother forty whacks;
When she saw what she had done
She gave her father forty-one!

after the acquittal of Lizzie Borden, in June 1893, from the charge of murdering her father and stepmother at Fall River, Massachusetts on 4 August 1892
popular rhyme

16 Lloyd George knew my father,
My father knew Lloyd George.

> two-line comic song, sung to the tune of 'Onward, Christian Soldiers' and possibly by Tommy Rhys Roberts (1910–75)

17 London, thou art of townes *A per se*.

> 'London' (poem of unknown authorship, previously attributed to William Dunbar, c.1465–c.1530)

18 London, thou art the flower of cities all!
Gemme of all joy, jasper of jocunditie.

> 'London' l. 16

19 Love me little, love me long,
Is the burden of my song.

> 'Love me little, love me long' (1569–70)

20 CHILD: Mamma, are Tories born wicked, or do they grow wicked afterwards?
MOTHER: They are born wicked, and grow worse.

> G. W. E. Russell *Collections and Recollections* (1898) ch. 10

21 Medicine for the soul.

inscription on the library of Ramses II at Thebes (c.1292–1225 BC)

> Diodorus Siculus *Bibliotheca Historica* 60–30 BC

22 The ministry of all the talents.

name given ironically to William Grenville's coalition of 1806, and also applied to later coalitions

> G. W. Cooke *The History of Party* (1837) vol. 3

23 Miss Buss and Miss Beale
Cupid's darts do not feel.

How different from us,
Miss Beale and Miss Buss.
*of the Headmistress of the North London Collegiate School
and the Principal of the Ladies' College, Cheltenham*
   rhyme, c.1884

1 Most Gracious Queen, we thee implore
To go away and sin no more,
But if that effort be too great,
To go away at any rate.
epigram on Caroline of Brunswick, wife of **GEORGE IV**
   letter from Francis Burton to Lord Colchester, 15 November
   1820; in *Diary and Correspondence of Lord Colchester* (1861)
   vol. 3

2 Multiplication is vexation,
Division is as bad;
The Rule of Three doth puzzle me,
And Practice drives me mad.
   Lean's Collectanea vol. 4 (1904) (possibly 16th-century)

3 My name is George Nathaniel Curzon,
I am a most superior person.
of Lord **CURZON**
   The Masque of Balliol (c.1870), in W. G. Hiscock *The Balliol
   Rhymes* (1939); see **BEECHING** 65:16, **SPRING-RICE** 769:2

4 The nature of God is a circle of which the
centre is everywhere and the circumference is
nowhere.
   said to have been traced to a lost treatise of Empedocles;
   quoted in the *Roman de la Rose*, and by St Bonaventura in
   Itinerarius Mentis in Deum ch. 5, closing line

5 The nearest thing to death in life
Is David Patrick Maxwell Fyfe,
Though underneath that gloomy shell
He does himself extremely well.
on Lord **KILMUIR**
   E. Grierson *Confessions of a Country Magistrate* (1972), said to
   have been current on the Northern circuit in the late 1930s

6 No beauty she doth miss,
When all her robes are on;
But beauty's self she is,
When all her robes are gone.
   'Madrigal', in F. Davison (ed.) *Poetical Rhapsody* (1602)

7 The noise, my dear! And the people!
*of the retreat from Dunkirk, May 1940; the saying has also
been attributed to Ernest Thesiger of the First World War*
   Anthony Rhodes *Sword of Bone* (1942) ch. 22

8 No more Latin, no more French,
No more sitting on a hard board bench.
No more beetles in my tea
Making googly eyes at me;
No more spiders in my bath
Trying hard to make me laugh.
children's rhyme for the end of term
   Iona and Peter Opie *Lore and Language of Schoolchildren*
   (1959) ch. 13

9 Not so much a programme, more a way of life!
   title of BBC television series, 1964

10 O Death, thou comest when I had thee least in
mind.
   Everyman (c.1509–19) l. 119

11 O God, if there be a God, save my soul, if I
have a soul!
*prayer of a common soldier before the battle of Blenheim,
1704*
   in *Notes and Queries* vol. 173, no. 15 (9 October 1937); quoted
   in John Henry Newman *Apologia pro Vita Sua* (1864)

12 Oh, the comfort—the inexpressible comfort of
feeling safe with a person, having neither to
weigh thoughts, nor measure words, but pouring
them all out, just as they are, chaff and grain
together; knowing that a faithful hand will take
and sift them—keep what is worth keeping—
and with the breath of kindness blow the rest
away.
   19th century saying, often attributed to George **ELIOT** or
   Dinah Mulock Craik (1826–87)

13 Once upon a time . . .
traditional opening to a story, especially a fairy story
   recorded from 1595

14 One Cartwright brought a Slave from Russia,
and would scourge him, for which he was
questioned: and it was resolved, That England
was too pure an Air for Slaves to breathe in.
   'In the 11th of Elizabeth' (17 November 1568–16 November
   1569), in John Rushworth *Historical Collections* (1680–1722) vol.
   2; see **COWPER** 256:9

15 On Waterloo's ensanguined plain
Full many a gallant man was slain,
But none, by sabre or by shot,
Fell half so flat as Walter Scott.
on Sir Walter **SCOTT**'s poem 'The Field of Waterloo' (1815)
   U. Pope-Hennessy *The Laird of Abbotsford* (1932) ch. 9

16 Peace, order, and good government.
   British North America Act 1867 sect. 91, introduction

17 A place within the meaning of the Act.
   usually taken to be a reference to the Betting Act 1853, sect.
   2, which banned off-course betting on horse-races

18 The plan is called 'Shock and Awe', and its goal
is 'the psychological destruction of the enemy's
will to fight'.
   in *New Yorker* 10 February 2003; see **ULLMAN AND WADE** 821:9

19 Please do not shoot the pianist. He is doing his
best.
printed notice in a dancing saloon
   Oscar Wilde *Impressions of America* 'Leadville' (c.1882–3)

20 Please to remember the Fifth of November,
Gunpowder Treason and Plot.
We know no reason why gunpowder treason
Should ever be forgot.
   traditional rhyme on the Gunpowder Plot (1605)

21 Prudence is the other woman in Gordon's life.
of Gordon **BROWN**
   unidentified aide, quoted in BBC News online (Budget
   Briefing), 20 March 1998

22 Psychological flaws.
on which, according to an unnamed source, Gordon **BROWN**
needed to 'get a grip'
   in *Observer* 18 January 1998; attributed to Alastair **CAMPBELL**
   by Bernard Ingham in minutes of the Parliamentary Select

Committee on Public Administration, 2 June 1998, but denied by Campbell in evidence to the Committee, 23 June 1998

1 *Puella Rigensis ridebat*
Quam tigris in tergo vehebat;
Externa profecta,
Interna revecta,
Risusque cum tigre manebat.

There was a young lady of Riga
Who smiled as she rode on a tiger;
They returned from the ride
With the lady inside,
And the smile on the face of the tiger.
variants exist from 1924 or earlier

2 The [*or* A] quick brown fox jumps over the lazy dog.
used by keyboarders to ensure that all letters of the alphabet are functioning
R. Hunter Middleton's introduction to *The Quick Brown Fox* (1945) by Richard H. Templeton Jr.

3 The rabbit has a charming face:
Its private life is a disgrace.
I really dare not name to you
The awful things that rabbits do.
'The Rabbit', in *The Week-End Book* (1925)

4 Raise the stone, and there thou shalt find me, cleave the wood and there am I.
Oxyrhynchus Papyri, in B. P. Grenfell and A. S. Hunt (eds.) *Sayings of Our Lord* (1897) Logion 5, l. 23

5 Say it ain't so, Joe.
'Shoeless' Joe Jackson and seven other Chicago players were charged with being bribed to lose the 1919 World Baseball Series
plea said to have been made by a boy as Jackson emerged from the hearing, September 1920

6 Says Tweed to Till—
'What gars ye rin sae still?'
Says Till to Tweed—
'Though ye rin with speed
And I rin slaw,
For ae man that ye droon
I droon twa'.
'Two Rivers' (traditional rhyme)

7 Science finds, industry applies, man conforms.
subtitle of guidebook to 1933 Chicago World's Fair

8 See the happy moron,
He doesn't give a damn,
I wish I were a moron,
My God! perhaps I am!
in *Eugenics Review* July 1929

9 Seven wealthy towns contend for HOMER dead
Through which the living HOMER begged his bread.
epilogue to *Aesop at Tunbridge; or, a Few Selected Fables in Verse* By No Person of Quality (1698); see HEYWOOD 398:4

10 Since first I saw your face, I resolved to honour and renown ye;
If now I be disdained, I wish my heart had never known ye.
What? I that loved and you that liked, shall we begin to wrangle?

No, no, no, my heart is fast, and cannot disentangle.
song set by Thomas Ford in *Music of Sundry Kinds* (1607)

11 So cryptic as to be almost meaningless. If there is a meaning, it is doubtless objectionable.
banning the film The Seashell and the Clergyman *(1929)*
The British Board of Film Censors; J. C. Robertson *Hidden Cinema* (1989) ch. 1

12 So long as there shall but one hundred of us remain alive, we will never subject ourselves to the dominion of the English. For it is not glory, it is not riches, neither is it honour, but it is freedom alone that we fight and contend for, which no honest man will lose but with his life.
to the Pope, asserting the independence of Scotland
'Declaration of Arbroath', a letter sent by the Scottish Parliament, 6 April 1320

13 So much chewing gum for the eyes.
small boy's definition of certain television programmes
James Beasley Simpson *Best Quotes of '50, '55, '56* (1957)

14 Sumer is icumen in,
Lhude sing cuccu!
Groweth sed, and bloweth med,
And springth the wude nu.
'Cuckoo Song' (c.1250), sung annually at Reading Abbey gateway and first recorded by John Fornset, a monk of Reading Abbey; see POUND 620:15

15 The Sun himself cannot forget
His fellow traveller.
on Sir Francis DRAKE
Wit's Recreations (1640) epigram no. 146

16 That blessed word Mesopotamia.
supposed to have greatly consoled a pious but illiterate old woman
traditional, from the 1860s; see also GARRICK 349:16

17 There is a lady sweet and kind,
Was never face so pleased my mind;
I did but see her passing by,
And yet I love her till I die.
found on the reverse of leaf 53 of 'Popish Kingdome or reigne of Antichrist', in Latin verse by Thomas Naogeorgus, and Englished by Barnabe Googe; printed in 1570; sometimes attributed to Thomas Forde

18 There is so much good in the worst of us,
And so much bad in the best of us,
That it hardly becomes any of us
To talk about the rest of us.
attributed, among others, to Edward Wallis Hoch (1849–1945) on the grounds of it having appeared in his Kansas publication, the *Marion Record*, though in fact disclaimed by him ('behooves' sometimes substituted for 'becomes')

19 There shall be a Scottish parliament.
first clause of the Scotland Act, 1998; see DEWAR 275:7

20 This is a rotten argument, but it should be good enough for their lordships on a hot summer afternoon.
annotation to a ministerial brief, said to have been read out inadvertently in the House of Lords
Lord Home *The Way the Wind Blows* (1976)

1 Though I yield to no one in my admiration for Mr Coolidge, I do wish he did not look as if he had been weaned on a pickle.

anonymous remark, in Alice Roosevelt Longworth Crowded Hours *(1933) ch. 21*

2 Too small to live in and too large to hang on a watch-chain.

Chiswick House described by a guest

Cecil Roberts And so to Bath *(1940) ch. 4*

3 To secure for the workers by hand or by brain the full fruits of their industry and the most equitable distribution thereof that may be possible upon the basis of the common ownership of the means of production, distribution, and exchange.

Clause Four of the Labour Party's Constitution of 1918 (revised 1929); the commitment to common ownership of services was largely removed in 1995; see **ANONYMOUS** *16:20*

4 We are putting passengers off in small boats . . . Engine room getting flooded . . . CQ.

CQD was the original SOS call for shipping

last signals sent from the Titanic, *15 April 1912*

5 Weep you no more, sad fountains;
What need you flow so fast?

lute song (1603) set to music by John Dowland, in New Oxford Book of Sixteenth-Century Verse *(1991)*

6 We hold these truths to be self-evident, that all men are created equal, that they are endowed by their Creator with certain unalienable rights, that among these are life, liberty and the pursuit of happiness.

The American Declaration of Independence, 4 July 1776; see **JEFFERSON** *431:6*

7 We want eight, and we won't wait.

on the construction of Dreadnoughts

George Wyndham, speech in The Times *29 March 1909*

8 Western wind, when will thou blow,
The small rain down can rain?
Christ, if my love were in my arms
And I in my bed again!

'Western Wind' (published 1790) in New Oxford Book of Sixteenth-Century Verse *(1991)*

9 When I was a little boy, I had but a little wit,
'Tis a long time ago, and I have no more yet;
Nor ever ever shall, until that I die,
For the longer I live the more fool am I.

Wit and Mirth, an Antidote against Melancholy (1684 ed.)

10 Where is the man who has the power and skill
To stem the torrent of a woman's will?
For if she will, she will, you may depend on't;
And if she won't, she won't; so there's an end on't.

inscription on the pillar erected on the mount in the Dane John Field, Canterbury, in Examiner *31 May 1829*

11 Whilst Adam slept, Eve from his side arose:
Strange his first sleep should be his last repose.

'The Consequence'

12 Who is in charge of the clattering train?

poem on Major Marindin's Report to the Board of Trade on the railway collision near Eastleigh

'Death and his Brother Sleep' in Punch *4 October 1890; see* **BEAVERBROOK** *64:1*

13 The whole is more than the sum of the parts.

traditional saying, probably deriving from Aristotle; see **ARISTOTLE** *27:4*

14 With a heart of furious fancies,
Whereof I am commander;
With a burning spear,
And a horse of air,
To the wilderness I wander.

'Tom o' Bedlam'

15 Would you like to sin
With Elinor Glyn
On a tigerskin?
Or would you prefer
To err
With her
On some other fur?

1907 rhyme, in A. Glyn Elinor Glyn *(1955) bk. 2, sect. 30*

16 Yet, if his majesty our sovereign lord
Should of his own accord
Friendly himself invite,
And say 'I'll be your guest tomorrow night',
How should we stir ourselves, call and command
All hands to work! . . .
But at the coming of the King of Heaven
All's set at six and seven:
We wallow in our sin.
Christ cannot find a chamber in the inn.
We entertain Him always like a stranger,
And as at first still lodge Him in the manger.

from Christ Church MS

17 You should make a point of trying every experience once, excepting incest and folk-dancing.

Arnold Bax (1883–1953), quoting 'a sympathetic Scot' in Farewell My Youth *(1943)*

18 You were a premature anti-Fascist.

interviewer for Yale Classics Department in 1946, on hearing that the young Bernard Knox had fought with the International Brigade in the Spanish Civil War

Bernard Knox 'Premature Anti-Fascist' (Bill Susman Lecture Series, New York, 1998)

FRENCH

19 *Ça ira.*

Things will work out.

refrain of 'Carillon national', popular song of the French Revolution (c. July 1790), translated by William Doyle; the phrase is believed to originate with Benjamin **FRANKLIN**, *who may have uttered it in 1776 when asked for news of the American Revolution*

20 *Cet animal est très méchant,*
Quand on l'attaque il se défend.

This animal is very bad; when attacked it defends itself.

'La Ménagerie' (1868 song) by 'Théodore P. K.'

1 *Chevalier sans peur et sans reproche.*

Fearless, blameless knight.

> description in contemporary chronicles of Pierre Bayard
> (1476–1524)

2 *Il y avait un jeune homme de Dijon,*
Qui n'avait que peu de religion.
Il dit: 'Quant à moi,
Je déteste tous les trois,
Le Père, et le Fils, et le Pigeon.'

There was a young man of Dijon,
Who had only a little religion,
He said: 'As for me,
I detest all the three,
The Father, the Son, and the Pigeon.'

> *The Norman Douglas Limerick Book* (1969, privately printed,
> 1928, as *Some Limericks*) introduction

3 RIDDLE: *Je suis le capitaine de vingt-quatre soldats, et*
sans moi Paris serait pris?
ANSWER: *A.*

RIDDLE: I am the captain of twenty-four soldiers,
and without me Paris would be taken?
ANSWER: A [i.e. 'Paris' minus 'a' = *pris* taken].

> the saying ' With twenty-six lead soldiers [the characters of
> the alphabet set up for printing] I can conquer the world'
> may derive from this riddle, but probably arose
> independently
> Hugh Rowley *Puniana: or, Thoughts wise and otherwise* (1867)

4 *Laissez-nous-faire.*

Allow us to do [it].

> remark dating from c.1664, in *Journal Oeconomique* Paris, April
> 1751: 'Monsieur Colbert assembled several deputies of
> commerce at his house to ask what could be done for
> commerce; the most rational and the least flattering among
> them answered him in one word: "Laissez-nous-faire"'; see
> **ARGENSON** 26:11, **QUESNAY** 651:16

5 *L'amour est aveugle; l'amitié ferme les yeux.*

Love is blind; friendship closes its eyes.

> proverbial saying; see **PROVERBS** 638:6

6 *Le monde est plein de fous, et qui n'en veut pas voir*
Doit se tenir tout seul, et casser son miroir.

The world is full of fools, and he who would
see none should live alone and smash his mirror.

> adaptation from an original form attributed to Claude Le
> Petit (1640–65) in *Discours satiriques* (1686)

7 *L'ordre règne à Varsovie.*

Order reigns in Warsaw.

> after the brutal suppression of an uprising, the newspaper
> *Moniteur* reported, 16 September 1831, 'L'ordre et la tranquillité
> sont entièrement rétablis dans la capitale [Order and calm are
> completely restored in the capital]'; on the same day Count
> Sebastiani, minister of foreign affairs, declared: 'La tranquillité
> règne à Varsovie [Peace reigns in Warsaw]'

8 *Nous n'irons plus aux bois, les lauriers sont coupés.*

We'll to the woods no more,
The laurels all are cut.

> old nursery rhyme, quoted by Théodore de Banville in *Les
> Cariatides, les stalactites* (1842–6); translated by A. E.
> Housman in *Last Poems* (1922) introductory

9 *Revenons à ces moutons.*

Let us get back to these sheep [i.e. 'Let us get
back to the subject'].

> *Maistre Pierre Pathelin* l. 1191 (often quoted as 'Retournons à
> nos moutons [Let us return to our sheep]')

10 *Si le Roi m'avait donné,*
Paris, sa grand'ville,
Et qu'il me fallût quitter
L'amour de ma mie,
Je dirais au roi Henri:
'Reprenez votre Paris:
J'aime mieux ma mie, au gué,
J'aime mieux ma mie.'

If the king had given me Paris, his great city,
and if I were required to give up my darling's
love, I would say to King Henry: 'Take your
Paris back; I prefer my darling, by the ford, I
prefer my darling.'

> popular song, attributed to Antoine de Navarre (1518–62);
> quoted in this form by Molière in *Le Misanthrope* act 1, sc. 2

11 *Toujours perdrix!*

Always partridge!

> *attributed to a confessor of* **HENRI IV**, *who rebuked the king*
> *for his sexual liaisons and thereafter was served nothing but*
> *partridge*
> G. Büchmann *Geflügelte Worte* (1874 ed.)

12 *Tout passe, tout casse, tout lasse.*

Everything passes, everything perishes,
everything palls.

> Charles Cahier *Quelques six mille proverbes* (1856) no. 1718

GERMAN

13 *Arbeit macht frei.*

Work liberates.

> words inscribed on the gates of Dachau concentration camp,
> 1933, and subsequently on those of Auschwitz

14 *Jedem das Seine.*

To each his own.

> *often quoted as 'Everyone gets what he deserves'*
> inscription on the gate of Buchenwald concentration camp,
> c. 1937; see **BOLD** 131:8

15 *Kommt der Krieg ins Land*
Gibt's Lügen wie Sand.

When war enters a country
It produces lies like sand.

> epigraph to Arthur Ponsonby *Falsehood in Wartime* (1928)

GREEK

16 Let no one enter who does not know geometry
[mathematics].

> *inscription on* **PLATO**'s *door, probably at the Academy at*
> *Athens*
> Elias Philosophus *In Aristotelis Categorias Commentaria*; in A.
> Busse (ed.) *Commentaria in Aristotelem Graeca* (1900) vol. 18,
> pt. 1

17 Nothing in excess.

> *inscribed on the temple of Apollo at Delphi*
> variously ascribed to the Seven Wise Men; see **PROVERBS**
> 637:8

18 The very best thing for a person is health,
Second good looks and third honest wealth,

the fourth is to be in the prime of your life
With people around you who cause you no
strife.
drinking song, quoted in Plato *Gorgias* 451e

1 Whenever God prepares evil for a man, He first
damages his mind, with which he deliberates.
scholiastic annotation to Sophocles's *Antigone* l. 622; see
PROVERBS 647:18

LATIN

2 *Adeste, fideles,*
laeti triumphantes;
venite, venite in Bethlehem;
natum videte regem angelorum . . .
venite, adoremus Dominum.

O come, all ye faithful,
Joyful and triumphant,
O come ye, O come ye to Bethlehem;
Come and behold him,
Born the King of angels:
O come, let us adore him . . . Christ the Lord!
French or German hymn (*c.*1743) in *Murray's Hymnal* (1852);
translation based on that of F. Oakeley (1841)

3 *Ave Caesar, morituri te salutant.*

Hail Caesar, those who are about to die salute
you.
gladiators saluting the Roman Emperor
Suetonius *Lives of the Caesars* 'Claudius' ch. 21

4 *Ave verum corpus,*
natum ex Maria Virgine.

Hail the true body, born of the Virgin Mary.
Eucharistic hymn, probably dating from the 14th century

5 *Caveant consules ne quid res publica detrimenti*
capiat.

Let the consuls see to it that no harm come to
the state.
senatorial 'ultimate decree' in the Roman Republic; see
Cicero *Pro Milone* ch. 70

6 *Cras amet qui nunquam amavit, quique amavit cras*
amet!

Let those love now, who never loved before:
Let those who always loved, now love the more.
Pervigilium Veneris (translated by Thomas Parnell, 1722)

7 *Gaudeamus igitur,*
Juvenes dum sumus
Post jucundam juventutem,
Post molestam senectutem,
Nos habebit humus.

Let us then rejoice,
While we are young.
After the pleasures of youth
And the burdens of old age
Earth will hold us.
medieval students' song, traced to 1267, but revised in the
18th century

8 *Meum est propositum*
In taberna mori,
Ut sint vina proxima
Morientis ori.
Tunc cantabunt laetius

Angelorum chori:
'Sit Deus propitius
Huic potatori!'

I desire to end my days in a tavern drinking,
May some Christian hold for me the glass when
I am shrinking;
That the Cherubim may cry, when they see me
sinking,
'God be merciful to a soul of this gentleman's
way of thinking.'
The Arch-poet (fl. 1159–67) 'Estuans intrinsecus ira vehementi'
(translated by Leigh Hunt)

9 *Omnia dispono solus meritos[que] corono. Quos*
scelus exercet me judice poena coercet.

I alone dispose of all things and crown the just.
Those who follow crime I judge and punish.
around the mandorla enclosing the figure of Christ
inscription on the western portal of St-Lazare, Autun; carved
by Gislebertus, c.1130

10   *Pereat, qui crastina curat!*
Mors aurem vellens 'vivite' ait, 'venio.'

Away with him who heeds the morrow! Death,
plucking the ear, cries: 'Live; I come!'
Copa l. 37, formerly attributed to **VIRGIL**, (translated by H.
Rushton Fairclough)

11 *Quidquid agis, prudenter agas, et respice finem.*

Whatever you do, do cautiously, and look to the
end.
Gesta Romanorum no. 103

12 *Sic transit gloria mundi.*

Thus passes the glory of the world.
said during the coronation of a new Pope, while flax is
burned to represent the transitoriness of earthly glory
used at the coronation of Alexander V in Pisa, 7 July 1409,
but earlier in origin; see **THOMAS À KEMPIS** 804:14

13 *Vox et praeterea nihil.*

A voice and nothing more.
describing a nightingale
Plutarch *Moralia* sect. 233a, no. 15

OLD ENGLISH

14 *Hige sceal þe heardra, heorte þe cenre,*
mod sceal þe mare, þe ure mægen lytlað.

Thought shall be the harder, heart the keener,
courage the greater, as our might lessens.
The Battle of Maldon (translated by R. K. Gordon, 1926)

15 *Hwæt! wē Gārdena in gēardagum*
þēodcyninga þrym gefrūnon,
hū ðā æþelingas ellen fremedon.

Listen!
        The fame of Danish kings
in days gone by, the daring feats
worked by those heroes are well known to us.
Beowulf, translated by Kevin Crossley-Holland

16 *þæs oferēode, þisses swā mæg.*

That passed over, so may this.
Deor

1 King Harold was killed and Earl Leofwine his brother and Earl Gyrth his brother . . . and the French remained masters of the field.
Anglo-Saxon Chronicle for 1066

2 There was no single hide nor a yard of land nor indeed was one ox or one cow or one pig left out, that was not put down in his record.
of William the Conqueror's commissioning of the Domesday Book
Anglo-Saxon Chronicle for 1087

3 Men said openly that Christ slept and His saints.
of England during the civil war between Stephen and Matilda
Anglo-Saxon Chronicle for 1137

OLD NORSE

4 *Deyr fé, deyja frændr,*
deyr sjalfr et sama;
en orðstirr deyr aldrigi
hveims sér góðar getr.

Cattle die, kinsmen die,
the self must also die;
but glory never dies,
for the man who is able to achieve it.
Hávamál ('Sayings of the High One'), c.10th century

5 The morning work has been unequal; I have spun twelve ells of yarn, and you have killed Kjartan.
Laxdæla Saga (c.12th century); the words of Gudrun

6 I did the worst to him I loved the most.
Laxdæla Saga (c.12th century); the words of Gudrun

Jean Anouilh 1910–87
French dramatist. See also HELLMAN 390:6

7 *Dieu est avec tout le monde . . . Et, en fin de compte, il est toujours avec ceux qui ont beaucoup d'argent et de grosses armées.*

God is on everyone's side . . . And, in the last analysis, he is on the side of those with plenty of money and large armies.
L'Alouette [The Lark] (1953); see **BUSSY-RABUTIN** 182:16, **VOLTAIRE** 834:16

8 *Maintenant le ressort est bandé. Cela n'a plus qu'à se dérouler tout seul. C'est cela qui est commode dans la tragédie. On donne le petit coup de pouce pour que cela démarre.*

The spring is wound up tight. It will uncoil of itself. That is what is so convenient in tragedy. The least little turn of the wrist will do the job. Anything will set it going.
Antigone (1944, translated by Lewis Galantiere, 1957)

9 *C'est propre, la tragédie. C'est reposant, c'est sûr.*
Tragedy is clean, it is restful, it is flawless.
Antigone (1944, translated by Lewis Galantiere, 1957)

10 *Il y a l'amour bien sûr. Et puis il y a la vie, son ennemie.*

There is love of course. And then there's life, its enemy.
Ardèle (1949)

11 *Vous savez bien que l'amour, c'est avant tout le don de soi!*

You know very well that love is, above all, the gift of oneself!
Ardèle (1949)

12 *Mourir, mourir . . . Mourir ce n'est rien. Commence donc par vivre. C'est moins drôle et c'est plus long.*

Dying is nothing. So start by living. It's less fun and it lasts longer.
Roméo et Jeannette (1946) act 3

13 *Il y a aura toujours un chien perdu quelquepart qui m'empêchera d'être heureux.*

There will always be a lost dog somewhere that will prevent me from being happy.
La Sauvage [The Restless Heart] (1938) act 3

Christopher Anstey 1724–1805
English writer

14 If ever I ate a good supper at night,
I dreamed of the devil, and waked in a fright.
The New Bath Guide (1766) Letter 4 'A Consultation of the Physicians'

15 You may go to Carlisle's, and to Almack's too;
And I'll give you my head if you find such a host,
For coffee, tea, chocolate, butter, and toast:
How he welcomes at once all the world and his wife,
And how civil to folk he ne'er saw in his life.
The New Bath Guide (1766) Letter 13 'A Public Breakfast'

F. Anstey (Thomas Anstey Guthrie)
1856–1934
English writer

16 Drastic measures is Latin for a whopping.
Vice Versa (1882) ch. 7

Susan Brownell Anthony 1820–1906
American feminist and political activist

17 Men, their rights, and nothing more; women, their rights, and nothing less.
motto of The Revolution, 8 January 1868

18 Join the union, girls, and together say, 'Equal Pay for Equal Work!'
in The Revolution 8 October 1869

19 Marriage, to women as to men, must be a luxury, not a necessity; an incident of life, not all of it.
speech, 1875

Minna Antrim 1861–1950
American writer

20 A fool bolts pleasure, then complains of moral indigestion.
Naked Truth and Veiled Allusions (1902)

Apelles
Greek painter of the 4th century BC

1 *Nulla dies sine linea.*

Not a day without a line.
proverbial summary of his philosophy
Pliny the Elder *Historia Naturalis* bk. 35, sect. 36

Guillaume Apollinaire 1880–1918
French poet. On Apollinaire: see **LOGUE** 498:10

2 *Les souvenirs sont cors de chasse*
Dont meurt le bruit parmi le vent.

Memories are hunting horns
Whose sound dies on the wind.
'Cors de Chasse' (1912)

3 *Sous le pont Mirabeau coule la Seine.*
Et nos amours, faut-il qu'il m'en souvienne?
La joie venait toujours après la peine.
Vienne la nuit, sonne l'heure,
Les jours s'en vont, je demeure.

Under Mirabeau Bridge flows the Seine.
And our loves, must I remember them?
Joy always came after pain.
Let night come, ring out the hour,
The days go by, I remain.
'Le Pont Mirabeau' (1912)

4 When man wanted to make a machine that
would walk he created the wheel, which does
not resemble a leg.
Les Mamelles de Tirésias (1918)

5 *On ne peut pas porter partout le cadavre de son père.*
One can't carry one's father's corpse about
everywhere.
Les peintres cubistes (1965) 'Méditations esthétiques: Sur la
peinture' pt. 1

Edward Appleton 1892–1965
English physicist

6 I do not mind what language an opera is sung in
so long as it is a language I don't understand.
in *Observer* 28 August 1955

Thomas Gold Appleton 1812–84
American epigrammatist

7 Good Americans, when they die, go to Paris.
Oliver Wendell Holmes *The Autocrat of the Breakfast Table*
(1858) ch. 6; see **PROVERBS** 633:16, **WILDE** 855:23

8 A Boston man is the east wind made flesh.
attributed

Arabian Nights Entertainments, or the Thousand and one Nights
A collection of stories written in Arabic

9 Who will change old lamps for new ones? . . .
new lamps for old ones?
'The History of Aladdin'

10 Open Sesame!
'The History of Ali Baba'

William Arabin 1773–1841
English judge

11 If ever there was a case of clearer evidence than
this of persons acting together, this case is that
case.
H. B. Churchill *Arabiniana* (1843)

12 Prisoner, God has given you good abilities,
instead of which you go about the country
stealing ducks.
also attributed to a Revd Mr Alderson, in Frederick Pollock
Essays in the Law (1922)

13 They will steal the very teeth out of your
mouth as you walk through the streets. *I know it*
from experience.
on the citizens of Uxbridge
Sir W. Ballantine *Some Experiences of a Barrister's Life* (1882)
vol. 1, ch. 6

Yasser Arafat 1929–2004
Palestinian statesman, President 1996–2004

14 Palestine is the cement that holds the Arab
world together, or it is the explosive that blows
it apart.
in *Time* 11 November 1974

Louis Aragon 1897–1982
French poet, essayist, and novelist

15 *Ô mois des floraisons mois des métamorphoses*
Mai qui fut sans nuage et Juin poignardé
Je n'oublierai jamais les lilas ni les roses
Ni ceux que le printemps dans ses plis a gardé.

O month of flowerings, month of
metamorphoses,
May without cloud and June that was stabbed,
I shall never forget the lilac and the roses
Nor those whom spring has kept in its folds.
'Les lilas et les roses' (1940)

Diane Arbus 1923–71
American photographer

16 A photograph is a secret about a secret. The
more it tells you the less you know.
Patricia Bosworth *Diane Arbus: a Biography* (1985)

John Arbuthnot 1667–1735
Scottish physician and pamphleteer

17 Law is a bottomless pit.
The History of John Bull (1712) title of first pamphlet

18 Curle (who is one of the new terrors of Death)
has been writing letters to every body for
memoirs of his life.
letter to Jonathan Swift, 13 January 1733, in H. Williams (ed.)
The Correspondence of Jonathan Swift vol. 4 (1965); see
LYNDHURST 506:1, **WETHERELL** 849:6

Archilochus
Greek poet of the 7th century BC

19 Not for me a tall and dandy captain with a
shaven chin,

flaunting all affectedly his dainty lovelocks as he
struts;
I'd prefer one short and bandy-legged, with a
heart within
stout and good, and firmly planted on his feet,
and full of guts.
> E. Diehl (ed.) *Anthologia Lyrica Graeca* (3rd ed., 1949–52) vol.
> 1, no. 60, translated by A. R. Burn

1 The fox knows many things—the hedgehog one
big one.
> E. Diehl (ed.) *Anthologia Lyrica Graeca* (3rd ed., 1949–52) vol.
> 1, no. 103; see **BERLIN** 73:9

Archimedes *c.*287–212 BC
Greek mathematician and inventor

2 Eureka! [I've got it!]
> Vitruvius Pollio *De Architectura* bk. 9, preface, sect. 10

3 Give me but one firm spot on which to stand,
and I will move the earth.
> *on the action of a lever*
> Pappus *Synagoge* bk. 8, proposition 10, sect. 11

Elizabeth Arden *c.*1880–1966
**Canadian-born American businesswoman. On Arden: see
RUBINSTEIN 672:2**

4 Nothing that costs only a dollar is worth having.
> attributed; in *Fortune* October 1973

Robert Ardrey 1908–80
American dramatist and evolutionist

5 Not in innocence, and not in Asia, was mankind
born.
> *African Genesis* (1961)

Hannah Arendt 1906–75
American political philosopher

6 It was as though in those last minutes he was
summing up the lessons that this long course in
human wickedness had taught us—the lesson of
the fearsome, word-and-thought-defying *banality
of evil.*
> *of Adolf Eichmann, responsible for the administration of the
> Nazi concentration camps*
> *Eichmann in Jerusalem* (1963) ch. 15

7 Only crime and the criminal, it is true, confront
us with the perplexity of radical evil; but only
the hypocrite is really rotten to the core.
> *On Revolution* (1963) ch. 2, pt. 5

8 The most radical revolutionary will become a
conservative on the day after the revolution.
> in *New Yorker* 12 September 1970

9 Under conditions of tyranny it is far easier to
act than to think.
> W. H. Auden *A Certain World* (1970)

Comte d'Argenson (Marc Pierre de Voyer d'Argenson) 1696–1764
French statesman; founder of the École Militaire, Paris

10 DESFONTAINES: I must live.
D'ARGENSON: I do not see the necessity.
> *on Desfontaines having produced a pamphlet satirizing
> D'Argenson, his benefactor*
> Voltaire *Alzire* (1736) 'Discours Préliminaire' footnote, in
> *Oeuvres Complètes Théâtre* (1877) vol. 2

Marquis d'Argenson (René Louis de Voyer d'Argenson) 1694–1757
French politician and political essayist

11 *Laisser-faire.*
No interference.
> *Mémoires et Journal Inédit du Marquis d'Argenson* (1858 ed.)
> vol. 5; see **ANONYMOUS** 22:4, **QUESNAY** 651:16

Ludovico Ariosto 1474–1533
Italian poet and dramatist

12 *Natura il fece, e poi roppe la stampa.*
Nature made him, and then broke the mould.
> *Orlando Furioso* (1532) canto 10, st. 84

Aristophanes *c.*450–*c.*385 BC
Greek comic dramatist

13 How about 'Cloudcuckooland'?
> *naming the capital city of the Birds*
> *The Birds* (414 BC) l. 819

14 This Second Logic then, I mean the Worse one,
They teach to talk unjustly, and—prevail.
> *The Clouds* (423 BC) l. 113; see **MILTON** 542:3

15 The old are in a second childhood.
> *The Clouds* (423 BC) l. 1417

16 But he was contented there, is contented here.
> *on* **SOPHOCLES** (there = *on earth and* here = *in Hades*)
> *The Frogs* (405 BC) l. 82

17 Brekekekex koax koax.
> *cry of the Frogs*
> *The Frogs* (405 BC) l. 209 and *passim*

18 You have all the characteristics of a popular
politician: a horrible voice, bad breeding and a
vulgar manner.
> *The Knights* (424 BC) l. 217

19 You will never make a crab walk straight.
> *Peace* l. 1083

20 Under every stone lurks a politician.
> *playing on the Greek proverb 'Under every stone lurks a
> scorpion'*
> *Thesmophoriazusae* l. 530

Aristotle 384–322 BC
**Greek philosopher and scientist. On Aristotle: see DANTE
264:17; see also ASCHAM 33:10**

21 Now, we may say that the most important
subjects about which all men deliberate and

deliberative orators harangue, are five in number, to wit: ways and means, war and peace, the defence of the country, imports and exports, legislation.
The Art of Rhetoric bk. 1, 1359b 19–23

1 Wit is educated insolence.
The Art of Rhetoric bk. 2, 1389b 12

2 All use metaphors in conversation, as well as proper and appropriate words.
The Art of Rhetoric bk. 3, 1404b 2

3 All men by nature desire knowledge.
Metaphysics bk. 1, ch. 1, 980a 22

4 Whenever anything which has several parts is such that the whole is something over and above its parts, and not just the sum of them all, like a heap, then it always has some cause.
Metaphysics 1045a 10f; see **ANONYMOUS** 21:13

5 Every art and every investigation, and likewise every practical pursuit or undertaking, seems to aim at some good: hence it has been well said that the Good is That at which all things aim.
Nicomachean Ethics bk. 1, 1094a 1–3

6 Therefore, the good of man must be the end [i.e. objective] of the science of politics.
Nicomachean Ethics bk. 1, 1094b 6–7

7 The end of this science [ethics] is not knowledge but action.
Nicomachean Ethics bk. 1 1095a; see **CARLYLE** 200:22

8 The Good of man is the active exercise of his soul's faculties in conformity with excellence or virtue . . . Moreover this activity must occupy a complete lifetime; for one swallow does not make spring, nor does one fine day; and similarly one day or a brief period of happiness does not make a man supremely blessed and happy.
Nicomachean Ethics bk. 1, 1098a 16–20

9 Neither by nature, then, nor contrary to nature do the virtues arise in us; nature gives us the capacity to receive them, and this capacity is brought to maturity by habit.
often quoted in the form 'We are what we repeatedly do'
Nicomachean Ethics bk. 2, 1103a 25

10 We learn an art or craft by doing the things that we shall have to do when we have learnt it.
often quoted as 'What we have to learn to do, we learn by doing'
Nicomachean Ethics bk. 2, 1103a 30

11 Now some think that all justice is of this sort, because that which is by nature is unchangeable and has everywhere the same force (as fire burns both here and in Persia), while they see change in the things recognized as just.
Nicomachean Ethics bk. 5, 1134b 26

12 The prudent man aspires not to pleasure, but to the absence of pain.
Nicomachean Ethics bk. 7, 1152b 15

13 In a word, everything that we choose we choose for the sake of something else—except happiness, which is an end.
Nicomachean Ethics bk. 10, 1177a 2–10

14 We make war that we may live in peace.
Nicomachean Ethics bk. 10, 1177b 5–6 (translated by M. Ostwald); see **VEGETIUS** 826:2

15 Politicians also have no leisure, because they are always aiming at something beyond political life itself, power and glory, or happiness.
Nicomachean Ethics bk. 10, 1177b 12–14

16 Even if our contact with eternal beings is slight, none the less because of its surpassing value this knowledge is a greater pleasure than our knowledge of everything around us.
On the Parts of Animals bk. 1, ch. 5, 644b 31; see **THOMAS AQUINAS** 805:10

17 In a sense the soul is all existing things.
On the Soul bk. 3, ch. 8, 431b 21

18 Man differs from other animals in that he is the most imitative of creatures, and he learns his earliest lessons by imitation. Also inborn in all of us is the instinct to enjoy works of imitation. What happens in actual experience is evidence of this; for we enjoy looking at the most accurate representations of things which in themselves we find painful to see, such as the forms of the lowest animals and of corpses.
Poetics ch. 4, 1448b (translated by T. S. Dorsch)

19 Tragedy is thus an imitation of an action that is worth serious attention, complete in itself and of some amplitude . . . by means of pity and fear bringing about the purgation of such emotions.
Poetics ch. 6, 1449b 24–8

20 A whole is that which has a beginning, a middle, and an end.
Poetics ch. 7, 1450b 26–7

21 So poetry is something more philosophical and more worthy of serious attention than history, for while poetry is concerned with universal truth, history treats of particular facts . . . The particular facts of the historian are what, say, Alcibiades did, or what happened to him.
Poetics ch. 9, 1451b 5–6

22 Probable impossibilities are to be preferred to improbable possibilities.
Poetics ch. 24, 1460a 26–7; see **AGATHON** 9:11

23 Sophocles said that he drew men as they ought to be, whereas Euripides drew them as they are.
Poetics ch. 25, 1460b 33–4

24 Man is by nature a political animal.
the literal meaning of the Greek is 'an animal which lives in cities'
Politics bk. 1, 1253a 2–3

25 He who is unable to live in society, or who has no need because he is sufficient for himself, must be either a beast or a god.
Politics bk. 1, 1253a 27–9; see **BACON** 46:32

1 Nature does nothing without purpose or uselessly.
Politics bk. 1, 1256b 20–21

2 The guest will judge better of a feast than the cook.
Politics bk. 3, 1282a 20

3 For if liberty and equality, as is thought by some, are chiefly to be found in democracy, they will be best attained when all persons alike share in the government to the utmost.
Politics bk. 4, 1291b 35

4 Where some people are very wealthy and others have nothing, the result will be either extreme democracy or absolute oligarchy, or despotism will come from either of those excesses.
Politics bk. 4, 1296a 1–3

5 No tyrant need fear till men begin to feel confident in each other.
Politics bk. 5, 1314a

6 The basis of a democratic state is liberty.
Politics bk. 6, 1317b

7 Whereas then a rattle is a suitable occupation for infant children, education serves as a rattle for young people when older.
Politics bk. 8, 1340b 29–31

8 *Amicus Plato, sed magis amica veritas.*
Plato is dear to me, but dearer still is truth.
Latin translation of a Greek original ascribed to Aristotle

9 The roots of education are bitter, but the fruit is sweet.
Diogenes Laertius *Lives of Philosophers* bk. 5, sect. 18

10 When he was asked 'What is a friend?' he said 'One soul inhabiting two bodies.'
Diogenes Laertius *Lives of Philosophers* bk. 5, sect. 20

11 This realization, according to [Aristotle], is twofold. Either it is potential, as that of Hermes in the wax, provided the wax be adapted to receive the proper mouldings, or as that of the statue implicit in the bronze; or again it is determinate, which is the case with the completed figure of Hermes or the finished statue.
Diogenes Laertius *Lives of the Philosophers* bk. 5, sect. 33

12 I lived uncertain, I die doubtful: O thou Being of beings, have mercy upon me!
attributed last words, probably apocryphal; a Latin version was current in the early 17th century

Lewis Addison Armistead 1817–63
American army officer

13 Give them the cold steel, boys!
during the American Civil War, 1863
attributed

Harry Armstrong 1879–1951
American songwriter

14 There's an old mill by the stream, Nellie Dean, Where we used to sit and dream, Nellie Dean.

And the waters as they flow
Seem to murmur sweet and low,
'You're my heart's desire; I love you, Nellie Dean.'
'Nellie Dean' (1905 song)

John Armstrong 1709–79
Scottish poet and physician

15 'Tis not for mortals always to be blest.
The Art of Preserving Health (1744) bk. 4, l. 260

16 'Tis not too late tomorrow to be brave.
The Art of Preserving Health (1744) bk. 4, l. 460

Louis Armstrong 1901–71
American singer and jazz musician

17 If you still have to ask . . . shame on you.
when asked what jazz is
Max Jones et al. *Salute to Satchmo* (1970); see **MISQUOTATIONS** 548:8

18 All music is folk music, I ain't never heard no horse sing a song.
in *New York Times* 7 July 1971

Neil Armstrong 1930–
American astronaut; first man on the moon

19 Houston, Tranquillity Base here. The Eagle has landed.
radio message as the lunar module touched down
in *The Times* 21 July 1969

20 That's one small step for a man, one giant leap for mankind.
landing on the moon
in *New York Times* 21 July 1969; interference in the transmission obliterated 'a'

Robert Armstrong 1927–
British civil servant; Head of the Civil Service, 1981–7

21 It contains a misleading impression, not a lie. It was being economical with the truth.
during the 'Spycatcher' trial in New South Wales
in *Daily Telegraph* 19 November 1986; see **BURKE** 175:10, **CLARK** 233:12, **TWAIN** 820:4

Arnald-Amaury d. 1225
French abbot of Cîteaux

22 Kill them all; God will recognize his own.
when asked how the true Catholics could be distinguished from the heretics at the massacre of Béziers, 1209
Jonathan Sumption *The Albigensian Crusade* (1978)

Peter Arno *see* Cartoon captions 205:17

Edwin Arnold 1832–1904
English poet and journalist

23 Nor ever once ashamed
So we be named

Press-men; Slaves of the Lamp; Servants of
Light.
'The Tenth Muse' (1895) st. 18

George Arnold 1834–65

American humorist

1 The living need charity more than the dead.
'The Jolly Old Pedagogue' (1866)

Matthew Arnold 1822–88

English poet and essayist; son of Thomas ARNOLD

2 And we forget because we must
And not because we will.
'Absence' (1852)

3 A bolt is shot back somewhere in our breast,
And a lost pulse of feeling stirs again.
The eye sinks inward, and the heart lies plain,
And what we mean, we say, and what we
would, we know.
'The Buried Life' (1852) l. 84

4 The Sea of Faith
Was once, too, at the full, and round earth's
shore
Lay like the folds of a bright girdle furled.
But now I only hear
Its melancholy, long, withdrawing roar,
Retreating, to the breath
Of the night-wind, down the vast edges drear
And naked shingles of the world.
'Dover Beach' (1867) l. 21

5 Ah, love, let us be true
To one another!
'Dover Beach' (1867) l. 29

6 And we are here as on a darkling plain
Swept with confused alarms of struggle and
flight,
Where ignorant armies clash by night.
'Dover Beach' (1867) l. 35

7 Be neither saint nor sophist-led, but be a man.
Empedocles on Etna (1852) act 1, sc. 2, l. 136

8 Is it so small a thing
To have enjoyed the sun,
To have lived light in the spring,
To have loved, to have thought, to have done.
Empedocles on Etna (1852) act 1, sc. 2, l. 397

9 Because thou must not dream, thou needst not
then despair!
Empedocles on Etna (1852) act 1, sc. 2, l. 426

10 Come to me in my dreams, and then
By day I shall be well again!
For then the night will more than pay
The hopeless longing of the day.
'Faded Leaves' (1855) no. 5 (first published, 1852, as 'Longing')

11 Come, dear children, let us away;
Down and away below!
'The Forsaken Merman' (1849) l. 1

12 Now the great winds shorewards blow;
Now the salt tides seawards flow;

Now the wild white horses play,
Champ and chafe and toss in the spray.
'The Forsaken Merman' (1849) l. 4

13 Sand-strewn caverns, cool and deep,
Where the winds are all asleep;
Where the spent lights quiver and gleam;
Where the salt weed sways in the stream;
'The Forsaken Merman' (1849) l. 35

14 Where great whales come sailing by,
Sail and sail, with unshut eye,
Round the world for ever and aye.
'The Forsaken Merman' (1849) l. 43

15 Creep into thy narrow bed,
Creep, and let no more be said!
Vain thy onset! all stands fast.
Thou thyself must break at last.

Let the long contention cease!
Geese are swans, and swans are geese.
Let them have it how they will!
Thou art tired; best be still.
'The Last Word' (1867)

16 Calm soul of all things! make it mine
To feel, amid the city's jar,
That there abides a peace of thine,
Man did not make, and cannot mar.
'Lines written in Kensington Gardens' (1852)

17 He spoke, and loosed our heart in tears.
He laid us as we lay at birth
On the cool flowery lap of earth.
of William **WORDSWORTH**
'Memorial Verses, April 1850' (1852) l. 47

18 Ere the parting hour go by,
Quick, thy tablets, Memory!
'A Memory Picture' (1849)

19 With aching hands and bleeding feet
We dig and heap, lay stone on stone;
We bear the burden and the heat
Of the long day, and wish 'twere done.
Not till the hours of light return,
All we have built do we discern.
'Morality' (1852); see **BIBLE** 102:11

20 Say, has some wet bird-haunted English lawn
Lent it the music of its trees at dawn?
'Parting' (1852) l. 19

21 Hark! ah, the Nightingale!
The tawny-throated!
Hark! from that moonlit cedar what a burst!
What triumph! hark—what pain!
'Philomela' (1853) l. 1

22 Eternal Passion!
Eternal Pain!
of the nightingale
'Philomela' (1853) l. 31

23 Cruel, but composed and bland,
Dumb, inscrutable and grand,
So Tiberius might have sat,
Had Tiberius been a cat.
'Poor Matthias' (1885) l. 40

1 Her cabined ample Spirit,
It fluttered and failed for breath.
To-night it doth inherit
The vasty hall of death.
'Requiescat' (1853)

2 Not deep the Poet sees, but wide.
'Resignation' (1849) l. 214

3 Yet they, believe me, who await
No gifts from chance, have conquered fate.
'Resignation' (1849) l. 247

4 Not milder is the general lot
Because our spirits have forgot,
In action's dizzying eddy whirled,
The something that infects the world.
'Resignation' (1849) l. 275

5 Coldly, sadly descends
The autumn evening. The Field
Strewn with its dank yellow drifts
Of withered leaves, and the elms,
Fade into dimness apace,
Silent;—hardly a shout
From a few boys late at their play!
'Rugby Chapel, November 1857' (1867)

6 Go, for they call you, Shepherd, from the hill.
'The Scholar-Gipsy' (1853) l. 1

7 All the live murmur of a summer's day.
'The Scholar-Gipsy' (1853) l. 20

8 Tired of knocking at Preferment's door.
'The Scholar-Gipsy' (1853) l. 35

9 Crossing the stripling Thames at Bab-lock-hithe.
'The Scholar-Gipsy' (1853) l. 74

10 The line of festal light in Christ-Church hall.
'The Scholar-Gipsy' (1853) l. 129

11 Thou waitest for the spark from heaven! and we,
Light half-believers in our casual creeds . . .
Who hesitate and falter life away,
And lose to-morrow the ground won to-day—
Ah, do not we, Wanderer, await it too?
'The Scholar-Gipsy' (1853) l. 171

12 O born in days when wits were fresh and clear,
And life ran gaily as the sparkling Thames;
Before this strange disease of modern life,
With its sick hurry, its divided aims,
Its heads o'ertaxed, its palsied hearts, was rife—
Fly hence, our contact fear!
'The Scholar-Gipsy' (1853) l. 201

13 Still nursing the unconquerable hope,
Still clutching the inviolable shade.
'The Scholar-Gipsy' (1853) l. 211

14 Resolve to be thyself: and know, that he
Who finds himself, loses his misery.
'Self-Dependence' (1852) l. 31

15 Others abide our question. Thou art free.
We ask and ask: Thou smilest and art still,
Out-topping knowledge.
'Shakespeare' (1849)

16 And thou, who didst the stars and sunbeams
know,

Self-schooled, self-scanned, self-honoured, self-
secure,
Didst tread on Earth unguessed at.
'Shakespeare' (1849)

17 Truth sits upon the lips of dying men.
'Sohrab and Rustum' (1853) l. 656

18 But the majestic river floated on,
Out of the mist and hum of that low land,
Into the frosty starlight.
'Sohrab and Rustum' (1853) l. 875

19 The longed-for dash of waves is heard, and wide
His luminous home of waters opens, bright
And tranquil, from whose floor the new-bathed
stars
Emerge, and shine upon the Aral Sea.
'Sohrab and Rustum' (1853) l. 889

20 For rigorous teachers seized my youth,
And purged its faith, and trimmed its fire,
Showed me the high, white star of Truth,
There bade me gaze, and there aspire.
'Stanzas from the Grande Chartreuse' (1855) l. 67

21 Wandering between two worlds, one dead,
The other powerless to be born,
With nowhere yet to rest my head,
Like these, on earth I wait forlorn.
'Stanzas from the Grande Chartreuse' (1855) l. 85

22 What helps it now, that Byron bore,
With haughty scorn which mocked the smart,
Through Europe to the Aetolian shore
The pageant of his bleeding heart?
That thousands counted every groan,
And Europe made his woe her own?
'Stanzas from the Grande Chartreuse' (1855) l. 133

23 Still bent to make some port he knows not
where,
Still standing for some false impossible shore.
'A Summer Night' (1852) l. 68

24 The signal-elm, that looks on Ilsley downs,
The Vale, the three lone weirs, the youthful
Thames.
'Thyrsis' (1866) l. 14

25 And that sweet City with her dreaming spires.
of Oxford
'Thyrsis' (1866) l. 19; see **RAPHAEL** 655:11

26 So have I heard the cuckoo's parting cry,
From the wet field, through the vext garden-
trees,
Come with the volleying rain and tossing
breeze:
'The bloom is gone, and with the bloom go I.'
'Thyrsis' (1866) l. 57

27 Too quick despairer, wherefore wilt thou go?
Soon will the high Midsummer pomps come on,
Soon will the musk carnations break and swell.
'Thyrsis' (1866) l. 61

28 The foot less prompt to meet the morning dew,
The heart less bounding at emotion new,

And hope, once crushed, less quick to spring
again.
'Thyrsis' (1866) l. 138

1 Who saw life steadily, and saw it whole:
The mellow glory of the Attic stage;
Singer of sweet Colonus, and its child.
of **SOPHOCLES**
'To a Friend' (1849)

2 France, famed in all great arts, in none supreme.
'To a Republican Friend—Continued' (1849)

3 Yes! in the sea of life enisled,
With echoing straits between us thrown,
Dotting the shoreless watery wild,
We mortal millions live *alone*.
'To Marguerite—Continued' (1852) l. 1

4 A God, a God their severance ruled!
'To Marguerite—Continued' (1852) l. 22

5 And bade betwixt their shores to be
The unplumbed, salt, estranging sea.
'To Marguerite—Continued' (1852) l. 24

6 Nor bring, to see me cease to live,
Some doctor full of phrase and fame,
To shake his sapient head and give
The ill he cannot cure a name.
'A Wish' (1867)

7 And sigh that one thing only has been lent
To youth and age in common—discontent.
'Youth's Agitations' (1852)

8 Our society distributes itself into Barbarians,
Philistines, and Populace; and America is just
ourselves, with the Barbarians quite left out, and
the Populace nearly.
Culture and Anarchy (1869) preface

9 The pursuit of perfection, then, is the pursuit of
sweetness and light . . . He who works for
sweetness and light united, works to make
reason and the will of God prevail.
Culture and Anarchy (1869) ch. 1; see **FORSTER** 337:19, **SWIFT**
782:2

10 The men of culture are the true apostles of
equality.
Culture and Anarchy (1869) ch. 1

11 When I want to distinguish clearly the
aristocratic class from the Philistines proper, or
middle class, [I] name the former, in my own
mind *the Barbarians*.
Culture and Anarchy (1869) ch. 3

12 Marching where it likes, meeting where it likes,
bawling what it likes, breaking what it likes—to
this vast residuum we may with great propriety
give the name of Populace.
of the working class
Culture and Anarchy (1869) ch. 3

13 Hebraism and Hellenism—between these two
points of influence moves our world.
Culture and Anarchy (1869) ch. 4

14 No man, who knows nothing else, knows even
his Bible.
Culture and Anarchy (1869) ch. 5

15 Nothing could moderate, in the bosom of the
great English middle class, their passionate,
absorbing, almost blood-thirsty clinging to life.
Essays in Criticism First Series (1865) preface

16 Whispering from her towers the last
enchantments of the Middle Age . . . Home of
lost causes, and forsaken beliefs, and unpopular
names, and impossible loyalties!
of Oxford
Essays in Criticism First Series (1865) preface; see **BEERBOHM**
66:2

17 The gloom, the smoke, the cold, the strangled
illegitimate child! . . . And the final
touch,—short, bleak and inhuman: *Wragg is in
custody*.
*prompted by a newspaper report of the murder of her
illegitimate child by a girl named Wragg*
Essays in Criticism First Series (1865) 'The Function of Criticism
at the Present Time'

18 I am bound by my own definition of criticism: *a
disinterested endeavour to learn and propagate the
best that is known and thought in the world.*
Essays in Criticism First Series (1865) 'The Function of Criticism
at the Present Time'

19 Philistinism!—We have not the expression in
English. Perhaps we have not the word because
we have so much of the thing.
Essays in Criticism First Series (1865) 'Heinrich Heine'

20 The great apostle of the Philistines, Lord
Macaulay.
Essays in Criticism First Series (1865) 'Joubert'

21 The absence, in this country, of any force of
educated literary and scientific opinion.
Essays in Criticism First Series (1865) 'The Literary Influence of
Academies'

22 In poetry, no less than in life, he is 'a beautiful
and ineffectual angel, beating in the void his
luminous wings in vain'.
Essays in Criticism Second Series (1888) 'Shelley' (quoting
from his own essay on Byron in the same work)

23 More and more mankind will discover that we
have to turn to poetry to interpret life for us, to
console us, to sustain us. Without poetry, our
science will appear incomplete; and most of
what now passes with us for religion and
philosophy will be replaced by poetry.
Essays in Criticism Second Series (1888) 'The Study of Poetry'

24 The difference between genuine poetry and the
poetry of Dryden, Pope, and all their school, is
briefly this: their poetry is conceived and
composed in their wits, genuine poetry is
conceived and composed in the soul.
Essays in Criticism Second Series (1888) 'Thomas Gray'

25 Poetry is at bottom a criticism of life.
Essays in Criticism Second Series (1888) 'Wordsworth'

26 His expression may often be called bald . . . but
it is bald as the bare mountain tops are bald,
with a baldness full of grandeur.
Essays in Criticism Second Series (1888) 'Wordsworth'

1 I am past thirty, and three parts iced over.
Howard Foster Lowry (ed.) The Letters of Matthew Arnold to Arthur Hugh Clough (1932) 12 February 1853

2 Terms like grace, new birth, justification . . . terms, in short, which with St Paul are literary terms, theologians have employed as if they were scientific terms.
Literature and Dogma (1873) ch. 1

3 The true meaning of religion is thus not simply morality, but morality touched by emotion.
Literature and Dogma (1873) ch. 1

4 Conduct is three-fourths of our life and its largest concern.
Literature and Dogma (1873) ch. 1

5 But there remains the question: what righteousness really is. The method and secret and sweet reasonableness of Jesus.
Literature and Dogma (1873) ch. 12

6 So we have the Philistine of genius in religion—Luther; the Philistine of genius in politics—Cromwell; the Philistine of genius in literature—Bunyan.
Mixed Essays (1879) 'Lord Falkland'

7 Wordsworth says somewhere that wherever Virgil seems to have composed 'with his eye on the object', Dryden fails to render him. Homer invariably composes 'with his eye on the object', whether the object be a moral or a material one: Pope composes with his eye on his style, into which he translates his object, whatever it is.
On Translating Homer (1861) Lecture 1

8 Of these two literatures [French and German], as of the intellect of Europe in general, the main effort, for now many years, has been a *critical* effort; the endeavours, in all branches of knowledge—theology, philosophy, history, art, science—to see the object as in itself it really is.
On Translating Homer (1861) Lecture 2

9 He [the translator] will find one English book and one only, where, as in the *Iliad* itself, perfect plainness of speech is allied with perfect nobleness; and that book is the Bible.
On Translating Homer (1861) Lecture 3

10 Nothing has raised more questioning among my critics than these words—noble, the grand style . . . I think it will be found that the grand style arises in poetry, when a noble nature, poetically gifted, treats with simplicity or with severity a serious subject.
On Translating Homer. Last Words (1862)

11 Have something to say, and say it as clearly as you can. That is the only secret of style.
G. W. E. Russell Collections and Recollections (1898) ch. 13

Samuel James Arnold 1774–1852

English organist and composer

12 England, home and beauty.
'The Death of Nelson' (1811 song)

Thomas Arnold 1795–1842

English historian and educator; Headmaster of Rugby School from 1828; father of Matthew ARNOLD

13 My object will be, if possible, to form Christian men, for Christian boys I can scarcely hope to make.
on appointment to the Headmastership of Rugby School
letter to Revd John Tucker, 2 March 1828; Arthur Penrhyn Stanley *The Life and Correspondence of Thomas Arnold* (1844) vol. 1, ch. 2

14 What we must look for here is, 1st, religious and moral principles: 2ndly, gentlemanly conduct: 3rdly, intellectual ability.
address to the praepostors [prefects] of Rugby School
Arthur Penrhyn Stanley *The Life and Correspondence of Thomas Arnold* (1844) vol. 1, ch. 3

15 As for rioting, the old Roman way of dealing with that is always the right one; flog the rank and file, and fling the ringleaders from the Tarpeian rock.
from an unpublished letter written before 1828, quoted by Matthew **ARNOLD** in *Cornhill Magazine* August 1868 'Anarchy and Authority'

16 It is quite awful to watch the strength of evil in such young minds, and how powerless is every effort against it. It would give the vainest man alive a very fair notion of his own insufficiency, to see how little he can do and how his most earnest addresses are as a cannon ball on a bolster.
David Newsome *Godliness and Good Learning* (1961)

17 My love for any place, or person, or institution, is exactly the measure of my desire to reform them.
David Newsome *Godliness and Good Learning* (1961); see **TUSA** 819:16

Raymond Aron 1905–83

French sociologist and political journalist

18 *La pensée politique, en France, est rétrospective ou utopique.*

Political thought, in France, is retrospective or utopian.
The Opium of the Intellectuals (1955) ch. 1

Antonin Artaud 1896–1948

French actor, director, and dramatic theorist

19 *Il faut nous laver de la littérature. Nous voulons être hommes avant tout, être humains.*

We must wash literature off ourselves. We want to be men above all, to be human.
Les Oeuvres et les Hommes (unpublished MS, 17 May 1922)

Lev A. Artsimovich 1909–73

Russian physicist

20 The joke definition according to which 'Science is the best way of satisfying the curiosity of

individuals at government expense' is more or less correct.

in Novy Mir January 1967

1 If one proposed to the Royal Society a two-wheeled vehicle for personal transportation, they would immediately conclude that it was impossible because it is clearly and absolutely unstable.

on the conservatism of scientific bodies

attributed

Roger Ascham 1515–68

English scholar, writer, and courtier; he was tutor to Princess Elizabeth (later ELIZABETH I) and may also have taught Lady Jane GREY

2 I said . . . how, and why, young children, were sooner allured by love, than driven by beating, to attain good learning.

The Schoolmaster (1570) preface

3 There is no such whetstone, to sharpen a good wit and encourage a will to learning, as is praise.

The Schoolmaster (1570) bk. 1

4 Mark all mathematical heads which be only and wholly bent on these sciences, how solitary they be themselves, how unfit to live with others, and how unapt to serve the world.

The Schoolmaster (1570) bk. 1

5 To laugh, to lie, to flatter, to face
Four ways in court to win men grace.

The Schoolmaster (1570) bk. 1

6 Learning teacheth more in one year than experience in twenty.

The Schoolmaster (1570) bk. 1

7 We know by experience itself, that . . . we find out but a short way, by long wandering.

The Schoolmaster (1570) bk. 1

8 *Inglese Italianato, è un diavolo incarnato*, that is to say, you remain men in shape and fashion, but become devils in life and condition.

of Englishmen travelling in Italy
The Schoolmaster (1570) bk. 1

9 What toys, the daily reading of such a book, may work in the will of a young gentleman, or a young maid . . . wise men can judge, and honest men do pity.

of Malory's Le Morte D'Arthur as unsuitable reading for the young
The Schoolmaster (1570) bk. 1

10 He that will write well in any tongue, must follow this counsel of Aristotle, to speak as the common people do, to think as wise men do; and so should every man understand him, and the judgement of wise men allow him.

Toxophilus (1545) 'To all gentlemen and yeomen of England'; summarizing a passage in Aristotle Topics bk. 2, ch. 2

John Ashcroft 1942–

American Republican politician, US Attorney General 2001–4

11 We may never know why he turned his back on our country and our values, but we cannot ignore that he did. Youth is not absolution for treachery.

on John Walker Lindh, an American who fought for the Taliban
in Newsweek 28 January 2002

Daisy Ashford 1881–1972

English child author

12 Mr Salteena was an elderly man of 42.

The Young Visiters (1919) ch. 1

13 I am not quite a gentleman but you would hardly notice it but can't be helped anyhow.

The Young Visiters (1919) ch. 1

14 Bernard always had a few prayers in the hall and some whiskey afterwards as he was rarther pious but Mr Salteena was not very addicted to prayers so he marched up to bed.

The Young Visiters (1919) ch. 3

15 It was a sumpshous spot all done up in gold with plenty of looking glasses.

The Young Visiters (1919) ch. 5

16 Oh I see said the Earl but my own idear is that these things are as piffle before the wind.

The Young Visiters (1919) ch. 5

17 My life will be sour grapes and ashes without you.

The Young Visiters (1919) ch. 8

Isaac Asimov 1920–92

Russian-born biochemist and science fiction writer

18 The three fundamental Rules of Robotics . . . One, a robot may not injure a human being, or, through inaction, allow a human being to come to harm . . . Two . . . a robot must obey the orders given it by human beings except where such orders would conflict with the First Law . . . three, a robot must protect its own existence as long as such protection does not conflict with the First or Second Laws.

I, Robot (1950) 'Runaround'

19 When, however, the lay public rallies around an idea that is denounced by distinguished but elderly scientists and supports that idea with great fervour and emotion—the distinguished but elderly scientists are then, after all, probably right.

corollary to Arthur C. CLARKE's law; see CLARKE 233:14
Arthur C. Clarke 'Asimov's Corollary' in K. Frazier (ed.) Paranormal Borderlands of Science (1981)

20 The first law of dietetics seems to be: if it tastes good, it's bad for you.

attributed

Anne Askew 1521–46

English Protestant martyr and writer

1 Like as the armèd knight
  Appointed to the field,
  With this world will I fight,
  And faith shall be my shield . . .

  I am not she that list
  My anchor to let fall,
  For every drizzling mist
  My ship substantial.
  'The Ballad which Anne Askew made and sang when she was
  in Newgate' (1546)

Elizabeth Asquith (Princess Antoine Bibesco) 1897–1945

**British daughter of Herbert Henry ASQUITH and Margot
ASQUITH**

2 Kitchener is a great poster.
  More Memories (1933) ch. 6

Herbert Asquith, Earl of Oxford and Asquith 1852–1928

**British Liberal statesman, Prime Minister 1908–16; husband
of Margot ASQUITH and father of Elizabeth ASQUITH. On
Asquith: see BONHAM CARTER 132:9**

3 We had better wait and see.
  *phrase used repeatedly in speeches in 1910, referring to the
  rumour that the House of Lords was to be flooded with new
  Liberal peers to ensure the passage of the Finance Bill*
  Roy Jenkins *Asquith* (1964)

4 We shall never sheathe the sword which we have
  not lightly drawn until Belgium recovers in full
  measure all and more than all that she has
  sacrificed, until France is adequately secured
  against the menace of aggression, until the
  rights of the smaller nationalities of Europe are
  placed upon an unassailable foundation, and
  until the military domination of Prussia is
  wholly and finally destroyed.
  speech at the Guildhall, London, 9 November 1914, in *The
  Times* 10 November 1914

5 Youth would be an ideal state if it came a little
  later in life.
  in *Observer* 15 April 1923

6 It is fitting that we should have buried the
  Unknown Prime Minister by the side of the
  Unknown Soldier.
  of Andrew BONAR LAW
  Robert Blake *The Unknown Prime Minister* (1955)

7 [The War Office kept three sets of figures:] one
  to mislead the public, another to mislead the
  Cabinet, and the third to mislead itself.
  Alistair Horne *Price of Glory* (1962) ch. 2

Margot Asquith 1864–1945

**British political hostess; wife of Herbert ASQUITH and
mother of Elizabeth ASQUITH**

8 The *t* is silent, as in *Harlow.*
  to Jean Harlow, who had been mispronouncing 'Margot'
  T. S. Matthews *Great Tom* (1973) ch. 7

9 Lord Birkenhead is very clever but sometimes
  his brains go to his head.
  in *Listener* 11 June 1953 'Margot Oxford' by Lady Violet
  Bonham Carter

10 He can't see a belt without hitting below it.
  of LLOYD GEORGE
  in *Listener* 11 June 1953 'Margot Oxford' by Lady Violet
  Bonham Carter

Mary Astell 1668–1731

English poet and feminist

11   Their sophistry I can control
  Who falsely say that women have no soul.
  'Ambition' (written 1684) l. 7

12 Happy am I who out of danger sit,
  Can see and pity them who wade thro it;
  Need take no thought my treasure to dispose,
  What I ne'er had I cannot fear to lose.
  'Awake my Lute' l. 18

13 Our opposers usually miscall our quickness of
  thought, fancy and flash, and christen their own
  heaviness by the specious names of judgement
  and solidity; but it is easy to retort upon them
  the reproachful ones of dullness and stupidity.
  An Essay in Defence of the Female Sex (1696)

14 Fetters of gold are still fetters, and the softest
  lining can never make them so easy as liberty.
  An Essay in Defence of the Female Sex (1696); see BACON 45:26

15 If all men are born free, how is it that all
  women are born slaves?
  Some Reflections upon Marriage (1706 ed.) preface

16 If marriage be such a blessed state, how comes
  it, may you say, that there are so few happy
  marriages? Now in answer to this, it is not to be
  wondered that so few succeed; we should rather
  be surprised to find so many do, considering
  how imprudently men engage, the motives they
  act by, and the very strange conduct they
  observe throughout.
  Some Reflections upon Marriage (1700) preface

17 'Tis less to be wondered at that women marry
  off in haste, for if they took time to consider
  and reflect upon it, they seldom would.
  Some Reflections upon Marriage (1700)

Jacob Astley 1579–1652

English soldier and royalist

18 O Lord! thou knowest how busy I must be this
  day: if I forget thee, do not thou forget me.
  prayer before the Battle of Edgehill, 1642
  Philip Warwick *Memoires* (1701)

1 Gentlemen, ye may now sit and play, for you have done all your work, if you fall not out among yourselves.

to enemy officers, after being captured at Stow-on-the-Wold, 1646

R. Field *Stow-on-the-Wold, 1646* (1992)

Nancy Astor 1879–1964

American-born British Conservative politician. See also CHURCHILL 231:4

2 I married beneath me, all women do.

in *Dictionary of National Biography 1961–1970* (1981)

Kemal Atatürk 1881–1938

Turkish general and statesman, President 1923–38

3 There is no difference between the Johnnies and the Mehmets to us where they lie side by side in this country of ours. You, the mothers, who sent their sons from faraway countries, wipe away your tears. Your sons are now lying in our bosom and are in peace. After having lost their lives on this land, they have become our sons as well.

address to a group of visiting Australians at Anzac Cove, Gallipoli, 1934; subsequently inscribed on the memorial there, and on the Atatürk memorials in Canberra and Wellington

Brooks Atkinson 1894–1984

American journalist and critic

4 After each war there is a little less democracy to save.

Once Around the Sun (1951) 7 January

Farid al-Din Attar d. c.1220

Persian poet

5 The conference of the birds.

title of book of poems

David Attenborough 1926–

English naturalist and broadcaster

6 I'm not over-fond of animals. I am merely astounded by them.

in *Independent* 14 January 1995

Clement Attlee 1883–1967

British Labour statesman, Prime Minister 1945–51. See also DE GAULLE 271:11

7 The voice we heard was that of Mr Churchill but the mind was that of Lord Beaverbrook.

a Daily Express headline had reported Churchill as predicting 'Gestapo in Britain if Socialists win'

speech on radio, 5 June 1945; Francis Williams *A Prime Minister Remembers* (1961); see **BIBLE** 80:7

8 Few thought he was even a starter
There were many who thought themselves smarter
But he ended PM

CH and OM
An earl and a knight of the garter.

describing himself in a letter to Tom Attlee, 8 April 1956

Kenneth Harris *Attlee* (1982)

9 [Russian Communism is] the illegitimate child of Karl Marx and Catherine the Great.

speech at Aarhus University, 11 April 1956, in *The Times* 12 April 1956

10 Democracy means government by discussion, but it is only effective if you can stop people talking.

speech at Oxford, 14 June 1957, in *The Times* 15 June 1957

11 A monologue is not a decision.

to Winston CHURCHILL, who had complained that a matter had been raised several times in Cabinet

Francis Williams *A Prime Minister Remembers* (1961) ch. 7

Margaret Atwood 1939–

Canadian novelist

12 The threshold of a new house is a lonely place.

The Handmaid's Tale (1985)

13 Nobody dies from lack of sex. It's lack of love we die from.

The Handmaid's Tale (1986)

Henriette Auber 1773–1862

English hymn-writer

14 Our blest Redeemer, ere he breathed
His tender last farewell,
A Guide, a Comforter, bequeathed
With us to dwell.

He came in tongues of living flame,
To teach, convince, subdue;
All-powerful as the wind he came,
As viewless too.

'Our blest Redeemer, ere he breathed' (1829 hymn)

John Aubrey 1626–97

English antiquary and biographer

15 The Bishop sometimes would take the key of the wine-cellar, and he and his chaplain [Lushington] would go and lock themselves in and be merry. Then first he lays down his episcopal hat—*There lies the Doctor.* Then he puts off his gown—*There lies the Bishop.* Then 'twas, *Here's to thee, Corbet,* and *Here's to thee, Lushington.*

Brief Lives 'Richard Corbet'

16 How these curiosities would be quite forgot, did not such idle fellows as I am put them down.

Brief Lives 'Venetia Digby'

17 He was wont to say that if he had read as much as other men, he should have known no more than other men.

Brief Lives 'Thomas Hobbes'

18 As they were reading of inscribing and circumscribing figures, said he, I will show you

how to inscribe a triangle in a quadrangle. Bring a pig into the quadrangle and I will set the college dog at him, and he will take the pig by the ear, then I come and take the dog by the tail and the hog by the tail, and so there you have a triangle in a quadrangle; *quod erat faciendum*.
Brief Lives 'Ralph Kettel'

1 His harmonical and ingenious soul did lodge in a beautiful and well proportioned body. He was a spare man.
Brief Lives 'John Milton'

2 Oval face. His eye a dark grey. He had auburn hair. His complexion exceeding fair—he was so fair that they called him *the lady of* Christ's College.
Brief Lives 'John Milton'

3 He pronounced the letter R (*littera canina*) very hard—a certain sign of a satirical wit.
Brief Lives 'John Milton'

4 Sciatica: he cured it, by boiling his buttock.
Brief Lives 'Sir Jonas Moore'

5 She was when a child much against the Bishops, and prayed to God to take them to him, but afterwards was reconciled to them. Prayed aloud, as the hypocritical fashion then was, and was overheard.
Brief Lives 'Katherine Philips'

6 Sir Walter, being strangely surprised and put out of his countenance at so great a table, gives his son a damned blow over the face. His son, as rude as he was, would not strike his father, but strikes over the face the gentleman that sat next to him and said 'Box about: 'twill come to my father anon'.
Brief Lives 'Sir Walter Raleigh'

7 He was a handsome, well-shaped man: very good company, and of a very ready and pleasant smooth wit.
Brief Lives 'William Shakespeare'

8 Anno 1670, not far from Cirencester, was an apparition; being demanded whether a good spirit or a bad? returned no answer, but disappeared with a curious perfume and most melodious twang. Mr W. Lilly believes it was a fairy.
Miscellanies (1696) 'Apparitions'

Auctoritates Aristotelis

A compilation of medieval propositions drawn from diverse classical and other sources (ed. J. Hamesse, 1974)

9 *Consuetudo est altera natura.*
Habit is second nature.

10 *Contra negantem principia non est disputandum.*
You cannot argue with someone who denies the first principles.

11 *Deus et natura nihil faciunt frustra.*
God and nature do nothing in vain.

12 *Ignorantia excusat peccatum.*
Ignorance excuses from sin.

13 *Melius est esse quam non esse.*
It is better to be than not to be.

14 *Natura dat unicuique quod sibi conveniens est.*
Nature gives to each what is appropriate.

15 *Natura desiderat semper quod melius est.*
Nature always desires what is better.

16 *Non est idem bonus homo et bonus civis.*
A good man and a good citizen are not the same thing.

17 *Omnes homines naturaliter scire desiderant.*
All men naturally desire to know.

18 *Oportet inquisitores veritatis non esse inimicos.*
There should be no enmity among seekers after truth.

19 *Parentes plus amant filios quam e converso.*
Parents love their children more than children love their parents.

20 *Signum scientis est posse docere.*
The touchstone of knowledge is the ability to teach.

21 *Silentium mulieri praestat ornatum.*
Silence is a woman's finest ornament.

22 *Tempus est mensura motus rerum mobilium.*
Time is the measure of movement.

W. H. Auden 1907–73

English poet. On Auden: see ORWELL 587:21

23 Blessed Cecilia, appear in visions
To all musicians, appear and inspire:
Translated Daughter, come down and startle
Composing mortals with immortal fire.
Anthem for St Cecilia's Day (1941) pt. 1

24 I'll love you, dear, I'll love you
Till China and Africa meet
And the river jumps over the mountain
And the salmon sing in the street,

I'll love you till the ocean
Is folded and hung up to dry
And the seven stars go squawking
Like geese about the sky.
'As I Walked Out One Evening' (1940)

25 The glacier knocks in the cupboard,
The desert sighs in the bed,
And the crack in the teacup opens
A lane to the land of the dead.
'As I Walked Out One Evening' (1940)

26   Make intercession
For the treason of all clerks.
'At the Grave of Henry James' (1945); see BENDA 69:11

27 August for the people and their favourite islands.
title of poem (1936)

28 The desires of the heart are as crooked as corkscrews

Not to be born is the best for man.
'Death's Echo' (1937); see **SOPHOCLES** 761:17

1 Happy the hare at morning, for she cannot read
The Hunter's waking thoughts.
Dog beneath the Skin (with Christopher **ISHERWOOD**, 1935) act 2, sc. 2

2 To save your world you asked this man to die:
Would this man, could he see you now, ask why?
'Epitaph for the Unknown Soldier' (1955)

3 When he laughed, respectable senators burst
with laughter,
And when he cried the little children died in the
streets.
'Epitaph on a Tyrant' (1940); see **MOTLEY** 562:13

4 Stop all the clocks, cut off the telephone,
Prevent the dog from barking with a juicy bone,
Silence the pianos and with muffled drum
Bring out the coffin, let the mourners come.
'Funeral Blues' (1936)

5 He was my North, my South, my East and
West,
My working week and my Sunday rest,
My noon, my midnight, my talk, my song;
I thought that love would last for ever: I was
wrong.
'Funeral Blues' (1936)

6 To us he is no more a person
now but a whole climate of opinion.
'In Memory of Sigmund Freud' (1940) st. 17

7 The mercury sank in the mouth of the dying
day.
What instruments we have agree
The day of his death was a dark cold day.
'In Memory of W. B. Yeats' (1940) pt. 1

8 You were silly like us; your gift survived it all:
The parish of rich women, physical decay,
Yourself. Mad Ireland hurt you into poetry.
'In Memory of W. B. Yeats' (1940) pt. 2

9 For poetry makes nothing happen: it survives
In the valley of its saying where executives
Would never want to tamper.
'In Memory of W. B. Yeats' (1940) pt. 2

10 Earth, receive an honoured guest:
William Yeats is laid to rest.
Let the Irish vessel lie
Emptied of its poetry.
'In Memory of W. B. Yeats' (1940) pt. 3

11 In the nightmare of the dark
All the dogs of Europe bark,
And the living nations wait,
Each sequestered in its hate;
Intellectual disgrace
Stares from every human face,
And the seas of pity lie
Locked and frozen in each eye.
'In Memory of W. B. Yeats' (1940) pt. 3

12 Time that with this strange excuse
Pardoned Kipling and his views,

And will pardon Paul Claudel,
Pardons him for writing well.
'In Memory of W. B. Yeats' (1940) pt. 3

13 In the deserts of the heart
Let the healing fountain start,
In the prison of his days
Teach the free man how to praise.
'In Memory of W. B. Yeats' (1940) pt. 3

14 Look, stranger, at this island now.
title of poem (1936)

15 Lay your sleeping head, my love,
Human on my faithless arm.
'Lullaby' (1940)

16 About suffering they were never wrong,
The Old Masters: how well they understood
Its human position; how it takes place
While someone else is eating or opening a
window or just walking dully along.
'Musée des Beaux Arts' (1940)

17 They never forgot
That even the dreadful martyrdom must run its
course
Anyhow in a corner, some untidy spot
Where the dogs go on with their doggy life and
the torturer's horse
Scratches its innocent behind on a tree.
'Musée des Beaux Arts' (1940)

18 To the man-in-the-street, who, I'm sorry to say,
Is a keen observer of life,
The word 'Intellectual' suggests straight away
A man who's untrue to his wife.
New Year Letter (1941) l. 1277 n.

19 This is the Night Mail crossing the Border,
Bringing the cheque and the postal order,
Letters for the rich, letters for the poor,
The shop at the corner, the girl next door.
Pulling up Beattock, a steady climb:
The gradient's against her, but she's on time.
Past cotton-grass and moorland boulder,
Shovelling white steam over her shoulder.
'Night Mail' (1936) pt. 1

20 Letters of thanks, letters from banks,
Letters of joy from girl and boy,
Receipted bills and invitations
To inspect new stock or to visit relations,
And applications for situations,
And timid lovers' declarations,
And gossip, gossip from all the nations.
'Night Mail' (1936) pt. 3

21 And make us as Newton was, who in his garden
watching
The apple falling towards England, became
aware
Between himself and her of an eternal tie.
'O Love, the interest itself' (1936)

22 Private faces in public places
Are wiser and nicer
Than public faces in private places.
Orators (1932) dedication

1 Out on the lawn I lie in bed,
Vega conspicuous overhead.
'Out on the lawn I lie in bed' (1936)

2 O what is that sound which so thrills the ear
Down in the valley drumming, drumming?
Only the scarlet soldiers, dear,
The soldiers coming.
'O what is that sound' (1936)

3 Some thirty inches from my nose
The frontier of my Person goes,
And all the untilled air between
Is private *pagus* or demesne.
Stranger, unless with bedroom eyes
I beckon you to fraternize,
Beware of rudely crossing it:
I have no gun, but I can spit.
'Prologue: the Birth of Architecture' (1966) postscript

4 My Dear One is mine as mirrors are lonely.
'The Sea and the Mirror' (1944) pt. 2 (Miranda)

5 I and the public know
What all schoolchildren learn,
Those to whom evil is done
Do evil in return.
'September 1, 1939' (1940)

6 But who can live for long
In an euphoric dream;
Out of the mirror they stare,
Imperialism's face
And the international wrong.
'September 1, 1939' (1940)

7 All I have is a voice
To undo the folded lie,
The romantic lie in the brain
Of the sensual man-in-the-street
And the lie of Authority
Whose buildings grope the sky:
There is no such thing as the State
And no one exists alone;
Hunger allows no choice
To the citizen or the police;
We must love one another or die.
'September 1, 1939' (1940)

8 A shilling life will give you all the facts.
title of poem (1936)

9 Each year brings new problems of Form and
Content,
new foes to tug with: at Twenty I tried to
vex my elders, past Sixty it's the young whom
I hope to bother.
'Shorts I' (1969)

10 A poet's hope: to be,
like some valley cheese,
local, but prized elsewhere.
'Shorts II' (1976)

11 Harrow the house of the dead; look shining at
New styles of architecture, a change of heart.
'Sir, No Man's Enemy' (1930)

12 To-morrow for the young the poets exploding
like bombs,

The walks by the lake, the weeks of perfect
communion;
To-morrow the bicycle races
Through the suburbs on summer evenings: but
to-day the struggle.
'Spain 1937' (1937) st. 20

13 The stars are dead; the animals will not look:
We are left alone with our day, and the time is
short and
History to the defeated
May say Alas but cannot help or pardon.
'Spain 1937' (1937) st. 23

14 To ask the hard question is simple.
title of poem (1933)

15 Was he free? Was he happy? The question is
absurd:
Had anything been wrong, we should certainly
have heard.
'The Unknown Citizen' (1940)

16 The sky is darkening like a stain;
Something is going to fall like rain,
And it won't be flowers.
'The Witnesses' (1935) l. 67

17 All sin tends to be addictive, and the terminal
point of addiction is what is called damnation.
A Certain World (1970) 'Hell'

18 Man is a history-making creature who can
neither repeat his past nor leave it behind.
The Dyer's Hand (1963) 'D. H. Lawrence'

19 When I find myself in the company of scientists,
I feel like a shabby curate who has strayed by
mistake into a drawing room full of dukes.
The Dyer's Hand (1963) 'The Poet and the City'

20 Some books are undeservedly forgotten; none
are undeservedly remembered.
The Dyer's Hand (1963) 'Reading'

21 Art is born of humiliation.
Stephen Spender *World Within World* (1951) ch. 2

22 My face looks like a wedding-cake left out in the
rain.
Humphrey Carpenter *W. H. Auden* (1981) pt. 2, ch. 6

23 Nothing I wrote in the thirties saved one Jew
from Auschwitz.
attributed

Émile Augier 1820–89
French poet and dramatist

24 MARQUIS: *Mettez un canard sur un lac au milieu des
cygnes, vous verrez qu'il regrettera sa mare et finira
par y retourner.*
MONTRICHARD: *La nostalgie de la boue!*

MARQUIS: Put a duck on a lake in the midst of
some swans, and you'll see he'll miss his pond
and eventually return to it.
MONTRICHARD: Longing to be back in the mud!
Le Mariage d'Olympe (1855) act 1, sc. 1

St Augustine of Hippo AD 354–430

Roman Christian theologian. On Augustine: see **ISIDORE** 426:4; see also **PRAYERS** 623:8

1 The works of Creation are described as being completed in six days, the same formula for a day being repeated six times. The reason for this is that six is the number of perfection.
The City of God bk. 9, ch. 30

2 *Tu excitas, ut laudare te delectet, quia fecisti nos, ad te et inquietum est cor nostrum, donec requiescat in te.*
You stir man to take pleasure in praising you, because you have made us for yourself, and our heart is restless until it rests in you.
Confessions (AD 397–8) bk. 1, ch. 1

3 *Nondum amabam, et amare amabam . . . quaerebam quid amarem, amans amare.*
I loved not yet, yet I loved to love . . . I sought what I might love, loving to love.
Confessions (AD 397–8) bk. 3, ch. 1

4 *Et illa erant fercula, in quibus mihi esurienti te inferebantur sol et luna.*
And these were the dishes wherein to me, hunger-starven for thee, the sun and moon were served up.
Confessions (AD 397–8) bk. 3, ch. 6

5 When he was reading, he drew his eyes along over the leaves, and his heart searched into the sense, but his voice and tongue were silent.
of St Ambrose
Confessions (AD 397–8) bk. 6, ch. 3

6 *Da mihi castitatem et continentiam, sed noli modo.*
Give me chastity and continency—but not yet!
Confessions (AD 397–8) bk. 8, ch. 7

7 *Tu non poteris quod isti, quod istae?*
Are you not able to do what these men and women have done?
Confessions (AD 397–8) bk. 8, ch. 11

8 *Tolle lege, tolle lege.*
Take up and read, take up and read.
Confessions (AD 397–8) bk. 8, ch. 12

9 Although it is part of my nature, I cannot understand all that I am. This means, then, that the mind is too narrow to contain itself entirely. But where is that part of it which it does not itself contain?
Confessions (AD 397–8) bk. 10, ch. 8

10 *Sero te amavi, pulchritudo tam antiqua et tam nova, sero te amavi! et ecce intus eras et ego foris, et ibi te quaerebam.*
Too late came I to love thee, O thou Beauty both so ancient and so fresh, yea too late came I to love thee. And behold, thou wert within me, and I out of myself, where I made search for thee.
Confessions (AD 397–8) bk. 10, ch. 27

11 *Continentiam iubes; da quod iubes et iube quod vis.*
You command continence; give what you command, and command what you will.
Confessions (AD 397–8) bk. 10, ch. 29

12 Poetry is devil's wine.
Contra Academicos

13 *Securus iudicat orbis terrarum.*
The verdict of the world is conclusive.
Contra Epistulam Parmeniani bk. 3 ch. 24

14 *Salus extra ecclesiam non est.*
There is no salvation outside the church.
De Baptismo contra Donatistas bk. 4, ch. 17, sect. 24; see **CYPRIAN** 263:14

15 I have, however, often observed this fact of human behaviour, that with certain people, when sexuality is repressed avarice seems to grow in its place.
De Bono Viduitatis sect. 26

16 *Audi partem alteram.*
Hear the other side.
De Duabus Animabus contra Manicheos ch. 14

17 Hence, a devout Christian must avoid astrologers and all impious soothsayers, especially when they tell the truth, for fear of leading his soul into error by consorting with demons and entangling himself with the bonds of such association.
De Genesi ad Litteram bk. 2, ch. 17, sect. 37; see **MISQUOTATIONS** 547:16

18 *Dilige et quod vis fac.*
Love and do what you will.
often quoted as 'Ama et fac quod vis'
In Epistolam Joannis ad Parthos (AD 413) tractatus 7, sect. 8

19 *Multi quidem facilius se abstinent ut non utantur, quam temperent ut bene utantur.*
To many, total abstinence is easier than perfect moderation.
On the Good of Marriage (AD 401) ch. 21

20 *Martyres veros non faciat poena sed causa.*
True martyrdom is not determined by the penalty suffered, but by the cause.
Epistle 89 in Alois Goldbacher *S. Aureli Augustini Hipponensis Episcopi Epistulae* (1895) vol. 2

21 *Cum dilectione hominum et odio vitiorum.*
With love for mankind and hatred of sins.
often quoted as 'Love the sinner but hate the sin'
letter 211 in J.-P. Migne (ed.) *Patrologiae Latinae* (1845) vol. 33; see **POPE** 614:9

22 *Roma locuta est; causa finita est.*
Rome has spoken; the case is concluded.
traditional summary of words found in *Sermons* (Antwerp, 1702) no. 131, sect. 10

23 *De vitiis nostris scalam nobis facimus, si vitia ipsa calcamus.*
We make ourselves a ladder out of our vices if we trample the vices themselves underfoot.
sermon no. 176 ('On the Ascension of the Lord' no. 1) in J.-P. Migne (ed.) *Patrologiae Latinae* (1845) vol. 38

1 It is a singing to the praise of God. If you praise God, and do not sing, you utter no hymn. If you sing, and praise no God, you utter no hymn. If you praise anything which does not pertain to the praise of God, though in singing you praise, you utter no hymn.

defining a hymn

note to Psalm 148; J. R. Watson *The English Hymn: a Critical and Historical Study* (1997) ch. 1

Augustus 63 BC–AD 14

first Roman emperor, nephew of Julius CAESAR

2 Quintilius Varus, give me back my legions.

on Varus' loss of three legions in battle with Germanic tribes, AD 9

Suetonius *Lives of the Caesars* 'Divus Augustus' sect. 23

3 *Festina lente.*

Make haste slowly.

Suetonius *Lives of the Caesars* 'Divus Augustus' sect. 25; see PROVERBS 638:13

4 He could boast that he inherited it brick and left it marble.

referring to the city of Rome

Suetonius *Lives of the Caesars* 'Divus Augustus' sect. 28

5 That they would pay at the Greek Kalends.

meaning never; the Greeks did not use calends in reckoning time

Suetonius *Lives of the Caesars* 'Divus Augustus' sect. 87

Aung San Suu Kyi 1945–

Burmese political leader

6 Real freedom is freedom from fear, and unless you can live free from fear you cannot live a dignified human life.

undated interview with the BBC; transcript on BBC World Service website

Marcus Aurelius AD 121–180

Roman emperor from AD 161

7 You will give yourself this [rest], if you do every act of your life as though it were your last.

Meditations bk. 2, sect. 5; see KEN 459:14

8 Nowhere can a man find a quieter or more untroubled retreat than in his own soul.

Meditations bk. 4, sect. 3

9 Everything is fitting for me, my universe, which fits thy purpose. Nothing in its good time is too early or too late for me; everything is fruit for me which thy seasons, Nature, bear; from thee, in thee, to thee, are all things. The poet sings 'Dear city of Cecrops', and you will not say 'Dear city of God'?

Meditations bk. 4, sect. 23

10 The universe is truly in love with its task of fashioning whatever is next to be.

Meditations bk. 4, sect. 36

11 Time is a violent torrent; no sooner is a thing brought to sight than it is swept by and another takes its place, and this too will be swept away.

Meditations bk. 4, sect. 43; see HERACLITUS 393:3

12 Be like a headland of rock on which the waves break incessantly: but it stands fast and around it the seething of the waters sinks to rest.

Meditations bk. 4, sect. 49

13 Nothing happens to anybody which he is not fitted by nature to bear.

Meditations bk. 5, sect. 18

14 Sexual intercourse . . . is merely internal attrition and the spasmodic excretion of mucus.

Meditations bk 6, sect. 13

15 Shame on the soul, to falter on the road of life while the body still perseveres.

Meditations bk. 6, sect. 29

16 Every instant of time is a pinprick of eternity. All things are petty, easily changed, vanishing away.

Meditations bk. 6, sect. 36

17 He who sees what is now has seen all things, whatsoever comes to pass from everlasting and whatsoever shall be unto everlasting time.

Meditations bk. 6, sect. 37

18 An angry look on the face is wholly against nature.

Meditations bk. 7, sect. 24

19 The art of living is more like wrestling than dancing, for it requires that we should stand ready and firm to meet onsets which are sudden and unexpected.

Meditations bk. 7, sect. 61

20 To change your mind and to follow him who sets you right is to be nonetheless the free agent that you were before.

Meditations bk. 8, sect. 16

21 Mankind have been created for the sake of one another. Either instruct them, therefore, or endure them.

Meditations bk. 8, sect. 59

22 Whatever befalls you was prepared for you beforehand from eternity, and the thread of causes was spinning from everlasting both your existence and this which befalls you.

Meditations bk. 10, sect. 5

23 Waste no more time arguing what a good man should be. Be one.

Meditations bk. 10, sect. 16

24 The unripe grape, the ripe, and the dried. All things are changes, not into nothing, but into that which is not at present.

Meditations bk. 11, sect. 35

25 Man, you have been a citizen in this world city, what does it matter whether for five years or fifty?

Meditations bk. 12, sect. 36

Decius Magnus Ausonius c.AD 309–392

Roman poet

1 *Nemo bonus Britto est.*

No good man is a Briton.
Epigrams 119

Jane Austen 1775–1817

English novelist. On Austen: see **HARDING** 380:5, **MITFORD** 551:6, **SCOTT** 689:28; see also **CLARKE** 234:1

2 Miss Bates stood in the very worst predicament in the world for having much of the public favour; and she had no intellectual superiority to make atonement for herself, or frighten those who might hate her, into outward respect.
Emma (1816) ch. 3

3 An egg boiled very soft is not unwholesome.
Emma (1816) ch. 3

4 One half of the world cannot understand the pleasures of the other.
Emma (1816) ch. 9

5 The folly of people's not staying comfortably at home when they can! . . . five dull hours in another man's house, with nothing to say or to hear that was not said and heard yesterday, and may not be said and heard again tomorrow . . . four horses and four servants taken out for nothing but to convey five idle, shivering creatures into colder rooms and worse company than they might have had at home.
Emma (1816) ch. 13

6 The sooner every party breaks up the better.
Emma (1816) ch. 25

7 Surprises are foolish things. The pleasure is not enhanced, and the inconvenience is often considerable.
Emma (1816) ch. 26

8 A mind lively and at ease, can do with seeing nothing, and can see nothing that does not answer.
Emma (1816) ch. 27

9 One has no great hopes from Birmingham. I always say there is something direful in the sound.
Emma (1816) ch. 36

10 One of Edward's Mistresses was Jane Shore, who has had a play written about her, but it is a tragedy and therefore not worth reading.
The History of England (written 1791)

11 Nothing can be said in his vindication, but that his abolishing Religious Houses and leaving them to the ruinous depredations of time has been of infinite use to the landscape of England in general.
of HENRY VIII
The History of England (written 1791)

12 It was too pathetic for the feelings of Sophia and myself—we fainted Alternately on a Sofa.
Love and Freindship (written 1790) 'Letter the 8th'

13 There is not one in a hundred of either sex who is not taken in when they marry. Look where I will, I see that it *is* so; and I feel that it *must* be so, when I consider that it is, of all transactions, the one in which people expect most from others, and are least honest themselves.
Mansfield Park (1814) ch. 5

14 We do not look in great cities for our best morality.
Mansfield Park (1814) ch. 9

15 A large income is the best recipe for happiness I ever heard of. It certainly may secure all the myrtle and turkey part of it.
Mansfield Park (1814) ch. 22

16 Shakespeare one gets acquainted with without knowing how. It is part of an Englishman's constitution. His thoughts and beauties are so spread abroad that one touches them everywhere, one is intimate with him by instinct.
Mansfield Park (1814) ch. 34

17 We have all a better guide in ourselves, if we would attend to it, than any other person can be.
Mansfield Park (1814) ch. 42

18 Let other pens dwell on guilt and misery. I quit such odious subjects as soon as I can.
Mansfield Park (1814) ch. 48

19 'Oh! it is only a novel! . . . only Cecilia, or Camilla, or Belinda:' or, in short, only some work in which the most thorough knowledge of human nature, the happiest delineation of its varieties, the liveliest effusions of wit and humour are conveyed to the world in the best chosen language.
Northanger Abbey (1818) ch. 5

20 Oh! who can ever be tired of Bath?
Northanger Abbey (1818) ch. 10

21 Where people wish to attach, they should always be ignorant. To come with a well-informed mind, is to come with an inability of administering to the vanity of others, which a sensible person would always wish to avoid. A woman especially, if she have the misfortune of knowing any thing, should conceal it as well as she can.
Northanger Abbey (1818) ch. 14

22 From politics, it was an easy step to silence.
Northanger Abbey (1818) ch. 14

23 A country like this, where . . . every man is surrounded by a neighbourhood of voluntary spies, and where roads and newspapers lay every thing open.
Northanger Abbey (1818) ch. 34

24 Sir Walter Elliot, of Kellynch-hall, in Somersetshire, was a man who, for his own amusement, never took up any book but the Baronetage; there he found occupation for an idle hour, and consolation in a distressed one.
Persuasion (1818) ch. 1

1 She had been forced into prudence in her youth, she learned romance as she grew older—the natural sequel of an unnatural beginning.
Persuasion (1818) ch. 4

2 She ventured to hope he did not always read only poetry; and to say, that she thought it was the misfortune of poetry, to be seldom safely enjoyed by those who enjoyed it completely; and that the strong feelings which alone could estimate it truly, were the very feelings which ought to taste it but sparingly.
Persuasion (1818) ch. 11

3 'My idea of good company, Mr Elliot, is the company of clever, well-informed people, who have a great deal of conversation; that is what I call good company.' 'You are mistaken,' said he gently, 'that is not good company, that is the best.'
Persuasion (1818) ch. 16

4 Men have had every advantage of us in telling their own story. Education has been theirs in so much higher a degree; the pen has been in their hands.
Persuasion (1818) ch. 23; see **HARDY** 380:13

5 All the privilege I claim for my own sex . . . is that of loving longest, when existence or when hope is gone.
Persuasion (1818) ch. 23

6 It was, perhaps, one of those cases in which advice is good or bad only as the event decides.
Persuasion (1818) ch. 23

7 Pride and prejudice.
title of novel (1813); see **BURNEY** 176:23

8 It is a truth universally acknowledged, that a single man in possession of a good fortune, must be in want of a wife.
Pride and Prejudice (1813) ch. 1, opening words

9 She was a woman of mean understanding, little information, and uncertain temper.
Pride and Prejudice (1813) ch. 1

10 May I ask whether these pleasing attentions proceed from the impulse of the moment, or are the result of previous study?
Pride and Prejudice (1813) ch. 14

11 Mr Collins had only to change from Jane to Elizabeth—and it was soon done—done while Mrs Bennet was stirring the fire.
Pride and Prejudice (1813) ch. 15

12 In his library he had been always sure of leisure and tranquillity; and though prepared . . . to meet with folly and conceit in every other room in the house, he was used to be free of them there.
Pride and Prejudice (1813) ch. 15

13 From this day you must be a stranger to one of your parents.—Your mother will never see you again if you do *not* marry Mr Collins, and I will never see you again if you *do*.
Pride and Prejudice (1813) ch. 20

14 Without thinking highly either of men or matrimony, marriage had always been her object; it was the only honourable provision for well-educated young women of small fortune, and however uncertain of giving happiness, must be their pleasantest preservative from want.
Pride and Prejudice (1813) ch. 22

15 What is the difference in matrimonial affairs, between the mercenary and the prudent move? Where does discretion end, and avarice begin?
Pride and Prejudice (1813) ch. 27

16 Loss of virtue in a female is irretrievable . . . one false step involves her in endless ruin.
Pride and Prejudice (1813) ch. 47

17 Are the shades of Pemberley to be thus polluted?
Pride and Prejudice (1813) ch. 56

18 You ought certainly to forgive them as a Christian, but never to admit them in your sight, or allow their names to be mentioned in your hearing.
Pride and Prejudice (1813) ch. 57

19 For what do we live, but to make sport for our neighbours, and laugh at them in our turn?
Pride and Prejudice (1813) ch. 57

20 Think only of the past as its remembrance gives you pleasure.
Pride and Prejudice (1813) ch. 58

21 An annuity is a very serious business.
Sense and Sensibility (1811) vol. 1, ch. 2

22 On every formal visit a child ought to be of the party, by way of provision for discourse.
Sense and Sensibility (1811) vol. 2, ch. 6

23 A person and face, of strong, natural, sterling insignificance, though adorned in the first style of fashion.
Sense and Sensibility (1811) vol. 2, ch. 11

24 It is not time or opportunity that is to determine intimacy; it is disposition alone. Seven years would be insufficient to make some people acquainted with each other, and seven days are more than enough for others.
Sense and Sensibility (1811) vol. 2, ch. 12

25 To be so bent on marriage, to pursue a man merely for the sake of situation, is a sort of thing that shocks me; I cannot understand it. Poverty is a great evil; but to a woman of education and feeling it ought not, it cannot be the greatest.
The Watsons (c.1804)

26 We met . . . Dr Hall in such very deep mourning that either his mother, his wife, or himself must be dead.
letter to Cassandra Austen, 17 May 1799, in R. W. Chapman (ed.) *Jane Austen's Letters* (1952)

27 How horrible it is to have so many people killed!—And what a blessing that one cares for none of them!
letter to Cassandra Austen, 31 May 1811, after the battle of

Albuera, 16 May 1811, in R. W. Chapman (ed.) *Jane Austen's Letters* (1952)

1 I suppose all the world is sitting in judgement upon the Princess of Wales's letter. Poor woman, I shall support her as long as I can, because she *is* a woman and because I hate her husband.

letter to Martha Lloyd, 16 February 1813; *Selected Letters* (1985)

2 3 or 4 families in a country village is the very thing to work on.

letter to Anna Austen, 9 September 1814, in R. W. Chapman (ed.) *Jane Austen's Letters* (1952)

3 I think I may boast myself to be, with all possible vanity, the most unlearned and uninformed female who ever dared to be an authoress.

letter, 11 December 1815, in R. W. Chapman (ed.) *Jane Austen's Letters* (1952)

4 What should I do with your strong, manly, spirited sketches, full of variety and glow?—How could I possibly join them on to the little bit (two inches wide) of ivory on which I work with so fine a brush, as produces little effect after much labour?

letter to J. Edward Austen, 16 December 1816, in R. W. Chapman (ed.) *Jane Austen's Letters* (1952)

5 Single women have a dreadful propensity for being poor—which is one very strong argument in favour of matrimony.

letter to Fanny Knight, 13 March 1817, in R. W. Chapman (ed.) *Jane Austen's Letters* (1952)

6 He and I should not in the least agree of course, in our ideas of novels and heroines;—pictures of perfection as you know make me sick and wicked.

letter to Fanny Knight, 23 March 1817, in R. W. Chapman (ed.) *Jane Austen's Letters* (1952)

7 I am going to take a heroine whom no-one but myself will much like.

on starting Emma

J. E. Austen-Leigh *A Memoir of Jane Austen* (1926 ed.)

8 When I asked if there was anything she wanted, her answer was that she wanted nothing but death.

her sister Cassandra's account of Jane Austen in her last illness

Cassandra Austen, letter to Fanny Knight, July 1817, in R. W. Chapman (ed.) *Jane Austen's Letters* (1952)

J. L. Austin 1911–60
English philosopher

9 In such cases we should not know what to say. This is when we say 'words fail us' and mean this literally. We should need new words. The old ones just would not fit. They aren't meant to cover this kind of case.

on being asked how one might describe the predicament of the character in KAFKA*'s* Metamorphosis *who wakes to*

find himself transformed into a giant cockroach; see **KAFKA** 452:3

Isaiah Berlin 'Austin and the Early Beginnings of Oxford Philosophy' in *Essays on J. L. Austin* (1973)

10 When asked to state his 'criterion' of philosophical correctness, [he] replied that, well, if you could get a collection of 'more or less cantankerous colleagues' all to accept something after argument, that, he thought, would be 'a bit of a criterion'.

G. J. Warnock 'Saturday Mornings' in *Essays on J. L. Austin* (1973)

Earl of Avon *see* **Anthony Eden**

Revd Awdry (Wilbert Vere Awdry) 1911–97
English writer of children's books

11 You've a lot to learn about trucks, little Thomas. They are silly things and must be kept in their place. After pushing them about here for a few weeks you'll know almost as much about them as Edward. Then you'll be a Really Useful Engine.

Thomas the Tank Engine (1946)

12 I should like my epitaph to say, 'He helped people see God in the ordinary things of life, and he made children laugh.'

in *Independent* 22 March 1997, obituary

Alan Ayckbourn 1939–
English dramatist

13 My mother used to say, Delia, if S-E-X ever rears its ugly head, close your eyes before you see the rest of it.

Bedroom Farce (1978) act 2

14 This place, you tell them you're interested in the arts, you get messages of sympathy.

Chorus of Disapproval (1986) act 2

A. J. Ayer 1910–89
English philosopher

15 No moral system can rest solely on authority.

The Humanist Outlook (1968) introduction

16 The criterion which we use to test the genuineness of apparent statements of fact is the criterion of verifiability. We say that a sentence is factually significant to any given person, if, and only if, he knows how to verify the proposition which it purports to express—that is, if he knows what observations would lead him, under certain conditions, to accept the proposition as being true, or reject it as being false.

Language, Truth, and Logic (1936) ch. 1

17 If now I . . . say 'Stealing money is wrong,' I produce a sentence which has no factual meaning—that is, expresses no proposition which can be either true or false. It is as if I had

written 'Stealing money!!'—where the shape and thickness of the exclamation marks show, by a suitable convention, that a special sort of moral disapproval is the feeling which is being expressed.
Language, Truth, and Logic (1936) ch. 6

1 We offer the theist the same comfort as we gave to the moralist. His assertions cannot possibly be valid, but they cannot be invalid either. As he says nothing at all about the world, he cannot justly be accused of saying anything false, or anything for which he has insufficient grounds. It is only when the theist claims that in asserting the existence of a transcendent god he is expressing a genuine proposition that we are entitled to disagree with him.
Language, Truth, and Logic (1936) ch. 6

2 Why should you mind being wrong if someone can show you that you are?
attributed

Ayesha fl. 1492
Moorish princess, mother of the last Sultan of Granada

3 You do well to weep as a woman over what you could not defend as a man.
reproach to her son Boabdil (Muhammad XI), who had surrendered Granada to Ferdinand and Isabella
traditional attribution; Washington Irving *The Alhambra* (1832; rev. ed. 1851) ch. 18

Pam Ayres 1947–
English writer of humorous verse

4 Medicinal discovery,
It moves in mighty leaps,
It leapt straight past the common cold
And gave it us for keeps.
'Oh no, I got a cold' (1976)

Robert Aytoun 1570–1638
Scottish poet and courtier

5 I loved thee once. I'll love no more,
Thine be the grief, as is the blame;
Thou art not what thou wast before,
What reason I should be the same?
'To an Inconstant Mistress'

W. E. Aytoun 1813–65
Scottish lawyer and writer of ballads

6 'He is coming! he is coming!'
Like a bridegroom from his room,
Came the hero from his prison
To the scaffold and the doom.
'The Execution of Montrose' (1849) st. 14

7 The grim Geneva ministers
With anxious scowl drew near,
As you have seen the ravens flock
Around the dying deer.
'The Execution of Montrose' (1849) st. 17

8 The deep, unutterable woe
Which none save exiles feel.
'The Island of the Scots' (1849) st. 12

9 The earth is all the home I have,
The heavens my wide roof-tree.
'The Wandering Jew' (1867) l. 49

 **B b**

Charles Babbage 1791–1871
English mathematician and inventor; pioneer of machine computing. See also LOVELACE 501:14

10 Improvements succeeded each other so rapidly, that machines which had never been finished were abandoned in the hands of their makers, because new improvements had superseded their utility.
On the Economy of Manufactures (1832)

11 Propose to an Englishman any principle, or any instrument, however admirable, and you will observe that the whole effort of the English mind is directed to find a difficulty, a defect, or an impossibility in it. If you speak to him of a machine for peeling a potato, he will pronounce it impossible: if you peel a potato with it before his eyes, he will declare it useless, because it will not slice a pineapple.
Thoughts on the Principle of Taxation (3rd ed. 1852) preface

12 Every moment dies a man,
Every moment 1 1/16 is born.
parody of **TENNYSON**'s 'Vision of Sin', in an unpublished letter to the poet, in *New Scientist* 4 December 1958; see **TENNYSON** 801:2

Isaac Babel 1894–1940
Russian short-story writer

13 A phrase is born into the world both good and bad at the same time. The secret lies in a slight, an almost invisible twist. The lever should rest in your hand, getting warm, and you can only turn it once, not twice.
Guy de Maupassant (1932)

14 No iron can stab the heart with such force as a full stop put just at the right place.
Guy de Maupassant (1932)

15 On Sabbath eves I am oppressed . . . O the rotted Talmuds of my childhood! O the dense melancholy of memories!
Red Cavalry (1926) 'Gedali' (translated by Walter Morison)

16 The bee of sorrow had stung his heart.
Red Cavalry (1926) 'Pan Apolek' (translated by Walter Morison)

17 Both of us looked on the world as a meadow in May—a meadow traversed by women and horses.
Red Cavalry (1926) 'The Story of a Horse' (translated by Walter Morison)

1 Your language becomes clear and strong, not when you can no longer add a sentence, but when you can no longer take away from it.
  P. Blake and M. Hayward (eds.) *Dissonant Voices in Soviet Literature* (1961)

Lauren Bacall 1924–

American actress

2 Imagination is the highest kite that can fly.
  Lauren Bacall by Myself (1979)

3 I think your whole life shows in your face and you should be proud of that.
  in *Daily Telegraph* 2 March 1988

Johann Sebastian Bach 1685–1750

German composer. On Bach: see **BEECHAM** 65:14, **BEETHOVEN** 66:9, **FRY** 345:24

4 There is nothing to it. You only have to hit the right notes at the right time and the instrument plays itself.
  when complimented on his organ playing
  K. Geiringer *The Bach Family* (1954)

Francis Bacon 1561–1626

English lawyer, courtier, philosopher, and essayist. On Bacon: see **JONSON** 447:4, **STRACHEY** 778:10, **WALTON** 839:15

5 For all knowledge and wonder (which is the seed of knowledge) is an impression of pleasure in itself.
  The Advancement of Learning (1605) bk. 1, ch. 1, sect. 3

6 Look abroad into universality.
  The Advancement of Learning (1605) bk. 1, ch. 3, sect. 6

7 So let great authors have their due, as time, which is the author of authors, be not deprived of his due, which is further and further to discover truth.
  The Advancement of Learning (1605) bk. 1, ch. 4, sect. 12

8 If a man will begin with certainties, he shall end in doubts; but if he will be content to begin with doubts, he shall end in certainties.
  The Advancement of Learning (1605) bk. 1, ch. 5, sect. 8

9 [Knowledge is] a rich storehouse for the glory of the Creator and the relief of man's estate.
  The Advancement of Learning (1605) bk. 1, ch. 5, sect. 11

10 Antiquities are history defaced, or some remnants of history which have casually escaped the shipwreck of time.
  The Advancement of Learning (1605) bk. 2, ch. 2, sect. 1

11 Poesy was ever thought to have some participation of divineness, because it doth raise and erect the mind, by submitting the shows of things to the desires of the mind; whereas reason doth buckle and bow the mind unto the nature of things.
  The Advancement of Learning (1605) bk. 2, ch. 4, sect. 2

12 The knowledge of man is as the waters, some descending from above, and some springing from beneath; the one informed by the light of nature, the other inspired by divine revelation.
  The Advancement of Learning (1605) bk. 2, ch. 5, sect. 1

13 They are ill discoverers that think there is no land, when they can see nothing but sea.
  The Advancement of Learning (1605) bk. 2, ch. 7, sect. 5

14 Words are the tokens current and accepted for conceits, as moneys are for values.
  The Advancement of Learning (1605) bk. 2, ch. 16, sect. 3

15 A dance is a measured pace, as a verse is a measured speech.
  The Advancement of Learning (1605) bk. 2, ch. 16, sect. 5

16 But men must know, that in this theatre of man's life it is reserved only for God and angels to be lookers on.
  The Advancement of Learning (1605) bk. 2, ch. 20, sect. 8

17 Did not one of the fathers in great indignation call poesy *vinum daemonum*?
  vinum daemonum = *the wine of devils*
  The Advancement of Learning (1605) bk. 2, ch. 22, sect. 13; see **AUGUSTINE** 39:12

18 All good moral philosophy is but an handmaid to religion.
  The Advancement of Learning (1605) bk. 2, ch. 22, sect. 14

19 It is in life as it is in ways, the shortest way is commonly the foulest, and surely the fairer way is not much about.
  The Advancement of Learning (1605) bk. 2, ch. 23, sect. 45

20 Alonso of Aragon was wont to say in commendation of old age, that age appears to be best in four things,—old wood best to burn, old wine to drink, old friends to trust, and old authors to read.
  Apophthegms New and Old (1625) no. 97

21 That all things are changed, and that nothing really perishes, and that the sum of matter remains exactly the same, is sufficiently certain.
  Cogitationes de Natura Rerum Cogitatio 5 in J. Spedding (ed.) *The Works of Francis Bacon* vol. 5 (1858)

22 *Antiquitas saeculi juventus mundi.*
  Ancient times were the youth of the world.
  De Dignitate et Augmentis Scientiarum (1623) bk. 1 (translated by Gilbert Watts, 1640)

23 *Divitiae bona ancilla, pessima domina.*
  Riches are a good handmaid, but the worst mistress.
  De Dignitate et Augmentis Scientiarum (1623) bk. 6, ch. 3, pt. 3 'The Antitheta of Things' no. 6 (translated by Gilbert Watts, 1640)

24 *Silentium, stultorum virtus.*
  Silence is the virtue of fools.
  De Dignitate et Augmentis Scientiarum (1623) bk. 6, ch. 3, pt. 3 'The Antitheta of Things' no. 31 (translated by Gilbert Watts, 1640)

25 I hold every man a debtor to his profession.
  The Elements of the Common Law (1596) preface

26 Why should a man be in love with his fetters, though of gold?
  Essay of Death para. 4 in *The Remaines of . . . Lord Verulam* (1648); see **ASTELL** 34:14

1 He is the fountain of honour.
An Essay of a King (1642); attribution doubtful; see **BAGEHOT** 50:8

2 Prosperity is the blessing of the Old Testament, adversity is the blessing of the New.
Essays (1625) 'Of Adversity'

3 The pencil of the Holy Ghost hath laboured more in describing the afflictions of Job than the felicities of Solomon.
Essays (1625) 'Of Adversity'

4 Prosperity doth best discover vice, but adversity doth best discover virtue.
Essays (1625) 'Of Adversity'

5 I had rather believe all the fables in the legend, and the Talmud, and the Alcoran, than that this universal frame is without a mind.
Essays (1625) 'Of Atheism'

6 A little philosophy inclineth man's mind to atheism, but depth in philosophy bringeth men's minds about to religion.
Essays (1625) 'Of Atheism'

7 They that deny a God destroy man's nobility; for certainly man is of kin to the beasts by his body; and, if he be not of kin to God by his spirit, he is a base and ignoble creature.
Essays (1625) 'Of Atheism'

8 Virtue is like a rich stone, best plain set.
Essays (1625) 'Of Beauty'

9 There is no excellent beauty that hath not some strangeness in the proportion.
Essays (1625) 'Of Beauty'

10 He said it that knew it best.
referring to **DEMOSTHENES**
Essays (1625) 'Of Boldness'; see **DEMOSTHENES** 273:1

11 In civil business; what first? boldness; what second and third? boldness: and yet boldness is a child of ignorance and baseness.
Essays (1625) 'Of Boldness'; see **DANTON** 265:18, **DEMOSTHENES** 273:1

12 Boldness is an ill keeper of promise.
Essays (1625) 'Of Boldness'

13 Houses are built to live in and not to look on; therefore let use be preferred before uniformity, except where both may be had.
Essays (1625) 'Of Building'

14 Light gains make heavy purses.
Essays (1625) 'Of Ceremonies and Respects'

15 He that is too much in anything, so that he giveth another occasion of satiety, maketh himself cheap.
Essays (1625) 'Of Ceremonies and Respects'

16 Books will speak plain when counsellors blanch.
Essays (1625) 'Of Counsel'

17 [Some] there be that can pack the cards and yet cannot play well; so there are some that are good in canvasses and factions, that are otherwise weak men.
Essays (1625) 'Of Cunning'

18 I knew one that when he wrote a letter he would put that which was most material in the postscript, as if it had been a bymatter.
Essays (1625) 'Of Cunning'; see **STEELE** 770:14

19 Nothing doth more hurt in a state than that cunning men pass for wise.
Essays (1625) 'Of Cunning'

20 Men fear death as children fear to go in the dark; and as that natural fear in children is increased with tales, so is the other.
Essays (1625) 'Of Death'

21 Revenge triumphs over death; love slights it; honour aspireth to it; grief flieth to it.
Essays (1625) 'Of Death'

22 It is as natural to die as to be born; and to a little infant, perhaps, the one is as painful as the other.
Essays (1625) 'Of Death'

23 Death . . . openeth the gate to good fame, and extinguisheth envy.
Essays (1625) 'Of Death'

24 I knew a wise man that had it for a by-word, when he saw men hasten to a conclusion. 'Stay a little, that we may make an end the sooner.'
Essays (1625) 'Of Dispatch'

25 To choose time is to save time.
Essays (1625) 'Of Dispatch'

26 It is a miserable state of mind to have few things to desire, and many things to fear.
Essays (1625) 'Of Empire'; see **BLAKE** 128:9

27 Riches are for spending.
Essays (1625) 'Of Expense'

28 A man ought warily to begin charges which once begun will continue.
Essays (1625) 'Of Expense'

29 There is little friendship in the world, and least of all between equals.
Essays (1625) 'Of Followers and Friends'

30 Chiefly the mould of a man's fortune is in his own hands.
Essays (1625) 'Of Fortune'

31 If a man look sharply, and attentively, he shall see Fortune: for though she be blind, yet she is not invisible.
Essays (1625) 'Of Fortune'

32 It had been hard for him that spake it to have put more truth and untruth together, in a few words, than in that speech: 'Whosoever is delighted in solitude is either a wild beast, or a god.'
Essays (1625) 'Of Friendship'; see **ARISTOTLE** 27:25

33 A crowd is not company, and faces are but a gallery of pictures, and talk but a tinkling cymbal, where there is no love.
Essays (1625) 'Of Friendship'

34 It redoubleth joys, and cutteth griefs in halves.
Essays (1625) 'Of Friendship'

1 Cure the disease and kill the patient.
Essays (1625) 'Of Friendship'

2 God Almighty first planted a garden; and, indeed, it is the purest of human pleasures.
Essays (1625) 'Of Gardens'

3 Nothing is more pleasant to the eye than green grass kept finely shorn.
Essays (1625) 'Of Gardens'

4 If a man be gracious and courteous to strangers, it shows he is a citizen of the world.
Essays (1625) 'Of Goodness, and Goodness of Nature'

5 The inclination to goodness is imprinted deeply in the nature of man: insomuch, that if it issue not towards men, it will take unto other living creatures.
Essays (1625) 'Of Goodness, and Goodness of Nature'

6 Men in great place are thrice servants: servants of the sovereign or state, servants of fame, and servants of business.
Essays (1625) 'Of Great Place'

7 It is a strange desire to seek power and to lose liberty.
Essays (1625) 'Of Great Place'

8 The rising unto place is laborious, and by pains men come to greater pains; and it is sometimes base, and by indignities men come to dignities. The standing is slippery, and the regress is either a downfall, or at least an eclipse.
Essays (1625) 'Of Great Place'

9 Severity breedeth fear, but roughness breedeth hate. Even reproofs from authority ought to be grave, and not taunting.
Essays (1625) 'Of Great Place'

10 All rising to great place is by a winding stair.
Essays (1625) 'Of Great Place'

11 As the births of living creatures at first are ill-shapen, so are all innovations, which are the births of time.
Essays (1625) 'Of Innovations'

12 He that will not apply new remedies must expect new evils; for time is the greatest innovator.
Essays (1625) 'Of Innovations'

13 The speaking in a perpetual hyperbole is comely in nothing but in love.
Essays (1625) 'Of Love'

14 It has been well said that 'the arch-flatterer with whom all the petty flatterers have intelligence is a man's self.'
Essays (1625) 'Of Love'; see **PLUTARCH** 610:8

15 He that hath wife and children hath given hostages to fortune; for they are impediments to great enterprises, either of virtue or mischief.
Essays (1625) 'Of Marriage and the Single Life'; see **LUCAN** 503:19

16 A single life doth well with churchmen, for charity will hardly water the ground where it must first fill a pool.
Essays (1625) 'Of Marriage and the Single Life'

17 Wives are young men's mistresses, companions for middle age, and old men's nurses.
Essays (1625) 'Of Marriage and the Single Life'

18 He was reputed one of the wise men that made answer to the question when a man should marry? 'A young man not yet, an elder man not at all.'
Essays (1625) 'Of Marriage and the Single Life'; see **PUNCH** 649:14

19 It is generally better to deal by speech than by letter.
Essays (1625) 'Of Negotiating'

20 New nobility is but the act of power, but ancient nobility is the act of time.
Essays (1625) 'Of Nobility'

21 The joys of parents are secret, and so are their griefs and fears.
Essays (1625) 'Of Parents and Children'

22 Children sweeten labours, but they make misfortunes more bitter.
Essays (1625) 'Of Parents and Children'

23 Fame is like a river, that beareth up things light and swollen, and drowns things weighty and solid.
Essays (1625) 'Of Praise'

24 Age will not be defied.
Essays (1625) 'Of Regimen of Health'

25 Revenge is a kind of wild justice, which the more man's nature runs to, the more ought law to weed it out.
Essays (1625) 'Of Revenge'

26 A man that studieth revenge keeps his own wounds green.
Essays (1625) 'Of Revenge'

27 Defer not charities till death; for certainly, if a man weigh it rightly, he that doth so is rather liberal of another man's than of his own.
Essays (1625) 'Of Riches'

28 The four pillars of government . . . (which are religion, justice, counsel, and treasure).
Essays (1625) 'Of Seditions and Troubles'

29 The surest way to prevent seditions (if the times do bear it) is to take away the matter of them.
Essays (1625) 'Of Seditions and Troubles'

30 Money is like muck, not good except it be spread.
Essays (1625) 'Of Seditions and Troubles'; see **PROVERBS** 639:4

31 The remedy is worse than the disease.
Essays (1625) 'Of Seditions and Troubles'

32 Studies serve for delight, for ornament, and for ability.
Essays (1625) 'Of Studies'

33 To spend too much time in studies is sloth.
Essays (1625) 'Of Studies'

34 Read not to contradict and confute, nor to believe and take for granted, nor to find talk and discourse, but to weigh and consider.
Essays (1625) 'Of Studies'

1 Some books are to be tasted, others to be swallowed, and some few to be chewed and digested.
Essays (1625) 'Of Studies'

2 Reading maketh a full man; conference a ready man; and writing an exact man.
Essays (1625) 'Of Studies'

3 Histories make men wise; poets, witty; the mathematics, subtile; natural philosophy, deep; moral, grave; logic and rhetoric, able to contend.
Essays (1625) 'Of Studies'

4 There is a superstition in avoiding superstition.
Essays (1625) 'Of Superstition'

5 Suspicions amongst thoughts are like bats amongst birds, they ever fly by twilight.
Essays (1625) 'Of Suspicion'

6 There is nothing makes a man suspect much, more than to know little.
Essays (1625) 'Of Suspicion'

7 Neither is money the sinews of war (as it is trivially said).
Essays (1625) 'Of the True Greatness of Kingdoms'; see **CICERO** 232:7

8 Neither will it be, that a people overlaid with taxes should ever become valiant and martial.
Essays (1625) 'Of the True Greatness of Kingdoms'

9 Travel, in the younger sort, is a part of education; in the elder, a part of experience. He that travelleth into a country before he hath some entrance into the language, goeth to school, and not to travel.
Essays (1625) 'Of Travel'

10 What is truth? said jesting Pilate; and would not stay for an answer.
Essays (1625) 'Of Truth'; see **BIBLE** 108:26

11 A mixture of a lie doth ever add pleasure.
Essays (1625) 'Of Truth'

12 It is not the lie that passeth through the mind, but the lie that sinketh in, and settleth in it, that doth the hurt.
Essays (1625) 'Of Truth'

13 The inquiry of truth, which is the love-making, or wooing of it, the knowledge of truth, which is the presence of it, and the belief of truth, which is the enjoying of it, is the sovereign good of human nature.
Essays (1625) 'Of Truth'

14 All colours will agree in the dark.
Essays (1625) 'Of Unity in Religion'

15 It was prettily devised of Aesop, 'The fly sat upon the axle-tree of the chariot-wheel and said, what a dust do I raise.'
Essays (1625) 'Of Vain-Glory'

16 In the youth of a state arms do flourish; in the middle age of a state, learning; and then both of them together for a time; in the declining age of a state, mechanical arts and merchandise.
Essays (1625) 'Of Vicissitude of Things'

17 Be so true to thyself as thou be not false to others.
Essays (1625) 'Of Wisdom for a Man's Self'; see **SHAKESPEARE** 700:6

18 It is the nature of extreme self-lovers, as they will set a house on fire, and it were but to roast their eggs.
Essays (1625) 'Of Wisdom for a Man's Self'; see **PROVERBS** 644:36

19 It is the wisdom of the crocodiles, that shed tears when they would devour.
Essays (1625) 'Of Wisdom for a Man's Self'

20 Young men are fitter to invent than to judge, fitter for execution than for counsel, and fitter for new projects than for settled business.
Essays (1625) 'Of Youth and Age'

21 God forbid that we should give out a dream of our own imagination for a pattern of the world.
The Great Instauration (1620) translated by J. Spedding

22 For they thought generally that he was a Prince as ordained, and sent down from heaven to unite and put to an end the long dissensions of the two houses; which although they had had, in the times of Henry the Fourth, Henry the Fifth, and a part of Henry the Sixth on the one side, and the times of Edward the Fourth on the other, lucid intervals and happy pauses; yet they did ever hang over the kingdom, ready to break forth into new perturbations and calamities.
History of King Henry VII (1622) para. 3 in J. Spedding (ed.) *The Works of Francis Bacon* vol. 6 (1858)

23 I have rather studied books than men.
A Letter of Advice . . . to the Duke of Buckingham, When he became Favourite to King James (1661)

24 I have taken all knowledge to be my province.
'To My Lord Treasurer Burghley' (1592) in J. Spedding (ed.) *The Letters and Life of Francis Bacon* vol. 1 (1861)

25 *Nam et ipsa scientia potestas est.*
For also knowledge itself is power.
Meditationes Sacrae (1597) 'Of Heresies'; see **PROVERBS** 637:9

26 I would live to study, and not study to live.
Memorial of Access to King James I (c.1622) in *Letters, Speeches, Charges, Advices, etc. of Francis Bacon* (1763)

27 God's first Creature, which was Light.
New Atlantis (1627)

28 The end of our foundation is the knowledge of causes, and secret motions of things; and the enlarging of the bounds of human Empire, to the effecting of all things possible.
New Atlantis (1627)

29 *Homo, Naturae minister et interpres.*
Man is Nature's agent and interpreter.
Novum Organum (1620) bk. 1, Aphorism 1 (translated by J. Spedding); see **WHEWELL** 850:4

30 *Subtilitas naturae subtilitatem sensus et intellectus multis partibus superat.*
The subtlety of nature is greater many times

over than the subtlety of the senses and understanding.
> *Novum Organum* (1620) bk. 1, Aphorism 10 (translated by J. Spedding)

1 *Quod enim mavult homo verum esse, id potius credit.*
For what a man would like to be true, that he more readily believes.
> *Novum Organum* (1620) bk. 1, Aphorism 49 (translated by J. Spedding); see **DEMOSTHENES** 272:18, **CAESAR** 192:17

2 *Magna ista scientiarum mater.*
That great mother of sciences.
> *of natural philosophy*
> *Novum Organum* (1620) bk. 1, Aphorism 80 (translated by J. Spedding)

3 *Vim et virtutem et consequentias rerum inventarum notare juvat; quae non in aliis manifestius occurrunt, quam in illis tribus quae antiquis incognitae, et quarum primordia, licet recentia, obscura et ingloria sunt: Artis nimirum Imprimendi, Pulveris Tormentarii, et Acus Nauticae. Haec enim tria rerum faciem et statum in orbe terrarum mutaverunt.*
It is well to observe the force and virtue and consequence of discoveries, and these are to be seen nowhere more conspicuously than in those three which were unknown to the ancients, and of which the origins, though recent, are obscure and inglorious; namely, printing, gunpowder, and the mariner's needle [compass] . . . these three have changed the whole face and state of things throughout the world.
> *Novum Organum* (1620) bk. 1, Aphorism 129 (translated by J. Spedding); see **CARLYLE** 199:22

4 *Natura enim non imperatur, nisi parendo.*
Nature cannot be ordered about, except by obeying her.
> *Novum Organum* (1620) bk. 1, Aphorism 129 (translated by J. Spedding)

5 Books must follow sciences, and not sciences books.
> *Resuscitatio* (1657) 'Proposition touching Amendment of Laws'

6 Wise nature did never put her precious jewels into a garret four stories high: and therefore . . . exceeding tall men had ever very empty heads.
> J. Spedding (ed.) *The Works of Francis Bacon* vol. 7 (1859) 'Additional Apophthegms' no. 17

7 Hope is a good breakfast, but it is a bad supper.
> J. Spedding (ed.) *The Works of Francis Bacon* vol. 7 (1859) 'Apophthegms contained in *Resuscitatio*' no. 36; see **PROVERBS** 634:43

8 Anger makes dull men witty, but it keeps them poor.
> *often attributed to Queen* **ELIZABETH I** *from a misreading of the text*
> J. Spedding (ed.) *The Works of Francis Bacon* vol. 7 (1859) 'Baconiana'

9 The world's a bubble; and the life of man
Less than a span.
> *The World* (1629)

10 Who then to frail mortality shall trust,
But limns the water, or but writes in dust.
> *The World* (1629)

11 What then remains, but that we still should cry,
Not to be born, or being born, to die?
> *The World* (1629)

12 There be three things which make a nation great and prosperous: a fertile soil, busy workshops, easy conveyance for men and goods from place to place.
> attributed; S. Platt (ed.) *Respectfully Quoted* (1989)

13 For my name and memory, I leave it to men's charitable speeches, and to foreign nations, and the next ages.
> will, 19 December 1625; J. Spedding (ed.) *The Letters and Life of Francis Bacon* vol. 7 (1874)

Francis Bacon 1909–92
Irish painter

14 Champagne for my real friends, real pain for my sham friends.
> in the 1950s; Michael Peppiatt *Francis Bacon* (1996)

15 What I see is a marvellous painting. But how are you going to make it? And, of course, as I don't know how to make it, I rely then on chance and accident making it for me.
> David Sylvester (ed.) *Interviews with Francis Bacon: the brutality of fact* (ed. 3, 1987)

Roger Bacon *c.*1220–*c.*92
English philosopher, scientist, Franciscan friar

16 If in other sciences we should arrive at certainty without doubt and truth without error, it behoves us to place the foundations of knowledge in mathematics.
> *Opus Majus* bk. 1, ch. 4

Lord Baden-Powell *see* Mottoes 563:5

Karl Baedeker 1801–59
German publisher

17 Oxford is on the whole more attractive than Cambridge to the ordinary visitor; and the traveller is therefore recommended to visit Cambridge first, or to omit it altogether if he cannot visit both.
> *Great Britain* (1887) Route 30 'From London to Oxford'

18 The traveller need have no scruple in limiting his donations to the smallest possible sums, as liberality frequently becomes a source of annoyance and embarrassment.
> *Northern Italy* (1895) 'Gratuities'

19 PASSPORTS. On arrival at a Syrian port the traveller's passport is sometimes asked for, but an ordinary visiting-card will answer the purpose equally well.
> *Palestine and Syria* (1876) 'Passports and Custom House'

Joan Baez 1941–

American singer and songwriter

1 The only thing that's been a worse flop than the organization of non-violence has been the organization of violence.

Daybreak (1970) 'What Would You Do If?'; see **PÉGUY** 602:4

Walter Bagehot 1826–77

English economist and essayist. See also **DISRAELI** 284:9

2 A constitutional statesman is in general a man of common opinion and uncommon abilities.

Biographical Studies (1881) 'Sir Robert Peel'

3 He believes, with all his heart and soul and strength, that there *is* such a thing as truth; he has the soul of a martyr with the intellect of an advocate.

Biographical Studies (1881) 'Mr Gladstone'

4 Capital must be propelled by self-interest; it cannot be enticed by benevolence.

Economic Studies (1880) ch. 2

5 The mystic reverence, the religious allegiance, which are essential to a true monarchy, are imaginative sentiments that no legislature can manufacture in any people.

The English Constitution (1867) 'The Cabinet'

6 In such constitutions [as England's] there are two parts . . . first, those which excite and preserve the reverence of the population—the *dignified* parts . . . and next, the *efficient* parts—those by which it, in fact, works and rules.

The English Constitution (1867) 'The Cabinet'

7 No orator ever made an impression by appealing to men as to their plainest physical wants, except when he could allege that those wants were caused by some one's tyranny.

The English Constitution (1867) 'The Cabinet'

8 The Crown is, according to the saying, the 'fountain of honour'; but the Treasury is the spring of business.

The English Constitution (1867) 'The Cabinet'; see **BACON** 46:1

9 A cabinet is a combining committee—a *hyphen* which joins, a *buckle* which fastens, the legislative part of the state to the executive part of the state.

The English Constitution (1867) 'The Cabinet'

10 It has been said that England invented the phrase, 'Her Majesty's Opposition'; that it was the first government which made a criticism of administration as much a part of the polity as administration itself. This critical opposition is the consequence of cabinet government.

The English Constitution (1867) 'The Cabinet'; see **HOBHOUSE** 401:12

11 *The Times* has made many ministries.

The English Constitution (1867) 'The Cabinet'

12 We often want, at the sudden occurrence of a grave tempest, to change the helmsman—to replace the pilot of the calm by the pilot of the storm.

The English Constitution (1867) 'The Cabinet'

13 It has been said, not truly, but with a possible approximation to truth, that in 1802 every hereditary monarch was insane.

The English Constitution (1867) 'Checks and Balances'

14 The soldier—that is, the great soldier—of to-day is not a romantic animal, dashing at forlorn hopes, animated by frantic sentiment, full of fancies as to a love-lady or a sovereign; but a quiet, grave man, busied in charts, exact in sums, master of the art of tactics, occupied in trivial detail; thinking, as the Duke of Wellington was said to do, *most* of the shoes of his soldiers; despising all manner of *éclat* and eloquence; perhaps, like Count Moltke, 'silent in seven languages'.

The English Constitution (1867) 'Checks and Balances'

15 The finest brute votes in Europe.

view of 'a cynical politician'; sometimes attributed to **DISRAELI**

The English Constitution (1867) 'The House of Commons'

16 The order of nobility is of great use, too, not only in what it creates, but in what it prevents. It prevents the rule of wealth—the religion of gold. This is the obvious and natural idol of the Anglo-Saxon.

The English Constitution (1867) 'The House of Lords'

17 The House of Commons lives in a state of perpetual potential choice: at any moment it can choose a ruler and dismiss a ruler. And therefore party is inherent in it, is bone of its bone, and breath of its breath.

The English Constitution (1867) 'The House of Commons'

18 An Opposition, on coming into power, is often like a speculative merchant whose bills become due. Ministers have to make good their promises, and they find a difficulty in so doing.

The English Constitution (1867) 'The House of Commons'

19 A severe though not unfriendly critic of our institutions said that 'the cure for admiring the House of Lords was to go and look at it.'

The English Constitution (1867) 'The House of Lords'

20 Nations touch at their summits.

The English Constitution (1867) 'The House of Lords'

21 As soon as we see that England is a disguised republic we must see too that the classes for whom the disguise is necessary must be tenderly dealt with.

The English Constitution (1867) 'Its History'

22 It is nice to trace how the actions of a retired widow and an unemployed youth become of such importance.

of Queen **VICTORIA** *and the future* **EDWARD VII**
The English Constitution (1867) 'The Monarchy'

23 Women—one half the human race at least—care fifty times more for a marriage than a ministry.

The English Constitution (1867) 'The Monarchy'

1 Royalty is a government in which the attention of the nation is concentrated on one person doing interesting actions. A Republic is a government in which that attention is divided between many, who are all doing uninteresting actions. Accordingly, so long as the human heart is strong and the human reason weak, Royalty will be strong because it appeals to diffused feeling, and Republics weak because they appeal to the understanding.
The English Constitution (1867) 'The Monarchy'

2 Throughout the greater part of his life George III was a kind of 'consecrated obstruction'.
The English Constitution (1867) 'The Monarchy'

3 There are arguments for not having a Court, and there are arguments for having a splendid Court; but there are no arguments for having a mean Court.
The English Constitution (1867) 'The Monarchy'

4 The Queen . . . must sign her own death-warrant if the two Houses unanimously send it up to her.
The English Constitution (1867) 'The Monarchy'

5 Above all things our royalty is to be reverenced, and if you begin to poke about it you cannot reverence it . . . Its mystery is its life. We must not let in daylight upon magic.
The English Constitution (1867) 'The Monarchy (continued)'

6 The Sovereign has, under a constitutional monarchy such as ours, three rights—the right to be consulted, the right to encourage, the right to warn.
The English Constitution (1867) 'The Monarchy (continued)'

7 The only fit material for a constitutional king is a prince who begins early to reign—who in his youth is superior to pleasure—who in his youth is willing to labour—who has by nature a genius for discretion. Such kings are among God's greatest gifts, but they are also among His rarest.
The English Constitution (1867) 'The Monarchy' (continued)

8 It is an inevitable defect, that bureaucrats will care more for routine than for results.
The English Constitution (1867) 'On Changes of Ministry'

9 The worst families are those in which the members never really speak their minds to one another; they maintain an atmosphere of unreality, and everyone always lives in an atmosphere of suppressed ill-feeling.
The English Constitution (ed. 2, 1872) introduction

10 No real English gentleman, in his secret soul, was ever sorry for the death of a political economist.
Estimates of some Englishmen and Scotchmen (1858) 'The First Edinburgh Reviewers'

11 Writers, like teeth, are divided into incisors and grinders.
Estimates of some Englishmen and Scotchmen (1858) 'The First Edinburgh Reviewers'

12 To a great experience one thing is essential, an experiencing nature.
Estimates of some Englishmen and Scotchmen (1858) 'Shakespeare—the Individual'

13 One of the greatest pains to human nature is the pain of a new idea.
Physics and Politics (1872) 'The Age of Discussion'

14 The most melancholy of human reflections, perhaps, is that, on the whole, it is a question whether the benevolence of mankind does most good or harm.
Physics and Politics (1872) 'The Age of Discussion'

15 The truth is that the propensity of man to imitate what is before him is one of the strongest parts of his nature.
Physics and Politics (1872) 'Nation-Making'

16 One of the most common defects of half-instructed minds is to think much of that in which they differ from others, and little of that in which they agree with others.
on the evils of sectarianism
in *Economist* 11 June 1870

17 The great breeding people had gone out and multiplied; colonies in every clime attest our success; French is the *patois* of Europe; English is the language of the world.
in *National Review* January 1856 'Edward Gibbon'

18 The purchaser [of a newspaper] desires an article which he can appreciate at sight; which he can lay down and say, 'An excellent article, very excellent; exactly *my own* sentiments.'
in *National Review* July 1856 'The Character of Sir Robert Peel'

19 He describes London like a special correspondent for posterity.
in *National Review* 7 October 1858 'Charles Dickens'

20 Wordsworth, Tennyson and Browning; or, pure, ornate, and grotesque art in English poetry.
in *National Review* November 1864, essay title

Abdul Baha 1844–1921

Persian co-founder (with his father **BAHA'ULLAH**) of the Baha'i faith

21 In this century, which is the century of light and the revelation of mysteries . . . it is well established that mankind and womankind as parts of composite humanity are coequal and that no difference in estimate is allowable, for all are human.
at a woman's suffrage meeting in New York, 1912; *The Promulgation of Universal Peace* (2nd ed., 1982)

22 Today, humanity is bowed down with trouble, sorrow and grief, no one escapes; the world is wet with tears; but, thank God, the remedy is at our doors. Let us turn our hands away from the world of matter and live in the spiritual world.
Paris Talks (1912) November 22

Baha'ullah 1817–92

Persian co-founder (with his son Abdul **BAHA**) of the Baha'i faith

1 No man shall attain the shores of the ocean of true understanding except he be detached from all that is in heaven and earth.
The Book of Certitude

Bahya ibn Paquda fl. 1080

Spanish-born Jewish philosopher

2 We are obliged to serve God both outwardly and inwardly. Outward service is expressed in the duties of the members, such as prayer, fasting, almsgiving, learning and teaching the Torah . . . all of which can be wholly performed by man's physical body. Inward service, however, is expressed in the duties of the heart, in the heart's assertion of the unity of God, in belief in him and in his Book, in constant obedience to him and fear of him, in humility before him, love for him and complete reliance upon him, submission to him and abstinence from the things hateful to him.
The Duties of the Heart introduction

3 You should know, O man, that the greatest enemy you have in the world is your inclination.
The Duties of the Heart ch. 5E

4 All virtues and duties are dependent on humility.
The Duties of the Heart ch. 6H

David Bailey 1938–

English photographer. See also **SLOGANS** 755:6

5 It takes a lot of imagination to be a good photographer. You need less imagination to be a painter, because you can invent things. But in photography everything is so ordinary; it takes a lot of looking before you learn to see the ordinary.
interview in *The Face* December 1984

Philip James Bailey 1816–1902

English poet

6 We should count time by heart-throbs.
Festus (1839) sc. 5

7 America, thou half-brother of the world;
With something good and bad of every land.
Festus (1839) sc. 10

Bruce Bairnsfather *see* Cartoon captions

205:19

Henry Williams Baker 1821–77

English clergyman and hymn-writer

8 Lord, thy word abideth,
And our footsteps guideth;
Who its truth believeth

Light and joy receiveth.
'Lord, thy word abideth' (1861 hymn)

9 The King of love my shepherd is,
Whose goodness faileth never;
I nothing lack if I am his
And he is mine for ever . . .

Perverse and foolish oft I strayed,
But yet in love he sought me,
And on his shoulder gently laid,
And home, rejoicing, brought me.
'The King of love my shepherd is' (1868 hymn)

Michael Bakunin 1814–76

Russian revolutionary and anarchist

10 The urge for destruction is also a creative urge!
Jahrbuch für Wissenschaft und Kunst (1842) 'Die Reaktion in Deutschland' (under the pseudonym 'Jules Elysard')

11 Everything will pass, and the world will perish but the Ninth Symphony will remain.
of **BEETHOVEN**'s *Ninth Symphony*
Edmund Wilson *To The Finland Station* (1940)

James Baldwin 1924–87

American novelist and essayist

12 Children have never been very good at listening to their elders, but they have never failed to imitate them. They must, they have no other models.
Nobody Knows My Name (1961) 'Fifth Avenue, Uptown: a letter from Harlem'

13 Anyone who has ever struggled with poverty knows how extremely expensive it is to be poor.
Nobody Knows My Name (1961) 'Fifth Avenue, Uptown: a letter from Harlem'

14 Freedom is not something that anybody can be given; freedom is something people take and people are as free as they want to be.
Nobody Knows My Name (1961) 'Notes for a Hypothetical Novel'

15 Money, it turned out, was exactly like sex, you thought of nothing else if you didn't have it and thought of other things if you did.
in *Esquire* May 1961 'Black Boy looks at the White Boy'

16 It comes as a great shock around the age of 5, 6 or 7 to discover that the flag to which you have pledged allegiance, along with everybody else, has not pledged allegiance to you. It comes as a great shock to see Gary Cooper killing off the Indians and, although you are rooting for Gary Cooper, that the Indians are you.
speaking for the proposition that 'The American Dream is at the expense of the American Negro'
speech at the Cambridge Union, England, 17 February 1965; in *New York Times Magazine* 7 March 1965

1 If they take you in the morning, they will be coming for us that night.

in *New York Review of Books* 7 January 1971 'Open Letter to my Sister, Angela Davis'

Stanley Baldwin 1867–1947

British Conservative statesman, Prime Minister 1923–4, 1924–9, 1935–7. On Baldwin: see **BEAVERBROOK** 63:13, **CHURCHILL** 230:10, **CURZON** 263:10, **TREVELYAN** 815:9; see also **KIPLING** 468:26

2 They [parliament] are a lot of hard-faced men who look as if they had done very well out of the war.

J. M. Keynes *Economic Consequences of the Peace* (1919) ch. 5

3 A platitude is simply a truth repeated until people get tired of hearing it.

speech in the House of Commons, 29 May 1924

4 There are three classes which need sanctuary more than others—birds, wild flowers, and Prime Ministers.

in *Observer* 24 May 1925

5 I think it is well also for the man in the street to realize that there is no power on earth that can protect him from being bombed. Whatever people may tell him, the bomber will always get through. The only defence is in offence, which means that you have to kill more women and children more quickly than the enemy if you want to save yourselves.

speech in the House of Commons, 10 November 1932

6 Since the day of the air, the old frontiers are gone. When you think of the defence of England you no longer think of the chalk cliffs of Dover; you think of the Rhine. That is where our frontier lies.

speech in the House of Commons, 30 July 1934

7 I shall be but a short time tonight. I have seldom spoken with greater regret, for my lips are not yet unsealed. Were these troubles over I would make a case, and I guarantee that not a man would go into the lobby against us.

on the Abyssinian crisis

speech in the House of Commons, 10 December 1935; see **MISQUOTATIONS** 548:11

8 This House today is a theatre which is being watched by the whole world. Let us conduct ourselves with that dignity which His Majesty is showing in this hour of his trial.

speech on the abdication of **EDWARD VIII**, House of Commons, 10 December 1936

9 Once I leave, I leave. I am not going to speak to the man on the bridge, and I am not going to spit on the deck.

resignation statement to the Cabinet, 28 May 1937

10 Do not run up your nose dead against the Pope or the NUM!

R. A. Butler *The Art of Memory* (1982) 'Iain Macleod'; see **MACMILLAN** 513:1

Arthur James Balfour 1848–1930

British Conservative statesman and Prime Minister 1902–5; nephew of Lord **SALISBURY**. On Balfour: see **CHURCHILL** 229:4, **CHURCHILL** 230:15, **LLOYD GEORGE** 496:12

11 It is unfortunate, considering that enthusiasm moves the world, that so few enthusiasts can be trusted to speak the truth.

letter to Mrs Drew, 19 May 1891; L. March-Phillips and B. Christian (eds.) *Some Hawarden Letters* (1917) ch. 7

12 The tyranny of majorities may be as bad as the tyranny of Kings . . . and I do not think that any rational or sober man will say that what is justifiable against a tyrannical King may not under certain circumstances be justifiable against a tyrannical majority.

watching the Belfast march past of Ulster Loyalists in 1893

in *Times* 5 April 1893

13 His Majesty's Government view with favour the establishment in Palestine of a national home for the Jewish people, and will use their best endeavours to facilitate the achievement of this object, it being clearly understood that nothing shall be done which may prejudice the civil and religious rights of existing non-Jewish communities in Palestine, or the rights and political status enjoyed by Jews in any other country.

known as the 'Balfour Declaration'

letter to Lord Rothschild, 2 November 1917

14 I make it a rule never to stare at people when they are in obvious distress.

on being asked what he thought of the behaviour of the German delegation at the signing of the Treaty of Versailles

Max Egremont *Balfour* (1980)

15 Zionism, be it right or wrong, good or bad, is rooted in age-long traditions, in present need, in future hopes, of far profounder import than the desires and prejudices of the seven hundred thousand Arabs who now inhabit that ancient land.

in August 1919; Max Egremont *Balfour* (1980)

16 Nothing matters very much and very few things matter at all.

Clodagh Anson *Book: discreet memoirs* (1931) ch. 13

17 Christianity, of course . . . but why journalism?

replying to Frank Harris, who had claimed that 'all the faults of the age come from Christianity and journalism'

Margot Asquith *Autobiography* (1920) vol. 1, ch. 10

18 I thought he was a young man of promise, but it appears he is a young man of promises.

of Winston **CHURCHILL**

Winston Churchill *My Early Life* (1930) ch. 17

19 I am more or less happy when being praised, not very uncomfortable when being abused, but I have moments of uneasiness when being explained.

K. Young *A. J. Balfour* (1963)

Ballads

1 There was a youth, and a well-beloved youth,
And he was an esquire's son,
He loved the bailiff's daughter dear,
That lived in Islington.
    'The Bailiff's Daughter of Islington'

2 All in the merry month of May,
When green buds they were swellin',
Young Jemmy Grove on his death-bed lay,
For love of Barbara Allen.
    'Barbara Allen's Cruelty'

3 O mother, mother, make my bed,
O make it saft and narrow:
My love has died for me to-day,
I'll die for him to-morrow.
    'Barbara Allen's Cruelty'

4 It fell about the Lammastide,
When the muir-men win their hay
The doughty Douglas bound him to ride
Into England, to drive a prey.
    'Battle of Otterburn'

5 There were twa sisters sat in a bour;
Binnorie, O Binnorie!
There came a knight to be their wooer,
By the bonnie milldams o' Binnorie.
    'Binnorie'

6 Ye Highlands and ye Lawlands,
O where hae ye been?
They hae slain the Earl of Murray,
And hae laid him on the green.
    'The Bonny Earl of Murray'

7 He was a braw gallant,
And he played at the gluve;
And the bonny Earl of Murray,
O he was the Queen's luve!

O lang will his Lady
Look owre the Castle Downe,
Ere she see the Earl of Murray
Come sounding through the town!
    'The Bonny Earl of Murray'

8 Fight on, my merry men all;
For why, my life is at an end;
Lord Percy sees my fall.
spoken by Earl Douglas
    'Chevy Chase'

9 Is there any room at your head, Sanders?
Is there any room at your feet?
Or any room at your twa sides,
Where fain, fain I would sleep?

There is na room at my head, Margaret,
There is na room at my feet;
My bed it is the cold, cold grave;
Among the hungry worms I sleep.
    'Clerk Sanders'

10 She hadna sailed a league, a league,
A league but barely three,
Till grim, grim grew his countenance
And gurly grew the sea.
    'The Daemon Lover'

11 'What hills are yon, yon pleasant hills,
The sun shines sweetly on?'—
'O yon are the hills o' Heaven,' he said,
'Where you will never won.'
    'The Daemon Lover'

12 Let me have length and breadth enough,
And under my head a sod;
That they may say when I am dead,
—*Here lies bold Robin Hood!*
    'The Death of Robin Hood'

13 There were three lords drinking at the wine
On the dowie dens o' Yarrow;
They made a compact them between
They would go fight tomorrow.
    'Dowie Dens of Yarrow'

14 O well's me o' my gay goss-hawk,
That he can speak and flee!
He'll carry a letter to my love,
Bring another back to me.
    'The Gay Goss Hawk'

15 I am a man upon the land,
I am a selkie in the sea;
When I am far and far from land,
My home it is the Sule Skerry.
    'The Great Selkie of Sule Skerry'

16 I wish I were where Helen lies,
Night and day on me she cries;
O that I were where Helen lies,
On fair Kirkconnell lea!

Curst be the heart that thought the thought,
And curst the hand that fired the shot,
When in my arms burd Helen dropt,
And died to succour me!
    'Helen of Kirkconnell'

17 Blair Atholl's mine, Jeanie,
Little Dunkeld is mine, lassie,
St Johnston's bower, and Huntingtower,
And all that's mine is thine, lassie.
    'Huntingtower'

18 Where are your eyes that looked so mild
When my poor heart you first beguiled?
Why did you run from me and the child?
Och, Johnny, I hardly knew ye!
    'Johnny, I hardly knew Ye'

19 I was but seven years auld
When my mither she did die;
My father married the ae warst woman
The warld did ever see.

For she has made me the laily worm
That lies at the fit o' the tree
And my sister Masery she's made
The machrel of the sea.

An' evry Saturday at noon
The machrel comes to me
An' she takes my laily head
An' lays it on her knee;
An' she kaims it wi' a siller kaim
An' washes 't in the sea.
    'The Laily Worm and the Machrel'

1 'What gat ye to your dinner, Lord Randal, my
  Son?
  What gat ye to your dinner, my handsome
  young man?'
  'I gat eels boil'd in broo'; mother, make my bed
  soon,
  For I'm weary wi' hunting, and fain wald lie
  down.'
  'Lord Randal'

2 This ae nighte, this ae nighte,
  —*Every nighte and alle,*
  Fire and fleet and candle-lighte,
  And Christe receive thy saule.
  fleet = *corruption of* flet, *meaning house-room*
  'Lyke-Wake Dirge'

3 From Brig o' Dread when thou may'st pass,
  —*Every nighte and alle,*
  To Purgatory fire thou com'st at last;
  And Christe receive thy saule.
  'Lyke-Wake Dirge'

4 If ever thou gavest meat or drink,
  —*Every nighte and alle,*
  The fire sall never make thee shrink
  And Christe receive thy saule.
  'Lyke-Wake Dirge'

5 When captains courageous whom death could
    not daunt,
  Did march to the siege of the city of Gaunt,
  They mustered their soldiers by two and by
    three,
  And the foremost in battle was Mary Ambree.
  'Mary Ambree'

6 For in my mind, of all mankind
  I love but you alone.
  'The Nut Brown Maid'

7 For I must to the greenwood go
  Alone, a banished man.
  'The Nut Brown Maid'

8 Marie Hamilton's to the kirk gane
  Wi' ribbons on her breast;
  The King thought mair o' Marie Hamilton
  Than he listen'd to the priest.
  'The Queen's Maries'

9 Yestreen the Queen had four Maries,
  The night she'll hae but three;
  There was Marie Seaton, and Marie Beaton,
  And Marie Carmichael, and me.
  'The Queen's Maries'

10 'O what is longer than the wave?
  And what is deeper than the sea?
  What is greener than the grass?
  And what is more wicked than a woman once
  was?'
  'Love is longer than the wave,
  And hell is deeper than the sea.
  Envy's greener than the grass,
  And the de'il more wicked than a woman e'er
  was.'

As soon as she the fiend did name,
He flew awa' in a bleezing flame.
  'Riddles Wisely Expounded'

11 There are twelve months in all the year,
  As I hear many men say,
  But the merriest month in all the year
  Is the merry month of May.
  'Robin Hood and the Widow's Three Sons'

12 Fight on, my men, sayes Sir Andrew Bartton,
  I am hurt but I am not slain;
  Ile lay mee downe and bleed a while
  And then Ile rise and fight againe.
  'Sir Andrew Bartton'

13 The king sits in Dunfermline town
  Drinking the blude-red wine.
  'Sir Patrick Spens'

14 To Noroway, to Noroway,
  To Noroway o'er the faem;
  The king's daughter o' Noroway,
  'Tis thou must bring her hame.
  'Sir Patrick Spens'

15 I saw the new moon late yestreen
  Wi' the auld moon in her arm;
  And if we gang to sea master,
  I fear we'll come to harm.
  'Sir Patrick Spens'

16 O lang, lang may the ladies sit,
  Wi' their fans into their hand,
  Before they see Sir Patrick Spens
  Come sailing to the strand!
  'Sir Patrick Spens'

17 Half-owre, half-owre to Aberdour,
  'Tis fifty fathoms deep;
  And there lies good Sir Patrick Spens,
  Wi' the Scots lords at his feet!
  'Sir Patrick Spens'

18 And she has kilted her green kirtle
  A little abune her knee;
  And she has braided her yellow hair
  A little abune her bree.
  'Tam Lin'

19 But what I ken this night, Tam Lin,
  Gin I had kent yestreen,
  I wad ta'en out thy heart o' flesh,
  And put in a heart o' stane.
  'Tam Lin'

20 She's mounted on her milk-white steed,
  She's ta'en true Thomas up behind.
  'Thomas the Rhymer'

21 And see ye not yon braid, braid road,
  That lies across the lily leven?
  That is the Path of Wickedness,
  Though some call it the Road to Heaven.
  'Thomas the Rhymer'

22 It was mirk, mirk night, there was nae starlight,
  They waded thro' red blude to the knee;
  For a' the blude that's shed on the earth
  Rins through the springs o' that countrie.
  'Thomas the Rhymer'

1 There were three ravens sat on a tree,
They were as black as they might be.
The one of them said to his make,
'Where shall we our breakfast take?'
'The Three Ravens'

2 God send every gentleman
Such hounds, such hawks, and such leman.
leman = *sweetheart*
'The Three Ravens'

3 As I was walking all alane,
I heard twa corbies making a mane:
The tane unto the tither did say,
'Where sall we gang and dine the day?'
'—In behint yon auld fail dyke
I wot there lies a new-slain knight;
And naebody kens that he lies there
But his hawk, his hound, and his lady fair.

'His hound is to the hunting gane,
His hawk to fetch the wild-fowl hame,
His lady's ta'en anither mate,
So we may make our dinner sweet.

'Ye'll sit on his white hause-bane,
And I'll pike out his bonny blue e'en:
Wi' ae lock o' his gowden hair
We'll theek our nest when it grows bare.'
corbies = *ravens;* fail = *turf;* hause = *neck;* theek = *thatch*
'The Twa Corbies'

4 The wind doth blow to-day, my love,
And a few small drops of rain;
I never had but one true love;
In cold grave she was lain.

I'll do as much for my true-love
As any young man may;
I'll sit and mourn all at her grave
For a twelvemonth and a day.
'The Unquiet Grave'

5 O waly, waly, up the bank,
And waly, waly, doun the brae,
And waly, waly, yon burn-side,
Where I and my Love wont to gae!
'Waly, Waly'

6 O waly, waly, gin love be bonnie
A little time while it is new!
But when 'tis auld it waxeth cauld,
And fades awa' like morning dew.
'Waly, Waly'

7 But had I wist, before I kist,
That love had been sae ill to win,
I had locked my heart in a case o' gowd,
And pinned it wi' a siller pin.

And O! if my young babe were born,
And set upon the nurse's knee;
And I mysel' were dead and gane,
And the green grass growing over me!
'Waly, Waly'

8 Tom Pearse, Tom Pearse, lend me your grey
  mare,
All along, down along, out along, lee.
For I want for to go to Widdicombe Fair,

Wi' Bill Brewer, Jan Stewer, Peter Gurney, Peter
  Davey, Dan'l Whiddon, Harry Hawk,
Old Uncle Tom Cobbleigh and all.
Old Uncle Tom Cobbleigh and all.
'Widdicombe Fair'

J. G. Ballard 1930–
British writer

9 A car crash harnesses elements of eroticism,
aggression, desire, speed, drama, kinaesthetic
factors, the stylizing of motion, consumer goods,
status—all these in one event. I myself see the
car crash as a tremendous sexual event really: a
liberation of human and machine libido (if there
is such a thing).
interview in *Penthouse* September 1970

10 Some refer to it as a cultural Chernobyl. I think
of it as a cultural Stalingrad.
of Euro Disney
in *Daily Telegraph* 2 July 1994; see **MNOUCHKINE** 551:14

Whitney Balliett 1926–2007
American writer

11 A critic is a bundle of biases held loosely
together by a sense of taste.
Dinosaurs in the Morning (1962) introductory note

12 The sound of surprise.
title of book on jazz (1959)

Honoré de Balzac 1799–1850
French novelist

13 *La prospérité porte avec elle une ivresse à laquelle les
hommes inférieurs ne résistent jamais.*
Prosperity brings with it an intoxication which
inferior men are unable to resist.
César Birotteau (1837) pt. 1

14 *L'homme n'est ni bon ni méchant, il naît avec des
instincts et des aptitudes.*
Man is neither good nor bad; he is born with
instincts and abilities.
La Comédie Humaine (1842) vol. 1, foreword

15 Equality may perhaps be a right, but no power
on earth can ever turn it into a fact.
La Duchesse de Langeais (1834)

16 *Affreuse condition de l'homme! il n'y a pas un de ses
bonheurs qui ne vienne d'une ignorance quelconque.*
How frightful is man's condition! There is not
one of his joys which does not come from some
ignorance or other.
Eugénie Grandet (1833) 'Portraits of Bourgeois' (translated by
Sylvia Raphael)

17 *La modestie, ou mieux la crainte, est une des
premières vertus de l'amour.*
Modesty, or rather a fear of being unworthy, is
one of the first virtues aroused by love.
Eugénie Grandet (1833) 'Provincial Love' (translated by Sylvia
Raphael)

1 He drew out the most delicious thin watch that Breguet had ever made. 'Fancy, it is eleven o'clock, I was up early'.
   Eugénie Grandet (1833)

2 A flow of words is a sure sign of duplicity.
   Letters of Two Brides (1841–42) pt. 1, letter 6

3 *La haine est un tonique, elle fait vivre, elle inspire la vengeance; mais la pitié tue, elle affaiblit encore notre faiblesse.*

   Hatred is a tonic, it makes one live, it inspires vengeance; but pity kills, it makes our weakness weaker.
   La Peau de Chagrin [The Wild Ass's Skin] (1831) ch. 1

4 *Le despotisme fait illégalement de grandes choses, la liberté ne se donne même pas la peine d'en faire légalement de très petites.*

   Despotism accomplishes great things illegally; liberty doesn't even go to the trouble of accomplishing small things legally.
   La Peau de Chagrin [The Wild Ass's Skin] (1831) ch. 3

5 If I'm not a genius, I'm done for.
   letter to his sister Laure, 1819; Graham Robb *Balzac* (1994) ch. 3

6 I am not deep, but I am very wide, and it takes time to walk round me.
   letter to Countess Maffei, 1837

George Bancroft 1800–91
American scholar and diplomat

7 Calvinism [in Switzerland] . . . established a religion without a prelate, a government without a king.
   History of the United States (1855 ed.) vol. 3, ch. 6

Tallulah Bankhead 1903–68
American actress

8 Cocaine habit-forming? Of course not. I ought to know. I've been using it for years.
   Tallulah (1952)

9 I'm as pure as the driven slush.
   in *Saturday Evening Post* 12 April 1947

10 I read Shakespeare and the Bible and I can shoot dice. That's what I call a liberal education.
   attributed

11 They used to shoot her through gauze. You should shoot me through linoleum.
   on Shirley Temple
   attributed

Joseph Banks 1743–1820
English botanist, who accompanied Captain **COOK** on his first voyage to the Pacific

12 I was awaked by the singing of the birds ashore . . . Their voices were certainly the most melodious wild music I have ever heard, almost imitating small bells but with the most tuneable silver sound imaginable.
   off the coast of New Zealand
   diary, 17 January 1770; J. C. Beaglehole (ed.) *The Endeavour Journal of Joseph Banks* (1962)

13 Who knows but that England may revive in New South Wales when it has sunk in Europe.
   letter to Governor Hunter, 30 March 1797

Théodore Faullain de Banville 1823–91
French poet

14 *Jeune homme sans mélancolie,*
   Blond comme un soleil d'Italie,
   Garde bien ta belle folie.

   Young man untroubled by melancholy, fair as an Italian sun, take good care of your fine carelessness.
   'A Adolphe Gaiffe' (1856)

15 LICENCES POÉTIQUES. *Il n'y en a pas.*

   POETIC LICENCE. There's no such thing.
   Petit traité de poésie française (1872) ch. 4

Imamu Amiri Baraka (Everett LeRoi Jones) 1934–
American poet and dramatist

16 A man is either free or he is not. There cannot be any apprenticeship for freedom.
   in *Kulchur* Spring 1962 'Tokenism'

17 God has been replaced, as he has all over the West, with respectability and airconditioning.
   Midstream (1963)

Yevgeny Baratynsky 1800–44
Russian poet

18 Providence has given human wisdom the choice between two fates: either hope and agitation, or hopelessness and calm.
   'Two Fates' (1823) (translated by Dmitri Obolensky)

Anna Laetitia Barbauld 1743–1825
English poet and literary editor

19 If e'er thy breast with freedom glowed,
   And spurned a tyrant's chain,
   Let not thy strong oppressive force
   A free-born mouse detain.
   'The Mouse's Petition to Doctor Priestley Found in the Trap where he had been confined all Night' (1773) l. 9

20 Beware, lest in the worm you crush
   A brother's soul you find.
   'The Mouse's Petition' (1773) l. 33

21 Yes, injured Woman! rise, assert thy right!
   'The Rights of Woman' (written c.1795, published 1825) l. 1

Mary Barber c.1690–1757

Irish poet

1 What is it our mammas bewitches
To plague us little boys with breeches?
'Written for My Son, and Spoken by Him at His First Putting on Breeches' (1731) l. 1

2 A husband's first praise is a Friend and
Protector:
Then change not these titles for Tyrant and
Hector.
'Conclusion of a Letter to the Revd Mr C—' (1734) l. 67

John Barbour c.1320–95

Scottish poet

3 Storys to rede ar delitabill,
Suppos that thai be nocht bot fabill.
The Bruce (1375) bk. 1, l. 1

4 A! fredome is a noble thing!
Fredome mayse man to haiff liking.
The Bruce (1375) bk. 1, l. 225

Alexander Barclay c.1475–1552

Scottish poet and priest

5 Thy bread is black, of ill sapour and taste,
And hard as flint because thou none should
waste,
That scant be thy teeth able it to break.
Dip it in pottage if thou no shift can make,
And though white and brown be both at one
price,
With brown shalt thou feed lest white might
make thee nice.
The lords will alway that people note and see
Between them and servants some diversity,
Though it to them turn to no profit at all;
If they have pleasure, the servant shall have
small.
Eclogues (1514) no. 2, l. 790

R. H. Barham ('Thomas Ingoldsby')

1788–1845

English clergyman and writer

6 Though I've always considered Sir Christopher
Wren,
As an architect, one of the greatest of men;
And, talking of Epitaphs,—much I admire his,
'Circumspice, si Monumentum requiris';
Which an erudite Verger translated to me,
'If you ask for his Monument, Sir-come-spy-see!'
The Ingoldsby Legends (First Series, 1840) 'The Cynotaph'; see **EPITAPHS** 319:10

7 What *was* to be done?—'twas perfectly plain
That they could not well hang the man over
again;
What *was* to be done?—The man was dead!
Nought *could* be done—nought could be said;
So—my Lord Tomnoddy went home to bed!
The Ingoldsby Legends (First Series, 1840) 'Hon. Mr Sucklethumbkin's Story'; see also **BROUGH** 160:7

8 The Jackdaw sat on the Cardinal's chair!
Bishop, and abbot, and prior were there;
Many a monk, and many a friar,
Many a knight, and many a squire,
With a great many more of lesser degree,—
In sooth a goodly company;
And they served the Lord Primate on bended
knee.
The Ingoldsby Legends (First Series, 1840) 'The Jackdaw of Rheims'

9 He cursed him in sleeping, that every night
He should dream of the devil, and wake in a
fright.
The Ingoldsby Legends (First Series, 1840) 'The Jackdaw of Rheims'

10 Never was heard such a terrible curse!
But what gave rise
To no little surprise,
Nobody seemed one penny the worse!
The Ingoldsby Legends (First Series, 1840) 'The Jackdaw of Rheims'

11 Heedless of grammar, they all cried, 'That's
him!'
The Ingoldsby Legends (First Series, 1840) 'The Jackdaw of Rheims'

12 Here's a corpse in the case with a sad swelled
face,
And a 'Crowner's Quest' is a queer sort of
thing!
in later editions: 'a Medical Crowner's a queer sort of thing!'
The Ingoldsby Legends (First Series, 1840) 'A Lay of St Gengulphus'

13 Now haste ye, my handmaidens, haste and see
How he sits there and glowers with his head on
his knee!
The Ingoldsby Legends (First Series, 1840) 'The Legend of Hamilton Tighe'

14 But wherever they live, or whenever they die
They'll never get rid of young Hamilton Tighe.
The Ingoldsby Legends (First Series, 1840) 'The Legend of Hamilton Tighe'

15 A servant's too often a negligent elf;
—If it's business of consequence, DO IT
YOURSELF!
The Ingoldsby Legends (Second Series, 1842) 'The Ingoldsby Penance!—Moral'

Sabine Baring-Gould 1834–1924

English clergyman

16 Onward, Christian soldiers,
Marching as to war,
With the cross of Jesus
Going on before.
'Onward, Christian Soldiers' (1864 hymn)

17 Through the night of doubt and sorrow
Onward goes the pilgrim band,
Singing songs of expectation,
Marching to the Promised Land.
'Through the night of doubt and sorrow' (1867 hymn); translated from the Danish of B. S. Ingemann (1789–1862)

Frederick R. Barnard

1 One picture is worth ten thousand words.
in *Printers' Ink* 10 March 1927

Julian Barnes 1946–

English novelist

2 Do not imagine that Art is something which is designed to give gentle uplift and self-confidence. Art is not a *brassière*. At least, not in the English sense. But do not forget that *brassière* is the French for life-jacket.
Flaubert's Parrot (1984) ch. 10

3 Books say: she did this because. Life says: she did this. Books are where things are explained to you; life is where things aren't.
Flaubert's Parrot (1984) ch. 13

4 Does history repeat itself, the first time as tragedy, the second time as farce? No, that's too grand, too considered a process. History just burps, and we taste again that raw-onion sandwich it swallowed centuries ago.
A History of the World in 10½ Chapters (1989) 'Parenthesis'; see **MARX** 526:8, **PROVERBS** 634:34

5 Love is just a system for getting someone to call you darling after sex.
Talking It Over (1991) ch. 16

Peter Barnes 1931–2004

English dramatist

6 CLAIRE: How do you know you're . . . God?
EARL OF GURNEY: Simple. When I pray to Him I find I'm talking to myself.
The Ruling Class (1969) act 1, sc. 4

William Barnes 1801–86

English poet and philologist

7 An' there vor me the apple tree
Do leän down low in Linden Lea.
Hwomely Rhymes (1859) 'My Orcha'd in Linden Lea'

8 But still the neäme do bide the seäme—
'Tis Pentridge—Pentridge by the river.
Hwomely Rhymes (1859) 'Pentridge by the River'

Richard Barnfield 1574–1627

English poet

9 The waters were his winding sheet, the sea was
made his tomb;
Yet for his fame the ocean sea, was not sufficient
room.
on the death of Sir John Hawkins
The Encomion of Lady Pecunia (1598) 'To the Gentlemen Readers'

10 My flocks feed not, my ewes breed not,
My rams speed not, all is amiss:
Love in dying, Faith is defying,
Heart's renying, causer of this.
'The Unknown Shepherd's Complaint' in Nicholas Ling (ed.)
England's Helicon (1600)

11 Man's life is well comparèd to a feast,
Furnished with choice of all variety;
To it comes Time; and as a bidden guest
He sets him down, in pomp and majesty;
The three-fold Age of man the waiters be.
Then with an earthen voider (made of clay)
Comes Death, and takes the table clean away.
'Man's life' (1598)

Phineas T. Barnum 1810–91

American showman. See also LINCOLN 494:11

12 There's a sucker born every minute.
attributed

Amelia E. Barr 1831–1919

American writer and journalist

13 The fate of love is that it always seems too little or too much.
The Belle of Bolling Green (1904) ch. 4

J. M. Barrie 1860–1937

Scottish writer and dramatist. On Barrie: see GUEDALLA 374:7, HOPE 406:21

14 His lordship may compel us to be equal upstairs, but there will never be equality in the servants' hall.
The Admirable Crichton (performed 1902, published 1914) act 1

15 One thinks more darkly down the left arm.
Peter Pan (1928) dedication

16 When the first baby laughed for the first time, the laugh broke into a thousand pieces and they all went skipping about, and that was the beginning of fairies.
Peter Pan (1928) act 1

17 Every time a child says 'I don't believe in fairies' there is a little fairy somewhere that falls down dead.
Peter Pan (1928) act 1

18 To die will be an awfully big adventure.
Peter Pan (1928) act 3; see **FROHMAN** 344:1

19 The man is not wholly evil: he has a Thesaurus in his cabin.
of Captain Hook
Peter Pan (1928) act 4

20 Do you believe in fairies? Say quick that you believe! If you believe, clap your hands!
Peter Pan (1928) act 4

21 That is ever the way. 'Tis all jealousy to the bride and good wishes to the corpse.
Quality Street (performed 1901, published 1913) act 1

22 Charm . . . it's a sort of bloom on a woman. If you have it, you don't need to have anything else; and if you don't have it, it doesn't much matter what else you have.
What Every Woman Knows (performed 1908, published 1918) act 1

1 There are few more impressive sights in the world than a Scotsman on the make.
   What Every Woman Knows (performed 1908, published 1918) act 2

2 The tragedy of a man who has found himself out.
   What Every Woman Knows (performed 1908, published 1918) act 4

3 To be born is to be wrecked on an island.
   preface to R. M. Ballantyne *The Coral Island* (1913 ed.)

Sebastian Barry 1955–
Irish writer and dramatist

4 Do you not feel that this island is moored only lightly to the sea-bed, and might be off for the Americas at any moment?
   Prayers of Sherkin (1991)

Ethel Barrymore 1879–1959
American actress

5 For an actress to be a success, she must have the face of a Venus, the brains of a Minerva, the grace of Terpsichore, the memory of a Macaulay, the figure of Juno, and the hide of a rhinoceros.
   George Jean Nathan *The Theatre in the Fifties* (1953)

Karl Barth 1886–1968
Swiss Protestant theologian

6 Men have never been good, they are not good and they never will be good.
   Christian Community (1948)

7 He will not be like an ant which has foreseen everything in advance, but like a child in a forest, or on Christmas Eve: one who is always rightly astonished by events, by the encounters and experiences which overtake him.
   of the justified man
   Church Dogmatics (1936)

Roland Barthes 1915–80
French writer and critic

8 What the public wants is the image of passion, not passion itself.
   Mythologies (1957) 'Le monde où l'on catche'

9 I think that cars today are almost the exact equivalent of the great Gothic cathedrals: I mean the supreme creation of an era, conceived with passion by unknown artists, and consumed in image if not in usage by a whole population which appropriates them as a purely magical object.
   Mythologies (1957) 'La nouvelle Citroën'

Bernard Baruch 1870–1965
American financier and presidential adviser

10 Let us not be deceived—we are today in the midst of a cold war.
   'cold war' was suggested to him by H. B. Swope, former editor of the New York World
   speech to South Carolina Legislature, 16 April 1947; in *New York Times* 17 April 1947

11 To me old age is always fifteen years older than I am.
   in *Newsweek* 29 August 1955

12 Vote for the man who promises least; he'll be the least disappointing.
   Meyer Berger *New York* (1960)

13 A political leader must keep looking over his shoulder all the time to see if the boys are still there. If they aren't still there, he's no longer a political leader.
   in *New York Times* 21 June 1965

Jacques Barzun 1907–
American historian and educationist

14 If it were possible to talk to the unborn, one could never explain to them how it feels to be alive, for life is washed in the speechless real.
   The House of Intellect (1959) ch. 6

Matsuo Basho 1644–94
Japanese poet

15 Early autumn—
   rice field, ocean,
   one green.
   translated by Lucien Stryk

16 Friends part
   forever—wild geese
   lost in cloud.
   translated by Lucien Stryk

17 How pleasant—
   just once *not* to see
   Fuji through mist.
   translated by Lucien Stryk

18 Old pond,
   leap-splash—
   a frog.
   translated by Lucien Stryk

19 Rainy days—
   silkworms droop
   on mulberries.
   translated by Lucien Stryk

20 Under the cherry—
   blossom soup,
   blossom salad.
   translated by Lucien Stryk

21 You, the butterfly—
   I, Chuang Tzu's
   dreaming heart.
   translated by Lucien Stryk; see **CHUANG TZU** 227:11

1 Days and months are travellers of eternity. So are the years that pass by.
The Narrow Road to the Deep North, translated by Nobuyuki Yuasa

2 Go to the pine if you want to learn about the pine.
Nobuyuki Yuasa (ed.) *Basho. The Narrow Road to the Deep North* (1966) introduction

William Basse d. *c*.1653
English poet

3 The first men that our Saviour dear
Did choose to wait upon him here,
Blest fishers were; and fish the last
Food was, that he on earth did taste:
I therefore strive to follow those
Whom he to follow him hath chose.
'The Angler's Song' (1653)

4 Renownèd Spenser, lie a thought more nigh
To learnèd Chaucer, and rare Beaumont lie
A little nearer Spenser, to make more room
For Shakespeare, in your threefold, fourfold tomb.
'On Mr Wm. Shakespeare' (1633)

Thomas Bastard 1566–1618
English poet

5 Age is deformed, youth unkind,
We scorn their bodies, they our mind.
Chrestoleros (1598) bk. 7, epigram 9

Edgar Bateman *and* George Le Brunn
British songwriters

6 Wiv a ladder and some glasses,
You could see to 'Ackney Marshes,
If it wasn't for the 'ouses in between.
'If it wasn't for the 'Ouses in between' (1894 song)

H. M. Bateman *see* Cartoon captions
205:12

Katherine Lee Bates 1859–1929
American writer and educationist

7 America! America!
God shed His grace on thee
And crown thy good with brotherhood
From sea to shining sea!
'America the Beautiful' (1893)

Jean Batten 1909–82
New Zealand aviator

8 Every flyer who ventures across oceans to distant lands is a potential explorer; in his or her breast burns the same fire that urged the adventurers of old to set forth in their sailing-ships for foreign lands.
Alone in the Sky (1979) ch. 18

Charles Baudelaire 1821–67
French poet and critic

9 *Le poète est semblable au prince des nuées*
Qui hante la tempête et se rit de l'archer;
Exilé sur le sol, au milieu des huées,
Ses ailes de géant l'empêchent de marcher.
The poet is like the prince of the clouds, who rides out the tempest and laughs at the archer. But when he is exiled on the ground, amidst the clamour, his giant's wings prevent him from walking.
Les fleurs du mal (1857) 'L'Albatross'—'Spleen et idéal' no. 2

10 *Hypocrite lecteur,—mon semblable,—mon frère.*
Hypocrite reader—my likeness—my brother.
Les fleurs du mal (1857) 'Au Lecteur'

11 *La nature est un temple où de vivants piliers*
Laissent parfois sortir de confuses paroles;
L'homme y passe à travers des forêts de symboles
Qui l'observent avec des regards familiers.
Nature is a temple, where, from living pillars, confused words are sometimes allowed to escape; here man passes, through forests of symbols, which watch him with looks of recognition.
Les fleurs du mal (1857) 'Correspondances' no. 4

12 *Là, tout n'est qu'ordre et beauté,*
Luxe, calme et volupté.
Everything there is simply order and beauty, luxury, peace and sensual indulgence.
Les fleurs du mal (1857) 'L'Invitation au voyage'—'Spleen et idéal' no. 56

13 *Quelle est cette île triste et noire? C'est Cythère,*
Nous dit-on, un pays fameux dans les chansons,
Eldorado banal de tous les vieux garçons.
Regardez, après tout, c'est un pauvre terre.
What sad, black isle is that? It's Cythera, so they say, a land celebrated in song, the banal Eldorado of all the old fools. Look, after all, it's a land of poverty.
Les fleurs du mal (1857) 'Un voyage à Cythère'—'Les fleurs du mal' no. 121

14 *Nous voulons, tant ce feu nous brûle le cerveau,*
Plonger au fond du gouffre, Enfer ou Ciel,
*   qu'importe?*
Au fond de l'Inconnu pour trouver du nouveau!
We want, this fire so burns our brain tissue, to drown in the abyss—heaven or hell, who cares? Through the unknown, we'll find the new.
Les fleurs du mal (1857) 'Le voyage' no. 126 (translated by Robert Lowell)

15 All that is beautiful and noble is the result of reason and calculation.
The Painter of Modern Life (1863) 'In Praise of Cosmetics'

16 What happened on the 2nd of December physically depoliticized me. You can no longer talk of generally held ideas. That the whole of Paris is Orleanist is beyond dispute, but that doesn't concern me. If I had voted, I could only have voted for myself.

letter to Narcisse Ancelle, 5 March 1852; in *Selected Letters of Charles Baudelaire* (tr. Rosemary Lloyd, 1986)

1 *Il y a dans tout changement quelque chose d'infâme et d'agréable à la fois, quelque chose qui tient de l'infidelité et du déménagement. Cela suffit à expliquer la Révolution Française.*

There is in all change something at once sordid and agreeable, which smacks of infidelity and household removals. This is sufficient to explain the French Revolution.

Journaux intimes (1887) 'Mon coeur mis à nu' no. 4 (translated by Christopher Isherwood)

2 *La croyance au progrès est une doctrine de paresseux, une doctrine de Belges. C'est l'individu qui compte sur ses voisins pour faire sa besogne.*

Belief in progress is a doctrine of idlers and Belgians. It is the individual relying upon his neighbours to do his work.

Journaux intimes (1887) 'Mon coeur mis à nu' no. 9 (translated by Christopher Isherwood)

3 There are as many kinds of beauty as there are habitual ways of seeking happiness.

The Salon of 1846 (1846) 'What is Romanticism?'

4 *Il faut épater le bourgeois.*

One must astonish the bourgeois.

attributed; also attributed to Privat d'Anglemont (c.1820–59) in the form '*Je les ai épatés, les bourgeois* [I flabbergasted them, the bourgeois]'

Jean Baudrillard 1929–2007
French sociologist and cultural critic

5 To love someone is to isolate him from the world, wipe out every trace of him, dispossess him of his shadow, drag him into a murderous future. It is to circle around the other like a dead star and absorb him into a black light.

Fatal Strategies (1983)

Yehuda Bauer 1926–
Czech-born Israeli historian

6 I come from a people who gave the ten commandments to the world. Time has come to strengthen them by three additional ones, which we ought to adopt and commit ourselves to: thou shalt not be a perpetrator; thou shalt not be a victim; and thou shalt never, but never, be a bystander.

speech to the German Bundestag, 1998, quoted in his own speech to the Stockholm International Forum on the Holocaust, 26 July 2000

L. Frank Baum 1856–1919
American writer

7 The road to the City of Emeralds is paved with yellow brick.

The Wonderful Wizard of Oz (1900) ch. 2; see **HARBURG** 380:1

Beverley Baxter 1891–1964
British journalist and Conservative politician

8 Beaverbrook is so pleased to be in the Government that he is like the town tart who has finally married the Mayor!

Henry Channon *Chips: the Diaries* (1967) 12 June 1940

Thomas Haynes Bayly 1797–1839
English poet and dramatist

9 Oh! no! we never mention her,
Her name is never heard;
My lips are now forbid to speak
That once familiar word.

'Oh! No! We Never Mention Her' (1844)

Beachcomber *see* J. B. Morton

Todd Beamer 1968–2001
American businessman

10 Let's roll.

heard by telephone operator as Beamer and other passengers were planning to storm the cockpit of the hijacked United Airlines Flight 93 on 11 September 2001; the plane crashed in Pennsylvania minutes later
in *Washington Post* 17 September 2001

James Beattie 1735–1803
Scottish philosopher and poet

11 Some deemed him wondrous wise, and some
believed him mad.

The Minstrel bk. 1 (1771) st. 16

12 Fancy a thousand wondrous forms descries
More wildly great than ever pencil drew,
Rocks, torrents, gulfs, and shapes of giant size,
And glittering cliffs on cliffs, and fiery ramparts rise.

The Minstrel bk. 1 (1771) st. 53

13 In the deep windings of the grove, no more
The hag obscene, and grisly phantom dwell;
Nor in the fall of mountain-stream, or roar
Of winds, is heard the angry spirit's yell.

The Minstrel bk. 2 (1774) st. 48

David Beatty 1871–1936
British Admiral of the Fleet, 1916–19

14 There's something wrong with our bloody ships today.

at the Battle of Jutland, 1916
Winston Churchill *The World Crisis 1916–1918* (1927) pt. 1

Topham Beauclerk 1739–80
English dandy

15 Then he does not wear them out in practice.

on hearing that a certain person was 'a man of good principles'
James Boswell *The Life of Samuel Johnson* (1791) 14 April 1778

Pierre-Augustin Caron de Beaumarchais 1732–99

French dramatist

1 *Aujourd'hui ce qui ne vaut pas la peine d'être dit, on le chante.*

Today if something is not worth saying, people sing it.

Le Barbier de Séville (1775) act 1, sc. 2

2 *Je me presse de rire de tout, de peur d'être obligé d'en pleurer.*

I hurry to laugh at everything, for fear of having to weep at it.

Le Barbier de Séville (1775) act 1, sc. 2

3 *Boire sans soif et faire l'amour en tout temps, madame, il n'y a que ça qui nous distingue des autres bêtes.*

Drinking when we are not thirsty and making love all year round, madam; that is all there is to distinguish us from other animals.

Le Mariage de Figaro (1784) act 2, sc. 21

4 *Si vous n'avez de çà pour garder un bon domestique, je ne suis pas assez bête, moi, pour renvoyer un si bon maître.*

If you haven't enough up here to keep a good servant, I'm not so stupid as to dismiss such a good master.

Le Mariage de Figaro (1784) act 2, sc. 21

5 *En fait d'amour, vois-tu, trop n'est pas même assez.*

With love, you see, even too much is not enough.

Le Mariage de Figaro (1784) act 4, sc. 1

6 *Parce que vous êtes un grand seigneur, vous vous croyez un grand génie! . . . Vous vous êtes donné la peine de naître, et rien de plus.*

Because you are a great lord, you believe yourself to be a great genius! . . . You took the trouble to be born, but no more.

Le Mariage de Figaro (1784) act 5, sc. 3

Francis Beaumont 1584–1616

English poet and dramatist

7 Nose, nose, jolly red nose,
Who gave thee this jolly red nose? . . .
Nutmegs and ginger, cinnamon and cloves,
And they gave me this jolly red nose.

The Knight of the Burning Pestle (c.1607) act 1

8　　　　What things have we seen,
Done at the Mermaid! heard words that have
　　been
So nimble, and so full of subtil flame,
As if that every one from whence they came,
Had meant to put his whole wit in a jest,
And had resolved to live a fool, the rest
Of his dull life.

'Letter to Ben Jonson'

9 Here are sands, ignoble things,
Dropt from the ruined sides of kings;

Here's a world of pomp and state,
Buried in dust, once dead by fate.

'On the Tombs in Westminster Abbey'

Francis Beaumont 1584–1616 *and* John Fletcher 1579–1625

English dramatists. See also **FLETCHER**

10 Those have most power to hurt us that we love.

The Maid's Tragedy (written 1610–11) act 5

11 PHILASTER: Oh, but thou dost not know
What 'tis to die.
BELLARIO: Yes, I do know, my Lord:
'Tis less than to be born; a lasting sleep;
A quiet resting from all jealousy,
A thing we all pursue; I know besides,
It is but giving over of a game,
That must be lost.

Philaster (written 1609) act 3

12 There is no other purgatory but a woman.

The Scornful Lady (1616) act 3

Lord Beaverbrook (Max Aitken, Lord Beaverbrook) 1879–1964

Canadian-born British newspaper proprietor and Conservative politician. On Beaverbrook: see **ATTLEE** 35:7, **BAXTER** 62:8, **KIPLING** 468:26

13 The Flying Scotsman is no less splendid a sight when it travels north to Edinburgh than when it travels south to London. Mr Baldwin denouncing sanctions was as dignified as Mr Baldwin imposing them.

in *Daily Express* 29 May 1937

14 He did not seem to care which way he travelled providing he was in the driver's seat.

of **LLOYD GEORGE**
The Decline and Fall of Lloyd George (1963) ch. 7

15 Now who is responsible for this work of development on which so much depends? To whom must the praise be given? To the boys in the back rooms. They do not sit in the limelight. But they are the men who do the work.

in *Listener* 27 March 1941

16 I ran the paper [*Daily Express*] purely for propaganda, and with no other purpose.

evidence to Royal Commission on the Press, 18 March 1948, in A. J. P. Taylor *Beaverbrook* (1972)

17 With the publication of his Private Papers in 1952, he committed suicide 25 years after his death.

of Earl **HAIG**
Men and Power (1956)

18 Our cock won't fight.

to Winston **CHURCHILL** *of* **EDWARD VIII**, *during the abdication crisis of 1936*
Frances Donaldson *Edward VIII* (1974) ch. 22

19 I have had two masters and one of them betrayed me.

of **BONAR LAW** *and* **CHURCHILL**
A. J. P. Taylor, letter, 16 December 1973; *Letters to Eva* (1991)

1 Who's in charge of the clattering train?
habitual question about an organization; see **ANONYMOUS** *21:12*
    A. Chisholm and M. Davie *Beaverbrook* (1992)

Carl Becker 1873–1945

American historian

2 The significance of man is that he is that part of the universe that asks the question, What is the significance of Man? He alone can stand apart imaginatively and, regarding himself and the universe in their eternal aspects, pronounce a judgement: The significance of man is that he is insignificant and is aware of it.
    Progress and Power (1936) ch. 3

Samuel Beckett 1906–89

Irish dramatist, novelist, and poet

3 It is suicide to be abroad. But what is it to be at home, Mr Tyler, what is it to be at home? A lingering dissolution.
    All That Fall (1957)

4 We could have saved sixpence. We have saved fivepence. (*Pause*) But at what cost?
    All That Fall (1957)

5 I shall state silence more competently than ever a better man spangled the butterflies of vertigo.
    A Dream of Fair to Middling Women (written 1932)

6 CLOV: Do you believe in the life to come?
HAMM: Mine was always that.
    Endgame (1958)

7 Let us pray to God . . . the bastard! He doesn't exist!
    Endgame (1958)

8 Perhaps my best years are gone . . . but I wouldn't want them back. Not with the fire that's in me now.
    Krapp's Last Tape (1959)

9 There is no use indicting words, they are no shoddier than what they peddle.
    Malone Dies (1958)

10 If I had the use of my body I would throw it out of the window.
    Malone Dies (1958)

11 The sun shone, having no alternative, on the nothing new.
    Murphy (1938)

12 His writing is not *about* something; it is that something itself.
    of James **JOYCE**
    Our Exagmination Round the Factification for Incamination of Work in Progress (1929)

13 To find a form that accommodates the mess, that is the task of the artist now.
    Proust (1961)

14 Where I am, I don't know, I'll never know, in the silence you don't know, you must go on, I can't go on, I'll go on.
    The Unnamable (1959)

15 Nothing to be done.
    Waiting for Godot (1955) act 1

16 There's a man all over for you, blaming on his boots the faults of his feet.
    Waiting for Godot (1955) act 1

17 One of the thieves was saved. (*Pause*) It's a reasonable percentage.
    Waiting for Godot (1955) act 1

18 ESTRAGON: Charming spot. Inspiring prospects. Let's go.
VLADIMIR: We can't.
ESTRAGON: Why not?
VLADIMIR: We're waiting for Godot.
    Waiting for Godot (1955) act 1

19 Nothing happens, nobody comes, nobody goes, it's awful!
    Waiting for Godot (1955) act 1

20 He can't think without his hat.
    Waiting for Godot (1955) act 1

21 VLADIMIR: That passed the time.
ESTRAGON: It would have passed in any case.
VLADIMIR: Yes, but not so rapidly.
    Waiting for Godot (1955) act 1

22 We are not saints, but we have kept our appointment. How many people can boast as much?
    Waiting for Godot (1955) act 2

23 We all are born mad. Some remain so.
    Waiting for Godot (1955) act 2

24 They give birth astride of a grave, the light gleams an instant, then it's night once more.
    Waiting for Godot (1955) act 2

25 Habit is a great deadener.
    Waiting for Godot (1955) act 2

26 Ever tried. Ever failed. No matter. Try again. Fail again. Fail better.
    Worstward Ho (1983)

27 I couldn't have done it otherwise, gone on I mean. I could not have gone on through the awful wretched mess of life without having left a stain upon the silence.
    Deirdre Bair *Samuel Beckett* (1978)

28 Even death is unreliable: instead of zero it may be some ghastly hallucination, such as the square root of minus one.
    attributed

William Beckford 1759–1844

English writer and collector. On Beckford: see **BORGES** 151:9

29 When he was angry, one of his eyes became so terrible, that no person could bear to behold it; and the wretch upon whom it was fixed, instantly fell backward, and sometimes expired. For fear, however, of depopulating his dominions and making his palace desolate, he but rarely gave way to his anger.
    Vathek (1782; 3rd ed., 1816) opening para.

1 He did not think, with the Caliph Omar Ben Adalaziz, that it was necessary to make a hell of this world to enjoy Paradise in the next.
   Vathek (1782; 3rd ed., 1816) para. 2

2 I am not over-fond of resisting temptation.
   Vathek (1782; 3rd ed., 1816) para. 215

Thomas Lovell Beddoes 1803–49
English poet and dramatist

3 If thou wilt ease thine heart
   Of love and all its smart,
   Then sleep, dear, sleep.
   Death's Jest Book 1825–8 (1850) act 2, sc. 2 'Dirge'

4 But wilt thou cure thine heart
   Of love and all its smart,
   Then die, dear, die.
   Death's Jest Book 1825–8 (1850) act 2, sc. 2 'Dirge'

5 I have a bit of FIAT in my soul,
   And can myself create my little world.
   Death's Jest Book 1825–8 (1850) act 5, sc. 1, l. 39

6 If there were dreams to sell,
   What would you buy?
   Some cost a passing bell;
   Some a light sigh,
   That shakes from Life's fresh crown
   Only a rose-leaf down.
   If there were dreams to sell,
   Merry and sad to tell,
   And the crier rung the bell,
   What would you buy?
   'Dream-Pedlary' (written 1830, published 1851)

The Venerable Bede AD 673–735
English historian and scholar; monk of Jarrow

7 If history records good things of good men, the thoughtful hearer is encouraged to imitate what is good.
   Ecclesiastical History of the English People preface

8 'Such,' he said, 'O King, seems to me the present life of men on earth, in comparison with that time which to us is uncertain, as if when on a winter's night you sit feasting with your ealdormen and thegns,—a single sparrow should fly swiftly into the hall, and coming in at one door, instantly fly out through another. In that time in which it is indoors it is indeed not touched by the fury of the winter, but yet, this smallest space of calmness being passed almost in a flash, from winter going into winter again, it is lost to your eyes. Somewhat like this appears the life of man; but of what follows or what went before, we are utterly ignorant.'
   Ecclesiastical History of the English People (translated by B. Colgrave, 1969) bk. 2, ch. 13

Harry Bedford *and* Terry Sullivan
British songwriters

9 I'm a bit of a ruin that Cromwell knocked about a bit.
   'It's a Bit of a Ruin that Cromwell Knocked about a Bit' (1920 song; written for Marie Lloyd)

Barnard Elliott Bee 1823–61
American Confederate general

10 There is Jackson with his Virginians, standing like a stone wall. Let us determine to die here, and we will conquer.
   referring to General T. J. ('Stonewall') JACKSON *at the battle of Bull Run, 21 July, 1861 (in which Bee himself was killed)*
   B. Perley Poore *Perley's Reminiscences* (1886) vol. 2, ch. 7

Thomas Beecham 1879–1961
English conductor

11 Like two skeletons copulating on a corrugated tin roof.
   describing the harpsichord
   Harold Atkins and Archie Newman *Beecham Stories* (1978)

12 The musical equivalent of the Towers of St Pancras Station.
   of ELGAR's *1st Symphony*
   Neville Cardus *Sir Thomas Beecham* (1961) p. 113

13 There are two golden rules for an orchestra: start together and finish together. The public doesn't give a damn what goes on in between.
   Harold Atkins and Archie Newman *Beecham Stories* (1978)

14 Too much counterpoint; what is worse, Protestant counterpoint.
   of J. S. BACH
   in *Guardian* 8 March 1971

15 Why do we have to have all these third-rate foreign conductors around—when we have so many second-rate ones of our own?
   L. Ayre *Wit of Music* (1966) p. 70

H. C. Beeching 1859–1919
English clergyman

16 First come I; my name is Jowett.
   There's no knowledge but I know it.
   I am Master of this college:
   What I don't know isn't knowledge.
   The Masque of Balliol (composed by and current among members of Balliol College in the late 1870s) in W. G. Hiscock (ed.) *The Balliol Rhymes* (1939); see ANONYMOUS 19:3, SPRING-RICE 769:2

Max Beerbohm 1872–1956
English critic, essayist, and caricaturist. On Beerbohm: see SHAW 742:19

17 Mankind is divisible into two great classes: hosts and guests.
   And Even Now (1920) 'Hosts and Guests'

18 I was not unpopular [at school] . . . It is Oxford that has made me insufferable.
   More (1899) 'Going Back to School'

1 Enter Michael Angelo. Andrea del Sarto appears for a moment at a window. Pippa passes.

Seven Men (1919) 'Savonarola Brown' act 3

2 The fading signals and grey eternal walls of that antique station, which, familiar to them and insignificant, does yet whisper to the tourist the last enchantments of the Middle Age.

Zuleika Dobson (1911) ch. 1; see **ARNOLD** 31:16

3 The dullard's envy of brilliant men is always assuaged by the suspicion that they will come to a bad end.

Zuleika Dobson (1911) ch. 4

4 DEEPLY REGRET INFORM YOUR GRACE LAST NIGHT TWO BLACK OWLS CAME AND PERCHED ON BATTLEMENTS REMAINED THERE THROUGH NIGHT HOOTING AT DAWN FLEW AWAY NONE KNOWS WHITHER AWAITING INSTRUCTIONS JELLINGS.

Zuleika Dobson (1911) ch. 14

5 PREPARE VAULT FOR FUNERAL MONDAY DORSET.

Zuleika Dobson (1911) ch. 14

6 Fate wrote her a most tremendous tragedy, and she played it in tights.

of Caroline of Brunswick, wife of **GEORGE IV**

The Yellow Book (1894) vol. 3

Ethel Lynn Beers 1827–79
American poet

7 All quiet along the Potomac to-night,
No sound save the rush of the river,
While soft falls the dew on the face of the dead—
The picket's off duty forever.

'The Picket Guard' (1861) st. 6; see **MCCLELLAN** 509:11

Ludwig van Beethoven 1770–1827
German composer. On Beethoven: see **BAKUNIN** 52:11

8 *Muss es sein? Es muss sein.*

Must it be? It must be.

String Quartet in F Major, Opus 135, epigraph

9 The immortal god of harmony.

of J. S. **BACH**

letter to Breitkopf und Härtel, 22 April 1801; Michael Hamburger (ed.) *Beethoven: Letters, Journals and Correspondence* (1951)

10 I shall seize fate by the throat; it shall certainly never wholly overcome me.

letter to Franz Wegeler, 16 November 1801, in A. C. Kalischer (ed.) *Beethoven's Letters* (1909)

11 I like honesty and sincerity; and I maintain that an artist should not be shabbily treated.

often quoted as 'No one should drive a hard bargain with an artist'

letter to C. F. Peters, 5 June 1822, in E. Anderson *Letters of Beethoven* (1961)

12 I shall hear in heaven.

attributed last words, almost certainly apocryphal but current since the mid nineteenth century

Isabella Beeton 1836–65
English writer on cookery

13 The housekeeper must consider herself as the immediate representative of her mistress, and bring, to the management of the household, all those qualities of honesty, industry, and vigilance, in the same degree as if she were at the head of her own family . . . Cleanliness, punctuality, order, and method, are essentials in the character of a housekeeper.

Book of Cookery and Household Management (1861) ch. 2

Brendan Behan 1923–64
Irish dramatist

14 PAT: He was an Anglo-Irishman.
MEG: In the blessed name of God what's that?
PAT: A Protestant with a horse.

Hostage (1958) act 1

15 When I came back to Dublin, I was courtmartialled in my absence and sentenced to death in my absence, so I said they could shoot me in my absence.

Hostage (1958) act 1

16 We're here because we're queer
Because we're queer because we're here.

Hostage (1958) act 3; see **MILITARY SAYINGS, SLOGANS, AND SONGS** 535:17

17 *on being asked 'What was the message of your play' after a performance of* The Hostage:

Message? Message? What the hell do you think I am, a bloody postman?

Dominic Behan *My Brother Brendan* (1965); see **GOLDWYN** 365:22

18 There's no such thing as bad publicity except your own obituary.

Dominic Behan *My Brother Brendan* (1965); see **PROVERBS** 626:27

Aphra Behn 1640–89
English dramatist, poet, and novelist

19 Oh, what a dear ravishing thing is the beginning of an Amour!

The Emperor of the Moon (1687) act 1, sc. 1

20 Love ceases to be a pleasure, when it ceases to be a secret.

The Lover's Watch (1686) 'Four o' Clock. General Conversation'

21 All I ask, is the privilege for my masculine part the poet in me . . . If I must not, because of my sex, have this freedom . . . I lay down my quill, and you shall hear no more of me.

preface to *The Lucky Chance* (1686)

22 Since man with that inconstancy was born,
To love the absent, and the present scorn,
Why do we deck, why do we dress
For such a short-lived happiness?
Why do we put attraction on,
Since either way 'tis we must be undone?

Lycidus (1688) 'To Alexis, in Answer to his Poem against Fruition'

1 I owe a duty, where I cannot love.
The Moor's Revenge (1677) act 3, sc. 3

2 Be just, my lovely swain, and do not take
Freedoms you'll not to me allow;
Or give Amynta so much freedom back
That she may rove as well as you.
Let us then love upon the honest square,
Since interest neither have designed.
For the sly gamester, who ne'er plays me fair,
Must trick for trick expect to find.
Poems upon Several Occasions (1684) 'To Lysander, on some Verses he writ, and asking more for his Heart than 'twas worth'

3 A brave world, Sir, full of religion, knavery, and change: we shall shortly see better days.
The Roundheads (1682) act 1, sc. 1

4 Variety is the soul of pleasure.
The Rover pt. 2 (1681) act 1; see **COWPER** 256:12

5 Come away; poverty's catching.
The Rover pt. 2 (1681) act 1

6 Money speaks sense in a language all nations understand.
The Rover pt. 2 (1681) act 3

7 Do you not daily see fine clothes, rich furniture, jewels and plate are more inviting than beauty unadorned?
The Rover pt. 2 (1681) act 4

8 The soft, unhappy sex.
The Wandering Beauty (1698) para. 1

John Hay Beith *see* Ian Hay

Lord Belhaven 1656–1708
Scottish politician

9 Good God! What, is this an entire surrender?
culmination of a speech opposing the Union with England
speech in the Scottish Parliament, 2 November 1706

Alexander Graham Bell 1847–1922
Scottish inventor of the telephone

10 Mr Watson—come here—I want to see you.
to his assistant, Thomas Watson; the first words spoken on the telephone, 10 March 1876
James Mackay *Sounds Out of Silence* (1997) ch. 6

Clive Bell 1881–1964
English art critic

11 I will try to account for the degree of my aesthetic emotion. That, I conceive, is the function of the critic.
Art (1914) pt. 3, ch. 3

12 Only reason can convince us of those three fundamental truths without a recognition of which there can be no effective liberty: that what we believe is not necessarily true; that what we like is not necessarily good; and that all questions are open.
Civilization (1928) ch. 5

George Bell 1883–1958
English clergyman, Bishop of Chichester

13 The policy is obliteration, openly acknowledged. This is not a justifiable act of war.
of the saturation bombing of Berlin
speech, House of Lords, 9 February 1944

Gertrude Bell 1868–1926
English traveller, archaeologist, and government servant

14 The world of adventure and of enterprise, dark with hurrying storms, glittering in raw sunlight, an unanswered question and unanswerable doubt hidden in the fold of every hill.
on travel in the desert
Syria: The Desert and the Sown (1907)

Francis Bellamy 1856–1931
American clergyman and editor

15 I pledge allegiance to the flag of the United States of America and to the republic for which it stands, one nation under God, indivisible, with liberty and justice for all.
The Pledge of Allegiance to the Flag (1892)

St Robert Bellarmine 1542–1621
Italian cardinal and theologian

16 Nobody can remember more than seven of anything.
reason for omitting the eight beatitudes from his catechism
John Bossy *Christianity in the West 1400–1700* (1985)

Hilaire Belloc 1870–1953
British poet, essayist, historian, novelist, and Liberal politician

17 Child! do not throw this book about;
Refrain from the unholy pleasure
Of cutting all the pictures out!
Preserve it as your chiefest treasure.
A Bad Child's Book of Beasts (1896) dedication

18 I shoot the Hippopotamus
With bullets made of platinum,
Because if I use leaden ones
His hide is sure to flatten 'em.
A Bad Child's Book of Beasts (1896) 'The Hippopotamus'; see **FORSTER** 337:15

19 And mothers of large families (who claim to common sense)
Will find a Tiger well repay the trouble and expense.
A Bad Child's Book of Beasts (1896) 'The Tiger'

20 Believing Truth is staring at the sun
Which but destroys the power that could perceive.
So naught of our poor selves can be at one
With burning Truth, nor utterly believe.
'Believing Truth is staring at the sun' (1938)

21 Physicians of the Utmost Fame
Were called at once; but when they came

They answered, as they took their Fees,
'There is no Cure for this Disease.'
Cautionary Tales (1907) 'Henry King'

1 And always keep a-hold of Nurse
For fear of finding something worse.
Cautionary Tales (1907) 'Jim'

2 Sir! you have disappointed us!
We had intended you to be
The next Prime Minister but three:
The stocks were sold; the Press was squared;
The Middle Class was quite prepared.
But as it is! . . . My language fails!
Go out and govern New South Wales!
Cautionary Tales (1907) 'Lord Lundy'

3 Matilda told such Dreadful Lies,
It made one Gasp and Stretch one's Eyes.
Cautionary Tales (1907) 'Matilda'

4 For every time She shouted 'Fire!'
They only answered 'Little Liar!'
Cautionary Tales (1907) 'Matilda'

5 She was not really bad at heart,
But only rather rude and wild:
She was an aggravating child.
Cautionary Tales (1907) 'Rebecca'

6 Of Courtesy, it is much less
Than Courage of Heart or Holiness,
Yet in my Walks it seems to me
That the Grace of God is in Courtesy.
'Courtesy' (1910)

7 Here richly, with ridiculous display,
The Politician's corpse was laid away.
While all of his acquaintance sneered and
    slanged
I wept: for I had longed to see him hanged.
'Epitaph on the Politician Himself' (1923)

8 I said to Heart, 'How goes it ?' Heart replied:
'Right as a Ribstone Pippin!' But it lied.
'The False Heart' (1910)

9 I'm tired of Love: I'm still more tired of Rhyme.
But Money gives me pleasure all the time.
'Fatigued' (1923)

10 Strong brother in God and last companion,
    Wine.
'Heroic Poem upon Wine' (1926)

11 Remote and ineffectual Don
That dared attack my Chesterton.
'Lines to a Don' (1910)

12 Whatever happens we have got
The Maxim Gun, and they have not.
The Modern Traveller (1898) pt. 6

13 The Llama is a woolly sort of fleecy hairy goat,
With an indolent expression and an undulating
    throat
Like an unsuccessful literary man.
More Beasts for Worse Children (1897) 'The Llama'

14 The Microbe is so very small
You cannot make him out at all.

But many sanguine people hope
To see him through a microscope.
More Beasts for Worse Children (1897) 'The Microbe'

15 Oh! let us never, never doubt
What nobody is sure about!
More Beasts for Worse Children (1897) 'The Microbe'

16 Lord Finchley tried to mend the Electric Light
Himself. It struck him dead: And serve him
    right!
It is the business of the wealthy man
To give employment to the artisan.
More Peers (1911) 'Lord Finchley'

17 Like many of the Upper Class
He liked the Sound of Broken Glass.
New Cautionary Tales (1930) 'About John'; see **WAUGH** 842:11

18 The accursed power which stands on Privilege
(And goes with Women, and Champagne, and
    Bridge)
Broke—and Democracy resumed her reign:
(Which goes with Bridge, and Women and
    Champagne).
'On a Great Election' (1923)

19 I am a sundial, and I make a botch
Of what is done much better by a watch.
'On a Sundial' (1938)

20 When I am dead, I hope it may be said:
'His sins were scarlet, but his books were read.'
'On His Books' (1923)

21 Pale Ebenezer thought it wrong to fight,
But Roaring Bill (who killed him) thought it
    right.
'The Pacifist' (1938)

22 The great hills of the South Country
They stand along the sea;
And it's there walking in the high woods
That I could wish to be,
And the men that were boys when I was a boy
Walking along with me.
'The South Country' (1910)

23 When I am living in the Midlands
That are sodden and unkind . . .
And the great hills of the South Country
Come back into my mind.
'The South Country' (1910)

24 Do you remember an Inn,
Miranda?
Do you remember an Inn?
'Tarantella' (1923)

25 And the fleas that tease in the High Pyrenees
And the wine that tasted of the tar?
'Tarantella' (1923)

26 Balliol made me, Balliol fed me,
Whatever I had she gave me again:
And the best of Balliol loved and led me.
God be with you, Balliol men.
'To the Balliol Men Still in Africa' (1910)

27 There's nothing worth the wear of winning,
But laughter and the love of friends.
Verses (1910) 'Dedicatory Ode'

1 Is there no Latin word for Tea? Upon my soul, if I had known that I would have let the vulgar stuff alone.
On Nothing (1908) 'On Tea'

Saul Bellow 1915–2005
American novelist

2 If I am out of my mind, it's all right with me, thought Moses Herzog.
Herzog (1961), opening words

3 It is sometimes necessary to repeat what we all know. All mapmakers should place the Mississippi in the same location, and avoid originality.
Mr Sammler's Planet (1969)

4 Art has something to do with the achievement of stillness in the midst of chaos. A stillness which characterizes prayer, too, and the eye of the storm . . . an arrest of attention in the midst of distraction.
George Plimpton *Writers at Work* (1967) 3rd series

Du Belloy (Pierre-Laurent Buirette du Belloy)
1725–75
French dramatist

5 *Plus je vis d'étrangers, plus j'aimai ma patrie.*
The more foreigners I saw, the more I loved my homeland.
Le Siège de Calais (1765) act 2, sc. 3

Robert Benchley 1889–1945
American humorist. See also **FILM LINES** 328:24

6 The biggest obstacle to professional writing is the necessity for changing a typewriter ribbon.
Chips off the old Benchley (1949) 'Learn to Write'

7 The surest way to make a monkey of a man is to quote him.
My Ten Years in a Quandary (1936)

8 In America there are two classes of travel—first class, and with children.
Pluck and Luck (1925)

9 It took me fifteen years to discover that I had no talent for writing, but I couldn't give it up because by that time I was too famous.
Nathaniel Benchley *Robert Benchley* (1955) ch. 1

10 STREETS FLOODED. PLEASE ADVISE.
telegram sent on arriving in Venice
R. E. Drennan (ed.) *Wits End* (1973) 'Robert Benchley'

Julien Benda 1867–1956
French philosopher and novelist

11 *La trahison des clercs.*
The treachery of the intellectuals.
title of book (1927)

Peter Benenson 1921–2005
English founder of Amnesty International

12 Better to light a candle than curse the darkness.
at a Human Rights Day ceremony, 10 December 1961; see **PROVERBS** 627:38

Stephen Vincent Benét 1898–1943
American poet and novelist

13 I have fallen in love with American names,
The sharp, gaunt names that never get fat,
The snakeskin-titles of mining-claims,
The plumed war-bonnet of Medicine Hat,
Tucson and Deadwood and Lost Mule Flat.
'American Names' (1927)

14 I shall not rest quiet in Montparnasse.
I shall not lie easy at Winchelsea.
You may bury my body in Sussex grass,
You may bury my tongue at Champmédy.
I shall not be there, I shall rise and pass.
Bury my heart at Wounded Knee.
'American Names' (1927)

15 And kept his heart a secret to the end
From all the picklocks of biographers.
*of Robert E. **LEE***
John Brown's Body (1928)

16 We thought we were done with these things but we were wrong.
We thought, because we had power, we had wisdom.
'Litany for Dictatorships' (1935)

William Rose Benét 1886–1950
American poet

17 Blake saw a treefull of angels at Peckham Rye,
And his hands could lay hold on the tiger's terrible heart.
Blake knew how deep is Hell, and Heaven how high,
And could build the universe from one tiny part.
'Mad Blake' (1918); see **BLAKE** 128:13

Judah Benjamin 1811–84
American politician and lawyer

18 The gentleman will please remember that when his half-civilized ancestors were hunting the wild boar in Silesia, mine were princes of the earth.
in reply to a taunt by a Senator of German descent
B. Perley Poore *Perley's Reminiscences* (1886)

Tony Benn (Anthony Wedgwood Benn)
1925–
British Labour politician

19 Not a reluctant peer but a persistent commoner.
at a Press Conference, 23 November 1960

20 Some of the jam we thought was for tomorrow, we've already eaten.
attributed, 1969; see **CARROLL** 203:6

1 It is as wholly wrong to blame Marx for what was done in his name, as it is to blame Jesus for what was done in his.
Alan Freeman *The Benn Heresy* (1982) 'Interview with Tony Benn'

2 A faith is something you die for; a doctrine is something you kill for: there is all the difference in the world.
in *Observer* 16 April 1989 'Sayings of the Week'

3 *questions habitually asked by Tony Benn on meeting somebody in a position of power:*
What power have you got? Where did you get it from? In whose interests do you exercise it? To whom are you accountable? How do we get rid of you?
'The Independent Mind', lecture at Nottingham, 18 June 1993

4 If you file your waste-paper basket for 50 years, you have a public library.
in *Daily Telegraph* 5 March 1994

5 A quotation is what a speaker wants to say—unlike a soundbite which is all that an interviewer allows you to say.
letter to Antony Jay, August 1996

George Bennard 1873–1958
American Methodist minister and hymn-writer

6 I will cling to the old rugged cross,
And exchange it some day for a crown.
'The Old Rugged Cross' (1913 hymn)

Alan Bennett 1934–
English dramatist and actor

7 I have never understood this liking for war. It panders to instincts already catered for within the scope of any respectable domestic establishment.
Forty Years On (1969) act 1

8 Memories are not shackles, Franklin, they are garlands.
Forty Years On (1969) act 2

9 Standards are always out of date. That is what makes them standards.
Forty Years On (1969) act 2

10 Sapper, Buchan, Dornford Yates, practitioners in that school of Snobbery with Violence that runs like a thread of good-class tweed through twentieth-century literature.
Forty Years On (1969) act 2

11 We started off trying to set up a small anarchist community, but people wouldn't obey the rules.
Getting On (1972) act 1

12 To be Prince of Wales is not a position. It is a predicament.
The Madness of King George (1995 film); in the 1992 play *The Madness of George III* the line was 'To be heir to the throne . . .'

13 People always complain about muck-raking biographers saying 'Leave us our heroes.' 'Leave us our villains' is just as important.
of an attempt to rehabilitate **HAIG**
diary, 11 February 1996

Arnold Bennett 1867–1931
English novelist

14 His opinion of himself, having once risen, remained at 'set fair'.
The Card (1911) ch. 1

15 'What great cause is he identified with?' 'He's identified . . . with the great cause of cheering us all up.'
The Card (1911) ch. 12

16 The price of justice is eternal publicity.
Things that have Interested Me (2nd series, 1923) 'Secret Trials'

17 A cause may be inconvenient, but it's magnificent. It's like champagne or high heels, and one must be prepared to suffer for it.
The Title (1918) act 1

18 Being a husband is a whole-time job. That is why so many husbands fail. They cannot give their entire attention to it.
The Title (1918) act 1

19 Journalists say a thing that they know isn't true, in the hope that if they keep on saying it long enough it *will* be true.
The Title (1918) act 1

20 Literature's always a good card to play for Honours.
The Title (1918) act 3

Jill Bennett 1931–90
English actress; fourth wife of John OSBORNE

21 Never marry a man who hates his mother, because he'll end up hating you.
in *Observer* 12 September 1982 'Sayings of the Week'

A. C. Benson 1862–1925
English writer

22 Land of Hope and Glory, Mother of the Free,
How shall we extol thee who are born of thee?
Wider still and wider shall thy bounds be set;
God who made thee mighty, make thee mightier yet.
'Land of Hope and Glory' written to be sung as the Finale to **ELGAR**'s *Coronation Ode* (1902)

Stella Benson 1892–1933
English novelist

23 Call no man foe, but never love a stranger.
This is the End (1917)

Henry A. Bent 1926–
American chemist

1 The important point is not the bigness of Avogadro's number but the bigness of Avogadro.

Avogadro's number is equal to 6.023 x 10²³ (named after the Italian chemist and physicist Amedeo Avogadro (1776–1856), who in 1811 formulated a law for deriving molecular weights)

The Second Law (1965)

Jeremy Bentham 1748–1832
English philosopher and jurist, the first major proponent of utilitarianism

2 Right . . . is the child of law: from real laws come real rights; but from imaginary laws, from laws of nature, fancied and invented by poets, rhetoricians, and dealers in moral and intellectual poisons, come imaginary rights, a bastard brood of monsters.

Anarchical Fallacies in J. Bowring (ed.) *Works* vol. 2 (1843)

3 Natural rights is simple nonsense: natural and imprescriptible rights, rhetorical nonsense—nonsense upon stilts.

Anarchical Fallacies in J. Bowring (ed.) *Works* vol. 2 (1843)

4 The greatest happiness of the greatest number is the foundation of morals and legislation.

Bentham claimed to have acquired the 'sacred truth' either from Joseph PRIESTLEY or Cesare Beccaria (1738–94)

The Commonplace Book in J. Bowring (ed.) *Works* vol. 10 (1843); see **HUTCHESON** 422:10

5 I do really take it for an indisputable truth, and a truth that is one of the corner stones of political science—the more strictly we are watched, the better we behave.

Farming Defended (1797)

6 The Fool had stuck himself up one day, with great gravity, in the King's throne; with a stick, by way of a sceptre, in one hand, and a ball in the other: being asked what he was doing? he answered *'reigning'*. Much of the same sort of reign, I take it would be that of our Author's [Blackstone's] Democracy.

A Fragment on Government (1776) ch. 2, para. 34, footnote (e)

7 All punishment is mischief: all punishment in itself is evil.

Principles of Morals and Legislation (1789) ch. 13, para. 2

8 The question is not, Can they reason? nor, Can they talk? but, Can they suffer?

Principles of Morals and Legislation (1789) ch. 17

9 Every law is contrary to liberty.

Principles of the Civil Code (1843)

10 Publicity is the very soul of justice. It is the keenest spur to exertion, and the surest of all guards against improbity.

Publicity in the Courts of Justice (1843)

11 As to the evil which results from a censorship, it is impossible to measure it, because it is impossible to tell where it ends.

Theory of Legislation (1864) 'Principles of the Penal Code' pt. 4, ch. 2

12 He rather hated the ruling few than loved the suffering many.

of James Mill, father of John Stuart MILL

H. N. Pym (ed.) *Memories of Old Friends, being Extracts from the Journals and Letters of Caroline Fox* (1882) p. 113, 7 August 1840

13 Prose is when all the lines except the last go on to the end. Poetry is when some of them fall short of it.

M. St. J. Packe *The Life of John Stuart Mill* (1954) bk. 1, ch. 2

Edmund Clerihew Bentley 1875–1956
English writer, inventor of the comic verse form, the 'clerihew'

14 The Art of Biography
Is different from Geography.
Geography is about Maps,
But Biography is about Chaps.

Biography for Beginners (1905) introduction

15 What I like about Clive
Is that he is no longer alive.
There is a great deal to be said
For being dead.

Biography for Beginners (1905) 'Clive'

16 Sir Humphrey Davy
Abominated gravy.
He lived in the odium
Of having discovered Sodium.

Biography for Beginners (1905) 'Sir Humphrey Davy'

17 John Stuart Mill,
By a mighty effort of will,
Overcame his natural *bonhomie*
And wrote 'Principles of Political Economy'.

Biography for Beginners (1905) 'John Stuart Mill'

18 Sir Christopher Wren
Said, 'I am going to dine with some men.
If anybody calls
Say I am designing St Paul's.'

Biography for Beginners (1905) 'Sir Christopher Wren'

19 George the Third
Ought never to have occurred.
One can only wonder
At so grotesque a blunder.

More Biography (1929) 'George the Third'

Eric Bentley 1916–
American dramatist and writer

20 Ours is the age of substitutes: instead of language, we have jargon; instead of principles, slogans; and, instead of genuine ideas, Bright Ideas.

in *New Republic* 29 December 1952

Richard Bentley 1662–1742

English classical scholar

1 I hold it as certain, that no man was ever written out of reputation but by himself.
   William Warburton (ed.) *The Works of Alexander Pope* (1751) vol. 4

2 It is a pretty poem, Mr Pope, but you must not call it Homer.
   when pressed by POPE *to comment on 'My Homer' [i.e. his translation of* HOMER'*s* Iliad]
   John Hawkins (ed.) *The Works of Samuel Johnson* (1787) vol. 4 'The Life of Pope'

3 It would be port if it could.
   on claret
   R. C. Jebb *Bentley* (1902) ch. 12

Lloyd Bentsen 1921–2006

American Democratic politician

4 *responding to Dan Quayle's claim to have 'as much experience in the Congress as Jack* KENNEDY *had when he sought the presidency':*
   Senator, I served with Jack Kennedy. I knew Jack Kennedy. Jack Kennedy was a friend of mine. Senator, you're no Jack Kennedy.
   in the vice-presidential debate, 5 October 1988

Pierre-Jean de Béranger 1780–1857

French poet

5 *Nos amis, les ennemis.*
   Our friends, the enemy.
   'L'Opinion de ces demoiselles' (written 1815) in *Chansons de De Béranger* (1832)

6 *Il était un roi d'Yvetot*
   Peu connu dans l'histoire.
   There was a king of Yvetot
   Little known to history.
   'Le Roi d'Yvetot' (written 1813) in *Chansons de De Béranger* (1832)

Lord Charles Beresford 1846–1919

British politician

7 VERY SORRY CAN'T COME. LIE FOLLOWS BY POST.
   telegram to the Prince of Wales, on being summoned to dine at the eleventh hour
   Ralph Nevill *The World of Fashion 1837–1922* (1923) ch. 5; see PROUST

Henri Bergson 1859–1941

French philosopher

8 The present contains nothing more than the past, and what is found in the effect was already in the cause.
   L'Évolution créatrice [Creative Evolution] (1907) ch. 1

9 *L'élan vital.*
   The vital spirit.
   L'Évolution créatrice [Creative Evolution] (1907) ch. 2 (section title)

10 Only those ideas which least belong to us can be adequately expressed in words.
   Time and Free Will (1910) ch. 2

George Berkeley 1685–1753

Irish philosopher and Anglican bishop. On Berkeley: see BYRON 189:12, JOHNSON 440:10, SMITH 758:3

11 They are neither finite quantities, or quantities infinitely small, nor yet nothing. May we not call them the ghosts of departed quantities?
   on NEWTON'*s infinitesimals*
   The Analyst (1734) sect. 35

12 [Tar water] is of a nature so mild and benign and proportioned to the human constitution, as to warm without heating, to cheer but not inebriate.
   Siris (1744) para. 217; see COWPER 256:19

13 Truth is the cry of all, but the game of the few.
   Siris (1744) para. 368

14 The same principles which at first lead to scepticism, pursued to a certain point bring men back to common sense.
   Three Dialogues between Hylas and Philonous (1734) Dialogue 3

15 Yet so it is we see the illiterate bulk of mankind that walk the high-road of plain common sense, and are governed by the dictates of nature, for the most part easy and undisturbed.
   A Treatise Concerning the Principles of Human Knowledge (1710) introduction, sect. 1

16 We have first raised a dust and then complain we cannot see.
   A Treatise Concerning the Principles of Human Knowledge (1710) introduction, sect. 3

17 All the choir of heaven and furniture of earth—in a word, all those bodies which compose the mighty frame of the world—have not any subsistence without a mind.
   A Treatise Concerning the Principles of Human Knowledge (1710) pt. 1, sect. 6

18 Westward the course of empire takes its way;
   The first four acts already past,
   A fifth shall close the drama with the day:
   Time's noblest offspring is the last.
   'On the Prospect of Planting Arts and Learning in America' (1752) st. 6.

Irving Berlin (Israel Baline) 1888–1989

American songwriter

19 Must you dance ev'ry dance
   With the same fortunate man?
   You have danced with him since the music began.
   Won't you change partners and dance with me?
   'Change Partners' (1938 song) in *Carefree*

20 Heaven—I'm in Heaven—And my heart beats so that I can hardly speak;
   And I seem to find the happiness I seek
   When we're out together dancing cheek-to-cheek.
   'Cheek-to-Cheek' (1935 song) in *Top Hat*

1 God bless America,
  Land that I love,
  Stand beside her and guide her
  Thru the night with a light from above.
  From the mountains to the prairies,
  To the oceans white with foam,
  God bless America,
  My home sweet home.
    'God Bless America' (1939 song)

2 There may be trouble ahead,
  But while there's moonlight and music and love
    and romance,
  Let's face the music and dance.
    'Let's Face the Music and Dance' (1936 song) in *Follow the
    Fleet*

3 A pretty girl is like a melody
  That haunts you night and day.
    'A Pretty Girl is like a Melody' (1919 song)

4 The song is ended (but the melody lingers on).
    title of song (1927)

5 There's no business like show business.
    title of song in *Annie Get Your Gun* (1946)

6 I'm dreaming of a white Christmas,
  Just like the ones I used to know,
  Where the tree-tops glisten
  And children listen
  To hear sleigh bells in the snow.
    'White Christmas' (1942 song) in *Holiday Inn*

7 Listen, kid, take my advice, never hate a song
  that has sold half a million copies.
    to Cole **PORTER**, of the song 'Rosalie'
    Philip Furia *Poets of Tin Pan Alley* (1990)

Isaiah Berlin 1909–97
Latvian-born British philosopher

8 Injustice, poverty, slavery, ignorance—these may
  be cured by reform or revolution. But men do
  not live only by fighting evils. They live by
  positive goals, individual and collective, a vast
  variety of them, seldom predictable, at times
  incompatible.
    Four Essays on Liberty (1969) 'Political Ideas in the Twentieth
    Century'

9 There exists a great chasm between those, on
  one side, who relate everything to a single
  central vision . . . and, on the other side, those
  who pursue many ends, often unrelated and
  even contradictory . . . The first kind of
  intellectual and artistic personality belongs to the
  hedgehogs, the second to the foxes.
    The Hedgehog and the Fox (1953) sect. 1; see **ARCHILOCHUS**
    26:1

10 Liberty is liberty, not equality or fairness or
  justice or human happiness or a quiet
  conscience.
    Two Concepts of Liberty (1958)

11 Few new truths have ever won their way against
  the resistance of established ideas save by being
  overstated.
    Vico and Herder (1976)

12 Rousseau was the first militant lowbrow.
    in *Observer* 9 November 1952

Hector Berlioz 1803–69
French composer

13 Time is a great teacher but unfortunately it kills
  all its pupils.
    attributed; in *Almanach des lettres françaises et étrangères*
    (1924) 11 May

J. D. Bernal 1901–71
Irish-born physicist

14 Men will not be content to manufacture life:
  they will want to improve on it.
    The World, the Flesh and the Devil (1929)

Georges Bernanos 1888–1948
French novelist and essayist

15 The wish for prayer is a prayer in itself.
    Journal d'un curé de campagne (1936) ch. 2

16 Hell, madam, is to love no more.
    Journal d'un curé de campagne (1936) ch. 2

Bernard of Chartres d. *c.*1130
French philosopher

17 We are like dwarfs on the shoulders of giants,
  so that we can see more than they, and things at
  a greater distance, not by virtue of any
  sharpness of sight on our part, or any physical
  distinction, but because we are carried high and
  raised up by their giant size.
    John of Salisbury *The Metalogicon* (1159) bk. 3, ch. 4, quoted
    in R. K. Merton *On the Shoulders of Giants* (1965) ch. 9; see
    COLERIDGE 241:23, **NEWTON** 574:7

St Bernard of Clairvaux 1090–1153
**French theologian, monastic reformer, and abbot. See also
CASWALL 206:14**

18 You will find something more in woods than in
  books. Trees and stones will teach you that
  which you can never learn from masters.
    Epistles no. 106; see **SHAKESPEARE** 696:15, **WORDSWORTH**
    869:14

19 I am a kind of chimaera of my age, neither
  cleric nor layman.
    Epistles no. 250

20 *Liberavi animam meam.*
  I have freed my soul.
    Epistles no. 371

21 In the cloister, under the eyes of the brethren
  who read there, what profit is there in those
  ridiculous monsters, in that marvellous and
  deformed beauty, that beautiful deformity? To
  what purpose are those unclean apes, those
  fierce lions, those monstrous centaurs, those
  half-men, those striped tigers, those fighting
  knights, those hunters winding their horns.

Many bodies are there seen under one head, or again, many heads to a single body. Here is a four-footed beast with a serpent's tail; there, a fish with a beast's head. Here again the forepart of a horse trails half a goat behind it, or a horned beast bears the hind quarters of a horse. In short so many and so marvellous are the varieties of diverse shapes on every hand, that we are more tempted to read in the marble than in our books, and to spend the whole day in wondering at these things rather than in meditating the law of God. For God's sake, if men are not ashamed of these follies, why at least do they not shrink from the expense?

letter to William, Abbot of St-Thierry, c.1125

1 I spoke; and at once the Crusaders have multiplied to infinity. Villages and towns are now deserted. You will scarcely find one man for every seven women. Everywhere you see widows whose husbands are still alive.

of the effects of his preaching the Second Crusade
letter to Pope Eugenius III, 1146

2 Will the light only shine if it is in a candelabrum of gold or silver?

on Pope Urban II's conferring the title of Lux Mundi [*light of the world*] *on the abbey of Cluny*
attributed

Claude Bernard 1813–78

French physiologist

3 Observation is a passive science, experimentation an active science.

An Introduction to the Study of Experimental Medicine (1865, translated by Henry Copley Green, 1949)

4 [The science of life] is a superb and dazzlingly lighted hall which may be reached only by passing through a long and ghastly kitchen.

An Introduction to the Study of Experimental Medicine (1865, translated by Henry Copley Green, 1949)

5 By a marvellous compensation, science, in humbling our pride, proportionately increases our power.

An Introduction to the Study of Experimental Medicine (1865, translated by Henry Copley Green, 1949)

Bill Bernbach 1911–82

American advertising executive

6 A great ad campaign will make a bad product fail faster. It will get more people to know it's bad.

Bill Bernbach said (1989)

Eric Berne 1910–70

American psychiatrist

7 Games people play: the psychology of human relationships.

title of book (1964)

8 Human life [as] . . . a process of filling in time until the arrival of death, or Santa Claus, with

very little choice, if any, of what kind of business one is going to transact during the long wait, is a commonplace but not the final answer.

Games People Play (1964) ch. 18

Lord Berners 1883–1950

English composer, artist, and writer

9 He's always backing into the limelight.

of T. E. **LAWRENCE**
oral tradition; see also **SHAW** 742:21

Tim Berners-Lee 1955–

English computer scientist

10 It was always difficult to predict how fast it was going to take off or whether it would crash. We just kept our fingers crossed.

referring to the early days of the World Wide Web
in CIO December 1999

Yogi Berra 1925–

American baseball player

11 The future ain't what it used to be.

attributed

12 If people don't want to come out to the ball park, nobody's going to stop 'em.

of baseball games
attributed

13 It ain't over till it's over.

comment on National League pennant race, 1973, quoted in many versions

14 It was déjà vu all over again.

attributed

Wendell Berry 1934–

American poet and novelist

15 I come into the peace of wild things
who do not tax their lives with forethought
of grief. I come into the presence of still water.
And I feel above me the day-blind stars
waiting with their light.

'The Peace of Wild Things' (1968)

16 Our hair
turns white with our ripening
as though to fly away in some
coming wind, bearing the seed
of what we know.

'Ripening' (1980)

17 Radiances know him. Grown lighter
than breath, he is set free
in our remembering. Grown brighter
than vision, he goes dark
into the life of the hill
that holds his peace.

'Three Elegiac Poems' (1969)

18 The earth is what we all have in common.

The Unsettling of America (1977) ch. 7

John Berryman 1914–72

American poet

1   People will take balls,
Balls will be lost always, little boy,
And no one buys a ball back.
'The Ball Poem' (1948)

2 We must travel in the direction of our fear.
'A Point of Age' (1942)

3 Life, friends, is boring. We must not say so . . .
And moreover my mother told me as a boy
(repeatingly) 'Ever to confess you're bored
means you have no
Inner Resources.' I conclude now I have no
inner resources, because I am heavy bored.
77 Dream Songs (1964) no. 14

4 I seldom go to films. They are too exciting,
said the Honourable Possum.
77 Dream Songs (1964) no. 53

Pierre Berton 1920–2004

Canadian writer

5 The march of social progress is like a long and
straggling parade, with the seers and prophets at
its head and a smug minority bringing up the
rear.
The Smug Minority (1968)

6 Somebody who knows how to make love in a
canoe.
definition of a Canadian
in Toronto Star, Canadian Magazine 22 December 1973

Charles Best fl. 1602

English poet

7 Look how the pale Queen of the silent night
Doth cause the Ocean to attend upon her,
And he, as long as she is in his sight,
With his full tide is ready her to honour.
'Of the Moon' (1602) in N. Ault (ed.) Elizabethan Lyrics from
the Original Texts (1925)

Theobald von Bethmann Hollweg

1856–1921

German statesman, Chancellor 1909–17

8 Just for a word 'neutrality'—a word which in
wartime has so often been disregarded—just for
a scrap of paper, Great Britain is going to make
war on a kindred nation who desires nothing
better than to be friends with her.
summary of a report by Sir Edward Goschen to Sir Edward
GREY
British Documents on Origins of the War 1898–1914 (1926) vol.
11; The Diary of Edward Goschen 1900–1914 (1980) Appendix B
discusses the contentious origins of this statement

John Betjeman 1906–84

English poet

9 He sipped at a weak hock and seltzer
As he gazed at the London skies

Through the Nottingham lace of the curtains
Or was it his bees-winged eyes?
He rose, and he put down The Yellow Book.
He staggered—and, terrible-eyed,
He brushed past the palms on the staircase
And was helped to a hansom outside.
'The Arrest of Oscar Wilde at the Cadogan Hotel' (1937)

10 And girls in slacks remember Dad,
And oafish louts remember Mum,
And sleepless children's hearts are glad,
And Christmas-morning bells say 'Come!'
Even to shining ones who dwell
Safe in the Dorchester Hotel.
And is it true? And is it true,
This most tremendous tale of all,
Seen in a stained-glass window's hue,
A Baby in an ox's stall?
The Maker of the stars and sea
Become a Child on earth for me?
'Christmas' (1954)

11 Oh! Chintzy, Chintzy cheeriness,
Half dead and half alive!
'Death in Leamington' (1931)

12 Spirits of well-shot woodcock, partridge, snipe
Flutter and bear him up the Norfolk sky.
'Death of King George V' (1937)

13 Old men who never cheated, never doubted,
Communicated monthly, sit and stare
At the new suburb stretched beyond the run-way
Where a young man lands hatless from the air.
'Death of King George V' (1937)

14 Phone for the fish-knives, Norman
As Cook is a little unnerved;
You kiddies have crumpled the serviettes
And I must have things daintily served.
'How to get on in Society' (1954)

15 The Church's Restoration
In eighteen-eighty-three
Has left for contemplation
Not what there used to be.
'Hymn' (1931)

16 Think of what our Nation stands for,
Books from Boots' and country lanes,
Free speech, free passes, class distinction,
Democracy and proper drains.
Lord, put beneath Thy special care
One-eighty-nine Cadogan Square.
'In Westminster Abbey' (1940)

17 Stony seaboard, far and foreign,
Stony hills poured over space,
Stony outcrop of the Burren,
Stones in every fertile place,
Little fields with boulders dotted,
Grey-stone shoulders saffron-spotted,
Stone-walled cabins thatched with reeds,
Where a Stone Age people breeds
The last of Europe's stone age race.
'Ireland with Emily' (1945)

18 Belbroughton Road is bonny, and pinkly bursts
the spray

Of prunus and forsythia across the public way.
'May-Day Song for North Oxford' (1945); see **SONGS,**
SPIRITUALS, AND SHANTIES 763:4

1 Gaily into Ruislip Gardens
Runs the red electric train,
With a thousand Ta's and Pardon's
Daintily alights Elaine;
Hurries down the concrete station
With a frown of concentration,
Out into the outskirt's edges
Where a few surviving hedges
Keep alive our lost Elysium—rural Middlesex
again.
'Middlesex' (1954)

2 Official designs are aggressively neuter,
The Puritan work of an eyeless computer.
'The Newest Bath Guide' (1974)

3 Pam, I adore you, Pam, you great big
mountainous sports girl,
Whizzing them over the net, full of the strength
of five.
'Pot Pourri from a Surrey Garden' (1940)

4 The gas was on in the Institute,
The flare was up in the gymn,
A man was running a mineral line,
A lass was singing a hymn,
When Captain Webb the Dawley man,
Captain Webb from Dawley,
Came swimming along in the old canal
That carries the bricks to Lewley.
'A Shropshire Lad' (1940)

5 Come, friendly bombs, and fall on Slough!
It isn't fit for humans now,
There isn't grass to graze a cow.
Swarm over, Death!
'Slough' (1937)

6 Miss J. Hunter Dunn, Miss J. Hunter Dunn,
Furnish'd and burnish'd by Aldershot sun.
'A Subaltern's Love-Song' (1945)

7 Love-thirty, love-forty, oh! weakness of joy,
The speed of a swallow, the grace of a boy,
With carefullest carelessness, gaily you won,
I am weak from your loveliness, Joan Hunter
Dunn.
Miss Joan Hunter Dunn, Miss Joan Hunter
Dunn,
How mad I am, sad I am, glad that you won.
'A Subaltern's Love-Song' (1945)

8 The dread of beatings! Dread of being late!
And, greatest dread of all, the dread of games!
Summoned by Bells (1960) ch. 7

9 Broad of Church and 'broad of Mind',
Broad before and broad behind,
A keen ecclesiologist,
A rather dirty Wykehamist.
'The Wykehamist' (1931)

10 Ghastly good taste, or a depressing story of the
rise and fall of English architecture.
title of book (1933)

Bruno Bettelheim 1903–90

Austrian-born American psychologist

11 The most extreme agony is to feel that one has
been utterly forsaken.
Surviving and other essays (1979)

Aneurin Bevan 1897–1960

British Labour politician. On Bevan: see **BEVIN** 77:14

12 This island is made mainly of coal and
surrounded by fish. Only an organizing genius
could produce a shortage of coal and fish at the
same time.
speech at Blackpool, 24 May 1945, in *Daily Herald* 25 May
1945

13 No amount of cajolery, and no attempts at
ethical or social seduction, can eradicate from
my heart a deep burning hatred for the Tory
Party . . . So far as I am concerned they are
lower than vermin.
speech at Manchester, 4 July 1948, in *The Times* 5 July 1948

14 The language of priorities is the religion of
Socialism.
speech at Labour Party Conference in Blackpool, 8 June 1949,
in *Report of the 48th Annual Conference* (1949)

15 He does not talk the language of the 20th
century but that of the 18th. He is still fighting
Blenheim all over again. His only answer to a
difficult situation is send a gun-boat.
of Winston **CHURCHILL**
speech at Labour Party Conference, Scarborough, 2 October
1951, in *Daily Herald* 3 October 1951

16 We know what happens to people who stay in
the middle of the road. They get run down.
in *Observer* 6 December 1953

17 Damn it all, you can't have the crown of thorns
and the thirty pieces of silver.
on his position in the Labour Party, c.1956
Michael Foot *Aneurin Bevan* (1973) vol. 2, ch. 13

18 I am not going to spend any time whatsoever in
attacking the Foreign Secretary . . . If we
complain about the tune, there is no reason to
attack the monkey when the organ grinder is
present.
during a debate on the Suez crisis
in the House of Commmons, 16 May 1957

19 If you carry this resolution you will send
Britain's Foreign Secretary naked into the
conference chamber.
speaking against a motion proposing unilateral nuclear
disarmament by the UK at Labour Party Conference in
Brighton, 3 October 1957
in *Daily Herald* 4 October 1957

20 I know that the right kind of leader for the
Labour Party is a desiccated calculating machine
who must not in any way permit himself to be
swayed by indignation. If he sees suffering,
privation or injustice he must not allow it to
move him, for that would be evidence of the
lack of proper education or of absence of self-

control. He must speak in calm and objective accents and talk about a dying child in the same way as he would about the pieces inside an internal combustion engine.
generally taken as referring to Hugh GAITSKELL, *although Bevan specifically denied it in an interview with Robin Day on 28 April 1959*
Michael Foot *Aneurin Bevan* (1973) vol. 2, ch. 11

1 This so-called affluent society is an ugly society still. It is a vulgar society. It is a meretricious society. It is a society in which priorities have gone all wrong.
speech in Blackpool, 29 November 1959

2 I read the newspapers avidly. It is my one form of continuous fiction.
in *The Times* 29 March 1960

3 I stuffed their mouths with gold.
of his handling of the consultants during the establishment of the National Health Service
Brian Abel-Smith *The Hospitals 1800–1948* (1964) ch. 29

4 Listening to a speech by Chamberlain is like paying a visit to Woolworth's: everything in its place and nothing above sixpence.
Michael Foot *Aneurin Bevan* (1962) vol. 1, ch. 8

William Henry Beveridge 1879–1963
British economist and social reformer

5 Ignorance is an evil weed, which dictators may cultivate among their dupes, but which no democracy can afford among its citizens.
Full Employment in a Free Society (1944) pt. 7

6 Want is one only of five giants on the road of reconstruction . . . the others are Disease, Ignorance, Squalor and Idleness.
Social Insurance and Allied Services (1942) pt. 7

7 I have a thousand things to do.
his last words, in *Oxford Mail* 18 March 1963

Ernest Bevin 1881–1951
British Labour politician and trade unionist. On Bevin: see FOOT 336:7

8 The most conservative man in this world is the British Trade Unionist when you want to change him.
speech, 8 September 1927, in *Report of Proceedings of the Trades Union Congress* (1927)

9 I hope you will carry no resolution of an emergency character telling a man with a conscience like Lansbury what he ought to do . . . It is placing the Executive in an absolutely wrong position to be taking your conscience round from body to body to be told what you ought to do with it.
of the Labour politician George Lansbury (1859–1940); often quoted as 'hawking his conscience round the Chancelleries of Europe'
in *Labour Party Conference Report* (1935)

10 There never has been a war yet which, if the facts had been put calmly before the ordinary

folk, could not have been prevented . . . The common man, I think, is the great protection against war.
speech in the House of Commons, 23 November 1945

11 My [foreign] policy is to be able to take a ticket at Victoria Station and go anywhere I damn well please.
in *Spectator* 20 April 1951

12 If you open that Pandora's Box, you never know what Trojan 'orses will jump out.
on the Council of Europe
Roderick Barclay *Ernest Bevin and the Foreign Office* (1975) ch. 3

13 I didn't ought never to have done it. It was you, Willie, what put me up to it.
to Lord Strang, after officially recognizing Communist China
C. Parrott *Serpent and Nightingale* (1977) ch. 3

14 *on the observation that Aneurin* BEVAN *was sometimes his own worst enemy:*
Not while I'm alive 'e ain't!
also attributed to Bevin of Herbert MORRISON
Roderick Barclay *Ernest Bevin and the Foreign Office* (1975)

Theodore Beza 1519–1605
French Calvinist theologian

15 It is the peculiarity of the Church of God . . . to endure blows, not to give them; but yet you will be pleased to remember, that it is an anvil on which many a hammer has been broken.
reply to the King of Navarre after the massacre of the Huguenots at Vassey in March 1562
G. de Félice *Histoire des protestants de France* (1851) bk. 2, ch. 5; see MACLAREN 512:1, PROVERBS 629:2

Bhagavadgita
Hindu poem composed between the 2nd century BC and the 2nd century AD and incorporated into the Mahabharata
textual translations are those of J. Mascaro, 1978

16 As the Spirit of our mortal body wanders on in childhood, and youth and old age, the Spirit wanders on to a new body: of this the sage has no doubts.
ch. 2, v. 13

17 If any man thinks he slays, and if another thinks he is slain, neither knows the ways of truth. The Eternal in man cannot kill: the Eternal in man cannot die.
He is never born, and he never dies. He is in Eternity, he is for evermore. Never-born and eternal, beyond times gone or to come, he does not die when the body dies.
ch. 2, v. 19; see EMERSON 314:11, UPANISHADS 822:9

18 As a man leaves an old garment and puts on one that is new, the spirit leaves his mortal body and puts on one that is new.
ch. 2, v. 22

19 Invisible before birth are all beings and after death invisible again. They are seen between two unseens. Why in this truth find sorrow?
ch. 2, v. 28

1 Set thy heart upon thy work but never upon its reward. Work not for a reward: but never cease to do thy work.

Do thy work in the peace of Yoga and, free from selfish desires, be not moved in success or in failure. Yoga is evenness of mind—a peace that is ever the same.

ch. 2, v. 47

2 When in recollection he withdraws all his senses from the attractions of the pleasures of sense, even as a tortoise withdraws all its limbs, then his is a serene wisdom.

ch. 2, v. 58

3 And do thy duty, even if it be humble, rather than another's, even if it be great. To die in one's duty is life: to live in another's is death.

ch. 3, v. 35

4 I [Krishna] am all-powerful Time which destroys all things, and I have come here to slay these men. Even if thou dost not fight, all the warriors facing thee shall die.

ch. 11, v. 32; see **OPPENHEIMER** 585:14

5 Only by love can men see me, and know me, and come unto me.

He who works for me, who loves me, whose End Supreme I am, free from attachment to all things, and with love for all creation, he in truth comes unto me.

ch. 11, v. 54

6 God dwells in the heart of all beings, Arjuna: thy God dwells in thy heart. And his power of wonder moves all things—puppets in a play of shadows—whirling them onwards on the stream of time.

ch. 18, v. 61

7 Leave all things behind, and come unto me for thy salvation. I will make thee free from the bondage of sins. Fear no more.

ch. 18, v. 66

Benazir Bhutto 1953–2007

Pakistani stateswoman, Prime Minister 1988–90 and 1993–96; assassinated

8 Every dictator uses religion as a prop to keep himself in power.

interview on *60 Minutes*, CBS-TV, 8 August 1986

The Bible (Authorized Version, 1611)

the translator of the original texts into Latin (see the **BIBLE (VULGATE)**) was St **JEROME**; many English phrases in the Authorized Version, such as 'fight the good fight', 'the powers that be', and 'the spirit is willing', derive from William **TYNDALE**'s translation of the early 16th century. See also **BOOK OF COMMON PRAYER** (Psalms)

9 Upon the setting of that bright Occidental Star, Queen Elizabeth of most happy memory.

The Epistle Dedicatory

10 The appearance of Your Majesty, as of the Sun in his strength.

The Epistle Dedicatory

11 Translation it is that openeth the window, to let in the light; that breaketh the shell, that we may eat the kernel; that putteth aside the curtain, that we may look into the most holy place; that removeth the cover of the well, that we may come by the water.

The Translators to the Reader

OLD TESTAMENT: GENESIS

12 In the beginning God created the heaven and the earth. And the earth was without form, and void; and darkness was upon the face of the deep. And the Spirit of God moved upon the face of the waters.

And God said, Let there be light: and there was light.

Genesis ch. 1, v. 1; see **BYRON** 189:10

13 And the evening and the morning were the first day.

Genesis ch. 1, v. 5

14 And God saw that it was good.

Genesis ch. 1, v. 10

15 And God made two great lights; the greater light to rule the day, and the lesser light to rule the night.

Genesis ch. 1, v. 16

16 And God said, Let us make man in our image, after our likeness: and let them have dominion over the fish of the sea, and over the fowl of the air, and over the cattle, and over all the earth and over every creeping thing that creepeth upon the earth.

Genesis ch. 1, v. 26

17 Male and female created he them.

Genesis ch. 1, v. 27

18 Be fruitful, and multiply, and replenish the earth, and subdue it.

Genesis ch. 1, v. 28

19 And the Lord God formed man of the dust of the ground, and breathed into his nostrils the breath of life; and man became a living soul.

And the Lord God planted a garden eastward in Eden.

Genesis ch. 2, v. 7

20 And out of the ground made the Lord God to grow every tree that is pleasant to the sight, and good for food; the tree of life also in the midst of the garden, and the tree of knowledge of good and evil.

Genesis ch. 2, v. 9

21 But of the tree of the knowledge of good and evil, thou shalt not eat of it: for in the day that thou eatest thereof thou shalt surely die.

Genesis ch. 2, v. 17

22 It is not good that the man should be alone; I will make him an help meet for him.

Genesis ch. 2, v. 18

1 And the Lord God caused a deep sleep to fall upon Adam, and he slept: and he took one of his ribs, and closed up the flesh instead thereof; And the rib, which the Lord God had taken from man, made he a woman.
Genesis ch. 2, v. 21

2 This is now bone of my bones, and flesh of my flesh: she shall be called Woman, because she was taken out of Man.
Genesis ch. 2, v. 23; see **MILTON** 544:8

3 Therefore shall a man leave his father and his mother, and shall cleave unto his wife: and they shall be one flesh.
Genesis ch. 2, v. 24

4 Now the serpent was more subtil than any beast of the field.
Genesis ch. 3, v. 1

5 Ye shall be as gods, knowing good and evil.
Genesis ch. 3, v. 5

6 And they sewed fig leaves together, and made themselves aprons.
And they heard the voice of the Lord God walking in the garden in the cool of the day.
'And made themselves breeches' in the Geneva Bible, 1560, known for that reason as the 'Breeches Bible'
Genesis ch. 3, v. 7

7 The woman whom thou gavest to be with me, she gave me of the tree, and I did eat.
Genesis ch. 3, v. 12

8 What is this that thou hast done?
Genesis ch. 3, v. 13

9 The serpent beguiled me, and I did eat.
Genesis ch. 3, v. 13

10 It shall bruise thy head, and thou shalt bruise his heel.
Genesis ch. 3, v. 15

11 In sorrow thou shalt bring forth children.
Genesis ch. 3, v. 16

12 In the sweat of thy face shalt thou eat bread.
Genesis ch. 3, v. 19

13 For dust thou art, and unto dust shalt thou return.
Genesis ch. 3, v. 19; see **LONGFELLOW** 499:14

14 Am I my brother's keeper?
Genesis ch. 4, v. 9

15 The voice of thy brother's blood crieth unto me from the ground.
Genesis ch. 4, v. 10

16 My punishment is greater than I can bear.
Genesis ch. 4, v. 13

17 And the Lord set a mark upon Cain.
Genesis ch. 4, v. 15

18 And Cain went out from the presence of the Lord, and dwelt in the land of Nod, on the east of Eden.
Genesis ch. 4, v. 16

19 And Enoch walked with God: and he was not; for God took him.
Genesis ch. 5, v. 24

20 And all the days of Methuselah were nine hundred sixty and nine years: and he died.
Genesis ch. 5, v. 27

21 There were giants in the earth in those days; and also after that, when the sons of God came in unto the daughters of men, and they bare children to them, the same became mighty men which were of old, men of renown.
Genesis ch. 6, v. 4

22 There went in two and two unto Noah into the Ark, the male and the female.
Genesis ch. 7, v. 9

23 But the dove found no rest for the sole of her foot.
Genesis ch. 8, v. 9

24 For the imagination of man's heart is evil from his youth.
Genesis ch. 8, v. 21

25 While the earth remaineth, seedtime and harvest, and cold and heat, and summer and winter, and day and night shall not cease.
Genesis ch. 8, v. 22

26 At the hand of every man's brother will I require the life of man.
Genesis ch. 9, v. 5

27 Whoso sheddeth man's blood, by man shall his blood be shed.
Genesis ch. 9, v. 6

28 I do set my bow in the cloud, and it shall be for a token of a covenant between me and the earth. And it shall come to pass, when I bring a cloud over the earth, that the bow shall be seen in the cloud.
Genesis ch. 9, v. 13

29 Even as Nimrod the mighty hunter before the Lord.
Genesis ch. 10, v. 9

30 Let there be no strife, I pray thee, between thee and me . . . for we be brethren.
Genesis ch. 13, v. 8

31 An horror of great darkness fell upon him.
Genesis ch. 15, v. 12

32 Thou shalt be buried in a good old age.
Genesis ch. 15, v. 15

33 His [Ishmael's] hand will be against every man, and every man's hand against him.
Genesis ch. 16, v. 12

34 Now Abraham and Sarah were old and well stricken in age; and it ceased to be with Sarah after the manner of women.
Genesis ch. 18, v. 11

35 Shall not the Judge of all the earth do right.
Genesis ch. 18, v. 25

36 But his [Lot's] wife looked back from behind him, and she became a pillar of salt.
Genesis ch. 19, v. 26

37 Take now thy son, thine only son Isaac, whom thou lovest.
Genesis ch. 22, v. 2

1 My son, God will provide himself a lamb.
  Genesis ch. 22, v. 8

2 Behold behind him a ram caught in a thicket by his horns.
  Genesis ch. 22, v. 13

3 Esau selleth his birthright for a mess of pottage.
  Genesis ch. 25: chapter heading in Geneva Bible, 1560

4 Esau was a cunning hunter, a man of the field; and Jacob was a plain man, dwelling in tents.
  Genesis ch. 25, v. 27

5 And he sold his birthright unto Jacob.
  Genesis ch. 25, v. 33

6 Behold, Esau my brother is a hairy man, and I am a smooth man.
  Genesis ch. 27, v. 11

7 The voice is Jacob's voice, but the hands are the hands of Esau.
  Genesis ch. 27, v. 22

8 Thy brother came with subtilty, and hath taken away thy blessing.
  Genesis ch. 27, v. 35

9 And he dreamed, and behold a ladder set up on the earth, and the top of it reached to heaven: and behold the angels of God ascending and descending on it.
  Genesis ch. 28, v. 12

10 Surely the Lord is in this place; and I knew it not.
  Genesis ch. 28, v. 16

11 This is none other but the house of God, and this is the gate of heaven.
  Genesis ch. 28, v. 17

12 And Jacob served seven years for Rachel; and they seemed unto him but a few days, for the love he had to her.
  Genesis ch. 29, v. 20

13 The Lord watch between me and thee, when we are absent one from another.
  Genesis ch. 31, v. 49

14 I will not let thee go, except thou bless me.
  Genesis ch. 32, v. 26

15 For I have seen God face to face, and my life is preserved.
  Genesis ch. 32, v. 30

16 Now Israel loved Joseph more than all his children, because he was the son of his old age; and he made him a coat of many colours.
  Genesis ch. 37, v. 3

17 Behold, your sheaves stood round about, and made obeisance to my sheaf.
  Genesis ch. 37, v. 7

18 Behold, this dreamer cometh.
  Genesis ch. 37, v. 19

19 Some evil beast hath devoured him.
  Genesis ch. 37, v. 20

20 And she caught him by his garment, saying, Lie with me; and he left his garment in her hand, and fled.
  Genesis ch. 39, v. 12

21 And the lean and the ill favoured kine did eat up the first seven fat kine.
  Genesis ch. 41, v. 20

22 And the thin ears devoured the seven good ears.
  Genesis ch. 41, v. 24

23 Jacob saw that there was corn in Egypt.
  Genesis ch. 42, v. 1

24 Ye are spies; to see the nakedness of the land ye are come.
  Genesis ch. 42, v. 9

25 My son shall not go down with you; for his brother is dead, and he is left alone: if mischief befall him by the way in which ye go, then shall ye bring down my grey hairs with sorrow to the grave.
  Genesis ch. 42, v. 38

26 Ye shall eat the fat of the land.
  Genesis ch. 45, v. 18

27 See that ye fall not out by the way.
  Genesis ch. 45, v. 24

28 Few and evil have the days of the years of my life been.
  Genesis ch. 47, v. 9

29 Unstable as water, thou shalt not excel.
  Genesis ch. 49, v. 4

EXODUS

30 She took for him an ark of bulrushes, and daubed it with slime.
  Exodus ch. 2, v. 3

31 Who made thee a prince and a judge over us?
  Exodus ch. 2, v. 14

32 I have been a stranger in a strange land.
  Exodus ch. 2, v. 22

33 Behold, the bush burned with fire, and the bush was not consumed.
  Exodus ch. 3, v. 2

34 Put off thy shoes from off thy feet, for the place whereon thou standest is holy ground.
  Exodus ch. 3, v. 5

35 And Moses hid his face; for he was afraid to look upon God.
  Exodus ch. 3, v. 6

36 A land flowing with milk and honey.
  Exodus ch. 3, v. 8

37 I AM THAT I AM.
  Exodus ch. 3, v. 14

38 The Lord God of your fathers, the God of Abraham, the God of Isaac, and the God of Jacob.
  Exodus ch. 3, v. 15

39 But I am slow of speech, and of a slow tongue.
  Exodus ch. 4, v. 10

1 I know not the Lord, neither will I let Israel go.
Exodus ch. 5, v. 2

2 And I will harden Pharaoh's heart, and multiply my signs and my wonders in the land of Egypt.
Exodus ch. 7, v. 3

3 Aaron's rod swallowed up their rods.
And he hardened Pharaoh's heart, that he hearkened not.
Exodus ch. 7, v. 12

4 Let my people go.
Exodus ch. 7, v. 16

5 Stretch out thine hand toward heaven, that there may be darkness over the land of Egypt, even darkness which may be felt.
Exodus ch. 10, v. 21

6 Your lamb shall be without blemish.
Exodus ch. 12, v. 5

7 And they shall eat the flesh in that night, roast with fire, and unleavened bread; and with bitter herbs they shall eat it.
Eat not of it raw, nor sodden at all with water, but roast with fire; his head with his legs, and with the purtenance thereof.
Exodus ch. 12, v. 8

8 Ye shall eat it in haste; it is the Lord's passover.
Exodus ch. 12, v. 11

9 For I will pass through the land of Egypt this night, and will smite all the firstborn in the land of Egypt, both man and beast.
Exodus ch. 12, v. 12

10 And Pharaoh rose up in the night, he, and all his servants, and all the Egyptians; and there was a great cry in Egypt; for there was not a house where there was not one dead.
Exodus ch. 12, v. 30

11 And they spoiled the Egyptians.
Exodus ch. 12, v. 36

12 And the Lord went before them by day in a pillar of a cloud, to lead them the way; and by night in a pillar of fire, to give them light.
Exodus ch. 13, v. 21

13 The Lord is a man of war.
Exodus ch. 15, v. 3

14 Would to God we had died by the hand of the Lord in the land of Egypt, when we sat by the flesh pots, and when we did eat bread to the full.
Exodus ch. 16, v. 3

15 I am the Lord thy God, which have brought thee out of the land of Egypt, out of the house of bondage.
Thou shalt have no other gods before me.
Thou shalt not make unto thee any graven image, or any likeness of any thing that is in heaven above, or that is in the earth beneath, or that is in the water under the earth.
Exodus ch. 20, v. 2

16 I the Lord thy God am a jealous God, visiting the iniquity of the fathers upon the children unto the third and fourth generation of them that hate me.
Exodus ch. 20, v. 5; see **BOOK OF COMMON PRAYER** 136:20, **FRENCH** 342:8

17 Thou shalt not take the name of the Lord thy God in vain.
Exodus ch. 20, v. 7

18 Remember the sabbath day, to keep it holy.
Six days shalt thou labour, and do all thy work:
But the seventh day is the sabbath of the Lord thy God: in it thou shalt not do any work.
Exodus ch. 20, v. 8

19 For in six days the Lord made heaven and earth, the sea, and all that in them is, and rested the seventh day: wherefore the Lord blest the sabbath day, and hallowed it.
Exodus ch. 20, v. 11

20 Honour thy father and thy mother: that thy days may be long upon the land which the Lord thy God giveth thee.
Thou shalt not kill.
Thou shalt not commit adultery.
Thou shalt not steal.
Thou shalt not bear false witness against thy neighbour.
Thou shalt not covet thy neighbour's house, thou shalt not covet thy neighbour's wife, nor his manservant, nor his maidservant, nor his ox, nor his ass, nor any thing that is thy neighbour's.
Exodus ch. 20, v. 12; see **BOOK OF COMMON PRAYER** 137:1

21 Life for life,
Eye for eye, tooth for tooth, hand for hand, foot for foot,
Burning for burning, wound for wound, stripe for stripe.
Exodus ch. 21, v. 23

22 And thou shalt put in the breastplate of judgement the Urim and the Thummim.
sacred symbols worn on the breastplate of the high priest
Exodus ch. 28, v. 30

23 These be thy gods, O Israel.
Exodus ch. 32, v. 4

24 I will not go up in the midst of thee; for thou art a stiffnecked people: lest I consume thee in the way.
Exodus ch. 33, v. 3

25 There shall no man see me and live.
Exodus ch. 33, v. 20

LEVITICUS

26 And the swine, though he divide the hoof, and be cloven-footed, yet he cheweth not the cud.
Leviticus ch. 11, v. 7

27 Let him go for a scapegoat into the wilderness.
Leviticus ch. 16, v. 10

28 Ye shall therefore keep my statutes and my judgments: which if a man do, he shall live in them: I am the Lord.
Leviticus ch. 18, v. 5; see **TALMUD** 789:16

1 Thou shalt love thy neighbour as thyself.
Leviticus ch. 19, v. 18; see **BIBLE** 102:17

NUMBERS

2 The Lord bless thee, and keep thee:
The Lord make his face shine upon thee, and be gracious unto thee:
The Lord lift up his countenance upon thee, and give thee peace.
Numbers ch. 6, v. 24

3 These are the names of the men which Moses sent to spy out the land.
Numbers ch. 13, v. 16

4 And there we saw the giants, the sons of Anak, which come of the giants: and we were in our own sight as grasshoppers, and so we were in their sight.
Numbers ch. 13, v. 33

5 And Israel smote him with the edge of the sword, and possessed his land.
Numbers ch. 21, v. 24

6 He whom thou blessest is blessed, and he whom thou cursest is cursed.
Numbers ch. 22, v. 6

7 God is not a man, that he should lie.
Numbers ch. 23, v. 19

8 What hath God wrought!
quoted by Samuel **MORSE** *in the first electric telegraph message, 24 May 1844*
Numbers ch. 23, v. 23

9 I called thee to curse mine enemies, and, behold, thou hast altogether blessed them these three times.
Numbers ch. 24, v. 10

10 Be sure your sin will find you out.
Numbers ch. 32, v. 23

DEUTERONOMY

11 I call heaven and earth to witness against you this day.
Deuteronomy ch. 4, v. 26

12 Remember that thou wast a servant in the land of Egypt, and that the Lord thy God brought thee out thence through a mighty hand and by a stretched out arm.
Deuteronomy ch. 5, v. 15

13 Hear, O Israel: The Lord our God is one Lord.
Deuteronomy ch. 6, v. 4; see **SIDDUR** 750:5

14 If there arise among you a prophet, or a dreamer of dreams . . . Thou shalt not hearken.
Deuteronomy ch. 13, v. 1

15 If thy brother, the son of thy mother, or thy son, or thy daughter, or the wife of thy bosom, or thy friend, which is as thine own soul, entice thee secretly . . . Thou shalt not consent.
Deuteronomy ch. 13, v. 6

16 The secret things belong unto the Lord our God.
Deuteronomy ch. 29, v. 29

17 I have set before you life and death, blessing and cursing: therefore choose life that both thou and thy seed may live.
Deuteronomy ch. 30, v. 19

18 He found him in a desert land, and in the waste howling wilderness; he led him about, he instructed him, he kept him as the apple of his eye.
Deuteronomy ch. 32, v. 10

19 For they are a very froward generation, children in whom is no faith.
Deuteronomy ch. 32, v. 20

20 I will heap mischiefs upon them; I will spend mine arrows upon them.
Deuteronomy ch. 32, v. 23

21 The eternal God is thy refuge, and underneath are the everlasting arms.
Deuteronomy ch. 33, v. 27

22 No man knoweth of his [Moses's] sepulchre unto this day.
Deuteronomy ch. 34, v. 6

JOSHUA

23 As I was with Moses, so I will be with thee: I will not fail thee, nor forsake thee.
Joshua ch. 1, v. 5

24 Be strong and of a good courage; be not afraid, neither be thou dismayed: for the Lord thy God is with thee, whithersoever thou goest.
Joshua ch. 1, v. 9

25 This line of scarlet thread.
Joshua ch. 2, v. 18

26 All the Israelites passed over on dry ground.
Joshua ch. 3, v. 17

27 When the people heard the sound of the trumpet, and the people shouted with a great shout, that the wall fell down flat, so that the people went up into the city.
Joshua ch. 6, v. 20

28 Let them live; but let them be hewers of wood and drawers of water unto all the congregation.
Joshua ch. 9, v. 21

29 Sun, stand thou still upon Gibeon; and thou, Moon, in the valley of Ajalon.
Joshua ch. 10, v. 12

30 I am going the way of all the earth.
Joshua ch. 23, v. 14

JUDGES

31 He delivered them into the hands of spoilers.
Judges ch. 2, v. 14

32 Then Jael Heber's wife took a nail of the tent, and took an hammer in her hand, and went softly unto him, and smote the nail into his temples, and fastened it into the ground: for he was fast asleep and weary.
Judges ch. 4, v. 21

33 I arose a mother in Israel.
Judges ch. 5, v. 7

1 The stars in their courses fought against Sisera.
Judges ch. 5, v. 20

2 He asked water, and she gave him milk; she brought forth butter in a lordly dish.
Judges ch. 5, v. 25

3 At her feet he bowed, he fell, he lay down.
Judges ch. 5, v. 27

4 The mother of Sisera looked out at a window, and cried through the lattice, Why is his chariot so long in coming? why tarry the wheels of his chariots?
Judges ch. 5, v. 28

5 The Lord is with thee, thou mighty man of valour.
Judges ch. 6, v. 12 (spoken to Gideon)

6 The Spirit of the Lord came upon Gideon, and he blew a trumpet.
Judges ch. 6, v. 34

7 The host of Midian was beneath him in the valley.
Judges ch. 7, v. 8

8 Is not the gleaning of the grapes of Ephraim better than the vintage of Abi-ezer?
Judges ch. 8, v. 2

9 Faint, yet pursuing.
Judges ch. 8, v. 4

10 Let fire come out of the bramble and devour the cedars of Lebanon.
Judges ch. 9, v. 15

11 Then said they unto him, Say now Shibboleth: and he said Sibboleth: for he could not frame to pronounce it right. Then they took him, and slew him.
Judges ch. 12, v. 6

12 Out of the eater came forth meat, and out of the strong came forth sweetness.
Judges ch. 14, v. 14

13 If ye had not plowed with my heifer, ye had not found out my riddle.
Judges ch. 14, v. 18

14 He smote them hip and thigh.
Judges ch. 15, v. 8 (Samson)

15 With the jawbone of an ass, heaps upon heaps, with the jaw of an ass have I slain a thousand men.
Judges ch. 15, v. 16

16 The Philistines be upon thee, Samson.
Judges ch. 16, v. 9

17 He wist not that the Lord was departed from him.
Judges ch. 16, v. 20

18 He did grind in the prison house.
Judges ch. 16, v. 21

19 The dead which he slew at his death were more than they which he slew in his life.
Judges ch. 16, v. 30

20 In those days there was no king in Israel, but every man did that which was right in his own eyes.
Judges ch. 17, v. 6

21 From Dan even to Beer-sheba.
Judges ch. 20, v. 1

22 The people arose as one man.
Judges ch. 20, v. 8

RUTH

23 Intreat me not to leave thee, or to return from following after thee: for whither thou goest, I will go; and where thou lodgest, I will lodge: thy people shall be my people, and thy God my God:
Where thou diest, will I die, and there will I be buried: the Lord do so to me, and more also, if ought but death part thee and me.
Ruth ch. 1, v. 16

I SAMUEL

24 All the increase of thy house shall die in the flower of their age.
I Samuel ch. 2, v. 33

25 The Lord called Samuel: and he answered, Here am I.
I Samuel ch. 3, v. 4

26 Speak, Lord; for thy servant heareth.
I Samuel ch. 3, v. 9

27 The ears of every one that heareth it shall tingle.
I Samuel ch. 3, v. 11

28 Quit yourselves like men, and fight.
I Samuel ch. 4, v. 9

29 And she named the child I-chabod, saying, The glory is departed from Israel.
I Samuel ch. 4, v. 21; see **BROWNING** 168:8

30 And the asses of Kish Saul's father were lost. And Kish said to Saul his son, Take now one of the servants with thee, and arise, go seek the asses.
I Samuel ch. 9, v. 3; see **MILTON** 544:23

31 Is Saul also among the prophets?
I Samuel ch. 10, v. 11

32 God save the king.
I Samuel ch. 10, v. 24

33 A man after his own heart.
I Samuel ch. 13, v. 14

34 I did but taste a little honey with the end of the rod that was in mine hand, and, lo, I must die.
I Samuel ch. 14, v. 43

35 To obey is better than sacrifice, and to hearken than the fat of rams.
I Samuel ch. 15, v. 22

36 For rebellion is as the sin of witchcraft.
I Samuel ch. 15, v. 23

37 For the Lord seeth not as man seeth: for man looketh on the outward appearance, but the Lord looketh on the heart.
I Samuel ch. 16, v. 7

1 Now he was ruddy, and withal of a beautiful countenance, and goodly to look to.
I Samuel ch. 16, v. 12 (David)

2 I know thy pride, and the naughtiness of thine heart.
I Samuel ch. 17, v. 28

3 Let no man's heart fail because of him.
I Samuel ch. 17, v. 32

4 Go, and the Lord be with thee.
I Samuel ch. 17, v. 37

5 And he took his staff in his hand and chose him five smooth stones out of the brook.
I Samuel ch. 17, v. 40

6 Am I a dog, that thou comest to me with staves?
I Samuel ch. 17, v. 43

7 Saul hath slain his thousands, and David his ten thousands.
I Samuel ch. 18, v. 7; see **PORTEUS** 619:23

8 David therefore departed thence, and escaped to the cave Adullam: and when his brethren and all his father's house heard it, they went down thither to him.
And every one that was in distress, and every one that was in debt, and every one that was discontented, gathered themselves unto him.
I Samuel ch. 22, v. 1; see **BRIGHT** 157:5

9 And Saul said, God hath delivered him into mine hand.
I Samuel ch. 23, v. 7

10 Behold, I have played the fool, and have erred exceedingly.
I Samuel ch. 26, v. 21

II SAMUEL

11 The beauty of Israel is slain upon thy high places: how are the mighty fallen!
Tell it not in Gath, publish it not in the streets of Askelon; lest the daughters of the Philistines rejoice, lest the daughters of the uncircumcised triumph.
Ye mountains of Gilboa, let there be no dew, neither let there be rain, upon you, nor fields of offerings: for there the shield of the mighty is vilely cast away.
II Samuel ch. 1, v. 19 (David's lament for Saul and Jonathan)

12 Saul and Jonathan were lovely and pleasant in their lives, and in their death they were not divided: they were swifter than eagles, they were stronger than lions.
Ye daughters of Israel, weep over Saul, who clothed you in scarlet, with other delights, who put on ornaments of gold upon your apparel.
II Samuel ch. 1, v. 23

13 I am distressed for thee, my brother Jonathan: very pleasant hast thou been unto me: thy love to me was wonderful, passing the love of women.
How are the mighty fallen, and the weapons of war perished!
II Samuel ch. 1, v. 26

14 And David danced before the Lord with all his might.
II Samuel ch. 6, v. 14

15 Set ye Uriah in the forefront of the hottest battle.
II Samuel ch. 10, v. 15

16 The poor man had nothing, save one little ewe lamb.
II Samuel ch. 12, v. 3

17 Thou art the man.
II Samuel ch. 12, v. 7

18 While the child was yet alive, I fasted and wept . . . But now he is dead, wherefore should I fast? can I bring him back again? I shall go to him but he shall not return to me.
II Samuel ch. 12, v. 22

19 For we needs must die, and are as water spilt on the ground, which cannot be gathered up again; neither doth God respect any person.
II Samuel ch. 14, v. 14

20 Come out, come out, thou bloody man, and thou man of Belial.
II Samuel ch. 16, v. 7

21 And the king was much moved, and went up to the chamber over the gate, and wept: and as he went, thus he said, O my son Absalom, my son, my son Absalom! would God I had died for thee, O Absalom, my son, my son!
II Samuel ch. 18, v. 33

22 By my God have I leaped over a wall.
II Samuel ch. 22, v. 30; see **BOOK OF COMMON PRAYER** 140:7

23 David . . . the sweet psalmist of Israel.
II Samuel ch. 23, v. 1

24 Went in jeopardy of their lives.
II Samuel ch. 23, v. 17

I KINGS

25 And Zadok the priest took an horn of oil out of the tabernacle, and anointed Solomon. And they blew the trumpet; and all the people said, God save king Solomon.
I Kings ch. 1, v. 39

26 Then will I cut off Israel out of the land which I have given them; and this house, which I have hallowed for my name, will I cast out of my sight; and Israel shall be a proverb and a byword among all people.
I Kings ch. 9, v. 7

27 And when the queen of Sheba had seen all Solomon's wisdom . . . there was no more spirit in her.
I Kings ch. 10, v. 4

28 Behold, the half was not told me.
I Kings ch. 10, v. 7

29 Once in three years came the navy of Tharshish, bringing gold, and silver, ivory, and apes, and peacocks.
I Kings ch. 10, v. 22; see **MASEFIELD** 527:3

1 But king Solomon loved many strange women.
I Kings ch. 11, v. 1

2 My little finger shall be thicker than my father's loins.
I Kings ch. 12, v. 10

3 My father hath chastised you with whips, but I will chastise you with scorpions.
I Kings ch. 12, v. 11

4 To your tents, O Israel: now see to thine own house, David.
I Kings ch. 12, v. 16

5 He slept with his fathers.
I Kings ch. 14, v. 20

6 He went and dwelt by the brook Cherith, that is before Jordan.
And the ravens brought him bread and flesh in the morning, and bread and flesh in the evening; and he drank of the brook.
I Kings ch. 17, v. 5 (Elijah)

7 An handful of meal in a barrel, and a little oil in a cruse.
I Kings ch. 17, v. 12

8 How long halt ye between two opinions?
I Kings ch. 18, v. 21

9 He is talking, or he is pursuing, or he is in a journey, or peradventure he sleepeth, and must be awaked.
I Kings ch. 18, v. 27

10 There is a sound of abundance of rain.
I Kings ch. 18, v. 41

11 There ariseth a little cloud out of the sea, like a man's hand.
I Kings ch. 18, v. 44

12 He girded up his loins, and ran before Ahab.
I Kings ch. 18, v. 46

13 He himself went a day's journey into the wilderness, and came and sat down under a juniper tree.
I Kings ch. 19, v. 4

14 But the Lord was not in the wind: and after the wind an earthquake; but the Lord was not in the earthquake:
And after the earthquake a fire: but the Lord was not in the fire: and after the fire a still small voice.
I Kings ch. 19, v. 11

15 Elijah passed by him, and cast his mantle upon him.
I Kings ch. 19, v. 19

16 A vineyard, which was in Jezreel.
I Kings ch. 21, v. 1

17 And Ahab spake unto Naboth, saying, Give me thy vineyard, that I may have it for a garden of herbs, because it is near unto my house.
I Kings ch. 21, v. 2

18 Hast thou found me, O mine enemy?
I Kings ch. 21, v. 20

19 I saw all Israel scattered upon the hills, as sheep that have not a shepherd.
I Kings ch. 22, v. 17

20 Feed him with bread of affliction and with water of affliction, until I come in peace.
I Kings ch. 22, v. 27

21 And a certain man drew a bow at a venture, and smote the king of Israel between the joints of the harness.
I Kings ch. 22, v. 34

II KINGS

22 Elijah went up by a whirlwind into heaven.
And Elisha saw it, and he cried, My father, my father, the chariot of Israel, and the horsemen thereof.
II Kings ch. 2, v. 11

23 The spirit of Elijah doth rest on Elisha.
II Kings ch. 2, v. 15

24 Go up, thou bald head.
II Kings ch. 2, v. 23 (the children to Elisha)

25 Is it well with the child? And she answered, It is well.
II Kings ch. 4, v. 26

26 There is death in the pot.
II Kings ch. 4, v. 40

27 He shall know that there is a prophet in Israel.
II Kings ch. 5, v. 8

28 Are not Abana and Pharpar, rivers of Damascus, better than all the waters of Israel?
II Kings ch. 5, v. 12 (Naaman)

29 I bow myself in the house of Rimmon.
II Kings ch. 5, v. 18

30 Whence comest thou, Gehazi?
II Kings ch. 5, v. 25

31 Is thy servant a dog, that he should do this great thing?
II Kings ch. 8, v. 13

32 Is it peace? And Jehu said, What hast thou to do with peace? turn thee behind me.
II Kings ch. 9, v. 18

33 The driving is like the driving of Jehu, the son of Nimshi; for he driveth furiously.
II Kings ch. 9, v. 20

34 She painted her face, and tired her head, and looked out at a window.
II Kings ch. 9, v. 30 (Jezebel)

35 Had Zimri peace, who slew his master?
II Kings ch. 9, v. 31

36 Who is on my side? who?
II Kings ch. 9, v. 32

37 They found no more of her than the skull, and the feet, and the palms of her hands.
II Kings ch. 9, v. 35

38 Thou trustest upon the staff of this bruised reed, even upon Egypt, on which if a man lean, it will go into his hand, and pierce it.
II Kings ch. 18, v. 21

I CHRONICLES

1 For we are strangers before thee, and sojourners, as were all our fathers: our days on the earth are as a shadow, and there is none abiding.
I Chronicles ch. 29, v. 15

2 He died in a good old age, full of days, riches, and honour.
I Chronicles ch. 29, v. 28

NEHEMIAH

3 Every one with one of his hands wrought in the work, and with the other hand held a weapon.
Nehemiah ch. 4, v. 17

ESTHER

4 And if I perish, I perish.
Esther ch. 4, v. 16

5 Yet all this availeth me nothing, so long as I see Mordecai the Jew sitting at the king's gate.
Esther ch. 5, v. 13

6 So they hanged Haman on the gallows that he had prepared for Mordecai.
Esther ch. 7, v. 10

7 Thus shall it be done to the man whom the king delighteth to honour.
Esther ch. 6, v. 9

JOB

8 There was a man in the land of Uz, whose name was Job.
Job ch. 1, v. 1

9 And the Lord said unto Satan, Whence comest thou? Then Satan answered the Lord, and said, From going to and fro in the earth, and from walking up and down in it.
Job ch. 1, v. 7

10 Doth Job fear God for naught?
Job ch. 1, v. 9

11 The Lord gave, and the Lord hath taken away; blessed be the name of the Lord.
Job ch. 1, v. 21

12 All that a man hath will he give for his life.
Job ch. 2, v. 4

13 And he took him a potsherd to scrape himself withal.
Job ch. 2, v. 8

14 Curse God, and die.
Job ch. 2, v. 9

15 Let the day perish wherein I was born, and the night in which it was said, There is a man child conceived.
Job ch. 3, v. 3

16 For now should I have lain still and been quiet, I should have slept: then had I been at rest,
With kings and counsellors of the earth, which built desolate places for themselves.
Job ch. 3, v. 13

17 There the wicked cease from troubling, and there the weary be at rest.
Job ch. 3, v. 17

18 Wherefore is light given to him that is in misery, and life unto the bitter in soul?
Job ch. 3, v. 20

19 Then a spirit passed before my face; the hair of my flesh stood up.
Job ch. 4, v. 15

20 Shall mortal man be more just than God? shall a man be more pure than his maker?
Job ch. 4, v. 17

21 Man is born unto trouble, as the sparks fly upward.
Job ch. 5, v. 7

22 My days are swifter than a weaver's shuttle.
Job ch. 7, v. 6

23 He shall return no more to his house, neither shall his place know him any more.
Job ch. 7, v. 10

24 Let me alone, that I may take comfort a little, Before I go whence I shall not return, even to the land of darkness and the shadow of death.
Job ch. 10, v. 20

25 A land . . . where the light is as darkness.
Job ch. 10, v. 22

26 Canst thou by searching find out God?
Job ch. 11, v. 7

27 No doubt but ye are the people, and wisdom shall die with you.
Job ch. 12, v. 2

28 With the ancient is wisdom; and in length of days understanding.
Job ch. 12, v. 12

29 Though he slay me, yet will I trust in him: but I will maintain mine own ways before him.
Job ch. 13, v. 15

30 Man that is born of a woman is of few days, and full of trouble.
He cometh forth like a flower, and is cut down: he fleeth also as a shadow, and continueth not.
Job ch. 14, v. 1; see **BOOK OF COMMON PRAYER** 139:8

31 Miserable comforters are ye all.
Job ch. 16, v. 2

32 I also could speak as ye do: if your soul were in my soul's stead.
Job ch. 16, v. 4

33 I am escaped with the skin of my teeth.
Job ch. 19, v. 20

34 I know that my redeemer liveth, and that he shall stand at the latter day upon the earth:
And though after my skin worms destroy this body, yet in my flesh shall I see God.
Job ch. 19, v. 25

35 Ye should say, Why persecute we him, seeing the root of the matter is found in me?
Job ch. 19, v. 28

36 But where shall wisdom be found?
Job ch. 28, v. 12

1 The price of wisdom is above rubies.
Job ch. 28, v. 18

2 I was eyes to the blind, and feet was I to the lame.
Job ch. 29, v. 15

3 He hath cast me into the mire, and I am become like dust and ashes.
Job ch. 30, v. 19

4 For I know that thou wilt bring me to death, and to the house appointed for all living.
Job ch. 30, v. 23

5 I am a brother to dragons, and a companion to owls.
Job ch. 30, v. 29

6 Great men are not always wise.
Job ch. 32, v. 9

7 Who is this that darkeneth counsel by words without knowledge?
Job ch. 38, v. 2

8 Where wast thou when I laid the foundations of the earth? declare, if thou hast understanding.
Job ch. 38, v. 4

9 When the morning stars sang together, and all the sons of God shouted for joy.
Job ch. 38, v. 7

10 When I made the cloud the garment thereof, and thick darkness a swaddlingband for it.
of the sea
Job ch. 38 v. 9; see **ANDREWES** 15:14, **ELIOT** 309:24

11 Hath the rain a father? or who hath begotten the drops of dew?
Job ch. 38, v. 28

12 Canst thou bind the sweet influences of Pleiades, or loose the bands of Orion?
Job ch. 38, v. 31

13 He saith among the trumpets, Ha, ha; and he smelleth the battle afar off, the thunder of the captains, and the shouting.
Job ch. 39, v. 25

14 Behold now behemoth, which I made with thee; he eateth grass as an ox.
Job ch. 40, v. 15

15 He is the chief of the ways of God: he that made him can make his sword to approach unto him.
Job ch. 40, v. 19

16 The shady trees cover him with their shadow; the willows of the brook compass him about.
Job ch. 40, v. 22

17 Canst thou draw out leviathan with an hook?
Job ch. 41, v. 1

18 I have heard of thee by the hearing of the ear: but now mine eye seeth thee.
Job ch. 42, v. 5

19 So the Lord blessed the latter end of Job more than his beginning.
Job ch. 42, v. 12

PROVERBS

20 Surely in vain the net is spread in the sight of any bird.
Proverbs ch. 1, v. 17; see **PROVERBS** 636:3

21 For whom the Lord loveth he correcteth.
Proverbs ch. 3, v. 12

22 Length of days is in her right hand; and in her left hand riches and honour.
Proverbs ch. 3, v. 16

23 Her ways are ways of pleasantness, and all her paths are peace.
Proverbs ch. 3, v. 17; see **SPRING-RICE** 769:1

24 Wisdom is the principal thing; therefore get wisdom: and with all thy getting get understanding.
Proverbs ch. 4, v. 7

25 The path of the just is as the shining light, that shineth more and more unto the perfect day.
Proverbs ch. 4, v. 18

26 For the lips of a strange woman drop as an honeycomb, and her mouth is smoother than oil:
But her end is bitter as wormwood, sharp as a two-edged sword.
Her feet go down to death; her steps take hold on hell.
Proverbs ch. 5, v. 3

27 Go to the ant thou sluggard; consider her ways, and be wise.
Proverbs ch. 6, v. 6

28 How long wilt thou sleep, O sluggard? When wilt thou arise out of thy sleep?
So shall thy poverty come as one that travelleth, and thy want as an armed man.
Yet a little sleep, a little slumber, a little folding of the hands to sleep.
Proverbs ch. 6, v. 9

29 Can a man take fire in his bosom, and his clothes not be burned?
Proverbs ch. 6, v. 27

30 Come, let us take our fill of love until the morning: let us solace ourselves with loves.
For the goodman is not at home, he is gone a long journey.
Proverbs ch. 7, v. 18

31 He goeth after her straightway, as an ox goeth to the slaughter.
Proverbs ch. 7, v. 22

32 Wisdom hath builded her house, she hath hewn out her seven pillars.
Proverbs ch. 9, v. 1; see **LAWRENCE** 484:8

33 Stolen waters are sweet, and bread eaten in secret is pleasant.
Proverbs ch. 9, v. 17; see **PROVERBS** 643:40

34 A wise son maketh a glad father: but a foolish son is the heaviness of his mother.
Proverbs ch. 10, v. 1

35 The destruction of the poor is their poverty.
Proverbs ch. 10, v. 15

1 He that is surety for a stranger shall smart for it.
Proverbs ch. 11, v. 15

2 As a jewel of gold in a swine's snout, so is a fair woman which is without discretion.
Proverbs ch. 11, v. 22

3 A virtuous woman is a crown to her husband.
Proverbs ch. 12, v. 4

4 A righteous man regardeth the life of his beast: but the tender mercies of the wicked are cruel.
Proverbs ch. 12, v. 10

5 Lying lips are abomination to the Lord.
Proverbs ch. 12, v. 22; see ANONYMOUS 16:3

6 Hope deferred maketh the heart sick: but when the desire cometh, it is a tree of life.
Proverbs ch. 13, v. 12; see PROVERBS 634:41

7 The way of transgressors is hard.
Proverbs ch. 13, v. 15

8 The desire accomplished is sweet to the soul.
Proverbs ch. 13, v. 19

9 He that spareth his rod hateth his son.
Proverbs ch. 13, v. 24; see PROVERBS 643:28

10 Even in laughter the heart is sorrowful.
Proverbs ch. 14, v. 13

11 In all labour there is profit.
Proverbs ch. 14, v. 23

12 Righteousness exalteth a nation.
Proverbs ch. 14, v. 34

13 A soft answer turneth away wrath.
Proverbs ch. 15, v. 1; see PROVERBS 643:18

14 A merry heart maketh a cheerful countenance.
Proverbs ch. 15, v. 13

15 Better is a dinner of herbs where love is, than a stalled ox and hatred therewith.
'Better is a mess of pottage with love, than a fat ox with evil will' in Matthew's Bible (1535)
Proverbs ch. 15, v. 17; see PROVERBS 627:27

16 A word spoken in due season, how good is it!
Proverbs ch. 15, v. 23

17 Pride goeth before destruction, and an haughty spirit before a fall.
Proverbs ch. 16, v. 18; see PROVERBS 642:5

18 He that is slow to anger is better than the mighty; and he that ruleth his spirit than he that taketh a city.
Proverbs ch. 16, v. 32

19 He that repeateth a matter separateth very friends.
Proverbs ch. 17, v. 9

20 A friend loveth at all times, and a brother is born for adversity.
Proverbs ch. 17, v. 17

21 A merry heart doeth good like a medicine.
Proverbs ch. 17, v. 22

22 A wounded spirit who can bear?
Proverbs ch. 18, v. 14

23 There is a friend that sticketh closer than a brother.
Proverbs ch. 18, v. 24; see KIPLING 467:14

24 Wine is a mocker, strong drink is raging.
Proverbs ch. 20, v. 1

25 Every fool will be meddling.
Proverbs ch. 20, v. 3

26 Even a child is known by his doings.
Proverbs ch. 20, v. 11

27 The hearing ear, and the seeing eye, the Lord hath made even both of them.
Proverbs ch. 20, v. 12

28 It is naught, it is naught, saith the buyer: but when he is gone his way, then he boasteth.
Proverbs ch. 20, v. 14

29 It is better to dwell in a corner of the housetop, than with a brawling woman in a wide house.
Proverbs ch. 21, v. 9

30 A good name is rather to be chosen than great riches.
Proverbs ch. 22, v. 1

31 Train up a child in the way he should go: and when he is old, he will not depart from it.
Proverbs ch. 22, v. 6

32 Remove not the ancient landmark, which thy fathers have set.
Proverbs ch. 22, v. 28

33 Look not thou upon the wine when it is red, when it giveth his colour in the cup ... At the last it biteth like a serpent, and stingeth like an adder.
Proverbs ch. 23, v. 31

34 The heart of kings is unsearchable.
Proverbs ch. 25, v. 3

35 A word fitly spoken is like apples of gold in pictures of silver.
Proverbs ch. 25, v. 11

36 Whoso boasteth himself of a false gift is like clouds and wind without rain.
Proverbs ch. 25, v. 14

37 Withdraw thy foot from thy neighbour's house; lest he be weary of thee, and so hate thee.
Proverbs ch. 25, v. 17

38 If thine enemy be hungry, give him bread to eat; and if he be thirsty, give him water to drink. For thou shalt heap coals of fire upon his head, and the Lord shall reward thee.
Proverbs ch. 25, v. 21

39 As cold waters to a thirsty soul, so is good news from a far country.
Proverbs ch. 25, v. 25

40 Answer not a fool according to his folly, lest thou also be like unto him.
Answer a fool according to his folly, lest he be wise in his own conceit.
Proverbs ch. 26, v. 4

41 As a dog returneth to his vomit, so a fool returneth to his folly.
Proverbs ch. 26, v. 11; see PROVERBS 630:11

1 Seest thou a man wise in his own conceit? There is more hope of a fool than of him.
Proverbs ch. 26, v. 12

2 The sluggard is wiser in his own conceit than seven men that can render a reason.
Proverbs ch. 26, v. 16

3 Boast not thyself of to morrow; for thou knowest not what a day may bring forth.
Proverbs ch. 27, v. 1

4 Open rebuke is better than secret love.
Proverbs ch. 27, v. 5

5 Faithful are the wounds of a friend.
Proverbs ch. 27, v. 6

6 A continual dropping in a very rainy day and a contentious woman are alike.
Proverbs ch. 27, v. 15

7 The wicked flee when no man pursueth: but the righteous are bold as a lion.
Proverbs ch. 28, v. 1

8 He that maketh haste to be rich shall not be innocent.
Proverbs ch. 28, v. 20

9 A fool uttereth all his mind.
Proverbs ch. 29, v. 11

10 Where there is no vision, the people perish.
Proverbs ch. 29, v. 18

11 Give me neither poverty nor riches; feed me with food convenient for me.
Proverbs ch. 30, v. 8

12 There be three things which are too wonderful for me, yea, four which I know not:
The way of an eagle in the air; the way of a serpent upon a rock; the way of a ship in the midst of the sea; and the way of a man with a maid.
Proverbs ch. 30, v. 18

13 Give strong drink unto him that is ready to perish, and wine unto those that be of heavy hearts.
Proverbs ch. 31, v. 6

14 Who can find a virtuous woman? for her price is far above rubies.
Proverbs ch. 31, v. 10

15 Strength and honour are her clothing; and she shall rejoice in time to come.
quoted by the Archbishop of Canterbury at the funeral of Queen ELIZABETH *the Queen Mother, 9 April 2002, from the New Revised Standard Version: 'Strength and dignity are her clothing, and she laughs at the time to come'*
Proverbs ch. 31, v. 25

ECCLESIASTES

16 Vanity of vanities, saith the Preacher, vanity of vanities; all is vanity.
What profit hath a man of all his labour which he taketh under the sun?
One generation passeth away, and another generation cometh.
Ecclesiastes ch. 1, v. 2; see BIBLE (VULGATE) 120:7

17 All the rivers run into the sea; yet the sea is not full.
Ecclesiastes ch. 1, v. 7

18 All things are full of labour; man cannot utter it: the eye is not satisfied with seeing, nor the ear filled with hearing.
Ecclesiastes ch. 1, v. 8

19 The thing that hath been, it is that which shall be; and that which is done is that which shall be done: and there is no new thing under the sun.
Ecclesiastes ch. 1, v. 9; see PROVERBS 644:34

20 All is vanity and vexation of spirit.
Ecclesiastes ch. 1, v. 14

21 He that increaseth knowledge increaseth sorrow.
Ecclesiastes ch. 1, v. 18

22 Wisdom excelleth folly, as far as light excelleth darkness.
Ecclesiastes ch. 2, v. 13

23 To every thing there is a season, and a time to every purpose under the heaven:
A time to be born, and a time to die; a time to plant, and a time to pluck up that which is planted;
A time to kill, and a time to heal; a time to break down, and a time to build up;
A time to weep, and a time to laugh; a time to mourn, and a time to dance;
A time to cast away stones, and a time to gather stones together; a time to embrace, and a time to refrain from embracing;
A time to get, and a time to lose; a time to keep, and a time to cast away;
A time to rend, and a time to sew; a time to keep silence, and a time to speak;
A time to love, and a time to hate; a time of war, and a time of peace.
Ecclesiastes ch. 3, v. 1; see PROVERBS 644:19

24 For that which befalleth the sons of men befalleth beasts; even one thing befalleth them: as the one dieth, so dieth the other; yea, they have all one breath; so that a man hath no preeminence above a beast: for all is vanity.
Ecclesiastes ch. 3, v. 19

25 Wherefore I praised the dead which are already dead more than the living which are yet alive.
Ecclesiastes ch. 4, v. 2

26 A threefold cord is not quickly broken.
Ecclesiastes ch. 4, v. 12; see BURKE 172:18

27 God is in heaven, and thou upon earth: therefore let thy words be few.
Ecclesiastes ch. 5, v. 2

28 The sleep of a labouring man is sweet.
Ecclesiastes ch. 5, v. 12; see BUNYAN 171:16

29 The heart of the wise is in the house of mourning, but the heart of fools is in the house of mirth.
Ecclesiastes ch. 7, v. 4

1 As the crackling of thorns under a pot, so is the laughter of a fool.
Ecclesiastes ch. 7, v. 6

2 Better is the end of a thing than the beginning thereof.
Ecclesiastes ch. 7, v. 8

3 Say not thou, What is the cause that the former days were better than these? for thou dost not enquire wisely concerning this.
Ecclesiastes ch. 7, v. 10

4 In the day of prosperity be joyful, but in the day of adversity consider.
Ecclesiastes ch. 7, v. 14

5 God hath made man upright; but they have sought out many inventions.
Ecclesiastes ch. 7, v. 29

6 There is no man that hath power over the spirit to retain the spirit; neither hath he power in the day of death; there is no discharge in that war.
Ecclesiastes ch. 8, v. 8

7 A man hath no better thing under the sun, than to eat, and to drink, and to be merry.
Ecclesiastes ch. 8, v. 15; see BIBLE 92:22, BIBLE 105:14, PROVERBS 630:47

8 A living dog is better than a dead lion.
Ecclesiastes ch. 9, v. 4; see PROVERBS 637:49

9 Go thy way, eat thy bread with joy, and drink thy wine with a merry heart; for God now accepteth thy works.
Ecclesiastes ch. 9, v. 7

10 Whatsoever thy hand findeth to do, do it with thy might; for there is no work, nor device, nor knowledge, nor wisdom, in the grave, whither thou goest.
Ecclesiastes ch. 9, v. 10

11 The race is not to the swift, nor the battle to the strong.
Ecclesiastes ch. 9, v. 11; see DAVIDSON 267:15, PAGE 591:15, PROVERBS 642:17

12 He that diggeth a pit shall fall into it.
Ecclesiastes ch. 10, v. 8

13 Woe to thee, O land, when thy king is a child, and thy princes eat in the morning!
Ecclesiastes ch. 10, v. 16; see SHAKESPEARE 731:19

14 Wine maketh merry: but money answereth all things.
Ecclesiastes ch. 10, v. 19

15 Cast thy bread upon the waters: for thou shalt find it after many days.
Ecclesiastes ch. 11, v. 1

16 In the place where the tree falleth, there it shall be.
Ecclesiastes ch. 11, v. 3; see PROVERBS 626:36

17 He that observeth the wind shall not sow; and he that regardeth the clouds shall not reap.
Ecclesiastes ch. 11, v. 4

18 Truly the light is sweet, and a pleasant thing it is for the eyes to behold the sun.
Ecclesiastes ch. 11, v. 7

19 Rejoice, O young man, in thy youth; and let thy heart cheer thee in the days of thy youth.
Ecclesiastes ch. 11, v. 9

20 Remember now thy Creator in the days of thy youth, while the evil days come not, nor the years draw nigh, when thou shalt say, I have no pleasure in them;
While the sun, or the light, or the moon, or the stars, be not darkened, nor the clouds return after the rain:
In the day when the keepers of the house shall tremble, and the strong men shall bow themselves, and the grinders cease because they are few, and those that look out of the windows be darkened,
And the doors shall be shut in the streets, when the sound of the grinding is low, and he shall rise up at the voice of the bird, and all the daughters of music shall be brought low;
Also when they shall be afraid of that which is high, and fears shall be in the way, and the almond tree shall flourish, and the grasshopper shall be a burden, and desire shall fail: because man goeth to his long home, and the mourners go about the streets:
Or ever the silver cord be loosed, or the golden bowl be broken, or the pitcher be broken at the fountain, or the wheel broken at the cistern.
Then shall the dust return to the earth as it was: and the spirit shall return unto God who gave it.
Ecclesiastes ch. 12, v. 1

21 Of making many books there is no end; and much study is a weariness of the flesh.
Ecclesiastes ch. 12, v. 12

22 Fear God, and keep his commandments: for this is the whole duty of man.
For God shall bring every work into judgement, with every secret thing, whether it be good, or whether it be evil.
Ecclesiastes ch. 12, v. 13

SONG OF SOLOMON

23 The song of songs, which is Solomon's.
Let him kiss me with the kisses of his mouth: for thy love is better than wine.
Song of Solomon ch. 1, v. 1

24 I am black, but comely, O ye daughters of Jerusalem,
as the tents of Kedar, as the curtains of Solomon.
Song of Solomon ch. 1, v. 5

25 A bundle of myrrh is my wellbeloved unto me; he shall lie all night betwixt my breasts.
Song of Solomon ch. 1, v. 13

26 I am the rose of Sharon, and the lily of the valleys.
Song of Solomon ch. 2, v. 1

27 Rise up, my love, my fair one, and come away.
For, lo, the winter is past, the rain is over and gone;

The flowers appear on the earth; the time of the singing of birds is come, and the voice of the turtle is heard in our land.
Song of Solomon ch. 2, v. 10

1 Take us the foxes, the little foxes, that spoil the vines.
Song of Solomon ch. 2, v. 15

2 My beloved is mine, and I am his: he feedeth among the lilies.
Until the day break, and the shadows flee away.
Song of Solomon ch. 2, v. 16

3 By night on my bed I sought him whom my soul loveth.
Song of Solomon ch. 3, v. 1

4 Behold, thou art fair, my love; behold, thou art fair; thou hast doves' eyes within thy locks: thy hair is as a flock of goats, that appear from mount Gilead.
Thy teeth are like a flock of sheep that are even shorn, which came up from the washing; whereof every one bear twins, and none is barren among them.
Thy lips are like a thread of scarlet, and thy speech is comely: thy temples are like a piece of a pomegranate within thy locks.
Thy neck is like the tower of David builded for an armoury, whereon there hang a thousand bucklers, all shields of mighty men.
Thy two breasts are like two young roes that are twins, which feed among the lilies.
Song of Solomon ch. 4, v. 1

5 Thou art all fair, my love; there is no spot in thee.
Song of Solomon ch. 4, v. 7

6 A garden inclosed is my sister, my spouse; a spring shut up, a fountain sealed.
Song of Solomon ch. 4, v. 12

7 Awake, O north wind; and come, thou south; blow upon my garden, that the spices thereof may flow out. Let my beloved come into his garden, and eat his pleasant fruits.
Song of Solomon ch. 4, v. 16

8 I sleep, but my heart waketh: it is the voice of my beloved that knocketh, saying, Open to me, my sister, my love, my dove, my undefiled.
Song of Solomon ch. 5, v. 2

9 The watchmen that went about the city found me, they smote me, they wounded me; the keepers of the walls took away my veil from me.
I charge you, O daughters of Jerusalem, if ye find my beloved, that ye tell him, that I am sick of love.
What is thy beloved more than another beloved, O thou fairest among women?
Song of Solomon ch. 5, v. 7

10 His hands are as gold rings set with the beryl: his belly is as bright ivory overlaid with sapphires.

His legs are as pillars of marble, set upon sockets of fine gold: his countenance is as Lebanon, excellent as the cedars.
His mouth is most sweet: yea, he is altogether lovely. This is my beloved, and this is my friend, O daughters of Jerusalem.
Song of Solomon ch. 5, v. 14

11 Who is she that looketh forth as the morning, fair as the moon, clear as the sun, and terrible as an army with banners?
Song of Solomon ch. 6, v. 10

12 Return, return, O Shulamite; return, return, that we may look upon thee.
Song of Solomon ch. 6, v. 13

13 How beautiful are thy feet with shoes, O prince's daughter!
Song of Solomon ch. 7, v. 1

14 Thy navel is like a round goblet, which wanteth not liquor: thy belly is like an heap of wheat set about with lilies.
Song of Solomon ch. 7, v. 2

15 Thy neck is as a tower of ivory; thine eyes like the fishpools in Heshbon.
Song of Solomon ch. 7, v. 4

16 Set me as a seal upon thine heart, as a seal upon thine arm: for love is strong as death; jealousy is cruel as the grave.
Song of Solomon ch. 8, v. 6

17 Many waters cannot quench love, neither can the floods drown it: if a man would give all the substance of his house for love, it would utterly be contemned.
Song of Solomon ch. 8, v. 7

18 Make haste, my beloved, and be thou like to a roe or to a young hart upon the mountains of spices.
Song of Solomon ch. 8, v. 14

ISAIAH

19 The daughter of Zion is left as a cottage in a vineyard, as a lodge in a garden of cucumbers, as a besieged city.
Isaiah ch. 1, v. 8

20 Though your sins be as scarlet, they shall be as white as snow.
Isaiah ch. 1, v. 18

21 They shall beat their swords into plowshares, and their spears into pruninghooks: nation shall not lift up sword against nation, neither shall they learn war any more.
Isaiah ch. 2, v. 4; see **RENDALL** 658:7. Micah ch. 4, v. 3, Joel ch. 3, v. 10 have same image

22 What mean ye that ye beat my people to pieces, and grind the faces of the poor?
Isaiah ch. 3, v. 15

23 My well-beloved hath a vineyard in a very fruitful hill.
Isaiah ch. 5, v. 1

1 And he looked that it should bring forth grapes, and it brought forth wild grapes.
Isaiah ch. 5, v. 2

2 And he looked for judgement, but behold oppression; for righteousness, but behold a cry.
Isaiah ch. 5, v. 7

3 Woe unto them that join house to house, that lay field to field, till there be no place.
Isaiah ch. 5, v. 8

4 Woe unto them that call evil good, and good evil.
Isaiah ch. 5, v. 20

5 For all this his anger is not turned away, but his hand is stretched out still.
Isaiah ch. 5, v. 25

6 In the year that king Uzziah died I saw also the Lord sitting upon a throne, high and lifted up, and his train filled the temple.
Above it stood the seraphims: each one had six wings; with twain he covered his face, and with twain he covered his feet, and with twain he did fly.
And one cried unto another, and said, Holy, holy, holy, is the Lord of hosts: the whole earth is full of his glory.
Isaiah ch. 6, v. 1

7 Then said I, Woe is me! for I am undone; because I am a man of unclean lips, and I dwell in the midst of a people of unclean lips.
Isaiah ch. 6, v. 5

8 Then flew one of the seraphims unto me, having a live coal in his hand, which he had taken with the tongs from off the altar.
And he laid it upon my mouth, and said, Lo, this hath touched thy lips.
Isaiah ch. 6, v. 6

9 Whom shall I send, and who will go for us? Then said I, Here am I; send me.
Isaiah ch. 6, v. 8

10 Then said I, Lord, how long?
Isaiah ch. 6, v. 11

11 Behold, a virgin shall conceive, and bear a son, and shall call his name Immanuel.
Butter and honey shall he eat, that he may know to refuse the evil, and choose the good.
Isaiah ch. 7, v. 14

12 Sanctify the Lord of hosts himself; and let him be your fear, and let him be your dread.
And he shall be for a sanctuary; but for a stone of stumbling and for a rock of offence to both the houses of Israel.
Isaiah ch. 8, v. 13

13 The people that walked in darkness have seen a great light: they that dwell in the land of the shadow of death, upon them hath the light shined.
Thou hast multiplied the nation, and not increased the joy: they joy before thee according

to the joy in harvest, and as men rejoice when they divide the spoil.
Isaiah ch. 9, v. 2; see **SCOTTISH METRICAL PSALMS** 690:12

14 For unto us a child is born, unto us a son is given: and the government shall be upon his shoulder: and his name shall be called Wonderful, Counsellor, The mighty God, The everlasting Father, The Prince of Peace.
Of the increase of his government and peace there shall be no end.
Isaiah ch. 9, v. 6

15 The zeal of the Lord of hosts will perform this.
Isaiah ch. 9, v. 7

16 And there shall come forth a rod out of the stem of Jesse, and a branch shall grow out of his roots:
And the spirit of the Lord shall rest upon him, the spirit of wisdom and understanding, the spirit of counsel and might, the spirit of knowledge and of the fear of the Lord.
Isaiah ch. 11, v. 1

17 The wolf also shall dwell with the lamb, and the leopard shall lie down with the kid; and the calf and the young lion and the fatling together; and a little child shall lead them.
Isaiah ch. 11, v. 6

18 And the lion shall eat straw like the ox.
And the sucking child shall play on the hole of the asp, and the weaned child shall put his hand on the cockatrice' den.
They shall not hurt nor destroy in all my holy mountain: for the earth shall be full of the knowledge of the Lord, as the waters cover the sea.
Isaiah ch. 11, v. 7

19 And the wild beasts of the islands shall cry in their desolate houses, and dragons in their pleasant palaces.
Isaiah ch. 13, v. 22

20 How art thou fallen from heaven, O Lucifer, son of the morning!
Isaiah ch. 14, v. 12

21 Watchman, what of the night? Watchman, what of the night?
The watchman said, The morning cometh, and also the night.
Isaiah ch. 21, v. 11

22 Let us eat and drink; for to morrow we shall die.
Isaiah ch. 22, v. 13; see **BIBLE** 90:7, **BIBLE** 105:14, **PROVERBS** 630:47

23 In this mountain shall the Lord of hosts make unto all people a feast of fat things, a feast of wine on the lees, of fat things full of marrow, of wine on the lees well refined.
Isaiah ch. 25, v. 6

24 He will swallow up death in victory; and the Lord God will wipe away tears from off all faces.
Isaiah ch. 25, v. 8

1 For precept must be upon precept, precept upon precept; line upon line, line upon line; here a little, and there a little.

Isaiah ch. 28, v. 10

2 We have made a covenant with death, and with hell are we at agreement.

Isaiah ch. 28, v. 15; see **GARRISON** 350:1

3 The bread of adversity, and the waters of affliction.

Isaiah ch. 30, v. 20

4 This is the way, walk ye in it.

Isaiah ch. 30, v. 21

5 And a man shall be as an hiding place from the wind, and a covert from the tempest; as rivers of water in a dry place, as the shadow of a great rock in a weary land.

Isaiah ch. 32, v. 2

6 And thorns shall come up in her palaces, nettles and brambles in the fortresses thereof: and it shall be an habitation of dragons, and a court for owls.

Isaiah ch. 34, v. 13

7 The wild beasts of the desert shall also meet with the wild beasts of the island, and the satyr shall cry to his fellow; the screech owl also shall rest there, and find for herself a place of rest.

Isaiah ch. 34, v. 14

8 The wilderness and the solitary place shall be glad for them; and the desert shall rejoice, and blossom as the rose.

Isaiah ch. 35, v. 1

9 Strengthen ye the weak hands, and confirm the feeble knees.

Isaiah ch. 35, v. 3

10 Then shall the lame man leap as an hart, and the tongue of the dumb sing: for in the wilderness shall waters break out, and streams in the desert.

Isaiah ch. 35, v. 6

11 They shall obtain joy and gladness, and sorrow and sighing shall flee away.

Isaiah ch. 35, v. 10

12 Set thine house in order: for thou shalt die, and not live.

Isaiah ch. 38, v. 1

13 I shall go softly all my years in the bitterness of my soul.

Isaiah ch. 38, v. 15

14 Comfort ye, comfort ye my people, saith your God.
Speak ye comfortably to Jerusalem, and cry unto her, that her warfare is accomplished.

Isaiah ch. 40, v. 1

15 The voice of him that crieth in the wilderness, Prepare ye the way of the Lord, make straight in the desert a highway for our God.
Every valley shall be exalted, and every mountain and hill shall be made low: and the

crooked shall be made straight, and the rough places plain:
And the glory of the Lord shall be revealed, and all flesh shall see it together: for the mouth of the Lord hath spoken it.

Isaiah ch. 40, v. 3; see **BIBLE** 98:15

16 The voice said, Cry. And he said, What shall I cry? All flesh is grass, and all the goodliness thereof is as the flower of the field:
The grass withereth, the flower fadeth: because the spirit of the Lord bloweth upon it: surely the people is grass.

Isaiah ch. 40, v. 6; see **BIBLE** 117:1

17 He shall feed his flock like a shepherd: he shall gather the lambs with his arm, and carry them in his bosom, and shall gently lead those that are with young.

Isaiah ch. 40, v. 11

18 The nations are as a drop of a bucket, and are counted as the small dust of the balance: behold, he taketh up the isles as a very little thing.

Isaiah ch. 40, v. 15

19 Have ye not known? have ye not heard? hath it not been told you from the beginning?

Isaiah ch. 40, v. 21

20 But they that wait upon the Lord shall renew their strength: they shall mount up with wings as eagles; they shall run, and not be weary; and they shall walk, and not faint.

Isaiah ch. 40, v. 31

21 A bruised reed shall he not break, and the smoking flax shall he not quench.

Isaiah ch. 42, v. 3

22 Woe unto him that striveth with his maker! Let the potsherd strive with the potsherds of the earth. Shall the clay say to him that fashioneth it, What makest thou?

Isaiah ch. 45, v. 9

23 I have chosen thee in the furnace of affliction.

Isaiah ch. 48, v. 10

24 O that thou hadst hearkened to my commandments! then had thy peace been as a river, and thy righteousness as the waves of the sea.

Isaiah ch. 48, v. 18

25 There is no peace, saith the Lord, unto the wicked.

Isaiah ch. 48, v. 22

26 Can a woman forget her sucking child, that she should not have compassion on the son of her womb? yea, they may forget, yet will I not forget thee.

Isaiah ch. 49, v. 15

27 How beautiful upon the mountains are the feet of him that bringeth good tidings, that publisheth peace; that bringeth good tidings of

good, that publisheth salvation; that saith unto Zion, Thy God reigneth!

Isaiah ch. 52, v. 7

1 For they shall see eye to eye, when the Lord shall bring again Zion.

Break forth into joy, sing together, ye waste places of Jerusalem: for the Lord hath comforted his people, he hath redeemed Jerusalem.

Isaiah ch. 52, v. 8

2 Who hath believed our report? and to whom is the arm of the Lord revealed?

Isaiah ch. 53, v. 1

3 He is despised and rejected of men; a man of sorrows, and acquainted with grief: and we hid as it were our faces from him; he was despised, and we esteemed him not.

Surely he hath borne our griefs, and carried our sorrows.

Isaiah ch. 53, v. 3

4 But he was wounded for our transgressions, he was bruised for our iniquities: the chastisement of our peace was upon him; and with his stripes we are healed.

All we like sheep have gone astray; we have turned every one to his own way; and the Lord hath laid on him the iniquity of us all.

He was oppressed, and he was afflicted, yet he opened not his mouth: he is brought as a lamb to the slaughter, and as a sheep before her shearers is dumb, so he openeth not his mouth.

Isaiah ch. 53, v. 5

5 He was cut off out of the land of the living.

Isaiah ch. 53, v. 8

6 He was numbered with the transgressors; and he bare the sin of many, and made intercession for the transgressors.

Isaiah ch. 53, v. 12

7 Ho, every one that thirsteth, come ye to the waters, and he that hath no money; come ye, buy, and eat; yea, come, buy wine and milk without money and without price.

Wherefore do ye spend money for that which is not bread? and your labour for that which satisfieth not?

Isaiah ch. 55, v. 1

8 Seek ye the Lord while he may be found, call ye upon him while he is near.

Isaiah ch. 55, v. 6

9 For my thoughts are not your thoughts, neither are your ways my ways, saith the Lord.

Isaiah ch. 55, v. 8

10 Instead of the thorn shall come up the fir tree, and instead of the brier shall come up the myrtle tree.

Isaiah ch. 55, v. 13

11 I will give them an everlasting name, that shall not be cut off.

Isaiah ch. 56, v. 5

12 Mine house shall be called an house of prayer for all people.

Isaiah ch. 56, v. 7; see **BIBLE** 102:13

13 The righteous perisheth, and no man layeth it to heart.

Isaiah ch. 57, v. 1

14 Peace to him that is far off, and to him that is near.

Isaiah ch. 57, v. 19

15 Is not this the fast that I have chosen? to loose the bands of wickedness, to undo the heavy burdens, and to let the oppressed go free, and that ye break every yoke?

Isaiah ch. 58, v. 6

16 Then shall thy light break forth as the morning, and thine health shall spring forth speedily.

Isaiah ch. 58, v. 8

17 They make haste to shed innocent blood.

Isaiah ch. 59, v. 7

18 Arise, shine; for thy light is come, and the glory of the Lord is risen upon thee.

Isaiah ch. 60, v. 1

19 The Spirit of the Lord God is upon me . . . To bind up the brokenhearted, to proclaim liberty to the captives, and the opening of the prison to them that are bound;

To proclaim the acceptable year of the Lord, and the day of vengeance of our God; to comfort all that mourn.

Isaiah ch. 61, v. 1

20 To give unto them beauty for ashes, the oil of joy for mourning, the garment of praise for the spirit of heaviness.

Isaiah ch. 61, v. 3

21 All our righteousnesses are as filthy rags; and we all do fade as a leaf.

Isaiah ch. 64, v. 6

22 Stand by thyself, come not near to me; for I am holier than thou.

Isaiah ch. 65, v. 5

23 For, behold, I create new heavens and a new earth.

Isaiah ch. 65, v. 17

JEREMIAH

24 Can a maid forget her ornaments, or a bride her attire?

Jeremiah ch. 2, v. 32

25 This people hath a revolting and a rebellious heart.

Jeremiah ch. 5, v. 23

26 The prophets prophesy falsely, and the priests bear rule by their means; and my people love to have it so: and what will ye do in the end thereof?

Jeremiah ch. 5, v. 31

27 They have healed also the hurt of the daughter of my people slightly, saying, Peace, peace; when there is no peace.

Jeremiah ch. 6, v. 14

1 The harvest is past, the summer is ended, and we are not saved.
Jeremiah ch. 8, v. 20

2 Is there no balm in Gilead?
Jeremiah ch. 8, v. 22

3 Can the Ethiopian change his skin, or the leopard his spots?
Jeremiah ch. 13, v. 23; see **PROVERBS** 637:18

4 Woe is me, my mother, that thou hast borne me a man of strife and a man of contention to the whole earth!
Jeremiah ch. 15, v. 10

5 The heart is deceitful above all things, and desperately wicked.
Jeremiah ch. 17, v. 9

6 As the partridge sitteth on eggs, and hatcheth them not; so he that getteth riches, and not by right, shall leave them in the midst of his days.
Jeremiah ch. 17, v. 11

7 Behold, I will make thee a terror to thyself, and to all thy friends.
Jeremiah ch. 20, v. 4

LAMENTATIONS

8 How doth the city sit solitary, that was full of people!
Lamentations ch. 1, v. 1

9 Is it nothing to you, all ye that pass by? behold, and see if there be any sorrow like unto my sorrow.
Lamentations ch. 1, v. 12

10 And I said, My strength and my hope is perished from the Lord:
Remembering mine affliction and my misery, the wormwood and the gall.
Lamentations ch. 3, v. 18

11 It is good for a man that he bear the yoke in his youth.
Lamentations ch. 3, v. 27

12 He giveth his cheek to him that smiteth him.
Lamentations ch. 3, v. 30

13 O Lord, thou hast seen my wrong: judge thou my cause.
Lamentations ch. 4, v. 59

EZEKIEL

14 As is the mother, so is her daughter.
Ezekiel ch. 16, v. 44; see **PROVERBS** 637:34

15 The fathers have eaten sour grapes, and the children's teeth are set on edge.
Ezekiel ch. 18, v. 2

16 When the wicked man turneth away from his wickedness that he hath committed, and doeth that which is lawful and right, he shall save his soul alive.
Ezekiel ch. 18, v. 27

17 The king of Babylon stood at the parting of the ways.
Ezekiel ch. 21, v. 21

18 Thou art like a young lion of the nations, and thou art as a whale in the seas.
Ezekiel bk. 32, v. 2; see **MELVILLE** 531:11

19 The hand of the Lord was upon me, and carried me out in the spirit of the Lord, and set me down in the midst of the valley which was full of bones.
Ezekiel ch. 37, v. 1

20 Can these bones live?
Ezekiel ch. 37, v. 3

21 Again he said unto me, Prophesy upon these bones, and say unto them, O ye dry bones, hear the word of the Lord.
Ezekiel ch. 37, v. 4

DANIEL

22 To you it is commanded, O peoples, nations, and languages,
That at what time ye hear the sound of the cornet, flute, harp, sackbut, psaltery, dulcimer, and all kinds of music, ye fall down and worship the golden image that Nebuchadnezzar the king hath set up:
And whoso falleth not down and worshippeth shall the same hour be cast into the midst of a burning fiery furnace.
Daniel ch. 3, v. 4

23 Shadrach, Meshach, and Abed-nego, ye servants of the most high God, come forth and come hither.
Daniel ch. 3, v. 26

24 In the same hour came forth fingers of a man's hand, and wrote over against the candlestick upon the plaister of the wall of the king's palace.
Daniel ch. 5, v. 5

25 And this is the writing that was written, MENE, MENE, TEKEL, UPHARSIN.
This is the interpretation of the thing: MENE; God hath numbered thy kingdom, and finished it.
TEKEL; Thou art weighed in the balances and art found wanting.
PERES; Thy kingdom is divided, and given to the Medes and Persians.
Daniel ch. 5, v. 25

26 Now, O king, establish the decree, and sign the writing, that it be not changed, according to the law of the Medes and Persians, which altereth not.
Daniel ch. 6, v. 8

27 The Ancient of days did sit, whose garment was white as snow, and the hair of his head like the pure wool: his throne was like the fiery flame, and his wheels as burning fire.
A fiery stream issued and came forth from behind him: thousand thousands ministered unto him, and ten thousand times ten thousand stood before him: the judgement was set, and the books were opened.
Daniel ch. 7, v. 9

1 O Daniel, a man greatly beloved.
  Daniel ch. 10, v. 11

2 Many shall run to and fro, and knowledge shall be increased.
  Daniel ch. 12, v. 4

HOSEA

3 Like people, like priest.
  Hosea ch. 4, v. 9; see **PROVERBS** 637:35

4 They have sown the wind, and they shall reap the whirlwind.
  Hosea ch. 8, v. 7; see **PROVERBS** 645:1

5 I drew them . . . with bands of love.
  Hosea ch. 11, v. 4

JOEL

6 That which the palmerworm hath left hath the locust eaten.
  Joel ch. 1, v. 4

7 I will restore to you the years that the locust hath eaten, the cankerworm, and the caterpillar, and the palmerworm, my great army which I sent among you.
  Joel ch. 2, v. 25

8 And it shall come to pass afterward, that I will pour out my spirit upon all flesh; and your sons and your daughters shall prophesy, your old men shall dream dreams, your young men shall see visions.
  Joel ch. 2, v. 28

9 Multitudes, multitudes in the valley of decision: for the day of the Lord is near in the valley of decision.
  Joel ch. 3, v. 14

AMOS

10 Can two walk together, except they be agreed?
  Amos ch. 3, v. 3

11 Shall there be evil in a city, and the Lord hath not done it?
  Amos ch. 3, v. 6

12 I have overthrown some of you, as God overthrew Sodom and Gomorrah, and ye were as a firebrand plucked out of the burning.
  Amos ch. 4, v. 11

MICAH

13 But thou, Bethlehem Ephratah, though thou be little among the thousands of Judah, yet out of thee shall he come forth unto me that is to be ruler in Israel.
  Micah ch. 5, v. 2

14 What doth the Lord require of thee, but to do justly, and to love mercy, and to walk humbly with thy God?
  Micah ch. 6, v. 8

NAHUM

15 Woe to the bloody city! it is all full of lies and robbery; the prey departeth not.
  Nahum ch. 3, v. 1

HABAKKUK

16 Write the vision, and make it plain upon tables, that he may run that readeth it.
  Habakkuk ch. 2, v. 2; see also **KEBLE** 459:2

ZEPHANIAH

17 Woe to her that is filthy and polluted, to the oppressing city!
  Zephaniah ch. 3, v. 1

HAGGAI

18 Ye have sown much, and bring in little; ye eat but ye have not enough . . . and he that earneth wages earneth wages to put it into a bag with holes.
  Haggai ch. 1, v. 6

MALACHI

19 But unto you that fear my name shall the Sun of righteousness arise with healing in his wings.
  Malachi ch. 4, v. 2; see **WESLEY** 847:9

APOCRYPHA

20 The first wrote, Wine is the strongest. The second wrote, The king is strongest. The third wrote, Women are strongest: but above all things Truth beareth away the victory.
  I Esdras ch. 3, v. 10

21 Great is Truth, and mighty above all things.
  I Esdras ch. 4, v. 41; see **BIBLE (VULGATE)** 120:19

22 Nourish thy children, O thou good nurse; stablish their feet.
  II Esdras ch. 2, v. 25

23 For the world has lost his youth, and the times begin to wax old.
  II Esdras ch. 14, v. 10

24 I shall light a candle of understanding in thine heart, which shall not be put out.
  II Esdras ch. 14, v. 25; see **LATIMER** 482:16

25 The ear of jealousy heareth all things.
  Wisdom of Solomon ch. 1, v. 10

26 Let us crown ourselves with rosebuds, before they be withered.
  Wisdom of Solomon ch. 2, v. 8

27 Through envy of the devil came death into the world.
  Wisdom of Solomon ch. 2, v. 24

28 But the souls of the righteous are in the hand of God, and there shall no torment touch them.
  In the sight of the unwise they seemed to die: and their departure is taken for misery,
  And their going from us to be utter destruction: but they are in peace.
  For though they be punished in the sight of men, yet is their hope full of immortality.
  And having been a little chastised, they shall be greatly rewarded: for God proved them, and found them worthy for himself.
  Wisdom of Solomon ch. 3, v. 1

29 And in the time of their visitation they shall shine, and run to and fro like sparks among the stubble.
  Wisdom of Solomon ch. 3, v. 7

1 He, being made perfect in a short time, fulfilled a long time.
Wisdom of Solomon ch. 4, v. 13

2 We fools accounted his life madness, and his end to be without honour:
How is he numbered among the children of God, and his lot is among the saints!
Wisdom of Solomon ch. 5, v. 4

3 Even so we in like manner, as soon as we were born, began to draw to our end.
Wisdom of Solomon ch. 5, v. 13

4 For the hope of the ungodly . . . passeth away as the remembrance of a guest that tarrieth but a day.
Wisdom of Solomon ch. 5, v. 14

5 And love is the keeping of her laws; and the giving heed unto her laws is the assurance of incorruption.
Wisdom of Solomon ch. 6, v. 18

6 For the same things uttered in Hebrew, and translated into another tongue, have not the same force in them: and not only these things, but the law itself, and the prophets, and the rest of the books, have no small difference, when they are spoken in their own language.
Ecclesiasticus: The Prologue

7 For the Lord is full of compassion and mercy, long-suffering, and very pitiful, and forgiveth sins, and saveth in time of affliction.
Ecclesiasticus ch. 2, v. 11

8 We will fall into the hands of the Lord, and not into the hands of men: for as his majesty is, so is his mercy.
Ecclesiasticus ch. 2, v. 18

9 Be not curious in unnecessary matters: for more things are shewed unto thee than men understand.
Ecclesiasticus ch. 3, v. 23

10 Be not ignorant of any thing in a great matter or a small.
Ecclesiasticus ch. 5, v. 15

11 A faithful friend is the medicine of life.
Ecclesiasticus ch. 6, v. 16

12 Laugh no man to scorn in the bitterness of his soul.
Ecclesiasticus ch. 7, v. 11

13 Miss not the discourse of the elders.
Ecclesiasticus ch. 8, v. 9

14 Open not thine heart to every man.
Ecclesiasticus ch. 8, v. 19

15 Forsake not an old friend; for the new is not comparable to him; a new friend is as new wine; when it is old, thou shalt drink it with pleasure.
Ecclesiasticus ch. 9, v. 10

16 Many kings have sat down upon the ground; and one that was never thought of hath worn the crown.
Ecclesiasticus ch. 11, v. 5

17 Judge none blessed before his death.
Ecclesiasticus ch. 11, v. 28; see **SOLON** 760:10

18 He that toucheth pitch shall be defiled therewith.
Ecclesiasticus ch. 13, v. 1; see **PROVERBS** 634:11

19 For how agree the kettle and the earthen pot together?
Ecclesiasticus ch. 13, v. 2

20 When a rich man is fallen, he hath many helpers: he speaketh things not to be spoken, and yet men justify him: the poor man slipped, and yet they rebuked him too; he spake wisely, and could have no place.
Ecclesiasticus ch. 14, v. 22

21 When thou hast enough, remember the time of hunger.
Ecclesiasticus ch. 18, v. 25

22 Be not made a beggar by banqueting upon borrowing.
Ecclesiasticus ch. 18, v. 33

23 He that contemneth small things shall fall by little and little.
Ecclesiasticus ch. 19, v. 1

24 A merchant shall hardly keep himself from doing wrong.
Ecclesiasticus ch. 26, v. 29

25 Many have fallen by the edge of the sword: but not so many as have fallen by the tongue.
Ecclesiasticus ch. 28, v. 18

26 And weigh thy words in a balance, and make a door and bar for thy mouth.
Ecclesiasticus ch. 28, v. 25

27 Envy and wrath shorten the life.
Ecclesiasticus ch. 30, v. 24

28 Leave off first for manners' sake.
Ecclesiasticus ch. 31, v. 17

29 Wine is as good as life to a man, if it be drunk moderately: what life is then to a man that is without wine? for it was made to make men glad.
Ecclesiasticus ch. 31, v. 27

30 Leave not a stain in thine honour.
Ecclesiasticus ch. 33, v. 22

31 Honour a physician with the honour due unto him for the uses which ye may have of him: for the Lord hath created him.
Ecclesiasticus ch. 38, v. 1

32 He that sinneth before his Maker, let him fall into the hand of the physician.
Ecclesiasticus ch. 38, v. 15

33 The wisdom of a learned man cometh by opportunity of leisure: and he that hath little business shall become wise.
Ecclesiasticus ch. 38, v. 24

34 How can he get wisdom . . . whose talk is of bullocks?
Ecclesiasticus ch. 38, v. 25

1 Let us now praise famous men, and our fathers that begat us.
Ecclesiasticus ch. 44, v. 1

2 Such as did bear rule in their kingdoms.
Ecclesiasticus ch. 44, v. 3

3 Such as found out musical tunes, and recited verses in writing:
Rich men furnished with ability, living peaceably in their habitations.
Ecclesiasticus ch. 44, v. 5

4 There be of them, that have left a name behind them.
Ecclesiasticus ch. 44, v. 8

5 And some there be, which have no memorial . . . and are become as though they had never been born . . .
But these were merciful men, whose righteousness hath not been forgotten . . .
Their seed shall remain for ever, and their glory shall not be blotted out.
Their bodies are buried in peace; but their name liveth for evermore.
Ecclesiasticus ch. 44, v. 9

6 As the flower of roses in the spring of the year, as lilies by the rivers of waters, and as the branches of the frankincense tree in the time of summer.
Ecclesiasticus ch. 50, v. 8

7 Get learning with a great sum of money, and get much gold by her.
Ecclesiasticus ch. 51, v. 28

8 It is a foolish thing to make a long prologue, and to be short in the story itself.
II Maccabees ch. 2, v. 32

9 When he was at the last gasp.
II Maccabees ch. 7, v. 9

NEW TESTAMENT: ST MATTHEW

10 There came wise men from the east to Jerusalem,
Saying, Where is he that is born King of the Jews? for we have seen his star in the east, and are come to worship him.
St Matthew ch. 2, v. 1

11 They presented unto him gifts; gold, and frankincense, and myrrh.
St Matthew ch. 2, v. 11

12 They departed into their own country another way.
St Matthew ch. 2, v. 12

13 In Rama was there a voice heard, lamentation, and weeping, and great mourning, Rachel weeping for her children, and would not be comforted, because they are not.
St Matthew ch. 2, v. 18; referring to Jeremiah ch. 31, v. 15

14 Repent ye: for the kingdom of heaven is at hand.
St Matthew ch. 3, v. 2

15 The voice of one crying in the wilderness, Prepare ye the way of the Lord, make his paths straight.
St Matthew ch. 3, v. 3; see BIBLE 93:15

16 John had his raiment of camel's hair, and a leathern girdle about his loins; and his meat was locusts and wild honey.
St Matthew ch. 3, v. 4

17 O generation of vipers, who hath warned you to flee from the wrath to come?
St Matthew ch. 3, v. 7

18 And now also the axe is laid unto the root of the trees.
St Matthew ch. 3, v. 10

19 This is my beloved Son, in whom I am well pleased.
St Matthew ch. 3, v. 17

20 Man shall not live by bread alone, but by every word that proceedeth out of the mouth of God.
St Matthew ch. 4, v. 4, echoing Deuteronomy ch. 8, v. 3; see PROVERBS 638:15, STEVENSON 776:2

21 Thou shalt not tempt the Lord thy God.
St Matthew ch. 4, v. 7, echoing Deuteronomy ch. 6, v. 16

22 The devil taketh him up into an exceeding high mountain, and sheweth him all the kingdoms of the world, and the glory of them.
St Matthew ch. 4, v. 8

23 Angels came and ministered unto him.
St Matthew ch. 4, v. 11

24 Follow me, and I will make you fishers of men.
St Matthew ch. 4, v. 19

25 Blessed are the poor in spirit: for theirs is the kingdom of heaven.
Blessed are they that mourn: for they shall be comforted.
Blessed are the meek: for they shall inherit the earth.
Blessed are they which do hunger and thirst after righteousness: for they shall be filled.
Blessed are the merciful: for they shall obtain mercy.
Blessed are the pure in heart: for they shall see God.
Blessed are the peacemakers: for they shall be called the children of God.
St Matthew ch. 5, v. 3; see SMITH 756:17

26 Ye are the salt of the earth: but if the salt have lost his savour, wherewith shall it be salted?
St Matthew ch. 5, v. 13

27 Ye are the light of the world. A city that is set on an hill cannot be hid.
St Matthew ch. 5, v. 14

28 Let your light so shine before men, that they may see your good works.
St Matthew ch. 5, v. 16

29 Think not that I am come to destroy the law, or the prophets: I am come not to destroy, but to fulfil.
St Matthew ch. 5, v. 17

1 Except your righteousness shall exceed the righteousness of the scribes and Pharisees, ye shall in no case enter into the kingdom of heaven.
St Matthew ch. 5, v. 20

2 Whosoever shall say, Thou fool, shall be in danger of hell fire.
St Matthew ch. 5, v. 22

3 Till thou hast paid the uttermost farthing.
St Matthew ch. 5, v. 26

4 Swear not at all; neither by heaven; for it is God's throne:
Nor by the earth; for it is his footstool.
St Matthew ch. 5, v. 34

5 Resist not evil: but whosoever shall smite thee on thy right cheek, turn to him the other also.
St Matthew ch. 5, v. 39

6 Whosoever shall compel thee to go a mile, go with him twain.
St Matthew ch. 5, v. 41

7 He maketh his sun to rise on the evil and on the good, and sendeth rain on the just and on the unjust.
St Matthew ch. 5, v. 45; see **BOWEN** 153:16

8 For if ye love them which love you, what reward have ye? do not even the publicans the same?
St Matthew ch. 5, v. 46

9 Be ye therefore perfect, even as your Father which is in heaven is perfect.
St Matthew ch. 5, v. 48

10 When thou doest alms, let not thy left hand know what thy right hand doeth.
That thine alms may be in secret: and thy Father which seeth in secret himself shall reward you openly.
St Matthew ch. 6, v. 3

11 Use not vain repetitions, as the heathen do: for they think that they shall be heard for their much speaking.
St Matthew ch. 6, v. 7

12 After this manner therefore pray ye: Our Father which art in heaven, Hallowed be thy name.
Thy kingdom come. Thy will be done in earth, as it is in heaven.
Give us this day our daily bread.
And forgive us our debts, as we forgive our debtors.
And lead us not into temptation, but deliver us from evil: For thine is the kingdom, and the power, and the glory, for ever. Amen.
St Matthew ch. 6, v. 9; see **BOOK OF COMMON PRAYER** 133:7, **MISSAL** 549:17

13 Lay not up for yourselves treasures upon earth, where moth and rust doth corrupt, and where thieves break through and steal:
But lay up for yourselves treasures in heaven.
St Matthew ch. 6, v. 19

14 Where your treasure is, there will your heart be also.
St Matthew ch. 6, v. 21

15 No man can serve two masters . . . Ye cannot serve God and mammon.
St Matthew ch. 6, v. 24; see **PROVERBS** 648:14

16 Is not the life more than meat, and the body than raiment?
Behold the fowls of the air: for they sow not, neither do they reap, nor gather into barns.
St Matthew ch. 6, v. 25

17 Which of you by taking thought can add one cubit unto his stature?
St Matthew ch. 6, v. 27

18 Consider the lilies of the field, how they grow; they toil not, neither do they spin:
And yet I say unto you, That even Solomon in all his glory was not arrayed like one of these.
St Matthew ch. 6, v. 28

19 Seek ye first the kingdom of God, and his righteousness; and all these things shall be added unto you.
St Matthew ch. 6, v. 33

20 Take therefore no thought for the morrow: for the morrow shall take thought for the things of itself. Sufficient unto the day is the evil thereof.
St Matthew ch. 6, v. 34; see **PROVERBS** 643:49

21 Judge not, that ye be not judged.
St Matthew ch. 7, v. 1; see **PROVERBS** 636:48

22 Why beholdest thou the mote that is in thy brother's eye, but considerest not the beam that is in thine own eye?
St Matthew ch. 7, v. 3

23 Neither cast ye your pearls before swine.
St Matthew ch. 7, v. 6; see **PROVERBS** 630:16

24 Ask, and it shall be given you; seek, and ye shall find; knock, and it shall be opened unto you.
St Matthew ch. 7, v. 7; see **PROVERBS** 642:40

25 Every one that asketh receiveth; and he that seeketh findeth.
St Matthew ch. 7, v. 8

26 Or what man is there of you, whom if his son ask bread, will he give him a stone?
St Matthew ch. 7, v. 9

27 Therefore all things whatsoever ye would that men should do to you, do ye even so to them: for this is the law and the prophets.
St Matthew ch. 7, v. 12

28 Wide is the gate, and broad is the way, that leadeth to destruction, and many there be that go in thereat.
St Matthew ch. 7, v. 13

29 Strait is the gate, and narrow is the way, which leadeth unto life, and few there be that find it.
St Matthew ch. 7, v. 14

30 Beware of false prophets, which come to you in sheep's clothing, but inwardly they are ravening wolves.
St Matthew ch. 7, v. 15

1 Do men gather grapes of thorns, or figs of thistles?
St Matthew ch. 7, v. 16

2 By their fruits ye shall know them.
St Matthew ch. 7, v. 20

3 The winds blew, and beat upon that house; and it fell not: for it was founded upon a rock.
St Matthew ch. 7, v. 25

4 Every one that heareth these sayings of mine, and doeth them not, shall be likened unto a foolish man, which built his house upon the sand:
And the rain descended, and the floods came, and the winds blew, and beat upon that house; and it fell: and great was the fall of it.
St Matthew ch. 7, v. 27

5 For he taught them as one having authority, and not as the scribes.
St Matthew ch. 7, v. 29

6 Lord I am not worthy that thou shouldest come under my roof.
St Matthew ch. 8, v. 8; see **MISSAL** 549:20

7 I am a man under authority, having soldiers under me: and I say to this man, Go, and he goeth; and to another, Come, and he cometh; and to my servant, Do this, and he doeth it.
St Matthew ch. 8, v. 9

8 I have not found so great faith, no, not in Israel.
St Matthew ch. 8, v. 10

9 But the children of the kingdom shall be cast out into outer darkness: there shall be weeping and gnashing of teeth.
St Matthew ch. 8, v. 12

10 The foxes have holes, and the birds of the air have nests; but the Son of man hath not where to lay his head.
St Matthew ch. 8, v. 20

11 Let the dead bury their dead.
St Matthew ch. 8, v. 22; see **LONGFELLOW** 499:16, **PROVERBS** 637:23

12 The whole herd of swine ran violently down a steep place into the sea, and perished in the waters.
St Matthew ch. 8, v. 32

13 He saw a man, named Matthew, sitting at the receipt of custom: and he saith unto him, Follow me. And he arose and followed him.
St Matthew ch. 9, v. 9

14 Why eateth your Master with publicans and sinners?
St Matthew ch. 9, v. 11

15 They that be whole need not a physician, but they that are sick.
St Matthew ch. 9, v. 12

16 I am not come to call the righteous, but sinners to repentance.
St Matthew ch. 9, v. 13

17 Neither do men put new wine into old bottles.
St Matthew ch. 9, v. 17; see **PROVERBS** 647:45

18 Thy faith hath made thee whole.
St Matthew ch. 9, v. 22

19 The maid is not dead, but sleepeth.
St Matthew ch. 9, v. 24

20 He casteth out devils through the prince of the devils.
St Matthew ch. 9, v. 34

21 The harvest truly is plenteous, but the labourers are few.
St Matthew ch. 9, v. 37

22 Go rather to the lost sheep of the house of Israel.
St Matthew ch. 10, v. 6

23 Freely ye have received, freely give.
St Matthew ch. 10, v. 8

24 When ye depart out of that house or city, shake off the dust of your feet.
St Matthew ch. 10, v. 14

25 Be ye therefore wise as serpents, and harmless as doves.
St Matthew ch. 10, v. 16

26 The disciple is not above his master, nor the servant above his lord.
St Matthew ch. 10, v. 24

27 Are not two sparrows sold for a farthing? and one of them shall not fall on the ground without your Father.
The very hairs of your head are all numbered. Fear ye not therefore, ye are of more value than many sparrows.
St Matthew ch. 10, v. 29; see **BIBLE** 105:13

28 I came not to send peace, but a sword.
St Matthew ch. 10, v. 34

29 A man's foes shall be they of his own household.
St Matthew ch. 10, v. 36

30 He that findeth his life shall lose it: and he that loseth his life for my sake shall find it.
St Matthew ch. 10, v. 39

31 Whosoever shall give to drink unto one of these little ones a cup of cold water only in the name of a disciple, verily I say unto you, he shall in no wise lose his reward.
St Matthew ch. 10, v. 42

32 Art thou he that should come, or do we look for another?
St Matthew ch. 11, v. 3

33 What went ye out into the wilderness to see? A reed shaken with the wind?
But what went ye out for to see? A man clothed in soft raiment? . . .
But what went ye out for to see? A prophet? yea, I say unto you, and more than a prophet.
St Matthew ch. 11, v. 7

34 We have piped unto you, and ye have not danced; we have mourned unto you, and ye have not lamented.
St Matthew ch. 11, v. 17

1 Wisdom is justified of her children.
St Matthew ch. 11, v. 19

2 Come unto me, all ye that labour and are heavy laden, and I will give you rest.
Take my yoke upon you, and learn of me; for I am meek and lowly in heart: and ye shall find rest unto your souls.
For my yoke is easy, and my burden is light.
St Matthew ch. 11, v. 28

3 He that is not with me is against me.
St Matthew ch. 12, v. 30 and St Luke ch. 11, v. 23

4 The blasphemy against the Holy Ghost shall not be forgiven unto men.
St Matthew ch. 12, v. 31

5 The tree is known by his fruit.
St Matthew ch. 12, v. 33; see **PROVERBS** 645:34

6 Out of the abundance of the heart the mouth speaketh.
St Matthew ch. 12, v. 34; see **PROVERBS** 641:26

7 Every idle word that men shall speak, they shall give account thereof in the day of judgement.
St Matthew ch. 12, v. 36

8 An evil and adulterous generation seeketh after a sign.
St Matthew ch. 12, v. 39

9 Behold, a greater than Solomon is here.
St Matthew ch. 12, v. 42

10 When the unclean spirit is gone out of a man, he walketh through dry places, seeking rest, and findeth none.
Then he saith, I will return into my house from whence I came out; and when he is come, he findeth it empty, swept, and garnished.
St Matthew ch. 12, v. 43

11 Then goeth he, and taketh with himself seven other spirits more wicked than himself, and they enter in and dwell there: and the last state of that man is worse than the first.
St Matthew ch. 12, v. 45

12 Behold my mother and my brethren!
St Matthew ch. 12, v. 49

13 Behold, a sower went forth to sow;
And when he sowed, some seeds fell by the wayside, and the fowls came and devoured them up:
Some fell upon stony places, where they had not much earth: and forthwith they sprung up, because they had no deepness of earth:
And when the sun was up, they were scorched; and because they had no root, they withered away.
And some fell among thorns; and the thorns sprang up and choked them:
But other fell into good ground, and brought forth fruit, some an hundredfold, some sixtyfold, some thirtyfold.
St Matthew ch. 13, v. 3

14 He also that received the seed among the thorns is he that heareth the word; and the care of this world, and the deceitfulness of riches, choke the word, and he becometh unfruitful.
St Matthew ch. 13, v. 22

15 The kingdom of heaven is like to a grain of mustard seed, which a man took, and sowed in his field:
Which indeed is the least of all seeds: but when it is grown, it is the greatest among herbs, and becometh a tree, so that the birds of the air come and lodge in the branches thereof.
St Matthew ch. 13, v. 31

16 The kingdom of heaven is like unto a merchant man, seeking goodly pearls:
Who, when he had found one pearl of great price, went and sold all that he had, and bought it.
St Matthew ch. 13, v. 45

17 A prophet is not without honour, save in his own country, and in his own house.
St Matthew ch. 13, v. 57; see **PROVERBS** 642:9

18 In the fourth watch of the night Jesus went unto them, walking on the sea.
St Matthew ch. 14, v. 25

19 Be of good cheer; it is I; be not afraid.
St Matthew ch. 14, v. 27

20 O thou of little faith, wherefore didst thou doubt?
St Matthew ch. 14, v. 31

21 Not that which goeth into the mouth defileth a man; but that which cometh out of the mouth, this defileth a man.
St Matthew ch. 15, v. 11

22 They be blind leaders of the blind. And if the blind lead the blind, both shall fall into the ditch.
St Matthew ch. 15, v. 14; see **PROVERBS** 646:44

23 Truth, Lord: yet the dogs eat of the crumbs which fall from their masters' table.
St Matthew ch. 15, v. 27

24 When it is evening, ye say, It will be fair weather: for the sky is red.
St Matthew ch. 16, v. 2

25 Ye can discern the face of the sky; but can ye not discern the signs of the times?
St Matthew ch. 16, v. 3

26 Thou art Peter, and upon this rock I will build my church; and the gates of hell shall not prevail against it.
St Matthew ch. 16, v. 18

27 Get thee behind me, Satan.
St Matthew ch. 16, v. 23

28 If ye have faith as a grain of mustard seed, ye shall say unto this mountain, Remove hence to yonder place; and it shall remove.
St Matthew ch. 17, v. 20; see **PROVERBS** 632:2

29 Except ye be converted, and become as little children, ye shall not enter into the kingdom of heaven.
St Matthew ch. 18, v. 3

1 Whoso shall receive one such little child in my name receiveth me.
But whoso shall offend one of these little ones which believe in me, it were better for him that a millstone were hanged about his neck, and that he were drowned in the depth of the sea.
St Matthew ch. 18, v. 5

2 If thine eye offend thee, pluck it out, and cast it from thee: it is better for thee to enter into life with one eye, rather than having two eyes to be cast into hell fire.
St Matthew ch. 18, v. 9

3 For where two or three are gathered together in my name, there am I in the midst of them.
St Matthew ch. 18, v. 20

4 Lord, how oft shall my brother sin against me, and I forgive him? till seven times?
Jesus saith unto him I say not unto thee, Until seven times: but Until seventy times seven.
St Matthew ch. 18, v. 21

5 What therefore God hath joined together, let not man put asunder.
St Matthew ch. 19, v. 6; see BOOK OF COMMON PRAYER 139:3

6 If thou wilt be perfect, go and sell that thou hast, and give to the poor, and thou shalt have treasure in heaven.
St Matthew ch. 19, v. 21

7 He went away sorrowful: for he had great possessions.
St Matthew ch. 19, v. 22

8 It is easier for a camel to go through the eye of a needle, than for a rich man to enter into the kingdom of God.
St Matthew ch. 19, v. 24. See also St Luke ch. 18, v. 24

9 With men this is impossible; but with God all things are possible.
St Matthew ch. 19, v. 26; see PROVERBS 626:21

10 But many that are first shall be last; and the last shall be first.
St Matthew ch. 19, v. 30

11 These last have wrought but one hour, and thou hast made them equal unto us, which have borne the burden and heat of the day.
St Matthew ch. 20, v. 12

12 I will give unto this last, even as unto thee. Is it not lawful for me to do what I will with mine own?
St Matthew ch. 20, v. 14

13 It is written, My house shall be called the house of prayer; but ye have made it a den of thieves.
St Matthew ch. 21, v. 13; see BIBLE 94:12

14 For many are called, but few are chosen.
St Matthew ch. 22, v. 14; see PROVERBS 638:26

15 Render therefore unto Caesar the things which are Caesar's; and unto God the things that are God's.
St Matthew ch. 22, v. 21; see CRASHAW 259:10

16 For in the resurrection they neither marry, nor are given in marriage.
St Matthew ch. 22, v. 30

17 Thou shalt love the Lord thy God with all thy heart, and with all thy soul, and with all thy mind.
This is the first and great commandment.
And the second is like unto it, Thou shalt love thy neighbour as thyself.
St Matthew ch. 22, v. 38; see BIBLE 82:1

18 Woe unto you, scribes and Pharisees, hypocrites! for ye pay tithe of mint and anise and cummin, and have omitted the weightier matters of the law, judgement, mercy, and faith: these ought ye to have done, and not to leave the other undone.
St Matthew ch. 23, v. 23

19 Ye blind guides, which strain at a gnat, and swallow a camel.
St Matthew ch. 23, v. 24

20 Ye are like unto whited sepulchres, which indeed appear beautiful outward, but are within full of dead men's bones, and of all uncleanness.
St Matthew ch. 23, v. 27

21 O Jerusalem, Jerusalem, thou that killest the prophets, and stonest them which are sent unto thee, how often would I have gathered thy children together, even as a hen gathereth her chickens under her wings, and ye would not!
St Matthew ch. 23, v. 37

22 Ye shall hear of wars and rumours of wars: see that ye be not troubled: for all these things must come to pass but the end is not yet.
St Matthew ch. 24, v. 6

23 For nation shall rise against nation, and kingdom against kingdom.
St Matthew ch. 24, v. 7

24 When ye therefore shall see the abomination of desolation, spoken of by Daniel the prophet, stand in the holy place.
St Matthew ch. 24, v. 15, referring to Daniel ch. 12, v. 11

25 Wheresoever the carcase is, there will the eagles be gathered together.
St Matthew ch. 24, v. 28; see PROVERBS 647:10

26 Heaven and earth shall pass away, but my words shall not pass away.
St Matthew ch. 24, v. 35

27 For as in the days that were before the flood they were eating and drinking, marrying and giving in marriage, until the day that Noe entered into the ark,
And knew not until the flood came, and took them all away; so shall also the coming of the Son of Man be.
St Matthew ch. 24, v. 38

28 One shall be taken, and the other left.
St Matthew ch. 24, v. 40

1 Watch therefore: for ye know not what hour your Lord doth come.
St Matthew ch. 24, v. 42

2 Well done, thou good and faithful servant: thou hast been faithful over a few things, I will make thee a ruler over many things: enter thou into the joy of thy lord.
St Matthew ch. 25, v. 21

3 Lord, I knew thee that thou art an hard man, reaping where thou hast not sown, and gathering where thou hast not strawed.
St Matthew ch. 25, v. 24

4 Unto every one that hath shall be given, and he shall have abundance: but from him that hath not shall be taken away even that which he hath.
St Matthew ch. 25, v. 29

5 And he shall set the sheep on his right hand, but the goats on the left.
St Matthew ch. 25, v. 33

6 For I was an hungred, and ye gave me meat: I was thirsty and ye gave me drink: I was a stranger, and ye took me in:
Naked, and ye clothed me: I was sick, and ye visited me: I was in prison, and ye came unto me.
St Matthew ch. 25, v. 35

7 Inasmuch as ye have done it unto one of the least of these my brethren, ye have done it unto me.
St Matthew ch. 25, v. 40

8 There came unto him a woman having an alabaster box of very precious ointment, and poured it on his head, as he sat at meat.
St Matthew ch. 26, v. 7

9 To what purpose is this waste?
For this ointment might have been sold for much, and given to the poor.
St Matthew ch. 26, v. 8 (St John ch. 12, v. 5 attributes this to Judas Iscariot)

10 What will ye give me, and I will deliver him unto you? And they covenanted with him [Judas Iscariot] for thirty pieces of silver. ·
St Matthew ch. 26, v. 15

11 It had been good for that man if he had not been born.
St Matthew ch. 26, v. 24

12 Jesus took bread, and blessed it, and brake it, and gave it to the disciples, and said, Take, eat; this is my body.
St Matthew ch. 26, v. 26

13 This night, before the cock crow, thou shalt deny me thrice.
St Matthew ch. 26, v. 34 (to St Peter)

14 Though I should die with thee, yet will I not deny thee.
St Matthew ch. 26, v. 35 (St Peter)

15 If it be possible, let this cup pass from me.
St Matthew ch. 26, v. 39

16 What, could ye not watch with me one hour?
St Matthew ch. 26, v. 40

17 Watch and pray, that ye enter not into temptation: the spirit indeed is willing but the flesh is weak.
St Matthew ch. 26, v. 41

18 Friend, wherefore art thou come?
St Matthew ch. 26, v. 50

19 All they that take the sword shall perish with the sword.
St Matthew ch. 26, v. 52; see **PROVERBS** 634:24

20 Thy speech bewrayeth thee.
Then began he [St Peter] to curse and to swear, saying, I know not the man. And immediately the cock crew.
St Matthew ch. 26, v. 73

21 He [Pilate] took water, and washed his hands before the multitude, saying, I am innocent of the blood of this just person: see ye to it.
St Matthew ch. 27, v. 24

22 His blood be on us, and on our children.
St Matthew ch. 27, v. 25

23 He saved others; himself he cannot save.
St Matthew ch. 27, v. 42

24 Eli, Eli, lama sabachthani? . . . My God, my God, why hast thou forsaken me?
St Matthew ch. 27, v. 46; see **BOOK OF COMMON PRAYER** 140:15

25 And, lo, I am with you alway, even unto the end of the world.
St Matthew ch. 28, v. 20

ST MARK

26 The sabbath was made for man, and not man for the sabbath.
St Mark ch. 2, v. 27

27 How can Satan cast out Satan?
St Mark ch. 3, v. 23; see **SORLEY** 764:2

28 If a house be divided against itself, that house cannot stand.
St Mark ch. 3, v. 25; see **LINCOLN** 493:10, **PROVERBS** 634:46

29 He that hath ears to hear, let him hear.
St Mark ch. 4, v. 9

30 With what measure ye mete, it shall be measured to you.
St Mark ch. 4, v. 24

31 My name is Legion: for we are many.
St Mark ch. 5, v. 9

32 Jesus, immediately knowing in himself that virtue had gone out of him, turned him about in the press, and said, Who touched my clothes?
St Mark ch. 5, v. 30

33 I see men as trees, walking.
St Mark ch. 8, v. 24

34 For what shall it profit a man, if he shall gain the whole world, and lose his own soul?
St Mark ch. 8, v. 36; see **BOLT** 131:21

1 Lord, I believe; help thou mine unbelief.
St Mark ch. 9, v. 24

2 Suffer the little children to come unto me, and forbid them not: for of such is the kingdom of God.
St Mark ch. 10, v. 14

3 Beware of the scribes, which love to go in long clothing, and love salutations in the marketplaces,
And the chief seats in the synagogues, and the uppermost rooms at feasts:
Which devour widows' houses, and for a pretence make long prayers.
St Mark ch. 12, v. 38

4 And there came a certain poor widow, and she threw in two mites.
St Mark ch. 12, v. 42

5 Watch ye therefore: for ye know not when the master of the house cometh . . . Lest coming suddenly he find you sleeping.
St Mark ch. 13, v. 35

6 Go ye into all the world, and preach the gospel to every creature.
St Mark ch. 16, v. 15

ST LUKE

7 Hail, thou that art highly favoured, the Lord is with thee: blessed art thou among women.
St Luke ch. 1, v. 28 (the angel to the Virgin Mary); see **PRAYERS** 623:1

8 And Mary said,
My soul doth magnify the Lord,
And my spirit hath rejoiced in God my Saviour.
For he hath regarded the low estate of his handmaiden: for, behold, from henceforth all generations shall call me blessed.
St Luke ch. 1, v. 46, known as the Magnificat; v. 47 reads 'Tell out my soul, the greatness of the Lord' in *The New English Bible*; see **BIBLE (VULGATE)** 120:10

9 He hath shewed strength with his arm; he hath scattered the proud in the imagination of their hearts.
He hath put down the mighty from their seats, and exalted them of low degree.
He hath filled the hungry with good things; and the rich he hath sent empty away.
St Luke ch. 1, v. 51 (the Magnificat)

10 To give light to them that sit in darkness and in the shadow of death, to guide our feet into the way of peace.
St Luke ch. 1, v. 79

11 And it came to pass in those days, that there went out a decree from Caesar Augustus, that all the world should be taxed.
St Luke ch. 2, v. 1

12 She brought forth her firstborn son, and wrapped him in swaddling clothes, and laid him in a manger; because there was no room for them in the inn.
And there were in the same country shepherds abiding in the field, keeping watch over their flock by night.
And, lo, the angel of the Lord came upon them, and the glory of the Lord shone round about them: and they were sore afraid.
St Luke ch. 2, v. 7

13 Behold, I bring you good tidings of great joy.
St Luke ch. 2, v. 10 (the angel to the shepherds)

14 Glory to God in the highest, and on earth peace, good will toward men.
St Luke ch. 2, v. 14 (the angels to the shepherds); see **MISSAL** 549:8

15 But Mary kept all these things, and pondered them in her heart.
St Luke ch. 2, v. 19

16 Lord, now lettest thou thy servant depart in peace, according to thy word.
St Luke ch. 2, v. 29 (Simeon); see **BIBLE (VULGATE)** 120:12

17 A light to lighten the Gentiles, and the glory of thy people Israel.
St Luke ch. 2, v. 32 (Simeon)

18 Yea, a sword shall pierce through thy own soul also.
St Luke ch. 2, v. 35 (Simeon to the Virgin Mary)

19 Wist ye not that I must be about my Father's business?
St Luke ch. 2, v. 49

20 And the devil, taking him up into a high mountain, shewed unto him all the kingdoms of the world in a moment of time.
St Luke ch. 4, v. 5

21 Physician, heal thyself.
St Luke ch. 4, v. 23; see **PROVERBS** 641:35

22 Master, we have toiled all the night, and have taken nothing: nevertheless at thy word I will let down the net.
St Luke ch. 5, v. 5 (St Peter)

23 No man . . . having drunk old wine straightway desireth new: for he saith, The old is better.
St Luke ch. 5, v. 39

24 Woe unto you, when all men shall speak well of you!
St Luke ch. 6, v. 26

25 Love your enemies, do good to them which hate you.
St Luke ch. 6, v. 27

26 Give, and it shall be given unto you; good measure, pressed down, and shaken together, and running over, shall men give into your bosom.
St Luke ch. 6, v. 38

27 Her sins, which are many, are forgiven; for she loved much.
St Luke ch. 7, v. 47

28 No man, having put his hand to the plough, and looking back, is fit for the kingdom of God.
St Luke ch. 9, v. 62

1 For the labourer is worthy of his hire.
St Luke ch. 10, v. 7; see **PROVERBS** 637:10

2 I beheld Satan as lightning fall from heaven.
St Luke ch. 10, v. 18

3 Blessed are the eyes which see the things which
ye see:
For I tell you, that many prophets and kings
have desired to see those things which ye see,
and have not seen them; and to hear those
things which ye hear, and have not heard them.
St Luke ch. 10, v. 23

4 A certain man went down from Jerusalem to
Jericho, and fell among thieves.
St Luke ch. 10, v. 30

5 He passed by on the other side.
St Luke ch. 10, v. 31

6 He took out two pence, and gave them to the
host, and said unto him, Take care of him; and
whatsoever thou spend more, when I come
again, I will repay thee.
St Luke ch. 10, v. 35

7 Go, and do thou likewise.
St Luke ch. 10, v. 37

8 But Martha was cumbered about much serving,
and came to him, and said, Lord, dost thou not
care that my sister hath left me to serve alone?
bid her therefore that she help me.
St Luke ch. 10, v. 40

9 Mary hath chosen that good part, which shall
not be taken away from her.
St Luke ch. 10, v. 42

10 When a strong man armed keepeth his palace,
his goods are in peace. But when a stronger
than he shall come upon him, and overcome
him, he taketh from him all his armour wherein
he trusted, and divideth his spoils.
St Luke ch. 11, v. 21

11 No man, when he hath lighted a candle, putteth
it in a secret place, neither under a bushel, but
on a candlestick, that they which come in may
see the light.
St Luke ch. 11, v. 33

12 Woe unto you, lawyers! for ye have taken away
the key of knowledge.
St Luke ch. 11, v. 52

13 Are not five sparrows sold for two farthings, and
not one of them is forgotten before God?
St Luke ch. 12, v. 6; see **BIBLE** 100:27

14 Soul, thou hast much goods laid up for many
years; take thine ease, eat, drink, and be merry.
St Luke ch. 12, v. 19; see **BIBLE** 90:7, **BIBLE** 92:22

15 Thou fool, this night thy soul shall be required
of thee.
St Luke ch. 12, v. 20

16 Let your loins be girded about, and your lights
burning.
St Luke ch. 12, v. 35

17 For unto whomsoever much is given, of him
shall be much required.
St Luke ch. 12, v. 48; see **FIELDING** 326:12

18 When thou art bidden of any man to a
wedding, sit not down in the highest room; lest
a more honourable man than thou be bidden of
him;
And he that bade thee and him come and say to
thee, Give this man place; and thou begin with
shame to take the lowest room.
St Luke ch. 14, v. 8

19 Friend, go up higher.
St Luke ch. 14, v. 10

20 For whosoever exalteth himself shall be abased;
and he that humbleth himself shall be exalted.
St Luke ch. 14, v. 11; St Matthew ch. 23, v. 12 is similar

21 They all with one consent began to make excuse
. . . I pray thee have me excused.
St Luke ch. 14, v. 18

22 I have married a wife, and therefore I cannot
come.
St Luke ch. 14, v. 20

23 Go out quickly into the streets and lanes of the
city, and bring in hither the poor, and the
maimed, and the halt, and the blind.
St Luke ch. 14, v. 21

24 Go out into the highways and hedges, and
compel them to come in.
St Luke ch. 14, v. 23

25 For which of you, intending to build a tower,
sitteth not down first, and counteth the cost,
whether he have sufficient to finish it?
St Luke ch. 14, v. 28

26 Leave the ninety and nine in the wilderness.
St Luke ch. 15, v. 4

27 Rejoice with me; for I have found my sheep
which was lost.
St Luke ch. 15, v. 6

28 Joy shall be in heaven over one sinner that
repenteth, more than over ninety and nine just
persons, which need no repentance.
St Luke ch. 15, v. 7

29 The younger son gathered all together, and took
his journey into a far country, and there wasted
his substance with riotous living.
St Luke ch. 15, v. 13

30 He would fain have filled his belly with the
husks that the swine did eat: and no man gave
unto him.
And when he came to himself, he said, How
many hired servants of my father's have bread
enough and to spare, and I perish with hunger!
St Luke ch. 15, v. 16

31 I will arise and go to my father, and will say
unto him, Father, I have sinned against heaven,
and before thee,
And am no more worthy to be called thy son:
make me as one of thy hired servants.
St Luke ch. 15, v. 18

1 Bring hither the fatted calf, and kill it.
  St Luke ch. 15, v. 23

2 This my son was dead, and is alive again; he was lost, and is found.
  St Luke ch. 15, v. 24

3 And the Lord commended the unjust steward, because he had done wisely: for the children of this world are in their generation wiser than the children of light.
  St Luke ch. 16, v. 8

4 Make to yourselves friends of the mammon of unrighteousness; that, when ye fail, they may receive you into everlasting habitations.
  St Luke ch. 16, v. 9

5 He that is faithful in that which is least is faithful also in much.
  St Luke ch. 16, v. 10

6 There was a certain rich man, which was clothed in purple and fine linen, and fared sumptuously every day:
  And there was a certain beggar named Lazarus, which was laid at his gate, full of sores,
  And desiring to be fed with the crumbs which fell from the rich man's table: moreover the dogs licked his sores.
  And it came to pass that the beggar died, and was carried by the angels into Abraham's bosom.
  St Luke ch. 16, v. 19

7 Between us and you there is a great gulf fixed.
  St Luke ch. 16, v. 26

8 If they hear not Moses and the prophets, neither will they be persuaded, though one rose from the dead.
  St Luke ch. 16, v. 31

9 The kingdom of God is within you.
  St Luke ch. 17, v. 21

10 Remember Lot's wife.
  St Luke ch. 17, v. 32

11 Men ought always to pray, and not to faint.
  St Luke ch. 18, v. 1

12 God, I thank thee, that I am not as other men are.
  St Luke ch. 18, v. 11

13 God be merciful to me a sinner.
  St Luke ch. 18, v. 13

14 Out of thine own mouth will I judge thee.
  St Luke ch. 19, v. 22

15 If these should hold their peace, the stones would immediately cry out.
  St Luke ch. 19, v. 40

16 If thou hadst known, even thou, at least in this thy day, the things which belong unto thy peace! but now they are hid from thine eyes.
  St Luke ch. 19, v. 42

17 And when they heard it, they said, God forbid.
  St Luke ch. 20, v. 16

18 He shall show you a large upper room furnished.
  St Luke ch. 22, v. 12

19 I am among you as he that serveth.
  St Luke ch. 22, v. 27

20 Nevertheless, not my will, but thine, be done.
  St Luke ch. 22, v. 42

21 And the Lord turned, and looked upon Peter.
  St Luke ch. 22, v. 61

22 For if they do these things in a green tree, what shall be done in the dry?
  St Luke ch. 23, v. 31

23 Father, forgive them: for they know not what they do.
  St Luke ch. 23, v. 34

24 Lord, remember me when thou comest into thy kingdom.
  St Luke ch. 23, v. 42 (the Penitent Thief)

25 To day shalt thou be with me in paradise.
  St Luke ch. 23, v. 43 (to the Penitent Thief)

26 Father, into thy hands I commend my spirit.
  St Luke ch. 23, v. 46; see **BOOK OF COMMON PRAYER** 141:15

27 He was a good man, and a just.
  St Luke ch. 23, v. 50 (Joseph of Arimathea)

28 Why seek ye the living among the dead?
  St Luke ch. 24, v. 5

29 Their words seemed to them as idle tales.
  St Luke ch. 24, v. 11

30 Abide with us: for it is toward evening, and the day is far spent.
  St Luke ch. 24, v. 29; see **LYTE** 506:4

31 Did not our heart burn within us, while he talked with us by the way?
  St Luke ch. 24, v. 32 (the disciples on the road to Emmaus)

32 He was known of them in breaking of bread.
  St Luke ch. 24, v. 35

33 They gave him a piece of a broiled fish, and of an honeycomb.
  St Luke ch. 24, v. 42

ST JOHN

34 In the beginning was the Word, and the Word was with God, and the Word was God.
  St John ch. 1, v. 1; see **MISSAL** 550:2

35 All things were made by him; and without him was not any thing made that was made.
  St John ch. 1, v. 3

36 And the light shineth in darkness; and the darkness comprehended it not.
  St John ch. 1, v. 5

37 There was a man sent from God, whose name was John.
  St John ch. 1, v. 6

38 He was not that Light, but was sent to bear witness of that Light.
  That was the true Light, which lighteth every man that cometh into the world.
  St John ch. 1, v. 8

1 He was in the world, and the world was made by him, and the world knew him not.
He came unto his own, and his own received him not.
St John ch. 1, v. 10

2 And the Word was made flesh, and dwelt among us, (and we beheld his glory, the glory as of the only begotten of the Father,) full of grace and truth.
St John ch. 1, v. 14; see **MISSAL** 550:3

3 No man hath seen God at any time.
St John ch. 1, v. 18

4 I baptize with water: but there standeth one among you, whom ye know not;
He it is, who coming after me is preferred before me, whose shoe's latchet I am not worthy to unloose.
St John ch. 1, v. 26 (St John the Baptist)

5 Behold the Lamb of God, which taketh away the sin of the world.
St John ch. 1, v. 29; see **MISSAL** 549:19

6 Can there any good thing come out of Nazareth?
St John ch. 1, v. 46

7 Behold an Israelite indeed, in whom is no guile!
St John ch. 1, v. 47

8 Woman, what have I to do with thee? mine hour is not yet come.
St John ch. 2, v. 4

9 Every man at the beginning doth set forth good wine; and when men have well drunk, then that which is worse: but thou hast kept the good wine until now.
St John ch. 2, v. 10

10 When he had made a scourge of small cords, he drove them all out of the temple.
St John ch. 2, v. 15

11 Verily, verily, I say unto thee, Except a man be born again, he cannot see the kingdom of God.
St John ch. 3, v. 3

12 The wind bloweth where it listeth, and thou hearest the sound thereof, but canst not tell whence it cometh, and whither it goeth.
St John ch. 3, v. 8

13 God so loved the world, that he gave his only begotten Son, that whosoever believeth in him should not perish, but have everlasting life.
St John ch. 3, v. 16

14 Men loved darkness rather than light, because their deeds were evil.
St John ch. 3, v. 19

15 God is a Spirit: and they that worship him must worship him in spirit and in truth.
St John ch. 4, v. 24

16 Except ye see signs and wonders, ye will not believe.
St John ch. 4, v. 48

17 Rise, take up thy bed, and walk.
St John ch. 5, v. 8

18 He was a burning and a shining light.
St John ch. 5, v. 35

19 Search the scriptures; for in them ye think ye have eternal life: and they are which testify of me.
St John ch. 5, v. 39

20 There is a lad here, which hath five barley loaves, and two small fishes: but what are they among so many?
St John ch. 6, v. 9

21 Gather up the fragments that remain, that nothing be lost.
St John ch. 6, v. 12

22 Verily, verily, I say unto you . . . my Father giveth you the true bread from heaven.
For the bread of God is he which cometh down from heaven, and giveth life to the world.
St John ch. 6, v. 32

23 I am the bread of life: he that cometh to me shall never hunger; and he that believeth on me shall never thirst.
St John ch. 6, v. 35

24 Him that cometh to me I will in no wise cast out.
St John ch. 6, v. 37

25 Verily, verily, I say unto you, He that believeth on me hath everlasting life.
St John ch. 6, v. 47

26 It is the spirit that quickeneth.
St John ch. 6, v. 63

27 And the scribes and the Pharisees brought unto him a woman taken in adultery.
St John ch. 8, v. 3

28 He that is without sin among you, let him first cast a stone at her.
St John ch. 8, v. 7

29 Neither do I condemn thee: go, and sin no more.
St John ch. 8, v. 11

30 And ye shall know the truth, and the truth shall make you free.
St John ch. 8, v. 32

31 Ye are of your father the devil, and the lusts of your father ye will do. He was a murderer from the beginning, and abode not in the truth, because there is no truth in him. When he speaketh a lie, he speaketh of his own: for he is a liar, and the father of it.
St John ch. 8, v. 44

32 The night cometh, when no man can work.
St John ch. 9, v. 4

33 He is of age; ask him: he shall speak for himself.
St John ch. 9, v. 21

34 One thing I know, that, whereas I was blind, now I see.
St John ch. 9, v. 25

1 I am the door.
St John ch. 10, v. 9

2 I am the good shepherd: the good shepherd giveth his life for the sheep.
St John ch. 10, v. 11

3 The hireling fleeth, because he is an hireling, and careth not for the sheep.
St John ch. 10, v. 13

4 Other sheep I have, which are not of this fold.
St John ch. 10, v. 16

5 Though ye believe not me, believe the works.
St John ch. 10, v. 38

6 I am the resurrection, and the life.
St John ch. 11, v. 25

7 Jesus wept.
St John ch. 11, v. 35; see **HUGO** 419:8

8 It is expedient for us, that one man should die for the people.
St John ch. 11, v. 50 (Caiaphas)

9 The poor always ye have with you.
St John ch. 12, v. 8

10 Lord, dost thou wash my feet?
St John ch. 13, v. 6 (St Peter)

11 That thou doest, do quickly.
St John ch. 13, v. 27

12 Let not your heart be troubled.
St John ch. 14, v. 1

13 In my Father's house are many mansions . . . I go to prepare a place for you.
St John ch. 14, v. 2

14 I am the way, the truth, and the life: no man cometh unto the Father, but by me.
St John ch. 14, v. 6

15 Have I been so long time with you, and yet hast thou not known me, Philip?
St John ch. 14, v. 9

16 Judas saith unto him, not Iscariot.
St John ch. 14, v. 22

17 Peace I leave with you, my peace I give unto you: not as the world giveth, give I unto you.
St John ch. 14, v. 27

18 Greater love hath no man than this, that a man lay down his life for his friends.
St John ch. 15, v. 13; see **JOYCE** 448:22, **THORPE** 810:5

19 Ye have not chosen me, but I have chosen you.
St John ch. 15, v. 16

20 It is expedient for you that I go away: for if I go not away, the Comforter will not come unto you.
St John ch. 16, v. 7

21 I have yet many things to say unto you, but ye cannot bear them now.
St John ch. 16, v. 12

22 A little while, and ye shall not see me: and again, a little while, and ye shall see me, because I go to the Father.
St John ch. 16, v. 16

23 In the world ye shall have tribulation: but be of good cheer; I have overcome the world.
St John ch. 16, v. 33

24 While I was with them in the world, I kept them in thy name: those that thou gavest me I have kept, and none of them is lost but the son of perdition.
St John ch. 17, v. 12

25 Put up thy sword into the sheath.
St John ch. 18, v. 11 (to St Peter)

26 Pilate saith unto him, What is truth?
St John ch. 18, v. 38; see **BACON** 48:10

27 Now Barabbas was a robber.
St John ch. 18, v. 40; see **CAMPBELL** 195:20

28 A place called the place of a skull, which is called in the Hebrew Golgotha.
St John ch. 19, v. 17

29 And Pilate wrote a title and put it on the cross. And the writing was, JESUS OF NAZARETH THE KING OF THE JEWS.
St John ch. 19, v. 19

30 What I have written I have written.
St John ch. 19, v. 22 (Pilate)

31 Woman, behold thy son! . . .
Behold thy mother!
St John ch. 19, v. 26 (to the Virgin Mary and, traditionally, St John)

32 I thirst.
St John ch. 19, v. 28

33 It is finished.
St John ch. 19, v. 30; see **BIBLE (VULGATE)** 120:16

34 The first day of the week cometh Mary Magdalene early, when it was yet dark, unto the sepulchre, and seeth the stone taken away from the sepulchre.
St John ch. 20, v. 1

35 So they ran both together: and the other disciple did outrun Peter, and came first to the sepulchre.
St John ch. 20, v. 4

36 They have taken away my Lord, and I know not where they have laid him.
St John ch. 20, v. 13 (St Mary Magdalene)

37 Jesus saith unto her, Woman, why weepest thou? whom seekest thou? She supposing him to be the gardener saith unto him, Sir, if thou have borne him hence, tell me where thou hast laid him, and I will take him away.
St John ch. 20, v. 15

38 Touch me not.
St John ch. 20, v. 17 (to St Mary Magdalene); see **BIBLE (VULGATE)** 120:17

39 Except I shall see in his hands the print of the nails, and put my finger into the print of the nails, and thrust my hand into his side, I will not believe.
St John ch. 20, v. 25 (St Thomas)

1 Be not faithless, but believing.
St John ch. 20, v. 27 (to St Thomas)

2 Thomas answered and said unto him, My Lord and my God.
St John ch. 20, v. 28

3 Thomas, because thou hast seen me, thou hast believed: blessed are they that have not seen, and yet have believed.
St John ch. 20, v. 29

4 Simon Peter saith unto them, I go a fishing.
St John ch. 21, v. 3

5 Simon, son of Jonas, lovest thou me more than these? . . . Feed my lambs.
St John ch. 21, v. 15

6 Feed my sheep.
St John ch. 21, v. 16

7 Lord, thou knowest all things; thou knowest that I love thee.
St John ch. 21, v. 17 (St Peter)

8 When thou wast young, thou girdedst thyself, and walkedst whither thou wouldest: but when thou shalt be old, thou shalt stretch forth thy hands, and another shall gird thee, and carry thee whither thou wouldest not.
St John ch. 21, v. 18 (to St Peter)

9 Peter, turning about, seeth the disciple whom Jesus loved following; which also leaned on his breast at supper, and said Lord, which is he that betrayeth thee?
St John ch. 21, v. 20 (tradionally St John)

10 Jesus saith unto him, If I will that he tarry till I come, what is that to thee?
St John ch. 21, v. 22 (to St Peter, of St John)

ACTS OF THE APOSTLES

11 Ye men of Galilee, why stand ye gazing up into heaven?
Acts of the Apostles ch. 1, v. 11

12 And suddenly there came a sound from heaven as of a rushing mighty wind, and it filled all the house where they were sitting.
And there appeared unto them cloven tongues like as of fire.
Acts of the Apostles ch. 2, v. 2

13 Parthians, and Medes, and Elamites, and the dwellers in Mesopotamia, and in Judaea, and Cappadocia, in Pontus, and Asia,
Phrygia, and Pamphylia, in Egypt, and in the parts of Libya about Cyrene, and strangers of Rome, Jews and proselytes,
Cretes and Arabians, we do hear them speak in our tongues the wonderful works of God.
Acts of the Apostles ch. 2, v. 9

14 And all that believed were together, and had all things common.
Acts of the Apostles ch. 2, v. 44

15 Silver and gold have I none; but such as I have give I thee.
Acts of the Apostles ch. 3, v. 6

16 Walking, and leaping, and praising God.
Acts of the Apostles ch. 3, v. 8

17 It is not reason that we should leave the word of God, and serve tables.
Acts of the Apostles ch. 6, v. 2

18 The witnesses laid down their clothes at a young man's feet, whose name was Saul.
Acts of the Apostles ch. 7, v. 58

19 Saul was consenting unto his death.
Acts of the Apostles ch. 8, v. 1

20 Thy money perish with thee, because thou hast thought that the gift of God may be purchased with money.
Acts of the Apostles ch. 8, v. 20 (to Simon Magus)

21 Saul, Saul, why persecutest thou me?
Acts of the Apostles ch. 9, v. 4

22 It is hard for thee to kick against the pricks.
Acts of the Apostles ch. 9, v. 5

23 The street which is called Straight.
Acts of the Apostles ch. 9, v. 11

24 Dorcas: this woman was full of good works.
Acts of the Apostles ch. 9, v. 36

25 He fell into a trance,
And saw heaven opened, and a certain vessel descending unto him, as it had been a great sheet knit at the four corners, and let down to the earth:
Wherein were all manner of four-footed beasts of the earth, and wild beasts, and creeping things, and fowls of the air.
Acts of the Apostles ch. 10, v. 10

26 What God hath cleansed, that call not thou common.
Acts of the Apostles ch. 10, v. 15

27 God is no respecter of persons.
Acts of the Apostles ch. 10, v. 34

28 He was eaten of worms, and gave up the ghost.
Acts of the Apostles ch. 12, v. 23

29 The gods are come down to us in the likeness of men.
Acts of the Apostles ch. 14, v. 11

30 We also are men of like passions with you.
Acts of the Apostles ch. 14, v. 15

31 Come over into Macedonia, and help us.
Acts of the Apostles ch. 16, v. 9

32 What must I do to be saved?
Acts of the Apostles ch. 16, v. 30

33 The Jews which believed not, moved with envy, took unto them certain lewd fellows of the baser sort, and gathered a company, and set all the city on an uproar.
Acts of the Apostles ch. 17, v. 5

34 Those that have turned the world upside down are come hither also;
Whom Jason hath received: and these all do contrary to the decrees of Caesar, saying that there is another king, one Jesus.
Acts of the Apostles ch. 17, v. 6

1 What will this babbler say?
Acts of the Apostles ch. 17, v. 18

2 For all the Athenians and strangers which were there spent their time in nothing else, but either to tell, or to hear some new thing.
Acts of the Apostles ch. 17, v. 21

3 Ye men of Athens, I perceive that in all things ye are too superstitious.
For as I passed by, and beheld your devotions, I found an altar with this inscription, TO THE UNKNOWN GOD. Whom therefore ye ignorantly worship, him declare I unto you.
Acts of the Apostles ch. 17, v. 22

4 God that made the world and all things therein, seeing that he is Lord of Heaven and earth, dwelleth not in temples made with hands.
Acts of the Apostles ch. 17, v. 24

5 For in him we live, and move, and have our being.
Acts of the Apostles ch. 17, v. 28

6 We have not so much as heard whether there be any Holy Ghost.
Acts of the Apostles ch. 19, v. 2

7 All with one voice about the space of two hours cried out, Great is Diana of the Ephesians.
Acts of the Apostles ch. 19, v. 34

8 I go bound in the spirit unto Jerusalem.
Acts of the Apostles ch. 20, v. 22

9 It is more blessed to give than to receive.
Acts of the Apostles ch. 20, v. 35; see **PROVERBS** 636:12

10 But Paul said, I am a man which am a Jew of Tarsus, a city in Cilicia, a citizen of no mean city.
Acts of the Apostles ch. 21, v. 39

11 And the chief captain answered, With a great sum obtained I this freedom. And Paul said, But I was free born.
Acts of the Apostles ch. 22, v. 28

12 A conscience void of offence toward God, and toward men.
Acts of the Apostles ch. 24, v. 16

13 I appeal unto Caesar.
Acts of the Apostles ch. 25, v. 11

14 Hast thou appealed unto Caesar? unto Caesar shalt thou go.
Acts of the Apostles ch. 25, v. 12

15 Paul, thou art beside thyself; much learning doth make thee mad.
Acts of the Apostles ch. 26, v. 24

16 For this thing was not done in a corner.
Acts of the Apostles ch. 26, v. 26

17 Almost thou persuadest me to be a Christian.
Acts of the Apostles ch. 26, v. 28

18 I would to God, that not only thou, but also all that hear me this day, were both almost, and altogether such as I am, except these bonds.
Acts of the Apostles ch. 26, v. 29

ROMANS

19 Without ceasing I make mention of you always in my prayers.
Romans ch. 1, v. 9

20 I am debtor both to the Greeks, and to the Barbarians; both to the wise, and to the unwise.
Romans ch. 1, v. 14

21 The just shall live by faith.
Romans ch. 1, v. 17

22 Worshipped and served the creature more than the Creator.
Romans ch. 1, v. 25

23 Patient continuance in well doing.
Romans ch. 2, v. 7

24 A law unto themselves.
Romans ch. 2, v. 14

25 Let God be true, but every man a liar.
Romans ch. 3, v. 4

26 Let us do evil, that good may come.
Romans ch. 3, v. 8

27 For all have sinned, and come short of the glory of God.
Romans ch. 3, v. 23

28 For where no law is, there is no transgression.
Romans ch. 4, v. 15

29 Who against hope believed in hope, that he might become the father of many nations.
Romans ch. 4, v. 18 (of Abraham)

30 Hope maketh not ashamed; because the love of God is shed abroad in our hearts by the Holy Ghost which is given unto us.
Romans ch. 5, v. 5

31 Where sin abounded, grace did much more abound.
Romans ch. 5, v. 20

32 Shall we continue in sin, that grace may abound?
God forbid. How shall we, that are dead to sin, live any longer in sin?
Romans ch. 6, v. 1

33 We also should walk in newness of life.
Romans ch. 6, v. 4

34 Christ being raised from the dead dieth no more; death hath no more dominion over him.
For in that he died, he died unto sin once: but in that he liveth, he liveth unto God.
Romans ch. 6, v. 9; see **THOMAS** 805:14

35 The wages of sin is death.
Romans ch. 6, v. 23

36 Is the law sin? God forbid. Nay, I had not known sin, but by the law.
Romans ch. 7, v. 7

37 For the good that I would I do not: but the evil which I would not, that I do.
Romans ch. 7, v. 19; see **OVID** 590:13

38 O wretched man that I am! who shall deliver me from the body of this death?
Romans ch. 7, v. 24

1 They that are after the flesh do mind the things of the flesh; but they that are after the Spirit the things of the Spirit.
For to be carnally minded is death.
> Romans ch. 8, v. 5

2 For ye have not received the spirit of bondage again to fear; but ye have received the Spirit of adoption, whereby we cry, Abba, Father.
> Romans ch. 8, v. 15

3 We are the children of God:
And if the children, then heirs; heirs of God, and joint-heirs with Christ.
> Romans ch. 8, v. 16

4 For we know that the whole creation groaneth and travaileth in pain together until now.
> Romans ch. 8, v. 22

5 All things work together for good to them that love God.
> Romans ch. 8, v. 28

6 If God be for us, who can be against us?
> Romans ch. 8, v. 31

7 For I am persuaded, that neither death, nor life, nor angels, nor principalities, nor powers, nor things present, nor things to come,
Nor height, nor depth, nor any other creature, shall be able to separate us from the love of God, which is in Christ Jesus our Lord.
> Romans ch. 8, v. 38

8 Shall the thing formed say to him that formed it, Why hast thou made me thus?
Hath not the potter power over the clay, of the same lump to make one vessel unto honour, and another unto dishonour?
> Romans ch. 9, v. 20

9 I beseech you therefore, brethren, by the mercies of God, that ye present your bodies a living sacrifice, holy, acceptable unto God.
> Romans ch. 12, v. 1

10 Rejoice with them that do rejoice, and weep with them that weep.
> Romans ch. 12, v. 15

11 Mind not high things, but condescend to men of low estate. Be not wise in your own conceits.
> Romans ch. 12, v. 16

12 Vengeance is mine; I will repay, saith the Lord.
> Romans ch. 12, v. 19

13 Be not overcome of evil, but overcome evil with good.
> Romans ch. 12, v. 21

14 Let every soul be subject unto the higher powers . . . the powers that be are ordained of God.
> Romans ch. 13, v. 1

15 Render therefore to all their dues: tribute to whom tribute is due; custom to whom custom; fear to whom fear; honour to whom honour.
Owe no man anything, but to love one another: for he that loveth another hath fulfilled the law.
> Romans ch. 13, v. 7

16 Now it is high time to awake out of sleep: for now is our salvation nearer than when we believed.
The night is far spent, the day is at hand: let us therefore cast off the works of darkness, and let us put on the armour of light.
> Romans ch. 13, v. 11

17 Make not provision for the flesh, to fulfil the lusts thereof.
> Romans ch. 13, v. 14

18 Doubtful disputations.
> Romans ch. 14, v. 1

19 Let every man be fully persuaded in his own mind.
> Romans ch. 14, v. 5

20 Salute one another with an holy kiss.
> Romans ch. 16, v. 16

I CORINTHIANS

21 The foolishness of preaching to save them that believe.
> I Corinthians ch. 1, v. 21

22 For the Jews require a sign, and the Greeks seek after wisdom.
> I Corinthians ch. 1, v. 22

23 We preach Christ crucified, unto the Jews a stumbling-block, and unto the Greeks foolishness.
> I Corinthians ch. 1, v. 23

24 God hath chosen the foolish things of the world to confound the wise; and God hath chosen the weak things of the world to confound the things which are mighty.
> I Corinthians ch. 1, v. 27

25 But as it is written, Eye hath not seen, nor ear heard, neither have entered into the heart of man, the things which God hath prepared for them that love him.
> I Corinthians ch. 2, v. 9

26 I have planted, Apollos watered; but God gave the increase.
> I Corinthians ch. 3, v. 6

27 Stewards of the mysteries of God.
> I Corinthians ch. 4, v. 1

28 We are made a spectacle unto the world, and to angels.
> I Corinthians ch. 4, v. 9

29 Absent in body, but present in spirit.
> I Corinthians ch. 5, v. 3

30 Know ye not that a little leaven leaveneth the whole lump?
> I Corinthians ch. 5, v. 6

31 Christ our passover is sacrificed for us:
Therefore let us keep the feast, not with the old leaven, neither with the leaven of malice and wickedness; but with the unleavened bread of sincerity and truth.
> I Corinthians ch. 5, v. 7

1 Your body is the temple of the Holy Ghost.
I Corinthians ch. 6, v. 19

2 It is better to marry than to burn.
I Corinthians ch. 7, v. 9; see **PROVERBS** 627:40

3 The unbelieving husband is sanctified by the wife.
I Corinthians ch. 7, v. 14

4 The fashion of this world passeth away.
I Corinthians ch. 7, v. 31

5 Knowledge puffeth up, but charity edifieth.
I Corinthians ch. 8, v. 1

6 Who goeth a warfare any time at his own charges? who planteth a vineyard, and eateth not of the fruit thereof?
I Corinthians ch. 9, v. 7

7 I am made all things to all men.
I Corinthians ch. 9, v. 22

8 Know ye not that they which run in a race run all, but one receiveth the prize.
I Corinthians ch. 9, v. 24

9 Now they do it to obtain a corruptible crown; but we an incorruptible.
I therefore so run, not as uncertainly; so fight I, not as one that beateth the air.
But I keep under my body, and bring it into subjection; lest that by any means, when I have preached to others, I myself should be a castaway.
I Corinthians ch. 9, v. 25

10 All things are lawful for me, but all things are not expedient.
I Corinthians ch. 10, v. 23

11 For the earth is the Lord's and the fulness thereof.
I Corinthians ch. 10, v. 26; see **BOOK OF COMMON PRAYER** 141:1

12 Doth not even nature itself teach you, that if a man have long hair, it is a shame unto him?
But if a woman have long hair, it is a glory to her.
I Corinthians ch. 11, v. 14

13 Now there are diversities of gifts, but the same Spirit.
I Corinthians ch. 12, v. 4

14 Though I speak with the tongues of men and of angels, and have not charity, I am become as sounding brass, or a tinkling cymbal.
And though I have the gift of prophecy, and understand all mysteries, and all knowledge; and though I have all faith; so that I could remove mountains; and have not charity, I am nothing.
And though I bestow all my goods to feed the poor, and though I give my body to be burned, and have not charity, it profiteth me nothing.
Charity suffereth long, and is kind; charity envieth not; charity vaunteth not itself, is not puffed up,
Doth not behave itself unseemly, seeketh not her own, is not easily provoked, thinketh no evil;
Rejoiceth not in iniquity, but rejoiceth in the truth;
Beareth all things, believeth all things, hopeth all things, endureth all things.
Charity never faileth: but whether there be prophecies, they shall fail; whether there be tongues, they shall cease; whether there be knowledge, it shall vanish away.
For we know in part, and we prophesy in part.
But when that which is perfect is come, then that which is in part shall be done away.
When I was a child, I spake as a child, I understood as a child, I thought as a child: but when I became a man, I put away childish things.
For now we see through a glass, darkly; but then face to face: now I know in part; but then shall I know even as also I am known.
And now abideth faith, hope, charity, these three; but the greatest of these is charity.
I Corinthians ch. 13, v. 1

15 If the trumpet give an uncertain sound, who shall prepare himself to the battle?
I Corinthians ch. 14, v. 8

16 Except ye utter by the tongue words easy to be understood, how shall it be known what is spoken? for ye shall speak into the air.
I Corinthians ch. 14, v. 9; see **BUNYAN** 171:3

17 Let all things be done decently and in order.
I Corinthians ch. 14, v. 40

18 Last of all he was seen of me also, as of one born out of due time.
For I am the least of the apostles, that am not meet to be called an apostle, because I persecuted the church of God.
But by the grace of God I am what I am.
I Corinthians ch. 15, v. 8

19 I laboured more abundantly than they all: yet not I, but the grace of God which was with me.
I Corinthians ch. 15, v. 10

20 If in this life only we have hope in Christ, we are of all men most miserable.
I Corinthians ch. 15, v. 19

21 But now is Christ risen from the dead, and become the first fruits of them that slept.
For since by man came death, by man came also the resurrection of the dead.
For as in Adam all die, even so in Christ shall all be made alive.
I Corinthians ch. 15, v. 20

22 The last enemy that shall be destroyed is death.
I Corinthians ch. 15, v. 26; 'The last enemy' was the title of a book (1942) by Richard Hillary (1919–43)

23 If after the manner of men I have fought with beasts at Ephesus, what advantageth it me, if the dead rise not? let us eat and drink; for to morrow we die.
I Corinthians ch. 15, v. 32; see **BIBLE** 90:7, **BIBLE** 92:22, **BIBLE** 105:14

1 Evil communications corrupt good manners.
I Corinthians ch. 15, v. 33; see **PROVERBS** 631:36

2 One star differeth from another star in glory.
I Corinthians ch. 15, v. 41

3 So also is the resurrection of the dead. It is sown in corruption; it is raised in incorruption.
I Corinthians ch. 15, v. 42

4 The first man is of the earth, earthy.
I Corinthians ch. 15, v. 47

5 Behold, I shew you a mystery; We shall not all sleep, but we shall all be changed,
In a moment, in the twinkling of an eye, at the last trump; for the trumpet shall sound, and the dead shall be raised incorruptible, and we shall be changed.
For this corruptible must put on incorruption, and this mortal must put on immortality.
I Corinthians ch. 15, v. 51

6 O death, where is thy sting? O grave, where is thy victory?
I Corinthians ch. 15, v. 55; see **MILITARY SAYINGS, SLOGANS, AND SONGS** 535:15

II CORINTHIANS

7 Our sufficiency is of God;
Who also hath made us able ministers of the new testament; not of the letter, but of the spirit: for the letter killeth, but the spirit giveth life.
II Corinthians ch. 3, v. 5

8 We have this treasure in earthen vessels.
II Corinthians ch. 4, v. 7

9 We know that if our earthly house of this tabernacle were dissolved, we have a building of God, an house not made with hands, eternal in the heavens.
II Corinthians ch. 5, v. 1; see **BROWNING** 165:8

10 For he saith, I have found thee in a time accepted, and in the day of salvation have I succoured thee: behold, now is the accepted time; behold, now is the day of salvation.
II Corinthians ch. 6, v. 2

11 As having nothing, and yet possessing all things.
II Corinthians ch. 6, v. 10

12 God loveth a cheerful giver.
II Corinthians ch. 9, v. 7

13 For ye suffer fools gladly, seeing ye yourselves are wise.
II Corinthians ch. 11, v. 19

14 Are they Hebrews? so am I. Are they Israelites? so am I. Are they the seed of Abraham? so am I.
Are they ministers of Christ? (I speak as a fool) I am more.
II Corinthians ch. 11, v. 22

15 Of the Jews five times received I forty stripes save one.
Thrice was I beaten with rods, once was I stoned, thrice I suffered shipwreck, a night and a day have I been in the deep;
In weariness and painfulness, in watchings often, in hunger and thirst, in fastings often, in cold and nakedness.
Beside those things that are without, that which cometh upon me daily, the care of all the churches.
II Corinthians ch. 11, v. 24

16 In journeyings often, in perils of waters, in perils of robbers, in perils by mine own countrymen, in perils by the heathen, in perils of the city, in perils in the wilderness, in perils in the sea, in perils among false brethren.
II Corinthians ch. 11, v. 26

17 I knew a man in Christ above fourteen years ago (whether in the body, I cannot tell; or whether out of the body, I cannot tell: God knoweth)—such an one caught up to the third heaven.
II Corinthians ch. 12, v. 2

18 There was given to me a thorn in the flesh, the messenger of Satan to buffet me.
II Corinthians ch. 12, v. 7

19 My strength is made perfect in weakness.
II Corinthians ch. 12, v. 9

GALATIANS

20 The right hands of fellowship.
Galatians ch. 2, v. 9

21 It is written, that Abraham had two sons, the one by a bondmaid, the other by a freewoman. But he who was of the bondwoman was born after the flesh; but he of the freewoman was by promise.
Which things are an allegory.
Galatians ch. 4, v. 22

22 Ye are fallen from grace.
Galatians ch. 5, v. 4

23 But the fruit of the Spirit is love, joy, peace, longsuffering, gentleness, goodness, faith, Meekness, temperance.
Galatians ch. 5, v. 22

24 Bear ye one another's burdens.
Galatians ch. 6, v. 2; see **WINTHROP** 860:17

25 Be not deceived; God is not mocked: for whatsoever a man soweth, that shall he also reap.
Galatians ch. 6, v. 7; see **PROVERBS** 626:43

26 Let us not be weary in well doing: for in due season we shall reap, if we faint not.
Galatians ch. 6, v. 9; 'Be not weary in well doing' in II Thessalonians ch. 3, v. 13

27 Ye see how large a letter I have written unto you with mine own hand.
Galatians ch. 6, v. 11

EPHESIANS

28 [Christ] came and preached peace to you which were afar off, and to them that were nigh.
Ephesians ch. 2, v. 17

29 Unto me, who am less than the least of all saints, is this grace given, that I should preach

among the Gentiles the unsearchable riches of Christ.
Ephesians ch. 3, v. 8

1 I bow my knees unto the Father of our Lord Jesus Christ,
Of whom the whole family in heaven and earth is named,
That he would grant you, according to the riches of his glory, to be strengthened with might by his Spirit in the inner man.
Ephesians ch. 3, v. 14

2 The love of Christ, which passeth knowledge.
Ephesians ch. 3, v. 19

3 Now unto him that is able to do exceeding abundantly above all that we ask or think, according to the power that worketh in us,
Unto him be glory in the church by Christ Jesus throughout all ages, world without end. Amen.
Ephesians ch. 3, v. 20

4 I therefore, the prisoner of the Lord, beseech you that ye walk worthy of the vocation wherewith ye are called.
Ephesians ch. 4, v. 1

5 He gave some, apostles; and some, prophets; and some, evangelists; and some, pastors and teachers;
For the perfecting of the saints, for the work of the ministry, for the edifying of the body of Christ:
Till we all come in the unity of the faith, and of the knowledge of the Son of God, unto a perfect man, unto the measure of the stature of the fulness of Christ:
That we henceforth be no more children, tossed to and fro, and carried about with every wind of doctrine, by the sleight of men, and cunning craftiness, whereby they lie in wait to deceive.
Ephesians ch. 4, v. 11

6 We are members one of another.
Ephesians ch. 4, v. 25

7 Be ye angry and sin not: let not the sun go down upon your wrath.
Ephesians ch. 4, v. 26; see **PROVERBS** 639:37

8 Fornication, and all uncleanness, or covetousness, let it not be once named among you, as becometh saints;
Neither filthiness, nor foolish talking, nor jesting, which are not convenient.
Ephesians ch. 5, v. 3

9 Let no man deceive you with vain words: for because of these things cometh the wrath of God upon the children of disobedience.
Ephesians ch. 5, v. 6

10 See then that ye walk circumspectly, not as fools, but as wise,
Redeeming the time, because the days are evil.
Ephesians ch. 5, v. 15

11 Be not drunk with wine, wherein is excess; but be filled with the Spirit;

Speaking to yourselves in psalms and hymns and spiritual songs, singing and making melody in your heart to the Lord.
Ephesians ch. 5, v. 18

12 Ye fathers, provoke not your children to wrath.
Ephesians ch. 6, v. 4

13 Not with eyeservice, as menpleasers.
Ephesians ch. 6, v. 6

14 Put on the whole armour of God.
Ephesians ch. 6, v. 11

15 For we wrestle not against flesh and blood, but against principalities, against powers, against the rulers of the darkness of this world, against spiritual wickedness in high places.
Wherefore take unto you the whole armour of God, that ye may be able to withstand in the evil day, and having done all, to stand.
Stand therefore, having your loins girt about with truth, and having on the breastplate of righteousness;
And your feet shod with the preparation of the gospel of peace;
Above all, taking the shield of faith, wherewith ye shall be able to quench all the fiery darts of the wicked.
Ephesians ch. 6, v. 12

PHILIPPIANS

16 For me to live is Christ, and to die is gain.
Philippians ch. 1, v. 21

17 Having a desire to depart, and to be with Christ; which is far better.
Philippians ch. 1, v. 23

18 Let this mind be in you, which was also in Christ Jesus:
Who, being in the form of God, thought it not robbery to be equal with God:
But made himself of no reputation, and took upon him the form of a servant and was made in the likeness of men.
Philippians ch. 2, v. 5

19 God hath also highly exalted him, and given him a name which is above every name:
That at the name of Jesus every knee should bow, of things in heaven, and things in earth, and things under the earth.
Philippians ch. 2, v. 9; see **NOEL** 576:18

20 Work out your own salvation with fear and trembling.
Philippians ch. 2, v. 12

21 If any other man thinketh that he hath whereof he might trust in the flesh, I more:
Circumcised the eighth day, of the stock of Israel, of the tribe of Benjamin, an Hebrew of the Hebrews; as touching the law, a Pharisee.
Philippians ch. 3, v. 4

22 But what things were gain to me, those I counted loss for Christ.
Philippians ch. 3, v. 7

1 Forgetting those things which are behind, and reaching forth unto those things which are before,
I press toward the mark.
Philippians ch. 3, v. 13

2 Whose God is their belly, and whose glory is in their shame.
Philippians ch. 3, v. 19

3 Rejoice in the Lord alway: and again I say, Rejoice.
Philippians ch. 4, v. 4

4 The peace of God, which passeth all understanding, shall keep your hearts and minds through Christ Jesus.
Philippians ch. 4, v. 7; see **JAMES I** 429:3

5 Whatsoever things are true, whatsoever things are honest, whatsoever things are just, whatsoever things are pure, whatsoever things are lovely, whatsoever things are of good report; if there be any virtue and if there be any praise, think on these things.
Philippians ch. 4, v. 8

6 I can do all things through Christ which strengtheneth me.
Philippians ch. 4, v. 13

COLOSSIANS

7 For by him were all things created, that are in heaven, and that are in earth, visible and invisible, whether they be thrones, or dominions, or principalities, or powers.
Colossians ch. 1, v. 16; see **MILTON** 543:22

8 Set your affection on things above, not on things on the earth.
Colossians ch. 3, v. 2

9 Ye have put off the old man with his deeds:
And have put on the new man, which is renewed in knowledge after the image of him that created him:
Where there is neither Greek nor Jew, circumcision nor uncircumcision, Barbarian, Scythian, bond nor free: but Christ is all, and in all.
Colossians ch. 3, v. 9

10 Husbands, love your wives, and be not bitter against them.
Colossians ch. 3, v. 19

11 Let your speech be alway with grace, seasoned with salt.
Colossians ch. 4, v. 6

I THESSALONIANS

12 We give thanks to God always for you all, making mention of you in our prayers;
Remembering without ceasing your work of faith and labour of love, and patience of hope in our Lord Jesus Christ.
I Thessalonians ch. 1, v. 2

13 Study to be quiet, and to do your own business.
I Thessalonians ch. 4, v. 11

14 But let us, who are of the day, be sober, putting on the breastplate of faith and love; and for an helmet, the hope of salvation.
I Thessalonians ch. 5, v. 8

15 Rejoice evermore. Pray without ceasing. In everything give thanks.
I Thessalonians ch. 5, v. 16

16 Prove all things; hold fast that which is good.
1 Thessalonians ch. 5, v. 21

II THESSALONIANS

17 If any would not work, neither should he eat.
II Thessalonians ch. 3, v. 10; see **PROVERBS** 635:27

I TIMOTHY

18 Sinners; of whom I am chief.
I Timothy ch. 1, v. 15

19 A bishop then must be blameless, the husband of one wife, vigilant, sober, of good behaviour, given to hospitality, apt to teach;
Not given to wine, no striker, not greedy of filthy lucre; but patient, not a brawler, not covetous.
I Timothy ch. 3, v. 2

20 Refuse profane and old wives' fables, and exercise thyself rather unto godliness.
I Timothy ch. 4, v. 7

21 Use a little wine for thy stomach's sake.
I Timothy ch. 5, v. 23

22 For we brought nothing into this world, and it is certain we can carry nothing out.
I Timothy ch. 6, v. 7

23 The love of money is the root of all evil.
I Timothy ch. 6, v. 10; see **PROVERBS** 639:2, **SUDRAKA** 779:16

24 Fight the good fight of faith, lay hold on eternal life.
I Timothy ch. 6, v. 12; see **MONSELL** 554:1

II TIMOTHY

25 For God hath not given us the spirit of fear; but of power, and of love, and of a sound mind.
II Timothy ch. 1, v. 7

26 Hold fast the form of sound words.
II Timothy ch. 1, v. 13

27 Be instant in season, out of season.
II Timothy ch. 4, v. 2

28 I have fought a good fight, I have finished my course, I have kept the faith.
II Timothy ch. 4, v. 7

TITUS

29 Unto the pure all things are pure.
Titus ch. 1, v. 15; see **LAWRENCE** 483:11, **PROVERBS** 645:31

HEBREWS

30 God, who at sundry times and in divers manners spake in time past unto the fathers by the prophets,
Hath in these last days spoken unto us by his Son, whom he hath appointed heir of all things, by whom he also made the worlds:

Who being the brightness of his glory, and the express image of his person, and upholding all things by the word of his power, when he had by himself purged our sins, sat down on the right hand of the Majesty on high.
Hebrews ch. 1, v. 1

1 Without shedding of blood is no remission.
Hebrews ch. 9, v. 22

2 It is a fearful thing to fall into the hands of the living God.
Hebrews ch. 10, v. 31

3 Faith is the substance of things hoped for, the evidence of things not seen.
Hebrews ch. 11, v. 1

4 For he looked for a city which hath foundations, whose maker and builder is God.
Hebrews ch. 11, v. 10

5 These all died in faith, not having received the promises, but having seen them afar off, and were persuaded of them, and embraced them, and confessed that they were strangers and pilgrims on the earth.
Hebrews ch. 11, v. 13

6 Of whom the world was not worthy.
Hebrews ch. 11, v. 38

7 Wherefore seeing we also are compassed about with so great a cloud of witnesses, let us lay aside every weight, and the sin which doth so easily beset us, and let us run with patience the race that is set before us,
Looking unto Jesus the author and finisher of our faith; who for the joy that was set before him endured the cross, despising the shame, and is set down at the right hand of God.
Hebrews ch. 12, v. 1

8 Whom the Lord loveth he chasteneth.
Hebrews ch. 12, v. 6

9 The spirits of just men made perfect.
Hebrews ch. 12, v. 23

10 Let brotherly love continue.
Hebrews ch. 13, v. 1

11 Be not forgetful to entertain strangers: for thereby some have entertained angels unawares.
Hebrews ch. 13, v. 2

12 Jesus Christ the same yesterday, and to day, and for ever.
Hebrews ch. 13, v. 8

13 For here have we no continuing city, but we seek one to come.
Hebrews ch. 13, v. 14

14 To do good and to communicate forget not.
Hebrews ch. 13, v. 16

JAMES

15 Let patience have her perfect work.
James ch. 1, v. 4

16 Blessed is the man that endureth temptation: for when he is tried, he shall receive the crown of life.
James ch. 1, v. 12

17 Every good gift and every perfect gift is from above, and cometh down from the Father of lights, with whom is no variableness, neither shadow of turning.
James ch. 1, v. 17

18 Be swift to hear, slow to speak, slow to wrath: For the wrath of man worketh not the righteousness of God.
Wherefore lay apart all filthiness and superfluity of naughtiness, and receive with meekness the engrafted word, which is able to save your souls,
For if any be a hearer of the word, and not a doer, he is like unto a man beholding his natural face in a glass:
For he beholdeth himself, and goeth his way, and straightway forgetteth what manner of man he was.
James ch. 1, v. 19

19 But be ye doers of the word, and not hearers only, deceiving your own selves.
James ch. 1, v. 22

20 If any man among you seem to be religious, and bridleth not his tongue, but deceiveth his own heart, this man's religion is vain.
James ch. 1, v. 26

21 Pure religion and undefiled before God and the Father is this, To visit the fatherless and widows in their affliction, and to keep himself unspotted from the world.
James ch. 1, v. 27

22 Faith without works is dead.
James ch. 2, v. 20

23 How great a matter a little fire kindleth.
James ch. 3, v. 5

24 The tongue can no man tame; it is an unruly evil.
James ch. 3, v. 8

25 Doth a fountain send forth at the same place sweet water and bitter?
James ch. 3, v. 11

26 For what is your life? It is even a vapour, that appeareth for a little time, and then vanisheth away.
James ch. 4, v. 14

27 Ye have heard of the patience of Job.
James ch. 5, v. 11

28 Let your yea be yea; and your nay, nay.
James ch. 5, v. 12

29 The effectual fervent prayer of a righteous man availeth much.
James ch. 5, v. 16

I PETER

30 Jesus Christ: Whom having not seen, ye love; in whom, though now ye see him not, yet believing, ye rejoice with joy unspeakable and full of glory.
I Peter ch. 1, v. 7

1 All flesh is as grass, and all the glory of man as the flower of grass. The grass withereth, and the flower thereof falleth away.
I Peter ch. 1, v. 24; see **BIBLE** 93:16

2 As newborn babes, desire the sincere milk of the word, that ye may grow thereby:
If so be ye have tasted that the Lord is gracious.
I Peter ch. 2, v. 2

3 But ye are a chosen generation, a royal priesthood, an holy nation, a peculiar people.
I Peter ch. 2, v. 9

4 Abstain from fleshly lusts, which war against the soul.
I Peter ch. 2, v. 11

5 Honour all men. Love the brotherhood. Fear God. Honour the king.
I Peter ch. 2, v. 17

6 For what glory is it, if, when ye be buffeted for your faults, ye shall take it patiently? but if, when ye do well, and suffer for it, ye take it patiently, this is acceptable with God.
I Peter ch. 2, v. 20

7 Ye were as sheep going astray; but are now returned unto the Shepherd and Bishop of your souls.
I Peter ch. 2, v. 25

8 The ornament of a meek and quiet spirit.
I Peter ch. 3, v. 4

9 Giving honour unto the wife, as unto the weaker vessel.
I Peter ch. 3, v. 7

10 Not rendering evil for evil, or railing for railing: but contrariwise blessing.
I Peter ch. 3, v. 9

11 The end of all things is at hand.
I Peter ch. 4, v. 7

12 Charity shall cover the multitude of sins.
I Peter ch. 4, v. 8; see **PROVERBS** 628:43

13 Be sober, be vigilant; because your adversary the devil, as a roaring lion, walketh about, seeking whom he may devour.
I Peter ch. 5, v. 8

II PETER

14 And the day star arise in your hearts.
II Peter ch. 1, v. 19

15 The dog is turned to his own vomit again.
II Peter ch. 2, v. 22

I JOHN

16 If we say that we have no sin, we deceive ourselves, and the truth is not in us.
I John ch. 1, v. 8

17 But whoso hath this world's good, and seeth his brother have need, and shutteth up his bowels of compassion from him, how dwelleth the love of God in him?
I John ch. 3, v. 17

18 He that loveth not knoweth not God; for God is love.
I John ch. 4, v. 8

19 There is no fear in love; but perfect love casteth out fear.
I John ch. 4, v. 18; see **CONNOLLY** 248:12

20 If a man say, I love God, and hateth his brother, he is a liar: for he that loveth not his brother whom he hath seen, how can he love God whom he hath not seen?
I John ch. 4, v. 20

III JOHN

21 He that doeth good is of God: but he that doeth evil hath not seen God.
III John v. 11

REVELATION

22 John to the seven churches which are in Asia: Grace be unto you, and peace, from him which is, and which was, and which is to come.
Revelation ch. 1, v. 4

23 Behold, he cometh with clouds; and every eye shall see him, and they also which pierced him: and all kindreds of the earth shall wail because of him. Even so, Amen.
I am Alpha and Omega, the beginning and the ending, saith the Lord.
Revelation ch. 1, v. 7

24 I was in the Spirit on the Lord's day, and heard behind me a great voice as of a trumpet.
Revelation ch. 1, v. 10

25 What thou seest, write in a book, and send it unto the seven churches which are in Asia.
Revelation ch. 1, v. 11

26 Being turned, I saw seven golden candlesticks.
Revelation ch. 1, v. 12

27 His head and his hairs were white like wool, as white as snow; and his eyes were as a flame of fire;
And his feet like unto fine brass, as if they burned in a furnace; and his voice as the sound of many waters.
And he had in his right hand seven stars: and out of his mouth went a sharp two-edged sword: and his countenance was as the sun shineth in his strength.
And when I saw him, I fell at his feet as dead.
Revelation ch. 1, v. 14

28 I am he that liveth, and was dead; and, behold, I am alive for evermore, Amen; and have the keys of hell and of death.
Revelation ch. 1, v. 18

29 I have somewhat against thee, because thou hast left thy first love.
Revelation ch. 2, v. 4

30 Be thou faithful unto death, and I will give thee a crown of life.
Revelation ch. 2, v. 10

31 I will not blot out his name out of the book of life.
Revelation ch. 3, v. 5

32 I will write upon him my new name.
Revelation ch. 3, v. 12

1 I know thy works, that thou art neither cold nor hot: I would thou wert cold or hot.
So then, because thou art lukewarm, and neither cold nor hot, I will spew thee out of my mouth.
Revelation ch. 3, v. 15; see COWLEY 254:16

2 Behold, I stand at the door, and knock.
Revelation ch. 3, v. 20

3 And he that sat was to look upon like a jasper and a sardine stone: and there was a rainbow round about the throne, in sight like unto an emerald.
Revelation ch. 4, v. 3

4 And before the throne there was a sea of glass like unto crystal: and in the midst of the throne, and round about the throne, were four beasts full of eyes before and behind.
Revelation ch. 4, v. 6

5 They were full of eyes within: and they rest not day and night, saying, Holy, holy, holy, Lord God Almighty, which was, and is, and is to come.
Revelation ch. 4, v. 8; see BOOK OF COMMON PRAYER 137:14, MISSAL 549:16

6 Thou hast created all things, and for thy pleasure they are and were created.
Revelation ch. 4, v. 11

7 Who is worthy to open the book, and to loose the seals thereof?
Revelation ch. 5, v. 2

8 The four beasts and four and twenty elders fell down before the Lamb, having every one of them harps, and golden vials full of odours, which are the prayers of saints.
Revelation ch. 5, v. 8

9 He went forth conquering, and to conquer.
Revelation ch. 6, v. 2

10 And I looked, and behold a pale horse: and his name that sat on him was Death.
Revelation ch. 6, v. 8

11 The kings of the earth, and the great men, and the rich men, and the chief captains, and the mighty men, and every bondman, and every free man, hid themselves in the dens and in the rocks of the mountains;
And said to the mountains and rocks, Fall on us, and hide us from the face of him that sitteth upon the throne, and from the wrath of the Lamb:
For the great day of his wrath is come; and who shall be able to stand?
Revelation ch. 6, v. 15

12 A great multitude, which no man could number, of all nations, and kindreds, and people, and tongues, stood before the throne, and before the Lamb.
Revelation ch. 7, v. 9

13 And all the angels stood round about the throne, and about the elders and the four beasts, and fell before the throne on their faces, and worshipped God.
Revelation ch. 7, v. 11

14 And one of the elders answered, saying unto me, What are these which are arrayed in white robes? and whence came they?
Revelation ch. 7, v. 13

15 These are they which came out of great tribulation, and have washed their robes, and made them white in the blood of the Lamb.
Revelation ch. 7, v. 14; see LINDSAY 495:1

16 They shall hunger no more, neither thirst any more; neither shall the sun light on them, nor any heat.
Revelation ch. 7, v. 16

17 God shall wipe away all tears from their eyes.
Revelation ch. 7, v. 17

18 And when he had opened the seventh seal, there was silence in heaven about the space of half an hour.
Revelation ch. 8, v. 1

19 And the name of the star is called Wormwood.
Revelation ch. 8, v. 11

20 And in those days shall men seek death, and shall not find it; and shall desire to die, and death shall flee from them.
Revelation ch. 9, v. 6

21 And there were stings in their tails.
Revelation ch. 9, v. 10

22 It was in my mouth sweet as honey: and as soon as I had eaten it, my belly was bitter.
Revelation ch. 10, v. 10

23 And there appeared a great wonder in heaven; a woman clothed with the sun, and the moon under her feet, and upon her head a crown of twelve stars.
Revelation ch. 12, v. 1

24 And there was war in heaven: Michael and his angels fought against the dragon; and the dragon fought and his angels.
Revelation ch. 12, v. 7

25 Who is like unto the beast? who is able to make war with him?
Revelation ch. 13, v. 4

26 And that no man might buy or sell, save he that had the mark, or the name of the beast, or the number of his name.
Revelation ch. 13, v. 17

27 Let him that hath understanding count the number of the beast: for it is the number of a man; and his number is Six hundred threescore and six.
Revelation ch. 13, v. 18

28 And I heard a voice from heaven, as the voice of many waters, and as the voice of a great thunder: and I heard the voice of harpers harping with their harps:
And they sung as it were a new song . . . and no man could learn that song but the hundred and forty and four thousand, which were redeemed from the earth.
Revelation ch. 14, v. 2

1 Babylon is fallen, is fallen, that great city.
Revelation ch. 14, v. 8

2 And the smoke of their torment ascendeth up for ever and ever: and they have no rest day or night, who worship the beast and his image.
Revelation ch. 14, v. 11

3 Blessed are the dead which die in the Lord from henceforth: Yea, saith the Spirit, that they may rest from their labours; and their works do follow them.
Revelation ch. 14, v. 13

4 And I saw as it were a sea of glass mingled with fire.
Revelation ch. 15, v. 2

5 Behold, I come as a thief.
Revelation ch. 16, v. 15

6 And he gathered them together into a place called in the Hebrew tongue Armageddon.
Revelation ch. 16, v. 16

7 I will shew unto thee the judgement of the great whore that sitteth upon many waters.
Revelation ch. 17, v. 1

8 And upon her forehead was a name written, MYSTERY, BABYLON THE GREAT, THE MOTHER OF HARLOTS AND ABOMINATIONS OF THE EARTH.
Revelation ch. 17, v. 5

9 And a mighty angel took up a stone like a great millstone, and cast it into the sea, saying, Thus with violence shall that great city Babylon be thrown down, and shall be found no more at all.
Revelation ch. 18, v. 21

10 And I saw heaven opened, and behold a white horse; and he that sat upon him was called Faithful and True.
Revelation ch. 19, v. 11

11 And he hath on his vesture and on his thigh a name written, KING OF KINGS, AND LORD OF LORDS.
Revelation ch. 19, v. 16

12 And he laid hold on the dragon, that old serpent, which is the Devil, and Satan, and bound him a thousand years.
Revelation ch. 20, v. 2

13 And I saw a great white throne.
Revelation ch. 20, v. 11

14 And the sea gave up the dead which were in it; and death and hell delivered up the dead which were in them: and they were judged every man according to their works.
Revelation ch. 20, v. 13

15 And I saw a new heaven and a new earth: for the first heaven and the first earth were passed away; and there was no more sea.
And I John saw the holy city, new Jerusalem, coming down from God out of heaven, prepared as a bride adorned for her husband.
Revelation ch. 21, v. 1

16 And God shall wipe away all tears from their eyes; and there shall be no more death, neither sorrow, nor crying, neither shall there be any more pain: for the former things are passed away.
And he that sat upon the throne said, Behold, I make all things new. And he said unto me, Write: for these words are true and faithful.
Revelation ch. 21, v. 4; see **POUND** 620:17

17 I will give unto him that is athirst of the fountain of the water of life freely.
Revelation ch. 21, v. 6

18 The street of the city was pure gold.
Revelation ch. 21, v. 21

19 And the gates of it shall not be shut at all by day: for there shall be no night there.
Revelation ch. 21, v. 25

20 And he shewed me a pure river of water of life, clear as crystal, proceeding out of the throne of God and of the Lamb.
Revelation ch. 22, v. 1

21 And the leaves of the tree were for the healing of the nations.
Revelation ch. 22, v. 2

22 And, behold, I come quickly.
Revelation ch. 22, v. 12

23 For without are dogs, and sorcerers, and whoremongers, and murderers, and idolaters, and whosoever loveth and maketh a lie.
Revelation ch. 22, v. 15

24 Amen. Even so, come, Lord Jesus.
Revelation ch. 22, v. 20

The Bible (Vulgate)

the principal Latin version of the Bible, prepared mainly by St **JEROME** in the late 4th century

25 *Dominus illuminatio mea, et salus mea, quem timebo?*

The Lord is the source of my light and my safety, so whom shall I fear?
Psalm 26, v. 1; see **BOOK OF COMMON PRAYER** 141:9, **MOTTOES** 563:8

26 *Cor meum eructavit.*

My heart has uttered.
Psalm 44, v. 1 (Psalm 45, v. 1 in the Authorized Version); see **BOOK OF COMMON PRAYER** 142:12

27 *Asperges me hyssopo, et mundabor; lavabis me, et super nivem dealbabor.*

You will sprinkle me with hyssop, and I shall be made clean; you will wash me and I shall be made whiter than snow.
Psalm 51, v. 7 (Psalm 52, v. 7 in the Authorized Version); see **BOOK OF COMMON PRAYER** 143:6

28 *Dominabitur a mari usque ad mare.*

He shall have dominion from sea to sea.
Psalm 71, v. 8 (Psalm 72, v. 8 in the Authorized Version); see **MOTTOES** 563:2

29 *Cantate Domino canticum novum, quia mirabilia fecit.*

Sing to the Lord a new song, because he has done marvellous things.
> Psalm 97, v. 1 (Psalm 98, v. 1 in the Authorized Version); see **BOOK OF COMMON PRAYER** 146:11

1 *Jubilate Deo, omnis terra; servite Domino in laetitia.*
Sing joyfully to God, all the earth; serve the Lord with gladness.
> Psalm 99, v. 2 (Psalm 100, v. 2 in the Authorized Version); see **BOOK OF COMMON PRAYER** 146:15

2 *Beatus vir qui timet Dominum, in mandatis ejus volet nimis!*
Happy is the man who fears the Lord, who is only too willing to follow his orders.
> Psalm 111, v. 1 (Psalm 112, v. 1 in the Authorized Version)

3 *Non nobis, Domine, non nobis; sed nomini tuo da gloriam.*
Not unto us, Lord, not unto us; but to thy name give glory.
> Psalm 113 (second part), v. 1 (Psalm 115, v. 1 in the Authorized Version); see **BOOK OF COMMON PRAYER** 148:4

4 *Laudate Dominum, omnes gentes; laudate eum, omnes populi.*
Praise the Lord, all nations; praise him, all people.
> Psalm 116, v. 1 (Psalm 117, v. 1 in the Authorized Version)

5 *Nisi Dominus aedificaverit domum, in vanum laboraverunt qui aedificant eam.*
Nisi Dominus custodierit civitatem, frustra vigilat qui custodit eam.
Unless the Lord has built the house, its builders have laboured in vain. Unless the Lord guards the city, the watchman watches in vain.
> Psalm 126, v. 1 (Psalm 127, v. 1 in the Authorized Version); see **BOOK OF COMMON PRAYER** 149:2, **MOTTOES** 563:13

6 *De profundis clamavi ad te, Domine; Domine, exaudi vocem meam.*
Up from the depths I have cried to thee, Lord; Lord, hear my voice.
> Psalm 129, v. 1 (Psalm 130, v. 1 in the Authorized Version); see **BOOK OF COMMON PRAYER** 149:7

7 *Vanitas vanitatum, dixit Ecclesiastes; vanitas vanitatum, et omnia vanitas.*
Vanity of vanities, said the preacher; vanity of vanities, and everything is vanity.
> Ecclesiastes ch. 1, v. 2; see **BIBLE** 89:16, **MÉNAGE** 531:15

8 *Rorate, coeli, desuper, et nubes pluant Justum; aperiatur terra, et germinet Salvatorem.*
Drop down dew, heavens, from above, and let the clouds rain down righteousness; let the earth be opened, and a saviour spring to life.
> Isaiah ch. 45, v. 8

9 *Benedicite, omnia opera Domini, Domino; laudate et superexaltate eum in secula.*
Bless the Lord, all the works of the Lord; praise him and exalt him above all things for ever.
> Daniel ch. 3, v. 57; see **BOOK OF COMMON PRAYER** 133:12

10 *Magnificat anima mea Dominum; Et exsultavit spiritus meus in Deo salutari meo.*

My soul doth magnify the Lord: and my spirit hath rejoiced in God my Saviour.
> St Luke ch. 1, v. 46; see **BIBLE** 104:8

11 *Esurientes implevit bonis, et divites dimisit inanes.*
He hath filled the hungry with good things: and the rich he hath sent empty away.
> St Luke ch. 1, v. 53; see **BIBLE** 104:9

12 *Nunc dimittis servum tuum, Domine, secundum verbum tuum in pace.*
Lord, now lettest thou thy servant depart in peace: according to thy word.
> St Luke ch. 2, v. 29; see **BIBLE** 104:16

13 *Pax Vobis.*
Peace be unto you.
> St Luke ch. 24, v. 36

14 *Quo vadis?*
Where are you going?
> St John ch. 16, v. 5

15 *Ecce homo.*
Behold the man.
> St John ch. 19, v. 5

16 *Consummatum est.*
It is achieved.
> St John ch. 19, v. 30; see **BIBLE** 108:33

17 *Noli me tangere.*
Do not touch me.
> St John ch. 20, v. 17; see **BIBLE** 108:38

18 *Sicut modo geniti infantes, rationabile, sine dolo lac concupiscite.*
After the fashion of newborn babes, desire the sincere milk of the word.
> I Peter ch. 2, v. 2; see **BIBLE** 117:2

19 *Magna est veritas, et praevalet.*
Great is truth, and it prevails.
> III Esdras ch. 4, v. 41; see **BIBLE** 96:21, **BROOKS** 160:6

Isaac Bickerstaffe 1733–c.1808
Irish dramatist

20 Perhaps it was right to dissemble your love,
But—why did you kick me downstairs?
> 'An Expostulation' (1789); see **CARROLL** 202:1

21 There was a jolly miller once,
Lived on the river Dee;
He worked and sang from morn till night;
No lark more blithe than he.
> *Love in a Village* (a comic opera with music by Thomas Arne, 1762) act 1, sc. 2

22 And this the burthen of his song,
For ever used to be,
I care for nobody, not I,
If no one cares for me.
> *Love in a Village* (1762) act 1, sc. 2

E. H. Bickersteth 1825–1906
English clergyman

23 Peace, perfect peace, in this dark world of sin?
The Blood of Jesus whispers peace within.
> *Songs in the House of Pilgrimage* (1875) 'Peace, perfect peace'

Francis Biddle 1886–1968
American lawyer and judge, Attorney-General 1941-7, senior American judge at the Nuremberg Trials

1 The Constitution has never greatly bothered any wartime President.
In Brief Authority (1962)

Ambrose Bierce 1842–c.1914
American writer

2 ALLIANCE, *n*. In international politics, the union of two thieves who have their hands so deeply inserted in each other's pocket that they cannot separately plunder a third.
The Cynic's Word Book (1906)

3 APPLAUSE, *n*. The echo of a platitude.
The Cynic's Word Book (1906)

4 BATTLE, *n*. A method of untying with the teeth a political knot that would not yield to the tongue.
The Cynic's Word Book (1906)

5 CALAMITY, *n*. . . . Calamities are of two kinds: misfortune to ourselves, and good fortune to others.
The Cynic's Word Book (1906)

6 CONSERVATIVE, *n*. A statesman who is enamoured of existing evils, as distinguished from the Liberal, who wishes to replace them with others.
The Cynic's Word Book (1906)

7 HISTORY, *n*. An account, mostly false, of events, mostly unimportant, which are brought about by rulers, mostly knaves, and soldiers, mostly fools.
The Cynic's Word Book (1906)

8 PEACE, *n*. In international affairs, a period of cheating between two periods of fighting.
The Devil's Dictionary (1911)

9 PREJUDICE, *n*. A vagrant opinion without visible means of support.
The Devil's Dictionary (1911)

10 SAINT, *n*. A dead sinner revised and edited.
The Devil's Dictionary (1911)

Roger Bigod, Earl of Norfolk
1245–1306
English peer, Marshal of England, 1270-1301

11 EDWARD I: By God, earl, you shall either go or hang.
BIGOD: By God, O King, I will neither go nor hang!
on the King's requiring the barons to invade France through Gascony while he himself took command in Flanders, 24 February 1297
Harry Rothwell (ed.) *The Chronicle of Walter of Guisbrough* Camden Society Series 3, vol. 89 (1957)

Steve Biko 1946–77
South African anti-apartheid campaigner

12 The liberal must understand that the days of the Noble Savage are gone; that the blacks do not need a go-between in this struggle for their own emancipation. No true liberal should feel any resentment at the growth of black consciousness. Rather, all true liberals should realize that the place for their fight for justice is within their white society. The liberals must realize that they themselves are oppressed if they are true liberals and therefore they must fight for their own freedom and not that of the nebulous 'they' with whom they can hardly claim identification. The liberal must apply himself with absolute dedication to the idea of educating his white brothers.
'Black Souls in White Skins?' (written 1970), in *Steve Biko—I Write What I Like* (1978); see **DRYDEN** 295:15

Josh Billings (Henry Wheeler Shaw) 1818–85
American humorist

13 Love iz like the meazles; we kant have it bad but onst, and the latter in life we hav it the tuffer it goes with us.
Josh Billings' Wit and Humour (1874)

Maeve Binchy 1940–
Irish novelist

14 It's not perfect, but to me on balance Right Now is a lot better than the Good Old Days.
In *Irish Times* 15 November 1997

Laurence Binyon 1869–1943
English poet

15 They shall grow not old, as we that are left grow old.
Age shall not weary them, nor the years condemn.
At the going down of the sun and in the morning
We will remember them.
regularly recited as part of the ritual for Remembrance Day parades
'For the Fallen' (1914)

16 Now is the time for the burning of the leaves.
'The Ruins' (1942)

Bion c.325–c.255 BC
Greek popular philosopher, born in Olbia, Scythia

17 I mourn Adonis: 'Fair Adonis is dead'.
'Epitaph on Adonis'; see **SHELLEY** 743:8

18 Boys throw stones at frogs for fun, but the frogs don't die for 'fun', but in sober earnest.
Plutarch *Moralia*

Nigel Birch 1906–81
British Conservative politician

1 My God! They've shot our fox!
on hearing of the resignation of Hugh Dalton, Labour Chancellor of the Exchequer, after the leak of Budget secrets
comment, 13 November 1947; Harold Macmillan *Tides of Fortune* (1969) ch. 3

Lord Birkenhead *see* **F. E. Smith**

Earle Birney 1904–95
Canadian poet

2 We French, we English, never lost our civil war,
endure it still, a bloodless civil bore;
no wounded lying about, no Whitman wanted.
It's only by our lack of ghosts we're haunted.
'Can.Lit.' (1962)

Augustine Birrell 1850–1933
British politician and essayist

3 That great dust-heap called 'history'.
Obiter Dicta (1884) 'Carlyle'; see **TROTSKY** 817:6

Harrison Birtwistle 1934–
English composer and clarinettist

4 You can't stop. Composing's not voluntary, you know. There's no choice, you're not free. You're landed with an idea and you have responsibility to that idea.
in *Observer* 14 April 1996 'Sayings of the Week'

Billy Bishop 1894–1956
Canadian fighter pilot

5 This flying is the most wonderful invention. A man ceases to be human up there. He feels that nothing is impossible.
letter to his parents from Netheravon, England, 1 September 1915; W. Arthur Bishop *The Courage of the Early Morning* (1965)

Elizabeth Bishop 1911–79
American poet

6 The state with the prettiest name,
the state that floats in brackish water,
held together by mangrove roots.
'Florida' (1946)

7 This iceberg cuts its facets from within.
Like jewelry from a grave
it saves itself perpetually and adorns
only itself.
'The Imaginary Iceberg' (1946)

8 Topography displays no favourites; North's as near as West.
More delicate than the historians' are the map-makers' colours.
'The Map' (1946)

9 The armoured cars of dreams, contrived to let us do
so many a dangerous thing.
'Sleeping Standing Up' (1946)

10 Lullaby.
Let nations rage,
let nations fall.
The shadow of the crib makes an enormous cage
upon the wall.
'Songs for a Coloured Singer' (1946)

11 If she speaks of a chair you can practically sit on it.
of Marianne **MOORE**
notebook, c.1934/5; D. Kalstone *Becoming a Poet* (1989)

12 I am overcome by my own amazing sloth . . . Can you please forgive me and believe that it is really because I want to do something well that I don't do it at all?
letter to Marianne Moore, 25 February 1937

13 I am sorry for people who can't write letters. But I suspect also that you and I . . . love to write them because it's kind of like working without really doing it.
letter to Kit and Ilse Barker, 5 September 1953

Otto von Bismarck 1815–98
German statesman, Chancellor of the German Empire 1871–90, known as the 'Iron Chancellor'. On Bismarck: see **TAYLOR** 791:13, **TENNIEL** 792:17; see also **MISQUOTATIONS** 548:6

14 If the Princess can leave the Englishwoman at home and become a Prussian, then she may be a blessing to the country.
on the marriage of Victoria, Princess Royal, to Prince Frederick William of Prussia
letter, c.1857; Hannah Pakula *An Uncommon Woman: The Empress Frederick* (1996)

15 The secret of politics? Make a good treaty with Russia.
in 1863, when first in power
A. J. P. Taylor *Bismarck* (1955) ch. 7

16 Politics is the art of the possible.
in conversation with Meyer von Waldeck, 11 August 1867, in H. Amelung *Bismarck-Worte* (1918); see **BUTLER** 183:5, **GALBRAITH** 347:15, **MEDAWAR** 530:1

17 Let us . . . put Germany in the saddle! She will know well enough how to ride!
in 1867; Alan Palmer *Bismarck* (1976) ch. 9

18 We will not go to Canossa.
during his quarrel with Pope Pius IX regarding papal authority over German subjects, in allusion to the Emperor Henry IV's submission to Pope Gregory VII at Canossa in Modena in 1077
speech to the Reichstag, 14 May 1872

19 Not worth the healthy bones of a single Pomeranian grenadier.
of possible German involvement in the Balkans; see **HARRIS** *383:1*
speech to the Reichstag, 5 December 1876

1 Whoever speaks of Europe is wrong, [it is] a geographical concept.

marginal note on a letter from the Russian Chancellor Gorchakov, November 1876; see **METTERNICH** 533:10

2 I do not regard the procuring of peace as a matter in which we should play the role of arbiter between different opinions . . . more that of an honest broker who really wants to press the business forward.

speech to the Reichstag, 19 February 1878, in Ludwig Hahn (ed.) *Fürst Bismarck. Sein politisches Leben und Wirken* vol. 3 (1881)

3 This policy cannot succeed through speeches, and shooting-matches, and songs; it can only be carried out through blood and iron.

speech in the Prussian House of Deputies, 28 January 1886, in *Fürst Bismarck als Redner. Vollständige Sammlung der parlamentarischen Reden* (1885–91) vol. 15; in a speech on 30 September 1862, Bismarck had used the form 'Iron and blood' (in *Fürst Bismarck. Sein politisches Leben und Wirken* (1878) vol. 4)

4 If there is ever another war in Europe, it will come out of some damned silly thing in the Balkans.

attributed by Herr Ballen and quoted by Winston S. **CHURCHILL** in the House of Commons, 16 August 1945

5 A lath of wood painted to look like iron.

describing Lord **SALISBURY**

attributed, but vigorously denied by Sidney Whitman in *Personal Reminiscences of Prince Bismarck* (1902) ch. 14

6 The old Jew! That is the man.

of **DISRAELI** *at the Congress of Berlin*

attributed

James Black 1924–

Scottish analytical pharmacologist; winner of the Nobel prize for medicine

7 In the culture I grew up in you did your work and you did not put your arm around it to stop other people from looking—you took the earliest possible opportunity to make knowledge available.

on modern scientific research

in *Daily Telegraph* 11 December 1995

Valentine Blacker 1728–1823

Irish soldier

8 Put your trust in God, my boys, and keep your powder dry.

often attributed to Oliver **CROMWELL** *himself*

'Oliver's Advice' in E. Hayes *Ballads of Ireland* (1856) vol. 1; see **PROVERBS** 642:14

William Blackstone 1723–80

English jurist

9 Man was formed for society.

Commentaries on the Laws of England (1765) introduction, sect. 2; see **ARISTOTLE** 27:25

10 The king never dies.

Commentaries on the Laws of England (1765) bk. 1, ch. 7

11 The royal navy of England hath ever been its greatest defence and ornament; it is its ancient and natural strength; the floating bulwark of the island.

Commentaries on the Laws of England (1765) bk. 1, ch. 13; see **COVENTRY** 253:8

12 A third subordinate right of every Englishman is that of applying to the courts of justice for redress of injuries.

Commentaries on the Laws of England (1765) bk. 2, ch. 1

13 That the king can do no wrong, is a necessary and fundamental principle of the English constitution.

Commentaries on the Laws of England (1765) bk. 3, ch. 17

14 It is better that ten guilty persons escape than one innocent suffer.

Commentaries on the Laws of England (1765) bk. 4, ch. 27

Robert Blair 1699–1746

Scottish poet

15 Oft, in the lone church-yard at night I've seen,
The schoolboy with a satchel in his hand,
Whistling aloud to keep his courage up . . .
Sudden he starts! and hears, or thinks he hears,
The sound of something purring at his heels;
Full fast he flies, and dares not look behind him,
Till out of breath, he overtakes his fellows.

The Grave (1743) l. 57; see **COLERIDGE** 241:7

16 Smiled like yon knot of cowslips on the cliff,
Not to be come at by the willing hand.

The Grave (1753) l. 523

Tony Blair 1953–

British Labour statesman, Prime Minister 1997–2007. On Blair: see **SHORT** 750:1; see also **BUSH** 182:13

17 Labour is the party of law and order in Britain today. Tough on crime and tough on the causes of crime.

as Shadow Home Secretary

speech at the Labour Party Conference, 30 September 1993

18 Ask me my three main priorities for Government, and I tell you: education, education and education.

speech at the Labour Party Conference, 1 October 1996; see **MICHELET** 534:3

19 We are not the masters. The people are the masters. We are the servants of the people . . . What the electorate gives, the electorate can take away.

addressing Labour MPs on the first day of the new Parliament, 7 May 1997; see **BURKE** 175:19

in *Guardian* 8 May 1997

20 She was the People's Princess, and that is how she will stay . . . in our hearts and in our memories forever.

on hearing of the death of **DIANA**, *Princess of Wales, 31 August 1997*

in *The Times* 1 September 1997

1 This is not a time for soundbites.
of the final stage of the Northern Irish negotiations
Belfast, 8 April 1998, in *Irish Times* 11 April 1998

2 This is not a battle betweeen the United States and terrorism, but between the free and democratic world and terrorism. We therefore here in Britain stand shoulder to shoulder with our American friends in this hour of tragedy and we, like them, will not rest until this evil is driven from our world.
in Downing Street, London, 11 September 2001

3 The state of Africa is a scar on the conscience of the world.
speech to Labour Party Conference, 2 October 2001

4 PRESENTER: [Is Britain] prepared to send troops to commit themselves, to pay the blood price?
TONY BLAIR: Yes. What is important though is that at moments of crisis they [the USA] . . . need to know, 'Are you prepared to commit, are you prepared to be there when the shooting starts?'
interview on BBC2 *Hotline to the President* 8 September 2002

5 This is not the time to falter.
speech in the House of Commons, 18 March 2003

6 However much the right hon. gentleman may dance around the ring beforehand, at some point, he will come within the reach of a big clunking fist.
to David Cameron, the House of Commons, 15 November 2006

Eubie Blake (James Hubert Blake) 1883–1983
American ragtime pianist

7 If I'd known I was gonna live this long, I'd have taken better care of myself.
on reaching the age of 100
in *Observer* 13 February 1983 'Sayings of the Week'

William Blake 1757–1827
English artist and poet, whose poems mark the beginning of romanticism. On Blake: see BENÉT 69:17

8 When Sir Joshua Reynolds died
All Nature was degraded:
The King dropped a tear into the Queen's ear;
And all his pictures faded.
Annotations to The Works of Sir Joshua Reynolds 'When Sir Joshua Reynolds died' (c.1808)

9 To see a world in a grain of sand
And a heaven in a wild flower,
Hold infinity in the palm of your hand
And eternity in an hour.
'Auguries of Innocence' (c.1803) l. 1

10 A robin red breast in a cage
Puts all Heaven in a rage.
'Auguries of Innocence' (c.1803) l. 5

11 A dog starved at his master's gate
Predicts the ruin of the State.
A horse misused upon the road

Calls to Heaven for human blood.
Each outcry of the hunted hare
A fibre from the brain does tear.
A skylark wounded in the wing,
A cherubim does cease to sing.
'Auguries of Innocence' (c.1803) l. 9

12 He who shall hurt the little wren
Shall never be beloved by men
He who the ox to wrath has moved
Shall never be by woman loved.
'Auguries of Innocence' (c.1803) l. 29

13 The caterpillar on the leaf
Repeats to thee thy mother's grief.
Kill not the moth nor butterfly,
For the Last Judgement draweth nigh.
'Auguries of Innocence' (c.1803) l. 37

14 A truth that's told with bad intent
Beats all the lies you can invent.
'Auguries of Innocence' (c.1803) l. 53

15 Man was made for joy and woe;
And when this we rightly know
Thro' the world we safely go.
'Auguries of Innocence' (c.1803) l. 56

16 The strongest poison ever known
Came from Caesar's laurel crown.
'Auguries of Innocence' (c.1803) l. 97

17 If the Sun and Moon should doubt,
They'd immediately go out.
To be in a passion you good may do,
But no good if a passion is in you.
'Auguries of Innocence' (c.1803) l. 109

18 The whore and gambler, by the State
Licensed, build that nation's fate.
The harlot's cry from street to street
Shall weave old England's winding sheet.
'Auguries of Innocence' (c.1803) l. 113

19 Every night and every morn
Some to misery are born,
Every morn and every night
Some are born to sweet delight.
Some are born to sweet delight,
Some are born to endless night.
'Auguries of Innocence' (c.1803) l. 119

20 God appears and God is Light
To those poor souls who dwell in night
But does a human form display
To those who dwell in realms of day.
'Auguries of Innocence' (c.1803) l. 129

21 Does the eagle know what is in the pit?
Or wilt thou go ask the mole:
Can wisdom be put in a silver rod?
Or love in a golden bowl?
The Book of Thel (1789) plate i 'Thel's Motto'

22   Everything that lives,
Lives not alone, nor for itself.
The Book of Thel (1789) plate 3, l. 26

23 The Vision of Christ that thou dost see
Is my vision's greatest enemy;

Thine has a great hook nose like thine,
Mine has a snub nose like to mine.
The Everlasting Gospel (c.1818) (a) l. 1

1 Both read the Bible day and night,
But thou read'st black where I read white.
The Everlasting Gospel (c.1818) (a) l. 13

2 Was Jesus gentle, or did he
Give any marks of gentility?
When twelve years old he ran away
And left his parents in dismay.
The Everlasting Gospel (c.1818) (b) l. 1

3 Was Jesus humble or did he
Give any proofs of humility
Boast of high things with humble tone
And give with charity a stone.
The Everlasting Gospel (c.1818) (d) l. 1

4 Humility is only doubt
And does the sun and moon blot out
Rooting over with thorns and stems
The buried soul and all its gems
This life's dim windows of the soul
Distorts the heavens from pole to pole
And leads you to believe a lie
When you see with, not through, the eye.
The Everlasting Gospel (c.1818) (d) l. 99

5 Was Jesus chaste? or did he
Give any lessons of chastity?
The morning blushed fiery red:
Mary was found in adulterous bed.
The Everlasting Gospel (c.1818) (e) l. 1

6 Jesus was sitting in Moses' chair,
They brought the trembling woman there.
Moses commands she be stoned to death,
What was the sound of Jesus breath?
He laid His hand on Moses' Law:
The ancient Heavens, in silent awe
Writ with curses from pole to pole,
All away began to roll.
The Everlasting Gospel (c.1818) (e) l. 7

7 I am sure this Jesus will not do
Either for Englishman or Jew.
The Everlasting Gospel (c.1818) (f) l. 1

8 Mutual Forgiveness of each vice,
Such are the Gates of Paradise.
For the Sexes: The Gates of Paradise 'Mutual Forgiveness of each Vice' [prologue]

9 Truly, my Satan, thou art but a dunce,
And dost not know the garment from the man;
Every harlot was a virgin once,
Nor can'st thou ever change Kate into Nan.

Tho' thou art worshipped by the names divine
Of Jesus and Jehovah, thou art still
The Son of Morn in weary Night's decline,
The lost traveller's dream under the hill.
For the Sexes: The Gates of Paradise 'To the Accuser who is The God of This World' [epilogue]; see **YOUNG** 876:26

10 Wisdom is sold in the desolate market where
none come to buy.
The Four Zoas 'Night the Second'

11 I must create a system, or be enslaved by
another man's.
I will not reason and compare: my business is to
create.
Jerusalem (1815) 'Chapter 1' (plate 10, l. 20)

12   Near mournful
Ever weeping Paddington.
Jerusalem (1815) 'Chapter 1' (plate 12, l. 27)

13 The fields from Islington to Marybone,
To Primrose Hill and Saint John's Wood
Were builded over with pillars of gold;
And there Jerusalem's pillars stood.
Jerusalem (1815) 'To the Jews' (plate 27, l. 1) "The fields from Islington to Marybone"

14 For a tear is an intellectual thing;
And a sigh is the sword of an Angel King
And the bitter groan of the martyr's woe
Is an arrow from the Almighty's bow!
Jerusalem (1815) 'To the Deists' (plate 52, l. 25) "I saw a Monk of Charlemaine"

15 He who would do good to another, must do it
in minute particulars
General good is the plea of the scoundrel,
hypocrite and flatterer:
For Art and Science cannot exist but in minutely
organized particulars.
Jerusalem (1815) 'Chapter 3' (plate 55, l. 60)

16 I give you the end of a golden string;
Only wind it into a ball:
It will lead you in at Heaven's gate,
Built in Jerusalem's wall.
Jerusalem (1815) 'To the Christians' (plate 77) "I give you the end of a golden string"

17 England! awake! awake! awake!
Jerusalem thy sister calls!
Why wilt thou sleep the sleep of death,
And close her from thy ancient walls?
Jerusalem (1815) 'To the Christians' (plate 77) "England! awake!
. . . "

18 And now the time returns again:
Our souls exult, and London's towers,
Receive the Lamb of God to dwell
In England's green and pleasant bowers.
Jerusalem (1815) 'To the Christians' (plate 77)

19 It is easier to forgive an enemy than to forgive a
friend.
Jerusalem (1815) 'Chapter 4' (plate 91, l. 1)

20 I care not whether a man is good or evil; all that
I care
Is whether he is a wise man or a fool. Go! put
off holiness
And put on Intellect.
Jerusalem (1815) 'Chapter 4' (plate 91, l. 54)

21   May God us keep
From Single vision and Newton's sleep!
'Letter to Thomas Butts, 22 November 1802'

22 O why was I born with a different face?
Why was I not born like the rest of my race?
'Letter to Thomas Butts, 16 August 1803'

1 Without contraries is no progression. Attraction and repulsion, reason and energy, love and hate, are necessary to human existence.
The Marriage of Heaven and Hell (1790–3) 'The Argument'

2 Energy is Eternal Delight.
The Marriage of Heaven and Hell (1790–3) 'The voice of the Devil'

3 The reason Milton wrote in fetters when he wrote of Angels and God, and at liberty when of Devils and Hell, is because he was a true Poet, and of the Devil's party without knowing it.
The Marriage of Heaven and Hell (1790–3) 'The voice of the Devil' (note)

4 The road of excess leads to the palace of wisdom.
The Marriage of Heaven and Hell (1790–3) 'Proverbs of Hell'

5 Prudence is a rich, ugly, old maid courted by Incapacity.
The Marriage of Heaven and Hell (1790–3) 'Proverbs of Hell'

6 He who desires but acts not, breeds pestilence.
The Marriage of Heaven and Hell (1790–3) 'Proverbs of Hell'

7 A fool sees not the same tree that a wise man sees.
The Marriage of Heaven and Hell (1790–3) 'Proverbs of Hell'

8 Eternity is in love with the productions of time.
The Marriage of Heaven and Hell (1790–3) 'Proverbs of Hell'

9 Bring out number weight and measure in a year of dearth.
The Marriage of Heaven and Hell (1790–3) 'Proverbs of Hell'

10 No bird soars too high, if he soars with his own wings.
The Marriage of Heaven and Hell (1790–3) 'Proverbs of Hell'

11 If the fool would persist in his folly he would become wise.
The Marriage of Heaven and Hell (1790–3) 'Proverbs of Hell'

12 Prisons are built with stones of Law, brothels with bricks of Religion.
The Marriage of Heaven and Hell (1790–3) 'Proverbs of Hell'

13 The pride of the peacock is the glory of God.
The lust of the goat is the bounty of God.
The wrath of the lion is the wisdom of God.
The nakedness of woman is the work of God.
The Marriage of Heaven and Hell (1790–3) 'Proverbs of Hell'

14 The tygers of wrath are wiser than the horses of instruction.
The Marriage of Heaven and Hell (1790–3) 'Proverbs of Hell'

15 You never know what is enough unless you know what is more than enough.
The Marriage of Heaven and Hell (1790–3) 'Proverbs of Hell'

16 Damn braces: Bless relaxes.
The Marriage of Heaven and Hell (1790–3) 'Proverbs of Hell'

17 Exuberance is beauty.
The Marriage of Heaven and Hell (1790–3) 'Proverbs of Hell'

18 Sooner murder an infant in its cradle than nurse unacted desires.
The Marriage of Heaven and Hell (1790–3) 'Proverbs of Hell'

19 Truth can never be told so as to be understood, and not be believed.
The Marriage of Heaven and Hell (1790–3) 'Proverbs of Hell'

20 How do you know but every bird that cuts the airy way
Is an immense world of delight, closed by your senses five?
The Marriage of Heaven and Hell (1790–3) 'A Memorable Fancy' plate 7

21 Then I asked: 'Does a firm persuasion that a thing is so, make it so?'
He replied: 'All Poets believe that it does, and in ages of imagination this firm persuasion removed mountains; but many are not capable of a firm persuasion of anything.'
The Marriage of Heaven and Hell (1790–3) 'A Memorable Fancy' plates 12–13

22 If the doors of perception were cleansed everything would appear to man as it is, infinite.
The Marriage of Heaven and Hell (1790–3) 'A Memorable Fancy' plate 14

23 I was in a printing house in Hell, and saw the method in which knowledge is transmitted from generation to generation.
The Marriage of Heaven and Hell (1790–3) 'A Memorable Fancy' plates 15–17

24 And did those feet in ancient time
Walk upon England's mountains green?
And was the holy Lamb of God
On England's pleasant pastures seen?

And did the Countenance Divine
Shine forth upon our clouded hills?
And was Jerusalem builded here
Among these dark Satanic mills?

Bring me my bow of burning gold:
Bring me my arrows of desire:
Bring me my spear: O clouds, unfold!
Bring me my chariot of fire.

I will not cease from mental fight,
Nor shall my sword sleep in my hand,
Till we have built Jerusalem,
In England's green and pleasant land.
Milton (1804–10) preface 'And did those feet in ancient time'

25 Mock on, mock on Voltaire, Rousseau:
Mock on, mock on: tis all in vain!
You throw the sand against the wind,
And the wind blows it back again.
MS Note-Book

26 The atoms of Democritus
And Newton's particles of light
Are sands upon the Red sea shore,
Where Israel's tents do shine so bright.
MS Note-Book

27 To forgive enemies H— does pretend,
Who never in his life forgave a friend.
MS Note-Book

28 The errors of a wise man make your rule
Rather than the perfections of a fool.
MS Note-Book

1 Great things are done when men and mountains
  meet;
  This is not done by jostling in the street.
  MS Note-Book

2 He who binds to himself a joy
  Doth the winged life destroy;
  But he who kisses the joy as it flies
  Lives in Eternity's sunrise.
  MS Note-Book 'Several Questions Answered'—"He who binds
  to himself a joy"

3 What is it men in women do require?
  The lineaments of gratified desire.
  What is it women do in men require?
  The lineaments of gratified desire.
  MS Note-Book 'Several Questions Answered'—"What is it men
  in women do require"

4 The sword sung on the barren heath,
  The sickle in the fruitful field:
  The sword he sung a song of death,
  But could not make the sickle yield.
  MS Note-Book

5 Never pain to tell thy love
  Love that never told can be;
  For the gentle wind does move
  Silently, invisibly.
  MS Note-Book

6 Piping down the valleys wild,
  Piping songs of pleasant glee,
  On a cloud I saw a child,
  And he laughing said to me.

  'Pipe a song about a Lamb!'
  So I piped with merry cheer.
  'Piper pipe that song again;'
  So I piped: he wept to hear.
  Songs of Innocence (1789) introduction

7 When my mother died I was very young,
  And my father sold me while yet my tongue
  Could scarcely cry "weep! 'weep! 'weep! 'weep!'
  So your chimneys I sweep, and in soot I sleep.
  Songs of Innocence (1789) 'The Chimney Sweeper'

8 To Mercy, Pity, Peace, and Love,
  All pray in their distress.
  Songs of Innocence (1789) 'The Divine Image'

9 For Mercy has a human heart,
  Pity a human face,
  And Love, the human form divine,
  And Peace, the human dress.
  Songs of Innocence (1789) 'The Divine Image'; see **BLAKE** 128:6

10 Then cherish pity, lest you drive an angel from
   your door.
   Songs of Innocence (1789) 'Holy Thursday'

11 Little Lamb who made thee?
   Dost thou know who made thee?
   Gave thee life and bid thee feed.
   By the stream and o'er the mead;
   Gave thee clothing of delight,
   Softest clothing woolly bright;
   Gave thee such a tender voice,
   Making all the vales rejoice!
   Songs of Innocence (1789) 'The Lamb'

12 My mother bore me in the southern wild,
   And I am black, but O! my soul is white;
   White as an angel is the English child:
   But I am black as if bereaved of light.
   Songs of Innocence (1789) 'The Little Black Boy'

13 When the voices of children are heard on the
   green
   And laughing is heard on the hill.
   Songs of Innocence (1789) 'Nurse's Song'

14 Can I see another's woe,
   And not be in sorrow too?
   Can I see another's grief,
   And not seek for kind relief?
   Songs of Innocence (1789) 'On Another's Sorrow'

15 Hear the voice of the Bard!
   Who present, past, and future, sees.
   Songs of Experience (1794) introduction

16 Ah, Sun-flower! weary of time,
   Who countest the steps of the Sun;
   Seeking after that sweet golden clime
   Where the traveller's journey is done.

   Where the Youth pined away with desire,
   And the pale Virgin shrouded in snow:
   Arise from their graves and aspire,
   Where my Sun-flower wishes to go.
   Songs of Experience (1794) 'Ah, Sun-flower!'

17 Love seeketh not itself to please,
   Nor for itself hath any care;
   But for another gives its ease,
   And builds a Heaven in Hell's despair.
   Songs of Experience (1794) 'The Clod and the Pebble'

18 Love seeketh only Self to please,
   To bind another to its delight,
   Joys in another's loss of ease,
   And builds a Hell in Heaven's despite.
   Songs of Experience (1794) 'The Clod and the Pebble'

19 Am not I
   A fly like thee?
   Or art not thou
   A man like me?
   Songs of Experience (1794) 'The Fly'

20 My mother groaned! my father wept.
   Into the dangerous world I leapt:
   Helpless, naked, piping loud;
   Like a fiend hid in a cloud.
   Songs of Experience (1794) 'Infant Sorrow'

21 Children of the future age,
   Reading this indignant page:
   Know that in a former time
   Love! sweet love! was thought a crime.
   Songs of Experience (1794) 'A Little Girl Lost'

22 I was angry with my friend;
   I told my wrath, my wrath did end.
   I was angry with my foe:
   I told it not, my wrath did grow.
   Songs of Experience (1794) 'A Poison Tree'

1 In the morning glad I see,
My foe outstretched beneath the tree
Songs of Experience (1794) 'A Poison Tree'

2 O Rose, thou art sick!
The invisible worm
That flies in the night,
In the howling storm:

Has found out thy bed
Of crimson joy:
And his dark secret love
Does thy life destroy.
Songs of Experience (1794) 'The Sick Rose'

3 Tyger Tyger, burning bright,
In the forests of the night;
What immortal hand or eye,
Could frame thy fearful symmetry?
Songs of Experience (1794) 'The Tiger'

4 What the hand dare seize the fire?

And what shoulder, and what art,
Could twist the sinews of thy heart?
And when thy heart began to beat,
What dread hand? and what dread feet?
Songs of Experience (1794) 'The Tiger'

5 When the stars threw down their spears
And watered heaven with their tears:
Did he smile his work to see?
Did he who made the Lamb make thee?
Songs of Experience (1794) 'The Tiger'

6 Cruelty has a human heart,
And Jealousy a human face;
Terror the human form divine,
And Secrecy the human dress.
'A Divine Image'; etched but not included in *Songs of Experience* (1794); see **BLAKE** 127:9

7 Vision or Imagination is a Representation of what Eternally Exists, Really and Unchangeably.
A Vision of the Last Judgement (1810) in *MS Note-Book*

8 What it will be questioned when the sun rises do you not see a round disc of fire somewhat like a guinea O no no I see an innumerable company of the heavenly host crying Holy, Holy, Holy is the Lord God Almighty.
A Vision of the Last Judgement (1810) in *MS Note-Book*; see **BIBLE** 118:5

9 He who has few things to desire cannot have many to fear.
Annotations to Bacon's 'Essays' (c. 1798); see **BACON** 46:26

10 Intuition of truth, not preceded by perceptible meditation, is genius.
Annotations to Lavater's 'Aphorisms on Man' (c.1788); see **LAVATER** 483:6

11 The tree which moves some to tears of joy is in the eyes of others only a green thing that stands in the way.
letter to Rev. Dr Trusler, 23 August 1799

12 The ruins of time build mansions in eternity.
letter to William Hayley, 6 May 1800

13 A tree filled with angels, bright wings bespangling every bough like stars.
Blake's first vision on Peckham Rye as a boy; see **BENÉT** 69:17
Alexander Gilchrist *The Life of William Blake* (1863)

Susanna Blamire 1747–94
English poet

14 I've gotten a rock, I've gotten a reel,
I've gotten a wee bit spinning-wheel;
An' by the whirling rim I've found
How the weary, weary warl goes round.
'I've Gotten a Rock, I've Gotten a Reel' (c.1790) l. 1

15 Should we miss but a tree where we used to be playing,
Or find the wood cut where we sauntered a-Maying,—
If the yew-seat's away, or the ivy's a-wanting,
We hate the fine lawn and the new-fashioned planting.
Each thing called improvement seems blackened with crimes,
If it tears up one record of blissful old times.
'When Home We Return' (c.1790) l. 7

Jean Joseph Louis Blanc 1811–82
French utopian socialist

16 In the Saint-Simonian doctrine, the problem of the distribution of benefits is resolved by this famous saying: *To each according to his ability; to each ability according to its fruits.*
Blanc cites Saint-Simon in order to disagree with his ideas
Organisation du travail (1841 ed.); see **MARX** 526:5, **MORELLY** 559:18

Lesley Blanch 1904–2007
English writer

17 She was an Amazon. Her whole life was spent riding at breakneck speed towards the wilder shores of love.
of Jane Digby El Mezrab (1807–81)
The Wilder Shores of Love (1954) pt. 2, ch. 1

Danny Blanchflower 1926–93
English footballer

18 The great fallacy is that the game is first and last about winning. It is nothing of the kind. The game is about glory, it is about doing things in style and with a flourish, about going out and beating the lot, not waiting for them to die of boredom.
attributed, 1972

Fanny Blankers-Koen 1918–2004
Dutch athlete

19 When I competed, no one ever thought it would be possible to make money from doing something you enjoyed so much.
quoted in *Independent* 27 January 2004 (obituary)

Philip Paul Bliss 1838–76
American evangelist

1 Hold the fort, for I am coming.
suggested by a flag message from General **SHERMAN**; *see* **SHERMAN** 749:8
Gospel Hymns and Sacred Songs (1875) no. 14

Hans Blix 1928–
Swedish diplomat

2 We have not found any smoking guns.
of weapons inspections in Iraq
in *Newsweek* 20 January 2003

Karen Blixen *see* Isak Dinesen

Alexander Blok 1880–1921
Russian poet

3 When rowan leaves are dank and rusting
And rowan berries red as blood,
When in my palm the hangman's thrusting
The final nail with bony thud . . .
Then, through the blood and weeping, stretches
My dying sight to space remote;
I see upon the river's reaches
Christ sailing to me in a boat.
'Autumn Love' (1907) (translated by Maurice Bowra)

4 The wind plays up; snow flutters down.
Twelve men are marching through the town.
'The Twelve' (1918) (translated by Jon Stallworthy and Peter France)

5 Caps tilted, fag drooping, every one
looks like a jailbird on the run.
'The Twelve' (1918) (translated by Jon Stallworthy and Peter France)

6 So they march with sovereign tread
Behind them limps the hungry dog,
and wrapped in wild snow at their head
carrying a blood-red flag—
soft-footed where the blizzard swirls,
invulnerable where bullets crossed—
crowned with a crown of snowflake pearls,
a flowery diadem of frost,
ahead of them goes Jesus Christ.
'The Twelve' (1918) (translated by Jon Stallworthy and Peter France)

Reginald Blomfield 1856–1942
English architect

7 Architecture should be at the head of the arts, not at the foot of the professions.
R. N. Shaw and T. G. Jackson (eds.) *Architecture* (1892)

Gebhard Lebrecht Blücher 1742–1819
Prussian field marshal

8 *Was für Plunder!*
What rubbish!
of London, as seen from the Monument in June 1814
Evelyn Princess Blücher *Memoirs of Prince Blücher* (1932); *see* **MISQUOTATIONS** 549:3

Judy Blume 1938–
American writer

9 Are you there God? It's me, Margaret.
I just told my mother I want a bra.
Please help me grow God. You know where.
I want to be like everyone else.
Are You There God? It's Me, Margaret (1970)

Edmund Blunden 1896–1974
English poet

10 All things they have in common being so poor,
And their one fear, Death's shadow at the door.
'Almswomen' (1920)

11 I am for the woods against the world,
But are the woods for me?
'The Kiss' (1931)

12 I have been young, and now am not too old;
And I have seen the righteous forsaken,
His health, his honour and his quality taken.
This is not what we were formerly told.
'Report on Experience' (1929); *see* **BOOK OF COMMON PRAYER** 141:25

13 This was my country and it may be yet,
But something flew between me and the sun.
'The Resignation' (1928)

Wilfrid Scawen Blunt 1840–1922
English poet

14 To the Grafton Gallery to look at . . . the Post-Impressionist pictures sent over from Paris . . . The drawing is on the level of that of an untaught child of seven or eight years old, the sense of colour that of a tea-tray painter, the method that of a schoolboy who wipes his fingers on a slate after spitting on them . . . These are not works of art at all, unless throwing a handful of mud against a wall may be called one. They are the works of idleness and impotent stupidity, a pornographic show.
My Diaries (1920) 15 November 1910

Robert Bly 1926–
American poet

15 Terror just before death,
Shoulders torn, shot
From helicopters, the boy
Tortured with the telephone generator,
'I felt sorry for him
And blew his head off with a shotgun.'
These instants become crystals,
Particles
The grass cannot dissolve. Our own gaiety
Will end up
In Asia, and in your cup you will look down
And see
Black Starfighters.
We were the ones we intended to bomb!
'Driving Through Minnesota During the Hanoi Bombings' (1968)

1 Alive, we are like a sleek black water beetle.
Skating across still water in any direction
We choose, and soon to be swallowed
Suddenly from beneath.
'Night' (1962)

2 Every modern male has, lying at the bottom of
his psyche, a large, primitive being covered with
hair down to his feet. Making contact with this
Wild Man is the step the Eighties male or the
Nineties male has yet to take.
Iron John (1990)

Ronald Blythe 1922–

English writer

3 An industrial worker would sooner have a £5
note but a countryman must have praise.
Akenfield (1969)

4 With full-span lives having become the norm,
people may need to learn how to be aged as
they once had to learn how to be adult.
The View in Winter (1979)

Boccaccio 1313–75

Italian writer, poet, and humanist

5 *E infinite volte avvenne che, andando due preti con
una croce per alcuno, si misero tre o quatro bare,
da'portatori portate, di dietro a quella: e, dove un
morto credevano avere i preti a seppilire, n'avevano
sei o otto e tal fiate pii.*

And times without number it happened that two
priests would be on their way to bury someone,
holding a cross before them, only to find that
bearers carrying three or four additional biers
would fall in behind them; so that whereas the
priests had thought they only had one burial to
attend to, they in fact had six or eight, and
sometimes more.
during the Black Death
Decameron (1348–58) introduction

6 *Fosse grandissime nelle quali a centinaia si
mettevano i sopravegnenti; e in quelle stivati, come si
mettono le mercantie nelle navi a suolo a suolo.*

They dug for each graveyard a huge trench, in
which they laid the corpses as they arrived by
hundreds at a time, piling them up tier upon tier
as merchandise is stowed in a ship.
Decameron (1348–58) introduction

7 *In tanto che molto volte nelle cose da lui fatte si
truova che il visivo denso degli uomini vi prese
errore, quello credendo esser vero che era dipinto.*

Mortal sight was often puzzled, face to face with
his creations, and took the painted thing for the
actual object.
of the painting of Giotto (c.1267–1337)
Decameron (1348–58) bk. 6

John Ernest Bode 1816–74

English clergyman

8 O Jesus, I have promised
To serve thee to the end;
Be thou for ever near me,
My Master and my Friend.
'O Jesus, I have promised' (1869 hymn); written for the
confirmation of Bode's three children

9 O let me hear thee speaking
In accents clear and still,
Above the storms of passion,
The murmurs of self-will.
'O Jesus, I have promised' (1869 hymn)

Ivan F. Boesky 1937–

American businessman

10 Greed is all right . . . Greed is healthy. You can
be greedy and still feel good about yourself.
commencement address, Berkeley, California, 18 May 1986;
see **FILM LINES** 328:10

Boethius c.AD 476–524

Roman statesman and philosopher

11 *Nam in omni adversitate fortunae infelicissimum est
genus infortunii, fuisse felicem.*

For in every ill-turn of fortune the most
unhappy sort of unfortunate man is the one
who has been happy.
De Consolatione Philosophiae bk. 2, prose 4; see **CHAUCER**
221:5, **DANTE** 264:18, **TENNYSON** 796:24

Louise Bogan 1897–1970

American poet

12 Women have no wilderness in them,
They are provident instead,
Content in the tight hot cell of their hearts
To eat dusty bread.
'Women' (1923)

Humphrey Bogart 1899–1957

American actor. See **CATCHPHRASES** 207:4, **FILM LINES**
328:11, **FILM LINES** 328:14, **FILM LINES** 329:13

13 PLEASE FENCE ME IN BABY THE WORLD'S TOO BIG OUT
HERE AND I DON'T LIKE IT WITHOUT YOU.
telegram to Lauren **BACALL**
Lauren Bacall *By Myself* (1978)

John B. Bogart *see* Charles A. Dana 264:3

Niels Bohr 1885–1962

Danish physicist and pioneer in quantum physics

14 Anybody who is not shocked by this subject has
failed to understand it.
of quantum mechanics
attributed; in *Nature* 23 August 1990

15 Never express yourself more clearly than you
think.
Abraham Pais *Einstein Lived Here* (1994)

1 One of the favourite maxims of my father was the distinction between the two sorts of truths, profound truths recognized by the fact that the opposite is also a profound truth, in contrast to trivialities where opposites are obviously absurd.
S. Rozental *Niels Bohr* (1967)

Nicolas Boileau 1636–1711
French critic and poet

2 *Enfin Malherbe vint, et, le premier en France,*
Fit sentir dans les vers une juste cadence.
At last came Malherbe, and he was the first in France to give poetry a proper flow.
L'Art poétique (1674) canto 1, l. 131

3 *Un sot trouve toujours un plus sot qui l'admire.*
A fool can always find a greater fool to admire him.
L'Art poétique (1674) canto 1, l. 232

4 *Qu'en un lieu, qu'en un jour, un seul fait accompli*
Tienne jusqu'à la fin le théâtre rempli.
Let a single completed action, all in one place, all in one day, keep the theatre packed to the end of your play.
L'Art poétique (1674) canto 3, l. 45

5 *Si j'écris quatre mots, j'en effacerai trois.*
Of every four words I write, I strike out three.
Satire (2). *A M. Molière* (1665)

Eavan Boland 1944–
Irish poet

6 Imagine how they stood there, what they stood with
that their possessions may become our power.
Cardboard. Iron. Their hardships parcelled in them.
'The Emigrant Irish' (1987)

7 I think of what great art removes:
Hazard and death, the future and the past.
'From the painting *Back from Market* by Chardin' (1967)

Alan Bold 1943–
Scottish poet

8 This happened near the core
Of a world's culture. This
Occurred among higher things.
This was a philosophical conclusion.
Everybody gets what he deserves.
'June 1967 at Buchenwald' (1969); see **ANONYMOUS** 22:14

9 Scotland, land of the omnipotent No.
'A Memory of Death' (1969)

10 Our job is to try
To change things.
After Hiroshima
You ask a poet to sing.
'Recitative' (1965)

Henry St John, Lord Bolingbroke
1678–1751
English politician, diplomatist, and author

11 They make truth serve as a stalking-horse to error.
Letters on the Study and Use of History (1752) No. 4, pt. 1

12 They [Thucydides and Xenophon] maintained the dignity of history.
Letters on the Study and Use of History (1752) No. 5, pt. 2

13 Nations, like men, have their infancy.
On the Study of History letter 5, in *Works* (1809) vol. 3

14 Truth lies within a little and certain compass, but error is immense.
Reflections upon Exile (1716)

15 What a world is this, and how does fortune banter us!
letter to Jonathan Swift, 3 August 1714, in Harold Williams (ed.) *Correspondence of Jonathan Swift* (1963) vol. 2

16 The great mistake is that of looking upon men as virtuous, or thinking that they can be made so by laws.
comment (c.1728), in Joseph Spence *Observations, Anecdotes, and Characters* (1820, ed. J. M. Osborn, 1966) Anecdote 882

Heinrich Böll 1917–85
German novelist and short-story writer

17 Soon can mean in one second, Soon can mean in one year. Soon is a terrible word. This Soon compresses the future, shrinks it, offers no certainty, no certainty whatever, it stands for absolute uncertainty. Soon is nothing and Soon is a lot. Soon is everything. Soon is death . . .
The Train was on Time (1949)

18 Happiness washes away many things, just as suffering washes away many things.
The Train was on Time (1949)

Robert Bolt 1924–95
English dramatist

19 A man for all seasons.
title of play (1960); see **WHITTINGTON** 853:5

20 This country's planted thick with laws from coast to coast—Man's laws, not God's—and if you cut them down—and you're just the man to do it—d'you really think you could stand upright in the winds that would blow then?
A Man for All Seasons (1960) act 1

21 It profits a man nothing to give his soul for the whole world . . . But for Wales—!
A Man for All Seasons (1960) act 2; see **BIBLE** 103:34

Edmund Bolton c.1575–c.1633
English poet

22 The withered primrose by the mourning river,
The faded summer's sun from weeping fountains,

The light-blown bubble vanished for ever,
The molten snow upon the naked mountains,
Are emblems that the treasures we up-lay
Soon wither, vanish, fade, and melt away.
'A Palinode' (1600)

Elizabeth Patterson Bonaparte
1785–1879

American-born wife of Jérôme Bonaparte, youngest brother
of **NAPOLEON I**

1 Even quarrels with one's husband are preferable
to the ennui of a solitary existence.
Eugene L. Didier *The Life and Letters of Madame Bonaparte*
(1879)

Laetitia Bonaparte 1750–1836

French mother of **NAPOLEON I**

2 *Pourvu que ça dure!*

Let's hope it lasts!
on her son **NAPOLEON I** *becoming Emperor, 1804*
attributed, possibly apocryphal

Andrew Bonar Law 1858–1923

Canadian-born British Conservative statesman, Prime
Minister 1922–3. On Bonar Law: see **ASQUITH** 34:6,
BEAVERBROOK 63:19

3 There are things stronger than parliamentary
majorities. I can imagine no length of resistance
to which Ulster will not go, in which I shall not
be ready to support them.
at a Unionist meeting at Blenheim in 1912
Robert Blake *The Unknown Prime Minister* (1955)

4 In war it is necessary not only to be active but
to seem active.
letter to Asquith, 1916; Robert Blake *The Unknown Prime
Minister* (1955)

5 If I am a great man, then all great men are
frauds.
Lord Beaverbrook *Politicians and the War* (1932)

St Bonaventura (Giovanni di Fidanza)
1221–74

Italian Franciscan theologian

6 Reason is the natural image of the Creator.
Itinerarium Mentis in Deum

Carrie Jacobs Bond 1862–1946

American songwriter

7 When you come to the end of a perfect day.
'A Perfect Day' (1910 song)

David Bone 1874–1959

Scottish naval officer and writer

8 It's 'Damn you, Jack — I'm all right!' with you
chaps.
Brassbounder (1910) ch. 3

Violet Bonham Carter 1887–1969

British Liberal politician

9 HOW DARE YOU BECOME PRIME MINISTER WHEN I'M
AWAY GREAT LOVE CONSTANT THOUGHT VIOLET.
telegram to her father, H. H. **ASQUITH**, *7 April 1908*
Mark Bonham Carter and Mark Pottle (eds.) *Lantern Slides*
(1996)

Dietrich Bonhoeffer 1906–45

German Lutheran theologian and martyr

10 I have come to the conclusion that I have made
a mistake in coming to America. I must live
through this difficult period of our national
history with the Christian people of Germany. I
shall have no right to participate in the
reconstruction of Christian life in Germany after
the war if I do not share the trials of this time
with my people.
letter to Reinhold Niebuhr, July 1939

11 In me there is darkness, but with you there is
light.
prayer written for fellow-prisoners in a Nazi prison, 1943
Letters and Papers from Prison (1971)

12 It is the nature, and the advantage, of strong
people that they can bring out the crucial
questions and form a clear opinion about them.
The weak always have to decide between
alternatives that are not their own.
Widerstand und Ergebung (Resistance and Submission, 1951)
'Ein paar Gedanken über Verschiedenes'

13 Jesus is there only for others . . . God in human
form! not . . . in the Greek divine-human form
of 'man in himself', but 'the man for others',
and therefore the crucified.
Widerstand und Ergebung (Resistance and Submission, 1951)
'Entwurf einer Arbeit'

St Boniface 680–754

Anglo-Saxon missionary

14 In your parishes, it is said, the evil of
drunkenness has greatly increased . . . This evil
indeed is peculiar to the heathen and to our
race. For neither the Franks, nor the Gauls, nor
the Lombards, nor the Romans, nor the Greeks
have it.
*letter to Cuthbert, Archbishop of Canterbury, 747; in The
English Correspondence of St Boniface* (1911)

The Book of Common Prayer 1662

15 It hath been the wisdom of the Church of
England, ever since the first compiling of her
Publick Liturgy, to keep the mean between the
two extremes, of too much stiffness in refusing,
and of too much easiness in admitting any
variation from it.
The Preface

1 There was never any thing by the wit of man so well devised, or so sure established, which in continuance of time hath not been corrupted.
The Preface Concerning the Service of the Church

2 Dearly beloved brethren, the Scripture moveth us in sundry places to acknowledge and confess our manifold sins and wickedness; and that we should not dissemble nor cloke them before the face of Almighty God our heavenly Father; but confess them with an humble, lowly, penitent, and obedient heart.
Morning Prayer Sentences of the Scriptures

3 I pray and beseech you, as many as are here present, to accompany me with a pure heart, and humble voice, unto the throne of the heavenly grace.
Morning Prayer Sentences of the Scriptures

4 We have erred, and strayed from thy ways like lost sheep. We have followed too much the devices and desires of our own hearts.
Morning Prayer General Confession

5 We have left undone those things which we ought to have done; And we have done those things which we ought not to have done; And there is no health in us.
Morning Prayer General Confession

6 Restore thou them that are penitent; According to thy promises declared unto mankind in Christ Jesu our Lord. And grant, O most merciful Father, for his sake; That we may hereafter live a godly, righteous, and sober life.
Morning Prayer General Confession

7 And forgive us our trespasses, As we forgive them that trespass against us.
Morning Prayer The Lord's Prayer; see **BIBLE** 99:12, **MISSAL** 549:17

8 Glory be to the Father, and to the Son: and to the Holy Ghost; As it was in the beginning, is now, and ever shall be: world without end. Amen.
Morning Prayer Gloria; see **MISSAL** 546:19

9 We praise thee, O God: we acknowledge thee to be the Lord.
All the earth doth worship thee: the Father everlasting.
To thee all Angels cry aloud: the Heavens, and all the Powers therein.
To thee Cherubin, and Seraphin: continually do cry,
Holy, Holy, Holy: Lord God of Sabaoth;
Heaven and earth are full of the Majesty: of thy Glory.
The glorious company of the Apostles: praise thee.
The goodly fellowship of the Prophets: praise thee.
The noble army of Martyrs: praise thee.
Morning Prayer Te Deum; see **PRAYERS** 623:8

10 When thou hadst overcome the sharpness of death: thou didst open the Kingdom of Heaven to all believers.
Morning Prayer Te Deum

11 Day by day: we magnify thee;
And we worship thy Name: ever world without end.
Vouchsafe, O Lord: to keep us this day without sin.
O Lord, have mercy upon us: have mercy upon us.
O Lord, let thy mercy lighten upon us: as our trust is in thee.
O Lord, in thee have I trusted: let me never be confounded.
Morning Prayer Te Deum; see **PRAYERS** 623:9

12 O all ye Works of the Lord, bless ye the Lord.
Morning Prayer Benedicite

13 O ye Waters that be above the Firmament, bless ye the Lord.
Morning Prayer Benedicite

14 O ye Showers, and Dew, bless ye the Lord: praise him, and magnify him for ever.
O ye Winds of God, bless ye the Lord: praise him, and magnify him for ever.
Morning Prayer Benedicite

15 O ye Dews, and Frosts, bless ye the Lord: praise him, and magnify him for ever.
O ye Frost and Cold, bless ye the Lord: praise him and magnify him for ever.
O ye Ice and Snow, bless ye the Lord: praise him and magnify him for ever.
O ye Nights, and Days, bless ye the Lord: praise him, and magnify him for ever.
Morning Prayer Benedicite

16 O let the Earth bless the Lord: yea, let it praise him, and magnify him for ever.
Morning Prayer Benedicite

17 O all ye Green Things upon the Earth, bless ye the Lord: praise him, and magnify him for ever.
Morning Prayer Benedicite

18 O ye Whales, and all that move in the Waters, bless ye the Lord: praise him, and magnify him for ever.
Morning Prayer Benedicite

19 I believe in God the Father Almighty, Maker of heaven and earth:
And in Jesus Christ his only Son our Lord, Who was conceived by the Holy Ghost, Born of the Virgin Mary, Suffered under Pontius Pilate, Was crucified, dead, and buried, He descended into hell; The third day he rose again from the dead, He ascended into heaven, And sitteth on the right hand of God the Father Almighty; From thence he shall come to judge the quick and the dead.
I believe in the Holy Ghost; The holy Catholic Church; The Communion of Saints; The

Forgiveness of sins; The Resurrection of the body, And the life everlasting. Amen.
Morning Prayer The Apostles' Creed; see **BOOK OF COMMON PRAYER** 137:2, **MISSAL** 549:11

1 Give peace in our time, O Lord.
Morning Prayer Versicle

2 O God, who art the author of peace and lover of concord, in knowledge of whom standeth our eternal life, whose service is perfect freedom; Defend us thy humble servants in all assaults of our enemies.
Morning Prayer The Second Collect, for Peace

3 Grant that this day we fall into no sin, neither run into any kind of danger.
Morning Prayer The Third Collect, for Grace

4 In Quires and Places where they sing, here followeth the Anthem.
Morning Prayer rubric following Third Collect

5 Endue her plenteously with heavenly gifts; grant her in health and wealth long to live.
Morning Prayer Prayer for the Queen's Majesty

6 Almighty God, the fountain of all goodness.
Morning Prayer Prayer for the Royal Family

7 Almighty and everlasting God, who alone workest great marvels; Send down upon our Bishops, and Curates, and all Congregations committed to their charge, the healthful Spirit of thy grace; and that they may truly please thee, pour upon them the continual dew of thy blessing.
Morning Prayer Prayer for the Clergy and People

8 Almighty God, who hast given us grace at this time with one accord to make our common supplications unto thee; and dost promise, that when two or three are gathered together in thy Name thou wilt grant their requests: Fulfil now, O Lord, the desires and petitions of thy servants, as may be most expedient for them.
Morning Prayer Prayer of St Chrysostom

9 O God, from whom all holy desires, all good counsels, and all just works do proceed; Give unto thy servants that peace which the world cannot give.
Evening Prayer Second Collect

10 Lighten our darkness, we beseech thee, O Lord; and by thy great mercy defend us from all perils and dangers of this night.
Evening Prayer Third Collect

11 Whosoever will be saved: before all things it is necessary that he hold the Catholic Faith.
At Morning Prayer Athanasian Creed 'Quicunque vult'

12 And the Catholic Faith is this: That we worship one God in Trinity, and Trinity in Unity; Neither confounding the Persons: nor dividing the Substance.
At Morning Prayer Athanasian Creed 'Quicunque vult'

13 There are not three incomprehensibles, nor three uncreated: but one uncreated, and one incomprehensible.
At Morning Prayer Athanasian Creed 'Quicunque vult'

14 Perfect God, and perfect Man: of a reasonable soul and human flesh subsisting;
Equal to the Father, as touching his Godhead: and inferior to the Father, as touching his Manhood.
At Morning Prayer Athanasian Creed 'Quicunque vult'

15 Have mercy upon us miserable sinners.
The Litany

16 From all evil and mischief; from sin, from the crafts and assaults of the devil; from thy wrath, and from everlasting damnation,
Good Lord, deliver us.
The Litany

17 From envy, hatred, and malice, and from all uncharitableness,
Good Lord, deliver us.
The Litany

18 From all the deceits of the world, the flesh, and the devil,
Good Lord, deliver us.
The Litany

19 From lightning and tempest; from plague, pestilence, and famine; from battle and murder, and from sudden death,
Good Lord, deliver us.
The Litany; see **NASHE** 569:3

20 By thine Agony and bloody Sweat; by thy Cross and Passion; by thy precious Death and Burial; by thy glorious Resurrection and Ascension; and by the coming of the Holy Ghost,
Good Lord, deliver us.
The Litany

21 In all time of our tribulation; in all time of our wealth; in the hour of death, and in the day of judgement,
Good Lord, deliver us.
The Litany

22 That it may please thee to illuminate all Bishops, Priests, and Deacons, with true knowledge and understanding of thy Word; and that both by their preaching and living they may set it forth, and show it accordingly;
We beseech thee to hear us, good Lord.
The Litany

23 That it may please thee to strengthen such as do stand; and to comfort and help the weak-hearted; and to raise up them that fall; and finally to beat down Satan under our feet;
We beseech thee to hear us, good Lord.
The Litany

24 That it may please thee to preserve all that travel by land or by water, all women labouring of child, all sick persons, and young children; and to shew thy pity upon all prisoners and captives;

We beseech thee to hear us, good Lord.
The Litany; see **SWIFT** 783:7

1 Defend, and provide for, the fatherless children, and widows, and all that are desolate and oppressed.
The Litany

2 That it may please thee to give and preserve to our use the kindly fruits of the earth, so as in due time we may enjoy them;
We beseech thee to hear us, good Lord.
The Litany

3 O God, merciful Father, that despisest not the sighing of a contrite heart, not the desire of such as be sorrowful; Mercifully assist our prayers that we make before thee in all our troubles and adversities, whensoever they oppress us.
The Litany

4 O God, whose nature and property is ever to have mercy and to forgive, receive our humble petitions; and though we be tied and bound with the chain of our sins, yet let the pitifulness of thy great mercy loose us; for the honour of Jesus Christ, our Mediator and Advocate.
Prayers . . . upon Several Occasions A prayer

5 O God, the Creator and Preserver of all mankind, we humbly beseech thee for all sorts and conditions of men.
Prayers . . . upon Several Occasions 'Collect or Prayer for all Conditions of Men'

6 We pray for the good estate of the Catholick Church; that it may be so guided and governed by thy good Spirit, that all who profess and call themselves Christians may be led into the way of truth.
Prayers . . . upon Several Occasions 'Collect or Prayer for all Conditions of Men'

7 We commend to thy fatherly goodness all those, who are any ways afflicted, or distressed, in mind, body, or estate; that it may please thee to comfort and relieve them, according to their several necessities, giving them patience under their sufferings, and a happy issue out of all their afflictions.
Prayers . . . upon Several Occasions 'Collect or Prayer for all Conditions of Men'

8 We bless thee for our creation, preservation, and all the blessings of this life; but above all, for thine inestimable love in the redemption of the world by our Lord Jesus Christ; for the means of grace, and for the hope of glory.
Thanksgivings General Thanksgiving

9 O God our heavenly Father, who by thy gracious providence dost cause the former and the latter rain to descend upon the earth, that it may bring forth fruit for the use of man; We give thee humble thanks that it hath pleased thee, in our great necessity, to send us at the last a joyful rain upon thine inheritance, and to refresh it when it was dry.
Thanksgivings For Rain

10 Almighty God, give us grace that we may cast away the works of darkness, and put upon us the armour of light, now in the time of this mortal life, in which thy Son Jesus Christ came to visit us in great humility.
Collects The first Sunday in Advent

11 Blessed Lord, who hast caused all holy Scriptures to be written for our learning; Grant that we may in such wise hear them, read, mark, learn, and inwardly digest them, that by patience, and comfort of thy holy Word, we may embrace, and ever hold fast the blessed hope of everlasting life.
Collects The second Sunday in Advent

12 That whereas, through our sins and wickedness, we are sore let and hindered in running the race that is set before us, thy bountiful grace and mercy may speedily help and deliver us.
Collects The fourth Sunday in Advent

13 O Lord, we beseech thee mercifully to receive the prayers of thy people which call upon thee; and grant that they may both perceive and know what things they ought to do, and also may have grace and power faithfully to fulfil the same.
Collects The first Sunday after the Epiphany

14 O God, who knowest us to be set in the midst of so many and great dangers, that by reason of the frailty of our nature we cannot always stand upright; Grant to us such strength and protection, as may support us in all dangers, and carry us through all temptations.
Collects The fourth Sunday after the Epiphany

15 Almighty and everlasting God, who hatest nothing that thou hast made, and dost forgive the sins of all them that are penitent.
Collects Ash Wednesday

16 Almighty God, who seest that we have no power of ourselves to help ourselves; Keep us both outwardly in our bodies, and inwardly in our souls; that we may be defended from all adversities which may happen to the body, and from all evil thoughts which may assault and hurt the soul.
Collects The second Sunday in Lent

17 We humbly beseech thee, that, as by thy special grace preventing us thou dost put into our minds good desires, so by thy continued help we may bring the same to good effect.
Collects Easter-Day

18 Grant us so to put away the leaven of malice and wickedness, that we may alway serve thee in pureness of living and truth.
Collects The first Sunday after Easter

19 O Almighty God, who alone canst order the unruly wills and affections of sinful men; Grant unto thy people, that they may love the thing

which thou commandest, and desire that which thou dost promise; that so, among the sundry and manifold changes of the world, our hearts may surely there be fixed, where true joys are to be found.
Collects The fourth Sunday after Easter

1 We beseech thee, leave us not comfortless; but send to us thine Holy Ghost to comfort us, and exalt us unto the same place whither our Saviour Christ is gone before.
Collects Sunday after Ascension Day

2 God, who as at this time didst teach the hearts of thy faithful people, by the sending to them the light of thy Holy Spirit; Grant us by the same Spirit to have a right judgement in all things.
Collects Whit-Sunday

3 Because through the weakness of our mortal nature we can do no good thing without thee, grant us the help of thy grace, that in keeping of thy commandments we may please thee, both in will and deed.
Collects The first Sunday after Trinity

4 O God, the protector of all that trust in thee, without whom nothing is strong, nothing is holy; Increase and multiply upon us thy mercy; that, thou being our ruler and guide, we may so pass through things temporal, that we finally lose not the things eternal.
Collects The fourth Sunday after Trinity

5 Grant, O Lord, we beseech thee, that the course of this world may be so peaceably ordered by thy governance, that thy Church may joyfully serve thee in all godly quietness.
Collects The fifth Sunday after Trinity

6 O God, who hast prepared for them that love thee such good things as pass man's understanding; Pour into our hearts such love toward thee, that we, loving thee above all things, may obtain thy promises, which exceed all that we can desire.
Collects The sixth Sunday after Trinity

7 Lord of all power and might, who art the author and giver of all good things; Graft in our hearts the love of thy Name, increase in us true religion, nourish us with all goodness, and of thy great mercy keep us in the same.
Collects The seventh Sunday after Trinity

8 Pour down upon us the abundance of thy mercy; forgiving us those things whereof our conscience is afraid.
Collects The twelfth Sunday after Trinity

9 O God, forasmuch as without thee we are not able to please thee; Mercifully grant, that thy Holy Spirit may in all things direct and rule our hearts.
Collects The nineteenth Sunday after Trinity

10 Grant, we beseech thee, merciful Lord, to thy faithful people pardon and peace, that they may be cleansed from all their sins, and serve thee with a quiet mind.
Collects The one and twentieth Sunday after Trinity

11 Lord, we beseech thee to keep thy household the Church in continual godliness.
Collects The two and twentieth Sunday after Trinity

12 Grant that those things which we ask faithfully we may obtain effectually.
Collects The three and twentieth Sunday after Trinity

13 Stir up, we beseech thee, O Lord, the wills of thy faithful people; that they, plenteously bringing forth the fruit of good works, may of thee be plenteously rewarded.
Collects The five and twentieth Sunday after Trinity

14 Give us grace, that, being not like children carried away with every blast of vain doctrine, we may be established in the truth of thy holy Gospel.
Collects St Mark's Day

15 O Almighty God, who hast knit together thine elect in one communion and fellowship, in the mystical body of thy Son Christ our Lord; Grant us grace so to follow thy blessed Saints in all virtuous and godly living, that we may come to those unspeakable joys, which thou hast prepared for them that unfeignedly love thee.
Collects All Saints' Day

16 And if any of those be an open and notorious evil liver, or have done any wrong to his neighbours by word or deed, so that the Congregation be thereby offended; the Curate, having knowledge thereof, shall call him and advertise him, that in any wise he presume not to come to the Lord's Table.
Holy Communion introductory rubric

17 Until he have openly declared himself to have truly repented and amended his former naughty life.
Holy Communion introductory rubric

18 The Table, at the Communion-time having a fair white linen cloth upon it, shall stand in the Body of the Church, or in the Chancel.
Holy Communion introductory rubric

19 Almighty God, unto whom all hearts be open, all desires known, and from whom no secrets are hid; Cleanse the thoughts of our hearts by the inspiration of thy Holy Spirit, that we may perfectly love thee, and worthily magnify thy holy Name.
Holy Communion The Collect

20 I the Lord thy God am a jealous God, and visit the sins of the fathers upon the children unto the third and fourth generation of them that hate me.
the phrase 'sins of the fathers' is also used in the Douay/ Rheims Bible (1609) in Numbers ch. 14, v. 18
Holy Communion The Ten Commandments; see **BIBLE** 81:16

21 Incline our hearts to keep this law.
Holy Communion The Ten Commandments (response)

1 Thou shalt do no murder.
Holy Communion The Ten Commandments; see **BIBLE** 81:20

2 I believe in one God the Father Almighty, Maker of heaven and earth, And of all things visible and invisible:
And in one Lord Jesus Christ, the only-begotten Son of God, Begotten of his Father before all worlds, God of God, Light of Light, Very God of very God, Begotten, not made, Being of one substance with the Father, By whom all things were made.
Holy Communion Nicene Creed; see **BOOK OF COMMON PRAYER** 133:19, **MISSAL** 549:11

3 And I believe in the Holy Ghost, the Lord and giver of life, Who proceedeth from the Father and the Son, Who with the Father and the Son together is worshipped and glorified, Who spake by the Prophets. And I believe one Catholick and Apostolick Church.
Holy Communion Nicene Creed; see **MISSAL** 549:11

4 Let us pray for the whole state of Christ's Church militant here in earth.
Holy Communion Prayer for the Church Militant

5 We humbly beseech thee most mercifully to accept our alms and oblations, and to receive these our prayers, which we offer unto thy Divine Majesty; beseeching thee to inspire continually the universal Church with the spirit of truth, unity, and concord: And grant, that all they that do confess thy holy Name may agree in the truth of thy holy Word, and live in unity, and godly love.
Holy Communion Prayer for the Church Militant

6 Grant unto her [the Queen's] whole Council, and to all that are put in authority under her, that they may truly and indifferently minister justice.
Holy Communion Prayer for the Church Militant

7 Give grace, O heavenly Father, to all Bishops and Curates, that they may both by their life and doctrine set forth thy true and lively Word.
Holy Communion Prayer for the Church Militant

8 We most humbly beseech thee of thy goodness, O Lord, to comfort and succour all them, who in this transitory life are in trouble, sorrow, need, sickness, or any other adversity. And we also bless thy holy Name for all thy servants departed this life in thy faith and fear.
Holy Communion Prayer for the Church Militant

9 Ye that do truly and earnestly repent you of your sins, and are in love and charity with your neighbours, and intend to lead a new life, following the commandments of God, and walking from henceforth in his holy ways; Draw near with faith, and take this holy Sacrament to your comfort; and make your humble confession to Almighty God, meekly kneeling upon your knees.
Holy Communion The Invitation

10 We do earnestly repent, And are heartily sorry for these our misdoings; The remembrance of them is grievous unto us; The burden of them is intolerable.
Holy Communion General Confession

11 Hear what comfortable words our Saviour Christ saith unto all that truly turn to him.
Holy Communion Comfortable Words (preamble)

12 Lift up your hearts.
Holy Communion versicles and responses; see **MISSAL** 549:14

13 It is meet and right so to do.
Holy Communion versicles and responses

14 It is very meet, right, and our bounden duty, that we should at all times, and in all places, give thanks unto thee, O Lord, Holy Father, Almighty, Everlasting God.
Therefore with Angels and Archangels, and with all the company of heaven, we laud and magnify thy glorious Name; evermore praising thee, and saying, Holy, holy, holy, Lord God of hosts, heaven and earth are full of thy glory: Glory be to thee, O Lord most High.
Holy Communion Hymn of Praise; see **BIBLE** 118:5, **MISSAL** 549:16

15 Almighty God, our heavenly Father, who of thy tender mercy didst give thine only Son Jesus Christ to suffer death upon the cross for our redemption; who made there (by his one oblation of himself once offered) a full, perfect, and sufficient sacrifice, oblation, and satisfaction, for the sins of the whole world.
Holy Communion Prayer of Consecration

16 Who, in the same night that he was betrayed, took Bread; and, when he had given thanks, he brake it, and gave it to his disciples, saying, Take, eat, this is my Body which is given for you: Do this in remembrance of me. Likewise after supper he took the Cup; and, when he had given thanks, he gave it to them, saying, Drink ye all of this; for this is my Blood of the New Testament, which is shed for you and for many for the remission of sins: Do this, as oft as ye shall drink it, in remembrance of me.
Holy Communion Prayer of Consecration

17 Although we be unworthy, through our manifold sins, to offer unto thee any sacrifice, yet we beseech thee to accept this our bounden duty and service; not weighing our merits, but pardoning our offences.
Holy Communion First Prayer of Oblation

18 We are very members incorporate in the mystical body of thy Son, which is the blessed company of all faithful people; and are also heirs through hope of thy everlasting kingdom.
'Father of all, We give you thanks and praise, that when we were still far off you met us in your Son and brought us home. Dying and living, he declared your love, gave us grace, and opened the gate of glory' in Alternative Service Book *Post-Communion prayer*
Holy Communion Second (alternative) Prayer of Oblation

1 The blessing of God Almighty, the Father, the Son, and the Holy Ghost, be amongst you and remain with you always.
Holy Communion The Blessing

2 Assist us mercifully, O Lord, in these our supplications and prayers, and dispose the way of thy servants towards the attainment of everlasting salvation; that, among all the changes and chances of this mortal life, they may ever be defended by thy most gracious and ready help.
Holy Communion Collects after the Offertory

3 Prevent us, O Lord, in all our doings with thy most gracious favour, and further us with thy continual help; that in all our works, begun, continued, and ended in thee, we may glorify thy holy Name.
Holy Communion Collects after the Offertory

4 Those things, which for our unworthiness we dare not, and for our blindness we cannot ask, vouchsafe to give us, for the worthiness of thy Son Jesus Christ our Lord.
Holy Communion Collects after the Offertory

5 It is expedient that Baptism be administered in the vulgar tongue.
Public Baptism of Infants introductory rubric

6 O merciful God, grant that the old Adam in this Child may be so buried, that the new man may be raised up in him.
Public Baptism of Infants Invocation of blessing on the child

7 It is your part and duty also . . . to walk answerably to your Christian calling, and as becometh the children of light.
Baptism of Such as are of Riper Years Priest's final address

8 QUESTION: Who gave you this Name?
ANSWER: My Godfathers and Godmothers in my Baptism; wherein I was made a member of Christ, the child of God, and an inheritor of the kingdom of heaven.
Catechism

9 I should renounce the devil and all his works, the pomps and vanity of this wicked world, and all the sinful lusts of the flesh.
Catechism

10 QUESTION: What dost thou chiefly learn by these Commandments?
ANSWER: I learn two things: my duty towards God, and my duty to my Neighbour.
Catechism

11 My duty towards my Neighbour, is to love him as myself, and to do to all men, as I would they should do unto me.
Catechism

12 To submit myself to all my governors, teachers, spiritual pastors and masters.
Catechism

13 To keep my hands from picking and stealing, and my tongue from evil-speaking, lying, and slandering.
Catechism

14 Not to covet nor desire other men's goods; but to learn and labour truly to get mine own living, and to do my duty in that state of life, unto which it shall please God to call me.
Catechism

15 QUESTION: How many Sacraments hath Christ ordained in his Church?
ANSWER: Two only, as generally necessary to salvation, that is to say, Baptism, and the Supper of the Lord.
QUESTION: What meanest thou by this word *Sacrament*?
ANSWER: I mean an outward and visible sign of an inward and spiritual grace.
Catechism

16 Our help is in the name of the Lord;
Who hath made heaven and earth.
Order of Confirmation

17 Lord, hear our prayers.
And let our cry come unto thee.
Order of Confirmation

18 Defend, O Lord, this thy Child [*or* this thy Servant] with thy heavenly grace, that he may continue thine for ever; and daily increase in thy holy Spirit more and more, until he come unto thy everlasting kingdom.
Order of Confirmation

19 If any of you know cause, or just impediment, why these two persons should not be joined together in holy Matrimony, ye are to declare it. This is the first [*second*, or *third*] time of asking.
Solemnization of Matrimony The Banns

20 Dearly beloved, we are gathered together here in the sight of God, and in the face of this congregation, to join together this Man and this Woman in holy Matrimony.
Solemnization of Matrimony Exhortation

21 Which holy estate Christ adorned and beautified with his presence, and first miracle that he wrought, in Cana of Galilee; and is commended of Saint Paul to be honourable among all men: and therefore not by any to be enterprised, nor taken in hand, unadvisedly, lightly, or wantonly, to satisfy men's carnal lusts and appetites, like brute beasts that have no understanding.
Solemnization of Matrimony Exhortation

22 First, It was ordained for the procreation of children, to be brought up in the fear and nurture of the Lord, and to the praise of his holy Name.
Solemnization of Matrimony Exhortation

23 If any man can shew any just cause, why they may not lawfully be joined together, let him now speak, or else hereafter for ever hold his peace.
Solemnization of Matrimony Exhortation

24 Wilt thou have this Woman to thy wedded wife, to live together after God's ordinance in the holy estate of Matrimony? Wilt thou love her,

THE BOOK OF COMMON PRAYER

comfort her, honour, and keep her in sickness and in health; and, forsaking all other, keep thee only unto her, so long as ye both shall live?
Solemnization of Matrimony Betrothal

1 I *N.* take thee *M.* to my wedded husband, to have and to hold from this day forward, for better for worse, for richer for poorer, in sickness and in health, to love, cherish, and to obey, till death us do part, according to God's holy ordinance; and thereto I give thee my troth.
the man having used the words 'I plight thee my troth' and not having promised 'to obey'; the woman may also omit the promise 'to obey'
Solemnization of Matrimony Betrothal

2 With this Ring I thee wed, with my body I thee worship, and with all my worldly goods I thee endow.
'All that I am I give to you, and all that I have I share with you' in the Alternative Service Book
Solemnization of Matrimony Wedding

3 Those whom God hath joined together let no man put asunder.
Solemnization of Matrimony Wedding; see **BIBLE** 102:5

4 Forasmuch as *M.* and *N.* have consented together in holy wedlock, and have witnessed the same before God and this company, and thereto have given and pledged their troth either to other, and have declared the same by giving and receiving of a Ring, and by joining of hands; I pronounce that they be Man and Wife together.
Solemnization of Matrimony Minister's Declaration

5 Peace be to this house, and to all that dwell in it.
The Visitation of the Sick

6 Unto God's gracious mercy and protection we commit thee.
The Visitation of the Sick

7 The Office ensuing is not to be used for any that die unbaptized, or excommunicate, or have laid violent hands upon themselves.
The Burial of the Dead introductory rubric

8 Man that is born of a woman hath but a short time to live, and is full of misery.
The Burial of the Dead First Anthem; see **BIBLE** 86:30

9 In the midst of life we are in death.
The Burial of the Dead First Anthem; see **MUMFORD** 565:1

10 Forasmuch as it hath pleased Almighty God of his great mercy to take unto himself the soul of our dear brother here departed, we therefore commit his body to the ground; earth to earth, ashes to ashes, dust to dust; in sure and certain hope of the Resurrection to eternal life, through our Lord Jesus Christ; who shall change our vile body, that it may be like unto his glorious body, according to the mighty working, whereby he is able to subdue all things to himself.
The Burial of the Dead Interment

11 Blessed is the man that hath not walked in the counsel of the ungodly, nor stood in the way of sinners: and hath not sat in the seat of the scornful.
Psalm 1, v. 1

12 Why do the heathen so furiously rage together: and why do the people imagine a vain thing?
Psalm 2, v. 1

13 Thou shalt bruise them with a rod of iron: and break them in pieces like a potter's vessel.
Psalm 2, v. 9

14 Blessed are all they that put their trust in him.
Psalm 2, v. 12

15 Stand in awe, and sin not: commune with your own heart, and in your chamber, and be still.
Psalm 4, v. 4

16 Lord, lift thou up: the light of thy countenance upon us.
Psalm 4, v. 7

17 I will lay me down in peace, and take my rest.
Psalm 4, v. 9

18 Make thy way plain before my face.
Psalm 5, v. 8

19 Let them perish through their own imaginations.
Psalm 5, v. 11

20 I am weary of my groaning; every night wash I my bed: and water my couch with my tears.
Psalm 6, v. 6

21 Away from me, all ye that work vanity.
Psalm 6, v. 8

22 Out of the mouth of very babes and sucklings hast thou ordained strength, because of thine enemies.
*Psalm 8, v. 2; see **PROVERBS** 641:27*

23 What is man, that thou art mindful of him: and the son of man, that thou visitest him?
Thou madest him lower than the angels: to crown him with glory and worship.
Psalm 8, v. 4

24 Up, Lord, and let not man have the upper hand.
Psalm 9, v. 19

25 He that said in his heart, Tush, I shall never be cast down: there shall no harm happen unto me.
Psalm 10, v. 6

26 Upon the ungodly he shall rain snares, fire and brimstone, storm and tempest: this shall be their portion to drink.
Psalm 11, v. 7

27 How long wilt thou forget me, O Lord, for ever: how long wilt thou hide thy face from me?
Psalm 13, v. 1

28 The fool hath said in his heart: There is no God. They are corrupt, and become abominable in their doings: there is none that doeth good, no not one.
Psalm 14, v. 1

29 They are all gone out of the way, they are altogether become abominable.
Psalm 14, v. 4

1 Lord, who shall dwell in thy tabernacle: or who shall rest upon thy holy hill?
Even he, that leadeth an uncorrupt life: and doeth the thing which is right, and speaketh the truth from his heart.
He that hath used no deceit in his tongue, nor done evil to his neighbour: and hath not slandered his neighbour.
Psalm 15, v. 1

2 He that sweareth unto his neighbour, and disappointeth him not: though it were to his own hindrance.
He that hath not given his money upon usury: nor taken reward against the innocent.
Whoso doeth these things: shall never fall.
Psalm 15, v. 5

3 The lot is fallen unto me in a fair ground: yea, I have a goodly heritage.
'The lines are fallen unto me in pleasant places' in the Bible (Authorized Version, 1611) Psalm 16, v. 6
Psalm 16, v. 7

4 Thou shalt not leave my soul in hell: neither shalt thou suffer thy Holy One to see corruption.
Psalm 16, v. 11

5 He rode upon the cherubims, and did fly: he came flying upon the wings of the wind.
Psalm 18, v. 10

6 At the brightness of his presence his clouds removed: hailstones, and coals of fire.
Psalm 18, v. 12

7 With the help of my God I shall leap over the wall.
Psalm 18, v. 29; see **BIBLE** 84:22

8 The heavens declare the glory of God: and the firmament sheweth his handy-work.
Psalm 19, v. 1

9 There is neither speech nor language: but their voices are heard among them.
Their sound is gone out into all lands: and their words into the ends of the world.
In them hath he set a tabernacle for the sun: which cometh forth as a bridegroom out of his chamber, and rejoiceth as a giant to run his course.
Psalm 19, v. 3

10 The statutes of the Lord are right, and rejoice the heart: the commandment of the Lord is pure, and giveth light unto the eyes.
Psalm 19, v. 8

11 The judgements of the Lord are true, and righteous altogether.
More to be desired are they than gold, yea, than much fine gold: sweeter also than honey, and the honey-comb.
Psalm 19, v. 10; see **LINCOLN** 494:5

12 Let the words of my mouth, and the meditation of my heart: be alway acceptable in thy sight, O Lord: my strength, and my redeemer.
Psalm 19, v. 14

13 Some put their trust in chariots, and some in horses: but we will remember the Name of the Lord our God.
Psalm 20, v. 7

14 They intended mischief against thee: and imagined such a device as they are not able to perform.
Psalm 21, v. 11

15 My God, my God, look upon me; why hast thou forsaken me: and art so far from my health, and from the words of my complaint?
O my God, I cry in the day-time, but thou hearest not: and in the night-season also I take no rest.
Psalm 22, v. 1

16 But as for me, I am a worm, and no man: a very scorn of men, and the out-cast of the people.
All they that see me laugh me to scorn: they shoot out their lips, and shake their heads, saying,
He trusted in God, that he would deliver him: let him deliver him, if he will have him.
Psalm 22, v. 6

17 Many oxen are come about me: fat bulls of Basan close me in on every side.
Psalm 22, v. 12

18 I am poured out like water, and all my bones are out of joint: my heart also in the midst of my body is even like melting wax.
Psalm 22, v. 14

19 They pierced my hands and my feet; I may tell all my bones: they stand staring and looking upon me.
They part my garments among them: and cast lots upon my vesture.
Psalm 22, v. 17

20 The Lord is my shepherd: therefore can I lack nothing.
He shall feed me in a green pasture: and lead me forth beside the waters of comfort.
'The Lord is my shepherd; I shall not want. / He maketh me to lie down in green pastures: he leadeth me beside the still waters' in the Bible (Authorized Version, 1611)
Psalm 23, v. 1; see **HERBERT** 395:1, **SCOTTISH METRICAL PSALMS** 690:9

21 Yea, though I walk through the valley of the shadow of death, I will fear no evil: for thou art with me; thy rod and thy staff comfort me.
Thou shalt prepare a table before me against them that trouble me: thou hast anointed my head with oil, and my cup shall be full.
But thy loving-kindness and mercy shall follow me all the days of my life: and I will dwell in the house of the Lord for ever.
Psalm 23, v. 4; see **SCOTTISH METRICAL PSALMS** 690:9

1 The earth is the Lord's, and all that therein is: the compass of the world, and they that dwell therein.
'The earth is the Lord's, and the fulness thereof' in the Bible (Authorized Version, 1611)
Psalm 24, v. 1

2 Lift up your heads, O ye gates, and be ye lift up, ye everlasting doors: and the King of glory shall come in.
Who is the King of glory: it is the Lord strong and mighty, even the Lord mighty in battle.
Psalm 24, v. 7

3 Even the Lord of hosts, he is the King of glory.
Psalm 24, v. 10

4 O remember not the sins and offences of my youth.
Psalm 25, v. 6

5 Deliver Israel, O God: out of all his troubles.
Psalm 25, v. 21

6 Examine me, O Lord, and prove me: try out my reins and my heart.
Psalm 26, v. 2

7 I will wash my hands in innocency, O Lord: and so will I go to thine altar;
That I may shew the voice of thanksgiving: and tell of all thy wondrous works.
Psalm 26, v. 6

8 My foot standeth right: I will praise the Lord in the congregation.
Psalm 26, v. 12

9 The Lord is my light, and my salvation; whom then shall I fear: the Lord is the strength of my life; of whom then shall I be afraid?
Psalm 27, v. 1; see **BIBLE (VULGATE)** 119:25

10 Teach me thy way, O Lord: and lead me in the right way, because of mine enemies.
Psalm 27, v. 13

11 I should utterly have fainted: but that I believe verily to see the goodness of the Lord in the land of the living.
Psalm 27, v. 15

12 The voice of the Lord breaketh the cedar-trees: yea, the Lord breaketh the cedars of Libanus.
He maketh them also to skip like a calf: Libanus also, and Sirion, like a young unicorn.
Psalm 29, v. 5

13 The Lord shall give strength unto his people: the Lord shall give his people the blessing of peace.
Psalm 29, v. 10

14 Heaviness may endure for a night, but joy cometh in the morning.
Psalm 30, v. 5

15 Into thy hands I commend my spirit.
Psalm 31, v. 6; see **BIBLE** 106:26

16 Blessed is the man unto whom the Lord imputeth no sin: and in whose spirit there is no guile.

For while I held my tongue: my bones consumed away through my daily complaining.
Psalm 32, v. 2

17 Great plagues remain for the ungodly: but whoso putteth his trust in the Lord, mercy embraceth him on every side.
Psalm 32, v. 11

18 Sing unto the Lord a new song: sing praises lustily unto him with a good courage.
Psalm 33, v. 3

19 O taste and see, how gracious the Lord is: blessed is the man that trusteth in him.
Psalm 34, v. 8

20 The lions do lack, and suffer hunger: but they who seek the Lord shall want no manner of thing that is good.
Psalm 34, v. 10

21 Keep thy tongue from evil: and thy lips, that they speak no guile.
Eschew evil, and do good: seek peace, and ensue it.
Psalm 34, v. 13

22 They rewarded me evil for good: to the great discomfort of my soul.
Psalm 35, v. 12

23 O deliver my soul from the calamities which they bring on me, and my darling from the lions.
Psalm 35, v. 17

24 Fret not thyself because of the ungodly.
Psalm 37, v. 1

25 I have been young, and now am old: and yet saw I never the righteous forsaken, nor his seed begging their bread.
Psalm 37, v. 25; see **BLUNDEN** 129:12

26 I myself have seen the ungodly in great power: and flourishing like a green bay-tree.
Psalm 37, v. 36

27 I held my tongue, and spake nothing: I kept silence, yea, even from good words; but it was pain and grief to me.
Psalm 39, v. 3

28 Lord, let me know mine end, and the number of my days: that I may be certified how long I have to live.
Psalm 39, v. 5

29 For man walketh in a vain shadow, and disquieteth himself in vain: he heapeth up riches, and cannot tell who shall gather them.
Psalm 39, v. 7

30 I waited patiently for the Lord: and he inclined unto me, and heard my calling.
He brought me also out of the horrible pit, out of the mire and clay: and set my feet upon the rock, and ordered my goings.
Psalm 40, v. 1

31 In the volume of the book it is written of me, that I should fulfil thy will, O my God.
Psalm 40, v. 10

1 Thou art my helper and redeemer: make no long tarrying, O my God.
Psalm 40, v. 21

2 Blessed is he that considereth the poor and needy: the Lord shall deliver him in the time of trouble.
Psalm 41, v. 1

3 Yea, even mine own familiar friend, whom I trusted: who did also eat of my bread, hath laid great wait for me.
'. . . hath lifted up his heel against me' in the Bible (Authorized Version, 1611)
Psalm 41, v. 9

4 Like as the hart desireth the water-brooks: so longeth my soul after thee, O God.
My soul is a thirst for God, yea, even for the living God.
'As the hart panteth after the water brooks, so panteth my soul after thee, O God. / My soul thirsteth for God, the living God' in the Bible (Authorized Version, 1611)
Psalm 42, v. 1; see TATE 790:14

5 Why art thou so full of heaviness, O my soul: and why art thou so disquieted within me?
Psalm 42, v. 6

6 One deep calleth another, because of the noise of the water-pipes: all thy waves and storms are gone over me.
Psalm 42, v. 9

7 I will say unto the God of my strength, Why hast thou forgotten me: why go I thus heavily, while the enemy oppresseth me?
My bones are smitten asunder as with a sword: while mine enemies that trouble me cast me in the teeth;
Namely, while they say daily unto me: Where is now thy God?
Psalm 42, v. 11

8 Give sentence with me, O God, and defend my cause against the ungodly people: O deliver me from the deceitful and wicked man.
Psalm 43, v. 1

9 O send out thy light and thy truth, that they may lead me: and bring me unto thy holy hill, and to thy dwelling.
And that I may go unto the altar of God, even unto the God of my joy and gladness: and upon the harp will I give thanks unto thee, O God, my God.
Psalm 43, v. 3

10 O put thy trust in God: for I will yet give him thanks, which is the help of my countenance, and my God.
Psalm 43, v. 6

11 We have heard with our ears, O God, our fathers have told us: what thou hast done in their time of old.
Psalm 44, v. 1

12 My heart is inditing of a good matter: I speak of the things which I have made unto the King.

My tongue is the pen: of a ready writer.
Psalm 45, v. 1; see BIBLE (VULGATE) 119:26

13 Thou hast loved righteousness, and hated iniquity: wherefore God, even thy God, hath anointed thee with the oil of gladness above thy fellows.
Psalm 45, v. 8

14 Kings' daughters were among thy honourable women: upon thy right hand did stand the queen in a vesture of gold, wrought about with divers colours.
Psalm 45, v. 10

15 The King's daughter is all glorious within: her clothing is of wrought gold.
Psalm 45, v. 14

16 Instead of thy fathers thou shalt have children: whom thou mayest make princes in all lands.
Psalm 45, v. 17

17 God is our hope and strength: a very present help in trouble. Therefore will we not fear, though the earth be moved: and though the hills be carried into the midst of the sea.
Psalm 46, v. 1; see ANONYMOUS 16:3

18 The heathen make much ado, and the kingdoms are moved: but God hath shewed his voice, and the earth shall melt away.
The Lord of hosts is with us: the God of Jacob is our refuge.
Psalm 46, v. 6

19 He maketh wars to cease in all the world: he breaketh the bow, and knappeth the spear in sunder, and burneth the chariots in the fire.
Be still then, and know that I am God: I will be exalted among the heathen, and I will be exalted in the earth.
Psalm 46, v. 9

20 O clap your hands together, all ye people: O sing unto God with the voice of melody.
Psalm 47, v. 1

21 He shall subdue the people under us: and the nations under our feet.
Psalm 47, v. 3

22 God is gone up with a merry noise: and the Lord with the sound of the trump.
Psalm 47, v. 5

23 For lo, the kings of the earth: are gathered, and gone by together.
They marvelled to see such things: they were astonished, and suddenly cast down.
Psalm 48, v. 3

24 Thou shalt break the ships of the sea: through the east-wind.
Psalm 48, v. 6

25 Walk about Sion, and go round about her: and tell the towers thereof.
Mark well her bulwarks, set up her houses: that ye may tell them that come after.
Psalm 48, v. 11

1 Man will not abide in honour: seeing he may be compared unto the beasts that perish.
Psalm 49, v. 12

2 All the beasts of the forest are mine: and so are the cattle upon a thousand hills.
Psalm 50, v. 10

3 Thinkest thou that I will eat bulls' flesh: and drink the blood of goats?
Psalm 50, v. 13

4 Wash me throughly from my wickedness: and cleanse me from my sin.
For I acknowledge my faults: and my sin is ever before me.
Against thee only have I sinned, and done this evil in thy sight.
Psalm 51, v. 2

5 Behold, I was shapen in wickedness: and in sin hath my mother conceived me.
Psalm 51, v. 5

6 Thou shalt purge me with hyssop, and I shall be clean: thou shalt wash me, and I shall be whiter than snow.
Thou shalt make me hear of joy and gladness: that the bones which thou hast broken may rejoice.
Psalm 51, v. 7; see **BIBLE (VULGATE)** 119:27

7 Make me a clean heart, O God: and renew a right spirit within me.
Cast me not away from thy presence: and take not thy holy Spirit from me.
O give me the comfort of thy help again: and stablish me with thy free Spirit.
Psalm 51, v. 10

8 Deliver me from blood-guiltiness, O God.
Psalm 51, v. 14

9 Thou shalt open my lips, O Lord: and my mouth shall shew thy praise.
For thou desirest no sacrifice, else would I give it thee: but thou delightest not in burnt-offerings.
The sacrifice of God is a troubled spirit: a broken and contrite heart, O God, shalt thou not despise.
O be favourable and gracious unto Sion: build thou the walls of Jerusalem.
Psalm 51, v. 15

10 O that I had wings like a dove: for then would I flee away, and be at rest.
Psalm 55, v. 6

11 It was even thou, my companion: my guide, and mine own familiar friend.
We took sweet counsel together: and walked in the house of God as friends.
Psalm 55, v. 14

12 The words of his mouth were softer than butter, having war in his heart: his words were smoother than oil, and yet they be very swords.
Psalm 55, v. 22

13 Thou tellest my flittings; put my tears into thy bottle: are not these things noted in thy book?
Psalm 56, v. 8

14 Under the shadow of thy wings shall be my refuge, until this tyranny be over-past.
Psalm 57, v. 1

15 God shall send forth his mercy and truth: my soul is among lions.
And I lie even among the children of men, that are set on fire: whose teeth are spears and arrows, and their tongue a sharp sword.
Set up thyself, O God, above the heavens: and thy glory above all the earth.
Psalm 57, v. 4

16 They have laid a net for my feet, and pressed down my soul: they have digged a pit before me, and are fallen into the midst of it themselves.
Psalm 57, v. 7

17 Awake up, my glory; awake, lute and harp: I myself will awake right early.
Psalm 57, v. 9

18 They are as venomous as the poison of a serpent: even like the deaf adder that stoppeth her ears;
Which refuseth to hear the voice of the charmer: charm he never so wisely.
Psalm 58, v. 4

19 Gilead is mine, and Manasses is mine: Ephraim also is the strength of my head; Judah is my law-giver;
Philistia, be thou glad of me.
Psalm 60, v. 7

20 Moab is my wash-pot; over Edom will I cast out my shoe.
Psalm 60, v. 8

21 Their delight is in lies; they give good words with their mouth, but curse with their heart.
Psalm 62, v. 4

22 As for the children of men, they are but vanity: the children of men are deceitful upon the weights, they are altogether lighter than vanity itself.
O trust not in wrong and robbery, give not yourselves unto vanity: if riches increase, set not your heart upon them.
Psalm 62, v. 9

23 God spake once, and twice I have also heard the same: that power belongeth unto God;
And that thou, Lord, art merciful: for thou rewardest every man according to his work.
Psalm 62, v. 11

24 My soul thirsteth for thee, my flesh also longeth after thee: in a barren and dry land where no water is.
Psalm 63, v. 2

25 These also that seek the hurt of my soul: they shall go under the earth.

Let them fall upon the edge of the sword: that they may be a portion for foxes.
Psalm 63, v. 10

1 Thou, O God, art praised in Sion: and unto thee shall the vow be performed in Jerusalem.
Thou that hearest the prayer: unto thee shall all flesh come.
Psalm 65, v. 1

2 Thou that art the hope of all the ends of the earth, and of them that remain in the broad sea.
Who in his strength setteth fast the mountains: and is girded about with power.
Who stilleth the raging of the sea: and the noise of his waves, and the madness of the people.
Psalm 65, v. 5

3 Thou crownest the year with thy goodness: and thy clouds drop fatness.
They shall drop upon the dwellings of the wilderness: and the little hills shall rejoice on every side.
The folds shall be full of sheep: the valleys also shall stand so thick with corn, that they shall laugh and sing.
Psalm 65, v. 12

4 God be merciful unto us, and bless us: and shew us the light of his countenance, and be merciful unto us;
That thy way may be known upon earth: thy saving health among all nations.
Let the people praise thee, O God: yea, let all the people praise thee.
Psalm 67, v. 1

5 Then shall the earth bring forth her increase: and God, even our own God, shall give us his blessing.
Psalm 67, v. 6

6 Let God arise, and let his enemies be scattered: let them also that hate him flee before him.
Psalm 68, v. 1

7 O sing unto God, and sing praises unto his name: magnify him that rideth upon the heavens, as it were upon an horse; praise him in his name JAH, and rejoice before him.
He is a Father of the fatherless, and defendeth the cause of the widows: even God in his holy habitation.
He is the God that maketh men to be of one mind in an house, and bringeth the prisoners out of captivity: but letteth the runagates continue in scarceness.
O God, when thou wentest forth before the people: when thou wentest through the wilderness,
The earth shook, and the heavens dropped at the presence of God.
Psalm 68, v. 4

8 The Lord gave the word: great was the company of the preachers.
Kings with their armies did flee, and were discomfited: and they of the household divided the spoil.
Though ye have lien among the pots, yet shall ye be as the wings of a dove: that is covered with silver wings, and her feathers like gold.
Psalm 68, v. 11

9 Why hop ye so, ye high hills? this is God's hill, in which it pleaseth him to dwell.
Psalm 68, v. 16

10 Thou art gone up on high, thou hast led captivity captive, and received gifts for men.
Psalm 68, v. 18

11 The zeal of thine house hath even eaten me.
Psalm 69, v. 9

12 Thy rebuke hath broken my heart; I am full of heaviness: I looked for some to have pity on me, but there was no man, neither found I any to comfort me.
They gave me gall to eat: and when I was thirsty they gave me vinegar to drink.
Psalm 69, v. 21

13 Let their habitation be void: and no man to dwell in their tents.
Psalm 69, v. 26

14 Let them be wiped out of the book of the living: and not be written among the righteous.
Psalm 69, v. 29

15 Let them be ashamed and confounded that seek after my soul: let them be turned backward and put to confusion that wish me evil.
Let them for their reward be soon brought to shame: that cry over me, There, there.
Psalm 70, v. 2

16 I am become as it were a monster unto many: but my sure trust is in thee.
Psalm 71, v. 6

17 Cast me not away in the time of age: forsake me not when my strength faileth me.
Psalm 71, v. 8

18 The mountains also shall bring peace: and the little hills righteousness unto the people.
Psalm 72, v. 3

19 His dominion shall be also from the one sea to the other: and from the flood unto the world's end.
They that dwell in the wilderness shall kneel before him: his enemies shall lick the dust.
The Kings of Tharsis and of the isles shall give presents: the kings of Arabia and Saba shall bring gifts.
All kings shall fall down before him: all nations shall do him service.
Psalm 72, v. 8

20 He shall live, and unto him shall be given of the gold of Arabia.
Psalm 72, v. 15

21 Then thought I to understand this: but it was too hard for me.

Until I went into the sanctuary of God: then understood I the end of these men.
Psalm 73, v. 15

1 O deliver not the soul of thy turtle-dove unto the multitude of the enemies: and forget not the congregation of the poor for ever.
Psalm 74, v. 20

2 For promotion cometh neither from the east, nor from the west: nor yet from the south.
Psalm 75, v. 7

3 In Jewry is God known: his Name is great in Israel.
At Salem is his tabernacle: and his dwelling in Sion.
Psalm 76, v. 1

4 I have considered the days of old: and the years that are past.
Psalm 77, v. 5

5 Hear my law, O my people: incline your ears unto the words of my mouth.
I will open my mouth in a parable: I will declare hard sentences of old;
Which we have heard and known: and such as our fathers have told us.
Psalm 78, v. 1

6 Not to be as their forefathers, a faithless and stubborn generation: a generation that set not their heart aright, and whose spirit cleaveth not stedfastly unto God.
Psalm 78, v. 9

7 He divided the sea, and let them go through: he made the waters to stand on an heap.
Psalm 78, v. 14

8 He rained down manna also upon them for to eat: and gave them food from heaven.
So man did eat angels' food: for he sent them meat enough.
Psalm 78, v. 25

9 So the Lord awaked as one out of sleep: and like a giant refreshed with wine.
Psalm 78, v. 66

10 Turn us again, O God: shew the light of thy countenance, and we shall be whole.
Psalm 80, v. 3

11 Sing we merrily unto God our strength: make a cheerful noise unto the God of Jacob.
Take the psalm, bring hither the tabret: the merry harp with the lute.
Blow up the trumpet in the new-moon: even in the time appointed, and upon our solemn feast-day.
Psalm 81, v. 1

12 I have said, Ye are gods: and ye are all children of the most Highest.
But ye shall die like men: and fall like one of the princes.
Psalm 82, v. 6

13 O how amiable are thy dwellings: thou Lord of hosts!

My soul hath a desire and longing to enter into the courts of the Lord: my heart and my flesh rejoice in the living God.
Yea, the sparrow hath found her an house, and the swallow a nest where she may lay her young: even thy altars, O Lord of hosts, my King and my God.
Psalm 84, v. 1; see **SCOTTISH METRICAL PSALMS** 690:10

14 Blessed is the man whose strength is in thee: in whose heart are thy ways.
Who going through the vale of misery use it for a well: and the pools are filled with water.
They will go from strength to strength.
Psalm 84, v. 5

15 For one day in thy courts: is better than a thousand.
I had rather be a door-keeper in the house of my God: than to dwell in the tents of ungodliness.
Psalm 84, v. 10

16 Wilt thou not turn again, and quicken us: that thy people may rejoice in thee?
Psalm 85, v. 6

17 Mercy and truth are met together: righteousness and peace have kissed each other.
Truth shall flourish out of the earth: and righteousness hath looked down from heaven.
Psalm 85, v. 10

18 Very excellent things are spoken of thee: thou city of God.
Psalm 87, v. 2

19 Lord, thou hast been our refuge: from one generation to another.
Before the mountains were brought forth, or ever the earth and the world were made: thou art God from everlasting, and world without end.
Psalm 90, v. 1

20 For a thousand years in thy sight are but as yesterday: seeing that is past as a watch in the night.
As soon as thou scatterest them they are even as a sleep: and fade away suddenly like the grass.
In the morning it is green, and groweth up: but in the evening it is cut down, dried up, and withered.
Psalm 90, v. 4

21 The days of our age are threescore years and ten; and though men be so strong that they come to fourscore years: yet is their strength then but labour and sorrow; so soon passeth it away, and we are gone.
Psalm 90, v. 10

22 So teach us to number our days: that we may apply our hearts unto wisdom.
Psalm 90, v. 12

23 For he shall deliver thee from the snare of the hunter and from the noisome pestilence.

He shall defend thee under his wings, and thou shalt be safe under his feathers: his faithfulness and truth shall be thy shield and buckler.
Psalm 91, v. 3

1 Thou shalt not be afraid for any terror by night: nor for the arrow that flieth by day;
For the pestilence that walketh in darkness: nor for the sickness that destroyeth in the noon-day.
A thousand shall fall beside thee, and ten thousand at thy right hand: but it shall not come nigh thee.
Psalm 91, v. 5

2 For thou, Lord, art my hope: thou hast set thine house of defence very high.
There shall no evil happen unto thee: neither shall any plague come nigh thy dwelling.
For he shall give his angels charge over thee: to keep thee in all thy ways.
They shall bear thee in their hands: that thou hurt not thy foot against a stone.
Thou shalt go upon the lion and adder: the young lion and the dragon shalt thou tread under thy feet.
Psalm 91, v. 9

3 With long life will I satisfy him: and shew him my salvation.
Psalm 91, v. 16

4 The Lord is King, and hath put on glorious apparel: the Lord hath put on his apparel, and girded himself with strength.
He hath made the round world so sure: that it cannot be moved.
Psalm 93, v. 1

5 The floods are risen, O Lord, the floods have lift up their voice: the floods lift up their waves.
The waves of the sea are mighty, and rage horribly: but yet the Lord, who dwelleth on high, is mightier.
Thy testimonies, O Lord, are very sure: holiness becometh thine house for ever.
Psalm 93, v. 4

6 He that planted the ear, shall he not hear: or he that made the eye, shall he not see?
Psalm 94, v. 9

7 O come, let us sing unto the Lord: let us heartily rejoice in the strength of our salvation.
Let us come before his presence with thanksgiving: and shew ourselves glad in him with psalms.
Psalm 95, v. 1

8 In his hand are all the corners of the earth: and the strength of the hills is his also.
The sea is his, and he made it: and his hands prepared the dry land.
O come, let us worship and fall down: and kneel before the Lord our Maker.
For he is the Lord our God: and we are the people of his pasture, and the sheep of his hand.
To-day if ye will hear his voice, harden not your hearts: as in the provocation, and as in the day of temptation in the wilderness;
When your fathers tempted me: proved me, and saw my works.
Forty years long was I grieved with this generation, and said It is a people that do err in their hearts, for they have not known my ways;
Unto whom I sware in my wrath: that they should not enter into my rest.
Psalm 95, v. 4

9 Ascribe unto the Lord the honour due unto his Name: bring presents, and come into his courts.
O worship the Lord in the beauty of holiness: let the whole earth stand in awe of him.
Psalm 96, v. 8

10 The Lord is King, the earth may be glad thereof: yea, the multitude of the isles may be glad thereof.
Psalm 97, v. 1

11 O sing unto the Lord a new song: for he hath done marvellous things.
With his own right hand, and with his holy arm: hath he gotten himself the victory.
Psalm 98, v. 1; see **BIBLE (VULGATE)** 119:29

12 Praise the Lord upon the harp: sing to the harp with a psalm of thanksgiving.
With trumpets also, and shawms: O shew yourselves joyful before the Lord the King.
Psalm 98, v. 6

13 With righteousness shall he judge the world: and the people with equity.
Psalm 98, v. 10

14 The Lord is King, be the people never so impatient: he sitteth between the cherubims, be the earth never so unquiet.
Psalm 99, v. 1

15 O be joyful in the Lord, all ye lands: serve the Lord with gladness, and come before his presence with a song.
Be ye sure that the Lord he is God: it is he that hath made us, and not we ourselves; we are his people, and the sheep of his pasture.
Psalm 100, v. 1; see **BIBLE (VULGATE)** 120:1

16 I am become like a pelican in the wilderness: and like an owl that is in the desert.
I have watched, and am even as it were a sparrow: that sitteth alone upon the house-top.
Psalm 102, v. 6

17 Thou, Lord, in the beginning hast laid the foundation of the earth: and the heavens are the work of thy hands.
They shall perish, but thou shalt endure: they all shall wax old as doth a garment;
And as a vesture shalt thou change them, and they shall be changed: but thou art the same, and thy years shall not fail.
Psalm 102, v. 25

18 Praise the Lord, O my soul: and forget not all his benefits.
Psalm 103, v. 2

1 The Lord is full of compassion and mercy: long-suffering, and of great goodness.
He will not alway be chiding: neither keepeth he his anger for ever.
Psalm 103, v. 8

2 For look how high the heaven is in comparison of the earth: so great is his mercy also toward them that fear him.
Look how wide also the east is from the west: so far hath he set our sins from us.
Yea, like as a father pitieth his own children: even so is the Lord merciful unto them that fear him.
For he knoweth whereof we are made: he remembereth that we are but dust.
Psalm 103, v. 11

3 The days of man are but as grass: for he flourisheth as a flower of a field.
For as soon as the wind goeth over it, it is gone: and the place thereof shall know it no more.
Psalm 103, v. 15

4 Who layeth the beams of his chambers in the waters: and maketh the clouds his chariot, and walketh upon the wings of the wind.
He maketh his angels spirits: and his ministers a flaming fire.
He laid the foundations of the earth: that it never should move at any time.
Thou coveredst it with the deep like as with a garment: the waters stand in the hills.
Psalm 104, v. 3

5 Thou hast set them their bounds which they shall not pass: neither turn again to cover the earth.
He sendeth the springs into the rivers: which run among the hills.
All beasts of the field drink thereof: and the wild asses quench their thirst.
Beside them shall the fowls of the air have their habitation: and sing among the branches.
Psalm 104, v. 9

6 He bringeth forth grass for the cattle: and green herb for the service of men;
That he may bring food out of the earth, and wine that maketh glad the heart of man: and oil to make him a cheerful countenance, and bread to strengthen man's heart.
The trees of the Lord also are full of sap: even the cedars of Libanus which he hath planted.
Psalm 104, v. 14

7 The high hills are a refuge for the wild goats: and so are the stony rocks for the conies.
He appointed the moon for certain seasons: and the sun knoweth his going down.
Psalm 104, v. 18

8 Thou makest darkness that it may be night: wherein all the beasts of the forest do move.
The lions roaring after their prey: do seek their meat from God.
Psalm 104, v. 20

9 There go the ships, and there is that Leviathan: whom thou hast made to take his pastime therein.
Psalm 104, v. 26

10 The earth shall tremble at the look of him: if he do but touch the hills, they shall smoke.
Psalm 104, v. 32

11 He had sent a man before them: even Joseph, who was sold to be a bond-servant;
Whose feet they hurt in the stocks: the iron entered into his soul.
Psalm 105, v. 17

12 The king sent, and delivered him: the prince of the people let him go free.
He made him lord also of his house: and ruler of all his substance;
That he might inform his princes after his will: and teach his senators wisdom.
Psalm 105, v. 20

13 Yea, they thought scorn of that pleasant land: and gave no credence to his word;
But murmured in their tents: and hearkened not unto the voice of the Lord.
Psalm 106, v. 24

14 Thus were they stained with their own works: and went a whoring with their own inventions.
Psalm 106, v. 38

15 Such as sit in darkness, and in the shadow of death: being fast bound in misery and iron.
Psalm 107, v. 10

16 Their soul abhorred all manner of meat: and they were even hard at death's door.
Psalm 107, v. 18

17 They that go down to the sea in ships: and occupy their business in great waters;
These men see the works of the Lord: and his wonders in the deep.
Psalm 107, v. 23

18 They reel to and fro, and stagger like a drunken man: and are at their wit's end.
So when they cry unto the Lord in their trouble: he delivereth them out of their distress.
For he maketh the storm to cease: so that the waves thereof are still.
Then are they glad, because they are at rest: and so he bringeth them unto the haven where they would be.
Psalm 107, v. 27

19 The Lord said unto my Lord: Sit thou on my right hand, until I make thine enemies thy footstool.
Psalm 110, v. 1

20 Thou art a Priest for ever after the order of Melchisedech.
Psalm 110, v. 4

21 The fear of the Lord is the beginning of wisdom: a good understanding have all they that do thereafter; the praise of it endureth for ever.
Psalm 111, v. 10

1 A good man is merciful, and lendeth: and will guide his words with discretion.
For he shall never be moved: and the righteous shall be had in everlasting remembrance.
Psalm 112, v. 5

2 He maketh the barren woman to keep house: and to be a joyful mother of children.
Psalm 113, v. 8

3 When Israel came out of Egypt: and the house of Jacob from among the strange people,
Judah was his sanctuary: and Israel his dominion.
The sea saw that, and fled: Jordan was driven back.
The mountains skipped like rams: and the little hills like young sheep.
Psalm 114, v. 1

4 Not unto us, O Lord, not unto us, but unto thy Name give the praise.
Psalm 115, v. 1; see **BIBLE (VULGATE)** 120:3

5 They have mouths, and speak not: eyes have they, and see not.
They have ears, and hear not: noses have they, and smell not.
They have hands, and handle not: feet have they, and walk not: neither speak they through their throat.
Psalm 115, v. 5

6 The snares of death compassed me round about: and the pains of hell gat hold upon me.
Psalm 116, v. 3

7 And why? thou hast delivered my soul from death: mine eyes from tears, and my feet from falling.
Psalm 116, v. 8

8 I said in my haste, All men are liars.
Psalm 116, v. 10

9 I will pay my vows now in the presence of all his people: right dear in the sight of the Lord is the death of his saints.
Psalm 116, v. 13

10 The right hand of the Lord hath the pre-eminence: the right hand of the Lord bringeth mighty things to pass.
Psalm 118, v. 16

11 The same stone which the builders refused: is become the head-stone in the corner.
This is the Lord's doing: and it is marvellous in our eyes.
This is the day which the Lord hath made: we will rejoice and be glad in it.
Psalm 118, v. 22

12 Blessed be he that cometh in the Name of the Lord: we have wished you good luck, ye that are of the house of the Lord.
Psalm 118, v. 26

13 The law of thy mouth is dearer unto me: than thousands of gold and silver.
Psalm 119, v. 72

14 Thy word is a lantern unto my feet: and a light unto my paths.
Psalm 119, v. 105

15 Woe is me that I am constrained to dwell with Mesech: and to have my habitation among the tents of Kedar.
Psalm 120, v. 4

16 I labour for peace, but when I speak unto them therof: they make them ready to battle.
Psalm 120, v. 6

17 I will lift up mine eyes unto the hills: from whence cometh my help.
My help cometh even from the Lord: who hath made heaven and earth.
He will not suffer thy foot to be moved: and he that keepeth thee will not sleep.
Behold, he that keepeth Israel: shall neither slumber nor sleep.
The Lord himself is thy keeper: the Lord is thy defence upon thy right hand;
So that the sun shall not burn thee by day: neither the moon by night.
Psalm 121, v. 1; see **SCOTTISH METRICAL PSALMS** 690:11

18 The Lord shall preserve thy going out, and thy coming in: from this time forth for evermore.
Psalm 121, v. 8

19 I was glad when they said unto me: We will go into the house of the Lord.
Our feet shall stand in thy gates: O Jerusalem.
Jerusalem is built as a city: that is at unity in itself.
For thither the tribes go up, even the tribes of the Lord.
Psalm 122, v. 1

20 O pray for the peace of Jerusalem: they shall prosper that love thee.
Peace be within thy walls: and plenteousness with thy palaces.
Psalm 122, v. 6

21 If the Lord himself had not been on our side, now may Israel say: if the Lord himself had not been on our side, when men rose up against us;
They had swallowed us up quick: when they were so wrathfully displeased at us.
Psalm 124, v. 1

22 Our soul is escaped even as a bird out of the snare of the fowler: the snare is broken, and we are delivered.
Our help standeth in the Name of the Lord: who hath made heaven and earth.
Psalm 124, v. 6; see **BOOK OF COMMON PRAYER** 138:16

23 The hills stand about Jerusalem: even so standeth the Lord round about his people, from this time forth for evermore.
Psalm 125, v. 2

24 When the Lord turned again the captivity of Sion: then were we like unto them that dream.

Then was our mouth filled with laughter: and our tongue with joy.
> Psalm 126, v. 1

1 Turn our captivity, O Lord: as the rivers in the south.
They that sow in tears: shall reap in joy.
He that now goeth on his way weeping, and beareth forth good seed: shall doubtless come again with joy, and bring his sheaves with him.
> Psalm 126, v. 5

2 Except the Lord build the house: their labour is but lost that build it.
Except the Lord keep the city: the watchman waketh but in vain.
> Psalm 127, v. 1; see **BIBLE (VULGATE)** 120:5

3 Like as the arrows in the hand of the giant: even so are the young children.
Happy is the man that hath his quiver full of them: they shall not be ashamed when they speak with their enemies in the gate.
> Psalm 127, v. 5

4 Thy wife shall be as the fruitful vine: upon the walls of thine house.
Thy children like the olive-branches: round about thy table.
> Psalm 128, v. 3

5 Many a time have they fought against me from my youth up: may Israel now say.
> Psalm 129, v. 1

6 But they have not prevailed against me.
The plowers plowed upon my back: and made long furrows.
> Psalm 129, v. 2

7 Out of the deep have I called unto thee, O Lord: Lord, hear my voice.
O let thine ears consider well: the voice of my complaint.
If thou, Lord, wilt be extreme to mark what is done amiss: O Lord, who may abide it?
> Psalm 130, v. 1; see **BIBLE (VULGATE)** 120:6

8 My soul fleeth unto the Lord: before the morning watch, I say, before the morning watch.
> Psalm 130, v. 6

9 Lord, I am not high-minded: I have no proud looks.
I do not exercise myself in great matters: which are too high for me.
> Psalm 131, v. 1

10 Behold, how good and joyful a thing it is: brethren, to dwell together in unity!
> Psalm 133, v. 1

11 He smote divers nations: and slew mighty kings;
Sehon king of the Amorites, and Og the king of Basan: and all the kingdoms of Canaan;
And gave their land to be an heritage: even an heritage unto Israel his people.
> Psalm 135, v. 10

12 O give thanks unto the Lord, for he is gracious: and his mercy endureth for ever.
> Psalm 136, v. 1; see **MILTON** 540:1

13 By the waters of Babylon we sat down and wept: when we remembered thee, O Sion.
As for our harps, we hanged them up: upon the trees that are therein.
> Psalm 137, v. 1

14 How shall we sing the Lord's song: in a strange land?
If I forget thee, O Jerusalem: let my right hand forget her cunning.
> Psalm 137, v. 4

15 O Lord, thou hast searched me out, and known me: thou knowest my down-sitting, and mine up-rising; thou understandest my thoughts long before.
> Psalm 139, v. 1

16 Such knowledge is too wonderful and excellent for me: I cannot attain unto it.
> Psalm 139, v. 5

17 If I climb up into the heaven, thou art there: if I go down to hell, thou art there also.
If I take the wings of the morning: and remain in the uttermost parts of the sea;
Even there also shall thy hand lead me: and thy right hand shall hold me.
> Psalm 139, v. 7

18 I will give thanks unto thee, for I am fearfully and wonderfully made.
> Psalm 139, v. 13

19 Thine eyes did see my substance, yet being imperfect: and in thy book were all my members written;
Which day by day were fashioned: when as yet there were none of them.
> Psalm 139, v. 15

20 Try me, O God, and seek the ground of my heart: prove me, and examine my thoughts.
> Psalm 139, v. 23

21 Let the lifting up of my hands be an evening sacrifice.
Set a watch, O Lord, before my mouth: and keep the door of my lips.
> Psalm 141, v. 2

22 Let the ungodly fall into their own nets together: and let me ever escape them.
> Psalm 141, v. 11

23 Enter not into judgement with thy servant: for in thy sight shall no man living be justified.
> Psalm 143, v. 2

24 Save me, and deliver me from the hand of strange children: whose mouth talketh of vanity, and their right hand is a right hand of iniquity.
That our sons may grow up as the young plants: and that our daughters may be as the polished corners of the temple.
> Psalm 144, v. 11

1 The Lord upholdeth all such as fall: and lifteth up all those that are down.
Psalm 145, v. 14

2 Thou givest them their meat in due season. Thou openest thine hand: and fillest all things living with plenteousness.
Psalm 145, v. 15

3 O put not your trust in princes, nor in any child of man: for there is no help in them.
Psalm 146, v. 2

4 The Lord looseth men out of prison: the Lord giveth sight to the blind.
Psalm 146, v. 7

5 The Lord careth for the strangers; he defendeth the fatherless and widow: as for the way of the ungodly, he turneth it upside down.
Psalm 146, v. 9

6 A joyful and pleasant thing it is to be thankful. The Lord doth build up Jerusalem: and gather together the out-casts of Israel.
He healeth those that are broken in heart: and giveth medicine to heal their sickness.
He telleth the number of the stars: and calleth them all by their names.
Psalm 147, v. 1

7 He hath no pleasure in the strength of an horse: neither delighteth he in any man's legs.
Psalm 147, v. 10

8 He giveth snow like wool: and scattereth the hoar-frost like ashes.
He casteth forth his ice like morsels: who is able to abide his frost?
Psalm 147, v. 16

9 Praise the Lord upon earth: ye dragons, and all deeps;
Fire and hail, snow and vapours: wind and storm, fulfilling his word.
Psalm 148, v. 7

10 Young men and maidens, old men and children, praise the Name of the Lord: for his Name only is excellent, and his praise above heaven and earth.
Psalm 148, v. 12

11 Let the saints be joyful with glory: let them rejoice in their beds.
Let the praises of God be in their mouth: and a two-edged sword in their hands;
To be avenged of the heathen: and to rebuke the people;
To bind their kings in chains: and their nobles with links of iron.
Psalm 149, v. 5; see **MACAULAY** *508:3*

12 Praise him upon the well-tuned cymbals: praise him upon the loud cymbals.
Let every thing that hath breath: praise the Lord.
Psalm 150, v. 5

13 Be pleased to receive into thy Almighty and most gracious protection the persons of us thy servants, and the Fleet in which we serve.
Forms of Prayer to be Used at Sea First Prayer

14 That we may be . . . a security for such as pass on the seas upon their lawful occasions.
Forms of Prayer to be Used at Sea First Prayer

15 We therefore commit his body to the deep, to be turned into corruption, looking for the resurrection of the body (when the Sea shall give up her dead).
Forms of Prayer to be Used at Sea At the Burial of their Dead at Sea

16 Come, Holy Ghost, our souls inspire,
And lighten with celestial fire.
Thou the anointing Spirit art,
Who dost thy seven-fold gifts impart.
Ordering of Priests 'Veni, Creator Spiritus'; translation by Bishop John Cosin, 1627, from the c.9th century original, possibly by Rabanus Maurus (776–856)

17 Holy Scripture containeth all things necessary to salvation.
Articles of Religion (1562) no. 6

18 Man is very far gone from original righteousness.
Articles of Religion (1562) no. 9

19 It is a thing plainly repugnant to the Word of God, and the custom of the Primitive Church, to have publick Prayer in the Church, or to minister the Sacraments in a tongue not understanded of the people.
Articles of Religion (1562) no. 24

20 The sacrifices of Masses, in the which it was commonly said, that the Priest did offer Christ for the quick and the dead, to have remission of pain or guilt, were blasphemous fables, and dangerous deceits.
Articles of Religion (1562) no. 31

21 The Bishop of Rome hath no jurisdiction in this Realm of England.
Articles of Religion (1562) no. 37

22 It is lawful for Christian men, at the commandment of the Magistrate, to wear weapons, and serve in the wars.
Articles of Religion (1562) no. 37

23 The Riches and Goods of Christians are not common, as touching the right, title, and possession of the same, as certain Anabaptists do falsely boast.
Articles of Religion (1562) no. 38

24 A Man may not marry his Mother.
A Table of Kindred and Affinity

John Wilkes Booth 1838–65
American actor and assassin

25 *Sic semper tyrannis!* The South is avenged.
having shot President **LINCOLN**, *14 April 1865*
in New York Times *15 April 1865; the second part of the*

statement does not appear in any contemporary source, and is possibly apocryphal; see **MOTTOES** 563:19

1 Useless! Useless!
last words; Philip van Doren Stern *The Man Who Killed Lincoln* (1939)

Paul Booth

2 Who put the colours in the rainbow?
Who put the salt into the sea?
Who put the cold into the snowflake?
Who made you and me?
Who put the hump upon the camel?
Who put the neck on the giraffe? . . .
God made all of these.
'Who put the colours in the rainbow?'

William Booth 1829–1912

English religious leader; founder of the Salvation Army, 1878. On Booth: see **LINDSAY** 495:1

3 The submerged tenth.
defined by Booth as 'three million men, women, and children, a vast despairing multitude in a condition nominally free, but really enslaved'
In Darkest England (1890) pt. 1, title of ch. 2

Frances Boothby fl. 1670

English dramatist

4 I'm hither come, but what d'ye think to say?
A woman's pen presents you with a play:
Who smiling told me I'd be sure to see
That once confirmed, the house would empty be.
Marcelia (1670) prologue

Robert Boothby 1900–86

British Conservative politician

5 *You* speak for Britain!
*to Arthur Greenwood, acting Leader of the Labour Party, after Neville **CHAMBERLAIN** had failed to announce an ultimatum to Germany; perhaps taking up an appeal already voiced by Leo **AMERY***
Harold Nicolson, diary, 2 September 1939; see **AMERY** 14:6

James H. Boren 1925–

American bureaucrat

6 Guidelines for bureaucrats: (1) When in charge, ponder. (2) When in trouble, delegate. (3) When in doubt, mumble.
in *New York Times* 8 November 1970

Jorge Luis Borges 1899–1986

Argentinian writer

7 The universe (which others call the Library) is composed of an indefinite, perhaps an infinite number of hexagonal galleries.
Ficciones (1956) 'The Library of Babel'

8 On those remote pages [of the *Celestial Emporium of Benevolent Knowledge*] it is written

that animals are divided into (a) those that belong to the Emperor, (b) embalmed ones, (c) those that are trained, (d) suckling pigs, (e) mermaids, (f) fabulous ones, (g) stray dogs, (h) those that are included in this classification, (i) those that tremble as if they were mad, (j) innumerable ones, (k) those drawn with a very fine camel's hair brush, (l) others, (m) those that have just broken a flower vase, (n) those that resemble flies from a distance.
Other Inquisitions (1966)

9 The original is unfaithful to the translation.
*of Henley's translation of **BECKFORD***'s Vathek
Sobre el 'Vathek' de William Beckford (1943)

10 The Falklands thing was a fight between two bald men over a comb.
application of a proverbial phrase
in *Time* 14 February 1983

Cesare Borgia *see* Mottoes 563:3

George Borrow 1803–81

English writer

11 There's night and day, brother, both sweet things; sun, moon, and stars, brother, all sweet things: there's likewise a wind on the heath. Life is very sweet, brother; who would wish to die?
Lavengro (1851) ch. 25

12 Let no one sneer at the bruisers of England—what were the gladiators of Rome, or the bull-fighters of Spain, in its palmiest days, compared to England's bruisers?
Lavengro (1851) ch. 26

13 A losing trade, I assure you, sir: literature is a drug.
Lavengro (1851) ch. 30

14 Fear God, and take your own part.
The Romany Rye (1857) ch. 16

15 The English have forgot that they ever conquered the Welsh, but some ages will elapse before the Welsh forget that the English have conquered them.
Wild Wales (1854) ch. 49

Pierre Bosquet 1810–61

French general

16 *C'est magnifique, mais ce n'est pas la guerre.*
It is magnificent, but it is not war.
on the charge of the Light Brigade at Balaclava, 25 October 1854
Cecil Woodham-Smith *The Reason Why* (1953) ch. 12

John Collins Bossidy 1860–1928

American oculist

17 And this is good old Boston,
The home of the bean and the cod,
Where the Lowells talk to the Cabots

And the Cabots talk only to God.

verse spoken at Holy Cross College alumni dinner in Boston, Massachusetts, 1910, in *Springfield Sunday Republican* 14 December 1924

Jacques-Bénigne Bossuet 1627–1704

French preacher

1 *L'Angleterre, ah, la perfide Angleterre, que le rempart de ses mers rendait inaccessible aux Romains, la foi du Sauveur y est abordée.*

England, ah, faithless England, which the protection afforded by its seas rendered inaccessible to the Romans, the faith of the Saviour spread even there.

first sermon on the feast of the Circumcision, in *Oeuvres de Bossuet* (1816) vol. 11; see **XIMÉNÈZ** 872:2

James Boswell 1740–95

Scottish lawyer; companion and biographer of Samuel **JOHNSON**. On Boswell: see **MACAULAY 506:17, WALPOLE 837:23**; see also **MACAULAY 507:10**

2 I think there is a blossom about me of something more distinguished than the generality of mankind.

Boswell's London Journal (ed. F. A. Pottle, 1950) 20 January 1763

3 I am, I flatter myself, completely a citizen of the world. In my travels through Holland, Germany, Switzerland, Italy, Corsica, France, I never felt myself from home.

Journal of a Tour to the Hebrides (ed. F. A. Pottle, 1936) 14 August 1773; see also **BACON** 47:4, **SOCRATES** 760:7

4 We [Boswell and Johnson] are both *Tories*; both convinced of the utility of monarchical power, and both lovers of that reverence and affection for a sovereign which constitute loyalty, a principle which I take to be absolutely extinguished in Britain.

Journal of a Tour to the Hebrides (ed. F. A. Pottle, 1936) 13 September 1773

5 A page of my Journal is like a cake of portable soup. A little may be diffused into a considerable portion.

Journal of a Tour to the Hebrides (ed. F. A. Pottle, 1936) 13 September 1773

6 I have never yet exerted ambition in rising in the state. But sure I am, no man has made his way better to the best company.

Journal of a Tour to the Hebrides (ed. F. A. Pottle, 1936) 16 September 1773

7 JOHNSON: Well, we had a good talk.
BOSWELL: Yes, Sir; you tossed and gored several persons.

The Life of Samuel Johnson (1791) Summer 1768

8 A man, indeed, is not genteel when he gets drunk; but most vices may be committed very genteelly: a man may debauch his friend's wife genteelly: he may cheat at cards genteelly.

The Life of Samuel Johnson (1791) 6 April 1775

Horatio Bottomley 1860–1933

English newspaper proprietor and financier

9 *reply to a prison visitor who asked if he were sewing:*
No, reaping.

S. T. Felstead *Horatio Bottomley* (1936) ch. 16

10 What poor education I have received has been gained in the University of Life.

speech at the Oxford Union, 2 December 1920; Beverley Nichols 25 (1926) ch. 7

Lucien Bouchard 1938–

Canadian lawyer and politician, Premier of Quebec 1996–2001

11 Canada is divisible because it's not a real country. Canada is two nations, two peoples, two territories and this one is ours and we're keeping it!

when asked, after the 1995 Quebec referendum on independence, why he felt no guilt about having Quebec separate from the rest of Canada

statement at a press conference, January 1996

Dion Boucicault (Dionysius Lardner Boursiquot) 1820–90

Irish dramatist

12 Men talk of killing time, while time quietly kills them.

London Assurance (1841) act 2, sc. 1; see **SITWELL** 753:16

Antoine Boulay de la Meurthe 1761–1840

French statesman

13 *C'est pire qu'un crime, c'est une faute.*
It is worse than a crime, it is a blunder.

on hearing of the execution of the Duc d'Enghien, captured in Baden by Napoleon's forces, in 1804

C.-A. Sainte-Beuve *Nouveaux Lundis* (1870) vol. 12

Harold Edwin Boulton 1859–1935

English songwriter

14 Devon, glorious Devon!

'Glorious Devon' (1902)

15 Speed, bonnie boat, like a bird on the wing,
'Onward,' the sailors cry;
Carry the lad that's born to be king,
Over the sea to Skye.

'Skye Boat Song' (1908)

Matthew Boulton 1728–1809

English engineer

16 I sell here, Sir, what all the world desires to have—POWER.

speaking to **BOSWELL** *of his engineering works*

James Boswell *Life of Samuel Johnson* (1791) 22 March 1776

Henri Bourassa 1868–1952

Canadian journalist and Liberal politician

1 We have in our country the patriotism of Ontarians, the patriotism of Quebecers and the patriotism of westerners . . . but there is no Canadian patriotism, and there will not be a Canadian nation as long as we do not have a Canadian patriotism.
speech, the Canadian Club of Toronto, 22 January 1907

F. W. Bourdillon 1852–1921

English poet

2 The night has a thousand eyes,
And the day but one.
Among the Flowers (1878) 'Light'; see LYLY 505:22

Paul Bourget 1852–1935

French writer

3 We had better live as we think, otherwise sooner or later we shall end up by thinking as we have lived.
Le Démon de Midi (1914)

4 Ideas are to literature what light is to painting.
La Physiologie de l'Amour Moderne (1890)

Louis Bousquet

French songwriter

5 *Nous en rêvons la nuit, nous y pensons le jour,*
Ce n'est que Madelon, mais pour nous, c'est l'amour.
We dream of her by night, we think of her by day,
It's only Madelon, but for us, it's love.
'Quand Madelon' (1914), French soldiers' song of the First World War

E. E. Bowen 1836–1901

English schoolmaster

6 Forty years on, when afar and asunder
Parted are those who are singing to-day.
'Forty Years On' (Harrow School Song, published 1886)

Elizabeth Bowen 1899–1973

British novelist and short-story writer, born in Ireland

7 My family got their position and drew their power from a situation that shows an inherent wrong. In the grip of that situation, England and Ireland each turned to the other a closed, harsh, distorted face—a face that, in each case, their lovers would hardly know.
Bowen's Court (afterword, ed. 2, 1964)

8 The innocent are so few that two of them seldom meet—when they do, their victims lie strewn around.
The Death of the Heart (1938) pt. 1, ch. 8

9 There is no end to the violations committed by children on children, quietly talking alone.
The House in Paris (1935) pt. 1, ch. 2

10 Fate is not an eagle, it creeps like a rat.
The House in Paris (1935) pt. 2, ch. 2

11 Jealousy is no more than feeling alone against smiling enemies.
The House in Paris (1935) pt. 2, ch. 8

12 I could wish that the English kept history in mind more, that the Irish kept it in mind less.
'Notes on Eire' 9 November 1949

13 A high altar on the move.
of Edith SITWELL
V. Glendinning Edith Sitwell (1981) ch. 25

Lord Bowen 1835–94

English judge

14 The man on the Clapham omnibus.
the average man
in Law Reports (1903); attributed

15 When I hear of an 'equity' in a case like this, I am reminded of a blind man in a dark room—looking for a black hat—which isn't there.
John Alderson Foote Pie-Powder (1911)

16 The rain, it raineth on the just
And also on the unjust fella:
But chiefly on the just, because
The unjust steals the just's umbrella.
Walter Sichel Sands of Time (1923) ch. 4; see BIBLE 99:7

David Bowie (David Jones) 1947–

English rock musician

17 Ground control to Major Tom.
'Space Oddity' (1969 song)

William Lisle Bowles 1762–1850

English clergyman and poet

18 The cause of Freedom is the cause of God!
A Poetical Address to the Right Honourable Edmund Burke (1791) l. 78

Maurice Bowra 1898–1971

English scholar and literary critic

19 I'm a man more dined against than dining.
John Betjeman Summoned by Bells (1960) ch. 9; see SHAKESPEARE 715:20

Boy George 1961–

English pop singer and songwriter

20 Sex has never been an obsession with me. It's just like eating a bag of crisps. Quite nice, but nothing marvellous. Sex is not simply black and white. There's a lot of grey.
in Sun 21 October 1982

Mary Elizabeth Braddon 1837–1915

English novelist

21 It is worse than a crime, Violet; it is an impropriety.
Vixen (1879) vol. 2, ch. 15

John Bradford *c.*1510–55

English Protestant martyr

1 But for the grace of God there goes John
Bradford.

*on seeing a group of criminals being led to their execution;
usually quoted as 'There but for the grace of God go I'
in Dictionary of National Biography (1917–)*

F. H. Bradley 1846–1924

English philosopher

2 Metaphysics is the finding of bad reasons for
what we believe upon instinct; but to find these
reasons is no less an instinct.

Appearance and Reality (1893) preface

3 The world is the best of all possible worlds, and
everything in it is a necessary evil.

Appearance and Reality (1893) preface

4 Where everything is bad it must be good to
know the worst.

Appearance and Reality (1893) preface

Omar Bradley 1893–1981

American general

5 The way to win an atomic war is to make
certain it never starts.

speech on Armistice Day, 1948

6 We have grasped the mystery of the atom and
rejected the Sermon on the Mount.

*speech on Armistice Day, 1948
Collected Writings (1967) vol. 1*

7 The world has achieved brilliance without
wisdom, power without conscience. Ours is a
world of nuclear giants and ethical infants.

*speech on Armistice Day, 1948
Collected Writings (1967) vol. 1*

Don Bradman 1908–2001

Australian cricketer

8 Bowl fast, bowl faster. When you play Test
cricket you don't give Englishmen an inch. Play
it tough, all the way. Grind them into the dust.

Jack Fingleton Batting from Memory (1981)

John Bradshaw 1602–59

English judge at the trial of CHARLES I

9 Rebellion to tyrants is obedience to God.

*suppositious epitaph; Henry S. Randall Life of Thomas Jefferson
(1865) vol. 3, appendix 4; see MOTTOES 563:17*

Anne Bradstreet *c.*1612–72

English-born American poet

10 Thou ill-form'd offspring of my feeble brain,
Who after birth did'st by my side remain,
Till snatched from thence by friends, less wise
  than true
Who thee abroad expos'd to public view,

Made thee in rags, halting to th' press to trudge,
Where errors were not lessened (all may judge)
At thy return my blushing was not small,
My rambling brat (in print) should mother call.

'The Author to her Book' (1650)

11 I am obnoxious to each carping tongue,
Who says my hand a needle better fits,
A poet's pen, all scorn, I should thus wrong;
For such despite they cast on female wits:
If what I do prove well, it won't advance,
They'll say it's stolne, or else, it was by chance.

'The Prologue' (1650)

12 Let Greeks be Greeks, and Women what they
  are,
Men have precedency, and still excel.

'The Prologue' (1650)

13 This mean and unrefinèd stuff of mine,
Will make your glistering gold but more to
  shine.

'The Prologue' (1650)

14 Authority without wisdom is like a heavy axe
without an edge, fitter to bruise than polish.

The Tenth Muse (1650) 'Meditations Divine and Moral'

Ernest Bramah (Ernest Bramah Smith)

1868–1942

English writer

15 'Your insight is clear and unbiased,' said the
gracious Sovereign. 'But however entrancing it is
to wander unchecked through a garden of bright
images, are we not enticing your mind from
another subject of almost equal importance?'

Kai Lung's Golden Hours (1922) ch. 10

16 It is a mark of insincerity of purpose to spend
one's time in looking for the sacred Emperor in
the low-class tea-shops.

The Wallet of Kai Lung (1900)

James Bramston *c.*1694–1744

English clergyman and poet

17 What's not destroyed by Time's devouring hand?
Where's Troy, and where's the Maypole in the
  Strand?

The Art of Politics (1729) l. 71

Louis D. Brandeis 1856–1941

American jurist and Supreme Court Justice

18 If we would guide by the light of reason, we
must let our minds be bold.

dissenting opinion in Jay Burns Baking Co. v. Bryan (1924)

19 Those who won our independence . . . believed
liberty to be the secret of happiness and courage
to be the secret of liberty.

in Whitney v California (1927)

20 Fear of serious injury alone cannot justify
suppression of free speech and assembly. Men
feared witches and burned women. It is the

function of speech to free men from the bondage of irrational fears.
in Whitney v. California (1927)

1 The greatest dangers to liberty lurk in insidious encroachment by men of zeal, well-meaning but without understanding.
dissenting opinion in Olmstead v. United States (1928)

2 Publicity is justly commended as a remedy for social and industrial diseases. Sunlight is said to be the best of disinfectants; electric light the most efficient policeman.
Other People's Money (1914)

Willy Brandt 1913–92

German statesman, Chancellor of West Germany 1969–74

3 We want to risk more democracy.
speech to parliament after his election as Chancellor, 28 October 1969

4 Where mass hunger reigns, we cannot speak of peace.
World Armament and World Hunger (1986)

Joseph Brant (Thayendanegea) 1742–1807

American-born Canadian Mohawk leader

5 I bow to no man for I am considered a prince among my own people. But I will gladly shake your hand.
on being presented to **GEORGE III**
attributed

Georges Braque 1882–1963

French painter

6 Art is meant to disturb, science reassures.
Le Jour et la nuit: Cahiers 1917–52

7 Truth exists; only lies are invented.
Le Jour et la nuit: Cahiers 1917–52

Richard Brathwaite c.1588–1673

English poet

8 To Banbury came I, O profane one!
Where I saw a Puritane-one
Hanging of his cat on Monday
For killing of a mouse on Sunday.
Barnabee's Journal (1638) pt. 1, st. 4

John W. Bratton *and* James B. Kennedy

British songwriters

9 If you go down in the woods today
You're sure of a big surprise
If you go down in the woods today
You'd better go in disguise
For every Bear that ever there was
Will gather there for certain because,
Today's the day the Teddy Bears have their
Picnic.
'The Teddy Bear's Picnic' (1932 song)

Werner von Braun 1912–77

German-born American rocket engineer

10 Don't tell me that man doesn't belong out there. Man belongs wherever he wants to go—and he'll do plenty well when he gets there.
on space
in Time 17 February 1958

11 Basic research is what I am doing when I don't know what I am doing.
R. L. Weber A Random Walk in Science (1973)

Bertolt Brecht 1898–1956

German dramatist. See also **HARE** 382:6

12 Terrible is the temptation to be good.
The Caucasian Chalk Circle (1948)

13 Hesitating doesn't matter if only you win out.
The Good Woman of Setzuan (1938) prologue

14 No one can be good for long when goodness is not in demand.
The Good Woman of Setzuan (1938) sc. 2

15 The aim of science is not to open the door to infinite wisdom, but to set a limit to infinite error.
The Life of Galileo (1939) sc. 9

16 ANDREA: Unhappy the land that has no heroes!
. . .
GALILEO: No. Unhappy the land that needs heroes.
The Life of Galileo (1939) sc. 13

17 Don't be afraid of death so much as an inadequate life.
The Mother (1957) sc. 10

18 One observes, they have gone too long without a war here. Where is morality to come from in such a case, I ask? Peace is nothing but slovenliness, only war creates order.
Mother Courage (1939) sc. 1

19 Because I don't trust him, we are friends.
Mother Courage (1939) sc. 3

20 The finest plans are always ruined by the littleness of those who ought to carry them out, for the Emperors can actually do nothing.
Mother Courage (1939) sc. 6

21 War always finds a way.
Mother Courage (1939) sc. 6

22 Don't tell me peace has broken out, when I've just bought some new supplies.
Mother Courage (1939) sc. 8

23 The resistible rise of Arturo Ui.
title of play (1941)

24 Oh, the shark has pretty teeth, dear,
And he shows them pearly white.
Just a jackknife has Macheath, dear
And he keeps it out of sight.
The Threepenny Opera (1928) prologue

25 Food comes first, then morals.
The Threepenny Opera (1928) act 2, sc. 3

1 What is robbing a bank compared with founding a bank?
 The Threepenny Opera (1928) act 3, sc. 3

2 Who built Thebes of the seven gates?
 In the books you will find the names of kings.
 Did the kings haul up the lumps of rock? . . .
 Where, the evening that the wall of China was finished
 Did the masons go?
 'Questions From A Worker Who Reads' (1935)

3 Would it not be easier
 In that case for the government
 To dissolve the people
 And elect another?
 on the uprising against the Soviet occupying forces in East Germany in 1953
 'The Solution' (1953)

4 Truly, I'm living in a time of darkness.
 'To Those Born Later' (1939)

5 Yes, we went, as often changing countries as changing shoes
 Through the wars of the classes, despairing
 Each time we found an abuse, and no sense of outrage.
 'To Those Born Later' (1939)

Gerald Brenan 1894–1987
British travel writer and novelist

6 Those who have some means think that the most important thing in the world is love. The poor know that it is money.
 Thoughts in a Dry Season (1978); see **BALDWIN** 52:13

7 You can't get at the truth by writing history; only the novelist can do that.
 in *Times Literary Supplement* 28 November 1986

William J. Brennan Jr. 1906–97
American lawyer and judge, US Supreme Court justice, a leading proponent of the view that the Constitution needed to be adapted to the needs of each generation

8 The nation's future depends upon leaders trained through wide exposure to that robust exchange of ideas which discovers truth 'out of a multitude of tongues'.
 Supreme Court decision on *Keyishian v. Board of Regents of the University of the State of New York et al.* (1967); see **HAND** 379:6

Sydney Brenner 1927–
South African-born biologist

9 A modern computer hovers between the obsolescent and the nonexistent.
 attributed in *Science* 5 January 1990

Jane Brereton (née Hughes) 1685–1740
English poet

10 The picture, placed the busts between,
 Adds to the thought much strength:

Wisdom and Wit are little seen,
 But Folly's at full length.
 'On Mr Nash's Picture at Full Length, between the Busts of Sir Isaac Newton and Mr Pope' (1744)

Nicholas Breton *c.*1545–1626
English writer and poet

11 We rise with the lark and go to bed with the lamb.
 The Court and Country (1618) para. 8

12 I wish my deadly foe, no worse
 Than want of friends, and empty purse.
 'A Farewell to Town' (1577)

13 Much ado there was, God wot;
 He would love and she would not.
 'Phillida and Coridon' (1600)

14 Come little babe, come silly soul,
 Thy father's shame, thy mother's grief,
 Born as I doubt to all our dole,
 And to thy self unhappy chief.
 'A Sweet Lullaby' (1597)

Aristide Briand 1862–1932
French statesman

15 The high contracting powers solemnly declare . . . that they condemn recourse to war and renounce it . . . as an instrument of their national policy towards each other . . . The settlement or the solution of all disputes or conflicts of whatever nature or of whatever origin they may be which may arise . . . shall never be sought by either side except by pacific means.
 draft, 20 June 1927, later incorporated into the Kellogg Pact, 1928, in *Le Temps* 13 April 1928

Percy Williams Bridgeman 1882–1961
American physicist

16 The scientific method, as far as it is a method, is nothing more than doing one's damnedest with one's mind, no holds barred.
 Reflections of a Physicist (1955)

Edward Bridges 1892–1969
English civil servant, Cabinet Secretary and Head of the Civil Service

17 I confidently expect that we shall continue to be grouped with mothers-in-law and Wigan Pier as one of the recognized objects of ridicule.
 of civil servants
 Portrait of a Profession (1950)

Robert Bridges 1844–1930
English poet

18 All my hope on God is founded.
 'All my hope on God is founded' (1899 hymn)

19 When men were all asleep the snow came flying,

In large white flakes falling on the city brown,
Stealthily and perpetually settling and loosely
    lying,
Hushing the latest traffic of the drowsy town.
'London Snow' (1890)

John Bright 1811–89

English Liberal politician and reformer

1 The angel of death has been abroad throughout
the land; you may almost hear the beating of his
wings.
on the effects of the war in the Crimea
    speech in the House of Commons, 23 February 1855

2 A gigantic system of outdoor relief for the
aristocracy of Great Britain.
of British foreign policy
    speech at Birmingham, 29 October 1858; G. Barnett Smith
    Life and Speeches of John Bright (1881) vol. 1, ch. 16

3 I am for 'Peace, retrenchment, and reform', the
watchword of the great Liberal party 30 years
ago.
    speech at Birmingham, 28 April 1859, in *The Times* 29 April
    1859; the phrase occurs earlier in Samuel Warren *Ten
    Thousand a Year* (1841) bk. 7, ch. 1 as 'An immense yellow
    banner . . . "Peace! Retrenchment!! Reform!!"'

4 England is the mother of Parliaments.
    speech at Birmingham, 18 January 1865, in *The Times* 19
    January 1865

5 The right hon Gentleman . . . has retired into
what may be called his political Cave of
Adullam—and he has called about him every
one that was in distress and every one that was
discontented.
referring to Robert LOWE, *leader of the dissident Whigs
opposed to the Reform Bill of 1866*
    speech in the House of Commons, 13 March 1866; see BIBLE
    84:8

6 Force is not a remedy.
    speech to the Birmingham Junior Liberal Club, 16 November
    1880, in *The Times* 17 November 1880

7 The knowledge of the ancient languages is
mainly a luxury.
    letter in *Pall Mall Gazette* 30 November 1886

Anthelme Brillat-Savarin 1755–1826

French jurist and gourmet

8 Tell me what you eat and I will tell you what
you are.
    The Physiology of Taste (1825) aphorism no. 4; see FEUERBACH
    325:15

9 The discovery of a new dish does more for
human happiness than the discovery of a star.
    The Physiology of Taste (1825) aphorism no. 9

10 Cooking is the most ancient of the arts, for
Adam was born hungry.
    The Physiology of Taste (1825) pt. 1

11 Your true amateur *sips* his wine; as he lingers
over each separate mouthful, he obtains from
each the sum total of pleasure which he would

have experienced had he emptied his glass at a
single draught.
    The Physiology of Taste (1825) pt. 2

Vera Brittain 1893–1970

English writer

12 Meek wifehood is no part of my profession;
I am your friend, but never your possession.
    'Married Love' (1926)

13 Politics are usually the executive expression of
human immaturity.
    Rebel Passion (1964)

Paul Broca 1824–80

French surgeon

14 The great regions of the mind correspond to the
great regions of the brain.
    at the Société Anatomique, August 1861

Russell Brockbank *see* Cartoon

captions 205:8

Joseph Brodsky 1940–96

Russian-born American poet

15 As a form of moral insurance, at least, literature
is much more dependable than a system of
beliefs or a philosophical doctrine.
    'Uncommon Visage', Nobel lecture 1987, in *On Grief and
    Reason* (1996)

Tom Brokaw 1940–

American journalist

16 We don't just have egg on our face. We have
omelette all over our suits.
*on the networks' premature calls of a win in Florida in the
presidential election, first to Al* GORE *and then to George W.*
BUSH
    in *Atlanta Constitution-Journal* 9 November 2000 (online
    edition)

Alexander Brome 1620–66

English poet

17 I have been in love, and in debt, and in drink,
This many and many a year.
    Songs and Other Poems (2nd ed., 1664) pt. 1 'The Mad Lover'

18 Come, blessed peace, we once again implore,
And let our pains be less, or power more.
    Songs and Other Poems (1661) 'The Riddle' (written 1644)

Jacob Bronowski 1908–74

Polish-born mathematician and humanist

19 The world can only be grasped by action, not by
contemplation . . . The hand is the cutting edge
of the mind.
    The Ascent of Man (1973) ch. 3

1 The essence of science: ask an impertinent question, and you are on the way to a pertinent answer.
The Ascent of Man (1973) ch. 4

2 The wish to hurt, the momentary intoxication with pain, is the loophole through which the pervert climbs into the minds of ordinary men.
The Face of Violence (1954) ch. 5

3 Therapy has become what I think of as the tenth American muse.
attributed

Charlotte Brontë 1816–55

English novelist; daughter of Patrick **BRONTË**, sister of Emily **BRONTË**

4 Conventionality is not morality. Self-righteousness is not religion. To attack the first is not to assail the last. To pluck the mask from the face of the Pharisee, is not to lift an impious hand to the Crown of Thorns.
Jane Eyre (2nd ed., 1848) preface

5 There was no possibility of taking a walk that day.
Jane Eyre (1847) ch. 1, opening words

6 Prejudices, it is well known, are most difficult to eradicate from the heart whose soil has never been loosened or fertilised by education.
Jane Eyre (1847) ch. 29

7 As his curate, his comrade, all would be right . . . There would be recesses in my mind which would be only mine, to which he never came; and sentiments growing there, fresh and sheltered, which his austerity could never blight, nor his measured warrior-march trample down. But as his wife . . . forced to keep the fire of my nature continually low, to compel it to burn inwardly and never utter a cry . . . *this* would be unendurable.
Jane, of St John Rivers
Jane Eyre (1847) ch. 34

8 Reader, I married him.
Jane, of Mr Rochester
Jane Eyre (1847) ch. 38

9 Of late years an abundant shower of curates has fallen upon the North of England.
Shirley (1849) ch. 1

10 Be a governess! Better be a slave at once!
Shirley (1849) ch. 13

11 It is rustic all through. It is moorish, and wild, and knotty as a root of heath.
on the setting of Emily **BRONTË**'s *Wuthering Heights*
in Charlotte's preface to the 1850 edition

12 We wove a web in childhood,
A web of sunny air;
We dug a spring in infancy
Of water pure and fair;
We sowed in youth a mustard seed,
We cut an almond rod;

We are now grown up to riper age—
Are they withered in the sod?
'We wove a web in childhood' (written 1835)

13 I shall soon be 30—and I have done nothing yet . . . I feel as if we were all buried here.
letter to Ellen Nussey, 24 March 1845; *The Letters of Charlotte Brontë* (1995) vol. 1

14 You are not to suppose any of the characters in *Shirley* intended as literal portraits . . . We only suffer reality to *suggest*, never to *dictate*.
letter to Ellen Nussey, 16 November 1849, in Elizabeth Gaskell *The Life of Charlotte Bronte* (1857) ch. 18

Emily Brontë 1818–48

English novelist and poet; daughter of Patrick **BRONTË**, sister of Charlotte **BRONTË**. On Brontë: see **BRONTË** 158:11

15 No coward soul is mine,
No trembler in the world's storm-troubled sphere:
I see Heaven's glories shine,
And faith shines equal, arming me from fear.
'No coward soul is mine' (1846)

16 Oh! dreadful is the check—intense the agony—
When the ear begins to hear, and the eye begins to see;
When the pulse begins to throb, the brain to think again;
The soul to feel the flesh, and the flesh to feel the chain.
'The Prisoner' (1846)

17 Cold in the earth—and fifteen wild Decembers,
From those brown hills, have melted into spring.
'Remembrance' (1846)

18 Proud people breed sad sorrows for themselves.
Wuthering Heights (1847) ch. 7

19 My love for Linton is like the foliage in the woods; time will change it, I'm well aware, as winter changes the trees—My love for Heathcliff resembles the eternal rocks beneath:—a source of little visible delight, but necessary.
Wuthering Heights (1847) ch. 9

20 The tyrant grinds down his slaves and they don't turn against him; they crush those beneath them.
Wuthering Heights (1847) ch. 11

21 I lingered round them, under that benign sky: watched the moths fluttering among the heath and hare-bells; listened to the soft wind breathing through the grass; and wondered how any one could ever imagine unquiet slumbers for the sleepers in that quiet earth.
Wuthering Heights (1847), closing words

Patrick Brontë 1777–1861

English clergyman, born in Ireland, perpetual curate of Haworth, Yorkshire from 1820; father of Charlotte **BRONTË** and Emily **BRONTË**

22 Charlotte has been writing a book, and it is much better than likely.
to his younger daughters, on first reading Jane Eyre; *in a*

letter of August 1850, Mrs Gaskell gives the wording as 'Charlotte has been writing a book—and it is better than I expected'
> Elizabeth Gaskell *The Life of Charlotte Brontë* (1857)

1 No quailing, Mrs Gaskell! no drawing back!
apropos her undertaking to write the life of Charlotte
BRONTË
> letter from Mrs Gaskell to Ellen Nussey, 24 July 1855, in J. A. V. Chapple and A. Pollard (eds.) *The Letters of Mrs Gaskell* (1966) no. 257

Frances Brooke 1724–89
Canadian novelist and writer

2 The road from Quebec to Montreal is almost a continued street, the villages being numerous, and so extended along the banks of the river St. Lawrence as to leave scarce a space without houses in view; except where here or there a river, wood, or mountain intervenes, as if to give a more pleasing variety to the scene.
> *The History of Emily Montague* (1769)

Henry Brooke 1703–83
Irish poet and dramatist

3 For righteous monarchs,
Justly to judge, with their own eyes should see;
To rule o'er freemen, should themselves be free.
> *Earl of Essex* (performed 1750, published 1761) act 1; see **JOHNSON** 444:2

Rupert Brooke 1887–1915
English poet. On Brooke: see **CORNFORD** 252:3, **JAMES** 430:9, **LEAVIS** 486:18

4 Blow out, you bugles, over the rich Dead!
There's none of these so lonely and poor of old,
But, dying, has made us rarer gifts than gold.
These laid the world away; poured out the red
Sweet wine of youth; gave up the years to be
Of work and joy, and that unhoped serene, That
    men call age; and those that would have been,
Their sons, they gave, their immortality.
> 'The Dead' (1914)

5 . . . The cool kindliness of sheets, that soon
Smooth away trouble; and the rough male kiss
Of blankets.
> 'The Great Lover' (1914)

6 Just now the lilac is in bloom,
All before my little room.
> 'The Old Vicarage, Grantchester' (1915)

7 Unkempt about those hedges blows
An English unofficial rose.
> 'The Old Vicarage, Grantchester' (1915)

8 Curates, long dust, will come and go
On lissom, clerical, printless toe;
And oft between the boughs is seen
The sly shade of a Rural Dean.
> 'The Old Vicarage, Grantchester' (1915)

9 God! I will pack, and take a train,
And get me to England once again!

For England's the one land, I know,
Where men with Splendid Hearts may go.
> 'The Old Vicarage, Grantchester' (1915)

10 For Cambridge people rarely smile,
Being urban, squat, and packed with guile.
> 'The Old Vicarage, Grantchester' (1915)

11 Stands the Church clock at ten to three?
And is there honey still for tea?
> 'The Old Vicarage, Grantchester' (1915)

12 Now, God be thanked Who has matched us with
    His hour,
And caught our youth, and wakened us from
    sleeping,
With hand made sure, clear eye, and sharpened
    power,
To turn, as swimmers into cleanness leaping.
> 'Peace' (1914)

13 If I should die, think only this of me:
That there's some corner of a foreign field
That is for ever England. There shall be
In that rich earth a richer dust concealed;
A dust whom England bore, shaped, made
    aware,
Gave, once, her flowers to love, her ways to
    roam,
A body of England's, breathing English air,
Washed by the rivers, blest by suns of home.

And think, this heart, all evil shed away,
A pulse in the eternal mind, no less
Gives somewhere back the thoughts by England
    given;
Her sights and sounds; dreams happy as her day;
And laughter, learnt of friends; and gentleness,
In hearts at peace, under an English heaven.
> 'The Soldier' (1914)

14 History repeats itself; historians repeat one another.
> letter to Geoffrey Keynes, 4 June 1906; see **PROVERBS** 634:34

Anita Brookner 1928–
English novelist and art historian

15 Good women always think it is their fault when someone else is being offensive. Bad women never take the blame for anything.
> *Hotel du Lac* (1984) ch. 7

16 I have reached the age when a woman begins to perceive that she is growing into the person she least plans to resemble: her mother.
> *Incidents in the Rue Laugier* (1995) ch. 1

17 They were privileged children . . . they would always expect to be greeted with smiles.
> *Lewis Percy* (1989) ch. 9

18 Dr Weiss, at forty, knew that her life had been ruined by literature.
> *A Start in Life* (1981) ch. 1

Gwendolyn Brooks 1917–2000

American poet

1 Exhaust the little moment. Soon it dies.
And be it gash or gold it will not come
Again in this identical disguise.
'Exhaust the little moment' (1949)

2 Abortions will not let you forget.
You remember the children you got that you did
not get . . .
'The Mother' (1945)

3 The time
cracks into furious flower. Lifts its face
all unashamed. And sways in wicked grace.
'The Second Sermon on the Warpland' (1968)

J. Brooks

4 A four-legged friend, a four-legged friend,
He'll never let you down.
sung by Roy Rogers about his horse Trigger
'A Four Legged Friend' (1952)

Phillips Brooks 1835–93

American clergyman

5 O little town of Bethlehem,
How still we see thee lie!
Above thy deep and dreamless sleep
The silent stars go by.
Yet in thy dark streets shineth
The everlasting light;
The hopes and fears of all the years
Are met in thee to-night.
'O Little Town of Bethlehem' (1868 hymn)

Thomas Brooks 1608–80

English Puritan divine

6 For (*magna est veritas et praevalebit*) great is truth,
and shall prevail.
The Crown and Glory of Christianity (1662); see **BIBLE**
(VULGATE) 120:19

Robert Barnabas Brough 1828–60

English satirical writer

7 My Lord Tomnoddy is thirty-four;
The Earl can last but a few years more.
My Lord in the Peers will take his place:
Her Majesty's councils his words will grace.
Office he'll hold and patronage sway;
Fortunes and lives he will vote away;
And what are his qualifications?—ONE!
He's the Earl of Fitzdotterel's eldest son.
Songs of the Governing Classes (1855) 'My Lord Tomnoddy'; see
also **BARHAM** 58:7

Lord Brougham 1778–1868

Scottish lawyer and politician; Lord Chancellor. On
Brougham: see **MELBOURNE** 530:15

8 All we see about us, King, Lords, and
Commons, the whole machinery of the State, all
the apparatus of the system, and its varied
workings, end in simply bringing twelve good
men into a box.
in the House of Commons, 7 February 1828

9 The schoolmaster is abroad! and I trust more to
the schoolmaster, armed with his primer, than I
do to the soldier in full military array, for
upholding and extending the liberties of his
country.
*sometimes quoted as 'Look out, gentlemen, the
schoolmaster is abroad!', which Brougham is said to have
used in a speech at the Mechanics' Instute, London, in 1825*
in the House of Commons, 29 January 1828

10 Education makes a people easy to lead, but
difficult to drive; easy to govern, but impossible
to enslave.
attributed

Heywood Broun 1888–1939

American journalist

11 Men build bridges and throw railroads across
deserts, and yet they contend successfully that
the job of sewing on a button is beyond them.
Accordingly, they don't have to sew buttons.
Seeing Things at Night (1921) 'Holding a Baby'

12 Posterity is as likely to be wrong as anybody
else.
Sitting on the World (1924) 'The Last Review'

13 Everybody favours free speech in the slack
moments when no axes are being ground.
in New York World 23 October 1926

14 Just as every conviction begins as a whim so
does every emancipator serve his apprenticeship
as a crank. A fanatic is a great leader who is just
entering the room.
in New York World 6 February 1928

Heywood Hale Broun 1918–

American actor

15 Sports do not build character. They reveal it.
attributed; James Michener Sports in America (1976)

Christy Brown 1932–81

Irish writer

16 Painting became everything to me . . . Through
it I made articulate all that I saw and felt,
all that went on inside the mind that was housed
within my useless body like a prisoner in a cell.
My Left Foot (1954)

Gordon Brown 1951–

British Labour statesman, Chancellor of the Exchequer
1997–2007, and Prime Minister from 2007. On Brown: see
ANONYMOUS 19:21, **ANONYMOUS** 19:22

17 Ideas which stress the growing importance of
international cooperation and new theories of
economic sovereignty across a wide range of

areas—macroeconomics, the environment, the growth of post neo-classical endogenous growth theory and the symbiotic relationships between growth and investment in people and infrastructure.

New Labour Economics speech, September 1994, 'winner' of the ironic Plain English No Nonsense Award for 1994

1 It is about time we had an end to the old Britain, where all that matters is the privileges you were born with, rather than the potential you actually have.

speech, 25 May 2000

2 I'm a father, that's what matters most. Nothing matters more.

on the birth of his son John
in *Observer* 19 October 2003

3 I learned from my mother and father that for every opportunity there was an obligation, for every demand a duty, for every chance given, a contribution to be made. And when they said to me that for every right there was a responsibility, for them that was not just words. What they meant was quite simple and straightforward, for me my moral compass.

speech, Labour Party Conference, 26 September 2005, in *Guardian* 26 September 2005 (electronic edition)

H. Rap Brown (Hubert Geroid Brown)
1943–
American Black Power leader

4 I say violence is necessary. It is as American as cherry pie.

speech at Washington, 27 July 1967, in *Washington Post* 28 July 1967

Henry Box Brown b. 1815
American escaped slave

5 I entered the world a slave—in the midst of a country whose most honoured writings declare that all men have a right to liberty.

Narrative of the Life of Henry Box Brown (1851)

John Brown 1715–66
English clergyman and writer

6 I have seen some extracts from Johnson's Preface to his 'Shakespeare' . . . No feeling nor pathos in him! Altogether upon the high horse, and blustering about Imperial Tragedy!

letter to Garrick, 27 October 1765, in *The Private Correspondence of David Garrick* (1831) vol. 1

John Brown 1800–59
American abolitionist. On Brown: see SONGS, SPIRITUALS, AND SHANTIES 763:1

7 Now, if it is deemed necessary that I should forfeit my life for the furtherance of the ends of justice, and mingle my blood further with the blood of my children, and with the blood of

millions in this slave country whose rights are disregarded by wicked, cruel, and unjust enactments, I say let it be done.

last speech to the court, 2 November 1859, in *The Life, Trial and Execution of Captain John Brown* (1859)

8 I, John Brown, am now quite certain that the crimes of this guilty land will never be purged away but with blood.

written on the day of his execution, 2 December 1859, in R. J. Hinton *John Brown and His Men* (1894) ch. 12

9 This *is* a beautiful country!

last words as he rode to the gallows, seated on his coffin at his execution on 2 December 1859

Joseph Brown 1821–94
American politician and Confederate supporter; Governor of Georgia during the Civil War

10 I entered into this Revolution to contribute my mite to sustain the rights of states and prevent the consolidation of the Government, and I am *still* a rebel . . . no matter who may be in power.

refusing to accept the Confederate President Jefferson **DAVIS**'s *call for a day of national fasting*
in 1863; Geoffrey C. Ward *The Civil War* (1991)

Lew Brown (Louis Brownstein) 1893–1958
American songwriter

11 Life is just a bowl of cherries.

title of song (1931)

T. E. Brown 1830–97
Manx schoolmaster and poet

12 A garden is a lovesome thing, God wot!

'My Garden' (1893)

Thomas Brown 1663–1704
English satirist

13 A little before you made a leap into the dark.

Letters from the Dead to the Living (1702) 'Answer to Mr Joseph Haines'; see **HOBBES** 401:11

14 I do not love thee, Dr Fell.
The reason why I cannot tell;
But this I know, and know full well,
I do not love thee, Dr Fell.

written while an undergraduate at Christ Church, Oxford, of which Dr Fell was Dean
A. L. Hayward (ed.) *Amusements Serious and Comical by Tom Brown* (1927); see **MARTIAL** 524:4, **WATKYNS** 841:4

Cecil Browne 1932–
American businessman

15 But not so odd
As those who choose
A Jewish God,
But spurn the Jews.

reply to verse by William Norman Ewer; see **EWER** 322:2

Sir Thomas Browne 1605–82

English writer and physician

1 He who discommendeth others obliquely commendeth himself.
Christian Morals (1716) pt. 1, sect. 34

2 As for that famous network of Vulcan, which enclosed Mars and Venus, and caused that unextinguishable laugh in heaven, since the gods themselves could not discern it, we shall not pry into it.
The Garden of Cyrus (1658) ch. 2

3 Life itself is but the shadow of death, and souls departed but the shadows of the living: all things fall under this name. The sun itself is but the dark *simulacrum,* and light but the shadow of God.
The Garden of Cyrus (1658) ch. 4

4 Flat and flexible truths are beat out by every hammer; but Vulcan and his whole forge sweat to work out Achilles his armour.
The Garden of Cyrus (1658) ch. 5

5 The quincunx of heaven runs low, and 'tis time to close the five ports of knowledge.
The Garden of Cyrus (1658) ch. 5

6 All things began in order, so shall they end, and so shall they begin again; according to the ordainer of order and mystical mathematics of the city of heaven.
The Garden of Cyrus (1658) ch. 5

7 Nor will the sweetest delight of gardens afford much comfort in sleep; wherein the dullness of that sense shakes hands with delectable odours; and though in the bed of Cleopatra, can hardly with any delight raise up the ghost of a rose.
The Garden of Cyrus (1658) ch. 5

8 Though Somnus in Homer be sent to rouse up Agamemnon, I find no such effects in these drowsy approaches of sleep. To keep our eyes open longer were but to act our Antipodes. The huntsmen are up in America, and they are already past their first sleep in Persia. But who can be drowsy at that hour which freed us from everlasting sleep? or have slumbering thoughts at that time, when sleep itself must end, and as some conjecture all shall awake again?
The Garden of Cyrus (1658) ch. 5

9 Old mortality, the ruins of forgotten times.
Hydriotaphia (Urn Burial, 1658) Epistle Dedicatory

10 With rich flames and hired tears they solemnized their obsequies.
Hydriotaphia (Urn Burial, 1658) ch. 3

11 Men have lost their reason in nothing so much as their religion, wherein stones and clouts make martyrs.
Hydriotaphia (Urn Burial, 1658) ch. 4

12 Were the happiness of the next world as closely apprehended as the felicities of this, it were a martyrdom to live.
Hydriotaphia (Urn Burial, 1658) ch. 4

13 The long habit of living indisposeth us for dying.
Hydriotaphia (Urn Burial, 1658) ch. 5

14 What song the Syrens sang, or what name Achilles assumed when he hid himself among women, though puzzling questions, are not beyond all conjecture.
Hydriotaphia (Urn Burial, 1658) ch. 5

15 But to subsist in bones, and be but pyramidally extant, is a fallacy in duration.
Hydriotaphia (Urn Burial, 1658) ch. 5

16 Generations pass while some trees stand, and old families last not three oaks.
Hydriotaphia (Urn Burial, 1658) ch. 5

17 To be nameless in worthy deeds exceeds an infamous history.
Hydriotaphia (Urn Burial, 1658) ch. 5

18 The iniquity of oblivion blindly scattereth her poppy, and deals with the memory of men without distinction to merit perpetuity.
Hydriotaphia (Urn Burial, 1658) ch. 5

19 The night of time far surpasseth the day, and who knows when was the equinox?
Hydriotaphia (Urn Burial, 1658) ch. 5

20 Man is a noble animal, splendid in ashes, and pompous in the grave.
Hydriotaphia (Urn Burial, 1658) ch. 5

21 Ready to be any thing, in the ecstasy of being ever.
Hydriotaphia (Urn Burial, 1658) ch. 5

22 At my devotion I love to use the civility of my knee, my hat, and hand.
Religio Medici (1643) pt. 1, sect. 3

23 Many from . . . an inconsiderate zeal unto truth, have too rashly charged the troops of error, and remain as trophies unto the enemies of truth.
Religio Medici (1643) pt. 1, sect. 6

24 A man may be in as just possession of truth as of a city, and yet be forced to surrender.
Religio Medici (1643) pt. 1, sect. 6

25 As for those wingy mysteries in divinity and airy subtleties in religion, which have unhinged the brains of better heads, they never stretched the *pia mater* of mine; methinks there be not impossibilities enough in religion for an active faith.
Religio Medici (1643) pt. 1, sect. 9

26 I love to lose myself in a mystery, to pursue my reason to an *O altitudo!*
Religio Medici (1643) pt. 1, sect. 9

27 Who can speak of eternity without a solecism, or think thereof without an ecstasy? Time we may comprehend, 'tis but five days elder than ourselves.
Religio Medici (1643) pt. 1, sect. 11

28 I have often admired the mystical way of Pythagoras, and the secret magic of numbers.
Religio Medici (1643) pt. 1, sect. 12

1 We carry within us the wonders we seek without us: there is all Africa and her prodigies in us.
Religio Medici (1643) pt. 1, sect. 15; see **PLINY** 609:16

2 All things are artificial, for nature is the art of God.
Religio Medici (1643) pt. 1, sect. 16

3 Obstinacy in a bad cause, is but constancy in a good.
Religio Medici (1643) pt. 1, sect. 25

4 Persecution is a bad and indirect way to plant religion.
Religio Medici (1643) pt. 1, sect. 25

5 Not wrung from speculations and subtleties, but from common sense, and observation; not picked from the leaves of any author, but bred among the weeds and tares of mine own brain.
Religio Medici (1643) pt. 1, sect. 36

6 I am not so much afraid of death, as ashamed thereof; 'tis the very disgrace and ignominy of our natures, that in a moment can so disfigure us that our nearest friends, wife, and children, stand afraid and start at us.
Religio Medici (1643) pt. 1, sect. 40

7 Certainly there is no happiness within this circle of flesh, nor is it in the optics of these eyes to behold felicity; the first day of our Jubilee is death.
Religio Medici (1643) pt. 1, sect. 44

8 He forgets that he can die who complains of misery, we are in the power of no calamity, while death is in our own.
Religio Medici (1643) pt. 1, sect. 44

9 All places, all airs make unto me one country: I am in England, everywhere, and under any meridian.
Religio Medici (1643) pt. 2, sect. 1

10 If there be any among those common objects of hatred I do condemn and laugh at, it is that great enemy of reason, virtue and religion, the multitude, that numerous piece of monstrosity, which taken asunder seem men, and the reasonable creatures of God; but confused together, make but one great beast, and a monstrosity more prodigious than Hydra.
Religio Medici (1643) pt. 2, sect. 1

11 But how shall we expect charity towards others when we are so uncharitable to ourselves?
Religio Medici (1643) pt. 2, sect. 4

12 This trivial and vulgar way of coition; it is the foolishest act a wise man commits in all his life, nor is there any thing that will more deject his cooled imagination, when he shall consider what an odd and unworthy piece of folly he hath committed.
Religio Medici (1643) pt. 2, sect. 9

13 Sure there is music even in the beauty, and the silent note which Cupid strikes, far sweeter than

the sound of an instrument. For there is music wherever there is a harmony, order or proportion; and thus far we may maintain the music of the spheres; for those well-ordered motions, and regular paces, though they give no sound unto the ear, yet to the understanding they strike a note most full of harmony.
Religio Medici (1643) pt. 2, sect. 9

14 We all labour against our own cure, for death is the cure of all diseases.
Religio Medici (1643) pt. 2, sect. 9

15 For the world, I count it not an inn, but an hospital, and a place, not to live, but to die in.
Religio Medici (1643) pt. 2, sect. 11

16 There is surely a piece of divinity in us, something that was before the elements, and owes no homage unto the sun.
Religio Medici (1643) pt. 2, sect. 11

17 We term sleep a death, and yet it is waking that kills us, and destroys those spirits which are the house of life.
Religio Medici (1643) pt. 2, sect. 12

18 Half our days we pass in the shadow of the earth; and the brother of death exacteth a third part of our lives.
S. Wilkin (ed.) *Sir Thomas Browne's Works* (1835) vol. 4, p. 355 'On Dreams'

19 That children dream not in the first half year, that men dream not in some countries, are to me sick men's dreams, dreams out of the ivory gate, and visions before midnight.
S. Wilkin (ed.) *Sir Thomas Browne's Works* (1835) vol. 4 'On Dreams'

William Browne 1692–1774

English physician and writer

20 The King to Oxford sent a troop of horse,
For Tories own no argument but force:
With equal skill to Cambridge books he sent,
For Whigs admit no force but argument.
reply to Trapp's epigram on **GEORGE I**, in J. Nichols *Literary Anecdotes* vol. 3 (1812); see **TRAPP** 814:17

Elizabeth Barrett Browning 1806–61

English poet; wife of Robert **BROWNING**. On Browning: see **FITZGERALD** 332:1

21 Some people always sigh in thanking God.
Aurora Leigh (1857) bk. 1, l. 445

22 The works of women are symbolical.
We sew, sew, prick our fingers, dull our sight,
Producing what? A pair of slippers, sir,
To put on when you're weary.
Aurora Leigh (1857) bk. 1, l. 456

23   We have hearts within,
Warm, live, improvident, indecent hearts.
Aurora Leigh (1857) bk. 3, l. 461

24 Nay, if there's room for poets in this world
A little overgrown (I think there is)

Their sole work is to represent the age,
Their age, not Charlemagne's.
Aurora Leigh (1857) bk. 5, l. 200

1 And Camelot to minstrels seemed as flat
As Fleet Street to our poets.
Aurora Leigh (1857) bk. 5, l. 212

2 For say a foolish thing but oft enough . . .
. . . the same thing
Shall pass at last for absolutely wise,
And not with fools exclusively.
Aurora Leigh (1857) bk. 6, l. 4

3 The devil's most devilish when respectable.
Aurora Leigh (1857) bk. 7, l. 105

4 Earth's crammed with heaven,
And every common bush afire with God.
Aurora Leigh (1857) bk. 7, l. 821

5 And kings crept out again to feel the sun.
'Crowned and Buried' (1844) st. 11

6 Do ye hear the children weeping, O my
brothers,
Ere the sorrow comes with years?
'The Cry of the Children' (1844) st. 1

7 And lips say, 'God be pitiful,'
Who ne'er said, 'God be praised.'
'The Cry of the Human' (1844) st. 1

8 I tell you, hopeless grief is passionless.
'Grief' (1844)

9 Or from Browning some 'Pomegranate', which,
if cut deep down the middle,
Shows a heart within blood-tinctured, of a
veined humanity.
'Lady Geraldine's Courtship' (1844) st. 41

10 'Yes,' I answered you last night;
'No,' this morning, sir, I say.
Colours seen by candle-light
Will not look the same by day.
'The Lady's Yes' (1844)

11 What was he doing, the great god Pan,
Down in the reeds by the river?
'A Musical Instrument' (1862)

12 The true gods sigh for the cost and pain,—
For the reed which grows nevermore again
As a reed with the reeds in the river.
'A Musical Instrument' (1862)

13 How do I love thee? Let me count the ways.
I love thee to the depth and breadth and height
My soul can reach, when feeling out of sight
For the ends of Being and ideal Grace.
Sonnets from the Portuguese (1850) no. 43

14 I love thee with the breath,
Smiles, tears, of all my life!—and if God choose,
I shall but love thee better after death.
Sonnets from the Portuguese (1850) no. 43

15 Thou large-brained woman and large-hearted
man.
'To George Sand—A Desire' (1844)

Frederick 'Boy' Browning 1896–1965
English soldier

16 I think we might be going a bridge too far.
*expressing reservations about the Arnhem 'Market Garden'
operation to Field Marshal* **MONTGOMERY**
on 10 September 1944; R. E. Urquhart *Arnhem* (1958)

Robert Browning 1812–89
**English poet; husband of Elizabeth Barrett BROWNING. On
Browning: see BAGEHOT 51:20, BROWNING 164:9, WILDE
855:2, WILDE 855:8**

17 The high that proved too high, the heroic for
earth too hard,
The passion that left the ground to lose itself in
the sky,
Are music sent up to God by the lover and the
bard;
Enough that he heard it once: we shall hear it
by-and-by.
'Abt Vogler' (1864) st. 10

18 . . . I feel for the common chord again . . .
The C Major of this life.
'Abt Vogler' (1864) st. 12

19 Ah, but a man's reach should exceed his grasp,
Or what's a heaven for?
'Andrea del Sarto' (1855) l. 97

20 Still, what an arm! and I could alter it:
But all the play, the insight and the stretch—
Out of me, out of me!
'Andrea del Sarto' (1855) l. 115

21 One who never turned his back but marched
breast forward,
Never doubted clouds would break,
Never dreamed, though right were worsted,
wrong would triumph,
Held we fall to rise, are baffled to fight better,
Sleep to wake.
Asolando (1889) 'Epilogue'

22 Greet the unseen with a cheer!
Asolando (1889) 'Epilogue'

23 There spoke up a brisk little somebody,
Critic and whippersnapper, in a rage
To set things right.
referring to the poet Alfred Austin (1835–1913)
Balaustion's Adventure (1871) l. 306

24 Just when we are safest, there's a sunset-touch,
A fancy from a flower-bell, some one's death,
A chorus-ending from Euripides.
'Bishop Blougram's Apology' (1855) l. 182

25 The grand Perhaps!
'Bishop Blougram's Apology' (1855) l. 190

26 Our interest's on the dangerous edge of things.
The honest thief, the tender murderer,
The superstitious atheist, demirep
That loves and saves her soul in new French
books.
'Bishop Blougram's Apology' (1855) l. 395

1 You, for example, clever to a fault,
The rough and ready man who write apace,
Read somewhat seldomer, think perhaps even
    less.
'Bishop Blougram's Apology' (1855) l. 420

2 He said true things, but called them by wrong
names.
'Bishop Blougram's Apology' (1855) l. 996

3 Shrewd was that snatch from out the corner
    South
He graced his carrion with, God curse the same!
'The Bishop Orders his Tomb' (1845) l. 18

4 And have I not Saint Praxed's ear to pray
Horses for ye, and brown Greek manuscripts,
And mistresses with great smooth marbly limbs?
—That's if ye carve my epitaph aright.
'The Bishop Orders his Tomb' (1845) l. 73

5 And then how I shall lie through centuries,
And hear the blessed mutter of the mass,
And see God made and eaten all day long,
And feel the steady candle-flame, and taste
Good strong thick stupefying incense-smoke!
'The Bishop Orders his Tomb' (1845) l. 80

6 Boot, saddle, to horse, and away!
'Boot and Saddle' (1842)

7 And I turn the page, and I turn the page,
Not verse now, only prose!
'By the Fireside' (1855) st. 2

8 When earth breaks up and heaven expands,
How will the change strike me and you
In the house not made with hands?
'By the Fireside' (1855) st. 27; see BIBLE 113:9

9 Oh, the little more, and how much it is!
And the little less, and what worlds away!
'By the Fireside' (1855) st. 39

10 Setebos, Setebos, and Setebos!
'Thinketh, He dwelleth i' the cold o' the moon.
'Caliban upon Setebos' (1864) l. 24; see SHAKESPEARE 733:19

11 'Let twenty pass, and stone the twenty-first,
Loving not, hating not, just choosing so.
'Caliban upon Setebos' (1864) l. 102

12 Dauntless the slug-horn to my lips I set,
And blew. *'Childe Roland to the Dark Tower came.'*
'Childe Roland to the Dark Tower Came' (1855) st. 34; see
SHAKESPEARE 716:5

13 We loved, sir—used to meet:
How sad and bad and mad it was—
But then, how it was sweet!
'Confessions' (1864) st. 9

14 Stung by the splendour of a sudden thought.
'A Death in the Desert' (1864) l. 59

15 . . . Progress, man's distinctive mark alone,
Not God's, and not the beasts': God is, they are,
Man partly is and wholly hopes to be.
'A Death in the Desert' (1864) l. 586

16 Open my heart and you will see
Graved inside of it, 'Italy'.
'De Gustibus' (1855) pt. 2, l. 43

17   'Tis well averred,
A scientific faith's absurd.
'Easter-Day' (1850) l. 123

18 Karshish, the picker-up of learning's crumbs,
The not-incurious in God's handiwork.
'An Epistle . . . of Karshish' (1855)

19 Beautiful Evelyn Hope is dead!
'Evelyn Hope' (1855)

20 If you get simple beauty and naught else,
You get about the best thing God invents.
'Fra Lippo Lippi' (1855) l. 217

21   This world's no blot for us,
Nor blank; it means intensely, and means good:
To find its meaning is my meat and drink.
'Fra Lippo Lippi' (1855) l. 313

22 This is our master, famous calm and dead,
Borne on our shoulders.
'A Grammarian's Funeral' (1855) l. 27

23 Yea, but we found him bald too, eyes like lead,
Accents uncertain:
'Time to taste life,' another would have said,
'Up with the curtain!'
'A Grammarian's Funeral' (1855) l. 53

24 He said, 'What's time? Leave Now for dogs and
    apes!
Man has Forever.'
'A Grammarian's Funeral' (1855) l. 83

25 That low man seeks a little thing to do,
Sees it and does it:
This high man, with a great thing to pursue,
Dies ere he knows it.
That low man goes on adding one to one,
His hundred's soon hit.
This high man, aiming at a million,
Misses an unit.
'A Grammarian's Funeral' (1855) l. 113

26 He settled *Hoti's* business—let it be!
Properly based *Oun*—
Gave us the doctrine of the enclitic *De,*
Dead from the waist down.
'A Grammarian's Funeral' (1855) l. 129

27 Oh, to be in England
Now that April's there,
And whoever wakes in England
Sees, some morning, unaware,
That the lowest boughs and the brushwood
    sheaf
Round the elm-tree bole are in tiny leaf,
While the chaffinch sings on the orchard bough
In England—now!
'Home-Thoughts, from Abroad' (1845); see CUMMINGS 262:6

28 That's the wise thrush; he sings each song twice
    over,
Lest you should think he never could recapture
The first fine careless rapture!
'Home-Thoughts, from Abroad' (1845)

29 Nobly, nobly Cape Saint Vincent to the North-
west died away;

Sunset ran, one glorious blood-red, reeking into
  Cadiz Bay.
  'Home-Thoughts, from the Sea' (1845)

1 'Here and here did England help me: how can I
  help England?'—say,
  Whoso turns as I, this evening, turn to God to
  praise and pray,
  While Jove's planet rises yonder, silent over
  Africa.
  'Home-Thoughts, from the Sea' (1845)

2   'With this same key
  Shakespeare unlocked his heart,' once more!
  Did Shakespeare? If so, the less Shakespeare he!
  'House' (1876); see WORDSWORTH 869:2

3 How they brought the good news from Ghent
  to Aix.
  title of poem (1845)

4 I sprang to the stirrup, and Joris, and he;
  I galloped, Dirck galloped, we galloped all three.
  'How they brought the Good News from Ghent to Aix' (1845)
  l. 1

5 A man can have but one life and one death,
  One heaven, one hell.
  'In a Balcony' (1855) l. 13

6 'You're wounded!' 'Nay,' the soldier's pride
  Touched to the quick, he said:
  'I'm killed, Sire!' And his chief beside,
  Smiling the boy fell dead.
  'Incident of the French Camp' (1842) st. 5

7 Ignorance is not innocence but sin.
  The Inn Album (1875) canto 5

8 The swallow has set her six young on the rail,
  And looks sea-ward.
  'James Lee's Wife' (1864) pt. 3, st. 1

9 Who knows but the world may end tonight?
  'The Last Ride Together' (1855) st. 2

10 Had I said that, had I done this,
  So might I gain, so might I miss.
  Might she have loved me? just as well
  She might have hated, who can tell!
  'The Last Ride Together' (1855) st. 4

11 'Tis an awkward thing to play with souls,
  And matter enough to save one's own.
  'A Light Woman' (1855) st. 12

12 Just for a handful of silver he left us,
  Just for a riband to stick in his coat.
  deploring WORDSWORTH's *abandoning of his radical views*
  'The Lost Leader' (1845)

13 We that had loved him so, followed him,
  honoured him,
  Lived in his mild and magnificent eye,
  Learned his great language, caught his clear
  accents,
  Made him our pattern to live and to die!
  Shakespeare was of us, Milton was for us,
  Burns, Shelley, were with us—they watch from
  their graves!
  'The Lost Leader' (1845)

14 Never glad confident morning again!
  'The Lost Leader' (1845)

15 Kentish Sir Byng stood for his King,
  Bidding the crop-headed Parliament swing.
  'Marching Along' (1842)

16 Marched them along, fifty-score strong,
  Great-hearted gentlemen, singing this song.
  God for King Charles! Pym and such carles
  To the Devil that prompts 'em their treasonous
  parles!
  'Marching Along' (1842)

17 A tap at the pane, the quick sharp scratch
  And blue spurt of a lighted match,
  And a voice less loud, through its joys and fears,
  Than the two hearts beating each to each!
  'Meeting at Night' (1845)

18 Ah, did you once see Shelley plain,
  And did he stop and speak to you
  And did you speak to him again?
  How strange it seems, and new!
  'Memorabilia' (1855)

19 That's my last Duchess painted on the wall,
  Looking as if she were alive.
  'My Last Duchess' (1842) l. 1

20   She had
  A heart—how shall I say?—too soon made glad,
  Too easily impressed; she liked whate'er
  She looked on, and her looks went everywhere.
  'My Last Duchess' (1842) l. 21

21 Never the time and the place
  And the loved one all together!
  'Never the Time and the Place' (1883)

22   What's come to perfection perishes.
  Things learned on earth, we shall practise in
  heaven:
  Works done least rapidly, Art most cherishes.
  'Old Pictures in Florence' (1855) st. 17

23 Dante, who loved well because he hated,
  Hated wickedness that hinders loving.
  'One Word More' (1855) st. 5

24 Measure your mind's height by the shade it
  casts!
  Paracelsus (1835) pt. 3, l. 821

25 I give the fight up: let there be an end,
  A privacy, an obscure nook for me.
  I want to be forgotten even by God.
  Paracelsus (1835) pt. 5, l. 363

26 Round the cape of a sudden came the sea,
  And the sun looked over the mountain's rim:
  And straight was a path of gold for him,
  And the need of a world of men for me.
  'Parting at Morning' (1849)

27 It was roses, roses, all the way.
  'The Patriot' (1855)

28 The air broke into a mist with bells.
  'The Patriot' (1855)

29 Sun-treader, life and light be thine for ever!
  of SHELLEY
  Pauline (1833) l. 151

1 Rats!
 They fought the dogs and killed the cats,
 And bit the babies in the cradles,
 And ate the cheeses out of the vats,
 And licked the soup from the cooks' own ladles,
 Split open the kegs of salted sprats,
 Made nests inside men's Sunday hats,
 And even spoiled the women's chats
 By drowning their speaking
 With shrieking and squeaking
 In fifty different sharps and flats.
   'The Pied Piper of Hamelin' (1842) st. 2

2 So munch on, crunch on, take your nuncheon,
 Breakfast, supper, dinner, luncheon!
   'The Pied Piper of Hamelin' (1842) st. 7

3 The year's at the spring
 And day's at the morn;
 Morning's at seven;
 The hill-side's dew-pearled;
 The lark's on the wing;
 The snail's on the thorn:
 God's in his heaven—
 All's right with the world!
   Pippa Passes (1841) pt. 1, l. 221; see **PROVERBS** 633:10

4 All service ranks the same with God—
 With God, whose puppets, best and worst,
 Are we: there is no last nor first.
   Pippa Passes (1841) epilogue

5 That moment she was mine, mine, fair,
 Perfectly pure and good.
   'Porphyria's Lover' (1842) l. 36

6   All her hair
 In one long yellow string I wound
 Three times her little throat around,
 And strangled her. No pain felt she;
 I am quite sure she felt no pain.
   'Porphyria's Lover' (1842) l. 38

7 Fear death?—to feel the fog in my throat,
 The mist in my face.
   'Prospice' (1864)

8 I was ever a fighter, so—one fight more,
 The best and the last!
 I would hate that death bandaged my eyes, and
   forbore,
 And bade me creep past.
 No! let me taste the whole of it, fare like my
   peers
 The heroes of old,
 Bear the brunt, in a minute pay glad life's
   arrears
 Of pain, darkness and cold.
   'Prospice' (1864)

9 Grow old along with me!
 The best is yet to be,
 The last of life, for which the first was made.
   'Rabbi Ben Ezra' (1864) st. 1

10 Fancies that broke through language and
   escaped.
   'Rabbi Ben Ezra' (1864) st. 25

11 Time's wheel runs back or stops: potter and clay
   endure.
   'Rabbi Ben Ezra' (1864) st. 27

12 O lyric Love, half-angel and half-bird.
   The Ring and the Book (1868-9) bk. 1, l. 1391

13   So, Pietro craved an heir,
 (The story always old and always new).
   The Ring and the Book (1868-9) bk. 2, l. 213

14   Go practise if you please
 With men and women: leave a child alone
 For Christ's particular love's sake!
   The Ring and the Book (1868-9) bk. 3, l. 88

15 In the great right of an excessive wrong.
   The Ring and the Book (1868-9) bk. 3, l. 1055

16 Faultless to a fault.
   The Ring and the Book (1868-9) bk. 9, l. 1175

17 White shall not neutralize the black, nor good
 Compensate bad in man, absolve him so:
 Life's business being just the terrible choice.
   The Ring and the Book (1868-9) bk. 10, l. 1235

18 Gr-r-r—there go, my heart's abhorrence!
 Water your damned flowerpots, do!
 If hate killed men, Brother Lawrence,
 God's blood, would not mine kill you!
   'Soliloquy of the Spanish Cloister' (1842) st. 1

19 There's a great text in Galatians,
 Once you trip on it, entails
 Twenty-nine distinct damnations,
 One sure, if another fails.
   'Soliloquy of the Spanish Cloister' (1842) st. 7

20 Sidney's self, the starry paladin.
   Sordello (1840) bk. 1, l. 69

21 Still more labyrinthine buds the rose.
   Sordello (1840) bk. 1, l. 476

22   Any nose
 May ravage with impunity a rose.
   Sordello (1840) bk. 6, l. 881

23 He looked at her, as a lover can;
 She looked at him, as one who awakes:
 The past was a sleep, and her life began.
   'The Statue and the Bust' (1855) l. 28

24 And the sin I impute to each frustrate ghost
 Is—the unlit lamp and the ungirt loin,
 Though the end in sight was a vice, I say.
   'The Statue and the Bust' (1863 revision) l. 246

25 Oh Galuppi, Baldassaro, this is very sad to find!
 I can hardly misconceive you; it would prove me
   deaf and blind;
 But although I take your meaning, 'tis with such
   a heavy mind!
   'A Toccata of Galuppi's' (1855) st. 1

26 Hark, the dominant's persistence till it must be
   answered to!
   'A Toccata of Galuppi's' (1855) st. 8

27 Then they left you for their pleasure: till in due
   time, one by one,
 Some with lives that came to nothing, some
   with deeds as well undone,

Death stepped tacitly and took them where they
never see the sun.
'A Toccata of Galuppi's' (1855) st. 10

1 In you come with your cold music till I creep
through every nerve.
'A Toccata of Galuppi's' (1855) st. 11

2 Dust and ashes, dead and done with, Venice
spent what Venice earned.
'A Toccata of Galuppi's' (1855) st. 12

3 What of soul was left, I wonder, when the
kissing had to stop?
'A Toccata of Galuppi's' (1855) st. 14

4 Dear dead women, with such hair, too—what's
become of all the gold
Used to hang and brush their bosoms? I feel
chilly and grown old.
'A Toccata of Galuppi's' (1855) st. 15

5 I would that you were all to me,
You that are just so much, no more.
'Two in the Campagna' (1855) st. 8

6   I pluck the rose
And love it more than tongue can speak—
Then the good minute goes.
'Two in the Campagna' (1855) st. 10

7 What's become of Waring
Since he gave us all the slip?
Waring (1842) pt. 1, l. 1

8 Ichabod, Ichabod,
The glory is departed!
Waring (1842) pt. 6, l. 99; see **BIBLE** 83:29

9 Or, who in Moscow, toward the Czar,
With the demurest of footfalls,
Over the Kremlin's pavement bright
With serpentine and syenite,
Steps, with five other Generals.
Waring (1842) pt. 6, l. 109

10 Let's contend no more, Love,
Strive nor weep:
All be as before, Love,
—Only sleep!
'A Woman's Last Word' (1855) st. 1

11 Ay, dead! and were yourself alive, good Fitz,
How to return your thanks would pass my wits.
Kicking you seems the common lot of curs—
While more appropriate greeting lends you
grace:
Surely to spit there glorifies your face—
Spitting from lips once sanctified by Hers.
rejoinder to Edward **FITZGERALD**, *who had 'thanked God my
wife was dead'*
in *Athenaeum* 13 July 1889; see **FITZGERALD** 332:1

12 When it was written, God and Robert Browning
knew what it meant; now only God knows.
on Sordello
attributed; see **KLOPSTOCK** 469:11

Lenny Bruce 1925–66
American comedian

13 The liberals can understand everything but
people who don't understand them.
John Cohen (ed.) *The Essential Lenny Bruce* (1967)

14 I'll die young, but it's like kissing God.
on his drug addiction
attributed

Robert Bruce 1554–1631
Scottish minister and laird of Kinnaird

15 Now, God be with you, my children: I have
breakfasted with you and shall sup with my
Lord Jesus Christ this night.
Robert Fleming *The Fulfilling of the Scripture* (3rd ed., 1693)

Beau Brummell (George Bryan Brummell)
1778–1840
English dandy

16 Who's your fat friend?
referring to the Prince of Wales, later **GEORGE IV**
Capt. Jesse *Life of George Brummell* (1844) vol. 1

17 [Brummell] used to say that, whether it was
summer or winter, he always liked to have the
morning well-aired before he got up.
Charles Macfarlane *Reminiscences of a Literary Life* (1917) ch. 27

18 No perfumes, but very fine linen, plenty of it,
and country washing.
Memoirs of Harriette Wilson (1825) vol. 1

Frank Bruno 1961–
English boxer

19 Boxing's just show business with blood.
in *Guardian* 20 November 1991

20 Know what I mean, Harry?
*supposed to have been said in interview with sports
commentator Harry Carpenter, possibly apocryphal*

Giordano Bruno 1548–1600
Italian philosopher

21 He is glorified not in one, but in countless suns,
not in a single earth, a single world, but in a
thousand thousand, I say in an infinity of
worlds.
On the Infinite Universe and Worlds (1584) 'Introductory
Epistle'

Mary Brunton 1778–1818
Scottish novelist

22 The tranquil current of domestic happiness
affords no materials for narrative.
Self-Control (1811) vol. 2

William Jennings Bryan 1860–1925

American Democratic politician

1 You shall not press down upon the brow of labour this crown of thorns, you shall not crucify mankind upon a cross of gold.

opposing the gold standard

speech at the Democratic National Convention, Chicago, 1896, in *The First Battle. A Story of the Campaign of 1896* (1896) vol. 1, ch. 10

Bill Bryson 1951–

American travel writer

2 I had always thought that once you grew up you could do anything you wanted—stay up all night or eat ice-cream straight out of the container.

The Lost Continent (1989)

3 What an odd thing tourism is. You fly off to a strange land, eagerly abandoning all the comforts of home, and then expend vast quantities of time and money in a largely futile attempt to recapture the comforts that you wouldn't have lost if you hadn't left home in the first place.

Neither Here Nor There (1991)

Zbigniew Brzezinski 1928–

American politician

4 Russia can be an empire or a democracy, but it cannot be both.

in *Foreign Affairs* March/April 1994 'The Premature Partnership'

Martin Buber 1878–1965

Austrian-born religious philosopher and Zionist

5 Through the Thou a person becomes I.

I and Thou (1923)

John Buchan (Lord Tweedsmuir) 1875–1940

Scottish novelist and brother of O. **DOUGLAS**; Governor-General of Canada, 1935–40

6 There may be Peace without Joy, and Joy without Peace, but the two combined make Happiness.

Memory-Hold-the-Door (1940) ch. 5

7 It's a great life if you don't weaken.

Mr Standfast (1919) ch. 5

8 Have you ever considered what a diabolical weapon that can be—using all the channels of modern publicity to poison and warp men's minds? It is the most dangerous thing on earth . . . Happily, in the long run it defeats itself, but only after it has sown the world with mischief.

The Three Hostages (1924) ch. 4

9 An atheist is a man who has no invisible means of support.

H. E. Fosdick *On Being a Real Person* (1943) ch. 10

Frank Buchman 1878–1961

American evangelist; founder of the Moral Re-Armament movement

10 I thank heaven for a man like Adolf Hitler, who built a front line of defence against the anti-Christ of Communism.

in *New York World-Telegram* 26 August 1936

11 There is enough in the world for everyone's need, but not enough for everyone's greed.

Remaking the World (1947)

Georg Büchner 1813–37

German dramatist

12 Enjoy yourself—that's the best way to pray.

Danton's Death (1835) act 1, sc. 5

13 That's the only difference between men that I've been able to discover. Everyone acts according to his nature—in other words he does what does him good.

Danton's Death (1835) act 1, sc. 6

14 That damned argument: something cannot become nothing, there's the misery. Creation has become so broad, there's no emptiness. Everything is packed and swarming. The void has destroyed itself; creation is its wound.

Danton's Death (1835) act 3, sc. 7

Gene Buck (Edward Eugene Buck) 1885–1957 *and* Herman Ruby 1891–1959

15 That Shakespearian rag,—
Most intelligent, very elegant.

'That Shakespearian Rag' (1912 song); see **ELIOT** 311:9

John Sheffield, 1st Duke of Buckingham and Normanby 1648–1721

English poet and politician

16 Reject that vulgar error which appears
So fair, of making perfect characters,
There's no such thing in Nature, and you'll draw
A faultless monster which the world ne'er saw.

An Essay upon Poetry (1682) l. 232

17 Learn to write well, or not to write at all.

'An Essay upon Satire' (1689)

George Villiers, 2nd Duke of Buckingham 1628–87

English courtier and writer. On Buckingham: see **DRYDEN** 294:20, **POPE** 615:6

18 The world is made up for the most part of fools and knaves, both irreconcilable foes to truth.

The Dramatic Works (1715) vol. 2 'To Mr Clifford On his Humane Reason'

19 What a devil is the plot good for, but to bring in fine things?

The Rehearsal (1672) act 3, sc. 1

20 Ay, now the plot thickens very much upon us.

The Rehearsal (1672) act 3, sc. 2

1 My legs, the emblem of my various thought,
Show to what sad distraction I am brought.
The Rehearsal (1672) act 3, sc. 5

H. J. Buckoll 1803–71

English clergyman; master at Rugby School from 1826

2 Lord, dismiss us with Thy blessing,
Thanks for mercies past receive.
Pardon all, their faults confessing;
Time that's lost may all retrieve.
Psalms and Hymns for the Use of Rugby School Chapel (1850)
'Lord, Dismiss us with Thy Blessing'

J. B. Buckstone 1802–79

English comedian and dramatist

3 And we won't go home till morning.
Billy Taylor (performed 1829) act 1, sc. 2

Comte de Buffon (George-Louis Leclerc) 1707–88

French naturalist

4 Style is the man himself.
Discours sur le style (address given to the Académie Française,
25 August 1753); see **PROVERBS** 643:46

5 Genius is only a greater aptitude for patience.
Hérault de Séchelles *Voyage à Montbar* (1803); see **CARLYLE**
199:23

Edward Bullard 1907–80

English geophysicist

6 Rutherford was a disaster. He started the
'something for nothing' tradition . . . the notion
that research can always be done on the cheap
. . . The war taught us differently. If you want
quick and effective results you must put the
money in.
P. Grosvenor and J. McMillan *The British Genius* (1973); see
RUTHERFORD 676:5

Arthur Buller 1874–1944

British-born Canadian botanist and mycologist

7 There was a young lady named Bright,
Whose speed was far faster than light;
She set out one day
In a relative way
And returned on the previous night.
'Relativity' in *Punch* 19 December 1923

Gerald Bullett 1893–1958

English writer

8 My Lord Archbishop, what a scold you are!
And when your man is down how bold you are!
Of charity how oddly scant you are!
How Lang, O Lord, how full of Cantuar!
*on the role of Cosmo Gordon Lang, Archbishop of
Canterbury, in the abdication of* **EDWARD VIII**
composed *c.*1936

Bernhard von Bülow 1849–1929

German statesman, Chancellor of Germany 1900–9

9 We desire to throw no one into the shade [in
East Asia], but we also demand our own place in
the sun.
in the Reichstag, 6 December 1897, in *Graf Bülows Reden*
(1903); see **WILHELM II** 856:21

Edward Robert Bulwer, Earl of Lytton *see* Owen Meredith

Edward George Bulwer-Lytton (1st Baron Lytton) 1803–73

British novelist and politician

10 From the petty droppings of the well of
manners, the fossilized incrustations of national
character are formed.
England and the English (1833) vol. 1, ch. 2

11 Here Stanley meets,—how Stanley scorns, the
glance!
The brilliant chief, irregularly great,
Frank, haughty, rash,—the Rupert of Debate!
on Edward Stanley, 14th Earl of **DERBY**
The New Timon (1846) pt. 1, sect. 3, l. 202; see **DISRAELI**
284:6

12 Out-babying Wordsworth and out-glittering
Keats.
on **TENNYSON**
The New Timon (1846) pt. 2, sect. 1, l. 62

13 It was a dark and stormy night.
Paul Clifford (1830), opening words

14 Beneath the rule of men entirely great
The pen is mightier than the sword.
Richelieu (1839) act 2, sc. 2, l. 307; see **BURTON** 181:12,
PROVERBS 641:32

15 In science, read, by preference, the newest
works; in literature, the oldest.
Caxtoniana (1863) 'Hints on Mental Culture'

16 There is no man so friendless but what he can
find a friend sincere enough to tell him
disagreeable truths.
What will he do with it? (1857) vol. 1, bk. 3, ch. 15

Alfred 'Poet' Bunn *c.*1796–1860

English theatrical manager and librettist

17 I dreamed that I dwelt in marble halls
With vassals and serfs at my side.
The Bohemian Girl (1843) act 2 'The Gipsy Girl's Dream'

Basil Bunting 1900–85

English poet

18 Praise the green earth. Chance has appointed
her
home, workshop, larder, middenpit.
Her lousy skin scabbed here and there by
cities provides us with name and nation.
'Attis: or, Something Missing' (1931) pt. 1

1 Dance tiptoe, bull,
black against may.
Ridiculous and lovely
chase hurdling shadows
morning into noon.
  'Briggflatts' (1965) pt. 1

Luis Buñuel 1900–83

Spanish film director. See also **FILM TITLES** 331:3

2 Thanks to God, I am still an atheist.
  in *Le Monde* 16 December 1959

John Bunyan 1628–88

English writer and Nonconformist preacher. On Bunyan: see **ARNOLD** 32:6; see also **TWAIN** 819:19

3 Words easy to be understood do often hit the mark; when high and learned ones do only pierce the air.
  The Holy City (1665) 'The Epistle to Four Sorts of Readers' 'To the Learned Reader'; see **BIBLE** 112:16

4 As I walked through the wilderness of this world.
  The Pilgrim's Progress (1678) pt. 1, opening words

5 The name of the slough was Despond.
  The Pilgrim's Progress (1678) pt. 1

6 CHRISTIAN: Gentlemen, Whence came you, and whither do you go?
FORMALIST AND HYPOCRISY: We were born in the land of Vainglory, and we are going for praise to Mount Sion.
  The Pilgrim's Progress (1678) pt. 1

7 It is an hard matter for a man to go down into the valley of Humiliation . . . and to catch no slip by the way.
  The Pilgrim's Progress (1678) pt. 1

8 A foul Fiend coming over the field to meet him; his name is Apollyon.
  The Pilgrim's Progress (1678) pt. 1

9 It beareth the name of Vanity-Fair, because the town where 'tis kept, is lighter than vanity.
  The Pilgrim's Progress (1678) pt. 1; see **BOOK OF COMMON PRAYER** 143:22

10 Hanging is too good for him, said Mr Cruelty.
  The Pilgrim's Progress (1678) pt. 1

11 Yet my great-grandfather was but a water-man, looking one way, and rowing another: and I got most of my estate by the same occupation.
  The Pilgrim's Progress (1678) pt. 1; see **BURTON** 181:7

12 They are for religion when in rags and contempt; but I am for him when he walks in his golden slippers, in the sunshine and with applause.
  The Pilgrim's Progress (1678) pt. 1

13 A castle, called Doubting Castle, the owner whereof was Giant Despair.
  The Pilgrims Progress (1678) pt.1

14 Now Giant Despair had a wife, and her name was Diffidence.
  The Pilgrim's Progress (1678) pt. 1

15 They came to the Delectable Mountains.
  The Pilgrim's Progress (1678) pt. 1

16 Sleep is sweet to the labouring man.
  The Pilgrim's Progress (1678) pt. 1; see **BIBLE** 89:28

17 Then I saw that there was a way to Hell, even from the gates of heaven.
  The Pilgrim's Progress (1678) pt. 1

18 So I awoke, and behold it was a dream.
  The Pilgrim's Progress (1678) pt. 1

19 A man that could look no way but downwards, with a muckrake in his hand.
  The Pilgrim's Progress (1684) pt. 2; see **ROOSEVELT** 667:22

20 One leak will sink a ship, and one sin will destroy a sinner.
  The Pilgrim's Progress (1684) pt. 2

21 He that is down needs fear no fall,
He that is low no pride.
He that is humble ever shall
Have God to be his guide.
  The Pilgrim's Progress (1684) pt. 2 'Shepherd Boy's Song'

22 Difficulties, lions, or Vanity-Fair, he feared not at all: 'twas only sin, death, and Hell that was to him a terror.
  of Mr Fearing
  The Pilgrim's Progress (1684) pt. 2

23 A man there was, tho' some did count him mad,
The more he cast away, the more he had.
  The Pilgrim's Progress (1684) pt. 2

24 Mercy . . . laboured much for the poor . . . an ornament to her profession.
  The Pilgrim's Progress (1684) pt. 2

25 Who would true valour see,
Let him come hither;
One here will constant be,
Come wind, come weather.
There's no discouragement
Shall make him once relent
His first avowed intent
To be a pilgrim.

Who so beset him round
With dismal stories,
Do but themselves confound—
His strength the more is.
  The Pilgrim's Progress (1684) pt. 2

26 The last words of Mr Despondency were, Farewell night, welcome day. His daughter went through the river singing, but none could understand what she said.
  The Pilgrim's Progress (1684) pt. 2

27 I am going to my Fathers, and tho' with great difficulty I am got hither, yet now I do not repent me of all the trouble I have been at to arrive where I am. My sword, I give to him that shall succeed me in my pilgrimage, and my courage and skill to him that can get it. My marks and scars I carry with me, to be a witness

for me, that I have fought his battles, who will
now be my rewarder.
Mr Valiant-for-Truth
> *The Pilgrim's Progress* (1684) pt. 2

1 So he passed over, and the trumpets sounded for
him on the other side.
Mr Valiant-for-Truth
> *The Pilgrim's Progress* (1684) pt. 2

2 I have formerly lived by hearsay and faith, but
now I go where I shall live by sight, and shall be
with Him in whose company I delight myself.
Mr Standfast
> *The Pilgrim's Progress* (1684) pt. 2

Samuel Dickinson Burchard 1812–91
American Presbyterian minister

3 We are Republicans and don't propose to leave
our party and identify ourselves with the party
whose antecedents are rum, Romanism, and
rebellion.
> speech at the Fifth Avenue Hotel, New York, 29 October
> 1884, in *New York World* 30 October 1884

Julie Burchill 1960–
English journalist and writer. See also ANONYMOUS 17:17

4 Now, at last, this sad, glittering century has an
image worthy of it: a wandering, wondering
girl, a silly Sloane turned secular saint, coming
home in her coffin to RAF Northolt like the
good soldier she was.
of DIANA, Princess of Wales
> in *Guardian* 2 September 1997

James Bland Burges 1752–1824
English poet

5 Pandora's box, whence flew dispersed
All the dire mischiefs which mankind have
cursed.
> *The Dragon Knight* (1816) canto 7

Anthony Burgess 1917–93
English novelist and critic

6 A clockwork orange.
> title of novel (1962)

7 It was the afternoon of my eighty-first birthday,
and I was in bed with my catamite when Ali
announced that the archbishop had come to see
me.
> *Earthly Powers* (1980), opening words

8 He said it was artificial respiration, but now I
find I am to have his child.
> *Inside Mr Enderby* (1963) pt. 1, ch. 4

9 The US presidency is a Tudor monarchy plus
telephones.
> George Plimpton (ed.) *Writers at Work* (4th Series, 1977)

Gelett Burgess 1866–1951
American humorist and illustrator

10 I never saw a Purple Cow,
I never hope to see one;
But I can tell you, anyhow,
I'd rather see than be one!
> *The Burgess Nonsense Book* (1914) 'The Purple Cow'

11 Ah, yes! I wrote the 'Purple Cow'—
I'm sorry, now, I wrote it!
But I can tell you anyhow,
I'll kill you if you quote it!
> *The Burgess Nonsense Book* (1914) 'Confessional'

Lord Burghley *see* William Cecil

John William Burgon 1813–88
English clergyman; Dean of Chichester from 1876

12 Match me such marvel, save in Eastern clime,—
A rose-red city—half as old as Time!
> *Petra* (1845) l. 131; see PLOMER 610:6, ROGERS 665:14

John Burgoyne 1722–92
English general and dramatist

13 You have only, when before your glass, to keep
pronouncing to yourself nimini-pimini—the lips
cannot fail of taking their plie.
plie = curve
> *The Heiress* (1786) act 3, sc. 2

Edmund Burke 1729–97
**Irish-born Whig politician and man of letters. On Burke: see
GOLDSMITH 364:18, JOHNSON 443:21, PAINE 592:18, PAINE
592:19; see also MISQUOTATIONS 548:4**

14 The conduct of a losing party never appears
right: at least it never can possess the only
infallible criterion of wisdom to vulgar
judgements—success.
> *Letter to a Member of the National Assembly* (1791)

15 Those who have been once intoxicated with
power, and have derived any kind of emolument
from it, even though for but one year, can never
willingly abandon it.
> *Letter to a Member of the National Assembly* (1791)

16 Tyrants seldom want pretexts.
> *Letter to a Member of the National Assembly* (1791)

17 You can never plan the future by the past.
> *Letter to a Member of the National Assembly* (1791)

18 The king, and his faithful subjects, the lords and
commons of this realm,—the triple cord, which
no man can break.
> *A Letter to a Noble Lord* (1796); see BIBLE 89:26

19 Many have been taught to think that
moderation, in a case like this, is a sort of
treason.
> *Letter to the Sheriffs of Bristol* (1777)

20 Between craft and credulity, the voice of reason
is stifled.
> *Letter to the Sheriffs of Bristol* (1777)

1 Liberty too must be limited in order to be possessed.
Letter to the Sheriffs of Bristol (1777)

2 Nothing in progression can rest on its original plan. We may as well think of rocking a grown man in the cradle of an infant.
Letter to the Sheriffs of Bristol (1777)

3 Among a people generally corrupt, liberty cannot long exist.
Letter to the Sheriffs of Bristol (1777)

4 There is, however, a limit at which forbearance ceases to be a virtue.
Observations on a late Publication on the Present State of the Nation (2nd ed., 1769)

5 It is a general popular error to imagine the loudest complainers for the public to be the most anxious for its welfare.
Observations on a late Publication on the Present State of the Nation (2nd ed., 1769)

6 It is the nature of all greatness not to be exact; and great trade will always be attended with considerable abuses.
On American Taxation (1775)

7 Falsehood has a perennial spring.
On American Taxation (1775)

8 To tax and to please, no more than to love and to be wise, is not given to men.
On American Taxation (1775); see **PROVERBS** 640:41

9 I have in general no very exalted opinion of the virtue of paper government.
On Conciliation with America (1775)

10 The concessions of the weak are the concessions of fear.
On Conciliation with America (1775)

11 When we speak of the commerce with our colonies, fiction lags after truth; invention is unfruitful, and imagination cold and barren.
On Conciliation with America (1775)

12 The use of force alone is but *temporary*. It may subdue for a moment; but it does not remove the necessity of subduing again; and a nation is not governed, which is perpetually to be conquered.
On Conciliation with America (1775)

13 Nothing less will content me, than *whole America*.
On Conciliation with America (1775)

14 All Protestantism, even the most cold and passive, is a sort of dissent. But the religion most prevalent in our northern colonies is a refinement on the principle of resistance; it is the dissidence of dissent, and the Protestantism of the Protestant religion.
On Conciliation with America (1775)

15 I do not know the method of drawing up an indictment against an whole people.
On Conciliation with America (1775)

16 It is not, what a lawyer tells me I *may* do; but what humanity, reason, and justice, tells me I ought to do.
On Conciliation with America (1775)

17 Freedom and not servitude is the cure of anarchy; as religion, and not atheism, is the true remedy for superstition.
On Conciliation with America (1775)

18 Every human benefit, every virtue and every prudent act, is founded on compromise.
On Conciliation with America (1775)

19 Instead of a standing revenue, you will have therefore a perpetual quarrel.
On Conciliation with America (1775)

20 Parties must ever exist in a free country.
On Conciliation with America (1775)

21 Slavery they can have anywhere. It is a weed that grows in every soil.
On Conciliation with America (1775)

22 Deny them this participation of freedom, and you break that sole bond, which originally made, and must still preserve the unity of the empire.
On Conciliation with America (1775)

23 It is the love of the people; it is their attachment to their government, from the sense of the deep stake they have in such a glorious institution, which gives you your army and your navy, and infuses into both that liberal obedience, without which your army would be a base rabble, and your navy nothing but rotten timber.
On Conciliation with America (1775)

24 Magnanimity in politics is not seldom the truest wisdom; and a great empire and little minds go ill together.
On Conciliation with America (1775)

25 By adverting to the dignity of this high calling, our ancestors have turned a savage wilderness into a glorious empire: and have made the most extensive, and the only honourable conquests; not by destroying, but by promoting the wealth, the number, the happiness of the human race.
On Conciliation with America (1775)

26 No passion so effectually robs the mind of all its powers of acting and reasoning as fear.
On the Sublime and Beautiful (1757) pt. 2, sect. 2

27 Custom reconciles us to everything.
On the Sublime and Beautiful (1757) pt. 4, sect. 18

28 I flatter myself that I love a manly, moral, regulated liberty as well as any gentleman.
Reflections on the Revolution in France (1790)

29 Whenever our neighbour's house is on fire, it cannot be amiss for the engines to play a little on our own.
Reflections on the Revolution in France (1790)

30 A state without the means of some change is without the means of its conservation.
Reflections on the Revolution in France (1790)

1 Make the Revolution a parent of settlement, and not a nursery of future revolutions.
Reflections on the Revolution in France (1790)

2 People will not look forward to posterity, who never look backward to their ancestors.
Reflections on the Revolution in France (1790)

3 Those who attempt to level never equalize.
Reflections on the Revolution in France (1790)

4 Whatever each man can separately do, without trespassing upon others, he has a right to do for himself; and he has a right to a fair portion of all which society, with all its combinations of skill and force, can do in his favour.
Reflections on the Revolution in France (1790)

5 Government is a contrivance of human wisdom to provide for human *wants*. Men have a right that these wants should be provided for by this wisdom.
Reflections on the Revolution in France (1790)

6 I thought ten thousand swords must have leapt from their scabbards to avenge even a look that threatened her with insult.
of **MARIE-ANTOINETTE**
Reflections on the Revolution in France (1790)

7 The age of chivalry is gone.— That of sophisters, economists, and calculators, has succeeded; and the glory of Europe is extinguished for ever.
Reflections on the Revolution in France (1790)

8 The unbought grace of life, the cheap defence of nations, the nurse of manly sentiment and heroic enterprise, is gone!
Reflections on the Revolution in France (1790)

9 This barbarous philosophy, which is the offspring of cold hearts and muddy understandings.
Reflections on the Revolution in France (1790)

10 In the groves of *their* academy, at the end of every vista, you see nothing but the gallows.
Reflections on the Revolution in France (1790); see **HORACE** 410:22

11 Kings will be tyrants from policy when subjects are rebels from principle.
Reflections on the Revolution in France (1790)

12 Learning will be cast into the mire, and trodden down under the hoofs of a swinish multitude.
Reflections on the Revolution in France (1790)

13 Because half a dozen grasshoppers under a fern make the field ring with their importunate chink, whilst thousands of great cattle, reposed beneath the shadow of the British oak, chew the cud and are silent, pray do not imagine that those who make the noise are the only inhabitants of the field.
Reflections on the Revolution in France (1790)

14 Man is by his constitution a religious animal; atheism is against not only our reason, but our instincts.
Reflections on the Revolution in France (1790); see **ARISTOTLE** 27:24

15 A perfect democracy is therefore the most shameless thing in the world.
Reflections on the Revolution in France (1790)

16 Society is indeed a contract . . . it becomes a partnership not only between those who are living, but between those who are living, those who are dead, and those who are to be born.
Reflections on the Revolution in France (1790)

17 Nobility is a graceful ornament to the civil order. It is the Corinthian capital of polished society.
Reflections on the Revolution in France (1790)

18 Superstition is the religion of feeble minds.
Reflections on the Revolution in France (1790)

19 He that wrestles with us strengthens our nerves, and sharpens our skill. Our antagonist is our helper.
Reflections on the Revolution in France (1790)

20 Our patience will achieve more than our force.
Reflections on the Revolution in France (1790)

21 By hating vices too much, they come to love men too little.
Reflections on the Revolution in France (1790)

22 We begin our public affections in our families. No cold relation is a zealous citizen.
Reflections on the Revolution in France (1790)

23 Good order is the foundation of all good things.
Reflections on the Revolution in France (1790)

24 Nothing turns out to be so oppressive and unjust as a feeble government.
Reflections on the Revolution in France (1790)

25 Every politician ought to sacrifice to the graces; and to join compliance with reason.
Reflections on the Revolution in France (1790)

26 Never, no never, did Nature say one thing and Wisdom say another.
Third Letter . . . on the Proposals for Peace with the Regicide Directory (1797)

27 Ambition can creep as well as soar.
Third Letter . . . on the Proposals for Peace . . . (1797)

28 And having looked to government for bread, on the very first scarcity they will turn and bite the hand that fed them.
Thoughts and Details on Scarcity (1800)

29 To complain of the age we live in, to murmur at the present possessors of power, to lament the past, to conceive extravagant hopes of the future, are the common dispositions of the greatest part of mankind.
Thoughts on the Cause of the Present Discontents (1770)

30 I am not one of those who think that the people are never in the wrong. They have been so, frequently and outrageously, both in other countries and in this. But I do say, that in all disputes between them and their rulers, the presumption is at least upon a par in favour of the people.
Thoughts on the Cause of the Present Discontents (1770)

1 The power of the crown, almost dead and rotten as Prerogative, has grown up anew, with much more strength, and far less odium, under the name of Influence.
Thoughts on the Cause of the Present Discontents (1770)

2 We must soften into a credulity below the milkiness of infancy to think all men virtuous. We must be tainted with a malignity truly diabolical, to believe all the world to be equally wicked and corrupt.
Thoughts on the Cause of the Present Discontents (1770)

3 When ... [people] imagine that their food is only a cover for poison, and when they neither love nor trust the hand that serves it, it is not the name of the roast beef of old England that will persuade them to sit down to the table that is spread for them.
Thoughts on the Cause of the Present Discontents (1770)

4 When bad men combine, the good must associate; else they will fall, one by one, an unpitied sacrifice in a contemptible struggle.
Thoughts on the Cause of the Present Discontents (1770); see **MISQUOTATIONS** 548:4

5 Of this stamp is the cant of *Not men, but measures*; a sort of charm by which many people get loose from every honourable engagement.
Thoughts on the Cause of the Present Discontents (1770); see **CANNING** 197:5, **GOLDSMITH** 365:2

6 It is therefore our business carefully to cultivate in our minds, to rear to the most perfect vigour and maturity, every sort of generous and honest feeling that belongs to our nature. To bring the dispositions that are lovely in private life into the service and conduct of the commonwealth;
Thoughts on the Cause of the Present Discontents (1770)

7 So to be patriots, as not to forget we are gentlemen.
Thoughts on the Cause of the Present Discontents (1770)

8 Laws, like houses, lean on one another.
A Tract on the Popery Laws (planned c.1765) ch. 3, pt. 1 in *The Works* vol. 5 (1812)

9 In all forms of Government the people is the true legislator.
A Tract on the Popery Laws ch. 3, pt. 1 in *The Works* vol. 5 (1812)

10 Falsehood and delusion are allowed in no case whatsoever: But, as in the exercise of all the virtues, there is an economy of truth.
Two Letters on the Proposals for Peace with the Regicide Directory (1796) pt. 1; see **ARMSTRONG** 28:21

11 All men that are ruined are ruined on the side of their natural propensities.
Two Letters on the Proposals for Peace with the Regicide Directory (9th ed., 1796)

12 Example is the school of mankind, and they will learn at no other.
Two Letters on the Proposals for Peace with the Regicide Directory (9th ed., 1796)

13 The greater the power, the more dangerous the abuse.
speech on the Middlesex Election, 7 February 1771, in *The Speeches* (1854)

14 The fire-bell at midnight disturbs your sleep, but it keeps you from being burned in your bed.
speech on the Jury Bill, 7 March 1771, in P. Langford (ed.) *Writings and Speeches of Edmund Burke* (1981) vol. 2

15 Your representative owes you, not his industry only, but his judgement; and he betrays, instead of serving you, if he sacrifices it to your opinion.
speech, 3 November 1774, in *Speeches at his Arrival at Bristol* (1774)

16 People crushed by law have no hopes but from power. If laws are their enemies, they will be enemies to laws; and those, who have much to hope and nothing to lose, will always be dangerous, more or less.
letter to Charles James Fox, 8 October 1777, in *The Correspondence of Edmund Burke* vol. 3 (1961)

17 Bad laws are the worst sort of tyranny.
Speech at Bristol, previous to the Late Election (1780)

18 Individuals pass like shadows; but the commonwealth is fixed and stable.
speech, House of Commons, 11 February 1780

19 The people are the masters.
speech, House of Commons, 11 February 1780; see **BLAIR** 123:19

20 Not merely a chip of the old 'block', but the old block itself.
on the younger **PITT**'s maiden speech, February 1781
N. W. Wraxall *Historical Memoirs of My Own Time* (1904 ed.) pt. 2

21 Every other conqueror of every other description has left some monument, either of state or beneficence, behind him. Were we to be driven out of India this day, nothing would remain to tell that it had been possessed, during the inglorious period of our dominion, by anything better than the orang-outang or the tiger.
speech on Fox's East India Bill, House of Commons, 1 December 1783

22 Your governor [Warren Hastings] stimulates a rapacious and licentious soldiery to the personal search of women, lest these unhappy creatures should avail themselves of the protection of their sex to secure any supply for their necessities.
speech on Fox's East India Bill, House of Commons, 1 December 1783

23 The people never give up their liberties but under some delusion.
speech at County Meeting of Buckinghamshire, 1784, attributed in E. Latham *Famous Sayings* (1904), with 'except' substituted for 'but'

24 Religious persecution may shield itself under the guise of a mistaken and over-zealous piety.
speech, 18 February 1788, in E. A. Bond (ed.) *Speeches ... in the Trial of Warren Hastings* (1859) vol. 1

1 An event has happened, upon which it is difficult to speak, and impossible to be silent.
   speech, 5 May 1789, in E. A. Bond (ed.) *Speeches . . . in the Trial of Warren Hastings* (1859) vol. 2

2 At last dying in the last dyke of prevarication.
   speech, 7 May 1789, in E. A. Bond (ed.) *Speeches . . . in the Trial of Warren Hastings* (1859) vol. 2

3 Old religious factions are volcanoes burnt out.
   speech on the Petition of the Unitarians, 11 May 1792, in *The Works* vol. 5 (1812); see DISRAELI 284:26

4 Dangers by being despised grow great.
   speech on the Petition of the Unitarians, 11 May 1792, in *The Works* vol. 5 (1812)

5 There is but one law for all, namely, that law which governs all law—the law of our Creator, the law of humanity, justice, equity, the law of nature and of nations.
   speech, 28 May 1794, in E. A. Bond (ed.) *Speeches . . . in the Trial of Warren Hastings* (1859) vol. 4

6 The cold neutrality of an impartial judge.
   J. P. Brissot *To his Constituents* (1794) 'Translator's Preface' (written by Burke)

7 The silent touches of time.
   letter to William Smith, 29 January 1795, in *The Correspondence of Edmund Burke* vol. 8 (1969)

8 Somebody has said, that a king may make a nobleman but he cannot make a gentleman.
   letter to William Smith, 29 January 1795, in *The Correspondence of Edmund Burke* vol. 8 (1969)

9 His virtues were his arts.
   inscription on the pedestal of the statue of the Marquis of Rockingham in Wentworth Park

10 Those who carry on great public schemes must be proof against the most fatiguing delays, the most mortifying disappointments, the most shocking insults, and, worst of all, the presumptuous judgements of the ignorant upon their designs.
   attributed; Benjamin Ward Richardson 'A Biographical Dissertation' ch. 4 in Edwin Chadwick *The Health of Nations* (1887)

Johnny Burke 1908–64

American songwriter

11 Every time it rains, it rains
   Pennies from heaven.
   Don't you know each cloud contains
   Pennies from heaven?
   'Pennies from Heaven' (1936 song)

12 Like Webster's Dictionary, we're Morocco bound.
   The Road to Morocco (1942 film) title song

Frances Hodgson Burnett 1849–1924

English-born American novelist

13 When Mary Lennox was sent to Misselthwaite Manor to live with her uncle, everybody said she was the most disagreeable-looking child ever seen.
   The Secret Garden (1911), opening words

Thomas E. Burnett Jnr 1963–2001

American businessman

14 I love you, honey. I know we're all going to die—but there's three of us who are going to do something about it.
   final phone call to his wife from the hijacked Flight 93, which crashed south of Pittsburgh, 11 September 2001
   in *Independent* 13 September 2001; see MCEWAN 510:14

Fanny Burney (Mme d'Arblay) 1752–1840

English novelist and diarist

15 A little alarm now and then keeps life from stagnation.
   Camilla (1796) bk. 3, ch. 11

16 There is nothing upon the face of the earth so insipid as a medium. Give me love or hate! a friend that will go to jail for me, or an enemy that will run me through the body!
   Camilla (1796) bk. 3, ch. 12

17 It's a delightful thing to think of perfection; but it's vastly more amusing to talk of errors and absurdities.
   Camilla (1796) bk. 3, ch. 12

18 Vice is detestable; I banish all its appearances from my coteries; and I would banish its reality, too, were I sure I should then have any thing but empty chairs in my drawing-room.
   Camilla (1796) bk. 5, ch. 6

19 The cure of a romantic first flame is a better surety to subsequent discretion, than all the exhortations of all the fathers, and mothers, and guardians, and maiden aunts in the universe.
   Camilla (1796) bk. 5, ch. 6

20 O, we all acknowledge our faults, now; 'tis the mode of the day: but the acknowledgement passes for current payment; and therefore we never amend them.
   Camilla (1796) bk. 6, ch. 2

21 No man is in love when he marries. He may have loved before; I have even heard he has sometimes loved after: but at the time never. There is something in the formalities of the matrimonial preparations that drive away all the little cupidons.
   Camilla (1796) bk. 6, ch. 10

22 Travelling is the ruin of all happiness! There's no looking at a building here after seeing Italy.
   Cecilia (1782) bk. 4, ch. 2

23 'The whole of this unfortunate business,' said Dr Lyster, 'has been the result of PRIDE AND PREJUDICE.'
   Cecilia (1782) bk. 10, ch. 10

24 'Do you come to the play without knowing what it is?' 'O yes, Sir, yes, very frequently; I have no time to read play-bills; one merely comes to meet one's friends, and show that one's alive.'
   Evelina (1778) Letter 20

1 The freedom with which Dr Johnson condemns whatever he disapproves is astonishing.
Diary and Letters of Madame D'Arblay (1842) pt. 2 (23 August 1778)

2 The delusive seduction of martial music.
Joyce Hemlow et al. (eds.) *Journals and Letters of Fanny Burney* vol. 5 (1975) 'Paris Journal'

3 Such a set of tittle tattle, prittle prattle visitants! Oh dear! I am so sick of the ceremony and fuss of these fall lall people! So much dressing—chit chat—complimentary nonsense—In short, a country town is my detestation.
diary, 17 July 1768, in *Early Journals and Letters of Fanny Burney* (ed. L. E. Troide, 1988) vol. 1

4 O! how short a time does it take to put an end to a woman's liberty!
of a wedding
diary, 20 July 1768, in *Early Journals and Letters of Fanny Burney* (ed. L. E. Troide, 1988) vol. 1

John Burns 1858–1943
British Liberal politician

5 The Thames is liquid history.
to an American who had compared the Thames disparagingly with the Mississippi
in *Daily Mail* 25 January 1943

Robert Burns 1759–96
Scottish poet. See also **SONGS, SPIRITUALS, AND SHANTIES** 762:1

6 O thou! whatever title suit thee,
Auld Hornie, Satan, Nick, or Clootie.
'Address to the Deil' (1786)

7 Address to the unco guid.
title of poem, 1787

8 Then gently scan your brother man,
Still gentler sister woman;
Tho' they may gang a kennin wrang,
To step aside is human.
'Address to the Unco Guid' (1787)

9 Ae fond kiss, and then we sever;
Ae fareweel, and then for ever!
'Ae fond Kiss' (1792)

10 Flow gently, sweet Afton, among thy green braes,
Flow gently, I'll sing thee a song in thy praise.
'Afton Water' (1792)

11 Should auld acquaintance be forgot
And never brought to mind?
'Auld Lang Syne' (1796)

12 We'll tak a cup o' kindness yet,
For auld lang syne.
'Auld Lang Syne' (1796)

13 Auld Scotland has a raucle tongue.
raucle *meaning 'rash, impetuous'*
'The Author's Earnest Cry' (1786)

14 Freedom and Whisky gang thegither!
'The Author's Earnest Cry and Prayer' (1786) l. 185

15 Ay waukin, Oh,
Waukin still and weary:
Sleep I can get nane,
For thinking on my dearie.
'Ay Waukin O' (1790)

16 Ye banks and braes o' bonny Doon,
How can ye bloom sae fresh and fair;
How can ye chant, ye little birds,
And I sae weary fu' o' care!
'The Banks o' Doon' (1792)

17 And my fause luver stole my rose,
But ah! he left the thorn wi' me.
'The Banks o' Doon' (1792)

18 Thou minds me o' departed joys,
Departed, never to return.
'The Banks o' Doon' (1792)

19 O saw ye bonnie Lesley,
As she gaed o'er the border?
She's gane, like Alexander,
To spread her conquests farther.
To see her is to love her,
And love but her for ever;
For Nature made her what she is
And never made anither!
'Bonnie Lesley' (1798)

20 Gin a body meet a body
Comin thro' the rye,
Gin a body kiss a body
Need a body cry?
'Comin thro' the rye' (1796)

21 Contented wi' little and cantie wi' mair,
Whene'er I forgather wi' Sorrow and Care,
I gie them a skelp, as they're creeping alang,
Wi' a cog o' gude swats and an auld Scotish sang.
'Contented wi' little' (1796)

22 Th' expectant wee-things, toddlin', stacher through
To meet their Dad, wi' flichterin' noise an' glee.
'The Cotter's Saturday Night' (1786) st. 3

23 They never sought in vain that sought the Lord aright.
'The Cotter's Saturday Night' (1786) st. 6

24 The healsome porritch, chief of Scotia's food.
'The Cotter's Saturday Night' (1786) st. 11

25 The sire turns o'er, wi' patriarchal grace,
The big ha'-Bible, ance his father's pride.
'The Cotter's Saturday Night' (1786) st. 12

26 From scenes like these old Scotia's grandeur springs,
That makes her loved at home, revered abroad:
Princes and Lords are but the breath of kings,
'An honest man's the noblest work of God.'
'The Cotter's Saturday Night' (1786) st. 19; see **POPE** 617:8

27 I wasna fou, but just had plenty.
'Death and Dr Hornbook' (1787) st. 3

28 On ev'ry hand it will allow'd be,
He's just—nae better than he shou'd be.
'A Dedication to G[avin] H[amilton]' (1786) l. 25

1 There's threesome reels, there's foursome reels,
There's hornpipes and strathspeys, man,
But the ae best dance e'er cam to the land
Was, the deil's awa wi' th'Exciseman.
'The Deil's awa wi' th'Exciseman' (1792)

2 Perhaps it may turn out a sang;
Perhaps, turn out a sermon.
'Epistle to a Young Friend' (1786) st. 1

3 I waive the quantum o' the sin;
The hazard of concealing;
But och! it hardens a' within,
And petrifies the feeling!
'Epistle to a Young Friend' (1786) st. 6

4 An atheist-laugh's a poor exchange
For Deity offended!
'Epistle to a Young Friend' (1786) st. 9

5 Gie me ae spark o' Nature's fire,
That's a' the learning I desire.
'Epistle to J. L[aprai]k' (1786) st. 13

6 For thus the royal mandate ran,
When first the human race began,
'The social, friendly, honest man,
Whate'er he be,
'Tis he fulfils great Nature's plan,
And none but he.'
'To the same [John Lapraik]' st. 15

7 The rank is but the guinea's stamp,
The man's the gowd for a' that!
'For a' that and a' that' (1790)

8 A man's a man for a' that.
'For a' that and a' that' (1790)

9 Green grow the rashes, O,
Green grow the rashes, O;
The sweetest hours that e'er I spend,
Are spent among the lasses, O.
'Green Grow the Rashes' (1787); see **SONGS, SPIRITUALS, AND
SHANTIES** 762:13

10 Auld nature swears, the lovely dears
Her noblest work she classes, O;
Her prentice han' she tried on man,
An' then she made the lasses, O.
'Green Grow the Rashes' (1787)

11 O, gie me the lass that has acres o' charms,
O, gie me the lass wi' the weel-stockit farms.
'Hey for a Lass wi' a Tocher' (1799)

12 Here, some are thinkin' on their sins,
An' some upo' their claes.
'The Holy Fair' (1786) st. 10

13 There's some are fou o' love divine;
There's some are fou o' brandy.
'The Holy Fair' (1786) st. 27

14 O L--d thou kens what zeal I bear,
When drinkers drink, and swearers swear,
And singin' there, and dancin' here,
Wi' great an' sma';
For I am keepet by thy fear,
Free frae them a'.
But yet—O L--d—confess I must—

At times I'm fash'd wi' fleshly lust . . .
O L--d—yestreen—thou kens—wi' Meg—
Thy pardon I sincerely beg!
O may 't ne'er be a living plague,
To my dishonour!
And I'll ne'er lift a lawless leg
Again upon her.
'Holy Willie's Prayer' (1785)

15 There's death in the cup—so beware!
'Inscription on a Goblet' (published 1834)

16 It was a' for our rightfu' King
We left fair Scotland's strand.
'It was a' for our Rightfu' King' (1796)

17 Corn rigs, an' barley rigs,
An' corn rigs are bonnie.
'It was upon a Lammas Night' (1796)

18 John Anderson my jo, John,
When we were first acquent,
Your locks were like the raven,
Your bonny brow was brent.
'John Anderson my Jo' (1790)

19 I once was a maid, tho' I cannot tell when,
And still my delight is in proper young men.
'The Jolly Beggars' (1799) l. 57, also known as 'Love and
Liberty—A Cantata'

20 Partly wi' LOVE o'ercome sae sair,
And partly she was drunk.
'The Jolly Beggars' (1799) l. 183

21 A fig for those by law protected!
LIBERTY's a glorious feast!
Courts for cowards were erected,
Churches built to please the PRIEST.
'The Jolly Beggars' (1799) l. 254

22 Life is all a VARIORUM,
We regard not how it goes;
Let them cant about DECORUM,
Who have characters to lose.
'The Jolly Beggars' (1799) l. 270

23 Some have meat and cannot eat,
Some can not eat that want it:
But we have meat and we can eat,
Sae let the Lord be thankit.
'The Kirkudbright Grace' (1790), also known as 'The Selkirk
Grace'

24 I've seen sae mony changefu' years,
On earth I am a stranger grown:
I wander in the ways of men,
Alike unknowing and unknown.
'Lament for James, Earl of Glencairn' (1793)

25 May coward shame distain his name,
The wretch that dares not die!
'McPherson's Farewell' (1788)

26   Nature's law,
That man was made to mourn!
'Man was made to Mourn' (1786) st. 4

27 Man's inhumanity to man
Makes countless thousands mourn!
'Man was made to Mourn' (1786) st. 7

1 O Death! the poor man's dearest friend,
The kindest and the best!
'Man was made to Mourn' (1786) st. 11

2 Go fetch to me a pint o' wine,
An' fill it in a silver tassie.
'My Bonnie Mary' (1790)

3 My heart's in the Highlands, my heart is not
here;
My heart's in the Highlands a-chasing the deer;
Chasing the wild deer, and following the roe,
My heart's in the Highlands, wherever I go.
'My Heart's in the Highlands' (1790)

4 My love she's but a lassie yet.
title of poem, 1787

5 The minister kiss'd the fiddler's wife,
An' could na preach for thinkin' o't.
'My Love She's but a Lassie yet' (1790)

6 The wan moon sets behind the white wave,
And time is setting with me, Oh.
'Open the door to me, Oh' (1793)

7 O whistle, an' I'll come to you, my lad:
O whistle, an' I'll come to you, my lad:
Tho' father and mither should baith gae mad,
O whistle, and I'll come to you, my lad.
'O Whistle, an' I'll come to you, my Lad' (1788); see **FLETCHER**
335:13

8 O, my Luve's like a red, red rose
That's newly sprung in June;
O my Luve's like the melodie
That's sweetly play'd in tune.
'A Red Red Rose' (1796), derived from various folk-songs

9 Scots, wha hae wi' Wallace bled,
Scots, wham Bruce has aften led,
Welcome to your gory bed,—
Or to victorie.
Now's the day, and now's the hour;
See the front o' battle lour;
See approach proud Edward's power,
Chains and slaverie.
'Robert Bruce's March to Bannockburn' (1799), also known as
'Scots, Wha Hae'

10 Liberty's in every blow!
Let us do—or die!!!
'Robert Bruce's March to Bannockburn' (1799)

11 Good Lord, what is man! for as simple he looks,
Do but try to develop his hooks and his crooks,
With his depths and his shallows, his good and
his evil,
All in all he's a problem must puzzle the devil.
'Sketch' inscribed to Charles James Fox (1800)

12 This day Time winds th'exhausted chain,
To run the twelvemonth's length again.
'Sketch. New Year's Day. To Mrs Dunlop' (1789)

13 His ancient, trusty, drouthy crony,
Tam lo'ed him like a vera brither;
They had been fou for weeks thegither.
'Tam o' Shanter' (1791) l. 42

14 Kings may be blest, but Tam was glorious,
O'er a' the ills o' life victorious!
'Tam o' Shanter' (1791) l. 57

15 But pleasures are like poppies spread,
You seize the flow'r, its bloom is shed;
Or like the snow falls in the river,
A moment white—then melts for ever.
'Tam o' Shanter' (1791) l. 59

16 Nae man can tether time or tide.
'Tam o' Shanter' (1791) l. 67

17 Inspiring, bold John Barleycorn,
What dangers thou canst make us scorn!
Wi' tippenny, we fear nae evil;
Wi' usquebae, we'll face the devil!
'Tam o' Shanter' (1791) l. 105

18 As Tammie glowr'd, amaz'd, and curious,
The mirth and fun grew fast and furious.
'Tam o' Shanter' (1791) l. 143

19 Tam tint his reason a' thegither,
And roars out—'Weel done, Cutty-sark!'
'Tam o' Shanter' (1791) l. 185

20 Ah Tam! ah Tam! thou'll get thy fairin'!
In hell they'll roast thee like a herrin!
'Tam o' Shanter' (1791) l. 201

21 A man may drink and no be drunk;
A man may fight and no be slain;
A man may kiss a bonnie lass,
And aye be welcome back again.
'There was a Lass' (1788)

22 Fair fa' your honest, sonsie face,
Great chieftain o' the puddin'-race!
Aboon them a' ye tak your place,
Painch, tripe, or thairm:
Weel are ye wordy o' a grace
As lang's my arm.
'To a Haggis' (1787)

23 O wad some Pow'r the giftie gie us
To see oursels as others see us!
It wad frae mony a blunder free us,
And foolish notion.
'To a Louse' (1786)

24 Wee, sleekit, cow'rin', tim'rous beastie,
O what a panic's in thy breastie!
Thou need na start awa sae hasty,
Wi' bickering brattle!
I wad be laith to rin an' chase thee,
Wi' murd'ring pattle!
'To a Mouse' (1786)

25 I'm truly sorry Man's dominion
Has broken Nature's social union,
An' justifies that ill opinion
Which makes thee startle,
At me, thy poor, earth-born companion,
An' fellow-mortal!
'To a Mouse' (1786)

26 The best laid schemes o' mice an' men
Gang aft a-gley.
'To a Mouse' (1786); see **PROVERBS** 627:25

27 Come, Firm Resolve, take thou the van,
Thou stalk o' carl-hemp in man!
And let us mind, faint heart ne'er wan

A lady fair;
Wha does the utmost that he can,
Will whyles do mair.
'To Dr Blacklock' (1800)

1 Some rhyme a neebor's name to lash;
Some rhyme (vain thought!) for needfu' cash;
Some rhyme to court the countra clash,
An' raise a din;
For me, an aim I never fash;
I rhyme for fun.
'To J. S[mith]' (1786) st. 5

2 An' fareweel dear, deluding woman,
The joy of joys!
'To J. S[mith]' (1786) st. 14

3 Their sighan', cantan', grace-proud faces,
Their three-mile prayers, and half-mile graces.
'To the Rev. John M'Math' (1808)

4 We labour soon, we labour late,
To feed the titled knave, man;
And a' the comfort we're to get,
Is that ayont the grave, man.
'The Tree of Liberty' (1838)

5 His lockèd, lettered, braw brass collar,
Shew'd him the gentleman and scholar.
'The Twa Dogs' (1786) l. 13

6 An' there began a lang digression
About the lords o' the creation.
'The Twa Dogs' (1786) l. 45

7 Rejoiced they were na men, but dogs.
'The Twa Dogs' (1786) l. 236

8 All in this mottie, misty clime,
I backward mus'd on wasted time,
How I had spent my youthfu' prime
An' done nae-thing,
But stringing blethers up to rhyme
For fools to sing.
'The Vision' (1785)

9 What can a young lassie, what shall a young
lassie,
What can a young lassie do wi' an auld man?
'What can a Young Lassie do wi' an Auld Man' (1792)

10 It is the moon, I ken her horn,
That's blinkin in the lift sae hie;
She shines sae bright to wyle us hame,
But by my sooth she'll wait a wee!
'Willie Brew'd a Peck o' Maut' (1790)

11 The Poetic Genius of my country found me as
the prophetic bard Elijah did Elisha—at the
plough; and threw her inspiring mantle over me.
She bade me sing the loves, the joys, the rural
scenes and rural pleasures of my native soil, in
my native tongue; I tuned my wild, artless
notes, as she inspired.
preface to *Poems* (1787 2nd ed.)

12 Don't let the awkward squad fire over me.
said shortly before his death; A. Cunningham *The Works of
Robert Burns; with his Life* vol. 1 (1834)

Aaron Burr 1756–1836
American politician

13 Law is whatever is boldly asserted and plausibly
maintained.
James Parton *The Life and Times of Aaron Burr* (1857);
attributed

William S. Burroughs 1914–97
American novelist

14 Junk is the ideal product . . . the ultimate
merchandise. No sales talk necessary. The client
will crawl through a sewer and beg to buy.
The Naked Lunch (1959) introduction

15 The face of 'evil' is always the face of total
need.
The Naked Lunch (1959) introduction

16 In homosexual sex you know exactly what the
other person is feeling, so you are identifying
with the other person completely. In
heterosexual sex you have no idea what the
other person is feeling.
Victor Bockris *With William Burroughs: A Report from the
Bunker* (1981) 'On Men'

17 Love? What is it? Most natural painkiller. What
there is . . . LOVE.
final entry in his journal, 1 August 1997, the day before he
died; in *New Yorker* 18 August 1997

Benjamin Hapgood Burt 1880–1950
American songwriter

18 One evening in October, when I was one-third
sober,
An' taking home a 'load' with manly pride;
My poor feet began to stutter, so I lay down in
the gutter,
And a pig came up an' lay down by my side;
Then we sang 'It's all fair weather when good
fellows get together,'
Till a lady passing by was heard to say:
'You can tell a man who "boozes" by the
company he chooses'
And the pig got up and slowly walked away.
'The Pig Got Up and Slowly Walked Away' (1933 song)

19 When you're all dressed up and no place to go.
title of song (1913)

Nat Burton

20 There'll be bluebirds over the white cliffs of
Dover,
Tomorrow, just you wait and see.
'The White Cliffs of Dover' (1941 song)

Richard Burton 1821–90

English explorer, anthropologist, and translator

1 Don't be frightened; I am recalled. Pay, pack, and follow at convenience.

note to his wife, 19 August 1871, on being replaced as British Consul to Damascus

Isabel Burton *Life of Captain Sir Richard F. Burton* (1893) vol. 1, ch. 21

Robert Burton 1577–1640

English clergyman and scholar

2 All my joys to this are folly,
Naught so sweet as Melancholy.
The Anatomy of Melancholy (1621–51) 'The Author's Abstract of Melancholy'

3 I write of melancholy, by being busy to avoid melancholy.
The Anatomy of Melancholy (1621–51) 'Democritus to the Reader'

4 They lard their lean books with the fat of others' works.
The Anatomy of Melancholy (1621–51) 'Democritus to the Reader'

5 A loose, plain, rude writer . . . I call a spade a spade.
The Anatomy of Melancholy (1621–51) 'Democritus to the Reader'

6 I had not time to lick it into form, as she [a bear] doth her young ones.
The Anatomy of Melancholy (1621–51) 'Democritus to the Reader'

7 Like watermen, that row one way and look another.
The Anatomy of Melancholy (1621–51) 'Democritus to the Reader'; see **BUNYAN** 171:11

8 All poets are mad.
The Anatomy of Melancholy (1621–51) 'Democritus to the Reader'; see **WORDSWORTH** 868:22

9 A nightingale . . . dies for shame if another bird sings better.
The Anatomy of Melancholy (1621–51) pt. 1, sect. 2, member 3, subsect. 6

10 What, if a dear year come or dearth, or some loss? And were it not that they are loath to lay out money on a rope, they would be hanged forthwith, and sometimes die to save charges.
The Anatomy of Melancholy (1621–51) pt. 1, sect. 2, member 3, subsect. 12

11 I may not here omit those two main plagues, and common dotages of human kind, wine and women, which have infatuated and besotted myriads of people. They go commonly together.
The Anatomy of Melancholy (1621–51) pt. 1, sect. 2, member 3, subsect. 13

12 *Hinc quam sit calamus saevior ense patet.*
From this it is clear how much the pen is worse than the sword.
The Anatomy of Melancholy (1621–51) pt. 1, sect. 2, member 4, subsect. 4; see **BULWER-LYTTON** 170:14, **PROVERBS** 641:32

13 See one promontory (said Socrates of old), one mountain, one sea, one river, and see all.
The Anatomy of Melancholy (1621–51) pt. 1, sect. 2, member 4, subsect. 7

14 One was never married, and that's his hell: another is, and that's his plague.
The Anatomy of Melancholy (1621–51) pt. 1, sect. 2, member 4, subsect. 7

15 Who cannot give good counsel? 'tis cheap, it costs them nothing.
The Anatomy of Melancholy (1621–51) pt. 2, sect. 3, member 3, subsect. 1

16 What is a ship but a prison?
The Anatomy of Melancholy (1621–51) pt. 2, sect. 3, member 4, subsect. 1; see **JOHNSON** 439:12

17 All places are distant from Heaven alike.
The Anatomy of Melancholy (1621–51) pt. 2, sect. 3, member 4, subsect. 1

18 'Let me not live,' saith Aretine's Antonia, 'if I had not rather hear thy discourse than see a play!'
The Anatomy of Melancholy (1621–51) pt. 3, sect. 1, member 1, subsect. 1

19 To enlarge or illustrate this power and effect of love is to set a candle in the sun.
The Anatomy of Melancholy (1621–51) pt. 3, sect. 2, member 1, subsect. 2; see **SIDNEY** 750:10, **YOUNG** 876:15

20 No cord nor cable can so forcibly draw, or hold so fast, as love can do with a twined thread.
The Anatomy of Melancholy (1621–51) pt. 3, sect. 2, member 1, subsect. 2

21 To these crocodile's tears they will add sobs, fiery sighs, and sorrowful countenance, pale colour, leanness.
The Anatomy of Melancholy (1621–51) pt. 3, sect. 2, member 2, subsect. 4

22 Diogenes struck the father when the son swore.
The Anatomy of Melancholy (1621–51) pt. 3, sect. 2, member 5, subsect. 5

23 One religion is as true as another.
The Anatomy of Melancholy (1621–51) pt. 3, sect. 4, member 2, subsect. 1

24 Be not solitary, be not idle.
The Anatomy of Melancholy (1621–51), closing words

Wilhelm Busch 1832–1908

German satirical poet and illustrator

25 *Ach, das war ein schlimmes Ding,*
Wie es Max und Moritz ging!
Drum ist hier, was sie getrieben,
Abgemalt und aufgeschrieben.

Oh, that was a bad business,
What happened to Max and Moritz!
Which is why their doings are here
Pictured and written down.
Max und Moritz (1865)

26 *Vater werden ist nicht schwer*
Vater sein dagegen sehr.

Becoming a father isn't difficult,

But it's very difficult to be a father.
Julchen (1877)

Hermann Busenbaum 1600–68
German theologian

1 *Cum finis est licitus, etiam media sunt licita.*

The end justifies the means.
Medulla Theologiae Moralis (1650); literally 'When the end is allowed, the means also are allowed'; see **PROVERBS** 631:3

Barbara Bush 1925–
American wife of George **BUSH**; First Lady, 1989–93

2 Somewhere out in this audience may even be someone who will one day follow in my footsteps, and preside over the White House as the President's spouse. I wish him well!
remarks at Wellesley College Commencement, 1 June 1990

George Bush 1924–
American Republican statesman, 41st President of the US 1989–93; father of George W. **BUSH**

3 Oh, the vision thing.
responding to the suggestion that he turn his attention from short-term campaign objectives and look to the longer term.
in *Time* 26 January 1987

4 Read my lips: no new taxes.
campaign pledge on taxation
in *New York Times* 19 August 1988

5 I'm President of the United States, and I'm not going to eat any more broccoli!
in *New York Times* 23 March 1990

6 And now, we can see a new world coming into view. A world in which there is the very real prospect of a new world order.
speech, in *New York Times* 7 March 1991

7 [It is] time to turn our attention to pressing challenges like . . . how to make American families more like the Waltons and a little bit less like the Simpsons.
speech, Neenah, Wisconsin, 27 July 1992

George W. Bush 1946–
American Republican statesman, 43rd President of the US 2001–9; son of George **BUSH**. See also **PAGE** 591:15

8 We will make no distinction between terrorists who committed these acts and those who harbour them.
after the terrorist attacks of 11 September
televised address, 12 September 2001

9 Today we feel what Franklin Roosevelt called the warm courage of national unity. This unity against terror is now extending across the world.
address in Washington National Cathedral, 14 September 2001, at the day of mourning for those killed in the terrorist attacks of 11 September
in *Times* 15 September 2001; see **ROOSEVELT** 667:6

10 This crusade, this war on terrorism is going to take a while.
the President later retracted his use of the word 'crusade'
at a White House press conference, 16 September 2001

11 States like these . . . constitute an axis of evil, arming to threaten the peace of this world.
of Iraq, Iran, and North Korea
State of the Union address, in *Newsweek* 11 February 2002

12 Brownie, you're doing a heck of a job.
to Michael Brown, then Director of the Federal Emergency Managemenet Agency, in the aftermath of Hurricane Katrina's devastation of New Orleans
comment in speech, Alabama, 2 September 2005; in *New York Times* 3 September 2005

13 Yo, Blair. How are you doing?
the President addresses Tony **BLAIR** *during a break in the G8 summit in St Petersburg, Russia, 17 July 2006; a microphone had been left on*
in *Guardian* 18 July 2006

Comte de Bussy-Rabutin 1618–93
French soldier and poet

14 *L'amour vient de l'aveuglement,*
L'amitié de la connaissance.

Love comes from blindness,
Friendship from knowledge.
Histoire Amoureuse des Gaules: Maximes d'Amour (1665) pt. 1; see **PROVERBS** 638:6

15 *L'absence est à l'amour ce qu'est au feu le vent;*
Il éteint le petit, il allume le grand.

Absence is to love what wind is to fire;
It extinguishes the small, it kindles the great.
Histoire Amoureuse des Gaules: Maximes d'Amour (1665) pt. 2; see **FRANCIS** 340:18, **LA ROCHEFOUCAULD** 482:3

16 As you know, God is usually on the side of the big squadrons against the small.
letter to the Comte de Limoges, 18 October 1677, in *Lettres de . . . Comte de Bussy* (1697) vol. 4; see **ANOUILH** 24:7, **PROVERBS** 642:10, **TACITUS** 787:12, **VOLTAIRE** 834:16

Joseph Butler 1692–1752
English bishop and theologian

17 It has come, I know not how, to be taken for granted, by many persons, that Christianity is not so much as a subject of inquiry; but that it is, now at length, discovered to be fictitious.
The Analogy of Religion (1736) 'Advertisement'

18 But to us, probability is the very guide of life.
The Analogy of Religion (1736) 'Introduction'; see **CICERO** 231:19

19 Everything is what it is, and not another thing.
preface to *Fifteen Sermons preached at the Rolls Chapel* (ed. 2, 1729)

20 Things and actions are what they are, and the consequences of them will be what they will be: why then should we desire to be deceived?
Fifteen Sermons preached at the Rolls Chapel (1726) no. 7

1 Sir, the pretending to extraordinary revelations and gifts of the Holy Ghost is a horrid thing—a very horrid thing.

to John **WESLEY**, 16 August 1739; John Wesley *Journal* (ed. N. Curnock) note

Nicholas Murray Butler 1862–1947

American President of Columbia University, 1901–45

2 An expert is one who knows more and more about less and less.

Commencement address at Columbia University (attributed)

R. A. ('Rab') Butler 1902–82

British Conservative politician

3 REPORTER: Mr Butler, would you say that this [Anthony Eden] is the best Prime Minister we have?

R. A. BUTLER: Yes.

interview at London Airport, 8 January 1956; R. A. Butler *The Art of the Possible*

4 I think a Prime Minister has to be a butcher and know the joints. That is perhaps where I have not been quite competent, in knowing all the ways that you can cut up a carcass.

in *Listener* 28 June 1966

5 Politics is the Art of the Possible. That is what these pages show I have tried to achieve—not more—and that is what I have called my book.

The Art of the Possible (1971); see **BISMARCK** 122:16

6 In politics you must always keep running with the pack. The moment that you falter and they sense that you are injured, the rest will turn on you like wolves.

Dennis Walters *Not Always with the Pack* (1989)

Samuel Butler 1612–80

English poet

7 He'd run in debt by disputation,
And pay with ratiocination.

Hudibras pt. 1 (1663), canto 1, l. 77

8 For rhetoric he could not ope
His mouth, but out there flew a trope.

Hudibras pt. 1 (1663), canto 1, l. 81

9 A Babylonish dialect
Which learned pedants much affect.

Hudibras pt. 1 (1663), canto 1, l. 93

10 What ever sceptic could inquire for;
For every why he had a wherefore.

Hudibras pt. 1 (1663), canto 1, l. 131

11 He knew what's what, and that's as high
As metaphysic wit can fly.

Hudibras pt. 1 (1663), canto 1, l. 149

12 Such as take lodgings in a head
That's to be let unfurnished.

Hudibras pt. 1 (1663), canto 1, l. 159

13 And still be doing, never done:
As if Religion were intended
For nothing else but to be mended.

Hudibras pt. 1 (1663), canto 1, l. 202

14 Compound for sins, they are inclined to,
By damning those they have no mind to.

Hudibras pt. 1 (1663), canto 1, l. 213

15 The trenchant blade, Toledo trusty,
For want of fighting was grown rusty,
And eat into it self, for lack
Of some body to hew and hack.

Hudibras pt. 1 (1663), canto 1, l. 357

16 For rhyme the rudder is of verses,
With which like ships they steer their courses.

Hudibras pt. 1 (1663), canto 1, l. 457

17 Great actions are not always true sons
Of great and mighty resolutions.

Hudibras pt. 1 (1663), canto 1, l. 877

18 Cleric before, and Lay behind;
A lawless linsy-woolsy brother,
Half of one order, half another.

Hudibras pt. 1 (1663), canto 3, l. 1226

19 Learning, that cobweb of the brain,
Profane, erroneous, and vain.

Hudibras pt. 1 (1663), canto 3, l. 1339

20 She that with poetry is won,
Is but a desk to write upon.

Hudibras pt. 2 (1664), canto 1, l. 591

21 Love is a boy, by poets styled,
Then spare the rod, and spoil the child.

Hudibras pt. 2 (1664), canto 1, l. 843; see **PROVERBS** 643:28

22 Oaths are but words, and words but wind.

Hudibras pt. 2 (1664), canto 2, l. 107

23 For truth is precious and divine
Too rich a pearl for carnal swine.

Hudibras pt. 2 (1664) canto 2, l. 263

24 Doubtless the pleasure is as great
Of being cheated, as to cheat.
As lookers-on feel most delight,
That least perceive a juggler's sleight;
And still the less they understand,
The more th' admire his sleight of hand.

Hudibras pt. 2 (1664), canto 3, l. 1

25 What makes all doctrines plain and clear?
About two hundred pounds a year.
And that which was proved true before,
Prove false again? Two hundred more.

Hudibras pt. 3 (1680), canto 1, l. 1277

26 He that complies against his will,
Is of his own opinion still.

Hudibras pt. 3 (1680), canto 3, l. 547; see **PROVERBS** 634:5

27 For Justice, though she's painted blind,
Is to the weaker side inclined.

Hudibras pt. 3 (1680), canto 3, l. 709

28 For money has a power above
The stars and fate, to manage love.

Hudibras pt. 3 (1680) 'The Lady's Answer to the Knight' l. 131

29 All love at first, like generous wine,
Ferments and frets, until 'tis fine;

But when 'tis settled on the lee,
And from th' impurer matter free,
Becomes the richer still, the older,
And proves the pleasanter, the colder.
Genuine Remains (1759) 'Miscellaneous Thoughts'

1 The law can take a purse in open court,
Whilst it condemns a less delinquent for't.
Genuine Remains (1759) 'Miscellaneous Thoughts'

Samuel Butler 1835–1902
English novelist

2 It has been said that though God cannot alter the past, historians can; it is perhaps because they can be useful to Him in this respect that He tolerates their existence.
Erewhon Revisited (1901) ch. 14; see **AGATHON** 9:10

3 All animals, except man, know that the principal business of life is to enjoy it.
The Way of All Flesh (1903) ch. 19

4 The advantage of doing one's praising for oneself is that one can lay it on so thick and exactly in the right places.
The Way of All Flesh (1903) ch. 34

5 Young as he was, his instinct told him that the best liar is he who makes the smallest amount of lying go the longest way.
The Way of All Flesh (1903) ch. 39

6 'Tis better to have loved and lost than never to have lost at all.
The Way of All Flesh (1903) ch. 67; see **TENNYSON** 795:9

7 It was very good of God to let Carlyle and Mrs Carlyle marry one another and so make only two people miserable instead of four.
Letters between Samuel Butler and Miss E. M. A. Savage 1871–1885 (1935) 21 November 1884

8 All progress is based upon a universal innate desire on the part of every organism to live beyond its income.
Notebooks (1912) ch. 1

9 The history of art is the history of revivals.
Notebooks (1912) ch. 8

10 An apology for the Devil: It must be remembered that we have only heard one side of the case. God has written all the books.
Notebooks (1912) ch. 14

11 A definition is the enclosing a wilderness of idea within a wall of words.
Notebooks (1912) ch. 14

12 To live is like to love — all reason is against it, and all healthy instinct for it.
Notebooks (1912) ch. 14

13 The public buys its opinions as it buys its meat, or takes in its milk, on the principle that it is cheaper to do this than to keep a cow. So it is, but the milk is more likely to be watered.
Notebooks (1912) ch. 17

14 You can do very little with faith, but you can do nothing without it.
Notebooks (1912) ch. 20

15 The three most important things a man has are, briefly, his private parts, his money, and his religious opinions.
Further Extracts from Notebooks (1934)

16 Jesus! with all thy faults I love thee still.
Further Extracts from Notebooks (1934)

17 Conscience is thoroughly well-bred and soon leaves off talking to those who do not wish to hear it.
Further Extracts from Notebooks (1934)

18 Yet meet we shall, and part, and meet again Where dead men meet, on lips of living men.
'Not on sad Stygian shore' (1904)

19 Dusty, cobweb-covered, maimed, and set at naught,
Beauty crieth in an attic, and no man regardeth.
O God! O Montreal!
'Psalm of Montreal', in *Spectator* 18 May 1878

William Butler 1535–1618
English physician

20 Doubtless God could have made a better berry, but doubtless God never did.
of the strawberry
Izaak Walton *The Compleat Angler* (3rd ed., 1661) pt. 1, ch. 5

Mary Butts 1890–1937
English writer

21 I was told that desire for learning in women was against the will of God.
The Crystal Cabinet (1937) ch. 20

A. S. Byatt 1936–
English novelist

22 Didactic rushes of information were a great shortcoming in returning travellers.
Angels and Insects (1992) 'Morpho Eugenia'

23 That is the main thing, to be alive. As long as you are alive, everything is surprising, rightly seen.
Angels and Insects (1992) 'Morpho Eugenia'

24 What literature can and should do is change the people who teach the people who don't read the books.
interview in *Newsweek* 5 June 1995

25 Ms. Rowling's magic world has no place for the numinous.
in *New York Times* 7 July 2003

William Byrd 1543–1623
English composer

26 The exercise of singing is delightful to Nature, and good to preserve the health of man. It doth strengthen all parts of the breast, and doth open the pipes.
Psalms, Sonnets and Songs (1588)

27 Tallis is dead, and music dies.
'Ye Sacred Muses'

John Byrom 1692–1763

English poet

1 I am content, I do not care,
Wag as it will the world for me.
'Careless Content' (1773)

2 Christians, awake! Salute the happy morn,
Whereon the Saviour of the world was born.
Hymn (c.1750)

3 Some say, that Signor Bononcini,
Compared to Handel's a mere ninny;
Others aver, that to him Handel
Is scarcely fit to hold a candle.
Strange! that such high dispute should be
'Twixt Tweedledum and Tweedledee.
'On the Feuds between Handel and Bononcini' (1727)

4 God bless the King, I mean the Faith's Defender;
God bless—no harm in blessing—the Pretender;
But who Pretender is, or who is King,
God bless us all—that's quite another thing.
'To an Officer in the Army, Extempore, Intended to allay the Violence of Party-Spirit' (1773)

Lord Byron 1788–1824

English poet. On Byron: see **ARNOLD** 30:22, **LAMB** 476:10; see also **CAMPBELL** 195:20

5 Proud Wellington, with eagle beak so curled,
That nose, the hook where he suspends the world!
'The Age of Bronze' (1823) st. 13

6 For what were all these country patriots born?
To hunt, and vote, and raise the price of corn?
'The Age of Bronze' (1823) st. 14

7 Year after year they voted cent per cent
Blood, sweat, and tear-wrung millions—why? for rent!
'The Age of Bronze' (1823) st. 14; see **CHURCHILL** 229:12

8 Did'st ever see a gondola? . . .
It glides along the water looking blackly,
Just like a coffin clapt in a canoe.
Beppo (1818) st. 19

9 In short, he was a perfect cavaliero,
And to his very valet seemed a hero.
Beppo (1818) st. 33; see **CORNUEL** 252:7

10 His heart was one of those which most enamour us,
Wax to receive, and marble to retain.
Beppo (1818) st. 34

11 Our cloudy climate, and our chilly women.
Beppo (1818) st. 49

12 A pretty woman as was ever seen,
Fresh as the Angel o'er a new inn door.
Beppo (1818) st. 57

13 Where the virgins are soft as the roses they twine,
And all, save the spirit of man, is divine.
The Bride of Abydos (1813) canto 1, st. 1

14 Such was Zuleika, such around her shone
The nameless charms unmarked by her alone—
The light of love, the purity of grace,
The mind, the Music breathing from her face,
The heart whose softness harmonized the whole,
And oh! that eye was in itself a Soul!
The Bride of Abydos (1813) canto 1, st. 6

15   I have looked out
In the vast desolate night in search of him;
And when I saw gigantic shadows in
The umbrage of the walls of Eden, chequered
By the far-flashing of the cherubs' swords,
I watched for what I thought his coming: for
With fear rose longing in my heart to know
What 'twas which shook us all—but nothing came.
Cain (1821) act 1, sc. 1, l. 266

16 Adieu, adieu! my native shore
Fades o'er the waters blue.
Childe Harold's Pilgrimage (1812–18) canto 1, st. 13

17 Lo! where the Giant on the mountain stands,
His blood-red tresses deep'ning in the sun,
With death-shot glowing in his fiery hands,
And eye that scorcheth all it glares upon.
Childe Harold's Pilgrimage (1812–18) canto 1, st. 39

18 Here all were noble, save Nobility.
Childe Harold's Pilgrimage (1812–18) canto 1, st. 85

19 Cold is the heart, fair Greece! that looks on thee,
Nor feels as lovers o'er the dust they loved;
Dull is the eye that will not weep to see
Thy walls defaced, thy mouldering shrines removed
By British hands.
Childe Harold's Pilgrimage (1812–18) canto 2, st. 15

20 None are so desolate but something dear,
Dearer than self, possesses or possessed
A thought, and claims the homage of a tear.
Childe Harold's Pilgrimage (1812–18) canto 2, st. 24

21 Dark Sappho! could not verse immortal save
That breast imbued with such immortal fire?
Could she not live who life eternal gave?
Childe Harold's Pilgrimage (1812–18) canto 2, st. 39

22 Fair Greece! sad relic of departed worth!
Immortal, though no more! though fallen, great!
Childe Harold's Pilgrimage (1812–18) canto 2, st. 73

23 Hereditary bondsmen! know ye not
Who would be free themselves must strike the blow?
Childe Harold's Pilgrimage (1812–18) canto 2, st. 76

24 What is the worst of woes that wait on age?
What stamps the wrinkle deeper on the brow?
To view each loved one blotted from life's page,
And be alone on earth, as I am now.
Childe Harold's Pilgrimage (1812–18) canto 2, st. 98

25 Once more upon the waters! yet once more!
And the waves bound beneath me as a steed
That knows his rider.
Childe Harold's Pilgrimage (1812–18) canto 3, st. 2

1 The wandering outlaw of his own dark mind.
   Childe Harold's Pilgrimage (1812–18) canto 3, st. 3

2   Years steal
   Fire from the mind as vigour from the limb;
   And life's enchanted cup but sparkles near the
      brim.
   Childe Harold's Pilgrimage (1812–18) canto 3, st. 8

3 Where rose the mountains, there to him were
      friends;
   Where rolled the ocean, thereon was his home;
   Where a blue sky, and glowing clime, extends,
   He had the passion and the power to roam.
   Childe Harold's Pilgrimage (1812–18) canto 3, st. 13

4 The very knowledge that he lived in vain,
   That all was over on this side the tomb,
   Had made Despair a smilingness assume.
   Childe Harold's Pilgrimage (1812–18) canto 3, st. 16

5 There was a sound of revelry by night,
   And Belgium's capital had gathered then
   Her beauty and her chivalry, and bright
   The lamps that shone o'er fair women and brave
      men;
   A thousand hearts beat happily; and when
   Music arose with its voluptuous swell,
   Soft eyes looked love to eyes which spake again,
   And all went merry as a marriage bell;
   But hush! hark! a deep sound strikes like a rising
      knell!
   Childe Harold's Pilgrimage (1812–18) canto 3, st. 21

6 On with the dance! let joy be unconfined;
   No sleep till morn, when Youth and Pleasure
      meet
   To chase the glowing Hours with flying feet.
   Childe Harold's Pilgrimage (1812–18) canto 3, st. 22

7 He rushed into the field, and, foremost fighting,
      fell.
   Childe Harold's Pilgrimage (1812–18) canto 3, st. 23

8   But life will suit
   Itself to Sorrow's most detested fruit,
   Like to the apples on the Dead Sea's shore,
   All ashes to the taste.
   Childe Harold's Pilgrimage (1812–18) canto 3, st. 34

9 Quiet to quick bosoms is a hell.
   Childe Harold's Pilgrimage (1812–18) canto 3, st. 42

10 To fly from, need not be to hate, mankind.
   Childe Harold's Pilgrimage (1812–18) canto 3, st. 69

11 I live not in myself, but I become
   Portion of that around me; and to me,
   High mountains are a feeling, but the hum
   Of human cities torture.
   Childe Harold's Pilgrimage (1812–18) canto 3, st. 72

12 His love was passion's essence:—as a tree
   On fire by lightning, with ethereal flame
   Kindled he was, and blasted.
   of Jean-Jacques ROUSSEAU
   Childe Harold's Pilgrimage (1812–18) canto 3, st. 78

13 Sapping a solemn creed with solemn sneer.
   of Edward GIBBON
   Childe Harold's Pilgrimage (1812–18) canto 3, st. 107

14 I have not loved the world, nor the world me;
   I have not flattered its rank breath, nor bowed
   To its idolatries a patient knee.
   Childe Harold's Pilgrimage (1812–18) canto 3, st. 113

15 I stood in Venice, on the Bridge of Sighs:
   A palace and a prison on each hand.
   Childe Harold's Pilgrimage (1812–18) canto 4, st. 1

16   I stood
   Among them, but not of them; in a shroud
   Of thoughts which were not their thoughts.
   Childe Harold's Pilgrimage (1812–18) canto 3, st. 113

17 The moon is up, and yet it is not night;
   Sunset divides the sky with her—a sea
   Of glory streams along the Alpine height
   Of blue Friuli's mountains; Heaven is free
   From clouds, but of all colours seems to be
   Melted to one vast Iris of the West,
   Where the day joins the past eternity.
   Childe Harold's Pilgrimage (1812–18) canto 4, st. 27

18 Italia! oh Italia! thou who hast
   The fatal gift of beauty.
   Childe Harold's Pilgrimage (1812–18) canto 4, st. 42

19 Oh Rome! my country! city of the soul!
   Childe Harold's Pilgrimage (1812–18) canto 4, st. 78

20 Alas! our young affections run to waste,
   Or water but the desert.
   Childe Harold's Pilgrimage (1812–18) canto 4, st. 120

21 Of its own beauty is the mind diseased.
   Childe Harold's Pilgrimage (1812–18) canto 4, st. 122

22 Time, the avenger! unto thee I lift
   My hands, and eyes, and heart, and crave of
      thee a gift.
   Childe Harold's Pilgrimage (1812–18) canto 4, st. 130

23 But I have lived, and have not lived in vain:
   My mind may lose its force, my blood its fire,
   And my frame perish even in conquering pain;
   But there is that within me which shall tire
   Torture and Time, and breathe when I expire.
   Childe Harold's Pilgrimage (1812–18) canto 4, st. 137

24 *There* were his young barbarians all at play,
   There was their Dacian mother— he, their sire,
   Butchered to make a Roman holiday.
   Childe Harold's Pilgrimage (1812–18) canto 4, st. 141

25 A ruin—yet what ruin! from its mass
   Walls, palaces, half-cities, have been reared.
   Childe Harold's Pilgrimage (1812–18) canto 4, st. 143

26 While stands the Coliseum, Rome shall stand;
   When falls the Coliseum, Rome shall fall;
   And when Rome falls—the World.
   Childe Harold's Pilgrimage (1812–18) canto 4, st. 145

27   The Lord of the unerring bow,
   The God of life, and poesy, and light.
   Childe Harold's Pilgrimage (1812–18) canto 4, st. 161

28 Oh! that the desert were my dwelling-place,
   With one fair spirit for my minister,
   That I might all forget the human race,
   And, hating no one, love but only her!
   Childe Harold's Pilgrimage (1812–18) canto 4, st. 177

1 There is a pleasure in the pathless woods,
There is a rapture on the lonely shore,
There is society, where none intrudes,
By the deep sea, and music in its roar:
I love not man the less, but nature more.
Childe Harold's Pilgrimage (1812–18) canto 4, st. 178

2 Roll on, thou deep and dark blue Ocean—roll!
Ten thousand fleets sweep over thee in vain;
Man marks the earth with ruin—his control
Stops with the shore.
Childe Harold's Pilgrimage (1812–18) canto 4, st. 179

3 Without a grave, unknelled, uncoffined, and
unknown.
Childe Harold's Pilgrimage (1812–18) canto 4, st. 179

4 Dark-heaving;—boundless, endless, and
sublime—
The image of eternity.
of the sea
Childe Harold's Pilgrimage (1812–18) canto 4, st. 183

5 The glory and the nothing of a name.
'Churchill's Grave' (1816)

6 Such hath it been—shall be—beneath the sun
The many still must labour for the one.
The Corsair (1814) canto 1, st. 8

7 There was a laughing devil in his sneer,
That raised emotions both of rage and fear;
And where his frown of hatred darkly fell,
Hope withering fled, and Mercy sighed farewell!
The Corsair (1814) canto 1, st. 9

8 Deep in my soul that tender secret dwells,
Lonely and lost to light for evermore,
Save when to thine my heart responsive swells,
Then trembles into silence as before.
The Corsair (1814) canto 1, st. 14 'Medora's Song'

9   The spirit burning but unbent,
May writhe, rebel—the weak alone repent!
The Corsair (1814) canto 2, st. 10

10 Oh! too convincing—dangerously dear—
In woman's eye the unanswerable tear!
The Corsair (1814) canto 2, st. 15

11   And she for him had given
Her all on earth, and more than all in heaven!
The Corsair (1814) canto 3, st. 17

12 He left a Corsair's name to other times,
Linked with one virtue, and a thousand crimes.
The Corsair (1814) canto 3, st. 24

13 Slow sinks, more lovely ere his race be run,
Along Morea's hills the setting sun;
Not, as in northern climes, obscurely bright,
But one unclouded blaze of living light.
'The Curse of Minerva' (1812) l. 1 and *The Corsair* (1814) canto
3, st. 1

14 A land of meanness, sophistry, and mist.
of Scotland
'The Curse of Minerva' (1812) l. 138

15 Each breeze from foggy mount and marshy
plain
Dilutes with drivel every drizzly brain,

Till, burst at length, each wat'ry head o'erflows,
Foul as their soil, and frigid as their snows.
of Scotland
'The Curse of Minerva' (1812) l. 139

16 The Assyrian came down like the wolf on the
fold,
And his cohorts were gleaming in purple and
gold;
And the sheen of their spears was like stars on
the sea,
When the blue wave rolls nightly on deep
Galilee.
'The Destruction of Sennacherib' (1815) st. 1

17 For the Angel of Death spread his wings on the
blast,
And breathed in the face of the foe as he passed.
'The Destruction of Sennacherib' (1815) st. 3

18 And Coleridge, too, has lately taken wing,
But, like a hawk encumbered with his hood,
Explaining metaphysics to the nation—
I wish he would explain his explanation.
Don Juan (1819–24) canto 1, dedication st. 2

19 The intellectual eunuch Castlereagh.
Don Juan (1819–24) canto 1, dedication st. 11

20 My way is to begin with the beginning.
Don Juan (1819–24) canto 1, st. 7

21 But—Oh! ye lords of ladies intellectual,
Inform us truly, have they not hen-pecked you
all?
Don Juan (1819–24) canto 1, st. 22

22 Married, charming, chaste, and twenty-three.
Don Juan (1819–24) canto 1, st. 59

23 What men call gallantry, and gods adultery,
Is much more common where the climate's
sultry.
Don Juan (1819–24) canto 1, st. 63

24 Christians have burnt each other, quite
persuaded
That all the Apostles would have done as they
did.
Don Juan (1819–24) canto 1, st. 83

25 He thought about himself, and the whole earth,
Of man the wonderful, and of the stars,
And how the deuce they ever could have birth;
And then he thought of earthquakes, and of
wars,
How many miles the moon might have in girth,
Of air-balloons, and of the many bars
To perfect knowledge of the boundless skies;
And then he thought of Donna Julia's eyes.
Don Juan (1819–24) canto 1, st. 92

26 A little still she strove, and much repented,
And whispering 'I will ne'er consent'—
consented.
Don Juan (1819–24) canto 1, st. 117

27 'Twas strange that one so young should thus
concern
His brain about the action of the sky;

If *you* think 'twas philosophy that this did,
I can't help thinking puberty assisted.
Don Juan (1819–24) canto 1, st. 93

1 Sweet is revenge—especially to women.
Don Juan (1819–24) canto 1, st. 124

2 Pleasure's a sin, and sometimes sin's a pleasure.
Don Juan (1819–24) canto 1, st. 133

3 Man's love is of man's life a thing apart,
'Tis woman's whole existence.
Don Juan (1819–24) canto 1, st. 194; see **AMIS** 14:14

4 A panoramic view of hell's in training,
After the style of Virgil and of Homer,
So that my name of Epic's no misnomer.
Don Juan (1819–24) canto 1, st. 200

5 Prose poets like blank-verse, I'm fond of rhyme,
Good workmen never quarrel with their tools.
Don Juan (1819–24) canto 1, st. 201

6 So for a good old-gentlemanly vice,
I think I must take up with avarice.
Don Juan (1819–24) canto 1, st. 216

7 There's nought, no doubt, so much the spirit
calms
As rum and true religion.
Don Juan (1819–24) canto 2, st. 34

8 A solitary shriek, the bubbling cry
Of some strong swimmer in his agony.
Don Juan (1819–24) canto 2, st. 53

9 Let us have wine and women, mirth and
laughter,
Sermons and soda-water the day after.
Don Juan (1819–24) canto 2, st. 178

10 Man, being reasonable, must get drunk;
The best of life is but intoxication.
Don Juan (1819–24) canto 2, st. 179

11 They looked up to the sky, whose floating glow
Spread like a rosy ocean, vast and bright;
They gazed upon the glittering sea below,
Whence the broad moon rose circling into sight;
They heard the wave's splash, and the wind so
low,
And saw each other's dark eyes darting light
Into each other—and, beholding this,
Their lips drew near, and clung into a kiss.
Don Juan (1819–24) canto 2, st. 185

12 And thus they form a group that's quite antique,
Half naked, loving, natural, and Greek.
Don Juan (1819–24) canto 2, st. 194

13 Alas! the love of women! it is known
To be a lovely and a fearful thing!
Don Juan (1819–24) canto 2, st. 199

14 In her first passion woman loves her lover,
In all the others all she loves is love.
Don Juan (1819–24) canto 3, st. 3

15 Love and marriage rarely can
combine,
Although they both are born in the same clime;
Marriage from love, like vinegar from wine—

A sad, sour, sober beverage—by time
Is sharpened from its high celestial flavour,
Down to a very homely household savour.
Don Juan (1819–24) canto 3, st. 5

16 Think you, if Laura had been Petrarch's wife,
He would have written sonnets all his life?
Don Juan (1819–24) canto 3, st. 8

17 All tragedies are finished by a death,
All comedies are ended by a marriage;
The future states of both are left to faith.
Don Juan (1819–24) canto 3, st. 9

18 Dreading that climax of all human ills,
The inflammation of his weekly bills.
Don Juan (1819–24) canto 3, st. 35

19 . . . He was the mildest mannered
man
That ever scuttled ship or cut a throat.
Don Juan (1819–24) canto 3, st. 41

20 But Shakespeare also says, 'tis very silly
'To gild refinèd gold, or paint the lily.'
Don Juan (1819–24) canto 3, st. 76; see **SHAKESPEARE** 714:11

21 The isles of Greece, the isles of Greece!
Where burning Sappho loved and sung,
Where grew the arts of war and peace,
Where Delos rose, and Phoebus sprung!
Eternal summer gilds them yet,
But all, except their sun, is set!
Don Juan (1819–24) canto 3, st. 86 (1)

22 The mountains look on Marathon—
And Marathon looks on the sea;
And musing there an hour alone,
I dreamed that Greece might still be free.
Don Juan (1819–24) canto 3, st. 86 (3)

23 For what is left the poet here?
For Greeks a blush—for Greece a tear.
Don Juan (1819–24) canto 3, st. 86 (6)

24 Earth! render back from out thy breast
a remnant of our Spartan dead!
Of the three hundred grant but three,
To make a new Thermopylae!
Don Juan (1819–24) canto 3, st. 86 (7)

25 Milton's the prince of poets—so we say;
A little heavy, but no less divine.
Don Juan (1819–24) canto 3, st. 91

26 A drowsy frowzy poem, called the 'Excursion',
Writ in a manner which is my aversion.
Don Juan (1819–24) canto 3, st. 94

27 We learn from Horace, Homer sometimes
sleeps;
We feel without him: Wordsworth sometimes
wakes.
Don Juan (1819–24) canto 3, st. 98; see **HORACE** 409:14

28 Ave Maria! 'tis the hour of prayer!
Ave Maria! 'tis the hour of love!
Don Juan (1819–24) canto 3, st. 103; see **PRAYERS** 623:1

29 Now my sere fancy 'falls into the yellow
Leaf,' and imagination droops her pinion,
And the sad truth which hovers o'er my desk

Turns what was once romantic to burlesque.
Don Juan (1819–24) canto 4, st. 3; see **BYRON** 190:21,
SHAKESPEARE 722:16

1 And if I laugh at any mortal thing,
'Tis that I may not weep.
Don Juan (1819–24) canto 4, st. 4

2 'Whom the gods love die young' was said of
yore.
And many deaths do they escape by this.
Don Juan (1819–24) canto 4, st. 12; see **MENANDER** 531:16

3   I've stood upon Achilles' tomb,
And heard Troy doubted; time will doubt of
Rome.
Don Juan (1819–24) canto 4, st. 101

4 When amatory poets sing their loves
In liquid lines mellifluously bland,
And pair their rhymes as Venus yokes her doves.
They little think what mischief is in hand.
Don Juan (1819–24) canto 5, st. 1

5 And is this blood, then, formed but to be shed?
Can every element our elements mar?
And air—earth—water—fire live—and we dead?
We, whose minds comprehend all things?
Don Juan (1819–24) canto 5, st. 39

6 . . . That all-softening, overpowering knell,
The tocsin of the soul—the dinner bell.
Don Juan (1819–24) canto 5, st. 49

7 Why don't they knead two virtuous souls for life
Into that moral centaur, man and wife?
Don Juan (1819–24) canto 5, st. 158

8 There is a tide in the affairs of women,
Which, taken at the flood, leads—God knows
where.
Don Juan (1819–24) canto 6, st. 2; see **SHAKESPEARE** 713:28

9 A lady of a 'certain age', which means
Certainly aged.
Don Juan (1819–24) canto 6, st. 69

10 'Let there be light!' said God, and there was
light!'
'Let there be blood!' says man, and there's a sea!
Don Juan (1819–24) canto 7, st. 41; see **BIBLE** 78:12

11 Read your own hearts and Ireland's present
story,
Then feed her famine fat with Wellesley's glory.
Don Juan (1819–24) canto 8, st. 125

12 When Bishop Berkeley said 'there was no
matter',
And proved it—'twas no matter what he said.
Don Juan (1819–24) canto 11, st. 1; **JOHNSON** 440:10

13 And, after all, what is a lie? 'Tis but
The truth in masquerade.
Don Juan (1819–24) canto 11, st. 37

14 'Tis strange the mind, that very fiery particle,
Should let itself be snuffed out by an article.
on **KEATS** *'who was killed off by one critique'*
Don Juan (1819–24) canto 11, st. 60

15 For talk six times with the same single lady,
And you may get the wedding dresses ready.
Don Juan (1819–24) canto 12, st. 59

16   Merely innocent flirtation,
Not quite adultery, but adulteration.
Don Juan (1819–24) canto 12, st. 63

17 Now hatred is by far the longest pleasure;
Men love in haste, but they detest at leisure.
Don Juan (1819–24) canto 13, st. 4; see **PROVERBS** 638:33

18 Cervantes smiled Spain's chivalry away.
Don Juan (1819–24) canto 13, st. 11

19 The English winter—ending in July,
To recommence in August.
Don Juan (1819–24) canto 13, st. 42

20 Society is now one polished horde,
Formed of two mighty tribes, the *Bores* and
Bored.
Don Juan (1819–24) canto 13, st. 95

21 Of all the horrid, hideous notes of woe,
Sadder than owl-songs or the midnight blast,
Is that portentous phrase, 'I told you so.'
Don Juan (1819–24) canto 14, st. 50

22 'Tis strange—but true; for truth is always
strange;
Stranger than fiction.
Don Juan (1819–24) canto 14, st. 101; see **PROVERBS** 645:36

23 All present life is but an Interjection,
An 'Oh!' or 'Ah!' of joy or misery,
Or a 'Ha! ha!' or 'Bah!'—a yawn, or 'Pooh!'
Of which perhaps the latter is most true.
Don Juan (1819–24) canto 15, st. 1

24 A lovely being, scarcely formed or moulded,
A rose with all its sweetest leaves yet folded.
Don Juan (1819–24) canto 15, st. 43

25 'Tis wonderful what fable will not do!
'Tis said it makes reality more bearable:
But what's reality? Who has its clue?
Philosophy? No; she too much rejects.
Religion? Yes; but which of all her sects?
Don Juan (1819–24) canto 15, st. 89

26 How little do we know that which we are!
How less what we may be!
Don Juan (1819–24) canto 15, st. 99

27 The worlds beyond this world's perplexing waste
Had more of her existence for in her
There was a depth of feeling to embrace
Thoughts, boundless, deep, but silent too as
space.
Don Juan (1819–24) canto 16, st. 48

28   The mind can make
Substance, and people planets of its own
With beings brighter than have been, and give
A breath to forms which can outlive all flesh.
'The Dream' (1816) st. 1

29   I'll publish, right or wrong:
Fools are my theme, let satire be my song.
English Bards and Scotch Reviewers (1809) l. 5

30 A man must serve his time to every trade
Save censure—critics all are ready made.
Take hackneyed jokes from Miller, got by rote,
With just enough of learning to misquote.
English Bards and Scotch Reviewers (1809) l. 63

1 Each country Book-club bows the knee to Baal,
And, hurling lawful Genius from the throne,
Erects a shrine and idol of its own.
English Bards and Scotch Reviewers (1809) l. 138

2 Who, both by precept and example, shows
That prose is verse, and verse is merely prose,
Convincing all by demonstration plain,
Poetic souls delight in prose insane;
And Christmas stories tortured into rhyme,
Contain the essence of the true sublime.
of **WORDSWORTH**
English Bards and Scotch Reviewers (1809) l. 241

3 Be warm, but pure; be amorous, but be chaste.
English Bards and Scotch Reviewers (1809) l. 306

4 The petrifactions of a plodding brain.
English Bards and Scotch Reviewers (1809) l. 416

5 Then let Ausonia, skilled in every art
To soften manners, but corrupt the heart,
Pour her exotic follies o'er the town,
To sanction Vice, and hunt Decorum down.
Ausonia = Italy
English Bards and Scotch Reviewers (1809) l. 618

6 He nursed the pinion which impelled the steel.
English Bards and Scotch Reviewers (1809) l. 846

7 Let simple Wordsworth chime his childish verse,
And brother Coleridge lull the babe at nurse.
English Bards and Scotch Reviewers (1809) l. 917

8 And glory, like the phoenix midst her fires,
Exhales her odours, blazes, and expires.
English Bards and Scotch Reviewers (1809) l. 959

9 Dusky like night, but night with all her stars,
Or cavern sparkling with its native spars;
With eyes that were a language and a spell,
A form like Aphrodite's in her shell,
With all her loves around her on the deep,
Voluptuous as the first approach of sleep.
'The Island' (1823) canto 2, st. 7

10 Friendship is Love without his wings!
'L'Amitié est l'amour sans ailes' (written 1806, published 1831)

11 So he has cut his throat at last!—He! Who?
The man who cut his country's long ago.
on Castlereagh's suicide, c.1822
'Epigram on Lord Castlereagh'

12 Sorrow is knowledge: they who know the most
Must mourn the deepest o'er the fatal truth,
The Tree of Knowledge is not that of Life.
Manfred (1817) act 1, sc. 1, l. 10

13 How beautiful is all this visible world!
How glorious in its action and itself!
But we, who name ourselves its sovereigns, we,
Half dust, half deity, alike unfit
To sink or soar, with our mixed essence make
A conflict of its elements, and breathe
The breath of degradation and of pride.
Manfred (1817) act 1, sc. 2, l. 37

14 I linger yet with nature, for the night
Hath been to me a more familiar face
Than that of man; and in her starry shade

Of dim and solitary loveliness
I learned the language of another world.
Manfred (1817) act 3, sc. 4, l. 2

15 Old man! 'tis not so difficult to die.
Manfred (2nd ed., 1819) act 3, sc. 4, l. 151

16   You have deeply ventured;
But all must do so who would greatly win.
Marino Faliero (1821) act 1, sc. 2

17 'Tis done—but yesterday a King!
And armed with Kings to strive—
And now thou art a nameless thing:
So abject—yet alive!
'Ode to Napoleon Bonaparte' (1814) st. 1

18 The arbiter of others' fate
A suppliant for his own!
'Ode to Napoleon Bonaparte' (1814) st. 5

19 The Cincinnatus of the West.
of George **WASHINGTON**
'Ode to Napoleon Bonaparte' (1814) st. 19

20 It is not in the storm nor in the strife
We feel benumbed, and wish to be no more,
But in the after-silence on the shore,
When all is lost, except a little life.
'On hearing that Lady Byron was ill' (written 1816)

21 My days are in the yellow leaf;
The flowers and fruits of love are gone;
The worm, the canker, and the grief
Are mine alone!
'On This Day I Complete my Thirty-Sixth Year' (1824); see
BYRON 188:29, **SHAKESPEARE** 722:16

22 My hair is grey, but not with years,
Nor grew it white
In a single night,
As men's have grown from sudden fears.
The Prisoner of Chillon (1816) st. 1

23 And the whole earth would henceforth be
A wider prison unto me.
The Prisoner of Chillon (1816) st. 12

24 Remember thee! Aye, doubt it not;
Thy husband too shall think of thee;
By neither shalt thou be forgot,
Thou false to him, thou fiend to me!
reply to Lady Caroline **LAMB** *who had written 'Remember
me!' in a book belonging to Byron*
'Remember Thee! Remember Thee!' (1813)

25 She walks in beauty, like the night
Of cloudless climes and starry skies;
And all that's best of dark and bright
Meet in her aspect and her eyes:
Thus mellowed to that tender light
Which heaven to gaudy day denies.
'She Walks in Beauty' (1815) st. 1

26 A mind at peace with all below,
A heart whose love is innocent!
'She Walks in Beauty' (1815)

27 Born in the garret, in the kitchen bred,
Promoted thence to deck her mistress' head.
'A Sketch from Private Life' (1816)

1 Eternal spirit of the chainless mind!
Brightest in dungeons, Liberty! thou art.
'Sonnet on Chillon' (1816)

2 Chillon! thy prison is a holy place.
'Sonnet on Chillon' (1816)

3   May none those marks efface!
For they appeal from tyranny to God.
'Sonnet on Chillon' (1816)

4 So, we'll go no more a-roving
So late into the night,
Though the heart be still as loving,
And the moon be still as bright.
'So we'll go no more a-roving' (written 1817)

5 There's not a joy the world can give like that it
takes away.
'Stanzas for Music' (1816)

6 Oh, talk not to me of a name great in story;
The days of our youth are the days of our
glory;
And the myrtle and ivy of sweet two-and-twenty
Are worth all your laurels, though ever so
plenty.
'Stanzas Written on the Road between Florence and Pisa,
November 1821'

7 I knew it was love, and I felt it was glory.
'Stanzas Written on the Road between Florence and Pisa,
November 1821'

8 I am ashes where once I was fire.
'To the Countess of Blessington' (written 1823)

9 Still I can't contradict, what so oft has been said,
'Though women are angels, yet wedlock's the
devil.'
'To Eliza' (1806)

10 And when we think we lead, we are most led.
The Two Foscari (1821) act 2, sc. 1, l. 361

11 The angels all were singing out of tune,
And hoarse with having little else to do,
Excepting to wind up the sun and moon,
Or curb a runaway young star or two.
The Vision of Judgement (1822) st. 2

12 And when the gorgeous coffin was laid low,
It seemed the mockery of hell to fold
The rottenness of eighty years in gold.
on the burial of GEORGE III
The Vision of Judgement (1822) st. 10

13 In whom his qualities are reigning still,
Except that household virtue, most uncommon,
Of constancy to a bad, ugly woman.
The Vision of Judgement (1822) st. 12

14 As he drew near, he gazed upon the gate
Ne'er to be entered more by him or Sin,
With such a glance of supernatural hate,
As made Saint Peter wish himself within;
He pattered with his keys at a great rate,
And sweated through his apostolic skin:
Of course his perspiration was but ichor,
Or some such other spiritual liquor.
The Vision of Judgement (1822) st. 25

15 Yet still between his Darkness and his Brightness
There passed a mutual glance of great
politeness.
The Vision of Judgement (1822) st. 35

16   Satan met his ancient friend
With more hauteur, as might an old Castilian
Poor noble meet a mushroom rich civilian.
The Vision of Judgement (1822) st. 36

17 And when the tumult dwindled to a calm,
I left him practising the hundredth psalm.
The Vision of Judgement (1822) st. 106

18 When we two parted
In silence and tears,
Half broken-hearted
To sever for years,
Pale grew thy cheek and cold,
Colder thy kiss.
'When we two parted' (1816)

19 If I should meet thee
After long years,
How should I greet thee?—
With silence and tears.
'When we two parted' (1816)

20 Near this spot are deposited the remains of one
who possessed beauty without vanity, strength
without insolence, courage without ferocity, and
all the virtues of Man, without his vices.
'Inscription on the Monument of a Newfoundland Dog'
(1808)

21 The man is mad, Sir, mad, frightful as a
Mandrake, and lean as a rutting Stag, and all
about a bitch not worth a Bank token.
of the Revd Robert Bland
letter to John Cam Hobhouse, 16 November 1811; in L. A.
Marchand (ed.) Byron's Letters and Journals vol. 2 (1973)

22 My Princess of Parallelograms.
of his future wife Annabella Milbanke, a keen amateur
mathematician; Byron explains: 'Her proceedings are quite
rectangular, or rather we are two parallel lines prolonged to
infinity side by side but never to meet'
letter to Lady Melbourne, 18 October 1812; in L. A. Marchand
(ed.) Byron's Letters and Journals vol. 2 (1973)

23 The place is very well and quiet and the children
only scream in a low voice.
letter to Lady Melbourne, 21 September 1813, in L. A.
Marchand (ed.) Byron's Letters and Journals vol. 3 (1974)

24 We have progressively improved into a less
spiritual species of tenderness—but the seal is
not yet fixed though the wax is preparing for the
impression.
of his relationship with Lady Frances Webster
letter to Lady Melbourne, 14 October 1813; in L. A. Marchand
(ed.) Byron's Letters and Journals vol. 3 (1974)

25 I by no means rank poetry high in the scale of
intelligence—this may look like affectation—but
it is my real opinion—it is the lava of the
imagination whose eruption prevents an
earthquake.
letter to Annabella Milbanke, 29 November 1813, in L. A.
Marchand (ed.) Byron's Letters and Journals vol. 3 (1974)

1 I prefer the talents of action—of war—of the senate—or even of science—to all the speculations of those mere dreamers of another existence.
letter to Annabella Milbanke, 29 November 1813, in L. A. Marchand (ed.) *Byron's Letters and Journals* vol. 3 (1974)

2 What is hope? nothing but the paint on the face of Existence; the least touch of truth rubs it off, and then we see what a hollow-cheeked harlot we have got hold of.
letter to Thomas Moore, 28 October 1815, in L. A. Marchand (ed.) *Byron's Letters and Journals* vol. 4 (1975)

3 Like other parties of the kind, it was first silent, then talky, then argumentative, then disputatious, then unintelligible, then altogethery, then inarticulate, and then drunk.
letter to Thomas Moore, 31 October 1815, in L. A. Marchand (ed.) *Byron's Letters and Journals* vol. 4 (1975)

4 Wordsworth—stupendous genius! damned fool! These poets run about their ponds though they cannot fish.
fragment of a letter to James Hogg, recorded in the diary of Henry Crabb Robinson, 1 December 1816; in L. A. Marchand (ed.) *Byron's Letters and Journals* vol. 5 (1976)

5 Love in this part of the world is no sinecure.
letter to John Murray from Venice, 27 December 1816, in L. A. Marchand (ed.) *Byron's Letters and Journals* vol. 5 (1976)

6 I hate things all *fiction* . . . there should always be some foundation of fact for the most airy fabric and pure invention is but the talent of a liar.
letter to John Murray from Venice, 2 April 1817; in L. A. Marchand (ed.) *Byron's Letters and Journals* vol. 5 (1976)

7 Without means, without connection, without character . . . he beat them all, in all he ever attempted.
of Richard Brinsley **SHERIDAN**
letter to Thomas Moore, 1 June 1818, in L. A. Marchand (ed.) *Byron's Letters and Journals* vol. 6 (1978)

8 Is it not *life*, is it not *the thing*?—Could any man have written it—who has not lived in the world?—and tooled in a post-chaise? in a hackney coach? in a gondola? Against a wall? in a court carriage? in a *vis-à-vis*?—on a table?—and under it?
of Don Juan
letter to Douglas Kinnaird, 26 October 1819; in L. A. Marchand (ed.) *Byron's Letters and Journals* vol. 6 (1978)

9 The reading or non-reading a book—will never keep down a single petticoat.
letter to Richard Hoppner, 29 October 1819, in L. A. Marchand (ed.) *Byron's Letters and Journals* vol. 6 (1978)

10 Such writing is a sort of mental masturbation—he is always f—gg—g his *imagination*.—I don't mean that he is indecent but viciously soliciting his own ideas into a state which is neither poetry nor any thing else but a Bedlam vision produced by raw pork and opium.
of **KEATS**
letter to John Murray, 9 November 1820; in L. A. Marchand (ed.) *Byron's Letters and Journals* vol. 7 (1979)

11 I awoke one morning and found myself famous.
on the instantaneous success of Childe Harold
Thomas Moore *Letters and Journals of Lord Byron* (1830) vol. 1

12 You should have a softer pillow than my heart.
to his wife, who had rested her head on his breast
E. C. Mayne (ed.) *The Life and Letters of Anne Isabella, Lady Noel Byron* (1929) ch. 11

James Branch Cabell 1879–1958
American novelist and essayist

13 The optimist proclaims that we live in the best of all possible worlds; and the pessimist fears this is true.
The Silver Stallion (1926) bk. 4, ch. 26

Caecilius Statius d. after 166 BC
Roman comic dramatist, born in Gaul

14 *Serit arbores, quae alteri saeclo prosint.*
He plants the trees to serve another age.
Synephebi; quoted in Cicero 'De Senectute'

Augustus Caesar *see* Augustus

Irving Caesar 1895–1996
American songwriter

15 Picture you upon my knee,
Just tea for two and two for tea.
'Tea for Two' (1925 song)

Julius Caesar 100–44 BC
Roman general and statesman. See also **PLUTARCH** 610:12

16 *Gallia est omnis divisa in partes tres.*
Gaul as a whole is divided into three parts.
De Bello Gallico bk. 1, sect. 1, opening words

17 Men are nearly always willing to believe what they wish.
De Bello Gallico bk. 3, sect. 18; see **BACON** 49:1, **DEMOSTHENES** 272:18

18 Caesar's wife must be above suspicion.
divorcing his wife Pompeia after unfounded allegations were made against her
oral tradition, based on Plutarch *Parallel Lives* 'Julius Caesar' ch. 10, sect. 9; see **PROVERBS** 628:30

19 Caesar had rather be first in a village than second at Rome.
Francis Bacon *The Advancement of Learning* pt. 2, ch. 23, sect. 36; based on Plutarch *Parallel Lives* 'Julius Caesar' ch. 11: 'I should rather be first among these people than second at Rome'

20 Thou hast Caesar and his fortune with thee.
Plutarch *Parallel Lives* 'Julius Caesar' ch. 38, sect. 3 (translated by T. North, 1579; literally 'You are carrying Caesar, and his fortune is in the same boat')

1 *Iacta alea est.*

The die is cast.

at the crossing of the Rubicon, the boundary beyond which he was forbidden to lead his army

Suetonius *Lives of the Caesars* 'Divus Julius' sect. 32; originally spoken in Greek, Plutarch *Parallel Lives* 'Pompey' ch. 60, sect. 2

2 *Veni, vidi, vici.*

I came, I saw, I conquered.

inscription displayed in Caesar's Pontic triumph, according to Suetonius *Lives of the Caesars* 'Divus Julius' sect. 37; or, according to Plutarch *Parallel Lives* 'Julius Caesar' ch. 50, sect. 2, written in a letter by Caesar, announcing the victory of Zela, 47 BC, which concluded the Pontic campaign

3 *Et tu, Brute?*

You too, Brutus?

traditional rendering of Suetonius *Lives of the Caesars* 'Divus Julius' sect. 82: 'Some have written that when Marcus Brutus rushed at him, he said in Greek, "You too, my child?"'; see **SHAKESPEARE** 712:17

John Cage 1912–92

American composer, pianist, and writer

4   I have nothing to say
               and I am saying it and that is poetry.

'Lecture on nothing' (1961)

James Cagney *see* Misquotations 549:7

James M. Cain 1892–1977

American novelist

5 The postman always rings twice.

title of novel (1934)

Pedro Calderón de La Barca 1600–81

Spanish dramatist and poet

6 . . . *Aun en sueños*
no se pierde el hacer bien.

Even in dreams good works are not wasted.

La Vida es Sueño (1636) 'Segunda Jornada' l. 2146

7 *¿Qué es la vida? Un frenesí.*
¿Qué es la vida? Una ilusión,
una sombra, una ficción,
y el mayor bien es pequeño;
que toda la vida es sueño,
y los sueños, sueños son.

What is life? a frenzy. What is life? An illusion, a shadow, a fiction. And the greatest good is of slight worth, as all life is a dream, and dreams are dreams.

La Vida es Sueño (1636) 'Segunda Jornada' l. 2183; see **MONTAIGNE** 555:17

Caligula (Gaius Julius Caesar Germanicus) AD 12–41

Roman emperor from AD 37. See also ACCIUS 1:7

8 *Utinam populus Romanus unam cervicem haberet!*

Would that the Roman people had but one neck!

Suetonius *Lives of the Caesars* 'Gaius Caligula' sect. 30

9 *Ita feri ut se mori sentiat.*

Strike him so that he can feel that he is dying.

Suetonius *Lives of the Caesars* 'Gaius Caligula' sect. 30

James Callaghan 1912–2005

British Labour statesman, Prime Minister 1976–9. See also MISQUOTATIONS 547:8

10 You cannot now, if you ever could, spend your way out of a recession.

speech at Labour Party Conference, 28 September 1976

11 You never reach the promised land. You can march towards it.

in a television interview, 20 July 1978

12 I had known it was going to be a 'winter of discontent'.

television interview, 8 February 1979; in *Daily Telegraph* 9 February 1979; see **NEWSPAPER HEADLINES AND LEADERS** 573:25

13 It's the first time in recorded history that turkeys have been known to vote for an early Christmas.

in the debate resulting in the fall of the Labour government, when the pact between Labour and the Liberals had collapsed, and the Scottish and Welsh Nationalists had also withdrawn their support

in the House of Commons, 28 March 1979

14 There are times, perhaps once every thirty years, when there is a sea-change in politics. It then does not matter what you say or what you do. There is a shift in what the public wants and what it approves of. I suspect there is now such a sea-change—and it is for Mrs Thatcher.

during the election campaign of 1979

Kenneth O. Morgan *Callaghan* (1997)

Callimachus c.305–c.240 BC

Greek poet and scholar

15 Someone spoke of your death, Heraclitus. It
    brought me
Tears, and I remembered how often together
We ran the sun down with talk.

R. Pfeiffer (ed.) *Callimachus* (1949–53) Epigram 2; translated by Peter Jay; see **CORY** 252:13

16 I abhor, too, the roaming lover, nor do I drink from every well; I loathe all things held in common.

R. Pfeiffer (ed.) *Callimachus* (1949–53) Epigram 28; see **HORACE** 412:14

17 A great book is like great evil.

R. Pfeiffer (ed.) *Callimachus* (1949–53) Fragment 465; see **PROVERBS** 633:27

18 I sing nothing that is not attested.

fragment 617, translated by C. A. Trypanis

Charles Alexandre de Calonne

1734–1802

French statesman

1 *Madame, si c'est possible, c'est fait; impossible? cela se fera.*

Madam, if a thing is possible, consider it done; the impossible? that will be done.

in J. Michelet *Histoire de la Révolution Française* (1847) vol. 1, pt. 2, sect. 8; see **MILITARY SAYINGS, SLOGANS, AND SONGS** 535:6, **NANSEN** 567:8

C. S. Calverley (born Blayds) 1831–84

English writer

2 The farmer's daughter hath soft brown hair; (*Butter and eggs and a pound of cheese*)
And I met with a ballad, I can't say where,
Which wholly consisted of lines like these.
'Ballad' (1872)

3 O Beer! O Hodgson, Guinness, Allsopp, Bass!
Names that should be on every infant's tongue!
'Beer' (1861)

4 For I've read in many a novel that, unless they've souls that grovel,
Folks *prefer* in fact a hovel to your dreary marble halls.
'In the Gloaming' (1872); see **BUNN** 170:17

5 How Eugene Aram, though a thief, a liar, and a murderer,
Yet, being intellectual, was amongst the noblest of mankind.
'Of Reading' (1861); see **HOOD** 405:14

Italo Calvino 1923–85

Italian novelist and short-story writer

6 The gaze of dogs who don't understand and who don't know that they may be right not to understand.
Il Barone Rampante [The Baron in the Trees] (1957) ch. 10

7 Revolutionaries are more formalistic than conservatives.
Il Barone Rampante [The Baron in the Trees] (1957) ch. 28

8 A classic is a book that has never finished saying what it has to say.
'Why Read the Classics?' in *L'Espresso* 28 June 1981

Helder Camara 1909–99

Brazilian priest

9 When I give food to the poor they call me a saint. When I ask why the poor have no food they call me a communist.
attributed

Pierre, Baron de Cambronne

1770–1842

French general

10 *La Garde meurt, mais ne se rend pas.*
The Guards die but do not surrender.
attributed to Cambronne when called upon to surrender at
Waterloo, 1815, but later denied by him; an alternative version is that he replied: 'Merde! [Shit!]', known in French as the 'mot de Cambronne'
H. Houssaye *La Garde meurt et ne se rend pas* (1907)

Lord Camden 1714–94

British Whig politician; Lord Chancellor, 1766–70

11 Taxation and representation are inseparable . . . whatever is a man's own, is absolutely his own; no man hath a right to take it from him without his consent either expressed by himself or representative; whoever attempts to do it, attempts an injury; whoever does it, commits a robbery; he throws down and destroys the distinction between liberty and slavery.
on the taxation of Americans by the British parliament
speech in the House of Lords, 10 February 1766; see **OTIS** 589:9

David Cameron 1966–

British Conservative politician

12 We—the people in suits—often see hoodies as aggressive, the uniform of a rebel army of gangsters. But hoodies are more defensive than offensive. They're a way to stay invisible in the street.
speech to Centre for Social Justice, 10 July 2006, in BBC News (online edition) 10 July 2006; see **COAKER** 237:9

Julia Margaret Cameron 1815–79

English photographer

13 I longed to arrest all beauty that came before me.
Annals of my Glass House (1874)

Alastair Campbell 1957–

British journalist, Press Secretary to the Prime Minister (Tony **BLAIR**) 1997–2003. See also **ANONYMOUS** 19:22

14 Labour spin doctors aren't supposed to like Tory MPs. But Alan Clark was an exceptional man.
in *Mirror* 8 September 1999

Jane Montgomery Campbell 1817–78

English hymn-writer

15 We plough the fields, and scatter
The good seed on the land,
But it is fed and watered
By God's almighty hand;
He sends the snow in winter,
The warmth to swell the grain,
The breezes and the sunshine,
And soft refreshing rain.
'We plough the fields, and scatter' (1861 hymn); translated from the German of Matthias Claudius (1740–1815)

Mrs Patrick Campbell (Beatrice Stella

Tanner) 1865–1940

English actress. On Campbell: see WOOLLCOTT 864:16

1 The deep, deep peace of the double-bed after
the hurly-burly of the chaise-longue.
on her recent marriage
Alexander Woollcott *While Rome Burns* (1934) 'The First Mrs
Tanqueray'

2 It doesn't matter what you do in the bedroom as
long as you don't do it in the street and frighten
the horses.
Daphne Fielding *The Duchess of Jermyn Street* (1964) ch. 2

Roy Campbell 1901–57

South African poet

3   Giraffes!—a People
Who live between the earth and skies,
Each in his lone religious steeple,
Keeping a lighthouse with his eyes.
'Dreaming Spires' (1946)

4 You praise the firm restraint with which they
write—
I'm with you there, of course:
They use the snaffle and the curb all right,
But where's the bloody horse?
'On Some South African Novelists' (1930)

Thomas Campbell 1777–1844

Scottish poet

5 Let us think of them that sleep,
Full many a fathom deep,
By thy wild and stormy steep,
Elsinore!
'Battle of the Baltic' (1809)

6 O leave this barren spot to me!
Spare, woodman, spare the beechen tree.
'The Beech-Tree's Petition' (1800); see MORRIS 560:10

7 To-morrow let us do or die!
'Gertrude of Wyoming' (1809) pt. 3, st. 37

8 On the green banks of Shannon, when Sheelah
was nigh,
No blithe Irish lad was so happy as I;
No harp like my own could so cheerily play,
And wherever I went was my poor dog Tray.
'The Harper' (1799)

9 On Linden, when the sun was low,
All bloodless lay the untrodden snow,
And dark as winter was the flow
Of Iser, rolling rapidly.
'Hohenlinden' (1802)

10 A chieftain to the Highlands bound
Cries, 'Boatman, do not tarry!
And I'll give thee a silver pound
To row us o'er the ferry.'
'Lord Ullin's Daughter' (1809)

11 O, I'm the chief of Ulva's isle
And this Lord Ullin's daughter.
'Lord Ullin's Daughter' (1809)

12 'Tis distance lends enchantment to the view,
And robes the mountain in its azure hue.
Pleasures of Hope (1799) pt. 1, l. 7; see PROVERBS 630:6

13 Hope, for a season, bade the world farewell,
And Freedom shrieked—as Kosciuszko fell!
Pleasures of Hope (1799) pt. 1, l. 381

14 What millions died—that Caesar might be great!
Pleasures of Hope (1799) pt. 2, l. 174

15 What though my wingèd hours of bliss have
been,
Like angel-visits, few and far between?
Pleasures of Hope (1799) pt. 2, l. 375

16 An original something, fair maid, you would
win me
To write—but how shall I begin?
For I fear I have nothing original in me—
Excepting Original Sin.
'To a Young Lady, Who Asked Me to Write Something
Original for Her Album' (1843)

17 Day her sultry fires had wasted.
'The Turkish Lady'

18 Ye Mariners of England
That guard our native seas,
Whose flag has braved, a thousand years
The battle and the breeze.
'Ye Mariners of England' (1801)

19 With thunders from her native oak
She quells the floods below.
'Ye Mariners of England' (1801)

20 Now Barabbas was a publisher.
alteration of Bible verse; also attributed, wrongly, to BYRON
attributed, in Samuel Smiles *A Publisher and his Friends:
Memoir and Correspondence of the late John Murray* (1891) vol.
1, ch. 14; see BIBLE 108:27

Thomas Campion 1567–1620

English poet and musician

21 My sweetest Lesbia let us live and love,
And though the sager sort our deeds reprove,
Let us not weigh them: Heav'n's great lamps do
dive
Into their west, and straight again revive,
But soon as once set is our little light,
Then must we sleep one ever-during night.
A Book of Airs (1601) no. 1 'My sweetest Lesbia' (translation of
Catullus *Carmina* no. 5); see CATULLUS 210:6

22 When to her lute Corinna sings,
Her voice revives the leaden strings,
And both in highest notes appear,
As any challenged echo clear.
But when she doth of mourning speak,
Ev'n with her sighs the strings do break.
A Book of Airs (1601) no. 6

23 Good thoughts his only friends,
His wealth a well-spent age,
The earth his sober inn
And quiet pilgrimage.
A Book of Airs (1601) no. 18

24 There is a garden in her face
Where roses and white lilies grow;

A heavenly paradise is that place,
Wherein all pleasant fruits do flow.
There cherries grow, which none may buy
Till 'Cherry ripe' themselves do cry.

The Fourth Book of Airs (c.1617) no. 7; music by Richard Alison,
who published the song in *An Hour's Recreation in Music*
(1606)

1 Rose-cheeked Laura, come;
Sing thou smoothly with thy beauty's
Silent music, either other
Sweetly gracing.

'Rose-cheeked Laura' (1602)

2 Kind are her answers,
But her performance keeps no day;
Breaks time, as dancers
From their own music when they stray.

The Third Book of Airs (1617) no. 7

Albert Camus 1913–60
French novelist, dramatist, and essayist

3 *Intellectuel = celui qui se dédouble.*
An intellectual is someone whose mind watches
itself.

Carnets, 1935–42 (1962)

4 Politics and the fate of mankind are formed by
men without ideals and without greatness.

Carnets, 1935–42 (1962)

5 You know what charm is: a way of getting the
answer yes without having asked any clear
question.

The Fall (1956)

6 We are all special cases. We all want to appeal
against something! Everyone insists on his
innocence, at all costs, even if it means accusing
the rest of the human race and heaven.

The Fall (1956)

7 We seldom confide in those who are better than
ourselves.

The Fall (1956)

8 I'll tell you a great secret, my friend. Don't wait
for the last judgement. It happens every day.

The Fall (1956)

9 Sisyphus, proletarian of the gods, powerless and
rebellious, knows the whole extent of his
wretched condition; it is what he thinks of
during his descent. The lucidity that was to
constitute his torture at the same time crowns
his victory. There is no fate that cannot be
surmounted by scorn.

The Myth of Sisyphus (1942) (translated by Justin O'Brien)

10 Integrity has no need of rules.

The Myth of Sisyphus (1942)

11 The struggle itself towards the heights is enough
to fill a human heart. One must imagine that
Sisyphus is happy.

The Myth of Sisyphus (1942)

12 What is a rebel? A man who says no.

The Rebel (1951)

13 All modern revolutions have ended in a
reinforcement of the State.

The Rebel (1951)

14 Every revolutionary ends as an oppressor or a
heretic.

The Rebel (1951)

15 Virtue cannot separate itself from reality
without becoming a principle of evil.

The Rebel (1951)

16 When the imagination sleeps, words are emptied
of their meaning.

Resistance, Rebellion and Death (1961) 'Reflections on the
Guillotine'

17 Mother died today. Or perhaps it was yesterday, I
don't know.

The Stranger (1944), opening words

18 Martha: 'What is autumn?' Jan: 'A second spring,
where every leaf is a flower.'

Théâtre, récits, nouvelles (1967) 'Le Malentendu' (1944)

19 One sometimes sees more clearly in the man
who lies than in the man who tells the truth.
Truth, like the light, blinds. Lying, on the other
hand, is a beautiful twilight, which gives to each
object its value.

attributed; Lord Trevelyan *Diplomatic Channels* (1973)

20 What I know most surely about morality and
the duty of man I owe to sport.

often quoted as ' . . . I owe to football'
Herbert R. Lottman *Albert Camus* (1979)

21 Without work, all life goes rotten, but when
work is soulless, life stifles and dies.

attributed; E. F. Schumacher *Good Work* (1979)

Elias Canetti 1905–94
Bulgarian-born writer and novelist

22 There is nothing that man fears more than the
touch of the unknown.

Crowds and Power (1960)

23 Secrecy lies at the very core of power.

Crowds and Power (1960)

24 All the things one has forgotten scream for help
in dreams.

The Human Province (1973)

George Canning 1770–1827
British Tory statesman, Prime Minister 1827

25 In matters of commerce the fault of the Dutch
Is offering too little and asking too much.
The French are with equal advantage content,
So we clap on Dutch bottoms just twenty per
cent.

*dispatch, in cipher, to the English ambassador at the Hague,
31 January 1826*

Sir Harry Poland *Mr Canning's Rhyming 'Dispatch' to Sir Charles
Bagot* (1905)

1 A steady patriot of the world alone,
The friend of every country but his own.
on the Jacobin
'New Morality' (1821) l. 113; see **DISRAELI** 285:7, **OVERBURY** 589:15

2 And finds, with keen discriminating sight,
Black's not so black;—nor white so very white.
'New Morality' (1821) l. 199

3 Give me the avowed, erect and manly foe;
Firm I can meet, perhaps return the blow;
But of all plagues, good Heaven, thy wrath can send,
Save me, oh, save me, from the candid friend.
'New Morality' (1821) l. 207

4 Pitt is to Addington
As London is to Paddington.
'The Oracle' (c.1803)

5 Away with the cant of 'Measures not men'!—the idle supposition that it is the harness and not the horses that draw the chariot along. If the comparison must be made, if the distinction must be taken, men are everything, measures comparatively nothing.
speech on the Army estimates, 8 December 1802, in *Speeches of . . . Canning* (1828) vol. 2; the phrase 'measures not men' may be found as early as 1742 (in a letter from Chesterfield to Dr Chevenix, 6 March); see **BURKE** 175:5, **GOLDSMITH** 365:2

6 I called the New World into existence, to redress the balance of the Old.
speech on the affairs of Portugal, in House of Commons 12 December 1826

7 You well know how soon one of these stupendous masses, now reposing on their shadows in perfect stillness, would upon any call of patriotism or of necessity, assume the likeness of an animated thing, instinct with life and motion: how soon it would ruffle, as it were its swelling plumage, how quickly it would put forth all its beauty and its bravery, collect its scattered elements of strength and waken its dormant thunder . . . Such is England herself; while apparently passive and motionless, she silently concentrates the power to be put forth on an adequate occasion.
on the men-of-war lying at anchor in the harbour
speech at Plymouth, 12 December 1823; in R. W. Seton-Watson *Britain in Europe 1789–1914* (1945)

Hughie Cannon 1877–1912
American songwriter

8 Won't you come home Bill Bailey, won't you come home?
'Bill Bailey, Won't You Please Come Home' (1902 song)

Moya Cannon 1956–
Irish poet

9 Our windy, untidy loft
where old people had flung up old junk
they'd thought might come in handy
ploughs, ladles, bears, lions, a clatter of heroes.
'The Stars' (1997)

Eric Cantona 1966–
French footballer

10 When seagulls follow a trawler, it is because they think sardines will be thrown into the sea.
to the media at the end of a press conference, 31 March 1995

Robert Capa 1913–54
Hungarian-born American photojournalist

11 If your pictures aren't good enough, you aren't close enough.
Russell Miller *Magnum: Fifty years at the Front Line of History* (1997)

Truman Capote 1924–84
American writer and novelist. On Capote: see **VIDAL** 827:16

12 Other voices, other rooms.
title of novel (1948)

Al Capp (Alfred Gerard Caplin) 1907–79
American cartoonist

13 A product of the untalented, sold by the unprincipled to the utterly bewildered.
of abstract art
in *National Observer* 1 July 1963; see **ZAPPA** 877:13

Francesco Caracciolo 1752–99
Neapolitan diplomat

14 In England there are sixty different religions, and only one sauce.
attributed

Ethna Carbery 1866–1902
Irish poet

15 I met the Love-Talker one eve in the glen,
He was handsomer than any of our handsome young men,
His eyes were blacker than the sloe, his voice sweeter far
Than the crooning of old Kevin's pipes beyond in Coolnagar.
'The Love-Talker' (1902)

16 Oh, Kathaleen Ní Houlihan, your road's a thorny way,
And 'tis a faithful soul would walk the flints with you for aye,
Would walk the sharp and cruel flints until his locks grew grey.
'The Passing of the Gael' (1902)

17 Young Rody MacCorley goes to die
On the Bridge of Toome today.
'Rody MacCorley' (1902)

Ernesto Cardenal 1925–

Nicaraguan poet

1 While classes exist no one is free
We are not born to be slaves
or to be masters.
We are born to be brothers and sisters.
What is capitalism but buying and selling of
people?
'Canto Nacional' (1972) translated by Dinah Livingstone

2 When you get the nomination, the prize, the
promotion,
think of the ones who died.
When you are at the reception, delegation,
commission,
think of the ones who died.
When you have won the election and the crowd
congratulates you,
think of the ones who died.
'For Those Dead Our Dead' translated by Dinah Livingstone

3 When they asked Joan of Arc at her trial
whether God loved the English, she replied:
'God does not love the English *in* France.' And
this is the mystery of our vocation. God also
loves the man who is dictator of Nigaragua, but
he does not love him *as* the dictator of
Nigaragua.
of Anastasio **SOMOZA**
Vida en el Amor (1970) 'Will of God' translated by Dinah
Livingstone

Neville Cardus 1889–1975

English critic and writer

4 If everything else in this nation of ours were
lost but cricket—her Constitution and the laws
of England of Lord Halsbury—it would be
possible to reconstruct from the theory and
practice of cricket all the eternal Englishness
which has gone to the establishment of that
Constitution and the laws aforesaid.
Cricket (1930)

Richard Carew 1555–1620

English poet

5 Will you have all in all for prose and verse? Take
the miracle of our age, Sir Philip Sidney.
William Camden *Remains concerning Britain* (1614) 'The
Excellency of the English Tongue'

Thomas Carew c.1595–1640

English poet and courtier

6 He that loves a rosy cheek,
Or a coral lip admires,
Or, from star-like eyes, doth seek
Fuel to maintain his fires;
As old Time makes these decay,
So his flames must waste away.
'Disdain Returned' (1640)

7 The Muses' garden with pedantic weeds
O'erspread, was purged by thee; the lazy seeds

Of servile imitation thrown away,
And fresh invention planted.
'An Elegy upon the Death of Dr John Donne' (1640)

8 Here lies a king, that ruled as he thought fit
The universal monarchy of wit.
'An Elegy upon the Death of Dr John Donne' (1640)

9 The purest soul that e'er was sent
Into a clayey tenement.
'Epitaph On the Lady Mary Villiers' (1640)

10 Good to the poor, to kindred dear,
To servants kind, to friendship clear,
To nothing but herself severe.
'Inscription on the Tomb of Lady Mary Wentworth' (1640)

11 So though a virgin, yet a bride
To every Grace, she justified
A chaste polygamy, and died.
'Inscription on the Tomb of Lady Mary Wentworth' (1640)

12 Though a stranger to this place,
Bewail in theirs thine own hard case:
For thou perhaps at thy return
Mayst find thy darling in an urn.
'On the Lady Mary Villiers' (1640)

13 Ask me no more where Jove bestows,
When June is past, the fading rose;
For in your beauty's orient deep
These flowers, as in their causes, sleep.
'A Song' (1640)

14 Ask me no more whither doth haste
The nightingale when May is past;
For in your sweet dividing throat
She winters and keeps warm her note.
'A Song' (1640)

15 Ask me no more if east or west
The Phoenix builds her spicy nest;
For unto you at last she flies,
And in your fragrant bosom dies.
'A Song' (1640)

16 When thou, poor excommunicate
From all the joys of love, shalt see
The full reward and glorious fate
Which my strong faith shall purchase me,
Then curse thine own inconstancy.
'To My Inconstant Mistress' (1640)

George Carey 1935–

English Anglican churchman; Archbishop of Canterbury
1991–2002

17 We must recall that the Church is always 'one
generation away from extinction.'
Working Party Report *Youth A Part: Young People and the
Church* (1996) foreword

Henry Carey c.1687–1743

English comic dramatist and songwriter. See also **SONGS,
SPIRITUALS, AND SHANTIES** 762:9

18 Let your little verses flow
Gently, sweetly, row by row;
Let the verse the subject fit,

Little subject, little wit.
'Namby-Pamby: or, A Panegyric on the New Versification'
(1725)

1 As an actor does his part,
So the nurses get by heart
Namby-pamby's little rhymes,
Little jingle, little chimes.
'Namby-Pamby' (1725)

2 Of all the girls that are so smart
There's none like pretty Sally,
She is the darling of my heart,
And she lives in our alley.
'Sally in our Alley' (1729)

James B. Carey 1911–73

American labour leader

3 I don't think that makes any difference. A door-opener for the Communist party is worse than a member of the Communist party. When someone walks like a duck, swims like a duck, and quacks like a duck, he's a duck.
of Communist affiliations during the MCCARTHY *era*
in *New York Times* 3 September 1948; see HARRIS 383:2

Jane Carlyle (née Welsh) 1801–66

Scottish wife of Thomas CARLYLE. On Carlyle: see BUTLER 184:7

4 I am not at all the sort of person you and I took me for.
letter to Thomas Carlyle, 7 May 1822, in C. R. Sanders et al.
(eds.) *Collected Letters of Thomas and Jane Welsh Carlyle* (1970)
vol. 2

Thomas Carlyle 1795–1881

Scottish historian and political philosopher. On Carlyle: see BUTLER 184:7, CLOUGH 237:8

5 A witty statesman said, you might prove anything by figures.
Chartism (1839) ch. 2

6 Surely of all 'rights of man', this right of the ignorant man to be guided by the wiser, to be, gently or forcibly, held in the true course by him, is the indisputablest.
Chartism (1839) ch. 6

7 In epochs when cash payment has become the sole nexus of man to man.
Chartism (1839) ch. 6

8 The foul sluggard's comfort: 'It will last my time.'
Critical and Miscellaneous Essays (1838) 'Count Cagliostro.
Flight Last'

9 Thou wretched fraction, wilt thou be the ninth part even of a tailor?
Critical and Miscellaneous Essays (1838) 'Francia'; see PROVERBS
639:50

10 The Golden Calf of Self-love soon waxes to be a burning Phalaris bull, which reduces its father and adorer to ashes.
German Romance (1827) note to translation of RICHTER's
Schmelzle's Journey to Flætz

11 Experience is the best of schoolmasters, only the school fees are heavy.
Miscellaneous Essays (1838) 'Goethe's Helena'

12 What is all knowledge too but recorded experience, and a product of history; of which, therefore, reasoning and belief, no less than action and passion, are essential materials?
Critical and Miscellaneous Essays (1838) 'On History'

13 History is the essence of innumerable biographies.
Critical and Miscellaneous Essays (1838) 'On History'

14 A well-written Life is almost as rare as a well-spent one.
Critical and Miscellaneous Essays (1838) 'Jean Paul Friedrich
Richter'

15 There is no life of a man, faithfully recorded, but is a heroic poem of its sort, rhymed or unrhymed.
Critical and Miscellaneous Essays (1838) 'Sir Walter Scott'

16 Under all speech that is good for anything there lies a silence that is better. Silence is deep as Eternity; speech is shallow as Time.
Critical and Miscellaneous Essays (1838) 'Sir Walter Scott'

17 To the very last he [Napoleon] had a kind of idea; that, namely, of *La carrière ouverte aux talents*, The tools to him that can handle them.
Critical and Miscellaneous Essays (1838) 'Sir Walter Scott' (*La
carrière . . .* Career open to the talents)

18 It can be said of him, when he departed, he took a man's life along with him.
Critical and Miscellaneous Essays (1838) 'Sir Walter Scott'

19 This idle habit of 'accounting for the moral sense' . . . The moral sense, thank God, is a thing you will never 'account for' . . . By no greatest happiness principle, greatest nobleness principle, or any principle whatever, will you make that in the least clearer than it already is.
Critical and Miscellaneous Essays (1838) 'Shooting Niagara: and
After?'

20 It is the Age of Machinery, in every outward and inward sense of that word.
Critical and Miscellaneous Essays (1838) 'Signs of the Times'

21 The Bible-Society . . . is found, on inquiry, to be . . . a machine for converting the Heathen.
Critical and Miscellaneous Essays (1838) 'Signs of the Times'

22 The three great elements of modern civilization, Gunpowder, Printing, and the Protestant Religion.
Critical and Miscellaneous Essays (1838) 'The State of German
Literature'; see BACON 49:3

23 'Genius' (which means transcendent capacity of taking trouble, first of all).
History of Frederick the Great (1858–65) bk. 4, ch. 3; see
BUFFON 170:5, PROVERBS 632:45

24 A whiff of grapeshot.
History of the French Revolution (1837) vol. 1, bk. 5, ch. 3

25 History a distillation of rumour.
History of the French Revolution (1837) vol. 1, bk. 7, ch. 5

1 The difference between Orthodoxy or My-doxy
and Heterodoxy or Thy-doxy.
History of the French Revolution (1837) vol. 2, bk. 4, ch. 2; see
WARBURTON 839:18

2 The seagreen Incorruptible.
describing **ROBESPIERRE**
History of the French Revolution (1837) vol. 2, bk. 4, ch. 4

3 France was long a despotism tempered by
epigrams.
History of the French Revolution (1837) vol. 3, bk. 7, ch. 7

4 Aristocracy of the Moneybag.
History of the French Revolution (1837) vol. 3, bk. 7, ch. 7

5 Worship is transcendent wonder.
On Heroes, Hero-Worship, and the Heroic (1841) 'The Hero as
Divinity'

6 I hope we English will long maintain our *grand
talent pour le silence.*
On Heroes, Hero-Worship, and the Heroic (1841) 'The Hero as
King'

7 In books lies the *soul* of the whole Past Time;
the articulate audible voice of the Past, when
the body and material substance of it has
altogether vanished like a dream.
On Heroes, Hero-Worship, and the Heroic (1841) 'The Hero as
Man of Letters'

8 The true University of these days is a collection
of books.
On Heroes, Hero-Worship, and the Heroic (1841) 'The Hero as
Man of Letters'

9 One life; a little gleam of time between two
eternities.
On Heroes, Hero-Worship, and the Heroic (1841) 'The Hero as
Man of Letters'

10 Adversity is sometimes hard upon a man; but for
one man who can stand prosperity, there are a
hundred that will stand adversity.
On Heroes, Hero-Worship, and the Heroic (1841) 'The Hero as
Man of Letters'

11 Maid-servants, I hear people complaining, are
getting instructed in the 'ologies'.
Inaugural Address at Edinburgh, 2 April 1866, on being installed
as Rector of the University

12 A Parliament speaking through reporters to
Buncombe and the twenty-seven millions mostly
fools.
Latter-Day Pamphlets (1850) 'Parliaments'; see **WALKER** 836:9

13 The Dismal Science.
on political economy
Latter-Day Pamphlets (1850) 'The Present Time'

14 Little other than a redtape talking-machine, and
unhappy bag of parliamentary eloquence.
describing himself
Latter-Day Pamphlets (1850) 'The Present Time'

15 Transcendental moonshine.
*on the influence of a romantic imagination in motivating
Sterling to enter the priesthood*
The Life of John Sterling (1851) pt. 1, ch. 15

16 There is always hope in a man that actually and
earnestly works: in Idleness alone is there
perpetual despair.
Past and Present (1843) bk. 3, ch. 11

17 Captains of industry.
Past and Present (1843) bk. 4, ch. 4 (title)

18 He who first shortened the labour of copyists by
device of *Movable Types* was disbanding hired
armies, and cashiering most Kings and Senates,
and creating a whole new democratic world: he
had invented the art of printing.
Sartor Resartus (1834) bk. 1, ch. 5

19 Man is a tool-using animal . . . Without tools he
is nothing, with tools he is all.
Sartor Resartus (1834) bk. 1, ch. 5; see **FRANKLIN** 341:11

20 Whoso has sixpence is sovereign (to the length
of sixpence) over all men; commands cooks to
feed him, philosophers to teach him, kings to
mount guard over him,—to the length of
sixpence.
Sartor Resartus (1834) bk. 1, ch. 5

21 Language is called the garment of thought:
however, it should rather be, language is the
flesh-garment, the body, of thought.
Sartor Resartus (1834) bk. 1, ch. 11; see **FORKEL** 337:14

22 The end of man is an action and not a thought,
though it were the noblest.
Sartor Resartus (1834) bk. 2, ch. 6; see **ARISTOTLE** 27:7

23 The everlasting No.
Sartor Resartus (1834) bk. 2, ch. 7 (title)

24 Be no longer a chaos, but a world, or even
worldkin. Produce! Produce! Were it but the
pitifullest infinitesimal fraction of a product,
produce it in God's name! 'Tis the utmost thou
hast in thee: out with it, then.
Sartor Resartus (1834) bk. 2, ch. 9

25 Does it not stand on record that the English
Queen Elizabeth, receiving a deputation of
eighteen tailors, address them with a 'Good
morning, gentlemen both!'
Sartor Resartus (1834) bk. 3, ch. 11, quoting an imaginary work
by Diogenes Teufelsdröctch; see **PROVERBS** 639:50

26 What a sad want I am in of libraries, of books
to gather facts from! Why is there not a
Majesty's library in every county town? There is
a Majesty's jail and gallows in every one.
diary, 18 May 1832

27 A good book is the purest essence of a human
soul.
speech in support of the London Library, 24 June 1840, in F.
Harrison *Carlyle and the London Library* (1907)

28 'Gad! she'd better!'
on hearing that Margaret Fuller 'accept[ed] the universe'
William James *Varieties of Religious Experience* (1902) lecture 2

29 Macaulay is well for a while, but one wouldn't
live under Niagara.
R. M. Milnes *Notebook* (1838)

30 Cobden is an inspired bagman, who believes in a
calico millennium.
T. W. Reid *Life, Letters and Friendships of Richard Monckton*
(1890) vol. 1, ch. 10

31 If Jesus Christ were to come to-day, people
would not even crucify him. They would ask

him to dinner, and hear what he had to say, and make fun of it.

D. A. Wilson *Carlyle at his Zenith* (1927)

Stokely Carmichael 1941–98
American Black Power leader

1 The only position for women in SNCC is prone.

response to a question about the position of women

at a Student Nonviolent Coordinating Committee conference, November 1964

Stokely Carmichael 1941–98 *and* Charles Vernon Hamilton 1929–
American Black Power leaders

2 The adoption of the concept of Black Power is one of the most legitimate and healthy developments in American politics and race relations in our time. . . . It is a call for black people in this country to unite, to recognize their heritage, to build a sense of community. It is a call for black people to begin to define their own goals, to lead their own organizations and to support those organizations. It is a call to reject the racist institutions and values of this society.

Black Power (1967)

Andrew Carnegie 1835–1919
American industrialist and philanthropist. See also **PROVERBS** 632:41

3 The man who dies . . . rich dies disgraced.

in *North American Review* June 1889 'Wealth'

Dale Carnegie 1888–1955
American writer and lecturer

4 How to win friends and influence people.

title of book (1936)

Julia A. Carney 1823–1908

5 Little drops of water,
Little grains of sand,
Make the mighty ocean
And the beauteous land.

'Little Things' (1845)

Caroline of Ansbach 1683–1737
German princess, Queen Consort of Great Britain and Ireland from 1727, wife of **GEORGE II**. See also **GEORGE II** 352:9, **WALPOLE** 838:14

6 My dear firstborn is the greatest ass, and the greatest liar, and the greatest *canaille*, and the greatest beast in the whole world, and I heartily wish he was out of it.

of her eldest son, Frederick, Prince of Wales, father of **GEORGE III**

in *Dictionary of National Biography* (1917–)

Joseph Edwards Carpenter 1813–85
English poet and songwriter

7 What are the wild waves saying
Sister, the whole day long,
That ever amid our playing,
I hear but their low lone song?

'What are the Wild Waves Saying?' (1850 song)

Emily Carr 1871–1945
Canadian artist

8 You come into the world alone and you go out of the world alone yet it seems to me you are more alone while living than even going and coming.

Hundreds and Thousands: The Journals of Emily Carr (1966) 16 July 1933

9 A picture equals a movement in space.

Hundreds and Thousands: The Journals of Emily Carr (1966) August 1935

J. L. Carr 1912–94
English novelist

10 *You* have not had thirty years' experience . . . *You* have had one year's experience 30 times.

The Harpole Report (1972)

Lewis Carroll (Charles Lutwidge Dodgson) 1832–98
English writer and mathematician

11 'What is the use of a book', thought Alice, 'without pictures or conversations?'

Alice's Adventures in Wonderland (1865) ch. 1

12 'Curiouser and curiouser!' cried Alice.

Alice's Adventures in Wonderland (1865) ch. 2

13 How doth the little crocodile
Improve his shining tail,
And pour the waters of the Nile
On every golden scale!

Alice's Adventures in Wonderland (1865) ch. 2; see **WATTS** 841:11

14 How cheerfully he seems to grin,
How neatly spreads his claws,
And welcomes little fishes in
With gently smiling jaws!

Alice's Adventures in Wonderland (1865) ch. 2

15 EVERYBODY has won, and all must have prizes.

Alice's Adventures in Wonderland (1865) ch. 3

16 'I'll be judge, I'll be jury,' said cunning old Fury;
'I'll try the whole cause, and condemn you to death.'

Alice's Adventures in Wonderland (1865) ch. 3

17 'You are old, Father William,' the young man said,
'And your hair has become very white;
And yet you incessantly stand on your head—
Do you think, at your age, it is right?'

Alice's Adventures in Wonderland (1865) ch. 5; see **SOUTHEY** 764:14

1 'I have answered three questions, and that is
   enough,'
Said his father; 'don't give yourself airs!
Do you think I can listen all day to such stuff?
Be off, or I'll kick you downstairs!'
   Alice's Adventures in Wonderland (1865) ch. 5; see
   BICKERSTAFFE 120:20

2 'If everybody minded their own business,' said
   the Duchess in a hoarse growl, 'the world would
   go round a good deal faster than it does.'
   Alice's Adventures in Wonderland (1865) ch. 6

3 Speak roughly to your little boy,
And beat him when he sneezes;
He only does it to annoy,
Because he knows it teases.
   Alice's Adventures in Wonderland (1865) ch. 6

4 This time it vanished quite slowly, beginning
   with the end of the tail, and ending with the
   grin, which remained some time after the rest of
   it had gone.
   the Cheshire Cat
   Alice's Adventures in Wonderland (1865) ch. 6

5 'Then you should say what you mean,' the
   March Hare went on. 'I do,' Alice hastily replied;
   'at least—at least I mean what I say—that's the
   same thing, you know.' 'Not the same thing a
   bit!' said the Hatter. 'Why, you might just as
   well say that "I see what I eat" is the same thing
   as "I eat what I see!" '
   Alice's Adventures in Wonderland (1865) ch. 7

6 Twinkle, twinkle, little bat!
How I wonder what you're at!
Up above the world you fly!
Like a teatray in the sky.
   Alice's Adventures in Wonderland (1865) ch. 7; see **TAYLOR AND
   TAYLOR** 791:16

7 'Take some more tea,' the March Hare said to
   Alice, very earnestly. 'I've had nothing yet,' Alice
   replied in an offended tone, 'so I can't take
   more.' 'You mean you can't take *less*,' said the
   Hatter: 'it's very easy to take *more* than nothing.'
   Alice's Adventures in Wonderland (1865) ch. 7

8 Off with her head!
   the Queen of Hearts
   Alice's Adventures in Wonderland (1865) ch. 8

9 Everything's got a moral, if you can only find it.
   Alice's Adventures in Wonderland (1865) ch. 9

10 Take care of the sense, and the sounds will take
   care of themselves.
   Alice's Adventures in Wonderland (1865) ch. 9; see **PROVERBS**
   644:2

11 'That's nothing to what I could say if I chose,'
   the Duchess replied.
   Alice's Adventures in Wonderland (1865) ch. 9

12 'That's the reason they're called lessons,' the
   Gryphon remarked: 'because they lessen from
   day to day.'
   Alice's Adventures in Wonderland (1865) ch. 9

13 'Will you walk a little faster?' said a whiting to a
   snail,

'There's a porpoise close behind us, and he's
   treading on my tail.'
   Alice's Adventures in Wonderland (1865) ch. 10

14 Will you, won't you, will you, won't you, will
   you join the dance?
   Alice's Adventures in Wonderland (1865) ch. 10

15 'Tis the voice of the Lobster: I heard him
   declare
   'You have baked me too brown, I must sugar
   my hair.'
   Alice's Adventures in Wonderland (1865) ch. 10; see **WATTS**
   841:17

16 Soup of the evening, beautiful Soup!
   Alice's Adventures in Wonderland (1865) ch. 10

17 'Where shall I begin, please your Majesty?' he
   asked. 'Begin at the beginning,' the King said,
   gravely, 'and go on till you come to the end:
   then stop.'
   Alice's Adventures in Wonderland (1865) ch. 12

18 'That's not a regular rule: you invented it just
   now.'
   'It's the oldest rule in the book,' said the King.
   'Then it ought to be Number One,' said Alice.
   Alice's Adventures in Wonderland (1865) ch. 12

19 No! No! Sentence first—verdict afterwards.
   Alice's Adventures in Wonderland (1865) ch. 12

20 What a comfort a Dictionary is!
   Sylvie and Bruno Concluded (1893)

21 'Twas brillig, and the slithy toves
Did gyre and gimble in the wabe;
All mimsy were the borogoves,
And the mome raths outgrabe.
'Beware the Jabberwock, my son!
The jaws that bite, the claws that catch!'
   Through the Looking-Glass (1872) ch. 1

22 And as in uffish thought he stood,
The Jabberwock, with eyes of flame,
Came whiffling through the tulgey wood,
And burbled as it came!

One, two! One, two! And through and through
The vorpal blade went snicker-snack!
He left it dead, and with its head
He went galumphing back.

'And hast thou slain the Jabberwock?
Come to my arms, my beamish boy!
O frabjous day! Callooh! Callay!'
He chortled in his joy.
   Through the Looking-Glass (1872) ch. 1

23 Curtsey while you're thinking what to say. It
   saves time.
   Through the Looking-Glass (1872) ch. 2

24 Now, *here*, you see, it takes all the running *you*
   can do, to keep in the same place. If you want
   to get somewhere else, you must run at least
   twice as fast as that!
   Through the Looking-Glass (1872) ch. 2

25 Speak in French when you can't think of the
   English for a thing.
   Through the Looking-Glass (1872) ch. 2

1 If you think we're wax-works, you ought to pay, you know. Wax-works weren't made to be looked at for nothing. Nohow!
Through the Looking-Glass (1872) ch. 4

2 'Contrariwise,' continued Tweedledee, 'if it was so, it might be; and if it were so, it would be: but as it isn't, it ain't. That's logic.'
Through the Looking-Glass (1872) ch. 4

3 The Walrus and the Carpenter
Were walking close at hand;
They wept like anything to see
Such quantities of sand:
'If this were only cleared away,'
They said, 'it would be grand!'

'If seven maids with seven mops
Swept it for half a year,
Do you suppose,' the Walrus said,
'That they could get it clear?'
'I doubt it,' said the Carpenter,
And shed a bitter tear.
Through the Looking-Glass (1872) ch. 4

4 'The time has come,' the Walrus said,
'To talk of many things:
Of shoes—and ships—and sealing wax—
Of cabbages—and kings—
And why the sea is boiling hot—
And whether pigs have wings.'
Through the Looking-Glass (1872) ch. 4

5 But answer came there none—
And this was scarcely odd because
They'd eaten every one.
Through the Looking-Glass (1872) ch. 4; see **SCOTT** 688:6

6 The rule is, jam to-morrow and jam yesterday—but never jam today.
Through the Looking-Glass (1872) ch. 5; see **BENN** 69:20

7 'It's a poor sort of memory that only works backwards,' the Queen remarked.
Through the Looking-Glass (1872) ch. 5

8 Why, sometimes I've believed as many as six impossible things before breakfast.
Through the Looking-Glass (1872) ch. 5

9 With a name like yours, you might be any shape, almost.
Through the Looking-Glass (1872) ch. 6

10 They gave it me,—for an un-birthday present.
Through the Looking-Glass (1872) ch. 6

11 'There's glory for you!' 'I don't know what you mean by "glory",' Alice said. 'I meant, "there's a nice knock-down argument for you!" ' 'But "glory" doesn't mean "a nice knock-down argument",' Alice objected. 'When *I* use a word,' Humpty Dumpty said in a rather scornful tone, 'it means just what I choose it to mean—neither more nor less.'
Through the Looking-Glass (1872) ch. 6

12 'The question is,' said Humpty Dumpty, 'which is to be master—that's all.'
Through the Looking-Glass (1872) ch. 6; see **SHAWCROSS** 742:24

13 You see it's like a portmanteau—there are two meanings packed up into one word.
Through the Looking-Glass (1872) ch. 6

14 'I can repeat poetry as well as other folk if it comes to that—' 'Oh, it needn't come to that!' Alice hastily said.
Through the Looking-Glass (1872) ch. 6

15 The little fishes of the sea,
They sent an answer back to me.

The little fishes' answer was
'We cannot do it, Sir, because—'
Through the Looking-Glass (1872) ch. 6

16 He's an Anglo-Saxon Messenger—and those are Anglo-Saxon attitudes.
Through the Looking-Glass (1872) ch. 7

17 The other Messenger's called Hatta. I must have *two* you know—to come and go. One to come, and one to go.
Through the Looking-Glass (1872) ch. 7

18 'There's nothing like eating hay when you're faint' . . . 'I didn't say there was nothing *better*,' the King replied, 'I said there was nothing *like* it.'
Through the Looking-Glass (1872) ch. 7

19 It's as large as life, and twice as natural!
Through the Looking-Glass (1872) ch. 7

20 It's my own invention.
the White Knight
Through the Looking-Glass (1872) ch. 8

21 He said, 'I look for butterflies
That sleep among the wheat:
I make them into mutton-pies,
And sell them in the street.'
Through the Looking-Glass (1872) ch. 8

22 Or madly squeeze a right-hand foot
Into a left-hand shoe.
Through the Looking-Glass (1872) ch. 8

23 No admittance till the week after next!
Through the Looking-Glass (1872) ch. 9

24 It isn't etiquette to cut any one you've been introduced to. Remove the joint.
Through the Looking-Glass (1872) ch. 9

25 Un-dish-cover the fish, or dishcover the riddle.
Through the Looking-Glass (1872) ch. 9

26 What I tell you three times is true.
The Hunting of the Snark (1876) 'Fit the First: The Landing'

27 He would answer to 'Hi!' or to any loud cry,
Such as 'Fry me!' or 'Fritter-my-wig!'
The Hunting of the Snark (1876) 'Fit the First: The Landing'

28 His intimate friends called him 'Candle-ends',
And his enemies, 'Toasted-cheese'.
The Hunting of the Snark (1876) 'Fit the First: The Landing'

29 'What's the good of *Mercator's* North Poles and Equators,
Tropics, Zones and Meridian lines?'
So the Bellman would cry: and the crew would reply,

'They are merely conventional signs!'
The Hunting of the Snark (1876) 'Fit the Second: The Bellman's Speech'

1 But the principal failing occurred in the sailing,
And the Bellman, perplexed and distressed,
Said he *had* hoped, at least, when the wind blew due East,
That the ship would *not* travel due West!
The Hunting of the Snark (1876) 'Fit the Second: The Bellman's Speech'

2 But oh, beamish nephew, beware of the day,
If your Snark be a Boojum! For then
You will softly and suddenly vanish away,
And never be met with again!
The Hunting of the Snark (1876) 'Fit the Third: The Baker's Tale'

3 They sought it with thimbles, they sought it with care;
They pursued it with forks and hope;
They threatened its life with a railway-share;
They charmed it with smiles and soap.
The Hunting of the Snark (1876) 'Fit the Fifth: The Beaver's Lesson'

4 For the Snark *was* a Boojum, you see.
The Hunting of the Snark (1876) 'Fit the Eighth: The Vanishing'

5 I never loved a dear Gazelle—
Nor anything that cost me much:
High prices profit those who sell,
But why should I be fond of such?
Phantasmagoria (1869) 'Theme with Variations'; see **MOORE** 558:14

6 He thought he saw an Elephant,
That practised on a fife:
He looked again, and found it was
A letter from his wife.
'At length I realize,' he said,
'The bitterness of life!'
Sylvie and Bruno (1889) ch. 5

7 Long and painful experience has taught me one great principle in managing business for other people, viz., if you want to inspire confidence, *give plenty of statistics*.
C. L. Dodgson *Three Years in a Curatorship by One Whom It Has Tried* (1886)

William Herbert Carruth 1859–1924

8 Some call it evolution,
And others call it God.
'Each In His Own Tongue' (1908)

Edward Carson 1854–1935
British lawyer and politician

9 I now enter into compact with you, and with the help of God you and I joined together . . . will yet defeat the most nefarious conspiracy that has ever been hatched against a free people . . . We must be prepared . . . the morning Home Rule passes, ourselves to become responsible for the government of the Protestant Province of Ulster.
speech at Craigavon, 23 September 1911

10 From the day I first entered parliament up to the present, devotion to the union has been the guiding star of my political life.
in *Dictionary of National Biography* (1917–)

Rachel Carson 1907–64
American zoologist

11 Over increasingly large areas of the United States, spring now comes unheralded by the return of the birds, and the early mornings are strangely silent where once they were filled with the beauty of bird song.
The Silent Spring (1962)

Angela Carter 1940–92
English novelist

12 Comedy is tragedy that happens to *other* people.
Wise Children (1991) ch. 4

13 If *Miss* means respectably unmarried, and *Mrs* respectably married, then *Ms* means nudge, nudge, wink, wink.
'The Language of Sisterhood' in Christopher Ricks (ed.) *The State of the Language* (1980); see **MONTY PYTHON'S FLYING CIRCUS** 556:18

Henry Carter d. 1806

14 True patriots we; for be it understood,
We left our country for our country's good . . .
And none will doubt but that our emigration
Has proved most useful to the British nation.
prologue, written for, but not recited at, the opening of the Playhouse, Sydney, New South Wales, 16 January 1796, when the actors were principally convicts
A. W. Jose and H. J. Carter (eds.) *The Australian Encyclopaedia* (1927); previously attributed to George Barrington (b. 1755); see **FITZGEFFREY** 330:16

Howard Carter 1874–1939
English archaeologist

15 Yes, wonderful things.
when asked what he could see on first looking into the tomb of Tutankhamun, 26 November 1922; his notebook records the words as 'Yes, it is wonderful'
The Tomb of Tut-ankh-amen (1933)

James Earl 'Jimmy' Carter 1924–
American Democratic statesman, 39th President of the US 1977–81

16 I'm Jimmy Carter, and I'm going to be your next president.
I'll Never Lie to You (1976); see **GORE** 366:7

17 I've looked on a lot of women with lust. I've committed adultery in my heart many times. This is something that God recognizes I will do—and I have done it—and God forgives me for it.
in *Playboy* November 1976

Sydney Carter 1915–2004

English folk-song writer

1 It's God they ought to crucify
Instead of you and me,
I said to the carpenter
A-hanging on the tree.
'Friday Morning' (1967)

2 I danced in the morning
When the world was begun
And I danced in the moon
And the stars and the sun
And I came down from heaven
And I danced on the earth—
At Bethlehem I had my birth.
Dance then wherever you may be,
I am the Lord of the Dance, said he,
And I'll lead you all, wherever you may be
And I'll lead you all in the dance, said he.
'Lord of the Dance' (1967)

3 One more step along the world I go.
'One More Step'

Jacques Cartier 1491–1557

French navigator and explorer

4 *J'estime mieux que autrement, que c'est la terre que Dieu donne à Caïn.*
I am rather inclined to believe that this is the land God gave to Cain.
on discovering the northern shore of the Gulf of St Lawrence (now Labrador and Quebec) in 1534; after the murder of Abel, Cain was exiled to the desolate land of Nod (see BIBLE 79:18)
La Première Relation; H. P. Biggar (ed.) The Voyages of Jacques Cartier (1924)

Henri Cartier-Bresson 1908–2004

French photographer and artist

5 The decisive moment.
title of book (1952); see RETZ 658:10

6 To me, photography is the simultaneous recognition, in a fraction of a second, of the significance of an event as well as of a precise organisation of forms which give that event its proper expression.
The Decisive Moment (1952)

Barbara Cartland 1901–2000

English writer

7 After forty a woman has to choose between losing her figure or her face. My advice is to keep your face, and stay sitting down.
Libby Purves 'Luncheon à la Cartland'; in The Times 6 October 1993; similar remarks have been attributed since c.1980

Cartoon captions

8 Fog in Channel—Continent isolated.
newspaper placard in cartoon, Round the Bend with Brockbank

(1948) by the British cartoonist Russell Brockbank (1913–79); the phrase 'Continent isolated' was quoted as already current by John Gunther Inside Europe (1938)

9 It's a naïve domestic Burgundy without any breeding, but I think you'll be amused by its presumption.
caption in New Yorker 27 March 1937, by James **THURBER**

10 MOTHER: It's broccoli, dear.
CHILD: I say it's spinach, and I say the hell with it.
cartoon caption in New Yorker 8 December 1928

11 It's our *own* story *exactly*! He bold as a hawk, she soft as the dawn.
caption in New Yorker 25 February 1939, by James **THURBER**; see **LOVER** 502:11

12 The man who . . .
illustrating social gaffes resulting from snobbery
opening words of the caption for a series of cartoons (first appearing in 1912) by H. M. Bateman (1887–1970)

13 No son—they're not the same—devolution takes longer.
father to his son, who is reading a book on evolution
caption to cartoon by Scottish cartoonist Ewen Bain (1925–89) in Scots Independent January 1978

14 On the Internet, nobody knows you're a dog.
cartoon caption in New Yorker 5 July 1993, by the American cartoonist Peter Steiner (1940–)

15 The price of petrol has been raised by a penny. Official.
a torpedoed sailor with oil-stained face lying on a raft; the message was intended to be a warning against wasting petrol, but it was taken by some as suggesting that lives were being put at risk for profit
caption in Daily Mirror 3 March 1942; cartoon by Philip Zec (1909–83) and caption by 'Cassandra' (William Connor, 1909–67).

16 We have met the enemy and he is us.
the cartoon-strip character, Pogo the opossum, looking at litter under a tree; used as an Earth Day poster in 1971
Pogo cartoon, 1970, by the American cartoonist Walt Kelly (1913–73); see **PERRY** 604:7

17 Well, back to the old drawing board.
a civilian designer, plans under his arm, turns away from a crashed plane, as service personnel look on in horror or rush forward
caption to a cartoon in the New Yorker, 1 March 1941, by the American cartoonist Peter Arno (1904–68)

18 Well, if I called the wrong number, why did you answer the phone?
caption in New Yorker 5 June 1937, by James **THURBER**

19 Well, if you knows of a better 'ole, go to it.
Old Bill and a friend in a shellhole under fire
caption in Fragments from France (1915), by the British cartoonist Bruce Bairnsfather (1888–1959)

John Cartwright 1740–1824

English political reformer

20 One man shall have one vote.
The People's Barrier Against Undue Influence (1780) ch. 1 'Principles, maxims, and primary rules of politics' no. 68

Elizabeth Tanfield Cary 1585–1639
English woman of letters, poet, and dramatist

1 I know I could enchain him with a smile:
And lead him captive with a gentle word,
I scorn my look should ever man beguile,
Or other speech, than meaning to afford.
The Tragedy of Mariam (1613)

Joyce Cary 1888–1957
Irish novelist and short-story writer

2 Sara could commit adultery at one end and
weep for her sins at the other, and enjoy both
operations at once.
The Horse's Mouth (1944)

Giovanni Jacopo Casanova 1725–98
Italian adventurer

3 Marriage is a sacrament which I detest . . .
Because it is the tomb of love.
History of my Life (1990, tr. W. R. Trask) vol. 9, ch. 8

4 I have lived as a philosopher and I die as a
Christian.
last words; *The Memoirs of Casanova* (1937) p. 492

Roger Casement 1864–1916
Irish nationalist; executed for treason in 1916. On Casement:
see **YEATS** 873:13

5 Self-government is our right, a thing born in us
at birth, a thing no more to be doled out to us,
or withheld from us, by another people than the
right to life itself—than the right to feel the sun,
or smell the flowers, or to love our kind.
statement at the conclusion of his trial, the Old Bailey,
London, 29 June 1916

6 Where all your rights become only an
accumulated wrong; where men must beg with
bated breath for leave to subsist in their own
land, to think their own thoughts, to sing their
own songs, to garner the fruits of their own
labours . . . then surely it is a braver, a saner and
truer thing, to be a rebel in act and deed against
such circumstances as these than tamely to
accept it as the natural lot of men.
statement at the conclusion of his trial, the Old Bailey,
London, 29 June 1916

Johnny Cash 1932–2003
American singer and songwriter

7 It was a real slow walk in a real sad rain.
'Drive On' (1993)

A. M. Cassandre 1901–68
French illustrator

8 A good poster is a visual telegram.
attributed

Mary Cassatt 1844–1926
American artist

9 Why do people so love to wander? I think the
civilized parts of the world will suffice for me in
the future.
letter to Louisine Havemeyer, 11 February 1911

Barbara Castle 1910–2002
British Labour politician

10 I will fight for what I believe in until I drop
dead. And that's what keeps you alive.
in *Guardian* 14 January 1998

Ted Castle 1907–79
English journalist

11 In place of strife.
*title of Government White Paper, 17 January 1969, suggested
by Castle to his wife, Barbara* **CASTLE***, then Secretary of
State for Employment*
Barbara Castle, diary, 15 January 1969

Fidel Castro 1927–
Cuban statesman, Prime Minister 1959–76 and President
since 1976

12 *La historia me absolverá.*
History will absolve me.
title of pamphlet (1953)

13 Capitalism is using its money; we socialists
throw it away.
in *Observer* 8 November 1964 'Sayings of the Week'

Edward Caswall 1814–78
English hymn-writer

14 Jesu, the very thought of Thee
With sweetness fills the breast.
translation of 'Jesu dulcis memoria, dans vera cordis
gaudia', *usually attributed to St* **BERNARD**
'Jesu, the very thought of thee' (1849 hymn)

15 My God, I love Thee; not because
I hope for heaven thereby.
'My God, I Love Thee' (1849 hymn); translation of 'O deus ego
amo te, nec amo te ut salves me'; usually attributed to St
Francis Xavier (1506–52)

16 See, amid the winter's snow,
Born for us on earth below,
See, the Lamb of God appears,
Promised from eternal years!
Hail, thou ever-blessèd morn!
Hail, redemption's happy dawn!
Sing through all Jerusalem:
Christ is born in Bethlehem!
'See, amid the winter's snow' (1858 hymn)

17 When morning gilds the skies.
Title of hymn (1854)

☐ **Catchphrases** *see* box opposite. *See also*
LAUREL 483:1

Catchphrases

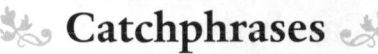

1 CECIL: After you, Claude.
CLAUDE: No, after you, Cecil.
ITMA (BBC radio programme, 1939–49), written by Ted Kavanagh (1892–1958)

2 Am I bovvered?
teenager Lauren, in *The Catherine Tate Show* (2004–), created by Catherine Tate (1968–)

3 And now for something completely different.
Monty Python's Flying Circus (BBC TV programme, 1969–74)

4 Anyone for tennis?
said to be typical of drawing-room comedies, much associated with Humphrey Bogart (1899–1957); perhaps from George Bernard Shaw 'Anybody on for a game of tennis?' *Misalliance* (1914)

5 Are you sitting comfortably? Then I'll begin.
sometimes 'Then we'll begin'
Listen with Mother (BBC radio programme for children, 1950–82), used by Julia Lang (1921–)

6 The butler did it!
a solution for detective stories
Nigel Rees, in *Sayings of the Century* (1984), quotes a correspondent who recalls hearing it at a cinema *c.*1916 but the origin of the phrase has not been traced

7 Can I do you now, sir?
spoken by 'Mrs Mopp'
ITMA (BBC radio programme, 1939–49), written by Ted Kavanagh (1892–1958)

8 Can you hear me, mother?
used by Sandy Powell (1900–82)

9 Come on! Come on!
habitual adjuration by Jeremy PAXMAN to contestants on *University Challenge* on BBC2 (1994–)

10 The day war broke out.
customary preamble to radio monologues in the role of a Home Guard
used by Robb Wilton (1881–1957) from *c.*1940

11 Didn't she [*or* he *or* they] do well?
used by Bruce Forsyth (1928–) in 'The Generation Game' on BBC Television, 1973 onwards

12 Does my bum look big in this?
used by Arabella Weir in *The Fast Show* on BBC Television 1994–97

13 Don't forget the diver.
spoken by 'The Diver'; based on 'a memory of the pier at New Brighton where Tommy Handley used to go as a child . . . A man in a bathing suit . . . whined "Don't forget the diver, sir."'
ITMA (BBC radio programme, 1939–49), written by Ted Kavanagh (1892–1958)

14 Don't have nightmares. Do sleep well.
habitual closing words for BBC1's *Crimewatch* (1984–), spoken by Nick Ross

15 Eat my shorts!
The Simpsons (American TV series, 1990–), created by Matt Groening

16 Ee, it was agony, Ivy.
Ray's a Laugh (BBC radio programme, 1949–61), written by Ted Ray (1906–77)

17 Evening, all.
opening words spoken by Jack Warner as Sergeant Dixon in *Dixon of Dock Green* (BBC television series, 1956–76), written by Ted Willis (1918–)

18 Everybody wants to get inta the act!
used by Jimmy Durante (1893–1980)

19 An everyday story of country folk.
introduction to *The Archers* (BBC radio serial, 1950 onwards), written by Geoffrey Webb and Edward J. Mason

20 George—don't do that.
used by Joyce GRENFELL as a recurring line in monologues about a nursery school, from the 1950s

21 Give him the money, Barney.
Have a Go! (BBC radio quiz programme, 1946–67), used by Wilfred Pickles (1904–78)

22 A good idea—son.
Educating Archie, 1950–3 BBC radio comedy series, written by Eric Sykes (1923–) and Max Bygraves (1922–)

23 Good morning, sir—was there something?
used by Sam Costa in radio comedy series *Much-Binding-in-the-Marsh*, written by Richard Murdoch (1907–90) and Kenneth Horne (1900–69), started 2 January 1947

24 Good night and good luck.
habitual sign-off by the broadcaster Ed MURROW

25 Goodnight, children . . . everywhere.
closing words normally spoken by 'Uncle Mac' in the 1930s and 1940s
on *Children's Hour* (BBC Radio programme); written by Derek McCulloch (1892–1978)

26 Have you read any good books lately?
used by Richard Murdoch in radio comedy series *Much-Binding-in-the-Marsh*, written by Richard Murdoch (1907–90) and Kenneth Horne (1900–69), started 2 January 1947

27 Hello, good evening, and welcome.
used by David FROST in 'The Frost Programme' on ITV Television, 1966 onwards

28 Here come de judge.
from the song-title 'Here comes the judge' (1968); written by Dewey 'Pigmeat' Markham, Dick Alen, Bob Astor, and Sarah Harvey

29 Here's one I made earlier.
culmination to directions for making a model out of empty yoghurt pots, coat-hangers, and similar domestic items
children's BBC television programme *Blue Peter*, 1963 onwards

30 He shoots! He scores!
used by Foster William Hewitt (1902–85), Canadian broadcaster, at ice-hockey games; first said over the radio 4 April 1933 at the game between the Toronto Maple Leafs and the Boston Bruins

31 I didn't get where I am today without . . . .
used by the manager C. J. in BBC television series *The Fall and Rise of Reginald Perrin*, 1976–80); based on David Nobbs *The Death of Reginald Perrin* (1975)

continued

Catchphrases *continued*

1 I don't like this game, let's play another game—let's play doctor and nurses.
phrase first used by Bluebottle in 'The Phantom Head-Shaver' in *The Goon Show* (BBC radio series) 15 October 1954, written by Spike **MILLIGAN**; the catchphrase was often 'I do not like this game'

2 I don't mind if I do.
spoken by 'Colonel Chinstrap'
ITMA (BBC radio programme, 1939–49), written by Ted Kavanagh (1892–1958)

3 I go—I come back.
spoken by 'Ali Oop'
ITMA (BBC radio programme, 1939–49), written by Ted Kavanagh (1892–1958)

4 I have a cunning plan.
Baldrick's habitual overoptimistic promise in *Blackadder II* (1987 television series), written by Richard Curtis and Ben Elton (1959–)

5 I'm Bart Simpson: who the hell are you?
The Simpsons (American TV series, 1990–), created by Matt Groening

6 I'm in charge.
used by Bruce Forsyth (1928–) in 'Sunday Night at the London Palladium' on ITV, 1958 onwards

7 I'm worried about Jim.
frequent line in *Mrs Dale's Diary*, BBC radio series 1948–69

8 It all depends what you mean by . . .
habitually used by C. E. M. Joad (1891–1953) when replying to questions on 'The Brains Trust' (formerly 'Any Questions'), BBC radio (1941–8)

9 It's a good thing.
customary form of approbation in the areas of home decorating and cooking from US businesswoman Martha Stewart (1941–)

10 It's being so cheerful as keeps me going.
spoken by 'Mona Lott'
ITMA (BBC radio programme, 1939–49), written by Ted Kavanagh (1892–1958)

11 I've arrived and to prove it I'm here!
Educating Archie, 1950–3 BBC radio comedy series, written by Eric Sykes (1923–) and Max Bygraves (1922–)

12 I've started so I'll finish.
said when a contestant's time runs out while a question is being put
Magnus Magnusson (1929–2007) *Mastermind*, BBC television (1972–97)

13 Just like that!
used by Tommy Cooper (1921–84)

14 Keep on truckin'.
used by Robert Crumb (1943–) in cartoons from c.1972

15 Left hand down a bit!
The Navy Lark (BBC radio series, 1959–77), written by Laurie Wyman

16 Let's be careful out there.
Hill Street Blues (television series, 1981 onwards), written by Steven Bochco and Michael Kozoll

17 Meredith, we're in!
originating in a stage sketch by Fred Kitchen (1872–1950), *The Bailiff* (1907); J. P. Gallagher *Fred Karno* (1971) ch. 9

18 Mind my bike!
used by Jack Warner (1895–1981) in the BBC radio series *Garrison Theatre*, 1939 onwards

19 Nice to see you—to see you, nice.
used by Bruce Forsyth (1928–) in 'The Generation Game' on BBC Television, 1973 onwards

20 Oh, calamity!
used by Robertson Hare (1891–1979)

21 Ohhh, I don't *believe* it!
Victor Meldrew in *One Foot in the Grave* (BBC television series, 1989–), written by David Renwick

22 Once again we stop the mighty roar of London's traffic.
In Town Tonight (BBC radio series, 1933–60) preamble

23 Pass the sick bag, Alice.
used by John **JUNOR**; in *Sunday Express* and elsewhere, from 1980 or earlier

24 Phone a friend.
advice to contestants by Chris Tarrant, host of the ITV quiz show *Who Wants to be a Millionaire* (1998–)

25 Seriously, though, he's doing a grand job!
popularized by David **FROST** in 'That Was The Week That Was', on BBC Television, 1962-3; originally deriving from a sketch written for Roy Kinnear

26 Shome mishtake, shurely?
in *Private Eye* magazine, 1980s

27 So farewell then . . .
frequent opening of poems by 'E. J. Thribb' in Private Eye magazine, usually as an obituary
1970s onwards

28 Take me to your leader.
from science-fiction stories

29 The truth is out there.
The X Files (American television series, 1993–), created by Chris Carter

30 Very interesting . . . but stupid.
Rowan and Martin's Laugh-In (American television series, 1967–73), written by Dan Rowan (1922–87) and Dick Martin (1923–2008)

31 The weekend starts here.
Ready, Steady, Go, British television series, c.1963

32 We have ways of making you talk.
perhaps originating in the line 'We have ways of making men talk' in *Lives of a Bengal Lancer* (1935 film), written by Waldemar Young et al.

33 What's up, Doc?
Bugs Bunny cartoons, written by Tex Avery (1907–80) from c.1940

34 Who loves ya, baby?
used by Telly Savalas (1926–) in American TV series *Kojak* (1973-8)

35 Without hesitation, deviation, or repetition.
instruction for contestants' monologues on the panel show *Just a Minute* (BBC Radio, 1967–); coined by producer Ian Messiter (1920–99)

continued

Catchphrases *continued*

1 Yeah but no but yeah but no.
Vicky Pollard's habitual protest
  spoken by Matt Lucas, in the BBC comedy *Little Britain* (2003–), written and performed by Matt Lucas and David Walliams

2 You are the weakest link . . . goodbye.
  catchphrase used by Anne Robinson on the television game-show *The Weakest Link* (2000–)

3 You bet your sweet bippy.
  Rowan and Martin's Laugh-In (American television series, 1967–73), written by Dan Rowan (1922–87) and Dick Martin (1923–2008)

4 You might very well think that. I couldn't possibly comment.
the Chief Whip's habitual response to questioning
  House of Cards (televised 1990); written by Michael Dobbs (1948–)

5 You're going to like this . . . not a lot . . . but you'll like it!
  used by Paul Daniels (1938–) in his conjuring act, especially on television from 1981 onwards

6 You rotten swines. I told you I'd be deaded.
  phrase first used by Bluebottle in 'Hastings Flyer' in *The Goon Show* (BBC radio series) 3 January 1956, written by Spike **MILLIGAN**

7 Your starter for ten.
  phrase often used by Bamber Gascoigne (1935–) in *University Challenge* (ITV quiz series, 1962–87)

8 You silly twisted boy.
  phrase first used in 'The Dreaded Batter Pudding Hurler' in *The Goon Show* (BBC radio series) 12 October 1954, written by Spike **MILLIGAN**

A Catechism of Christian Doctrine

1898

Popularly known as the 'Penny Catechism'

9 Who made you? God made me.
Why did God make you? God made me to know Him, love him, and serve Him in this world, and to be happy with Him for ever in the next.
  ch. 1

Willa Cather 1873–1947

American novelist

10 Oh, the Germans classify, but the French arrange!
  Death Comes For the Archbishop (1927)

11 Where there is great love there are always miracles.
  Death Comes for the Archbishop (1927)

12 Men travel faster now, but I do not know if they go to better things.
  Death Comes for the Archbishop (1927)

13 That is happiness: to be dissolved into something complete and great.
on her gravestone in Jaffrey, New Hampshire
  My Ántonia (1918) bk 1, ch 2

14 Winter lies too long in country towns; hangs on until it is stale and shabby, old and sullen.
  My Ántonia (1918) bk 2, ch 7

15 I like trees because they seem more resigned to the way they have to live than other things do.
  O Pioneers! (1913) pt. 2, ch. 4

16 The heart of another is a dark forest, always, no matter how close it has been to one's own.
  The Professor's House (1925) ch. 8; see **TURGENEV** 819:2

17 I tell you there is such a thing as creative hate!
  The Song of the Lark (1915)

Catherine the Great 1729–96

Russian monarch, Empress from 1762

18 *Moi, je serai autocrate: c'est mon métier. Et le bon Dieu me pardonnera: c'est son métier.*

I shall be an autocrat: that's my trade. And the good Lord will forgive me: that's his.
  attributed; see **HEINE** 389:17

Cato the Elder ('the Censor') 234–149 BC

Roman statesman, orator, and writer

19 *Delenda est Carthago.*

Carthage must be destroyed.
words concluding every speech Cato made in the Senate
  Pliny the Elder *Naturalis Historia* bk. 15, ch. 74

20 A farm is like a man—however great the income, if there is extravagance but little is left.
  On Agriculture bk 2, sect. 6

21 Even though work stops, expenses run on.
  On Agriculture bk 39, sect. 2

22 *Rem tene; verba sequentur.*

Grasp the subject, the words will follow.
  Caius Julius Victor *Ars Rhetorica* 'De inventione'

Carrie Chapman Catt 1859–1947

American feminist

23 No written law has ever been more binding than unwritten custom supported by popular opinion.
speech at Senate hearing on woman's suffrage, 13 February 1900
  Why We Ask for the Submission of an Amendment (1900)

24 When a just cause reaches its flood-tide . . . whatever stands in the way must fall before its overwhelming power.
  speech at Stockholm, *Is Woman Suffrage Progressing?* (1911)

Catullus *c.*84–*c.*54 BC

Roman poet. On Catullus: see **TENNYSON** 793:14

1 *Cui dono lepidum novum libellum*
Arido modo pumice expolitum?

To whom shall I give my nice new little book
polished dry with pumice?
Carmina no. 1

2   *Namque tu solebas*
Meas esse aliquid putare nugas.

For you used to think my trifles were worth
something.
Carmina no. 1

3 *Plus uno maneat perenne saeclo.*

May it live and last for more than a century.
Carmina no. 1

4 *Lugete, O Veneres Cupidinesque,*
Et quantum est hominum venustiorum.
Passer mortuus est meae puellae,
Passer, deliciae meae puellae.

Mourn, you powers of Charm and Desire, and
all you who are endowed with charm. My lady's
sparrow is dead, the sparrow which was my
lady's darling.
Carmina no. 3; see **MILLAY** 537:3

5 *Qui nunc it per iter tenebricosum*
Illuc, unde negant redire quemquam.

Now he goes along the darksome road, thither
whence they say no one returns.
Carmina no. 4

6 *Vivamus, mea Lesbia, atque amemus,*
Rumoresque senum severiorum
Omnes unius aestimemus assis.
Soles occidere et redire possunt:
Nobis cum semel occidit brevis lux
Nox est perpetua una dormienda.

Let us live, my Lesbia, and let us love, and let us
reckon all the murmurs of more censorious old
men as worth one farthing. Suns can set and
come again: for us, when once our brief light
has set, one everlasting night is to be slept.
Carmina no. 5; see **CAMPION** 195:21, **JONSON** 446:12

7 *Da mi basia mille, deinde centum,*
Dein mille altera, dein secunda centum,
Deinde usque altera mille, deinde centum.

Give me a thousand kisses, then a hundred, then
another thousand, then a second hundred, then
yet another thousand, then a hundred.
Carmina no. 5

8 *Miser Catulle, desinas ineptire,*
Et quod vides perisse perditum ducas.

Poor Catullus, drop your silly fancies, and what
you see is lost let it be lost.
Carmina no. 8

9 *Paene insularum, Sirmio, insularumque*
Ocelle.

Sirmio, bright eye of peninsulas and islands.
Carmina no. 31; see **TENNYSON** 793:14

10 *Nam risu inepto res ineptior nulla est.*

For there is nothing sillier than a silly laugh.
Carmina no. 39; see **CHESTERFIELD** 223:8, **CONGREVE** 246:26

11 *Iam ver egelidos refert tepores.*

Now Spring restores balmy warmth.
Carmina no. 46

12 *Gratias tibi maximas Catullus*
Agit pessimus omnium poeta,
Tanto pessimus omnium poeta,
Quanto tu optimus omnium's patronum.

Catullus gives you warmest thanks,
And he the worst of poets ranks;
As much the worst of bards confessed,
As you of advocates the best.
letter of thanks to **CICERO**
Carmina no. 49 (translated by Sir William Marris)

13 *Ille mi par esse deo videtur,*
Ille, si fas est, superare divos,
Qui sedens adversus identidem te
Spectat et audit
Dulce ridentem, misero quod omnis
Eripit sensus mihi.

Like a god he seems to me, above the gods, if
so may be, who sitting often close to you may
see and hear you sweetly laughing, which
snatches away all the senses from poor me.
Carmina no. 51 (a translation of Sappho); see **SAPPHO** 680:22

14 *Caeli, Lesbia nostra, Lesbia illa,*
Illa Lesbia, quam Catullus unam
Plus quam se atque suos amavit omnes,
Nunc in quadriviis et angiportis
Glubit magnanimos Remi nepotes.

O Caelius, our Lesbia, that Lesbia whom
Catullus once loved uniquely, more than himself
and more than all his own, now at the
crossroads and in the alleyways has it off with
the high-minded descendants of Remus.
Carmina no. 58

15 *Ut flos in saeptis secretus nascitur hortis,*
Ignotus pecori, nullo contusus aratro,
Quem mulcent aurae, firmat sol, educat imber;
Multi illum pueri, multae optavere puellae.

As a flower grows concealed in an enclosed
garden, unknown to the cattle, bruised by no
plough, and which the breezes caress, the sun
makes strong, and the rain brings out; many
boys and many girls long for it.
Carmina no. 62

16 *Sed mulier cupido quod dicit amanti,*
In vento et rapida scribere oportet aqua.

But what a woman says to her lusting lover is
best to write in wind and swift-flowing water.
Carmina no. 70

17 *Desine de quoquam quicquam bene velle mereri,*
Aut aliquem fieri posse putare pium.

Give up wanting to deserve any thanks from
anyone, or thinking that anybody can be
grateful.
Carmina no. 73

1 *Siqua recordanti benefacta priora voluptas*
Est homini, cum se cogitat esse pium.

If a man can take any pleasure in recalling the thought of kindnesses done, when he thinks that he has been a true friend.
Carmina no. 76

2 *Difficile est longum subito deponere amorem.*
Difficile est, verum hoc qualubet efficias.

It is difficult suddenly to lay aside a long-cherished love. It is difficult; but you should accomplish it, one way or another.
Carmina no. 76

3 *Si vitam puriter egi.*

If I have led a pure life.
Carmina no. 76

4 *O di, reddite mi hoc pro pietate mea.*

O gods, grant me this in return for my piety.
Carmina no. 76

5 *Odi et amo: quare id faciam, fortasse requiris.*
Nescio, sed fieri sentio et excrucior.

I hate and I love: why I do so you may well ask. I do not know, but I feel it happen and am in agony.
Carmina no. 85

6 *Multas per gentes et multa per aequora vectus*
Advenio has miseras, frater, ad inferias,
Ut te postremo donarem munere mortis
Et mutam nequiquam alloquerer cinerem . . .
Nunc tamen interea haec prisco quae more parentum
Tradita sunt tristi munere ad inferias,
Accipe fraterno multum manantia fletu,
Atque in perpetuum, frater, ave atque vale.

By many lands and over many a wave
I come, my brother, to your piteous grave,
To bring you the last offering in death
And o'er dumb dust expend an idle breath . . .
Yet take these gifts, brought as our fathers bade
For sorrow's tribute to the passing shade;
A brother's tears have wet them o'er and o'er;
And so, my brother, hail, and farewell evermore!
Carmina no. 101 (translated by Sir William Marris); see
TENNYSON 793:14

7 *At non effugies meos iambos.*

But you shall not escape my iambics.
R. A. B. Mynors (ed.) *Catulli Carmina* (1958) Fragment 3

Charles Causley 1917–2003

English poet and schoolmaster

8 Watch where he comes walking
Out of the Christmas flame,
Dancing, double-talking:
Herod is his name.
'Innocents' Song' (1961)

9 Timothy Winters comes to school
With eyes as wide as a football-pool,
Ears like bombs and teeth like splinters:
A blitz of a boy is Timothy Winters.
'Timothy Winters' (1957)

Constantine Cavafy 1863–1933

Greek poet

10 Body, remember not only how much you were loved,
not only the beds you lay on,
but also those desires glowing openly
in eyes that looked at you,
trembling for you in voices.
'Body, Remember' (1918)

11 When you set out for Ithaka
ask that your way be long.
'Ithaka' (1911) (translated by E. Keeley and P. Sherrard)

12 Ithaka gave you the splendid journey.
Without her you would not have set out.
She hasn't anything else to give you.
'Ithaka' (1911)

13 What are we waiting for, gathered in the market-place?
The barbarians are to arrive today.
'Waiting for the Barbarians' (1904) (translated by E. Keeley and P. Sherrard)

14 And now, what will become of us without the barbarians?
Those people were a kind of solution.
'Waiting for the Barbarians' (1904)

15 New places you will not find, you will not find another sea
The city will follow you.
'The Town' (1911) (translated by E. Keeley and P. Sherrard)

Edith Cavell 1865–1915

English nurse, executed by the Germans for assisting in the escape of British soldiers from occupied Belgium

16 Standing, as I do, in view of God and eternity, I realize that patriotism is not enough. I must have no hatred or bitterness towards anyone.
on the eve of her execution
in *The Times* 23 October 1915

Margaret Cavendish (Duchess of Newcastle) c.1624–74

English woman of letters

17 Greek, Latin poets, I could never read,
Nor their historians, but our English Speed;
I could not steal their wit, nor plots out take;
All my plays' plots, my own poor brain did make.
Plays (1662) 'To the Readers'

18 Marriage is the grave or tomb of wit.
Plays (1662) 'Nature's Three Daughters' pt. 2, act 5, sc. 20

19 If Nature had not befriended us with beauty, and other good graces, to help us to insinuate our selves into men's affections, we should have been more enslaved than any other of Nature's creatures she hath made.
Sociable Letters (1664)

20 But for the most part, women are not educated as they should be, I mean those of quality; oft

their education is only to dance, sing, and fiddle, to write complimental letters, to read romances, to speak some languages that is not their native . . . their parents take more care of their feet than their head, more of their words than their reason.

Sociable Letters (1664)

Count Cavour (Camillo Benso di Cavour) 1810–61

Italian statesman, first Premier (in 1861) of a united Italy

1 We are ready to proclaim throughout Italy this great principle: a free church in a free state.

speech, 27 March 1861, in William de la Rive *Reminiscences of the Life and Character of Count Cavour* (1862) ch. 13

William Caxton c.1421–91

first English printer

2 The worshipful father and first founder and embellisher of ornate eloquence in our English, I mean Master Geoffrey Chaucer.

Caxton's edition (c.1478) of Chaucer's translation of Boethius *De Consolacione Philosophie* epilogue

3 It is notoriously known through the universal world that there be nine worthy and the best that ever were. That is to wit three paynims, three Jews, and three Christian men. As for the paynims they were . . . the first Hector of Troy . . . the second Alexander the Great; and the third Julius Caesar . . . As for the three Jews . . . the first was Duke Joshua . . . the second David, King of Jerusalem; and the third Judas Maccabaeus . . . And sith the said Incarnation . . . was first the noble Arthur . . . The second was Charlemagne or Charles the Great . . . and the third and last was Godfrey of Bouillon.

Thomas Malory *Le Morte D'Arthur* (1485) prologue

4 I, according to my copy, have done set it in imprint, to the intent that noble men may see and learn the noble acts of chivalry, the gentle and virtuous deeds that some knights used in those days.

Thomas Malory *Le Morte D'Arthur* (1485) prologue

Lord Edward Cecil 1867–1918

English soldier and civil servant

5 An agreement between two men to do what both agree is wrong.

definition of a compromise
letter, 3 September 1911; Kenneth Rose *The Later Cecils* (1975) ch. 7

Lord Hugh Cecil 1869–1956

British Conservative politician and clergyman, Provost of Eton

6 There is no more ungraceful figure than that of a humanitarian with an eye to the main chance.

of the Liberal statesman Henry Campbell Bannerman (1836–1908)
in *The Times* 24 June 1901

Robert Cecil 1563–1612

English courtier and statesman, son of William CECIL, Lord Burghley

7 Rest content, and give heed to one that hath sorrowed in the bright lustre of a court, and gone heavily even on the best-seeming fair ground . . . I know it bringeth little comfort on earth; and he is, I reckon, no wise man that looketh this way to Heaven.

letter to John Harington; Algernon Cecil *A Life of Robert Cecil* (1915) ch. 12

William Cecil (Lord Burghley) 1520–98

English courtier and politician, father of Robert CECIL. On Cecil: see ELIZABETH I 311:27, ELIZABETH I 312:8, ELIZABETH I 312:9

8 What! all this for a song?

to Queen ELIZABETH I, on being ordered to make a gratuity of £100 to SPENSER in return for some poems
Edmund Spenser *The Faerie Queene* (1751) 'The Life of Mr Edmund Spenser' by Thomas Birch

Paul Celan 1920–70

German poet

9 A man lives in the house he plays with his
  vipers he writes
he writes when it grows dark to Deutschland
  your golden hair Margareta
Your ashen hair Shulamith we shovel a grave in
  the air there you won't lie too cramped.

'Deathfugue' (written 1944)

10 He shouts play death more sweetly this Death is
  a master from Deutschland
he shouts scrape your strings darker you'll rise
  then as smoke to the sky
you'll have a grave then in the clouds there you
  won't lie too cramped.

'Deathfugue' (written 1944)

11 *Der Tod ist ein Meister aus Deutschland.*

Death is a master from Germany.

'Deathfugue' (written 1944)

12 There's nothing in the world for which a poet will give up writing, not even when he is a Jew and the language of his poems is German.

letter to relatives, 2 August 1948

Susannah Centlivre c.1669–1723

English actress and dramatist

13 For he or she, who drags the marriage chain,
And finds in spouse occasion to complain,
Should hide their frailties with a lover's care,
And let th'ill-judging world conclude 'em fair;
Better th'offence ne'er reach the offender's ear.
For they who sin with caution, whilst concealed,
Grow impudently careless, when revealed.

The Artifice (1722) act 5, sc. 3

14 The real Simon Pure.

A Bold Stroke for a Wife (1718) act 5, sc. 1

1 Nothing to be done without a bribe I find, in love as well as law.
The Perjured Husband (1700) act 3, sc. 2

2 The carping malice of the vulgar world; who think it a proof of sense to dislike every thing that is writ by Women.
The Platonic Lady (1707) dedication

Cervantes (Miguel de Cervantes Saavedra)
1547–1616
Spanish novelist and dramatist. On Cervantes: see BYRON 189:18

3 *El Caballero de la Triste Figura.*
The Knight of the Doleful Countenance.
Don Quixote (1605) pt. 1, ch. 19

4 *El pan comido y la compañía deshecha.*
With the bread eaten up, up breaks the company.
Don Quixote (1605) pt. 2, ch. 7

5 *No todos podemos ser frailes, y muchos son los caminos por donde lleva Dios a los suyos al cielo: religión es la caballería.*
We cannot all be friars, and many are the ways by which God leads his own to eternal life. Knight-errantry *is* religion.
to Sancho, on his asking whether, to get to heaven, we ought not all to become monks
Don Quixote (1605) pt. 2, ch. 8

6 *Es un entreverado loco, lleno de lúcidos intervalos.*
He's a muddle-headed fool, with frequent lucid intervals.
Don Quixote (1605) pt. 2, ch. 18 (Don Lorenzo of Don Quixote)

7 *Dos linajes solos hay en el mundo, como decía una abuela mía, que son el tener y el no tener.*
There are only two families in the world, as a grandmother of mine used to say: the haves and the have-nots.
Don Quixote (1605) pt. 2, ch. 20

8 *Digo, paciencia y barajar.*
What I say is, patience, and shuffle the cards.
Don Quixote (1605) pt. 2, ch. 23

9 *La diligencia es madre de la buena ventura y la pereza, su contrario, jamás llegó al término que pide un buen deseo.*
Diligence is the mother of good fortune, and idleness, its opposite, never led to good intention's goal.
Don Quixote (1605) pt. 2, ch. 43

10 Alas! all music jars when the soul's out of tune.
Don Quixote (1615) pt. 2, ch. 44; extra line added by Peter Motteux (1660–1718) in his translation of 1700-3, and not in Cervantes' original text

11 *Bien haya el que inventó el sueño, capa que cubre todos los humanos pensamientos, manjar que quita la hambre, agua que ahuyenta la sed, fuego que calienta el frío, frío que templa el ardor, y, finalmente, moneda general con que todas las cosas se compran, balanza y peso que iguala al pastor con el rey y al simple con el discreto.*
Blessings on him who invented sleep, the mantle that covers all human thoughts, the food that satisfies hunger, the drink that slakes thirst, the fire that warms cold, the cold that moderates heat, and, lastly, the common currency that buys all things, the balance and weight that equalizes the shepherd and the king, the simpleton and the sage.
Don Quixote (1605) pt. 2, ch. 68

12 *Morir cuerdo, y vivir loco.*
To die in wisdom, having lived in folly.
Don Quixote's epitaph
Don Quixote (1605) pt. 2, ch. 74

13 *Una cosa es alabar la disciplina y otra el darse con ella, y, en efecto.*
It is one thing to praise discipline, and another to submit to it.
Coloquio de los Perros (The Dialogue of the Dogs) in *Novelas Ejemplares* (1613)

14 *Los buenos pintores imitan la naturaleza, pero los malos la vomitan.*
Good painters imitate nature, bad ones spew it up.
El Licenciado Vidriera in *Novelas Ejemplares* (1613)

15 *Puesto ya el pie en el estribo.*
With one foot already in the stirrup.
apprehending his own imminent death
Los Trabajos de Persiles y Sigismunda (1617) preface

Paul Cézanne 1839–1906
French painter

16 Treat nature in terms of the cylinder, the sphere, the cone, all in perspective.
letter to Emile Bernard, 1904; Emile Bernard *Paul Cézanne* (1925)

17 I will astonish Paris with an apple.
Gustave Geffroy *Claude Monet: His Life, His Times, His Works* (1894)

18 Monet is only an eye, but what an eye!
attributed

John Chalkhill *c.*1600–42
English poet

19 Oh, the gallant fisher's life,
It is the best of any
'Tis full of pleasure, void of strife,
And 'tis beloved of many.
'Piscator's Song', in Izaak Walton *The Compleat Angler* (1653-76)

Jason Chamberlain fl. 1811
American clergyman

20 Morals and manners will rise or decline with our attention to grammar.
inaugural address, University of Vermont, 1811

Joseph Chamberlain 1836–1914

British Liberal politician, father of Neville **CHAMBERLAIN**

1 In politics, there is no use looking beyond the next fortnight.

> letter from A. J. Balfour to 3rd Marquess of Salisbury, 24 March 1886; A. J. Balfour *Chapters of Autobiography* (1930) ch. 16; see **WILSON** 859:6

2 Provided that the City of London remains, as it is at present, the clearing-house of the world, any other nation may be its workshop.

> speech at the Guildhall, 19 January 1904, in *The Times* 20 January 1904; see **DISRAELI** 284:4

3 The day of small nations has long passed away. The day of Empires has come.

> speech at Birmingham, 12 May 1904, in *The Times* 13 May 1904

Neville Chamberlain 1869–1940

British Conservative statesman, Prime Minister 1937–40, son of Joseph **CHAMBERLAIN**. On Chamberlain: see **BEVAN** 77:4; see also **BOOTHBY** 151:5

4 In war, whichever side may call itself the victor, there are no winners, but all are losers.

> speech at Kettering, 3 July 1938, in *The Times* 4 July 1938

5 How horrible, fantastic, incredible it is that we should be digging trenches and trying on gas-masks here because of a quarrel in a far away country between people of whom we know nothing.

> *on Germany's annexation of the Sudetenland*
> radio broadcast, 27 September 1938, in *The Times* 28 September 1938

6 This is the second time in our history that there has come back from Germany to Downing Street peace with honour. I believe it is peace for our time.

> speech from 10 Downing Street, 30 September 1938, in *The Times* 1 October 1938; see **DISRAELI** 285:8, **RUSSELL** 675:19

7 This morning, the British Ambassador in Berlin handed the German government a final Note stating that, unless we heard from them by eleven o'clock that they were prepared at once to withdraw their troops from Poland, a state of war would exist between us. I have to tell you now that no such undertaking has been received, and that consequently this country is at war with Germany.

> radio broadcast, 3 September 1939

8 Whatever may be the reason—whether it was that Hitler thought he might get away with what he had got without fighting for it, or whether it was that after all the preparations were not sufficiently complete—however, one thing is certain—he missed the bus.

> speech at Central Hall, Westminster, 4 April 1940, in *The Times* 5 April 1940

Haddon Chambers 1860–1921

English dramatist

9 The long arm of coincidence.

> *Captain Swift* (1888) act 2

Jack Chambers 1931–78

Canadian painter

10 When you are interested in life more than you are in painting, then your paintings can come to life.

> William Withrow *Contemporary Painting in Canada* (1972)

William Chambers 1726–96

British architect

11 In the constructive part of architecture, the ancients were no great proficients.

> *Treatise on Decorative Civil Architecture* (ed. 3, 1791)

Nicolas-Sébastien Chamfort 1741–94

French writer

12 *La plus perdue de toutes les journées est celle où l'on n'a pas ri.*

Of all days, the one most surely wasted is the one on which one has not laughed.

> *Maximes et Pensées* (1796) ch. 1

13 *Voulez-vous voir à quel point chaque état de la société corrompt les hommes? Examinez ce qu'ils sont quand ilsen ont éprouvé plus long-temps l'influence, c'est-à-dire dans la vieillesse. Voyez ce que c'est qu'un vieux courtisan, un vieux prêtre, un vieux juge, un vieux procureur, un vieux chirurgien.*

If you would find to what extent each condition of society can corrupt a man, examine what he is when he has undergone that influence for the longest possible time, that is to say, when he is old. See what an old courtier is like, an old priest, an old judge, an old solicitor, an old surgeon.

> *Maximes et Pensées* (1796) ch. 2

14 *Vivre est une maladie dont le sommeil nous soulage toutes les 16 heures. C'est un palliatif. La mort est le remède.*

Living is an illness to which sleep provides relief every sixteen hours. It's a palliative. The remedy is death.

> *Maximes et Pensées* (1796) ch. 2

15 *Des qualités trop supérieures rendent souvent un homme moins propre à la société. On ne va pas au marché avec des lingots; on y va avec de l'argent ou de la petite monnaie.*

Qualities too elevated often unfit a man for society. We don't take ingots with us to market; we take silver or small change.

> *Maximes et Pensées* (1796) ch. 3

16 *En amour, tout est vrai, tout est faux; et c'est la seule chose sur laquelle on ne puisse pas dire une absurdité.*

In love, everything is true, everything is false; and it is the one subject on which one cannot express an absurdity.
Maximes et Pensées (1796) ch. 6

1 *L'amour, tel qu'il existe dans la société, n'est que l'échange de deux fantaisies et le contact de deux épidermes.*

Love, in the form in which it exists in society, is nothing but the exchange of two fantasies and the superficial contact of two bodies.
Maximes et Pensées (1796) ch. 6

2 *Je dirais volontiers des métaphysiciens ce que Scaliger disait des Basques, on dit qu'ils s'entendent, mais je n'en crois rien.*

I am tempted to say of metaphysicians what Scaliger used to say of the Basques: they are said to understand one another, but I don't believe a word of it.
Maximes et Pensées (1796) ch. 7

3 *On n'est point un homme d'esprit pour avoir beaucoup d'idées, comme on n'est pas un bon Général poue avoir beaucoup de soldats.*

A man is not necessarily intelligent because he has plenty of ideas, any more than he is a good general because he has plenty of soldiers.
Maximes et Pensées (1796) ch. 7

4 *Les pauvres sont les nègres de l'Europe.*

The poor are Europe's blacks.
Maximes et Pensées (1796) ch. 8

5 *Sois mon frère, ou je te tue.*

Be my brother, or I kill you.
his interpretation of 'Fraternité ou la mort [*Fraternity or death*]'
P. R. Anguis (ed.) *Oeuvres Complètes* (1824) vol. 1 'Notice Historique sur la Vie et les Écrits de Chamfort'; see **POLITICAL SLOGANS AND SONGS** 613:1

6 *La postérité n'est pas autre chose qu'un public qui succède à un autre: or, vous voyez ce que c'est le public d'à présent.*

Posterity is no more than one public which follows another. Now, you see what the public is today!
Caractère et anecdotes (1953) vol. 2, p. 99

John Chandler 1806–76
English clergyman

7 Conquering kings their titles take
From the foes they captive make.
hymn (1837); translation from a Latin original: '*Victis sibi cognomina sumant tyranni gentibus . . .* '

Raymond Chandler 1888–1959
American writer of detective fiction

8 It was a blonde. A blonde to make a bishop kick a hole in a stained glass window.
Farewell, My Lovely (1940) ch. 13

9 A big hard-boiled city with no more personality than a paper cup.
of Los Angeles
The Little Sister (1949) ch. 26

10 Crime isn't a disease, it's a symptom. Cops are like a doctor that gives you aspirin for a brain tumour.
The Long Good-Bye (1953) ch. 47

11 Down these mean streets a man must go who is not himself mean, who is neither tarnished nor afraid.
in *Atlantic Monthly* December 1944 'The Simple Art of Murder'

12 If my books had been any worse, I should not have been invited to Hollywood, and if they had been any better, I should not have come.
letter to Charles W. Morton, 12 December 1945, in Dorothy Gardiner and Katherine S. Walker *Raymond Chandler Speaking* (1962)

13 Would you convey my compliments to the purist who reads your proofs and tell him or her that I write in a sort of broken-down patois which is something like the way a Swiss waiter talks, and that when I split an infinitive, God damn it, I split it so it will stay split.
letter to Edward Weeks, 18 January 1947, in F. MacShane *Life of Raymond Chandler* (1976) ch. 7

14 When in doubt have a man come through the door with a gun in his hand.
attributed

Coco Chanel (Gabrielle Bonheur) 1883–1971
French couturière

15 You ask if they were happy. This is not a characteristic of a European. To be contented—that's for the cows.
A. Madsen *Coco Chanel* (1990) ch. 35

16 Youth is something very new: twenty years ago no one mentioned it.
Marcel Haedrich *Coco Chanel, Her Life, Her Secrets* (1971)

Henry ('Chips') Channon 1897–1958
American-born British Conservative politician and diarist

17 What is more dull than a discreet diary? One might just as well have a discreet soul.
diary, 26 July 1935

Charlie Chaplin (Charles Spencer Chaplin) 1889–1977
English film actor and director

18 All I need to make a comedy is a park, a policeman and a pretty girl.
My Autobiography (1964) ch. 10

19 Words are cheap. The biggest thing you can say is 'elephant'.
on the universality of silent films
B. Norman *The Movie Greats* (1981)

Arthur Chapman 1873–1935

American poet

1 Out where the handclasp's a little stronger,
  Out where the smile dwells a little longer,
  That's where the West begins.
  Out Where the West Begins (1916)

George Chapman *c.*1559–1634

English scholar, poet, and dramatist

2 Man is a torch borne in the wind; a dream
  But of a shadow, summed with all his substance.
  Bussy D'Ambois (1607–8) act 1, sc. 1

3 Who to himself is law, no law doth need,
  Offends no law, and is a king indeed.
  Bussy D'Ambois (1607–8) act 2, sc. 1

4   Oh my fame,
  Live in despite of murder!
  Bussy D'Ambois (1607–8) act 5, sc. 3

5 There is no danger to a man, that knows
  What life and death is; there's not any law,
  Exceeds his knowledge; neither is it lawful
  That he should stoop to any other law,
  He goes before them, and commands them all,
  That to himself is a law rational.
  The Conspiracy of Charles, Duke of Byron (1608) act 3, sc. 3

6 Come, come, dear Night, Love's mart of kisses,
  Sweet close of his ambitious line,
  The fruitful summer of his blisses,
  Love's glory doth in darkness shine.
  O come, soft rest of cares, come Night,
  Come naked Virtue's only tire,
  The reapèd harvest of the light,
  Bound up in sheaves of sacred fire.
  Hero and Leander (1598)

7 We have watered our houses in Helicon.
  occasionally misread 'We have watered our horses in Helicon', following an 1814 edition
  May-Day (1611) act 3, sc. 3

8 I am ashamed the law is such an ass.
  Revenge for Honour (1654) act 3, sc. 2; see DICKENS 280:6

9 They're only truly great who are truly good.
  Revenge for Honour (1654) act 5, sc. 2, last line

10 A poem, whose subject is not truth, but things like truth.
  The Revenge of Bussy D'Ambois (1613) dedication

11 Danger, the spur of all great minds.
  The Revenge of Bussy D'Ambois (1613) act 5, sc. 1

12 And let a scholar all Earth's volumes carry,
   He will be but a walking dictionary.
   The Tears of Peace (1609) l. 530

John Jay Chapman 1862–1933

American essayist and poet

13 It is necessary to destroy reputations when they are lies. Peace be to their ashes. But war and fire until they be ashes.
   Between Elections (1900)

14 The present in New York is so powerful that the past is lost.
   Emerson and Other Essays (rev. ed. 1909), preface

Charles I 1600–49

British monarch, King of England, Scotland, and Ireland from 1625, son of JAMES I and father of CHARLES II. On Charles I: see MARVELL 525:6

15 Never make a defence or apology before you be accused.
   letter to Lord Wentworth, 3 September 1636, in Sir Charles Petrie (ed.) *Letters of King Charles I* (1935)

16 I see all the birds are flown.
   after attempting to arrest five members of the Long Parliament (PYM, Hampden, Haselrig, Holles, and Strode)
   in the House of Commons, 4 January 1642

17 Sweet-heart, now they will cut off thy father's head. Mark, child, what I say: they will cut off my head, and perhaps make thee a king. But mark what I say: you must not be a king, so long as your brothers Charles and James do live.
   said to Prince Henry
   Reliquiae Sacrae Carolinae (1650)

18 You manifestly wrong even the poorest ploughman, if you demand not his free consent.
   The King's Reasons for declining the jurisdiction of the High Court of Justice, 21 January 1649, in S. R. Gardiner Constitutional Documents of the Puritan Revolution (1906 ed.)

19 As to the King, the laws of the land will clearly instruct you for that . . . For the people; and truly I desire their liberty and freedom, as much as any body: but I must tell you, that their liberty and freedom consists in having the government of those laws, by which their life and their goods may be most their own; 'tis not for having share in government [sirs] that is nothing pertaining to 'em. A subject and a sovereign are clean different things.
   speech on the scaffold, 30 January 1649; J. Rushworth Historical Collections pt. 4, vol. 2 (1701)

20 If I would have given way to an arbitrary way, for to have all laws changed according to the power of the sword, I needed not to have come here; and therefore I tell you (and I pray God it be not laid to your charge) that I am the martyr of the people.
   speech on the scaffold, 30 January 1649; J. Rushworth Historical Collections pt. 4, vol. 2 (1701)

21 I die a Christian, according to the profession of the Church of England, as I found it left me by my father.
   speech on the scaffold, 30 January 1649; J. Rushworth Historical Collections pt. 4, vol. 2 (1701)

22 I go from a corruptible to an incorruptible crown, where no disturbance can be, no disturbance in the world.
   speech on the scaffold, 30 January 1649; J. Rushworth Historical Collections pt. 4, vol. 2 (1701)

1 Remember—.

last words, giving his George (insignia of the Order of the Garter) to Bishop Juxon

 speech on the scaffold, 30 January 1649

Charles II 1630–85

British monarch, King of England, Scotland and Ireland from 1660, son of **CHARLES I**. On Charles: see **DEFOE** 271:1, **EPITAPHS** 317:16, **ROCHESTER** 664:18, **SELLAR AND YEATMAN** 692:4

2 Better than a play.

on the debates in the House of Lords on Lord Ross's Divorce Bill, 1670

 A. Bryant *King Charles II* (1931)

3 He [Charles II] said once to myself, he was no atheist, but he could not think God would make a man miserable only for taking a little pleasure out of the way.

 Bishop Gilbert Burnet *History of My Own Time* (1724) vol. 1, bk. 2, p. 93

4 He [Lauderdale] told me, the king spoke to him to let that [Presbytery] go, for it was not a religion for gentlemen.

 Bishop Gilbert Burnet *History of My Own Time* (1724) vol. 1, bk. 2

5 His nonsense suits their nonsense.

said of Woolly, afterwards Bishop of Clonfert ('a very honest man, but a very great blockhead') who had gone from house to house trying to persuade Nonconformists to go to church

 Bishop Gilbert Burnet *History of My Own Time* (1724) vol. 1, bk. 2

6 I am sure no man in England will take away my life to make you King.

to his brother James

 William King *Political & Literary Anecdotes* (1818)

7 I am weary of travelling and am resolved to go abroad no more. But when I am dead and gone I know not what my brother will do: I am much afraid that when he comes to wear the crown he will be obliged to travel again.

on the difference between himself and his brother (later James II)

 attributed

8 It is upon the navy under the good Providence of God that the safety, honour, and welfare of this realm do chiefly depend.

 'Articles of War' preamble (probably a popular paraphrase); Geoffrey Callender *The Naval Side of British History* (1952) pt. 1, ch. 8

9 This is very true: for my words are my own, and my actions are my ministers'.

*reply to Lord **ROCHESTER**'s epitaph on him*

 Thomas Hearne: *Remarks and Collections* (1885–1921) 17 November 1706; see **EPITAPHS** 317:16

10 He had been, he said, an unconscionable time dying; but he hoped that they would excuse it.

 Lord Macaulay *History of England* (1849) vol. 1, ch. 4

11 Let not poor Nelly starve.

*last words, referring to Nell **GWYN**, his mistress*

 Bishop Gilbert Burnet *History of My Own Time* (1724) vol. 1, bk. 3

Charles V 1500–58

Spanish monarch, Holy Roman Emperor, 1519–56; King of Spain from 1516

12 To God I speak Spanish, to women Italian, to men French, and to my horse—German.

 attributed; Lord Chesterfield *Letters to his Son* (ed. Dobrée, 1932) vol. 4

Charles, Prince of Wales 1948–

Heir apparent to the British throne; son of **ELIZABETH II** and former husband of **DIANA**, Princess of Wales

13 *when asked if he was 'in love':*

 Yes . . . whatever that may mean.

after the announcement of his engagement

 interview, 24 February 1981; see **DUFFY** 298:14

14 A monstrous carbuncle on the face of a much-loved and elegant friend.

on the proposed extension to the National Gallery

 speech to the Royal Institute of British Architects, 30 May 1984, in *The Times* 31 May 1984; see **SPENCER** 766:7

15 I just come and talk to the plants, really—very important to talk to them, they respond I find.

 television interview, 21 September 1986

Pierre Charron 1541–1603

French philosopher and theologian

16 The true science and study of man is man.

 De la Sagesse (1601) bk. 1, preface; see **POPE** 616:29

Salmon Portland Chase 1808–73

American lawyer and politician

17 The Constitution, in all its provisions, looks to an indestructible Union composed of indestructible States.

 decision in Texas v. White, 1868, in *Cases Argued and Decided in the Supreme Court of the United States* (1926) bk. 19

François-René Chateaubriand

(Vicomte de Chateaubriand) 1768–1848

French writer and diplomat

18 The original writer is not he who refrains from imitating others, but he who can be imitated by none.

 Le Génie du Christianisme (1802) pt. 2, bk. 1, ch. 3

19 Moments of crisis produce in man a redoubling of life.

 Mémoires d'outre-tombe (1849–50)

Geoffrey Chaucer c.1343–1400

English poet. On Chaucer: see **CAXTON** 212:2, **DRYDEN** 297:20, **DUNBAR** 299:11, **LYDGATE** 505:15, **SPENSER** 768:7, **WARD** 839:19

line references are to The Riverside Chaucer (ed. F. N. Robinson, 1987)

1 Ful craftier to pley she was
Than Athalus, that made the game
First of the ches, so was his name.
The Book of the Duchess l. 662

2 Whan that Aprill with his shoures soote
The droghte of March hath perced to the roote.
The Canterbury Tales 'The General Prologue' l. 1

3 And smale foweles maken melodye,
That slepen al the nyght with open ye
(So priketh hem nature in hir corages),
Thanne longen folk to goon on pilgrimages.
The Canterbury Tales 'The General Prologue' l. 9

4 He loved chivalrie,
Trouthe and honour, fredom and curteisie.
The Canterbury Tales 'The General Prologue' l. 45

5 He was a verray, parfit gentil knyght.
The Canterbury Tales 'The General Prologue' l. 72

6 He was as fressh as is the month of May.
The Canterbury Tales 'The General Prologue' l. 92

7 Curteis he was, lowely, and servysable,
And carf biforn his fader at the table.
The Canterbury Tales 'The General Prologue' l. 99

8 Hire gretteste ooth was but by Seinte Loy.
The Canterbury Tales 'The General Prologue' l. 120

9 Ful weel she soong the service dyvyne,
Entuned in hir nose ful semely;
And Frenssh she spak ful faire and fetisly,
After the scole of Stratford atte Bowe,
For Frenssh of Parys was to hire unknowe.
The Canterbury Tales 'The General Prologue' l. 122

10 She wolde wepe, if that she saugh a mous
Kaught in a trappe, if it were deed or bledde.
Of smale houndes hadde she that she fedde
With rosted flessh, or milk and wastel-breed.
But soore wepte she if oon of hem were deed.
The Canterbury Tales 'The General Prologue' l. 144

11 Of smal coral aboute hire arm she bar
A peire of bedes, gauded al with grene,
And theron heng a brooch of gold ful sheene,
On which ther was first write a crowned A,
And after *Amor vincit omnia*.
The Canterbury Tales 'The General Prologue' l. 158; see **VIRGIL** 832:10

12 He yaf nat of that text a pulled hen,
That seith that hunters ben nat hooly men.
The Canterbury Tales 'The General Prologue' l. 177

13 Somwhat he lipsed, for his wantownesse,
To make his Englissh sweete upon his tonge.
The Canterbury Tales 'The General Prologue' l. 264

14 A Clerk there was of Oxenford also,
That unto logyk hadde longe ygo.
As leene was his hors as is a rake,

And he was nat right fat, I undertake,
But looked holwe, and therto sobrely.
The Canterbury Tales 'The General Prologue' l. 285

15 For hym was levere have at his beddes heed
Twenty bookes, clad in blak or reed,
Of Aristotle and his philosophie
Than robes riche, or fithele, or gay sautrie.
But al be that he was a philosophre,
Yet hadde he but litel gold in cofre.
The Canterbury Tales 'The General Prologue' l. 293

16 And gladly wolde he lerne and gladly teche.
The Canterbury Tales 'The General Prologue' l. 308

17 Nowher so bisy a man as he ther nas,
And yet he semed bisier than he was.
The Canterbury Tales 'The General Prologue' l. 321

18 For he was Epicurus owene sone.
The Canterbury Tales 'The General Prologue' l. 336

19 Housbondes at chirche dore she hadde fyve,
Withouten oother compaignye in youthe—
But thereof nedeth nat to speke as nowthe.
The Canterbury Tales 'The General Prologue' l. 460

20 This noble ensample to his sheep he yaf,
That first he wroghte, and afterward he taughte.
The Canterbury Tales 'The General Prologue' l. 496

21 If gold ruste, what shall iren do?
The Canterbury Tales 'The General Prologue' l. 500

22 But Cristes loore and his apostels twelve
He taughte; but first he folwed it hymselve.
The Canterbury Tales 'The General Prologue' l. 527

23 His nosethirles blake were and wyde.
A swerd and a bokeler bar he by his syde.
His mouth as greet was as a greet forneys.
He was a janglere and a goliardeys,
And that was moost of synne and harlotries.
The Canterbury Tales 'The General Prologue' l. 557

24 A Somonour was ther with us in that place,
That hadde a fyr-reed cherubynnes face,
For saucefleem he was, with eyen narwe.
As hoot he was and lecherous as a sparwe.
The Canterbury Tales 'The General Prologue' l. 623

25 Wel loved he garleek, oynons, and eek lekes,
And for to drynken strong wyn, reed as blood.
The Canterbury Tales 'The General Prologue' l. 634

26 His walet, biforn him in his lappe,
Bretful of pardoun, comen from Rome al hoot.
The Canterbury Tales 'The General Prologue' l. 686

27 He hadde a croys of latoun ful of stones,
And in a glas he hadde pigges bones.
But with thise relikes, whan that he fond
A povre person dwellynge upon lond,
Upon a day he gat hym moore moneye
Than that the person gat in monthes tweye;
And thus, with feyned flaterye and japes,
He made the person and the peple his apes.
The Canterbury Tales 'The General Prologue' l. 699

28 O stormy peple! Unsad and evere untrewe!
The Canterbury Tales 'The Clerk's Tale' l. 995

29 Grisilde is deed, and eek hire pacience,
And bothe atones buryed in Ytaille;

For which I crie in open audience
No wedded man so hardy be t'assaille
His wyves pacience in trust to fynde
Grisildis, for in certein he shal faille.
The Canterbury Tales 'The Clerk's Tale: Lenvoy de Chaucer'
l. 1177

1 Ye archewyves, stondeth at defense,
Syn ye be strong as is a greet camaille;
Ne suffreth nat that men yow doon offense.
And sklendre wyves, fieble as in bataille,
Beth egre as is a tygre yond in Ynde;
Ay clappeth as a mille, I yow consaille.
The Canterbury Tales 'The Clerk's Tale: Lenvoy de Chaucer'
l. 1195

2 Be ay of chiere as light as leef on lynde,
And lat hym care, and wepe, and wrynge, and
waille!
The Canterbury Tales 'The Clerk's Tale: Lenvoy de Chaucer'
l. 1211

3 Love wol nat been constreyned by maistrye.
When maistrie comth, the God of Love anon
Beteth his wynges, and farewel, he is gon!
Love is a thyng as any spirit free.
The Canterbury Tales 'The Franklin's Tale' l. 764

4 Wommen, of kynde, desiren libertee,
And nat to been constreyned as a thral;
And so doon men, if I sooth seyen shal.
The Canterbury Tales 'The Franklin's Tale' l. 768

5 Til that the brighte sonne loste his hewe;
For th'orisonte hath reft the sonne his lyght—
This is as muche to seye as it was nyght.
The Canterbury Tales 'The Franklin's Tale' l. 1016

6 Trouthe is the hyeste thyng that man may kepe.
The Canterbury Tales 'The Franklin's Tale' l. 1479

7 And therefore, at the kynges court, my brother,
Ech man for hymself, ther is noon oother.
The Canterbury Tales 'The Knight's Tale' l. 1181

8 And whan a beest is deed he hath no peyne;
But man after his deeth moot wepe and pleyne.
The Canterbury Tales 'The Knight's Tale' l. 1319

9 The bisy larke, messager of day.
The Canterbury Tales 'The Knight's Tale' l. 1491

10 For pitee renneth soone in gentil herte.
The Canterbury Tales 'The Knight's Tale' l. 1761

11 The smylere with the knyf under the cloke.
The Canterbury Tales 'The Knight's Tale' l. 1999

12 Up roos the sonne, and up roos Emelye.
The Canterbury Tales 'The Knight's Tale' l. 2273

13 What is this world? what asketh men to have?
Now with his love, now in his colde grave.
The Canterbury Tales 'The Knight's Tale' l. 2777

14 She is mirour of alle curteisye.
The Canterbury Tales 'The Man of Law's Tale' l. 166

15 Lat take a cat, and fostre hym wel with milk
And tendre flessh, and make his couche of silk,
And lay hym seen a mous go by the wal,
Anon he weyveth milk and flessh and al,
And every deyntee that is in that hous,
Swich appetit hath he to ete a mous.
The Canterbury Tales 'The Manciple's Tale' l. 175

16 Kepe wel they tonge, and thenk upon the crowe.
The Canterbury Tales 'The Manciple's Tale' l. 362

17 And what is bettre than wisedoom? Womman.
And
what is bettre than a good womman? Nothyng.
The Canterbury Tales 'The Tale of Melibee' l. 1107

18 She was a prymerole, a piggesnye,
For any lord to leggen in his bedde,
Or yet for any good yeman to wedde.
The Canterbury Tales 'The Miller's Tale' l. 3268

19 Derk was the nyght as pich, or as the cole,
And at the wyndow out she putte hir hole,
And Absolon, hym fil no bet be wers,
But with his mouth he kiste hir naked ers
Ful savourly, er he were war of this.
Abak he stirte, and thoughte it was amys,
For wel he wiste a woman hath no berd.
He felte a thyng al rough and long yherd,
And seyde, 'Fy! allas! what have I to do?'
'Tehee!' quod she, and clapte the wyndow to.
The Canterbury Tales 'The Miller's Tale' l. 3730

20 For certein, whan that Fortune list to flee,
Ther may no man the cours of hire withholde.
The Canterbury Tales 'The Monk's Tale' l. 1995

21 Ful wys is he that kan hymselven knowe!
The Canterbury Tales 'The Monk's Tale' l. 2139

22 Redeth the grete poete of Ytaille
That highte Dant, for he kan al devyse
Fro point to point; nat o word wol he faille.
The Canterbury Tales 'The Monk's Tale' l. 2460

23 His coomb was redder than the fyn coral,
And batailled as it were a castel wal;
His byle was blak, and as the jeet it shoon;
Lyk asure were his legges and his toon;
His nayles whitter than the lylye flour,
And lyk the burned gold was his colour,
This gentil cok hadde in his governaunce
Sevene hennes for to doon al his plesaunce,
Whiche were his sustres and his paramours,
And wonder lyk to hym, as of colours;
Of whiche the faireste hewed on hir throte
Was cleped fair damoysele Pertelote.
The Canterbury Tales 'The Nun's Priest's Tale' l. 2859

24 Mordre wol out; that se we day by day.
The Canterbury Tales 'The Nun's Priest's Tale' l. 3052; see
PROVERBS 639:20

25 Whan that the month in which the world bigan,
That highte March, whan God first maked man.
The Canterbury Tales 'The Nun's Priest's Tale' l. 3187

26 And on a Friday fil al this meschaunce.
The Canterbury Tales 'The Nun's Priest's Tale' l. 3341

27 Thanne peyne I me to strecche forth the nekke,
And est and west upon the peple I bekke.
The Canterbury Tales 'The Pardoner's Prologue' l. 395

28 O wombe! O bely! O stynkyng cod
Fulfilled of dong and of corrupcioun!
The Canterbury Tales 'The Pardoner's Tale' l. 534

1 And lightly as it comth, so wol we spende.
The Canterbury Tales 'The Pardoner's Tale' l. 781

2 Yet in oure asshen olde is fyr yreke.
The Canterbury Tales 'The Reeve's Prologue' l. 3882

3 The gretteste clerkes been noght wisest men.
The Canterbury Tales 'The Reeve's Tale' l. 4054

4 So was hir joly whistle wel ywet.
The Canterbury Tales 'The Reeve's Tale' l. 4155

5 Thou lookest as thou woldest fynde an hare,
For evere upon the ground I se thee stare.
The Canterbury Tales 'Prologue to Sir Thopas' l. 696

6 He hadde a semely nose.
The Canterbury Tales 'Sir Thopas' l. 729

7 'By God,' quod he, 'for pleynly, at a word,
Thy drasty rymyng is nat worth a toord!'
The Canterbury Tales 'Sir Thopas' l. 929

8 Experience, though noon auctoritee
Were in this world, is right ynogh for me
To speke of wo that is in mariage.
The Canterbury Tales 'The Wife of Bath's Prologue' l. 1

9 Yblessed be god that I have wedded fyve!
Welcome the sixte, whan that evere he shal.
For sothe, I wol nat kepe me chaast in al.
Whan myn housbonde is fro the world ygon,
Som Cristen man shall wedde me anon.
The Canterbury Tales 'The Wife of Bath's Prologue' l. 44

10 And after wyn on Venus moste I thynke,
For al so siker as cold engendreth hayl,
A likerous mouth moste han a likerous tayl.
The Canterbury Tales 'The Wife of Bath's Prologue' l. 464

11 But—Lord Crist!—what that it remembreth me
Upon my yowthe, and on my jolitee,
It tikleth me aboute myn herte roote.
Unto this day it dooth myn herte boote
That I have had my world as in my time.
The Canterbury Tales 'The Wife of Bath's Prologue' l. 469

12 And for to se, and eek for to be seye
Of lusty folk.
The Canterbury Tales 'The Wife of Bath's Prologue' l. 552

13 But yet I hadde alwey a coltes tooth.
Gat-tothed I was, and that bicam me weel.
The Canterbury Tales 'The Wife of Bath's Prologue' l. 602

14 Of which mayde anon, maugree hir heed,
By verray force, he rafte hire maydenhed.
The Canterbury Tales 'The Wife of Bath's Tale' l. 887

15 Wommen desiren to have sovereynetee
As wel over hir housbond as hir love.
The Canterbury Tales 'The Wife of Bath's Tale' l. 1038

16 Venus clerk Ovide,
That hath ysowen wonder wide
The grete god of Loves name.
The House of Fame l. 1487

17 And as for me, though that I konne but lyte,
On bokes for to rede I me delyte,
And to hem yive I feyth and ful credence,
And in myn herte have hem in reverence
So hertely, that ther is game noon

That fro my bokes maketh me to goon,
But yt be seldom on the holyday,
Save, certeynly, whan that the month of May
Is comen, and that I here the foules synge,
And that the floures gynnen for to sprynge,
Farewel my bok and my devocioun!
The Legend of Good Women 'The Prologue' l. 29

18 Of al the floures in the mede,
Thanne love I most thise floures white and rede,
Swiche as men callen daysyes in our toun.
The Legend of Good Women 'The Prologue' l. 41

19 That wel by reson men it calle may
The 'dayesye,' or elles the 'ye of day,'
The emperice and flour of floures alle.
The Legend of Good Women 'The Prologue' l. 183

20 And she was fayr as is the rose in May.
The Legend of Good Women 'Cleopatra' l. 613

21 That lyf so short,
the craft so long to lerne,
Th'assay so hard, so sharp the conquerynge.
The Parliament of Fowls l. 1; see **HIPPOCRATES** 399:13,
PROVERBS 626:35

22 Thou shalt make castels thanne in Spayne
And dreme of joye, all but in vayne.
The Romaunt of the Rose l. 2573

23 O blynde world, O blynde entencioun!
How often falleth al the effect contraire
Of surquidrie and foul presumpcioun;
For kaught is proud, and kaught is debonaire.
This Troilus is clomben on the staire,
And litel weneth that he moot descenden;
But alday faileth thing that fooles wenden.
Troilus and Criseyde bk. 1, l. 211

24 For evere it was, and evere it shal byfalle,
That Love is he that alle thing may bynde,
For may no man fordon the lawe of kynde.
Troilus and Criseyde bk. 1, l. 236

25 But love a womman that she woot it nought,
And she wol quyte it that thow shalt nat fele;
Unknowe, unkist, and lost, that is unsought.
Troilus and Criseyde bk. 1, l. 807

26 O wynd, O wynd, the weder gynneth clere.
Troilus and Criseyde bk. 2, l. 2

27 Ye knowe ek that in forme of speche is chaunge
Withinne a thousand yeer, and wordes tho
That hadden pris, now wonder nyce and
straunge
Us thinketh hem, and yet thei spake hem so.
Troilus and Criseyde bk. 2, l. 22

28 So longe mote ye lyve, and alle proude,
Til crowes feet be growe under youre yë.
Troilus and Criseyde bk. 2, l. 402

29 And we shall speek of the somwhat, I trowe,
Whan thow art gon, to don thyn eris glowe!
Troilus and Criseyde bk. 2, l. 1021

30 God loveth, and to love wol nought werne,
And in this world no lyves creature
Withouten love is worth, or may endure.
Troilus and Criseyde bk. 3, l. 12

1 It is nought good a slepyng hound to wake.
Troilus and Criseyde bk. 3, l. 764; see **PROVERBS** 637:20

2 For I have seyn of a ful misty morwe
Folowen ful ofte a myrie someris day.
Troilus and Criseyde bk. 3, l. 1060

3 Right as an aspes leef she gan to quake.
Troilus and Criseyde bk. 3, l. 1200

4 And as the newe abaysed nyghtyngale,
That stynteth first whan she bygynneth to synge.
Troilus and Criseyde bk. 3, l. 1233

5 For of fortunes sharpe adversitee
The worst kynde of infortune is this,
A man to han ben in prosperitee,
And it remembren, whan it passed is.
Troilus and Criseyde bk. 3, l. 1625; see **BOETHIUS** 130:11, **DANTE** 264:18

6 Oon ere it herde, at tother out it wente.
Troilus and Criseyde bk. 4, l. 434

7 But manly sette the world on six and sevene;
And if thow deye a martyr, go to hevene!
Troilus and Criseyde bk. 4, l. 622

8 For tyme ylost may nought recovered be.
Troilus and Criseyde bk. 4, l. 1283

9 Ye, fare wel al the snow of ferne yere!
Troilus and Criseyde bk. 5, l. 1176

10 Ek gret effect men write in place lite;
Th' entente is al, and nat the lettres space.
Troilus and Criseyde bk. 5, l. 1629

11 Go, litel bok, go, litel myn tragedye,
Ther God thi makere yet, er that he dye,
So sende myght to make in som comedye!
But litel bok, no makyng thow n'envie,
But subgit be to alle poesye;
And kis the steppes, where as thow seest pace
Virgile, Ovide, Omer, Lucan, and Stace.
And for ther is so gret diversite
In Englissh and in writyng of oure tonge,
So prey I God that non myswrite the,
Ne the mysmetre for defaute of tonge;
And red wherso thow be, or elles songe,
That thow be understonde, God I biseche!
Troilus and Criseyde bk. 5, l. 1786; see **STEVENSON** 777:4

12 And whan that he was slayn in this manere,
His lighte goost ful blisfully is went
Up to the holughnesse of the eighthe spere,
In convers letyng everich element;
And ther he saugh, with ful avysement
The erratik sterres, herkenyng armonye
With sownes ful of hevenyssh melodie.
And down from thennes faste he gan avyse
This litel spot of erthe, that with the se
Embraced is, and fully gan despise
This wrecched world, and held al vanite
To respect of the pleyn felicite
That is in hevene above.
Troilus and Criseyde bk. 5, l. 1811

13 O yonge, fresshe folkes, he or she,
In which that love up groweth with youre age.

Repeyreth hom fro worldly vanyte,
And of youre herte up casteth the visage
To thilke God that after his ymage
Yow made, and thynketh al nys but a faire,
This world that passeth soone as floures faire.
And loveth hym the which that right for love
Upon a crois, our soules for to beye,
First start, and roos, and sit in hevene above;
For he nyl falsen no wight, dar I seye,
That wol his herte al holly on hym leye.
And syn he best to love is, and most meke,
What nedeth feynede loves for to seke?
Troilus and Criseyde bk. 5, l. 1835

14 Lo here, of payens corsed olde rites!
Lo here, what alle hire goddes may availle!
Lo here, thise wrecched worldes appetites!
Lo here, the fyn and guerdoun for travaille
Of Jove, Appollo, of Mars, of swich rascaille!
Troilus and Criseyde bk. 5, l. 1849

15 O moral Gower, this book I directe
To the.
Troilus and Criseyde bk. 5, l. 1856

16 Flee fro the prees, and dwelle with sothfastnesse.
'Truth: Balade de Bon Conseyle' l. 1

17 Forth, pilgrim, forth! Forth, beste, out of thy stal!
Know thy contree, look up, thank God of al;
Hold the heye wey, and lat thy gost thee lede,
And trowth thee shal delivere, it is no drede.
'Truth: Balade de Bon Conseyle' l. 18

Anton Chekhov 1860–1904
Russian dramatist and short-story writer

18 If a lot of cures are suggested for a disease, it means that the disease is incurable.
The Cherry Orchard (1904) act 1 (translated by Elisaveta Fen)

19 The Lord God has given us vast forests, immense fields, wide horizons; surely we ought to be giants, living in such a country as this.
The Cherry Orchard (1904) act 2 (translated by Elisaveta Fen)

20 To begin to live in the present, we must first atone for our past and be finished with it, and we can only atone for it by suffering, by extraordinary, unceasing exertion.
The Cherry Orchard (1904) act 2 (translated by Elisaveta Fen)

21 MEDVEDENKO: Why do you wear black all the time?
MASHA: I'm in mourning for my life, I'm unhappy.
The Seagull (1896) act 1

22 NINA: Your play's hard to act, there are no living people in it.
TREPLEV: Living people! We should show life neither as it is nor as it ought to be, but as we see it in our dreams.
The Seagull (1896) act 1

23 Women can't forgive failure.
The Seagull (1896) act 2

1 I'm a seagull. No, that's wrong. Remember you shot a seagull? A man happened to come along, saw it and killed it, just to pass the time. A plot for a short story.
The Seagull (1896) act 4

2 Man must work by the sweat of his brow whatever his class, and that should make up the whole meaning and purpose of his life and happiness and contentment.
The Three Sisters (1901) act 1 (translated by Elisaveta Fen)

3 People who don't even notice whether it's summer or winter are lucky! If I lived in Moscow I don't think I'd care what the weather was like.
The Three Sisters (1901) act 2 (translated by Elisaveta Fen)

4 Life isn't finished for us yet! We're going to live! . . . Maybe, if we wait a little longer, we shall find out why we live, why we suffer.
The Three Sisters (1901) act 4 (translated by Elisaveta Fen)

5 Forests keep disappearing, rivers dry up, wild life's become extinct, the climate's ruined and the land grows poorer and uglier every day.
Uncle Vanya (1897) act 1

6 When a woman isn't beautiful, people always say, 'You have lovely eyes, you have lovely hair.'
Uncle Vanya (1897) act 3

7 A writer must be as objective as a chemist: he must abandon the subjective line; he must know that dung-heaps play a very reasonable part in a landscape, and that evil passions are as inherent in life as good ones.
letter to M. V. Kiselev, 14 January 1887, in L. S. Friedland (ed.) *Anton Chekhov: Letters on the Short Story* . . . (1964)

8 Medicine is my lawful wife and literature is my mistress. When I get tired of one I spend the night with the other.
letter to A. S. Suvorin, 11 September 1888, in L. S. Friedland (ed.) *Anton Chekhov: Letters on the Short Story* . . . (1964)

9 Brevity is the sister of talent.
letter to Alexander Chekhov, 11 April 1889, in L. S. Friedland (ed.) *Anton Chekhov: Letters on the Short Story* . . . (1964)

10 I couldn't stand a happiness that went on morning noon and night . . . I promise to be a splendid husband, but give me a wife who, like the moon, does not rise every night in my sky.
on being urged to marry
letter, 23 March 1895; Donald Rayfield *Anton Chekhov* (1997)

11 Between 'God exists' and 'There is no God' lies a whole enormous field which a true sage has great difficulty in crossing. But a Russian knows only one of these two extremes and the middle between them doesn't interest him, which is why he knows nothing or very little . . . A good man's indifference is as good as any religion.
diary, 1897; Donald Rayfield *Anton Chekhov* (1997)

12 Women deprived of the company of men pine, men deprived of the company of women become stupid.
Notebooks (1921)

13 Love, friendship, respect do not unite people as much as common hatred for something.
Notebooks (1921)

14 If in the first act you have hung a pistol on the wall, then in the following one it should be fired. Otherwise don't put it there.
I. Ya. Gurlyand 'Reminiscences of A. P. Chekhov, in *Teatr i iskusstvo* 11 July 1904

15 It's been so long since I've had champagne.
last words, after which he slowly drank the glass and died
Henri Troyat *Chekhov* (1984)

Apsley Cherry-Garrard 1882–1959
English polar explorer

16 For a joint scientific and geographical piece of organization, give me Scott; for a winter journey, Wilson; for a dash to the Pole and nothing else, Amundsen: and if I am in the devil of a hole and want to get out of it, give me Shackleton every time.
The Worst Journey in the World (1923); see **MISQUOTATIONS** 549:4

Mary Chesnut 1823–86
American diarist and Confederate supporter

17 Atlanta is gone. That agony is over. There is no hope but we will try to have no fear.
after the fall of Atlanta to **SHERMAN**'s *army in 1864*
Geoffrey C. Ward *The Civil War* (1991) ch. 4

Lord Chesterfield (Philip Dormer Stanhope, Earl of Chesterfield) 1694–1773
English writer and politician. On Chesterfield: see **JOHNSON** 439:3, **WALPOLE** 838:4

18 Unlike my subject will I frame my song,
It shall be witty and it sha'n't be long.
epigram on 'Long' Sir Thomas Robinson in the *Dictionary of National Biography* (1917–) vol. 17

19 In scandal, as in robbery, the receiver is always thought as bad as the thief.
Advice to his Son (1775) 'Rules for Conversation: Private Scandal'

20 In matters of religion and matrimony I never give any advice; because I will not have anybody's torments in this world or the next laid to my charge.
Letters to Arthur Charles Stanhope, Esq. (1817) 12 October 1765

21 Religion is by no means a proper subject of conversation in a mixed company.
Letters . . . to his Godson and Successor (1890) Letter 142

22 Cunning is the dark sanctuary of incapacity.
Letters . . . to his Godson and Successor (1890) 'Letter . . . to be delivered after his own death'

23 The knowledge of the world is only to be acquired in the world, and not in a closet.
Letters to his Son (1774) 4 October 1746

24 An injury is much sooner forgotten than an insult.
Letters to his Son (1774) 9 October 1746

1 Courts and camps are the only places to learn the world in.
Letters to his Son (1774) 2 October 1747

2 Take the tone of the company that you are in.
Letters to his Son (1774) 16 October 1747

3 Do as you would be done by is the surest method that I know of pleasing.
Letters to his Son (1774) 16 October 1747

4 I recommend to you to take care of minutes: for hours will take care of themselves.
Letters to his Son (1774) 6 November 1747; see **LOWNDES** 503:12

5 Advice is seldom welcome; and those who want it the most always like it the least.
Letters to his Son (1774) 29 January 1748

6 Wear your learning, like your watch in a private pocket: and do not merely pull it out and strike it, merely to show that you have one.
Letters to his Son (1774) 22 February 1748

7 Speak of the moderns without contempt, and of the ancients without idolatry.
Letters to his Son (1774) 27 February 1748

8 In my mind, there is nothing so illiberal and so ill-bred, as audible laughter.
Letters to his Son (1774) 9 March 1748; see **CATULLUS** 210:10, **CONGREVE** 246:26

9 Wrongs are often forgiven, but contempt never is. Our pride remembers it for ever.
Letters to his Son (1774) 1 July 1748

10 Women, then, are only children of a larger growth.
Letters to his Son (1774) 5 September 1748; see **DRYDEN** 295:10

11 We read every day, with astonishment, things which we see every day without surprise.
Letters to his Son (1774) 13 September 1748

12 It must be owned, that the Graces do not seem to be natives of Great Britain; and I doubt, the best of us here have more of rough than polished diamond.
Letters to his Son (1774) 18 November 1748

13 Idleness is only the refuge of weak minds.
Letters to his Son (1774) 20 July 1749

14 Putting moral virtues at the highest, and religion at the lowest, religion must still be allowed to be a collateral security, at least, to virtue; and every prudent man will sooner trust to two securities than to one.
Letters to his Son (1774) 8 January 1750

15 It is commonly said, and more particularly by Lord Shaftesbury, that ridicule is the best test of truth.
Letters to his Son (1774) 6 February 1752; see **SHAFTESBURY** 693:19

16 Knowledge may give weight, but accomplishments give lustre, and many more people see than weigh.
Maxims, in *Letters to his Son* (3rd ed., 1774) vol. 4

17 The chapter of knowledge is a very short, but the chapter of accidents is a very long one.
letter to Solomon Dayrolles, 16 February 1753, in M. Maty (ed.) *Miscellaneous Works* vol. 2 (1778) no. 79

18 I converse with my equals, my vegetables, which I find in a flourishing condition.
letter to Solomon Dayrolles, 1 August 1754, in Lord Mahon (ed.) *The Letters of Philip Dormer Stanhope, Earl of Chesterfield* (1845) vol. 4

19 I . . . could not help reflecting in my way upon the singular ill-luck of this my dear country, which, as long as ever I remember it, and as far back as I have read, has always been governed by the only two or three people, out of two or three millions, totally incapable of governing, and unfit to be trusted.
in *The World* 7 October 1756; M. Maty (ed.) *Miscellaneous Works* vol. 2 (1778) 'Miscellaneous Pieces' no. 45

20 Tyrawley and I have been dead these two years; but we don't choose to have it known.
James Boswell *Life of Samuel Johnson* (1934 ed.) vol. 2, 3 April 1773

21 The pleasure is momentary, the position ridiculous, and the expense damnable.
of sex
attributed

22 Give Dayrolles a chair.
last words, to his godson Dayrolles; W. H. Craig *Life of Lord Chesterfield* (1907)

G. K. Chesterton 1874–1936

English essayist, novelist, and poet. On Chesterton: see **BELLOC** 68:11, **EPITAPHS** 319:6

23 Are they clinging to their crosses, F. E. Smith?
satirizing F. E. SMITH's response to the Welsh Disestablishment Bill
'Antichrist' (1915)

24 Talk about the pews and steeples
And the Cash that goes therewith!
But the souls of Christian peoples . . .
Chuck it, Smith!
'Antichrist' (1915)

25 The gallows in my garden, people say,
Is new and neat and adequately tall.
I tie the noose on in a knowing way
As one that knots his necktie for a ball;
But just as all the neighbours—on the wall—
Are drawing a long breath to shout 'Hurray!'
The strangest whim has seized me . . . . After all
I think I will not hang myself today.
'Ballade of Suicide' (1915)

26 I tell you naught for your comfort,
Yea, naught for your desire,
Save that the sky grows darker yet
And the sea rises higher.
The Ballad of the White Horse (1911) bk. 1

27 For the great Gaels of Ireland
Are the men that God made mad,
For all their wars are merry,
And all their songs are sad.
The Ballad of the White Horse (1911) bk. 2

1 The thing on the blind side of the heart,
On the wrong side of the door,
The green plant groweth, menacing
Almighty lovers in the Spring;
There is always a forgotten thing,
And love is not secure.
The Ballad of the White Horse (1911) bk. 3

2 When fishes flew and forests walked
And figs grew upon thorn,
Some moment when the moon was blood
Then surely I was born.

With monstrous head and sickening cry
And ears like errant wings,
The devil's walking parody
On all four-footed things.
'The Donkey' (1900)

3 Fools! For I also had my hour;
One far fierce hour and sweet:
There was a shout about my ears,
And palms before my feet.
'The Donkey' (1900)

4 They died to save their country and they only
saved the world.
'English Graves' (1922)

5 Why do you rush through the fields in trains,
Guessing so much and so much.
Why do you flash through the flowery meads,
Fat-head poet that nobody reads;
And why do you know such a frightful lot
About people in gloves and such?
'The Fat White Woman Speaks' (1933); an answer to Frances
Cornford; see **CORNFORD** 252:2

6 From all that terror teaches,
From lies of tongue and pen,
From all the easy speeches
That comfort cruel men,
From sale and profanation
Of honour and the sword,
From sleep and from damnation,
Deliver us, good Lord!
'A Hymn' (1915)

7 White founts falling in the courts of the sun,
And the Soldan of Byzantium is smiling as they
run.
'Lepanto' (1915)

8 The cold queen of England is looking in the
glass;
The shadow of the Valois is yawning at the
Mass.
'Lepanto' (1915)

9 The last and lingering troubadour to whom the
bird has sung,
That once went singing southward when all the
world was young.
'Lepanto' (1915)

10 Strong gongs groaning as the guns boom far,
Don John of Austria is going to the war.
'Lepanto' (1915)

11 The folk that live in Liverpool, their heart is in
their boots;

They go to hell like lambs, they do, because the
hooter hoots.
'Me Heart' (1914)

12 Before the Roman came to Rye or out to Severn
strode,
The rolling English drunkard made the rolling
English road.
A reeling road, a rolling road, that rambles
round the shire,
And after him the parson ran, the sexton and
the squire;
'The Rolling English Road' (1914)

13 A merry road, a mazy road, and such as we did
tread
The night we went to Birmingham by way of
Beachy Head.
'The Rolling English Road' (1914)

14 For there is good news yet to hear and fine
things to be seen,
Before we go to Paradise by way of Kensal
Green.
'The Rolling English Road' (1914)

15 Smile at us, pay us, pass us; but do not quite
forget.
For we are the people of England, that never
have spoken yet.
'The Secret People' (1915)

16 We only know the last sad squires ride slowly
towards the sea,
And a new people takes the land: and still it is
not we.
'The Secret People' (1915)

17 God made the wicked Grocer
For a mystery and a sign,
That men might shun the awful shops
And go to inns to dine.
'The Song Against Grocers' (1914)

18 He keeps a lady in a cage
Most cruelly all day,
And makes her count and calls her 'Miss'
Until she fades away.
'The Song Against Grocers' (1914)

19 Tea, although an Oriental,
Is a gentleman at least;
Cocoa is a cad and coward,
Cocoa is a vulgar beast.
'Song of Right and Wrong' (1914)

20 Lancashire merchants whenever they like
Can water the beer of a man in Klondike
Or poison the meat of a man in Bombay;
And that is the meaning of Empire Day.
'Songs of Education: II Geography' (1922)

21 And Noah he often said to his wife when he sat
down to dine,
'I don't care where the water goes if it doesn't
get into the wine.'
'Wine and Water' (1914)

1 An adventure is only an inconvenience rightly considered. An inconvenience is only an adventure wrongly considered.
   All Things Considered (1908) 'On Running after one's Hat'

2 AM IN MARKET HARBOROUGH. WHERE OUGHT I TO BE?
   telegram sent to his wife in London
   Autobiography (1936)

3 Literature is a luxury; fiction is a necessity.
   The Defendant (1901) 'A Defence of Penny Dreadfuls'

4 The rich are the scum of the earth in every country.
   The Flying Inn (1914) ch. 15

5 Happiness is a mystery like religion, and should never be rationalized.
   Heretics (1905) ch. 7

6 We make our friends; we make our enemies; but God makes our next-door neighbour.
   Heretics (1905) ch. 14

7 Bigotry may be roughly defined as the anger of men who have no opinions.
   Heretics (1905) ch. 20

8 After the first silence the small man said to the other: 'Where does a wise man hide a pebble?' And the tall man answered in a low voice: 'On the beach.'
   The small man nodded, and after a short silence said: 'Where does a wise man hide a leaf?' And the other answered: 'In the forest.'
   The Innocence of Father Brown (1911)

9 One sees great things from the valley; only small things from the peak.
   The Innocence of Father Brown (1911)

10 Thieves respect property. They merely wish the property to become their property that they may more perfectly respect it.
   The Man who was Thursday (1908) ch. 4

11 The poor have sometimes objected to being governed badly; the rich have always objected to being governed at all.
   The Man who was Thursday (1908) ch. 11

12 Tradition means giving votes to the most obscure of all classes, our ancestors. It is the democracy of the dead.
   Orthodoxy (1908) ch. 4

13 Democrats object to men being disqualified by the accident of birth; tradition objects to their being disqualified by the accident of death.
   Orthodoxy (1908) ch. 4

14 All conservatism is based upon the idea that if you leave things alone you leave them as they are. But you do not. If you leave a thing alone you leave it to a torrent of change.
   Orthodoxy (1908) ch. 7

15 It isn't that they can't see the solution. It is that they can't see the problem.
   The Scandal of Father Brown (1935)

16 They say travel broadens the mind; but you must have the mind.
   'The Shadow of the Shark' (1921)

17 Lying in bed would be an altogether perfect and supreme experience if only one had a coloured pencil long enough to draw on the ceiling.
   Tremendous Trifles (1909) 'On Lying in Bed'

18 The whole object of travel is not to set foot on foreign land; it is at last to set foot on one's own country as a foreign land.
   Tremendous Trifles (1909) 'The Riddle of the Ivy'

19 Hardy went down to botanize in the swamp, while Meredith climbed towards the sun. Meredith became, at his best, a sort of daintily dressed Walt Whitman: Hardy became a sort of village atheist brooding and blaspheming over the village idiot.
   The Victorian Age in Literature (1912)

20 He could not think up to the height of his own towering style.
   of **TENNYSON**
   The Victorian Age in Literature (1912) ch. 3

21 The Christian ideal has not been tried and found wanting. It has been found difficult; and left untried.
   What's Wrong with the World (1910) pt. 1 'The Unfinished Temple'

22 The prime truth of woman, the universal mother . . . that if a thing is worth doing, it is worth doing badly.
   What's Wrong with the World (1910) pt. 4 'Folly and Female Education'

23 To be clever enough to get all that money, one must be stupid enough to want it.
   The Wisdom of Father Brown (1914)

24 Journalism largely consists in saying 'Lord Jones Dead' to people who never knew that Lord Jones was alive.
   The Wisdom of Father Brown (1914)

25 Democracy means government by the uneducated, while aristocracy means government by the badly educated.
   in *New York Times* 1 February 1931, pt. 5

26 When men stop believing in God they don't believe in nothing; they believe in anything.
   widely attributed, although not traced in his works; first recorded as 'The first effect of not believing in God is to believe in anything' in Emile Cammaerts *Chesterton: The Laughing Prophet* (1937)

Maurice Chevalier 1888–1972
French singer and actor

27 Considering the alternative, it's not too bad at all.
   on being asked what he felt about the advancing years, on his seventy-second birthday
   Michael Freedland *Maurice Chevalier* (1981)

Joseph Benedict 'Ben' Chifley
1885–1951

Australian Labor statesman, Prime Minister 1945–9

1 We have a great objective—the light on the hill—which we aim to reach by working for the betterment of mankind not only here but anywhere we may give a helping hand.
    speech to the Annual Conference of the New South Wales branch of the Australian Labor Party, 12 June 1949

Lydia Maria Child 1802–80

American abolitionist and suffragist

2 We first crush people to the earth, and then claim the right of trampling on them forever, because they are prostrate.
    An Appeal on Behalf of That Class of Americans Called Africans (1833)

3 Woman stock is rising in the market. I shall not live to see women vote, but I'll come and rap at the ballot box.
    letter to Sarah Shaw, 3 August 1856

Erskine Childers 1870–1922

British writer and Irish nationalist

4 The riddle of the sands.
    title of novel (1903)

5 Come closer, boys. It will be easier for you.
    last words to the firing squad at his execution
    Burke Wilkinson The Zeal of the Convert (1976) ch. 26

William Chillingworth 1602–44

English theologian

6 The Bible and the Bible only is the religion of Protestants.
    The Religion of Protestants (1637)

7 I once knew a man out of courtesy help a lame dog over a stile, and he for requital bit his fingers.
    The Religion of Protestants (1637)

Jacques Chirac 1932–

French statesman, Prime Minister 1974–6 and 1986–8, President 1995–2007

8 For its part, France wants you to take part in this great undertaking.
    on European Monetary Union
    speech to both Houses of Parliament, 15 May 1996

9 You have been very rude, and I have never been spoken to like this before.
    to Tony BLAIR at the EU enlargement summit in Brussels
    in Guardian online 29 October 2002

10 It is not well-brought-up behaviour. They missed a good opportunity to keep quiet.
    criticizing the support from Central and Eastern European states for the Anglo-American stance on Iraq
    in The Times 19 February 2003

Thomas O. Chisholm 1866–1960

11 Great is thy faithfulness! Great is thy faithfulness!
    Morning by morning new mercies I see;
    All I have needed thy hand has provided.
    Great is thy faithfulness, Lord, unto me.
    'Great is thy faithfulness' (hymn)

Rufus Choate 1799–1859

American lawyer and politician

12 Its constitution the glittering and sounding generalities of natural right which make up the Declaration of Independence.
    letter to the Maine Whig State Central Committee, 9 August 1856, in S. G. Brown The Works of Rufus Choate with a Memoir of his Life (1862) vol. 1; see EMERSON 315:21

Duc de Choiseul 1719–85

French politician

13 A minister who moves about in society is in a position to read the signs of the times even in a festive gathering, but one who remains shut up in his office learns nothing.
    Jack F. Bernard Talleyrand (1973)

Noam Chomsky 1928–

American linguistics scholar

14 The notion 'grammatical' cannot be identified with 'meaningful' or 'significant' in any semantic sense. Sentences (1) and (2) are equally nonsensical, but . . . only the former is grammatical.
    (1) Colourless green ideas sleep furiously.
    (2) Furiously sleep ideas green colourless.
    Syntactic Structures (1957) ch. 2

15 The empiricist view is so deep-seated in our way of looking at the human mind that it almost has the character of a superstition.
    radio discussion, in Listener 30 May 1968

16 As soon as questions of will or decision or reason or choice of action arise, human science is at a loss.
    television interview, in Listener 6 April 1978

17 The Internet is an élite organization; most of the population of the world has never even made a phone call.
    on the limitations of the World Wide Web
    in Observer 18 February 1996

Jean Chrétien 1934–

Canadian Liberal statesman, Prime Minister 1993–2003

18 Leadership means making people feel good.
    in Toronto Star 7 June 1984

19 The art of politics is learning to walk with your back to the wall, your elbows high, and a smile on your face. It's a survival game played under the glare of lights.
    Straight from the Heart (1985)

Agatha Christie 1890–1976
English writer of detective fiction

1 War settles *nothing* . . . to *win* a war is as disastrous as to lose one!
   An Autobiography (1977) pt. 10

2 He [Hercule Poirot] tapped his forehead. 'These little grey cells. It is "up to them".'
   The Mysterious Affair at Styles (1920) ch. 10

3 I'm a sausage machine, a perfect sausage machine.
   G. C. Ramsey *Agatha Christie* (1972)

Christina of Denmark, Duchess of Milan 1522–90
Danish princess

4 If I had two heads, I would happily place one at the disposal of the King of England.
   on the possibility of marrying **HENRY VIII**
   attributed in varying forms since the 19th century

David Christy 1802–*c*.68

5 Cotton is King; or, the economical relations of slavery.
   title of book, 1855

Chuang Tzu (Zhuangzi) *c*.369–286 BC
Chinese philosopher

6 Without them [feelings] there would not be I. And without me who will experience them? They are right near by. But we don't know what causes them. It seems there is a True Lord who does so, but there is no indication of his existence.
   Chuang Tzu ch. 2

7 When one is at ease with himself, one is near Tao.
   Chuang Tzu ch. 2

8 The sage harmonizes the right and wrong and rests in natural equalization. This is called following two courses at the same time.
   Chuang Tzu ch. 2

9 The universe and I exist together, and all things and I are one.
   Chuang Tzu ch. 2

10 The sage has the sun and moon by his side. He grasps the universe under the arm. He blends everything into a harmonious whole, casts aside whatever is confused or obscured, and regards the humble as honourable.
   Chuang Tzu ch. 2

11 Once I, Chang Chou, dreamed that I was a butterfly and was happy as a butterfly. I was conscious that I was quite pleased with myself but I did not know that I was Chou. Suddenly I awoke and there I was, visibly Chou. I do not know whether it was Chou dreaming that he was a butterfly or the butterfly dreaming that it was Chou.
   Chuang Tzu ch. 2; see **BASHO** 60:21

12 If the Universe is hidden in the universe itself, then there can be no escape from it. This is the great truth of things in general.
   Chuang Tzu ch. 6

13 Tao has reality and evidence but no action or physical form. It may be transmitted but cannot be received. It may be obtained but cannot be seen. It is based in itself, rooted in itself. Before heaven and earth came into being, Tao existed by itself from all time.
   Chuang Tzu ch. 6

14 Those who are contented and at ease when the occasion comes and live in accord with the course of Nature cannot be affected by sorrow or joy. This is what the ancients called release from bondage. Those who cannot release themselves are so because they are bound by material things.
   Chuang Tzu ch. 6

15 Do not be the possessor of fame. Do not be the storehouse of schemes. Do not take over the function of things. Do not be the master of knowledge [to manipulate things]. Personally realize the infinite to the highest degree and travel in the realm of which there is no sign. Exercise fully what you have received from Nature without any subjective viewpoint. In one word; be absolutely vacuous.
   Chuang Tzu ch. 7

16 The mind of the perfect man is like a mirror. It does not lean forward or backward in its response to things. It responds to things but conceals nothing of its own. Therefore it is able to deal with things without injury to [its reality].
   Chuang Tzu ch. 7

Mary, Lady Chudleigh (née Leigh)
1656–1710
English poet

17 'Tis hard we should be by the men despised,
   Yet kept from knowing what would make us prized;
   Debarred from knowledge, banished from the schools,
   And with the utmost industry bred fools.
   The Ladies Defence (1701)

18 Wife and Servant are the same,
   But only differ in the name.
   Poems (1703) 'To the Ladies'

19 Then shun, oh! shun that wretched state
   And all the fawning flatterers hate:
   Value yourselves, and men despise
   You must be proud if you'll be wise.
   on marriage
   Poems (1703) 'To the Ladies'

Francis Pharcellus Church *see*
Newspaper headlines

Charles Churchill 1731–64

English poet

1 Though by whim, envy, or resentment led,
They damn those authors whom they never
read.
The Candidate (1764) l. 57

2 The danger chiefly lies in acting well;
No crime's so great as daring to excel.
An Epistle to William Hogarth (1763) l. 51

3   Be England what she will,
With all her faults, she is my country still.
The Farewell (1764) l. 27; see **COWPER** 256:10

4 It can't be Nature, for it is not sense.
The Farewell (1764) l. 200

5 And adepts in the speaking trade
Keep a cough by them ready made.
The Ghost (1763) bk. 2, l. 545

6 Just to the windward of the law.
The Ghost (1763) bk. 3, l. 56

7 . . . He for subscribers baits his hook,
And takes your cash; but where's the book?
No matter where; wise fear, you know,
Forbids the robbing of a foe;
But what, to serve our private ends,
Forbids the cheating of our friends?
satirizing Samuel JOHNSON
The Ghost (1763) bk. 3, l. 801

8 A joke's a very serious thing.
The Ghost (1763) bk. 4, l. 1386

9 Happy, thrice happy now the savage race,
Since Europe took their gold, and gave them
grace!
Pastors she sends to help them in their need,
Some who can't write, with others who can't
read.
Gotham (1764) bk. 1, l. 67

10 Old-age, a second child, by Nature cursed
With more and greater evils than the first,
Weak, sickly, full of pains; in ev'ry breath
Railing at life, and yet afraid of death.
Gotham (1764) bk. 1, l. 215

11 Keep up appearances; there lies the test;
The world will give thee credit for the rest.
Outward be fair, however foul within;
Sin if thou wilt, but then in secret sin.
Night (1761) l. 311

12 Stay out all night, but take especial care
That Prudence bring thee back to early prayer
As one with watching and with study faint,
Reel in a drunkard, and reel out a saint.
Night (1761) l. 321

13 Grave without thought, and without feeling gay.
on pretentious poets
The Prophecy of Famine (1763) l. 60

14   No merit but mere knack of rhyme,
Short gleams of sense, and satire out of time.
The Prophecy of Famine (1763) l. 81

15 Apt Alliteration's artful aid.
The Prophecy of Famine (1763) l. 86

16 He sickened at all triumphs but his own.
*of Thomas Franklin, Professor of Greek at Cambridge
University*
The Rosciad (1761) l. 64

17 To mischief trained, e'en from his mother's
womb,
Grown old in fraud, tho' yet in manhood's
bloom.
Adopting arts, by which gay villains rise,
And reach the heights, which honest men
despise;
Mute at the bar, and in the senate loud,
Dull 'mongst the dullest, proudest of the proud;
A pert, prim prater of the northern race,
Guilt in his heart, and famine in his face.
of Alexander Wedderburn, later Lord Loughborough
The Rosciad (1761) l. 69

18 But, spite of all the criticizing elves,
Those who would make us feel, must feel
themselves.
The Rosciad (1761) l. 961

19 Where he falls short, 'tis Nature's fault alone;
Where he succeeds, the merit's all his own.
of the actor, Thomas Sheridan
The Rosciad (1761) l. 1025

Lord Randolph Churchill 1849–94

British Conservative politician, father of Winston CHURCHILL

20 The forest laments in order that Mr Gladstone
may perspire.
on GLADSTONE's hobby of felling trees
speech on Financial Reform, delivered in Blackpool, 24
January 1884, in F. Banfield (ed.) *Life and Speeches of Lord
Randolph Churchill* (1884)

21 I decided some time ago that if the G. O. M.
went for Home Rule, the Orange card would be
the one to play. Please God it may turn out the
ace of trumps and not the two.
G. O. M. = Grand Old Man (GLADSTONE)
letter to Lord Justice FitzGibbon, 16 February 1886, in Robert
Rhodes James *Lord Randolph Churchill* (1959) ch. 8

22 Ulster will fight; Ulster will be right.
public letter, 7 May 1886, in R. F. Foster *Lord Randolph
Churchill* (1981)

23 An old man in a hurry.
on GLADSTONE
address to the electors of South Paddington, 19 June 1886; in
W. S. Churchill *Lord Randolph Churchill* (1906) vol. 2

24 All great men make mistakes. Napoleon forgot
Blücher, I forgot Goschen.
*when Lord Randolph suddenly resigned the position of
Chancellor of the Exchequer in 1886, GOSCHEN had been
appointed in his place*
Leaves from the Notebooks of Lady Dorothy Nevill (1907)

1 I never could make out what those damned dots [decimal points] meant.
  W. S. Churchill *Lord Randolph Churchill* (1906) vol. 2

Winston Churchill 1874–1965

British Conservative statesman, Prime Minister 1940–5, 1951–5; son of Lord Randolph **CHURCHILL**. On Churchill: see **ATTLEE** 35:7, **BALFOUR** 53:18, **BEVAN** 76:15, **DE VALERA** 275:2, **MURROW** 566:6; see also **JOHNSON** 443:19, **SPEARS** 765:16

2 It cannot in the opinion of His Majesty's Government be classified as slavery in the extreme acceptance of the word without some risk of terminological inexactitude.
  speech in the House of Commons, 22 February 1906

3 Business carried on as usual during alterations on the map of Europe.
  on the self-adopted 'motto' of the British people
  speech at Guildhall, 9 November 1914, *Complete Speeches* (1974) vol. 3

4 The difference between him and Arthur is that Arthur is wicked and moral, Asquith is good and immoral.
  comparing H. H. ASQUITH with Arthur BALFOUR
  E. T. Raymond *Mr Balfour* (1920)

5 The whole map of Europe has been changed . . . but as the deluge subsides and the waters fall short we see the dreary steeples of Fermanagh and Tyrone emerging once again.
  speech in the House of Commons, 16 February 1922

6 Anyone can rat, but it takes a certain amount of ingenuity to re-rat.
  on rejoining the Conservatives twenty years after leaving them for the Liberals, c.1924
  Kay Halle *Irrepressible Churchill* (1966)

7 I remember, when I was a child, being taken to the celebrated Barnum's circus, which contained an exhibition of freaks and monstrosities, but the exhibit on the programme which I most desired to see was the one described as 'The Boneless Wonder'. My parents judged that that spectacle would be too revolting and demoralizing for my youthful eyes, and I have waited 50 years to see the boneless wonder sitting on the Treasury Bench.
  of Ramsay MACDONALD
  speech in the House of Commons, 28 January 1931

8 [The Government] go on in strange paradox, decided only to be undecided, resolved to be irresolute, adamant for drift, solid for fluidity, all-powerful to be impotent.
  speech in the House of Commons, 12 November 1936

9 Dictators ride to and fro upon tigers which they dare not dismount. And the tigers are getting hungry.
  letter, 11 November 1937, in *Step by Step* (1939); see **PROVERBS** 634:26

10 The utmost he [Neville Chamberlain] has been able to gain for Czechoslovakia and in the matters which were in dispute has been that the German dictator, instead of snatching his victuals from the table, has been content to have them served to him course by course.
  speech in the House of Commons, 5 October 1938

11 I cannot forecast to you the action of Russia. It is a riddle wrapped in a mystery inside an enigma.
  radio broadcast, 1 October 1939, in *Into Battle* (1941)

12 I have nothing to offer but blood, toil, tears and sweat.
  speech in the House of Commons, 13 May 1940; see **BYRON** 185:7

13 What is our policy? . . . to wage war against a monstrous tyranny, never surpassed in the dark, lamentable catalogue of human crime.
  speech in the House of Commons, 13 May 1940

14 What is our aim? . . . Victory, victory at all costs, victory in spite of all terror; victory, however long and hard the road may be; for without victory, there is no survival.
  speech in the House of Commons, 13 May 1940

15 We shall not flag or fail. We shall go on to the end. We shall fight in France, we shall fight on the seas and oceans, we shall fight with growing confidence and growing strength in the air, we shall defend our island, whatever the cost may be. We shall fight on the beaches, we shall fight on the landing grounds, we shall fight in the fields and in the streets, we shall fight in the hills; we shall never surrender.
  speech in the House of Commons, 4 June 1940

16 Let us therefore brace ourselves to our duty, and so bear ourselves that, if the British Empire and its Commonwealth lasts for a thousand years, men will still say, 'This was their finest hour.'
  speech in the House of Commons, 18 June 1940

17 Never in the field of human conflict was so much owed by so many to so few.
  on the Battle of Britain
  speech in the House of Commons, 20 August 1940; see **TREVELYAN** 815:10

18 No one can guarantee success in war, but only deserve it.
  letter to Lord Wavell, 26 November 1940, in *The Second World War* vol. 2 (1949) ch. 27; see **ADDISON** 4:12

19 Give us the tools and we will finish the job.
  radio broadcast, 9 February 1941, in *Complete Speeches* (1974) vol. 6

20 When I warned them [the French Government] that Britain would fight on alone whatever they did, their generals told their Prime Minister and his divided Cabinet, 'In three weeks England will have her neck wrung like a chicken.' Some chicken! Some neck!
  speech to Canadian Parliament, 30 December 1941, in *Complete Speeches* (1974) vol. 6

21 A medal glitters, but it also casts a shadow.
  a reference to the envy caused by the award of honours
  in 1941; Kenneth Rose *King George V* (1983) p. 7

1 Now this is not the end. It is not even the beginning of the end. But it is, perhaps, the end of the beginning.

on the Battle of Egypt

speech at the Mansion House, London, 10 November 1942, in *The End of the Beginning* (1943)

2 We make this wide encircling movement in the Mediterranean, having for its primary object the recovery of the command of that vital sea, but also having for its object the exposure of the underbelly of the Axis, especially Italy, to heavy attack.

speech in the House of Commons, 11 November 1942; see **MISQUOTATIONS** 548:18

3 National compulsory insurance for all classes for all purposes from the cradle to the grave.

radio broadcast, 21 March 1943, in *Complete Speeches* (1974) vol. 7

4 There is no finer investment for any community than putting milk into babies.

radio broadcast, 21 March 1943, in *Complete Speeches* (1974) vol. 7

5 The empires of the future are the empires of the mind.

speech at Harvard, 6 September 1943, in *Onwards to Victory* (1944)

6 From Stettin in the Baltic to Trieste in the Adriatic an iron curtain has descended across the Continent.

'iron curtain' previously had been applied by others to the Soviet Union or her sphere of influence, e.g. Ethel Snowden Through Bolshevik Russia (1920), Dr GOEBBELS Das Reich (25 February 1945), and by Churchill himself in a cable to President TRUMAN (4 June 1945)

speech at Westminster College, Fulton, Missouri, 5 March 1946, in *Complete Speeches* (1974) vol. 7

7 Democracy is the worst form of Government except all those other forms that have been tried from time to time.

speech in the House of Commons, 11 November 1947

8 This is the sort of English up with which I will not put.

Ernest Gowers *Plain Words* (1948) 'Troubles with Prepositions'

9 Naval tradition?. Monstrous. Nothing but rum, sodomy, prayers, and the lash.

often quoted as 'rum, sodomy, and the lash', as in Peter Gretton Former Naval Person (1968)

Harold Nicolson, diary, 17 August 1950

10 The candle in that great turnip has gone out.

in reply to the comment 'One never hears of BALDWIN nowadays — he might as well be dead'

Harold Nicolson: Diaries and Letters 1945–62 (1968) diary 17 August 1950

11 To jaw-jaw is always better than to war-war.

speech at White House, 26 June 1954, in *New York Times* 27 June 1954

12 I have never accepted what many people have kindly said—namely, that I inspired the nation . . . It was the nation and the race dwelling all round the globe that had the lion's heart. I had

the luck to be called upon to give the roar. I also hope that I sometimes suggested to the lion the right place to use his claws.

speech at Westminster Hall, 30 November 1954

13 I have taken more out of alcohol than alcohol has taken out of me.

Quentin Reynolds *By Quentin Reynolds* (1964) ch. 11

14 In defeat unbeatable: in victory unbearable.

of Lord MONTGOMERY

Edward Marsh *Ambrosia and Small Beer* (1964) ch. 5

15 Like a powerful graceful cat walking delicately and unsoiled across a rather muddy street.

of BALFOUR's moving from ASQUITH's Cabinet to that of LLOYD GEORGE

Great Contemporaries (1937)

16 *of the career of Lord CURZON:*

The morning had been golden; the noontide was bronze; and the evening lead. But all were solid, and each was polished till it shone after its fashion.

Great Contemporaries (1937)

17 Courage is rightly esteemed the first of human qualities because as has been said, it is the quality which guarantees all others.

Great Contemporaries (1937)

18 Headmasters have powers at their disposal with which Prime Ministers have never yet been invested.

My Early Life (1930) ch. 2

19 Mr Gladstone read Homer for fun, which I thought served him right.

My Early Life (1930) ch. 2

20 It is a good thing for an uneducated man to read books of quotations.

My Early Life (1930) ch. 9

21 In war: resolution. In defeat: defiance. In victory: magnanimity. In peace: goodwill.

The Second World War vol. 1 (1948) epigraph, which according to Edward Marsh in *A Number of People* (1939), occurred to Churchill shortly after the conclusion of the First World War

22 The loyalties which centre upon number one are enormous. If he trips he must be sustained. If he makes mistakes they must be covered. If he sleeps he must not be wantonly disturbed. If he is no good he must be pole-axed. But this last extreme process cannot be carried out every day; and certainly not in the days just after he has been chosen.

The Second World War (1949) vol. 2, ch. 1

23 If Hitler invaded hell I would make at least a favourable reference to the devil in the House of Commons.

The Second World War (1950) vol. 3, ch. 20

24 I did not suffer from any desire to be relieved of my responsibilities. All I wanted was compliance with my wishes after reasonable discussion.

The Second World War (1951) vol. 4, ch. 5

1 Jellicoe was the only man on either side who could lose the war in an afternoon.
The World Crisis (1927) pt. 1, ch. 5

2 The ability to foretell what is going to happen tomorrow, next week, next month, and next year. And to have the ability afterwards to explain why it didn't happen.
describing the qualifications desirable in a prospective politician
B. Adler *Churchill Wit* (1965)

3 I am fond of pigs. Dogs look up to us. Cats look down on us. Pigs treat us as equals.
attributed, in M. Gilbert *Never Despair* (1988)

4 NANCY ASTOR: If I were your wife I would put poison in your coffee!
CHURCHILL: And if I were your husband I would drink it.
Consuelo Vanderbilt Balsan *Glitter and Gold* (1952)

5 A remarkable example of modern art. It certainly combines force with candour.
on the notorious 80th birthday portrait by Graham Sutherland, later destroyed by Lady Churchill
Martin Gilbert *Churchill: A Life* (1991)

6 The only recorded instance in history of a rat swimming *towards* a sinking ship.
of a former Conservative who proposed to stand as a Liberal
Leon Harris *The Fine Art of Political Wit* (1965)

7 A sheep in sheep's clothing.
of Clement ATTLEE
Lord Home *The Way the Wind Blows* (1976) ch. 6; see GOSSE 366:13

8 Take away that pudding—it has no theme.
Lord Home *The Way the Wind Blows* (1976) ch. 16

Count Galeazzo Ciano 1903–44

Italian fascist politician; son-in-law of MUSSOLINI

9 *La vittoria trova cento padri, e nessuno vuole riconoscere l'insuccesso.*
Victory has a hundred fathers, but defeat is an orphan.
literally 'no-one wants to recognise defeat as his own'
Diary (1946) vol. 2, 9 September 1942

Colley Cibber 1671–1757

English dramatist, actor, and theatre manager

10 Oh! how many torments lie in the small circle of a wedding-ring!
The Double Gallant (1707) act 1, sc. 2

11 Off with his head—so much for Buckingham.
Richard III (1700) act 4 (adapted from Shakespeare); see SHAKESPEARE 731:21

12 Perish the thought!
Richard III (1700) act 5 (adapted from Shakespeare)

13 Conscience avaunt, Richard's himself again:
Hark! the shrill trumpet sounds, to horse, away,
My soul's in arms, and eager for the fray.
Richard III (1700) act 5 (adapted from Shakespeare)

14 Stolen sweets are best.
The Rival Fools (1709) act 1, sc. 1; see PROVERBS 643:39

Cicero (Marcus Tullius Cicero) 106–43 BC

Roman statesman, orator, and writer. On Cicero: see CATULLUS 210:12, DICKENS 277:27; see also MISQUOTATIONS 547:5

15 *Dicit enim tamquam in Platonis politeia, non tamquam in Romuli faece sententiam.*
For he delivers his opinions as though he were living in Plato's Republic rather than among the dregs of Romulus.
of M. Porcius Cato, the Younger
Ad Atticum bk. 2, letter 1, sect. 8

16 *Sed nescio quo modo nihil tam absurde dici potest quod non dicatur ab aliquo philosophorum.*
There is nothing so absurd but some philosopher has said it.
De Divinatione bk. 2, ch. 119

17 *Vulgo enim dicitur: Iucundi acti labores.*
For it is commonly said: completed labours are pleasant.
De Finibus bk. 2, ch. 105

18 *Salus populi suprema est lex.*
The good of the people is the chief law.
De Legibus bk. 3, ch. 8; see SELDEN 691:16

19 From this followed the corollary, that many sensations are probable, that is, though not amounting to a full perception they are yet possessed of a certain distinctness and clearness, and so can direct the conduct of the wise man.
De Natura Deorum bk. 1, ch. 5; see BUTLER 182:18

20 'Ipse dixit.' 'Ipse' autem erat Pythagoras.
'He himself said', and this 'himself' was Pythagoras.
De Natura Deorum bk. 1, ch. 10

21 *Summum bonum.*
The highest good.
De Officiis bk. 1, ch. 5

22 For of all gainful professions, nothing is better, nothing more pleasing, nothing more delightful, nothing better becomes a well-bred man than agriculture.
De Officiis bk. 1, ch. 42

23 *Cedant arma togae, concedant laurea laudi.*
Let war yield to peace, laurels to paeans.
De Officiis bk. 1, ch. 77

24 *Nescire autem quid ante quam natus sis acciderit, id est semper esse puerum.*
To be ignorant of what occurred before you were born is to remain forever a child.
De Oratore ch. 34, para. 120

25 *Mens cuiusque is est quisque.*
The spirit is the true self.
De Republica bk. 6, ch. 26

26 *Nihil est enim illi principio deo, qui omnem mundum regit, quod quidem in terris fiat, acceptius quam* *concilia coetusque hominum iure sociati, quae civitates appellantur.*

For there is nothing that happens on earth that is more welcome to that supreme God who rules the whole universe than the institutions and congregations of men united by a sense of right, which are called states.
De Republica bk. 6, ch. 13

1 *Quousque tandem abutere, Catilina, patientia nostra?*

How long will you abuse our patience, Catiline?
In Catilinam Speech 1, ch. 1

2 *O tempora, O mores!*

Oh, the times! Oh, the manners!
In Catilinam Speech 1, ch. 1

3 *Abiit, excessit, evasit, erupit.*

He departed, he withdrew, he strode off, he broke forth.
In Catilinam Speech 2, ch. 1

4 *Civis Romanus sum.*

I am a Roman citizen.
In Verrem Speech 5, ch. 147; see **KENNEDY** 460:13, **PALMERSTON** 595:3

5 *Quamquam bonum te timor faciebat, non diuturnus magister officii.*

However it was fear — no lasting teacher of duty — that made you good.
Second Philippic ch. 36

6 *Quod di omen avertant.*

May the gods avert this omen.
Third Philippic ch. 35

7 *Nervos belli, pecuniam infinitam.*

The sinews of war, unlimited money.
Fifth Philippic ch. 5; see **BACON** 48:7, **FARQUHAR** 324:11

8 *Silent enim leges inter arma.*

Laws are silent in time of war.
Pro Milone ch. 11

9 *Cui bono?*

To whose profit?
Pro Roscio Amerino ch. 84 and *Pro Milone* ch. 12, sect. 32, quoting L. Cassius Longinus Ravilla

10 *Id quod est praestantissimum maximeque optabile omnibus sanis et bonis et beatis, cum dignitate otium.*

The thing which is the most outstanding and chiefly to be desired by all healthy and good and well-off persons, is leisure with honour.
Pro Sestio ch. 98

11 *Errare mehercule malo cum Platone . . . quam cum istis vera sentire.*

I would rather be wrong, by God, with Plato . . . than be correct with those men.
on Pythagoreans
Tusculanae Disputationes bk. 1, ch. 39

12 *Et morbi perniciosiores pluresque sunt animi quam corporis.*

Diseases of the soul are both more dangerous and more numerous than those of the body.
Tusculanae Disputationes bk. 3, ch. 3

13 *O fortunatam natam me consule Romam!*

O happy Rome, born when I was consul!
Juvenal *Satires* poem 10, l. 122

14 *Laudandum adulescentum, ornandum, tollendum.*

The young man should be praised, decorated, and got rid of.
of Octavian, the future Emperor **AUGUSTUS**
referred to in a letter from Decimus Brutus to Cicero; *Epistulae ad Familiares* bk. 11, sect. 20

E. M. Cioran 1911–95
Romanian-born French philosopher

15 Without the possibility of suicide, I would have killed myself long ago.
in *Independent* 2 December 1989

16 I do nothing, granted. But I see the hours pass—which is better than trying to fill them.
in *Guardian* 11 May 1993

Claire Clairmont 1798–1879
English lover of BYRON and stepsister of Mary SHELLEY

17 I shall ever remember the gentleness of your manners and the wild originality of your countenance.
letter to Lord Byron, 16 April 1816; M. K. Stocking (ed.) *The Clairmont Correspondence* (1995)

John Clare 1793–1864
English poet of the natural world; certified insane in 1837, he spent the rest of his life in an asylum

18 When badgers fight and everyone's a foe.
'Badger' (written c.1836)

19 He could not die when the trees were green, For he loved the time too well.
'The Dying Child'

20 My life hath been one chain of contradictions, Madhouses, prisons, whore-shops.
'Child Harold' (written 1841) l. 146

21 They took me from my wife, and to save trouble
I wed again, and made the error double.
'Child Harold' (written 1841) l. 152

22 God hath often saw
Things here too dirty for the light of day;
For in a madhouse there exists no law
Now stagnant grows my too refinèd clay;
I envy birds their wings to fly away.
'Child Harold' (written 1841) l. 158

23 Pale death, the grand physician, cures all pain;
The dead rest well who lived for joys in vain.
'Child Harold' (written 1841) l. 215

24 Hopeless hope hopes on and meets no end, Wastes without springs and homes without a friend.
'Child Harold' (written 1841) l. 1018

25 A quiet, pilfering, unprotected race.
'The Gipsy Camp' (1841)

1 I am—yet what I am, none cares or knows;
  My friends forsake me like a memory lost:
  I am the self-consumer of my woes.
  'I Am' (1848)

2 I long for scenes where man hath never trod
  A place where woman never smiled or wept
  There to abide with my Creator God
  And sleep as I in childhood sweetly slept,
  Untroubling and untroubled where I lie
  The grass below, above, the vaulted sky.
  'I Am' (1848)

3 The present is the funeral of the past,
  And man the living sepulchre of life.
  'The present is the funeral of the past' (written 1845)

4 Summers pleasures they are gone like to visions
    every one
  And the cloudy days of autumn and of winter
    cometh on
  I tried to call them back but unbidden they are
    gone
  Far away from heart and eye and for ever far
    away.
  'Remembrances'

Edward Hyde, Earl of Clarendon

1609–74

English statesman and historian

5 Without question, when he first drew the sword,
  he threw away the scabbard.
  of Hampden
    The History of the Rebellion (1703, ed. W. D. Macray, 1888) vol.
    3, bk. 7, sect. 84; see **PROVERBS** 647:20

6 He had a head to contrive, a tongue to
  persuade, and a hand to execute any mischief.
  of Hampden
    The History of the Rebellion (1703, ed. W. D. Macray, 1888) vol.
    3, bk. 7, sect. 84; see **GIBBON** 354:13

7 He . . . would, with a shrill and sad accent,
  ingeminate the word *Peace, Peace*.
  of FALKLAND
    The History of the Rebellion (1703, ed. W. D. Macray, 1888) vol.
    3, bk. 7, sect. 233

8 So enamoured on peace that he would have
  been glad the King should have bought it at any
  price.
  of FALKLAND
    The History of the Rebellion (1703, ed. W. D. Macray, 1888) vol.
    3, bk. 7, sect. 233

9 He will be looked upon by posterity as a brave
  bad man.
  of CROMWELL
    The History of the Rebellion (1703, ed. W. D. Macray, 1888) vol.
    6, bk. 15, closing words

Claribel (Mrs Charlotte Alington Barnard)

1840–69

English writer of ballads

10 I cannot sing the old songs
   I sang long years ago,

For heart and voice would fail me,
  And foolish tears would flow.
  'The Old Songs' (1865)

Alan Clark 1928–99

**British Conservative politician, son of Kenneth CLARK. On
Clark: see CAMPBELL**

11 There are no true friends in politics. We are all
   sharks circling, and waiting, for traces of blood
   to appear in the water.
   diary, 30 November 1990

12 Our old friend economical . . . with the *actualité*.
   *under cross-examination at the Old Bailey during the Matrix
   Churchill case*
     in Independent 10 November 1992; see **ARMSTRONG** 28:21

Kenneth Clark 1903–83

English art historian, father of Alan CLARK

13 It's a curious fact that the all-male religions have
   produced no religious imagery—in most cases
   have positively forbidden it. The great religious
   art of the world is deeply involved with the
   female principle.
   Civilisation (1969) ch. 7

Arthur C. Clarke 1917–2008

English science fiction writer

14 When a distinguished but elderly scientist states
   that something is possible, he is almost certainly
   right. When he states that something is
   impossible, he is very probably wrong.
   Profiles of the Future (1962) ch. 2; see **ASIMOV** 33:19

15 Any sufficiently advanced technology is
   indistinguishable from magic.
   Profiles of the Future (1962) ch. 2

16 How inappropriate to call this planet Earth
   when it is clearly Ocean.
   in Nature 8 March 1990

Austin Clarke 1896–1974

Irish poet, dramatist, and novelist

17 For the house of the planter
   Is known by the trees.
   'The Planter's Daughter' (1929)

18 And O! She was the Sunday
   In every week.
   'The Planter's Daughter' (1929)

Grant Clarke 1891–1931 *and* Edgar Leslie 1885–1976

19 He'd have to get under, get out and get under
   And fix up his automobile.
   He'd Have to Get Under—Get Out and Get Under (1913 song)

James Stanier Clarke c.1765–1834

English clergyman, chaplain and private secretary to Prince
Leopold of Coburg

1 Perhaps when you again appear in print you
may choose to dedicate your volumes to Prince
Leopold: any historical romance, illustrative of
the history of the august House of Coburg,
would just now be very interesting.
> letter to Jane Austen, 27 March 1816, in R. W. Chapman (ed.)
> *Jane Austen's Letters* (1952)

John Clarke d. 1658

English schoolmaster

2 He that would thrive
Must rise at five;
He that hath thriven
May lie till seven.
> *Paraemiologia Anglo-Latina* (1639) 'Diligentia'

Claudian 370–c.404

Alexandrian-born Roman poet

3 *Ille Caledoniis posuit qui castra pruinis.*
He who pitched his camp among the Caledonian
frosts.
> *of the Roman general Theodosius the Elder*
> *De quatro consulate Honorii Augustii* ch. 8, l. 26

4 *Erret, et extremos alter scrutetur Hiberos:*
Plus habet hic vitae, plus habet ille viae.
Let who will be a wanderer and explore farthest
Spain: such may have more of a journey: this
man has more of a life.
> *of the old man of Verona who never left his home*
> *De Sene Veronensi*

Appius Claudius Caecus fl. 312–279 BC

Roman censor, orator, and prose writer

5 *Faber est suae quisque fortunae.*
Each man is the smith of his own fortune.
> Sallust *Ad Caesarem Senem de Re Publica Oratio* ch. 1, sect. 2;
> see **PROVERBS** 631:28

Matthias Claudius 1740–1815

German poet

6 *'s ist leider Krieg—und ich begehre*
Nicht schuld daran zu sein!
Alas, it is war, and I have no wish to carry the
guilt for it.
> *Warsong*

7 *Was sollt ich machen, wenn im Schlaf mit Grämen*
Und blutig, bleich und blass,
Die Geister Erschlagnen zu mir kämen,
Und vor mir weinten, was?
What should I do if in fretful sleep
The ghosts of the slaughtered were to appear,
Bloody, pale, and wan, and weep
In front of me, what should I do?
> *Warsong*

Karl von Clausewitz 1780–1831

Prussian soldier and military theorist

8 Everything is very simple in war, but the
simplest thing is difficult. These difficulties
accumulate and produce a friction which no
man can imagine exactly who has not seen war.
> *On War* (1832–4) bk. 1, ch. 7, tr. J. J. Graham

9 The general unreliability of all information
presents a special problem in war: all action
takes place, so to speak, in a kind of twilight,
which, like fog or moonlight, often tends to
make things seem grotesque and larger than
they really are.
> *often alluded to by the phrase 'fog of war'*
> *On War* (1832–4) bk 2, ch. 2, tr. M. Howard and P. Paret

10 The closer these practical probabilities drive war
toward the absolute, the more the belligerent
states are involved and drawn into its vortex, the
clearer appear the connections between its
separate actions, and the more imperative the
need not to take the first step without
considering the last.
> *On War* (1832–4) bk. 8, ch. 3, tr. M. Howard and P. Paret

11 War is nothing but a continuation of politics
with the admixture of other means.
> *commonly rendered as 'War is the continuation of politics*
> *by other means'*
> *On War* (1832–4) bk. 8, ch. 6, sect. B

Henry Clay 1777–1852

American politician. On Clay: see **GLASCOCK** 360:16

12 If you wish to avoid foreign collision, you had
better abandon the ocean.
> speech in the House of Representatives, 22 January 1812, in C.
> Colton *The Life, Correspondence and Speeches of Henry Clay*
> (1864) vol. 5

13 The gentleman [Josiah Quincy] can not have
forgotten his own sentiment, uttered even on the
floor of this House, 'peaceably if we can,
forcibly if we must'.
> speech in Congress, 8 January 1813, in C. Colton (ed.) *The*
> *Works of Henry Clay* (1904) vol. 1

14 The arts of power and its minions are the same
in all countries and in all ages. It marks a victim;
denounces it; and excites the public odium and
the public hatred, to conceal its own abuses and
encroachments.
> speech in the Senate, 14 March 1834, in C. Colton (ed.) *The*
> *Works of Henry Clay* (1904) vol. 5

15 I had rather be right than be President.
> *to Senator Preston of South Carolina, 1839*
> attributed; S. W. McCall *Life of Thomas Brackett Reed* (1914)
> ch. 14

16 It has been my invariable rule to do all for the
Union. If any man wants the key of my heart,
let him take the key of the Union, and that is
the key to my heart.
> speech in Norfolk, 22 April 1844; Robert V. Rimini *Henry Clay*
> (1991)

Philip 'Tubby' Clayton 1885–1972
Australian-born English clergyman, founder of Toc H

1 CHAIRMAN: What is service?
CANDIDATE: The rent we pay for our room on earth.
admission ceremony of Toc H, a society founded after the First World War to provide Christian fellowship and social service
Tresham Lever *Clayton of Toc H* (1971)

Clearchus *c.*450–401 BC
Spartan officer

2 I will go with you and suffer whatever I must suffer. For I consider that you are my country and my friends and comrades; and with you, I think I shall be honoured wherever I may be, but without you I am not able either to help a friend or hurt an enemy. Where you go, there I will go also: that is my resolve.
speech to his soldiers after the death of Cyrus at the battle of Cunaxa, 401 BC
Xenophon *Anabasis* bk. 1, ch. 3, sect. 6

Eldridge Cleaver 1935–98
American political activist

3 Too much agreement kills a chat.
Soul on Ice (1968) 'Letters from Prison'

4 What we're saying today is that you're either part of the solution or you're part of the problem.
speech in San Francisco, 1968, in R. Scheer *Eldridge Cleaver, Post Prison Writings and Speeches* (1969)

John Cleland 1710–89
English writer

5 Truth! stark naked truth, is the word.
Memoirs of a Woman of Pleasure a.k.a. *Fanny Hill* (1749) vol. 1

Georges Clemenceau 1841–1929
French statesman, Prime Minister of France 1906–9, 1917–20. See also **SAYINGS** 685:7

6 War is too serious a matter to entrust to military men.
attributed to Clemenceau, e.g. in Hampden Jackson *Clemenceau and the Third Republic* (1946), but also to Briand and Talleyrand; see **DE GAULLE** 271:11

7 My home policy: I wage war; my foreign policy: I wage war. All the time I wage war.
speech to French Chamber of Deputies, 8 March 1918, in *Discours de Guerre* (1968)

8 It is easier to make war than to make peace.
speech at Verdun, 20 July 1919, in *Discours de Paix* (1938)

9 What do you expect when I'm between two men of whom one [Lloyd George] thinks he is Napoleon and the other [Woodrow Wilson] thinks he is Jesus Christ?
to André Tardieu, on being asked why he always gave in to **LLOYD GEORGE** *at the Paris Peace Conference, 1918*
James Lees-Milne *Harold Nicolson* (1980) vol. 1, ch. 7, letter from Nicolson to his wife, 20 May 1919

Clement XIII 1693–1769
Italian cleric; Pope 1758–69

10 *Sint ut sunt aut non sint.*
Let them be as they are or not be at all.
replying to a request for changes in the constitutions of the Society of Jesus
J. A. M. Crétineau-Joly *Clément XIV et les Jésuites* (1847)

Cleopatra 69–30 BC
Egyptian monarch, Queen from 47 BC

11 I will not be triumphed over.
Livy *Ab Urbe Condita* bk. 133 (fragment 54)

Grover Cleveland 1837–1908
American Democratic statesman, 22nd and 24th President of the US 1885–9 and 1893–7

12 I have considered the pension list of the republic a roll of honour.
Veto of Dependent Pension Bill, 5 July 1888, in *A Compilation of the Messages and Papers of the Presidents* vol. 11 (1897)

13 The lessons of paternalism ought to be unlearned and the better lesson taught that, while the people should patriotically and cheerfully support their government, its functions do not include the support of the people.
inaugural address, 4 March 1893, in *New York Times* 5 March 1893

Harlan Cleveland 1918–2008
American government official

14 The revolution of rising expectations.
phrase coined, 1950; Arthur Schlesinger *A Thousand Days* (1965) ch. 16

John Cleveland 1613–58
English poet. See also **EPITAPHS** 318:8

15 Had Cain been Scot, God would have changed his doom
Nor forced him wander, but confined him home.
'The Rebel Scot' (1647)

Clarice Cliff 1899–1972
English ceramic artist

16 Women today want continual change, they will have colour and plenty of it. Colour seems to radiate happiness and the spirit of modern life and movement, and I cannot put too much of it into my designs to please women.
in 1930; Leonard Griffin *Clarice Cliff: the Art of the Bizarre* (1999)

Hillary Rodham Clinton 1947–

American lawyer and politician, wife of Bill **CLINTON**, First Lady of the US 1993–2001

1 I am not standing by my man, like Tammy Wynette. I am sitting here because I love him, I respect him, and I honour what he's been through and what we've been through together.
interview on *60 Minutes*, CBS-TV, 27 January 1992

2 I could have stayed home and baked cookies and had teas. But what I decided was to fulfil my profession, which I entered before my husband was in public life.
comment on questions raised by rival Democratic contender Edmund G. Brown Jr.; in *Albany Times-Union* 17 March 1992

3 The great story here . . . is this vast right-wing conspiracy that has been conspiring against my husband since the day he announced for president.
interview on *Today* (NBC television), 27 January 1998

4 Although we weren't able to shatter that highest, hardest glass ceiling this time, thanks to you, it has about 18 million cracks in it.
speech to her supporters, conceding the Democratic party presidential nomination to Barack **OBAMA**, 7 June 2008

William Jefferson ('Bill') Clinton 1946–

American Democratic statesman, 42nd President of the US 1993–2001; husband of Hillary Rodham **CLINTON**

5 I experimented with marijuana a time or two. And I didn't like it, and I didn't inhale.
in *Washington Post* 30 March 1992

6 The comeback kid!
description of himself after coming second in the New Hampshire primary in the 1992 presidential election (since 1952, no presidential candidate had won the election without first winning in New Hampshire)
Michael Barone and Grant Ujifusa *The Almanac of American Politics 1994*

7 I did not have sexual relations with that woman.
television interview, in *Daily Telegraph* 27 January 1998

8 It depends on what the meaning of 'is' is.
videotaped evidence to the grand jury; tapes broadcast 21 September 1998
in *Guardian* 22 September 1998

9 The American people have spoken—but it's going to take a little while to determine exactly what they said.
on the US presidential election
in *Mail on Sunday* 12 November 2000; see **SALISBURY** 678:16

Lord Clive 1725–74

British general and colonial administrator; Governor of Bengal. On Clive: see **BENTLEY** 71:15

10 By God, Mr Chairman, at this moment I stand astonished at my own moderation!
reply during Parliamentary cross-examination, 1773
G. R. Gleig *The Life of Robert, First Lord Clive* (1848) ch. 29

11 I feel that I am reserved for some end or other.
when his pistol twice failed to fire, while attempting to take his own life
G. R. Gleig *The Life of Robert, First Lord Clive* (1848) ch. 1

Arthur Hugh Clough 1819–61

English poet. On Clough: see **SWINBURNE** 786:3

12 Rome, believe me, my friend, is like its own Monte Testaceo,
Merely a marvellous mass of broken and castaway wine-pots.
Amours de Voyage (1858) canto 1, pt. 2

13 I do not like being moved: for the will is excited; and action
Is a most dangerous thing: I tremble for something factitious,
Some malpractice of heart and illegitimate process;
We are so prone to these things with our terrible notions of duty.
Amours de Voyage (1858) canto 2, pt. 11

14 Whither depart the souls of the brave that die in the battle,
Die in the lost, lost fight, for the cause that perishes with them?
Amours de Voyage (1858) canto 5, pt. 6

15 Good, too, Logic, of course; in itself, but not in fine weather.
The Bothie of Tober-na-Vuolich (1848) pt. 2, l. 249

16 Grace is given of God, but knowledge is bought in the market.
The Bothie of Tober-na-Vuolich (1848) pt. 4, l. 159

17 Afloat. We move: Delicious! Ah,
What else is like the gondola?
Dipsychus (1865) sc. 5

18 I drive through the street, and I care not a d–mn;
The people they stare, and they ask who I am;
And if I should chance to run over a cad,
I can pay for the damage if ever so bad.
Dipsychus (1865) sc. 5

19 My pleasure of thought is the pleasure of thinking
How pleasant it is to have money, heigh ho!
How pleasant it is to have money.
Dipsychus (1865) sc. 5

20 And almost every one when age,
Disease, or sorrows strike him,
Inclines to think there is a God,
Or something very like Him.
Dipsychus (1865) sc. 6

21 Thou shalt have one God only; who
Would be at the expense of two?
'The Latest Decalogue' (1862); see **BIBLE** 81:15

22 Thou shalt not kill; but need'st not strive Officiously to keep alive.
'The Latest Decalogue' (1862)

1 Do not adultery commit;
Advantage rarely comes of it.
'The Latest Decalogue' (1862)

2 Thou shalt not steal; an empty feat,
When it's so lucrative to cheat.
'The Latest Decalogue' (1862)

3 Thou shalt not covet; but tradition
Approves all forms of competition.
'The Latest Decalogue' (1862)

4 'Tis better to have fought and lost,
Than never to have fought at all.
'Peschiera' (1854); see **TENNYSON** 795:9

5 Say not the struggle naught availeth,
The labour and the wounds are vain,
The enemy faints not, nor faileth,
And as things have been, things remain.
'Say not the struggle naught availeth' (1855)

6 If hopes were dupes, fears may be liars.
'Say not the struggle naught availeth' (1855)

7 In front the sun climbs slow, how slowly,
But westward, look, the land is bright.
'Say not the struggle naught availeth' (1855)

8 What shall we do without you? Think where we
are. Carlyle has led us all out into the desert,
and he has left us there.
parting words to Ralph Waldo **EMERSON**, *15 July 1848*
E. E. Hale *James Russell Lowell and his Friends* (1889) ch. 9

Vernon Coaker 1953–

British Labour politician

9 Cameron's empty idea seems to be 'let's hug a
hoodie', whatever they have done.
*commenting on the text of a forthcoming speech by David
Cameron: see* **CAMERON** 194:12; *in Observer 9 July 2006*

Kurt Cobain 1967–94

American rock singer, guitarist, and songwriter. See also
YOUNG AND BLACKBURN 877:5

10 I'd rather be dead than cool.
'Stay Away' (1991 song)

Thomas W. Cobb fl. 1820

American politician

11 If you persist, the Union will be dissolved. You
have kindled a fire which all the waters of the
ocean cannot put out, which seas of blood can
only extinguish.
*to James Tallmadge, on his amendment to the bill to admit
Missouri to the Union as a slave state in 1820*
Robert V. Remini *Henry Clay* (1991) ch. 11

William Cobbett 1762–1835

English political reformer and radical journalist

12 From a very early age, I had imbibed the
opinion, that it was every man's duty to do all
that lay in his power to leave his country as
good as he had found it.
Political Register 22 December 1832

13 Nouns of number, or multitude, such as Mob,
Parliament, Rabble, House of Commons,
Regiment, Court of King's Bench, Den of
Thieves, and the like.
English Grammar (1817) letter 17 'Syntax as Relating to
Pronouns'

14 But what is to be the fate of the great wen of
all? The monster, called . . . 'the metropolis of
the empire'?
of London
Rural Rides: The Kentish Journal in *Cobbett's Weekly Political
Register* 5 January 1822, vol. 40

Alison Cockburn (née Rutherford) 1713–94

Scottish poet and songwriter

15 I've seen the smiling of Fortune beguiling,
I've felt all its favours and found its decay;
Sweet was its blessing, kind its caressing,
But now it is fled, fled far, far away.
'The Flowers of the Forest' (1765); see **ELLIOT** 313:13

16 O fickle Fortune, why this cruel sporting?
Why thus torment us poor sons of day?
Nae mair your smiles can cheer me, nae mair
your frowns can fear me,
For the flowers of the forest are a' wade away.
wade = weeded (*often quoted as 'For the flowers of the
forest are withered away'*)
'The Flowers of the Forest' (1765)

Bruce Cockburn 1945–

Canadian singer and songwriter

17 Got to kick at the darkness 'til it bleeds daylight.
'Lovers in a Dangerous Time' (1984 song)

Claud Cockburn 1904–81

British writer and journalist

18 Small earthquake in Chile. Not many dead.
*claimed as the winning entry for a dullest headline
competition at* The Times (*the headline in question has
never been traced, and may well be apocryphal*)
In Time of Trouble (1956) ch. 10

Jean Cocteau 1889–1963

French dramatist and film director

19 History is a combination of reality and lies. The
reality of History becomes a lie. The unreality
of the fable becomes the truth.
Journal d'un inconnu (1953) 'De la prééminence des fables'

20 Life is a horizontal fall.
Opium (1930)

21 Victor Hugo was a madman who thought he
was Victor Hugo.
Opium (1930)

22 Being tactful in audacity is knowing how far one
can go too far.
Le Rappel à l'ordre (1926) 'Le Coq et l'Arlequin'

23 If it has to choose who is to be crucified, the
crowd will always save Barabbas.
Le Rappel à l'ordre (1926) 'Le Coq et l'Arlequin'

1 My method is simple: not to bother about poetry. It must come of its own accord. Merely whispering its name drives it away.
on 26 August 1945; *Professional Secrets* (1972)

J. M. Coetzee 1940–
South African novelist

2 He thought of himself as a termite boring its way through a rock. There seemed nothing to do but live.
The Life and Times of Michael K (1983) pt. 1

George M. Cohan 1878–1942
American songwriter, dramatist, and producer

3 Over there, over there,
Send the word, send the word over there
That the Yanks are coming, the Yanks are coming,
The drums rum-tumming everywhere.
So prepare, say a prayer,
Send the word, send the word to beware.
We'll be over, we're coming over
And we won't come back till it's over, over there.
'Over There' (1917 song)

4 I'm a Yankee Doodle Dandy,
A Yankee Doodle, do or die;
A real live nephew of my Uncle Sam's,
Born on the fourth of July.
I've got a Yankee Doodle sweetheart,
She's my Yankee Doodle joy.
Yankee Doodle came to London,
Just to ride the ponies;
I am the Yankee Doodle Boy.
'Yankee Doodle Boy' (1904 song); see **SONGS, SPIRITUALS, AND SHANTIES** 763:17

5 I don't care what you say about me, as long as you say *something* about me, and as long as you spell my name right.
to a newspaperman who wanted some information about Broadway Jones in 1912
John McCabe *George M. Cohan* (1973)

Leonard Cohen 1934–
Canadian singer and writer

6 Some say that no one ever leaves Montreal, for that city, like Canada itself, is designed to preserve the past, a past that happened somewhere else.
The Favourite Game (1963) bk. 2, ch. 19

7 A woman watches her body uneasily, as though it were an unreliable ally in the battle for love.
The Favourite Game (1963) bk. 3, ch. 8

8 I don't consider myself a pessimist. I think of a pessimist as someone who is waiting for it to rain. And I feel soaked to the skin.
in *Observer* 2 May 1993 'Sayings of the Week'

Aston Cokayne 1608–84
English poet

9 Sydney, whom we yet admire
Lighting our little torches at his fire.
Funeral Elegies, no. 1 'On the Death of my very good Friend Mr Michael Drayton' (1658)

Edward Coke 1552–1634
English jurist

10 How long soever it hath continued, if it be against reason, it is of no force in law.
The First Part of the Institutes of the Laws of England (1628) bk. 1, ch. 10, sect. 80

11 Reason is the life of the law, nay the common law itself is nothing else but reason.
The First Part of the Institutes of the Laws of England (1628) bk. 2, ch. 6, sect. 138

12 Law . . . is the perfection of reason.
The First Part of the Institutes of the Laws of England (1628) bk. 2, ch. 6, sect. 138

13 The gladsome light of Jurisprudence.
The First Part of the Institutes of the Laws of England (1628) 'Epilogus', closing words

14 For a man's house is his castle, *et domus sua cuique est tutissimum refugium* [and each man's home is his safest refuge].
The Third Part of the Institutes of the Laws of England (1628) ch. 73; see **PROVERBS** 631:7

15 Six hours in sleep, in law's grave study six,
Four spend in prayer, the rest on Nature fix.
translation of a quotation from Justinian *The Pandects* (or *Digest*) bk. 2, ch. 4 'De in Jus Vocando'; see **JONES** 445:12

16 They [corporations] cannot commit treason, nor be outlawed, nor excommunicate, for they have no souls.
The Reports of Sir Edward Coke (1658) vol. 5, pt. 10 'The case of Sutton's Hospital'; see **PROVERBS** 629:21, **THURLOW** 810:14

17 Magna Charta is such a fellow, that he will have no sovereign.
on the Lords' Amendment to the Petition of Right, 17 May 1628
J. Rushworth *Historical Collections* (1659) vol. 1

Jean-Baptiste Colbert 1619–83
French statesman, chief minister to **LOUIS XIV** 1665–83

18 It is a 'beautiful maxim' that it is necessary to save five *sous* on unessential things, and to pour out millions when it is a question of your glory.
letter to Louis XIV, 1666

19 The art of taxation consists in so plucking the goose as to obtain the largest possible amount of feathers with the smallest possible amount of hissing.
attributed

Stephen Colbert 1964–
American satirist

20 Truth that comes from the gut, not books.
definition of 'truthiness'; the word was later picked by the

The Colbert Report 17 October 2005

David Coleman 1926–

British sports commentator

1 He just can't believe what isn't happening to him.

in *Guardian* 24 December 1980 'Sports Quotes of the Year'

Hartley Coleridge 1796–1849

English poet; eldest son of Samuel Taylor COLERIDGE

2 But what is Freedom? Rightly understood,
A universal licence to be good.
'Liberty' (1833)

3 She is not fair to outward view
As many maidens be;
Her loveliness I never knew
Until she smiled on me.
Oh! then I saw her eye was bright,
A well of love, a spring of light.
'She is not fair' (1833)

Mary Coleridge 1861–1907

English poet, novelist, and essayist

4 Egypt's might is tumbled down
Down a-down the deeps of thought;
Greece is fallen and Troy town,
Glorious Rome hath lost her crown,
Venice' pride is nought.

But the dreams their children dreamed
Fleeting, unsubstantial, vain
Shadowy as the shadows seemed
Airy nothing, as they deemed,
These remain.
'Egypt's might is tumbled down' (1908); see **SHAKESPEARE** 727:3

Samuel Taylor Coleridge 1772–1834

**English poet, critic, and philosopher, father of Hartley
COLERIDGE. On Coleridge: see BYRON 187:18, BYRON 190:7,
HAZLITT 386:2, HUNT 421:11, LAMB 477:8, SHELLEY 744:14**

5 O softly tread, said Christabel.
'Christabel' (1816) pt. 1, l. 164

6 Behold! her bosom and half her side—
A sight to dream of, not to tell!
'Christabel' (1816) pt. 1, l. 252

7 A little child, a limber elf,
Singing, dancing to itself,
A fairy thing with red round cheeks,
That always finds, and never seeks,
Makes such a vision to the sight
As fills a father's eyes with light.
'Christabel' (1816) pt. 2, conclusion, l. 656

8 I see them all so excellently fair,
I see, not feel, how beautiful they are!
'Dejection: an Ode' (1802) st. 2

9 O Lady! we receive but what we give,
And in our life alone does Nature live.
'Dejection: an Ode' (1802) st. 4

10 For hope grew round me, like the twining vine,
And fruits, and foliage, not my own, seemed mine.
'Dejection: an Ode' (1802) st. 6

11 But oh! each visitation
Suspends what nature gave me at my birth,
My shaping spirit of imagination.
'Dejection: an Ode' (1802) st. 6; see **COLERIDGE** 241:20

12 And the Devil did grin, for his darling sin
Is pride that apes humility.
'The Devil's Thoughts' (1799)

13 And what if all animated nature
Be but organic harps diversely framed,
That tremble into thought, as o'er them sweeps,
Plastic and vast, one intellectual breeze,
At once the soul of each, and god of all?
'The Eolian Harp' (1796) l. 44

14 What is an Epigram? a dwarfish whole,
Its body brevity, and wit its soul.
'Epigram' (1809)

15 O, lift one thought in prayer for S. T. C.;
That he who many a year with toil of breath
Found death in life, may here find life in death.
'Epitaph for Himself' (1834)

16 Forth from his dark and lonely hiding-place
(Portentous sight!) the owlet Atheism,
Sailing on obscene wings athwart the noon,
Drops his blue-fringèd lids, and holds them close,
And hooting at the glorious sun in Heaven,
Cries out, 'Where is it?'
'Fears in Solitude' (1798)

17 The frost performs its secret ministry,
Unhelped by any wind.
'Frost at Midnight' (1798) l. 1

18 Sea, and hill, and wood,
With all the numberless goings-on of life,
Inaudible as dreams!
'Frost at Midnight' (1798) l. 11

19 The thin blue flame
Lies on my low-burnt fire, and quivers not;
Only that film, which fluttered on the grate,
Still flutters there, the sole unquiet thing
'Frost at Midnight' (1798) l. 13

20 For I was reared
In the great city, pent 'mid cloisters dim,
And saw nought love but the sky and stars.
But *thou*, my babe! shalt wander like a breeze
By lakes and sandy shores, beneath the crags
Of ancient mountain, and beneath the clouds,
Which image in their bulk both lakes and shores
And mountain crags.
'Frost at Midnight' (1798) l. 51

21 Therefore all seasons shall be sweet to thee.
'Frost at Midnight' (1798) l. 65

1   Whether the eave-drops fall
Heard only in the trances of the blast,
Or if the secret ministry of frost
Shall hang them up in silent icicles,
Quietly shining to the quiet moon.
    'Frost at Midnight' (1798) l. 70

2 O struggling with the darkness all the night,
And visited all night by troops of stars.
    'Hymn before Sunrise, in the Vale of Chamouni' (1809) l. 30

3 On awaking he . . . instantly and eagerly wrote
down the lines that are here preserved. At this
moment he was unfortunately called out by a
person on business from Porlock.
    'Kubla Khan' (1816) preliminary note; see **SMITH** 757:21

4 In Xanadu did Kubla Khan
A stately pleasure-dome decree:
Where Alph, the sacred river, ran
Through caverns measureless to man
Down to a sunless sea.
So twice five miles of fertile ground
With walls and towers were girdled round.
    'Kubla Khan' (1816)

5 A savage place! as holy and enchanted
As e'er beneath a waning moon was haunted
By woman wailing for her demon-lover!
And from this chasm, with ceaseless turmoil
    seething,
As if this earth in fast thick pants were
    breathing,
A mighty fountain momently was forced.
    'Kubla Khan' (1816)

6 It was a miracle of rare device,
A sunny pleasure-dome with caves of ice.
    'Kubla Khan' (1816)

7 And 'mid this tumult Kubla heard from far
Ancestral voices prophesying war!
    'Kubla Khan' (1816)

8 A damsel with a dulcimer
In a vision once I saw:
It was an Abyssinian maid,
And on her dulcimer she played,
Singing of Mount Abora.
    'Kubla Khan' (1816)

9 And all who heard should see them there,
And all should cry, Beware! Beware!
His flashing eyes, his floating hair!
Weave a circle round him thrice,
And close your eyes with holy dread,
For he on honey-dew hath fed,
And drunk the milk of Paradise.
    'Kubla Khan' (1816)

10 All thoughts, all passions, all delights,
Whatever stirs this mortal frame,
All are but ministers of Love,
And feed his sacred flame.
    'Love' (1800)

11 With Donne, whose muse on dromedary trots,
Wreathe iron pokers into true-love knots.
Rhyme's sturdy cripple, fancy's maze and clue,

Wit's forge and fire-blast, meaning's press and
    screw.
    'On Donne's Poetry' (1818)

12 It is an ancient Mariner,
And he stoppeth one of three.
'By thy long grey beard and glittering eye,
Now wherefore stopp'st thou me?'
    'The Rime of the Ancient Mariner' (1798) pt. 1

13 He holds him with his glittering eye—
The Wedding-Guest stood still.
    'The Rime of the Ancient Mariner' (1798) pt. 1

14 The Wedding-Guest sat on a stone:
He cannot choose but hear.
    'The Rime of the Ancient Mariner' (1798) pt. 1

15 The Wedding-Guest here beat his breast,
For he heard the loud bassoon.
    'The Rime of the Ancient Mariner' (1798) pt. 1

16 And ice, mast-high, came floating by,
As green as emerald.
    'The Rime of the Ancient Mariner' (1798) pt. 1

17 'God save thee, ancient Mariner!
From the fiends that plague thee thus!—
Why look'st thou so?'—With my cross-bow
I shot the Albatross.
    'The Rime of the Ancient Mariner' (1798) pt. 1

18 Nor dim nor red, like God's own head,
The glorious Sun uprist.
    'The Rime of the Ancient Mariner' (1798) pt. 2

19 We were the first that ever burst
Into that silent sea.
    'The Rime of the Ancient Mariner' (1798) pt. 2

20 As idle as a painted ship
Upon a painted ocean.
    'The Rime of the Ancient Mariner' (1798) pt. 2

21 Water, water, everywhere,
And all the boards did shrink;
Water, water, everywhere,
Nor any drop to drink.

The very deep did rot: O Christ!
That ever this should be!
Yes, slimy things did crawl with legs
Upon the slimy sea.
    'The Rime of the Ancient Mariner' (1798) pt. 2

22 *Her* lips were red, *her* looks were free,
Her locks were yellow as gold:
Her skin was white as leprosy,
The Night-mare LIFE-IN-DEATH was she,
Who thicks man's blood with cold.
    'The Rime of the Ancient Mariner' (1798) pt. 3

23 The Sun's rim dips; the stars rush out;
At one stride comes the dark.
    'The Rime of the Ancient Mariner' (1798) pt. 3

24 The hornèd Moon, with one bright star
Within the nether tip.
    'The Rime of the Ancient Mariner' (1798) pt. 3; see
    WORDSWORTH 864:20

25 I fear thee, ancient Mariner!
I fear thy skinny hand!

And thou art long, and lank, and brown,
As is the ribbed sea-sand.
'The Rime of the Ancient Mariner' (1798) pt. 4

1 Alone, alone, all, all alone,
Alone on a wide wide sea!
And never a saint took pity on
My soul in agony.
'The Rime of the Ancient Mariner' (1798) pt. 4

2 And a thousand thousand slimy things
Lived on; and so did I.
'The Rime of the Ancient Mariner' (1798) pt. 4

3 A spring of love gushed from my heart,
And I blessed them unaware.
'The Rime of the Ancient Mariner' (1798) pt. 4

4 Oh Sleep! it is a gentle thing,
Beloved from pole to pole.
To Mary Queen the praise be given!
She sent the gentle sleep from Heaven,
That slid into my soul.
'The Rime of the Ancient Mariner' (1798) pt. 5

5 We were a ghastly crew.
'The Rime of the Ancient Mariner' (1798) pt. 5

6 It ceased; yet still the sails made on
A pleasant noise till noon,
A noise like of a hidden brook
In the leafy month of June,
That to the sleeping woods all night
Singeth a quiet tune.
'The Rime of the Ancient Mariner' (1798) pt. 5

7 Like one, that on a lonesome road
Doth walk in fear and dread,
And having once turned round walks on,
And turns no more his head;
Because he knows, a frightful fiend
Doth close behind him tread.
'The Rime of the Ancient Mariner' (1798) pt. 6; see **BLAIR** 123:15

8 No voice; but oh! the silence sank
Like music on my heart.
'The Rime of the Ancient Mariner' (1798) pt. 6

9 I pass, like night, from land to land;
I have strange power of speech.
'The Rime of the Ancient Mariner' (1798) pt. 7

10 He prayeth well, who loveth well
Both man and bird and beast.

He prayeth best, who loveth best
All things both great and small.
'The Rime of the Ancient Mariner' (1798) pt. 7

11 He went like one that hath been stunned,
And is of sense forlorn:
A sadder and a wiser man,
He rose the morrow morn.
'The Rime of the Ancient Mariner' (1798) pt. 7

12 So for the mother's sake the child was dear,
And dearer was the mother for the child.
'Sonnet to a Friend Who Asked How I Felt When the Nurse First Presented My Infant to Me' (1797)

13 Well, they are gone, and here must I remain,
This lime-tree bower my prison!
'This Lime-Tree Bower my Prison' (1800) l. 1

14   A charm
For thee, my gentle-hearted Charles, to whom
No sound is dissonant which tells of life.
of Charles **LAMB**
'This Lime-Tree Bower my Prison' (1800) l. 74

15 Work without hope draws nectar in a sieve,
And hope without an object cannot live.
'Work without Hope' (1828)

16 He who begins by loving Christianity better than
Truth will proceed by loving his own sect or
church better than Christianity, and end by
loving himself better than all.
Aids to Reflection (1825) 'Moral and Religious Aphorisms' no. 25

17 Evidences of Christianity! I am weary of the
word. Make a man feel the want of it; rouse
him, if you can, to the self-knowledge of his
need of it; and you may safely trust it to his
own Evidence.
Aids to Reflection (1825) 'Conclusion'

18 If a man could pass through Paradise in a
dream, and have a flower presented to him as a
pledge that his soul had really been there, and if
he found the flower in his hand when he
awoke—Aye! and what then?
Anima Poetae (E. H. Coleridge ed., 1895)

19 Until you understand a writer's ignorance,
presume yourself ignorant of his understanding.
Biographia Literaria (1817) ch. 12

20 The primary imagination I hold to be the living
Power and prime Agent of all human
Perception, and as a repetition in the finite mind
of the eternal act of creation in the infinite I AM.
Biographia Literaria (1817) ch. 13

21 That willing suspension of disbelief for the
moment, which constitutes poetic faith.
Biographia Literaria (1817) ch. 14

22 Our *myriad-minded* Shakespeare.
Footnote. *Anēr myrionous*, a phrase which I have
borrowed from a Greek monk, who applies it to
a Patriarch of Constantinople.
Biographia Literaria (1817) ch. 15

23 The dwarf sees farther than the giant, when he
has the giant's shoulder to mount on.
The Friend (1818) vol. 2 'On the Principles of Political
Knowledge'; see **BERNARD** 73:17, **NEWTON** 574:7

24 Iago's soliloquy— the motive-hunting of
motiveless malignity.
The Literary Remains of Samuel Taylor Coleridge (1836) bk. 2
'Notes on the Tragedies of Shakespeare: Othello'

25 State policy, a cyclops with one eye, and that in
the back of the head!
On the Constitution of the Church and State (1839)

26 Reviewers are usually people who would have
been poets, historians, biographers, &c., if they
could; they have tried their talents at one or at
the other, and have failed; therefore they turn
critics.
Seven Lectures on Shakespeare and Milton (delivered 1811–12,
published 1856) Lecture 1; see **DISRAELI** 286:5

1 You abuse snuff! Perhaps it is the final cause of the human nose.
   Table Talk (1835) 4 January 1823

2 To see him act, is like reading Shakespeare by flashes of lightning.
   of Edmund Kean
   Table Talk (1835) 27 April 1823

3 Prose = words in their best order;—poetry = the *best* words in the best order.
   Table Talk (1835) 12 July 1827

4 The man's desire is for the woman; but the woman's desire is rarely other than for the desire of the man.
   Table Talk (1835) 23 July 1827

5 Poetry is certainly something more than good sense, but it must be good sense at all events; just as a palace is more than a house, but it must be a house, at least.
   Table Talk (1835) 9 May 1830

6 Swift was *anima Rabelaisii habitans in sicco*—the soul of Rabelais dwelling in a dry place.
   Table Talk (1835) 15 June 1830

7 In politics, what begins in fear usually ends in folly.
   Table Talk (1835) 5 October 1830

8 If men could learn from history, what lessons it might teach us! But passion and party blind our eyes, and the light which experience gives is a lantern on the stern, which shines only on the waves behind us!
   Table Talk (1835) 18 December 1831

9 That passage is what I call the sublime dashed to pieces by cutting too close with the fiery four-in-hand round the corner of nonsense.
   on lines excluded from his own poem Limbo, *written 1817*
   Table Talk (1835) 20 January 1834

10 Shakespeare . . . is of no age—nor of any religion, or party or profession. The body and substance of his works came out of the unfathomable depths of his own oceanic mind.
   Table Talk (1835) 15 March 1834

11 Bygone images and scenes of early life have stolen into my mind, like breezes blown from the spice-islands of Youth and Hope—those twin realities of this phantom world!
   Table Talk (1835) 10 July 1834

12 Summer has set in with its usual severity.
   Alfred Ainger (ed.) *Letters of Charles Lamb* (1888) vol. 2, letter to Vincent Novello, 9 May 1826

Colette (Sidonie-Gabrielle Colette) 1873–1954
French novelist

13 The world of the emotions that are so lightly called physical.
   Le Blé en herbe (1923)

14 Her childhood, then her adolescence, had taught her patience, hope, silence and the easy

manipulation of the weapons and virtues of all prisoners.
   Chéri (1920) pt. 2 (translated by Janet Flanner, 1930)

15 Let's buy a pack of cards, good wine, bridge scores, knitting needles, all the paraphernalia needed to fill an enormous void, everything needed to hide that horror—the old woman.
   Chéri (1920) pt. 2 (translated by Janet Flanner, 1930)

16 Free women are not women at all.
   Claudine in Paris (1901)

17 If we want to be sincere, we must admit that there is a well-nourished love and an ill-nourished love. And the rest is literature.
   The Last of Chéri (1926) (translated by Viola Gerard Garvin)

18 It is wise to apply the oil of refined politeness to the mechanism of friendship.
   The Pure and the Impure (1932) ch. 9

19 You will do foolish things, but do them with enthusiasm.
   advice to her daughter
   attributed in *New York Times* 26 November 1977

Mary Collier c.1690–c.1762
English washerwoman and poet

20 Though we all day with care our work attend,
   Such is our fate, we know not when 'twill end.
   When evening's come, you homeward take your way;
   We, till our work is done, are forced to stay.
   The Woman's Labour (1739)

21 So the industrious bees do hourly strive
   To bring their loads of honey to the hive;
   Their sordid owners always reap the gains,
   And poorly recompense their toils and pains.
   The Woman's Labour (1739)

22 The greatest heroes that the world can know,
   To *women* their original must owe.
   'The Three Wise Sentences, from the First Book of Esdras' (1740) l. 132

William Collingbourne d. 1484
English landowner; conspirator against Richard III

23 The Cat, the Rat, and Lovell our dog
   Rule all England under a hog.
   referring to Sir William Catesby (d. 1485), Sir Richard Ratcliffe (d. 1485), Lord Lovell (1454–c.1487), whose crest was a dog, and King Richard III, whose emblem was a wild boar
   Robert Fabyan *The Concordance of Chronicles* (ed. H. Ellis, 1811)

Lord Collingwood 1748–1810
English admiral

24 Now, gentlemen, let us do something today which the world may talk of hereafter.
   before the Battle of Trafalgar, 21 October 1805
   G. L. Newnham Collingwood (ed.) *A Selection from the Correspondence of Lord Collingwood* (1828) vol. 1

R. G. Collingwood 1889–1943

English philosopher and archaeologist

1 Perfect freedom is reserved for the man who lives by his own work and in that work does what he wants to do.

Speculum Mentis (1924); see **GILL** 358:16

Charles Collins

English songwriter

2 Any old iron, any old iron,
Any any old old iron?
You look neat
Talk about a treat,
You look dapper from your napper to your feet.
Dressed in style, brand new tile,
And your father's old green tie on,
But I wouldn't give you tuppence for your old watch chain;
Old iron, old iron?

'Any Old Iron' (1911 song, with E. A. Sheppard and Fred Terry); the second line often sung 'Any any any old iron?'

3 My old man said, 'Follow the van,
Don't dilly-dally on the way!'
Off went the cart with the home packed in it,
I walked behind with my old cock linnet.
But I dillied and dallied, dallied and dillied,
Lost the van and don't know where to roam.
You can't trust the 'specials' like the old time 'coppers'
When you can't find your way home.

'Don't Dilly-Dally on the Way' (1919 song, with Fred Leigh); popularized by Marie Lloyd

Michael Collins 1890–1922

Irish revolutionary

4 That volley which we have just heard is the only speech which it is proper to make over the grave of a dead Fenian.

at the funeral of Thomas Ashe, who had died in prison while on hunger strike

Glasnevin cemetery, 30th September 1917

5 Think—what I have got for Ireland? Something which she has wanted these past seven hundred years. Will anyone be satisfied at the bargain? Will anyone? I tell you this—early this morning I signed my death warrant. I thought at the time how odd, how ridiculous—a bullet may just as well have done the job five years ago.

on signing the treaty establishing the Irish Free State; he was shot from ambush in the following year

letter, 6 December 1921, in T. R. Dwyer *Michael Collins and the Treaty* (1981) ch. 4

6 We've been waiting seven hundred years, you can have the seven minutes.

arriving at Dublin Castle for the handover by British forces on 16 January 1922, and being told that he was seven minutes late

Tim Pat Coogan *Michael Collins* (1990); attributed

7 My own fellow-countymen won't kill me.

before leaving for Cork where he was ambushed and killed, 20 August 1922

James Mackay *Michael Collins* (1996)

Tim Collins 1960–

British soldier

8 I expect you to rock their world. Wipe them out if that is what they choose. But if you are ferocious in battle remember to be magnanimous in victory.

speech to the men under his command on arrival in Iraq, 20 March 2003

Wilkie Collins 1824–89

English novelist

9 Women can resist a man's love, a man's fame, a man's personal appearance, and a man's money, but they cannot resist a man's tongue when he knows how to talk to them.

The Woman in White (1860) 'The Second Epoch' pt. 5

William Collins 1721–59

English poet

10 To fair Fidele's grassy tomb
Soft maids and village hinds shall bring
Each opening sweet of earliest bloom,
And rifle all the breathing spring.

'Dirge' (1744); occasionally included in 18th-century performances of Shakespeare's *Cymbeline*

11 Now air is hushed, save where the weak-eyed bat,
With short shrill shriek flits by on leathern wing,
Or where the beetle winds
His small but sullen horn,
As oft he rises 'midst the twilight path,
Against the pilgrim borne in heedless hum.

'Ode to Evening' (1747)

12 How sleep the brave, who sink to rest,
By all their country's wishes blest!

'Ode Written in the Year 1746' (1748)

13 By fairy hands their knell is rung,
By forms unseen their dirge is sung.

'Ode Written in the Year 1746' (1748)

14 With eyes up-raised, as one inspired,
Pale Melancholy sate retired,
And from her wild sequestered seat,
In notes by distance made more sweet,
Poured thro' the mellow horn her pensive soul.

'The Passions, an Ode for Music' (1747)

15 Love of peace, and lonely musing,
In hollow murmurs died away.

'The Passions, an Ode for Music' (1747)

16 Too nicely Jonson knew the critic's part,
Nature in him was almost lost in Art.

'Verses addressed to Sir Thomas Hanmer' (1743)

George Colman, the Elder 1732–94 *and* David Garrick 1717–79

English dramatists

1 Love and a cottage! Eh, Fanny! Ah, give me indifference and a coach and six!
The Clandestine Marriage (1766) act 1; see **KEATS** 455:12

George Colman, the Younger

1762–1836

English dramatist

2 Oh, London is a fine town,
A very famous city,
Where all the streets are paved with gold,
And all the maidens pretty.
The Heir at Law (performed 1797, published 1808) act 1, sc. 2

3 Says he, 'I am a handsome man, but I'm a gay deceiver.'
Love Laughs at Locksmiths (1808) act 2; see **PROVERBS** 638:7

4 My father was an eminent button maker . . . but I had a soul above buttons . . . I panted for a liberal profession.
New Hay at the Old Market (1795) sc. 1

5 Johnson's style was grand and Gibbon's elegant; the stateliness of the former was sometimes pedantic, and the polish of the latter was occasionally finical. Johnson marched to kettle-drums and trumpets; Gibbon moved to flute and hautboys: Johnson hewed passages through the Alps, while Gibbon levelled walks through parks and gardens.
Random Records (1830) vol. 1

6 As the lone Angler, patient man,
At Mewry-Water, or the Banne,
Leaves off, against his placid wish,
Impaling worms to torture fish.
The Lady of the Wreck (1813) canto 2, st. 18

7 And, on the label of the stuff,
He wrote this verse;
Which one would think was clear enough,
And terse:—
When taken,
To be well shaken.
'The Newcastle Apothecary' (1797)

John Robert Colombo 1936–

Canadian writer

8 Canada could have enjoyed:
English government,
French culture,
and American know-how.

Instead it ended up with:
English know-how,
French government,
and American culture.
'O Canada' (1965)

Charles Caleb Colton c.1780–1832

English clergyman and writer

9 When you have nothing to say, say nothing.
Lacon (1820) vol. 1, no. 183

10 Examinations are formidable even to the best prepared, for the greatest fool may ask more than the wisest man can answer.
Lacon (1820) vol. 1, no. 322

11 If you would be known, and not know, vegetate in a village; if you would know, and not be known, live in a city.
Lacon (1820) vol. 1, no. 334

12 Man is an embodied paradox, a bundle of contradictions.
Lacon (1820) vol. 1, no. 408

St Colum Cille ?521–597

Irish cleric and missionary, founder of Iona

13 To every cow her calf, to every book its copy.
traditionally attributed

Christopher Columbus 1451–1506

Italian-born Spanish explorer

14 To speak, in conclusion, only of what has been done during this hurried voyage, their Highnesses will see that I can give them as much gold as they desire, if they will give me a little assistance
letter to Luis De Sant' Angel, 15 February 1493, referrring to Ferdinand and Isabella of Spain

Betty Comden 1919–2006 *and* Adolph Green 1915–2002

15 New York, New York,—a helluva town.
New York, New York (1945 song)

16 The party's over, it's time to call it a day.
'The Party's Over' (1956); see **CROSLAND** 261:6

Henry Steele Commager 1902–98

American historian

17 It was observed half a century ago that what is a stone wall to a layman, to a corporate lawyer is a triumphant arch. Much the same might be said of civil rights and freedoms. To the layman the Bill of Rights seems to be a stone wall against the misuse of power. But in the hands of a congressional committee, or often enough of a judge, it turns out to be so full of exceptions and qualifications that it might be a whole series of arches.
'The Right to Dissent' in *Current History* October 1955; see **DUNNE** 300:3

Denis Compton 1918–97

English cricketer

1 I couldn't bat for the length of time required to score 500. I'd get bored and fall over.

to Brian Lara, who had recently scored 501 not out, a world record in first-class cricket

in *Daily Telegraph* 27 June 1994

Ivy Compton-Burnett 1884–1969

English novelist

2 Time has too much credit . . . It is not a great healer. It is an indifferent and perfunctory one. Sometimes it does not heal at all. And sometimes when it seems to, no healing has been necessary.

Darkness and Day (1951) ch. 7; see **PROVERBS** 645:18

3 Being cruel to be kind is just ordinary cruelty with an excuse made for it . . . And it is right that it should be more resented, as it is.

Daughters and Sons (1937) ch. 6

4 Well, of course, people are only human . . . But it really does not seem much for them to be.

A Family and a Fortune (1939) ch. 2

5 There are different kinds of wrong. The people sinned against are not always the best.

The Mighty and their Fall (1961) ch. 7

6 A leopard does not change his spots, or change his feeling that spots are rather a credit.

More Women than Men (1933) ch. 4; see **PROVERBS** 637:18

7 My point is that it [wickedness] is not punished, and that is why it is natural to be guilty of it. When it is likely to be punished, most of us avoid it.

in *Orion* (1945) 'A Conversation between I. Compton-Burnett and M. Jourdain'

8 There's not much to say. I haven't been at all deedy.

on being asked about herself

in *The Times* 30 August 1969

Auguste Comte 1798–1857

French philosopher

9 M. Comte used to reproach his early English admirers with maintaining the 'conspiracy of silence' concerning his later performances.

J. S. Mill *Auguste Comte and Positivism* (1865)

Prince de Condé (the Great Condé)

1621–86

French general

10 *Silence! Voilà l'ennemi!*

Hush! Here comes the enemy!

as the Jesuit preacher Louis Bourdaloue mounted the pulpit at St Sulpice

P. M. Lauras *Bourdaloue: sa vie et ses oeuvres* (1881) vol. 2

Marquis de Condorcet 1743–94

French philosopher

11 As one meditates about the nature of the moral sciences one really cannot avoid the conclusion that since, like the physical sciences, they rest upon observation of the facts, they ought to follow the same methods, acquire a language no less exact and precise, and so attain to the same degree of certainty. If some being alien to our species were to set himself to study us he would find no difference between these two studies, and would examine human society as we do that of bees or beavers.

Discours prononcé dans l'Académie Française 21 February 1782; A. Condorcet O'Connor and M. F. Arago (eds.) *Oeuvres de Condorcet* vol. 1 (1847–9)

Confucius (K'ung Fu-tzu) 551–479 BC

Chinese philosopher, whose ideas about the importance of practical moral values, collected by his disciples in the *Analects*, formed the basis of the philosophy of Confucianism

textual translations of the Analects *are those of Wing-Tsit Chan, 1963*

12 Is it not a pleasure to learn and to repeat or practice from time to time what has been learned? Is it not delightful to have friends coming from afar? Is one not a superior man if he does not feel hurt even though he does not feel recognized?

Analects ch. 1, v. 1

13 When a man's father is alive, look at the bent of his will. When his father is dead, look at his conduct. If for three years [of mourning] he does not change from the way of his father, he may be called filial.

Analects ch. 1, v. 11

14 A ruler who governs his state by virtue is like the north polar star, which remains in its place while all the other stars revolve around it.

Analects ch. 2, v. 1

15 At fifteen my mind was set on learning. At thirty my character had been formed. At forty I had no more perplexities. At fifty I knew the Mandate of Heaven. At sixty I was at ease with whatever I heard. At seventy I could follow my heart's desire without transgressing moral principles.

Analects ch. 2, v. 4

16 A man who reviews the old so as to find out the new is qualified to teach others.

Analects ch. 2, v. 11

17 The superior man is broadminded but not partisan; the inferior man is partisan but not broadminded.

Analects ch. 2, v. 14

18 A superior man in dealing with the world is not for anything or against anything. He follows righteousness as the standard.

Analects ch. 4, v. 10

1 The Way of our Master is none other than conscientiousness and altruism.
the 'one thread' of Confucius' doctrines
   Analects ch. 4, v. 15

2 The superior man understands righteousness; the inferior man understands profit.
   Analects ch. 4, v. 16

3 Man is born with uprightness. If one loses it he will be lucky if he escapes with his life.
   Analects ch. 6, v. 17

4 The man of wisdom delights in water; the man of humanity delights in mountains. The man of wisdom is active; the man of humanity is tranquil. The man of wisdom enjoys happiness; the man of humanity enjoys long life.
   Analects ch. 6, v. 21

5 The superior man extensively studies literature and restrains himself with the rules of propriety. Thus he will not violate the Way.
   Analects ch. 6, v. 25

6 I transmit but do not create. I believe in and love the ancients.
   Analects ch. 7, v. 1

7 Set your will on the Way. Have a firm grasp on virtue. Rely on humanity. Find recreation in the arts.
   Analects ch. 7, v. 6

8 Let a man be stimulated by poetry, established by the rules of propriety, and perfected by music.
   Analects ch. 8, v. 8

9 I have never yet seen anyone whose desire to build up his moral power was as strong as sexual desire.
   Analects ch. 9, v. 17; translated by Arthur Waley

10 The commander of three armies may be taken away but the will of even a common man may not be taken away from him.
   Analects ch. 9, v. 25

11 If we are not yet able to serve man, how can we serve spiritual beings? . . . If we do not yet know about life how can we know about death?
   Analects ch. 11, v. 11

12 To go too far is the same as not to go far enough.
   Analects ch. 11, v. 15

13 No state can exist without the confidence of the people.
   Analects ch. 12, v. 7

14 If you desire what is good, the people will be good. The character of a ruler is like wind and that of the people is like grass. In whatever direction the wind blows the grass always bends.
   Analects ch. 12, v. 19

15 The way of the superior man is threefold, but I have not been able to attain it. The man of wisdom has no perplexities; the man of

humanity has no worry; the man of courage has no fear.
   Analects ch. 14, v. 30

16 It is the word altruism. Do not do to others what you do not want them to do to you.
replying to Tzu-hung's question 'Is there one word which can serve as the guiding principle for conduct throughout life?'
   Analects ch. 15, v. 23

17 It is man that can make the Way great, and not the Way that can make man great.
   Analects ch. 15, v. 28

18 In education there should be no class distinction.
   Analects ch. 15, v. 38

19 By nature men are alike. Through practice they have become far apart.
   Analects ch. 17, v. 2

20 Only the most intelligent and the most stupid do not change.
   Analects ch. 17, v. 3

21 Does Heaven say anything? The four seasons run their course and all things are produced. Does Heaven say anything?
   Analects ch. 17, v. 19

22 Women and servants are most difficult to deal with. If you are familiar with them, they cease to be humble. If you keep a distance from them, they resent it.
   Analects ch. 17, v. 25

23 Wherever you go, go with all your heart.
   Shu Jing pt. 5, bk. 9, ch. 6

William Congreve 1670–1729
English dramatist

24 It is the business of a comic poet to paint the vices and follies of human kind.
   The Double Dealer (1694) epistle dedicatory

25 Retired to their tea and scandal, according to their ancient custom.
   The Double Dealer (1694) act 1, sc. 1

26 There is nothing more unbecoming a man of quality than to laugh; Jesu, 'tis such a vulgar expression of the passion!
   The Double Dealer (1694) act 1, sc. 4; see **CATULLUS** 210:10, **CHESTERFIELD** 223:8

27 Tho' marriage makes man and wife one flesh, it leaves 'em still two fools.
   The Double Dealer (1694) act 2, sc. 3

28 See how love and murder will out.
   The Double Dealer (1694) act 4, sc. 6; see **PROVERBS** 639:20

29 No mask like open truth to cover lies,
As to go naked is the best disguise.
   The Double Dealer (1694) act 5, sc. 6

30 I am always of the opinion with the learned, if they speak first.
   Incognita (1692)

1 Has he not a rogue's face? . . . a hanging-look to me . . . has a damned Tyburn-face, without the benefit o' the Clergy.

Love for Love (1695) act 2, sc. 7

2 I came upstairs into the world; for I was born in a cellar.

Love for Love (1695) act 2, sc. 7

3 I know that's a secret, for it's whispered every where.

Love for Love (1695) act 3, sc. 3

4 He that first cries out stop thief, is often he that has stolen the treasure.

Love for Love (1695) act 3, sc. 14

5 Women are like tricks by sleight of hand,
Which, to admire, we should not understand.

Love for Love (1695) act 4, sc. 21

6 A branch of one of your antediluvian families, fellows that the flood could not wash away.

Love for Love (1695) act 5, sc. 2

7 Aye, 'tis well enough for a servant to be bred at an University. But the education is a little too pedantic for a gentleman.

Love for Love (1695) act 5, sc. 3

8 Music has charms to sooth a savage breast.

The Mourning Bride (1697) act 1, sc. 1

9 Heaven has no rage, like love to hatred turned,
Nor Hell a fury, like a woman scorned.

The Mourning Bride (1697) act 3, sc. 8; see **PROVERBS** 634:31

10 In my conscience I believe the baggage loves me, for she never speaks well of me herself, nor suffers any body else to rail at me.

The Old Bachelor (1693) act 1, sc. 1

11 Man was by Nature Woman's cully made:
We never are, but by ourselves, betrayed.

The Old Bachelor (1693) act 3, sc. 1

12 Bilbo's the word, and slaughter will ensue.

The Old Bachelor (1693) act 3, sc. 7

13 If this be not love, it is madness, and then it is pardonable.

The Old Bachelor (1693) act 3, sc. 10

14 There is in true beauty, as in courage, somewhat which narrow souls cannot dare to admire.

The Old Bachelor (1693) act 4, sc. 3

15 Eternity was in that moment.

The Old Bachelor (1693) act 4, sc. 7

16 SHARPER: Thus grief still treads upon the heels of pleasure:
Married in haste, we may repent at leisure.
SETTER: Some by experience find those words mis-placed:
At leisure married, they repent in haste.

The Old Bachelor (1693) act 5, sc. 1; see **BYRON** 189:17, **PROVERBS** 638:33

17 Courtship to marriage, as a very witty prologue to a very dull play.

The Old Bachelor (1693) act 5, sc. 10

18 They come together like the Coroner's Inquest, to sit upon the murdered reputations of the week.

The Way of the World (1700) act 1, sc. 1

19 I always take blushing either for a sign of guilt, or of ill breeding.

The Way of the World (1700) act 1, sc. 9

20 Say what you will, 'tis better to be left than never to have been loved.

The Way of the World (1700) act 2, sc. 1; see **PROVERBS** 645:23, **TENNYSON** 795:9

21 Here she comes i' faith full sail, with her fan spread and streamers out, and a shoal of fools for tenders.

The Way of the World (1700) act 2, sc. 4

22 WITWOUD: Madam, do you pin up your hair with all your letters?
MILLAMANT: Only with those in verse, Mr Witwoud. I never pin up my hair with prose.

The Way of the World (1700) act 2, sc. 4

23 Beauty is the lover's gift.

The Way of the World (1700) act 2, sc. 4

24 A little disdain is not amiss; a little scorn is alluring.

The Way of the World (1700) act 3, sc. 5

25 O, nothing is more alluring than a levee from a couch in some confusion.

The Way of the World (1700) act 4, sc. 1

26 Don't let us be familiar or fond, nor kiss before folks, like my Lady Fadler and Sir Francis: nor go to Hyde-Park together the first Sunday in a new chariot, to provoke eyes and whispers, and then never be seen there together again; as if we were proud of one another the first week, and ashamed of one another ever after . . . Let us be very strange and well-bred: Let us be as strange as if we had been married a great while, and as well-bred as if we were not married at all.

The Way of the World (1700) act 4, sc. 5

27 These articles subscribed, if I continue to endure you a little longer, I may by degrees dwindle into a wife.

The Way of the World (1700) act 4, sc. 5

28 I hope you do not think me prone to any iteration of nuptials.

The Way of the World (1700) act 4, sc. 12

29 Careless she is with artful care,
Affecting to seem unaffected.

'Amoret'

30 Music alone with sudden charms can bind
The wand'ring sense, and calm the troubled mind.

'Hymn to Harmony'

31 Would I were free from this restraint,
Or else had hopes to win her;
Would she could make of me a saint,
Or I of her a sinner.

'Pious Selinda Goes to Prayers' (song)

1 I confess freely to you, I could never look long upon a monkey, without very mortifying reflections.
letter to John Dennis, 10 July 1695

Gerry Conlon 1954–

Northern Irish member of the Guildford Four, the first to be released from prison

2 The life sentence goes on. It's like a runaway train that you can't just get off.
of life after his conviction was quashed by the Court of Appeal
in Irish Post 13 September 1997

James M. Connell 1852–1929

Irish socialist songwriter

3 The people's flag is deepest red;
It shrouded oft our martyred dead.
'The Red Flag' (1889) in H. E. Piggott *Songs that made History* (1937) ch. 6

4 Then raise the scarlet standard high!
Within its shade we'll live or die.
Tho' cowards flinch and traitors sneer,
We'll keep the red flag flying here.
'The Red Flag' (1889) in H. E. Piggott *Songs that made History* (1937) ch. 6

Billy Connolly 1942–

Scottish comedian

5 Marriage is a wonderful invention; but, then again, so is a bicycle repair kit.
Duncan Campbell *Billy Connolly* (1976)

6 I don't want a Stormont. I don't want a wee pretendy government in Edinburgh.
on the prospective Scottish Parliament; often quoted as 'a wee pretendy Parliament'
interview on *Breakfast with Frost* (BBC TV), 9 February 1997

Cyril Connolly 1903–74

English writer

7 Whom the gods wish to destroy they first call promising.
Enemies of Promise (1938) ch. 13; see **PROVERBS** 647:18

8 There is no more sombre enemy of good art than the pram in the hall.
Enemies of Promise (1938) ch. 14

9 The Mandarin style . . . is beloved by literary pundits, by those who would make the written word as unlike as possible to the spoken one. It is the style of those writers whose tendency is to make their language convey more than they mean or more than they feel, it is the style of most artists and all humbugs.
Enemies of Promise (1938) ch. 20

10 Imprisoned in every fat man a thin one is wildly signalling to be let out.
The Unquiet Grave (1944) pt. 2; see **ORWELL** 586:21

11 Our memories are card-indexes consulted, and then put back in disorder by authorities whom we do not control.
The Unquiet Grave (1944) pt. 3

12 Perfect fear casteth out love.
remark to Philip Toynbee during the Blitz
in *Observer* 1 December 1974; obituary notice by Toynbee; see **BIBLE** 117:19

13 It is closing time in the gardens of the West and from now on an artist will be judged only by the resonance of his solitude or the quality of his despair.
in *Horizon* December 1949–January 1950

James Connolly 1868–1916

Irish labour leader and nationalist; executed after the Easter Rising, 1916

14 The worker is the slave of capitalist society, the female worker is the slave of that slave.
The Re-conquest of Ireland (1915)

15 The time for Ireland's battle is NOW, the place for Ireland's battle is HERE.
in *The Workers' Republic* 22 January 1916

Jimmy Connors 1952–

American tennis player

16 New Yorkers love it when you spill your guts out there. Spill your guts at Wimbledon and they make you stop and clean it up.
at Flushing Meadow
in *Guardian* 24 December 1984 'Sports Quotes of the Year'

Joseph Conrad (Teodor Josef Konrad Korzeniowski) 1857–1924

Polish-born English novelist. See also SPENSER 767:10

17 As I waited I thought that there's nothing like a confession to make one look mad; and that of all confessions a written one is the most detrimental all round. Never confess! Never, never!
Chance (1913) ch. 7

18 The opening was barred by a black bank of clouds, and the tranquil waterway leading to the uttermost ends of the earth flowed sombre under an overcast sky—seemed to lead into the heart of an immense darkness.
Heart of Darkness (1902) ch. 1, opening words

19 The conquest of the earth, which mostly means the taking it away from those who have a different complexion or slightly flatter noses than ourselves, is not a pretty thing when you look into it.
Heart of Darkness (1902) ch. 1

20 We live, as we dream—alone.
Heart of Darkness (1902) ch. 1

21 Exterminate all the brutes!
Heart of Darkness (1902) ch. 2

1 The horror! The horror!
Heart of Darkness (1902) ch. 3

2 Mistah Kurtz—he dead.
Heart of Darkness (1902) ch. 3

3 A man that is born falls into a dream like a man who falls into the sea. If he tries to climb out into the air as inexperienced people endeavour to do, he drowns.
Lord Jim (1900) ch. 20

4 To the destructive element submit yourself, and with the exertions of your hands and feet in the water make the deep, deep sea keep you up.
Lord Jim (1900) ch. 20

5 My task which I am trying to achieve is by the power of the written word, to make you hear, to make you feel—it is, before all, to make you *see*. That—and no more, and it is everything.
The Nigger of the Narcissus (1897) preface

6 Action is consolatory. It is the enemy of thought and the friend of flattering illusions.
Nostromo (1904) pt. 1, ch. 6

7 It's only those who do nothing that make no mistakes, I suppose.
Outcast of the Islands (1896) pt. 3, ch. 2

8 The terrorist and the policeman both come from the same basket.
The Secret Agent (1907) ch. 4

9 Only in men's imagination does every truth find an effective and undeniable existence. Imagination, not invention, is the supreme master of art, as of life.
Some Reminiscences (1912) ch. 1

10 The scrupulous and the just, the noble, humane, and devoted natures; the unselfish and the intelligent may begin a movement—but it passes away from them. They are not the leaders of a revolution. They are its victims.
Under Western Eyes (1911) pt. 2, ch. 3

11 A belief in a supernatural source of evil is not necessary; men alone are quite capable of every wickedness.
Under Western Eyes (1911) pt. 2, ch. 4

12 I remember my youth and the feeling that will never come back any more—the feeling that I could last for ever, outlast the sea, the earth, and all men; the deceitful feeling that lures us on to joys, to perils, to love, to vain effort—to death; the triumphant conviction of strength, the heat of life in the handful of dust, the glow in the heart that with every year grows dim, grows cold, grows small, and expires—and expires, too soon, too soon—before life itself.
Youth (1902); see **ELIOT** 311:3

13 For me, writing—*the only possible writing*—is just simply the conversion of nervous force into phrases.
letter, October 1903

Shirley Conran 1932–
English writer

14 Life is too short to stuff a mushroom.
Superwoman (1975)

Henry Constable 1562–1613
English poet

15 I did not know that thou wert dead before;
I did not feel the grief I did sustain;
The greater stroke astonisheth the more;
Astonishment takes from us sense of pain.
I stood amazed when others' tears begun,
And now begin to weep when they have done.
'To Sir Philip Sidney's Soul' (1595)

John Constable 1776–1837
English painter, many of whose best-known paintings were inspired by the landscape of his native Suffolk

16 I am just returned . . . with a deep conviction of Sir Joshua Reynolds' observation that there is no easy way of becoming a good painter. It can only be obtained by long contemplation and incessant labour.
letter to John Dunthorne, 29 May 1802; R. G. W. Clive *John Constable* (1903); see **REYNOLDS** 659:9

17 The sound of water escaping from mill-dams, etc., willows, old rotten planks, slimy posts, and brickwork . . . those scenes made me a painter and I am grateful.
letter to John Fisher, 23 October 1821, in C. R. Leslie *Memoirs of the Life of John Constable* (1843) ch. 5

18 A gentleman's park—is my aversion. It is not beauty because it is not nature.
of Fonthill
letter to John Fisher, 7 October 1822, in *Correspondence* (1968) vol. 6

19 In Claude's landscape all is lovely—all amiable—all is amenity and repose;—the calm sunshine of the heart.
lecture, 2 June 1836, in C. R. Leslie *Memoirs of the Life of John Constable* (1843) ch. 18

20 There is nothing ugly; *I never saw an ugly thing in my life*: for let the form of an object be what it may,—light, shade, and perspective will always make it beautiful.
C. R. Leslie *Memoirs of the Life of John Constable* (1843) ch. 17

Benjamin Constant (Henri Benjamin Constant de Rebecque) 1767–1834
French novelist, political philosopher, and politician

21 Art for art's sake, with no purpose, for any purpose perverts art. But art achieves a purpose which is not its own.
describing a conversation with Crabb Robinson about the latter's work on **KANT'S** *aesthetics*
Journal intime 11 February 1804, in *Revue Internationale* 10 January 1887; see **COUSIN** 253:6

Constantine the Great c.AD 288–337

Roman emperor from AD 306

1 *In hoc signo vinces.*

In this sign shalt thou conquer.

traditional form of Constantine's vision (AD 312), reported in Greek as 'By this, conquer', in Eusebius *Life of Constantine* bk. 1, ch. 28

Constitution of the United States

1787

the first ten amendments are known as the Bill of Rights

2 Representatives and direct taxes shall be apportioned among the several States which may be included within this Union, according to their respective numbers, which shall be determined by adding to the whole number of free persons, including those bound to service for a term of years, and excluding Indians not taxed, three fifths of all other persons.

article 1, sect. 2

3 He shall from time to time give to the Congress information of the state of the Union, and recommend to their consideration such measures as he shall judge necessary and expedient.

article 2, sect. 3 'President shall communicate to Congress'

4 Congress shall make no law respecting an establishment of religion, or prohibiting the free exercise thereof; or abridging the freedom of speech, or of the press; or the right of the people peaceably to assemble, and to petition the government for a redress of grievances.

First Amendment (1791)

5 A well-regulated militia, being necessary to the security of a free State, the right of the people to keep and bear arms, shall not be infringed.

Second Amendment (1791)

6 Nor shall any person subject for the same offense to be twice put in jeopardy of life or limb; nor shall be compelled in any criminal case to be a witness against himself, nor be deprived of life, liberty, or property, without due process of law.

Fifth Amendment (1791)

7 Excessive bail shall not be required, nor excessive fines imposed, nor cruel and unusual punishment inflicted.

Eighth Amendment (1791)

A. J. Cook 1885–1931

English labour leader; Secretary of the Miners' Federation of Great Britain, 1924–31

8 Not a penny off the pay, not a second on the day.

often quoted with 'minute' substituted for 'second'

speech at York, 3 April 1926, in *The Times* 5 April 1926

Eliza Cook 1818–89

English poet

9 Better build schoolrooms for 'the boy', Than cells and gibbets for 'the man'.

'A Song for the Ragged Schools' (1853)

James Cook 1728–79

English explorer

10 Ambition leads me not only farther than any other man has been before me, but as far as I think it possible for man to go.

diary 30 January 1774

Robin Cook 1946–2005

British Labour politician, Foreign Secretary 1997–2003

11 Our foreign policy must have an ethical dimension and must support the demands of other people for the democratic rights on which we insist for ourselves.

mission statement by the new Foreign Secretary, 12 May 1997

in *The Times* 13 May 1997

12 Why is it now so urgent that we should take military action to disarm a military capacity that has been there for 20 years, and which we helped to create?

resigning from the government over Iraq

speech in the House of Commons, 17 March 2003

Calvin Coolidge 1872–1933

American Republican statesman, 30th President of the US 1923–9. On Coolidge: see **ANONYMOUS 21:1, LIPPMANN 495:9, PARKER 596:15**

13 There is no right to strike against the public safety by anybody, anywhere, any time.

telegram to Samuel Gompers, 14 September 1919

14 Civilization and profits go hand in hand.

speech in New York, 27 November 1920, in *New York Times* 28 November 1920

15 The chief business of the American people is business.

speech in Washington, 17 January 1925, in *New York Times* 18 January 1925

16 That man has offered me unsolicited advice for six years, all of it bad.

in 1928, when asked to support the Presidential nomination of his eventual successor Herbert **HOOVER**

Donald R. McCoy *Calvin Coolidge: the Quiet President* (1967)

17 *when asked by Mrs Coolidge what a sermon had been about:*

'Sins,' he said. 'Well, what did he say about sin?' 'He was against it.'

John H. McKee *Coolidge: Wit and Wisdom* (1933); perhaps apocryphal

18 They hired the money, didn't they?

on war debts incurred by England and others

John H. McKee *Coolidge: Wit and Wisdom* (1933)

1 Nothing in the world can take the place of persistence. Talent will not; nothing is more common than unsuccessful men with talent. Genius will not; unrewarded genius is almost a proverb. Education will not; the world is full of educated derelicts. Persistence and determination are omnipotent. The slogan 'press on' has solved and always will solve the problems of the human race.
> attributed in the programme of a memorial service for Coolidge in 1933

Duff Cooper, Lord Norwich 1890–1954
British Conservative politician, diplomat, and writer

2 Your two stout lovers frowning at one another across the hearth rug, while your small, but perfectly formed one kept the party in a roar.
> letter to Lady Diana Manners, later his wife, October 1914; in Artemis Cooper *Durable Fire* (1983)

Elizabeth Cooper fl. 1730
English writer and dramatist

3 Regularity and Decorum. 'Tis what we women-authors, in particular, have been thought greatly deficient in; and I should be concerned to find it an objection not to be removed.
> preface to *The Rival Widows* (1735)

Susie Cooper 1902–95
English ceramic designer and manufacturer

4 Pottery . . . is a practical and lasting form of art. Not everyone can afford original paintings, but most people can afford pottery.
> in *Evening Sentinel* 16 September 1971

5 The space you leave behind is as important as the space you fill.
> Ann Eatwell and Andrew Casey (eds.) *Susie Cooper: a Pioneer of Modern Design* (2002)

Wendy Cope 1945–
English poet

6 Making cocoa for Kingsley Amis.
> title of poem (1986)

7 I used to think all poets were Byronic—
Mad, bad and dangerous to know.
And then I met a few. Yes it's ironic—
I used to think all poets were Byronic.
They're mostly wicked as a ginless tonic
And wild as pension plans.
> 'Triolet' (1986); see **LAMB** 476:10

Aaron Copland 1900–90
American composer, pianist, and conductor

8 The whole problem can be stated quite simply by asking, 'Is there a meaning to music?' My answer to that would be, 'Yes.' And 'Can you state in so many words what the meaning is?' My answer to that would be, 'No.'
> *What to Listen for in Music* (1939)

Richard Corbet 1582–1635
English poet and prelate; Chaplain to James I

9 Farewell, rewards and Fairies,
Good housewives now may say,
For now foul sluts in dairies
Do fare as well as they.
> 'The Fairies' Farewell'

10 Who of late for cleanliness,
Finds sixpence in her shoe?
> 'The Fairies' Farewell'

11 By which we note the Fairies
Were of the old profession;
Their songs were Ave Marys,
Their dances were procession.
> 'The Fairies' Farewell'

12 I wish thee all thy mother's graces,
Thy father's fortunes, and his places.
I wish thee friends, and one at Court,
Not to build on, but support;
To keep thee, not in doing many
Oppressions, but from suffering any.
> 'To his Son, Vincent Corbet'

Pierre Corneille 1606–84
French dramatist. On Corneille: see JOHNSON 444:13

13 *A vaincre sans péril, on triomphe sans gloire.*
To conquer without risk is to triumph without glory.
> *Le Cid* (1637) act 2, sc. 2

14 *Faites votre devoir et laissez faire aux dieux.*
Do your duty, and leave the outcome to the Gods.
> *Horace* (1640) act 2, sc. 8

15 *Un premier mouvement ne fut jamais un crime.*
A first impulse was never a crime.
> *Horace* (1640) act 5, sc. 3; see **MONTROND** 556:12

Cornelius Nepos *c.*110–24 BC
Roman biographer

16 All this he said with so steady a voice and countenance, that he seemed to be passing, not out of life, but merely from one house to another.
> *Life of Atticus* ch. 22

Ralph Cornes

17 Computers are anti-Faraday machines. He said he couldn't understand anything until he could count it, while computers count everything and understand nothing.
> in *Guardian* 28 March 1991

Bernard Cornfeld 1927–95
American businessman

18 Do you sincerely want to be rich?
> *stock question to salesmen*
> C. Raw et al. *Do You Sincerely Want to be Rich?* (1971)

Frances Cornford (née Darwin) 1886–1960

English poet; wife of Francis M. **CORNFORD**

1 How long ago Hector took off his plume,
   Not wanting that his little son should cry,
   Then kissed his sad Andromache goodbye —
   And now we three in Euston waiting-room.
   'Parting in Wartime' (1948)

2 O fat white woman whom nobody loves,
   Why do you walk through the fields in gloves
     . . .
   Missing so much and so much?
   'To a Fat Lady seen from the Train' (1910); see **CHESTERTON**
   224:5

3 A young Apollo, golden-haired,
   Stands dreaming on the verge of strife,
   Magnificently unprepared
   For the long littleness of life.
   of Rupert **BROOKE**
   'Youth' (1910)

Francis M. Cornford 1874–1943

English academic; husband of Frances **CORNFORD**

4 Every public action, which is not customary,
   either is wrong, or, if it is right, is a dangerous
   precedent. It follows that nothing should ever be
   done for the first time.
   Microcosmographia Academica (1908) ch. 7

5 Another sport which wastes unlimited time is
   comma-hunting. Once start a comma and the
   whole pack will be off, full cry, especially if they
   have had a literary training . . . But comma-
   hunting is so exciting as to be a little dangerous.
   When attention is entirely concentrated on
   punctuation, there is some fear that the conduct
   of business may suffer, and a proposal get
   through without being properly obstructed on
   its demerits. It is therefore wise, when a kill has
   been made, to move at once for adjournment.
   Microcosmographia Academica (1908) ch. 8

6 That branch of the art of lying which consists in
   very nearly deceiving your friends without quite
   deceiving your enemies.
   of propaganda
   Microcosmographia Academica (1922 ed.)

Mme Cornuel 1605–94

French society hostess

7 No man is a hero to his valet.
   Lettres de Mlle Aïssé à Madame C (1787) Letter 13 'De Paris,
   1728'; see **BYRON** 185:9, **PROVERBS** 640:6

Coronation Service 1689

8 We present you with this Book, the most
   valuable thing that this world affords. Here is
   wisdom; this is the royal Law; these are the
   lively Oracles of God.
   The Presenting of the Holy Bible; L. G. Wickham Legge
   English Coronation Records (1901)

Correggio (Antonio Allegri Correggio)

c.1489–1534

Italian painter

9 *Son pittore ancor io!*
   I, too, am a painter!
   on seeing Raphael's St Cecilia at Bologna, c.1525
   L. Pungileoni *Memorie Istoriche de . . . Correggio* (1817) vol. 1

Gregory Corso 1930–2001

American poet

10 O God, and the wedding! All her family and her
    friends
    and only a handful of mine all scroungy and
    bearded
    just wait to get at the drinks and food.
    'Marriage' (1960)

William Cory (Johnson) 1823–92

English poet; assistant master at Eton College, 1845–72

11 Jolly boating weather,
    And a hay harvest breeze,
    Blade on the feather,
    Shade off the trees
    Swing, swing together
    With your body between your knees.
    'Eton Boating Song' in *Eton Scrap Book* (1865); E. Parker
    Floreat (1923)

12 Nothing in life shall sever
    The chain that is round us now.
    'Eton Boating Song' in *Eton Scrap Book* (1865); E. Parker
    Floreat (1923)

13 They told me, Heraclitus, they told me you
    were dead,
    They brought me bitter news to hear and bitter
    tears to shed.
    I wept as I remembered how often you and I
    Had tired the sun with talking and sent him
    down the sky.
    'Heraclitus' (1858); translation of Callimachus 'Epigram 2'; see
    CALLIMACHUS 193:15

Bill Cosby 1937–

American comedian and actor

14 The heart of marriage is memories.
    Love and Marriage (1989)

Charles Cotton 1630–87

English poet

15 The shadows now so long do grow,
    That brambles like tall cedars show,
    Molehills seem mountains, and the ant
    Appears a monstrous elephant.
    'Evening Quatrains' (1689) st. 3

John Cotton 1584–1652

English-born New England puritan preacher and theologian

1 If you pinch the sea of its liberty, though it be walls of stone or brass, it will beat them down.
'Limitations of Government'; Perry Miller *The American Puritans* (1956)

2 There is never peace where full liberty is not given, nor never stable peace where more than full liberty is granted.
'Limitations of Government'; Perry Miller *The American Puritans* (1956)

Baron Pierre de Coubertin 1863–1937

French sportsman and educationist

3 The important thing in life is not the victory but the contest; the essential thing is not to have won but to have fought well.
speech at a government banquet in London, 24 July 1908, in T. A. Cook *Fourth Olympiad* (1909)

Émile Coué 1857–1926

French psychologist. On Coué: see **INGE** 424:19

4 Every day, in every way, I am getting better and better.
to be said 15 to 20 times, morning and evening
De la suggestion et de ses applications (1915)

Douglas Coupland 1961–

Canadian writer

5 Generation X: tales for an accelerated culture.
title of book (1991)

Victor Cousin 1792–1867

French philosopher

6 We must have religion for religion's sake, morality for morality's sake, as with art for art's sake ... the beautiful cannot be the way to what is useful, or to what is good, or to what is holy; it leads only to itself.
Du Vrai, du beau, et du bien [Sorbonne lecture, 1818] (1853) pt. 2; see **CONSTANT** 249:21

Jacques Cousteau 1910–97

French naval officer and underwater explorer. See also **EPITAPHS** 317:2

7 Mankind has probably done more damage to the earth in the 20th century than in all of previous human history.
'Consumer Society is the Enemy' in *New Perspectives Quarterly* Summer 1996

Thomas Coventry 1578–1640

English judge

8 The dominion of the sea, as it is an ancient and undoubted right of the crown of England, so it is the best security of the land ... The wooden walls are the best walls of this kingdom.
wooden walls = ships
speech to the Judges, 17 June 1635, in J. Rushworth *Historical*

Collections (1680) vol. 2; see **BLACKSTONE** 123:11, **THEMISTOCLES** 804:10

Noël Coward 1899–1973

English dramatist, actor, and composer

9 Dance, dance, dance, little lady!
Leave tomorrow behind.
'Dance, Little Lady' (1928 song)

10 Don't let's be beastly to the Germans
When our Victory is ultimately won.
'Don't Let's Be Beastly to the Germans' (1943 song)

11 There's sand in the porridge and sand in the bed,
And if this is pleasure we'd rather be dead.
'The English Lido' (1928)

12 I believe that since my life began
The most I've had is just
A talent to amuse.
'If Love Were All' (1929 song)

13 I'll see you again,
Whenever spring breaks through again.
'I'll See You Again' (1929 song)

14 Mad about the boy.
title of song (1932)

15 Mad dogs and Englishmen
Go out in the midday sun.
The Japanese don't care to,
The Chinese wouldn't dare to,
The Hindus and Argentines sleep firmly from twelve to one,
But Englishmen detest a siesta.
'Mad Dogs and Englishmen' (1931 song)

16 Don't put your daughter on the stage, Mrs Worthington,
Don't put your daughter on the stage.
'Mrs Worthington' (1935 song)

17 Poor little rich girl.
title of song (1925)

18 Someday I'll find you,
Moonlight behind you,
True to the dream I am dreaming.
'Someday I'll Find You' (1930 song)

19 The Stately Homes of England,
How beautiful they stand,
To prove the upper classes
Have still the upper hand.
'The Stately Homes of England' (1938 song); see **HEMANS** 390:15

20 There are bad times just around the corner,
There are dark clouds travelling through the sky
And it's no good whining
About a silver lining
For we know from experience that they won't roll by.
'There are Bad Times Just Around the Corner' (1953 song); see **PROVERBS** 631:15

21 I believe we should all behave quite differently if we lived in a warm, sunny climate all the time.
Brief Encounter (1945)

1 Very flat, Norfolk.
   Private Lives (1930) act 1

2 Extraordinary how potent cheap music is.
   Private Lives (1930) act 1

3 Certain women should be struck regularly, like gongs.
   Private Lives (1930) act 3

4 Dear 338171 (May I call you 338?).
   letter to T. E. Lawrence, 25 August 1930

5 Just say the lines and don't trip over the furniture.
   advice on acting
   D. Richards *The Wit of Noël Coward* (1968)

6 Television is for appearing on, not looking at.
   D. Richards *The Wit of Noël Coward* (1968)

7 Two wise acres and a cow.
   of Edith SITWELL, *Osbert* SITWELL, *and Sacheverell Sitwell*
   John Pearson *Façades* (1978) ch. 10; see POLITICAL SLOGANS AND SONGS 613:11

Abraham Cowley 1618–67

English poet and essayist. On Cowley: see ADDISON 4:9, DRYDEN 297:22, POPE 617:21

8 The thirsty earth soaks up the rain,
   And drinks, and gapes for drink again.
   The plants suck in the earth, and are
   With constant drinking fresh and fair.
   'Drinking' (1656)

9 Fill all the glasses there, for why
   Should every creature drink but I,
   Why, man of morals, tell me why?
   'Drinking' (1656)

10 God the first garden made, and the first city Cain.
   Essays, in Verse and Prose (1668) 'The Garden'; see COWPER 256:8

11 Hence, ye profane; I hate ye all;
   Both the great vulgar, and the small.
   Essays, in Verse and Prose (1668) 'Of Greatness' (translation of Horace Odes bk. 3, no. 1); see HORACE 412:14

12 This only grant me, that my means may lie
   Too low for envy, for contempt too high.
   Essays, in Verse and Prose (1668) 'Of Myself'

13 Acquaintance I would have, but when't depends
   Not on the number, but the choice of friends.
   Essays, in Verse and Prose (1668) 'Of Myself'

14 Love in her sunny eyes does basking play;
   Love walks the pleasant mazes of her hair;
   Love does on both her lips for ever stray;
   And sows and reaps a thousand kisses there.
   In all her outward parts Love's always seen;
   But, oh, he never went within.
   The Mistress: or . . . Love Verses (1647) 'The Change'

15 The world's a scene of changes, and to be
   Constant, in Nature were inconstancy.
   The Mistress: or . . . Love Verses (1647) 'Inconstancy'

16 Lukewarmness I account a sin
   As great in love as in religion.
   The Mistress: or . . . Love Verses (1647) 'The Request'; see BIBLE 118:1

17   The stings,
   The crowd, and buzz, and murmurings
   Of this great hive, the city.
   The Mistress: or . . . Love Verses (1647) 'The Wish'

18 Nothing so soon the drooping spirits can raise
   As praises from the men, whom all men praise.
   'Ode upon a Copy of Verses of My Lord Broghill's' (1663)

19 Poet and Saint! to thee alone are given
   The two most sacred names of earth and Heaven.
   'On the Death of Mr Crashaw' (1656)

20 Life is an incurable disease.
   'To Dr Scarborough' (1656) st. 6

Hannah Cowley (née Parkhouse)
1743–1809

English dramatist

21 Five minutes! Zounds! I have been five minutes too late all my life-time!
   The Belle's Stratagem (1780) act 1, sc. 1

22 Vanity, like murder, will out.
   The Belle's Stratagem (1780) act 1, sc. 4

23 But what is woman?—only one of Nature's agreeable blunders.
   Who's the Dupe? (1779) act 2; see NIETZSCHE 575:10

William Cowper 1731–1800

English poet

24 No voice divine the storm allayed,
   No light propitious shone;
   When snatched from all effectual aid,
   We perished, each alone:
   But I beneath a rougher sea,
   And whelmed in deeper gulfs than he.
   'The Castaway' (written 1799) l. 61

25 Grief is itself a med'cine.
   'Charity' (1782) l. 159

26 He found it inconvenient to be poor.
   of a burglar
   'Charity' (1782) l. 189

27 A tale should be judicious, clear, succinct;
   The language plain, and incidents well linked;
   Tell not as new what ev'ry body knows,
   And new or old, still hasten to a close.
   'Conversation' (1782) l. 235

28 The pipe with solemn interposing puff,
   Makes half a sentence at a time enough;
   The dozing sages drop the drowsy strain,
   Then pause, and puff—and speak, and pause again.
   'Conversation' (1782) l. 245

29 Pernicious weed! whose scent the fair annoys,
   Unfriendly to society's chief joys.
   on tobacco
   'Conversation' (1782) l. 251

30 His wit invites you by his looks to come,
   But when you knock it never is at home.
   'Conversation' (1782) l. 303

1 . . . Thousands, careless of the damning sin,
 Kiss the book's outside who ne'er look within.
 on oath-taking
 'Expostulation' (1782) l. 388

2 The man that hails you Tom or Jack,
 And proves by thumps upon your back
 How he esteems your merit,
 Is such a friend, that one had need
 Be very much his friend indeed
 To pardon or to bear it.
 'Friendship' (1782) l. 169

3 Damned below Judas; more abhorred than he
 was.
 'Hatred and vengeance, my eternal portion' (written c.1774)

4 Man disavows, and Deity disowns me.
 'Hatred and vengeance, my eternal portion' (written c.1774)

5 Men deal with life, as children with their play,
 Who first misuse, then cast their toys away.
 'Hope' (1782) l. 127

6 Could he with reason murmur at his case,
 Himself sole author of his own disgrace?
 'Hope' (1782) l. 316

7 And differing judgements serve but to declare
 That truth lies somewhere, if we knew but
 where.
 'Hope' (1782) l. 423

8 John Gilpin was a citizen
 Of credit and renown,
 A train-band captain eke was he
 Of famous London town.
 'John Gilpin' (1785) l. 1

9 My sister and my sister's child,
 Myself and children three,
 Will fill the chaise; so you must ride
 On horseback after we.
 'John Gilpin' (1785) l. 13

10 O'erjoy'd was he to find
 That, though on pleasure she was bent,
 She had a frugal mind.
 'John Gilpin' (1785) l. 30

11 Beware of desperate steps. The darkest day
 (Live till tomorrow) will have passed away.
 'The Needless Alarm' (written c.1790) l. 132

12 God moves in a mysterious way
 His wonders to perform;
 He plants his footsteps in the sea,
 And rides upon the storm.
 Olney Hymns (1779) 'Light Shining out of Darkness'

13 Behind a frowning providence
 He hides a smiling face.
 Olney Hymns (1779) 'Light Shining out of Darkness'

14 Hark, my soul! it is the Lord;
 'Tis thy Saviour, hear his word;
 Jesus speaks, and speaks to thee;
 'Say, poor sinner, lov'st thou me?'
 Olney Hymns (1779) 'Lovest Thou Me?'

15 There is a fountain filled with blood
 Drawn from Emmanuel's veins,

And sinners, plunged beneath that flood,
 Lose all their guilty stains.
 Olney Hymns (1779) 'Praise for the Fountain Opened'

16 Oh! for a closer walk with God,
 A calm and heav'nly frame;
 A light to shine upon the road
 That leads me to the Lamb!
 Olney Hymns (1779) 'Walking with God'

17 My dog! what remedy remains,
 Since, teach you all I can,
 I see you, after all my pains,
 So much resemble man!
 'On a Spaniel called Beau, killing a young bird' (written 1793)

18 Toll for the brave—
 The brave! that are no more:
 All sunk beneath the wave,
 Fast by their native shore.
 'On the Loss of the Royal George' (written 1782)

19 His sword was in the sheath,
 His fingers held the pen,
 When Kempenfeld went down
 With twice four hundred men.
 'On the Loss of the Royal George' (written 1782)

20 Oh, fond attempt to give a deathless lot
 To names ignoble, born to be forgot!
 'On Observing Some Names of Little Note Recorded in the
 Biographia Britannica' (1782)

21 Thy morning bounties ere I left my home,
 The biscuit, or confectionary plum.
 'On the Receipt of My Mother's Picture out of Norfolk' (1798)
 l. 60

22 Me howling winds drive devious, tempest-tossed,
 Sails ripped, seams op'ning wide, and compass
 lost.
 'On the Receipt of My Mother's Picture out of Norfolk' (1798)
 l. 102

23 I shall not ask Jean Jacques Rousseau,
 If birds confabulate or no.
 'Pairing Time Anticipated' (1795)

24 The poplars are felled, farewell to the shade
 And the whispering sound of the cool
 colonnade.
 'The Poplar-Field' (written 1784)

25 Oh, laugh or mourn with me the rueful jest,
 A cassocked huntsman and a fiddling priest!
 'The Progress of Error' (1782) l. 110

26 Remorse, the fatal egg by pleasure laid.
 'The Progress of Error' (1782) l. 239

27 How much a dunce that has been sent to roam
 Excels a dunce that has been kept at home.
 'The Progress of Error' (1782) l. 415

28 Thou god of our idolatry, the press . . .
 Thou fountain, at which drink the good and
 wise;
 Thou ever-bubbling spring of endless lies;
 Like Eden's dread probationary tree,
 Knowledge of good and evil is from thee.
 'The Progress of Error' (1782) l. 461

1 He likes the country, but in truth must own,
Most likes it, when he studies it in town.
'Retirement' (1782) l. 573

2   Philologists, who chase
A panting syllable through time and space,
Start it at home, and hunt it in the dark,
To Gaul, to Greece, and into Noah's ark.
'Retirement' (1782) l. 691

3 Admirals extolled for standing still,
Or doing nothing with a deal of skill.
'Table Talk' (1782) l. 192

4 Freedom has a thousand charms to show,
That slaves, howe'er contented, never know.
'Table Talk' (1782) l. 260

5 I sing the sofa.
The Task (1785) bk. 1 'The Sofa' l. 1

6 Thus first necessity invented stools,
Convenience next suggested elbow-chairs,
And luxury the accomplished sofa last.
The Task (1785) bk. 1 'The Sofa' l. 86

7 The nurse sleeps sweetly, hired to watch the
sick,
Whom, snoring, she disturbs.
The Task (1785) bk. 1 'The Sofa' l. 89

8 God made the country, and man made the
town.
The Task (1785) bk. 1 'The Sofa' l. 749; see COWLEY 254:10,
PROVERBS 633:7

9 Slaves cannot breathe in England, if their lungs
Receive our air, that moment they are free;
They touch our country, and their shackles fall.
The Task (1785) bk. 2 'The Timepiece' l. 40; see ANONYMOUS
19:14

10 England, with all thy faults, I love thee still—
My country!
The Task (1785) bk. 2 'The Timepiece' l. 206; see CHURCHILL
228:3

11 There is a pleasure in poetic pains
Which only poets know.
The Task (1785) bk. 2 'The Timepiece' l. 285

12 Variety's the very spice of life,
That gives it all its flavour.
The Task (1785) bk. 2 'The Timepiece' l. 606; see BEHN 67:4,
PROVERBS 646:2

13 I was a stricken deer, that left the herd
Long since.
The Task (1785) bk. 3 'The Garden' l. 108; see SHAKESPEARE
702:25

14 Great contest follows, and much learned dust
Involves the combatants.
The Task (1785) bk. 3 'The Garden' l. 161

15 Defend me, therefore, common sense, say I,
From reveries so airy, from the toil
Of dropping buckets into empty wells,
And growing old in drawing nothing up!
The Task (1785) bk. 3 'The Garden' l. 187

16   Newton, childlike sage!
Sagacious reader of the works of God.
The Task (1785) bk. 3 'The Garden' l. 252

17   Detested sport,
That owes its pleasures to another's pain.
of hunting
The Task (1785) bk. 3 'The Garden' l. 326

18 Studious of laborious ease.
The Task (1785) bk. 3 'The Garden' l. 361

19 Now stir the fire, and close the shutters fast,
Let fall the curtains, wheel the sofa round,
And, while the bubbling and loud-hissing urn
Throws up a steamy column, and the cups,
That cheer but not inebriate, wait on each,
So let us welcome peaceful evening in.
The Task (1785) bk. 4 'The Winter Evening' l. 34; see BERKELEY
72:12

20 'Tis pleasant through the loopholes of retreat
To peep at such a world; to see the stir
Of the great Babel, and not feel the crowd.
The Task (1785) bk. 4 'The Winter Evening' l. 88

21 I crown thee king of intimate delights,
Fire-side enjoyments, home-born happiness.
The Task (1785) bk. 4 'The Winter Evening' l. 139

22 A Roman meal . . .
. . . a radish and an egg.
The Task (1785) bk. 4 'The Winter Evening' l. 168

23 The slope of faces, from the floor to th' roof,
(As if one master-spring controlled them all),
Relaxed into a universal grin.
of the theatre
The Task (1785) bk. 4 'The Winter Evening' l. 202

24 Shaggy, and lean, and shrewd, with pointed ears
And tail cropped short, half lurcher and half cur.
The Task (1785) bk. 5 'The Winter Morning Walk' l. 45

25 But war's a game, which, were their subjects
wise,
Kings would not play at.
The Task (1785) bk. 5 'The Winter Morning Walk' l. 187

26   Knowledge dwells
In heads replete with thoughts of other men;
Wisdom in minds attentive to their own.
The Task (1785) bk. 6 'The Winter Walk at Noon' l. 89

27 Knowledge is proud that he has learned so
much;
Wisdom is humble that he knows no more.
The Task (1785) bk. 6 'The Winter Walk at Noon' l. 96

28 Nature is but a name for an effect,
Whose cause is God.
The Task (1785) bk. 6 'The Winter Walk at Noon' l. 223

29 A cheap but wholesome salad from the brook.
The Task (1785) bk. 6 'The Winter Walk at Noon' l. 304

30 I would not enter on my list of friends
(Tho' graced with polished manners and fine
sense,
Yet wanting sensibility) the man
Who needlessly sets foot upon a worm.
The Task (1785) bk. 6 'The Winter Walk at Noon' l. 560

31 The parson knows enough who knows a duke.
'Tirocinium' (1785) l. 403

1   Tenants of life's middle state,
Securely placed between the small and great.
> 'Tirocinium' (1785) l. 807

2   He has no hope that never had a fear.
> 'Truth' (1782) l. 298

3   But what is man in his own proud esteem?
Hear him, himself the poet and the theme;
A monarch clothed with majesty and awe,
His mind his kingdom and his will his law.
> 'Truth' (1782) l. 403

4   I am monarch of all I survey,
My right there is none to dispute;
From the centre all round to the sea
I am lord of the fowl and the brute.
> 'Verses Supposed to be Written by Alexander Selkirk' (1782);
> see **DEFOE** 270:15

5   Oh! I could thresh his old jacket till I made his
pension jingle in his pockets.
> *on Samuel* **JOHNSON**'s *inadequate treatment of* Paradise
> Lost
>> letter to the Revd William Unwin, 31 October 1779; J. King
>> and C. Ryskamp (eds.) *Letters and Prose Writings of William
>> Cowper* vol. 1 (1979)

6   Our severest winter, commonly called the spring.
> letter to the Revd William Unwin, 8 June 1783, in J. King and
> C. Ryskamp (eds.) *Letters and Prose Writings of William Cowper*
> vol. 2 (1981)

7   You must always understand, my dear, that
when poets talk of cottages and hermitages, and
such like matters, they mean a house with six
sashes in front, two comfortable parlours, a
smart staircase and three bed-chambers of
convenient dimensions; in short, exactly such a
house as this.
> letter to Lady Hesketh, 26 November 1786, in J. King and C.
> Ryskamp (eds.) *Letters and Prose Writings of William Cowper*
> vol. 2 (1981)

George Crabbe 1754–1832

English poet

8   'What is a church?'—Our honest sexton tells,
''Tis a tall building, with a tower and bells.'
> *The Borough* (1810) Letter 2 'The Church' l. 11

9   Virtues neglected then, adored become,
And graces slighted, blossom on the tomb.
> *The Borough* (1810) Letter 2 'The Church' l. 133

10   The Town small-talk flows from lip
to lip;
Intrigues half-gathered, conversation-scraps,
Kitchen-cabals, and nursery-mishaps.
> *The Borough* (1810) Letter 3 'The Vicar' l. 70

11   Habit with him was all the test of truth,
'It must be right: I've done it from my youth.'
> *The Borough* (1810) Letter 3 'The Vicar' l. 138

12   And need and misery, vice and danger bind
In sad alliance each degraded mind.
> *The Borough* (1810) Letter 18 'The Poor and Their Dwellings'
> l. 352

13   There anchoring, Peter chose from man to hide,
There hang his head, and view the lazy tide
In its hot slimy channel slowly glide;
Where the small eels that left the deeper way
For the warm shore, within the shallows play;
Where gaping mussels, left upon the mud,
Slope their slow passage to the fallen flood;—
Here dull and hopeless he'd lie down and trace
How sidelong crabs had scrawled their crooked
race.
> *The Borough* (1810) Letter 22 'Peter Grimes' l. 185

14   He nursed the feelings these dull scenes
produce,
And loved to stop beside the opening sluice;
Where the small stream, confined in narrow
bound,
Ran with a dull, unvaried, sad'ning sound;
Where all presented to the eye or ear,
Oppressed the soul! with misery, grief, and fear.
> *The Borough* (1810) Letter 22 'Peter Grimes' l. 199

15   One was a female, who had grievous ill
Wrought in revenge, and she enjoy'd it still . . .
Sullen she was, and threatening; in her eye
Glared the stern triumph that she dared to die.
> *The Borough* (1810) Letter 23 'Prisons' l. 208

16   Lo! the poor toper whose untutored sense,
Sees bliss in ale, and can with wine dispense;
Whose head proud fancy never taught to steer,
Beyond the muddy ecstasies of beer.
> 'Inebriety' (in imitation of Pope, 1775) pt. 1, l. 132; see **POPE**
> 616:20

17   With awe, around these silent walks I tread;
These are the lasting mansions of the dead.
> 'The Library' (1808) l. 105

18   Lo! all in silence, all in order stand,
And mighty folios first, a lordly band;
Then quartos their well-ordered ranks maintain,
And light octavos fill a spacious plain;
See yonder, ranged in more frequented rows,
A humbler band of duodecimos.
> 'The Library' (1808) l. 128

19   Fashion, though Folly's child, and guide of fools,
Rules e'en the wisest, and in learning rules.
> 'The Library' (1808) l. 167

20   Coldly profane and impiously gay.
> 'The Library' (1808) l. 265

21   The murmuring poor, who will not fast in
peace.
> 'The Newspaper' (1785) l. 158

22   A master passion is the love of news.
> 'The Newspaper' (1785) l. 279

23   Our farmers round, well pleased with constant
gain,
Like other farmers, flourish and complain.
> 'The Parish Register' (1807) pt. 1, l. 273

24   The one so worn as you behold,
So thin and pale—is yet of gold.
> *these lines were printed by Crabbe's son from a paper
> which he had found wrapped round his mother's wedding-
> ring (with 'ring' instead of 'one')*
>> 'A Ring to Me Cecilia Sends' (written c.1813–14)

1 He tried the luxury of doing good.
Tales of the Hall (1819) 'Boys at School' l. 139; see **GARTH** 350:2, **GOLDSMITH** 364:23

2 'The game,' said he, 'is never lost till won.'
Tales of the Hall (1819) 'Gretna Green' l. 334

3 The face the index of a feeling mind.
Tales of the Hall (1819) 'Lady Barbara' l. 124

4 Secrets with girls, like loaded guns with boys,
Are never valued till they make a noise.
Tales of the Hall (1819) 'The Maid's Story' l. 84

5 Yes, thus the Muses sing of happy swains,
Because the Muses never knew their pains:
They boast their peasants' pipes, but peasants now
Resign their pipes and plod behind the plough.
The Village (1783) bk. 1, l. 21

6 I grant indeed that fields and flocks have charms,
For him that gazes or for him that farms.
The Village (1783) bk. 1, l. 39

7   I paint the cot,
As truth will paint it, and as bards will not.
The Village (1783) bk. 1, l. 53

8 Where Plenty smiles—alas! she smiles for few,
And those who taste not, yet behold her store,
Are as the slaves that dig the golden ore,
The wealth around them makes them doubly poor.
The Village (1783) bk. 1, l. 136

9 The cold charities of man to man.
The Village (1783) bk. 1, l. 245

10 A potent quack, long versed in human ills,
Who first insults the victim whom he kills;
Whose murd'rous hand a drowsy bench protect,
And whose most tender mercy is neglect.
The Village (1783) bk. 1, l. 282

Maurice James Craig 1919–

Irish poet and architectural historian

11 O the bricks they will bleed and the rain it will weep
And the damp Lagan fog lull the city to sleep;
It's to hell with the future and live on the past:
May the Lord in His mercy be kind to Belfast.
based on the traditional refrain 'May God in His mercy look down on Belfast'
'Ballad to a Traditional Refrain' (1974)

Hart Crane 1899–1932

American poet

12 Stars scribble on our eyes the frosty sagas,
The gleaming cantos of unvanquished space.
'Cape Hatteras' (1930)

13 Cowslip and shad-blow, flaked like tethered foam
Around bared teeth of stallions, bloomed that spring.
'Cape Hatteras' (1930)

14 We have seen
The moon in lonely alleys make
A grail of laughter of an empty ash can.
'Chaplinesque' (1926)

15 The apple on its bough is her desire,—
Shining suspension, mimic of the sun.
'Garden Abstract' (1926)

16 Ah, madame! truly it's not right
When one isn't the real Gioconda,
To adapt her methods and deportment
For snaring the poor world in a blue funk.
'Locutions des Pierrots' (1933)

17   So the 20th Century—so
whizzed the Limited—roared by and left
three men, still hungry on the tracks, ploddingly
watching the tail lights wizen and converge, slipping
gimleted and neatly out of sight.
'The River' (1930)

18 O Sleepless as the river under thee,
Vaulting the sea, the prairies' dreaming sod,
Unto us lowliest sometime sweep, descend
And of the curveship lend a myth to God.
'To Brooklyn Bridge' (1930)

19 You who desired so much—in vain to ask—
Yet fed your hunger like an endless task,
Dared dignify the labor, bless the quest—
Achieved that stillness ultimately best,
Being, of all, least sought for: Emily, hear!
'To Emily Dickinson' (1927)

Stephen Crane 1871–1900

American writer

20 The red badge of courage.
title of novel (1895)

Thomas Cranmer 1489–1556

English Anglican prelate and martyr; Archbishop of Canterbury from 1553. On Cranmer: see **HENRY VIII** 392:2

21 This was the hand that wrote it [his recantation], therefore it shall suffer first punishment.
at the stake, Oxford, 21 March 1556
John Richard Green *A Short History of the English People* (1874) ch. 7, sect. 2

Richard Crashaw c.1612–49

English poet. On Crashaw: see **COWLEY** 254:19

22 Lord, what is man? Why should he cost thee
So dear? What had his ruin lost thee?
Lord, what is man, that thou hast overbought
So much a thing of nought?
'Caritas Nimia, or The Dear Bargain' (1648)

23 *Nympha pudica Deum vidit, et erubuit.*
The conscious water saw its God, and blushed.
literally, 'the chaste nymph saw . . . '; the translation above is attributed to **DRYDEN***, when a schoolboy*
Epigrammata Sacra (1634) 'Aquae in vinum versae [Water

changed into wine]'; the translation is discussed in *Notes and Queries* 4th series (1869) vol. 4

1 Love's passives are his activ'st part.
The wounded is the wounding heart.
'The Flaming Heart upon the Book of Saint Teresa' (1652) l. 73

2 By all the eagle in thee, all the dove.
'The Flaming Heart upon the Book of Saint Teresa' (1652) l. 95

3 Love, thou art absolute sole Lord
Of life and death.
'Hymn to the Name and Honour of the Admirable Saint Teresa' (1652) l. 1

4 Poor World (said I) what wilt thou do
To entertain this starry stranger?
Is this the best thou canst bestow?
A cold, and not too cleanly, manger?
Contend, ye powers of heav'n and earth
To fit a bed for this huge birth.
'Hymn of the Nativity' (1652)

5 Welcome, all wonders in one sight!
Eternity shut in a span.
'Hymn of the Nativity' (1652)

6 Lo here a little volume, but large book.
'On a Prayer book' (1646)

7 It is love's great artillery
Which here contracts itself and comes to lie
Close couched in your white bosom.
'On a Prayer book' (1646)

8 I would be married, but I'd have no wife,
I would be married to a single life.
'On Marriage' (1646)

9 Two walking baths; two weeping motions;
Portable, and compendious oceans.
'Saint Mary Magdalene, or The Weeper' (1652) st. 19

10 All is Caesar's; and what odds
So long as Caesar's self is God's?
Steps to the Temple (1646) 'Mark 12'; see **BIBLE** 102:15

11 And when life's sweet fable ends,
Soul and body part like friends;
No quarrels, murmurs, no delay;
A kiss, a sigh, and so away.
'Temperance' (1652)

12 Whoe'er she be,
That not impossible she
That shall command my heart and me.
'Wishes to His (Supposed) Mistress' (1646)

Julia Crawford *c.*1800–*c.*55
Irish poet and composer

13 Kathleen Mavourneen! the grey dawn is breaking,
The horn of the hunter is heard on the hill.
'Kathleen Mavourneen' in *Metropolitan Magazine*, London (1835)

Robert Crawford 1959–
Scottish poet

14 In Scotland we live between and across languages.
Identifying Poets (1993)

Crazy Horse (Ta-Sunko-Witko) *c.*1849–77
Sioux chief

15 One does not sell the earth upon which the people walk.
Dee Brown *Bury My Heart at Wounded Knee* (1970) ch. 12

Donald Creighton 1902–79
Canadian historian

16 The historian's first task is the elucidation of character.
Towards the Discovery of Canada (1972)

Mandell Creighton 1843–1901
English prelate

17 No people do so much harm as those who go about doing good.
in *The Life and Letters of Mandell Creighton* by his wife (1904) vol. 2

Michel Guillaume Jean de Crèvecoeur 1735–1813
French-born immigrant to America

18 What then is the American, this new man? He is either a European, or the descendant of a European, hence that strange mixture of blood, which you will find in no other country . . . Here individuals of all nations are melted into a new race of men, whose labours and posterity will one day cause great changes in the world.
Letters from an American Farmer (1782)

Ranulphe Crewe 1558–1646
English judge

19 And yet time hath his revolution; there must be a period and an end to all temporal things, *finis rerum*, an end of names and dignities and whatsoever is terrene; and why not of De Vere? Where is Bohun, where's Mowbray, where's Mortimer? Nay, which is more and most of all, where is Plantagenet? They are entombed in the urns and sepulchres of mortality. And yet let the name and dignity of De Vere stand so long as it pleaseth God.
speech in Oxford Peerage Case, 22 March 1626; in *Dictionary of National Biography* (1917–) vol. 5; see **TECUMSEH** 792:11

Francis Crick 1916–2004
English biophysicist

20 We have discovered the secret of life!
on the discovery of the structure of DNA, 1953
James D. Watson *The Double Helix* (1968)

1 'You' your joys and your sorrows, your memories and ambitions, your sense of personal identity and free will, are in fact no more than the behaviour of a vast assembly of nerve cells and their associated molecules.
The Astonishing Hypothesis: The Scientific Search for the Soul (1994) ch. 1

2 Almost all aspects of life are engineered at the molecular level, and without understanding molecules we can only have a very sketchy understanding of life itself.
What Mad Pursuit (1988) ch. 5

Francis Crick 1916–2004 *and* James D. Watson 1928–

English biophysicist; American biologist

3 It has not escaped our notice that the specific pairing we have postulated immediately suggests a possible copying mechanism for the genetic material.
proposing the double helix as the structure of DNA, and hence the chemical mechanism of heredity
in *Nature* 25 April 1953

Quentin Crisp 1908–99

English writer and actor

4 There was no need to do any housework at all. After the first four years the dirt doesn't get any worse.
The Naked Civil Servant (1968) ch. 15

5 An autobiography is an obituary in serial form with the last instalment missing.
The Naked Civil Servant (1968) ch. 29

Julian Critchley 1930–2000

British Conservative politician and journalist

6 The only safe pleasure for a parliamentarian is a bag of boiled sweets.
in *Listener* 10 June 1982

Richmal Crompton (Richmal Crompton Lamburn) 1890–1969

English writer of books for children

7 I'll thcream and thcream and thcream till I'm thick. I can.
Violet Elizabeth's habitual threat
Still—William (1925) ch. 8

Oliver Cromwell 1599–1658

English Parliamentary general and statesman, Lord Protector of the Commonwealth from 1653. On Cromwell:
see ARNOLD 32:6, BLACKER 123:8, CLARENDON 233:9, DRYDEN 295:22, MILTON 545:17, POPE 617:10; see also MISQUOTATIONS 548:22

8 A few honest men are better than numbers.
letter to William Spring, September 1643, in Thomas Carlyle *Oliver Cromwell's Letters and Speeches* (2nd ed., 1846)

9 I would rather have a plain russet-coated captain that knows what he fights for, and loves what he knows, than that which you call 'a gentleman' and is nothing else.
letter to William Spring, September 1643, in Thomas Carlyle *Oliver Cromwell's Letters and Speeches* (2nd ed., 1846)

10 Cruel necessity.
on the execution of CHARLES I
Joseph Spence *Anecdotes* (1820)

11 It has pleased God to bless our endeavours at Drogheda . . . I believe we put to the sword the whole number of the defendants.
letter to Bradshaw, September 1649

12 I beseech you, in the bowels of Christ, think it possible you may be mistaken.
letter to the General Assembly of the Kirk of Scotland, 3 August 1650, in Thomas Carlyle *Oliver Cromwell's Letters and Speeches* (1845)

13 The dimensions of this mercy are above my thoughts. It is, for aught I know, a crowning mercy.
letter to William Lenthall, Speaker of the Parliament of England, 4 September 1651, in Thomas Carlyle *Oliver Cromwell's Letters and Speeches* (1845)

14 You have sat too long here for any good you have been doing. Depart, I say, and let us have done with you. In the name of God, go!
addressing the Rump Parliament, 20 April 1653; oral tradition, based on Bulstrode Whitelock *Memorials of the English Affairs* (1732 ed.); see AMERY 14:7

15 Take away that fool's bauble, the mace.
at the dismissal of the Rump Parliament, 20 April 1653; in Bulstrode Whitelock *Memorials of the English Affairs* (1732 ed.); see MISQUOTATIONS 548:20

16 It's a maxim not to be despised, 'Though peace be made, yet it's interest that keeps peace.'
speech to Parliament, 4 September 1654, in Thomas Carlyle *Oliver Cromwell's Letters and Speeches* (1845)

17 Necessity hath no law. Feigned necessities, imaginary necessities . . . are the greatest cozenage that men can put upon the Providence of God, and make pretences to break known rules by.
speech to Parliament, 12 September 1654, in Thomas Carlyle *Oliver Cromwell's Letters and Speeches* (1845); see PROVERBS 639:28

18 Your poor army, those poor contemptible men, came up hither.
speech to Parliament, 21 April 1657, in Thomas Carlyle *Oliver Cromwell's Letters and Speeches* (1845); see ANONYMOUS 17:3

19 You have accounted yourselves happy on being environed with a great ditch from all the world besides.
speech to Parliament, 25 January 1658, in Thomas Carlyle *Oliver Cromwell's Letters and Speeches* (1845)

20 Hell or Connaught.
summary of the choice offered to the Catholic population of Ireland, transported to the western counties to make room for settlers
traditionally attributed

1 My design is to make what haste I can to be gone.

last words; John Morley *Oliver Cromwell* (1900) bk. 5, ch. 10

Walter Cronkite 1916–

American broadcaster and journalist, anchorman for CBS television, 1962–81

2 It seems now more certain than ever that the bloody experience of Vietnam is to end in a stalemate.

after visiting Vietnam; see **JOHNSON** 435:8

CBS special television report, 27 February 1968; quoted in D. Halberstam *The Powers That Be* (1979)

Bing Crosby 1903–77

American singer and film actor. See also **EPITAPHS** 318:10

3 Where the blue of the night
Meets the gold of the day,
Someone waits for me.

'Where the Blue of the Night meets the Gold of the Day' (1931 song, with Roy Turk and Fred Ahlert)

Anthony Crosland 1918–77

British Labour politician

4 Total abstinence and a good filing system are not now the right signposts to the socialist Utopia; or at least, if they are, some of us will fall by the wayside.

The Future of Socialism (1956)

5 If it's the last thing I do, I'm going to destroy every fucking grammar school in England. And Wales, and Northern Ireland.

c.1965, while Secretary of State for Education and Science
Susan Crosland *Tony Crosland* (1982)

6 The party's over.

cutting back central government's support for rates, as Minister of the Environment in the 1970s
Anthony Sampson *The Changing Anatomy of Britain* (1982); see **COMDEN AND GREEN** 244:16

Amanda Cross (Carolyn G. Heilbrun) 1926–2003

American crime writer and academic

7 In former days, everyone found the assumption of innocence so easy; today we find fatally easy the assumption of guilt.

Poetic Justice (1970)

Douglas Cross

American songwriter

8 I left my heart in San Francisco
High on a hill it calls to me.
To be where little cable cars climb half-way to the stars,
The morning fog may chill the air—
I don't care!

'I Left My Heart in San Francisco' (1954 song)

Richard Assheton, Lord Cross 1823–1914

British Conservative politician

9 I hear a smile.

when the House of Lords laughed at his speech in favour of Spiritual Peers
G. W. E. Russell *Collections and Recollections* (1898) ch. 29

Richard Crossman 1907–74

British Labour politician. On Crossman: see **DALTON** 264:1

10 While there is death there is hope.

on the death of Hugh **GAITSKELL** *in 1963; according to Crossman, this was a favourite phrase of Harold* **LASKI**
Tam Dalyell *Dick Crossman* (1989)

11 The Civil Service is profoundly deferential — 'Yes, Minister! No, Minister! If you wish it, Minister!'

Diaries of a Cabinet Minister vol. 1 (1975) 22 October 1964

Samuel Crossman 1624–83

English clergyman

12 My song is love unknown,
My saviour's love for me,
Love to the loveless shown,
That they might lovely be.
O, who am I,
That for my sake
My Lord should take
Frail flesh and die?

'My song is love unknown' (1664); set to music as a hymn from 1868, and by John Ireland in 1919

Crowfoot c.1830–90

Blackfoot chief

13 A little while and I will be gone from among you, whither I cannot tell. From nowhere we came, into nowhere we go. What is life? It is a flash of a firefly in the night. It is a breath of a buffalo in the winter time. It is as the little shadow that runs across the grass and loses itself in the sunset.

attributed farewell to his people, 25 April 1890; John Peter Turner The North-West Mounted Police: 1873–93 (1950); see **HAGGARD** 376:3

Aleister Crowley 1875–1947

English diabolist

14 Do what thou wilt shall be the whole of the Law.

Book of the Law (1909) l. 40; see **RABELAIS** 652:10

Ralph Cudworth 1617–88

English Puritan divine and scholar

15 Some who are far from atheists, may make themselves merry with that conceit of thousands of spirits dancing at once upon a needle's point.

The True Intellectual System of the Universe (1678)

Nicholas Culpeper 1616–54

English physician

1 God gave tyrants in his wrath, and will take them away in his displeasure.
A Physical Directory (1649)

Richard Cumberland 1631–1718

English divine

2 It is better to wear out than to rust out.
George Horne *The Duty of Contending for the Faith* (1786); see
PROVERBS 627:41

e. e. cummings (Edward Estlin Cummings) 1894–1962

American poet

3 anyone lived in a pretty how town
(with up so floating many bells down)
spring summer autumn winter
he sang his didn't he danced his did.
50 Poems (1949) no. 29

4 'next to of course god america i
love you land of the pilgrims' and so forth oh
say can you see by the dawn's early my
country 'tis of centuries come and go
and are no more what of it we should worry
in every language even deafanddumb
thy sons acclaim your glorious name by gorry
by jingo by gee by gosh by gum.
is 5 (1926) p. 62

5 Humanity i love you because
when you're hard up you pawn your
intelligence to buy a drink.
'La Guerre' no. 2 (1925)

6 o to be a metope
now that triglyph's here.
'Memorabilia' (1926); see **BROWNING** 165:27

7 a politician is an arse upon
which everyone has sat except a man.
1 x 1 (1944) no. 10

8 plato told
him: he couldn't
believe it (jesus
told him; he
wouldn't believe
it) lao
tsze
certainly told
him, and general
(yes
mam)
sherman.
1 x 1 (1944) no. 13

9 pity this busy monster, manunkind,
not. Progress is a comfortable disease.
1 x 1 (1944) no. 14

10 We doctors know
a hopeless case if—listen: there's a hell

of a good universe next door; let's go.
1 x 1 (1944) no. 14

11 when man determined to destroy
himself he picked the was
of shall and finding only why
smashed it into because.
1 x 1 (1944) no. 26

12 i like my body when it is with your
body. It is so quite new a thing.
Muscles better and nerves more.
'Sonnets–Actualities' no. 8 (1925)

13 the Cambridge ladies who live in furnished souls
are unbeautiful and have comfortable minds.
'Sonnets–Realities' no. 1 (1923)

William Thomas Cummings 1903–45

American priest

14 There are no atheists in the foxholes.
Carlos P. Romulo *I Saw the Fall of the Philippines* (1943) ch. 15

Allan Cunningham 1784–1842

Scottish poet

15 A wet sheet and a flowing sea,
A wind that follows fast
And fills the white and rustling sail
And bends the gallant mast.
'A Wet Sheet and a Flowing Sea' (1825)

16 It's hame and it's hame, hame fain wad I be,
O, hame, hame, hame to my ain countree!
'It's hame and It's hame', in James Hogg *Jacobite Relics of Scotland* (1819) vol. 1; in his notes, Hogg says he took it from R. H. Cromek's *Remains of Nithsdale and Galloway Song* (1810) and supposes that it owed much to Cunningham

J. V. Cunningham 1911–85

American poet

17 And all's coherent.
Search in this gloss
No text inherent:
The text was loss.
The gain is gloss.
'To the Reader' (1947)

Mario Cuomo 1932–

American Democratic politician

18 You campaign in poetry. You govern in prose.
in *New Republic*, Washington, DC, 8 April 1985

Don Cupitt 1934–

English theologian

19 Christmas is the Disneyfication of Christianity.
in *Independent* 19 December 1996

Marie Curie 1867–1934

Polish-born French physicist

20 In science, we must be interested in things, not in persons.
to an American journalist, c.1904, after she and her

husband Pierre had shared the Nobel Prize for Physics with
A.-H. Becquerel

    Eve Curie *Madame Curie* (1937)

1 Nothing in life is to be feared, it is only to be
understood.

    attributed

Allen Curnow 1911–2001

New Zealand poet and critic

2 Simply by sailing in a new direction
You could enlarge the world.

    'Landfall in Unknown Seas' (1943)

3 The sailor lives, and stands beside us, paying
Out into time's wave
The stain of blood that writes an island story.

    'Landfall in Unknown Seas' (1943)

John Philpot Curran 1750–1817

Irish judge

4 The condition upon which God hath given
liberty to man is eternal vigilance; which
condition if he break, servitude is at once the
consequence of his crime, and the punishment
of his guilt.

    speech on the right of election of the Lord Mayor of Dublin,
10 July 1790, in Thomas Davis (ed.) *Speeches* (1845)

5 Like the silver plate on a coffin.

    describing Robert **PEEL**'s smile

    quoted by Daniel O'Connell, House of Commons, 26 February
1835

Edwina Currie 1946–

British Conservative politician

6 I wasn't even in the index.

    on the omission of their affair from John **MAJOR**'s
autobiography

    in *The Times* 28 September 2002

John Curtin 1885–1945

Australian Labor statesman, Prime Minister 1941–5

7 Australia looks to America, free of any pangs as
to our traditional links or kinship with the
United Kingdom.

    *of the threat from Japan, and British reluctance to recall
Australian troops from the Middle East*

    in *Herald* (Melbourne) 27 December 1941

Michael Curtiz 1888–1962

Hungarian-born American film director

8 Bring on the empty horses!

    while directing The Charge of the Light Brigade *(1936
film)*

    David Niven *Bring on the Empty Horses* (1975) ch. 6

Lord Curzon 1859–1925

British Conservative politician; Viceroy of India 1898–1905.
On Curzon: see ANONYMOUS 19:3, CHURCHILL 230:16, NEHRU
569:14

9 When a group of Cabinet Ministers begins to
meet separately and to discuss independent
action, the death-tick is audible in the rafters.

    in November 1922, shortly before the fall of **LLOYD GEORGE**'s
Coalition Government

    David Gilmour *Curzon* (1994)

10 Not even a public figure. A man of no
experience. And of the utmost insignificance.

    of Stanley **BALDWIN**, *appointed Prime Minister in 1923 in
succession to* **BONAR LAW**

    Harold Nicolson *Curzon: the Last Phase* (1934)

11 Dear me, I never knew that the lower classes
had such white skins.

    *supposedly said by Curzon when watching troops bathing
during the First World War*

    K. Rose *Superior Person* (1969)

12 Gentlemen do not take soup at luncheon.

    E. L. Woodward *Short Journey* (1942) ch. 7

Astolphe Louis Léonard, Marquis de Custine 1790–1857

French writer and traveller

13 This empire, vast as it is, is only a prison to
which the emperor holds the key.

    of Russia

    La Russie en 1839; at Peterhof, 23 July 1839

St Cyprian c.AD 200–258

Roman writer and martyr; Bishop of Carthage

14 He cannot have God for his father who has not
the church for his mother.

    De Ecclesiae Catholicae Unitate sect. 6; see **AUGUSTINE** 39:14

15 *Fratres nostros non esse lugendos arcessitione
dominica de saeculo liberatos, cum sciamus non
amitti sed praemitti.*

Our brethren who have been freed from the
world by the summons of the Lord should not
be mourned, since we know that they are not
lost but sent before.

    De Mortalite ch. 20 (ed. M. L. Hannam, 1933); see **NORTON**
577:8, **ROGERS** 665:13

16 There cannot be salvation for any, except in the
Church.

    Epistle Ad Pomponium, De Virginibus sect. 4; see **AUGUSTINE**
39:14, **CYPRIAN** 263:14

Dd

Hugh Dalton 1887–1962
British Labour politician

1 He is loyal to his own career but only incidentally to anything or anyone else.
of Richard **CROSSMAN**
diary, 17 September 1941

Tam Dalyell 1932–
Scottish-born Labour politician

2 Under the new Bill, shall I still be able to vote on many matters in relation to West Bromwich but not West Lothian, as I was under the last Bill, and will my right hon. Friend [James Callaghan, MP for Cardiff] be able to vote on many matters in relation to Carlisle but not Cardiff?
formulation of the 'West Lothian question', identifying the constitutional anomaly that would arise if devolved assemblies were established for Scotland and for Wales but not for England
in the House of Commons, 3 November 1977

Charles A. Dana 1819–97
American newspaper editor

3 If a dog bites a man it is not news, but if a man bites a dog it is.
often attributed to the American journalist John B. Bogart (1848–1921)
attributed, in *Bookman* February 1917; earlier sources do not attribute to a specific individual

Samuel Daniel 1563–1619
English poet and dramatist

4 And look, how Thames, enriched with many a flood . . .
Glides on, with pomp of waters, unwithstood,
Unto the ocean.
The Civil Wars (1595) bk. 2, st. 7

5 Custom that is before all law, Nature that is above all art.
A Defence of Rhyme (1603)

6 Care-charmer Sleep, son of the sable Night,
Brother to Death, in silent darkness born.
Delia (1592) Sonnet 54; see **FLETCHER** 335:12, **SHELLEY** 746:5

7 Tiring thy wits and toiling to no end,
But to attain that idle smoke of praise.
Musophilus (1599) l. 1

8 And who, in time, knows whither we may vent
The treasure of our tongue, to what strange shores
This gain of our best glory shall be sent,

T'enrich unknowing nations with our stores?
What worlds in th'yet unformed Occident
May come refined with th'accents that are ours?
Musophilus (1599) l. 957

9   But years hath done this wrong,
To make me write too much, and live too long.
Philotas (1605) 'To the Prince' (dedication) l. 108

10 Tis strange to see the humour of these men
These great aspiring spirits, that should be wise.
Philotas (1605) act 1, sc. 2, l. 350

11   Princes in this case
Do hate the traitor, though they love the treason.
The Tragedy of Cleopatra (1594) act 4, sc. 1; see **DRYDEN** 295:19

Dante Alighieri 1265–1321
Italian poet whose epic poem *The Divine Comedy* describes his spiritual journey through Hell and Purgatory, and finally to Paradise. On Dante: see **BROWNING** 166:23

12 *Nel mezzo del cammin di nostra vita*
Mi ritrovai per una selva oscura
che la diritta via era smarrita.
In the middle of the journey of our life I came to myself within a dark wood where the straight way was lost.
Divina Commedia 'Inferno' canto 1, l. 1

13 PER ME SI VA NELLA CITTÀ DOLENTE,
PER ME SI VA NELL' ETERNO DOLORE,
PER ME SI VA TRA LA PERDUTA GENTE . . .
LASCIATE OGNI SPERANZA VOI CH'ENTRATE!
Through me is the way to the sorrowful city.
Through me is the way to eternal suffering.
Through me is the way to join the lost people . . . Abandon all hope, you who enter!
inscription at the entrance to Hell
Divina Commedia 'Inferno' canto 3, l. 1

14 *Non ragioniam di lor, ma guarda, e passa.*
Let us not speak of them, but look, and pass on.
Divina Commedia 'Inferno' canto 3, l. 51

15 *Il gran rifiuto.*
The great refusal.
Divina Commedia 'Inferno' canto 3, l. 60

16 *Onorate l'altissimo poeta.*
Honour the greatest poet.
of **VIRGIL**
Divina Commedia 'Inferno' canto 4, l. 80

17 *Il maestro di color che sanno.*
The master of those who know.
of **ARISTOTLE**
Divina Commedia 'Inferno' canto 4, l. 131

18 . . . *Nessun maggior dolore,*
Che ricordarsi del tempo felice
Nella miseria.
There is no greater pain than to remember a happy time when one is in misery.
Divina Commedia 'Inferno' canto 5, l. 121; see **BOETHIUS** 130:11, **TENNYSON** 796:24

1 *Galeotto fu il libro e chi lo scrisse:*
Quel giorno più non vi leggemmo avante.

A Galeotto [a pander] was the book and writer too: that day we did not read any more.
Divina Commedia 'Inferno' canto 5, l. 137

2 *Siete voi qui, ser Brunetto?*

Are *you* here, Advocate Brunetto?
of Brunetto Latini, an old and respected friend of Dante, encountered in hell
Divina Commedia 'Inferno' canto 15, l. 30

3 *La cara e buona imagine paterna.*

The dear and kindly paternal image.
Divina Commedia 'Inferno' canto 15, l. 83

4 *Considerate la vostra semenza:*
Fatti non foste a viver come bruti,
Ma per seguir virtute e conoscenza.

Consider your origins: you were not made to live as brutes, but to follow virtue and knowledge.
Divina Commedia 'Inferno' canto 26, l. 118

5 *Lamenti saettaron me diversi,*
Che di pietà ferrati avean li strali.

Strange lamentations assailed me that had their shafts barbed with pity.
Divina Commedia 'Inferno' canto 29, l. 43

6 *E quindi uscimmo a riveder le stelle.*

Thence we came forth to see the stars again.
Divina Commedia 'Inferno' canto 34, l. 139

7 *O dignitosa coscienza e netta,*
Come t'è picciol fallo amaro morso!

O pure and noble conscience, how bitter a sting to thee is a little fault!
Divina Commedia 'Purgatorio' canto 3, l. 8

8 *Questa montagna è tale,*
Che sempre al cominciar di sotto è grave;
E quant' uom più va su, e men fa male.

This mountain is such that it is always hard at the start below and the higher one goes it is less toilsome.
Divina Commedia 'Purgatorio' canto 4, l. 88

9 *Che ti fa ciò che quivi pispiglia?*
Vien dietro a me, e lascia dir le genti.

What is it to thee what they whisper there? Come after me and let the people talk.
Divina Commedia 'Purgatorio' canto 5, l. 12

10 *Rade volte risurge per li rami*
L'umana probitate; e questo vole
Quei che la dà, perché da lui si chiami.

Rarely does human worth rise through the branches, and this He wills also who gives it, that it may be sought from Him.
Divina Commedia 'Purgatorio' canto 7, l. 121

11 *O vana gloria dell'umane posse*
Com'poco verde in su la cima dura
se non è giunta dall'etati grosse!

Credette Cimabue nella pittura
tener lo campo, ed ora ha Giotto il grido
si che la fama di colui è oscura.

O vain renown of human enterprise, no longer lasting than the greenery of the trees, unless succeeded by an uncouth age.
In painting Cimabue was thought to hold the field; now Giotto has the palm, so that he has obscured the other's fame.
Divina Commedia 'Purgatorio' canto 11, l. 91

12 *Non è il mondan romore altro che un fiato*
di vento, ch'or vien quinci ed or qien quindi,
e muta nome perchè muta lato.

The reputation which the world bestows is like the wind, that shifts now here now there, its name changed with the quarter whence it blows.
Divina Commedia 'Purgatorio' canto 11, l. 100

13 *Men che dramma*
Di sangue m'è rimaso, che no tremi;
Conosco i segni dell' antica fiamma.

Less than a drop of blood remains in me that does not tremble; I recognize the signals of the ancient flame.
Divina Commedia 'Purgatorio' canto 30, l. 46; see **VIRGIL** 829:20

14 *Puro e disposto a salire alle stelle.*

Pure and ready to mount to the stars.
Divina Commedia 'Purgatorio' canto 33, l. 145

15 *E'n la sua volontade è nostra pace.*

In His will is our peace.
Divina Commedia 'Paradiso' canto 3, l. 85

16 *Tu proverai sì come sa di sale*
Lo pane altrui, e com'è duro calle
Lo scendere e'l salir per l'altrui scale.

You shall find out how salt is the taste of another man's bread, and how hard is the way up and down another man's stairs.
Divina Commedia 'Paradiso' canto 17, l. 58

17 *L'amor che muove il sole e l'altre stelle.*

The love that moves the sun and the other stars.
Divina Commedia 'Paradiso' canto 33, l. 145

Georges Jacques Danton 1759–94

French revolutionary leader and orator, executed on the orders of his former ally **ROBESPIERRE**. See also **STENDHAL** 771:15

18 *De l'audace, et encore de l'audace, et toujours de l'audace!*

Boldness, and again boldness, and always boldness!
speech to the Legislative Committee of General Defence, 2 September 1792, in *Le Moniteur* 4 September 1792; see **BACON** 46:11

19 Kings and emperors threaten us, but now you have thrown down the gauntlet to them. That gauntlet is the head of a king.
speech to the inhabitants of Liège and Hainault, 31 January 1793, in Robert Christophe *Danton* (1967)

1 Thou wilt show my head to the people: it is worth showing.
to his executioner, 5 April 1794
Thomas Carlyle *History of the French Revolution* (1837) vol. 3, bk. 6, ch. 2

Joe Darion 1917–2001
American songwriter

2 Dream the impossible dream.
'The Impossible Dream' (1965 song)

George Darley 1795–1846
Irish-born poet

3 O blest unfabled Incense Tree,
That burns in glorious Araby.
'Nepenthe' (1835) l. 147

Bill Darnell
Canadian environmentalist

4 Make it a *green* peace.
at a meeting of the Don't Make a Wave Committee, which preceded the formation of Greenpeace
in Vancouver, 1970; Robert Hunter *The Greenpeace Chronicle* (1979); see **HUNTER** 422:2

Clarence Darrow 1857–1938
American lawyer, noted counsel for the defence

5 I do not consider it an insult, but rather a compliment to be called an agnostic. I do not pretend to know where many ignorant men are sure—that is all that agnosticism means.
speech at the trial of John Thomas Scopes for teaching Darwin's theory of evolution in school, 15 July 1925, in *The World's Most Famous Court Trial* (1925) ch. 4

6 I would like to see a time when man loves his fellow man and forgets his colour or his creed. We will never be civilized until that time comes. I know the Negro race has a long road to go. I believe that the life of the Negro race has been a life of tragedy, of injustice, of oppression. The law has made him equal, but man has not.
speech in Detroit, 19 May 1926

7 When I was a boy I was told that anybody could become President. I'm beginning to believe it.
Irving Stone *Clarence Darrow for the Defence* (1941)

Charles Darwin 1809–82
English natural historian and geologist, proponent of the theory of evolution by natural selection; grandson of Erasmus DARWIN, father of Francis DARWIN. On Darwin: see HUXLEY 423:12

8 Disinterested love for all living creatures, the most noble attribute of man.
The Descent of Man (1871) ch. 3

9 The highest possible stage in moral culture is when we recognize that we ought to control our thoughts.
The Descent of Man (1871) ch. 4

10 False views, if supported by some evidence, do little harm, for everyone takes a salutary pleasure in proving their falseness.
The Descent of Man (1871) ch. 21

11 A hairy quadruped, furnished with a tail and pointed ears, probably arboreal in its habits.
on man's probable ancestors
The Descent of Man (1871) ch. 21

12 Man with all his noble qualities . . . still bears in his bodily frame the indelible stamp of his lowly origin.
The Descent of Man (1871), closing words

13 I have called this principle, by which each slight variation, if useful, is preserved, by the term of Natural Selection.
On the Origin of Species (1859) ch. 3

14 We will now discuss in a little more detail the Struggle for Existence.
On the Origin of Species (1859) ch. 3

15 The expression often used by Mr Herbert Spencer of the Survival of the Fittest is more accurate [than 'Struggle for Existence'], and is sometimes equally convenient.
On the Origin of Species (1869 ed.) ch. 3; see **SPENCER** 765:22

16 From the war of nature, from famine and death, the most exalted object which we are capable of conceiving, namely, the production of the higher animals, directly follows.
On the Origin of Species (1859) ch. 3

17 There is grandeur in this view of life.
On the Origin of Species (1859) ch. 14

18 From so simple a beginning endless forms most beautiful and most wonderful have been, and are being, evolved.
On the Origin of Species (1859) ch. 14

19 What a book a devil's chaplain might write on the clumsy, wasteful, blundering, low, and horridly cruel works of nature!
letter to J. D. Hooker, 13 July 1856, in *Correspondence of Charles Darwin* vol. 6 (1990)

20 Animals, whom we have made our slaves, we do not like to consider our equal.
Notebook B (1837–8) in P. H. Barrett et al. (eds.) *Charles Darwin's Notebooks 1836–1844* (1987)

21 He who understands baboon [will] would do more towards metaphysics than Locke.
Notebook M (16 August 1838) in P. H. Barrett et al. (eds.) *Charles Darwin's Notebooks 1836–1844* (1987)

22 With me the horrid doubt always arises whether the convictions of man's mind which has been developed from the mind of the lower animals, are of any value or at all trustworthy.
Francis Darwin (ed.) *The Life and Letters of Charles Darwin* (1887) ch. 3

Erasmus Darwin 1731–1802

English physician; grandfather of Charles **DARWIN**, great-grandfather of Francis **DARWIN**

1 A fool . . . is a man who never tried an experiment in his life.
> F. V. Barry (ed.) *Maria Edgeworth: Chosen Letters* (1931) To Sophy Ruxton, 9 March 1792

2 No, Sir, because I have time to think before I speak, and don't ask impertinent questions.
when asked if he found his stammering very inconvenient
> 'Reminiscences of My Father's Everyday Life', an appendix by Francis Darwin to his edition of Charles Darwin *Autobiography* (1877)

Erasmus Darwin 1804–81

English physician, brother of Charles **DARWIN**

3 In fact the *a priori* reasoning is so entirely satisfactory to me that if the facts won't fit in, why so much the worse for the facts is my feeling.
after reading The Origin of Species
> letter to Charles Darwin, 23 November 1859; F. Darwin (ed.) *The Life of Charles Darwin* (1902)

Francis Darwin 1848–1925

English botanist; son of Charles **DARWIN**, great-grandson of Erasmus **DARWIN**

4 In science the credit goes to the man who convinces the world, not to the man to whom the idea first occurs.
> in *Eugenics Review* April 1914 'Francis Galton'

Charles D'Avenant 1656–1714

English dramatist and political economist

5 Custom, that unwritten law,
By which the people keep even kings in awe.
> *Circe* (1677) act 2, sc. 3

William D'Avenant 1606–68

English dramatist and poet

6 In every grave make room, make room!
The world's at an end, and we come, we come.
> *The Law against Lovers* (1673) act 3, sc. 1 'Viola's Song'

7 Had laws not been, we never had been blamed;
For not to know we sin is innocence.
> 'The Philosopher's Disquisition directed to the Dying Christian' (1672) st. 76

8 So nature, when she fruit designs, thinks fit
By beauteous blossoms to proceed to it;
And whilst she does accomplish all the spring,
Birds to her secret operations sing.
> 'Poem to the King's most Sacred Majesty' (1663)

9 For I must go where lazy Peace
Will hide her drowsy head;
And, for the sport of kings, increase
The number of the dead.
> 'The Soldier Going to the Field' (1673); see **SOMERVILLE** 760:18, **SURTEES** 781:6

10 The lark now leaves his wat'ry nest
And, climbing, shakes his dewy wings.
> 'Song: The Lark' (1638)

Elizabeth David 1913–92

English cook and writer

11 Good food is always a trouble and its preparation should be regarded as a labour of love.
> *French Country Cooking* (1951) introduction

12 The cooking of the Mediterranean shores, endowed with all the natural resources, the colour and flavour of the South, is a blend of tradition and brilliant improvisation. The Latin genius flashes from the kitchen pans.
> *Mediterranean Food* (1950) introduction

13 In Europe, spices were the jewels and furs and brocades of the kitchen and the still-room.
> *Spices, Salt and Aromatics in the English Kitchen* (1970) preface

John Davidson 1857–1909

Scottish poet

14 A runnable stag, a kingly crop.
> 'A Runnable Stag' (1906)

15 In anguish we uplift
A new unhallowed song:
The race is to the swift,
The battle to the strong.
> 'War Song' (1899) st. 1; see **BIBLE** 90:11

John Davies 1569–1626

English poet

16 Wedlock, indeed, hath oft compared been
To public feasts where meet a public rout,
Where they that are without would fain go in
And they that are within would fain go out.
> 'A Contention Betwixt a Wife, a Widow, and a Maid for Precedence' (1608) l. 193

17 Skill comes so slow, and life so fast doth fly,
We learn so little and forget so much.
> 'Nosce Teipsum' (1599) st. 19

18 For this, the wisest of all moral men
Said *he knew nought, but that he nought did know;*
And the great mocking master mocked not then,
When he said, *Truth was buried deep below.*
> 'Nosce Teipsum' (1599) st. 20; see **MILTON** 544:27, **SOCRATES** 759:15

19 I know my life's a pain and but a span,
I know my sense is mocked in every thing;
And to conclude, I know myself a man,
Which is a proud and yet a wretched thing.
> 'Nosce Teipsum' (1599) st. 45

20 This wondrous miracle did Love devise,
For dancing is love's proper exercise.
> 'Orchestra, or a Poem of Dancing' (1596) st. 18

21 What makes the vine about the elm to dance
With turnings, windings, and embracements round?

What makes the lodestone to the north advance
His subtle point, as if from thence he found
His chief attractive virtue to redound?
Kind nature first doth cause all things to love;
Love makes them dance, and in just order move.
'Orchestra, or a Poem of Dancing' (1596) st. 56

1 Since all the world's great fortune and affairs
Forward and backward rapt and whirlèd are,
According to the music of the spheres;
And Chance herself her nimble feet upbears
On a round slippery wheel, that rolleth aye.
And turns all states with her imperious sway;
'Orchestra, or a Poem of Dancing' (1596) st. 60

Robertson Davies 1913–95
Canadian novelist

2 A great many complimentary things have been
said about the faculty of memory, and if you
look in a good quotation book you will find
them neatly arranged.
The Enthusiasms of Robertson Davies (1990)

3 I see Canada as a country torn between a very
northern, rather extraordinary, mystical spirit
which it fears and its desire to present itself to
the world as a Scotch banker.
The Enthusiasms of Robertson Davies (1990)

Scrope Davies c.1783–1852
English conversationalist

4 Babylon in all its desolation is a sight not so
awful as that of the human mind in ruins.
ADDISON, in The Spectator no. 421 (3 July 1712), also
remarked of 'a distracted person' that 'Babylon in ruins is
not so melancholy a spectacle'
letter to Thomas Raikes, May 1835, in *A Portion of the Journal
kept by Thomas Raikes* (1856) vol. 2; see **BIBLE** 119:1, **DOYLE**
292:12

W. H. Davies 1871–1940
Welsh poet

5 And hear the pleasant cuckoo, loud and long—
The simple bird that thinks two notes a song.
'April's Charms' (1916)

6 A rainbow and a cuckoo's song
May never come together again;
May never come
This side the tomb.
'A Great Time' (1914)

7 It was the Rainbow gave thee birth,
And left thee all her lovely hues.
'Kingfisher' (1910)

8 What is this life if, full of care,
We have no time to stand and stare.
'Leisure' (1911)

9 Sweet Stay-at-Home, sweet Well-content,
Thou knowest of no strange continent:
Thou hast not felt thy bosom keep
A gentle motion with the deep.
'Sweet Stay-At-Home' (1913)

Bette Davis *see* **Epitaphs** 319:9, **Film lines**
328:3, **Film lines** 328:6, **Film lines** 329:22

Jefferson Davis 1808–89
American statesman, President of the Confederate states
1861–5. On Davis: see **YANCEY** 872:5

10 If the Confederacy fails, there should be written
on its tombstone: *Died of a Theory.*
in 1865; Geoffrey C. Ward *The Civil War* (1991) ch. 5

Sammy Davis Jnr. 1925–90
American entertainer

11 Being a star has made it possible for me to get
insulted in places where the average Negro
could never *hope* to go and get insulted.
Yes I Can (1965) pt. 3, ch. 23

Thomas Davis 1814–45
Irish poet and nationalist. On Davis: see **FERGUSON** 325:6

12 But the land of their heart's hope they never
saw more,
For in far, foreign fields, from Dunkirk to
Belgrade
Lie the soldiers and chiefs of the Irish Brigade.
'The Battle-Eve of the Brigade' (1846)

13 And then I prayed I yet might see
Our fetters rent in twain,
And Ireland, long a province, be
A Nation once again.
'A Nation Once Again' (1846)

14 Come in the evening, or come in the morning,
Come when you're looked for, or come without
warning.
'The Welcome' (1846)

15 But—hark!—some voice like thunder spake:
The West's awake! the West's awake!
'The West's Asleep' (1846)

16 This country of ours is no sandbank, thrown up
by some recent caprice of earth. It is an ancient
land, honoured in the archives of civilisation,
traceable into antiquity by its piety, its valour,
and its sufferings. Every great European race has
sent its stream to the river of Irish mind.
Literary and Historical Essays (1846)

17 If we live influenced by wind, and sun, and tree,
and not by the passions and deeds of the past,
we are a thriftless and hopeless people.
Literary and Historical Essays (1846)

Michael Davitt 1846–1905
Irish nationalist

18 An Englishman of the strongest type moulded
for an Irish purpose.
of Charles Stewart **PARNELL**
The Fall of Feudalism in Ireland (1906)

Richard Dawkins 1941–

English evolutionary biologist and science writer

1 [Natural selection] has no vision, no foresight, no sight at all. If it can be said to play the role of watchmaker in nature, it is the *blind* watchmaker.
The Blind Watchmaker (1986) ch. 1; see **PALEY** 593:8

2 However many ways there may be of being alive, it is certain that there are vastly more ways of being dead.
The Blind Watchmaker (1986) ch. 1

3 The essence of life is statistical improbability on a colossal scale.
The Blind Watchmaker (1986) ch. 11

4 They are in you and in me; they created us, body and mind; and their preservation is the ultimate rationale for our existence . . . they go by the name of genes, and we are their survival machines.
The Selfish Gene (1976) ch. 2

Christopher Dawson 1889–1970

English historian of ideas and social culture

5 As soon as men decide that all means are permitted to fight an evil, then their good becomes indistinguishable from the evil that they set out to destroy.
The Judgement of the Nations (1942)

Lord Dawson of Penn 1864–1945

English physician to King **GEORGE V**

6 The King's life is moving peacefully towards its close.
bulletin, drafted on a menu card at Buckingham Palace on the eve of the king's death, 20 January 1936, in Kenneth Rose *King George V* (1983) ch. 10

C. Day-Lewis 1904–72

English poet and critic

7 Do not expect again a phoenix hour,
The triple-towered sky, the dove complaining,
Sudden the rain of gold and heart's first ease
Traced under trees by the eldritch light of sundown.
'From Feathers to Iron' (1935)

8 Tempt me no more; for I
Have known the lightning's hour,
The poet's inward pride,
The certainty of power.
The Magnetic Mountain (1933) pt. 3, no. 24

9 And when the Treaty emptied the British jails,
A haggard woman returned and Dublin went wild to greet her.
But still it was not enough: an iota
Of compromise, she cried, and the Cause fails.
'Remembering Con Markievicz' (1970)

10 Selfhood begins with a walking away,
And love is proved in the letting go.
'Walking Away' (1962)

11 It is the logic of our times,
No subject for immortal verse—
That we who lived by honest dreams
Defend the bad against the worse.
'Where are the War Poets?' (1943)

James Dean *see* Film titles 331:10

John Dean 1938–

American lawyer and White House counsel during the Watergate affair

12 We have a cancer within, close to the Presidency, that is growing.
from the [Nixon] Presidential Transcripts, 21 March 1973

Seamus Deane 1940–

Irish poet and novelist

13 Meningitis. It was a word you had to bite on to say it. It had a fright and a hiss in it.
Reading in the Dark (1996)

Percy Dearmer 1867–1936

English clergyman

14 He who would valiant be
'Gainst all disaster,
Let him in constancy
Follow the Master.
'He who would valiant be', hymn after John Bunyan; see **BUNYAN** 171:25

15 Jesu, good above all other,
Gentle Child of gentle Mother,
In a stable born our Brother,
Give us grace to persevere.
'Jesu, good above all other' (1906 hymn)

Simone de Beauvoir 1908–86

French novelist and feminist

16 It is not in giving life but in risking life that man is raised above the animal; that is why superiority has been accorded in humanity not to the sex that brings forth but to that which kills.
The Second Sex (1949) vol. 1, pt. 2, ch. 1

17 One is not born a woman: one becomes one.
The Second Sex (1949) vol. 2, pt. 1, ch. 1

18 Few tasks are more like the torture of Sisyphus than housework, with its endless repetition . . . The housewife wears herself out marking time: she makes nothing, simply perpetuates the present.
The Second Sex (1949) pt. 5, ch. 1

Louis de Bernières 1954–

English novelist and short-story writer

19 The human heart likes a little disorder in its geometry.
Captain Corelli's Mandolin (1994) ch. 26

Edward de Bono 1933–

British writer and physician

1 Some people are aware of another sort of thinking which ... leads to those simple ideas that are obvious only after they have been thought of ... the term 'lateral thinking' has been coined to describe this other sort of thinking; 'vertical thinking' is used to denote the conventional logical process.
   The Use of Lateral Thinking (1967) foreword

Eugene Victor Debs 1855–1926

American socialist

2 When great changes occur in history, when great principles are involved, as a rule the majority are wrong. The minority are right.
   speech at his trial for sedition in Cleveland, Ohio, 11 September 1918; in *Speeches* (1928); see **DILLON** 283:8

3 While there is a lower class, I am in it; while there is a criminal element, I am of it; while there is a soul in prison, I am not free.
   speech at his trial for sedition in Cleveland, Ohio, 14 September 1918; in *Liberator* November 1918

Stephen Decatur 1779–1820

American naval officer

4 Our country! In her intercourse with foreign nations, may she always be in the right; but our country, right or wrong.
   Decatur's toast at Norfolk, Virginia, April 1816, in A. S. Mackenzie *Life of Stephen Decatur* (1846) ch. 14; see **ADAMS** 3:16, **SCHURZ** 687:9

Daniel Defoe 1660–1731

English novelist and journalist; his novel *Robinson Crusoe* (1719) was based on the real-life adventures of Alexander Selkirk (1676–1721), who had been marooned on the uninhabited Pacific island of Juan Fernandez between 1704 and 1709

5 We must distinguish between a man of polite learning and a mere scholar: the first is a gentleman and what a gentleman should be; the last is a mere book-case, a bundle of letters, a head stuffed with the jargon of languages, a man that understands every body but is understood by no body.
   The Complete English Gentleman (written 1728–9) ch. 5

6 We not only dig our graves with our teeth.
   Conjugal Lewdness (1727) ch. 12; see **SMILES** 755:17

7 Why then should women be denied the benefits of instruction? If knowledge and understanding had been useless additions to the sex, God almighty would never have given them capacities.
   An Essay Upon Projects (1697) 'Of Academies: An Academy for Women'

8 Things as certain as death and taxes, can be more firmly believed.
   History of the Devil (1726) bk. 2, ch. 6; see **FRANKLIN** 341:10

9 Vice came in always at the door of necessity, not at the door of inclination.
   Moll Flanders (1721)

10 Give me not poverty lest I steal.
   Review vol. 8, no. 75 (15 September 1711); later incorporated into *Moll Flanders* (1721)

11 He told me ... that mine was the middle state, or what might be called the upper station of low life, which he had found by long experience was the best state in the world, the most suited to human happiness.
   Robinson Crusoe (1719)

12 I never saw them afterwards, or any sign of them, except three of their hats, one cap, and two shoes that were not fellows.
   on his shipmates
   Robinson Crusoe (1719, ed. J. D. Crowley, 1972)

13 It happened one day, about noon, going towards my boat, I was exceedingly surprised with the print of a man's naked foot on the shore, which was very plain to be seen in the sand. I stood like one thunderstruck, or as if I had seen an apparition.
   Robinson Crusoe (1719)

14 My man Friday.
   Robinson Crusoe (1719)

15 My island was now peopled, and I thought my self very rich in subjects; and it was a merry reflection which I frequently made, how like a king I looked.
   Robinson Crusoe (1719); see **COWPER** 257:4

16 The best of men cannot suspend their fate:
The good die early, and the bad die late.
   'Character of the late Dr S. Annesley' (1697)

17 We loved the doctrine for the teacher's sake.
   'Character of the late Dr S. Annesley' (1697)

18 Nature has left this tincture in the blood,
That all men would be tyrants if they could.
   The History of the Kentish Petition (1712–13) addenda, l. 11

19 Actions receive their tincture from the times,
And as they change are virtues made or crimes.
   A Hymn to the Pillory (1703) l. 29

20 Fools out of favour grudge at knaves in place.
   The True-Born Englishman (1701) introduction, l. 7

21 Wherever God erects a house of prayer,
The Devil always builds a chapel there;
And 'twill be found, upon examination,
The latter has the largest congregation.
   The True-Born Englishman (1701) pt. 1, l. 1; see **PROVERBS** 647:7

22 In their religion they are so uneven,
That each one goes his own by-way to heaven.
   The True-Born Englishman (1701) pt. 1, l. 104

23 From this amphibious ill-born mob began
That vain, ill-natured thing, an Englishman.
   The True Born Englishman (1701) pt.1, l. 132

24 Your Roman-Saxon-Danish-Norman English.
   The True-Born Englishman (1701) pt. 1, l. 139; **TENNYSON** 801:3

1 His lazy, long, lascivious reign.
of CHARLES II
The True-Born Englishman (1701) pt. 1, l. 236

2 Great families of yesterday we show,
And lords whose parents were the Lord knows
who.
The True-Born Englishman (1701) pt. 1, l. 374

3 And of all plagues with which mankind are
curst,
Ecclesiastic tyranny's the worst.
The True-Born Englishman (1701) pt. 2, l. 299

4 When kings the sword of justice first lay down,
They are no kings, though they possess the
crown.
Titles are shadows, crowns are empty things,
The good of subjects is the end of kings.
The True-Born Englishman (1701) pt. 2, l. 313

5 The power of nations is not now measured, as it
has been, by prowess, gallantry, and conduct.
'Tis the wealth of nations that makes them
great.
in *A Review of the Affairs of France* 19 April 1705

Edgar Degas 1834–1917

French artist

6 Art is vice. You don't marry it legitimately, you
rape it.
Paul Lafond *Degas* (1918)

Charles de Gaulle 1890–1970

French soldier and statesman, wartime organizer of the Free French movement; head of government 1944–6 and President 1959–69. On de Gaulle: see SPEARS 765:16

7 France has lost a battle. But France has not lost
the war!
proclamation, 18 June 1940, in *Discours, messages et déclarations du Général de Gaulle* (1941)

8 Faced by the bewilderment of my countrymen,
by the disintegration of a government in thrall
to the enemy, by the fact that the instututions of
my country are incapable, at the moment, of
functioning, I General de Gaulle, a French
soldier and military leader, realize that I now
speak for France.
speech in London, 19 June 1940

9 Since they whose duty it was to wield the sword
of France have let it fall shattered to the ground,
I have taken up the broken blade.
speech, 13 July 1940, in *Discours et Messages* (1942)

10 *Je vous ai compris.*
I have understood you.
speech to French colonists at Algiers, 4 June 1958, in *Discours et Messages* vol. 3 (1970); by 1962 Algeria had achieved independence

11 Politics are too serious a matter to be left to the
politicians.
replying to ATTLEE's remark that 'De Gaulle is a very good soldier and a very bad politician'
Clement Attlee *A Prime Minister Remembers* (1961) ch. 4; see CLEMENCEAU 235:6

12 *Europe des patries.*
A Europe of nations.
widely associated with De Gaulle, c.1962, and taken as encapsulating his views, although perhaps not coined by him
J. Lacouture *De Gaulle: the Ruler* (1991)

13 How can you govern a country which has 246
varieties of cheese?
Ernest Mignon *Les Mots du Général* (1962)

14 Since a politician never believes what he says, he
is quite surprised to be taken at his word.
Ernest Mignon *Les Mots du Général* (1962)

15 Treaties, you see, are like girls and roses: they
last while they last.
speech at Elysée Palace, 2 July 1963, in André Passeron *De Gaulle parle 1962–6* (1966)

16 *Vive Le Québec Libre.*
Long Live Free Quebec.
speech in Montreal, 24 July 1967, in *Discours et messages* (1970)

17 *Toute ma vie, je me suis fait une certaine idée de la France.*
All my life I have thought of France in a certain
way.
War Memoirs (1955) vol. 1

18 And now she is like everyone else.
on the death of his daughter, who had been born with Down's syndrome
Jean Lacouture *De Gaulle* (1965)

19 One does not put Voltaire in the Bastille.
when asked to arrest SARTRE, in the 1960s
in *Encounter* June 1975

Thomas Dekker 1570–1641

English dramatist

20 That great fishpond (the sea).
The Honest Whore (1604) pt. 1, act 1, sc. 2

21   The best of men
That e'er wore earth about him, was a sufferer,
A soft, meek, patient, humble, tranquil spirit,
The first true gentleman that ever breathed.
The Honest Whore (1604) pt. 1, act 1, sc. 2

22 Golden slumbers kiss your eyes,
Smiles awake you when you rise:
Sleep, pretty wantons, do not cry,
And I will sing a lullaby.
Rock them, rock them, lullaby.
Patient Grissil (1603) act 4, sc. 2

Walter de la Mare 1873–1956

English poet and novelist

23 Ann, Ann!
Come! quick as you can!
There's a fish that *talks*
In the frying-pan.
'Alas, Alack' (1913)

24 Oh, no man knows
Through what wild centuries

Roves back the rose.
'All That's Past' (1912)

1 He is crazed with the spell of far Arabia,
They have stolen his wits away.
'Arabia' (1912)

2 But beauty vanishes; beauty passes;
However rare—rare it be;
'Epitaph' (1912)

3 Look thy last on all things lovely,
Every hour.
'Fare Well' (1918)

4 Hi! handsome hunting man
Fire your little gun.
Bang! Now the animal
Is dead and dumb and done.
Nevermore to peep again, creep again, leap
again,
Eat or sleep or drink again, Oh, what fun!
'Hi!' (1930)

5 Three jolly gentlemen,
In coats of red,
Rode their horses
Up to bed.
'The Huntsmen' (1913)

6 'Is there anybody there?' said the Traveller,
Knocking on the moonlit door;
And his horse in the silence champed the grasses
Of the forest's ferny floor.
'The Listeners' (1912)

7 'Tell them I came, and no one answered,
That I kept my word,' he said.
'The Listeners' (1912)

8 Ay, they heard his foot upon the stirrup,
And the sound of iron on stone,
And how the silence surged softly backward,
When the plunging hoofs were gone.
'The Listeners' (1912)

9 What is the world, O soldiers?
It is I:
I, this incessant snow,
This northern sky;
Soldiers, this solitude
Through which we go
Is I.
'Napoleon' (1906)

10 Softly along the road of evening,
In a twilight dim with rose,
Wrinkled with age, and drenched with dew,
Old Nod, the shepherd, goes.
'Nod' (1912)

11 Slowly, silently, now the moon
Walks the night in her silver shoon.
'Silver' (1913)

12 Behind the blinds I sit and watch
The people passing—passing by;
And not a single one can see
My tiny watching eye.
'The Window' (1913)

Shelagh Delaney 1939–

English dramatist

13 Women never have young minds. They are born
three thousand years old.
A Taste of Honey (1959) act 1, sc. 2

Frederick Delius 1862–1934

English composer, of German and Scandinavian descent

14 It is only that which cannot be expressed
otherwise that is worth expressing in music.
in *Sackbut* September 1920 'At the Crossroads'

Agnes de Mille 1908–93

American dancer and choreographer

15 The truest expression of a people is in its dances
and its music. Bodies never lie.
in *New York Times Magazine* 11 May 1975

Democritus c.460–c.370 BC

Greek philosopher

16 By convention there is colour, by convention
sweetness, by convention bitterness, but in
reality there are atoms and space.
fragment 125

17 The animal needing something knows how
much it needs, the man does not.
fragment 198

Demosthenes c.384–c.322 BC

Greek orator and Athenian statesman

18 Nothing is easier than self-deceit. For what each
man wishes, that he also believes to be true.
Third Olynthiac sect. 19; see **BACON** 49:1, **CAESAR** 192:17

19 What worse change can any one bring against
an orator than that his words and his sentiments
do not tally?
On the Crown

20 You, Athenians, possessing unsurpassed
resources—fleet, infantry, cavalry, revenue—have
never to this very day employed them aright,
and yet you carry on war with Philip exactly as
a barbarian boxes. The barbarian, when struck,
always clutches the place; hit him on the other
side and there go his hands. He neither knows
nor cares how to parry a blow or how to watch
his adversary.
First Philippic ch. 40

21 Excessive dealings with tyrants are not good for
the security of free states.
Second Philippic ch. 21

22 There is one safeguard known generally to the
wise, which is an advantage and security to all,
but especially to democracies against
despots—suspicion.
Second Philippic ch. 24

1 When asked what was first in oratory, [he] replied to his questioner, 'action,' what second, 'action,' and again third, 'action'.
Cicero Brutus *ch. 37, sect. 142*

Jack Dempsey 1895–1983

American boxer

2 Honey, I just forgot to duck.
to his wife, on losing the World Heavyweight title, 23 September 1926; after a failed attempt on his life in 1981, Ronald REAGAN *quipped 'I forgot to duck'*
J. and B. P. Dempsey *Dempsey* (1977)

Deng Xiaoping 1904–97

Chinese Communist statesman, from 1977 paramount leader of China

3 It doesn't matter if a cat is black or white, as long as it catches mice.
in the early 1960s; in Daily Telegraph *20 February 1997, obituary*

John Denham 1615–69

English poet

4 Thames, the most loved of all the Ocean's sons,
By his old sire, to his embraces runs,
Hasting to pay his tribute to the Sea,
Like mortal life to meet eternity.
'Cooper's Hill' (1642)

5 Now every leaf and every moving breath
Presents a foe, and every foe a death.
'Cooper's Hill' (1642)

6 Youth, what man's age is like to be doth show;
We may our ends by our beginnings know.
'Of Prudence' (1668) l. 225

7 Old Mother Wit, and Nature gave
Shakespeare and Fletcher all they have;
In Spenser, and in Jonson, Art,
Of slower Nature got the start.
'On Mr Abraham Cowley' (1667)

8 Such is our pride, our folly, or our fate,
That few, but such as cannot write, translate.
'To Richard Fanshaw' (1648)

Lord Denman 1779–1854

English politician and lawyer; Lord Chief Justice, 1832–50

9 Trial by jury itself, instead of being a security to persons who are accused, will be a delusion, a mockery, and a snare.
on a case involving the fraudulent omission of sixty names from the list of jurors in Dublin
speech in the House of Lords, 4 September 1844; in E. W. Cox (ed.) Reports of Cases in Criminal Law *(1846) vol. 1*

Lord Denning 1899–1999

English judge

10 To every subject of this land, however powerful, I would use Thomas Fuller's words over three

hundred years ago, 'Be ye never so high, the law is above you.'
in a High Court ruling against the Attorney-General, January 1977; see FULLER *346:15*

11 The keystone of the rule of law in England has been the independence of judges. It is the only respect in which we make any real separation of powers.
The Family Story (1981)

John Dennis 1657–1734

English critic, poet, and dramatist

12 A man who could make so vile a pun would not scruple to pick a pocket.
in The Gentleman's Magazine *(1781) editorial note*

13 The great design of art is to restore the decays that happened to human nature by the fall, by restoring order.
The Grounds of Criticism in Poetry (1704) ch. 2

14 Damn them! They will not let my play run, but they steal my thunder!
on hearing his new thunder effects used at a performance of Macbeth, *following the withdrawal of one of his own plays after only a short run*
William S. Walsh *A Handy-Book of Literary Curiosities* (1893)

Christine de Pisan 1364–c.1430

Italian writer, resident in France from 1369

15 Where true love is, it showeth; it will not feign.
'The Epistle of Othea to Hector'

Thomas De Quincey 1785–1859

English essayist and critic

16 The burden of the incommunicable.
Confessions of an English Opium Eater (1856 ed.) pt. 1

17 Oxford Street, stony-hearted stepmother, thou that listenest to the sighs of orphans, and drinkest the tears of children.
Confessions of an English Opium Eater (1822, ed. 1856) pt. 1

18 A duller spectacle this earth of ours has not to show than a rainy Sunday in London.
Confessions of an English Opium Eater (1822, ed. 1856) pt. 2

19 Thou hast the keys of Paradise, oh just, subtle, and mighty opium!
Confessions of an English Opium Eater (1822, ed. 1856) pt. 2

20 Books, we are told, propose to *instruct* or to *amuse*. Indeed! . . . The true antithesis to knowledge, in this case, is not *pleasure*, but *power*. All that is literature seeks to communicate power; all that is not literature, to communicate knowledge.
De Quincey adds that he is indebted for this distinction to 'many years' conversation with Mr WORDSWORTH'
Letters to a Young Man whose Education has been Neglected no. 3, in the London Magazine *January–July 1823*

21 Murder considered as one of the fine arts.
title of essay in Blackwood's Magazine *February 1827*

22 If once a man indulges himself in murder, very soon he comes to think little of robbing; and

from robbing he comes next to drinking and sabbath-breaking, and from that to incivility and procrastination.

'On Murder Considered as One of the Fine Arts' (Supplementary Paper) in *Blackwood's Magazine* November 1839

1 There is first the literature of *knowledge*, and secondly, the literature of *power*.

review of the *Works of Pope* (1847 ed.) in *North British Review* August 1848, vol. 9

Edward Stanley, 14th Earl of Derby

1799–1869

British Conservative statesman, Prime Minister 1852, 1858–9, 1866–8. On Derby: see **BULWER-LYTTON** 170:11, **DISRAELI** 284:6

2 The duty of an Opposition [is] very simple . . . to oppose everything, and propose nothing.

quoting 'Mr Tierney, a great Whig authority' in the House of Commons, 4 June 1841

3 Meddle and muddle.

summarizing Lord John **RUSSELL**'s foreign policy Speech on the Address, House of Lords, 4 February 1864

Jacques Derrida 1930–2004

Algerian-born French philosopher and critic

4 *Il n'y a pas de hors-texte.*
There is nothing outside of the text.

Of Grammatology (1967)

5 *Il y a plus affaire à interpréter les interprétations qu'à interpréter les choses. Montaigne.*
We need to interpret interpretations more than to interpret things. Montaigne.

Writing and Difference (1967) 'Structure, Sign and Play in the Discourse of the Human Sciences' translated by Alan Bass: epigraph; see **MONTAIGNE** 555:26

René Descartes 1596–1650

French philosopher and mathematician. On Descartes: see **RYLE** 676:9

6 The reading of good books is like a conversation with the best men of past centuries—in fact like a prepared conversation, in which they reveal only the best of their thoughts.

Le Discours de la méthode (1637) pt. 1

7 Common sense is the best distributed commodity in the world, for every man is convinced that he is well supplied with it.

Le Discours de la méthode (1637) pt. 1

8 For it is not enough to have a good mind; the main thing is to use it well.

Le Discours de la méthode (1637) pt. 1

9 *Je pense, donc je suis.*
I think, therefore I am.

usually quoted as, 'Cogito, ergo sum', from the 1641 Latin edition
Le Discours de la méthode (1637) pt. 4

10 I could not possibly exist with the nature I actually have, that is, one endowed with the idea

of God, unless there really is a God; the very God, I mean, of whom I have an idea.

Meditationes (ed. 2, 1642) pt. 3

11 It is contrary to reason to say that there is a vacuum or space in which there is absolutely nothing.

Principia Philosophiae (1644) pt. 2, sect. 16 (translated by E. S. Haldane and G. R. T. Ross)

Camille Desmoulins 1760–94

French revolutionary; a supporter of **DANTON**, he was executed with him

12 Clemency is also a revolutionary measure.

in *Le Vieux Cordelier* 15 December 1793

13 My age is that of the *bon Sansculotte Jésus*; an age fatal to Revolutionists.

reply given at his trial
Thomas Carlyle *History of the French Revolution* (1837) bk. 6, ch. 2

Septimus Despencer (Ralph Butler)

14 Dear me, our postilion has been struck by lightning.

reported phrase from a Magyar-English Manual of Conversation
Little Missions (1932) ch. 4

Philippe Néricault Destouches

1680–1754

French dramatist

15 *Les absents ont toujours tort.*
The absent are always in the wrong.

L'Obstacle imprévu (1717) act 1, sc. 6

Buddy De Sylva 1895–1950 *and* Lew Brown 1893–1958

16 The moon belongs to everyone,
The best things in life are free,
The stars belong to everyone,
They gleam there for you and me.

'The Best Things in Life are Free' (1927 song); see **PROVERBS** 627:24

Eamonn de Valera 1882–1975

American-born Irish statesman, Taoiseach 1937–48, 1951–4, and 1957–9, and President of the Republic of Ireland 1959–73. On de Valera: see **LLOYD GEORGE** 496:20

17 Whenever I wanted to know what the Irish people wanted, I had only to examine my own heart and it told me straight off what the Irish people wanted.

speech in Dáil Éireann, 6 January 1922

18 Further sacrifice of life would now be in vain . . . Military victory must be allowed to rest for the moment with those who have destroyed the Republic.

message to the Republican armed forces, 24 May 1923

1 That Ireland which we dreamed of would be the home of a people who valued material wealth only as a basis of right living, of a people who were satisfied with frugal comfort and devoted their leisure to the things of the spirit; a land whose countryside would be bright with cosy homesteads, whose fields and villages would be joyous with sounds of industry, the romping of sturdy children, the contests of athletic youths, the laughter of comely maidens; whose firesides would be the forums of the wisdom of serene old age.

St Patrick's Day broadcast, 17 March 1943

2 Mr Churchill is proud of Britain's stand alone, after France had fallen, and before America had entered the war. Could he not find in his heart the generosity to acknowledge that there is a small nation that stood alone, not for one year or two, but for several hundred years, against aggression; that endured spoliation, famines, massacres in endless succession; that was clubbed many times into insensibility but each time, on returning consciousness, took up the fight anew; a small nation that could never be got to accept defeat and has never surrendered her soul?

radio broadcast, 16 May 1945

Edward De Vere, Earl of Oxford *see* Oxford

Robert Devereux, Earl of Essex *see* Essex

Bernard De Voto 1897–1955
American writer

3 The proper union of gin and vermouth is a great and sudden glory; it is one of the happiest marriages on earth, and one of the shortest lived.

in *Harper's Magazine* December 1949

Peter De Vries 1910–93
American novelist and humorist

4 Gluttony is an emotional escape, a sign something is eating us.

Comfort Me With Apples (1956)

5 It is the final proof of God's omnipotence that he need not exist in order to save us.

The Mackerel Plaza (1958) ch. 1

6 The value of marriage is not that adults produce children but that children produce adults.

The Tunnel of Love (1954) ch. 8

Donald Dewar 1937–2000
Scottish Labour politician; First Minister for Scotland from 1999

7 'There shall be a Scottish parliament.' Through long years, those words were first a hope, then a belief, then a promise. Now they are a reality.

at the official opening of the Scottish Parliament
speech, 1 July 1999; see **ANONYMOUS** 20:19

James Dewar 1842–1923
Scottish physicist

8 Minds are like parachutes. They only function when they are open.

attributed

Lord Dewar 1864–1930
Scottish industrialist

9 [There are] only two classes of pedestrians in these days of reckless motor traffic—the quick, and the dead.

George Robey *Looking Back on Life* (1933) ch. 28

George Dewey 1837–1917
American naval officer

10 You may fire when you are ready, Gridley.

to the captain of his flagship at Manila, 1 May 1898, during the Spanish-American War
in *Autobiography* (1913) ch. 15

Sergei Diaghilev 1872–1929
Russian ballet impresario

11 *Étonne-moi.*
Astonish me.

to Jean **COCTEAU**
Wallace Fowlie (ed.) *Journals of Jean Cocteau* (1956) ch. 1

12 Tchaikovsky thought of committing suicide for fear of being discovered as a homosexual, but today, if you are a composer and *not* homosexual, you might as well put a bullet through your head.

Vernon Duke *Listen Here!* (1963)

Diana, Princess of Wales 1961–97
British princess, former wife of CHARLES, Prince of Wales. On Diana: see BLAIR 123:20, DUFFY 298:14, ELIZABETH II 313:4, JOHN AND TAUPIN 434:7, SPENCER 766:5

13 I'd like to be a queen in people's hearts but I don't see myself being Queen of this country.

interview on *Panorama*, BBC1 TV, 20 November 1995

14 There were three of us in this marriage, so it was a bit crowded.

interview on *Panorama*, BBC1 TV, 20 November 1995

Diane de Poitiers 1499–1566
French mistress of Henry II of France

15 *Adieu doulx baisers colombins.*
Adieu ce qu'en secret faisons

Quand entre nous deux nous jouons.
Farewell sweet kisses, pigeon-wise,
With lip and tongue; farewell again
The secret sports betwixt us twain.
'To Henry II Upon His Leaving for a Trip' (c.1552)

Porfirio Diaz 1830–1915

Mexican revolutionary and statesman, President of Mexico
1877–80, 1884–1911

1 Poor Mexico, so far from God and so close to
the United States.
attributed

Charles Dibdin 1745–1814

English songwriter and dramatist

2 Did you ever hear of Captain Wattle?
He was all for love, and a little for the bottle.
'Captain Wattle and Miss Roe' (1797)

3 For a soldier I listed, to grow great in fame,
And be shot at for sixpence a-day.
'Charity' (1791)

4 In every mess I finds a friend,
In every port a wife.
'Jack in his Element' (1790)

5 But the standing toast that pleased the most
Was—The wind that blows, the ship that goes,
And the lass that loves a sailor!
'The Lass that Loves a Sailor' (1811)

6 Here, a sheer hulk, lies poor Tom Bowling,
The darling of our crew.
'Tom Bowling' (1790)

Thomas Dibdin 1771–1841

English songwriter

7 Oh! what a snug little Island,
A right little, tight little Island!
'The Snug Little Island' (1833)

Charles Dickens 1812–70

English novelist. On Dickens: see **BAGEHOT** 51:19

BARNABY RUDGE

8 Something will come of this. I hope it mayn't be
human gore.
Simon Tappertit
Barnaby Rudge (1841) ch. 4

9 There are strings . . . in the human heart that
had better not be wibrated.
Mr Tappertit
Barnaby Rudge (1841) ch. 22

BLEAK HOUSE

10 Jarndyce and Jarndyce still drags its dreary length
before the Court, perennially hopeless.
Bleak House (1853) ch. 1

11 This is a London particular . . . A fog, miss.
Bleak House (1853) ch. 3

12 Telescopic philanthropy.
Bleak House (1853) ch. 4, chapter heading

13 The wind's in the east . . . I am always conscious
of an uncomfortable sensation now and then
when the wind is blowing in the east.
Mr Jarndyce
Bleak House (1853) ch. 6

14 He wos wery good to me, he wos!
Jo
Bleak House (1853) ch. 11

15 He is celebrated, almost everywhere, for his
Deportment.
Caddy Jellyby of Mr Turveydrop
Bleak House (1853) ch. 14

16 You are a human boy, my young friend. A
human boy. O glorious to be a human boy! . . .
O running stream of sparkling joy
To be a soaring human boy!
Mr Chadband
Bleak House (1853) ch. 19

17 Jobling, there *are* chords in the human mind.
Mr Guppy
Bleak House (1853) ch. 20

18 'It is,' says Chadband, 'the ray of rays, the sun
of suns, the moon of moons, the star of stars. It
is the light of Terewth.'
Bleak House (1853) ch. 25

19 It's my old girl that advises. She has the head.
But I never own to it before her. Discipline must
be maintained.
Mr Bagnet
Bleak House (1853) ch. 27

20 The old conspiracy to make me happy!
Esther
Bleak House (1853) ch. 35; see **UPDIKE** 822:20

21 The one great principle of the English law is, to
make business for itself.
Bleak House (1853) ch. 39

22 Dead, your Majesty, Dead, my lords and
gentlemen. Dead, Right Reverends and Wrong
Reverends of every Order. Dead, men and
women, born with heavenly compassion in your
hearts. And dying thus around us, every day.
on the death of Jo
Bleak House (1853) ch. 47

23 I call them the Wards in Jarndyce. They are
caged up with all the others. With Hope, Joy,
Youth, Peace, Rest, Life, Dust, Ashes, Waste,
Want, Ruin, Despair, Madness, Death, Cunning,
Folly, Words, Wigs, Rags, Sheepskin, Plunder,
Precedent, Jargon, Gammon, and Spinach!
Miss Flite's birds
Bleak House (1853) ch. 60

THE CHIMES

24 O let us love our occupations,
Bless the squire and his relations,
Live upon our daily rations,
And always know our proper stations.
The Chimes (1844) 'The Second Quarter'

A CHRISTMAS CAROL

1 'Bah,' said Scrooge. 'Humbug!'
A Christmas Carol (1843) stave 1

2 I am the Ghost of Christmas Past.
A Christmas Carol (1843) stave 2

3 'God bless us every one!' said Tiny Tim, the last of all.
A Christmas Carol (1843) stave 3

4 It *was* a turkey! He could never have stood upon his legs, that bird. He would have snapped 'em off short in a minute, like sticks of sealing-wax.
A Christmas Carol (1843) stave 5

DAVID COPPERFIELD

5 I am a lone lorn creetur . . . and everythink goes contrairy with me.
Mrs Gummidge
David Copperfield (1850) ch. 3

6 She's been thinking of the old 'un!
Mr Peggotty of Mrs Gummidge
David Copperfield (1850) ch. 3

7 Barkis is willin'.
David Copperfield (1850) ch. 5

8 Experientia does it—as papa used to say.
Mrs Micawber
David Copperfield (1850) ch. 11; see TACITUS 787:13

9 I have known him come home to supper with a flood of tears, and a declaration that nothing was now left but a jail; and go to bed making a calculation of the expense of putting bow-windows to the house, 'in case anything turned up,' which was his favourite expression.
of Mr Micawber
David Copperfield (1850) ch. 11

10 Annual income twenty pounds, annual expenditure nineteen nineteen six, result happiness. Annual income twenty pounds, annual expenditure twenty pounds nought and six, result misery.
Mr Micawber
David Copperfield (1850) ch. 12

11 Mr. Dick had been for upwards of ten years endeavouring to keep King Charles the First out of the Memorial; but he had been constantly getting into it, and was there now.
David Copperfield (1850) ch. 14

12 The mistake was made of putting some of the trouble out of King Charles's head into my head.
Mr Dick
David Copperfield (1850) ch. 17

13 We are so very 'umble.
Uriah Heep
David Copperfield (1850) ch. 17

14 I only ask for information.
Miss Rosa Dartle
David Copperfield (1850) ch. 20

15 It was as true . . . as taxes is. And nothing's truer than them.
Mr Barkis
David Copperfield (1850) ch. 21; see FRANKLIN 341:10

16 What a world of gammon and spinnage it is, though, ain't it!
Miss Mowcher
David Copperfield (1850) ch. 22

17 I assure you she's the dearest girl.
Mr Traddles
David Copperfield (1850) ch. 27

18 Accidents will occur in the best-regulated families.
Mr Micawber
David Copperfield (1850) ch. 28; see PROVERBS 626:4

19 'People can't die, along the coast,' said Mr Peggotty, 'except when the tide's pretty nigh out. They can't be born, unless it's pretty nigh in—not properly born, till flood. He's a going out with the tide.'
David Copperfield (1850) ch. 30

20 Mrs Crupp had indignantly assured him that there wasn't room to swing a cat there; but, as Mr Dick justly observed to me, sitting down on the foot of the bed, nursing his leg, 'You know, Trotwood, I don't want to swing a cat. I never do swing a cat. Therefore, what does that signify to *me!*'
David Copperfield (1850) ch. 35

21 It's only my child-wife.
of Dora
David Copperfield (1850) ch. 44

22 Circumstances beyond my individual control.
Mr Micawber
David Copperfield (1850) ch. 49

23 I'm Gormed—and I can't say no fairer than that!
Mr Peggotty
David Copperfield (1850) ch. 63

DOMBEY AND SON

24 He's tough, ma'am, tough is J.B. Tough, and devilish sly!
Major Bagstock
Dombey and Son (1848) ch. 7

25 Papa! What's money?
Paul Dombey
Dombey and Son (1848) ch. 8

26 There was no light nonsense about Miss Blimber . . . she was dry and sandy with working in the graves of deceased languages. None of your live languages for Miss Blimber. They must be dead—stone dead—and then Miss Blimber dug them up like a Ghoul.
Dombey and Son (1848) ch. 11

27 If I could have known Cicero, and been his friend, and talked with him in his retirement at Tusculum (beau-ti-ful Tusculum), I could have died contented.
Mrs Blimber
Dombey and Son (1848) ch. 11

1 In the Proverbs of Solomon you will find the following words, 'May we never want a friend in need, nor a bottle to give him!' When found, make a note of.
Captain Cuttle
   Dombey and Son (1848) ch. 15

2 What the waves were always saying.
   Dombey and Son (1848) title of ch. 16

3 Cows are my passion.
Mrs Skewton
   Dombey and Son (1848) ch. 21

4 If you could see my legs when I take my boots off, you'd form some idea of what unrequited affection is.
Mr Toots
   Dombey and Son (1848) ch. 48

GREAT EXPECTATIONS

5 Your sister is given to government.
Joe Gargery
   Great Expectations (1861) ch. 7

6 'He calls the knaves, Jacks, this boy,' said Estella with disdain, before our first game was out.
   Great Expectations (1861) ch. 8

7 In the little world in which children have their existence, whosoever brings them up, there is nothing so finely perceived and so finely felt, as injustice.
   Great Expectations (1861) ch. 8

8 Her bringing me up by hand, gave her no right to bring me up by jerks.
   Great Expectations (1861) ch. 8

9 It is a most miserable thing to feel ashamed of home.
   Great Expectations (1861) ch. 14

10 On the Rampage, Pip, and off the Rampage, Pip; such is Life!
Joe Gargery
   Great Expectations (1861) ch. 15

11 He wishes me most particular to write *what larks*. He says you will understand.
message from Joe Gargery to Pip
   Great Expectations (1861) ch. 27

HARD TIMES

12 Now, what I want is, Facts . . . Facts alone are wanted in life.
Mr Gradgrind
   Hard Times (1854) bk. 1, ch. 1

LITTLE DORRIT

13 Whatever was required to be done, the Circumlocution Office was beforehand with all the public departments in the art of perceiving—HOW NOT TO DO IT.
   Little Dorrit (1857) bk. 1, ch. 10

14 There's milestones on the Dover Road!
Mr F.'s Aunt
   Little Dorrit (1857) bk. 1, ch. 23

15 As to marriage on the part of a man, my dear, Society requires that he should retrieve his fortunes by marriage. Society requires that he should gain by marriage. Society requires that he should found a handsome establishment by marriage. Society does not see, otherwise, what he has to do with marriage.
Mrs Merdle
   Little Dorrit (1857) bk. 1, ch. 33

16 Father is rather vulgar, my dear. The word Papa, besides, gives a pretty form to the lips. Papa, potatoes, poultry, prunes, and prism, are all very good words for the lips: especially prunes and prism.
Mrs General
   Little Dorrit (1857) bk. 2, ch. 5

17 Once a gentleman, and always a gentleman.
Rigaud
   Little Dorrit (1857) bk. 2, ch. 28

MARTIN CHUZZLEWIT

18 Affection beaming in one eye, and calculation shining out of the other.
Mrs Todgers
   Martin Chuzzlewit (1844) ch. 8

19 Charity and Mercy. Not unholy names, I hope?
Mr Pecksniff
   Martin Chuzzlewit (1844) ch. 9

20 Here's the rule for bargains: 'Do other men, for they would do you.' That's the true business precept.
Jonas Chuzzlewit
   Martin Chuzzlewit (1844) ch. 11

21 'Mrs Harris,' I says, 'leave the bottle on the chimley-piece, and don't ask me to take none, but let me put my lips to it when I am so dispoged.'
Mrs Gamp
   Martin Chuzzlewit (1844) ch. 19

22 Some people . . . may be Rooshans, and others may be Prooshans; they are born so, and will please themselves. Them which is of other naturs thinks different.
Mrs Gamp
   Martin Chuzzlewit (1844) ch. 19

23 Brought reg'lar and draw'd mild.
Mrs Gamp on her 'half a pint of porter'
   Martin Chuzzlewit (1844) ch. 25

24 He'd make a lovely corpse.
Mrs Gamp
   Martin Chuzzlewit (1844) ch. 25

25 'Sairey,' says Mrs Harris, 'sech is life. Vich likeways is the hend of all things!'
Mrs Gamp
   Martin Chuzzlewit (1844) ch. 29

26 'The Ankworks package . . . I wish it was in Jonadge's belly, I do,' cried Mrs Gamp; appearing to confound the prophet with the whale in this miraculous aspiration.
   Martin Chuzzlewit (1844) ch. 40

1 'Who deniges of it?' Mrs Gamp enquired.
Martin Chuzzlewit (1844) ch. 49

2 No, Betsey! Drink fair, wotever you do!
Mrs Gamp
Martin Chuzzlewit (1844) ch. 49

3 The words she spoke of Mrs Harris, lambs could
not forgive . . . nor worms forget.
Mrs Gamp
Martin Chuzzlewit (1844) ch. 49

4 Farewell! Be the proud bride of a ducal coronet,
and forget me! . . . Unalterably, never yours,
Augustus.
Augustus Moddle
Martin Chuzzlewit (1844) ch. 54

NICHOLAS NICKLEBY

5 United Metropolitan Improved Hot Muffin and
Crumpet Baking and Punctual Delivery
Company.
Nicholas Nickleby (1839) ch. 2

6 EDUCATION.—At Mr Wackford Squeers's Academy,
Dotheboys Hall, at the delightful village of
Dotheboys, near Greta Bridge in Yorkshire,
Youth are boarded, clothed, booked, furnished
with pocket-money, provided with all necessaries,
instructed in all languages living and dead,
mathematics, orthography, geometry, astronomy,
trigonometry, the use of the globes, algebra,
single stick (if required), writing, arithmetic,
fortification, and every other branch of classical
literature. Terms, twenty guineas per annum. No
extras, no vacations, and diet unparalleled.
Nicholas Nickleby (1839) ch. 3

7 He had but one eye, and the popular prejudice
runs in favour of two.
Mr Squeers
Nicholas Nickleby (1839) ch. 4

8 Here's richness!
Mr Squeers
Nicholas Nickleby (1839) ch. 5

9 Subdue your appetites my dears, and you've
conquered human natur.
Mr Squeers
Nicholas Nickleby (1839) ch. 5

10 C-l-e-a-n, clean, verb active, to make bright, to
scour. W-i-n, win, d-e-r, der, winder, a casement.
When the boy knows this out of the book, he
goes and does it.
Mr Squeers
Nicholas Nickleby (1839) ch. 8

11 As she frequently remarked when she made any
such mistake, it would be all the same a
hundred years hence.
Mrs Squeers
Nicholas Nickleby (1839) ch. 9

12 There are only two styles of portrait painting;
the serious and the smirk.
Miss La Creevy
Nicholas Nickleby (1839) ch. 10

13 Sir, My pa requests me to write to you, the
doctors considering it doubtful whether he will
ever recuvver the use of his legs which prevents
his holding a pen.
Fanny Squeers
Nicholas Nickleby (1839) ch. 15

14 I pity his ignorance and despise him.
Fanny Squeers
Nicholas Nickleby (1839) ch. 15

15 'It's very easy to talk,' said Mrs Mantalini. 'Not
so easy when one is eating a demnition egg,'
replied Mr Mantalini; 'for the yolk runs down
the waistcoat, and yolk of egg does not match
any waistcoat but a yellow waistcoat, demmit.'
Nicholas Nickleby (1839) ch. 17

16 Language was not powerful enough to describe
the infant phenomenon.
Nicholas Nickleby (1839) ch. 23

17 The unities, sir . . . are a completeness—a kind
of universal dovetailedness with regard to place
and time.
Mr Curdle
Nicholas Nickleby (1839) ch. 24

18 She's the only sylph I ever saw, who could stand
upon one leg, and play the tambourine on her
other knee, like a sylph.
Mr Crummles
Nicholas Nickleby (1839) ch. 25

19 Bring in the bottled lightning, a clean tumbler,
and a corkscrew.
The Gentleman in the Small-clothes
Nicholas Nickleby (1839) ch. 49

20 All is gas and gaiters.
The Gentleman in the Small-clothes
Nicholas Nickleby (1839) ch. 49

21 My life is one demd horrid grind!
Mr Mantalini
Nicholas Nickleby (1839) ch. 64

22 He has gone to the demnition bow-wows.
Mr Mantalini
Nicholas Nickleby (1839) ch. 64

THE OLD CURIOSITY SHOP

23 Codlin's the friend, not Short.
Codlin
The Old Curiosity Shop (1841) ch. 19

24 I never nursed a dear Gazelle, to glad me with
its soft black eye, but when it came to know me
well, and love me, it was sure to marry a
market-gardener.
Dick Swiveller
The Old Curiosity Shop (1841) ch. 56; see **MOORE** 558:14

25 It was a maxim with Foxey—our revered father,
gentlemen—'Always suspect everybody.'
Sampson Brass
The Old Curiosity Shop (1841) ch. 66

OLIVER TWIST

1 Please, sir, I want some more.
Oliver
> *Oliver Twist* (1838) ch. 2

2 Known by the *sobriquet* of 'The artful Dodger'.
> *Oliver Twist* (1838) ch. 8

3 There is a passion for hunting something deeply implanted in the human breast.
> *Oliver Twist* (1838) ch. 10

4 I only know two sorts of boys. Mealy boys, and beef-faced boys.
Mr Grimwig
> *Oliver Twist* (1838) ch. 14

5 Oh, Mrs Corney, what a prospect this opens! What a opportunity for a jining of hearts and house-keepings!
Bumble
> *Oliver Twist* (1838) ch. 27

6 'If the law supposes that,' said Mr Bumble . . . 'the law is a ass—a idiot.'
Bumble
> *Oliver Twist* (1838) ch. 51; see **CHAPMAN** 216:8

OUR MUTUAL FRIEND

7 A literary man—*with* a wooden leg.
Mr Boffin, of Silas Wegg
> *Our Mutual Friend* (1865) bk. 1, ch. 5

8 Professionally he declines and falls, and as a friend he drops into poetry.
Mr Boffin, of Silas Wegg
> *Our Mutual Friend* (1865) bk. 1, ch. 5

9 Meaty jelly, too, especially when a little salt, which is the case when there's ham, is mellering to the organ.
Silas Wegg
> *Our Mutual Friend* (1865) bk. 1, ch. 5

10 There is in the Englishman a combination of qualities, a modesty, an independence, a responsibility, a repose, combined with an absence of everything calculated to call a blush into the cheek of a young person, which one would seek in vain among the Nations of the Earth.
Mr Podsnap
> *Our Mutual Friend* (1865) bk. 1, ch. 11

11 I think . . . that it is the best club in London.
Mr Twemlow, on the House of Commons
> *Our Mutual Friend* (1865) bk. 2, ch. 3

12 He'd be sharper than a serpent's tooth, if he wasn't as dull as ditch water.
Fanny Cleaver
> *Our Mutual Friend* (1865) bk. 3, ch. 10

13 I want to be something so much worthier than the doll in the doll's house.
Bella
> *Our Mutual Friend* (1865) bk. 4, ch. 5

PICKWICK PAPERS

14 He had used the word in its Pickwickian sense . . . He had merely considered him a humbug in a Pickwickian point of view.
Mr Blotton
> *Pickwick Papers* (1837) ch. 1

15 Kent, sir—everybody knows Kent—apples, cherries, hops, and women.
Jingle
> *Pickwick Papers* (1837) ch. 2

16 I wants to make your flesh creep.
The Fat Boy
> *Pickwick Papers* (1837) ch. 8

17 'It's always best on these occasions to do what the mob do.' 'But suppose there are two mobs?' suggested Mr Snodgrass. 'Shout with the largest,' replied Mr Pickwick.
> *Pickwick Papers* (1837) ch. 13

18 Battledore and shuttlecock's a wery good game, vhen you an't the shuttlecock and two lawyers the battledores, in which case it gets too excitin' to be pleasant.
Mr Weller
> *Pickwick Papers* (1837) ch. 20

19 Be wery careful o' vidders all your life.
Mr Weller
> *Pickwick Papers* (1837) ch. 20

20 Poverty and oysters always seem to go together.
Sam Weller
> *Pickwick Papers* (1837) ch. 22

21 'Do you spell it with a "V" or a "W"?' inquired the judge. 'That depends upon the taste and fancy of the speller, my Lord,' replied Sam [Weller].
> *Pickwick Papers* (1837) ch. 34

22 'Little to do, and plenty to get, I suppose?' said Sergeant Buzfuz, with jocularity. 'Oh, quite enough to get, sir, as the soldier said ven they ordered him three hundred and fifty lashes,' replied Sam. 'You must not tell us what the soldier, or any other man, said, sir,' interposed the judge; 'it's not evidence.'
> *Pickwick Papers* (1837) ch. 34; see **PROVERBS** 646:30

23 A good uniform must work its way with the women, sooner or later.
The Gentleman in Blue
> *Pickwick Papers* (1837) ch. 37

24 'And a bird-cage, sir,' says Sam. 'Veels vithin veels, a prison in a prison.'
> *Pickwick Papers* (1837) ch. 40

25 The have-his-carcase, next to the perpetual motion, is vun of the blessedest things as wos ever made.
Sam Weller
> *Pickwick Papers* (1837) ch. 43

26 Anythin' for a quiet life, as the man said wen he took the sitivation at the lighthouse.
Sam Weller
> *Pickwick Papers* (1837) ch. 43; see **MIDDLETON** 534:7

1 'Never . . . see . . . a dead postboy, did you?'
inquired Sam . . . 'No,' rejoined Bob, 'I never
did.' 'No!' rejoined Sam triumphantly. 'Nor never
vill; and there's another thing that no man never
see, and that's a dead donkey.'
Pickwick Papers (1837) ch. 51

SKETCHES BY BOZ

2 Minerva House . . . where some twenty girls . . .
acquired a smattering of everything, and a
knowledge of nothing.
Sketches by Boz (1839) Tales, ch. 3 'Sentiment'

A TALE OF TWO CITIES

3 It was the best of times, it was the worst of
times, it was the age of wisdom, it was the age
of foolishness, it was the epoch of belief, it was
the epoch of incredulity, it was the season of
Light, it was the season of Darkness, it was the
spring of hope, it was the winter of despair, we
had everything before us, we had nothing before
us, we were all going direct to Heaven, we were
all going direct the other way.
A Tale of Two Cities (1859) bk. 1, ch. 1, opening words

4 A likely thing . . . If it was ever intended that I
should go across salt water, do you suppose
Providence would have cast my lot in an island?
Miss Pross
A Tale of Two Cities (1859) bk. 1, ch. 4

5 If you must go flopping yourself down, flop in
favour of your husband and child, and not in
opposition to 'em.
Jerry Cruncher
A Tale of Two Cities (1859) bk. 2, ch. 1

6 'It is possible—that it may not come, during our
lives . . . We shall not see the triumph.' 'We shall
have helped it,' returned madame.
Monsieur and Madame Defarge
A Tale of Two Cities (1859) bk. 2, ch. 16

7 It is a far, far better thing that I do, than I have
ever done; it is a far, far better rest that I go to,
than I have ever known.
Sydney Carton's thoughts on the scaffold
A Tale of Two Cities (1859) bk. 3, ch. 15

8 'And if you was to walk through the bedrooms
now, you'd see the ragged mouldy bedclothes
a-heaving and a-heaving like seas. And a-heaving
and a-heaving with what?' he says. 'Why, with
the rats under 'em'.
'Tom Tiddler's Ground' in *All the Year Round* 12 December
1861

9 My faith in the people governing is, on the
whole, infinitesimal; my faith in The People
governed is, on the whole, illimitable.
speech at Birmingham and Midland Institute, 27 September
1869, in K. J. Fielding (ed.) *Speeches of Charles Dickens* (1960)

Emily Dickinson 1830–86

American poet. On Dickinson: see CRANE 258:19

10 After great pain, a formal feeling comes.
'After great pain, a formal feeling comes' (1862)

11 Because I could not stop for Death—
He kindly stopped for me—
The Carriage held but just Ourselves—
And Immortality.
'Because I could not stop for Death' (c.1863)

12 Since then—'tis Centuries—and yet
Feels shorter than the Day
I first surmised the Horses Heads
Were toward Eternity.
'Because I could not stop for Death' (c.1863)

13 There is no Frigate like a Book
To take us Lands away
Nor any Coursers like a Page
Of prancing Poetry.
'A Book (2)' (c.1873)

14 The Bustle in a House
The Morning after Death
Is solemnest of industries
Enacted upon Earth—
The Sweeping up the Heart
And putting Love away
We shall not want to use again
Until Eternity.
'The Bustle in a House' (c.1866)

15 What fortitude the Soul contains,
That it can so endure
The accent of a coming Foot—
The opening of a Door.
'Elysium is as far as to' (c.1882)

16 Heaven is what I cannot reach
The apple on the tree
'Forbidden Fruit' (c.1861)

17 There interposed a Fly—
With Blue—uncertain stumbling Buzz—
Between the light—and me—
And then the Windows failed—and then
I could not see to see.
'I heard a Fly buzz—when I died' (c.1862)

18 It comes, without a consternation—
Dissolves—the same—
But leaves a sumptuous destitution—
Without a name.
'It comes, without a consternation' (c. 1876)

19 Parting is all we know of heaven,
And all we need of hell.
'My life closed twice before its close'

20 The Soul selects her own Society—
Then—shuts the Door—
To her divine Majority—
Present no more.
'The Soul selects her own Society' (c.1862)

21 Success is counted sweetest
By those who ne'er succeed.
To comprehend a nectar
Requires sorest need.
'Success is counted sweetest' (1859)

22 There's a certain Slant of light,
Winter Afternoons—

That oppresses like the Heft
Of Cathedral Tunes—
'There's a certain Slant of light' (c.1861)

1 They shut me up in prose—
As when a little girl
They put me in the closet—
Because they liked me 'still'.
'They shut me up in prose' (c.1862)

2 This is my letter to the world
That never wrote to me.
'This is my letter to the world' (c.1862)

3 This quiet Dust was Gentlemen and Ladies
And Lads and Girls—
Was laughter and ability and Sighing
And Frocks and Curls.
'This quiet Dust was Gentlemen and Ladies' (c.1864)

4 Will you tell me my fault, frankly as to yourself,
for I had rather wince, than die. Men do not call
the surgeon to commend the bone, but to set it,
Sir.
letter to T. W. Higginson, July 1862

5 Friday I tasted life. It was a vast morsel. A
Circus passed the house—still I feel the red in
my mind though the drums are out. The Lawn
is full of south and the odors tangle, and I hear
to-day for the first time the river in the tree.
letter to Mrs J. G. Holland, May 1866, in T. H. Johnson (ed.)
The Letters of Emily Dickinson vol. 2 (1958)

John Dickinson 1732–1808
American politician, lawyer, and pamphleteer

6 We have counted the cost of this contest, and
find nothing so dreadful as voluntary slavery . . .
Our cause is just, our union is perfect.
*declaration of reasons for taking up arms against England,
presented to Congress, 8 July 1775*
C. J. Stillé *The Life and Times of John Dickinson* (1891) ch. 5

7 Then join hand in hand, brave Americans all,—
By uniting we stand, by dividing we fall.
'The Liberty Song' (1768), in *The Writings of John Dickinson*
vol. 1 (1895); see **PROVERBS** 646:1

Paul Dickson 1939–
American writer

8 Rowe's Rule: the odds are five to six that the
light at the end of the tunnel is the headlight of
an oncoming train.
in *Washingtonian* November 1978; see **LOWELL** 503:10

Bo Diddley 1928–2008
American rock musician

9 I've never got paid. A dude with a pencil is
worse than a cat with a machine gun.
on his failure to receive royalties
in *Galveston County Daily News* 17 September 1999

Denis Diderot 1713–84
French philosopher and man of letters

10 *Et des boyaux du dernier prêtre
Serrons le cou du dernier roi.*
And [with] the guts of the last priest
Let's shake the neck of the last king.
Dithrambe sur fête de rois; see **MESLIER** 533:7

11 Poetry wants something enormous, barbarous,
savage.
Discours de la poésie dramatique (1758)

12 There are two sorts of laws, those of absolute
equity and universality, and the bizarre ones
which owe their autonomy only to blindness or
to the force of circumstance. The latter merely
cover the man who is breaking them with a
passing disgrace, which time then transfers to
the judges and the nations, on whom it remains
forever.
Oeuvres romanesques (ed. H. Bénac, revised L. Perol, 1981)
translated by Peter France

13 The first vows sworn by two creatures of flesh
and blood were made at the foot of a rock that
was crumbling to dust; they called as witness to
their constancy a heaven which never stays the
same for one moment; everything within them
and around them was changing, and they
thought their hearts were exempt from
vicissitudes. Children!
Oeuvres romanesques (ed. H. Bénac, revised L. Perol, 1981)
translated by Peter France

14 *L'esprit de l'escalier.*
Staircase wit.
*the witty riposte one thinks of only when one has left the
drawing-room and is already on the way downstairs*
Paradoxe sur le Comédien (written 1773–8, published 1830)

15 Be a hypocrite, if you like, but don't talk like
one.
Rameau's Nephew (written 1761)

16 See this egg. It is with this that all the schools of
theology and all the temples of the earth are to
be overturned.
on how life develops from an insensitive mass
Le Rêve de d'Alembert (written 1769, published 1830) pt. 1

17 Oh Richardson! thou singular genius.
Isaac D'Israeli *Curiosities of Literature* (1849 ed.)

Joan Didion 1934–
American writer

18 Was there ever in anyone's life span a point free
in time, devoid of memory, a night when choice
was any more than the sum of all the choices
gone before?
Run River (1963) ch. 4

19 When we start deceiving ourselves into thinking
not that we want something or need something,
not that it is a pragmatic necessity for us to have
it, but that it is a *moral imperative* that we have
it, then is when we join the fashionable

madmen, and then is when the thin whine of hysteria is heard in the land, and then is when we are in bad trouble.
Slouching towards Bethlehem (1968) 'On Morality'

1 We tell ourselves stories in order to live.
The White Album (1979)

John G. Diefenbaker 1895–1979

Canadian Progressive Conservative statesman, Prime Minister 1957–63

2 There can be no dedication to Canada's future without a knowledge of its past.
in *Toronto Star* 9 October 1964

Howard Dietz 1896–1983

American songwriter

3 *Ars gratia artis.*
Art for art's sake.
motto of Metro-Goldwyn-Mayer film studios, apparently intended to say 'Art is beholden to the artists'
Bosley Crowthier *The Lion's Share* (1957); see **CONSTANT** 249:21

Wentworth Dillon, Lord Roscommon *c.*1633–85

Irish poet and critic

4 Men ever had, and ever will have leave,
To coin new words well suited to the age:
Words are like leaves, some wither every year,
And every year a younger race succeeds.
Art of Poetry (1680) l. 73; see **HORACE** 408:19

5 But words once spoke can never be recalled.
Art of Poetry (1680) l. 438; see **HORACE** 410:14

6 Choose an author as you choose a friend.
Essay on Translated Verse (1684) l. 96

7 Immodest words admit of no defence,
For want of decency is want of sense.
Essay on Translated Verse (1684) l. 113

8 The multitude is always in the wrong.
Essay on Translated Verse (1684) l. 183; see **DEBS** 270:2, **IBSEN** 424:5

Ernest Dimnet 1866–1954

French priest, writer, and lecturer

9 Architecture, of all the arts, is the one which acts the most slowly, but the most surely, on the soul.
What We Live By (1932) pt. 2, ch. 12

Isak Dinesen (Karen Blixen) 1885–1962

Danish novelist and short-story writer

10 Out of Africa.
title of book (1937); see **PROVERBS** 644:17

11 A herd of elephant . . . pacing along as if they had an appointment at the end of the world.
Out of Africa (1937) pt. 1, ch. 1

12 The giraffe, in their queer, inimitable, vegetative gracefulness . . . a family of rare, long-stemmed, speckled gigantic flowers slowly advancing.
Out of Africa (1937) pt. 1, ch. 1

13 What is man, when you come to think upon him, but a minutely set, ingenious machine for turning, with infinite artfulness, the red wine of Shiraz into urine?
Seven Gothic Tales (1934) 'The Dreamers'

Diogenes *c.*400–*c.*325 BC

Greek Cynic philosopher. On Diogenes: see ALEXANDER 12:2

14 Alexander . . . asked him if he lacked anything. 'Yes,' said he, 'that I do: that you stand out of my sun a little.'
Plutarch *Parallel Lives* 'Alexander' ch. 14, sect. 4 (translated by T. North, 1579)

15 This is Plato's man.
presenting Plato's disciples with a plucked chicken after **PLATO** defined Man as 'a two-footed, featherless animal'; Plato subsequently added 'with broad flat nails'
Diogenes Laertius *Lives of the Philosophers*

16 I am looking for a man.
on his reason for taking around a lamp in daylight; the context implies 'a good man', but often quoted as 'an honest man'
Diogenes Laertius *Lives of the Philosophers*

17 To get practice in being refused.
on being asked why he was begging for alms from a statue
Diogenes Laertius *Lives of the Philosophers*

Dionysius of Halicarnassus fl. 30–7 BC

Greek historian, resident in Rome from 30 BC

18 History is philosophy from examples.
Ars Rhetorica ch. 11, sect. 2

Pseudo-Dionysius fl. 6th century

unidentified author of theological and Neoplatonist works

19 The most holy mysteries are set forth in two modes: one by means of similar and sacred representations akin to their nature, and the other through unlike forms designed with every possible discordance and difference.
The Celestial Hierarchies

Paul Dirac 1902–84

British theoretical physicist

20 It is more important to have beauty in one's equations than to have them fit experiment . . . It seems that if one is working from the point of view of getting beauty in one's equations, and if one has a really sound insight, one is on a sure line of progress. If there is not complete agreement between the results of one's work and experiment, one should not allow oneself to be too discouraged, because the discrepancy may well be due to minor features that are not

properly taken into account and that will get cleared up with further developments of the theory.

in *Scientific American* May 1963

Walt Disney 1901–66

American animator and film producer

1 I don't know, fellows, I guess I'm getting too old for animation.

on seeing rushes from The Jungle Book *(1967 film)*
Richard Schickel *The Disney Version* (1986)

2 Fancy being remembered around the world for the invention of a mouse!

during his last illness
Leonard Mosley *Disney's World* (1985)

Benjamin Disraeli, Lord Beaconsfield 1804–81

British Tory statesman and novelist, Prime Minister 1868, 1874–80. On Disraeli: see **SALISBURY** 678:12, **SALISBURY** 678:17

3 Though I sit down now, the time will come when you will hear me.

maiden speech in the House of Commons, 7 December 1837

4 The Continent will [not] suffer England to be the workshop of the world.

speech, House of Commons, 15 March 1838; see **CHAMBERLAIN** 214:2

5 Thus you have a starving population, an absentee aristocracy, and an alien Church, and in addition the weakest executive in the world. That is the Irish Question.

speech, House of Commons, 16 February 1844

6 The noble Lord is the Prince Rupert of Parliamentary discussion.

of Edward Stanley, later Lord **DERBY**
speech, House of Commons, 24 April 1844; see **BULWER-LYTTON** 170:11

7 The right hon. Gentleman caught the Whigs bathing, and walked away with their clothes.

on Sir Robert **PEEL***'s abandoning protection in favour of free trade, traditionally the policy of the Whig Opposition*
speech, House of Commons, 28 February 1845

8 Protection is not a principle, but an expedient.

speech, House of Commons, 17 March 1845

9 A Conservative Government is an organized hypocrisy.

BAGEHOT, *quoting Disraeli in* The English Constitution (1867) 'The House of Lords', *elaborated on the theme with the words 'so much did the ideas of its "head" differ from the sensations of its "tail"'*
speech, House of Commons, 17 March 1845

10 He traces the steam-engine always back to the tea-kettle.

of Robert **PEEL**
speech, House of Commons, 11 April 1845

11 Justice is truth in action.

speech, House of Commons, 11 February 1851

12 I read this morning an awful, though monotonous, manifesto in the great organ of public opinion, which always makes me tremble: Olympian bolts; and yet I could not help fancying amid their rumbling terrors I heard the plaintive treble of the Treasury Bench.

speech, House of Commons, 13 February 1851

13 Petulance is not sarcasm, and . . . insolence is not invective.

speech, House of Commons, 16 December 1852

14 England does not love coalitions.

speech, House of Commons, 16 December 1852

15 Finality is not the language of politics.

speech, House of Commons, 28 February 1859

16 It was a melancholy day for human nature when that stupid Lord Anson, after beating about for three years, found himself again at Greenwich. The circumnavigation of our globe was accomplished, but the illimitable was annihilated and a fatal blow [dealt] to all imagination.

written 1860, in *Reminiscences* (ed. H. and M. Swartz, 1975) ch. 6

17 You are not going, I hope, to leave the destinies of the British Empire to prigs and pedants.

speech, House of Commons, 5 February 1863

18 Party is organized opinion.

speech at Oxford, 25 November 1864, in *The Times* 26 November 1864

19 Man, my Lord, is a being born to believe.

speech at Oxford, 25 November 1864, in *The Times* 26 November 1864

20 Is man an ape or an angel? Now I am on the side of the angels.

speech at Oxford, 25 November 1864, in *The Times* 26 November 1864; see **HUXLEY** 423:16

21 Assassination has never changed the history of the world.

speech, House of Commons, 1 May 1865

22 I had to prepare the mind of the country, and . . . to educate our party.

speech at Edinburgh, 29 October 1867, in *The Times* 30 October 1867

23 Change is inevitable in a progressive country. Change is constant.

speech at Edinburgh, 29 October 1867, in *The Times* 30 October 1867

24 There can be no economy where there is no efficiency.

Address to his Constituents, 1 October 1868, in *The Times* 3 October 1868

25 I believe that without party Parliamentary government is impossible.

speech at Manchester, 3 April 1872, in *The Times* 4 April 1872

26 You behold a range of exhausted volcanoes.

of the Treasury Bench
speech at Manchester, 3 April 1872, in *The Times* 4 April 1872; see **BURKE** 176:3

27 Increased means and increased leisure are the two civilizers of man.

speech at Manchester, 3 April 1872, in *The Times* 4 April 1872

1 A University should be a place of light, of liberty, and of learning.
  speech, House of Commons, 11 March 1873

2 An author who speaks about his own books is almost as bad as a mother who talks about her own children.
  at a banquet given in Glasgow on his installation as Lord Rector, 19 November 1873, in *The Times* 20 November 1873

3 Upon the education of the people of this country the fate of this country depends.
  speech, House of Commons, 15 June 1874

4 He is a great master of gibes and flouts and jeers.
  of the Marquess of **SALISBURY**
  speech, House of Commons, 5 August 1874

5 Mr Gladstone not only appeared but rushed into the debate . . . the new members trembled and fluttered like small birds when a hawk is in the air.
  of **GLADSTONE** *in the House of Commons, 15 March 1875*
  letter to Queen Victoria, March 1875; Roy Jenkins *Gladstone* (1995)

6 Coffee house babble.
  on the Bulgarian Atrocities, 1876; see **GLADSTONE**
  in R. W. Seton-Watson *Britain in Europe 1789–1914* (1955)

7 Cosmopolitan critics, men who are the friends of every country save their own.
  speech at Guildhall, 9 November 1877, in *The Times* 10 November 1877; see **CANNING** 197:1, **OVERBURY** 589:15

8 Lord Salisbury and myself have brought you back peace—but a peace I hope with honour.
  speech on returning from the Congress of Berlin, 16 July 1878, in *The Times* 17 July 1878; see **CHAMBERLAIN** 214:6, **RUSSELL** 675:19

9 A sophistical rhetorician, inebriated with the exuberance of his own verbosity.
  of **GLADSTONE**
  in *The Times* 29 July 1878

10 One of the greatest of Romans, when asked what were his politics, replied, *Imperium et Libertas*. That would not make a bad programme for a British Ministry.
  speech at Mansion House, London, 10 November 1879, quoting a paraphrase of Tacitus by Winston Churchill (c.1620–88) *Divi Britannici* (1675): 'Here the two great interests Imperium & Libertas, res olim insociabiles (saith Tacitus), began to incounter each other'; see **TACITUS** 786:18

11 The key of India is London.
  speech, House of Commons, 4 March 1881

12 Take away that emblem of mortality.
  on being offered an air cushion to sit on, 1881
  Robert Blake *Disraeli* (1966) ch. 32

13 No it is better not. She would only ask me to take a message to Albert.
  on his death-bed, declining a proposed visit from Queen **VICTORIA**
  Robert Blake *Disraeli* (1966) ch. 32

14 I will not go down to posterity talking bad grammar.
  while correcting proofs of his last Parliamentary speech, 31 March 1881
  Robert Blake *Disraeli* (1966) ch. 32

15 No Government can be long secure without a formidable Opposition.
  Coningsby (1844) bk. 2, ch. 1

16 A government of statesmen or of clerks? Of Humbug or Humdrum?
  Coningsby (1844) bk. 2, ch. 4

17 'A sound Conservative government,' said Taper, musingly. 'I understand: Tory men and Whig measures.'
  Coningsby (1844) bk. 2, ch. 6

18 Youth is a blunder; Manhood a struggle; Old Age a regret.
  Coningsby (1844) bk. 3, ch. 1

19 It seems to me a barren thing this Conservatism—an unhappy cross-breed, the mule of politics that engenders nothing.
  Coningsby (1844) bk. 3, ch. 5; see **POWER** 622:8

20 Where can we find faith in a nation of sectaries?
  Coningsby (1844) bk. 4, ch. 13

21 Man is only truly great when he acts from the passions.
  Coningsby (1844) bk. 4, ch. 13

22 With words we govern men.
  Contarini Fleming (1832) pt. 1, ch. 21

23 Read no history: nothing but biography, for that is life without theory.
  Contarini Fleming (1832) pt. 1, ch. 23; see **EMERSON** 315:3

24 The practice of politics in the East may be defined by one word—dissimulation.
  Contarini Fleming (1832) pt. 5, ch. 10

25 His Christianity was muscular.
  Endymion (1880) ch. 14

26 An insular country, subject to fogs, and with a powerful middle class, requires grave statesmen.
  Endymion (1880) ch. 37

27 As for our majority . . . one is enough.
  Endymion (1880) ch. 64

28 'Sensible men are all of the same religion.' 'And pray what is that?' . . . 'Sensible men never tell.'
  Endymion (1880) ch. 81; see **SHAFTESBURY** 693:17

29 The sweet simplicity of the three per cents.
  Endymion (1880) ch. 91; see **STOWELL** 778:8

30 I believe they went out, like all good things, with the Stuarts.
  Endymion (1880) ch. 99

31 Debt is the prolific mother of folly and of crime.
  Henrietta Temple (1837) bk. 2, ch. 1

32 Time is the great physician.
  Henrietta Temple (1837) bk. 6, ch. 9; see **PROVERBS** 645:18

33 They mean well; their feelings are strong, but their hearts are in the right place.
  The Infernal Marriage (1834) pt. 1, 1 (of the Furies)

1 The blue ribbon of the turf.
of the Derby
Lord George Bentinck (1852) ch. 26

2 London: a nation, not a city.
Lothair (1870) ch. 27

3 The gondola of London.
a hansom cab
Lothair (1870) ch. 27

4 When a man fell into his anecdotage it was a sign for him to retire from the world.
Lothair (1870) ch. 28

5 You know who the critics are? The men who have failed in literature and art.
Lothair (1870) ch. 35; see **COLERIDGE** 241:26

6 'Two nations; between whom there is no intercourse and no sympathy; who are as ignorant of each other's habits, thoughts, and feelings, as if they were dwellers in different zones, or inhabitants of different planets; who are formed by a different breeding, are fed by a different food, are ordered by different manners, and are not governed by the same laws.' 'You speak of—' said Egremont, hesitatingly, 'THE RICH AND THE POOR.'
Sybil (1845) bk. 2, ch. 5; see **FOSTER** 338:19

7 Mr Kremlin himself was distinguished for ignorance, for he had only one idea,—and that was wrong.
Sybil (1845) bk. 4, ch. 5; see **JOHNSON** 440:23

8 I was told that the Privileged and the People formed Two Nations.
Sybil (1845) bk. 4, ch. 8

9 The Youth of a Nation are the trustees of Posterity.
Sybil (1845) bk. 6, ch. 13

10 That fatal drollery called a representative government.
Tancred (1847) bk. 2, ch. 13

11 A majority is always the best repartee.
Tancred (1847) bk. 2, ch. 14

12 The East is a career.
Tancred (1847) bk. 2, ch. 14

13 London is a modern Babylon.
Tancred (1847) bk. 5, ch. 5

14 Experience is the child of Thought, and Thought is the child of Action. We cannot learn men from books.
Vivian Grey (1826) bk. 5, ch. 1

15 All power is a trust . . . from the people, and for the people, all springs, and all must exist.
Vivian Grey (1826) bk. 6, ch. 7; see **DRYDEN** 294:17

16 All Paradise opens! Let me die eating ortolans to the sound of soft music!
The Young Duke (1831) bk. 1, ch. 10; see **SMITH** 758:27

17 'The age of chivalry is past,' said May Dacre. 'Bores have succeeded to dragons.'
The Young Duke (1831) bk. 2, ch. 5

18 Damn your principles! Stick to your party.
attributed to Disraeli and believed to have been said to Edward **BULWER-LYTTON**
E. Latham *Famous Sayings and their Authors* (1904)

19 Everyone likes flattery; and when you come to Royalty you should lay it on with a trowel.
to Matthew **ARNOLD**
G. W. E. Russell *Collections and Recollections* (1898) ch. 23

20 I am dead; dead, but in the Elysian fields.
to a peer, on his elevation to the House of Lords
W. Monypenny and G. Buckle *Life of Benjamin Disraeli* vol. 5 (1920) ch. 13

21 I have climbed to the top of the greasy pole.
on becoming Prime Minister
W. Monypenny and G. Buckle *Life of Benjamin Disraeli* vol. 4 (1916) ch. 16

22 I never deny; I never contradict; I sometimes forget.
said to Lord Esher of his relations with Queen **VICTORIA**
Elizabeth Longford *Victoria R. I* (1964) ch. 27

23 Never complain and never explain.
J. Morley *Life of William Ewart Gladstone* (1903) vol. 1; see **FISHER** 330:9, **HUBBARD** 417:13

24 The palace is not safe when the cottage is not happy.
Robert Blake *Disraeli* (1966)

25 Palmerston is now seventy. If he could prove evidence of his potency in his electoral address he'd sweep the country.
to the suggestion that capital could be made from one of Palmerston's affairs
Hesketh Pearson *Dizzy* (1951); attributed, probably apocryphal

26 Pray remember, Mr Dean, no dogma, no Dean.
W. Monypenny and G. Buckle *Life of Benjamin Disraeli* vol. 4 (1916) ch. 10

27 The school of Manchester.
describing the free trade politics of Cobden and **BRIGHT**
Robert Blake *Disraeli* (1966) ch. 10

28 There are three kinds of lies: lies, damned lies and statistics.
attributed to Disraeli in Mark Twain *Autobiography* (1924) vol. 1; anonymous versions of this occur earlier, e.g. in *Economic Journal* June 1892

29 We came here for fame.
to John **BRIGHT**, *in the House of Commons*
Robert Blake *Disraeli* (1966) ch. 4

30 When I want to read a novel, I write one.
W. Monypenny and G. Buckle *Life of Benjamin Disraeli* vol. 6 (1920) ch. 17; see **PUNCH** 650:4

Isaac D'Israeli 1766–1848

English literary historian; father of Benjamin **DISRAELI**

31 He wreathed the rod of criticism with roses.
of Pierre Bayle
Curiosities of Literature (9th ed., 1834) vol. 1

William Chatterton Dix 1837–98

English clergyman

32 Alleluia! sing to Jesus,
His the sceptre, his the throne;

Alleluia! his the triumph,
His the victory alone:
Hark! the songs of peaceful Zion
Thunder like a mighty flood;
Jesus, out of every nation,
Hath redeemed us by his blood.
'Alleluia! sing to Jesus' (1867 hymn)

1 As with gladness men of old
Did the guiding star behold.
'As with gladness men of old' (1861 hymn)

Henry Austin Dobson 1840–1921

English poet, biographer, and essayist

2 All passes. Art alone
Enduring stays to us;
The Bust outlasts the throne,—
The Coin, Tiberius.
'Ars Victrix' (1876); translation of Gautier's 'L'Art'; see **GAUTIER** 350:14

3 Fame is a food that dead men eat,—
I have no stomach for such meat.
'Fame is a Food' (1906)

4 The ladies of St James's!
They're painted to the eyes;
Their white it stays for ever,
Their red it never dies:
But Phyllida, my Phyllida!
Her colour comes and goes;
It trembles to a lily, —
It wavers to a rose.
'The Ladies of St James's' (1883)

5 Time goes, you say? Ah no!
Alas, Time stays, *we* go.
'The Paradox of Time' (1877)

Ken Dodd 1927–

English comedian

6 Freud's theory was that when a joke opens a window and all those bats and bogeymen fly out, you get a marvellous feeling of relief and elation. The trouble with Freud is that he never had to play the old Glasgow Empire on a Saturday night after Rangers and Celtic had both lost.
in *Guardian* 30 April 1991; quoted in many, usually much contracted, forms since the mid-1960s

Philip Doddridge 1702–51

English Nonconformist divine

7 O God of Bethel, by whose hand
Thy people still are fed,
Who through this weary pilgrimage
Hast all our fathers led.
Hymns (1755) 'O God of Bethel'

Bubb Dodington, Lord Melcombe

1691–1762

English politician

8 Love thy country, wish it well,
Not with too intense a care,
'Tis enough, that when it fell,
Thou its ruin didst not share.
'Ode' (written 1761) in Joseph Spence *Anecdotes* (1820)

Dogen Kigen 1200–53

Japanese Buddhist monk

9 Because it is intrinsically the verification of practice, there is no end to verification; because it is the practice of verification, there is no beginning to practice.
often quoted as 'There is no beginning to practice nor end to enlightenment; there is no beginning to enlightenment nor end to practice'
William R. LaFleur (ed.) *Dogen Studies* (1985)

10 To study the self is to forget the self. To forget the self is to be authenticated by the myriad things.
often quoted as ' . . . to become one with the ten thousand things'
William R. LaFleur (ed.) *Dogen Studies* (1985)

Aelius Donatus

Roman grammarian of the 4th century AD

11 *Pereant, inquit, qui ante nos nostra dixerunt.*
Confound those who have said our remarks before us.
St Jerome *Commentary on Ecclesiastes* bk 1; J. P. Migne *Patrologiae Latinae* vol. 23

J. P. Donleavy 1926–

Irish-American novelist

12 When you don't have any money, the problem is food. When you have money, it's sex. When you have both it's health.
The Ginger Man (1955) ch. 5

John Donne 1572–1631

English metaphysical poet, clergyman, and preacher. On Donne: see **CAREW** 198:7, **COLERIDGE** 240:11, **JAMES I** 429:3, **JONSON** 447:2, **MCEWAN** 510:13, **WALTON** 839:14
Verse dates are those of composition

13 And new philosophy calls all in doubt,
The element of fire is quite put out;
The sun is lost, and th'earth, and no man's wit
Can well direct him, where to look for it.
An Anatomy of the World: The First Anniversary (1611) l. 205

14 She, she is dead; she's dead; when thou know'st this,
Thou know'st how dry a cinder this world is.
An Anatomy of the World: The First Anniversary (1611) l. 427

15 Love built on beauty, soon as beauty, dies.
Elegies 'The Anagram' (c.1595)

1 No spring, nor summer beauty hath such grace,
As I have seen in one autumnal face.
Elegies 'The Autumnal' (c.1600)

2 Whoever loves, if he do not propose
The right true end of love, he's one that goes
To sea for nothing but to make him sick.
Elegies 'Love's Progress' (c.1600)

3 By our first strange and fatal interview,
By all desires which thereof did ensue.
Elegies 'On His Mistress' (c.1600)

4 Nurse, O my love is slain; I saw him go
O'er the white Alps, alone; I saw him, I,
Assailed, fight, taken, stabbed, bleed, fall, and
die.
Elegies 'On His Mistress' (c.1600)

5   We easily know
By this these angels from an evil sprite,
They set our hairs, but these our flesh upright.
Elegies 'To His Mistress Going to Bed' (c.1595)

6 License my roving hands, and let them go,
Behind, before, above, between, below.
O my America, my new found land,
My kingdom, safeliest when with one man
manned.
Elegies 'To His Mistress Going to Bed' (c.1595)

7 Hail, Bishop Valentine, whose day this is,
All the air is thy Diocese.
'An Epithalamion . . . on the Lady Elizabeth and Count
Palatine being Married on St Valentine's Day' (1613)

8 At the round earth's imagined corners, blow
Your trumpets, angels, and arise, arise
From death, you numberless infinities
Of souls, and to your scattered bodies go.
Holy Sonnets (1609) no. 4 (ed. J. Carey, 1990)

9 All whom war, dearth, age, agues, tyrannies,
Despair, law, chance, hath slain.
Holy Sonnets (1609) no. 4 (ed. J. Carey, 1990)

10 Death be not proud, though some have called
thee
Mighty and dreadful, for thou art not so,
For, those, whom thou think'st, thou dost
overthrow,
Die not, poor death, nor yet canst thou kill me.
Holy Sonnets (1609) no. 6 (ed. J. Carey, 1990)

11 One short sleep past, we wake eternally,
And death shall be no more; Death thou shalt
die.
Holy Sonnets (1609) no. 6 (ed. J. Carey, 1990)

12 Batter my heart, three-personed God; for, you
As yet but knock, breathe, shine, and seek to
mend.
Holy Sonnets (after 1609) no. 10 (ed. J. Carey, 1990)

13 Take me to you, imprison me, for I
Except you enthral me, never shall be free,
Nor ever chaste, except you ravish me.
Holy Sonnets (after 1609) no. 10 (ed. J. Carey, 1990)

14 I am a little world made cunningly
Of elements, and an angelic sprite.
Holy Sonnets (after 1609) no. 15 (ed. J. Carey, 1990)

15 What if this present were the world's last night?
Holy Sonnets (after 1609) no. 19 (ed. J. Carey, 1990)

16 To see God only, I go out of sight:
And to 'scape stormy days, I choose
An everlasting night.
'A Hymn to Christ, at the Author's last going into Germany'
(1619)

17 Since I am coming to that holy room,
Where, with thy choir of saints for evermore,
I shall be made thy music; as I come
I tune the instrument here at the door,
And what I must do then, think now before.
'Hymn to God my God, in my Sickness' (1623)

18 Wilt thou forgive that sin where I begun,
Which is my sin, though it were done before?
Wilt thou forgive those sins, through which I
run
And do them still: though still I do deplore?
When thou hast done, thou hast not done,
For, I have more.
'A Hymn to God the Father' (1623)

19   Her pure and eloquent blood
Spoke in her cheeks, and so distinctly wrought,
That one might almost say, her body thought.
Of the Progress of the Soul: The Second Anniversary (1612) l. 244

20 So, of a lone unhaunted place possessed,
Did this soul's second inn, built by the guest,
This living buried man, this quiet mandrake,
rest.
'The Progress of the Soul' (1601) st. 16

21 Nature's great masterpiece, an elephant,
The only harmless great thing.
'The Progress of the Soul' (1601) st. 39

22   On a huge hill,
Cragged, and steep, Truth stands, and he that
will
Reach her, about must, and about must go.
Satire no. 3 (1594–5) l. 79

23 Air and angels.
title of poem, *Songs and Sonnets*

24   Just such disparity
As is 'twixt air and angels' purity,
'Twixt women's love, and men's will ever be.
Songs and Sonnets 'Air and Angels'

25 All other things, to their destruction draw,
Only our love hath no decay;
This, no tomorrow hath, nor yesterday,
Running it never runs from us away,
But truly keeps his first, last, everlasting day.
Songs and Sonnets 'The Anniversary'

26 Come live with me, and be my love,
And we will some new pleasures prove
Of golden sands, and crystal brooks,
With silken lines, and silver hooks.
Songs and Sonnets 'The Bait'; see **MARLOWE** 522:20, **RALEGH**
653:13

27 A naked thinking heart, that makes no show,
Is to a woman, but a kind of ghost.
Songs and Sonnets 'The Blossom' l. 27

1 For God's sake hold your tongue, and let me love.
Songs and Sonnets 'The Canonization'

2 Dear love, for nothing less than thee
Would I have broke this happy dream,
It was a theme
For reason, much too strong for fantasy.
Songs and Sonnets 'The Dream' ('Dear love, for nothing less than thee')

3 So, if I dream I have you, I have you,
For, all our joys are but fantastical.
Songs and Sonnets 'The Dream' ('Image of her whom I love')

4 Where, like a pillow on a bed,
A pregnant bank swelled up, to rest
The violet's reclining head,
Sat we two, one another's best.
Songs and Sonnets 'The Ecstasy'

5 So must pure lovers' souls descend
T'affections, and to faculties,
Which sense may reach and apprehend,
Else a great prince in prison lies.
Songs and Sonnets 'The Ecstasy'

6 Oh wrangling schools, that search what fire
Shall burn this world, had none the wit
Unto this knowledge to aspire,
That this her fever might be it?
Songs and Sonnets 'A Fever'

7 I wonder by my troth, what thou, and I
Did, till we loved, were we not weaned till then?
But sucked on country pleasures, childishly?
Or snorted we in the seven sleepers den?
Songs and Sonnets 'The Good-Morrow'

8 And now good morrow to our waking souls,
Which watch not one another out of fear.
Songs and Sonnets 'The Good-Morrow'

9 Stand still, and I will read to thee
A lecture, love, in love's philosophy.
Songs and Sonnets 'A Lecture in the Shadow'

10 I long to talk with some old lover's ghost,
Who died before the god of love was born.
Songs and Sonnets 'Love's Deity'

11 'Tis the year's midnight, and it is the day's.
Songs and Sonnets 'A Nocturnal upon St Lucy's Day'

12 The world's whole sap is sunk:
The general balm th'hydroptic earth hath drunk.
Songs and Sonnets 'A Nocturnal upon St Lucy's Day'

13 When my grave is broke up again
Some second guest to entertain,
(For graves have learnt that woman-head
To be to more than one a bed)
And he that digs it, spies
A bracelet of bright hair about the bone,
Will he not let us alone?
Songs and Sonnets 'The Relic'

14 Go, and catch a falling star,
Get with child a mandrake root,
Tell me, where all past years are,
Or who cleft the Devil's foot,

Teach me to hear mermaids singing.
Songs and Sonnets 'Song: Go and catch a falling star'

15 And swear
No where
Lives a woman true and fair.
Songs and Sonnets 'Song: Go and catch a falling star'

16 Busy old fool, unruly sun,
Why dost thou thus,
Through windows, and through curtains call on us?
Must to thy motions lovers' seasons run?
Songs and Sonnets 'The Sun Rising'

17 Love, all alike, no season knows, nor clime,
Nor hours, days, months, which are the rags of time.
Songs and Sonnets 'The Sun Rising'

18 This bed thy centre is, these walls thy sphere.
Songs and Sonnets 'The Sun Rising'

19 I am two fools, I know,
For loving, and for saying so
In whining poetry.
Songs and Sonnets 'The Triple Fool'

20 I have done one braver thing
Than all the Worthies did,
And yet a braver thence doth spring,
Which is, to keep that hid.
Songs and Sonnets 'The Undertaking'

21 Thy firmness makes my circle just,
And makes me end, where I begun.
Songs and Sonnets 'A Valediction: forbidding mourning'

22   O more than moon,
Draw not up seas to drown me in thy sphere,
Weep me not dead, in thine arms, but forbear
To teach the sea what it may do too soon.
Songs and Sonnets 'A Valediction: of Weeping'

23 Sir, more than kisses, letters mingle souls.
'To Sir Henry Wotton' (1597-8)

24 And seeing the snail, which everywhere doth roam,
Carrying his own house still, still is at home,
Follow (for he is easy paced) this snail,
Be thine own palace, or the world's thy gaol.
'To Sir Henry Wotton' (1597-8)

25 Whensoever my affliction assails me, methinks I have the keys of my prison in mine own hand, and no remedy presents itself so soon to my heart, as mine own sword.
on suicide
Biathanatos (1608)

26 We have a winding sheet in our mother's womb, which grows with us from our conception, and we come into the world, wound up in that winding sheet, for we come to seek a grave.
Death's Duel (1632)

27 That which we call life, is but *hebdomada mortium*, a week of death, seven days, seven periods of our life spent in dying, a dying seven times over; and there is an end.
Death's Duel (1632)

1 There we leave you, in that blessed dependancy, to hang upon him that hangs upon the Cross, there bathe in his tears, there suck at his wounds, and lie down in peace in his grave, till he vouchsafe you a resurrection, and an ascension into that Kingdom, which he hath prepared for you, with the inestimable price of his incorruptible blood. Amen.

Death's Duel (1632)

2 My God, my God, thou art a direct God, may I not say a literal God, a God that wouldst be understood literally and according to the plain sense of all that thou sayest? But thou art also . . . a figurative, a metaphorical God too.

Devotions upon Emergent Occasions (1624) 'Expostulation XIX'

3 But I do nothing upon my self, and yet I am mine own Executioner.

Devotions upon Emergent Occasions (1624) 'Meditation XII'

4 No man is an Island, entire of it self; every man is a piece of the Continent, a part of the main; if a clod be washed away by the sea, Europe is the less, as well as if a promontory were, as well as if a manor of thy friends or of thine own were; any man's death diminishes me, because I am involved in Mankind; And therefore never send to know for whom the bell tolls; it tolls for thee.

Devotions upon Emergent Occasions (1624) 'Meditation XVII'; 'For whom the bell tolls' was the title of a novel (1940) by Ernest **HEMINGWAY**

5 From this I testify her holy cheerfulness, and religious alacrity, (one of the best evidences of a good conscience), that as she came to this place, God's house of Prayer . . . she ever hastened her family, and her company hither, with that cheerful provocation, For God's sake let's go, For God's sake let's be there at the Confession.

A Sermon of Commemoration of the Lady Danvers [mother of George Herbert] (1627)

6 As soon as there were two, there was pride.

LXXX Sermons (1640) 19 December 1619

7 This love of place and precedency rocks us in our cradles, it lies down with us in our graves.

LXXX Sermons (1640) 19 December 1619

8 [Death] comes equally to us all, and makes us all equal when it comes. The ashes of an Oak in the Chimney, are no epitaph of that Oak, to tell me how high or how large that was; It tells me not what flocks it sheltered while it stood, nor what men it hurt when it fell.

LXXX Sermons (1640) 8 March 1621/2

9 When a whirlwind hath blown the dust of the Churchyard into the Church, and the man sweeps out the dust of the Church into the Churchyard, who will undertake to sift those dusts again, and to pronounce, This is the Patrician, this is the noble flower, and this the yeomanly, this the Plebeian bran.

LXXX Sermons (1640) 8 March 1621/2

10 I throw myself down in my Chamber, and I call in, and invite God, and his Angels thither, and when they are there, I neglect God and his Angels, for the noise of a fly, for the rattling of a coach, for the whining of a door.

LXXX Sermons (1640) 12 December 1626 'At the Funeral of Sir William Cokayne'

11 A memory of yesterday's pleasures, a fear of tomorrow's dangers, a straw under my knee, a noise in mine ear, a light in mine eye, an anything, a nothing, a fancy, a chimera in my brain, troubles me in my prayer. So certainly is there nothing, nothing in spiritual things, perfect in this world.

LXXX Sermons (1640) 12 December 1626 'At the Funeral of Sir William Cokayne'

12 Poor intricated soul! Riddling, perplexed, labyrinthical soul!

LXXX Sermons (1640) 25 January 1628/9

13 They shall awake as Jacob did, and say as Jacob said, *Surely the Lord is in this place*, and *this is no other but the house of God, and the gate of heaven*, And into that gate they shall enter, and in that house they shall dwell, where there shall be no Cloud nor Sun, no darkness nor dazzling, but one equal light, no noise nor silence, but one equal music, no fears nor hopes, but one equal possession, no foes nor friends, but one equal communion and identity, no ends nor beginnings, but one equal eternity.

XXVI Sermons (1660) 29 February 1627/8

14 John Donne, Anne Donne, Un-done.

in a letter to his wife, on being dismissed from the service of his father-in-law, Sir George More

Izaak Walton *The Life of Dr Donne* (first printed in *LXXX Sermons*, 1640)

Ariel Dorfman 1942–

Chilean writer

15 Responsibility without power, the fate of the secretary through the ages.

Reader (1995) act 1; see **KIPLING** 468:26, **STOPPARD** 777:14

Fedor Dostoevsky 1821–81

Russian novelist

16 If you were to destroy in mankind the belief in immortality, not only love but every living force maintaining the life of the world would at once be dried up.

The Brothers Karamazov (1879–80) bk. 2, ch. 6

17 Beauty is mysterious as well as terrible. God and devil are fighting there, and the battlefield is the heart of man.

The Brothers Karamazov (1879–80) bk. 3, ch. 3

18 If the devil doesn't exist, but man has created him, he has created him in his own image and likeness.

The Brothers Karamazov (1879–80) bk. 5, ch. 4

19 Too high a price is asked for harmony; it's beyond our means to pay so much to enter. And so I hasten to give back my entrance ticket . . .

It's not God that I don't accept, Alyosha, only I most respectfully return Him the ticket.
The Brothers Karamazov (1879–80) bk. 5, ch. 4

1 Imagine that you are creating a fabric of human destiny with the object of making men happy in the end, giving them peace and rest at last, but that it was essential and inevitable to torture to death only one tiny creature . . . and to found that edifice on its unavenged tears, would you consent to be the architect on those conditions?
The Brothers Karamazov (1879–80) bk. 5, ch. 4

2 Men reject their prophets and slay them, but they love their martyrs and honour those whom they have slain.
The Brothers Karamazov (1879–80) bk. 6, ch. 3

3 Power is given only to him who dares to stoop and take it . . . one must have the courage to dare.
Crime and Punishment (1866) pt. 5, ch. 4 (translated by David Magarshak)

4 I wanted to murder, for my own satisfaction . . . At that moment I did not care a damn whether I would become the benefactor of someone, or would spend the rest of my life like a spider catching them all in my web and sucking the living juices out of them.
Crime and Punishment (1866) pt. 5, ch. 4 (translated by David Magarshak)

5 To crush, to annihilate a man utterly, to inflict on him the most terrible punishment so that the most ferocious murderer would shudder at it beforehand, one need only give him work of an absolutely, completely useless and irrational character.
House of the Dead (1862) pt. 1, ch. 1 (translated by Constance Garnett)

6 Beauty will save the world.
The Idiot (1868) pt. 3, ch. 5

7 In despair there are the most intense enjoyments, especially when one is very acutely conscious of the hopelessness of one's position.
Notes from Underground (1864) pt. 1, ch. 2 (translated by Andrew R. McAndrew)

8 What man wants is simply *independent* choice, whatever that independence may cost and wherever it may lead.
Notes from Underground (1864) pt. 1, ch. 7 (translated by Constance Garnett)

Lord Alfred Douglas 1870–1945

English poet and intimate of Oscar **WILDE**

9 I am the Love that dare not speak its name.
'Two Loves' (1896)

Gavin Douglas *c.*1475–1522

Scottish poet and prelate

10 And all small fowlys singis on the spray:
Welcum the lord of lycht and lamp of day.
Eneados (1553) bk. 12, prologue l. 251

James Douglas, Earl of Morton

*c.*1516–81

Scottish courtier

11 Here lies he who neither feared nor flattered any flesh.
of John **KNOX**, *said as he was buried, 26 November 1572*
George R. Preedy *The Life of John Knox* (1940) ch. 7

Keith Douglas 1920–44

English poet

12 Remember me when I am dead
And simplify me when I'm dead.
'Simplify me when I'm Dead' (1941)

13 But she would weep to see today
how on his skin the swart flies move;
the dust upon the paper eye
and the burst stomach like a cave.

For here the lover and killer are mingled
who had one body and one heart.
And death, who had the soldier singled
has done the lover mortal hurt.
'Vergissmeinnicht, 1943'

Norman Douglas 1868–1952

Scottish-born novelist and essayist

14 You can tell the ideals of a nation by its advertisements.
South Wind (1917) ch. 6

15 To find a friend one must close one eye. To keep him—two.
South Wind (1917) ch. 11

16 Many a man who thinks to found a home discovers that he has merely opened a tavern for his friends.
South Wind (1917) ch. 20

O. Douglas (Anna Buchan) 1877–1948

Scottish writer, sister of John **BUCHAN**

17 It is wonderful how much news there is when people write every other day; if they wait for a month, there is nothing that seems worth telling.
Penny Plain (1920)

18 I know heaps of quotations, so I can always make quite a fair show of knowledge.
The Setons (1917)

Alec Douglas-Home *see* Lord Home

Frederick Douglass *c.*1818–95

American former slave and civil rights campaigner

19 Every tone [of the songs of the slaves] was a testimony against slavery, and a prayer to God for deliverance from chains.
Narrative of the Life of Frederick Douglass (1845) ch. 2

1 The life of the nation is secure only while the nation is honest, truthful, and virtuous.
  speech on the 23rd anniversary of Emancipation in the District of Columbia, Washington DC, April 1885

Lorenzo Dow 1777–1834
American divine

2 You will be damned if you do—And you will be damned if you don't.
  on the Calvinist doctrine of 'Particular Election'
  Reflections on the Love of God (1836) ch. 6

Ernest Dowson 1867–1900
English poet

3 I have forgot much, Cynara! gone with the wind,
  Flung roses, roses, riotously, with the throng,
  Dancing, to put thy pale, lost lilies out of mind;
  But I was desolate and sick of an old passion,
  Yea, all the time, because the dance was long:
  I have been faithful to thee, Cynara! in my fashion.
  'Non Sum Qualis Eram' (1896) (also known as 'Cynara'); see
  HORACE 413:12

4 They are not long, the weeping and the laughter,
  Love and desire and hate.
  'Vitae Summa Brevis' (1896)

5 They are not long, the days of wine and roses.
  'Vitae Summa Brevis' (1896)

Arthur Conan Doyle 1859–1930
Scottish-born writer of detective fiction

6 Singularity is almost invariably a clue. The more featureless and commonplace a crime is, the more difficult is it to bring it home.
  The Adventures of Sherlock Holmes (1892) 'The Boscombe Valley Mystery'

7 It is my belief, Watson, founded upon my experience, that the lowest and vilest alleys in London do not present a more dreadful record of sin than does the smiling and beautiful countryside.
  The Adventures of Sherlock Holmes (1892) 'The Copper Beeches'

8 A man should keep his little brain attic stocked with all the furniture that he is likely to use, and the rest he can put away in the lumber room of his library, where he can get it if he wants it.
  The Adventures of Sherlock Holmes (1892) 'The Five Orange Pips'

9 It is quite a three-pipe problem, and I beg that you won't speak to me for fifty minutes.
  The Adventures of Sherlock Holmes (1892) 'The Red-Headed League'

10 You see, but you do not observe.
  The Adventures of Sherlock Holmes (1892) 'Scandal in Bohemia'

11 The giant rat of Sumatra, a story for which the world is not yet prepared.
  The Case-Book of Sherlock Holmes (1927) 'The Sussex Vampire'

12 Of all ruins that of a noble mind is the most deplorable.
  His Last Bow (1917) 'The Dying Detective'; see **DAVIES** 268:4

13 Good old Watson! You are the one fixed point in a changing age.
  His Last Bow (1917) title story

14 You know my method. It is founded upon the observation of trifles.
  The Memoirs of Sherlock Holmes (1894) 'The Crooked Man'

15 'Excellent,' I cried. 'Elementary,' said he.
  The Memoirs of Sherlock Holmes (1894) 'The Crooked Man'; see **MISQUOTATIONS** 547:11

16 Ex-Professor Moriarty of mathematical celebrity . . . is the Napoleon of crime, Watson.
  The Memoirs of Sherlock Holmes (1894) 'The Final Problem'

17 'Is there any other point to which you would wish to draw my attention?'
  'To the curious incident of the dog in the night-time.'
  'The dog did nothing in the night-time.'
  'That was the curious incident,' remarked Sherlock Holmes.
  The Memoirs of Sherlock Holmes (1894) 'Silver Blaze'

18 What one man can invent another can discover.
  The Return of Sherlock Holmes (1905) 'The Dancing Men'

19 Detection is, or ought to be, an exact science, and should be treated in the same cold and unemotional manner. You have attempted to tinge it with romanticism, which produces much the same effect as if you worked a love-story or an elopement into the fifth proposition of Euclid.
  The Sign of Four (1890) ch. 1

20 How often have I said to you that when you have eliminated the impossible, whatever remains, *however improbable*, must be the truth?
  The Sign of Four (1890) ch. 6

21 You know my methods. Apply them.
  The Sign of Four (1890) ch. 6

22 It is the unofficial force—the Baker Street irregulars.
  The Sign of Four (1890) ch. 8

23 London, that great cesspool into which all the loungers and idlers of the Empire are irresistibly drained.
  A Study in Scarlet (1888) ch. 1

24 It is a capital mistake to theorize before you have all the evidence. It biases the judgement.
  A Study in Scarlet (1888) ch. 3

25 Where there is no imagination there is no horror.
  A Study in Scarlet (1888) ch. 5

26 From the astrologer came the astronomer, from the alchemist the chemist, from the mesmerist the experimental psychologist. The quack of yesterday is the professor of tomorrow.
  Tales of Terror and Mystery (1922) 'The Leather Funnel'

1 The vocabulary of 'Bradshaw' is nervous and terse, but limited.
   The Valley of Fear (1915) ch. 1

2 Mediocrity knows nothing higher than itself, but talent instantly recognizes genius.
   The Valley of Fear (1915) ch. 1

3 What of the bow?
   The bow was made in England,
   Of true wood, of yew wood,
   The wood of English bows.
   The White Company (1891) 'Song of the Bow'

Francis Doyle 1810–88

English poet

4 Last night, among his fellow roughs,
   He jested, quaffed, and swore.
   'The Private of the Buffs' (1866)

Margaret Drabble 1939–

English novelist

5 England's not a bad country . . . It's just a mean, cold, ugly, divided, tired, clapped-out, post-imperial, post-industrial slag-heap covered in polystyrene hamburger cartons.
   A Natural Curiosity (1989)

6 Perhaps the rare and simple pleasure of being seen for what one is compensates for the misery of being it.
   A Summer Bird-Cage (1963) ch. 7

Francis Drake c.1540–96

English sailor and explorer. On Drake: see **ANONYMOUS** 20:15

7 There must be a beginning of any great matter, but the continuing unto the end until it be thoroughly finished yields the true glory.
   dispatch to Francis Walsingham, 17 May 1587, in *Navy Records Society* vol. 11 (1898)

8 The singeing of the King of Spain's Beard.
   on the expedition to Cadiz, 1587
   Francis Bacon *Considerations touching a War with Spain* (1629)

9 I must have the gentleman to haul and draw with the mariner, and the mariner with the gentleman . . . I would know him, that would refuse to set his hand to a rope, but I know there is not any such here.
   J. S. Corbett *Drake and the Tudor Navy* (1898) vol. 1, ch. 9

10 There is plenty of time to win this game, and to thrash the Spaniards too.
   when news of the Armada was brought while he was playing bowls on Plymouth Hoe
   attributed, in *Dictionary of National Biography* (1917–) vol. 5

Joseph Rodman Drake 1795–1820

American poet

11 Forever float that standard sheet!
   Where breathes the foe but falls before us,
   With Freedom's soil beneath our feet,
   And Freedom's banner streaming o'er us?
   'The American Flag' in *New York Evening Post* 29 May 1819 (also attributed to Fitz-Greene Halleck)

Michael Drayton 1563–1631

English poet

12 Ill news hath wings, and with the wind doth go,
   Comfort's a cripple and comes ever slow.
   The Barons' Wars (1603) canto 2, st. 28

13 Thus when we fondly flatter our desires,
   Our best conceits do prove the greatest liars.
   The Barons' Wars (1603) canto 6, st. 94

14 Since there's no help, come let us kiss and part,
   Nay, I have done: you get no more of me,
   And I am glad, yea glad with all my heart,
   That thus so cleanly, I myself can free,
   Shake hands for ever, cancel all our vows,
   And when we meet at any time again,
   Be it not seen in either of our brows,
   That we one jot of former love retain.
   Idea (1619) Sonnet 61

15 That shire which we the Heart of England well
   may call.
   of Warwickshire
   Poly-Olbion (1612–22) Song 13, l. 2

16 But when the bowels of the earth were sought,
   And men her golden entrails did espy,
   This mischief then into the world was brought,
   This framed the mint which coined our misery.

   Then lofty pines were by ambition hewn,
   And men sea-monsters swam the brackish flood
   In wainscot tubs to seek out worlds unknown,
   For certain ill to leave assuréd good.
   The Shepherd's Garland (1593) Eclogue 8

17 For that fine madness still he did retain
   Which rightly should possess a poet's brain.
   on **MARLOWE**
   'To Henry Reynolds, of Poets and Poesy' (1627) l. 109

18 Next these, learn'd Jonson, in this list I bring,
   Who had drunk deep of the Pierian spring.
   'To Henry Reynolds, of Poets and Poesy' (1627) l. 129; see **POPE** 615:28

19 Fair stood the wind for France
   When we our sails advance,
   Nor now to prove our chance
   Longer will tarry.
   To the Cambro-Britons (1619) 'Agincourt'

William Drennan 1754–1820

Irish physcian, poet, and political reformer

20 Nor one feeling of vengeance presume to defile
   The cause, or the men, of the Emerald Isle.
   Erin (1795) st. 3

John Drinkwater 1882–1937

English poet and dramatist

1   Deep is the silence, deep
On moon-washed apples of wonder.
'Moonlit Apples' (1917)

William Driver 1803–86

American sailor

2 I name thee Old Glory.
saluting a new flag hoisted on his ship, the Charles
Doggett
attributed

Henry Drummond 1851–97

Scottish theological writer

3 There are reverent minds who ceaselessly scan
the fields of Nature and the books of Science in
search of gaps—gaps which they will fill up with
God. As if God lived in gaps?
The Ascent of Man (1894) ch. 10

Thomas Drummond 1797–1840

British government official; Under-secretary of State for
Ireland, 1835–40

4 Property has its duties as well as its rights.
letter to the Earl of Donoughmore, 22 May 1838, in R. Barry
O'Brien *Thomas Drummond . . . Life and Letters* (1889)

William Drummond of Hawthornden 1585–1649

Scottish poet

5 Phoebus, arise,
And paint the sable skies,
With azure, white, and red.
'Song: Phoebus, arise' (1614)

6   A morn
Of bright carnations did o'erspread her face.
'Sonnet: Alexis here she stayed' (1614)

7 In all nations it is observed that there are some
families fatal to the ruin of the Commonwealth
and some persons fatal to the ruin of the house
and race of which they are descended.
Agnes Mure *Scottish Pageant* (1946) vol. 1

John Dryden 1631–1700

English poet, critic, and dramatist. On Dryden: see **ARNOLD
31:24**, **ARNOLD 32:7**, **JOHNSON 436:20**, **MACAULAY 507:22**;
see also **CRASHAW 258:23**

8 Then Israel's monarch, after Heaven's own heart,
His vigorous warmth did, variously, impart
To wives and slaves: and, wide as his command,
Scattered his Maker's image through the land.
Absalom and Achitophel (1681) pt. 1, l. 7

9 Whate'er he did was done with so much ease,
In him alone, 'twas natural to please.
Absalom and Achitophel (1681) pt. 1, l. 27

10 Plots, true or false, are necessary things,
To raise up commonwealths and ruin kings.
Absalom and Achitophel (1681) pt. 1, l. 83

11 Of these the false Achitophel was first,
A name to all succeeding ages curst.
For close designs and crooked counsels fit,
Sagacious, bold, and turbulent of wit,
Restless, unfixed in principles and place,
In power unpleased, impatient of disgrace;
A fiery soul, which working out its way,
Fretted the pigmy body to decay.
Absalom and Achitophel (1681) pt. 1, l. 150

12 A daring pilot in extremity;
Pleased with the danger, when the waves went
high
He sought the storms; but for a calm unfit.
Absalom and Achitophel (1681) pt. 1, l. 159

13 Great wits are sure to madness near allied,
And thin partitions do their bounds divide.
Absalom and Achitophel (1681) pt. 1, l. 163

14 Why should he, with wealth and honour blest,
Refuse his age the needful hours of rest?
Punish a body which he could not please;
Bankrupt of life, yet prodigal of ease?
And all to leave what with his toil he won
To that unfeathered two-legged thing, a son.
Absalom and Achitophel (1681) pt. 1, l. 165

15 In friendship false, implacable in hate:
Resolved to ruin or to rule the state.
Absalom and Achitophel (1681) pt. 1, l. 173

16 The people's prayer, the glad diviner's theme,
The young men's vision and the old men's
dream!
Absalom and Achitophel (1681) pt. 1, l. 238

17 All empire is no more than power in trust.
Absalom and Achitophel (1681) pt. 1, l. 411; see **DISRAELI** 286:15

18 Better one suffer, than a nation grieve.
Absalom and Achitophel (1681) pt. 1, l. 416

19 But far more numerous was the herd of such
Who think too little and who talk too much.
Absalom and Achitophel (1681) pt. 1, l. 533

20 A man so various that he seemed to be
Not one, but all mankind's epitome.
Stiff in opinions, always in the wrong;
Was everything by starts, and nothing long.
But, in the course of one revolving moon:
Was chemist, fiddler, statesman, and buffoon.
of 'Zimri', figure representing George Villiers, 2nd Duke of
BUCKINGHAM
Absalom and Achitophel (1681) pt. 1, l. 545

21 In squandering wealth was his peculiar art:
Nothing went unrewarded, but desert.
Beggared by fools, whom still he found too late:
He had his jest, and they had his estate.
Absalom and Achitophel (1681) pt. 1, l. 559

22 Youth, beauty, graceful action seldom fail:
But common interest always will prevail:

And pity never ceases to be shown
To him, who makes the people's wrongs his
   own.
Absalom and Achitophel (1681) pt. 1, l. 723

1 For who can be secure of private right,
If sovereign sway may be dissolved by might?
Nor is the people's judgement always true:
The most may err as grossly as the few.
Absalom and Achitophel (1681) pt. 1, l. 779

2 Never was patriot yet, but was a fool.
Absalom and Achitophel (1681) pt. 1, l. 968

3 Beware the fury of a patient man.
Absalom and Achitophel (1681) pt. 1, l. 1005

4 Happy, happy, happy pair!
None but the brave,
None but the brave,
None but the brave deserves the fair.
Alexander's Feast (1697) l. 4; see **PROVERBS** 640:15

5 Drinking is the soldier's pleasure;
Rich the treasure;
Sweet the pleasure;
Sweet is pleasure after pain.
Alexander's Feast (1697) l. 57

6 War, he sung, is toil and trouble;
Honour but an empty bubble.
Never ending, still beginning,
Fighting still, and still destroying,
If the world be worth thy winning,
Think, oh think, it worth enjoying.
Alexander's Feast (1697) l. 97

7 Revenge, revenge! Timotheus cries.
Alexander's Feast (1697) l. 131

8 Errors, like straws, upon the surface flow;
He who would search for pearls must dive
   below.
All for Love (1678) prologue

9   Give, you gods,
Give to your boy, your Caesar,
The rattle of a globe to play withal,
This gewgaw world, and put him cheaply off:
I'll not be pleased with less than Cleopatra.
All for Love (1678) act 2, sc. 1

10 Men are but children of a larger growth;
Our appetites as apt to change as theirs,
And full as craving too, and full as vain.
All for Love (1678) act 4, sc. 1; see **CHESTERFIELD** 223:10

11 By viewing nature, nature's handmaid art,
Makes mighty things from small beginnings
   grow:
Thus fishes first to shipping did impart,
Their tail the rudder, and their head the prow.
Annus Mirabilis (1667) st. 155

12 An horrid stillness first invades the ear,
And in that silence we the tempest fear.
Astraea Redux (1660) l. 7

13 Death, in itself, is nothing; but we fear,
To be we know not what, we know not where.
Aureng-Zebe (1675) act 4, sc. 1

14 Refined himself to soul, to curb the sense
And made almost a sin of abstinence.
'The Character of a Good Parson' (1700) l. 10

15 I am as free as nature first made man,
Ere the base laws of servitude began,
When wild in woods the noble savage ran.
The Conquest of Granada (1670) pt. 1, act 1, sc. 1

16 Forgiveness to the injured does belong;
But they ne'er pardon, who have done the
   wrong.
The Conquest of Granada (1670) pt. 2, act 1, sc. 2

17 Thou strong seducer, opportunity!
The Conquest of Granada (1670) pt. 2, act 4, sc. 3

18 Bold knaves thrive without one grain of sense,
But good men starve for want of impudence.
Constantine the Great (1684) epilogue

19 She hugged the offender, and forgave the
   offence.
Cymon and Iphigenia (1700) l. 367; see **AUGUSTINE** 39:21,
DRYDEN 295:30

20 Better to hunt in fields, for health unbought,
Than fee the doctor for a nauseous draught.
The wise, for cure, on exercise depend;
God never made his work, for man to mend.
Epistle 'To my honoured kinsman John Driden' (1700) l. 92

21 Even victors are by victories undone.
Epistle 'To my honoured kinsman John Driden' (1700) l. 164

22 For he was great, ere fortune made him so.
on the death of Oliver **CROMWELL**
Heroic Stanzas (1659) st. 6

23 For truth has such a face and such a mien
As to be loved needs only to be seen.
The Hind and the Panther (1687) pt. 1, l. 33

24 My manhood, long misled by wandering fires,
Followed false lights.
The Hind and the Panther (1687) pt. 1, l. 72

25 Reason to rule, but mercy to forgive:
The first is law, the last prerogative.
The Hind and the Panther (1687) pt. 1, l. 261

26 Either be wholly slaves or wholly free.
The Hind and the Panther (1687) pt. 2, l. 285

27 Much malice mingled with a little wit
Perhaps may censure this mysterious writ.
The Hind and the Panther (1687) pt. 3, l. 1

28 For present joys are more to flesh and blood
Than a dull prospect of a distant good.
The Hind and the Panther (1687) pt. 3, l. 364

29 By education most have been misled;
So they believe, because they so were bred.
The priest continues what the nurse began,
And thus the child imposes on the man.
The Hind and the Panther (1687) pt. 3, l. 389

30 T'abhor the makers, and their laws approve,
Is to hate traitors and the treason love.
The Hind and the Panther (1687) pt. 3, l. 706; see **AUGUSTINE**
39:21, **DRYDEN** 295:19

1 For those whom God to ruin has designed,
He fits for fate, and first destroys their mind.
The Hind and the Panther (1687) pt. 3, l. 1093; see
ANONYMOUS 23:1, **PROVERBS** 647:18

2 And love's the noblest frailty of the mind.
The Indian Emperor (1665) act 2, sc. 2; see **SHADWELL** 693:13

3 Repentance is the virtue of weak minds.
The Indian Emperor (1665) act 3, sc. 1

4 For all the happiness mankind can gain
Is not in pleasure, but in rest from pain.
The Indian Emperor (1665) act 4, sc. 1

5 That fairy kind of writing which depends only
upon the force of imagination.
King Arthur (1691) dedication

6 War is the trade of kings.
King Arthur (1691) act 2, sc. 2

7 Fairest Isle, all isles excelling,
Seat of pleasures, and of loves;
Venus here will choose her dwelling,
And forsake her Cyprian groves.
King Arthur (1691) act 5 'Song of Venus'; see **WESLEY** 847:17

8 Ovid, the soft philosopher of love.
Love Triumphant (1694) act 2, sc. 1

9 All human things are subject to decay,
And, when fate summons, monarchs must obey.
MacFlecknoe (1682) l. 1

10 The rest to some faint meaning make pretence,
But Shadwell never deviates into sense.
Some beams of wit on other souls may fall,
Strike through and make a lucid interval;
But Shadwell's genuine night admits no ray,
His rising fogs prevail upon the day.
MacFlecknoe (1682) l. 19

11 Thy genius calls thee not to purchase fame
In keen iambics, but mild anagram:
Leave writing plays, and choose for thy
command
Some peaceful province in Acrostic Land.
There thou mayest wings display and altars
raise,
And torture one poor word ten thousand ways.
MacFlecknoe (1682) l. 203

12 I am resolved to grow fat and look young till
forty, and then slip out of the world with the
first wrinkle and the reputation of five-and-
twenty.
The Maiden Queen (1668) act 3, sc. 1

13 I am to be married within these three days;
married past redemption.
Marriage à la Mode (1672) act 1, sc. 1

14 We loathe our manna, and we long for quails.
The Medal (1682) l. 131

15 But treason is not owned when 'tis descried;
Successful crimes alone are justified.
The Medal (1682) l. 207

16 Whatever is, is in its causes just.
Oedipus (with Nathaniel Lee, 1679) act 3, sc. 1; see **POPE** 616:28

17 But love's a malady without a cure.
Palamon and Arcite (1700) bk. 2, l. 110

18 Fool, not to know that love endures no tie,
And Jove but laughs at lovers' perjury.
Palamon and Arcite (1700) bk. 2, l. 148; see **OVID** 589:21,
PROVERBS 636:47

19 And Antony, who lost the world for love.
Palamon and Arcite (1700) bk. 2, l. 607

20 Repentance is but want of power to sin.
Palamon and Arcite (1700) bk. 3, l. 813

21 Like pilgrims to th'appointed place we tend;
The world's an inn, and death the journey's end.
Palamon and Arcite (1700) bk. 3, l. 887

22 But 'tis the talent of our English nation,
Still to be plotting some new reformation.
'The Prologue at Oxford, 1680' (prologue to Nathaniel Lee
Sophonisba, 2nd ed., 1681)

23 So poetry, which is in Oxford made
An art, in London only is a trade.
'Prologue to the University of Oxon . . . at the Acting of *The
Silent Woman*' (1673)

24 Joy ruled the day, and Love the night.
The Secular Masque (1700) l. 81

25 All, all of a piece throughout;
Thy chase had a beast in view;
Thy wars brought nothing about;
Thy lovers were all untrue.
'Tis well an old age is out,
And time to begin a new.
The Secular Masque (1700) l. 92

26 For secrets are edged tools,
And must be kept from children and from fools.
Sir Martin Mar-All (1667) act 2, sc. 2

27 From harmony, from heavenly harmony
This universal frame began:
From harmony to harmony
Through all the compass of the notes it ran,
The diapason closing full in Man.
A Song for St Cecilia's Day (1687) st. 1

28 What passion cannot Music raise and quell?
A Song for St Cecilia's Day (1687) st. 2

29 The soft complaining flute.
A Song for St Cecilia's Day (1687) st. 4

30 The trumpet shall be heard on high,
The dead shall live, the living die,
And Music shall untune the sky.
A Song for St Cecilia's Day (1687) 'Grand Chorus'

31 There is a pleasure sure,
In being mad, which none but madmen know!
The Spanish Friar (1681) act 1, sc. 1

32 And, dying, bless the hand that gave the blow.
The Spanish Friar (1681) act 2, sc. 2

33 The dial spoke not, but it made shrewd signs,
And pointed full upon the stroke of murder.
The Spanish Friar (1681) act 4, sc. 2

34 Mute and magnificent, without a tear.
Threnodia Augustalis (1685) st. 2

1 Freedom which in no other land will thrive,
Freedom an English subject's sole prerogative.
Threnodia Augustalis (1685) st. 10

2   Wit will shine
Through the harsh cadence of a rugged line.
'To the Memory of Mr Oldham' (1684)

3 Thou youngest virgin-daughter of the skies,
Made in the last promotion of the blest.
'To the pious Memory of . . . Mrs Anne Killigrew' (1686) l. 1

4 And he, who servilely creeps after sense,
Is safe, but ne'er will reach an excellence.
Tyrannic Love (1669) prologue

5 All delays are dangerous in war.
Tyrannic Love (1669) act 1, sc. 1

6 Happy the man, and happy he alone,
He, who can call to-day his own:
He who, secure within, can say,
Tomorrow do thy worst, for I have lived today.
translation of Horace *Odes* bk. 3, no. 29; see **HORACE** 413:8,
SMITH 758:20

7 Not Heaven itself upon the past has power;
But what has been, has been, and I have had my
   hour.
translation of Horace *Odes* bk. 3, no. 29

8 Look round the habitable world! how few
Know their own good; or knowing it, pursue.
translation of Juvenal *Satires* no. 10

9 She knows her man, and when you rant and
   swear,
Can draw you to her *with a single hair.*
translation of Persius *Satires* no. 5, l. 246

10 Arms, and the man I sing, who, forced by fate,
And haughty Juno's unrelenting hate,
Expelled and exiled, left the Trojan shore.
translation of Virgil *Aeneid* (*Aeneis*, 1697) bk. 1, l. 1; see **VIRGIL**
828:10

11 We must beat the iron while it is hot, but we
may polish it at leisure.
Aeneis (1697) dedication; see **PROVERBS** 643:45

12 Every age has a kind of universal genius, which
inclines those that live in it to some particular
studies.
An Essay of Dramatic Poesy (1668)

13 The famous rules, which the French call *Des
Trois Unitez*, or, the Three Unities, which ought
to be observed in every regular play; namely, of
Time, Place, and Action.
An Essay of Dramatic Poesy (1668)

14 A thing well said will be wit in all languages.
An Essay of Dramatic Poesy (1668)

15 He was naturally learn'd; he needed not the
spectacles of books to read Nature: he looked
inwards, and found her there . . . He is many
times flat, insipid; his comic wit degenerating
into clenches, his serious swelling into bombast.
But he is always great.
on SHAKESPEARE
An Essay of Dramatic Poesy (1668)

16 He invades authors like a monarch; and what
would be theft in other poets, is only victory in
him.
on Ben **JONSON**
An Essay of Dramatic Poesy (1668)

17 If by the people you understand the multitude,
the *hoi polloi*, 'tis no matter what they think;
they are sometimes in the right, sometimes in
the wrong: their judgement is a mere lottery.
An Essay of Dramatic Poesy (1668)

18 [Shakespeare] is the very Janus of poets; he
wears almost everywhere two faces; and you
have scarce begun to admire the one, ere you
despise the other.
Essay on the Dramatic Poetry of the Last Age (1672)

19 What judgement I had increases rather than
diminishes; and thoughts, such as they are, come
crowding in so fast upon me, that my only
difficulty is to choose or reject; to run them into
verse or to give them the other harmony of
prose.
Fables Ancient and Modern (1700) preface

20 'Tis sufficient to say, according to the proverb,
that here is God's plenty.
of **CHAUCER**
Fables Ancient and Modern (1700) preface

21 [Chaucer] is a perpetual fountain of good sense.
Fables Ancient and Modern (1700) preface

22 One of our late great poets is sunk in his
reputation, because he could never forgive any
conceit which came in his way; but swept like a
drag-net, great and small. There was plenty
enough, but the dishes were ill-sorted; whole
pyramids of sweetmeats, for boys and women;
but little of solid meat for men.
on Abraham **COWLEY**
Fables Ancient and Modern (1700) preface

23 Sure the poet . . . spewed up a good lump of
clotted nonsense at once.
Notes and Observations on the Empress of Morocco [by Elkanah
Settle] (1674) 'The First Act'

24 How easy it is to call rogue and villain, and that
wittily! But how hard to make a man appear a
fool, a blockhead, or a knave, without using any
of those opprobrious terms! To spare the
grossness of the names, and to do the thing yet
more severely, is to draw a full face, and to
make the nose and cheeks stand out, and yet
not to employ any depth of shadowing.
Of Satire (1693)

25 A man may be capable, as Jack Ketch's wife said
of his servant, of a plain piece of work, a bare
hanging; but to make a malefactor die sweetly
was only belonging to her husband.
Of Satire (1693)

26 Cousin Swift, you will never be a poet.
Samuel Johnson *Lives of the English Poets* (1779–81) 'Dryden'

Alexander Dubček 1921–92

Czechoslovak statesman, First Secretary of the Czechoslovak Communist Party 1968–9; he was removed from office following the Soviet invasion of 1968

1 In the service of the people we followed such a policy that socialism would not lose its human face.

in *Rudé Právo* 19 July 1968; a resolution by the party group in the Ministry of Foreign Affairs, 1968, referred to Czechoslovakian foreign policy acquiring 'its own defined face'; in *Rudé Právo* 14 March 1968

Joachim Du Bellay 1522–60

French poet

2 *France, mère des arts, des armes et des lois.*

France, mother of arts, of warfare, and of laws.
Les Regrets (1558) sonnet no. 9

3 *Heureux qui comme Ulysse a fait un beau voyage*
Ou comme celui–là qui conquit la toison,
Et puis est retourné, plein d'usage et raison,
Vivre entre ses parents le reste de son âge!

Happy he who like Ulysses has made a great journey, or like that man who won the Fleece and then came home, full of experience and good sense, to live the rest of his time among his family!
Les Regrets (1558) Sonnet no. 31

4 *Plus que le marbre dur me plaît l'ardoise fine,*
Plus mon Loire Gaulois, que le Tibre Latin,
Plus mon petit Lyré, que le mont Palatin,
Et plus que l'air marin la douceur angevine.

I love thin slate more than hard marble, my Gallic Loire more than the Latin Tiber, my little Liré more than the Palatine Hill, and more than the sea air the sweetness of Anjou.
Les Regrets (1558) Sonnet no. 31

W. E. B. Du Bois 1868–1963

American social reformer and political activist

5 The cost of liberty is less than the price of repression.
John Brown (1909) ch. 13

6 The problem of the twentieth century is the problem of the colour line—the relation of the darker to the lighter races of men in Asia and Africa, in America and the islands of the sea.
The Souls of Black Folk (1905) ch. 2

7 Herein lies the tragedy of the age: not that men are poor . . . not that men are wicked . . . but that men know so little of men.
The Souls of Black Folk (1905) ch. 12

8 One thing alone I charge you. As you live, believe in life!
last message, written 26 June, 1957, and read at his funeral, 1963, in *Journal of Negro History* April 1964

Stephen Duck 1705–56

English poet and clergyman

9 Let those who feast at ease on dainty fare,
Pity the reapers, who their feasts prepare.
'The Thresher's Labour' (1730)

10 Like Sisyphus, our work is never done;
Continually rolls back the restless stone.
'The Thresher's Labour' (1730)

Mme Du Deffand (Marie de Vichy-Chamrond) 1697–1780

French literary hostess

11 *La distance n'y fait rien; il n'y a que le premier pas qui coûte.*

The distance is nothing; it is only the first step that is difficult.
commenting on the legend that St Denis, carrying his head in his hands, walked two leagues
letter to Jean Le Rond d'Alembert, 7 July 1763, in Gaston Maugras *Trois mois à la cour de Frédéric* (1886); see **PROVERBS** 636:27

Helen, Lady Dufferin 1807–67

Irish writer

12 Is the cabin still left standing? Has the rich man need of all?
Is the children's birthplace taken now within the new park wall?
'The Emigrant Ship'

George Duffield 1818–88

American Presbyterian minister

13 Stand up!—stand up for Jesus!
Ye soldiers of the Cross.
'Stand Up, Stand Up for Jesus' (1858 hymn); the opening line inspired by the dying words of the American evangelist, Dudley Atkins Tyng; see **TYNG** 821:8

Carol Ann Duffy 1965–

English poet

14 Whatever 'in love' means,
true love is talented.
Someone vividly gifted in love has gone.
*on the death of **DIANA**, Princess of Wales*
'September, 1997' (1997); see **CHARLES** 217:13

Charles Gavan Duffy 1816–1903

Irish nationalist and (later) Australian politician

15 I am still an Irish rebel to the backbone and the spinal marrow, a rebel for the same reason that John Hampden and Algernon Sidney, George Washington and Charles Carrol of Carroltown, were rebels—because tyranny had supplanted the law.
arriving in Australia in 1856
Cyril Pearl *The Three Lives of Gavan Duffy* (1979)

Georges Duhamel 1884–1966
French novelist

1 I have too much respect for the idea of God to make it responsible for such an absurd world.
  Le désert de Bièvres (1937)

John Foster Dulles 1888–1959
American international lawyer and Republican politician, Secretary of State from 1953

2 The ability to get to the verge without getting into the war is the necessary art . . . We walked to the brink and we looked it in the face.
  in *Life* 16 January 1956; see **STEVENSON** 774:24

Alexandre Dumas ('Dumas père') 1802–70
French novelist and dramatist

3 *Cherchons la femme.*
  Let us look for the woman.
  attributed to Joseph Fouché (1763–1820) in the form 'Cherchez la femme'
    Les Mohicans de Paris [The Mohicans of Paris] (1854–5) *passim*

4 *Tous pour un, un pour tous.*
  All for one, one for all.
    Les Trois Mousquetaires [The Three musketeers] (1844) ch. 9

Alexandre Dumas ('Dumas fils') 1824–95
French writer

5 All generalizations are dangerous, even this one.
  attributed

Daphne Du Maurier 1907–89
English novelist

6 Last night I dreamt I went to Manderley again.
  Rebecca (1938), opening words

Charles François du Périer Dumouriez 1739–1823
French general

7 The courtiers who surround him have forgotten nothing and learnt nothing.
  of Louis XVIII, at the time of the Declaration of Verona, September 1795; quoted by **NAPOLEON I** *in his Declaration to the French on his return from Elba, 1815*
    Examen impartial d'un Écrit intitulé Déclaration de Louis XVIII (1795); see **TALLEYRAND** 788:19

Paul Lawrence Dunbar 1872–1906
American poet

8 I know why the caged bird sings!
  adopted by Maya **ANGELOU** *as the title of her autobiography, 1969*
    'Sympathy' st. 3; see **WEBSTER** 844:22

William Dunbar c.1465–c.1513
Scottish poet and priest. See also **ANONYMOUS** 18:17

9 All women of us suld have honouring,
  Service and love above all other thing.
    'In Praise of Women'

10 I that in heill wes and gladnes
  Am trublit now with gret seiknes
  And feblit with infirmitie:
  Timor mortis conturbat me.
  Timor . . . = *The fear of death troubles me;* makaris = *makers, i.e. poets*
    'Lament for the Makaris'

11 He hes done petuously devour,
  The noble Chaucer, of makaris flouir,
  The Monk of Bery, and Gower, all three;
  Timor mortis conturbat me.
    'Lament for the Makaris'

12 All love is lost but upon God alone.
    'The Merle and the Nightingale' st. 2

Isadora Duncan 1878–1927
American dancer and teacher

13 *Adieu, mes amis. Je vais à la gloire.*
  Farewell, my friends. I go to glory.
  last words before her scarf caught in a car wheel, breaking her neck
    Mary Desti *Isadora Duncan's End* (1929) ch. 25

Henry Dundas 1742–1811
Scottish-born politician

14 When it is said that no alternative is left to the New Englanders but to starve or rebel, this is not the fact, for there is another way, to submit.
  the word 'starvation' was said to have been coined in relation to this speech, and Dundas became known as 'Starvation Dundas'
    in the House of Commons, 1775

Ian Dunlop 1940–
British art historian

15 The shock of the new: seven historic exhibitions of modern art.
  title of book (1972)

Douglas Dunn 1942–
Scottish poet

16 In a country like this
  Our ghosts outnumber us . . .
    'At Falkland Palace' (1988)

17 My poems should be Clyde-built, crude and sure,
  With images of those dole-deployed
  To honour the indomitable Reds,
  Clydesiders of slant steel and angled cranes;
  A poetry of nuts and bolts, born, bred,
  Embattled by the Clyde, tight and impure.
    'Clydesiders' (1974)

1 They ruined us. They conquered continents.
We filled their uniforms. We cruised the seas.
We worked their mines and made their histories.
You work, we rule, they said. We worked; they
  ruled.
They fooled the tenements. All men were
  fooled.
'Empires' (1979)

2 I am light with meditation, religiose
And mystic with a day of solitude.
'Reading Pascal in the Lowlands' (1985)

Finlay Peter Dunne 1867–1936
American humorous writer

3 A law, Hinnissey, that might look like a wall to
you or me wud look like a triumphal arch to
th'expeeryenced eye iv a lawyer.
'Mr Dooley on the Power of the Press' in *American Magazine*
no. 62 1906; see **COMMAGER** 244:17

Sean Dunne 1956–97
Irish poet

4 The country wears their going like a scar,
Today their relatives save to support and
Send others in planes for the new diaspora.
'Letter from Ireland' (1991)

John Dunning, Lord Ashburton
1731–83
English lawyer and politician

5 The influence of the Crown has increased, is
increasing, and ought to be diminished.
resolution passed in the House of Commons, 6 April 1780

Richard Duppa 1770–1831
English artist and writer

6 In language, the ignorant have prescribed laws to
the learned.
Maxims (1830) no. 252

Marguerite Duras 1914–96
French writer

7 Fear is my main point of reference. Causing fear
is what constitutes evil.
Emily L. (1987)

8 Men like women who write. Even though they
don't say so. A writer is a foreign country.
Practicalities (1987) 'The M. D. Uniform'

Paul Durcan 1944–
Irish poet

9 Poetry's another word
For losing everything
Except purity of heart.
'Christmas Day' (1996)

10   Some of us made it
To the forest edge, but many of us did not

Make it, although their unborn children did—
Such as you whom the camp commandant
  branded
Sid Vicious of the Sex Pistols. Jesus, break his
  fall:
There—but for the clutch of luck—go we all.
'The Death by Heroin of Sid Vicious' (1980)

Ray Durem 1915–63
American poet

11 Some of my best friends are white boys.
when I meet 'em
I treat 'em
just the same as if they was people.
'Broadminded' (written 1951)

Albrecht Dürer 1471–1528
German painter and engraver

12 He that would be a painter must have a natural
turn thereto. Love and delight therein are better
teachers of the Art of Painting than compulsion
is.
Third Book of Human Proportions (written c.1512–3)
introduction; William Martin Conway *Literary remains of
Albrecht Dürer* (1889)

John George Lambton, Lord Durham 1792–1840
English Whig politician

13 £40,000 a year a moderate income—such a one
as a man *might jog on with*.
Herbert Maxwell (ed.) *The Creevey Papers* (1903) vol. 2, from a
letter from Mr Creevey to Miss Elizabeth Ord, 13 September
1821

14 I expected to find a contest between a
government and a people: I found two nations
warring in the bosom of a single state.
of Canada
Report of the Affairs of British North America (1839)

Leo Durocher 1906–91
American baseball coach

15 I called off his players' names as they came
marching up the steps behind him . . . All nice
guys. They'll finish last. Nice guys. Finish last.
*casual remark at a practice ground in the presence of a
number of journalists, July 1946, generally quoted as 'Nice
guys finish last'*
Nice Guys Finish Last (1975) pt. 1

Lawrence Durrell 1912–90
English novelist, poet, and travel writer

16 I love to feel events overlapping each other,
crawling over one another like wet crabs in a
basket.
Balthazar (1958) pt. 1

17 No history much? Perhaps. Only this ominous
Dark beauty flowering under veils,

Trapped in the spectrum of a dying style:
A village like an instinct left to rust,
Composed around the echo of a pistol-shot.
'Sarajevo' (1951)

Friedrich Dürrenmatt 1921–90

Swiss dramatist and novelist

1 Truth is such a difficult problem that most
people don't see any problem in it at all.
'The Bridge' (1981) in *Friedrich Dürrenmatt: Selected Writings*
(2006) vol. 3, tr. Joel Agee

Ian Dury 1942–2000

English rock singer and songwriter

2 Sex and drugs and rock and roll.
title of song (1977)

Andrea Dworkin 1946–2005

American feminist and writer

3 Seduction is often difficult to distinguish from
rape. In seduction, the rapist bothers to buy a
bottle of wine.
speech to women at Harper & Row, 1976; in *Letters from a
War Zone* (1988)

Edward Dyer d. 1607

English poet

4 Silence augmenteth grief, writing increaseth
rage,
Staled are my thoughts, which loved and lost,
the wonder of our age.
previously attributed to Fulke **GREVILLE**
'Elegy on the Death of Sir Philip Sidney' (1593)

5 My mind to me a kingdom is.
Such perfect joy therein I find
That it excels all other bliss
That world affords or grows by kind.
Though much I want which most would have,
Yet still my mind forbids to crave.
'In praise of a contented mind' (1588), attributed

John Dyer 1700–58

Welsh clergyman and poet

6 The care of sheep, the labours of the loom,
And arts of trade, I sing.
The Fleece (1757) bk. 1, l. 1

7 Industry,
Which dignifies the artist, lifts the swain,
And the straw cottage to a palace turns.
The Fleece (1757) bk. 3, l. 332

8 But transient is the smile of fate:
A little rule, a little sway,
A sunbeam in a winter's day,
Is all the proud and mighty have
Between the cradle and the grave.
Grongar Hill (1726) l. 88

9 The town and village, dome and farm,
Each give each a double charm,
As pearls upon an Ethiop's arm.
Grongar Hill (1726) l. 111

10 The pilgrim oft
At dead of night, mid his orison hears
Aghast the voice of Time, disparting tow'rs.
The Ruins of Rome (1740) l. 38

John Dyer

English poet

11 And he that will this health deny,
Down among the dead men let him lie.
'Down among the Dead Men' (c.1700)

Bob Dylan (Robert Zimmerman) 1941–

American singer and songwriter

12 How many roads must a man walk down
Before you can call him a man? . . .
The answer, my friend, is blowin' in the wind,
The answer is blowin' in the wind.
'Blowin' in the Wind' (1962 song)

13 They're selling postcards of the hanging.
'Desolation Row' (1965 song)

14 Praise be to Nero's Neptune
The Titanic sails at dawn
And everybody's shouting
'Which Side Are You On?'
And Ezra Pound and T. S. Eliot
Fighting in the captain's tower
While calypso singers laugh at them
And fishermen hold flowers.
'Desolation Row' (1965 song)

15 I saw ten thousand talkers whose tongues were
all broken,
I saw guns and sharp swords, in the hands of
young children . . .
And it's a hard rain's a gonna fall.
'A Hard Rain's A Gonna Fall' (1963 song)

16 Money doesn't talk, it swears.
'It's Alright, Ma (I'm Only Bleeding)' (1965 song)

17 She takes just like a woman, yes, she does
She makes love just like a woman, yes, she does
And she aches just like a woman
But she breaks like a little girl.
'Just Like a Woman' (1966 song)

18 How does it feel
To be on your own
With no direction home
Like a complete unknown
Like a rolling stone?
'Like a Rolling Stone' (1965 song)

19 She knows there's no success like failure
And that failure's no success at all.
'Love Minus Zero / No Limit' (1965 song)

20 Hey! Mr Tambourine Man, play a song for me.
I'm not sleepy and there is no place I'm going
to.
'Mr Tambourine Man' (1965 song)

1 Ah, but I was so much older then,
I'm younger than that now.
'My Back Pages' (1964 song)

2 Señor, señor, do you know where we're headin'?
Lincoln County Road or Armageddon?
'Señor (Tale of Yankee Power)' (1978 song)

3 All that foreign oil controlling American soil.
'Slow Train' (1979 song)

4 The times they are a-changin'.
title of song (1964)

5 Come mothers and fathers,
Throughout the land
And don't criticize
What you can't understand.
'The Times They Are A-Changing' (1964 song)

6 But I can't think for you
You'll have to decide,
Whether Judas Iscariot
Had God on his side.
'With God on our Side' (1963 song)

Amelia Earhart 1898–1937

American aviator; her aircraft was lost over the Pacific
Ocean during a round-the-world flight

7 Courage is the price that Life exacts for granting
peace,
The soul that knows it not, knows no release
From little things.
'Courage' (1927)

8 The best mascot is a good mechanic.
Mary S. Lovell The Sound of Wings (1989)

George Eastman 1854–1932

American inventor and manufacturer of photographic
equipment

9 To my friends. My work is done—why wait?
suicide note, 14 March 1932, Elizabeth Brayer George Eastman
(2006)

Clint Eastwood see Film lines 328:9

Abba Eban 1915–2002

Israeli diplomat

10 History teaches us that men and nations behave
wisely once they have exhausted all other
alternatives.
speech in London, 16 December 1970, in The Times 17
December 1970

Fred Ebb 1932–2004

American songwriter

11 Money makes the world go around.
'Money Money' (1965 song), from the musical Cabaret

Marie von Ebner-Eschenbach

1830–1916

Austrian writer

12 Fear not those who argue but those who dodge.
Aphorisms (1905)

Arthur Eddington 1882–1944

English astrophysicist

13 We do not argue with the critic who urges that
the stars are not hot enough for this process; we
tell him to go and find a hotter place.
on the formation of heavier elements by nuclear reactions
The Internal Constitution of the Stars (1926)

14 Let us draw an arrow arbitrarily. If as we follow
the arrow we find more and more of the
random element in the world, then the arrow is
pointing towards the future; if the random
element decreases the arrow points towards the
past . . . I shall use the phrase 'time's arrow' to
express this one-way property of time which has
no analogue in space.
The Nature of the Physical World (1928) ch. 4

15 If an army of monkeys were strumming on
typewriters they might write all the books in the
British Museum.
The Nature of the Physical World (1928); see WILENSKY 856:20

16 If someone points out to you that your pet
theory of the universe is in disagreement with
Maxwell's equations—then so much the worse
for Maxwell's equations. If it is found to be
contradicted by observation—well, these
experimentalists do bungle things sometimes.
But if your theory is found to be against the
second law of thermodynamics I can give you
no hope; there is nothing for it but to collapse
in deepest humiliation.
The Nature of the Physical World (1928) ch. 14

17 I am standing on the threshold about to enter a
room. It is a complicated business. In the first
place I must shove against an atmosphere
pressing with a force of fourteen pounds on
every square inch of my body. I must make sure
of landing on a plank travelling at twenty miles
a second round the sun— a fraction of a second
too early or too late, the plank would be miles
away. I must do this whilst hanging from a
round planet, head outward into space, and with
a wind of aether blowing at no one knows how
many miles a second through every interstice of
my body.
The Nature of the Physical World (1928) ch. 15

18 I ask you to look both ways. For the road to a
knowledge of the stars leads through the atom;
and important knowledge of the atom has been
reached through the stars.
Stars and Atoms (1928) Lecture 1

Mary Baker Eddy 1821–1910

American religious leader and founder of the Christian Science movement

1 Jesus of Nazareth was the most scientific man that ever trod the globe. He plunged beneath the material surface of things, and found the spiritual cause.
  Science and Health with Key to the Scriptures (1875)

2 Disease is an experience of so-called mortal mind. It is fear made manifest on the body.
  Science and Health with Key to the Scriptures (1875)

Anthony Eden, Earl of Avon

1897–1977

British Conservative statesman, Prime Minister 1955–7. On Eden: see **MUGGERIDGE** 564:6

3 We are in an armed conflict; that is the phrase I have used. There has been no declaration of war.
  on the Suez crisis
    speech in the House of Commons, 1 November 1956

4 Long experience has taught me that to be criticized is not always to be wrong.
  during the Suez crisis
    speech at Lord Mayor's Guildhall banquet; in *Daily Herald* 10 November 1956

Clarissa Eden 1920–

English wife of Anthony **EDEN**

5 For the past few weeks I have really felt as if the Suez Canal was flowing through my drawing-room.
    speech at Gateshead, 20 November 1956

Marriott Edgar 1880–1951

British actor and writer

6 There's a famous seaside place called Blackpool,
  That's noted for fresh air and fun,
  And Mr and Mrs Ramsbottom
  Went there with young Albert, their son.
    'The Lion and Albert' (1932)

Maria Edgeworth 1767–1849

English-born Irish novelist

7 Well! some people talk of morality, and some of religion, but give me a little snug property.
    The Absentee (1812) ch. 2

8 It was her settled purpose to make the Irish and Ireland ridiculous and contemptible to Lord Colambre; to disgust him with his native country; to make him abandon the wish of residing on his own estate. To confirm him an absentee was her object.
    The Absentee (1812) ch. 7

9 We cannot judge either of the feelings or of the character of men with perfect accuracy, from their actions or their appearance in public; it is from their careless conversation, their half-finished sentences, that we may hope with the greatest probability of success to discover their real character.
    Castle Rackrent (1800) preface

10 Business was his aversion; pleasure was his business.
    The Contrast (1804) ch. 2

11 What a misfortune it is to be born a woman! . . . Why seek for knowledge, which can prove only that our wretchedness is irremediable? If a ray of light break in upon us, it is but to make darkness more visible; to show us the new limits, the Gothic structure, the impenetrable barriers of our prison.
    Leonora (1806) Letter 1

12 Man is to be held only by the *slightest* chains, with the idea that he can break them at pleasure, he submits to them in sport.
    Letters for Literary Ladies (1795) 'Letters of Julia and Caroline' no. 1

Richard Lovell Edgeworth 1744–1817

Irish landowner and writer, father of Maria **EDGEWORTH**

13 We hear from good authority that the King was much pleased with Castle Rackrent—he rubbed his hands and said what—what—I know something now of my Irish subjects.
    letter to D. A. Beaufort, 26 April 1800

Thomas Alva Edison 1847–1931

American inventor

14 The horseless vehicle is the coming wonder.
    interview, in *New York World* 17 November 1895

15 Genius is one per cent inspiration, ninety-nine per cent perspiration.
    said c.1903, in *Harper's Monthly Magazine* September 1932; see **BUFFON** 170:5

16 For most of my life I refused to work at any problem unless its solution seemed to be capable of being put to commercial use.
    interview, in *New York Sun* February 1917

James Edmeston 1791–1867

English architect and hymn-writer

17 Lead us, Heavenly Father, lead us
  O'er the world's tempestuous sea;
  Guard us, guide us, keep us, feed us,
  For we have no help but Thee;
  Yet possessing every blessing,
  If our God our Father be.
    'Lead us, heavenly Father, lead us' (1821)

John Maxwell Edmonds 1875–1958

English classicist

18 When you go home, tell them of us and say,
  'For your tomorrows these gave their today.'
    Inscriptions Suggested for War Memorials (1919); see **EPITAPHS** 320:3

St Edmund of Abingdon c.1175–1240

English scholar and churchman, Archbishop of Canterbury from 1233

1 Study as if you were to live for ever; live as if you were to die tomorrow.

John Crozier *St Edmund of Abingdon* (1982)

Edward III 1312–77

English monarch, King from 1327. See also **MOTTOES** 563:10

2 Also say to them, that they suffre hym this day to wynne his spurres, for if god be pleased, I woll this journey be his, and the honoure therof.

speaking of the Black Prince at Crécy, 1346; commonly quoted as 'Let the boy win his spurs'

The Chronicle of Froissart (translated by Sir John Bourchier, Lord Berners, 1523–5) ch. 130

Edward VII 1841–1910

British monarch, King of the United Kingdom from 1901. On Edward: see **NEWSPAPER HEADLINES AND LEADERS** 573:22

3 I thought everyone must know that a *short* jacket is always worn with a silk hat at a private view in the morning.

to Frederick Ponsonby, who had proposed accompanying him in a tailcoat

Philip Magnus *Edward VII* (1964) ch. 19

Edward VIII, afterwards Duke of Windsor 1894–1972

British prince and monarch; eldest son of **GEORGE V**, he succeeded his father in 1936, but abdicated after eleven months in order to marry an American divorcee, Mrs Wallis Simpson (later the Duchess of **WINDSOR**). On Edward: see **BEAVERBROOK** 63:18, **GEORGE V** 353:1, **HARDIE** 380:3, **MARY** 526:16, **MARY** 526:17, **NEWSPAPER HEADLINES AND LEADERS** 573:17

4 These works brought all these people here. Something should be done to get them at work again.

speaking at the derelict Dowlais Iron and Steel Works, 18 November 1936

in *Western Mail* 19 November 1936; see **MISQUOTATIONS** 548:19

5 At long last I am able to say a few words of my own . . . you must believe me when I tell you that I have found it impossible to carry the heavy burden of responsibility and to discharge my duties as King as I would wish to do without the help and support of the woman I love.

radio broadcast following his abdication, 11 December 1936, in The Times 12 December 1936

6 The thing that impresses me most about America is the way parents obey their children.

in *Look* 5 March 1957

Jonathan Edwards 1703–58

American theologian

7 Of all Insects no one is more wonderful than the spider especially with Respect to their sagacity and admirable way of working . . . I . . . once saw a very large spider to my surprise swimming in the air . . . and others have assured me that they often have seen spiders fly, the appearance is truly very pretty and pleasing.

The Flying Spider—Observations by Jonathan Edwards when a boy 'Of Insects' in *Andover Review* vol. 13 (1890); see **LOWELL** 503:7

8 The bodies of those that made such a noise and tumult when alive, when dead, lie as quietly among the graves of their neighbours as any others.

Sermon on procrastination (*Miscellaneous Discourses*) in *Works* (1834) vol. 2

Oliver Edwards 1711–91

English lawyer

9 I have tried too in my time to be a philosopher; but, I don't know how, cheerfulness was always breaking in.

James Boswell *Life of Samuel Johnson* (1791) 17 April 1778

10 For my part now, I consider supper as a turnpike through which one must pass, in order to get to bed.

BOSWELL notes: 'I am not absolutely sure but this was my own suggestion, though it is truly in the character of Edwards'

James Boswell *Life of Samuel Johnson* (1791) 17 April 1778

Richard Edwards c.1523–66

English poet and dramatist

11 The falling out of faithful friends, renewing is of love.

The Paradise of Dainty Devices (1576) 'Amantium Irae'; see **PROVERBS** 642:15

Sarah Egerton 1670–1723

English poet

12 From the first dawn of life unto the grave, Poor womankind's in every state a slave.

'The Emulation' (1703)

13 We will our rights in learning's world maintain; Wit's empire now shall know a female reign.

'The Emulation' (1703)

Paul Ralph Ehrlich 1932–

American biologist

14 The first rule of intelligent tinkering is to save all the parts.

in *Saturday Review* 5 June 1971

John Ehrlichman 1925–99

American Presidential assistant to Richard **NIXON**

1 I think we ought to let him hang there. Let him twist slowly, slowly in the wind.

Richard NIXON had withdrawn his support for Patrick Gray, nominated as director of the FBI, although Gray himself had not been informed

in a telephone conversation with John Dean; in *Washington Post* 27 July 1973

Max Ehrmann 1872–1945

American writer

2 Go placidly amid the noise and the haste, and remember what peace there may be in silence.

often wrongly dated to 1692, the date of foundation of a church in Baltimore whose vicar circulated the poem in 1956

'Desiderata' (1948)

Joseph von Eichendorff 1788–1857

German poet

3 *Wem Gott will rechte Gunst erweisen, Den schickt er in die weite Welt.*

Those whom God wishes to show true favour He sends out into the great wide world.

Der frohe Wandersmann (1826)

Einhard *c.*770–840

Frankish chronicler, friend and biographer of Charlemagne

4 He was large and strong and of lofty stature, though not disproportionately tall; the upper part of his head was round, his eyes very large and animated, nose a little long, hair fair, and face laughing and merry. Thus his appearance was always stately and dignified, whether he was standing or sitting; although his neck was somewhat short, and his belly rather prominent; but the symmetry of the rest of his body concealed these defects.

of Charlemagne

The Life of Charlemagne (ed. S. Painter, 1960)

Albert Einstein 1879–1955

German-born theoretical physicist; originator of the theory of relativity. On Einstein: see **ANONYMOUS** 18:1, **SQUIRE** 769:9

5 Science without religion is lame, religion without science is blind.

Science, Philosophy and Religion: a Symposium (1941) ch. 13

6 $E = mc^2$.

the usual form of Einstein's original statement: 'If a body releases the energy L in the form of radiation, its mass is decreased by L/V²'

in *Annalen der Physik* 18 (1905)

7 God is subtle but he is not malicious.

remark made during a week at Princeton beginning 9 May 1921, later carved above the fireplace of the Common Room of Fine Hall (the Mathematical Institute), Princeton University; R. W. Clark *Einstein* (1973) ch. 14

8 I am convinced that *He* [God] does not play dice.

often quoted as: 'God does not play dice'

letter to Max Born, 4 December 1926; in *Einstein und Born Briefwechsel* (1969)

9 If my theory of relativity is proven correct, Germany will claim me as a German and France will declare that I am a citizen of the world. Should my theory prove untrue, France will say that I am a German and Germany will declare that I am a Jew.

address at the Sorbonne, Paris, possibly early December 1929, in *New York Times* 16 February 1930

10 I never think of the future. It comes soon enough.

in an interview, given on the *Belgenland*, December 1930

11 The eternal mystery of the world is its comprehensibility . . . The fact that it is comprehensible is a miracle.

usually quoted as 'The most incomprehensible fact about the universe is that it is comprehensible'

in *Franklin Institute Journal* March 1936 'Physics and Reality'

12 Some recent work by E. Fermi and L. Szilard, which has been communicated to me in manuscript, leads me to expect that the element uranium may be turned into a new and important source of energy in the immediate future. Certain aspects of the situation which has arisen seem to call for watchfulness and, if necessary, quick action on the part of the Administration.

warning of the possible development of an atomic bomb, and leading to the setting up of the Manhattan Project

letter to Franklin **ROOSEVELT**, 2 August 1939, drafted by Leo Szilard and signed by Einstein

13 The unleashed power of the atom has changed everything save our modes of thinking and we thus drift toward unparalleled catastrophe.

telegram to prominent Americans, 24 May 1946, in *New York Times* 25 May 1946

14 If *A* is a success in life, then *A* equals *x* plus *y* plus *z*. Work is *x*; *y* is play; and *z* is keeping your mouth shut.

in *Observer* 15 January 1950

15 Common sense is nothing more than a deposit of prejudices laid down in the mind before you reach eighteen.

Lincoln Barnett *The Universe and Dr Einstein* (1950 ed.)

16 The grand aim of all science [is] to cover the greatest number of empirical facts by logical deduction from the smallest possible number of hypotheses or axioms.

Lincoln Barnett *The Universe and Dr Einstein* (1950 ed.)

17 If I would be a young man again and had to decide how to make my living, I would not try to become a scientist or scholar or teacher. I would rather choose to be a plumber or a peddler in the hope to find that modest degree of independence still available under present circumstances.

in *Reporter* 18 November 1954

1 The distinction between past, present and future is only an illusion, however persistent.
letter to Michelangelo Besso, 21 March 1955

2 Nationalism is an infantile sickness. It is the measles of the human race.
Helen Dukas and Banesh Hoffman *Albert Einstein, the Human Side* (1979)

3 One must divide one's time between politics and equations. But our equations are much more important to me.
C. P. Snow 'Einstein' in M. Goldsmith et al. (eds.) *Einstein* (1980)

4 When I was young, I found out that the big toe always ends up making a hole in a sock. So I stopped wearing socks.
to Philippe Halsman; A. P. French *Einstein: A Centenary Volume* (1979)

Carlos Eire 1950–

Cuban writer

5 The world changed while I slept, and much to my surprise, no one had consulted me.
Waiting for Snow in Havana (2003) ch. 1

Dwight D. Eisenhower 1890–1969

American Republican statesman, 34th President of the US 1953–61

6 This world in arms is not spending money alone. It is spending the sweat of its labourers, the genius of its scientists, the hopes of its children.
speech in Washington, 16 April 1953, in *Public Papers of Presidents 1953* (1960)

7 I just will not—I *refuse*—to get into the gutter with that guy.
explaining why he did not try to restrain Senator **MCCARTHY**
in 1953; in *American National Biography* (online edition) 'Joseph McCarthy'

8 You have broader considerations that might follow what you might call the 'falling domino' principle. You have a row of dominoes set up. You knock over the first one, and what will happen to the last one is that it will go over very quickly. So you have the beginning of a disintegration that would have the most profound influences.
speech at press conference, 7 April 1954, in *Public Papers of Presidents 1954* (1960)

9 I think that people want peace so much that one of these days governments had better get out of the way and let them have it.
broadcast discussion, 31 August 1959, in *Public Papers of Presidents 1959* (1960)

10 In preparing for battle I have always found that plans are useless, but planning is indispensable.
Richard Nixon *Six Crises* (1962); attributed

Alfred Eisenstaedt 1898–1995

German-born American photographer and photojournalist

11 It's more important to click with people than to click the shutter
in *Life* 24 August 1995 (electronic edition), obituary

Eleazar of Worms 1176–1238

Jewish rabbi

12 No crown carries such royalty with it as doth humility; no monument gives such glory as an unsullied name; no worldly gain can equal that which comes from observing God's laws.
Sefer Rokeah

13 The highest sacrifice is a broken and contrite heart; the highest wisdom is that which is found in the Torah; the noblest of all ornaments is modesty; and the most beautiful thing that man can do, is to forgive a wrong.
Sefer Rokeah; see **BOOK OF COMMON PRAYER** 143:7

14 If the means of thy support in life be measured out scantily to thee, remember that thou hast to be thankful and grateful even for the mere privilege to breathe, and that thou must look upon that suffering as a test of thy piety and a preparation for better things.
Sefer Rokeah

Edward Elgar 1857–1934

English composer. On Elgar: see **BEECHAM** 65:12; see also **SHELLEY** 746:10

15 To my friends pictured within.
Enigma Variations (1899) dedication

16 *Bramo assai, poco spero, nulla chieggio.*
I essay much, I hope little, I ask nothing.
inscribed at the end of *Enigma Variations* (1899); see **TASSO** 790:10

17 This is what I hear all day—the trees are singing my music—or have I sung theirs?
letter to Jaeger, 11 July 1900; Michael Kennedy *Life of Elgar* (1968)

18 There is music in the air.
R. J. Buckley *Sir Edward Elgar* (1905) ch. 4

George Eliot (Mary Ann Evans) 1819–80

English novelist. On Eliot: see **GASKELL** 350:10; see also **ANONYMOUS** 19:12

19 Our deeds determine us, as much as we determine our deeds; and until we know what has been or will be the peculiar combination of outward with inward facts, which constitute a man's critical actions, it will be better not to think ourselves wise about his character.
Adam Bede (1859) ch. 29

20 He was like a cock who thought the sun had risen to hear him crow.
Adam Bede (1859) ch. 33

21 The beginning of hardship is like the first taste of bitter food—it seems for a moment

unbearable; yet, if there is nothing else to satisfy our hunger, we take another bite and find it possible to go on.
Adam Bede (1859) ch. 36

1 Deep, unspeakable suffering may well be called a baptism, a regeneration, the initiation into a new state.
Adam Bede (1859) ch. 42

2 We hand folks over to God's mercy, and show none ourselves.
Adam Bede (1859) ch. 42

3 The mother's yearning, that completest type of the life in another life which is the essence of real human love, feels the presence of the cherished child even in the debased, degraded man.
Adam Bede (1859) ch. 43

4 We cannot reform our forefathers.
Adam Bede (1859) ch. 53

5 Vanity is as ill at ease under indifference as tenderness is under a love which it cannot return.
Daniel Deronda (1876) bk. 1 ch. 10

6 Gossip is a sort of smoke that comes from the dirty tobacco-pipes of those who diffuse it: it proves nothing but the bad taste of the smoker.
Daniel Deronda (1876) bk. 2, ch. 13

7 A difference of taste in jokes is a great strain on the affections.
Daniel Deronda (1876) bk. 2, ch. 15

8 There is a great deal of unmapped country within us which would have to be taken into account in an explanation of our gusts and storms.
Daniel Deronda (1876) bk. 3, ch. 24

9 Friendships begin with liking or gratitude—roots that can be pulled up.
Daniel Deronda (1876) bk. 4, ch. 32

10 Half the sorrows of women would be averted if they could repress the speech they know to be useless; nay, the speech they have resolved not to make.
Felix Holt (1866) ch. 2

11 There is no private life which has not been determined by a wider public life.
Felix Holt (1866) ch. 3

12 An election is coming. Universal peace is declared, and the foxes have a sincere interest in prolonging the lives of the poultry.
Felix Holt (1866) ch. 5

13 Speech is often barren; but silence also does not necessarily brood over a full nest. Your still fowl, blinking at you without remark, may all the while be sitting on one addled egg; and when it takes to cackling will have nothing to announce but that addled delusion.
Felix Holt (1866) ch. 15

14 A woman can hardly ever choose . . . she is dependent on what happens to her. She must

take meaner things, because only meaner things are within her reach.
Felix Holt (1866) ch. 27

15 'Abroad', that large home of ruined reputations.
Felix Holt (1866) epilogue

16 Debasing the moral currency.
The Impressions of Theophrastus Such (1879) essay title

17 Blessed is the man who, having nothing to say, abstains from giving us wordy evidence of the fact.
The Impressions of Theoprastus Such (1879) ch. 4

18 Many Theresas have been born who found for themselves no epic life wherein there was a constant unfolding of far-resonant action; perhaps only a life of mistakes, the offspring of a certain spiritual grandeur ill-matched with the meanness of opportunity; perhaps a tragic failure which found no sacred poet and sank unwept into oblivion.
Middlemarch (1871–2) Prelude

19 Pride helps us; and pride is not a bad thing when it only urges us to hide our own hurts, not to hurt others.
Middlemarch (1871–2) bk. 1, ch. 6

20 A woman dictates before marriage in order that she may have an appetite for submission afterwards.
Middlemarch (1871–2) bk. 1, ch. 9

21 He said he should prefer not to know the sources of the Nile, and that there should be some unknown regions preserved as hunting-grounds for the poetic imagination.
Middlemarch (1871–2) bk. 1, ch. 9

22 Among all forms of mistake, prophecy is the most gratuitous.
Middlemarch (1871–2) bk. 1, ch. 10

23 Plain women he regarded as he did the other severe facts of life, to be faced with philosophy and investigated by science.
Middlemarch (1871–2) bk. 1, ch. 11 (Lydgate)

24 Any one watching keenly the stealthy convergence of human lots, sees a slow preparation of effects from one life on another, which tells like a calculated irony on the indifference or the frozen stare with which we look at our unintroduced neighbour.
Middlemarch (1871–2) bk. 1, ch. 11

25 Fred's studies are not very deep . . . he is only reading a novel.
Middlemarch (1871–2) bk 1, ch. 11

26 If we had a keen vision and feeling of all ordinary human life, it would be like hearing the grass grow and the squirrel's heart beat, and we should die of that roar which lies on the other side of silence.
Middlemarch (1871–2) bk. 2, ch. 20

27 We do not expect people to be deeply moved by what is not unusual. That element of tragedy

which lies in the very fact of frequency, has not yet wrought itself into the coarse emotion of mankind.

Middlemarch (1871–2) bk. 2, ch. 20

1 A woman, let her be as good as she may, has got to put up with the life her husband makes for her.

Middlemarch (1871–2) bk. 3, ch. 25

2 A man is seldom ashamed of feeling that he cannot love a woman so well when he sees a certain greatness in her: nature having intended greatness for men.

Middlemarch (1871–2) bk. 4, ch. 39

3 'I am going to London,' said Dorothea. 'How can you always live in a street? And you will be so poor.'

Middlemarch (1871–2) bk. 8, ch. 84

4 Anger and jealousy can no more bear to lose sight of their objects than love.

The Mill on the Floss (1860) bk. 1, ch. 10

5 Our instructed vagrancy, which has hardly time to linger by the hedgerows, but runs away early to the tropics, and is at home with palms and banyans—which is nourished on books of travel, and stretches the theatre of its imagination to the Zambesi.

The Mill on the Floss (1860) bk. 3, ch. 9

6 The dead level of provincial existence.

The Mill on the Floss (1860) bk. 5, ch. 3

7 The happiest women, like the happiest nations, have no history.

The Mill on the Floss (1860) bk. 6, ch. 3; see **MONTESQUIEU** 556:7

8 'Character' says Novalis, in one of his questionable aphorisms—'character is destiny.'

The Mill on the Floss (1860) bk. 6, ch. 6; see **HERACLITUS** 393:1, **NOVALIS** 577:10

9 An ass may bray a good while before he shakes the stars down.

Romola (1863) bk. 3, ch. 50

10 In every parting there is an image of death.

Scenes of Clerical Life (1858) 'Amos Barton' ch. 10

11 Cruelty, like every other vice, requires no motive outside itself—it only requires opportunity.

Scenes of Clerical Life (1858) 'Janet's Repentance' ch. 13

12 Errors look so very ugly in persons of small means—one feels they are taking quite a liberty in going astray; whereas people of fortune may naturally indulge in a few delinquencies.

Scenes of Clerical Life (1858) 'Janet's Repentance' ch. 25

13 Oh may I join the choir invisible
Of those immortal dead who live again
In minds made better by their presence.

'Oh May I Join the Choir Invisible' (1867)

14 Life is too precious to be spent in this weaving and unweaving of false impressions, and it is better to live quietly under some degree of

misrepresentation than to attempt to remove it by the uncertain process of letter-writing.

letter to Mrs Peter Taylor, 8 June 1856, in G. S. Haight (ed.) *The George Eliot Letters* vol. 2 (1954)

15 Whatever may be the success of my stories, I shall be resolute in preserving my incognito, having observed that a *nom de plume* secures all the advantages without the disagreeables of reputation.

letter to William Blackwood, 4 February 1857, in G. S. Haight (ed.) *The George Eliot Letters* vol. 3 (1954)

16 If art does not enlarge men's sympathies, it does nothing morally.

letter to Charles Bray, 5 July 1859, in G. S. Haight (ed.) *The George Eliot Letters* vol. 3 (1954)

17 Beginnings are always troublesome . . . Even Macaulay's few pages of introduction to his 'Introduction' in the English History are the worst bit of writing in the book.

letter to Sara Hennell, 15 August 1859, in G. S. Haight (ed.) *The George Eliot Letters* vol. 3 (1954)

18 The idea of God, so far as it has been a high spiritual influence, is the ideal of a goodness entirely human.

letter to the Hon. Mrs H. F. Ponsonby, 10 December 1874, in G. S. Haight (ed.) *The George Eliot Letters* vol. 6 (1956)

19 She, stirred somewhat beyond her wont, and taking as her text the three words which have been used so often as the inspiring trumpet-calls of men—the words *God, Immortality, Duty*—pronounced, with terrible earnestness, how inconceivable was the *first*, how unbelievable the *second*, and yet how peremptory and absolute the third. Never, perhaps, have sterner accents affirmed the sovereignty of impersonal and unrecompensing Law.

F. W. H. Myers 'George Eliot', in *Century Magazine* November 1881

T. S. Eliot (Thomas Stearns Eliot) 1888–1965

American-born British poet, critic, and dramatist. On Eliot: see LEAVIS 486:19

20 Because I do not hope to turn again
Because I do not hope
Because I do not hope to turn.

Ash-Wednesday (1930) pt. 1

21 Teach us to care and not to care
Teach us to sit still.

Ash-Wednesday (1930) pt. 1

22 Lady, three white leopards sat under a juniper-tree
In the cool of the day.

Ash-Wednesday (1930) pt. 2

23 What is hell?
Hell is oneself,
Hell is alone, the other figures in it
Merely projections. There is nothing to escape from
And nothing to escape to. One is always alone.

The Cocktail Party (1950) act 1, sc. 3; see **SARTRE** 681:14

1 Success is relative:
It is what we can make of the mess we have
   made of things.
The Family Reunion (1939) pt. 2, sc. 3

2 Round and round the circle
Completing the charm
So the knot be unknotted
The cross be uncrossed
The crooked be made straight
And the curse be ended.
The Family Reunion (1939) pt. 2, sc. 3

3 Time present and time past
Are both perhaps present in time future,
And time future contained in time past.
Four Quartets 'Burnt Norton' (1936) pt. 1

4 Footfalls echo in the memory
Down the passage which we did not take
Towards the door we never opened
Into the rose-garden.
Four Quartets 'Burnt Norton' (1936) pt. 1

5   Human kind
Cannot bear very much reality.
Four Quartets 'Burnt Norton' (1936) pt. 1.

6 At the still point of the turning world.
Four Quartets 'Burnt Norton' (1936) pt. 2

7   Words strain,
Crack and sometimes break, under the burden,
Under the tension, slip, slide, perish,
Decay with imprecision, will not stay in place,
Will not stay still.
Four Quartets 'Burnt Norton' (1936) pt. 5

8 In my beginning is my end.
Four Quartets 'East Coker' (1940) pt. 1; see **MARY** 527:2

9 That was a way of putting it—not very
   satisfactory:
A periphrastic study in a worn-out poetical
   fashion,
Leaving one still with the intolerable wrestle
With words and meanings. The poetry does not
   matter.
Four Quartets 'East Coker' (1940) pt. 2

10 The houses are all gone under the sea.
The dancers are all gone under the hill.
Four Quartets 'East Coker' (1940) pt. 2

11 O dark dark dark. They all go into the dark,
The vacant interstellar spaces, the vacant into
   the vacant.
Four Quartets 'East Coker' (1940) pt. 3

12 The wounded surgeon plies the steel
That questions the distempered part;
Beneath the bleeding hands we feel
The sharp compassion of the healer's art
Resolving the enigma of the fever chart.
Four Quartets 'East Coker' (1940) pt. 4

13   Each venture
Is a new beginning, a raid on the inarticulate
With shabby equipment always deteriorating
In the general mess of imprecision of feeling.
Four Quartets 'East Coker' (1940) pt. 5

14   I think that the river
Is a strong brown god—sullen, untamed and
   intractable.
Four Quartets 'The Dry Salvages' (1941) pt. 1

15   The communication
Of the dead is tongued with fire beyond the
   language of the living.
Four Quartets 'Little Gidding' (1942) pt. 1

16 Ash on an old man's sleeve
Is all the ash the burnt roses leave.
Four Quartets 'Little Gidding' (1942) pt. 2

17 This is the death of air.
Four Quartets 'Little Gidding' (1942) pt. 2

18 Since our concern was speech, and speech
   impelled us
To purify the dialect of the tribe
And urge the mind to aftersight and foresight.
Four Quartets 'Little Gidding' (1942) pt. 2

19 We shall not cease from exploration
And the end of all our exploring
Will be to arrive where we started
And know the place for the first time.
Four Quartets 'Little Gidding' (1942) pt. 5

20 What we call the beginning is often the end
And to make an end is to make a beginning.
The end is where we start from.
Four Quartets 'Little Gidding' (1942) pt. 5

21   So, while the light fails
On a winter's afternoon, in a secluded chapel
History is now and England.
Four Quartets 'Little Gidding' (1942) pt. 5

22 And all shall be well and
All manner of thing shall be well
When the tongues of flame are in-folded
Into the crowned knot of fire
And the fire and the rose are one.
Four Quartets 'Little Gidding' (1942) pt. 5; see **JULIAN** 449:6

23 Here I am, an old man in a dry month
Being read to by a boy, waiting for rain.
'Gerontion' (1920)

24 The word within a word, unable to speak a
   word,
Swaddled with darkness.
'Gerontion' (1920); see **ANDREWES** 15:14, **BIBLE** 87:10

25 After such knowledge, what forgiveness?
'Gerontion' (1920)

26 Tenants of the house,
Thoughts of a dry brain in a dry season.
'Gerontion' (1920)

27 We are the hollow men
We are the stuffed men
Leaning together
Headpiece filled with straw. Alas!
'The Hollow Men' (1925)

28 *Here we go round the prickly pear*
Prickly pear prickly pear
Here we go round the prickly pear
At five o'clock in the morning.

Between the idea
And the reality
Between the motion
And the act
Falls the Shadow.
'The Hollow Men' (1925)

1 This is the way the world ends
Not with a bang but a whimper.
'The Hollow Men' (1925)

2 A cold coming we had of it,
Just the worst time of the year
For a journey, and such a long journey:
The ways deep and the weather sharp,
The very dead of winter.
'Journey of the Magi' (1927); see **ANDREWES** 15:15

3   I had seen birth and death
But had thought they were different.
'Journey of the Magi' (1927)

4 An alien people clutching their gods.
'Journey of the Magi' (1927)

5 Let us go then, you and I,
When the evening is spread out against the sky
Like a patient etherized upon a table.
'The Love Song of J. Alfred Prufrock' (1917); see **LEWIS** 491:20

6 In the room the women come and go
Talking of Michelangelo.
'The Love Song of J. Alfred Prufrock' (1917)

7 The yellow fog that rubs its back upon the
window-panes.
'The Love Song of J. Alfred Prufrock' (1917)

8 I have measured out my life with coffee spoons.
'The Love Song of J. Alfred Prufrock' (1917)

9 I should have been a pair of ragged claws
Scuttling across the floors of silent seas.
'The Love Song of J. Alfred Prufrock' (1917)

10 I have seen the moment of my greatness flicker,
And I have seen the eternal Footman hold my
coat, and snicker,
And in short, I was afraid.
'The Love Song of J. Alfred Prufrock' (1917)

11 No! I am not Prince Hamlet, nor was meant to
be;
Am an attendant lord, one that will do
To swell a progress, start a scene or two,
Advise the prince.
'The Love Song of J. Alfred Prufrock' (1917)

12 I grow old . . . I grow old . . .
I shall wear the bottoms of my trousers rolled.
'The Love Song of J. Alfred Prufrock' (1917)

13 Shall I part my hair behind? Do I dare to eat a
peach?
I shall wear white flannel trousers, and walk
upon the beach.
I have heard the mermaids singing, each to each.
I do not think that they will sing to me.
'The Love Song of J. Alfred Prufrock' (1917); see **DONNE**
289:14

14 I am aware of the damp souls of housemaids
Sprouting despondently at area gates.
'Morning at the Window' (1917)

15 Polyphiloprogenitive
The sapient sutlers of the Lord.
'Mr Eliot's Sunday Morning Service' (1919)

16 Yet we have gone on living,
Living and partly living.
Murder in the Cathedral (1935) pt. 1

17 The last temptation is the greatest treason:
To do the right deed for the wrong reason.
Murder in the Cathedral (1935) pt. 1

18 Clear the air! clean the sky! wash the wind! take
the stone from stone, take the skin from the
arm, take the muscle from bone, and wash
them.
Murder in the Cathedral (1935) pt. 2

19 The Naming of Cats is a difficult matter,
It isn't just one of your holiday games;
You may think at first I'm as mad as a hatter
when I tell you, a cat must have THREE
DIFFERENT NAMES.
Old Possum's Book of Practical Cats (1939) 'The Naming of
Cats'

20 He always has an alibi, and one or two to spare:
At whatever time the deed took place—MACAVITY
WASN'T THERE!
Old Possum's Book of Practical Cats (1939) 'Macavity: the
Mystery Cat'

21 The winter evening settles down
With smell of steaks in passageways.
Six o'clock.
The burnt-out ends of smoky days.
'Preludes' (1917)

22 Midnight shakes the memory
As a madman shakes a dead geranium.
'Rhapsody on a Windy Night' (1917)

23 Where is the wisdom we have lost in
knowledge?
Where is the knowledge we have lost in
information?
The Rock (1934) pt. 1

24 And the wind shall say: 'Here were decent
godless people:
Their only monument the asphalt road
And a thousand lost golf balls.'
The Rock (1934) pt. 1

25 Birth, and copulation, and death.
That's all the facts when you come to brass
tacks.
Sweeney Agonistes (1932) 'Fragment of an Agon'

26 I gotta use words when I talk to you.
Sweeney Agonistes (1932) 'Fragment of an Agon'

27 The nightingales are singing near
The Convent of the Sacred Heart,

And sang within the bloody wood
When Agamemnon cried aloud
And let their liquid siftings fall

To stain the stiff dishonoured shroud.
'Sweeney among the Nightingales' (1919)

1 April is the cruellest month, breeding
Lilacs out of the dead land.
The Waste Land (1922) pt. 1

2 I read, much of the night, and go south in the
winter.
The Waste Land (1922) pt. 1

3 I will show you fear in a handful of dust.
The Waste Land (1922) pt. 1; see **CONRAD** 249:12

4 Madame Sosostris, famous clairvoyante,
Had a bad cold, nevertheless
Is known to be the wisest woman in Europe,
With a wicked pack of cards.
The Waste Land (1922) pt. 1

5 A crowd flowed over London Bridge, so many,
I had not thought death had undone so many.
The Waste Land (1922) pt. 1

6 The Chair she sat in, like a burnished throne,
Glowed on the marble.
The Waste Land (1922) pt. 2; see **SHAKESPEARE** 694:22

7 And still she cried, and still the world pursues,
'Jug Jug' to dirty ears.
The Waste Land (1922) pt. 2; see **LYLY** 505:21

8 I think we are in rats' alley
Where the dead men lost their bones.
The Waste Land (1922) pt. 2

9 O O O O that Shakespeherian Rag—
It's so elegant
So intelligent.
The Waste Land (1922) pt. 2; see **BUCK AND RUBY** 169:15

10 Hurry up please it's time.
The Waste Land (1922) pt. 2

11 But at my back from time to time I hear
The sound of horns and motors, which shall
bring
Sweeney to Mrs Porter in the spring.
O the moon shone bright on Mrs Porter
And on her daughter
They wash their feet in soda water.
The Waste Land (1922) pt. 3; see **MARVELL** 525:12

12 At the violet hour, when the eyes and back
Turn upward from the desk, when the human
engine waits
Like a taxi throbbing waiting.
The Waste Land (1922) pt. 3

13 I Tiresias, old man with wrinkled dugs.
The Waste Land (1922) pt. 3

14 One of the low on whom assurance sits
As a silk hat on a Bradford millionaire.
The Waste Land (1922) pt. 3

15 When lovely woman stoops to folly and
Paces about her room again, alone,
She smoothes her hair with automatic hand,
And puts a record on the gramophone.
The Waste Land (1922) pt. 3; see **GOLDSMITH** 365:14

16 Phlebas the Phoenician, a fortnight dead,
Forgot the cry of gulls, and the deep sea swell

And the profit and loss.
The Waste Land (1922) pt. 4

17 Who is the third who walks always beside you?
When I count, there are only you and I together
But when I look ahead up the white road
There is always another one walking beside you.
The Waste Land (1922) pt. 5

18 These fragments I have shored against my ruins.
The Waste Land (1922) pt. 5

19 Shantih, shantih, shantih.
The Waste Land (1922) closing words; see **UPANISHADS** 822:7

20 Webster was much possessed by death
And saw the skull beneath the skin.
'Whispers of Immortality' (1919)

21 The only way of expressing emotion in the form
of art is by finding an 'objective correlative'; in
other words, a set of objects, a situation, a chain
of events which shall be the formula of that
particular emotion; such that when the external
facts, which must terminate in sensory
experience, are given, the emotion is
immediately evoked.
The Sacred Wood (1920) 'Hamlet and his Problems'

22 Immature poets imitate; mature poets steal.
The Sacred Wood (1920) 'Philip Massinger'

23 Someone said: 'The dead writers are remote
from us because we *know* so much more than
they did.' Precisely, and they are that which we
know.
The Sacred Wood (1920) 'Tradition and Individual Talent'

24 In the seventeenth century a dissociation of
sensibility set in, from which we have never
recovered; and this dissociation, as is natural,
was due to the influence of the two most
powerful poets of the century, Milton and
Dryden.
Selected Essays (1932) 'The Metaphysical Poets' (1921)

25 Poets in our civilization, as it exists at present,
must be *difficult*.
Selected Essays (1932) 'The Metaphysical Poets' (1921)

26 To me . . . [*The Waste Land*] was only the relief
of a personal and wholly insignificant grouse
against life; it is just a piece of rhythmical
grumbling.
The Waste Land (ed. Valerie Eliot, 1971) epigraph

Elizabeth I 1533–1603

English monarch, Queen of England and Ireland from 1558;
daughter of **HENRY VIII** and younger sister of **MARY I**. On
Elizabeth: see **BIBLE** 78:9; see also **BACON** 49:8, **MOTTOES**
563:18

27 This judgement I have of you that you will not
be corrupted by any manner of gift and that
you will be faithful to the state; and that
without respect of my private will you will give
me that counsel which you think best.
to William **CECIL**, *appointing him her Secretary of State in
1558*
Conyers Read *Mr Secretary Cecil and Queen Elizabeth* (1955)

1 The queen of Scots is this day leichter of a fair son, and I am but a barren stock.

to her ladies, June 1566, in Sir James Melville Memoirs of His Own Life *(1827 ed.)*

2 I am your anointed Queen. I will never be by violence constrained to do anything. I thank God that I am endued with such qualities that if I were turned out of the Realm in my petticoat, I were able to live in any place in Christome.

speech to Members of Parliament, 5 November 1566, in J. E. Neale Elizabeth I and her Parliaments 1559–1581 *(1953) pt. 3, ch. 1*

3 I love, and yet am forced to seem to hate;
I do, yet dare not say I ever meant;
I seem stark mute, but inwardly do prate.

'On Monsieur's Departure' (c. 1582)

4 I know what it is to be a subject, what to be a Sovereign, what to have good neighbours, and sometimes meet evil-willers.

speech to a Parliamentary deputation at Richmond, 12 November 1586, in Sir John Neale Elizabeth I and her Parliaments 1584–1601 *(1957, from a report 'which the Queen herself heavily amended in her own hand'; see* **MISQUOTATIONS** *548:1*

5 I will make you shorter by the head.

to the leaders of her Council, who were opposing her course towards **MARY** Queen of Scots

F. Chamberlin Sayings of Queen Elizabeth *(1923)*

6 I know I have the body of a weak and feeble woman, but I have the heart and stomach of a king, and of a king of England too; and think foul scorn that Parma or Spain, or any prince of Europe, should dare to invade the borders of my realm.

speech to the troops at Tilbury on the approach of the Armada, 1588, in Lord Somers A Third Collection of Scarce and Valuable Tracts *(1751)*

7 The daughter of debate, that eke discord doth sow.

on **MARY** Queen of Scots

George Puttenham (ed.) The Art of English Poesie *(1589) bk. 3, ch. 20*

8 My lord, we make use of you, not for your bad legs, but for your good head.

to William **CECIL**, *who suffered from gout*

F. Chamberlin Sayings of Queen Elizabeth *(1923)*

9 I do entreat heaven daily for your longer life, else will my people and myself stand in need of cordials too. My comfort hath been in my people's happiness and their happiness in thy discretion.

to William **CECIL** *on his death-bed, 1598*

F. Chamberlin Sayings of Queen Elizabeth *(1923)*

10 Though God hath raised me high, yet this I count the glory of my crown: that I have reigned with your loves.

The Golden Speech, 1601, in The Journals of All the Parliaments . . . Collected by Sir Simonds D'Ewes *(1682)*

11 To be a king and wear a crown is a thing more glorious to them that see it than it is pleasant to them that bear it.

The Golden Speech, 1601, in Leah S. Marcus et al. (eds.) Elizabeth I: collected works *(2000) 'Commons journal of Haywood Townsend, MP'*

12 God may pardon you, but I never can.

to the dying Countess of Nottingham, who had supposedly prevented an appeal from the former royal favourite the Earl of **ESSEX** *against his death sentence from reaching the Queen; the story is almost certainly apocryphal*

David Hume The History of England under the House of Tudor *(1759) vol. 2, ch. 7*

13 Must! Is *must* a word to be addressed to princes? Little man, little man! thy father, if he had been alive, durst not have used that word.

to Robert **CECIL**, *on his saying she must go to bed, shortly before her death*

J. R. Green A Short History of the English People *(1874) ch. 7;* Dodd's Church History of England *vol. 3 (ed. M. A. Tierney, 1840) adds: 'but thou knowest I must die, and that maketh thee so presumptuous'*

14 If thy heart fails thee, climb not at all.

lines after Sir Walter **RALEGH**, *written on a window-pane*

Thomas Fuller Worthies of England *vol. 1; see* **RALEGH** *654:5*

15 I think that, at the worst, God has not yet ordained that England shall perish.

F. Chamberlin Sayings of Queen Elizabeth *(1923)*

16 I would not open windows into men's souls.

oral tradition, in J. B. Black Reign of Elizabeth 1558–1603 *(1936); the words very possibly originating in a letter drafted by* **BACON**

17 Like strawberry wives, that laid two or three great strawberries at the mouth of their pot, and all the rest were little ones.

describing the tactics of the Commission of Sales, in their dealings with her

Francis Bacon Apophthegms New and Old *(1625) no. 54*

18 Madam I may not call you; mistress I am ashamed to call you; and so I know not what to call you; but howsoever, I thank you.

to the wife of the Archbishop of Canterbury, the Queen disapproving of marriage among the clergy

Sir John Harington A Brief View of the State of the Church of England *(1653)*

19 My Lord, I had forgot the fart.

to Edward de Vere, Earl of **OXFORD**, *on his return from seven years self-imposed exile, occasioned by the acute embarrassment to himself of breaking wind in the presence of the Queen*

John Aubrey Brief Lives *'Edward de Vere'*

20 'Twas God the word that spake it,
He took the bread and brake it;
And what the word did make it;
That I believe, and take it.

answer on being asked her opinion of Christ's presence in the Sacrament

S. Clarke The Marrow of Ecclesiastical History *(1675) pt. 2, bk. 1 'The Life of Queen Elizabeth'*

21 All my possessions for a moment of time.

last words; attributed, but almost certainly apocryphal

Elizabeth II 1926–

British monarch, Queen of the United Kingdom from 1952; daughter of **GEORGE VI** and Queen **ELIZABETH** the Queen Mother, mother of Prince **CHARLES** and Princess **ANNE**. On Elizabeth: see **GRIGG** 373:6, **PHILIP** 605:15

1 I declare before you all that my whole life, whether it be long or short, shall be devoted to your service and the service of our great Imperial family to which we all belong.
broadcast speech, as Princess Elizabeth, to the Commonwealth from Cape Town, 21 April 1947, in *The Times* 22 April 1947

2 I think everybody really will concede that on this, of all days, I should begin my speech with the words 'My husband and I'.
speech at Guildhall, London, on her 25th wedding anniversary
in *The Times* 21 November 1972

3 In the words of one of my more sympathetic correspondents, it has turned out to be an 'annus horribilis'.
speech at Guildhall, London, 24 November 1992

4 I for one believe that there are lessons to be drawn from her life and from the extraordinary and moving reaction to her death.
*broadcast from Buckingham Palace on the evening before the funeral of **DIANA**, Princess of Wales, 5 September 1997*
in *The Times* 6 September 1997

Queen Elizabeth, the Queen Mother

1900–2002

British Queen Consort of **GEORGE VI**, mother of **ELIZABETH II**

5 I'm glad we've been bombed. It makes me feel I can look the East End in the face.
to a London policeman, 13 September 1940
John Wheeler-Bennett *King George VI* (1958) pt. 3, ch. 6

6 The Princesses would never leave without me and I couldn't leave without the King, and the King will never leave.
on the suggestion that the royal family be evacuated during the Blitz
Penelope Mortimer *Queen Elizabeth* (1986) ch. 25

7 How small and selfish is sorrow. But it bangs one about until one is senseless.
*letter to Edith **SITWELL**, shortly after the death of **GEORGE VI***
Victoria Glendinning *Edith Sitwell* (1983) ch. 25

Elizabeth, Countess von Arnim

1866–1941

Australian-born British writer

8 Guests can be, and often are, delightful, but they should never be allowed to get the upper hand.
All the Dogs in My Life (1936)

Alf Ellerton

British songwriter

9 Belgium put the kibosh on the Kaiser.
title of song (1914)

John Ellerton 1826–93

English clergyman

10 The day Thou gavest, Lord, is ended,
The darkness falls at Thy behest.
Hymn (1870), the first line borrowed from an earlier, anonymous hymn

Duke Ellington 1899–1974

American jazz pianist, composer, and band-leader. See also **MILLS** 537:17

11 Playing 'Bop' is like scrabble with all the vowels missing.
in *Look* 10 August 1954

Emily Elizabeth Steele Elliot 1836–97

English hymn-writer

12 O come to my heart, Lord Jesus!
There is room in my heart for thee.
'Thou didst leave thy throne and thy kingly crown' (1870 hymn)

Jane Elliot 1727–1805

Scottish poet

13 I've heard them lilting, at the ewe milking.
Lasses a' lilting, before dawn of day;
But now they are moaning, on ilka green loaning;
The flowers of the forest are a' wede away.
'The Flowers of the Forest' (1769), the most popular version of the traditional lament for the Battle of Flodden in 1513; see **COCKBURN** 237:15

Charlotte Elliott 1789–1871

English hymn-writer

14 Just as I am, without one plea
But that Thy blood was shed for me,
And that Thou bidd'st me come to Thee,
O Lamb of God, I come!
Invalid's Hymn Book (1834) 'Just as I am'

15 'Christian! seek not yet repose,'
Hear thy guardian angel say;
Thou art in the midst of foes—
'Watch and pray.'
Morning and Evening Hymns (1836) 'Christian! seek not yet repose'; see **BIBLE** 103:17

Ebenezer Elliott 1781–1849

English poet known as the 'Corn Law Rhymer'

16 What is a communist? One who hath yearnings
For equal division of unequal earnings.
'Epigram' (1850)

17 When wilt thou save the people?
Oh, God of Mercy! when?
The people, Lord, the people!
Not thrones and crowns, but men!
'The People's Anthem' (1850)

18 The meanest thing to which we bid adieu,
Loses its meanness in the parting hour.
The Village Patriarch (1829) bk. 9, sect. 3

1 Stop! For the gate hangs well that hinders none;
Refresh, and pay, then stoutly travel on!
often quoted in the form 'The gate hangs high and hinders none / Refresh and pay and travel on'
'Win-hill'

George Ellis 1753–1815

English poet and journalist

2 Snowy, Flowy, Blowy,
Showery, Flowery, Bowery,
Hoppy, Croppy, Droppy,
Breezy, Sneezy, Freezy.
'The Twelve Months'

Havelock Ellis (Henry Havelock Ellis)

1859–1939

English sexologist

3 What we call 'progress' is the exchange of one nuisance for another nuisance.
Impressions and Comments (1914) 31 July 1912

4 All civilization has from time to time become a thin crust over a volcano of revolution.
Little Essays of Love and Virtue (1922) ch. 7

Thomas Edward Ellis 1859–99

British Liberal politician and Welsh nationalist

5 Over and above all, we shall work for a Legislature, elected by the manhood and womanhood of Wales.
speech at Bala, 1890

Henry Elston (Friar Elstow) fl. 1517–59

English Franciscan friar

6 With thanks to God we know the way to heaven, to be as ready by water as by land, and therefore we care not which way we go.
when threatened with drowning by **HENRY VIII**
John Stow *The Annals of England* (1615); see **GILBERT** 356:8

Paul Éluard 1895–1952

French poet

7 *L'espoir ne fait pas de poussière.*
Hope raises no dust.
'Ailleurs, ici, partout' (1946)

8 *Adieu tristesse*
Bonjour tristesse
Tu es inscrite dans les lignes du plafond.
Farewell sadness
Good-day sadness
You are inscribed in the lines of the ceiling.
'À peine défigurée' (1932)

Buchi Emecheta 1944–

Nigerian writer

9 I am a woman and a woman of Africa. I am a daughter of Nigeria and if she is in shame, I shall stay and mourn with her in shame.
Destination Biafra (1982)

10 The whole world seemed so unequal, so unfair. Some people were created with all the good things ready-made for them, others were just created like mistakes. God's mistakes.
Second-Class Citizen (1974) ch.9

Ralph Waldo Emerson 1803–82

American philosopher and poet. See also CLOUGH 237:8

11 If the red slayer think he slays,
Or if the slain think he is slain,
They know not well the subtle ways
I keep, and pass, and turn again.
'Brahma' (1867); see **LANG** 478:10, **UPANISHADS** 822:9

12 I am the doubter and the doubt.
'Brahma' (1867)

13 By the rude bridge that arched the flood,
Their flag to April's breeze unfurled,
Here once the embattled farmers stood,
And fired the shot heard round the world.
'Concord Hymn' (1837)

14 Things are in the saddle,
And ride mankind.
'Ode' inscribed to W. H. Channing (1847)

15 He builded better than he knew;—
The conscious stone to beauty grew.
'The Problem' (1847)

16 The frolic architecture of the snow.
'The Snowstorm' (1847)

17 When Duty whispers low, *Thou must,*
The youth replies, *I can.*
'Voluntaries' no. 3 (1867)

18 Make yourself necessary to someone.
The Conduct of Life (1860) 'Considerations by the way'

19 All sensible people are selfish, and nature is tugging at every contract to make the terms of it fair.
The Conduct of Life (1860) 'Considerations by the way'

20 Art is a jealous mistress.
The Conduct of Life (1860) 'Wealth'

21 The louder he talked of his honour, the faster we counted our spoons.
The Conduct of Life (1860) 'Worship'; see **JOHNSON** 439:22, **SHAW** 741:5

22 People seem not to see that their opinion of the world is also a confession of character.
The Conduct of Life (1860) 'Worship'

23 I feel in regard to this aged England . . . that she sees a little better on a cloudy day, and that, in storm of battle and calamity, she has a secret vigour and a pulse like a cannon.
speech at Manchester, November 1847 in *English Traits* (1883 ed.)

24 Nothing great was ever achieved without enthusiasm.
Essays (1841) 'Circles'

25 The only reward of virtue is virtue; the only way to have a friend is to be one.
Essays (1841) 'Friendship'

1 We need books of this tart cathartic virtue, more than books of political science or of private economy.
on **PLUTARCH**'s Lives
Essays (1841) 'Heroism'

2 It was a high counsel that I once heard given to a young person, 'Always do what you are afraid to do.'
Essays (1841) 'Heroism'

3 There is properly no history; only biography.
Essays (1841) 'History'; see **DISRAELI** 285:23

4 In skating over thin ice, our safety is in our speed.
Essays (1841) 'Prudence'

5 Whoso would be a man must be a nonconformist.
Essays (1841) 'Self-Reliance'

6 A foolish consistency is the hobgoblin of little minds, adored by little statesmen and philosophers and divines. With consistency a great soul has simply nothing to do.
Essays (1841) 'Self-Reliance'

7 Is it so bad, then, to be misunderstood? Pythagoras was misunderstood, and Socrates, and Jesus, and Luther, and Copernicus, and Galileo, and Newton, and every pure and wise spirit that ever took flesh. To be great is to be misunderstood.
Essays (1841) 'Self-Reliance'

8 To fill the hour—that is happiness.
Essays. Second Series (1844) 'Experience'

9 Every man is wanted, and no man is wanted much.
Essays. Second Series (1844) 'Nominalist and Realist'

10 Language is fossil poetry.
Essays. Second Series (1844) 'The Poet'

11 What is a weed? A plant whose virtues have not been discovered.
Fortune of the Republic (1878)

12 Every hero becomes a bore at last.
Representative Men (1850) 'Uses of Great Men'

13 Hitch your wagon to a star.
Society and Solitude (1870) 'Civilization'

14 We boil at different degrees.
Society and Solitude (1870) 'Eloquence'

15 America is a country of young men.
Society and Solitude (1870) 'Old Age'

16 No man can have society upon his own terms. If he seeks it, he must serve it too.
Journal 28 May 1833

17 There never was a child so lovely but his mother was glad to get asleep.
Journal 1836

18 People say law, but they mean wealth.
Journal 9 October 1841

19 I spoke of friendship, but my friends and I are fishes in our habit. As for taking Thoreau's arm, I should as soon take the arm of an elm tree.
Journal August 1848

20 I hate quotations. Tell me what you know.
Journals and Miscellaneous Notebooks (1961) May 1849

21 Glittering generalities! They are blazing ubiquities.
on *Rufus* **CHOATE**
attributed; see **CHOATE** 226:12

22 If a man write a better book, preach a better sermon, or make a better mouse-trap than his neighbour, tho' he build his house in the woods, the world will make a beaten path to his door.
attributed to Emerson in Sarah S. B. Yule *Borrowings* (1889); Mrs Yule states in *The Docket* February 1912 that she copied this in her handbook from a lecture delivered by Emerson; the quotation was the occasion of a long controversy owing to Elbert **HUBBARD**'s claim to its authorship

Robert Emmet 1778–1803

Irish nationalist, executed for treason. On Emmet: see **MOORE** 558:12

23 Let no man write my epitaph . . . When my country takes her place among the nations of the earth, *then*, and *not till then*, let my epitaph be written.
speech from the dock when condemned to death, 19 September 1803

William Empson 1906–84

English poet and literary critic

24 There is a Supreme God in the ethnological section;
A hollow toad shape, faced with a blank shield.
He needs his belly to include the Pantheon,
Which is inserted through a hole behind.
'Homage to the British Museum' (1935)

25 Waiting for the end, boys, waiting for the end.
'Just a smack at Auden' (1940)

26 You don't want madhouse and the whole thing there.
'Let it Go' (1955)

27 Slowly the poison the whole blood stream fills.
It is not the effort nor the failure tires.
The waste remains, the waste remains and kills.
'Missing Dates' (1935)

28 The central function of imaginative literature is to make you realize that other people act on moral convictions different from your own.
Milton's God (1981) ch. 7

29 Seven types of ambiguity.
title of book (1930)

30 Learning French is some trouble, but after that you have a clear and beautiful language; in English the undergrowth is part of the language.
in *Spectator* 14 June 1935

Friedrich Engels 1820–95

German socialist; founder, with Karl **MARX**, of modern Communism. See also **MARX AND ENGELS**

31 *Der Staat wird nicht 'abgeschafft', er stirbt ab.*
The State is not 'abolished', *it withers away.*
Anti-Dühring (1878) pt. 3, ch. 2

1 Naturally, the workers are perfectly free; the manufacturer does not force them to take his materials and his cards, but he says to them . . . 'If you don't like to be frizzled in my frying-pan, you can take a walk into the fire'.
The Condition of the Working Class in England in 1844 (1892) ch. 7

Thomas Dunn English 1819–1902
American physician, lawyer, and writer

2 Oh! don't you remember sweet Alice, Ben Bolt, Sweet Alice, whose hair was so brown,
Who wept with delight when you gave her a smile,
And trembled with fear at your frown?
'Ben Bolt' (1885)

Ennius 239–169 BC
Roman writer. On Ennius: see **HORACE 414:13**

3 *O Tite tute Tati tibi tanta tyranne tulisti!*
O tyrant Titus Tatius, what a lot you brought upon yourself!
Annals bk. 1 (l. 104 in O. Skutsch (ed.) *Annals of Q. Ennius*, 1985)

4 *Moribus antiquis res stat Romana virisque.*
The Roman state survives by its ancient customs and its manhood.
Annals bk. 5 (l. 156 in O. Skutsch (ed.) *Annals of Q. Ennius*, 1985)

5 *Unus homo nobis cunctando restituit rem.*
One man by delaying put the state to rights for us.
referring to the Roman general Fabius Cunctator ('The Delayer')
Annals bk. 12 (l. 363 in O. Skutsch (ed.) *Annals of Q. Ennius*, 1985)

6 *At tuba terribili sonitu taratantara dixit.*
And the trumpet in terrible tones went taratantara.
Annals (l. 451 in O. Skutsch (ed.) *Annals of Q. Ennius*, 1985)

Ephelia
English 17th-century poet

7 And yet I love this false, this worthless man,
With all the passion that a woman can;
Dote on his imperfections, though I spy
Nothing to love; I love, and know not why.
Female Poems (1679) 'To one that asked me why I loved J.G.'

Nora Ephron 1941–
American screenwriter and director. See also **FILM LINES 328:18**

8 The anecdote is a particularly dehumanising sort of descriptive narrative.
Scribble, Scribble (1978)

Epictetus *c.*AD 50–120
Phrygian Stoic philosopher

9 It is neither death, nor exile, nor toil, nor any such thing that is the cause of our doing, or of our not doing, anything, but only our opinions and the decisions of our will.
often quoted as 'Not things, but opinions about things, trouble men'
The Discourses bk. 1, ch. 11

10 Everything has two handles, by one of which it ought to be carried and by the other not.
The Encheiridion sect. 43

Epicurus 341–271 BC
Greek philosopher

11 Death, therefore, the most awful of evils, is nothing to us, seeing that, when we are death is not come, and when death is come, we are not.
Diogenes Laertius *Lives of Eminent Philosophers* bk. 10, sect. 125

12 Of all the means which wisdom acquires to ensure happiness throughout the whole of life, by far the most important is friendship.
Diogenes Laertius *Lives of Eminent Philosophers* bk. 10, sect. 148

□ **Epitaphs** *see* **box opposite.** *See also* **CATHER 209:13, SPENSER 767:10**

Jacob Epstein 1880–1959
American-born British sculptor. On Epstein: see **ANONYMOUS 17:7, ANONYMOUS 18:1**

13 Why don't they stick to murder and leave art to us?
on hearing that his statue of Lazarus in New College chapel, Oxford, kept **KHRUSHCHEV** *awake at night*
attributed

Olaudah Equiano *c.*1745–*c.*97
African writer and former slave

14 We are . . . a nation of dancers, singers and poets.
of the Ibo people
Narrative of the Life of Olaudah Equiano (1789) ch. 1

15 When I recovered a little I found some black people about me . . . I asked them if we were not to be eaten by those white men with horrible looks, red faces, and loose hair.
Narrative of the Life of Olaudah Equiano (1789) ch. 3

16 The worth of a soul cannot be told.
Narrative of the Life of Olaudah Equiano (1789) ch. 10

Erasmus (Desiderius Erasmus) *c.*1469–1536
Dutch Christian humanist

17 *In regione caecorum rex est luscus.*
In the country of the blind the one-eyed man is king.
Adages bk. 3, century 4, no. 96; see **PROVERBS 636:2**

18 In a free state, tongues too should be free.
The Education of a Christian Prince (1516)

19 *Omnium horarum hominem.*
A man of all hours.
of Sir Thomas **MORE***; see* **WHITTINGTON 853:5**
In Praise of Folly (1509) prefatory letter

continued

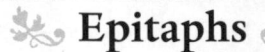 Epitaphs

1 The body of
Benjamin Franklin, printer,
(Like the cover of an old book,
Its contents worn out,
And stripped of its lettering and gilding)
Lies here, food for worms!
Yet the work itself shall not be lost,
For it will, as he believed, appear once more
In a new
And more beautiful edition,
Corrected and amended
By its Author!

> Benjamin **FRANKLIN**'s epitaph for himself (1728); see **TURGOT** 819:7

2 Commander Jacques-Yves Cousteau has
rejoined the world of silence.

> *announcement by the Cousteau Foundation, Paris, 25 June 1997;* **COUSTEAU** (1910–97) *published* The Silent World *in 1953*
>> in *Daily Telegraph* 26 June 1997

3 *Coelorum perrupit claustra.*

He broke the barriers of the heavens.

> Latin epitaph of the German-born English astronomer William Herschel (1738–1822), at Upton, near Windsor

4 *Et in Arcadia ego.*

And I too in Arcadia.

> tomb inscription, of disputed meaning, often depicted in classical paintings, notably by **POUSSIN** in 1655; E. Panofsky 'Et in Arcadia ego' in R. K. Klibansky and H. J. Paton (eds.) *Philosophy and History: Essays Presented to E. Cassirer* (1936)

5 Excuse my dust.

> *Dorothy* **PARKER** (1893–1967); *suggested epitaph for herself* (1925)
>> Alexander Woollcott *While Rome Burns* (1934) 'Our Mrs Parker'

6 *Ex umbris et imaginibus in veritatem.*

From shadows and types to the reality.

> *John Henry* **NEWMAN** (1801–90)
>> motto on his memorial tablet, in Owen Chadwick *Newman* (1983)

7 Farewell, great painter of mankind!
Who reached the noblest point of art,
Whose pictured morals charm the mind
And through the eye correct the heart.

> *epitaph on William Hogarth (1697–1764)*
>> monument in Chiswick churchyard (1772), by David **GARRICK**

8 Free at last, free at last
Thank God almighty
We are free at last.

> *epitaph of Martin Luther* **KING** (1929–68), *Atlanta, Georgia*
>> anonymous spiritual, with which he ended his 'I have a dream' speech; see **KING** 463:11

9 From Moses to Moses there was none like
unto Moses.

> later inscription on the tomb of the Jewish scholar Moses **MAIMONIDES** (1135–1204)

10 God damn you all: I told you so.

> *H. G.* **WELLS**' *suggestion for his own epitaph, in conversation with Ernest Barker, 1939*
>> Ernest Barker *Age and Youth* (1953)

11 God give me work till my life shall end
And life till my work is done.

> *epitaph of Winifred* **HOLTBY** (1898–1935)
>> Vera Brittain *Testament of Friendship: the Story of Winifred Holtby* (1940); see **SWAN** 781:25

12 Good friend, for Jesu's sake forbear
To dig the dust enclosed here.
Blest be the man that spares these stones,
And curst be he that moves my bones.

> *William* **SHAKESPEARE** (1564–1616)
>> inscription on his grave, Stratford upon Avon, probably composed by himself

13 Go, tell the Spartans, thou who passest by,
That here obedient to their laws we lie.

> *epitaph for the 300 Spartans killed at Thermopylae, 480 BC*
>> attributed to **SIMONIDES**; Herodotus *Histories* bk. 7, ch. 228

14 Hereabouts died a very gallant gentleman,
Captain L. E. G. Oates of the Inniskilling
Dragoons. In March 1912, returning from the
Pole, he walked willingly to his death in a
blizzard to try and save his comrades, beset by
hardships.

> *epitaph on cairn erected in the Antarctic, 15 November 1912, by E. L. Atkinson (1882–1929) and Apsley Cherry-Garrard (1882–1959)*
>> Apsley Cherry-Garrard *The Worst Journey in the World* (1922); see **OATES** 582:16

15 Here lie I, Martin Elginbrodde:
Hae mercy o' my soul, Lord God;
As I wad do, were I Lord God,
And ye were Martin Elginbrodde.

> George MacDonald *David Elginbrod* (1863) bk. 1, ch. 13

16 Here lies a great and mighty king
Whose promise none relies on;
He never said a foolish thing,
Nor ever did a wise one.

> *of* **CHARLES II** (1630–85); *an alternative first line reads:* 'Here lies our sovereign lord the King'
>> John Wilmot, Earl of Rochester 'The King's Epitaph'; in C. E. Doble et al. *Thomas Hearne: Remarks and Collections* (1885–1921) 17 November 1706; see **CHARLES II** 217:9

continued

Epitaphs *continued*

1 Here lies a poor woman who always was tired,
For she lived in a place where help wasn't
hired.
Her last words on earth were, Dear friends I
am going
Where washing ain't done nor sweeping nor
sewing,
And everything there is exact to my wishes,
For there they don't eat and there's no washing
of dishes . . .
Don't mourn for me now, don't mourn for me
never,
For I'm going to do nothing for ever and ever.
*epitaph in Bushey churchyard, before 1860; destroyed by
1916*

2 Here lies a valiant warrior
Who never drew a sword;
Here lies a noble courtier
Who never kept his word;
Here lies the Earl of Leicester
Who governed the estates
Whom the earth could never living love,
And the just heaven now hates.
of Robert Dudley, Earl of Leicester (c.1532–88)
*attributed to Ben JONSON in Silvester Tissington A Collection
of Epitaphs and Monumental Inscriptions (1857)*

3 Here lies Fred,
Who was alive and is dead:
Had it been his father,
I had much rather;
Had it been his brother,
Still better than another;
Had it been his sister,
No one would have missed her;
Had it been the whole generation,
Still better for the nation:
But since 'tis only Fred,
Who was alive and is dead,—
There's no more to be said.
of Frederick Louis, Prince of Wales (1707–1751), son of
GEORGE II *and* **CAROLINE** *of Ansbach*
in Horace Walpole Memoirs of George II (1847) vol. 1

4 Here lies Groucho Marx—and lies and lies and
lies. P.S. He never kissed an ugly girl.
his own suggestion for his epitaph
B. Norman The Movie Greats (1981)

5 Here lies one whose name was writ in water.
epitaph for himself by John KEATS (1795–1821)
*Richard Monckton Milnes Life, Letters and Literary Remains of
John Keats (1848) vol. 2; see SHAKESPEARE 711:5*

6 Here lies that peerless paper peer Lord Peter,
Who broke the laws of God and man and
metre.
epitaph for Patrick ('Peter'), Lord Robertson (1794–1855)
by John Gibson LOCKHART
The Journal of Sir Walter Scott (1890) vol. 1

7 Here lies W. C. Fields. I would rather be living
in Philadelphia.
W. C. **FIELDS'** *suggested epitaph for himself, in Vanity Fair
June 1925*

8 Here lies wise and valiant dust,
Huddled up, 'twixt fit and just:
Strafford, who was hurried hence
'Twixt treason and convenience.
He spent his time here in a mist,
A Papist, yet a Calvinist . . .
Riddles lie here, or in a word,
Here lies blood; and let it lie
Speechless still, and never cry.
John **CLEVELAND** *(1613–58) 'Epitaph on the Earl of Strafford'
(1647)*

9 Here Skugg
Lies snug
As a bug
In a rug.
*letter to Georgiana Shipley on the death of her squirrel,
26 September 1772; skugg = squirrel*
Benjamin **FRANKLIN**, *in W. B. Willcox (ed.) Papers of
Benjamin Franklin vol. 19 (1975)*

10 He was an average guy who could carry a
tune.
Bing **CROSBY**'s *suggested epitaph for himself*
in Newsweek 24 October 1977

11 His foe was folly and his weapon wit.
W. S. **GILBERT** *(1836–1911)*
inscription by Anthony **HOPE** *on memorial on the Victoria
Embankment, London, 1915*

12 *Hodie mihi, cras tibi.*
It is my lot today, yours tomorrow.
traditional inscription on gravestones

13 I will return. And I will be millions.
inscription on the tomb of Eva **PERÓN** *(1919–52), Buenos
Aires*

14 John Le Mesurier wishes it to be known that
he conked out on November 15th. He sadly
misses family and friends.
*obituary notice on the death of John Le Mesurier (1912–83),
in The Times 16 November 1983*

15 Life is a jest; and all things show it.
I thought so once; but now I know it.
John **GAY** *(1685–1732)*
'My Own Epitaph' (1720)

16 Long night succeeds thy little day
Oh blighted blossom! can it be,
That this grey stone and grassy clay
Have closed our anxious care of thee?
Thomas Love **PEACOCK**'s *epitaph on his daughter
Margaret, who died at the age of three*
H. Cole (ed.) Works of Peacock (1875)

continued

Epitaphs *continued*

1 Love made me poet,
And this I writ;
My heart did do it,
And not my wit.

> Elizabeth, Lady Tanfield (c.1565–1628); epitaph for her husband, in Burford Parish Church, Oxfordshire

2 My friend, judge not me,
Thou seest I judge not thee.
Betwixt the stirrup and the ground
Mercy I asked, mercy I found.

> *epitaph for 'A gentleman falling off his horse [who] brake his neck'*
> William Camden *Remains Concerning Britain* (1605) 'Epitaphs'

3 My sledge and anvil lie declined
My bellows too have lost their wind
My fire's extinct, my forge decayed,
And in the dust my vice is laid
My coals are spent, my iron's gone
My nails are drove, my work is done.

> *blacksmith's epitaph*
> in Nettlebed churchyard, commemorating William Strange, d. 6 June 1746

4 *Olivarii Goldsmith,*
Poetae, Physici, Historici,
Qui nullum fere scribendi genus
Non tetigit,
Nullum quod tetigit non ornavit.

> To Oliver Goldsmith, A Poet, Naturalist, and Historian, who left scarcely any style of writing untouched, and touched none that he did not adorn.

> *epitaph on GOLDSMITH (1728–74) by Samuel JOHNSON*
> James Boswell *Life of Samuel Johnson* (1791) 22 June 1776

5 O rare Ben Jonson.

> inscription on the tomb of Ben JONSON in Westminster Abbey

6 Poor G.K.C., his day is past—
Now God will know the truth at last.

> *mock epitaph for G. K. CHESTERTON, by E. V. Lucas (1868–1938)*
> Dudley Barker *G. K. Chesterton* (1973)

7 *Quod nunc es fueram, famosus in orbe, viator,*
et quod nunc ego sum, tuque futurus eris.

> What thou art now, wayfarer, world-renowned,
> I was: what I am now, so shall thou be.

> *epitaph written for himself by ALCUIN (c.735–804)*
> translated by Helen Waddell *Mediaeval Latin Lyrics* (1929)

8 Rest in peace. The mistake shall not be repeated.

> inscription on the cenotaph at Hiroshima, Japan

9 She did it the hard way.

> *epitaph of Bette Davis (1908–89), chosen by herself*
> James Spada *More Than a Woman* (1993)

10 *Si monumentum requiris, circumspice.*

> If you seek a monument, gaze around.

> inscription in St Paul's Cathedral, London, attributed to the son of Sir Christopher Wren (1632–1723), its architect; see **BARHAM** 58:6

11 A soldier of the Great War known unto God.

> *standard epitaph for the unidentified dead of World War One*
> adopted by the War Graves Commission

12 Their name liveth for evermore.

> *standard inscription on the Stone of Sacrifice in each military cemetery of World War One, proposed by Rudyard KIPLING as a member of the War Graves Commission*
> Charles Carrington *Rudyard Kipling* (rev. ed. 1978); see **BIBLE** 98:5, **SASSOON** 682:12

13 Timothy has passed . . .

> *message on his Internet web page announcing the death of Timothy LEARY, 31 May 1996*
> in *Guardian* 1 June 1996

14 *Ubi saeva indignatio ulterius cor lacerare nequit.*

> Where fierce indignation can no longer tear his heart.

> *Jonathan SWIFT (1667–1745)*
> Shane Leslie *The Skull of Swift* (1928) ch. 15; see **YEATS** 875:2

15 Underneath this sable hearse
Lies the subject of all verse;
Sidney's sister, Pembroke's mother,
Death, ere thou hast slain another,
Fair and learn'd, and good as she,
Time shall throw a dart at thee.

> William Browne (c.1590–1643) 'Epitaph on the Countess Dowager of Pembroke' (1623)

16 Under this stone, Reader, survey
Dead Sir John Vanbrugh's house of clay.
Lie heavy on him, Earth! for he
Laid many heavy loads on thee!

> Abel Evans (1679–1737) 'Epitaph on Sir John Vanbrugh, Architect of Blenheim Palace'

17 We must know,
We will know.

> *David HILBERT (1862–1943)*
> epitaph on his tombstone, Göttingen; Constance Reid *Hilbert* (1970) ch. 25

18 Were there but a few hearts and intellects like hers this earth would already become the hoped-for heaven.

> *epitaph (1859) inscribed by John Stuart MILL on the tomb of his wife, Harriet (d. 1858), at the cemetery of St Véran, near Avignon*
> M. St J. Packe *Life of John Stuart Mill* (1954) bk. 7, ch. 3

continued

Epitaphs *continued*

1 What Cato did, and Addison approved,
Cannot be wrong.
lines found on the desk of Eustace Budgell (1686–1737),
after he, too, had taken his own life
> Colley Cibber *Lives of the Poets* (1753) vol. 5 'Life of Eustace
> Budgell'

2 What wee gave, wee have;
What wee spent, wee had;
What wee kept, wee lost.
epitaph on Edward Courtenay, Earl of Devonshire (d. 1419)
and his wife
> at Tiverton, in Thomas Westcote *A View of Devonshire in*
> *1630* (ed. G. Oliver and P. Jones, 1845); variants appear in

Tristram Risdon *Survey of the County of Devon* (1714) and
Edmund Spenser *The Shepherd's Calendar* (1579)

3 When you go home, tell them of us and say,
'For your tomorrow we gave our today.'
Kohima memorial to the Burma campaign of the Second
World War, from a poem by John Maxwell **EDMONDS**; in
recent years used at Remembrance Day parades in the UK;
see **BINYON** 121:15, **EDMONDS** 303:18

4 Without you, Heaven would be too dull to
bear,
And Hell would not be Hell if you are there.
epitaph for Maurice **BOWRA**
John **SPARROW**, in *Times Literary Supplement* 30 May 1975

Erasmus *continued*

5 Man's mind is so formed that it is far more
susceptible to falsehood than to truth.
In Praise of Folly (1509)

6 It is wisdom in prosperity, when all is as thou
wouldst have it, to fear and suspect the worst.
Proverbs or Adages (1545 ed.) fol. 31

Ludwig Erhard 1897–1977

German statesman, Chancellor of West Germany (1963–6)

7 Without Britain Europe would remain only a
torso.
remark on West German television, 27 May 1962; in *The Times*
28 May 1962

Susan Ertz 1894–1985

American writer

8 Millions long for immortality who don't know
what to do with themselves on a rainy Sunday
afternoon.
Anger in the Sky (1943)

Lord Esher 1913–

English architect and planner

9 When politicians and civil servants hear the
word 'culture' they feel for their blue pencils.
speech, House of Lords, 2 March 1960; see **JOHST** 445:4

Phil Esposito 1942–

Canadian ice-hockey player

10 This was more emotional than winning the
Stanley Cup. A Stanley Cup's for your team and
your city, but beating Russia is for your country.
on Team Canada beating the USSR in ice hockey in 1972
in *Globe and Mail* 2 October 1972

Robert Devereux, Earl of Essex

1566–1601

English soldier, courtier, and royal favourite; executed for
treason. See also **ELIZABETH I** 312:12

11 Reasons are not like garments, the worse for
wearing.
letter to Lord Willoughby, 4 January 1599, in *Notes and*
Queries 10th Series, vol. 2 (1904)

Henri Estienne 1531–98

French printer and publisher

12 *Si jeunesse savait; si vieillesse pouvait.*
If youth knew; if age could.
Les Prémices (1594) bk. 4, epigram 4

George Etherege c.1635–91

English dramatist

13 I walk within the purlieus of the Law.
Love in a Tub (1664) act 1, sc. 3; see **TENNYSON** 795:25

14 When love grows diseased, the best thing we
can do is put it to a violent death; I cannot
endure the torture of a lingering and
consumptive passion.
The Man of Mode (1676) act 2, sc. 2

15 Writing, Madam, 's a mechanic part of wit! A
gentleman should never go beyond a song or a
billet.
The Man of Mode (1676) act 4, sc. 1

16 Fear not, though love and beauty fail,
My reason shall my heart direct:
Your kindness now will then prevail,
And passion turn into respect:
Chloris, at worst, you'll in the end
But change your Lover for a friend.
New Academy of Compliments (1671) 'Chloris, 'tis not in your
power'

Euclid fl. *c.*300 BC

Greek mathematician, whose work on geometry was the
standard until other kinds of geometry were discovered in
the nineteenth century

17 *Quod erat demonstrandum.*
Which was to be proved.
often abbreviated to QED
> Latin translation from the Greek of *Elementa* bk. 1,
> proposition 5 and *passim*

18 A line is length without breadth.
Elementa bk. 1, definition 2

19 There is no 'royal road' to geometry.
addressed to Ptolemy I, in Proclus *Commentary on the First*

Book of Euclid's Elementa prologue, pt. 2; see **PROVERBS** 644:31

Eugénie 1826–1920

Spanish wife of Napoleon III, Empress of the French

1 I see in every single article of this peace a little egg, a nucleus of more wars.

of the Treaty of Versailles, 1919
Harold Kurtz *The Empress Eugénie* (1964)

Infanta Eulalia of Spain 1864–1958

Spanish princess

2 We could not go anywhere without sending word ahead so that life might be put on parade for us.

Court Life from Within (1915)

Euripides *c.*485–*c.*406 BC

Greek dramatist. On Euripides: see ARISTOTLE 27:23

3 Never shall I say that marriage brings more joy than pain.

Alcestis l. 238

4 Be happy, drink, think each day your own as you live it and leave the rest to fortune.

Alcestis l. 788

5 Nothing have I found stronger than Necessity.

Alcestis l. 965

6 Mere cleverness is not wisdom.

Bacchae l. 395

7 The divine will manifests itself in many forms, and the gods bring many things to pass against our expectations.
What we thought would happen remains unfulfilled,
while the god has found a way to accomplish the unexpected.
And that is what has happened here.

Bacchae l. 1388; the same lines conclude Euripides' plays *Alcestis, Andromache,* and *Helen*

8 What we know and understand to be noble we fail to carry out, some from laziness, others because they give precedence to some other pleasure than honour.

Hippolytus l. 380

9 My tongue swore, but my mind's unsworn.

Hippolytus lamenting his breaking of an oath
Hippolytus l. 612

10 Better a life of wretchedness than a noble death.

Iphigenia in Tauris l. 1252

11 Men say of us that we live a life free from danger at home while they fight wars. How wrong they are! I would rather stand three times in the battle line than bear one child.

Medea l. 247

12 When passions come upon men in strength beyond due measure their gift is neither one of glory nor of greatness.

Medea l. 627

13 May temperance befriend me, the gods' most lovely gift.

Medea l. 636

14 O sleep's enchantment, friend and helper against sickness.

Orestes l. 211

15 The man is to be envied who has been fortunate in his children, and has avoided dire calamity.

Orestes l. 542

16 You mention a slave's condition; not to say what one thinks.

The Phoenician Women l. 392

17 Man's best possession is a sympathetic wife.

fragment no. 164; Augustus Nauck *Tragicorum Graecorum Fragmenta*

John Evelyn 1620–1706

English diarist

18 This knight was indeed a valiant Gent: but not a little given to romance, when he spake of himself.

of the royalist Sir Lewis Dyve (1599–1669)
E. S. de Beer (ed.) *Diary of John Evelyn* (1955) 6 September 1651

19 Mulberry Garden, now the only place of refreshment about the town for persons of the best quality to be exceedingly cheated at.

E. S. de Beer (ed.) *Diary of John Evelyn* (1955) 10 May 1654

20 That miracle of a youth, Mr Christopher Wren.

E. S. de Beer (ed.) *Diary of John Evelyn* (1955) 11 July 1654

21 I saw Hamlet Prince of Denmark played, but now the old play began to disgust this refined age.

E. S. de Beer (ed.) *Diary of John Evelyn* (1955) 26 November 1661

22 God grant mine eyes may never behold the like, who now saw above ten thousand houses all in one flame.

of the Great Fire of London
E. S. de Beer (ed.) *Diary of John Evelyn* (1955) 2 September 1666

Lord Eversley *see* Charles Shaw-Lefevre

Gavin Ewart 1916–95

English poet

23 The path of true love isn't smooth,
the ruffled feathers sex can soothe
ruffle again—for couples never
spend all their lives in bed together.

'24th March 1986' (1987)

24 Is it Colman's smile
That makes life worth while
Or Crawford's significant form?
Is it Lombard's lips
Or Mae West's hips
That carry you through the storm?

'Verse from an Opera' (1939)

William Norman Ewer 1885–1977
English writer

1 I gave my life for freedom—This I know:
For those who bade me fight had told me so.
'Five Souls' (1917)

2 How odd
Of God
To choose
The Jews.
Week-End Book (1924); see **BROWNE** 161:15

Winifred Ewing 1929–
Scottish Nationalist politician

3 The Scottish Parliament which adjourned on 25
March in the year 1707 is hereby reconvened.
opening speech, as oldest member of the new Parliament
in Scottish Parliament 12 May 1999

Frederick William Faber 1814–63
English Church of England clergyman and Roman Catholic
priest

4 Faith of our Fathers! living still
In spite of dungeon, fire, and sword:
Oh, how our hearts beat fast with joy
Whene'er they hear that glorious word.

Faith of our Fathers! Holy Faith!
We will be true to thee till death.
'Faith of our Fathers'

5 Faith of our Fathers! Mary's prayers
Shall win our country back to thee
And by the truth that comes from God
England shall then indeed be free.
'Faith of our Fathers'

6 My God, how wonderful Thou art!
Thy Majesty how bright!
Oratory Hymns (1854) 'The Eternal Father'

7 There's a wideness in God's mercy
Like the wideness of the sea.
Oratory Hymns (1854) 'Souls of men, why will ye scatter'

8 Dark night hath come down on us, Mother!
and we
Look out for thy shining, sweet Star of the Sea!
'O Purest of Creatures'

Quintus Fabius Maximus c.275–203 BC
Roman politician and general

9 To be turned from one's course by men's
opinions, by blame, and by misrepresentation
shows a man unfit to hold an office.
Plutarch *Parallel Lives* 'Fabius Maximus'

Robert Fabyan d. 1513
English chronicler

10 King Henry [I] being in Normandy, after some
writers, fell from or with his horse, whereof he
caught his death; but Ranulphe says he took a
surfeit by eating of a lamprey, and thereof died.
The New Chronicles of England and France (1516) vol. 1, ch. 229

11 The Duke of Clarence . . . then being a prisoner
in the Tower, was secretly put to death and
drowned in a barrel of Malmesey wine within
the said Tower.
The New Chronicles of England and France (1516) vol. 2 '1478';
'malvesye' for 'malmesey' in early editions

Clifton Fadiman 1904–99
American critic

12 Milk's leap toward immortality.
of cheese
Any Number Can Play (1957)

13 The mama of dada.
of Gertrude **STEIN**
Party of One (1955)

Émile Faguet 1847–1916
French writer and critic

14 It would be equally reasonable to say that sheep
are born carnivorous, and everywhere nibble
grass.
in response to Rousseau (see **ROUSSEAU** *670:14)*
summarizing the view of Joseph de Maistre; *Politiques et
Moralistes du Dix-Neuvième Siècle* (1899)

Thomas Fairfax 1621–71
English Parliamentary general

15 Human probabilities are not sufficient grounds
to make war upon a neighbour nation.
*in 1650, refusing to lead an invasion of Scotland after the
proclamation there of* **CHARLES II** *as king*
in *Dictionary of National Biography* (1917–)

Lucius Cary, Lord Falkland 1610–43
English royalist politician. On Falkland: see **CLARENDON**
233:7, CLARENDON 233:8

16 When it is not necessary to change, it is
necessary not to change.
Discourses of Infallibility (1660) 'A Speech concerning
Episcopacy' delivered in 1641

Frantz Fanon 1925–61
French West Indian psychoanalyst and writer

17 To speak means to be in a position to use a
certain syntax, to grasp the morphology of this
or that language, but it means above all to
assume a culture, to support the weight of a
civilization.
Black Skin, White Masks (1952) ch. 1

1 Leave this Europe where they are never done talking of Man, yet murder men everywhere they find them.
  The Wretched of the Earth (1961)

2 The shape of Africa resembles a revolver, and Zaire is the trigger.
  attributed

Richard Fanshawe 1605–66
English diplomat and translator

3 Ten years the world upon him falsely smiled,
  Sheathing in fawning looks the deadly knife
  Long aimed at his head; that so beguiled
  It more securely might bereave his life:
  Then threw him to a scaffold from a throne.
  Much doctrine lies under this little stone.
  The Faithful Shepherd (1648) 'The Fall'; translation of G. B. Guarini's *Il pastor fido*, 1589

U. A. Fanthorpe 1929–
English poet

4 There is a kind of love called maintenance,
  Which stores the WD40 and knows when to use it.
  'Atlas' (1995)

5 Now, children, the poet. He is less exciting.
  All he brandishes is a ball-point,
  Which he plays with on unastonishing paper.
  'Painter and Poet' (1995)

6   But I too was planted by water,
  Born with the tune of Gloucestershire in my head,
  Knowing our English as much the language of heaven
  As Jerome's tawdry Latin, pagan patter,
  That Jesus and His fishers never spoke.
  They say it cannot be translated into our tongue it is so rude. It is not so rude as they are false liars. For the Greek tongue agreeth more with the English than with the Latin. And the properties of the Hebrew tongue agreeth a thousand times more with the English than with the Latin.
  'Tyndale in Darkness' (1995); see **TYNDALE** 821:5

Michael Faraday 1791–1867
English physicist and chemist

7 The most prominent requisite to a lecturer, though perhaps not really the most important, is a good delivery; for though to all true philosophers science and nature will have charms innumerable in every dress, yet I am sorry to say that the generality of mankind cannot accompany us one short hour unless the path is strewed with flowers.
  Advice to a Lecturer (1960); from his letters and notebook written at age 21

8 Nothing is too wonderful to be true, if it be consistent with the laws of nature, and in such things as these, experiment is the best test of such consistency.
  diary, 19 March 1849; *Faraday's Diary* (1934 ed.) vol. 5

9 Tyndall, I must remain plain Michael Faraday to the last; and let me now tell you, that if I accepted the honour which the Royal Society desires to confer upon me, I would not answer for the integrity of my intellect for a single year.
  on being offered the Presidency of the Royal Society
  J. Tyndall *Faraday as a Discoverer* (1868) 'Illustrations of Character'

10 Why sir, there is every possibility that you will soon be able to tax it!
  *to **GLADSTONE**, when asked about the usefulness of electricity*
  W. E. H. Lecky *Democracy and Liberty* (1899 ed.)

Wallace Fard c.1891–1934
American religious leader, founder of the Nation of Islam

11 The blue-eyed devil white man.
  Malcolm X with Alex Haley *The Autobiography of Malcolm X* (1965); see **MALCOLM X** 517:8

Eleanor Farjeon 1881–1965
English writer for children

12 Morning has broken
  Like the first morning,
  Blackbird has spoken
  Like the first bird.
  Children's Bells (1957) 'A Morning Song (for the First Day of Spring)'

Herbert Farjeon 1887–1945
English writer and theatre critic

13 For I've danced with a man.
  I've danced with a man
  Who—well, you'll never guess.
  I've danced with a man who's danced with a girl
  Who's danced with the Prince of Wales!
  'I've danced with a man who's danced with a girl'; first written for Elsa Lanchester and sung at private parties; later sung on stage by Mimi Crawford (1928)

James Farley 1888–1976
American Democratic politician

14 As Maine goes, so goes Vermont.
  *after predicting correctly that Franklin **ROOSEVELT** would carry all but two states in the election of 1936; see **POLITICAL SLOGANS AND SONGS** 612:4*
  statement to the press, 4 November 1936

Edward Farmer c.1809–76
English poet

15 I have no pain, dear mother, now;
  But oh! I am so dry:
  Just moisten poor Jim's lips once more;
  And, mother, do not cry!
  'The Collier's Dying Child'; see **ANONYMOUS** 18:2

Farouk 1920–65

Egyptian monarch, King 1936–52

1 The whole world is in revolt. Soon there will be only five Kings left—the King of England, the King of Spades, the King of Clubs, the King of Hearts and the King of Diamonds.
said to Lord Boyd-Orr at a conference in Cairo, 1948; *As I Recall* (1966) ch. 21

George Farquhar 1678–1707

Irish dramatist

2 I have fed purely upon ale; I have eat my ale, drank my ale, and I always sleep upon ale.
The Beaux' Stratagem (1707) act 1, sc. 1

3 My Lady Bountiful.
The Beaux' Stratagem (1707) act 1, sc. 1

4 There is no scandal like rags, nor any crime so shameful as poverty.
The Beaux' Stratagem (1707) act 1, sc. 1

5 There's some diversion in a talking blockhead; and since a woman must wear chains, I would have the pleasure of hearing 'em rattle a little.
The Beaux' Stratagem (1707) act 2, sc. 2

6 I believe they talked of me, for they laughed consumedly.
The Beaux' Stratagem (1707) act 3, sc. 1

7 'Twas for the good of my country that I should be abroad.—Anything for the good of one's country—I'm a Roman for that.
The Beaux' Stratagem (1707) act 3, sc. 2

8 Spare all I have, and take my life.
The Beaux' Stratagem (1707) act 5, sc. 2

9 Grant me some wild expressions, Heavens, or I shall burst— . . . Words, words or I shall burst.
The Constant Couple (1699) act 5, sc. 3

10 Charming women can true converts make, We love the precepts for the teacher's sake.
The Constant Couple (1699) act 5, sc. 3; see **DEFOE** 270:17

11 Money is the sinews of love, as of war.
Love and a Bottle (1698) act 2, sc. 1; see **CICERO** 232:7

12 Poetry's a mere drug, Sir.
Love and a Bottle (1698) act 3, sc. 2; see **LOWELL** 502:15

David Glasgow Farragut 1801–70

American naval officer and Union admiral

13 Damn the torpedoes! Full speed ahead.
at the battle of Mobile Bay, 5 August 1864, during the American Civil War (torpedoes = mines)
A. T. Mahan *Great Commanders: Admiral Farragut* (1892) ch. 10

William Faulkner 1897–1962

American novelist. See also **FILM TITLES** 331:7

14 The past is never dead. It's not even past.
Requiem for a Nun (1951) act 1

15 Yes, he thought, between grief and nothing I will take grief.
The Wild Palms (1931) 'Wild Palms'

16 He made the books and he died.
his own 'sum and history of my life'
letter to Malcolm Cowley, 11 February 1949

17 I believe man will not merely endure, he will prevail. He is immortal, not because he, alone among creatures, has an inexhaustible voice but because he has a soul, a spirit capable of compassion and sacrifice and endurance.
Nobel Prize acceptance speech, Stockholm, 10 December 1950

18 The writer's only responsibility is to his art. He will be completely ruthless if he is a good one. He has a dream. It anguishes him so much he must get rid of it. He has no peace until then. Everything goes by the board . . . If a writer has to rob his mother, he will not hesitate; the *Ode on a Grecian Urn* is worth any number of old ladies.
in *Paris Review* Spring 1956

19 A man shouldn't fool with booze until he's fifty; then he's a damn fool if he doesn't.
James M. Webb and A. Wigfall Green *William Faulkner of Oxford* (1965)

John Fawcett 1740–1817

English Baptist theologian

20 Blest be the tie that binds
Our hearts in Jesu's love.
'Blest be the tie that binds'

Guy Fawkes 1570–1606

English conspirator in the Gunpowder Plot, 1605

21 A desperate disease requires a dangerous remedy.
6 November 1605, in *Dictionary of National Biography* (1917–); see **PROVERBS** 629:40, **SHAKESPEARE** 703:23

Dianne Feinstein 1933–

American Democratic politician

22 Toughness doesn't have to come in a pinstripe suit.
in *Time* 4 June 1984

Federico Fellini 1920–93

Italian film director

23 All art is autobiographical; the pearl is the oyster's autobiography.
in *Atlantic Monthly* December 1965

James Fenton 1949–

English poet

24 It is not what they built. It is what they knocked down.
It is not the houses. It is the spaces between the houses.
It is not the streets that exist. It is the streets that no longer exist.
German Requiem (1981)

1 Yes
You have come upon the fabled lands where
   myths
Go when they die.
'The Pitt-Rivers Museum' (1983)

2 Windbags can be right. Aphorists can be wrong.
It is a tough world.
in *Times* 21 February 1985

Edna Ferber 1887–1968

American writer

3 Perhaps too much of everything is as bad as too
little.
Giant (1952) ch. 6

4 Roast Beef, Medium, is not only a food. It is a
philosophy.
Roast Beef, Medium (1911) foreword

5 Being an old maid is like death by drowning, a
really delightful sensation after you cease to
struggle.
R. E. Drennan *Wit's End* (1973)

Samuel Ferguson 1810–86

Irish poet

6 I walked through Ballinderry in the springtime,
When the bud was on the tree,
And I said, in every fresh-ploughed field
   beholding
The sowers striding free,
Scattering broadcast forth the corn in golden
   plenty
On the quick, seed-clasping soil
Even such, this day, among the fresh-stirred
   hearts of Erin,
Thomas Davis, is thy toil.
'Lament for the Death of Thomas Davis'

7 As I heard the sweet lark sing
In the clear air of the day.
'The Lark in the Clear Air'

Robert Fergusson 1750–74

Scottish poet

8 For thof ye had as wise a snout on
As Shakespeare or Sir Isaac Newton,
Your judgement fouk woud hae a doubt on,
I'll tak my aith,
Till they could see ye wi' a suit on
O' gude Braid Claith.
'Braid Claith' (1773)

9 The Lawyers may revere that tree
Where thieves so oft have swung,
Since, by the Law's most wise decree,
Her thieves are never hung.
'Epigram on a Lawyer's desiring one of the Tribe to look with
respect to a Gibbet' (1779)

Pierre de Fermat 1601–65

French mathematician

10 *Cuius rei demonstrationem mirabilem sane detexi
hanc marginis exiguitas non caperet.*

I have a truly marvellous demonstration of this
proposition which this margin is too narrow to
contain.
*of 'Fermat's last theorem', written in the margin of his copy
of* Diophantus' Arithmetica, *and subsequently published by
his son in 1670 in an edition of the book containing
Fermat's annotations*
Simon Singh *Fermat's Last Theorem* (1997)

Enrico Fermi 1901–54

Italian-born American atomic physicist. On Fermi: see
ALVAREZ 14:2

11 If I could remember the names of all these
particles I'd be a botanist.
R. L. Weber *More Random Walks in Science* (1973)

12 Whatever Nature has in store for mankind,
unpleasant as it may be, men must accept, for
ignorance is never better than knowledge.
Laura Fermi *Atoms in the Family* (1955)

13 But where is everybody?
*on the existence of extra-terrestrials, known as the Fermi
paradox*
attributed, c.1950

Kathleen Ferrier 1912–53

English contralto

14 Now I'll have eine kleine Pause.
last words; Gerald Moore *Am I Too Loud?* (1962)

Ludwig Feuerbach 1804–72

German philosopher

15 *Der Mensch ist, was er isst.*
Man is what he eats.
Jacob Moleschott *Lehre der Nahrungsmittel: Für das Volk* (1850)
'Advertisement'; see **BRILLAT-SAVARIN** 157:8, **PROVERBS** 647:38

Paul Feyerabend 1924–94

Austrian philosopher

16 The time is overdue for adding the separation of
state and science to the by now customary
separation of state and church. Science is only
one of the many instruments man has invented
to cope with his surroundings. It is not the only
one, it is not infallible, and it has become too
powerful, too pushy, and too dangerous to be
left on its own.
Against Method (1975)

Richard Phillips Feynman 1918–88

American theoretical physicist

17 The world looks so different after learning
science. For example, trees are made of air,

primarily. When they are burned, they go back to air, and in the flaming heat is released the flaming heat of the sun which was bound in to convert the air into tree.

speech to the 15th annual meeting of the National Science Teachers Association, New York City, 1966

1 For a successful technology, reality must take precedence over public relations, for nature cannot be fooled.

appendix to the *Rogers Commission Report on the Space Shuttle Challenger Accident* 6 June 1986

2 What I cannot create, I do not understand.
attributed

Eugene Field 1850–95
American poet and journalist

3 But I, when I undress me
Each night, upon my knees,
Will ask the Lord to bless me,
With apple pie and cheese.
'Apple Pie and Cheese' (1889)

4 Wynken, Blynken, and Nod one night
Sailed off in a wooden shoe—
Sailed on a river of crystal light,
Into a sea of dew.
'Wynken, Blynken, and Nod' (1889)

5 He played the King as though under momentary apprehension that someone else was about to play the ace.
of Creston Clarke as King Lear
review attributed to Field, in the *Denver Tribune* c.1880

Frank Field 1942–
British Labour politician

6 The archbishop is usually to be found nailing his colours to the fence.
of Archbishop RUNCIE; a similar comment has been recorded on A. J. BALFOUR, c.1904
attributed in *Crockfords 1987/88* (1987)

Helen Fielding 1958–
English writer

7 I will not . . . sulk about having no boyfriend, but develop inner poise and authority and sense of self as woman of substance, complete *without* boyfriend, as best way to obtain boyfriend.
Bridget Jones's Diary (1996)

Henry Fielding 1707–54
English novelist and dramatist. On Fielding: see
RICHARDSON 660:17

8 It hath been often said, that it is not death, but dying, which is terrible.
Amelia (1751) bk. 3, ch. 4

9 The dusky night rides down the sky,
And ushers in the morn;
The hounds all join in glorious cry,

The huntsman winds his horn:
And a-hunting we will go.
Don Quixote in England (1733) act 2, sc. 5 'A-Hunting We Will Go'

10 Oh! The roast beef of England,
And old England's roast beef.
The Grub Street Opera (1731) act 3, sc. 3

11 He in a few minutes ravished this fair creature, or at least would have ravished her, if she had not, by a timely compliance, prevented him.
Jonathan Wild (1743) bk. 3, ch. 7

12 To whom nothing is given, of him can nothing be required.
Joseph Andrews (1742) bk. 2, ch. 8; see **BIBLE** 105:17

13 I describe not men, but manners; not an individual, but a species.
Joseph Andrews (1742) bk. 3, ch. 1

14 Public schools are the nurseries of all vice and immorality.
Joseph Andrews (1742) bk. 3, ch. 5

15 A lottery is a taxation
Upon all the fools in creation
And Heaven be praised
It is easily rais'd,
Credulity's always in fashion.
The Lottery (1732) sc. 1

16 Love and scandal are the best sweeteners of tea.
Love in Several Masques (1728) act 4, sc. 11

17 Map me no maps, sir, my head is a map, a map of the whole world.
Rape upon Rape (1730) act 2, sc. 5

18 Thwackum was for doing justice, and leaving mercy to heaven.
Tom Jones (1749) bk. 3, ch. 10

19 What is commonly called love, namely the desire of satisfying a voracious appetite with a certain quantity of delicate white human flesh.
Tom Jones (1749) bk. 6, ch. 1

20 O! more than Gothic ignorance.
Tom Jones (1749) bk. 7, ch. 3

21 The only supernatural agents which can in any manner be allowed to us moderns, are ghosts; but of these I would advise an author to be extremely sparing. These are indeed like arsenic, and other dangerous drugs in physic, to be used with the utmost caution; nor would I advise the introduction of them at all in those works, or by those authors, to which or to whom a horse-laugh in the reader would be any great prejudice or mortification.
Tom Jones (1749) bk. 8, ch. 1

22 His designs were strictly honourable, as the phrase is; that is, to rob a lady of her fortune by way of marriage.
Tom Jones (1749) bk. 11, ch. 4

23 That monstrous animal, a husband and wife.
Tom Jones (1749) bk. 15, ch. 9

1 When a man lays the foundation of his own ruin, others will, I am afraid, be too apt to build upon it.
  Tom Jones (1749) bk. 18, ch. 10

2 All Nature wears one universal grin.
  Tom Thumb the Great (1731) act 1, sc. 1

3 When I'm not thanked at all, I'm thanked enough,
  I've done my duty, and I've done no more.
  Tom Thumb the Great (1731) act 1, sc. 3

Dorothy Fields 1905–74
American songwriter

4 A fine romance with no kisses.
  A fine romance, my friend, this is.
  'A Fine Romance' (1936 song)

5 Grab your coat, and get your hat,
  Leave your worry on the doorstep,
  Just direct your feet
  To the sunny side of the street.
  'On the Sunny Side of the Street' (1930 song)

W. C. Fields (William Claude Dukenfield) 1880–1946
American humorist. On Fields: see **ROSTEN** 670:8; see also **EPITAPHS** 318:7

6 Never give a sucker an even break.
  title of a W. C. Fields film (1941); the catchphrase (Fields's own) is said to have originated in the musical comedy *Poppy* (1923); see **PROVERBS** 639:35

7 Some weasel took the cork out of my lunch.
  You Can't Cheat an Honest Man (1939 film)

8 It ain't a fit night out for man or beast.
  adopted by Fields but claimed by him not to be original; letter, 8 February 1944, in *W. C. Fields by Himself* (1974) pt. 2

9 Fish fuck in it.
  on being asked why he never drank water
  attributed

10 Hell, I never vote *for* anybody. I always vote *against*.
  Robert Lewis Taylor *W. C. Fields* (1950); see **ADAMS** 2:9

☐ **Film lines** *see* **box overleaf.** *See also* **ALLEN, FIELDS, GARBO, LAUREL, PRÉVERT, WEST**

☐ **Film titles** *see* **box on page 331**

Alain Finkielkraut
French philosopher

11 Civilized people must get off their high horse and learn with humble lucidity that they too are an indigenous variety.
  describing **LÉVI-STRAUSS***'s views*
  The Undoing of Thought (1988)

12 In a world which has lost its transcendental significance, cultural identity serves to sanction those barbarous traditions which God is no longer in a position to endorse. Fanaticism is indefensible when it appeals to heaven, but beyond reproach when it is grounded in antiquity and cultural distinctiveness.
  The Undoing of Thought (1988)

Ronald Firbank 1886–1926
English novelist

13 'O! help me, heaven,' she prayed, 'to be decorative and to do right!'
  The Flower Beneath the Foot (1923) ch. 2

14 There was a pause—just long enough for an angel to pass, flying slowly.
  Vainglory (1915) ch. 6

15 The world is disgracefully managed, one hardly knows to whom to complain.
  Vainglory (1915) ch. 10

L'Abbé Edgeworth de Firmont 1745–1807
Irish-born priest, confessor to **LOUIS XVI**

16 *Fils de Saint Louis, montez au ciel.*
  Son of Saint Louis, ascend to heaven.
  to **LOUIS XVI** *as he mounted the steps of the guillotine, 1793*
  attributed

Michael Fish 1944–
English weather forecaster

17 A woman rang to say she heard there was a hurricane on the way. Well don't worry, there isn't.
  weather forecast on the night before serious gales in southern England
  BBC TV, 15 October 1987

Andrew Fisher 1862–1928
Australian Labor statesman, Prime Minister 1908–9, 1910–13, 1914–15

18 Australians will stand beside our own to help and defend her to our last man and our last shilling.
  speech in Colac, 31 July 1914, reported in *Argus* 3 August 1914

H. A. L. Fisher 1856–1940
English historian

19 Men wiser and more learned than I have discerned in history a plot, a rhythm, a predetermined pattern. These harmonies are concealed from me. I can see only one emergency following upon another as wave follows upon wave.
  A History of Europe (1935)

20 Purity of race does not exist. Europe is a continent of energetic mongrels.
  A History of Europe (1935) ch. 1

❧ Film lines ❧

1 Anyway, Ma, I made it . . . Top of the world!
White Heat (1949 film) written by Ivan Goff (1910–) and Ben Roberts (1916–84); last lines; spoken by James Cagney

2 Cancel the kitchen scraps for lepers and orphans. No more merciful beheadings. And call off Christmas!
Robin Hood, Prince of Thieves (1991 film) written by Pen Densham and John Watson; spoken by Alan Rickman

3 Don't let's ask for the moon! We have the stars!
Now, Voyager (1942 film), from the novel (1941) by Olive Higgins Prouty (1882–1974); spoken by Bette Davis

4 Either he's dead, or my watch has stopped.
A Day at the Races (1937 film) written by Robert Pirosh, George Seaton, and George Oppenheimer; spoken by Groucho **MARX**

5 E.T. phone home.
E.T. (1982 film) written by Melissa Mathison (1950–)

6 Fasten your seat-belts, it's going to be a bumpy night.
All About Eve (1950 film) written by Joseph L. Mankiewicz (1909–); spoken by Bette Davis

7 Follow the money.
All the President's Men (1976 film), written by William Goldman; spoken by Hal Holbrook as Deep Throat to Bob Woodward

8 Frankly, my dear, I don't give a damn!
Gone with the Wind (1939 film) written by Sidney Howard; spoken by Clark Gable; see **MITCHELL** 551:4

9 Go ahead, make my day.
Sudden Impact (1983 film) written by Joseph C. Stinson (1947–); spoken by Clint Eastwood

10 Greed—for lack of a better word—is good. Greed is right. Greed works.
Wall Street (1987 film) written by Stanley Weiser and Oliver Stone (1946–); see **BOESKY** 130:10

11 Here's looking at you, kid.
Casablanca (1942 film) written by Julius J. Epstein (1909–2001), Philip G. Epstein (1909–52), and Howard Koch (1902–95); spoken by Humphrey Bogart to Ingrid Bergman

12 I could have had class. I could have been a contender.
On the Waterfront (1954 film) written by Budd **SCHULBERG**; spoken by Marlon Brando

13 I fear we have only awakened a sleeping giant, and his reaction will be terrible.
of the attack on Pearl Harbor
Tora! Tora! Tora! (1970 film) written by Larry Forrester, Hideo Oguni, and Ryuzo Kikushima; said by the Japanese admiral Isoroku **YAMAMOTO**, although there is no evidence that Yamamoto used these words; see **YAMAMOTO** 872:3

14 If she can stand it, I can. Play it!
usually quoted as 'Play it again, Sam'
Casablanca (1942 film) written by Julius J. Epstein (1909–2001), Philip G. Epstein (1909–52), and Howard Koch (1902–95); spoken by Humphrey Bogart; see **MISQUOTATIONS** 548:14

15 If you can't leave in a taxi you can leave in a huff. If that's too soon, you can leave in a minute and a huff.
Duck Soup (1933 film) written by Bert Kalmar (1884–1947), Harry Ruby (1895–1974), Arthur Sheekman (1891–1978), and Nat Perrin; spoken by Groucho **MARX**

16 If you carry a 00 number it means you're licensed to kill, not get killed.
Dr No (1962 film) written by Richard Maibaum, Johanna Harwood, and Berkely Mather, and based on the novel by Ian **FLEMING**; spoken by Bernard Lee as 'M'; see **FLEMING** 334:17

17 I'll be back.
The Terminator (1984 film) written by James Cameron (1954–) and Gale Anne Hurd; spoken by Arnold Schwarzenegger; see **TAGLINES FOR FILMS** 788:4

18 I'll have what she's having.
woman to waiter, seeing Sally acting an orgasm
When Harry Met Sally (1989 film) written by Nora Ephron (1941–)

19 I love the smell of napalm in the morning. It smells like victory.
Apocalypse Now (1979 film) written by John Milius and Francis Ford Coppola (1939–); spoken by Robert Duvall

20 In Italy for thirty years under the Borgias they had warfare, terror, murder, bloodshed—they produced Michelangelo, Leonardo da Vinci and the Renaissance. In Switzerland they had brotherly love, five hundred years of democracy and peace and what did that produce . . . ? The cuckoo clock.
The Third Man (1949 film); words added by Orson **WELLES** to Graham **GREENE**'s screenplay

21 I see dead people.
The Sixth Sense (1999 film) written by Manoj Night Shyamalan; spoken by Haley Joel Osment

22 It's a funny old world—a man's lucky if he gets out of it alive.
You're Telling Me (1934 film) written by Walter de Leon and Paul M. Jones; spoken by W. C. **FIELDS**; see **THATCHER** 804:6

23 DRIFTWOOD (*Groucho Marx*): It's all right. That's—that's in every contract. That's—that's what they call a sanity clause.
FIORELLO (*Chico Marx*): You can't fool me. There ain't no Sanity Claus.
Night at the Opera (1935 film) written by George S. Kaufman (1889–1961) and Morrie Ryskind (1895–1985)

24 Let's get out of these wet clothes and into a dry Martini.
line coined in the 1920s by Robert **BENCHLEY**'s press agent and adopted by Mae **WEST** in *Every Day's a Holiday* (1937 film)

continued

Film lines *continued*

1 Let's go to work.

> *Reservoir Dogs* (1992 film) written and directed by Quentin Tarantino; spoken by Lawrence Tierney

2 Lunch? You gotta be kidding. Lunch is for wimps.

> *Wall Street* (1987 film) written by Stanley Weiser and Oliver Stone (1946–)

3 Madness! Madness!

> *The Bridge on the River Kwai* (1957 film of the novel by Pierre Boulle) written by Carl Foreman (1914–84), closing line

4 Major Strasser has been shot. Round up the usual suspects.

> *Casablanca* (1942 film) written by Julius J. Epstein (1909–2001), Philip G. Epstein (1909–52), and Howard Koch (1902–95); spoken by Claude Rains

5 The man you love to hate.

> anonymous billing for Erich von Stroheim in the film *The Heart of Humanity* (1918)

6 Man your ships, and may the force be with you.

> *Star Wars* (1977 film) written by George Lucas (1944–)

7 Marriage isn't a word . . . it's a *sentence*!

> *The Crowd* (1928 film) written by King Vidor (1895–1982)

8 Maybe just whistle. You know how to whistle, don't you, Steve? You just put your lips together and blow.

> *To Have and Have Not* (1944 film) written by Jules Furthman (1888–1960) and William **FAULKNER**; spoken by Lauren **BACALL**

9 EUNICE GRAYSON: Mr—?

SEAN CONNERY: Bond. James Bond.

> *Dr No* (1962 film) written by Richard Maibaum, Johanna Harwood, and Berkely Mather, and based on the novel by Ian **FLEMING**

10 Mr Kane was a man who got everything he wanted, and then lost it. Maybe Rosebud was something he couldn't get or something he lost. Anyway, it wouldn't have explained anything. I don't think any word can explain a man's life. No, I guess Rosebud is just a piece in a jigsaw puzzle, a missing piece.

> *Citizen Kane* (1941 film) written by Herman J. Mankiewicz (1897–1953) and Orson **WELLES**

11 My momma always said life was like a box of chocolates . . . you never know what you're gonna get.

> *Forrest Gump* (1994 film) written by Eric Roth, based on the novel (1986) by Winston Groom; spoken by Tom Hanks

12 Nature, Mr Allnutt, is what we are put into this world to rise above.

> *The African Queen* (1951 film) written by James Agee 1909–55; spoken by Katharine Hepburn; not in the novel by C. S. Forester

13 Of all the gin joints in all the towns in all the world, she walks into mine.

> *Casablanca* (1942 film) written by Julius J. Epstein (1909–2001), Philip G. Epstein (1909–52), and Howard Koch (1902–95); spoken by Humphrey Bogart

14 Oh no, it wasn't the aeroplanes. It was Beauty killed the Beast.

> *King Kong* (1933 film) written by James Creelman (1901–41) and Ruth Rose, final words

15 The pellet with the poison's in the vessel with the pestle. The chalice from the palace has the brew that is true.

> *The Court Jester* (1955 film) written by Norman Panama (1914–) and Melvin Frank (1913–88); spoken by Danny Kaye

16 Remember, you're fighting for this woman's honour . . . which is probably more than she ever did.

> *Duck Soup* (1933 film) written by Bert Kalmar (1884–1947), Harry Ruby (1895–1974), Arthur Sheekman (1891–1978), and Nat Perrin; spoken by Groucho **MARX**

17 The son of a bitch stole my watch!

> *The Front Page* (1931 film), from the play (1928) by Charles MacArthur (1895–1956) and Ben **HECHT**

18 That was a little bit more information than I needed to know.

> *Pulp Fiction* (1994 film) written by Quentin Tarantino (1963–); spoken by Uma Thurman

19 To infinity and beyond.

> *Toy Story* (1995) written by Joel Cohen, et al.; spoken by Buzz Lightyear

20 Toto, I've a feeling we're not in Kansas any more.

> *The Wizard of Oz* (1939 film) written by Noel Langley (1911–80), Florence Ryerson, and Edgar Allan Wolfe; spoken by Judy Garland

21 GERRY: We can't get married at all . . . I'm a man.

OSGOOD: Well, nobody's perfect.

> *Some Like It Hot* (1959 film) written by Billy **WILDER** and I. A. L. Diamond; closing words spoken by Jack Lemmon and Joe E. Brown

22 What a dump!

> *Beyond the Forest* (1949 film) written by Lenore Coffee (?1897–1984); line spoken by Bette Davis, entering a room

23 What have the Romans ever done for us?

> *Monty Python's Life of Brian* (1983 film) written by John Cleese, Graham Chapman, Eric Idle, Michael Palin, Terry Gilliam, and Terry Jones

24 When the legend becomes fact, print the legend.

> *The Man who Shot Liberty Valance* (1962 film) written by Willis Goldbeck and James Warner Bellah; see **JOHNSON** 434:16

continued

Film lines *continued*

1 Why, a four-year-old child could understand this report. Run out and find me a four-year-old child. I can't make head or tail of it.
Duck Soup (1933 film) written by Bert Kalmar (1884–1947), Harry Ruby (1895–1974), Arthur Sheekman (1891–1978), and Nat Perrin; spoken by Groucho **MARX**

2 NINOTCHKA: Why should you carry other people's bags?
PORTER: Well, that's my business, Madame.
NINOTCHKA: That's no business. That's social injustice.
PORTER: That depends on the tip.
Ninotchka (1939 film) written by Charles Brackett (1892–1969), Billy **WILDER**, and Walter Reisch (1903–1983)

3 You finally, really did it—you maniacs! You blew it up! Damn you! Damn you all to hell!
Planet of the Apes (1968 film) written by Michael Wilson and Rod Serling; spoken by Charlton Heston

4 You're going out a youngster but you've *got* to come back a star.
42nd Street (1933 film) written by James Seymour and Rian James

5 You're here to stay until the rustle in your dying throat relieves you!
Beau Hunks (1931 film; re-named *Beau Chumps* for British audiences) written by H. M. Walker; addressed to **LAUREL** and Hardy

6 JOE GILLIS: You used to be in pictures. You used to be big.
NORMA DESMOND: I am big. It's the pictures that got small.
Sunset Boulevard (1950 film) written by Charles Brackett (1892–1969), Billy **WILDER**, and D. M. Marshman Jr

John Arbuthnot Fisher 1841–1920
British admiral

7 The best scale for an experiment is 12 inches to a foot.
Memories (1919)

8 Sack the lot!
on government overmanning and overspending
letter to *The Times*, 2 September 1919

9 Never contradict
Never explain
Never apologize.
letter to *The Times*, 5 September 1919; see **DISRAELI** 286:23, **HUBBARD** 417:13

10 Yours till Hell freezes.
letter to George Lambert, 5 April 1909, in A. J. Marder *Fear God and Dread Nought* (1956) vol. 2, pt. 1, ch. 2, but not original, as described in F. Ponsonby *Reflections of Three Reigns* (1951): 'Once an officer in India wrote to me and ended his letter "Yours till Hell freezes". I used this forcible expression in a letter to Fisher, and he adopted it'

Marve Fisher
American songwriter

11 I like Chopin and Bizet, and the voice of Doris Day,
Gershwin songs and old forgotten carols.
But the music that excels is the sound of oil wells
As they slurp, slurp, slurp into the barrels.
'An Old-Fashioned Girl' (1954 song)

12 I want an old-fashioned house
With an old-fashioned fence
And an old-fashioned millionaire.
'An Old-Fashioned Girl' (1954 song)

R. A. Fisher 1890–1962
English statistician and geneticist

13 The best causes tend to attract to their support the worst arguments.
Statistical Methods and Scientific Inference (1956)

14 It was Darwin's chief contribution, not only to Biology but to the whole of natural science, to have brought to light a process by which contingencies *a priori* improbable are given, in the process of time, an increasing probability, until it is their non-occurrence, rather than their occurrence, which becomes highly improbable.
sometimes quoted as 'Natural selection is a mechanism for generating an exceedingly high degree of improbability'
'Retrospect of the criticisms of the Theory of Natural Selection' in Julian Huxley *Evolution as a Process* (1954)

Albert H. Fitz

15 You are my honey, honeysuckle, I am the bee.
'The Honeysuckle and the Bee' (1901 song)

Charles Fitzgeffrey c.1575–1638
English poet

16 And bold and hard adventures t' undertake,
Leaving his country for his country's sake.
Sir Francis Drake (1596) st. 213; see **CARTER** 204:14

Edward Fitzgerald 1809–83
English scholar and poet

17 Awake! for Morning in the bowl of night
Has flung the stone that puts the stars to flight:
And Lo! the Hunter of the East has caught
The Sultan's turret in a noose of light.
The Rubáiyát of Omar Khayyám (1859) st. 1

continued

Film titles

1 Back to the future.
written by Robert Zemeckis and Bob Gale, 1985

2 Close encounters of the third kind.
written by Steven Spielberg (1947–), 1977

3 The discreet charm of the bourgeoisie.
written by Luis **BUÑUEL**, 1972

4 The Empire strikes back.
written by George Lucas (1944–), 1980

5 Every which way but loose.
written by Jeremy Joe Kronsberg, 1978; starring Clint Eastwood

6 The good, the bad, and the ugly.
written by Age Scarpelli, Luciano Vincenzoni (1926–), and Sergio Leone (1921–), 1966

7 The long hot summer.
based on stories by William FAULKNER
written by Irving Ravetch and Harriet Frank, 1958; 'The Long Summer' is the title of bk. 3 of Faulkner's *The Hamlet* (1940)

8 Naughty but nice.
written by Jerry Wald (1911–62) and Richard Macaulay, 1939; see **ADVERTISING SLOGANS** 8:7

9 Never on Sunday.
written by Jules Dassin (1911–), 1959

10 Rebel without a cause.
written by R. M. Lindner (1914–56), 1959, based on his book (1944); starring James Dean

11 Sunday, bloody Sunday.
written by Penelope Gilliatt (1933–), 1971

12 Suppose they gave a war and nobody came?
written by Don McGuire and Hal Captain, 1969; 'Suppose They Gave a War and No One Came?' was the title of a piece by Charlotte Keyes in *McCall's* October 1966; see **GINSBERG** 358:21, **SANDBURG** 680:7

13 Sweet smell of success.
written by Ernest Lehman (1920–), 1957

Edward Fitzgerald *continued*

14 Each morn a thousand roses brings, you say;
Yes, but where leaves the rose of yesterday?
The Rubáiyát of Omar Khayyám (4th ed., 1879) st. 9

15 Here with a loaf of bread beneath the bough,
A flask of wine, a book of verse—and Thou
Beside me singing in the wilderness—
And wilderness is paradise enow.
The Rubáiyát of Omar Khayyám (1859) st. 11; 'And wilderness is paradise enow' in 4th ed., (1879) st. 12

16 Ah, take the cash in hand and waive the rest;
Oh, the brave music of a *distant* drum!
The Rubáiyát of Omar Khayyám (1859) st. 12; 'Ah, take the cash and let the credit go, / Nor heed the rumble of a distant drum!' in 4th ed., (1879) st. 13

17 I sometimes think that never blows so red
The rose as where some buried Caesar bled.
The Rubáiyát of Omar Khayyám (1859) st. 18

18 Dust into dust, and under dust, to lie,
Sans wine, sans song, sans singer, and—sans End!
The Rubáiyát of Omar Khayyám (1859) st. 23

19 One thing is certain, and the rest is lies;
The flower that once hath blown for ever dies.
The Rubáiyát of Omar Khayyám (1859) st. 26; 'The flower that once hath blown for ever dies' in 4th ed., (1879) st. 63

20 Ah, fill the cup:—what boots it to repeat
How time is slipping underneath our feet:
Unborn TOMORROW, and dead YESTERDAY,
Why fret about them if TODAY be sweet!
The Rubáiyát of Omar Khayyám (1859) st. 37

21 'Tis all a chequer-board of nights and days
Where Destiny with Men for pieces plays:
Hither and thither moves, and mates, and slays,
And one by one back in the closet lays.
The Rubáiyát of Omar Khayyám (1859) st. 49; 'But helpless pieces of the game he plays / Upon this chequerboard of

nights and days; / Hither and thither moves, and checks, and slays, / And one by one back in the closet lays' in 4th ed., (1879) st. 69

22 The ball no question makes of Ayes and Noes,
But here or there as strikes the player goes;
And he that tossed you down into the field,
He knows about it all—HE knows—HE knows!
The Rubáiyát of Omar Khayyám (4th ed., 1879) st. 70

23 The moving finger writes; and, having writ,
Moves on: nor all thy piety nor wit
Shall lure it back to cancel half a line,
Nor all thy tears wash out a word of it.
The Rubáiyát of Omar Khayyám (1859) st. 51; 'all your tears' in 4th ed. (1879) st. 71

24 That inverted bowl we call The Sky.
The Rubáiyát of Omar Khayyám (1859) st. 52; 'they call the Sky' in 4th ed. (1879) st. 72

25 They sneer at me for leaning all awry;
What! did the hand then of the potter shake?
The Rubáiyát of Omar Khayyám (4th ed., 1879) st. 86

26 Who *is* the potter, pray, and who the pot?
The Rubáiyát of Omar Khayyám (1859) st. 60

27 Indeed the idols I have loved so long
Have done my credit in this world much wrong:
Have drowned my glory in a shallow cup
And sold my reputation for a song.
The Rubáiyát of Omar Khayyám (4th ed., 1879) st. 93

28 Alas, that spring should vanish with the rose!
That youth's sweet-scented manuscript should close!
The Rubáiyát of Omar Khayyám (1859) st. 72

29 And when Thyself with shining foot shall pass
Among the guests star-scattered on the grass,
And in thy joyous errand reach the spot
Where I made one—turn down an empty glass!
The Rubáiyát of Omar Khayyám (1859) st. 75; 'And when like her, O Saki, you shall pass / Among the guests star-scattered

on the grass / And in your joyous errand reach . . . ' in 4th
ed., (1879) st. 101

1 Mrs Browning's death is rather a relief to me, I
must say: no more Aurora Leighs, thank God! A
woman of real genius, I know; but what is the
upshot of it all? She and her sex had better mind
the kitchen and their children; and perhaps the
poor: except in such things as little novels, they
only devote themselves to what men do much
better, leaving that which men do worse or not
at all.
> letter to W. H. Thompson, 15 July 1861, in A. M. and A. B.
> Terhune (eds.) *Letters of Edward Fitzgerald* (1980) vol. 2; see
> **BROWNING** 168:11

2 Taste is the feminine of genius.
> letter to J. R. Lowell, October 1877, in A. M. and A. B. Terhune
> (eds.) *Letters of Edward Fitzgerald* (1980) vol. 4

F. Scott Fitzgerald 1896–1940
American novelist

3 Let me tell you about the very rich. They are
different from you and me.
> *to which Ernest* **HEMINGWAY** *replied, 'Yes, they have more
> money' (in* Esquire *August 1936 'The Snows of Kilimanjaro')*
> *All the Sad Young Men* (1926) 'Rich Boy'

4 The beautiful and damned.
> title of novel (1922)

5 At eighteen our convictions are hills from which
we look; at forty-five they are caves in which we
hide.
> 'Bernice Bobs her Hair' (1920)

6 The test of a first-rate intelligence is the ability
to hold two opposed ideas in the mind at the
same time, and still retain the ability to function.
> 'The Crack-Up' in *Esquire* February 1936

7 No grand idea was ever born in a conference,
but a lot of foolish ideas have died there.
> Edmund Wilson (ed.) *The Crack-Up* (1945) 'Note-Books E'

8 Show me a hero and I will write you a tragedy.
> Edmund Wilson (ed.) *The Crack-Up* (1945) 'Note-Books E'

9 You can stroke people with words.
> Edmund Wilson (ed.) *The Crack-Up* (1945) 'Note-Books O'

10 I've been drunk for about a week now, and I
thought it might sober me up to sit in a library.
> *The Great Gatsby* (1925) ch. 3

11 'What'll we do with ourselves this afternoon?'
cried Daisy, 'and the day after that, and the next
thirty years?'
> *The Great Gatsby* (1925) ch. 7

12 Her voice is full of money.
> *The Great Gatsby* (1925) ch. 7

13 They were careless people, Tom and
Daisy—they smashed up things and creatures
and then retreated back into their money or
their vast carelessness, or whatever it was that
kept them together, and let other people clean
up the mess they had made.
> *The Great Gatsby* (1925) ch. 9

14 In a real dark night of the soul it is always three
o'clock in the morning.
> 'Handle with Care' in *Esquire* March 1936; see **MISQUOTATIONS**
> 547:13

15 See that little stream—we could walk to it in
two minutes. It took the British a month to
walk it—a whole empire walking very slowly,
dying in front and pushing forward behind. And
another empire walked very slowly backward a
few inches a day, leaving the dead like a million
bloody rugs.
> *Tender is the Night* (1934)

16 There are no second acts in American lives.
> Edmund Wilson (ed.) *The Last Tycoon* (1941) 'Hollywood, etc.'

17 An author ought to write for the youth of his
own generation, the critics of the next, and the
schoolmasters of ever after.
> letter to the Booksellers' Convention, April 1920; Andrew
> Turnbull (ed.) *Selected Letters of F. Scott Fitzgerald* (1963)

18 All good writing is *swimming under water* and
holding your breath.
> letter (undated) to his daughter, Frances Scott Fitzgerald;
> Andrew Turnbull (ed.) *Selected Letters of F. Scott Fitzgerald*
> (1963)

Penelope Fitzgerald 1916–2000
English novelist and biographer

19 Duty is what no-one else will do at the moment.
> *Offshore* (1979) ch. 1

Robert Fitzsimmons 1862–1917
New Zealand boxer

20 The bigger they are, the further they have to
fall.
> *prior to a fight*
> in *Brooklyn Daily Eagle* 11 August 1900; see **PROVERBS** 628:4

Bud Flanagan 1896–1968
English comedian

21 Underneath the Arches,
I dream my dreams away,
Underneath the Arches,
On cobble-stones I lay.
> 'Underneath the Arches' (1932 song)

Michael Flanders 1922–75 *and* Donald Swann 1923–94
English songwriters

22 Have Some Madeira, M'dear.
> title of song (c.1956)

23 Mud! Mud! Glorious mud!
Nothing quite like it for cooling the blood.
So, follow me, follow,
Down to the hollow,
And there let us wallow
In glorious mud.
> 'The Hippopotamus' (1952)

24 Eating people is wrong!
> 'The Reluctant Cannibal' (1956 song); adopted as the title of
> a novel (1959) by Malcolm Bradbury

Thomas Flatman 1637–88

English poet

1 There's an experienced rebel, Time,
   And in his squadrons Poverty;
   There's Age that brings along with him
   A terrible artillery:
   And if against all these thou keep'st thy crown,
   Th'usurper Death will make thee lay it down.
   'The Defiance' (1686)

2 But princes (like the wondrous Enoch) should be
   free
   From Death's unbounded tyranny,
   And when their godlike race is run,
   And nothing glorious left undone,
   Never submit to Fate, but only disappear.
   'On the Much Lamented Death of Our Late Sovereign Lord
   King Charles II' (1686)

Gustave Flaubert 1821–80

French novelist

3 *Il la croyait heureuse; et elle lui en voulait de ce
   calme si bien assis, de cette pesanteur sereine, du
   bonheur même qu'elle lui donnait.*

   He took it for granted that she was content; and
   she resented his settled calm, his serene dullness,
   the very happiness she herself brought him.
   Madame Bovary (1857) pt. 1 , ch. 7 (translated by F.
   Steegmuller)

4 *La parole humaine est comme un chaudron fêlé où
   nous battons des mélodies à faire danser les ours,
   quand on voudrait attendrir les étoiles.*

   Human speech is like a cracked kettle on which
   we tap crude rhythms for bears to dance to,
   while we long to make music that will melt the
   stars.
   Madame Bovary (1857) pt. 1, ch. 12 (translated by F.
   Steegmuller)

5 *Alors elle se rappela les héoïns des livres qu'elle
   avait lus, et la légion lyrique de ces femmes adultères
   se mit à chanter dans sa mémoire avec des voix de
   soeurs qui la charmaient.*

   She remembered the heroines of novels she had
   read, and the lyrical legion of those adulterous
   women began to sing in her memory with
   sisterly voices that enchanted her.
   Madame Bovary (1857) pt. 2 , ch. 9 (translated by F.
   Steegmuller)

6 *Emma ressemblait à toutes les maîtresses; et le
   charme de la noveauté, peu à peu tombant comme un
   vêtement, laissait voir à nu l'éternelle monotonie de
   la passion, qui a toujours les mêmes formes et la
   même langage.*

   Emma was like all his other mistresses; and as
   the charm of novelty gradually slipped from her
   like a piece of her clothing, he saw revealed in
   all its nakedness the eternal monotony of
   passion, which always assumes the same forms
   and always speaks the same language.
   Madame Bovary (1857) pt. 2, ch. 12 (translated by F.
   Steegmuller)

7 *Le dénigrement de ceux que nous aimons toujours
   nous en détache quelque peu. Il ne faut pas toucher
   aux idoles: la dorure en reste aux mains.*

   Casting aspersions on those we love always does
   something to loosen our ties. We shouldn't
   maltreat our idols: the gilt comes off in our
   hands.
   Madame Bovary (1857) pt. 3, ch. 6 (translated by F.
   Steegmuller)

8 *Une pareille aisance de manières, cette simplicité, qui
   est un raffinement, et où les naifs aperçoivent
   l'expression d'une sympathie instantée.*

   Naturalness and ease of manner—a product of
   sophistication which the gullible interpret as a
   sign of instant affinity.
   A Sentimental Education (1869) pt. 1, ch. 5 (translated by
   Douglas Parmée)

9 *Pour plaire aux femmes, il faut étaler une
   insouciance de bouffon ou des fureurs de tragédie!
   Elles se moquent de nous quand on leur dit qu'on les
   aime, simplement!*

   To please women you either have to be carefree
   and play the fool or else be tragic and
   passionate. When you say to them quite simply
   that you love them, women laugh at you.
   A Sentimental Education (1869) pt. 3, ch. 3 (translated by
   Douglas Parmée)

10 *Tous les deux ne trouvaient plus rien à se dire. Il y a
   un moment, dans les séparations, où la personne
   aimée n'est déja plus avec nous.*

   Neither could find anything to say. There comes
   a moment during leave-taking when the loved
   one is no longer with us.
   A Sentimental Education (1869) pt. 3, ch. 6 (translated by
   Douglas Parmée)

11 From time to time, in the towns, I open a
   newspaper. Things seem to be going at a dizzy
   rate. We are dancing not on a volcano, but on
   the rotten seat of a latrine.
   letter to Louis Bouilhet, 14 November 1850, in M. Nadeau
   (ed.) *Correspondence 1846–51* (1964) (translated by F.
   Steegmuller)

12 What a heavy oar the pen is, and what a strong
   current ideas are to row in!
   letter to Louise Colet, 23 October 1851, in *Letters of Gustave
   Flaubert* (1980) vol. 1 (translated by F. Steegmuller)

13 It is splendid to be a great writer, to put men
   into the frying pan of your words and make
   them pop like chestnuts.
   letter to Louise Colet, 3 November 1851, in *Letters of Gustave
   Flaubert* (1980) vol. 1 (translated by F. Steegmuller)

14 Prose was born yesterday—this is what we must
   tell ourselves. Poetry is pre-eminently the
   medium of past literatures. All the metrical
   combinations have been tried but nothing like
   this can be said of prose.
   letter to Louise Colet, 24 April 1852, in M. Nadeau (ed.)
   Correspondence 1852 (1964)

1 You can calculate the worth of a man by the number of his enemies, and the importance of a work of art by the harm that is spoken of it.
   letter to Louise Colet, 14 June 1853, in M. Nadeau (ed.) *Correspondence 1853–56* (1964)

2 Poetry is a subject as precise as geometry.
   letter to Louise Colet, 14 August 1853, in M. Nadeau (ed.) *Correspondence 1853–56* (1964)

3 Style is life! It is the very life-blood of thought!
   letter to Louise Colet, 7 September 1853, in M. Nadeau (ed.) *Correspondence 1853–56* (1964)

4 The artist must be in his work as God is in creation, invisible and all-powerful; one must sense him everywhere but never see him.
   letter to Mademoiselle Leroyer de Chantepie, 18 March 1857, in M. Nadeau (ed.) *Correspondence 1857–64* (1965)

5 Books are made not like children but like pyramids . . . and they're just as useless! and they stay in the desert! . . . Jackals piss at their foot and the bourgeois climb up on them.
   letter to Ernest Feydeau, November/December 1857, in M. Nadeau (ed.) *Correspondence 1857–64* (1965)

6 Human life is a sad show, undoubtedly: ugly, heavy and complex. Art has no other end, for people of feeling, than to conjure away the burden and bitterness.
   letter to Amelie Bosquet, July 1864, in M. Nadeau (ed.) *Correspondence 1857–64* (1965)

7 Success is a consequence and must not be an end.
   letter to George Sand, 1876, no. 309 in A. L. McKenzie (ed.) *The George Sand–Gustave Flaubert Letters* (1922)

8 *Madame Bovary, c'est moi.*
   Madame Bovary is myself.
   attributed

James Elroy Flecker 1884–1915

English poet

9 West of these out to seas colder than the Hebrides
   I must go
   Where the fleet of stars is anchored and the young
   Star captains glow.
   'The Dying Patriot' (1913)

10 The dragon-green, the luminous, the dark, the serpent-haunted sea.
   'The Gates of Damascus' (1913)

11 We are the Pilgrims, master; we shall go Always a little further.
   The Golden Journey to Samarkand (1913) pt. 1, 'Epilogue'

12 For lust of knowing what should not be known, We take the Golden Road to Samarkand.
   The Golden Journey to Samarkand (1913) pt. 1, 'Epilogue'

13 I have seen old ships sail like swans asleep Beyond the village which men still call Tyre, With leaden age o'ercargoed, dipping deep For Famagusta and the hidden sun That rings black Cyprus with a lake of fire.
   'Old Ships' (1915)

14 O friend unseen, unborn, unknown, Student of our sweet English tongue, Read out my words at night, alone: I was a poet, I was young.
   'To a Poet a Thousand Years Hence' (1910)

Richard Flecknoe d. *c*.1678

Irish poet

15 Still-born Silence! thou that art Floodgate of the deeper heart.
   'Invocation of Silence' (1653)

Ian Fleming 1908–64

English thriller writer. See also **FILM LINES 328:16, FILM LINES 329:9, MISQUOTATIONS 548:7**

16 A medium Vodka dry Martini—with a slice of lemon peel. Shaken and not stirred.
   ordered by James Bond
   Dr No (1958) ch. 14

17 The licence to kill for the Secret Service, the double-0 prefix, was a great honour.
   Dr No (1958); see **FILM LINES 328:16**

Marjory Fleming 1803–11

English child writer

18 A direful death indeed they had That would put any parent mad But she was more than usual calm She did not give a singel dam.
   Journals, Letters and Verses (ed. A. Esdaile, 1934)

19 The most devilish thing is 8 times 8 and 7 times 7 it is what nature itselfe cant endure.
   Journals, Letters and Verses (ed. A. Esdaile, 1934)

20 To-day I pronunced a word which should never come out of a lady's lips it was that I called John a Impudent Bitch.
   Journals, Letters and Verses (ed. A. Esdaile, 1934)

21 Sentiment is what I am not acquainted with.
   Journals, Letters and Verses (ed. A. Esdaile, 1934)

22 O lovely O most charming pug Thy graceful air and heavenly mug . . . His noses cast is of the roman He is a very pretty weoman I could not get a rhyme for roman And was obliged to call it weoman.
   'Sonnet'

Robert, Marquis de Flers 1872–1927 *and* Arman de Caillavet 1869–1915

French dramatists

23 Democracy is the name we give the people whenever we need them.
   L'habit vert act 1, sc. 12, in *La petite Illustration série théâtre* 31 May 1913

Andrew Fletcher of Saltoun 1655–1716

Scottish patriot and anti-Unionist

1 If a man were permitted to make all the ballads, he need not care who should make the laws of a nation.

'An Account of a Conversation concerning a Right Regulation of Government for the Good of Mankind. In a Letter to the Marquis of Montrose' (1704) in *Political Works* (1732) pt. 7

2 The sea is the only empire which can naturally belong to us. Conquest is not our interest, much less to consume our people and treasure in conquering for others.

'A Discourse of Government with relation to Militias' in *Political Works* (1732)

3 The Scots deserve no pity, if they voluntarily surrender their united and separate interests to the mercy of an united Parliament, where the English have so vast a majority . . . their 45 Scots members may dance round to all eternity, in this trap of their own making.

State of the Controversy betwixt United and Separate Parliaments (1706)

4 Lord have mercy on my poor country that is so barbarously oppressed.

last words, September 1716

John Fletcher 1579–1625

English dramatist. See also BEAUMONT AND FLETCHER, SHAKESPEARE, HENRY VIII

5 Best while you have it use your breath,
There is no drinking after death.

The Bloody Brother, or Rollo Duke of Normandy (with Ben Jonson and others, performed *c*.1616;) act 2, sc. 2 'Song'

6 And he that will go to bed sober,
Falls with the leaf still in October.

The Bloody Brother act 2, sc. 2 'Song'

7 Three merry boys, and three merry boys,
And three merry boys are we,
As ever did sing in a hempen string
Under the Gallows-Tree.

The Bloody Brother act 3, sc. 2

8 Death hath so many doors to let out life.

The Custom of the Country (with Massinger) act 2, sc. 2; see **MASSINGER** 527:12, **SENECA** 692:20, **WEBSTER** 844:11

9 Our acts our angels are, or good or ill,
Our fatal shadows that walk by us still.

The Honest Man's Fortune epilogue

10 Are you at ease now? Is your heart at rest?
Now you have got a shadow, an umbrella
To keep the scorching world's opinion
From your fair credit.

Rule a Wife and Have a Wife (performed 1624) act 3, sc. 1

11 Daisies smell-less, yet most quaint,
And sweet thyme true,
Primrose first born child of Ver,
Merry Springtime's Harbinger.

Two Noble Kinsmen (with Shakespeare) act 1, sc. 1

12 Care-charming Sleep, thou easer of all woes,
Brother to Death.

Valentinian (performed *c*.1610;–14) act 5, sc. 7 'Song'; see **DANIEL** 264:6, **SHELLEY** 746:5

13 Whistle and she'll come to you.

Wit Without Money act 4, sc. 4; see **BURNS** 179:7

14 Charity and beating begins at home.

Wit Without Money act 5, sc. 2; see **PROVERBS** 628:42

Phineas Fletcher 1582–1650

English clergyman and poet

15 Drop, drop, slow tears,
And bathe those beauteous feet,
Which brought from Heaven
The news and Prince of Peace.

Poetical Miscellanies (1633) 'An Hymn'

16 In your deep floods
Drown all my faults and fears;
Not let His eye
See sin, but through my tears.

Poetical Miscellanies (1633) 'An Hymn'

17 Poorly (poor man) he lived; poorly (poor man) he died.

The Purple Island (1633) canto 1, st. 19

18 Love is like linen often changed, the sweeter.

Sicelides (performed 1614) act 3, sc. 5

Matthew Flinders 1774–1814

English explorer

19 It is necessary, however, to geographical precision, that so soon as New Holland and New South Wales were known to form one land, there should be a general name applicable to the whole.

on his acceptance of the name 'Terra Australis'
A Voyage to Terra Australis (1814) introduction

20 Had I permitted myself any innovation upon the original term, it would have been to convert it into Australia; as being more agreeable to the ear, and an assimilation to the names of the other great portions of the earth.

A Voyage to Terra Australis (1814) introduction (note)

21 A poor dried up land afflicted by fever and flies and fit only for a college of monks whose religious zeal might cope with the suffocating heat and mosquitoes.

of Cotton's Island
A Voyage to Terra Australis (1814)

22 [I was] induced to go to sea against the wishes of friends from reading *Robinson Crusoe*.

in *The Naval Chronicle* 1814

Jean-Pierre Claris de Florian 1755–94

French writer and poet

23 *Plaisir d'amour ne dure qu'un moment,*
Chagrin d'amour dure toute la vie.

Love's pleasure lasts but a moment;

Love's sorrow lasts all through life.
Célestine (1784); see **MALORY** 517:20

Dario Fo 1926–
Italian dramatist

1 *Non si paga, non si paga.*
We won't pay, we won't pay.
title of play (1975; translated by Lino Pertile in 1978 as 'We Can't Pay? We Won't Pay!' and performed in London in 1981 as 'Can't Pay? Won't Pay!'); see **POLITICAL SLOGANS AND SONGS** 612:12

Ferdinand Foch 1851–1929
French general and Marshal

2 My centre is giving way, my right is retreating, situation excellent, I am attacking.
message during the first Battle of the Marne, September 1914
R. Recouly *Foch* (1919) ch. 6

3 This is not a peace treaty, it is an armistice for twenty years.
at the signing of the Treaty of Versailles, 1919
Paul Reynaud *Mémoires* (1963) vol. 2

J. Foley 1906–70
British songwriter

4 Old soldiers never die,
They simply fade away.
'Old Soldiers Never Die' (1920 song); copyrighted by Foley but possibly a 'folk-song' from the First World War; see **PROVERBS** 640:33

Jane Fonda 1937–
American actress

5 A man has every season, while a woman has only the right to spring.
in *Daily Mail* 13 September 1989

Bernard le Bovier de Fontenelle
1657–1757
French man of letters

6 Do you believe that you have humiliated me by teaching me that the earth goes round the sun? I swear to you that my self-esteem has not diminished on that account.
Discourse on the Plurality of Worlds (1686) 'First Evening'

Michael Foot 1913–
British Labour politician

7 A speech from Ernest Bevin on a major occasion had all the horrific fascination of a public execution. If the mind was left immune, eyes and ears and emotions were riveted.
Aneurin Bevan (1962) vol. 1, ch. 13

8 Think of it! A second Chamber selected by the Whips. A seraglio of eunuchs.
speech in the House of Commons, 3 February 1969

9 It is not necessary that every time he rises he should give his famous imitation of a semi-house-trained polecat.
of Norman **TEBBIT**
speech in the House of Commons, 2 March 1978

Samuel Foote 1720–77
English actor and dramatist

10 Born in a cellar . . . and living in a garret.
The Author (1757) act 2

11 God's revenge against vanity.
to David **GARRICK**, *who had asked him what he thought of a heavy shower of rain falling on the day of the* **SHAKESPEARE** *Jubilee, organized by and chiefly starring Garrick himself*
W. Cooke *Memoirs of Samuel Foote* (1805) vol. 2

12 He is not only dull in himself, but the cause of dullness in others.
on a dull law lord
James Boswell *Life of Samuel Johnson* (1791) 1783; see **SHAKESPEARE** 707:5

13 So she went into the garden to cut a cabbage-leaf to make an apple-pie; and at the same time a great she-bear coming up the street, pops its head into the shop. 'What! no soap?' So he died, and she very imprudently married the barber; and there were present the Picninnies, and the Joblillies, and the Garyulies, and the grand Panjandrum himself, with the little round button at top; and they all fell to playing the game of catch as catch can, till the gun powder ran out at the heels of their boots.
nonsense composed to test the vaunted memory of the actor Charles Macklin (1697?–1797)
Maria Edgeworth *Harry and Lucy* (1825) vol. 2

Miss C. F. Forbes 1817–1911
English writer

14 The sense of being well-dressed gives a feeling of inward tranquillity which religion is powerless to bestow.
R. W. Emerson *Letters and Social Aims* (1876)

Anna Ford 1943–
English journalist and broadcaster

15 Let's face it, there are no plain women on television.
in *Observer* 23 September 1979

Gerald Ford 1909–2006
American Republican statesman, 38th President of the US 1974–7. On Ford: see **JOHNSON** 435:11

16 If the Government is big enough to give you everything you want, it is big enough to take away everything you have.
John F. Parker *If Elected* (1960)

17 I am a Ford, not a Lincoln.
on taking the vice-presidential oath, 6 December 1973
in *Washington Post* 7 December 1973

1 Our long national nightmare is over. Our Constitution works; our great Republic is a Government of laws and not of men.

on being sworn in as President, 9 August 1974

G. J. Lankevich *Gerald R. Ford* (1977); see **ADAMS** 3:2

Henry Ford 1863–1947

American car manufacturer and businessman

2 Any customer can have a car painted any colour that he wants so long as it is black.

on the Model T Ford, 1909

Henry Ford with Samuel Crowther *My Life and Work* (1922) ch. 2

3 History is more or less bunk.

in *Chicago Tribune* 25 May 1916 (interview with Charles N. Wheeler)

4 What we call evil is simply ignorance bumping its head in the dark.

in *Observer* 16 March 1930

John Ford 1586–after 1639

English dramatist

5 Tempt not the stars, young man, thou canst not play
With the severity of fate.

The Broken Heart (1633) act 1, sc. 3

6 I am . . . a mushroom
On whom the dew of heaven drops now and then.

The Broken Heart (1633) act 1, sc. 3

7 The joys of marriage are the heaven on earth,
Life's paradise, great princess, the soul's quiet,
Sinews of concord, earthly immortality,
Eternity of pleasures; no restoratives
Like to a constant woman.

The Broken Heart (1633) act 2, sc. 2

8 He hath shook hands with time.

The Broken Heart (1633) act 5, sc. 2; see **WESLEY** 848:7

9   Tell us, pray, what devil
This melancholy is, which can transform
Men into monsters.

The Lady's Trial (1639) act 3, sc. 1

10 Brother, even by our mother's dust, I charge you,
Do not betray me to your mirth or hate;
Love me, or kill me, brother.

'Tis Pity She's a Whore (1633) act 1, sc. 2

11 View but her face, and in that little round,
You may observe a world of variety.

'Tis Pity She's a Whore (1633) act 2

Lena Guilbert Ford 1870–1918

American poet

12 Keep the Home-fires burning,
While your hearts are yearning,
Though your lads are far away
They dream of Home.

There's a silver lining
Through the dark cloud shining;
Turn the dark cloud inside out,
Till the boys come Home.

'Till the Boys Come Home!' (1914 song); music by Ivor Novello; see **PROVERBS** 631:15

Howell Forgy 1908–83

American naval chaplain

13 Praise the Lord and pass the ammunition.

at Pearl Harbor, 7 December 1941, while Forgy moved along a line of sailors passing ammunition by hand to the deck

in *New York Times* 1 November 1942; later the title of a song by Frank Loesser, 1942

Johann Nicolaus Forkel 1749–1818

German organist and music historian

14 Language is the garment of thought, just as melody is the garment of harmony.

Allgemeine Geschichte der Musik (1788) vol. 1, ch. 24; see **CARLYLE** 200:21

Nathan Bedford Forrest *see* Misquotations 547:15

E. M. Forster 1879–1970

English novelist. On Forster: see **MANSFIELD** 520:7

15 American women shoot the hippopotamus with eyebrows made of platinum.

Abinger Harvest (1936) 'Mickey and Minnie'; see **BELLOC** 67:18

16 It is not that the Englishman can't feel—it is that he is afraid to feel. He has been taught at his public school that feeling is bad form. He must not express great joy or sorrow, or even open his mouth too wide when he talks—his pipe might fall out if he did.

Abinger Harvest (1936) 'Notes on English Character'

17 Yes—oh dear yes—the novel tells a story.

Aspects of the Novel (1927) ch. 2

18 The test of a round character is whether it is capable of surprising in a convincing way. If it never surprises, it is flat. If it does not convince, it is flat pretending to be round.

on fictional characters

Aspects of the Novel (1927) ch. 4

19 A dogged attempt to cover the universe with mud, an inverted Victorianism, an attempt to make crossness and dirt succeed where sweetness and light failed.

of James **JOYCE***'s* Ulysses

Aspects of the Novel (1927) ch. 6; see **ARNOLD** 31:9, **SWIFT** 782:2

20 It is a period between two wars—the long week-end it has been called.

The Development of English Prose between 1918 and 1939 (1945)

21 Railway termini. They are our gates to the glorious and the unknown. Through them we pass out into adventure and sunshine, to them, alas! we return.

Howards End (1910) ch. 2

1 To trust people is a luxury in which only the wealthy can indulge; the poor cannot afford it.

Howards End (1910) ch. 5

2 Personal relations are the important thing for ever and ever, and not this outer life of telegrams and anger.

Howards End (1910) ch. 19

3 Only connect! . . . Only connect the prose and the passion, and both will be exalted, and human love will be seen at its height.

Howards End (1910) ch. 22

4 Of all means to regeneration Remorse is surely the most wasteful. It cuts away healthy tissue with the poisoned. It is a knife that probes far deeper than the evil.

Howards End (1910) ch. 41

5 It's the worst thing that can ever happen to you in all your life, and you've got to mind it . . . They'll come saying, 'Bear up—trust to time.' No, no; they're wrong. Mind it.

The Longest Journey (1907) ch. 5

6 The so-called white races are really pinko-grey.

A Passage to India (1924) ch. 7

7 Nothing in India is identifiable, the mere asking of a question causes it to disappear or to merge in something else.

A Passage to India (1924) ch. 8

8 Pathos, piety, courage—they exist, but are identical, and so is filth. Everything exists, nothing has value.

A Passage to India (1924) ch. 14

9 Where there is officialism every human relationship suffers.

A Passage to India (1924) ch. 24

10 Like all gossip—it's merely one of those half-alive things that try to crowd out real life.

A Passage to India (1924) ch. 31

11 God si [is] Love. Is this the final message of India?

A Passage to India (1924) ch. 33

12 If I had to choose between betraying my country and betraying my friend, I hope I should have the guts to betray my country.

Two Cheers for Democracy (1951) 'What I Believe'

13 So Two cheers for Democracy: one because it admits variety and two because it permits criticism. Two cheers are quite enough: there is no occasion to give three. Only Love the Beloved Republic deserves that.

Two Cheers for Democracy (1951) 'What I Believe'; see SWINBURNE 785:16

Venantius Fortunatus c.AD 530–c.610

Frankish poet and priest; Bishop of Poitiers from AD 599

14 *Pange, lingua, gloriosi*
Proelium certaminis.

Sing, my tongue, of the battle in the glorious struggle.

Passiontide hymn, most commonly sung as: 'Sing, my tongue, the glorious battle'

'Pange lingua gloriosi'; see THOMAS AQUINAS 805:4

15 *Vexilla regis prodeunt,*
Fulget crucis mysterium;
Qua vita mortem pertulit,
Et morte vitam protulit.

The banners of the king advance, the mystery of the cross shines bright; where his life went through with death, and from death brought forth life.

hymn, usually sung as 'The royal banners forward go'

'Vexilla Regis'

16 *Regnavit a ligno Deus.*

God reigned from the wood.

'Vexilla Regis'

Harry Emerson Fosdick 1878–1969

American Baptist minister

17 I renounce war for its consequences, for the lies it lives on and propagates, for the undying hatred it arouses, for the dictatorships it puts in the place of democracy, for the starvation that stalks after it.

Armistice Day Sermon in New York, 1933, in *The Secret of Victorious Living* (1934)

Charles Foster 1828–1904

American politician

18 Isn't this a billion dollar country?

responding to a Democratic gibe about a 'million dollar Congress'

at the 51st Congress; also attributed to Thomas B. Reed, who reported the exchange in *North American Review* March 1892, vol. 154

John Foster 1770–1843

English Baptist minister

19 But the two classes [the educated and the uneducated] so beheld in contrast, might they not seem to belong to two different nations?

Essay on the Evils of Popular Ignorance (1820); see DISRAELI 286:6, DISRAELI 286:8

20 They [the wealthy] are in a religious diving-bell; religion is not circumambient, but a little is conveyed down into the worldly depth, where they breathe by a sort of artificial inlet—a tube.

Journal Item 420 in *Life and Correspondence* (1846)

Stephen Collins Foster 1826–64

American songwriter

21 Beautiful dreamer, wake unto me,
Starlight and dewdrop are waiting for thee.

'Beautiful Dreamer' (1864 song)

22 Gwine to run all night!
Gwine to run all day!

I'll bet my money on de bobtail nag—
Somebody bet on de bay.
'De Camptown Races' (1850) chorus

1 I dream of Jeanie with the light brown hair,
Floating, like a vapour, on the soft summer air.
'Jeanie with the Light Brown Hair' (1854)

2 Way down upon the Swanee River,
Far, far, away,
There's where my heart is turning ever;
There's where the old folks stay.
'The Old Folks at Home' (1851)

3 All the world is sad and dreary
Everywhere I roam,
Oh! darkies, how my heart grows weary,
Far from the old folks at home.
'The Old Folks at Home' (1851) chorus

Charles Fourier 1772–1837
French social theorist

4 The extension of women's rights is the basic
principle of all social progress.
Théorie des Quatre Mouvements (1808) vol. 2, ch. 4

H. W. Fowler 1858–1933
English lexicographer and grammarian

5 The English speaking world may be divided into
(1) those who neither know nor care what a split
infinitive is; (2) those who do not know, but care
very much; (3) those who know and condemn;
(4) those who know and approve; and (5) those
who know and distinguish. Those who neither
know nor care are the vast majority and are a
happy folk, to be envied by most of the
minority classes.
Modern English Usage (1926)

H. W. Fowler 1858–1933 *and* F. G. Fowler 1870–1918
English lexicographers and grammarians

6 Pretentious quotations being the surest road to
tedium.
The King's English (1906)

Norman Fowler 1938–
British Conservative politician

7 I have a young family and for the next few years
I should like to devote more time to them.
often quoted as 'spend more time with my family'
resignation letter to the Prime Minister, in *Guardian* 4 January
1990; see **THATCHER** 804:3

William Fowler *c.*1560–1612
Scottish writer and courtier

8 Your beauty was the first that won the place,
And scaled the walls of my undaunted heart,
Which, captive now, pines in a caitive case,
Unkindly met with rigour for desert;–

Yet not the less your servant shall abide,
In spite of rude repulse or silent pride.
The Tarantula of Love sonnet 9

Caroline Fox d. 1774
English wife of Henry Fox, Lord **HOLLAND**, and mother of
Charles James **FOX**

9 That little boy will be a thorn in Charles's side
as long as he lives.
seeing in the young William **PITT** *a prospective rival for her
son Charles James* **FOX**
attributed

Charles James Fox 1749–1806
English Whig politician, son of Henry Fox, Lord **HOLLAND**.
On Fox: see **SHAW-LEFEVRE** 742:25

10 He was uniformly of an opinion which, though
not a popular one, he was ready to aver, that the
right of governing was not property but a trust.
on **PITT** *the Younger's scheme of Parliamentary Reform,
1785*
J. L. Hammond *Charles James Fox* (1903) ch. 4

11 How much the greatest event it is that ever
happened in the world! and how much the best!
on the fall of the Bastille
letter to Richard Fitzpatrick, 30 July 1789, in Lord John Russell
Life and Times of C. J. Fox vol. 2 (1859)

12 I die happy.
last words, Lord John Russell *Life and Times of C. J. Fox* vol. 3
(1860) ch. 69

George Fox 1624–91
English founder of the Society of Friends (Quakers)

13 I saw also that there was an ocean of darkness
and death, but an infinite ocean of light and
love, which flowed over the ocean of darkness.
Journal 1647

14 I told them I lived in the virtue of that life and
power that took away the occasion of all wars.
*on being offered a captaincy in the army of the
Commonwealth, against the forces of the King*
Journal 1651

15 I . . . espied three steeple-house spires, and they
struck at my life.
on seeing the spires of Lichfield
Journal 1651

16 Walk cheerfully over the world, answering that
of God in every one.
Journal 1656

17 Be still and cool in thy own mind and spirit
from thy own thoughts, and then thou wilt feel
the principle of God to turn thy mind to the
Lord God.
Journal 1658

18 All bloody principles and practices, we, as to our
own particulars, do utterly deny, with all
outward wars and strife and fightings with
outward weapons, for any end or under any

pretence whatsoever. And this is our testimony to the whole world.
Journal 1661

Henry Fox *see* Lord Holland

Michael J. Fox 1961–
Canadian actor

1 It's all about losing your brain without losing your mind.
on his fight against Parkinson's disease
in *The Times* 16 September 2000

Terry Fox 1958–81
Canadian runner, whose right leg was amputated because of cancer

2 I'm not a dreamer . . . but I believe in miracles. I have to.
planning a fund-raising run across Canada; he completed two thirds of his 'Marathon of Hope'
letter to the Canadian Cancer Society, 15 October 1979

Janet Frame 1924–2004
New Zealand writer

3 For your own good is a persuasive argument that will eventually make a man agree to his own destruction.
Faces in the Water (1961) ch. 4

Anatole France (Jacques-Anatole-François Thibault) 1844–1924
French novelist and man of letters

4 Man is so made that he can only find relaxation from one kind of labour by taking up another.
The Crime of Sylvestre Bonnard (1881)

5 In every well-governed state, wealth is a sacred thing; in democracies it is the only sacred thing.
L'Île des pingouins (1908) pt. 6, ch. 2

6 Christianity has done a great deal for love by making a sin of it.
Le Jardin d'Épicure (1895)

7 A throne, what is a throne? Is it four pieces of wood covered in velvet? No! A throne is a man, and that man is I!
Le Lys rouge (1894) ch. 3

8 They [the poor] have to labour in the face of the majestic equality of the law, which forbids the rich as well as the poor to sleep under bridges, to beg in the streets, and to steal bread.
Le Lys rouge (1894) ch. 7

9 Without lies humanity would perish of despair and boredom.
La Vie en fleur (1922)

10 The good critic is he who relates the adventures of his soul in the midst of masterpieces.
La Vie littéraire (1888) dedicatory letter

11 It is by acts and not by ideas that people live.
La Vie littéraire (1888) 'Sérénus'

12 Make hatred hated!
to public school teachers
speech in Tours, August 1919; Carter Jefferson *Anatole France: The Politics of Scepticism.*

13 You think you are dying for your country; you die for the industrialists.
in *L'Humanité* 18 July 1922

14 When a thing has been said and well said, have no scruple: take it and copy it.
'The Creed', in Jean Jacques Brousson and John Pollock *Anatole France Himself: A Boswellian Record* (1925)

Francis I 1494–1547
French monarch, King from 1515

15 *De toutes choses ne m'est demeuré que l'honneur et la vie qui est saulve.*
Of all I had, only honour and life have been spared.
letter to his mother following his defeat at Pavia, 1525; see
MISQUOTATIONS 547:1
in *Collection des Documents Inédits sur l'Histoire de France* (1847) vol. 1

St Francis of Assisi 1181–1226
Italian monk, founder of the Franciscan Order

16 Praised be You, my Lord, with all your creatures,
especially Sir Brother Sun,
Who is the day and through whom You give us light.
'The Canticle of Brother Sun'

17 Lord, make me an instrument of Your peace!
Where there is hatred let me sow love;
Where there is injury, pardon;
Where there is doubt, faith;
Where there is despair, hope;
Where there is darkness, light;
Where there is sadness, joy.
O divine Master, grant that I may not so much seek
To be consoled as to console;
To be understood as to understand;
To be loved as to love.
'Prayer of St Francis' (attributed)

St Francis de Sales 1567–1622
French bishop of Geneva; leader of the Counter-Reformation

18 Big fires flare up in a wind, but little ones are blown out unless they are carried in under cover.
Introduction à la vie dévote (1609) pt. 3, ch. 34; see **BUSSY-RABUTIN** 182:15, **LA ROCHEFOUCAULD** 482:3

19 *On a beau dire, mais le coeur parle au coeur, et la langue ne parle qu'aux oreilles.*
It has been said in vain, but heart speaks to heart, whereas language only speaks to the ears.
letter to the Archbishop of Bourges, 5 October 1604, in

Oeuvres de Saint François de Sales (1834) vol. 3; see **MOTTOES** 563:6

Anne Frank 1929–45

German-born Jewish diarist

1 I want to go on living even after death!
diary, 4 April 1944

Felix Frankfurter 1882–1965

American judge

2 It is a fair summary of history to say that the safeguards of liberty have been forged in controversies involving not very nice people.
dissenting opinion in United States v. Rabinowitz (1950)

Benjamin Franklin 1706–90

American politician, inventor, and scientist. On Franklin: see **TURGOT** 819:7; see also **ANONYMOUS** 21:19, **EPITAPHS** 317:1, **EPITAPHS** 318:9, **TOASTS** 812:2

3 Remember that time is money.
Advice to a Young Tradesman (1748); see **PROVERBS** 645:19

4 Some are weather-wise, some are otherwise.
Poor Richard's Almanac (1735) February

5 Necessity never made a good bargain.
Poor Richard's Almanac (1735) April

6 At twenty years of age, the will reigns; at thirty, the wit; and at forty, the judgement.
Poor Richard's Almanac (1741) June

7 He that lives upon hope will die fasting.
Poor Richard's Almanac (1758) preface

8 We must indeed all hang together, or, most assuredly, we shall all hang separately.
at the signing of the Declaration of Independence, 4 July 1776 (possibly not original); P. M. Zall Ben Franklin (1980)

9 There never was a good war, or a bad peace.
letter to Josiah Quincy, 11 September 1783, in Works (1882) vol. 10

10 In this world nothing can be said to be certain, except death and taxes.
letter to Jean Baptiste Le Roy, 13 November 1789, in Works of Benjamin Franklin (1817) ch. 6.; see **DEFOE** 270:8, **PROVERBS** 640:18

11 Man is a tool-making animal.
James Boswell Life of Samuel Johnson (1791) 7 April 1778; see **CARLYLE** 200:19

12 What is the use of a new-born child?
when asked what was the use of a new invention
J. Parton Life and Times of Benjamin Franklin (1864) pt. 4, ch. 17

Rosalind Franklin 1920–58

English physical chemist and molecular biologist

13 You look at science (or at least talk of it) as some sort of demoralizing invention of man, something apart from real life, and which must be cautiously guarded and kept separate from everyday existence. But science and everyday life cannot and should not be separated.
letter to her father, summer 1940; Brenda Maddox Rosalind Franklin: the Dark Lady of DNA (2002) ch. 4

Lord Franks 1905–92

English philosopher and administrator

14 The Pentagon, that immense monument to modern man's subservience to the desk.
in Observer 30 November 1952

15 A secret in the Oxford sense: you may tell it to only one person at a time.
in Sunday Telegraph 30 January 1977

Tommy Franks 1945–

American general

16 This will be a campaign unlike any other in history. A campaign characterized by shock, by surprise, by flexibility, by the employment of precise munitions on a scale never before seen, and by the application of overwhelming force.
*encapsulated in the phrase 'shock and awe', originally deriving from a Pentagon briefing document by Harlan Ullman and James P. Wade; see **ULLMAN AND WADE** 821:9*
briefing in Qatar, 22 March 2003

Dawn Fraser 1937–

Australian swimmer

17 I hated the easy assumption that girls had to be slower than boys.
attributed; Colin Jarman Guinness Dictionary of Sports Quotations (1990)

Malcolm Fraser 1930–

Australian Liberal statesman, Prime Minister 1975–83

18 Life is not meant to be easy.
*5th Alfred Deakin Lecture, 20 July 1971; see **SHAW** 739:13*

James George Frazer 1854–1941

Scottish anthropologist

19 The golden bough.
title of book (1890–1915); from William Pitt's 1743 translation of Virgil Aeneid bk. 6: 'A mighty tree, that bears a golden bough'

Frederick the Great 1712–86

Prussian monarch, King from 1740. On Frederick: see **NAPOLEON I** 567:13; see also **NAPOLEON I** 568:6

20 Philosophers should be the teachers of the world and the teachers of princes. They must think logically and we must act logically.
letter to Christian Wolff, 23 May 1740; T. C. W. Blanning Culture of Power (2002) ch. 6

21 All religions are just as good as each other, so long as the people who practise them are honest, and even if the Turks and heathens came and wanted to populate this country, then we would build mosques and temples for them.
official reply to an enquiry from the General Directory on the civic rights of Roman Catholics, June 1740; T. C. W. Blanning Culture of Power (2002) ch. 6

22 All religions must be tolerated and the sole concern of officials is to ensure that one denomination does not interfere with another, for here everyone can seek salvation in the manner that seems best to him.

scribbled in the margin of an official reply to an enquiry from the General Directory on the civic rights of Roman Catholics, June 1740; T. C. W. Blanning *Culture of Power* (2002) ch. 6

1 Rascals, would you live for ever?

to hesitant Guards at Kolin, 18 June 1757
attributed

2 Drive out prejudices through the door, and they will return through the window.

letter to Voltaire, 19 March 1771, in *Oeuvres Complètes* (1790) vol. 12; see **PROVERBS** 647:40

3 To see just how bad contemporary taste in Germany is, just visit any theatre. There you will see the abominable plays of Shakespeare being performed in German translations and the audiences deriving great pleasure from these ridiculous farces which merit only to be performed in front of savages in Canada.

Sur la littérature allemande (1780), trans. T. C. W. Blanning

4 My people and I have come to an agreement which satisfies us both. They are to say what they please, and I am to do what I please.

his interpretation of benevolent despotism
attributed

Cathy Freeman 1973–
Australian athlete

5 I was so angry because they were denying they had done anything wrong, denying that a whole generation was stolen.

of official response to concerns about the 'stolen generation' of Aboriginal children forcibly removed from their families
interview in *Daily Telegraph* 16 July 2000

E. A. Freeman 1823–92
English historian. On Freeman: see **ROGERS** 666:1

6 History is past politics, and politics is present history.

Methods of Historical Study (1886)

John Freeth c.1731–1808
English poet

7 The loss of America what can repay?
New colonies seek for at Botany Bay.

'Botany Bay' in *New London Magazine* (1786)

Marilyn French 1929–
American writer

8 The truth is that it is not the sins of the fathers that descend unto the third generation, but the sorrows of the mothers.

Her Mother's Daughter (1987); see **BOOK OF COMMON PRAYER** 136:20

9 Whatever they may be in public life, whatever their relations with men, in their relations with women, all men are rapists, and that's all they are. They rape us with their eyes, their laws, and their codes.

The Women's Room (1977)

10 'I hate discussions of feminism that end up with who does the dishes,' she said. So do I. But at the end, there are always the damned dishes.

The Women's Room (1977)

Percy French 1854–1920
Irish songwriter

11 Come back, Paddy Reilly, to Ballyjamesduff;
Come home, Paddy Reilly, to me.

'Come Back, Paddy Reilly'

12 Oh Mary, this London's a wonderful sight,
With the people all working by day and by night
. . .
But for all I found there, I might as well be
Where the Mountains of Mourne sweep down
to the sea.

'The Mountains of Mourne'

John Hookham Frere 1769–1846
English poet

13 The feathered race with pinions skim the air—
Not so the mackerel, and still less the bear!

'The Progress of Man' (1798) canto 1, l. 34

14 Ah! who has seen the mailed lobster rise,
Clap her broad wings, and soaring claim the
skies?

'The Progress of Man' (1798) canto 1, l. 44

Sigmund Freud 1856–1939
Austrian psychiatrist; originator of psychoanalysis. On Freud: see **AUDEN** 37:6, **DODD** 287:6; see also **RIVIERE** 663:2

15 Anatomy is destiny.

Collected Writings (1924) vol. 5

16 The interpretation of dreams is the royal road to a knowledge of the unconscious activities of the mind.

The Interpretation of Dreams (2nd ed., 1909) ch. 7, sect. E; see **MISQUOTATIONS** 547:10

17 Intolerance of groups is often, strangely enough, exhibited more strongly against small differences than against fundamental ones.

Moses and Monotheism (1938)

18 Analogies decide nothing, that is true, but they can make one feel more at home.

New Introductory Lectures on Psychoanalysis (1933)

19 Being totally honest with oneself is a good exercise.

letter to Wilhelm Fliess, 15 October 1897, in Jeffrey Moussaieff Mason (tr.) *The Complete Letters of Sigmund Freud to Wilhelm Fliess* (1985)

20 'Itzig, where are you riding to?' 'Don't ask me, ask the horse.'

letter to Wilhelm Fliess, 7 July 1898, in *Origins of Psychoanalysis* (1950)

1 The great question that has never been answered
and which I have not yet been able to answer,
despite my thirty years of research into the
feminine soul, is 'What does a woman want?'
  letter to Marie Bonaparte, in Ernest Jones *Sigmund Freud: Life
  and Work* (1955) vol. 2, pt. 3, ch. 16

2 All that matters is love and work.
  attributed

3 Frozen anger.
  his definition of depression
  attributed

Nancy Friday 1937–
American writer

4 The older I get the more of my mother I see in
myself.
  My Mother, My Self (1977) ch.1

5 It was the promise of men, that around each
corner there was yet another man, more
wonderful than the last, that sustained me. You
see, I had men confused with life . . . You can't
get what I wanted from a man, not in this life.
  My Mother, My Self (1977) ch.8

Betty Friedan 1921–2006
American feminist

6 The problem that has no name.
  *being the fact that American women are kept from growing
  to their full human capacities*
  The Feminine Mystique (1963) ch. 14

7 It is easier to live through someone else than to
become complete yourself.
  The Feminine Mystique (1963) ch. 14

8 Today the problem that has no name is how to
juggle work, love, home and children.
  The Second Stage (1987); see **DOUGLAS** 291:9

Milton Friedman 1912–2006
American economist and exponent of monetarism; policy
adviser to President **REAGAN** 1981–9. See also **SAYINGS**
685:13

9 There is an invisible hand in politics that
operates in the opposite direction to the invisible
hand in the market. In politics, individuals who
seek to promote only the public good are led by
an invisible hand to promote special interests
that it was no part of their intention to
promote.
  Bright Promises, Dismal Performance: An Economist's Protest
  (1983)

10 Inflation is the one form of taxation that can be
imposed without legislation.
  in *Observer* 22 September 1974

11 Thank heavens we do not get all of the
government that we are made to pay for.
  attributed; quoted by Lord Harris of High Cross in the House
  of Lords, 24 November 1994

Brian Friel 1929–
Irish dramatist

12 Two such wonderful phrases—'I understand
perfectly' and 'That is a lie'—a précis of life,
aren't they?
  The Communication Cord (1983)

13 Do you want the whole countryside to be
laughing at us?—women of our years?—mature
women, *dancing*?
  Dancing at Lughnasa (1990)

Elisabeth Frink 1930–93
English sculptor and graphic artist. On Frink: see **POPE-
HENNESSY** 618:27

14 I feel that as religion is a vocation for many
people—and nuns and monks are solitary
people—so art is a comparable vocation for
artists because of the solitariness of our work.
  Elisabeth Frink: Sculpture, Catalogue Raisonné (1984)

15 I have focused on the male because to me he is
a subtle combination of sensuality and strength
with vulnerability.
  Elisabeth Frink: Sculpture, Catalogue Raisonné (1984)

Max Frisch 1911–91
Swiss novelist and dramatist

16 *Jeder Bürger ist strafbar, genaugenommen, von einem
gewissen Einkommen an.*

Strictly speaking, every citizen above a certain
level of income is guilty of some offence.
  The Fire Raisers (1953) sc. 3, translated by Michael Bullock

17 CHORFÜHRER: *Der, um zu wissen, was droht,
Zeitungen liest*
*Täglich zum Frühstück entrüstet
Über ein fernes Ereignis,
Täglich beliefert mit Deutung,
Die ihm das eigene Sinnen erspart,
Täglich erfahrend, was gestern geschah,
Schwerlich durchschaut er, was eben geschieht
Unter dem eigenen Dach:—*
CHOR: *Unveröffentlichtes!*

CHORUS LEADER: He who, in order to know
What danger threatens, reads papers,
Each day at breakfast indignant
Over some distant disaster,
Each day given explanations
That spare him the need to think,
Each day informed of what happened the day
  before,
He finds it hard to perceive what is happening
  now
Beneath his own roof—
CHORUS: Unpublished!
  The Fire Raisers (1953) sc. 3, translated by Michael Bullock

18 Technology . . . the knack of so arranging the
world that we need not experience it.
  Homo Faber (1957) pt. 2

Charles Frohman 1860–1915
American theatrical manager

1 Why fear death? It is the most beautiful
adventure in life.
last words, before drowning in the Lusitania, 7 May 1915
I. F. Marcosson and D. Frohman *Charles Frohman* (1916) ch. 19;
see **BARRIE** 59:18

Erich Fromm 1900–80
American philosopher and psychologist

2 Immature love says: 'I love you because I need
you.' Mature love says: 'I need you because I
love you.'
The Art of Loving (1956) ch. 2

3 In the nineteenth century the problem was that
God is dead; in the twentieth century the
problem is that *man is dead*. In the nineteenth
century inhumanity meant cruelty; in the
twentieth century it means schizoid self-
alienation. The danger of the past was that men
became slaves. The danger of the future is that
men may become robots.
The Sane Society (1955) ch. 9

David Frost 1939–
English broadcaster and writer. See also **CATCHPHRASES**
207:27, CATCHPHRASES 208:25

4 Having one child makes you a parent; having
two you are a referee.
in *Independent* 16 September 1989

Robert Frost 1874–1963
American poet

5 I have been one acquainted with the night.
'Acquainted with the Night' (1928)

6 . . . Life is too much like a pathless wood
Where your face burns and tickles with the
cobwebs
Broken across it, and one eye is weeping
From a twig's having lashed across it open.
'Birches' (1916)

7 I'd like to get away from earth awhile
And then come back to it and begin over.
May no fate wilfully misunderstand me
And half grant what I wish and snatch me away
Not to return. Earth's the right place for love:
I don't know where it's likely to go better.
'Birches' (1916)

8 Most of the change we think we see in life
Is due to truths being in and out of favour.
'The Black Cottage' (1914)

9 Forgive, O Lord, my little jokes on Thee
And I'll forgive Thy great big one on me.
'Cluster of Faith' (1962)

10 And nothing to look backward to with pride,
And nothing to look forward to with hope.
'The Death of the Hired Man' (1914)

11 'Home is the place where, when you have to go
there,
They have to take you in.'
'I should have called it
Something you somehow haven't to deserve.'
'The Death of the Hired Man' (1914)

12 They cannot scare me with their empty spaces
Between stars—on stars where no human race
is.
I have it in me so much nearer home
To scare myself with my own desert places.
'Desert Places' (1936)

13 Some say the world will end in fire,
Some say in ice.
From what I've tasted of desire
I hold with those who favour fire.
But if it had to perish twice,
I think I know enough of hate
To say that for destruction ice
Is also great
And would suffice.
'Fire and Ice' (1923)

14 The land was ours before we were the land's.
She was our land more than a hundred years
Before we were her people.
'The Gift Outright' (1942)

15 Happiness makes up in height for what it lacks
in length.
title of poem (1942)

16 And were an epitaph to be my story
I'd have a short one ready for my own.
I would have written of me on my stone:
I had a lover's quarrel with the world.
'The Lesson for Today' (1942)

17 Something there is that doesn't love a wall,
That sends the frozen-ground-swell under it.
'Mending Wall' (1914)

18 My apple trees will never get across
And eat the cones under his pines, I tell him.
He only says, 'Good fences make good
neighbours.'
'Mending Wall' (1914)

19 Before I built a wall I'd ask to know
What I was walling in or walling out,
And to whom I was like to give offence.
'Mending Wall' (1914)

20 I never dared be radical when young
For fear it would make me conservative when
old.
'Precaution' (1936)

21 No memory of having starred
Atones for later disregard,
Or keeps the end from being hard.
'Provide Provide' (1936)

22 Two roads diverged in a wood, and I—
I took the one less travelled by,
And that has made all the difference.
'The Road Not Taken' (1916)

1 We dance round in a ring and suppose,
But the Secret sits in the middle and knows.
  'The Secret Sits' (1942)

2 I've broken Anne of gathering bouquets.
It's not fair to the child. It can't be helped
  though:
Pressed into service means pressed out of shape.
  'The Self-Seeker' (1914)

3 The woods are lovely, dark and deep.
But I have promises to keep,
And miles to go before I sleep,
And miles to go before I sleep.
  'Stopping by Woods on a Snowy Evening' (1923)

4 'Men work together', I told him from the heart,
'Whether they work together or apart'.
  'The Tuft of Flowers' (1913)

5 The figure a poem makes. It begins in delight
and ends in wisdom. The figure is the same as
for love.
  Collected Poems (1939) 'The Figure a Poem Makes'

6 A momentary stay against confusion.
  of poetry
  Collected Poems (1939) 'The Figure a Poem Makes'

7 No tears in the writer, no tears in the reader. No
surprise for the writer, no surprise for the
reader.
  Collected Poems (1939) 'The Figure a Poem Makes'

8 Like a piece of ice on a hot stove the poem
must ride on its own melting. A poem may be
worked over once it is in being, but may not be
worried into being.
  Collected Poems (1939) 'The Figure a Poem Makes'

9 Poetry is a way of taking life by the throat.
  Elizabeth S. Sergeant *Robert Frost* (1960) ch. 18

10 You can be a little ungrammatical if you come
from the right part of the country.
  in *Atlantic Monthly* January 1962

11 I'd as soon write free verse as play tennis with
the net down.
  Edward Lathem *Interviews with Robert Frost* (1966)

12 Poetry is what is lost in translation. It is also
what is lost in interpretation.
  Louis Untermeyer *Robert Frost* (1964)

Christopher Fry 1907–2005
English dramatist

13 The dark is light enough.
  title of play (1954)

14 I do not know why the necessity of God
Should feed on grief; but it seems so.
  The Firstborn (1948) act 3, sc. 2

15 The lady's not for burning.
  title of play (1949); see **THATCHER** 803:16

16   What after all
Is a halo? It's only one more thing to keep clean.
  The Lady's not for Burning (1949) act 1

17 Where in this small-talking world can I find
A longitude with no platitude?
  The Lady's not for Burning (1949) act 3

18   The best
Thing we can do is to make wherever we're
  lost in
Look as much like home as we can.
  The Lady's not for Burning (1949) act 3

19 The human heart can go to the lengths of God.
  A Sleep of Prisoners (1951)

20 Poetry is the language in which man explores his
own amazement.
  in *Time* 3 April 1950

Elizabeth Fry 1780–1845
English Quaker prison reformer

21 Does capital punishment tend to the security of
the people?
  By no means. It hardens the hearts of men,
and makes the loss of life appear light to them;
and it renders life insecure, inasmuch as the law
holds out that property is of greater value than
life.
  note found among her papers; Rachel E. Cresswell and
  Katharine Fry *Memoir of the Life of Elizabeth Fry* (1848)

22 Punishment is not for revenge, but to lessen
crime and reform the criminal.
  note found among her papers; Rachel E. Cresswell and
  Katharine Fry *Memoir of the Life of Elizabeth Fry* (1848)

Roger Fry 1866–1934
English art critic

23 Art is significant deformity.
  Virginia Woolf *Roger Fry* (1940) ch. 8

24 Bach almost persuades me to be a Christian.
  Virginia Woolf *Roger Fry* (1940) ch. 11

Mary E. Frye 1905–2004
American housewife and poet

25 Do not stand at my grave and weep:
I am not there. I do not sleep.
I am a thousand winds that blow.
I am the diamond glints on snow.
I am the sunlight on ripened grain.
I am the gentle autumn's rain.
When you awaken in the morning's hush,
I am the swift uplifting rush
Of quiet birds in circled flight.
I am the soft stars that shine at night.
Do not stand at my grave and cry;
I am not there, I did not die.
  *quoted in letter left by British soldier Stephen Cummins
  when killed by the IRA, March 1989*
  originally circulated privately from 1932 on

Carlos Fuentes 1928–
Mexican novelist and writer

26 New York: building itself up out of its own
disintegration, its inevitable destiny as the city
for everyone, energetic, tireless, brutal,
murderous city of the entire world, where we all

recognize ourselves and see our worst and our best.
The Crystal Frontier (1994) title story

1 In Eden the only wealth is nakedness and unawareness.
The Orange Tree (1994) 'The Two Americas'

Athol Fugard 1932–
South African dramatist

2 Caring. Not the most exciting of words, is it? Almost as humble as a tool. But that is the Alchemist's Stone of human endeavour.
Dimetos (1975) act 1, sc. 4

Francis Fukuyama 1952–
American historian

3 What we may be witnessing is not just the end of the Cold War but the end of history as such: that is, the end point of man's ideological evolution and the universalism of Western liberal democracy.
in *Independent* 20 September 1989

J. William Fulbright 1905–95
American politician

4 The Soviet Union has indeed been our greatest menace, not so much because of what it has done, but because of the excuses it has provided us for our failures.
in *Observer* 21 December 1958 'Sayings of the Year'

R. Buckminster Fuller 1895–1983
American designer and architect

5 Either war is obsolete or men are.
in *New Yorker* 8 January 1966

6 God, to me, it seems,
is a verb
not a noun,
proper or improper.
No More Secondhand God (1963) (untitled poem written in 1940); see **HUGO** 419:1

7 Now there is one outstandingly important fact regarding Spaceship Earth, and that is that no instruction book came with it.
Operating Manual for Spaceship Earth (1969) ch. 4

Thomas Fuller 1608–61
English preacher and historian

8 But our captain counts the Image of God nevertheless his image, cut in ebony as if done in ivory.
The Holy State and the Profane State (1642) bk. 2 'The Good Sea-Captain'

9 Know most of the rooms of thy native country before thou goest over the threshold thereof.
The Holy State and the Profane State (1642) bk. 3 'Of Travelling'

10 Anger is one of the sinews of the soul.
The Holy State and the Profane State (1642) bk. 3 'Of Anger'

11 Light (God's eldest daughter) is a principal beauty in building.
The Holy State and the Profane State (1642) bk. 3 'Of Building'

12 He was one of a lean body and visage, as if his eager soul, biting for anger at the clog of his body, desired to fret a passage through it.
The Holy State and the Profane State (1642) bk. 5 'Life of the Duke of Alva'

Thomas Fuller 1654–1734
English writer and physician

13 A stumble may prevent a fall.
Gnomologia (1732) no. 424

14 Action is the proper fruit of knowledge.
Gnomologia (1732) no. 732

15 Be you never so high, the law is above you.
Gnomologia (1732) no. 943; see **DENNING** 273:10

16 He that plants trees loves others beside himself.
Gnomologia (1732) no. 2247

17 Poor men's reasons are not heard.
Gnomologia (1732) no. 3897

18 The soul is not where it lives, but where it loves.
Gnomologia (1732) no. 4761

19 We are all Adam's children but silk makes the difference.
Gnomologia (1732) no. 5425

20 Ask counsel of the ancients, what is best; but of the moderns, what is fittest.
Introductio ad Prudentiam (1727) pt. 2, no. 1869

Alfred Funke 1869–1941
German writer

21 *Gott strafe England!*
God punish England!
Schwert und Myrte (1914); see **POLITICAL SLOGANS AND SONGS** 612:19

David Maxwell Fyfe *see* Lord Kilmuir

Rose Fyleman 1877–1957
English writer for children

22 There are fairies at the bottom of our garden!
Fairies and Chimneys (1918) 'The Fairies' (first published in *Punch* 23 May 1917)

Clark Gable *see* Film lines 328:8

Thomas Gainsborough 1727–88

English painter

1 Damn gentlemen. There is not such a set of enemies to a real artist in the world as they are, if not kept at a proper distance.

> letter to the musician William Jackson, 2 September 1767; Mary Woodall (ed.) *The Letters of Thomas Gainsborough* (1961)

2 Recollect that painting and punctuality mix like oil and vinegar, and that genius and regularity are utter enemies, and must be to the end of time.

> speech to the Edward Stratford, 1 May 1772; Mary Woodall (ed.) *The Letters of Thomas Gainsborough* (1961)

3 Damn the fellow, how various he is!

> *of Joshua* REYNOLDS

> in 1782, attributed; William B. Boulton *Thomas Gainsborough* (1905)

4 We are all going to Heaven, and Vandyke is of the company.

> attributed last words, in William B. Boulton *Thomas Gainsborough* (1905) ch. 9

Thomas Gaisford 1779–1855

English classicist; Dean of Christ Church, Oxford, from 1831

5 Nor can I do better, in conclusion, than impress upon you the study of Greek literature, which not only elevates above the vulgar herd, but leads not infrequently to positions of considerable emolument.

> Christmas Day Sermon in the Cathedral, Oxford, in W. Tuckwell *Reminiscences of Oxford* (2nd ed., 1907)

Hugh Gaitskell 1906–63

British Labour politician. On Gaitskell: see BEVAN 76:20

6 There are some of us . . . who will fight and fight and fight again to save the Party we love.

> speech at Labour Party Conference, 5 October 1960, in *Report of 59th Annual Conference*

7 It means the end of a thousand years of history.

> *on a European federation*

> speech at Labour Party Conference, 3 October 1962, in *Report of 61st Annual Conference*

Gaius (or Caius) *c.*AD 110–*c.*180

Roman jurist

8 *Damnosa hereditas.*

Ruinous inheritance.

> *The Institutes* bk. 2, ch. 163

J. K. Galbraith 1908–2006

Canadian-born American economist

9 The affluent society.

> title of book (1958)

10 These are the days when men of all social disciplines and all political faiths seek the comfortable and the accepted; when the man of controversy is looked upon as a disturbing

influence; when originality is taken to be a mark of instability; and when, in minor modification of the scriptural parable, the bland lead the bland.

> *The Affluent Society* (1958) ch. 1, sect. 3

11 The greater the wealth, the thicker will be the dirt.

> *The Affluent Society* (1958) ch. 18, sect. 2

12 The salary of the chief executive of the large corporation is not a market reward for achievement. It is frequently in the nature of a warm personal gesture by the individual to himself.

> *Annals of an Abiding Liberal* (1979)

13 Trickle-down theory—the less than elegant metaphor that if one feeds the horse enough oats, some will pass through to the road for the sparrows.

> *The Culture of Contentment* (1992)

14 Meetings are held because men seek companionship or, at a minimum, wish to escape the tedium of solitary duties.

> *The Great Crash 1929* (1954)

15 Politics is not the art of the possible. It consists in choosing between the disastrous and the unpalatable.

> speech to President Kennedy, 2 March 1962, in *Ambassador's Journal* (1969); see BISMARCK 122:16

Galen AD 129–199

Greek physician who attempted to systematize the whole of medicine, making important discoveries in anatomy and physiology

16 The chief merit of language is clearness, and we know that nothing detracts so much from this as do unfamiliar terms.

> *On the Natural Faculties* bk. 1, sect. 1

17 If anyone wishes to observe the works of nature, he should put his trust not in books of anatomy but in his own eyes.

> *On the Usefulness of the Parts of the Body* bk. 2 [1, 72] sect. 3

Galileo Galilei 1564–1642

Italian astronomer and physicist

18 Philosophy is written in that great book which ever lies before our eyes—I mean the universe . . . This book is written in mathematical language and its characters are triangles, circles and other geometrical figures, without whose help . . . one wanders in vain through a dark labyrinth.

> *often quoted as 'The book of nature is written . . . '*

> *The Assayer* (1623)

19 SALVIATI: Now you see how easy it is to understand.

SAGREDO: So are all truths, once they are discovered.

often quoted as 'All truths are easy to understand, once they are discovered; the point is, to discover them'

Dialogue Concerning the two Chief World Systems (1632) 'The Second Day' translated by Stillman Drake

1 *Eppur si muove.*

But it does move.

after his recantation, that the earth moves around the sun, in 1632

attributed; Baretti *Italian Library* (1757) is possibly the earliest appearance of the phrase

2 In disputes about natural phenomena one must begin not with the authority of Scriptural passage but with sensory experience and necessary demonstrations. For the Holy Scripture and nature derive equally from the Godhead, the former as the dictation of the Holy Spirit and the latter as the most obedient executrix of God's orders.

letter to Christina Lotharinga, Arch-Duchess of Tuscany; P. MacHamer (ed.) *Cambridge Companion to Galileo* (1998)

John Galsworthy 1867–1933

English novelist

3 He was afflicted by the thought that where Beauty was, nothing ever ran quite straight, which, no doubt, was why so many people looked on it as immoral.

In Chancery (1920) pt. 1, ch. 13

4 A man of action forced into a state of thought is unhappy until he can get out of it.

Maid in Waiting (1931) ch. 3

John Galt 1779–1839

Scottish writer

5 From the lone shieling of the misty island
Mountains divide us, and the waste of seas—
Yet still the blood is strong, the heart is
   Highland,
And we in dreams behold the Hebrides!

'Canadian Boat Song' translated from the Gaelic in *Blackwoods Edinburgh Magazine* September 1829 'Noctes Ambrosianae' no. 46, and later attributed to Galt

Ray Galton 1930– *and* Alan Simpson 1929–

English scriptwriters

6 I came in here in all good faith to help my country. I don't mind giving a reasonable amount [of blood], but a pint . . . why that's very nearly an armful.

Hancock's Half Hour 'The Blood Donor' (1961 BBC television programme); words spoken by Tony Hancock

George Gamow 1904–68

Russian-born American physicist

7 We do not know why they [elementary particles] have the masses they do; we do not know why

they transform into another the way they do; we do not know anything! The one concept that stands like the Rock of Gibraltar in our sea of confusion is the Pauli [exclusion] principle.

in *Scientific American* July 1959

8 With five free parameters, a theorist could fit the profile of an elephant.

attributed; in *Nature* 21 June 1990

Indira Gandhi 1917–84

Indian stateswoman, Prime Minister 1966–77 and 1980–4

9 I cannot understand how anyone can be an Indian and not be proud—the richness and infinite variety of our composite heritage, the magnificence of the people's spirit, equal to any disaster or burden, firm in their faith . . . even in poverty and hardship.

paper found after her death, *Remembered Moments* (1987)

10 I have lived a long life and I am proud that I spent the whole of my life in the service of my people. I am only proud of this and of nothing else. I shall continue to serve until my last breath and when I die, I can say, that every drop of my blood will invigorate India and strengthen it.

speech, Bhubaneshwar, 30 October 1984 (the night before she was assassinated); *Selected Speeches* (1986) vol. 5

Mahatma Gandhi (Mohandas Karamchand Gandhi) 1869–1948

Indian nationalist and spiritual leader, who pursued a policy of nonviolent civil disobedience against British rule in India; assassinated January 1948. On Gandhi: see NAIDU 567:3, NEHRU 569:10; see also SAYINGS 684:17

11 What difference does it make to the dead, the orphans and the homeless, whether the mad destruction is wrought under the name of totalitarianism or the holy name of liberty or democracy?

Non-Violence in Peace and War (1942) vol. 1, ch. 142

12 The moment the slave resolves that he will no longer be a slave, his fetters fall. He frees himself and shows the way to others. Freedom and slavery are mental states.

Non-Violence in Peace and War (1949) vol. 2, ch. 5

13 Non-violence is the first article of my faith. It is also the last article of my creed.

speech at Shahi Bag, 18 March 1922, on a charge of sedition, in *Young India* 23 March 1922

14 In my humble opinion, non-cooperation with evil is as much a duty as is cooperation with good.

speech in Ahmadabad, 23 March 1922

15 *on being asked what he thought of modern civilization:*

That would be a good idea.

while visiting England in 1930

E. F. Schumacher *Good Work* (1979)

1 We must be the change we wish to see in the world.
>not traced in Gandhi's writings, but said to be a favourite saying; attributed (1989) in *Yale Book of Quotations*

Greta Garbo (Greta Lovisa Gustafsson) 1905–90

Swedish film actress. See also TAGLINES FOR FILMS 788:3

2 I want to be alone.
>*Grand Hotel* (1932 film), the phrase already being associated with Garbo

Frederico García Lorca *see* Lorca

Gabriel García Márquez 1928–

Colombian novelist

3 Necessity has the face of a dog.
>*In Evil Hour* (1968)

Richard Gardiner b. *c.*1533

English writer

4 Sowe Carrets in your Gardens, and humbly praise God for them, as for a singular and great blessing.
>*Profitable Instructions for the Manuring, Sowing and Planting of Kitchen Gardens* (1599)

Ed Gardner 1901–63

American radio comedian

5 Opera is when a guy gets stabbed in the back and, instead of bleeding, he sings.
>in *Duffy's Tavern* (US radio programme, 1940s)

James A. Garfield 1831–81

American Republican statesman, 20th President of the US 1881. On Garfield: see THAYER 804:9

6 Fellow-citizens: God reigns, and the Government at Washington lives!
>speech on the assassination of President Lincoln, 17 April 1865; in *Death of President Garfield* (1881)

Giuseppe Garibaldi 1807–82

Italian patriot and military leader

7 Men, I'm getting out of Rome. Anyone who wants to carry on the war against the outsiders, come with me. I can offer you neither honours nor wages; I offer you hunger, thirst, forced marches, battles and death. Anyone who loves his country, follow me.
>Giuseppe Guerzoni *Garibaldi* (1882) vol. 1 (not a verbatim record)

John Nance Garner 1868–1967

American Democratic politician; vice-president 1933–41

8 The vice-presidency isn't worth a pitcher of warm piss.
>O. C. Fisher *Cactus Jack* (1978) ch. 11

David Garrick 1717–79

English actor-manager. On Garrick: see FOOTE 336:11, GOLDSMITH 364:17, GOLDSMITH 364:19, GOLDSMITH 364:20, JOHNSON 436:27; see also COLMAN AND GARRICK, EPITAPHS 317:7

9 They smile with the simple, and feed with the poor.
>*Florizel and Perdita* (performed 1756) act 2, sc. 1; see JOHNSON 440:16

10 Heart of oak are our ships,
Heart of oak are our men:
We always are ready;
Steady, boys, steady;
We'll fight and we'll conquer again and again.
>*Harlequin's Invasion* (1759) 'Heart of Oak' (song)

11 Here lies Nolly Goldsmith, for shortness called Noll,
Who wrote like an angel, but talked like poor Poll.
>'Impromptu Epitaph' (written 1773/4); see GOLDSMITH 364:17, JOHNSON 443:1

12 A fellow-feeling makes one wond'rous kind.
>'An Occasional Prologue on Quitting the Theatre' 10 June 1776

13 Are these the choice dishes the Doctor has sent us?
Is this the great poet whose works so content us?
This Goldsmith's fine feast, who has written fine books?
Heaven sends us good meat, but the Devil sends cooks.
>'On Doctor Goldsmith's Characteristical Cookery' (1777)

14 Prologues precede the piece—in mournful verse;
As undertakers—walk before the hearse.
>prologue to Arthur Murphy's *The Apprentice* (1756)

15 Kitty, a fair, but frozen maid,
Kindled a flame I still deplore.
>'A Riddle' (1762)

16 He could make men weep or tremble by his varied utterances of the word 'Mesopotamia'.
>*on the moving voice of the English Methodist preacher George Whitefield (1714–70); Garrick is also said to have remarked 'I would give a hundred guineas if I could say "Oh" like Mr Whitefield'*
>A. C. H. Seymour *The Life and Times of Selina, Countess of Huntingdon* (1840) ch. 33; see also ANONYMOUS 20:16

William Lloyd Garrison 1805–79

American anti-slavery campaigner

17 I am in earnest—I will not equivocate—I will not excuse—I will not retreat a single inch—and I will be heard!
>in *The Liberator* 1 January 1831 'Salutatory Address'

18 Our country is the world—our countrymen are all mankind.
>*The Liberator* 15 December 1837 'Prospectus'

1 The compact which exists between the North and the South is 'a covenant with death and an agreement with hell'.
resolution adopted by the Massachusetts Anti-Slavery Society, 27 January 1843, in Archibald H. Grimke *William Lloyd Garrison: The Abolitionist* (1891) ch. 16; see **BIBLE** 93:2

Samuel Garth 1661–1719
English poet and physician

2 Hard was their lodging, homely was their food;
For all their luxury was doing good.
'Claremont' (1715) l. 148; see **CRABBE** 258:1, **GOLDSMITH** 364:23

3 A barren superfluity of words.
The Dispensary (1699) canto 2, l. 82

George Gascoigne *c.*1534–77
English soldier and poet

4 The carrion crow, that loathsome beast,
Which cries against the rain.
'Gascoigne's Good Morrow' (1573)

5 As busy brains must beat on tickle toys,
As rash invention breeds a raw device,
So sudden falls do hinder hasty joys;
And as swift baits do fleetest fish entice,
So haste makes waste.
'No haste but good' (1573); see **PROVERBS** 633:48

Elizabeth Gaskell 1810–65
English novelist

6 A man . . . is *so* in the way in the house!
Cranford (1853) ch. 1

7 Economy was always 'elegant', and money-spending always 'vulgar' and ostentatious—a sort of sour-grapeism, which made us very peaceful and satisfied.
Cranford (1853) ch. 1

8 I'll not listen to reason . . . Reason always means what someone else has got to say.
Cranford (1853) ch. 14

9 That kind of patriotism which consists in hating all other nations.
Sylvia's Lovers (1863) ch. 1

10 It is a noble grand book, whoever wrote it—but Miss Evans' life taken at the best construction, does so jar against the beautiful book that one cannot help hoping against hope.
on first hearing of the true identity of 'George **ELIOT***', author of* Adam Bede
letter to George Smith, 4 August 1859; *The Letters of Mrs Gaskell* (1966)

11 I look at them as a child looks at a cake,—with glittering eyes and watering mouth, imagining the pleasure that awaits him!
on the books she was planning to read
letter to George Smith, 4 August 1859; *The Letters of Mrs Gaskell* (1966)

Paul Gauguin 1848–1903
French painter

12 A hint—don't paint too much direct from nature. Art is an abstraction! study nature then brood on it and treasure the creation which will result, which is the only way to ascend towards God—to create like our Divine Master.
letter to Emile Schuffenecker, 14 August 1888; *Paul Gauguin: Letters to his wife and friends* (1946, ed. Maurice Malingue, trans. Henry J. Stenning)

Alan Gaunt 1935–
English hymn-writer

13 We pray for peace,
But not the easy peace
Built on complacency
And not the truth of God.
'We pray for peace' (hymn)

Théophile Gautier 1811–72
French poet, novelist, and critic

14 *Toute passe.—L'art robuste
Seul à l'éternité,
Le Buste
Survit à la cité.*
Everything passes. Robust art alone is eternal, the bust survives the city.
'L'Art' (1857); see **DOBSON** 287:2

15 *Il était impossible de tromper sur la note cette chatte dilettante.*
The dilettante in fur was not to be deceived.
of his cat's response to a high-pitched human voice
Ménagerie intime (1869); quoted in Agnes Repplier *The Fireside Sphinx* (1901) ch. 8

Gavarni (Guillaume Sulpice Chevalier) 1804–66
French lithographer

16 *Les enfants terribles.*
The little terrors.
title of a series of prints (1842)

John Gay 1685–1732
English poet and dramatist. On Gay: see **JOHNSON** 436:21; see also **EPITAPHS** 318:15

17 How, like a moth, the simple maid
Still plays about the flame!
The Beggar's Opera (1728) act 1, sc. 4, air 4

18 Our Polly is a sad slut! nor heeds what we have taught her.
I wonder any man alive will ever rear a daughter!
The Beggar's Opera (1728) act 1, sc. 8, air 7

19 Do you think your mother and I should have lived comfortably so long together, if ever we had been married?
The Beggar's Opera (1728) act 1, sc. 8

1 Can Love be controlled by advice?
   The Beggar's Opera (1728) act 1, sc. 8, air 8

2 Money, wife, is the true fuller's earth for reputations, there is not a spot or a stain but what it can take out.
   The Beggar's Opera (1728) act 1, sc. 9

3 The comfortable estate of widowhood, is the only hope that keeps up a wife's spirits.
   The Beggar's Opera (1728) act 1, sc. 10

4 If with me you'd fondly stray.
   Over the hills and far away.
   The Beggar's Opera (1728) act 1, sc. 13, air 16; **NURSERY RHYMES** 582:6, **STEVENSON** 777:6

5 Women and wine should life employ.
   Is there ought else on earth desirous?
   The Beggar's Opera (1728) act 2, sc. 1, air 19

6 If the heart of a man is deprest with cares,
   The mist is dispelled when a woman appears.
   The Beggar's Opera (1728) act 2, sc. 3, air 21

7 Youth's the season made for joys;
   Love is then our duty.
   The Beggar's Opera (1728) act 2, sc. 4, air 22

8 In one respect indeed, our employment may be reckoned dishonest, because, like great Statesmen, we encourage those who betray their friends.
   The Beggar's Opera (1728) act 2, sc. 10

9 How happy could I be with either,
   Were t'other dear charmer away!
   The Beggar's Opera (1728) act 2, sc. 13, air 35

10 She who has never loved, has never lived.
   The Captives (1724) act 2, sc. 2

11 A woman's friendship ever ends in love.
   Dione (1720) act 4, sc. 6

12 Whence is thy learning? Hath thy toil
   O'er books consumed the midnight oil?
   Fables (1727) introduction, l. 15; see **QUARLES** 651:9

13 Envy's a sharper spur than pay,
   No author ever spared a brother,
   Wits are gamecocks to one another.
   Fables (1727) 'The Elephant and the Bookseller' l. 74

14 And when a lady's in the case,
   You know, all other things give place.
   Fables (1727) 'The Hare and Many Friends' l. 41

15 Those who in quarrels interpose,
   Must often wipe a bloody nose.
   Fables (1727) 'The Mastiffs' l. 1

16 An open foe may prove a curse,
   But a pretended friend is worse.
   Fables (1727) 'The Shepherd's Dog and the Wolf' l. 33

17 I know you lawyers can, with ease,
   Twist words and meanings as you please;
   That language, by your skill made pliant,
   Will bend to favour ev'ry client.
   Fables (1738) 'The Dog and the Fox' l. 1

18 Studious of elegance and ease,
   Myself alone I seek to please.
   Fables (1738) 'The Man, the Cat, the Dog, and the Fly' l. 127

19 But flattery never seems absurd;
   The flattered always takes your word.
   Fables (1727) 'The Painter Who Pleased Everybody and Nobody' l. 7

20 That politician tops his part,
   Who readily can lie with art.
   Fables (1738) 'The Squire and his Cur' l. 27

21 Give me, kind heaven, a private station,
   A mind serene for contemplation.
   Fables (1738) 'The Vulture, the Sparrow, and Other Birds' l. 69

22 Praising all alike, is praising none.
   'A Letter to a Lady' (1714) l. 114

23 An inconstant woman, tho' she has no chance to be very happy, can never be very unhappy.
   'Polly' (1729) act 1, sc. 14

24 All in the Downs the fleet was moored,
   The streamers waving in the wind,
   When black-eyed Susan came aboard.
   'Sweet William's Farewell to Black-Eyed Susan' (1720)

25 They'll tell thee, sailors, when away,
   In ev'ry port a mistress find.
   'Sweet William's Farewell to Black-Eyed Susan' (1720)

26 Adieu, she cries! and waved her lily hand.
   'Sweet William's Farewell to Black-Eyed Susan' (1720)

27 A miss for pleasure, and a wife for breed.
   'The Toilette' (1716)

Noel Gay (Richard Moxon Armitage)
1898–1954
English songwriter

28 I'm leaning on a lamp post at the corner of the street,
   In case a certain little lady comes by.
   'Leaning on a Lamp Post' (1937); sung by George Formby in the film *Father Knew Best*

Eric Geddes 1875–1937
British politician and administrator

29 The Germans, if this Government is returned, are going to pay every penny; they are going to be squeezed as a lemon is squeezed—until the pips squeak.
   speech at Cambridge, 10 December 1918, in *Cambridge Daily News* 11 December 1918

Frank Gehry 1929–
Canadian-born American architect

30 People ask me if I'm an artist or an architect.
   But I think they're the same.
   in *Toronto Star* 4 September 1987

Bob Geldof 1954– *and* Midge Ure
1953–
Irish rock musician; Scottish rock musician

31 Do they know it's Christmas?
   title of song (1984)

Martha Gellhorn 1908–98

American journalist

1 *of the defeat of the Spanish Republic:*

I daresay we all became more competent press tourists because of it, since we never again cared so much. You can only love one war; afterward, I suppose, you do your duty.

The Honeyed Peace (1953)

2 Never believe governments, not any of them, not a word they say; keep an untrusting eye on all they do.

in obituary, *Daily Telegraph* 17 February 1998

Jean Genet 1910–86

French novelist, poet, and dramatist

3 What we need is hatred. From it our ideas are born.

The Blacks (1959); epigraph

4 Are you there . . . Africa of the millions of royal slaves, deported Africa, drifting continent, are you there? Slowly you vanish, you withdraw into the past, into the tales of castaways, colonial museums, the works of scholars.

The Blacks (1959)

5 Anyone who hasn't experienced the ecstasy of betrayal knows nothing about ecstasy at all.

Prisoner of Love (1986)

Genghis Khan (Temujin) 1162–1227

Mongol ruler, who took the name Genghis Khan ('ruler of all') in 1206

6 Happiness lies in conquering one's enemies, in driving them in front of oneself, in taking their property, in savouring their despair, in outraging their wives and daughters.

Witold Rodzinski *The Walled Kingdom: A History of China* (1979)

George I 1660–1727

British monarch, King of Great Britain and Ireland from 1714. On George I: see **JOHNSON** 441:15, **LANDOR** 478:6

7 I hate all Boets and Bainters.

John Campbell *Lives of the Chief Justices* (1849) 'Lord Mansfield'; the remark 'I hate bainting and boetry too!' is attributed to **GEORGE II** in John Ireland *Hogarth Illustrated* (1791)

George II 1683–1760

British monarch, King of Great Britain and Ireland from 1727, husband of **CAROLINE** of Ansbach. On George II: see **LANDOR** 478:6; see also **GEORGE I** 352:7

8 We are come for your good, for all your goods.

speech at Portsmouth, probably 1716, in Joseph Spence *Anecdotes* (ed. J. M. Osborn, 1966) no. 903

9 *Non, j'aurai des maîtresses.*

No, I shall have mistresses.

when Queen **CAROLINE**, *on her deathbed in 1737, urged him to marry again; the Queen replied, 'Ah! mon dieu! cela n'empêche pas* [*Oh, my God! That won't make any difference*]*'*

John Hervey *Memoirs of the Reign of George II* (1848) vol. 2.

10 Mad, is he? Then I hope he will *bite* some of my other generals.

replying to the Duke of Newcastle, who had complained that General **WOLFE** *was a madman*

Henry Beckles Willson *Life and Letters of James Wolfe* (1909) ch. 17

George III 1738–1820

British monarch, King of Great Britain and Ireland from 1760. On George III: see **BAGEHOT** 51:2, **BENTLEY** 71:19, **BYRON** 191:12, **LANDOR** 478:6, **SHELLEY** 746:14, **WALPOLE** 838:9; see also **EDGEWORTH** 303:13

11 Born and educated in this country, I glory in the name of Briton.

The King's Speech on Opening the Session House of Lords, 18 November 1760

12 Was there ever such stuff as great part of Shakespeare? Only one must not say so! But what think you?—what?—Is there not sad stuff? what?—what?

to Fanny Burney, in *Diary and Letters of Madame d'Arblay* vol. 2 (1842) diary, 19 December 1785

George IV 1762–1830

British monarch, King of Great Britain and Ireland from 1820. On George IV: see **AUSTEN** 43:1, **BRUMMELL** 168:16, **HUNT** 421:17, **LANDOR** 478:6; see also **TOASTS** 812:6

13 Harris, I am not well; pray get me a glass of brandy.

on first seeing Caroline of Brunswick, his future wife

Earl of Malmesbury *Diaries and Correspondence* (1844) vol. 3, 5 April 1795

George V 1865–1936

British monarch, King of Great Britain and Ireland from 1910, father of **EDWARD VIII** and **GEORGE VI**, and husband of Queen **MARY**. On George V: see **BETJEMAN** 75:12, **DAWSON OF PENN** 269:6, **NICOLSON** 575:4

14 I venture to allude to the impression which seemed generally to prevail among their brethren across the seas, that the Old Country must wake up if she intends to maintain her old position of pre-eminence in her Colonial trade against foreign competitors.

reprinted in 1911 with the title Wake up, England

speech at Guildhall, 5 December 1901, in Harold Nicolson *King George V* (1952)

15 I have many times asked myself whether there can be more potent advocates of peace upon earth through the years to come than this massed multitude of silent witnesses to the desolation of war.

> message read at Terlincthun Cemetery, Boulogne, 13 May 1922, in *The Times* 15 May 1922

1 After I am dead, the boy will ruin himself in twelve months.

> *of his son, the future* **EDWARD VIII**
>
> Keith Middlemas and John Barnes *Baldwin* (1969) ch. 34

2 *on H. G.* **WELLS***'s comment on 'an alien and uninspiring court':*

I may be uninspiring, but I'll be damned if I'm an alien!

> Sarah Bradford *George VI* (1989); attributed

3 My father was frightened of his mother; I was frightened of my father, and I am damned well going to see to it that my children are frightened of me.

> attributed in Randolph S. Churchill *Lord Derby* (1959), but said by Kenneth Rose in *George V* (1983) to be almost certainly apocryphal; see **MORSHEAD** 561:17

4 Bugger Bognor.

> *on his deathbed in 1936, when someone remarked 'Cheer up, your Majesty, you will soon be at Bognor again.'; alternatively, a comment made in 1929, when it was proposed that the town be named Bognor Regis on account of the king's convalescence there after a serious illness*
>
> probably apocryphal; Kenneth Rose *King George V* (1983) ch. 9

5 How's the Empire?

> *said to his private secretary on the morning of his death*
>
> letter from Lord Wigram, 31 January 1936, in J. E. Wrench *Geoffrey Dawson and Our Times* (1955) ch. 28

George VI 1895–1952

British monarch, King of Great Britain and Northern Ireland from 1936. See also HASKINS 384:3

6 Personally I feel happier now that we have no allies to be polite to and to pamper.

> to Queen Mary, 27 June 1940, in John Wheeler-Bennett *King George VI* (1958) pt. 3, ch. 6

7 Abroad is bloody.

> W. H. Auden *A Certain World* (1970) 'Royalty'; see **MITFORD** 551:9

8 The family firm.

> *description of the British monarchy*
>
> attributed

Dan George 1899–1981

Canadian native chief and actor

9 When the white man came we had the land and they had the bibles; now they have the land and we have the bibles.

> Gerald Walsh *Indians in Transition: An Inquiry Approach* (1971)

Daniel George (Daniel George Bunting)

English writer

10 O Freedom, what liberties are taken in thy name!

> *The Perpetual Pessimist* (1963); see **ROLAND** 666:9

David Lloyd George *see* David Lloyd George

Geronimo *c.*1829–1909

Apache chief

11 Once I moved about like the wind. Now I surrender to you and that is all.

> surrendering to General Crook, 25 March 1886; Dee Brown *Bury My Heart at Wounded Knee* (1970) ch. 17

Ira Gershwin 1896–1983

American songwriter. See also HEYWARD AND GERSHWIN

12 A foggy day in London Town
Had me low and had me down.
I viewed the morning with alarm,
The British Museum had lost its charm.
How long, I wondered, could this thing last?
But the age of miracles hadn't passed,
For, suddenly, I saw you there
And through foggy London town the sun was shining everywhere.

> 'A Foggy Day' (1937 song) in *Damsel in Distress*

13 I don't think I'll fall in love today.

> title of song (1928, from *Treasure Girl*); see **CHESTERTON** 223:25

14 I got rhythm.

> title of song (1930, from *Girl Crazy*)

15 In time the Rockies may crumble,
Gibraltar may tumble,
They're only made of clay,
But our love is here to stay.

> 'Love is Here to Stay' (1938 song) in *The Goldwyn Follies*

16 Holding hands at midnight
'Neath a starry sky,
Nice work if you can get it,
And you can get it if you try.

> 'Nice Work If You Can Get It' (1937 song) in *Damsel in Distress*

17 Ev'ry corner that you turn you meet a notable
With a statement that is eminently quotable!

> 'Of Thee I Sing' (title of song and show, 1931)

18 They all laughed at Christopher Columbus
When he said the world was round
They all laughed when Edison recorded sound
They all laughed at Wilbur and his brother
When they said that man could fly;
They told Marconi
Wireless was a phony—
It's the same old cry!

> 'They All Laughed' (1937 song)

19 A good lyric should be rhymed conversation.

> Philip Furia *Ira Gershwin* (1966)

Gervase of Canterbury c.1141–c.1210

English monastic chronicler

1 Him, therefore, they retained, on account of his lively genius and good reputation, and dismissed the others.
on the appointment of William of Sens as architect of the new work at Canterbury cathedral in 1174
Chronica Gervasii; F. Woodman *The Architectural History of Canterbury Cathedral* (1981)

J. Paul Getty 1892–1976

American industrialist

2 If you can actually count your money, then you are not really a rich man.
in *Observer* 3 November 1957

Giuseppe Giacosa 1847–1906 *and* Luigi Illica 1857–1919

Italian librettists

3 *Che gelida manina.*
Your tiny hand is frozen.
Rodolfo to Mimi
La Bohème (1896) act 1; music by Puccini

Edward Gibbon 1737–94

English historian. On Gibbon: see **BYRON** 186:13, **COLMAN** 244:5, **GLOUCESTER** 360:18

4 The various modes of worship, which prevailed in the Roman world, were all considered by the people as equally true; by the philosopher, as equally false; and by the magistrate, as equally useful. And thus toleration produced not only mutual indulgence, but even religious concord.
The Decline and Fall of the Roman Empire (1776–88) ch. 2

5 In elective monarchies, the vacancy of the throne is a moment big with danger and mischief.
The Decline and Fall of the Roman Empire (1776–88) ch. 3

6 History . . . is, indeed, little more than the register of the crimes, follies, and misfortunes of mankind.
The Decline and Fall of the Roman Empire (1776–88) ch. 3; see **VOLTAIRE** 834:10

7 Twenty-two acknowledged concubines, and a library of sixty-two thousand volumes, attested the variety of his inclinations, and from the productions which he left behind him, it appears that the former as well as the latter were designed for use rather than ostentation. [Footnote] By each of his concubines the younger Gordian left three or four children. His literary productions were by no means contemptible.
The Decline and Fall of the Roman Empire (1776–88) ch. 7

8 All taxes must, at last, fall upon agriculture.
quoting Artaxerxes, in *The Decline and Fall of the Roman Empire* (1776–88) ch. 8

9 Whenever the offence inspires less horror than the punishment, the rigour of penal law is obliged to give way to the common feelings of mankind.
The Decline and Fall of the Roman Empire (1776–88) ch. 14

10 The duty of an historian does not call upon him to interpose his private judgement in this nice and important controversy.
The Decline and Fall of the Roman Empire (1776–88) ch. 15

11 Corruption, the most infallible symptom of constitutional liberty.
The Decline and Fall of the Roman Empire (1776–88) ch. 21

12 The courage of a soldier is found to be the cheapest and most common quality of human nature.
The Decline and Fall of the Roman Empire (1776–1788) ch. 25

13 In every deed of mischief he had a heart to resolve, a head to contrive, and a hand to execute.
of Comnenus
The Decline and Fall of the Roman Empire (1776–88) ch. 48; see **CLARENDON** 233:6

14 Our sympathy is cold to the relation of distant misery.
The Decline and Fall of the Roman Empire (1776–88) ch. 49

15 There is nothing perhaps more adverse to nature and reason than to hold in obedience remote countries and foreign nations in opposition to their inclination and interest.
The Decline and Fall of the Roman Empire (1776–88) ch. 49

16 Persuasion is the resource of the feeble; and the feeble can seldom persuade.
The Decline and Fall of the Roman Empire (1776–88) ch. 68

17 All that is human must retrograde if it does not advance.
The Decline and Fall of the Roman Empire (1776–88) ch. 71

18 The satirist may laugh, the philosopher may preach, but Reason herself will respect the prejudices and habits which have been consecrated by the experience of mankind.
Memoirs of My Life (1796) ch. 1

19 To the University of Oxford I acknowledge no obligation; and she will as cheerfully renounce me for a son, as I am willing to disclaim her for a mother. I spent fourteen months at Magdalen College: they proved the fourteen months the most idle and unprofitable of my whole life.
Memoirs of My Life (1796) ch. 3

20 Their dull and deep potations excused the brisk intemperance of youth.
on the dons at Oxford
Memoirs of My Life (1796) ch. 3

21 Dr— well remembered that he had a salary to receive, and only forgot that he had a duty to perform.
Memoirs of My Life (1796) ch. 3

22 It was here that I suspended my religious inquiries (aged 17).
Memoirs of My Life (1796) ch. 4

23 I saw and loved.
Memoirs of My Life (1796) ch. 4

1 I sighed as a lover, I obeyed as a son.
  Memoirs of My Life (1796) ch. 4 n.

2 Crowds without company, and dissipation without pleasure.
  of London
  Memoirs of My Life (1796) ch. 5

3 The captain of the Hampshire grenadiers . . . has not been useless to the historian of the Roman empire.
  of his own army service
  Memoirs of My Life (1796) ch. 5

4 It was at Rome, on the fifteenth of October, 1764, as I sat musing amidst the ruins of the Capitol, while the barefoot friars were singing vespers in the Temple of Jupiter, that the idea of writing the decline and fall of the city first started to my mind.
  Memoirs of My Life (1796) ch. 6 n.

5 I will not dissemble the first emotions of joy on the recovery of my freedom, and, perhaps, the establishment of my fame. But my pride was soon humbled, and a sober melancholy was spread over my mind, by the idea that I had taken an everlasting leave of an old and agreeable companion, and that whatsoever might be the future date of my History, the life of the historian must be short and precarious.
  on the completion of The Decline and Fall of the Roman Empire
  Memoirs of My Life (1796) ch. 8

6 My English text is chaste, and all licentious passages are left in the obscurity of a learned language.
  parodied as 'decent obscurity' in the Anti-Jacobin, 1797–8
  Memoirs of My Life (1796) ch. 8

7 The abbreviation of time, and the failure of hope, will always tinge with a browner shade the evening of life.
  Memoirs of My Life (1796) ch. 8

Orlando Gibbons 1583–1625
English organist and composer

8 The silver swan, who, living had no note,
  When death approached unlocked her silent throat.
  The First Set of Madrigals and Motets of Five Parts (1612) 'The Silver Swan'

Stella Gibbons 1902–89
English novelist

9 When the sukebind hangs heavy from the wains.
  Cold Comfort Farm (1932) ch. 5

10 Something nasty in the woodshed.
  Cold Comfort Farm (1932) ch. 10

Wolcott Gibbs 1902–58
American critic

11 Backward ran sentences until reeled the mind.
  satirizing the style of Time *magazine*
  in *New Yorker* 28 November 1936 'Time . . . Fortune . . . Life . . . Luce'

Kahlil Gibran 1883–1931
Lebanese-born American writer and painter

12 Are you a politician who says to himself: 'I will use my country for my own benefit'? . . . Or are you a devoted patriot, who whispers in the ear of his inner self: 'I love to serve my country as a faithful servant.'
  The New Frontier (1931), translated by Anthony R. Ferris in *The Voice of the Master* (1958); see **KENNEDY** 460:10

13 And ever has it been that love knows not its own depth until the hour of separation.
  The Prophet (1923) 'The Coming of the Ship'

14 Your children are not your children.
  They are the sons and daughters of Life's longing for itself.
  They came through you but not from you
  And though they are with you yet they belong not to you.
  You may give them your love but not your thoughts,
  For they have their own thoughts.
  You may house their bodies but not their souls.
  The Prophet (1923) 'On Children'

15 You shall be together when the white wings of death scatter your days.
  Ay, you shall be together even in the silent memory of God.
  But let there be spaces in your togetherness,
  And let the winds of the heavens dance between you.
  The Prophet (1923) 'On Marriage'

16 Work is love made visible.
  The Prophet (1923) 'On Work'

17 An exaggeration is a truth that has lost its temper.
  Sand and Foam (1926)

Wilfrid Wilson Gibson 1878–1962
English poet

18 Nor feel the heart-break in the heart of things.
  'Lament' (1918)

André Gide 1869–1951
French novelist and critic

19 In the realm of the emotions, the real is indistinguishable from the imaginary.
  The Counterfeiters (1925) pt. 1, ch. 8

20 The whole effect of Christianity was to transfer the drama onto the moral plane.
  The Counterfeiters (1925) pt. 1, ch. 13 (tr. Dorothy Bussy)

1 One doesn't discover new lands without consenting to lose sight of the shore for a very long time.
The Counterfeiters (1925) pt. 3, ch. 15 (tr. Dorothy Bussy)

2 Oh, if only we could lean over the soul we love and see as in a mirror the image we cast there!
La Porte Étroite (Strait is the Gate, 1909) pt. 2, translated by Dorothy Bussy

3 Ah, this, that we call happiness, how intimate a part of the soul it is, and of what little importance are the outside elements which seem to go to its making!
La Porte Étroite (Strait is the Gate, 1909) pt. 5, translated by Dorothy Bussy

4 True kindness presupposes the faculty of imagining as one's own the sufferings and joys of others.
Pretexts (1959) 'Portraits and Aphorisms'

5 In life one corrects *oneself*—one improves *oneself*—so people say; but one can't correct what one *does*. It's the power of revising that makes writing such a colourless affair.
The Vatican Cellars (1914) bk. 2, ch. 6, translated by Dorothy Bussy

6 The great secret of Stendhal, his great shrewdness, consisted in writing *at once* . . . thought charged with emotion.
Journal (1939) vol. 3, 3 September 1937 (translated by Justin O'Brien)

7 Hugo—alas!
when asked who was the greatest 19th-century poet
Claude Martin *La Maturité d'André Gide* (1977)

Humphrey Gilbert *c.*1537–83

English explorer

8 We are as near to heaven by sea as by land!
Richard Hakluyt *Third and Last Volume of the Voyages . . . of the English Nation* (1600); see **ELSTON** 314:6

W. S. Gilbert (Sir William Schwenck Gilbert)

1836–1911

English writer of comic and satirical verse, best known as a librettist who collaborated on light operas with the composer Sir Arthur Sullivan. On Gilbert: see EPITAPHS 318:11

9 Then they began to sing
That extremely lovely thing,
'*Scherzando! ma non troppo ppp.*'
The 'Bab' Ballads (1869) 'Story of Prince Agib'

10 That celebrated,
Cultivated,
Underrated
Nobleman,
The Duke of Plaza Toro!
The Gondoliers (1889) act 1

11 Of that there is no manner of doubt—
No probable, possible shadow of doubt—
No possible doubt whatever.
The Gondoliers (1889) act 1

12 But the privilege and pleasure
That we treasure beyond measure
Is to run on little errands for the Ministers of State.
The Gondoliers (1889) act 2

13 Take a pair of sparkling eyes,
Hidden, ever and anon,
In a merciful eclipse.
The Gondoliers (1889) act 2

14 When every one is somebodee,
Then no one's anybody.
The Gondoliers (1889) act 2

15 Bow, bow, ye lower middle classes!
Bow, bow, ye tradesmen, bow, ye masses.
Iolanthe (1882) act 1

16 The Law is the true embodiment
Of everything that's excellent.
It has no kind of fault or flaw,
And I, my Lords, embody the Law.
Iolanthe (1882) act 1

17 Hearts just as pure and fair
May beat in Belgrave Square
As in the lowly air
Of Seven Dials.
Iolanthe (1882) act 1

18 I often think it's comical
How Nature always does contrive
That every boy and every gal,
That's born into the world alive,
Is either a little Liberal,
Or else a little Conservative!
Iolanthe (1882) act 2

19 When in that House MPs divide,
If they've a brain and cerebellum too,
They have to leave that brain outside,
And vote just as their leaders tell 'em to.
Iolanthe (1882) act 2

20 The prospect of a lot
Of dull MPs in close proximity,
All thinking for themselves is what
No man can face with equanimity.
Iolanthe (1882) act 2

21 The House of Peers, throughout the war,
Did nothing in particular,
And did it very well.
Iolanthe (1882) act 2

22 When you're lying awake with a dismal headache, and repose is taboo'd by anxiety,
I conceive you may use any language you choose to indulge in, without impropriety.
Iolanthe (1882) act 2

23 For you dream you are crossing the Channel, and tossing about in a steamer from Harwich—
Which is something between a large bathing machine and a very small second class carriage.
Iolanthe (1882) act 2

24 The shares are a penny, and ever so many are taken by Rothschild and Baring,

And just as a few are allotted to you, you awake
with a shudder despairing.
Iolanthe (1882) act 2

1 A wandering minstrel I—
A thing of shreds and patches.
Of ballads, songs and snatches,
And dreamy lullaby!
The Mikado (1885) act 1; see **SHAKESPEARE** 703:16

2 I can trace my ancestry back to a protoplasmal
primordial atomic globule. Consequently, my
family pride is something in-conceivable. I can't
help it. I was born sneering.
The Mikado (1885) act 1

3 As some day it may happen that a victim must
be found,
I've got a little list—I've got a little list
Of society offenders who might well be under
ground
And who never would be missed—who never
would be missed!
The Mikado (1885) act 1

4 The idiot who praises, with enthusiastic tone,
All centuries but this, and every country but his
own.
The Mikado (1885) act 1; see **CANNING** 197:1, **DISRAELI** 285:7,
OVERBURY 589:15

5 Three little maids from school are we,
Pert as a schoolgirl well can be,
Filled to the brim with girlish glee.
The Mikado (1885) act 1

6 Three little maids who, all unwary,
Come from a ladies' seminary.
The Mikado (1885) act 1

7 Modified rapture!
The Mikado (1885) act 1

8 Awaiting the sensation of a short, sharp shock,
From a cheap and chippy chopper on a big black
block.
The Mikado (1885) act 1

9 Here's a how-de-doo!
The Mikado (1885) act 2

10 Here's a state of things!
The Mikado (1885) act 2

11 My object all sublime
I shall achieve in time—
To let the punishment fit the crime—
The punishment fit the crime.
The Mikado (1885) act 2

12 I have a left shoulder-blade that is a miracle of
loveliness. People come miles to see it. My right
elbow has a fascination that few can resist.
The Mikado (1885) act 2

13 Something lingering, with boiling oil in it, I
fancy.
The Mikado (1885) act 2

14 Merely corroborative detail, intended to give
artistic verisimilitude to an otherwise bald and
unconvincing narrative.
The Mikado (1885) act 2

15 The flowers that bloom in the spring,
Tra la,
Have nothing to do with the case.
The Mikado (1885) act 2

16 On a tree by a river a little tom-tit
Sang 'Willow, titwillow, titwillow!'
And I said to him, 'Dicky-bird, why do you sit
Singing Willow, titwillow, titwillow?'
The Mikado (1885) act 2

17 There's a fascination frantic
In a ruin that's romantic;
Do you think you are sufficiently decayed?
The Mikado (1885) act 2

18 If you're anxious for to shine in the high
aesthetic line as a man of culture rare.
Patience (1881) act 1

19 The meaning doesn't matter if it's only idle
chatter of a transcendental kind.
Patience (1881) act 1

20 An attachment à la Plato for a bashful young
potato, or a not too French French bean!
Patience (1881) act 1

21 If you walk down Piccadilly with a poppy or a
lily in your medieval hand.
Patience (1881) act 1

22 Francesca di Rimini, miminy, piminy,
Je-ne-sais-quoi young man!
Patience (1881) act 2

23 A greenery-yallery, Grosvenor Gallery,
Foot-in-the-grave young man!
Patience (1881) act 2

24 I'm called Little Buttercup—dear Little
Buttercup,
Though I could never tell why.
HMS Pinafore (1878) act 1

25 What, never?
No, never!
What, *never*?
Hardly ever!
HMS Pinafore (1878) act 1

26 Though 'Bother it' I may
Occasionally say,
I never use a big, big D—
HMS Pinafore (1878) act 1

27 And so do his sisters, and his cousins and his
aunts!
His sisters and his cousins,
Whom he reckons up by dozens,
And his aunts!
HMS Pinafore (1878) act 1

28 I cleaned the windows and I swept the floor,
And I polished up the handle of the big front
door.
I polished up that handle so carefullee
That now I am the Ruler of the Queen's Navee!
HMS Pinafore (1878) act 1

1 I always voted at my party's call,
And I never thought of thinking for myself at
all.
HMS Pinafore (1878) act 1

2 Stick close to your desks and never go to sea,
And you all may be Rulers of the Queen's
Navee!
HMS Pinafore (1878) act 1

3 He is an Englishman!
For he himself has said it,
And it's greatly to his credit,
That he is an Englishman!
HMS Pinafore (1878) act 2

4 For he might have been a Roosian,
A French, or Turk, or Proosian,
Or perhaps Ital-ian!
But in spite of all temptations
To belong to other nations,
He remains an Englishman!
HMS Pinafore (1878) act 2

5 It is, it is a glorious thing
To be a Pirate King.
The Pirates of Penzance (1879) act 1

6 I'm very good at integral and differential
calculus,
I know the scientific names of beings
animalculous;
In short, in matters vegetable, animal, and
mineral,
I am the very model of a modern Major-
General.
The Pirates of Penzance (1879) act 1

7 About binomial theorem I'm teeming with a lot
of news,
With many cheerful facts about the square on
the hypotenuse.
The Pirates of Penzance (1879) act 1

8 When constabulary duty's to be done,
A policeman's lot is not a happy one.
The Pirates of Penzance (1879) act 2

9 Man is Nature's sole mistake!
Princess Ida (1884) act 2

10 He combines the manners of a Marquis with the
morals of a Methodist.
Ruddigore (1887) act 1

11 Some word that teems with hidden
meaning—like Basingstoke.
Ruddigore (1887) act 2

12 This particularly rapid, unintelligible patter
Isn't generally heard, and if it is it doesn't
matter.
Ruddigore (1887) act 2

13 I was a pale young curate then.
The Sorcerer (1877) act 1

14 She may very well pass for forty-three
In the dusk with a light behind her!
Trial by Jury (1875)

15 'Tis ever thus with simple folk—an accepted wit
has but to say 'Pass the mustard', and they roar
their ribs out!
The Yeoman of the Guard (1888) act 2

Eric Gill 1882–1940
English sculptor, engraver, and typographer

16 That state is a state of slavery in which a man
does what he likes to do in his spare time and in
his working time that which is required of him.
Art-nonsense and Other Essays (1929) 'Slavery and Freedom';
see **COLLINGWOOD** 243:1

Andrew Gilligan 1968–
English journalist

17 I have spoken to a British official who was
involved in the preparation of the dossier, and
he told me that until the week before it was
published, the draft dossier produced by the
intelligence services added little to what was
already publicly known. He said: [Voiceover]: 'It
was transformed in the week before it was
published, to make it sexier'.
BBC Radio 4 *Today* programme, 29 May 2003; in *Guardian* 27
June 2003

Charlotte Perkins Gilman 1860–1935
American writer and feminist

18 The labour of women in the house, certainly
enables men to produce more wealth than they
otherwise could; and in this way women are
economic factors in society. But so are horses.
Women and Economics (1898) ch. 1

19 There is no female mind. The brain is not an
organ of sex. As well speak of a female liver.
Women and Economics (1898) ch. 8

20 Work first—love next.
letter to G. Houghton Gilman, 26 July 1899, in Mary A. Hill
(ed.) *A Journey from Within: the love letters of Charlotte Perkins
Gilman* (1995)

Allen Ginsberg 1926–97
American poet and novelist

21 What if someone gave a war & Nobody came?
Life would ring the bells of Ecstasy and Forever
be Itself again.
'Graffiti' (1972); see **FILM TITLES** 331:12, **SANDBURG** 680:7

22 I saw the best minds of my generation destroyed
by madness, starving hysterical naked,
dragging themselves through the negro streets at
dawn looking for an angry fix,
angelheaded hipsters burning for the ancient
heavenly connection to the starry dynamo in
the machinery of the night.
Howl (1956)

23 What thoughts I have of you tonight, Walt
Whitman, for I walked
down the sidestreets under the trees with a
headache self-

conscious looking at the full moon.
'A Supermarket in California' (1956)

1 What peaches and what penumbras! Whole families shopping at night! Aisles full of husbands! Wives in the avocados, babies in the tomatoes!—and you, Garcia Lorca what were you doing down by the watermelons?
'A Supermarket in California' (1956)

2 Ah, dear father, graybeard, lonely old courage-teacher, what
America did you have when Charon quit poling his ferry and you
got out on a smoking bank and stood watching the boat
disappear on the black waters of Lethe?
on Walt **WHITMAN**
'A Supermarket in California' (1956)

3 I'm tired, and I have to go to sleep.
last words, before lapsing into a final coma
in *Athens News* 9 April 1997

Nikki Giovanni 1943–

American poet

4 it's a sex object if you're pretty
and no love
or love and no sex if you're fat
'Woman Poem' (1970)

George Gipp 1895–1920

American footballer

5 Tell them to go in there with all they've got and win just one for the Gipper.
the catchphrase 'Win one for the Gipper' was later used by Ronald **REAGAN**, *who played Gipp in the 1940 film* Knute Rockne, All American
Knut Rockne 'Gipp the Great' in *Collier's* 22 November 1930

Giraldus Cambrensis (Gerald of Wales)

*c.*1146–*c.*1223

Welsh cleric and historian

6 The well of poisons brims over in the East.
The History and Topography of Ireland pt. 1, ch. 32

7 The Isle of Man . . . is equidistant from the north of Ireland and Britain. There was a great controversy in antiquity concerning the question, to which of the two countries should the island properly belong? . . . All agreed that since it allowed poisonous reptiles to live in it, it should belong to Britain.
The History and Topography of Ireland pt. 2, ch. 48

Jean Giraudoux 1882–1944

French dramatist

8 As soon as war is declared it will be impossible to hold the poets back. Rhyme is still the most effective drum.
La Guerre de Troie n'aura pas lieu (1935) act 2, sc. 4 (translated by Christopher Fry as *Tiger at the Gates*, 1955)

9 All of us here know there's no better way of exercising the imagination than the study of law. No poet ever interpreted nature as freely as a lawyer interprets the truth.
La Guerre de Troie n'aura pas lieu (1935) act 2, sc. 5

George Gissing 1857–1903

English novelist

10 Mr Quarmby laughed in a peculiar way, which was the result of long years of mirth-subdual in the Reading-room.
New Grub Street (1891)

Rudolph Giuliani 1944–

American Republican politician, Mayor of New York 1993–2001

11 The number of casualties will be more than any of us can bear.
in the aftermath of the terrorist attacks which destroyed the World Trade Center in New York, and damaged the Pentagon, 11 September 2001
in *Times* 12 September 2001

Edna Gladney

American philanthropist

12 There are no illegitimate children, only illegitimate parents.
MGM paid her a large sum for the line for the 1941 film based on her life, 'Blossoms in the Dust'
A. Loos *Kiss Hollywood Good-Bye* (1978)

W. E. Gladstone 1809–98

British Liberal statesman. Prime Minister 1868–74, 1880–5, 1886, 1892–4. On Gladstone: see ANONYMOUS 17:14, BAGEHOT 50:3, CHURCHILL 228:20, CHURCHILL 228:21, CHURCHILL 228:23, DISRAELI 285:5, DISRAELI 285:9, LABOUCHERE 474:14, SELLAR AND YEATMAN 692:7, VICTORIA 827:10, VICTORIA 827:12

13 Ireland, Ireland! that cloud in the west, that coming storm.
letter to his wife, 12 October 1845

14 This is the negation of God erected into a system of Government.
A Letter to the Earl of Aberdeen on the State Prosecutions of the Neapolitan Government (1851)

15 Finance is, as it were, the stomach of the country, from which all the other organs take their tone.
article on finance, 1858, in H. C. G. Matthew Gladstone 1809–1874 (1986) ch. 5

16 I am come among you 'unmuzzled'.
speech in Manchester, 18 July 1865, after his parliamentary defeat at Oxford University; see **PALMERSTON** 595:6
John Morley *Life of Gladstone* (1903) vol. 2

17 You cannot fight against the future. Time is on our side.
speech on the Reform Bill, in House of Commons, 27 April 1866

1 My mission is to pacify Ireland.
on receiving news that he was to form his first cabinet, 1st December 1868
> H. C. G. Matthew *Gladstone 1809–1874* (1986) ch. 5

2 Let the Turks now carry away their abuses in the only possible manner, namely by carrying off themselves . . . one and all, bag and baggage, shall I hope clear out from the province they have desolated and profaned.
Bulgarian Horrors and the Question of the East (1876); see **DISRAELI** 285:6

3 [An] Established Clergy will always be a Tory Corps d'Armée.
letter to Bishop Goodwin, 8 September 1881

4 It is perfectly true that these gentlemen wish to march through rapine to disintegration and dismemberment of the Empire, and, I am sorry to say, even to the placing of different parts of the Empire in direct hostility one with the other.
on the Irish Land League
> speech at Knowsley, 27 October 1881, in *The Times*, 28 October 1881

5 There never was a Churchill from John of Marlborough down that had either morals or principles.
in conversation in 1882, recorded by Captain R. V. Briscoe; R. F. Foster Lord Randolph Churchill (1981)

6 Ideal perfection is not the true basis of English legislation. We look at the attainable; we look at the practical, and we have too much English sense to be drawn away by those sanguine delineations of what might possibly be attained in Utopia, from a path which promises to enable us to effect great good for the people of England.
speech on the Reform Bill, in House of Commons, 28 February 1884

7 I would tell them of my own intention to keep my counsel . . . and I will venture to recommend them, as an old Parliamentary hand, to do the same.
speech, House of Commons, 21 January 1886

8 This, if I understand it, is one of those golden moments of our history, one of those opportunities which may come and may go, but which rarely returns.
speech on the Second Reading of the Home Rule Bill, in House of Commons, 7 June 1886

9 I will venture to say, that upon the one great class of subjects, the largest and the most weighty of them all, where the leading and determining considerations that ought to lead to a conclusion are truth, justice, and humanity—upon these, gentlemen, all the world over, I will back the masses against the classes.
speech in Liverpool, 28 June 1886, in The Times 29 June 1886

10 The blubbering Cabinet.
of the colleagues who wept at his final Cabinet meeting
> diary, 1 March 1894; note

11 What that Sicilian mule was to me, I have been to the Queen.
of a mule on which Gladstone rode, which he 'could neither love nor like', although it had rendered him 'much valuable service'
> memorandum, 20 March 1894; H. C. G. Matthew *The Gladstone Diaries* vol. 8 (1994)

12 The God-fearing and God-sustaining University of Oxford. I served her, perhaps mistakenly, but to the best of my ability.
farewell message, just before his death, May 1898
> Roy Jenkins *Gladstone* (1995)

13 I absorb the vapour and return it as a flood.
on public speaking
> Lord Riddell *Some Things That Matter* (1927 ed.)

14 It is not a Life at all. It is a Reticence, in three volumes.
on J. W. Cross's Life of George Eliot
> E. F. Benson *As We Were* (1930) ch. 6

15 [Money should] fructify in the pockets of the people.
> H. G. C. Matthew *Gladstone 1809–1874* (1986)

Thomas Glascock
American politician

16 No, sir! I am his adversary, and choose not to subject myself to his fascination.
when Thomas Glascock of Georgia took his seat in the US Senate, a mutual friend expressed the wish to introduce him to Henry CLAY of Virginia
> Robert V. Remini *Henry Clay* (1991) ch. 6

Hannah Glasse fl. 1747
English cook

17 Take your hare when it is cased.
cased = skinned
> *The Art of Cookery Made Plain and Easy* (1747) ch. 1; see **PROVERBS** 632:18

William Henry, Duke of Gloucester
1743–1805
British prince, brother of **GEORGE III**

18 Another damned, thick, square book! Always scribble, scribble, scribble! Eh! Mr Gibbon?
> Henry Best *Personal and Literary Memorials* (1829); D. M. Low *Edward Gibbon* (1937) notes alternative attributions to the Duke of Cumberland and King George III

Jean-Luc Godard 1930–
French film director

19 Photography is truth. The cinema is truth 24 times per second.
> *Le Petit Soldat* (1960 film)

20 *Ce n'est pas une image juste, c'est juste une image.*
This is not a just image, it is just an image.
> Colin MacCabe *Godard: Images, Sounds, Politics* (1980)

21 GEORGES FRANJU: Movies should have a beginning, a middle and an end.

JEAN-LUC GODARD: Certainly, but not necessarily in that order.
> in *Time* 14 September 1981; see **ARISTOTLE** 27:20

A. D. Godley 1856–1925

English classicist

1 What is this that roareth thus?
Can it be a Motor Bus?
Yes, the smell and hideous hum
Indicat Motorem Bum!...
How shall wretches live like us
Cincti Bis Motoribus?
Domine, defende nos
Contra hos Motores Bos!
> letter to C. R. L. Fletcher, 10 January 1914, in *Reliquiae* (1926) vol. 1

Sidney Godolphin 1610–43

English poet

2 Or love me less, or love me more
And play not with my liberty;
Either take all, or all restore,
Bind me at least, or set me free.
> 'Song'

William Godwin 1756–1836

English social philosopher and novelist; husband of Mary **WOLLSTONECRAFT** and father of Mary **SHELLEY**

3 Perfectibility is one of the most unequivocal characteristics of the human species.
> *An Enquiry concerning the Principles of Political Justice* (1793) bk. 1, ch. 2

4 Love of our country is another of those specious illusions, which have been invented by impostors in order to render the multitude the blind instruments of their crooked designs.
> *An Enquiry concerning the Principles of Political Justice* (1793) bk. 5, ch. 16

5 It is a most mistaken way of teaching men to feel they are brothers, by imbuing their mind with perpetual hatred.
> *on the subject of war*
> *An Enquiry concerning the Principles of Political Justice* (1793) bk. 5, ch. 18

6 What . . . can be more shameless than for society to make an example of those whom she has goaded to the breach of order, instead of amending her own institutions which, by straining order into tyranny, produced the mischief?
> *on the penal laws*
> *An Enquiry concerning the Principles of Political Justice* (1793) bk. 7, ch. 3

Joseph Goebbels 1897–1945

German Nazi leader

7 We can manage without butter but not, for example, without guns. If we are attacked we can only defend ourselves with guns not with butter.
> speech in Berlin, 17 January 1936, in *Deutsche Allgemeine Zeitung* 18 January 1936; see **GOERING** 361:9

8 Making noise is an effective means of opposition.
> Ernest K. Bramsted *Goebbels and National Socialist Propaganda 1925-45* (1965)

Hermann Goering 1893–1946

German Nazi leader. See also **JOHST** 445:4

9 We have no butter . . . but I ask you—would you rather have butter or guns? . . . preparedness makes us powerful. Butter merely makes us fat.
> speech at Hamburg, 1936, in W. Frischauer *Goering* (1951) ch. 10; see **GOEBBELS** 361:7

10 I herewith commission you to carry out all preparations with regard to . . . a *total solution* of the Jewish question in those territories of Europe which are under German influence.
> instructions to Heydrich, 31 July 1941, in W. L. Shirer *The Rise and Fall of the Third Reich* (1962) bk. 5, ch. 27; see **HEYDRICH** 397:17

Johann Wolfgang von Goethe
1749–1832

German poet, novelist, and dramatist

11 *Was man in der Jugend wünscht,*
hat man im Alter die Fülle.
What one wishes for in youth, one has in abundance in old age.
> *Dictung und Wahrheit* pt. 2 (Poetry and Truth, 1812) motto

12 *Glücklich allein*
Ist die Seele, die liebt.
Only the soul that loves is happy.
> *Egmont* (1788) 'Clärchens Lied'

13 *Es irrt der Mensch, so lang er strebt.*
Man will err while yet he strives.
> *Faust* pt. 1 (1808) 'Prolog im Himmel'

14 *Welch Schauspiel! Aber ach, ein Schauspiel nur!*
What a show! But alas, only a show!
> *Faust* pt. 1 (1808) 'Nacht'

15 *Was du ererbt von deinen Vätern hast,*
Erwirb es, um es zu besitzen.
What you have inherited from your fathers
Work on, that you may possess it.
> *Faust* pt. 1 (1808) 'Nacht'

16 *Zwei Seelen wohnen, ach! in meiner Brust.*
Two souls dwell, alas! in my breast.
> *Faust* pt. 1 (1808) 'Vor dem Thor'

17 *Ich bin der Geist der stets verneint.*
I am the spirit that always denies.
> *Faust* pt. 1 (1808) 'Studierzimmer'

18 *Der Teufel ist ein egoist.*
The devil is an egotist.
> *Faust* pt. 1 (1808) 'Studierzimmer'

19 *Entbehren sollst Du! sollst entbehren!*
Das ist der ewige Gesang.

Deny yourself! You must deny yourself!
That is the song that never ends.
Faust pt. 1 (1808) 'Studierzimmer'

1 *Grau, teurer Freund, ist alle Theorie*
Und grün des Lebens goldner Baum.

All theory, dear friend, is grey, but the golden
tree of actual life springs ever green.
Faust pt. 1 (1808) 'Studierzimmer'

2 *Sobald du' dir vertraust, sobald weisst du zu leben.*

Just trust yourself and you'll learn the art of
living.
Faust pt. 1 (1808) 'Studierzimmer'

3 *O nein! die Kraft ist schwach,*
allein die Lust ist gross.

O no! the strength is weak but the desire is
great.
Faust pt. 1 (1808) 'Auerbachs Keller in Leipzig'

4 *Meine Ruh' ist hin,*
Mein Herz ist schwer.

My peace is gone,
My heart is heavy.
Faust pt. 1 (1808) 'Gretchen am Spinnrad'

5 *Das ist der Weisheit letzter Schluss:*
Nur der verdient sich Freiheit wie das Leben,
Der täglich sie erobern muss.

This is wisdom's final thought:
Freedom alone he earns as well as life
Who day by day must conquer them anew.
Faust pt. 2 (1832) act 5 'Grosser Vorhof des Palastes'

6 *Die Tat ist alles, nichts der Ruhm.*

The deed is all, the glory nothing.
Faust pt. 2 (1832) 'Hochgebirg'

7 *Das Ewig-Weibliche zieht uns hinan.*

Eternal Woman draws us upward.
Faust pt. 2 (1832) 'Hochgebirg' closing words

8 *Du musst herrschen und gewinnen,*
Oder dienen und verlieren,
Leiden oder triumphieren
Amboss oder Hammer sein.

You must be master and win, or serve and lose,
grieve or triumph, be the anvil or the hammer.
Der Gross-Cophta (1791) act 2

9 *Wenn es eine Freude ist das Gute zu geniessen, so ist*
es eine grössere das Bessere zu empfinden, und in der
Kunst ist das Beste gut genug.

Since it is a joy to have the benefit of what is
good, it is a greater one to experience what is
better, and in art the best is good enough.
Italienische Reise (1816–17) 3 March 1787

10 *Der Aberglaube ist die Poesie des Lebens.*

Superstition is the poetry of life.
Maximen und Reflexionen (1819) 'Literatur und Sprache' no.
908

11 *Wer fremde Sprachen nicht kennt, weiss nichts von*
seiner eigenen.

He who does not know foreign languages knows
nothing of his own.
Maximen und Reflexionen (1821) pt. 2, no. 91

12 *Es bildet ein Talent sich in der Stille,*
Sich ein Charakter in dem Strom der Welt.

Talent develops in quiet places, character in the
full current of human life.
Torquato Tasso (1790) act 1, sc. 2

13 *Die Wahlverwandtschaften.*

Elective affinities.
title of novel (1809)

14 *Ach, ich bin des Treibens müde!*

Oh, how I am tired of the struggle!
Wandrers Nachtlied (1821)

15 *Über allen Gipfeln*
Ist Ruh'.

Over all the mountain tops is peace.
Wandrers Nachtlied (1821)

16 *Denn niemand glaube die ersten Eindrücke der*
Jugend verwinden zu können.

Let no one think that he can conquer the first
impressions of his youth.
Wilhelm Meisters Lehrjare (1795–6) bk. 2, ch. 9 (translated by
Carlyle)

17 *Wer nie sein Brot mit Tränen ass,*
Wer nie die kummervollen Nächte
Auf seinem Bette weinend sass,
Der kennt euch nicht, ihr himmlischen Mächte.

Who never ate his bread in sorrow,
Who never spent the darksome hours
Weeping and watching for the morrow
He knows ye not, ye heavenly powers.
Wilhelm Meisters Lehrjahre (1795–6) bk. 2, ch. 13 (translated by
Carlyle)

18 *Kennst du das Land, wo die Zitronen blühn?*
Im dunklen Laub die Gold-Orangen glühn,
Ein sanfter Wind vom blauen Himmel weht,
Die Myrte still und hoch der Lorbeer steht—
Kennst du es wohl?
Dahin! Dahin
Möcht ich mit dir, o mein Geliebter, ziehn!

Know you the land where the lemon-trees
bloom? In the dark foliage the gold oranges
glow; the myrtle is still and the laurel stands
tall—do you know it well? There, there, I would
go, O my beloved, with thee!
Wilhelm Meisters Lehrjahre (1795–6) bk. 3, ch. 1

19 If I love you, what does that matter to you!
Wilhelm Meisters Lehrjahre (1795–6) bk. 4, ch. 9

20 *Nur, wer die Sehnsucht kennt,*
Weiss, was ich leide!

None but the lonely heart
Knows what I suffer!
Wilhelm Meisters Lehrjahre (1795–6) bk. 4, ch. 11 'Mignons
Lied'

21 *Wenn wir, sagtest Du, die Menschen nur nehmen,*
wie sie sind, so machen wir sie schlechter; wenn wir
sie behandeln, als wären sie, was sie sein sollten so
bringen wir sie dahin, wohin sie zu bringen sind.

When we take people, thou wouldst say, merely
as they are, we make them worse; when we

treat them as if they were what they should be, we improve them as far as they can be improved.

sometimes quoted as 'Treat a man as he is, and that is what he remains. Treat a man as he can be, and that is what he becomes'
    Wilhelm Meisters Lehrjare (1795–6) bk. 8, ch. 4, translated by Carlyle

1 *Ohne Hast, aber ohne Rast.*
Without haste, but without rest.
    Zahme Xenien (with Schiller, 1796) sect. 2, no. 6, l. 281

2 *Willst du ins Unendliche schreiten,*
Geh nur im Endlichen nach allen Seiten.
If you wish to advance into the infinite, explore the finite in all directions.
    epigram, in David Luke *Goethe: Selected Verse* (1964)

3 For the rest of it, the last and greatest art is to limit and isolate oneself.
    J. P. Eckermann *Conversations with Goethe in the Last Years of his Life* (1836–48) 20 April 1825

4 Classicism is health, romanticism is disease.
    J. P. Eckermann *Conversations with Goethe in the Last Years of his Life* (1836–48) 2 April 1829

5 I do not know myself, and God forbid that I should.
    J. P. Eckermann *Conversations with Goethe in the Last Years of his Life* (1836–48) 10 April 1829; see **PROVERBS** 637:8

6 *Mehr Licht!*
More light!
    abbreviated version of 'Macht doch den zweiten Fensterladen auch auf, damit mehr Licht hereinkomme [Open the second shutter, so that more light can come in]')
    last words; K. W. Müller *Goethes letzte literarische Thätigkeit* (1832)

Oliver St John Gogarty 1878–1957
Irish writer and surgeon

7 I said, 'It is most extraordinary weather for this time of year!' He replied, 'Ah, it isn't this time of year at all.'
    It Isn't This Time of Year at All (1954)

8 Golden stockings you had on
In the meadow where you ran.
    'Golden Stockings'

9 Only the Lion and the Cock;
As Galen says, withstand Love's shock.
So, dearest, do not think me rude
If I yield now to lassitude,
But sympathize with me. I know
You would not have me roar or crow.
    'After Galen' (1957)

Nikolai Gogol 1809–52
Russian writer

10 As you pass from the tender years of youth into harsh and embittered manhood, make sure you take with you on your journey all the human emotions! Don't leave them on the road, for you will not pick them up afterwards!
    Dead Souls (1842) pt. 1, ch. 6 (translated by David Magarshak)

11 A land that does not like doing things by halves.
    of Russia
    Dead Souls (1842) pt. 1, ch. 11 (translated by David Magarshak)

12 [Are not] you too, Russia, speeding along like a spirited *troika* that nothing can overtake? . . . Everything on earth is flying past, and looking askance, other nations and states draw aside and make way.
    Dead Souls (1842) pt. 1, ch. 11 (translated by David Magarshak)

Isaac Goldberg 1887–1938

13 Diplomacy is to do and say
The nastiest thing in the nicest way.
    in *The Reflex* October 1927

Whoopi Goldberg 1949–
American actress

14 I dislike this idea that if you're a black person in America then you must be called an African-American. I'm not an African. I'm an American. Just call me black, if you want to call me anything.
    in *Irish Times* 25 April 1998 'Quotes of the Week'

William Golding 1911–93
English novelist

15 Nothing is so impenetrable as laughter in a language you don't understand.
    An Egyptian Journal (1985)

16 Anyone who moved through those years without understanding that man produces evil as a bee produces honey, must have been blind or wrong in the head.
    of the Second World War
    The Hot Gates (1965) 'Fable'

Emma Goldman 1869–1940
American anarchist

17 Anarchism, then, really, stands for the liberation of the human mind from the dominion of religion; the liberation of the human body from the dominion of property; liberation from the shackles and restraints of government.
    Anarchism and Other Essays (1910)

Carlo Goldoni 1707–93
Italian dramatist

18 A wise traveller never despises his own country.
    Pamela (1749) act 1, sc. 16

James Goldsmith 1933–97
British financier and politician

19 When you marry your mistress you create a job vacancy.
    marrying Lady Annabel Birley in 1978
    G. Wansell *Tycoon* (1987)

Oliver Goldsmith 1728–74

Irish writer, poet, and dramatist. On Goldsmith: see
EPITAPHS 319:4, **GARRICK** 349:11, **GARRICK** 349:13, **JOHNSON**
441:6

1 Sweet Auburn, loveliest village of the plain.
The Deserted Village (1770) l. 1

2 Ill fares the land, to hast'ning ills a prey,
Where wealth accumulates, and men decay;
Princes and lords may flourish, or may fade;
A breath can make them, as a breath has made;
But a bold peasantry, their country's pride,
When once destroyed, can never be supplied.
The Deserted Village (1770) l. 51

3 How happy he who crowns in shades like these,
A youth of labour with an age of ease.
The Deserted Village (1770) l. 99

4 The loud laugh that spoke the vacant mind.
The Deserted Village (1770) l. 122; see **CHESTERFIELD** 223:8

5 A man he was to all the country dear,
And passing rich with forty pounds a year.
Remote from towns he ran his godly race,
Nor e'er had changed nor wished to change his
place.
The Deserted Village (1770) l. 141

6 Truth from his lips prevailed with double sway,
And fools, who came to scoff, remained to pray.
The Deserted Village (1770) l. 179

7 A man severe he was, and stern to view;
I knew him well, and every truant knew;
Well had the boding tremblers learned to trace
The day's disasters in his morning face;
Full well they laughed with counterfeited glee,
At all his jokes, for many a joke had he.
The Deserted Village (1770) l. 197

8 The village all declared how much he knew;
'Twas certain he could write and cypher too.
The Deserted Village (1770) l. 207

9 In arguing too, the parson owned his skill,
For e'en though vanquished, he could argue still;
While words of learned length, and thund'ring
sound
Amazed the gazing rustics ranged around,
And still they gazed, and still the wonder grew,
That one small head could carry all he knew.
The Deserted Village (1770) l. 211

10 How wide the limits stand
Between a splendid and a happy land.
The Deserted Village (1770) l. 267

11 In all the silent manliness of grief.
The Deserted Village (1770) l. 384

12 I see the rural virtues leave the land.
The Deserted Village (1770) l. 398

13 Thou source of all my bliss, and all my woe,
That found'st me poor at first, and keep'st me
so.
of poetry
The Deserted Village (1770) l. 413

14 Man wants but little here below,
Nor wants that little long.
'Edwin and Angelina, or the Hermit' (1766); see **HOLMES**
403:14, **YOUNG** 876:25

15 The doctor found, when she was dead,—
Her last disorder mortal.
'Elegy on Mrs Mary Blaize' (1759)

16 The man recovered of the bite,
The dog it was that died.
'Elegy on the Death of a Mad Dog' (1766)

17 Our Garrick's a salad; for in him we see
Oil, vinegar, sugar, and saltness agree.
Retaliation (1774) l. 11; see **GARRICK** 349:11

18 Too nice for a statesman, too proud for a wit.
of Edmund **BURKE**
Retaliation (1774) l. 32

19 An abridgement of all that was pleasant in man.
of David **GARRICK**
Retaliation (1774) l. 94

20 On the stage he was natural, simple, affecting;
'Twas only that when he was off he was acting.
of David **GARRICK**
Retaliation (1774) l. 101

21 Of praise a mere glutton, he swallowed what
came,
And the puff of a dunce he mistook it for fame.
of David **GARRICK**
Retaliation (1774) l. 101

22 When they talked of their Raphaels, Correggios,
and stuff,
He shifted his trumpet, and only took snuff.
of Joshua **REYNOLDS**
Retaliation (1774) l. 145

23 Or press the bashful stranger to his food,
And learn the luxury of doing good.
The Traveller (1764) l. 21; see **CRABBE** 258:1, **GARTH** 350:2

24 Such is the patriot's boast, where'er we roam,
His first, best country ever is, at home.
The Traveller (1764) l. 73

25 And honour sinks where commerce long
prevails.
The Traveller (1764) l. 92

26 Pride in their port, defiance in their eye,
I see the lords of human kind pass by.
The Traveller (1764) l. 327

27 Laws grind the poor, and rich men rule the law.
The Traveller (1764) l. 386

28 How small, of all that human hearts endure,
That part which laws or kings can cause or cure!
The Traveller (1764) l. 429; see **JOHNSON** 438:4

29 The true use of speech is not so much to
express our wants as to conceal them.
The Bee no. 3 (20 October 1759) 'On the Use of Language'

30 Friendship is a disinterested commerce between
equals; love, an abject intercourse between
tyrants and slaves.
The Good-Natured Man (1768) act 1

1 Don't let us make imaginary evils, when you know we have so many real ones to encounter.
The Good-Natured Man (1768) act 1

2 Measures not men, have always been my mark.
The Good Natured Man (1768) act 2; see **BURKE** 175:5, **CANNING** 197:5

3 Let schoolmasters puzzle their brain,
With grammar, and nonsense, and learning,
Good liquor, I stoutly maintain,
Gives genius a better discerning.
She Stoops to Conquer (1773) act 1, sc. 1 'Song'

4 The very pink of perfection.
She Stoops to Conquer (1773) act 1

5 I'll be with you in the squeezing of a lemon.
She Stoops to Conquer (1773) act 1

6 Your worship must not tell the story of Ould Grouse in the gun-room.
She Stoops to Conquer (1773) act 2

7 This is Liberty-Hall, gentlemen.
She Stoops to Conquer (1773) act 2

8 The first blow is half the battle.
She Stoops to Conquer (1773) act 2

9 A man who leaves home to mend himself and others is a philosopher; but he who goes from country to country, guided by a blind impulse of curiosity, is a vagabond.
The Citizen of the World (1762)

10 I was ever of opinion, that the honest man who married and brought up a large family, did more service than he who continued single and only talked of population.
The Vicar of Wakefield (1766) ch. 1

11 I . . . chose my wife, as she did her wedding gown, not for a fine glossy surface, but such qualities as would wear well.
The Vicar of Wakefield (1766) ch. 1

12 All our adventures were by the fire-side, and all our migrations from the blue bed to the brown.
The Vicar of Wakefield (1766) ch. 1

13 The virtue which requires to be ever guarded is scarce worth the sentinel.
The Vicar of Wakefield (1766) ch. 5; see **MILTON** 545:24

14 When lovely woman stoops to folly
And finds too late that men betray,
What charm can soothe her melancholy,
What art can wash her guilt away?
The Vicar of Wakefield (1766) ch. 24; see **ELIOT** 311:15

15 There is no arguing with Johnson; for when his pistol misses fire, he knocks you down with the butt end of it.
James Boswell *Life of Samuel Johnson* (1791) 26 October 1769

16 As I take my shoes from the shoemaker, and my coat from the tailor, so I take my religion from the priest.
James Boswell *Life of Samuel Johnson* (1791) 9 April 1773

Barry Goldwater 1909–98
American Republican politician

17 I would remind you that extremism in the defence of liberty is no vice! And let me remind you also that moderation in the pursuit of justice is no virtue!
accepting the presidential nomination, 16 July 1964, in *New York Times* 17 July 1964

Sam Goldwyn (Samuel Goldfish) 1882–1974
American film producer. On Goldwyn: see HAND 379:7

18 Gentlemen, include me out.
resigning from the Motion Picture Producers and Distributors of America, October 1933
Michael Freedland *The Goldwyn Touch* (1986) ch. 10

19 That's the way with these directors, they're always biting the hand that lays the golden egg.
Alva Johnston *The Great Goldwyn* (1937) ch. 1

20 A verbal contract isn't worth the paper it is written on.
Alva Johnston *The Great Goldwyn* (1937) ch. 1

21 Any man who goes to a psychiatrist should have his head examined.
Norman Zierold *Moguls* (1969) ch. 3

22 Pictures are for entertainment, messages should be delivered by Western Union.
Arthur Marx *Goldwyn* (1976) ch. 15; see **BEHAN** 66:17

Ivan Goncharov 1812–91
Russian novelist

23 No devastating or redeeming fires have ever burnt in my life . . . My life began by flickering out.
Oblomov (1859) pt. 2, ch. 4 (translated by David Magarshak)

24 You lost your ability for doing things in childhood . . . It all began with your inability to put on your socks and ended by your inability to live.
Oblomov (1859) pt. 4, ch. 2 (translated by David Magarshak)

Maud Gonne (Maud Gonne MacBride) 1867–1953
Irish nationalist and actress

25 The Famine Queen.
*of Queen **VICTORIA***
in *L'Irlande libre* 1900

Amy Goodman 1957–
American journalist

26 Go to where the silence is and say something.
accepting an award from Columbia University for her coverage of the 1991 massacre in East Timor by Indonesian troops
in *Columbia Journalism Review* March/April 1994

Barnabe Googe 1540–94

English poet

1 Fair face show friends
When riches do abound:
Come time of proof,
Farewell, they must away.
'Of Money' (1563)

Thomas Goold 1766–1846

Irish lawyer and politician

2 The God of nature never intended that Ireland
should be a province, and by God she never will.
speech opposing the Act of Union at a meeting of the Irish
Bar, 9 December 1799

Mikhail Sergeevich Gorbachev 1931–

Soviet statesman, General Secretary of the Communist
Party of the USSR 1985–91 and President 1988–91. On
Gorbachev: see **GROMYKO** 373:13, **THATCHER** 803:22,
ZHVANETSKY 877:16

3 The guilt of Stalin and his immediate entourage
before the Party and the people for the mass
repressions and lawlessness they committed is
enormous and unforgivable.
speech on the seventieth anniversary of the Russian
Revolution, 2 November 1987

4 The idea of restructuring [perestroika] . . .
combines continuity and innovation, the
historical experience of Bolshevism and the
contemporaneity of socialism.
speech on the seventieth anniversary of the Russian
Revolution, 2 November 1987

Adam Lindsay Gordon 1833–70

Australian poet

5 Life is mostly froth and bubble,
Two things stand like stone,
Kindness in another's trouble,
Courage in your own.
Ye Wearie Wayfarer (1866) 'Fytte 8'

Mack Gordon 1904–59

American songwriter

6 Pardon me boy is that the Chattanooga Choo-
choo,
Track twenty nine,
Boy you can gimme a shine.
I can afford to board a Chattanooga Choo-choo,
I've got my fare and just a trifle to spare.
You leave the Pennsylvania station 'bout a
quarter to four,
Read a magazine and then you're in Baltimore,
Dinner in the diner nothing could be finer
Than to have your ham'n eggs in Carolina.
'Chattanooga Choo-choo' (1941 song)

Albert Gore Jr. 1948–

American Democratic politician, Vice-President 1993–2001;
presidential candidate in 2000

7 I am Al Gore, and I used to be the next
president of the United States of America.
addressing Bocconi University in Milan
in Newsweek 19 March 2001; see **CARTER** 204:16

Eva Gore-Booth 1870–1926

Irish poet

8 The little waves of Breffny go stumbling through
my soul.
'The Waves of Breffny' (1920)

Maxim Gorky 1868–1936

Russian writer and revolutionary

9 The proletarian state must bring up thousands of
excellent 'mechanics of culture', 'engineers of
the soul'.
speech at the Writers' Congress 1934; see **KENNEDY** 460:14,
STALIN 769:15

Stuart Gorrell 1902–63

American songwriter

10 Georgia, Georgia, no peace I find,
Just an old sweet song keeps Georgia on my
mind.
'Georgia on my Mind' (1930 song)

George Joachim, Lord Goschen 1831–1907

British Liberal Unionist politician. On Goschen: see
CHURCHILL 228:24

11 I have the courage of my opinions, but I have
not the temerity to give a political blank cheque
to Lord Salisbury.
speech in the House of Commons, 19 February 1884

Edmund Gosse 1849–1928

English poet and man of letters

12 The theory, coarsely enough, and to my Father's
great indignation, was defined by a hasty press
as being this—that God hid the fossils in the
rocks in order to tempt geologists into infidelity.
on Philip Gosse's fundamentalist interpretation of geology
(in Omphalos, 1857), subsequently applied to evolution
Father and Son (1907) ch. 5

13 A sheep in sheep's clothing.
of the 'woolly-bearded poet' Sturge **MOORE**
F. Greenslet Under the Bridge (1943) ch. 10; see **CHURCHILL**
231:7

Glenn Gould 1932–82

Canadian pianist and composer

14 The purpose of art is the lifelong construction
of a state of wonder.
commencement address, York University, Toronto, 6
November 1982

Stephen Jay Gould 1941–2002
American palaeontologist

1 A man does not attain the status of Galileo merely because he is persecuted; he must also be right.
Ever since Darwin (1977)

2 Life is a copiously branching bush, continually pruned by the grim reaper of extinction, not a ladder of predictable progress.
Wonderful Life (1989) ch. 1

3 Science is an integral part of culture. It's not this foreign thing, done by an arcane priesthood. It's one of the glories of human intellectual tradition.
in *Independent* 24 January 1990

John Gower c.1330–1408
English poet

4 It hath and schal ben evermor
That love is maister wher he wile.
Confessio Amantis (1386–90) prologue, l. 34

Goya (Francisco José de Goya y Lucientes) 1746–1828
Spanish painter

5 *No se puede mirar.*
One cannot look at this.
The Disasters of War (1863) title of etching, no. 26

6 *El sueño de la razón produce monstruos.*
The dream of reason produces monsters.
Los Caprichos (1799) plate 43 (title)

Baltasar Gracián 1601–58
Spanish philosopher

7 Never open the door to the least of evils, for many other, greater ones lurk outside.
The Art of Worldly Wisdom (translated by Christopher Maurer, 1994)

8 Renew your brilliance. It is the privilege of the Phoenix. Excellence grows old and so does fame. Custom wears down our admiration, and a mediocre novelty can conquer the greatest eminence in its old age. So be reborn in courage, in intellect, in happiness, and in all else. Dare to renew your brilliance, dawning many times, like the sun, only changing your surroundings. Withhold it and make people miss it; renew it and make them applaud.
The Art of Worldly Wisdom (translated by Christopher Maurer, 1994)

9 Don't express your ideas too clearly. Most people think little of what they understand, and venerate what they do not.
The Art of Worldly Wisdom (translated by Christopher Maurer, 1994)

Clementina Stirling Graham 1782–1877
Scottish writer

10 The best way to get the better of temptation is just to yield to it.
Mystifications (1859) 'Soirée at Mrs Russel's'; see **WILDE** 855:9

D. M. Graham 1911–99
British broadcaster

11 That this House will in no circumstances fight for its King and Country.
motion worded by Graham for a debate at the Oxford Union, of which he was Librarian, 9 February 1933 (passed by 275 votes to 153)

Harry Graham 1874–1936
English writer and journalist

12 Weep not for little Léonie
Abducted by a French Marquis!
Though loss of honour was a wrench
Just think how it's improved her French.
More Ruthless Rhymes for Heartless Homes (1930) 'Compensation'

13 O'er the rugged mountain's brow
Clara threw the twins she nursed,
And remarked, 'I wonder now
Which will reach the bottom first?'
Ruthless Rhymes for Heartless Homes (1899) 'Calculating Clara'

14 'There's been an accident,' they said,
'Your servant's cut in half; he's dead!'
'Indeed!' said Mr Jones, 'and please,
Send me the half that's got my keys.'
Ruthless Rhymes for Heartless Homes (1899) 'Mr Jones' (attributed to 'G.W.')

15 Billy, in one of his nice new sashes,
Fell in the fire and was burnt to ashes;
Now, although the room grows chilly,
I haven't the heart to poke poor Billy.
Ruthless Rhymes for Heartless Homes (1899) 'Tender-Heartedness'

James Graham *see* Marquess of Montrose

Martha Graham 1894–1991
American dancer, teacher, and choreographer

16 Dance is the hidden language of the soul.
Blood Memory (1991)

17 Dancing appears glamorous, easy, delightful. But the path to the paradise of achievement is not easier than any other. There is fatigue so great that the body cries, even in its sleep.
Blood Memory (1991)

Kenneth Grahame 1859–1932
Scottish-born writer

18 The curate faced the laurels—hesitatingly. But Aunt Maria flung herself on him. 'O Mr

Hodgitts!' I heard her cry, 'you are brave! for my sake do not be rash!' He was not rash.
The Golden Age (1895) 'The Burglars'

1 There is *nothing*—absolutely nothing—half so much worth doing as simply messing about in boats.
The Wind in the Willows (1908) ch. 1

2 The poetry of motion! The *real* way to travel! The *only* way to travel! Here today—in next week tomorrow! Villages skipped, towns and cities jumped—always somebody else's horizon!
The Wind in the Willows (1908) ch. 2; see **KAUFMAN AND ANTHONY** 453:11

3 O bliss! O poop-poop! O my!
The Wind in the Willows (1908) ch. 2

4 The clever men at Oxford
Know all that there is to be knowed.
But they none of them know one half as much
As intelligent Mr Toad!
The Wind in the Willows (1908) ch. 10

James Grainger *c.*1721–66
English physician and man of letters

5 What is fame? an empty bubble;
Gold? a transient, shining trouble.
'Solitude' (1755) l. 96

6 　　　　Knock off the chains
Of heart-debasing slavery; give to man,
Of every colour and of every clime,
Freedom, which stamps him image of his God.
The Sugar Cane (1764) bk. 4

Phil Gramm 1942–
American Republican politician

7 I did not come to Washington to be loved, and I have not been disappointed.
Michael Barone and Grant Ujifusa *The American Political Almanac* 1994

Bernie Grant 1944–2000
British Labour politician

8 The police were to blame for what happened on Sunday night and what they got was a bloody good hiding.
after a riot in which a policeman was killed
speech as leader of Haringey Council outside Tottenham Town Hall, 8 October 1985

Cary Grant 1904–86
British-born American actor

9 QUESTION: HOW OLD CARY GRANT?
ANSWER: OLD CARY GRANT FINE. HOW YOU?
telegram exchange; R. Schickel *Cary Grant* (1983)

George P. Grant 1918–88
Canadian social philosopher

10 What is so endearing about the young French Canadians revolting against their tradition is that

they sometimes write as if Voltaire's *Candide* had come off the press last week instead of two hundred years ago.
Technology and Empire: Perspectives on North America (1969) 'Canadian Fate and Imperialism'

Robert Grant 1785–1838
British lawyer and politician

11 O worship the King, all-glorious above;
O gratefully sing his power and his love:
Our Shield and Defender, the Ancient of Days,
Pavilioned in splendour, and girded with praise.
'O worship the King, all glorious above' (1833 hymn)

Ulysses S. Grant 1822–85
American Unionist general and statesman, 18th President of the US 1869-77

12 No terms except unconditional and immediate surrender can be accepted. I propose to move immediately upon your works.
to Simon Bolivar Buckner, under siege at Fort Donelson, 16 February 1862; in P. C. Headley *The Life and Campaigns of General U. S. Grant* (1869) ch. 6

13 I purpose to fight it out on this line, if it takes all summer.
dispatch to Washington, from head-quarters in the field, 11 May 1864, in P. C. Headley *The Life and Campaigns of General U. S. Grant* (1869) ch. 23

14 The war is over—the rebels are our countrymen again.
preventing his men from cheering after **LEE***'s surrender at Appomattox*
on 9 April, 1865

15 Let us have peace.
letter to General Joseph R. Hawkey, 29 May 1868, accepting the presidential nomination, in P. C. Headley *The Life and Campaigns of General U. S. Grant* (1869) ch. 29

16 I know no method to secure the repeal of bad or obnoxious laws so effective as their stringent execution.
inaugural address, 4 March 1869, in P. C. Headley *The Life and Campaigns of General U. S. Grant* (1869) ch. 29

17 Let no guilty man escape, if it can be avoided
. . . No personal consideration should stand in the way of performing a public duty.
on the implication of his private secretary in a tax fraud
endorsement of a letter relating to the Whiskey Ring received 29 July 1875, in E. P. Oberholtzer *History of the United States Since the Civil War* (1937) vol. 3, ch. 19

George Granville, Lord Lansdowne
1666–1735
English poet and dramatist

18 Bright as the day, and like the morning, fair,
Such Cloe is . . . and common as the air.
'Cloe' (1712)

19 Cowards in scarlet pass for men of war.
The She Gallants (1696) act 5

Günter Grass 1927–

German novelist, poet, and dramatist

1 The citizen's first duty is unrest.
  The Citizen's First Duty address delivered 1967; in *Speak Out!*
  (1968)

2 I want to warn against this time-honoured
  means of dealing with the past; I prefer, myself,
  to keep the wound open.
  Dokumente zur politischen Wirkung (1968)

3 In those days, when every male who could stand
  half-way erect was being shipped to Verdun to
  undergo a radical change of posture from the
  vertical to the eternal horizontal.
  The Tin Drum (1959) bk. 1 'Moth and Light Bulb', translated
  by Ralph Manheim

4 Only too soon it became clear to me that in this
  world of ours every Rasputin has his Goethe,
  that every Rasputin draws a Goethe or if you
  prefer every Goethe a Rasputin in his wake, or
  even makes one if need be, in order to be able
  to condemn him later on.
  The Tin Drum (1959) bk. 1 'Rasputin and the Alphabet',
  translated by Ralph Manheim

Henry Grattan 1746–1820

Irish nationalist leader

5 The thing he proposes to buy is what cannot be
  sold—liberty.
  *speech in the Irish Parliament against the proposed union,
  16 January 1800*
    in *Dictionary of National Biography* (1917–)

6 The Channel forbids union, the ocean forbids
  separation.
  quoted by W. E. **GLADSTONE**, speech, House of Commons, 8
  April 1886

Arthur Percival Graves 1846–1931

Irish songwriter

7 Trottin' to the fair,
  Me and Moll Maloney,
  Seated, I declare
  On a single pony.
  'Ridin' Double'

John Woodcock Graves 1795–1886

English huntsman and songwriter

8 D'ye ken John Peel with his coat so grey?
  D'ye ken John Peel at the break of the day?
  D'ye ken John Peel when he's far far away
  With his hounds and his horn in the morning?
  an alternative version 'coat so gay' is often sung
    'John Peel' (1820)

9 Yes, I ken John Peel and Ruby too,
  Ranter and Ringwood, Bellman and True;
  From a find to a check, from a check to a view,
  From a view to a death in the morning.
  'John Peel' (1820)

Robert Graves 1895–1985

English poet

10 Beware, madam, of the witty devil,
   The arch intriguer who walks disguised
   In a poet's cloak, his gay tongue oozing evil.
   'Beware, Madam!'

11 There's a cool web of language winds us in,
   Retreat from too much joy or too much fear.
   'The Cool Web' (1927)

12 Truth-loving Persians do not dwell upon
   The trivial skirmish fought near Marathon.
   'The Persian Version' (1945)

13 Love is a universal migraine.
   A bright stain on the vision
   Blotting out reason.
   'Symptoms of Love'

14 Goodbye to all that.
   title of autobiography (1929)

15 If there's no money in poetry, neither is there
   poetry in money.
   speech at London School of Economics, 6 December 1963

John Gray 1951–

16 Men are from Mars, women are from Venus.
   title of book (1992)

John Chipman Gray 1839–1915

American lawyer

17 Dirt is only matter out of place; and what is a
   blot on the escutcheon of the Common Law
   may be a jewel in the crown of the Social
   Republic.
   Restraints on the Alienation of Property (2nd ed., 1895) preface

Patrick, Lord Gray d. 1612

18 A dead woman bites not.
   pressing for the execution of **MARY** *Queen of Scots in 1587*
   oral tradition; quoted as 'Mortua non mordet [Being dead, she
   will bite no more]' in A. Darcy's 1625 translation of William
   Camden's *Annals of the Reign of Queen Elizabeth* (1615) vol. 1;
   see **PROVERBS** 629:34

Thomas Gray 1716–71

English poet. On Gray: see **JOHNSON** 436:22, **JOHNSON**
441:12, **JOHNSON** 442:29, **WOLFE** 862:17

19 Ruin seize thee, ruthless King!
   Confusion on thy banners wait.
   The Bard (1757) l. 1

20 Loose his beard, and hoary hair
   Streamed, like a meteor, to the troubled air.
   The Bard (1757) l. 19; see **MILTON** 541:26

21 Weave the warp, and weave the woof,
   The winding-sheet of Edward's race.
   The Bard (1757) l. 49

22 In gallant trim the gilded vessel goes;
   Youth on the prow, and Pleasure at the helm.
   'The Bard' (1757) l. 73

1 The curfew tolls the knell of parting day,
The lowing herd wind slowly o'er the lea,
The ploughman homeward plods his weary way,
And leaves the world to darkness and to me.

Now fades the glimmering landscape on the
sight,
And all the air a solemn stillness holds,
Save where the beetle wheels his droning flight,
And drowsy tinklings lull the distant folds.
Elegy Written in a Country Churchyard (1751) l. 1

2 Save that from yonder ivy-mantled tow'r,
The moping owl does to the moon complain.
Elegy Written in a Country Churchyard (1751) l. 9

3 Beneath those rugged elms, that yew-tree's
shade,
Where heaves the turf in many a mouldering
heap,
Each in his narrow cell for ever laid,
The rude forefathers of the hamlet sleep.
Elegy Written in a Country Churchyard (1751) l. 13

4 Let not ambition mock their useful toil,
Their homely joys, and destiny obscure;
Nor grandeur hear with a disdainful smile,
The short and simple annals of the poor.

The boast of heraldry, the pomp of pow'r,
And all that beauty, all that wealth e'er gave,
Awaits alike th' inevitable hour,
The paths of glory lead but to the grave.
Elegy Written in a Country Churchyard (1751) l. 29

5 Can storied urn or animated bust
Back to its mansion call the fleeting breath?
Can honour's voice provoke the silent dust,
Or flatt'ry soothe the dull cold ear of death?
Elegy Written in a Country Churchyard (1751) l. 41

6 Full many a gem of purest ray serene,
The dark unfathomed caves of ocean bear:
Full many a flower is born to blush unseen,
And waste its sweetness on the desert air.

Some village-Hampden, that with dauntless
breast
The little tyrant of his fields withstood;
Some mute inglorious Milton here may rest,
Some Cromwell guiltless of his country's blood.
Elegy Written in a Country Churchyard (1751) l. 53

7 Forbad to wade through slaughter to a throne,
And shut the gates of mercy on mankind.
Elegy Written in a Country Churchyard (1751) l. 67

8 Far from the madding crowd's ignoble strife,
Their sober wishes never learned to stray;
Along the cool sequestered vale of life
They kept the noiseless tenor of their way.
Elegy Written in a Country Churchyard (1751) l. 73

9 Here rests his head upon the lap of Earth
A youth to fortune and to fame unknown.
Fair Science frowned not on his humble birth,
And Melancholy marked him for her own.
Elegy Written in a Country Churchyard (1751) l. 117

10 Ye distant spires, ye antique towers,
That crown the wat'ry glade.
Ode on a Distant Prospect of Eton College (1747) l. 1

11 Alas, regardless of their doom,
The little victims play!
No sense have they of ills to come,
Nor care beyond to-day.
Ode on a Distant Prospect of Eton College (1747) l. 51

12 To each his suff'rings, all are men,
Condemned alike to groan;
The tender for another's pain,
Th' unfeeling for his own.
Ode on a Distant Prospect of Eton College (1747) l. 91

13 Thought would destroy their paradise.
No more; where ignorance is bliss,
'Tis folly to be wise.
Ode on a Distant Prospect of Eton College (1747) l. 98; see
PROVERBS 647:8

14 Demurest of the tabby kind,
The pensive Selima reclined.
'Ode on the Death of a Favourite Cat' (1748)

15 What female heart can gold despise?
What cat's averse to fish?
'Ode on the Death of a Favourite Cat' (1748)

16 A favourite has no friend!
'Ode on the Death of a Favourite Cat' (1748)

17 Not all that tempts your wand'ring eyes
And heedless hearts, is lawful prize;
Nor all, that glisters, gold.
'Ode on the Death of a Favourite Cat' (1748)

18 The Attic warbler pours her throat,
Responsive to the cuckoo's note,
The untaught harmony of spring.
'Ode on the Spring' (1748) l. 5

19 In thy green lap was Nature's darling laid.
of SHAKESPEARE
The Progress of Poesy (1757) l. 84

20 Nor second he, that rode sublime
Upon the seraph-wings of ecstasy,
The secrets of th' abyss to spy.
He passed the flaming bounds of place and
time:
The living throne, the sapphire-blaze,
Where angels tremble, while they gaze,
He saw; but blasted with excess of light,
Closed his eyes in endless night.
of MILTON
The Progress of Poesy (1757) l. 95

21 Thoughts, that breathe, and words, that burn.
The Progress of Poesy (1757) l. 110

22 Beyond the limits of a vulgar fate,
Beneath the good how far—but far above the
great.
The Progress of Poesy (1757) l. 122

23 Too poor for a bribe, and too proud to
importune,
He had not the method of making a fortune.
'Sketch of his own Character' (written 1761)

1 The language of the age is never the language of poetry, except among the French, whose verse, where the thought or image does not support it, differs in nothing from prose.
   letter to Richard West, 8 April 1742, in H. W. Starr (ed.) *Correspondence of Thomas Gray* (1971) vol. 1

2 It has been usual to catch a mouse or two (for form's sake) in public once a year.
   on refusing the Laureateship
   letter to William Mason, 19 December 1757; in H. W. Starr (ed.) *Correspondence of Thomas Gray* (1971) vol. 2

3 I shall be but a shrimp of an author.
   letter to Horace Walpole, 25 February 1768, in H. W. Starr (ed.) *Correspondence of Thomas Gray* (1971) vol. 3

4 Any fool may write a most valuable book by chance, if he will only tell us what he heard and saw with veracity.
   letter to Horace Walpole, 25 February 1768, in H. W. Starr (ed.) *Correspondence of Thomas Gray* (1971) vol. 3

Horace Greeley 1811–72
American founder and editor of the *New York Tribune*

5 Go West, young man, and grow up with the country.
   Hints toward Reforms (1850); see **NEWSPAPER HEADLINES AND LEADERS** 573:11

Matthew Green 1696–1737
English poet

6 They politics like ours profess,
   The greater prey upon the less.
   The Grotto (1732) l. 69

7 To cure the mind's wrong bias, spleen,
   Some recommend the bowling-green,
   Some, hilly walks; all, exercise.
   The Spleen (1737) l. 89

8 Or to some coffee-house I stray
   For news, the manna of a day.
   The Spleen (1737) l. 168

9 By happy alchemy of mind
   They turn to pleasure all they find.
   The Spleen (1737) l. 610

Graham Greene 1904–91
English novelist. See also MISQUOTATIONS 549:1

10 Catholics and Communists have committed great crimes, but at least they have not stood aside, like an established society, and been indifferent. I would rather have blood on my hands than water like Pilate.
   The Comedians (1966) pt. 3, ch. 4

11 He gave her a bright fake smile; so much of life was a putting-off of unhappiness for another time. Nothing was ever lost by delay.
   The Heart of the Matter (1948) bk. 1, pt. 1, ch. 1

12 Against the beautiful and the clever and the successful, one can wage a pitiless war, but not against the unattractive.
   The Heart of the Matter (1948) bk. 1, pt. 1, ch. 2

13 They had been corrupted by money, and he had been corrupted by sentiment. Sentiment was the more dangerous, because you couldn't name its price. A man open to bribes was to be relied upon below a certain figure, but sentiment might uncoil in the heart at a name, a photograph, even a smell remembered.
   The Heart of the Matter (1948) bk. 1, pt. 1, ch. 2

14 In human relations kindness and lies are worth a thousand truths.
   The Heart of the Matter (1948) bk. 1, pt. 2, ch. 4

15 Point me out the happy man and I will point you out either egotism, selfishness, evil—or else an absolute ignorance.
   The Heart of the Matter (1948) bk. 2, pt. 1, ch. 1

16 He felt the loyalty we all feel to unhappiness—the sense that that is where we really belong.
   The Heart of the Matter (1948) bk. 2, pt. 2, ch. 1

17 His hilarity was like a scream from a crevasse.
   The Heart of the Matter (1948) bk. 3, pt. 1, ch. 1

18 There is always one moment in childhood when the door opens and lets the future in.
   The Power and the Glory (1940) pt. 1, ch. 1

19 Innocence always calls mutely for protection, when we would be so much wiser to guard ourselves against it: innocence is like a dumb leper who has lost his bell, wandering the world meaning no harm.
   The Quiet American (1955) pt. 1, ch. 3

20 I never knew a man who had better motives for all the trouble he caused.
   The Quiet American (1955) pt. 1, ch. 4

21 Rooms don't change, ornaments stand where you place them: only the heart decays.
   The Quiet American (1955) pt. 4, ch. 1

22 Success is more dangerous than failure, the ripples break over a wider coastline.
   in *The Independent* 4 April 1991

Nancy Greene 1943–
Canadian alpine skier

23 You have to have a real love of your sport to carry you through all the bad times, you still want to ski even when things aren't working.
   in *Vancouver Sun* 23 November 1999

Robert Greene c.1560–92
English poet and dramatist

24 Hangs in the uncertain balance of proud time.
   Friar Bacon and Friar Bungay (1594) act 3, sc. 1

25 Ah! what is love! It is a pretty thing,
   As sweet unto a shepherd as a king,
   And sweeter too;
   For kings have cares that wait upon a crown,
   And cares can make the sweetest love to frown.
   'The Shepherd's Wife's Song' (1590)

1 For there is an upstart crow, beautified with our feathers, that with his tiger's heart wrapped in a player's hide, supposes he is as well able to bumbast out a blank verse as the best of you; and being an absolute *Johannes fac totum*, is in his own conceit the only Shake-scene in a country.
Groatsworth of Wit Bought with a Million of Repentance (1592); see **SHAKESPEARE** 710:5

Alan Greenspan 1926–

American economist, Chairman of the US Federal Reserve, 1987–2006

2 How do we know when irrational exuberance has unduly escalated asset values?
speech in Washington, 5 December 1996

3 An infectious greed seemed to grip much of our business community.
of the late 1990s
in *New York Times* 17 July 2002 (online edition)

Germaine Greer 1939–

Australian feminist

4 The female eunuch.
title of book (1970)

5 Women have very little idea of how much men hate them.
The Female Eunuch (1970)

Gregory the Great c.AD 540–604

Roman cleric, Pope from 590

6 *Non Angli sed Angeli.*
Not Angles but Angels.
on seeing English slaves in Rome
oral tradition, based on Bede *Historia Ecclesiastica* bk. 2, sect. 1: 'Responsum est, quod Angli vocarentur. At ille: "Bene," inquit; "nam et angelicam habent faciem, et tales angelorum in caelis decet esse coheredes" [They answered that they were called Angles. "It is well," he said, "for they have the faces of angels, and such should be the co-heirs of the angels of heaven"]'

Gregory VII c.1020–85

Italian cleric, Pope from 1073

7 *Dilexi iustitiam et odi iniquitatem, propterea morior in exilio.*
I have loved justice and hated iniquity: therefore I die in exile.
last words, at Salerno, following his conflict with the Emperor Henry IV; J. W. Bowden *The Life and Pontificate of Gregory VII* (1840) vol. 2, bk. 3, ch. 20

Stephen Grellet 1773–1855

French Quaker and missionary

8 I expect to pass through this world but once; any good thing therefore that I can do, or any kindness that I can show to any fellow-creature, let me do it now; let me not defer or neglect it, for I shall not pass this way again.
attributed; some of the many other claimants to authorship are given in John o' London *Treasure Trove* (1925)

Joyce Grenfell 1910–79

English comedy actress and writer. See also **CATCHPHRASES** 207:20

9 Stately as a galleon, I sail across the floor,
Doing the Military Two-step, as in the days of yore . . .
So gay the band,
So giddy the sight,
Full evening dress is a must,
But the zest goes out of a beautiful waltz
When you dance it bust to bust.
'Stately as a Galleon' (1978 song)

Julian Grenfell 1888–1915

English soldier and poet

10 And Life is Colour and Warmth and Light
And a striving evermore for these;
And he is dead, who will not fight;
And who dies fighting has increase.
'Into Battle' in *The Times* 28 May 1915

George Grenville 1712–70

British Whig statesman, Prime Minister 1763–5. On Grenville: see **WALPOLE** 838:8

11 A wise government knows how to enforce with temper, or to conciliate with dignity.
speaking against the expulsion of John **WILKES**
in the House of Commons, 3 February 1769

Jean-Baptiste-Louis Gresset 1709–77

French poet and dramatist

12 *Les sots sont ici-bas pour nos menus plaisirs.*
Fools are here below for our minor pleasures.
Le Méchant (1747) act 2, sc. 1

Wayne Gretzky 1961–

Canadian ice-hockey player

13 I skate to where the puck is going to be, not where it's been.
attributed, 1985; John Robert Colombo *Colombo's New Canadian Quotations* (1987)

Frances Greville (née Macartney) c.1724–89

Irish poet

14 Far as distress the soul can wound
'Tis pain in each degree;
Bliss goes but to a certain bound,
Beyond is agony.
'A Prayer for Indifference' (1759)

Fulke Greville, Lord Brooke 1554–1628

English poet, writer, and politician. See also **DYER** 301:4

15 Life is a top which whipping Sorrow driveth.
Caelica (1633) 'The earth with thunder torn, with fire blasted'

16 O wearisome condition of humanity!
Born under one law, to another bound;

Vainly begot, and yet forbidden vanity;
Created sick, commanded to be sound.
Mustapha (1609) act 5, sc. 4

Edward Grey, Lord Grey of Fallodon 1862–1933

British Liberal politician, Foreign Secretary 1905–16

1 The lamps are going out all over Europe; we shall not see them lit again in our lifetime.
on the eve of the First World War
25 Years (1925) vol. 2, ch. 18

Lady Jane Grey 1537–54

English monarch, great-niece of **HENRY VIII**, queen of England 9–19 June 1553

2 One of the greatest benefits that God ever gave me is that he sent me so sharp and severe parents and so gentle a schoolmaster.
Roger Ascham *The Schoolmaster* (1570) bk. 1

Arthur Griffith 1871–1922

Irish statesman

3 The Irish leader who would connive in the name of Home Rule at the acceptance of any measure which alienated for a day—for an hour—for one moment of time—a square inch of the soil of Ireland would act the part of a traitor and would deserve a traitor's fate.
in *Sinn Féin* 21 February 1914

4 We have brought back the flag; we have brought back the evacuation of Ireland after 700 years by British troops and the formation of an Irish army. We have brought back to Ireland her full rights.
when moving acceptance of the Treaty in the Dáil, December 1921

Mervyn Griffith-Jones 1909–79

British lawyer

5 Is it a book you would even wish your wife or your servants to read?
of D. H. LAWRENCE's Lady Chatterley's Lover, while appearing for the prosecution at the Old Bailey, 20 October 1960
in *The Times* 21 October 1960

John Grigg 1924–2001

English writer and journalist, who as Lord Altrincham disclaimed his hereditary title in 1963

6 The personality conveyed by the utterances which are put into her mouth is that of a priggish schoolgirl, captain of the hockey team, a prefect, and a recent candidate for confirmation. It is not thus that she will be able to come into her own as an independent and distinctive character.
of Queen ELIZABETH II
in *National and English Review* August 1957

7 Autobiography is now as common as adultery and hardly less reprehensible.
in *Sunday Times* 28 February 1962

Nicholas Grimald 1519–62

English poet

8 Of all the heavenly gifts that mortal men commend,
What trusty treasure in the world can countervail a friend?
'Of Friendship' (1557)

Jacob Grimm 1785–1863 *and* Wilhelm Grimm 1786–1859

German philologists and folklorists

9 And so the little girl grew up: her skin was as white as snow, her cheeks as rosy as the blood, and her hair as black as ebony.
Kinder- und Hausmärchen [Fairytales and Household Stories] (1812–14) 'Snow White'

10 Mirror, mirror on the wall,
Who is the fairest of them all?
Kinder- und Hausmärchen [Fairytales and Household Stories] (1812–14) 'Snow White'

11 Rapunzel, Rapunzel, let down your hair.
Kinder- und Hausmärchen [Fairytales and Household Stories] (1812–14) 'Rapunzel'

Joseph ('Jo') Grimond 1913–93

British Liberal politician, Leader of the Liberal Party 1956–67

12 In bygone days, commanders were taught that when in doubt, they should march their troops towards the sound of gunfire. I intend to march my troops towards the sound of gunfire.
speech to the Liberal Party Assembly, 14 September 1963

Andrei Gromyko 1909–89

Soviet statesman, President of the USSR 1985–8

13 Comrades, this man has a nice smile, but he's got iron teeth.
of Mikhail GORBACHEV
speech to Soviet Communist Party Central Committee, 11 March 1985

George Grossmith 1847–1912

English actor, singer, and writer

14 You should see me dance the Polka,
You should see me cover the ground,
You should see my coat-tails flying,
As I jump my partner round.
'See me Dance the Polka' (c.1887 song)

George Grossmith 1847–1912 *and* Weedon Grossmith 1854–1919

English writers

15 What's the good of a home if you are never in it?
The Diary of a Nobody (1894) ch. 1

1 I . . . recognized her as a woman who used to work years ago for my old aunt at Clapham. It only shows how small the world is.
The Diary of a Nobody (1894) ch. 2

2 I left the room with silent dignity, but caught my foot in the mat.
The Diary of a Nobody (1894) ch. 12

3 I am a poor man, but I would gladly give ten shillings to find out who sent me the insulting Christmas card I received this morning.
The Diary of a Nobody (1894) ch. 13

Andrew Grove 1936–
Hungarian-born American businessman

4 Only the paranoid survive.
dictum on which he has long run his company, the Intel Corporation
in *New York Times* 18 December 1994

Philip Guedalla 1889–1944
English historian and biographer

5 Any stigma, as the old saying is, will serve to beat a dogma.
Masters and Men (1923) 'Ministers of State'; see **PROVERBS** 636:17

6 The little ships, the unforgotten Homeric catalogue of *Mary Jane* and *Peggy IV*, of *Folkestone Belle*, *Boy Billy*, and *Ethel Maud*, of *Lady Haig* and *Skylark* . . . the little ships of England brought the Army home.
on the evacuation of Dunkirk
Mr Churchill (1941) ch. 7

7 The cheerful clatter of Sir James Barrie's cans as he went round with the milk of human kindness.
Supers and Supermen (1920) 'Some Critics'

8 The work of Henry James has always seemed divisible by a simple dynastic arrangement into three reigns: James I, James II, and the Old Pretender.
Supers and Supermen (1920) 'Some Critics'

Edgar A. Guest 1881–1959
American writer, journalist, and poet

9 The best of all the preachers are the men who live their creeds.
'Sermons we See' (1926)

Ernesto ('Che') Guevara 1928–67
Argentinian revolutionary and guerrilla leader

10 The Revolution is made by man, but man must forge his revolutionary spirit from day to day.
Socialism and Man in Cuba (1968)

François Guizot 1787–1874
French historian and politician. See also **SAYINGS** 685:7

11 Humanity cannot for long dispense with greatness.
in 1832; E. Percy *The Heresy of Democracy* (1954)

Nubar Gulbenkian 1896–1972
British industrialist and philanthropist

12 The best number for a dinner party is two—myself and a dam' good head waiter.
in *Daily Telegraph* 14 January 1965

Nikolai Gumilev 1886–1921
Russian poet

13 Our freedom is but a light that breaks through from another world.
'The Tram that Lost its Way' (1921) (translated by Dmitri Obolensky)

Thom Gunn 1929–2004
English poet

14 My thoughts are crowded with death
and it draws so oddly on the sexual
that I am confused
confused to be attracted
by, in effect, my own annihilation.
'In Time of Plague' (1992)

15 Their relationship consisted
In discussing if it existed.
'Jamesian' (1992)

Dorothy Frances Gurney 1858–1932
English poet

16 The kiss of the sun for pardon,
The song of the birds for mirth,
One is nearer God's Heart in a garden
Than anywhere else on earth.
'God's Garden' (1913)

Ivor Gurney 1890–1937
English poet

17 I paid the prices of life
Standing where Rome immortal heard October's strife,
A war poet whose right of honour cuts falsehood like a knife.
'Poem for End' (c.1922–5)

18 War told me truth: I have Severn's right of maker,
As of Cotswold: war told me: I was elect, I was born fit
To praise the three hundred feet depth of every acre
Between Tewkesbury and Stroudway, Side and Wales Gate.
'While I Write' (c.1922–5)

John Hampden Gurney 1802–62
English clergyman

19 Ye holy angels bright,
Who wait at God's right hand,
Or through the realms of light
Fly at your Lord's command,

Assist our song,
Or else the theme
Too high doth seem
For mortal tongue.

> 'Ye holy angels bright' (1838 hymn); based on a poem by
> Richard Baxter (1615–91)

1 My soul, bear thou thy part,
Triumph in God above,
And with a well-tuned heart
Sing thou the songs of love.

> 'Ye holy angels bright' (1838 hymn)

Woody Guthrie (Woodrow Wilson Guthrie)
1912–67

American folksinger and songwriter

2 This land is your land, this land is my land,
From California to the New York Island.
From the redwood forest to the Gulf Stream
waters
This land was made for you and me.

> 'This Land is Your Land' (1956 song)

Nell Gwyn 1650–87

**English actress and courtesan. On Gwyn: see CHARLES II
217:11, PEPYS 603:10**

3 Pray, good people, be civil. I am the Protestant
whore.

> at Oxford, during the anti-Catholic ferment at the time of the
> Popish Plot, 1681; in B. Bevan *Nell Gwyn* (1969) ch. 13

Peter John Gzowski 1934–2002

Canadian broadcaster

4 We need spring. We need it desperately and,
usually, we need it before God is willing to give
it to us.

> Peter Gzowski's Spring Tonic (1979)

William Habington 1605–54

English poet

5 Direct your eyesight inward, and you'll find
A thousand regions in your mind
Yet undiscover'd. Travel them, and be
Expert in home cosmography.

> 'To my honoured friend Sir Ed. P. Knight', in *Castara* (1634)

6 Cast me upon some naked shore,
Where I may track
Only the print of some sad wrack,
If thou be there, though the seas roar
I shall no gentler calm implore.

> 'Vias tuas Domine demonstra mihi' in *Castara: The Third Part*
> (1640)

Hadrian AD 76–138

Roman emperor from 117. See also YOURCENAR 877:6

7 *Animula vagula blandula,*
Hospes comesque corporis,
Quae nunc abibis in loca
Pallidula rigida nudula,
Nec ut soles dabis iocos!

Ah! gentle, fleeting, wav'ring sprite,
Friend and associate of this clay!
To what unknown region borne,
Wilt thou now wing thy distant flight?
No more with wonted humour gay,
But pallid, cheerless, and forlorn.

> J. W. Duff (ed.) *Minor Latin Poets* (1934); translated by Byron
> as 'Adrian's Address to His Soul When Dying'; see POPE 614:1

Ernst Haeckel 1834–1919

German biologist and philosopher

8 Ontogenesis, or the development of the
individual, is a short and quick recapitulation of
phylogenesis, or the development of the tribe to
which it belongs, determined by the laws of
inheritance and adaptation.

> *this discredited theory is often summarized as, 'ontogeny*
> *recapitulates phylogeny'*
> The History of Creation (1868)

Hafiz c.1325–c.90

Persian poet

9 Ho, saki, haste, the beaker bring,
Fill up, and pass it round the ring;
Love seemed at first an easy thing—
But ah! the hard awakening.

> 'Love's Awakening' c. 1368–9, translated by A. J. Arberry

Haggadah

**the text recited at the Seder on the first two nights of the
Jewish Passover**

10 This is the bread of poverty which our fathers
ate in the land of Egypt. Let all who are hungry
come and eat; let all who are in need come to
our Passover feast. Now we are here; next year
may we be in the land of Israel! Now we are
slaves; next year may we be free!

> *The narration*

11 It is this promise which has stood by our fathers
and by us. For it is not simply a matter of one
man rising up against us to destroy us. Rather,
in every generation men have risen up against us
to destroy us, but the Holy One, blessed be he,
has saved us from their hands.

> *In every generation*

12 Rabban Gamaliel says: 'Whoever does not
mention the following three things at Passover
has not fulfilled his duty—the Passover sacrifice,
unleavened bread, and bitter herbs.'

> *The three essentials of the Seder*

1 Therefore, we are duty-bound to thank, praise, laud, glorify, exalt, honour, bless, extol, and adore him who performed all these miracles for our fathers and for us. He has brought us out from slavery to freedom, from sorrow to joy, from mourning to holiday, from darkness to great light, and from bondage to redemption. Let us, then, sing before him a new song. Hallelujah!
Praise to the Redeemer of Israel

2 Next year in Jerusalem!
Accepted

H. Rider Haggard 1856–1925

English writer. On Haggard: see **STEPHEN** 772:4

3 Out of the dark we came, into the dark we go . . . Life is nothing. Life is all. It is the hand with which we hold off death. It is the glow-worm that shines in the night-time and is black in the morning; it is the white breath of the oxen in winter; it is the little shadow that runs across the grass and loses itself at sunset.
King Solomon's Mines (1886) ch. 5; see **CROWFOOT** 261:13

4 She who must be obeyed.
She (1887) ch. 6 and *passim*

C. F. S. Hahnemann *see* Mottoes 563:20

Earl Haig 1861–1928

British general, Commander in France, 1915–18. On Haig: see **BEAVERBROOK** 63:17

5 A very weak-minded fellow I am afraid, and, like the feather pillow, bears the marks of the last person who has sat on him!
describing the 17th Earl of Derby
letter to Lady Haig, 14 January 1918; in R. Blake *Private Papers of Douglas Haig* (1952) ch. 16

6 Every position must be held to the last man: there must be no retirement. With our backs to the wall, and believing in the justice of our cause, each one of us must fight on to the end.
order to British troops, 12 April 1918; A. Duff Cooper *Haig* (1936) vol. 2, ch. 23

Quintin Hogg, Lord Hailsham
1907–2001

British Conservative politician

7 A great party is not to be brought down because of a scandal by a woman of easy virtue and a proved liar.
in a BBC television interview on the Profumo affair, in *The Times* 14 June 1963

8 The elective dictatorship.
title of the Dimbleby Lecture, 19 October 1976

9 The English and, more latterly, the British, have the habit of acquiring their institutions by chance or inadvertence, and shedding them in a fit of absent-mindedness.
'The Granada Guildhall Lecture 1987' 10 November 1987; see **SEELEY** 691:4

Hakuin 1686–1769

Japanese monk, writer and artist; founder of modern Japanese Zen

10 If someone claps his hand a sound arises. Listen to the sound of the single hand!
often quoted as, 'What is the sound of one hand clapping?'
attributed

J. B. S. Haldane 1892–1964

Scottish mathematical biologist

11 Now, my own suspicion is that the universe is not only queerer than we suppose, but queerer than we *can* suppose . . . I suspect that there are more things in heaven and earth than are dreamed of, or can be dreamed of, in any philosophy.
Possible Worlds and Other Essays (1927) 'Possible Worlds'; see **SHAKESPEARE** 700:27

12 If my mental processes are determined wholly by the motions of atoms in my brain, I have no reason for supposing that my beliefs are true. They may be sound chemically, but that does not make them sound logically. And hence I have no reason for supposing my brain to be composed of atoms.
Possible Worlds (1927) 'When I am Dead'

13 The Creator, if He exists, has a special preference for beetles.
on observing that there are 400,000 species of beetle on this planet, but only 8,000 species of mammals
report of lecture, 7 April 1951, in *Journal of the British Interplanetary Society* (1951) vol. 10

14 No-one could study mathematics intensively for more than five hours a day and remain sane.
in *Perspectives in Biology and Medicine* (1966) 'An Autobiography in Brief'

H. R. Haldeman 1929–93

American Presidential assistant to Richard **NIXON**

15 Once the toothpaste is out of the tube, it is awfully hard to get it back in.
to John Dean on the Watergate affair, 8 April 1973, in *Hearings Before the Select Committee on Presidential Campaign Activities of US Senate: Watergate and Related Activities* (1973) vol. 4

Edward Everett Hale 1822–1909

American Unitarian clergyman; Senate chaplain for 1903

16 'Do you pray for the senators, Dr Hale?' 'No, I look at the senators and I pray for the country.'
Van Wyck Brooks *New England Indian Summer* (1940)

Matthew Hale 1609–76

English judge

17 Christianity is part of the laws of England.
William Blackstone's summary of Hale's words (Taylor's case, 1676) in *Commentaries* (1769) vol. 4; Holdsworth's *History of English Law* (1937 ed.) vol. 8 traces the origin of the expression to Sir John Prisot (d. 1460)

Nathan Hale 1755–76

American revolutionary

1 Every kind of service necessary to the public good becomes honourable by being necessary.
letter to William Hull, 10 September 1776

2 I only regret that I have but one life to lose for my country.
last words, prior to his execution by the British for spying, 22 September 1776
Henry Phelps Johnston *Nathan Hale, 1776* (1914) ch. 7; see **ADDISON** 4:18

Sarah Josepha Hale 1788–1879

American writer

3 Mary had a little lamb,
Its fleece was white as snow,
And everywhere that Mary went
The lamb was sure to go.
Poems for Our Children (1830) 'Mary's Little Lamb'

Judah Ha-Levi *c.*1075–1141

Jewish poet and philosopher, born in Spain

4 Israel amidst the nations is like the heart amidst the organs; it is the most sick and the most healthy of them all.
The Kuzari 2.36

5 I understand the difference between the God and the Lord and I see how great is the difference between the God of Abraham and the God of Aristotle.
The Kuzari 4.16

George Savile, Lord Halifax ('the Trimmer') 1633–95

English politician and essayist

6 Love is a passion that hath friends in the garrison.
Advice to a Daughter (1688) 'Behaviour and Conversation'

7 This innocent word *Trimmer* signifieth no more than this, that if men are together in a boat, and one part of the company would weigh it down on one side, another would make it lean as much to the contrary.
Character of a Trimmer (1685, printed 1688)

8 Men in business are in as much danger from those that work under them, as from those that work against them.
Political, Moral, and Miscellaneous Thoughts and Reflections (1750) 'Instruments of State: Ministers'

9 A known liar should be outlawed in a well-ordered government.
Political, Moral, and Miscellaneous Thoughts and Reflections (1750) 'Miscellaneous: Lying'

10 Anger is never without an argument, but seldom with a good one.
Political, Moral, and Miscellaneous Thoughts and Reflections (1750) 'Of Anger'

11 After a revolution, you see the same men in the drawing-room, and within a week the same flatterers.
Political, Moral, and Miscellaneous Thoughts and Reflections (1750) 'Of Courts'

12 There is . . . no fundamental, but that *every supreme power must be arbitrary.*
Political, Moral, and Miscellaneous Thoughts and Reflections (1750) 'Of Fundamentals'

13 It is in a disorderly government as in a river, the lightest things swim at the top.
Political, Moral, and Miscellaneous Thoughts and Reflections (1750) 'Of Government'

14 The best definition of the best government is, that it has no inconveniences but such as are supportable; but inconveniences there must be.
Political, Moral, and Miscellaneous Thoughts and Reflections (1750) 'Of Government'

15 Malice is of a low stature, but it hath very long arms.
Political, Moral, and Miscellaneous Thoughts and Reflections (1750) 'Of Malice and Envy'

16 The best party is but a kind of conspiracy against the rest of the nation.
Political, Moral, and Miscellaneous Thoughts and Reflections (1750) 'Of Parties'

17 When the people contend for their liberty, they seldom get anything by their victory but new masters.
Political, Moral, and Miscellaneous Thoughts and Reflections (1750) 'Of Prerogative, Power and Liberty'

18 Power is so apt to be insolent and Liberty to be saucy, that they are very seldom upon good terms.
Political, Moral, and Miscellaneous Thoughts and Reflections (1750) 'Of Prerogative, Power and Liberty'

19 Men are not hanged for stealing horses, but that horses may not be stolen.
Political, Moral, and Miscellaneous Thoughts and Reflections (1750) 'Of Punishment'

20 Wherever a knave is not punished, an honest man is laughed at.
Political, Moral, and Miscellaneous Thoughts and Reflections (1750) 'Of Punishment'

21 State business is a cruel trade; good nature is a bungler in it.
Political, Moral, and Miscellaneous Thoughts and Reflections (1750) 'Wicked Ministers'

22 The struggling for knowledge hath a pleasure in it like that of wrestling with a fine woman.
Political, Moral, and Miscellaneous Thoughts and Reflections (1750) 'Miscellaneous Thoughts and Reflections'

23 To the question, What shall we do to be saved in this World? there is no other answer but this, Look to your Moat.
A Rough Draft of a New Model at Sea (1694)

24 Lord Rochester was made Lord president: which being a post superior in rank, but much inferior both in advantage and credit to that he held formerly, drew a jest from Lord Halifax . . . he

had heard of many kicked down stairs, but
never of any that was kicked up stairs before.
Gilbert Burnet *History of My Own Time* (written 1683–6) vol. 1
(1724)

Joseph Hall 1574–1656
English bishop

1 Lo, all princes and monarchs dance with us in
the same ring.
Epistles (1608) vol. 2, decad. 2, no. 9

2 I first adventure, follow me who list
And be the second English satirist.
Virgidemiae (1597) prologue

3 Perfection is the child of Time.
Works (1625)

Radclyffe Hall 1883–1943
English novelist

4 The well of loneliness
title of novel (1928), an exploration of a lesbian relationship
which caused outrage at the time, and was banned in Britain
for many years

5 You're neither unnatural, nor abominable, nor
mad; you're as much a part of what people call
nature as anyone else; only you're unexplained
as yet—you've not got your niche in creation.
of lesbianism
The Well of Loneliness (1928) bk. 2, ch. 20, sect. 3

Fitz-Greene Halleck 1790–1867
American poet

6 They love their land because it is their own,
And scorn to give aught other reason why;
Would shake hands with a king upon his throne,
And think it kindness to his Majesty.
'Connecticut' (1847)

7 Green be the turf above thee,
Friend of my better days!
None knew thee but to love thee,
Nor named thee but to praise.
'On the Death of Joseph Rodman Drake' (1820)

Friedrich Halm 1806–71
German dramatist

8 *Zwei Seelen und ein Gedanke,*
Zwei Herzen und ein Schlag!

Two souls with but a single thought,
Two hearts that beat as one.
Der Sohn der Wildnis (1842) act 2; translated by Maria Lovell as
Ingomar the Barbarian (1854)

Margaret Halsey 1910–97
American writer

9 The English never smash in a face. They merely
refrain from asking it to dinner.
With Malice Toward Some (1938) pt. 3

W. F. ('Bull') Halsey 1882–1959
American admiral

10 The Third Fleet's sunken and damaged ships
have been salvaged and are retiring at high speed
toward the enemy.
*on hearing claims that the Japanese had virtually
annihilated the US fleet*
report, 14 October 1944; E. B. Potter *Bull Halsey* (1985) ch. 17

Alexander Hamilton c.1755–1804
American politician, US Secretary to the Treasury, 1789–95

11 A national debt, if it is not excessive, will be to
us a national blessing.
letter to Robert Morris, 30 April 1781, in John C. Hamilton
(ed.) *Works of Alexander Hamilton* vol. 1 (1850)

William Hamilton 1788–1856
Scottish metaphysician

12 Truth, like a torch, the more it's shook it shines.
Discussions on Philosophy (1852) title page (epigram)

13 On earth there is nothing great but man; in man
there is nothing great but mind.
Lectures on Metaphysics and Logic (ed. Mamsel and Veitch,
1859) vol. 1; attributed in a Latin form to Favorinus in Pico di
Mirandola (1463–94) *Disputationes Adversus Astrologiam
Divinatricem* (ed. E. Garin, 1946) bk. 3, ch. 27

Oscar Hammerstein II 1895–1960
American songwriter

14 Fish got to swim and birds got to fly
I got to love one man till I die,
Can't help lovin' dat man of mine.
'Can't Help Lovin' Dat Man of Mine' (1927 song) in *Showboat*

15 Climb ev'ry mountain, ford ev'ry stream
Follow ev'ry rainbow, till you find your dream.
'Climb Ev'ry Mountain' (1959 song) in *The Sound of Music*

16 I'm gonna wash that man right outa my hair.
title of song (1949) in *South Pacific*

17 June is bustin' out all over.
title of song (1945) in *Carousel*

18 The last time I saw Paris
Her heart was warm and gay,
I heard the laughter of her heart in ev'ry street
café.
'The Last Time I saw Paris' (1941 song) in *Lady Be Good*

19 The corn is as high as an elephant's eye,
An' it looks like it's climbin' clear up to the sky.
'Oh, What a Beautiful Mornin' ' (1943 song) in *Oklahoma!*

20 Ol' man river, dat ol' man river,
He must know sumpin', but don't say nothin',
He jus' keeps rollin',
He jus' keeps rollin' along.
'Ol' Man River' (1927 song) in *Showboat*

21 Some enchanted evening,
You may see a stranger,
You may see a stranger,
Across a crowded room.
'Some Enchanted Evening' (1949 song) in *South Pacific*

1 The hills are alive with the sound of music,
With songs they have sung for a thousand years.
The hills fill my heart with the sound of music,
My heart wants to sing ev'ry song it hears.
'The Sound of Music' (1959 title-song in show)

2 There is nothin' like a dame.
title of song (1949) in *South Pacific*

3 I'm as corny as Kansas in August,
High as a flag on the Fourth of July!
'A Wonderful Guy' (1949 song) in *South Pacific*

4 You'll never walk alone.
title of song (1945) in *Carousel*

5 You've got to be taught to be afraid
Of people whose eyes are oddly made,
Of people whose skin is a different shade.
You've got to be carefully taught.
'You've Got to be Carefully Taught' (1949 song) in *South Pacific*

Learned Hand 1872–1961
American judge

6 Right conclusions are more likely to be gathered
out of a multitude of tongues, than through any
kind of authoritative selection. To many this is,
and will always be, folly; but we have staked
upon it our all.
in *United States v. Associated Press* 1943; see **BRENNAN** 156:8

7 A self-made man may prefer a self-made name.
on Samuel Goldfish's changing his name to Samuel
GOLDWYN
Bosley Crowther *Lion's Share* (1957) ch. 7

George Frederick Handel 1685–1759
German-born composer and organist, resident in England
from 1712

8 I have read my Bible very well, and shall choose
for myself.
on being sent the texts of the anthems for the 1727
coronation by the bishops
Charles Burney *An Account of the Musical Performances in
Westminster-Abbey* (1785) 'Sketch of the Life of Handel'

9 Whether I was in my body or out of my body
as I wrote it I know not. God knows.
of the 'Hallelujah Chorus' in his *Messiah*; echoing St Paul
Romain Rolland *A Musical Tour Through the Land of the Past*
(1922); see **BIBLE** 113:17

Kate Hankey 1834–1911
English evangelist

10 Tell me the old, old story
Of unseen things above,
Of Jesus and his glory,
Of Jesus and his love.
'Tell me the old, old story' (1867 hymn)

Brian Hanrahan 1949–
English journalist

11 I counted them all out and I counted them all
back.
*on the number of British aeroplanes joining the raid on Port
Stanley in the Falkland Islands*
BBC broadcast report, 1 May 1982, in *Battle for the Falklands*
(1982)

Lorraine Hansberry 1930–65
American dramatist

12 Though it be a thrilling and marvellous thing to
be merely young and gifted in such times, it is
doubly so, doubly dynamic—to be young, gifted
and *black*.
*To be young, gifted and black: Lorraine Hansberry in her own
words* (1969) adapted by Robert Nemiroff; see **IRVINE** 425:20

Rick Hansen 1957–
Canadian wheelchair athlete

13 My disability is that I cannot use my legs. My
handicap is your negative perception of that
disability, and thus of me.
Rick Hansen: Man in Motion (1987, with Jim Taylor)

Edmond Haraucourt 1856–1941
French poet

14 *Partir c'est mourir un peu,*
C'est mourir à ce qu'on aime:
On laisse un peu de soi-même
En toute heure et dans tout lieu.

To go away is to die a little, it is to die to that
which one loves: everywhere and always, one
leaves behind a part of oneself.
Seul (1891) 'Rondel de l'Adieu'

Otto Harbach 1873–1963
American songwriter

15 Now laughing friends deride tears I cannot hide,
So I smile and say 'When a lovely flame dies,
Smoke gets in your eyes.'
'Smoke Gets in your Eyes' (1933 song)

E. Y. ('Yip') Harburg 1898–1981
American songwriter

16 Brother can you spare a dime?
title of song (1932)

17 Say, it's only a paper moon,
Sailing over a cardboard sea.
'It's Only a Paper Moon' (1933 song, with Billy Rose)

18 Wanna cry, wanna croon.
Wanna laugh like a loon.
It's that Old Devil Moon in your eyes.
'Old Devil Moon' (1946 song) in *Finian's Rainbow*

19 Somewhere over the rainbow
Way up high,

There's a land that I heard of
Once in a lullaby.
'Over the Rainbow' (1939 song) in *The Wizard of Oz*

1 Follow the yellow brick road.
'We're Off to See the Wizard' (1939 song) in *The Wizard of Oz*; see **BAUM** 62:7, **JOHN AND TAUPIN** 434:9

William Harcourt 1827–1904
British Liberal politician

2 We are all socialists now.
during the passage of Lord **GOSCHEN***'s 1888 budget, noted for the reduction of the national debt*
attributed; Hubert Bland 'The Outlook' in G. B. Shaw (ed.) *Fabian Essays in Socialism* (1889)

Keir Hardie 1856–1915
Scottish Labour politician, first leader of both the Independent Labour Party (1893) and the Labour Party (1906)

3 From his childhood onward this boy will be surrounded by sycophants and flatterers by the score—[*Cries of* 'Oh, oh!']—and will be taught to believe himself as of a superior creation. [*Cries of* 'Oh, oh!'] A line will be drawn between him and the people whom he is to be called upon some day to reign over. In due course, following the precedent which has already been set, he will be sent on a tour round the world, and probably rumours of a morganatic alliance will follow—[*Loud cries of* 'Oh, oh!' *and* 'Order!']—and the end of it all will be that the country will be called upon to pay the bill. [*Cries of* Divide!]
of the future **EDWARD VIII**
speech in the House of Commons, 28 June 1894

4 Woman, even more than the working class, is the great unknown quantity of the race.
speech at Bradford, 11 April 1914

D. W. Harding 1906–
British psychologist and critic

5 Regulated hatred.
title of an article on the novels of Jane **AUSTEN**
in *Scrutiny* March 1940

Warren G. Harding 1865–1923
American Republican statesman, 29th President of the US 1921–3

6 America's present need is not heroics, but healing; not nostrums but normalcy; not revolution, but restoration.
speech at Boston, 14 May 1920, in Frederick E. Schortemeier *Rededicating America* (1920) ch. 17

7 I must utter my belief in the divine inspiration of the founding fathers.
inaugural address, 4 March 1921

Philip Yorke, Lord Hardwicke
1690–1764
English judge. On Hardwicke: see **PULTENEY** 649:13

8 His doubts are better than most people's certainties.
of Lord Dirleton's Law Doubts (1698)
James Boswell *Life of Samuel Johnson* (1791)

Godfrey Harold Hardy 1877–1947
English mathematician

9 Beauty is the first test: there is no permanent place in the world for ugly mathematics.
A Mathematician's Apology (1940)

Thomas Hardy 1840–1928
English novelist and poet

10 A local thing called Christianity.
The Dynasts (1904) pt. 1, act 1, sc. 6

11 War makes rattling good history; but Peace is poor reading.
The Dynasts (1904) pt. 1, act 2, sc. 5

12 Far from the madding crowd.
title of novel (1874); see **GRAY** 370:8

13 It is hard for a woman to define her feelings in language which is chiefly made by men to express theirs.
Far from the Madding Crowd (1874) ch. 81; see **AUSTEN** 42:4

14 Done because we are too menny.
Jude the Obscure (1896) pt. 6, ch. 2

15 Dialect words—those terrible marks of the beast to the truly genteel.
The Mayor of Casterbridge (1886) ch. 20

16 She whose youth had seemed to teach that happiness was but the occasional episode in a general drama of pain.
The Mayor of Casterbridge (1886) ch. 45, closing words

17 The regular resource of people who don't go enough into the world to live a novel is to write one.
A Pair of Blue Eyes (1873) ch. 12

18 It was at present a place perfectly accordant with man's nature—neither ghastly, hateful, nor ugly: neither commonplace, unmeaning, nor tame; but, like man, slighted and enduring; and withal singularly colossal and mysterious in its swarthy monotony. As with some persons who have long lived a past, solitude seemed to look out of its countenance. It had a lonely face, suggesting tragical possibilities.
of Egdon Heath
The Return of the Native (1878) bk. 1, ch. 1

19 Human beings, in their generous endeavour to construct a hypothesis that shall not degrade a First Cause, have always hesitated to conceive a dominant power of a lower moral quality than their own.
The Return of the Native (1878) bk. 6, ch. 1

1 A novel is an impression, not an argument.
Tess of the D'Urbervilles (5th ed., 1892) preface

2 Why it was that upon this beautiful feminine tissue, sensitive as gossamer, and practically blank as snow as yet, there should have been traced such a coarse pattern as it was doomed to receive; why so often the coarse appropriates the finer thus, the wrong man the woman, the wrong woman the man, many thousand years of analytical philosophy have failed to explain to our sense of order.
Tess of the D'Urbervilles (1891) ch. 11

3 The two forces were at work here as everywhere, the inherent will to enjoy, and the circumstantial will against enjoyment.
Tess of the D'Urbervilles (1891) ch. 43

4 'Justice' was done, and the President of the Immortals (in Aeschylean phrase) had ended his sport with Tess.
Tess of the D'Urbervilles (1891) ch. 59, closing words

5 Good, but not religious-good.
Under the Greenwood Tree (1872) ch. 2

6 It was one of those sequestered spots outside the gates of the world . . . where, from time to time, dramas of a grandeur and unity truly Sophoclean are enacted in the real, by virtue of the concentrated passions and closely knit interdependence of the lives therein.
The Woodlanders (1887) ch. 1

7 The business of the poet and novelist is to show the sorriness underlying the grandest things, and the grandeur underlying the sorriest things.
notebook entry for 19 April 1885, in Florence Hardy *The Early Life of Thomas Hardy 1840–91* (1928) ch. 13

8 When the Present has latched its postern behind
   my tremulous stay,
And the May month flaps its glad green leaves
   like wings,
Delicate-filmed as new-spun silk, will the
   neighbours say,
'He was a man who used to notice such things'?
'Afterwards' (1917)

9 The bower we shrined to Tennyson,
Gentlemen,
Is roof-wrecked; damps there drip upon
Sagged seats, the creeper-nails are rust,
The spider is sole denizen.
'An Ancient to Ancients' (1922)

10 'Peace upon earth!' was said. We sing it,
And pay a million priests to bring it.
After two thousand years of mass
We've got as far as poison-gas.
'Christmas: 1924' (1928)

11 In a solitude of the sea
Deep from human vanity,
And the Pride of Life that planned her, stilly
   couches she.
'Convergence of the Twain' (1914); poem on the loss of the *Titanic*

12 Over the mirrors meant
To glass the opulent
The sea-worm crawls—grotesque, slimed, dumb,
   indifferent.
'Convergence of the Twain' (1914)

13 The Immanent Will that stirs and urges
   everything.
'Convergence of the Twain' (1914)

14 An aged thrush, frail, gaunt, and small,
In blast-beruffled plume.
'The Darkling Thrush' (1902)

15 So little cause for carollings
Of such ecstatic sound
Was written on terrestrial things
Afar or nigh around,
That I could think there trembled through
His happy good-night air
Some blessed Hope, whereof he knew
And I was unaware.
'The Darkling Thrush' (1902)

16 If way to the Better there be, it exacts a full
   look at the worst.
'De Profundis' (1902)

17 Well, World, you have kept faith with me,
Kept faith with me;
Upon the whole you have proved to be
Much as you said you were.
'He Never Expected Much' (1928)

18 I am the family face;
Flesh perishes, I live on,
Projecting trait and trace
Through time to times anon,
And leaping from place to place
Over oblivion.
'Heredity' (1917)

19 Only a man harrowing clods
In a slow silent walk
With an old horse that stumbles and nods
Half asleep as they stalk.
'In Time of "The Breaking of Nations" ' (1917)

20 Yonder a maid and her wight
Come whispering by:
War's annals will cloud into night
Ere their story die.
'In Time of "The Breaking of Nations" ' (1917)

21 Yes; quaint and curious war is!
You shoot a fellow down
You'd treat if met where any bar is,
Or help to half-a-crown.
'The Man he Killed' (1909)

22 What of the faith and fire within us
Men who march away
Ere the barn-cocks say
Night is growing grey,
To hazards whence no tears can win us;
What of the faith and fire within us
Men who march away?
'Men Who March Away' (1914)

23 In the third-class seat sat the journeying boy
And the roof-lamp's oily flame

Played down on his listless form and face,
Bewrapt past knowing to what he was going,
Or whence he came.
'Midnight on the Great Western' (1917)

1 Woman much missed, how you call to me, call
to me.
'The Voice' (1914)

2 This is the weather the cuckoo likes,
And so do I.
'Weathers' (1922)

3 And drops on gate-bars hang in a row,
And rooks in families homeward go,
And so do I.
'Weathers' (1922)

4 When I set out for Lyonnesse,
A hundred miles away,
The rime was on the spray,
And starlight lit my lonesomeness
When I set out for Lyonnesse
A hundred miles away.
'When I set out for Lyonnesse' (1914)

5 If this sort of thing continues no more novel-
writing for me. A man must be a fool to
deliberately stand up and be shot at.
of a hostile review of Tess of the D'Urbervilles, *1891*
Florence Hardy *The Early Life of Thomas Hardy* (1928)

David Hare 1947–
English actor and dramatist

6 What's courage? Failure of planning, that's all.
Bertolt Brecht *Mother Courage and her Children* (1995 version
for the National Theatre)

7 War's like love. It finds a way.
Bertolt Brecht *Mother Courage and Her Children* (1995 version
for the National Theatre); see **BRECHT** 155:21, **PROVERBS** 638:11

Julius Hare 1795–1855 *and* Augustus Hare 1792–1834
English writers and clergymen

8 The ancients dreaded death: the Christian can
only fear dying.
Guesses at Truth (1827) Series 1

Maurice Evan Hare 1886–1967
English limerick writer

9 There once was a man who said, 'Damn!
It is borne in upon me I am
An engine that moves
In predestinate grooves,
I'm not even a bus, I'm a tram.'
'Limerick' (1905)

W. F. Hargreaves 1846–1919
British songwriter

10 I'm Burlington Bertie
I rise at ten thirty and saunter along like a toff,

I walk down the Strand with my gloves on my
hand,
Then I walk down again with them off.
'Burlington Bertie from Bow' (1915 song)

11 I acted so tragic the house rose like magic,
The audience yelled 'You're sublime.'
They made me a present of Mornington
Crescent
They threw it a brick at a time.
'The Night I Appeared as Macbeth' (1922 song)

John Harington d. 1582
English poet

12 There was a battle fought of late,
Yet was the slaughter small;
The strife was, whether I should write,
Or send nothing at all.
Of one side were the captains' names
Short Time and Little Skill;
One fought alone against them both,
Whose name was Great Good-will.
'To his mother' (written 1540)

John Harington 1561–1612
English writer and courtier

13 When I make a feast,
I would my guests should praise it, not the
cooks.
Epigrams (1618) bk. 1, no. 5

14 Treason doth never prosper, what's the reason?
For if it prosper, none dare call it treason.
Epigrams (1618) bk. 4, no. 5

David Ormsby Gore, Lord Harlech 1918–85
British diplomat; Ambassador to Washington, 1961–5

15 Britain will be honoured by historians more for
the way she disposed of an empire than for the
way in which she acquired it.
in *New York Times* 28 October 1962, sect. 4

Harold II c.1019–66
English monarch, King 1066

16 He will give him seven feet of English ground,
or as much more as he may be taller than other
men.
*his offer to Harald Hardrada of Norway, invading England,
before the battle of Stamford Bridge*
King Harald's Saga sect. 91, in Snorri Sturluson *Heimskringla*
(c.1260, first translated by Samuel Laing as *History of the
Norse Kings*, 1844)

Jimmy Harper, Will E. Haines, *and* Tommy Connor

17 The biggest aspidistra in the world.
title of song (1938); popularized by Gracie Fields

Arthur Harris 1892–1984

British Air Force Marshal, Commander-in-Chief of Bomber Command, 1942–5

1 I would not regard the whole of the remaining cities of Germany as worth the bones of one British Grenadier.

supporting the continued strategic bombing of German cities

> letter to Norman Bottomley, deputy Chief of Air Staff, 29 March 1945; Max Hastings *Bomber Command* (1979); see **BISMARCK** 122:19

Joel Chandler Harris 1848–1908

American writer

2 Hit look lak sparrer-grass, hit feel like sparrer-grass, hit tas'e lak sparrer-grass, en I bless ef 'taint sparrer-grass.

> *Nights with Uncle Remus* (1883) ch. 27; see **CAREY** 199:3

3 All by my own-alone self.

> *Nights with Uncle Remus* (1883) ch. 36

4 Bred en bawn in a brier-patch!

> *Uncle Remus and His Legends of the Old Plantation* (1881) 'How Mr Rabbit was too Sharp for Mr Fox'

5 Lounjun 'roun' en suffer'n'.

> *Uncle Remus and His Legends of the Old Plantation* (1881) 'Mr Wolf tackles Old Man Tarrypin'

6 Tar-baby ain't sayin' nuthin', en Brer Fox, he lay low.

> *Uncle Remus and His Legends of the Old Plantation* (1881) 'The Wonderful Tar-Baby Story'

Wilson Harris 1921–

Guyanese novelist, poet, and critic

7 When one dreams, one dreams alone. When one writes a book, one is alone.

> in *Bomb* (82) Winter 2002–3

Tony Harrison 1937–

English poet

8 The ones we choose to love become our anchor when the hawser of the blood-tie's hacked, or frays.

> *v* (1985)

Josephine Hart 1942–

Irish novelist

9 Damaged people are dangerous. They know they can survive.

> *Damage* (1991) ch. 12

Lorenz Hart 1895–1943

American songwriter

10 I'm wild again
Beguiled again
A simpering, whimpering child again,
Bewitched, bothered, and bewildered am I.

> 'Bewitched' (1941 song) in *Pal Joey* (1941)

11 When love congeals
It soon reveals
The faint aroma of performing seals,
The double crossing of a pair of heels.
I wish I were in love again!

> 'I Wish I Were in Love Again' (1937 song) in *Babes in Arms*

12 I get too hungry for dinner at eight.
I like the theatre, but never come late.
I never bother with people I hate.
That's why the lady is a tramp.

> 'The Lady is a Tramp' (1937 song) in *Babes in Arms*

13 In a mountain greenery
Where God paints the scenery—
Just two crazy people together.

> 'Mountain Greenery' (1926 song)

14 Thou swell! Thou witty!
Thou sweet! Thou grand!
Wouldst kiss me pretty?
Wouldst hold my hand?

> 'Thou Swell' (1927 song)

Bret Harte 1836–1902

American poet

15 And on that grave where English oak and holly
And laurel wreaths entwine
Deem it not all a too presumptuous folly,—
This spray of Western pine!

> 'Dickens in Camp' (1870)

16 If, of all words of tongue and pen,
The saddest are, 'It might have been,'
More sad are these we daily see:
'It is, but hadn't ought to be!'

> 'Mrs Judge Jenkins' (1867); see **WHITTIER** 853:3

17 And he smiled a kind of sickly smile, and curled up on the floor,
And the subsequent proceedings interested him no more.

> 'The Society upon the Stanislaus' (1868) st. 7

18 All you know about it [luck] for certain is that it's bound to change.

> 'The Outcasts of Poker Flat' (1871) in *The Luck of the Roaring Camp and Other Stories* (1922)

David Hartley 1731–1813

English Whig politician

19 That the slave trade is contrary to the laws of God and to the rights of men.

> *proposing its abolition in the House of Commons in 1776*
> Charles Stuart *A Memoir of Granville Sharp* (1836)

L. P. Hartley 1895–1972

English novelist

20 The past is a foreign country: they do things differently there.

> *The Go-Between* (1953) prologue (opening words); see **MORLEY** 560:2

F. W. Harvey b. 1888
English poet

1 From troubles of the world
I turn to ducks
Beautiful comical things.
'Ducks' (1919)

Molly Haskell 1940–
American writer and film critic

2 Being alone and liking it is, for a woman, an act
of treachery, an infidelity far more threatening
than adultery.
Love and Other Infectious Diseases (1990)

Minnie Louise Haskins 1875–1957
English teacher and writer

3 And I said to the man who stood at the gate of
the year: 'Give me a light that I may tread safely
into the unknown.'
And he replied:
'Go out into the darkness and put your hand
into the Hand of God. That shall be to you
better than light and safer than a known way.'
quoted by **GEORGE VI** *in his Christmas broadcast, 1939*
Desert (1908) 'God Knows'

Edwin Hatch 1835–89
English clergyman and scholar

4 Breathe on me, Breath of God,
Fill me with life anew,
That I may love what thou dost love,
And do what thou wouldst do.
'Breathe on me, Breath of God' (1878 hymn)

Helen Hathaway 1893–1932
American writer

5 More tears have been shed over men's lack of
manners than their lack of morals.
Manners for Men (1928)

Charles Haughey 1925–2006
Irish Fianna Fáil statesman, Taoiseach 1979–81, 1982, and
1987–92. On Haughey: see **O'BRIEN** 583:3

6 It was a bizarre happening, an unprecedented
situation, a grotesque situation, an almost
unbelievable mischance.
*on the series of events leading to the resignation of the
Attorney General; the acronym* GUBU (*grotesque,
unbelievable, bizarre, and unprecedented*) *was subsequently
coined by Conor Cruise* **O'BRIEN** *to describe Haughey's style
of government*
at a press conference in 1982; T. Ryle Dwyer *Charlie: the
Political Biography of Charles Haughey* (1987) ch. 12

Václav Havel 1936–
Czech dramatist and statesman, President of
Czechoslovakia 1989–92 and of the Czech Republic
1993–2003

7 Truth is not merely what we are thinking, but
also why, to whom and under what
circumstances we say it.
Temptation (1985)

8 I really do inhabit a system in which words are
capable of shaking the entire structure of
government, where words can prove mightier
than ten military divisions.
speech in Germany accepting a peace prize, October 1989, in
Independent 9 December 1989

Zahi Hawass 1947–
Egyptian archaeologist

9 There is an ancient Egyptian saying that 'Man
fears time, and time fears the pyramids,' but this
is no longer true. The pyramids must fear time,
too.
in *New York Times* 10 August 1997

Stephen Hawes d. *c.*1523
English poet

10 After the day there cometh the dark night;
For though the day be never so long,
At last the bells ringeth to evensong.
The Pastime of Pleasure (1509) ch. 42, st. 10

R. S. Hawker 1803–75
English clergyman and poet

11 And have they fixed the where and when?
And shall Trelawny die?
Here's twenty thousand Cornish men
Will know the reason why!
*the last three lines have been in existence since the
imprisonment by James II, in 1688, of seven bishops,
including Trelawny, Bishop of Bristol*
'The Song of the Western Men'

Jacquetta Hawkes 1910–96
English archaeologist and writer

12 Every age has the Stonehenge it deserves—or
desires.
in *Antiquity* no. 41, 1967

13 I was conscious of this vanished being and
myself as part of an unbroken stream of
consciousness . . . With an imaginative effort it is
possible to see the eternal present in which all
days, all the seasons of the plain, stand in
enduring unity.
discovering a Neanderthal skeleton
in *New York Times Biographical Service* 21 March 1996

Stephen Hawking 1942–

English theoretical physicist

1 Each equation . . . in the book would halve the sales.
A Brief History of Time (1988)

2 In effect, we have redefined the task of science to be the discovery of laws that will enable us to predict events up to the limits set by the uncertainty principle.
A Brief History of Time (1988) ch. 11

3 What is it that breathes fire into the equations and makes a universe for them to describe . . . Why does the universe go to all the bother of existing?
A Brief History of Time (1988)

4 If we find the answer to that [why it is that we and the universe exist], it would be the ultimate triumph of human reason—for then we would know the mind of God.
A Brief History of Time (1988) ch. 11

5 I think computer viruses should count as life. Maybe it says something about human nature, that the only form of life we have created so far is purely destructive.
'Life in the Universe', undated lecture on www.hawking.org (September 2008)

Nathaniel Hawthorne 1804–64

American novelist

6 Amid the fluctuating waves of our social life, somebody is always at the drowning-point.
The House of the Seven Gables (1851) ch. 2

7 Dr Johnson's morality was as English an article as a beefsteak.
Our Old Home (1863) 'Lichfield and Uttoxeter'

8 The scarlet letter.
title of novel (1850)

9 America is now given over to a damned mob of scribbling women.
letter, 1855; Caroline Ticknor *Hawthorne and his Publisher* (1913)

Lord Charles Hay *c.*1700–60

Scottish army officer

10 Gentlemen of France, fire first.
said before the Battle of Fontenoy, 1745, a battle in the war of the Austrian Succession, which resulted in a victory for the French over Austria and her allies
Voltaire *Siècle de Louis XIV* (1751), where the wording is given as 'Gentlemen of the French guards, open fire'

Ian Hay (John Hay Beith) 1876–1952

Scottish novelist and dramatist

11 War is hell, and all that, but it has a good deal to recommend it. It wipes out all the small nuisances of peace-time.
The First Hundred Thousand (1915)

12 What do you mean, funny? Funny-peculiar or funny ha-ha?
The Housemaster (1938) act 3

13 The dawn of legibility in his handwriting has revealed his utter inability to spell.
attributed; perhaps used in a dramatization of *The Housemaster* (1938)

Franz Joseph Haydn 1732–1809

Austrian composer

14 But all the world understands my language.
on being advised by **MOZART**, *in 1790, not to visit England because he knew too little of the world and too few languages*
Rosemary Hughes *Haydn* (1950) ch. 6

Alfred Hayes 1911–85

American songwriter

15 I dreamed I saw Joe Hill last night
Alive as you and me.
Says I, 'But Joe, you're ten years dead.'
'I never died,' says he.
'I Dreamed I Saw Joe Hill Last Night' (1936 song); see **HILL** 398:14

J. Milton Hayes 1884–1940

English writer

16 There's a one-eyed yellow idol to the north of Khatmandu,
There's a little marble cross below the town,
There's a broken-hearted woman tends the grave of Mad Carew,
And the Yellow God forever gazes down.
The Green Eye of the Yellow God (1911)

Eliza Haywood *c.*1693–1756

English actress, dramatist, and novelist

17 One has no sooner left off one's bib and apron, than people cry—'Miss will soon be married!'—and this man, and that man, is presently picked out for a husband. Mighty ridiculous! they want to deprive us of all the pleasures of life, just when one begins to have a relish for them.
The History of Miss Betty Thoughtless (1751)

William Hazlitt 1778–1830

English essayist. On Hazlitt: see **STEVENSON** 776:4

18 Any one is to be pitied, who has just sense enough to perceive his deficiencies.
Characteristics (1823) no. 213

19 Every man, in his own opinion, forms an exception to the ordinary rules of morality.
Characteristics (1823) no. 305

20 His sayings are generally like women's letters; all the pith is in the postscript.
of Charles **LAMB**
Conversations of James Northcote (1826–7)

1 Wit is the salt of conversation, not the food.
Lectures on the English Comic Writers (1819) 'On Wit and Humour'

2 He talked on for ever; and you wished him to talk on for ever.
of **COLERIDGE**
Lectures on the English Poets (1818) 'On the Living Poets'

3 So have I loitered my life away, reading books, looking at pictures, going to plays, hearing, thinking, writing on what pleased me best. I have wanted only one thing to make me happy, but wanting that have wanted everything.
Literary Remains (1836) 'My First Acquaintance with Poets'

4 By despising all that has preceded us, we teach others to despise ourselves.
'On Reading New Books' in *Monthly Magazine* 1827

5 The greatest test of courage I can conceive is to speak the truth in the House of Commons.
'On the Difference between Writing and Speaking'; in *London Magazine* July 1820

6 The dupe of friendship, and the fool of love; have I not reason to hate and to despise myself? Indeed I do; and chiefly for not having hated and despised the world enough.
The Plain Speaker (1826) 'On the Pleasure of Hating'

7 The love of liberty is the love of others; the love of power is the love of ourselves.
Political Essays (1819) 'The Times Newspaper'

8 There is nothing good to be had in the country, or if there is, they will not let you have it.
The Round Table (1817) 'Observations on Mr Wordsworth's Poem *The Excursion*'

9 Comedy naturally wears itself out—destroys the very food on which it lives; and by constantly and successfully exposing the follies and weaknesses of mankind to ridicule, in the end leaves itself nothing worth laughing at.
The Round Table (1817) 'On Modern Comedy'

10 The art of pleasing consists in being pleased.
The Round Table (1817) 'On Manner'

11 A nickname is the heaviest stone that the devil can throw at a man.
Sketches and Essays (1839) 'Nicknames'

12 We must overact our part in some measure, in order to produce any effect at all.
Sketches and Essays (1839) 'On Cant and Hypocrisy'

13 Rules and models destroy genius and art.
Sketches and Essays (1839) 'On Taste'

14 No one ever approaches perfection except by stealth, and unknown to himself.
Sketches and Essays (1839) 'On Taste'

15 Death cancels everything but truth; and strips a man of everything but genius and virtue. It is a sort of natural canonization.
The Spirit of the Age (1825) 'Lord Byron'

16 The present is an age of talkers, and not of doers; and the reason is, that the world is growing old. We are so far advanced in the Arts and Sciences, that we live in retrospect, and dote on past achievement.
The Spirit of the Age (1825) 'Mr Coleridge'

17 He writes as fast as they can read, and he does not write himself down . . . His worst is better than any other person's best.
The Spirit of the Age (1825) 'Sir Walter Scott'

18 His works (taken together) are almost like a new edition of human nature. This is indeed to be an author!
The Spirit of the Age (1825) 'Sir Walter Scott'

19 Mr Wordsworth's genius is a pure emanation of the Spirit of the Age. Had he lived in any other period of the world, he would never have been heard of.
The Spirit of the Age (1825) 'Mr Wordsworth'

20 You will hear more good things on the outside of a stagecoach from London to Oxford than if you were to pass a twelvemonth with the undergraduates, or heads of colleges, of that famous university.
Table Talk vol. 1 (1821) 'The Ignorance of the Learned'

21 Danger is a good teacher, and makes apt scholars.
Table Talk vol. 1 (1821) 'The Indian Jugglers'

22 The English (it must be owned) are rather a foul-mouthed nation.
Table Talk vol. 2 (1822) 'On Criticism'

23 We can scarcely hate any one that we know.
Table Talk vol. 2 (1822) 'On Criticism'

24 Give me the clear blue sky over my head, and the green turf beneath my feet, a winding road before me, and a three hours' march to dinner—and then to thinking! It is hard if I cannot start some game on these lone heaths.
Table Talk vol. 2 (1822) 'On Going a Journey'

25 Well, I've had a happy life.
last words; W. C. Hazlitt *Memoirs of William Hazlitt* (1867)

Bessie Head 1937–86

South African-born writer

26 And if the white man thought that Asians were a low, filthy nation, Asians could still smile with relief—at least, they were not Africans. And if the white man thought that Africans were a low, filthy nation, Africans in southern Africa could still smile—at least, they were not bushmen. They all have their monsters.
Maru (1971) pt. 1

27 Love is mutually feeding each other, not one living on another like a ghoul.
A Question of Power (1973)

Denis Healey 1917–

British Labour politician, husband of Edna HEALEY. See also PHILLIPS 606:7

28 I warn you there are going to be howls of anguish from the 80,000 people who are rich

enough to pay over 75% [tax] on the last slice of their income.
speech at Labour Party Conference, 1 October 1973

1 Like being savaged by a dead sheep.
*on being criticized by Geoffrey **HOWE** in the House of Commons*
in the House of Commons, 14 June 1978

Edna Healey 1918–

English writer, wife of Denis **HEALEY**

2 She has no hinterland; in particular she has no sense of history.
*of Margaret **THATCHER***
Denis Healey *The Time of My Life* (1989)

Timothy Michael Healy 1855–1931

Irish nationalist politician

3 **REDMOND**: Gladstone is now master of the Party!
HEALY: Who is to be mistress of the Party?
*at the meeting of the Irish Parliamentary Party on 6 December 1890, when the Party split over **PARNELL**'s involvement in the O'Shea divorce; Healy's reference to Katherine O'Shea was particularly damaging to Parnell*
Robert Kee *The Laurel and the Ivy* (1993)

4 The Sinns won in three years what we did not win in forty. You cannot make revolutions with rosewater, or omelettes without breaking eggs.
letter to his brother; Frank Callanan T. M. Healy (1996)

Seamus Heaney 1939–

Irish poet

5 All agog at the plasterer on his ladder
Skimming our gable and writing our name there
With his trowel point, letter by strange letter.
'Alphabets' (1987)

6 And found myself thinking: if it were nowadays,
This is how Death would summon Everyman.
'A Call' (1996)

7 How culpable was he
That last night when he broke
Our tribe's complicity?
'Now you're supposed to be
An educated man,'
I hear him say. 'Puzzle me
The right answer to that one.'
'Casualty' (1979)

8 History says, *Don't hope*
On this side of the grave.
But then, once in a lifetime
The longed-for tidal wave
Of justice can rise up
And hope and history rhyme.
The Cure at Troy (version of **SOPHOCLES**' *Philoctetes*, 1990)

9 Between my finger and my thumb
The squat pen rests.
I'll dig with it.
'Digging' (1966)

10 Me waiting until I was nearly fifty
To credit marvels.
'Fosterling' (1991)

11 The annals say: when the monks of Clonmacnoise
Were all at prayers inside the oratory
A ship appeared above them in the air.
'Lightenings viii' (1991)

12 And then the ox would lurch against the gong
And deaden it and I would feel my tongue
Like the dropped gangplank of a cattle truck,
Trampled and rattled, running piss and muck.
'Mycenae Lookout' (1995); see **AESCHYLUS** 6:12

13 Don't be surprised
If I demur, for, be advised
My passport's green.
No glass of ours was ever raised
To toast *The Queen*.
rebuking the editors of The Penguin Book of Contemporary British Poetry *for including him among its authors*
Open Letter (Field Day pamphlet no. 2, 1983)

14 Who would connive
in civilised outrage
yet understand the exact
and tribal, intimate revenge.
'Punishment' (1975)

15 Until, on Vinegar Hill, the fatal conclave.
Terraced thousands died, shaking scythes at cannon.
'Requiem for the Croppies' (1969)

16 My heart besieged by anger, my mind a gap of danger,
I walked among their old haunts, the home ground where they bled;
And in the dirt lay justice like an acorn in the winter
Till its oak would sprout in Derry where the thirteen men lay dead.
of Bloody Sunday, Londonderry, 30 January 1972
'The Road to Derry'

17   HERE IS THE NEWS,
Said the absolute speaker. Between him and us
A great gulf was fixed where pronunciation
Reigned tyrannically
'A Sofa in the Forties' (1996)

18   The famous
Northern reticence, the tight gag of place
And times: yes, yes. Of the 'wee six' I sing
Where to be saved you only must save face
And whatever you say, you say nothing.
'Whatever You Say Say Nothing' (1975)

19 If revolution is the kicking down of a rotten door, evolution is more like pushing the stone from the mouth of the tomb. There is an Easter energy about it, a sense of arrival rather than wreckage.
in Observer 12 April 1998

1 No death outside my immediate family has left me more bereft. No death in my lifetime has hurt poets more.
funeral oration for Ted HUGHES, 3 November 1998, in *Guardian* 4 November 1998

William Randolph Hearst 1863–1951
American newspaper publisher and tycoon

2 The day when this nation ceases to shape its foreign policy primarily for the safety and welfare of the American people will be the day on which its national doom is sealed—and its international doom too.
in *San Francisco Examiner* 7 May 1924

3 You furnish the pictures and I'll furnish the war.
message to the artist Frederic Remington in Havana, Cuba, during the Spanish-American War of 1898
attributed

Edward Heath 1916–
British Conservative statesman, Prime Minister 1970–4

4 The unpleasant and unacceptable face of capitalism.
on the Lonrho affair
in the House of Commons, 15 May 1973

5 Rejoice, rejoice, rejoice.
telephone call to his office on hearing of Margaret THATCHER's fall from power in 1990
attributed; in *Daily Telegraph* 24 September 1998 (online edition)

John Heath-Stubbs 1918–2006
English poet

6 Venerable Mother Toothache
Climb down from the white battlements,
Stop twisting in your yellow fingers
The fourfold rope of nerves;
And tomorrow I will give you a tot of whisky
To hold in your cupped hands,
A garland of anise flowers,
And three cloves like nails.
'A Charm Against the Toothache' (1954)

Reginald Heber 1783–1826
English clergyman and hymn writer; Bishop of Calcutta from 1823

7 Brightest and best of the sons of the morning,
Dawn on our darkness and lend us thine aid;
Star of the east, the horizon adorning,
Guide where our infant Redeemer is laid.
'Brightest and best of the sons of the morning' (1827 hymn)

8 From Greenland's icy mountains,
From India's coral strand,
Where Afric's sunny fountains
Roll down their golden sand.
'From Greenland's icy mountains' (1821 hymn)

9 What though the spicy breezes
Blow soft o'er Ceylon's isle;

Though every prospect pleases,
And only man is vile:
In vain with lavish kindness
The gifts of God are strown;
The heathen in his blindness
Bows down to wood and stone.
'From Greenland's icy mountains' (1821 hymn); Heber later altered 'Ceylon's isle' to 'Java's isle'; see KIPLING 465:14

10 Holy, Holy, Holy! Lord God Almighty!
Early in the morning our song shall rise to thee:
Holy, Holy, Holy! merciful and mighty!
God in Three Persons, blessèd Trinity!

Holy, Holy, Holy! all the saints adore thee,
Casting down their golden crowns around the glassy sea,
Cherubim and Seraphim falling down before thee,
Which wert, and art, and evermore shalt be.
'Holy, Holy, Holy! Lord God Almighty!' (1826 hymn)

Ben Hecht 1894–1964
American screenwriter. See also FILM LINES 329:17

11 [Goldwyn] filled the room with wonderful panic and beat at your mind like a man in front of a slot machine, shaking it for a jackpot.
A. Scott Berg *Goldwyn* (1989) ch. 15

G. W. F. Hegel 1770–1831
German idealist philosopher. See also MARX 526:8

12 Gangrenous limbs cannot be cured with lavender water.
The German Constitution (1798–1802) pt. 9 'The growth of states in the rest of Europe', translated by M. Knox; see PROVERBS 642:23

13 What experience and history teach is this—that nations and governments have never learned anything from history, or acted upon any lessons they might have drawn from it.
Lectures on the Philosophy of World History: Introduction (1830, translated by H. B. Nisbet, 1975) introduction

14 It is easier to perceive the shortcomings of individuals, states, and the course of world affairs than to understand their true impact.
Lectures on the Philosophy of World History: Introduction (1830, translated by H. B. Nisbet, 1975)

15 Only in the state does man have a rational existence . . . Man owes his entire existence to the state, and has his being within it alone. Whatever worth and spiritual reality he possesses are his solely by virtue of the state.
Lectures on the Philosophy of World History: Introduction (1830, translated by H. B. Nisbet, 1975)

16 It is a land of desire for all those who are weary of the historical arsenal of old Europe.
of America
Lectures on the Philosophy of World History: Introduction (1830, translated by H. B. Nisbet, 1975)

17 In history, we are concerned with what has been and what is; in philosophy, however, we are concerned not with what belongs exclusively to

the past or to the future, but with that which *is*, both now and eternally—in short, with reason.

Lectures on the Philosophy of World History: Introduction (1830, translated by H. B. Nisbet, 1975)

1 What is rational is actual and what is actual is rational.

Philosophy of Right (1821, translated by T. M. Knox, 1952)

2 When philosophy paints its grey on grey, then has a shape of life grown old. By philosophy's grey on grey it cannot be rejuvenated but only understood. The owl of Minerva spreads its wings only with the falling of the dusk.

Philosophy of Right (1821, translated by T. M. Knox, 1952)

3 Thus to be independent of public opinion is the first formal condition of achieving anything great or rational whether in life or in science. Great achievement is assured, however, of subsequent recognition and grateful acceptance by public opinion, which in due course will make it one of its own prejudices.

Philosophy of Right (1821, translated by T. M. Knox, 1952) sect. 318

Heikhalot Rabbati

Jewish mystical text of c.5th–6th century AD

4 I may tell them the mysteries that are hidden and concealed, the wonders of the weaving of the web on which depends the perfection and glory of the world . . . the wonders of the path of the celestial ladder, one end of which rests on earth and the other by the right foot of the Throne of Glory.

16:1

Christoph Hein 1944–

German writer

5 I don't know what a personal gift is. I think if I really gave someone a personal gift, it would scare him to death. I don't know what a personal gift for myself would be, either. But I'm sure that if it were really personal, I would burst into tears. At least I'd know then what sort of person I am.

The Distant Lover (1982) ch. 10, translated by Krishna Winston

Piet Hein 1905–96

Danish poet and cartoonist

6 Problems worthy
of attack
prove their worth
by hitting back.

'Problems' (1969)

Heinrich Heine 1797–1856

German poet

7   *Dort, wo man Bücher*
Verbrennt, verbrennt man auch am Ende Menschen.

Wherever books will be burned, men also, in the end, are burned.

Almansor (1823) l. 245

8 *Auf Flügeln des Gesanges.*
On wings of song.

title of song (1823)

9 *Ich weiss nicht, was soll es bedeuten,*
Dass ich so traurig bin;
Ein Märchen aus alten Zeiten,
Das kommt mir nicht aus dem Sinn.

I know not why I am so sad; I cannot get out of my head a fairy-tale of olden times.

'Die Lorelei' (1826–31)

10 *Es ist eine alte Geschichte,*
Doch bleibt sie immer neu.

It is so old a story,
Yet somehow always new.

Lyrisches Intermezzo (1823) no. 39 (translated by Hal Draper)

11 Wild, dark times are rumbling towards us, and the prophet who wishes to write a new apocalypse will have to invent entirely new beasts, and beasts so terrible that the ancient animal symbols of Saint John will seem like cooing doves and cupids in comparison.

Lutezia (1855)

12 *Sie hatten sich beide so herzlich lieb,*
Spitzbübin war sie, er war ein Dieb.

They loved each other beyond belief—
She was a strumpet, he was a thief.

Neue Gedichte (1852) 'Ein Weib' (translated by Louis Untermeyer, 1938)

13 What then is music? . . . It exists between thought and phenomenon, like a twilight medium, it stands between spirit and matter, related to and yet different from both; it is spirit, but spirit governed by time; it is matter, but matter that can manage without space.

On the French Stage: Intimate letters to August Lewald (1857)

14 It may be that the stars of heaven appear to us fair and pure simply because we are at such a distance from them, and know nothing of their private life.

The Romantic School (1833)

15 *Hört ihr das Glöckchen klingeln? Kniet nieder—Man*
bringt die Sakramente einem sterbenden Gotte.

Do you hear the little bell tinkle? Kneel down. They are bringing the sacraments to a dying god.

Zur Geschichte der Religion und Philosophie in Deutschland (1834) bk. 2, closing words

16 Maximilien Robespierre was nothing but the hand of Jean Jacques Rousseau, the bloody hand that drew from the womb of time the body whose soul Rousseau had created.

Zur Geschichte der Religion und Philosophie in Deutschland (1834) bk. 3, para. 3

17 *Dieu me pardonnera, c'est son métier.*
God will pardon me, it is His trade.

on his deathbed, Alfred Meissner *Heinrich Heine. Erinnerungen* (1856) ch. 5; see **CATHERINE** 209:18

Werner Heisenberg 1901–76

German mathematical physicist

1 An expert is someone who knows some of the worst mistakes that can be made in his subject and who manages to avoid them.

Der Teil und das Ganze (1969) ch. 17 (translated by A. J. Pomerans as *Physics and Beyond*, 1971)

2 *on Felix Bloch's stating that space was the field of linear operations:*

Nonsense. Space is blue and birds fly through it.

Felix Bloch 'Heisenberg and the early days of quantum mechanics' in *Physics Today* December 1976

Joseph Heller 1923–99

American novelist

3 There was only one catch and that was Catch-22, which specified that a concern for one's own safety in the face of dangers that were real and immediate was the process of a rational mind . . . Orr would be crazy to fly more missions and sane if he didn't, but if he was sane he had to fly them. If he flew them he was crazy and didn't have to; but if he didn't want to he was sane and had to.

Catch-22 (1961) ch. 5

4 Some men are born mediocre, some men achieve mediocrity, and some men have mediocrity thrust upon them. With Major Major it had been all three.

Catch-22 (1961) ch. 9; see **SHAKESPEARE** 735:24

5 When I read something saying I've not done anything as good as *Catch-22* I'm tempted to reply, 'Who has?'

in *The Times* 9 June 1993

Lillian Hellman 1905–84

American dramatist. On Hellman: see **MCCARTHY** 509:8

6 Propaganda is a soft weapon: hold it in your hands too long, and it will move about like a snake, and strike the other way.

The Lark (1955), adapted from *L'Alouette* by Jean **ANOUILH**

7 I cannot and will not cut my conscience to fit this year's fashions.

letter to John S. Wood, 19 May 1952, in *US Congress Committee Hearing on Un-American Activities* (1952) pt. 8

Leona Helmsley c.1920–2007

American hotelier

8 Only the little people pay taxes.

comment made to her housekeeper in 1983, and reported at her trial for tax evasion

in *New York Times* 12 July 1989

Héloise c.1098–1164

French abbess, lover of **ABELARD**

9 God knows I never sought anything in you except yourself; I wanted simply you, nothing of yours.

letter to Peter Abelard, c.1132; Betty Radice *The Letters of Abelard and Heloise* (1974)

10 My heart was not in me but with you, and now, even more, if it is not with you it is nowhere.

letter to Peter Abelard, c.1132; Betty Radice *The Letters of Abelard and Heloise* (1974)

Helvétius (Claude Arien Helvétius) 1715–71

French philosopher. On Helvétius: see **MISQUOTATIONS** 547:20

11 [We must] substitute the language of interest for the tone of injury. Do not complain, appeal to interest.

De l'esprit (1758) 'Discours 2' ch. 15

12 *L'éducation nous faisait ce que nous sommes.*

Education made us what we are.

De l'esprit (1758) 'Discours 3' ch. 30

13 When prejudice commands, reason is silent.

De l'homme (1773)

Felicia Hemans 1793–1835

English poet. On Hemans: see **SCOTT** 690:3

14 The boy stood on the burning deck
Whence all but he had fled;
The flame that lit the battle's wreck
Shone round him o'er the dead.

'Casabianca' (1849)

15 The stately homes of England,
How beautiful they stand!
Amidst their tall ancestral trees,
O'er all the pleasant land.

'The Homes of England' (1849); see **COWARD** 253:19

John Heming 1556–1630 *and* Henry Condell d. 1627

English joint editors of the First Folio

16 Well! it is now public, and you will stand for your privileges we know: to read, and censure. Do so, but buy it first. That doth best commend a book, the stationer says.

First Folio Shakespeare (1623) preface

17 Who, as he was a happy imitator of Nature, was a most gentle expresser of it. His mind and hand went together: And what he thought, he uttered with that easiness, that we have scarce received from him a blot.

First Folio Shakespeare (1623) preface; see **JONSON** 447:3, **POPE** 617:24

Ernest Hemingway 1899–1961

American novelist. See also **DONNE** 290:4, **FITZGERALD** 332:3, **JACKSON** 427:3, **STEIN** 771:6

1 Where do the noses go? I always wondered where the noses would go.
For Whom the Bell Tolls (1940) ch. 7

2 But did thee feel the earth move?
For Whom the Bell Tolls (1940) ch. 13

3 Paris is a movable feast.
A Movable Feast (1964) epigraph

4 All things truly wicked start from an innocence.
A Movable Feast (1964) ch. 20

5 The sun also rises.
title of novel (1926)

6 Grace under pressure.
when asked what he meant by 'guts' in an interview with Dorothy **PARKER**
in *New Yorker* 30 November 1929

7 The most essential gift for a good writer is a built-in, shock-proof shit detector. This is the writer's radar, and all great writers have had it.
in *Paris Review* Spring 1958

8 Hesitation increases in relation to risk in equal proportion to age.
A. E. Hotchner *Papa Hemingway* (1966) pt. 1, ch. 3

Jimi Hendrix (James Marshall Hendrix) 1942–70

American rock musician

9 Purple haze is in my brain
Lately things don't seem the same.
'Purple Haze' (1967 song)

Arthur W. D. Henley

10 Nobody loves a fairy when she's forty.
title of song (1934)

W. E. Henley 1849–1903

English poet and dramatist. On Henley: see **WILDE** 856:11

11 A deal of Ariel, just a streak of Puck,
Much Antony, of Hamlet most of all,
And something of the Shorter-Catechist.
of Robert Louis **STEVENSON**
'In Hospital' (1888)

12 Out of the night that covers me,
Black as the Pit from pole to pole,
I thank whatever gods may be
For my unconquerable soul.

In the fell clutch of circumstance,
I have not winced nor cried aloud:
Under the bludgeonings of chance
My head is bloody, but unbowed.
'Invictus. In Memoriam R.T.H.B.' (1888)

13 It matters not how strait the gate,
How charged with punishments the scroll,

I am the master of my fate:
I am the captain of my soul.
'Invictus. In Memoriam R.T.H.B.' (1888)

14 What have I done for you,
England, my England?
'Pro Rege Nostro' (1900); see **MACDONELL** 510:12

15 Or ever the knightly years were gone
With the old world to the grave,
I was a King in Babylon
And you were a Christian slave.
'To W. A.' (1888)

Peter Hennessy 1947–

English historian

16 The model of a modern Prime Minister would be a kind of grotesque composite freak—someone with the dedication to duty of a Peel, the physical energy of a Gladstone, the detachment of a Salisbury, the brains of an Asquith, the balls of a Lloyd George, the word-power of a Churchill, the administrative gifts of an Attlee, the style of a Macmillan, the managerialism of a Heath, and the sleep requirements of a Thatcher. Human beings do not come like that.
The Hidden Wiring (1995); see **GILBERT** 358:6

Henri IV (of Navarre) 1553–1610

French monarch, King of France from 1589

17 I want there to be no peasant in my kingdom so poor that he is unable to have a chicken in his pot every Sunday.
Hardouin de Péréfixe *Histoire de Henry le Grand* (1681); see **HOOVER** 406:14

18 Hang yourself, brave Crillon; we fought at Arques and you were not there.
traditional form given by Voltaire to a letter from Henri to Crillon, 20 September 1597; Henri's actual words, as given in *Lettres missives de Henri IV, Collection des documents inédits de l'histoire de France* vol. 4 (1847) were 'My good man, Crillon, hang yourself for not having been at my side last Monday at the greatest event that's ever been seen and perhaps ever will be seen'

19 *Paris vaut bien une messe.*

Paris is well worth a mass.
attributed to Henri IV; alternatively to his minister Sully, in conversation with Henri

20 The wisest fool in Christendom.
of **JAMES I** *of England*
attributed both to Henri IV and Sully

Henry I 1068–1135

English monarch, King from 1100

21 An illiterate king is a crowned ass.
described as a proverbial usage on the part of Henry by William of Malmesbury in *De Gestis Regum Anglorum*, and probably first coined by Count Foulques II of Anjou, c.950

Henry II 1133–89
English monarch, King from 1154

1 Will no one rid me of this turbulent priest?
of Thomas Becket, Archbishop of Canterbury, murdered in Canterbury Cathedral, December 1170

oral tradition, conflating a number of variant forms, including G. Lyttelton *History of the Life of King Henry the Second* (1769) pt. 4: 'so many cowardly and ungrateful men in his court, none of whom would revenge him of the injuries he sustained from one turbulent priest'

Henry VIII 1491–1547
English monarch, King from 1509. On Henry VIII: see
AUSTEN 41:11, **CHRISTINA** 227:4, **MORE** 559:6

2 That man hath the sow by the right ear.
of Thomas **CRANMER,** *June 1529*

Acts and Monuments of John Foxe ['Foxe's Book of Martyrs'] (1570)

3 The King found her so different from her picture . . . that . . . he swore they had brought him a Flanders mare.
of Anne of Cleves

Tobias Smollett *A Complete History of England* (3rd ed., 1759) vol. 6

Henry of Huntingdon *c.*1084–1155
English chronicler

4 They beheaded priests at the very altar, and then cutting off the heads of the crucifixes on the roodbeams they put the priest's head on the trunk of the crucifix, and the head of the crucifix on the trunk of the priest.
description of atrocities occurring during the invasion of King David of Scotland in 1138

Historia Anglorum (ed. T. Arnold, Rolls series, 1879)

5 A new kind of monster, compounded of purity and corruption, a monk and a knight.
of Henry of Blois (1101–71), bishop of Winchester and brother of King Stephen

Historia Anglorum (ed. T. Arnold, Rolls series, 1879)

Matthew Henry 1662–1714
English divine

6 The better day, the worse deed.
An Exposition on the Old and New Testament (1710) Genesis ch. 3, v. 6, gloss 2; see **PROVERBS** 627:36

7 He rolls it under his tongue as a sweet morsel.
An Exposition on the Old and New Testament (1710) Psalm 36, v. 2, gloss 1

8 They that die by famine die by inches.
An Exposition on the Old and New Testament (1710) Psalm 59, v. 15, gloss 5 (referring incorrectly to v. 13)

O. Henry (William Sydney Porter) 1862–1910
American short-story writer

9 It was beautiful and simple as all truly great swindles are.
Gentle Grafter (1908) 'Octopus Marooned'

10 It looked like a good thing, but wait till I tell you.
Whirligigs (1910) 'The Ransom of Red Chief'

11 Turn up the lights; I don't want to go home in the dark.
last words, quoting the song 'I'm afraid to come home in the dark' (1907) by Harry Williams (1874–1924)

Charles Alphonso Smith *O. Henry Biography* (1916) ch. 9

Patrick Henry 1736–99
American statesman

12 Caesar had his Brutus—Charles the First, his Cromwell—and George the Third—('Treason,' cried the Speaker) . . . *may profit by their example. If this be treason, make the most of it.*
speech in the Virginia assembly, May 1765, in William Wirt *Patrick Henry* (1818) sect. 2

13 I am not a Virginian, but an American.
in [John Adams's] Notes of Debates in the Continental Congress, Philadelphia, 6 September 1774; in L. H. Butterfield (ed.) *Diary and Autobiography of John Adams* (1961) vol. 2

14 I know not what course others may take; but as for me, give me liberty, or give me death!
speech in Virginia Convention, 23 March 1775, in William Wirt *Patrick Henry* (1818) sect. 4

Philip Henry 1631–96
English clergyman

15 All this, and heaven too!
in Matthew Henry *Life of Mr Philip Henry* (1698) ch. 5

Joseph Henshaw 1603–79
English divine; Bishop of Peterborough from 1663

16 One doth but breakfast here, another dines, he that liveth longest doth but sup; we must all go to bed in another world.
Horae Succisivae (1631) pt. 1

Barbara Hepworth 1903–75
English sculptor

17 I rarely draw what I see—I draw what I feel in my body.
Drawings from a Sculptor's Landscape (1966)

18 Carving is interrelated masses conveying an emotion: a perfect relationship between the mind and the colour, light and weight which is the stone, made by the hand which feels.
Herbert Read (ed.) *Unit One* (1934)

Heraclitus *c.*540–*c.*480 BC
Greek philosopher

19 If you do not expect it, you will not find out the unexpected.
On the Universe fragment 7 (translated by W. H. S. Jones)

20 War is the father of all and the king of all.
On the Universe fragment 44 (translated by W. H. S. Jones)

21 It would not be better if things happened to men just as they wish.
On the Universe fragment 104

1 A man's character is his fate.
On the Universe fragment 121 (translated by W. H. S. Jones); see **ELIOT** 308:8, **NOVALIS** 577:10

2 A hidden connection is stronger than an obvious one.
Hippolytus Refutatio vol. 9, bk. 9, sect. 5

3 Everything flows and nothing stays.
Plato *Cratylus* 402a; see **AURELIUS** 40:11

4 You can't step twice into the same river.
Plato *Cratylus* 402a

5 The road up and the road down are one and the same.
H. Diels and W. Kranz *Die Fragmente der Vorsokratiker* (7th ed., 1954) fragment 60

6 Eyes and ears are bad witnesses to men if they have souls that understand not their language.
often quoted as 'poor witnesses to people if they have uncultured souls'
H. Ritter and L. Preller *Historia Philosophiae Graecae* (1898) fragment 42

7 I have searched myself.
Philip Wheelwright *Heraclitus* (1959) fragment 8

8 The people should fight for their law as for their city wall.
Philip Wheelwright *Heraclitus* (1959) fragment 82

Lord Herbert of Cherbury 1583–1648

English philosopher and poet; brother of George HERBERT

9 Now that the April of your youth adorns
The garden of your face.
'Ditty: Now that the April' (1665)

A. P. Herbert (Sir Alan Patrick Herbert)

1890–1971

English writer and humorist

10 Don't let's go to the dogs tonight,
For mother will be there.
'Don't Let's Go to the Dogs Tonight' (1926)

11 The Farmer will never be happy again;
He carries his heart in his boots;
For either the rain is destroying his grain
Or the drought is destroying his roots.
'The Farmer' (1922)

12 As my poor father used to say
In 1863,
Once people start on all this Art
Goodbye, moralitee!
'Lines for a Worthy Person' (1930)

13 This high official, all allow,
Is grossly overpaid;
There wasn't any Board, and now
There isn't any Trade.
'The President of the Board of Trade' (1922)

14 Nothing is wasted, nothing is in vain:
The seas roll over but the rocks remain.
Tough at the Top (operetta *c.*1949)

15 Holy deadlock.
title of novel (1934)

16 People must not do things for fun. We are not here for fun. There is no reference to fun in any Act of Parliament.
Uncommon Law (1935) 'Is it a Free Country?'

17 The critical period in matrimony is breakfast-time.
Uncommon Law (1935) 'Is Marriage Lawful?'

18 'Was the cow crossed?'
'No, your worship, it was an open cow.'
on an attempt to write a cheque on a cow
Uncommon Law (1935) 'The Negotiable Cow'

19 The Common Law of England has been laboriously built about a mythical figure—the figure of 'The Reasonable Man'.
Uncommon Law (1935) 'The Reasonable Man'

George Herbert 1593–1633

English metaphysical poet and clergyman

20 Whereas my birth and spirit rather took
The way that takes the town;
Thou didst betray me to a lingering book,
And wrap me in a gown.
'Affliction (1)' (1633) l. 37

21 Now I am here, what thou wilt do with me
None of my books will show:
I read, and sigh, and wish I were a tree;
For then I should grow
To fruit or shade: at least some bird would trust
Her household to me, and I should be just.
'Affliction (1)' (1633) l. 55

22 Ah, my dear God! though I am clean forgot,
Let me not love Thee, if I love Thee not.
'Affliction (1)' (1633) l. 65

23 We are the trees, whom shaking fastens more.
'Affliction (V)' (1633) l. 20

24 Love is that liquor sweet and most divine,
Which my God feels as blood; but I, as wine.
'The Agonie' (1633) l. 17

25 Let all the world in ev'ry corner sing
My God and King.
'Antiphon: Let all the world in ev'ry corner sing' (1633)

26 Hearken unto a Verser, who may chance
Rhyme thee to good, and make a bait of pleasure.
A verse may find him, who a sermon flies,
And turn delight into a sacrifice.
'The Church Porch' (1633) st. 1

27 Judge not the preacher, for he is thy Judge:
If thou mislike him, thou conceiv'st him not.
God calleth preaching folly. Do not grudge
To pick out treasures from an earthen pot.
The worst speaks something good: if all want sense,
God takes a text, and preacheth patience.
'The Church Porch' (1633) st. 72

28 I struck the board, and cried, 'No more.
I will abroad.'
What? shall I ever sigh and pine?

My lines and life are free; free as the road,
Loose as the wind, as large as store.
'The Collar' (1633)

1 Away; take heed:
I will abroad.
Call in thy death's-head there: tie up thy fears.
'The Collar' (1633)

2 But as I raved and grew more fierce and wild
At every word,
Methought I heard one calling, 'Child';
And I replied, 'My Lord.'
'The Collar' (1633)

3 O that thou shouldst give dust a tongue
To cry to thee,
And then not hear it crying!
'Denial' (1633) l. 16

4 I got me flowers to strew Thy way;
I got me boughs off many a tree:
But Thou wast up by break of day,
And brought'st Thy sweets along with Thee.
'Easter' (1633)

5 Teach me, my God and King,
In all things Thee to see,
And what I do in any thing
To do it as for Thee.
'The Elixir' (1633)

6 A man that looks on glass,
On it may stay his eye;
Or if he pleaseth, through it pass,
And then the heaven espy.
'The Elixir' (1633)

7 A servant with this clause
Makes drudgery divine:
Who sweeps a room as for Thy laws
Makes that and th' action fine.
'The Elixir' (1633)

8 Oh that I were an orange-tree,
That busy plant!
Then I should ever laden be,
And never want
Some fruit for Him that dressed me.
'Employment: He that is weary, let him sit' (1633)

9 Who would have thought my shrivelled heart
Could have recovered greenness?
'The Flower' (1633)

10 And now in age I bud again,
After so many deaths I live and write;
I once more smell the dew and rain,
And relish versing.
'The Flower' (1633)

11 Lovely enchanting language, sugar-cane,
Honey of roses!
'The Forerunners' (1633)

12 Who says that fictions only and false hair
Become a verse? Is there in truth no beauty?
Is all good structure in a winding stair?
'Jordan (1)' (1633)

13 I made a posy while the day ran by:
Here will I smell my remnant out, and tie

My life within this band.
But Time did beckon to the flowers, and they
By noon most cunningly did steal away,
And withered in my hand.
'Life' (1633)

14 Love bade me welcome: yet my soul drew back,
Guilty of dust and sin.
But quick-eyed Love, observing me grow slack
From my first entrance in,
Drew nearer to me, sweetly questioning,
If I lacked any thing.
'Love: Love bade me welcome' (1633)

15 'You must sit down,' says Love, 'and taste my
meat.'
So I did sit and eat.
'Love: Love bade me welcome' (1633)

16 For us the winds do blow,
The earth doth rest, heaven move, and fountains
flow.
Nothing we see, but means our good,
As our delight or as our treasure:
The whole is either our cupboard of food,
Or cabinet of pleasure.
'Man' (1633)

17 When boys go first to bed,
They step into their voluntary graves.
'Mortification' (1633)

18 Prayer: prayer the Church's banquet.
title of poem (1633)

19 Exalted manna, gladness of the best,
Heaven in ordinary, man well drest,
The Milky Way, the bird of Paradise,
Church-bells beyond the stars heard, the soul's
blood,
The land of spices; something understood.
'Prayer: Prayer the Church's banquet' (1633)

20 When God at first made man,
Having a glass of blessings standing by;
Let us (said he) pour on him all we can:
Let the world's riches, which dispersed lie,
Contract into a span.
'The Pulley' (1633)

21 He would adore my gifts instead of Me,
And rest in Nature, not the God of Nature:
So both should losers be.
'The Pulley' (1633)

22 Yet let him keep the rest,
But keep them with repining restlessness:
Let him be rich and weary, that at least,
If goodness lead him not, yet weariness
May toss him to My breast.
'The Pulley' (1633)

23 But who does hawk at eagles with a dove?
'The Sacrifice' (1633) l. 91

24 Man stole the fruit, but I must climb the tree.
'The Sacrifice' (1633) l. 202

25 Lord, with what care Thou hast begirt us round!
Parents first season us: then schoolmasters

Deliver us to laws; they send us bound
To rules of reason, holy messengers,
Pulpits and Sundays, sorrow dogging sin,
Afflictions sorted, anguish of all sizes,
Fine nets and stratagems to catch us in,
Bibles laid open, millions of surprises.
'Sin: Lord, with what care Thou hast begirt us round!' (1633)

1 The God of love my Shepherd is,
And He that doth me feed:
While He is mine, and I am His,
What can I want or need?
'The 23rd Psalm' (1633); see **BOOK OF COMMON PRAYER** 140:20

2 Sweet day, so cool, so calm, so bright,
The bridal of the earth and sky,
The dew shall weep thy fall to-night;
For thou must die.
Sweet rose, whose hue angry and brave
Bids the rash gazer wipe his eye:
Thy root is ever in its grave,
And thou must die.
Sweet spring, full of sweet days and roses,
A box where sweets compacted lie;
My music shows ye have your closes,
And all must die.
'Virtue' (1633)

3 Only a sweet and virtuous soul,
Like seasoned timber, never gives;
But though the whole world turn to coal,
Then chiefly lives.
'Virtue' (1633)

4 He that makes a good war makes a good peace.
Outlandish Proverbs (1640) no. 420

5 He that lives in hope danceth without music.
Outlandish Proverbs (1640) no. 1006; see **PROVERBS** 634:10

Johann Gottfried von Herder

1744–1803

German critic and philosopher

6 I am not here to think, but to be, feel, live!
Bernhard Suphan (ed.) J. G. Herder *Sämmtliche Werke* (1877–1913)

Hermetic Corpus

A collection of religious and philosophical writings of the mid-1st to late 3rd century AD, ascribed in the medieval period to Hermes Trismegistus

7 Because of man God changes and turns into the form of man.
Jean-Pierre Mahé *The Way of Hermes* (1999) 'Fragmenta Hermetica 21'

Herodotus *c.*485–*c.*425 BC

Greek historian

8 No one is stupid enough to prefer war to peace; in peace sons bury their fathers and in war fathers bury their sons. However, I suppose the god must have wanted this to happen.
Histories bk. 1 sect. 87

9 If one were to order all mankind to choose the best set of rules in the world, each group would, after due consideration, choose its own customs; each group regards its own as being by far the best.
Histories bk. 3 sect. 38

10 Father, your visitor is going to corrupt you if you don't get up and leave.
comment attributed to Gorgo, young daughter of Cleomenes, King of Sparta, on Aristagoras' attempts to bribe her father
Histories bk. 5 sect. 51

11 The man who has planned badly, if fortune is on his side, may have had a stroke of luck; but his plan was a bad one nonetheless.
Histories bk. 7, sect. 10

12 If the Persians hide the sun, the battle will be in shade rather than sunlight.
comment attributed to Dieneces of Sparta, on being told that the Persians were so numerous that their arrows when shot hid the sun
Histories bk. 7 sect. 226

13 The most hateful torment for men is to have knowledge of everything but power over nothing.
Histories bk. 9 sect. 16

Robert Herrick 1591–1674

English poet and clergyman

14 Here a little child I stand,
Heaving up my either hand;
Cold as paddocks though they be,
Here I lift them up to Thee,
For a benison to fall
On our meat, and on us all. Amen.
'Another Grace for a Child' (1647)

15 I sing of brooks, of blossoms, birds, and bowers:
Of April, May, of June, and July-flowers.
I sing of May-poles, Hock-carts, wassails, wakes,
Of bride-grooms, brides, and of their bridal-cakes.
'The Argument of his Book' from *Hesperides* (1648)

16 And once more yet (ere I am laid out dead)
Knock at a star with my exalted head.
'The Bad Season Makes the Poet Sad' (1648)

17 Cherry-ripe, ripe, ripe, I cry,
Full and fair ones; come and buy:
If so be, you ask me where
They do grow? I answer, there,
Where my Julia's lips do smile;
There's the land, or cherry-isle.
'Cherry-Ripe' (1648)

18 Get up, sweet Slug-a-bed, and see
The dew bespangling herb and tree.
'Corinna's Going a-Maying' (1648)

19 Then while time serves, and we are but decaying;
Come, my Corinna, come, let's go a-Maying.
'Corinna's Going a-Maying' (1648)

1 A sweet disorder in the dress
Kindles in clothes a wantonness:
A lawn about the shoulders thrown
Into a fine distraction . . .
A careless shoe-string, in whose tie
I see a wild civility:
Do more bewitch me, than when Art
Is too precise in every part.
'Delight in Disorder' (1648)

2 Love is a circle that doth restless move
In the same sweet eternity of love.
'Love What It Is' (1648)

3 Her eyes the glow-worm lend thee,
The shooting-stars attend thee;
And the elves also,
Whose little eyes glow,
Like the sparks of fire, befriend thee.
'The Night-Piece, to Julia' (1648)

4 Night makes no difference 'twixt the Priest and
Clerk;
Joan as my Lady is as good i' th' dark.
'No Difference i' th' Dark' (1648)

5 Made us nobly wild, not mad.
'An Ode for him [Ben Jonson]' (1648)

6 And yet each verse of thine
Out-did the meat, out-did the frolic wine.
'An Ode for him [Ben Jonson]' (1648)

7 Fain would I kiss my Julia's dainty leg,
Which is as white and hairless as an egg.
'On Julia's Legs' (1648)

8 Praise they that will times past, I joy to see
My self now live: this age best pleaseth me.
'The Present Time Best Pleaseth' (1648)

9 But, for Man's fault, then was the thorn,
Without the fragrant rose-bud, born;
But ne'er the rose without the thorn.
'The Rose' (1647)

10 A little saint best fits a little shrine,
A little prop best fits a little vine,
As my small cruse best fits my little wine.
'A Ternary of Littles, upon a Pipkin of Jelly sent to a Lady'
(1648)

11 For my Embalming (Sweetest) there will be
No Spices wanting, when I'm laid by thee.
'To Anthea: Now is the Time' (1648)

12 Bid me to live, and I will live
Thy Protestant to be:
Or bid me love, and I will give
A loving heart to thee.
'To Anthea, Who May Command Him Anything' (1648)

13 Bid me despair, and I'll despair,
Under that cypress tree:
Or bid me die, and I will dare
E'en Death, to die for thee.

Thou art my life, my love, my heart,
The very eyes of me:
And hast command of every part,
To live and die for thee.
'To Anthea, Who May Command Him Anything' (1648)

14 Fair daffodils, we weep to see
You haste away so soon.
'To Daffodils' (1648)

15 We have short time to stay, as you,
We have as short a Spring;
As quick a growth to meet decay,
As you or any thing.
'To Daffodils' (1648)

16 If any thing delight me for to print
My book, 'tis this; that Thou, my God, art in't.
'To God' (1647)

17 Gather ye rosebuds while ye may,
Old Time is still a-flying:
And this same flower that smiles to-day,
To-morrow will be dying.
'To the Virgins, to Make Much of Time' (1648)

18 Then be not coy, but use your time;
And while ye may, go marry:
For having lost but once your prime,
You may for ever tarry.
'To the Virgins, to Make Much of Time' (1648)

19 Whenas in silks my Julia goes,
Then, then (methinks) how sweetly flows
That liquefaction of her clothes.
Next, when I cast mine eyes and see
That brave vibration each way free;
O how that glittering taketh me!
'Upon Julia's Clothes' (1648)

20 So smooth, so sweet, so silvery is thy voice,
As, could they hear, the damned would make no
noise,
But listen to thee (walking in thy chamber)
Melting melodious words, to lutes of amber.
'Upon Julia's Voice' (1648)

21 To work a wonder, God would have her shown,
At once, a bud, and yet a rose full-blown.
'The Virgin Mary' (1647)

William Herschel *see* Epitaphs 317:3

Lord Hervey 1696–1743

**English politician and writer. On Hervey: see MONTAGU
554:12, POPE 614:24**

22 Whoever would lie usefully should lie seldom.
Memoirs of the Reign of George II (ed. J. W. Croker, 1848) vol.
1, ch. 19

23 I am fit for nothing but to carry candles and set
chairs all my life.
letter to Robert Walpole, 1737, in *Memoirs of the Reign of
George II* (ed. J. W. Croker, 1848) vol. 2, ch. 40

Alexander Herzen 1812–70

Russian writer and revolutionary

24 Art, and the summer lightning of individual
happiness: these are the only real goods we
have.
Sobranie sochinenii v tridtsati tomakh (Moscow, 1954–66) vol.
16, p. 135, translated by Isaiah Berlin

Theodor Herzl 1860–1904

Hungarian-born journalist, dramatist, and Zionist leader

1 At Basle I founded the Jewish state.
  of the first Zionist congress, held in Basle in 1897
    diary, 3 September 1897

Hesiod

Greek poet of c.700 BC

2 Then potter is potter's enemy, and
  craftsman is craftsman's
  rival; tramp is jealous of tramp
  and singer of singer.
    Works and Days l.25, translated by R. Lattimore

3 The half is greater than the whole.
    Works and Days l. 40

4 The fool learns by suffering.
    Works and Days l. 218

5 Often a whole city is paid punishment
  for one bad man.
    Works and Days l. 240, translated by R. Lattimore

6 The man who does evil to another does evil
  to himself,
  and the evil counsel is most evil
  for him who counsels it.
    Works and Days l. 265, translated by R. Lattimore

7 Between us and excellence, the gods have placed
  the sweat of our brows.
    Works and Days l. 289

8 When the bottle has just been opened, and
    when
  it's giving out, drink deep;
  be sparing when it's half-full; but it's useless
  to spare the fag end.
    Works and Days l. 368, translated by R. Lattimore

Hermann Hesse 1877–1962

German novelist and poet

9 If you hate a person, you hate something in him
  that is part of yourself. What isn't part of
  ourselves doesn't disturb us.
    Demian (1919) ch. 6

10 One never reaches home, but wherever friendly
  paths intersect the whole world looks like home
  for a time.
    Demian (1919) ch. 7

11 The bourgeois prefers comfort to pleasure,
  convenience to liberty, and a pleasant
  temperature to the deathly inner consuming fire.
    Der Steppenwolf (1927) 'Tractat vom Steppenwolf', translated
    by Basil Creighton

12 Humour has always something bourgeois in it.
    Der Steppenwolf (1927) 'Tractat vom Steppenwolf'

13 *Das Glück ist ein Wie, kein Was; ein Talent, kein
  Objekt.*
  Happiness is a how, not a what; a talent, not an
  object.
    attributed

Gordon Hewart 1870–1943

British lawyer and politician

14 A long line of cases shows that it is not merely
  of some importance, but is of fundamental
  importance that justice should not only be done,
  but should manifestly and undoubtedly be seen
  to be done.
    Rex v Sussex Justices, 9 November 1923, in *Law Reports King's
    Bench Division* (1924) vol. 1

Foster William Hewitt *see* Catchphrases

207:30

John Hewitt 1907–87

Northern Irish poet

15 We would be strangers in the Capitol;
  this is our country also, no-where else;
  and we shall not be outcast on the world.
    'The Colony' (1950)

16 I'm an Ulsterman, of planter stock. I was born
  in the island of Ireland, so secondarily I'm an
  Irishman. I was born in the British archipelago
  and English is my native tongue, so I am British.
  The British archipelago consists of offshore
  islands to the continent of Europe, so I'm
  European. This is my hierarchy of values and so
  far as I am concerned, anyone who omits one
  step in that sequence of values is falsifying the
  situation.
    in *The Irish Times* 4 July 1974

Reinhard Heydrich 1904–42

German Nazi leader

17 Now the rough work has been done we begin
  the period of finer work. We need to work in
  harmony with the civil administration. We count
  on you gentlemen as far as the final solution is
  concerned.
    on the planned mass murder of all European Jews; see
    GOERING *361:10*
      speech in Wannsee, 20 January 1942

Du Bose Heyward 1885–1940 *and* Ira Gershwin 1896–1983

American songwriters

18 It ain't necessarily so,
  It ain't necessarily so,
  De t'ings dat yo' li'ble
  To read in de Bible
  It ain't necessarily so.
    'It ain't necessarily so' (1935 song) in *Porgy and Bess*

19 Summer time an' the livin' is easy,
  Fish are jumpin' an' the cotton is high.
  Oh, yo' daddy's rich, and yo' ma' is good-
    lookin',
  So hush, little baby, don' yo' cry.
    'Summertime' (1935 song) in *Porgy and Bess*

1 A woman is a sometime thing.
title of song (1935) in *Porgy and Bess*

John Heywood *c.*1497–*c.*1580

English dramatist

2 All a green willow, willow;
All a green willow is my garland.
'The Green Willow'; see **SHAKESPEARE** 729:10

3 I never heard thy fire once spark,
I never heard thy dog once bark.
I never heard once in thy house
So much as one peep of one mouse.
I never heard thy cat once mew.
These praises are not small nor few.
'A quiet neighbour' (1556)

Thomas Heywood *c.*1574–1641

English dramatist

4 Seven cities warred for Homer, being dead,
Who, living, had no roof to shroud his head.
'The Hierarchy of the Blessed Angels' (1635); see **ANONYMOUS** 20:9

J. R. Hicks 1904–89

English economist

5 The best of all monopoly profits is a quiet life.
Econometrica (1935) 'The Theory of Monopoly'

David Hilbert 1862–1943

German mathematician. See also **EPITAPHS** 319:17

6 The importance of a scientific work can be measured by the number of previous publications it makes it superfluous to read.
attributed; Lewis Wolpert *The Unnatural Nature of Science* (1993)

Hildegard of Bingen 1098–1179

German abbess, scholar, composer, and mystic

7 Listen now! a king sat on his throne, high pillars before him splendidly adorned and set on pediments of ivory . . . Then the king chose to lift a small feather from the ground, and he commanded it to fly just as the king himself wished. But a feather does not fly of its own accord, it is borne up by the air. So too I am not imbued with human doctrine or strong powers . . . Rather, I depend entirely on God's help.
often summarized 'Thus am I a feather on the breath of God'
letter to Odo of Soissons, 1148, in *Selected Writings* (2001, translated by M. Atherton)

8 I, a mere female and a fragile vessel, speak these things not from me but from the serene Light.
letter to Elizabeth of Schönau, 1152–6, in *Selected Writings* (2001, translated by M. Atherton)

Aaron Hill 1685–1750

English poet and dramatist

9 Tender-handed stroke a nettle,
And it stings you for your pains;
Grasp it like a man of mettle,
And it soft as silk remains.
'Verses Written on a Window in Scotland'

Christopher Hill 1912–2003

English historian

10 Only very slowly and late have men come to realize that unless freedom is universal it is only extended privilege.
Century of Revolution (1961)

Geoffrey Hill 1932–

English poet

11   Poetry
Unearths from among the speechless dead

Lazarus mystified, common man
Of death. The lily rears its gouged face
From the provided loam.
'History as Poetry' (1968)

12 She kept the siege. And every day
We watched her brooding over death
Like a strong bird above its prey.
The room filled with the kettle's breath.
'In Memory of Jane Fraser' (1959)

13 I love my work and my children. God
Is distant, difficult. Things happen.
Too near the ancient troughs of blood
Innocence is no earthly weapon.
'Ovid in the Third Reich' (1968)

Joe Hill (Joel Hägglund) 1879–1915

Swedish-born American labour leader and songwriter. On Hill: see **HAYES** 385:15

14 You will eat, bye and bye,
In that glorious land above the sky;
Work and pray, live on hay,
You'll get pie in the sky when you die.
'Preacher and the Slave' in *Songs of the Workers* (Industrial Workers of the World, 1911)

15 I will die like a true-blue rebel. Don't waste any time in mourning—organize.
before his death by firing squad
farewell telegram to Bill Haywood, 18 November 1915, in *Salt Lake (Utah) Tribune* 19 November 1915

Pattie S. Hill 1868–1946

American educationist

16 Happy birthday to you.
title of song (1935)

Rowland Hill 1744–1833

English clergyman

1 He did not see any reason why the devil should have all the good tunes.
E. W. Broome *The Rev. Rowland Hill* (1881) ch. 7; see **PROVERBS** 647:24

Edmund Hillary 1919–2008

New Zealand mountaineer

2 Well, we knocked the bastard off!
on conquering Mount Everest, 1953
Nothing Venture, Nothing Win (1975) ch. 10; see **MALLORY** 517:17

Fred Hillebrand 1893–1963

3 Home James, and don't spare the horses.
title of song (1934)

Hillel 'The Elder' c.60 BC–c.AD 9

Jewish scholar and teacher

4 What is hateful to you do not to your neighbour: that is the whole Torah.
in *Talmud* Shabbat 31a

5 Be of the disciples of Aaron, loving peace and pursuing peace, loving mankind and bringing them nigh to the Law.
in *Talmud* Mishnah 'Pirqei Avot' 1:12

6 A name made great is a name destroyed.
in *Talmud* Mishnah 'Pirqei Avot' 1:13

7 If I am not for myself who is for me? and being for my own self what am I? If not now when?
in *Talmud* Mishnah 'Pirqei Avot' 1:14

8 Keep not aloof from the congregation.
in *Talmud* Mishnah 'Pirqei Avot' 2:5

9 Say not, When I have leisure I will study; perchance thou wilt never have leisure.
in *Talmud* Mishnah 'Pirqei Avot' 2:5

James Hilton 1900–54

English novelist

10 Nothing really wrong with him—only anno domini, but that's the most fatal complaint of all, in the end.
Goodbye, Mr Chips (1934) ch. 1

Paris Hilton 1981–

American heiress

11 Dress cute wherever you go. Life is too short to blend in.
Confessions of an Heiress (2004)

Hippocleides

Greek aristocrat of 6th century BC Athens

12 Hippocleides doesn't care.
on being told that he had ruined his marriage chances with the daughter of a tyrant, concluding a dance by standing on his head and gesticulating with his legs
Herodotus *Histories* bk. 6, sect. 129

Hippocrates c.460–357 BC

Greek physician

13 Life is short, the art long.
often quoted as 'Ars longa, vita brevis', after **SENECA***'s rendering in* De Brevitate Vitae *sect. 1*
Aphorisms sect. 1, para. 1 (translated by W. H. S. Jones); see **CHAUCER** 220:21, **LONGFELLOW** 499:15, **PROVERBS** 626:35

14 Extreme remedies are most appropriate for extreme diseases.
Aphorisms sect. 1, para. 6 (translated by W. H. S. Jones); see **PROVERBS** 629:40

15 When two pains occur together, but not in the same place, the more violent obscures the other.
Aphorisms sect. 2, para. 46 (translated by W. H. S. Jones)

16 I swear by Apollo the physician, by Asclepius, by Health, by Panacea and by all the gods and goddesses, making them my witnesses, that I will carry out, according to my ability and judgement, this oath and this indenture.
The Hippocratic Oath (translated by W. H. S. Jones)

17 I will use treatment to help the sick according to my ability and judgement, but never with a view to injury or wrong-doing. Neither will I administer a poison to anybody when asked to do so, nor will I suggest such a course.
The Hippocratic Oath (translated by W. H. S. Jones)

18 I will not use the knife, not even, verily, on sufferers from stone but I will give place to such as are craftsmen therein.
The Hippocratic Oath (translated by W. H. S. Jones)

19 And whatsoever I shall see or hear in the course of my profession, as well as outside my profession in my intercourse with men, if it be what should not be published abroad, I will never divulge holding such things to be holy secrets.
The Hippocratic Oath (translated by W. H. S. Jones)

20 Time is that wherein there is opportunity, and opportunity is that wherein there is no great time.
Precepts ch. 1 (translated by W. H. S. Jones, 1923)

21 Healing is a matter of time, but it is sometimes also a matter of opportunity.
Precepts ch. 1 (translated by W. H. S. Jones, 1923)

Emperor Hirohito 1901–89

Japanese monarch, Emperor from 1926

22 The war situation has developed not necessarily to Japan's advantage.
announcing Japan's surrender, in a broadcast to his people after atom bombs had destroyed Hiroshima and Nagasaki
on 15 August 1945

Damien Hirst 1965–

English artist

1 It's amazing what you can do with an E in A-level art, twisted imagination and a chainsaw.
after winning the 1995 Turner Prize
in *Observer* 3 December 1995 'Sayings of the Week'

Alfred Hitchcock 1899–1980

English-born film director

2 Actors are cattle.
in *Saturday Evening Post* 22 May 1943

3 If I made Cinderella, the audience would immediately be looking for a body in the coach.
in *Newsweek* 11 June 1956

4 Television has brought back murder into the home—where it belongs.
in *Observer* 19 December 1965

5 There is no terror in a bang, only in the anticipation of it.
Leslie Halliwell (ed.) *Halliwell's Filmgoer's Companion* (1984); attributed

Adolf Hitler 1889–1945

German dictator. On Hitler: see **BUCHMAN** 169:10, **CHAMBERLAIN** 214:8

6 The broad mass of a nation . . . will more easily fall victim to a big lie than to a small one.
Mein Kampf (1925) vol. 1, ch. 10

7 The night of the long knives.
referring to the massacre of Ernst Roehm and his associates by Hitler on 29–30 June 1934 (subsequently associated with Harold MACMILLAN's Cabinet dismissals of 13 July 1962)
S. H. Roberts *The House Hitler Built* (1937) pt. 2, ch. 3

8 I go the way that Providence dictates with the assurance of a sleepwalker.
speech in Munich, 15 March 1936, in Max Domarus (ed.) *Hitler: Reden und Proklamationen 1932–1945* (1962)

9 It is the last territorial claim which I have to make in Europe, but it is the claim from which I will not recede and which, God-willing, I will make good.
on the Sudetenland
speech at Berlin Sportpalast, 26 September 1938; in Max Domarus (ed.) *Hitler: Reden und Proklamationen 1932–1945* (1962)

10 With regard to the problem of the Sudeten Germans, my patience is now at an end!
speech at Berlin Sportpalast, 26 September 1938, in Max Domarus (ed.) *Hitler: Reden und Proklamationen 1932–1945* (1962)

11 Is Paris burning?
on 25 August 1944, in Larry Collins and Dominique Lapierre *Is Paris Burning?* (1965) ch. 5

Lady Ho fl. 300 BC

Chinese poet

12 When a pair of magpies fly together
They do not envy the pair of phoenixes.
'A Song of Magpies'; K. Rexroth and Chung (eds.) *The Orchid Boat: Women Poets of China* (1972)

Thomas Hobbes 1588–1679

English philosopher. On Hobbes: see **AUBREY** 35:17, **SWIFT** 784:3

13 Laughter is nothing else but sudden glory arising from some sudden conception of some eminency in ourselves, by comparison with the infirmity of others, or with our own formerly.
Human Nature (1650) ch. 9, sect. 13

14 By art is created that great Leviathan, called a commonwealth or state, (in Latin *civitas*) which is but an artificial man . . . and in which, the sovereignty is an artificial soul.
Leviathan (1651) introduction

15 True and False are attributes of speech, not of things. And where speech is not, there is neither Truth nor Falsehood.
Leviathan (1651) pt. 1, ch. 4

16 In Geometry (which is the only science that it hath pleased God hitherto to bestow on mankind) men begin at settling the significations of their words; which . . . they call Definitions.
Leviathan (1651) pt. 1, ch. 4

17 Words are wise men's counters, they do but reckon by them: but they are the money of fools, that value them by the authority of an Aristotle, a Cicero, or a Thomas, or any other doctor whatsoever, if but a man.
Leviathan (1651) pt. 1, ch. 4

18 Riches, knowledge and honour are but several sorts of power.
Leviathan (1651) pt. 1, ch. 8

19 The power of a man, to take it universally, is his present means, to obtain some future apparent good; and is either original or instrumental.
Leviathan (1651) pt. 1, ch. 10

20 I put for a general inclination of all mankind, a perpetual and restless desire of power after power, that ceaseth only in death.
Leviathan (1651) pt. 1, ch. 11

21 They that approve a private opinion, call it opinion; but they that mislike it, heresy: and yet heresy signifies no more than private opinion.
Leviathan (1651) pt. 1, ch. 11

22 During the time men live without a common power to keep them all in awe, they are in that condition which is called war; and such a war as is of every man against every man.
Leviathan (1651) pt. 1, ch. 13

23 For as the nature of foul weather, lieth not in a shower or two of rain; but in an inclination thereto of many days together: so the nature of war consisteth not in actual fighting, but in the known disposition thereto during all the time there is no assurance to the contrary.
Leviathan (1651) pt. 1, ch. 13

24 No arts; no letters; no society; and which is worst of all, continual fear and danger of violent

death; and the life of man, solitary, poor, nasty, brutish, and short.
Leviathan (1651) pt. 1, ch. 13

1 Force, and fraud, are in war the two cardinal virtues.
Leviathan (1651) pt. 1, ch. 13

2 Liberties . . . depend on the silence of the law.
Leviathan (1651) pt. 2, ch. 16

3 They that are discontented under *monarchy*, call it *tyranny*; and they that are displeased with *aristocracy*, call it *oligarchy*: so also, they which find themselves grieved under a *democracy*, call it *anarchy*, which signifies the want of government; and yet I think no man believes, that want of government, is any new kind of government.
Leviathan (1651) pt. 2, ch. 19

4 To accuse requires less eloquence (such is man's nature) than to excuse.
Leviathan (1651) pt. 2, ch. 19

5 Whereas some have attributed the dominion [of the family] to the man only, as being of the more excellent sex; they misreckon in it. For there is not always that difference of strength, or prudence between the man and the woman, as that the right can be determined without war.
Leviathan (1651) pt. 2, ch. 20

6 A man's conscience and his judgement is the same thing; and as the judgement, so also the conscience, may be erroneous.
Leviathan (1651) pt. 2, ch. 29

7 For it is with the mysteries of our religion, as with wholesome pills for the sick, which swallowed whole, have the virtue to cure; but chewed, are for the most part cast up again without effect.
Leviathan (1651) pt. 3, ch. 32

8 The papacy is not other than the ghost of the deceased Roman Empire, sitting crowned upon the grave thereof.
Leviathan (1651) pt. 4, ch. 47

9 The praise of ancient authors proceeds not from the reverence of the dead, but from the competition, and mutual envy of the living.
Leviathan (1651) 'A Review and Conclusion'

10 And hereupon it was my mother dear
Did bring forth twins at once, both me, and fear.
often quoted as 'Fear and I were born twins'; his mother's fear was of the Spanish Armada
The Life of Thomas Hobbes . . . written by himself (1680)

11 I am about to take my last voyage, a great leap in the dark.
last words, attributed (see **VANBRUGH** 823:19), but with no authoritative source; a contemporary version is: 'On his death bed he should say that he was 91 years finding out a hole to go out of this world, and at length found it', Anthony Wood diary, 10 December 1679, in Andrew Clark (ed.) *The Life and Times of Anthony Wood* vol. 2 (1892)

John Cam Hobhouse, Lord Broughton 1786–1869
English politician

12 It is said to be very hard on his majesty's ministers to raise objections to this proposition. For my own part, I think it is more hard on his majesty's opposition (a laugh) to compel them to take this course.
speech, House of Commons, 10 April 1826; see **BAGEHOT** 50:10

Eric Hobsbawm 1917–
British historian

13 This was the kind of war which existed in order to produce victory parades.
of the Falklands War
in *Marxism Today* January 1983

Margaret Hoby 1571–1633
English diarist

14 This day I bestowed too much time in the garden, and thereby was worse able to perform spiritual duties.
diary, 6 April 1605; Dorothy M. Meads (ed.) *Diary of Lady Margaret Hoby* (1930)

David Hockney 1937–
English artist

15 Art has to move you and design does not, unless it's a good design for a bus.
in *Guardian* 26 October 1988

Dorothy Hodgkin 1910–94
British chemist

16 I'm really an experimentalist. I used to say, I think with my hands. I just like manipulation. I began to like it as a child and it's continued to be a pleasure.
Lewis Wolpert and Alison Richards *A Passion for Science* (1988) ch. 6

17 I was captured for life by chemistry and by crystals.
Georgina Ferry *Dorothy Hodgkin* (1998) ch. 1

Ralph Hodgson 1871–1962
English poet

18 'Twould ring the bells of Heaven
The wildest peal for years,
If Parson lost his senses
And people came to theirs,
And he and they together
Knelt down with angry prayers
For tamed and shabby tigers
And dancing dogs and bears,
And wretched, blind, pit ponies,
And little hunted hares.
'Bells of Heaven' (1917)

1 Time, you old gipsy man,
  Will you not stay,
  Put up your caravan
  Just for one day?
  'Time, You Old Gipsy Man' (1917)

Al Hoffman 1902–60 *and* Dick Manning 1912–

2 Takes two to tango.
  title of song (1952); see **PROVERBS** 636:42

August Heinrich Hoffman (Hoffman von Fallersleben) 1798–1874
German poet

3 *Deutschland über alles.*
  Germany above all.
  title of poem (1841)

Heinrich Hoffmann 1809–94
German writer for children

4 Augustus was a chubby lad;
  Fat ruddy cheeks Augustus had:
  And everybody saw with joy
  The plump and hearty, healthy boy.
  He ate and drank as he was told,
  And never let his soup get cold.
  But one day, one cold winter's day,
  He screamed out, 'Take the soup away!
  O take the nasty soup away!
  I won't have any soup today.'
  Struwwelpeter (1848) 'Augustus'

5 But fidgety Phil,
  He won't sit still.
  Struwwelpeter (1848) 'Fidgety Philip'

6 Look at little Johnny there,
  Little Johnny Head-In-Air!
  Struwwelpeter (1848) 'Johnny Head-In-Air'; see **PUDNEY** 648:34

7 The door flew open, in he ran,
  The great, long, red-legged scissor-man.
  Struwwelpeter (1848) 'The Little Suck-a-Thumb'

8 Snip! Snap! Snip! They go so fast.
  That both his thumbs are off at last.
  Struwwelpeter (1848) 'The Little Suck-a-Thumb'

9 The hare sits snug in leaves and grass,
  And laughs to see the green man pass.
  Struwwelpeter (1848) 'The Man Who Went Out Shooting'

10 And now she's trying all she can,
  To shoot the sleepy, green-coat man.
  Struwwelpeter (1848) 'The Man Who Went Out Shooting'

11 The hare's own child, the little hare.
  Struwwelpeter (1848) 'The Man Who Went Out Shooting'

12 Anything to me is sweeter
  Than to see Shock-headed Peter.
  Struwwelpeter (1848) 'Shock-Headed Peter' (title poem)

Gerard Hoffnung 1925–59
English humorist

13 Standing among savage scenery, the hotel offers stupendous revelations. There is a French widow in every bedroom, affording delightful prospects.
  supposedly quoting a letter from a Tyrolean landlord
  speech at the Oxford Union, 4 December 1958

Hugo von Hofmannsthal 1874–1929
Austrian poet and writer

14 We have fewer friends than we imagine, but more than we know.
  Book of Friends (1922)

Lancelot Hogben 1895–1975
English scientist

15 This is not the age of pamphleteers. It is the age of the engineers. The spark-gap is mightier than the pen. Democracy will not be salvaged by men who talk fluently, debate forcefully and quote aptly.
  Science for the Citizen (1938) epilogue; see **PROVERBS** 641:32

James Hogg 1770–1835
Scottish poet and writer. See also **SONGS, SPIRITUALS, AND SHANTIES** 762:1, **SONGS, SPIRITUALS, AND SHANTIES** 762:9

16 Where the pools are bright and deep
  Where the gray trout lies asleep,
  Up the river and o'er the lea
  That's the way for Billy and me.
  'A Boy's Song' (1838)

17 Cock up your beaver, and cock it fu' sprush;
  We'll over the Border and gi'e them a brush;
  There's somebody there we'll teach better behaviour.
  Hey, Johnnie lad, cock up your beaver!
  'Cock Up Your Beaver' in *Jacobite Relics of Scotland* Second Series (1821)

18 We'll o'er the water, we'll o'er the sea,
  We'll o'er the water to Charlie;
  Come weel, come wo, we'll gather and go,
  And live or die wi' Charlie.
  'O'er the Water to Charlie' in *Jacobite Relics of Scotland* Second Series (1821)

19 Bird of the wilderness,
  Blithesome and cumberless,
  Sweet be thy matin o'er moorland and lea!
  'The Skylark'

20 The private memoirs and confessions of a justified sinner.
  title of novel (1824)

Paul Henri, Baron d'Holbach 1723–89
French philosopher

21 Art is only Nature operating with the aid of the instruments she has made.
  Système de la Nature (1780 ed.) pt. 1, ch. 1

1 If ignorance of nature gave birth to the Gods, knowledge of nature is destined to destroy them.
Système de la Nature (1770) pt. 2, ch. 1

Johann Christian Friedrich Hölderlin 1770–1843

German lyric poet

2 *So zu harren und was zu thun indess und zu sagen? Weiss ich nicht und wozu Dichter in durftiger Zeit?*

Always waiting and what to do or to say in the meantime
I don't know, and who wants poets at all in lean years?
'Bread and Wine' (1800–01), translated by Michael Hamburger in *Poems and Fragments* (1994)

3 *Alles Getrennte findet sich wieder.*

All that is divided will find itself again.
Hyperion

Billie Holiday (Eleanor Fagan) 1915–59

American singer. See also **ALLEN** 13:6

4 Mama may have, papa may have,
But God bless the child that's got his own!
That's got his own.
'God Bless the Child' (1941 song, with Arthur Herzog Jnr)

5 Mom and Pop were just a couple of kids when they got married. He was eighteen, she was sixteen, and I was three.
Lady Sings the Blues (1956, with William Duffy) ch. 1, opening words

Henry Fox, Lord Holland 1705–74

English Whig politician, father of Charles James **FOX**. On Holland: see **WALPOLE** 838:6

6 If Mr Selwyn calls again, shew him up: if I am alive I shall be delighted to see him; and if I am dead he would like to see me.
during his last illness
J. H. Jesse *George Selwyn and his Contemporaries* (1844) vol. 3

Henry Scott Holland 1847–1918

English theologian and preacher

7 Death is nothing at all; it does not count. I have only slipped away into the next room.
sermon preached on Whitsunday 1910, in *Facts of the Faith* (1919) 'The King of Terrors'

Stanley Holloway 1890–1982

English actor and singer

8 Sam, Sam, pick up tha' musket.
'Pick Up Tha' Musket' (1930 recorded monologue)

John H. Holmes 1879–1964

American Unitarian minister

9 This, now, is the judgement of our scientific age—the third reaction of man upon the universe! This universe is not hostile, nor yet is it friendly. It is simply indifferent.
The Sensible Man's View of Religion (1932) ch. 4

Oliver Wendell Holmes 1809–94

American physician, poet, and essayist

10 Every now and then a man's mind is stretched by a new idea or sensation, and never shrinks back to its former dimensions.
Autocrat of the Breakfast Table (1891) ch. 11

11 It is the province of knowledge to speak and it is the privilege of wisdom to listen.
The Poet at the Breakfast-Table (1872) ch. 10

12 Fate tried to conceal him by naming him Smith.
of Samuel Francis **SMITH**
'The Boys' (1858)

13 Lean, hungry, savage anti-everythings.
'A Modest Request' (1848)

14 Man wants but little drink below,
But wants that little strong.
'A Song of other Days' (1848); see **GOLDSMITH** 364:14

15 Blank cheques of intellectual bankruptcy.
definition of catchphrases
attributed

Oliver Wendell Holmes Jr. 1841–1935

American lawyer and Supreme Court Justice

16 We pause to . . . recall what our country has done for each of us and to ask ourselves what we can do for our country in return.
speech, Keene, New Hampshire, 30 May 1884; see **KENNEDY** 460:10

17 It is better to be seventy years young than forty years old!
reply to invitation from Julia Ward **HOWE** *to her seventieth birthday party, 27 May 1889*
Laura Richards and Maud Howe Elliott *Julia Ward Howe* (1916) vol. 2

18 Certitude is not the test of certainty. We have been cocksure of many things that were not so.
'Natural Law' (1918)

19 The most stringent protection of free speech would not protect a man falsely shouting fire in a theatre and causing a panic . . . The question in every case is whether the words used are used in such circumstances and are of such a nature as to create a clear and present danger that they will bring about the substantive evils that Congress has a right to prevent.
sometimes quoted as, 'shouting fire in a crowded theatre'
in *Schenck v. United States* (1919)

20 The minute a phrase becomes current it becomes an apology for not thinking accurately to the end of the sentence.
letter to Harold Laski, 2 July 1917

21 But I have long thought that if you knew a column of advertisements by heart, you could achieve unexpected felicities with them. You can get a happy quotation anywhere if you have the eye.

  letter to Harold Laski, 31 May 1923

Winifred Holtby 1898–1935

British novelist and journalist. See also **EPITAPHS** 317:11

1 The crown of life is neither happiness nor annihilation; it is understanding.

  Vera Brittain *Testament of Friendship: the Story of Winifred Holtby* (1940)

Miroslav Holub 1923–98

Czech poet

2 But above all
  we have
  the ability
  to sort peas,
  to cup water in our hands,
  to seek
  the right screw
  under the sofa
  for hours.

  'Wings' (1967)

John Home 1722–1808

Scottish dramatist

3 My name is Norval; on the Grampian hills
  My father feeds his flocks.

  Douglas (1756) act 2, sc. 1

4 Like Douglas conquer, or like Douglas die.

  Douglas (1756) act 5

Alec Douglas-Home, Lord Home 1903–95

British Conservative statesman, Prime Minister 1963–4

5 As far as the fourteenth earl is concerned, I suppose Mr Wilson, when you come to think of it, is the fourteenth Mr Wilson.

  replying to Harold **WILSON**'s *remark (on Home's becoming leader of the Conservative party) that 'the whole [democratic] process has ground to a halt with a fourteenth Earl'*

  in *Daily Telegraph* 22 October 1963

Homer

Greek poet of the 8th century BC. On Homer: see
ANONYMOUS 20:9, **ARNOLD** 32:7, **HORACE** 409:14, **KEATS** 457:6

6 Achilles' cursed anger sing, O goddess, that son of Peleus, which started a myriad sufferings for the Achaeans.

  The Iliad bk. 1, l. 1; see **POPE** 617:14

7 Agamemnon, King of Men.

  The Iliad, passim

8 In silence trailing away
  by the shore of the tumbling clamorous
    whispering sea.

  The Iliad bk. 1, l. 34

9 Winged words.

  The Iliad bk. 1, l. 201

10 The son of Kronos [Zeus] spoke, and nodded with his darkish brows, and immortal locks fell forward from the lord's deathless head, and he made great Olympus tremble.

  The Iliad bk. 1, l. 528

11 It is no cause for anger that the Trojans and the well-greaved Achaeans have suffered for so long over *such* a woman: she is wondrously like the immortal goddesses to look upon.

  of Helen

  The Iliad bk. 3, l. 156

12 Son of Atreus, what manner of speech has escaped the barrier of your teeth?

  The Iliad bk. 4, l. 350

13   Very like leaves
  upon this earth are the generations of men—
  old leaves, cast on the ground by wind, young
    leaves
  the greening forest bears when spring comes in.

  The Iliad bk. 6, l. 146

14 Always to be best, and to be distinguished above the rest.

  The Iliad bk. 6, l. 208

15 As he said this, Hector held out his arms
  to take his baby. But the child squirmed round
  on the nurse's bosom and begain to wail,
  terrified by his father's great war helm.

  The Iliad bk. 6, l. 466

16 Smiling through her tears.

  The Iliad bk. 6, l. 484

17 Hateful to me as the gates of Hades is that man who hides one thing in his heart and speaks another.

  The Iliad bk. 9, l. 312

18 This is the one best omen, to fight in defence of one's country.

  The Iliad bk. 12, l. 243

19 He lay great and greatly fallen, forgetful of his horsemanship.

  The Iliad bk. 16, l. 776

20 It lies in the lap of the gods.

  The Iliad bk. 17, l. 514 and elsewhere

21 They ran, one fleeing, and one pursuing. In front a good man fled, but one mightier far pursued him swiftly; for it was not for beast of sacrifice or for bull's hide that they strove, such as are men's prizes for swiftness of foot, but it was for the life of horse-taming Hector that they ran.

  Achilles and Hector

  The Iliad bk. 22, l. 156

22 Great Priam entered in, and coming close to Achilles, clasped in his hands his knees, and kissed his hands, the terrible, man-slaying hands that had slain his many sons.

  The Iliad bk. 24, l. 477

1   This is the way
the gods ordained the destiny of men,
to bear such burdens in our lives, while they
feel no affliction.
  The Iliad bk. 24, l. 525

2 Tell me, Muse, of the man of many devices,
who wandered far and wide after he had sacked
Troy's sacred city, and saw the towns of many
men and knew their mind.
  of Odysseus
  The Odyssey bk. 1, l. 1

3 Early-born rosy-fingered dawn.
  The Odyssey bk. 2, l. 1 and *passim*

4 Athene sent them a following breeze, a strong
west wind that whistled over the wine-dark sea.
  The Odyssey bk. 2, l. 420

5 There is nothing more shameless than the
accursed belly; it thrusts itself upon a man's
mind in spite of his afflictions.
  The Odyssey bk. 7, l. 219; see **POPE** 618:1

6 I would rather be tied to the soil as another
man's serf, even a poor man's, who hadn't much
to live on himself, than be King of all these the
dead and destroyed.
  The Odyssey bk. 11, l. 489

7 Come hither, renowned Odysseus, hither, you
pride and glory of all Achaea! Pause with your
ship; listen to our song. Never has any man
passed this way in his dark vessel and left
unheard the honey-sweet music from our lips;
first he has taken his delight, then gone on his
way a wiser man. We know of all the sorrows
in the wide land of Troy that Argives and
Trojans bore because the gods would needs have
it so; we know of all things that come to pass
on the fruitful earth.
  the Sirens
  The Odyssey bk. 12, l. 184

8 Have patience, heart. Once you endured worse
than this.
  The Odyssey bk. 20, l. 18

Arthur Honegger 1892–1955
Swiss composer

9 The first requirement for a composer is to be
dead.
  Je suis compositeur (1951)

Thomas Hood 1799–1845
English poet and humorist

10 Take her up tenderly,
Lift her with care;
Fashioned so slenderly,
Young, and so fair!
  'The Bridge of Sighs' (1844)

11 Or was there a dearer one
Still, and a nearer one
Yet, than all other?
  'The Bridge of Sighs' (1844)

12 The bleak wind of March
Made her tremble and shiver;
But not the dark arch,
Or the black flowing river.
  'The Bridge of Sighs' (1844)

13 Mad from life's history,
Glad to death's mystery,
Swift to be hurled—
Anywhere, anywhere,
Out of the world!
  'The Bridge of Sighs' (1844)

14 Two stern-faced men set out from Lynn,
Through the cold and heavy mist;
And Eugene Aram walked between,
With gyves upon his wrist.
  'The Dream of Eugene Aram' (1829)

15 Ben Battle was a soldier bold,
And used to war's alarms:
But a cannon-ball took off his legs,
So he laid down his arms!
  'Faithless Nelly Gray' (1826)

16 For here I leave my second leg,
And the Forty-second Foot!
  'Faithless Nelly Gray' (1826)

17 They went and told the sexton, and
The sexton tolled the bell.
  'Faithless Sally Brown' (1826)

18 I remember, I remember,
The house where I was born,
The little window where the sun
Came peeping in at morn.
  'I Remember' (1826)

19 But evil is wrought by want of thought,
As well as want of heart!
  'The Lady's Dream' (1844)

20 Home-made dishes that drive one from home.
  Miss Kilmansegg and her Precious Leg (1841–3) 'Her Misery'

21 No sun—no moon!
No morn—no noon
No dawn—no dusk—no proper time of day.
  'No!' (1844)

22 No warmth, no cheerfulness, no healthful ease,
No comfortable feel in any member—
No shade, no shine, no butterflies, no bees,
No fruits, no flowers, no leaves, no birds,—
November!
  'No!' (1844)

23 I saw old Autumn in the misty morn
Stand shadowless like Silence, listening
To silence.
  'Ode: Autumn' (1823)

24 Some minds improve by travel, others, rather
Resemble copper wire, or brass,
Which gets the narrower by going farther!
  'Ode to Rae Wilson, Esq.'

25 She stood breast high amid the corn,
Clasped by the golden light of morn,
Like the sweetheart of the sun,

Who many a glowing kiss had won.
'Ruth' (1827); see **KEATS** 456:10

1 With fingers weary and worn,
With eyelids heavy and red,
A woman sat, in unwomanly rags,
Plying her needle and thread—
Stitch! stitch! stitch!
In poverty, hunger, and dirt.
And still with a voice of dolorous pitch
She sang the 'Song of the Shirt'.
'The Song of the Shirt' (1843)

2 Oh! God! that bread should be so dear,
And flesh and blood so cheap!
'The Song of the Shirt' (1843)

3 What is a modern poet's fate?
To write his thoughts upon a slate;
The critic spits on what is done,
Gives it a wipe—and all is gone.
'To the Reviewers', dedication of *Whims and Oddities* (1826)

4 There are three things which the public will
always clamour for, sooner or later: namely,
novelty, novelty, novelty.
Announcement of Comic Annual for 1836, in 'Quote . . . Unquote'
newsletter January 2001

5 The sedate, sober, silent, serious, sad-coloured
sect.
of Quakers
Comic Annual (1839) 'The Doves and the Crows'

6 Holland . . . lies so low they're only saved by
being dammed.
Up the Rhine (1840) 'Letter from Martha Penny to Rebecca
Page'

Richard Hooker *c.*1554–1600
English theologian

7 He that goeth about to persuade a multitude,
that they are not so well governed as they ought
to be, shall never want attentive and favourable
hearers.
Of the Laws of Ecclesiastical Polity (1593) bk. 1, ch. 1, sect. 1

8 Of Law there can be no less acknowledged, than
that her seat is the bosom of God, her voice the
harmony of the world: all things in heaven and
earth do her homage, the very least as feeling
her care, and the greatest as not exempted from
her power.
Of the Laws of Ecclesiastical Polity (1593) bk. 1, ch. 16, sect. 8

9 Alteration though it be from worse to better
hath in it inconveniences, and those weighty.
Of the Laws of Ecclesiastical Polity (1593) bk. 4, ch. 14, sect. 1;
see **JOHNSON** 435:16

10 In truth for the greatest part such silly things,
that very easiness doth make them hard to be
disputed of in serious manner.
of recent innovations in church rites and ceremonies
Of the Laws of Ecclesiastical Polity bk. 5 (1597) 'Dedication to
Archbishop Whitgift'

Ellen Sturgis Hooper 1816–41
American poet

11 I slept, and dreamed that life was beauty;
I woke, and found that life was duty.
'Beauty and Duty' (1840)

Herbert Hoover 1874–1964
American Republican statesman, 31st President of the US
1929–33. On Hoover: see **COOLIDGE** 250:16

12 Our country has deliberately undertaken a great
social and economic experiment, noble in motive
and far-reaching in purpose.
on the Eighteenth Amendment enacting Prohibition
letter to Senator W. H. Borah, 23 February 1928; in Claudius
O. Johnson Borah of Idaho (1936) ch. 21

13 The American system of rugged individualism.
speech in New York City, 22 October 1928, in New Day (1928)
p. 154

14 The slogan of progress is changing from the full
dinner pail to the full garage.
*sometimes paraphrased as, 'a car in every garage and a
chicken in every pot'*
speech, 22 October 1928; see **HENRI IV** 391:17

15 Words without actions are the assassins of
idealism.
attributed, in Capital Times (Madison, Wisconsin) 15 April 1930

16 The grass will grow in the streets of a hundred
cities, a thousand towns.
*on proposals 'to reduce the protective tariff to a competitive
tariff for revenue'*
speech, 31 October 1932, in State Papers of Herbert Hoover
(1934) vol. 2

17 Older men declare war. But it is youth who
must fight and die.
speech at the Republican National Convention, Chicago, 27
June 1944, in Addresses upon the American Road (1946)

Alec Derwent Hope 1907–2000
Australian poet

18 Lost in the blue unfriendliness of space.
'The Death of the Bird' (1948)

Anthony Hope (Anthony Hope Hawkins)
1863–1933
English novelist. See also **EPITAPHS** 318:11

19 Economy is going without something you do
want in case you should, some day, want
something you probably won't want.
The Dolly Dialogues (1894) no. 12

20 'You oughtn't to yield to temptation.' 'Well,
somebody must, or the thing becomes absurd,'
said I.
The Dolly Dialogues (1894) no. 14

21 Oh, for an hour of Herod!
*at the first night of J. M. **BARRIE**'s Peter Pan in 1904*
Denis Mackail The Story of JMB (1941) ch. 17

Bob Hope 1903–2003

American comedian

1 A bank is a place that will lend you money if you can prove that you don't need it.

In Alan Harrington *Life in the Crystal Palace* (1959) 'The Tyranny of Farms'

Francis Hope 1938–74

British journalist and poet

2 And scribbled lines like fallen hopes
On backs of tattered envelopes.

'Instead of a Poet' (1965)

Laurence Hope (Adela Florence Nicolson)
1865–1904

English-born Indian poet

3 Pale hands I loved beside the Shalimar,
Where are you now? Who lies beneath your spell?

The Garden of Kama (1901) 'Kashmiri Song'

4 Less than the dust, beneath thy Chariot wheel,
Less than the rust, that never stained thy Sword
. . .
Less than the need thou hast in life of me.
Even less am I.

The Garden of Kama (1901) 'Less than the Dust'

Gerard Manley Hopkins 1844–89

English poet and priest

5 Not, I'll not, carrion comfort, Despair, not feast on thee;
Not untwist—slack they may be—these last strands of man
In me or, most weary, cry *I can no more.* I can;
Can something, hope, wish day come, not choose not to be.

'Carrion Comfort' (written 1885)

6 Towery city and branchy between towers;
Cuckoo-echoing, bell-swarmèd, lark-charmèd,
rook-racked, river-rounded.

'Duns Scotus's Oxford' (written 1879)

7 The world is charged with the grandeur of God.
It will flame out like shining from shook foil . . .
Generations have trod, have trod, have trod;
And all is seared with trade; bleared, smeared with toil;
And wears man's smudge and shares man's smell: the soil
Is bare now, nor can foot feel, being shod.

'God's Grandeur' (written 1877)

8   Because the Holy Ghost over the bent
World broods with warm breast and with ah!
bright wings.

'God's Grandeur' (written 1877)

9 Elected Silence, sing to me
And beat upon my whorlèd ear,

Pipe me to pastures still and be
The music that I care to hear.

'The Habit of Perfection' (written 1866)

10 Palate, the hutch of tasty lust,
Desire not to be rinsed with wine.

'The Habit of Perfection' (written 1866)

11 I have desired to go
Where springs not fail,
To fields where flies no sharp and sided hail
And a few lilies blow.

'Heaven-Haven' (written 1864)

12 What would the world be, once bereft
Of wet and wildness? Let them be left,
O let them be left, wildness and wet;
Long live the weeds and the wilderness yet.

'Inversnaid' (written 1881)

13 No worst, there is none. Pitched past pitch of grief,
More pangs will, schooled at forepangs, wilder wring.
Comforter, where, where is your comforting?

'No worst, there is none' (written 1885)

14 O the mind, mind has mountains; cliffs of fall
Frightful, sheer, no-man-fathomed. Hold them cheap
May who ne'er hung there.

'No worst, there is none' (written 1885)

15   All
Life death does end and each day dies with sleep.

'No worst, there is none' (written 1885)

16 Glory be to God for dappled things.

'Pied Beauty' (written 1877)

17 All things counter, original, spare, strange;
Whatever is fickle, freckled (who knows how?)
With swift, slow; sweet, sour; adazzle, dim;
He fathers-forth whose beauty is past change:
Praise him.

'Pied Beauty' (written 1877)

18 The glassy peartree leaves and blooms, they brush
The descending blue; that blue is all in a rush
With richness.

'Spring' (written 1877)

19 Márgarét, áre you gríeving
Over Goldengrove unleaving?

'Spring and Fall: to a young child' (written 1880)

20 Áh! ás the heart grows older
It will come to such sights colder
By and by, nor spare a sigh
Though worlds of wanwood leafmeal lie;
And yet you *will* weep and know why.

'Spring and Fall: to a young child' (written 1880)

21 It ís the blight man was born for,
It is Margaret you mourn for.

'Spring and Fall: to a young child' (written 1880)

22   This piece-bright paling shuts the spouse

Christ home, Christ and his mother and all his
hallows.
'The Starlight Night' (written 1877)

1 I am all at once what Christ is, since he was
what I am, and
This Jack, joke, poor potsherd, patch,
matchwood, immortal diamond,
Is immortal diamond.
'That Nature is a Heraclitean Fire' (written 1888)

2 Thou art indeed just, Lord, if I contend
With thee; but, sir, so what I plead is just.
Why do sinners' ways prosper? and why must
Disappointment all I endeavour end?
'Thou art indeed just, Lord' (written 1889)

3 Birds build—but not I build; no, but strain,
Time's eunuch, and not breed one work that
wakes.
Mine, O thou lord of life, send my roots rain.
'Thou art indeed just, Lord' (written 1889); see **HOPKINS**
408:11

4 I caught this morning morning's minion,
kingdom of daylight's dauphin, dapple-dawn-
drawn Falcon.
'The Windhover' (written 1877)

5   My heart in hiding
Stirred for a bird,—the achieve of, the mastery
of the thing!
'The Windhover' (written 1877)

6   I did say yes
O at lightning and lashed rod;
Thou heardst me truer than tongue confess
Thy terror, O Christ, O God.
'The Wreck of the Deutschland' (written 1876) pt. 1

7 On Saturday sailed from Bremen,
American-outward-bound,
Take settler and seamen, tell men with women,
Two hundred souls in the round.
'The Wreck of the Deutschland' (written 1876) pt. 2

8 Time has three dimensions and one positive
pitch or direction. It is therefore not so much
like any river or any sea as like the Sea of
Galilee, which has the Jordan running through it
and giving a current to the whole.
'Creation and Redemption The Great Sacrifice' (written 1881),
in Christopher Devlin (ed.) *The Sermons and Devotional
Writings of Gerard Manley Hopkins* (1959) ch. 8

9 To lift up the hands in prayer gives God glory,
but a man with a dungfork in his hand, a
woman with a slop-pail, give him glory too. He
is so great that all things give him glory if you
mean they should.
G. Roberts (ed.) *Gerard Manley Hopkins. Selected Prose* (1980)
'The Principle or Foundation' (1882)

10 I am surprised you should say fancy and
aesthetic tastes have led me to my present state
of mind; these would be better satisfied in the
Church of England, for bad taste is always
meeting one in the accessories of Catholicism.
on his adoption of the Catholic faith
letter to his father, 16 October 1866; in G. Roberts (ed.)
Gerard Manley Hopkins. Selected Prose (1980)

11 The fine pleasure is not to do a thing but to feel
that you could . . . If I could but get on, if I
could but produce a work I should not mind its
being buried, silenced, and going no further; but
it kills me to be time's eunuch and never to
beget.
letter to Robert Bridges, 1 September 1885, in C. C. Abbott
(ed.) *The Correspondence of Gerard Manley Hopkins and Robert
Bridges* (1935); see **HOPKINS** 408:3

Joseph Hopkinson 1770–1842
American politician

12 Hail, Columbia! happy land!
Hail, ye heroes! heaven-born band!
'Hail, Columbia!' in *Porcupine's Gazette* 20 April 1798

Edward Hopper 1882–1967
American artist

13 Maybe I'm not very human. What I wanted to
do was to paint sunlight on the side of the
house.
interview with Lloyd Goodrich, 20 April 1946; S. Wagstaff
(ed.) *Edward Hopper* (2004)

Horace (Quintus Horatius Flaccus) 65–8 BC
Roman poet

14   *Ut turpiter atrum*
Desinat in piscem mulier formosa superne.
So that what is a beautiful woman on top ends
in a black and ugly fish.
Ars Poetica l. 3

15   '*Pictoribus atque poetis*
Quidlibet audendi semper fuit aequa potestas.'
Scimus, et hanc veniam petimusque damusque
vicissim.
'Painters and poets alike have always had licence
to dare anything.' We know that, and we both
claim and permit others this indulgence.
Ars Poetica l. 9

16 *Inceptis gravibus plerumque et magna professis*
Purpureus, late qui splendeat, unus et alter
Adsuitur pannus.
Works of serious purpose and grand promises
often have a purple patch or two stitched on, to
shine far and wide.
Ars Poetica l. 14

17   *Brevis esse laboro,*
Obscurus fio.
I strive to be brief, and I become obscure.
Ars Poetica l. 25

18 *Dixeris egregie notum si callida verbum*
Reddiderit iunctura novum.
You will have written exceptionally well if, by
skilful arrangement of your words, you have
made an ordinary one seem original.
Ars Poetica l. 47

19   *Licuit semperque licebit*
Signatum praesente nota producere nomen.

Ut silvae foliis pronos mutantur in annos,
Prima cadunt: ita verborum vetus interit aetas,
Et iuvenum ritu florent modo nata vigentque.

It has ever been, and ever will be, permitted to issue words stamped with the mint-mark of the day. As forests change their leaves with each year's decline, and the earliest drop off: so with words, the old race dies, and like the young of human kind, the new-born bloom and thrive.
Ars Poetica l. 58; see **DILLON** 283:4

1 *Multa renascentur quae iam cecidere, cadentque*
Quae nunc sunt in honore vocabula, si volet usus,
Quem penes arbitrium est et ius et norma loquendi.

Many terms which have now dropped out of favour will be revived, and those that are at present respectable will drop out, if usage so choose, with whom lies the decision, the judgement, and the rule of speech.
Ars Poetica l. 70

2 *Grammatici certant et adhuc sub iudice lis est.*

Scholars dispute, and the case is still before the courts.
Ars Poetica l. 78

3 *Proicit ampullas et sesquipedalia verba.*

He throws aside his paint-pots and his words a foot and a half long.
Ars Poetica l. 97; see **WELLS** 846:20

4   *Si vis me flere, dolendum est*
Primum ipsi tibi.

If you want me to weep, you must first feel grief yourself.
Ars Poetica l. 102

5 *Difficile est proprie communia dicere.*

It is hard to utter common notions in an individual way.
Ars Poetica l. 128

6 *Parturient montes, nascetur ridiculus mus.*

Mountains will go into labour, and a silly little mouse will be born.
Ars Poetica l. 139

7 *Non fumum ex fulgore, sed ex fumo dare lucem*
Cogitat.

His thinking does not produce smoke after the flame, but light after smoke.
Ars Poetica l. 143

8 *Semper ad eventum festinat et in medias res*
Non secus ac notas auditorem rapit.

He always hurries to the main event and whisks his audience into the middle of things as though they knew already.
Ars Poetica l. 148

9   *Quae*
Despererat tractata nitescere posse, relinquit.

What he fears he cannot make attractive with his touch he abandons.
Ars Poetica l. 149

10 *Difficilis, querulus, laudator temporis acti*
Se puero, castigator censorque minorum.

Tiresome, complaining, a praiser of past times, when he was a boy, a castigator and censor of the young generation.
Ars Poetica l. 173

11   *Vos exemplaria Graeca*
Nocturna versate manu, versate diurnu.

You should turn the pages of your Greek models by night and by day.
Ars Poetica l. 268

12 *Omne tulit punctum qui miscuit utile dulci,*
Lectorem delectando pariterque monendo.

He has gained every point who has mixed profit with pleasure, by delighting the reader at the same time as instructing him.
Ars Poetica l. 343

13 *Verum ubi plura nitent in carmine, non ego paucis*
Offendar maculis.

When many beauties grace a poem, I shall not take offence at a few faults.
Ars Poetica l. 351

14 *Indignor quandoque bonus dormitat Homerus.*

I'm aggrieved when sometimes even excellent Homer nods.
Ars Poetica l. 359; see **BYRON** 188:27, **PROVERBS** 634:38

15 *Ut pictura poesis.*

A poem is like a painting.
Ars Poetica l. 361

16   *Mediocribus esse poetis*
Non homines, non di, non concessere columnae.

Not gods, nor men, nor even booksellers have put up with poets being second-rate.
Ars Poetica l. 372

17 *Condo et compono quae mox depromere possim.*

I put together and collect things which I will soon be able to draw upon.
Epistles bk. 1, no. 1, l. 12

18 *Nullius addictus iurare in verba magistri,*
Quo me cumque rapit tempestas, deferor hospes.

Not bound to swear allegiance to any master, wherever the wind takes me I travel as a visitor.
Epistles bk. 1, no. 1, l. 14; see **MOTTOES** 563:14

19 *Virtus est vitium fugere, et sapientia prima*
stultitia caruisse.

To flee vice is the beginning of virtue, and to have got rid of folly is the beginning of wisdom.
Epistles bk. 1, no. 1, l. 41

20 *Condicio dulcis sine pulvere palmae.*

The happy state of winning the palm without the dust of racing.
Epistles bk. 1, no. 1, l. 51

21 *O cives, cives, quarenda pecunia primum est;*
Virtus post nummos.

Citizens, citizens, the first thing to acquire is money. Cash before conscience!
Epistles bk. 1, no. 1, l. 53

1 *Si possis recte, si non, quocumque modo rem.*

If possible honestly, if not, somehow, make money.

Epistles bk. 1, no. 1, l. 66; see **POPE** 617:17

2 *Olim quod vulpes aegroto cauta leoni*
Respondit referam: 'quia me vestigia terrent,
Omnia te adversum spectantia, nulla retrorsum.'

Let me remind you what the wary fox said once upon a time to the sick lion: 'Because those footprints scare me, all directed your way, none coming back.'

explaining why he did not follow popular opinion
Epistles bk. 1, no. 1, l. 73; see **AESOP** 9:2

3 *Quidquid delirant reges plectuntur Achivi.*

Whatever madness their kings commit, the Greeks take the beating.

Epistles bk. 1, no. 2, l. 14

4 *Nos numerus sumus et fruges consumere nati.*

We are just statistics, born to consume resources.

Epistles bk. 1, no. 2, l. 27

5 *Dimidium facti qui coepit habet: sapere aude.*

To have begun is half the job: dare to know.

Epistles bk. 1, no. 2, l. 40

6 *Ira furor brevis est.*

Anger is a short madness.

Epistles bk. 1, no. 2, l. 62

7 *Omnem crede diem tibi diluxisse supremum.*
Grata superveniet quae non sperabitur hora.
Me pinguem et nitidum bene curata cute vises
Cum ridere voles Epicuri de grege porcum.

Believe each day that has dawned is your last. Some hour to which you have not been looking forward will prove lovely. As for me, if you want a good laugh, you will come and find me fat and sleek, in excellent condition, one of Epicurus's herd of pigs.

Epistles bk. 1, no. 4, l. 13

8 *Nil admirari prope res est una, Numici,*
Solaque quae possit facere et servare beatum.

To marvel at nothing is just about the one and only thing, Numicius, that can make a man happy and keep him that way.

Epistles bk. 1, no. 6, l. 1; see **POPE** 617:18

9 *Naturam expelles furca, tamen usque recurret.*

You may drive out nature with a pitchfork, yet she'll be constantly running back.

Epistles bk. 1, no. 10, l. 24; see **PROVERBS** 647:40

10 *Caelum non animum mutant qui trans mare currunt.*
Strenua nos exercet inertia: navibus atque
Quadrigis petimus bene vivere. Quod petis hic est,
Est Ulubris, animus si te non deficit aequus.

They change their clime, not their frame of mind, who rush across the sea. We strain at achieving nothing: we seek happiness in boats and carriage rides. What you seek is here, at

Ulubrae, so long as peace of mind does not desert you.

Epistles bk. 1, no. 11, l. 27

11 *Concordia discors.*

Discordant harmony.

Epistles bk. 1, no. 12, l. 19

12 *Hae latebrae dulces et, iam si credis, amoenae*
Incolumem tibi me praestant septembribus horis.

This retreat, so sweet—yes, believe me, so bewitching—keeps me, my friend, in sound health in September's heat.

Epistles bk. 1, no. 16, l. 15

13 *Principibus placuisse viris non ultima laus est.*
Non cuivis homini contingit adire Corinthum.

It is not the least praise to have pleased leading men. Not everyone is lucky enough to get to Corinth.

Epistles bk. 1, no. 17, l. 35

14 *Et semel emissum volat irrevocabile verbum.*

And once sent out a word takes wing beyond recall.

Epistles bk. 1, no. 18, l. 71; see **DILLON** 283:5

15 *Nam tua res agitur, paries cum proximus ardet.*

For it is your business, when the wall next door catches fire.

Epistles bk. 1, no. 18, l. 84

16 *Fallentis semita vitae.*

The pathway of a life unnoticed.

Epistles bk. 1, no. 18, l. 103

17 *Nulla placere diu nec vivere carmina possunt*
Quae scribuntur aquae potoribus.

No verse can give pleasure for long, nor last, that is written by drinkers of water.

Epistles bk. 1, no. 19, l. 2

18 *O imitatores, servum pecus.*

O imitators, you slavish herd.

Epistles bk. 1, no. 19, l. 19

19 *Scribimus indocti doctique poemata passim.*

Skilled or unskilled, we all scribble poems.

Epistles bk. 2, no. 1, l. 117; see **POPE** 617:23

20 *Sic leve, sic parvum est, animum quod laudis avarum*
Subruit aut reficit.

How light, how small is the thing which casts down or restores a mind greedy for praise.

Epistles bk. 2, no. 1, l. 181

21 *Si foret in terris, rideret Democritus.*

If he were on earth, Democritus would laugh at the sight.

Epistles bk. 2, no. 1, l. 194

22 *Atque inter silvas Academi quaerere verum.*

And seek for truth in the groves of Academe.

Epistles bk. 2, no. 2, l. 45

23 *Caedimur et totidem plagis consumimus hostem*
Lento Samnites ad lumina prima duello.

We belabour each other, and with tit for tat use

up our foe, like Samnites, in a long-drawn bout,
till the first lamps are lighted.

of literary battles

Epistles bk. 2, no. 2, l. 97

1 *Multa fero, ut placem genus irritabile vatum.*

I have to put up with a lot, to please the touchy
breed of poets.

Epistles bk. 2, no. 2, l. 102

2 *Quid te exempta iuvat spinis de pluribus una?*
Vivere si recte nescis, decede peritis.
Lusisti satis, edisti satis atque bibisti:
Tempus abire tibi est.

What pleasure does it give to be rid of one
thorn out of many? If you don't know how to
live right, give way to those who are expert at it.
You have had enough fun, eaten and drunk
enough: it is time for you to go.

Epistles bk. 2, no. 2, l. 212

3 *Beatus ille, qui procul negotiis,*
Ut prisca gens mortalium,
Paterna rura bubus exercet suis,
Solutus omni faenore.

Happy the man who, far away from business,
like the race of men of old, tills his ancestral
fields with his own oxen, unbound by any
interest to pay.

Epodes epode 2, l. 1

4 *Quodsi me lyricis vatibus inseres,*
Sublimi feriam sidera vertice.

And if you include me among the lyric poets,
I'll hold my head so high it'll strike the stars.

Odes bk. 1, no. 1, l. 35

5 *Animae dimidium meae.*

Half my own soul.

of VIRGIL

Odes bk. 1, no. 3, l. 8

6 *Illi robur et aes triplex*
Circa pectus erat, qui fragilem truci
Commisit pelago ratem
Primus.

Oak was round his breast, and triple bronze,
who first launched his frail boat on the rough
sea.

Odes bk. 1, no. 3, l. 9

7 *Pallida Mors aequo pulsat pede pauperum tabernas*
Regumque turris.

Pale Death breaks into the cottages of the poor
as into the castles of kings.

Odes bk. 1, no. 4, l. 13

8 *Vitae summa brevis spem nos vetat incohare longam.*

Life's short span forbids us to enter on far-
reaching hopes.

Odes bk. 1, no. 4, l. 15

9 *Quis multa gracilis te puer in rosa*
Perfusus liquidis urget odoribus
Grato, Pyrrha, sub antro?
Cui flavam religas comam?

What slim youngster soaked in perfumes
is hugging you now, Pyrrha, on a bed of roses
deep in your lovely cave? For whom
are you tying up your blonde hair?

Odes bk. 1, no. 5, l. 1

10 *Simplex munditiis.*

Plain in thy neatness.

Odes bk. 1, no. 5, l. 5, translated by John **MILTON**

11 *Nil desperandum.*

Never despair.

Odes bk. 1, no. 7, l. 27

12 *Cras ingens iterabimus aequor.*

Tomorrow we shall sail again on the vast ocean.

Odes bk. 1, no. 7, l. 32

13 *Quid sit futurum cras fuge quaerere et*
Quem Fors dierum cumque dabit lucro
Appone.

Drop the question what tomorrow may bring,
and count as profit every day that Fate allows
you.

Odes bk. 1, no. 9, l. 13

14 *Nunc et latentis proditor intumo*
Gratus puellae risus ab angulo
Pignusque dereptum lacertis
Aut digito male pertinaci.

Now is the time for the lovely laugh from the
secret corner
giving away the girl in her hiding-place,
and for the token snatched from her arm
or finger feebly resisting.

Odes bk. 1, no. 9, l. 21

15 *Tu ne quaesieris, scire nefas, quem mihi, quem tibi*
Finem di dederint.

Do not try to find out—we're forbidden to
know—what end the gods may bestow on me or
you.

Odes bk. 1, no. 11, l. 1

16   *Dum loquimur, fugerit invida*
Aetas: carpe diem, quam minimum credula postero.

While we're talking, envious time is fleeing:
seize the day, put no trust in the future.

Odes bk. 1, no. 11, l. 7

17 *Felices ter et amplius*
Quos irrupta tenet copula nec malis
Divulsus querimoniis
Suprema citius solvet amor die.

Thrice blessed (and more) are they whom an
unbroken bond holds and whose love, never
strained by nasty quarrels, will not slip until
their dying day.

written above the main entrance to Harvard Yard

Odes bk. 1, no. 13, l. 17

18 *O matre pulchra filia pulchrior.*

Daughter lovelier than your lovely mother.

Odes bk. 1, no. 16, l. 1

19 *Integer vitae scelerisque purus.*

Wholesome of life and free of crimes.

Odes bk. 1, no. 22, l. 1

1 *Dulce ridentem Lalagen amabo,*
Dulce loquentem.

I will go on loving Lalage, who laughs so
sweetly and talks so sweetly.

> Odes bk. 1, no. 22, l. 23; see **CATULLUS** 210:13, **SAPPHO** 680:22

2 *Parcus deorum cultor et infrequens.*

A grudging and irregular worshipper of the
gods.

> Odes bk. 1, no. 34, l. 1

3 *Nunc est bibendum, nunc pede libero*
Pulsanda tellus.

Now for drinking, now the Earth must shake
beneath a lively foot.

> Odes bk. 1, no. 37, l. 1

4 *Persicos odi, puer, apparatus.*

I hate all that Persian gear, boy.

> Odes bk. 1, no. 38, l. 1

5 *Mitte sectari rosa quo locorum*
Sera moretur.

Stop looking for the place where a late rose may
yet linger.

> Odes bk. 1, no. 38, l. 3

6 *Aequam memento rebus in arduis*
Servare mentem.

When the going gets rough, remember to keep
calm.

> Odes bk. 2, no. 3, l. 1

7 *Omnes eodem cogimur.*

We are all gathered to the same place.

> Odes bk. 2, no. 3, l. 25

8 *Auream quisquis mediocritatem*
Diligit.

Whoever loves the golden mean.

> Odes bk. 2, no. 10, l. 5

9   *Neque semper arcum*
Tendit Apollo.

Apollo does not always stretch his bow.

> Odes bk. 2, no. 10, l. 19

10 *Eheu fugaces, Postume, Postume,*
Labuntur anni.

Ah me, Postumus, Postumus, the fleeting years
are slipping by.

> Odes bk. 2, no. 14, l. 1; see **SMART** 755:15

11   *Nihil est ab omni*
Parte beatum.

Nothing is an unmixed blessing.

> Odes bk. 2, no. 16, l. 27

12 *Tu secanda marmora*
Locas sub ipsum funus et sepulchri
Immemor struis domos.

But you, though in the very shadow of death,
place contracts for cutting marble slabs, and
build houses without giving a thought to your
tomb.

> Odes bk. 2, no. 18, l. 17

13 *Credite posteri.*

Believe me, you who come after me!

> Odes bk. 2, no. 19, l. 2

14 *Odi profanum vulgus et arceo;*
Favete linguis; carmina non prius
Audita Musarum sacerdos
Virginibus puerisque canto.

I hate the common herd and keep them off.
Hush your tongues; as a priest of the Muses, I
sing songs never heard before to virgin girls and
boys.

> Odes bk. 3, no. 1, l. 1; see **CALLIMACHUS** 193:16, **COWLEY** 254:11

15   *Aequa lege Necessitas*
Sortitur insignis et imos;
Omne capax movet urna nomen.

Necessity with her impartial law picks out by lot
both high and humble.
All names are shaken in that capacious urn.

> Odes bk. 3, no. 1, l. 14

16 *Post equitem sedet atra Cura.*

Black Care sits behind the horseman.

> Odes bk. 3, no. 1, l. 40

17 *Dulce et decorum est pro patria mori.*

Lovely and honourable it is to die for one's
country.

> Odes bk. 3, no. 2, l. 13; see **OWEN** 591:6, **POUND** 621:5

18 *Iustum et tenacem propositi virum*
Non civium ardor prava iubentium,
Non vultus instantis tyranni
Mente quatit solida.

The just man having a firm grasp of his
intentions, neither the heated passions of his
fellow men ordaining something awful, nor a
tyrant staring him in the face, will shake in his
convictions.

> Odes bk. 3, no. 3, l. 1

19 *Si fractus illabatur orbis,*
Impavidum ferient ruinae.

If the world should break and fall on him, its
ruins would strike him unafraid.

> Odes bk. 3, no. 3, l. 7; see **ADDISON** 5:2, **POPE** 614:16

20 *Auditis an me ludit amabilis*
insania?

Do you hear? or does some seductive madness
mock me?

> Odes bk. 3, no. 4, l. 5

21   *Opaco*
Pelion imposuisse Olympo.

To pile Pelion on top of shady Olympus.

> Odes bk. 3, no. 4, l. 52

22 *Vis consili expers mole ruit sua.*

Force, unaided by judgement, collapses through
its own weight.

> Odes bk. 3, no. 4, l. 65

1 *Dis te minorem quod geris, imperas.*
You rule because you hold yourself inferior to
the gods.
Odes bk. 3, no. 6, l. 5

2 *Damnosa quid non imminuit dies?*
Aetas parentum peior avis tulit
Nos nequiores, mox daturos
Progeniem vitiosiorem.
What do the ravages of time not injure? Our
parents' age (worse than our grandparents') has
produced us, more worthless still, who will soon
give rise to a yet more vicious generation.
Odes bk. 3, no. 6, l. 45

3 *Splendide mendax et in omne virgo*
Nobilis aevum.
Gloriously deceitful and a virgin renowned for
ever.
of the Danaid Hypermestra
Odes bk. 3, no. 11, l. 35

4 *O fons Bandusiae, splendidior vitro.*
O spring of Bandusia, brighter than glass.
Odes bk. 3, no. 13, l. 1

5 *Magnas inter opes inops.*
A beggar amidst great riches.
Odes bk. 3, no. 16, l. 28

6 *Vixi puellis nuper idoneus*
Et militavi non sine gloria;
Nunc arma defunctumque bello
barbiton hic paries habebit.
Till now I have lived my life without complaints
from girls, and campaigned with my share of
honours.
Now my armour and my lyre—its wars are
over—
will hang on this wall.
Odes bk. 3, no. 26, l. 1

7 *Fumum et opes strepitumque Romae.*
The smoke and wealth and din of Rome.
Odes bk. 3, no. 29, l. 12

8 *Ille potens sui*
Laetusque deget, cui licet in diem
Dixisse Vixi: cras vel atra
Nube polum pater occupato
Vel sole puro.
That man shall live as his own master and in
happiness who can say each day 'I have lived':
tomorrow let the Father fill the sky with a black
cloud or clear sunshine.
Odes bk. 3, no. 29, l. 41; see **DRYDEN** 297:6

9 *Exegi monumentum aere perennius.*
I have erected a monument more lasting than
bronze.
Odes bk. 3, no. 30, l. 1

10 *Non omnis moriar.*
I shall not altogether die.
Odes bk. 3, no. 30, l. 6

11 *Usque ego postera*
Crescam laude recens, dum Capitolium

Scandet cum tacita virgine pontifex.
My fame will grow,
ever renewed in time to come, as long as
the priest climbs the Capitol with the silent
Virgin.
Odes bk. 3, no. 30, l. 7

12 *Non sum qualis eram bonae*
Sub regno Cinarae.
I am not as I was when good Cinara was my
queen.
Odes bk. 4, no. 1, l. 3; see **DOWSON** 292:3

13 *Sed cur heu, Ligurine, cur*
Manat rara meas lacrima per genas?
Cur facunda parum decoro
Inter verba cadit lingua silentio?
Nocturnis ego somniis
Iam captum teneo iam volucrem sequor
Te per gramina Martii
Campi, te per aquas, dure, volubilis.
But why, Ligurinus, oh why,
is that tear trickling down my cheek?
Why does my glib tongue
fall shamefully silent as I speak?
At night in my dreams sometimes I catch
and hold you, sometimes I pursue you as you
run
over the grass of the Campus Martius
or swim, so hard of heart, the rolling waves.
Odes bk. 4, no. 1, l. 33

14 *Quod spiro et placeo, si placeo, tuum est.*
That I make poetry and give pleasure (if I give
pleasure) are because of you.
Odes bk. 4, no. 3, l. 24

15 *Merses profundo: pulchrior evenit.*
Plunge it in deep water: it comes up more
beautiful.
Odes bk. 4, no. 4, l. 65

16 *Occidit, occidit*
Spes omnis et fortuna nostri
Nominis Hasdrubale interempto.
All our hope is fallen, fallen, and the luck of our
name lost with Hasdrubal.
Odes bk. 4, no. 4, l. 70

17 *Diffugere nives, redeunt iam gramina campis*
Arboribusque comae.
The snows have fled, now grass returns to the
fields and leaves to the trees.
Odes bk. 4, no. 7, l. 1

18 *Immortalia ne speres, monet annus et almum*
Quae rapit hora diem.
The year and the hour which robs us of the fair
day warn us not to hope for things to last for
ever.
Odes bk. 4, no. 7, l. 7

19 *Frigora mitescunt Zephyris, ver proterit aestas*
Interitura, simul
Pomifer Autumnus fruges effuderit, et mox
Bruma recurrit iners.

The cold melts in the Zephyrs, Summer
   tramples on the heels
of Spring, and will die the moment
Autumn laden with fruit pours out her crops,
   and soon
sluggish Winter comes running back.
   Odes bk. 4, no. 7, l. 9

1 *Damna tamen celeres reparant caelestia lunae;*
Nos ubi decidimus
Quo pius Aeneas, quo dives Tullus et Ancus,
Pulvis et umbra sumus.

Swift moons make good their losses in the sky,
but when we go down to be
with pious Aeneas, wealthy Tullus, and Ancus,
we are dust and shadow.
   Odes bk. 4, no. 7, l. 13

2 *Dignum laude virum Musa vetat mori.*

The man worthy of praise the Muse forbids to
die.
   Odes bk. 4, no. 8, l. 28

3 *Vixere fortes ante Agamemnona*
Multi; sed omnes illacrimabiles
Urgentur ignotique longa
Nocte, carent quia vate sacro.

Many brave men lived before Agamemnon's
time; but they are all, unmourned and unknown,
covered by the long night, because they lack
their sacred poet.
   Odes bk. 4, no. 9, l. 25; see **PROVERBS** 628:21

4 *Non possidentem multa vocaveris*
Recte beatum: rectius occupat
Nomen beati, qui deorum
Muneribus sapienter uti
Duramque callet pauperiem pati
Peiusque leto flagitium timet.

It is not he who has many possessions that you
should call blessed: he more rightly deserves that
name who knows how to use the gods' gifts
wisely and to endure harsh poverty, and who
fears dishonour more than death.
   Odes bk. 4, no. 9, l. 45

5 *Misce stultitiam consiliis brevem:*
Dulce est desipere in loco.

Mix a little foolishness with your prudence: it's
good to be silly at the right moment.
   Odes bk. 4, no. 12, l. 27

6 *Qui fit, Maecenas, ut nemo, quam sibi sortem*
Seu ratio dederit seu fors obiecerit, illa
Contentus vivat, laudet diversa sequentis?

How is it, Maecenas, that no one lives contented
with his lot, whether he has planned it for
himself or fate has flung him into it, but yet he
praises those who follow different paths?
   Satires bk. 1, no. 1, l. 1

7 *Quamquam ridentem dicere verum*
Quid vetat?

Why should truth not be impress'd
Beneath the cover of a jest.
   Satires bk 1, no. 1, l. 24

8 *. . . Mutato nomine de te*
Fabula narratur.

Change the name and it's about you, that story.
   Satires bk. 1, no. 1, l. 69

9 *Est modus in rebus.*

There is moderation in everything.
   Satires bk. 1, no. 1, l. 106; see **PROVERBS** 638:43, **PROVERBS**
644:27

10 *Hoc genus omne.*

All that tribe.
   Satires bk. 1, no. 2, l. 2

11 *. . . Ab ovo*
Usque ad mala.

From the egg right through to the apples.
   from the start to the finish of a meal
   Satires bk. 1, no. 3, l. 6

12 *Quis paria esse fere placuit peccata, laborant*
Cum ventum ad verum est: sensus moresque
   repugnant
Atque ipsa Utilitas, iusti prope mater et aequi.

Those whose creed is that all sins are much on a
par are at a loss when they come to face facts.
Feelings and customs rebel, and expediency itself
is the mother of justice and equity.
   Satires bk. 1, no. 3, l. 96

13 *Etiam disiecti membra poetae.*

Even though broken up, the limbs of a poet.
   of **ENNIUS**
   Satires bk. 1, no. 4, l. 62

14 *. . . Ad unguem*
Factus homo.

An accomplished man to his fingertips.
   Satires bk. 1, no. 5, l. 32

15 *. . . Credat Iudaeus Apella,*
Non ego.

Let Apella the Jew believe it; I shan't.
   Satires bk. 1, no. 5, l. 100

16   *Ridiculum acri*
Fortius et melius magnas plerumque secat res.

Humour very often cuts the knot of serious
questions more trenchantly and successfully than
severity.
   Satires bk. 1, no. 10, l. 14

17 *In silvam . . . ligna feras insanius.*

It's insane to carry timber to the forest.
   Satires bk. 1, no. 10, l. 34

18 *Solventur risu tabulae, tu missus abibis.*

The case will be dismissed with a laugh. You
will get off scot-free.
   Satires bk. 2, no. 1, l. 86 (translated by H. R. Fairclough)

19 *Par nobile fratrum.*

A noble pair of brothers.
   Satires bk. 2, no. 3, l. 243 (i.e. notorious villains)

20 *Hoc erat in votis: modus agri non ita magnus,*
Hortus ubi et tecto vicinus iugis aquae fons
Et paulum silvae super his foret.

This was among my prayers: a piece of land not so very large, where a garden should be and a spring of ever-flowing water near the house, and a bit of woodland as well as these.

Satires bk. 2, no. 6, l. 1; see **MALLET** 517:16, **SWIFT** 783:24

1 *O noctes cenaeque deum!*

O nights and feasts divine!

Satires bk. 2, no. 6, l. 65

2 *Responsare cupidinibus, contemnere honores*
Fortis, et in se ipso totus, teres, atque rotundus.

Strong enough to answer back to desires, to despise honours, and a whole man in himself, polished and well-rounded.

Satires bk. 2, no. 7, l. 85

Samuel Horsley 1733–1806

English bishop

3 In this country . . . the individual subject . . . 'has nothing to do with the laws but to obey them'.

defending a maxim he had used earlier in committee
speech, House of Lords, 13 November 1795

A. E. Housman 1859–1936

English poet and classicist

4 Oh who is that young sinner with the handcuffs on his wrists?
And what has he been after that they groan and shake their fists?
And wherefore is he wearing such a conscience-stricken air?
Oh they're taking him to prison for the colour of his hair.

first drafted in summer 1895, following the trial and imprisonment of Oscar **WILDE**
Collected Poems (1939) 'Additional Poems' no. 18

5 The Grizzly Bear is huge and wild;
He has devoured the infant child.
The infant child is not aware
He has been eaten by the bear.

'Infant Innocence' (1938)

6 And how am I to face the odds
Of man's bedevilment and God's?
I, a stranger and afraid
In a world I never made.

Last Poems (1922) no. 12

7 The candles burn their sockets,
The blinds let through the day,
The young man feels his pockets
And wonders what's to pay.

Last Poems (1922) no. 21

8 These, in the day when heaven was falling,
The hour when earth's foundations fled,
Followed their mercenary calling
And took their wages and are dead.

Their shoulders held the sky suspended;
They stood, and earth's foundations stay;
What God abandoned, these defended,
And saved the sum of things for pay.

Last Poems (1922) no. 37 'Epitaph on an Army of Mercenaries'

9 For nature, heartless, witless nature,
Will neither care nor know
What stranger's feet may find the meadow
And trespass there and go,
Nor ask amid the dews of morning
If they are mine or no.

Last Poems (1922) no. 40

10 Life, to be sure, is nothing much to lose;
But young men think it is, and we were young.

More Poems (1936) no. 36

11 Loveliest of trees, the cherry now
Is hung with bloom along the bough,
And stands about the woodland ride
Wearing white for Eastertide.

A Shropshire Lad (1896) no. 2

12 And since to look at things in bloom
Fifty springs are little room,
About the woodlands I will go
To see the cherry hung with snow.

A Shropshire Lad (1896) no. 2

13 Clay lies still, but blood's a rover;
Breath's a ware that will not keep.
Up, lad: when the journey's over
There'll be time enough to sleep.

A Shropshire Lad (1896) no. 4

14 And naked to the hangman's noose
The morning clocks will ring
A neck God made for other use
Than strangling in a string.

A Shropshire Lad (1896) no. 9

15 When I was one-and-twenty
I heard a wise man say,
'Give crowns and pounds and guineas
But not your heart away;
Give pearls away and rubies,
But keep your fancy free.'
But I was one-and-twenty,
No use to talk to me.

A Shropshire Lad (1896) no. 13

16 In summertime on Bredon
The bells they sound so clear;
Round both the shires they ring them
In steeples far and near,
A happy noise to hear.

Here of a Sunday morning
My love and I would lie,
And see the coloured counties,
And hear the larks so high
About us in the sky.

A Shropshire Lad (1896) no. 21

17 The lads in their hundreds to Ludlow come in for the fair,
There's men from the barn and the forge and the mill and the fold,
The lads for the girls and the lads for the liquor are there,
And there with the rest are the lads that will never be old.

A Shropshire Lad (1896) no. 23

1 On Wenlock Edge the wood's in trouble;
His forest fleece the Wrekin heaves;
The wind it plies the saplings double,
And thick on Severn snow the leaves.
A Shropshire Lad (1896) no. 31

2 The gale, it plies the saplings double,
It blows so hard, 'twill soon be gone:
To-day the Roman and his trouble
Are ashes under Uricon.
A Shropshire Lad (1896) no. 31

3 From far, from eve and morning
And yon twelve-winded sky,
The stuff of life to knit me
Blew hither: here am I.
A Shropshire Lad (1896) no. 32

4 Into my heart an air that kills
From yon far country blows:
What are those blue remembered hills,
What spires, what farms are those?

That is the land of lost content,
I see it shining plain,
The happy highways where I went
And cannot come again.
A Shropshire Lad (1896) no. 40

5 And bound for the same bourn as I,
On every road I wandered by,
Trod beside me, close and dear,
The beautiful and death-struck year.
A Shropshire Lad (1896) no. 41

6 Shot? so quick, so clean an ending?
Oh that was right, lad, that was brave.
A Shropshire Lad (1896) no. 44

7 Oh soon, and better so than later
After long disgrace and scorn,
You shot dead the household traitor,
The soul that should not have been born.
A Shropshire Lad (1896) no. 44

8 Clunton and Clunbury,
Clungunford and Clun,
Are the quietest places
Under the sun.
A Shropshire Lad (1896) no. 50 (epigraph)

9 By brooks too broad for leaping
The lightfoot boys are laid;
The rose-lipt girls are sleeping
In fields where roses fade.
A Shropshire Lad (1896) no. 54

10 Say, for what were hop-yards meant,
Or why was Burton built on Trent?
Oh many a peer of England brews
Livelier liquor than the Muse,
And malt does more than Milton can
To justify God's ways to man.
Ale, man, ale's the stuff to drink
For fellows whom it hurts to think.
A Shropshire Lad (1896) no. 62; see **MILTON** 541:10

11 I tell the tale that I heard told.
Mithridates, he died old.
A Shropshire Lad (1896) no. 62

12 Three minutes' thought would suffice to find
this out; but thought is irksome and three
minutes is a long time.
D. Iunii Iuvenalis Saturae (1905) preface

13 A year or two ago . . . I received from America a
request that I would define poetry. I replied that
I could no more define poetry than a terrier can
define a rat, but that I thought we both
recognized the object by the symptoms which it
provokes in us.
The Name and Nature of Poetry (1933)

14 Cambridge has seen many strange sights. It has
seen Wordsworth drunk and Porson sober. It is
now destined to see a better scholar than
Wordsworth and a better poet than Porson
betwixt and between.
speech at University College, London, 29 March 1911, in R. W.
Chambers *Man's Unconquerable Mind* (1939)

Samuel Houston 1793–1863
American politician and military leader

15 The North is determined to preserve this Union.
They are not a fiery, impulsive people as you
are, for they live in colder climates. But when
they begin to move in a given direction . . . they
move with the steady momentum and
perseverance of a mighty avalanche.
in 1861, warning the people of Texas against secession
Geoffrey C. Ward *The Civil War* (1991) ch. 1

John Howard 1939–
Australian statesman, Prime Minister 1996–2007

16 I want people to reflect on the loss of life. I
want them to reflect on what it means in terms
of the loss of innocence . . . in relation to this
country's dealings with different parts of the
world.
on the Bali bombing, 12 October 2002
interview on Australian television (Channel Ten News), 14
October 2002

Geoffrey Howe 1926–
British Conservative politician. On Howe: see HEALEY 387:1

17 It is rather like sending your opening batsmen to
the crease only for them to find the moment
that the first balls are bowled that their bats
have been broken before the game by the team
captain.
*on the difficulties caused him as Foreign Secretary by
Margaret **THATCHER**'s anti-European views*
resignation speech as Deputy Prime Minister, in the House of
Commons, 13 November 1990

18 The time has come for others to consider their
own response to the tragic conflict of loyalties
with which I have myself wrestled for perhaps
too long.
resignation speech
in the House of Commons, 13 November 1990

Gordie Howe 1928–

Canadian ice-hockey player

1 All pro athletes are bilingual. They speak English and profanity.

   in *Toronto Star* 27 May 1975

Joseph Howe 1804–73

Canadian journalist and politician

2 Yes, gentlemen, come what will, while I live, Nova Scotia shall have the blessing of an open and unshackled press.

   spoken at his trial in Halifax, Nova Scotia, for publishing, in the Novascotian *newspaper, a libellous editorial on corruption in government*
   'Address to the Jury' May 1835

Julia Ward Howe 1819–1910

American Unitarian lay preacher

3 Mine eyes have seen the glory of the coming of the Lord:
   He is trampling out the vintage where the grapes of wrath are stored;
   He hath loosed the fateful lightning of his terrible swift sword:
   His truth is marching on.

   The Grapes of Wrath *was the title of a novel (1939) by John* STEINBECK
   'Battle Hymn of the Republic' (1862)

James Howell c.1594–1666

Welsh-born English man of letters

4 Some hold translations not unlike to be The wrong side of a Turkey tapestry.

   Familiar Letters (1645–55) bk. 1, no. 6

5 One hair of a woman can draw more than a hundred pair of oxen.

   Familiar Letters (1645–55) bk. 2, no. 4; see **PROVERBS** 627:12

6 The Netherlands have been for many years, as one may say, the very cockpit of Christendom.

   Instructions for Foreign Travel (1642)

Frankie Howerd (Francis Alex Howard) 1922–92

English comedian

7 Such cruel glasses.

   of the broadcaster and interviewer Robin Day
   in *That Was The Week That Was* (BBC television series, from 1963)

Mary Howitt 1799–1888

English writer for children

8 Buttercups and daisies,
   Oh, the pretty flowers;
   Coming ere the springtime,
   To tell of sunny hours.

   'Buttercups and Daisies' (1838)

9 'Will you walk into my parlour?' said a spider to a fly:
   ''Tis the prettiest little parlour that ever you did spy.'

   'The Spider and the Fly' (1834)

Edmond Hoyle 1672–1769

English writer on card-games

10 When in doubt, win the trick.

   Hoyle's Games Improved (ed. Charles Jones, 1790) 'Twenty-four Short Rules for Learners'; though attributed to Hoyle, this may well have been an editorial addition by Jones, since it is not found in earlier editions

Fred Hoyle 1915–2001

English astrophysicist

11 Space isn't remote at all. It's only an hour's drive away if your car could go straight upwards.

   in *Observer* 9 September 1979 'Sayings of the Week'

12 There is a coherent plan to the universe, though I don't know what it's a plan for.

   attributed

Elbert Hubbard 1859–1915

American writer. See also **EMERSON** 315:22

13 Never explain—your friends do not need it and your enemies will not believe you anyway.

   The Motto Book (1907); see **WODEHOUSE** 862:4

14 Life is just one damned thing after another.

   Philistine December 1909; often attributed to Frank Ward O'Malley

15 Editor: a person employed by a newspaper, whose business it is to separate the wheat from the chaff, and to see that the chaff is printed.

   The Roycroft Dictionary (1914)

Frank McKinney ('Kin') Hubbard 1868–1930

American humorist

16 It's no disgrace t'be poor, but it might as well be.

   Short Furrows (1911)

Howard Hughes Jr. 1905–76

American industrialist, aviator, and film producer

17 That man's ears make him look like a taxi-cab with both doors open.

   of Clark Gable
   Charles Higham and Joel Greenberg *Celluloid Muse* (1969)

Jimmy Hughes *and* Frank Lake

18 You'll get no promotion this side of the ocean,
   So cheer up, my lads, Bless 'em all!
   Bless 'em all! Bless 'em all! The long and the short and the tall.

   'Bless 'Em All' (1940 song)

Langston Hughes 1902–67
American writer and poet

1 I, too, sing America.

I am the darker brother.
They send me to eat in the kitchen
When company comes.
But I laugh,
And eat well,
And grow strong.

Tomorrow
I'll sit at the table
When company comes
Nobody'll dare
Say to me,
'Eat in the kitchen'
Then.

Besides, they'll see how
beautiful I am
And be ashamed,—

I, too, am America.
'I, Too' in *Survey Graphic* March 1925

2 I've known rivers:
I've known rivers ancient as the world and older
than the flow of human blood in human
veins.
'The Negro Speaks of Rivers' (1921)

3 I bathed in the Euphrates when dawns were
young.
I built my hut near the Congo and it lulled me
to sleep.
I looked upon the Nile and raised the pyramids
above it.
I heard the singing of the Mississippi when Abe
Lincoln went down to New Orleans, and I've
seen its muddy bosom turn all golden in the
sunset.
'The Negro Speaks of Rivers' (1921)

4 'It's powerful,' he said.
'What?'
'That one drop of Negro blood—because just
one drop of black blood makes a man coloured.
One drop—you are a Negro!'
Simple Takes a Wife (1953)

5 I got the Weary Blues
And I can't be satisfied.
'Weary Blues' (1926)

Robert Hughes 1938–
Australian writer

6 What the convict system bequeathed to later
Australian generations was not the sturdy,
skeptical independence . . . but an intense
concern with social and political respectability.
The idea of the 'convict stain', a moral blot
soaked into our fabric, dominated all argument
about Australian selfhood by the 1840s.
The Fatal Shore (1987) introduction

Ted Hughes 1930–98
English poet. On Hughes: see **HEANEY** 388:1

7 Daylong this tomcat lies stretched flat
As an old rough mat, no mouth and no eyes,
Continual wars and wives are what
Have tattered his ears and battered his head.
'Esther's Tomcat' (1960)

8 It took the whole of Creation
To produce my foot, my each feather:
Now I hold Creation in my foot.
'Hawk Roosting' (1960)

9 Fourteen centuries have learned,
From charred remains, that what took place
When Alexandria's library burned
Brain-damaged the human race.
'Hear it Again' (1997)

10   I saw the horses:
Huge in the dense grey—ten together—
Megalith-still. They breathed, making no move,
With draped manes and tilted hind-hooves,
Making no sound.
I passed: not one snorted or jerked its head.
Grey silent fragments
Of a grey silent world.
'The Horses' (1957)

11 . . . With a sudden sharp hot stink of fox,
It enters the dark hole of the head.
'The Thought-Fox' (1957)

12 Ten years after your death
I meet on a page of your journal, as never
before,
The shock of your joy.
'Visit' (1998)

13 Grape is my mulatto mother
In this frozen whited country.
'Wino' (1967)

Thomas Hughes 1822–96
English lawyer, politician, and writer

14 'I don't care a straw for Greek particles, or the
digamma, no more does his mother. What is he
sent to school for? . . . If he'll only turn out a
brave, helpful, truth-telling Englishman, and a
gentleman, and a Christian, that's all I want,'
thought the Squire.
Tom Brown's Schooldays (1857) pt. 1, ch. 4

15 He never wants anything but what's right and
fair; only when you come to settle what's right
and fair, it's everything that he wants and
nothing that you want. And that's his idea of a
compromise. Give me the Brown compromise
when I'm on his side.
Tom Brown's Schooldays (1857) pt. 2, ch. 2

16 It's more than a game. It's an institution.
of cricket
Tom Brown's Schooldays (1857) pt. 2, ch. 7

Victor Hugo 1802–85

French poet, novelist, and dramatist. On Hugo: see **COCTEAU** 237:21, **GIDE** 356:7

1 *Le mot, c'est le Verbe, et le Verbe, c'est Dieu.*

The word is the Verb, and the Verb is God.
Contemplations (1856) bk. 1, no. 8

2 *Souffrons, mais souffrons sur les cimes.*

If suffer we must, let's suffer on the heights.
Contemplations (1856) bk. 5, no. 26 'Les Malheureux'

3 *On résiste à l'invasion des armées; on ne résiste pas à l'invasion des idées.*

A stand can be made against invasion by an army; no stand can be made against invasion by an idea.
Histoire d'un Crime (written 1851-2, published 1877) pt. 5, sect. 10; see **SAYINGS** 685:12

4 *La symétrie, c'est l'ennui, et l'ennui est le fond même du deuil. Le désespoir bâille.*

Symmetry is tedious, and tedium is the very basis of mourning. Despair yawns.
Les Misérables (1862) vol. 2, bk. 4, ch. 1

5 *Ôtez Time is money, que reste-t-il de l'Angleterre? ôtez Cotton is king, que reste-t-il de l'Amerique?*

Take away *time is money*, and what is left of England? take away *cotton is king*, and what is left of America?
Les Misérables (1862) 'Marius' bk. 4 ch. 4

6 *Étourdir de grelots l'esprit qui veut penser.*

To daze with little bells the spirit that would think.
Le Roi s'amuse (1833) act 2, sc. 2

7 *La popularité? C'est la gloire en gros sous.*

Popularity? It is glory's small change.
Ruy Blas (1838)

8 *Jésus a pleuré, Voltaire a souri; c'est de cette larme divine et de ce sourire humain qu'est faite la douceur de la civilisation actuelle. (Applaudissements prolongés.)*

Jesus wept; Voltaire smiled. Of that divine tear and of that human smile the sweetness of present civilisation is composed. (*Hearty applause.*)
transcript of centenary oration on **VOLTAIRE**, 30 May 1878, *Centenaire de Voltaire* (1878); see **BIBLE** 108:7

Hui-neng 638–713

Chinese philosopher, 6th Zen Patriarch
textual translations are those of Wong Mou-Lam, 1969

9 There is no Bodhi-tree,
Nor stand of mirror bright.
Since all is void,
Where can the dust alight?
Platform Scripture ch. 1

10 When you are thinking of neither good nor evil, what is at that particular moment, Venerable Sir, your real nature [original face]?
Platform Scripture ch. 1

11 When a pennant was blown about by the wind, two Bhikkus [monks] entered into a dispute as to what it was that was in motion, the wind or the pennant. As they could not settle their difference I submitted to them that it was neither, and that what actually moved was their own mind.
Platform Scripture ch. 1

12 Should we be so fortunate as to be followers of the Sudden School in this life,
In a sudden we shall see the Bhagavat of our Essence of Mind.
He who seeks the Buddha [from without] by practising certain doctrines
Knows not where the real Buddha is to be found.
He who is able to realize the Truth within his own mind
Has sown the seed of Buddhahood.
Platform Scripture ch. 1

Basil Hume 1923–99

English cardinal and Roman Catholic Archbishop of Westminster

13 It is harder for some people to believe that God loves them than to believe that he exists.
in *Guardian* 18 June 1999

David Hume 1711–76

Scottish philosopher, economist, and historian, uncle of David **HUME**. On Hume: see **SMITH** 758:3; see also **QUINE** 652:2

14 Custom, then, is the great guide of human life.
An Enquiry Concerning Human Understanding (1748) sect. 5, pt. 1

15 The great advantage of the mathematical sciences above the moral consists in this, that the ideas of the former, being sensible, are always clear and determinate.
An Enquiry Concerning Human Understanding (1748) sect. 7, pt. 1

16 If we take in our hand any volume; of divinity or school metaphysics, for instance; let us ask, *Does it contain any abstract reasoning concerning quantity or number?* No. *Does it contain any experimental reasoning, concerning matter of fact and existence?* No. Commit it then to the flames: for it can contain nothing but sophistry and illusion.
An Enquiry Concerning Human Understanding (1748) sect. 12, pt. 3

17 We soon learn that there is nothing mysterious or supernatural in the case, but that all proceeds from the usual propensity of mankind towards the marvellous, and that, though this inclination may at intervals receive a check from sense and learning, it can never be thoroughly extirpated from human nature.
An Enquiry Concerning Human Understanding (1748) 'Of Miracles' pt. 2

1 The Christian religion not only was at first attended with miracles, but even at this day cannot be believed by any reasonable person without one. Mere reason is insufficient to convince us of its veracity: and whoever is moved by faith to assent to it, is conscious of a continued miracle in his own person, which subverts all the principles of his understanding, and gives him a determination to believe what is most contrary to custom and experience.
An Enquiry Concerning Human Understanding (1748) 'Of Miracles' pt. 2

2 Avarice, the spur of industry, is so obstinate a passion, and works its way through so many real dangers and difficulties, that it is not likely to be scared by an imaginary danger, which is so small that it scarcely admits of calculation.
Essays: Moral and Political (1741–2) 'Of Civil Liberty'

3 Money . . . is none of the wheels of trade: it is the oil which renders the motion of the wheels more smooth and easy.
Essays: Moral and Political (1741–2) 'Of Money'

4 How many frivolous quarrels and disgusts are there, which people of common prudence endeavour to forget, when they lie under the necessity of passing their lives together; but which would soon inflame into the most deadly hatred, were they pursued to the utmost, under the prospect of an easy separation?
Essays: Moral and Political (1741–2) 'Of Polygamy and Divorces'

5 Nothing is more surprising to those who consider human affairs with a philosophical eye, than to see the easiness with which the many are governed by the few, and to observe the implicit submission with which men resign their own sentiments and passions to those of their rulers.
Essays: Moral and Political (1741–2) 'Of the First Principles of Government'

6 A little miss, dressed in a new gown for a dancing-school ball, receives as complete enjoyment as the greatest orator, who triumphs in the splendour of his eloquence, while he governs the passions and resolutions of a numerous assembly.
Essays: Moral and Political (1741–2) 'The Sceptic'

7 Should it be said, that, by living under the dominion of a prince, which one might leave, every individual has given a tacit assent to his authority . . . We may as well assert, that a man by remaining in a vessel, freely consents to the dominion of the master; though he was carried on board while asleep, and must leap into the ocean, and perish, the moment he leaves her.
Essays, Moral, Political, and Literary (ed. T. H. Green and T. H. Grose, 1875) 'Of the Original Contract' (1748)

8 In all ages of the world, priests have been enemies of liberty.
Essays, Moral, Political, and Literary (ed. T. H. Green and T. H. Grose, 1875) 'Of the Parties of Great Britain' (1741–2)

9 The heart of man is made to reconcile the most glaring contradictions.
Essays, Moral, Political, and Literary (ed. T. H. Green and T. H. Grose, 1875) 'Of the Parties of Great Britain' (1741–2)

10 In all matters of opinion and science . . . the difference between men is . . . oftener found to lie in generals than in particulars; and to be less in reality than in appearance. An explanation of the terms commonly ends the controversy, and the disputants are surprised to find that they had been quarrelling, while at bottom they agreed in their judgement.
Essays, Moral, Political, and Literary (ed. T. H. Green and T. H. Grose, 1875) 'Of the Standard of Taste' (1757)

11 Beauty is no quality in things themselves. It exists merely in the mind which contemplates them.
Essays, Moral, Political, and Literary (ed. T. H. Green and T. H. Grose, 1875) 'Of the Standard of Taste' (1757)

12 The life of man is of no greater importance to the universe than that of an oyster.
Essays, Moral, Political, and Literary (ed. T. H. Green and T. H. Grose, 1875) 'On Suicide' (1783)

13 A propensity to hope and joy is real riches: one to fear and sorrow, real poverty.
Essays Moral, Political, and Literary (ed. T. H. Green and T. H. Grose, 1875) 'The Sceptic' (1741–2)

14 Opposing one species of superstition to another, set them a quarrelling; while we ourselves, during their fury and contention, happily make our escape into the calm, though obscure, regions of philosophy.
Four Dissertations (1757) 'The Natural History of Religion' sect. 15

15 Never literary attempt was more unfortunate than my Treatise of Human Nature. It fell *dead-born from the press.*
My Own Life (1777) ch. 1

16 It is a just political maxim, that every man must be supposed a knave.
Political Discourses (1751) essay 6

17 Poets . . . though liars by profession, always endeavour to give an air of truth to their fictions.
A Treatise upon Human Nature (1739) bk. 1, pt. 3

18 Reason is, and ought only to be the slave of the passions, and can never pretend to any other office than to serve and obey them.
A Treatise upon Human Nature (1739) bk. 2, pt. 3

19 It is not contrary to reason to prefer the destruction of the whole world to the scratching of my finger.
A Treatise upon Human Nature (1739) bk. 2, pt. 3

20 In every system of morality, which I have hitherto met with, I have always remarked, that the author proceeds for some time in the ordinary way of reasoning, and establishes the being of a god, or makes observations concerning human affairs; when of a sudden I am surprized to find that instead of the usual

copulations of proposition, *is* and *is not*, I meet with no proposition that is not connected with an *ought* or an *ought not*. This change is imperceptible; but it is, however, of the last consequence.
A Treatise upon Human Nature (1739) bk. 3, pt. 1

David Hume 1757–1838
Scottish jurist and judge, nephew of David **HUME**

1 Every court of criminal justice must have the power of correcting the greatest and most dangerous of all abuses of the forms of law,—that of the protracted imprisonment of the accused, untried, perhaps not intended ever to be tried, nay, it may be, not informed of the nature of the charge against him, or the name of the accuser.
Commentaries on the Law of Scotland, Respecting Crimes (1819) vol. 2, ch. 4 'Of Liberation on the Act 1701, c. 6'

Hubert Humphrey 1911–78
American Democratic politician

2 Here we are the way politics ought to be in America, the politics of happiness, the politics of purpose and the politics of joy.
speech in Washington, 27 April 1968, in *New York Times* 28 April 1968

G. W. Hunt *c.*1829–1904
English composer of music-hall songs

3 We don't want to fight, but, by jingo if we do,
We've got the ships, we've got the men, we've got the money too.
We've fought the Bear before, and while Britons shall be true,
The Russians shall not have Constantinople.
'We Don't Want to Fight' (1878 music hall song)

Leigh Hunt 1784–1859
English poet and essayist. On Hunt: see **SHELLEY** 744:15

4 Abou Ben Adhem (may his tribe increase!)
Awoke one night from a deep dream of peace,
And saw, within the moonlight in his room,
Making it rich, and like a lily in bloom,
An angel writing in a book of gold:—
Exceeding peace had made Ben Adhem bold,
And to the presence in the room he said,
'What writest thou?'—The vision raised its head,
And with a look made of all sweet accord,
Answered, 'The names of those who love the Lord.'
'Abou Ben Adhem' (1838)

5 Write me as one that loves his fellow-men.
'Abou Ben Adhem' (1838)

6 The laughing queen that caught the world's great hands.
referring to Cleopatra
'The Nile' (1818)

7 Jenny kissed me when we met,
Jumping from the chair she sat in;
Time, you thief, who love to get
Sweets into your list, put that in:
Say I'm weary, say I'm sad,
Say that health and wealth have missed me,
Say I'm growing old, but add,
Jenny kissed me.
'Rondeau' (1838)

8 Stolen sweets are always sweeter,
Stolen kisses much completer,
Stolen looks are nice in chapels,
Stolen, stolen, be your apples.
'Song of Fairies Robbing an Orchard' (1830)

9 The two divinest things this world has got,
A lovely woman in a rural spot!
'The Story of Rimini' (1816) canto 3, l. 257

10 Places of nestling green, for poets made.
'The Story of Rimini' (1816) canto 3, l. 290

11 His forehead was prodigious—a great piece of placid marble; and his fine eyes, in which all the activity of his mind seemed to concentrate, moved under it with a sprightly ease, as if it was pastime to them to carry all that thought.
of **COLERIDGE**
Autobiography (1850) ch. 16

12 Poetry, in the most comprehensive application of the term, I take to be the flower of any kind of experience, rooted in truth, and issuing forth into beauty.
The Story of Rimini (1832 ed.) preface

13 The pretension is nothing; the performance every thing. A good apple is better than an insipid peach.
The Story of Rimini (1832 ed.) preface

14 A mere gossiping entertainment: a few child's squalls, a few mumbled amens, and a few mumbled cakes, and a few smirks accompanied by a few fees.
on the christening of his godson
letter to Marianne Kent, February 1806; in T. L. Hunt *Correspondence of Leigh Hunt* (1862) vol. 1

15 Never lay yourself open to what is called conviction: you might as well open your waistcoat to receive a knock-down blow.
in *The Examiner* 6 March 1808 'Rules for the Conduct of Newspaper Editors'

16 A playful moderation in politics is just as absurd as a remonstrative whisper to a mob.
in *The Examiner* 6 March 1808 'Rules for the Conduct of Newspaper Editors'

17 This Adonis in loveliness was a corpulent man of fifty.
of the Prince Regent, later **GEORGE IV**
in *The Examiner* 22 March 1812

18 A pleasure so exquisite as almost to amount to pain.
on receiving 'a glorious batch of Examiners'
letter to Alexander Ireland, 2 June 1848, in T. L. Hunt *Correspondence of Leigh Hunt* (1862) vol. 2

Anne Hunter 1742–1821

Scottish poet

1 My mother bids me bind my hair
  With bands of rosy hue,
  Tie up my sleeves with ribbons rare,
  And lace my bodice blue.
   'A Pastoral Song' (1794)

Robert Hunter 1941–2005

Canadian writer

2 The word *Greenpeace* had a ring to it—it
  conjured images of Eden; it said ecology and
  antiwar in two syllables; it fit easily into even a
  one-column headline.
   Warriors of the Rainbow (1979); see **DARNELL** 266:4

William Hunter 1718–83

Scottish obstetrician

3 Some physiologists will have it that the stomach
  is a mill;—others, that it is a fermenting
  vat;—others again that it is a stew-pan;—but in
  my view of the matter, it is neither a mill, a
  fermenting vat, nor a stew-pan—but a *stomach*,
  gentlemen, a *stomach*.
   MS note from his lectures, in J. A. Paris *A Treatise on Diet*
   (1824) epigraph

Herman Hupfeld 1894–1951

American songwriter

4 You must remember this, a kiss is still a kiss,
  A sigh is just a sigh;
  The fundamental things apply,
  As time goes by.
   'As Time Goes By' (1931 song); see **MISQUOTATIONS** 548:14

Zora Neale Hurston c.1901–60

American writer

5 I do not weep at the world—I am too busy
  sharpening my oyster knife.
   How It Feels to Be Colored Me (1928)

John Huss c.1372–1415

Bohemian preacher and reformer

6 *O sancta simplicitas!*
  O holy simplicity!
   *at the stake, seeing an aged peasant bringing a bundle of
   twigs to throw on the pile*
   J. W. Zincgreff and J. L. Weidner *Apophthegmata* (Amsterdam,
   1653) pt. 3; see **JEROME** 433:4

Saddam Hussein 1937–2006

Iraqi statesman, President 1979–2003; following his
overthrow he was brought to trial and executed in 2006

7 The mother of battles.
   *popular interpretation of his description of the approaching
   Gulf War; in* The Times *7 January 1991 it was reported that*

*he had no intention of relinquishing Kuwait and was ready
for the 'mother of all wars'*
   speech in Baghdad, 6 January 1991

8 Baghdad is determined to force the Mongols of
  our age to commit suicide at its gates.
   in *Independent* 18 January 2003

Francis Hutcheson 1694–1746

Scottish philosopher

9 Wisdom denotes the pursuing of the best ends
  by the best means.
   An Inquiry into the Original of our Ideas of Beauty and Virtue
   (1725) Treatise 1, sect. 5, subsect. 16

10 That action is best, which procures the greatest
  happiness for the greatest numbers.
   An Inquiry into the Original of our Ideas of Beauty and Virtue
   (1725) Treatise 2, sect. 3, subsect. 8; see **BENTHAM** 71:4

Lord Hutton 1931–

British judge, Lord Chief Justice for Northern Ireland

11 I make it clear that it will be for me to decide as
  I think right within my terms of reference the
  matters which will be the subject of my
  investigation.
   statement on the terms of the inquiry into the death of Dr
   David Kelly, 21 July 2003

Aldous Huxley 1894–1963

English novelist

12 There are few who would not rather be taken in
  adultery than in provincialism.
   Antic Hay (1923) ch. 10

13 Brave new world.
   title of novel (1932); see **SHAKESPEARE** 734:4

14 The proper study of mankind is books.
   Crome Yellow (1921) ch. 28; see **POPE** 616:29

15 Too much consistency is as bad for the mind as
  it is for the body. Consistency is contrary to
  nature, contrary to life. The only completely
  consistent people are the dead.
   Do What You Will (1929) 'Wordsworth in the Tropics'

16 The end cannot justify the means, for the simple
  and obvious reason that the means employed
  determine the nature of the ends produced.
   Ends and Means (1937) ch. 1

17 So long as men worship the Caesars and
  Napoleons, Caesars and Napoleons will duly
  arise and make them miserable.
   Ends and Means (1937) ch. 8

18 Chastity—the most unnatural of all the sexual
  perversions.
   Eyeless in Gaza (1936) ch. 27

19 Several excuses are always less convincing than
  one.
   Point Counter Point (1928) ch. 1

20 Most human beings have an almost infinite
  capacity for taking things for granted.
   Themes and Variations (1950) 'Variations on a Philosopher'

1 A million million spermatozoa,
All of them alive:
Out of their cataclysm but one poor Noah
Dare hope to survive.

And among that billion minus one
Might have chanced to be
Shakespeare, another Newton, a new Donne—
But the One was Me.

'Fifth Philosopher's Song' (1920)

2 Beauty for some provides escape,
Who gain a happiness in eyeing
The gorgeous buttocks of the ape
Or Autumn sunsets exquisitely dying.

'Ninth Philosopher's Song' (1920)

Julian Huxley 1887–1975

English biologist

3 Operationally, God is beginning to resemble not a ruler but the last fading smile of a cosmic Cheshire cat.

Religion without Revelation (1957 ed.) ch. 3; see **CARROLL** 202:4

T. H. Huxley 1825–95

English biologist and surgeon, a leading supporter of Darwinism

4 Most of my colleagues [in the Metaphysical Society] were -*ists* of one sort or another; and, however kind and friendly they might be, I, the man without a rag of a label to cover himself with, could not fail to have some of the uneasy feelings which must have beset the historical fox when, after leaving the trap in which his tail remained, he presented himself to his normally elongated companions. So I took thought, and invented what I conceived to be the appropriate title of 'agnostic'.

Collected Essays (1893–4) 'Agnosticism'

5 The great tragedy of Science—the slaying of a beautiful hypothesis by an ugly fact.

Collected Essays (1893–4) 'Biogenesis and Abiogenesis'

6 Science is nothing but trained and organized common sense, differing from the latter only as a veteran may differ from a raw recruit: and its methods differ from those of common sense only as far as the guardsman's cut and thrust differ from the manner in which a savage wields his club.

Collected Essays (1893–4) 'The Method of Zadig'

7 If some great Power would agree to make me always think what is true and do what is right, on condition of being turned into a sort of clock and wound up every morning before I got out of bed, I should instantly close with the offer.

Collected Essays (1893–4) 'On Descartes' *Discourse on Method*' (written 1870)

8 If a little knowledge is dangerous, where is the man who has so much as to be out of danger?

Collected Essays vol. 3 (1895) 'On Elementary Instruction in Physiology' (written 1877)

9 Patience and tenacity of purpose are worth more than twice their weight of cleverness.

Collected Essays vol. 3 (1895) 'On Medical Education' (address at University College, 1870)

10 The chessboard is the world; the pieces are the phenomena of the universe; the rules of the game are what we call the laws of Nature. The player on the other side is hidden from us. We know that his play is always fair, just, and patient. But also we know, to our cost, that he never overlooks a mistake, or makes the smallest allowance for ignorance.

Lay Sermons, Addresses, and Reviews (1870) 'A Liberal Education'

11 The necessity of making things plain to uninstructed people was one of the very best means of clearing up the obscure corners in one's own mind.

Man's Place in Nature (1894 ed.) preface

12 My reflection, when I first made myself master of the central idea of the 'Origin', was, How extremely stupid not to have thought of that!

'On the Reception of the "Origin of Species"' in F. Darwin *Life and Letters of Charles Darwin* vol. 2 (1888) ch. 5

13 It is the customary fate of new truths to begin as heresies and to end as superstitions.

Science and Culture and Other Essays (1881) 'The Coming of Age of the Origin of Species'

14 Irrationally held truths may be more harmful than reasoned errors.

Science and Culture and Other Essays (1881) 'The Coming of Age of the Origin of Species'

15 Logical consequences are the scarecrows of fools and the beacons of wise men.

Science and Culture and Other Essays (1881) 'On the Hypothesis that Animals are Automata'

16 I asserted—and I repeat—that a man has no reason to be ashamed of having an ape for his grandfather. If there were an ancestor whom I should feel shame in recalling it would rather be a *man*—a man of restless and versatile intellect—who, not content with an equivocal success in his own sphere of activity, plunges into scientific questions with which he has no real acquaintance, only to obscure them by an aimless rhetoric, and distract the attention of his hearers from the real point at issue by eloquent digressions and skilled appeals to religious prejudice.

replying to Bishop Samuel **WILBERFORCE** *in the debate on* **DARWIN**'*s theory of evolution; see* **WILBERFORCE** 853:16

meeting of the British Association in Oxford, 30 June 1860; letter from J. R. Green to Professor Boyd Dawkins in Leonard Huxley (ed.) *Life and Letters of Thomas Henry Huxley* (1900)

17 I am too much of a sceptic to deny the possibility of anything.

letter to Herbert Spencer, 22 March 1886, in Leonard Huxley *Life and Letters of Thomas Henry Huxley* (1900) vol. 2, ch. 8

1 The deepest sin against the human mind is to believe things without evidence.
  attributed

Edward Hyde *see* Earl of Clarendon

Dolores Ibarruri ('La Pasionaria')
1895–1989
Spanish Communist leader

2 *Il vaut mieux mourir debout que de vivre à genoux!*
  It is better to die on your feet than to live on your knees.
  also attributed to Emiliano **ZAPATA**
    speech in Paris, 3 September 1936, in *L'Humanité* 4 September 1936

3 *No pasarán.*
  They shall not pass.
    radio broadcast, Madrid, 19 July 1936, in *Speeches and Articles 1936–38* (1938); see **MILITARY SAYINGS, SLOGANS, AND SONGS** 535:11

Henrik Ibsen 1828–1906
Norwegian dramatist

4 The worst enemy of truth and freedom in our society is the compact majority. Yes, the damned, compact, liberal majority.
  An Enemy of the People (1882) act 4

5 The majority never has right on its side.
  An Enemy of the People (1882) act 4; see **DILLON** 283:8

6 You should never have your best trousers on when you go out to fight for freedom and truth.
  An Enemy of the People (1882) act 5

7 Mother, give me the sun.
  Ghosts (1881) act 3

8 But good God, people don't do such things!
  Hedda Gabler (1890) act 4

9 Castles in the air—they are so easy to take refuge in. And easy to build, too.
  The Master Builder (1892) act 3

10 What ought a man to be? Well, my short answer is 'himself'.
  Peer Gynt (1867) act 4

11 Take the life-lie away from the average man and straight away you take away his happiness.
  The Wild Duck (1884) act 5

12 On the contrary.
  last words, after a nurse had said that he 'seemed to be a little better'
  Michael Meyer *Ibsen* (1967)

Ice-T 1958–
American rap musician

13 Passion makes the world go round. Love just makes it a safer place.
  The Ice Opinion (as told to Heidi Sigmund, 1994) ch. 4

St Ignatius Loyola 1491–1556
Spanish theologian, founder of the Jesuits

14 Teach us, good Lord, to serve Thee as Thou deservest:
  To give and not to count the cost;
  To fight and not to heed the wounds;
  To toil and not to seek for rest;
  To labour and not to ask for any reward
  Save that of knowing that we do Thy will.
  'Prayer for Generosity' (1548)

I-Hsüan d. 867
Chinese monk and Zen master

15 Seekers of the Way. In Buddhism no effort is necessary. All one has to do is to do nothing except to move his bowels, urinate, put on his clothing, eat his meals, and lie down if he is tired. The stupid will laugh at him, but the wise will understand.
  Recorded Conversations of Zen Master I-Hsüan v. 5

16 Kill anything that you happen on. Kill the Buddha if you happen to meet him . . . Kill your parents or relatives if you happen to meet them. Only then can you be free, not bound by material things, and absolutely free and at ease.
  Recorded Conversations of Zen Master I-Hsüan v. 6

Francis Iles 1893–1970
English crime writer

17 It was not until several weeks after he had decided to murder his wife that Dr Bickleigh took any active steps in the matter. Murder is a serious business.
  Malice Aforethought (1931), opening words

Ivan Illich 1926–2002
American sociologist

18 In a consumer society there are inevitably two kinds of slaves: the prisoners of addiction and the prisoners of envy.
  Tools for Conviviality (1973) ch. 3

Charles Inge 1868–1957

19 This very remarkable man
  Commends a most practical plan:
  You can do what you want
  If you don't think you can't,
  So don't think you can't think you can.
  'On Monsieur Coué' (1928); see **COUÉ** 253:4

William Ralph Inge 1860–1954

English writer and clergyman; Dean of St. Paul's, 1911–34

1 The enemies of Freedom do not argue; they shout and they shoot.
  End of an Age (1948) ch. 4

2 The effect of boredom on a large scale in history is underestimated. It is a main cause of revolutions, and would soon bring to an end all the static Utopias and the farmyard civilization of the Fabians.
  End of an Age (1948) ch. 6

3 To become a popular religion, it is only necessary for a superstition to enslave a philosophy.
  Idea of Progress (Romanes Lecture delivered at Oxford, 27 May 1920)

4 It takes in reality only one to make a quarrel. It is useless for the sheep to pass resolutions in favour of vegetarianism, while the wolf remains of a different opinion.
  Outspoken Essays: First Series (1919) 'Patriotism'

5 A man may build himself a throne of bayonets, but he cannot sit on it.
  a similar image was used by Boris **YELTSIN** *at the time of the failed military coup in Russia, August 1991*
  Philosophy of Plotinus (1923) vol. 2, Lecture 22

Jean Ingelow 1820–97

English poet

6 Play uppe 'The Brides of Enderby'.
  'The High Tide on the Coast of Lincolnshire, 1571' (1863)

7 'Cusha! Cusha! Cusha!' calling
  E'er the early dews were falling,
  Farre away I heard her song.
  'The High Tide on the Coast of Lincolnshire, 1571' (1863)

8 But each will mourn her own (she saith)
  And sweeter woman ne'er drew breath
  Than my sonne's wife, Elizabeth.
  'The High Tide on the Coast of Lincolnshire, 1571' (1863)

Robert G. Ingersoll 1833–99

American agnostic

9 An honest God is the noblest work of man.
  The Gods (1876) pt. 1; see **POPE** 617:8

10 In nature there are neither rewards nor punishments—there are consequences.
  Some Reasons Why (1881) pt. 8 'The New Testament'

11 I believe it was Magellan who said, 'The Church says the earth is flat; but I have seen its shadow on the moon, and I have more confidence even in a shadow than the Church'.
  'Individuality' (lecture, 1873); see **MISQUOTATIONS** 547:21

John Kells Ingram 1823–1907

Irish social philosopher and songwriter

12 They rose in dark and evil days.
  'The Memory of the Dead' (1843)

13 Who fears to speak of Ninety-Eight?
  Who blushes at the name?
  'The Memory of the Dead' (1843)

J. A. D. Ingres 1780–1867

French painter

14 *Le dessin est la probité de l'art.*
  Drawing is the true test of art.
  Pensées d'Ingres (1922)

15 Make copies, young man, many copies. You can only become a good artist by copying the masters.
  to Degas; A. Vollard Souvenirs d'un marchand de tableaux (1937)

Eugène Ionesco 1912–94

French dramatist

16 *C'est une chose anormale de vivre.*
  Living is abnormal.
  Le Rhinocéros (1959) act 1

17 *Tu ne prévois les événements que lorsqu'ils sont déjà arrivés.*
  You can only predict things after they have happened.
  Le Rhinocéros (1959) act 3

18 *Un fonctionnaire ne plaisante pas.*
  A civil servant doesn't make jokes.
  Tueur sans gages (The Killer, 1958) act 1

St Irenaeus c.AD 130–c.200

Greek theologian

19 *Gloria Dei vivens homo.*
  A living man is the glory of God.
  Against the Heresies bk. 4, ch. 20

Weldon J. Irvine

American songwriter

20 Young, gifted and black.
  title of song (1969); see **HANSBERRY** 379:12

Washington Irving 1783–1859

American writer

21 A sharp tongue is the only edged tool that grows keener with constant use.
  The Sketch Book (1820) 'Rip Van Winkle'

22 There is a certain relief in change, even though it be from bad to worse . . . it is often a comfort to shift one's position and be bruised in a new place.
  Tales of a Traveller (1824) 'To the Reader'

23 The almighty dollar, that great object of universal veneration throughout our land.
  in *New Yorker* 12 November 1836 'The Creole Village'

Anne Ingram, Lady Irwin c.1696–1764

English poet

24 A female mind like a rude fallow lies;
  No seed is sown, but weeds spontaneous rise.

As well might we expect, in winter, spring,
As land untilled a fruitful crop should bring.
'An Epistle to Mr Pope. Occasioned by his Characters of
Women' in the *Gentleman's Magazine* (1736)

1 Untaught the noble end of glorious truth,
Bred to deceive even from their earliest youth.
'An Epistle to Mr Pope. Occasioned by his Characters of
Women' in the *Gentleman's Magazine* (1736)

Christopher Isherwood 1904–86

English novelist. See also AUDEN 37:1

2 The common cormorant (or shag)
Lays eggs inside a paper bag,
You follow the idea, no doubt?
It's to keep the lightning out.

But what these unobservant birds
Have never thought of, is that herds
Of wandering bears might come with buns
And steal the bags to hold the crumbs.
'The Common Cormorant' (written *c*.1925)

3 I am a camera with its shutter open, quite
passive, recording, not thinking.
Goodbye to Berlin (1939) 'Berlin Diary' Autumn 1930

St Isidore of Seville *c*.560–636

Spanish archbishop and Doctor of the Church

4 However Augustine surpassed the zeal of all
these by his genius and wisdom. For he wrote
so much that no one is able in the days and
nights even to read his books, far less to write
them.
Etymologies bk. 6, ch. 7, sect. 3

Alec Issigonis 1906–88

Turkish-born British engineer, designer of the Morris Minor
(1948) and the Mini (1959)

5 A camel is a horse designed by a committee.
on his dislike of working in teams
in *Guardian* 14 January 1991 'Notes and Queries'; attributed

Charles Ives 1874–1954

American composer

6 Beauty in music is too often confused with
something that lets the ears lie back in an easy
chair.
Joseph Machlis *Introduction to Contemporary Music* (1963)

Alija Izetbegović 1925–2003

Bosnian statesman, President of Bosnia and Herzegovina
1990–2003

7 And to my people I say, this may not be a just
peace, but it is more just than a continuation of
war.
*after signing the Dayton accord with representatives of
Serbia and Croatia*
in Dayton, Ohio, 21 November 1995

Eddie Izzard 1962–

English comedian

8 'Cake or death?' 'Cake, please.'
*imagining how a Church of England Inquisition might have
worked*
Dress to Kill (stage show, San Francisco, 1998)

Andrew Jackson 1767–1845

American Democratic statesman, 7th President of the US
1829–37

9 Our Federal Union: it must be preserved.
toast given on the Jefferson Birthday Celebration, 13 April
1830; in Thomas Hart Benton *Thirty Years' View* (1856) vol. 1

10 Each public officer who takes an oath to support
the constitution swears that he will support it as
he understands it, and not as it is understood by
others.
vetoing the bill to re-charter the Bank of the United States
Presidential message, 10 July 1832, in H. S. Commager (ed.)
Documents of American History vol. 1 (1963)

Jesse Jackson 1941–

American Democratic politician and clergyman

11 When I look out at this convention, I see the
face of America, red, yellow, brown, black, and
white. We are all precious in God's sight—the
real rainbow coalition.
speech at Democratic National Convention, Atlanta, 19 July
1988

12 She sat down in order that we all might stand
up—and the walls of segregation came down.
of the civil rights activist Rosa Parks
in *BBC News* (online edition) 25 October 2005

Mahalia Jackson 1911–72

American singer

13 It's easy to be independent when you've got
money. But to be independent when you haven't
got a thing—that's the Lord's test.
Movin' On Up (with Evan McLoud Wylie 1966) ch. 1

Michael Jackson 1958–

American pop singer

14 Before you judge me, try hard to love me, look
within your heart
Then ask,—have you seen my childhood?
'Childhood' (1995 song)

Robert H. Jackson 1892–1954

American lawyer and judge

15 That four great nations, flushed with victory and
stung with injury, stay the hands of vengeance

and voluntarily submit their captive enemies to the judgement of the law, is one of the most significant tributes that Power has ever paid to Reason.

opening statement for the prosecution at Nuremberg
before the International Military Tribunal in Nuremberg, 21 November 1945

Thomas Jonathan 'Stonewall' Jackson 1824–63

American Confederate general. On Jackson: see BEE 65:10

1 Always mystify, mislead, and surprise the enemy, if possible.

his strategic motto during the Civil War
M. Miner and H. Rawson *American Heritage Dictionary of American Quotations* (1997)

2 My duty is to obey orders.
attributed

3 Let us cross over the river and rest under the shade of the trees.
Across the River and into the Trees *was the title of a novel* (1950) *by Ernest* **HEMINGWAY**
last words; M. Miner and H. Rawson *American Heritage Dictionary of American Quotations* (1997)

Harriet Jacobs 1813–97

American abolitionist and writer

4 Reader, be assured this narrative is no fiction.
Incidents in the Life of a Slave Girl (1860) preface

Joe Jacobs 1896–1940

American boxing manager

5 We was robbed!
after Jack Sharkey beat Max Schmeling (of whom Jacobs was manager) in the heavyweight title fight, 21 June 1932
Peter Heller *In This Corner* (1975)

6 I should of stood in bed.
after leaving his sick-bed to attend the World Baseball Series in Detroit, 1935, and betting on the losers
John Lardner *Strong Cigars* (1951)

Jacopone da Todi *c.*1230–1306

Italian Franciscan lay brother

7 *Stabat Mater dolorosa,*
Iuxta crucem lacrimosa,
Dum pendebat filius.

At the cross her station keeping,
Stood the mournful Mother weeping,
Where he hung, the dying Lord.
'Stabat Mater dolorosa', ascribed also to Pope Innocent III and others (translation based on that of E. Caswall in *Lyra Catholica*, 1849)

Mick Jagger 1943– *and* Keith Richards 1943–

English rock musicians

8 Get off of my cloud.
title of song (1966)

9 Mother needs something today to calm her down,
And though she's not really ill,
There's a little yellow pill:
She goes running for the shelter
Of a mother's little helper,
And it helps her on her way,
Gets her through her busy day.
'Mother's Little Helper' (1966 song)

10 I can't get no satisfaction
I can't get no girl reaction.
'(I Can't Get No) Satisfaction' (1965 song)

11 Ev'rywhere I hear the sound of marching, charging feet, boy,
'Cause summer's here and the time is right for fighting in the street, boy.
But what can a poor boy do
Except to sing for a rock 'n' roll band,
'Cause in sleepy London town
There's just no place for a street fighting man!
'Street Fighting Man' (1968 song)

12 Please allow me to introduce myself
I'm a man of wealth and taste.
'Sympathy for the Devil' (1968 song)

13 Pleased to meet you, hope you guess my name
But what's puzzling you
Is the nature of my game.
'Sympathy for the Devil' (1968 song)

Richard Jago 1715–81

English poet

14 With leaden foot time creeps along
While Delia is away.
'Absence'

Jaina Sutras

Indian tradition, founded in the 6th century BC
textual translations are those of H. Jacobi, 1884

15 He believes in soul, believes in the world, believes in reward, believes in action . . . these are all the causes of sin, which must be comprehended and renounced.
Ācārāṇga Sutra bk. 1, lecture 1, lesson 1, v. 5

16 There are some who, of a truth, know this [causing injury] to be the bondage, the delusion, the death, the hell.
Ācārāṇga Sutra bk. 1, lecture 1, lesson 2, v. 4

17 He who sees by himself, needs no instruction. But the miserable, afflicted fool who delights in pleasures and whose miseries do not cease, is turned round in the whirl of pains.
Ācārāṇga Sutra bk. 1, lecture 2, lesson 3, v. 6

18 The world is greatly troubled by women.
Ācārāṇga Sutra bk. 1, lecture 2, lesson 4, v. 3

19 A wise man should avoid wrath, pride, deceit, greed, love, hate, delusion, conception, birth, death, hell, animal existence, and pain.
Ācārāṇga Sutra bk. 1, lecture 3, lesson 4, v. 4

1 All breathing, existing, living, sentient creatures should not be slain, nor treated with violence, nor abused, nor tormented, nor driven away. This is the pure, unchangeable, eternal law.
Ācārāṅga Sutra bk. 1, lecture 4, lesson 1, v 1.

2 All the professors, conversant with pain, preach renunciation.
Ācārāṅga Sutra bk. 1, lecture 4, lesson 3, v. 2

3 Four things of paramount value are difficult to obtain here by a living being: human birth, instruction in the Law, belief in it, and energy in self-control.
Uttarādhyayana lecture 3, v. 1

4 These two ways of life ending with death have been declared: death with one's will and death against one's will.
Death against one's will is that of ignorant men . . . death with one's will is that of wise men.
Uttarādhyayana lecture 5, v. 2

5 There are five causes which render wholesome discipline impossible: egoism, delusion, carelessness, illness, and idleness.
Uttarādhyayana lecture 11, v. 3

6 He who adopts the law in the intention to live as a monk, should live in company, upright, and free from desire; he should abandon his former connections, and not longing for pleasures, he should wander about as an unknown beggar; then he is a true monk.
Uttarādhyayana lecture 15, v. 1

7 By the adoration of the twenty-four Jinas the soul arrives at purity of faith.
Uttarādhyayana lecture 29, v. 9

8 By renouncing his body he acquires the pre-eminent virtues of the Siddhas, by the possession of which he goes to the highest region of the universe, and becomes absolutely happy.
Uttarādhyayana lecture 29, v. 38

9 A monk destroys by austerities the bad karma which he had acquired by love and hatred.
Uttarādhyayana lecture 30, v. 1

10 There are three ways of committing sins: by one's own activity, by commission, by approval.
Sūtrakritāṅga bk. 1, lecture 1, ch. 3, v. 26

11 This is the quintessence of wisdom: not to kill anything. Know this to be the legitimate conclusion from the principle of the reciprocity with regard to non-killing.
Sūtrakritāṅga bk. 1, lecture 1, ch. 4, v. 10

12 Exert and control yourself! For it is not easy to walk on ways where there are minutely small animals.
Sūtrakritāṅga bk. 1, lecture 2, ch. 1, v. 11

13 Know this to be thus as I [Mahāvīra] have told you, because I am the Saviour.
Sūtrakritāṅga bk. 1, lecture 16, v. 6

14 This creed of the Nirgranthas [Jains] is true, supreme, excellent, full of virtues, right, pure, it removes doubts, it is the road to perfection, liberation, Nirvana.
Sūtrakritāṅga bk. 2, lecture 7, v. 15

Jalal ad-Din ar-Rumi 1207–73

Persian poet and Sufi mystic

15 In it is what is in it.
title of a collection of discourses, in Persian *Fihi ma Fihi*

16 Each of us touches one place
and understands the whole in that way.
The palm and the fingers feeling in the dark are how the senses explore the reality of the elephant.
If each of us held a candle there,
and if we went in together,
we could see it.
on the inferences drawn by men touching different parts of an elephant in the dark; see **SANA'I** *679:18*
Mathnawi bk. 3 (1259–69)

17 Listen to the story told by the reed,
of being separated.
'Since I was cut from the reedbed,
I have made this crying sound.
Anyone apart from someone he loves
understands what I say.'
'The Reed Flute's Song', tr. Coleman Barks

18 I go into the Muslim mosque and the Jewish synagogue and the Christian church and I see one altar.
Coleman Barks and John Moyne (eds.) *The Essential Rumi* (1999)

19 The result of my life is not more than three words:
I was raw, I became ripe, I burnt—
attributed; AnneMarie Schimmel *The Triumphal Sun: a Study of the Works of Jalaloddin Rumi* (1980)

James I (James VI of Scotland) 1566–1625

British monarch, King of Scotland from 1567 and of England from 1603, father of CHARLES I. On James: see HENRI IV 391:20

20 A branch of the sin of drunkenness, which is the root of all sins.
A Counterblast to Tobacco (1604)

21 A custom loathsome to the eye, hateful to the nose, harmful to the brain, dangerous to the lungs, and in the black, stinking fume thereof, nearest resembling the horrible Stygian smoke of the pit that is bottomless.
A Counterblast to Tobacco (1604)

22 No bishop, no King.
to a deputation of Presbyterians from the Church of Scotland, seeking religious tolerance in England
W. Barlow *Sum and Substance of the Conference* (1604)

23 The state of monarchy is the supremest thing upon earth; for kings are not only God's lieutenants upon earth, and sit upon God's throne, but even by God himself they are called gods.
speech to Parliament, 21 March 1610, in *Works* (1616)

1 The king is truly *parens patriae*, the politique father of his people.
speech to Parliament, 21 March 1610, in *Works* (1616)

2 I will govern according to the common weal, but not according to the common will.
December, 1621, in J. R. Green *History of the English People* vol. 3 (1879) bk. 7, ch. 4

3 Dr Donne's verses are like the peace of God; they pass all understanding.
remark recorded by Archdeacon Plume (1630–1704); see BIBLE 115:4

4 I made the carles lords, but who made the carlines ladies?
E. Grenville Murray *Embassies and Foreign Courts* (1855) ch. 14

James V 1512–42
Scottish monarch, King from 1513

5 It came with a lass, and it will pass with a lass.
of the crown of Scotland, on learning of the birth of MARY Queen of Scots, December 1542
Robert Lindsay of Pitscottie (c.1500–65) *History of Scotland* (1728)

Evan James 1809–78
Welsh bard

6 The land of my fathers, how fair is thy fame.
'Land of My Fathers' (1856), translated by W. G. Rothery

7 Wales, Wales, sweet are thy hills and vales,
Thy speech, thy song,
To thee belong,
O may they live ever in Wales.
'Land of My Fathers' (1856)

Henry James 1843–1916
American novelist, brother of William JAMES. On James: see GUEDALLA 374:8, MAUGHAM 528:5, WELLS 846:18

8 The ever-importunate murmur, 'Dramatize it, dramatize it!'
The Altar of the Dead (1909 ed.) preface

9 The Story is just the spoiled child of art.
The Ambassadors (1909 ed.) preface

10 Live all you can; it's a mistake not to. It doesn't so much matter what you do in particular, so long as you have your life. If you haven't had that, what *have* you had?
The Ambassadors (1903) bk. 5, ch. 11

11 The balloon of experience is in fact of course tied to the earth, and under that necessity we swing, thanks to a rope of remarkable length, in the more or less commodious car of the imagination; but it is by the rope we know where we are, and from the moment that cable is cut we are at large and unrelated.
The American (1909 ed.) preface

12 The historian, essentially, wants more documents than he can really use; the dramatist only wants more liberties than he can really take.
The Aspern Papers (1909 ed.) preface

13 Most English talk is a quadrille in a sentry-box.
The Awkward Age (1899) bk. 5, ch. 19

14 Vereker's secret, my dear man—the general intention of his books: the string the pearls were strung on, the buried treasure, the figure in the carpet.
The Figure in the Carpet (1896) ch. 11

15 One might enumerate the items of high civilization, as it exists in other countries, which are absent from the texture of American life, until it should become a wonder to know what was left. No State, in the European sense of the word, and indeed barely a specific national name. No sovereign, no court, no personal loyalty, no aristocracy, no church, no clergy, no army, no diplomatic service, no country gentlemen, no palaces, no castles, nor manors, nor old country houses, nor parsonages, nor thatched cottages, nor ivied ruins; no cathedrals nor abbeys, nor little Norman churches; no great universities nor public schools—no Oxford, nor Eton, nor Harrow; no literature, no novels, no museums, no pictures, no political society, no sporting class—no Epsom nor Ascot! . . . The natural remark in the almost lurid light of such an indictment, would be that if these things are left out, everything is left out.
Hawthorne (1879) ch. 2

16 He was worse than provincial—he was parochial.
of THOREAU
Hawthorne (1879) ch. 4

17 The black and merciless things that are behind the great possessions.
The Ivory Tower (1917) notes

18 Cats and monkeys—monkeys and cats—all human life is there!
The Madonna of the Future (1879) vol. 1; see ADVERTISING SLOGANS 7:3

19 We work in the dark—we do what we can—we give what we have. Our doubt is our passion and our passion is our task. The rest is the madness of art.
'The Middle Years' (short story, 1893)

20 Experience is never limited, and it is never complete; it is an immense sensibility, a kind of huge spider-web of the finest silken threads suspended in the chamber of consciousness, and catching every air-borne particle in its tissue.
Partial Portraits (1888) 'The Art of Fiction'

21 What is character but the determination of incident? What is incident but the illustration of character?
Partial Portraits (1888) 'The Art of Fiction'

22 The house of fiction has in short not one window, but a million . . . but they are, singly or together, as nothing without the posted presence of the watcher.
The Portrait of a Lady (1908 ed.) preface

1 The note I wanted; that of the strange and sinister embroidered on the very type of the normal and easy.
Prefaces (1909) 'The Altar of the Dead'

2 The fatal futility of Fact.
The Spoils of Poynton (1909 ed.) preface

3 The time-honoured bread-sauce of the happy ending.
Theatricals (1894) 2nd series

4 The turn of the screw.
title of novel (1898)

5 We were alone with the quiet day, and his little heart, dispossessed, had stopped.
The Turn of the Screw (1898)

6 There is no difficulty in beginning; the trouble is to leave off!
in 1891; Leon Edel (ed.) *The Diary of Alice James* (1965)

7 I could come back to America . . . to die—but never, never to live.
letter to Mrs William James, 1 April 1913, in Leon Edel (ed.) *Letters* vol. 4 (1984)

8 The war has used up words.
in *New York Times* 21 March 1915

9 Of course, of course.
on hearing that Rupert **BROOKE** *had died on a Greek island*
C. Hassall *Rupert Brooke* (1964) ch. 14

10 Summer afternoon—summer afternoon . . . the two most beautiful words in the English language.
Edith Wharton *A Backward Glance* (1934) ch. 10

11 So here it is at last, the distinguished thing!
on experiencing his first stroke
Edith Wharton *A Backward Glance* (1934) ch. 14

P. D. James 1920–

English writer of detective stories

12 What the detective story is about is not murder but the restoration of order.
in *Face* December 1986

13 I had an interest in death from an early age. It fascinated me. When I heard 'Humpty Dumpty sat on a wall,' I thought, 'Did he fall or was he pushed?'
in *Paris Review* 1995

William James 1842–1910

American philosopher; brother of Henry JAMES

14 There is no more miserable human being than one in whom nothing is habitual but indecision.
The Principles of Psychology (1890) vol. 1, ch. 4

15 The art of being wise is the art of knowing what to overlook.
The Principles of Psychology (1890) vol. 2, ch. 22

16 There is no worse lie than a truth misunderstood by those who hear it.
The Varieties of Religious Experience (1902)

17 Man, biologically considered, and whatever else he may be into the bargain, is simply the most formidable of all the beasts of prey, and, indeed, the only one that preys systematically on its own species.
in *Atlantic Monthly* December 1904

18 The moral flabbiness born of the exclusive worship of the bitch-goddess *success*.
letter to H. G. Wells, 11 September 1906, in *Letters* (1920) vol. 2

19 Hogamus, higamous
Man is polygamous
Higamus, hogamous
Woman monogamous.
in *Oxford Book of Marriage* (1990)

Randall Jarrell 1914–65

American poet

20 From my mother's sleep I fell into the State,
And I hunched in its belly till my wet fur froze.
Six miles from earth, loosed from its dream of life,
I woke to black flak and the nightmare fighters.
When I died they washed me out of the turret with a hose.
'The Death of the Ball Turret Gunner' (1945)

21 The firelight of a long, blind, dreaming story
Lingers upon your lips; and I have seen
Firm, fixed forever in your closing eyes,
The Corn King beckoning to his Spring Queen.
'A Girl in a Library' (1951)

22 In bombers named for girls, we burned
The cities we had learned about in school—
Till our lives wore out; our bodies lay among
The people we had killed and never seen.
When we lasted long enough they gave us medals;
When we died they said, 'Our casualties were low.'
'Losses' (1963)

23 Art is long and critics are the insects of a day.
A Sad Heart at the Supermarket (1962) 'Poets, Critics, and Readers'

Maria Jastrzebska 1953–

Polish-born British poet

24 I do
And then again
She does
And then sometimes
Neither of us
Wears any trousers at all.
'Which of Us Wears the Trousers'

Douglas Jay 1907–96

British Labour politician. See also POLITICAL SLOGANS AND SONGS 612:15

25 In the case of nutrition and health, just as in the case of education, the gentleman in Whitehall

really does know better what is good for people than the people know themselves.

The Socialist Case (1939) ch. 30

Jean Paul *see* Johann Paul Friedrich Richter

James Jeans 1877–1946

English astronomer, physicist, and mathematician

1 Taking a very gloomy view of the future of the human race, let us suppose that it can only expect to survive for two thousand million years longer, a period about equal to the past age of the earth. Then, regarded as a being destined to live for three-score years and ten, humanity, although it has been born in a house seventy years old, is itself only three days old.

Eos (1928)

2 If we assume that the last breath of, say, Julius Caesar has by now become thoroughly scattered through the atmosphere, then the chances are that each of us inhales one molecule of it with every breath we take.

An Introduction to the Kinetic Theory of Gases (1940)

3 Life exists in the universe only because the carbon atom possesses certain exceptional properties.

The Mysterious Universe (1930) ch. 1

4 From the intrinsic evidence of his creation, the Great Architect of the Universe now begins to appear as a pure mathematician.

The Mysterious Universe (1930) ch. 5

Thomas Jefferson 1743–1826

American Democratic Republican statesman, 3rd President of the US 1801–9. See also MOTTOES 563:17

5 When in the course of human events, it becomes necessary for one people to dissolve the political bonds which have connected them with another, and to assume among the powers of the earth the separate and equal station to which the laws of nature and of Nature's God entitle them, a decent respect to the opinions of mankind requires that they should declare the causes which impel them to the separation.

American Declaration of Independence, 4 July 1776, preamble

6 We hold these truths to be sacred and undeniable; that all men are created equal and independent, that from that equal creation they derive rights inherent and inalienable, among which are the preservation of life, and liberty, and the pursuit of happiness.

'Rough Draft' of the American Declaration of Independence, in J. P. Boyd et al. *Papers of Thomas Jefferson* (1950) vol. 1; see **ANONYMOUS** 21:6

7 Our liberty depends on freedom of the press, and that cannot be limited without being lost.

letter to James Currie, 28 January 1786, in *Papers of Thomas Jefferson* (1954) vol. 9

8 Experience declares that man is the only animal which devours his own kind, for I can apply no

milder term to the governments of Europe, and to the general prey of the rich on the poor.

letter to Colonel Edward Carrington, 16 January 1787, in *Papers of Thomas Jefferson* (1955) vol. 11

9 A little rebellion now and then is a good thing.

letter to James Madison, 30 January 1787, in *Papers of Thomas Jefferson* (1955) vol. 11

10 State a moral case to a ploughman and a professor. The former will decide it as well, and often better than the latter, because he has not been led astray by artificial rules.

letter to Peter Carr, 10 August 1787, in *Papers of Thomas Jefferson* (1955) vol. 12

11 The tree of liberty must be refreshed from time to time with the blood of patriots and tyrants. It is its natural manure.

letter to W. S. Smith, 13 November 1787, in *Papers of Thomas Jefferson* (1955) vol. 12

12 I think our governments will remain virtuous for many centuries; as long as they are chiefly agricultural; and this will be as long as there shall be vacant lands in any part of America. When they get piled upon one another in large cities, as in Europe, they will become corrupt as in Europe.

letter to James Madison, 20 December 1787, in *Papers of Thomas Jefferson* (1955) vol. 12

13 Whenever a man has cast a longing eye on them [official positions], a rottenness begins in his conduct.

letter to Tench Coxe, 21 May 1799, in P. L. Ford (ed.) *Writings of Thomas Jefferson* (1896) vol. 7

14 Though the will of the majority is in all cases to prevail, that will to be rightful must be reasonable; . . . the minority possess their equal rights, which equal law must protect, and to violate would be oppression.

first inaugural address, 4 March 1801

15 Would the honest patriot, in the full tide of successful experiment, abandon a government which has so far kept us free and firm?

first inaugural address, 4 March 1801

16 Peace, commerce, and honest friendship with all nations—entangling alliances with none.

first inaugural address, 4 March 1801

17 Freedom of religion; freedom of the press, and freedom of person under the protection of *habeas corpus*, and trial by juries impartially selected. These principles form the bright constellation which has gone before us, and guided our steps through an age of revolution and reformation.

first inaugural address, 4 March 1801

18 I have learned to expect that it will rarely fall to the lot of imperfect man to retire from this station with the reputation and the favour which bring him into it.

first inaugural address, 4 March 1801

1 If a due participation of office is a matter of right, how are vacancies to be obtained? Those by death are few; by resignation none.
letter to E. Shipman and others, 12 July 1801, in P. L. Ford (ed.) *Writings of Thomas Jefferson* (1897) vol. 8; see **MISQUOTATIONS** 547:14

2 When a man assumes a public trust, he should consider himself as public property.
to Baron von Humboldt, 1807, in B. L. Rayner *Life of Jefferson* (1834)

3 Nothing can now be believed which is seen in a newspaper. Truth itself becomes suspicious by being put into that polluted vehicle.
letter to John Norvell, 14 June 1807, in *The Portable Thomas Jefferson* (1977)

4 But though an old man, I am but a young gardener.
letter to Charles Willson Peale, 20 August 1811, in *Thomas Jefferson's Garden Book* (1944)

5 And so we have gone on, and so we shall go on, puzzled and prospering beyond example in the history of man.
letter to John Adams, 21 January 1812, in L. J. Coppin (ed.) *Adams–Jefferson Letters* (1959)

6 I agree with you that there is a natural aristocracy among men. The grounds of this are virtue and talents.
letter to John Adams, 28 October 1813, in P. L. Ford (ed.) *Writings of Thomas Jefferson* (1898) vol. 9

7 If a nation expects to be ignorant and free, in a state of civilization, it expects what never was and never will be.
letter to Colonel Charles Yancey, 6 January 1816, in P. L. Ford (ed.) *Writings of Thomas Jefferson* (1899) vol. 10

8 Nothing gives one person so great advantage over another, as to remain always cool and unruffled under all circumstances.
letter to Francis Wayles Eppes, 21 May 1816, in Jerry Holmes (ed.) *Thomas Jefferson: A Chronology of His Thoughts* (2002)

9 Banking establishments are more dangerous than standing armies.
letter to John Taylor, 28 May 1816, in T. Jefferson Randolph (ed.) *Memoirs, Correspondence & Private Papers of T. Jefferson* (1829) vol. 3

10 We have the wolf by the ears; and we can neither hold him, nor safely let him go. Justice is in one scale, and self-preservation in the other.
on slavery
letter to John Holmes, 22 April 1820; in A. A. Lipscome and A. E. Berg (eds.) *Writings of Thomas Jefferson* (1903) vol. 15

11 I know no safe depository of the ultimate powers of the society but the people themselves; and if we think them not enlightened enough to exercise their control with a wholesome discretion, the remedy is not to take it from them, but to inform their discretion by education.
letter to William Charles Jarvis, 28 September 1820, in P. L. Ford (ed.) *Writings of Thomas Jefferson* (1899) vol. 10

12 To attain all this [universal republicanism], however, rivers of blood must yet flow, and years of desolation pass over; yet the object is worth rivers of blood, and years of desolation.
letter to John Adams, 4 September 1823, in P. L. Ford *Writings of Thomas Jefferson* (1899) vol. 10; see **POWELL** 622:2, **VIRGIL** 830:4

13 Millions of innocent men, women, and children, since the introduction of Christianity, have been burnt, tortured, fined, imprisoned; yet we have not advanced one inch towards uniformity [of opinion]. What has been the effect of coercion? To make one half the world fools, and the other half hypocrites.
Notes on the State of Virginia (1781–5) Query 17

14 Indeed I tremble for my country when I reflect that God is just.
Notes on the State of Virginia (1781–5) Query 18

15 No duty the Executive had to perform was so trying as to put the right man in the right place.
J. B. MacMaster *History of the People of the United States* (1883–1913) vol. 2, ch. 13

16 This is the Fourth?
last words, on 4 July 1826

Francis, Lord Jeffrey 1773–1850
Scottish critic

17 This will never do.
on **WORDSWORTH**'s The Excursion (1814)
in *Edinburgh Review* November 1814

David Jenkins 1925–
English theologian; Bishop of Durham 1984–94

18 I am not clear that God manoeuvres physical things . . . After all, a conjuring trick with bones only proves that it is as clever as a conjuring trick with bones.
on the Resurrection
in 'Poles Apart' (BBC radio, 4 October 1984)

Roy Jenkins 1920–2003
British politician; co-founder of the Social Democratic Party, 1981

19 The politics of the left and centre of this country are frozen in an out-of-date mould which is bad for the political and economic health of Britain and increasingly inhibiting for those who live within the mould. Can it be broken?
speech to Parliamentary Press Gallery, 9 June 1980, in *The Times* 10 June 1980

Elizabeth Jennings 1926–2001
English poet

20 I hate a word like 'pets': it sounds so much Like something with no living of its own.
'My Animals' (1966)

Soame Jenyns 1704–87
English politician and writer

1 Those who profess outrageous zeal for the liberty and prosperity of their country, and at the same time infringe her laws, affront her religion and debauch her people, are but despicable quacks.
A Free Enquiry into the Nature and Origin of Evil (1757) Letter 5

2 Thousands are collected from the idle and the extravagant for seeing dogs, horses, men and monkeys perform feats of activity, and, in some places, for the privilege only of seeing one another.
Works (1790) vol. 2 'Thoughts on the National Debt'

St Jerome *c*.AD 342–420
Roman Christian monk and scholar; translator of the original Bible texts into Latin (see BIBLE (VULGATE)). On Jerome: see TYNDALE 821:4

3 *Aliorum vulnus nostra sit cautio.*
Let us take warning from another's wound.
letter 54, To Furia, AD 394

4 *Venerationi mihi semper fuit non verbosa rusticitas, sed sancta simplicitas.*
I have revered always not crude verbosity, but holy simplicity.
letter 57, To Pammachius; see HUSS 422:6

5 *Romanus orbis ruit et tamen cervix nostra erecta non flectitur.*
The Roman world is falling, yet we hold our heads erect instead of bowing our necks.
letter 60, To Heliodorus, AD 396

6 *Cotidie morimur, cotidie commutamur, et tamen aeternos esse nos credimus.*
Every day we die, every day we are changed, and yet we believe ourselves to be eternal.
letter 60, To Heliodorus, AD 396

7 *Fiunt, non nascuntur Christiani.*
Christians are not born but made.
letter 107, To Laeta, AD 403

8 Holy writ is the scripture of peoples, for it is made, that all peoples should know it.
attributed, in J. Forshall and F. Madden (eds.) *The Holy Bible . . . in the Earliest English Versions* (1850) vol. 1 'The Prologue' [probably by John Purvey, *c*.1353–*c*.1428] ch. 15

Jerome K. Jerome 1859–1927
English novelist and dramatist

9 It is impossible to enjoy idling thoroughly unless one has plenty of work to do.
Idle Thoughts of an Idle Fellow (1886) 'On Being Idle'

10 The passing of the third floor back.
title of story (1907) and play (1910)

11 I want a house that has got over all its troubles; I don't want to spend the rest of my life bringing up a young and inexperienced house.
They and I (1909) ch. 11

12 It is a most extraordinary thing, but I never read a patent medicine advertisement without being impelled to the conclusion that I am suffering from the particular disease therein dealt with in its most virulent form.
Three Men in a Boat (1889) ch. 1

13 I like work: it fascinates me. I can sit and look at it for hours. I love to keep it by me: the idea of getting rid of it nearly breaks my heart.
Three Men in a Boat (1889) ch. 15

William Jerome 1865–1932
American songwriter

14 Any old place I can hang my hat is home sweet home to me.
title of song (1901)

Douglas Jerrold 1803–57
English dramatist and journalist

15 Religion's in the heart, not in the knee.
The Devil's Ducat (1830) act 1, sc. 3

16 The best thing I know between France and England is—the sea.
The Wit and Opinions of Douglas Jerrold (1859) 'The Anglo-French Alliance'

17 Earth is here so kind, that just tickle her with a hoe and she laughs with a harvest.
of Australia
The Wit and Opinions of Douglas Jerrold (1859) 'A Land of Plenty'

John Jewel 1522–71
English Protestant clergyman and bishop

18 In old time we had treen chalices and golden priests, but now we have treen priests and golden chalices.
Certain Sermons Preached Before the Queen's Majesty (1609)

Steve Jobs 1955–
American computer executive

19 It turns out people want keyboards. When Apple first started out, people couldn't type. We realized: Death would eventually take care of this.
interview, 28 May 2003

John XXIII (Angelo Giuseppe Roncalli)
1881–1963
Italian cleric, Pope from 1958

20 If civil authorities legislate for or allow anything that is contrary to that order and therefore contrary to the will of God, neither the laws made or the authorizations granted can be binding on the consciences of the citizens, since God has more right to be obeyed than man.
Pacem in Terris (1963)

21 [In the universal *Declaration of Human Rights* (December, 1948)] in most solemn form, the

dignity of a person is acknowledged to all human beings; and as a consequence there is proclaimed, as a fundamental right, the right of free movement in search for truth and in the attainment of moral good and of justice, and also the right to a dignified life.
Pacem in Terris (1963)

1 I want to throw open the windows of the Church so that we can see out and the people can see in.
attributed

John of Salisbury *c.*1115–80

English ecclesiastical scholar; supporter of Thomas Becket

2 The brevity of our life, the dullness of our senses, the torpor of our indifference, the futility of our occupation, suffer us to know but little: and that little is soon shaken and then torn from the mind by that traitor to learning, that hostile and faithless stepmother to memory, oblivion.
Prologue to the Policraticus (ed. C. C. I. Webb, 1909) vol. 1, translated by Helen Waddell

St John of the Cross 1542–91

Spanish mystic and poet. See also MISQUOTATIONS 547:13

3 *Muero porque no muero.*
I die because I do not die.
the same words occur in St TERESA of Ávila 'Versos nacidos del fuego del amor de Dios' (c.1571–3)
'Coplas del alma que pena por ver a Dios' (c.1578)

4 *Con un no saber sabiendo.*
With a knowing ignorance.
'Coplas hechas sobre un éxtasis de alta contemplación'

Elton John 1947– *and* Bernie Taupin 1950–

English pop singer and songwriter; songwriter

5 It seems to me you lived your life
Like a candle in the wind.
Never knowing who to cling to
When the rain set in.
And I would have liked to have known you
But I was just a kid
The candle burned out long before
Your legend ever did.
Goodbye Norma Jean.
of Marilyn MONROE
'Candle in the Wind' (song, 1973); see MEREDITH 532:12

6 Even when you died
Oh the press still hounded you.
'Candle in the Wind' (song, 1973)

7 Goodbye England's rose;
May you ever grow in our hearts.
rewritten for and sung at the funeral of DIANA, Princess of Wales, 7 September 1997
'Candle in the Wind' (song, revised version, 1997)

8 And it seems to me you lived your life
Like a candle in the wind:

Never fading with the sunset
When the rain set in.
And your footsteps will always fall here
On England's greenest hills;
Your candle's burned out long before
Your legend ever will.
'Candle in the Wind' (song, revised version, 1997)

9 Goodbye yellow brick road.
title of song (1973); see HARBURG 380:1

John Paul II 1920–2005

Polish cleric, Pope from 1978

10 Love is never defeated, and I could add, the history of Ireland proves it.
speech in Galway, 30 September 1979

11 It would be simplistic to say that Divine Providence caused the fall of communism. It fell by itself as a consequence of its own mistakes and abuses. It fell by itself because of its own inherent weaknesses.
when asked if the fall of the USSR could be ascribed to God
Carl Bernstein and Marco Politi *His Holiness: John Paul II and the Hidden History of our Time* (1996)

12 The tree was already rotten. I just gave it a good shake and the rotten apples fell.
of the Soviet Union
Carl Bernstein and Marco Politi *His Holiness: John Paul II and the Hidden History of our Time* (1996)

13 Let me go to the house of the Father.
last words, spoken in Polish
in *Independent* 19 September 2005

Amryl Johnson 1944–2001

Trinidadian poet

14 for . . . I am
Black
And I am
Angry
My name is
Midnight
Without
Pity.
'Midnight Without Pity' (1982)

Amy Johnson 1903–41

English aviator

15 Had I been a man I might have explored the Poles, or climbed Mount Everest, but as it was, my spirit found outlet in the air.
Margot Asquith (ed.) *Myself When Young* (1938)

Dorothy Johnson 1905–84

16 If the myth gets bigger than the man, print the myth.
Indian Country (1953) 'The Man Who Shot Liberty Valance';
see FILM LINES 329:24

Hiram Johnson *see* **Sayings** 685:20

Linton Kwesi Johnson 1952–
Jamaican-born poet

1 Brothers and sisters rocking,
a dread beat pulsing fire, burning.
'Dread Beat an Blood' (1975)

2 Cold lights hurting, breaking, hurting;
fire in the head and a dread beat bleeding,
beating fire: dread.
'Dread Beat an Blood' (1975)

Lyndon Baines Johnson 1908–73
American Democratic statesman, 36th President of the US 1963–9

3 I am a free man, an American, a United States Senator, and a Democrat, in that order.
in *Texas Quarterly* Winter 1958

4 All I have I would have given gladly not to be standing here today.
following the assassination of J. F. KENNEDY
first speech to Congress as President, 27 November 1963, in *Public Papers of ... Lyndon B. Johnson 1963–64* vol. 1

5 In your time we have the opportunity to move not only toward the rich society and the powerful society, but upward to the Great Society.
speech at University of Michigan, 22 May 1964, in *Public Papers of ... Lyndon B. Johnson 1963–64* vol. 1

6 We still seek no wider war.
speech on radio and television, 4 August 1964, in *Public Papers of ... Lyndon B. Johnson 1963–64* vol. 2

7 We are not about to send American boys 9 or 10,000 miles away from home to do what Asian boys ought to be doing for themselves.
speech at Akron University, 21 October 1964, in *Public Papers of ... Lyndon B. Johnson 1963–64* vol. 2; see **ROOSEVELT** 667:10

8 If I've lost Walter Cronkite I've lost Mr Average Citizen.
in 1968, after hearing Walter Cronkite's comment on the position in Vietnam (now often quoted as ' . . . I've lost the country'); see CRONKITE 261:2
to his press secretary George Christian; reported in D. Halberstam *The Powers That Be* (1979)

9 I don't want loyalty. I want *loyalty*. I want him to kiss my ass in Macy's window at high noon and tell me it smells like roses. I want his pecker in my pocket.
discussing a prospective assistant
David Halberstam *The Best and the Brightest* (1972) ch. 20

10 Better to have him inside the tent pissing out, than outside pissing in.
of J. Edgar Hoover
David Halberstam *The Best and the Brightest* (1972) ch. 20

11 So dumb he can't fart and chew gum at the same time.
of Gerald FORD
Richard Reeves *A Ford, not a Lincoln* (1975) ch. 2

Pauline Johnson (Tekahionwake) 1861–1913
Canadian poet

12 For soft is the song my paddle sings.
'The Song My Paddle Sings'

Philander Chase Johnson 1866–1939
American journalist and humorist

13 Cheer up! the worst is yet to come!
in *Everybody's Magazine* May 1920

Philip Johnson 1906–2005
American architect

14 Architecture is the art of how to waste space.
New York Times 27 December 1964

Samuel Johnson 1709–84
English poet, critic, and lexicographer. On Johnson: see BOSWELL 152:4, BROWN 161:6, BURNEY 177:1, CHURCHILL 228:7, COLMAN 244:5, COWPER 257:5, GOLDSMITH 365:15, HAWTHORNE 385:7, KNOWLES 469:15, MACAULAY 506:17, PEMBROKE 602:11, SMOLLETT 759:10, WALPOLE 837:23; see also EPITAPHS 319:4, SWIFT 784:16

15 In all pointed sentences, some degree of accuracy must be sacrificed to conciseness.
'The Bravery of the English Common Soldier' in *The British Magazine* January 1760

16 Change is not made without inconvenience, even from worse to better.
A Dictionary of the English Language (1755) preface; see **HOOKER** 406:9

17 I am not yet so lost in lexicography as to forget that words are the daughters of earth, and that things are the sons of heaven. Language is only the instrument of science, and words are but the signs of ideas: I wish, however, that the instrument might be less apt to decay, and that signs might be permanent, like the things which they denote.
A Dictionary of the English Language (1755) preface; see **MADDEN** 514:3

18 Every quotation contributes something to the stability or enlargement of the language.
on citations of usage in a dictionary
A Dictionary of the English Language (1755) preface

19 But these were the dreams of a poet doomed at last to wake a lexicographer.
A Dictionary of the English Language (1755) preface

20 If the changes we fear be thus irresistible, what remains but to acquiesce with silence, as in the other insurmountable distresses of humanity? It remains that we retard what we cannot repel, that we palliate what we cannot cure.
A Dictionary of the English Language (1755) preface

21 *Dull.* To make dictionaries is dull work.
A Dictionary of the English Language (1755) 'dull' (8th definition)

22 *Excise.* A hateful tax levied upon commodities.
A Dictionary of the English Language (1755)

1 *Lexicographer.* A writer of dictionaries, a harmless drudge.
   A Dictionary of the English Language (1755)

2 *Network.* Anything reticulated or decussated at equal distances, with interstices between the intersections.
   A Dictionary of the English Language (1755)

3 *Oats.* A grain, which in England is generally given to horses, but in Scotland supports the people.
   A Dictionary of the English Language (1755)

4 *Patron.* Commonly a wretch who supports with insolence, and is paid with flattery.
   A Dictionary of the English Language (1755)

5 *Pension.* Pay given to a state hireling for treason to his country.
   A Dictionary of the English Language (1755)

6 The only end of writing is to enable the readers better to enjoy life, or better to endure it.
   A Free Enquiry (1757, ed. D. Greene, 1984)

7 When two Englishmen meet, their first talk is of the weather.
   in *The Idler* no. 11 (24 June 1758)

8 Among the calamities of war may be jointly numbered the diminution of the love of truth, by the falsehoods which interest dictates and credulity encourages.
   in *The Idler* no. 30 (11 November 1758); see SAYINGS 685:20

9 Promise, large promise, is the soul of an advertisement.
   in *The Idler* no. 40 (20 January 1759)

10 He whom nature has made weak, and idleness keeps ignorant, may yet support his vanity by the name of a critic.
   in *The Idler* no. 61 (9 June 1759)

11 The true art of memory is the art of attention.
   in *The Idler* no. 74 (15 September 1759)

12 I directed them to bring a bundle [of hay] into the room, and slept upon it in my riding coat. Mr Boswell, being more delicate, laid himself sheets with hay over and under him, and lay in linen like a gentleman.
   A Journey to the Western Islands of Scotland (1775) 'Glenelg'

13 At seventy-seven it is time to be in earnest.
   A Journey to the Western Islands of Scotland (1775) 'Col'

14 A hardened and shameless tea-drinker, who has for twenty years diluted his meals with only the infusion of this fascinating plant; whose kettle has scarcely time to cool; who with tea amuses the evening, with tea solaces the midnight, and with tea welcomes the morning.
   review in the *Literary Magazine* vol. 2, no. 13 (1757)

15 About things on which the public thinks long it commonly attains to think right.
   Lives of the English Poets (1779–81) 'Addison'

16 Whoever wishes to attain an English style, familiar but not coarse, and elegant but not ostentatious, must give his days and nights to the volumes of Addison.
   Lives of the English Poets (1779–81) 'Addison'

17 The great source of pleasure is variety. Uniformity must tire at last, though it be uniformity of excellence. We love to expect; and, when expectation is disappointed or gratified, we want to be again expecting.
   Lives of the English Poets (1779–81) 'Butler'

18 The true genius is a mind of large general powers, accidentally determined to some particular direction.
   Lives of the English Poets (1779–81) 'Cowley'

19 Language is the dress of thought.
   Lives of the English Poets (1779–81) 'Cowley'; see POPE 616:3, WESLEY 848:10

20 The father of English criticism.
   Lives of the English Poets (1779–81) 'Dryden'

21 This play . . . was first offered to Cibber and his brethren at Drury-Lane, and rejected; it being then carried to Rich had the effect, as was ludicrously said, of making Gay *rich*, and Rich *gay*.
   of GAY's The Beggar's Opera
   Lives of the English Poets (1779–81) 'John Gay'

22 In the character of his Elegy I rejoice to concur with the common reader; for by the common sense of readers uncorrupted with literary prejudices . . . must be finally decided all claim to poetical honours.
   Lives of the English Poets (1779–81) 'Gray'

23 An exotic and irrational entertainment, which has been always combated, and always has prevailed.
   of Italian opera
   Lives of the English Poets (1779–81) 'Hughes'

24 We are perpetually moralists, but we are geometricians only by chance. Our intercourse with intellectual nature is necessary; our speculations upon matter are voluntary and at leisure.
   Lives of the English Poets (1779–81) 'Milton'

25 An acrimonious and surly republican.
   Lives of the English Poets (1779–81) 'Milton'

26 He that runs against Time has an antagonist not subject to casualties.
   Lives of the English Poets (1779–81) 'Pope'

27 I am disappointed by that stroke of death, which has eclipsed the gaiety of nations and impoverished the public stock of harmless pleasure.
   on the death of GARRICK
   Lives of the English Poets (1779–81) 'Edmund Smith'

28 He washed himself with oriental scrupulosity.
   Lives of the English Poets (1779–81) 'Swift'

29 Friendship is not always the sequel of obligation.
   Lives of the English Poets (1779–81) 'James Thomson'

1 Nothing can please many, and please long, but just representations of general nature.
   Plays of William Shakespeare . . . (1765) preface

2 He that tries to recommend him by select quotations, will succeed like the pedant in Hierocles, who, when he offered his house to sale, carried a brick in his pocket as a specimen.
   of **SHAKESPEARE**
   Plays of William Shakespeare . . . (1765) preface; see **SWIFT** 782:4

3 Love is only one of many passions; and . . . it has no great influence upon the sum of life.
   Plays of William Shakespeare . . . (1765) preface

4 Shakespeare has united the powers of exciting laughter and sorrow not only in one mind but in one composition . . . That this is a practice contrary to the rules of criticism will be readily allowed; but there is always an appeal open from criticism to nature.
   Plays of William Shakespeare . . . (1765) preface

5 A quibble is to Shakespeare, what luminous vapours are to the traveller; he follows it at all adventures, it is sure to lead him out of his way and sure to engulf him in the mire.
   Plays of William Shakespeare . . . (1765) preface

6 We fix our eyes upon his graces, and turn them from his deformities, and endure in him what we should in another loathe or despise.
   of **SHAKESPEARE**
   Plays of William Shakespeare . . . (1765) preface

7 I have always suspected that the reading is right, which requires many words to prove it wrong; and the emendation wrong, that cannot without so much labour appear to be right.
   Plays of William Shakespeare . . . (1765) preface

8 Notes are often necessary, but they are necessary evils.
   Plays of William Shakespeare . . . (1765) preface

9 Lawful and settled authority is very seldom resisted when it is well employed.
   in The Rambler no. 50 (8 September 1750)

10 It is better to suffer wrong than to do it, and happier to be sometimes cheated than not to trust.
   in The Rambler no. 79 (18 December 1750)

11 No place affords a more striking conviction of the vanity of human hopes, than a public library.
   in The Rambler no. 106 (23 March 1751)

12 I have laboured to refine our language to grammatical purity, and to clear it from colloquial barbarisms, licentious idioms, and irregular combinations.
   in The Rambler no. 208 (14 March 1752)

13 Ye who listen with credulity to the whispers of fancy, and pursue with eagerness the phantoms of hope; who expect that age will perform the promises of youth, and that the deficiencies of the present day will be supplied by the morrow;

attend to the history of Rasselas prince of Abyssinia.
   Rasselas (1759) ch. 1

14 The business of a poet, said Imlac, is to examine, not the individual, but the species; to remark general properties and appearances: he does not number the streaks of the tulip, or describe the different shades in the verdure of the forest.
   Rasselas (1759) ch. 10

15 He [the poet] must write as the interpreter of nature, and the legislator of mankind, and consider himself as presiding over the thoughts and manners of future generations; as a being superior to time and place.
   Rasselas (1759) ch. 10; see **SHELLEY** 747:14

16 Human life is everywhere a state in which much is to be endured, and little to be enjoyed.
   Rasselas (1759) ch. 11

17 Marriage has many pains, but celibacy has no pleasures.
   Rasselas (1759) ch. 26

18 Example is always more efficacious than precept.
   Rasselas (1759) ch. 30

19 I consider this mighty structure as a monument of the insufficiency of human enjoyments.
   of the Pyramids
   Rasselas (1759) ch. 32

20 Integrity without knowledge is weak and useless, and knowledge without integrity is dangerous and dreadful.
   Rasselas (1759) ch. 41

21 There is perhaps no class of men, to whom the precept given by the Apostle to his converts against too great confidence in their understandings, may be more properly inculcated, than those who are dedicated to the profession of literature.
   Sermons (1788) no. 8

22 He [God] will not leave his promises unfulfilled, nor his threats unexecuted . . . Neither can he want power to execute his purposes; he who spoke, and the world was made, can speak again, and it will perish.
   Sermons (1788) no. 10

23 How is it that we hear the loudest yelps for liberty among the drivers of negroes?
   Taxation No Tyranny (1775)

24 A generous and elevated mind is distinguished by nothing more certainly than an eminent degree of curiosity.
   dedication of his English translation of Fr. J. Lobo's Voyage to Abyssinia (1735), signed 'the editor' but attributed to Johnson in James Boswell Life of Samuel Johnson (1791) 1734

25 There Poetry shall tune her sacred voice,
   And wake from ignorance the Western World.
   Demetrius forecasting the Renaissance
   Irene (1749) act 4, sc. 1, l. 122

1 Here falling houses thunder on your head,
And here a female atheist talks you dead.
London (1738) l. 17

2 Of all the griefs that harrass the distressed,
Sure the most bitter is a scornful jest;
Fate never wounds more deep the gen'rous
heart,
Than when a blockhead's insult points the dart.
London (1738) l. 166

3 The stage but echoes back the public voice.
The drama's laws the drama's patrons give,
For we that live to please, must please to live.
'Prologue spoken at the Opening of the Theatre in Drury
Lane' (1747)

4 How small of all that human hearts endure,
That part which laws or kings can cause or cure.
Still to ourselves in every place consigned,
Our own felicity we make or find.
lines added to Oliver Goldsmith's *The Traveller* (1764) l. 429;
see **GOLDSMITH** 364:28

5 Let observation with extensive view,
Survey mankind, from China to Peru.
The Vanity of Human Wishes (1749) l. 1

6 There mark what ills the scholar's life assail,
Toil, envy, want, the patron, and the jail.
The Vanity of Human Wishes (1749) l. 159

7 A frame of adamant, a soul of fire,
No dangers fright him, and no labours tire.
of Charles XII of Sweden
The Vanity of Human Wishes (1749) l. 193

8 His fall was destined to a barren strand,
A petty fortress, and a dubious hand;
He left the name, at which the world grew pale,
To point a moral, or adorn a tale.
of Charles XII of Sweden
The Vanity of Human Wishes (1749) l. 219

9 Enlarge my life with multitude of days,
In health, in sickness, thus the suppliant prays;
Hides from himself his state, and shuns to know,
That life protracted is protracted woe.
Time hovers o'er, impatient to destroy,
And shuts up all the passages of joy.
The Vanity of Human Wishes (1749) l. 255

10 In life's last scene what prodigies surprise,
Fears of the brave, and follies of the wise?
From Marlb'rough's eyes the streams of dotage
flow,
And Swift expires a driv'ler and a show.
The Vanity of Human Wishes (1749) l. 315

11 Must helpless man, in ignorance sedate,
Roll darkling down the torrent of his fate?
The Vanity of Human Wishes (1749) l. 345

12 Still raise for good the supplicating voice,
But leave to heaven the measure and the choice.
The Vanity of Human Wishes (1749) l. 351

13 A lawyer has no business with the justice or
injustice of the cause which he undertakes,
unless his client asks his opinion, and then he is
bound to give it honestly. The justice or injustice
of the cause is to be decided by the judge.
James Boswell *Journal of a Tour to the Hebrides* (1785) 15
August 1773

14 Let him go abroad to a distant country; let him
go to some place where he is *not* known. Don't
let him go to the devil where he is known!
*Boswell having asked if someone should commit suicide to
avoid certain disgrace*
James Boswell *Tour to the Hebrides* (1785) 18 August 1773

15 I have, all my life long, been lying till noon; yet
I tell all young men, and tell them with great
sincerity, that nobody who does not rise early
will ever do any good.
James Boswell *Tour to the Hebrides* (1785) 14 September 1773

16 I inherited a vile melancholy from my father,
which has made me mad all my life, at least not
sober.
James Boswell *Tour to the Hebrides* (1785) 16 September 1773;
see **JOHNSON** 443:19

17 I am always sorry when any language is lost,
because languages are the pedigree of nations.
James Boswell *Tour to the Hebrides* (1785) 18 September 1773

18 I do not much like to see a Whig in any dress;
but I hate to see a Whig in a parson's gown.
James Boswell *Tour to the Hebrides* (1785) 24 September 1773

19 A cucumber should be well sliced, and dressed
with pepper and vinegar, and then thrown out,
as good for nothing.
James Boswell *Tour to the Hebrides* (1785) 5 October 1773

20 I am sorry I have not learned to play at cards. It
is very useful in life: it generates kindness and
consolidates society.
James Boswell *Tour to the Hebrides* (1785) 21 November 1773

21 JOHNSON: I had no notion that I was wrong or
    irreverent to my tutor.
BOSWELL: That, Sir, was great fortitude of mind.
JOHNSON: No, Sir; stark insensibility.
James Boswell *Life of Samuel Johnson* (1791) 31 October 1728

22 Sir, we are a nest of singing birds.
of Pembroke College, Oxford
James Boswell *Life of Samuel Johnson* (1791) 1730

23 He was a vicious man, but very kind to me. If
you call a dog *Hervey*, I shall love him.
of his former patron Henry Hervey
James Boswell *Life of Samuel Johnson* (1791) 1737

24 My old friend, Mrs Carter, could make a
pudding, as well as translate Epictetus.
James Boswell *Life of Samuel Johnson* (1791) Spring 1738

25 Tom Birch is as brisk as a bee in conversation;
but no sooner does he take a pen in his hand,
than it becomes a torpedo to him, and benumbs
all his faculties.
James Boswell *Life of Samuel Johnson* (1791) 1743

26 I'll come no more behind your scenes, David;
for the silk stockings and white bosoms of your
actresses excite my amorous propensities.
to **GARRICK**; *John* **WILKES** *recalled the remark in the form:*

'the silk stockings and white bosoms of your actresses do make my genitals to quiver'
James Boswell *Life of Samuel Johnson* (1791) 1750

1 A man may write at any time, if he will set himself doggedly to it.
James Boswell *Life of Samuel Johnson* (1791) March 1750

2 A fly, Sir, may sting a stately horse and make him wince; but one is but an insect, and the other is a horse still.
James Boswell *Life of Samuel Johnson* (1791) 1754

3 This man I thought had been a Lord among wits; but, I find, he is only a wit among Lords.
of Lord **CHESTERFIELD**
James Boswell *Life of Samuel Johnson* (1791) 1754

4 They teach the morals of a whore, and the manners of a dancing master.
of the Letters *of Lord* **CHESTERFIELD**
James Boswell *Life of Samuel Johnson* (1791) 1754

5 I had done all that I could; and no man is well pleased to have his all neglected, be it ever so little.
James Boswell *Life of Samuel Johnson* (1791) letter to Lord Chesterfield, 7 February 1755

6 The shepherd in Virgil grew at last acquainted with Love, and found him a native of the rocks.
James Boswell *Life of Samuel Johnson* (1791) letter to Lord Chesterfield, 7 February 1755

7 Is not a Patron, my Lord, one who looks with unconcern on a man struggling for life in the water, and, when he has reached ground, encumbers him with help? The notice which you have been pleased to take of my labours, had it been early, had been kind; but it has been delayed till I am indifferent, and cannot enjoy it; till I am solitary, and cannot impart it; till I am known, and do not want it.
James Boswell *Life of Samuel Johnson* (1791) letter to Lord Chesterfield, 7 February 1755

8 There are two things which I am confident I can do very well: one is an introduction to any literary work, stating what it is to contain, and how it should be executed in the most perfect manner; the other is a conclusion, shewing from various causes why the execution has not been equal to what the author promised to himself and to the public.
James Boswell *Life of Samuel Johnson* (1791) 1755

9 Ignorance, madam, pure ignorance.
on being asked why he had defined pastern *as the 'knee' of a horse*
James Boswell *Life of Samuel Johnson* (1791) 1755

10 I have protracted my work till most of those whom I wished to please have sunk into the grave; and success and miscarriage are empty sounds.
James Boswell *Life of Samuel Johnson* (1791) 1755

11 If a man does not make new acquaintance as he advances through life, he will soon find himself left alone. A man, Sir, should keep his friendship in constant repair.
James Boswell *Life of Samuel Johnson* (1791) 1755

12 No man will be a sailor who has contrivance enough to get himself into a jail; for being in a ship is being in a jail, with the chance of being drowned . . . A man in a jail has more room, better food, and commonly better company.
James Boswell *Life of Samuel Johnson* (1791) 16 March 1759; see **BURTON** 181:16

13 No, Sir, I am not a botanist; and (alluding, no doubt, to his near sightedness) should I wish to become a botanist, I must first turn myself into a reptile.
James Boswell *Life of Samuel Johnson* (1791) 20 July 1762

14 BOSWELL: I do indeed come from Scotland, but I cannot help it . . .
JOHNSON: That, Sir, I find, is what a very great many of your countrymen cannot help.
James Boswell *Life of Samuel Johnson* (1791) 16 May 1763

15 Yes, Sir, many men, many women, and many children.
on Dr Blair's asking whether any man of a modern age could have written Ossian
James Boswell *Life of Samuel Johnson* (1791) 24 May 1763; see also **JOHNSON** 441:10, **JOHNSON** 443:15

16 I did not think he ought to be shut up. His infirmities were not noxious to society. He insisted on people praying with him; and I'd as lief pray with Kit Smart as any one else. Another charge was, that he did not love clean linen; and I have no passion for it.
James Boswell *Life of Samuel Johnson* (1791) 24 May 1763

17 You *may* abuse a tragedy, though you cannot write one. You may scold a carpenter who has made you a bad table, though you cannot make a table. It is not your trade to make tables.
on literary criticism
James Boswell *Life of Samuel Johnson* (1791) 25 June 1763

18 I am afraid he has not been in the inside of a church for many years; but he never passes a church without pulling off his hat. This shows that he has good principles.
of Dr John Campbell
James Boswell *Life of Samuel Johnson* (1791) 1 July 1763

19 Great abilities are not requisite for an historian . . . imagination is not required in any high degree.
James Boswell *Life of Samuel Johnson* (1791) 6 July 1763

20 The noblest prospect which a Scotchman ever sees, is the high road that leads him to England!
James Boswell *Life of Samuel Johnson* (1791) 6 July 1763

21 A man ought to read just as inclination leads him; for what he reads as a task will do him little good.
James Boswell *Life of Samuel Johnson* (1791) 14 July 1763

22 But if he does really think that there is no distinction between virtue and vice, why, Sir,

when he leaves our houses, let us count our spoons.

James Boswell *Life of Samuel Johnson* (1791) 14 July 1763; see **EMERSON** 314:21

1 All the arguments which are brought to represent poverty as no evil, show it to be evidently a great evil. You never find people labouring to convince you that you may live very happily upon a plentiful fortune.

James Boswell *Life of Samuel Johnson* (1791) 20 July 1763

2 Truth, Sir, is a cow, that will yield such people [sceptics] no more milk, and so they are gone to milk the bull.

James Boswell *Life of Samuel Johnson* (1791) 21 July 1763

3 Young men have more virtue than old men; they have more generous sentiments in every respect.

James Boswell *Life of Samuel Johnson* (1791) 21 July 1763

4 In my early years I read very hard. It is a sad reflection, but a true one, that I knew almost as much at eighteen as I do now.

James Boswell *Life of Samuel Johnson* (1791) 21 July 1763

5 Why, Sir, Sherry is dull, naturally dull; but it must have taken him a great deal of pains to become what we now see him. Such an excess of stupidity, Sir, is not in Nature.

of Thomas Sheridan

James Boswell *Life of Samuel Johnson* (1791) 28 July 1763

6 It is burning a farthing candle at Dover, to shew light at Calais.

on Thomas Sheridan's influence on the English language

James Boswell *Life of Samuel Johnson* (1791) 28 July 1763; see **YOUNG** 876:15

7 A woman's preaching is like a dog's walking on his hinder legs. It is not done well; but you are surprised to find it done at all.

James Boswell *Life of Samuel Johnson* (1791) 31 July 1763

8 We could not have had a better dinner had there been a *Synod of Cooks*.

James Boswell *Life of Samuel Johnson* (1791) 5 August 1763

9 Don't, Sir, accustom yourself to use big words for little matters. It would *not* be *terrible*, though I *were* to be detained some time here.

when Boswell said it would be 'terrible' if Johnson should not be able to return speedily from Harwich

James Boswell *Life of Samuel Johnson* (1791) 6 August 1763

10 I refute it *thus*.

*on Boswell observing of Bishop **BERKELEY**'s theory of the non-existence of matter that though they were satisfied it was not true, they were unable to refute it, Johnson struck his foot against a large stone, till he rebounded from it, with these words*

James Boswell *Life of Samuel Johnson* (1791) 6 August 1763

11 Sir John, Sir, is a very unclubbable man.

of Sir John Hawkins

James Boswell *Life of Samuel Johnson* (1791) Spring 1764

12 That all who are happy, are equally happy, is not true. A peasant and a philosopher may be equally *satisfied*, but not equally *happy*. Happiness

consists in the multiplicity of agreeable consciousness.

James Boswell *Life of Samuel Johnson* (1791) February 1766

13 Our tastes greatly alter. The lad does not care for the child's rattle, and the old man does not care for the young man's whore.

James Boswell *Life of Samuel Johnson* (1791) Spring 1766

14 It was not for me to bandy civilities with my Sovereign.

James Boswell *Life of Samuel Johnson* (1791) February 1767

15 There was as great a difference between them as between a man who knew how a watch was made, and a man who could tell the hour by looking on the dial-plate.

James Boswell *Life of Samuel Johnson* (1791) Spring 1768

16 Let me smile with the wise, and feed with the rich.

*responding to **GARRICK***

James Boswell *Life of Samuel Johnson* (1791) 6 October 1769; see **GARRICK** 349:9

17 We *know* our will is free, and *there's* an end on't.

James Boswell *Life of Samuel Johnson* (1791) 16 October 1769

18 In the description of night in Macbeth, the beetle and the bat detract from the general idea of darkness,—inspissated gloom.

James Boswell *Life of Samuel Johnson* (1791) 16 October 1769

19 Most schemes of political improvement are very laughable things.

James Boswell *Life of Samuel Johnson* (1791) 26 October 1769

20 It matters not how a man dies, but how he lives. The act of dying is not of importance, it lasts so short a time.

James Boswell *Life of Samuel Johnson* (1791) 26 October 1769

21 Burton's *Anatomy of Melancholy*, he said, was the only book that ever took him out of bed two hours sooner than he wished to rise.

James Boswell *Life of Samuel Johnson* (1791) 1770

22 Want of tenderness, he always alleged, was want of parts, and was no less a proof of stupidity than depravity.

James Boswell *Life of Samuel Johnson* (1791) 1770

23 That fellow seems to me to possess but one idea, and that is a wrong one.

of a chance-met acquaintance

James Boswell *Life of Samuel Johnson* (1791) 1770; see **DISRAELI** 286:7

24 Johnson observed, that 'he did not care to speak ill of any man behind his back, but he believed the gentleman was an *attorney*.'

James Boswell *Life of Samuel Johnson* (1791) 1770

25 The triumph of hope over experience.

of a man who remarried immediately after the death of a wife with whom he had been unhappy

James Boswell *Life of Samuel Johnson* (1791) 1770

26 Every man has a lurking wish to appear considerable in his native place.

James Boswell *Life of Samuel Johnson* (1791) letter to Sir Joshua Reynolds, 17 July 1771

1 It is so far from being natural for a man and woman to live in a state of marriage, that we find all the motives which they have for remaining in that connection, and the restraints which civilized society imposes to prevent separation, are hardly sufficient to keep them together.

   James Boswell *Life of Samuel Johnson* (1791) 31 March 1772

2 Nobody can write the life of a man, but those who have eat and drunk and lived in social intercourse with him.

   James Boswell *Life of Samuel Johnson* (1791) 31 March 1772

3 If a sovereign oppresses his people to a great degree, they will rise and cut off his head. There is a remedy in human nature against tyranny, that will keep us safe under every form of government.

   James Boswell *Life of Samuel Johnson* (1791) 31 March 1772

4 Why, Sir, if you were to read Richardson for the story, your impatience would be so much fretted that you would hang yourself.

   James Boswell *Life of Samuel Johnson* (1791) 6 April 1772

5 Grief is a species of idleness.

   letter to Mrs Thrale, 17 March 1773, in R. W. Chapman (ed.) *Letters of Samuel Johnson* (1952) vol. 1

6 He has, indeed, done it very well; but it is a foolish thing well done.

   on **GOLDSMITH**'s apology in the London Chronicle for physically assaulting Thomas Evans, who had published a damaging open letter to Goldsmith in the London Packet 24 March 1773

   James Boswell *Life of Samuel Johnson* (1791) 3 April 1773

7 All intellectual improvement arises from leisure.

   James Boswell *Life of Samuel Johnson* (1791) 13 April 1773

8 ELPHINSTON: What, have you not read it through? JOHNSON: No, Sir, do *you* read books *through*?

   James Boswell *Life of Samuel Johnson* (1791) 19 April 1773

9 Read over your compositions, and where ever you meet with a passage which you think is particularly fine, strike it out.

   quoting a college tutor

   James Boswell *Life of Samuel Johnson* (1791) 30 April 1773

10 I hope I shall never be deterred from detecting what I think a cheat, by the menaces of a ruffian ['Ossian'].

   James Boswell *Life of Samuel Johnson* (1791) letter to James Macpherson, 20 January 1775; see also **JOHNSON** 439:15

11 There are few ways in which a man can be more innocently employed than in getting money.

   James Boswell *Life of Samuel Johnson* (1791) 27 March 1775

12 He was dull in a new way, and that made many people think him *great*.

   of Thomas **GRAY**

   James Boswell *Life of Samuel Johnson* (1791) 28 March 1775

13 I never think I have hit hard, unless it rebounds.

   James Boswell *Life of Samuel Johnson* (1791) 2 April 1775

14 Fleet-street has a very animated appearance; but I think the full tide of human existence is at Charing-Cross.

   James Boswell *Life of Samuel Johnson* (1791) 2 April 1775

15 George the First knew nothing, and desired to know nothing; did nothing, and desired to do nothing; and the only good thing that is told of him is, that he wished to restore the crown to its hereditary successor.

   James Boswell *Life of Samuel Johnson* (1791) 6 April 1775

16 It is wonderful, when a calculation is made, how little the mind is actually employed in the discharge of any profession.

   James Boswell *Life of Samuel Johnson* (1791) 6 April 1775

17 The greatest part of a writer's time is spent in reading, in order to write: a man will turn over half a library to make one book.

   James Boswell *Life of Samuel Johnson* (1791) 6 April 1775

18 Patriotism is the last refuge of a scoundrel.

   James Boswell *Life of Samuel Johnson* (1791) 7 April 1775

19 Knowledge is of two kinds. We know a subject ourselves, or we know where we can find information upon it.

   James Boswell *Life of Samuel Johnson* (1791) 18 April 1775

20 Politics are now nothing more than means of rising in the world.

   James Boswell *Life of Samuel Johnson* (1791) 18 April 1775

21 Players, Sir! I look upon them as no better than creatures set upon tables and joint-stools to make faces and produce laughter, like dancing dogs.

   James Boswell *Life of Samuel Johnson* (1791) 1775

22 In lapidary inscriptions a man is not upon oath.

   James Boswell *Life of Samuel Johnson* (1791) 1775

23 There is now less flogging in our great schools than formerly, but then less is learned there; so that what the boys get at one end they lose at the other.

   James Boswell *Life of Samuel Johnson* (1791) 1775

24 Nothing odd will do long. *Tristram Shandy* did not last.

   James Boswell *Life of Samuel Johnson* (1791) 20 March 1776

25 There is nothing which has yet been contrived by man, by which so much happiness is produced as by a good tavern or inn.

   James Boswell *Life of Samuel Johnson* (1791) 21 March 1776; see **SHENSTONE** 747:19

26 Marriages would in general be as happy, and often more so, if they were all made by the Lord Chancellor, upon a due consideration of characters and circumstances, without the parties having any choice in the matter.

   James Boswell *Life of Samuel Johnson* (1791) 22 March 1776

27 He is gone, and we are going.

   on the death of her son, Harry

   letter to Mrs Thrale, 25 March 1776, in R. W. Chapman (ed.) *Letters of Samuel Johnson* (1952) vol. 3

1 Questioning is not the mode of conversation among gentlemen. It is assuming a superiority.
James Boswell *Life of Samuel Johnson* (1791) 25 March 1776

2 If a madman were to come into this room with a stick in his hand, no doubt we should pity the state of his mind; but our primary consideration would be to take care of ourselves. We should knock him down first, and pity him afterwards.
James Boswell *Life of Samuel Johnson* (1791) 3 April 1776

3 We would all be idle if we could.
James Boswell *Life of Samuel Johnson* (1791) 1776

4 No man but a blockhead ever wrote, except for money.
James Boswell *Life of Samuel Johnson* (1791) 5 April 1776

5 A man who has not been in Italy, is always conscious of an inferiority, from his not having seen what it is expected a man should see.
James Boswell *Life of Samuel Johnson* (1791) 11 April 1776

6 BOSWELL: Sir, what is poetry?
JOHNSON: Why Sir, it is much easier to say what it is not. We all *know* what light is; but it is not easy to *tell* what it is.
James Boswell *Life of Samuel Johnson* (1791) 12 April 1776

7 Sir, you have but two topics, yourself and me. I am sick of both.
James Boswell *Life of Samuel Johnson* (1791) May 1776

8 If I had no duties, and no reference to futurity, I would spend my life in driving briskly in a post-chaise with a pretty woman.
James Boswell *Life of Samuel Johnson* (1791) 19 September 1777

9 Depend upon it, Sir, when a man knows he is to be hanged in a fortnight, it concentrates his mind wonderfully.
on the execution of Dr Dodd for forgery, 27 June 1777
James Boswell *Life of Samuel Johnson* (1791) 19 September 1777

10 When a man is tired of London, he is tired of life.
James Boswell *Life of Samuel Johnson* (1791) 20 September 1777

11 All argument is against it; but all belief is for it.
of the existence of ghosts
James Boswell *Life of Samuel Johnson* (1791) 31 March 1778

12 John Wesley's conversation is good, but he is never at leisure. He is always obliged to go at a certain hour. This is very disagreeable to a man who loves to fold his legs and have out his talk, as I do.
James Boswell *Life of Samuel Johnson* (1791) 31 March 1778

13 Every man thinks meanly of himself for not having been a soldier, or not having been at sea.
James Boswell *Life of Samuel Johnson* (1791) 10 April 1778

14 Johnson had said that he could repeat a complete chapter of 'The Natural History of Iceland', from the Danish of Horrebow, the whole of which was exactly thus:—'CHAP. LXXII. *Concerning snakes*. There are no snakes to be met with throughout the whole island.'
James Boswell *Life of Samuel Johnson* (1791) 13 April 1778

15 The more contracted that power is, the more easily it is destroyed. A country governed by a despot is an inverted cone.
James Boswell *Life of Samuel Johnson* (1791) 14 April 1778

16 So it is in travelling; a man must carry knowledge with him, if he would bring home knowledge.
James Boswell *Life of Samuel Johnson* (1791) 17 April 1778

17 Sir, the insolence of wealth will creep out.
James Boswell *Life of Samuel Johnson* (1791) 18 April 1778

18 All censure of a man's self is oblique praise. It is in order to shew how much he can spare.
James Boswell *Life of Samuel Johnson* (1791) 25 April 1778

19 I have always said, the first Whig was the Devil.
James Boswell *Life of Samuel Johnson* (1791) 28 April 1778

20 Mutual cowardice keeps us in peace. Were one half of mankind brave and one half cowards, the brave would be always beating the cowards. Were all brave, they would lead a very uneasy life; all would be continually fighting: but being all cowards, we go on very well.
James Boswell *Life of Samuel Johnson* (1791) 28 April 1778

21 Were it not for imagination, Sir, a man would be as happy in the arms of a chambermaid as of a Duchess.
James Boswell *Life of Samuel Johnson* (1791) 9 May 1778

22 Madam, before you flatter a man so grossly to his face, you should consider whether or not your flattery is worth his having.
remark to Hannah MORE
Charlotte Barrett (ed.) *Diary and Letters of Madame D'Arblay* [Fanny Burney] (1842) vol. 1, pt. 2, August 1778

23 Claret is the liquor for boys; port, for men; but he who aspires to be a hero (smiling) must drink brandy.
James Boswell *Life of Samuel Johnson* (1791) 7 April 1779

24 A man who exposes himself when he is intoxicated, has not the art of getting drunk.
James Boswell *Life of Samuel Johnson* (1791) 24 April 1779

25 Worth seeing, yes; but not worth going to see.
on the Giant's Causeway
James Boswell *Life of Samuel Johnson* (1791) 12 October 1779

26 If you are idle, be not solitary; if you are solitary, be not idle.
James Boswell *Life of Samuel Johnson* (1791) letter to Boswell, 27 October 1779; see BURTON 181:24

27 Among the anfractuosities of the human mind, I know not if it may not be one, that there is a superstitious reluctance to sit for a picture.
James Boswell *Life of Samuel Johnson* (1791) 1780

28 Every man has a right to utter what he thinks truth, and every other man has a right to knock him down for it. Martyrdom is the test.
James Boswell *Life of Samuel Johnson* (1791) 1780

29 They are forced plants, raised in a hot-bed; and they are poor plants; they are but cucumbers after all.
of Thomas Gray's Odes
James Boswell *Life of Samuel Johnson* (1791) 1780

1 No man was more foolish when he had not a pen in his hand, or more wise when he had.

of Oliver GOLDSMITH

James Boswell *Life of Samuel Johnson* (1791) 1780; see GARRICK 349:11

2 If a man talks of his misfortunes there is something in them that is not disagreeable to him; for where there is nothing but pure misery, there never is any recourse to the mention of it.

James Boswell *Life of Samuel Johnson* (1791) 1780

3 Mrs Montagu has dropt me. Now, Sir, there are people whom one should like very well to drop, but would not wish to be dropped by.

James Boswell *Life of Samuel Johnson* (1791) March 1781

4 This merriment of parsons is mighty offensive.

James Boswell *Life of Samuel Johnson* (1791) March 1781

5 We are not here to sell a parcel of boilers and vats, but the potentiality of growing rich, beyond the dreams of avarice.

at the sale of Thrale's brewery

James Boswell *Life of Samuel Johnson* (1791) 6 April 1781; see MOORE 557:5

6 Classical quotation is the *parole* of literary men all over the world.

James Boswell *Life of Samuel Johnson* (1791) 8 May 1781

7 Why, that is, because, dearest, you're a dunce.

to Miss Monckton, later Lady Corke, who said that STERNE's *writings affected her*

James Boswell *Life of Samuel Johnson* (1791) May 1781

8 Sir, I have two very cogent reasons for not printing any list of subscribers;—one, that I have lost all the names,—the other, that I have spent all the money.

James Boswell *Life of Samuel Johnson* (1791) May 1781

9 Always, Sir, set a high value on spontaneous kindness. He whose inclination prompts him to cultivate your friendship of his own accord, will love you more than one whom you have been at pains to attach to you.

James Boswell *Life of Samuel Johnson* (1791) May 1781

10 A wise Tory and a wise Whig, I believe, will agree. Their principles are the same, though their modes of thinking are different.

James Boswell *Life of Samuel Johnson* (1791) May 1781, written statement given to Boswell

11 I hate a fellow whom pride, or cowardice, or laziness drives into a corner, and who does nothing when he is there but sit and *growl*; let him come out as I do, and *bark*.

of Jeremiah Markland

James Boswell *Life of Samuel Johnson* (1791) 10 October 1782

12 Resolve not to be poor: whatever you have, spend less. Poverty is a great enemy to human happiness; it certainly destroys liberty, and it makes some virtues impracticable, and others extremely difficult.

James Boswell *Life of Samuel Johnson* (1791) letter to Boswell, 7 December 1782

13 How few of his friends' houses would a man choose to be at when he is sick.

James Boswell *Life of Samuel Johnson* (1791) 1783

14 There is a wicked inclination in most people to suppose an old man decayed in his intellects. If a young or middle-aged man, when leaving a company, does not recollect where he laid his hat, it is nothing; but if the same inattention is discovered in an old man, people will shrug up their shoulders, and say, 'His memory is going.'

James Boswell *Life of Samuel Johnson* (1791) 1783

15 A man might write such stuff for ever, if he would *abandon* his mind to it.

of Ossian

James Boswell *Life of Samuel Johnson* (1791) 1783; see also JOHNSON 439:15

16 Sir, there is no settling the point of precedency between a louse and a flea.

on the relative merits of two minor poets

James Boswell *Life of Samuel Johnson* (1791) 1783

17 When I observed he was a fine cat, saying, 'Why yes, Sir, but I have had cats whom I liked better than this'; and then as if perceiving Hodge to be out of countenance, adding, 'but he is a very fine cat, a very fine cat indeed.'

James Boswell *Life of Samuel Johnson* (1791) 1783

18 Clear your mind of cant.

James Boswell *Life of Samuel Johnson* (1791) 15 May 1783

19 The black dog I hope always to resist, and in time to drive, though I am deprived of almost all those that used to help me . . . When I rise my breakfast is solitary, the black dog waits to share it, from breakfast to dinner he continues barking, except that Dr Brocklesby for a little keeps him at a distance . . . Night comes at last, and some hours of restlessness and confusion bring me again to a day of solitude. What shall exclude the black dog from a habitation like this?

on his attacks of melancholia; more recently associated with Winston CHURCHILL, *who used the phrase 'black dog' when alluding to his own periodic bouts of depression*

letter to Mrs Thrale, 28 June 1783, in R. W. Chapman (ed.) *Letters of Samuel Johnson* (1952) vol. 3

20 As I know more of mankind I expect less of them, and am ready now to call a man *a good man*, upon easier terms than I was formerly.

James Boswell *Life of Samuel Johnson* (1791) September 1783

21 If a man were to go by chance at the same time with Burke under a shed, to shun a shower, he would say—'this is an extraordinary man.'

on Edmund BURKE

James Boswell *Life of Samuel Johnson* (1791) 15 May 1784

22 It is as bad as bad can be: it is ill-fed, ill-killed, ill-kept, and ill-drest.

on the roast mutton he had been served at an inn

James Boswell *Life of Samuel Johnson* (1791) 3 June 1784

23 JOHNSON: As I cannot be sure that I have fulfilled the conditions on which salvation is granted, I am afraid I may be one of those who shall be damned (looking dismally).

DR ADAMS: What do you mean by damned?
JOHNSON: (passionately and loudly) Sent to Hell, Sir, and punished everlastingly.
James Boswell *Life of Samuel Johnson* (1791) 12 June 1784

1 Milton, Madam, was a genius that could cut a Colossus from a rock; but could not carve heads upon cherry-stones.
to Hannah MORE, *who had expressed a wonder that the poet who had written* Paradise Lost *should write such poor sonnets*
James Boswell *Life of Samuel Johnson* (1791) 13 June 1784

2 It might as well be said 'Who drives fat oxen should himself be fat.'
parodying Henry BROOKE
James Boswell *Life of Samuel Johnson* (1791) June 1784; see BROOKE 159:3

3 Sir, I have found you an argument; but I am not obliged to find you an understanding.
James Boswell *Life of Samuel Johnson* (1791) June 1784

4 No man is a hypocrite in his pleasures.
James Boswell *Life of Samuel Johnson* (1791) June 1784; see POPE 615:15

5 Talking of the Comedy of 'The Rehearsal,' he said, 'It has not wit enough to keep it sweet.' This was easy;—he therefore caught himself, and pronounced a more rounded sentence; 'It has not vitality enough to preserve it from putrefaction.'
James Boswell *Life of Samuel Johnson* (1791) June 1784

6 Who can run the race with Death?
James Boswell *Life of Samuel Johnson* (1791) letter to Dr Burney, 2 August 1784

7 Dictionaries are like watches, the worst is better than none, and the best cannot be expected to go quite true.
James Boswell *Life of Samuel Johnson* (1791) letter to Francesco Sastres, 21 August 1784

8 Sir, I look upon every day to be lost, in which I do not make a new acquaintance.
James Boswell *Life of Samuel Johnson* (1791) November 1784

9 I will be conquered; I will not capitulate.
on his illness
James Boswell *Life of Samuel Johnson* (1791) November 1784

10 Long-expected one-and-twenty,
Ling'ring year, at length is flown;
Pride and pleasure, pomp and plenty,
Great [Sir John], are now your own.
James Boswell *Life of Samuel Johnson* (1791) December 1784

11 An odd thought strikes me:—we shall receive no letters in the grave.
James Boswell *Life of Samuel Johnson* (1791) December 1784

12 Abstinence is as easy to me, as temperance would be difficult.
William Roberts (ed.) *Memoirs of the Life and Correspondence of Mrs Hannah More* (1834) vol. 1

13 Corneille is to Shakespeare ... as a clipped hedge is to a forest.
Hester Lynch Piozzi *Anecdotes of ... Johnson* (1786)

14 Difficult do you call it, Sir? I wish it were impossible.
on the performance of a celebrated violinist
William Seward *Supplement to the Anecdotes of Distinguished Persons* (1797)

15 [Goldsmith] seeming to repine at the success of Beattie's Essay on Truth—'Here's such a stir (said he) about a fellow that has written one book, and I have written many.' Ah, Doctor (says his friend [Johnson]), there go two-and-forty sixpences you know to one guinea.
Hester Lynch Piozzi *Anecdotes of ... Johnson* (1786)

16 He hated a fool, and he hated a rogue, and he hated a whig; he was a very good hater.
of Bathurst
Hester Lynch Piozzi *Anecdotes of ... Johnson* (1786)

17 I dogmatise and am contradicted, and in this conflict of opinions and sentiments I find delight.
on his conversation in taverns
John Hawkins *Life of Samuel Johnson* (1787) p. 87

18 *Iam moriturus.*
I who am about to die.
to Francesco Sastres, shortly before his death on 13 December 1784, in John Hawkins *Life of Samuel Johnson* (1787); see ANONYMOUS 23:3

19 If the man who turnips cries,
Cry not when his father dies,
'Tis a proof that he had rather
Have a turnip than his father.
burlesque of Lope de Vega's lines 'si a quien los leones vence [He who can conquer a lion ...]', which he said were 'founded on a trivial conceit'
Hester Lynch Piozzi *Anecdotes of ... Johnson* (1786)

20 It is very strange, and very melancholy, that the paucity of human pleasures should persuade us ever to call hunting one of them.
Hester Lynch Piozzi *Anecdotes of ... Johnson* (1786)

21 Love is the wisdom of the fool and the folly of the wise.
William Cooke *Life of Samuel Foote* (1805) vol. 2

22 A man is in general better pleased when he has a good dinner upon his table, than when his wife talks Greek.
John Hawkins (ed.) *The Works of Samuel Johnson* (1787) 'Apophthegms, Sentiments, Opinions, etc.' vol. 11

23 Of music Dr Johnson used to say that it was the only sensual pleasure without vice.
in European Magazine (1795)

24 One day at Streatham ... a young gentleman called to him suddenly, and I suppose he thought disrespectfully, in these words: 'Mr Johnson, would you advise me to marry?' 'I would advise no man to marry, Sir,' returns for answer in a very angry tone Dr Johnson, 'who is not likely to propagate understanding.'
Hester Lynch Piozzi *Anecdotes of ... Johnson* (1786)

25 Was there ever yet anything written by mere man that was wished longer by its readers,

excepting *Don Quixote, Robinson Crusoe*, and the *Pilgrim's Progress*?
Hester Lynch Piozzi *Anecdotes of . . . Johnson* (1786)

1 What is written without effort is in general read without pleasure.
William Seward *Biographia* (1799)

Samuel Johnson 1822–82
American nonconformist minister

2 City of God, how broad and far.
title of hymn (1864)

Tom Johnston 1881–1965
Scottish Labour politician

3 They have barred us by barbed wire fences from the bens and glens: the peasant has been ruthlessly swept aside to make room for the pheasant, and the mountain hare now brings forth her young on the hearthstone of the Gael!
Our Scots Noble Families (1909); see **ROSS** 668:16

Hanns Johst 1890–1978
German dramatist; his play about Albert Schlageter, executed in 1923 for sabotage by French occupying forces, was very popular with the Nazi leadership

4 Whenever I hear the word culture . . . I release the safety-catch of my Browning!
often attributed to Hermann **GOERING**, *and quoted as 'Whenever I hear the word culture, I reach for my pistol!'* *Schlageter* (1933) act 1, sc. 1

Jean de Joinville *c.*1224–1319
French historian, biographer of Louis IX of France

5 Just like the writer who has finished his book and illuminates it with gold and azure, so the king illuminated his kingdom with the beautiful abbeys he made.
The Life of St Louis

Al Jolson (Asa Yoelson) 1886–1950
American singer. See also **LEWIS AND YOUNG** 492:11

6 You think that's noise—you ain't heard nuttin' yet!
in a café, competing with the din from a neighbouring building site, in 1906; subsequently an aside in the 1927 film The Jazz Singer
Martin Abramson *The Real Story of Al Jolson* (1950) (later the title of a Jolson song, 1919, in the form 'You Ain't Heard Nothing Yet')

Henry Arthur Jones 1851–1929 *and* Henry Herman 1832–94
English dramatists

7 O God! Put back Thy universe and give me yesterday.
The Silver King (1907) act 2, sc. 4

John Paul Jones 1747–92
American admiral

8 I have not yet begun to fight.
when asked whether he had lowered his flag, as his ship was sinking, 23 September 1779
Mrs Reginald De Koven *Life and Letters of John Paul Jones* (1914) vol. 1

LeRoi Jones *see* Imamu Amiri Baraka

Mary Harris 'Mother' Jones *c.*1837–1930
Irish-born American labour activist

9 Pray for the dead and fight like hell for the living!
The Autobiography of Mother Jones (1925)

Steve Jones 1944–
English geneticist

10 The Admiralty sent the *Beagle* to South America with Darwin on board not because they were interested in evolution but because they knew that the first step to understanding (and, with luck, controlling) the world was to make a map of it. The same is true of the genes.
The Language of the Genes (1993)

11 Sex and taxes are in many ways the same. Tax does to cash what males do to genes. It dispenses assets among the population as a whole. Sex, not death, is the great leveller.
speech to the Royal Society; in *Independent* 25 January 1997

William Jones 1746–94
English jurist

12 Seven hours to law, to soothing slumber seven, Ten to the world allot, and *all* to Heaven.
lines in substitution for Sir Edward Coke's lines 'Six hours in sleep . . . ', in Lord Teignmouth *Life of Sir W. Jones* (1835) vol. 2; see **COKE** 238:15

Erica Jong 1942–
American novelist

13 The zipless fuck is absolutely pure. It is free of ulterior motives. There is no power game. The man is not 'taking' and the woman is not 'giving' . . . The zipless fuck is the purest thing there is. And it is rarer than the unicorn.
Fear of Flying (1973) ch. 1

14 Jealousy is all the fun you *think* they had.
How to Save Your Own Life (1977)

Ben Jonson *c.*1573–1637
English dramatist and poet. On Jonson: see **DRYDEN** 297:16, **EPITAPHS** 319:5, **MILTON** 539:31; see also **EPITAPHS** 318:2

15   We will eat our mullets, Soused in high-country wines, sup pheasants' eggs,

And have our cockles boiled in silver shells;
Our shrimps to swim again, as when they lived,
In a rare butter made of dolphins' milk,
Whose cream does look like opals.
The Alchemist (1610) act 4, sc. 1

1 Neither do thou lust after that tawney weed
tobacco.
Bartholomew Fair (1614) act 2, sc. 6

2 PEOPLE: The Voice of Cato is the voice of Rome.
CATO: The voice of Rome is the consent of
heaven!
Catiline his Conspiracy (1611) act 3, sc. 1

3 Queen and huntress, chaste and fair,
Now the sun is laid to sleep,
Seated in thy silver chair,
State in wonted manner keep:
Hesperus entreats thy light,
Goddess, excellently bright.
Cynthia's Revels (1600) act 5, sc. 3

4 Still to be neat, still to be drest,
As you were going to a feast;
Still to be powdered, still perfumed,
Lady, it is to be presumed,
Though art's hid causes are not found,
All is not sweet, all is not sound.
Epicene (1609) act 1, sc. 1

5 I do utter as good things every hour, if they
were collected and observed, as either of 'em.
Epicene (1609) act 2, sc. 3

6   Blind Fortune still
Bestows her gifts on such as cannot use them.
Every Man out of His Humour (1599) act 2, sc. 2

7 Detraction is but baseness' varlet;
And apes are apes, though clothed in scarlet.
The Poetaster (1601) act 5, sc. 1; see **PROVERBS** 626:28

8 'Twas only fear first in the world made gods.
Sejanus (1603) act 2, sc. 2

9   I glory
More in the cunning purchase of my wealth
Than in the glad possession.
Volpone (1606) act 1, sc. 1

10 I have been at my book, and am now past the
craggy paths of study, and come to the flowery
plains of honour and reputation.
Volpone (1606) act 2, sc. 1

11 Calumnies are answered best with silence.
Volpone (1606) act 2, sc. 2

12 Suns, that set, may rise again;
But if once we lose this light,
'Tis with us perpetual night.
Volpone (1606) act 3, sc. 5; see **CATULLUS** 210:6

13 Our drink shall be prepared gold and amber;
Which we will take, until my roof whirl around
With the *vertigo*: and my dwarf shall dance.
Volpone (1606) act 3, sc. 5

14 Come, my Celia, let us prove,
While we can, the sports of love.
Volpone (1606) act 3, sc. 5; see **CATULLUS** 210:6

15   Honour! tut, a breath,
There's no such thing in nature; a mere term
Invented to awe fools.
Volpone (1606) act 3, sc. 7

16 You have a gift, sir, (thank your education),
Will never let you want, while there are men,
And malice, to breed causes.
to a lawyer
Volpone (1606) act 5, sc. 1

17 Rest in soft peace, and, asked, say here doth lie
Ben Jonson his best piece of poetry.
'On My First Son' (1616)

18 This figure that thou here seest put,
It was for gentle Shakespeare cut,
Wherein the graver had a strife
With Nature, to out-do the life:
O could he but have drawn his wit
As well in brass, as he has hit
His face; the print would then surpass
All that was ever writ in brass:
But since he cannot, reader, look
Not on his picture, but his book.
on the portrait of **SHAKESPEARE**
First Folio Shakespeare (1623) 'To the Reader'

19 Follow a shadow, it still flies you;
Seem to fly it, it will pursue:
So court a mistress, she denies you;
Let her alone, she will court you.
Say, are not women truly then
Styled but the shadows of us men?
'That Women are but Men's Shadows' (1616)

20 Drink to me only with thine eyes,
And I will pledge with mine;
Or leave a kiss but in the cup,
And I'll not look for wine.
'To Celia' (1616)

21 In small proportions we just beauty see,
And in short measures life may perfect be.
'To the Immortal Memory ... of ... Sir Lucius Carey and Sir
H. Morison' (1640)

22   Soul of the Age!
The applause, delight, the wonder of our stage!
'To the Memory of My Beloved, the Author, Mr William
Shakespeare' (1623)

23   How far thou didst our Lyly
outshine,
Or sporting Kyd, or Marlowe's mighty line.
'To the Memory of ... Shakespeare' (1623)

24 Thou hadst small Latin, and less Greek.
'To the Memory of ... Shakespeare' (1623)

25 He was not of an age, but for all time!
'To the Memory of ... Shakespeare' (1623)

26 Sweet Swan of Avon! What a sight it were
To see thee in our waters yet appear,
And make those flights upon the banks of
Thames
That so did take Eliza, and our James!
'To the Memory of ... Shakespeare' (1623)

27 Thou art not, Penshurst, built to envious show
Of touch or marble, nor canst boast a row

Of polished pillars, or a roof of gold;
Thou hast no lantern whereof tales are told,
Or stair, or courts; but standst an ancient pile,
And these grudged at, art reverenced the while.
'To Penshurst' (1616) l. 1

1 The blushing apricot and woolly peach
Hang on thy walls, that every child may reach.
'To Penshurst' (1616) l. 43

2 Donne, for not keeping of accent, deserved
hanging . . . Shakespeare wanted art.
in *Conversations with William Drummond of Hawthornden*
(written 1619) no. 3

3 The players have often mentioned it as an
honour to Shakespeare that in his writing,
whatsoever he penned, he never blotted out a
line. My answer hath been 'Would he had
blotted a thousand' . . . But he redeemed his
vices with his virtues. There was ever more in
him to be praised than to be pardoned.
Timber, or Discoveries made upon Men and Matter (1641) l. 658
'De Shakespeare Nostrati'; see **HEMING AND CONDELL** 390:17,
POPE 617:24

4 The fear of every man that heard him was, lest
he should make an end.
on Francis **BACON**
Timber, or Discoveries made upon Men and Matter (1641) l. 906
'Dominus Verulamius'

5 Talking and eloquence are not the same: to
speak, and to speak well, are two things.
Timber, or Discoveries made upon Men and Matter (1641) l. 1882
'Praecept[a] Element[aria]'

6 As the multitude call timber-trees, promiscuously
growing, a wood or forest; so am I bold to
entitle these lesser poems, of later growth, by
this of Underwood, out of the analogy they
hold to the Forest in my former book.
The Underwood (1640) 'To the Reader'; see **STEVENSON** 777:3

Janis Joplin 1943–70
American singer

7 Fourteen heart attacks and he had to die in my
week. In MY week.
when ex-President **EISENHOWER***'s death prevented her
photograph appearing on the cover of* Newsweek
in *New Musical Express* 12 April 1969

8 Onstage I make love to twenty-five thousand
people, then I go home alone.
in *New Yorker* 14 August 1971

Thomas Jordan *c.*1612–85
English poet and dramatist

9 They plucked communion tables down
And broke our painted glasses;
They threw our altars to the ground
And tumbled down the crosses.
They set up Cromwell and his heir—
The Lord and Lady Claypole—
Because they hated Common Prayer,
The organ and the maypole.
'How the War began' (1664)

Joseph II 1741–90
Austrian monarch, Holy Roman Emperor

10 Too beautiful for our ears, and much too many
notes, dear Mozart.
of The Abduction from the Seraglio (*1782*)
attributed; Franz Xaver Niemetschek *Life of Mozart* (1798)

Chief Joseph (Hinmaton-Yalaktit)
*c.*1840–1904
Nez Percé chief

11 From where the sun now stands I will fight no
more forever.
speech at the end of the Nez Percé war in 1877; Dee Brown
Bury My Heart at Wounded Knee (1970) ch. 13

12 Good words do not last long unless they
amount to something. Words do not pay for my
dead people.
on a visit to Washington in 1879; Chester Anders Fee *Chief
Joseph* (1936)

Jenny Joseph 1932–
English poet

13 When I am an old woman I shall wear purple
With a red hat which doesn't go, and doesn't
suit me.
And I shall spend my pension on brandy and
summer gloves
And satin sandals, and say we've got no money
for butter.
'Warning' (1974)

Benjamin Jowett 1817–93
**English classicist; Master of Balliol College, Oxford, from
1870. On Jowett: see BEECHING 65:16**

14 The lie in the soul is a true lie.
introduction to his translation (1871) of Plato's *Republic* bk. 2

15 Nowhere probably is there more true feeling,
and nowhere worse taste, than in a churchyard.
Evelyn Abbott and Lewis Campbell (eds.) *Letters of Benjamin
Jowett* (1899) ch. 6

16 One man is as good as another until he has
written a book.
Evelyn Abbott and Lewis Campbell (eds.) *Life and Letters of
Benjamin Jowett* (1897) vol. 1

James Joyce 1882–1941
**Irish novelist and modernist writer. On Joyce: see BECKETT
64:12, FORSTER 337:19, LAWRENCE 484:6, WOOLF 864:13**

17 His soul swooned slowly as he heard the snow
falling faintly through the universe and faintly
falling, like the descent of their last end, upon
all the living and the dead.
Dubliners (1914) 'The Dead'

18 Dear, dirty Dublin.
Dubliners (1914) 'A Little Cloud'

1 riverrun, past Eve and Adam's, from swerve of shore to bend of bay, brings us by a commodious vicus of recirculation back to Howth Castle and Environs.
Finnegans Wake (1939) pt. 1, opening words

2 That ideal reader suffering from an ideal insomnia.
Finnegans Wake (1939) pt. 1

3 All moanday, tearsday, wailsday, thumpsday, frightday, shatterday till the fear of the Law.
Finnegans Wake (1939) pt. 2

4 Three quarks for Muster Mark!
Finnegans Wake (1939) pt. 2

5 A portrait of the artist as a young man.
title of book (1916)

6 Once upon a time and a very good time it was there was a moocow coming down along the road and this moocow that was down along the road met a nicens little boy named baby tuckoo.
A Portrait of the Artist as a Young Man (1916) ch. 1, opening words

7 Poor Parnell! he cried loudly. My dead king!
A Portrait of the Artist as a Young Man (1916) ch. 1

8 When the soul of a man is born in this country, there are nets flung at it to hold it back from flight. You talk to me of nationality, language, religion. I shall try to fly by those nets.
A Portrait of the Artist as a Young Man (1916) ch. 5

9 Ireland is the old sow that eats her farrow.
A Portrait of the Artist as a Young Man (1916) ch. 5

10 The artist, like the God of the creation, remains within or behind or beyond or above his handiwork, invisible, refined out of existence, indifferent, paring his fingernails.
A Portrait of the Artist as a Young Man (1916) ch. 5

11 The only arms I allow myself to use, silence, exile, and cunning.
A Portrait of the Artist as a Young Man (1916) ch. 5

12 By an epiphany he meant a sudden spiritual manifestation, whether in vulgarity of speech or of gesture or in a memorable phase of the mind itself. He believed that it was for the man of letters to recover these epiphanies with extreme care, seeing that they themselves are the most delicate and evanescent of moments.
Stephen Hero (1944) ch. 25 (part of a first draft of *A Portrait of the Artist as a Young Man*)

13 Stately, plump Buck Mulligan came from the stairhead, bearing a bowl of lather on which a mirror and a razor lay crossed.
Ulysses (1922)

14 The snotgreen sea. The scrotumtightening sea.
Ulysses (1922)

15 It is a symbol of Irish art. The cracked lookingglass of a servant.
Ulysses (1922)

16 I fear those big words, Stephen said, which make us so unhappy.
Ulysses (1922)

17 History, Stephen said, is a nightmare from which I am trying to awake.
Ulysses (1922)

18 Mr Leopold Bloom ate with relish the inner organs of beasts and fowls. He liked thick giblet soup, nutty gizzards, a stuffed roast heart, liverslices fried with crustcrumbs, fried hencod's roes. Most of all he liked grilled mutton kidneys which gave to his palate a fine tang of faintly scented urine.
Ulysses (1922)

19 He . . . saw the dark tangled curls of his bush floating, floating hair of the stream around the limp father of thousands, a languid floating flower.
Ulysses (1922)

20 Come forth, Lazarus! And he came fifth and lost the job.
Ulysses (1922)

21 Plenty to see and hear and feel yet. Feel live warm beings near you. They aren't going to get me this innings. Warm beds: warm full blooded life.
Ulysses (1922)

22 Greater love than this, he said, no man hath that a man lay down his wife for his friend. Go thou and do likewise. Thus, or words to that effect, saith Zarathustra, sometime regius professor of French letters to the university of Oxtail.
Ulysses (1922); see **BIBLE** 108:18

23 The heaventree of stars hung with humid nightblue fruit.
Ulysses (1922)

24 O, father forsaken,
Forgive your son!
'Ecce Puer'

25 Writing in English is the most ingenious torture ever devised for sins committed in previous lives. The English reading public explains the reason why.
letter, 5 September 1918; Richard Ellmann (ed.) *Selected Letters of James Joyce* (1975)

William Joyce (Lord Haw-Haw) 1906–46
American-born wartime broadcaster from Nazi Germany, executed for treason

26 Germany calling! Germany calling!
habitual introduction to propaganda broadcasts to Britain during the Second World War

Juan Carlos I 1938–
Spanish monarch, King from 1975

27 I will neither abdicate the Crown nor leave Spain. Whoever rebels will provoke a new civil war and will be responsible.
on the occasion of the attempted coup in 1981
television broadcast at 1.15 a.m., 24 February 1981

Judah ben Samuel the Hasid d. 1217

Jewish mystic

1 In thy intercourse with non-Jews, be careful to be as wholly sincere as in that with Jews. In most places, Jews are not unlike Christians in their morals and usages.
Sefer Hasidim

2 There are three [sorts of people] for whom we should sternly close our hearts: a cruel person who commits vile things; the fool who rushes into ruin in spite of warning; and the ingrate. Ingratitude is the blackest of faults.
Sefer Hasidim

3 Sweet hymns shall be my chant and woven songs.
For Thou art all for which my spirit longs—
To be within the shadow of Thy hand
And all Thy mystery to understand.
The while Thy glory is upon my tongue,
My inmost heart with love of Thee is wrung.
'Hymn of Glory'

Jack Judge 1878–1938 *and* Harry Williams 1874–1924

British songwriters

4 It's a long way to Tipperary,
It's a long way to go;
It's a long way to Tipperary,
To the sweetest girl I know!
Goodbye, Piccadilly,
Farewell, Leicester Square,
It's a long, long way to Tipperary,
But my heart's right there!
'It's a Long Way to Tipperary' (1912 song)

Julian of Norwich 1343–after 1416

English mystic and anchorite

5 He showed me something small, no bigger than a hazelnut, lying in the palm of my hand, as it seemed to me, and it was as round as a ball. I looked at it with the eye of my understanding, and thought: What can this be? I was amazed that it could last, for I thought that because of its littleness it would suddenly have fallen into nothing. And I was answered in my understanding: It lasts and always will, because God loves it; and thus every thing has being through the love of God.
Revelations of Divine Love (the long text) ch. 5

6 Sin is behovely, but all shall be well and all shall be well and all manner of thing shall be well.
behovely = *expedient, necessary*
Revelations of Divine Love (the long text) ch. 27, Revelation 13; see **ELIOT** 309:22

7 Wouldest thou wit thy Lord's meaning in this thing? Wit it well: Love was his meaning. Who shewed it thee? Love. What shewed He thee? Love. Wherefore shewed it He? for Love . . .

Thus was I learned that Love is our Lord's meaning.
Revelations of Divine Love (the long text) ch. 86, Revelation 16

8 The Holy Ghost moveth ne'er a thing against charity, for if He did, He would be contrary to His own self for He is all charity.
Margery Kempe *The Book of Margery Kempe* (1436) bk. 1, ch. 18

Julian the Apostate *c.*AD 332–363

Roman emperor from AD 360

9 *Vicisti, Galilaee.*
You have won, Galilean.
supposed dying words; a late embellishment of Theodoret *Ecclesiastical History* (AD *c.*450) bk. 3, ch. 25; see **SWINBURNE** 785:19

Carl Gustav Jung 1875–1961

Swiss psychologist

10 A more or less superficial layer of the unconscious is undoubtedly personal. I call it the *personal unconscious*. But this personal unconscious rests upon a deeper layer, which does not derive from personal experience and is not a personal acquisition but is inborn. This deeper layer I call the *collective unconscious* . . . The contents of the personal unconscious are chiefly the *feeling-toned complexes* . . . The contents of the collective unconscious, on the other hand, are known as *archetypes*.
Eranos Jahrbuch (1934)

11 A man who has not passed through the inferno of his passions has never overcome them.
Memories, Dreams, Reflections (1962) ch. 9

12 As far as we can discern, the sole purpose of human existence is to kindle a light in the darkness of mere being.
Memories, Dreams, Reflections (1962) ch. 11

13 Every form of addiction is bad, no matter whether the narcotic be alcohol or morphine or idealism.
Memories, Dreams, Reflections (1962) ch. 12

14 The meeting of two personalities is like the contact of two chemical substances: if there is any reaction, both are transformed.
Modern Man in Search of a Soul (1933)

15 The afternoon of human life must also have a significance of its own and cannot be merely a pitiful appendage to life's morning.
The Stages of Life (1930)

16 Man needs difficulties; they are necessary for health.
'The Transcendent Function' (1916) para. 143, in *The Structure and Dynamics of the Psyche* (1960)

17 If there is anything that we wish to change in the child, we should first examine it and see whether it is not something that could better be changed in ourselves.
'Vom Werden der Persönlichkeit' (1932)

Jung Chang 1952–

Chinese writer

1 At the age of fifteen my grandmother became the concubine of a warlord general.
Wild Swans (1991), opening words

'Junius'

English 18th-century pseudonymous writer

2 The liberty of the press is the *Palladium* of all the civil, political, and religious rights of an Englishman.
The Letters of Junius (1772 ed.) 'Dedication to the English Nation'

3 There is a holy mistaken zeal in politics as well as in religion. By persuading others, we convince ourselves.
in *Public Advertiser* 19 December 1769, letter 35

4 As for Mr Wedderburne, there is something about him, which even treachery cannot trust.
in *Public Advertiser* 22 June 1771, letter 49

John Junor 1919–97

Scottish journalist. See also **CATCHPHRASES** 208:23

5 Such a graceful exit. And then he had to go and do this on the doorstep.
on Harold **WILSON**'s 'Lavender List' (*the honours list he drew up on resigning the British premiership in 1976*)
in *Observer* 23 January 1990

Donald Justice 1925–2004

American poet

6 Men at forty
Learn to close softly
The doors to rooms they will not be
Coming back to.
'Men at Forty' (1967)

Justinian AD 483–565

Roman emperor from AD 527

7 Justice is the constant and perpetual wish to render to every one his due.
Institutes bk. 1, ch. 1, para. 1

8 Solomon, I have vanquished thee.
at the dedication of Hagia Sophia in Constantinople, 27 December AD 537
attributed (according to a late tradition)

Claude Jutra 1930–86

Canadian film director

9 I can face death, but I cannot face watching myself disappear from within . . . I don't know who I am anymore.
from a conversation with the founder of The Right to Die Society about his Alzheimer's disease, a few months before his suicide
in *Homemaker's Magazine* November–December 1991

Juvenal c.AD 60–c.130

Roman satirist

10 *Semper ego auditor tantum?*
Must I always be a mere listener?
Satires no. 1, l. 1

11 *Difficile est saturam non scribere.*
It's hard not to write satire.
Satires no. 1, l. 30

12 *Probitas laudatur et alget.*
Honesty is praised and left to shiver.
Satires no. 1, l. 74 (translation by G. G. Ramsay)

13 *Si natura negat, facit indignatio versum.*
Even if nature says no, indignation makes me write verse.
Satires no. 1, l. 79

14 *Quidquid agunt homines, votum timor ira voluptas Gaudia discursus nostri farrago libelli est.*
Everything mankind does, their hope, fear, rage, pleasure, joys, business, are the hotch-potch of my little book.
Satires no. 1, l. 85

15 *Quis tulerit Gracchos de seditione querentes?*
Who would put up with the Gracchi complaining about subversion?
Satires no. 2, l. 24

16 *Dat veniam corvis, vexat censura columbis.*
Our censor's rule condemns the doves while acquitting the ravens.
Satires no. 2, l. 63 (translated by Niall Rudd)

17 *Nemo repente fuit turpissimus.*
No one ever suddenly became depraved.
Satires no. 2, l. 83

18 *Iam pridem Syrus in Tiberim defluxit Orontes Et linguam et mores.*
The Syrian Orontes has now for long been pouring into the Tiber, with its own language and ways of behaving.
Satires no. 3, l. 62

19 *Grammaticus, rhetor, geometres, pictor, aliptes, Augur, schoenobates, medicus, magus, omnia novit Graeculus esuriens: in caelum iusseris ibit.*
Scholar, public speaker, geometrician, painter, physical training instructor, diviner of the future, rope-dancer, doctor, magician, the hungry little Greek can do everything: send him to—heaven (and he'll go there).
Satires no. 3, l. 76

20 *Nil habet infelix paupertas durius in se Quam quod ridiculos homines facit.*
The misfortunes of poverty carry with them nothing harder to bear than that it makes men ridiculous.
Satires no. 3, l. 152

21 *Haud facile emergunt quorum virtutibus obstat Res angusta domi.*

They do not easily rise out of obscurity whose talents straitened circumstances obstruct at home.
Satires no. 3, l. 164

1 . . . *Omnia Romae*
Cum pretio.

Everything in Rome has its price.
Satires no. 3, l. 183

2 *Rara avis in terris nigroque simillima cycno.*

A rare bird on this earth, like nothing so much as a black swan.
Satires no. 6, l. 165

3 *Hoc volo, sic iubeo, sit pro ratione voluntas.*

I will have this done, so I order it done; let my will replace reasoned judgement.
Satires no. 6, l. 223

4 *Nulla fere causa est, in qua non femina litem moverit.*

There's hardly a case that comes to court that is not inspired by a woman.
Satires no. 6, l. 242 (translated by Niall Rudd)

5 *'Pone seram, cohibe.' Sed quis custodiet ipsos Custodes? Cauta est et ab illis incipit uxor.*

'Bolt her in, keep her indoors.' But who is to guard the guards themselves? Your wife is prudent and begins with them.
Satires no. 6, l. 347

6 *Tenet insanabile multos Scribendi cacoethes et aegro in corde senescit.*

Many suffer from the incurable disease of writing, and it becomes chronic in their sick minds.
Satires no. 7, l. 51

7 *Occidit miseros crambe repetita magistros.*

Re-hashed cabbage wore out the wretched teachers.
Satires no. 7, l. 154

8 *Qui praeceptorem sancti volvere parentis Esse loco.*

They thought that the teacher should have the role of a revered parent.
Satires no. 7, l. 209

9 *Nobilitas sola est atque unica virtus.*

Virtue is the one and only nobility.
Satires no, 8, l. 20

10 *Summum crede nefas animam praeferre pudori Et propter vitam vivendi perdere causas.*

Count it the greatest sin to prefer mere existence to honour, and for the sake of life to lose the reasons for living.
Satires no. 8, l. 83

11 *Cantabit vacuus coram latrone viator.*

Travel light and you can sing in the robber's face.
Satires no. 10, l. 22

12 . . . *Verbosa et grandis epistula venit A Capreis.*

A huge wordy letter came from Capri.
on the Emperor **TIBERIUS**'s letter to the Senate, which caused the downfall of Sejanus in AD 31
Satires no. 10, l. 71

13 . . . *Duas tantum res anxius optat, Panem et circenses.*

Only two things does he [the modern citizen] anxiously wish for—bread and circuses.
Satires no. 10, l. 80

14 *Expende Hannibalem: quot libras in duce summo Invenies?*

Weigh Hannibal: how many pounds will you find in that great general?
Satires no. 10, l. 147

15 . . . *I, demens, et saevas curre per Alpes Ut pueris placeas et declamatio fias.*

Off you go, madman, and hurry across the horrible Alps, duly to delight schoolboys and become a subject for practising speech-making.
on Hannibal
Satires no. 10, l. 166

16 *Mors sola fatetur Quantula sint hominum corpuscula.*

Death alone reveals how small are men's poor bodies.
on Hannibal
Satires no. 10, l. 172

17 *Orandum est ut sit mens sana in corpore sano.*

One should pray for a sound mind in a sound body.
Satires no. 10, l. 356

18 *Voluptates commendat rarior usus.*

The less we indulge our pleasures the more we enjoy them.
Satires no. 11, l. 208 (translated by Niall Rudd)

19 . . . *Prima est haec ultio, quod se Iudice nemo nocens absolvitur.*

This is the first of punishments, that no guilty man is acquitted if judged by himself.
Satires no. 13, l. 2

20 *Quippe minuti Semper et infirmi est animi exiguique voluptas Ultio.*

Indeed, revenge is always the pleasure of a paltry, feeble, tiny mind.
Satires no. 13, l. 189

21 *Maxima debetur puero reverentia, siquid Turpe paras, nec tu pueri contempseris annos.*

A child is owed the greatest respect; if you ever have something disgraceful in mind, don't ignore your son's tender years.
Satires no. 14, l. 47

Kk

Pauline Kael 1919–2001
American film critic

1 The words 'Kiss Kiss Bang Bang' which I saw on an Italian movie poster, are perhaps the briefest statement imaginable of the basic appeal of movies.
    Kiss Kiss Bang Bang (1968) 'Note on the Title'

Franz Kafka 1883–1924
Czech novelist, who wrote in German

2 There are two cardinal human sins from which all others derive: impatience and indolence. Perhaps there is only one cardinal sin: impatience. Because of impatience we were driven out of Paradise; because of impatience we cannot return.
    Collected Aphorisms no. 3, in *Shorter Works* vol. 1 (1973)

3 When Gregor Samsa awoke one morning from uneasy dreams he found himself transformed in his bed into a gigantic insect.
    The Metamorphosis (1915) ch. 1, opening words; see **AUSTIN** 43:9

4 Was he an animal, that music could capture him so completely? It seemed to him that he was being shown the way to the longed for, unknown, nourishment.
    The Metamorphosis (1915) ch. 3

5 Someone must have traduced Joseph K., for without having done anything wrong he was arrested one fine morning.
    The Trial (1925) ch. 1

6 You may object that it is not a trial at all; you are quite right, for it is only a trial if I recognize it as such.
    The Trial (1925) ch. 2

7 It's often better to be in chains than to be free.
    The Trial (1925) ch. 8

8 'It is not necessary to accept everything as true, we must only accept it as necessary.'
    'A melancholy conclusion . . . It turns lying into a universal principle.'
    The Trial (1925) ch. 9

9 A book must be the axe for the frozen sea within us.
    letter, 27 January 1904

10 I think you should only read those books which bite and sting you.
    letter to Oskar Pollack, 27 June 1904

11 Don't despair, not even over the fact that you don't despair.
    diary, 21 July 1913, in Max Brod (ed.) *The Diaries of Franz Kafka* (1948)

Frida Kahlo 1907–54
Mexican painter

12 I paint my own reality.
    Hayden Herrera *Frida* (1983)

13 Feet, why do I need them if I have wings to fly?
    after the amputation of her right leg due to gangrene
    diary entry, 1953; Martha Zamora *Frida Kahlo: the Brush of Anguish* (1990)

14 I hope for a happy exit and I hope never to come back.
    last diary entry; Martha Zamora *Frida Kahlo: the Brush of Anguish* (1990)

Gus Kahn 1886–1941 *and* Raymond B. Egan 1890–1952
American songwriters

15 There's nothing surer,
    The rich get rich and the poor get children.
    In the meantime, in between time,
    Ain't we got fun.
    'Ain't We Got Fun' (1921 song)

Kamo no Chomei 1155–1216
Japanese poet

16 Ceaselessly the river flows, and yet the water is never the same, while in the still pools the shifting foam gathers and is gone, never staying for a moment. Even so is man and his habitation.
    Hojoki [The Ten Foot Square Hut] translated by A. L. Sadler

Immanuel Kant 1724–1804
German philosopher

17 Two things fill the mind with ever new and increasing wonder and awe, the more often and the more seriously reflection concentrates upon them: the starry heaven above me and the moral law within me.
    Critique of Practical Reason (1788)

18 Nothing in the world—indeed nothing even beyond the world—can possibly be conceived which could be called good without qualification except a *good will*.
    Foundation of the Metaphysics of Morals (1785) sect. 1

19 I am never to act otherwise than so that I could also will that my maxim should become a universal law.
    Fundamental Principles of the Metaphysics of Ethics (1785) sect. 1 (translated by T. K. Abbott)

20 There is an imperative which commands a certain conduct immediately, without having as its condition any other purpose to be attained by it. This imperative is Categorical . . . This imperative may be called that of Morality.
    Fundamental Principles of the Metaphysics of Ethics (1785) sect. 2 (translated by T. K. Abbott)

1 Whoever wills the end, wills also (so far as reason decides his conduct) the means in his power which are indispensably necessary thereto.
Fundamental Principles of the Metaphysics of Ethics (1785) sect. 2 (translated by T. K. Abbott)

2 Happiness is not an ideal of reason but of imagination.
Fundamental Principles of the Metaphysics of Ethics (1785) sect. 2 (translated by T. K. Abbott)

3 So act as to treat humanity, whether in thine own person or in that of any other, in every case as an end withal, never as means only.
Fundamental Principles of the Metaphysics of Ethics (1785) sect. 2 (translated by T. K. Abbott)

4 Out of the crooked timber of humanity no straight thing can ever be made.
Idee zu einer allgemeinen Geschichte in weltbürgerlicher Absicht (1784) proposition 6

5 Dare to know! Have the courage to use your own reason! This is the motto of the Enlightenment.
What is Enlightenment? (1784)

Donna Karan 1948–
American fashion designer and businesswoman

6 Sometimes fashion moves from the moment to the moment to the moment. But where is the integrity in design?
in *Detroit News* February 2000

Alphonse Karr 1808–90
French novelist and journalist

7 *Si l'on veut abolir la peine de mort en ce cas, que MM les assassins commencent.*
In that case, if we are to abolish the death penalty, let the murderers take the first step.
Les Guêpes January 1849 (6th series, 1859)

8 *Plus ça change, plus c'est la même chose.*
The more things change, the more they are the same.
Les Guêpes January 1849 (6th series, 1859)

George S. Kaufman 1889–1961
American dramatist

9 Satire is what closes Saturday night.
Scott Meredith *George S. Kaufman and his Friends* (1974) ch. 6

Gerald Kaufman 1930–
British Labour politician

10 The longest suicide note in history.
on the Labour Party manifesto New Hope for Britain (1983)
Denis Healey *The Time of My Life* (1989) ch. 23

Paul Kaufman *and* Mike Anthony
American songwriters

11 Poetry in motion.
title of song (1960); see **GRAHAME** 368:2

Christoph Kaufmann 1753–95
German man of letters

12 *Sturm und Drang.*
Storm and stress.
title suggested by Kaufmann for a romantic drama of the American War of Independence by the German dramatist, F. M. Klinger (1775), and thereafter given to a period of literary ferment which prevailed in Germany during the latter part of the 18th century

Kenneth Kaunda 1924–
Zambian statesman, President 1964–91

13 Westerners have aggressive problem-solving minds; Africans experience people.
attributed, 1990

Patrick Kavanagh 1904–67
Irish poet

14 Clay is the word and clay is the flesh
Where the potato-gatherers like mechanized scarecrows move
Along the side-fall of the hill—Maguire and his men.
'The Great Hunger' (1947)

15   The weak, washy way of true tragedy—
A sick horse nosing around the meadow for a clean place to die.
'The Great Hunger' (1947)

16 I hate what every poet hates in spite
Of all the solemn talk of contemplation.
Oh, Alexander Selkirk knew the plight
Of being king and government and nation.
A road, a mile of kingdom, I am king
Of banks and stones and every blooming thing.
'Inniskeen Road: July Evening' (1936); see **COWPER** 257:4

Alan Kay 1940–
American computer scientist

17 The best way to predict the future is to invent it.
in 1971, at the Palo Alto Research Center

Danny Kaye *see* **Film lines** 329:15

Paul Keating 1944–
Australian Labor statesman, Prime Minister 1991–6

18 Even as it [Great Britain] walked out on you and joined the Common Market, you were still looking for your MBEs and your knighthoods, and all the rest of the regalia that comes with it. You would take Australia right back down the time tunnel to the cultural cringe where you have always come from.
addressing Australian Conservative supporters of Great Britain
speech, House of Representatives (Australia) 27 February 1992; see **PHILLIPS** 606:5

John Keats 1795–1821

English poet. On Keats: see **BULWER-LYTTON** 170:12, **BYRON** 189:14, **BYRON** 192:10, **LOCKHART** 498:2, **YEATS** 873:10; see also **EPITAPHS** 318:5

1 Bright star, would I were steadfast as thou art.
   first line of sonnet (written 1819)

2 The imagination of a boy is healthy, and the mature imagination of a man is healthy; but there is a space of life between, in which the soul is in a ferment, the character undecided, the way of life uncertain, the ambition thick-sighted: thence proceeds mawkishness.
   Endymion (1818) preface

3 A thing of beauty is a joy for ever.
   Endymion (1818) bk. 1, l. 1; see **ROWLAND** 671:10

4 St Agnes' Eve—Ah, bitter chill it was!
   The owl, for all his feathers, was a-cold;
   The hare limped trembling through the frozen grass,
   And silent was the flock in woolly fold.
   'The Eve of St Agnes' (1820) st. 1

5 The sculptured dead, on each side, seem to freeze,
   Emprisoned in black, purgatorial rails.
   'The Eve of St Agnes' (1820) st. 2

6 The silver, snarling trumpets 'gan to chide.
   'The Eve of St Agnes' (1820) st. 4

7 And soft adorings from their loves receive
   Upon the honeyed middle of the night.
   'The Eve of St Agnes' (1820) st. 6

8 Out went the taper as she hurried in;
   Its little smoke, in pallid moonshine, died.
   'The Eve of St Agnes' (1820) st. 23

9 A casement high and triple-arched there was,
   All garlanded with carven imag'ries
   Of fruits, and flowers, and bunches of knot-grass,
   And diamonded with panes of quaint device,
   Innumerable of stains and splendid dyes,
   As are the tiger-moth's deep-damasked wings.
   'The Eve of St Agnes' (1820) st. 24

10   By degrees
   Her rich attire creeps rustling to her knees.
   'The Eve of St Agnes' (1820) st. 26

11 Trembling in her soft and chilly nest.
   'The Eve of St Agnes' (1820) st. 27

12 As though a rose should shut, and be a bud again.
   'The Eve of St Agnes' (1820) st. 27

13 And still she slept an azure-lidded sleep,
   In blanchèd linen, smooth, and lavendered,
   While he from forth the closet brought a heap
   Of candied apple, quince, and plum, and gourd;
   With jellies soother than the creamy curd,
   And lucent syrops, tinct with cinnamon;
   Manna and dates, in argosy transferred
   From Fez; and spiced dainties, every one,
   From silken Samarcand to cedared Lebanon.
   'The Eve of St Agnes' (1820) st. 30

14 He played an ancient ditty, long since mute,
   In Provence called, 'La belle dame sans mercy.'
   'The Eve of St Agnes' (1820) st. 33; see also **KEATS** 455:9

15 And they are gone: aye, ages long ago
   These lovers fled away into the storm.
   'The Eve of St Agnes' (1820) st. 42

16 Fanatics have their dreams, wherewith they weave
   A paradise for a sect.
   'The Fall of Hyperion' (written 1819) l. 1

17 The poet and the dreamer are distinct,
   Diverse, sheer opposite, antipodes.
   The one pours out a balm upon the world,
   The other vexes it.
   'The Fall of Hyperion' (written 1819) l. 199

18 Ever let the fancy roam,
   Pleasure never is at home.
   'Fancy' (1820) l. 1

19 O sweet Fancy! let her loose;
   Summer's joys are spoilt by use.
   'Fancy' (1820) l. 9

20 Deep in the shady sadness of a vale
   Far sunken from the healthy breath of morn,
   Far from the fiery noon, and eve's one star,
   Sat grey-haired Saturn, quiet as a stone.
   'Hyperion: A Fragment' (1820) bk. 1, l. 1

21   No stir of air was there,
   Not so much life as on a summer's day
   Robs not one light seed from the feathered grass,
   But where the dead leaf fell, there did it rest.
   'Hyperion: A Fragment' (1820) bk. 1, l. 7

22 That large utterance of the early gods!
   'Hyperion: A Fragment' (1820) bk. 1, l. 51

23 As when, upon a trancèd summer-night,
   Those green-robed senators of mighty woods,
   Tall oaks, branch-charmèd by the earnest stars,
   Dream, and so dream all night without a stir.
   'Hyperion: A Fragment' (1820) bk. 1, l. 72

24 And still they were the same bright, patient stars.
   'Hyperion: A Fragment' (1820) bk. 1, l. 353

25 Knowledge enormous makes a god of me.
   'Hyperion: A Fragment' (1820) bk. 3, l. 113

26 I had a dove and the sweet dove died;
   And I have thought it died of grieving:
   O, what could it grieve for? Its feet were tied,
   With a silken thread of my own hand's weaving.
   'I had a dove and the sweet dove died' (written 1818)

27 So the two brothers and their murdered man
   Rode past fair Florence.
   'Isabella; or, The Pot of Basil' (1820) st. 27

28 And she forgot the stars, the moon, and sun,
   And she forgot the blue above the trees,
   And she forgot the dells where waters run,

And she forgot the chilly autumn breeze;
She had no knowledge when the day was done,
And the new morn she saw not: but in peace
Hung over her sweet Basil evermore,
And moistened it with tears unto the core.
'Isabella; or, The Pot of Basil' (1820) st. 53

1   'For cruel 'tis,' said she,
'To steal my Basil-pot away from me.'
'Isabella; or, The Pot of Basil' (1820) st. 62

2   And then there crept
A little noiseless noise among the leaves,
Born of the very sigh that silence heaves.
'I stood tip-toe upon a little hill' (1817) l. 10

3 Here are sweet peas, on tip-toe for a flight.
'I stood tip-toe upon a little hill' (1817) l. 57

4 Oh, what can ail thee knight at arms
Alone and palely loitering?
The sedge has withered from the lake
And no birds sing!
'La belle dame sans merci' (1820) st. 1

5 I see a lily on thy brow
With anguish moist and fever dew,
And on thy cheeks a fading rose
Fast withereth too.
'La belle dame sans merci' (1820) st. 3

6 I met a lady in the meads
Full beautiful, a faery's child
Her hair was long, her foot was light
And her eyes were wild.
'La belle dame sans merci' (1820) st. 4

7 She looked at me as she did love
And made sweet moan.
'La belle dame sans merci' (1820) st. 5

8 I set her on my pacing steed
And nothing else saw all day long
For sidelong would she bend and sing
A faery's song.
'La belle dame sans merci' (1820) st. 6

9 . . . La belle dame sans merci
Thee hath in thrall.
'La belle dame sans merci' (1820) st. 10; see also **KEATS** 454:14

10 I saw their starved lips in the gloam
With horrid warning gapèd wide
And I awoke and found me here
On the cold hill's side.
'La belle dame sans merci' (1820) st. 11

11 She was a gordian shape of dazzling hue,
Vermilion-spotted, golden, green, and blue;
Striped like a zebra, freckled like a pard,
Eyed like a peacock, and all crimson barred.
'Lamia' (1820) pt. 1, l. 47

12 Love in a hut, with water and a crust,
Is—Love, forgive us!—cinders, ashes, dust;
Love in a palace is perhaps at last
More grievous torment than a hermit's fast.
'Lamia' (1820) pt. 2, l. 1; see **COLMAN AND GARRICK** 244:1

13   Do not all charms fly
At the mere touch of cold philosophy?
'Lamia' (1820) pt. 2, l. 229

14 Philosophy will clip an Angel's wings,
Conquer all mysteries by rule and line,
Empty the haunted air, and gnomèd mine—
Unweave a rainbow.
'Lamia' (1820) pt. 2, l. 234

15 Souls of poets dead and gone,
What Elysium have ye known,
Happy field or mossy cavern,
Choicer than the Mermaid Tavern?
Have ye tippled drink more fine
Than mine host's Canary wine?
'Lines on the Mermaid Tavern' (1820)

16 Thou still unravished bride of quietness,
Thou foster-child of silence and slow time.
'Ode on a Grecian Urn' (1820) st. 1

17 What men or gods are these? What maidens loth?
What mad pursuit? What struggle to escape?
What pipes and timbrels? What wild ecstasy?
'Ode on a Grecian Urn' (1820) st. 1

18 Heard melodies are sweet, but those unheard
Are sweeter.
'Ode on a Grecian Urn' (1820) st. 2

19 For ever wilt thou love, and she be fair!
'Ode on a Grecian Urn' (1820) st. 2

20 For ever piping songs for ever new.
'Ode on a Grecian Urn' (1820) st. 3

21 For ever warm and still to be enjoyed,
For ever panting, and for ever young;
All breathing human passion far above,
That leaves a heart high-sorrowful and cloyed,
A burning forehead, and a parching tongue.
'Ode on a Grecian Urn' (1820) st. 3

22 Who are these coming to the sacrifice?
To what green altar, O mysterious priest,
Lead'st thou that heifer lowing at the skies?
'Ode on a Grecian Urn' (1820) st. 4

23 O Attic shape! Fair attitude!
'Ode on a Grecian Urn' (1820) st. 5

24 Thou, silent form, dost tease us out of thought
As doth eternity: Cold Pastoral!
'Ode on a Grecian Urn' (1820) st. 5

25 'Beauty is truth, truth beauty,'—that is all
Ye know on earth, and all ye need to know.
'Ode on a Grecian Urn' (1820) st. 5

26 No, no, go not to Lethe, neither twist
Wolf's-bane, tight-rooted, for its poisonous wine.
'Ode on Melancholy' (1820) st. 1

27 Nor let the beetle, nor the death-moth be
Your mournful Psyche.
'Ode on Melancholy' (1820) st. 1

28 But when the melancholy fit shall fall
Sudden from heaven like a weeping cloud,
That fosters the droop-headed flowers all,

And hides the green hill in an April shroud;
Then glut thy sorrow on a morning rose,
Or on the rainbow of the salt sand-wave,
Or on the wealth of globèd peonies.
'Ode on Melancholy' (1820) st. 2

1 She dwells with Beauty—Beauty that must die;
And Joy, whose hand is ever at his lips
Bidding adieu; and aching Pleasure nigh,
Turning to poison while the bee-mouth sips:
Ay, in the very temple of Delight
Veiled Melancholy has her sovran shrine,
Though seen of none save him whose strenuous
tongue
Can burst Joy's grape against his palate fine;
His soul shall taste the sadness of her might,
And be among her cloudy trophies hung.
'Ode on Melancholy' (1820) st. 3

2 My heart aches, and a drowsy numbness pains
My sense, as though of hemlock I had drunk,
Or emptied some dull opiate to the drains
One minute past, and Lethe-wards had sunk.
'Ode to a Nightingale' (1820) st. 1

3 O, for a draught of vintage! that hath been
Cooled a long age in the deep-delvèd earth,
Tasting of Flora and the country green.
'Ode to a Nightingale' (1820) st. 2

4 O for a beaker full of the warm South,
Full of the true, the blushful Hippocrene,
With beaded bubbles winking at the brim,
And purple-stainèd mouth;
That I might drink, and leave the world unseen,
And with thee fade away into the forest dim.
'Ode to a Nightingale' (1820) st. 2

5 Fade far away, dissolve, and quite forget
What thou among the leaves hast never known,
The weariness, the fever, and the fret.
'Ode to a Nightingale' (1820) st. 3

6 Where youth grows pale, and spectre-thin, and
dies.
'Ode to a Nightingale' (1820) st. 3

7 Away! away! for I will fly to thee,
Not charioted by Bacchus and his pards,
But on the viewless wings of Poesy,
Though the dull brain perplexes and retards:
Already with thee! tender is the night.
'Ode to a Nightingale' (1820) st. 4

8 Fast fading violets covered up in leaves;
And mid-May's eldest child,
The coming musk-rose, full of dewy wine,
The murmurous haunt of flies on summer eves.
'Ode to a Nightingale' (1820) st. 5

9 Darkling I listen; and, for many a time
I have been half in love with easeful Death,
Called him soft names in many a musèd rhyme,
To take into the air my quiet breath;
Now more than ever seems it rich to die,
To cease upon the midnight with no pain.
'Ode to a Nightingale' (1820) st. 6

10 Thou wast not born for death, immortal bird!
No hungry generations tread thee down;

The voice I hear this passing night was heard
In ancient days by emperor and clown:
Perhaps the self-same song that found a path
Through the sad heart of Ruth, when, sick for
home,
She stood in tears amid the alien corn;
The same that oft-times hath
Charmed magic casements, opening on the foam
Of perilous seas, in faery lands forlorn.
'Ode to a Nightingale' (1820) st. 7

11 Forlorn! the very word is like a bell
To toll me back from thee to my sole self!
Adieu! the fancy cannot cheat so well
As she is famed to do, deceiving elf.
'Ode to a Nightingale' (1820) st. 8

12 Was it a vision, or a waking dream?
Fled is that music:—do I wake or sleep?
'Ode to a Nightingale' (1820) st. 8

13 'Mid hushed, cool-rooted flowers, fragrant-eyed,
Blue, silver-white, and budded Tyrian.
'Ode to Psyche' (1820) st. 1

14 Much have I travelled in the realms of gold,
And many goodly states and kingdoms seen.
'On First Looking into Chapman's Homer' (1817)

15 Then felt I like some watcher of the skies
When a new planet swims into his ken;
Or like stout Cortez when with eagle eyes
He stared at the Pacific—and all his men
Looked at each other with a wild surmise—
Silent, upon a peak in Darien.
'On First Looking into Chapman's Homer' (1817)

16 Mortality
Weighs heavily on me like unwilling sleep.
'On Seeing the Elgin Marbles' (1817)

17 The poetry of earth is never dead:
When all the birds are faint with the hot sun,
And hide in cooling trees, a voice will run
From hedge to hedge about the new-mown
mead.
'On the Grasshopper and Cricket' (1817)

18 O for ten years, that I may overwhelm
Myself in poesy; so I may do the deed
That my own soul has to itself decreed.
'Sleep and Poetry' (1817) l. 96

19 They swayed about upon a rocking horse,
And thought it Pegasus.
'Sleep and Poetry' (1817) l. 186

20 And they shall be accounted poet kings
Who simply tell the most heart-easing things.
'Sleep and Poetry' (1817) l. 267

21 Turn the key deftly in the oilèd wards,
And seal the hushèd casket of my soul.
'Sonnet to Sleep' (written 1819)

22 Season of mists and mellow fruitfulness,
Close bosom-friend of the maturing sun;
Conspiring with him how to load and bless
With fruit the vines that round the thatch-eaves
run.
'To Autumn' (1820) st. 1

1 Who hath not seen thee oft amid thy store?
Sometimes whoever seeks abroad may find
Thee sitting careless on a granary floor,
Thy hair soft-lifted by the winnowing wind;
Or on a half-reaped furrow sound asleep,
Drowsed with the fume of poppies while thy
hook
Spares the next swath and all its twinèd flowers.
'To Autumn' (1820) st. 2

2 Where are the songs of Spring? Ay, where are
they?
Think not of them, thou hast thy music too.
'To Autumn' (1820) st. 3

3 Then in a wailful choir the small gnats mourn
Among the river sallows, borne aloft
Or sinking as the light wind lives or dies.
'To Autumn' (1820) st. 3

4 The red-breast whistles from a garden-croft;
And gathering swallows twitter in the skies.
'To Autumn' (1820) st. 3

5 How soon the film of death obscured that eye,
Whence genius wildly flashed.
'To Chatterton' (written 1815); see also **WORDSWORTH** 868:22

6 Aye on the shores of darkness there is light,
And precipices show untrodden green,
There is a budding morrow in midnight,
There is a triple sight in blindness keen.
'To Homer' (written 1818)

7 To one who has been long in city pent,
'Tis very sweet to look into the fair
And open face of heaven.
'To one who has been long in city pent' (1817); see **MILTON** 544:4

8 When I have fears that I may cease to be
Before my pen has gleaned my teeming brain.
'When I have fears that I may cease to be' (written 1818)

9 When I behold, upon the night's starred face
Huge cloudy symbols of a high romance.
'When I have fears that I may cease to be' (written 1818)

10   Then on the shore
Of the wide world I stand alone and think
Till love and fame to nothingness do sink.
'When I have fears that I may cease to be' (written 1818)

11 A long poem is a test of invention which I take
to be the polar star of poetry, as fancy is the
sails, and imagination the rudder.
letter to Benjamin Bailey, 8 October 1817, in H. E. Rollins (ed.) *Letters of John Keats* (1958) vol. 1

12 I am certain of nothing but the holiness of the
heart's affections and the truth of
imagination—what the imagination seizes as
beauty must be truth—whether it existed before
or not.
letter to Benjamin Bailey, 22 November 1817, in H. E. Rollins (ed.) *Letters of John Keats* (1958) vol. 1; see **KEATS** 455:25

13 O for a life of sensations rather than of
thoughts!
letter to Benjamin Bailey, 22 November 1817, in H. E. Rollins (ed.) *Letters of John Keats* (1958) vol. 1

14 A man should have the fine point of his soul
taken off to become fit for this world.
letter to J. H. Reynolds, 22 November 1817, in H. E. Rollins (ed.) *Letters of John Keats* (1958) vol. 1

15 Negative Capability, that is when man is capable
of being in uncertainties, mysteries, doubts,
without any irritable reaching after fact and
reason—Coleridge, for instance, would let go by
a fine isolated verisimilitude caught from the
penetralium of mystery, from being incapable of
remaining content with half knowledge.
letter to George and Thomas Keats, 21 December 1817, in H. E. Rollins (ed.) *Letters of John Keats* (1958) vol. 1

16 There is nothing stable in the world—uproar's
your only music.
letter to George and Thomas Keats, 13 January 1818, in H. E. Rollins (ed.) *Letters of John Keats* (1958) vol. 1

17 For the sake of a few fine imaginative or
domestic passages, are we to be bullied into a
certain philosophy engendered in the whims of
an egotist?
on the overbearing influence of **WORDSWORTH** *upon his contemporaries*
letter to J. H. Reynolds, 3 February 1818, in H. E. Rollins (ed.) *Letters of John Keats* (1958) vol. 1

18 We hate poetry that has a palpable design upon
us—and if we do not agree, seems to put its
hand in its breeches pocket. Poetry should be
great and unobtrusive, a thing which enters into
one's soul, and does not startle it or amaze it
with itself, but with its subject.
letter to J. H. Reynolds, 3 February 1818, in H. E. Rollins (ed.) *Letters of John Keats* (1958) vol. 1

19 Almost any man may, like the spider, spin from
his own inwards his own airy citadel.
letter to J. H. Reynolds, 19 February 1818, in H. E. Rollins (ed.) *Letters of John Keats* (1958) vol. 1

20 If poetry comes not as naturally as the leaves to
a tree it had better not come at all.
letter to John Taylor, 27 February 1818, in H. E. Rollins (ed.) *Letters of John Keats* (1958) vol. 1

21 Scenery is fine—but human nature is finer.
letter to Benjamin Bailey, 13 March 1818, in H. E. Rollins (ed.) *Letters of John Keats* (1958) vol. 1

22 It is impossible to live in a country which is
continually under hatches . . . Rain! Rain! Rain!
letter to J. H. Reynolds from Devon, 10 April 1818, in H. E. Rollins (ed.) *Letters of John Keats* (1958) vol. 1

23 I am in that temper that if I were under water I
would scarcely kick to come to the top.
letter to Benjamin Bailey, 25 May 1818, in H. E. Rollins (ed.) *Letters of John Keats* (1958) vol. 1

24 O the flummery of a birth place! Cant! Cant!
Cant! It is enough to give a spirit the guts-ache.
letter to John Hamilton Reynolds, 11 July 1818 in M. B. Forman (ed.) *Letters of John Keats* (1952)

25 I do think better of womankind than to suppose
they care whether Mister John Keats five feet
high likes them or not.
letter to Benjamin Bailey, 18 July 1818, in H. E. Rollins (ed.) *Letters of John Keats* (1958) vol. 1

1 There is an awful warmth about my heart like a load of immortality.
   letter to J. H. Reynolds, 22 September 1818, in H. E. Rollins (ed.) *Letters of John Keats* (1958) vol. 1

2 In Endymion, I leaped headlong into the sea, and thereby have become better acquainted with the soundings, the quicksands, and the rocks, than if I had stayed upon the green shore, and piped a silly pipe, and took tea and comfortable advice.
   letter to James Hessey, 8 October 1818, in H. E. Rollins (ed.) *Letters of John Keats* (1958) vol. 1

3 As to the poetical character itself, (I mean that sort of which, if I am any thing, I am a member; that sort distinguished from the Wordsworthian or egotistical sublime; which is a thing *per se* and stands alone) it is not itself—it has no self ... It has as much delight in conceiving an Iago as an Imogen.
   letter to Richard Woodhouse, 27 October 1818, in H. E. Rollins (ed.) *Letters of John Keats* (1958) vol. 1

4 The roaring of the wind is my wife and the stars through the window pane are my children.
   letter to George and Georgiana Keats, 24 October 1818, in H. E. Rollins (ed.) *Letters of John Keats* (1958) vol. 1

5 I have come to this resolution—never to write for the sake of writing, or making a poem, but from running over with any little knowledge or experience which many years of reflection may perhaps give me—otherwise I shall be dumb.
   letter to B. R. Haydon, 8 March 1819, in H. E. Rollins (ed.) *Letters of John Keats* (1958) vol. 2

6 I go among the fields and catch a glimpse of a stoat or a fieldmouse peeping out of the withered grass—The creature hath a purpose and its eyes are bright with it—I go amongst the buildings of a city and I see a man hurrying along—to what? The Creature has a purpose and his eyes are bright with it.
   letter to George and Georgiana Keats, 19 March 1819, in H. E. Rollins (ed.) *Letters of John Keats* (1958) vol. 2

7 Call the world if you please 'The vale of soul-making'.
   letter to George and Georgiana Keats, 21 April 1819, in H. E. Rollins (ed.) *Letters of John Keats* (1958) vol. 2

8 I have met with women whom I really think would like to be married to a poem and to be given away by a novel.
   letter to Fanny Brawne, 8 July 1819, in H. E. Rollins (ed.) *Letters of John Keats* (1958) vol. 2

9 I have two luxuries to brood over in my walks, your loveliness and the hour of my death. O that I could have possession of them both in the same minute.
   letter to Fanny Brawne, 25 July 1819, in H. E. Rollins (ed.) *Letters of John Keats* (1958) vol. 2

10 Fine writing is next to fine doing the top thing in the world.
   letter to J. H. Reynolds, 24 August 1819, in H. E. Rollins (ed.) *Letters of John Keats* (1958) vol. 2

11 All clean and comfortable I sit down to write.
   letter to George and Georgiana Keats, 17 September 1819, in H. E. Rollins (ed.) *Letters of John Keats* (1958) vol. 2

12 The only means of strengthening one's intellect is to make up one's mind about nothing—to let the mind be a thoroughfare for all thoughts. Not a select party.
   letter to George and Georgiana Keats, 24 September 1819, in H. E. Rollins (ed.) *Letters of John Keats* (1958) vol. 2

13 If you should have a boy do not christen him John ... 'Tis a bad name and goes against a man. If my name had been Edmund I should have been more fortunate.
   letter to George and Georgiana Keats, 13 January 1820, in H. E. Rollins (ed.) *Letters of John Keats* (1958) vol. 2

14 'If I should die,' said I to myself, 'I have left no immortal work behind me—nothing to make my friends proud of my memory—but I have loved the principle of beauty in all things, and if I had had time I would have made myself remembered.'
   letter to Fanny Brawne, c.February 1820, in H. E. Rollins (ed.) *Letters of John Keats* (1958) vol. 2

15 I wish you could invent some means to make me at all happy without you. Every hour I am more and more concentrated in you; every thing else tastes like chaff in my mouth.
   letter to Fanny Brawne, August 1820, in H. E. Rollins (ed.) *Letters of John Keats* (1958) vol. 2

16 'Load every rift' of your subject with ore.
   letter to Shelley, August 1820, in H. E. Rollins (ed.) *Letters of John Keats* (1958) vol. 2; see **SPENSER** 767:12

17 I shall soon be laid in the quiet grave—thank God for the quiet grave—O! I can feel the cold earth upon me—the daisies growing over me—O for this quiet—it will be my first.
   letter from Joseph Severn to John Taylor, 6 March 1821, in H. E. Rollins (ed.) *Letters of John Keats* (1958) vol. 2

18 In disease Medical Men guess: if they cannot ascertain a disease, they call it nervous.
   J. A. Gere and John Sparrow (eds.) *Geoffrey Madan's Notebooks* (1981); attributed

John Keats 1920–
American journalist

19 All this is so much hoopla, because our automobiles are so poorly designed as to be unsafe at *any* speed, and more speed simply increases the danger.
   The Insolent Chariots (1958) ch. 4

John Keble 1792–1866
English clergyman; leader of the Oxford Movement

20 Blessed are the pure in heart,
   For they shall see our God,
   The secret of the Lord is theirs,
   Their soul is Christ's abode.
   The Christian Year (1827) 'Blessed are the pure in heart'

21 New every morning is the love
   Our wakening and uprising prove;

Through sleep and darkness safely brought,
Restored to life, and power, and thought.
The Christian Year (1827) 'Morning'

1 The trivial round, the common task,
Would furnish all we ought to ask.
The Christian Year (1827) 'Morning'

2 There is a book, who runs may read,
Which heavenly truth imparts,
And all the lore its scholars need,
Pure eyes and Christian hearts.
The Christian Year (1827) 'Septuagesima'; see **BIBLE** 96:16

3 The voice that breathed o'er Eden,
That earliest wedding-day,
The primal marriage blessing,
It hath not passed away.
'Holy Matrimony' (1857 hymn)

4 If the Church of England were to fail, it would
be found in my parish.
D. Newsome *The Parting of Friends* (1966) ch. 8, pt. 3

Brian Keenan *see* **Koran** 471:8

Helen Keller 1880–1968

American writer and social reformer, blind and deaf from
the age of 19 months

5 Life is either a daring adventure or nothing.
Let Us Have Faith (1940)

6 The mystery of language was revealed to me. I
knew then that 'w-a-t-e-r' meant the wonderful
cool something that was flowing over my hand.
That living word awakened my soul, gave it
light, joy, set it free!
The Story of My Life (1902) ch. 4

7 Everything has its wonders, even darkness and
silence, and I learn, whatever state I may be in,
therein to be content.
The Story of My Life (1902) ch. 22

Frank B. Kellogg *see* **Briand** 156:15

Hugh Kelly 1739–77

Irish dramatist

8 Of all the stages in a woman's life, none is so
dangerous as the period between her
acknowledgment of a passion for a man, and the
day set apart for her nuptials.
Memoirs of a Magdalen (1767, ed. 1782)

9 Your people of refined sentiments are the most
troublesome creatures in the world to deal with.
False Delicacy (performed 1768) act 5, sc. 1

Ned Kelly 1855–80

Australian outlaw

10 Such is life.
last words, before being hanged, 11 November 1880
Frank Clune *The Kelly Hunters* (1955)

Thomas Kelly 1769–1855

Irish clergyman and hymn-writer

11 The head that once was crowned with thorns
Is crowned with glory now.
'The head that once was crowned with thorns' (1820 hymn)

Walt Kelly *see* **Cartoon captions** 205:16

Lord Kelvin 1824–1907

British physicist and natural philosopher

12 When you can measure what you are speaking
about, and express it in numbers, you know
something about it; but when you cannot
measure it, when you cannot express it in
numbers, your knowledge is of a meagre and
unsatisfactory kind: it may be the beginning of
knowledge, but you have scarcely, in your
thoughts, advanced to the stage of *science*,
whatever the matter may be.
*often quoted as 'If you cannot measure it, then it is not
science'*
Popular Lectures and Addresses vol. 1 (1889) 'Electrical Units of
Measurement', delivered 3 May 1883

Thomas à Kempis *see* **Thomas à Kempis**

Thomas Ken 1637–1711

English divine; Bishop of Bath and Wells, 1684–91, and
formerly chaplain to **CHARLES II**

13 Awake, my soul, and with the sun
Thy daily stage of duty run.
Shake off dull sloth, and joyful rise
To pay thy morning sacrifice.
'Morning Hymn' in Winchester College *Manual of Prayers*
(1695) but already in use by 1674

14 Redeem thy mis-spent time that's past,
And live this day as if thy last.
'Morning Hymn' (1709 ed.) v. 2; see **AURELIUS** 40:7

15 All praise to thee, my God, this night,
For all the blessings of the light;
Keep me, O keep me, King of Kings,
Beneath thy own almighty wings.
*the first line later changed to 'Glory to thee, my God this
night'*
'Evening Hymn' in Winchester College *Manual of Prayers*
(1695) but already in use by 1674

16 Teach me to live, that I may dread
The grave as little as my bed.
'Evening Hymn' (1695) v. 3

Jaan Kenbrovin *and* William Kellette

17 I'm forever blowing bubbles.
title of song (1919)

Florynce Kennedy 1916–2000

American lawyer

18 If men could get pregnant, abortion would be a
sacrament.
in *Ms.* March 1973

1 When you want to get to the suites, start in the streets.
her rule for political activism
attributed; in *Los Angeles Times* 28 December 2000 (obituary)

Jimmy Kennedy *and* Michael Carr

British songwriters

2 We're gonna hang out the washing on the Siegfried Line.
title of song (1939)

John Fitzgerald Kennedy 1917–63

American Democratic statesman, 35th President of the US 1961–3; assassinated while riding in a motorcade in Dallas, Texas, he was succeeded as President by Lyndon **JOHNSON**. On Kennedy: see **BENTSEN** 72:4; see also **ONASSIS** 585:6

3 Don't buy a single vote more than necessary. I'll be damned if I'm going to pay for a landslide.
telegraphed message from his father, read at a Gridiron dinner in Washington, 15 March 1958, and almost certainly JFK's invention; J. F. Cutler *Honey Fitz* (1962)

4 We stand today on the edge of a new frontier.
speech accepting the Democratic nomination in Los Angeles, 15 July 1960, in *Vital Speeches* 1 August 1960

5 Let the word go forth from this time and place, to friend and foe alike, that the torch has been passed to a new generation of Americans—born in this century, tempered by war, disciplined by a hard and bitter peace.
inaugural address, 20 January 1961, in *Vital Speeches* 1 February 1961

6 Let every nation know, whether it wishes us well or ill, that we shall pay any price, bear any burden, meet any hardship, support any friend, oppose any foe to assure the survival and the success of liberty.
inaugural address, 20 January 1961, in *Vital Speeches* 1 February 1961

7 If a free society cannot help the many who are poor, it cannot save the few who are rich.
inaugural address, 20 January 1961, in *Vital Speeches* 1 February 1961

8 Let us never negotiate out of fear. But let us never fear to negotiate.
inaugural address, 20 January 1961, in *Vital Speeches* 1 February 1961

9 All this will not be finished in the first 100 days. Nor will it be finished in the first 1,000 days, nor in the life of this Administration, nor even perhaps in our lifetime on this planet. But let us begin.
inaugural address, 20 January 1961, in *Vital Speeches* 1 February 1961

10 And so, my fellow Americans: ask not what your country can do for you—ask what you can do for your country. My fellow citizens of the world: ask not what America will do for you, but what together we can do for the freedom of man.
inaugural address, 20 January 1961, in *Vital Speeches* 1 February 1961; see **GIBRAN** 355:12, **HOLMES** 403:16

11 Mankind must put an end to war or war will put an end to mankind.
speech to United Nations General Assembly, 25 September 1961, in *New York Times* 26 September 1961

12 No one has been barred on account of his race from fighting or dying for America—there are no 'white' or 'coloured' signs on the foxholes or graveyards of battle.
Message to Congress on proposed Civil Rights Bill, 19 June 1963, in *New York Times* 20 June 1963

13 *Ich bin ein Berliner.*
I am a Berliner.
speech in West Berlin, 26 June 1963, in *New York Times* 27 June 1963; see **CICERO** 232:4

14 In free society art is not a weapon . . . Artists are not engineers of the soul.
speech at Amherst College, Mass., 26 October 1963, in *New York Times* 27 October 1963; see **GORKY** 366:9, **STALIN** 769:15

15 It was involuntary. They sank my boat.
on being asked how he became a war hero
Arthur M. Schlesinger Jr. *A Thousand Days* (1965) ch. 4

Joseph P. Kennedy 1888–1969

American financier and diplomat; father of J. F. **KENNEDY**

16 We're going to sell Jack like soapflakes.
when his son John made his bid for the Presidency
John H. Davis *The Kennedy Clan* (1984) ch. 23

17 When the going gets tough, the tough get going.
also attributed to Knute Rockne
J. H. Cutler *Honey Fitz* (1962); see **PROVERBS** 646:47

Robert Kennedy 1925–68

American Democratic politician, son of Joseph **KENNEDY** and Rose **KENNEDY**, brother of John Fitzgerald **KENNEDY**. See also **AESCHYLUS** 6:13

18 One-fifth of the people are against everything all the time.
speech, University of Pennsylvania, 6 May 1964; in *Philadelphia Inquirer* 7 May 1964

19 Each time a man stands up for an ideal, or acts to improve the lot of others, or strikes out against injustice, he sends forth a tiny ripple of hope, and crossing each other from a million different centres of energy and daring those ripples build a current which can sweep down the mightiest walls of oppression and resistance.
speech, Cape Town, 6 June 1966

20 For every ten men who are willing to face the guns of an enemy there is only one willing to brave the disapproval of his fellow, the censure of his colleagues, the wrath of his society. Moral courage is a rarer commodity than bravery in battle or great intelligence.
speech, Cape Town, 7 June 1966

21 There is a Chinese curse which says 'May he live in interesting times.' Like it or not we live in interesting times. They are times of danger and

uncertainty; but they are also more open to the creative energy of men than any other time in history.

speech, Cape Town, 6 June 1966; see **SAYINGS** 685:2

Rose Kennedy 1890–1995

American wife of Joseph **KENNEDY**, mother of John Fitzgerald **KENNEDY** and Robert **KENNEDY**

1 Now Teddy must run.

to her daughter, on hearing of the assassination of Robert **KENNEDY**

in *The Times* 24 January 1995 (obituary); attributed, perhaps apocryphal

Kenojuak Ashevak 1927–

Canadian Inuit sculptor and artist

2 A piece of paper from the outside world is as thin as the shell of a snowbird's egg.

Eskimo Artist: Kenojuak (1962 film)

Jomo Kenyatta 1891–1978

Kenyan statesman, Prime Minister of Kenya 1963 and President 1964–78

3 The African is conditioned, by the cultural and social institutions of centuries, to a freedom of which Europe has little conception, and it is not in his nature to accept serfdom forever. He realizes that he must fight unceasingly for his own emancipation; for without this he is doomed to remain the prey of rival imperialisms.

Facing Mount Kenya (1938); conclusion

Lady Caroline Keppel b. 1735

English poet

4 What's this dull town to me?
Robin's not near.
He whom I wished to see,
Wished for to hear;
Where's all the joy and mirth
Made life a heaven on earth?
O! they're all fled with thee,
Robin Adair.

'Robin Adair' (c.1750)

Jack Kerouac 1922–69

American novelist

5 The beat generation.

phrase coined in the course of a conversation; in Playboy June 1959

Jean Kerr 1923–2003

American writer

6 As someone pointed out recently, if you can keep your head when all about you are losing theirs, it's just possible you haven't grasped the situation.

Please Don't Eat the Daisies (1957) introduction; see **KIPLING** 466:5

7 I feel about airplanes the way I feel about diets. It seems to me that they are wonderful things for other people to go on.

The Snake Has All the Lines (1958)

8 I'm tired of all this nonsense about beauty being only skin-deep. That's deep enough. What do you want—an adorable pancreas?

The Snake has all the Lines (1958)

William Kethe d. 1594

Scottish Calvinist

9 All people that on earth do dwell,
Sing to the Lord with cheerful voice.

'All people that on earth do dwell' in *Fourscore and Seven Psalms of David* (Geneva, 1561; later known as the Geneva Psalter); usually sung to the tune 'Old Hundredth', and often known by that name

10 The Lord, ye know, is God indeed;
Without our aid he did us make;
We are his folk, he doth us feed,
And for his sheep he doth us take.

O enter then his gates with praise,
Approach with joy his courts unto;
Praise, laud, and bless his name always,
For it is seemly so to do.

'All people that on earth do dwell' in *Fourscore and Seven Psalms of David* (Geneva, 1561; later known as the Geneva Psalter)

Ralph Kettell 1563–1643

English scholar, President of Trinity College, Oxford, from 1599

11 Here is Hey for Garsington! and Hey for Cuddesdon! and Hey Hockley! but here's nobody cries, Hey for God Almighty!

sermon at Garsington Revel, in Oliver Lawson Dick (ed.) Aubrey's Brief Lives *(1949) 'Ralph Kettell'*

Thomas Kettle 1880–1916

Irish economist and poet

12 Ireland is a small but insuppressible island half an hour nearer the sunset than Great Britain.

'On Crossing the Irish Sea'

Francis Scott Key 1779–1843

American lawyer and verse-writer

13 'Tis the star-spangled banner; O long may it wave
O'er the land of the free, and the home of the brave!

'The Star-Spangled Banner' (1814)

John Maynard Keynes 1883–1946

English economist

14 I work for a Government I despise for ends I think criminal.

letter to Duncan Grant, 15 December 1917, in British Library Add. MSS *57931 fo. 119*

1 Like Odysseus, the President looked wiser when he was seated.
of Woodrow **WILSON**
The Economic Consequences of the Peace (1919) ch. 3

2 Lenin was right. There is no subtler, no surer means of overturning the existing basis of society than to debauch the currency. The process engages all the hidden forces of economic law on the side of destruction, and does it in a manner which not one man in a million is able to diagnose.
The Economic Consequences of the Peace (1919) ch. 6

3 I do not know which makes a man more conservative—to know nothing but the present, or nothing but the past.
The End of Laissez-Faire (1926) pt. 1

4 This extraordinary figure of our time, this syren, this goat-footed bard, this half-human visitor to our age from the hag-ridden magic and enchanted woods of Celtic antiquity.
Essays in Biography (1933) 'Mr Lloyd George'

5 *In the long run* we are all dead.
A Tract on Monetary Reform (1923) ch. 3

Ruhollah Khomeini 1900–89
Iranian Shiite Muslim leader

6 If laws are needed, Islam has established them all. There is no need . . . after establishing a government, to sit down and draw up laws.
Islam and Revolution: Writings and Declarations of Imam Khomeini (1981) 'Islamic Government'

7 I would like to inform all the intrepid Muslims in the world that the author of the book entitled *The Satanic Verses*, which has been compiled, printed and published in opposition to Islam, the Prophet and the Qur'an, as well as those publishers who were aware of its contents, have been declared *madhur el dam* [those whose blood must be shed]. I call on all zealous Muslims to execute them quickly, wherever they find them, so that no-one will dare to insult Islam again. Whoever is killed in this path will be regarded as a martyr.
fatwa against Salman **RUSHDIE**, issued 14 February 1989; Malise Ruthven A Satanic Affair (1990) ch. 5; see **WESKER** 847:5

Nikita Khrushchev 1894–1971
Soviet statesman, Premier 1958–64. See also **EPSTEIN** 316:13

8 If anyone believes that our smiles involve abandonment of the teaching of Marx, Engels and Lenin he deceives himself. Those who wait for that must wait until a shrimp learns to whistle.
speech in Moscow, 17 September 1955, in New York Times 18 September 1955

9 Whether you like it or not, history is on our side. We will bury you.
speech to Western diplomats at reception in Moscow for Polish leader Mr Gomulka, 18 November 1956, in The Times 19 November 1956

10 If one cannot catch the bird of paradise, better take a wet hen.
in Time 6 January 1958

Amir Khusrau 1253–1325
Persian poet

11 If there is a paradise on earth, it is this, it is this, it is this.
inscribed on the wall of the Diwan-i-Khas [the hall of special audience] in the Red Fort at Delhi

Sören Kierkegaard 1813–55
Danish philosopher

12 Far from idleness being the root of evil, rather it is the true good.
Either/Or (1843) pt. 1, ch. 6 'Crop Rotation'

13 Once a man acts in a decisive sense and comes out into reality, existence can get a grip on him and providence educate him.
Journals (tr. A. Dru, 1958) 1850

Kitty Kiernan d. 1945
Irish fiancée of Michael **COLLINS**

14 I felt, if we were ever to part, it would be easier for us both, especially for me, to do it soon, because later it would be bitter for me. But I'd love you just the same.
letter to Michael Collins, 1921; L. O'Broin (ed.) The Letters of Michael Collins and Kitty Kiernan (1983)

Joyce Kilmer 1886–1918
American poet

15 I think that I shall never see
A poem lovely as a tree.
'Trees' (1914); see **NASH** 568:22

16 Poems are made by fools like me,
But only God can make a tree.
'Trees' (1914)

David Maxwell Fyfe, Lord Kilmuir 1900–67
British Conservative politician and lawyer. On Kilmuir: see **ANONYMOUS** 19:5

17 Loyalty is the Tory's secret weapon.
Anthony Sampson Anatomy of Britain (1962) ch. 6

Francis Kilvert 1840–79
English clergyman and diarist

18 Of all noxious animals, too, the most noxious is a tourist. And of all tourists the most vulgar, ill-bred, offensive and loathsome is the British tourist.
W. Plomer (ed.) Selections from the Diary of the Rev. Francis Kilvert (1938–40) 5 April 1870

1 It is a fine thing to be out on the hills alone. A man can hardly be a beast or a fool alone on a great mountain.

W. Plomer (ed.) *Selections from the Diary* . . . 29 May 1871

Benjamin Franklin King 1857–94

American poet

2 Nothing to do but work,
Nothing to eat but food,
Nothing to wear but clothes
To keep one from going nude.

'The Pessimist'

3 Nowhere to go but out,
Nowhere to come but back.

'The Pessimist'

Henry King 1592–1669

English poet; Bishop of Chichester from 1642

4 Sleep on (my Love!) in thy cold bed
Never to be disquieted.
My last Good-night! Thou wilt not wake
Till I thy fate shall overtake:
Till age, or grief, or sickness must
Marry my body to that dust
It so much loves; and fill the room
My heart keeps empty in thy tomb.
Stay for me there: I will not fail
To meet thee in that hollow vale.

'An Exequy' (1657) l. 81 (written for his wife Anne, d. 1624)

5 But hark! My pulse, like a soft drum
Beats my approach, tells thee I come.

'An Exequy' (1657) l. 111

Martin Luther King 1929–68

American Baptist minister and civil rights leader;
assassinated in Memphis, Tennessee

6 I want to be the white man's brother, not his brother-in-law.

in *New York Journal-American* 10 September 1962

7 Judicial decrees may not change the heart; but they can restrain the heartless.

speech in Nashville, Tennessee, 27 December 1962, in James Melvin Washington (ed.) *A Testament of Hope: The Essential Writings of Martin Luther King, Jr.* (1986) ch. 22

8 Injustice anywhere is a threat to justice everywhere.

letter from Birmingham Jail, Alabama, 16 April 1963, in *Atlantic Monthly* August 1963

9 The Negro's great stumbling block in the stride toward freedom is not the White Citizens Councillor or the Ku Klux Klanner but the white moderate who is more devoted to order than to justice; who prefers a negative peace which is the absence of tension to a positive peace which is the presence of justice.

letter from Birmingham Jail, Alabama, 16 April 1963, in *Atlantic Monthly* August 1963

10 If a man hasn't discovered something he will die for, he isn't fit to live.

speech in Detroit, 23 June 1963, in James Bishop *The Days of Martin Luther King* (1971) ch. 4

11 I have a dream that one day on the red hills of Georgia the sons of former slaves and the sons of former slave owners will be able to sit down together at the table of brotherhood . . .
I have a dream that my four little children will one day live in a nation where they will not be judged by the colour of their skin but by the content of their character.

speech at Civil Rights March in Washington, 28 August 1963, in *New York Times* 29 August 1963

12 We must learn to live together as brothers or perish together as fools.

speech at St Louis, 22 March 1964, in *St Louis Post-Dispatch* 23 March 1964

13 Cowardice asks the question, 'Is it safe?'
Expediency asks the question, 'Is it politic?'
Vanity asks the question, 'Is it popular?' But Conscience asks the question, 'Is it right?'

speech, 1967; in *Autobiography of Martin Luther King Jr.* (1999) ch. 30

14 We shall overcome because the arc of a moral universe is long, but it bends toward justice.

sermon at the National Cathedral, Washington, 31 March 1968, in James Melvin Washington *A Testament of Hope* (1991); see **OBAMA** 583:1, **PARKER** 596:23,

15 I just want to do God's will. And he's allowed me to go up to the mountain. And I've looked over, and I've seen the promised land . . . So I'm happy tonight. I'm not worried about anything. I'm not fearing any man.

on the day before his assassination

speech in Memphis, 3 April 1968, in *New York Times* 4 April 1968

16 The means by which we live have outdistanced the ends for which we live. Our scientific power has outrun our spiritual power. We have guided missiles and misguided men.

Strength to Love (1963) ch. 7

17 A riot is at bottom the language of the unheard.

Where Do We Go From Here? (1967) ch. 4

Stephen King 1947–

American writer

18 Terror . . . often arises from a pervasive sense of disestablishment; that things are in the unmaking.

Danse Macabre (1981)

Stoddard King 1889–1933

British songwriter

19 There's a long, long trail awinding
Into the land of my dreams.

'There's a Long, Long Trail' (1913 song)

William King 1650–1729

Irish cleric

1 The cry of the whole people is loud for bread;
God knows what will be the consequence; many
are starved, and I am afraid many more will be.
view of the Archbishop of Dublin in 1720
Daniel Corkery *The Hidden Ireland* (1925)

William Lyon Mackenzie King

1874–1950

Canadian Liberal statesman, Prime Minister 1921–6,
1926–30, and 1935–48

2 If some countries have too much history, we
have too much geography.
speech, Canadian House of Commons, 18 June 1936

3 Not necessarily conscription, but conscription if
necessary.
speech, Canadian House of Commons, 7 July 1942

Charles Kingsley 1819–75

English writer and clergyman. On Kingsley: see **STUBBS**
779:8

4 Be good, sweet maid, and let who will be clever;
Do noble things, not dream them, all day long.
'A Farewell' (1858)

5 Do the work that's nearest,
Though it's dull at whiles,
Helping, when we meet them,
Lame dogs over stiles.
'The Invitation. To Tom Hughes' (1856)

6 And such a port for mariners I ne'er shall see
again
As the pleasant isle of Avès, beside the Spanish
Main.
'The Last Buccaneer' (1857)

7 Welcome, wild North-easter!
Shame it is to see
Odes to every zephyr;
Ne'er a verse to thee.
'Ode to the North-East Wind' (1858)

8 'Tis the hard grey weather
Breeds hard English men.
'Ode to the North-East Wind' (1858)

9 Come; and strong within us
Stir the Vikings' blood;
Bracing brain and sinew;
Blow, thou wind of God!
'Ode to the North-East Wind' (1858)

10 'O Mary, go and call the cattle home,
And call the cattle home,
And call the cattle home,
Across the sands of Dee.'
The western wind was wild and dank with
foam,
And all alone went she.
'The Sands of Dee' (1858)

11 And never home came she.
'The Sands of Dee' (1858)

12 Three fishers went sailing away to the west,
Away to the west as the sun went down;
Each thought on the woman who loved him the
best,
And the children stood watching them out of
the town.
'The Three Fishers' (1858)

13 For men must work, and women must weep,
And there's little to earn, and many to keep,
Though the harbour bar be moaning.
'The Three Fishers' (1858)

14 When all the world is young, lad,
And all the trees are green;
And every goose a swan, lad,
And every lass a queen;
Then hey for boot and horse, lad,
And round the world away:
Young blood must have its course, lad,
And every dog his day.
'Young and Old' (from *The Water Babies*, 1863)

15 We have used the Bible as if it was a constable's
handbook—an opium-dose for keeping beasts of
burden patient while they are being overloaded.
Letters to the Chartists no. 2; see **MARX** 526:3

16 Eustace is a man no longer; he is become a
thing, a tool, a Jesuit.
Westward Ho! (1855) ch. 23

Hugh Kingsmill (Hugh Kingsmill Lunn)

1889–1949

English man of letters

17 What still alive at twenty-two,
A clean upstanding chap like you?
Sure, if your throat 'tis hard to slit,
Slit your girl's, and swing for it.
'Two Poems, after A. E. Housman' (1933) no. 1

18 But bacon's not the only thing
That's cured by hanging from a string.
'Two Poems, after A. E. Housman' (1933) no. 1

19 Snobbishness . . . is the desire for what divides
men, and the inability to value what unites
them.
D. H. Lawrence (1938) ch. 2

20 God's apology for relations.
of friends
Michael Holroyd *The Best of Hugh Kingsmill* (1970)
introduction

Barbara Kingsolver 1955–

American writer

21 Marriage is one long fit of compromise, deep
and wide.
The Poisonwood Bible (1998) bk. 5 'Exodus'

Neil Kinnock 1942–

British Labour politician, Leader of the Labour Party
1983–92

22 *during the Falklands War, replying to a heckler who said
that Mrs* **THATCHER** *'showed guts'*
It's a pity others had to leave theirs on the

ground at Goose Green to prove it.
television interview, 6 June 1983

1 If Margaret Thatcher wins on Thursday, I warn you not to be ordinary, I warn you not to be young, I warn you not to fall ill, and I warn you not to grow old.
on the prospect of a Conservative re-election
speech at Bridgend, 7 June 1983

2 Why am I the first Kinnock in a thousand generations to be able to get to a university?
later plagiarized by the American politician Joe Biden
speech in party political broadcast, 21 May 1987

Alfred Kinsey 1894–1956
American zoologist and sex researcher

3 The only unnatural sex act is that which you cannot perform.
in Time 21 January 1966

Rudyard Kipling 1865–1936
English writer and poet. On Kipling: see STEPHEN 772:4; see also EPITAPHS 319:12

4 When you've shouted 'Rule Britannia', when you've sung 'God save the Queen'—
When you've finished killing Kruger with your mouth.
'The Absent-Minded Beggar' (1899) st. 1

5 He's an absent-minded beggar and his weaknesses are great—
But we and Paul must take him as we find him—
He is out on active service, wiping something off a slate—
And he's left a lot o' little things behind him!
'The Absent-Minded Beggar' (1899) st. 1

6 England's on the anvil—hear the hammers ring—
Clanging from the Severn to the Tyne!
Never was a blacksmith like our Norman King—
England's being hammered, hammered, hammered into line!
'The Anvil' (1927)

7 Seek not to question other than
The books I leave behind.
'The Appeal' (1940)

8 Oh, East is East, and West is West, and never the twain shall meet,
Till Earth and Sky stand presently at God's great Judgement Seat;
But there is neither East nor West, Border, nor Breed, nor Birth,
When two strong men stand face to face, tho' they come from the ends of earth!
'The Ballad of East and West' (1892); see PROVERBS 630:43

9 Four things greater than all things are,—
Women and Horses and Power and War.
'The Ballad of the King's Jest' (1892)

10 Foot—foot—foot—foot—sloggin' over Africa—
(Boots—boots—boots—boots—movin' up and down again!)
'Boots' (1903)

11 If any question why we died,
Tell them, because our fathers lied.
'Common Form' (1919)

12 The Devil whoops, as he whooped of old: 'It's clever, but is it Art?'
'The Conundrum of the Workshops' (1892)

13 For they're hangin' Danny Deever, you can hear the Dead March play,
The regiment's in 'ollow square—they're hangin' him to-day;
They've taken of his buttons off an' cut his stripes away,
An' they're hangin' Danny Deever in the mornin'.
'Danny Deever' (1892)

14 The 'eathen in 'is blindness bows down to wood an' stone;
'E don't obey no orders unless they is 'is own.
'The 'Eathen' (1896); see HEBER 388:9

15 And what should they know of England who only England know?
'The English Flag' (1892)

16 I could not dig: I dared not rob:
Therefore I lied to please the mob.
Now all my lies are proved untrue
And I must face the men I slew.
What tale shall serve me here among
Mine angry and defrauded young?
'Epitaphs of the War: A Dead Statesman' (1919)

17 My son was killed while laughing at some jest. I would I knew
What it was, and it might serve me in a time when jests are few.
'Epitaphs of the War: A Son' (1919)

18 The female of the species is more deadly than the male.
'The Female of the Species' (1919); see PROVERBS 632:9

19 So 'ere's *to* you, Fuzzy-Wuzzy, at your 'ome in the Soudan;
You're a pore benighted 'eathen but a first-class fightin' man.
'Fuzzy-Wuzzy' (1892)

20 We're poor little lambs who've lost our way,
Baa! Baa! Baa!
We're little black sheep who've gone astray,
Baa-aa-aa!
Gentlemen-rankers out on the spree,
Damned from here to Eternity,
God ha' mercy on such as we,
Baa! Yah! Bah!
'Gentlemen-Rankers' (1892)

21 We have done with Hope and Honour, we are lost to Love and Truth,
We are dropping down the ladder rung by rung,
And the measure of our torment is the measure of our youth.

God help us, for we knew the worst too young!
'Gentlemen-Rankers' (1892)

1 Our England is a garden, and such gardens are not made
By singing:—'Oh, how beautiful!' and sitting in the shade,
While better men than we go out and start their working lives
At grubbing weeds from gravel paths with broken dinner-knives.
'The Glory of the Garden' (1911)

2 As it will be in the future, it was at the birth of Man—
There are only four things certain since Social Progress began:—
That the Dog returns to his Vomit and the Sow returns to her Mire,
And the burnt Fool's bandaged finger goes wabbling back to the Fire.
'The Gods of the Copybook Headings' (1927)

3 Though I've belted you and flayed you,
By the livin' Gawd that made you,
You're a better man than I am, Gunga Din!
'Gunga Din' (1892)

4 What is a woman that you forsake her,
And the hearth-fire and the home-acre,
To go with the old grey Widow-maker?
'Harp Song of the Dane Women' (1906)

5 If you can keep your head when all about you
Are losing theirs and blaming it on you;
If you can trust yourself when all men doubt you,
But make allowance for their doubting too;
If you can wait and not be tired by waiting,
Or being lied about, don't deal in lies,
Or being hated, don't give way to hating,
And yet don't look too good, nor talk too wise;
If you can dream—and not make dreams your master;
If you can think—and not make thoughts your aim,
If you can meet with triumph and disaster
And treat those two impostors just the same...
'If—' (1910)

6 If you can talk with crowds and keep your virtue,
Or walk with Kings—nor lose the common touch,
If neither foes nor loving friends can hurt you,
If all men count with you, but none too much;
If you can fill the unforgiving minute
With sixty seconds' worth of distance run,
Yours is the Earth and everything that's in it,
And—which is more—you'll be a Man, my son!
'If—' (1910)

7 There are nine and sixty ways of constructing tribal lays,
And—every—single—one—of—them—is—right!
'In the Neolithic Age' (1893)

8 Old days! the wild geese are flighting,
Head to the storm as they faced it before.
'The Irish Guards'

9 Then ye returned to your trinkets; then ye contented your souls
With the flannelled fools at the wicket or the muddied oafs at the goals.
'The Islanders' (1903)

10 I've taken my fun where I've found it,
An' now I must pay for my fun.
'The Ladies' (1896)

11 For the Colonel's Lady an' Judy O'Grady
Are sisters under their skins!
'The Ladies' (1896)

12 And Ye take mine honour from me if Ye take away the sea!
'The Last Chantey' (1896)

13 Down to Gehenna or up to the Throne,
He travels the fastest who travels alone.
L'Envoi to *The Story of the Gadsbys* (1890), 'The Winners'; see **PROVERBS** 634:17

14 By the old Moulmein Pagoda, lookin' eastward to the sea,
There's a Burma girl a-settin', and I know she thinks o' me;
For the wind is in the palm-trees, an' the temple-bells they say:
'Come you back, you British soldier; come you back to Mandalay!'
'Mandalay' (1892)

15 On the road to Mandalay,
Where the flyin'-fishes play,
An' the dawn comes up like thunder outer China 'crost the Bay!
'Mandalay' (1892)

16 Ship me somewheres east of Suez, where the best is like the worst,
Where there aren't no Ten Commandments an' a man can raise a thirst.
'Mandalay' (1892)

17 They shall not return to us, the resolute, the young,
The eager and whole-hearted whom we gave:
But the men who left them thriftily to die in their own dung,
Shall they come with years and honour to the grave?
'Mesopotamia' (1917)

18 Dawn off the Foreland—the young flood making
Jumbled and short and steep—
Black in the hollows and bright where it's breaking—
Awkward water to sweep.
'Mines reported in the fairway,
'Warn all traffic and detain.
' 'Sent up *Unity*, *Claribel*, *Assyrian*, *Stormcock*, and *Golden Gain*.'
'Mine Sweepers' (1915)

19 'Have you news of my boy Jack?'
Not this tide.

'When d'you think that he'll come back?'
Not with this wind blowing, and this tide.
 'My Boy Jack' (1916)

1 And the end of the fight is a tombstone white,
    with the name of the late deceased,
And the epitaph drear: 'A fool lies here who
    tried to hustle the East.'
 The Naulahka (1892) ch. 5

2 A Nation spoke to a Nation,
A Throne sent word to a Throne:
'Daughter am I in my mother's house,
But mistress in my own.
The gates are mine to open,
As the gates are mine to close,
And I abide by my Mother's House.'
Said our Lady of the Snows.
 'Our Lady of the Snows' (1898)

3 The toad beneath the harrow knows
Exactly where each tooth-point goes;
The butterfly upon the road
Preaches contentment to that toad.
 'Pagett, MP' (1886)

4 There is sorrow enough in the natural way
From men and women to fill our day;
But when we are certain of sorrow in store,
Why do we always arrange for more?
*Brothers and Sisters, I bid you beware
Of giving your heart to a dog to tear.*
 'The Power of the Dog' (1909)

5 The tumult and the shouting dies—
The captains and the kings depart—
Still stands Thine ancient Sacrifice,
An humble and a contrite heart.
Lord God of Hosts, be with us yet,
Lest we forget—lest we forget!
 'Recessional' (1897)

6 Far-called our navies melt away—
On dune and headland sinks the fire—
Lo, all our pomp of yesterday
Is one with Nineveh, and Tyre!
 'Recessional' (1897)

7 Such boasting as the Gentiles use,
Or lesser breeds without the Law.
 'Recessional' (1897)

8 For frantic boast and foolish word—
Thy mercy on Thy People, Lord.
 'Recessional' (1897)

9 How far is St. Helena from the field of
    Austerlitz?
 'A St. Helena Lullaby' (1910)

10 Five and twenty ponies,
Trotting through the dark—
Brandy for the Parson,
'Baccy for the Clerk;
Laces for a lady, letters for a spy,
Watch the wall, my darling, while the
    Gentlemen go by!
 'A Smuggler's Song' (1906)

11 Them that asks no questions isn't told a lie.
Watch the wall, my darling, while the
    Gentlemen go by!
 'A Smuggler's Song' (1906)

12 If blood be the price of admiralty,
Lord God, we ha' paid in full!
 'The Song of the Dead' (1896)

13 Or little, lost, Down churches praise
The Lord who made the hills.
 'Sussex' (1903)

14 One man in a thousand, Solomon says,
Will stick more close than a brother.
 'The Thousandth Man' (1910); see **BIBLE** 88:23

15 For the sin ye do by two and two ye must pay
    for one by one!
 'Tomlinson' (1892)

16 Makin' mock o' uniforms that guard you while
    you sleep.
 'Tommy' (1892)

17 Then it's Tommy this, an' Tommy that, an'
    'Tommy 'ow's yer soul?'
But it's 'Thin red line of 'eroes' when the drums
    begin to roll.
 'Tommy' (1892); see **RUSSELL** 676:1

18 Of all the trees that grow so fair,
Old England to adorn,
Greater are none beneath the Sun,
Than Oak, and Ash, and Thorn.
 'A Tree Song' (1906)

19 A fool there was and he made his prayer
(Even as you and I!)
To a rag and a bone and a hank of hair
(We called her the woman who did not care)
But the fool he called her his lady fair—
(Even as you and I!)
 'The Vampire' (1897) st. 1

20 They shut the road through the woods
Seventy years ago.
Weather and rain have undone it again,
And now you would never know
There was once a road through the woods.
 'The Way through the Woods' (1910)

21 It is always a temptation to a rich and lazy
    nation,
To puff and look important and to say:-
'Though we know we should defeat you, we
    have not the time to meet you,
We will therefore pay you cash to go away.'
And that is called paying the Dane-geld;
But we've proved it again and again,
That if once you have paid him the Dane-geld
You never get rid of the Dane.
 'What Dane-geld means' (1911)

22 And only the Master shall praise us, and only
    the Master shall blame;
And no one shall work for money, and no one
    shall work for fame,
But each for the joy of the working, and each,
    in his separate star,

Shall draw the Thing as he sees It for the God
   of Things as They are!
'When Earth's Last Picture is Painted' (1896)

1 When 'Omer smote 'is bloomin' lyre,
He'd 'eard men sing by land an' sea;
An' what he thought 'e might require,
'E went an' took—the same as me!
'When 'Omer smote 'is bloomin' lyre' (1896)

2 Take up the White Man's burden—
Send forth the best ye breed—
Go, bind your sons to exile
To serve your captives' need.
'The White Man's Burden' (1899)

3 When you're wounded and left on Afghanistan's
   plains
And the women come out to cut up what
   remains
Just roll to your rifle and blow out your brains
An' go to your Gawd like a soldier.
'The Young British Soldier' (1892)

4 Lalun is a member of the most ancient
profession in the world.
In Black and White (1888) 'On the City Wall'; see **REAGAN**
656:11

5 They settled things by making up a saying,
'What the Bandar-log think now the Jungle will
think later': and that comforted them a great
deal.
The Jungle Book (1894) 'Kaa's Hunting'; see **PROVERBS** 646:24

6 'We be of one blood, thou and I', Mowgli
answered.
The Jungle Book (1894) 'Kaa's Hunting'

7 The motto of all the mongoose family is, 'Run
and find out.'
The Jungle Book (1894) 'Rikki-Tikki-Tavi'

8 He walked by himself, and all places were alike
to him.
Just So Stories (1902) 'The Cat that Walked by Himself'

9 And he went back through the Wet Wild
Woods, waving his wild tail and walking by his
wild lone. But he never told anybody.
Just So Stories (1902) 'The Cat that Walked by Himself'

10 One Elephant—a new Elephant—an Elephant's
Child—who was full of 'satiable curtiosity.
Just So Stories (1902) 'The Elephant's Child'

11 The great grey-green, greasy, Limpopo River, all
set about with fever trees.
Just So Stories (1902) 'The Elephant's Child'

12 I keep six honest serving-men
(They taught me all I knew);
Their names are What and Why and When
And How and Where and Who.
Just So Stories (1902) 'The Elephant's Child'

13 You must *not* forget the suspenders, Best
Beloved.
Just So Stories (1902) 'How the Whale got his Throat'

14 And the small 'Stute Fish said in a small 'stute
voice, 'Noble and generous Cetacean, have you

ever tasted Man?' 'No,' said the Whale. 'What is
it like?' 'Nice,' said the small 'Stute Fish. 'Nice
but nubbly.'
Just So Stories (1902) 'How the Whale got his Throat'

15 He had his Mummy's leave to paddle, or else he
would never have done it, because he was a man
of infinite-resource-and-sagacity.
Just So Stories (1902) 'How the Whale got his Throat'

16 Little Friend of all the World.
Kim's nickname
Kim (1901) ch. 1

17 He was the greatest, as he was the hugest, of
the war correspondents . . . and he always
opened his conversation with the news that
there would be trouble in the Balkans in the
spring.
The Light that Failed (1891) ch. 4

18 The man who would be king.
title of short story (1888)

19 He swathed himself in quotations—as a beggar
would enfold himself in the purple of Emperors.
Many Inventions (1893) 'The Finest Story in the World'

20 Take my word for it, the silliest woman can
manage a clever man; but it takes a very clever
woman to manage a fool.
the view of Mrs Hauksbee
Plain Tales from the Hills (1888) 'Three and—an Extra'

21 Now this is the Law of the Jungle—as old and
   as true as the sky;
And the Wolf that shall keep it may prosper, but
   the Wolf that shall break it must die.
The Second Jungle Book (1895) 'The Law of the Jungle'

22 My Daemon was with me in the *Jungle Books*,
Kim, and both Puck books, and good care I took
to walk delicately lest he should withdraw. I
know that he did not, because when these books
were finished they said so themselves with,
almost, the water-hammer click of a tap turned
off.
Something of Myself (1937)

23 I gloat!
Stalky & Co. (1899)

24 A Flopshus Cad, an Outrageous Stinker, a Jelly-
bellied Flag-flapper.
Stalky & Co. (1899)

25 'Tisn't beauty, so to speak, nor good talk
necessarily. It's just It. Some women'll stay in a
man's memory if they once walked down a
street.
Traffics and Discoveries (1904) 'Mrs Bathurst'

26 Power without responsibility: the prerogative of
the harlot throughout the ages.
*summing up Lord **BEAVERBROOK**'s political standpoint vis-à-
vis the Daily Express, and quoted by Stanley **BALDWIN**, 18
March 1931*
in *Kipling Journal* vol. 38, no. 180, December 1971; see
DORFMAN 290:15, **STOPPARD** 777:14

Henry Kissinger 1923–

German-born American statesman, Secretary of State
1973–7

1 The conventional army loses if it does not win.
The guerrilla wins if he does not lose.
in Foreign Affairs January 1969

2 Power is the great aphrodisiac.
in New York Times 19 January 1971

3 We are the President's men.
M. and B. Kalb *Kissinger* (1974) ch. 7

Lord Kitchener 1850–1916

British soldier and statesman; Secretary of State for War
from the outbreak of the First World War in 1914. On
Kitchener: see **ASQUITH** 34:2; see also **MILITARY SAYINGS,
SLOGANS, AND SONGS** 535:19

4 You are ordered abroad as a soldier of the King
to help our French comrades against the
invasion of a common enemy . . . In this new
experience you may find temptations both in
wine and women. You must entirely resist both
temptations, and, while treating all women with
perfect courtesy, you should avoid any intimacy.
Do your duty bravely. Fear God. Honour the
King.
message to soldiers of the British Expeditionary Force (1914),
in The Times 19 August 1914

5 I don't mind your being killed, but I object to
your being taken prisoner.
to the Prince of Wales during the First World War
in Journals and Letters of Reginald Viscount Esher (1938) vol. 3,
18 December 1914

Paul Klee 1879–1940

German-Swiss painter

6 Art does not reproduce the visible; rather, it
makes visible.
Inward Vision (1958) 'Creative Credo' (1920)

7 An active line on a walk, moving freely without
a goal. A walk for walk's sake. The agent is a
point that shifts position.
Pedagogical Sketchbook (1925)

8 Colour has taken hold of me; no longer do I
have to chase after it. I know that it has hold of
me for ever. That is the significance of this
blessed moment.
on a visit to Tunis in 1914
Herbert Read A Concise History of Modern Painting (1968)

Heinrich von Kleist 1777–1811

German dramatist

9 *Man hat viel beissend abgefasste Schriften,
Die, dass ein Gott sei, nicht gestehen wollen;
Jedoch den Teufel hat, soviel ich weiss,
Kein Atheist noch bündig wegbewiesen.*

We've had some very caustic writings
Unwilling to concede that God exists.

However, the devil, so far as I'm aware
No atheist has yet quite proved away.
The Broken Jug (1808) sc. 11, translated by David Constantine

10 *Meinst Du, das Glück werd'immerdar, wie jüngst,
Mit einem Kranz den Ungehorsam lohnen?
Den Sieg nicht mag ich, der, ein Kind des Zufalls,
Mir von der Bank fällt; das Gesetz will ich,
Die Mutter meiner Krone, aufrecht halten,
Die ein Geschlecht von Siegen mir erzeugt.*

Do you suppose that Fortune always will
Crown disobedience with laurels, as lately?
I do not want a victory that is
The bastard child of chance. I want
The law upheld which is the mother of my
crown
To bear me a whole family of victories.
The Prince of Homburg (1821) act 5, sc. 5, translated by David
Constantine

Friedrich Klopstock 1724–1803

German poet

11 God and I both knew what it meant once; now
God alone knows.
on the meaning of a passage in one of his poems
C. Lombroso *The Man of Genius* (1891) pt. 1, ch. 2; see
BROWNING 168:12

Charles Knight *and* Kenneth Lyle

British songwriters

12 When there's trouble brewing,
When there's something doing,
Are we downhearted?
No! Let 'em all come!
'Here we are! Here we are again!!' (1914 song)

Frank H. Knight 1885–1973

American economist

13 Costs merely register competing attractions.
Risk, Uncertainty and Profit (1921)

L. C. Knights 1906–97

English critic and academic

14 How many children had Lady Macbeth?
satirizing an over-realistic approach to criticism
title of essay (1933)

Mary Knowles 1733–1807

English Quaker

15 He gets at the substance of a book directly; he
tears out the heart of it.
*on Samuel **JOHNSON***
James Boswell *The Life of Samuel Johnson* (1791) 15 April 1778

John Knox *c.*1505–72

Scottish Protestant reformer. On Knox: see **DOUGLAS** 291:11

1 The first blast of the trumpet against the monstrous regiment of women.
regiment = *rule*
title of pamphlet (1558)

2 *Un homme avec Dieu est toujours dans la majorité.*
A man with God is always in the majority.
inscription on the Reformation Monument, Geneva

Ronald Knox 1888–1957

English writer and Roman Catholic priest

3 When suave politeness, tempering bigot zeal,
Corrected *I believe* to *One does feel.*
'Absolute and Abitofhell' (1913)

4 There once was a man who said, 'God
Must think it exceedingly odd
If he finds that this tree
Continues to be
When there's no one about in the Quad.'
*to which came the anonymous reply: 'Dear Sir, / Your
astonishment's odd / I am always about in the Quad. / And
that's why the tree / Will continue to be, / Since observed
by / Yours faithfully, / God'*
Langford Reed *Complete Limerick Book* (1924)

5 The baby doesn't understand English and the Devil knows Latin.
on being asked to perform a baptism in English
Evelyn Waugh *Ronald Knox* (1959) pt. 1, ch. 5

6 A loud noise at one end and no sense of responsibility at the other.
definition of a baby
attributed

Vicesimus Knox 1752–1821

English writer

7 All sensible people agree in thinking that large seminaries of young ladies, though managed with all the vigilance and caution which human abilities can exert, are in danger of great corruption.
Liberal Education (1780) sect. 27 'On the literary education of women'

8 Can anything be more absurd than keeping women in a state of ignorance, and yet so vehemently to insist on their resisting temptation?
Mary Wollstonecraft *A Vindication of the Rights of Woman* (1792) ch. 7

Ted Koehler

American songwriter

9 Stormy weather,
Since my man and I ain't together.
'Stormy Weather' (1933 song)

Arthur Koestler 1905–83

Hungarian-born writer

10 One may not regard the world as a sort of metaphysical brothel for emotions.
Darkness at Noon (1940) 'The Second Hearing' pt. 7

11 God seems to have left the receiver off the hook, and time is running out.
The Ghost in the Machine (1967) ch. 18

12 A writer's ambition should be . . . to trade a hundred contemporary readers for ten readers in ten years' time and for one reader in a hundred years.
in *New York Times Book Review* 1 April 1951

Helmut Kohl 1930–

German statesman, Chancellor of West Germany (1982–90) and first postwar Chancellor of united Germany (1990–8)

13 The policy of European integration is in reality a question of war and peace in the 21st century.
speech at Louvain University, 2 February 1996

Johann Georg Kohl 1808–78

German travel writer

14 We had now entered the notorious county of Tipperary, in which more murders and assaults are committed in one year than in the whole Kingdom of Saxony in five.
Ireland, Scotland and England (1844); see **TROLLOPE** 816:12

Käthe Kollwitz 1867–1945

German sculptor and graphic artist

15 As you, the children of my body, have been my tasks, so too are my other works.
letter to her son Hans, 21 February 1915

16 I have never done any work cold . . . I have always worked with my blood, so to speak.
letter to her son Hans, 16 April 1917

The Koran

textual translations are those of A. J. Arberry, 1964

17 In the Name of God, the Merciful, the Compassionate.
sura 1

18 Praise belongs to God, the Lord of all Being,
the All-merciful, the All-compassionate,
the Master of the Day of Doom.
sura 1

19 Thee only we serve; to Thee alone we pray for succour.
Guide us in the straight path,
the path of those whom Thou hast blessed,
not of those against whom Thou art wrathful,
nor of those who are astray.
sura 1

20 That is the Book [the Koran], wherein is no doubt,

a guidance to the godfearing
who believe in the Unseen.
   sura 2

1 And if you are in doubt concerning that We have
sent down on Our servant [Muhammad], then
   bring a sura
like it, and call your witnesses, apart from
God, if you are truthful.
And if you do not—and you will not—then
fear the Fire, whose fuel is men and stones,
prepared for unbelievers.
   sura 2

2 True piety is this:
to believe in God, and the Last Day,
the angels, the Book, and the Prophets,
to give of one's substance, however cherished,
to kinsmen, and orphans,
the needy, the traveller, beggars,
and to ransom the slave,
to perform the prayer, to pay the alms.
   sura 2

3 The month of Ramadan, wherein the Koran
was sent down to be a guidance
to the people, and as clear signs
of the Guidance and the Salvation
So let those of you, who are present
at the month, fast it.
   sura 2

4 And fight in the way of God with those
who fight with you, but aggress not: God loves
not the aggressors.
   sura 2

5 No compulsion is there in religion.
   sura 2

6 God is the protector of the believers;
He brings them forth from the shadows
into the light.
   sura 2

7 God has
permitted trafficking, and forbidden usury.
   sura 2

8 Say to the unbelievers: 'You shall be
overthrown, and mustered into Gehenna—
an evil cradling!'
   sura 3; 'An evil cradling' was the title of a book (1992) by
   Brian Keenan (1905-)

9 The true religion with God is Islam.
   sura 3

10 Abraham in truth was not a Jew,
neither a Christian; but he was a Muslim
and one pure of faith; certainly he was never
of the idolaters.
   sura 3

11 Say: 'We believe in God, and that which has
   been sent
down on us, and sent down on Abraham and
   Ishmael,
Isaac and Jacob, and the Tribes, and in that
   which was

given to Moses and Jesus, and the Prophets of
   their
Lord; we make no division between any of
   them, and
to Him we surrender.'
   sura 3

12 Whoso desires another religion than Islam, it
   shall
not be accepted of him; in the next world he
   shall
be among the losers.
   sura 3

13 Every soul shall taste of death; you shall surely
be paid in full your wages on the Day
of Resurrection.
   sura 3

14 Men are the managers of the affairs of women.
   sura 4

15 Righteous women are therefore obedient,
guarding the secret for God's guarding.
And those you fear may be rebellious
admonish; banish them to their couches,
and beat them.
   sura 4

16 So let them fight in the way of God who
sell the present life for the world to come;
and whosoever fights in the way of God
and is slain, or conquers, We shall bring him
a mighty wage.
   sura 4

17 How is it with you, that you do not fight
in the way of God, and for the men,
women, and children who, being abased,
say, 'Our Lord, bring us forth from this city
whose people are evildoers, and appoint to us
a protector from Thee, and appoint to us
from Thee a helper?'
   sura 4

18 Whatever good visits thee, it is of God;
whatever evil visits thee is of thyself.
   sura 4

19 What, do they not ponder the Koran?
If it had been from other than God
surely they would have found in it much
inconsistency.
   sura 4

20 God—
there is no God but He.
He will surely gather you
to the Resurrection Day,
no doubt of it.
And who is truer in tidings than God?
   sura 4

21 To God belongs all that is in the heavens
and in the earth, and God encompasses
everything.
   sura 4

22 Souls are very
prone to avarice. If you do good

and are godfearing, surely God is aware of the
   things you do.

   sura 4; 'Men's souls are naturally inclined to covetousness;
   but if ye be kind towards women and fear to wrong them,
   God is well acquainted with what ye do' in George Sale's
   translation, 1734

1 The Messiah, Jesus son of Mary,
   was only the Messenger of God.

   sura 4

2 Today I have perfected your religion
   for you, and I have completed My blessing
   upon you and I have approved Islam for
   your religion.

   sura 5

3 Whoso slays a soul not to retaliate for a soul
   slain, nor for corruption done in the land,
   shall be as if he had slain mankind altogether.

   sura 5

4 And we have sent down to thee the Book
   with the truth, confirming the Book
   that was before it, and assuring it.

   sura 5

5 He originates
   creation, then He brings it back again
   that He may recompense those who believe
   and do deeds of righteousness, justly.

   sura 10

6 Glory be to Him, who carried His servant by
      night
   from the Holy Mosque to the Further Mosque
   the precincts of which We have blessed,
   that We might show him some of Our signs.

   sura 17

7 Perform the prayer
   at the sinking of the sun to the darkening of the
      night
   and the recital of dawn.

   sura 17

8 Even so We have sent it down
   as an Arabic Koran, and We
   have turned about in it something
   of threats, that haply they may be
   godfearing, or it may arouse in
   them remembrance.

   sura 20

9 And do thou purify
   My House [Kaaba] for those that shall go
      about it
   and those that stand, for those that bow
   and prostrate themselves;
   and proclaim among men the Pilgrimage.

   sura 22

10 The flesh of them shall not reach God,
   neither their blood, but godliness from you
   shall reach him.

   of the beasts of sacrifice

   sura 22; sometimes translated as 'It is not their meat nor
   their blood that reaches Allah'

11 He
   named you Muslims

aforetime and in this, that the Messenger
might be a witness against you, and that
you might be witnesses against mankind.

   sura 22

12 God is the Light of the heavens and the earth;
   the likeness of His Light is as a niche
   wherein is a lamp . . .
   kindled from a Blessed Tree,
   an olive that is neither of the East nor of the
      West
   whose oil wellnigh would shine, even if no fire
      touched it;
   Light upon Light.

   sura 24

13 Muhammad is not the father of any one
   of your men, but the Messenger of God,
   and the Seal of the Prophets

   sura 33

14 God knows the Unseen in the heavens and the
      earth;
   He knows the thoughts within the breasts.
   It is He who appointed you viceroys in the
      earth.

   sura 35

15 The sending down of the Book is from God
   the All-mighty, the All-wise.
   We have sent down to thee the Book with the
      truth;
   so worship God, making thy religion
   His sincerely.

   sura 39

16 Not equal are the good deed and the evil deed.
   Repel with that which is fairer
   and behold, he between whom and thee
   there is enmity shall be as if he were
   a loyal friend.

   sura 41; 'Good and evil shall not be held equal. Turn away evil
   with that which is better; and behold the man between
   whom and thyself there was enmity, shall become, as it
   were, thy warmest friend' in George Sale's translation, 1734

17 It belongs not to any mortal that
   God should speak to him, except
   by revelation, or from behind
   a veil,
   or that He should send a messenger
   and he reveal whatsoever He will,
   by His leave.

   sura 42

18 Surely,
   unto God all things come home.

   sura 42

19 And those who are slain in the way of God, He
   will not send their works astray,
   He will guide them, and dispose their minds
      aright,
   and He will admit them to Paradise,
   that He has made known to them.

   sura 47

20 It is He who has sent his Messenger with
   the guidance and the religion of truth, that

He may uplift it above every religion.
sura 48

1 Muhammed is the Messenger of God,
and those who are with him are hard
against the unbelievers, merciful
one to another.
sura 48

2 Thou seest them
bowing, prostrating, seeking bounty
from God and good pleasure. Their
mark is on their faces, the trace of
prostration. That is their likeness
in the Torah, and their likeness
in the Gospel.
of believers
sura 48

3 O mankind, We have created you
male and female, and appointed you
races and tribes, that you may know
one another.
sura 49

4 By the glorious Koran!
sura 50

5 We indeed created man; and We know
what his soul whispers within him,
and We are nearer to him than the
jugular vein.
sura 50

6 He [God] is the First and the Last, the Outward
and the Inward.
sura 57

7 He is God
the Creator, the Maker, the Shaper,
To Him belong the Names Most Beautiful.
sura 59

8 On that day [the Day of Judgement] you shall
be exposed, not one secret
of yours concealed.
Then as for him who is given his book in his
right hand,
he shall say, 'Here, take and read my book!
Certainly
I thought that I should encounter my
reckoning.' So he
shall be in a pleasing life
in a lofty Garden,
its clusters nigh to gather.
sura 69

9 Recite: In the Name of thy Lord who created
created Man of a blood-clot.
sura 96

Gene Kranz 1933–
American lead flight director for NASA Mission Control

10 Failure is not an option.
announcement to ground crew in Houston, 14 April 1970, as
Apollo 13 approached the critical earth-to-moon decision
loop; this version was used in the film Apollo 13 (1995),
though his actual words were 'This crew is coming home'
title of autobiography, 2000

Karl Kraus 1874–1936
Austrian satirist

11 How is the world ruled and how do wars start?
Diplomats tell lies to journalists and then believe
what they read.
Aphorisms and More Aphorisms (1909)

12 There is no unhappier creature on earth than a
fetishist who yearns to embrace a woman's shoe
and has to embrace the whole woman.
Aphorisms and More Aphorisms (1909)

13 A journalist is stimulated by a deadline. He
writes worse when he has time.
Pro Domo et Mundo (1912) pt. 4

14 What good is speed if the brain has oozed out
on the way?
in *Die Fackel* September 1909 'The Discovery of the North
Pole'

Jiddu Krishnamurti d. 1986
Indian spiritual philosopher

15 Religion is the frozen thought of men out of
which they build temples.
in *Observer* 22 April 1928 'Sayings of the Week'

16 Truth is a pathless land, and you cannot
approach it by any path whatsoever, by any
religion, by any sect.
speech in Holland, 3 August 1929

17 Happiness is a state of which you are
unconscious, of which you are not aware. The
moment you are aware that you are happy, you
cease to be happy . . . You want to be
consciously happy; the moment you are
consciously happy, happiness is gone.
Penguin Krishnamurti Reader (1970) 'Questions and Answers'

Kris Kristofferson 1936–
American actor

18 Freedom's just another word for nothin' left to
lose,
Nothin' ain't worth nothin', but it's free.
'Me and Bobby McGee' (1969 song, with Fred Foster)

Leopold Kronecker 1823–91
German mathematician

19 God made the integers, all the rest is the work
of man.
Jahresberichte der Deutschen Mathematiker Vereinigung

Paul Kruger 1825–1904
**South African soldier and statesman, President of Transvaal
1883-99**

20 A bill of indemnity . . . for raid by Dr Jameson
and the British South Africa Company's troops.
The amount falls under two heads—first,
material damage, total of claim, £677,938 3s.

3*d.*—second, moral or intellectual damage, total of claim, £1,000,000.
> telegram on behalf of the South African Republic, communicated to the House of Commons by Joseph Chamberlain, 18 February 1897

Joseph Wood Krutch 1893–1970
American critic and naturalist

1 The most serious charge which can be brought against New England is not Puritanism but February.
> *The Twelve Seasons* (1949) 'February'

Stanley Kubrick 1928–99
American film director

2 The great nations have always acted like gangsters, and the small nations like prostitutes.
> in *Guardian* 5 June 1963

Satish Kumar 1937–
Indian writer

3 Lead me from death to life, from falsehood to truth.
Lead me from despair to hope, from fear to trust.
Lead me from hate to love, from war to peace.
Let peace fill our heart, our world, our universe.
> 'Prayer for Peace' (1981); adapted from the UPANISHADS; see UPANISHADS 822:7

Milan Kundera 1929–
Czech novelist

4 The struggle of man against power is the struggle of memory against forgetting.
> *The Book of Laughter and Forgetting* (1979) pt. 1, ch. 2

5 The unbearable lightness of being.
> title of novel (1984)

6 None among us is superman enough to escape kitsch completely. No matter how we scorn it, kitsch is an integral part of the human condition.
> *The Unbearable Lightness of Being* (1984) pt. 6, ch. 12

7 Mankind's true moral test, its fundamental test (which lies deeply buried from view) consists of its attitudes towards those who are at its mercy: animals.
> *The Unbearable Lightness of Being* (1984) pt. 7, ch. 2

Hanif Kureishi 1954–
English novelist and screenwriter

8 My name is Karim Amir, and I am an Englishman born and bred, almost.
> *The Buddha of Suburbia* (1990) pt. 1, ch. 1, opening words

9 Everyone looks at you . . . and thinks: an Indian boy, how exotic, how interesting, what stories of aunties and elephants we'll hear now from him. And you're from Orpington.
> *The Buddha of Suburbia* (1990) pt. 2, ch. 9

Thomas Kyd 1558–94
English dramatist

10 My son—and what's a son? A thing begot Within a pair of minutes, thereabout, A lump bred up in darkness.
> *The Spanish Tragedy* (1592) act 3, sc. 11, The Third Addition (1602 ed.) l. 5

11 It grew a gallows and did bear our son, It bore thy fruit and mine.
> *The Spanish Tragedy* (1592) act 3, sc. 12, The Fourth Addition (1602 ed.) l. 70

12 For what's a play without a woman in it?
> *The Spanish Tragedy* (1592) act 4, sc. 1, l. 97

13 Hieronimo is mad again.
> alternative title given to *The Spanish Tragedy* in 1615

 **L l**

Henry Labouchere 1831–1912
British politician

14 He [Labouchere] did not object to the old man always having a card up his sleeve, but he did object to his insinuating that the Almighty had placed it there.
> on GLADSTONE's *'frequent appeals to a higher power'*
> Earl Curzon *Modern Parliamentary Eloquence* (1913); another version is: 'Who cannot refrain from perpetually bringing an ace down his sleeve, even when he has only to play fair to win the trick', letter in A. L. Thorold *The Life of Henry Labouchere* (1913) ch. 15

Jean de la Bruyère 1645–96
French satiric moralist

15 We love well only once, the first time. The loves which follow are less involuntary.
> *The Characters, or The Manners of the Age* (1688) 'Of the Heart'

16 We must laugh before we are happy, for fear of dying without having laughed at all.
> *The Characters, or The Manners of the Age* (1688) 'Of the Heart'

17 The onset and the waning of love make themselves felt in the uneasiness experienced at being alone together.
> *The Characters, or The Manners of the Age* (1688) 'Of the Heart'

18 The people have little intelligence, the great no heart . . . if I had to choose I should have no hesitation: I would be of the people.
> *The Characters, or The Manners of the Age* (1688) 'Of the Great'

19 Man has but three events in his life: to be born, to live, and to die. He is not conscious of his birth, he suffers at his death and he forgets to live.
> *The Characters, or The Manners of the Age* (1688) 'Of Man'

1 Between good sense and good taste there is the same difference as between cause and effect.
The Characters, or The Manners of the Age (1688) 'Of Judgement'

2 A pious man is one who would be an atheist if the king were.
The Characters, or The Manners of the Age (1688) 'Of Fashion'

3 Everything has been said, and we are more than seven thousand years of human thought too late.
The Characters, or The Manners of the Age (1688) 'The Works of the Mind'

4 Making a book is a craft, as is making a clock; it takes more than wit to become an author.
The Characters, or The Manners of the Age (1688) 'The Works of the Mind'

Nivelle de la Chaussée 1692–1754
French dramatist

5 *Quand tout le monde a tort, tout le monde a raison.*
When everyone is wrong, everyone is right.
La Gouvernante (1747) act 1, sc. 3

James Lackington 1746–1815
English bookseller

6 At last, by singing and repeating enthusiastic amorous hymns, and ignorantly applying particular texts of scripture, I got my imagination to the proper pitch, and thus was I born again in an instant.
Memoirs (1792 ed.) Letter 6

Pierre Choderlos de Laclos 1741–1803
French soldier and writer

7 Monsieur de Valmont, with an illustrious name, a large fortune, and many agreeable qualities, early realized that to achieve influence in society no more is required than to practise the arts of adulation and ridicule with equal skill.
Les Liaisons Dangereuses (1782) letter 32

8 Our intentions make blackguards of us all; our weakness in carrying them out we call probity.
Les Liaisons Dangereuses (1782) letter 66

9 He cannot rate me very high if he thinks he is worth my fidelity!
Les Liaisons Dangereuses (1782) letter 113

10 A man enjoys the happiness he feels, a woman the happiness she gives.
Les Liaisons Dangereuses (1782) letter 130

11 If you will allow me, at my age, a reflection that is scarcely ever made at yours, I must say that if one only knew where one's true happiness lay one would never look for it outside the limits prescribed by the law and by religion.
Les Liaisons Dangereuses (1782) letter 171

Madame de La Fayette 1634–93
French novelist

12 One reproaches a lover, but can one reproach a husband, when his only fault is that he no longer loves?
The Princess of Clèves (1678) pt. 4

Jean de la Fontaine 1621–95
French poet and fabulist

13 *Je plie et ne romps pas.*
I bend and I break not.
Fables bk. 1 (1668) 'Le Chêne et le Roseau'

14 *C'est double plaisir de tromper le trompeur.*
It is doubly pleasing to trick the trickster.
Fables bk. 2 (1668) 'Le Coq et le Renard'

15 *Aide-toi, le ciel t'aidera.*
Help yourself, and heaven will help you.
Fables bk. 6 (1668) 'Le Chartier Embourbé'; see **PROVERBS** 633:6

16 *La mort ne surprend point le sage,*
Il est toujours prêt à partir.
Death never takes the wise man by surprise; he is always ready to go.
Fables bk. 8 (1678–9) 'Death and the Dying Man'; see **MONTAIGNE** 554:21

17 *Il connaît l'univers et ne se connaît pas.*
He knows the universe and does not know himself.
Fables bk. 8 (1678–9) 'Democritus and the Abderites'

18 *Rien ne pèse tant qu'un secret;*
Le porter loin est difficile aux dames:
Et je sais même sur ce fait
Bon nombre d'hommes qui sont femmes.
Nothing weighs so heavy as a secret; women find it difficult to carry one far. And I know a lot of men who are just like women about this.
Fables bk. 8 (1678–9) 'The Women and the Secret'

19 *Ventre affamé n'a point d'oreilles.*
A hungry stomach has no ears.
Fables bk. 9 (1678–9) 'The Kite and the Nightingale'

20 *Aucun chemin des fleurs ne conduit à la gloire.*
No path of flowers leads to glory.
Fables bk. 10 (1694) 'The Two Adventurers and the Talisman'

21 *Certain renard voulut, dit-on, se faire loup. Hé! qui peut dire que pour le métier de mouton jamais aucun loup ne soupire?*
A certain fox, it is said, wanted to become a wolf. Ah! who can say why no wolf has ever craved the life of a sheep?
Fables Choisies (1693 ed.) bk. 7, no. 9

Jules Laforgue 1860–87
French poet

22 *Ah! que la vie est quotidienne.*
Oh, what a day-to-day business life is.
Complainte sur certains ennuis (1885)

1 History is a gaudy old nightmare who does not suspect that the best jokes are the shortest.
Mélanges posthumes (1903)

Fiorello La Guardia 1882–1947
American politician

2 When I make a mistake, it's a beaut!
on the appointment of Herbert O'Brien as a judge in 1936
William Manners *Patience and Fortitude* (1976)

John Lahr 1941–
American critic

3 Criticism is a life without risk.
Light Fantastic (1996)

4 I know in an existential sense that life can change on a dime . . . something has instantly and inexorably changed in American life.
in the aftermath of the terrorist attacks which destroyed the World Trade Center in New York, and damaged the Pentagon
'Forever Changed', online correspondence with August Wilson in *Slate*, posted 11 September 2001

R. D. Laing 1927–89
Scottish psychiatrist

5 The divided self.
title of book (1960) on schizophrenia

6 Madness need not be all breakdown. It may also be break-through.
The Politics of Experience (1967) ch. 6

Alphonse de Lamartine 1790–1869
French poet

7 *Borné dans sa nature, infini dans ses vœux,*
L'homme est un dieu tombé qui se souvient des cieux.
Limited in his nature, infinite in his desires, man is a fallen god who remembers heaven.
'L'Homme' (1820)

8 *Un seul être vous manque, et tout est dépeuplé.*
Only one being is wanting, and your whole world is bereft of people.
'L'Isolement' (1820)

9 *Ô temps! suspend ton vol, et vous, heures propices!*
Suspendez votre cours.
O Time! arrest your flight, and you, propitious hours, stay your course.
Le Lac (1820) st. 6

Lady Caroline Lamb 1785–1828
English wife of William Lamb, Lord **MELBOURNE**. On Lamb: see **BYRON** 190:24

10 Mad, bad, and dangerous to know.
of **BYRON**, *after their first meeting at a ball*
diary, March 1812; in Elizabeth Jenkins *Lady Caroline Lamb* (1932) ch. 6

Charles Lamb 1775–1834
English writer. On Lamb: see **HAZLITT** 385:20

11 If the husband be a man with whom you have lived on a friendly footing before marriage,—if you did not come in on the wife's side,—if you did not sneak into the house in her train, but were an old friend in first habits of intimacy before their courtship was so much as thought on,—look about you . . . Every long friendship, every old authentic intimacy, must be brought into their office to be new stamped with their currency, as a sovereign Prince calls in the good old money that was coined in some reign before he was born or thought of, to be new marked and minted with the stamp of his authority, before he will let it pass current in the world.
Essays of Elia (1823) 'A Bachelor's Complaint of the Behaviour of Married People'

12 Ceremony is an invention to take off the uneasy feeling which we derive from knowing ourselves to be less the object of love and esteem with a fellow-creature than some other person is. It endeavours to make up, by superior attentions in little points, for that invidious preference which it is forced to deny in the greater.
Essays of Elia (1823) 'A Bachelor's Complaint of the Behaviour of Married People'

13 Presents, I often say, endear Absents.
Essays of Elia (1823) 'A Dissertation upon Roast Pig'

14 The human species, according to the best theory I can form of it, is composed of two distinct races, *the men who borrow,* and *the men who lend.*
Essays of Elia (1823) 'The Two Races of Men'

15 Your *borrowers of books*—those mutilators of collections, spoilers of the symmetry of shelves, and creators of odd volumes.
Essays of Elia (1823) 'The Two Races of Men'

16 Not many sounds in life . . . exceed in interest a knock at the door.
Essays of Elia (1823) 'Valentine's Day'

17 Books think for me.
Last Essays of Elia (1833) 'Detached Thoughts on Books and Reading'

18 Things in books' clothing.
Last Essays of Elia (1833) 'Detached Thoughts on Books and Reading'

19 [A pun] is a pistol let off at the ear; not a feather to tickle the intellect.
Last Essays of Elia (1833) 'Popular Fallacies' no. 9

20 For thy sake, Tobacco, I
Would do any thing but die.
'A Farewell to Tobacco' l. 122

21   Gone before
To that unknown and silent shore.
'Hester' (1803) st. 7

22 I have had playmates, I have had companions,
In my days of childhood, in my joyful school-days,—
All, all are gone, the old familiar faces.
'The Old Familiar Faces'

1 A child's a plaything for an hour.
'Parental Recollections' (1809); often attributed to Lamb's sister Mary

2 I have something more to do than feel.
on the death of his mother, at his sister Mary's hands
letter to S. T. Coleridge, 27 September 1796, in E. W. Marrs (ed.) *Letters of Charles and Mary Lamb* (1975) vol. 1

3 Cultivate simplicity, Coleridge.
letter to S. T. Coleridge, 8 November 1796, in E. W. Marrs (ed.) *Letters of Charles and Mary Lamb* (1975) vol. 1

4 The man must have a rare recipe for melancholy, who can be dull in Fleet Street.
letter to Thomas Manning, 15 February 1802, in E. W. Marrs (ed.) *Letters of Charles and Mary Lamb* (1976) vol. 2

5 Nursed amid her noise, her crowds, her beloved smoke—what have I been doing all my life, if I have not lent out my heart with usury to such scenes?
of London
letter to Thomas Manning, 15 February 1802, in E. W. Marrs (ed.) *Letters of Charles and Mary Lamb* (1976) vol. 2

6 Nothing puzzles me more than time and space; and yet nothing troubles me less, as I never think about them.
letter to Thomas Manning, 2 January 1810, in E. W. Marrs (ed.) *Letters of Charles and Mary Lamb* (1978) vol. 3

7 This very night I am going to leave off tobacco! Surely there must be some other world in which this unconquerable purpose shall be realized.
letter to Thomas Manning, 26 December 1815, in E. W. Marrs (ed.) *Letters of Charles and Mary Lamb* (1978) vol. 3

8 An Archangel a little damaged.
of COLERIDGE
letter to Wordsworth, 26 April 1816, in E. W. Marrs (ed.) *Letters of Charles and Mary Lamb* (1978) vol. 3

9 Fanny Kelly's divine plain face.
of the actress and singer Fanny Kelly (1790–1882)
letter to Mary Wordsworth, 18 February 1818, in Henry H. Harper (ed.) *Letters of Charles Lamb* (1905) vol. 4

10 The ever-haunting importunity Of business?
letter to Bernard Barton, 11 September 1822, in Henry H. Harper (ed.) *Letters of Charles Lamb* (1905) vol. 4

11 When my sonnet was rejected, I exclaimed, 'Damn the age; I will write for Antiquity!'
letter to B. W. Proctor, 22 January 1829, in *Works* (1912) vol. 6

12 The greatest pleasure I know, is to do a good action by stealth, and to have it found out by accident.
'Table Talk by the late Elia' in *The Athenaeum* 4 January 1834

13 I toiled after it, sir, as some men toil after virtue.
on being asked 'how he had acquired his power of smoking at such a rate'
Thomas Noon Talfourd *Memoirs of Charles Lamb* (1892)

Constant Lambert 1905–51
English composer

14 The whole trouble with a folk song is that once you have played it through there is nothing

much you can do except play it over again and play it rather louder.
Music Ho! (1934) ch. 3

15 The average English critic is a don *manqué*, hopelessly parochial when not exaggeratedly teutonophile, over whose desk must surely hang the motto (presumably in Gothic lettering) 'Above all no enthusiasm'.
in *Opera* December 1950; see **TALLEYRAND** 788:17

John Lambert 1619–83
English soldier and Parliamentary supporter

16 The quarrel is now between light and darkness, not who shall rule, but whether we shall live or be preserved or no. Good words will not do with the cavaliers.
speech in the Parliament of 1656 supporting the rule of the major-generals
in *Dictionary of National Biography* (1917–)

John George Lambton *see* Lord Durham

George Lamming 1927–
Barbados-born novelist and poet

17 In the castle of my skin.
title of novel (1953)

Norman Lamont 1942–
British Conservative politician, Chancellor 1990–3. See also MISQUOTATIONS 547:18

18 Rising unemployment and the recession have been the price that we've had to pay to get inflation down. [Labour shouts] That is a price well worth paying.
speech in the House of Commons, 16 May 1991

19 We give the impression of being in office but not in power.
as a backbencher
speech in the House of Commons, 9 June 1993

Giuseppe di Lampedusa 1896–1957
Italian writer

20 If we want things to stay as they are, things will have to change.
The Leopard (1957)

21 Love. Of course, love. Flames for a year, ashes for thirty.
The Leopard (1957)

Osbert Lancaster 1908–86
English writer and cartoonist

22 Fan-vaulting . . . from an aesthetic standpoint frequently belongs to the 'Last-supper-carved-on-a-peach-stone' class of masterpiece.
Pillar to Post (1938) 'Perpendicular'

23 All over the country the latest and most scientific methods of mass-production are being utilized to turn out a stream of old oak beams, leaded window-panes and small discs of bottle-glass, all structural devices which our ancestors lost no time in abandoning as soon as an increase in wealth and knowledge enabled them to do so.

Pillar to Post (1938) 'Stockbroker's Tudor'

Letitia Elizabeth Landon (L. E. L.)
1802–38

English writer

1 Few, save the poor, feel for the poor.
'The Poor'

2 She was so changed, the soft carnation cloud
Once mantling o'er her cheek . . .
Had faded into paleness, broken by
Bright burning blushes, torches of the tomb.
'Sad is the tale' (1818)

Walter Savage Landor 1775–1864
English poet

3 I strove with none; for none was worth my strife;
Nature I loved, and, next to Nature, Art.
'Dying Speech of an Old Philosopher' (1853)

4 Ireland never was contented . . .
Say you so? You are demented.
Ireland was contented when
All could use the sword and pen,
And when Tara rose so high
That her turrets split the sky.
'Ireland never was contented' (1853)

5 Ah, what avails the sceptred race!
Ah, what the form divine!
'Rose Aylmer' (1806)

6 George the First was always reckoned
Vile, but viler George the Second;
And what mortal ever heard
Any good of George the Third?
When from earth the Fourth descended
God be praised the Georges ended!
epigram in *The Atlas*, 28 April 1855; earlier versions are discussed in *Notes and Queries* 3 May 1902

7 There are no fields of amaranth on this side of the grave.
Imaginary Conversations 'Aesop and Rhodope' in *Works of Walter Savage Landor* (1846) vol. 2

8 I shall dine late; but the dining-room will be well-lighted, the guests few and select. I neither am, nor ever shall be, popular.
of the Edinburgh Review *on his* Hellenics
in April 1850, J. Forster *Walter Savage Landor: a Biography* (1869)

Andrew Lang 1844–1912
Scottish man of letters

9 St Andrews by the Northern sea,
A haunted town it is to me!
'Almae Matres' (1884)

10 If the wild bowler thinks he bowls,
Or if the batsman thinks he's bowled,
They know not, poor misguided souls,
They too shall perish unconsoled.
I am the batsman and the bat,
I am the bowler and the ball.
'Brahma'; see **EMERSON** 314:11

11 They hear like ocean on a western beach
The surge and thunder of the Odyssey.
'The Odyssey' (1881)

12 He uses statistics as a drunken man uses lamp posts—for support rather than illumination.
Alan L. Mackay *Harvest of a Quiet Eye* (1977); attributed

Susanne Langer 1895–1985
American philosopher

13 Art is the objectification of feeling, and the subjectification of nature.
Mind (1967) vol. 1

William Langland c.1330–c.1400
English poet

14 In a somer seson, whan softe was the sonne.
The Vision of Piers Plowman B text (ed. A. V. C. Schmidt, 1987) prologue l. 1

15 Ac on a May morwenynge on Malverne hilles
Me bifel a ferly, of Fairye me thoghte.
The Vision of Piers Plowman B text (ed. A. V. C. Schmidt, 1987) prologue l. 5; ' . . . Me biful for to slepe, for werynesse of-walked' in C text (ed. D. Pearsall, 1978) prologue l. 7

16 A faire feeld ful of folk fond I ther bitwene—
Of alle manere of men, the meene and the riche,
Werchynge and wandrynge as the world asketh.
The Vision of Piers Plowman B text (ed. A. V. C. Schmidt, 1987) prologue l. 17

17 Brewesters and baksters, bochiers and cokes—
For thise are men on this molde that moost harm wercheth
To the povere peple.
The Vision of Piers Plowman B text (ed. A. V. C. Schmidt, 1987) Passus 3, l. 79; 'As bakeres and breweres, bocheres and cokes; / For thyse men don most harm to the mene peple' in C text (ed. D. Pearsall, 1978) Passus 3, l. 80

18 *Parum lauda; vitupera parcius.*
Be sparing in praise, and more so in blame.
The Vision of Piers Plowman B text (ed. A. V. C. Schmidt, 1987) Passus 11, l. 106; the saying is attributed to Seneca by some medieval scholars

19 Suffraunce is a soverayn vertue, and a swift vengeaunce.
Who suffreth moore than God?
The Vision of Piers Plowman B text (ed. A. V. C. Schmidt, 1987) Passus 11, l. 378

20 Grammer, the ground of al.
The Vision of Piers Plowman B text (ed. A. V. C. Schmidt, 1987) Passus 15, l. 370

21 Innocence is next God, and nyght and day it crieth
'Vengeaunce! Vengeaunce! Forgyve be it nevere

That shente us and shedde oure blood!'
The Vision of Piers Plowman B text (ed. A. V. C. Schmidt, 1987)
Passus 17, l. 289

1 'After sharpest shoures,' quath Pees 'most shene
   is the sonne;
Is no weder warmer than after watry cloudes.'
Pees = *Peace*
The Vision of Piers Plowman B text (ed. A. V. C. Schmidt, 1987)
Passus 18, l. 411

Stephen Langton d. 1228
English cleric, Archbishop of Canterbury

2 *Veni, Sancte Spiritus,*
Et emitte coelitus
Lucis tuae radium.

Come, Holy Spirit, and send out from heaven
the beam of your light.
The 'Golden Sequence' for Whit Sunday (also attributed to
several others, notably Pope Innocent III)

3 *Lava quod est sordidum,*
Riga quod est aridum,
Sana quod est saucium.
Flecte quod est rigidum,
Fove quod est frigidum,
Rege quod est devium.

Wash what is dirty, water what is dry, heal what
is wounded. Bend what is stiff, warm what is
cold, guide what goes off the road.
The 'Golden Sequence' for Whit Sunday

Emilia Lanier 1569–1645
English-born poet

4 And since all arts at first from Nature came,
That goodly creature, mother of perfection,
Whom Jove's almighty hand at first did frame,
Taking both her and hers in his protection:
Why should not she now grace my barren
   muse,
And in a woman all defects excuse.
'The Dedications' (1611)

5 The walks put on their summer liveries,
And all things else did hold like similes:
The trees with leaves, with fruits, with flowers
   clad,
Embrac'd each other, seeming to be glad.
'The Description of Cookham' (1611)

Lao Tzu c.604–c.531 BC
Chinese philosopher; founder of Taoism
textual translations are those of Wing-Tsit Chan, 1963

6 The Tao [Way] that can be told of is not the
   eternal Tao;
The name that can be named is not the eternal
   name.
The Nameless is the origin of Heaven and
   Earth;
The Named is the mother of all things.
Tao-te Ching ch. 1

7 Front and back follow each other.
Therefore the sage manages affairs without
   action
And spreads doctrines without words.
Tao-te Ching ch. 2

8 Heaven and earth are not humane
They regard all things as straw dogs.
The sage is not humane.
He regards all people as straw dogs.
Tao-te Ching ch. 5

9 Thirty spokes are united around the hub to
   make a wheel,
But it is on its non-being that the utility of the
   carriage depends.
Clay is moulded to form a utensil,
But it is on its non-being that the utility of the
   utensil depends.
Doors and windows are cut out to make a
   room,
But it is on its non-being that the utility of the
   room depends.
Therefore turn being into advantage, and non-
   being into utility.
non-being *sometimes translated* hole
Tao-te-Ching ch. 11

10 The best [rulers] are those whose existence is
   [merely] known by the people.
The next best are those who are loved and
   praised.
The next are those who are feared.
And the next are those who are reviled . . .
[The great rulers] accomplish their task; they
   complete their work.
Nevertheless their people say that they simply
   follow Nature.
*often quoted as, 'A leader is best when people barely know
he exists . . . He acts without unnecessary speech, and
when the work is done the people say "We did it ourselves"'*
Tao-te Ching ch. 17

11 Let people hold on to these:
Manifest plainness,
Embrace simplicity,
Reduce selfishness,
Have few desires.
Tao-te Ching ch. 19

12 The thing that is called Tao is eluding and
   vague.
Vague and eluding, there is in it the form.
Eluding and vague, in it are things.
Deep and obscure, in it is the essence.
The essence is very real; in it are evidences.
Tao-te Ching ch. 21

13 I call it Tao.
If forced to give it a name, I shall call it Great.
Now being great means functioning everywhere.
Functioning everywhere means far-reaching.
Being far-reaching means returning to the
   original point.
Therefore Tao is great.
Tao-te Ching ch. 25

1 A good traveller leaves no track or trace.
often quoted as 'A good traveller has no fixed plans'
Tao Te Ching ch. 27

2 He who knows others is wise;
He who knows himself is enlightened.
He who conquers others has physical strength.
He who conquers himself is strong.
Tao-te Ching ch. 33

3 The man of superior virtue is not [conscious of]
his virtue,
And in this way he really possesses virtue.
The man of inferior virtue never loses [sight of]
his virtue,
And in this way he loses his virtue.
Tao-te Ching ch. 38

4 Reversion is the action of the Tao.
Weakness is the function of the Tao.
All things in the world come from being.
And being comes from non-being.
Tao-te Ching ch. 40

5 Tao produced the One.
The One produced the two.
The two produced the three.
And the three produced the ten thousand things.
The ten thousand things carry the yin and
embrace the yang,
and through the blending of the material force
they achieve harmony.
Tao-te Ching ch. 42

6 One may know the world without going out of
doors.
One may see the Way of Heaven without
looking through windows.
The further one goes, the less one knows.
Tao-te Ching ch. 47

7 The pursuit of learning is to increase day after
day.
The pursuit of Tao is to decrease day after day.
It is to decrease and further decrease until one
reaches the point of taking no action.
No action is undertaken, and yet nothing is left
undone.
Tao-te Ching ch. 48

8 He who knows does not speak.
He who speaks does not know.
Tao-te Ching ch. 56

9 The more laws and orders are made prominent,
The more thieves and bandits there will be.
Tao-te Ching ch. 57; see **PROVERBS** 639:10

10 The female always overcomes the male by
tranquillity,
And by tranquillity she is underneath.
Tao-te Ching ch. 61

11 A tower of nine storeys begins with a heap of
earth.
The journey of a thousand *li* starts from where
one stands.
Tao-te Ching ch. 64

12 Heaven's net is indeed vast.
Though its meshes are wide, it misses nothing.
Tao-te Ching ch. 73

13 There is nothing softer and weaker than water,
And yet there is nothing better for attacking
hard and strong things.
For this reason there is no substitute for it.
All the world knows that the weak overcomes
the strong and the soft overcomes the hard.
But none can practise it.
Tao-te Ching ch. 78

14 The sage does not accumulate for himself.
The more he uses for others, the more he has
himself.
The more he gives to others, the more he
possesses of his own.
The Way of Heaven is to benefit others and not
to injure.
The Way of the sage is to act but not to
compete.
Tao-te Ching ch. 81

Dionysius Lardner 1793–1859
Irish scientific writer

15 Men might as well project a voyage to the moon
as attempt to employ steam navigation against
the stormy North Atlantic Ocean.
speech to the British Association for the Advancement of
Science, 1838

Ring Lardner 1885–1933
American writer

16 Are you lost daddy I arsked tenderly.
Shut up he explained.
The Young Immigrunts (1920) ch. 10

James Larkin 1867–1947
Irish labour leader

17 Hell has no terror for me. I have lived there.
Thirty six years of hunger and poverty have
been my portion. They cannot terrify me with
hell. Better to be in hell with Dante and Davitt
than to be in heaven with Carson and Murphy.
in 1913, during the 'Dublin lockout' labour dispute
Ulick O'Connor *The Troubles* (rev. ed., 1996)

Philip Larkin 1922–85
English poet

18 Sexual intercourse began
In nineteen sixty-three
(Which was rather late for me) —
Between the end of the *Chatterley* ban
And the Beatles' first LP.
'Annus Mirabilis' (1974)

19 Time has transfigured them into
Untruth. The stone fidelity
They hardly meant has come to be
Their final blazon, and to prove

Our almost-instinct almost true:
What will survive of us is love.
'An Arundel Tomb' (1964)

1 What are days for?
Days are where we live.
'Days' (1964)

2 Life is first boredom, then fear.
Whether or not we use it, it goes.
'Dockery & Son' (1964)

3 And that will be England gone,
The shadows, the meadows, the lanes,
The guildhalls, the carved choirs.
There'll be books; it will linger on
In galleries; but all that remains
For us will be concrete and tyres.
'Going, Going' (1974)

4 Rather than words comes the thought of high
 windows:
The sun-comprehending glass,
And beyond it, the deep blue air, that shows
Nothing, and is nowhere, and is endless.
'High Windows' (1974)

5 Nothing, like something, happens anywhere.
'I Remember, I Remember' (1955)

6 Never such innocence,
Never before or since,
As changed itself to past
Without a word—the men
Leaving the gardens tidy,
The thousands of marriages
Lasting a little while longer:
Never such innocence again.
'MCMXIV' (1964)

7 I listen to money singing. It's like looking down
From long french windows at a provincial town,
The slums, the canal, the churches ornate and
 mad
In the evening sun. It is intensely sad.
'Money' (1974)

8 Perhaps being old is having lighted rooms
Inside your head, and people in them, acting.
People you know, yet can't quite name.
'The Old Fools' (1974)

9 They fuck you up, your mum and dad.
They may not mean to, but they do.
They fill you with the faults they had
And add some extra, just for you.
'This Be The Verse' (1974)

10 Man hands on misery to man.
It deepens like a coastal shelf.
Get out as early as you can,
And don't have any kids yourself.
'This Be The Verse' (1974)

11 Why should I let the toad *work*
Squat on my life?
Can't I use my wit as a pitchfork
And drive the brute off?
'Toads' (1955)

12 Give me your arm, old toad;
Help me down Cemetery Road.
'Toads Revisited' (1964)

13 I thought of London spread out in the sun,
Its postal districts packed like squares of wheat.
'The Whitsun Weddings' (1964)

14 A beginning, a muddle, and an end.
on the 'classic formula' for a novel
in New Fiction no. 15, January 1978; see **ARISTOTLE** 27:20

15 Deprivation is for me what daffodils were for
Wordsworth.
Required Writing (1983); see **WORDSWORTH** 866:8

16 I am afraid the compulsion to write poems left
me about seven years ago, since when I have
written virtually nothing. Naturally this is a
disappointment, but I would sooner write no
poems than bad poems.
letter, 11 August 1984; Anthony Thwaite (ed.) *Selected Letters
of Philip Larkin* (1992)

Duc de la Rochefoucauld 1613–80
French moralist

17 Passion often makes a fool of the wisest man,
and often makes the greatest fools wise.
Maxims (1678) no. 6

18 We are all strong enough to bear the
misfortunes of others.
Maxims (1678) no. 19

19 Self-interest, which blinds some people, brings
light to others.
Maxims (1678) no. 40

20 There is no disguise which can hide love for
long where it exists, or feign it where it does
not.
Maxims (1678) no. 70

21 It is more shameful to doubt one's friends than
to be duped by them.
Maxims (1678) no. 84

22 Everyone complains of his memory, and no one
complains of his judgement.
Maxims (1678) no. 89

23 There are good marriages, but no delightful
ones.
Maxims (1678) no. 113

24 A weak mind is the only defect out of our
power to mend.
Maxims (1678) no. 130

25 There are people whose defects become them,
and others who are ill served by their good
qualities.
Maxims (1678) no. 155

26 The glory of great men should always be
measured against the means they used to acquire
it.
Maxims (1678) no. 157

27 Hypocrisy is a tribute which vice pays to virtue.
Maxims (1678) no. 218

1 The height of cleverness is to be able to conceal it.
Maxims (1678) no. 245

2 There is scarcely a single man sufficiently aware to know all the evil he does.
Maxims (1678) no. 269

3 Absence diminishes commonplace passions and increases great ones, as the wind extinguishes candles and kindles fire.
Maxims (1678) no. 276; see **BUSSY-RABUTIN** 182:15, **FRANCIS** 340:18

4 Pride, which inspires us with so much envy, is sometimes of use toward the moderating of it too.
Maxims (1678) no. 281

5 In most of mankind gratitude is merely a secret hope for greater favours.
Maxims (1678) no. 298; see **WALPOLE** 838:16

6 We often forgive those who bore us, but we cannot forgive those whom we bore.
Maxims (1678) no. 304

7 The accent of one's birthplace lingers in the mind and in the heart as it does in one's speech.
Maxims (1678) no. 342

8 People by whom one must not be bored are almost always boring.
Maxims (1678) no. 352

9 It is easier to know man in general than to know one man in particular.
Maxims (1678) no. 436

10 The same force which serves to resist love also makes it strong and lasting; and weak people, who are always shaken by passions, are almost never fulfilled by them.
Maxims (1678) no. 477

11 In the misfortune of our best friends, we always find something which is not displeasing to us.
Réflexions ou Maximes Morales (1665) maxim 99

12 One is never as unhappy as one thinks, nor as happy as one hopes.
Sentences et Maximes de Morale (Dutch edition, 1664) maxim 128

Duc de la Rochefoucauld-Liancourt

1747–1827

French social reformer

13 LOUIS XVI: *C'est une grande révolte.*
LA ROCHEFOUCAULD-LIANCOURT: *Non, Sire, c'est une grande révolution.*
LOUIS XVI: It is a big revolt.
LA ROCHEFOUCAULD-LIANCOURT: No, Sir, it is a big revolution.
on a report reaching Versailles of the Fall of the Bastille, 1789
F. Dreyfus *La Rochefoucauld-Liancourt* (1903) ch. 2, sect. 3

Harold Laski 1893–1950

British Labour politician. See also CROSSMAN 261:10

14 That state of resentful coma that . . . dons dignify by the name of research.
letter to Oliver Wendell Holmes Jr., 10 October 1922

Hugh Latimer *c.*1485–1555

English Protestant martyr

15 *Gutta cavat lapidem, non vi sed saepe cadendo.*
The drop of rain maketh a hole in the stone, not by violence, but by oft falling.
The Second Sermon preached before the King's Majesty (19 April 1549); see **OVID** 590:4, **PROVERBS** 629:20

16 Be of good comfort Master Ridley, and play the man. We shall this day light such a candle by God's grace in England, as (I trust) shall never be put out.
last words, prior to being burned for heresy, 16 October 1555
John Foxe *Actes and Monuments* (1570 ed.); see **BIBLE** 96:24

William Laud 1573–1645

English churchman, Archbishop of Canterbury from 1633; executed for treason

17 Lord I am coming as fast as I can, I know I must pass through the shadow of death, before I can come to see thee; But it is but *Umbra Mortis,* a mere shadow of death, a little darkness upon nature; but thou by thy merits and passion, hast broke through the jaws of death; the Lord receive my soul, and have mercy upon me, and bless this kingdom with peace and plenty, and with brotherly love and charity, that there may not be this effusion of Christian blood amongst them, for Jesus Christ his sake, if it be thy will.
at the scaffold, in Peter Heylin Cyprianus Anglicus *(1668)*

Harry Lauder (Hugh MacLennan)

1870–1950

Scottish music-hall entertainer. See also MORRISON 561:9

18 Keep right on to the end of the road,
Keep right on to the end.
Tho' the way be long, let your heart be strong,
Keep right on round the bend.
'The End of the Road' (1924 song)

19 I love a lassie, a bonnie, bonnie lassie,
She's as pure as the lily in the dell.
She's as sweet as the heather, the bonnie bloomin' heather—
Mary, ma Scotch Bluebell.
'I Love a Lassie' (1905 song)

20 Roamin' in the gloamin',
On the bonnie banks o' Clyde.
'Roamin' in the Gloamin'' (1911 song)

Stan Laurel (Arthur Stanley Jefferson)
1890–1965
American film comedian, born in Britain

1 Another nice mess you've gotten me into.

often 'another fine mess'

Another Fine Mess (1930 film) and many other Laurel and Hardy films; spoken by Oliver Hardy

William L. Laurence 1888–1977
American journalist

2 At first it was a giant column that soon took the shape of a supramundane mushroom.

on the first atomic explosion in New Mexico, 16 July 1945

in New York Times 26 September 1945

Wilfrid Laurier 1841–1919
Canadian Liberal statesman, Prime Minister 1896–1911

3 Had I been born on the banks of the Saskatchewan, I would myself have shouldered a musket to fight against the neglect of governments and the shameless greed of speculators.

addressing meeting in the Champ de Mars, Montreal, 22 November 1885; O.D. Skelton Life and Letters of Sir Wilfrid Laurier (1921)

4 The nineteenth century was the century of the United States. I think we can claim that it is Canada that shall fill the twentieth century.

speech in Ottawa, 18 January 1904; see **TRUDEAU** 817:11

5 Quebec does not have opinions, only sentiments.

Mason Wade The French Canadians: 1760–1967 (1968)

Johann Kaspar Lavater 1741–1801
Swiss theologian

6 The discovery of truth, by slow progressive meditation, is wisdom.

Aphorisms on Man (c.1788) no. 93; see **BLAKE** 128:10

7 Trust not him with your secrets, who, when left alone in the room, turns over your papers.

Aphorisms on Man (c.1788) no. 439

8 The public seldom forgive twice.

Aphorisms on Man (c.1788) no. 596

Emily Lawless 1845–1913
Irish poet

9 She said, 'God knows they owe me nought,
I tossed them to the foaming sea,
I tossed them to the howling wastes,
Yet still their love comes home to me.'

'After Aughrim'

10 There's famine in the land, its grip is tightening still!
There's trouble, black and bitter, on every side I glance.

'An Exile's Mother'

D. H. Lawrence 1885–1930
English novelist and poet. On Lawrence: see GRIFFITH-JONES 373:5, ROBINSON 664:5, ZERN 877:15

11 To the Puritan all things are impure, as somebody says.

Etruscan Places (1932) 'Cerveteri'; see **BIBLE** 115:29

12 John Thomas says good-night to Lady Jane, a little droopingly, but with a hopeful heart.

Lady Chatterley's Lover (1928) ch. 19

13 Pornography is the attempt to insult sex, to do dirt on it.

Phoenix (1936) 'Pornography and Obscenity' ch. 3

14 Never trust the artist. Trust the tale. The proper function of a critic is to save the tale from the artist who created it.

Studies in Classic American Literature (1923) ch. 1

15 Be a good animal, true to your instincts.

The White Peacock (1911) pt. 2, ch. 2

16 Don't you find it a beautiful clean thought, a world empty of people, just uninterrupted grass, and a hare sitting up?

Women in Love (1920) ch. 11

17 Is it the secret of the long-nosed Etruscans?
The long-nosed, sensitive-footed, subtly-smiling Etruscans
Who made so little noise outside the cypress groves?

'Cypresses' (1923)

18 How beastly the bourgeois is
Especially the male of the species.

'How Beastly the Bourgeois Is' (1929)

19 Men! The only animal in the world to fear!

'Mountain Lion' (1923)

20 I never saw a wild thing
Sorry for itself.

'Self-Pity' (1929)

21 Now it is autumn and the falling fruit
And the long journey towards oblivion . . .
Have you built your ship of death, O have you?
O build your ship of death, for you will need it.

'Ship of Death' (1932)

22 A snake came to my water-trough
On a hot, hot day, and I in pyjamas for the heat,
To drink there.

'Snake' (1923)

23 And so, I missed my chance with one of the lords
Of life.
And I have something to expiate:
A pettiness.

'Snake' (1923)

24 Not I, not I, but the wind that blows through me!

'Song of a Man who has Come Through' (1917)

25 When I read Shakespeare I am struck with wonder
That such trivial people should muse and thunder

In such lovely language.
'When I Read Shakespeare' (1929)

1 Curse the blasted, jelly-boned swines, the slimy, the belly-wriggling invertebrates, the miserable sodding rotters, the flaming sods, the snivelling, dribbling, dithering, palsied, pulse-less lot that make up England today. They've got white of egg in their veins, and their spunk is that watery it's a marvel they can breed. They *can* nothing but frog-spawn—the gibberers! God, how I hate them!
letter to Edward Garnett, 3 July 1912, in H. T. Moore (ed.) *Collected Letters of D. H. Lawrence* (1962) vol. 1

2 Tragedy ought really to be a great kick at misery.
letter to A. W. McLeod, 6 October 1912, in H. T. Moore (ed.) *Collected Letters of D. H. Lawrence* (1962) vol. 1

3 Australia has a marvellous sky and air and blue clarity, and a hoary sort of land beneath it, like a Sleeping Princess on whom the dust of ages has settled.
letter to Jan Juta, 20 May 1922; *Letters and Works* (1987) vol. 4

4 The dead don't die. They look on and help.
letter to J. Middleton Murry, 2 February 1923, in H. T. Moore (ed.) *Collected Letters of D. H. Lawrence* (1962) vol. 2

5 I want to go south, where there is no autumn, where the cold doesn't crouch over one like a snow-leopard waiting to pounce. The heart of the North is dead, and the fingers of cold are corpse fingers.
letter to J. Middleton Murry, 3 October 1924, in H. T. Moore (ed.) *Collected Letters of D. H. Lawrence* (1962) vol. 2

6 My God, what a clumsy *olla putrida* James Joyce is! Nothing but old fags and cabbage-stumps of quotations from the Bible and the rest, stewed in the juice of deliberate, journalistic dirty-mindedness.
letter to Aldous and Maria Huxley, 15 August 1928, in H. T. Moore (ed.) *Collected Letters of D. H. Lawrence* (1962) vol. 2

T. E. Lawrence ('Lawrence of Arabia')
1888–1935
English soldier and writer. On Lawrence: see BERNERS 74:9

7 Many men would take the death-sentence without a whimper to escape the life-sentence which fate carries in her other hand.
The Mint (1955) pt. 1, ch. 4

8 The seven pillars of wisdom.
title of book (1926); see BIBLE 87:32

9 I loved you, so I drew these tides of men into
   my hands and wrote my will across the sky in
   stars
To earn you freedom, the seven pillared worthy
   house, that your eyes might be shining for me
When we came.
The Seven Pillars of Wisdom (1926) dedication

10 Surely the sex business isn't worth all this damned fuss? I've met only a handful of people who cared a biscuit for it.
on reading Lady Chatterley's Lover
   Christopher Hassall *Edward Marsh* (1959)

Laws of Manu
a code of Hindu religious law, dating in its present form from the 1st century BC
textual translations are those of W. Doniger with B. K. Smith, 1991

11 The very birth of a priest [brahmin] is the eternal physical form of religion; for he is born for the sake of religion and is fit to become one with ultimate reality.
ch. 1, v. 98

12 The man who gives him [the pupil] the benefit of the revealed canon . . . should be known as his guru.
ch. 1, v. 149

13 Since people in the other three stages of life are supported every day by the knowledge and the food of the householder, therefore the householder stage of life is the best.
ch. 3, v. 78

14 You can never get meat without violence to creatures with the breath of life, and the killing of creatures with the breath of life does not get you to heaven; therefore you should not eat meat.
ch. 5, v. 48

15 A girl, a young woman, or even an old woman should not do anything independently, even in [her own] house.
In childhood a woman should be under her father's control, in youth under her husband's, and when her husband is dead, under her sons'.
ch. 5, v. 147

16 There is no difference at all between the goddesses of good fortune . . . who live in houses and women . . . who are the lamps of their houses, worthy of reverence and greatly blessed because of their progeny.
ch. 9, v. 26

17 'Let there be mutual absence of infidelity until death'; this should be known as the supreme duty of a man and a woman, in a nutshell.
ch. 9, v. 101

18 All of those castes who are excluded from the world of those who were born from the mouth, arms, thighs and feet (of the primordial Man) are traditionally regarded as aliens.
ch. 10, v. 45

19 Manu has said that non-violence, truth, not stealing, purification, and the suppression of the sensory powers is the duty of the four classes, in a nutshell.
ch. 10, v. 63

Irving Layton 1912–2006
Canadian poet

1 An aphorism
should be
like a burr:
sting,
stick,
and leave
a little soreness
afterwards.
The Whole Bloody Bird (1969) 'Aphs'

2 We love in another's soul
whatever of ourselves
we can deposit in it;
the greater the deposit,
the greater the love.
The Whole Bloody Bird (1969) 'Aphs'

Emma Lazarus 1849–87
American poet

3 Give me your tired, your poor,
Your huddled masses yearning to breathe free,
The wretched refuse of your teeming shore,
Send these, the homeless, tempest-tossed, to me:
I lift my lamp beside the golden door.
inscription on the Statue of Liberty, New York
'The New Colossus' (1883)

Edmund Leach 1910–89
English anthropologist

4 Far from being the basis of the good society, the family, with its narrow privacy and tawdry secrets, is the source of all our discontents.
BBC Reith Lectures, 1967, in *Listener* 30 November 1967

Stephen Leacock 1869–1944
Canadian humorist

5 The parent who could see his boy as he really is, would shake his head and say: 'Willie, is no good; I'll sell him.'
Essays and Literary Studies (1916) 'Lot of a Schoolmaster'

6 Advertising may be described as the science of arresting human intelligence long enough to get money from it.
Garden of Folly (1924) 'The Perfect Salesman'

7 I am what is called a *professor emeritus*—from the Latin *e*, 'out', and *meritus*, 'so he ought to be'.
Here are my Lectures (1938) ch. 14

8 A sportsman is a man who, every now and then, simply has to get out and kill something. Not that he's cruel. He wouldn't hurt a fly. It's not big enough.
My Remarkable Uncle (1942)

9 Lord Ronald said nothing; he flung himself from the room, flung himself upon his horse and rode madly off in all directions.
Nonsense Novels (1911) 'Gertrude the Governess'

10 A decision of the courts decided that the game of golf may be played on Sunday, not being a game within the view of the law, but being a form of moral effort.
Over the Footlights (1923) 'Why I Refuse to Play Golf'

Mary Leapor 1722–46
English poet

11 In spite of all romantic poets sing,
This gold, my dearest, is an useful thing.
'Mira to Octavia'

12 Woman, a pleasing but a short-lived flower,
Too soft for business and too weak for power:
A wife in bondage, or neglected maid:
Despised, if ugly; if she's fair, betrayed.
'An Essay on Woman'

Edward Lear 1812–88
English artist and writer of humorous verse

13 Who, or why, or which, or what,
Is the Akond of Swat?
'The Akond of Swat' (1888)

14 There was an Old Man with a beard,
Who said, 'It is just as I feared!—
Two Owls and a Hen,
Four Larks and a Wren,
Have all built their nests in my beard!'
A Book of Nonsense (1846)

15 On the coast of Coromandel
Where the early pumpkins blow,
In the middle of the woods,
Lived the Yonghy-Bonghy-Bó.
'The Courtship of the Yonghy-Bonghy-Bó' (1871); see **SITWELL** 753:17

16 The Dong with a luminous nose.
title of poem (1871)

17 When awful darkness and silence reign
Over the great Gromboolian plain.
'The Dong with a Luminous Nose' (1871)

18 When storm-clouds brood on the towering heights
Of the Hills of the Chankly Bore.
'The Dong with a Luminous Nose' (1871)

19 Far and few, far and few,
Are the lands where the Jumblies live;
Their heads are green, and their hands are blue,
And they went to sea in a Sieve.
'The Jumblies' (1871)

20 And they bought an Owl, and a useful Cart,
And a pound of Rice, and a Cranberry Tart,
And a hive of silvery Bees.
And they bought a Pig, and some green Jackdaws,
And a lovely Monkey with lollipop paws,
And forty bottles of Ring-Bo-Ree,
And no end of Stilton Cheese.
'The Jumblies' (1871)

21 Nasticreechia Krorluppia.
More Nonsense (1872) 'Nonsense Botany'

1 There was an old man of Thermopylae,
Who never did anything properly.
More Nonsense (1872) 'One Hundred Nonsense Pictures and
Rhymes'

2 Till Mrs Discobbolos said
'Oh! W! X! Y! Z!
It has just come into my head—
Suppose we should happen to fall!!!!
Darling Mr Discobbolos?'
'Mr and Mrs Discobbolos' (1871)

3 'How pleasant to know Mr Lear!'
Who has written such volumes of stuff!
Some think him ill-tempered and queer,
But a few think him pleasant enough.
Nonsense Songs (1871) preface

4 Old Foss is the name of his cat:
His body is perfectly spherical,
He weareth a runcible hat.
Nonsense Songs (1871) preface

5 The Owl and the Pussy-Cat went to sea
In a beautiful pea-green boat.
They took some honey, and plenty of money,
Wrapped up in a five-pound note.
The Owl looked up to the Stars above
And sang to a small guitar,
'Oh lovely Pussy! O Pussy, my love,
What a beautiful Pussy you are.'
'The Owl and the Pussy-Cat' (1871)

6 Pussy said to the Owl, 'You elegant fowl!
How charmingly sweet you sing!
O let us be married! too long we have tarried:
But what shall we do for a ring?'
They sailed away for a year and a day,
To the land where the Bong-tree grows,
And there in a wood a Piggy-wig stood
With a ring at the end of his nose.
'The Owl and the Pussy-Cat' (1871)

7 'Dear Pig, are you willing to sell for one shilling
Your ring?' Said the Piggy, 'I will.'
'The Owl and the Pussy-Cat' (1871)

8 They dined on mince, and slices of quince,
Which they ate with a runcible spoon;
And hand in hand, on the edge of the sand,
They danced by the light of the moon.
'The Owl and the Pussy-Cat' (1871)

9 The Pobble who has no toes
Had once as many as we;
When they said, 'Some day you may lose them
all';—
He replied,—'Fish fiddle de-dee!'
'The Pobble Who Has No Toes' (1871)

10 He has gone to fish, for his Aunt Jobiska's
Runcible Cat with crimson whiskers!
'The Pobble Who Has No Toes' (1871)

11 'But the longer I live on this Crumpetty Tree
The plainer than ever it seems to me
That very few people come this way
And that life on the whole is far from gay!'
Said the Quangle-Wangle Quee.
'The Quangle-Wangle's Hat' (1871)

Timothy Leary 1920–96

American psychologist and drug pioneer, who became a
figurehead for the hippy drug culture. See also EPITAPHS
319:13

12 If you take the game of life seriously, if you
take your nervous system seriously, if you take
your sense organs seriously, if you take the
energy process seriously, you must turn on, tune
in and drop out.
lecture, June 1966, in *The Politics of Ecstasy* (1968) ch. 21

13 The PC is the LSD of the '90s.
remark made in the early 1990s; in *Guardian* 1 June 1996

14 Why not? Why not? Why not? Yeah.
last words, in *Independent* 1 June 1996

Mary Elizabeth Lease 1853–1933

American writer, lecturer, and suffragist

15 Kansas had better stop raising corn and begin
raising hell.
E. J. James et al. *Notable American Women 1607–1950* (1971)
vol. 2; recorded in slightly varying forms

F. R. Leavis 1895–1978

English literary critic

16 The common pursuit.
title of book (1952)

17 The few really great—the major novelists . . . are
significant in terms of the human awareness
they promote; awareness of the possibilities of
life.
The Great Tradition (1948) ch. 1

18 He energized the Garden-Suburb ethos with a
certain original talent and the vigour of a
prolonged adolescence . . . rather like Keats's
vulgarity with a Public School accent.
of Rupert **BROOKE**
New Bearings in English Poetry (1932) ch. 2

19 Self-contempt, well-grounded.
on the foundation of T. S. **ELIOT**'s *work*
in *Times Literary Supplement* 21 October 1988 (quoted by
Christopher Ricks in a BBC radio talk); see MILTON 544:2

Fran Lebowitz 1946–

American writer

20 There is no such thing as inner peace. There is
only nervousness or death.
Metropolitan Life (1978)

21 The best fame is a writer's fame: it's enough to
get a table at a good restaurant, but not enough
that you get interrupted when you eat.
in *Observer* 30 May 1993 'Sayings of the Week'

Stanislaw Lec 1909–66

Polish writer

22 Is it progress if a cannibal uses knife and fork?
Unkempt Thoughts (1962)

John le Carré (David John Moore Cornwell)
1931–

English thriller writer

1 The spy who came in from the cold.
    title of novel (1963)

Le Corbusier (Charles-Édouard Jeanneret)
1887–1965

French architect

2 *Une maison est une machine-à-habiter.*
    A house is a machine for living in.
    Vers une architecture (1923); see **TOLSTOY** 813:16

3 A hundred times I have thought: New York is a
    catastrophe, and fifty times: it is a beautiful
    catastrophe.
    When the Cathedrals were White (1947) 'The Fairy Catastrophe'

4 This frightful word [function] was born under
    other skies than those I have loved—those where
    the sun reigns supreme.
    Stephen Gardiner *Le Corbusier* (1974) introduction

Alexandre Auguste Ledru-Rollin
1807–74

French politician

5 Ah well! I am their leader, I really had to follow
    them!
    E. de Mirecourt *Les Contemporains* vol. 14 (1857) 'Ledru-Rollin'

Francis Ledwidge 1891–1917
Irish poet

6 He shall not hear the bittern cry
    In the wild sky where he is lain,
    Nor voices of the sweeter birds
    Above the wailing of the rain.
    'Lament for Thomas MacDonagh'

Gypsy Rose Lee (Rose Louise Hovick)
1914–70

American striptease artiste

7 God is love, but get it in writing.
    attributed

Harper Lee 1926–
American novelist

8 Shoot all the bluejays you want, if you can hit
    'em, but remember it's a sin to kill a
    mockingbird.
    To Kill a Mockingbird (1960) ch. 10

Henry Lee ('Light-Horse Harry') 1756–1818
American soldier and politician, father of Robert E. LEE

9 A citizen, first in war, first in peace, and first in
    the hearts of his countrymen.
    Funeral Oration on the death of General Washington (1800)

Laurie Lee 1914–97
English writer

10 I was set down from the carrier's cart at the age
    of three; and there with a sense of
    bewilderment and terror my life in the village
    began.
    Cider with Rosie (1959)

Nathaniel Lee c.1653–92
English dramatist

11 When the sun sets, shadows, that showed at
    noon
    But small, appear most long and terrible.
    Oedipus (with John Dryden, 1679) act 4, sc. 1

12 When Greeks joined Greeks, then was the tug
    of war!
    The Rival Queens (1677) act 4, sc. 2; see **PROVERBS** 646:38

13 The lust of power,
    Like glory boy, it licenses to kill,
    A strong temptation, to do bravely ill.
    Sophonisba (1676) act 1, sc. 1

14 Man, false man, smiling, destructive man.
    Theodosius (1680) act 3, sc. 2

15 They called me mad, and I called them mad,
    and damn them, they outvoted me.
    R. Porter *A Social History of Madness* (1987), introduction;
    attributed

Robert E. Lee 1807–70
American Confederate general, son of Henry LEE

16 It is well that war is so terrible. We should grow
    too fond of it.
    after the battle of Fredericksburg, December 1862
    attributed

17 I have fought against the people of the North
    because I believed they were seeking to wrest
    from the South its dearest rights. But I have
    never cherished toward them bitter or vindictive
    feelings, and I have never seen the day when I
    did not pray for them.
    Geoffrey C. Ward *The Civil War* (1991) ch. 5

18 *refusing an offer to write his memoirs:*
    I should be trading on the blood of my men.
    attributed, perhaps apocryphal

19 Strike the tent.
    attributed last words

Richard Le Gallienne 1866–1947
English poet

20 The cry of the Little Peoples goes up to God in
    vain,
    For the world is given over to the cruel sons of
    Cain.
    'The Cry of the Little Peoples' (1899)

Ursula K. Le Guin 1929–
American fantasy and science fiction writer

1 Love doesn't just sit there, like a stone, it has to be made, like bread; remade all the time, made new.
The Lathe of Heaven (1971) ch. 10

Ernest Lehman *see* Film titles 331:13

Tom Lehrer 1928–
American satirical singer-songwriter and mathematician

2 Plagiarize! Let no one else's work evade your eyes,
Remember why the good Lord made your eyes.
'Lobachevski' (1953 song)

3 Poisoning pigeons in the park.
song title, 1953

4 It is sobering to consider that when Mozart was my age he had already been dead for a year.
N. Shapiro (ed.) *An Encyclopedia of Quotations about Music* (1978)

Gottfried Wilhelm Leibniz 1646–1716
German philosopher

5 It is God who is the ultimate reason of things, and the knowledge of God is no less the beginning of science than his essence and will are the beginning of beings.
Letter on a General Principle Useful in Explaining the Laws of Nature (1687)

6 It is the knowledge of necessary and eternal truths which distinguishes us from mere animals, and gives us *Reason* and the sciences, raising us to knowledge of ourselves and of God. It is this in us which we call the rational soul or *Mind*.
The Monadology (1714) sect. 29 (translated by R. Latta)

7 *Nihil est sine ratione.*
There is nothing without a reason.
Studies in Physics and the Nature of Body (1671)

8 *Eadem sunt quorum unum potest substitui alteri salva veritate.*
Two things are identical if one can be substituted for the other without affecting the truth.
'Table de définitions' (1704) in L. Coutourat (ed.) *Opuscules et fragments inédits de Leibniz* (1903)

9 We should like Nature to go no further; we should like it to be finite, like our mind; but this is to ignore the greatness and majesty of the Author of things.
letter to S. Clarke, 1715, translated by M. Morris and G. H. R. Parkinson in *Leibniz: Philosophical Writings* (1973)

Fred W. Leigh d. 1924
British songwriter

10 Can't get away to marry you today,
My wife won't let me!
'Waiting at the Church (My Wife Won't Let Me)' (1906 song)

11 Why am I always the bridesmaid,
Never the blushing bride?
'Why Am I Always the Bridesmaid?' (1917 song, with Charles Collins and Lily Morris); see **PROVERBS** 626:24

Vivien Leigh 1913–67
English actress

12 Shaw is like a train. One just speaks the words and sits in one's place. But Shakespeare is like bathing in the sea—one swims where one wants.
letter from Harold Nicolson to Vita Sackville-West, 1 February 1956

Curtis E. LeMay 1906–90
American air-force officer

13 They've got to draw in their horns and stop their aggression, or we're going to bomb them back into the Stone Age.
on the North Vietnamese
Mission with LeMay (1965)

Ninon de Lenclos 1620–1705
French courtesan

14 How often have I told you, that love seldom dies of hunger, but frequently of satiety?
letter 41 to the Marquis de Sevigné, *The Memoirs of Ninon de L'Enclos* (1778)

Lenin (Vladimir Ilich Ulyanov) 1870–1924
Russian revolutionary and first Premier of the Soviet Union, 1918–24. See also **KEYNES** 462:2, **MISQUOTATIONS** 547:6

15 Imperialism is the monopoly stage of capitalism.
Imperialism as the Last Stage of Capitalism (1916) ch. 7 'Briefest possible definition of imperialism'

16 While the State exists, there can be no freedom. When there is freedom there will be no State.
State and Revolution (1919) ch. 5

17 What is to be done?
title of pamphlet (1902); originally the title of a novel (1863) by N. G. Chernyshevsky

18 Communism is Soviet power plus the electrification of the whole country.
Report to 8th Congress, 1920, in *Collected Works* (ed. 5) vol. 42

19 Who? Whom? [i.e. Who masters whom?]
definition of political science, meaning 'Who will outstrip whom?'
in *Polnoe Sobranie Sochinenii* vol. 44 (1970) 17 October 1921 and elsewhere

20 A good man fallen among Fabians.
of George Bernard **SHAW**
Arthur Ransome *Six Weeks in Russia in 1919* (1919) 'Notes of Conversations with Lenin'

21 Liberty is precious—so precious that it must be rationed.
Sidney and Beatrice Webb *Soviet Communism* (1936)

John Lennon 1940–80

English pop singer and songwriter. See also **LENNON AND MCCARTNEY**

1 Happiness is a warm gun.
  title of song (1968); see **ADVERTISING SLOGANS** 7:28

2 Imagine there's no heaven,
  It's easy if you try,
  No hell below us,
  Above us only sky.
  'Imagine' (1971 song)

3 Will the people in the cheaper seats clap your
  hands? All the rest of you, if you'll just rattle
  your jewellery.
  at the Royal Variety Performance, 4 November 1963, in R.
  Colman *John Winston Lennon* (1984) pt. 1, ch. 11

4 We're more popular than Jesus now; I don't
  know which will go first—rock 'n' roll or
  Christianity.
  of The Beatles
  interview in *Evening Standard* 4 March 1966

John Lennon 1940–80 *and* Paul McCartney 1942–

English pop singers and songwriters. See also **LENNON, MCCARTNEY**

5 Back in the USSR.
  title of song (1968)

6 For I don't care too much for money,
  For money can't buy me love.
  'Can't Buy Me Love' (1964 song)

7 Eleanor Rigby picks up the rice in the church
    where a wedding has been,
  Lives in a dream.
  Waits at the window, wearing the face that she
    keeps in a jar by the door,
  Who is it for?
  All the lonely people, where do they all come
    from?
  'Eleanor Rigby' (1966 song)

8 Give peace a chance.
  title of song (1969)

9 It's been a hard day's night,
  And I've been working like a dog.
  'A Hard Day's Night' (1964 song)

10 Strawberry fields forever.
  title of song (1967)

11 She's got a ticket to ride, but she don't care.
  'Ticket to Ride' (1965 song)

12 Will you still need me, will you still feed me,
  When I'm sixty four?
  'When I'm Sixty Four' (1967 song)

13 Oh I get by with a little help from my friends,
  Mm, I get high with a little help from my
    friends.
  'With a Little Help From My Friends' (1967 song)

Dan Leno (George Galvin) 1860–1904

English entertainer

14 Ah! what is man? Wherefore does he why?
  Whence did he whence? Whither is he
  withering?
  Dan Leno Hys Booke (1901) ch. 1

William Lenthall 1591–1662

English politician, Speaker of the House of Commons

15 I have neither eye to see, nor tongue to speak
  here, but as the House is pleased to direct me.
  to **CHARLES I**, *on being asked if he had seen any of the five
  MPs whom the King had ordered to be arrested, 4 January
  1642*
  John Rushworth *Historical Collections. The Third Part* vol. 2
  (1692); see **LINCOLN** 494:7

Leonardo da Vinci 1452–1519

Italian painter and designer

16 Whoever in discussion adduces authority uses
  not intellect but rather memory.
  Edward McCurdy (ed. and trans.) *Leonardo da Vinci's
  Notebooks* (1906) bk. 1

17 Life well spent is long.
  Edward McCurdy (ed. and trans.) *Leonardo da Vinci's
  Notebooks* (1906) bk. 1

18 Iron rusts from disuse; stagnant water loses its
  purity and in cold weather becomes frozen; even
  so does inaction sap the vigour of the mind.
  Edward McCurdy (ed. and trans.) *Leonardo da Vinci's
  Notebooks* (1906) bk. 1

19 Human subtlety . . . will never devise an
  invention more beautiful, more simple or more
  direct than does Nature, because in her
  inventions nothing is lacking, and nothing is
  superfluous.
  Edward McCurdy (ed. and trans.) *Leonardo da Vinci's
  Notebooks* (1906) bk. 1

20 Perspective is the bridle and rudder of painting.
  Irma Richter (ed.) *Selections from the Notebooks of Leonardo
  da Vinci* (World's Classics, 1952)

21 The span of a man's outspread arms is equal to
  his height.
  Irma Richter (ed.) *Selections from the Notebooks of Leonardo
  da Vinci* (World's Classics, 1952)

22 Every man at three years old is half his height.
  Irma A. Richter (ed.) *Selections from the Notebooks of Leonardo
  da Vinci* (World's Classics, 1952)

23 The poet ranks far below the painter in the
  representation of visible things, and far below
  the musician in that of invisible things.
  Irma A. Richter (ed.) *Selections from the Notebooks of Leonardo
  da Vinci* (World's Classics, 1952)

Mikhail Lermontov 1814–41
Russian novelist and poet

1 The love of savages isn't much better than the love of noble ladies; ignorance and simple-heartedness can be as tiresome as coquetry.
A Hero of our Time (1840) 'Bella' (translated by Philip Longworth)

2 Of two close friends, one is always the slave of the other.
A Hero of our Time (1840) 'Princess Mary' (translated by Philip Longworth)

3 Ever since I lived and entered into action, fate has somehow led me to the climax of other people's dramas, as if no one could die, no one could despair without me. I have always been the essential character of the fifth act.
A Hero of our Time (1840) 'Princess Mary' (translated by Philip Longworth)

4 I am like a man yawning at a ball; the only reason he does not go home to bed is that his carriage has not arrived yet.
A Hero of our Time (1840) 'Princess Mary' (translated by Philip Longworth)

5 No, I'm not Byron, it's my role
To be an undiscovered wonder,
Like him, a persecuted wand'rer,
But furnished with a Russian soul.
'No, I'm not Byron' (1832) (translated by Alan Myers)

Alan Jay Lerner 1918–86
American songwriter

6 Don't let it be forgot
That once there was a spot
For one brief shining moment that was known
As Camelot.
now particularly associated with the White House of John F.
KENNEDY; *see* **ONASSIS** 585:6
'Camelot' (1960 song)

7 I'm getting married in the morning,
Ding! dong! the bells are gonna chime.
Pull out the stopper;
Let's have a whopper;
But get me to the church on time!
'Get me to the Church on Time' (1956 song) in *My Fair Lady*

8 Why can't a woman be more like a man?
Men are so honest, so thoroughly square;
Eternally noble, historically fair;
Who, when you win, will always give your back
a pat.
Why can't a woman be like that?
'A Hymn to Him' (1956 song) in *My Fair Lady*

9 We met at nine.
We met at eight.
I was on time.
No, you were late.
Ah yes! I remember it well.
'I Remember it Well' (1958 song) in *Gigi*

10 I've grown accustomed to the trace
Of something in the air;
Accustomed to her face.
'I've Grown Accustomed to her Face' (1956 song) in *My Fair Lady*

11 The rain in Spain stays mainly in the plain.
'The Rain in Spain' (1956 song) in *My Fair Lady*

12 In Hertford, Hereford, and Hampshire,
Hurricanes hardly happen.
'The Rain in Spain' (1956 song) in *My Fair Lady*

13 Thank heaven for little girls!
For little girls get bigger every day.
'Thank Heaven for Little Girls' (1958 song) in *Gigi*

14 All I want is a room somewhere,
Far away from the cold night air,
With one enormous chair;
Oh, wouldn't it be loverly?
'Wouldn't it be Loverly' (1956 song) in *My Fair Lady*

15 Oozing charm from every pore,
He oiled his way around the floor.
'You Did It' (1956 song) in *My Fair Lady*

Doris Lessing 1919–
English writer

16 There's only one real sin, and that is to persuade oneself that the second-best is anything but the second-best.
The Golden Notebook (1962)

17 When old settlers say 'One has to understand the country,' what they mean is, 'You have to get used to our ideas about the native.'
The Grass is Singing (1950) ch. 1

18 What of October, that ambiguous month, the month of tension, the unendurable month?
Martha Quest (1952) pt. 4, sect. 1

G. E. Lessing 1729–81
German dramatist and critic

19 *Gestern liebt' ich,*
Heute leid' ich,
Morgen sterb' ich:
Dennoch denk' ich
Heut und morgen
Gern an gestern.

Yesterday I loved, today I suffer, tomorrow I die: but I still think fondly, today and tomorrow, of yesterday.
'Lied aus dem Spanischen' (1780)

20 *Ein einziger dankbarer Gedanke gen Himmel ist das vollkommenste Gebet.*

One single grateful thought raised to heaven is the most perfect prayer.
Minna von Barnhelm (1767) act 2, sc. 7

21 If God were to hold out enclosed in His right hand all Truth, and in His left hand just the active search for Truth, though with the condition that I should always err therein, and He should say to me: Choose! I should humbly take His left hand and say: Father! Give me this one; absolute Truth belongs to Thee alone.
Eine Duplik (1778) pt. 1

Winifred Mary Letts 1882–1972
English writer

1 I saw the spires of Oxford
As I was passing by,
The grey spires of Oxford
Against a pearl-grey sky;
My heart was with the Oxford men
Who went abroad to die.
'The Spires of Oxford' (1916)

Lord Leverhulme 1851–1925
English industrialist and philanthropist

2 Half the money I spend on advertising is wasted,
and the trouble is I don't know which half.
David Ogilvy *Confessions of an Advertising Man* (1963)

Ada Leverson 1865–1936
English novelist

3 He seemed at ease and to have the look of the
last gentleman in Europe.
of Oscar **WILDE**
Letters to the Sphinx (1930)

Denise Levertov 1923–97
English-born American poet

4 Images
split the truth
in fractions.
'A Sequence' (1961)

5 two by two in the ark of
the ache of it.
'The Ache of Marriage' (1964)

René Lévesque 1922–87
Canadian politician, founder of Parti Québecois

6 Outside Quebec, I don't find two great cultures.
I feel like a foreigner. First and foremost, I am a
Québecois, and second—with a rather growing
sense of doubt—a Canadian.
in *Toronto Star* 1 June 1963

Primo Levi 1919–87
Italian novelist and poet

7 Our language lacks words to express this
offence, the demolition of a man.
of a year spent in Auschwitz
If This is a Man (1958)

Bernard Levin 1928–2004
English journalist

8 Whom the mad would destroy, they first make
gods.
of **MAO ZEDONG** *in 1967*
Levin quoting himself in *The Times* 21 September 1987; see
PROVERBS 647:18

Duc de Lévis 1764–1830
French soldier and writer

9 *Noblesse oblige.*
Nobility has its obligations.
Maximes et Réflexions (1812 ed.) 'Morale: Maximes et
Préceptes' no. 73

10 *Gouverner, c'est choisir.*
To govern is to choose.
Maximes et Réflexions (1812 ed.) 'Politique: Maximes de
Politique' no. 19

Claude Lévi-Strauss 1908–
French social anthropologist

11 Language is a form of human reason, and has
its reasons which are unknown to man.
The Savage Mind (1962) ch. 9; see **PASCAL** 598:7

12 The purpose of myth is to provide a logical
model capable of overcoming a contradiction (an
impossible achievement if, as it happens, the
contradiction is real).
Structural Anthropology (1968) ch. 11

G. H. Lewes 1817–78
English man of letters; common-law husband of George
ELIOT

13 Murder, like talent, seems occasionally to run in
families.
The Physiology of Common Life (1859) ch. 12

14 The pen, in our age, weighs heavier in the social
scale than the sword of a Norman Baron.
Ranthorpe (1847) epilogue; see **PROVERBS** 641:32

C. S. Lewis 1898–1963
English novelist, religious writer, and literary scholar

15 No one ever told me that grief felt so like fear.
A Grief Observed (1961)

16 Every one says forgiveness is a lovely idea, until
they have something to forgive.
Mere Christianity (1952) bk. 3, ch. 7

17 We have trained them [men] to think of the
Future as a promised land which favoured
heroes attain—not as something which everyone
reaches at the rate of sixty minutes an hour,
whatever he does, whoever he is.
The Screwtape Letters (1942) no. 25

18 She's the sort of woman who lives for
others—you can always tell the others by their
hunted expression.
The Screwtape Letters (1942) no. 26

19 A young man who wishes to remain a sound
atheist cannot be too careful of his reading.
Surprised by Joy (1955)

20 For twenty years I've stared my level best
To see if evening—any evening—would suggest
A patient etherized upon a table;
In vain. I simply wasn't able.
on contemporary poetry
'A Confession' (1964); see **ELIOT** 310:5

1 Often when I pray I wonder if I am not posting letters to a non-existent address.
letter to Arthur Greeves, 24 December 1930

2 Courage is not simply *one* of the virtues but the form of every virtue at the testing point.
Cyril Connolly *The Unquiet Grave* (1944) ch. 3

3 He that but looketh on a plate of ham and eggs to lust after it, hath already committed breakfast with it in his heart.
letter, 10 March 1954

David Lewis 1909–81
Canadian politician

4 Louder voices: the corporate welfare bums.
title of book, 1972

Esther Lewis (Clark) fl. 1747–89
English poet

5 Are simple women only fit
To dress, to darn, to flower, or knit,
To mind the distaff, or the spit?
Why are the needle and the pen
Thought incompatible by men?
'A Mirror for Detractors' (1754) l. 146

George Cornewall Lewis 1806–63
British Liberal politician and writer

6 Life would be tolerable but for its amusements.
in *The Times* 18 September 1872; see **SURTEES** 781:15

Gwyneth Lewis 1959–
Welsh poet

7 *Creu gwir fel gwydr o ffwrnais awen.*
Creating truth like glass from inspiration's furnace.
Welsh words inscribed outside the Welsh Millennium Centre in Cardiff, 2004

8 In these stones horizons sing.
English words inscribed outside the Welsh Millennium Centre in Cardiff, 2004

Robert Lewis
American pilot

9 It just seems impossible to comprehend. Just how many did we kill? I honestly have the feeling of groping for words to explain this or I might say 'my God, what have we done?' If I live a hundred years I'll never quite get those few minutes out of my mind.
on the bombing of Hiroshima
log book of the Enola Gay, 6 August 1945

Sam M. Lewis 1885–1959 *and* Joe Young 1889–1939
American songwriters

10 How 'ya gonna keep 'em down on the farm (after they've seen Paree)?
title of song (1919)

11 Mammy, Mammy, look at me. Don't you know me? I'm your little baby.
'My Mammy' (1918 song); sung by Al **JOLSON**

Sinclair Lewis 1885–1951
American novelist

12 Our American professors like their literature clear and cold and pure and very dead.
The American Fear of Literature (Nobel Prize Address, 12 December 1930), in H. Frenz *Literature 1901–1967* (1969)

13 To George F. Babbitt, as to most prosperous citizens of Zenith, his motor car was poetry and tragedy, love and heroism. The office was his pirate ship but the car his perilous excursion ashore.
Babbitt (1922) ch. 3

14 She did her work with the thoroughness of a mind which reveres details and never quite understands them.
Babbitt (1922) ch. 18

15 It can't happen here.
title of novel (1935)

Wyndham Lewis 1882–1957
English novelist, painter, and critic

16 Gertrude Stein's prose-song is a cold, black suet-pudding . . . Cut it at any point, it is the same thing . . . all fat, without nerve.
of Three Lives (1909)
Time and Western Man (1927)

17 Angels in jumpers.
describing the figures in Stanley **SPENCER**'s *paintings*
attributed

Ludwig Lewisohn 1882–1955
German-born novelist

18 There are philosophies which are unendurable not because men are cowards, but because they are men.
The Modern Drama (1916)

George Leybourne d. 1884
English songwriter

19 He'd fly through the air with the greatest of ease,
A daring young man on the flying trapeze.
'The Flying Trapeze' (1868 song)

Liberace (Wladziu Valentino Liberace) 1919–87
American showman

20 When the reviews are bad I tell my staff that they can join me as I cry all the way to the bank.
Autobiography (1973) ch. 2; originally reported in the form: 'He [Liberace] begins to belabour the critics announcing that *he* doesn't mind what they say but that poor George [his

brother] "cried all the way to the bank"', in *Collier's* 17 September 1954

Libosus of Vaga
Roman Bishop present at Council of Carthage, 256 AD

1 The Lord says in the gospel; 'I am the Truth'. He does not say 'I am custom'. Therefore, when the truth is made manifest, custom must give way to truth.
  St Augustine of Hippo *On Baptism* bk. 3, ch. 6, sect. 9; see **BIBLE** 108:14

Georg Christoph Lichtenberg 1742–99
German scientist and drama critic

2 The journalists have constructed for themselves a little wooden chapel, which they also call the Temple of Fame, in which they put up and take down portraits all day long and make such a hammering you can't hear yourself speak.
  A. Leitzmann *Georg Christoph Lichtenberg Aphorismen* (1904)

3 There is a great deal of difference between *still* believing something, and *again* believing it.
  Notebook E no. 8 1775–6 in *Aphorisms* (1990)

A. J. Liebling 1904–63
American writer

4 Freedom of the press is guaranteed only to those who own one.
  'The Wayward Press: Do you belong in Journalism?' (1960)

Gordon Lightfoot 1938–
Canadian singer and songwriter

5 Does any one know where the love of God goes
When the waves turn the minutes to hours?
  'The Wreck of the Edmund Fitzgerald' (1976 song)

Charles-Joseph, Prince de Ligne
1735–1814
Belgian soldier

6 *Le congrès ne marche pas, il danse.*
  The Congress makes no progress; it dances.
  Auguste de la Garde-Chambonas *Souvenirs du Congrès de Vienne* (1820) ch. 1

Beatrice Lillie 1894–1989
Canadian-born comedienne

7 Never darken my Dior again!
  to a waiter who had spilled soup down her neck
  in *Every Other Inch a Lady* (1973) ch. 14

George Lillo 1693–1739
Flemish-born dramatist

8 There's sure no passion in the human soul,
But finds its food in music.
  The Fatal Curiosity (1736) act 1, sc. 2

Abraham Lincoln 1809–65
American statesman, 16th President of the US 1861–5. On Lincoln: see **BOOTH** 150:25, **STANTON** 770:3

9 To give victory to the right, not bloody bullets, but peaceful ballots only, are necessary.
  speech, 18 May 1858, in R. P. Basler (ed.) *Collected Works of Abraham Lincoln* (1953) vol. 2; see **MISQUOTATIONS** 547:3

10 'A house divided against itself cannot stand.' I believe this government cannot endure permanently, half slave and half free.
  speech, 16 June 1858, in R. P. Basler (ed.) *Collected Works . . .* (1953) vol. 2; see **BIBLE** 103:28

11 What is conservatism? Is it not adherence to the old and tried, against the new and untried?
  speech, 27 February 1860, in R. P. Basler (ed.) *Collected Works . . .* (1953) vol. 3

12 Let us have faith that right makes might, and in that faith, let us, to the end, dare to do our duty as we understand it.
  speech, 27 February 1860, in R. P. Basler (ed.) *Collected Works . . .* (1953) vol. 3

13 I take the official oath to-day with no mental reservations, and with no purpose to construe the Constitution or laws by any hypercritical rules.
  first inaugural address, 4 March 1861, in R. P. Basler (ed.) *Collected Works . . .* (1953) vol. 4

14 The mystic chords of memory, stretching from every battlefield and patriot grave to every living heart and hearthstone all over this broad land, will yet swell the chorus of the Union when again touched, as surely they will be, by the better angels of our nature.
  first inaugural address, 4 March 1861

15 I think the necessity of being *ready* increases. Look to it.
  the whole of a letter to Governor Andrew Curtin of Pennsylvania, 8 April 1861, in R. P. Basler (ed.) *Collected Works . . .* (1953) vol. 4

16 He who does *something* at the head of one regiment, will eclipse him who does *nothing* at the head of a hundred.
  letter to Major-General David Hunter, 31 December 1861, in R. P. Basler (ed.) *Collected Works . . .* (1953) vol. 5

17 My paramount object in this struggle is to save the Union . . . If I could save the Union without freeing any slave, I would do it; and if I could save it by freeing all the slaves, I would do it; and if I could save it by freeing some and leaving others alone, I would also do that . . . I have here stated my purpose according to my views of official duty and I intend no modification of my oft-expressed personal wish that all men everywhere could be free.
  letter to Horace Greeley, 22 August 1862, in R. P. Basler (ed.) *Collected Works . . .* (1953) vol. 5

18 In giving freedom to the slave, we assure freedom to the free—honourable alike in what we give and what we preserve. We shall nobly

save, or meanly lose, the last, best hope of earth.
> Annual Message to Congress, 1 December 1862, in R. P. Basler (ed.) *Collected Works . . .* (1953) vol. 5

1 Fourscore and seven years ago our fathers brought forth upon this continent a new nation, conceived in liberty, and dedicated to the proposition that all men are created equal . . . In a larger sense we cannot dedicate, we cannot consecrate, we cannot hallow this ground. The brave men, living and these dead, who struggled here, have consecrated it far above our power to add or detract. The world will little note, nor long remember, what we say here, but it can never forget what they did here. It is for us, the living, rather to be dedicated here to the unfinished work which they who fought here have thus far so nobly advanced . . . we here highly resolve that the dead shall not have died in vain, that this nation, under God, shall have a new birth of freedom; and that government of the people, by the people, and for the people, shall not perish from the earth.

the Lincoln Memorial inscription reads 'by the people, for the people'
> address at the dedication of the National Cemetery at Gettysburg, 19 November 1863, as reported the following day, in R. P. Basler (ed.) *Collected Works . . .* (1953) vol. 7; see **WEBSTER** 843:21

2 The President tonight has a dream:—He was in a party of plain people, and, as it became known who he was, they began to comment on his appearance. One of them said:—'He is a very common-looking man.' The President replied:—'The Lord prefers common-looking people. That is the reason he makes so many of them.'
> John Hay *Letters of John Hay and Extracts from Diary* (1908) vol. 1, 23 December 1863

3 I claim not to have controlled events, but confess plainly that events have controlled me.
> letter to A. G. Hodges, 4 April 1864, in R. P. Basler (ed.) *Collected Works . . .* (1953) vol. 7

4 It is not best to swap horses when crossing streams.
> reply to National Union League, 9 June 1864, in R. P. Basler (ed.) *Collected Works . . .* (1953) vol. 7; see **PROVERBS** 630:18

5 Fondly do we hope, fervently do we pray, that this mighty scourge of war may speedily pass away. Yet, if God wills that it continue until all the wealth piled by the bond-man's two hundred and fifty years of unrequited toil shall be sunk, and until every drop of blood drawn with the lash shall be paid by another drawn with the sword, as was said three thousand years ago, so still it must be said, 'The judgements of the Lord are true and righteous altogether.'
> second inaugural address, 4 March 1865, in R. P. Basler (ed.) *Collected Works . . .* (1953) vol. 8; see **BOOK OF COMMON PRAYER** 140:11

6 With malice toward none; with charity for all; with firmness in the right, as God gives us to see the right, let us strive on to finish the work we are in: to bind up the nation's wounds; to care for him who shall have borne the battle, and for his widow and his orphan, to do all which may achieve and cherish a just and lasting peace among ourselves, and with all nations.
> second inaugural address, 4 March 1865, in R. P. Basler (ed.) *Collected Works . . .* (1953) vol. 8

7 As President, I have no eyes but constitutional eyes; I cannot see you.
> attributed reply to the South Carolina Commissioners; see **LENTHALL** 489:15

8 I have always found that mercy bears richer fruits than strict justice.
> remark to Joseph Gillespie, in letter from Gillespie to *Herald and Torch Light* [Hagerstown, MD] 15 March 1876

9 People who like this sort of thing will find this the sort of thing they like.
judgement of a book
> G. W. E. Russell *Collections and Recollections* (1898) ch. 30

10 So you're the little woman who wrote the book that made this great war!
*on meeting Harriet Beecher **STOWE**, author of* Uncle Tom's Cabin
> Carl Sandburg *Abraham Lincoln: The War Years* (1936) vol. 2, ch. 39

11 You may fool all the people some of the time; you can even fool some of the people all the time; but you can't fool all of the people all the time.
*also attributed to Phineas **BARNUM***
> Alexander K. McClure *Lincoln's Yarns and Stories* (1904)

Charles Lindbergh 1902–74
American aviator, who in 1927 made the first solo transatlantic flight

12 I was astonished at the effect my successful landing in France had on the nations of the world. To me, it was like a match lighting a bonfire.
> *Autobiography of Values* (1978)

R. M. Lindner *see* Film titles 331:10

J. A. Lindon
13 Points
Have no parts or joints
How then can they combine
To form a line?
> M. Gardner *Wheels, Life and Other Mathematical Amusements* (1983)

Audrey Erskine Lindop fl. 1959
14 The singer not the song.
> title of novel (1959), from the title of a West Indian calypso

Vachel Lindsay 1879–1931
American poet

15 Then I saw the Congo, creeping through the black,

Cutting through the forest with a golden track.
'The Congo' pt. 1 (1914)

1 Booth led boldly with his big bass drum—
(Are you washed in the blood of the Lamb?)
'General William Booth Enters into Heaven' (1913); see **BIBLE**
118:15

2 Booth died blind and still by faith he trod,
Eyes still dazzled by the ways of God.
'General William Booth Enters into Heaven' (1913)

Graham Linehan *and* Arthur Mathews
Irish writers

3 It's great being a priest, isn't it, Ted?
'Good Luck, Father Ted' (1994), episode from *Father Ted*
(Channel 4 TV, 1994–8)

Eric Linklater 1899–1974
Scottish novelist

4 'There won't be any revolution in America,' said
Isadore. Nikitin agreed. 'The people are all too
clean. They spend all their time changing their
shirts and washing themselves. You can't feel
fierce and revolutionary in a bathroom.'
Juan in America (1931) bk. 5, pt. 3

Art Linkletter 1912–
American broadcaster and humorist

5 The four stages of man are infancy, childhood,
adolescence and obsolescence.
A Child's Garden of Misinformation (1965) ch. 8

George Linley 1798–1865
English songwriter

6 Among our ancient mountains,
And from our lovely vales,
Oh, let the prayer re-echo:
'God bless the Prince of Wales!'
'God Bless the Prince of Wales' (1862 song); translated from
the Welsh original by J. C. Hughes (1837–87)

Lin Yutang 1895–1976
Chinese writer and philologist

7 A good traveller is one who does not know
where he is going to, and a perfect traveller does
not know where he came from.
The Importance of Living (1938) ch. 11

8 [The traveller can] get the greatest joy of travel
even without going to the mountains, by staying
at home and watching and going about the field
to watch a sailing cloud, or a dog, or a hedge,
or a lonely tree.
The Importance of Living (1938) ch. 11

Walter Lippmann 1889–1974
American journalist

9 Mr Coolidge's genius for inactivity is developed
to a very high point. It is far from being an
indolent activity. It is a grim, determined, alert
inactivity which keeps Mr Coolidge occupied
constantly. Nobody has ever worked harder at
inactivity, with such force of character, with
such unremitting attention to detail, with such
conscientious devotion to the task.
Men of Destiny (1927)

10 The final test of a leader is that he leaves behind
him in other men the conviction and the will to
carry on.
in *New York Herald Tribune* 14 April 1945

Joseph Lister 1827–1912
English surgeon

11 There are people who do not object to eating a
mutton chop—people who do not even object to
shooting a pheasant . . . —and yet who consider
it something monstrous to introduce under the
skin of a guinea pig a little inoculation of some
microbe to ascertain its action.
in *British Medical Journal* (1897) vol. 1, p. 317

Richard Littledale 1833–90
English clergyman

12 Come down, O Love divine,
Seek thou this soul of mine,
And visit it with thine own ardour glowing;
O Comforter, draw near,
Within my heart appear,
And kindle it, thy holy flame bestowing.

O let it freely burn,
Till earthly passion turn
To dust and ashes in its heat consuming.
'Come down, O Love divine' (1867 hymn); translation of
'Discendi, Amor santo' by Bianco da Siena (c.1350–1434)

13 Let holy charity
Mine outward vesture be,
And lowliness become mine inner clothing;
True lowliness of heart,
Which takes the humbler part,
And o'er its own shortcomings weeps with
loathing.
'Come down, O Love divine' (1867 hymn)

Joan Littlewood 1914–2002 *and* Charles Chilton 1914–

14 Oh what a lovely war.
title of stage show (1963)

Maxim Litvinov 1876–1951
Soviet diplomat

15 Peace is indivisible.
note to the Allies, 25 February 1920; A. U. Pope *Maxim
Litvinoff* (1943)

Penelope Lively 1933–

English novelist

1 Language tethers us to the world; without it we spin like atoms.
Moon Tiger (1987)

2 We are walking lexicons. In a single sentence of idle chatter we preserve Latin, Anglo-Saxon, Norse; we carry a museum inside our heads, each day we commemorate peoples of whom we have never heard.
Moon Tiger (1987)

David Livingstone 1813–73

Scottish missionary and explorer

3 No permanent elevation of a people can be effected without commerce.
in *Quarterly Review* April 1861

Ken Livingstone 1945–

British Labour politician, Mayor of London 2000–8

4 If voting changed anything, they'd abolish it.
title of book, 1987

Livy (Titus Livius) 59 BC–AD 17

Roman historian

5 *Vae victis.*
Down with the defeated!
cry (already proverbial) of the Gallic King, Brennus, on capturing Rome in 390 BC
Ab Urbe Condita bk. 5, ch. 48, sect. 9

6 War is just, Samnites, to those for whom it is necessary.
Ab Urbe Condita bk. 9, ch. 1, sect. 10

7 *Pugna magna victi sumus.*
We were defeated in a great battle.
announcement of disaster for the Romans in Hannibal's ambush at Lake Trasimene in 217 BC
Ab Urbe Condita bk. 22, ch. 7, sect. 8

8 The worst kind of shame is that caused by parsimony or poverty.
Ab Urbe Condita bk. 34, ch. 4, sect. 13

Richard Llewellyn (Richard Llewellyn Lloyd) 1907–83

Welsh novelist and dramatist

9 How green was my valley.
title of book (1939)

Robert Lloyd 1733–64

English poet

10 Alone from Jargon born to rescue Law,
From precedent, grave hum, and formal saw!
To strip chicanery of its vain pretence,
And marry Common Law to Common Sense!
'The Law-Student' (1762); on Lord **MANSFIELD**, Lord Chief Justice, 1756–88

11 All the art of Imitation,
Is pilf'ring from the first creation.
'Shakespeare' (1762)

David Lloyd George 1863–1945

British Liberal statesman, Prime Minister 1916–22. On Lloyd George: see **ASQUITH** 34:10, **CLEMENCEAU** 235:9, **KEYNES** 462:4

12 The leal and trusty mastiff which is to watch over our interests, but which runs away at the first snarl of the trade unions . . . A mastiff? It is the right hon. Gentleman's poodle.
*on the House of Lords and A. J. **BALFOUR** respectively in the House of Commons, 26 June 1907*

13 A fully-equipped duke costs as much to keep up as two Dreadnoughts; and dukes are just as great a terror and they last longer.
speech at Newcastle, 9 October 1909, in *The Times* 11 October 1909

14 The great peaks of honour we had forgotten—Duty, Patriotism, and—clad in glittering white—the great pinnacle of Sacrifice, pointing like a rugged finger to Heaven.
speech at Queen's Hall, London, 19 September 1914, in *The Times* 20 September 1914

15 At eleven o'clock this morning came to an end the cruellest and most terrible war that has ever scourged mankind. I hope we may say that thus, this fateful morning, came to an end all wars.
speech in the House of Commons, 11 November 1918; see **WELLS** 846:25

16 What is our task? To make Britain a fit country for heroes to live in.
speech at Wolverhampton, 23 November 1918, in *The Times* 25 November 1918

17 Unless I am mistaken, by the steps we have taken [in Ireland] we have murder by the throat.
speech at the Mansion House, 9 November 1920; Frank Owen *Tempestuous Journey* (1954) ch. 28

18 The world is becoming like a lunatic asylum run by lunatics.
in *Observer* 8 January 1933; see **ROWLAND** 671:12

19 A politician was a person with whose politics you did not agree. When you did agree, he was a statesman.
speech at Central Hall, Westminster, 2 July 1935, in *The Times* 3 July 1935

20 Negotiating with de Valera . . . is like trying to pick up mercury with a fork.
*to which **DE VALERA** replied, 'Why doesn't he use a spoon?'*
M. J. MacManus *Eamon de Valera* (1944) ch. 6

21 Sufficient conscience to bother him, but not sufficient to keep him straight.
*of Ramsay **MACDONALD***
A. J. Sylvester *Life with Lloyd George* (1975)

Liz Lochhead 1947–

Scottish poet and dramatist

1 I wouldn't thank you for a Valentine
I won't wake up early wondering if the
postman's been.
Should 10 red-padded satin hearts arrive with a
sticky sickly saccharine
Sentiments in very vulgar verses I wouldn't
wonder if you meant them.
'I Wouldn't Thank You for a Valentine' (1985)

John Locke 1632–1704

English philosopher, a founder of empiricism and political
liberalism

2 New opinions are always suspected, and usually
opposed, without any other reason but because
they are not already common.
An Essay concerning Human Understanding (1690) 'Dedicatory
Epistle'

3 The commonwealth of learning is not at this
time without master-builders, whose mighty
designs, in advancing the sciences, will leave
lasting monuments to the admiration of
posterity . . . in an age that produces such
masters as the great Huygenius and the
incomparable Mr Newton . . . 'tis ambition
enough to be employed as an under-labourer in
clearing ground a little, and removing some of
the rubbish that lies in the way of knowledge.
An Essay concerning Human Understanding (1690) 'Epistle to
the Reader'

4 General propositions are seldom mentioned in
the huts of Indians: much less are they to be
found in the thoughts of children.
An Essay concerning Human Understanding (1690) bk. 1, ch. 2,
sect. 11

5 Nature never makes excellent things for mean or
no uses.
An Essay concerning Human Understanding (1690) bk. 2, ch. 1,
sect. 15

6 No man's knowledge here can go beyond his
experience.
An Essay concerning Human Understanding (1690) bk. 2, ch. 1,
sect. 19

7 It is one thing to show a man that he is in error,
and another to put him in possession of truth.
An Essay concerning Human Understanding (1690) bk. 4, ch. 7,
sect. 11

8 There are very few lovers of truth, for truth-
sake, even among those who persuade
themselves that they are so. How a man may
know, whether he be so, in earnest, is worth
enquiry; and I think, there is this one unerring
mark of it, viz. the not entertaining any
proposition with greater assurance than the
proofs it is built on will warrant. Whoever goes
beyond this measure of assent, it is plain,
receives not truth in the love of it, loves not
truth for truth-sake, but for some other by-end.
An Essay concerning Human Understanding (1690) bk. 4, ch. 19,
sect. 1

9 Reason is natural revelation, whereby the eternal
Father of light, and fountain of all knowledge
communicates to mankind that portion of truth
which he has laid within the reach of their
natural faculties.
An Essay concerning Human Understanding (1690) bk. 4, ch. 19,
sect. 4

10 Crooked things may be as stiff and unflexible as
straight: and men may be as positive in error as
in truth.
An Essay concerning Human Understanding (1690) bk. 4, ch. 19,
sect. 11

11 All men are liable to error; and most men are,
in many points, by passion or interest, under
temptation to it.
An Essay concerning Human Understanding (1690) bk. 4, ch.
20, sect. 17

12 Whatsoever . . . [man] removes out of the state
that nature hath provided and left it in, he hath
mixed his labour with, and joined to it
something that is his own, and thereby makes it
his property.
Second Treatise of Civil Government (1690) ch. 5, sect. 27

13 [That] ill deserves the name of confinement
which hedges us in only from bogs and
precipices. So that, however it may be mistaken,
the end of law is, not to abolish or restrain, but
to preserve and enlarge freedom.
Second Treatise of Civil Government (1690) ch. 6, sect. 57

14 Man . . . hath by nature a power . . . to preserve
his property—that is, his life, liberty, and
estate—against the injuries and attempts of
other men.
Second Treatise of Civil Government (1690) ch. 7, sect. 87

15 Man being . . . by nature all free, equal, and
independent, no one can be put out of this
estate, and subjected to the political power of
another, without his own consent.
Second Treatise of Civil Government (1690) ch. 8, sect. 95

16 The only way by which any one divests himself
of his natural liberty and puts on the bonds of
civil society is by agreeing with other men to
join and unite into a community.
Second Treatise of Civil Government (1690) ch. 8, sect. 95

17 The great and chief end, therefore, of men's
uniting into commonwealths, and putting
themselves under government, is the
preservation of their property.
Second Treatise of Civil Government (1690) ch. 9, sect. 124

18 The rod, which is the only instrument of
government that tutors generally know, or ever
think of, is the most unfit of any to be used in
education.
Some Thoughts Concerning Education (5th ed., 1705) sect. 47

19 You would think him a very foolish fellow, that
should not value a virtuous, or a wise man,
infinitely before a great scholar.
Some Thoughts Concerning Education (5th ed., 1705) sect. 147

20 Wherever law ends, tyranny begins.
Two Treatises of Government (1689) ch. 18, no. 202

Frederick Locker-Lampson 1821–95

English writer of light verse

1 And many are afraid of God—
And more of Mrs Grundy.
'The Jester's Plea' (1868); see **MORTON** 562:9

John Gibson Lockhart 1794–1854

Scottish writer and critic. See also **EPITAPHS** 318:6

2 It is a better and a wiser thing to be a starved
apothecary than a starved poet; so back to the
shop Mr John, back to 'plasters, pills, and
ointment boxes.'
reviewing Keats's Endymion
in Blackwood's Edinburgh Magazine August 1818

3 Barring drink and the girls, I ne'er heard of a
sin:
Many worse, better few, than bright, broken
Maginn.
'Epitaph for William Maginn (1794–1842)', in William Maginn
Miscellanies (1885) vol. 1, p. xviii

David Lodge 1935–

English novelist

4 Literature is mostly about having sex and not
much about having children. Life is the other
way round.
The British Museum is Falling Down (1965) ch. 4

5 Morris read through the letter. Was it a shade
too fulsome? No, that was another law of
academic life: it is impossible to be excessive in
flattery of one's peers.
Small World (1984) pt. 3, ch. 1

Thomas Lodge 1558–1625

English man of letters

6 Love in my bosom like a bee
Doth suck his sweet;
Now with his wings he plays with me,
Now with his feet.
Within mine eyes he makes his nest,
His bed amidst my tender breast;
My kisses are his daily feast,
And yet he robs me of my rest.
Ah, wanton, will ye?
'Love in my bosom like a bee' (1590)

7 Love guards the roses of thy lips
And flies about them like a bee;
If I approach he forward skips,
And if I kiss he stingeth me.
'Love guards the roses of thy lips' (1593)

Frank Loesser 1910–69

American songwriter

8 See what the boys in the back room will have
And tell them I'm having the same.
'Boys in the Back Room' (1939 song)

9 Isn't it grand! Isn't it fine! Look at the cut, the
style, the line!

The suit of clothes is altogether, but altogether
it's altogether
The most remarkable suit of clothes that I have
ever seen.
'The King's New Clothes' (1952 song); from the film Hans
Christian Andersen; see **ANDERSEN** 15:4

Christopher Logue 1926–

English poet

10 Come to the edge.
We might fall.
Come to the edge.
It's too high!
COME TO THE EDGE!
And they came
and he pushed
and they flew . . .
on **APOLLINAIRE**
'Come to the edge' (1969)

11 I, Christopher Logue, was baptized the year
Many thousands of Englishmen,
Fists clenched, their bellies empty,
Walked day and night on the capital city.
'The Song of Autobiography' (1996)

Jack London 1876–1916

American novelist

12 The call of the wild.
title of novel (1903)

Huey Long 1893–1935

American Democratic politician

13 For the present you can just call me the
Kingfish.
Every Man a King (1933)

Henry Wadsworth Longfellow

1807–82

American poet

14 I shot an arrow into the air,
It fell to earth, I knew not where.
'The Arrow and the Song' (1845)

15 Thou, too, sail on, O Ship of State!
Sail on, O Union, strong and great!
Humanity with all its fears,
With all the hopes of future years,
Is hanging breathless on thy fate!
'The Building of the Ship' (1849)

16 Between the dark and the daylight,
When the night is beginning to lower,
Comes a pause in the day's occupations,
That is known as the Children's Hour.
'The Children's Hour' (1859)

17 For thine own purpose, thou hast sent
The strife and the discouragement!
Christus: A Mystery (1872) pt. 2 'The Golden Legend' 'A Village
Church' l. 1077

1 The cares that infest the day
Shall fold their tents, like the Arabs,
And as silently steal away.
'The Day is Done' (1844)

2 If you would hit the mark, you must aim a little
above it;
Every arrow that flies feels the attraction of
earth.
'Elegiac Verse' (1880)

3 This is the forest primeval.
Evangeline (1847) introduction

4 Sorrow and silence are strong, and patient
endurance is godlike.
Evangeline (1847) pt. 2, l. 60

5 The shades of night were falling fast,
As through an Alpine village passed
A youth, who bore, 'mid snow and ice,
A banner with the strange device,
Excelsior!
'Excelsior' (1841)

6 Giotto's tower,
The lily of Florence blossoming in stone.
'Giotto's Tower' (1866)

7 I like that ancient Saxon phrase, which calls
The burial-ground God's-Acre!
'God's-Acre' (1841)

8 The holiest of all holidays are those
Kept by ourselves in silence and apart;
The secret anniversaries of the heart.
'Holidays' (1877)

9 The heights by great men reached and kept
Were not attained by sudden flight,
But they, while their companions slept,
Were toiling upward in the night.
'The Ladder of Saint Augustine' (1850)

10 Standing, with reluctant feet,
Where the brook and river meet.
'Maidenhood' (1841)

11 A boy's will is the wind's will
And the thoughts of youth are long, long
thoughts.
'My Lost Youth' (1858)

12 *Emigravit* is the inscription on the tombstone
where he lies;
Dead he is not, but departed,—for the artist
never dies.
on Albrecht Dürer
'Nuremberg' (1844)

13 Not in the clamour of the crowded street,
Not in the shouts and plaudits of the throng,
But in ourselves, are triumph and defeat.
'The Poets' (1876)

14 Tell me not, in mournful numbers,
Life is but an empty dream!
For the soul is dead that slumbers,
And things are not what they seem.
Life is real! Life is earnest!
And the grave is not its goal;

Dust thou art, to dust returnest,
Was not spoken of the soul.
'A Psalm of Life' (1838); see **BIBLE** 79:13

15 Art is long, and Time is fleeting,
And our hearts, though stout and brave,
Still, like muffled drums, are beating
Funeral marches to the grave.
'A Psalm of Life' (1838); see **HIPPOCRATES** 399:13

16 Trust no Future, howe'er pleasant!
Let the dead Past bury its dead!
Act,—act in the living Present!
Heart within, and God o'erhead!
'A Psalm of Life' (1838); see **BIBLE** 100:11

17 Lives of great men all remind us
We can make our lives sublime,
And, departing, leave behind us
Footprints on the sands of time.
'A Psalm of Life' (1838)

18 Let us, then, be up and doing,
With a heart for any fate;
Still achieving, still pursuing,
Learn to labour and to wait.
'A Psalm of Life' (1838)

19 Into each life some rain must fall,
Some days must be dark and dreary.
'The Rainy Day' (1842)

20 Though the mills of God grind slowly, yet they
grind exceeding small;
Though with patience He stands waiting, with
exactness grinds He all.
'Retribution' (1870), translation of Friedrich von Logau
(1604–55) *Sinngedichte* (1654) no. 3224; see **PROVERBS**
638:39

21 A Lady with a Lamp shall stand
In the great history of the land,
A noble type of good,
Heroic womanhood.
*on Florence **NIGHTINGALE***
'Santa Filomena' (1857)

22 By the shore of Gitche Gumee,
By the shining Big-Sea-Water,
Stood the wigwam of Nokomis,
Daughter of the Moon, Nokomis.
The Song of Hiawatha (1855) 'Hiawatha's Childhood'

23 Dark behind it rose the forest,
Rose the black and gloomy pine-trees,
Rose the firs with cones upon them;
Bright before it beat the water,
Beat the clear and sunny water,
Beat the shining Big-Sea-Water.
The Song of Hiawatha (1855) 'Hiawatha's Childhood'

24 From the waterfall he named her,
Minnehaha, Laughing Water.
The Song of Hiawatha (1855) 'Hiawatha and Mudjekeewis'

25 Listen, my children, and you shall hear
Of the midnight ride of Paul Revere,
On the eighteenth of April in Seventy-five.
Tales of a Wayside Inn pt. 1 (1863) 'The Landlord's Tale: Paul
Revere's Ride'

1 One if by land and two if by sea;
And I on the opposite shore will be,
Ready to ride and sound the alarm.
  Tales of a Wayside Inn pt. 1 (1863) 'The Landlord's Tale: Paul
  Revere's Ride'; see **REVERE** 658:14

2 The fate of a nation was riding that night.
  Tales of a Wayside Inn pt. 1 (1863) 'The Landlord's Tale: Paul
  Revere's Ride'

3 Ships that pass in the night, and speak each
  other in passing;
Only a signal shown and a distant voice in the
  darkness;
So on the ocean of life we pass and speak one
  another,
Only a look and a voice; then darkness again
  and a silence.
  Tales of a Wayside Inn pt. 3 (1874) 'The Theologian's Tale:
  Elizabeth' pt. 4

4 Under a spreading chestnut tree
The village smithy stands;
The smith, a mighty man is he,
With large and sinewy hands;
And the muscles of his brawny arms
Are strong as iron bands.
  'The Village Blacksmith' (1839)

5 Each morning sees some task begin,
Each evening sees it close;
Something attempted, something done,
Has earned a night's repose.
  'The Village Blacksmith' (1839)

6 It was the schooner Hesperus,
That sailed the wintry sea;
And the skipper had taken his little daughter,
To bear him company.
  'The Wreck of the Hesperus' (1839)

7 There was a little girl
Who had a little curl
Right in the middle of her forehead,
When she was good
She was very, very good,
But when she was bad she was horrid.
  *composed for, and sung to, his second daughter while a
  babe in arms, c.1850*
  B. R. Tucker-Macchetta *The Home Life of Henry W. Longfellow*
  (1882) ch. 5

8 The square root of half a number of bees, and
also eight-ninths of the whole, alighted on the
jasmines, and a female buzzed responsive to the
hum of the male inclosed at night in a water-lily.
O, beautiful damsel, tell me the number of bees.
  Kavanagh (1849) ch. 4

Longinus on the Sublime

Greek literary treatise of unknown authorship and date

9 Sublimity is the echo of a noble mind.
  sect. 9

Michael Longley 1939–

Irish poet

10 I am travelling from one April to another.
It is the same train between the same
  embankments.
Gorse fires are smoking, but primroses burn
And celandines and white may and gorse
  flowers.
  'Gorse Fires' (1991)

11 Astrologers or three wise men
Who may shortly be setting out
For a small house up the Shankill
Or the Falls, should pause on their way
To buy gifts at Jim Gibson's shop,
Dates and chestnuts and tambourines.
  'The Greengrocer' (1979)

Alice Roosevelt Longworth 1884–1980

American daughter of Theodore ROOSEVELT

12 If you haven't got anything good to say about
anyone come and sit by me.
  maxim embroidered on a cushion in her home
  Michael Teague *Mrs L: Conversations with Alice Roosevelt
  Longworth* (1981)

Anita Loos 1893–1981

American writer

13 Gentlemen prefer blondes.
  title of book (1925)

14 So this gentleman said a girl with brains ought
to do something with them besides think.
  Gentlemen Prefer Blondes (1925) ch. 1

15 So I really think that American gentlemen are
the best after all, because kissing your hand may
make you feel very very good but a diamond
and safire bracelet lasts forever.
  Gentlemen Prefer Blondes (1925) ch. 4; see **ADVERTISING
  SLOGANS** 7:15, **ROBIN** 663:15

16 So then Dr Froyd said that all I needed was to
cultivate a few inhibitions and get some sleep.
  Gentlemen Prefer Blondes (1925) ch. 5

Federico García Lorca 1899–1936

**Spanish poet and dramatist, killed by nationalists in the
Spanish Civil War. On Lorca: see READ 656:5**

17 *A las cinco de la tarde.*
Eran las cinco en punto de la tarde.
Un niño trajo la blanca sábana
a las cinco de la tarde.

At five in the afternoon.
It was exactly five in the afternoon.
A boy brought the white sheet
at five in the afternoon.
  Llanto por Ignacio Sánchez Mejías (1935) 'La Cogida y la
  muerte'

18 *Verde que te quiero verde.*
Verde viento. Verdes ramas.

El barco sobre la mar
y el caballo en la montaña.

Green how I want you green.
Green wind.
Green boughs.
The ship on the sea
and the horse on the mountain.

Romance sonámbulo (1924-7)

Edward N. Lorenz 1917–2008

American meteorologist

1 Predictability: Does the flap of a butterfly's
wings in Brazil set off a tornado in Texas?

title of paper given to the American Association for the
Advancement of Science, Washington, 29 December 1979;
James Gleick *Chaos* (1988)

Konrad Lorenz 1903–89

Austro-German zoologist

2 It is a good morning exercise for a research
scientist to discard a pet hypothesis every day
before breakfast. It keeps him young.

Das Sogenannte Böse (1963; translated by Marjorie Latzke as
On Aggression, 1966) ch. 2

Louis XIV (the 'Sun King') 1638–1715

French monarch, King from 1643

3 *L'État c'est moi.*

I am the State.

before the Parlement de Paris, 13 April 1655

probably apocryphal; J. A. Dulaure *Histoire de Paris* (1834)
vol. 6

4 *J'ai failli attendre.*

I was nearly kept waiting.

attribution queried, among others, by E. Fournier in *L'Esprit
dans l'Histoire* (1857) ch. 48

5 *Toutes les fois que je donne une place vacante, je fais
cent mécontents et un ingrat.*

Every time I create an appointment, I create a
hundred malcontents and one ingrate.

Voltaire *Siècle de Louis XIV* (1768 ed.) vol. 2, ch. 26

6 *Il n'y a plus de Pyrénées.*

The Pyrenees are no more.

on the accession of his grandson to the throne of Spain,
1700

attributed to Louis by Voltaire in *Siècle de Louis XIV* (1753) ch.
26, but to the Spanish Ambassador to France in the *Mercure
Galant* (Paris) November 1700

7 It means I'm growing old when ladies declare
war on me.

following the accession of Queen Anne, Britain declared war
on France

Gila Curtis *The Life and Times of Queen Anne* (1972); attributed

Louis XV 1710–74

French monarch, King from 1715

8 Are the streets being paved with gold over there?
I fully expect to awake one morning in Versailles

to see the walls of the fortress rising above the
horizon.

on the costs of fortifying Louisbourg on Cape Breton Island,
Canada, c.1745

attributed

Louis XVI 1754–93

**French monarch, King from 1774; deposed in 1789 on the
outbreak of the French Revolution and executed in 1793. On
Louis: see FIRMONT 327:16; see also LA ROCHEFOUCAULD-
LIANCOURT 482:13**

9 *diary entry for 14 July 1789, the day of the storming of the*
Bastille:

Rien.

Nothing.

Simon Schama *Citizens* (1989) ch. 10

Louis XVIII 1755–1824

French monarch, King from 1814; titular king from 1795

10 *Rappelez-vous bien qu'il n'est aucun de vous qui
n'ait dans sa giberne le bâton de maréchal du duc de
Reggio; c'est à vous à l'en faire sortir.*

Remember that there is not one of you who
does not carry in his cartridge-pouch the
marshal's baton of the duke of Reggio; it is up
to you to bring it forth.

speech to Saint-Cyr cadets, 9 August 1819, in *Moniteur
Universel* 10 August 1819

11 *L'exactitude est la politesse des rois.*

Punctuality is the politeness of kings.

attributed in *Souvenirs de J. Lafitte* (1844) bk. 1, ch. 3; see
PROVERBS 642:11

Joe Louis 1914–81

American boxer

12 He can run. But he can't hide.

of Billy Conn, his opponent, before a heavyweight title fight,
19 June 1946

Louis: My Life Story (1947)

Louis Philippe 1773–1850

French monarch, King 1830–48

13 Died, has he? Now I wonder what he meant by
that?

of **TALLEYRAND**

attributed, perhaps apocryphal

Ada Lovelace 1815–52

English mathematican, daughter of Lord BYRON

14 The Analytical Engine weaves algebraic patterns
just as the Jacquard loom weaves flowers and
leaves.

of **BABBAGE**'s mechanical computer

Luigi Menabrea *Sketch of the Analytical Engine invented by
Charles Babbage* (1843), translated and annotated by Ada
Lovelace, Note A

Richard Lovelace 1618–58

English poet

1 Lucasta that bright northern star.
'Amyntor from Beyond the Sea to Alexis' (1649)

2 Forbear, thou great good husband, little ant.
'The Ant' (1660)

3 When Love with unconfinèd wings
Hovers within my gates.
'To Althea, From Prison' (1649)

4 When thirsty grief in wine we steep,
When healths and draughts go free,
Fishes, that tipple in the deep,
Know no such liberty.
'To Althea, From Prison' (1649)

5 Stone walls do not a prison make,
Nor iron bars a cage;
Minds innocent and quiet take
That for an hermitage.
If I have freedom in my love,
And in my soul am free;
Angels alone, that soar above,
Enjoy such liberty.
'To Althea, From Prison' (1649)

6 Tell me not, Sweet, I am unkind,
That from the nunnery
Of thy chaste breast, and quiet mind,
To war and arms I fly.

True; a new mistress now I chase,
The first foe in the field;
And with a stronger faith embrace
A sword, a horse, a shield.
'To Lucasta, Going to the Wars' (1649)

7 Yet this inconstancy is such,
As you too shall adore;
I could not love thee, Dear, so much,
Loved I not honour more.
'To Lucasta, Going to the Wars' (1649)

Bernard Lovell 1913–

English astronomer

8 Youth is vivid rather than happy, but memory
always remembers the happy things.
in *The Times* 20 August 1993

James Lovell 1928–

American astronaut

9 Houston, we've had a problem.
on Apollo 13 space mission, 14 April 1970
in *The Times* 15 April 1970

Samuel Lover 1797–1868

Irish writer

10 When once the itch of literature comes over a
man, nothing can cure it but the scratching of a
pen.
Handy Andy (1842) ch. 36

11 Young Rory O'More courted Kathaleen bawn,
He was bold as a hawk, and she soft as the
dawn.
'Rory O'More' (1837 song); see **CARTOON CAPTIONS** 205:11

David Low 1891–1963

New Zealand-born British political cartoonist

12 Colonel Blimp.
cartoon creation, proponent of reactionary establishment
opinions

Robert Lowe, Lord Sherbrooke
1811–92

British Liberal politician. On Lowe: see **BRIGHT** 157:5; see
also **MISQUOTATIONS** 548:24

13 The Chancellor of the Exchequer is a man
whose duties make him more or less of a taxing
machine. He is intrusted with a certain amount
of misery which it is his duty to distribute as
fairly as he can.
speech, House of Commons, 11 April 1870

Amy Lowell 1874–1925

American poet

14 And the softness of my body will be guarded by
embrace
By each button, hook, and lace.
For the man who should loose me is dead,
Fighting with the Duke in Flanders,
In a pattern called a war.
Christ! What are patterns for?
'Patterns' (1916)

15 All books are either dreams or swords,
You can cut, or you can drug, with words.
'Sword Blades and Poppy Seed' (1914); see **FARQUHAR** 324:12

James Russell Lowell 1819–91

American poet

16 An' you've gut to git up airly
Ef you want to take in God.
The Biglow Papers (First Series, 1848) no. 1 'A Letter'

17 There comes Poe with his raven like Barnaby
Rudge,
Three-fifths of him genius, and two-fifths sheer
fudge.
'A Fable for Critics' (1848) l. 1215; see **POE** 610:19

18 Blessèd are the horny hands of toil!
'A Glance Behind the Curtain' (1844); see **SALISBURY** 679:1

19 Once to every man and nation comes the
moment to decide,
In the strife of Truth with Falsehood, for the
good or evil side.
'The Present Crisis' (1845)

20 Truth forever on the scaffold, Wrong forever on
the throne,—
Yet that scaffold sways the future, and, behind
the dim unknown,

Standeth God within the shadow, keeping watch
above his own.
'The Present Crisis' (1845)

1 May is a pious fraud of the almanac.
'Under the Willows' (1869) l. 21

2 There is no good in arguing with the inevitable.
The only argument available with an east wind
is to put on your overcoat.
Democracy and other Addresses (1887) 'Democracy'

Robert Lowell 1917–77
American poet

3 My eyes have seen what my hand did.
'Dolphin' (1973)

4 Terrible that old life of decency
without unseemly intimacy
or quarrels, when the unemancipated woman
still had her Freudian papa and maids!
'During Fever' (1959)

5 Their monument sticks like a fishbone
in the city's throat.
'For the Union Dead' (1964)

6 At forty-five,
What next, what next?
At every corner,
I meet my Father,
my age, still alive.
'Middle Age' (1964)

7 I saw the spiders marching through the air,
Swimming from tree to tree that mildewed day
In latter August when the hay
Came creaking to the barn.
'Mr Edwards and the Spider' (1950); see **EDWARDS** 304:7

8   This is death.
To die and know it. This is the Black Widow,
death.
'Mr Edwards and the Spider' (1950)

9 The Lord survives the rainbow of His will.
'The Quaker Graveyard in Nantucket' (1950)

10 If we see light at the end of the tunnel,
It's the light of the oncoming train.
'Since 1939' (1977); see **DICKSON** 282:8

11 None of the wilder subtleties
of grace or art will sweeten these
stiff quatrains shovelled out four-square.
of hymns as contrasted with poetry and the Bible
'Waking Early Sunday Morning' (1967)

William Lowndes 1652–1724
English politician

12 Take care of the pence, and the pounds will
take care of themselves.
Lord Chesterfield *Letters to his Son* (1774) 5 February 1750 ('for

the pounds . . . ' in an earlier letter, 6 November 1747); see
CARROLL 202:10, **CHESTERFIELD** 223:4, **PROVERBS** 644:2

L. S. Lowry 1887–1976
English painter

13 I'm a simple man, and I use simple materials.
Mervyn Levy *Paintings of L. S. Lowry* (1975)

Malcolm Lowry 1909–57
English novelist

14 How alike are the groans of love to those of the
dying.
Under the Volcano (1947) ch. 12

Mina Loy 1882–1966
English-born American poet and artist

15 [Be] *Brave* and deny at the outset—that pathetic
clap-trap war cry *Woman is the equal of man* for
She is NOT! . . . Leave off looking to men to find
out what you are *not*—Seek within yourselves to
find out what you *are*.
'Feminist Manifesto' (1914, unpublished) in Virginia M. Kovidis
Mina Loy (1980)

Lucan (Marcus Annaeus Lucanus) AD 39–65
Roman poet

16   *Quis iustius induit arma*
Scire nefas, magno se iudice quisque tuetur:
Victrix causa deis placuit, sed victa Catoni.

It is not granted to know which man took up
arms with more right on his side. Each pleads
his cause before a great judge: the winning
cause pleased the gods, but the losing one
pleased Cato.
Pharsalia bk. 1, l. 128

17 *Stat magni nominis umbra.*

There stands the ghost of a great name.
of Pompey
Pharsalia bk. 1, l. 135

18 *Nil actum credens, dum quid superesset agendum.*

Thinking nothing done while anything remained
to be done.
Pharsalia bk. 2, l. 657; see **ROGERS** 665:12

19   *Coniunx*
Est mihi, sunt nati: dedimus tot pignora fatis.

I have a wife, I have sons: we have given so
many hostages to the fates.
Pharsalia bk. 6, l. 661; see **BACON** 47:15

20 *Jupiter est quodcumque vides, quocumque moveris.*

Jupiter is whatever you see, whichever way you
move.
Pharsalia bk. 9, l. 580

George Lucas *see* Film lines 329:6, Film titles 331:4

Clare Booth Luce 1903–87
American diplomat, politician, and writer

1 Much of . . . his global thinking is, no matter how you slice it, still globaloney.
speech to the House of Representatives, February 1943

Lucilius (Gaius Lucilius) *c*.180–102 BC
Roman poet

2 *Maior erat natu; non omnia possumus omnes.*
He was greater in years; we cannot all do everything.
Macrobius *Saturnalia* bk. 6, ch. 1, sect. 35; see **VIRGIL** 832:8

Lucretius (Titus Lucretius Carus) *c*.94–55 BC
Roman poet. On Lucretius: see **VIRGIL** 832:18

3 *Aeneadum genetrix, divumque hominumque voluptas.*
Mother of Aeneas' race; pleasure of gods and mortals alike.
of Venus
De Rerum Natura bk. 1, l. 1

4 *Ergo vivida vis animi pervicit, et extra*
Processit longe flammantia moenia mundi
Atque omne immensum peragravit, mente animoque.
So the vital strength of his spirit won through, and he made his way far outside the flaming walls of the world and ranged over the measureless whole, both in mind and spirit.
on EPICURUS
De Rerum Natura bk. 1, l. 72

5 *Tantum religio potuit suadere malorum.*
So much wrong could religion induce.
De Rerum Natura bk. 1, l. 101

6 *Lucida tela diei.*
Clear shafts of day.
De Rerum Natura bk. 1, l. 147

7 . . . *Nil posse creari*
De nilo.
Nothing can be created out of nothing.
De Rerum Natura bk. 1, l. 155

8 *Sed veluti pueris absinthia taetra medentes*
Cum dare conantur, prius oras pocula circum
Contingit mellis duci flavoque liquore.
For as with children, when the doctors try
To give them loathsome wormwood, first they smear
Sweet yellow honey on the goblet's rim.
De Rerum Natura bk. 1, l. 936

9 *Suave, mari magno turbantibus aequora ventis,*
E terra magnum alterius spectare laborem.
Non quia vexari quemquamst iucunda voluptas,
Sed quibus ipse malis careas quia cernere suave est.
Lovely it is, when the winds are churning up the waves on the great sea, to gaze out from the land on the great efforts of someone else; not because it's an enjoyable pleasure that somebody is in difficulties, but because it's lovely to realize what troubles you are yourself spared.
De Rerum Natura bk. 2, l. 1

10 *Augescunt aliae gentes, aliae minuuntur,*
Inque brevi spatio mutantur saecla animantum
Et quasi cursores vitai lampada tradunt.
Some races increase, others are reduced, and in a short while the generations of living creatures are changed and like runners relay the torch of life.
De Rerum Natura bk. 2, l. 8

11 *Nil igitur mors est ad nos neque pertinet hilum,*
Quandoquidem natura animi mortalis habetur.
Death therefore is nothing to us nor does it concern us a scrap, seeing that the nature of the spirit we possess is something mortal.
De Rerum Natura bk. 3, l. 830

12 *Vitaque mancipio, nulli datur, omnibus usu.*
And life is given to none freehold, but it is leasehold for all.
De Rerum Natura bk. 3, l. 971

13 *Scire licet nobis nil esse in morte timendum*
Nec miserum fieri qui non est posse neque hilum
Differre an nullo fuerit iam tempore natus,
Mortalem vitam mors cum immortalis ademit.
We can know there is nothing to be feared in death, that one who is not cannot be made unhappy, and that it matters not a scrap whether one might ever have been born at all, when death that is immortal has taken over one's mortal life.
De Rerum Natura bk. 3, l. 866

14 *Cur non ut plenus vitae conviva recedis*
Aequo animoque capis securam, stulte, quietem?
Why not, like a banqueter fed full of life, withdraw with contentment and rest in peace, you fool?
De Rerum Natura bk. 3, l. 938

15 *Medio de fonte leporum*
Surgit amari aliquid quod in ipsis floribus angat.
From the midst of the fountain of delights rises something bitter that chokes them all amongst the flowers.
De Rerum Natura bk. 4, l. 1133

Fray Luis de León *c*.1527–91
Spanish poet and religious writer

16 *Que descansada vida*
la del que huye el mundanal ruido,
y sigue la escondida
senda, por donde han ido
los pocos sabios que en el mundo han sido!
What a relaxed life is that which flees the worldly clamour, and follows the hidden path

down which have gone the few wise men there have been in the world!

'Vida Retirada'

1 *Dicebamus hesterno die . . .*

We were saying yesterday . . .

on resuming a lecture at Salamanca University in 1577, after five years' imprisonment

attributed, among others, by A. F. G. Bell in *Luis de León* (1925) ch. 8

Alison Lurie 1926–

American novelist

2 There's a rule, I think. You get what you want in life, but not your second choice too.

Real People (1969) 'July 5'

Martin Luther 1483–1546

German Protestant theologian. On Luther: see ARNOLD 32:6

3 *Esto peccator et pecca fortiter, sed fortius fide et gaude in Christo.*

Be a sinner and sin strongly, but more strongly have faith and rejoice in Christ.

letter to Melanchthon, 1521, in *Epistolae* (Jena, 1556) vol. 1, folio 345 verso

4 Here stand I. I can do no other. God help me. Amen.

speech at the Diet of Worms, 18 April 1521; attributed

5 If I had heard that as many devils would set on me in Worms as there are tiles on the roofs, I should none the less have ridden there.

to the Princes of Saxony, 21 August 1524, in *Sämmtliche Schriften* vol. 16 (1745) ch. 10, sect. 1, no. 763:15

6 There will be little dogs, with golden hair, shining like precious stones.

sermon on the resurrection, Easter Sunday, 1544

7 For, where God built a church, there the devil would also build a chapel . . . In such sort is the devil always God's ape.

Colloquia Mensalia (1566) ch. 2 (translated by H. Bell as *Martin Luther's Divine Discourses*, 1652); see PROVERBS 647:7

8 *Eine feste Burg ist unser Gott,*
Ein gute Wehr und Waffen.

A safe stronghold our God is still,
A trusty shield and weapon.

'Eine feste Burg ist unser Gott' (1529); translated by Thomas Carlyle

9 The confidence and faith of the heart alone make both God and an idol.

Large Catechism (1529) 'The First Commandment'

10 Whatever your heart clings to and confides in, that is really your God.

Large Catechism (1529) 'The First Commandment'

11 So our Lord God commonly gives riches to those gross asses to whom He vouchsafes nothing else.

Tischreden oder Colloquia (collected by J. Aurifaber, 1566) ch. 4

12 *Wer nicht liebt Wein, Weib und Gesang,*
Der bleibt ein Narr sein Leben lang.

Who loves not woman, wine, and song
Remains a fool his whole life long.

attributed (later inscribed in the Luther room in the Wartburg, but with no proof of authorship)

Edwin Lutyens 1869–1944

English architect

13 There will never be great architects or great architecture without great patrons.

in *Country Life* 8 May 1915

Rosa Luxemburg 1871–1919

German revolutionary

14 *Freiheit ist immer nur Freiheit des anders Denkenden.*

Freedom is always and exclusively freedom for the one who thinks differently.

Die Russische Revolution (1918) sect. 4

John Lydgate c.1370–c.1451

English poet

15 Sithe off oure language he was the lodesterre.

of CHAUCER

The Fall of Princes (1431–8) prologue l. 252

16 Comparisouns doon offte gret greuaunce.

The Fall of Princes (1431–8) bk. 3, l. 2188; see PROVERBS 629:16

17 Woord is but wynd; leff woord and tak the dede.

Secrets of Old Philosophers l. 1224

18 Love is mor than gold or gret richesse.

The Story of Thebes pt. 3, l. 2716

John Lyly c.1554–1606

English poet and dramatist

19 CAMPASPE: Were women never so fair, men would be false.

APELLES: Were women never so false, men would be fond.

Campaspe (1584) act 3, sc. 3

20 Cupid and my Campaspe played
At cards for kisses, Cupid paid.

Campaspe (1584) act 3, sc. 5

21 What bird so sings, yet so does wail?
O 'tis the ravished nightingale.
Jug, jug, jug, jug, tereu, she cries,
And still her woes at midnight rise.

Campaspe (1584) act 5, sc. 1; see ELIOT 311:7

22 Night hath a thousand eyes.

The Maydes Metamorphosis (1600) act 3, sc. 1

23 If all the earth were paper white
And all the sea were ink
'Twere not enough for me to write
As my poor heart doth think.

'If all the earth were paper white'; see NURSERY RHYMES 579:5

Lord Lyndhurst 1772–1863

English politician and lawyer; three times Lord Chancellor

1 Campbell has added another terror to death.

on Lord Campbell's Lives of the Lord Chancellors *being written without the consent of heirs or executors*

E. Bowen-Rowlands *Seventy-Two Years At the Bar* (1924) ch. 10; see **ARBUTHNOT** 25:18, **TREE** 815:5, **WETHERELL** 849:6

Jonathan Lynn 1943– *and* Antony Jay 1930–

English writers

2 I think it will be a clash between the political will and the administrative won't.

Yes Prime Minister (1987) vol. 2

Lysander d. 395 BC

Greek general

3 Deceive boys with toys, but men with oaths.

Plutarch *Parallel Lives* 'Lysander' ch. 8; see **PLUTARCH** 610:13

Henry Francis Lyte 1793–1847

English hymn-writer

4 Abide with me: fast falls the eventide;
The darkness deepens; Lord, with me abide.

'Abide with Me' (probably written in 1847); see **BIBLE** 106:30

5 Change and decay in all around I see;
O Thou, who changest not, abide with me.

'Abide with Me' (probably written in 1847)

6 Praise my soul, the King of heaven;
To his feet thy tribute bring.
Ransomed, healed, restored, forgiven,
Who like me his praise should sing?

'Praise, my soul, the King of heaven' (1834 hymn)

7 Father-like, he tends and spares us.

'Praise, my soul, the King of heaven' (1834 hymn)

George Lyttelton, Lord Lyttelton 1709–73

English politician and man of letters

8 Seek to be good, but aim not to be great;
A woman's noblest station is retreat.

'Advice to a Lady' (1773)

Humphrey Lyttelton 1922–2008

English jazz musician and broadcaster

9 As we journey through life, discarding baggage along the way, we should keep an iron grip, to the very end, on the capacity for silliness. It preserves the soul from desiccation.

It Just Occurred to Me (2006)

E. R. Bulwer, Lord Lytton *see* Owen Meredith

Douglas MacArthur 1880–1964

American general, commander of US (later Allied) forces in the SW Pacific during the Second World War. On MacArthur: see **TRUMAN** 817:23

10 I came through and I shall return.

on reaching Australia, 20 March 1942, having broken through Japanese lines en route from Corregidor
in *New York Times* 21 March 1942

11 In war, indeed, there can be no substitute for victory.

in *Congressional Record* 19 April 1951, vol. 97, pt. 3

Rose Macaulay 1881–1958

English novelist

12 Love's a disease. But curable.

Crewe Train (1926)

13 'Take my camel, dear,' said my aunt Dot, as she climbed down from this animal on her return from High Mass.

The Towers of Trebizond (1956), opening words

Thomas Babington Macaulay 1800–59

English politician and historian. On Macaulay: see **ARNOLD** 31:20, **CARLYLE** 200:29, **SMITH** 758:18

14 In order that he might rob a neighbour whom he had promised to defend, black men fought on the coast of Coromandel, and red men scalped each other by the Great Lakes of North America.

Biographical Essays (1857) 'Frederic the Great'

15 The gallery in which the reporters sit has become a fourth estate of the realm.

Essays Contributed to the Edinburgh Review (1843) vol. 1 'Hallam'

16 He knew that the essence of war is violence, and that moderation in war is imbecility.

Essays Contributed to the Edinburgh Review (1843) vol. 1 'John Hampden'

17 The gigantic body, the huge massy face, seamed with the scars of disease, the brown coat, the black worsted stockings, the grey wig with the scorched foretop, the dirty hands, the nails bitten and pared to the quick.

Essays Contributed to the Edinburgh Review (1843) vol. 1 'Samuel Johnson'

18 Out of his surname they have coined an epithet for a knave, and out of his Christian name a synonym for the Devil.

Essays Contributed to the Edinburgh Review (1843) vol. 1 'Machiavelli'

1 As civilization advances, poetry almost necessarily declines.
Essays Contributed to the Edinburgh Review (1843) vol. 1 'Milton'

2 If men are to wait for liberty till they become wise and good in slavery, they may indeed wait for ever.
Essays Contributed to the Edinburgh Review (1843) vol. 1 'Milton'

3 They esteemed themselves rich in a more precious treasure, and eloquent in a more sublime language, nobles by the right of an earlier creation, and priests by the imposition of a mightier hand.
of the Puritans
Essays Contributed to the Edinburgh Review (1843) vol. 1 'Milton'

4 We know no spectacle so ridiculous as the British public in one of its periodical fits of morality.
Essays Contributed to the Edinburgh Review (1843) vol. 1 'Moore's Life of Lord Byron'

5 We have heard it said that five per cent is the natural interest of money.
Essays Contributed to the Edinburgh Review (1843) vol. 1 'Southey's Colloquies'

6 With the dead there is no rivalry. In the dead there is no change. Plato is never sullen. Cervantes is never petulant. Demosthenes never comes unseasonably. Dante never stays too long. No difference of political opinion can alienate Cicero. No heresy can excite the horror of Bossuet.
Essays Contributed to the Edinburgh Review (1843) vol. 2 'Lord Bacon'

7 An acre in Middlesex is better than a principality in Utopia.
Essays Contributed to the Edinburgh Review (1843) vol. 2 'Lord Bacon'

8 The highest intellects, like the tops of mountains, are the first to catch and to reflect the dawn.
Essays Contributed to the Edinburgh Review (1843) vol. 2 'Sir James Mackintosh'

9 The history of England is emphatically the history of progress.
Essays Contributed to the Edinburgh Review (1843) vol. 2 'Sir James Mackintosh'

10 Biographers, translators, editors, all, in short, who employ themselves in illustrating the lives or writings of others, are peculiarly exposed to the *Lues Boswelliana*, or disease of admiration.
Essays Contributed to the Edinburgh Review (1843) vol. 2 'William Pitt, Earl of Chatham'

11 On the day of the accession of George the Third, the ascendancy of the Whig party terminated; and on that day the purification of the Whig party began.
Essays Contributed to the Edinburgh Review (1843) vol. 2 'William Pitt, Earl of Chatham'

12 The conformation of his mind was such that whatever was little seemed to him great, and whatever was great seemed to him little.
Essays Contributed to the Edinburgh Review (1843) vol. 2 'Horace Walpole'

13 Every schoolboy knows who imprisoned Montezuma, and who strangled Atahualpa.
Essays Contributed to the Edinburgh Review (1843) vol. 3 'Lord Clive'; see **TAYLOR** 792:3

14 The Chief Justice was rich, quiet, and infamous.
Essays Contributed to the Edinburgh Review (1843) vol. 3 'Warren Hastings'

15 That temple of silence and reconciliation where the enmities of twenty generations lie buried.
of Westminster Abbey
Essays Contributed to the Edinburgh Review (1843) vol. 3 'Warren Hastings'

16 She [the Roman Catholic Church] may still exist in undiminished vigour when some traveller from New Zealand shall, in the midst of a vast solitude, take his stand on a broken arch of London Bridge to sketch the ruins of St Paul's.
Essays Contributed to the Edinburgh Review (1843) vol. 3 'Von Ranke'; see **WALPOLE** 837:19

17 She [the Church of Rome] thoroughly understands what no other church has ever understood, how to deal with enthusiasts.
Essays Contributed to the Edinburgh Review (1843) vol. 3 'Von Ranke'

18 Persecution produced its natural effect on them [Puritans and Calvinists]. It found them a sect; it made them a faction.
History of England vol. 1 (1849) ch. 1

19 It was a crime in a child to read by the bedside of a sick parent one of those beautiful collects which had soothed the griefs of forty generations of Christians.
*of the **BOOK OF COMMON PRAYER***
History of England vol. 1 (1849) ch. 2

20 The Puritan hated bear-baiting, not because it gave pain to the bear, but because it gave pleasure to the spectators.
History of England vol. 1 (1849) ch. 2

21 The English Bible, a book which, if everything else in our language should perish, would alone suffice to show the whole extent of its beauty and power.
T. F. Ellis (ed.) *Miscellaneous Writings of Lord Macaulay* (1860) 'John Dryden' (1828)

22 His imagination resembled the wings of an ostrich. It enabled him to run, though not to soar.
T. F. Ellis (ed.) *Miscellaneous Writings of Lord Macaulay* (1860) 'John Dryden' (1828)

23 This province of literature is a debatable line. It lies on the confines of two distinct territories . . . It is sometimes fiction. It is sometimes theory.
of history
T. F. Ellis (ed.) *Miscellaneous Writings of Lord Macaulay* (1860) vol. 1 'History' (1828)

1 History begins in novel and ends in essay.
   T. F. Ellis (ed.) *Miscellaneous Writings of Lord Macaulay* (1860)
   vol. 1 'History' (1828)

2 Till Skiddaw saw the fire that burned on Gaunt's
     embattled pile,
   And the red glare on Skiddaw roused the
     burghers of Carlisle.
   'The Armada' (1833)

3 Obadiah Bind-their-kings-in-chains-and-their-
   nobles-with-links-of-iron.
   'The Battle of Naseby' (1824) fictitious author's name; see
   BOOK OF COMMON PRAYER 150:11

4 Oh, wherefore come ye forth in triumph from
     the north,
   With your hands, and your feet, and your
     raiment all red?
   'The Battle of Naseby' (1824)

5 And the Man of Blood was there, with his long
     essenced hair,
   And Astley, and Sir Marmaduke, and Rupert of
     the Rhine.
   'The Battle of Naseby' (1824)

6 By those white cliffs I never more must see,
   By that dear language which I spake like thee,
   Forget all feuds, and shed one English tear
   O'er English dust. A broken heart lies here.
   'A Jacobite's Epitaph' (1845)

7 Gay are the Martian Calends:
   December's Nones are gay:
   But the proud Ides, when the squadron rides,
   Shall be Rome's whitest day!
   Lays of Ancient Rome (1842) 'The Battle of Lake Regillus' st. 1

8 Those trees in whose grim shadow
   The ghastly priest doth reign,
   The priest who slew the slayer,
   And shall himself be slain.
   Lays of Ancient Rome (1842) 'The Battle of Lake Regillus' st. 10

9 Let no man stop to plunder,
   But slay, and slay, and slay;
   The Gods who live for ever
   Are on our side to-day.
   Lays of Ancient Rome (1842) 'The Battle of Lake Regillus' st. 35

10 Lars Porsena of Clusium
   By the nine gods he swore
   That the great house of Tarquin
   Should suffer wrong no more.
   Lays of Ancient Rome (1842) 'Horatius' st. 1

11 The harvests of Arretium,
   This year, old men shall reap.
   This year, young boys in Umbro
   Shall plunge the struggling sheep;
   And in the vats of Luna,
   This year, the must shall foam
   Round the white feet of laughing girls
   Whose sires have marched to Rome.
   Lays of Ancient Rome (1842) 'Horatius' st. 8

12 But by the yellow Tiber
   Was tumult and affright.
   Lays of Ancient Rome (1842) 'Horatius' st. 13

13 And how can man die better
   Than facing fearful odds,
   For the ashes of his fathers,
   And the temples of his Gods?
   Lays of Ancient Rome (1842) 'Horatius' st. 27

14 Now who will stand on either hand,
   And keep the bridge with me?
   Lays of Ancient Rome (1842) 'Horatius' st. 29

15 Then none was for a party;
   Then all were for the state;
   Then the great man helped the poor,
   And the poor man loved the great:
   Then lands were fairly portioned;
   Then spoils were fairly sold:
   The Romans were like brothers
   In the brave days of old.
   Lays of Ancient Rome (1842) 'Horatius' st. 32

16 But hark! the cry is Astur
   And lo! the ranks divide,
   And the great Lord of Luna
   Comes with his stately stride.
   Lays of Ancient Rome (1842) 'Horatius' st. 42

17 Was none who would be foremost
   To lead such dire attack;
   But those behind cried 'Forward!'
   And those before cried 'Back!'
   Lays of Ancient Rome (1842) 'Horatius' st. 50

18 Oh, Tiber! father Tiber
   To whom the Romans pray,
   A Roman's life, a Roman's arms,
   Take thou in charge this day!
   Lays of Ancient Rome (1842) 'Horatius' st. 59

19 And even the ranks of Tuscany
   Could scarce forbear to cheer.
   Lays of Ancient Rome (1842) 'Horatius' st. 60

20 With weeping and with laughter
   Still is the story told,
   How well Horatius kept the bridge
   In the brave days of old.
   Lays of Ancient Rome (1842) 'Horatius' st. 70

21 On the left side goes Remus,
   With wrists and fingers red,
   And in his hand a boar-spear,
   And on the point a head—
   A wrinkled head and aged,
   With silver beard and hair,
   And holy fillets round it,
   Such as the pontiffs wear—
   The head of ancient Camers,
   Who spoke the words of doom:
   'The children to the Tiber,
   The mother to the tomb.'
   Lays of Ancient Rome (1842) 'The Prophecy of Capys'

22 Thank you, madam, the agony is abated.
   aged four, having had hot coffee spilt over his legs
   G. O. Trevelyan *Life and Letters of Lord Macaulay* (1876) ch. 1

23 We must at present do our best to form a class
   who may be interpreters between us and the
   millions whom we govern; a class of persons,

Indian in blood and colour, but English in taste, in opinions, in morals, and in intellect.
> minute, as Member of Supreme Council of India, 2 February 1835, in W. Nassan Lees *Indian Musalmàns* (1871)

1 How odd that people of sense should find any pleasure in being accompanied by a beast who is always spoiling conversation.
> *of dogs*
> G. O. Trevelyan *Life and Letters of Macaulay* (1876) ch. 14

Anthony McAuliffe 1898–1975
American general

2 Nuts!
> *replying to the German demand for surrender at Bastogne, Belgium, 22 December 1944*
> in *New York Times* 28 December 1944

Norman McCaig 1910–96
Scottish poet

3 Who owns this landscape?
The millionaire who bought it or
the poacher staggering downhill in the early
  morning
with a deer on his back?
> 'A Man in Assynt' (1969)

Joseph McCarthy 1908–57
American politician and anti-Communist agitator. On McCarthy: see **EISENHOWER** 306:7, **WELCH** 845:13

4 I have here in my hand a list of two hundred and five [people] that were known to the Secretary of State as being members of the Communist Party and who nevertheless are still working and shaping the policy of the State Department.
> speech at Wheeling, West Virginia, 9 February 1950

5 McCarthyism is Americanism with its sleeves rolled.
> speech in Wisconsin, 1952, in Richard Rovere *Senator Joe McCarthy* (1973)

Mary McCarthy 1912–89
American novelist

6 Europe is the unfinished negative of which America is the proof.
> *On the Contrary* (1961) 'America the Beautiful'

7 If someone tells you he is going to make a 'realistic decision', you immediately understand that he has resolved to do something bad.
> *On the Contrary* (1961) 'American Realist Playwrights'

8 Every word she writes is a lie, including 'and' and 'the'.
> *on Lillian* **HELLMAN**
> in *New York Times* 16 February 1980

Linda McCartney 1941–98
American photographer, wife of Paul **MCCARTNEY**

9 I don't eat anything with a face.
> quoted in *BBC News* (online edition) 19 April 1998; obituary

Paul McCartney 1942–
English pop singer and songwriter. See also **LENNON AND MCCARTNEY**

10 You cannot reheat a soufflé.
> *discounting rumours of a Beatles reunion*
> attributed; L. Botts *Loose Talk* (1980)

George B. McClellan 1826–85
American Union general and politician

11 All quiet along the Potomac.
> *said at the time of the American Civil War*
> attributed; see **BEERS** 66:7

Ewan MacColl 1915–89
English folksinger and songwriter

12 Dirty old town.
> *of Salford*
> title of song, 1950

13 And I used to sleep standing on my feet
As we hunted for the shoals of herring.
> 'The Shoals of Herring' (1960 song)

P. D. McCormick c.1834–1916
Australian musician

14 In joyful strains then let us sing
Advance Australia fair.
> *the national anthem of Australia, from 1984*
> 'Advance Australia Fair' (c.1878 song)

Horace McCoy 1897–1955
American novelist

15 They shoot horses don't they.
> title of novel (1935)

John McCrae 1872–1918
Canadian poet and military physician

16 In Flanders fields the poppies blow
Between the crosses, row on row,
That mark our place; and in the sky
The larks, still bravely singing, fly
Scarce heard amid the guns below.
> 'In Flanders Fields' (1915)

17 To you from failing hands we throw
The torch; be yours to hold it high.
If ye break faith with us who die
We shall not sleep, though poppies grow.
In Flanders fields.
> 'In Flanders Fields' (1915)

Carson McCullers 1917–67
American writer

18 The heart is a lonely hunter.
> title of novel (1940); from the line by Fiona McLeod (William Sharp) (1855–1905) 'The Lonely Hunter' (1896) st. 6: 'My heart is a lonely hunter that hunts on a lonely hill'

Hugh MacDiarmid (Christopher Murray Grieve) 1892–1978

Scottish poet and nationalist

1 Scotland small? Our multiform, our infinite
  Scotland *small*?
  Only as a patch of hillside may be a cliché
  corner
  To a fool who cries 'Nothing but heather!' . . .
    Direadh 1 (1974)

2 I'll ha'e nae hauf-way hoose, but aye be whaur
  Extremes meet—it's the only way I ken
  To dodge the curst conceit o' bein' richt
  That damns the vast majority o' men.
    A Drunk Man Looks at the Thistle (1926)

3 He's no a man ava',
  And lacks a proper pride,
  Gin less than a' the world
  Can ser' him for a bride!
    A Drunk Man Looks at the Thistle (1926)

4 Hold a glass of pure water to the eye of the
  sun!
  . . . This is the nearest analogy to the essence of
  human life
  Which is even more difficult to see.
  Dismiss anything you can see more easily;
  It is not alive—it is not worth seeing.
    'The Glass of Pure Water' (1962)

5 The rose of all the world is not for me.
  I want for my part
  Only the little white rose of Scotland
  That smells sharp and sweet—and breaks the
  heart.
    'The Little White Rose' (1934)

George MacDonald 1824–1905

Scottish writer and poet. See also **EPITAPHS 317:15**

6 Where did you come from, baby dear?
  Out of the everywhere into here.
    At the Back of the North Wind (1871) ch. 33 'Song'

7 So, then, as darkness had no beginning, neither
  will it ever have an end . . . Where the light
  cannot come, there abideth the darkness. The
  light doth but hollow a mine out of the infinite
  extension of the darkness. And ever upon the
  steps of the light treadeth the darkness; yea,
  springeth in fountains and wells amidst it, from
  the secret channels of its mighty sea.
    Phantastes (1858) ch. 8

John A. Macdonald 1815–91

Scottish-born Canadian Liberal-Conservative statesman,
Prime Minister 1867–73 and 1878–91

8 When fortune empties her chamberpot on your
  head, smile—and say 'we are going to have a
  summer shower'.
    spoken c.1875 when Leader of the Opposition

9 A British subject I was born, and a British
  subject I will die.
    speech, 17 February 1891, in Toronto *Empire* 18 February 1891

Ramsay MacDonald 1866–1937

British Labour statesman, Prime Minister 1924, 1931–5. On
MacDonald: see **CHURCHILL 229:7, LLOYD GEORGE 496:21,
NICOLSON 575:2**

10 We hear war called murder. It is not: it is
  suicide.
    in *Observer* 4 May 1930

11 Tomorrow every Duchess in London will be
  wanting to kiss me!
    after forming the National Government, 25 August 1931
    Viscount Snowden *An Autobiography* (1934) vol. 2

A. G. MacDonell 1889–1941

Scottish writer

12 England, their England.
    title of novel (1933); see **HENLEY** 391:14

Ian McEwan 1948–

English novelist

13 Shakespeare would have grasped wave functions,
  Donne would have understood complementarity
  and relative time. They would have been excited.
  What richness! They would have plundered this
  new science for their imagery. And they would
  have educated their audiences too. But you 'arts'
  people, you're not only ignorant of these
  magnificent things, you're rather proud of
  knowing nothing.
    The Child in Time (1987) ch. 2

14 I love you . . . That is what they were all saying
  down their phones, from the hijacked planes and
  the burning towers. There is only love, and then
  oblivion. Love was all they had to set against the
  hatred of their murderers.
    of the last messages received from those trapped by
    terrorist attack in buildings and planes, 11 September 2001
    in *Guardian* 15 September 2001; see **BURNETT** 176:14

William McGonagall c.1825–1902

Scottish writer of doggerel verse

15 Beautiful Railway Bridge of the Silv'ry Tay!
  Alas, I am very sorry to say
  That ninety lives have been taken away
  On the last Sabbath day of 1879,
  Which will be remembered for a very long time.
    'The Tay Bridge Disaster'

Patrick McGoohan 1928–2009, George Markstein, and David Tomblin

American actor; scriptwriters

16 I am not a number, I am a free man!
    Number Six, in *The Prisoner* (TV series 1967–68); additional
    title sequence from the second episode onwards

Roger McGough 1937–

English poet

17 Let me die a youngman's death
  Not a clean & in-between-

The-sheets, holy-water death,
Not a famous-last-words
Peaceful out-of-breath death.
'Let Me Die a Youngman's Death' (1967)

1 And though poets I admire have published
poems
Whose imperfections reflect our own decay,
I could never begin a poem; 'When I am dead'
In case it tempted Fate, and Fate gave way.
'When I am Dead' (1982); see **ROSSETTI** 669:9

Jimmie McGregor 1932–

Scottish singer and songwriter

2 Oh, he's football crazy, he's football mad
And the football it has robbed him o' the wee
bit sense he had.
And it would take a dozen skivvies, his clothes
to wash and scrub,
Since our Jock became a member of that terrible
football club.
'Football Crazy' (1960 song)

Niccolò Machiavelli 1469–1527

Italian political philosopher and Florentine statesman. On
Machiavelli: see **MACAULAY** 506:18

3 If . . . sometimes you need to conceal a fact
with words, do it in such a way that it does not
become known, or, if it does become known,
that you have a ready and quick defence.
'Advice to Raffaello Girolami when he went as Ambassador to
the Emperor' (October 1522) in *Machiavelli: The Chief Works
and Others* (translated by Allan Gilbert, 1965)

4 It is necessary for him who lays out a state and
arranges laws for it to presuppose that all men
are evil and that they are always going to act
according to the wickedness of their spirits
whenever they have free scope.
Discourse upon the First Ten Books of Livy (written 1513–17) bk.
1, ch. 3 (translated by Allan Gilbert)

5 The cause of the bad and of the good fortune
of men is the way in which their method of
working fits the times.
Discourse upon the First Ten Books of Livy (written 1513–17) bk.
3, ch. 9 (translated by Allan Gilbert)

6 Men should be either treated generously or
destroyed, because they take revenge for slight
injuries—for heavy ones they cannot.
The Prince (written 1513) ch. 3 (translated by Allan Gilbert)

7 This leads to a debate: is it better to be loved
than feared, or the reverse? The answer is that it
is desirable to be both, but because it is difficult
to join them together, it is much safer for a
prince to be feared than loved, if he is to fail in
one of the two.
The Prince (written 1513) ch. 8 (translated by Allan Gilbert)

8 Let no one oppose this belief of mine with that
well-worn proverb: 'He who builds on the
people builds on mud.'
The Prince (written 1513) ch. 9 (translated by Allan Gilbert)

9 It is the nature of men to feel as much obligated
for benefits they confer as for those they receive.
The Prince (written 1513) ch. 10 (translated by Allan Gilbert)

10 Since, then, a prince is necessitated to play the
animal well, he chooses among the beasts the
fox and the lion, because the lion does not
protect himself from traps; the fox does not
protect himself from wolves. The prince must
be a fox, therefore, to recognize the traps and a
lion to frighten the wolves.
The Prince (written 1513) ch. 18 (translated by Allan Gilbert)

11 As to the actions of all men, and especially
those of princes, against whom charges cannot
be brought in court, everybody looks at their
result.
The Prince (written 1513) ch. 18 (translated by Allan Gilbert)

12 He [the prince] holds to what is right when he
can but knows how to do wrong when he must.
The Prince (written 1513) ch. 18 (translated by Allan Gilbert)

13 So long as the great majority of men are not
deprived of either property or honour, they are
satisfied.
The Prince (written 1513) ch. 19 (translated by Allan Gilbert)

14 There is no other way for securing yourself
against flatteries except that men understand
that they do not offend you by telling you the
truth; but when everybody can tell you the
truth, you fail to get respect.
The Prince (written 1513) ch. 23 (translated by Allan Gilbert)

Claude McKay 1890–1948

American poet and novelist

15 If we must die, let it not be like hogs
Hunted and penned in an inglorious spot,
While round us bark the mad and hungry dogs,
Making their mock at our accursed lot.
'If We Must Die' (1922)

16 Like men we'll face the murderous, cowardly
pack,
Pressed to the wall, dying, but fighting back!
'If We Must Die' (1922)

Compton Mackenzie 1883–1972

English novelist

17 Women do not find it difficult nowadays to
behave like men, but they often find it extremely
difficult to behave like gentlemen.
Literature in My Time (1933) ch. 22

James Mackintosh 1765–1832

Scottish philosopher and historian

18 Men are never so good or so bad as their
opinions.
Dissertation on the Progress of Ethical Philosophy (1830) sect. 6
'Jeremy Bentham'

19 The Commons, faithful to their system,
remained in a wise and masterly inactivity.
Vindiciae Gallicae (1791) sect. 1

Alexander Maclaren 1826–1910

Scottish divine

1 'The Church is an anvil which has worn out many hammers', and the story of the first collision is, in essentials, the story of all.
Expositions of Holy Scripture: Acts of the Apostles (1907) ch. 4; see **BEZA** 77:15, **PROVERBS** 629:2

Don McLean 1945–

American songwriter

2 Something touched me deep inside
The day the music died.
on the death of Buddy Holly
'American Pie' (1972 song)

3 So, bye, bye, Miss American Pie,
Drove my Chevy to the levee
But the levee was dry.
Them good old boys was drinkin' whiskey and rye
Singin' 'This'll be the day that I die.'
'American Pie' (1972 song)

Archibald MacLeish 1892–1982

American poet and public official

4 A Poem should be palpable and mute
As a globed fruit.
'Ars Poetica' (1926)

5 A poem should be wordless
As the flight of birds.
'Ars Poetica' (1926)

6 A poem should not mean
But be.
'Ars Poetica' (1926)

Murdoch McLennan fl. 1715

Scottish poet

7 There's some say that we wan, some say that they wan,
Some say that nane wan at a', man;
But one thing I'm sure, that at Sheriffmuir
A battle there was which I saw, man:
And we ran, and they ran, and they ran, and we ran,
And we ran; and they ran awa', man!
'Sheriffmuir' in J. Woodfall Ebsworth (ed.) *Roxburghe Ballads* vol. 6 (1889)

Iain Macleod 1913–70

British Conservative politician. On Macleod: see **SALISBURY** 679:5

8 It is some measure of the tightness of the magic circle on this occasion that neither the Chancellor of the Exchequer nor the Leader of the House of Commons had any inkling of what was happening.
*of the 'evolvement' of Alec Douglas-*HOME *as Conservative leader after the resignation of Harold* MACMILLAN
in *The Spectator* 17 January 1964

Marshall McLuhan 1911–80

Canadian communications scholar

9 The new electronic interdependence recreates the world in the image of a global village.
The Gutenberg Galaxy (1962)

10 The medium is the message.
Understanding Media (1964) ch. 1 (title)

11 Television brought the brutality of war into the comfort of the living room. Vietnam was lost in the living rooms of America—not the battlefields of Vietnam.
in *Montreal Gazette* 16 May 1975

12 Advertising is the greatest art form of the twentieth century.
in *Advertising Age* 3 September 1976

13 Gutenberg made everybody a reader. Xerox makes everybody a publisher.
in *Guardian Weekly* 12 June 1977

Comte de MacMahon 1808–93

French soldier and statesman, President of the Third Republic 1873–9

14 *J'y suis, j'y reste.*
Here I am, and here I stay.
at the taking of the Malakoff fortress during the Crimean War, 8 September 1855
G. Hanotaux *Histoire de la France Contemporaine* (1903–8) vol. 2, ch. 1, sect. 1; MacMahon later denied that he had expressed himself in such 'lapidary form'

Harold Macmillan 1894–1986

British Conservative statesman, Prime Minister 1957–63. On Macmillan: see **THORPE** 810:5; see also **HITLER** 400:7

15 We . . . are Greeks in this American empire . . . We must run the Allied Forces HQ as the Greeks ran the operations of the Emperor Claudius.
to Richard CROSSMAN *in 1944*
in *Sunday Telegraph* 9 February 1964

16 Forever poised between a cliché and an indiscretion.
on the life of a Foreign Secretary
in *Newsweek* 30 April 1956

17 Let us be frank about it: most of our people have never had it so good.
'*You Never Had It So Good' was the Democratic Party slogan during the 1952 US election campaign*
speech at Bedford, 20 July 1957, in *The Times* 22 July 1957

18 I thought the best thing to do was to settle up these little local difficulties, and then turn to the wider vision of the Commonwealth.
on leaving for a Commonwealth tour, following the resignation of the Chancellor of the Exchequer and others
statement at London airport, 7 January 1958; in *The Times* 8 January 1958

19 The wind of change is blowing through this continent, and, whether we like it or not, this

growth of [African] national consciousness is a political fact.

> speech at Cape Town, 3 February 1960, in *Pointing the Way* (1972)

1 There are three bodies no sensible man directly challenges: the Roman Catholic Church, the Brigade of Guards and the National Union of Mineworkers.

> in *Observer* 22 February 1981; see **BALDWIN** 53:10

2 First of all the Georgian silver goes, and then all that nice furniture that used to be in the saloon. Then the Canalettos go.

on privatization

> speech to the Tory Reform Group, 8 November 1985, in *The Times* 9 November 1985; see **MISQUOTATIONS** 548:17

3 The opposition of events.

on his biggest problem; popularly quoted as, 'Events, dear boy. Events'

> David Dilks *The Office of Prime Minister in Twentieth Century Britain* (1993)

Robert McNamara 1916–

American Democratic politician, Secretary of Defense during the Vietnam War

4 I don't object to it's being called 'McNamara's War' . . . It is a very important war and I am pleased to be identified with it and do whatever I can to win it.

> in *New York Times* 25 April 1964

5 We . . . acted according to what we thought were the principles and traditions of this nation. We were wrong. We were terribly wrong.

*of the conduct of the Vietnam War by the **KENNEDY** and **JOHNSON** administrations*

> speaking in Washington, just before the twentieth anniversary of the American withdrawal from Vietnam; in *Daily Telegraph* (electronic edition) 10 April 1995

6 Military force—especially when wielded by an outside power—cannot bring order in a country that cannot govern itself.

> in *Daily Telegraph* (electronic edition) 10 April 1995

Louis MacNeice 1907–63

British poet, born in Belfast

7 Better authentic mammon than a bogus god.

> *Autumn Journal* (1939)

8 It's no go the merrygoround, it's no go the rickshaw,
All we want is a limousine and a ticket for the peepshow.

> 'Bagpipe Music' (1938)

9 The glass is falling hour by hour, the glass will fall for ever,
But if you break the bloody glass you won't hold up the weather.

> 'Bagpipe Music' (1938)

10 So they were married—to be the more together—
And found they were never again so much together,

Divided by the morning tea,
By the evening paper,
By children and tradesmen's bills.

> 'Les Sylphides' (1941)

11 Time was away and somewhere else,
There were two glasses and two chairs
And two people with the one pulse
(Somebody stopped the moving stairs):
Time was away and somewhere else.

> 'Meeting Point' (1941)

12 I am not yet born; O fill me
With strength against those who would freeze my
humanity.

> 'Prayer Before Birth' (1944)

13 Let them not make me a stone and let them not spill me,
Otherwise kill me.

> 'Prayer Before Birth' (1944)

14 The sunlight on the garden
Hardens and grows cold,
We cannot cage the minute
Within its net of gold.

> 'Sunlight on the Garden' (1938)

15 By a high star our course is set,
Our end is Life. Put out to sea.

> 'Thalassa' (1964)

16 I would have a poet able-bodied, fond of talking, a reader of the newspapers, capable of pity and laughter, informed in economics, appreciative of women, involved in personal relationships, actively interested in politics, susceptible to physical impressions.

> *Modern Poetry* (1938)

Robert MacNeil 1931–

Canadian writer

17 Parents can plant magic in a child's mind through certain words spoken with some thrilling quality of voice, some uplift of the heart and spirit.

> *Wordstruck* (1989)

William Macpherson of Cluny 1926–

Scottish lawyer

18 For the purposes of our Inquiry the concept of institutional racism which we apply consists of:
The collective failure of an organisation to provide an appropriate and professional service to people because of their colour, culture, or ethnic origin. It can be seen or detected in processes, attitudes and behaviour which amount to discrimination through unwitting prejudice, ignorance, thoughtlessness and racist stereotyping which disadvantage minority ethnic people.

> *The Stephen Lawrence Inquiry: Report* (February 1999) ch. 6

Geoffrey Madan 1895–1947

English bibliophile

1 The great tragedy of the classical languages is to have been born twins.
Geoffrey Madan's Notebooks (1981)

2 The dust of exploded beliefs may make a fine sunset.
Livre sans nom: Twelve Reflections (privately printed 1934) no. 12

Samuel Madden 1686–1765

Irish poet

3 Words are men's daughters, but God's sons are things.
Boulter's Monument (1745) l. 377; see **JOHNSON** 435:17

Winnie Madikizela-Mandela 1934–

South African political activist; former wife of Nelson **MANDELA**

4 With that stick of matches, with our necklace, we shall liberate this country.
speech in black townships, 14 April 1986, in *Guardian* 15 April 1986

James Madison 1751–1836

American Democratic Republican statesman, 4th President of the US 1809–17

5 Liberty is to faction what air is to fire, an aliment without which it instantly expires. But it could not be less folly to abolish liberty, which is essential to political life, because it nourishes faction than it would be to wish the annihilation of air, which is essential to animal life, because it imparts to fire its destructive agency.
The Federalist (1787) no. 10

6 The diversity in the faculties of men, from which the rights of property originate, is not less an insuperable obstacle to a uniformity of interests. The protection of these faculties is the first object of government. From the protection of different and unequal faculties of acquiring property, the possession of different degrees and kinds of property immediately results.
The Federalist (1787) no. 10

7 If men were angels, no government would be necessary.
The Federalist (1788) no. 51

8 I believe there are more instances of the abridgement of freedom of the people by gradual and silent encroachments of those in power than by violent and sudden usurpations.
speech in Virginia Convention, 16 June 1788

9 The class of citizens who provide at once their own food and their own raiment, may be viewed as the most truly independent and happy.
'Republican Distribution of Citizens' in *National Gazette* 5 March 1792, in R. Ketcham (ed.) *Selected Writings of James Madison* (2006)

10 No nation could preserve its freedom in the midst of continual warfare.
Political Observations [pamphlet published in Philadelphia] 20 April 1795, in R. Ketcham (ed.) *Selected Writings of James Madison* (2006)

11 The advancement and diffusion of knowledge . . . is the only guardian of true liberty.
letter to George Thomson, 30 June 1825, *Letters and other Writings of James Madison* (1865) vol. 3

Madonna 1958–

American pop singer and actress

12 Being blonde is definitely a different state of mind. I can't really put my finger on it, but the artifice of being blonde has some incredible sort of sexual connotation.
in *Rolling Stone* 23 March 1989

Gaeus Cilnius Maecenas d. 8 BC

Roman statesman

13 Never allow any innovation in religion, because the peace of the state depends on it.
attributed; M. F. Wiles *Archetypal Heresy* (1996)

Maurice Maeterlinck 1862–1949

Belgian poet, dramatist, and essayist

14 *Il n'y a pas de morts.*
There are no dead.
L'Oiseau bleu (1909) act 4

John Gillespie Magee 1922–41

American airman, member of the Royal Canadian Airforce

15 Oh! I have slipped the surly bonds of earth
And danced the skies on laughter-silvered wings.
'High Flight' (1943); see **REAGAN** 656:17

16 And, while with silent lifting mind I've trod
The high, untrespassed sanctity of space,
Put out my hand and touched the face of God.
'High Flight' (1943); see **REAGAN** 656:17

William Connor Magee 1821–91

English clergyman, Bishop of Peterborough and Archbishop of York

17 It would be better that England should be free than that England should be compulsorily sober.
speech on the Intoxicating Liquor Bill, House of Lords, 2 May 1872

Ferdinand Magellan *see* Misquotations

547:21

Magna Carta

Political charter signed by King John at Runnymede, 1215

18 *Quod Anglicana ecclesia libera sit.*
That the English Church shall be free.
Clause 1

1 *Nullius liber homo capiatur, vel imprisonetur, aut dissaisiatur, aut utlagetur, aut exuletur, aut aliquo modo destruatur, nec super eum ibimus, nec super eum mittemus, nisi per legale judicium parium suorum vel per legem terrae.*

No free man shall be taken or imprisoned or dispossessed, or outlawed or exiled, or in any way destroyed, nor will we go upon him, nor will we send against him except by the lawful judgement of his peers or by the law of the land.

Clause 39

2 *Nulli vendemus, nulli negabimus aut differemus, rectum aut justitiam.*

To no man will we sell, or deny, or delay, right or justice.

Clause 40; see **SAYINGS** 684:32

René Magritte 1898–1967

Belgian surrealist painter

3 The mind loves the unknown. It loves images whose meaning is unknown, since the meaning of the mind itself is unknown.

Suzy Gablik *Magritte* (1970) ch. 1

Mahāyāna Buddhist texts

a tradition which emerged in India around the 1st century AD, which later spread to China, Japan, and elsewhere

4 Homage to thee, Perfect Wisdom,
Boundless and transcending thought!
All thy limbs are without blemish,
Faultless those who Thee discern.

'Hymn to Perfect Wisdom' by Rahulabhadra (c.150 AD)

5 This all-knowledge of the Tathagata has come forth from the perfection of wisdom. The physical personality of the Tathagata, on the other hand, is the result of the skill in means of the perfection of wisdom.

Perfect Wisdom in 8,000 Lines (c.100 BC–100 AD) ch. 3, v. 58

6 Where there is no perception, appellation, conception, or conventional expression, there one speaks of 'perfect wisdom'.

Perfect Wisdom in 8,000 Lines (c.100 BC–100 AD) ch. 7, v. 177

7 A Bodhisattva who is full of pity and concerned with the welfare of all beings, who dwells in friendliness, compassion, sympathetic joy and even mindedness.

Perfect Wisdom in 8,000 Lines (c.100 BC–100 AD) ch. 20, v. 373

8 A glow-worm, or some other luminous animal, does not think that its light could illuminate the Continent of Jambudvipa [India], or radiate over it. Just so the Disciples and Pratyekabuddhas do not think that they should, after winning full enlightenment lead all beings to Nirvana. But the sun, when it has arisen, radiates its light over the whole of Jambudvipa. Just so a Bodhisattva, after he has accomplished the practices which

lead to the full enlightenment of Buddhahood, leads countless beings to Nirvana.

Large Sutra on Perfect Wisdom (in 25,000 lines) (c.50–200 AD) v. 41

9 Form is emptiness and the very emptiness is form; emptiness does not differ from form, nor does form differ from emptiness; whatever is form, that is emptiness, whatever is emptiness, that is form.

Heart Sutra (4th century AD) v. 3

10 One should know the Prajnaparamita as the great spell, the spell of great knowledge, the utmost spell, the unequalled spell, allayer of all suffering, in truth,—for what could go wrong? By the Prajnaparamita has this spell been delivered. It runs like this: gone, gone, gone beyond, gone altogether beyond, O what an awakening, all hail!

Heart Sutra (4th century AD) v. 8

11 This saying has been taught by the Tathagata in a hidden sense: 'Those who know the discourse on dharma as a raft should forsake dharmas, and how much more so non-dharmas.'

Diamond Sutra (4th century AD) v. 6

12 Those who by my form did see me,
And those who followed me by my voice,
Wrong are the efforts they engaged in,
Me those people will not see.

Diamond Sutra (4th century AD) v. 26a

13 As stars, a fault of vision, as a lamp,
A mock show, dew drops, or a bubble,
A dream, a lightning flash, or cloud,
So we should view what is conditioned.

Diamond Sutra (4th century AD) v. 32a

14 Foolish common people do not understand that what is seen is merely their own mind.

Lankāvatāra Sutra (c.4th century AD) p. 90

15 The road to Buddhahood is open to all.
At all times have all living beings the Germ of Buddhahood in them.

Ratnagotravibhāga (c.3th century AD) v. 28

16 When I rain down the rain of Dharma,
Then all this world is well refreshed . . .
And then, refreshed, just like the plants,
The world will burst forth into blossoms.

Lotus Sutra pt. 5, v. 36

17 In the world deluded by ignorance, the supreme all-knowing one,
The Tathagata, the great physician, appears, full of compassion.

Lotus Sutra pt. 5, v. 60

18 There is no triad of vehicles, but here there is only one vehicle.

Lotus Sutra pt. 5, v. 82

19 [The Happy Land] which is the world system of the Lord Amitabha [Buddha of Infinite Light], is rich and prosperous, comfortable, fertile, delightful and crowded with many gods and men.

Pure Land Sutra ch. 15

1 All beings are irreversible from the supreme enlightenment if they hear the name of the Lord Amitabha, and, on hearing it, with one single thought only raise their hearts to him with a resolve connected with serene faith.
Larger Pure Land Sutra ch. 26

2 Sons or daughters of good family, who may desire to see that Tathagata Amitabha in this very life . . . should dedicate their store of merit to being reborn therein [Sukhāvatī].
Larger Pure Land Sutra ch. 27

3 Universally Good is present in all lands
Sitting on a jewelled lotus throne, beheld by all;
He manifests all psychic powers
And is able to enter infinite meditations.
Flower Garland Sutra (c.2nd century AD) bk. 3

Gustav Mahler 1860–1911
Austrian composer

4 Fortissimo at last!
on seeing Niagara Falls
K. Blaukopf *Gustav Mahler* (1973) ch. 8

5 The symphony must be like the world. It must embrace everything.
remark to Sibelius, Helsinki, 1907; K. and H. Blaukopf (eds.) *Mahler: his life, work and world* (1976)

Derek Mahon 1941–
Irish poet

6 'I am just going outside and may be some time.'
The others nod, pretending not to know.
At the heart of the ridiculous, the sublime.
Antarctica (1985) title poem; see OATES 582:16

7 Somewhere beyond the scorched gable end and the burnt-out buses
there is a poet indulging
his wretched rage for order.
'Rage for Order' (1978)

Norman Mailer 1923–2007
American novelist and essayist

8 So we think of Marilyn who was every man's love affair with America, Marilyn Monroe who was blonde and beautiful and had a sweet little rinky-dink of a voice and all the cleanliness of all the clean American backyards.
Marilyn (1973)

9 A modern democracy is a tyranny whose borders are undefined; one discovers how far one can go only by travelling in a straight line until one is stopped.
The Presidential Papers (1964) preface

10 The world stood like a playing card on edge . . .
One looked at the buildings one passed and wondered if one was to see them again.
looking back at the week of the Cuban Missile Crisis
The Presidential Papers (1964)

11 All the security around the American president is just to make sure the man who shoots him gets caught.
in *Sunday Telegraph* 4 March 1990

Maimonides (Moses ben Maimon) 1135–1204
Jewish philosopher and Rabbinic scholar, born in Spain. See also EPITAPHS 317:9

12 The basic tenets of our Torah and its fundamental principles are thirteen in number: *The first fundamental principle* is the existence of the Creator. There is a being who exists in the most perfect mode of existence, and he is the cause of the existence of all other beings.
Commentary on the Mishnah Sanhedrin 10 (Heleq)

13 When I find the road narrow, and can see no other way of teaching a well established truth except by pleasing one intelligent man and displeasing ten thousand fools—I prefer to address myself to the man.
The Guide for the Perplexed, introduction

14 Know that for the human mind there are certain objects of perception which are within the scope of its nature and capacity; on the other hand, there are, amongst things which actually exist, certain objects which the mind can in no way and by no means grasp: the gates of perception are closed against it.
The Guide for the Perplexed ch. 31

15 Man's love of God is identical with his knowledge of Him.
The Guide for the Perplexed ch. 51

16 Astrology is a disease, not a science.
Laws of Repentance

17 He who visits the sick is as though he would take away part of his sickness and lighten his pain.
Mishneh Torah bk. 14 'Judges' ch. 14, no. 4

Henry Maine 1822–88
English jurist

18 The movement of the progressive societies has hitherto been a movement *from Status to Contract*.
Ancient Law (1861) ch. 5

19 So great is the ascendancy of the Law of Actions in the infancy of Courts of Justice, that substantive law has at first the look of being gradually secreted in the interstices of procedure; and the early lawyer can only see the law through the envelope of its technical forms.
Dissertations on Early Law and Custom (1883) ch. 11

20 War appears to be as old as mankind, but peace is a modern invention.
lecture delivered in Cambridge, 1887, in *International Law* (1888)

21 Except the blind forces of Nature, nothing moves in this world which is not Greek in its origin.
Village Communities (3rd ed., 1876)

Joseph de Maistre 1753–1821

French writer and diplomat

1 *Toute nation a le gouvernement qu'elle mérite.*

Every country has the government it deserves.
Lettres et Opuscules Inédits (1851) vol. 1, letter 53 (15 August 1811)

John Major 1943–

British Conservative statesman, Prime Minister 1990–7. On Major: see **CURRIE** 263:6

2 If the policy isn't hurting, it isn't working.
on controlling inflation
speech in Northampton, 27 October 1989; see **POLITICAL SLOGANS AND SONGS** 613:19

3 Society needs to condemn a little more and understand a little less.
interview with *Mail on Sunday* 21 February 1993

4 Fifty years on from now, Britain will still be the country of long shadows on county [cricket] grounds, warm beer, invincible green suburbs, dog lovers, and—as George Orwell said—old maids bicycling to Holy Communion through the morning mist.
speech to the Conservative Group for Europe, 22 April 1993; see **ORWELL** 587:7

5 It is time to get back to basics: to self-discipline and respect for the law, to consideration for others, to accepting responsibility for yourself and your family, and not shuffling it off on the state.
speech to the Conservative Party Conference, 8 October 1993

Bernard Malamud 1914–86

American novelist and short-story writer

6 There's no such thing as an unpolitical man, especially a Jew.
The Fixer (1966) ch. 9

7 Levin wanted friendship and got friendliness; he wanted steak and they offered spam.
A New Life (1961)

Malcolm X 1925–65

American civil rights campaigner

8 The white man was *created* a devil, to bring chaos upon this earth.
speech, *c.*1953; Malcolm X with Alex Haley *The Autobiography of Malcolm X* (1965); see **FARD** 323:11

9 If you're born in America with a black skin, you're born in prison.
in an interview, June 1963

10 You can't separate peace from freedom because no one can be at peace unless he has his freedom.
speech in New York, 7 January 1965, *Malcolm X Speaks* (1965)

11 We are not speaking of any *individual* white man. We are speaking of the *collective* white man's *historical* record. We are speaking of the collective white man's cruelties, and evils, and greeds, that have seen him *act* like a devil toward the non-white man.
Malcolm X with Alex Haley *The Autobiography of Malcolm X* (1965)

Stéphane Mallarmé 1842–98

French poet

12 *La chair est triste, hélas! et j'ai lu tous les livres.*
The flesh, alas, is wearied; and I have read all the books there are.
'Brise Marin' (1887)

13 *Prélude à l'après-midi d'un faune.*
Prelude to the afternoon of a faun.
title of poem (c.1865)

14 *Un coup de dés jamais n'abolira le hasard.*
A throw of the dice will never eliminate chance.
title of poem (1897)

15 *Il se promène, lisant au livre de lui-même.*
He strolls, reading the book of himself.
'Hamlet et Fortinbras' in *La Revue blanche* 15 July 1896

David Mallet (Malloch) *c.*1705–65

Scottish poet

16 O grant me, Heaven, a middle state,
Neither too humble nor too great;
More than enough, for nature's ends,
With something left to treat my friends.
'Imitation of Horace'; see **HORACE** 414:20

George Leigh Mallory 1886–1924

English mountaineer

17 Because it's there.
on being asked why he wanted to climb Mount Everest (Mallory was lost on Everest in the following year)
in *New York Times* 18 March 1923

Thomas Malory d. 1471

English writer whose major work, *Le Morte D'Arthur*, was a prose translation of the legends of King Arthur, selected from French and other sources. See also **ASCHAM** 33:9, **CAXTON** 212:4

18 Whoso pulleth out this sword of this stone and anvil is rightwise King born of all England.
Le Morte D'Arthur (finished 1470, printed by Caxton 1485) bk. 1, ch. 4

19 The questing beast . . . had in shape like a serpent's head and a body like a leopard, buttocked like a lion and footed like a hart. And in his body there was such a noise as it had been twenty couple of hounds questing, and such noise that beast made wheresomever he went.
questing = *yelping*
Le Morte D'Arthur (1485) bk. 9, ch. 12

20 God defend me, said Dinadan, for the joy of love is too short, and the sorrow thereof, and what cometh thereof, dureth over long.
Le Morte D'Arthur (1485) bk. 10, ch. 56; see **FLORIAN** 335:23

1 Thus endeth the story of the Sangreal, that was briefly drawn out of French into English, the which is a story chronicled for one of the truest and the holiest that is in this world.
Le Morte D'Arthur (1485) bk. 17, ch. 23

2 Therefore all ye that be lovers call unto your remembrance the month of May, like as did Queen Guenevere, for whom I make here a little mention, that while she lived she was a true lover, and therefore she had a good end.
Le Morte D'Arthur (1485) bk. 18, ch. 25

3 Wherefore, madam, I pray you kiss me and never no more. Nay, said the queen, that shall I never do, but abstain you from such works: and they departed. But there was never so hard an hearted man but he would have wept to see the dolour that they made.
Le Morte D'Arthur (1485) bk. 21, ch. 10

4 Thou wert never matched of earthly knight's hand; and thou wert the courteoust knight that ever bare shield; and thou wert the truest friend to thy lover that ever bestrad horse; and thou wert the truest lover of a sinful man that ever loved woman; and thou wert the kindest man that ever struck with sword; and thou wert the goodliest person that ever came among press of knights; and thou wert the meekest man and the gentlest that ever ate in hall among ladies; and thou wert the sternest knight to thy mortal foe that ever put spear in the rest.
to Sir Launcelot
Le Morte D'Arthur (1485) bk. 21, ch. 13

5 And many men say that there is written upon his tomb this verse: *Hic iacet Arthurus, rex quondam rexque futurus* [Here lies Arthur, the once and future king].
Le Morte d'Arthur (1485) bk. 31, ch. 7

David Malouf 1934–
Australian writer

6 I am a B-b-british object!
Remembering Babylon (1993), spoken by Gemmy Fairly using the words of James Morrill; see **MORRILL** 560:6

André Malraux 1901–76
French novelist, essayist, and art critic

7 *La condition humaine.*
The human condition.
title of book (1933)

8 *Il n'y a pas cinquante manières de combattre, il n'y en a qu'une, c'est d'être vainqueur. Ni la révolution ni la guerre ne consistent à se plaire à soi-même.*
There are not fifty ways of fighting, there's only one, and that's to win. Neither revolution nor war consists in doing what one pleases.
L'Espoir (1937) pt. 2, sect. 2, ch. 12

9 *L'homme sait que le monde n'est pas à l'échelle humaine; et il voudrait qu'il le fût.*

Man knows that the world is not made on a human scale; and he wishes that it were.
Les Noyers d'Altenburg (1945) pt. 2, ch. 3

10 *L'art est un anti-destin.*
Art is a revolt against fate.
Les Voix du silence (1951) pt. 4, ch. 7

Thomas Robert Malthus 1766–1834
English political economist

11 Population, when unchecked, increases in a geometrical ratio. Subsistence only increases in an arithmetical ratio.
Essay on the Principle of Population (1798) ch. 1

12 The proper check to population, moral restraint.
Essay on the Principle of Population (1798) ch. 2

13 The perpetual struggle for room and food.
Essay on the Principle of Population (1798) ch. 3

Lord Mancroft 1914–87
British Conservative politician

14 Cricket—a game which the English, not being a spiritual people, have invented in order to give themselves some conception of eternity.
Bees in Some Bonnets (1979)

W. R. Mandale

15 Up and down the City Road,
In and out the Eagle,
That's the way the money goes—
Pop goes the weasel!
'Pop Goes the Weasel' (1853 song); also attributed to Charles Twiggs

Nelson Mandela 1918–
South African political activist and statesman, President 1994–99

16 I have dedicated my life to this struggle of the African people. I have fought against white domination, and I have fought against black domination. I have cherished the ideal of a democratic and free society in which all persons live together in harmony with equal opportunities. It is an ideal which I hope to live for, and to see realized. But my lord, if needs be, it is an ideal for which I am prepared to die.
speech at his trial in Pretoria, 20 April 1964, which he quoted on his release in Cape Town, 11 February 1990 (he had been sentenced to life imprisonment as an activist for the African National Congress)

17 I stand here before you not as a prophet but as a humble servant of you, the people. Your tireless and heroic sacrifices have made it possible for me to be here today. I therefore place the remaining years of my life in your hands.
speech in Cape Town, 11 February 1990

18 No one is born hating another person because of the colour of his skin, or his background, or

his religion. People must learn to hate, and if they can learn to hate, they can be taught to love, for love comes more naturally to the human heart than its opposite.
Long Walk to Freedom (1994)

1 True reconciliation does not consist in merely forgetting the past.
speech, 7 January 1996

Peter Mandelson 1953–
British Labour politician

2 Before this campaign started, it was said that I was facing political oblivion, my career in tatters . . . They underestimated me, because I am a fighter and not a quitter.
on winning back his Hartlepool seat in the General Election
speech, 8 June 2001

Osip Mandelstam 1892–1938
Russian poet

3 The age is rocking the wave
with human grief
to a golden beat, and an adder
is breathing in time with it in the grass.
'The Age' (1923) (translated by C. M. Bowra)

4 Cruel and feeble, you'll look back
with the smile of a half-wit:
an animal that could run once,
staring at its own tracks.
'The Age' (1923) (translated by C. M. Bowra)

5 Only in war our fate has consummation,
And divination too will perish then.
'Tristia' (1919) (translated by C. M. Bowra)

John Streeter Manifold 1915–85
Australian poet and writer on music

6 Down under we send soldiers and wool abroad but keep poets and wine at home.
attributed, *Selected Verse* (1948)

Manilius (Marcus Manilius)
Roman poet of the 1st century AD

7 *Eripuitque Jovi fulmen viresque tonandi,
et sonitum ventis concessit, nubibus ignem.*

And snatched from Jove the lightning shaft and power to thunder, and attributed the noise to the winds, the flame to the clouds.
of human intelligence
Astronomica bk. 1, l. 104; see **TURGOT** 819:7

Mrs Manley 1663–1724
English novelist and dramatist

8 No time like the present.
The Lost Lover (1696) act 4, sc. 1

Horace Mann 1796–1859
American educationist

9 The object of punishment is, prevention from evil; it never can be made impulsive to good.
Lectures and Reports on Education (1867 ed.) lecture 7

10 Lost, yesterday, somewhere between Sunrise and Sunset, two golden hours, each set with sixty diamond minutes. No reward is offered, for they are gone forever.
'Lost, Two Golden Hours' in *Common School Journal*
November 1844

Thomas Mann 1875–1955
German novelist

11 *Unsere Fähigkeit zum Ekel ist, wie ich anmerken möchte, desto grösser, je lebhafter unsere Begierde ist, das heisst: je inbrünstiger wir eigentlich der Welt und ihren Darbietungen anhangen.*

Our capacity for disgust, let me observe, is in proportion to our desires; that is in proportion to the intensity of our attachment to the things of this world.
The Confessions of Felix Krull (1954) pt. 1, ch. 5 (translated by Denver Lindley)

12 *Die Zeit hat in Wirklichkeit keine Einschnitte, es gibt kein Gewitter oder Drommetengetön beim Beginn eines neuen Monats oder Jahres, und selbst bei dem eines neuen Säkulums sind es nur wir Menschen, die schiessen und läuten.*

Time has no divisions to mark its passage, there is never a thunderstorm or blare of trumpets to announce the beginning of a new month or year. Even when a new century begins it is only we mortals who ring bells and fire off pistols.
The Magic Mountain (1924) ch. 4, sect. 4 (translated by H. T. Lowe-Porter)

13 *Warten heisst: Voraneilen, heisst: Zeit und Gegenwart nicht als Geschenk, sondern nur als Hindernis empfinden, ihren Eigenwert verneinen und vernichten und sie im Geist überspringen. Warten, sagt man, sei langweilig. Es ist jedoch ebensowohl oder sogar eigentlich kurzweilig, indem es Zeitmengen verschlingt, ohne sie um ihrer selbst willen zu leben und auszunutzen.*

And waiting means hurrying on ahead, it means regarding time and the present moment not as a boon, but an obstruction; it means making their actual content null and void, by mentally overleaping them. Waiting we say is long. We might just as well—or more accurately—say it is short, since it consumes whole spaces of time without our living them or making any use of them as such.
The Magic Mountain (1924) ch. 5, sect. 5 (translated by H. T. Lowe-Porter)

14 *Die Sprach is Gesittung selbst . . . Das Wort, selbst das widersprechendste, ist so verbindend . . . Aber die Wortlosigkeit vereinsamt.*

Speech is civilisation itself. The word, even the most contradictory word, preserves contact—it is silence which isolates.

The Magic Mountain (1924) ch. 6 (translated by H. T. Lowe-Porter)

1 *Wir kommen aus dem Dunkel und gehen ins Dunkel, dazwischen liegen Erlebnisse; aber Anfang und Ende, Geburt und Tod, werden von uns nicht erlebt, sie haben keinen subjektiven Charakter, sie fallen als Vorgänge ganz ins Gebiet des Objektiven, so ist es damit.*

We come out of the dark and go into the dark again, and in between lie the experiences of our life. But the beginning and end, birth and death, we do not experience; they have no subjective character, they fall entirely in the category of objective events, and that's that.

The Magic Mountain (1924) ch. 6, sect. 8 (translated by H. T. Lowe-Porter)

2 *Unser Sterben ist mehr eine Angelegenheit der Weiterlebenden als unserer selbst.*

A man's dying is more the survivors' affair than his own.

The Magic Mountain (1924) ch. 6, sect. 8 (translated by H. T. Lowe-Porter)

3 *Die Zeit ist das Element der Erzählung, wie sie das Element des Lebens ist,—unlösbar damit verbunden, wie mit den Körpern im Raum. Sie ist auch das Element der Musik, als welche die Zeit misst und gliedert, sie kurzweilig und kostbar auf einmal macht.*

For time is the medium of narration, as it is the medium of life. Both are inextricably bound up with it, as are bodies in space. Similarly, time is the medium of music; music divides, measures, articulates time, and can shorten it, yet enhance its value, both at once.

The Magic Mountain (1924) ch. 7, sect. 1 (translated by H. T. Lowe-Porter)

4 *Das kühlt, das klärt, dem zuge der stunden hält eine bestimmte Gemütsverfassung nicht ungewandelt stand.*

Time cools, time clarifies; no mood can be maintained quite unaltered through the course of hours.

The Magic Mountain (1924) ch. 7 (translated by H. T. Lowe-Porter)

5 In our time the destiny of man presents its meanings in political terms.

attributed; quoted in Archibald MacLeish 'Public Speech and Private Speech in Poetry' in *Yale Review* Spring 1938

John Manners, Duke of Rutland

1818–1906

English Tory politician and writer

6 Let wealth and commerce, laws and learning die,
But leave us still our old nobility!

England's Trust (1841) pt. 3, l. 227

Katherine Mansfield (Kathleen Mansfield Beauchamp) 1888–1923

New Zealand-born short-story writer

7 E. M. Forster never gets any further than warming the teapot. He's a rare fine hand at that. Feel this teapot. Is it not beautifully warm? Yes, but there ain't going to be no tea.

Journal (1927) May 1917

8 I'm a writer first and a woman after.

letter to John Middleton Murry, July 1917

9 Whenever I prepare for a journey I prepare as though for death. Should I never return, all is in order.

Journal (1927) 29 January 1922

William Murray, Lord Mansfield

1705–93

Scottish lawyer and politician. On Mansfield: see LLOYD 496:10

10 The constitution does not allow reasons of state to influence our judgements: God forbid it should! We must not regard political consequences; however formidable soever they might be: if rebellion was the certain consequence, we are bound to say '*fiat justitia, ruat caelum*'.

Rex v. Wilkes, 8 June 1768, in *The English Reports* (1909) vol. 98; see ADAMS 3:16, WATSON 841:8

11 Consider what you think justice requires, and decide accordingly. But never give your reasons; for your judgement will probably be right, but your reasons will certainly be wrong.

advice to a newly appointed colonial governor ignorant in the law

John Lord Campbell *The Lives of the Chief Justices of England* (1849) vol. 2, ch. 40

Richard Mant 1776–1848

Irish divine and ecclesiastical historian

12 Bright the vision that delighted
Once the sight of Judah's seer;
Sweet the countless tongues united
To entrance the prophet's ear.

'Bright the vision that delighted' (1837 hymn)

Alessandro Manzoni 1785–1873

Italian novelist, dramatist, and poet

13 *Il primero svegliarsi, dopo una sciagura, e in impiccio, é un momento molto amaro. La mente, appena risentita ricorre all' idee abituali della vita tranquilla antecedente; ma il pensiero del nuovo stato di cose le si affacia subito sgarbatamente.*

The arousing from sleep, after a recent misfortune, is a bitter moment; the mind at first habitually recurs to its previous tranquillity, but is soon depressed by the thought of the contrast that awaits it.

The Betrothed (1825–42) ch. 2

1 *La sposina ne fu l'idolo, il trastullo, la vittima.*

The young bride was the idol, the amusement, the victim of the evening.

The Betrothed (1825-42) ch. 10

Mao Zedong 1893–1976

Chinese statesman, effective leader of the Chinese Communist Party from the time of the Long March (1934-5), and Chairman of the Communist Party of the Chinese People's Republic 1949-76

2 Politics is war without bloodshed while war is politics with bloodshed.

lecture, 1938, in *Selected Works* (1965) vol. 2

3 Every Communist must grasp the truth, 'Political power grows out of the barrel of a gun'.

speech, 6 November 1938, in *Selected Works* (1965) vol. 2

4 The atom bomb is a paper tiger which the United States reactionaries use to scare people. It looks terrible, but in fact it isn't . . . All reactionaries are paper tigers.

interview, 1946, in *Selected Works* (1961) vol. 4

5 Letting a hundred flowers blossom and a hundred schools of thought contend is the policy for promoting progress in the arts and the sciences and a flourishing socialist culture in our land.

speech in Peking, 27 February 1957, in *Quotations of Chairman Mao* (1966)

Diego Maradona 1960–

Argentine football player

6 The goal was scored a little bit by the hand of God, another bit by head of Maradona.

on his controversial goal against England in the 1986 World Cup

in *Guardian* 1 July 1986

René Maran 1887–1960

French novelist, born in Martinique

7 Life is short. Work is for those who will never be able to understand life. Idleness cannot degrade a man. To the discriminating eye it differs from laziness.

Batouala (1921) ch. 1, translated by Alvah C. Bessie

8 Ah, the whites! Their malignity and their omniscience—that was what made them terrifying!

Batouala (1921) ch. 2, translated by Alvah C. Bessie

Marco Polo c.1254–c.1324

Italian traveller, who with his father and uncle travelled to China and the court of Kublai Khan

9 I have not told even half of the things that I have seen.

when asked if he wished to deny any of his stories of his travels

attributed, but probably apocryphal

William Learned Marcy 1786–1857

American politician

10 The politicians of New York . . . see nothing wrong in the rule, that to the victor belong the spoils of the enemy.

speech to the Senate, 25 January 1832, in James Parton *Life of Andrew Jackson* (1860) vol. 3, ch. 29

Princess Margaret 1930–2002

British princess, sister of **ELIZABETH II**

11 Mindful of the Church's teaching that Christian marriage is indissoluble, and conscious of my duty to the Commonwealth, I have resolved to put these considerations before any others.

announcing her decision not to marry a divorced man, Group Captain Peter Townsend

statement from Clarence House, 31 October 1955; in *The Times* 1 November 1955

Marguerite of Angoulême 1492–1549

French writer, sister of **FRANCIS I** and Queen of Navarre

12 Though jealousy be produced by love, as ashes are by fire, yet jealousy extinguishes love as ashes smother the flame.

Heptameron (1558) 'Novel 48, the Fifth Day'

Lynn Margulis 1938–

American biologist

13 Gaia is a tough bitch. People think the earth is going to die and they have to save it, that's ridiculous . . . There's no doubt that Gaia can compensate for our output of greenhouse gases, but the environment that's left will not be happy for any people.

in *New York Times Biographical Service* January 1996

Marie-Antoinette 1755–93

Austrian princess and French Queen consort of **LOUIS XVI**, executed during the French Revolution

14 *Qu'ils mangent de la brioche.*

Let them eat cake.

on being told that her people had no bread

attributed, but much older; in his *Confessions* (1740) Rousseau refers to a similar remark being a well-known saying; another version is: '*Que ne mangent-ils de la croûte de pâté?* [Why don't they eat pastry?]' attributed to Marie-Thérèse (1638–83), wife of Louis XIV, in Louis XVIII *Relation d'un Voyage à Bruxelles et à Coblentz en 1791* (1823)

Edwin Markham 1852–1940

American poet

15 A thing that grieves not and that never hopes, Stolid and stunned, a brother to the ox?

'The Man with the Hoe' (1899)

Johnny Marks 1909–85

American songwriter

16 Rudolph, the Red-Nosed Reindeer Had a very shiny nose,

And if you ever saw it,
You would even say it glows.
'Rudolph, the Red-Nosed Reindeer' (1949 song)

Leo Marks 1920–2001

English cryptographer and screenwriter

1 The life that I have
Is all that I have
And the life that I have
Is yours.
The love that I have
Of the life that I have
Is yours and yours and yours.
*given to the British secret agent Violette Szabo (1921–45),
for use with the Special Operations Executive*
'The Life that I Have' (written 1943)

Sarah, Duchess of Marlborough

1660–1744

British favourite of Queen Anne and wife of John Churchill, 1st Duke of Marlborough and noted general

2 The Duke returned from the wars today and did
pleasure me in his top-boots.
oral tradition, attributed in various forms; I. Butler *Rule of
Three* (1967) ch. 7

3 If I were young and handsome as I was, instead
of old and faded as I am, and you could lay the
empire of the world at my feet, you should
never share the heart and hand that once
belonged to John, Duke of Marlborough.
refusing an offer of marriage from the Duke of Somerset
W. S. Churchill *Marlborough: His Life and Times* vol. 4 (1938)
ch. 39

Bob Marley 1945–81

Jamaican reggae musician and songwriter

4 Get up, stand up
Stand up for your rights
Get up, stand up
Never give up the fight.
'Get up, Stand up' (1973 song)

5 I shot the sheriff
But I swear it was in self-defence
I shot the sheriff
And they say it is a capital offence.
'I Shot the Sheriff' (1974 song)

Christopher Marlowe 1564–93

**English dramatist and poet. On Marlowe: see DRAYTON
293:17, JONSON 446:23; see also ANONYMOUS 18:4**

6 I'll have them fly to India for gold,
Ransack the ocean for orient pearl.
Doctor Faustus (1604) act 1, sc. 1

7 Why, this is hell, nor am I out of it.
Doctor Faustus (1604) act 1, sc. 3

8 Hell hath no limits nor is circumscribed
In one self place, where we are is Hell,

And to be short, when all the world dissolves,
And every creature shall be purified,
All places shall be hell that are not heaven.
Doctor Faustus (1604) act 2, sc. 1

9 Was this the face that launched a thousand
ships,
And burnt the topless towers of Ilium?
Sweet Helen, make me immortal with a kiss!
Doctor Faustus (1604) act 5, sc. 1

10 Now hast thou but one bare hour to live,
And then thou must be damned perpetually.
Stand still, you ever-moving spheres of heaven,
That time may cease, and midnight never come.
Doctor Faustus (1604) act 5, sc. 2

11 *O lente lente currite noctis equi.*
The stars move still, time runs, the clock will
strike,
The devil will come, and Faustus must be
damned.
O I'll leap up to my God: who pulls me down?
See, see, where Christ's blood streams in the
firmament.
One drop would save my soul, half a drop, ah
my Christ.
Doctor Faustus (1604) act 5, sc. 2; see OVID 589:17

12 Cut is the branch that might have grown full
straight,
And burnèd is Apollo's laurel bough,
That sometime grew within this learned man.
Doctor Faustus (1604) epilogue

13 My men, like satyrs grazing on the lawns,
Shall with their goat feet dance an antic hay.
Edward II (1593) act 1, sc. 1

14 Tell Isabel the Queen, I looked not thus,
When for her sake I ran at tilt in France.
Edward II (1593) act 5, sc. 5

15 Where both deliberate, the love is slight;
Who ever loved that loved not at first sight?
Hero and Leander (1598) First Sestiad, l. 175; see SHAKESPEARE
697:17

16 I count religion but a childish toy,
And hold there is no sin but ignorance.
The Jew of Malta (c.1592) prologue

17 Thus methinks should men of judgement frame
Their means of traffic from the vulgar trade,
And, as their wealth increaseth, so enclose
Infinite riches in a little room.
The Jew of Malta (c.1592) act 1, sc. 1

18 As for myself, I walk abroad o' nights
And kill sick people groaning under walls:
Sometimes I go about and poison wells.
The Jew of Malta (c.1592) act 2, sc. 3

19 BARNARDINE: Thou hast committed—
BARABAS: Fornication? But that was in another
country: and besides, the wench is dead.
The Jew of Malta (c.1592) act 4, sc. 1

20 Come live with me, and be my love,
And we will all the pleasures prove,

That valleys, groves, hills and fields,
Woods or steepy mountain yields.
'The Passionate Shepherd to his Love'; see **DONNE** 288:26,
RALEGH 653:13

1 By shallow rivers, to whose falls
Melodious birds sing madrigals.
'The Passionate Shepherd to his Love'

2 With milk-white harts upon an ivory sled
Thou shalt be drawn amidst the frozen pools,
And scale the icy mountains' lofty tops,
Which with thy beauty will be soon resolved.
Tamburlaine the Great (1590) pt. 1, act 1, sc. 2

3 Our swords shall play the orators for us.
Tamburlaine the Great (1590) pt. 1, act 1, sc. 2

4 Accurst be he that first invented war.
Tamburlaine the Great (1590) pt. 1, act 2, sc. 4

5 Is it not passing brave to be a king,
And ride in triumph through Persepolis?
Tamburlaine the Great (1590) pt. 1, act 2, sc. 5

6   The ripest fruit of all,
That perfect bliss and sole felicity,
The sweet fruition of an earthly crown.
Tamburlaine the Great (1590) pt. 1, act 2, sc. 7

7 Virtue is the fount whence honour springs.
Tamburlaine the Great (1590) pt. 1, act 4, sc. 4

8 Now walk the angels on the walls of heaven,
As sentinels to warn th' immortal souls,
To entertain divine Zenocrate.
Tamburlaine the Great (1590) pt. 2, act 2, sc. 4

9 More childish valorous than manly wise.
Tamburlaine the Great (1590) pt. 2, act 4, sc. 1

10 Holla, ye pampered jades of Asia!
What, can ye draw but twenty miles a day . . . ?
Tamburlaine the Great (1590) pt. 2, act 4, sc. 3; see
SHAKESPEARE 707:14

Don Marquis 1878–1937
American poet and journalist

11 procrastination is the
art of keeping
up with yesterday.
archy and mehitabel (1927) 'certain maxims of archy'

12 an optimist is a guy
that has never had
much experience.
archy and mehitabel (1927) 'certain maxims of archy'

13 it s cheerio
my deario that
pulls a lady through.
archy and mehitabel (1927) 'cheerio, my deario'

14 I have got you out here
in the great open spaces
where cats are cats.
archy and mehitabel (1927) 'mehitabel has an adventure'

15 but wotthehell archy wotthehell
jamais triste archy jamais triste
that is my motto.
archy and mehitabel (1927) 'mehitabel sees paris'

16 did you ever
notice that when
a politician
does get an idea
he usually
gets it all wrong.
archys life of mehitabel (1933) 'archygrams'

17 Writing a book of poetry is like dropping a rose
petal down the Grand Canyon and waiting for
the echo.
E. Anthony *O Rare Don Marquis* (1962)

18 The art of newspaper paragraphing is to stroke
a platitude until it purrs like an epigram.
E. Anthony *O Rare Don Marquis* (1962)

John Marriot 1780–1825
English clergyman

19 Thou, whose eternal Word
Chaos and darkness heard,
And took their flight,
Hear us, we humbly pray,
And, where the Gospel-day
Sheds not its glorious ray,
Let there be light!
'almighty' substituted for 'eternal' from 1861
'Thou, whose eternal Word' (hymn written c.1813)

Frederick Marryat 1792–1848
English naval captain and novelist

20 If you please, ma'am, it was a very little one.
the nurse, excusing her illegitimate baby
Mr Midshipman Easy (1836) ch. 3

21 All zeal . . . all zeal, Mr Easy.
Mr Midshipman Easy (1836) ch. 9

Arthur Marshall 1910–89
English journalist and former schoolmaster

22 What, knocked a tooth out? Never mind, dear,
laugh it off, laugh it off; it's all part of life's rich
pageant.
The Games Mistress (recorded monologue, 1937)

John Marshall 1755–1835
American jurist

23 [The] government of the United States has been
emphatically termed a government of laws, and
not of men.
in *Marbury v. Madison* (1803); see **ADAMS** 3:2

24 The power to tax involves the power to destroy.
in *McCulloch v. Maryland* (1819)

25 The people made the Constitution, and the
people can unmake it. It is the creature of their
own will, and lives only by their will.
in *Cohens v. Virginia* (1821)

Thomas R. Marshall 1854–1925
American politician

1 What this country needs is a really good 5-cent
cigar.
in *New York Tribune* 4 January 1920, pt. 7

Thurgood Marshall 1908–93
American civil rights lawyer and Supreme Court judge

2 We must never forget that the only real source
of power that we as judges can tap is the
respect of the people.
in *Chicago Tribune* 15 August 1981

Martial *c.*AD 40–*c.*104
Roman epigrammatist, born in Spain

3 *Non est, crede mihi, sapientis dicere 'Vivam':*
Sera nimis vita est crastina: vive hodie.

Believe me, wise men don't say 'I shall live to do
that', tomorrow's life's too late; live today.
Epigrammata bk. 1, no. 15

4 *Non amo te, Sabidi, nec possum dicere quare:*
Hoc tantum possum dicere, non amo te.

I don't love you, Sabidius, and I can't tell you
why; all I can tell you is this, that I don't love
you.
Epigrammata bk. 1, no. 32; see **BROWN** 161:14, **WATKYNS** 841:4

5 *Laudant illa sed ista legunt.*

They praise those works, but read these.
Epigrammata bk. 4, no. 49

6   *Bonosque*
Soles effugere atque abire sentit,
Qui nobis pereunt et imputantur.

Each of us feels the good days speed and depart,
and they're lost to us and counted against us.
Epigrammata bk. 5, no. 20

7 *Mollia non rigidus caespes tegat ossa; nec illi,*
Terra, gravis fueris: non fuit illa tibi.

Not hard be the turf that covers her soft bones,
be not heavy upon her, earth; she was not heavy
upon you.
on a dead child
Epigrammata bk. 5, no. 34, l. 9

8 *Thais habet nigros, niveos Laecania dentes.*
Quae ratio est? emptos haec habet, illa suos.

Thais' teeth are black, Laecania's snow-white.
The reason? The one has those she bought, the
other her own.
Epigrammata bk. 5, no. 43

9 *Non est vivere, sed valere vita est.*

Life's not just being alive, but being well.
Epigrammata bk. 6, no. 70

10 *Vitam quae faciant beatiorem,*
Iucundissime Martialis, haec sunt:
Res non parta labore sed relicta;
non ingratus ager, focus perennis.

The things that make life happier, most genial

Martial, are these: means not acquired by labour,
but bequeathed; fields not unkindly, an ever-
blazing hearth.
Epigrammata bk. 10, no. 47; see **SURREY** 780:13

11 *Difficilis facilis, iucundus acerbus es idem:*
Nec tecum possum vivere nec sine te.

Difficult or easy, pleasant or bitter, you are the
same you: I cannot live with you—or without
you.
Epigrammata bk. 12, no. 46(47); see **ADDISON** 5:4

12 *Rus in urbe.*

Country in the town.
Epigrammata bk. 12, no. 57

Harriet Martineau 1802–76
English writer

13 The sum and substance of female education in
America, as in England, is training women to
consider marriage as the sole object in life, and
to pretend that they do not think so.
Society in America (1837)

Andrew Marvell 1621–78
English metaphysical poet and politician

14 Where the remote Bermudas ride
In the ocean's bosom unespied.
'Bermudas' (c.1653)

15 He hangs in shades the orange bright,
Like golden lamps in a green night.
'Bermudas' (c.1653)

16 And makes the hollow seas, that roar,
Proclaim the ambergris on shore.
'Bermudas' (c.1653)

17 Echo beyond the Mexique Bay.
'Bermudas' (c.1653)

18 My love is of a birth as rare
As 'tis for object strange and high:
It was begotten by Despair
Upon Impossibility.

Magnanimous Despair alone
Could show me so divine a thing,
Where feeble Hope could ne'er have flown
But vainly flapped its tinsel wing.
'The Definition of Love' (1681)

19 As lines (so loves) oblique may well
Themselves in every angle greet:
But ours so truly parallel,
Though infinite, can never meet.

Therefore the love which us doth bind,
But Fate so enviously debars,
Is the conjunction of the mind,
And opposition of the stars.
'The Definition of Love' (1681)

20 So architects do square and hew,
Green trees that in the forest grew.
'A Dialogue between the Soul and the Body' (1681)

1 Choosing each stone, and poising every weight,
Trying the measures of the breadth and height;
Here pulling down, and there erecting new,
Founding a firm state by proportions true.
  'The First Anniversary of the Government under His Highness
  the Lord Protector, 1655' l. 245

2 How vainly men themselves amaze
To win the palm, the oak, or bays.
  'The Garden' (1681) st. 1

3 The gods, that mortal beauty chase,
Still in a tree did end their race.
Apollo hunted Daphne so,
Only that she might laurel grow.
And Pan did after Syrinx speed,
Not as a nymph, but for a reed.
  'The Garden' (1681) st. 4

4 What wondrous life is this I lead!
Ripe apples drop about my head;
The luscious clusters of the vine
Upon my mouth do crush their wine;
The nectarine, and curious peach,
Into my hands themselves do reach;
Stumbling on melons, as I pass,
Ensnared with flowers, I fall on grass.
  'The Garden' (1681) st. 5

5 Annihilating all that's made
To a green thought in a green shade.
  'The Garden' (1681) st. 6

6 *He* nothing common did or mean
Upon that memorable scene:
But with his keener eye
The axe's edge did try.
  on the execution of **CHARLES I**
  'An Horatian Ode upon Cromwell's Return from Ireland'
  (written 1650) l. 57

7 So much one man can do,
That does both act and know.
  'An Horatian Ode upon Cromwell's Return from Ireland'
  (written 1650) l. 75

8 Ye country comets, that portend
No war, nor prince's funeral.
  'The Mower to the Glow-worms' (1681)

9 Had it lived long, it would have been
Lilies without, roses within.
  'The Nymph Complaining for the Death of her Fawn' (1681)
  l. 91

10 Had we but world enough, and time,
This coyness, lady, were no crime.
  'To His coy Mistress' (1681) l. 1

11   I would
Love you ten years before the flood:
And you should, if you please, refuse
Till the conversion of the Jews.
My vegetable love should grow
Vaster than empires, and more slow.
  'To His coy Mistress' (1681) l. 7

12 But at my back I always hear
Time's wingèd chariot hurrying near:

And yonder all before us lie
Deserts of vast eternity.
  'To His Coy Mistress' (1681) l. 21; see **ELIOT** 311:11

13   Then worms shall try
That long preserved virginity:
And your quaint honour turn to dust;
And into ashes all my lust.
The grave's a fine and private place,
But none, I think, do there embrace.
  'To His Coy Mistress' (1681) l. 27

14 Let us roll all our strength, and all
Our sweetness, up into one ball:
And tear our pleasures with rough strife,
Thorough the iron gates of life.
Thus, though we cannot make our sun
Stand still, yet we will make him run.
  'To His Coy Mistress' (1681) l. 41

15 He is translation's thief that addeth more,
As much as he that taketh from the store
Of the first author.
  'To His Worthy Friend Dr Witty' (1651)

16 Oh thou, that dear and happy isle
The garden of the world ere while,
Thou paradise of four seas,
Which heaven planted us to please,
But, to exclude the world, did guard
With watery if not flaming sword;
What luckless apple did we taste,
To make us mortal, and thee waste?
  'Upon Appleton House' (1681) st. 41

17 But now the salmon-fishers moist
Their leathern boats begin to hoist;
And, like Antipodes in shoes,
Have shod their heads in their canoes.
How tortoise-like, but not so slow,
These rational amphibii go!
  'Upon Appleton House' (1681) st. 97

Holt Marvell (Eric Maschwitz) 1901–69

English songwriter

18 A cigarette that bears a lipstick's traces,
An airline ticket to romantic places;
And still my heart has wings
These foolish things
Remind me of you.
  'These Foolish Things Remind Me of You' (1935 song)

Chico Marx 1891–1961

**American film comedian, brother of Groucho MARX. See
also FILM LINES 328:23**

19 I wasn't kissing her, I was just whispering in her
mouth.
  on being discovered by his wife with a chorus girl
  Groucho Marx and Richard J. Anobile *Marx Brothers Scrapbook*
  (1973) ch. 24

Groucho Marx 1890–1977

American film comedian, brother of Chico MARX. On Marx: see SLOGANS 755:7; see also EPITAPHS 318:4, FILM LINES 328:4, FILM LINES 328:15, FILM LINES 328:23, FILM LINES 329:16, FILM LINES 330:1

1 PLEASE ACCEPT MY RESIGNATION. I DON'T WANT TO BELONG TO ANY CLUB THAT WILL ACCEPT ME AS A MEMBER.

   Groucho and Me (1959) ch. 26

2 I never forget a face, but in your case I'll be glad to make an exception.

   Leo Rosten *People I have Loved, Known or Admired* (1970) 'Groucho'

Karl Marx 1818–83

German political philosopher; founder of modern Communism. On Marx: see BENN 70:1, SCHUMPETER 687:6, SLOGANS 755:7

3 Religion is the sigh of the oppressed creature, the heart of a heartless world . . . It is the opium of the people.

   A Contribution to the Critique of Hegel's Philosophy of Right (1843–4) introduction; see KINGSLEY 464:15

4 Mankind always sets itself only such problems as it can solve; since, looking at the matter more closely, it will always be found that the task itself arises only when the material conditions for its solution already exist or are at least in the process of formation.

   A Contribution to the Critique of Political Economy (1859) preface (translated by D. McLellan)

5 From each according to his abilities, to each according to his needs.

   Critique of the Gotha Programme (written 1875, but of earlier origin); see BLANC 128:16, MORELLY 559:18; an earlier version is: 'The formula of Communism, as propounded by Cabet, may be expressed thus:—"the duty of each is according to his faculties; his right according to his wants"', in *North British Review* (1849) vol 10

6 And even when a society has got upon the right track for the discovery of the natural laws of its movement—and it is the ultimate aim of this work, to lay bare the economic law of motion of modern society—it can neither clear by bold leaps, nor remove by legal enactments, the obstacles offered by the successive phases of its normal development. But it can shorten and lessen the birth-pangs.

   Das Kapital (1st German ed., 1867) preface (25 July 1865)

7 Centralization of the means of production, and socialization of labour at last reach a point where they become incompatible with their capitalist integument. This integument is burst asunder. The knell of capitalist private property sounds. The expropriators are expropriated.

   Das Kapital (1867) ch. 32

8 Hegel says somewhere that all great events and personalities in world history reappear in one fashion or another. He forgot to add: the first time as tragedy, the second as farce.

   The Eighteenth Brumaire of Louis Bonaparte (1852) sect. 1; the origin of the Hegel reference is uncertain, but see HEGEL 388:13

9 The philosophers have only interpreted the world in various ways; the point is to change it.

   Theses on Feuerbach (written 1845, published 1888) no. 11

10 What I did that was new was to prove . . . that the class struggle necessarily leads to the dictatorship of the proletariat.

   the phrase 'dictatorship of the proletariat' had been used earlier in the Constitution of the World Society of Revolutionary Communists (1850), signed by Marx and others
   letter to Georg Weydemeyer 5 March 1852; Marx claimed that the phrase had been coined by Auguste Blanqui (1805–81), but it has not been found in this form in Blanqui's work

11 All I know is that I am not a Marxist.

   attributed in a letter from Friedrich Engels to Conrad Schmidt, 5 August 1890; in Karl Marx and Friedrich Engels *Correspondence* (1934)

Karl Marx 1818–83 *and* Friedrich Engels 1820–95

German political philosopher and German socialist

12 A spectre is haunting Europe—the spectre of Communism.

   The Communist Manifesto (1848) opening words

13 The history of all hitherto existing society is the history of class struggles.

   The Communist Manifesto (1848) pt. 1

14 The proletarians have nothing to lose but their chains. They have a world to win. WORKING MEN OF ALL COUNTRIES, UNITE!

   commonly rendered as 'Workers of the world, unite!'
   The Communist Manifesto (1848), closing words (from the 1888 translation by Samuel Moore, edited by Engels)

Mary I (Mary Tudor) 1516–58

English monarch, Queen from 1553; elder daughter of HENRY VIII and sister of ELIZABETH I

15 When I am dead and opened, you shall find 'Calais' lying in my heart.

   Holinshed's Chronicles vol. 4 (1808); see SELLAR AND YEATMAN 692:2

Queen Mary 1867–1953

British princess, Queen Consort of GEORGE V

16 All *this* thrown away for *that*.

   on returning home to Marlborough House, London after the abdication of her son, King EDWARD VIII, December 1936
   David Duff *George and Elizabeth* (1983) ch. 10

17 I do not think you have ever realised the shock, which the attitude you took up caused your family and the whole nation. It seemed inconceivable to those who had made such sacrifices during the war that you, as their King, refused a lesser sacrifice.

   letter to the Duke of Windsor (formerly EDWARD VIII), July 1938, in J. Pope-Hennessy *Queen Mary* (1959) ch. 7

Mary, Queen of Scots 1542–87

Scottish monarch, Queen 1542–67; as a prisoner in England she became a focus of Catholic plots and was eventually executed. On Mary: see **ELIZABETH I** 312:1, **GRAY** 369:18, **JAMES V** 429:5

1 Look to your consciences and remember that the theatre of the world is wider than the realm of England.

to the commissioners appointed to try her at Fotheringhay, 13 October 1586

Antonia Fraser *Mary Queen of Scots* (1969) ch. 25

2 *En ma fin git mon commencement.*

In my end is my beginning.

motto embroidered with an emblem of her mother, Mary of Guise, and quoted in a letter from William Drummond of Hawthornden to Ben Jonson in 1619; see **ELIOT** 309:8

John Masefield 1878–1967

English poet

3 Quinquireme of Nineveh from distant Ophir
Rowing home to haven in sunny Palestine,
With a cargo of ivory,
And apes and peacocks,
Sandalwood, cedarwood, and sweet white wine.

'Cargoes' (1903); see **BIBLE** 84:29

4 Dirty British coaster with a salt-caked smoke stack,
Butting through the Channel in the mad March days,
With a cargo of Tyne coal,
Road-rails, pig lead,
Firewood, ironware, and cheap tin trays.

'Cargoes' (1903)

5 O Christ, the plough, O Christ, the laughter
Of holy white birds flying after.

'The Everlasting Mercy' (1911)

6 I must go down to the seas again, to the lonely sea and the sky,
And all I ask is a tall ship and a star to steer her by,
And the wheel's kick and the wind's song and the white sail's shaking,
And a grey mist on the sea's face and a grey dawn breaking.

'Sea Fever' (1902)

7 I must go down to the sea again, for the call of the running tide
Is a wild call and a clear call that may not be denied.

'Sea Fever' (1902)

Donald Mason 1913–

American naval officer

8 Sighted sub, sank same.

on sinking a Japanese submarine in the Atlantic region (the first US naval success in the war)

radio message, 28 January 1942; in *New York Times* 27 February 1942

Philip Massinger 1583–1640

English dramatist

9 Ambition, in a private man a vice,
Is in a prince the virtue.

The Bashful Lover (licensed 1636, published 1655) act 1, sc. 2

10   Pray enter
You are learned Europeans and we worse
Than ignorant Americans.

The City Madam (licensed 1632, published 1658) act 3, sc. 3

11 Oh that thou hadst like others been all words,
And no performance.

The Parliament of Love (1624) act 4, sc. 2

12 Death has a thousand doors to let out life:
I shall find one.

A Very Woman (licensed 1634, published 1655) act 5, sc. 4; see **FLETCHER** 335:8, **SENECA** 692:20, **WEBSTER** 844:11

Cotton Mather 1662–1728

American puritan preacher and divine, son of Increase **MATHER**

13 I write the wonders of the Christian religion, flying from the depravations of Europe, to the American strand: and, assisted by the Holy Author of that religion, I do, with all conscience of truth, required therein by Him, who is the Truth itself, report the wonderful displays of His infinite power, wisdom, goodness, and faithfulness, wherewith His Divine Providence hath irradiated an Indian wildnerness.

introduction to Magnalia Christi Americana *(1702), opening line*

14 Every man will have his own style which will distinguish him as much as his gait.

Manuductio ad Ministerium (1726) 'Of Style'

15 That there is a Devil is a thing doubted by none but such as are under the influences of the Devil. For any to deny the being of a Devil must be from an ignorance or profaneness worse than diabolical.

The Wonders of the Invisible World (1693)

Increase Mather 1639–1723

American puritan divine and writer, father of Cotton **MATHER**

16 Now as usually providence so ordereth that they who have been speaking all their lives long shall not say much when they come to die.

The Life and Death of . . . Mr Richard Mather (1670)

17 Thunder is the voice of God, and, therefore, to be dreaded.

Remarkable Providences (1684)

James Mathew 1830–1908

Irish judge

18 In England, justice is open to all—like the Ritz Hotel.

R. E. Megarry *Miscellany-at-Law* (1955); see **ANONYMOUS** 17:9

Henri Matisse 1869–1954
French painter

1 What I dream of is an art of balance, of purity and serenity devoid of troubling or depressing subject matter . . . a soothing, calming influence on the mind, rather like a good armchair which provides relaxation from physical fatigue.
Notes d'un peintre (1908)

2 To give yourself completely to what you're doing while simultaneously watching yourself do it—that's the hardest of all for those who do work by instinct.
letter to Amélie Matisse, 31 March 1912, in Hilary Spurling *Matisse the Master* vol. 2 (2005)

3 I want anyone tired, worn down, driven to the limits of endurance, to find calm and repose in my painting.
in *Cahiers d'aujourdhui* 4 April 1913, in Hilary Spurling *Matisse the Master* vol. 2 (2005) ch. 1

Leonard Matlovich d. 1988
American Air Force Sergeant

4 When I was in the military, they gave me a medal for killing two men and a discharge for loving one.
attributed

W. Somerset Maugham 1874–1965
English novelist

5 Poor Henry, he's spending eternity wandering round and round a stately park and the fence is just too high for him to peep over and they're having tea just too far away for him to hear what the countess is saying.
of Henry **JAMES**
Cakes and Ale (1930) ch. 11

6 The most useful thing about a principle is that it can always be sacrificed to expediency.
The Circle (1921) act 3

7 It is not true that suffering ennobles the character; happiness does that sometimes, but suffering, for the most part, makes men petty and vindictive.
The Moon and Sixpence (1919) ch. 17

8 A woman can forgive a man for the harm he does her, but she can never forgive him for the sacrifices he makes on her account.
The Moon and Sixpence (1919) ch. 41

9 Like all weak men he laid an exaggerated stress on not changing one's mind.
Of Human Bondage (1915) ch. 39

10 People ask you for criticism, but they only want praise.
Of Human Bondage (1915) ch. 50

11 Money is like a sixth sense without which you cannot make a complete use of the other five.
Of Human Bondage (1915) ch. 51

12 I [Death] was astonished to see him in Baghdad, for I had an appointment with him tonight in Samarra.
Sheppey (1933) act 3; see **O'HARA** 583:15

13 Dying is a very dull, dreary affair. And my advice to you is to have nothing whatever to do with it.
to his nephew Robin, in 1965
Robin Maugham *Conversations with Willie* (1978)

Bill Mauldin 1921–2003
American cartoonist

14 I feel like a fugitive from th' law of averages.
cartoon caption in *Up Front* (1945)

Guy de Maupassant 1850–93
French novelist and short-story writer

15 *L'esprit de l'homme est capable de tout.*
The mind of man is capable of anything.
'La Chevelure' (The Tress of Hair, 1884)

André Maurois 1885–1967
French writer

16 Growing old is no more than a bad habit which a busy man has no time to form.
The Art of Living (1940) ch. 8

James Maxton 1885–1946
British Labour politician

17 All I say is, if you cannot ride two horses you have no right in the circus.
opposing disaffiliation of the Scottish Independent Labour Party from the Labour Party; usually quoted as, ' . . . no right in the bloody circus'
in *Daily Herald* 12 January 1931; see **PROVERBS** 635:23

James Clerk Maxwell 1831–79
Scottish physicist

18 Scientific truth should be presented in different forms, and should be regarded as equally scientific whether it appears in the robust form and the vivid colouring of a physical illustration, or in the tenuity and paleness of a symbolic expression.
attributed; in *Physics Teacher* December 1969

Theresa May 1956–
British Conservative politician

19 You know what some people call us: the nasty party.
speech to the Conservative Conference, 7 October 2002

Vladimir Mayakovsky 1893–1930
Russian poet

20 If you wish—
. . . I'll be irreproachably tender;

not a man, but—a cloud in trousers!
'The Cloud in Trousers' (1915) (translated by Samuel Charteris)

1 Not a sound. The universe sleeps, resting a huge
ear on its paw with mites of stars.
'The Cloud in Trousers' (1915) (translated by Samuel Charteris)

2 In our language rhyme is a barrel. A barrel of
dynamite. The line is a fuse. The line smoulders
to the end and explodes; and the town is blown
sky-high in a stanza.
'Conversation with an Inspector of Taxes about Poetry' (1926)
(translated by Dmitri Obolensky)

3 Oh for just
one
more conference
regarding the eradication of all conferences!
'In Re Conferences'; Herbert Marshall (ed.) *Mayakovsky* (1965)

4 To us love says humming that the heart's stalled
motor has begun working again.
'Letter from Paris to Comrade Kostorov on the Nature of
Love' (1928) (translated by Samuel Charteris)

5 Ours is the land.
The air—ours.
Ours the diamond mines of stars.
And we will never,
never!
Allow anyone,
anyone!
To ravage our land with shells,
to tear our air with sharpened spear points.
'Revolution: a Poet's Chronicle' (1917) (translated by C. M.
Bowra)

6 The love boat has crashed against the everyday.
You and I, we are quits, and there is no point in
listing mutual pains, sorrows, and hurts.
*from an unfinished poem found among Mayakovsky's
papers, a variant of which he quoted in his suicide letter*
letter 12 April 1930

Louis B. Mayer 1885–1957
Russian-born American film executive, head of MGM

7 We've got more stars than there are in the
heavens, all of them except for that damned
Mouse over at Disney.
Sheridan Morley and Ruth Leon *Gene Kelly* (1996)

Jonathan Mayhew 1720–66
American divine

8 Rulers have no authority from God to do
mischief.
*A Discourse Concerning Unlimited Submission and Non-
Resistance to the Higher Powers* (1750)

9 As soon as the prince sets himself up above the
law, he loses the king in the tyrant; he does to
all intents and purpose unking himself.
*A Discourse Concerning Unlimited Submission and Non-
Resistance to the Higher Powers* (1750)

Ernst Mayr 1904–2005
German-born American evolutionary biologist

10 There is more to biology than rats, *Drosophila*,
Caenorhabditis, and *E. coli*.
foreword to Lynn Margulis and Dorion Sagan *Acquiring
Genomes: A Theory of the Origins of Species* (2003)

Giuseppe Mazzini 1805–72
Italian nationalist leader

11 Insurrection—by means of guerrilla bands—is
the true method of warfare for all nations
desirous of emancipating themselves from a
foreign yoke.
General Instructions for the Members of Young Italy (1833)
sect. 4

12 A nation is the universality of citizens speaking
the same tongue.
in *La Giovine Italia*, 1832

Margaret Mead 1901–78
American anthropologist

13 The knowledge that the personalities of the two
sexes are socially produced is congenial to every
programme that looks forward towards a
planned order of society. It is a two-edged
sword.
Sex and Temperament in Three Primitive Societies (1935) pt. 4
'Conclusion'

14 Never doubt that a small group of thoughtful
committed citizens can change the world. In
fact, it's the only thing that ever has.
attributed; Mary Bowman-Kruhm *Margaret Mead: a biography*
(2003)

Shepherd Mead 1914–
American advertising executive

15 How to succeed in business without really
trying.
title of book (1952)

Hughes Mearns 1875–1965
American writer

16 As I was walking up the stair
I met a man who wasn't there.
He wasn't there again today.
I wish, I wish he'd stay away.
lines written for *The Psycho-ed*, an amateur play, in
Philadelphia, 1910 (set to music in 1939 as 'The Little Man
Who Wasn't There')

Peter Medawar 1915–87
English immunologist and writer

17 If a scientist were to cut his ear off, no one
would take it as evidence of a heightened
sensibility.
'J. B. S.' (1968)

1 If politics is the art of the possible, research is surely the art of the soluble. Both are immensely practical-minded affairs.

in *New Statesman* 19 June 1964; see **BISMARCK** 122:16

2 During the 1950s, the first great age of molecular biology, the English Schools of Oxford and particularly of Cambridge produced more than a score of graduates of quite outstanding ability—much more brilliant, inventive, articulate and dialectically skilful than most young scientists; right up in the Watson class. But Watson had one towering advantage over all of them: in addition to being extremely clever he had something important to be clever *about*.

review of James D. **WATSON**'s *The Double Helix* in *New York Review of Books* 28 March 1968

Catherine de' Medici 1518–89

Italian-born queen consort of Henri II of France

3 A false report, if believed during three days, may be of great service to a government.

Isaac D'Israeli *Curiosities of Literature* 2nd series (1849) vol. 2; perhaps apocryphal

Cosimo de' Medici 1389–1464

Italian statesman and banker, founder of the Medici family's power in Florence

4 We read that we ought to forgive our enemies; but we do not read that we ought to forgive our friends.

speaking of what **BACON** *refers to as 'perfidious friends'*
Francis Bacon *Apophthegms* (1625) no. 206

Lorenzo de' Medici 1449–92

Italian statesman and poet, patron of the arts

5 *Quanto è bella giovinezza*
Che si fugge tuttavia!
Chi vuol esser lieto sia:
Di doman non ci è certezza.

How beautiful is youth, that is always slipping away! Whoever wants to be happy, let him be so: of tomorrow there's no knowing.

'Trionfo di Bacco e di Arianna'

Mehmed II 1430–81

Ottoman sultan, conqueror of Constantinople in 1453

6 The spider weaves the curtains in the palace of the Caesars;
The owl calls the watches in the towers of Afrasiab.

quoting an anonymous Persian poet at the ruins of the Old Sacred Palace in Constantinople, 1453
attributed; Steven Runciman *Fall of Constantinople* (1965) ch. 11

Golda Meir 1898–1978

Israeli stateswoman, Prime Minister 1969–74

7 Those that perished in Hitler's gas chambers were the last Jews to die without standing up to defend themselves.

speech to United Jewish Appeal Rally, New York, 11 June 1967

8 Pessimism is a luxury that a Jew can never allow himself.

in *Observer* 29 December 1974

Nellie Melba (Helen Porter Mitchell) 1861–1931

Australian operatic soprano

9 The first rule of opera is the first rule of life, a very simple and possibly unexciting rule, for which I shall receive no thanks. That is, see to everything yourself.

Melodies and Memories (1925) ch. 27

10 Art is not national. It is international. Music is not written in red, white and blue; it is written with the heart's blood of the composer.

Melodies and Memories (1925) ch. 28

11 Sing 'em muck! It's all they can understand!

advice to Dame Clara Butt, prior to her departure for Australia
W. H. Ponder *Clara Butt* (1928) ch. 12

William Lamb, Lord Melbourne 1779–1848

British Whig statesman, Prime Minister 1834, 1835–41; husband of Lady Caroline LAMB. See also ANONYMOUS 17:13

12 Universities never reform themselves; everyone knows that.

speech, House of Lords, 11 April 1837

13 Damn it! Another Bishop dead! I believe they die to vex me.

attributed; Lord David Cecil *Lord M* (1954) ch. 4

14 God help the Minister that meddles with art!

Lord David Cecil *Lord M* (1954) ch. 3

15 If left out he would be dangerous, but if taken in, he would be simply destructive.

when forming his second administration, Melbourne omitted the former Lord Chancellor, **BROUGHAM**
Lord David Cecil *Lord M* (1954) ch. 4

16 I wish I was as cocksure of anything as Tom Macaulay is of everything.

Lord Cowper's preface to *Lord Melbourne's Papers* (1889)

17 Now, is it to lower the price of corn, or isn't it? It is not much matter which we say, but mind, we must all say *the same*.

attributed; Walter Bagehot *The English Constitution* (1867) ch. 1

18 Things have come to a pretty pass when religion is allowed to invade the sphere of private life.

on hearing an evangelical sermon
G. W. E. Russell *Collections and Recollections* (1898) ch. 6

1 What all the wise men promised has not happened, and what all the d—d fools said would happen has come to pass.
of the Catholic Emancipation Act (1829)
H. Dunckley *Lord Melbourne* (1890) ch. 9

2 What I like about the Order of the Garter is that there is no damned merit about it.
Lord David Cecil *The Young Melbourne* (1939)

3 What I want is men who will support me when I am in the wrong.
replying to a politician who said 'I will support you as long as you are in the right'
Lord David Cecil *Lord M* (1954) ch. 4

4 When in doubt what should be done, do nothing.
Lord David Cecil *Lord M* (1954) ch. 1

David Mellor 1949–

British Conservative politician and broadcaster

5 I do believe the popular press is drinking in the last chance saloon.
interview on *Hard News* (Channel 4), 21 December 1989

Herman Melville 1819–91

American novelist and poet

6 That Calvinistic sense of innate depravity and original sin from whose visitations, in some shape or other, no deeply thinking mind is always and wholly free.
Hawthorne and His Mosses (1850)

7 Fame is an accident; merit a thing absolute.
Mardi (1849) ch. 126

8 Call me Ishmael.
Moby Dick (1851) ch. 1, opening words

9 Meditation and water are wedded for ever.
Moby Dick (1851) ch. 1

10 A whaleship was my Yale College and my Harvard.
Moby Dick (1851) ch. 24

11 Thou art as a lion of the waters and as a dragon of the sea.
Moby Dick (1851) ch. 82; see **BIBLE** 95:18

12 To produce a mighty book, you must choose a mighty theme.
Moby Dick (1851) ch. 104

13 Towards thee I roll, thou all-destroying but unconquering whale . . . from hell's heart I stab at thee.
Moby Dick (1851) ch. 135

14 War being the greatest of evils, all its accessories necessarily partake of the same character.
Omoo (1846) ch. 29

Gilles Ménage 1613–92

French scholar

15 *Comme nous nous entretenions de ce qui pouvait rendre heureux, je lui dis; Sanitas sanitatum, et omnia sanitas.*

While we were discussing what could make one happy, I said to him: *Sanitas sanitatum et omnia sanitas* [Health of healths and everything is health].
from a conversation with Jean-Louis Guez de Balzac (1594–1654), in *Ménagiana* (1693); **BIBLE** (**VULGATE**) 120:7

Menander 342–c.292 BC

Greek comic dramatist

16 Whom the gods love dies young.
Dis Exapaton fragment 4, in F. H. Sandbach (ed.) *Menandri Reliquiae Selectae* (1990); see **BYRON** 189:2, **PROVERBS** 647:17

17 We live, not as we wish to, but as we can.
The Lady of Andros in *Menander: the Principal Fragments* (translated by F. G. Allinson, 1951)

Mencius *see* Meng-tzu

H. L. Mencken 1880–1956

American journalist and literary critic

18 Love is the delusion that one woman differs from another.
Chrestomathy (1949) ch. 30; see **SHAW** 740:20

19 Puritanism. The haunting fear that someone, somewhere, may be happy.
Chrestomathy (1949) ch. 30

20 Democracy is the theory that the common people know what they want, and deserve to get it good and hard.
A Little Book in C major (1916)

21 Conscience: the inner voice which warns us that someone may be looking.
A Little Book in C major (1916)

22 It is now quite lawful for a Catholic woman to avoid pregnancy by a resort to mathematics, though she is still forbidden to resort to physics and chemistry.
Notebooks (1956) 'Minority Report'

23 There is always a well-known solution to every human problem—neat, plausible, and wrong.
Prejudices 2nd series (1920)

Moses Mendelssohn 1729–86

German-born Jewish philosopher

24 To put it in one word: I believe that Judaism knows nothing of revealed religion, in the sense in which this is understood by Christians. The Israelites possess divine legislation.
Jerusalem (1783) pt. 2

Meng-tzu (Mencius) 371–289 BC

Chinese philosopher

25 All men have the mind which cannot bear [to see the suffering of] others.
The Book of Mencius bk. 2, pt. A, v. 6

26 It is useless to talk to those who do violence to their own nature, and it is useless to do anything

with those who throw themselves away. To speak what is against propriety and righteousness is to do violence to oneself. To say that one cannot abide by humanity and follow righteousness is to throw oneself away.
The Book of Mencius bk. 4, pt. A, v. 10

1 The great man is the one who does not lose his [originally good] child's heart.
The Book of Mencius bk. 4, pt. B, v. 12

2 If you let people follow their feelings [original nature], they will be able to do good. This is what is meant by saying that human nature is good.
The Book of Mencius bk. 6, pt. A, v. 6

3 Moral principles please our minds as beef and mutton and pork please our mouths.
The Book of Mencius bk. 6, pt. A, v. 7

4 All things are already complete in oneself. There is no greater joy than to examine oneself and be sincere. When in ones's conduct one vigorously exercises altruism, humanity is not far to seek, but right by him.
The Book of Mencius bk. 7, pt. A, v. 4

Robert Gordon Menzies 1894–1978

Australian Liberal statesman, Prime Minister 1939–41 and 1949–66

5 What Great Britain calls the Far East is to us the near north.
in *Sydney Morning Herald* 27 April 1939

David Mercer 1928–80

English dramatist

6 A suitable case for treatment.
title of television play (1962); later filmed as *Morgan—A Suitable Case for Treatment* (1966)

Johnny Mercer 1909–76

American songwriter

7 You've got to ac-cent-tchu-ate the positive
Elim-my-nate the negative
Latch on to the affirmative
Don't mess with Mister In-between.
'Ac-cent-tchu-ate the Positive' (1944 song)

8 Jeepers Creepers—where you get them peepers?
'Jeepers Creepers' (1938 song)

9 Make it one for my baby
And one more for the road.
'One For My Baby' (1943 song)

10 That old black magic.
title of song (1942)

George Meredith 1828–1909

English novelist and poet. On Meredith: see **WILDE** 855:2, **WILDE** 855:8

11 'Tis Ireland gives England her soldiers, her generals too.
Diana of the Crossways (1885) ch. 2

12 The light of every soul burns upward. Of course, most of them are candles in the wind. Let us allow for atmospheric disturbance.
Diana of the Crossways (1885) ch. 39; see **JOHN AND TAUPIN** 434:5

13 A dainty rogue in porcelain.
The Egoist (1879) ch. 5

14 Cynicism is intellectual dandyism without the coxcomb's feathers.
The Egoist (1879) ch. 7

15 Kissing don't last: cookery do!
The Ordeal of Richard Feverel (1859) ch. 28

16 Speech is the small change of silence.
The Ordeal of Richard Feverel (1859) ch. 34

17 The lark ascending.
title of poem (1881)

18 She whom I love is hard to catch and conquer,
Hard, but O the glory of the winning were she won!
'Love in the Valley' st. 2

19 When her mother tends her before the laughing mirror,
Tying up her laces, looping up her hair,
Often she thinks, were this wild thing wedded,
More love should I have, and much less care.
'Love in the Valley' st. 3

20 On a starred night Prince Lucifer uprose.
Tired of his dark dominion swung the fiend . . .
He reached a middle height, and at the stars,
Which are the brain of heaven, he looked, and sank.
Around the ancient track marched, rank on rank,
The army of unalterable law.
'Lucifer in Starlight' (1883)

21 Not till the fire is dying in the grate,
Look we for any kinship with the stars.
Modern Love (1862) st. 4

22 Ah, what a dusty answer gets the soul
When hot for certainties in this our life!
Modern Love (1862) st. 50

23 Enter these enchanted woods,
You who dare.
'The Woods of Westermain' (1883)

Owen Meredith (Edward Robert Bulwer Lytton, Lord Lytton) 1831–91

English poet and statesman, Viceroy of India 1876–80

24 Genius does what it must, and Talent does what it can.
'Last Words of a Sensitive Second-Rate Poet' (1868)

Bob Merrill 1921–98

American songwriter and composer

25 How much is that doggie in the window?
title of song (1953)

26 People who need people are the luckiest people in the world.
'People who Need People' (1964 song)

James Merrill 1926–95

American poet

1 Each thirteenth year he married. When he died
There were already several chilled wives
In sable orbit—rings, cars, permanent waves.
We'd felt him warming up for a green bride.

He could afford it. He was 'in his prime'
And three score ten. But money was not time.
'The Broken Home' (1966)

2 Always that same old story—
Father Time and Mother Earth,
a marriage on the rocks.
'The Broken Home' (1966)

Dixon Lanier Merritt 1879–1972

American editor

3 Oh, a wondrous bird is the pelican!
His bill will hold more than his belican.
He can take in his beak
Enough food for a week
But I'm damned if I see how the helican.
adapted from the original in *Nashville Banner* 22 April 1913

W. S. Merwin 1927–

American poet

4 Sometimes it is inconceivable that I should be
the age I am.
'The Child' (1968)

5 This is the black sea-brute bulling through wave-
wrack,
Ancient as ocean's shifting hills.
'Leviathan' (1956)

6 The sea curling
Star-climbed, wind-combed, cumbered with itself
still
As at first it was, is the hand not yet contented
Of the Creator. And he waits for the world to
begin.
'Leviathan' (1956)

Jean Meslier c.1664–1733

French priest; his *Testament*, an atheistic treatise, became
known only after his death

7 I remember, on this matter, the wish made once
by an ignorant, uneducated man . . . He said he
wished . . . that all the great men in the world
and all the nobility could be hanged, and
strangled with the guts of priests. For myself . . .
I wish I could have the strength of Hercules to
purge the world of all vice and sin, and to have
the pleasure of destroying all those monsters of
error and sin [priests] who make all the peoples
of the world groan so pitiably.
*often quoted as 'I should like . . . the last of the kings to be
strangled with the guts of the last priest'*
Testament (ed. R. Charles, 1864) vol. 1, ch. 2; see **DIDEROT**
282:10

Ian Messiter *see* Catchphrases 208:35

Methodist Service Book 1975

8 I am no longer my own, but yours. Put me to
what you will, rank me with whom you will;
put me to doing, put me to suffering; let me be
employed for you or laid aside for you, exalted
for you or brought low for you; let me be full,
let me be empty; let me have all things, let me
have nothing.
The Covenant Prayer (based on the words of Richard Alleine
in the First Covenant Service, 1782)

Prince Metternich 1773–1859

Austrian statesman

9 The word 'freedom' means for me not a point
of departure but a genuine point of arrival. The
point of departure is defined by the word
'order'. Freedom cannot exist without the
concept of order.
Mein Politisches Testament in *Aus Metternich's Nachgelassenen
Papieren* (ed. A. von Klinkowström, 1880) vol. 7

10 Italy is a geographical expression.
discussing the Italian question with **PALMERSTON** *in 1847*
Mémoires, Documents, etc. de Metternich publiés par son fils
(1883) vol. 7

11 I feel obliged to call to the supporters of the
social uprising: Citizens of a dream-world,
nothing is altered. On 14 March 1848, there was
merely one man fewer.
of his own downfall
Aus Metternich's Nachgelassenen Papieren (ed. A. von
Klinkowström, 1880) vol. 8

12 The Emperor is everything, Vienna is nothing.
letter to Count Bombelles, 5 June 1848, in *Aus Metternich's
Nachgelassenen Papieren* (ed. A. von Klinkowström, 1880)
vol. 8

13 *L'erreur n'a jamais approché de mon esprit.*
Error has never approached my spirit.
addressed to Guizot in 1848, in François Pierre G. Guizot
Mémoires (1858–67) vol. 4

Charlotte Mew 1869–1928

English poet

14 She sleeps up in the attic there
Alone, poor maid. 'Tis but a stair
Betwixt us. Oh! my God! the down,
The soft young down of her, the brown,
The brown of her—her eyes, her hair, her hair!
'The Farmer's Bride' (1916)

Michelangelo 1475–1564

Italian sculptor, painter, architect, and poet

15 The marble not yet carved can hold the form
Of every thought the greatest artist has.
Sonnet 15, translated by Elizabeth Jennings

16 Love is a beautiful image
Imagined or seen within the heart,

The friend of virtue and gentility.
Sonnet 38, translated by Robert J. Clements

1 I've finished that chapel I was painting. The Pope is quite satisfied.
on completing the ceiling of the Sistine chapel
letter to his father, October 1512; E. H. Ramsden (ed.) *The Letters of Michelangelo* (1963)

2 Trifles make perfection, and perfection is no trifle.
attributed; Samuel Smiles Self-Help (1859) ch. 5

Jules Michelet 1798–1874
French historian

3 What is the first part of politics? Education. The second? Education. And the third? Education.
Le Peuple (1846); see BLAIR 123:18

4 England is an empire, Germany is a nation, a race, France is a person.
Histoire de France (1833–1867)

Adam Mickiewicz 1798–1855
Polish poet and dramatist

5 To these fields, painted with various grain, gilded with wheat, silvered with rye.
Pan Tadeusz (1834) bk. 1, l. 17, translated by W. Weintraub

William Julius Mickle 1735–88
Scottish poet

6 For there's nae luck about the house,
There's nae luck at a',
There's little pleasure in the house
When our gudeman's awa.
'The Mariner's Wife' (1769)

Thomas Middleton c.1580–1627
English dramatist

7 Anything for a quiet life.
title of play (written c.1620, possibly with John Webster); see DICKENS 280:26

8 I could not get the ring without the finger.
The Changeling (with William Rowley, c.1622) act 3, sc. 4

9 My study's ornament, thou shell of death,
Once the bright face of my betrothèd lady.
The Revenger's Tragedy (1607) act 1, sc. 1 (previously attributed to Cyril Tourneur, c.1575–1626)

10 Nine coaches waiting—hurry, hurry, hurry.
The Revenger's Tragedy (1607) act 2, sc. 1

11 Does the silk-worm expend her yellow labours
For thee? for thee does she undo herself?
The Revenger's Tragedy (1607) act 3, sc. 5

12 Mingle, mingle, mingle, you that mingle may.
The Witch act 5, sc. 3

Bette Midler 1945–
American actress

13 When it's three o'clock in New York, it's still 1938 in London.
attributed

Midrash
ancient commentary on the Hebrew scriptures, dating from the 2nd century AD

14 The Holy One, blessed be He, makes ladders by which He makes one go up, and another go down.
Leviticus Rabbah 8:1

15 The Holy One, blessed be He, waits for the nations of the world in the hope that they will repent, and be brought beneath His wings.
Numbers Rabbah 10:1

16 Whatever you think of your friend, he thinks the same of you.
Sifre Deuteronomy, piska 24

17 The words of Torah are likened to fire. Just as fire was given from heaven, so were the words of Torah given from heaven . . . just as fire lives forever, so do the words of Torah live forever.
Sifre Deuteronomy, piska 343

18 Should a person tell you there is wisdom among the nations, believe it . . . if he tells you that there is Torah among the nations, do not believe it.
Lamentations Rabbah 2:13

19 When a person enters the world his hands are clenched as though to say, 'The whole world is mine, I shall inherit it'; but when he takes leave of it his hands are spread open as though to say, 'I have inherited nothing from the world.'
Ecclesiastes Rabbah 5:14

20 A man cannot say to the Angel of Death, 'Wait for me until I make up my accounts.'
Ecclesiastes Rabbah 8:8

21 While God's face is above, His heart is below.
Song of Songs Rabbah 4:4

Ludwig Mies van der Rohe 1886–1969
German-born architect and designer. See also PROVERBS 637:19

22 God is in the details.
in New York Times 19 August 1969; also attributed to Aby Warburg (1866–1929)

George Mikes 1912–87
Hungarian-born writer

23 On the Continent people have good food; in England people have good table manners.
How to be an Alien (1946)

24 An Englishman, even if he is alone, forms an orderly queue of one.
How to be an Alien (1946) p. 44

William Porcher Miles 1822–96

25 'Vote early and vote often,' the advice openly displayed on the election banners in one of our northern cities.
in the House of Representatives, 31 March 1858

Military sayings, slogans, and songs

1 Action this day.
annotation as used by Winston Churchill at the Admiralty in 1940

2 All present and correct.
King's Regulations (Army) Report of the Orderly Sergeant to the Officer of the Day

3 Any officer who shall behave in a scandalous manner, unbecoming the character of an officer and a gentleman shall . . . be CASHIERED.
Articles of War (1872) 'Disgraceful Conduct' Article 79; the Naval Discipline Act, 10 August 1860, Article 24, uses the words 'conduct unbecoming the character of an Officer'

4 Are we downhearted? No!
expression much taken up by British soldiers during the First World War

5 Conduct . . . to the prejudice of good order and military discipline.
Army Discipline and Regulation Act (1879) Section 40

6 The difficult we do immediately; the impossible takes a little longer.
US Armed Forces' slogan; see **CALONNE** 194:1, **NANSEN** 567:8, **PROVERBS** 630:2

7 Every person subject to military law who . . . spreads reports calculated to create unnecessary alarm or despondency . . . shall . . . be liable to suffer penal servitude.
Army Act (1879); see **PENIAKOFF** 602:12

8 Fifty million Frenchmen can't be wrong.
saying popular with American servicemen during the First World War; later associated with Mae **WEST** and Texas Guinan (1884–1933), it was also the title of a 1927 song by Billy Rose and Willie Raskin

9 From the halls of Montezuma,
To the shores of Tripoli,
We fight our country's battles,
On the land as on the sea.
'The Marines' Hymn' (1847)

10 If it moves, salute it; if it doesn't move, pick it up; and if you can't pick it up, paint it.
1940s saying, in Paul Dickson *The Official Rules* (1978)

11 *Ils ne passeront pas.*
They shall not pass.
slogan used by the French army at the defence of Verdun in 1916; variously attributed to Marshal **PÉTAIN** and to General Robert Nivelle, and taken up by the Republicans in the Spanish Civil War in the form '*No pasarán!*'; see **IBARRURI** 424:3

12 Lions led by donkeys.
attributed to Max Hoffman (1869–1927) in Alan Clark *The Donkeys* (1961); this attribution has not been traced elsewhere, and the phrase is of much earlier origin: 'Unceasingly they had drummed into them the utterance of *The Times*: "You are lions led by packasses"' was said of French troops defeated by Prussians, in Francisque Sarcey *Paris during the Siege* (1871)

13 Loose lips sink ships.
American Second World war security slogan

14 Mademoiselle from Armenteers,
Hasn't been kissed for forty years,
Hinky, dinky, parley-voo.
song of the First World War, variously attributed to Edward Rowland and to Harry Carlton

15 O Death, where is thy sting-a-ling-a-ling,
O grave, thy victory?
The bells of Hell go ting-a-ling-a-ling
For you but not for me.
'For You But Not For Me', in S. Louis Guiraud (ed.) *Songs That Won the War* (1930); see **BIBLE** 113:6

16 She was poor but she was honest
Victim of a rich man's game.
First he loved her, then he left her,
And she lost her maiden name . . .

It's the same the whole world over,
It's the poor wot gets the blame,
It's the rich wot gets the gravy.
Ain't it all a bleedin' shame?
'She was Poor but she was Honest' (sung by British soldiers in the First World War)

17 We're here
Because
We're here.
sung to the tune of 'Auld Lang Syne', in John Brophy and Eric Partridge *Songs and Slang of the British Soldier 1914–18* (1930)

18 What's the use of worrying?
It never was worth while,
So, pack up your troubles in your old kit-bag,
And smile, smile, smile.
'Pack up your Troubles' (1915 song), written by George Asaf (1880–1951)

19 Your country needs you.
slogan on First World War recruitment poster, 1914, showing Lord **KITCHENER** pointing, designed by Alfred Leete (1882–1933)

20 Your King and Country need you.
recruitment slogan for First World War, coined by Eric Field, July 1914; *Advertising* (1959); see **RUBENS** 672:1

John Stuart Mill 1806–73

English philosopher and economist. On Mill: see **BENTLEY** 71:17; see also **EPITAPHS** 319:18

21 No great improvements in the lot of mankind are possible, until a great change takes place in the fundamental constitution of their modes of thought.
Autobiography (1873) ch. 7

22 Each is the only safe guardian of his own rights and interests.
Considerations on Representative Government (1861) ch. 3

23 The Conservatives . . . being by the law of their existence the stupidest party.
Considerations on Representative Government (1861) ch. 7 n.

24 I will call no being good, who is not what I mean when I apply that epithet to my fellow-

creatures; and if such a being can sentence me to hell for not so calling him, to hell I will go.
Examination of Sir William Hamilton's Philosophy (1865) ch. 7

1 Bad men need nothing more to compass their ends, than that good men should look on and do nothing.
Inaugural Address at St Andrew's (1867); see **MISQUOTATIONS** 548:4

2 The only purpose for which power can be rightfully exercised over any member of a civilized community, against his will, is to prevent harm to others. His own good, either physical or moral, is not a sufficient warrant.
On Liberty (1859) ch. 1

3 The only freedom which deserves the name, is that of pursuing our own good in our own way.
On Liberty (1859) ch. 1

4 If all mankind minus one were of one opinion, and only one person were of the contrary opinion, mankind would be no more justified in silencing that one person, than he, if he had the power, would be justified in silencing mankind.
On Liberty (1859) ch. 2

5 The peculiar evil of silencing the expression of opinion is, that it is robbing the human race; posterity as well as the existing generation; those who dissent from the opinion, still more than those who hold it. If the opinion is right, they are deprived of the opportunity of exchanging error for truth: if wrong, they lose, what is almost as great a benefit, the clearer perception and livelier impression of truth, produced by its collision with error.
On Liberty (1859) ch. 2

6 A party of order or stability, and a party of progress or reform, are both necessary elements of a healthy state of political life.
On Liberty (1859) ch. 2

7 The liberty of the individual must be thus far limited; he must not make himself a nuisance to other people.
On Liberty (1859) ch. 3

8 Liberty consists in doing what one desires.
On Liberty (1859) ch. 5

9 A State which dwarfs its men, in order that they may be more docile instruments in its hands even for beneficial purposes, will find that with small men no great thing can really be accomplished.
On Liberty (1859) ch. 5

10 Demand for commodities is not demand for labour.
Principles of Political Economy (1848) bk. 1, ch. 5

11 The principle which regulates the existing social relations between the two sexes—the legal subordination of one sex to the other—is wrong in itself, and now one of the chief hindrances to human improvement.
The Subjection of Women (1869) ch. 1

12 What is now called the nature of women is an eminently artificial thing—the result of forced repression in some directions, unnatural stimulation in others.
The Subjection of Women (1869) ch. 1

13 No slave is a slave to the same lengths, and in so full a sense of the word, as a wife is.
The Subjection of Women (1869) ch. 2

14 The laws of most countries are far worse than the people who execute them, and many of them are only able to remain laws by being seldom or never carried into effect. If married life were all that it might be expected to be, looking to the laws alone, society would be a hell upon earth.
The Subjection of Women (1869) ch. 2

15 The true virtue of human beings is fitness to live together as equals; claiming nothing for themselves but what they as freely concede to everyone else; regarding command of any kind as an exceptional necessity, and in all cases a temporary one.
The Subjection of Women (1869) ch. 2

16 It is better to be a human being dissatisfied than a pig satisfied; better to be Socrates dissatisfied than a fool satisfied.
Utilitarianism (1863) ch. 2

17 The most important thing women have to do is to stir up the zeal of women themselves.
letter to Alexander Bain, 14 July 1869, in Hugh S. R. Elliot (ed.) *Letters of John Stuart Mill* vol. 2 (1910)

18 My work is done.
last words, W. L. Courtney *Life of John Stuart Mill* (1889) ch. 9

Edna St Vincent Millay 1892–1950
American poet

19 Childhood is the kingdom where nobody dies. Nobody that matters, that is.
'Childhood is the Kingdom where Nobody dies' (1934)

20 Down, down, down into the darkness of the grave
Gently they go, the beautiful, the tender, the kind;
Quietly they go, the intelligent, the witty, the brave.
I know. But I do not approve. And I am not resigned.
'Dirge Without Music' (1928)

21 My candle burns at both ends;
It will not last the night;
But ah, my foes, and oh, my friends—
It gives a lovely light.
A Few Figs From Thistles (1920) 'First Fig'

22 Euclid alone
Has looked on Beauty bare. Fortunate they
Who, though once only and then but far away,
Have heard her massive sandal set on stone.
The Harp-Weaver and Other Poems (1923) sonnet 22

1 Justice denied in Massachusetts.
relating to the trial of Sacco and **VANZETTI** *and their execution on 22 August 1927*
  title of poem (1928)

2 The sun that warmed our stooping backs and
  withered the weeds uprooted—
We shall not feel it again.
We shall die in darkness, and be buried in the
  rain.
  'Justice Denied in Massachusetts' (1928)

3 Death devours all lovely things;
Lesbia with her sparrow
Shares the darkness—presently
Every bed is narrow.
  'Passer Mortuus Est' (1921); see **CATULLUS** 210:4

Alice Duer Miller 1874–1942
American writer

4 I am American bred,
I have seen much to hate here—much to forgive,
But in a world where England is finished and
  dead,
I do not wish to live.
  The White Cliffs (1940)

Arthur Miller 1915–2005
American dramatist. On Miller: see **NEWSPAPER HEADLINES AND LEADERS** 573:7

5 A suicide kills two people, Maggie, that's what
  it's for!
  After the Fall (1964) act 2

6 Death of a salesman.
  title of play (1949)

7 The world is an oyster, but you don't crack it
  open on a mattress.
  Death of a Salesman (1949) act 1

8 Willy Loman never made a lot of money. His
  name was never in the paper. He's not the finest
  character that ever lived. But he's a human
  being, and a terrible thing is happening to him.
  So attention must be paid.
  Death of a Salesman (1949) act 1

9 He's a man way out there in the blue, riding on
  a smile and a shoeshine. And when they start
  not smiling back—that's an earthquake . . . A
  salesman is got to dream, boy. It comes with the
  territory.
  Death of a Salesman (1949) 'Requiem'

10 The car, the furniture, the wife, the
  children—everything has to be disposable.
  Because you see the main thing today
  is—shopping.
  The Price (1968) act 1

11 This is Red Hook, not Sicily . . . This is the
  gullet of New York swallowing the tonnage of
  the world.
  A View from the Bridge (1955) act 1

12 A good newspaper, I suppose, is a nation talking
  to itself.
  in *Observer* 26 November 1961

Henry Miller 1891–1980
American novelist

13 Every man with a bellyful of the classics is an
  enemy to the human race.
  Tropic of Cancer (1934)

Jonathan Miller 1934–
English writer and director

14 In fact, I'm not really a *Jew*. Just Jew-*ish*. Not the
  whole hog, you know.
  Beyond the Fringe (1960 review) 'Real Class'

Spike Milligan (Terence Alan Milligan) 1918–2002
Irish comedian. See also **CATCHPHRASES** 208:1, **CATCHPHRASES** 209:6, **CATCHPHRASES** 209:8

15 Money couldn't buy friends but you got a better
  class of enemy.
  Puckoon (1963) ch. 6

A. J. Mills, Fred Godfrey, and Bennett Scott
British songwriters

16 Take me back to dear old Blighty.
  title of song (1916)

Irving Mills 1894–1985

17 It don't mean a thing
If it ain't got that swing.
  'It Don't Mean a Thing' (1932 song; music by Duke **ELLINGTON**)

Henry Hart Milman 1791–1868
English clergyman

18 Ride on! ride on in majesty!
The wingèd squadrons of the sky
Look down with sad and wond'ring eyes
To see the approaching sacrifice.
  'Ride on! ride on in majesty!' (1827 hymn)

A. A. Milne 1882–1956
English writer for children

19 The more he looked inside the more Piglet
  wasn't there.
  The House at Pooh Corner (1928) ch. 1

20 'I don't *want* him,' said Rabbit. 'But it's always
  useful to know where a friend-and-relation *is*,
  whether you want him or whether you don't.'
  The House at Pooh Corner (1928) ch. 3

21 He respects Owl, because you can't help
  respecting anybody who can spell TUESDAY, even
  if he doesn't spell it right; but spelling isn't

everything. There are days when spelling
Tuesday simply doesn't count.
The House at Pooh Corner (1928) ch. 5

1 When you are a Bear of Very Little Brain, and
you Think of Things, you find sometimes that a
Thing which seemed very Thingish inside you is
quite different when it gets out into the open
and has other people looking at it.
The House at Pooh Corner (1928) ch. 6

2 They're changing guard at Buckingham Palace—
Christopher Robin went down with Alice.
Alice is marrying one of the guard.
'A soldier's life is terrible hard,'
Says Alice.
When We Were Very Young (1924) 'Buckingham Palace'

3 James James
Morrison Morrison
Weatherby George Dupree
Took great
Care of his Mother,
Though he was only three.
James James
Said to his Mother,
'Mother,' he said, said he;
'You must never go down to the end of the
town, if you don't go down with me.'
When We Were Very Young (1924) 'Disobedience'

4 There once was a Dormouse who lived in a bed
Of delphiniums (blue) and geraniums (red),
And all the day long he'd a wonderful view
Of geraniums (red) and delphiniums (blue).
When We Were Very Young (1924) 'The Dormouse and the
Doctor'

5 The King asked
The Queen, and
The Queen asked
The Dairymaid:
'Could we have some butter for
The Royal slice of bread?'
When We Were Very Young (1924) 'The King's Breakfast'

6 And some of the bigger bears try to pretend
That they came round the corner to look for a
friend;
And they try to pretend that nobody cares
Whether you walk on the lines or squares.
When We Were Very Young (1924) 'Lines and Squares'

7 *What* is the matter with Mary Jane?
She's perfectly well and she hasn't a pain,
And it's lovely rice pudding for dinner again!
What *is* the matter with Mary Jane?
When We Were Very Young (1924) 'Rice Pudding'

8 Little Boy kneels at the foot of the bed,
Droops on the little hands little gold head.
Hush! Hush! Whisper who dares!
Christopher Robin is saying his prayers.
When We Were Very Young (1924) 'Vespers'; see **MORTON**
562:4

9 Isn't it funny
How a bear likes honey?

Buzz! Buzz! Buzz!
I wonder why he does?
Winnie-the-Pooh (1926) ch. 1

10 'Pathetic,' he [Eeyore] said. 'That's what it is.
Pathetic.'
Winnie-the-Pooh (1926) ch. 6

11 Time for a little something.
Winnie-the-Pooh (1926) ch. 6

12 My spelling is Wobbly. It's good spelling but it
Wobbles, and the letters get in the wrong places.
Winnie-the-Pooh (1926) ch. 6

13 Owl hasn't exactly got Brain, but he Knows
Things.
Winnie-the-Pooh (1926) ch. 9

14 Eeyore was saying to himself, 'This writing
business. Pencils and what-not. Over-rated, if
you ask me. Silly stuff. Nothing in it.'
Winnie-the-Pooh (1926) ch. 10

Lord Milner 1854–1925
British colonial administrator

15 If we believe a thing to be bad, and if we have a
right to prevent it, it is our duty to try to
prevent it and to damn the consequences.
speech in Glasgow, 26 November 1909, in *The Times* 27
November 1909

John Milton 1608–74
English poet and polemicist. On Milton: see **AUBREY** 36:1,
AUBREY 36:2, **AUBREY** 36:3, **BLAKE** 126:3, **BYRON** 188:25,
GRAY 370:20, **JOHNSON** 436:25, **JOHNSON** 444:1, **TENNYSON**
798:16, **WORDSWORTH** 866:16

16 Such sweet compulsion doth in music lie.
'Arcades' (1645) l. 68

17 Blest pair of Sirens, pledges of heaven's joy,
Sphere-born harmonious sisters, Voice, and
Verse.
'At a Solemn Music' (1645)

18 Where the bright seraphim in burning row
Their loud uplifted angel trumpets blow.
'At a Solemn Music' (1645)

19 Above the smoke and stir of this dim spot,
Which men call earth.
Comus (1637) l. 5

20 Yet some there be that by due steps aspire
To lay their just hands on that golden key
That opes the palace of eternity.
Comus (1637) l. 12

21 An old and haughty nation proud in arms.
Comus (1637) l. 33

22 And the gilded car of day
His glowing axle doth allay
In the steep Atlantic stream.
Comus (1637) l. 95

23 What hath night to do with sleep?
Comus (1637) l. 122

24 Come, knit hands, and beat the ground,
In a light fantastic round.
Comus (1637) l. 143

1 Calling shapes and beckoning shadows dire,
And airy tongues, that syllable men's names
On sands, and shores, and desert wildernesses.
  Comus (1637) l. 207

2 Sweet Echo, sweetest nymph that liv'st unseen
Within thy airy shell
By slow Meander's margent green,
And in the violet-embroidered vale.
  Comus (1637) l. 230

3 Virtue could see to do what Virtue would
By her own radiant light, though sun and moon
Were in the flat sea sunk.
  Comus (1637) l. 373

4 Yet where an equal poise of hope and fear
Does arbitrate the event, my nature is
That I incline to hope, rather than fear,
And gladly banish squint suspicion.
  Comus (1637) l. 410

5 'Tis chastity, my brother, chastity:
She that has that, is clad in complete steel.
  Comus (1637) l. 420; see **SHAKESPEARE** 700:12

6 How charming is divine philosophy!
Not harsh and crabbèd, as dull fools suppose,
But musical as is Apollo's lute.
  Comus (1637) l. 475

7 Storied of old in high immortal verse
Of dire chimeras and enchanted isles,
And rifted rocks whose entrance leads to hell.
  Comus (1637) l. 516

8 And filled the air with barbarous dissonance.
  Comus (1637) l. 550

9   Against the threats
Of malice or of sorcery, or that power
Which erring men call chance, this I hold firm,
Virtue may be assailed, but never hurt,
Surprised by unjust force, but not enthralled.
  Comus (1637) l. 586

10 Those budge doctors of the Stoic fur.
  Comus (1637) l. 707

11 Sabrina fair,
Listen where thou art sitting
Under the glassy, cool, translucent wave,
In twisted braids of lilies knitting
The loose train of thy amber-dropping hair.
  Comus (1637) l. 859 'Song'

12 Thus I set my printless feet
O'er the cowslip's velvet head,
That bends not as I tread.
  Comus (1637) l. 897

13 Hence, vain deluding joys,
The brood of folly without father bred.
  'Il Penseroso' (1645) l. 1

14 Come, pensive nun, devout and pure,
Sober, steadfast, and demure.
  'Il Penseroso' (1645) l. 31

15 Sweet bird that shunn'st the noise of folly,
Most musical, most melancholy!
  'Il Penseroso' (1645) l. 61

16 Where glowing embers through the room
Teach light to counterfeit a gloom,
Far from all resort of mirth,
Save the cricket on the hearth.
  'Il Penseroso' (1645) l. 79

17 Or bid the soul of Orpheus sing
Such notes as warbled to the string,
Drew iron tears down Pluto's cheek.
  'Il Penseroso' (1645) l. 105

18 Where more is meant than meets the ear.
  'Il Penseroso' (1645) l. 120

19 Hide me from day's garish eye.
  'Il Penseroso' (1645) l. 141; see **NEWMAN** 572:17

20 And storied windows richly dight,
Casting a dim religious light.
  'Il Penseroso' (1645) l. 159

21 Hence, loathèd Melancholy,
Of Cerberus, and blackest Midnight born,
In Stygian cave forlorn
'Mongst horrid shapes, and shrieks, and sights
  unholy.
  'L'Allegro' (1645) l. 1

22 So buxom, blithe, and debonair.
  of Euphrosyne [Mirth], one of the three Graces
  'L'Allegro' (1645) l. 24

23 Nods, and becks, and wreathèd smiles.
  'L'Allegro' (1645) l. 28

24 Sport that wrinkled Care derides,
And Laughter holding both his sides.
Come, and trip it as ye go
On the light fantastic toe.
  'L'Allegro' (1645) l. 31

25 Right against the eastern gate,
Where the great sun begins his state.
  'L'Allegro' (1645) l. 59

26 And the milkmaid singeth blithe,
And the mower whets his scythe,
And every shepherd tells his tale
Under the hawthorn in the dale.
  'L'Allegro' (1645) l. 65

27 Meadows trim with daisies pied,
Shallow brooks, and rivers wide.
  'L'Allegro' (1645) l. 75

28 Where perhaps some beauty lies,
The cynosure of neighbouring eyes.
  'L'Allegro' (1645) l. 79

29 Then to the spicy nut-brown ale.
  'L'Allegro' (1645) l. 100

30 Towered cities please us then,
And the busy hum of men.
  'L'Allegro' (1645) l. 117

31 Such sights as youthful poets dream
On summer eves by haunted stream.
Then to the well-trod stage anon,
If Jonson's learnèd sock be on,
Or sweetest Shakespeare fancy's child,
Warble his native wood-notes wild.
  'L'Allegro' (1645) l. 129

1 Let us with a gladsome mind
Praise the Lord, for he is kind,
For his mercies ay endure,
Ever faithful, ever sure.
'Let us with a gladsome mind' (1645); paraphrase of Psalm
136; see **BOOK OF COMMON PRAYER** 149:12

2 Yet once more, O ye laurels, and once more
Ye myrtles brown, with ivy never sere.
'Lycidas' (1638) l. 1

3 Bitter constraint, and sad occasion dear,
Compels me to disturb your season due;
For Lycidas is dead, dead ere his prime,
Young Lycidas, and hath not left his peer:
Who would not sing for Lycidas?
'Lycidas' (1638) l. 6

4 He must not float upon his watery bier
Unwept, and welter to the parching wind,
Without the meed of some melodious tear.
'Lycidas' (1638) l. 12

5 For we were nursed upon the self-same hill.
'Lycidas' (1638) l. 23

6 Were it not better done as others use,
To sport with Amaryllis in the shade,
Or with the tangles of Neaera's hair?
Fame is the spur that the clear spirit doth raise
(That last infirmity of noble mind)
To scorn delights, and live laborious days.
'Lycidas' (1638) l. 67

7 Comes the blind Fury with th' abhorrèd shears,
And slits the thin-spun life.
'Lycidas' (1638) l. 75

8 Fame is no plant that grows on mortal soil.
'Lycidas' (1638) l. 78

9 Last came, and last did go,
The pilot of the Galilean lake,
Two massy keys he bore of metals twain
(The golden opes, the iron shuts amain).
'Lycidas' (1638) l. 108

10   Their lean and flashy songs
Grate on their scrannel pipes of wretched straw,
The hungry sheep look up, and are not fed.
'Lycidas' (1638) l. 123

11 But that two-handed engine at the door
Stands ready to smite once, and smite no more.
'Lycidas' (1638) l. 130

12 Bring the rathe primrose that forsaken dies,
The tufted crow-toe, and pale jessamine.
'Lycidas' (1638) l. 142

13 Look homeward angel now, and melt with ruth.
'Lycidas' (1638) l. 163

14 So sinks the day-star in the ocean bed,
And yet anon repairs his drooping head,
And tricks his beams, and with new spangled
ore,
Flames in the forehead of the morning sky.
'Lycidas' (1638) l. 168

15 Through the dear might of Him that walked the
waves.
'Lycidas' (1638) l. 173

16 While the still morn went out with sandals grey.
'Lycidas' (1638) l. 187

17 At last he rose, and twitched his mantle blue:
Tomorrow to fresh woods, and pastures new.
'Lycidas' (1638) l. 192

18 What needs my Shakespeare for his honoured
bones,
The labour of an age in pilèd stones.
'On Shakespeare' (1632)

19 O fairest flower no sooner blown but blasted,
Soft silken primrose fading timelessly.
'On the Death of a Fair Infant Dying of a Cough' (1673) st. 1

20 For what can war, but endless war still breed?
'On the Lord General Fairfax at the Siege of Colchester'
(written 1648)

21 This is the month, and this the happy morn
Wherein the son of heaven's eternal king,
Of wedded maid, and virgin mother born,
Our great redemption from above did bring.
'On the Morning of Christ's Nativity' (1645) st. 1

22 The star-led wizards haste with odours sweet.
'On the Morning of Christ's Nativity' (1645) st. 4

23 It was the winter wild,
While the heaven-born-child
All meanly wrapped in the rude manger lies;
Nature in awe to him
Had doffed her gaudy trim,
With her great master so to sympathize.
'On the Morning of Christ's Nativity' (1645) 'The Hymn' st. 1

24 The helmèd cherubim
And sworded seraphim
Are seen in glittering ranks with wings
displayed.
'On the Morning of Christ's Nativity' (1645) 'The Hymn' st. 11

25 Ring out, ye crystal spheres,
Once bless our human ears
(If ye have power to touch our senses so),
And let your silver chime
Move in melodious time;
And let the base of heaven's deep organ blow,
And with your ninefold harmony
Make up full consort to the angelic symphony.
'On the Morning of Christ's Nativity' (1645) 'The Hymn' st. 13

26 Time will run back, and fetch the age of gold.
'On the Morning of Christ's Nativity' (1645) 'The Hymn' st. 14

27 And hell itself will pass away,
And leave her dolorous mansions to the peering
day.
'On the Morning of Christ's Nativity' (1645) 'The Hymn' st. 14

28 Swinges the scaly horror of his folded tail.
'On the Morning of Christ's Nativity' (1645) 'The Hymn' st. 18

29 The oracles are dumb,
No voice or hideous hum
Runs through the archèd roof in words
deceiving.
Apollo from his shrine
Can no more divine,
With hollow shriek the steep of Delphos leaving.
'On the Morning of Christ's Nativity' (1645) 'The Hymn' st. 19

1 So when the sun in bed,
Curtained with cloudy red,
Pillows his chin upon an orient wave.
'On the Morning of Christ's Nativity' (1645) 'The Hymn' st. 26

2 Time is our tedious song should here have
ending.
'On the Morning of Christ's Nativity' (1645) 'The Hymn' st. 27

3 New *Presbyter* is but old *Priest* writ large.
'On the New Forcers of Conscience under the Long Parliament' (1646)

4 Fly envious Time, till thou run out thy race,
Call on the lazy leaden-stepping hours.
'On Time' (1645)

5 If any ask for him, it shall be said,
Hobson has supped, and's newly gone to bed.
'On the University Carrier' (1645)

6 Rhyme being . . . but the invention of a
barbarous age, to set off wretched matter and
lame metre.
Paradise Lost (1667) 'The Verse' (preface, added 1668)

7 The troublesome and modern bondage of
rhyming.
Paradise Lost (1667) 'The Verse' (preface, added 1668)

8 Of man's first disobedience, and the fruit
Of that forbidden tree, whose mortal taste
Brought death into the world, and all our woe,
With loss of Eden.
Paradise Lost (1667) bk. 1, l. 1

9 Things unattempted yet in prose or rhyme.
Paradise Lost (1667) bk. 1, l. 16

10   What in me is dark
Illumine, what is low raise and support;
That to the height of this great argument
I may assert eternal providence,
And justify the ways of God to men.
Paradise Lost (1667) bk. 1, l. 22; see **HOUSMAN** 416:10, **POPE** 616:15

11 The infernal serpent; he it was, whose guile
Stirred up with envy and revenge, deceived
The mother of mankind.
Paradise Lost (1667) bk. 1, l. 34

12 No light, but rather darkness visible
Served only to discover sights of woe.
Paradise Lost (1667) bk. 1, l. 63

13   What though the field be lost?
All is not lost; the unconquerable will,
And study of revenge, immortal hate,
And courage never to submit or yield.
Paradise Lost (1667) bk. 1, l. 105

14 To do aught good never will be our task,
But ever to do ill our sole delight.
Paradise Lost (1667) bk. 1, l. 159

15 And out of good still to find means of evil.
Paradise Lost (1667) bk. 1, l. 165

16 What reinforcement we may gain from hope;
If not, what resolution from despair.
Paradise Lost (1667) bk. 1, l. 190

17   The will
And high permission of all-ruling heaven

Left him at large to his own dark designs,
That with reiterated crimes he might
Heap on himself damnation.
Paradise Lost (1667) bk. 1, l. 211

18 The mind is its own place, and in itself
Can make a heaven of hell, a hell of heaven.
Paradise Lost (1667) bk. 1, l. 254

19 Better to reign in hell, than serve in heaven.
Paradise Lost (1667) bk. 1, l. 263

20 His spear, to equal which the tallest pine
Hewn on Norwegian hills, to be the mast
Of some great admiral, were but a wand,
He walked with to support uneasy steps
Over the burning marl.
Paradise Lost (1667) bk. 1, l. 292

21 Thick as autumnal leaves that strew the brooks
In Vallombrosa, where the Etrurian shades
High overarched imbower.
Paradise Lost (1667) bk. 1, l. 302

22 First Moloch, horrid king besmeared with blood
Of human sacrifice, and parents' tears.
Paradise Lost (1667) bk. 1, l. 392

23 Astarte, queen of heaven, with crescent horns.
Paradise Lost (1667) bk. 1, l. 439

24   Thammuz came next behind,
Whose annual wound in Lebanon allured
The Syrian damsels to lament his fate
In amorous ditties all a summer's day,
While smooth Adonis from his native rock
Ran purple to the sea.
Paradise Lost (1667) bk. 1, l. 446

25   And when night
Darkens the streets, then wander forth the sons
Of Belial, flown with insolence and wine.
Paradise Lost (1667) bk. 1, l. 500

26 The imperial ensign, which full high advanced
Shone like a meteor streaming to the wind.
Paradise Lost (1667) bk. 1, l. 536; see **GRAY** 369:20

27 A shout that tore hell's concave, and beyond
Frighted the reign of Chaos and old Night.
Paradise Lost (1667) bk. 1, l. 542

28   Who overcomes
By force, hath overcome but half his foe.
Paradise Lost (1667) bk. 1, l. 648

29   Mammon led them on,
Mammon, the least erected spirit that fell
From heaven, for even in heaven his looks and
    thoughts
Were always downward bent, admiring more
The riches of heaven's pavement, trodden gold,
Than aught divine or holy else enjoyed
In vision beatific.
Paradise Lost (1667) bk. 1, l. 678

30   Let none admire
That riches grow in hell; that soil may best
Deserve the precious bane.
Paradise Lost (1667) bk. 1, l. 690

31   From morn
To noon he fell, from noon to dewy eve,

A summer's day; and with the setting sun
Dropped from the zenith like a falling star.
Paradise Lost (1667) bk. 1, l. 742

1   Pandemonium, the high capital
Of Satan and his peers.
Paradise Lost (1667) bk. 1, l. 756

2 High on a throne of royal state, which far
Outshone the wealth of Ormuz and of Ind,
Or where the gorgeous East with richest hand
Showers on her kings barbaric pearl and gold,
Satan exalted sat, by merit raised
To that bad eminence.
Paradise Lost (1667) bk. 2, l. 1

3 Belial, in act more graceful and humane;
A fairer person lost not heaven; he seemed
For dignity composed and high exploit:
But all was false and hollow; though his tongue
Dropped manna, and could make the worse
 appear
The better reason.
Paradise Lost (1667) bk. 2, l. 109; see **ARISTOPHANES** 26:14

4 To perish rather, swallowed up and lost
In the wide womb of uncreated night,
Devoid of sense and motion?
Paradise Lost (1667) bk. 2, l. 149

5 Thus Belial with words clothed in reason's garb
Counselled ignoble ease, and peaceful sloth,
Not peace.
Paradise Lost (1667) bk. 2, l. 226

6 Our torments also may in length of time
Become our elements.
Paradise Lost (1667) bk. 2, l. 274

7   With grave
Aspect he rose, and in his rising seemed
A pillar of state; deep on his front engraven
Deliberation sat and public care;
And princely counsel in his face yet shone,
Majestic though in ruin.
Paradise Lost (1667) bk. 2, l. 300

8   To sit in darkness here
Hatching vain empires.
Paradise Lost (1667) bk. 2, l. 377

9 And through the palpable obscure find out
His uncouth way.
Paradise Lost (1667) bk. 2, l. 406

10   Long is the way
And hard, that out of hell leads up to light.
Paradise Lost (1667) bk. 2, l. 432

11 For eloquence the soul, song charms the sense.
Paradise Lost (1667) bk. 2, l. 556

12 Of good and evil much they argued then,
Of happiness and final misery,
Passion and apathy, and glory and shame,
Vain wisdom all, and false philosophy.
Paradise Lost (1667) bk. 2, l. 562

13 A gulf profound as that Serbonian bog.
Paradise Lost (1667) bk. 2, l. 592

14 O'er many a frozen, many a fiery alp,
Rocks, caves, lakes, fens, bogs, dens, and shades
 of death,
A universe of death, which God by curse
Created evil.
Paradise Lost (1667) bk. 2, l. 620

15   Black it stood as night,
Fierce as ten Furies, terrible as hell,
And shook a dreadful dart.
Paradise Lost (1667) bk. 2, l. 670

16 Incensed with indignation Satan stood
Unterrified, and like a comet burned
That fires the length of Ophiuchus huge
In the Arctic sky, and from his horrid hair
Shakes pestilence and war.
Paradise Lost (1667) bk. 2, l. 707

17   Chaos umpire sits,
And by decision more embroils the fray
By which he reigns; next him high arbiter
Chance governs all.
Paradise Lost (1667) bk. 2, l. 907

18 Unless th'Almighty Maker them ordain
His dark materials to create more worlds.
Paradise Lost (1667) bk. 2, l. 915; see **PULLMAN** 649:11

19 Sable-vested Night, eldest of things.
Paradise Lost (1667) bk. 2, l. 962

20 With ruin upon ruin, rout on rout,
Confusion worse confounded.
Paradise Lost (1667) bk. 2, l. 995

21 So he with difficulty and labour hard
Moved on, with difficulty and labour he.
Paradise Lost (1667) bk. 2, l. 1021

22 Die he or justice must.
Paradise Lost (1667) bk. 3, l. 210; see **ANDREWES** 15:13

23 Dark with excessive bright.
Paradise Lost (1667) bk. 3, l. 380

24 So on this windy sea of land, the fiend
Walked up and down alone bent on his prey.
Paradise Lost (1667) bk. 3, l. 440

25 Into a limbo large and broad, since called
The Paradise of Fools, to few unknown.
Paradise Lost (1667) bk. 3, l. 495

26 Hypocrisy, the only evil that walks
Invisible, except to God alone.
Paradise Lost (1667) bk. 3, l. 683

27   At whose sight all the stars
Hide their diminished heads.
Paradise Lost (1667) bk. 4, l. 34

28 Warring in heaven against heaven's matchless
 king.
Paradise Lost (1667) bk. 4, l. 41

29 Me miserable! which way shall I fly
Infinite wrath, and infinite despair?
Which way I fly is hell; myself am hell.
Paradise Lost (1667) bk. 4, l. 73

30 Farewell remorse! All good to me is lost;
Evil, be thou my good.
Paradise Lost (1667) bk. 4, l. 109

1 Thence up he flew, and on the tree of life,
The middle tree and highest there that grew,
Sat like a cormorant.
Paradise Lost (1667) bk. 4, l. 194

2 Groves whose rich trees wept odorous gums and
balm,
Others whose fruit burnished with golden rind
Hung amiable, Hesperian fables true,
If true, here only.
Paradise Lost (1667) bk. 4, l. 248

3 Flowers of all hue, and without thorn the rose.
Paradise Lost (1667) bk. 4, l. 256

4 　　　Not that fair field
Of Enna, where Proserpine gathering flowers
Herself a fairer flower by gloomy Dis
Was gathered, which cost Ceres all that pain.
Paradise Lost (1667) bk. 4, l. 268

5 For contemplation he and valour formed,
For softness she and sweet attractive grace,
He for God only, she for God in him.
Paradise Lost (1667) bk. 4, l. 297

6 Yielded with coy submission, modest pride,
And sweet reluctant amorous delay.
Paradise Lost (1667) bk. 4, l. 310

7 Adam, the goodliest man of men since born
His sons, the fairest of her daughters Eve.
Paradise Lost (1667) bk. 4, l. 323

8 　　　These two
Emparadised in one another's arms
The happier Eden, shall enjoy their fill
Of bliss on bliss.
Paradise Lost (1667) bk. 4, l. 505

9 Now came still evening on, and twilight grey
Had in her sober livery all things clad.
Paradise Lost (1667) bk. 4, l. 598

10 　　　Now glowed the firmament
With living sapphires: Hesperus that led
The starry host, rode brightest, till the moon
Rising in clouded majesty, at length
Apparent queen unveiled her peerless light,
And o'er the dark her silver mantle threw.
Paradise Lost (1667) bk. 4, l. 604

11 With thee conversing I forget all time.
Paradise Lost (1667) bk. 4, l. 639

12 Millions of spiritual creatures walk the earth
Unseen, both when we wake, and when we
sleep.
Paradise Lost (1667) bk. 4, l. 677

13 　　　Nor turned I ween
Adam from his fair spouse, nor Eve the rites
Mysterious of connubial love refused.
Paradise Lost (1667) bk. 4, l. 741

14 　　　Sleep on
Blest pair; and O yet happiest if ye seek
No happier state, and know to know no more.
Paradise Lost (1667) bk. 4, l. 773

15 　　　Him there they found
Squat like a toad, close at the ear of Eve.
Paradise Lost (1667) bk. 4, l. 799

16 But wherefore thou alone? Wherefore with thee
Came not all hell broke loose?
Paradise Lost (1667) bk. 4, l. 917

17 My fairest, my espoused, my latest found,
Heaven's last best gift, my ever new delight.
Paradise Lost (1667) bk. 5, l. 18

18 Best image of myself and dearer half.
Paradise Lost (1667) bk. 5, l. 95

19 She turns, on hospitable thoughts intent.
Paradise Lost (1667) bk. 5, l. 332

20 　　　Nor jealousy
Was understood, the injured lover's hell.
Paradise Lost (1667) bk. 5, l. 449

21 　　　What if earth
Be but the shadow of heaven, and things therein
Each to other like, more than on earth is
thought?
Paradise Lost (1667) bk. 5, l. 574

22 Hear all ye angels, progeny of light,
Thrones, dominations, princedoms, virtues,
powers.
Paradise Lost (1667) bk. 5, l. 600; see **BIBLE** 115:7

23 Mystical dance, which yonder starry sphere
Of planets and of fixed in all her wheels
Resembles nearest, mazes intricate,
Eccentric intervolved, yet regular
Then most, when most irregular they seem,
And in their motions harmony divine
So smoothes her charming tones, that God's
own ear
Listens delighted.
Paradise Lost (1667) bk. 5, l. 620

24 Satan, so call him now, his former name
Is heard no more in heaven.
Paradise Lost (1667) bk. 5, l. 658

25 Servant of God, well done, well hast thou
fought
The better fight, who single has maintained
Against revolted multitudes the cause
Of truth, in word mightier than they in arms.
Paradise Lost (1667) bk. 6, l. 29

26 　　　Still govern thou my song,
Urania, and fit audience find, though few.
Paradise Lost (1667) bk. 7, l. 30

27 　　　There Leviathan
Hugest of living creatures, on the deep
Stretched like a promontory sleeps or swims,
And seems a moving land, and at his gills
Draws in, and at his trunk spouts out a sea.
Paradise Lost (1667) bk. 7, l. 412

28 The planets in their stations listening stood,
While the bright pomp ascended jubilant.
Open, ye everlasting gates, they sung,
Open, ye heavens, your living doors; let in
The great creator from his work returned
Magnificent, his six days' work, a world.
Paradise Lost (1667) bk. 7, l. 563; see **BOOK OF COMMON
PRAYER** 141:2

29 　　　In solitude
What happiness? who can enjoy alone,

Or all enjoying, what contentment find?
Paradise Lost (1667) bk. 8, l. 364

1   So absolute she seems
And in herself complete, so well to know
Her own, that what she wills to do or say
Seems wisest, virtuousest, discreetest, best.
Paradise Lost (1667) bk. 8, l. 547

2   Oft-times nothing profits more
Than self esteem, grounded on just and right
Well managed.
Paradise Lost (1667) bk. 8, l. 571; see LEAVIS 486:19

3 The serpent subtlest beast of all the field.
Paradise Lost (1667) bk. 9, l. 86

4 As one who long in populous city pent,
Where houses thick and sewers annoy the air,
Forth issuing on a summer's morn to breathe
Among the pleasant villages and farms
Adjoined, from each thing met conceives delight.
Paradise Lost (1667) bk. 9, l. 445; see KEATS 457:7

5 God so commanded, and left that command
Sole daughter of his voice; the rest, we live
Law to our selves, our reason is our law.
Paradise Lost (1667) bk. 9, l. 652

6   Her rash hand in evil hour
Forth reaching to the fruit, she plucked, she ate:
Earth felt the wound, and Nature from her seat
Sighing through all her works gave signs of woe
That all was lost.
Paradise Lost (1667) bk. 9, l. 780

7 O fairest of creation, last and best
Of all God's works.
Paradise Lost (1667) bk. 9, l. 896

8   Flesh of flesh,
Bone of my bone thou art, and from thy state
Mine never shall be parted, bliss or woe.
Paradise Lost (1667) bk. 9, l. 914; see BIBLE 79:2

9   What thou art is mine;
Our state cannot be severed, we are one,
One flesh; to lose thee were to lose my self.
Paradise Lost (1667) bk. 9, l. 957

10 . . . Yet I shall temper so
Justice with mercy.
Paradise Lost (1667) bk. 10, l. 77

11   He hears
On all sides, from innumerable tongues
A dismal universal hiss, the sound
Of public scorn.
Paradise Lost (1667) bk. 10, l. 506

12 This novelty on earth, this fair defect
Of nature?
Paradise Lost (1667) bk. 10, l. 891

13 Demoniac frenzy, moping melancholy
And moon-struck madness.
Paradise Lost (1667) bk. 11, l. 485

14   The evening star,
Love's harbinger.
Paradise Lost (1667) bk. 11, l. 588

15   For now I see
Peace to corrupt no less than war to waste.
Paradise Lost (1667) bk. 11, l. 783

16 O goodness infinite, goodness immense!
That all this good of evil shall produce,
And evil turn to good; more wonderful
Than that which by creation first brought forth
Light out of darkness!
Paradise Lost (1667) bk. 12, l. 469

17   Then wilt thou not be loath
To leave this Paradise, but shalt possess
A paradise within thee, happier far.
Paradise Lost (1667) bk. 12, l. 585

18 In me is no delay; with thee to go,
Is to stay here; without thee here to stay,
Is to go hence unwilling; thou to me
Art all things under heaven, all places thou,
Who for my wilful crime art banished hence.
Paradise Lost (1667) bk. 12, l. 615

19 They looking back, all the eastern side beheld
Of Paradise, so late their happy seat.
Paradise Lost (1667) bk. 12, l. 641

20 The world was all before them, where to choose
Their place of rest, and Providence their guide:
They hand in hand, with wandering steps and
    slow,
Through Eden took their solitary way.
Paradise Lost (1667) bk. 12, l. 646

21 Of whom to be dispraised were no small praise.
Paradise Regained (1671) bk. 3, l. 56

22 But on occasion's forelock watchful wait.
Paradise Regained (1671) bk. 3, l. 173

23 He who seeking asses found a kingdom.
of Saul
Paradise Regained (1671) bk. 3, l. 242; see BIBLE 83:30

24   The childhood shows the man,
As morning shows the day.
Paradise Regained (1671) bk. 4, l. 220; see WORDSWORTH
866:18

25 Athens, the eye of Greece, mother of arts
And eloquence.
Paradise Regained (1671) bk. 4, l. 240

26 See there the olive grove of Academe,
Plato's retirement, where the Attic bird
Trills her thick-warbled notes the summer long.
Paradise Regained (1671) bk. 4, l. 244

27 The first and wisest of them all professed
To know this only, that he nothing knew.
Paradise Regained (1671) bk. 4, l. 293; see DAVIES 267:18,
SOCRATES 759:15

28 Deep-versed in books and shallow in himself.
Paradise Regained (1671) bk. 4, l. 327

29 But headlong joy is ever on the wing.
'The Passion' (1645) st. 1

30 A little onward lend thy guiding hand.
Samson Agonistes (1671) l. 1

31 Ask for this great deliverer now, and find him
Eyeless in Gaza at the mill with slaves.
Samson Agonistes (1671) l. 40

1 O dark, dark, dark, amid the blaze of noon,
Irrecoverably dark, total eclipse
Without all hope of day!
Samson Agonistes (1671) l. 80

2 The sun to me is dark
And silent as the moon,
When she deserts the night
Hid in her vacant interlunar cave.
Samson Agonistes (1671) l. 86

3 To live a life half dead, a living death.
Samson Agonistes (1671) l. 100

4   Apt words have power to swage
The tumours of a troubled mind.
Samson Agonistes (1671) l. 184

5 Just are the ways of God,
And justifiable to men;
Unless there be who think not God at all.
Samson Agonistes (1671) l. 293

6 What boots it at one gate to make defence,
And at another to let in the foe?
Samson Agonistes (1671) l. 560

7 Yet beauty, though injurious, hath strange power,
After offence returning, to regain
Love once possessed.
Samson Agonistes (1671) l. 1003

8 Like that self-begotten bird
In the Arabian woods embossed,
That no second knows nor third,
And lay erewhile a holocaust.
Samson Agonistes (1671) l. 1699

9   Samson hath quit himself
Like Samson, and heroically hath finished
A life heroic.
Samson Agonistes (1671) l. 1709

10 Nothing is here for tears, nothing to wail.
Samson Agonistes (1671) l. 1721

11 And calm of mind, all passion spent.
Samson Agonistes (1671) l. 1758

12 Time the subtle thief of youth.
Sonnet 7 'How soon hath time' (1645)

13 Licence they mean when they cry liberty;
For who loves that, must first be wise and good.
Sonnet 12 'I did but prompt the age' (1673)

14 When I consider how my light is spent,
E're half my days, in this dark world and wide,
And that one talent which is death to hide
Lodged with me useless.
Sonnet 16 'When I consider how my light is spent' (1673)

15 Doth God exact day-labour, light denied,
I fondly ask; but patience to prevent
That murmur, soon replies, God doth not need
Either man's work or his own gifts, who best
Bear his mild yoke, they serve him best, his state
Is kingly. Thousands at his bidding speed
And post o'er land and ocean without rest:
They also serve who only stand and wait.
Sonnet 16 'When I consider how my light is spent' (1673)

16 Methought I saw my late espousèd saint
Brought to me like Alcestis from the grave.
Sonnet 19 'Methought I saw my late espousèd saint' (1673)

17 Cromwell, our chief of men.
'To the Lord General Cromwell' (written 1652)

18   Peace hath her victories
No less renowned than war.
'To the Lord General Cromwell' (written 1652)

19 He who would not be frustrate of his hope to
write well hereafter in laudable things, ought
himself to be a true poem.
An Apology for Smectymnuus (1642) introduction

20 They who have put out the people's eyes,
reproach them of their blindness.
An Apology for Smectymnuus (1642)

21 For this is not the liberty which we can hope,
that no grievance ever should arise in the
Commonwealth, that let no man in this world
expect; but when complaints are freely heard,
deeply considered, and speedily reformed, then
is the utmost bound of civil liberty attained that
wise men look for.
Areopagitica (1644)

22 As good almost kill a man as kill a good book:
who kills a man kills a reasonable creature,
God's image; but he who destroys a good book,
kills reason itself, kills the image of God, as it
were in the eye.
Areopagitica (1644)

23 A good book is the precious life-blood of a
master spirit, embalmed and treasured up on
purpose to a life beyond life.
Areopagitica (1644)

24 I cannot praise a fugitive and cloistered virtue,
unexercised and unbreathed, that never sallies
out and sees her adversary, but slinks out of the
race, where that immortal garland is to be run
for, not without dust and heat . . . that which
purifies us is trial, and trial is by what is
contrary.
Areopagitica (1644); see **GOLDSMITH** 365:13

25 Here the great art lies, to discern in what the
law is to be to restraint and punishment, and in
what things persuasion only is to work.
Areopagitica (1644)

26 If we think to regulate printing, thereby to
rectify manners, we must regulate all recreations
and pastimes, all that is delightful to man . . .
And who shall silence all the airs and madrigals,
that whisper softness in chambers?
Areopagitica (1644)

27 From that time ever since, the sad friends of
Truth, such as durst appear, imitating the careful
search that Isis made for the mangled body of
Osiris, went up and down gathering up limb by
limb still as they could find them. We have not
yet found them all, Lords and Commons, nor
ever shall do, till her Master's second coming;
He shall bring together every joint and member,

and shall mould them into an immortal feature of loveliness and perfection.
Areopagitica (1644)

1 To be still searching what we know not, by what we know, still closing up truth to truth as we find it (for all her body is homogeneal and proportional), this is the golden rule in theology as well as in arithmetic, and makes up the best harmony in a church.
Areopagitica (1644)

2 God is decreeing to begin some new and great period in his Church, even to the reforming of Reformation itself. What does he then but reveal Himself to his servants, and as his manner is, first to his Englishmen?
Areopagitica (1644)

3 A city of refuge, the mansion-house of liberty.
of London
Areopagitica (1644)

4 Where there is much desire to learn, there of necessity will be much arguing, much writing, many opinions; for opinion in good men is but knowledge in the making.
Areopagitica (1644) p. 31

5 Give me the liberty to know, to utter, and to argue freely according to conscience, above all liberties.
Areopagitica (1644)

6 Though all the winds of doctrine were let loose to play upon the earth, so Truth be in the field, we do injuriously by licensing and prohibiting to misdoubt her strength. Let her and Falsehood grapple; who ever knew Truth put to the worse, in a free and open encounter?
Areopagitica (1644)

7 Let not England forget her precedence of teaching nations how to live.
The Doctrine and Discipline of Divorce (1643) 'To the Parliament of England'

8 What I have spoken, is the language of that which is not called amiss *The good old Cause.*
The Ready and Easy Way to Establish a Free Commonwealth (2nd ed., 1660); see WORDSWORTH 867:20

9 This manner of writing [prose] wherein knowing myself inferior to myself . . . I have the use, as I may account it, but of my left hand.
The Reason of Church Government (1642) bk. 2, introduction

10 The land had once enfranchised herself from this impertinent yoke of prelaty, under whose inquisitorious and tyrannical duncery no free and splendid wit can flourish.
The Reason of Church Government (1642) bk. 2, introduction

11 Beholding the bright countenance of truth in the quiet and still air of delightful studies.
The Reason of Church Government (1642) bk. 2, introduction

12 None can love freedom heartily, but good men; the rest love not freedom, but licence.
The Tenure of Kings and Magistrates (1649)

13 No man who knows aught, can be so stupid to deny that all men naturally were born free.
The Tenure of Kings and Magistrates (1649)

Comte de Mirabeau 1749–91
French revolutionary

14 War is the national industry of Prussia.
attributed to Mirabeau by Albert Sorel (1842–1906), based on Mirabeau's introduction to *De la monarchie prussienne sous Frédéric le Grand* (1788)

☐ **Misquotations** *see* **box opposite**

The Missal
The Latin Eucharistic liturgy used by the Roman Catholic Church up to 1964

15 *Asperges me, Domine, hyssopo, et mundabor.*

Sprinkle me with hyssop, O Lord, and I shall be cleansed.
Anthem at Sprinkling the Holy Water; see **BOOK OF COMMON PRAYER** 143:6

16 *Dominus vobiscum.*
Et cum spiritu tuo.

The Lord be with you.
And with thy spirit.
The Ordinary of the Mass

17 *In Nomine Patris, et Filii, et Spiritus Sancti.*

In the Name of the Father, and of the Son, and of the Holy Ghost.
The Ordinary of the Mass

18 *Introibo ad altare Dei.*

I will go unto the altar of God.
The Ordinary of the Mass; see **BOOK OF COMMON PRAYER** 141:7

19 *Gloria Patri, et Filio, et Spiritui Sancto. Sicut erat in principio, et nunc, et semper, et in saecula saeculorum.*

Glory be to the Father, and to the Son, and to the Holy Ghost. As it was in the beginning, is now, and ever shall be, world without end.
The Ordinary of the Mass 'The Doxology'; see **BOOK OF COMMON PRAYER** 133:8

20 *Confiteor Deo omnipotenti . . . quia peccavi nimis cogitatione, verbo, et opere, mea culpa, mea culpa, mea maxima culpa.*

I confess to almighty God . . . that I have sinned exceedingly in thought, word, and deed, through my fault, through my fault, through my most grievous fault.
The Ordinary of the Mass

21 *Kyrie eleison . . . Christe eleison.*

Lord, have mercy upon us . . . Christ, have mercy upon us.
The Ordinary of the Mass

continued

Misquotations

1 All is lost save honour.
> popular summary of the words of **FRANCIS I** of France in a letter to his mother following his defeat at Pavia, 1525; see **FRANCIS I** 340:15

2 All rowed fast, but none so fast as stroke.
> *popular summary of the following passage: 'His blade struck the water a full second before any other: the lad had started well. Nor did he flag as the race wore on . . . as the boats began to near the winning-post, his oar was dipping into the water nearly* twice as often as any other' Desmond Coke (1879–1931) *Sandford of Merton* (1903) ch. 12

3 The ballot is stronger than the bullet.
> popular version of a speech by **LINCOLN**, 18 May 1858; see **LINCOLN** 493:9

4 Beam me up, Scotty.
> *supposedly the form in which Captain Kirk habitually requested to be returned from a planet to the Starship* Enterprise; *in fact the nearest equivalent found is 'Beam us up, Mr Scott'* Gene Roddenberry *Star Trek* (1966 onwards) 'Gamesters of Triskelion'

5 The budget should be balanced, the treasury should be refilled, public debt should be reduced, the arrogance of officialdom should be tempered and controlled, assistance to foreign lands should be curtailed lest Rome should become bankrupt, the mobs should be forced to work and not depend on government for subsistence.
> attributed to **CICERO** in *Congressional Record* 25 April 1968, but not traced in his works

6 The capitalists will sell us the rope with which to hang them.
> attributed to **LENIN**, but not found in his published works; I. U. Annenkov, in 'Remembrances of Lenin' includes a manuscript note attributed to Lenin: 'They [capitalists] will furnish credits which will serve us for the support of the Communist Party in their countries and, by supplying us materials and technical equipment which we lack, will restore our military industry necessary for our future attacks against our suppliers. To put it in other words, they will work on the preparation of their own suicide', in *Novyi Zhurnal/New Review* September 1961

7 Come with me to the Casbah.
> *often attributed to Charles Boyer (1898–1978) in the film* Algiers *(1938), but the line does not in fact occur* L. Swindell *Charles Boyer* (1983)

8 Crisis? What Crisis?
> *Sun* headline, 11 January 1979, summarizing James **CALLAGHAN**'s remark: 'I don't think other people in the world would share the view there is mounting chaos', interview at London Airport, 10 January 1979

9 Dark forces at work.
> *popular summary of comment attributed to Queen* **ELIZABETH II** *by former royal butler Paul Burrell, reported in the* Daily Mirror *as: 'There are powers at work in this country about which we have no knowledge'* in *The Times* 7 November 2002

10 Dreams are the royal road to the unconscious.
> popular summary of **FREUD**'s *The Interpretation of Dreams* (2nd ed., 1909); see **FREUD** 342:16

11 Elementary, my dear Watson, elementary.
> *remark attributed to Sherlock Holmes, but not found in this form in any book by Arthur Conan* **DOYLE**, *first found in P.G.* **WODEHOUSE** Psmith Journalist *(1915)* attributed; see **DOYLE** 292:15

12 England and America are two countries divided by a common language.
> attributed in this and other forms to George Bernard **SHAW**, but not found in Shaw's published writings; see **WILDE** 854:13

13 Faith, the dark night of the soul.
> St **JOHN** of the Cross *Complete Works* (1864), translated by David Lewis, vol. 1, bk. 1, ch. 3; the phrase appears in the translator's chapter heading for the poem: '*Noche oscura* [Dark night]' in *The Ascent of Mount Carmel* (1578–80)

14 Few die and none resign.
> popular summary of a letter of Thomas **JEFFERSON**, 1801; see **JEFFERSON** 432:1

15 Git thar fustest with the mostest.
> attributed to the American Confederate general Nathan Bedford Forrest (1821–77), though there is no evidence that non-standard speech was characteristic of Forrest, and the form 'Get there first with the most men' is also found

16 The good Christian should beware of mathematicians, and all those who make empty prophecies. The danger already exists that mathematicians have made a covenant with the Devil to darken the spirit and to confine man in the bonds of Hell.
> mistranslation of St **AUGUSTINE**'s *De Genesi ad Litteram*; the Latin word 'mathematicus' means both 'mathematician' and 'astrologer'; see **AUGUSTINE** 39:17

17 A good day to bury bad news.
> popular misquotation of Jo **MOORE**'s email of 11 September 2001; see **MOORE** 557:11

18 The green shoots of recovery.
> popular misquotation of the Chancellor's upbeat assessment of the economic situation: 'The green shoots of economic spring are appearing once again', Norman **LAMONT**, speech at Conservative Party Conference, 9 October 1991

19 Hug a hoodie.
> Vernon Coaker's summary of a speech by David Cameron calling for more understanding of apparently threatening young people (see **CAMERON** 194:12, **COAKER** 237:9)

20 I disapprove of what you say, but I will defend to the death your right to say it.
> *to* **HELVÉTIUS**, *following the burning of* De l'esprit *in 1759* attributed to **VOLTAIRE**, but in fact a later summary of his attitude by S. G. Tallentyre in *The Friends of Voltaire* (1907); see **VOLTAIRE** 835:9

21 I have seen the shadow of the Earth on the moon, and I have more faith in the shadow than the church.
> *opposing the view that the earth was flat* attributed to the Portuguese navigator Ferdinand Magellan (c. 1480–1521), but not traced before the mid nineteenth century; see **INGERSOLL** 425:11, **SAVAGE** 682:18

continued

Misquotations *continued*

1 In trust I have found treason.

traditional concluding words of a speech by **ELIZABETH I** to a Parliamentary deputation at Richmond, 12 November 1586; see **ELIZABETH I** 312:4

2 I paint with my prick.

attributed to Pierre Auguste **RENOIR**; possibly an inversion of 'It's with my brush that I make love', A. André *Renoir* (1919)

3 I think there is a world market for maybe five computers.

commonly attributed to Thomas **WATSON** Snr., but not traced; stated by IBM to derive from a misunderstanding of an occasion on 28 April 1953 when Thomas Watson Jnr. informed a meeting of IBM stockholders that 'we expected to get orders for five machines, we came home with orders for 18'

4 It is necessary only for the good man to do nothing for evil to triumph.

attributed (in a number of forms) to **BURKE**, but not found in his writings; see **BURKE** 175:4, see also **MILL** 536:1

5 It's life, Jim, but not as we know it.

late 20th century saying associated with the television series *Star Trek* (1966–), created by Gene **RODDENBERRY**; the saying does not occur in the series but derives from the 1987 song 'Star Trekkin' ' sung by The Firm

6 Laws are like sausages. It's better not to see them being made made.

attributed to **BISMARCK**, but not traced and probably apocryphal

7 Licensed to kill.

popular description of the status of Secret Service agent James Bond, 007, in the novels of Ian **FLEMING**; 'The licence to kill for the Secret Service, the double-o prefix, was a great honour' *Dr No* (1958)

8 Man, if you gotta ask you'll never know.

alternative version of Louis **ARMSTRONG**'s response when asked what jazz was; see **ARMSTRONG** 28:17

9 Me Tarzan, you Jane.

Johnny Weissmuller (1904–84) summing up his role in Tarzan, the Ape Man (1932 film)

in *Photoplay Magazine* June 1932; the words do not occur in the film or in the original novel by Edgar Rice Burroughs

10 Mind has no sex.

summarizing the view of Mary **WOLLSTONECRAFT**; see **WOLLSTONECRAFT** 863:6

11 My lips are sealed.

popular version of **BALDWIN**'s speech on the Abyssinian crisis, 10 December 1935; see **BALDWIN** 53:7

12 No plan survives first contact with the enemy.

popular version of Helmuth von **MOLTKE**; see **MOLTKE** 553:5

13 Once aboard the lugger and the maid is mine.

popular version of the line: 'I want you to assist me in forcing her on board the lugger; once there, I'll frighten her into marriage'

John Benn Johnstone (1803–91) *The Gipsy Farmer* (performed 1845)

14 Play it again, Sam.

in the film Casablanca, *written by Julius J. Epstein et al., Humphrey Bogart says, 'If she can stand it, I can. Play it!'; earlier in the film Ingrid Bergman says, 'Play it, Sam. Play As Time Goes By.'*

Casablanca (1942 film); see **FILM LINES** 328:14, **HUPFELD** 422:4

15 Praise from Sir Hubert is praise indeed.

popular version of 'Approbation from Sir Hubert Stanley . . . '; see **MORTON** 562:8

16 Put me back on my bike.

commonly quoted as the last words of the English cyclist Tom SIMPSON, after collapsing on Mont Ventoux in the Tour de France; see SIMPSON 753:4

William Fotheringham *Put Me Back on My Bike* (2002) ch. 2

17 Selling off the family silver.

popular summary of Harold **MACMILLAN**'s attack on privatization, 8 November 1985; see **MACMILLAN** 513:2

18 The soft underbelly of Europe.

popular version of **CHURCHILL**'s words in the House of Commons, 11 November 1942; see **CHURCHILL** 230:2

19 Something must be done.

popular version of **EDWARD VIII**'s words at the derelict Dowlais Iron and Steel Works, 18 November 1936; see **EDWARD VIII** 304:4

20 Take away these baubles.

popular version of **CROMWELL**'s words at the dismissal of the Rump Parliament, 20 April 1653; see **CROMWELL** 260:15

21 The time you enjoy wasting is not wasted time.

frequently attributed to Bertrand RUSSELL, but in fact Laurence J. PETER commenting on a quotation from Russell

Laurence J. Peter *Quotations for Our Time* (1977)

22 Warts and all.

popular summary of CROMWELL's instructions to the court painter Lely: 'Mr Lely, I desire you would use all your skill to paint my picture truly like me, and not flatter me at all; but remark all these roughnesses, pimples, warts, and everything as you see me; otherwise I will never pay a farthing for it'

Horace Walpole *Anecdotes of Painting in England* vol. 3 (1763) ch. 1

23 We are the masters now.

popular misquotation of Hartley **SHAWCROSS**'s speech in the House of Commons, 2 April 1946; see **SHAWCROSS** 742:24

24 We must educate our masters.

popular summary of Robert LOWE's speech on the passing of the Reform Bill: 'I believe it will be absolutely necessary that you should prevail on our future masters to learn their letters'

speech, House of Commons, 15 July 1867

continued

Misquotations *continued*

1 We must guard even our enemies against injustice.

Graham **GREENE**'s version of Thomas **PAINE**'s *Dissertation on the First Principles of Government*; see **PAINE** 592:17

2 We trained hard . . . but it seemed that every time we were beginning to form up into teams we would be reorganized. I was to learn later in life that we tend to meet any new situation by reorganizing; and a wonderful method it can be for creating the illusion of progress while producing confusion, inefficiency, and demoralization.

late 20th century saying, frequently attributed to **TACITUS** Arbiter (d. AD 65), but not found in his works

3 *Was für plündern!*

What a place to plunder!

misquotation of the comment of **BLÜCHER** on London, as

seen from the Monument in June 1814; see **BLÜCHER** 129:8

4 When disaster strikes and all hope is gone, get down on your knees and pray for Shackleton.

paraphrase of a comment by Apsley **CHERRY-GARRARD**; see **CHERRY-GARRARD** 222:16

5 The white heat of technology.

popular version of Harold **WILSON**'s speech at the Labour Party Conference, 1 October 1963; see **WILSON** 859:5

6 Why don't you come up and see me sometime?

alteration of Mae **WEST**'s invitation in the film *She Done Him Wrong* (1933); see **WEST** 848:15

7 You dirty rat!

associated with James Cagney (1899–1986), but not used by him in any film; in a speech at the American Film Institute banquet, 13 March 1974, Cagney said, 'I never said "Mmm, you dirty rat!"'

Cagney by Cagney (1976)

The Missal *continued*

8 *Gloria in excelsis Deo, et in terra pax hominibus bonae voluntatis. Laudamus te, benedicimus te, adoramus te, glorificamus te.*

Glory be to God on high, and on earth peace to men of good will. We praise thee, we bless thee, we adore thee, we glorify thee.

The Ordinary of the Mass; see **BIBLE** 104:14

9 *Oremus.*

Let us pray.

The Ordinary of the Mass

10 *Deo gratias.*

Thanks be to God.

The Ordinary of the Mass

11 *Credo in unum Deum, Patrem omnipotentem, factorem coeli et terrae, visibilium omnium et invisibilium.*

I believe in one God, the Father almighty, maker of heaven and earth, and of all things visible and invisible.

The Ordinary of the Mass 'The Nicene Creed'; see **BOOK OF COMMON PRAYER** 133:19

12 *Deum de Deo, lumen de lumine, Deum verum de Deo vero.*

God of God, light of light; true God of true God.

The Ordinary of the Mass 'The Nicene Creed'

13 *Et incarnatus est de Spiritu Sancto, ex Maria Virgine;* ET HOMO FACTUS EST.

And became incarnate by the Holy Ghost, of the Virgin Mary; AND WAS MADE MAN.

The Ordinary of the Mass 'The Nicene Creed'

14 *Sursum corda.*

Lift up your hearts.

The Ordinary of the Mass; see **BOOK OF COMMON PRAYER** 137:12

15 *Dignum et justum est.*

It is right and fitting.

The Ordinary of the Mass; see **BOOK OF COMMON PRAYER** 137:14

16 *Sanctus, sanctus, sanctus, Dominus Deus Sabaoth. Pleni sunt coeli et terra gloria tua. Hosanna in excelsis. Benedictus qui venit in nomine Domini.*

Holy, holy, holy, Lord God of Hosts. Heaven and earth are full of thy glory. Hosanna in the highest. Blessed is he that cometh in the name of the Lord.

The Ordinary of the Mass; see **BIBLE** 118:5, **BOOK OF COMMON PRAYER** 137:14

17 *Pater noster, qui es in coelis, sanctificetur nomen tuum; adveniat regnum tuum; fiat voluntas tua sicut in coelo, et in terra . . . sed libera nos a malo.*

Our Father, who art in heaven, hallowed be thy name; thy kingdom come; thy will be done on earth, as it is in heaven . . . but deliver us from evil.

The Ordinary of the Mass; see **BIBLE** 99:12

18 *Pax Domini sit semper vobiscum.*

The peace of the Lord be always with you.

The Ordinary of the Mass

19 *Agnus Dei, qui tollis peccata mundi, miserere nobis. Agnus Dei, qui tollis peccata mundi, dona nobis pacem.*

Lamb of God, who takest away the sins of the world, have mercy on us. Lamb of God, who takest away the sins of the world, give us peace.

The Ordinary of the Mass; see **BIBLE** 107:5

20 *Domine, non sum dignus ut intres sub tectum meum; sed tantum dic verbo, et sanabitur anima mea.*

Lord, I am not worthy that thou shouldst enter under my roof; but say only the word, and my soul shall be healed.

The Ordinary of the Mass; see **BIBLE** 100:6

1 *Ite missa est.*

Go, you are dismissed.

commonly interpreted as 'Go, the Mass is ended'
The Ordinary of the Mass

2 *In principio erat Verbum, et Verbum erat apud Deum, et Deus erat Verbum.*

In the beginning was the Word, and the Word was with God, and the Word was God.
The Ordinary of the Mass; see BIBLE 106:34

3 VERBUM CARO FACTUM EST.

THE WORD WAS MADE FLESH.
The Ordinary of the Mass; see BIBLE 107:2

4 *Requiem aeternam dona eis, Domine: et lux perpetua luceat eis.*

Grant them eternal rest, O Lord; and let perpetual light shine on them.
Order of Mass for the Dead

5 *Dies irae, dies illa,*
Solvet saeclum in favilla,
Teste David cum Sibylla.

That day, the day of wrath, will turn the universe to ashes, as David foretells (and the Sibyl too).
Order of Mass for the Dead 'Sequentia' l. 1; *commonly known as* Dies Irae *and sometimes attributed to Thomas of Celano (c.1190–1260)*

6 *Tuba mirum spargens sonum*
Per sepulcra regionum,
Coget omnes ante thronum.

Mors stupebit et natura,
Cum resurget creatura
Iudicanti responsura.

Liber scriptus proferetur,
In quo totum continetur
Unde mundus iudicetur.

The trumpet will fling out a wonderful sound through the tombs of all regions, it will drive everyone before the throne. Death will be aghast and so will nature, when creation rises again to make answer to the judge. The written book will be brought forth, in which everything is included whereby the world will be judged.
Order of Mass for the Dead 'Sequentia' l. 7

7 *Rex tremendae maiestatis,*
Qui salvandos salvas gratis,
Salva me, fons pietatis!

O King of tremendous majesty, who freely saves those who should be saved, save me, O source of pity!
Order of Mass for the Dead 'Sequentia' l. 22

8 *Inter oves locum praesta*
Et ab haedis me sequestra
Statuens in parte dextra.

Among the sheep set me a place and separate me from the goats, standing me on the right-hand side.
Order of Mass for the Dead 'Sequentia' l. 43

9 *Requiescant in pace.*

May they rest in peace.
Order of Mass for the Dead

10 *O felix culpa, quae talem ac tantum meruit habere Redemptorem.*

O happy fault, which has earned such a mighty Redeemer.
'Exsultet' on Holy Saturday

Mistinguett 1875–1956
French actress

11 A kiss can be a comma, a question mark or an exclamation point. That's basic spelling that every woman ought to know.
in *Theatre Arts* December 1955

Adrian Mitchell 1932–
English poet, novelist, and dramatist

12 Most people ignore most poetry
because
most poetry ignores most people.
Poems (1964)

Elma Mitchell 1919–2000
Scottish poet

13   Even the simplest poem
May destroy your immunity to human emotions.
All poems must carry a Government warning.
  Words
Can seriously affect your heart.
'This Poem . . . ' (1987)

14 Women reminded him of lilies and rose.
Me they remind rather of blood and soap,
Armed with a warm rag, assaulting noses,
Ears, neck and mouth and all the secret places.
'Thoughts After Ruskin' (1976)

John Mitchell 1785–1859
English soldier

15 The most important political question on which modern times have to decide is the policy that must now be pursued, in order to maintain the security of Western Europe against the overgrown power of Russia.
Thoughts on Tactics (1838)

Joni Mitchell (Roberta Joan Anderson) 1945–
Canadian singer and songwriter

16 They paved paradise
And put up a parking lot,
With a pink hotel,
A boutique, and a swinging hot spot.
'Big Yellow Taxi' (1970 song)

17 I've looked at life from both sides now,
From win and lose and still somehow

It's life's illusions I recall;
I really don't know life at all.
'Both Sides Now' (1967 song)

1 We are stardust,
We are golden,
And we got to get ourselves
Back to the garden.
'Woodstock' (1969 song)

Margaret Mitchell 1900–49
American novelist

2 Always providing you have enough courage—or money—you can do without a reputation.
Gone with the Wind (1936) ch. 9

3 Death and taxes and childbirth! There's never any convenient time for any of them.
Gone with the Wind (1936) ch. 38

4 I wish I could care what you do or where you go but I can't . . . My dear, I don't give a damn.
Gone with the Wind (1936) ch. 63; see FILM LINES 328:8

5 After all, tomorrow is another day.
Gone with the Wind (1936) ch. 63, closing words

Mary Russell Mitford 1787–1855
English novelist and dramatist

6 Till *Pride and Prejudice* showed what a precious gem was hidden in that unbending case, she was no more regarded in society than a poker or a fire-screen, or any other thin upright piece of wood or iron that fills its corner in peace and quietness. The case is very different now; she is still a poker—but a poker of whom every one is afraid.
of Jane AUSTEN
letter to Sir William Elford, 3 April 1815, in R. Brimley Johnson (ed.) *The Letters of Mary Russell Mitford* (1925)

Nancy Mitford 1904–73
English writer

7 Love in a cold climate.
title of book (1949); see SOUTHEY 764:23

8 'Always be civil to the girls, you never know who they may marry' is an aphorism which has saved many an English spinster from being treated like an Indian widow.
Love in a Cold Climate (1949) pt. 1, ch. 2; see AILESBURY 9:16

9 Frogs . . . are slightly better than Huns or Wops, but abroad is unutterably bloody and foreigners are fiends.
The Pursuit of Love (1945) ch. 15; see GEORGE VI 353:7

François Mitterrand 1916–96
French socialist statesman, President of France 1981–95

10 She has the eyes of Caligula, but the mouth of Marilyn Monroe.
of Margaret THATCHER, *briefing his new European Minister Roland Dumas*
in *Observer* 25 November 1990

Wilson Mizner 1876–1933
American dramatist

11 Be nice to people on your way up because you'll meet 'em on your way down.
Alva Johnston *The Legendary Mizners* (1953) ch. 4

12 If you steal from one author, it's plagiarism; if you steal from many, it's research.
Alva Johnston *The Legendary Mizners* (1953) ch. 4

13 A trip through a sewer in a glass-bottomed boat.
of Hollywood; reworked by Mayor Jimmy Walker into 'A reformer is a guy who rides through a sewer in a glass-bottomed boat'
Alva Johnston *The Legendary Mizners* (1953) ch. 4

Ariane Mnouchkine 1934–
French theatre director

14 A cultural Chernobyl.
of Euro Disney
in *Harper's Magazine* July 1992; see BALLARD 56:10

Emilio Mola 1887–1937
Spanish nationalist general

15 Fifth column.
an extra body of supporters claimed by General Mola in a broadcast as being within Madrid when he besieged the city with four columns of Nationalist forces
in *New York Times* 16 and 17 October 1936

Molière (Jean-Baptiste Poquelin) 1622–73
French comic dramatist

16 *Présentez toujours le devant au monde.*
Always present your front to the world.
L'Avare (1669) act 3, sc. 1

17 *Il faut manger pour vivre et non pas vivre pour manger.*
One should eat to live, and not live to eat.
L'Avare (1669) act 3, sc. 1

18 *Tout ce qui n'est point prose est vers; et tout ce qui n'est point vers est prose.*
All that is not prose is verse; and all that is not verse is prose.
Le Bourgeois Gentilhomme (1671) act 2, sc. 4

19 M. JOURDAIN: *Quoi? quand je dis: 'Nicole, apportez-moi mes pantoufles, et me donnez mon bonnet de nuit', c'est de la prose?*
MAÎTRE DE PHILOSOPHIE: *Oui, Monsieur.*
M. JOURDAIN: *Par ma foi! il y a plus de quarante ans que je dis de la prose sans que j'en susse rien.*
M. JOURDAIN: What? when I say: 'Nicole, bring me my slippers, and give me my night-cap,' is that prose?
PHILOSOPHY TEACHER: Yes, Sir.
M. JOURDAIN: Good heavens! For more than forty years I have been speaking prose without knowing it.
Le Bourgeois Gentilhomme (1671) act 2, sc. 4

1 *Ah, la belle chose que de savoir quelque chose.*
Ah, it's a lovely thing, to know a thing or two.
Le Bourgeois Gentilhomme (1671) act 2, sc. 4

2 *C'est une étrange entreprise que celle de faire rire les honnêtes gens.*
It's an odd job, making decent people laugh.
La Critique de l'école des femmes (1663) sc. 6

3 *Je voudrais bien savoir si la grande règle de toutes les règles n'est pas de plaire.*
I shouldn't be surprised if the greatest rule of all weren't to give pleasure.
La Critique de l'école des femmes (1663) sc. 6

4 *On ne meurt qu'une fois, et c'est pour si longtemps!*
One dies only once, and it's for such a long time!
Le Dépit amoureux (performed 1656, published 1662) act 5, sc. 3

5 *Qui vit sans tabac n'est pas digne de vivre.*
He who lives without tobacco is not worthy to live.
Don Juan (performed 1665) act 1, sc. 1

6 *Je vis de bonne soupe et non de beau langage.*
It's good food and not fine words that keeps me alive.
Les Femmes savantes (1672) act 2, sc. 7

7 *Guenille, si l'on veut: ma guenille m'est chère.*
Rags and tatters, if you like: I am fond of my rags and tatters.
Les Femmes savantes (1672) act 2, sc. 7

8 *Un sot savant est sot plus qu'un sot ignorant.*
A knowledgeable fool is a greater fool than an ignorant fool.
Les Femmes savantes (1672) act 4, sc. 3

9 *Les livres cadrent mal avec le mariage.*
Reading and marriage don't go well together.
Les Femmes savantes (1672) act 5, sc. 3

10 *Que diable allait-il faire dans cette galère?*
What the devil was he doing in that galley?
Les Fourberies de Scapin (1671) act 2, sc. 11

11 *Vous l'avez voulu, Georges Dandin, vous l'avez voulu.*
You've asked for it, Georges Dandin, you've asked for it.
Georges Dandin (1668) act 1, sc. 9

12 GÉRONTE: *Il me semble que vous les placez autrement qu'ils ne sont: que le coeur est du côté gauche, et le foie du côté droit.*
SGANARELLE: *Oui, cela était autrefois ainsi, mais nous avons changé tout cela, et nous faisons maintenant la médecine d'une méthode toute nouvelle.*
GÉRONTE: It seems to me you are locating them wrongly: the heart is on the left and the liver is on the right.
SGANARELLE: Yes, in the old days that was so, but we have changed all that, and we now practise medicine by a completely new method.
Le Médecin malgré lui (1667) act 2, sc. 4

13 *Il faut, parmi le monde, une vertu traitable.*
What's needed in this world is an accommodating sort of virtue.
Le Misanthrope (1666) act 1, sc. 1

14 *Et c'est une folie à nulle autre seconde,*
De vouloir se mêler de corriger le monde.
Of all human follies there's none could be greater
Than trying to render our fellow-men better.
Le Misanthrope (1666) act 1, sc. 1

15 *On doit se regarder soi-même, un fort long temps,*
Avant que de songer à condamner les gens.
One should look long and carefully at oneself before one considers judging others.
Le Misanthrope (1666) act 3, sc. 4

16 *C'est un homme expéditif, qui aime à dépêcher ses malades; et quand on a à mourir, cela se fait avec lui le plus vite du monde.*
He's an expeditious man, who likes to hurry his patients along; and when you have to die, he sees to that quicker than anyone.
Monsieur de Pourceaugnac (1670) act 1, sc. 5

17 *Ils commencent ici par faire pendre un homme et puis ils lui font son procès.*
Here [in Paris] they hang a man first, and try him afterwards.
Monsieur de Pourceaugnac (1670) act 1, sc. 5

18 *Je te dis que le marriage est une chose sainte et sacrée: et que c'est faire en honnêtes gens, que de débuter par là.*
I tell you that marriage is holy and sacred, and to start out by getting married is to behave in a proper fashion.
Les Précieuses Ridicules (1659) sc. 4

19 *Les gens de qualité savent tout sans avoir jamais rien appris.*
People of quality know everything without ever having been taught anything.
Les Précieuses ridicules (1660) sc. 9

20 *Assassiner c'est le plus court chemin.*
Assassination is the quickest way.
Le Sicilien (1668) sc. 12

21 *Ah, pour être dévot, je n'en suis pas moins homme.*
I am not the less human for being devout.
Le Tartuffe (performed 1664, published 1669) act 3, sc. 3

22 *On est aisement dupé par ce qu'on aime.*
One is easily fooled by that which one loves.
Le Tartuffe (1669) act 4, sc. 3

23 *Le ciel défend, de vrai, certains contentements,*
Mais on trouve avec lui des accommodements.
God, it is true, does some delights condemn,
But 'tis not hard to come to terms with Him.
Le Tartuffe (1669) act 4, sc. 5

24 *Le scandale du monde est ce qui fait l'offense,*
Et ce n'est pas pécher que pécher en silence.
It is public scandal that constitutes offence, and to sin in secret is not to sin at all.
Le Tartuffe (1669) act 4, sc. 5

1 *Les envieux mourrount, mais non jamais l'envie.*
The envious may die, but envy, never.
Le Tartuffe (1669) act 5, sc. 3

2 *L'homme est, je vous l'avoue, un méchant animal.*
Man, I can assure you, is a nasty creature.
Le Tartuffe (1669) act 5, sc. 6

3 *Il m'est permis de reprendre mon bien où je le trouve.*
It is permitted me to take good fortune where I
find it.
in J. L. Le Gallois *La Vie de Molière* (1704) p. 14

Mary Mollineux (née Southworth) 1651–95
English Quaker and poet

4 How sweet is harmless solitude!
What can its joys control?
Tumults and noise may not intrude,
To interrupt the soul.
'Solitude' (1670)

Helmuth von Moltke 1800–91
Prussian military commander. On Moltke: see **BAGEHOT**
50:14

5 No plan of operations reaches with any
certainty beyond the first encounter with the
enemy's main force.
Kriegsgechichtiche Einzelschriften (1880); see **MISQUOTATIONS**
548:12

6 Strategy is a system of expedients; it is more
than a mere scholarly discipline.
D. J. Hughes (ed.) *Moltke on the Art of War* (1993) ch. 3

7 Everlasting peace is a dream, and not even a
pleasant one; and war is a necessary part of
God's arrangement of the world ... Without
war the world would deteriorate into
materialism.
letter to Dr J. K. Bluntschli, 11 December 1880 (translated by
Mary Herms), in *Helmuth von Moltke as a Correspondent* (1893)

Walter Mondale 1928–
American Democratic politician

8 When I hear your new ideas I'm reminded of
that ad, 'Where's the beef?'
in a televised debate with Gary Hart, 11 March 1984; see
ADVERTISING SLOGANS 8:28

Piet Mondrian 1872–1944
Dutch painter

9 The essence of painting has actually always been
to make it [the universal] plastically perceptible
through colour and line.
'Natural Reality and Abstract Reality' (written 1919)

10 In order to approach the spiritual in art, one
employs reality as little as possible ... This
explains logically why primary forms are
employed. Since these forms are abstract, an
abstract art comes into being.
Sketchbook II (1914)

James, Duke of Monmouth 1649–85
English illegitimate son of **CHARLES II**; leader of the failed
Monmouth rebellion against James II

11 Do not hack me as you did my Lord Russell.
to his executioner
T. B. Macaulay *History of England* vol. 1 (1849) ch. 5

Jean Monnet 1888–1979
French economist and diplomat; founder of the European
Community

12 Europe has never existed. It is not the addition
of national sovereignties in a conclave which
creates an entity. One must genuinely *create*
Europe.
Anthony Sampson *The New Europeans* (1968)

13 We should not create a nation Europe instead of
a nation France.
François Duchêne *Jean Monnet* (1994)

James Monroe 1758–1831
American Democratic Republican statesman, 5th President
of the US 1817–25

14 We owe it ... to the amicable relations existing
between the United States and those [European]
powers to declare that we should consider any
attempt on their part to extend their system to
any portion of this hemisphere as dangerous to
our peace and safety.
principle that became known as the 'Monroe Doctrine'
annual message to Congress, 2 December 1823

15 The American continents ... are henceforth not
to be considered as subjects for future
colonization by any European powers.
annual message to Congress, 2 December 1823

16 The Navy is the arm from which our
Government will always derive most aid in
support of our neutral rights. Every power
engaged in war will know the strength of our
naval force, the number of our ships of each
class, their condition, and the promptitude with
which we may bring them into service, and will
pay due consideration to that argument.
message to Congress, 30 January 1824, in *Writings* vol. 7
(1903)

Marilyn Monroe 1926–62
American actress. On Monroe: see **JOHN AND TAUPIN** 434:5,
MAILER 516:8, **NEWSPAPER HEADLINES AND LEADERS** 573:7

17 *when asked if she really had nothing on in a calendar
photograph:*
I had the radio on.
in *Time* 11 August 1952

18 *on being asked what she wore in bed:*
Chanel No. 5.
Pete Martin *Marilyn Monroe* (1956)

John Samuel Bewley Monsell 1811–75
Irish-born clergyman

1 Fight the good fight with all thy might.
'The Fight for Faith' (1863 hymn); see **BIBLE** 115:24

2 O worship the Lord in the beauty of holiness,
Bow down before him, his glory proclaim;
With gold of obedience and incense of
   lowliness,
Kneel and adore him: the Lord is his name.
'O Worship the Lord' (1863 hymn)

Lady Mary Wortley Montagu
1689–1762

English poet and letter-writer

3 But the fruit that can fall without shaking,
Indeed is too mellow for me.
'Answered, for Lord William Hamilton' in J. Dodsley (ed.) *A Collection of Poems* vol. 6 (1758)

4 Let this great maxim be my virtue's guide:
In part she is to blame, who has been tried,
He comes too near, that comes to be denied.
The Plain Dealer (27 April 1724) 'The Resolve'

5 And we meet with champagne and a chicken at
last.
Six Town Eclogues (1747) 'The Lover' l. 25

6 As Ovid has sweetly in parable told,
We harden like trees, and like rivers grow cold.
Six Town Eclogues (1747) 'The Lover' l. 47

7 In chains and darkness, wherefore should I stay,
And mourn in prison, while I keep the key?
'Verses on Self-Murder' in *The London Magazine* (1749)

8 General notions are generally wrong.
letter to her husband Edward Wortley Montagu, 28 March 1710, in Robert Halsband (ed.) *Complete Letters of Lady Mary Wortley Montagu* (1965) vol. 1

9 Men are vile inconstant toads.
letter to Anne Justice, c. 12 June 1710, in *Selected Letters* (1997)

10 Civility costs nothing and buys everything.
letter to her daughter Lady Bute, 30 May 1756, in Robert Halsband (ed.) *Complete Letters of Lady Mary Wortley Montagu* (1967) vol. 3

11 I have too much indulged my sedentary humour
and have been a rake in reading.
letter to her daughter Lady Bute, 11 April 1759, in Robert Halsband (ed.) *Complete Letters of Lady Mary Wortley Montagu* (1967) vol. 3

12 This world consists of men, women, and
Herveys.
'Herveys' being a reference to Lord **HERVEY**
attributed by Lord Wharncliffe in *Letters and Works of Lady Mary Wortley Montagu* (1837) vol. 1

13 People wish their enemies dead—but I do not; I
say give them the gout, give them the stone!
W. S. Lewis et al. (eds.) *Horace Walpole's Correspondence* (1973) vol. 35

C. E. Montague 1867–1928
English writer

14 War hath no fury like a non-combatant.
Disenchantment (1922) ch. 16

John Montague 1929–
Irish poet and writer

15   To grow
a second tongue, as
harsh a humiliation
as twice to be born.
'A Grafted Tongue' (1972)

16 Like dolmens round my childhood, the old
people.
'Like Dolmens Round my Childhood' (1972)

Montaigne (Michel Eyquem de Montaigne)
1533–92

French moralist and essayist

17 Man, a subject which is marvellously vain,
diverse, and like the waves of the sea.
Essays (1580, ed. M. Rat, 1958) bk. 1, ch. 1

18 If falsehood, like truth, had one face, we should
know better where we are, for we should then
take for certain the opposite of what the liar
tells us.
Essays (1580, ed. M. Rat, 1958) bk. 1, ch. 9

19 To make judgements about great and lofty
things, a soul of the same stature is needed;
otherwise we ascribe to them that vice which is
our own.
Essays (1580, ed. M. Rat, 1958) bk. 1, ch. 14

20 The thing I fear most is fear.
Essays (1580, ed. M. Rat, 1958) bk. 1, ch. 18; see **ROOSEVELT** 667:4

21 One should always have one's boots on, and be
ready to leave.
Essays (1580, ed. M. Rat, 1958) bk. 1, ch. 20; see **LA FONTAINE** 475:16

22 I want death to find me planting my cabbages,
but caring little for it, and even less about the
imperfections of my garden.
Essays (1580, ed. M. Rat, 1958) bk. 1, ch. 20

23 The ceaseless labour of your life is to build the
house of death.
Essays (1580, ed. M. Rat, 1958) bk. 1, ch. 20

24 The value of life lies not in the length of days
but in the use you make of them; he has lived
for a long time who has little lived. Whether
you have lived enough depends not on the
number of your years but on your will.
Essays (1580, ed. M. Rat, 1958) bk. 1, ch. 20

25 It should be noted that children at play are not
playing about; their games should be seen as
their most serious-minded activity.
Essays (1580, ed. M. Rat, 1958) bk. 1, ch. 23

26 Bees ransack flowers here and there, but then
they make honey, which is entirely theirs: it is
no longer thyme or marjoram. Similarly a boy
will transform and mix his borrowings.
Essays (1580, ed. M. Rat, 1958) bk. 1 ch. 26

1 If I am pressed to say why I loved him, I feel it can only be explained by replying: 'Because it was he; because it was me.'
of his friend Étienne de la Boétie
Essays (1580, ed. M. Rat, 1958) bk. 1, ch. 28

2 Everyone calls barbarism what is not customary to him.
Essays (1580, ed. M. Rat, 1958) bk. 1, ch. 31

3 The worth and value of a man is in his heart and his will; there lies his real honour. Valour is the strength, not of legs and arms, but of heart and soul.
Essays (1580, ed. M. Rat, 1958) bk. 1, ch. 31

4 There are some defeats more triumphant than victories.
Essays (1580, ed. M. Rat, 1958) bk. 1, ch. 31

5 Nothing is so firmly believed as that which we least know.
Essays (1580, ed. M. Rat, 1958) bk. 1, ch. 32

6 There is scarcely any less bother in the running of a family than in that of an entire state. And domestic business is no less importunate for being less important.
Essays (1580, ed. M. Rat, 1958) bk. 1, ch. 39

7 A man should keep for himself a little back shop, all his own, quite unadulterated, in which he establishes his true freedom and chief place of seclusion and solitude.
Essays (1580, ed. M. Rat, 1958) bk. 1, ch. 39

8 The greatest thing in the world is to know how to be oneself.
Essays (1580, ed. M. Rat, 1958) bk. 1, ch. 39

9 Fame and tranquillity can never be bedfellows.
Essays (1580, ed. M. Rat, 1958) bk. 1, ch. 39

10 Tortures are a dangerous invention, and seem to be a test of endurance rather than of truth.
Essays (1580, ed. M. Rat, 1958) bk. 2, ch. 5

11 *Mon métier et mon art c'est vivre.*
Living is my job and my art.
Essays (1580, ed. M. Rat, 1958) bk. 2, ch. 6

12 Virtue shuns ease as a companion . . . It demands a rough and thorny path.
Essays (1580, ed. M. Rat, 1958) bk. 2, ch. 11

13 Our religion is made so as to wipe out vices; it covers them up, nourishes them, incites them.
Essays (1580, ed. M. Rat, 1958) bk. 2, ch. 12

14 When I play with my cat, who knows whether she isn't amusing herself with me more than I am with her?
Essays (1580, ed. M. Rat, 1958) bk. 2, ch. 12

15 *Que sais-je?*
What do I know?
on the position of the sceptic
Essays (1580, ed. M. Rat, 1958) bk. 2, ch. 12

16 Man is quite insane. He wouldn't know how to create a maggot, and he creates gods by the dozen.
Essays (1580, ed. M. Rat, 1958) bk. 2, ch. 12

17 Those who have likened our life to a dream were more right, by chance, than they realised. We are awake while sleeping, and waking sleep.
Essays (1580, ed. M. Rat, 1958) bk. 2, ch. 12

18 The diversity of human events offers us infinite examples in all sorts of forms.
Essays (1580, ed. M. Rat, 1958) bk. 2, ch. 17

19 Pleasure chews and grinds us.
Essays (1580, ed. M. Rat, 1958) bk. 2, ch. 20

20 There never were in the world two opinions alike, no more than two hairs or two grains; the most universal quality is diversity.
Essays (1580, ed. M. Rat, 1958) bk. 2, ch. 37

21 Every man carries the entire form of the human condition.
Essays (1580, ed. M. Rat, 1958) bk. 3, ch. 2

22 Is it reasonable that even the arts should take advantage of and profit by our natural stupitidy and feebleness of mind?
Essays (1580, ed. M. Rat, 1958) bk. 3, ch. 4

23 Every man's ordure well to his own sense doth smell.
Essays (1580, ed. M. Rat, 1958) bk. 3, ch. 8, Florio's translation of 1603

24 There is no man, good as he may be, who, if all his thoughts and actions were submitted to the scrutiny of the laws, would not deserve hanging ten times in his life.
Essays (1580, ed. M. Rat, 1958) bk. 3, ch. 9

25 It could be said of me that in this book I have only made up a bunch of other men's flowers, providing of my own only the string that ties them together.
Essays (1580, ed. M. Rat, 1958) bk. 3, ch. 12

26 There is more business in interpreting interpretations than in interpreting things, and more books on books than on any other subject: all we do is gloss each other. All is a-swarm with commentaries: of authors there is a dearth.
Essays (1580, ed. M. Rat, 1958) bk. 3, ch. 13; see **DERRIDA** 274:5

Eugenio Montale 1896–1981

Italian poet

27 *Portami il girasole impazzito di luce.*
Bring me the sunflower, crazed with the love of light.
'Bring me the sunflower' (1925) tr. J. Galassi

28 *Felicità raggiunta, si cammina*
per te sul fil de lama.
Agli occhi sei barlume che vacilla
al piede, teso ghiaccio che s'incrina;
e dunque non ti tocchi chi piu t'ama.
Happiness, for you we walk on a knife edge. To the eyes you are a flickering light, to the feet, thin ice that cracks; and so may no one touch you who loves you.
'Felicità raggiunta' (1925)

Montesquieu (Charles-Louis de Secondat)
1689–1755
French political philosopher

1 *Ce corps malade ne se soutient pas par un régime doux et tempéré, mais par des remèdes violents, qu'il épuisent et le minent sans cesse.*

That huge distempered body does not support itself by a mild and temperate regimen; but by violent remedies, which are incessantly corroding and exhausting its strength.

of the Ottoman empire; see **NICHOLAS I** 574:15
Lettres Persanes (1721) no. 19 (translated by J. Ozell, 1722)

2 *Il faut pleurer les hommes à leur naissance, et non pas à leur mort.*

Men should be bewailed at their birth, and not at their death.

Lettres Persanes (1721) no. 40 (translated by J. Ozell, 1722)

3 *Si les triangles faisoient un Dieu, ils lui donneroient trois côtés.*

If the triangles were to make a God they would give him three sides.

Lettres Persanes (1721) no. 59 (translated by J. Ozell, 1722)

4 *Le succès de la plupart des choses dépend de bien savoir combien il faut de temps pour réussir.*

In most things success depends on knowing how long it takes to succeed.

Pensées et fragments inédits . . . vol. 1 (1901) no. 630

5 *Les grands seigneurs ont des plaisirs, le peuple a de la joie.*

Great lords have their pleasures, but the people have fun.

Pensées et fragments inédits . . . vol. 2 (1901) no. 992

6 *Les Anglais sont occupés; ils n'ont pas le temps d'être polis.*

The English are busy; they don't have time to be polite.

Pensées et fragments inédits . . . vol. 2 (1901) no. 1428

7 Happy the people whose annals are blank in history-books!

attributed to Montesquieu by Thomas Carlyle in *History of Frederick the Great* (1858–65) bk. 16, ch. 1; see **ELIOT** 308:7, **PROVERBS** 633:43

Lord Montgomery of Alamein
1887–1976
British field marshal. On Montgomery: see **CHURCHILL** **230:14**

8 *Here* we will stand and fight; there will be no further withdrawal. I have ordered that all plans and instructions dealing with further withdrawal are to be burnt, and at once. We will stand and fight *here*. If we can't stay here alive, then let us stay here dead.

speech in Cairo, 13 August 1942

9 Rule 1, on page 1 of the book of war, is: 'Do not march on Moscow' . . . [Rule 2] is: 'Do not go fighting with your land armies in China.'

speech in the House of Lords, 30 May 1962

Robert Montgomery 1807–55
English clergyman and poet

10 The solitary monk who shook the world.

Luther: a Poem (1842) ch. 3 'Man's Need and God's Supply'

11 And thou, vast ocean! on whose awful face Time's iron feet can print no ruin-trace.

The Omnipresence of the Deity (1830 ed.) pt. 1, l. 105

Casimir, Comte de Montrond
1768–1843
French diplomat

12 Have no truck with first impulses for they are always generous ones.

attributed, in Comte J. d'Estourmel *Derniers Souvenirs* (1860), where the alternative attribution to Talleyrand is denied; see **CORNEILLE** 251:15

13 If something pleasant happens to you, don't forget to tell it to your friends, to make them feel bad.

attributed, in Comte J. d'Estourmel *Derniers Souvenirs* (1860) p. 319

James Graham, Marquess of Montrose 1612–50
Scottish royalist general and poet

14 Let them bestow on every airth a limb.

'Lines written on the Window of his Jail the Night before his Execution'

15 He either fears his fate too much,
Or his deserts are small,
That puts it not unto the touch
To win or lose it all.

'My Dear and Only Love' (written c.1642)

16 But if thou wilt be constant then,
And faithful of thy word,
I'll make thee glorious by my pen,
And famous by my sword.

'My Dear and Only Love' (written c.1642)

Percy Montrose
American songwriter

17 In a cavern, in a canyon,
Excavating for a mine,
Dwelt a miner, Forty-niner,
And his daughter, Clementine.
Oh, my darling, oh my darling, oh my darling Clementine!
Thou art lost and gone for ever, dreadful sorry, Clementine.

'Clementine' (1884 song)

Monty Python's Flying Circus 1969–74
BBC TV programme, written by Graham Chapman (1941–89), John Cleese (1939–), Terry Gilliam (1940–), Eric Idle (1943–), Terry Jones (1942–), and Michael Palin (1943–). See also CATCHPHRASES 207:3, FILM LINES 329:23

18 Your wife interested in . . . *photographs*? Eh? Know what I mean—*photographs*? He asked him

knowingly . . . nudge nudge, snap snap, grin grin, wink wink, say no more.
Monty Python's Flying Circus (1969)

1 It's *not* pining—it's passed on! This parrot is no more! It has ceased to be! It's expired and gone to meet its maker! This is a late parrot! It's a stiff! Bereft of life it rests in peace—if you hadn't nailed it to the perch it would be pushing up the daisies! It's rung down the curtain and joined the choir invisible! THIS IS AN EX–PARROT!
Monty Python's Flying Circus (1969)

2 Nobody expects the Spanish Inquisition!
Monty Python's Flying Circus (1970)

Clement C. Moore 1779–1863
American writer

3 'Twas the night before Christmas, when all through the house
Not a creature was stirring, not even a mouse;
The stockings were hung by the chimney with care,
In hopes that St Nicholas soon would be there.
'A Visit from St Nicholas' (December 1823)

Edward Moore 1712–57
English dramatist

4 This is adding insult to injuries.
The Foundling (1748) act 5, sc. 5

5 I am rich beyond the dreams of avarice.
The Gamester (1753) act 2, sc. 2; see **JOHNSON** 443:5

George Moore 1852–1933
Irish novelist

6 A man travels the world in search of what he needs and returns home to find it.
The Brook Kerith (1916) ch. 11

Henry Moore 1898–1986
English sculptor and draughtsman

7 Sculpture in stone should look honestly like stone . . . to make it look like flesh and blood, hair and dimples is coming down to the level of the stage conjuror.
in *Architectural Association Journal* May 1930

8 The first hole made through a piece of stone is a revelation.
in *Listener* 18 August 1937

9 Sculpture is an art of the open air. Daylight, *sunlight*, is necessary to it, and for me its best setting and complement is nature. I would rather have a piece of my sculpture put in a landscape, almost any landscape, than in, or on, the most beautiful building I know.
A. D. B. Sylvester *Sculpture and Drawings by Henry Moore* (1951)

10 The secret of life is to have a task, something you devote your entire life to, something you bring everything to, every minute of the day for your whole life. And the most important thing is—it must be something you cannot possibly do!
attributed, in Donald Hall *Henry Moore* (1966) introduction

Jo Moore
British government adviser

11 It is now a very good day to get out anything we want to bury.
email sent in the aftermath of the terrorist action in America, 11 September 2001
in *Daily Telegraph* 10 October 2001; see also **MISQUOTATIONS** 547:17

Marianne Moore 1887–1972
American poet

12 She says 'Men are monopolists
of "stars, garters, buttons
and other shining baubles"—
unfit to be the guardians
of another person's happiness.'
'Marriage' (1935), referring to Miss M. Carey Thomas 'Men practically reserve for themselves stately funerals, splendid monuments, memorial statues, titles, honorary degrees, stars, garters, ribbons, buttons and other shining baubles, so valueless in themselves and yet so infinitely desirable because they are symbols of recognition by their fellow-craftsmen of difficult work well done', Founder's address, Mount Holyoke, 1921

13   O to be a dragon,
a symbol of the power of Heaven—of silkworm size or immense; at times invisible.
Felicitous phenomenon!
'O To Be a Dragon' (1959)

14 I, too, dislike it: there are things that are important beyond all this fiddle.
Reading it, however, with a perfect contempt for it, one discovers in it, after all, a place for the genuine.
'Poetry' (1935)

15 Imaginary gardens with real toads in them.
'Poetry' (1935)

16 My father used to say,
'Superior people never make long visits,
have to be shown Longfellow's grave
or the glass flowers at Harvard.'
'Silence' (1935)

17 Nor was he insincere in saying, 'Make my house your inn.'
Inns are not residences.
'Silence' (1935)

18 The passion for setting people right is in itself an afflictive disease.
Distaste which takes no credit to itself is best.
'Snakes, Mongooses. Snake-Charmers, and the Like' (1935)

19 I am troubled, I'm dissatisfied, I'm Irish.
'Spenser's Ireland' (1941)

20   It is a privilege to see so much confusion.
'The Steeple-Jack' (1935)

1 Omissions are not accidents.
   Complete Poems (1967) epigraph

2 I never knew anyone who had a passion for
   words who had as much difficulty in saying
   things as I do. I very seldom say them in a
   manner I like. If I do it's because I don't know
   I'm trying.
   George Plimpton (ed.) *The Writer's Chapbook* (1989)

Sturge Moore 1870–1944

English poet and engraver. On Moore: see GOSSE 366:13

3 Then, cleaving the grass, gazelles appear
   (The gentler dolphins of kindlier waves)
   With sensitive heads alert of ear;
   Frail crowds that a delicate hearing saves.
   'The Gazelles' (1904)

Thomas Moore 1779–1852

Irish musician and songwriter

4 Yet, who can help loving the land that has
      taught us
   Six hundred and eighty-five ways to dress eggs?
   The Fudge Family in Paris (1818) Letter 8, l. 64

5 Though an angel should write, still 'tis *devils*
   must print.
   The Fudges in England (1835) Letter 3, l. 65

6 Believe me, if all those endearing young charms,
   Which I gaze on so fondly today,
   Were to change by tomorrow, and fleet in my
      arms,
   Like fairy gifts fading away!
   Irish Melodies (1807) 'Believe me, if all those endearing young
   charms'

7 'Twas from Kathleen's eyes he flew,
   Eyes of most unholy blue!
   Irish Melodies (1807) 'By that Lake'

8 You may break, you may shatter the vase, if you
   will,
   But the scent of the roses will hang round it
   still.
   Irish Melodies (1807) 'Farewell!—but whenever'

9 The harp that once through Tara's halls
   The soul of music shed,
   Now hangs as mute on Tara's walls
   As if that soul were fled.
   Irish Melodies (1807) 'The harp that once through Tara's halls'

10 No, there's nothing half so sweet in life
   As love's young dream.
   Irish Melodies (1807) 'Love's Young Dream'

11 The Minstrel Boy to the war is gone,
   In the ranks of death you'll find him;
   His father's sword he has girded on,
   And his wild harp slung behind him.
   Irish Melodies (1807) 'The Minstrel Boy'

12 Oh! breathe not his name, let it sleep in the
   shade,
   Where cold and unhonoured his relics are laid.
   of Robert EMMET
   Irish Melodies (1807) 'Oh! breathe not his name'

13 'Tis the last rose of summer
   Left blooming alone;
   All her lovely companions
   Are faded and gone.
   Irish Melodies (1807) ''Tis the last rose of summer'

14 I never nursed a dear gazelle,
   To glad me with its soft black eye,
   But when it came to know me well,
   And love me, it was sure to die!
   Lalla Rookh (1817) 'The Fire-Worshippers' pt. 1, l. 283; see
   CARROLL 204:5, DICKENS 279:24, PAYN 600:9

15 Like Dead Sea fruits, that tempt the eye,
   But turn to ashes on the lips!
   Lalla Rookh (1817) 'The Fire-Worshippers' pt. 2, l. 484

16 Oft, in the stilly night,
   Ere Slumber's chain has bound me,
   Fond Memory brings the light
   Of other days around me.
   National Airs (1815) 'Oft in the Stilly Night'

Thomas Osbert Mordaunt 1730–1809

British soldier

17 One crowded hour of glorious life
   Is worth an age without a name.
   'A Poem, said to be written by Major Mordaunt during the
   last German War', in *The Bee, or Literary Weekly Intelligencer* 12
   October 1791

Hannah More 1745–1833

English writer of tracts

18 For you'll ne'er mend your fortunes, nor help
   the just cause,
   By breaking of windows, or breaking of laws.
   'An Address to the Meeting in Spa Fields' (1817) in H.
   Thompson *Life of Hannah More* (1838) appendix, no. 7; see
   PANKHURST 595:15

19 He liked those literary cooks
   Who skim the cream of others' books;
   And ruin half an author's graces
   By plucking bon-mots from their places.
   Florio (1786) pt. 1, l. 123

20   Did not God
   Sometimes withhold in mercy what we ask,
   We should be ruined at our own request.
   Moses in the Bulrushes (1782) pt. 1, l. 35

21 Whether we consider the manual industry of
   the poor, or the intellectual exertions of the
   superior classes, we shall find that diligent
   occupation, if not criminally perverted from its
   purposes, is at once the instrument of virtue
   and the secret of happiness. Man cannot be
   safely trusted with a life of leisure.
   Christian Morals (1813) vol. 2, ch. 23

22 The prevailing manners of an age depend more
   than we are aware, or are willing to allow, on
   the conduct of the women; this is one of the
   principal hinges on which the great machine of
   human society turns.
   Essays on Various Subjects . . . for Young Ladies (1777) 'On
   Dissipation'

1 How much it is to be regretted, that the British ladies should ever sit down contented to polish, when they are able to reform; to entertain, when they might instruct; and to dazzle for an hour, when they are candidates for eternity!

Essays on Various Subjects . . . for Young Ladies (1777) 'On Dissipation'

2 It is humbling to reflect, that in those countries in which the fondness for the mere persons of women is carried to the highest excess, they are slaves; and that their moral and intellectual degradation increases in direct proportion to the adoration which is paid to mere external charms.

Strictures on the Modern System of Female Education (1799) vol. 1, ch. 1

Thomas More 1478–1535

English scholar and saint; Lord Chancellor of England, 1529-32. On More: see ERASMUS 316:19, WHITTINGTON 853:5

3 Your sheep, that were wont to be so meek and tame, and so small eaters, now, as I hear say, be become so great devourers, and so wild, that they eat up and swallow down the very men themselves.

Utopia (1516) bk. 1

4 They define virtue as living according to nature; and God, they say, created us to that end. When an individual obeys the dictates of reason in choosing one thing and avoiding another, he is following nature.

Utopia (1516) bk. 2

5 Anyone who campaigns for public office becomes disqualified for holding any office at all.

Utopia (1516) bk. 2

6 Son Roper, I may tell thee I have no cause to be proud thereof [the King having entertained him at Chelsea], for if my head could wish him a castle in France it should not fail to go.

of HENRY VIII

William Roper *Life of Sir Thomas More*

7 We may not look at our pleasure to go to heaven in feather-beds; it is not the way.

William Roper *Life of Sir Thomas More*

8 If the parties will at my hands call for justice, then, all were it my father stood on the one side, and the Devil on the other, his cause being good, the Devil should have right.

William Roper *Life of Sir Thomas More*

9 In good faith, I rejoiced, son, that I had given the devil a foul fall, and that with those Lords I had gone so far, as without great shame I could never go back again.

William Roper *Life of Sir Thomas More*

10 'By god's body, master More, *Indignatio principis mors est* [The anger of the sovereign is death].' 'Is that all, my Lord?' quoth he [to the Duke of Norfolk]. 'Then in good faith is there no more difference between your grace and me, but that I shall die to-day, and you to-morrow.'

William Roper *Life of Sir Thomas More*

11 Son Roper, I thank our Lord the field is won.

William Roper *Life of Sir Thomas More*

12 Is not this house as nigh heaven as my own?

of the Tower of London

William Roper *Life of Sir Thomas More*

13 I cumber you good Margaret much, but I would be sorry, if it should be any longer than tomorrow, for it is S. Thomas even and the vtas of Saint Peter and therefore tomorrow long I to go to God, it were a day very meet and convenient for me. I never liked your manner toward me better than when you kissed me last for I love when daughterly love and dear charity hath no leisure to look to worldly courtesy. Fare well my dear child and pray for me, and I shall for you and all your friends that we may merrily meet in heaven.

vtas = *octave*

last letter to his daughter Margaret Roper, 5 July 1535, on the eve of his execution, in E. F. Rogers (ed.) *Correspondence of Sir Thomas More* (1947)

14 I pray you, master Lieutenant, see me safe up, and my coming down let me shift for my self.

of mounting the scaffold

William Roper *Life of Sir Thomas More*

15 Pluck up thy spirits, man, and be not afraid to do thine office; my neck is very short; take heed therefore thou strike not awry, for saving of thine honesty.

words addressed to the executioner; William Roper *Life of Sir Thomas More*

16 This hath not offended the king.

last words, lifting his beard aside after laying his head on the block

Francis Bacon *Apophthegms New and Old* (1625) no. 22

Thomas Morell 1703–84

English librettist

17 See, the conquering hero comes! Sound the trumpets, beat the drums!

Judas Maccabeus (1747) 'A chorus of youths' and *Joshua* (1748) pt. 3 (to music by Handel)

Morelly fl. 1755

French writer

18 *Tout Citoyen contribuera pour sa part à l'utilité publique selon ses forces, ses talens et son âge; c'est sur cela que seront réglés ses devoirs, conformément aux loix distributives.*

Every citizen will make his own contribution to the activities of the community according to his strength, his talent, and his age: it is on this basis that his duties will be determined, conforming with the distributive laws.

Code de la Nature (1755) pt. 4; see BLANC 128:16, MARX 526:5

Robin Morgan 1941–
American feminist

1 Sisterhood is powerful.
   title of book (1970)

Christopher Morley 1890–1957
American writer

2 Life is a foreign language: all men mispronounce it.
   Thunder on the Left (1925) ch. 14; see **HARTLEY** 383:20

Lord Morley 1838–1923
British Liberal politician and writer

3 The golden Gospel of Silence is effectively compressed in thirty fine volumes.
   on **CARLYLE**'s History of Frederick the Great (*1858–65*), Carlyle having written of his subject as 'that strong, silent man'
   Critical Miscellanies (1886) 'Carlyle'

4 You have not converted a man, because you have silenced him.
   On Compromise (1874) ch. 5

Countess Morphy (Marcelle Azra Forbes)
fl. 1930–50

5 The tragedy of English cooking is that 'plain' cooking cannot be entrusted to 'plain' cooks.
   English Recipes (1935)

James Morrill 1824–65
British sailor shipwrecked off the Great Barrier Reef in 1846, and adopted into an Aboriginal tribe

6 Don't shoot, mates, I'm a British object!
   finding a white community after 17 years, 25 January 1863, in *Australian Dictionary of Biography* online edition; see **MALOUF** 518:6

Charles Morris 1745–1838
English songwriter

7 But a house is much more to my mind than a tree,
   And for groves, O! a good grove of chimneys for me.
   'Country and Town' (1840)

Desmond Morris 1928–
English anthropologist

8 The city is not a concrete jungle, it is a human zoo.
   The Human Zoo (1969) introduction

9 There are one hundred and ninety-three living species of monkeys and apes. One hundred and ninety-two of them are covered with hair. The exception is a naked ape self-named *Homo sapiens*.
   The Naked Ape (1967) introduction

George Pope Morris 1802–64
American poet. See also **POLITICAL SLOGANS AND SONGS** 612:23

10 Woodman, spare that tree!
   Touch not a single bough!
   In youth it sheltered me,
   And I'll protect it now.
   'Woodman, Spare That Tree' (1830); see **CAMPBELL** 195:6

William Morris 1834–96
English writer, artist, and designer

11 What is this, the sound and rumour? What is this that all men hear,
   Like the wind in hollow valleys when the storm is drawing near,
   Like the rolling on of ocean in the eventide of fear?
   'Tis the people marching on.
   Chants for Socialists (1885) 'The March of the Workers'

12 The idle singer of an empty day.
   The Earthly Paradise (1868–70) 'An Apology'

13 Dreamer of dreams, born out of my due time,
   Why should I strive to set the crooked straight?
   The Earthly Paradise (1868–70) 'An Apology'

14 Forget six counties overhung with smoke,
   Forget the snorting steam and piston stroke,
   Forget the spreading of the hideous town;
   Think rather of the pack-horse on the down,
   And dream of London, small and white and clean,
   The clear Thames bordered by its gardens green.
   The Earthly Paradise (1868–70) 'Prologue: The Wanderers' l. 1

15 Had she come all the way for this,
   To part at last without a kiss?
   Yea, had she borne the dirt and rain
   That her own eyes might see him slain
   Beside the haystack in the floods?
   'The Haystack in the Floods' (1858) l. 1

16 And ever she sung from noon to noon,
   'Two red roses across the moon.'
   'Two Red Roses across the Moon' (1858)

17 Fellowship is heaven, and lack of fellowship is hell.
   A Dream of John Ball (1888) ch. 4

18 Have nothing in your houses that you do not know to be useful, or believe to be beautiful.
   Hopes and Fears for Art (1882) 'Making the Best of It'

19 The reward of labour is life.
   News from Nowhere (1891) ch. 15

20 I spend my life ministering to the swinish luxury of the rich.
   reported by Sir Lowthian Bell to Alfred Powell, c.1877; W.R. Lethaby *Philip Webb* (1935)

Herbert Morrison 1888–1965

British Labour politician

1 Work is the call. Work at war speed. Good-night—and go to it.

broadcast as Minister of Supply, 22 May 1940, in *Daily Herald* 23 May 1940

Herbert 'Herb' Morrison d. 1989

American radio announcer

2 It's bursting into flames . . . Oh, the humanity, and all the passengers!

eyewitness account of the Hindenburg airship bursting into flames
recorded broadcast, 6 May 1937

3 Listen folks, I'm going to have to stop for a minute, because I've lost my voice—This is the worst thing I've ever witnessed.

eyewitness account of the Hindenburg disaster
recorded broadcast, 6 May 1937

Jim Morrison 1943–71

American rock singer and songwriter

4 Five to one, baby, one in five,
No one here gets out alive . . .
They got the guns but we got the numbers
Gonna win, yeah, we're taking over.

'Five to One' (1968 song)

5 C'mon, baby, light my fire.

'Light My Fire' (1967 song, with Robby Krieger)

6 What have they done to the earth?
What have they done to our fair sister?
Ravaged and plundered and ripped her and did her,
Stuck her with knives in the side of the dawn,
And tied her with fences and dragged her down.
I hear a very gentle sound,
With your ear down to the ground:
WE WANT THE WORLD AND WE WANT IT NOW!

'When the Music's Over' (1967 song)

7 I'm interested in anything about revolt, disorder, chaos, especially activity that appears to have no meaning. It seems to me to be the road toward freedom.

in *Time* 24 January 1968

8 When you make your peace with authority, you become an authority.

Andrew Doe and John Tobler *In Their Own Words: The Doors* (1988)

R. F. Morrison

9 Just a wee deoch-an-doris,
Just a wee yin, that's a'.
Just a wee deoch-an-doris,
Before we gang awa'.
There's a wee wifie waitin',
In a wee but-an-ben;
If you can say

'It's a braw bricht moonlicht nicht',
Ye're a' richt, ye ken.

'Just a Wee Deoch-an-Doris' (1911 song); popularized by Harry **LAUDER**

Toni Morrison 1931–

American novelist

10 Grab this land! Take it, hold it, my brothers, make it, my brothers, shake it, squeeze it, turn it, twist it, beat it, kick it, whip it, stomp it, dig it, plough it, seed it, reap it, rent it, buy it, sell it, own it, build it, multiply it, and pass it on—Can you hear me? Pass it on!

Song of Solomon (1977) ch. 10

11 The unending problem of growing old was not how he changed, but how things did.

Tar Baby (1981) ch. 5

Van Morrison 1945–

Irish singer, songwriter, and musician

12 Music is spiritual. The music business is not.

in *The Times* 6 July 1990

Dwight Morrow 1873–1931

American lawyer, banker, and diplomat

13 The world is divided into people who do things and people who get the credit. Try, if you can, to belong to the first class. There's far less competition.

letter to his son, in Harold Nicolson *Dwight Morrow* (1935) ch. 3

14 Any party which takes credit for the rain must not be surprised if its opponents blame it for the drought.

attributed; William Safire *Safire's New Political Dictionary* (1993)

Samuel Morse 1791–1872

American inventor

15 What hath God wrought.

the first electric telegraph message, 24 May 1844; see **BIBLE**

Wayne Lyman Morse 1900–74

American Democratic politician

16 I believe that history will record that we have made a great mistake.

in the Senate debate on the Tonkin Gulf Resolution, which committed the United States to intervention in Vietnam; Morse was the only Senator to vote against the resolution
in *Congressional Record* 6–7 August 1964

Owen Morshead 1893–1977

English librarian

17 The House of Hanover, like ducks, produce bad parents—they trample on their young.

as Royal Librarian, in conversation with Harold **NICOLSON**, *biographer of* **GEORGE V**
Harold Nicolson, letter to Vita Sackville-West, 7 January 1949

John Mortimer 1923–2009
English novelist, barrister, and dramatist

1 At school I never minded the lessons. I just resented having to work terribly hard at playing.
A Voyage Round My Father (1971) act 1

2 No brilliance is needed in the law. Nothing but common sense, and relatively clean fingernails.
A Voyage Round My Father (1971) act 1

J. B. Morton ('Beachcomber') 1893–1975
English journalist

3 One disadvantage of being a hog is that at any moment some blundering fool may try to make a silk purse out of your wife's ear.
By the Way (1931)

4 Hush, hush,
Nobody cares!
Christopher Robin
Has
Fallen
Down-
Stairs.
By the Way (1931); see **MILNE** 538:8

5 Dr Strabismus (Whom God Preserve) of Utrecht has patented a new invention. It is an illuminated trouser-clip for bicyclists who are using main roads at night.
Morton's Folly (1933)

Jelly Roll Morton 1885–1941
American jazz pianist, composer, and bandleader

6 Jazz music is to be played sweet, soft, plenty rhythm.
Mister Jelly Roll (1950)

Rogers Morton 1914–79
American public relations officer

7 I'm not going to rearrange the furniture on the deck of the Titanic.
having lost five of the last six primaries as President **FORD**'s *campaign manager*
in *Washington Post* 16 May 1976

Thomas Morton c.1764–1838
English dramatist

8 Approbation from Sir Hubert Stanley is praise indeed.
A Cure for the Heartache (1797) act 5, sc. 2; see **MISQUOTATIONS** 548:15

9 Always ding, dinging Dame Grundy into my ears—what will Mrs Grundy zay? What will Mrs Grundy think?
Speed the Plough (1798) act 1, sc. 1; see **LOCKER-LAMPSON** 498:1

Edwin Moses 1955–
American athlete and Olympic champion hurdler

10 I don't really see the hurdles. I sense them like a memory.
attributed

Andrew Motion 1952–
English poet

11 Each sudden gust of light explains itself as flames, but neither they, nor even bombs redoubled on the hills tonight can quite include me in their fear. What does remains invisible, is lost in curt societies whose deaths become revenge by morning, and whose homes are nothing more than all they pity most.
'Leaving Belfast' (1978)

12 Beside the river, swerving under ground. your future tracked you, snapping at your heels: Diana, breathless, hunted by your own quick hounds.
'Mythology' (1997)

John Lothrop Motley 1814–77
American historian

13 As long as he lived, he was the guiding-star of a whole brave nation, and when he died the little children cried in the streets.
of William of Orange (1572–84)
The Rise of the Dutch Republic (1856) pt. 6, ch. 7; see **AUDEN** 37:3

14 Give us the luxuries of life, and we will dispense with its necessities.
Oliver Wendell Holmes *Autocrat of the Breakfast-Table* (1857–8) ch. 6

Motoori Norinaga 1730–1801
Japanese scholar and poet

15 If one should ask you concerning the spirit of a true Japanese, point to the wild cherry blossom shining in the sun.
attributed

Peter Motteux *see* Cervantes 213:10

☐ Mottoes *see* box opposite

Lord Mountbatten 1900–79
British sailor, soldier, and statesman. On Mountbatten: see **ZIEGLER** 878:1

16 Right, now I understand people think you're the Forgotten Army on the Forgotten Front. I've come here to tell you you're quite wrong. You're not the Forgotten Army on the Forgotten Front. No, make no mistake about it. Nobody's ever *heard* of you.
encouragement to troops when taking over as Supreme Allied Commander South-East Asia in late 1943
R. Hough *Mountbatten* (1980)

Mottoes

1 *Ad majorem Dei gloriam.*

To the greater glory of God.
    motto of the Society of Jesus

2 *A mari usque ad mare.*

From sea unto sea.
    motto of Canada; see **BIBLE (VULGATE)** 119:28

3 *Aut Caesar, aut nihil.*

Caesar or nothing.
    motto inscribed on the sword of Cesare Borgia (1476–1507)

4 Be happy while y'er leevin,
For y'er a lang time deid.
    Scottish motto for a house
    in *Notes and Queries* 9th series, vol. 8, 7 December 1901

5 Be prepared.
    *motto of the Scout Association, based on the ititials of
    the founder, Lord Baden-Powell*
    Robert Baden-Powell *Scouting for Boys* (1908) pt. 1

6 *Cor ad cor loquitur.*

Heart speaks to heart.
    motto of John Henry **NEWMAN**; see **FRANCIS** 340:19

7 Defence, not defiance.
    motto of the Volunteers Movement (1859)

8 *Dominus illuminatio mea.*

The Lord is my light.
    motto of the University of Oxford; **BIBLE (VULGATE)** 119:25

9 *Fiat justitia et pereat mundus.*

Let justice be done, though the world perish.
    motto of Ferdinand I (1503–64), Holy Roman Emperor;
    Johannes Manlius *Locorum Communium Collectanea* (1563)
    vol. 2 'De Lege: Octatum Praeceptum'; see **WATSON** 841:8

10 *Honi soit qui mal y pense.*

Evil be to him who evil thinks.
    motto of the Order of the Garter, originated by **EDWARD
    III**, probably on 23 April of 1348 or 1349; see **SELLAR AND
    YEATMAN** 691:25

11 *Laborare est orare.*

To work is to pray.
    *also found in the form 'Ora, lege, et labora [Pray, read,
    and work]'*
    traditional motto of the Benedictine order

12 *Nemo me impune lacessit.*

No one provokes me with impunity.
    motto of the Crown of Scotland and of all Scottish
    regiments

13 *Nisi Dominus frustra.*

In vain without the Lord.
    motto of the city of Edinburgh; see **BIBLE (VULGATE)** 120:5

14 *Nullius in verba.*

In the word of none.
    emphasizing reliance on experiment rather than authority
    motto of the Royal Society; see **HORACE** 409:18

15 *Palmam qui meruit, ferat.*

Let him who has won it bear the palm.
    adopted by Lord **NELSON** as his motto, from John Jortin
    (1698–1770) *Lusus Poetici* (3rd ed., 1748) 'Ad Ventos'

16 *Per ardua ad astra.*

Through struggle to the stars.
    motto of the Mulvany family, quoted and translated by
    Rider **HAGGARD** in *The People of the Mist* (1894) ch. 1; still in
    use as motto of the R.A.F., having been proposed by J. S.
    Yule in 1912 and approved by King **GEORGE V** in 1913

17 Rebellion to tyrants is obedience to God.
    motto of Thomas **JEFFERSON**, from John **BRADSHAW**; see
    BRADSHAW 154:9

18 *Semper eadem.*

Ever the same.
    motto of **ELIZABETH I**

19 *Sic semper tyrannis.*

Thus always to tyrants.
    motto of the State of Virginia; see **BOOTH** 150:25

20 *Similia similibus curantur.*

Like cures like.
    motto of homeopathic medicine, although not found in
    this form in the writings of C. F. S. Hahnemann (1755–1843);
    the Latin appears as an anonymous side-note in Paracelsus
    Opera Omnia (c.1490–1541, ed. 1658) vol. 1

21 They always get their man.
    unofficial motto of the Royal Canadian Mounted Police;
    attributed to John J. Healy (1840–1908), American
    newspaperman and whiskey trader, in 1877

22 They haif said: Quhat say they? Lat thame say.
    motto of the Earls Marischal of Scotland, inscribed at
    Marischal College, Aberdeen, 1593; a similarly defiant motto
    in Greek has been found engraved in remains from classical
    antiquity

23 Who dares wins.
    motto of the British Special Air Service regiment, from 1942

Wolfgang Amadeus Mozart 1756–91

Austrian composer. On Mozart: see **JOSEPH II** 447:10,
LEHRER 488:4, **SCHNABEL** 686:9

24 I am happier when I have something to
compose, for that, after all, is my sole delight
and passion.
    letter to his father Leopold, 11 October 1777; Emily Anderson
    (ed.) *Letters of Mozart and his Family* (1966) vol. 1

25 The happy medium—truth in all things—is no
longer either known or valued; to gain applause,
one must write things so inane that they may be
played on a barrel-organ, or so unintelligible that
no rational being can comprehend them, though
on that very account they are likely to please.
    letter to his father Leopold, 28 December 1782; *The Letters* (tr.
    Lady Wallace, 1865)

26 Melody is the essence of music. I compare a
good melodist to a fine racer, and counterpoints
to hack post-horses.
    remark to Michael Kelly, 1786; Michael Kelly *Reminiscences*
    (1826)

27 The whole, though it be long, stands almost
complete and finished in my mind, so that I can

survey it, like a fine picture or a beautiful statue, at a glance. Nor do I hear in my imagination the parts *successively*, but I hear them, as it were, all at once. What a delight this is I cannot tell!
on his method of composition
letter, Edward Holmes *The Life of Mozart* (1845)

Hosni Mubarak 1928–

Egyptian statesman, President since 1981

1 Instead of having one [Osama] bin Laden, we will have 100 bin Ladens.
on the probable result of a western invasion of Iraq
in *Newsweek* 14 April 2003

Robert Mugabe 1924–

African statesman, Prime Minister of Zimbabwe 1980–7, President 1987–

2 Cricket civilizes people and creates good gentlemen. I want everyone to play cricket in Zimbabwe; I want ours to be a nation of gentlemen.
in *Sunday Times* 26 February 1984

3 Blair, keep your England and let me keep my Zimbabwe.
at the Earth Summit in Johannesburg, 2 September 2002

Malcolm Muggeridge 1903–90

English journalist

4 Something beautiful for God.
title of book (1971); see **TERESA** 801:19

5 The orgasm has replaced the Cross as the focus of longing and the image of fulfilment.
Tread Softly (1966)

6 He was not only a bore; he bored for England.
of Anthony **EDEN**
Tread Softly (1966)

7 Good taste and humour . . . are a contradiction in terms, like a chaste whore.
in *Time* 14 September 1953

Edwin Muir 1887–1959

Scottish poet

8 What shall I call you? A fountain in a waste,
A well of water in a country dry,
Or anything that's honest and good, an eye
That makes the whole world bright.
'The Confirmation' (1943)

9 And without fear the lawless roads
Ran wrong through all the land.
'Hölderlin's Journey' (1937)

10 Barely a twelvemonth after
The seven days war that put the world to sleep,
Late in the evening the strange horses came.
'The Horses' (1956)

Frank Muir 1920–98

English writer and broadcaster

11 The thinking man's crumpet.
of Joan Bakewell
attributed

Jean Muir 1928–95

English fashion designer

12 Engineering with fabric.
her definition of dressmaking
in *The Times* 30 May 1995, obituary

Paul Muldoon 1951–

Irish poet

13 I thought of you tonight, *a leanbh*, lying there in your long barrow,
colder and dumber than a fish by Francisco de Herrera.
'Incantata' (1994)

14 The Volkswagen parked in the gap,
But gently ticking over.
You wonder if it's lovers
And not men hurrying back
Across two fields and a river.
'Ireland' (1980)

Robert Muldoon 1921–92

New Zealand statesman, Prime Minister 1975–84

15 When New Zealanders emigrate to Australia, it raises the average IQ of both countries.
attributed

H. J. Muller 1890–1967

American geneticist

16 To say, for example, that a man is made up of certain chemical elements is a satisfactory description only for those who intend to use him as a fertilizer.
Science and Criticism (1943)

Herbert J. Muller 1905–80

American historian

17 Few have heard of Fra Luca Pacioli, the inventor of double-entry bookkeeping; but he has probably had much more influence on human life than has Dante or Michelangelo.
Uses of the Past (1957) ch. 8

Wilhelm Müller 1794–1827

German poet

18 *Vom Abendrot zum Morgenlicht*
Ward mancher Kopf zum Greise.
Wer glaubt's? Und meiner ward es nicht
Auf dieser ganzen Reise.
Between dusk and dawn many a head has turned white. Who can believe it? And mine has not changed on all this long journey.
Die Winterreise (1823) bk. 2 'Der greise Kopf'

Ethel Watts Mumford et al. 1878–1940
American writer and humorist

1 In the midst of life we are in debt.
Altogether New Cynic's Calendar (1907); see **BOOK OF COMMON PRAYER** 139:9

Lewis Mumford 1895–1990
American sociologist

2 Every generation revolts against its fathers and makes friends with its grandfathers.
The Brown Decades (1931)

3 Our national flower is the concrete cloverleaf.
in *Quote Magazine* 8 October 1961

Mumonkan *c.*1228
a Japanese Zen textbook

4 A monk once asked Jōshū, 'Has a dog the Buddha-Nature?'
Jōshū answered, 'Mu!'
case 1

5 He [Buddha] held up a flower before the congregation of monks. At this time all were silent but the Venerable Kasyapa only smiled. The World-Honoured One said . . .
'Without relying upon words and letters, beyond all teaching as a special transmission, I pass this all on to Mahakasyapa.'
case 6

6 A monk asked Tōzan, 'What is the Buddha?'
He replied 'Three pounds of flax.'
case 18

7 A monk asked Ummon, 'What is the Buddha?'
'It is a shit-wiping stick,' replied Ummon.
case 21

8 A monk asked Jōshū, 'What did Daruma [Bodhidharma] come to China for?' Jōshū answered, 'The oak tree in the [temple] front garden.'
case 37

Edvard Munch 1863–1944
Norwegian painter and engraver

9 You should not paint the chair, but only what someone has felt about it.
written *c.*1891; R. Heller *Munch* (1984) ch. 4

10 I was walking with two friends and the sun set and the heavens suddenly turned to blood and my friends continued walking. I stopped by the fence, deathly tired. Over the cold blue fjord and city was a flaming reddish yellow, and I felt a huge scream course through nature.
his account of how he came to imagine The Scream
Poul Erik Tøjner *Edvard Munch in his own words* (2003)

Murasaki Shikibu *c.*978–*c.*1031
Japanese writer and courtier

11 Anything whatsoever may become the subject of a novel, provided only that it happens in this mundane life and not in some fairyland beyond our human ken.
The Tale of Genji

12 People who have become so precious that they go out of their way to try and be sensitive in the most unpromising situations, trying to capture every moment of interest, are bound to look ridiculous and superficial.
The Diary of Lady Murasaki (translated by Richard Bowring, 1996)

Iris Murdoch 1919–99
English novelist and philosopher

13 Dora Greenfield left her husband because she was afraid of him. She decided six months later to return to him for the same reason.
The Bell (1958) ch. 1

14 All our failures are ultimately failures in love.
The Bell (1958) ch. 19

15 Those who are caught in mental cages can often picture freedom, it just has no attractive power.
The Sea, The Sea (1978) ch. 6

16 One doesn't have to get anywhere in a marriage. It's not a public conveyance.
A Severed Head (1961) ch. 3

17 Love is the extremely difficult realisation that something other than oneself is real. Love, and so art and morals, is the discovery of reality.
'The Sublime and the Good' in *Chicago Review* 13 (1959)

18 Since reality is incomplete, art must not be too much afraid of incompleteness.
'Against Dryness' in *Encounter* January 1961

19 Anything that consoles is fake.
R. Harries *Prayer and the Pursuit of Happiness* (1985)

20 We live in a fantasy world, a world of illusion. The great task in life is to find reality.
in *The Times* 15 April 1983 'Profile'

21 I'm just wandering, I think of things and then they go away for ever.
in September 1996 on her inability to write; the following February it was announced that she was suffering from Alzheimer's disease
in *Times* 5 February 1997

C. W. Murphy *and* Will Letters

22 Has anybody here seen Kelly?
Kelly from the Isle of Man?
'Has Anybody Here Seen Kelly?' (1909 song)

Fred Murray
American songwriter

23 Ginger, you're balmy!
title of song (1910)

James Augustus Henry Murray

1837–1915

Scottish lexicographer, first Editor of the *Oxford English Dictionary*

1 I feel that in many respects I and my assistants are simply pioneers, pushing our way experimentally through an untrodden forest, where no white man's axe has been before us.
'Report on the Philological Society's Dictionary' (1884) in *Transactions of the Philological Society* 1882–4

Les A. Murray 1938–

Australian poet

2   The trouble
with being best man is, you don't get a chance to prove it.
The Boys Who Stole the Funeral (1989)

3 Nothing's said till it's dreamed out in words
And nothing's true that figures in words only.
The Daylight Moon (1987) 'Poetry and Religion'

4 Men must have legends, else they will die of strangeness.
The Ilex Tree (1965) 'The Noonday Axeman'

Ed Murrow 1908–65

American broadcaster and journalist. See also
CATCHPHRASES 207:24

5 No one can terrorize a whole nation, unless we are all his accomplices.
of Joseph **MCCARTHY**
'See It Now', broadcast, 7 March 1954

6 He mobilized the English language and sent it into battle to steady his fellow countrymen and hearten those Europeans upon whom the long dark night of tyranny had descended.
of Winston **CHURCHILL**
broadcast, 30 November 1954, in *In Search of Light* (1967)

7 Anyone who isn't confused doesn't really understand the situation.
on the Vietnam War
Walter Bryan *The Improbable Irish* (1969) ch. 1

Miyamoto Musashi 1584–1645

Japanese soldier

8 Do not let the enemy see your spirit.
Go Rin No Sho [*A Book of Five Rings*]

Alfred de Musset 1810–57

French poet and dramatist

9 *Je haïs comme la mort l'état de plagiaire;*
Mon verre n'est pas grand mais je bois dans mon verre.
I hate like death the situation of the plagiarist; the glass I drink from is not large, but at least it is my own.
La Coupe et les lèvres (1832)

10 *Malgré moi l'infini me tourmente.*
I can't help it, the idea of the infinite torments me.
'L'Espoir en Dieu' (1838)

11 *Le seul bien qui me reste au monde*
Est d'avoir quelquefois pleuré.
The only good thing left to me is that I have sometimes wept.
'Tristesse' (1841)

12 *Je suis venu trop tard dans un monde trop vieux.*
I have come too late into a world too old.
Rolla (1833)

Benito Mussolini 1883–1945

Italian Fascist dictator

13 We must leave exactly on time . . . From now on everything must function to perfection.
to a station-master
Giorgio Pini *Mussolini* (1939) vol. 2, ch. 6; an early report was: 'The first benefit of Benito Mussolini's direction in Italy begins to be felt when one crosses the Italian Frontier and hears "*Il treno arriva all'orario* [The train is arriving on time]"' Infanta Eulalia of Spain *Courts and Countries after the War* (1925)

A. J. Muste 1885–1967

American pacifist

14 If I can't love Hitler, I can't love at all.
at a Quaker meeting 1940; in *New York Times* 12 February 1967

15 There is no way to peace. Peace is the way.
in *New York Times* 16 November 1967

Vladimir Nabokov 1899–1977

Russian-born American novelist

16 Lolita, light of my life, fire of my loins. My sin, my soul. Lo-lee-ta: the tip of the tongue taking a trip of three steps down the palate to tap, at three, on the teeth. Lo. Lee. Ta.
Lolita (1955) ch. 1, opening words

17 You can always count on a murderer for a fancy prose style.
Lolita (1955) ch. 1

18 Life is a great surprise. I do not see why death should not be an even greater one.
Pale Fire (1962)

19 The cradle rocks above an abyss, and common sense tells us that our existence is but a brief crack of light between two eternities of darkness.
Speak, Memory (1951) ch. 1

Ralph Nader 1934–

American consumer protectionist

1 Unsafe at any speed.
title of book (1965); see **KEATS** 458:19

Nagarjuna *c.*AD 2nd century

Indian philosopher

2 The doctrine of the Buddha is taught with
reference to two truths—conventional truth and
ultimate truth.
Those who do not understand the difference
between these two truths do not understand the
profound essence of the doctrine of the Buddha.
Root Verses of the Middle Way ch. 24, v. 8

Sarojini Naidu 1879–1949

Indian politician

3 If only Bapu knew the cost of setting him up in
poverty!
of Mahatma **GANDHI**
A. Campbell-Johnson *Mission with Mountbatten* (1951) ch. 12

Shiva Naipaul 1945–85

Trinidadian writer

4 The Third World is an artificial construction of
the West—an ideological empire on which the
sun is always setting.
An Unfinished Journey (1986)

V. S. Naipaul 1932–

Trinidadian writer of Indian descent, resident in Britain since
1950, noted especially for his satirical novels

5 The world is what it is; men who are nothing,
who allow themselves to become nothing, have
no place in it.
A Bend in the River (1979 novel), opening sentence

Ian Nairn 1930–83

British architect

6 If what is called development is allowed to
multiply at the present rate, then by the end of
the century Great Britain will consist of isolated
oases of preserved monuments in a desert of
wire, concrete roads, cosy plots and bungalows
. . . Upon this new Britain the *Review* bestows a
name in the hope that it will stick—SUBTOPIA.
in *Architectural Review* June 1955

Lewis Namier 1888–1960

Polish-born British historian

7 No number of atrocities however horrible can
deprive a nation of its right to independence,
nor justify its being put under the heel of its
worst enemies and persecutors.
in 1919; Julia Namier *Lewis Namier* (1971)

Fridtjof Nansen 1861–1930

Norwegian polar explorer

8 Never stop because you are afraid—you are
never so likely to be wrong. Never keep a line of
retreat: it is a wretched invention. The difficult is
what takes a little time; the impossible is what
takes a little longer.
in *Listener* 14 December 1939; see **CALONNE** 194:1, **MILITARY
SAYINGS, SLOGANS, AND SONGS** 535:6

Napoleon I 1769–1821

French monarch, Emperor 1804–15. On Napoleon: see
BYRON 190:17, **WELLINGTON** 846:9; see also **DUMOURIEZ**
299:7

9 What I have done so far is nothing. I am only at
the beginning of the career that lies before me.
in May 1796; F. Furcet *The French Revolution 1770–1814* (1996)

10 Think of it, soldiers; from the summit of these
pyramids, forty centuries look down upon you.
*speech to the Army of Egypt on 21 July 1798, before the
Battle of the Pyramids*
Gaspard Gourgaud *Mémoires* (1823) vol. 2 'Égypte—Bataille
des Pyramides'

11 It [the Channel] is a mere ditch, and will be
crossed as soon as someone has the courage to
attempt it.
letter to Consul Cambacérès, 16 November 1803, in
Correspondance de Napoléon Ier (1858–69) vol. 9

12 Let us be masters of the Channel for six hours,
and we are masters of the world.
*c.*1803; J. R. Green *History of the English People* (1880) vol. 4,
ch. 9

13 Hats off, gentlemen. If he were still alive, we
should not be here.
to his officers, standing by the grave of **FREDERICK THE
GREAT** *in Berlin, 1806*
Nancy Mitford *Frederick the Great* (1970)

14 A prince who gets a reputation for good nature
in the first year of his reign, is laughed at in the
second.
letter to his brother Louis, King of Holland, 4 April 1807, in
Correspondance de Napoléon Ier (1858–69) vol. 15

15 It is easier to put up with unpleasantness from a
man of one's own way of thinking than from
one who takes an entirely different point of
view.
letter to J. Finckenstein, 14 April 1807, in *Mémoires et
Correspondance politique et militaire du Roi Joseph* (1854) vol. 3

16 I want the whole of Europe to have one
currency; it will make trading much easier.
letter to his brother Louis, 6 May 1807; Alistair Horne *How Far
from Austerlitz?* (1996)

17 Religion is an all-important matter in a public
school for girls. Whatever people say, it is the
mother's safeguard, and the husband's. What we
ask of education is not that girls should think,
but that they should believe.
'Note sur L'Établissement D'Écouen' 15 May 1807, in
Correspondance de Napoléon Ier (1858–69) vol. 15

18 In war, three-quarters turns on personal
character and relations; the balance of

manpower and materials counts only for the remaining quarter.

'Observations sur les affaires d'Espagne, Saint-Cloud, 27 août 1808' in *Correspondance de Napoléon Ier* (1858–69) vol. 17

1 It is a matter of great interest what sovereigns are doing; but as to what Grand Duchesses are doing—Who cares?

letter, 17 December 1811, in *Lettres inédits de Napoléon I* (1897) vol. 2

2 There is only one step from the sublime to the ridiculous.

to De Pradt, Polish ambassador, after the retreat from Moscow in 1812

D. G. De Pradt *Histoire de l'Ambassade dans le grand-duché de Varsovie en 1812* (1815); see **PAINE** 592:7, **PROVERBS** 632:42

3 *La France a plus besoin de moi que je n'ai besoin de la France.*

France has more need of me than I have need of France.

speech to the Corps Législatif, Paris, 31 December 1813

4 As to moral courage, I have very rarely met with two o'clock in the morning courage: I mean instantaneous courage.

E. A. de Las Cases *Mémorial de Ste-Hélène* (1823) vol. 1, pt. 2, 4–5 December 1815; see **THOREAU** 809:18

5 Nothing is more contrary to the organization of the mind, of the memory, and of the imagination . . . The new system of weights and measures will be a stumbling block and the source of difficulties for several generations . . . It's just tormenting the people with trivia!!!

on the introduction of the metric system

Mémoires . . . écrits à Ste-Hélène (1823–5) bk. 4, ch. 21, pt. 4

6 An army marches on its stomach.

attributed, but probably condensed from a long passage in E. A. de Las Cases *Mémorial de Ste-Hélène* (1823) vol. 4, 14 November 1816; also attributed to **FREDERICK THE GREAT**, in *Notes and Queries* 10 March 1866; see **PROVERBS** 626:34, **SELLAR AND YEATMAN** 692:6

7 As though he had 200,000 men.

when asked how to deal with the Pope

J. M. Robinson *Cardinal Consalvi* (1987); see **STALIN** 769:16

8 *La carrière ouverte aux talents.*

The career open to the talents.

Barry E. O'Meara *Napoleon in Exile* (1822) vol. 1

9 England is a nation of shopkeepers.

Barry E. O'Meara *Napoleon in Exile* (1822) vol. 2; see **ADAMS** 4:1, **PROVERBS** 631:6, **SMITH** 756:5

10 Not tonight, Josephine.

attributed, but probably apocryphal; the phrase does not appear in contemporary sources, but was current by the early twentieth century

11 *of* **TALLEYRAND**:

A pile of shit in a silk stocking.

attributed

Ogden Nash 1902–71

American humorous poet

12 The turtle lives 'twixt plated decks
Which practically conceal its sex.

I think it clever of the turtle
In such a fix to be so fertile.

'Autres Bêtes, Autres Moeurs' (1931)

13 The camel has a single hump;
The dromedary, two;
Or else the other way around,
I'm never sure. Are you?

'The Camel' (1936)

14 The cow is of the bovine ilk;
One end is moo, the other, milk.

'The Cow' (1931)

15 One would be in less danger
From the wiles of the stranger
If one's own kin and kith
Were more fun to be with.

'Family Court' (1931)

16 Beneath this slab
John Brown is stowed.
He watched the ads,
And not the road.

'Lather as You Go' (1942)

17 Do you think my mind is maturing late,
Or simply rotted early?

'Lines on Facing Forty' (1942)

18 Good wine needs no bush,
And perhaps products that people really want
    need no hard-sell or soft-sell TV push.
Why not?
Look at pot.

'Most Doctors Recommend or yours For Fast, Fast, Fast Relief' (1972); see **PROVERBS** 633:25

19 Any kiddie in school can love like a fool,
But hating, my boy, is an art.

'Plea for Less Malice Toward None' (1933)

20 Candy
Is dandy
But liquor
Is quicker.

'Reflections on Ice-breaking' (1931)

21 I test my bath before I sit,
And I'm always moved to wonderment
That what chills the finger not a bit
Is so frigid upon the fundament.

'Samson Agonistes' (1942)

22 I think that I shall never see
A billboard lovely as a tree.
Perhaps, unless the billboards fall,
I'll never see a tree at all.

'Song of the Open Road' (1933); see **KILMER** 462:15

23 Sure, deck your lower limbs in pants;
Yours are the limbs, my sweeting.
You look divine as you advance—
Have you seen yourself retreating?

'What's the Use?' (1940)

Thomas Nashe 1567–1601

English pamphleteer and dramatist

24 O, tis a precious apothegmatical Pedant, who will find matter enough to dilate a whole day of

the first invention of *Fy, fa, fum*, I smell the blood of an English-man.
> *Have with you to Saffron-walden* (1596); see **ANONYMOUS** 17:6, **SHAKESPEARE** 716:5

1 Beauty is but a flower
Which wrinkles will devour.
> *Summer's Last Will and Testament* (1600) l. 1588

2 Brightness falls from the air;
Queens have died young and fair;
Dust hath closed Helen's eye.
I am sick, I must die.
Lord have mercy on us.
> *Summer's Last Will and Testament* (1600) l. 1590

3 From winter, plague and pestilence, good lord, deliver us!
> *Summer's Last Will and Testament* (1600) l. 1878; see **BOOK OF COMMON PRAYER** 134:19

4 No leaf he wrote on but was like a burning-glass to set on fire all his readers.
> *of Pietro Aretino (1492–1556)*
> *The Unfortunate Traveller* (1594)

James Ball Naylor 1860–1945

5 King David and King Solomon
Led merry, merry lives,
With many, many lady friends,
And many, many wives;
But when old age crept over them—
With many, many qualms!—
King Solomon wrote the Proverbs
And King David wrote the Psalms.
> 'King David and King Solomon' (1935)

John Mason Neale 1818–66

English clergyman

6 All glory, laud, and honour
To thee, Redeemer, King,
To whom the lips of children
Made sweet hosannas ring.
> 'All glory, laud, and honour' (1859 hymn); translated from the Latin traditionally attributed to St Theodulph of Orleans, c.820

7 Good King Wenceslas looked out,
On the feast of Stephen;
When the snow lay round about,
Deep and crisp and even.
> 'Good King Wenceslas'

8 Jerusalem the golden,
With milk and honey blessed.
> 'Jerusalem the golden' (1858 hymn); translated from the Latin of Bernard of Cluny (fl. 1140)

Jawaharlal Nehru 1889–1964

Indian statesman, Prime Minister 1947–64

9 At the stroke of the midnight hour, while the world sleeps, India will awake to life and freedom.
> *immediately prior to Independence*
> speech to the Indian Constituent Assembly, 14 August 1947

10 The light has gone out of our lives and there is darkness everywhere.
> *following GANDHI's assassination*
> broadcast, 30 January 1948; Richard J. Walsh *Nehru on Gandhi* (1948) ch. 6

11 I may lose many things including my temper, but I do not lose my nerve.
> at a press conference in Delhi, 4 June 1958

12 Democracy and socialism are means to an end, not the end itself.
> 'Basic Approach'; written for private circulation and reprinted in Vincent Shean *Nehru: the Years of Power* (1960)

13 There is no easy walk-over to freedom anywhere, and many of us will have to pass through the valley of the shadow again and again before we reach the mountain-tops of our desire.
> 'From Lucknow to Tripuri' (1939)

14 After every other Viceroy has been forgotten, Curzon will be remembered because he restored all that was beautiful in India.
> *in conversation with Lord Swinton*
> Kenneth Rose *Superior Person* (1969)

15 I shall be the last Englishman to rule in India.
> J. K. Galbraith *A Life in Our Times* (1981)

A. S. Neill 1883–1973

Scottish teacher and educationist

16 If we have to have an exam at 11, let us make it one for humour, sincerity, imagination, character—and where is the examiner who could test such qualities.
> letter to *Daily Telegraph* 1957; in *Daily Telegraph* 25 September 1973

Horatio, Lord Nelson 1758–1805

British admiral. On Nelson: see **SOUTHEY** 764:22; see also **MOTTOES** 563:15

17 It is my turn now; and if I come back, it is yours.
> *exercising his privilege, as second lieutenant, to board a prize ship before the Master*
> Robert Southey *Life of Nelson* (1813) ch. 1

18 You must consider every man your enemy who speaks ill of your king: and . . . you must hate a Frenchman as you hate the devil.
> Robert Southey *Life of Nelson* (1813) ch. 3

19 Before this time to-morrow I shall have gained a peerage, or Westminster Abbey.
> *before the battle of the Nile, 1798*
> Robert Southey *Life of Nelson* (1813) ch. 5

20 I have only one eye,—I have a right to be blind sometimes . . . I really do not see the signal!
> *at the battle of Copenhagen, 1801*
> Robert Southey *Life of Nelson* (1813) ch. 7

21 In honour I gained them, and in honour I will die with them.
> *when asked to cover the stars on his uniform*
> Robert Southey *Life of Nelson* (1813) ch. 9

1 I believe my arrival was most welcome, not only to the Commander of the Fleet but almost to every individual in it.

> letter to Lady Hamilton, 1 October 1805, in Robert Southey *Life of Nelson* (1813) ch. 9

2 When I came to explain to them the *'Nelson touch'*, it was like an electric shock. Some shed tears, all approved—'It was new—it was singular—it was simple!'

> letter to Lady Hamilton, 1 October 1805, in Robert Southey *Life of Nelson* (1813) ch. 9

3 May the Great God, whom I worship, grant to my Country and for the benefit of Europe in general a great and glorious victory; and may no misconduct in anyone tarnish it; and may humanity after Victory be the predominant feature of the British Fleet. For myself, individually, I commit my life to Him who made me, and may His blessing light upon my endeavours for serving my Country faithfully. To Him I resign myself and the just cause which is entrusted to me to defend. Amen. Amen. Amen.

> *diary entry, on the eve of the battle of Trafalgar, 21 October 1805*
>
> Nicholas Harris Nicolas (ed.) *Dispatches and Letters of . . . Nelson* (1846) vol. 7, p. 139

4 England expects that every man will do his duty.

> *at the battle of Trafalgar, 21 October 1805*
>
> Robert Southey *Life of Nelson* (1813) ch. 9

5 This is too warm work, Hardy, to last long.

> *at the battle of Trafalgar, 21 October 1805*
>
> Robert Southey *Life of Nelson* (1813) ch. 9

6 Kiss me, Hardy.

> *at the battle of Trafalgar, 21 October 1805*
>
> Robert Southey *Life of Nelson* (1813) ch. 9

7 Thank God, I have done my duty.

> *last words, at the battle of Trafalgar, 21 October 1805*
>
> Robert Southey *Life of Nelson* (1813) ch. 9

Howard Nemerov 1920–91

American poet and novelist

8 praise without end the go-ahead zeal
  of whoever it was invented the wheel;
  but never a word for the poor soul's sake
  that thought ahead, and invented the brake.

> 'To the Congress of the United States, Entering Its Third Century' 26 February 1989

Nero AD 37–68

Roman emperor, from 54 AD

9 *Qualis artifex pereo!*

  What an artist dies with me!

> *last words before committing suicide*
>
> Suetonius *Lives of the Caesars* 'Nero' sect. 49

Pablo Neruda 1904–73

Chilean poet

10 *¿Por cuánto tiempo muere el hombre?*

  How long does a man spend dying?

> 'And How Long?' (1958)

11 *Y pronto, entre la ropa y el humo, sobre la mesa hundida,*
  como una barajada cantidad, queda el alma.

  Soon, caught between clothes and smoke, on the sunken floor,
  the soul's reduced to a shuffled pack,

> 'The Heights of Macchu Picchu' (1945) canto 2, translated by Nathaniel Tarn

12 *Déjame olvidar hoy esta dicha, que es más ancha que el mar,*
  porque el hombre es más ancho que el mar y que sus islas,
  y hay que caer en él como en un pozo para salir del fondo
  con un ramo de agua secreta y de verdades sumergidas.

  Today let me forget this happiness, wider than all the sea,
  because man is wider than all the sea and her necklace of islands
  and we must fall into him as down a well to clamber back with
  branches of secret water, recondite truths.

> 'The Heights of Macchu Picchu' (1945) canto 11, translated by Nathaniel Tarn

13 I have gone marking the blank atlas of your body
  with crosses of fire.
  My mouth went across: a spider, trying to hide.
  In you, behind you, timid, driven by thirst.

> 'I Have Gone Marking' (1924), translated by W. S. Merwin

14 *¡Venid a ver la sangre*
  Por las calles!

  Come and see the blood
  in the streets!

> 'I'm Explaining a Few Things' (1947)

15 I did not come to solve anything.
  I came here to sing
  and for you to sing with me.

> 'Let the Rail Splitter Awake' (1950) translated by Waldeen

16 *Es tan corto el amor, y es tan largo el olvido.*

  Love is so short, forgetting is so long.

> 'Tonight I Can Write' (1924)

Gérard de Nerval 1808–55

French poet

17 *Dieu est mort! le ciel est vide—*
  Pleurez! enfants, vous n'avez plus de père.

  God is dead! Heaven is empty—Weep, children, you no longer have a father.

> *Les Chimères* (1854) 'Le Christ aux Oliviers' epigraph (summarizing a passage in Jean Paul's *Blumen-Frucht-und Dornstücke* (1796–7) in which God's children are referred to as 'orphans')

1 *Je suis le ténébreux,—le veuf,—l'inconsolé,*
Le prince d'Aquitaine à la tour abolie:
Ma seule étoile est morte, et mon luth constellé
Porte le soleil noir de la mélancolie.

I am the darkly shaded, the bereaved, the
inconsolate, the prince of Aquitaine, with the
blasted tower. My only *star* is dead, and my star-
strewn lute carries on it the black *sun of
melancholy.*

    Les Chimères (1854) 'El Desdichado'

2 Why should a lobster be any more ridiculous
than a dog . . . or any other animal that one
chooses to take for a walk? I have a liking for
lobsters. They are peaceful, serious creatures.
They know the secrets of the sea, they don't
bark, and they don't gnaw upon one's monadic
privacy like dogs do. And Goethe had an
aversion to dogs, and he wasn't mad.

    *justifying his walking a lobster on a lead in the gardens of
the Palais Royal*
    T. Gautier *Portraits et Souvenirs Littéraires* (1875), translated by
Richard Holmes

Edith Nesbit 1858–1924

English writer for children and novelist

3 It is a curious thing that people only ask if you
are enjoying yourself when you aren't.
    Five of Us, and Madeline (1925)

4 The affection you get back from children is
sixpence given as change for a sovereign.
    Julia Briggs *A Woman of Passion* (1987)

John von Neumann 1903–57

**Hungarian-born American mathematician and computer
pioneer**

5 In mathematics you don't understand things. You
just get used to them.
    Gary Zukav *The Dancing Wu Li Masters* (1979)

Otto Neurath 1882–1945

German philosopher

6 We are like sailors who must rebuild their ship
on the open sea, never able to dismantle it in
dry-dock and to reconstruct it there out of the
best materials.
    'Protocol Sentences', in A. J. Ayer (ed.) *Logical Positivism*
    (1959)

Allan Nevins 1890–1971

American historian

7 The former Allies had blundered in the past by
offering Germany too little, and offering even
that too late, until finally Nazi Germany had
become a menace to all mankind.
    in *Current History* (New York) May 1935

Henry Newbolt 1862–1938

English lawyer, poet, and man of letters

8 'Take my drum to England, hang et by the
shore,

Strike et when your powder's runnin' low;
If the Dons sight Devon, I'll quit the port o'
    Heaven,
An' drum them up the Channel as we drummed
    them long ago.'
    'Drake's Drum' (1897)

9 Drake he's in his hammock till the great
    Armadas come.
(Capten, art tha sleepin' there below?)
Slung atween the round shot, listenin' for the
    drum,
An' dreamin' arl the time o' Plymouth Hoe.
    'Drake's Drum' (1897)

10 Now the sunset breezes shiver,
And she's fading down the river,
But in England's song for ever
She's the Fighting Téméraire.
    'The Fighting Téméraire' (1897)

11 'Qui procul hinc', the legend's writ,—
The frontier-grave is far away—
'Qui ante diem periit:
Sed miles, sed pro patria.'
    The Island Race (1898) 'Clifton Chapel'

12 There's a breathless hush in the Close to-night—
Ten to make and the match to win—
A bumping pitch and a blinding light,
An hour to play and the last man in.
And it's not for the sake of a ribboned coat,
Or the selfish hope of a season's fame,
But his Captain's hand on his shoulder smote—
'Play up! play up! and play the game!'
    'Vitaï Lampada' (1897)

Anthony Newley 1931–99 *and* Leslie Bricusse 1931–

13 Stop the world, I want to get off.
    title of musical (1961)

John Henry Newman 1801–90

**English theologian, priest, and Cardinal; a key figure in the
Oxford Movement, he converted to Roman Catholicism in
1845. See also EPITAPHS 317:6, MOTTOES 563:6, TOASTS 812:4**

14 It is very difficult to get up resentment towards
persons whom one has never seen.
    Apologia pro Vita Sua (1864) 'Mr Kingsley's Method of
    Disputation'

15 There is such a thing as legitimate warfare: war
has its laws; there are things which may fairly be
done, and things which may not be done . . . He
has attempted (as I may call it) to *poison the
wells.*
    Apologia pro Vita Sua (1864) 'Mr Kingsley's Method of
    Disputation'

16 Two and two only supreme and luminously self-
evident beings, myself and my Creator.
    Apologia pro Vita Sua (1864) 'History of My Religious Opinions
    to the Year 1833'

1 Growth [is] the only evidence of life.
Newman's summary of a doctrine of the biblical scholar Thomas Scott (1747–1821)
Apologia pro Vita Sua (1864) 'History of My Religious Opinions from 1833 to 1839'

2 It would be a gain to the country were it vastly more superstitious, more bigoted, more gloomy, more fierce in its religion than at present it shows itself to be.
Apologia pro Vita Sua (1864) 'History of My Religious Opinions from 1833 to 1839'

3 From the age of fifteen, dogma has been the fundamental principle of my religion: I know no other religion; I cannot enter into the idea of any other sort of religion; religion, as a mere sentiment, is to me a dream and a mockery.
Apologia pro Vita Sua (1864) 'History of My Religious Opinions from 1833 to 1839'

4 This is what the Church is said to want, not party men, but sensible, temperate, sober, well-judging persons, to guide it through the channel of no-meaning, between the Scylla and Charybdis of Aye and No.
Apologia pro Vita Sua (1864) 'History of My Religious Opinions from 1833 to 1839'

5 Ten thousand difficulties do not make one doubt.
Apologia pro Vita Sua (1864) 'Position of my Mind since 1845'

6 The all-corroding, all-dissolving scepticism of the intellect in religious enquiries.
Apologia pro Vita Sua (1864) 'Position of my Mind since 1845'

7 To live is to change, and to be perfect is to have changed often.
An Essay on the Development of Christian Doctrine (1845) sect. 2

8 It is almost a definition of a gentleman to say that he is one who never inflicts pain.
The Idea of a University (1852) 'Knowledge and Religious Duty'

9 She [the Catholic Church] holds that it were better for sun and moon to drop from heaven, for the earth to fail, and for all the many millions who are upon it to die of starvation in extremest agony, as far as temporal affliction goes, than that one soul, I will not say, should be lost, but should commit one single venial sin, should tell one wilful untruth . . . or steal one poor farthing without excuse.
Lectures on Anglican Difficulties (1852) Lecture 8

10 It is as absurd to argue men, as to torture them, into believing.
'The Usurpations of Reason' (1831) in Oxford University Sermons (1843) no. 4

11 And this is all that is known, and more than all—yet nothing to what the angels know—of the life of a servant of God, who sinned and repented, and did penance and washed out his sins, and became a Saint, and reigns with Christ in heaven.
Lives of the English Saints (1844–5) 'The Legend of Saint Bettelin'; though attributed to Newman, 'and more than all' may have been added by J. A. Froude (1818–94)

12 When men understand what each other mean, they see, for the most part, that controversy is either superfluous or hopeless.
'Faith and Reason, contrasted as Habits of Mind' (Epiphany, 1839) in Oxford University Sermons (1843) no. 10

13 May He support us all the day long, till the shades lengthen, and the evening comes, and the busy world is hushed, and the fever of life is over, and our work is done! Then in His mercy may He give us a safe lodging, and a holy rest, and peace at the last.
'Wisdom and Innocence' (19 February 1843) in Sermons Bearing on Subjects of the Day (1843) no. 20

14 Firmly I believe and truly
God is Three, and God is One;
And I next acknowledge duly
Manhood taken by the Son.
The Dream of Gerontius (1865)

15 Praise to the Holiest in the height,
And in the depth be praise;
In all his words most wonderful,
Most sure in all His ways.
The Dream of Gerontius (1865)

16 Lead, kindly Light, amid the encircling gloom,
Lead thou me on;
The night is dark, and I am far from home,
Lead thou me on.
Keep Thou my feet; I do not ask to see
The distant scene; one step enough for me.
'Lead, kindly Light' (1834)

17 I loved the garish day, and spite of fears,
Pride ruled my will: remember not past years.
'Lead, kindly Light' (1834); see MILTON 539:19

18 *We can believe what we choose.* We are answerable for what we choose to believe.
letter to Mrs William Froude, 27 June 1848, in C. S. Dessain (ed.) Letters and Diaries of John Henry Newman vol. 12 (1962)

19 To assert . . . that nothing is known because nothing is known luminously and exactly, seems to me saying that we do not see the stars because we cannot tell the number, size, or distance from each other.
letter to Charles Meynell, 9 May 1860, in C. S. Dessain (ed.) Letters and Diaries of John Henry Newman vol. 19 (1969)

☐ Newspaper headlines and leaders
see **box opposite**

Huey Newton 1942–89
American political activist

20 I suggested [in 1966] that we use the panther as our symbol and call our political vehicle the Black Panther Party. The panther is a fierce animal, but he will not attack until he is backed into a corner; then he will strike out.
Revolutionary Suicide (1973) ch. 16; see POLITICAL SLOGANS AND SONGS 613:7

Newspaper headlines and leaders

1 Believe it or not.
title of syndicated newspaper feature (from 1918), written by Robert L. Ripley (1893–1949)

2 British Rail, which last week predicted that it was ready for the worst the weather could do, now blames the near-total dislocation of its services on 'the wrong sort of snow'.
leader in Evening Standard *12 February 1991; see* **WORRALL** 870:6

3 Bush Wins It.
original headline in the Miami Herald *for 8 November 2000; changed in final edition to 'It's Not Over Yet'*
in Daily Telegraph *9 November 2000*

4 Crisis? What crisis?
summarizing an interview with James **CALLAGHAN**
headline in Sun, *11 January 1979; see* **MISQUOTATIONS** 547:8

5 Dewey defeats Truman.
anticipating the result of the Presidential election, which **TRUMAN** *won against expectation*
in Chicago Tribune *3 November 1948*

6 Downing Street's dodgy dossier of 'intelligence' about Iraq.
referring to a briefing document on Iraqi weaponry which was later withdrawn
leading article, Observer *9 February 2003*

7 Egghead weds hourglass.
on the marriage of Arthur **MILLER** *and Marilyn* **MONROE**
headline in Variety *1956; attributed*

8 The filth and the fury.
following a notorious interview with the Sex Pistols broadcast live on Thames Television
headline in Daily Mirror, *2 December 1976*

9 Freddie Starr ate my hamster.
headline in Sun *13 March 1986*

10 GOTCHA!
on the sinking of the General Belgrano
headline in Sun *4 May 1982*

11 Go West, young man, go West!
editorial in Terre Haute [Indiana] Express *(1851), by John L. B. Soule (1815–91); see* **GREELEY** 371:5

12 In that case, it might be worthwhile for the Czechoslovak government to consider whether they should exclude altogether the project, which has found favour in some quarters, of making Czechoslovakia a more homogeneous State, by the secession of that fringe of alien populations who are contiguous to the nation with which they are united by race.
referring to the Sudeten Germans
leader in The Times *7 September 1938*

13 Is THIS the most dangerous man in Britain?
headline beside a picture of Tony **BLAIR**, *attacking his perceived sympathy for the euro*
in The Sun *25 June 1998*

14 It *is* a moral issue.
leader following the resignation of Profumo
in The Times *11 June 1963; see* **HAILSHAM** 376:7

15 It's that man again . . . ! At the head of a cavalcade of seven black motor cars Hitler swept out of his Berlin Chancellery last night on a mystery journey.
headline in Daily Express *2 May 1939; the acronym ITMA became the title of a BBC radio show, from September 1939*

16 It's The Sun wot won it.
following the 1992 general election
headline in Sun *11 April 1992*

17 King's Moll Reno'd in Wolsey's home town.
US newspaper headline on the divorce proceedings of Wallis Simpson (later Duchess of **WINDSOR**) *in Ipswich*
Frances Donaldson Edward VIII *(1974) ch. 7*

18 Splendid isolation.
headline in The Times *22 January 1896, referring to a speech by the Canadian politician George Foster (1847–1931) 16 January 1896: 'In these somewhat troublesome days when the great Mother Empire stands splendidly isolated in Europe', in* Official Report of the Debates of the House of Commons of the Dominion of Canada *(1896) vol. 41*

19 Sticks nix hick pix.
front-page headline on the lack of enthusiasm for farm dramas among rural populations
in Variety *17 July 1935*

20 Unless the people—the people everywhere—come forward and petition, ay, thunder for reform.
leader on the Reform Bill, possibly written by Edward Sterling (1773–1847), resulting in the nickname 'The Thunderer'
in The Times *29 January 1831; the phrase 'we thundered out' had been used earlier, 11 February 1829*

21 Wall St. lays an egg.
crash headline, Variety *30 October 1929*

22 We shall not pretend that there is nothing in his long career which those who respect and admire him would wish otherwise.
on **EDWARD VII**'s *accession to the throne*
in The Times *23 January 1901, leading article*

23 Who breaks a butterfly on a wheel?
defending Mick Jagger after his arrest for cannabis possession
leader in The Times *1 June 1967, written by William Rees-Mogg; see* **POPE** 614:24

24 Whose finger do you want on the trigger?
referring to the atom bomb
headline in Daily Mirror *21 September 1951*

25 Winter of discontent.
headline in Sun *30 April 1979; see* **CALLAGHAN** 193:12, **SHAKESPEARE** 731:9

26 Yes, Virginia, there is a Santa Claus.
replying to a letter from eight-year-old Virginia O'Hanlon
editorial by Francis Pharcellus Church (1839–1906) in New York Sun, *21 September 1897*

Isaac Newton 1642–1727

English mathematician and physicist. On Newton: see
AUDEN 37:21, **BLAKE** 125:21, **BRERETON** 156:10, **COWPER**
256:16, **POPE** 615:22, **THOMSON** 808:20, **WORDSWORTH**
868:13

1 Whence is it that Nature does nothing in vain:
and whence arises all that order and beauty
which we see in the world? . . . does it not
appear from phenomena that there is a Being
incorporeal, living, intelligent, omnipresent, who
in infinite space, as it were in his Sensory, sees
the things themselves intimately, and thoroughly
perceives them, and comprehends them wholly.
Opticks (1730 ed.) bk. 3, pt. 1, question 28

2 The changing of bodies into light, and light into
bodies, is very conformable to the course of
Nature, which seems delighted with
transmutations.
Opticks (1730 ed.) bk. 3, pt. 1, question 30

3 *Corpus omne perseverare in statu suo quiescendi vel
movendi uniformiter in directum, nisi quatenus illud
a viribus impressis cogitur statum suum mutare.*

Every body continues in its state of rest, or of
uniform motion in a right line, unless it is
compelled to change that state by forces
impressed upon it.
Principia Mathematica (1687) Laws of Motion 1 (translated by
Andrew Motte, 1729)

4 *Mutationem motus proportionalem esse vi motrici
impressae et fieri secundum lineam rectam qua vis
illa imprimitur.*

The alteration of motion is ever proportional to
the motive force impressed; and is made in the
direction of the right line in which that force is
impressed.
Principia Mathematica (1687) Laws of Motion 2 (translated by
Andrew Motte, 1729)

5 *Actioni contrarium semper et aequalem esse
reactionem: sive corporum duorum actiones in se
mutuo semper esse aequales et in partes contrarias
dirigi.*

To every action there is always opposed an equal
reaction: or, the mutual actions of two bodies
upon each other are always equal, and directed
to contrary parts.
Principia Mathematica (1687) Laws of Motion 3 (translated by
Andrew Motte, 1729)

6 *Hypotheses non fingo.*

I do not feign hypotheses.
Principia Mathematica (1713 ed.) 'Scholium Generale'

7 If I have seen further it is by standing on the
shoulders of giants.
letter to Robert Hooke, 5 February 1676, in H. W. Turnbull
(ed.) *Correspondence of Isaac Newton* vol. 1 (1959); see
BERNARD 73:17, **COLERIDGE** 241:23

8 Philosophy is such an impertinently litigious lady
that a man has as good be engaged in law suits
as have to do with her.
letter to Edmond Halley, 20 June 1686, in H. W. Turnbull (ed.)
Correspondence of Isaac Newton vol. 2 (1960)

9 I don't know what I may seem to the world, but
as to myself, I seem to have been only like a
boy playing on the sea-shore and diverting
myself in now and then finding a smoother
pebble or a prettier shell than ordinary, whilst
the great ocean of truth lay all undiscovered
before me.
Joseph Spence *Anecdotes* (ed. J. Osborn, 1966) no. 1259

10 O Diamond! Diamond! thou little knowest the
mischief done!
*to a dog, who knocked over a candle which set fire to some
papers and thereby 'destroyed the almost finished labours
of some years'*
Thomas Maude *Wensley-Dale . . . a Poem* (1772) st. 23 n.;
probably apocryphal

11 By thinking on it continually.
on how he had discovered the law of gravity
attributed in Voltaire *Éléments de la philosophie de Newton* pt.
3, ch. 3 (Kehl ed. 1785–9); it did not appear in editions
published during **VOLTAIRE**'s lifetime

John Newton 1725–1807

English clergyman

12 Amazing grace! how sweet the sound
That saved a wretch like me!
I once was lost, but now am found,
Was blind, but now I see.
Olney Hymns (1779) 'Amazing grace'

13 Glorious things of thee are spoken,
Zion, city of our God!
Olney Hymns (1779) 'Glorious things of thee are spoken'

14 How sweet the name of Jesus sounds
In a believer's ear!
It soothes his sorrows, heals his wounds,
And drives away his fear.
Olney Hymns (1779) 'How sweet the name of Jesus sounds'

Nicholas I 1796–1855

Russian monarch, emperor from 1825

15 Turkey is a dying man. We may endeavour to
keep him alive, but we shall not succeed. He
will, he must die.
F. Max Müller (ed.) *Memoirs of Baron Stockmar* (translated by
G. A. M. Müller, 1873) vol. 2; see **MONTESQUIEU** 556:1

16 Russia has two generals in whom she can
confide—Generals Janvier [January] and Février
[February].
attributed; in *Punch* 10 March 1855

Nicias *c*.470–413 BC

Greek politician and Athenian general

17 Courage is the knowledge of what is and is not
to be feared.
literally 'what is to be dreaded or dared'
Plato *Laches* 195

18 For a city consists in men, and not in walls nor
in ships empty of men.
speech to the defeated Athenian army at Syracuse, 413 BC
Thucydides *History of the Peloponnesian Wars* bk. 7, sect. 77

Harold Nicolson 1886–1968

English diplomat, politician, and writer; husband of Vita
SACKVILLE-WEST

1 Ponderous and uncertain is that relation between pressure and resistance which constitutes the balance of power. The arch of peace is morticed by no iron tendons . . . One night a handful of dust will patter from the vaulting: the bats will squeak and wheel in sudden panic: nor can the fragile fingers of man then stay the rush and rumble of destruction.

> *Public Faces* (1932) ch. 6

2 I am haunted by mental decay such as I saw creeping over Ramsay MacDonald. A gradual dimming of the lights.

> diary, 28 April 1947, in *Diaries and Letters 1945–62* (1968)

3 To be a good diarist one must have a little snouty, sneaky mind.

> of Samuel **PEPYS**
>
> diary, 9 November 1947, in *Diaries and Letters 1945–62* (1968)

4 For seventeen years he did nothing at all but kill animals and stick in stamps.

> of King **GEORGE V**
>
> diary, 17 August 1949 in *Diaries and Letters 1945–62* (1968)

Reinhold Niebuhr 1892–1971

American theologian

5 Man's capacity for justice makes democracy possible, but man's inclination to injustice makes democracy necessary.

> *Children of Light and Children of Darkness* (1944) foreword

6 Our gadget-filled paradise suspended in a hell of international insecurity.

> *Pious and Secular America* (1957)

Martin Niemöller 1892–1984

German theologian

7 Ask the first man you meet what he means by defending freedom, and he'll tell you privately he means defending the standard of living.

> address at Augsburg, January 1958; James Bentley *Martin Niemöller* (1984)

8 When Hitler attacked the Jews I was not a Jew, therefore, I was not concerned. And when Hitler attacked the Catholics, I was not a Catholic, and therefore, I was not concerned. And when Hitler attacked the unions and the industrialists, I was not a member of the unions and I was not concerned. Then, Hitler attacked me and the Protestant church—and there was nobody left to be concerned.

> often quoted in the form 'In Germany they came first for the Communists, and I didn't speak up because I wasn't a Communist . . . ' and so on
>
> in *Congressional Record* 14 October 1968

Friedrich Nietzsche 1844–1900

German philosopher and writer

9 God's first blunder: Man didn't find the animals amusing,—he dominated them, and didn't even want to be an 'animal'.

> *Der Antichrist* (1888) aphorism 48

10 Woman was God's second blunder.

> *Der Antichrist* (1888) aphorism 48; see **COWLEY** 254:23

11 What I understand by 'philosopher': a terrible explosive in the presence of which everything is in danger.

> *Ecce Homo* (1908) 'Die Unzeitgemässen' sect. 3

12 God is dead: but considering the state the species Man is in, there will perhaps be caves, for ages yet, in which his shadow will be shown.

> *Die fröhliche Wissenschaft* (1882) bk. 3, sect. 108; see **PLATO** 609:2

13 Morality is the herd-instinct in the individual.

> *Die fröhliche Wissenschaft* (1882) bk. 3, sect. 116

14 The secret of reaping the greatest fruitfulness and the greatest enjoyment from life is *to live dangerously!*

> *Die fröhliche Wissenschaft* (1882) bk. 4, sect. 283

15 Insects sting, not out of malice, but because they too want to live: likewise our critics; they want, not to hurt us, but to take our blood.

> *Human All Too Human* (1879) 'Mixed Opinions and Maxims' no. 164

16 He who fights with monsters might take care lest he thereby become a monster. And if you gaze for long into an abyss, the abyss gazes also into you.

> *Jenseits von Gut und Böse* (1886) ch. 4, no. 146

17 The thought of suicide is a great source of comfort: with it a calm passage is to be made across many a bad night.

> *Jenseits von Gut und Böse* (1886) ch. 4, no. 157

18 Master-morality and slave-morality.

> *Jenseits von Gut und Böse* (1886) ch. 9, no. 260

19 *Ich lehre euch den Übermenschen. Der Mensch ist Etwas, das überwunden werden soll.*

> I teach you the superman. Man is something to be surpassed.

> *Thus Spake Zarathustra* (1883) prologue, sect. 3

20 One must have a chaos inside oneself to give birth to a dancing star.

> *Thus Spake Zarathustra* (1883) bk. 1, sect. 5

21 You are going to women? Do not forget the whip!

> *Thus Spake Zarathustra* (1883) bk. 1 'Von Alten und jungen Weiblein'

22 Whatever we have words for, that we have already got beyond.

> *Twilight of the Idols* (1889) 'Skirmishes of an Untimely Man'

23 At the base of all these aristocratic races the predator is not to be mistaken, the splendorous *blond beast*, avidly rampant for plunder and victory.

> *Zur Genealogie der Moral* (1887) 1st treatise, no. 11

Florence Nightingale 1820–1910

English nurse and medical reformer. On Nightingale: see
LONGFELLOW 499:21, **STRACHEY** 778:12

1 Were there none who were discontented with
what they have, the world would never reach
anything better.
Cassandra: an Essay (1860) pt. 2

2 It may seem a strange principle to enunciate as
the very first requirement in a Hospital that it
should do the sick no harm.
Notes on Hospitals (1863 ed.) preface

3 I would earnestly ask my sisters to keep clear of
both the jargons now current everywhere . . . of
the jargon, namely about the 'rights' of women,
which urges women to do all that men do . . .
merely because men do it, and without regard
to whether this *is* the best that women can do;
and of the jargon which urges women to do
nothing that men do, merely because they are
women . . . Woman should bring the best she
has, *whatever* that is . . . without attending to
either of these cries.
Notes on Nursing (1860)

4 What nursing has to do . . . is to put the patient
in the best condition for nature to act upon him.
Notes on Nursing (1860)

5 No *man*, not even a doctor, ever gives any other
definition of what a nurse should be than
this—'devoted and obedient.' This definition
would do just as well for a porter. It might even
do for a horse. It would not do for a policeman.
Notes on Nursing (1860)

6 It was a complete *non sequitur* that, because a
boy stole your watch, he should be supported
on your rates in jail, perhaps for life . . . That
the punishment of jail is not deterrent,
experience too sadly proves. But 'punishment' is,
perhaps, not a word in God's vocabulary at all,
and if so ought not to be in ours.
letter to Alex Devine, 28 August 1890; in Lynn McDonald (ed.)
Florence Nightingale in Society and Politics (2003) vol. 5

7 Too kind, too kind.
*on the Order of Merit being brought to her at her home, 5
December 1907*
E. Cook *Life of Florence Nightingale* (1913) vol. 2, pt. 7, ch. 9

Anaïs Nin 1903–77

French-born American writer

8 The very touch of the letter was as if you had
taken me all into your arms.
letter to Henry Miller, 6 August 1932

9 Anxiety is love's greatest killer. It creates the
failures. It makes others feel as you might when
a drowning man holds on to you. You want to
save him, but you know he will strangle you
with his panic.
diary, February 1947; *The Diary of Anaïs Nin* vol. 4 (1944-7)

Richard Milhous Nixon 1913–94

American Republican statesman, 37th President of the US
1969-74; re-elected in 1972, he resigned from office owing
to his involvement in the Watergate scandal. See also
ANONYMOUS 17:2

10 The great silent majority.
broadcast, 3 November 1969 in *New York Times* 4 November
1969

11 There can be no whitewash at the White House.
on Watergate
television speech, 30 April 1973, in *New York Times* 1 May 1973

12 I made my mistakes, but in all my years of
public life, I have never profited, never profited
from public service. I've earned every cent. And
in all of my years in public life I have never
obstructed justice . . . I welcome this kind of
examination because people have got to know
whether or not their President is a crook. Well,
I'm not a crook.
speech at press conference, 17 November 1973, in *New York
Times* 18 November 1973

13 This country needs good farmers, good
businessmen, good plumbers, good carpenters.
farewell address at White House, 9 August 1974, in *New York
Times* 10 August 1974

14 When the President does it, that means that it is
not illegal.
David Frost *I Gave Them a Sword* (1978) ch. 8

15 I brought myself down. I gave them a sword.
And they stuck it in.
television interview, 19 May 1977, in David Frost *I Gave Them a
Sword* (1978) ch. 10

Kwame Nkrumah 1900–72

Ghanaian statesman, Prime Minister 1957-60, President
1960-6

16 Freedom is not something that one people can
bestow on another as a gift. They claim it as
their own and none can keep it from them.
speech in Accra, 10 July 1953

17 We face neither East nor West: we face forward.
conference speech, Accra, 7 April 1960; *Axioms of Kwame
Nkrumah* (1967)

Caroline Maria Noel 1817–77

English hymn-writer

18 At the name of Jesus
Every knee shall bow,
Every tongue confess him
King of glory now.
'At the name of Jesus' (1861 hymn); see **BIBLE** 114:19

Thomas Noel 1799–1861

English poet

19 Rattle his bones over the stones;
He's only a pauper, whom nobody owns!
'The Pauper's Drive' (1841)

Charles Howard, Duke of Norfolk

1746–1815

English peer

1 I cannot be a good Catholic; I cannot go to heaven; and if a man is to go to the devil, he may as well go thither from the House of Lords as from any other place on earth.

Henry Best *Personal and Literary Memorials* (1829) ch. 18

Christopher North (John Wilson)

1785–1854

Scottish literary critic

2 Minds like ours, my dear James, must always be above national prejudices, and in all companies it gives me true pleasure to declare, that, as a people, the English are very little indeed inferior to the Scotch.

Blackwood's Magazine (October 1826) 'Noctes Ambrosianae' no. 20

3 His Majesty's dominions, on which the sun never sets.

Blackwood's Magazine (April 1829) 'Noctes Ambrosianae' no. 42; see **SCHILLER** 683:13

4 Laws were made to be broken.

Blackwood's Magazine (May 1830) 'Noctes Ambrosianae' no. 49

Lord North 1732–92

British statesman, Prime Minister 1770–82

5 Oh God! It is all over!

on receiving the news of Cornwallis's surrender at Yorktown, 19 October 1781

in *Dictionary of National Biography* (1917–)

Alfred Harmsworth, Lord Northcliffe 1865–1922

British newspaper proprietor. On Northcliffe: see
ANONYMOUS 17:12

6 The power of the press is very great, but not so great as the power of suppress.

office message, *Daily Mail* 1918; Reginald Rose and Geoffrey Harmsworth *Northcliffe* (1959) ch. 22

7 When I want a peerage, I shall buy it like an honest man.

Tom Driberg *Swaff* (1974) ch. 2

Caroline Norton (née Sheridan) 1808–77

English poet and songwriter

8 And all our calm is in that balm—
Not lost but gone before.

'Not Lost but Gone Before'; see **CYPRIAN** 263:15, **ROGERS** 665:13

Jack Norworth 1879–1959

American songwriter

9 Oh, shine on, shine on, harvest moon
Up in the sky.

I ain't had no lovin'
Since April, January, June, or July.

'Shine On, Harvest Moon' (1908 song)

Novalis (Friedrich von Hardenberg) 1772–1801

German poet and novelist

10 I often feel, and ever more deeply I realize, that Fate and character are the same conception.

often quoted as 'Character is destiny' or 'Character is fate'
Heinrich von Ofterdingen (1802) bk. 2; see **ELIOT** 308:8, **HERACLITUS** 393:1

11 Every Englishman is an island.

Fragmente (1929) no. 1496

12 A God-intoxicated man.

of **SPINOZA**
attributed

Alfred Noyes 1880–1958

English poet

13 Go down to Kew in lilac-time, in lilac-time, in lilac-time,
Go down to Kew in lilac-time (it isn't far from London!).

'The Barrel-Organ' (1904)

14 The wind was a torrent of darkness among the gusty trees,
The moon was a ghostly galleon tossed upon cloudy seas,
The road was a ribbon of moonlight over the purple moor,
And the highwayman came riding—
Riding—riding—
The highwayman came riding, up to the old inn-door.

'The Highwayman' (1907)

15 Look for me by moonlight;
Watch for me by moonlight;
I'll come to thee by moonlight, though hell should bar the way!

'The Highwayman' (1907)

Lord Nuffield 1877–1963

English motor manufacturer and philanthropist

16 *on seeing the Morris Minor prototype in 1945:*

It looks like a poached egg—we can't make that.
attributed

Sam Nunn 1938–

American Democratic politician

17 Don't ask, don't tell.

summary of the **CLINTON** administration's compromise policy on homosexuals serving in the armed forces, in *New York Times* 12 May 1993

Nursery rhymes

Citations given are generally for the first appearance of the rhyme. For detailed bibliographical descriptions and variants, see The Oxford Dictionary of Nursery Rhymes

18 A was an apple-pie;
B bit it;

C cut it.
John Eachard Some Observations (1671)

1 As I was going to St Ives
I met a man with seven wives.
Harley MS mid 18th century

2 Baa, baa, black sheep,
Have you any wool?
Yes, sir, yes, sir
Three bags full:
One for the master,
And one for the dame,
And one for the little boy
Who lives down the lane.
Tommy Thumb's Pretty Song Book (c.1744)

3 Boys and girls come out to play,
The moon doth shine as bright as day.
William King Useful Transactions in Philosophy (1708–9)

4 Bye, baby bunting,
Daddy's gone a hunting,
Gone to get a rabbit skin
To wrap the baby bunting in.
Gammer Gurton's Garland (1784)

5 The children in Holland take pleasure in making
What the children in England take pleasure in
   breaking.
traditional

6 Cock a doodle doo!
My dame has lost her shoe,
My master's lost his fiddlestick,
And knows not what to do.
The Most Cruel and Bloody Murder Committed by an Innkeeper's Wife (1606)

7 Cross-patch,
Draw the latch,
Sit by the fire and spin;
Take a cup,
And drink it up,
Then call your neighbours in.
Mother Goose's Melody (c.1765)

8 Curly locks, Curly locks,
Wilt thou be mine?
Thou shalt not wash dishes
Nor yet feed the swine.
But sit on a cushion
And sew a fine seam,
And feed upon strawberries,
Sugar and cream.
Infant Institutes (1797)

9 Dance to your daddy,
My little babby,
Dance to your daddy, my little lamb;
You shall have a fishy
In a little dishy,
You shall have a fishy when the boat comes in.
Vocal Harmony (c.1806)

10 Daffy-down-dilly is new come to town,
With a yellow petticoat, and a green gown.
Songs for the Nursery (1805)

11 Diddle, diddle, dumpling, my son John,
Went to bed with his trousers on.
Newest Christmas Box (c.1797)

12 Ding, dong, bell,
Pussy's in the well.
Mother Goose's Melody (c.1765)

13 Fiddle-de-dee, Fiddle-de-dee,
The fly shall marry the humble-bee.
'Fiddle-de-dee' (c.1803)

14 A frog he would a-wooing go,
'Heigh-ho!' says Rowley . . .

. . . while they were all a-merry-making,
'Heigh-ho!' says Rowley,
A cat and her kittens came tumbling in.
Thomas Ravenscroft Melismata (1611)

15 Georgie Porgie, pudding and pie,
Kissed the girls and made them cry;
When the boys came out to play,
Georgie Porgie ran away.
J. O. Halliwell (ed.) Nursery Rhymes (1844)

16 Goosey, goosey gander,
Whither shall I wander?
Upstairs and downstairs,
And in my lady's chamber.
There I met an old man
Who would not say his prayers.
I took him by the left leg
And threw him down the stairs.
Gammer Gurton's Garland (1784)

17 Grey goose and gander,
Waft your wings together,
And carry the good king's daughter
Over the one-strand river.
J. O. Halliwell (ed.) Nursery Rhymes (1844)

18 Hark! Hark! The dogs do bark,
The beggars are coming to town.
Some in rags, some in jags,
And one in a velvet gown.
Gammer Gurton's Garland (1784)

19 He began to bark,
And she began to cry,
Lawk a mercy on me,
This is none of I!
'There was a little woman', *Mansfield MS*, c.1775; Iona and
Peter Opie (eds.) *Oxford Dictionary of Nursery Rhymes* (new
edn. 1997)

20 Here am I,
Little Jumping Joan;
When nobody's with me
I'm all alone.
T. Hughes Adventures of Jumping Joan (advertised 1808)

21 Hey diddle diddle,
The cat and the fiddle,
The cow jumped over the moon;
The little dog laughed
To see such sport,
And the dish ran away with the spoon.
Mother Goose's Melody (c.1765)

1 Hickety, pickety, my black hen,
 She lays eggs for gentlemen.
  J. O. Halliwell (ed.) Nursery Rhymes (1853)

2 Hickory, dickory, dock,
 The mouse ran up the clock.
 The clock struck one,
 The mouse ran down,
 Hickory, dickory, dock.
  Tommy Thumb's Pretty Song Book (c.1744)

3 How many miles to Babylon?
 Threescore miles and ten.
 Can I get there by candle-light?
 Yes, and back again.
  Songs for the Nursery (1805)

4 Humpty Dumpty sat on a wall,
 Humpty Dumpty had a great fall;
 All the king's horses,
 And all the king's men,
 Couldn't put Humpty together again.
  MS addition to a copy of Mother Goose's Melody (c.1803)

5 If all the world were paper,
 And all the sea were ink,
 If all the trees were bread and cheese,
 What should we have to drink?
  Witt's Recreations (1641); see LYLY *505:23*

6 I had a little nut tree
 Nothing would it bear
 But a silver nutmeg
 And a golden pear;
 The King of Spain's daughter
 Came to visit me,
 And all for the sake
 Of my little nut tree.
  Newest Christmas Box (c.1797)

7 I'll tell you a story
 About Jack a Nory.
  Nurse Lovechild Jacky Nory's Story Book for all Little Masters and Misses (advertised December 1745)

8 I love little pussy,
 Her coat is so warm,
 And if I don't hurt her
 She'll do me no harm.
  Hints for the Formation of Infant Schools (1829)

9 I'm the king of the castle,
 Get down you dirty rascal.
  W. C. Hazlitt (ed.) Brand's Popular Antiquities (1870)

10 Jack and Jill went up the hill
 To fetch a pail of water;
 Jack fell down and broke his crown,
 And Jill came tumbling after.
  Mother Goose's Melody (c.1765)

11 Jack be nimble,
 Jack be quick,
 Jack jump over
 The candle stick.
  Douce MS, c.1815; J. O. Halliwell (ed.) Nursery Rhymes (1844)

12 Jack Sprat could eat no fat,
 His wife could eat no lean,
 And so between them both, you see,

They licked the platter clean.
  John Clarke Paroemiologia Anglo-Latina (1639)

13 Ladybird, ladybird,
 Fly away home,
 Your house is on fire
 And your children all gone;
 All except one
 And that's little Ann
 And she has crept under
 The warming pan.
  Tommy Thumb's Pretty Song Book (c.1744)

14 Lavender's blue, diddle, diddle,
 Lavender's green;
 When I am king, diddle, diddle,
 You shall be queen.
  J. Wright etc. Diddle Diddle (c.1680)

15 The lion and the unicorn
 Were fighting for the crown;
 The lion beat the unicorn
 All round the town.
 Some gave them white bread,
 And some gave them brown;
 Some gave them plum cake,
 And sent them out of town.
  MS inscription (c.1691) beside a woodcut of the royal arms in a bible in the Opie Collection; William King Useful Transactions in Philosophy (1708–9)

16 Little Bo-Peep has lost her sheep,
 And can't tell where to find them;
 Leave them alone, and they'll come home,
 And bring their tails behind them.
  Douce MS, c.1805; Gammer Gurton's Garland (1810)

17 Little Boy Blue,
 Come blow your horn,
 The sheep's in the meadow,
 The cow's in the corn;
 But where is the boy
 Who looks after the sheep?
 He's under a haycock,
 Fast asleep.
  The Famous Tommy Thumb's Little Story Book (c.1760)

18 Little Jack Horner
 Sat in the corner,
 Eating a Christmas pie;
 He put in his thumb,
 And pulled out a plum,
 And said, what a good boy am I!
  Henry Carey Namby Pamby (1725)

19 Little Miss Muffet
 Sat on a tuffet
 Eating her curds and whey;
 There came a big spider,
 Who sat down beside her
 And frightened Miss Muffet away.
  Songs for the Nursery (1805)

20 Little Polly Flinders
 Sat among the cinders,
 Warming her pretty little toes;
 Her mother came and caught her,
 And whipped her little daughter

For spoiling her nice new clothes.
  J. Harris *Original Ditties for the Nursery* (c.1805)

1 Little Tommy Tucker
Sings for his supper;
What shall we give him?
White bread and butter.
  Tommy Thumb's Pretty Song Book (c.1744)

2 London Bridge is broken down
My fair lady.
  Henry Carey *Namby Pamby* (1725)

3 Lucy Locket lost her pocket
Kitty Fisher found it.
  J. O. Halliwell (ed.) *Nursery Rhymes* (1842)

4 A man in the wilderness asked me,
How many strawberries grow in the sea?
I answered him, as I thought good,
As many red herrings as grow in the wood.
  Bodleian MS; Iona and Peter Opie (eds.) *The Oxford Dictionary of Nursery Rhymes* (new edn., 1997)

5 Mary, Mary, quite contrary,
How does your garden grow?
With silver bells and cockle shells
And pretty maids all in a row.
  Tommy Thumb's Pretty Song Book (c.1744)

6 Monday's child is fair of face,
Tuesday's child is full of grace,
Wednesday's child is full of woe,
Thursday's child has far to go,
Friday's child is loving and giving,
Saturday's child works hard for his living,
And the child that is born of the Sabbath day,
Is bonny, and blithe, and good and gay.
  A. E. Bray *Traditions of Devonshire* (1838)

7 My mother said that I never should
Play with the gypsies in the wood.
  Robert Graves *Less Familiar Nursery Rhymes* (1927)

8 The north wind doth blow,
And we shall have snow,
And what will poor robin do then?
                    Poor thing.
He'll sit in a barn,
To keep himself warm,
And hide his head under his wing.
                    Poor thing.
  Songs for the Nursery (1805)

9 Old King Cole
Was a merry old soul,
And a merry old soul was he;
He called for his pipe,
And he called for his bowl,
And he called for his fiddlers three.
  William King *Useful Transactions in Philosophy* (1708–9)

10 Old Mother Hubbard
Went to the cupboard
To fetch her poor dog a bone;
But when she came there
The cupboard was bare
And so the poor dog had none.
  Sarah Catherine Martin *The Comic Adventures of Old Mother Hubbard* (1805), based on a traditional rhyme

11 Old Mother Slipper Slopper jumped out of bed,
And out of the window she popped her head:
Oh! John, John, John, the grey goose is gone,
And the fox is off to his den O! . . .

. . . And the little ones picked the bones O!
  'A fox jumped up one winter's night' in *Gammer Gurton's Garland* (1810)

12 One a penny, two a penny,
Hot cross buns!
If your daughters do not like them,
Give them to your sons.
  Christmas Box (1797)

13 One flew east and one flew west,
And one flew over the cuckoo's nest.
  traditional American version of counting-out rhyme 'Intry mintry cutry corn'; Roger D. Abrahams *Jump-Rope Rhymes* (1969)

14 One, two
Buckle my shoe;
Three, four,
Knock at the door;
Five, six,
Pick up sticks.
Seven, eight,
Lay them straight;
Nine, ten
A big fat hen.
  Songs for the Nursery (1805)

15 Oranges and lemons
Say the bells of St. Clements . . .

. . . When will you pay me?
Say the bells of Old Bailey.

When I grow rich,
Say the bells of Shoreditch . . .

. . . Here comes a candle to light you to bed,
Here comes a chopper to chop off your head.
  Tommy Thumb's Pretty Song Book (c.1744)

16 Pat-a-cake, pat-a-cake, baker's man,
Bake me a cake as fast as you can;
Pat it and prick it, and mark it with B,
Put it in the oven for baby and me.
  Tom D'Urfey *The Campaigners* (1698)

17 Pease porridge hot,
Pease porridge cold,
Pease porridge in the pot
Nine days old.
  Newest Christmas Box (c.1797)

18 Peter Piper picked a peck of pickled pepper.
  Peter Piper's Practical Principles of Plain and Perfect Pronunciation (1813)

19 Polly put the kettle on,
We'll all have tea.
  Charles Dickens *Barnaby Rudge* (1841)

20 Pussy cat, pussy cat, where have you been?
I've been to London to look at the queen.
  Songs for the Nursery (1805)

21 The Queen of Hearts
She made some tarts,
All on a summer's day;

The Knave of Hearts
He stole the tarts,
And took them clean away.
'The Hive, A Collection of Scraps' in *The European Magazine*
April 1782

1 Rain, rain, go away,
Come again another day.
James Howell *Proverbs* (1659)

2 Ride a cock-horse to Banbury Cross,
To see a fine lady upon a white horse;
Rings on her fingers and bells on her toes,
And she shall have music wherever she goes.
Gammer Gurton's Garland (1784)

3 Ring-a-ring o'roses,
A pocket full of posies,
A-tishoo! A-tishoo!
We all fall down.
Kate Greenaway *Mother Goose* (1881)

4 Round and round the garden
Like a teddy bear.
orally collected, 1946–50; Iona and Peter Opie (eds.) *The
Oxford Dictionary of Nursery Rhymes* (new edn., 1997)

5 Rub-a-dub-dub,
Three men in a tub
And how do you think they got there?
The butcher, the baker,
The candlestick-maker,
They all jumped out of a rotten potato
'Twas enough to make a man stare.
Christmas Box vol. 2 (1798)

6 See-saw, Margery Daw,
Jacky shall have a new master;
Jacky shall have but a penny a day,
Because he can't work any faster.
Mother Goose's Melody (c.1765)

7 Simple Simon met a pieman,
Going to the fair;
Says Simple Simon to the pieman,
Let me taste your ware.
Simple Simon, chapbook advertisement, 1764

8 Sing a song of sixpence,
A pocket full of rye;
Four and twenty blackbirds,
Baked in a pie.

When the pie was opened,
The birds began to sing;
Was not that a dainty dish,
To set before the king?

The king was in his counting-house,
Counting out his money;
The queen was in the parlour,
Eating bread and honey.

The maid was in the garden,
Hanging out the clothes,
There came a little blackbird,
And snapped off her nose.
Tommy Thumb's Pretty Song Book (c.1744)

9 Solomon Grundy,
Born on a Monday,

Christened on Tuesday,
Married on Wednesday,
Took ill on Thursday,
Worse on Friday,
Died on Saturday,
Buried on Sunday:
This is the end
Of Solomon Grundy.
J. O. Halliwell *Nursery Rhymes* (1842)

10 Taffy was a Welshman, Taffy was a thief,
Taffy came to my house and stole a piece of
beef.
Nancy Cock's Pretty Song Book (c.1780)

11 Tell tale tit,
Your tongue shall be slit.
Mother Goose's Melody (1780)

12 There was a crooked man, and he walked a
crooked mile,
He found a crooked sixpence against a crooked
stile;
He bought a crooked cat, which caught a
crooked mouse,
And they all lived together in a little crooked
house.
J. O. Halliwell (ed.) *Nursery Rhymes* (1842)

13 There was a lady loved a swine,
Honey, quoth she,
Pig-hog wilt thou be mine?
Hoogh, quoth he.
Bodley MS, c.1620; Iona and Peter Opie (eds.) *The Oxford
Dictionary of Nursery Rhymes* (new edn, 1997)

14 There was a little man, and he had a little gun.
Tommy Thumb's Pretty Song Book (c.1744)

15 There was an old woman who lived in a shoe,
She had so many children she didn't know what
to do.
Gammer Gurton's Garland (1784)

16 This is the house that Jack built . . .
. . . This is the farmer sowing his corn,
That kept the cock that crowed in the morn,
That waked the priest all shaven and shorn,
That married the man all tattered and torn,
That kissed the maiden all forlorn,
That milked the cow with the crumpled horn,
That tossed the dog,
That worried the cat,
That killed the rat,
That ate the malt
That lay in the house that Jack built.
Nurse Truelove's New-Year's-Gift (1755)

17 This is the way the ladies ride.
Robert Chambers *The Popular Rhymes of Scotland* (1842)

18 This little pig went to market,
This little pig stayed at home,
This little pig had roast beef,
This little pig had none,
And this little pig cried, Wee-wee-wee-wee-wee, I
can't find my way home.
The Famous Tommy Thumb's Little Story Book (c.1760)

1 Three blind mice, see how they run!
They all ran after the farmer's wife,
Who cut off their tails with a carving knife,
Did you ever see such a thing in your life,
As three blind mice?
   Thomas Ravenscroft *Deuteromelia* (1609)

2 Three little kittens they lost their mittens.
   Eliza Follen *New Nursery Songs* (1853)

3 Three wise men of Gotham
Went to sea in a bowl:
And if the bowl had been stronger,
My song would have been longer.
   Mother Goose's Melody (c.1765)

4 Tinker,
Tailor,
Soldier,
Sailor,
Rich man,
Poor man,
Beggarman,
Thief.
   traditional fortune-telling rhyme for counting out objects
   such as cherry stones or daisy petals; Iona and Peter Opie
   (eds.) *The Oxford Dictionary of Nursery Rhymes* (new edn,
   1997)

5 To market, to market,
To buy a plum bun:
Home again, home again,
Market is done.
   John Florio *Worlde of Wordes* (1611 edn.), *Songs for the Nursery*
   (1805)

6 Tom he was a piper's son,
He learned to play when he was young,
But all the tune that he could play,
Was 'Over the hills and far away.'
   Tom, the Piper's Son (chapbooks, from c.1795); see **GAY** 351:4,
   STEVENSON 777:6

7 Tom, Tom, the piper's son,
Stole a pig and away he run;
The pig was eat
And Tom was beat
And Tom went howling down the street.
   Tom, the Piper's Son (chapbooks, from c.1795)

8 Twist about, turn about, jump Jim Crow.
   Humorous Adventures of Jump Jim Crow (c.1836)

9 Wee Willie Winkie runs through the town,
Upstairs and downstairs in his night-gown,
Rapping at the window, crying through the lock,
Are the children all in bed, for now it's eight
   o'clock.
   Cries of Banbury and London (c.1840); this traditional rhyme
   formed the basis for a longer poem by William Miller
   (1810–72) in *Whistle-Binkie; A Collection of Songs for the Social
   Circle* (1841)

10 What are little boys made of?
What are little boys made of?
Frogs and snails
And puppy-dogs' tails,
That's what little boys are made of.
What are little girls made of?
What are little girls made of?

Sugar and spice
And all that's nice,
That's what little girls are made of.
   J. O. Halliwell *Nursery Rhymes* (1844)

11 Where are you going to, my pretty maid? . . .
   . . . My face is my fortune, sir, she said.
Then I can't marry you, my pretty maid.
Nobody asked you, sir, she said.
   William Pryce *Archaeologica Cornu-Britannica* (1790)

12 Who killed Cock Robin?
I, said the Sparrow,
With my bow and arrow,
I killed Cock Robin.

Who saw him die?
I, said the Fly,
With my little eye,
I saw him die . . .

. . . All the birds of the air
Fell a-sighing and a-sobbing,
When they heard the bell toll
For poor Cock Robin.
   Tommy Thumb's Pretty Song Book (c.1744)

Bill Nye (Edgar Wilson Nye) 1850–96
American humorist

13 I have been told that Wagner's music is better
than it sounds.
   Mark Twain *Autobiography* (1924) vol. 1

Julius Nyerere 1922–99
**Tanzanian statesman, President of Tanganyika 1962–4 and
of Tanzania 1964–85**

14 Should we really let our people starve so we can
pay our debts?
   in *Guardian* 21 March 1985

Oo

Charles Edward Oakley 1832–65
English clergyman

15 Hills of the North, rejoice:
Rivers and mountain-spring,
Hark to the advent voice!
Valley and lowland, sing!
   'Hills of the North, rejoice' (1870 hymn)

Lawrence Oates 1880–1912
English polar explorer. On Oates: see EPITAPHS 317:14

16 I am just going outside and may be some time.
   Robert Falcon **SCOTT** diary entry, 16–17 March 1912 in *Scott's
   Last Expedition* (1913) ch. 20; see **EPITAPHS** 317:14, **MAHON**
   516:6

Barack Obama 1959–

American Democratic statesman, 44th President of the US from 2009. See also **POLITICAL SLOGANS AND SONGS** 613:21

1 The arc of history is long but it bends towards justice.
    speech, George Mason University, 2 February 2007, in *Guardian* 10 February 2007; see **KING** 463:14, **PARKER** 596:23

Conor Cruise O'Brien 1917–2008

Irish politician, writer, and journalist. See also **HAUGHEY** 384:6

2 The strength of these men was that each of them could look a Pearsean ghost in the eye . . . Each of them, in their youth, had done the thing the ghost asked them to do, in 1916 or 1919–21 or both. That was it; from now on they would do what seemed reasonable to themselves in the interests of the actual people inhabiting the island of Ireland and not of a personified abstraction, or of a disembodied voice, or of a ghost.
    *of Sean Lemass (1899–1971) and other senior Irish politicians in the 1960s; see **PEARSE** 601:3*
        Ancestral Voices (1994)

3 If I saw Mr Haughey buried at midnight at a crossroads, with a stake driven through his heart—politically speaking—I should continue to wear a clove of garlic round my neck, just in case.
    in *Observer* 10 October 1982

Edna O'Brien 1932–

Irish novelist and short-story writer

4 August is a wicked month.
    title of novel (1965)

Flann O'Brien (Brian O'Nolan *and* O Nuallain) 1911–66

Irish novelist and journalist

5 A pint of plain is your only man.
    At Swim-Two-Birds (1939) 'The Workman's Friend'

Sean O'Casey 1880–1964

Irish dramatist

6 I killin' meself workin', an' he shthruttin' about from mornin' till night like a paycock!
    Juno and the Paycock (1925) act 1

7 He's an oul' butty o' mine—oh, he's a darlin' man, a daarlin' man.
    Juno and the Paycock (1925) act 1

8 The whole worl's in a state o' chassis!
    Juno and the Paycock (1925) act 1

9 English literature's performing flea.
    *of P. G. **WODEHOUSE***
        P. G. Wodehouse *Performing Flea* (1953)

William of Occam c.1285–1349

English Franciscan friar and philosopher

10 *Entia non sunt multiplicanda praeter necessitatem.*
    No more things should be presumed to exist than are absolutely necessary.
    'Occam's Razor', an ancient philosophical principle often attributed to Occam but earlier in origin
        not found in this form in his writings, although he frequently used similar expressions, such as: *'Pluralitas non est ponenda sine necessitate* [Plurality should not be assumed unnecessarily]', *Quodlibeta (c.1324)* no. 5, question 1, art. 2

Daniel O'Connell 1775–1847

Irish nationalist leader and social reformer, elected to Parliament in 1828

11 I have given my advice to my countrymen, and whenever I feel it necessary I shall continue to do so, careless whether it pleases or displeases this House or any mad person out of it.
    in *Dictionary of National Biography* (1917–)

Bernard O'Donoghue 1945–

Irish poet and academic

12 We were terribly lucky to catch
    The Ceauşescus' execution, being
    By sheer chance that Christmas Day
    In the only house for twenty miles
    With satellite TV. We sat,
    Cradling brandies, by the fire
    Watching those two small, cranky autocrats
    Lying in snow against a blood-spattered wall,
    Hardly able to believe our good fortune.
    'Carolling' (1995)

☐ **Official advice** *see* **box overleaf**

David Ogilvy 1911–99

British-born advertising executive

13 The consumer isn't a moron; she is your wife.
    Confessions of an Advertising Man (1963) ch. 5

James Ogilvy, Lord Seafield 1664–1730

Scottish lawyer, Lord Chancellor of Scotland

14 Now there's ane end of ane old song.
    as he signed the engrossed exemplification of the Act of Union, 1706
        in *The Lockhart Papers* (1817) vol. 1

John O'Hara 1905–70

American writer

15 Appointment in Samarra.
    title of novel (1934); see **MAUGHAM** 528:12

16 An artist is his own fault.
    The Portable F. Scott Fitzgerald (1945) introduction

Official advice

1 Careless talk costs lives.
   Second World War security slogan (popularly inverted as 'careless lives cost talk')

2 Clunk, click, every trip.
   road safety campaign promoting the use of seat-belts, 1971

3 Coughs and sneezes spread diseases. Trap the germs in your handkerchief.
   Second World War health slogan (1942)

4 Dig for Victory.
   Second World War slogan; from a radio broadcast by Reginald Dorman-Smith (1899–1977), 3 October 1939: 'Let "Dig for Victory" be the motto of every one with a garden and of every able-bodied man and woman capable of digging an allotment in their spare time', in *The Times* 4 October 1939

5 Don't ask a man to drink and drive.
   UK road safety slogan, from 1964

6 Don't die of ignorance.
   Aids publicity campaign, 1987

7 Duck and cover.
   US advice in the event of a missile attack, c.1950; associated particularly with children's cartoon character 'Bert the Turtle'

8 Is your journey *really* necessary?
   slogan coined to discourage Civil Servants from going home for Christmas, 1939

9 Keep Britain tidy.
   issued by the Central Office of Information, 1950s

10 Make do and mend.
   wartime slogan, 1940s

11 Slip, slop, slap.
   sun protection slogan, meaning slip *on a T-shirt,* slop *on some suncream,* slap *on a hat*
   Australian health education programme, 1980s

12 Smoking can seriously damage your health.
   government health warning now required by British law to be printed on cigarette packets
   from early 1970s, in form 'Smoking can damage your health'

13 Stop-look-and-listen.
   road safety slogan, current in the US from 1912

14 *Taisez-vous! Méfiez-vous! Les oreilles ennemies vous écoutent.*
   Keep your mouth shut! Be on your guard! Enemy ears are listening to you.
   official notice in France, 1915

15 Tradition dictates that we have a lawn—but do we really need one? Why not increase the size of your borders or replace lawned areas with paving stones or gravel?
   Severn Trent Water 'The Gardener's Water Code' (1996)

Theodore O'Hara 1820–67

American poet

16 The bivouac of the dead.
   title of poem (1847)

17 Sons of the dark and bloody ground.
   popularized 'the dark and bloody ground' as a name for Kentucky
   'The Bivouac of the Dead' (1847) st. 1

Georgia O'Keefe 1887–1986

American painter

18 Filling a space in a beautiful way. That's what art means to me.
   in *Art News* December 1977

John O'Keeffe 1747–1833

Irish dramatist

19 Amo, amas, I love a lass,
   As a cedar tall and slender;
   Sweet cowslip's grace
   Is her nom'native case,
   And she's of the feminine gender.
   The Agreeable Surprise (1781) act 2, sc. 2

20 Fat, fair and forty were all the toasts of the young men.
   The Irish Mimic (1795) sc. 2

Dennis O'Kelly c.1720–87

Irish racehorse-owner

21 Eclipse first, the rest nowhere.
   comment at Epsom on the occasion of the horse Eclipse's first race, 3 May 1769; the Dictionary of National Biography *gives the occasion as the Queen's Plate at Winchester, 1769*
   in *Annals of Sporting* vol. 2 (1822)

Abraham Okpik d. 1997

Canadian Inuit spokesman

22 There are very few Eskimos, but millions of Whites, just like mosquitoes. It is something very special and wonderful to be an Eskimo—they are like the snow geese. If an Eskimo forgets his language and Eskimo ways, he will be nothing but just another mosquito.
   attributed, 1966

Bruce Oldfield 1950–

English fashion designer

23 Fashion is more usually a gentle progression of revisited ideas.
   in *Independent* 9 September 1989

William Oldys 1696–1761

English antiquary

24 Busy, curious, thirsty fly,
   Gently drink, and drink as I;

Freely welcome to my cup.
'The Fly' (1732)

Frederick Scott Oliver 1864–1934

Scottish writer

1 A wise politician will never grudge a genuflexion or a rapture if it is expected of him by prevalent opinion.
The Endless Adventure (1930) vol. 1, pt. 1, ch. 20

Laurence Olivier 1907–89

English actor and director

2 The tragedy of a man who could not make up his mind.
introduction to his 1948 screen adaptation of *Hamlet*

3 Shakespeare—the nearest thing in incarnation to the eye of God.
in *Kenneth Harris Talking To* (1971) 'Sir Laurence Olivier'

4 Acting is a masochistic form of exhibitionism. It is not quite the occupation of an adult.
in *Time* 3 July 1978

Frank Ward O'Malley *see* Hubbard

417:14

Omar *c.*581–644

Arab caliph, conqueror of Syria, Palestine, and Egypt

5 If these writings of the Greeks agree with the book of God, they are useless and need not be preserved; if they disagree, they are pernicious and ought to be destroyed.
on burning the library of Alexandria, AD *c.641*
Edward Gibbon *The Decline and Fall of the Roman Empire* (1776–88) ch. 51

Jacqueline Kennedy Onassis 1929–94

American wife of John F. **KENNEDY**, First Lady of the US 1961–3

6 There'll be great Presidents again—and the Johnsons are wonderful, they've been wonderful to me—but there'll never be another Camelot again.
in *Life* 6 December 1963; see **LERNER** 490:6

Eugene O'Neill 1888–1953

American dramatist

7 For de little stealin' dey gits you in jail soon or late. For de big stealin' dey makes you Emperor and puts you in de Hall o' Fame when you croaks.
The Emperor Jones (1921) sc. 1

8 The iceman cometh.
title of play (1946)

9 A long day's journey into night.
title of play (written 1940–1)

10 Mourning becomes Electra.
title of play (1931)

11 The sea hates a coward!
Mourning becomes Electra (1931) pt. 2, act 4

Yoko Ono 1933–

Japanese poet and songwriter

12 Woman is the nigger of the world.
remark made in a 1968 interview for *Nova* magazine and adopted by her husband John **LENNON** as the title of a song (1972); J. Robertson *Art and Music of John Lennon* (1990) ch. 11

Brian O'Nolan *see* Flann O'Brien

John Opie 1761–1807

English painter

13 I mix them with my brains, sir.
on being asked with what he mixed his colours
Samuel Smiles *Self-Help* (1859) ch. 4

J. Robert Oppenheimer 1904–67

American physicist

14 I remembered the line from the Hindu scripture, the *Bhagavad Gita* . . . 'I am become death, the destroyer of worlds.'
on the explosion of the first atomic bomb near Alamogordo, New Mexico, 16 July 1945
Len Giovannitti and Fred Freed *The Decision to Drop the Bomb* (1965); see **BHAGAVADGITA** 78:4

15 The physicists have known sin; and this is a knowledge which they cannot lose.
lecture at Massachusetts Institute of Technology, 25 November 1947, in *Open Mind* (1955) ch. 5

16 When you see something that is technically sweet, you go ahead and do it and you argue about what to do about it only after you have had your technical success. That is the way it was with the atomic bomb.
in *In the Matter of J. Robert Oppenheimer, USAEC Transcript of Hearing Before Personnel Security Board* (1954)

Egan O'Rahilly *c.*1675–1729

Irish poet

17 I shall go after the heroes, ay, into the clay— My fathers followed theirs before Christ was crucified.
'Last Lines' translated by Frank O'Connor

Susie Orbach 1946–

American psychotherapist

18 Fat is a feminist issue.
title of book (1978)

Roy Orbison 1936–88 *and* Joe Melson 1935–

American singers and songwriters

19 Only the lonely (know the way I feel).
title of song (1960)

Orchot Tzaddikim

Jewish ethical work [The Ways of the Righteous] of c.15th century

1 The thread on which the different good qualities of human beings are strung as pearls, is the fear of God. When the fastenings of this fear are unloosed, the pearls roll in all directions, and are lost one by one.
Orchot Tzaddikim

2 Be not blind, but open-eyed, to the great wonders of Nature, familiar, everyday objects though they be to thee. But men are more wont to be astonished at the sun's eclipse than at his unfailing rise.
Orchot Tzaddikim

3 Be grateful for, not blind to the many, many sufferings which thou art spared; thou art no better than those who have been searched out and racked by them.
Orchot Tzaddikim

Baroness Orczy (Mrs Montague Barstow)

1865–1947

Hungarian-born novelist

4 We seek him here, we seek him there,
Those Frenchies seek him everywhere.
Is he in heaven?—Is he in hell?
That demmed, elusive Pimpernel?
The Scarlet Pimpernel (1905) ch. 12

Orderic Vitalis 1075–c.1142

English-born Norman monk and chronicler

5 For the mangled bodies that had been the flower of the English nobility and youth covered the ground as far as the eye could see.
of the battlefield at Hastings after the Norman victory in 1066
Ecclesiastical History

6 For the fortifications called castles by the French were scarcely known in the English provinces.
explaining the weakness of the English resistance, despite their fighting prowess
Ecclesiastical History

Meta Orred

Scottish 19th-century writer and poet

7 In the gloaming, Oh my darling!
When the lights are dim and low,
And the quiet shadows falling
Softly come and softly go.
'In the Gloaming' (1877 song)

José Ortega y Gasset 1883–1955

Spanish writer and philosopher

8 I am I plus my surroundings, and if I do not preserve the latter I do not preserve myself.
Meditations on Quixote (1914)

9 Hatred is a feeling which leads to the extinction of values.
Meditations on Quixote (1914)

10 Civilization is nothing more than the effort to reduce the use of force to the last resort.
The Revolt of the Masses (1930) ch. 8

11 A revolution does not last more than fifteen years, the period which coincides with the flourishing of a generation.
The Revolt of the Masses (1930) ch. 10

Joe Orton 1933–67

English dramatist

12 I'd the upbringing a nun would envy . . . Until I was fifteen I was more familiar with Africa than my own body.
Entertaining Mr Sloane (1964) act 1

13 It's all any reasonable child can expect if the dad is present at the conception.
Entertaining Mr Sloane (1964) act 3

14 Reading isn't an occupation we encourage among police officers. We try to keep the paper work down to a minimum.
Loot (1967) act 2

15 You were born with your legs apart. They'll send you to the grave in a Y-shaped coffin.
What the Butler Saw (1969) act 1

George Orwell (Eric Blair) 1903–50

English novelist and essayist

16 Man is the only creature that consumes without producing.
Animal Farm (1945) ch. 1

17 Four legs good, two legs bad.
Animal Farm (1945) ch. 3

18 All animals are equal but some animals are more equal than others.
Animal Farm (1945) ch. 10

19 The creatures outside looked from pig to man, and from man to pig, and from pig to man again, but already it was impossible to say which was which.
Animal Farm (1945), closing words

20 Good prose is like a window-pane.
Collected Essays (1968) vol. 1 'Why I Write'

21 I'm fat, but I'm thin inside. Has it ever struck you that there's a thin man inside every fat man, just as they say there's a statue inside every block of stone?
Coming up For Air (1939) pt. 1, ch. 3; see **CONNOLLY** 248:10

22 Roast beef and Yorkshire, or roast pork and apple sauce, followed up by suet pudding and driven home, as it were, by a cup of mahogany-brown tea, have put you in just the right mood . . . In these blissful circumstances, what is it that you want to read about?
Naturally, about a murder.
Decline of the English Murder and other essays (1965) title essay, written 1946

1 Down and out in Paris and London.
   title of book (1933)

2 He was an embittered atheist (the sort of atheist who does not so much disbelieve in God as personally dislike Him), and took a sort of pleasure in thinking that human affairs would never improve.
   Down and Out in Paris and London (1933) ch. 30

3 Down here it was still the England I had known in my childhood: the railway cuttings smothered in wild flowers . . . the red buses, the blue policemen—all sleeping the deep, deep sleep of England, from which I sometimes fear that we shall never wake till we are jerked out of it by the roar of bombs.
   Homage to Catalonia (1938) ch. 14

4 Keep the aspidistra flying.
   title of novel (1936)

5 Advertising is the rattling of a stick inside a swill bucket.
   Keep the Aspidistra Flying (1936) ch. 3

6 England is not the jewelled isle of Shakespeare's much-quoted passage, nor is it the inferno depicted by Dr Goebbels. More than either it resembles a family, a rather stuffy Victorian family, with not many black sheep in it but with all its cupboards bursting with skeletons . . . A family with the wrong members in control.
   The Lion and the Unicorn (1941) pt. 1 'England Your England';
   see **SHAKESPEARE** 730:10

7 Old maids biking to Holy Communion through the mists of the autumn mornings . . . these are not only fragments, but *characteristic* fragments, of the English scene.
   The Lion and the Unicorn (1941) pt. 1 'England Your England';
   see **MAJOR** 517:4

8 Probably the battle of Waterloo *was* won on the playing-fields of Eton, but the opening battles of all subsequent wars have been lost there.
   The Lion and the Unicorn (1941) pt. 1 'England Your England';
   see **WELLINGTON** 846:13

9 It was a bright cold day in April, and the clocks were striking thirteen.
   Nineteen Eighty-Four (1949), opening words

10 BIG BROTHER IS WATCHING YOU.
   Nineteen Eighty-Four (1949) pt. 1, ch. 1

11 War is peace. Freedom is slavery. Ignorance is strength.
   Nineteen Eighty-Four (1949) pt. 1, ch. 1

12 Who controls the past controls the future: who controls the present controls the past.
   Nineteen Eighty-Four (1949) pt. 1, ch. 3

13 Don't you see that the whole aim of Newspeak is to narrow the range of thought? In the end we shall make thoughtcrime literally impossible, because there will be no words in which to express it.
   Nineteen Eighty-Four (1949) pt. 1, ch. 5

14 Freedom is the freedom to say that two plus two make four. If that is granted, all else follows.
   Nineteen Eighty-Four (1949) pt. 1, ch. 7

15 The Lottery, with its weekly pay-out of enormous prizes, was the one public event to which the proles paid serious attention . . . It was their delight, their folly, their anodyne, their intellectual stimulant . . . the prizes were largely imaginary. Only small sums were actually paid out, the winners of the big prizes being non-existent persons.
   Nineteen Eighty-Four (1949) pt. 1, ch. 8

16 Syme was not only dead, he was abolished, an un-person.
   Nineteen Eighty-Four (1949) pt. 2, ch. 5

17 *Doublethink* means the power of holding two contradictory beliefs in one's mind simultaneously, and accepting both of them.
   Nineteen Eighty-Four (1949) pt. 2, ch. 9

18 Power is not a means, it is an end. One does not establish a dictatorship in order to safeguard a revolution; one makes the revolution in order to establish the dictatorship.
   Nineteen Eighty-Four (1949) pt. 3, ch. 3

19 If you want a picture of the future, imagine a boot stamping on a human face—for ever.
   Nineteen Eighty-Four (1949) pt. 3, ch. 3

20 In a Lancashire cotton-town you could probably go for months on end without once hearing an 'educated' accent, whereas there can hardly be a town in the South of England where you could throw a brick without hitting the niece of a bishop.
   The Road to Wigan Pier (1937) ch. 7

21 The high-water mark, so to speak, of Socialist literature is W. H. Auden, a sort of gutless Kipling.
   The Road to Wigan Pier (1937) ch. 11

22 We of the sinking middle class . . . may sink without further struggles into the working class where we belong, and probably when we get there it will not be so dreadful as we feared, for, after all, we have nothing to lose but our aitches.
   The Road to Wigan Pier (1937) ch. 13

23 Serious sport has nothing to do with fair play. It is bound up with hatred, jealousy, boastfulness, disregard of all rules, and sadistic pleasure in witnessing violence: in other words it is war minus the shooting.
   Shooting an Elephant (1950) 'I Write as I Please'

24 The great enemy of clear language is insincerity. When there is a gap between one's real and one's declared aims, one turns as it were instinctively to long words and exhausted idioms, like a cuttlefish squirting out ink.
   Shooting an Elephant (1950) 'Politics and the English Language'

1 In our time, political speech and writing are largely the defence of the indefensible.
Shooting an Elephant (1950) 'Politics and the English Language'

2 Political language . . . is designed to make lies sound truthful and murder respectable, and to give an appearance of solidity to pure wind.
Shooting an Elephant (1950) 'Politics and the English Language'

3 Saints should always be judged guilty until they are proved innocent.
Shooting an Elephant (1950) 'Reflections on Gandhi'

4 If there is a wrong thing to do, it will be done, infallibly. One has come to believe in that as if it were a law of nature.
diary, 18 May 1941, in *Collected Essays, Journalism and Letters* (1968) vol. 2; see **PROVERBS** 635:5

5 Whatever is funny is subversive, every joke is ultimately a custard pie . . . A dirty joke is a sort of mental rebellion.
in *Horizon* September 1941 'The Art of Donald McGill'

6 If liberty means anything at all it means the right to tell people what they do not want to hear.
'The Freedom of the Press' (written 1944), in *Times Literary Supplement* 15 September 1972

7 The quickest way of ending a war is to lose it.
in *Polemic* May 1946 'Second Thoughts on James Burnham'

8 At 50, everyone has the face he deserves.
last words in his notebook, 17 April 1949, in *Collected Essays, Journalism and Letters . . .* (1968) vol. 4

Dorothy Osborne 1627–95

English letter-writer and (from 1654) wife of William TEMPLE

9 About six or seven o'clock, I walk out into a common that lies hard by the house, where a great many young wenches keep sheep and cows and sit in the shade singing of ballads . . . I talk to them, and find they want nothing to make them the happiest people in the world, but the knowledge that they are so.
Letters of Dorothy Osborne to William Temple (ed. G. C. Moore Smith, 1928) 2 June 1653

10 All letters, methinks, should be free and easy as one's discourse, not studied as an oration, nor made up of hard words like a charm.
letter to William Temple, September 1653

11 'Tis much easier sure to get a good fortune than a good husband, but whosoever marries without any consideration of fortune shall never be allowed to do it out of so reasonable an apprehension.
letter to William Temple, 4 February 1654

12 I do not see that it puts any value upon men when women marry them for love (as they term it); 'tis not their merit but our folly that is always presumed to cause it, and would it be any advantage to you to have your wife thought an indiscreet person?
letter to William Temple, 4 February 1654

13 Dr Taylor . . . says there is a great advantage to be gained in resigning up one's will to the command of another, because the same action which in itself is wholly indifferent if done upon our own choice, becomes an act of duty and religion if done in obedience to the command of any person whom nature, the laws, or our selves have given a power over us.
letter to William Temple, 19 February 1654

John Osborne 1929–94

English dramatist

14 Don't clap too hard—it's a very old building.
The Entertainer (1957) no. 7

15 But I have a go, lady, don't I? I 'ave a go. I do.
The Entertainer (1957) no. 7

16 Look back in anger.
title of play (1956); see **PAUL** 600:1

17 Oh heavens, how I long for a little ordinary human enthusiasm. Just enthusiasm—that's all. I want to hear a warm, thrilling voice cry out Hallelujah! Hallelujah! I'm alive!
Look Back in Anger (1956) act 1

18 They spend their time mostly looking forward to the past.
Look Back in Anger (1956) act 2, sc. 1

19 There aren't any good, brave causes left. If the big bang does come, and we all get killed off, it won't be in aid of the old-fashioned, grand design. It'll just be for the Brave New-nothing-very-much-thank-you. About as pointless and inglorious as stepping in front of a bus.
Look Back in Anger (1956) act 3, sc. 1

20 Royalty is the gold filling in a mouthful of decay.
'They call it cricket' in T. Maschler (ed.) *Declaration* (1957)

21 This is a letter of hate. It is for you my countrymen, I mean those men of my country who have defiled it. The men with manic fingers leading the sightless, feeble, betrayed body of my country to its death . . . damn you England.
in *Tribune* 18 August 1961

Arthur O'Shaughnessy 1844–81

English poet

22 We are the music makers,
We are the dreamers of dreams . . .
We are the movers and shakers
Of the world for ever, it seems.
'Ode' (1874)

23 For each age is a dream that is dying,
Or one that is coming to birth.
'Ode' (1874)

William Osler 1849–1919

Canadian-born physician

1 That man can interrogate as well as observe nature, was a lesson slowly learned in his evolution.
Aphorisms from his Bedside Teachings (1961)

2 One finger in the throat and one in the rectum makes a good diagnostician.
Aphorisms from his Bedside Teachings (1961)

3 The young physician starts life with twenty drugs for each disease, and the old physician ends life with one drug for twenty diseases.
Aphorisms from His Bedside Teachings and Writings (1950, ed. William Bennett Bean)

4 The natural man has only two primal passions, to get and beget.
Science and Immortality (1904) ch. 2

5 The desire to take medicine is perhaps the greatest feature which distinguishes man from animals.
H. Cushing *Life of Sir William Osler* (1925) vol. 1, ch. 14

John L. O'Sullivan 1813–95

American journalist and diplomat

6 The best government is that which governs least.
in *United States Magazine and Democratic Review* (1837) introduction; see **THOREAU** 809:3

7 A spirit of hostile interference against us . . . checking the fulfilment of our manifest destiny to overspread the continent allotted by Providence for the free development of our yearly multiplying millions.
on opposition to the annexation of Texas
in *United States Magazine and Democratic Review* (1845) vol. 17

8 A torchlight procession marching down your throat.
describing certain kinds of whisky
G. W. E. Russell *Collections and Recollections* (1898) ch. 19

James Otis 1725–83

American politician

9 Taxation without representation is tyranny.
associated with his attack on writs of assistance, 1761, and later a watchword of the American Revolution
in *Dictionary of American Biography* vol. 14; see **CAMDEN** 194:11

Thomas Otway 1652–85

English dramatist

10 And for an apple damn'd mankind.
The Orphan (1680) act 3

11 Angels are painted fair to look like you:
There's in you all that we believe of heaven;
Amazing brightness, purity, and truth,
Eternal joy, and everlasting love!
Venice Preserved (1682) act 1, sc. 1

12 No praying, it spoils business.
Venice Preserved (1682) act 2, sc. 1

13 Give but an Englishman his whore and ease,
Beef and a sea-coal fire, he's yours for ever.
Venice Preserved (1682) act 2, sc. 3

14 The curse of growing factions and divisions
Still vex your councils.
Venice Preserved (1682) act 4, sc. 2

Thomas Overbury 1581–1613

English poet and courtier

15 He disdains all things above his reach, and preferreth all countries before his own.
Miscellaneous Works (1632) 'An Affected Traveller'; see **CANNING** 197:1, **DISRAELI** 285:7, **GILBERT** 357:4

Ovid (Publius Ovidius Naso) 43 BC–c.AD 17

Roman poet. On Ovid: see **DRYDEN** 296:8, **QUINTILIAN** 652:7

16 *Et puer est et nudus Amor sine sordibus annos*
Et nullas vestes, ut sit apertus, habet.
Quid puerum Veneris pretio prostare iubetis?
Quo pretuim condat non habet ille sinum.

Love is a child and naked; he has years that know no meanness, and he has no clothes, so that he is open in his ways. Why do you bid Venus' child prostitute himself for a fee? He has no pockets in which to store it.
Amores bk. 1, no. 10, l. 15

17 *Lente currite noctis equi.*

Run slowly, horses of the night.
Amores bk. 1, no. 13, l. 40; see **MARLOWE** 522:11

18 *Procul omen abesto!*

Far be that fate from us!
Amores bk. 1, no. 14, l. 41

19 *Procul hinc, procul este, severae!*

Far hence, keep far from me, you grim women!
Amores bk. 2, no. 1, l. 3

20 *Spectatum veniunt, veniunt spectentur ut ipsae.*

The women come to see the show, they come to make a show themselves.
Ars Amatoria bk. 1, l. 99

21 *Iuppiter ex alto periuria ridet amantum.*

Jupiter from on high laughs at lovers' perjuries.
Ars Amatoria bk. 1, l. 633; see **DRYDEN** 296:18, **PROVERBS** 636:47

22 *Expedit esse deos, et, ut expedit, esse putemus.*

It is convenient that there be gods, and, as it is convenient, let us believe that there are.
Ars Amatoria bk. 1, l. 637; see **VOLTAIRE** 834:8

23 *Semibovemque virum semivirumque bovem.*

A man half-bull and a bull half-man.
of the minotaur
Ars Amatoria bk. 2, l. 24

24 *Forsitan et nostrum nomen miscebitur istis.*

Perhaps my name too will be linked with theirs.
on the names of famous poets
Ars Amatoria bk. 3, l. 339

1 *Nescioqua natale solum dulcedine cunctos*
  Ducit et inmemores non sinit esse sui.

  By what sweet charm I know not the native land
  draws all men nor allows them to forget her.
  Epistulae ex Ponto bk. 1, no. 3, l. 35

2 *Adde quod ingenuas didicisse fideliter artes*
  Emollit mores nec sinit esse feros.

  Add the fact that to have conscientiously studied
  the liberal arts refines behaviour and does not
  allow it to be savage.
  Epistulae Ex Ponto bk. 2, no. 9, l. 47

3 *Ut desint vires, tamen est laudanda voluntas.*

  Though the strength is lacking, yet the
  willingness is commendable.
  Epistulae Ex Ponto bk. 3, no. 4, l. 79

4 *Gutta cavat lapidem, consumitur anulus usu.*

  Dripping water hollows out a stone, a ring is
  worn away by use.
  Epistulae Ex Ponto bk. 4, no. 10, l. 5; see **LATIMER** *482:15,*
  PROVERBS *629:20*

5 *Chaos, rudis indigestaque moles.*

  Chaos, a rough and unordered mass.
  Metamorphoses bk. 1, l. 7

6 *Aurea prima sata est aetas, quae vindice nullo,*
  Sponte sua, sine lege fidem rectumque colebat.

  Golden was that first age, which, with no one to
  compel, without a law, of its own will, kept faith
  and did the right.
  Metamorphoses bk. 1, l. 89

7 *Inde genus durum sumus experiensque laborum,*
  Et documenta damus qua simus origine nati.

  Hence come the hardness of our race and our
  endurance of toil; and we give proof from what
  origin we are sprung.
  Metamorphoses bk. 1, l. 414; see **RALEGH** *653:17*

8 *Materiam superabat opus.*

  The workmanship surpasses the material.
  of the bronze doors made by Vulcan for the palace of
  Apollo
  Metamorphoses bk 2, l. 5

9 *Medio tutissimus ibis.*

  You will go most safely by the middle way.
  Metamorphoses bk. 2, l. 137

10 *Vixque tenet lacrimae, quia nil lacrimabile cerrit.*

  Envy can scarcely hold back her tears, when she
  sees nothing to cry about.
  Metamorphoses bk. 2, l. 795

11 *Inopem me copia fecit.*

  Plenty has made me poor.
  Metamorphoses bk. 3, l. 466

12 *Ipse docet quid agam; fas est et ab hoste doceri.*

  He himself teaches what I should do; it is right
  to be taught by the enemy.
  Metamorphoses bk. 4, l. 428

13 *Video meliora, proboque;*
  Deteriora sequor.

  I see the better things, and approve; I follow the
  worse.
  Metamorphoses bk. 7, l. 20; see **BIBLE** *110:37*

14 *Tempus edax rerum.*

  Time the devourer of everything.
  Metamorphoses bk. 15, l. 234

15 *Iamque opus exegi, quod nec Iovis ira, nec ignis,*
  Nec poterit ferrum, nec edax abolere vetustas.

  And now I have finished the work, which neither
  the wrath of Jove, nor fire, nor the sword, nor
  devouring age shall be able to destroy.
  Metamorphoses bk. 15, l. 871

16 *Principiis obsta; sero medicina paratur*
  Cum mala per longas convaluere moras.

  Stop it at the start, it's late for medicine to be
  prepared when disease has grown strong
  through long delays.
  Remedia Amoris l. 91; see **PERSIUS** *604:10*

17 *Qui finem quaeris amoris,*
  Cedet amor rebus; res age, tutus eris.

  You who seek an end of love, love will yield to
  business: be busy, and you will be safe.
  Remedia Amoris l. 143

18 *Perdiderint cum me duo crimina, carmen et error.*

  Although two crimes, a song and a mistake,
  have done me in.
  Tristia bk. 2, l. 207

19 *Teque, rebellatrix, tandem, Germania, magni*
  Triste caput pedibus supposuisse ducis!

  How you, rebellious Germany, laid your
  wretched head beneath the feet of the great
  general.
  Tristia bk. 3, no. 12, l. 47

20 *Sponte sua carmen numeros veniebat ad aptos,*
  Et quod temptabam dicere versus erat.

  Of its own accord my song would come in the
  right rhythms, and what I was trying to say was
  poetry.
  Tristia bk. 4, no. 10, l. 25; see **POPE** *614:17*

21 *Vergilium vidi tantum.*

  I have only glimpsed Virgil.
  Tristia bk. 4, no. 10, l. 51

John Owen *c.*1563–1622
Welsh epigrammatist

22 God and the doctor we alike adore
   But only when in danger, not before;
   The danger o'er, both are alike requited,
   God is forgotten, and the Doctor slighted.
   Epigrams; see **QUARLES** *651:5*

Robert Owen 1771–1858
Welsh-born socialist and philanthropist

23 All the world is queer save thee and me, and
   even thou art a little queer.
   to his partner W. Allen, on severing business relations at
   New Lanark, 1828
   attributed

Wilfred Owen 1893–1918

English poet

1 My subject is War, and the pity of War.
The Poetry is in the pity.
Preface (written 1918) in *Poems* (1963)

2 All a poet can do today is warn.
Preface (written 1918) in *Poems* (1963)

3 What passing-bells for these who die as cattle?
Only the monstrous anger of the guns.
'Anthem for Doomed Youth' (written 1917)

4 The shrill, demented choirs of wailing shells;
And bugles calling for them from sad shires.
'Anthem for Doomed Youth' (written 1917)

5 The pallor of girls' brows shall be their pall;
Their flowers the tenderness of patient minds,
And each slow dusk a drawing-down of blinds.
'Anthem for Doomed Youth' (written 1917)

6 If you could hear, at every jolt, the blood
Come gargling from the froth-corrupted lungs,
Obscene as cancer, bitter as the cud
Of vile, incurable sores on innocent tongues,—
My friend, you would not tell with such high
    zest
To children ardent for some desperate glory,
The old Lie: Dulce et decorum est
Pro patria mori.
'Dulce et Decorum Est' (1963 ed.); see **HORACE** 412:17

7 Was it for this the clay grew tall?
'Futility' (written 1918)

8 It seemed that out of battle I escaped
Down some profound dull tunnel, long since
    scooped
Through granites which titanic wars had
    groined.
'Strange Meeting' (written 1918)

9 'Strange friend,' I said, 'here is no cause to
    mourn.'
'None,' said that other, 'save the undone years,
The hopelessness. Whatever hope is yours,
Was my life also.'
'Strange Meeting' (written 1918)

10 I am the enemy you killed, my friend.
I knew you in this dark: for you so frowned
Yesterday through me as you jabbed and killed
    . . .
Let us sleep now.
'Strange Meeting' (written 1918)

Count Oxenstierna 1583–1654

Swedish statesman

11 Dost thou not know, my son, with how little
wisdom the world is governed?
letter to his son, 1648, in J. F. af Lundblad *Svensk Plutark* (1826) pt. 2; an alternative attribution quotes 'a certain Pope' (possibly Julius III, 1487–1555) saying: 'Thou little thinkest what *a little foolery governs the whole world!*', John Selden *Table Talk* (1689) 'Pope' no. 2

Edward de Vere, Earl of Oxford

1550–1604

English poet. See also **ELIZABETH I** 312:19

12 The labouring man, that tills the fertile soil,
And reaps the harvest fruit, hath not in deed
The gain, but pain; and if for all his toil
He gets the straw, the lord will have the seed.
'The labouring man, that tills the fertile soil' (1573) st. 1

13 So he that takes the pain to pen the book
Reaps not the gifts of goodly golden Muse;
But those gain that who on the work shall look,
And from the sour the sweet by skill doth
    choose.
For he that beats the bush the bird not gets,
But who sits still and holdeth fast the nets.
'The labouring man, that tills the fertile soil' (1573) st. 6

Vance Packard 1914–97

American writer and journalist

14 The hidden persuaders.
title of a study of the advertising industry (1957)

John Page 1743–1808

American politician

15 We know the race is not to the swift nor the
battle to the strong. Do you not think an angel
rides in the whirlwind and directs this storm.
quoted by George W. **BUSH** *in his first inaugural address, 20 January 2001*

    letter to Thomas Jefferson, 20 July 1776; see **ADDISON** 4:11, **BIBLE** 90:11

William Tyler Page 1868–1942

American public servant and writer

16 I believe in the United States of America as a
government of the people, by the people, for
the people, whose just powers are derived from
the consent of the governed; a democracy in a
republic; a sovereign Nation of many sovereign
States; a perfect Union, one and inseparable,
established upon those principles of freedom,
equality, justice, and humanity for which
American patriots sacrificed their lives and
fortunes. I therefore believe it is my duty to my
country to love it, to support its Constitution, to
obey its laws, to respect its flag, and to defend it
against all enemies.
American's Creed (prize-winning competition entry, 1918) in *Congressional Record* vol. 56; see **LINCOLN** 494:1

Lord George Paget 1818–80
English soldier

1 As far as it engendered excitement the finest run in Leicestershire could hardly bear comparison.
the second-in-command's view of the charge of the Light Brigade
    The Light Cavalry Brigade in the Crimea (1881) ch. 5

Camille Paglia 1947–
American writer and critic

2 There is no female Mozart because there is no female Jack the Ripper.
    in *International Herald Tribune* 26 April 1991

Marcel Pagnol 1895–1974
French dramatist and film-maker

3 Honour is like a match, you can only use it once.
    Marius (1946) act 4, sc. 5

4 It's better to choose the culprits than to seek them out.
    Topaze (1930) act 1

Thomas Paine 1737–1809
English political theorist

5 It is necessary to the happiness of man that he be mentally faithful to himself. Infidelity does not consist in believing, or in disbelieving, it consists in professing to believe what one does not believe.
    The Age of Reason pt. 1 (1794)

6 Any system of religion that has any thing in it that shocks the mind of a child cannot be a true system.
    The Age of Reason pt. 1 (1794)

7 The sublime and the ridiculous are often so nearly related, that it is difficult to class them separately. One step above the sublime, makes the ridiculous; and one step above the ridiculous, makes the sublime again.
    The Age of Reason pt. 2 (1795); see **NAPOLEON I** 568:2, **PROVERBS** 632:42

8 Government, even in its best state, is but a necessary evil; in its worst state, an intolerable one. Government, like dress, is the badge of lost innocence; the palaces of kings are built upon the ruins of the bowers of paradise.
    Common Sense (1776) ch. 1

9 Though we have been wise enough to shut and lock a door against absolute Monarchy, we at the same time have been foolish enough to put the crown in possession of the key.
    Common Sense (1776) ch. 1

10 Monarchy and succession have laid . . . the world in blood and ashes.
    Common Sense (1776) ch. 2

11 Freedom hath been hunted round the globe. Asia and Africa have long expelled her. Europe regards her like a stranger, and England hath given her warning to depart. O! receive the fugitive, and prepare in time an asylum for mankind.
to America
    Common Sense (1776) ch. 3

12 As to religion, I hold it to be the indispensable duty of government to protect all conscientious professors thereof, and I know of no other business which government hath to do therewith.
    Common Sense (1776) ch. 4

13 These are the times that try men's souls. The summer soldier and the sunshine patriot will, in this crisis, shrink from the service of their country; but he that stands it *now*, deserves the love and thanks of men and women.
    The Crisis (December 1776) introduction

14 If there must be trouble, let it be in my day, that my child may have peace.
    The Crisis (December 1776)

15 Wisdom is not the purchase of a day.
    The Crisis (December 1776)

16 The religion of humanity.
    The Crisis (November 1778)

17 He that would make his own liberty secure, must guard even his enemy from oppression; for if he violates this duty, he establishes a precedent that will reach to himself.
    Dissertation on First Principles of Government (1795); see **MISQUOTATIONS** 549:1

18 As he rose like a rocket, he fell like the stick.
on Edmund **BURKE***'s losing the debate on the French Revolution to Charles James* **FOX***, in the House of Commons*
    Letter to the Addressers on the late Proclamation (1792)

19 [He] is not affected by the reality of distress touching his heart, but by the showy resemblance of it striking his imagination. He pities the plumage, but forgets the dying bird.
on Edmund **BURKE***'s Reflections on the Revolution in France, 1790*
    The Rights of Man (1791)

20 Lay then the axe to the root, and teach governments humanity. It is their sanguinary punishments which corrupt mankind.
    The Rights of Man (1791)

21 The idea of hereditary legislators is as inconsistent as that of hereditary judges, or hereditary juries; and as absurd as an hereditary mathematician, or an hereditary wise man; and as ridiculous as an hereditary poet laureate.
    The Rights of Man (1791)

22 Persecution is not an original feature of *any* religion; but it is always the strongly marked feature of all law-religions, or religions established by law.
    The Rights of Man (1791)

23 If, from the more wretched parts of the old world, we look at those which are in an

advanced state of improvement, we still find the greedy hand of government thrusting itself into every corner and crevice of industry, and grasping the spoil of the multitude.
Rights of Man pt. 2 (1792)

1 I compare it [monarchy] to something kept behind a curtain, about which there is a great deal of bustle and fuss, and a wonderful air of seeming solemnity; but when, by any accident, the curtain happens to be open, and the company see what it is, they burst into laughter.
The Rights of Man pt. 2 (1792)

2 The Minister, whoever he at any time may be, touches it as with an opium wand, and it sleeps obedience.
of Parliament
The Rights of Man pt. 2 (1792)

3 When, in countries that are called civilized, we see age going to the workhouse and youth to the gallows, something must be wrong in the system of government.
The Rights of Man pt. 2 (1792)

4 My country is the world, and my religion is to do good.
The Rights of Man pt. 2 (1792)

5 I do not believe that any two men, on what are called doctrinal points, think alike who think at all. It is only those who have not thought that appear to agree.
The Rights of Man pt. 2 (1792)

6 A share in two revolutions is living to some purpose.
Eric Foner *Tom Paine and Revolutionary America* (1976) ch. 7

José de Palafox 1780–1847
Spanish general

7 *Guerra a cuchillo.*
War to the knife.
on 4 August 1808, at the siege of Saragossa, the French general Verdier sent a one-word suggestion: 'Capitulation'. Palafox replied 'Guerra y cuchillo [War and the knife]', later reported as above; it subsequently appeared, at the behest of Palafox himself, on survivors' medals
José Gòmez de Arteche y Moro *Guerra de la Independencia* (1875) vol. 2, ch. 4

William Paley 1743–1805
English theologian and philosopher

8 Suppose I had found a *watch* upon the ground, and it should be enquired how the watch happened to be in that place . . . the inference, we think, is inevitable; that the watch must have had a maker, that there must have existed, at some time and at some place or other, an artificer or artificers, who formed it for the purpose which we find it actually to answer; who comprehended its construction, and designed its use.
Natural Theology (1802) ch. 1; see **DAWKINS** 269:1

9 Who can refute a sneer?
Principles of Moral and Political Philosophy (1785) bk. 5, ch. 9

Pali Tripitaka
the earliest collection of Buddhist sacred texts, *c.* 2nd century BC

10 Is it fitting to consider what is impermanent, painful, and subject to change as, 'This is mine, this am I, this is my self'?
Vinaya, Mahāv. [*Book of Discipline*] 1, 6

11 I go, reverend one, to the Lord and to the doctrine and the Order of monks. May the Lord take me as a lay disciple from this day forth while life lasts, who have gone to him as a refuge.
He [Yasa] was the first layman in the world received by the triple utterance.
Vinaya, Mahāv. [*Book of Discipline*] 1, 7

12 1) Refraining from taking life. 2) Refraining from taking what is not given. 3) Refraining from incontinence. 4) Refraining from falsehood. 5) Refraining from strong drink, intoxicants, and liquor, which are occasions of carelessness.
The Five Precepts
Vinaya, Mahāv. [*Book of Discipline*] 1, 56

13 I [Buddha] directed my mind to the knowledge of the extinction of the outflows. I understood it as it really is: This is suffering, this its arising, this its stopping, this the course leading to its stopping.
Vinaya [*Book of Discipline*] 3, 6

14 Dhamma has been taught by me without making a distinction between esoteric and exoteric. For the Tathagata has not the closed fist of a teacher in respect of mental states.
Dīgha-nikāya [*Longer Collection*] pt. 2, p. 100

15 You [monks] should live as islands, unto yourselves, being your own refuge, with no one else as your refuge, with the Dhamma as an island, with the Dhamma as your refuge, with no other refuge.
some translations prefer 'lamps' to 'islands'
Dīgha-nikāya [*Longer Collection*] pt. 2, p. 100

16 'Now, monks, I declare to you: all conditioned things are of a nature to decay—strive on untiringly.' These were the Tathagata's last words.
Dīgha-nikāya [*Longer Collection*] pt. 2, p. 156

17 In regard to things that are past, future and present the Tathagata is a speaker at a suitable time, a speaker of fact, on what has bearing, of Dhamma, of Discipline. Therefore is he called Tathagata.
Dīgha-nikāya [*Longer Collection*] pt. 3, p. 135

18 Monks, I will teach you Dhamma—the Parable of the Raft—for crossing over, not for retaining.
Majjhima-nikāya [*Medium Collection*] pt. 1, p. 134

1 Precisely this do I teach, now as formerly: ill and the stopping of ill.
Majjhima-nikāya [Medium Collection] pt. 1, p. 140

2 Who sees Conditioned Genesis sees Dhamma; who sees Dhamma sees Conditioned Genesis.
Majjhima-nikāya [Medium Collection] pt. 1, p. 190; see **PALI TRIPITAKA** 594:7

3 It is called Nirvana because of the getting rid of craving.
Samyutta-nikāya [Kindred Sayings] pt. 1, p. 39

4 In the Sakyan clan there was born
A Buddha, peerless among men,
Conqueror of all, repelling Mara—
The Visioned One sees all.
Samyutta-nikāya [Kindred Sayings] pt. 1, p. 134

5 The instructed disciple of the Aryans well and wisely reflects on Conditioned Genesis itself: If this is that comes to be; from the arising of this that arises; if this is not that does not come to be; from the stopping of this that is stopped.
Samyutta-nikāya [Kindred Sayings] pt. 2, p. 64

6 If one does not behold any self or anything of the nature of self in the five groups of grasping (material shape, feeling, perception, the impulses, consciousness), one is an Arahant, the outflows extinguished.
Samyutta-nikāya [Kindred Sayings] pt. 3, p. 127

7 Whoso sees Dhamma sees me; whoso sees me sees Dhamma.
Samyutta-nikāya [Kindred Sayings] pt. 3, p. 120

8 To what extent is the world called 'empty' Lord? Because it is empty of self or what belongs to self, it is therefore said: 'The world is empty.'
Samyutta-nikāya [Kindred Sayings] pt. 4, p. 54

9 I teach Dhamma that is lovely at the beginning, lovely in the middle and lovely at the ending, with the spirit and the letter.
Samyutta-nikāya [Kindred Sayings] pt. 4, p. 315

10 Avoiding both these extremes, [indulgence of sense pleasures, devotion to self-mortification] the Tathagata has realized the Middle Path: it gives vision, it gives knowledge, and it leads to calm, to insight, to enlightenment, to Nirvana.
First Sermon of the Buddha
Samyutta-nikāya [Kindred Sayings] pt. 56, p. 11

11 The Noble Truth of Suffering is this: Birth is suffering, ageing is suffering; sickness is suffering; death is suffering; sorrow and lamentation, pain, grief and despair are suffering; association with the unpleasant is suffering; dissociation from the pleasant is suffering; not to get what one wants is suffering—in brief, the five aggregates of attachment are suffering.
First Sermon of the Buddha
Samyutta-nikāya [Kindred Sayings] pt. 56, p. 11

12 The Noble Truth of the Path leading to the Cessation of suffering is this: It is simply the Noble Eightfold Path, namely right view; right thought; right speech; right action; right livelihood; right effort; right mindfulness; right concentration.
First Sermon of the Buddha
Samyutta-nikāya [Kindred Sayings] pt. 56, p. 11

13 Bhikkhus [monks], all is burning.
Fire Sermon
Samyutta-nikāya [Kindred Sayings] pt. 35, p. 28

14 As the great ocean has but one taste, that of salt, so has this Dharma and Discipline but one taste, the taste of Freedom.
Anguttara-nikāya [Gradual Sayings] pt. 4, p. 203

15 What we are today comes from our thoughts of yesterday, and our present thoughts build our life of tomorrow: our life is the creation of our mind.
Dhammapada v. 1

16 For hate is not conquered by hate: hate is conquered by love. This is a law eternal.
Dhammapada v. 5

17 Even as rain breaks not through a well-thatched house, passions break not through a well-guarded mind.
Dhammapada v. 14

18 Who can trace the invisible path of the man who soars in the sky of liberation, the infinite Void without beginning, whose passions are peace and over whom pleasures have no power? His path is as difficult to trace as that of the birds in the air.
Dhammapada v. 93

19 If a man should conquer in battle a thousand and a thousand more, and another man should conquer himself, his would be the greater victory, because the greatest of victories is the victory over oneself.
Dhammapada v. 103

20 Because there is, monks, an unborn, not become, not made, uncompounded, therefore an escape can be shown for what is born, has become, is made, is compounded.
Udāna [Solemn Utterances] p. 81

21 I see no other single hindrance such as this hindrance of ignorance, obstructed by which mankind for a long long time runs on and circles on.
Itivuttaka [Thus Was Said] p. 8

22 The person who is searching for his own happiness should pull out the dart that he has stuck in himself, the arrow-head of grieving, of desiring, of despair.
Sutta-Nipāta [Woven Cadences] v. 592

23 Of all beings this one is perfect, this man is the pinnacle, the ultimate, the hero of creatures! This is the man who, from the forest of the Masters, will set the Wheel of Teaching turning—the roar of the lion, King of Beasts!
Sutta-Nipāta [Woven Cadences] v. 684

24 There are no waves in the depths of the sea: it is still, unbroken. It is the same with the monk.

He is still, without any quiver of desire, without a remnant on which to build pride and desire.
Sutta-Nipāta [Woven Cadences] v. 920

Sarah Palin 1964–

American Republican politician

1 What's the difference between a hockey mom and a pitbull? Lipstick.
speech to Republican Party convention, 3 September 2008

Henry John Temple, Lord Palmerston 1784–1865

British statesman, Prime Minister 1855–8, 1859–65. On Palmerston: see DISRAELI 286:25

2 We have no eternal allies and we have no perpetual enemies. Our interests are eternal and perpetual, and those interests it is our duty to follow.
speech, House of Commons, 1 March 1848

3 I therefore fearlessly challenge the verdict which this House . . . is to give . . . whether, as the Roman, in days of old, held himself free from indignity, when he could say *Civis Romanus sum*; so also a British subject, in whatever land he may be, shall feel confident that the watchful eye and the strong arm of England will protect him against injustice and wrong.
in the debate on the protection afforded to the Greek trader David Pacifico (1784–1854) who had been born a British subject at Gibraltar
speech, House of Commons, 25 June 1850; see CICERO 232:4

4 You may call it combination, you may call it the accidental and fortuitous concurrence of atoms.
on a projected Palmerston–Disraeli coalition
speech, House of Commons, 5 March 1857

5 We do not want Egypt any more than any rational man with an estate in the north of England and a residence in the south, would have wished to possess the inns on the north road. All he could want would have been that the inns should be well kept, always accessible, and furnishing him, when he came, with mutton chops and post horses.
letter to Earl Cowley, 25 November 1859, in Hon. Evelyn Ashley *Life of . . . Viscount Palmerston 1846–65* (1876) vol. 2, ch. 4

6 He is a dangerous man; keep him in Oxford and he is partially muzzled; but send him elsewhere and he will run wild.
of GLADSTONE; see GLADSTONE 359:16
c. 1865, John Morley *Life of Gladstone* (1903) vol. 1

7 How d'ye do, and how is the old complaint?
reputed to be his greeting to all those he did not know
A. West *Recollections* (1899) vol. 1, ch. 2

8 Lord Palmerston, with characteristic levity had once said that only three men in Europe had ever understood [the Schleswig-Holstein question], and of these the Prince Consort was

dead, a Danish statesman (unnamed) was in an asylum, and he himself had forgotten it.
R. W. Seton-Watson *Britain in Europe 1789–1914* (1937) ch. 11

9 What is merit? The opinion one man entertains of another.
T. Carlyle *Shooting Niagara: and After?* (1867) ch. 8

10 Yes we have. Humbug.
on being told there was no English word equivalent to sensibilité
attributed

11 Die, my dear Doctor, that's the last thing I shall do!
last words; E. Latham *Famous Sayings and their Authors* (1904)

Christabel Pankhurst 1880–1958

English suffragette; daughter of Emmeline Pankhurst

12 Never lose your temper with the Press or the public is a major rule of political life.
Unshackled (1959) ch. 5

13 We are here to claim our right as women, not only to be free, but to fight for freedom. That it is our right as well as our duty.
in *Votes for Women* 31 March 1911

Emmeline Pankhurst 1858–1928

English suffragette leader; founder of the Women's Social and Political Union, 1903

14 There is something that Governments care far more for than human life, and that is the security of property, and so it is through property that we shall strike the enemy . . . I say to the Government: You have not dared to take the leaders of Ulster for their incitement to rebellion. Take me if you dare.
speech at Albert Hall, 17 October 1912, in *My Own Story* (1914)

15 The argument of the broken window pane is the most valuable argument in modern politics.
George Dangerfield *The Strange Death of Liberal England* (1936) pt. 2, ch. 3, sect. 4; see MORE 558:18

Paracelsus (Theophrastus Phillipus Aureolus Bombastus von Hohenheim) *c.*1493–1541

Swiss physician

16 There can be no surgeon who is not also a physician . . . Where the physician is not also a surgeon he is an idol that is nothing but a painted monkey.
Walter Pagel *Paracelsus: An introduction to Philosophical Medicine in the Era of the Renaissance* (1958)

Mitchell Parish 1900–93

American songwriter

17 When the deep purple falls over sleepy garden walls,
And the stars begin to flicker in the sky,
Thru' the mist of a memory you wander back to me,

Breathing my name with a sigh.
'Deep Purple' (1939); words added to music (1934) by Peter de Rose

Charlie Parker 1920–55

American jazz saxophonist

1 Music is your own experience, your thoughts, your wisdom. If you don't live it, it won't come out of your horn.
Nat Shapiro and Nat Hentoff *Hear Me Talkin' to Ya* (1955)

Dorothy Parker 1893–1967

American critic and humorist. On Parker: see WOOLLCOTT 864:17; see also EPITAPHS 317:5

2 Oh, life is a glorious cycle of song,
A medley of extemporanea;
And love is a thing that can never go wrong;
And I am Marie of Roumania.
'Comment' (1937)

3 Four be the things I'd been better without:
Love, curiosity, freckles, and doubt.
'Inventory' (1937)

4 Men seldom make passes
At girls who wear glasses.
'News Item' (1937)

5 Why is it no one ever sent me yet
One perfect limousine, do you suppose?
Ah no, it's always just my luck to get
One perfect rose.
'One Perfect Rose' (1937)

6 If, with the literate, I am
Impelled to try an epigram,
I never seek to take the credit;
We all assume that Oscar said it.
'A Pig's-Eye View of Literature' (1937)

7 Guns aren't lawful;
Nooses give;
Gas smells awful;
You might as well live.
'Résumé' (1937)

8 Where's the man could ease a heart like a satin gown?
'The Satin Dress' (1937)

9 By the time you say you're his,
Shivering and sighing
And he vows his passion is
Infinite, undying—
Lady, make a note of this:
One of you is lying.
'Unfortunate Coincidence' (1937)

10 Sorrow is tranquillity remembered in emotion.
Here Lies (1939) 'Sentiment'; see WORDSWORTH 870:3

11 *House Beautiful* is play lousy.
review in *New Yorker*, 1933, in Phyllis Hartnoll *Plays and Players* (1984)

12 She ran the whole gamut of the emotions from A to B.
of Katharine Hepburn at a Broadway first night, 1933
attributed

13 There's a hell of a distance between wise-cracking and wit. Wit has truth in it; wise-cracking is simply callisthenics with words.
in *Paris Review* Summer 1956

14 GOOD WORK, MARY. WE ALL KNEW YOU HAD IT IN YOU.
telegram to Mrs Sherwood on the arrival of her baby
Alexander Woollcott *While Rome Burns* (1934) 'Our Mrs Parker'

15 How do they know?
on being told that Calvin COOLIDGE had died
Malcolm Cowley *Writers at Work* 1st Series (1958)

16 Hollywood money isn't money. It's congealed snow, melts in your hand, and there you are.
Malcolm Cowley *Writers at Work* 1st Series (1958)

17 You can lead a horticulture, but you can't make her think.
John Keats *You Might as well Live* (1970)

18 It serves me right for putting all my eggs in one bastard.
on her abortion
John Keats *You Might as well Live* (1970) pt. 2, ch. 3

19 *on hearing the doorbell or a ringing telephone:*
What fresh hell is this?
Marion Meade *What Fresh Hell Is This?* (1988)

Martin Parker d. c.1656

English balladmonger

20 You gentlemen of England
Who live at home at ease,
How little do you think
On the dangers of the seas.
'The Valiant Sailors'; J. O. Halliwell (ed.) *Early Naval Ballads* (Percy Society, 1841)

21   The times will not mend
Till the King enjoys his own again.
'Upon Defacing of Whitehall' (1671)

Ross Parker 1914–74 *and* Hugh Charles 1907–95

British songwriters

22 There'll always be an England
While there's a country lane.
'There'll always be an England' (1939 song)

Theodore Parker 1810–60

American Unitarian preacher

23 I do not pretend to understand the moral universe; the arc is a long one, my eye reaches but little ways; I cannot calculate the curve and complete the figure by the experience of sight; I can divine it by conscience. And from what I see I am sure it bends toward justice.
Ten Sermons on Religion (1853) 'Justice and the conscience'; see KING 463:14, OBAMA 583:1

Thomas Parker 1667–1732

English lawyer, Lord Chancellor

1 Let all people be at liberty to know what I found my judgment upon; that, so when I have given it in any cause, others might be at liberty to judge of me.
  in *Cann v. Cann* (1719)

Colin Murray Parkes 1928–

English psychiatrist

2 The pain of grief is just as much a part of life as the joy of love; it is, perhaps, the price we pay for love, the cost of commitment.
  usually quoted as 'Grief is the price we pay for love'
  Bereavement: Studies of Grief in Adult Life (1972)

Henry Parkes 1815–95

English-born Australian statesman

3 The crimson thread of kinship runs through us all.
  on Australian federation
  speech at banquet in Melbourne 6 February 1890; *The Federal Government of Australasia* (1890)

C. Northcote Parkinson 1909–93

English writer

4 Expenditure rises to meet income.
  The Law and the Profits (1960) ch. 1

5 Work expands so as to fill the time available for its completion.
  Parkinson's Law (1958) ch. 1

6 Time spent on any item of the agenda will be in inverse proportion to the sum involved.
  Parkinson's Law (1958) ch. 3

7 The man who is denied the opportunity of taking decisions of importance begins to regard as important the decisions he is allowed to take.
  Parkinson's Law (1958) ch. 10

Charles Stewart Parnell 1846–91

Irish nationalist leader. On Parnell: see **HEALY** 387:3

8 Why should Ireland be treated as a geographical fragment of England . . . Ireland is not a geographical fragment, but a nation.
  in the House of Commons, 26 April 1875

9 No man has a right to fix the boundary of the march of a nation; no man has a right to say to his country—thus far shalt thou go and no further.
  speech at Cork, 21 January 1885, in *The Times* 22 January 1885

Thomas Parnell 1679–1718

Anglo-Irish poet

10 And all that's madly wild, or oddly gay,
  We call it only pretty Fanny's way.
  'An Elegy: To an Old Beauty'

Tony Parsons 1953–

English critic and writer

11 I never saw a beggar yet who would recognise guilt if it bit him on his unwashed ass.
  Dispatches from the Front Line of Popular Culture (1994)

Blaise Pascal 1623–62

French mathematician, physicist, and moralist

12 *Je n'ai fait celle-ci plus longue que parce que je n'ai pas eu le loisir de la faire plus courte.*
  I have made this [letter] longer than usual, only because I have not had the time to make it shorter.
  Lettres Provinciales (1657) no. 16; see **THOREAU** 809:8

13 *La dernière chose qu'on trouve en faisant un ouvrage, est de savoir celle qu'il faut mettre la première.*
  The last thing one knows in constructing a work is what to put first.
  Pensées (1670, ed. L. Brunschvicg, 1909) sect. 1, no. 19

14 *Quand on voit le style naturel, on est tout étonné et ravi, car on s'attendait de voir un auteur, et on trouve un homme.*
  When we see a natural style, we are quite surprised and delighted, for we expected to see an author and we find a man.
  Pensées (1670, ed. L. Brunschvicg, 1909) sect. 1, no. 29

15 *Car enfin, qu'est-ce que l'homme dans la nature? Un néant à l'égard de l'infini, un tout à l'égard du néant, un milieu entre rien et tout.*
  For after all, what is man in nature? A nothing in respect of that which is infinite, an all in respect of nothing, a middle betwixt nothing and all.
  Pensées (1670, ed. L. Brunschvicg, 1909) sect. 2, no. 72

16 *Peu de chose nous console parce que peu de chose nous afflige.*
  A trifle consoles us because a trifle upsets us.
  Pensées (1670) no. 77

17 *Quelle vanité que la peinture, qui attire l'admiration par la ressemblance des choses dont on n'admire point les originaux.*
  How vain painting is, exciting admiration by its resemblance to things of which we do not admire the originals.
  Pensées (1670, ed. L. Brunschvicg, 1909) sect. 2, no. 134

18 *Tout le malheur des hommes vient d'une seule chose, qui est de ne savoir pas demeurer en repos dans une chambre.*
  All the misfortunes of men derive from one single thing, which is their inability to be at ease in a room.
  Pensées (1670, ed. L. Brunschvicg, 1909) sect. 2, no. 139

19 *Le nez de Cléopâtre: s'il eût été plus court, toute la face de la terre aurait changé.*
  Had Cleopatra's nose been shorter, the whole face of the world would have changed.
  Pensées (1670, ed. L. Brunschvicg, 1909) sect. 2, no. 162

1 *Le silence éternel de ces espaces infinis m'effraie.*

The eternal silence of these infinite spaces [the heavens] terrifies me.

Pensées (1670, ed. L. Brunschvicg, 1909) sect. 2, no. 206

2 *Le dernier acte est sanglant, quelque belle que soit la comédie en tout le reste; on jette enfin de la terre sur la tête, et en voilà pour jamais.*

The last act is bloody, however charming the rest of the play may be; they throw earth over your head, and it is finished forever.

Pensées (1670, ed. L. Brunschvicg, 1909) sect. 3, no. 210

3 *On mourra seul.*

We shall die alone.

Pensées (1670, ed. L. Brunschvicg, 1909) sect. 3, no. 211

4 *La dernière démarche de la raison est la reconnaître qu'il y a un infinité de choses qui la surpassent.*

The last proceeding of reason is to recognize that there is an infinity of things which are beyond it.

Pensées (1670) no. 220

5 *'Dieu est, ou il n'est pas.' Mais de quel côté pencherons-nous? . . . Pesons le gain et la perte, en prenant croix que Dieu est. Estimons ces deux cas: si vous gagnez, vous gagnez tout; si vous perdez, vous ne perdez rien. Gagez donc qu'il est, sans hésiter.*

'God is or he is not.' But to which side shall we incline? . . . Let us weigh the gain and the loss in wagering that God is. Let us estimate the two chances. If you gain, you gain all; if you lose, you lose nothing. Wager then without hesitation that he is.

known as Pascal's wager

Pensées (1670, ed. L. Brunschvicg, 1909) sect. 3, no. 233

6 *Incrédules les plus crédules.*

The sceptical are the most credulous.

Pensées (1670) no. 257

7 *Le coeur a ses raisons que la raison ne connaît point.*

The heart has its reasons which reason knows nothing of.

Pensées (1670, ed. L. Brunschvicg, 1909) sect. 4, no. 277

8 *L'homme n'est qu'un roseau, le plus faible de la nature; mais c'est un roseau pensant.*

Man is only a reed, the weakest thing in nature; but he is a thinking reed.

Pensées (1670, ed. L. Brunschvicg, 1909) sect. 6, no. 347

9 *L'éloquence continue ennuie.*

Continual eloquence is tedious.

Pensées (1670, ed. L. Brunschvicg, 1909) sect. 6, no. 355

10 *Le moi est haïssable.*

The self is hateful.

Pensées (1670, ed. L. Brunschvicg, 1909) sect. 7, no. 455

11 *Console-toi, tu ne me chercherais pas si tu ne m'avais trouvé.*

Comfort yourself, you would not seek me if you had not found me.

Pensées (1670, ed. L. Brunschvicg, 1909) sect. 7, no. 553

12 *Jamais on ne fait le mal si pleinement et si gaiement que quand on le fait par conscience.*

We never do evil so fully and cheerfully as when we do it out of conscience.

Pensées (1670, ed. L. Brunschvicg, 1909) no. 895

13 FEU. *Dieu d'Abraham, Dieu d'Isaac, Dieu de Jacob, non des philosophes et savants. Certitude. Certitude. Sentiment. Joie. Paix.*

FIRE. God of Abraham, God of Isaac, God of Jacob, not of the philosophers and scholars. Certainty. Certainty. Feeling. Joy. Peace.

on a paper, dated 23 November 1654, stitched into the lining of his coat and found after his death

Boris Pasternak 1890–1960
Russian novelist and poet

14 Man is born to live, not to prepare for life.

Doctor Zhivago (1958) pt. 2, ch. 9, sect. 14 (translated by Max Hayward and Manya Harari)

15 Most people experience love, without noticing that there is anything remarkable about it.

Doctor Zhivago (1958) pt. 2, ch. 13, sect. 10

16 I don't like people who have never fallen or stumbled. Their virtue is lifeless and it isn't of much value. Life hasn't revealed its beauty to them.

Doctor Zhivago (1958) pt. 2, ch. 13, sect. 12

17 Art always serves beauty, and beauty is the joy of possessing form, and form is the key to organic life since no living thing can exist without it.

Doctor Zhivago (1958) pt. 2, ch. 14, sect. 14

18 One day Lara went out and did not come back . . . She died or vanished somewhere, forgotten as a nameless number on a list which was afterwards mislaid.

Doctor Zhivago (1958) pt. 2, ch. 15, sect. 17

19 Yet the order of the acts is planned
And the end of the way inescapable.
I am alone; all drowns in the Pharisees'
    hypocrisy.
To live your life is not as simple as to cross a
    field.

Doctor Zhivago (1958) 'Zhivago's Poems: Hamlet'

20 As after a storm
The surf floods over the reeds,
So in his heart
Her image is submerged.

In the years of trial,
When life was inconceivable,
From the bottom of the sea the tide of destiny
Washed her up to him.

Doctor Zhivago (1958) 'Zhivago's Poems: Parting'

21 In time to come, I tell them, we'll be equal
to any living now. If cripples, then
no matter; we shall just have been run over
by 'New Man' in the wagon of his 'Plan'.

'When I Grow Weary' (1932) (translated by J. M. Cohen)

Louis Pasteur 1822–95
French chemist and bacteriologist

1 Where observation is concerned, chance favours only the prepared mind.
   address given on the inauguration of the Faculty of Science, University of Lille, 7 December 1854; in R. Vallery-Radot *La Vie de Pasteur* (1900) ch. 4

2 There are no such things as applied sciences, only applications of science.
   address, 11 September 1872, in *Comptes rendus des travaux du Congrès viticole et séricicole de Lyon, 9–14 septembre 1872*

3 Wine may well be considered the most healthful and most hygienic of beverages.
   Études sur le vin (1873) pt. 1, ch. 2

4 Science knows no country, because knowledge belongs to humanity.
   toast at banquet of the International Congress of Sericiculture, Milan, 1876, in Maurice B. Strauss *Familiar Medical Quotations* (1968)

5 *Le germe n'est rien, c'est le terrain qui est tout.*
   The microbe is nothing, the terrain is everything.
   on his deathbed, to Professor Rénon; Hans Seyle *The Stress of Life* (1956)

Walter Pater 1839–94
English essayist and critic

6 She is older than the rocks among which she sits; like the vampire, she has been dead many times, and learned the secrets of the grave.
   of the Mona Lisa
   Studies in the History of the Renaissance (1873) 'Leonardo da Vinci'

7 All art constantly aspires towards the condition of music.
   The Renaissance: Studies in Art and Poetry (1888) 'The School of Giorgione'

8 To burn always with this hard, gemlike flame, to maintain this ecstasy, is success in life.
   Studies in the History of the Renaissance (1873) 'Conclusion'

'Banjo' Paterson (Andrew Barton Paterson) 1864–1941
Australian poet

9 Once a jolly swagman camped by a billabong,
   Under the shade of a coolibah tree;
   And he sang as he watched and waited till his
      'Billy' boiled:
   'You'll come a-waltzing, Matilda, with me.'
   'Waltzing Matilda' (1903 song)

Sadashiv Kanoji Patil
Indian politician

10 The Prime Minister is like the great banyan tree. Thousands shelter beneath it, but nothing grows.
   *when asked in an interview who would be **NEHRU's** successor*
   J. K. Galbraith *A Life in Our Times* (1981)

Coventry Patmore 1823–96
English poet

11 The angel in the house.
   title of poem (1854–62)

12 'I saw you take his kiss!' ''Tis true.'
   'O modesty!' ''Twas strictly kept:
   He thought me asleep; at least, I knew
   He thought I thought he thought I slept.'
   The Angel in the House (1854–62) bk. 2, canto 8, 'The Kiss'

13 Some dish more sharply spiced than this
   Milk-soup men call domestic bliss.
   'Olympus' l. 15

14 He that but once too nearly hears
   The music of forfended spheres
   Is thenceforth lonely, and for all
   His days as one who treads the Wall
   Of China, and, on this hand, sees
   Cities and their civilities
   And, on the other, lions.
   The Victories of Love bk. 1 (1860) 'From Mrs Graham'

Alan Paton 1903–88
South African writer

15 Cry, the beloved country.
   title of novel (1948)

16 For it is the dawn that has come, as it has come for a thousand centuries, never failing. But when that dawn will come, of our emancipation, from the fear of bondage and the bondage of fear, why, that is a secret.
   Cry, The Beloved Country (1948), closing words

St Patrick fl. 5th cent.
Patron saint and Apostle of Ireland, of Romano-British parentage

17 Today I put on
   a terrible strength
   invoking the Trinity,
   confessing the Three
   with faith in the one
   as I face my Maker.
   'St Patrick's Breastplate', traditionally attributed to St Patrick; see **ALEXANDER** 12:9

18 Christ beside me,
   Christ before me,
   Christ behind me,
   Christ within me,
   Christ beneath me,
   Christ above me.
   'St Patrick's Breastplate'

Mark Pattison 1813–84
English educationist

19 In research the horizon recedes as we advance, and is no nearer at sixty than it was at twenty. As the power of endurance weakens with age, the urgency of the pursuit grows more intense . . . And research is always incomplete.
   Isaac Casaubon (1875) ch. 10

Leslie Paul 1905–85

Irish writer

1 Angry young man.
the phrase was later associated with John OSBORNE's *play*
Look Back in Anger (1956)
title of book (1951)

Wolfgang Pauli 1900–58

Austrian-born American physicist who worked chiefly in
Switzerland. On Pauli: see WEISSKOPF 845:10

2 I don't mind your thinking slowly: I mind your
publishing faster than you think.
attributed

Tom Paulin 1949–

English-born Northern Irish poet and critic

3 Now dream
of that sweet
equal republic
where the juniper
talks to the oak,
the thistle,
the bandaged elm,
and the jolly jolly chestnut.
'The Book of Juniper' (1983)

4 The owl of Minerva in a hired car.
'Desertmartin' (1983)

5 That stretch of water, it's always
There for you to cross over
To the other shore, observing
The light of cities on blackness.
'States' (1977)

Cesare Pavese 1908–50

Italian novelist, poet, and critic

6 Pity was always a waste of one's time.
Existence is terrible, pity won't change that.
It's better to keep quiet, jaws clenched.
'Fallen Women' (1950) tr. Geoffrey Buck

7 Waiting is still an occupation. It's having nothing
to wait for that is terrible.
Il Mestiere di Vivere (1952, translated as The Burning Brand,
1961) 15 September 1946

Jeremy Paxman 1950–

English journalist and broadcaster. See also CATCHPHRASES
207:9

8 Did you threaten to overrule him?
*question asked 14 times of the Conservative politician
Michael Howard, then Home Secretary, referring to the
sacking of a prison governor by Derek Lewis, Director of the
Prison Service*
interview, BBC2 Newsnight 13 May 1997

James Payn 1830–98

English writer

9 I had never had a piece of toast
Particularly long and wide,

But fell upon the sanded floor,
And always on the buttered side.
in *Chambers's Journal* 2 February 1884; see MOORE 558:14

J. H. Payne 1791–1852

American actor, dramatist, and songwriter

10 Home, sweet home.
title of song, from *Clari, or, The Maid of Milan* (1823 opera)

11 Mid pleasures and palaces though we may roam,
Be it ever so humble, there's no place like home.
Clari, or, The Maid of Milan (1823 opera) 'Home, Sweet Home';
see PROVERBS 644:46

Thomas Love Peacock 1785–1866

English novelist and poet. On Peacock: see SHELLEY 744:17;
see also EPITAPHS 318:16

12 The march of mind has marched in through my
back parlour shutters, and out again with my
silver spoons, in the dead of night . . . my house
has been broken open on the most scientific
principles.
Crotchet Castle (1831) ch. 17

13 Science is one thing, wisdom is another. Science
is an edged tool with which men play like
children and cut their own fingers.
Gryll Grange (1861) ch. 19

14 I almost think it is the ultimate destiny of
science to exterminate the human race.
Gryll Grange (1861) ch. 19

15 'I distinguish the picturesque and the beautiful,
and I add to them, in the laying out of grounds,
a third and distinct character, which I call
unexpectedness.'
'Pray, sir,' said Mr Milestone, 'by what name do
you distinguish this character, when a person
walks round the grounds for the second time?'
Headlong Hall (1816) ch. 4

16 Marriage may often be a stormy lake, but
celibacy is almost always a muddy horsepond.
Melincourt (1817) ch. 7

17 Not drunk is he, who from the floor
Can rise alone and still drink more;
But drunk is he, who prostrate lies,
Without the power to drink or rise.
The Misfortunes of Elphin (1829) pt. 1, ch. 3

18 Laughter is pleasant, but the exertion is too
much for me.
Nightmare Abbey (1818) ch. 5

19 Sir, I have quarrelled with my wife; and a man
who has quarrelled with his wife is absolved
from all duty to his country.
Nightmare Abbey (1818) ch. 11

20 The mountain sheep are sweeter,
But the valley sheep are fatter;
We therefore deemed it meeter
To carry off the latter.
'The War Song of Dinas Vawr' (1823)

Norman Vincent Peale 1898–1993

American religious broadcaster and writer

1 The power of positive thinking.

title of book (1952)

Patrick Pearse 1879–1916

Irish nationalist leader; executed after the Easter Rising. On Pearse: see **YEATS** 873:9

2 The fools, the fools, the fools, they have left us our Fenian dead, and while Ireland holds these graves Ireland unfree shall never be at peace.

oration over the grave of the Fenian Jeremiah O'Donovan Rossa, 1 August 1915

3 Here be ghosts that I have raised this Christmastide, ghosts of dead men that have bequeathed a trust to us living men. Ghosts are troublesome things in a house or in a family, as we knew even before Ibsen taught us. There is only one way to appease a ghost. You must do the thing it asks you. The ghosts of a nation sometimes ask very big things and they must be appeased, whatever the cost.

on Christmas Day, 1915; Conor Cruise O'Brien Ancestral Voices (1994); see **O'BRIEN** *583:2*

Hesketh Pearson 1887–1964

English actor and biographer

4 Misquotation is, in fact, the pride and privilege of the learned. A widely-read man never quotes accurately, for the rather obvious reason that he has read too widely.

Common Misquotations (1934) introduction

5 There is no stronger craving in the world than that of the rich for titles, except perhaps that of the titled for riches.

The Pilgrim Daughters (1961) ch. 6

Lester Pearson 1897–1972

Canadian diplomat and Liberal statesman, Prime Minister 1963–8

6 The grim fact is that we prepare for war like precocious giants and for peace like retarded pygmies.

speech in Toronto, 14 March 1955

7 This is the flag of the future, but it does not dishonour the past.

on Canada obtaining a flag of its own, a project Pearson successfully achieved

speech in the House of Commons, Ottawa, 15 December 1964

Pedro I (Pedro IV of Portugal) 1798–1834

Portuguese monarch, first Emperor of Brazil, 1822–31

8 As it is for the good of all and the general happiness of the nation, I am ready and willing. Tell the people I'm staying.

in response to a popular delegation, and in defiance of a decree from Lisbon requiring his return; commonly rendered 'Fico [I'm staying]'

letter to D. João VI, 9 January 1822; R. J. Barman Brazil (1988)

Robert Peel 1788–1850

British Conservative statesman, Prime Minister 1834–5, 1841–6. On Peel: see **CURRAN** 263:5, **DISRAELI** 284:7

9 There is not a single law connected with my name which has not had as its object some mitigation of the severity of the criminal law; some prevention of abuse in the exercise of it; or some security for its impartial administration.

speech, House of Commons, 1 May 1827

10 As minister of the Crown . . . I reserve to myself, distinctly and unequivocally, the right of adapting my conduct to the exigency of the moment, and to the wants of the country.

in the House of Commons, 30 March 1829

11 All my experience in public life is in favour of the employment of what the world would call young men instead of old ones.

to Wellington in 1829; Norman Gash Sir Robert Peel (ed. 2, 1986)

12 No man attached to his country could always acquiesce in the opinions of the majority.

speech, House of Commons, 26 June 1831

13 In the present times of political excitement, the exacerbation of angry and unsocial feelings might be much softened by the effects which the fine arts had ever produced upon the minds of men.

on the building of the new National Gallery

speech, House of Commons Committee of Supply—National Gallery, 23 July 1832, in Speeches vol. 2 (1853)

14 Of all vulgar arts of government, that of solving every difficulty which might arise by thrusting the hand into the public purse is the most delusory and contemptible.

in the House of Commons, 1834

George Peele c.1556–96

English dramatist and poet

15   Love is a thing.
It is a prick, it is a sting,
It is a pretty, pretty thing;
It is a fire, it is a coal
Whose flame creeps in at every hole.

The Hunting of Cupid (c.1591)

16 When as the rye reach to the chin,
And chopcherry, chopcherry ripe within,
Strawberries swimming in the cream,
And schoolboys playing in the stream,
Then O, then O, then O, my true love said,
Till that time come again,
She could not live a maid.

The Old Wive's Tale (1595) l. 75 'Song'

17 His golden locks time hath to silver turned;
O time too swift, O swiftness never ceasing!

Polyhymnia (1590) 'Sonnet'

1 His helmet now shall make a hive for bees.
Polyhymnia (1590) 'Sonnet'

2 Goddess, allow this aged man his right,
To be your beadsman now that was your knight.
Polyhymnia (1590) 'Sonnet'

Charles Péguy 1873–1914

French poet and essayist

3 He who does not bellow the truth when he knows the truth makes himself the accomplice of liars and forgers.
Basic Verities (1943) 'Lettre du Provincial' 21 December 1899

4 Tyranny is always better organised than freedom.
Basic Verities (1943) 'War and Peace'; see **BAEZ** 50:1

5 The sinner is at the heart of Christianity . . . No one is as competent as the sinner in matters of Christianity. No one, except a saint.
Basic Verities (1943) 'Un Nouveau théologien . . . ' (1911)

Pelé 1940–

Brazilian footballer

6 Football? It's the beautiful game.
attributed

Mary Herbert, Countess of Pembroke 1561–1621

English poet and translator, sister of Philip **SIDNEY**

7 Men drawn by worth a woman to obey.
'Even now that Care which on thy Crown attends' (poem addressed to Queen Elizabeth)

8 Sing what God doth, and do what men may sing.
'Even now that Care which on thy Crown attends' (poem addressed to Queen Elizabeth)

William Herbert, Lord Pembroke

*c.*1501–70

English peer

9 Out ye whores, to work, to work, ye whores, go spin.
Andrew Clark (ed.) 'Brief Lives' . . . by John Aubrey (1898) vol. 1 'William Herbert, 1st Earl of Pembroke'; see **SCOTT** 689:27

Henry Herbert, Lord Pembroke

*c.*1534–1601

English peer

10 A parliament can do any thing but make a man a woman, and a woman a man.
quoted by his son, the 4th Earl, in a speech on 11 April 1648, proving himself Chancellor of Oxford
in *Harleian Miscellany* (1745) vol. 5

Henry Herbert, Lord Pembroke

1734–94

English peer

11 Dr Johnson's sayings would not appear so extraordinary, were it not for his bow-wow way.
James Boswell *Life of Samuel Johnson* (1791) 27 March 1775; see **SCOTT** 689:28

Vladimir Peniakoff 1897–1951

Belgian soldier and writer

12 A message came on the wireless for me. It said: 'SPREAD ALARM AND DESPONDENCY'. So the time had come, I thought, Eighth Army was taking the offensive. The date was, I think, May 18th, 1942.
Private Army (1950) pt. 2, ch. 5; see **MILITARY SAYINGS, SLOGANS, AND SONGS** 535:7

William Penn 1644–1718

English Quaker; founder of Pennsylvania. See also **PRAYERS** 623:2

13 Much reading is an oppression of the mind, and extinguishes the natural candle; which is the reason of so many senseless scholars in the world.
Fruits of a Father's Love (1726) ch. 2, no. 19

14 No pain, no palm; no thorns, no throne; no gall, no glory; no cross, no crown.
No Cross, No Crown (1669 pamphlet); see **PROVERBS** 640:1

15 It is a reproach to religion and government to suffer so much poverty and excess.
Some Fruits of Solitude (1693) pt. 1, no. 52

16 Men are generally more careful of the breed of their horses and dogs than of their children.
Some Fruits of Solitude (1693) pt. 1, no. 85

17 Let the people think they govern and they will be governed.
Some Fruits of Solitude (1693) pt. 1, no. 337

18 The taking of a bribe or gratuity, should be punished with as severe penalties as the defrauding of the State.
Some Fruits of Solitude (1693) pt. 1, no. 384

19 To be furious in religion, is to be irreligiously religious.
Some Fruits of Solitude (1693) pt. 1, no. 533

20 It may be a green country town which will never be burnt and always be wholesome.
of his planned city of Philadelphia
letter of instructions to commissioners, 30 September 1681, in Samuel M Janney *The Life of William Penn* (!856)

Roger Penrose 1931–

English mathematician and theoretical physicist

21 Consciousness . . . is the phenomenon whereby the universe's very existence is made known.
The Emperor's New Mind (1989) ch. 10 'Conclusion'

Samuel Pepys 1633–1703

English diarist. On Pepys: see **NICOLSON** 575:3

1 And so to bed.
Diary 20 April 1660

2 I went out to Charing Cross, to see Major-general Harrison hanged, drawn, and quartered; which was done there, he looking as cheerful as any man could do in that condition.
Diary 13 October 1660

3 A good honest and painful sermon.
Diary 17 March 1661

4 If ever I was foxed it was now.
Diary 23 April 1661

5 It lessened my esteem of a king, that he should not be able to command the rain.
Diary 19 July 1662

6 I see it is impossible for the King to have things done as cheap as other men.
Diary 21 July 1662

7 My wife, who, poor wretch, is troubled with her lonely life.
Diary 19 December 1662

8 Most of their discourse was about hunting, in a dialect I understand very little.
Diary 22 November 1663

9 While we were talking came by several poor creatures carried by, by constables, for being at a conventicle . . . I would to God they would either conform, or be more wise, and not be catched!
Diary 7 August 1664

10 Pretty witty Nell.
of Nell **GWYN**
Diary 3 April 1665

11 I saw a dead corpse in a coffin lie in the close unburied—and a watch is constantly kept there, night and day, to keep the people in—the plague making us cruel as dogs one to another.
Diary 4 September 1665

12 Strange to see how a good dinner and feasting reconciles everybody.
Diary 9 November 1665

13 Strange to say what delight we married people have to see these poor fools decoyed into our condition.
Diary 25 December 1665

14 In the heighth of it [the plague] . . . bold people there were to go in sport to one another's burials. And in spite to well people, would breathe in the faces . . . of well people going by.
Diary 12 February 1666

15 Music and women I cannot but give way to, whatever my business is.
Diary 9 March 1666

16 To this very day, I cannot sleep at night, without great terrors of fire.
Diary 28 February 1667

17 But it is pretty to see what money will do.
Diary 21 March 1667

18 And so I betake myself to that course, which is almost as much as to see myself go into my grave—for which, and all the discomforts that will accompany my being blind, the good God prepare me!
Diary 31 May 1669, closing words

19 Memoirs are true and useful stars, whilst studied histories are those stars joined in constellations, according to the fancy of the poet.
J. R. Tanner (ed.) *Samuel Pepys's Naval Minutes* (1926)

S. J. Perelman 1904–79

American humorist

20 Crazy like a fox.
title of book (1944)

Shimon Peres 1923–

Israeli statesman

21 Television has made dictatorship impossible, but democracy unbearable.
at a Davos meeting, in *Financial Times* 31 January 1995

Pericles *c.*495–429 BC

Greek statesman and Athenian general

22 The spring has gone out of the year.
Funeral Oration, Athens, 439 BC; Aristotle *The Art of Rhetoric* bk. 1, 1365a 31–3

23 Our love of what is beautiful does not lead to extravagance; our love of the things of the mind does not make us soft.
Funeral Oration, Athens, 430 BC, in Thucydides *History of the Peloponnesian War* bk. 2, ch. 40, sect. 1 (translated by Rex Warner)

24 Taking everything together then, I declare that our city is an education to Greece.
of Athens
Thucydides *History of the Peloponnesian War* bk. 2, ch. 41

25 For famous men have the whole earth as their memorial.
Thucydides *History of the Peloponnesian War* bk. 2, ch. 43, sect. 3

26 Happiness depends on being free, and freedom depends on being courageous.
Thucydides *History of the Peloponnesian War* bk. 2, ch. 43, sect. 4

27 Your great glory is not to be inferior to what God has made you, and the greatest glory of a woman is to be least talked about by men, whether they are praising you or criticizing you.
Thucydides *History of the Peloponnesian War* bk. 2, ch. 45, sect. 2

28 Wait for the wisest of all counsellors, Time.
Plutarch *Parallel Lives* 'Pericles' sect. 18

Eva Perón 1919–52

Argentinian wife of Juan Perón. On Perón: see **EPITAPHS** 318:13

1 Keeping books on charity is capitalist nonsense! I just use the money for the poor. I can't stop to count it.
Fleur Cowles *Bloody Precedent: the Peron Story* (1952)

Charles Perrault 1628–1703

French poet and critic

2 'Anne, sister Anne, do you see nothing coming?' And her sister Anne replied, 'I see nothing but the sun showing up the dust, and the grass looking green.'
Histoires et contes du temps passé [Stories and Tales of Past Times] (1697) 'Bluebeard'

3 'Oh Grandmother! What big ears you have!' 'All the better to hear you with.'
Histoires et contes du temps passé [Stories and Tales of Past Times] (1697) 'Little Red Riding Hood'

4 It belongs to my lord the Marquis of Carabas.
Histoires et contes du temps passé [Stories and Tales of Past Times] (1697) 'Puss in Boots'

Edward Perronet 1726–92

English clergyman

5 All hail the power of Jesus' Name;
Let Angels prostrate fall;
Bring forth the royal diadem
To crown Him Lord of all.
'All hail the power of Jesus' Name' (1780 hymn)

Jimmy Perry 1923–

English writer and songwriter

6 Who do you think you are kidding, Mister Hitler?
If you think we're on the run?
We are the boys who will stop your little game
We are the boys who will make you think again.
'Who do you think you are kidding, Mister Hitler' (theme song of *Dad's Army*, BBC television, 1968–77)

Oliver Hazard Perry 1785–1819

American naval officer

7 We have met the enemy and they are ours.
reporting his victory over the British in the battle of Lake Erie, 10 September 1813; see **CARTOON CAPTIONS** 205:16

Persius (Aulus Persius Flaccus) AD 34–62

Roman poet

8 *Nec te quaesiveris extra.*
And don't consult anyone's opinions but your own.
Satires no. 1, l. 7

9 *Virtutem videant intabescantque relicta.*
Let them recognize virtue and rot for having lost it.
Satires no. 3, l. 38

10 *Venienti occurrite morbo.*
Confront disease at its onset.
Satires no. 3, l. 64; see **OVID** 590:16

11 *Quod satis est sapio mihi.*
What I know is enough for me.
Satires no. 3, l. 78

12 *Tecum habita: noris quam sit tibi curta supellex.*
Live with yourself: get to know how poorly furnished you are.
Satires no. 4, l. 52

Ted Persons

13 Things ain't what they used to be.
title of song (1941)

Max Perutz 1914–2002

Austrian-born scientist

14 The priest persuades humble people to endure their hard lot; the politician urges them to rebel against it; and the scientist thinks of a method that does away with the hard lot altogether.
Is Science Necessary (1989)

Henri Philippe Pétain 1856–1951

French soldier and statesman. See also **MILITARY SAYINGS, SLOGANS, AND SONGS** 535:11

15 To write one's memoirs is to speak ill of everybody except oneself.
in *Observer* 26 May 1946

Laurence J. Peter 1919–90

Canadian writer. See also **MISQUOTATIONS** 548:21

16 In a hierarchy every employee tends to rise to his level of incompetence.
The Peter Principle (1969) ch. 1

Petrarch (Francesco Petrarca) 1304–74

Italian poet. On Petrarch: see **BYRON** 188:16

17 *Voi ch' ascoltate in rime sparse il suono*
di quei sospiri ond'io nudriva 'l core
in sul mio primo giovenile errore,
quand' era in parte altr' uom da quel ch' i' sono.
O you who hear within these scattered verses the sound of sighs with which I fed my heart in my first errant youthful days when I in part was not the man I am today.
Canzoniere no. 1 (c.1352) translated by Mark Musa

18 *E del mio vaneggiar vergogna è 'l frutto*
e 'l pentersi, e 'l conoscer chiaramente
che quanto piace al mondo è breve sogno.
And the fruit of my vanity is shame, and repentance, and the clear knowledge that whatever the world finds pleasing, is but a brief dream.
Canzoniere no. 1 (c.1352)

19 *Italia mia, ben che 'l parlar sia indarno*
a le piaghe mortali

che nel bel corpo tuo sì spesse veggio.

Oh, my own Italy, though words be useless
to heal the mortal wounds
I see covering all your lovely body.

  Canzoniere no. 128 (c.1352) translated by Mark Musa

1 *Pace non trovo et non ò da far guerra,*
e temo et spero, et ardo et son un ghiaccio.

I find no peace, and I am not at war,
I fear and hope, and burn and I am ice.

  Canzoniere no. 134 (c.1352) translated by Mark Musa

2 *Altissimum regionis huius montem, quem non*
immerito Ventosum vocant, hodierno die, sola videndi
insignem loco altitudinem cupiditate ductus, ascendi.

Today I climbed the highest mountain in this
region, which is not improperly called Ventosus
(Windy). The only motive for my ascent was the
wish to see what so great a height had to offer.

  of Mont Ventoux in Provence, France

  letter to Dionisio da Borgo San Sepolcro c.1336; *Letters on*
  Familiar Matters bk. 4, no. 1 (translated by Mark Musa)

3 *Continue morimur, ego dum hec scribo, tu dum leges,*
alii dum audient, dumque non audient, ego quoque
dum hec leges moriar, tu moreris dum hec scribo,
ambo morimur, omnes morimur, semper morimur.

We are continually dying; I while I am writing
these words, you while you are reading them,
others when they hear them or fail to hear
them. I shall be dying when you read this, you
die while I write, we both are dying, we all are
dying, we are dying forever.

  letter to Philippe de Cabassoles c.1360; *Letters on Familiar*
  Matters bk. 24, no. 1 (translated by Morris Bishop)

Jamie Petrie *and* Peter Cunnah

British singers and songwriters

4 Things can only get better.

  title of song (1994); see **POLITICAL SLOGANS AND SONGS** 613:9

Petronius (Petronius Arbiter) d. AD 65

Roman satirist. On Petronius: see **TACITUS** 787:8; see also
MISQUOTATIONS 549:2

5 *Canis ingens, catena vinctus, in pariete erat pictus*
superque quadrata littera scriptum 'Cave canem.'

A huge dog, tied by a chain, was painted on the
wall and over it was written in capital letters
'Beware of the dog.'

  Satyricon 'Cena Trimalchionis' ch. 29, sect. 1

6 *Abiit ad plures.*

He's gone to join the majority.

  meaning the dead

  Satyricon 'Cena Trimalchionis' ch. 42, sect. 5; see **YOUNG**
  877:3

7 *Nam Sibyllam quidem Cumis ego ipse oculis meis*
vidi in ampulla pendere, et cum illi pueri dicerent:
Sibylla, ti theleis; respondebat illa: apothanein thelō.

I myself with my own eyes saw the Sibyl at
Cumae hanging in a flask; and when the boys

cried at her: ' Sibyl, Sibyl, what do you want?' 'I
would that I were dead,' she used to answer.

  Satyricon 'Cena Trimalchionis' ch. 48, sect. 8; see **ROSSETTI**
  669:24

8 *Horatii curiosa felicitas.*

Horace's careful felicity.

  Satyricon ch. 118, sect. 5

9 *Foeda est in coitu et brevis voluptas*
Et taedet Veneris statim peractae.

Delight of lust is gross and brief
And weariness treads on desire.

  A. Baehrens *Poetae Latini Minores* (1882) vol. 4, no. 101
  (translated by Helen Waddell)

Pheidippides d. 490 BC

Athenian messenger

10 Greetings, we win!

  dying words, having run back to Athens from Marathon
  with news of victory over the Persians

  Lucian bk. 3, ch. 64 'Pro Lapsu inter salutandum' para. 3

Edward John Phelps 1822–1900

American lawyer and diplomat

11 The man who makes no mistakes does not
usually make anything.

  speech at the Mansion House, London, 24 January 1889; in
  The Times 25 January 1889; see **PROVERBS** 635:25

Kim Philby (Harold Adrian Russell Philby)
1912–88

British intelligence officer and Soviet spy

12 To betray, you must first belong.

  in *Sunday Times* 17 December 1967

Philip, Duke of Edinburgh 1921–

British prince, Greek-born husband of **ELIZABETH II**

13 Gentlemen, I think it is about time we 'pulled
our fingers out' . . . If we want to be more
prosperous we've simply got to get down to it
and work for it. The rest of the world does not
owe us a living.

  speech in London, 17 October 1961

14 If you stay here much longer you'll all be slitty-
eyed.

  remark to Edinburgh University students in Peking, 16
  October 1986

15 Tolerance is the one essential ingredient . . . You
can take it from me that the Queen has the
quality of tolerance in abundance.

  his recipe for a successful marriage, during celebrations for
  their golden wedding anniversary

  in *The Times* 20 November 1997

John Woodward ('Jack') Philip
1840–1900

American naval captain in the Spanish–American war

1 Don't cheer, men; those poor devils are dying.
at the Battle of Santiago, 4 July 1898
in *Dictionary of American Biography* vol. 14 (1934) 'John Woodward Philip'

Ambrose Philips *c.*1675–1749
English poet

2 The flowers anew, returning seasons bring;
But beauty faded has no second spring.
The First Pastoral (1708) 'Lobbin' l. 47

3 There solid billows of enormous size,
Alps of green ice, in wild disorder rise.
'A Winter-Piece' in *The Tatler* 7 May 1709

Katherine Philips 1632–64
English poet. On Philips: see AUBREY 36:5

4 I did but see him, and he disappeared,
I did but touch the rosebud, and it fell;
A sorrow unforeseen and scarcely feared,
So ill can mortals their afflictions spell.
'On the Death of my First and Dearest Child, Hector Philips' (1655)

Arthur Angell Phillips 1900–85
Australian critic and editor

5 Above our writers—and other artists—looms the intimidating mass of Anglo-Saxon culture. Such a situation almost inevitably produces the characteristic Australian Cultural Cringe—appearing either as the Cringe Direct, or as the Cringe Inverted, in the attitude of the Blatant Blatherskite, the God's-Own-Country and I'm-a-better-man-than-you-are Australian bore.
Meanjin (1950) 'The Cultural Cringe'; see KEATING 453:18

Caryl Phillips 1958–
West Indian-born British novelist and dramatist

6 England has changed. These days it's difficult to tell who's from around here and who's not. Who belongs and who's a stranger.
A Distant Shore (2003)

Morgan Phillips 1902–63
British Labour politician

7 The Labour Party owes more to Methodism than to Marxism.
James Callaghan *Time and Chance* (1987) ch. 1; coined by Denis HEALEY as speechwriter for Phillips at the Socialist International Conference, Copenhagen, 1953

Pablo Picasso 1881–1973
Spanish painter

8 There is nothing more dangerous than justice in the hands of judges, and a paintbrush in the hands of a painter. Just think of the danger to society!
conversation, 1935; Herschel B. Chipp *Theories of Modern Art* (1968)

9 No, painting is not made to decorate apartments. It's an offensive and defensive weapon against the enemy.
interview with Simone Téry, 24 March 1945, in Alfred H. Barr *Picasso* (1946)

10 The artist is a receptacle for emotions that come from all over the place: from the sky, from the earth, from a scrap of paper, from a passing shape, from a spider's web.
Alfred H. Barr Jr. *Picasso: Fifty Years of his Art* (1946)

11 When I was the age of these children I could draw like Raphael: it took me many years to learn how to draw like these children.
to Herbert READ, when visiting an exhibition of childen's drawings
quoted in letter from Read to *The Times* 27 October 1956

12 I paint objects as I think them, not as I see them.
John Golding *Cubism* (1959)

13 God is really only another artist. He invented the giraffe, the elephant, and the cat. He has no real style. He just goes on trying other things.
F. Gilot and C. Lake *Life With Picasso* (1964) pt. 1

14 Every positive value has its price in negative terms . . . The genius of Einstein leads to Hiroshima.
F. Gilot and C. Lake *Life With Picasso* (1964) pt. 2

15 We all know that Art is not truth. Art is a lie that makes us realize truth.
Dore Ashton *Picasso on Art* (1972) 'Two statements by Picasso'

Pindar 518–438 BC
Greek lyric poet

16 Water is best. But gold shines like fire blazing in the night, supreme of lordly wealth.
Olympian Odes bk. 1, l. 1

17 I have many swift arrows in my quiver which speak to the wise, but for the crowd they need interpreters. The skilled poet is one who knows much through natural gift, but those who have learned their art chatter turbulently, like ravens, vainly, against the divine bird of Zeus.
Olympian Odes bk. 2, l. 83

18 My soul, do not seek immortal life, but exhaust the realm of the possible.
Pythian Odes bk. 3, l. 109

19 Creatures of a day, what is a man? What is he not? Mankind is a dream of a shadow. But when a god-given brightness comes, a radiant light rests on men, and a gentle life.
Pythian Odes bk. 8, l. 135

Harold Pinter 1930–2008

English dramatist

1 If only I could get down to Sidcup! I've been waiting for the weather to break. He's got my papers, this man I left them with, it's got it all down there, I could prove everything.
The Caretaker (1960) act 1

2 Apart from the known and the unknown, what else is there?
The Homecoming (1965) act 2, sc. 1

3 The weasel under the cocktail cabinet.
on being asked what his plays were about
J. Russell Taylor *Anger and After* (1962)

Luigi Pirandello 1867–1936

Italian dramatist and novelist

4 Six characters in search of an author.
title of play (1921)

Robert M. Pirsig 1928–

American writer

5 Zen and the art of motorcycle maintenance.
title of book (1974)

6 That's the classical mind at work, runs fine inside but looks dingy on the surface.
Zen and the Art of Motorcycle Maintenance (1974) pt. 3, ch. 26

Walter B. Pitkin 1878–1953

7 Life begins at forty.
title of book (1932); see **PROVERBS** 637:27

William Pitt, Earl of Chatham

1708–78

British Whig statesman, Prime Minister 1766–8. On Pitt: see WALPOLE 838:15

8 The atrocious crime of being a young man . . . I shall neither attempt to palliate nor deny.
speech, House of Commons, 2 March 1741

9 The poorest man may in his cottage bid defiance to all the forces of the Crown. It may be frail—its roof may shake—the wind may blow through it—the storm may enter—the rain may enter—but the King of England cannot enter!
speech, c. March 1763, in Lord Brougham *Historical Sketches of Statesmen in the Time of George III* First Series (1845) vol. 1

10 Unlimited power is apt to corrupt the minds of those who possess it.
speech, House of Lords, 9 January 1770; see **ACTON** 1:16

11 There is something behind the throne greater than the King himself.
speech, House of Lords, 2 March 1770

12 We have a Calvinistic creed, a Popish liturgy, and an Arminian clergy.
speech, House of Lords, 19 May 1772; Basil Williams *Life of William Pitt Earl of Chatham* (1913) vol. 2, ch. 24

13 You cannot conquer America.
speech, House of Lords, 18 November 1777

14 I invoke the genius of the Constitution!
speech, House of Lords, 18 November 1777

15 Any state is better than despair. Let us at least make one effort; and if we must fall, let us fall like men.
speech, House of Lords, 7 April 1778

16 Our watchword is security.
attributed

17 The parks are the lungs of London.
quoted by William Windham in the House of Commons, 30 June 1808

William Pitt 1759–1806

British Tory statesman, Prime Minister 1783–1801, 1804–6. On Pitt: see BURKE 175:20, CANNING 197:4, FOX 339:10, SCOTT 688:19

18 Necessity is the plea for every infringement of human freedom: it is the argument of tyrants; it is the creed of slaves.
speech, House of Commons, 18 November 1783

19 We must recollect . . . what it is we have at stake, what it is we have to contend for. It is for our property, it is for our liberty, it is for our independence, nay, for our existence as a nation; it is for our character, it is for our very name as Englishmen, it is for everything dear and valuable to man on this side of the grave.
on the rupture of the Peace of Amiens and the resumption of war with Napoleon
speech, 22 July 1803, in *Speeches of the Rt. Hon. William Pitt* (1806) vol. 4

20 England has saved herself by her exertions, and will, as I trust, save Europe by her example.
replying to a toast in which he had been described as the saviour of his country in the wars with France
R. Coupland *War Speeches of William Pitt* (1915)

21 Roll up that map; it will not be wanted these ten years.
of a map of Europe, on hearing of Napoleon's victory at Austerlitz, December 1805
Earl Stanhope *Life of the Rt. Hon. William Pitt* vol. 4 (1862) ch. 43

22 Oh, my country! how I leave my country!
also variously reported as 'How I love my country'; and 'My country! oh, my country!'; oral tradition reports: 'I think I could eat one of Bellamy's veal pies'
Earl Stanhope *Life of the Rt. Hon. William Pitt* vol. 3 (1879) ch. 43; Earl Stanhope *Life of the Rt. Hon. William Pitt* (1st ed.), vol. 4 (1862) ch. 43; and G. Rose *Diaries and Correspondence* (1860) vol. 2, 23 January 1806

Pius VII 1742–1823

Italian cleric, Pope from 1800

23 We are prepared to go to the gates of Hell—but no further.
*attempting to reach an agreement with **NAPOLEON I**, c.1800–1*
J. M. Robinson *Cardinal Consalvi* (1987)

Pius XII 1876–1958
Italian cleric; Pope from 1939

1 One Galileo in two thousand years is enough.
on being asked to proscribe the works of **TEILHARD DE CHARDIN**
attributed; Stafford Beer *Platform for Change* (1975)

Max Planck 1858–1947
German physicist

2 A new scientific truth does not triumph by convincing its opponents and making them see the light, but rather because its opponents eventually die, and a new generation grows up that is familiar with it.
A Scientific Autobiography (1949, translated by F. Gaynor)

Sylvia Plath 1932–63
American poet

3 A living doll, everywhere you look.
It can sew, it can cook,
It can talk, talk, talk.
'The Applicant' (1966)

4 Is there no way out of the mind?
'Apprehensions' (1971)

5 I have always been scared of *you*,
With your Luftwaffe, your gobbledygoo.
And your neat moustache
And your Aryan eye, bright blue.
Panzer-man, panzer-man, O You—
'Daddy' (1963)

6 Every woman adores a Fascist,
The boot in the face, the brute
Brute heart of a brute like you.
'Daddy' (1963)

7 The woman is perfected
Her dead
Body wears the smile of accomplishment.
opening lines of her last poem, written a week before her suicide
'Edge'

8 I am the ghost of an infamous suicide,
My own blue razor rusting in my throat.
O pardon the one who knocks for pardon at
Your gate, father—your hound-bitch, daughter, friend.
It was my love that did us both to death.
'Electra on Azalea Path' (1959)

9 Dying,
Is an art, like everything else.
'Lady Lazarus' (1963)

10 Out of the ash
I rise with my red hair
And I eat men like air.
'Lady Lazarus' (1963)

11 Love set you going like a fat gold watch.
The midwife slapped your footsoles, and your
bald cry

Took its place among the elements.
'Morning Song' (1965)

12 Widow. The word consumes itself.
'Widow' (1971)

Plato 429–347 BC
Greek philosopher. On Plato: see **DIOGENES** 283:15; see also **ANONYMOUS** 22:16

13 Socrates, he says, breaks the law by corrupting young men and not recognizing the gods that the city recognizes, but some other new deities.
Apologia 24b

14 Is that which is holy loved by the gods because it is holy, or is it holy because it is loved by the gods?
Euthyphro 10

15 It [rhetoric] doesn't involve expertise; all you need is a mind which is good at guessing, some courage, and a natural talent for interacting with people. The general term I use to refer to it is 'flattery'.
Gorgias 463b (translated by Robin Waterfield)

16 Searching and learning is a process of remembering . . . and I, believing this to be true, am ready to search with you what virtue is.
Meno 81d

17 Socrates, I shall not accuse you as I accuse others, of getting angry and cursing me when I tell them to drink the poison imposed by the authorities. I know you on the contrary in your time here to be the noblest and gentlest and best man of all who ever came here; and now I am sure you are not angry with me, for you know who are responsible, but with them.
spoken by Socrates' jailor
Phaedo 116c

18 This was the end, Echekrates, of our friend; a man of whom we may say that of all whom we met at that time he was the wisest and justest and best.
on the death of **SOCRATES**
Phaedo 118a

19 The country places and the trees won't teach me anything, and the people in the city do.
Phaedrus 230d

20 For what should a man live, if not for the pleasures of discourse?
Phaedrus 258e, translated by Benjamin Jowett

21 What I say is that 'just' or 'right' means nothing but what is in the interest of the stronger party.
spoken by Thrasymachus
The Republic bk. 1, 338c (translated by F. M. Cornford)

22 For our discussion is about no ordinary matter, but on the right way to conduct our lives.
The Republic bk. 1, 352d

23 Can we devise one of those lies—the kind which crop up as the occasion demands, which we were talking about not so long ago—so that with a single noble lie we can indocrinate the rulers themselves, preferably, but at least the rest of the community?

The Republic bk. 3, 414b (translated by Robin Waterfield)

1 And so with the objects of knowledge: these derive from the Good not only their power of being known, but their very being and reality; and Goodness is not the same thing as being, but even beyond being, surpassing it in dignity and power.

The Republic bk. 6, 509b (translated by F. M. Cornford)

2 Behold! human beings living in a underground den . . . Like ourselves . . . they see only their own shadows, or the shadows of one another, which the fire throws on the opposite wall of the cave.

The Republic bk. 7, 515b; see **NIETZSCHE** 575:12

3 The city in which those who are to rule are least eager to hold office must needs be the best governed and freest from strife.

The Republic bk. 7, 520

4 The blame is his who chooses: God is blameless.

The Republic bk. 10, 617e

5 But if we are guided by me we shall believe that the soul is immortal and capable of enduring all extremes of good and evil, and so we shall hold ever to the upward way and pursue righteousness with wisdom always and ever, that we may be dear to ourselves and to the gods both during our sojourn here and when we receive our reward.

The Republic bk. 10, 621c

6 Evils, Theodorus, can never pass away, for there must always remain something which is antagonistic to good. Having no place among the gods in heaven, of necessity they hover around the mortal nature and this earthly sphere. Wherefore we ought to fly away from earth to heaven as quickly as we can; and to fly away is to become like God, as far as this is possible; and to become like him is to become holy, just, and wise.

Theaetetus 176a (translated by Benjamin Jowett)

7 God is always doing geometry.

Plutarch *Moralia*

Plautus *c.*250–184 BC

Roman comic dramatist

8 *Lupus est homo homini, non homo, quom qualis sit non novit.*

A man is a wolf rather than a man to another man, when he hasn't yet found out what he's like.

often quoted as 'Homo homini lupus [*A man is a wolf to another man*]'

Asinaria l. 495; see **VANZETTI** 824:9

9 *Dictum sapienti sat est.*

A sentence is enough for a sensible man.

proverbially: 'Verbum sapienti sat est [*A word is enough for the wise*]', *and abbreviated to* 'verb. sap.'

Persa l. 729; see **PROVERBS** 647:34

10 LABRAX: *Immo edepol una littera plus sum quam medicus.*

GRIPUS: *Tum tu*
            Mendicus es?

LABRAX: *Tetigisti acu.*

LABRAX: One letter more than a medical man, that's what I am.

GRIPUS: Then you're a mendicant?

LABRAX: You've hit the point.

Rudens l. 1305

Pliny the Elder AD 23–79

Roman statesman and scholar, uncle of PLINY the Younger

11 *Scito enim conferentum auctores me deprehendisse a iuratissimis et proximis veteres transcriptos ad verbum neque nominatos.*

When collating authorities I have found that the most professedly reliable and modern writers have copied the old authors word for word, without acknowledgement.

preface to *Historia Naturalis*

12 *Solum ut inter ista certum sit, nihil esse certi.*

The only certainty is that nothing is certain.

Historia Naturalis bk. 2, sect. 5

13 *Bruta fulmina.*

Harmless thunderbolts.

Historia Naturalis bk. 2, sect. 113

14 *Ut non sit satis aestimare, parens melior homini an tristior noverca fuerit.*

So that it is far from easy to judge whether she has proved a kind parent to man or a harsh step-mother.

on nature

Historia Naturalis bk. 7, sect. 1

15 *Nemo mortalium omnibus horis sapit.*

No man is wise at all times.

Historia Naturalis bk. 7, sect. 40

16 *Semper aliquid novi Africam adferre.*

Africa always brings [us] something new.

originally referring to hybridization of African animals

Historia Naturalis bk. 8, sect. 42; see **PROVERBS** 644:17

17 *Optimumque est, ut volgo dixere, aliena insania frui.*

And the best plan is, as the popular saying was, to profit by the folly of others.

Historia Naturalis bk. 18, sect. 31

18 *Addito salis grano.*

With the addition of a grain of salt.

commonly quoted as 'Cum grano salis [*With a grain of salt*]'

Historia Naturalis bk. 23, sect. 149

19 *Dicere etiam solebat nullum esse librum tam malum ut non aliqua parte prodesset.*

[Pliny] always said that there was no book so bad that some good could not be got out of it.
Pliny the Younger *Letters* bk. 3, no. 5

Pliny the Younger c.AD 61–c.112

Roman senator and writer, nephew of PLINY the Elder

1 *Nihil est, inquis, quod scribam. At hoc ipsum scribe, nihil esse quod scribas, vel solum illud unde incipere priores solebant: 'Si vales, bene est; ego valeo.' Hoc mihi sufficit; est enim maximum.*

You say you have nothing to write about. Well, you can at least write about *that*—or else simply the phrase our elders used to start a letter with: 'If you are well, well and good; I am well.' That will do for me—it is all that matters.
letter to Fabius Justus, in *Letters* (Loeb ed., 1969) bk. 1, sect. 11

2 *Non enim excursus hic ejus, sed opus ipsum est.*

For this is not a digression from it, but the work itself.
Letters bk. 5, sect. 6

William Plomer 1903–73

British poet

3 Out of that bungled, unwise war
An alp of unforgiveness grew.
'The Boer War' (1960)

4 With first-rate sherry flowing into second-rate whores,
And third-rate conversation without one single pause:
Just like a young couple
Between the wars.
'Father and Son: 1939' (1945)

5 On a sofa upholstered in panther skin
Mona did researches in original sin.
'Mews Flat Mona' (1960)

6 A rose-red sissy half as old as time.
'Playboy of the Demi-World: 1938' (1945); see BURGON 172:12

Plutarch c.AD 46–c.120

Greek philosopher and biographer

7 For the mind does not require filling like a bottle, but rather, like wood, it only requires kindling to create in it an impulse to think independently and an ardent desire for the truth.
Moralia sect. 48c 'On Listening to Lectures'; see RABELAIS 652:12

8 Everybody is himself his own foremost and greatest flatterer.
Moralia sect. 49f 'How to Tell a Flatterer from a Friend'; see BACON 47:14

9 To break a treaty is contempt for the gods. But to outwit an enemy is not only just and glorious—but profitable and sweet.
often quoted in the form 'To deceive a friend is impious. But . . .'
Parallel Lives 'Agesilaus' sect. 9

10 I am writing biography, not history, and the truth is that the most brilliant exploits often tell us nothing of the virtues or vices of the men who performed them, while on the other hand a chance remark or a joke may reveal far more of a man's character than the mere feat of winning battles in which thousands fall, or of marshalling great armies, or laying siege to cities.
Parallel Lives 'Alexander' sect. 7

11 For we are told that when a certain man was accusing both of them to him, he [Caesar] said that he had no fear of those fat and long-haired fellows, but rather of those pale and thin ones.
Parallel Lives 'Anthony' sect. 11; see SHAKESPEARE 711:22

12 The man who is thought to have been the first to see beneath the surface of Caesar's public policy and to fear it, as one might fear the smiling surface of the sea.
of CICERO
Parallel Lives 'Julius Caesar' sect. 4

13 He who cheats with an oath acknowledges that he is afraid of his enemy, but that he thinks little of God.
Parallel Lives 'Lysander' sect. 8; see LYSANDER 506:3

Edgar Allan Poe 1809–49

American writer. On Poe: see LOWELL 502:17

14 I was a child and she was a child,
In this kingdom by the sea;
But we loved with a love which was more than love—
I and my Annabel Lee.
'Annabel Lee' (1849)

15 And so, all the night-tide, I lie down by the side
Of my darling, my darling, my life and my bride
In her sepulchre there by the sea,
In her tomb by the side of the sea.
'Annabel Lee' (1849)

16 Keeping time, time, time,
In a sort of Runic rhyme,
To the tintinnabulation that so musically wells
From the bells, bells, bells, bells.
'The Bells' (1849) st. 1

17 All that we see or seem
Is but a dream within a dream.
'A Dream within a Dream' (1849)

18 The fever called 'Living'
Is conquered at last.
'For Annie' (1849)

19 Once upon a midnight dreary, while I pondered, weak and weary,
Over many a quaint and curious volume of forgotten lore,
While I nodded, nearly napping, suddenly there came a tapping,
As of some one gently rapping, rapping at my chamber door.
'The Raven' (1845) st. 1

1 Eagerly I wished the morrow,—vainly had I
sought to borrow
From my books surcease of sorrow—sorrow for
the lost Lenore—
For the rare and radiant maiden whom the
angels name Lenore—
Nameless here for evermore.
'The Raven' (1845) st. 2

2 Ghastly, grim and ancient raven wandering from
the Nightly shore—
Tell me what thy lordly name is on the Night's
Plutonian shore!
'The Raven' (1845) st. 8

3 Take thy beak from out my heart, and take thy
form from off my door!
Quoth the Raven, 'Nevermore'.
'The Raven' (1845) st. 17

4 And his eyes have all the seeming of a demon's
that is dreaming.
'The Raven' (1845) st. 18

5   The glory that was Greece
And the grandeur that was Rome.
'To Helen' (1831)

6 It was down by the dank tarn of Auber,
In the ghoul-haunted woodland of Weir.
'Ulalume' (1847)

Henri Poincaré 1854–1912
French mathematician and philosopher of science

7 Science is built up of facts, as a house is built of
stones; but an accumulation of facts is no more
a science than a heap of stones is a house.
Science and Hypothesis (1905) ch. 9

John C. Polanyi 1929–
German-born Canadian scientist

8 When . . . we fear science, we really fear
ourselves. Human dignity is better served by
embracing knowledge.
accepting the Nobel Prize for Chemistry, 10 December 1986

□ Political slogans and songs *see* box
overleaf. *See also* **CONNELL** 248:3, **MARX AND
ENGELS** 526:14, **POTTIER** 620:14

Jackson Pollock 1912–56
American painter

9 There was a reviewer a while back who wrote
that my pictures didn't have any beginning or
any end. He didn't mean it as a compliment, but
it was. It was a fine compliment.
Francis V. O'Connor *Jackson Pollock* (1967)

Polybius *c*.200–*c*.118 BC
Greek historian

10 Those who know how to win are much more
numerous than those who know how to make
proper use of their victories.
History bk. 10

John Pomfret 1667–1702
English clergyman

11 We live and learn, but not the wiser grow.
'Reason' (1700) l. 112

Madame de Pompadour (Antoinette
Poisson, Marquise de Pompadour) 1721–64
French favourite of Louis XV of France

12 *Après nous le déluge.*
After us the deluge.
Madame du Hausset *Mémoires* (1824)

Pompey the Great 106–48 BC
Roman general and statesman

13 *Navigare necesse est, vivere non est.*
To sail is necessary; to live is not.
insisting on setting sail during a storm
Plutarch *Parallel Lives* 'Pompey' sect. 50

Alexander Pope 1688–1744
English poet. On Pope: see **ARNOLD 31:24, ARNOLD 32:7,
BENTLEY 72:2, BRERETON 156:10**

14 Poetic Justice, with her lifted scale,
Where, in nice balance, truth with gold she
weighs,
And solid pudding against empty praise.
The Dunciad (1742) bk. 1, l. 52

15 Or where the pictures for the page atone,
And Quarles is saved by beauties not his own.
The Dunciad (1742) bk. 1, l. 139

16 Gentle Dullness ever loves a joke.
The Dunciad (1742) bk. 2, l. 34

17 A brain of feathers, and a heart of lead.
The Dunciad (1742) bk. 2, l. 44

18 How little, mark! that portion of the ball,
Where, faint at best, the beams of science fall.
The Dunciad (1742) bk. 3, l. 83

19 All crowd, who foremost shall be damned to
Fame.
The Dunciad (1742) bk. 3, l. 158

20 Flow Welsted, flow! like thine inspirer, Beer,
Tho' stale, not ripe; tho' thin, yet never clear;
So sweetly mawkish, and so smoothly dull;
Heady, not strong; o'erflowing tho' not full.
The Dunciad (1742) bk. 3, l. 169

21 A wit with dunces, and a dunce with wits.
The Dunciad (1742) bk. 4, l. 90

continued

Political slogans and songs

1 All power to the Soviets.
workers in Petrograd, 1917

2 All the way with LBJ.
US Democratic Party campaign slogan, 1960

3 Are you now, or have you ever been, a member of the Communist Party?
from 1947, the question habitually put by the House Un-American Activities Committee (HUAC) to those appearing before it, now particularly associated with the McCarthy period of the 1950s

4 As Maine goes, so goes the nation.
American political saying, c.1840; see **FARLEY** 323:14

5 Ban the bomb.
US anti-nuclear slogan, adopted by the Campaign for Nuclear Disarmament, 1953 onwards

6 A bayonet is a weapon with a worker at each end.
British pacifist slogan (1940)

7 Better red than dead.
slogan of nuclear disarmament campaigners, late 1950s

8 A bigger bang for a buck.
Charles E. **WILSON**'s defence policy, in *Newsweek* 22 March 1954

9 The big tent.
slogan used by the American Republican Party to denote a policy of inclusiveness
recorded from 1990

10 Black is beautiful.
slogan of American civil rights campaigners, mid-1960s

11 Burn, baby, burn.
Black extremist slogan in use during the Los Angeles riots, August 1965

12 Can't pay, won't pay.
anti-Poll Tax slogan, c.1990; see **FO** 336:1

13 Don't sell America short.
popular version of saying attributed, c.1890s, to John Pierpont Morgan (1837–1913)

14 *Ein Reich, ein Volk, ein Führer.*
One realm, one people, one leader.
Nazi Party slogan, early 1930s

15 Fair shares for all, is Labour's call.
slogan for the North Battersea by-election, 1946, coined by Douglas JAY
Douglas Jay *Change and Fortune* (1980) ch. 7

16 Fifty-four forty, or fight!
slogan of expansionist Democrats in the US presidential campaign of 1844, in which the Oregon boundary definition was an issue (in 1846 the new Democratic president, James K. Polk, compromised on the 49th parallel with Great Britain)

17 Free by '93.
Scottish National Party, general election campaign, 1992

18 Give us back our eleven days.
protesting against the adoption of the Gregorian Calendar in 1752, and in this form associated with Hogarth's cartoon showing a rowdy Oxfordshire election of 1754
David Ewing Duncan *The Calendar* (1998)

19 *Gott strafe England!*
God punish England!
a common salutation in Germany in 1914 and the following years, often wrongly attributed to the poem *Hassgesang gegen England* (1914) by Ernst Lissauer (1882–1937), known as the 'Hymn of Hate'; see **FUNKE** 346:21

20 Hey, hey, LBJ, how many kids did you kill today?
anti-Vietnam marching slogan, 1960s

21 I like Ike.
*used when General **EISENHOWER** was first seen as a potential presidential nominee*
US button badge, 1947; coined by Henry D. Spalding (d. 1990)

22 I met wid Napper Tandy, and he took me by the hand,
And he said, 'How's poor ould Ireland, and how does she stand?'
She's the most disthressful country that iver yet was seen,
For they're hangin' men an' women for the wearin' o' the Green.
'The Wearin' o' the Green' (c.1795 ballad)

23 The iron-armed soldier, the true-hearted soldier,
The gallant old soldier of Tippecanoe.
*presidential campaign song for William Henry Harrison, 1840; see **POLITICAL SLOGANS AND SONGS** 613:12*
attributed to George Pope Morris (1802–64)

24 It'll play in Peoria.
catchphrase of the **NIXON** administration (early 1970s) meaning 'it will be acceptable to middle America', but originating in a standard music hall joke of the 1930s

25 It's morning again in America.
slogan for Ronald **REAGAN**'s election campaign, 1984; coined by Hal Riney (1932–); in *Newsweek* 6 August 1984

26 It's Scotland's oil.
Scottish National Party, 1972

27 It's the economy, stupid.
on a sign put up at the 1992 **CLINTON** presidential campaign headquarters by campaign manager James Carville

28 *Kraft durch Freude.*
Strength through joy.
German Labour Front slogan, from 1933; coined by Robert Ley (1890–1945)

29 Labour isn't working.
on poster showing a long queue outside an unemployment office
Conservative Party slogan 1978–9

30 Labour's double whammy.
Conservative Party election slogan 1992

continued

Political slogans and songs *continued*

1 *Liberté! Égalité! Fraternité!*

Freedom! Equality! Brotherhood!

motto of the French Revolution, but of earlier origin
the Club des Cordeliers passed a motion, 30 June 1793, 'that owners should be urged to paint on the front of their houses, in large letters, the words: Unity, indivisibility of the Republic, Liberty, Equality, Fraternity or death'; in *Journal de Paris* no. 182 (from 1795 the words 'or death' were dropped); see **CHAMFORT** 215:5

2 Life's better with the Conservatives. Don't let Labour ruin it.
Conservative Party election slogan, 1959

3 New Labour, new danger.
Conservative slogan, 1996

4 No surrender!
the defenders of the besieged city of Derry to the Jacobite army of James II, April 1689, adopted as a slogan of Protestant Ulster
Jonathan Bardon *A History of Ulster* (1992)

5 Not in my name.
protesters against the war in Iraq, 2003

6 The personal is political.
1970s feminist slogan, attributed to Carol Hanisch (1945–)

7 Power to the people.
slogan of the Black Panther movement, from *c*.1968 onwards; see **NEWTON** 572:20

8 So on the Twelfth I proudly wear the sash my father wore.
'The Sash My Father Wore', traditional Orange song

9 Things can only get better.
Labour campaign slogan, 1997; see **PETRIE AND CUNNAH** 605:4

10 Thirteen years of Tory misrule.
unofficial Labour party election slogan, also in the form 'Thirteen wasted years', 1964

11 Three acres and a cow.
regarded as the requirement for self-sufficiency; associated with the radical politician Jesse Collings (1831–1920) and his land reform campaign begun in 1885
Jesse Collings in the House of Commons, 26 January 1886, although used earlier by Joseph **CHAMBERLAIN** in a speech at Evesham (in *The Times* 17 November 1885), by which time it was already proverbial

12 Tippecanoe and Tyler, too.
presidential campaign song for William Henry Harrison, 1840
attributed to A. C. Ross (fl. 1840); see **POLITICAL SLOGANS AND SONGS** 612:23

13 'Tis bad enough in man or woman
To steal a goose from off a common;
But surely he's without excuse
Who steals the common from the goose.
'On Inclosures'; in *The Oxford Book of Light Verse* (1938)

14 Votes for women.
adopted when it proved impossible to use a banner with the longer slogan 'Will the Liberal Party Give Votes for Women?' made by Emmeline PANKHURST (1858–1928), Christabel PANKHURST (1880–1958), and Annie Kenney (1879–1953)
slogan of the women's suffrage movement, from 13 October 1905; Emmeline Pankhurst *My Own Story* (1914)

15 War will cease when men refuse to fight.
pacifist slogan, from *c*.1936 (often quoted as, 'Wars will cease . . . ')

16 We shall not be moved.
title of labour and civil rights song (1931) adapted from an earlier gospel hymn

17 We shall overcome.
title of song, originating from before the American Civil War, adapted as a Baptist hymn ('I'll Overcome Some Day', 1901) by C. Albert Tindley; revived in 1946 as a protest song by black tobacco workers, and in 1963 during the black Civil Rights Campaign

18 Would you buy a used car from this man?
campaign slogan directed against Richard **NIXON**, 1968

19 Yes it hurt, yes it worked.
Conservative Party slogan, 1996; see **MAJOR** 517:2

20 Yesterday's men (they failed before!).
Labour Party slogan, referring to the Conservatives, 1970; coined by David Kingsley, Dennis Lyons, and Peter Lovell-Davis

21 Yes, we can.
Barack **OBAMA** presidential campaign slogan, 2007–8; the slogan is also associated with the children's television character Bob the Builder (1999–)

Alexander Pope *continued*

22 Whate'er the talents, or howe'er designed,
We hang one jingling padlock on the mind.
The Dunciad (1742) bk. 4, l. 161

23 The Right Divine of Kings to govern wrong.
The Dunciad (1742) bk. 4, l. 187

24 With the same cement, ever sure to bind,
We bring to one dead level ev'ry mind.
Then take him to develop, if you can,
And hew the block off, and get out the man.
The Dunciad (1742) bk. 4, l. 267

25 Isles of fragrance, lily-silver'd vales.
The Dunciad (1742) bk. 4, l. 303

26   She marked thee there,
Stretched on the rack of a too easy chair,
And heard thy everlasting yawn confess
The pains and penalties of idleness.
The Dunciad (1742) bk. 4, l. 342

27 Thy truffles, Perigord! thy hams, Bayonne!
The Dunciad (1742) bk. 4, l. 558

28 Religion blushing veils her sacred fires,
And unawares Morality expires.
The Dunciad (1742) bk. 4, l. 649

29 Lo! thy dread empire, Chaos! is restored;
Light dies before thy uncreating word:
Thy hand, great Anarch! lets the curtain fall;

And universal darkness buries all.
The Dunciad (1742) bk. 4, l. 653

1 Vital spark of heav'nly flame!
Quit, oh quit this mortal frame:
Trembling, hoping, ling'ring, flying,
Oh the pain, the bliss of dying!
'The Dying Christian to his Soul' (1730); see **HADRIAN** 375:7

2 What beck'ning ghost, along the moonlight
shade
Invites my step, and points to yonder glade?
'Elegy to the Memory of an Unfortunate Lady' (1717) l. 1

3 Is it, in heav'n, a crime to love too well?
'Elegy to the Memory of an Unfortunate Lady' (1717) l. 6

4 Is there no bright reversion in the sky,
For those who greatly think, or bravely die?
'Elegy to the Memory of an Unfortunate Lady' (1717) l. 9

5 Ambition first sprung from your blest abodes;
The glorious fault of angels and of gods.
'Elegy to the Memory of an Unfortunate Lady' (1717) l. 13

6 On all the line a sudden vengeance waits,
And frequent hearses shall besiege your gates.
'Elegy to the Memory of an Unfortunate Lady' (1717) l. 37

7 Oh happy state! when souls each other draw,
When love is liberty, and nature, law.
'Eloisa to Abelard' (1717) l. 91

8 Of all affliction taught a lover yet,
'Tis sure the hardest science to forget!
'Eloisa to Abelard' (1717) l. 189

9 How shall I lose the sin, yet keep the sense,
And love th'offender, yet detest th'offence?
'Eloisa to Abelard' (1717) l. 191; see **AUGUSTINE** 39:21

10 How happy is the blameless Vestal's lot!
The world forgetting, by the world forgot.
'Eloisa to Abelard' (1717) l. 207

11 Eternal sunshine of the spotless mind!
'Eloisa to Abelard' (1717) l. 209

12 You beat your pate, and fancy wit will come:
Knock as you please, there's nobody at home.
'Epigram: You beat your pate' (1732)

13 I am his Highness' dog at Kew;
Pray, tell me sir, whose dog are you?
'Epigram Engraved on the Collar of a Dog which I gave to his
Royal Highness' (1738)

14 Sir, I admit your gen'ral rule
That every poet is a fool:
But you yourself may serve to show it,
That every fool is not a poet.
'Epigram from the French' (1732)

15 Shut, shut the door, good John! fatigued I said,
Tie up the knocker, say I'm sick, I'm dead,
The dog-star rages!
'An Epistle to Dr Arbuthnot' (1735) l. 1

16 You think this cruel? take it for a rule,
No creature smarts so little as a fool.
Let peals of laughter, Codrus! round thee break,
Thou unconcerned canst hear the mighty crack.
Pit, box, and gall'ry in convulsions hurled,

Thou stand'st unshook amidst a bursting world.
'An Epistle to Dr Arbuthnot' (1735) l. 83; see **ADDISON** 5:2,
HORACE 412:19

17 As yet a child, nor yet a fool to fame,
I lisped in numbers, for the numbers came.
'An Epistle to Dr Arbuthnot' (1735) l. 127; see **OVID** 590:20

18 The Muse but served to ease some friend, not
wife,
To help me through this long disease, my life.
'An Epistle to Dr Arbuthnot' (1735) l. 131

19 A painted mistress, or a purling stream.
'An Epistle to Dr Arbuthnot' (1735) l. 150; see **ADDISON** 4:28

20 Pretty! in amber to observe the forms
Of hairs, or straws, or dirt, or grubs, or worms;
The things, we know, are neither rich nor rare,
But wonder how the devil they got there?
'An Epistle to Dr Arbuthnot' (1735) l. 169

21 And he, whose fustian's so sublimely bad,
It is not poetry, but prose run mad.
'An Epistle to Dr Arbuthnot' (1735) l. 187

22 Damn with faint praise, assent with civil leer,
And without sneering, teach the rest to sneer;
Willing to wound, and yet afraid to strike,
Just hint a fault, and hesitate dislike.
of **ADDISON**
'An Epistle to Dr Arbuthnot' (1735) l. 201; see **WYCHERLEY**
871:14

23 But still the great have kindness in reserve,
He helped to bury whom he helped to starve.
of a noble patron
'An Epistle to Dr Arbuthnot' (1735) l. 247

24 'Satire or sense, alas! can Sporus feel?
Who breaks a butterfly upon a wheel?'
Yet let me flap this bug with gilded wings,
This painted child of dirt that stinks and stings.
of Lord **HERVEY**
'An Epistle to Dr Arbuthnot' (1735) l. 307; see **NEWSPAPER**
HEADLINES AND LEADERS 573:23

25 Unlearn'd, he knew no schoolman's subtle art,
No language, but the language of the heart.
of his own father
'An Epistle to Dr Arbuthnot' (1735) l. 398

26 Virtue she finds too painful an endeavour,
Content to dwell in decencies for ever.
Epistles to Several Persons 'To a Lady' (1735) l. 163

27 A very heathen in the carnal part,
Yet still a sad, good Christian at her heart.
Epistles to Several Persons 'To a Lady' (1735) l. 67

28 Chaste to her husband, frank to all beside,
A teeming mistress, but a barren bride.
Epistles to Several Persons 'To a Lady' (1735) l. 71

29 Still round and round the ghosts of Beauty
glide,
And haunt the places where their honour died.
See how the world its veterans rewards!
A youth of frolics, an old age of cards.
Epistles to Several Persons 'To a Lady' (1735) l. 241

1 And mistress of herself, though china fall.
Epistles to Several Persons 'To a Lady' (1735) l. 268

2 Woman's at best a contradiction still.
Epistles to Several Persons 'To a Lady' (1735) l. 270

3 Who shall decide, when doctors disagree?
Epistles to Several Persons 'To Lord Bathurst' (1733) l. 1

4 But thousands die, without or this or that,
Die, and endow a college, or a cat.
Epistles to Several Persons 'To Lord Bathurst' (1733) l. 97

5 The ruling passion, be it what it will,
The ruling passion conquers reason still.
Epistles to Several Persons 'To Lord Bathurst' (1733) l. 155; see
POPE 615:15

6 In the worst inn's worst room, with mat half-
hung,
The floors of plaister, and the walls of dung,
On once a flock-bed, but repaired with straw,
With tape-tied curtains, never meant to draw,
The George and Garter dangling from that bed
Where tawdry yellow strove with dirty red,
Great Villiers lies.
on the death of the 2nd Duke of **BUCKINGHAM**
Epistles to Several Persons 'To Lord Bathurst' (1733) l. 299

7 Consult the genius of the place in all.
Epistles to Several Persons 'To Lord Burlington' (1731) l. 57; see
VIRGIL 830:17

8 To rest, the cushion and soft Dean invite,
Who never mentions Hell to ears polite.
Epistles to Several Persons 'To Lord Burlington' (1731) l. 149

9 Another age shall see the golden ear
Imbrown the slope, and nod on the parterre,
Deep harvests bury all his pride has planned,
And laughing Ceres re-assume the land.
Epistles to Several Persons 'To Lord Burlington' (1731) l. 173

10 'Tis use alone that sanctifies expense,
And splendour borrows all her rays from sense.
Epistles to Several Persons 'To Lord Burlington' (1731) l. 179

11 To observations which ourselves we make,
We grow more partial for th'observer's sake.
Epistles to Several Persons 'To Lord Cobham' (1734) l. 11

12 Like following life thro' creatures you dissect,
You lose it in the moment you detect.
Epistles to Several Persons 'To Lord Cobham' (1734) l. 39

13 'Tis from high life high characters are drawn;
A saint in crape is twice a saint in lawn.
Epistles to Several Persons 'To Lord Cobham' (1734) l. 87

14 'Tis education forms the common mind,
Just as the twig is bent, the tree's inclined.
Epistles to Several Persons 'To Lord Cobham' (1734) l. 101; see
PROVERBS 626:39

15 Search then the Ruling Passion: There, alone,
The wild are constant, and the cunning known;
The fool consistent, and the false sincere.
Epistles to Several Persons 'To Lord Cobham' (1734) l. 174; see
POPE 615:5

16 Odious! in woollen! 'twould a saint provoke!
Epistles to Several Persons 'To Lord Cobham' (1734) l. 242

17 One would not, sure, be frightful when one's
dead—

And—Betty—give this cheek a little red.
Epistles to Several Persons 'To Lord Cobham' (1734) l. 246

18 Old politicians chew on wisdom past,
And totter on in business to the last.
Epistles to Several Persons 'To Lord Cobham' (1734) l. 248

19 Statesman, yet friend to Truth! of soul sincere,
In action faithful, and in honour clear;
Who broke no promise, served no private end,
Who gained no title, and who lost no friend.
Epistles to Several Persons 'To Mr Addison' (1720) l. 67

20 She went, to plain-work, and to purling brooks,
Old-fashioned halls, dull aunts, and croaking
rooks.
She went from op'ra, park, assembly, play,
To morning-walks, and prayers three hours a
day.
'Epistle to Miss Blount, on her leaving the Town, after the
Coronation [of King George I, 1715]' (1717)

21 Or o'er cold coffee trifle with the spoon,
Court the slow clock, and dine exact at noon.
'Epistle to Miss Blount, on her leaving the Town, after the
Coronation [of King George I, 1715]' (1717)

22 Nature, and Nature's laws lay hid in night.
God said, *Let Newton be!* and all was light.
'Epitaph: Intended for Sir Isaac Newton' (1730); see **SQUIRE**
769:9

23 Of manners gentle, of affections mild;
In wit, a man; simplicity, a child;
With native humour temp'ring virtuous rage,
Formed to delight at once and lash the age.
'Epitaph: On Mr Gay in Westminster Abbey' (1733)

24 Some are bewildered in the maze of schools,
And some made coxcombs Nature meant but
fools.
An Essay on Criticism (1711) l. 26

25 Some have at first for wits, then poets passed,
Turned critics next, and proved plain fools at
last.
An Essay on Criticism (1711) l. 36

26 First follow Nature, and your judgement frame
By her just standard, which is still the same:
Unerring Nature, still divinely bright,
One clear, unchanged, and universal light,
Life, force and beauty must to all impart,
At once the source and end and test of art.
An Essay on Criticism (1711) l. 68

27 Great wits sometimes may gloriously offend,
And rise to faults true critics dare not mend.
From vulgar bounds with brave disorder part
And snatch a grace beyond the reach of art.
An Essay on Criticism (1711) l. 152; see **ADDISON** 5:23

28 A little learning is a dangerous thing;
Drink deep, or taste not the Pierian spring:
There shallow draughts intoxicate the brain,
And drinking largely sobers us again.
An Essay on Criticism (1711) l. 215; see **DRAYTON** 293:18,
PROVERBS 637:40

29 Hills peep o'er hills, and Alps on Alps arise!
An Essay on Criticism (1711) l. 232

1 Whoever thinks a faultless piece to see,
Thinks what ne'er was, nor is, nor e'er shall be.
An Essay on Criticism (1711) l. 253

2 True wit is Nature to advantage dressed,
What oft was thought, but ne'er so well
expressed.
An Essay on Criticism (1711) l. 297

3 Expression is the dress of thought.
An Essay on Criticism (1711) l. 318; see **JOHNSON** 436:19,
WESLEY 848:10

4   As some to church repair,
Not for the doctrine, but the music there.
An Essay on Criticism (1711) l. 342

5 A needless Alexandrine ends the song,
That, like a wounded snake, drags its slow
length along.
An Essay on Criticism (1711) l. 356

6 True ease in writing comes from art, not
chance,
As those move easiest who have learned to
dance.
'Tis not enough no harshness gives offence,
The sound must seem an echo to the sense.
An Essay on Criticism (1711) l. 362

7 But when loud surges lash the sounding shore,
The hoarse, rough verse should like the torrent
roar.
When Ajax strives, some rock's vast weight to
throw,
The line too labours, and the words move slow.
An Essay on Criticism (1711) l. 368

8 What woeful stuff this madrigal would be,
In some starved hackney sonneteer, or me?
But let a Lord once own the happy lines,
How the wit brightens! how the style refines!
An Essay on Criticism (1711) l. 418

9 Some praise at morning what they blame at
night;
But always think the last opinion right.
An Essay on Criticism (1711) l. 430

10 To err is human; to forgive, divine.
An Essay on Criticism (1711) l. 525; see **PROVERBS** 645:25

11 All seems infected that th'infected spy,
As all looks yellow to the jaundiced eye.
An Essay on Criticism (1711) l. 558

12 Men must be taught as if you taught them not,
And things unknown proposed as things forgot.
An Essay on Criticism (1711) l. 574

13 The bookful blockhead, ignorantly read,
With loads of learned lumber in his head.
An Essay on Criticism (1711) l. 612

14 For fools rush in where angels fear to tread.
An Essay on Criticism (1711) l. 625; see **PROVERBS** 632:33

15 Eye Nature's walks, shoot Folly as it flies,
And catch the Manners living as they rise.
Laugh where we must, be candid where we can;
But vindicate the ways of God to man.
An Essay on Man Epistle 1 (1733) l. 13; see **MILTON** 541:10

16 Observe how system into system runs,
What other planets circle other suns.
An Essay on Man Epistle 1 (1733) l. 25

17 Pleased to the last, he crops the flowery food,
And licks the hand just raised to shed his blood.
An Essay on Man Epistle 1 (1733) l. 83

18 Who sees with equal eye, as God of all,
A hero perish, or a sparrow fall,
Atoms or systems into ruin hurled,
And now a bubble burst, and now a world.
An Essay on Man Epistle 1 (1733) l. 87

19 Hope springs eternal in the human breast:
Man never Is, but always To be blest.
An Essay on Man Epistle 1 (1733) l. 95; see **PROVERBS** 634:44

20 Lo! the poor Indian, whose untutored mind
Sees God in clouds, or hears him in the wind.
An Essay on Man Epistle 1 (1733) l. 99; see **CRABBE** 257:16

21 But thinks, admitted to that equal sky,
His faithful dog shall bear him company.
An Essay on Man Epistle 1 (1733) l. 111

22 Pride still is aiming at the blest abodes,
Men would be angels, angels would be gods.
An Essay on Man Epistle 1 (1733) l. 125

23 Why has not man a microscopic eye?
For this plain reason, man is not a fly.
An Essay on Man Epistle 1 (1733) l. 193

24 Die of a rose in aromatic pain?
An Essay on Man Epistle 1 (1733) l. 200; see **WINCHILSEA** 860:9

25 The spider's touch, how exquisitely fine!
Feels at each thread, and lives along the line.
An Essay on Man Epistle 1 (1733) l. 217

26 All are but parts of one stupendous whole,
Whose body, Nature is, and God the soul.
An Essay on Man Epistle 1 (1733) l. 267

27 All nature is but art, unknown to thee;
All chance, direction, which thou canst not see;
All discord, harmony, not understood;
All partial evil, universal good.
An Essay on Man Epistle 1 (1733) l. 289

28 And, spite of Pride, in erring Reason's spite,
One truth is clear, 'Whatever IS, is RIGHT.'
An Essay on Man Epistle 1 (1733) l. 293; see **DRYDEN** 296:16

29 Know then thyself, presume not God to scan;
The proper study of mankind is man.
Placed on this isthmus of a middle state,
A being darkly wise, and rudely great.
An Essay on Man Epistle 2 (1733) l. 1; see **CHARRON** 217:16,
HUXLEY 422:14

30 Created half to rise, and half to fall;
Great lord of all things, yet a prey to all;
Sole judge of truth, in endless error hurled;
The glory, jest, and riddle of the world!
An Essay on Man Epistle 2 (1733) l. 15

31 Go, teach Eternal Wisdom how to rule—
Then drop into thyself, and be a fool!
An Essay on Man Epistle 2 (1733) l. 29

32 Vice is a monster of so frightful mien,
As, to be hated, needs but to be seen;

Yet seen too oft, familiar with her face,
We first endure, then pity, then embrace.
An Essay on Man Epistle 2 (1733) l. 217

1 The learn'd is happy nature to explore,
The fool is happy that he knows no more.
An Essay on Man Epistle 2 (1733) l. 263

2 Behold the child, by Nature's kindly law
Pleased with a rattle, tickled with a straw.
An Essay on Man Epistle 2 (1733) l. 275

3 For forms of government let fools contest;
Whate'er is best administered is best.
An Essay on Man Epistle 3 (1733) l. 303

4 Thus God and nature linked the gen'ral frame,
And bade self-love and social be the same.
An Essay on Man Epistle 3 (1733) l. 317; *An Essay on Man*
Epistle 4 (1734) l. 396 is similar

5 Oh Happiness! our being's end and aim!
Good, pleasure, ease, content! whate'er thy
name:
That something still which prompts th' eternal
sigh,
For which we bear to live, or dare to die.
An Essay on Man Epistle 4 (1734) l. 1

6 Honour and shame from no condition rise;
Act well your part, there all the honour lies.
An Essay on Man Epistle 4 (1734) l. 183

7 What can ennoble sots, or slaves, or cowards?
Alas! Not all the blood of all the Howards.
An Essay on Man Epistle 4 (1734) l. 205

8 An honest man's the noblest work of God.
An Essay on Man Epistle 4 (1734) l. 248; see **BURNS** 177:26,
INGERSOLL 425:9

9 And more true joy Marcellus exil'd feels
Than Caesar with a senate at his heels.
An Essay on Man Epistle 4 (1734) l. 258

10 See Cromwell, damned to everlasting fame!
An Essay on Man Epistle 4 (1734) l. 284

11 Slave to no sect, who takes no private road,
But looks thro' Nature, up to Nature's God.
An Essay on Man Epistle 4 (1734) l. 331

12 Thou wert my guide, philosopher, and friend.
An Essay on Man Epistle 4 (1734) l. 380

13 All our knowledge is, ourselves to know.
An Essay on Man Epistle 4 (1734) l. 398

14 Achilles' wrath, to Greece the direful spring
Of woes unnumbered, heavenly goddess, sing!
translation of *The Iliad* (1715) bk. 1, l. 1; see **BENTLEY** 72:2,
HOMER 404:6

15 They cried, No wonder such celestial charms
For nine long years have set the world in arms;
What winning graces! what majestic mien!
She moves a goddess, and she looks a queen!
translation of *The Iliad* (1715) bk. 3, l. 205

16 Not to go back, is somewhat to advance,
And men must walk at least before they dance.
Imitations of Horace Horace bk. 1, Epistle 1 (1738) l. 53

17 Get place and wealth, if possible, with grace;
If not, by any means get wealth and place.
Imitations of Horace Horace bk. 1, Epistle 1 (1738) l. 103; see
HORACE 410:1

18 Not to admire, is all the art I know,
To make men happy, and to keep them so.
Imitations of Horace Horace bk. 1, Epistle 6 (1738) l. 1; see
HORACE 410:8

19 The worst of madmen is a saint run mad.
Imitations of Horace Horace bk. 1, Epistle 6 (1738) l. 27

20 Shakespeare (whom you and ev'ry play-house
bill
Style the divine, the matchless, what you will)
For gain, not glory, winged his roving flight,
And grew immortal in his own despite.
Imitations of Horace Horace bk. 2, Epistle 1 (1737) l. 69

21 Who now reads Cowley? if he pleases yet,
His moral pleases, not his pointed wit.
Imitations of Horace Horace bk. 2, Epistle 1 (1737) l. 75

22 The people's voice is odd,
It is, and it is not, the voice of God.
Imitations of Horace Horace bk. 2, Epistle 1 (1737) l. 89; see
ALCUIN 11:10

23 But those who cannot write, and those who can,
All rhyme, and scrawl, and scribble, to a man.
Imitations of Horace Horace bk. 2, Epistle 1 (1737) l. 187; see
HORACE 410:19

24 Ev'n copious Dryden, wanted, or forgot,
The last and greatest art, the art to blot.
Imitations of Horace Horace bk. 2, Epistle 1 (1737) l. 280; see
HEMING AND CONDELL 390:17, **JONSON** 447:3

25 There still remains, to mortify a wit,
The many-headed monster of the pit.
Imitations of Horace Horace bk. 2, Epistle 1 (1737) l. 304; see
SHAKESPEARE 698:10

26 The feast of reason and the flow of soul.
Imitations of Horace Horace bk. 2, Satire 1 (1734) l. 128

27 For I, who hold sage Homer's rule the best,
Welcome the coming, speed the going guest.
Imitations of Horace Horace bk. 2, Satire 2 (1734) l. 159;
'Speed the parting guest' in Pope's translation of *The Odyssey*
(1725–6) bk. 15, l. 84

28 Let humble Allen, with an awkward shame,
Do good by stealth, and blush to find it fame.
Imitations of Horace Epilogue to the Satires (1738) Dialogue 1,
l. 135

29 Ask you what provocation I have had?
The strong antipathy of good to bad.
Imitations of Horace Epilogue to the Satires (1738) Dialogue 2,
l. 197

30 Yes, I am proud; I must be proud to see
Men not afraid of God, afraid of me.
Imitations of Horace Epilogue to the Satires (1738) Dialogue 2,
l. 208

31 Ye gods! annihilate but space and time,
And make two lovers happy.
Martinus Scriblerus . . . or The Art of Sinking in Poetry ch. 11
(Miscellanies, 1727); possibly quoting another poet

32 Happy the man, whose wish and care
A few paternal acres bound,
Content to breathe his native air,
In his own ground.
'Ode on Solitude' (written c.1700, aged about twelve)

33 Thus let me live, unseen, unknown;
Thus unlamented let me die;

Steal from the world, and not a stone
Tell where I lie.
'Ode on Solitude' (written c.1700)

1 Hunger is insolent, and will be fed.
translation of *The Odyssey* (1725) bk. 7, l. 300; see **HOMER**
405:5

2 Where'er you walk, cool gales shall fan the
glade,
Trees, where you sit, shall crowd into a shade:
Where'er you tread, the blushing flow'rs shall
rise,
And all things flourish where you turn your
eyes.
Pastorals (1709) 'Summer' l. 73

3 To wake the soul by tender strokes of art,
To raise the genius, and to mend the heart;
To make mankind, in conscious virtue bold,
Live o'er each scene, and be what they behold:
For this the Tragic Muse first trod the stage.
Prologue to Addison's *Cato* (1713) l. 1

4 What dire offence from am'rous causes springs,
What mighty contests rise from trivial things.
The Rape of the Lock (1714) canto 1, l. 1

5 Now lap-dogs give themselves the rousing shake,
And sleepless lovers, just at twelve, awake.
The Rape of the Lock (1714) canto 1, l. 15

6 With varying vanities, from ev'ry part,
They shift the moving toyshop of their heart.
The Rape of the Lock (1714) canto 1, l. 100

7 Here files of pins extend their shining rows,
Puffs, powders, patches, bibles, billet-doux.
The Rape of the Lock (1714) canto 1, l. 137

8 Fair tresses man's imperial race insnare,
And beauty draws us with a single hair.
The Rape of the Lock (1714) canto 2, l. 27; see **PROVERBS**
627:12

9 Belinda smiled, and all the world was gay.
The Rape of the Lock (1714) canto 2, l. 52

10 Here thou, great Anna! whom three realms
obey,
Dost sometimes counsel take—and sometimes
tea.
The Rape of the Lock (1714) canto 3, l. 7

11 At ev'ry word a reputation dies.
The Rape of the Lock (1714) canto 3, l. 16; see **SHERIDAN**
748:25

12 The hungry judges soon the sentence sign,
And wretches hang that jury-men may dine.
The Rape of the Lock (1714) canto 3, l. 21

13 Let spades be trumps! she said, and trumps they
were.
The Rape of the Lock (1714) canto 3, l. 46

14 Coffee, (which makes the politician wise,
And see thro' all things with his half-shut eyes).
The Rape of the Lock (1714) canto 3, l. 117

15 Not louder shrieks to pitying heav'n are cast,
When husbands or when lapdogs breathe their
last.
The Rape of the Lock (1714) canto 3, l. 157

16 Where'er you walk, cool gales shall fan the
glade.
'Summer. The Second Pastoral'

17 Teach me to feel another's woe;
To hide the fault I see;
That mercy I to others show,
That mercy show to me.
'The Universal Prayer' (1738)

18 Here hills and vales, the woodland and the plain,
Here earth and water seem to strive again;
Not chaos-like together crushed and bruised,
But, as the world, harmoniously confused:
Where order in variety we see,
And where, though all things differ, all agree.
'Windsor Forest' (1711) l. 11

19 Party-spirit, which at best is but the madness of
many for the gain of a few.
letter to Edward Blount, 27 August 1714, in G. Sherburn (ed.)
Correspondence of Alexander Pope (1956) vol. 1

20 How often are we to die before we go quite off
this stage? In every friend we lose a part of
ourselves, and the best part.
letter to Jonathan Swift, 5 December 1732, in G. Sherburn
(ed.) *Correspondence of Alexander Pope* (1956) vol. 3

21 A man should never be ashamed to own he has
been in the wrong, which is but saying, in other
words, that he is wiser to-day than he was
yesterday.
Miscellanies (1727) vol. 2 'Thoughts on Various Subjects'

22 It is with narrow-souled people as with narrow-
necked bottles: the less they have in them, the
more noise they make in pouring it out.
Miscellanies (1727) vol. 2 'Thoughts on Various Subjects'

23 When men grow virtuous in their old age, they
only make a sacrifice to God of the devil's
leavings.
Miscellanies (1727) vol. 2 'Thoughts on Various Subjects'

24 The most positive men are the most credulous.
Miscellanies (1727) vol. 2 'Thoughts on Various Subjects'

25 All gardening is landscape-painting.
Joseph Spence *Anecdotes* (ed. J. Osborn, 1966) no. 606

26 Here am I, dying of a hundred good symptoms.
to George, Lord Lyttelton, 15 May 1744, in Joseph Spence
Anecdotes (ed. J. Osborn, 1966) no. 637

John Pope-Hennessy 1913–94
English art historian

27 I still recall, with something of a shock the
moment, at the end of the first sitting, when I
looked at what had been a lump of clay, and
found that a third person was in the room.
on sitting to Elizabeth **FRINK**
Learning to Look (1991)

Karl Popper 1902–94
Austrian-born philosopher

28 If we choose freedom, then we must be
prepared to perish along with it.
All Life is Problem Solving (1999) ch. 7, sect. 7; first published
in *Die Philosophie und die Wissenschaften* (1967)

1 I shall certainly admit a system as empirical or scientific only if it is capable of being *tested* by experience. These considerations suggest that not the *verifiability* but the *falsifiability* of a system is to be taken as a criterion of demarcation . . . *It must be possible for an empirical scientific system to be refuted by experience.*
> *The Logic of Scientific Discovery* (1934) ch. 1, sect. 6

2 We may become the makers of our fate when we have ceased to pose as its prophets.
> *The Open Society and its Enemies* (1945) introduction

3 We should therefore claim, in the name of tolerance, the right not to tolerate the intolerant.
> *The Open Society and Its Enemies* (1945) ch. 7

4 We must plan for freedom, and not only for security, if for no other reason than that only freedom can make security secure.
> *The Open Society and its Enemies* (1945) vol. 2, ch. 21

5 There is no history of mankind, there are only many histories of all kinds of aspects of human life. And one of these is the history of political power. This is elevated into the history of the world.
> *The Open Society and its Enemies* (1945) vol. 2, ch. 25

6 Science must begin with myths, and with the criticism of myths.
> 'The Philosophy of Science' in C. A. Mace (ed.) *British Philosophy in the Mid-Century* (1957)

7 On the pre-scientific level we hate the very idea that we may be mistaken. So we cling dogmatically to our conjectures, as long as possible. On the scientific level, we systematically search for our mistakes . . . Thus on the pre-scientific level, we are often ourselves destroyed, eliminated, with our false theories; we perish with our false theories. On the scientific level, we systematically try to eliminate our false theories—we try to let our false theories die in our stead.
> B. Magee (ed.) *Modern British Philosophy* (1971) 'Conversation with Karl Popper'

Cole Porter 1891–1964
American songwriter

8 But I'm always true to you, darlin', in my fashion.
Yes I'm always true to you, darlin', in my way.
> 'Always True to You in my Fashion' (1949 song)

9 In olden days a glimpse of stocking
Was looked on as something shocking
Now, heaven knows,
Anything goes.
> 'Anything Goes' (1934 song)

10 When they begin the Beguine
It brings back the sound of music so tender,
It brings back a night of tropical splendour,
It brings back a memory ever green.
> 'Begin the Beguine' (1935 song)

11 Oh, give me land, lots of land under starry skies above,
Don't fence me in.
Let me ride through the wide open country that I love,
Don't fence me in.
> 'Don't Fence Me In' (1944 song)

12 But how strange the change from major to minor
Every time we say goodbye.
> 'Every Time We Say Goodbye' (1944 song)

13 I get no kick from champagne,
Mere alcohol doesn't thrill me at all,
So tell me why should it be true
That I get a kick out of you?
> 'I Get a Kick Out of You' (1934 song) in *Anything Goes*

14 It was great fun,
But it was just one of those things.
> 'Just One of Those Things' (1935 song)

15 Birds do it, bees do it,
Even educated fleas do it.
Let's do it, let's fall in love.
> 'Let's Do It' (1954 song; words added to the 1928 original)

16 Miss Otis regrets (she's unable to lunch today).
> title of song (1934)

17 My heart belongs to Daddy.
> title of song (1938)

18 Night and day, you are the one,
Only you beneath the moon and under the sun.
> 'Night and Day' (1932 song) in *Gay Divorce*

19 Have you heard it's in the stars,
Next July we collide with Mars?
WELL, DID YOU EVAH! What a swell party this is.
> 'Well, Did You Evah?' (1940 song; revived for the film *High Society*, 1956)

20 You're the top! You're the Coliseum,
You're the top! You're the Louvre Museum,
You're a melody
From a symphony by Strauss,
You're a Bendel bonnet,
A Shakespeare sonnet,
You're Mickey Mouse!
> 'You're the Top' (1934 song) in *Anything Goes*

Hal Porter 1911–84
Australian writer

21 One wants to be alone, fundamentally, not to escape others but to escape oneself, the versions of self compelled into existence by others.
> *The Paper Chase* (1966)

Beilby Porteus 1731–1808
English poet and prelate

22 . . . One murder made a villain,
Millions a hero.
> *Death* (1759) l. 154; see **ROSTAND** 670:7, **YOUNG** 876:14

23 War its thousands slays, Peace its ten thousands.
> *Death* (1759) l. 179; see **BIBLE** 84:7

1   Teach him how to live,
And, oh! still harder lesson! how to die.
Death (1759) l. 319

Michael Portillo 1953–

British Conservative politician

2 You don't look tall if you surround yourself by short grasses.
on Iain Duncan SMITH
    in *Independent* 22 February 2003

Francis Pott 1832–1909

English clergyman

3 The strife is o'er, the battle done;
Now is the Victor's triumph won;
O let the song of praise be sung:
Alleluia!
    'The strife is o'er, the battle done' (1861 hymn); translation of 'Finita iam sunt praelia' (c.1695)

Beatrix Potter 1866–1943

English writer for children

4 In the time of swords and periwigs and full-skirted coats with flowered lappets—when gentlemen wore ruffles, and gold-laced waistcoats of paduasoy and taffeta—there lived a tailor in Gloucester.
    The Tailor of Gloucester (1903) p. 9

5 I am worn to a ravelling . . . I am undone and worn to a thread-paper, for I have NO MORE TWIST.
    The Tailor of Gloucester (1903)

6 It is said that the effect of eating too much lettuce is 'soporific'.
    The Tale of the Flopsy Bunnies (1909)

7 Don't go into Mr McGregor's garden: your father had an accident there, he was put into a pie by Mrs McGregor.
    The Tale of Peter Rabbit (1902)

Dennis Potter 1935–94

English television dramatist

8 Below my window . . . the blossom is out in full now . . . I *see* it is the whitest, frothiest, blossomiest blossom that there ever could be, and I can see it. Things are both more trivial than they ever were, and more important than they ever were, and the difference between the trivial and the important doesn't seem to matter. But the nowness of everything is absolutely wondrous.
    on his heightened awareness of things, in the face of his imminent death
        interview with Melvyn Bragg on Channel 4, March 1994, in *Seeing the Blossom* (1994)

9 Religion to me has always been the wound, not the bandage.
        interview with Melvyn Bragg on Channel 4, March 1994, in *Seeing the Blossom* (1994)

Stephen Potter 1900–69

English writer

10 *How to be one up*—how to make the other man feel that something has gone wrong, however slightly.
    Lifemanship (1950)

11 'Yes, but not in the South', with slight adjustments, will do for any argument about any place, if not about any person.
    Lifemanship (1950) p. 43

12 A good general rule is to state that the bouquet is better than the taste, and vice versa.
    on wine-tasting
        One-Upmanship (1952) ch. 14

13 The theory and practice of gamesmanship or The art of winning games without actually cheating.
    title of book (1947)

Eugène Pottier 1816–87

French politician

14 *Debout! les damnés de la terre!*
Debout! les forçats de la faim!
La raison tonne en son cratère,
C'est l'éruption de la fin . . .
Nous ne sommes rien, soyons tout!
C'est la lutte finale
Groupons-nous, et, demain,
L'Internationale
Sera le genre humain.

On your feet, you damned souls of the earth! On your feet, inmates of hunger's prison! Reason is rumbling in its crater, and its final eruption is on its way . . . We are nothing, let us be everything! This is the final conflict: let us form up and, tomorrow, the International will encompass the human race.
    'L'Internationale' (1871); in H. E. Piggot *Songs that made History* (1937) ch. 8

Ezra Pound 1885–1972

American poet

15 Winter is icummen in,
Lhude sing Goddamm,
Raineth drop and staineth slop,
And how the wind doth ramm!
Sing: Goddamm.
    'Ancient Music' (1917); see ANONYMOUS 20:14

16 With usura hath no man a house of good stone each block cut smooth and well fitting.
    Cantos (1954) no. 45

17 Tching prayed on the mountain and wrote MAKE IT NEW
on his bath tub.
    Cantos (1954) no. 53; see BIBLE 119:16

18 Hang it all, Robert Browning,
There can be but the one 'Sordello'.
    Draft of XXX Cantos (1930) no. 2

1 And even I can remember
A day when the historians left blanks in their
writings,
I mean for things they didn't know.
Draft of XXX Cantos (1930) no. 13

2 For three years, out of key with his time,
He strove to resuscitate the dead art
Of poetry; to maintain 'the sublime'
In the old sense. Wrong from the start.
Hugh Selwyn Mauberley (1920) 'E. P. Ode pour l'élection de son sépulcre' pt. 1

3 The age demanded an image
Of its accelerated grimace,
Something for the modern stage,
Not, at any rate, an Attic grace.
Hugh Selwyn Mauberley (1920) 'E. P. Ode . . .' pt. 2

4 Christ follows Dionysus,
Phallic and ambrosial
Made way for macerations;
Caliban casts out Ariel.
Hugh Selwyn Mauberley (1920) 'E. P. Ode . . .' pt. 3

5 Died some, pro patria,
non 'dulce' non 'et decor' . . .
walked eye-deep in hell
believing in old men's lies, the unbelieving
came home, home to a lie.
Hugh Selwyn Mauberley (1920) 'E. P. Ode . . .' pt. 4; see **HORACE** 412:17

6 There died a myriad,
And of the best, among them,
For an old bitch gone in the teeth,
For a botched civilization.
Hugh Selwyn Mauberley (1920) 'E. P. Ode . . .' pt. 5

7 The apparition of these faces in the crowd;
Petals on a wet, black bough.
'In a Station of the Metro' (1916)

8 O woe, woe,
People are born and die,
We also shall be dead pretty soon
Therefore let us act as if we were dead already.
Mr Housman's Message (1911)

9 The ant's a centaur in his dragon world.
Pisan Cantos (1948) no. 81

10 Pull down thy VANITY
Thou art a beaten dog beneath the hail,
A swollen magpie in a fitful sun,
Half black half white
Nor knowst'ou wing from tail.
Pisan Cantos (1948) no. 81

11 The leaves fall early this autumn, in wind.
The paired butterflies are already yellow with
August
Over the grass in the West garden;
They hurt me. I grow older.
If you are coming down through the narrows of
the river Kiang,
Please let me know beforehand,
And I will come out to meet you

As far as Cho-fu-Sa.
'The River Merchant's Wife' (1915); from the Chinese of Rihaku

12 He hath not heart for harping, nor in ring-
having
Nor winsomeness to wife, nor world's delight
Nor any whit else save the wave's slash,
Yet longing comes upon him to fare forth on
the water.
Bosque takes blossom, cometh beauty of berries.
'The Seafarer' (1912); from the Anglo-Saxon original

13 Music begins to atrophy when it departs too far
from the dance; that poetry begins to atrophy
when it gets too far from music.
The ABC of Reading (1934) 'Warning'

14 Literature is news that STAYS news.
The ABC of Reading (1934) ch. 2

15 Real education must ultimately be limited to one
who INSISTS on knowing, the rest is mere sheep-
herding.
The ABC of Reading (1934) ch. 8

16 Poetry must be *as well written as prose.*
letter to Harriet Monroe, January 1915, in D. D. Paige (ed.) *Selected Letters of Ezra Pound* (1950)

Nicolas Poussin 1594–1665

French painter. See also: **EPITAPHS** 317:4

17 An imitation in lines and colours on any surface
of all that is to be found under the sun.
of painting
letter to M. de Chambray, 1665; C. Jouamy (ed.) *Correspondance de Nicolas Poussin* (1911)

Anthony Powell 1905–2000

English novelist

18 Books do furnish a room.
title of novel (1971); see **SMITH** 758:13

19 A dance to the music of time.
title of novel sequence (1951–75), after the title given by the Italian art critic Giovanni Pietro Bellori (1613–96) to a painting by Nicolas **POUSSIN**, '*Le 4 stagioni che ballano al suono del tempo* [The four seasons dancing to the sound of time]'

20 He's so wet you could shoot snipe off him.
A Question of Upbringing (1951) ch. 1

21 Growing old is like being increasingly penalized
for a crime you haven't committed.
Temporary Kings (1973) ch. 1

Colin Powell 1937–

American general and Republican politician

22 First, we are going to cut it off, and then, we
are going to kill it.
strategy for dealing with the Iraqi Army in the Gulf War
at a press conference, 23 January 1991

Enoch Powell 1912–98
British Conservative politician

1 History is littered with the wars which everybody knew would never happen.
speech to the Conservative Party Conference, 19 October 1967, in *The Times* 20 October 1967

2 As I look ahead, I am filled with foreboding. Like the Roman, I seem to see 'the River Tiber foaming with much blood'.
speech at the Annual Meeting of the West Midlands Area Conservative Political Centre, Birmingham, 20 April 1968, in *Observer* 21 April 1968; see VIRGIL 830:4

3 Judas was paid! I am sacrificing my whole political life.
response to a heckler's call of 'Judas', having advised Conservatives to vote Labour at the coming general election
speech at Bull Ring, Birmingham, 23 February 1974

4 To write a diary every day is like returning to one's own vomit.
interview in *Sunday Times* 6 November 1977

5 For a politician to complain about the press is like a ship's captain complaining about the sea.
in *Guardian* 3 December 1984

6 All political lives, unless they are cut off in midstream at a happy juncture, end in failure, because that is the nature of politics and of human affairs.
Joseph Chamberlain (1977)

John Powell 1645–1713
English judge

7 Nothing is law that is not reason.
Lord Raymond's *Reports* (1765) vol. 2

John O'Connor Power 1848–1919
Irish lawyer and politician

8 The mules of politics: without pride of ancestry, or hope of posterity.
of the Liberal Unionists
H. H. Asquith *Memories and Reflections* (1928) vol. 1, ch. 16; see DISRAELI 285:19

Terry Pratchett 1948–
English science fiction writer

9 Personal isn't the same as important.
Men at Arms (1993)

10 Most modern fantasy just rearranges the furniture in Tolkien's attic.
Stan Nicholls (ed.) *Wordsmiths of Wonder* (1993)

11 An embuggerance.
announcing that he had been diagnosed with an early-onset form of Alzheimer's disease
on the website www.paulkidby.com/news 11 December 2007

□ **Prayers** *see* box opposite

Keith Preston 1884–1927
American poet

12 Of all the literary scenes
Saddest this sight to me:
The graves of little magazines
Who died to make verse free.
'The Liberators'

Jacques Prévert 1900–77
French poet and screenwriter

13 *C'est tellement simple, l'amour.*
Love is so simple.
Les Enfants du Paradis (1945 film)

Anthony Price 1928–
English thriller writer and editor

14 The Devil himself had probably redesigned Hell in the light of information he had gained from observing airport layouts.
The Memory Trap (1989)

Richard Price 1723–91
English nonconformist minister

15 Now, methinks, I see the ardour for liberty catching and spreading; a general amendment beginning in human affairs; the dominion of kings changed for the dominion of laws, and the dominion of priests giving way to the dominion of reason and conscience.
A Discourse on the Love of our Country (1790)

Katharine Susannah Prichard 1883–1969
Australian novelist and writer

16 To live was to suffer; but to take the storms of life with exultation, defying the gods with joy in it all, that was the great achievement!
Intimate Strangers (1937) ch. 5

Gerald Priestland 1927–91
English writer and journalist

17 Journalists belong in the gutter because that is where the ruling classes throw their guilty secrets.
on Radio London 19 May 1988; in *Observer* 22 May 1988

J. B. Priestley 1894–1984
English novelist, dramatist, and critic

18 The first fall of snow is not only an event, but it is a magical event. You go to bed in one kind of world and wake up to find yourself in another quite different, and if this is not enchantment, then where is it to be found?
Apes and Angels (1928) 'First Snow'

continued

🌿 Prayers 🌿

1 *Ave Maria, gratia plena, Dominus tecum: Benedicta tu in mulieribus, et benedictus fructus ventris tui, Jesus.*

Hail Mary, full of grace, the Lord is with thee: Blessed art thou among women, and blessed is the fruit of thy womb, Jesus.

'Ave Maria' or 'Hail Mary', also known as 'The Angelic Salutation', dating from the 11th century; see **BIBLE** 104:7

2 Death is only an horizon, and an horizon is only the limit of our sight.

traditional, sometimes attributed to William **PENN**

3 From ghoulies and ghosties and long-leggety beasties
And things that go bump in the night,
Good Lord, deliver us!

'The Cornish or West Country Litany', in Francis T. Nettleinghame *Polperro Proverbs and Others* (1926) 'Pokerwork Panels'

4 God be in my head,
And in my understanding;
God be in my eyes,
And in my looking;
God be in my mouth,
And in my speaking;
God be in my heart,
And in my thinking;
God be at my end,
And at my departing.

Sarum Missal (11th century)

5 Matthew, Mark, Luke, and John,
The bed be blest that I lie on.
Four angels to my bed,
Four angels round my head,
One to watch, and one to pray,
And two to bear my soul away.

traditional (the first two lines in Thomas Ady *A Candle in the Dark*, 1656)

6 Now I lay me down to sleep;
I pray the Lord my soul to keep.
If I should die before I wake,
I pray the Lord my soul to take.

first printed in a late edition of the *New England Primer* (1781)

7 *Salve, regina, mater misericordiae,*
Vita, dulcedo et spes nostra, salve!
Ad te clamamus exsules filii Evae,
Ad te suspiramus gementes et flentes
In hac lacrimarum valle.
Eia ergo, advocata nostra,
Illos tuos misericordes oculos ad nos converte.
Et Iesum, benedictum fructum ventris tui,
Nobis post hoc exsilium ostende,
O clemens, o pia,
O dulcis virgo Maria.

Hail holy queen, mother of mercy, hail our life, our sweetness, and our hope! To thee do we cry, poor banished children of Eve; to thee do we send up our sighs, mourning and weeping in this vale of tears. Turn then, most gracious advocate, thine eyes of mercy towards us; and after this our exile show unto us the blessed fruit of thy womb, Jesus, O clement, O loving, O sweet virgin Mary.

attributed to various 11th century authors; *Analecta Hymnica* vol. 50 (1907) p. 318

8 *Te Deum laudamus: Te Dominum confitemur.*

We praise thee, God: we own thee Lord.

'Te Deum'; hymn traditionally attributed to St **AMBROSE** and St **AUGUSTINE** in AD 387, though more recently to St Niceta (d. c.414); see **BOOK OF COMMON PRAYER** 133:9, **PRAYERS** 623:9

9 *In te Domine, speravi: non confundar in aeternum.*
Lord, I have set my hopes in thee, I shall not be destroyed for ever.

'Te Deum'; see **BOOK OF COMMON PRAYER** 133:11, **PRAYERS** 623:8

J. B. Priestley *continued*

10 Men are much better than their ordinary life allows them to be.

English Journey (1934) ch. 8

11 To say that these men paid their shillings to watch twenty-two hirelings kick a ball is merely to say that a violin is wood and catgut, that *Hamlet* is so much paper and ink. For a shilling the Bruddersford United AFC offered you Conflict and Art.

Good Companions (1929) bk. 1, ch. 1

12 I can't help feeling wary when I hear anything said about the masses. First you take their faces from 'em by calling 'em the masses and then you accuse 'em of not having any faces.

Saturn Over the Water (1961) ch. 2

13 This little steamer, like all her brave and battered sisters, is immortal. She'll go sailing proudly down the years in the epic of Dunkirk. And our great-grand-children, when they learn how we began this war by snatching glory out of defeat, and then swept on to victory, may also learn how the little holiday steamers made an excursion to hell and came back glorious.

radio broadcast, 5 June 1940, in *Listener* 13 June 1940

14 The weakness of American civilization, and perhaps the chief reason why it creates so much discontent, is that it is so curiously abstract. It is a bloodless extrapolation of a satisfying life . . . You dine off the advertiser's 'sizzling' and not the meat of the steak.

in *New Statesman* 10 December 1971

15 *on being awarded the Order of Merit in 1977:*

I've only two things to say about it. First I deserve it. Second, they've been too long about giving me it. There'll be another vacancy very soon.

in a radio interview, October 1977; John Braine *J. B. Priestley* (1978)

Joseph Priestley 1733–1804

English nonconformist minister. See also BENTHAM 71:4

1 Every man, when he comes to be sensible of his natural rights, and to feel his own importance, will consider himself as fully equal to any other person whatever.

An Essay on the First Principles of Government (1768) pt. 1

John Critchley Prince 1808–66

English poet

2 It came as a boon and a blessing to men,
The peaceful, the pure, the victorious PEN!

'The Pen and the Press'; see ADVERTISING SLOGANS 8:20

Matthew Prior 1664–1721

English poet

3 I court others in verse: but I love thee in prose:
And they have my whimsies, but thou hast my heart.

'A Better Answer' (1718)

4 Be to her virtues very kind;
Be to her faults a little blind;
Let all her ways be unconfined;
And clap your padlock—on her mind.

'An English Padlock' (1705) l. 79

5 Nobles and heralds, by your leave,
Here lies what once was Matthew Prior,
The son of Adam and of Eve,
Can Stuart or Nassau go higher?

'Epitaph' (1702)

6 The merchant, to secure his treasure,
Conveys it in a borrowed name:
Euphelia serves to grace my measure;
But Chloe is my real flame.

'An Ode' (1709)

7 He ranged his tropes, and preached up patience;
Backed his opinion with quotations.

'Paulo Purganti and his Wife' (1709) l. 138

8 Cured yesterday of my disease,
I died last night of my physician.

'The Remedy Worse than the Disease' (1727)

9 What is a King?—a man condemned to bear
The public burden of the nation's care.

Solomon (1718) bk. 3, l. 275

10 For, as our different ages move,
'Tis so ordained (would Fate but mend it!)
That I shall be past making love,
When she begins to comprehend it.

'To a Child of Quality of Five Years Old' (1704)

11 From ignorance our comfort flows,
The only wretched are the wise.

'To the Hon. Charles Montague' (1692) st. 9; see GRAY 370:13

12 No, no; for my virginity,
When I lose that, says Rose, I'll die:
Behind the elms last night, cried Dick,
Rose, were you not extremely sick?

'A True Maid' (1718)

13 They never taste who always drink;
They always talk, who never think.

'Upon this Passage in Scaligerana' (1740)

V. S. Pritchett 1900–97

English writer and critic

14 The principle of procrastinated rape is said to be the ruling one in all the great best-sellers.

The Living Novel (1946) 'Clarissa'

Procopius c.AD 499–565

Byzantine administrator and historian

15 So the church has become a spectacle of marvellous beauty, overwhelming to those who see it, but to those who know it by hearsay altogether incredible. For it soars on high to match the sky, and as if surging up from amongst the other buildings it stands on high and looks down on the remainder of the city.

of the church of the Hagia Sophia; see JUSTINIAN 450:8 *Buildings*

Adelaide Ann Procter 1825–64

English writer of popular verse

16 A lost chord.

title of poem (1858)

17 Seated one day at the organ,
I was weary and ill at ease,
And my fingers wandered idly
Over the noisy keys.

'A Lost Chord' (1858)

18 It may be that Death's bright Angel
Will speak in that chord again
It may be that only in Heaven
I shall hear that grand Amen.

'A Lost Chord' (1858)

Propertius c.50–after 16 BC

Roman poet

19 *Cynthia prima suis miserum me cepit ocellis,*
Contactum nullis ante cupidinibus.

Cynthia first, with her eyes, caught wretched me
Smitten before by no desires.

Elegies bk. 1, no. 1, l. 1

20 *Navita de ventis, de tauris narrat arator,*
Enumerat miles vulnera, pastor oves.

The seaman tells stories of winds, the ploughman of bulls; the soldier details his wounds, the shepherd his sheep.

Elegies bk. 2, no. 1, l. 43

21 *Quod si deficiant vires, audacia certe*
Laus erit: in magnis et voluisse sat est.

Even if strength fail, boldness at least will deserve praise: in great endeavours even to have had the will is enough.
> *Elegies* bk. 2, no. 10, l. 5

1 *Cedite Romani scriptores, cedite Grai!*
Nescioquid maius nascitur Iliade.

Make way, you Roman writers, make way, Greeks! Something greater than the Iliad is born.
> of *VIRGIL's* Aeneid
> *Elegies* bk. 2, no. 34, l. 65

Protagoras b. *c.*485 BC
Greek sophist

2 That man is the measure of all things.
> Plato *Theaetetus* 160d; see **PROVERBS** 638:18

Pierre-Joseph Proudhon 1809–65
French social reformer

3 *La propriété c'est le vol.*
Property is theft.
> *Qu'est-ce que la propriété?* (1840) ch. 1

Marcel Proust 1871–1922
French novelist
Textual translations are those of C. K. Scott-Moncrieff and S. Hudson, revised by T. Kilmartin, 1981

4 Remembrance of things past.
> translation by C. K. Scott-Moncrieff and S. Hudson of the title *À la recherche du temps perdu* [*In search of lost time*] (1913–27); see **SHAKESPEARE** 737:24

5 *Longtemps, je me suis couché de bonne heure.*
For a long time I used to go to bed early.
> *Du côté de chez Swann* (Swann's Way, 1913) vol. 1, p. 1

6 *Et tout d'un coup le souvenir m'est apparu. Ce goût c'était celui du petit morceau de madeleine que le dimanche matin à Combray . . . ma tante Léonie m'offrait après l'avoir trempé dans son infusion de thé ou de tilleul.*

And suddenly the memory revealed itself. The taste was that of the little piece of madeleine which on Sunday mornings at Combray . . . my aunt Léonie used to give me, dipping it first in her own cup of tea or tisane.
> *Du côté de chez Swann* (Swann's Way, 1913) vol. 1

7 *Et il ne fut plus question de Swann chez les Verdurin.*
After which there was no more talk of Swann at the Verdurins'.
> *Du côté de chez Swann* (Swann's Way, 1913) vol. 2

8 *Dire que j'ai gâché des années de ma vie, que j'ai voulu mourir, que j'ai eu mon plus grand amour, pour une femme qui ne me plaisait pas, qui n'était pas mon genre!*

To think that I've wasted years of my life, that I've longed to die, that I've experienced my greatest love for a woman who didn't appeal to me, who wasn't even my type!
> *Du côté de chez Swann* (Swann's Way, 1913) vol. 2

9 *On devient moral dès qu'on est malheureux.*
One becomes moral as soon as one is unhappy.
> *A l'ombre des jeunes filles en fleurs* (Within a Budding Grove, 1918) vol. 1

10 *Tout ce que nous connaissons de grand nous vient des nerveux. Ce sont eux et non pas d'autres qui ont fondé les religions et composé les chefs-d'œuvre. Jamais le monde ne saura tout ce qu'il leur doit et surtout ce qu'eux ont souffert pour le lui donner.*

Everything we think of as great has come to us from neurotics. It is they and they alone who found religions and create great works of art. The world will never realise how much it owes to them and what they have suffered in order to bestow their gifts on it.
> *Le Côté de Guermantes* (Guermantes Way, 1921) vol. 1

11 *Il n'y a rien comme le désir pour empêcher les choses qu'on dit d'avoir aucune ressemblance avec ce qu'on a dans la pensée.*

There is nothing like desire for preventing the things one says from bearing any resemblance to what one has in one's mind.
> *Le Côté de Guermantes* (Guermantes Way, 1921) vol. 2

12 *Un artiste n'a pas besoin d'exprimer directement sa pensée dans son ouvrage pour que celui-ci en reflète la qualité; on a même pu dire que la louange la plus haute de Dieu est dans la négation de l'athée qui trouve la Création assez parfaite pour se passer d'un créateur.*

An artist has no need to express his thought directly in his work for the latter to reflect its quality; it has even been said that the highest praise of God consists in the denial of Him by the atheist who finds creation so perfect that it can dispense with a creator.
> *Le Côté de Guermantes* (Guermantes Way, 1921) vol. 2

13 *La maladie est le plus écouté des médicins: à la bonté, au savoir on ne fait que promettre; on obéit à la souffrance.*

Illness is the doctor to whom we pay most heed; to kindness, to knowledge, we make promise only; pain we obey.
> *Sodome et Gomorrhe* (Cities of the Plain, 1922) vol. 1, pt. 2, ch. 1

14 *J'ai horreur des couchers de soleil, c'est romantique, c'est opéra.*
I have a horror of sunsets, they're so romantic, so operatic.
> *Sodome et Gomorrhe* (Cities of the Plain, 1922) vol. 1

15 *On ne guérit d'une souffrance qu'à condition de l'éprouver pleinement.*
We are healed of a suffering only by experiencing it to the full.
> *Albertine disparue* (The Sweet Cheat Gone, 1925) ch. 1

16 *Une de ces dépêches dont M. de Guermantes avait spirituellement fixé le modèle: 'Impossible venir, mensonge suit'.*

One of those telegrams of which M. de Guermantes had wittily fixed the formula: 'Cannot come, lie follows'.
Le Temps retrouvé (Time Regained, 1926) ch. 1; see **BERESFORD** 72:7

1 *Les vrais paradis sont les paradis qu'on a perdus.*
The true paradises are the paradises that we have lost.
Le Temps retrouvé (Time Regained, 1926) ch. 3

2 *Le bonheur seul est salutaire pour le corps, mais c'est le chagrin qui développe les forces de l'esprit.*
For if unhappiness develops the forces of the mind, happiness alone is salutary to the body.
Le Temps retrouvé (Time Regained, 1926) ch. 3, p. 259

Proverbs *See also* Sayings

Dates given are generally for the first written appearance of a form of the proverb in English; the proverb may well have been in spoken use much earlier, and in many cases is cited as 'an old saying' at that time. For more detailed information, see The Concise Oxford Dictionary of Proverbs

3 Absence makes the heart grow fonder.
mid 19th century; 1st century BC in Latin

4 Accidents will happen (in the best-regulated families).
mid 18th century; see **DICKENS** 277:18

5 Actions speak louder than words.
early 17th century

6 Adventures are to the adventurous.
mid 19th century

7 Adversity makes strange bedfellows.
mid 19th century; see **SHAKESPEARE** 733:25

8 After a storm comes a calm.
late 14th century

9 After dinner rest awhile, after supper walk a mile.
late 16th century

10 After the feast comes the reckoning.
early 17th century

11 The age of miracles is past.
late 16th century

12 All cats are grey in the dark.
mid 16th century

13 All good things must come to an end.
mid 15th century

14 All is fish that comes to the net.
early 16th century

15 All is grist that comes to the mill.
grist = corn which is to be ground
mid 17th century

16 All roads lead to Rome.
late 14th century; earlier in Latin

17 All's fair in love and war.
early 17th century

18 All's for the best in the best of all possible worlds.
early 20th century, from **VOLTAIRE**; see **VOLTAIRE** 833:10

19 All's well that ends well.
late 14th century

20 All that glitters is not gold.
early 13th century

21 All things are possible with God.
late 17th century; see **BIBLE** 102:9

22 All things come to those who wait.
early 16th century

23 All work and no play makes Jack a dull boy.
mid 17th century

24 Always a bridesmaid, never a bride.
early 20th century; see **LEIGH** 488:11

25 Another day, another dollar.
late 19th century

26 Any port in a storm.
mid 18th century

27 Any publicity is good publicity.
early 20th century; see **BEHAN** 66:18

28 An ape's an ape, a varlet's a varlet, though they be clad in silk or scarlet.
mid 16th century; 2nd century AD in Greek

29 Appearances are deceptive.
mid 17th century

30 Appetite comes with eating.
mid 17th century, from **RABELAIS**; see **RABELAIS** 652:8

31 An apple a day keeps the doctor away.
mid 19th century

32 The apple never falls far from the tree.
mid 19th century

33 April showers bring forth May flowers.
mid 16th century

34 An army marches on its stomach.
mid 19th century, variously attributed to **FREDERICK THE GREAT** the Great and **NAPOLEON I**; see **NAPOLEON I** 568:6

35 Art is long and life is short.
late 14th century, from **HIPPOCRATES**; see **CHAUCER** 220:21, **HIPPOCRATES** 399:13

36 As a tree falls, so shall it lie.
mid 16th century; see **BIBLE** 90:16

37 As good be an addled egg as an idle bird.
late 16th century

38 As the day lengthens, so the cold strengthens.
early 17th century

39 As the twig is bent, so is the tree inclined.
early 18th century, from **POPE**; see **POPE** 615:14

40 As you bake so shall you brew.
late 16th century

41 As you brew, so shall you bake.
late 16th century

42 As you make your bed, so you must lie upon it.
late 16th century, late 15th century in French

43 As you sow, so you reap.
late 15th century; see **BIBLE** 113:25

44 Ask a silly question and you get a silly answer.
early 14th century

1 Ask no questions and hear no lies.
late 18th century

2 Attack is the best form of defence.
late 18th century; see **SAYINGS** 684:3

3 A bad excuse is better than none.
mid 16th century

4 Bad money drives out good.
*known as Gresham's Law, after Sir Thomas Gresham
(c.1519–79), who formulated the principle, though not the
proverb, in 1558*
early 20th century

5 Bad news travels fast.
late 16th century

6 A bad penny always turns up.
mid 18th century

7 Bad things come in threes.
late 19th century

8 A bad workman blames his tools.
early 17th century; late 13th century in French

9 A barking dog never bites.
mid 16th century; 13th century in French

10 Barnaby bright, Barnaby bright, the longest day
and the shortest night.
*St Barnabas' Day, 11 June, in Old Style reckoned the longest
day of the year*
mid 17th century

11 Bear and forbear.
late 16th century

12 Beauty draws with a single hair.
late 16th century; see **HOWELL** 417:5, **POPE** 618:8

13 Beauty is in the eye of the beholder.
mid 18th century; 3rd century BC in Greek

14 Beauty is only skin deep.
early 17th century

15 Beggars can't be choosers.
mid 16th century

16 Be just before you're generous.
mid 18th century

17 Believe nothing of what you hear, and only half
of what you see.
mid 19th century

18 A bellowing cow soon forgets her calf.
late 19th century

19 The best doctors are Dr Diet, Dr Quiet, and Dr
Merryman.
mid 16th century

20 The best is the enemy of the good.
mid 19th century; see **VOLTAIRE** 834:2

21 The best of friends must part.
early 17th century

22 The best of men are but men at best.
late 17th century

23 The best things come in small packages.
late 19th century

24 The best things in life are free.
early 20th century, from **DE SYLVA AND BROWN**; see **DE SYLVA
AND BROWN** 274:16

25 The best-laid schemes of mice and men gang aft
agley.
late 18th century, from **BURNS**; see **BURNS** 179:26

26 Be the day weary or be the day long, at last it
ringeth to evensong.
early 16th century

27 Better a dinner of herbs than a stalled ox where
hate is.
mid 16th century; see **BIBLE** 88:15

28 Better a good cow than a cow of a good kind.
early 20th century

29 Better are small fish than an empty dish.
late 17th century

30 Better be an old man's darling than a young
man's slave.
mid 16th century

31 Better be envied than pitied.
mid 16th century; 5th century BC in Greek

32 Better be out of the world than out of the
fashion.
mid 17th century

33 Better be safe than sorry.
mid 19th century

34 Better late than never.
early 14th century; 1st century BC in Greek

35 Better one house spoiled than two.
of two wicked or foolish people joined in marriage
late 16th century

36 The better the day, the better the deed.
early 17th century

37 Better the devil you know than the devil you
don't know.
mid 19th century

38 Better to light one candle than to curse the
darkness.
motto of the American Christopher Society, founded 1945
mid 20th century; see **BENENSON** 69:12, **STEVENSON** 775:1

39 Better to live one day as a tiger than a thousand
years as a sheep.
early 19th century; see **TIPU** 811:9

40 Better to marry than to burn.
early 20th century; see **BIBLE** 112:2

41 Better to wear out than to rust out.
early 18th century; see **CUMBERLAND** 262:2, **SHAKESPEARE**
707:10

42 Better wed over the mixen than over the moor.
*mixen = midden; better to marry a neighbour than a
stranger*
early 17th century

43 Between two stools one falls to the ground.
late 14th century

44 Beware of an oak, it draws the stroke; avoid an
ash, it counts the flash; creep under the thorn, it
can save you from harm.
on where to shelter from lightning
late 19th century

1 Be what you would seem to be.
late 14th century

2 Big fish eat little fish.
early 13th century

3 Big fleas have little fleas upon their backs to bite them, and little fleas have lesser fleas, and so *ad infinitum*.
early 18th century, from **SWIFT**; see **SWIFT** 784:4

4 The bigger they are, the harder they fall.
early 20th century; see **FITZSIMMONS** 332:20

5 A bird in the hand is worth two in the bush.
mid 15th century; 13th century in Latin

6 A bird never flew on one wing.
early 18th century

7 Birds in their little nests agree.
early 18th century, from **WATTS**; see **WATTS** 841:16

8 Birds of a feather flock together.
mid 16th century

9 A bleating sheep loses a bite.
late 16th century

10 Blessed are the dead that the rain rains on.
early 17th century

11 Blessed is he who expects nothing, for he shall never be disappointed.
early 18th century

12 Blessings brighten as they take their flight.
mid 18th century

13 A blind man's wife needs no paint.
mid 17th century

14 Blood is thicker than water.
early 19th century

15 The blood of the martyrs is the seed of the Church.
mid 16th century; see **TERTULLIAN** 802:11

16 Blood will have blood.
mid 15th century; see **SHAKESPEARE** 721:12

17 Blood will tell.
mid 19th century

18 Blue are the hills that are far away.
late 19th century, northern in origin

19 Boys will be boys.
occasionally 'girls will be girls'
early 17th century

20 Brag is a good dog, but Holdfast is better.
early 18th century

21 Brave men lived before Agamemnon.
early 19th century; see **HORACE** 414:3

22 The bread never falls but on its buttered side.
mid 19th century

23 Brevity is the soul of wit.
early 17th century, from **SHAKESPEARE**; see **SHAKESPEARE** 701:2

24 A bully is always a coward.
early 19th century

25 A burnt child dreads the fire.
mid 13th century

26 The busiest men have the most leisure.
late 19th century

27 Business before pleasure.
mid 19th century

28 The buyer has need of a hundred eyes, the seller of but one.
mid 17th century

29 Buy in the cheapest market and sell in the dearest.
late 16th century

30 Caesar's wife must be above suspicion.
late 18th century; see **CAESAR** 192:18

31 Call no man happy till he dies.
mid 16th century; see **SOLON** 760:10

32 Candlemas day, put beans in the clay; put candles and candlesticks away.
late 17th century

33 Care killed the cat.
late 16th century; see **SHAKESPEARE** 727:33

34 A carpenter is known by his chips.
early 16th century

35 Catching's before hanging.
early 19th century

36 A cat in gloves catches no mice.
late 16th century; 14th century in French

37 A cat may look at a king.
mid 16th century

38 The cat would eat fish, but would not wet her feet.
early 13th century

39 A chain is no stronger than its weakest link.
mid 19th century

40 A change is as good as a rest.
late 19th century

41 Change the name and not the letter, change for the worse and not the better.
meaning that it is unlucky for a woman to marry a man whose surname begins with the same letter as her own
mid 19th century

42 Charity begins at home.
late 14th century; see **SHERIDAN** 748:29

43 Charity covers a multitude of sins.
early 17th century; see **BIBLE** 117:12

44 Cheats never prosper.
early 19th century

45 A cherry year, a merry year; a plum year, a dumb year.
late 17th century

46 The child is the father of the man.
early 19th century, from **WORDSWORTH**; see **WORDSWORTH** 866:18

47 Children and fools tell the truth.
mid 16th century; late 14th century in French

48 Children are certain cares, but uncertain comforts.
mid 17th century

1 Children should be seen and not heard.
originally applied specifically to (young) women
early 15th century

2 The church is an anvil which has worn out many hammers.
early 20th century; see **BEZA** 77:15, **MACLAREN** 512:1

3 Circumstances alter cases.
late 17th century

4 Civility costs nothing.
early 18th century; late 15th century in French

5 A civil question deserves a civil answer.
mid 19th century

6 A clean conscience is a good pillow.
early 18th century

7 Cleanliness is next to godliness.
late 18th century; see **WESLEY** 847:22

8 Clergymen's sons always turn out badly.
late 19th century

9 Clothes make the man.
early 15th century

10 The cobbler to his last and the gunner to his linstock.
mid 18th century

11 Cold hands, warm heart.
early 20th century

12 Come live with me and you'll know me.
early 20th century

13 Coming events cast their shadow before.
early 19th century

14 Common fame is seldom to blame.
mid 17th century

15 The company makes the feast.
mid 17th century

16 Comparisons are odious.
mid 15th century; see **LYDGATE** 505:16, **SHAKESPEARE** 727:28

17 Confess and be hanged.
late 16th century

18 Confession is good for the soul.
mid 17th century

19 Conscience makes cowards of us all.
early 17th century, from **SHAKESPEARE**; see **SHAKESPEARE** 702:3

20 Constant dropping wears away a stone.
mid 13th century, earlier in Greek; see **LATIMER** 482:15

21 Corporations have neither bodies to be punished nor souls to be damned.
mid 17th century; see **COKE** 238:16, **THURLOW** 810:14

22 Councils of war never fight.
mid 19th century

23 The course of true love never did run smooth.
late 16th century, from **SHAKESPEARE**; see **SHAKESPEARE** 725:23

24 Cowards may die many times before their death.
late 16th century, from **SHAKESPEARE**; see **SHAKESPEARE** 712:13

25 The cowl does not make the monk.
late 14th century

26 A creaking door hangs longest.
late 18th century

27 Crime doesn't pay.
later associated with the US radio crime series The Shadow *and the cartoon detective Dick Tracy*
late 19th century

28 Crosses are ladders that lead to heaven.
early 17th century

29 Curiosity killed the cat.
early 20th century

30 Curses, like chickens, come home to roost.
late 14th century

31 The customer is always right.
early 20th century; see **RITZ** 662:19

32 Cut your coat according to your cloth.
mid 16th century

33 The darkest hour is just before dawn.
mid 17th century

34 Dead men don't bite.
mid 16th century; 1st century AD in Greek; see **GRAY** 369:18

35 Dead men tell no tales.
mid 17th century

36 A deaf husband and a blind wife are always a happy couple.
late 16th century

37 Death is the great leveller.
early 18th century

38 Death pays all debts.
early 17th century; see **SHAKESPEARE** 733:29

39 Delays are dangerous.
late 16th century

40 Desperate diseases must have desperate remedies.
mid 16th century; see **FAWKES** 324:21, **HIPPOCRATES** 399:14, **SHAKESPEARE** 703:23

41 The devil can quote Scripture for his own ends.
late 16th century

42 The devil finds work for idle hands to do.
early 18th century; see **WATTS** 841:12

43 The devil is not so black as he is painted.
mid 16th century

44 The devil looks after his own.
early 18th century

45 The devil makes his Christmas pies of lawyers' tongues and clerks' fingers.
late 16th century

46 The devil's children have the devil's luck.
late 17th century

47 Devil take the hindmost.
early 17th century

48 The devil was sick, the Devil a saint would be; the Devil was well, the devil a saint was he.
'saint' is sometimes replaced by 'monk'
early 17th century, variant of a medieval Latin proverb

1 Diamond cuts diamond.
early 17th century

2 The difficult is done at once, the impossible takes a little longer.
late 19th century; see **MILITARY SAYINGS, SLOGANS, AND SONGS** 535:6

3 Diligence is the mother of good luck.
late 16th century

4 Dirty water will quench fire.
mid 16th century

5 Discretion is the better part of valour.
late 16th century, from **SHAKESPEARE**; see **SHAKESPEARE** 706:30

6 Distance lends enchantment to the view.
late 18th century, from **CAMPBELL**; see **CAMPBELL** 195:12

7 Divide and rule.
early 17th century

8 Do as I say, not as I do.
mid 16th century

9 Do as you would be done by.
late 16th century

10 Dog does not eat dog.
mid 16th century

11 The dog returns to its vomit.
late 14th century; see **BIBLE** 88:41

12 Dogs bark, but the caravan goes on.
late 19th century

13 A dog that will fetch a bone will carry a bone.
early 19th century

14 Do not meet troubles half-way.
late 19th century

15 Do not spoil the ship for a ha'porth of tar.
ship = a dialectal pronunciation of sheep, and the original literal sense was 'do not allow sheep to die for the lack of a trifling amount of tar', tar being used to protect sores and wounds on sheep from flies
early 17th century

16 Do not throw pearls to swine.
mid 14th century; see **BIBLE** 99:23

17 Don't care was made to care.
mid 20th century, from a traditional children's rhyme

18 Don't change horses in mid stream.
mid 19th century; see **LINCOLN** 494:4

19 Don't count your chickens before they are hatched.
late 16th century

20 Don't cross the bridge till you come to it.
mid 19th century

21 Don't cry before you're hurt.
mid 16th century; early 14th century in French

22 Don't cut off your nose to spite your face.
mid 16th century; mid 14th century in French

23 Don't go near the water until you learn how to swim.
mid 19th century

24 Don't halloo till you are out of the wood.
late 18th century

25 Don't put all your eggs in one basket.
mid 17th century

26 Don't put the cart before the horse.
early 16th century

27 Don't sell the skin till you have caught the bear.
late 16th century; see **WALLER** 836:16

28 Don't teach your grandmother to suck eggs.
early 18th century

29 Don't throw out your dirty water until you get in fresh.
late 15th century

30 Don't throw the baby out with the bathwater.
mid 19th century; early 17th century in German

31 A door must be either shut or open.
mid 18th century

32 Do right and fear no man.
mid 15th century

33 Do unto others as you would they should do unto you.
late 15th century

34 Dream of a funeral and you hear of a marriage.
mid 17th century

35 Dreams go by contraries.
early 15th century

36 A dripping June sets all in tune.
mid 18th century

37 Drive gently over the stones.
early 18th century

38 A drowning man will clutch at a straw.
mid 16th century

39 Eagles don't catch flies.
mid 16th century

40 The early bird catches the worm.
mid 17th century; see **SAYINGS** 684:31

41 The early man never borrows from the late man.
mid 17th century

42 Early to bed and early to rise, makes a man healthy, wealthy, and wise.
late 15th century

43 East is east, and west is west.
late 19th century, from **KIPLING**; see **KIPLING** 465:8

44 East, west, home's best.
mid 19th century

45 Easy come, easy go.
mid 17th century

46 Easy does it.
mid 19th century

47 Eat, drink and be merry, for tomorrow we die.
late 19th century; a conflation of two biblical sayings: see **BIBLE** 90:7, **BIBLE** 92:22

48 Eat to live, not live to eat.
late 14th century; see **SOCRATES** 759:16

49 Empty sacks will never stand upright.
mid 17th century

1 Empty vessels make the most sound.
early 15th century

2 The end crowns the work.
early 16th century

3 The end justifies the means.
late 16th century

4 England is the paradise of women, the hell of horses, and the purgatory of servants.
late 16th century; a similar proverb in French is found applied to Paris in the mid 16th century

5 England's difficulty is Ireland's opportunity.
mid 19th century

6 The English are a nation of shopkeepers.
early 19th century; see NAPOLEON I 568:9

7 An Englishman's home is his castle.
late 16th century; see COKE 238:14

8 An Englishman's word is his bond.
early 16th century

9 Enough is as good as a feast.
late 14th century

10 Enough is enough.
mid 16th century

11 Even a worm will turn.
mid 16th century

12 Everybody loves a lord.
late 19th century

13 Everybody's business is nobody's business.
early 17th century

14 Every bullet has its billet.
late 16th century; see WILLIAM III 857:4

15 Every cloud has a silver lining.
mid 19th century; see COWARD 253:20, FORD 337:12, WESTON AND LEE 849:5

16 Every cock will crow upon his own dunghill.
mid 13th century; 1st century AD in Latin

17 Every dog has his day.
mid 16th century

18 Every dog is allowed one bite.
based on the common law rule (dating at least from the 17th century) by which the keeper of a domestic animal was not liable for harm done by it unless he knew of its vicious propensities
early 20th century

19 Every elm has its man.
early 20th century

20 Every herring must hang by its own gill.
early 17th century

21 Every Jack has his Jill.
early 17th century

22 Every land has its own law.
early 17th century

23 Every little helps.
early 17th century

24 Every man for himself.
late 14th century

25 Every man for himself and God for us all.
mid 16th century

26 Every man for himself, and the Devil take the hindmost.
early 16th century

27 Every man has his price.
mid 18th century; see WALPOLE 838:13

28 Every man is the architect of his own fortune.
early 16th century; see CLAUDIUS 234:5

29 Every man to his taste.
late 16th century

30 Every man to his trade.
late 16th century

31 Everyone speaks well of the bridge which carries him over.
late 17th century

32 Everyone stretches his legs according to the length of his coverlet.
early 14th century

33 Every picture tells a story.
early 20th century; see ADVERTISING SLOGANS 7:22

34 Everything has an end.
late 14th century

35 Every tub must stand on its own bottom.
mid 16th century

36 Evil communications corrupt good manners.
early 15th century; see BIBLE 113:1

37 Evil doers are evil dreaders.
late 16th century

38 Example is better than precept.
early 15th century

39 The exception proves the rule.
mid 17th century

40 Experience is the best teacher.
late 16th century; see TACITUS 787:13

41 Experience is the father of wisdom.
mid 16th century

42 Experience keeps a dear school.
mid 18th century

43 Extremes meet.
mid 18th century; mid 17th century in French

44 The eye of a master does more work than both his hands.
mid 18th century

45 The eyes are the window of the soul.
mid 16th century

46 Fact is stranger than fiction.
mid 19th century

47 Facts are stubborn things.
early 18th century

48 Faint heart never won fair lady.
mid 16th century

49 Fair and softly goes far in a day.
mid 14th century

50 A fair exchange is no robbery.
mid 16th century

1 Fair play's a jewel.
early 19th century

2 Faith will move mountains.
late 19th century; see **BIBLE** 101:28

3 Familiarity breeds contempt.
late 14th century; 5th century AD in Latin

4 Far-fetched and dear-bought is good for ladies.
mid 14th century

5 A fault confessed is half redressed.
mid 16th century

6 Fear the Greeks bearing gifts.
late 19th century, from **VIRGIL**; see **VIRGIL** 829:6

7 February fill dyke, be it black or be it white.
mid 16th century

8 Feed a cold and starve a fever.
probably intended as two separate admonitions, but sometimes interpreted to mean that if you feed a cold you will have to starve a fever later
mid 19th century

9 The female of the species is more deadly than the male.
early 20th century, from **KIPLING**; see **KIPLING** 465:18

10 Fields have eyes and woods have ears.
early 13th century; see **SWIFT** 784:5

11 Fight fire with fire.
mid 19th century

12 Finders keepers (losers weepers).
early 19th century

13 Findings keepings.
mid 19th century

14 Fine feathers make fine birds.
late 16th century

15 Fine words butter no parsnips.
mid 17th century

16 Fingers were made before forks.
the form 'God made hands before knives' is found in the mid 16th century
mid 18th century

17 Fire is a good servant but a bad master.
early 17th century

18 First catch your hare.
early 19th century, early 14th century in Latin; see **GLASSE** 360:17

19 First come, first served.
late 14th century, late 13th century in French

20 The first duty of a soldier is obedience.
mid 19th century

21 First impressions are the most lasting.
early 18th century

22 First things first.
late 19th century

23 First thoughts are best.
early 20th century

24 The fish always stinks from the head downwards.
late 16th century

25 Fish and guests stink after three days.
late 16th century

26 A fool and his money are soon parted.
late 16th century

27 A fool at forty is a fool indeed.
early 18th century, from **YOUNG**; see **YOUNG** 876:12

28 A fool may give a wise man counsel.
mid 14th century

29 Fools and bairns should never see half-done work.
early 18th century

30 Fools ask questions that wise men cannot answer.
mid 17th century

31 Fools build houses and wise men live in them.
late 17th century

32 Fools for luck.
mid 19th century

33 Fools rush in where angels fear to tread.
from **POPE**, early 18th century; see **POPE** 616:14

34 For want of a nail the shoe was lost; for want of a shoe the horse was lost; and for want of a horse the man was lost.
early 17th century; late 15th century in French

35 Forewarned is forearmed.
early 16th century

36 Fortune favours fools.
mid 16th century

37 Fortune favours the brave.
late 14th century; see **TERENCE** 801:15, **VIRGIL** 831:8

38 Four eyes see more than two.
mid 16th century

39 A friend in need is a friend indeed.
mid 11th century; 5th century BC in Greek

40 From clogs to clogs is only three generations.
late 19th century

41 From shirtsleeves to shirtsleeves in three generations.
early 20th century; often attributed to Andrew **CARNEGIE** but not found in his writings

42 From the sublime to the ridiculous is only one step.
late 19th century; see **NAPOLEON I** 568:2, **PAINE** 592:7

43 From the sweetest wine, the tartest vinegar.
late 16th century

44 Full cup, steady hand.
early 11th century

45 Genius is an infinite capacity for taking pains.
late 19th century; see **CARLYLE** 199:23

46 Give a dog a bad name and hang him.
early 18th century

47 Give a man rope enough and he will hang himself.
mid 17th century

48 Give a thing, and take a thing, to wear the devil's gold ring.
late 16th century

1 Give and take is fair play.
late 18th century

2 Give credit where credit is due.
late 18th century

3 Give the Devil his due.
late 16th century

4 Go abroad and you'll hear news of home.
late 17th century

5 Go further and fare worse.
mid 16th century

6 God helps them that help themselves.
mid 16th century; early 15th century in French

7 God made the country and man made the town.
mid 17th century; see **COWLEY** 254:10, **COWPER** 256:8

8 God makes the back to the burden.
early 19th century

9 God never sends mouths but He sends meat.
late 14th century

10 God's in his heaven; all's right with the world.
from early 16th century in the form 'God is where he was';
now largely replaced by **BROWNING**; see **BROWNING** 167:3

11 God sends meat, but the Devil sends cooks.
mid 16th century

12 The gods send nuts to those who have no teeth.
early 20th century

13 God tempers the wind to the shorn lamb.
mid 17th century

14 Gold may be bought too dear.
mid 16th century

15 A golden key can open any door.
late 16th century

16 Good Americans when they die go to Paris.
mid 19th century, from Thomas Gold **APPLETON**; see
APPLETON 25:7

17 A good beginning makes a good ending.
early 14th century

18 The good die young.
late 17th century

19 Good fences make good neighbours.
mid 17th century

20 A good horse cannot be of a bad colour.
early 17th century

21 The good is the enemy of the best.
early 20th century; see **VOLTAIRE** 834:2

22 A good Jack makes a good Jill.
early 17th century

23 Good men are scarce.
early 17th century

24 Good seed makes a good crop.
late 16th century

25 Good wine needs no bush.
early 15th century; see **NASH** 568:18

26 The grass is always greener on the other side of
the fence.
mid 20th century

27 A great book is a great evil.
early 17th century; see **CALLIMACHUS** 193:17

28 The greater the sinner, the greater the saint.
late 18th century

29 The greater the truth, the greater the libel.
late 18th century

30 Great minds think alike.
early 17th century

31 Great oaks from little acorns grow.
late 14th century

32 A green Yule makes a fat churchyard.
meaning a mild winter
mid 17th century

33 The grey mare is the better horse.
mid 16th century

34 A guilty conscience needs no accuser.
late 14th century; earlier in Latin

35 Half a loaf is better than no bread.
mid 16th century

36 The half is better than the whole.
mid 16th century

37 Half the truth is often a whole lie.
mid 18th century

38 Handsome is as handsome does.
late 16th century; see **PROVERBS** 642:2

39 The hand that rocks the cradle rules the world.
mid 19th century, from **WALLACE**; see **WALLACE** 836:14

40 Hang a thief when he's young, and he'll no'
steal when he's old.
early 19th century

41 Hanging and wiving go by destiny.
mid 16th century

42 Happy is the bride that the sun shines on.
mid 17th century

43 Happy is the country which has no history.
early 19th century; see **MONTESQUIEU** 556:7

44 Happy's the wooing that is not long a-doing.
late 16th century

45 Hard cases make bad law.
mid 19th century

46 Hard words break no bones.
late 17th century

47 Haste is from the Devil.
mid 17th century

48 Haste makes waste.
late 14th century; see **GASCOIGNE** 350:5

49 Hasty climbers have sudden falls.
mid 15th century

50 Hawks will not pick out hawks' eyes.
late 16th century

51 He gives twice who gives quickly.
mid 16th century; see **PUBLILIUS** 648:30

52 He is a good dog who goes to church.
early 19th century

1 He laughs best who laughs last.
early 17th century

2 He lives long who lives well.
mid 16th century

3 He that cannot obey cannot command.
early 16th century

4 He that cannot pay, let him pray.
early 17th century

5 He that complies against his will is of his own opinion still.
late 17th century, from Samuel **BUTLER**; see **BUTLER** 183:26

6 He that drinks beer, thinks beer.
early 19th century

7 He that follows freits, freits will follow him.
freits = *omens*
early 18th century

8 He that goes a-borrowing, goes a-sorrowing.
late 15th century

9 He that has an ill name is half hanged.
early 15th century

10 He that lives in hope dances to an ill tune.
late 16th century

11 He that touches pitch shall be defiled.
early 14th century; see **BIBLE** 97:18

12 He that will not when he may, when he will he shall have nay.
early 11th century

13 He that will thrive must first ask his wife.
early 16th century

14 He that will to Cupar maun to Cupar.
early 18th century

15 He that would eat the fruit must climb the tree.
early 18th century

16 He that would go to sea for pleasure would go to hell for a pastime.
late 19th century

17 He travels fastest who travels alone.
late 19th century; see **KIPLING** 466:13

18 He who can does, he who cannot, teaches.
early 20th century, from **SHAW**; see **SHAW** 741:13

19 He who excuses, accuses himself.
early 17th century

20 He who fights and runs away, may live to fight another day.
mid 16th century

21 He who hesitates is lost.
early 18th century; see **ADDISON** 4:16

22 He who is absent is always in the wrong.
mid 17th century

23 He who laughs last, laughs longest.
early 20th century

24 He who lives by the sword dies by the sword.
mid 17th century; see **BIBLE** 103:19

25 He who pays the piper calls the tune.
late 19th century

26 He who rides a tiger is afraid to dismount.
late 19th century

27 He who sups with the Devil should have a long spoon.
late 14th century

28 He who wills the end, wills the means.
late 17th century

29 Hear all, see all, say nowt, tak'all, keep all, gie nowt, and if tha ever does owt for nowt do it for thysen.
early 15th century

30 Heaven protects children, sailors, and drunken men.
mid 19th century

31 Hell hath no fury like a woman scorned.
late 17th century, from **CONGREVE**; see **CONGREVE** 247:9

32 Help you to salt, help you to sorrow.
mid 17th century

33 The higher the monkey climbs the more he shows his tail.
late 14th century

34 History repeats itself.
mid 19th century

35 Home is home, as the Devil said when he found himself in the Court of Session.
early 19th century

36 Home is home though it's never so homely.
mid 16th century

37 Home is where the heart is.
late 19th century

38 Homer sometimes nods.
late 14th century, from **HORACE**; see **HORACE** 409:14

39 Honesty is the best policy.
early 17th century

40 Honey catches more flies than vinegar.
mid 17th century

41 Hope deferred makes the heart sick.
early 16th century; see **BIBLE** 88:6

42 Hope for the best and prepare for the worst.
mid 16th century

43 Hope is a good breakfast but a bad supper.
mid 17th century; see **BACON** 49:7

44 Hope springs eternal.
early 18th century, from **POPE**; see **POPE** 616:19

45 Horses for courses.
late 19th century

46 A house divided cannot stand.
mid 11th century; see **BIBLE** 103:28

47 Hunger drives the wolf out of the wood.
late 15th century

48 Hunger is the best sauce.
early 16th century

49 A hungry man is an angry man.
mid 17th century

50 Hurry no man's cattle.
early 19th century

1 The husband is always the last to know.
early 17th century

2 An idle brain is the devil's workshop.
early 17th century

3 Idle people have the least leisure.
late 17th century

4 Idleness is the root of all evil.
early 15th century; see PROVERBS 639:2

5 If anything can go wrong, it will.
commonly known as Murphy's Law
mid 20th century; said to have been invented by George
Nichols in 1949, based on a remark by his colleague Captain
E. Murphy; see ORWELL 588:4

6 If a thing's worth doing, it's worth doing well.
mid 18th century

7 If at first you don't succeed, try, try, try again.
mid 19th century

8 If Candlemas day be sunny and bright, winter
will have another flight; if Candlemas day be
cloudy with rain, winter is gone and won't come
again.
Candlemas Day = 2 February
late 17th century

9 If every man would sweep his own door-step
the city would soon be clean.
early 17th century

10 If ifs and ands were pots and pans, there'd be no
work for tinkers' hands.
mid 19th century

11 If in February there be no rain, 'tis neither good
for hay nor grain.
early 18th century

12 If it were not for hope, the heart would break.
mid 13th century

13 If Saint Paul's day be fair and clear, it will betide
a happy year.
late 16th century

14 If the cap fits, wear it.
early 18th century

15 If the mountain will not come to Mahomet,
Mahomet must go to the mountain.
early 17th century

16 If the shoe fits, wear it.
late 18th century

17 If the sky falls we shall catch larks.
mid 15th century

18 If there were no receivers, there would be no
thieves.
late 14th century

19 If two ride on a horse, one must ride behind.
late 16th century

20 If wishes were horses, beggars would ride.
early 17th century

21 If you can't beat them, join them.
beat *is usually replaced by* lick *in the US*
mid 20th century saying

22 If you can't be good, be careful.
early 20th century; the Latin form *Si non caste tamen caute* is
found from the mid 11th century

23 If you can't ride two horses at once, you
shouldn't be in the circus.
early 20th century, from MAXTON; see MAXTON 528:17

24 If you don't like the heat, get out of the
kitchen.
mid 20th century; see TRUMAN 817:18

25 If you don't make mistakes you don't make
anything.
late 19th century; see PHELPS 605:11

26 If you don't speculate, you can't accumulate.
mid 20th century

27 If you don't work you shan't eat.
mid 16th century; see BIBLE 115:17

28 If you gently touch a nettle it'll sting you for
your pains; grasp it like a lad of mettle, an' as
soft as silk remains.
late 16th century; see HILL 398:9

29 If you lie down with dogs, you will get up with
fleas.
late 16th century

30 If you pay peanuts, you get monkeys.
mid 20th century

31 If you play with fire you get burnt.
late 19th century

32 If you're born to be hanged then you'll never be
drowned.
late 16th century

33 If you run after two hares you will catch
neither.
early 16th century

34 If you want a thing done well, do it yourself.
mid 16th century

35 If you want peace, you must prepare for war.
mid 16th century; see VEGETIUS 826:2

36 If you want to live and thrive, let the spider run
alive.
mid 19th century

37 If you would be happy for a week take a wife; if
you would be happy for a month kill a pig; but
if you would be happy all your life plant a
garden.
mid 17th century; the saying exists in a variety of forms, but
marriage is nearly always given as one of the ephemeral
forms of happiness

38 If you would be well served, serve yourself.
mid 17th century

39 Ignorance of the law is no excuse for breaking
it.
early 15th century; see SELDEN 691:11

40 Ill gotten goods never thrive.
early 16th century

41 Ill weeds grow apace.
late 15th century

42 Imitation is the sincerest form of flattery.
early 19th century

1 In for a penny, in for a pound.
late 17th century

2 In the country of the blind the one eyed man is king.
early 16th century; see **ERASMUS** 316:17

3 In vain the net is spread in the sight of the bird.
late 14th century; see **BIBLE** 87:20

4 It is a long lane that has no turning.
early 17th century

5 It is a poor dog that's not worth whistling for.
mid 16th century

6 It is a poor heart that never rejoices.
mid 19th century

7 It is as cheap sitting as standing.
mid 17th century

8 It is a wise child that knows its own father.
late 16th century

9 It is best to be off with the old love before you are on with the new.
early 19th century

10 It is best to be on the safe side.
late 17th century

11 It is better to be born lucky than rich.
mid 17th century

12 It is better to give than to receive.
late 14th century; see **BIBLE** 110:9

13 It is better to travel hopefully than to arrive.
late 19th century, from **STEVENSON**; see **STEVENSON** 775:27

14 It is easier to pull down than to build up.
late 16th century

15 It is easier to raise the Devil than to lay him.
mid 17th century

16 It is easy to be wise after the event.
early 17th century

17 It is easy to find a stick to beat a dog.
mid 16th century

18 It is good to make a bridge of gold to a flying enemy.
late 16th century

19 It is idle to swallow the cow and choke on the tail.
mid 17th century

20 It is ill sitting at Rome and striving with the Pope.
early 17th century

21 It is merry in hall when beards wag all.
early 14th century

22 It is never too late to learn.
late 17th century

23 It is never too late to mend.
late 16th century

24 It is no use crying over spilt milk.
mid 17th century

25 It is not spring until you can plant your foot upon twelve daisies.
mid 19th century

26 It is not work that kills, but worry.
late 19th century

27 It is the first step that is difficult.
late 16th century; see **DU DEFFAND** 298:11

28 It is the last straw that breaks the camel's back.
mid 17th century

29 It is the pace that kills.
mid 19th century

30 It never rains but it pours.
early 18th century

31 It's an ill wind that blows nobody any good.
mid 16th century

32 It's a sin to steal a pin.
late 19th century

33 It's an ill bird that fouls its own nest.
mid 13th century

34 It's dogged as does it.
mid 19th century; see **TROLLOPE** 816:14

35 It's ill speaking between a full man and a fasting.
mid 17th century

36 It's ill waiting for dead men's shoes.
early 16th century

37 It's too late to shut the stable-door after the horse has bolted.
mid 14th century

38 It takes all sorts to make a world.
early 17th century

39 It takes three generations to make a gentleman.
early 19th century

40 It takes two to make a bargain.
late 16th century

41 It takes two to make a quarrel.
early 18th century

42 It takes two to tango.
mid 20th century, from **HOFFMAN AND MANNING**; see **HOFFMAN AND MANNING** 402:2

43 Jack is as good as his master.
early 18th century

44 Jack of all trades and master of none.
early 18th century

45 Jam tomorrow and jam yesterday, but never jam today.
late 19th century, from **CARROLL**; see **CARROLL** 203:6

46 Jouk and let the jaw go by.
jouk = *stoop*, jaw = *a rush of water*
early 18th century

47 Jove but laughs at lovers' perjury.
mid 16th century; see **DRYDEN** 296:18, **TIBULLUS** 811:1

48 Judge not, that ye be not judged.
late 15th century; see **BIBLE** 99:21

49 Keep a thing seven years and you'll always find a use for it.
early 17th century

50 Keep no more cats than will catch mice.
late 17th century

1 Keep your own fish-guts for your own sea-maws.
early 18th century

2 Keep your shop and your shop will keep you.
early 17th century

3 Killing no murder.
mid 17th century, from **SEXBY**; see **SEXBY** 693:4

4 The king can do no wrong.
mid 17th century

5 A king's chaff is worth more than other men's corn.
early 17th century

6 Kings have long arms.
mid 16th century

7 Kissing goes by favour.
early 17th century

8 Know thyself.
inscribed on the temple of Apollo at Delphi, in the form gnōthi sauton; Plato, in Protagoras 343 b, ascribes the saying to the Seven Wise Men
late 14th century; see **ANONYMOUS** 22:17, **GOETHE** 363:5

9 Knowledge is power.
late 16th century; see **BACON** 48:25

10 The labourer is worthy of his hire.
late 14th century; see **BIBLE** 105:1

11 The last drop makes the cup run over.
mid 17th century

12 Laugh and the world laughs with you, weep and you weep alone.
late 19th century, from **WILCOX**; see **WILCOX** 854:9

13 Lay-overs for meddlers.
late 18th century

14 Learning is better than house and land.
late 18th century

15 Least said, soonest mended.
mid 15th century

16 Lend your money and lose your friend.
late 15th century

17 Length begets loathing.
mid 18th century

18 The leopard does not change his spots.
mid 16th century; see **BIBLE** 95:3, **COMPTON-BURNETT** 245:6

19 Less is more.
mid 19th century, often associated with **MIES VAN DER ROHE**

20 Let sleeping dogs lie.
late 14th century

21 Let the buyer beware.
early 16th century

22 Let the cobbler stick to his last
mid 16th century

23 Let the dead bury the dead.
early 19th century; see **BIBLE** 100:11

24 Let them laugh that win.
mid 16th century

25 Let well alone.
late 16th century

26 A liar ought to have a good memory.
mid 16th century; 1st century AD in Latin

27 Life begins at forty.
early 20th century, from **PITKIN**; see **PITKIN** 607:7

28 Life isn't all beer and skittles.
mid 19th century

29 Light come, light go.
late 14th century

30 Lightning never strikes the same place twice.
mid 19th century

31 Like breeds like.
mid 16th century

32 Like father, like son.
mid 14th century

33 Like master, like man.
early 16th century

34 Like mother, like daughter.
early 14th century; see **BIBLE** 95:14

35 Like people, like priest.
late 16th century; see **BIBLE** 96:3

36 Like will to like.
early 15th century

37 Listeners never hear any good of themselves.
mid 17th century

38 Little birds that can sing and won't sing must be made to sing.
late 17th century

39 Little fish are sweet.
early 19th century

40 A little knowledge is a dangerous thing.
from **POPE**, early 18th century; see **POPE** 615:28

41 Little leaks sink the ship.
early 17th century

42 Little pitchers have large ears.
mid 16th century

43 A little pot is soon hot.
mid 16th century

44 Little strokes fell great oaks.
early 15th century

45 Little thieves are hanged, but great ones escape.
mid 17th century

46 Little things please little minds.
late 16th century

47 Live and learn.
early 17th century

48 Live and let live.
early 17th century

49 A live dog is better than a dead lion.
late 14th century; see **BIBLE** 90:8

50 Long and lazy, little and loud; fat and fulsome, pretty and proud.
late 16th century

51 The longest way round is the shortest way home.
mid 17th century

1 Long foretold, long last; short notice, soon past.
mid 19th century

2 Look before you leap.
mid 14th century

3 Lookers-on see most of the game.
early 16th century

4 Love and a cough cannot be hid.
early 16th century

5 Love begets love.
mid 17th century

6 Love is blind.
late 14th century; see ANONYMOUS 22:5

7 Love laughs at locksmiths.
early 19th century; see COLMAN 244:3

8 Love makes the world go round.
mid 19th century, from a traditional French song

9 Love me little, love me long.
early 16th century

10 Love me, love my dog.
early 16th century

11 Love will find a way.
early 17th century

12 Lucky at cards, unlucky in love.
mid 18th century

13 Make haste slowly.
late 16th century; see AUGUSTUS 40:3

14 Make hay while the sun shines.
mid 16th century

15 Man cannot live by bread alone.
late 19th century; see BIBLE 98:20

16 A man is as old as he feels, and a woman as old as she looks.
late 19th century

17 A man is known by the company he keeps.
mid 16th century

18 Man is the measure of all things.
mid 16th century; see PROTAGORAS 625:2

19 Manners maketh man.
mid 14th century; motto of William of Wykeham (1324–1404)

20 Man proposes, God disposes.
mid 15th century; see THOMAS À KEMPIS 804:17

21 Man's extremity is God's opportunity.
early 17th century

22 The man who is born in a stable is not a horse.
early 19th century

23 A man who is his own lawyer has a fool for his client.
early 19th century

24 Many a little makes a mickle.
mid 13th century

25 Many a mickle makes a muckle.
a popular corruption of 'Many a little makes a mickle'
late 18th century

26 Many are called but few are chosen.
late 19th century; see BIBLE 102:14

27 Many a true word is spoken in jest.
late 14th century

28 Many go out for wool and come home shorn.
late 16th century

29 Many hands make light work.
early 14th century

30 March comes in like a lion, and goes out like a lamb.
early 17th century

31 Marriage is a lottery.
mid 17th century

32 Marriages are made in heaven.
mid 16th century

33 Marry in haste and repent at leisure.
late 16th century; see CONGREVE 247:16

34 Marry in May, rue for aye.
late 17th century

35 May chickens come cheeping.
late 19th century

36 Meat and mass never hindered man.
early 17th century

37 Might is right.
early 14th century

38 The mill cannot grind with the water that is past.
early 17th century

39 The mills of God grind slowly, yet they grind exceeding small.
mid 17th century; translation of an anonymous verse in Sextus Empiricus *Adversus Mathematicos* bk. 1, sect. 287; see LONGFELLOW 499:20

40 Misery loves company.
late 16th century

41 Misfortunes never come singly.
early 14th century

42 A miss is as good as a mile.
the syntax has been distorted by abridgement: the original form was 'an inch in a miss is as good as an ell'
early 17th century

43 Moderation in all things.
mid 19th century; see HORACE 414:9

44 Monday's child is fair of face,
Tuesday's child is full of grace,
Wednesday's child is full of woe,
Thursday's child has far to go,
Friday's child is loving and giving,
Saturday's child works hard for its living,
And a child that's born on the Sabbath day
Is fair and wise and good and gay.
mid 19th century

45 Money can't buy happiness.
mid 19th century

46 Money has no smell.
early 20th century; see VESPASIAN 827:1

47 Money isn't everything.
early 20th century

1 Money is power.
mid 18th century

2 Money is the root of all evil.
mid 15th century; see **BIBLE** 115:23

3 A moneyless man goes fast through the market.
early 18th century; late 14th century in French

4 Money, like manure, does no good till it is spread.
early 19th century; see **BACON** 47:30

5 Money makes a man.
early 16th century

6 Money makes money.
late 16th century

7 Money makes the mare to go.
early 16th century

8 Money talks.
mid 17th century

9 More haste, less speed.
mid 14th century

10 The more laws, the more thieves and bandits.
late 16th century; see **LAO TZU** 480:9

11 More people know Tom Fool than Tom Fool knows.
mid 17th century

12 The more the merrier.
late 14th century

13 The more you get the more you want.
mid 14th century

14 The more you stir it the worse it stinks.
mid 16th century

15 Morning dreams come true.
mid 16th century

16 The mother of mischief is no bigger than a midge's wing.
early 17th century

17 A mouse may help a lion.
alluding to Aesop's fable of the lion and the rat
mid 16th century

18 Much cry and little wool.
late 15th century

19 Much would have more.
mid 14th century

20 Murder will out.
early 14th century; see **CHAUCER** 219:24

21 My son is my son till he gets him a wife, but my daughter's my daughter all the days of her life.
late 17th century

22 Nature abhors a vacuum.
mid 16th century; see **RABELAIS** 652:9

23 The nearer the bone, the sweeter the meat.
late 14th century

24 The nearer the church, the farther from God.
early 14th century

25 Near is my kirtle, but nearer is my smock.
mid 15th century

26 Near is my shirt, but nearer is my skin.
late 16th century

27 Necessity is the mother of invention.
mid 16th century

28 Necessity knows no law.
late 14th century; see **PUBLILIUS** 648:32

29 Needles and pins, needles and pins, when a man marries, his trouble begins.
mid 19th century

30 Needs must when the devil drives.
mid 15th century

31 Ne'er cast a clout till May be out.
early 18th century

32 Never bid the Devil good morrow until you meet him.
late 19th century

33 Never choose your women or linen by candlelight.
late 16th century

34 Never do evil that good may come of it.
late 16th century

35 Never give a sucker an even break.
early 20th century; see **FIELDS** 327:6

36 Never is a long time.
late 14th century

37 Never let the sun go down on your anger.
mid 17th century; see **BIBLE** 114:7

38 Never look a gift horse in the mouth.
early 16th century

39 Never marry for money, but marry where money is.
late 19th century; see **TENNYSON** 798:19

40 Never mention rope in the house of a man who has been hanged.
late 16th century

41 Never put off till tomorrow what you can do today.
late 14th century

42 Never send a boy to do a man's job.
early 20th century

43 Never speak ill of the dead.
mid 16th century; 6th century BC in Greek

44 Never tell tales out of school.
early 16th century

45 Never too old to learn.
early 16th century

46 Never trouble trouble till trouble troubles you.
late 19th century

47 New brooms sweep clean.
mid 16th century

48 New lords, new laws.
mid 16th century

49 Night brings counsel.
late 16th century

50 Nine tailors make a man.
the literal meaning is that a gentleman must select his attire from various sources; it is now also associated with

bell-ringing: tailors = tellers = *strokes, the number of strokes on the passing bell indicating the sex of the deceased*
early 17th century

1 No cross, no crown.
early 17th century; see **PENN** 602:14

2 No cure, no pay.
expression used on Lloyd's of London's Standard Form of Salvage Agreement
late 19th century

3 A nod's as good as a wink to a blind horse.
late 18th century

4 No foot, no horse.
in North America as 'no hoof, no horse'
mid 18th century

5 No man can serve two masters.
early 14th century; see **BIBLE** 99:15

6 No man is a hero to his valet.
mid 18th century; see **CORNUEL** 252:7

7 No money, no Swiss.
the Swiss were particularly noted as mercenaries
late 16th century; see **RACINE** 653:3

8 No moon, no man.
late 19th century

9 No names, no pack-drill.
early 20th century

10 No news is good news.
early 17th century

11 No one should be judge in his own cause.
mid 15th century

12 No pain, no gain.
late 16th century

13 No penny, no paternoster.
early 16th century

14 No smoke without fire.
late 14th century

15 None but the brave deserve the fair.
late 17th century, from **DRYDEN**; see **DRYDEN** 295:4

16 Nothing comes of nothing.
late 14th century

17 Nothing for nothing.
early 18th century

18 Nothing is certain but death and taxes.
early 18th century; see **DEFOE** 270:8, **FRANKLIN** 341:10

19 Nothing is certain but the unforeseen.
late 19th century

20 Nothing should be done in haste but gripping a flea.
mid 17th century

21 Nothing so bad but it might have been worse.
late 19th century

22 Nothing so bold as a blind mare.
early 17th century

23 Nothing succeeds like success.
mid 19th century

24 Nothing venture, nothing gain.
early 17th century

25 Nothing venture, nothing have.
late 14th century

26 No time like the present.
mid 16th century

27 Obey orders, if you break owners.
late 18th century

28 Of two evils choose the less.
late 14th century; similar sentiments are found in **ARISTOTLE** and **CICERO**

29 Offenders never pardon.
mid 17th century

30 Old habits die hard.
mid 18th century

31 An old poacher makes the best gamekeeper.
late 14th century

32 Old sins cast long shadows.
early 20th century

33 Old soldiers never die.
early 20th century; see **FOLEY** 336:4

34 The only good Indian is a dead Indian.
mid 19th century; see **SHERIDAN** 747:23

35 On Saint Thomas the Divine kill all turkeys, geese and swine.
St Thomas the Apostle's feast is on 21 December
mid 18th century

36 On the first of March, the crows begin to search.
mid 19th century

37 Once a—, always a—
the formula is found from the early 17th century

38 Once a priest, always a priest.
mid 19th century

39 Once a whore, always a whore.
early 17th century

40 Once bitten, twice shy.
mid 19th century

41 One cannot love and be wise.
early 16th century

42 One does not wash one's dirty linen in public.
early 19th century

43 One Englishman can beat three Frenchmen.
late 16th century

44 One for sorrow; two for mirth; three for a wedding, four for a birth.
referring to the number of magpies seen
mid 19th century

45 One for the mouse, one for the crow, one to rot, one to grow.
referring to sowing seed
mid 19th century

46 One funeral makes many.
late 19th century

47 One good turn deserves another.
early 15th century

1 One half of the world does not know how the other half lives.
early 17th century

2 One hand for oneself and one for the ship.
late 18th century

3 One hand washes the other.
late 16th century

4 One hour's sleep before midnight is worth two after.
mid 17th century

5 One law for the rich and another for the poor.
early 19th century

6 One man may steal a horse, while another may not look over a hedge.
mid 16th century

7 One man's loss is another man's gain.
early 16th century

8 One man's meat is another man's poison.
late 16th century

9 One might as well be hanged for a sheep as a lamb.
late 17th century

10 One nail drives out another.
mid 13th century; also found in **ARISTOTLE**

11 One picture is worth ten thousand words.
early 20th century; see **BARNARD** 59:1

12 One size does not fit all.
early 17th century

13 One step at a time.
mid 19th century

14 One story is good till another is told.
late 16th century

15 One swallow does not make a summer.
mid 16th century

16 One volunteer is worth two pressed men.
early 18th century

17 One wedding brings another.
mid 17th century

18 One white foot, buy him; two white feet, try him; three white feet, look well about him; four white feet, go without him.
on horse-dealing
late 19th century

19 One year's seeding makes seven years weeding.
late 19th century

20 Opportunity makes a thief.
early 13th century

21 Opportunity never knocks twice at any man's door.
mid 16th century

22 Other times, other manners.
late 16th century

23 An ounce of practice is worth a pound of precept.
late 16th century

24 Out of debt, out of danger.
mid 17th century

25 Out of sight, out of mind.
mid 13th century; see **THOMAS À KEMPIS** 804:20

26 Out of the fullness of the heart the mouth speaks.
late 14th century; see **BIBLE** 101:6

27 Out of the mouths of babes—.
late 19th century; see **BOOK OF COMMON PRAYER** 139:22

28 Parsley seed goes nine times to the Devil.
mid 17th century

29 Patience is a virtue.
late 14th century

30 Pay beforehand was never well served.
late 16th century

31 A peck of March dust is worth a king's ransom.
early 16th century

32 The pen is mightier than the sword.
late 16th century; see **BULWER-LYTTON** 170:14, **LEWES** 491:14

33 A penny saved is a penny earned.
mid 17th century

34 Penny wise and pound foolish.
early 17th century

35 Physician, heal thyself.
early 15th century; see **BIBLE** 104:21

36 The pitcher will go to the well once too often.
mid 14th century

37 Pity is akin to love.
early 17th century

38 A place for everything, and everything in its place.
mid 17th century; often associated with Samuel **SMILES** and Mrs Beeton

39 Please your eye and plague your heart.
early 17th century

40 Politics makes strange bedfellows.
mid 19th century

41 Possession is nine points of the law.
early 17th century

42 A postern door makes a thief.
mid 15th century

43 The post of honour is the post of danger.
early 16th century

44 Poverty is no disgrace, but it's a great inconvenience.
late 16th century

45 Poverty is not a crime.
late 16th century

46 Power corrupts.
late 19th century, now commonly used in allusion to **ACTON**; see **ACTON** 1:16

47 Practice makes perfect.
mid 16th century

48 Practise what you preach.
late 14th century

1 Praise the child, and you make love to the mother.
early 19th century

2 Pretty is as pretty does.
mid 19th century, American equivalent of **PROVERBS** 633:38

3 Prevention is better than cure.
early 17th century

4 Pride feels no pain.
early 17th century

5 Pride goes before a fall.
late 14th century; see **BIBLE** 88:17

6 Procrastination is the thief of time.
mid 18th century, from **YOUNG**; see **YOUNG** 876:20

7 Promises, like pie-crust, are made to be broken.
late 17th century

8 The proof of the pudding is in the eating.
early 14th century

9 A prophet is not without honour save in his own country.
late 15th century; see **BIBLE** 101:17

10 Providence is always on the side of the big battalions.
early 19th century; see **BUSSY-RABUTIN** 182:16, **VOLTAIRE** 834:16

11 Punctuality is the politeness of princes.
mid 19th century; see **LOUIS XVIII** 501:11

12 Punctuality is the soul of business.
mid 19th century

13 Put a stout heart to a stey brae.
stey = *steep*
late 16th century

14 Put your trust in God, and keep your powder dry.
attributed to Oliver **CROMWELL**
mid 19th century; see **BLACKER** 123:8

15 The quarrel of lovers is the renewal of love.
early 16th century; see **EDWARDS** 304:11

16 Quickly come, quickly go.
late 16th century

17 The race is not to the swift, nor the battle to the strong.
early 17th century; see **BIBLE** 90:11

18 Rain before seven, fine before eleven.
mid 19th century

19 Red sky at night, shepherd's delight; red sky in the morning, shepherd's warning.
late 14th century

20 A reed before the wind lives on, while mighty oaks do fall.
late 14th century

21 Revenge is a dish that can be eaten cold.
late 19th century

22 Revenge is sweet.
mid 16th century

23 Revolutions are not made with rose-water.
early 19th century; see **HEGEL** 388:12

24 The rich man has his ice in the summer and the poor man gets his in the winter.
early 20th century

25 A rising tide lifts all boats.
principally known in the United States; associated with the Kennedy family
mid 20th century

26 The road to hell is paved with good intentions.
late 16th century

27 The robin and the wren are God's cock and hen; the martin and the swallow are God's mate and marrow.
late 18th century

28 Robin Hood could brave all weathers but a thaw wind.
mid 19th century

29 A rolling stone gathers no moss.
mid 14th century

30 Rome was not built in a day.
mid 16th century

31 The rotten apple injures its neighbour.
mid 14th century

32 Safe bind, safe find.
mid 16th century

33 Saint Swithun's day, if thou be fair, for forty days it will remain; Saint Swithun's day, if thou bring rain, for forty days it will remain.
Saint Swithun's day is 15 July
early 17th century

34 Save us from our friends.
late 15th century

35 Scratch a Russian and you find a Tartar.
early 19th century; see **ZANGWILL** 877:9

36 The sea refuses no river.
early 17th century

37 Second thoughts are best.
late 16th century

38 See a pin and pick it up, all the day you'll have good luck; see a pin and let it lie, bad luck you'll have all day.
mid 19th century

39 Seeing is believing.
early 17th century

40 Seek and ye shall find.
early 16th century; see **BIBLE** 99:24

41 See no evil, hear no evil, speak no evil.
conventionally represented by the monkeys ('the three wise monkeys') covering their eyes, ears, and mouth respectively with their hands
early 20th century

42 Self-praise is no recommendation.
early 19th century

43 Self-preservation is the first law of nature.
early 17th century

44 September blow soft till the fruit's in the loft.
late 16th century

1 Set a beggar on horseback, and he'll ride to the Devil.
late 16th century

2 Set a thief to catch a thief.
mid 17th century

3 The sharper the storm, the sooner it's over.
late 19th century

4 The shoemaker's son always goes barefoot.
mid 16th century

5 A short horse is soon curried.
mid 14th century

6 Short reckonings make long friends.
early 16th century

7 Shrouds have no pockets.
mid 19th century

8 A shut mouth catches no flies.
late 16th century

9 Silence is a woman's best garment.
mid 16th century

10 Silence is golden.
mid 19th century

11 Silence means consent.
late 14th century

12 Sing before breakfast, cry before night.
early 17th century

13 Six hours sleep for a man, seven for a woman, and eight for a fool.
early 17th century

14 A slice off a cut loaf isn't missed.
late 16th century

15 Slow and steady wins the race.
mid 18th century

16 Slow but sure.
late 17th century

17 Small choice in rotten apples.
late 16th century

18 A soft answer turneth away wrath.
late 14th century; see BIBLE 88:13

19 Softly, softly, catchee monkey.
early 20th century

20 So many men, so many opinions.
late 14th century; see TERENCE 801:16

21 So many mists in March, so many frosts in May.
early 17th century

22 Something is better than nothing.
mid 16th century

23 The sooner begun, the sooner done.
late 16th century

24 Soon ripe, soon rotten.
late 14th century

25 Sow dry and set wet.
mid 17th century

26 A sow may whistle, though it has an ill mouth for it.
early 19th century

27 Spare at the spigot, and let out the bung-hole.
mid 17th century

28 Spare the rod and spoil the child.
early 11th century; see BIBLE 88:9, BUTLER 183:21

29 Spare well and have to spend.
mid 16th century

30 Speak as you find.
late 16th century

31 Speak not of my debts unless you mean to pay them.
mid 17th century

32 Speech is silver, but silence is golden.
mid 19th century

33 The squeaking wheel gets the grease.
mid 20th century

34 A stern chase is a long chase.
stern chase = a chase in which the pursuing ship follows directly in the wake of the pursued
early 19th century

35 Sticks and stones may break my bones, but words will never hurt me.
late 19th century

36 A still tongue makes a wise head.
mid 16th century

37 Still waters run deep.
early 15th century

38 A stitch in time saves nine.
early 18th century

39 Stolen fruit is sweet.
early 17th century

40 Stolen waters are sweet.
late 14th century; see BIBLE 87:33

41 Stone-dead hath no fellow.
mid 17th century

42 Straws tell which way the wind blows.
mid 17th century

43 A stream cannot rise above its source.
mid 17th century

44 Stretch your arm no further than your sleeve will reach.
mid 16th century

45 Strike while the iron is hot.
late 14th century; see DRYDEN 297:11

46 The style is the man.
early 20th century, from BUFFON; see BUFFON 170:4

47 Success has many fathers, while failure is an orphan.
mid 20th century; see CIANO 231:9

48 Sue a beggar and catch a louse.
mid 17th century

49 Sufficient unto the day is the evil thereof.
mid 18th century; see BIBLE 99:20

50 The sun loses nothing by shining into a puddle.
early 14th century, of Classical origin

51 Sussex won't be druv.
early 20th century

1 A swarm in May is worth a load of hay; a swarm in June is worth a silver spoon; but a swarm in July is not worth a fly.
beekeepers' saying
mid 17th century

2 Take care of the pence and the pounds will take care of themselves.
mid 18th century; see **LOWNDES** 503:12

3 Take the goods the gods provide.
late 17th century

4 A tale never loses in the telling.
mid 16th century

5 Talk is cheap.
mid 19th century

6 Talk of the Devil, and he is bound to appear.
mid 17th century

7 Tastes differ.
early 19th century

8 Tell the truth and shame the Devil.
mid 16th century

9 There are as good fish in the sea as ever came out of it.
late 16th century

10 There are more ways of killing a cat than choking it with cream.
mid 19th century

11 There are more ways of killing a dog than choking it with butter.
mid 19th century

12 There are more ways of killing a dog than hanging it.
late 17th century

13 There are no birds in last year's nest.
early 17th century

14 There are tricks in every trade.
early 17th century

15 There are two sides to every question.
early 19th century

16 There goes more to marriage than four bare legs in a bed.
mid 16th century

17 There is always something new out of Africa.
mid 16th century, from **PLINY**; see **PLINY** 609:16

18 There is a remedy for everything except death.
early 15th century

19 There is a time for everything.
late 14th century; see **BIBLE** 89:23

20 There is always a first time.
late 18th century

21 There is always room at the top.
early 20th century; see **WEBSTER** 844:5

22 There is an exception to every rule.
late 16th century

23 There is a time and place for everything.
early 16th century

24 There is honour among thieves.
early 19th century

25 There is luck in leisure.
late 17th century

26 There is luck in odd numbers.
late 16th century

27 There is measure in all things.
late 14th century; see **HORACE** 414:9

28 There is more than one way to skin a cat.
mid 19th century

29 There is no accounting for tastes.
late 18th century

30 There is no little enemy.
mid 17th century

31 There is no royal road to learning.
early 19th century; see **EUCLID** 320:19

32 There is nothing like leather.
late 17th century

33 There is nothing lost by civility.
late 19th century

34 There is nothing new under the sun.
late 16th century; see **BIBLE** 89:19

35 There is nothing so good for the inside of a man as the outside of a horse.
early 20th century

36 There is reason in the roasting of eggs.
mid 17th century; see **BACON** 48:18

37 There is safety in numbers.
late 17th century

38 There is truth in wine.
mid 16th century

39 There's many a good cock come out of a tattered bag.
late 19th century

40 There's many a good tune played on an old fiddle.
early 20th century

41 There's many a slip 'twixt cup and lip.
mid 16th century

42 There's no fool like an old fool.
mid 16th century

43 There's no great loss without some gain.
mid 17th century

44 There's none so blind as those who will not see.
mid 16th century

45 There's none so deaf as those who will not hear.
mid 16th century

46 There's no place like home.
late 16th century; see **PAYNE** 600:11

47 There's nowt so queer as folk.
early 20th century

48 They that dance must pay the fiddler.
mid 17th century

49 They that live longest, see most.
early 17th century

1 They that sow the wind, shall reap the whirlwind.
late 16th century; see **BIBLE** 96:4

2 Things past cannot be recalled.
late 15th century

3 Think first and speak afterwards.
mid 16th century

4 Third time lucky.
mid 19th century

5 The third time pays for all.
late 16th century

6 Those who hide can find.
early 15th century

7 Those who live in glass houses shouldn't throw stones.
mid 17th century

8 Those who play at bowls must look out for rubbers.
mid 18th century

9 Thought is free.
late 14th century

10 Threatened men live long.
mid 16th century

11 Three may keep a secret, if two of them are dead.
mid 16th century

12 Three removals are as bad as a fire.
mid 18th century

13 Three things are not to be trusted; a cow's horn, a dog's tooth, and a horse's hoof.
late 14th century

14 Thrift is a great revenue.
mid 17th century

15 Throw dirt enough, and some will stick.
mid 17th century

16 Time and tide wait for no man.
late 14th century

17 Time flies.
late 14th century; see **VIRGIL** 833:2

18 Time is a great healer.
late 14th century

19 Time is money.
late 16th century

20 Time will tell.
mid 16th century

21 Time works wonders.
late 16th century

22 Times change and we with time.
attributed to the Emperor Lothar I (795–855) in the form 'Omnia mutantur, nos et mutamur in illis [All things change, and we change with them]'; now sometimes quoted as 'Tempora mutantur . . . '
late 16th century

23 'Tis better to have loved and lost, than never to have loved at all.
early 18th century; see **CONGREVE** 247:20, **TENNYSON** 795:9

24 Today you; tomorrow me.
early 17th century

25 To err is human (to forgive divine).
late 16th century; see **POPE** 616:10

26 To know all is to forgive all.
mid 20th century; see **STAËL** 769:10

27 Tomorrow is another day.
early 16th century; see **MITCHELL** 551:5

28 Tomorrow never comes.
early 16th century

29 The tongue always returns to the sore tooth.
late 16th century

30 Too many cooks spoil the broth.
late 16th century

31 To the pure all things are pure.
mid 19th century; see **BIBLE** 115:29

32 Trade follows the flag.
late 19th century

33 Travel broadens the mind.
early 20th century

34 The tree is known by its fruit.
early 16th century; see **BIBLE** 101:5

35 A trouble shared is a trouble halved.
early 20th century

36 Truth is stranger than fiction.
early 19th century, from **BYRON**; see **BYRON** 189:22

37 Truth lies at the bottom of a well.
mid 16th century

38 Truth makes the Devil blush.
mid 20th century

39 Truth will out.
mid 15th century

40 Turkey, heresy, hops, and beer came into England all in one year.
late 16th century

41 Turn about is fair play.
mid 18th century

42 Two blacks don't make a white.
early 18th century

43 Two boys are half a boy, and three boys are no boy at all.
early 20th century

44 Two heads are better than one.
late 14th century

45 Two is company, but three is none.
often used with the alternative ending 'three's a crowd'
early 18th century

46 Two of a trade never agree.
early 17th century

47 Two wrongs don't make a right.
late 18th century; see **SZASZ** 786:16

48 The unexpected always happens.
late 19th century

49 Union is strength.
mid 17th century

1 United we stand, divided we fall.
late 18th century, from **DICKINSON**; see **DICKINSON** 282:7

2 Variety is the spice of life.
late 18th century, from **COWPER**; see **COWPER** 256:12

3 Virtue is its own reward.
early 16th century

4 The voice of the people is the voice of God.
early 15th century; see **ALCUIN** 11:10

5 Walls have ears.
late 16th century

6 Walnuts and pears you plant for your heirs.
mid 17th century

7 Wanton kittens make sober cats.
early 18th century

8 Waste not, want not.
late 18th century

9 A watched pot never boils.
mid 19th century

10 The way to a man's heart is through his stomach.
early 19th century

11 The weakest go to the wall.
early 16th century

12 Wedlock is a padlock.
late 17th century

13 Well begun is half done.
early 15th century

14 We must eat a peck of dirt before we die.
mid 18th century

15 We must learn to walk before we can run.
mid 14th century

16 What a neighbour gets is not lost.
mid 16th century

17 What can't be cured must be endured.
late 16th century

18 What can you expect from a pig but a grunt.
early 18th century

19 Whatever man has done, man may do.
mid 19th century

20 What everybody says must be true.
early 15th century

21 What goes up must come down.
early 20th century

22 What is got over the Devil's back is spent under his belly.
late 16th century

23 What is new cannot be true.
mid 17th century

24 What Manchester says today, the rest of England says tomorrow.
late 19th century; see **KIPLING** 468:5

25 What must be, must be.
late 14th century

26 What's bred in the bone will come out in the flesh.
late 15th century

27 What's done cannot be undone.
mid 15th century

28 What's sauce for the goose is sauce for the gander.
late 17th century

29 What the eye doesn't see, the heart doesn't grieve over.
mid 16th century; earlier in Latin

30 What the soldier said isn't evidence.
mid 19th century; see **DICKENS** 280:22

31 What you don't know can't hurt you.
late 16th century

32 What you have, hold.
mid 15th century

33 What you lose on the swings you gain on the roundabouts.
early 20th century

34 What you spend, you have.
early 14th century

35 What you've never had you never miss.
early 20th century

36 When Adam delved and Eve span, who was then the gentleman?
traditionally taken by John Ball as the text of his revolutionary sermon on the outbreak of the Peasants' Revolt, 1381
late 14th century; see **ROLLE** 666:12

37 When all fruit fails, welcome haws.
early 18th century

38 When Greek meets Greek, then comes the tug of war.
late 17th century; see **LEE** 487:12

39 When house and land are gone and spent, then learning is most excellent.
mid 18th century

40 When in doubt, do nowt.
late 19th century

41 When in Rome, do as the Romans do.
mid 16th century; see **AMBROSE** 14:4

42 When one door shuts, another opens.
late 16th century

43 When poverty comes in at the door, love flies out of the window.
early 17th century

44 When the blind lead the blind, both shall fall into the ditch.
late 9th century; see **BIBLE** 101:22

45 When the cat's away, the mice will play.
early 17th century

46 When the furze is in bloom, my love's in tune.
mid 18th century

47 When the going gets tough, the tough get going.
mid 20th century; see **KENNEDY** 460:17

48 When the gorse is out of bloom, kissing's out of fashion.
mid 19th century

1 When the oak is before the ash, then you will only get a splash; when the ash is before the oak, then you may expect a soak.
mid 19th century

2 When the wind is in the east, 'tis neither good for man nor beast.
early 17th century

3 When the wine is in, the wit is out.
late 14th century

4 When thieves fall out, honest men come by their own.
mid 16th century

5 When things are at the worst they begin to mend.
late 16th century

6 Where bees are, there is honey.
early 17th century

7 Where God builds a church, the Devil will build a chapel.
mid 16th century; see **LUTHER** 505:7

8 Where ignorance is bliss, 'tis folly to be wise.
mid 18th century, from **GRAY**; see **GRAY** 370:13

9 Where MacGregor sits at the head of the table.
mid 19th century

10 Where the carcase is, there shall the eagles be gathered together.
mid 16th century; see **BIBLE** 102:25

11 Where there's a will there's a way.
mid 17th century

12 Where there's muck there's brass.
late 17th century

13 While the grass grows, the steed starves.
mid 14th century

14 While there's life there's hope.
mid 16th century

15 While two dogs are fighting for a bone, a third runs away with it.
late 14th century

16 A whistling woman and a crowing hen are neither fit for God nor men.
early 18th century

17 Whom the Gods love die young.
mid 16th century; see **MENANDER** 531:16

18 Whom the gods would destroy, they first make mad.
early 17th century, earlier in Greek; see **ANONYMOUS** 23:1

19 Who says A must say B.
mid 19th century, usually North American

20 Whosoever draws his sword against the prince must throw the scabbard away.
early 17th century

21 Who won't be ruled by the rudder must be ruled by the rock.
mid 17th century

22 Why buy a cow when milk is so cheap?
mid 17th century

23 Why keep a dog and bark yourself?
late 16th century

24 Why should the devil have all the best tunes?
mid 19th century; see **HILL** 399:1

25 A wilful man must have his way.
early 19th century

26 Wilful waste makes woeful want.
early 18th century

27 Winter never rots in the sky.
early 17th century

28 The wish is father to the thought.
late 16th century, from **SHAKESPEARE**; see **SHAKESPEARE** 707:29

29 A woman, a dog, and a walnut tree, the more you beat them the better they be.
late 16th century

30 A woman and a ship ever want mending.
late 16th century; 2nd century BC in Latin

31 A woman's place is in the home.
mid 19th century

32 A woman's work is never done.
late 16th century

33 Wonders will never cease.
late 18th century

34 A word to the wise is enough.
early 16th century; see **PLAUTUS** 609:9

35 Work expands so as to fill the time available.
mid 20th century, from **PARKINSON**; see **PARKINSON** 597:5

36 The worth of a thing is what it will bring.
late 16th century

37 Yorkshire born and Yorkshire bred, strong in the arm and weak in the head.
the names of other (chiefly northern) English counties and towns are also used instead of Yorkshire
mid 19th century

38 You are what you eat.
mid 20th century; see **FEUERBACH** 325:15

39 You buy land, you buy stones; you buy meat, you buy bones.
late 17th century

40 You can drive out nature with a pitchfork but she keeps on coming back.
mid 16th century; see **FREDERICK THE GREAT** 342:2, **HORACE** 410:9

41 You can have too much of a good thing.
late 15th century

42 You can only die once.
mid 15th century

43 You can't make a silk purse out of a sow's ear.
early 16th century

44 You can't please everyone.
late 15th century

45 You can't put new wine in old bottles.
early 20th century; see **BIBLE** 100:17

46 You can't teach an old dog new tricks.
early 16th century

1 You can't tell a book by its cover.
early 20th century

2 You can't win them all.
mid 20th century

3 You can take a horse to the water, but you can't make him drink.
late 12th century

4 You can take the boy out of the country but you can't take the country out of the boy.
mid 20th century, usually North American

5 You cannot catch old birds with chaff.
late 15th century

6 You cannot get a quart into a pint pot.
late 19th century

7 You cannot get blood from a stone.
mid 17th century

8 You cannot have your cake and eat it.
mid 16th century

9 You cannot lose what you never had.
late 16th century

10 You cannot make an omelette without breaking eggs.
mid 19th century

11 You cannot make bricks without straw.
mid 17th century

12 You cannot put an old head on young shoulders.
late 16th century

13 You cannot run with the hare and hunt with the hounds.
mid 15th century

14 You cannot serve God and Mammon.
early 16th century; see **BIBLE** 99:15

15 You cannot shift an old tree without it dying.
early 16th century

16 You don't get something for nothing.
late 19th century

17 You never know what you can do till you try.
early 19th century

18 You never miss the water till the well runs dry.
early 17th century

19 Young folks think old folks to be fools, but old folks know young folks to be fools.
late 16th century

20 A young man married is a young man marred.
late 16th century; see **SHAKESPEARE** 694:5

21 Young men may die, but old men must die.
mid 16th century

22 Young saint, old devil.
early 15th century

23 You pays your money and you takes your choice.
mid 19th century

24 You should know a man seven years before you stir his fire.
early 19th century

25 Youth must be served.
early 19th century

26 You win a few, you lose a few.
mid 20th century

Pu Yi 1906–67

Chinese monarch, Emperor of China 1908–12; Japan's puppet emperor of Manchuria 1934–45

27 For the past 40 years I had never folded my own quilt, made my own bed, or poured out my own washing. I had never even washed my own feet or tied my shoes.
From Emperor to Citizen (1964)

Publilius Syrus

Roman freedman and writer of mimes of the 1st century BC

28 *Beneficium accipere libertatem est vendere.*
To accept a favour is to sell your freedom.
Sententiae no. 61, in J. and A. Duff *Minor Latin Poets* (Loeb ed., 1934)

29 *Formosa facies muta commendatio est.*
A beautiful face is a mute recommendation.
Sententiae no. 199, in J. and A. Duff *Minor Latin Poets*; translated by Thomas Tenison in *Baconiana* (1679) 'Ornamenta Rationalia' no. 12

30 *Inopi beneficium bis dat qui dat celeriter.*
He gives the poor man twice as much good who gives quickly.
proverbially 'Bis dat qui cito dat [*He gives twice who gives soon*]'
Sententiae no. 274, in J. and A. Duff *Minor Latin Poets*; see **PROVERBS** 633:51

31 *Iudex damnatur ubi nocens absolvitur.*
The judge is condemned when the guilty party is acquitted.
Sententiae no. 296, in J. and A. Duff *Minor Latin Poets*

32 *Necessitas dat legem non ipsa accipit.*
Necessity gives the law without itself acknowledging one.
proverbially 'Necessitas non habet legem [*Necessity has no law*]'
Sententiae no. 444, in J. and A. Duff *Minor Latin Poets*; see **CROMWELL** 260:17, **PROVERBS** 639:28

33 *Semper iratus plus se posse putat quam possit.*
Anger always thinks it has power beyond its power.
Sententiae no. 643, in J. and A. Duff *Minor Latin Poets*

John Pudney 1909–77

English poet and writer

34 Do not despair
For Johnny-head-in-air;
He sleeps as sound
As Johnny underground.
'For Johnny' (1942); see **HOFFMANN** 402:6

35 And keep your tears
For him in after years.

Better by far
For Johnny-the-bright-star,
To keep your head,
And see his children fed.
'For Johnny' (1942)

Augustus Welby Pugin 1812–52

English architect and designer

1 The two great rules for design are these: *1st, that there should be no features about a building which are not necessary for convenience, construction or propriety; 2nd, that all ornament should consist of the essential construction of the building.* The neglect of these two rules is the cause of all the bad architecture of the present time.
   True Principles (1841)

2 A man who remains any length of time in a modern Gothic room, and escapes without being wounded by some of its minutiae, may consider himself extremely fortunate.
   True Principles (1841)

3 I seek *antiquity not novelty.* I strive to *revive* not *invent.*
   letter to John Bloxam, 13 September 1840; *Collected Letters* (2001) vol. 1

4 There is nothing worth living for but Christian Architecture and a boat.
   in *The Builder* 1852 vol. 10

5 How can you expect to convert England if you use a cope like that?
   to an unidentified Catholic priest
   Bernard England *The Sequel to Catholic Emancipation* (1915)

6 Nothing can be more dangerous than looking at prints of buildings, and trying to imitate bits of them. These architectural books are as bad as the Scriptures in the hands of the Protestants.
   J. Mordaunt Crook *Dilemma of Style* (1987)

7 Yet notwithstanding the palpable impracticability of adapting Greek temples to our climate, habits and religion, we see the attempt and failure continuously made and repeated; post office, theatre, church, bath, reading-room, hotel, methodist chapel and turnpike gate, all the present the eternal sameness of a Grecian temple outraged in all its proportions and character.
   J. Mordaunt Crook *The Greek Revival* (1995)

Joseph Pulitzer 1847–1911

Hungarian-born American newspaper proprietor and editor

8 Our Republic and its press will rise or fall together.
   referring to the importance of media independence
   in *North American Review* May 1904

9 A cynical, mercenary, demagogic, corrupt press will produce in time a people as base as itself.
   inscribed on the gateway to the Columbia School of Journalism in New York
   W. J. Granberg *The World of Joseph Pulitzer* (1965)

10 A newspaper should have no friends.
   Don C. Seitz *Joseph Pulitzer: his life and letters* (1926) ch. 1

Philip Pullman 1946–

English writer

11 His dark materials.
   overall title for his fantasy trilogy (1996–2001), from Milton: see **MILTON** 542:18

12 'Thou shalt not' might reach the head, but it takes 'Once upon a time' to reach the heart.
   in *Independent* 18 July 1996

William Pulteney, Earl of Bath

1684–1764

English peer

13 For Sir Ph—p well knows
That innuendos
Will serve him no longer in verse or in prose,
Since twelve honest men have decided the cause,
And were judges of fact, tho' not judges of laws.
   on the unsuccessful prosecution of The Craftsman, *1729 by Philip Yorke, later Lord* **HARDWICKE**
   'The Honest Jury' (1729) st. 3

Punch 1841–1992

English humorous weekly periodical

14 Advice to persons about to marry.—'Don't.'
   4 January 1845; see **BACON** 47:18

15 You pays your money and you takes your choice.
   3 January 1846

16 The Half-Way House to Rome, Oxford.
   27 January 1849

17 Never do to-day what you can put off till to-morrow.
   22 December 1849

18 Who's 'im, Bill?
A stranger!
'Eave 'arf a brick at 'im.
   25 February 1854

19 What is Matter?—Never mind.
What is Mind?—No matter.
   14 July 1855

20 It ain't the 'unting as 'urts 'im, it's the 'ammer, 'ammer, 'ammer along the 'ard 'igh road.
   31 May 1856

21 Mun, a had na' been the-erre abune two hours when—*bang*—went saxpence!!!
   5 December 1868

22 Cats is 'dogs' and rabbits is 'dogs' and so's Parrots, but this 'ere 'Tortis' is a insect, so there ain't no charge for it.
   6 March 1869

23 Nothink for nothink 'ere, and precious little for sixpence.
   16 October 1869

1 Go directly—see what she's doing, and tell her she mustn't.
16 November 1872

2 There was one poor tiger that hadn't *got* a Christian.
3 April 1875

3 It's worse than wicked, my dear, it's vulgar.
Almanac (1876)

4 I never read books—I *write* them.
11 May 1878; see DISRAELI 286:30

5 I am not hungry; but thank goodness, I am greedy.
28 December 1878

6 BISHOP: Who is it that sees and hears all we do, and before whom even I am but as a crushed worm?
PAGE: The Missus, my Lord.
14 August 1880

7 Ah whiles hae ma doobts aboot the meenister.
11 December 1880

8 WIFE OF TWO YEARS' STANDING: Oh yes! I'm sure he's not so fond of me as at first. He's away so much, neglects me dreadfully, and he's so cross when he comes home. What *shall* I do?
WIDOW: Feed the brute!
31 October 1885

9 Nearly all our best men are dead! Carlyle, Tennyson, Browning, George Eliot!—I'm not feeling very well myself.
6 May 1893

10 Botticelli isn't a wine, you Juggins! Botticelli's a *cheese*!
6 June 1894

11 I'm afraid you've got a bad egg, Mr Jones. Oh no, my Lord, I assure you! Parts of it are excellent!
11 May 1895

12 Look here, Steward, if this is coffee, I want tea; but if this is tea, then I wish for coffee.
23 July 1902

13 Sometimes I sits and thinks, and then again I just sits.
24 October 1906

Al Purdy 1918–2000
Canadian poet and writer

14 Look here
You've never seen this country
it's not the way you thought it was
Look again.
of Canada
'The Country of the Young' (1976)

15 Looking into his eyes
it is possible to see the first hunters
(if you have your own vision)
after the last ice age.
'Inuit' (1967)

Alexander Pushkin 1799–1837
Russian poet

16 Storm-clouds whirl and storm-clouds scurry;
From behind them pale moonlight
Flickers where the snowflakes hurry.
Dark the sky and dark the night.
'Devils' (1830) (translated by C. M. Bowra)

17 From early youth his dedication
Was to a single occupation . . .
The science of the tender passion.
Eugene Onegin (1833) ch. 1, st. 8 (translated by Babette Deutsch)

18 A woman's love for us increases
The less we love her, sooth to say—
She stoops, she falls, her struggling ceases;
Caught fast, she cannot get away.
Eugene Onegin (1833) ch. 4, st. 1 (translated by Babette Deutsch)

19 A tedious season they await
Who hear November at the gate.
Eugene Onegin (1833) ch. 4, st. 40 (translated by Babette Deutsch)

20 Moscow: those syllables can start
A tumult in the Russian heart.
Eugene Onegin (1833) ch. 7, st. 36 (translated by Babette Deutsch)

21 A green oak grows by a curving shore;
And round that oak hangs a golden chain.
Ruslan and Lyudmila (1820) 'Prologue' (translated by Elisaveta Fen)

22 When trade and traffic and all the noise of town
Is dimmed, and on the streets and squares
The filmy curtain of the night sinks down
With sleep, the recompense of cares,
To me the darkness brings not sleep nor rest.
'Remembrances' (1828) (translated by R. M. Hewitt)

Israel Putnam 1718–90
American general

23 Men, you are all marksmen—don't one of you fire until you see the white of their eyes.
also attributed to William Prescott (1726–95)
at Bunker Hill, 1775, in R. Frothingham *History of the Siege of Boston* (1873) ch. 5

Mario Puzo 1920–99
American novelist

24 I'll make him an offer he can't refuse.
The Godfather (1969) ch. 1

25 A lawyer with his briefcase can steal more than a hundred men with guns.
The Godfather (1969) ch. 1

Barbara Pym 1913–80
English novelist

26 She experienced all the cosiness and irritation which can come from living with thoroughly nice people with whom one has nothing in common.
Less than Angels (1955) ch. 23

John Pym 1584–1643

English Parliamentary leader

1 To have granted liberties, and not to have liberties in truth and realities, is but to mock the kingdom.

pointing out the illusory nature of **CHARLES I**'s *promises*
in *Dictionary of National Biography* (1917–)

Pyrrhus 319–272 BC

Greek monarch, King of Epirus from 306 BC

2 One more such victory over the Romans and we are lost.

on defeating the Romans at Asculum, 279 BC
Plutarch *Parallel Lives* 'Pyrrhus' ch. 21, sect. 9

Pythagoras 580–500 BC

Greek philosopher

3 Choose rather to be strong in soul than strong of body.

Stobaeus *Sententiae*

Qianlong 1711–99

Chinese monarch, Emperor of China 1735-95

4 As your ambassador can see for himself we possess all things. I set no value on objects strange or ingenious, and have no use for your country's manufactures.

writing to **GEORGE III** *after the first British trade mission had reached Beijing*
'The First Edict' September 1793, in Pei-Kai Cheng, Michael Lestz, and Jonathan D. Spence (eds.) *The Search for Modern China: A Documentary Collection* (1999)

Francis Quarles 1592–1644

English poet

5 Our God and soldiers we alike adore
Ev'n at the brink of danger; not before:
After deliverance, both alike requited,
Our God's forgotten, and our soldiers slighted.

Divine Fancies (1632) 'Of Common Devotion'; see **OWEN** 590:22

6 I wish thee as much pleasure in the reading, as I had in the writing.

Emblems (1635) 'To the Reader'

7 The heart is a small thing, but desireth great matters. It is not sufficient for a kite's dinner, yet the whole world is not sufficient for it.

Emblems (1635) bk. 1, no. 12 'Hugo de Anima'

8 My soul, sit thou a patient looker-on;
Judge not the play before the play is done:
Her plot hath many changes; every day
Speaks a new scene; the last act crowns the play.

Emblems (1635) bk. 1, no. 15 'Respice Finem'

9 We spend our midday sweat, our midnight oil;
We tire the night in thought, the day in toil.

Emblems (1635) bk. 2, no. 2, l. 33; see **GAY** 351:12

10 Be wisely worldly, be not worldly wise.

Emblems (1635) bk. 2, no. 2, l. 46

11 Thou art my way; I wander, if thou fly;
Thou art my light; if hid, how blind am I!
Thou art my life; if thou withdraw, I die.

Emblems (1643) bk. 3, no. 7

12 He teaches to deny that faintly prays.

A Feast for Worms (1620) sect. 7, Meditation 7, l. 2

13 Man is man's A.B.C. There is none that can Read God aright, unless he first spell Man.

Hieroglyphics of the Life of Man (1638) no. 1, l. 1

14 Physicians of all men are most happy; what good success soever they have, the world proclaimeth, and what faults they commit, the earth covereth.

Hieroglyphics of the Life of Man (1638) no. 4; see **WRIGHT** 870:16

15 We'll cry both arts and learning down,
And hey! then up go we!

The Shepherd's Oracles (1646) Eclogue 11 'Song of Anarchus'

François Quesnay 1694–1774

French political economist

16 *Vous ne connaissez qu'une seule règle du commerce; c'est (pour me servir de vos propres termes) de laisser passer et de laisser faire tous les acheteurs et tous les vendeurs quelconques.*

You recognize but one rule of commerce; that is (to avail myself of your own terms) to allow free passage and freedom of action to all buyers and sellers whoever they may be.

letter from M. Alpha to Quesnay, 1767, in L. Salleron *François Quesnay et la Physiocratie* (1958) vol. 2; not found in Quesnay's own writings; see **ANONYMOUS** 22:4, **ARGENSON** 26:11

Arthur Quiller-Couch ('Q') 1863–1944

English writer and critic

17 The best is the best, though a hundred judges have declared it so.

Oxford Book of English Verse (1900) preface

18 All the old statues of Victory have wings: but Grief has no wings. She is the unwelcome lodger that squats on the hearthstone between us and the fire and will not move or be dislodged.

Armistice Day anniversary sermon, Cambridge, November 1923

Philippe Quinault 1635–88

French dramatist

19 *Qui n'a plus qu'un moment à vivre
N'a plus rien à dissimuler.*

Whoever has but a moment to live has nothing more to hide.

Atys (1676) act 1, sc. 6

W. V. O. Quine 1908–2000
American philosopher

1 On the doctrinal side, I do not see that we are farther along today than where [David] Hume left us. The Humean predicament is the human predicament.
Ontological Relativity and Other Essays (1969) ch. 3

2 It is the tension between the scientist's laws and his own attempted breaches of them that powers the engines of science and makes it forge ahead.
Quiddities (1987) p. 8 'Anomaly'

3 Students of the heavens are separable into astronomers and astrologers as readily as are the minor domestic ruminants into sheep and goats, but the separation of philosophers into sages and cranks seems to be more sensitive to frames of reference.
Theories and Things (1981) ch. 23

Quintilian *c.*AD 35–*c.*96
Roman rhetorician

4 The all-important gift of an orator is to respond to change and variety in things.
Institutio Oratoria bk. 2, ch. 13, sect. 2

5 *Satura quidem tota nostra est.*
Verse satire indeed is entirely our own.
meaning Roman as opposed to Greek
Institutio Oratoria bk. 10, ch. 1, sect. 93

6 *Ovidi Medea videtur mihi ostendere quantum ille vir praestare potuerit si ingenio suo imperare quam indulgere maluisset.*
The Medea of Ovid seems to me to show how much that man could have excelled had he chosen to rein in his cleverness rather than indulge it.
Institutio Oratoria bk. 10, ch. 1, sect. 98

The Qur'an *see* The Koran

François Rabelais *c.*1494–*c.*1553
French humanist, satirist, and physician

7 *L'appétit vient en mangeant.*
The appetite grows by eating.
Gargantua (1534) bk. 1, ch. 5; see **PROVERBS** 626:30

8 *Natura vacuum abhorret.*
Nature abhors a vacuum.
quoting, in Latin, an article of ancient wisdom
Gargantua (1534) bk. 1, ch. 5; see **PROVERBS** 639:22

9 *Fay ce que vouldras.*
Do what you like.
Gargantua (1534) bk. 1, ch. 57; see **CROWLEY** 261:14

10 *Quaestio subtilissima, utrum chimera in vacuo bombinans possit comedere secundas intentiones.*
A most subtle question: whether a chimera buzzing in a vacuum can devour second intentions.
Pantagruel bk. 2, ch. 7

11 A child is not a vase to be filled, but a fire to be lit.
attributed; see **PLUTARCH** 610:7

12 *Je vais quérir un grand peut-être ... Tirez le rideau, la farce est jouée.*
I am going to seek a great perhaps ... Bring down the curtain, the farce is played out.
last words, attributed, but probably apocryphal; Jean Fleury
Rabelais et ses oeuvres (1877) vol. 1, ch. 3, pt. 15

Yitzhak Rabin 1922–95
Israeli statesman and military leader, Prime Minister 1974–7 and 1992–5

13 We say to you today in a loud and a clear voice: enough of blood and tears. Enough.
to the Palestinians, at the signing of the Israel–Palestine Declaration
in Washington, 13 September 1993

Jean Racine 1639–99
French tragedian

14 *Je l'ai trop aimé pour ne le point haïr!*
I have loved him too much not to feel any hatred for him.
Andromaque (1667) act 2, sc. 1

15 *C'était pendant l'horreur d'une profonde nuit.*
It was during the horror of a deep night.
Athalie (1691) act 2, sc. 5

16 *Elle flotte, elle hésite; en un mot, elle est femme.*
She floats, she hesitates; in a word, she's a woman.
Athalie (1691) act 3, sc. 3

17 *Ce n'est plus une ardeur dans mes veines cachée:*
C'est Vénus tout entière à sa proie attachée.
It's no longer a burning within my veins: it's Venus entire latched onto her prey.
Phèdre (1677) act 1, sc. 3

1 *Dans le fond des forêts votre image me suit.*

Deep in the forest glade your picture chases me.

Phèdre (1677) act 2, sc. 2

2 *Tous les jours se levaient clairs et sereins pour eux.*

Every day dawned clear and untroubled for them.

Phèdre (1677) act 4, sc. 6

3 *Point d'argent, point de Suisse, et ma porte était close.*

No money, no service, and my door stayed shut.

Les Plaideurs (1668) act 1, sc. 1; see **PROVERBS** 640:7

4 *Sans argent l'honneur n'est qu'une maladie.*

Honour, without money, is just a disease.

Les Plaideurs (1668) act 1, sc. 1

5 *Passons au déluge, je vous prie.*

Let's move on to the Deluge, if you please.

Les Plaideurs (1668) act 3, sc. 1

Lord Radcliffe 1899–1977

British lawyer and public servant

6 Governments always tend to want not really a free press but a managed or well-conducted one.

in 1967; Peter Hennessy *What the Papers Never Said* (1985)

St Radegund 518–587

Frankish queen

7 If you shrink from consecrating me, and fear man more than God, the Shepherd will require His sheep's soul from your hand.

persuading Médard Bishop of Noyon to ordain her deaconess

Venantius Fortunatus *The Life of St Radegund*

James Rado 1939– and Gerome Ragni 1942–

American songwriters

8 When the moon is in the seventh house,
And Jupiter aligns with Mars,
Then peace will guide the planets,
And love will steer the stars;
This is the dawning of the age of Aquarius.

'Aquarius' (1967 song) in *Hair*

John Rae 1931–2006

English writer, teacher, and educationist

9 War is, after all, the universal perversion . . . war stories, the pornography of war.

The Custard Boys (1960) ch. 13

Thomas Rainborowe d. 1648

English soldier and parliamentarian

10 The poorest he that is in England hath a life to live as the greatest he.

during the Army debates at Putney, 29 October 1647, in C. H. Firth (ed.) *The Clarke Papers* vol. 1, Camden Society, New Series 49 (1891)

Craig Raine 1944–

English poet

11 In homes, a haunted apparatus sleeps,
that snores when you pick it up.

If the ghost cries, they carry it
to their lips and soothe it to sleep

with sounds. And yet, they wake it up
deliberately, but tickling it with a finger.

'A Martian sends a Postcard Home' (1979)

Kathleen Raine 1908–2003

English poet

12 He has married me with a ring, a ring of bright water
Whose ripples spread from the heart of the sea.

Ring of bright water *was used a a book title by Gavin Maxwell (1914–69)*

'The Marriage of Psyche' (1952)

Walter Ralegh c.1552–1618

English poet, explorer, and courtier. See also **AUBREY** 36:6

13 If all the world and love were young,
And truth in every shepherd's tongue,
These pretty pleasures might me move
To live with thee, and be thy love.

'Answer to Marlow'; see **DONNE** 288:26, **MARLOWE** 522:20

14 Now what is love? I pray thee, tell.
It is that fountain and that well,
Where pleasure and repentance dwell.

'A Description of Love'

15 Say to the court, it glows
And shines like rotten wood;
Say to the church, it shows
What's good, and doth no good:
If church and court reply,
Then give them both the lie.

'The Lie' (1608)

16 Tell zeal it wants devotion;
Tell love it is but lust;
Tell time it metes but motion;
Tell flesh it is but dust:
And wish them not reply,
For thou must give the lie.

'The Lie' (1608)

17 From thence our kind hard-hearted is, enduring pain and care;
Approving that our bodies of a stony nature are.

translation of Ovid *Metamorphoses* bk. 1, l. 414; see **OVID** 590:7

18 Only we die in earnest, that's no jest.

'On the Life of Man'

19 Give me my scallop-shell of quiet,
My staff of faith to walk upon,
My scrip of joy, immortal diet,
My bottle of salvation,
My gown of glory, hope's true gage,

And thus I'll take my pilgrimage.
'The Passionate Man's Pilgrimage' (1604)

1 Our passions are most like to floods and
streams;
The shallow murmur, but the deep are dumb.
'Sir Walter Ralegh to the Queen' (1655)

2 Three things there be that prosper all apace,
And flourish while they are asunder far;
But on a day, they meet all in a place,
And when they meet, they one another mar.

And they be these: the Wood, the Weed, the
Wag:
The Wood is that that makes the gallows tree;
The Weed is that that strings the hangman's bag;
The Wag, my pretty knave, betokens thee.
'Sir Walter Ralegh to his Son'

3 As you came from the holy land
Of Walsinghame,
Met you not with my true love
By the way as you came?

How shall I know your true love,
That have met many one
As I went to the holy land,
That have come, that have gone?
'Walsinghame'

4 But true love is a durable fire,
In the mind ever burning,
Never sick, never old, never dead,
From itself never turning.
'Walsinghame'

5 Fain would I climb, yet fear I to fall.
line written on a window-pane, in Thomas Fuller *History of
the Worthies of England* (1662) 'Devonshire'; see **ELIZABETH I**
312:14

6 Even such is Time, which takes in trust
Our youth, our joys, and all we have,
And pays us but with age and dust;
Who in the dark and silent grave,
When we have wandered all our ways,
Shuts up the story of our days:
And from which earth, and grave, and dust,
The Lord shall raise me up, I trust.
written the night before his death, and found in his Bible in
the Gate-house at Westminster

7 Whoso taketh in hand to frame any state or
government ought to presuppose that all men
are evil, and at occasions will show themselves
so to be.
The Cabinet-Council (1658) ch. 26

8 Whosoever commands the sea commands the
trade; whosoever commands the trade of the
world commands the riches of the world, and
consequently the world itself.
'A Discourse of the Invention of Ships, Anchors, Compass,
&c.'

9 [History] hath triumphed over time, which
besides it, nothing but eternity hath triumphed
over.
The History of the World (1614) preface

10 Whosoever, in writing a modern history, shall
follow truth too near the heels, it may happily
strike out his teeth.
The History of the World (1614) preface

11 O eloquent, just, and mighty Death! . . . thou
hast drawn together all the farstretched
greatness, all the pride, cruelty, and ambition of
man, and covered it all over with these two
narrow words, *Hic jacet* [Here lies].
The History of the World (1614) bk. 5, ch. 6

12 'Tis a sharp remedy, but a sure one for all ills.
on feeling the edge of the axe prior to his execution
D. Hume *History of Great Britain* (1754) vol. 1, ch. 4

13 So the heart be right, it is no matter which way
the head lies.
*at his execution, on being asked which way he preferred to
lay his head*
W. Stebbing *Sir Walter Raleigh* (1891) ch. 30

14 I have a long journey to take, and must bid the
company farewell.
last words; E. Thompson *Sir Walter Raleigh* (1935) ch. 26

Walter Raleigh 1861–1922
English lecturer and critic

15 In examinations those who do not wish to know
ask questions of those who cannot tell.
Laughter from a Cloud (1923) 'Some Thoughts on
Examinations'

16 I wish I loved the Human Race;
I wish I loved its silly face;
I wish I liked the way it walks;
I wish I liked the way it talks;
And when I'm introduced to one
I wish I thought *What Jolly Fun!*
'Wishes of an Elderly Man' (1923)

17 An anthology is like all the plums and orange
peel picked out of a cake.
letter to Mrs Robert Bridges, 15 January 1915

Srinivasa Ramanujan 1887–1920
Indian mathematician

18 *replying to G. H.* **HARDY**'s *suggestion that the number of a
taxi-cab* (1729) *was 'dull':*
No, it is a very interesting number; it is the
smallest number expressible as a sum of two
cubes in two different ways.
the two ways being 1^3+12^3 *and* 9^3+10^3
in *Proceedings of the London Mathematical Society* 26 May 1921

19 An equation for me has no meaning unless it
expresses a thought of God.
Robert Kanigel *The Man Who Knew Infinity* (1992)

Michael Ramsey 1904–88
**British clergyman, Archbishop of York (1956–61) and
Canterbury (1961–74)**

20 I should love to think of a black Archbishop of
York holding a mission to the University of

Oxford, and telling a future generation of the scandal and glory of the Church.

address at the Sheldonian Theatre, Oxford, February 1960, in *Introducing the Christian Faith* (1961); see also **SENTAMU** 692:22

Ayn Rand 1905–82

American writer

1 Civilization is the progress toward a society of privacy. The savage's noble existence is public, ruled by the laws of his tribe. Civilization is the process of setting man free from men.
The Fountainhead (1947)

John Randolph 1773–1833

American politician

2 Never were abilities so much below mediocrity so well rewarded; no, not when Caligula's horse was made Consul.
on John Quincy **ADAMS**'s *appointment of Richard Rush as Secretary of the Treasury*
speech, 1 February 1828

3 He is a man of splendid abilities but utterly corrupt. He shines and stinks like rotten mackerel by moonlight.
of Edward Livingston
W. Cabell Bruce *John Randolph of Roanoke* (1923) vol. 2

Ian Rankin 1960–

Scottish novelist

4 We can't really demolish it until they finish building it.
on the Scottish parliament building
in *Independent* 20 July 2002

John Crowe Ransom 1888–1974

American poet and critic

5 The lazy geese, like a snow cloud
Dripping their snow on the green grass,
Tricking and stopping, sleepy and proud,
Who cried in goose, alas.
'Bells for John Whiteside's Daughter' (1924)

6 Here lies a lady of beauty and high degree.
Of chills and fever she died, of fever and chills,
The delight of her husband, her aunts, an infant of three,
And of medicos marvelling sweetly on her ills.
'Here Lies a Lady' (1924)

7 Two evils, monstrous either one apart,
Possessed me, and were long and loath at going:
A cry of Absence, Absence, in the heart,
And in the wood the furious winter blowing.
'Winter Remembered' (1945)

Arthur Ransome 1884–1967

English novelist, writer for children, and journalist

8 BETTER DROWNED THAN DUFFERS IF NOT DUFFERS WONT DROWN.
Swallows and Amazons (1930) ch. 1

Raoul Glabar *c.*985–*c.*1046

French Cluniac monk and chronicler

9 After the above-mentioned millennium which is now about three years past, there occurred throughout the whole world . . . a rebuilding of church basilicas . . . It was as if the whole earth, having cast off the old by shaking itself, were clothing itself everywhere in a white robe of churches.
of the rebuilding of churches in the 11th century
Histories bk 3, ch. 4

Frederic Raphael 1931–

American-born novelist and screenwriter. See also **SMITH** 756:16

10 Your idea of fidelity is not having more than one man in bed at the same time.
Darling (1965) ch. 18

11 City of perspiring dreams.
of Cambridge
The Glittering Prizes (1976) ch. 3 ; see **ARNOLD** 30:25

Joe Raposo 1937–89

American songwriter

12 It's not that easy being green.
sung by the Kermit the frog
'Bein' Green', song from Jim Henson's *Sesame Street* (TV show, 1969–)

Dan Rather 1931–

American journalist

13 I worry that patriotism run amok will trample the very values that the country seeks to defend.
in *Independent* 18 May 2002

Gerald Ratner 1949–

English businessman

14 We even sell a pair of earrings for under £1, which is cheaper than a prawn sandwich from Marks & Spencers. But I have to say the earrings probably won't last as long.
speech to the Institute of Directors, Albert Hall, 23 April 1991

Terence Rattigan 1911–77

English dramatist

15 Giants can be surprised. And they can't move as fast as pygmies.
Adventure Story (1949) act 1, sc. 1

16 Do you know what 'le vice Anglais'—the English vice—really is? Not flagellation, not pederasty—whatever the French believe it to be. It's our refusal to admit our emotions. We think they demean us, I suppose.
In Praise of Love (1973) act 2

Gwen Raverat 1885–1957
English wood-engraver

1 Ladies were ladies in those days; they did not do things themselves.
Period Piece (1952) ch. 5

Herbert Read 1893–1968
English art historian

2 Do not judge this movement kindly. It is not just another amusing stunt. It is defiant—the desperate act of men too profoundly convinced of the rottenness of our civilization to want to save a shred of its respectability.
International Surrealist Exhibition Catalogue, New Burlington Galleries, London, 11 June–4 July 1936, introduction

3 Images of flight, of ragged claws 'scuttling across the floors of silent seas', of excoriated flesh, frustrated sex, the geometry of fear.
on twentieth-century British sculpture
introduction to catalogue of Venice Biennale, 1952; Richard Calvocoressi *British Sculpture in the Twentieth Century* (1981); see ELIOT 310:9

4 Art is . . . pattern informed by sensibility.
The Meaning of Art (1955) ch. 1

5 Lorca was killed, singing,
and Fox who was my friend.
The rhythm returns: the song
which has no end.
'The Heart Conscripted' (1938)

6 I saw him stab
And stab again
A well-killed Boche.
This is the happy warrior,
This is he . . .
Naked Warriors (1919) 'The Scene of War, 4. The Happy Warrior'; see WORDSWORTH 865:6

Charles Reade 1814–84
English novelist and dramatist

7 *Courage, mon ami, le diable est mort!*
Take courage, my friend, the devil is dead!
The Cloister and the Hearth (1861) ch. 24, and *passim*

8 Sow an act, and you reap a habit. Sow a habit and you reap a character. Sow a character, and you reap a destiny.
attributed; in *Notes and Queries* (9th Series) vol. 12, 17 October 1903

Nancy Reagan 1923–
American actress and wife of Ronald REAGAN, First Lady of the US, 1981–9. See also SLOGANS 755:8

9 A woman is like a teabag—only in hot water do you realize how strong she is.
in *Observer* 29 March 1981

10 If the President has a bully pulpit, then the First Lady has a white glove pulpit . . . more refined, restricted, ceremonial, but it's a pulpit all the same.
in *New York Times* 10 March 1988; see ROOSEVELT 668:1

Ronald Reagan 1911–2004
American Republican statesman, 40th President of the US 1981–9. See also DEMPSEY 273:2, GIPP 359:5

11 Politics is supposed to be the second oldest profession. I have come to realize that it bears a very close resemblance to the first.
at a conference in Los Angeles, 2 March 1977; in Bill Adler *Reagan Wit* (1981) ch. 5; see KIPLING 468:4

12 I paid for this microphone.
in 1980, debating for the Republican nomination against George BUSH; the moderator had ordered Reagan's microphone turned off when he asked for the participation of other candidates, and the refusal to allow this was held to be very damaging to Bush
Lou Cannon *Ronald Reagan* (1982)

13 *President CARTER had described a proposal for a national health insurance plan*
JIMMY CARTER: Governor Reagan, again, typically is against such a proposal.
RONALD REAGAN: There you go again!
as Republican challenger debating with President Carter in the 1980 presidential campaign; in *Times* 30 October 1980

14 You can tell a lot about a fellow's character by his way of eating jellybeans.
in *New York Times* 15 January 1981

15 An evil empire.
of the Soviet Union
speech to the National Association of Evangelicals, 8 March 1983; in *New York Times* 9 March 1983

16 We are especially not going to tolerate these attacks from outlaw states run by the strangest collection of misfits, Looney Tunes, and squalid criminals since the advent of the Third Reich.
speech following the hijack of a US plane, 8 July 1985, in *New York Times* 9 July 1985

17 We will never forget them, nor the last time we saw them this morning, as they prepared for the journey and waved goodbye and 'slipped the surly bonds of earth' to 'touch the face of God.'
after the loss of the space shuttle Challenger *with all its crew*
broadcast from the Oval Office, 28 January 1986; see MAGEE 514:15

18 Mr Gorbachev, tear down this wall!
at the Brandenburg Gate in West Berlin, 12 June 1987

19 We have listened to the wisdom in an old Russian maxim. And I'm sure you're familiar with it, Mr General Secretary. The maxim is . . . 'trust, but verify'.
to Mikhail Gorbachev at the signing of the INF treaty on arms limitation, 8 December 1987, and used frequently thereafter

20 I now begin the journey that will lead me into the sunset of my life.
statement to the American people revealing that he had Alzheimer's disease
in *Daily Telegraph* 5 January 1995

Erell Reaves

21 Lady of Spain, I adore you.
Right from the night I first saw you,

My heart has been yearning for you,
What else could any heart do?
'Lady of Spain' (1913 song)

Red Cloud (Mahpiua Luta) 1822–1909

Sioux chief

1 You have heard the sound of the white soldier's
axe upon the Little Piney. His presence here is
. . . an insult to the spirits of our ancestors. Are
we then to give up their sacred graves to be
ploughed for corn? Dakotas, I am for war!
speech at council at Fort Laramie, 1866; Charles A. Eastman
Indian Heroes and Great Chieftains (1918)

John Redmond 1856–1918

Irish politician and nationalist leader

2 *in the spring of 1914, having been asked if anything could
now prevent Home Rule:*

A European war might do it.
in *Dictionary of National Biography* (1917–)

Henry Reed 1914–86

English poet and dramatist

3 As we get older we do not get any younger.
Seasons return, and today I am fifty-five,
And this time last year I was fifty-four,
And this time next year I shall be sixty-two.
'Chard Whitlow (Mr Eliot's Sunday Evening Postscript)' (1946)

4 Today we have naming of parts. Yesterday,
We had daily cleaning. And tomorrow morning,
We shall have what to do after firing. But today,
Today we have naming of parts. Japonica
Glistens like coral in all of the neighbour
gardens,
And today we have naming of parts.
'Lessons of the War: 1, Naming of Parts' (1946)

5 They call it easing the Spring: it is perfectly easy
If you have any strength in your thumb: like the
bolt,
And the breech, and the cocking-piece, and the
point of balance,
Which in our case we have not got.
'Lessons of the War: 1, Naming of Parts' (1946)

6 We cannot learn to forget as sometimes we
learn to remember,
To compose an oblivion like a memory,
To capture carefully an empty future,
As we recapture, fragment by fragment, the
past.
'Tintagel' (1946)

7 And the sooner the tea's out of the way, the
sooner we can get out the gin, eh?
Private Life of Hilda Tablet (1954 radio play) in *Hilda Tablet and
Others* (1971)

8 Of course we've all *dreamed* of reviving the
castrati; but it's needed Hilda to take the first
practical steps towards making them a reality . . .
She's drawn up a list of well-known singers who

she thinks would benefit . . . It's only a question
of getting them to agree.
Private Life of Hilda Tablet (1954 radio play) in *Hilda Tablet and
Others* (1971)

9 I have known her pass the whole evening
without mentioning a single book, or *in fact
anything unpleasant*, at all.
A Very Great Man Indeed (1953 radio play) in *Hilda Tablet and
Others* (1971)

John Reed 1887–1920

American journalist and revolutionary

10 Ten days that shook the world.
title of book (1919)

Joseph Reed 1741–85

American Revolutionary politician

11 I am not worth purchasing, but such as I am,
the King of Great Britain is not rich enough to
do it.
*replying to an offer from Governor George Johnstone of
£10,000, and any office in the Colonies in the King's gift, if
he were able successfully to promote a Union between the
UK and the US*
reply as recorded in a declaration of Congress, 11 August
1778; the earliest version is: 'My influence is but small, but
were it as great as Governor Johnstone would insinuate, the
King of Great Britain has nothing within his gift that would
tempt me', reply to Mrs Elizabeth Ferguson, 21 June 1778; W.
B. Read *Life and Correspondence of Joseph Reed* (1847) vol. 1,
ch. 18

Max Reger 1873–1916

German composer

12 I am sitting in the smallest room of my house. I
have your review before me. In a moment it will
be behind me.
*responding to a savage review by Rudolph Louis in
Münchener Neueste Nachrichten, 7 February 1906*
Nicolas Slonimsky *Lexicon of Musical Invective* (1953)

Charles A. Reich 1928–

American jurist

13 The greening of America.
title of book (1970)

Keith Reid 1946–

English pop singer and songwriter

14 Her face, at first . . . just ghostly
Turned a whiter shade of pale.
'A Whiter Shade of Pale' (1967 song)

Thomas Reid 1710–96

Scottish philosopher

15 There is no greater impediment to the
advancement of knowledge than the ambiguity
of words.
Essays on the Intellectual Powers of Man essay 1, ch. 1

Lord Reith 1889–1971

British administrator and politician, first general manager (1922–7) and first director-general (1927–38) of the BBC

1 He who prides himself on giving what he thinks the public wants is often creating a fictitious demand for lower standards which he will then satisfy.
memo to Crawford Committee 1926; Andrew Boyle *Only the Wind Will Listen* (1972)

2 By the time the civil service has finished drafting a document to give effect to a principle, there may be little of the principle left.
Into the Wind (1949)

3 When people feel deeply, impartiality is bias.
Into the Wind (1949)

Erich Maria Remarque 1898–1970

German novelist

4 All quiet on the western front.
English title of *Im Westen nichts Neues* (1929 novel); see BEERS 66:7, MCCLELLAN 509:11

Ernest Renan 1823–92

French philologist and historian

5 Before French culture, German culture, Italian culture, there is human culture.
'Qu'est-ce qu'une nation', address given in 1882

Jules Renard 1864–1910

French novelist and dramatist

6 *Les bourgeois, ce sont les autres.*
The bourgeois are other people.
diary, 28 January 1890, in *Oeuvres Complètes* (1925–7) vol. 5

Montague John Rendall 1862–1950

English member of the first BBC Board of Governors

7 Nation shall speak peace unto nation.
motto of the BBC; see BIBLE 91:21

Jean Renoir 1894–1979

French film director

8 Is it possible to succeed without any act of betrayal?
My Life and My Films (1974) 'Nana'

Pierre Auguste Renoir 1841–1919

French painter. See also MISQUOTATIONS 548:2

9 *C'étaient des fous, mais ils avaient cette petite flamme qui ne s'éteint pas.*
They were madmen; but they had in them that little flame which is not to be snuffed out.
on the men of the French Commune
Jean Renoir *Renoir, My Father* (translated by R. and D. Weaver, 1962) ch. 12

Jean-François Paul de Gondi, Cardinal de Retz 1613–79

French cleric and politician

10 There is nothing in the world which does not have its decisive moment, and the masterpiece of good management is to recognize and grasp this moment.
Mémoires (1717) bk. 2

11 There are no small steps in great affairs.
Mémoires (1717) bk. 2

12 A man who does not trust himself will never really trust anybody.
Mémoires (1717) bk. 3

13 To reduce the force of envy is the greatest of all secrets.
Mémoires (1717) bk. 4

Paul Revere 1735–1818

American patriot. On Revere: see LONGFELLOW 499:25

14 [We agreed] that if the British went out by water, we would show two lanterns in the North Church steeple; and if by land, one as a signal; for we were apprehensive it would be difficult to cross the Charles River or get over Boston Neck.
signals to be used if the British troops moved out of Boston; see LONGFELLOW 500:1
arrangements agreed with the Charlestown Committee of Safety on 16 April, 1775

Charles Revson 1906–75

American businessman

15 In the factory we make cosmetics; in the store we sell hope.
A. Tobias *Fire and Ice* (1976)

Frederic Reynolds 1764–1841

English dramatist

16 It is better to have written a damned play, than no play at all—it snatches a man from obscurity.
The Dramatist (1789) act 1, sc. 1

Joshua Reynolds 1723–92

English painter. On Reynolds: see BLAKE 124:8, GAINSBOROUGH 347:3, GOLDSMITH 364:22, WALPOLE 838:1

17 Few have been taught to any purpose who have not been their own teachers.
Discourses on Art (ed. R. Wark, 1975) no. 2 (11 December 1769)

18 If you have great talents, industry will improve them: if you have but moderate abilities, industry will supply their deficiency.
Discourses on Art (ed. R. Wark, 1975) no. 2 (11 December 1769)

19 A mere copier of nature can never produce anything great.
Discourses on Art (ed. R. Wark, 1975) no. 3 (14 December 1770)

1 Could we teach taste or genius by rules, they would be no longer taste and genius.
  Discourses on Art (ed. R. Wark, 1975) no. 3 (14 December 1770)

2 The value and rank of every art is in proportion to the mental labour employed in it, or the mental pleasure produced by it.
  Discourses on Art (ed. R. Wark, 1975) no. 4 (10 December 1771)

3 Genius . . . is the child of imitation.
  Discourses on Art (ed. R. Wark, 1975) no. 6 (10 December 1774)

4 The mind is but a barren soil; a soil which is soon exhausted, and will produce no crop, or only one, unless it be continually fertilized and enriched with foreign matter.
  Discourses on Art (ed. R. Wark, 1975) no. 6 (10 December 1774)

5 Art in its perfection is not ostentatious; it lies hid, and works its effect, itself unseen.
  Discourses on Art (ed. R. Wark, 1975) no. 6 (10 December 1774)

6 It is the very same taste which relishes a demonstration in geometry, that is pleased with the resemblance of a picture to an original, and touched with the harmony of music.
  Discourses on Art (ed. R. Wark, 1975) no. 7 (10 December 1776)

7 I should desire that the last words which I should pronounce in this Academy, and from this place, might be the name of—Michael Angelo.
  Discourses on Art (ed. R. Wark, 1975) no. 15 (10 December 1790)

8 Distinction is what we all seek after, and the world does set a value on them [titles].
  written in 1791, C. R. Leslie *The Life and Times of Sir Joshua Reynolds* (1865) vol. 2, ch. 10

9 There is no easy way of becoming a good painter.
  John Constable, letter to John Dunthorne, 29 May 1802; R. G. W. Clive *John Constable* (1903); see **CONSTABLE** 249:16

Malvina Reynolds 1900–78
American songwriter

10 Little boxes on the hillside . . .
  And they're all made out of ticky-tacky
  And they all look just the same.
  on the tract houses in the hills to the south of San Francisco
  'Little Boxes' (1962 song)

Cecil Rhodes 1853–1902
South African statesman

11 Ask any man what nationality he would prefer to be, and ninety-nine out of a hundred will tell you that they would prefer to be Englishmen.
  Gordon Le Sueur *Cecil Rhodes* (1913)

12 So little done, so much to do.
  on the day of his death; Lewis Michell *Life of Rhodes* (1910) vol. 2, ch. 39; see **TENNYSON** 795:18

Jean Rhys (Ella Gwendolen Rees Williams) c.1890–1979
British novelist and short-story writer

13 We can't all be happy, we can't all be rich, we can't all be lucky—and it would be so much less fun if we were . . . Some must cry so that others may be able to laugh the more heartily.
  Good Morning, Midnight (1939) pt. 1

14 The perpetual hunger to be beautiful and that thirst to be loved which is the real curse of Eve.
  The Left Bank (1927) 'Illusion'

15 Only the hopeless are starkly sincere and . . . only the unhappy can either give or take sympathy.
  The Left Bank (1927) 'In the Rue de l'Arrivée'

16 The feeling of Sunday is the same everywhere, heavy, melancholy, standing still. Like when they say 'As it was in the beginning, is now, and ever shall be, world without end.'
  Voyage in the Dark (1934) ch. 4, pt. 1

17 A doormat in a world of boots.
  describing herself
  in *Guardian* 6 December 1990

David Ricardo 1772–1823
English economist

18 Rent is that portion of the earth, which is paid to the landlord for the use of the original and indestructible powers of the soil.
  On the Principles of Political Economy and Taxation (1817) ch. 2

Alice Caldwell Rice 1870–1942
American humorist

19 Life is made up of desires that seem big and vital one minute and little and absurd the next. I guess we get what's best for us in the end.
  A Romance of Billy-Goat Hill (1912) ch. 2

Grantland Rice 1880–1954
American sports writer

20 For when the One Great Scorer comes to mark against your name,
  He writes—not that you won or lost—but how you played the Game.
  'Alumnus Football' (1941)

21 All wars are planned by old men
  In council rooms apart.
  'The Two Sides of War' (1955)

22 Outlined against a blue-grey October sky, the Four Horsemen rode again. In dramatic lore they were known as Famine, Pestilence, Destruction, and Death. These are only aliases. Their real names are Stuhldreher, Miller, Crowley, and Layden. They formed the crest of the South Bend cyclone before which another fighting Army football team was swept over the precipice.

report of football match between US Military Academy at West Point NY and University of Notre Dame

in *New York Tribune* 19 October 1924

Stephen Rice 1637–1715

Irish lawyer

1 I will drive a coach and six horses through the Act of Settlement.

W. King *State of the Protestants of Ireland* (1672) ch. 3, sect. 8

Tim Rice 1944–

English songwriter

2 Prove to me that you're no fool
Walk across my swimming pool.

Jesus Christ Superstar (1970) 'Herod's Song'; music by Andrew Lloyd Webber

Mandy Rice-Davies 1944–

English model and showgirl

3 He would, wouldn't he?

on hearing that Lord Astor denied her allegations, concerning himself and his house parties at Cliveden

at the trial of Stephen Ward, 29 June 1963; in *Guardian* 1 July 1963

Adrienne Rich 1923–

American poet and critic

4 The thing I came for:
the wreck and not the story of the wreck
the thing itself and not the myth.

'Diving into the Wreck' (1973)

5 Memory says: Want to do right? Don't count on me.

'Eastern War Time' (1991)

6 I'm accused of child-death of drinking blood . . .
there is spit on my sleeve there are phonecalls in the night . . .

'Eastern War Time' (1991)

7 Our friends were not unearthly beautiful.
Nor spoke with tongues of gold; our lovers blundered
Now and again when most we sought perfection,
Or hid in cupboards when the heavens thundered.

'Ideal Landscape' (1955)

Ann Richards 1933–2006

American Democratic politician

8 Poor George, he can't help it—he was born with a silver foot in his mouth.

of George BUSH

keynote speech at the Democratic convention, 1988; in *Independent* 20 July 1988

Frank Richards (Charles Hamilton)
1876–1961

English writer for boys

9 The fat greedy owl of the Remove.

'Billy Bunter' in the *Magnet* (1909) vol. 3, no. 72 'The Greyfriars Photographer'

I. A. Richards 1893–1979

English literary critic

10 It [poetry] is capable of saving us; it is a perfectly possible means of overcoming chaos.

Science and Poetry (1926) ch. 7

Justin Richardson 1900–75

British poet

11 For years a secret shame destroyed my peace—
I'd not read Eliot, Auden or MacNeice.
But then I had a thought that brought me hope—
Neither had Chaucer, Shakespeare, Milton, Pope.

'Take Heart, Illiterates' (1966)

Samuel Richardson 1689–1761

English novelist. On Richardson: see DIDEROT 282:17, JOHNSON 441:4

12 I have known a bird actually starve itself, and die with grief, at its being caught and caged—But never did I meet with a lady who was so silly . . . And yet we must all own that it is more difficult to catch a bird than a lady.

Clarissa (1747–8) vol. 3, letter 75

13 Love gratified is love satisfied—and love satisfied is indifference begun.

Clarissa (1747–8) vol. 4, letter 23

14 The affair is over. Clarissa lives.

announcement by Lovelace of his successful seduction of Clarissa

Clarissa (1747–8) vol. 5, letter 22

15 A feeling heart is a blessing that no one, who has it, would be without; and it is a moral security of innocence; since the heart that is able to partake of the distress of another, cannot wilfully give it.

History of Sir Charles Grandison (1754) vol. 3, letter 32

16 I . . . am such a sorry pruner, though greatly luxuriant, that I am apt to add three pages for one I take away.

letter to Edward Young, c.1744

17 His spurious brat, Tom Jones.

of FIELDING

letter to Thomas Edwards, 21 February 1752

18 Instruction, Madam, is the pill; amusement is the gilding.

letter to Lady Echlin, 22 September 1755

Cardinal Richelieu 1585–1642
French cleric and statesman

1 If you give me six lines written by the hand of the most honest of men, I will find something in them which will hang him.
attributed

Mordecai Richler 1931–2001
Canadian writer

2 I'm world famous, Dr Parks said, all over Canada.
The Incomparable Atuk (1963)

3 Wherever I travel I'm too late. The orgy has moved elsewhere.
Shovelling Trouble (1972) 'A Sense of the Ridiculous'

Hans Richter 1843–1916
German conductor

4 Up with your damned nonsense will I put twice, or perhaps once, but sometimes always, by God, never.
attributed

Johann Paul Friedrich Richter ('Jean Paul') 1763–1825
German novelist

5 Providence has given to the French the empire of the land, to the English that of the sea, and to the Germans that of—the air!
Thomas Carlyle 'Jean Paul Friedrich Richter' in *Edinburgh Review* no. 91 (1827)

George Ridding 1828–1904
English Bishop of Southwell from 1884

6 I feel a feeling which I feel you all feel.
sermon in the London Mission, 1885; in G. W. E. Russell *Collections and Recollections* (1898) ch. 29

Laura Riding 1901–91
American poet and novelist

7 Without dressmakers to connect
The good-will of the body
With the purpose of the head,
We should be two worlds
Instead of a world and its shadow
The flesh.
'Because of Clothes' (1938)

8 Art, whose honesty must work through artifice, cannot avoid cheating truth.
Selected Poems: In Five Sets (1975) preface

Nicholas Ridley 1929–93
British Conservative politician

9 *of the European Community:*
This is all a German racket, designed to take over the whole of Europe.
in *Spectator* 14 July 1990

Louis Riel 1844–85
Canadian Métis political leader, executed for treason after leading a Métis rebellion

10 People say the native stands on the edge of a chasm. It is not he who stands on the edge of a chasm; his claims are not false. They are just . . . Every step the Indian takes is based on a profound sense of fairness.
diary, 6 May 1885

11 I have been hunted as an elk for fifteen years.
speaking at the end of his trial, 1 August 1885; *The Queen vs. Louis Riel* (1886)

12 Every day in which I have neglected to prepare myself to die was a day of mental alienation.
interview published in the *Regina Leader* shortly before his execution by hanging on 16 November 1885

Rig Veda
a collection of hymns in early Sanskrit, composed in the 2nd millenium BC

13 We meditate on the lovely light of the god, Savitri:
May it stimulate our thoughts!
The Gāyatrī bk. 3, hymn 62, v. 10

14 Whence this creation has arisen—perhaps it formed itself, or perhaps it did not—the one who looks down on it, in the highest heaven, only he knows—or perhaps he does not know.
Creation Hymn bk. 10, hymn 129, v. 7

15 When they divided the Man, into how many parts did they apportion him? What did they call his mouth, his two arms and thighs and feet?
His mouth became the Brahman; his arms were made into the Warrior, his thighs the People, and from his feet the Servants were born.
Hymn of Man bk. 10, hymn 190, v. 11

Rainer Maria Rilke 1875–1926
German poet

16 *Wer sass nicht bang vor seines Herzen Vorhang?*
Who has not sat nervously before the stage curtain of his heart?
Duineser Elegien no. 4

17　　　　　*Alles*
Ist nicht es selbst.
Everything is not itself.
Duineser Elegien no. 4

18 *Wer hat uns also umgedreht, dass wir,*
was wir auch tun, in jener Haltung sind
von einem, welcher fortgeht? Wie er auf
dem letzten Hügel, der ihm ganz sein Tal
noch einmal zeigt, sich wendet, anhält, weilt—,
So leben wir und nehmen immer Abschied.
Who's turned us around like this, so that we always,
do what we may, retain the attitude
of someone who's departing? Just as he,

on the last hill, that shows him all his valley
for the last time, will turn and stop and linger,
We live our lives, for ever taking leave.
: *Duineser Elegien* (translated by J. B. Leishman and Stephen
Spender, 1948) no. 8

1 *Wir haben, wo wir lieben, ja nur dies:*
einander lassen; denn dass wir uns halten,
das fällt uns leicht und ist nicht erst zu lernen.

We need in love to practise only this:
letting each other go. For holding on
comes easily; we do not need to learn it.
: *Requiem für eine Freundin* ('Requiem for a Friend')

2 *Er ist einer der bleibenden Boten,*
der noch weit in die Türen der Toten
Schalen mit rühmlichen Früchten hält.

He is one of the staying messengers
Who still holds far into the doors of the dead
bowls of fruit worthy of praise.
: 'Sonnets to Orpheus', first part (c.1922)

3 A work of art is good if it has grown out of
necessity.
: *Letters to a Young Poet* (1929) 17 February 1903 (translated by
Reginald Snell)

4 Works of art are of an infinite solitariness, and
nothing is less likely to bring us near to them
than criticism. Only love can apprehend and
hold them, and can be just towards them.
: *Letters to a Young Poet* (1929) 23 April 1903 (translated by
Reginald Snell)

5 Love consists in this, that two solitudes protect
and touch and greet each other.
: Two solitudes *was the title of a novel* (1945) *by Hugh*
MacLennan (1907–90)
: *Letters to a Young Poet* (1929) 14 May 1904 (translated by
Hugh MacLennan)

6 People have already had to rethink so many
concepts of motion, and they will also gradually
come to realize that what we call fate does not
come into us from the outside, but emerges
from us.
: *Letters to a Young Poet* (1929) 12 August 1904 (translated by
Stephen Mitchell)

7 I hold this to be the highest task for a bond
between two people: that each protects the
solitude of the other.
: letter to Paula Modersohn-Becker, 12 February 1902, in
Gesammelte Briefe (1904) vol. 1

8 I don't think of work, only of gradually
regaining my health through reading, rereading,
reflecting.
: letter, c.1911; Donald Prater *A Ringing Glass* (1986)

Arthur Rimbaud 1854–91
French poet

9 *Plus douce qu'aux enfants la chair des pommes*
surettes,
L'eau verte pénétra ma coque de sapin.

Sweeter than the flesh of tart apples to children,
the green water penetrates my wooden hull.
: 'Le Bâteau ivre' (1883)

10 . . . *Je me suis baigné dans le Poème*
De la Mer, infusé d'astres, et lactescent,
Dévorant les azurs verts.

I have bathed in the Poem of the Sea, steeped in
stars, and milky, devouring the green azures.
: 'Le Bâteau ivre' (1883)

11 *J'ai vu le soleil bas, taché d'horreurs mystiques*
Illuminant de longs figements violets,
Pareils à des acteurs de drames très-antiques.

I have seen the sun set, stained with mystic
horrors, illuminating the long violet [blood-]
clots, just like actors in very ancient plays.
: 'Le Bâteau ivre' (1883)

12 *Je regrette l'Europe aux anciens parapets!*

I pine for Europe of the ancient parapets!
: 'Le Bâteau ivre' (1883)

13 *Je m'en allais, les poings dans mes poches crevées;*
Mon paletot aussi devenait idéal.

I was walking along, hands in holey pockets; my
overcoat also was entering the realms of the
ideal.
: 'Ma Bohème' (1870)

14 *La vie est la farce à mener par tous.*

Life is the farce which everyone has to perform.
: *A Season in Hell* (1873)

15 *La vraie vie est absente.*

Real life is elsewhere.
: *A Season in Hell* (1873)

16 *A l'aurore, armés d'une ardente patience, nous*
entrerons aux splendides villes.

At dawn, armed with a burning patience, we
shall enter the splendid cities.
: *A Season in Hell* (1873)

17 *Ô saisons, ô châteaux!*
Quelle âme est sans défauts?
Ô saisons, ô châteaux,
J'ai fait la magique étude
Du bonheur, que nul n'élude.

O seasons, O castles! What soul is without fault?
I have made the magic study of good fortune
which not one eludes.
: 'Ô saisons, ô châteaux' (1872)

18 *A noir, E blanc, I rouge, U vert, O bleu: voyelles,*
Je dirais quelque jour vos naissances latentes . . .
I, pourpres, sang craché, rire des lèvres belles
Dans la colère ou les ivresses pénitentes.

A black, E white, I red, U green, O blue: vowels,
some day I will tell of the births that may be
yours. I, purples, coughed-up blood, laughter of
beautiful lips in anger or penitent drunkennesses.
: 'Voyelles' (1870)

César Ritz 1850–1918
Swiss hotel proprietor

19 *Le client n'a jamais tort.*

The customer is never wrong.
: R. Nevill and C. E. Jerningham *Piccadilly to Pall Mall* (1908);
see **PROVERBS** 629:31

Antoine de Rivarol 1753–1801

French man of letters

1 *Ce qui n'est pas clair n'est pas français.*
What is not clear is not French.
Discours sur l'Universalité de la Langue Française (1784)

Joan Riviere b. 1883

2 Civilization and its discontents.
title given to her translation of Sigmund **FREUD**'s *Das Unbehagen in der Kultur* (1930)

Alain Robbe-Grillet 1922–2008

French novelist

3 *De la commode à la table il y a six pas: trois pas jusqu'à la cheminée et trois autres ensuite. Il y a cinq pas de la table au coin du lit; quatre pas du lit à la commode. Le chemin qui va de la commode à la table n'est pas tout à fait rectiligne: il s'incurve légèrement pour passer plus près de la cheminée.*
From the chest of drawers to the table is six steps; three to the fireplace and three more after that. It is five steps from the table to the corner of the bed; four steps from the bed to the chest of drawers. The path from the chest of drawers to the table is not quite straight: it curves gently to pass nearer the fireplace.
In the Labyrinth (1959) translated by Christine Brooke-Rose

Lord Robbins 1898–1984

English economist

4 Economics is the science which studies human behaviour as a relationship between ends and scarce means which have alternative uses.
Essay on the Nature and Significance of Economic Science (1932) ch. 1, sect. 3

Robin Robertson 1955–

Scottish poet

5 then bite the tongue out by the root . . .
and chew, never swallow.
This is not sex, remember;
you are eating the sea.
'Oyster' (1997)

Maximilien Robespierre 1758–94

French revolutionary, who as leader of the radical Jacobins urged the execution of **LOUIS XVI** and initiated the Terror; on his fall from power he was guillotined. On Robespierre: see **CARLYLE** 200:2, **HEINE** 389:16

6 A man of high principle will be ready to sacrifice to the state his wealth, his life, his very nature—everything, indeed, except his honour.
Discours sur les peines infamantes August 1784, in *Oeuvres Complètes* vol. 1 (1910)

7 I am no courtier, nor moderator, nor Tribune, nor defender of the people: I am myself the people.
speech at the Jacobin Club, 27 April 1792; in G. Laurent (ed.) *Le Defénseur de la Constitution* (1939)

8 *Citoyens, vouliez-vous une revolution sans revolution?*
Citizens, would you want a revolution without revolution?
speech to the Convention, 5 November 1792

9 The general will rules in society as the private will governs each separate individual.
Lettres à ses commettans (2nd series) 5 January 1793

10 Any law which violates the inalienable rights of man is essentially unjust and tyrannical; it is not a law at all.
Déclaration des droits de l'homme 24 April 1793, article 6; this article, in slightly different form, is recorded as having figured in Robespierre's *Projet* of 21 April 1793

11 Any institution which does not suppose the people good, and the magistrate corruptible, is evil.
Déclaration des droits de l'homme 24 April 1793, article 25

12 Wickedness is the root of despotism as virtue is the essence of the Republic.
in the Convention, 7 May 1794; in C. Vellay (ed.) *Discours et Rapports de Robespierre* (1908)

13 One single will is necessary.
private note, in S. A. Berville and J. F. Barrière *Papiers inédits trouvés chez Robespierre* vol. 2 (1828) no. 44

14 Intimidation without virtue is disastrous; virtue without intimidation is powerless.
J. M. Thompson *The French Revolution* (1943); attributed

Leo Robin 1900–84

American songwriter

15 A kiss on the hand may be quite continental,
But diamonds are a girl's best friend.
'Diamonds are a Girl's Best Friend' (1949 song) from the film *Gentlemen Prefer Blondes*; see **LOOS** 500:15

16 Thanks for the memory.
title of song (with Ralph Rainger, 1937)

Elizabeth Robins 1862–1952

American writer

17 To say in print what she thinks is the last thing the woman novelist or journalist is so rash as to attempt . . . Her publishers are not women.
in 1908, as first president of the Women Writers' Suffrage League

Edwin Arlington Robinson 1869–1935

American poet

18 I shall have more to say when I am dead.
'John Brown' (1920)

19 Go to the western gate, Luke Havergal,
There where the vines cling crimson on the wall,
And in the twilight wait for what will come.
'Luke Havergal' (1896)

20 So on we worked, and waited for the light,
And went without meat, and cursed the bread;
And Richard Cory, one calm summer night,
Went home and put a bullet through his head.
'Richard Cory' (1897)

1 The world is not a 'prison house', but a kind of kindergarten, where millions of bewildered infants are trying to spell God with the wrong blocks.
Literature in the Making (1917)

John Robinson ?1576–1625

English pastor to the Pilgrim Fathers

2 The Lord has more truth yet to break forth out of his holy word.
alleged address to the departing pilgrims, 1620
in *Dictionary of National Biography* (1917–)

3 The Lutherans refuse to advance beyond what Luther saw, while the Calvinists stick fast where they were left by that great man of God, who saw not all things.
regretting the current state of the reformed churches, in the alleged address to the departing pilgrims, 1620
in *Dictionary of National Biography* (1917–)

John Robinson 1919–83

English theologian; Bishop of Woolwich, 1959-69

4 Honest to God.
title of book (1963)

5 I think Lawrence tried to portray this [sex] relation as in a real sense an act of holy communion. For him flesh was sacramental of the spirit.
as defence witness in the case against Penguin Books for publishing Lady Chatterley's Lover
in *The Times* 28 October 1960

Mary Robinson 1758–1800

English poet

6 Pavement slippery, people sneezing,
Lords in ermine, beggars freezing;
Titled gluttons dainties carving,
Genius in a garret starving.
'January, 1795'

Mary Robinson 1944–

Irish Labour stateswoman, President 1990-97

7 Instead of rocking the cradle, they rocked the system.
in her victory speech, paying tribute to the women of Ireland
in *The Times* 10 November 1990; see **WALLACE** 836:14

Boyle Roche 1743–1807

Irish politician

8 A disorderly set of people whom no king can govern and no God can please.
of the Ulster Protestants
attributed

9 Mr Speaker, I smell a rat; I see him forming in the air and darkening the sky; but I'll nip him in the bud.
attributed

John Wilmot, Lord Rochester 1647–80

English poet. See also **EPITAPHS** 317:16

10   'Is there then no more?'
She cries. 'All this to love and rapture's due;
Must we not pay a debt to pleasure too?'
'The Imperfect Enjoyment' (1680)

11 Love . . .
That cordial drop heaven in our cup has thrown
To make the nauseous draught of life go down.
'A Letter from Artemisia in the Town to Chloe in the Country' (1679)

12 An age in her embraces passed
Would seem a winter's day,
Where life and light with envious haste
Are torn and snatched away.
'The Mistress: A Song' (1691)

13 Kind jealous doubts, tormenting fears,
And anxious cares, when past,
Prove our hearts' treasure fixed and dear,
And make us blest at last.
'The Mistress: A Song' (1691)

14   Natural freedoms are but just:
There's something generous in mere lust.
'A Ramble in St James' Park' (1680)

15 Reason, an *ignis fatuus* of the mind,
Which leaves the light of nature, sense, behind.
'A Satire against Mankind' (1679) l. 11

16 Then Old Age, and Experience, hand in hand,
Lead him to Death, and make him understand
. . .
Huddled in dirt the reasoning engine lies,
Who was so proud, so witty and so wise.
'A Satire against Mankind' (1679) l. 25

17 For all men would be cowards if they durst.
'A Satire against Mankind' (1679) l. 158

18 A merry monarch, scandalous and poor.
'A Satire on King Charles II' (1697)

19 Love a woman? You're an ass!
'Tis a most insipid passion
To choose out for your happiness
The silliest part of God's creation.
'Song' (1680)

20 Ancient person, for whom I
All the flattering youth defy,
Long be it ere thou grow old,
Aching, shaking, crazy, cold;
But still continue as thou art,
Ancient person of my heart.
'A Song of a Young Lady to her Ancient Lover' (1691)

21 Ere time and place were, time and place were not;
Where primitive nothing something straight begot;
Then all proceeded from the great united what.
'Upon Nothing' (1680)

22 Matter, the wickedest offspring of thy race,
By form assisted, flew from thy embrace,
And rebel light obscured thy reverend dusky face.

With form and matter, time and place did join;
Body, thy foe, with these did leagues combine,
To spoil thy peaceful realm, and ruin all thy line.
'Upon Nothing' (1680)

John D. Rockefeller 1839–1937

American industrialist and philanthropist

1 The growth of a large business is merely a
survival of the fittest . . . The American beauty
rose can be produced in the splendour and
fragrance which bring cheer to its beholder only
by sacrificing the early buds which grow up
around it.
W. J. Ghent *Our Benevolent Feudalism* (1902); 'American
Beauty Rose' became the title of a 1950 song by Hal David
and others; see **DARWIN** 266:15, **SPENCER** 765:22

Gene Roddenberry 1921–91

American film producer. See also **MISQUOTATIONS** 547:4,
MISQUOTATIONS 548:5

2 These are the voyages of the starship *Enterprise*.
Its five-year mission . . . to boldly go where no
man has gone before.
Star Trek (television series, from 1966)

Anita Roddick 1942–2007

English businesswoman

3 I think that business practices would improve
immeasurably if they were guided by 'feminine'
principles—qualities like love and care and
intuition.
Body and Soul (1991)

Richard Rodgers 1902–79

American composer and songwriter

4 The sweetest sounds I'll ever hear
Are still inside my head.
The kindest words I'll ever know
Are waiting to be said.
The most entrancing sight of all
Is yet for me to see.
And the dearest love in all the world
Is waiting somewhere for me.
'The Sweetest Sounds' (1962 song) in *No Strings*

Theodore Roethke 1908–63

American poet

5 Thought does not crush to stone.
The great sledge drops in vain.
Truth never is undone;
Its shafts remain.
'The Adamant' (1941)

6 I have known the inexorable sadness of pencils,
Neat in their boxes, dolour of pad and paper-
weight,
All the misery of manilla folders and mucilage,
Desolation in immaculate public places.
'Dolour' (1948)

7 I remember the neckcurls, limp and damp, as
tendrils;
And her quick look, a sidelong pickerel smile;
And how, once startled into talk, the light
syllables leaped for her,
And she balanced in the delight of her thought.
'Elegy for Jane' (1953)

8 In a dark wood I saw—
I saw my several selves
Come running from the leaves,
Lewd, tiny, careless lives
That scuttled under stones,
Or broke, but would not go.
'The Exorcism' (1958)

9 The body and the soul know how to play
In that dark world where gods have lost thir
way.
'Four for Sir John Davies' (1953) no. 2

10   O who can be
Both moth and flame? The weak moth
blundering by.
Whom do we love? I thought I knew the truth;
Of grief I died, but no one knew my death.
'The Sequel' (1964)

Ginger Rogers *see* Thaves 804:8

Richard Rogers 1933–

British architect

11 You should be able to read a building. It should
be what it does.
Walter Neurath Memorial lecture, London University, March
1990

Samuel Rogers 1763–1855

English poet

12 Think nothing done while aught remains to do.
'Human Life' (1819) l. 49; see **LUCAN** 503:18

13 But there are moments which he calls his own,
Then, never less alone than when alone,
Those whom he loved so long and sees no
more,
Loved and still loves—not dead—but gone
before,
He gathers round him.
'Human Life' (1819) l. 755; see **CYPRIAN** 263:15, **NORTON** 577:8

14 By many a temple half as old as Time.
Italy (1838 ed.) epilogue; see **BURGON** 172:12

15 Go—you may call it madness, folly;
You shall not chase my gloom away.
There's such a charm in melancholy,
I would not, if I could, be gay.
'To —, 1814'

16 Mine be a cot beside the hill.
'A Wish' (1786)

17 It doesn't much signify whom one marries, for
one is sure to find next morning that it was
someone else.
Alexander Dyce (ed.) *Table Talk of Samuel Rogers* (1860)

Thorold Rogers 1823–90

English economic historian

1 See, ladling butter from alternate tubs
Stubbs butters Freeman, Freeman butters Stubbs.
STUBBS and FREEMAN both being historians
W. H. Hutton (ed.) *Letters of William Stubbs* (1904)

Will Rogers 1879–1935

American actor and humorist

2 There is only one thing that can kill the movies, and that is education.
Autobiography of Will Rogers (1949) ch. 6

3 Income Tax has made more Liars out of the American people than Golf.
The Illiterate Digest (1924) 'Helping the Girls with their Income Taxes'

4 Everything is funny as long as it is happening to Somebody Else.
The Illiterate Digest (1924) 'Warning to Jokers: lay off the prince'

5 Well, all I know is what I read in the papers.
in *New York Times* 30 September 1923

6 You can't say civilization don't advance, however, for in every war they kill you in a new way.
in *New York Times* 23 December 1929

7 Half our life is spent trying to find something to do with the time we have rushed through life trying to save.
letter in *New York Times* 29 April 1930

Mme Roland (Marie-Jeanne Philipon)

1754–93

French revolutionary

8 The more I see of men, the more I like dogs.
attributed, in *Notes and Queries* 5 September 1908; see
TOUSSENEL 814:3

9 *Ô liberté! Ô liberté! que de crimes on commet en ton nom!*

O liberty! O liberty! what crimes are committed in thy name!
last words, before being guillotined
A. de Lamartine *Histoire des Girondins* (1847) bk. 51, ch. 8; see
GEORGE 353:10

Frederick William Rolfe ('Baron Corvo')

1860–1913

English novelist

10 Pray for the repose of His soul. He was so tired.
Hadrian VII (1904) ch. 24

Romain Rolland 1866–1944

French writer

11 A hero is the one who does what he can. The others don't.
Jean-Christophe (1904–12) 'l'Adolescent'

Richard Rolle de Hampole c.1290–1349

English mystic

12 When Adam dalfe and Eve spane
Go spire if thou may spede,
Where was than the pride of man
That now merres his mede?
G. G. Perry *Religious Pieces* (Early English Text Society, Original Series no. 26, revised ed. 1914); see **PROVERBS** 646:36

Samuel Romilly 1757–1818

English lawyer and politician

13 A system which betrays the greatest distrust of the people must never look for popular support.
Observations on a late publication, intituled, Thoughts on executive justice (1786)

Pierre de Ronsard 1524–85

French poet

14 *Mignonne, allons voir si la rose,*
Qui, ce matin, avait déclose
Sa robe de pourpre au soleil,
A point perdu, cette vêprée,
Les plis de sa robe pourprée
Et son teint au vôtre pareil.

See, Mignonne, hath not the rose
That this morning did unclose
Her purple mantle to the light,
Lost, before the day be dead,
The glory of her raiment red,
Her colour, bright as yours is bright?
Odes, à Cassandre (1555) bk. 1, no. 17 (translated by Andrew Lang)

15 *Quand vous serez bien vieille, au soir, à la chandelle,*
Assise auprès du feu, dévidant et filant,
Direz, chantant mes vers, en vous émerveillant,
Ronsard me célébrait du temps que j'étais belle.

When you are very old, and sit in the candle-light at evening spinning by the fire, you will say, as you murmur my verses, a wonder in your eyes, 'Ronsard sang of me in the days when I was fair.'
Sonnets pour Hélène (1578) bk. 2, no. 42

Eleanor Roosevelt 1884–1962

American humanitarian and diplomat, wife of Franklin Delano **ROOSEVELT** and First Lady of the US. On Roosevelt: see **STEVENSON** 775:1

16 The basis of all good human behaviour is kindness.
Book of Common Sense Etiquette (1962) introduction

17 Is there anything we can do for you? For you are the one in trouble now.
to Harry **TRUMAN**, *who became President on the death of Franklin D.* **ROOSEVELT**
in conversation, 12 April 1945

18 I cannot believe that war is the best solution. No one won the last war, and no one will win the next war.
letter to Harry Truman, 22 March 1948

1 No one can make you feel inferior without your consent.
in *Catholic Digest* August 1960

Franklin Delano Roosevelt 1882–1945

American Democratic statesman, 32nd President of the US 1933-45, and husband of Eleanor ROOSEVELT

2 These unhappy times call for the building of plans that . . . build from the bottom up and not from the top down, that put their faith once more in the forgotten man at the bottom of the economic pyramid.
radio address, 7 April 1932, in *Public Papers* (1938) vol. 1

3 I pledge you, I pledge myself, to a new deal for the American people.
speech to the Democratic Convention in Chicago, 2 July 1932, accepting the presidential nomination; in *Public Papers* (1938) vol. 1

4 The only thing we have to fear is fear itself.
inaugural address, 4 March 1933, in *Public Papers* (1938) vol. 2; see **MONTAIGNE** 554:20

5 In the field of world policy I would dedicate this Nation to the policy of the good neighbour.
inaugural address, 4 March 1933, in *Public Papers* (1938) vol. 2

6 We face the arduous days that lie before us in the warm courage of national unity.
inaugural address, 4 March 1933; see **BUSH** 182:9

7 I have seen war . . . I hate war.
speech at Chautauqua, NY, 14 August 1936, in *Public Papers* (1938) vol. 5

8 I see one-third of a nation ill-housed, ill-clad, ill-nourished.
second inaugural address, 20 January 1937, in *Public Papers* (1941) vol. 6

9 We have always known that heedless self-interest was bad morals; we know now that it is bad economics.
second inaugural address, 20 January 1937

10 Your boys are not going to be sent into any foreign wars.
speech in Boston, 30 October 1940, in *Public Papers* (1941) vol. 9; see **JOHNSON** 435:7

11 We must be the great arsenal of democracy.
'Fireside Chat' radio broadcast, 29 December 1940, in *Public Papers* (1941) vol. 9

12 We look forward to a world founded upon four essential human freedoms. The first is freedom of speech and expression—everywhere in the world. The second is freedom of every person to worship God in his own way—everywhere in the world. The third is freedom from want . . . everywhere in the world. The fourth is freedom from fear . . . anywhere in the world.
message to Congress, 6 January 1941, in *Public Papers* (1941) vol. 9

13 Yesterday, December 7, 1941—a date which will live in infamy—the United States of America was suddenly and deliberately attacked by naval and air forces of the Empire of Japan.
address to Congress, 8 December 1941, in *Public Papers* (1950) vol. 10

14 Books can not be killed by fire. People die, but books never die. No man and no force can abolish memory . . . In this war, we know, books are weapons. And it is a part of your dedication always to make them weapons for man's freedom.
'Message to the Booksellers of America' 6 May 1942, in *Publisher's Weekly* 9 May 1942

15 Oh Lord, give us faith. Give us faith in Thee; faith in our sons; faith in each other; faith in our united crusade.
address to the nation, D-Day, 6 June 1944

16 The work, my friend, is peace. More than an end of this war—an end to the beginnings of all wars.
undelivered address for Jefferson Day, 13 April 1945 (the day after Roosevelt died) in *Public Papers* (1950) vol. 13

Theodore Roosevelt 1858–1919

American Republican statesman, 26th President of the US 1901-9

17 I wish to preach, not the doctrine of ignoble ease, but the doctrine of the strenuous life.
speech to the Hamilton Club, Chicago, 10 April 1899, in *Works* (Memorial edition, 1923-6) vol. 15

18 I am as strong as a bull moose and you can use me to the limit.
'Bull Moose' subsequently became the popular name of the Progressive Party
letter to Mark Hanna, 27 June 1900, in *Works* (Memorial edition, 1923-6) vol. 23

19 There is a homely old adage which runs: 'Speak softly and carry a big stick; you will go far.' If the American nation will speak softly, and yet build and keep at a pitch of the highest training a thoroughly efficient navy, the Monroe Doctrine will go far.
speech in Chicago, 3 April 1903, in *New York Times* 4 April 1903

20 A man who is good enough to shed his blood for the country is good enough to be given a square deal afterwards. More than that no man is entitled to, and less than that no man shall have.
speech at the Lincoln Monument, Springfield, Illinois, 4 June 1903, in *Addresses and Presidential Messages 1902-4* (1904)

21 You can no more make an agreement with those leaders of Colombia than you can nail currant jelly to the wall. And the failure to nail currant jelly to the wall is not due to the nail. It's due to the currant jelly.
at the time of the Panama revolution, 1903
attributed by Edmund Morris, John F. Kennedy Presidential Historians Forum, 5 March 2002

22 The men with the muck-rakes are often indispensable to the well-being of society; but only if they know when to stop raking the muck.
speech in Washington, 14 April 1906, in *Works* (Memorial edition, 1923-6) vol. 18; see **BUNYAN** 171:19

1 I have got such a bully pulpit!

his personal view of the presidency

in *Outlook* (New York) 27 February 1909; see **REAGAN** 656:10

2 It is not the critic who counts; not the man who points out how the strong man stumbles, or where the doer of deeds could have done better. The credit belongs to the man who is actually in the arena.

'Citizenship in a Republic', speech at the Sorbonne, Paris, 23 April 1910

3 We stand at Armageddon, and we battle for the Lord.

speech at the Republican National Convention, 18 June 1912

4 There is no room in this country for hyphenated Americanism . . . The one absolutely certain way of bringing this nation to ruin, of preventing all possibility of its continuing to be a nation at all, would be to permit it to become a tangle of squabbling nationalities.

speech in New York, 12 October 1915, in *Works* (Memorial edition, 1923–6) vol. 20

5 I have never used in peace or in war any such expression as 'hands across the sea', and I emphatically disapprove of what it signifies save in so far as it means cordial friendship between us and every other nation that acts in accordance with the standards that we deem just and right.

in *Metropolitan* October 1915; see **WEBBER** 843:12

6 One of our defects as a nation is a tendency to use what have been called 'weasel words'. When a weasel sucks eggs the meat is sucked out of the egg. If you use a 'weasel word' after another, there is nothing left of the other.

speech in St Louis, 31 May 1916

7 To announce that there must be no criticism of the president, or that we are to stand by the president, right or wrong, is not only unpatriotic and servile, but is morally treasonable to the American public.

in *Kansas City Star* 7 May 1918

Lord Rootes 1894–1964

English motor-car manufacturer

8 No other man-made device since the shields and lances of ancient knights fulfils a man's ego like an automobile.

attributed, 1958

Salvator Rosa 1615–73

Italian painter and etcher

9 *Aut tace aut loquere meliora silentio.*

Be silent, unless your speech is better than silence.

inscription on self portrait in the National Gallery, London

Lord Rosebery 1847–1929

British Liberal statesman, Prime Minister 1894–5

10 I have never known the sweets of place with power, but of place without power, of place with the minimum of power—that is a purgatory, and if not a purgatory it is a hell.

in *Spectator* 6 July 1895

11 It is beginning to be hinted that we are a nation of amateurs.

Rectorial Address at Glasgow University, 16 November 1900, in *The Times* 17 November 1900

12 I must plough my furrow alone.

on remaining outside the Liberal Party leadership

speech, 19 July 1901, in *The Times* 20 July 1901

13 There are two supreme pleasures in life. One is ideal, the other real. The ideal is when a man receives the seals of office from his Sovereign. The real pleasure comes when he hands them back.

Sir Robert Peel (1899)

Ethel Rosenberg 1916–53 *and* Julius Rosenberg 1918–53

American husband and wife; convicted of spying for the Russians

14 We are innocent . . . To forsake this truth is to pay too high a price even for the priceless gift of life.

petition for executive clemency, filed 9 January 1953, in Ethel Rosenberg *Death House Letters* (1953)

15 We are the first victims of American Fascism.

letter from Julius to Emanuel Bloch before the Rosenbergs' execution, 19 June 1953; in *Testament of Ethel and Julius Rosenberg* (1954)

A. C. Ross *see* Political slogans and songs

613:12

William Stewart Ross 1844–1906

Scottish secularist

16 And the wild hare brings forth her young
On the hearthstone of the Gael.

'Culloden' (1878); see **JOHNSTON** 445:3

Christina Rossetti 1830–94

English poet; sister of Dante Gabriel ROSSETTI

17 My heart is like a singing bird
Whose nest is in a watered shoot.

'A Birthday' (1862)

18 My heart is like an apple tree
Whose boughs are bent with thickset fruit.

'A Birthday' (1862)

19 Come to me in the silence of the night;
Come in the speaking silence of a dream;
Come with soft rounded cheeks and eyes as bright
As sunlight on a stream;

Come back in tears,
O memory, hope, love of finished years.
'Echo' (1862)

1 For there is no friend like a sister
In calm or stormy weather;
To cheer one on the tedious way,
To fetch one if one goes astray,
To lift one if one totters down,
To strengthen while one stands.
'Goblin Market' (1862)

2 In the bleak mid-winter
Frosty wind made moan,
Earth stood hard as iron,
Water like a stone;
Snow had fallen, snow on snow,
Snow on snow,
In the bleak mid-winter,
Long ago.
'Mid-Winter' (1875)

3 Oh roses for the flush of youth,
And laurel for the perfect prime;
But pluck an ivy branch for me
Grown old before my time.
'Oh roses for the flush of youth' (1862)

4 Remember me when I am gone away,
Gone far away into the silent land.
'Remember' (1862)

5 Better by far you should forget and smile
Than that you should remember and be sad.
'Remember' (1862)

6 O Earth, lie heavily upon her eyes;
Seal her sweet eyes weary of watching, Earth.
'Rest' (1862)

7 Silence more musical than any song.
'Rest' (1862)

8 Does the road wind up-hill all the way?
Yes, to the very end.
Will the day's journey take the whole long day?
From morn to night, my friend.
'Up-Hill' (1862)

9 When I am dead, my dearest,
Sing no sad songs for me;
Plant thou no roses at my head,
Nor shady cypress tree:
Be the green grass above me
With showers and dewdrops wet;
And if thou wilt, remember,
And if thou wilt, forget.
'When I am dead' (1862); see MCGOUGH 511:1

10 Our Indian Crown is in great measure the
trapping of a splendid misery.
letter to Amelia Heimann, 29 July 1880

Dante Gabriel Rossetti 1828–82

English poet and painter, brother of Christina ROSSETTI

11 Like the sweet apple which reddens upon the
topmost bough,
A-top on the topmost twig,—which the pluckers
forgot, somehow,—

Forgot it not, nay, but got it not, for none could
get it till now.
'Beauty: A Combination from Sappho' (1861); see SAPPHO
681:1

12 The blessed damozel leaned out
From the gold bar of Heaven;
Her eyes were deeper than the depth
Of waters stilled at even;
She had three lilies in her hand,
And the stars in her hair were seven.
'The Blessed Damozel' (1870) st. 1

13 Her hair that lay along her back
Was yellow like ripe corn.
'The Blessed Damozel' (1870) st. 2

14 As low as where this earth
Spins like a fretful midge.
'The Blessed Damozel' (1870) st. 6

15 And the souls mounting up to God
Went by her like thin flames.
'The Blessed Damozel' (1870) st. 7

16 'We two,' she said, 'will seek the groves
Where the lady Mary is,
With her five handmaidens, whose names
Are five sweet symphonies,
Cecily, Gertrude, Magdalen,
Margaret and Rosalys.'
'The Blessed Damozel' (1870) st. 18

17 Oh! clasp we to our hearts, for deathless dower,
This close-companioned inarticulate hour
When twofold silence was the song of love.
The House of Life (1881) pt. 1 'Silent Noon'

18 I do not see them here; but after death
God knows I know the faces I shall see,
Each one a murdered self, with low last breath.
'I am thyself,—what hast thou done to me?'
'And I—and I—thyself,' (lo! each one saith,)
'And thou thyself to all eternity!'
The House of Life (1881) pt. 2 'Lost Days'

19 Give honour unto Luke Evangelist;
For he it was (the aged legends say)
Who first taught Art to fold her hands and pray.
The House of Life (1881) pt. 2 'Old and New Art'

20 Look in my face; my name is Might-have-been;
I am also called No-more, Too-late, Farewell.
The House of Life (1881) pt. 2 'A Superscription'; see TRAILL
814:16

21 Sleepless with cold commemorative eyes.
The House of Life (1881) pt. 2 'A Superscription'

22 Unto the man of yearning thought
And aspiration, to do nought
Is in itself almost an act.
'Soothsay' (1881) st. 10

23 I have been here before,
But when or how I cannot tell:
I know the grass beyond the door,
The sweet keen smell,
The sighing sound, the lights around the shore.
'Sudden Light' (1870)

24 'I saw the Sibyl at Cumae'
(One said) 'with mine own eye.

She hung in a cage, and read her rune
To all the passers-by.
Said the boys, "What wouldst thou, Sibyl?"
She answered, "I would die." '
  translation of Petronius *Satyricon* 'Cena Trimalchionis' ch. 48, sect. 8; see **PETRONIUS** 605:7

Gioacchino Rossini 1792–1868
Italian composer

1 Wagner has lovely moments but awful quarters of an hour.
  to Emile Naumann, April 1867, in E. Naumann *Italienische Tondichter* (1883) vol. 4

Edmond Rostand 1868–1918
French dramatist

2 . . . *Un grand nez est proprement l'indice*
D'un homme affable, bon, courtois, spirituel,
Libéral, courageux, tel que je suis.

A large nose is in fact the sign of an affable man, good, courteous, witty, liberal, courageous, such as I am.
  Cyrano de Bergerac (1897) act 1, sc. 1

3 *Il y a malgré vous quelque chose*
Que j'emporte, et ce soir, quand j'entrerai chez Dieu,
Mon salut balaiera largement le seuil bleu,
Quelque chose que sans un pli, sans une tache,
J'emporte malgré vous . . . et c'est . . . Mon panache!

There is, in spite of you, something which I shall take with me. And tonight, when I go into God's house, my bow will make a wide sweep across the blue threshold. Something which, with not a crease, not a mark, I'm taking away in spite of you . . . and it's . . . My panache!
  Cyrano de Bergerac (1897) act 5, sc. 4

4 *Le seul rêve intéresse,*
Vivre sans rêve, qu'est-ce?

The dream, alone, is of interest. What is life, without a dream?
  La Princesse Lointaine (1895) act 1, sc. 4

Jean Rostand 1894–1977
French biologist

5 The biologist passes, the frog remains.
  sometimes quoted as 'Theories pass. The frog remains'
  Inquiétudes d'un biologiste (1967)

6 To be adult is to be alone.
  Pensées d'un biologiste (1954)

7 Kill a man, and you are an assassin. Kill millions of men, and you are a conqueror. Kill everyone, and you are a god.
  Pensées d'un biologiste (1939) p. 116; see **PORTEUS** 619:22, **YOUNG** 876:14

Leo Rosten 1908–97
American writer and social scientist

8 Any man who hates dogs and babies can't be all bad.
  of W. C. FIELDS, and often attributed to him
  speech at Masquers' Club dinner, 16 February 1939; letter in *Times Literary Supplement* 24 January 1975

Philip Roth 1933–
American novelist

9 A Jewish man with parents alive is a fifteen-year-old boy, and will remain a fifteen-year-old boy until *they die!*
  Portnoy's Complaint (1967)

10 Doctor, my doctor, what do you say, LET'S PUT THE ID BACK IN YID!
  Portnoy's Complaint (1967)

Claude-Joseph Rouget de Lisle 1760–1836
French soldier

11 *Allons, enfants de la patrie,*
Le jour de gloire est arrivé . . .
Aux armes, citoyens!
Formez vos battaillons!

Come, children of our country, the day of glory has arrived . . . To arms, citizens! Form your battalions!
  'La Marseillaise' (25 April 1792)

Charles Roupell
British lawyer

12 To play billiards well is a sign of an ill-spent youth.
  attributed, in D. Duncan *Life of Herbert Spencer* (1908) ch. 20

Jean-Jacques Rousseau 1712–78
French philosopher and novelist. On Rousseau: see **BERLIN** 73:12, **BLAKE** 126:25, **BYRON** 186:12, **HEINE** 389:16; see also **COWPER** 255:23

13 *Du contrat social.*
The social contract.
  title of book, *Du contrat social* (1762)

14 *L'homme est né libre, et partout il est dans les fers.*
Man was born free, and everywhere he is in chains.
  Du Contrat social (1762) ch. 1

15 *C'est le chemin des passions qui m'a conduit à la philosophie.*
It is the path of the passions which has led me to philosophy.
  Julie, ou la nouvelle Héloïse (1761) pt. 2, letter 3

16 *Laisse, mon ami, ces vains moralistes et rentre au fond de ton âme: c'est là que tu retrouveras toujours la source de ce feu sacré qui nous embrasa tant de fois de l'amour des sublimes vertus; c'est là que tu*

verras ce simulacre éternel du vrai beau dont la contemplation nous anime d'un saint enthousiasme.

Leave those vain moralists, my friend, and return to the depth of your soul: that is where you will always rediscover the source of the sacred fire which so often inflamed us with love of the sublime virtues; that is where you will see the eternal image of true beauty, the contemplation of which inspires us with a holy enthusiasm.

Julie, ou la nouvelle Héloïse (1761, ed. M. Launay, 1967) pt. 2, letter 11

1 *Dussé-je vivre des siècles entiers, le doux temps de ma jeunesse ne peut ni renaître pour moi, ni s'effacer de mon souvenir.*

Should I live for centuries, the sweet period of my youth would not be reborn, nor effaced from my memory.

Julie, ou la nouvelle Héloïse (1761) pt. 6, letter 7

Martin Joseph Routh 1755–1854

English classicist

2 You will find it a very good practice always to verify your references, sir!

John William Burgon *Lives of Twelve Good Men* (1888 ed.) vol. 1

Matthew Rowbottom, Richard Stannard, *and* The Spice Girls

(Melanie Brown, Victoria Adams, Geri Halliwell, Emma Bunton, *and* Melanie Chisholm)

English songwriters and English pop singers

3 Yo I'll tell you what I want, what I really really want
so tell me what you want, what you really really want.

'Wannabe' (1996 song)

Nicholas Rowe 1674–1718

English dramatist

4 When every eye was closed, and the pale moon
And stars alone, shone conscious of the theft.

'The Fair Penitent' (1703) act 1, sc. 1

5 At length the morn and cold indifference came.

The Fair Penitent (1703) act 1, sc. 1

6 Is this that haughty, gallant, gay Lothario?

The Fair Penitent (1703) act 5, sc. 1

7 Like Helen, in the night when Troy was sacked,
Spectatress of the mischief which she made.

The Fair Penitent (1703) act 5, sc. 1

8 Death is the privilege of human nature,
And life without it were not worth our taking.

The Fair Penitent (1703) act 5, sc. 1

Helen Rowland 1875–1950

American writer

9 A husband is what is left of a lover, after the nerve has been extracted.

A Guide to Men (1922)

10 Somehow a bachelor never quite gets over the idea that he is a thing of beauty and a boy forever.

A Guide to Men (1922); see **KEATS** 454:3

11 The follies which a man regrets most, in his life, are those which he didn't commit when he had the opportunity.

A Guide to Men (1922)

Richard Rowland *c.*1881–1947

American film producer

12 The lunatics have taken charge of the asylum.

on the take-over of United Artists by Charles **CHAPLIN** *and others*

Terry Ramsaye *A Million and One Nights* (1926) vol. 2, ch. 79; see **LLOYD GEORGE** 496:18

J. K. Rowling 1965–

English novelist and writer for children, creator of 'Harry Potter'. On Rowling: see **BYATT** 184:25

13 Harry Potter was a highly unusual boy in many ways.

Harry Potter and the Prisoner of Azkaban (1999), opening words

14 Poverty is a lot like childbirth—you know it is going to hurt before it happens, but you'll never know how much until you experience it.

in *Mail on Sunday* 16 June 2002

Maude Royden 1876–1956

English religious writer

15 The Church should go forward along the path of progress and be no longer satisfied only to represent the Conservative Party at prayer.

address at Queen's Hall, London, 16 July 1917, in *The Times* 17 July 1917

Naomi Royde-Smith *c.*1875–1964

English novelist and dramatist

16 I know two things about the horse
And one of them is rather coarse.

Weekend Book (1928)

Matthew Roydon fl. 1580–1622

English poet

17 A sweet attractive kind of grace,
A full assurance given by looks,
Continual comfort in a face,
The lineaments of Gospel books;
I trow that countenance cannot lie,
Whose thoughts are legible in the eye.

'An Elegy . . . for his Astrophill [Sir Philip Sidney]' (1593) st. 18

18 Was never eye, did see that face,
Was never ear, did hear that tongue,
Was never mind, did mind his grace,
That ever thought the travel long—
But eyes, and ears, and ev'ry thought,
Were with his sweet perfections caught.

'An Elegy . . . for his Astrophill' (1593) st. 19

Paul Alfred Rubens 1875–1917

English songwriter

1 Oh! we don't want to lose you but we think you ought to go
For your King and your Country both need you so.
'Your King and Country Want You' (1914 song); see **MILITARY SAYINGS, SLOGANS, AND SONGS** 535:20

Helena Rubinstein 1882–1965

Polish-born American beautician and businesswoman. See also **ADVERTISING SLOGANS** 7:9

2 With my product and her packaging we could have ruled the world.
of Elizabeth **ARDEN**
Lindy Woodhead *War Paint* (2003) ch. 6

Richard Rumbold *c.*1622–85

English republican conspirator

3 I never could believe that Providence had sent a few men into the world, ready booted and spurred to ride, and millions ready saddled and bridled to be ridden.
on the scaffold
T. B. Macaulay *History of England* vol. 1 (1849) ch. 1

Carol Rumens 1944–

English poet

4 A slow psalm of two nations
Mourning a common pain
—Hebrew and Arabic mingling
Their silver-rooted vine;
Olives and roses falling
To sweeten Palestine.
'A New Song' (1993)

5 It's simple, isn't it?
Never say the yes
you don't mean, but the no
you always meant, say that,
even if it's too late,
even if it kills you.
'A Woman of a Certain Age' (1993)

Rumi *see* Jalal ad-Din ar-Rumi

Donald Rumsfeld 1932–

American Republican politician and businessman, US Defense Secretary 2001–6

6 You're thinking of Europe as Germany and France. I don't. I think that's old Europe. If you look at the entire Nato Europe today, the centre of gravity is shifting to the east.
to journalists who asked him about European hostility to a possible war, 22 January 2003
in *Independent* 21 February 2003

Robert Runcie 1921–2000

English Anglican clergyman; Archbishop of Canterbury 1980–91. On Runcie: see **FIELD** 326:6

7 People are mourning on both sides of this conflict. In our prayers we shall quite rightly remember those who are bereaved in our own country and the relations of the young Argentinian soldiers who were killed. Common sorrow could do something to reunite those who were engaged in this struggle. A shared anguish can be a bridge of reconciliation. Our neighbours are indeed like us.
service of thanksgiving at the end of the Falklands war, St. Paul's Cathedral, London, 26 July 1982

8 In the middle ages people were tourists because of their religion, whereas now they are tourists because tourism is their religion.
speech in London, 6 December 1988

Damon Runyon 1884–1946

American writer

9 Guys and dolls.
title of book (1931)

10 'My boy,' he says, 'always try to rub up against money, for if you rub up against money long enough, some of it may rub off on you.'
in Cosmopolitan August 1929, 'A Very Honourable Guy'

11 I do see her in tough joints more than somewhat.
in Collier's 22 May 1930, 'Social Error'

12 I always claim the mission workers came out too early to catch any sinners on this part of Broadway. At such an hour the sinners are still in bed resting up from their sinning of the night before, so they will be in good shape for more sinning a little later on.
in Collier's 28 January 1933, 'The Idyll of Miss Sarah Brown'

13 I long ago come to the conclusion that all life is 6 to 5 against.
in Collier's 8 September 1934, 'A Nice Price'

14 You can keep the things of bronze and stone, and give me one man to remember me just once a year.
note to his friends shortly before he died
Ed Weiner *The Damon Runyon Story* (1948)

Salman Rushdie 1947–

Indian-born British novelist. On Rushdie: see **KHOMEINI** 462:7; see also **ADVERTISING SLOGANS** 8:7

15 Most of what matters in your life takes place in your absence.
Midnight's Children (1981) bk. 1

16 To understand just one life, you have to swallow the world.
Midnight's Children (1981) bk. 1

17 Every pickle-jar . . . contains, therefore, the most exalted of possibilities: the feasibility of the chutnification of history.
Midnight's Children (1981) bk. 3

1 The empire writes back with a vengeance.
  in Times *3 July 1982; see* FILM TITLES *331:4*

2 What is freedom of expression? Without the freedom to offend, it ceases to exist.
  in Weekend Guardian *10 February 1990*

Dean Rusk 1909–94
American politician; Secretary of State, 1961–9

3 We're eyeball to eyeball, and I think the other fellow just blinked.
  on the Cuban missile crisis, 24 October 1962
  in Saturday Evening Post *8 December 1962*

John Ruskin 1819–1900
English art and social critic

4 You hear of me, among others, as a respectable architectural man-milliner; and you send for me, that I may tell you the leading fashion.
  The Crown of Wild Olive *(1866) Lecture 2 'Traffic'*

5 Thackeray settled like a meat-fly on whatever one had got for dinner, and made one sick of it.
  Fors Clavigera *(1871–84) Letter 31, 1 July 1873*

6 I have seen, and heard, much of Cockney impudence before now; but never expected to hear a coxcomb ask two hundred guineas for flinging a pot of paint in the public's face.
  on WHISTLER's *Nocturne in Black and Gold*
  Fors Clavigera *(1871–84) Letter 79, 18 June 1877; see* WHISTLER *850:10*

7 No person who is not a great sculptor or painter can be an architect. If he is not a sculptor or painter, he can only be a *builder*.
  Lectures on Architecture and Painting *(1854) Lectures 1 and 2 (addenda)*

8 Life without industry is guilt, and industry without art is brutality.
  Lectures on Art *(1870) Lecture 3 'The Relation of Art to Morals' sect. 95*

9 What is poetry? . . . The suggestion, by the imagination, of noble grounds for the noble emotions.
  Modern Painters *(1856) vol. 3, pt. 4, ch. 1*

10 All violent feelings . . . produce in us a falseness in all our impressions of external things, which I would generally characterize as the 'Pathetic Fallacy'.
  Modern Painters *(1856) vol. 3, pt. 4, ch. 12*

11 There was always more in the world than men could see, walked they ever so slowly; they will see it no better for going fast.
  Modern Painters *(1856) vol. 3, pt. 4, ch. 17*

12 The first test of a truly great man is his humility.
  Modern Painters *(1856) vol. 3, pt. 4, ch. 16*

13 To see clearly is poetry, prophecy, and religion—all in one.
  Modern Painters *(1856) vol. 3, pt. 4 'Of Modern Landscape'*

14 Mountains are the beginning and the end of all natural scenery.
  Modern Painters *(1856) vol. 4, pt. 5, ch. 20*

15 There was a rocky valley between Buxton and Bakewell . . . You enterprised a railroad . . . you blasted its rocks away . . . And now, every fool in Buxton can be at Bakewell in half-an-hour, and every fool in Bakewell at Buxton.
  Praeterita *vol. 3 (1889) 'Joanna's Cave'*

16 Great nations write their autobiographies in three manuscripts;—the book of their deeds, the book of their words, and the book of their art.
  St Mark's Rest *(1884)*

17 All books are divisible into two classes, the books of the hour, and the books of all time.
  Sesame and Lilies *(1865) 'Of Kings' Treasuries'*

18 Be sure that you go to the author to get at his meaning, not to find yours.
  Sesame and Lilies *(1865) 'Of Kings' Treasuries'*

19 Which of us . . . is to do the hard and dirty work for the rest, and for what pay? Who is to do the pleasant and clean work, and for what pay?
  Sesame and Lilies *(1865) 'Of Kings' Treasuries'*

20 How long most people would look at the best book before they would give the price of a large turbot for it.
  Sesame and Lilies *(1865) 'Of Kings' Treasuries'*

21 We call ourselves a rich nation, and we are filthy and foolish enough to thumb each other's books out of circulating libraries!
  Sesame and Lilies *(1865) 'Of Kings' Treasuries'*

22 I believe the right question to ask, respecting all ornament, is simply this: Was it done with enjoyment—was the carver happy while he was about it?
  Seven Lamps of Architecture *(1849) 'The Lamp of Life' sect. 24*

23 Better the rudest work that tells a story or records a fact, than the richest without meaning.
  Seven Lamps of Architecture *(1849) 'The Lamp of Memory' sect. 7*

24 When we build, let us think that we build for ever.
  Seven Lamps of Architecture *(1849) 'The Lamp of Memory' sect. 10*

25 Remember that the most beautiful things in the world are the most useless; peacocks and lilies for instance.
  Stones of Venice *vol. 1 (1851) ch. 2, sect. 17*

26 Labour without joy is base. Labour without sorrow is base. Sorrow without labour is base. Joy without labour is base.
  Time and Tide *(1867) Letter 5*

27 Your honesty is *not* to be based either on religion or policy. Both your religion and policy must be based on *it*.
  Time and Tide *(1867) Letter 8*

1 The first duty of a State is to see that every child born therein shall be well housed, clothed, fed and educated, till it attain years of discretion.
Time and Tide (1867) Letter 13

2 Fine art is that in which the hand, the head, and the heart of man go together.
The Two Paths (1859) Lecture 2

3 Not only is there but one way of *doing* things rightly, but there is only one way of *seeing* them, and that is, seeing the whole of them.
The Two Paths (1859) Lecture 2

4 Nobody cares much at heart about Titian; only there is a strange undercurrent of everlasting murmur about his name, which means the deep consent of all great men that he is greater than they.
The Two Paths (1859) Lecture 2

5 It ought to be quite as natural and straightforward a matter for a labourer to take his pension from his parish, because he has deserved well of his parish, as for a man in higher rank to take his pension from his country, because he has deserved well of his country.
Unto this Last (1862) preface, p. xviii

6 The force of the guinea you have in your pocket depends wholly on the default of a guinea in your neighbour's pocket. If he did not want it, it would be of no use to you.
Unto this Last (1862) Essay 2, p. 40

7 Soldiers of the ploughshare as well as soldiers of the sword.
Unto this Last (1862) Essay 3, p. 102

8 Government and cooperation are in all things the laws of life; anarchy and competition the laws of death.
Unto this Last (1862) Essay 3, p. 102

9 Whereas it has long been known and declared that the poor have no right to the property of the rich, I wish it also to be known and declared that the rich have no right to the property of the poor.
Unto this Last (1862) Essay 3, p. 103

10 There is no wealth but life.
Unto this Last (1862) Essay 4, p. 156

11 The only letters it [his faith] can hold by at all are the old Evangelical formulae. If only the geologists would let me alone, I could do very well, but those dreadful hammers! I hear the clink of them at the end of every cadence of the Bible verses.
letter to Henry Acland, 24 May 1851

12 Remember that it is the glory of Gothic architecture that it can do *anything*.
J. Mordaunt Crook *Dilemma of Style* (1987)

Bertrand Russell 1872–1970
British philosopher and mathematician. See also
MISQUOTATIONS 548:21

13 Men who are unhappy, like men who sleep badly, are always proud of the fact.
The Conquest of Happiness (1930) ch. 1

14 Boredom is . . . a vital problem for the moralist, since half the sins of mankind are caused by the fear of it.
The Conquest of Happiness (1930) ch. 4

15 One of the symptoms of approaching nervous breakdown is the belief that one's work is terribly important, and that to take a holiday would bring all kinds of disaster.
The Conquest of Happiness (1930) ch. 5

16 One should as a rule respect public opinion in so far as is necessary to avoid starvation and to keep out of prison, but anything that goes beyond this is voluntary submission to an unnecessary tyranny.
The Conquest of Happiness (1930) ch. 9

17 A sense of duty is useful in work, but offensive in personal relations. People wish to be liked, not to be endured with patient resignation.
The Conquest of Happiness (1930) ch. 10

18 Of all forms of caution, caution in love is perhaps the most fatal to true happiness.
The Conquest of Happiness (1930) ch. 12

19 To be able to fill leisure intelligently is the last product of civilization.
The Conquest of Happiness (1930) ch. 14

20 What is wanted is not the will to believe, but the wish to find out, which is its exact opposite.
Free Thought and Official Propaganda (1922)

21 Work is of two kinds: first, altering the position of matter at or near the earth's surface relatively to other such matter; second, telling other people to do so. The first kind is unpleasant and ill paid; the second is pleasant and highly paid.
In Praise of Idleness and Other Essays (1986) title essay (1932)

22 To fear love is to fear life, and those who fear life are already three parts dead.
Marriage and Morals (1929) ch. 19

23 Mathematics may be defined as the subject in which we never know what we are talking about, nor whether what we are saying is true.
Mysticism and Logic (1918) ch. 4

24 The law of causality, I believe, like much that passes muster among philosophers, is a relic of a bygone age, surviving, like the monarchy, only because it is erroneously supposed to do no harm.
Mysticism and Logic (1918) ch. 9

25 Only on the firm foundation of unyielding despair, can the soul's habitation henceforth be safely built.
Philosophical Essays (1910) no. 2

1 Mathematics, rightly viewed, possesses not only truth, but supreme beauty—a beauty cold and austere, like that of sculpture.
Philosophical Essays (1910) no. 4

2 The man who has fed the chicken every day throughout its life at last wrings its neck instead, showing that a more refined view as to the uniformity of nature would have been useful to the chicken.
The Problems of Philosophy (1912) ch. 6

3 The man who has no tincture of philosophy goes through life imprisoned in the prejudices derived from common sense, from the habitual beliefs of his age or his nation, and from convictions which have grown up in his mind without the cooperation or consent of his deliberate reason.
The Problems of Philosophy (1912) ch. 15

4 The recrudescence of Puritanism.
title of essay, 1928

5 Every man, wherever he goes, is encompassed by a cloud of comforting convictions, which move with him like flies on a summer day.
Sceptical Essays (1928) 'Dreams and Facts'

6 The infliction of cruelty with a good conscience is a delight to moralists. That is why they invented Hell.
Sceptical Essays (1928) 'On the Value of Scepticism'

7 It is obvious that 'obscenity' is not a term capable of exact legal definition; in the practice of the Courts, it means 'anything that shocks the magistrate'.
Sceptical Essays (1928) 'The Recrudescence of Puritanism'

8 Next to enjoying ourselves, the next greatest pleasure consists in preventing others from enjoying themselves, or, more generally, in the acquisition of power.
Sceptical Essays (1928) 'The Recrudescence of Puritanism'

9 Man is a credulous animal, and must believe *something*; in the absence of good grounds for belief, he will be satisfied with bad ones.
Unpopular Essays (1950) 'An Outline of Intellectual Rubbish'

10 Fear is the main source of superstition, and one of the main sources of cruelty.
Unpopular Essays (1950) 'An Outline of Intellectual Rubbish'

11 'Change' is scientific, 'progress' is ethical; change is indubitable, whereas progress is a matter of controversy.
Unpopular Essays (1950) 'Philosophy and Politics'

12 The merit of speculations on the fourth dimension . . . is chiefly that they stimulate the imagination, and free the intellect from the shackles of the actual.
in *Mind* 13 October 1904

13 If I were to suggest that between the Earth and Mars there is a china teapot revolving about the sun in an elliptical orbit, nobody would be able to disprove my assertion provided I were careful to add that the teapot is too small to be revealed even by our most powerful telescopes. But if I were to go on to say that, since my assertion cannot be disproved, it is intolerable presumption on the part of human reason to doubt it, I should rightly be thought to be talking nonsense.
'Is There a God?', commissioned (but not published) by *The Illustrated Magazine*, 1952; first published in *Collected Papers* vol. 11 (1997)

14 Many people would sooner die than think. In fact they do.
attributed

Bob Russell *and* Bobby Scott 1937–90
American songwriters

15 He ain't heavy . . . he's my brother.
title of song (1969)

Dale Russell 1937–
Canadian palaeontologist

16 Dinosaurs are a touchstone that separates the mentality of children from that of adults.
An Odyssey in Time: the Dinosaurs of North America (1989)

Dora Russell 1894–1986
English feminist

17 We want better reasons for having children than not knowing how to prevent them.
Hypatia (1925) ch. 4

George William Russell *see* Æ

Lord John Russell 1792–1878
British Whig statesman, Prime Minister 1846–52, 1865–6.
On Russell: see DERBY 274:3

18 It is impossible that the whisper of a faction should prevail against the voice of a nation.
reply to an Address from a meeting of 150,000 persons at Birmingham on the defeat of the second Reform Bill, October 1831
S. Walpole *Life of Lord John Russell* (1889) vol. 1, ch. 7

19 If peace cannot be maintained with honour, it is no longer peace.
speech at Greenock, 19 September 1853, in *The Times* 21 September 1853; see **CHAMBERLAIN** 214:6, **DISRAELI** 285:8

20 Among the defects of the Bill, which were numerous, one provision was conspicuous by its presence and another by its absence.
speech to the electors of the City of London, April 1859, in *The Times* 9 April 1859

21 A proverb is one man's wit and all men's wisdom.
R. J. Mackintosh *Sir James Mackintosh* (1835) vol. 2, ch. 7

William Howard Russell 1820–1907

Irish journalist; war correspondent of *The Times*

1 They dashed on towards that thin red line tipped with steel.

of the Russians charging the British at the battle of Balaclava, 1854

> The British Expedition to the Crimea (1877); Russell's original dispatch read: 'That thin red streak topped with a line of steel' in *The Times* 14 November 1854; see **KIPLING** 467:17

Ernest Rutherford 1871–1937

New Zealand physicist. On Rutherford: see **BULLARD** 170:6

2 All science is either physics or stamp collecting.

> J. B. Birks *Rutherford at Manchester* (1962)

3 If your experiment needs statistics, you ought to have done a better experiment.

> Norman T. J. Bailey *The Mathematical Approach to Biology and Medicine* (1967)

4 It was quite the most incredible event that has ever happened to me in my life. It was almost as incredible as if you fired a 15-inch shell at a piece of tissue paper and it came back and hit you.

on the back-scattering effect of metal foil on alpha-particles

> E. N. da C. Andrade *Rutherford and the Nature of the Atom* (1964)

5 We haven't got the money, so we've got to think!

> in *Bulletin of the Institute of Physics* (1962) vol. 13 (as recalled by R. V. Jones)

Sue Ryder 1923–2000

English charity worker

6 I don't look for reward. Surely, according to God's judgement, our reward is when we die. We are all pilgrims on this earth.

after her peerage was awarded in 1979

> in *Daily Telegraph* 3 November 2000; obituary

Gilbert Ryle 1900–76

English philosopher

7 A myth is, of course, not a fairy story. It is the presentation of facts belonging to one category in the idioms appropriate to another. To explode a myth is accordingly not to deny the facts but to re-allocate them.

> *The Concept of Mind* (1949) introduction

8 Philosophy is the replacement of category-habits by category-disciplines.

> *The Concept of Mind* (1949) introduction

9 The dogma of the Ghost in the Machine.

on the mental-conduct concepts of **DESCARTES**

> *The Concept of Mind* (1949) ch. 1

Ss

Sa'adiah ben Joseph Gaon 882–942

Jewish philosopher

10 We enquire into and speculate on the teachings of our religion for two reasons: first, to find out for ourselves what we have learned as imparted knowledge from the prophets of God; and secondly, to be able to refute anyone who argues against us concerning anything to do with our religion.

> *The Book of Beliefs and Opinions* introduction, sect. 6

11 Even women and children and those with no aptitude for speculation can attain to a complete religion, for all men are on an equal footing as far as knowledge derived from the senses is concerned. Praised be God who in his wisdom ordered things thus.

> *The Book of Beliefs and Opinions* introduction, sect. 6

Rafael Sabatini 1875–1950

Italian-born British novelist

12 He was born with a gift of laughter and a sense that the world was mad. And that was all his patrimony.

> *Scaramouche* (1921) bk. 1, ch. 1

Thomas Sackville, Lord Dorset 1536–1608

English poet and dramatist

13 And old Saturnus, with his frosty face,
With chilling cold had pierced the tender green
. . .
The summer's beauty yields to winter's blast.

> *The Mirror for Magistrates* (1563) st. 1

14 Crookbacked he was, tooth-shaken, and blear-eyed,
Went on three feet, and sometime crept on four,
With old lame bones that rattled by his side,
His scalp all pilled and he with eld forlore;
His withered fist still knocking at Death's door,
Fumbling and drivelling as he draws his breath;
For brief, the shape and messenger of Death.

of Old Age

> *The Mirror for Magistrates* (1563) st. 48

Victoria ('Vita') Sackville-West 1892–1962

English writer and gardener; wife of Harold **NICOLSON**

15 The greater cats with golden eyes
Stare out between the bars.

Deserts are there, and different skies,
And night with different stars.
The King's Daughter (1929) pt. 2, no. 1

1 The country habit has me by the heart,
For he's bewitched for ever who has seen,
Not with his eyes but with his vision, Spring
Flow down the woods and stipple leaves with
sun.
The Land (1926) 'Winter'

Anwar al-Sadat 1918–81
Egyptian statesman, President 1970–81

2 Peace is much more precious than a piece of
land.
speech in Cairo, 8 March 1978

Marquis de Sade 1740–1814
French writer and soldier

3 Do not breed. Nothing gives less pleasure than
childbearing. Pregnancies are damaging to
health, spoil the figure, wither the charms, and
it's the cloud of uncertainty forever hanging
over these events that darkens a husband's
mood.
Juliette (1797) pt. 1

Sadi *c.*1213–91
Persian poet

4 I never complained at the vicissitudes of fortune,
nor murmured at the ordinances of Heaven,
excepting once, when my feet were bare, and I
had not the means of procuring myself shoes. I
entered the great mosque at Cufah with a heavy
heart when I beheld a man who had no feet. I
offered up praise and thanksgiving to God for
his bounty, and bore with patience the want of
shoes.
The Rose Garden (1258) ch. 3, Tale 19; see **SAYINGS** 684:23

5 Science is for the cultivation of religion, not for
worldly enjoyment.
The Rose Garden (1258)

Carl Sagan 1934–96
American scientist and writer

6 Extraordinary claims require extraordinary
evidence.
*Billions and Billions: Thoughts on Life and Death at the Brink of
the Millennium* (1997)

7 If you wish to make an apple pie from scratch,
you must first invent the universe.
Cosmos (1980) ch. 9

8 To me, it underscores our responsibility to deal
more kindly with one another, and to preserve
and cherish the pale blue dot, the only home
we've ever known.
of Earth as photographed by Voyager 1
Pale Blue Dot (1995)

Françoise Sagan 1935–2004
French novelist

9 To jealousy, nothing is more frightful than
laughter.
La Chamade (1965) ch. 9

Mohammed al-Sahhaf
Iraqi politician, Minister of Information in Saddam
HUSSEIN's government

10 Baghdad is safe, protected. There are no
American infidels in Baghdad.
press briefing during the war in Iraq
in *Sunday Telegraph* 13 April 2003

11 I now inform you that you are too far from
reality.
final briefing to the press in Baghdad
in *Sunday Telegraph* 13 April 2003

Charles-Augustin Sainte-Beuve
1804–69
French critic

12 *Et Vigny plus secret,*
Comme en sa tour d'ivoire, avant midi rentrait.
And Vigny more discreet, as if in his ivory
tower, returned before noon.
Les Pensées d'Août, à M. Villemain (1837)

Antoine de Saint-Exupéry 1900–44
French novelist

13 Grown-ups never understand anything for
themselves, and it is tiresome for children to be
always and forever explaining things to them.
Le Petit Prince (1943) ch. 1

14 It is only with the heart that one can see rightly;
what is essential is invisible to the eye.
Le Petit Prince (1943) ch. 21

15 Experience shows us that love does not consist
in gazing at each other but in looking together
in the same direction.
Terre des Hommes (translated as 'Wind, Sand and Stars', 1939)
ch. 8

Andrei Sakharov 1921–89
Russian nuclear physicist

16 Every day I saw the huge material, intellectual
and nervous resources of thousands of people
being poured into the creation of a means of
total destruction, something capable of
annihilating all human civilization. I noticed that
the control levers were in the hands of people
who, though talented in their own ways, were
cynical.
Sakharov Speaks (1974)

Saki (Hector Hugh Munro) 1870–1916
British short-story writer

1 Waldo is one of those people who would be enormously improved by death.
Beasts and Super-Beasts (1914) 'The Feast of Nemesis'

2 The people of Crete unfortunately make more history than they can consume locally.
Chronicles of Clovis (1911) 'The Jesting of Arlington Stringham'

3 The cook was a good cook, as cooks go; and as cooks go, she went.
Reginald (1904) 'Reginald on Besetting Sins'

4 Never be a pioneer. It's the Early Christian that gets the fattest lion.
Reginald (1904) 'Reginald's Choir Treat'

5 I always say beauty is only sin deep.
Reginald (1904) 'Reginald's Choir Treat'

6 Good gracious, you've got to educate him first. You can't expect a boy to be vicious till he's been to a good school.
Reginald in Russia (1910) 'The Baker's Dozen'

7 A little inaccuracy sometimes saves tons of explanation.
The Square Egg (1924) 'Clovis on the Alleged Romance of Business'

J. D. Salinger 1919–
American novelist and short-story writer

8 The catcher in the rye.
title of novel (1951), from a misquotation of **BURNS**: '"You know that song 'If a body catch a body comin' through the rye'? I'd like—" "It's 'If a body *meet* a body coming through the rye'!" old Phoebe said' *The Catcher in the Rye* (1951) ch. 22; see **BURNS** 177:20, **SALINGER** 678:11

9 Sex is something I really don't understand too hot. You never know *where* the hell you are. I keep making up these sex rules for myself, and then I break them right away.
The Catcher in the Rye (1951) ch. 9

10 Take most people, they're crazy about cars. They worry if they get a little scratch on them, and they're always talking about how many miles they get to a gallon . . . I don't even like *old* cars. I mean they don't even interest me. I'd rather have a goddam horse. A horse is at least *human*, for God's sake.
The Catcher in the Rye (1951) ch. 17

11 I keep picturing all these little kids playing some game in this big field of rye and all . . . I mean if they're running and they don't look where they're going I have to come out from somewhere and catch them. That's all I'd do all day. I'd just be the catcher in the rye.
The Catcher in the Rye (1951) ch. 22

Lord Salisbury (3rd Marquess of Salisbury) 1830–1903
British Conservative statesman, Prime Minister 1855-6, 1886–92, 1895–1902. On Salisbury: see BISMARCK 123:5, DISRAELI 285:8

12 Too clever by half.
of **DISRAELI**'s *amendment on Disestablishment*
speech, House of Commons, 30 March 1868; see **SALISBURY** 679:5

13 English policy is to float lazily downstream, occasionally putting out a diplomatic boathook to avoid collisions.
letter to Lord Lytton, 9 March 1877; in Lady Gwendolen Cecil *Life of Robert, Marquis of Salisbury* (1921–32) vol. 2

14 A great deal of misapprehension arises from the popular use of maps on a small scale. As with such maps you are able to put a thumb on India and a finger on Russia, some persons at once think that the political situation is alarming and that India must be looked to. If the noble Lord would use a larger map—say one on the scale of the Ordnance Map of England—he would find that the distance between Russia and British India is not to be measured by the finger and thumb, but by a rule.
speech, House of Commons, 11 June 1877

15 No lesson seems to be so deeply inculcated by the experience of life as that you never should trust experts. If you believe the doctors, nothing is wholesome: if you believe the theologians, nothing is innocent: if you believe the soldiers, nothing is safe. They all require to have their strong wine diluted by a very large admixture of insipid common sense.
letter to Lord Lytton, 15 June 1877; in Lady Gwendolen Cecil *Life of Robert, Marquis of Salisbury* (1921–32) vol. 2

16 One of the nuisances of the ballot is that when the oracle has spoken you never know what it means.
after the Renfrew by-election of October 1877; Andrew Roberts *Salisbury: Victorian Titan* (1999)

17 What with deafness, ignorance of French, and Bismarck's extraordinary mode of speech, Beaconsfield has the dimmest idea of what is going on—understands everything crossways—and imagines a perpetual conspiracy.
of **DISRAELI** *at the Congress of Berlin*
letter to Lady Salisbury, 23 June 1878

18 We are part of the community of Europe and we must do our duty as such.
speech at Caernarvon, 10 April 1888, in *The Times* 11 April 1888

19 Where property is in question I am guilty . . . of erecting individual liberty as an idol, and of resenting all attempts to destroy or fetter it; but when you pass from liberty to life, in no well-governed State, in no State governed according to the principles of common humanity, are the claims of mere liberty allowed to endanger the lives of the citizens.
speech in the House of Lords, 29 July 1897

1 Horny-handed sons of toil.
in *Quarterly Review* October 1873; later popularized in the US by Denis Kearney (1847–1907); see **LOWELL** 502:18

2 If I had to do literary work of an absorbing character, Oxford is the last place in which I should attempt to do it.
letter to William Sanday, 30 May 1900; Brock and Curthoys (ed.) *History of the University of Oxford* (2000) vol. 7, pt. 2, ch. 25

3 By office boys for office boys.
of the Daily Mail
H. Hamilton Fyfe *Northcliffe, an Intimate Biography* (1930) ch. 4

4 I rank myself no higher in the scheme of things than a policeman—whose utility would disappear if there were no criminals.
comparing his role in the Conservative Party with that of **GLADSTONE**
Lady Gwendolen Cecil *Biographical Studies . . . of Robert, Third Marquess of Salisbury* (1962)

Lord Salisbury (5th Marquess of Salisbury) 1893–1972
British Conservative politician

5 Too clever by half.
of Iain Macleod, Colonial Secretary 'in his relationship to the white communities of Africa'
in the House of Lords, 7 March 1961; see **SALISBURY** 678:12

Sallust (Gaius Sallustius Crispus) 86–35 BC
Roman historian

6 *Alieni appetens, sui profusus.*
Greedy for the property of others, extravagant with his own.
Catiline ch. 5

7 *Nam idem velle atque idem nolle, ea demum firma amicitia est.*
To like and dislike the same things, that is indeed true friendship.
Catiline ch. 20

8 *Quieta movere magna merces videbatur.*
To stir up undisputed matters seemed a great reward in itself.
Catiline ch. 21

9 *Esse quam videri bonus malebat.*
He preferred to be rather than to seem good.
of Cato
Catiline ch. 54

10 *Urbem venalem et mature perituram, si emptorem invenerit.*
A venal city ripe to perish, if a buyer can be found.
of Rome
Jugurtha ch. 35

11 *Punica fide.*
With Carthaginian trustworthiness.
meaning treachery
Jugurtha ch. 108, sect. 3

Sallustius fl. *c.*AD 363
Roman writer

12 These things never happened, but are always.
On the Gods and the World

Alex Salmond 1954–
Scottish Nationalist politician

13 Nobody ever celebrated Devolution Day.
asserting his belief in full independence
in *Independent* 2 April 1992

14 The Scottish parliament is our passport to independence.
outgoing speech as party leader to the Scottish Nationalist Party Conference
in *Guardian* 23 September 2000

Sambandar (Tirunanacampantar)
Tamil poet and saint of the 6th–7th century

15 Let us praise the tender feet worshipped by the gods, the feet of our Lord.
hymn to Shiva, from the Tevaram

Lord Samuel 1870–1963
British Liberal politician

16 A library is thought in cold storage.
A Book of Quotations (1947)

Paul A. Samuelson 1915–
American economist

17 The consumer, so it is said, is the king . . . each is a voter who uses his money as votes to get the things done that he wants done.
Economics (8th ed., 1970)

Sana'i d. *c.*1131
Persian poet

18 Each had but known one part, and no man all;
Hence into deadly error each did fall.
No way to know the All man's heart can find:
Can knowledge e'er accompany the blind?
on blind men's conclusions on touching different parts of an elephant
'The Blind Men and the Elephant'; see **JALAL** 428:16

George Sand (Amandine-Aurore Lucille Dupin, Baronne Dudevant) 1804–76
French novelist

19 We cannot tear out a single page of our life, but we can throw the book in the fire.
Mauprat (1837)

20 There is only one happiness in life, to love and be loved.
letter to Lina Calamatta, 31 March 1862

21 Faith is an excitement and an enthusiasm; it is a condition of intellectual magnificence to which

we must cling as to a treasure, and not squander on our way through life in the small coin of empty words, or in exact and priggish argument.
letter to Des Planches, 25 May 1866

1 Art for art's sake is an empty phrase. Art for the sake of the true, art for the sake of the good and the beautiful, that is the faith I am searching for.
letter to Alexandre Saint-Jean, 1872

Carl Sandburg 1878–1967
American poet

2 Hog Butcher for the World,
Tool Maker, Stacker of Wheat,
Player with Railroads and the Nation's Freight Handler;
Stormy, husky, brawling,
City of the Big Shoulders.
'Chicago' (1916)

3 When Abraham Lincoln was shovelled into the tombs,
he forgot the copperheads and the assassin . . .
in the dust, in the cool tombs.
'Cool Tombs' (1918)

4 The fog comes
on little cat feet.
It sits looking
over harbour and city
on silent haunches
and then moves on.
'Fog' (1916)

5 Pile the bodies high at Austerlitz and Waterloo.
Shovel them under and let me work—
I am the grass; I cover all.
'Grass' (1918)

6 I tell you the past is a bucket of ashes.
'Prairie' (1918)

7 Little girl . . . Sometime they'll give a war and nobody will come.
The People, Yes (1936); see **FILM TITLES** 331:12, **GINSBERG** 358:21

8 Poetry is the achievement of the synthesis of hyacinths and biscuits.
in *Atlantic Monthly* March 1923 'Poetry Considered'

9 Slang is a language that rolls up its sleeves, spits on its hands and goes to work.
in *New York Times* 13 February 1959

Henry 'Red' Sanders 1905–58
American football coach

10 Sure, winning isn't everything. It's the only thing.
in *Sports Illustrated* 26 December 1955; often attributed to Vince Lombardi

Lord Sandwich 1718–92
British politician and diplomat; First Lord of the Admiralty

11 If any man will draw up his case, and put his name at the foot of the first page, I will give

him an immediate reply. Where he compels me to turn over the sheet, he must wait my leisure.
N. W. Wraxall *Memoirs* (1884) vol. 1

Martha Sansom 1690–1736
English poet

12 Foolish eyes, thy streams give over,
Wine, not water, binds the lover:
At the table then be shining,
Gay coquette, and all designing.
'Song' (written *c*.1726)

George Santayana 1863–1952
Spanish-born philosopher and critic

13 Fanaticism consists in redoubling your effort when you have forgotten your aim.
The Life of Reason (1905) vol. 1, introduction

14 Those who cannot remember the past are condemned to repeat it.
The Life of Reason (1905) vol. 1, ch. 12

15 It takes patience to appreciate domestic bliss; volatile spirits prefer unhappiness.
The Life of Reason (1905) vol. 2, ch. 2

16 Music is essentially useless, as life is: but both have an ideal extension which lends utility to its conditions.
The Life of Reason (1905) vol. 4, ch. 4

17 Perhaps the only true dignity of man is his capacity to despise himself.
Little Essays (1920) 'Emotions of the Materialist'

18 There is no cure for birth and death save to enjoy the interval.
Soliloquies in England (1922) 'War Shrines'

Sappho
Greek lyric poet of the late 7th century BC. On Sappho: see **BYRON** 185:21

19 Beauty endures only for as long as it can be seen;
Goodness, beautiful today, will remain so tomorrow.
Josephine Balmer *Sappho: Poems and Fragments* (1992) fragment 119

20 Some say an army of cavalry or of infantry or a fleet of ships is the most beautiful thing on the black earth. But I say it is whatever one loves.
D. L. Page (ed.) *Lyrica Graeca Selecta* (1968) no. 16

21 I want neither the honey nor the bee.
D. L. Page (ed.) *Lyrica Graeca Selecta* (1968) no. 146

22 That man seems to me on a par with the gods who sits in your company and listens to you so close to him speaking sweetly and laughing sexily, such a thing makes my heart flutter in my breast, for when I see you even for a moment, then power to speak another word fails me, instead my tongue freezes into silence, and at once a gentle fire has caught throughout my

flesh, and I see nothing with my eyes, and there's a drumming in my ears, and sweat pours down me, and trembling seizes all of me, and I become paler than grass, and I seem to fail almost to the point of death in my very self.
D. L. Page (ed.) *Lyrica Graeca Selecta* (1968) no. 199; see **CATULLUS** 210:13

1 Just as the sweet-apple reddens on the high branch, high on the highest, and the apple-pickers missed it, or rather did not miss it out, but could not reach it.
describing a girl before her marriage
D. L. Page (ed.) *Lyrica Graeca Selecta* (1968) no. 224; see **ROSSETTI** 669:11

2 For in a house that serves the Muses there must be no lamentation: such a thing does not befit it.
sometimes described as her dying words
A. Weighall *Sappho of Lesbos* (1932)

John Singer Sargent 1856–1925
American painter. On Sargent: see ANONYMOUS 18:8

3 Every time I paint a portrait I lose a friend.
attributed; N. Bentley and E. Esar *Treasury of Humorous Quotations* (1951)

Leslie Sarony 1897–1985
English songwriter

4 Ain't it grand to be blooming well dead?
title of song (1932)

Nathalie Sarraute 1902–99
French novelist

5 Radio and television . . . have succeeded in lifting the manufacture of banality out of the sphere of handicraft and placed it in that of a major industry.
in *Times Literary Supplement* 10 June 1960

Patrick Sarsfield c.1655–93
Irish soldier and Jacobite supporter

6 Would to God this wound had been for Ireland.
last words, on being mortally wounded at the battle of Landen, 19 August 1693, while fighting for France
attributed

Jean-Paul Sartre 1905–80
French philosopher, novelist, dramatist, and critic. On Sartre: see DE GAULLE 271:19

7 *Quand les riches se font la guerre ce sont les pauvres qui meurent.*
When the rich wage war it's the poor who die.
Le Diable et le bon Dieu (1951) act 1, tableau 1

8 Nothingness haunts being.
Being and Nothingness (1943) pt. 1, ch. 1

9 Existence precedes and rules essence.
Being and Nothingness (1943) pt. 4, ch. 1

10 *Je suis condamné à être libre.*
I am condemned to be free.
Being and Nothingness (1943) pt. 4, ch. 1

11 Man, being condemned to be free carries the weight of the whole world on his shoulders; he is responsible for the world and himself as a way of being.
Being and Nothingness (1943) pt. 4, ch. 1

12 *L'homme est une passion inutile.*
Man is a useless passion.
Being and Nothingness (1943) pt. 4, ch. 2

13 Human life begins on the far side of despair.
The Flies (1943) act 3, sc. 2

14 *Alors, c'est ça l'Enfer. Je n'aurais jamais cru . . . Vous vous rappelez: le soufre, le bûcher, le gril . . . Ah! quelle plaisanterie. Pas besoin de gril, L'Enfer, c'est les Autres.*
So that's what Hell is: I'd never have believed it . . . Do you remember, brimstone, the stake, the gridiron? . . . What a joke! No need of a gridiron, Hell is other people.
Huis Clos (1944) sc. 5; see **ELIOT** 308:23

15 I hate victims who respect their executioners.
Loser Wins [*Les Séquestrés d'Altona*] (1960) act 1, sc. 1

16 If only one man should hate another, it would be sufficient for hatred to spread from one to another and overwhelm mankind.
Lucifer and the Lord (1952) act 1, sc. 3

17 *Comme tous les songe-creux, je confondis le désenchantement avec la vérité.*
Like all dreamers, I mistook disenchantment for truth.
Les Mots (1964) 'Écrire'

18 *Je confondis les choses avec leurs noms: c'est croire.*
I confused things with their names: that is belief.
Les Mots (1964) 'Écrire'

19 *Il n'y a pas de bon père, c'est la règle; qu'on n'en tienne pas grief aux hommes mais au lien de paternité qui est pourri. Faire des enfants, rien de mieux; en avoir, quelle iniquité!*
There is no good father, that's the rule. Don't lay the blame on men but on the bond of paternity, which is rotten. To beget children, nothing better; to *have* them, what iniquity!
Les Mots (1964) 'Lire'

20 *Les bons pauvres ne savent pas que leur office est d'exercer notre générosité.*
The poor don't know that their function in life is to exercise our generosity.
Les Mots (1964) 'Lire'

21 *Elle ne croyait à rien; seul, son scepticisme l'empêchait d'être athée.*
She believed in nothing; only her scepticism kept her from being an atheist.
Les Mots (1964) 'Lire'

1 My thought is *me*: that's why I can't stop. I exist by what I think . . . and I can't prevent myself from thinking.
  Nausea (1938) 'Monday'

2 I distrust the incommunicable: it is the source of all violence.
  'Qu'est-ce que la littérature?' in *Les Temps Modernes* July 1947, p. 106

3 *L'écrivain doit donc refuser de se laisser transformer en institution.*

  A writer must refuse, therefore, to allow himself to be transformed into an institution.
  refusing the Nobel Prize at Stockholm, 22 October 1964; in M. Contat and M. Rybalka (eds.) *Les Écrits de Sartre* (1970)

Siegfried Sassoon 1886–1967

English poet

4 If I were fierce, and bald, and short of breath,
  I'd live with scarlet Majors at the Base,
  And speed glum heroes up the line to death.
  'Base Details' (1918)

5 I'd like to see a Tank come down the stalls,
  Lurching to rag-time tunes, or 'Home, sweet
    Home',—
  And there'd be no more jokes in Music-halls
  To mock the riddled corpses round Bapaume.
  'Blighters' (1917)

6 Does it matter?—losing your sight? . . .
  There's such splendid work for the blind;
  And people will always be kind,
  As you sit on the terrace remembering
  And turning your face to the light.
  'Does it Matter?' (1918)

7 Soldiers are citizens of death's grey land,
  Drawing no dividend from time's tomorrows.
  'Dreamers' (1918)

8 You are too young to fall asleep for ever;
  And when you sleep you remind me of the
    dead.
  'The Dug-Out' (1919)

9 Everyone suddenly burst out singing;
  And I was filled with such delight
  As prisoned birds must find in freedom.
  'Everyone Sang' (1919)

10 The song was wordless; the singing will never
    be done.
  'Everyone Sang' (1919)

11 'Good-morning; good morning!' the General said
  When we met him last week on our way to the
    line.
  Now the soldiers he smiled at are most of 'em
    dead,
  And we're cursing his staff for incompetent
    swine.
  'He's a cheery old card,' grunted Harry to Jack
  As they slogged up to Arras with rifle and pack.

  But he did for them both by his plan of attack.
  'The General' (1918)

12 Here was the world's worst wound. And here
    with pride
  'Their name liveth for ever' the Gateway claims.
  Was ever an immolation so belied
  As these intolerably nameless names?
  'On Passing the New Menin Gate' (1928); see **EPITAPHS** 319:12

Cicely Saunders 1916–2005

English nurse and physician, founder of St Christopher's Hospice, London

13 Suffering is only intolerable when nobody cares.
  'The Management of Patients in the Terminal Stage' in *Cancer* 1960 vol. 6

14 Deception is not as creative as truth. We do best in life if we look at it with clear eyes, and I think that applies to coming up to death as well.
  of the Hospice movement
  in *Time* 5 September 1988

15 You matter because you are you, and you matter to the last moment of your life. We will do all that we can not only to help you die peacefully, but also to live until you die.
  quoted in Robert Twycross 'A Tribute to Dame Cicely Saunders', Memorial Service, 8 March 2006

Ferdinand de Saussure 1857–1913

Swiss linguistics scholar

16 In language there are only differences.
  Course in General Linguistics (1916)

17 Language can . . . be compared with a sheet of paper: thought is the front and sound the back; one cannot cut the front without cutting the back at the same time.
  Course in General Linguistics (1916)

Minot Judson Savage 1841–1918

American Unitarian minister

18   In the moon's eclipse,
  The earth's round shadow on its face I see!
  I read God's works, which are his book indeed,
  And trust the hint that falleth from his lips
  More than all man's infallibility.
  'Magellan' (1883); see **MISQUOTATIONS** 547:21

George Savile *see* Lord Halifax

Dorothy L. Sayers 1893–1957

English writer of detective fiction and scholar

19 A society in which consumption has to be artificially stimulated in order to keep production going is a society founded on trash and waste, and such a society is a house built upon sand.
  Creed or Chaos? (1947) ch. 6

20 I admit it is better fun to punt than to be punted, and that a desire to have all the fun is nine-tenths of the law of chivalry.
  Gaudy Night (1935) ch. 14

1 The worst sin—perhaps the only sin—passion can commit, is to be joyless.
Gaudy Night (1935) ch. 23

2 I always have a quotation for everything—it saves original thinking.
Have His Carcase (1932)

3 Perhaps it is no wonder that the women were first at the Cradle and last at the Cross. They had never known a man like this Man—there has never been such another . . . who never made arch jokes about them, never treated them either as 'The women, God help us', or 'The ladies, God bless them!'
Unpopular Opinions (1946) 'The Human-Not-Quite-Human'

☐ **Sayings** *see* **box overleaf**

Gerald Scarfe 1936–
English caricaturist

4 I find a particular delight in taking the caricature as far as I can. It satisfies me to stretch the human frame about and recreate it and yet keep a likeness.
Scarfe by Scarfe (1986)

Lord Scarman 1911–2004
British judge

5 A government above the law is a menace to be defeated.
Why Britain Needs a Written Constitution (1992)

Friedrich von Schelling 1775–1854
German philosopher

6 Architecture in general is frozen music.
Philosophie der Kunst (1809)

Elsa Schiaparelli 1896–1973
Italian-born French fashion designer

7 If I have become what I am, I owe it to two distinct things—poverty and Paris. Poverty forced me to work, and Paris gave me a liking for it and courage.
in Constellation March 1954

8 The daring is gone. No one can dream any more.
on fashions after her last collection in 1954
Palmer White *Elsa Schiaparelli: Empress of Paris Fashion* (1986) ch. 22

Ferdinand von Schill 1776–1809
Prussian soldier

9 *Leiber ein Ende mit Schrecken als ein Schreck ohne Ende.*
Better a terrible end than terror without end.
to his troops before attacking the kingdom of Westphalia, 1809; Heinrich von Treitschke History of Germany in the Nineteenth Century *(1915) vol. 1, p. 403*

Friedrich von Schiller 1759–1805
German dramatist and poet

10 *Freude, schöner Götterfunken,*
Tochter aus Elysium,
Wir betreten feuertrunken,
Himmlische, dein Heiligtum.
Deine Zauber binden wieder,
Was die Mode streng geteilt.
Joy, beautiful radiance of the gods, daughter of Elysium, we set foot in your heavenly shrine dazzled by your brilliance. Your charms re-unite what common use has harshly divided.
'An die Freude' (1785)

11 *Alle Menschen werden Brüder*
Wo dein sanfter Flügel weilt.
All men become brothers under your tender wing.
'An die Freude' (1785)

12 *Ein Augenblick, gelebt im Paradiese,*
Wird nicht zu teuer mit dem Tod gebüsst.
One moment spent in Paradise
Is not too dearly paid for with one's life.
Don Carlos (1787) act 1, sc. 5

13 *Die Sonne geht in meinem Staat nicht unter.*
The sun does not set in my dominions.
Philip II
Don Carlos (1787) act 1, sc. 6; see **NORTH** 577:3

14 *Dreiundzwanzig Jahre,*
Und nichts für die Unsterblichkeit getan!
Twenty-three years old,
and I've done nothing for my immortality!
Don Carlos (1787) act 2, sc. 2

15 *Oft sogar es ist weise, zu entdecken,*
Was nicht verschwiegen bleiben kann.
It is wise to disclose what cannot be concealed.
Don Carlos (1787) act 4, sc. 4

16 *Nur durch das Morgenthor des Schönen*
Drangst du in der Erkenntnis Land.
Only through beauty's gate, can you penetrate the land of knowledge.
'Die Künstler' (1789)

17 *Mit der Dummheit kämpfen Götter selbst vergebens.*
With stupidity the gods themselves struggle in vain.
The Maid of Orleans (1801) act 3, sc. 6

18 *Was ist der langen Rede kurzer Sinn?*
What is the brief meaning of the lengthy speech?
Die Piccolomini (1800) act 1, sc. 2

19 *Ich bin mein Himmel und meine Hölle.*
I am my heaven and my hell.
Die Räuber (1781)

20 *Die Weltgeschichte ist das Weltgericht.*
The world's history is the world's judgement.
'Resignation' (1786) st. 19

continued

🌿 Sayings 🌿

1 And this, too, shall pass away.
traditional saying said to be true for all times and situations; an early version is: 'The Sultan asked for a signet motto, that should hold good for Adversity or Prosperity. Solomon gave him—"This also shall pass away"' Edward Fitzgerald *Polonius* (1852)

2 Been there, done that, got the T-shirt.
'been there, done that' recorded from 1980s, expanded form from 1990s

3 The best defence is a good offence.
late 20th century American saying; see **PROVERBS** 627:2

4 Business is like a car: it will not run by itself except downhill.
American saying

5 Children: one is one, two is fun, three is a houseful.
American

6 Christ has no body now on earth but yours, no hands but yours, no feet but yours, yours are the eyes through which he looks compassion on this world, yours are the feet with which he is to go about doing good.
modern saying, often attributed to St **TERESA** of Ávila (1512–82), but not found in her writings

7 Close your eyes and think of England.
said to derive from a 1912 entry in the journal of Lady Hillingdon (1857–1940), but the journal has never been traced

8 A committee is a group of the unwilling, chosen from the unfit, to do the unnecessary.
various attributions (origin unknown)

9 *Corruptio optimi pessima.*
Corruption of the best becomes the worst.
Latin saying, found in English from the early 17th century

10 Daddy, what did you do in the Great War?
daughter to father in First World War recruiting poster

11 [Death is] nature's way of telling you to slow down.
life insurance proverb; in *Newsweek* 25 April 1960

12 The Devil is in the details.
late 20th century saying

13 Different strokes for different folks.
strokes = *comforting gestures of approval or congratulation*
of US origin, late 20th century saying

14 Do not fold, spindle or mutilate.
instruction on punched cards (1950s, and in differing forms from the 1930s)

15 Don't get mad, get even.
late 20th century saying

16 The enemy of my enemy is my friend.
late 20th century, said to be 'an old Arab proverb'

17 An eye for an eye makes the whole world blind.
modern saying, often attributed to Mahatma **GANDHI**

18 The family that prays together stays together.
motto devised by Al Scalpone for the Roman Catholic Family Rosary Crusade, 1947

19 Garbage in, garbage out.
in computing, incorrect or faulty input will always cause poor output; origin of the acronym GIGO

20 Give a man a fish, and you feed him for a day; show him how to catch fish, and you feed him for a lifetime.
mid 20th century saying, perhaps deriving from the Chinese proverb 'Who teaches me for a day is my father for a lifetime'

21 Give me a child for the first seven years, and you may do what you like with him afterwards.
attributed as a Jesuit maxim, in *Lean's Collectanea* vol. 3 (1903); see **SPARK** 765:10

22 Go to jail. Go directly to jail. Do not pass go. Do not collect £200.
instructions on 'Community Chest' card in the game 'Monopoly'; invented by Charles Brace Darrow (1889–1967) in 1931

23 I cried because I had no shoes, until I met a man who had no feet.
modern saying, deriving from a Persian original; see **SADI** 677:4

24 If it ain't broke, don't fix it.
Bert Lance (1931–) in *Nation's Business* May 1977

25 If life hands you lemons, make lemonade.
late 20th century saying

26 If you're not part of the solution, you're part of the problem.
late 20th century saying; see **CLEAVER** 235:4

27 *Il ne faut pas être plus royaliste que le roi.*
You mustn't be more of a royalist than the king.
saying from the time of Louis XVI; François René, Vicomte de Chateaubriand *De la monarchie selon la charte* (1816) ch. 81

28 I married my husband for life, not for lunch.
origin unknown

29 It's not a bug, it's a feature.
bug = *an error in a computer program or system*
late 20th century saying

30 It's not what you know, it's who you know.
late 20th century saying

31 It's the second mouse that gets the cheese.
modern addition to the proverb 'The early bird . . .'; see **PROVERBS** 630:40

32 Justice delayed is justice denied.
late 20th century saying; see **MAGNA CARTA** 515:2

33 Laughter is the best medicine.
late 20th century saying

34 Let's run it up the flagpole and see if anyone salutes it.
Reginald Rose *Twelve Angry Men* (1955); recorded as an established advertising expression in the 1960s

continued

Sayings *continued*

1 Life is a sexually transmitted disease.
   graffito found on the London Underground, in D. J. Enright (ed.) *The Faber Book of Fevers and Frets* (1989)

2 May you live in interesting times.
   modern saying said to derive from a Chinese curse, but likely to be apocryphal; see KENNEDY 460:21

3 Members [of civil service orders] rise from CMG (known sometimes in Whitehall as 'Call Me God') to the KCMG ('Kindly Call Me God') to—for a select few governors and super-ambassadors—the GCMG ('God Calls Me God').
   Anthony Sampson *Anatomy of Britain* (1962) ch. 18

4 *Nil carborundum illegitimi.*
   Don't let the bastards grind you down.
   cod Latin saying in circulation during the Second World War, though possibly of earlier origin; often quoted as '*nil carborundum*' or '*illegitimi non carborundum*'

5 Nostalgia isn't what it used to be.
   graffito; taken as title of book by Simone Signoret, 1978

6 Nothing is for ever.
   late 20th century saying

7 Not to be a republican at twenty is proof of want of heart; to be one at thirty is proof of want of head.
   often used in the form 'Not to be a socialist . . . '
   adopted by CLEMENCEAU, and attributed by him to GUIZOT

8 The opera ain't over 'til the fat lady sings.
   Dan Cook, in *Washington Post* 3 June 1978

9 *Post coitum omne animal triste.*
   After coition every animal is sad.
   post-classical saying

10 Sell in May and go away (come back on St Leger day).
   relating to the cycle of activity on the London Stock Exchange: trading was slack in the summer. The St Leger horse race is in early September
   late 20th century saying

11 *Se non è vero, è molto ben trovato.*
   If it is not true, it is a happy invention.
   common saying from the 16th century

12 There is one thing stronger than all the armies in the world; and that is an idea whose time has come.
   in flyer for *Nation* 15 April 1943; see HUGO 419:3

13 There's no such thing as a free lunch.
   colloquial axiom in US economics from the 1960s, much associated with Milton FRIEDMAN; recorded in form 'there ain't no such thing as a free lunch' from 1938, which gave rise to the acronym TANSTAAFL in Robert Heinlein's *The Moon is a Harsh Mistress* (1966) ch. 11

14 Thirty days hath September,
   April, June, and November;
   All the rest have thirty-one,
   Excepting February alone,
   And that has twenty-eight days clear
   And twenty-nine in each leap year.
   Stevins MS (c.1555)

15 To err is human but to really foul things up requires a computer.
   Farmers' Almanac for 1978 'Capsules of Wisdom'; see POPE 616:10

16 What goes around comes around.
   late 20th century saying

17 What matters is what works.
   late 20th century saying

18 What you see is what you get.
   a computing expression, from which the acronym wysiwyg *derives*
   late 20th century saying

19 When all you have is a hammer, everything looks like a nail.
   late 20th century saying, mainly North American

20 When war is declared, Truth is the first casualty.
   attributed to Hiram Johnson, speaking in the US Senate, 1918, but not recorded in his speech; the first recorded use is as epigraph to Arthur Ponsonby's *Falsehood in Wartime* (1928); see JOHNSON 436:8

21 A woman without a man is like a fish without a bicycle.
   late 20th century saying, sometimes attributed to Gloria STEINEM

Friedrich von Schiller *continued*

22 *Der Mohr hat seine Arbeit getan, der Mohr kann gehen.*
   The Moor has done his work, the Moor can go.
   usually misquoted as 'Der Mohr hat seine Schuldigkeit getan [*The Moor has done his duty*]'
   Die Verschwörung des Fiesco (1782) act 3, sc. 4

23 *Anklagen ist mein Amt und meine Sendung.*
   To accuse is my duty and my mission.
   Wallenstein (1800)

24 *Dem Mimen flicht die Nachwelt keine Kränze.*
   Posterity weaves no garlands for the actor.
   often quoted as 'no garlands for imitators'
   Wallenstein's Camp (1798) prologue

25 *Wir wollen sein ein einzig Volk von Brüdern*
   In keiner Not uns trennen und Gefahr.
   We would be a single nation of brothers
   Standing together in any hour of need or danger.
   Wilhelm Tell (1804) act 2, sc. 2

26 If man is ever to solve that problem of politics in practice he will have to approach it through the problem of the aesthetic, because it is only through Beauty that man makes his way to Freedom.
   On the Aesthetic Education of Man (1795) letter 2, para. 5

27 The most perfect of all works of art is true political freedom.
   On the Aesthetic Education of Man (1795) letter 2

1 One would need to be already wise, in order to love wisdom.

> *On the Aesthetic Education of Man* (1795) letter 8

2 Man plays only when he is in the full sense of the word a man, and he is only wholly Man when he is playing.

> *On the Aesthetic Education of Man* (1795) letter 15, para. 9

3 Just as nature began gradually to vanish from human life as experience . . . so we see it emerge in the world of the poet as an idea.

> *On the Naive and Sentimental in Literature* (1796), tr. H. Watanabe-O'Kelly

Arthur M. Schlesinger Jr. 1917–2007
American historian

4 The answer to the runaway Presidency is not the messenger-boy Presidency. The American democracy must discover a middle way between making the President a czar and making him a puppet.

> *The Imperial Presidency* (1973) preface

Moritz Schlick 1882–1936
German philosopher

5 The meaning of a proposition is the method of its verification.

> *Philosophical Review* (1936) vol. 45

Heinrich Schliemann 1822–90
German archaeologist

6 I have gazed upon the face of Agamemnon.

> *on discovering a gold mask at Mycenae, 1876; traditional version of his telegram to the minister at Athens: 'This one is very like the picture which my imagination formed of Agamemnon long ago'*
> W. M. Calder and D. A. Traill *Myth, Scandal, and History* (1986)

Artur Schnabel 1882–1951
Austrian-born pianist

7 I know two kinds of audiences only—one coughing, and one not coughing.

> *My Life and Music* (1961) pt. 2, ch. 10

8 The notes I handle no better than many pianists. But the pauses between the notes—ah, that is where the art resides!

> in *Chicago Daily News* 11 June 1958

9 Too easy for children, and too difficult for artists.

> *of Mozart's sonatas*
> Nat Shapiro (ed.) *Encyclopaedia of Quotations about Music* (1978); in *My Life and Music* (1961) Schnabel says: 'Children are given Mozart because of the small *quantity* of the notes; grown-ups avoid Mozart because of the great *quality* of the notes'

Arnold Schoenberg 1874–1951
Austrian-born American composer and musical theorist

10 If it is art, it is not for the masses. 'If it is for the masses it is not art' is a topic which is rather similar to a word of yourself.

> letter to W. S. Schlamm, 1 July 1945

11 I am delighted to add another unplayable work to the repertoire. I want the Concerto to be difficult and I want the little finger to become longer. I can wait.

> *of his Violin Concerto*
> Joseph Machlis *Introduction to Contemporary Music* (1963)

Arthur Schopenhauer 1788–1860
German philosopher

12 The ordinary man has no sense for general truths . . . the genius on the contrary, overlooks and neglects what is individual.

> *Parerga and Paralipomena* (1851)

13 Wealth is like sea-water; the more we have, the thirstier we become, and the same is true of fame.

> *Parerga and Paralipomena* (1851)

14 Every separation gives a foretaste of death, and every meeting a foretaste of the resurrection.

> 'Psychological Observations' (1851) in *Essays* (1897, tr. Mrs Rudolf Dircks)

15 The suicide wills life, and is only dissatisfied with the conditions under which it has presented itself to him.

> *The World as Will and Idea* (1819) bk. 4, sect. 69

Olive Schreiner 1855–1920
South African novelist and feminist

16 All that is buried is not dead.

> *The Story of an African Farm* (1883) vol. 1, pt. 1, ch. 13

Patricia Schroeder 1940–
American Democratic politician

17 Ronald Reagan . . . is attempting a great breakthrough in political technology—he has been perfecting the Teflon-coated Presidency. He sees to it that nothing sticks to him.

> speech in the US House of Representatives, 2 August 1983

Budd Schulberg 1914–
American writer. See also **FILM LINES** 328:12

18 What makes Sammy run?

> title of book (1941)

E. F. Schumacher 1911–77
German-born economist

19 It was not the power of the Spaniards that destroyed the Aztec Empire but the disbelief of the Aztecs in themselves.

> *Roots of Economic Growth* (1962)

1 Small is beautiful. A study of economics as if people mattered.
title of book (1973)

2 Call a thing immoral or ugly, soul-destroying or a degradation of man, a peril to the peace of the world or to the well-being of future generations: as long as you have not shown it to be 'uneconomic' you have not really questioned its right to exist, grow, and prosper.
Small is Beautiful (1973) pt. 1, ch. 3

3 The most striking thing about modern industry is that it requires so much and accomplishes so little. Modern industry seems to be inefficient to a degree that surpasses one's ordinary powers of imagination. Its inefficiency therefore remains unnoticed.
Small is Beautiful (1973) pt. 2, ch. 3

4 It is of little use trying to suppress terrorism if the production of deadly devices continues to be deemed a legitimate employment of man's creative powers.
Small is Beautiful (1973) epilogue

Robert Schumann 1810–56
German composer

5 Hats off, gentlemen—a genius!
of Chopin
'An Opus 2' (1831); H. Pleasants (ed.) *Schumann on Music* (1965)

J. A. Schumpeter 1883–1950
American economist

6 The cold metal of economic theory is in Marx's pages immersed in such a wealth of steaming phrases as to acquire a temperature not naturally its own.
Capitalism, Socialism and Democracy (1942)

7 The first thing a man will do for his ideals is lie.
History of Economic Analysis (1954) pt. 1, ch. 4, note 10

8 One servant is worth a thousand gadgets.
J. K. Galbraith *A Life in our Times* (1981) ch. 6

Carl Schurz 1829–1906
American soldier and politician

9 My country, right or wrong; if right, to be kept right; and if wrong, to be set right!
speech, US Senate, 29 February 1872, in *Congressional Globe* vol. 45; see **DECATUR** 270:4

Delmore Schwartz 1913–66
American poet

10 Dogs are Shakespearean, children are strangers. Let Freud and Wordsworth discuss the child, Angels and Platonists shall judge the dog.
'Dogs are Shakespearean, Children are Strangers' (1938)

11 The heavy bear who goes with me, A manifold honey to smear his face,

Clumsy and lumbering here and there, The central ton of every place, The hungry beating brutish one In love with candy, anger, and sleep, Crazy factotum, dishevelling all, Climbs the building, kicks the football, Boxes his brother in the hate-ridden city.
'The Heavy Bear Who Goes With Me' (1958)

Albert Schweitzer 1875–1965
Franco-German missionary

12 Late on the third day, at the very moment when, at sunset, we were making our way through a herd of hippopotamuses, there flashed upon my mind, unforeseen and unsought, the phrase, 'Reverence for Life'.
Aus meinem Leben und Denken (1933) ch. 13

13 Truth has no special time of its own. Its hour is now—always, and indeed then most truly when it seems most unsuitable to actual circumstances.
Zwischen Wasser und Urwald (On the Edge of the Primeval Forest, 1922) ch. 11

Kurt Schwitters 1887–1948
German painter

14 I am a painter and I nail my pictures together.
R. Hausmann *Am Anfang war Dada* (1972)

Scipio Africanus (Publius Cornelius Scipio Africanus Major) 236–*c.*184 BC
Roman general and politician

15 *Numquam se minus otiosum esse quam cum otiosus, nec minus solum quam cum solus esset.*
Never less idle than when wholly idle, nor less alone than when wholly alone.
Cicero *De Officiis* bk. 3, ch. 1

16 *Ingrata patria, ne ossa quidem mea habes.*
Ungrateful country, you do not even have my bones.
inscription chosen for his tomb, when dying in voluntary exile
Valerius Maximus *Memorable Doings and Sayings* (2000, tr. D. R. Shackleton Bailey) bk. 5, ch. 3

Alexander Scott *c.*1525–*c.*1584
Scottish poet

17 Love is ane fervent fire, Kindled without desire, Short pleasure, long displeasure; Repentance is the hire; And pure treasure without measure. Love is ane fervent fire.
'Lo, What it is to Love' (*c.*1568)

C. P. Scott 1846–1932
English journalist; editor of the *Manchester Guardian*, 1872–1929

18 Comment is free, but facts are sacred.
in *Manchester Guardian* 5 May 1921; see **STOPPARD** 777:17

1 *Television*? The word is half Greek, half Latin.
No good can come of it.
Asa Briggs *The BBC: the First Fifty Years* (1985)

Robert Falcon Scott 1868–1912

English polar explorer. On Scott: see **CHERRY-GARRARD**
222:16

2 Great God! this is an awful place.
of the South Pole
diary, 17 January 1912, in *Scott's Last Expedition* (1913) vol. 1,
ch. 18

3 Make the boy interested in natural history if you
can; it is better than games.
last letter to his wife, in *Scott's Last Expedition* (1913) vol. 1,
ch. 20

4 Had we lived, I should have had a tale to tell of
the hardihood, endurance, and courage of my
companions which would have stirred the heart
of every Englishman. These rough notes and
our dead bodies must tell the tale.
'Message to the Public' in late editions of *The Times* 11
February 1913, and those of the following day; in *Scott's Last
Expedition* (1913) vol. 1, ch. 20

5 For God's sake look after our people.
last diary entry, 29 March 1912, in *Scott's Last Expedition* (1913)
vol. 1, ch. 20

Sir Walter Scott 1771–1832

Scottish novelist and poet. On Scott: see **ANONYMOUS** 19:15,
CARLYLE 199:18, **HAZLITT** 386:17

6 The valiant Knight of Triermain
Rung forth his challenge-blast again,
But answer came there none.
The Bridal of Triermain (1813) canto 3, st. 10; see **CARROLL**
203:5

7 Come fill up my cup, come fill up my can,
Come saddle your horses, and call up your men;
Come open the West Port, and let me gang free,
And it's room for the bonnets of Bonny
Dundee!'
The Doom of Devorgoil (1830) act 2, sc. 2 'Bonny Dundee'; see
SCOTT 689:23

8 Yet seemed that tone, and gesture bland,
Less used to sue than to command.
The Lady of the Lake (1810) canto 1, st. 21; see **SHAKESPEARE**
730:3

9 He is gone on the mountain,
He is lost to the forest,
Like a summer-dried fountain,
When our need was the sorest.
The Lady of the Lake (1810) canto 3, st. 16

10 Respect was mingled with surprise,
And the stern joy which warriors feel
In foemen worthy of their steel.
The Lady of the Lake (1810) canto 5, st. 10

11 If thou would'st view fair Melrose aright,
Go visit it by the pale moonlight;
For the gay beams of lightsome day
Gild, but to flout, the ruins grey.
The Lay of the Last Minstrel (1805) canto 2, st. 1

12   For ne'er
Was flattery lost on poet's ear:
A simple race! they waste their toil
For the vain tribute of a smile.
The Lay of the Last Minstrel (1805) canto 4, closing words

13 It is the secret sympathy,
The silver link, the silken tie,
Which heart to heart, and mind to mind,
In body and in soul can bind.
The Lay of the Last Minstrel (1805) canto 5, st. 13

14 Breathes there the man, with soul so dead,
Who never to himself hath said,
This is my own, my native land!
The Lay of the Last Minstrel (1805) canto 6, st. 1

15 Despite those titles, power, and pelf,
The wretch, concentred all in self,
Living, shall forfeit fair renown,
And, doubly dying, shall go down
To the vile dust, from whence he sprung,
Unwept, unhonoured, and unsung.
The Lay of the Last Minstrel (1805) canto 6, st. 1

16 O Caledonia! stern and wild,
Meet nurse for a poetic child!
Land of brown heath and shaggy wood,
Land of the mountain and the flood,
Land of my sires! what mortal hand
Can e'er untie the filial band
That knits me to thy rugged strand!
The Lay of the Last Minstrel (1805) canto 6, st. 2

17 O! many a shaft, at random sent,
Finds mark the archer little meant!
And many a word, at random spoken,
May soothe or wound a heart that's broken.
The Lord of the Isles (1813) canto 5, st. 18

18 Had'st thou but lived, though stripped of power,
A watchman on the lonely tower.
Marmion (1808) introduction to canto 1, st. 8

19 Now is the stately column broke,
The beacon-light is quenched in smoke,
The trumpet's silver sound is still,
The warder silent on the hill!
on the death of William **PITT** *the Younger*
Marmion (1808) introduction to canto 1, st. 8

20 And come he slow, or come he fast,
It is but Death who comes at last.
Marmion (1808) canto 2, st. 30

21 O, young Lochinvar is come out of the west,
Through all the wide Border his steed was the
best.
Marmion (1808) canto 5, st. 12 ('Lochinvar' st. 1)

22 So faithful in love, and so dauntless in war,
There never was knight like the young
Lochinvar.
Marmion (1808) canto 5, st. 12 ('Lochinvar' st. 1)

23 For a laggard in love, and a dastard in war,
Was to wed the fair Ellen of brave Lochinvar.
Marmion (1808) canto 5, st. 12 ('Lochinvar' st. 2)

1 O come ye in peace here, or come ye in war,
Or to dance at our bridal, young Lord
Lochinvar?
Marmion (1808) canto 5, st. 12 ('Lochinvar' st. 3)

2 And now I am come, with this lost love of
mine,
To lead but one measure, drink one cup of
wine.
Marmion (1808) canto 5, st. 12 ('Lochinvar' st. 4)

3 O what a tangled web we weave,
When first we practise to deceive!
Marmion (1808) canto 6, st. 17

4 O Woman! in our hours of ease,
Uncertain, coy, and hard to please,
And variable as the shade
By the light quivering aspen made;
When pain and anguish wring the brow,
A ministering angel thou!
Marmion (1808) canto 6, st. 30; see **SHAKESPEARE** 704:18

5 The stubborn spear-men still made good
Their dark impenetrable wood,
Each stepping where his comrade stood,
The instant that he fell.
Marmion (1808) canto 6, st. 34

6 Still from the sire the son shall hear
Of the stern strife, and carnage drear,
Of Flodden's fatal field,
Where shivered was fair Scotland's spear,
And broken was her shield!
Marmion (1808) canto 6, st. 34

7 O, Brignal banks are wild and fair,
And Greta woods are green,
And you may gather garlands there
Would grace a summer queen.
Rokeby (1813) canto 3, st. 16

8 It's no fish ye're buying—it's men's lives.
The Antiquary (1816) ch. 11

9 Widowed wife, and married maid,
Betrothed, betrayer, and betrayed!
The Betrothed (1825) ch. 15

10 Vacant heart and hand, and eye,—
Easy live and quiet die.
The Bride of Lammermoor (1819) ch. 2

11 I live by twa trades . . . fiddle, sir, and spade;
filling the world, and emptying of it.
The Bride of Lammermoor (1819) ch. 24

12 Touch not the cat but a glove.
but = *without*
The Fair Maid of Perth (1828) ch. 34

13 It's ill taking the breeks aff a wild Highlandman.
The Fortunes of Nigel (1822) ch. 5

14 For three wild lads were we, brave boys,
And three wild lads were we;
Thou on the land, and I on the sand,
And Jack on the gallows-tree!
Guy Mannering (1815) ch. 34

15 The hour is come, but not the man.
The Heart of Midlothian (1818) ch. 4, title

16 Proud Maisie is in the wood,
Walking so early,
Sweet Robin sits in the bush,
Singing so rarely.
The Heart of Midlothian (1818) ch. 40

17 His morning walk was beneath the elms in the
churchyard; 'for death,' he said, 'had been his
next-door neighbour for so many years, that he
had no apology for dropping the acquaintance.'
A Legend of Montrose (1819) introduction

18 March, march, Ettrick and Teviotdale,
Why the deil dinna ye march forward in order?
March, march, Eskdale and Liddesdale,
All the Blue Bonnets are bound for the Border.
The Monastery (1820) ch. 25

19 It is fortunate for tale-tellers that they are not
tied down like theatrical writers to the unities of
time and place.
'Old Mortality' (*Tales of My Landlord* 1st series, 1816)

20 Ah! County Guy, the hour is nigh,
The sun has left the lea,
The orange flower perfumes the bower,
The breeze is on the sea.
Quentin Durward (1823) ch. 4

21 The ae half of the warld thinks the tither daft.
Redgauntlet (1824) 'Journal of Darsie Latimer' ch. 7

22 But with the morning cool repentance came.
Rob Roy (1817) ch. 12

23 Come fill up my cup, come fill up my cann,
Come saddle my horses, and call up my man;
Come open your gates, and let me gae free,
I daurna stay langer in bonny Dundee.
Rob Roy (1817) ch. 23; see **SCOTT** 688:7

24 There's a gude time coming.
Rob Roy (1817) ch. 32

25 The play-bill, which is said to have announced
the tragedy of Hamlet, the character of the
Prince of Denmark being left out.
commonly alluded to as 'Hamlet without the Prince'
The Talisman (1825) introduction; W. J. Parke *Musical Memories*
(1830) vol. 1 gives a similar anecdote from 1787

26 Turner's palm is as itchy as his fingers are
ingenious.
letter to James Skene, 30 April 1823; *Letters* (1934)

27 But I must say to the Muse of fiction, as the
Earl of Pembroke said to the ejected nun of
Wilton, 'Go spin, you jade, go spin'.
diary, 9 February 1826; see **PEMBROKE** 602:9

28 The Big Bow-Wow strain I can do myself like
any now going; but the exquisite touch, which
renders ordinary commonplace things and
characters interesting, from the truth of the
description and the sentiment, is denied to me.
on Jane **AUSTEN**
W. E. K. Anderson (ed.) *Journals of Sir Walter Scott* (1972) 14
March 1826; see **PEMBROKE** 602:11

29 I would like to be there, were it but to see how
the cat jumps.
W. E. K. Anderson (ed.) *Journals of Sir Walter Scott* (1972)
7 October 1826

1 The blockheads talk of my being like
Shakespeare—not fit to tie his brogues.
W. E. K. Anderson (ed.) Journals of Sir Walter Scott *(1972)*
11 December 1826

2 Were I my own man . . . I would refuse this
offer (with all gratitude); but as I am situated,
L.300 or L.400 a-year is not to be sneezed at.
on being offered the Laureateship
*letter to James Ballantyne, 24 August 1813; John Gibson
Lockhart* Memoirs of the Life of Sir Walter Scott *(1837–8)*

3 Too many flowers . . . too little fruit.
describing the work of Felicia HEMANS
letter to Joanna Baillie, 18 July 1823, in Letters *(Centenary ed.)
vol. 8*

4 We shall never learn to feel and respect our real
calling and destiny, unless we have taught
ourselves to consider every thing as moonshine,
compared with the education of the heart.
to J. G. Lockhart, August 1825, in Lockhart's Life of Sir Walter
Scott *vol. 6 (1837) ch. 2*

5 Their factions have been so long envenomed and
having so little ground to fight their battle in
that they [the Irish] are like people fighting with
daggers in a hogshead.
*letter to Joanna Baillie, 12 October 1825, in H. J. C. Grierson
(ed.)* Letters of Sir Walter Scott *vol. 9 (1935)*

6 No! This right hand shall work it all off.
on being offered help in paying his debts
Henry Cockburn Memorials of his Time *(1856) January 1826*

7 All men who have turned out worth anything
have had the chief hand in their own education.
*letter to J. G. Lockhart, c.16 June 1830, in H. J. C. Grierson
(ed.)* Letters of Sir Walter Scott *vol. 11 (1936)*

8 Why do you bother the poor? Leave them alone.
*quoted by Lord Melbourne in Queen Victoria, diary 20
February 1839, in Lord Esher (ed.)* Girlhood of Queen Victoria
(1912) vol. 2

Scottish Metrical Psalms 1650

9 The Lord's my shepherd, I'll not want.
He makes me down to lie
In pastures green: he leadeth me
the quiet waters by.
My soul he doth restore again;
and me to walk doth make
Within the paths of righteousness,
ev'n for his own name's sake.
Yea, though I walk in death's dark vale,
yet will I fear none ill:
For thou art with me; and thy rod
and staff me comfort still.
My table thou hast furnished
in presence of my foes;
My head thou dost with oil anoint,
and my cup overflows.
Psalm 23, v. 1; see BOOK OF COMMON PRAYER *140:20*

10 How lovely is thy dwelling-place,
O Lord of hosts, to me!
The tabernacles of thy grace
how pleasant, Lord, they be!
Psalm 84, v. 1; see BOOK OF COMMON PRAYER *145:13*

11 I to the hills will lift mine eyes
from whence doth come mine aid.
My safety cometh from the Lord,
who heav'n and earth hath made.
Psalm 121, v. 1; see BOOK OF COMMON PRAYER *148:17*

12 The race that long in darkness pined
have seen a glorious light.
Paraphrase 19; see BIBLE *92:13*

Edmund Hamilton Sears 1810–76
American minister

13 It came upon the midnight clear,
That glorious song of old,
From Angels bending near the earth
To touch their harps of gold;
'Peace on the earth, good will to man
From Heaven's all gracious King.'
The world in solemn stillness lay
To hear the angels sing.
The Christian Register (1850) 'That Glorious Song of Old'

George Seddon 1927–
Australian environmental scientist

14 The most important fact in the environmental
history of Australia is that it had a radically new
technology imposed upon it, suddenly, twice.
*attributed; quoted in G. Davison, J. Hirst, and S. Macintyre
(eds.)* Oxford Companion to Australian History *(2001)*

John Sedgwick 1813–64
American Union general

15 They couldn't hit an elephant at this distance.
*last words, immediately prior to being killed by enemy fire
at the battle of Spotsylvania in the American Civil War*
Robert Denney The Civil War Years *(1992)*

Charles Sedley c.1639–1701
English dramatist and poet

16 Ah, Chloris! that I now could sit
As unconcerned as when
Your infant beauty could beget
No pleasure, nor no pain!
'Child and Maiden' (1668)

17 Love still has something of the sea
From whence his mother rose.
'Love still has something'

18 Phyllis, without frown or smile,
Sat and knotted all the while.
'Phyllis Knotting' (1694)

19 Phyllis is my only joy,
Faithless as the winds or seas;
Sometimes coming, sometimes coy,
Yet she never fails to please.
'Song'

Alan Seeger 1888–1916

American poet

1 I have a rendezvous with Death
At some disputed barricade.
'I Have a Rendezvous with Death' (1916)

Pete Seeger 1919–

American folk singer and songwriter

2 Where have all the flowers gone?
title of song (1961)

3 Education is when you read the fine print;
experience is what you get when you don't.
L. Botts *Loose Talk* (1980)

John Seeley 1834–95

English historian

4 We [the English] seem, as it were, to have
conquered and peopled half the world in a fit of
absence of mind.
The Expansion of England (1883) Lecture 1

Sefer Yezirah

Hebrew esoteric text on cosmology, 3rd–6th century AD

5 Thirty-two wondrous paths were engraved by
Yah, the Lord of hosts, the God of Israel, the
living God, God Almighty . . . who . . . created
his world by three principles: by limit, by letter
and by number.
There are ten primordial numbers and twenty-
two fundamental letters.
1:1

Erich Segal *see* **Taglines for films** 788:8

Sei Shōnagon *c.*966–*c.*1013

Japanese diarist and writer

6 There is nothing in the whole world so painful
as feeling that one is not liked. It always seems
to me that people who hate me must be
suffering from some strange form of lunacy.
The Pillow Book of Sei Shōnagon

7 If writing did not exist, what terrible depressions
we should suffer from.
The Pillow Book of Sei Shōnagon

John Selden 1584–1654

English historian and antiquary

8 *Scrutamini scripturas* [Let us look at the
scriptures]. These two words have undone the
world.
Table Talk (1689) 'Bible Scripture'; see **BIBLE** 107:19

9 Old friends are best. King James used to call for
his old shoes; they were easiest for his feet.
Table Talk (1689) 'Friends'

10 Commonly we say a judgement falls upon a
man for something in him we cannot abide.
Table Talk (1689) 'God's Judgements'

11 Ignorance of the law excuses no man; not that
all men know the law, but because 'tis an excuse
every man will plead, and no man can tell how
to confute him.
Table Talk (1689) 'Law'; see **PROVERBS** 635:39

12 Take a straw and throw it up into the air, you
shall see by that which way the wind is.
Table Talk (1689) 'Libels'

13 Marriage is nothing but a civil contract.
Table Talk (1689) 'Marriage'

14 A king is a thing men have made for their own
sakes, for quietness' sake. Just as in a family one
man is appointed to buy the meat.
Table Talk (1689) 'Of a King'

15 There never was a merry world since the fairies
left off dancing, and the Parson left conjuring.
Table Talk (1689) 'Parson'

16 There is not anything in the world so much
abused as this sentence, *Salus populi suprema lex
esto.*
Table Talk (1689) 'People'; see **CICERO** 231:18

17 Pleasure is nothing else but the intermission of
pain.
Table Talk (1689) 'Pleasure'

18 Syllables govern the world.
Table Talk (1689) 'Power: State'

19 Preachers say, Do as I say, not as I do.
Table Talk (1689) 'Preaching'

Arthur Seldon 1916–2005

English economist

20 Government of the busy by the bossy for the
bully.
on over-government
Capitalism (1990)

W. C. Sellar 1898–1951 *and* R. J. Yeatman 1898–1968

British humorous writers

21 For every person who wants to teach there are
approximately thirty who don't want to
learn—much.
And Now All This (1932) introduction

22 1066 and all that.
title of book (1930)

23 History is not what you thought. *It is what you
can remember.*
1066 and All That (1930) 'Compulsory Preface'

24 The Roman Conquest was, however, a *Good
Thing*, since the Britons were only natives at the
time.
1066 and All That (1930) ch. 1

25 Edward III had very good manners . . . and
made the memorable epitaph: 'Honi soie qui
mal y pense' ('Honey, your silk stocking's
hanging down').
1066 and All That (1930) ch. 24; see **MOTTOES** 563:10

1 Are you Edmund Mortimer? If not, have you got him?
1066 and All That (1930) ch. 28

2 The cruel Queen died and a post-mortem examination revealed the word 'CALLOUS' engraved on her heart.
1066 and All That (1930) ch. 32; see MARY I 526:15

3 The Cavaliers (Wrong but Wromantic) and the Roundheads (Right but Repulsive).
1066 and All That (1930) ch. 35

4 Charles II was always very merry and was therefore not so much a king as a Monarch.
1066 and All That (1930) ch. 36; see ROCHESTER 664:18

5 The National Debt is a very Good Thing and it would be dangerous to pay it off, for fear of Political Economy.
1066 and All That (1930) ch. 38

6 Napoleon's armies always used to march on their stomachs shouting: 'Vive l'Intérieur!'
1066 and All That (1930) ch. 48; see NAPOLEON I 568:6

7 Gladstone . . . spent his declining years trying to guess the answer to the Irish Question; unfortunately whenever he was getting warm, the Irish secretly changed the Question.
1066 and All That (1930) ch. 57

8 AMERICA was thus clearly top nation, and History came to a .
1066 and All That (1930) ch. 62

Seneca ('the Younger') *c.*4 BC–AD 65
Roman philosopher and poet

9 The way is long if one follows precepts, but short and helpful if one follows patterns.
Epistulae ad Lucilium no. 6, sect. 5

10 A small debt makes a man your debtor; a large one, an enemy.
Epistulae ad Lucilium no. 19

11 If one does not know to which port one is sailing, no wind is favourable.
Epistulae ad Lucilium no. 71, sect. 3

12 Pain is an inconsiderable thing if not reinforced by opinion.
Epistulae ad Lucilium no. 78, sect. 13

13 You must want nothing if you wish to challenge Jupiter, who himself wants nothing.
Epistulae ad Lucilium no. 110, sect. 20

14 *Homines dum docent discunt.*
Even while they teach, men learn.
Epistulae Morales no. 7, sect. 8

15 They are not enemies when we acquire them; we make them so.
on slaves
Epistulae Morales no. 47, sect. 5

16 Eternal law has arranged nothing better than this, that it has given us one way in to life, but many ways out.
Epistulae Morales no. 70, sect. 14

17 The hour which gives us life begins to take it away.
Hercules Furens l. 874

18 Small sorrows speak; great ones are silent.
Hippolytus l. 607

19 Fire is the test of gold; adversity, of strong men.
Moral Essays 'On Providence' ch. 5, sect. 10

20 Anyone can stop a man's life, but no one his death; a thousand doors open on to it.
Phoenissae l. 152; see FLETCHER 335:8, WEBSTER 844:11

21 *Illi mors gravis incubat*
Qui notus nimis omnibus
Ignotus moritur sibi.

On him does death lie heavily who, but too well known to all, dies to himself unknown.
Thyestes chorus 2 (translated by F. J. Miller)

John Sentamu 1949–
Uganda-born Anglican clergyman, Archbishop of York from 2005

22 *referring to Archbishop Michael Ramsey's words 'I should love to think of a black Archbishop of York holding a mission here':*
Well here I am, and you have already acknowledged that fact!
sermon preached at his Inauguration as Archbishop of York, 30 November 2005; see also RAMSEY 654:20

Gitta Sereny 1923–
Hungarian-born British writer and journalist

23 *to Albert Speer, who having always denied knowledge of the Holocaust had said that he was at fault in having 'looked away':*
You cannot look away from something you don't know. If you looked away, then you knew.
recalled on BBC2 *Reputations*, 2 May 1996

Robert W. Service 1874–1958
Canadian poet

24 A promise made is a debt unpaid, and the trail has its own stern code.
'The Cremation of Sam McGee' (1907)

25 Ah! the clock is always slow;
It is later than you think.
'It Is Later Than You Think' (1921)

26 This is the law of the Yukon, that only the Strong shall thrive;
That surely the Weak shall perish, and only the Fit survive.
'The Law of the Yukon' (1907)

27 When we, the Workers, all demand: 'What are WE fighting for?' . . .
Then, then we'll end that stupid crime, that devil's madness—War.
'Michael' (1921)

28 Back of the bar, in a solo game, sat Dangerous Dan McGrew,

And watching his luck was his light-o'-love, the
lady that's known as Lou.
'The Shooting of Dan McGrew' (1907)

Vikram Seth 1952–

Indian writer

1 If we cannot eschew hatred, at least let us
eschew group hatred.
Two Lives (2005)

William Seward 1801–72

American politician

2 I know, and all the world knows, that
revolutions never go backward.
speech at Rochester, 25 October 1858, in *The Irrepressible
Conflict* (1858)

Anna Sewell 1820–78

English writer

3 *Only* ignorance! How can you talk about only
ignorance! Don't you know that it is the worst
thing in the world next to wickedness.
Black Beauty (1877) ch. 19

Edward Sexby d. 1658

English conspirator

4 Killing no murder briefly discourst in three
questions.
an apology for tyrannicide
title of pamphlet (1657)

Anne Sexton 1928–74

American poet

5 I was tired of being a woman,
tired of the spoons and the pots,
tired of my mouth and my breasts
tired of the cosmetics and silks . . .
I was tired of the gender of things.
'Consorting with angels' (1967)

6 God owns heaven
but He craves the earth.
'The Earth' (1975)

7 My sleeping pill is white.
It is a splendid pearl;
it floats me out of myself,
my stung skin as alien
as a loose bolt of cloth.
'Lullaby' (1960)

8 In a dream you are never eighty.
'Old' (1962)

9 But suicides have a special language.
Like carpenters they want to know *which tools*.
They never ask *why build*.
'Wanting to Die' (1966)

Ernest Shackleton 1874–1922

British explorer. On Shackleton: see **CHERRY-GARRARD
222:16, MISQUOTATIONS 549:4**

10 Ship and stores have gone—so now we'll go
home.
to his men on the loss of the Endurance, *27 October 1915*
South (1991 ed.)

11 Superhuman effort isn't worth a damn unless it
achieves results.
to his navigator Frank Worsley, 1916; F. P. Worsley *Endurance*
(1931)

Thomas Shadwell c.1642–92

English dramatist. On Shadwell: see **DRYDEN 296:10**

12 Words may be false and full of art,
Sighs are the natural language of the heart.
Psyche (1675) act 3

13 And wit's the noblest frailty of the mind.
A True Widow (1679) act 2, sc. 1; see **DRYDEN 296:2**

14 Every man loves what he is good at.
A True Widow (1679) act 5, sc. 1

Peter Shaffer 1926–

English dramatist

15 All my wife has ever taken from the
Mediterranean—from that whole vast intuitive
culture—are four bottles of Chianti to make into
lamps.
Equus (1973) act 1, sc. 18

Anthony Ashley Cooper, 1st Earl of Shaftesbury 1621–83

English statesman

16 Admit lords, and you admit all.
refusing the claims of Cromwell's House of Lords
in *Dictionary of National Biography* (1917–)

17 'People differ in their discourse and profession
about these matters, but men of sense are really
but of one religion.' . . . 'Pray, my lord, what
religion is that which men of sense agree in?'
'Madam,' says the earl immediately, 'men of
sense never tell it.'
Bishop Gilbert Burnet *History of My Own Time* vol. 1 (1724) bk.
2, ch. 1 n.; see **DISRAELI 285:28**

Anthony Ashley Cooper, 3rd Earl of Shaftesbury 1671–1713

English statesman and philosopher

18 How comes it to pass, then, that we appear such
cowards in reasoning, and are so afraid to stand
the test of ridicule?
A Letter Concerning Enthusiasm (1708) sect. 2

19 Truth, 'tis supposed, may bear all lights: and one
of those in which things are to be viewed, in
order to [attain] a thorough recognition is that

by which we discern whatever is liable to
ridicule in any subject.

Sensus Communis: an essay on the freedom of wit and humour
(1709) pt. 1, sect. 1; see CHESTERFIELD 223:15

William Shakespeare 1564–1616

English dramatist. On Shakespeare: see ARNOLD 30:15,
AUBREY 36:7, BASSE 61:4, BROWNING 166:2, COLERIDGE
241:22, DRYDEN 297:15, DRYDEN 297:18, GEORGE III 352:12,
GRAY 370:19, GREENE 372:1, JOHNSON 437:2, JOHNSON 437:4,
JOHNSON 437:5, JOHNSON 437:6, JONSON 446:18, JONSON
446:22, JONSON 446:24, JONSON 446:25, JONSON 446:26,
LAWRENCE 483:25, MILTON 539:31, MILTON 540:18, OLIVIER
585:3, POPE 617:20, SCOTT 690:1,, WALPOLE 837:13,
WORDSWORTH 869:2; see also EPITAPHS 317:12, FLETCHER
335:11

*The text and references are taken from the traditional Oxford
Standard Authors edition in one volume. The line number is given
without brackets where the scene is all verse up to the quotation
and the line number is certain, and in square brackets where prose
makes it variable. Where modern editors prefer alternative readings
or scene numbering, this is indicated in a note*

ALL'S WELL THAT ENDS WELL

1 Moderate lamentation is the right of the dead,
excessive grief the enemy to the living.

All's Well That Ends Well (1603–4) act 1, sc. 1, l. [52]

2   It were all one
That I should love a bright particular star
And think to wed it, he is so above me.

All's Well that Ends Well (1603–4) act 1, sc. 1, l. [97]

3 Our remedies oft in ourselves do lie
Which we ascribe to heaven.

All's Well that Ends Well (1603–4) act 1, sc. 1, l. [232]

4 It is like a barber's chair that fits all buttocks.

All's Well that Ends Well (1603–4) act 2, sc. 2, l. [18]

5 A young man married is a man that's marred.

All's Well that Ends Well (1603–4) act 2, sc. 3, l. [315]; see
PROVERBS 648:20

6 The flowery way that leads to the broad gate
and the great fire.

All's Well that Ends Well (1603–4) act 4, sc. 5, l. [58]; see
SHAKESPEARE 720:12

ANTONY AND CLEOPATRA

7 The triple pillar of the world transformed
Into a strumpet's fool.

Antony and Cleopatra (1606–7) act 1, sc. 1, l. 12

8 CLEOPATRA: If it be love indeed, tell me how
much.
ANTONY: There's beggary in the love that can be
reckoned.
CLEOPATRA: I'll set a bourn how far to be
beloved.
ANTONY: Then must thou needs find out new
heaven, new earth.

Antony and Cleopatra (1606–7) act 1, sc. 1, l. 14

9 Let Rome in Tiber melt, and the wide arch
Of the ranged empire fall. Here is my space.
Kingdoms are clay.

Antony and Cleopatra (1606–7) act 1, sc. 1, l. 33

10 I love long life better than figs.

Antony and Cleopatra (1606–7) act 1, sc. 2, l. [34]

11   On the sudden
A Roman thought hath struck him.

Antony and Cleopatra (1606–7) act 1, sc. 2, l. [90]

12 The nature of bad news infects the teller.

Antony and Cleopatra (1606–7) act 1, sc. 2, l. [103]

13 CHARMIAN: In each thing give him way, cross him
in nothing.
CLEOPATRA: Thou teachest like a fool; the way to
lose him.

Antony and Cleopatra (1606–7) act 1, sc. 3, l. 9

14 In time we hate that which we often fear.

Antony and Cleopatra (1606–7) act 1, sc. 3, l. 12

15 Eternity was in our lips and eyes,
Bliss in our brows bent.

Antony and Cleopatra (1606–7) act 1, sc. 3, l. 35

16 O! my oblivion is a very Antony,
And I am all forgotten.

Antony and Cleopatra (1606–7) act 1, sc. 3, l. 90

17 Give me to drink mandragora . . .
That I might sleep out this great gap of time
My Antony is away.

Antony and Cleopatra (1606–7) act 1, sc. 5, l. 4

18 O happy horse, to bear the weight of Antony!

Antony and Cleopatra (1606–7) act 1, sc. 5, l. 21

19   He's speaking now,
Or murmuring, 'Where's my serpent of old
Nile?'

Antony and Cleopatra (1606–7) act 1, sc. 5, l. 24

20   My salad days,
When I was green in judgment, cold in blood,
To say as I said then!

Antony and Cleopatra (1606–7) act 1, sc. 5, l. 73

21 I do not much dislike the matter, but
The manner of his speech.

Antony and Cleopatra (1606–7) act 2, sc. 2, l. 117

22 The barge she sat in, like a burnished throne,
Burned on the water; the poop was beaten gold,
Purple the sails, and so perfumed, that
The winds were love-sick with them, the oars
were silver,
Which to the tune of flutes kept stroke, and
made
The water which they beat to follow faster,
As amorous of their strokes. For her own
person,
It beggared all description.

Antony and Cleopatra (1606–7) act 2, sc. 2, l. [199]; see ELIOT
311:6

23   Antony,
Enthroned i' the market-place, did sit alone,
Whistling to the air; which, but for vacancy,
Had gone to gaze on Cleopatra too
And made a gap in nature.

Antony and Cleopatra (1606–7) act 2, sc. 2, l. [222]

24   I saw her once
Hop forty paces through the public street;
And having lost her breath, she spoke, and
panted

That she did make defect perfection,
And, breathless, power breathe forth.
Antony and Cleopatra (1606–7) act 2, sc. 2, l. [236]; some editions prefer 'pour breath forth'

1 Age cannot wither her, nor custom stale
Her infinite variety; other women cloy
The appetites they feed, but she makes hungry
Where most she satisfies; for vilest things
Become themselves in her, that the holy priests
Bless her when she is riggish.
Antony and Cleopatra (1606–7) act 2, sc. 2, l. [243]

2 I have not kept the square, but that to come
Shall all be done by the rule.
Antony and Cleopatra (1606–7) act 2, sc. 3, l. 6

3 I' the east my pleasure lies.
Antony and Cleopatra (1606–7) act 2, sc. 3, l. 40

4 Give me some music—music, moody food
Of us that trade in love.
Antony and Cleopatra (1606–7) act 2, sc. 5, l. 1

5 Give me mine angle; we'll to the river: there—
My music playing far off—I will betray
Tawny-finned fishes; my bended hook shall pierce
Their slimy jaws; and, as I draw them up,
I'll think them every one an Antony,
And say, 'Ah, ha!' you're caught.
Antony and Cleopatra (1606–7) act 2, sc. 5, l. 10

6 I laughed him out of patience; and that night
I laughed him into patience: and next morn,
Ere the ninth hour, I drunk him to his bed.
Antony and Cleopatra (1606–7) act 2, sc. 5, l. 19

7 LEPIDUS: What manner o' thing is your crocodile?
ANTONY: It is shaped, sir, like itself, and it is as
broad as it hath breadth; it is just so high as it
is, and moves with its own organs; it lives by
that which nourisheth it; and the elements
once out of it, it transmigrates.
Antony and Cleopatra (1606–7) act 2, sc. 7, l. [47]

8 Egypt, thou knew'st too well
My heart was to thy rudder tied by th' strings,
And thou shouldst tow me after.
Antony and Cleopatra (1606–7) act 3, sc. 9, l. 56

9 He wears the rose
Of youth upon him.
Antony and Cleopatra (1606–7) act 3, sc. 11, l. 20

10 I found you as a morsel, cold upon
Dead Caesar's trencher.
Antony and Cleopatra (1606–7) act 3, sc. 11, l. 116

11 Let's have one other gaudy night: call to me
All my sad captains; fill our bowls once more;
Let's mock the midnight bell.
Antony and Cleopatra (1606–7) act 3, sc. 11, l. 182

12 O! my fortunes have
Corrupted honest men.
Antony and Cleopatra (1606–7) act 4, sc. 5, l. 16

13 O infinite virtue! com'st thou smiling from
The world's great snare uncaught?
Antony and Cleopatra (1606–7) act 4, sc. 8, l. 17

14 The hearts
That spanieled me at heels, to whom I gave
Their wishes, do discandy, melt their sweets
On blossoming Caesar.
Antony and Cleopatra (1606–7) act 4, sc. 10, l. 33

15 The soul and body rive not more in parting
Than greatness going off.
Antony and Cleopatra (1606–7) act 4, sc. 11, l. 5

16 Sometimes we see a cloud that's dragonish;
A vapour sometime like a bear or lion,
A towered citadel, a pendant rock,
A forked mountain, or blue promontory
With trees upon 't, that nod unto the world
And mock our eyes with air.
Antony and Cleopatra (1606–7) act 4, sc. 12, l. 2

17 Unarm, Eros; the long day's task is done,
And we must sleep.
Antony and Cleopatra (1606–7) act 4, sc. 12, l. 35

18 Stay for me:
Where souls do couch on flowers, we'll hand in hand,
And with our sprightly port make the ghosts gaze;
Dido and her Aeneas shall want troops,
And all the haunt be ours.
Antony and Cleopatra (1606–7) act 4, sc. 12, l. 50

19 I am dying, Egypt, dying.
Antony and Cleopatra (1606–7) act 4, sc. 13, l. 18

20 A Roman by a Roman
Valiantly vanquished.
Antony and Cleopatra (1606–7) act 4, sc. 13, l. 57

21 O! withered is the garland of the war,
The soldier's pole is fall'n; young boys and girls
Are level now with men; the odds is gone,
And there is nothing left remarkable
Beneath the visiting moon.
Antony and Cleopatra (1606–7) act 4, sc. 13, l. 64

22 What's brave, what's noble,
Let's do it after the high Roman fashion,
And make death proud to take us.
Antony and Cleopatra (1606–7) act 4, sc. 13, l. 86

23 He words me, girls, he words me, that I should not
Be noble to myself.
Antony and Cleopatra (1606–7) act 5, sc. 2, l. 190

24 Finish, good lady; the bright day is done,
And we are for the dark.
Antony and Cleopatra (1606–7) act 5, sc. 2, l. 192

25 Antony
Shall be brought drunken forth, and I shall see
Some squeaking Cleopatra boy my greatness
I' the posture of a whore.
Antony and Cleopatra (1606–7) act 5, sc. 2, l. 217

26 My resolution's placed, and I have nothing
Of woman in me; now from head to foot
I am marble-constant, now the fleeting moon
No planet is of mine.
Antony and Cleopatra (1606–7) act 5, sc. 2, l. 237

1 I wish you all joy of the worm.
   Antony and Cleopatra (1606–7) act 5, sc. 2, l. [260]

2 Give me my robe, put on my crown; I have
   Immortal longings in me.
   Antony and Cleopatra (1606–7) act 5, sc. 2, l. [282]

3 I am fire and air; my other elements
   I give to baser life.
   Antony and Cleopatra (1606–7) act 5, sc. 2, l. [291]

4   Come, thou mortal wretch,
   With thy sharp teeth this knot intrinsicate
   Of life at once untie; poor venomous fool,
   Be angry, and dispatch. O! couldst thou speak,
   That I might hear thee call great Caesar ass
   Unpolicied.
   Antony and Cleopatra (1606–7) act 5, sc. 2, l. [305]

5 CHARMIAN: O eastern star!
   CLEOPATRA: Peace! peace!
   Dost thou not see my baby at my breast,
   That sucks the nurse asleep?
   Antony and Cleopatra (1606–7) act 5, sc. 2, l. [309]

6 Now boast thee, death, in thy possession lies
   A lass unparalleled.
   Antony and Cleopatra (1606–7) act 5, sc. 2, l. [317]

7   She looks like sleep,
   As she would catch a second Antony
   In her strong toil of grace.
   Antony and Cleopatra (1606–7) act 5, sc. 2, l. [347]; some
   editions prefer 'another Antony'

8 She hath pursued conclusions infinite
   Of easy ways to die.
   Antony and Cleopatra (1606–7) act 5, sc. 2, l. [356]

AS YOU LIKE IT

9 Fleet the time carelessly, as they did in the
   golden world.
   As You Like It (1599) act 1, sc. 1, l. [126]

10 Let us sit and mock the good housewife Fortune
   from her wheel, that her gifts may henceforth
   be bestowed equally.
   As You Like It (1599) act 1, sc. 2, l. [35]

11 Hereafter, in a better world than this,
   I shall desire more love and knowledge of you.
   As You Like It (1599) act 1, sc. 2, l. [301]

12 O, how full of briers is this working-day world!
   As You Like It (1599) act 1, sc. 3, l. [12]

13 We'll have a swashing and a martial outside,
   As many other mannish cowards have
   That do outface it with their semblances.
   As You Like It (1599) act 1, sc. 3, l. [123]

14   Are not these woods
   More free from peril than the envious court?
   Here feel we but the penalty of Adam,
   The seasons' difference; as, the icy fang
   And churlish chiding of the winter's wind,
   Which, when it bites and blows upon my body,
   Even till I shrink with cold, I smile and say,
   'This is no flattery.'
   As You Like It (1599) act 2, sc. 1, l. 3; some editions prefer
   'Here feel we not'

15 Sweet are the uses of adversity,
   Which like the toad, ugly and venomous,
   Wears yet a precious jewel in his head;
   And this our life, exempt from public haunt,
   Finds tongues in trees, books in the running
     brooks,
   Sermons in stones, and good in everything.
   As You Like It (1599) act 2, sc. 1, l. 12; see **BERNARD** 73:18

16 Unregarded age in corners thrown.
   As You Like It (1599) act 2, sc. 3, l. 42

17 Therefore my age is as a lusty winter,
   Frosty, but kindly.
   As You Like It (1599) act 2, sc. 3, l. 52

18 O good old man! how well in thee appears
   The constant service of the antique world,
   When service sweat for duty, not for meed!
   Thou art not for the fashion of these times,
   Where none will sweat but for promotion.
   As You Like It (1599) act 2, sc. 3, l. 56

19 Ay, now am I in Arden; the more fool I. When I
   was at home I was in a better place; but
   travellers must be content.
   As You Like It (1599) act 2, sc. 4, l. [16]

20 In thy youth thou wast as true a lover
   As ever sighed upon a midnight pillow.
   As You Like It (1599) act 2, sc. 4, l. [26]

21 Under the greenwood tree
   Who loves to lie with me,
   And turn his merry note
   Unto the sweet bird's throat,
   Come hither, come hither, come hither:
   Here shall he see
   No enemy
   But winter and rough weather.
   As You Like It (1599) act 2, sc. 5, l. 1

22 I can suck melancholy out of a song as a weasel
   sucks eggs.
   As You Like It (1599) act 2, sc. 5, l. [12]

23 Who doth ambition shun
   And loves to live i' the sun,
   Seeking the food he eats,
   And pleased with what he gets.
   As You Like It (1599) act 2, sc. 5, l. [38]

24 I met a fool i' the forest.
   As You Like It (1599) act 2, sc. 7, l. 12

25 And so, from hour to hour, we ripe and ripe,
   And then from hour to hour, we rot and rot:
   And thereby hangs a tale.
   As You Like It (1599) act 2, sc. 7, l. 26

26 A worthy fool! Motley's the only wear.
   As You Like It (1599) act 2, sc. 7, l. 34

27 All the world's a stage,
   And all the men and women merely players:
   They have their exits and their entrances;
   And one man in his time plays many parts,
   His acts being seven ages.
   As You Like It (1599) act 2, sc. 7, l. 139

28   At first the infant,
   Mewling and puking in the nurse's arms.

And then the whining schoolboy, with his
  satchel,
And shining morning face, creeping like snail
Unwillingly to school.
  As You Like It (1599) act 2, sc. 7, l. 143

1   Then a soldier,
Full of strange oaths, and bearded like the pard,
Jealous in honour, sudden and quick in quarrel,
Seeking the bubble reputation
Even in the cannon's mouth. And then the
  justice,
In fair round belly with good capon lined.
  As You Like It (1599) act 2, sc. 7, l. 149

2   The sixth age shifts
Into the lean and slippered pantaloon,
With spectacles on nose and pouch on side,
His youthful hose well saved a world too wide
For his shrunk shank.
  As You Like It (1599) act 2, sc. 7, l. 157

3   Last scene of all,
That ends this strange eventful history,
Is second childishness, and mere oblivion,
Sans teeth, sans eyes, sans taste, sans everything.
  As You Like It (1599) act 2, sc. 7, l. 163

4 Blow, blow, thou winter wind,
Thou art not so unkind
As man's ingratitude.
  As You Like It (1599) act 2, sc. 7, l. 174

5 Heigh-ho! sing, heigh-ho! unto the green holly:
Most friendship is feigning, most loving mere
  folly.
Then heigh-ho! the holly!
This life is most jolly.
  As You Like It (1599) act 2, sc. 7, l. 180

6 Run, run, Orlando: carve on every tree
The fair, the chaste, and unexpressive she.
  As You Like It (1599) act 3, sc. 2, l. 9

7 From the east to western Ind,
No jewel is like Rosalind.
  As You Like It (1599) act 3, sc. 2, l. [94] .

8 Let us make an honourable retreat; though not
with bag and baggage, yet with scrip and
scrippage.
  As You Like It (1599) act 3, sc. 2, l. [170]

9 O wonderful, wonderful, and most wonderful
wonderful! and yet again wonderful, and after
that, out of all whooping!
  As You Like It (1599) act 3, sc. 2, l. [202]

10 Do you not know I am a woman? when I think,
I must speak.
  As You Like It (1599) act 3, sc. 2, l. [265]

11 I do desire we may be better strangers.
  As You Like It (1599) act 3, sc. 2, l. [276]

12 JAQUES: I do not like her name.
  ORLANDO: There was no thought of pleasing you
  when she was christened.
  As You Like It (1599) act 3, sc. 2, l. [283]

13 Time travels in divers paces with divers persons.
I'll tell you who Time ambles withal, who Time

trots withal, who Time gallops withal, and who
Time stands still withal.
  As You Like It (1599) act 3, sc. 2, l. [328]

14 I am not a slut, though I thank the gods I am
foul.
  As You Like It (1599) act 3, sc. 3, l. [40]

15   Down on your knees,
And thank heaven, fasting, for a good man's
  love.
  As You Like It (1599) act 3, sc. 5, l. 57

16 I pray you, do not fall in love with me,
For I am falser than vows made in wine.
  As You Like It (1599) act 3, sc. 5, l. [72]

17 Dead shepherd, now I find thy saw of might:
'Who ever loved that loved not at first sight?'
  As You Like It (1599) act 3, sc. 5, l. [81]; see **MARLOWE** 522:15

18 Come, woo me, woo me; for now I am in a
holiday humour, and like enough to consent.
  As You Like It (1599) act 4, sc. 1, l. [70]

19 You were better speak first, and when you were
gravelled for lack of matter, you might take
occasion to kiss.
  As You Like It (1599) act 4, sc. 1, l. [75]

20 Men are April when they woo, December when
they wed: maids are May when they are maids,
but the sky changes when they are wives.
  As You Like It (1599) act 4, sc. 1, l. [153]

21 The horn, the horn, the lusty horn
Is not a thing to laugh to scorn.
  As You Like It (1599) act 4, sc. 2, l. [17]

22 Oh! how bitter a thing it is to look into
happiness through another man's eyes.
  As You Like It (1599) act 5, sc. 2, l. [48]

23 'Tis like the howling of Irish wolves against the
moon.
  As You Like It (1599) act 5, sc. 2, l. [120]

24 It was a lover and his lass,
With a hey, and a ho, and a hey nonino,
That o'er the green cornfield did pass,
In the spring time, the only pretty ring time,
When birds do sing, hey ding a ding, ding;
Sweet lovers love the spring.
  As You Like It (1599) act 5, sc. 3, l. [18]

25 A poor virgin, sir, an ill-favoured thing, sir, but
mine own.
  As You Like It (1599) act 5, sc. 4, l. [60]

26 The retort courteous . . . the quip modest . . .
the reply churlish . . . the reproof valiant . . . the
counter check quarrelsome . . . the lie
circumstantial . . . the lie direct.
  of the degrees of a lie
    As You Like It (1599) act 5, sc. 4, l. [96]; some editions prefer
    'the lie with circumstance'

27 Your 'if' is the only peace-maker; much virtue in
'if'.
  As You Like It (1599) act 5, sc. 4, l. [108]

28 He uses his folly like a stalking-horse, and under
the presentation of that he shoots his wit.
  As You Like It (1599) act 5, sc. 4, l. [112]

1 If it be true that 'good wine needs no bush', 'tis true that a good play needs no epilogue.
As You Like It (1599) act 5, sc. 4, epilogue l. [3]; see **PROVERBS** 633:25

CORIOLANUS

2 He's a very dog to the commonalty.
Coriolanus (1608) act 1, sc. 1, l. [29]

3 What's the matter, you dissentious rogues,
That, rubbing the poor itch of your opinion,
Make yourselves scabs?
Coriolanus (1608) act 1, sc. 1, l. [170]

4 　　　　He that depends
Upon your favours swims with fins of lead,
And hews down oaks with rushes.
Coriolanus (1608) act 1, sc. 1, l. 179

5 My gracious silence, hail!
Coriolanus (1608) act 2, sc. 1, l. [194]

6 Hear you this Triton of the minnows? mark you
His absolute 'shall'?
Coriolanus (1608) act 3, sc. 1, l. 88

7 What is the city but the people?
Coriolanus (1608) act 3, sc. 1, l. 198

8 You common cry of curs! whose breath I hate
As reek o' the rotten fens, whose loves I prize
As the dead carcases of unburied men
That do corrupt my air,—I banish you.
Coriolanus (1608) act 3, sc. 3, l. 118

9 　　　　Despising,
For you, the city, thus I turn my back:
There is a world elsewhere.
Coriolanus (1608) act 3, sc. 3, l. 131

10 　　　　The beast
With many heads butts me away.
Coriolanus (1608) act 4, sc. 1, l. 1; see **POPE** 617:25

11 Let me have war, say I; it exceeds peace as far as day does night; it's spritely, waking, audible, and full of vent. Peace is a very apoplexy, lethargy: mulled, deaf, sleepy, insensible; a getter of more bastard children than war's a destroyer of men.
Coriolanus (1608) act 4, sc. 5, l. [237]; some editions prefer 'spritely walking'

12 　　　　I think he'll be to Rome
As is the osprey to the fish, who takes it
By sovereignty of nature.
Coriolanus (1608) act 4, sc. 7, l. 33

13 　　　　Like a dull actor now,
I have forgot my part, and I am out,
Even to a full disgrace.
Coriolanus (1608) act 5, sc. 3, l. 40

14 　　　　O! a kiss
Long as my exile, sweet as my revenge!
Now, by the jealous queen of heaven, that kiss
I carried from thee, dear, and my true lip
Hath virgined it e'er since.
Coriolanus (1608) act 5, sc. 3, l. 44

15 　　　　Chaste as the icicle
That's curdied by the frost from purest snow,
And hangs on Dian's temple.
Coriolanus (1608) act 5, sc. 3, l. 65; some editions prefer 'candied by the frost'

16 If you have writ your annals true, 'tis there,
That, like an eagle in a dove-cote, I
Fluttered your Volscians in Corioli:
Alone I did it.
Coriolanus (1608) act 5, sc. 5, l. 114

CYMBELINE

17 If she be furnished with a mind so rare,
She is alone the Arabian bird, and I
Have lost the wager. Boldness be my friend!
Arm me, audacity.
Cymbeline (1609–10) act 1, sc. 6, l. 16

18 　　　　On her left breast
A mole cinque-spotted, like the crimson drops
I' the bottom of a cowslip.
Cymbeline (1609–10) act 2, sc. 2, l. 37

19 Hark! hark! the lark at heaven's gate sings,
And Phoebus 'gins arise,
His steeds to water at those springs
On chaliced flowers that lies;
And winking Mary-buds begin
To ope their golden eyes:
With everything that pretty is,
My lady sweet, arise!
Cymbeline (1609–10) act 2, sc. 3, l. [22]

20 　　　　I thought her
As chaste as unsunned snow.
Cymbeline (1609–10) act 2, sc. 5, l. 12

21 The natural bravery of your isle, which stands
As Neptune's park, ribbed and paled in
With rocks unscalable, and roaring waters.
Cymbeline (1609–10) act 3, sc. 1, l. 18; some editions prefer 'banks unscalable'

22 O, for a horse with wings!
Cymbeline (1609–10) act 3, sc. 2, l. [49]

23 Hath Britain all the sun that shines?
Cymbeline (1609–10) act 3, sc. 4, l. [139]

24 Fear no more the heat o' the sun,
Nor the furious winter's rages;
Thou thy worldly task hast done,
Home art gone and ta'en thy wages:
Golden lads and girls all must,
As chimney-sweepers, come to dust.
Cymbeline (1609–10) act 4, sc. 2, l. 258

25 No exorciser harm thee!
Nor no witchcraft charm thee!
Ghost unlaid forbear thee!
Nothing ill come near thee!
Quiet consummation have:
And renowned be thy grave!
Cymbeline (1609–10) act 4, sc. 2, l. 276

26 　　　　Hang there like fruit, my soul,
Till the tree die.
Cymbeline (1609–10) act 5, sc. 5, l. 263; some editions prefer act 5, sc. 6

HAMLET

27 You come most carefully upon your hour.
Hamlet (1601) act 1, sc. 1, l. 6

28 For this relief much thanks; 'tis bitter cold
And I am sick at heart.
Hamlet (1601) act 1, sc. 1, l. 8

1 Not a mouse stirring.
Hamlet (1601) act 1, sc. 1, l. 10

2 Look, where it comes again!
Hamlet (1601) act 1, sc. 1, l. 40

3 This bodes some strange eruption to our state.
Hamlet (1601) act 1, sc. 1, l. 69

4 In the most high and palmy state of Rome,
A little ere the mightiest Julius fell,
The graves stood tenantless and the sheeted
dead
Did squeak and gibber in the Roman streets.
Hamlet (1601) act 1, sc. 1, l. 113

5 And then it started like a guilty thing
Upon a fearful summons.
Hamlet (1601) act 1, sc. 1, l. 148; see **WORDSWORTH** 867:14

6 It faded on the crowing of the cock.
Some say that ever 'gainst that season comes
Wherein our Saviour's birth is celebrated,
The bird of dawning singeth all night long;
And then, they say, no spirit can walk abroad.
The nights are wholesome; then no planets
strike,
No fairy takes, nor witch hath power to charm,
So hallowed and so gracious is the time.
Hamlet (1601) act 1, sc. 1, l. 157

7 But, look, the morn, in russet mantle clad,
Walks o'er the dew of yon high eastern hill.
Hamlet (1601) act 1, sc. 1, l. 166

8 Though yet of Hamlet our dear brother's death
The memory be green.
Hamlet (1601) act 1, sc. 2, l. 1

9 Therefore our sometime sister, now our queen
. . .
Have we, as 'twere with a defeated joy,
With one auspicious and one dropping eye,
With mirth in funeral and with dirge in
marriage,
In equal scale weighing delight and dole,
Taken to wife.
Hamlet (1601) act 1, sc. 2, l. 8

10 The head is not more native to the heart,
The hand more instrumental to the brain,
Than is the throne of Denmark to thy father.
Hamlet (1601) act 1, sc. 2, l. 47; some editions prefer
'instrumental to the mouth'

11 A little more than kin, and less than kind.
Hamlet (1601) act 1, sc. 2, l. 65

12 Not so, my lord; I am too much i' the sun.
Hamlet (1601) act 1, sc. 2, l. 67

13 Good Hamlet, cast thy nighted colour off,
And let thine eye look like a friend on Denmark.
Hamlet (1601) act 1, sc. 2, l. 68

14 QUEEN: Thou know'st 'tis common; all that live
must die,
Passing through nature to eternity.
HAMLET: Ay, madam, it is common.
Hamlet (1601) act 1, sc. 2, l. 72

15 Seems, madam! Nay, it is; I know not 'seems'.
'Tis not alone my inky cloak, good mother,

Nor customary suits of solemn black,
Nor windy suspiration of forced breath,
No, nor the fruitful river in the eye,
Nor the dejected 'haviour of the visage,
Together with all forms, modes, shows of grief,
That can denote me truly.
Hamlet (1601) act 1, sc. 2, l. 76

16 But I have that within which passeth show;
These but the trappings and the suits of woe.
Hamlet (1601) act 1, sc. 2, l. 85

17 O! that this too too solid flesh would melt,
Thaw, and resolve itself into a dew;
Or that the Everlasting had not fixed
His canon 'gainst self-slaughter!
Hamlet (1601) act 1, sc. 2, l. 129

18 How weary, stale, flat, and unprofitable
Seem to me all the uses of this world.
Hamlet (1601) act 1, sc. 2, l. 133

19 Things rank and gross in nature
Possess it merely. That it should come to this!
Hamlet (1601) act 1, sc. 2, l. 136

20 So excellent a king; that was, to this,
Hyperion to a satyr: so loving to my mother,
That he might not beteem the winds of heaven
Visit her face too roughly.
Hamlet (1601) act 1, sc. 2, l. 139

21 Frailty, thy name is woman!
A little month; or ere those shoes were old
With which she followed my poor father's body,
Like Niobe, all tears; why she, even she,—
O God! a beast, that wants discourse of reason,
Would have mourned longer.
Hamlet (1601) act 1, sc. 2, l. 146

22 My father's brother, but no more like my father
Than I to Hercules.
Hamlet (1601) act 1, sc. 2, l. 152

23 It is not, nor it cannot come to good;
But break, my heart, for I must hold my tongue!
Hamlet (1601) act 1, sc. 2, l. 158

24 A truant disposition, good my lord.
Hamlet (1601) act 1, sc. 2, l. 169

25 Thrift, thrift, Horatio! the funeral baked meats
Did coldly furnish forth the marriage tables.
Hamlet (1601) act 1, sc. 2, l. 180

26 In my mind's eye, Horatio.
Hamlet (1601) act 1, sc. 2, l. 185

27 He was a man, take him for all in all,
I shall not look upon his like again.
Hamlet (1601) act 1, sc. 2, l. 187

28 But answer made it none.
Hamlet (1601) act 1, sc. 2, l. 215

29 A countenance more in sorrow than in anger.
Hamlet (1601) act 1, sc. 2, l. 231

30 All is not well;
I doubt some foul play.
Hamlet (1601) act 1, sc. 2, l. 254

1   Foul deeds will rise,
Though all the earth o'erwhelm them, to men's
    eyes.
Hamlet (1601) act 1, sc. 2, l. 256

2   Do not, as some ungracious pastors do,
Show me the steep and thorny way to heaven,
Whiles, like a puffed and reckless libertine,
Himself the primrose path of dalliance treads,
And recks not his own rede.
Hamlet (1601) act 1, sc. 3, l. 47

3   The friends thou hast, and their adoption tried,
Grapple them to thy soul with hoops of steel.
Hamlet (1601) act 1, sc. 3, l. 62

4   Costly thy habit as thy purse can buy,
But not expressed in fancy; rich, not gaudy;
For the apparel oft proclaims the man.
Hamlet (1601) act 1, sc. 3, l. 70; see **WESLEY** 848:10

5   Neither a borrower, nor a lender be;
For loan oft loses both itself and friend.
Hamlet (1601) act 1, sc. 3, l. 75

6   This above all: to thine own self be true,
And it must follow, as the night the day,
Thou canst not then be false to any man.
Hamlet (1601) act 1, sc. 3, l. 78; see **BACON** 48:17

7   You speak like a green girl,
Unsifted in such perilous circumstance.
Hamlet (1601) act 1, sc. 3, l. 101

8   Ay, springes to catch woodcocks.
Hamlet (1601) act 1, sc. 3, l. 115

9   It is a nipping and an eager air.
Hamlet (1601) act 1, sc. 4, l. 2

10 But to my mind,—though I am native here,
And to the manner born,—it is a custom
More honoured in the breach than the
    observance.
Hamlet (1601) act 1, sc. 4, l. 14

11 Angels and ministers of grace defend us!
Be thou a spirit of health or goblin damned,
Bring with thee airs from heaven or blasts from
    hell,
Be thy intents wicked or charitable,
Thou com'st in such a questionable shape
That I will speak to thee: I'll call thee Hamlet,
King, father; royal Dane, O! answer me.
Hamlet (1601) act 1, sc. 4, l. 39

12 What may this mean,
That thou, dead corse again in complete steel
Revisit'st thus the glimpses of the moon,
Making night hideous.
Hamlet (1601) act 1, sc. 4, l. 51; see **MILTON** 539:5

13 I do not set my life at a pin's fee;
And for my soul, what can it do to that,
Being a thing immortal as itself?
Hamlet (1601) act 1, sc. 4, l. 65

14 Unhand me, gentlemen,
By heaven! I'll make a ghost of him that lets
    me.
Hamlet (1601) act 1, sc. 4, l. 84

15 Something is rotten in the state of Denmark.
Hamlet (1601) act 1, sc. 4, l. 90

16 I am thy father's spirit;
Doomed for a certain term to walk the night.
Hamlet (1601) act 1, sc. 5, l. 9

17 List, list, O, list!
Hamlet (1601) act 1, sc. 5, l. 13

18 I could a tale unfold whose lightest word
Would harrow up thy soul, freeze thy young
    blood,
Make thy two eyes, like stars, start from their
    spheres,
Thy knotted and combinèd locks to part,
And each particular hair to stand on end,
Like quills upon the fretful porpentine.
Hamlet (1601) act 1, sc. 5, l. 15

19 Revenge his foul and most unnatural murder.
Hamlet (1601) act 1, sc. 5, l. 25

20 Murder most foul, as in the best it is;
But this most foul, strange, and unnatural.
Hamlet (1601) act 1, sc. 5, l. 27

21 O my prophetic soul!
My uncle!
Hamlet (1601) act 1, sc. 5, l. 40

22 Thus was I, sleeping, by a brother's hand,
Of life, of crown, of queen, at once dispatched;
Cut off even in the blossoms of my sin,
Unhouseled, disappointed, unaneled,
No reckoning made, but sent to my account
With all my imperfections on my head:
O, horrible! O, horrible! most horrible!
Hamlet (1601) act 1, sc. 5, l. 74

23 Remember thee!
Ay, thou poor ghost, while memory holds a seat
In this distracted globe.
Hamlet (1601) act 1, sc. 5, l. 95

24 O most pernicious woman!
O villain, villain, smiling, damnèd villain!
My tables,—meet it is I set it down,
That one may smile, and smile, and be a villain;
At least I'm sure it may be so in Denmark.
Hamlet (1601) act 1, sc. 5, l. 105

25 These are but wild and whirling words, my lord.
Hamlet (1601) act 1, sc. 5, l. 133

26 Well said, old mole! canst work i' the earth so
    fast?
Hamlet (1601) act 1, sc. 5, l. 162

27 There are more things in heaven and earth,
    Horatio,
Than are dreamt of in your philosophy.
Hamlet (1601) act 1, sc. 5, l. 166; see **HALDANE** 376:11

28 To put an antic disposition on.
Hamlet (1601) act 1, sc. 5, l. 172

29 Rest, rest, perturbèd spirit.
Hamlet (1601) act 1, sc. 5, l. 182

30 The time is out of joint; O cursèd spite,
That ever I was born to set it right!
Hamlet (1601) act 1, sc. 5, l. 188

1 By indirections find directions out.
Hamlet (1601) act 2, sc. 1, l. 66

2 Brevity is the soul of wit.
Hamlet (1601) act 2, sc. 2, l. 90; see **PROVERBS** 628:23

3   To define true madness,
What is't but to be nothing else but mad?
Hamlet (1601) act 2, sc. 2, l. 93

4 More matter with less art.
Hamlet (1601) act 2, sc. 2, l. 95

5 POLONIUS: What do you read, my lord?
HAMLET: Words, words, words.
Hamlet (1601) act 2, sc. 2, l. [195]

6 Though this be madness, yet there is method in't.
Hamlet (1601) act 2, sc. 2, l. [211]

7 POLONIUS: My honourable lord, I will most humbly take my leave of you.
HAMLET: You cannot, sir, take from me any thing that I will more willingly part withal; except my life, except my life, except my life.
Hamlet (1601) act 2, sc. 2, l. [221]

8 HAMLET: Then you live about her waist, or in the middle of her favours?
GUILDENSTERN: Faith, her privates, we.
HAMLET: In the secret parts of Fortune? O! most true; she is a strumpet.
Hamlet (1601) act 2, sc. 2, l. [240]

9 There is nothing either good or bad, but thinking makes it so.
Hamlet (1601) act 2, sc. 2, l. [259]

10 O God! I could be bounded in a nut-shell, and count myself a king of infinite space, were it not that I have bad dreams.
Hamlet (1601) act 2, sc. 2, l. [263]

11 It goes so heavily with my disposition that this goodly frame, the earth, seems to me a sterile promontory; this most excellent canopy, the air, look you, this brave o'erhanging firmament, this majestical roof fretted with golden fire, why, it appears no other thing to me but a foul and pestilent congregation of vapours. What a piece of work is a man! How noble in reason! how infinite in faculty! in form, in moving, how express and admirable! in action how like an angel! in apprehension how like a god! the beauty of the world! the paragon of animals! And yet, to me, what is this quintessence of dust? man delights not me; no, nor woman neither, though, by your smiling, you seem to say so.
Hamlet (1601) act 2, sc. 2, l. [316]; some editions omit 'firmament'

12 He that plays the king shall be welcome; his majesty shall have tribute of me.
Hamlet (1601) act 2, sc. 2, l. [341]

13 There is something in this more than natural, if philosophy could find it out.
Hamlet (1601) act 2, sc. 2, l. [392]

14 I am but mad north-north-west; when the wind is southerly, I know a hawk from a handsaw.
Hamlet (1601) act 2, sc. 2, l. [405]

15 The best actors in the world, either for tragedy, comedy, history, pastoral, pastoral-comical, historical-pastoral, tragical-historical, tragical-comical-historical-pastoral, scene individable, or poem unlimited.
Hamlet (1601) act 2, sc. 2, l. [424]

16 The play, I remember, pleased not the million; 'twas caviare to the general.
Hamlet (1601) act 2, sc. 2, l. [465]

17 Good my lord, will you see the players well bestowed? Do you hear, let them be well used; for they are the abstracts and brief chronicles of the time: after your death you were better have a bad epitaph than their ill report while you live.
Hamlet (1601) act 2, sc. 2, l. [553]

18 Use every man after his desert, and who should 'scape whipping?
Hamlet (1601) act 2, sc. 2, l. [561]

19 O, what a rogue and peasant slave am I.
Hamlet (1601) act 2, sc. 2, l. [584]

20 For Hecuba!
What's Hecuba to him or he to Hecuba
That he should weep for her?
Hamlet (1601) act 2, sc. 2, l. [592]

21   He would drown the stage with
            tears,
And cleave the general ear with horrid speech,
Make mad the guilty, and appal the free,
Confound the ignorant, and amaze, indeed,
The very faculties of eyes and ears.
Hamlet (1601) act 2, sc. 2, l. [596]

22 But I am pigeon-livered, and lack gall
To make oppression bitter.
Hamlet (1601) act 2, sc. 2, l. [613]

23   Bloody, bawdy villain!
Remorseless, treacherous, lecherous, kindless
            villain!
Hamlet (1601) act 2, sc. 2, l. [616]

24   I have heard,
That guilty creatures sitting at a play
Have by the very cunning of the scene
Been struck so to the soul that presently
They have proclaimed their malefactions;
For murder, though it have no tongue, will
            speak
With most miraculous organ.
Hamlet (1601) act 2, sc. 2, l. [625]

25   The play's the thing
Wherein I'll catch the conscience of the king.
Hamlet (1601) act 2, sc. 2, l. [641]

26 To be, or not to be: that is the question:
Whether 'tis nobler in the mind to suffer
The slings and arrows of outrageous fortune,
Or to take arms against a sea of troubles,
And by opposing end them? To die: to sleep;

No more; and, by a sleep to say we end
The heart-ache and the thousand natural shocks
That flesh is heir to, 'tis a consummation
Devoutly to be wished. To die, to sleep;
To sleep: perchance to dream: ay, there's the rub;
For in that sleep of death what dreams may come
When we have shuffled off this mortal coil,
Must give us pause.
Hamlet (1601) act 3, sc. 1, l. 56

1 For who would bear the whips and scorns of time,
The oppressor's wrong, the proud man's contumely,
The pangs of disprized love, the law's delay,
The insolence of office, and the spurns
That patient merit of the unworthy takes,
When he himself might his quietus make
With a bare bodkin?
And makes us rather bear those ills we have,
Than fly to others that we know not of?
Hamlet (1601) act 3, sc. 1, l. 70

2 The undiscovered country from whose bourn
No traveller returns.
Hamlet (1601) act 3, sc. 1, l. 79

3 Thus conscience doth make cowards of us all;
And thus the native hue of resolution
Is sicklied o'er with the pale cast of thought,
And enterprises of great pith and moment
With this regard their currents turn awry,
And lose the name of action.
Hamlet (1601) act 3, sc. 1, l. 83; see **PROVERBS** 629:19

4 Nymph, in thy orisons
Be all my sins remembered.
Hamlet (1601) act 3, sc. 1, l. 89

5 Get thee to a nunnery: why wouldst thou be a breeder of sinners?
Hamlet (1601) act 3, sc. 1, l. [124]

6 Be thou as chaste as ice, as pure as snow, thou shalt not escape calumny. Get thee to a nunnery, go; farewell.
Hamlet (1601) act 3, sc. 1, l. [142]

7 I have heard of your paintings too, well enough. God hath given you one face and you make yourselves another.
Hamlet (1601) act 3, sc. 1, l. [150]

8 I say, we will have no more marriages.
Hamlet (1601) act 3, sc. 1, l. [156]

9 O! what a noble mind is here o'erthrown:
The courtier's, soldier's, scholar's, eye, tongue, sword;
The expectancy and rose of the fair state,
The glass of fashion, and the mould of form,
The observèd of all observers, quite, quite, down!
Hamlet (1601) act 3, sc. 1, l. [159]

10 Now see that noble and most sovereign reason,
Like sweet bells jangled, out of tune and harsh.
Hamlet (1601) act 3, sc. 1, l. [166]

11 O! woe is me,
To have seen what I have seen, see what I see!
Hamlet (1601) act 3, sc. 1, l. [169]

12 Speak the speech, I pray you, as I pronounced it to you, trippingly on the tongue; but if you mouth it, as many of your players do, I had as lief the town-crier spoke my lines. Nor do not saw the air too much with your hand, thus; but use all gently.
Hamlet (1601) act 3, sc. 2, l. 1

13 I would have such a fellow whipped for o'erdoing Termagant; it out-herods Herod.
Hamlet (1601) act 3, sc. 2, l. 14

14 Suit the action to the word, the word to the action.
Hamlet (1601) act 3, sc. 2, l. [20]

15 To hold, as 'twere, the mirror up to nature.
Hamlet (1601) act 3, sc. 2, l. [25]

16 I have thought some of nature's journeymen had made men and not made them well, they imitated humanity so abominably.
Hamlet (1601) act 3, sc. 2, l. [38]

17 Give me that man
That is not passion's slave, and I will wear him
In my heart's core, ay, in my heart of heart,
As I do thee.
Hamlet (1601) act 3, sc. 2, l. [76]

18 The chameleon's dish: I eat the air, promise-crammed; you cannot feed capons so.
Hamlet (1601) act 3, sc. 2, l. [98]

19 Here's metal more attractive.
Hamlet (1601) act 3, sc. 2, l. [117]

20 For, O! for, O! the hobby-horse is forgot.
Hamlet (1601) act 3, sc. 2, l. [145]

21 Marry, this is miching mallecho; it means mischief.
Hamlet (1601) act 3, sc. 2, l. [148]

22 The lady doth protest too much, methinks.
Hamlet (1601) act 3, sc. 2, l. [242]

23 HAMLET: No, no, they do but jest, poison in jest; no offence i' the world.
KING: What do you call the play?
HAMLET: The Mouse-trap.
Hamlet (1601) act 3, sc. 2, l. [247]

24 Let the galled jade wince, our withers are unwrung.
Hamlet (1601) act 3, sc. 2, l. [256]

25 Why, let the stricken deer go weep,
The hart ungallèd play;
For some must watch, while some must sleep:
So runs the world away.
Hamlet (1601) act 3, sc. 2, l. [287]; see **COWPER** 256:13

26 You would play upon me; you would seem to know my stops; you would pluck out the heart of my mystery; you would sound me from my lowest note to the top of my compass.
Hamlet (1601) act 3, sc. 2, l. [387]

1 Very like a whale.
Hamlet (1601) act 3, sc. 2, l. [406]

2 They fool me to the top of my bent.
Hamlet (1601) act 3, sc. 2, l. [408]

3 'Tis now the very witching time of night,
When churchyards yawn and hell itself breathes
  out
Contagion to this world: now could I drink hot
  blood,
And do such bitter business as the day
Would quake to look on.
Hamlet (1601) act 3, sc. 2, l. [413]

4 Let me be cruel, not unnatural;
I will speak daggers to her, but use none.
Hamlet (1601) act 3, sc. 2, l. [420]

5 O! my offence is rank, it smells to heaven.
Hamlet (1601) act 3, sc. 3, l. 36

6 Now might I do it pat, now he is praying.
Hamlet (1601) act 3, sc. 3, l. 73

7 He took my father grossly, full of bread,
With all his crimes broad blown, as flush as
  May;
And how his audit stands who knows save
  heaven?
Hamlet (1601) act 3, sc. 3, l. 80

8 My words fly up, my thoughts remain below:
Words without thoughts never to heaven go.
Hamlet (1601) act 3, sc. 3, l. 97

9 You go not, till I set you up a glass
Where you may see the inmost part of you.
Hamlet (1601) act 3, sc. 4, l. 19

10 How now! a rat? Dead, for a ducat, dead!
Hamlet (1601) act 3, sc. 4, l. 23

11 A bloody deed! almost as bad, good mother,
As kill a king, and marry with his brother.
Hamlet (1601) act 3, sc. 4, l. 28

12 Thou wretched, rash, intruding fool, farewell!
I took thee for thy better.
Hamlet (1601) act 3, sc. 4, l. 31

13   Speak no more;
Thou turn'st mine eyes into my very soul.
Hamlet (1601) act 3, sc. 4, l. 88

14   Nay, but to live
In the rank sweat of an enseamèd bed,
Stewed in corruption, honeying and making love
Over the nasty sty.
Hamlet (1601) act 3, sc. 4, l. 91

15 A cut-purse of the empire and the rule,
That from a shelf the precious diadem stole,
And put it in his pocket!
Hamlet (1601) act 3, sc. 4, l. 99

16 A king of shreds and patches.
Hamlet (1601) act 3, sc. 4, l. 102; see **GILBERT** 357:1

17   Mother, for love of grace,
Lay not that flattering unction to your soul.
Hamlet (1601) act 3, sc. 4, l. 142

18 For in the fatness of these pursy times,
Virtue itself of vice must pardon beg.
Hamlet (1601) act 3, sc. 4, l. 153

19 Assume a virtue, if you have it not.
That monster, custom, who all sense doth eat,
Of habits devil, is angel yet in this.
Hamlet (1601) act 3, sc. 4, l. 160

20 I must be cruel only to be kind.
Hamlet (1601) act 3, sc. 4, l. 178

21 For 'tis the sport to have the enginer
Hoist with his own petar.
Hamlet (1601) act 3, sc. 4, l. 206

22 I'll lug the guts into the neighbour room.
Hamlet (1601) act 3, sc. 4, l. 212

23   Diseases desperate grown,
By desperate appliances are relieved,
Or not at all.
Hamlet (1601) act 4, sc. 2, l. 9; some editions prefer act 4, sc. 3; see **FAWKES** 324:21, **PROVERBS** 629:40

24 A certain convocation of politic worms are e'en
at him. Your worm is your only emperor for
diet.
Hamlet (1601) act 4, sc. 2, l. [21]; some editions prefer act 4, sc. 3

25 A man may fish with the worm that hath eat of
a king, and eat of the fish that hath fed of that
worm.
Hamlet (1601) act 4, sc. 2, l. [29]; some editions prefer act 4, sc. 3

26 We go to gain a little patch of ground,
That hath in it no profit but the name.
Hamlet (1601) act 4, sc. 4, l. 18

27 How all occasions do inform against me,
And spur my dull revenge!
Hamlet (1601) act 4, sc. 4, l. 32

28   Some craven scruple
Of thinking too precisely on the event.
Hamlet (1601) act 4, sc. 4, l. 40

29   Rightly to be great
Is not to stir without great argument,
But greatly to find quarrel in a straw
When honour's at the stake.
Hamlet (1601) act 4, sc. 4, l. 53

30 How should I your true love know
From another one?
By his cockle hat and staff,
And his sandal shoon.
Hamlet (1601) act 4, sc. 5, l. [23]

31 He is dead and gone, lady,
He is dead and gone,
At his head a grass-green turf;
At his heels a stone.
Hamlet (1601) act 4, sc. 5, l. [29]

32 Lord! we know what we are, but know not what
we may be.
Hamlet (1601) act 4, sc. 5, l. [43]

33 Come, my coach! Good-night, ladies; good-night,
sweet ladies; good-night, good-night.
Hamlet (1601) act 4, sc. 5, l. [72]

34 When sorrows come, they come not single spies,
But in battalions.
Hamlet (1601) act 4, sc. 5, l. [78]

1 There's such divinity doth hedge a king,
That treason can but peep to what it would.
Hamlet (1601) act 4, sc. 5, l. [123]

2 There's rosemary, that's for remembrance; pray,
love, remember: and there is pansies, that's for
thoughts.
Hamlet (1601) act 4, sc. 5, l. [174]

3 There's fennel for you, and columbines; there's
rue for you; and here's some for me; we may
call it herb of grace o' Sundays. O! you must
wear your rue with a difference. There's a daisy;
I would give you some violets, but they
withered all when my father died. They say he
made a good end,— For bonny sweet Robin is
all my joy.
Hamlet (1601) act 4, sc. 5, l. [179]

4 And where the offence is let the great axe fall.
Hamlet (1601) act 4, sc. 5, l. [218]

5 There is a willow grows aslant a brook,
That shows his hoar leaves in the glassy stream.
Hamlet (1601) act 4, sc. 7, l. 167

6 There with fantastic garlands did she come,
Of crow-flowers, nettles, daisies, and long
purples,
That liberal shepherds give a grosser name,
But our cold maids do dead men's fingers call
them.
Hamlet (1601) act 4, sc. 7, l. 169

7 There, on the pendent boughs her coronet
weeds
Clambering to hang, an envious sliver broke,
When down her weedy trophies and herself
Fell in the weeping brook. Her clothes spread
wide,
And, mermaid-like, awhile they bore her up;
Which time she chanted snatches of old tunes,
As one incapable of her own distress.
Hamlet (1601) act 4, sc. 7, l. 173

8 Too much of water hast thou, poor Ophelia,
And therefore I forbid my tears; but yet
It is our trick, nature her custom holds,
Let shame say what it will.
Hamlet (1601) act 4, sc. 7, l. 186

9 There is no ancient gentlemen but gardeners,
ditchers and grave-makers; they hold up Adam's
profession.
Hamlet (1601) act 5, sc. 1, l. [32]

10 FIRST CLOWN: What is he that builds stronger
than either the mason, the shipwright, or the
carpenter?
SECOND CLOWN: The gallows-maker; for that
frame outlives a thousand tenants.
Hamlet (1601) act 5, sc. 1, l. [44]

11 Cudgel thy brains no more about it, for your
dull ass will not mend his pace with beating.
Hamlet (1601) act 5, sc. 1, l. [61]

12 But age, with his stealing steps
Hath clawed me in his clutch,

And hath shipped me intil the land,
As if I had never been such.
Hamlet (1601) act 5, sc. 1, l. [77]; some editions prefer 'caught
me in his clutch' see **VAUX** 825:17

13 This might be the pate of a politician . . . one
that would circumvent God, might it not?
Hamlet (1601) act 5, sc. 1, l. [84]

14 The age is grown so picked that the toe of the
peasant comes so near the heel of the courtier,
he galls his kibe.
Hamlet (1601) act 5, sc. 1, l. [150]

15 Alas, poor Yorick. I knew him, Horatio; a fellow
of infinite jest, of most excellent fancy.
Hamlet (1601) act 5, sc. 1, l. [201]

16 To what base uses we may return, Horatio!
Hamlet (1601) act 5, sc. 1, l. [222]

17 Imperious Caesar, dead, and turned to clay,
Might stop a hole to keep the wind away.
Hamlet (1601) act 5, sc. 1, l. [235]; some editions prefer
'Imperial Caesar'

18   Lay her i' the earth;
And from her fair and unpolluted flesh
May violets spring! I tell thee, churlish priest,
A ministering angel shall my sister be,
When thou liest howling.
Hamlet (1601) act 5, sc. 1, l. [260]; see **SCOTT** 689:4

19 Sweets to the sweet: farewell!
Hamlet (1601) act 5, sc. 1, l. [265]

20 I loved Ophelia: forty thousand brothers
Could not, with all their quantity of love,
Make up my sum.
Hamlet (1601) act 5, sc. 1, l. [291]

21 There's a divinity that shapes our ends,
Rough-hew them how we will.
Hamlet (1601) act 5, sc. 2, l. 10

22 I once did hold it, as our statists do,
A baseness to write fair, and laboured much
How to forget that learning; but, sir, now
It did me yeoman's service.
Hamlet (1601) act 5, sc. 2, l. 33

23 Not a whit, we defy augury; there's a special
providence in the fall of a sparrow. If it be now,
'tis not to come; if it be not to come, it will be
now; if it be not now, yet it will come: the
readiness is all.
Hamlet (1601) act 5, sc. 2, l. [232]

24 A hit, a very palpable hit.
Hamlet (1601) act 5, sc. 2, l. [295]

25 Why, as a woodcock to mine own springe,
Osric;
I am justly killed with my own treachery.
Hamlet (1601) act 5, sc. 2, l. [320]

26   This fell sergeant, death,
Is swift in his arrest.
Hamlet (1601) act 5, sc. 2, l. [350]; some editions prefer 'strict
in his arrest'

27   Report me and my cause aright
To the unsatisfied.
Hamlet (1601) act 5, sc. 2, l. [353]

1 I am more an antique Roman than a Dane.
  Hamlet (1601) act 5, sc. 2, l. [355]

2 If thou didst ever hold me in thy heart,
  Absent thee from felicity awhile,
  And in this harsh world draw thy breath in pain,
  To tell my story.
  Hamlet (1601) act 5, sc. 2, l. [360]

3 The rest is silence.
  Hamlet (1601) act 5, sc. 2, l. [372]

4 Now cracks a noble heart. Good-night, sweet
    prince,
  And flights of angels sing thee to thy rest!
  Hamlet (1601) act 5, sc. 2, l. [373]

5 That Rosencrantz and Guildenstern are dead.
  Hamlet (1601) act 5, sc. 2, l. [385]

6   Let four captains
  Bear Hamlet, like a soldier, to the stage;
  For he was likely, had he been put on,
  To have proved most royally.
  Hamlet (1601) act 5, sc. 2, l. [409]

HENRY IV, PART 1

7 Let us be Diana's foresters, gentlemen of the
  shade, minions of the moon.
  Henry IV, Part 1 (1597) act 1, sc. 2, l. [28]

8 FALSTAFF: And is not my hostess of the tavern a
    most sweet wench?
  PRINCE: As the honey of Hybla, my old lad of
    the castle.
  Henry IV, Part 1 (1597) act 1, sc. 2, l. [44]

9 What, in thy quips and thy quiddities?
  Henry IV, Part 1 (1597) act 1, sc. 2, l. [50]

10 Shall there be gallows standing in England when
  thou art king, and resolution thus fobbed as it is
  with the rusty curb of old father antick, the law.
  Henry IV, Part 1 (1597) act 1, sc. 2, l. [66]

11 O! thou hast damnable iteration, and art, indeed,
  able to corrupt a saint.
  Henry IV, Part 1 (1597) act 1, sc. 2, l. [101]

12 If all the year were playing holidays,
  To sport would be as tedious as to work;
  But when they seldom come, they wished for
    come.
  Henry IV, Part 1 (1597) act 1, sc. 2, l. [226]

13 To put down Richard, that sweet lovely rose,
  And plant this thorn, this canker, Bolingbroke.
  Henry IV, Part 1 (1597) act 1, sc. 3, l. 175

14   O! the blood more stirs
  To rouse a lion than to start a hare.
  Henry IV, Part 1 (1597) act 1, sc. 3, l. 197

15 By heaven methinks it were an easy leap
  To pluck bright honour from the pale-faced
    moon,
  Or dive into the bottom of the deep,
  Where fathom-line could never touch the
    ground,
  And pluck up drownèd honour by the locks.
  Henry IV, Part 1 (1597) act 1, sc. 3, l. 201

16 Why, what a candy deal of courtesy
  This fawning greyhound then did proffer me!
  Henry IV, Part 1 (1597) act 1, sc. 3, l. 251

17 I know a trick worth two of that.
  Henry IV, Part 1 (1597) act 2, sc. 1, l. [40]

18 We have the receipt of fern-seed, we walk
  invisible.
  Henry IV, Part 1 (1597) act 2, sc. 1, l. [95]

19 Go hang thyself in thine own heir-apparent
  garters!
  Henry IV, Part 1 (1597) act 2, sc. 2, l. [49]

20 On, bacons, on!
  Henry IV, Part 1 (1597) act 2, sc. 2, l. [99]

21 It would be argument for a week, laughter for a
  month, and a good jest for ever.
  Henry IV, Part 1 (1597) act 2, sc. 2, l. [104]; some editions
  prefer act 2, sc. 3

22   Falstaff sweats to death
  And lards the lean earth as he walks along.
  Henry IV, Part 1 (1597) act 2, sc. 2, l. [119]; some editions
  prefer act 2, sc. 3

23 Out of this nettle, danger, we pluck this flower,
  safety.
  Henry IV, Part 1 (1597) act 2, sc. 3, l. [11]; some editions prefer
  act 2, sc. 4

24 I am not yet of Percy's mind, the Hotspur of
  the North; he that kills me some six or seven
  dozen of Scots at a breakfast, washes his hands,
  and says to his wife, 'Fie upon this quiet life! I
  want work.'
  Henry IV, Part 1 (1597) act 2, sc. 4, l. [116]; some editions
  prefer act 2, sc. 5

25 There live not three good men unhanged in
  England, and one of them is fat and grows old.
  Henry IV, Part 1 (1597) act 2, sc. 4, l. [146]; some editions
  prefer act 2, sc. 5

26 Call you that backing of your friends? A plague
  upon such backing! give me them that will face
  me.
  Henry IV, Part 1 (1597) act 2, sc. 4, l. [168]; some editions
  prefer act 2, sc. 5

27 Nay that's past praying for: I have peppered two
  of them: two I am sure I have paid, two rogues
  in buckram suits. I tell thee what, Hal, if I tell
  thee a lie, spit in my face, call me horse. Thou
  knowest my old ward; here I lay, and thus I bore
  my point. Four rogues in buckram let drive at
  me,—
  Henry IV, Part 1 (1597) act 2, sc. 4, l. [214]; some editions
  prefer act 2, sc. 5

28 These lies are like the father that begets them;
  gross as a mountain, open, palpable.
  Henry IV, Part 1 (1597) act 2, sc. 4, l. [253]; some editions
  prefer act 2, sc. 5

29 Give you a reason on compulsion! if reasons
  were as plentiful as blackberries I would give no
  man a reason upon compulsion, I.
  Henry IV, Part 1 (1597) act 2, sc. 4, l. [267]; some editions
  prefer act 2, sc. 5

1 Mark now, how a plain tale shall put you down.
Henry IV, Part 1 (1597) act 2, sc. 4, l. [285]; some editions prefer act 2, sc. 5

2 Instinct is a great matter, I was a coward on instinct.
Henry IV, Part 1 (1597) act 2, sc. 4, l. [304]; some editions prefer act 2, sc. 5

3 I will do it in King Cambyses' vein.
Henry IV, Part 1 (1597) act 2, sc. 4, l. [430]; some editions prefer act 2, sc. 5

4 There is a devil haunts thee in the likeness of a fat old man; a tun of man is thy companion.
Henry IV, Part 1 (1597) act 2, sc. 4, l. [498]; some editions prefer act 2, sc. 5

5 That roasted Manningtree ox with the pudding in his belly, that reverend vice, that grey iniquity, that father ruffian, that vanity in years.
Henry IV, Part 1 (1597) act 2, sc. 4, l. [504]; some editions prefer act 2, sc. 5

6 No, my good lord; banish Peto, banish Bardolph, banish Poins; but for sweet Jack Falstaff, kind Jack Falstaff, true Jack Falstaff, valiant Jack Falstaff, and therefore more valiant, being, as he is, old Jack Falstaff, banish not him thy Harry's company, banish not him thy Harry's company: banish plump Jack and banish all the world.
Henry IV, Part 1 (1597) act 2, sc. 4, l. [528]; some editions prefer act 2, sc. 5

7 O monstrous! but one half-pennyworth of bread to this intolerable deal of sack!
Henry IV, Part 1 (1597) act 2, sc. 4, l. [598]; some editions prefer act 2, sc. 5

8 GLENDOWER: At my nativity
The front of heaven was full of fiery shapes,
Of burning cressets; and at my birth
The frame and huge foundation of the earth
Shaked like a coward.
HOTSPUR: Why, so it would have done at the same season, if your mother's cat had but kittened.
Henry IV, Part 1 (1597) act 3, sc. 1, l. 13

9 GLENDOWER: I can call spirits from the vasty deep.
HOTSPUR: Why, so can I, or so can any man;
But will they come when you do call for them?
Henry IV, Part 1 (1597) act 3, sc. 1, l. [53]

10 I had rather be a kitten and cry mew
Than one of these same metre ballad-mongers.
Henry IV, Part 1 (1597) act 3, sc. 1, l. [128]

11 Now I perceive the devil understands Welsh.
Henry IV, Part 1 (1597) act 3, sc. 1, l. [233]

12 He was but as the cuckoo is in June,
Heard, not regarded.
Henry IV, Part 1 (1597) act 3, sc. 2, l. 75

13 My near'st and dearest enemy.
Henry IV, Part 1 (1597) act 3, sc. 2, l. 123

14 Company, villanous company, hath been the spoil of me.
Henry IV, Part 1 (1597) act 3, sc. 3, l. [10]

15 Thou knowest in the state of innocency Adam fell; and what should poor Jack Falstaff do in the days of villainy. Thou seest I have more flesh than another man, and therefore more frailty.
Henry IV, Part 1 (1597) act 3, sc. 3, l. [184]

16 I saw young Harry, with his beaver on,
His cushes on his thighs, gallantly armed,
Rise from the ground like feathered Mercury,
And vaulted with such ease into his seat,
As if an angel dropped down from the clouds,
To turn and wind a fiery Pegasus,
And witch the world with noble horsemanship.
Henry IV, Part 1 (1597) act 4, sc. 1, l. 104

17 Doomsday is near; die all, die merrily.
Henry IV, Part 1 (1597) act 4, sc. 1, l. 134

18 Tut, tut; good enough to toss; food for powder, food for powder; they'll fill a pit as well as better: tush, man, mortal men, mortal men.
Henry IV, Part 1 (1597) act 4, sc. 2, l. [72]

19 Greatness knows itself.
Henry IV, Part 1 (1597) act 4, sc. 3, l. 74

20   I could be well content
To entertain the lag-end of my life
With quiet hours.
Henry IV, Part 1 (1597) act 5, sc. 1, l. 23

21 Rebellion lay in his way, and he found it.
Henry IV, Part 1 (1597) act 5, sc. 1, l. 28

22 I would it were bed-time, Hal, and all well.
Henry IV, Part 1 (1597) act 5, sc. 1, l. [125]

23 Thou owest God a death.
Henry IV, Part 1 (1597) act 5, sc. 1, l. [126]; see **SHAKESPEARE** 707:22

24 Honour pricks me on. Yea, but how if honour prick me off when I come on? how then?
Henry IV, Part 1 (1597) act 5, sc. 1, l. [131]

25 What is honour? A word. What is that word, honour? Air. A trim reckoning! Who hath it? He that died o' Wednesday.
Henry IV, Part 1 (1597) act 5, sc. 1, l. [136]

26 Now, *Esperance*! Percy! and set on.
Henry IV, Part 1 (1597) act 5, sc. 2, l. 96

27 Two stars keep not their motion in one sphere.
Henry IV, Part 1 (1597) act 5, sc. 4, l. 65

28 But thought's the slave of life, and life time's fool;
And time, that takes survey of all the world,
Must have a stop.
Henry IV, Part 1 (1597) act 5, sc. 4, l. [81]

29   Poor Jack, farewell!
I could have better spared a better man.
Henry IV, Part 1 (1597) act 5, sc. 4, l. [103]

30 The better part of valour is discretion; in the which better part, I have saved my life.
Henry IV, Part I (1597) act 5, sc. 4, l. [121]; see **PROVERBS** 630:5

31 Lord, Lord, how this world is given to lying! I grant you I was down and out of breath; and so

was he; but we rose both at an instant, and fought a long hour by Shrewsbury clock.
Henry IV, Part 1 (1597) act 5, sc. 4, l. [148]

1 For my part, if a lie may do thee grace, I'll gild it with the happiest terms I have.
Henry IV, Part 1 (1597) act 5, sc. 4, l. [161]

HENRY IV, PART 2

2 Enter Rumour, painted full of tongues.
Henry IV, Part 2 (1597) act 1, sc. 1, stage direction

3   Rumour is a pipe
Blown by surmises, jealousies, conjectures,
And of so easy and so plain a stop
That the blunt monster with uncounted heads,
The still-discordant wavering multitude,
Can play upon it.
Henry IV, Part 2 (1597) induction, l. 15

4 Yet the first bringer of unwelcome news
Hath but a losing office, and his tongue
Sounds ever after as a sullen bell,
Remembered knolling a departed friend.
Henry IV, Part 2 (1597) act 1, sc. 1, l. 100

5 I am not only witty in myself, but the cause that wit is in other men.
Henry IV, Part 2 (1597) act 1, sc. 2, l. [10]; see **FOOTE** 336:12

6 It is the disease of not listening, the malady of not marking, that I am troubled withal.
Henry IV, Part 2 (1597) act 1, sc. 2, l. [139]

7 I am as poor as Job, my lord, but not so patient.
Henry IV, Part 2 (1597) act 1, sc. 2, l. [145]

8 CHIEF JUSTICE: God send the prince a better companion!
FALSTAFF: God send the companion a better prince! I cannot rid my hands of him.
Henry IV, Part 2 (1597) act 1, sc. 2, l. [227]

9 It was always yet the trick of our English nation, if they have a good thing, to make it too common.
Henry IV, Part 2 (1597) act 1, sc. 2, l. [244]

10 I would to God my name were not so terrible to the enemy as it is: I were better to be eaten to death with rust than to be scoured to nothing with perpetual motion.
Henry IV, Part 2 (1597) act 1, sc. 2, l. [247]; see **PROVERBS** 627:41

11 I can get no remedy against this consumption of the purse: borrowing only lingers and lingers it out, but the disease is incurable.
Henry IV, Part 2 (1597) act 1, sc. 2, l. [268]

12 Away, you scullion! you rampallion! you fustilarian! I'll tickle your catastrophe.
Henry IV, Part 2 (1597) act 2, sc. 1, l. [67]

13 Doth it not show vilely in me to desire small beer?
Henry IV, Part 2 (1597) act 2, sc. 2, l. [7]

14   Shall pack-horses,
And hollow pampered jades of Asia,
Which cannot go but thirty miles a day,

Compare with Caesars, and with Cannibals,
And Trojan Greeks?
Henry IV, Part 2 (1597) act 2, sc. 4, l. [176]; see **MARLOWE** 523:10

15 Thou whoreson little tidy Bartholomew boar-pig.
Henry IV, Part 2 (1597) act 2, sc. 4, l. [249]

16 Is it not strange that desire should so many years outlive performance?
Henry IV, Part 2 (1597) act 2, sc. 4, l. [283]

17 Uneasy lies the head that wears a crown.
Henry IV, Part 2 (1597) act 3, sc. 1, l. 31

18 There is a history in all men's lives,
Figuring the nature of the times deceased,
The which observed, a man may prophesy,
With a near aim, of the main chance of things
As yet not come to life, which in their seeds
And weak beginnings lie intreasurèd.
Henry IV, Part 2 (1597) act 3, sc. 1, l. 80

19 A soldier is better accommodated than with a wife.
Henry IV, Part 2 (1597) act 3, sc. 2, l. [73]

20 Most forcible Feeble.
Henry IV, Part 2 (1597) act 3, sc. 2, l. [181]

21 We have heard the chimes at midnight.
Henry IV, Part 2 (1597) act 3, sc. 2, l. [231]

22 I care not; a man can die but once; we owe God a death.
Henry IV, Part 2 (1597) act 3, sc. 2, l. [253]; see **SHAKESPEARE** 706:23

23 He that dies this year is quit for the next.
Henry IV, Part 2 (1597) act 3, sc. 2, l. [257]

24 When a' was naked, he was, for all the world, like a forked radish, with a head fantastically carved upon it with a knife.
Henry IV, Part 2 (1597) act 3, sc. 2, l. [335]

25 That I may justly say with the hook-nosed fellow of Rome, 'I came, saw, and overcame.'
Henry IV, Part 2 (1597) act 4, sc. 3, l. [44]; some editions prefer act 4, sc. 2; see **CAESAR** 193:2

26 A man cannot make him laugh; but that's no marvel; he drinks no wine.
Henry IV, Part 2 (1597) act 4, sc. 3, l. [95]; some editions prefer act 4, sc. 2

27 O polished perturbation! golden care!
Henry IV, Part 2 (1597) act 4, sc. 5, l. 22; some editions prefer act 4, sc. 3

28 This sleep is sound indeed; this is a sleep
That from this golden rigol hath divorced
So many English kings.
Henry IV, Part 2 (1597) act 4, sc. 5, l. 34; some editions prefer act 4, sc. 3

29 Thy wish was father, Harry, to that thought.
Henry IV, Part 2 (1597) act 4, sc. 5, l. 91; some editions prefer act 4, sc. 3; see **PROVERBS** 647:28

30   Commit
The oldest sins the newest kind of ways.
Henry IV, Part 2 (1597) act 4, sc. 5, l. 124; some editions prefer act 4, sc. 3

31 It hath been prophesied to me many years
I should not die but in Jerusalem,

Which vainly I supposed the Holy Land.
But bear me to that chamber; there I'll lie:
In that Jerusalem shall Harry die.
Henry IV, Part 2 (1597) act 4, sc. 5, l. 235; some editions prefer act 4, sc. 3

1 This is the English, not the Turkish court;
Not Amurath an Amurath succeeds,
But Harry, Harry.
Henry IV, Part 2 (1597) act 5, sc. 2, l. 47

2 My father is gone wild into his grave.
Henry IV, Part 2 (1597) act 5, sc. 2, l. 123

3 I speak of Africa and golden joys.
Henry IV, Part 2 (1597) act 5, sc. 3, l. [101]

4 I know thee not, old man: fall to thy prayers;
How ill white hairs become a fool and jester!
Henry IV, Part 2 (1597) act 5, sc. 5, l. [52]

5 Presume not that I am the thing I was.
Henry IV, Part 2 (1597) act 5, sc. 5, l. [61]

6 Falstaff shall die of a sweat, unless already a' be killed with your hard opinions.
Henry IV, Part 2 (1597) act 5, sc. 5, epilogue, l. [32]

HENRY V

7 O! for a Muse of fire, that would ascend
The brightest heaven of invention;
A kingdom for a stage, princes to act
And monarchs to behold the swelling scene.
Henry V (1599) chorus, l. 1

8   Can this cockpit hold
The vasty fields of France? or may we cram
Within this wooden O the very casques
That did affright the air at Agincourt?
Henry V (1599) chorus, l. 11

9 Consideration like an angel came,
And whipped the offending Adam out of him.
Henry V (1599) act 1, sc. 1, l. 28

10   For so work the honey-bees,
Creatures that by a rule in nature teach
The act of order to a peopled kingdom.
They have a king and officers of sorts;
Where some, like magistrates, correct at home,
Others, like merchants, venture trade abroad,
Others, like soldiers, armèd in their stings,
Make boot upon the summer's velvet buds;
Which pillage they with merry march bring home
To the tent-royal of their emperor:
Who, busied in his majesty, surveys
The singing masons building roofs of gold.
Henry V (1599) act 1, sc. 2, l. 187

11 When we have matched our rackets to these balls,
We will in France, by God's grace, play a set
Shall strike his father's crown into the hazard.
Henry V (1599) act 1, sc. 2, l. 261

12 Now all the youth of England are on fire,
And silken dalliance in the wardrobe lies.
Henry V (1599) act 2, chorus, l. 1

13 For now sits Expectation in the air
And hides a sword from hilts unto the point

With crowns imperial, crowns and coronets,
Promised to Harry and his followers.
Henry V (1599) act 2, chorus, l. 8

14 He's in Arthur's bosom, if ever man went to Arthur's bosom.
Henry V (1599) act 2, sc. 3, l. [9]

15 His nose was as sharp as a pen, and a' babbled of green fields.
Henry V (1599) act 2, sc. 3, l. [17]

16 Once more unto the breach, dear friends, once more;
Or close the wall up with our English dead!
In peace there's nothing so becomes a man
As modest stillness and humility:
But when the blast of war blows in our ears,
Then imitate the action of the tiger;
Stiffen the sinews, summon up the blood,
Disguise fair nature with hard-favoured rage;
Then lend the eye a terrible aspect.
Henry V (1599) act 3, sc. 1, l. 1; some editions prefer 'conjure up the blood'

17 I see you stand like greyhounds in the slips,
Straining upon the start. The game's afoot:
Follow your spirit; and, upon this charge
Cry 'God for Harry! England and Saint George!'
Henry V (1599) act 3, sc. 1, l. 31

18 Give them great meals of beef and iron and steel, they will eat like wolves and fight like devils.
Henry V (1599) act 3, sc. 7, l. [166]

19 The royal captain of this ruined band.
Henry V (1599) act 4, chorus, l. 29

20 A little touch of Harry in the night.
Henry V (1599) act 4, chorus, l. 47

21 The king's a bawcock, and a heart of gold,
A lad of life, an imp of fame,
Of parents good, of fist most valiant:
I kiss his dirty shoe, and from my heart-string
I love the lovely bully.
Henry V (1599) act 4, sc. 1, l. 44

22 If you would take the pains but to examine the wars of Pompey the Great, you shall find, I warrant you, that there is no tiddle-taddle nor pibble-pabble in Pompey's camp.
Henry V (1599) act 4, sc. 1, l. [69]

23 Though it appear a little out of fashion,
There is much care and valour in this Welshman.
Henry V (1599) act 4, sc. 1, l. [86]

24 I think the king is but a man, as I am: the violet smells to him as it doth to me.
Henry V (1599) act 4, sc. 1, l. [106]

25 I am afeard there are few die well that die in a battle; for how can they charitably dispose of any thing when blood is their argument?
Henry V (1599) act 4, sc. 1, l. [149]

26 Every subject's duty is the king's; but every subject's soul is his own.
Henry V (1599) act 4, sc. 1, l. [189]

1 Upon the king! let us our lives, our souls,
Our debts, our careful wives,
Our children, and our sins lay on the king!
Henry V (1599) act 4, sc. 1, l. [250]

2   What infinite heart's ease
Must kings neglect, that private men enjoy!
And what have kings that privates have not too,
Save ceremony, save general ceremony?
Henry V (1599) act 4, sc. 1, l. [256]

3 'Tis not the balm, the sceptre and the ball,
The sword, the mace, the crown imperial,
The intertissued robe of gold and pearl,
The farcèd title running 'fore the king,
The throne he sits on, nor the tide of pomp
That beats upon the high shore of this world,
No, not all these, thrice-gorgeous ceremony,
Not all these, laid in bed majestical,
Can sleep so soundly as the wretched slave,
Who with a body filled and vacant mind
Gets him to rest, crammed with distressful
    bread.
Henry V (1599) act 4, sc. 1, l. [280]

4 O God of battles! steel my soldiers' hearts;
Possess them not with fear; take from them now
The sense of reckoning, if the opposèd numbers
Pluck their hearts from them.
Henry V (1599) act 4, sc. 1, l. [309]

5 If we are marked to die, we are enow
To do our country loss; and if to live,
The fewer men, the greater share of honour.
Henry V (1599) act 4, sc. 3, l. 20

6 He which hath no stomach to this fight,
Let him depart; his passport shall be made,
And crowns for convoy put into his purse:
We would not die in that man's company
That fears his fellowship to die with us.
This day is called the feast of Crispian:
He that outlives this day and comes safe home,
Will stand a tip-toe when this day is named,
And rouse him at the name of Crispian.
Henry V (1599) act 4, sc. 3, l. 35

7 Then will he strip his sleeve and show his scars,
And say, 'These wounds I had on Crispin's day.'
Old men forget: yet all shall be forgot,
But he'll remember with advantages
What feats he did that day.
Henry V (1599) act 4, sc. 3, l. 47

8 And Crispin Crispian shall ne'er go by,
From this day to the ending of the world,
But we in it shall be rememberèd;
We few, we happy few, we band of brothers;
For he to-day that sheds his blood with me
Shall be my brother; be he ne'er so vile
This day shall gentle his condition:
And gentlemen in England, now a-bed
Shall think themselves accursed they were not
    here,

And hold their manhoods cheap whiles any
    speaks
That fought with us upon Saint Crispin's day.
Henry V (1599) act 4, sc. 3, l. 57

9   But now behold,
In the quick forge and working-house of
    thought,
How London doth pour out her citizens.
Henry V (1599) act 5, chorus, l. 22

10 Not for Cadwallader and all his goats.
Henry V (1599) act 5, sc. 1, l. [29]

11   The naked, poor, and manglèd Peace,
Dear nurse of arts, plenties, and joyful births.
Henry V (1599) act 5, sc. 2, l. 34

12 For these fellows of infinite tongue, that can
rhyme themselves into ladies' favours, they do
always reason themselves out again.
Henry V (1599) act 5, sc. 2, l. [162]

HENRY VI, PART 1

13 Hung be the heavens with black, yield day to
    night!
Henry VI, Part 1 (1592) act 1, sc. 1, l. 1

14 Expect Saint Martin's summer, halcyon days.
Henry VI, Part 1 (1592) act 1, sc. 2, l. 131

15   Unbidden guests
Are often welcomest when they are gone.
Henry VI, Part 1 (1592) act 2, sc. 2, l. 55

16 But in these nice sharp quillets of the law,
Good faith, I am no wiser than a daw.
Henry VI, Part 1 (1592) act 2, sc. 4, l. 17

17 From off this brier pluck a white rose with me.
Plantagenet
Henry VI, Part 1 (1592) act 2, sc. 4, l. 30

18 Pluck a red rose from off this thorn with me.
Somerset
Henry VI, Part 1 (1592) act 2, sc. 4, l. 33

19 I owe him little duty and less love.
Henry VI, Part 1 (1592) act 4, sc. 4, l. 34

20 She's beautiful and therefore to be wooed;
She is a woman, therefore to be won.
Henry VI, Part 1 (1592) act 5, sc. 3, l. 78; some editions prefer
act 5, sc. 5; see **SHAKESPEARE** 734:10

HENRY VI, PART 2

21 Is this the government of Britain's isle,
And this the royalty of Albion's king?
Henry VI, Part 2 (1592) act 1, sc. 3, l. [47]

22 Thrice is he armed that hath his quarrel just.
Henry VI, Part 2 (1592) act 3, sc. 2, l. 233

23 The gaudy, blabbing, and remorseful day
Is crept into the bosom of the sea.
Henry VI, Part 2 (1592) act 4, sc. 1, l. 1

24 I say it was never merry world in England since
gentlemen came up.
Henry VI, Part 2 (1592) act 4, sc. 2, l. [10]

25 CADE: There shall be in England seven halfpenny
    loaves sold for a penny; the three-hooped pot
    shall have ten hoops; and I will make it felony
    to drink small beer. All the realm shall be in

common, and in Cheapside shall my palfrey go to grass. And when I am king,—as king I will be,— . . . there shall be no money; all shall eat and drink on my score; and I will apparel them all in one livery, that they may agree like brothers, and worship me their lord.
DICK: The first thing we do, let's kill all the lawyers.

Henry VI, Part 2 (1592) act 4, sc. 2, l. [73]

1 Is not this a lamentable thing, that of the skin of an innocent lamb should be made parchment? that parchment, being scribbled o'er, should undo a man?

Henry VI, Part 2 (1592) act 4, sc. 2, l. [88]

2 And Adam was a gardener.

Henry VI, Part 2 (1592) act 4, sc. 2, l. [146]

3 Thou hast most traitorously corrupted the youth of the realm in erecting a grammar school: and whereas, before, our forefathers had no other books but the score and the tally, thou hast caused printing to be used; and, contrary to the king, his crown and dignity, thou hast built a paper-mill.

Henry VI, Part 2 (1592) act 4, sc. 7, l. [35]

4 Away with him! away with him! he speaks Latin.

Henry VI, Part 2 (1592) act 4, sc. 7, l. [62]

HENRY VI, PART 3

5 O tiger's heart wrapped in a woman's hide!

Henry VI, Part 3 (1592) act 1, sc. 4, l. 137

6 This battle fares like to the morning's war,
When dying clouds contend with growing light,
What time the shepherd, blowing of his nails,
Can neither call it perfect day nor night.

Henry VI, Part 3 (1592) act 2, sc. 5, l. 1

7 Gives not the hawthorn bush a sweeter shade
To shepherds, looking on their silly sheep,
Than doth a rich embroidered canopy
To kings that fear their subjects' treachery?

Henry VI, Part 3 (1592) act 2, sc. 5, l. 42

8 Why, I can smile, and murder whiles I smile.

Henry VI, Part 3 (1592) act 3, sc. 2, l. 182

9 I'll drown more sailors than the mermaid shall;
I'll slay more gazers than the basilisk;
I'll play the orator as well as Nestor,
Deceive more slyly than Ulysses could,
And, like a Sinon, take another Troy.
I can add colours to the chameleon,
Change shapes with Proteus for advantages,
And set the murderous Machiavel to school.
Can I do this, and cannot get a crown?
Tut, were it farther off, I'll pluck it down.

Henry VI, Part 3 (1592) act 3, sc. 2, l. 186

10 Peace! impudent and shameless Warwick, peace;
Proud setter up and puller down of kings.

Henry VI, Part 3 (1592) act 3, sc. 3, l. 156

11 A little fire is quickly trodden out,
Which, being suffered, rivers cannot quench.

Henry VI, Part 3 (1592) act 4, sc. 8, l. 7

12 Suspicion always haunts the guilty mind;
The thief doth fear each bush an officer.

Henry VI, Part 3 (1592) act 5, sc. 6, l. 11

HENRY VIII

13 Heat not a furnace for your foe so hot
That it do singe yourself.

Henry VIII (1613) act 1, sc. 1, l. 140; play written with John **FLETCHER**

14 Go with me, like good angels, to my end;
And, as the long divorce of steel falls on me,
Make of your prayers one sweet sacrifice,
And lift my soul to heaven.

Henry VIII (1613) act 2, sc. 1, l. 75

15   Heaven will one day open
The king's eyes, that so long have slept upon
This bold bad man.

Henry VIII (1613) act 2, sc. 2, l. [42]; see **SPENSER** 767:4

16 Orpheus with his lute made trees,
And the mountain-tops that freeze,
Bow themselves when he did sing.

Henry VIII (1613) act 3, sc. 1, l. 3

17 In sweet music is such art,
Killing care and grief of heart
Fall asleep, or hearing die.

Henry VIII (1613) act 3, sc. 1, l. 12

18   I shall fall
Like a bright exhalation in the evening,
And no man see me more.

Henry VIII (1613) act 3, sc. 2, l. 226

19 Farewell! a long farewell, to all my greatness!
This is the state of man: to-day he puts forth
The tender leaves of hope; to-morrow blossoms,
And bears his blushing honours thick upon him;
The third day comes a frost, a killing frost;
And, when he thinks, good easy man, full surely
His greatness is a-ripening, nips his root,
And then he falls, as I do. I have ventured,
Like little wanton boys that swim on bladders,
This many summers in a sea of glory,
But far beyond my depth.

Henry VIII (1613) act 3, sc. 2, l. 352

20   O how wretched
Is that poor man that hangs on princes' favours!
There is, betwixt that smile we would aspire to,
That sweet aspect of princes, and their ruin,
More pangs and fears than wars or women have;
And when he falls, he falls like Lucifer,
Never to hope again.

Henry VIII (1613) act 3, sc. 2, l. 367

21 A peace above all earthly dignities,
A still and quiet conscience.

Henry VIII (1613) act 3, sc. 2, l. 380

22 Cromwell, I charge thee, fling away ambition:
By that sin fell the angels.

Henry VIII (1613) act 3, sc. 2, l. 441

23 Love thyself last: cherish those hearts that hate thee;
Corruption wins not more than honesty.

Henry VIII (1613) act 3, sc. 2, l. 444

1 Had I but served my God with half the zeal
I served my king, he would not in mine age
Have left me naked to mine enemies.
Henry VIII (1613) act 3, sc. 2, l. 456; see **WOLSEY** 863:19

2 An old man, broken with the storms of state
Is come to lay his weary bones among ye;
Give him a little earth for charity.
Henry VIII (1613) act 4, sc. 2, l. 21; see **WOLSEY** 863:18

3 So may he rest; his faults lie gently on him!
Henry VIII (1613) act 4, sc. 2, l. 31

4 His promises were, as he then was, mighty;
But his performance, as he is now, nothing.
Henry VIII (1613) act 4, sc. 2, l. 41

5 Men's evil manners live in brass; their virtues
We write in water.
Henry VIII (1613) act 4, sc. 2, l. 45; see **EPITAPHS** 318:5

6 He was a scholar, and a ripe and good one;
Exceeding wise, fair-spoken, and persuading:
Lofty and sour to them that loved him not;
But, to those men that sought him, sweet as
summer.
Henry VIII (1613) act 4, sc. 2, l. 51

7 Those twins of learning that he raised in you,
Ipswich and Oxford!
Henry VIII (1613) act 4, sc. 2, l. 58

8 In her days every man shall eat in safety
Under his own vine what he plants; and sing
The merry songs of peace to all his neighbours.
Henry VIII (1613) act 5, sc. 5, l. 34; some editions prefer act 5,
sc. 4

9 Nor shall this peace sleep with her; but as when
The bird of wonder dies, the maiden phoenix,
Her ashes new-create another heir
As great in admiration as herself.
Henry VIII (1613) act 5, sc. 5, l. 40; some editions prefer act 5,
sc. 4

10 Some come to take their ease
And sleep an act or two.
Henry VIII (1613) act 5, epilogue, l. 2

JULIUS CAESAR

11 Hence! home, you idle creatures, get you home:
Is this a holiday?
Julius Caesar (1599) act 1, sc. 1, l. 1

12 You blocks, you stones, you worse than senseless
things!
O you hard hearts, you cruel men of Rome,
Knew you not Pompey?
Julius Caesar (1599) act 1, sc. 1, l. [39]

13 CAESAR: Who is it in the press that calls on me?
I hear a tongue, shriller than all the music,
Cry 'Caesar'. Speak; Caesar is turned to hear.
SOOTHSAYER: Beware the ides of March.
Julius Caesar (1599) act 1, sc. 2, l. 15

14 Brutus, I do observe you now of late:
I have not from your eyes that gentleness
And show of love as I was wont to have:
You bear too stubborn and too strange a hand
Over your friend that loves you.
Julius Caesar (1599) act 1, sc. 2, l. 32

15   Poor Brutus, with himself at war,
Forgets the shows of love to other men.
Julius Caesar (1599) act 1, sc. 2, l. 46

16 I was born free as Caesar; so were you:
We both have fed as well, and we can both
Endure the winter's cold as well as he.
Julius Caesar (1599) act 1, sc. 2, l. 97

17 He had a fever when he was in Spain,
And when the fit was on him, I did mark
How he did shake; 'tis true, this god did shake.
Julius Caesar (1599) act 1, sc. 2, l. 119

18   Ye gods, it doth amaze me,
A man of such a feeble temper should
So get the start of the majestic world,
And bear the palm alone.
Julius Caesar (1599) act 1, sc. 2, l. 128

19 Why, man, he doth bestride the narrow world
Like a Colossus; and we petty men
Walk under his huge legs, and peep about
To find ourselves dishonourable graves.
Men at some time are masters of their fates:
The fault, dear Brutus, is not in our stars,
But in ourselves, that we are underlings.
Julius Caesar (1599) act 1, sc. 2, l. 134

20 'Brutus' will start a spirit as soon as 'Caesar'.
Now in the names of all the gods at once,
Upon what meat doth this our Caesar feed,
That he is grown so great?
Julius Caesar (1599) act 1, sc. 2, l. 146

21 When could they say, till now, that talked of
Rome,
That her wide walls encompassed but one man?
Now is it Rome indeed and room enough,
When there is in it but one only man.
Julius Caesar (1599) act 1, sc. 2, l. 153

22 Let me have men about me that are fat;
Sleek-headed men and such as sleep o' nights;
Yond' Cassius has a lean and hungry look;
He thinks too much: such men are dangerous.
Julius Caesar (1599) act 1, sc. 2, l. 191; see **PLUTARCH** 610:11

23 Would he were fatter! but I fear him not:
Yet if my name were liable to fear,
I do not know the man I should avoid
So soon as that spare Cassius. He reads much;
He is a great observer.
Julius Caesar (1599) act 1, sc. 2, l. 197

24   He loves no plays,
As thou dost, Antony.
Julius Caesar (1599) act 1, sc. 2, l. 202

25 Such men as he be never at heart's ease,
Whiles they behold a greater than themselves,
And therefore are they very dangerous.
I rather tell thee what is to be feared
Than what I fear, for always I am Caesar.
Julius Caesar (1599) act 1, sc. 2, l. 207

26 'Tis very like: he hath the falling sickness.
Julius Caesar (1599) act 1, sc. 2, l. [255]

27 CASSIUS: Did Cicero say any thing?
CASCA: Ay, he spoke Greek.

CASSIUS: To what effect?

CASCA: Nay, an I tell you that, I'll ne'er look you i' the face again; but those that understood him smiled at one another and shook their heads; but, for mine own part, it was Greek to me.
Julius Caesar (1599) act 1, sc. 2, l. [288]

1   Yesterday the bird of night did sit,
Even at noon-day, upon the market-place,
Hooting and shrieking.
Julius Caesar (1599) act 1, sc. 3, l. 26

2 Cassius from bondage will deliver Cassius.
Julius Caesar (1599) act 1, sc. 3, l. 90

3 It is the bright day that brings forth the adder;
And that craves wary walking.
Julius Caesar (1599) act 2, sc. 1, l. 14

4 Between the acting of a dreadful thing
And the first motion, all the interim is
Like a phantasma, or a hideous dream.
Julius Caesar (1599) act 2, sc. 1, l. 63

5 Let us be sacrificers, but not butchers, Caius.
Julius Caesar (1599) act 2, sc. 1, l. 166

6 Let's carve him as a dish fit for the gods,
Not hew him as a carcass fit for hounds.
Julius Caesar (1599) act 2, sc. 1, l. 173

7 For he is superstitious grown of late,
Quite from the main opinion he held once
Of fantasy, of dreams, and ceremonies.
Julius Caesar (1599) act 2, sc. 1, l. 195

8 But when I tell him he hates flatterers,
He says he does, being then most flattered.
Julius Caesar (1599) act 2, sc. 1, l. 207

9   What! is Brutus sick,
And will he steal out of his wholesome bed
To dare the vile contagion of the night?
Julius Caesar (1599) act 2, sc. 1, l. 263

10 PORTIA: Dwell I but in the suburbs
Of your good pleasure? If it be no more,
Portia is Brutus' harlot, not his wife.
BRUTUS: You are my true and honourable wife,
As dear to me as are the ruddy drops
That visit my sad heart.
Julius Caesar (1599) act 2, sc. 1, l. 285

11 I grant I am a woman, but, withal,
A woman that Lord Brutus took to wife;
I grant I am a woman, but, withal,
A woman well-reputed, Cato's daughter.
Think you I am no stronger than my sex,
Being so fathered and so husbanded?
Julius Caesar (1599) act 2, sc. 1, l. 292

12 When beggars die, there are no comets seen;
The heavens themselves blaze forth the death of princes.
Julius Caesar (1599) act 2, sc. 2, l. 30

13 Cowards die many times before their deaths;
The valiant never taste of death but once.
Of all the wonders that I yet have heard,
It seems to me most strange that men should fear;

Seeing that death, a necessary end,
Will come when it will come.
Julius Caesar (1599) act 2, sc. 2, l. 32

14 See! Antony, that revels long o' nights,
Is notwithstanding up.
Julius Caesar (1599) act 2, sc. 2, l. 116

15 CAESAR: The ides of March are come.
SOOTHSAYER: Ay, Caesar; but not gone.
Julius Caesar (1599) act 3, sc. 1, l. 1

16 But I am constant as the northern star,
Of whose true-fixed and resting quality
There is no fellow in the firmament.
Julius Caesar (1599) act 3, sc. 1, l. 60

17 *Et tu, Brute?* Then fall, Caesar!
Julius Caesar (1599) act 3, sc. 1, l. 77; see CAESAR 193:3

18 Ambition's debt is paid.
Julius Caesar (1599) act 3, sc. 1, l. 83

19   How many ages hence
Shall this our lofty scene be acted o'er,
In states unborn, and accents yet unknown!
Julius Caesar (1599) act 3, sc. 1, l. 111

20 O mighty Caesar! dost thou lie so low?
Are all thy conquests, glories, triumphs, spoils,
Shrunk to this little measure?
Julius Caesar (1599) act 3, sc. 1, l. 148

21   Live a thousand years,
I shall not find myself so apt to die:
No place will please me so, no mean of death,
As here by Caesar, and by you cut off,
The choice and master spirits of this age.
Julius Caesar (1599) act 3, sc. 1, l. 159

22 O! pardon me, thou bleeding piece of earth,
That I am meek and gentle with these butchers;
Thou art the ruins of the noblest man
That ever livèd in the tide of times.
Julius Caesar (1599) act 3, sc. 1, l. 254

23   Caesar's spirit, ranging for revenge,
With Ate by his side, come hot from hell,
Shall in these confines, with a monarch's voice
Cry, 'Havoc!' and let slip the dogs of war.
Julius Caesar (1599) act 3, sc. 1, l. 270

24 Passion, I see, is catching.
Julius Caesar (1599) act 3, sc. 1, l. 283

25 Not that I loved Caesar less, but that I loved Rome more.
Julius Caesar (1599) act 3, sc. 2, l. [22]

26 As he was valiant, I honour him: but, as he was ambitious, I slew him.
Julius Caesar (1599) act 3, sc. 2, l. [27]

27 Who is here so base that would be a bondman? If any, speak; for him have I offended. Who is here so rude that would not be a Roman? If any, speak; for him have I offended. Who is here so vile that will not love his country? If any, speak; for him have I offended. I pause for a reply.
Julius Caesar (1599) act 3, sc. 2, l. [31]

28 Friends, Romans, countrymen, lend me your ears;

I come to bury Caesar, not to praise him.
The evil that men do lives after them,
The good is oft interrèd with their bones.
Julius Caesar (1599) act 3, sc. 2, l. [79]

1   The noble Brutus
Hath told you Caesar was ambitious;
If it were so, it was a grievous fault;
And grievously hath Caesar answered it.
Julius Caesar (1599) act 3, sc. 2, l. [83]

2 For Brutus is an honourable man;
So are they all, all honourable men.
Julius Caesar (1599) act 3, sc. 2, l. [88]

3 He was my friend, faithful and just to me:
But Brutus says he was ambitious;
And Brutus is an honourable man.
Julius Caesar (1599) act 3, sc. 2, l. [91]

4 When that the poor have cried, Caesar hath
          wept;
Ambition should be made of sterner stuff.
Julius Caesar (1599) act 3, sc. 2, l. [97]

5   On the Lupercal
I thrice presented him a kingly crown
Which he did thrice refuse: was this ambition?
Julius Caesar (1599) act 3, sc. 2, l. [101]

6 You all did love him once, not without cause.
Julius Caesar (1599) act 3, sc. 2, l. [108]

7 But yesterday the word of Caesar might
Have stood against the world; now lies he there,
And none so poor to do him reverence.
Julius Caesar (1599) act 3, sc. 2, l. [124]

8 If you have tears, prepare to shed them now.
Julius Caesar (1599) act 3, sc. 2, l. [174]

9 This was the most unkindest cut of all.
Julius Caesar (1599) act 3, sc. 2, l. [188]

10 O! what a fall was there, my countrymen;
Then I, and you, and all of us fell down,
Whilst bloody treason flourished over us.
Julius Caesar (1599) act 3, sc. 2, l. [195]

11 I am no orator, as Brutus is;
But, as you know me all, a plain, blunt man,
That love my friend.
Julius Caesar (1599) act 3, sc. 2, l. [221]

12 For I have neither wit, nor words, nor worth,
Action, nor utterance, nor power of speech,
To stir men's blood; I only speak right on;
I tell you that which you yourselves do know.
Julius Caesar (1599) act 3, sc. 2, l. [225]

13   But were I Brutus,
And Brutus Antony, there were an Antony
Would ruffle up your spirits, and put a tongue
In every wound of Caesar, that should move
The stones of Rome to rise and mutiny.
Julius Caesar (1599) act 3, sc. 2, l. [230]

14   He hath left you all his walks,
His private arbours, and new-planted orchards,
On this side Tiber; he hath left you,
And to your heirs for ever; common pleasures,
To walk abroad, and recreate yourselves.
Julius Caesar (1599) act 3, sc. 2, l. [252]

15 Here was a Caesar! when comes such another?
Julius Caesar (1599) act 3, sc. 2, l. [257]

16 Now let it work; mischief, thou art afoot,
Take thou what course thou wilt!
Julius Caesar (1599) act 3, sc. 2, l. [265]

17 Tear him for his bad verses, tear him for his bad
verses.
Julius Caesar (1599) act 3, sc. 3, l. [34]

18 He shall not live; look, with a spot I damn him.
Julius Caesar (1599) act 4, sc. 1, l. 6

19 This is a slight unmeritable man,
Meet to be sent on errands.
Julius Caesar (1599) act 4, sc. 1, l. 12

20 Let me tell you, Cassius, you yourself
Are much condemned to have an itching palm.
Julius Caesar (1599) act 4, sc. 3, l. 7; some editions prefer act
4, sc. 2

21 I had rather be a dog, and bay the moon,
Than such a Roman.
Julius Caesar (1599) act 4, sc. 3, l. 27; some editions prefer act
4, sc. 2

22 Do not presume too much upon my love;
I may do that I shall be sorry for.
Julius Caesar (1599) act 4, sc. 3, l. 63; some editions prefer act
4, sc. 2

23 There is no terror, Cassius, in your threats;
For I am armed so strong in honesty
That they pass by me as the idle wind,
Which I respect not.
Julius Caesar (1599) act 4, sc. 3, l. 66; some editions prefer
act 4, sc. 2

24 A friend should bear his friend's infirmities,
But Brutus makes mine greater than they are.
Julius Caesar (1599) act 4, sc. 3, l. 85; some editions prefer act
4, sc. 2

25 Cassius is aweary of the world;
Hated by one he loves; braved by his brother.
Julius Caesar (1599) act 4, sc. 3, l. 94; some editions prefer
act 4, sc. 2

26 O Cassius! you are yokèd with a lamb
That carries anger as the flint bears fire;
Who, much enforcèd, shows a hasty spark,
And straight is cold again.
Julius Caesar (1599) act 4, sc. 3, l. 109; some editions prefer
act 4, sc. 2

27 Good reasons must, of force, give place to
          better.
Julius Caesar (1599) act 4, sc. 3, l. 202; some editions prefer
act 4, sc. 2

28 There is a tide in the affairs of men,
Which, taken at the flood, leads on to fortune;
Omitted, all the voyage of their life
Is bound in shallows and in miseries.
Julius Caesar (1599) act 4, sc. 3, l. 217; some editions prefer
act 4, sc. 2; see **BYRON** 189:8

29 But for your words, they rob the Hybla bees,
And leave them honeyless.
Julius Caesar (1599) act 5, sc. 1, l. 34

30 Forever, and forever, farewell, Cassius!
If we do meet again, why, we shall smile!

If not, why then, this parting was well made.
Julius Caesar (1599) act 5, sc. 1, l. 118

1 O Julius Caesar! thou art mighty yet!
Thy spirit walks abroad, and turns our swords
In our own proper entrails.
Julius Caesar (1599) act 5, sc. 3, l. 94

2 Thy life hath had some smatch of honour in it.
Julius Caesar (1599) act 5, sc. 5, l. 46

3 This was the noblest Roman of them all;
All the conspirators save only he
Did that they did in envy of great Caesar;
He only in a general honest thought
And common good to all, made one of them.
His life was gentle, and the elements
So mixed in him that Nature might stand up
And say to all the world, 'This was a man!'
Julius Caesar (1599) act 5, sc. 5, l. 68

KING JOHN

4   Hadst thou rather be a Faulconbridge
And like thy brother, to enjoy thy land,
Or the reputed son of Coeur-de-Lion,
Lord of thy presence and no land beside.
King John (1591–8) act 1, sc. 1, l. 134

5 Mad world! mad kings! mad composition!
King John (1591–8) act 2, sc. 1, l. 561

6 Well, whiles I am a beggar, I will rail,
And say there is no sin, but to be rich;
And, being rich, my virtue then shall be,
To say there is no vice, but beggary.
King John (1591–8) act 2, sc. 1, l. 593

7 Old Time the clock-setter, that bald sexton,
Time.
King John (1591–8) act 3, sc. 1, l. 324

8 Bell, book, and candle shall not drive me back,
When gold and silver becks me to come on.
King John (1591–8) act 3, sc. 3, l. 12

9 Grief fills the room up of my absent child,
Lies in his bed, walks up and down with me,
Puts on his pretty looks, repeats his words,
Remembers me of all his gracious parts,
Stuffs out his vacant garments with his form:
Then have I reason to be fond of grief.
King John (1591–8) act 3, sc. 4, l. 93

10 Life is as tedious as a twice-told tale,
Vexing the dull ear of a drowsy man.
King John (1591–8) act 3, sc. 4, l. 108

11 To gild refinèd gold, to paint the lily,
To throw a perfume on the violet,
To smooth the ice, or add another hue
Unto the rainbow, or with taper light
To seek the beauteous eye of heaven to garnish,
Is wasteful and ridiculous excess.
King John (1591–8) act 4, sc. 2, l. 11; see **BYRON** 188:20

12 Another lean unwashed artificer
Cuts off his tale and talks of Arthur's death.
King John (1591–8) act 4, sc. 2, l. 201

13 How oft the sight of means to do ill deeds
Makes ill deeds done!
King John (1591–8) act 4, sc. 2, l. 219

14 Heaven take my soul, and England keep my
bones!
King John (1591–8) act 4, sc. 3, l. 10

15 This England never did, nor never shall,
Lie at the proud foot of a conqueror,
But when it first did help to wound itself.
Now these her princes are come home again,
Come the three corners of the world in arms,
And we shall shock them: nought shall make us
rue,
If England to itself do rest but true.
King John (1591–8) act 5, sc. 7, l. 112

KING LEAR

16 Nothing will come of nothing: speak again.
King Lear (1605–6) act 1, sc. 1, l. [92]

17 LEAR: So young, and so untender?
CORDELIA: So young, my lord, and true.
LEAR: Let it be so; thy truth then be thy dower:
For, by the sacred radiance of the sun,
The mysteries of Hecate and the night,
By all the operation of the orbs
From whom we do exist and cease to be,
Here I disclaim all my paternal care,
Propinquity and property of blood,
And as a stranger to my heart and me
Hold thee from this for ever.
King Lear (1605–6) act 1, sc. 1, l. [108]

18 Come not between the dragon and his wrath.
King Lear (1605–6) act 1, sc. 1, l. [124]

19   I want that glib and oily art
To speak and purpose not; since what I well
intend,
I'll do't before I speak.
King Lear (1605–6) act 1, sc. 1, l. [227]

20 It is no vicious blot nor other foulness,
No unchaste action, or dishonoured step,
That hath deprived me of your grace and
favour,
But even for want of that for which I am richer,
A still-soliciting eye, and such a tongue
That I am glad I have not, though not to have it
Hath lost me in your liking.
King Lear (1605–6) act 1, sc. 1, l. [230]

21 'Tis the infirmity of his age; yet he hath ever
but slenderly known himself.
King Lear (1605–6) act 1, sc. 1, l. 293

22   Why bastard? wherefore base?
When my dimensions are as well compact,
My mind as generous, and my shape as true,
As honest madam's issue?
King Lear (1605–6) act 1, sc. 2, l. 6

23 I grow, I prosper;
Now, gods, stand up for bastards!
King Lear (1605–6) act 1, sc. 2, l. 21

24 This is the excellent foppery of the world, that,
when we are sick in fortune,—often the surfeit
of our own behaviour,— we make guilty of our
own disasters the sun, the moon, and the stars;
as if we were villains by necessity, fools by

heavenly compulsion, knaves, thieves, and treachers by spherical predominance, drunkards, liars, and adulterers by an enforced obedience of planetary influence.
King Lear (1605-6) act 1, sc. 2, l. [132]

1 My father compounded with my mother under the dragon's tail, and my nativity was under *ursa major*; so that it follows I am rough and lecherous. 'Sfoot! I should have been that I am had the maidenliest star in the firmament twinkled on my bastardizing.
King Lear (1605-6) act 1, sc. 2, l. [144]

2 My cue is villanous melancholy, with a sigh like Tom o' Bedlam.
King Lear (1605-6) act 1, sc. 2, l. [151]

3 LEAR: Dost thou call me fool, boy?
FOOL: All thy other titles thou hast given away; that thou wast born with.
King Lear (1605-6) act 1, sc. 4, l. [163]

4 Who is it that can tell me who I am?
King Lear (1605-6) act 1, sc. 4, l. 230

5 Ingratitude, thou marble-hearted fiend,
More hideous, when thou show'st thee in a child,
Than the sea-monster.
King Lear (1605-6) act 1, sc. 4, l. [283]

6 How sharper than a serpent's tooth it is
To have a thankless child!
King Lear (1605-6) act 1, sc. 4, l. [312]

7 O! let me not be mad, not mad, sweet heaven;
Keep me in temper; I would not be mad!
King Lear (1605-6) act 1, sc. 5, l. [51]

8 Thou whoreson zed! thou unnecessary letter!
King Lear (1605-6) act 2, sc. 2, l. [68]

9 Goose, if I had you upon Sarum plain,
I'd drive ye cackling home to Camelot.
King Lear (1605-6) act 2, sc. 2, l. [88]

10 Down, thou climbing sorrow!
Thy element's below.
King Lear (1605-6) act 2, sc. 4, l. [57]

11 O, sir! you are old;
Nature in you stands on the very verge
Of her confine.
King Lear (1605-6) act 2, sc. 4, l. [148]

12 O reason not the need! Our basest beggars
Are in the poorest thing superfluous.
Allow not nature more than nature needs,
Man's life is cheap as beast's.
King Lear (1605-6) act 2, sc. 4, l. 264

13 I will do such things,—
What they are yet I know not,—but they shall be
The terrors of the earth.
King Lear (1605-6) act 2, sc. 4, l. [283]

14 No, I'll not weep:
I have full cause of weeping, but this heart
Shall break into a hundred thousand flaws
Or ere I'll weep. O fool! I shall go mad.
King Lear (1605-6) act 2, sc. 4, l. [286]

15 Contending with the fretful elements;
Bids the wind blow the earth into the sea,
Or swell the curlèd waters 'bove the main,
That things might change or cease.
King Lear (1605-6) act 3, sc. 1, l. 4

16 Blow, winds, and crack your cheeks! rage! blow!
You cataracts and hurricanoes, spout
Till you have drenched our steeples, drowned the cocks!
You sulphurous and thought-executing fires,
Vaunt-couriers to oak-cleaving thunderbolts,
Singe my white head! And thou, all-shaking thunder,
Strike flat the thick rotundity o' the world!
Crack nature's moulds, all germens spill at once
That make ingrateful man!
King Lear (1605-6) act 3, sc. 2, l. 1

17 Rumble thy bellyful! Spit, fire! Spout, rain!
Nor rain, wind, thunder, fire, are my daughters:
I tax not you, you elements, with unkindness.
King Lear (1605-6) act 3, sc. 2, l. 14

18 There was never yet fair woman but she made mouths in a glass.
King Lear (1605-6) act 3, sc. 2, l. [35]

19 No, I will be the pattern of all patience; I will say nothing.
King Lear (1605-6) act 3, sc. 2, l. [37]

20 I am a man
More sinned against than sinning.
King Lear (1605-6) act 3, sc. 2, l. [59]; see **BOWRA** 153:19

21 He that has a little tiny wit,
With hey, ho, the wind and the rain,
Must make content with his fortunes fit,
Though the rain it raineth every day.
King Lear (1605-6) act 3, sc. 2, l. [74]

22 O! that way madness lies; let me shun that.
King Lear (1605-6) act 3, sc. 4, l. 21

23 Poor naked wretches, wheresoe'er you are,
That bide the pelting of this pitiless storm,
How shall your houseless heads and unfed sides,
Your loopèd and windowed raggedness, defend you
From seasons such as these?
King Lear (1605-6) act 3, sc. 4, l. 28

24 Take physic, pomp;
Expose thyself to feel what wretches feel.
King Lear (1605-6) act 3, sc. 4, l. 33

25 Pillicock sat on Pillicock-hill:
Halloo, halloo, loo, loo!
King Lear (1605-6) act 3, sc. 4, l. [75]

26 Keep thy foot out of brothels, thy hand out of plackets, thy pen from lenders' books, and defy the foul fiend.
King Lear (1605-6) act 3, sc. 4, l. [96]

27 Thou art the thing itself; unaccommodated man is no more but such a poor, bare, forked animal as thou art. Off, off, you lendings! Come; unbutton here.
King Lear (1605-6) act 3, sc. 4, l. [109]

1 This is the foul fiend Flibbertigibbet: he begins
at curfew, and walks till the first cock; he gives
the web and the pin, squints the eye, and makes
the harelip; mildews the white wheat, and hurts
the poor creatures of earth.
King Lear (1605–6) act 3, sc. 4, l. [118]

2 The green mantle of the standing pool.
King Lear (1605–6) act 3, sc. 4, l. [136]

3 The prince of darkness is a gentleman.
King Lear (1605–6) act 3, sc. 4, l. [148]

4 Poor Tom's a-cold.
King Lear (1605–6) act 3, sc. 4, l. [151]

5 Child Roland to the dark tower came,
His word was still, Fie, foh, and fum,
I smell the blood of a British man.
King Lear (1605–6) act 3, sc. 4, l. [185]; see **BROWNING** 165:12,
NASHE 568:24

6   The little dogs and all,
Tray, Blanch, and Sweet-heart, see, they bark at
   me.
King Lear (1605–6) act 3, sc. 6, l. [65]

7 I am tied to the stake, and I must stand the
course.
King Lear (1605–6) act 3, sc. 7, l. [54]

8   Out, vile jelly!
Where is thy lustre now?
King Lear (1605–6) act 3, sc. 7, l. [83]

9 The lowest and most dejected thing of fortune,
Stands still in esperance, lives not in fear:
The lamentable change is from the best;
The worst returns to laughter.
King Lear (1605–6) act 4, sc. 1, l. 3

10   The worst is not,
So long as we can say, 'This is the worst.'
King Lear (1605–6) act 4, sc. 1, l. 27

11 As flies to wanton boys, are we to the gods;
They kill us for their sport.
King Lear (1605–6) act 4, sc. 1, l. 36

12 You are not worth the dust which the rude wind
Blows in your face.
King Lear (1605–6) act 4, sc. 2, l. 30

13   It is the stars,
The stars above us, govern our conditions.
King Lear (1605–6) act 4, sc. 3, l. [34]

14 Crowned with rank fumitor and furrow weeds,
With burdocks, hemlock, nettles, cuckoo-flowers,
Darnel, and all the idle weeds that grow
In our sustaining corn.
King Lear (1605–6) act 4, sc. 4, l. 3

15   How fearful
And dizzy 'tis to cast one's eyes so low!
The crows and choughs that wing the midway
   air
Show scarce so gross as beetles; half-way down
Hangs one that gathers samphire, dreadful trade!
Methinks he seems no bigger than his head.
The fishermen that walk upon the beach
Appear like mice.
King Lear (1605–6) act 4, sc. 6, l. 12

16 GLOUCESTER: Is't not the king?
LEAR: Ay, every inch a king.
King Lear (1605–6) act 4, sc. 6, l. [110]

17   Die: die for adultery! No:
The wren goes to't, and the small gilded fly
Does lecher in my sight.
Let copulation thrive.
King Lear (1605–6) act 4, sc. 6, l. [115]

18 LEAR: But to the girdle do the Gods inherit,
Beneath is all the fiends':
There's hell, there's darkness, there is the
   sulphurous pit,
Burning, scalding, stench, consumption; fie, fie,
   fie! pah, pah! Give me an ounce of civet, good
   apothecary, to sweeten my imagination; there's
   money for thee.
GLOUCESTER: O! let me kiss that hand!
LEAR: Let me wipe it first; it smells of mortality.
GLOUCESTER: O ruined piece of nature! This great
   world
Should so wear out to nought.
King Lear (1605–6) act 4, sc. 6, l. [129]

19 A man may see how this world goes with no
eyes. Look with thine ears: see how yond justice
rails upon yond simple thief. Hark, in thine ear:
change places; and, handy-dandy, which is the
justice, which is the thief?
King Lear (1605–6) act 4, sc. 6, l. [154]

20 Thou rascal beadle, hold thy bloody hand!
Why dost thou lash that whore? Strip thine own
   back;
Thou hotly lust'st to use her in that kind
For which thou whipp'st her.
King Lear (1605–6) act 4, sc. 6, l. 158

21   Get thee glass eyes;
And, like a scurvy politician, seem
To see the things thou dost not.
King Lear (1605–6) act 4, sc. 6, l. [175]

22 When we are born we cry that we are come
To this great stage of fools.
King Lear (1605–6) act 4, sc. 6, l. [187]

23 Thou art a soul in bliss; but I am bound
Upon a wheel of fire.
King Lear (1605–6) act 4, sc. 7, l. 46

24 I am a very foolish, fond old man,
Fourscore and upward, not an hour more or
   less;
And, to deal plainly,
I fear I am not in my perfect mind.
King Lear (1605–6) act 4, sc. 7, l. 60

25   Men must endure
Their going hence, even as their coming hither:
Ripeness is all.
King Lear (1605–6) act 5, sc. 2, l. 9

26   Come, let's away to prison;
We two alone will sing like birds i' the cage:
When thou dost ask me blessing, I'll kneel
   down,
And ask of thee forgiveness: and we'll live

And pray, and sing, and tell old tales, and laugh
At gilded butterflies.
King Lear (1605-6) act 5, sc. 3, l. 8; see **WEBSTER** 844:22

1 Talk of court news; and we'll talk with them
too,
Who loses, and who wins; who's in, who's out;
And take upon 's the mystery of things,
As if we were God's spies; and we'll wear out,
In a walled prison, packs and sets of great ones
That ebb and flow by the moon.
King Lear (1605-6) act 5, sc. 3, l. 14

2 Upon such sacrifices, my Cordelia,
The gods themselves throw incense.
King Lear (1605-6) act 5, sc. 3, l. 20

3 The gods are just, and of our pleasant vices
Make instruments to plague us.
King Lear (1605-6) act 5, sc. 3, l. [172]

4 The wheel is come full circle.
King Lear (1605-6) act 5, sc. 3, l. [176]

5 Howl, howl, howl, howl! O! you are men of
stones:
Had I your tongue and eyes, I'd use them so
That heaven's vaults should crack. She's gone for
ever!
King Lear (1605-6) act 5, sc. 3, l. [259]

6 KENT: Is this the promised end?
EDGAR: Or image of that horror?
ALBANY: Fall and cease?
King Lear (1605-6) act 5, sc. 3, l. [265]

7   Her voice was ever soft,
Gentle and low, an excellent thing in woman.
King Lear (1605-6) act 5, sc. 3, l. [274]

8 And my poor fool is hanged! No, no, no life!
Why should a dog, a horse, a rat, have life,
And thou no breath at all? Thou'lt come no
more,
Never, never, never, never, never!
Pray you, undo this button.
King Lear (1605-6) act 5, sc. 3, l. [307]

9 Vex not his ghost: O! let him pass; he hates him
That would upon the rack of this tough world
Stretch him out longer.
King Lear (1605-6) act 5, sc. 3, l. [314]

10 The oldest hath borne most: we that are young,
Shall never see so much, nor live so long.
King Lear (1605-6) act 5, sc. 3, l. [327]

LOVE'S LABOUR'S LOST

11 Cormorant devouring Time.
Love's Labour's Lost (1595) act 1, sc. 1, l. 4

12 At Christmas I no more desire a rose
Than wish a snow in May's new-fangled mirth;
But like of each thing that in season grows.
Love's Labour's Lost (1595) act 1, sc. 1, l. 105; some editions
prefer 'new-fangled shows'

13 This wimpled, whining, purblind, wayward boy,
This senior-junior, giant-dwarf, Dan Cupid.
Love's Labour's Lost (1595) act 3, sc. 1, l. [189]; some editions
prefer 'Signor Junior'

14 A wightly wanton with a velvet brow,
With two pitch balls stuck in her face for eyes.
Love's Labour's Lost (1595) act 3, sc. 1, l. [206]; some editions
prefer 'whitely wanton'

15 He hath not fed of the dainties that are bred in
a book; he hath not eat paper, as it were; he
hath not drunk ink.
Love's Labour's Lost (1595) act 4, sc. 2, l. [25]

16 Old Mantuan! old Mantuan! Who understandeth
thee not, loves thee not.
Love's Labour's Lost (1595) act 4, sc. 2, l. [102]

17 From women's eyes this doctrine I derive:
They are the ground, the books, the academes,
From whence doth spring the true Promethean
fire.
Love's Labour's Lost (1595) act 4, sc. 3, l. [302]; see
SHAKESPEARE 717:19

18 For valour, is not love a Hercules,
Still climbing trees in the Hesperides?
Love's Labour's Lost (1595) act 4, sc. 3, l. [340]

19 From women's eyes this doctrine I derive:
They sparkle still the right Promethean fire;
They are the books, the arts, the academes,
That show, contain, and nourish all the world.
Love's Labour's Lost (1595) act 4, sc. 3, l. [350]; see
SHAKESPEARE 717:17

20 They have been at a great feast of languages,
and stolen the scraps.
Love's Labour's Lost (1595) act 5, sc. 1, l. [39]

21 Taffeta phrases, silken terms precise.
Love's Labour's Lost (1595) act 5, sc. 2, l. 407

22 Henceforth my wooing mind shall be expressed
In russet yeas and honest kersey noes.
Love's Labour's Lost (1595) act 5, sc. 2, l. 413

23 A jest's prosperity lies in the ear
Of him that hears it, never in the tongue
Of him that makes it.
Love's Labour's Lost (1595) act 5, sc. 2, l. [869]

24 When daisies pied and violets blue
And lady-smocks all silver-white
And cuckoo-buds of yellow hue
Do paint the meadows with delight,
The cuckoo then, on every tree,
Mocks married men.
Love's Labour's Lost (1595) act 5, sc. 2, l. [902]

25 When icicles hang by the wall,
And Dick the shepherd, blows his nail,
And Tom bears logs into the hall,
And milk comes frozen home in pail,
When blood is nipped and ways be foul,
Then nightly sings the staring owl,
Tu-who;
Tu-whit, tu-who—a merry note,
While greasy Joan doth keel the pot.
Love's Labour's Lost (1595) act 5, sc. 2, l. [920]

26 The words of Mercury are harsh after the songs
of Apollo. You, that way: we, this way.
Love's Labour's Lost (1595) act 5, sc. 2, l. [938]

MACBETH

1 FIRST WITCH: When shall we three meet again
In thunder, lightning, or in rain?
SECOND WITCH: When the hurly-burly's done,
When the battle's lost and won.
THIRD WITCH: That will be ere the set of sun.
FIRST WITCH: Where the place?
SECOND WITCH: Upon the heath.
THIRD WITCH: There to meet with Macbeth.
FIRST WITCH: I come, Graymalkin!
SECOND WITCH: Paddock calls.
THIRD WITCH: Anon!
Macbeth (1606) act 1, sc. 1, l. 1

2 Fair is foul, and foul is fair:
Hover through the fog and filthy air.
Macbeth (1606) act 1, sc. 1, l. 11

3 What bloody man is that?
Macbeth (1606) act 1, sc. 2, l. 1

4 Till he unseamed him from the nave to the
chaps,
And fixed his head upon our battlements.
Macbeth (1606) act 1, sc. 2, l. 22

5 Bellona's bridegroom, lapped in proof,
Confronted him with self-comparisons,
Point against point, rebellious arm 'gainst arm,
Curbing his lavish spirit.
Macbeth (1606) act 1, sc. 2, l. 55

6 A sailor's wife had chestnuts in her lap,
And munched, and munched, and munched:
'Give me,' quoth I:
'Aroint thee, witch!' the rump-fed runnion cries.
Her husband's to Aleppo gone, master o' the
Tiger:
But in a sieve I'll thither sail,
And, like a rat without a tail,
I'll do, I'll do, and I'll do.
Macbeth (1606) act 1, sc. 3, l. 4

7 Sleep shall neither night nor day
Hang upon his pent-house lid.
He shall live a man forbid.
Weary se'nnights nine times nine
Shall he dwindle, peak, and pine:
Though his bark cannot be lost,
Yet it shall be tempest-tost.
Macbeth (1606) act 1, sc. 3, l. 19

8 The weird sisters, hand in hand,
Posters of the sea and land,
Thus do go about, about.
Macbeth (1606) act 1, sc. 3, l. 32

9 So foul and fair a day I have not seen.
Macbeth (1606) act 1, sc. 3, l. 38

10 What are these,
So withered, and so wild in their attire,
That look not like th' inhabitants o' the earth,
And yet are on 't?
Macbeth (1606) act 1, sc. 3, l. 39

11 If you can look into the seeds of time,
And say which grain will grow and which will
not,
Speak then to me, who neither beg nor fear
Your favours nor your hate.
Macbeth (1606) act 1, sc. 3, l. 58

12 Say, from whence
You owe this strange intelligence? or why
Upon this blasted heath you stop our way
With such prophetic greeting?
Macbeth (1606) act 1, sc. 3, l. 72

13 Or have we eaten on the insane root
That takes the reason prisoner?
Macbeth (1606) act 1, sc. 3, l. 84

14 What! can the devil speak true?
Macbeth (1606) act 1, sc. 3, l. 107

15 Two truths are told,
As happy prologues to the swelling act
Of the imperial theme.
Macbeth (1606) act 1, sc. 3, l. 127

16 Present fears
Are less than horrible imaginings;
My thought, whose murder yet is but fantastical,
Shakes so my single state of man that function
Is smothered in surmise, and nothing is
But what is not.
Macbeth (1606) act 1, sc. 3, l. 137

17 Come what come may,
Time and the hour runs through the roughest
day.
Macbeth (1606) act 1, sc. 3, l. 146

18 MALCOLM: Nothing in his life
Became him like the leaving it: he died
As one that had been studied in his death
To throw away the dearest thing he owed
As 'twere a careless trifle.
DUNCAN: There's no art
To find the mind's construction in the face;
He was a gentleman on whom I built
An absolute trust.
Macbeth (1606) act 1, sc. 4, l. 7

19 Glamis thou art, and Cawdor; and shalt be
What thou art promised. Yet I do fear thy
nature;
It is too full o' the milk of human kindness
To catch the nearest way; thou wouldst be great,
Art not without ambition; but without
The illness should attend it; what thou wouldst
highly,
That thou wouldst holily; wouldst not play false,
And yet wouldst wrongly win.
Macbeth (1606) act 1, sc. 5, l. [16]

20 The raven himself is hoarse
That croaks the fatal entrance of Duncan
Under my battlements. Come, you spirits
That tend on mortal thoughts! unsex me here,
And fill me from the crown to the toe top full
Of direst cruelty; make thick my blood,
Stop up the access and passage to remorse,
That no compunctious visitings of nature
Shake my fell purpose.
Macbeth (1606) act 1, sc. 5, l. [38]

1   Come to my woman's breasts,
And take my milk for gall, you murdering
     ministers.
Macbeth (1606) act 1, sc. 5, l. [47]

2   Come, thick night,
And pall thee in the dunnest smoke of hell,
That my keen knife see not the wound it makes,
Nor heaven peep through the blanket of the
     dark,
To cry 'Hold, hold!'
Macbeth (1606) act 1, sc. 5, l. [50]

3 Your face, my thane, is as a book where men
May read strange matters. To beguile the time,
Look like the time; bear welcome in your eye,
Your hand, your tongue: look like the innocent
     flower,
But be the serpent under't.
Macbeth (1606) act 1, sc. 5, l. [63]

4 This castle hath a pleasant seat; the air
Nimbly and sweetly recommends itself
Unto our gentle senses.
Macbeth (1606) act 1, sc. 6, l. 1

5   This guest of summer,
The temple-haunting martlet, does approve
By his loved mansionry that the heaven's breath
Smells wooingly here: no jutty, frieze,
Buttress, nor coign of vantage, but this bird
Hath made his pendent bed and procreant
     cradle.
Macbeth (1606) act 1, sc. 6, l. 3

6 If it were done when 'tis done, then 'twere well
It were done quickly: if the assassination
Could trammel up the consequence, and catch
With his surcease success; that but this blow
Might be the be-all and the end-all here,
But here, upon this bank and shoal of time,
We'd jump the life to come.
Macbeth (1606) act 1, sc. 7, l. 1

7   We but teach
Bloody instructions, which, being taught, return,
To plague the inventor.
Macbeth (1606) act 1, sc. 7, l. 8

8   Besides, this Duncan
Hath borne his faculties so meek, hath been
So clear in his great office, that his virtues
Will plead like angels trumpet-tongued, against
The deep damnation of his taking-off.
Macbeth (1606) act 1, sc. 7, l. 16

9 And pity, like a naked new-born babe,
Striding the blast, or heaven's cherubim, horsed
Upon the sightless couriers of the air,
Shall blow the horrid deed in every eye,
That tears shall drown the wind.
Macbeth (1606) act 1, sc. 7, l. 21

10   I have no spur
To prick the sides of my intent, but only
Vaulting ambition, which o'erleaps itself,
And falls on the other.
Macbeth (1606) act 1, sc. 7, l. 25

11 We will proceed no further in this business:
He hath honoured me of late; and I have
     bought
Golden opinions from all sorts of people.
Macbeth (1606) act 1, sc. 7, l. 31

12   Was the hope drunk,
Wherein you dressed yourself? hath it slept
     since,
And wakes it now, to look so green and pale
At what it did so freely? From this time
Such I account thy love.
Macbeth (1606) act 1, sc. 7, l. 35

13 Letting 'I dare not' wait upon 'I would,'
Like the poor cat i' the adage?
Macbeth (1606) act 1, sc. 7, l. 44

14 I dare do all that may become a man;
Who dares do more is none.
Macbeth (1606) act 1, sc. 7, l. 46

15 LADY MACBETH: I have given suck, and know
How tender 'tis to love the babe that milks me:
I would, while it was smiling in my face,
Have plucked my nipple from his boneless gums,
And dash'd the brains out, had I so sworn as
     you
Have done to this.
MACBETH: If we should fail,—
LADY MACBETH: We fail!
But screw your courage to the sticking-place,
And we'll not fail.
Macbeth (1606) act 1, sc. 7, l. 54

16   Bring forth men-children only;
For thy undaunted mettle should compose
Nothing but males.
Macbeth (1606) act 1, sc. 7, l. 72

17 False face must hide what the false heart doth
     know.
Macbeth (1606) act 1, sc. 7, l. 82

18   There's husbandry in heaven;
Their candles are all out.
Macbeth (1606) act 2, sc. 1, l. 4

19 Is this a dagger which I see before me,
The handle toward my hand? Come, let me
     clutch thee:
I have thee not, and yet I see thee still.
Art thou not, fatal vision, sensible
To feeling as to sight? or art thou but
A dagger of the mind, a false creation,
Proceeding from the heat-oppressed brain?
Macbeth (1606) act 2, sc. 1, l. 33

20   Witchcraft celebrates
Pale Hecate's offerings; and withered murder,
Alarumed by his sentinel, the wolf,
Whose howl's his watch, thus with his stealthy
     pace,
With Tarquin's ravishing strides, toward his
     design
Moves like a ghost.
Macbeth (1606) act 2, sc. 1, l. 49

21   The bell invites me.
Hear it not, Duncan; for it is a knell

That summons thee to heaven or to hell.
Macbeth (1606) act 2, sc. 1, l. 62

1 That which hath made them drunk hath made
me bold,
What hath quenched them hath given me fire.
Macbeth (1606) act 2, sc. 2, l. 1

2 It was the owl that shrieked, the fatal bellman,
Which gives the stern'st good-night.
Macbeth (1606) act 2, sc. 2, l. 4

3   The attempt and not the deed,
Confounds us.
Macbeth (1606) act 2, sc. 2, l. 12

4   Had he not resembled
My father as he slept I had done't.
Macbeth (1606) act 2, sc. 2, l. 14

5 . . . Wherefore could not I pronounce 'Amen'?
I had most need of blessing, and 'Amen'
Stuck in my throat.
Macbeth (1606) act 2, sc. 2, l. 32

6 Methought I heard a voice cry, 'Sleep no more!
Macbeth does murder sleep,' the innocent sleep,
Sleep that knits up the ravelled sleave of care,
The death of each day's life, sore labour's bath,
Balm of hurt minds, great nature's second
course,
Chief nourisher in life's feast.
Macbeth (1606) act 2, sc. 2, l. 36

7 Glamis hath murdered sleep, and therefore
Cawdor
Shall sleep no more, Macbeth shall sleep no
more!
Macbeth (1606) act 2, sc. 2, l. 43

8 MACBETH: I am afraid to think what I have done;
Look on't again I dare not.
LADY MACBETH: Infirm of purpose!
Give me the daggers. The sleeping and the dead
Are but as pictures; 'tis the eye of childhood
That fears a painted devil.
If he do bleed
I'll gild the faces of the grooms withal;
For it must seem their guilt.
Macbeth (1606) act 2, sc. 2, l. 53

9 Will all great Neptune's ocean wash this blood
Clean from my hand? No, this my hand will
rather
The multitudinous seas incarnadine,
Making the green one red.
Macbeth (1606) act 2, sc. 2, l. 61

10 A little water clears us of this deed.
Macbeth (1606) act 2, sc. 2, l. 68

11 Here's a knocking, indeed! If a man were porter
of hell-gate he should have old turning the key.
Knock, knock, knock! Who's there i' the name
of Beelzebub? Here's a farmer that hanged
himself on the expectation of plenty.
Macbeth (1606) act 2, sc. 3, l. 1

12 This place is too cold for hell. I'll devil-porter it
no further: I had thought to have let in some of
all professions, that go the primrose way to the
everlasting bonfire.
Macbeth (1606) act 2, sc. 3, l. [19]; see **SHAKESPEARE** 694:6

13 PORTER: Drink, sir, is a great provoker of three
things.
MACDUFF: What three things does drink especially
provoke?
PORTER: Marry, sir, nose-painting, sleep, and
urine. Lechery, sir, it provokes, and
unprovokes; it provokes the desire, but it takes
away the performance.
Macbeth (1606) act 2, sc. 3, l. [28]

14 The labour we delight in physics pain.
Macbeth (1606) act 2, sc. 3, l. [56]

15 The night has been unruly: where we lay
Our chimneys were blown down; and, as they
say,
Lamentings heard i' the air; strange screams of
death,
And prophesying with accents terrible
Of dire combustion and confused events
New-hatched to the woeful time. The obscure
bird
Clamoured the live-long night: some say the
earth
Was feverous and did shake.
Macbeth (1606) act 2, sc. 3, l. [60]

16 Confusion now hath made his masterpiece!
Most sacrilegious murder hath broke ope
The Lord's anointed temple, and stole thence
The life o' the building!
Macbeth (1606) act 2, sc. 3, l. [72]

17 Shake off this downy sleep, death's counterfeit,
And look on death itself! up, up, and see
The great doom's image!
Macbeth (1606) act 2, sc. 3, l. [83]

18 MACDUFF: Our royal master's murdered!
LADY MACBETH: Woe, alas!
What! in our house?
Macbeth (1606) act 2, sc. 3, l. [95]

19 Had I but died an hour before this chance,
I had lived a blessed time.
Macbeth (1606) act 2, sc. 3, l. [98]

20   Where we are,
There's daggers in men's smiles: the near in
blood,
The nearer bloody.
Macbeth (1606) act 2, sc. 3, l. [146]

21 A falcon, towering in her pride of place,
Was by a mousing owl hawked at and killed.
Macbeth (1606) act 2, sc. 4, l. 12

22 Thou hast it now: King, Cawdor, Glamis, all,
As the weird women promised; and, I fear,
Thou play'dst most foully for't.
Macbeth (1606) act 3, sc. 1, l. 1

23 BANQUO: Go not my horse the better,
I must become a borrower of the night
For a dark hour or twain.
MACBETH: Fail not our feast.
Macbeth (1606) act 3, sc. 1, l. 26

1 FIRST MURDERER: We are men, my liege.
MACBETH: Ay, in the catalogue ye go for men,
As hounds and greyhounds, mongrels, spaniels,
   curs,
Shoughs, water-rugs, and demi-wolves are clipt
All by the name of dogs.
   Macbeth (1606) act 3, sc. 1, l. 90

2 LADY MACBETH: Things without all remedy
Should be without regard: what's done is done.
MACBETH: We have scotched the snake, not killed
   it:
She'll close and be herself, whilst our poor
   malice
Remains in danger of her former tooth.
   Macbeth (1606) act 3, sc. 2, l. 11

3   Duncan is in his grave;
After life's fitful fever he sleeps well;
Treason has done his worst: nor steel, nor
   poison,
Malice domestic, foreign levy, nothing,
Can touch him further.
   Macbeth (1606) act 3, sc. 2, l. 22

4   Ere the bat hath flown
His cloistered flight, ere, to black Hecate's
   summons
The shard-borne beetle with his drowsy hums
Hath rung night's yawning peal, there shall be
   done
A deed of dreadful note.
   Macbeth (1606) act 3, sc. 2, l. 40

5   Come, seeling night,
Scarf up the tender eye of pitiful day,
And with thy bloody and invisible hand,
Cancel and tear to pieces that great bond
Which keeps me pale! Light thickens, and the
   crow
Makes wing to the rooky wood;
Good things of day begin to droop and drowse,
Whiles night's black agents to their preys do
   rouse.
   Macbeth (1606) act 3, sc. 2, l. 46

6 The west yet glimmers with some streaks of
   day:
Now spurs the lated traveller apace
To gain the timely inn.
   Macbeth (1606) act 3, sc. 3, l. 5

7 But now I am cabined, cribbed, confined,
   bound in
To saucy doubts and fears.
   Macbeth (1606) act 3, sc. 4, l. 24

8 Now good digestion wait on appetite,
And health on both!
   Macbeth (1606) act 3, sc. 4, l. 38

9 Thou canst not say I did it: never shake
Thy gory locks at me.
   Macbeth (1606) act 3, sc. 4, l. 50

10 What man dare, I dare;
Approach thou like the rugged Russian bear,
The armed rhinoceros or the Hyrcan tiger,

Take any shape but that, and my firm nerves
Shall never tremble.
   Macbeth (1606) act 3, sc. 4, l. 99

11 Stand not upon the order of your going.
   Macbeth (1606) act 3, sc. 4, l. 119

12 It will have blood, they say; blood will have
   blood:
Stones have been known to move and trees to
   speak;
Augurs and understood relations have
By maggot-pies and choughs and rooks brought
   forth
The secret'st man of blood.
   Macbeth (1606) act 3, sc. 4, l. 122; see **PROVERBS** 628:16

13   I am in blood
Stepped in so far that, should I wade no more,
Returning were as tedious as go o'er.
   Macbeth (1606) act 3, sc. 4, l. 136

14 You lack the season of all natures, sleep.
   Macbeth (1606) act 3, sc. 4, l. 141

15 Round about the cauldron go;
In the poisoned entrails throw.
Toad, that under cold stone
Days and nights hast thirty-one
Sweltered venom sleeping got,
Boil thou first i' the charmèd pot.
Double, double toil and trouble;
Fire burn and cauldron bubble.
   Macbeth (1606) act 4, sc. 1, l. 4

16 Eye of newt, and toe of frog,
Wool of bat, and tongue of dog,
Adder's fork, and blind-worm's sting,
Lizard's leg, and howlet's wing,
For a charm of powerful trouble,
Like a hell-broth boil and bubble.
   Macbeth (1606) act 4, sc. 1, l. 14

17 Liver of blaspheming Jew,
Gall of goat, and slips of yew
Slivered in the moon's eclipse,
Nose of Turk, and Tartar's lips,
Finger of birth-strangled babe
Ditch-delivered by a drab,
Make the gruel thick and slab.
   Macbeth (1606) act 4, sc. 1, l. 26

18   By the pricking of my thumbs,
Something wicked this way comes.
   Macbeth (1606) act 4, sc. 1, l. 44

19 MACBETH: How now, you secret, black, and
   midnight hags!
What is't you do?
WITCHES: A deed without a name.
   Macbeth (1606) act 4, sc. 1, l. 48

20 Be bloody, bold, and resolute; laugh to scorn
The power of man, for none of woman born
Shall harm Macbeth.
   Macbeth (1606) act 4, sc. 1, l. 79

21 But yet, I'll make assurance double sure,
And take a bond of fate.
   Macbeth (1606) act 4, sc. 1, l. 83

1 Macbeth shall never vanquished be until
Great Birnam wood to high Dunsinane hill
Shall come against him.
Macbeth (1606) act 4, sc. 1, l. 92

2 His flight was madness: when our actions do
not,
Our fears do make us traitors.
Macbeth (1606) act 4, sc. 2, l. 3

3   He loves us not;
He wants the natural touch.
Macbeth (1606) act 4, sc. 2, l. 8

4 SON: And must they all be hanged that swear and
lie?
LADY MACDUFF: Every one.
SON: Who must hang them?
LADY MACDUFF: Why, the honest men.
SON: Then the liars and swearers are fools, for
there are liars and swearers enow to beat the
honest men and hang up them.
Macbeth (1606) act 4, sc. 2, l. [51]

5 Stands Scotland where it did?
Macbeth (1606) act 4, sc. 3, l. 164

6 Give sorrow words: the grief that does not
speak
Whispers the o'er-fraught heart, and bids it
break.
Macbeth (1606) act 4, sc. 3, l. 209

7 He has no children. All my pretty ones?
Did you say all? O hell-kite! All?
What! all my pretty chickens and their dam,
At one fell swoop?
Macbeth (1606) act 4, sc. 3, l. 216

8 Out, damned spot! out, I say! One; two: why
then, 'tis time to do't. Hell is murky! Fie, my
lord, fie! a soldier, and afeard? What need we
fear who knows it, when none can call our
power to account? Yet who would have thought
the old man to have had so much blood in him?
Macbeth (1606) act 5, sc. 1, l. [38]

9 The Thane of Fife had a wife: where is she
now?
Macbeth (1606) act 5, sc. 1, l. [46]

10 All the perfumes of Arabia will not sweeten this
little hand.
Macbeth (1606) act 5, sc. 1, l. [56]

11 What's done cannot be undone.
Macbeth (1606) act 5, sc. 1, l. [74]

12 More needs she the divine than the physician.
Macbeth (1606) act 5, sc. 1, l. [81]

13   Now does he feel his title
Hang loose about him, like a giant's robe
Upon a dwarfish thief.
Macbeth (1606) act 5, sc. 2, l. 20

14 Bring me no more reports; let them fly all:
Till Birnam wood remove to Dunsinane
I cannot taint with fear.
Macbeth (1606) act 5, sc. 3, l. 1

15 The devil damn thee black, thou cream-faced
loon!

Where gott'st thou that goose look?
Macbeth (1606) act 5, sc. 3, l. 11

16 I have lived long enough: my way of life
Is fall'n into the sear, the yellow leaf;
And that which should accompany old age,
As honour, love, obedience, troops of friends,
I must not look to have.
Macbeth (1606) act 5, sc. 3, l. 22; see **BYRON** 188:29, **BYRON**
190:21

17 Canst thou not minister to a mind diseased?
Pluck from the memory a rooted sorrow,
Raze out the written troubles of the brain,
And with some sweet oblivious antidote
Cleanse the stuffed bosom of that perilous stuff
Which weighs upon the heart?
Macbeth (1606) act 5, sc. 3, l. 37

18 Throw physic to the dogs; I'll none of it.
Macbeth (1606) act 5, sc. 3, l. 47

19 The cry is still, 'They come'.
Macbeth (1606) act 5, sc. 5, l. 2

20 I have almost forgot the taste of fears.
Macbeth (1606) act 5, sc. 5, l. 9

21 I have supped full with horrors.
Macbeth (1606) act 5, sc. 5, l. 13

22 She should have died hereafter;
There would have been a time for such a word,
To-morrow, and to-morrow, and to-morrow,
Creeps in this petty pace from day to day,
To the last syllable of recorded time;
And all our yesterdays have lighted fools
The way to dusty death. Out, out, brief candle!
Life's but a walking shadow, a poor player,
That struts and frets his hour upon the stage,
And then is heard no more; it is a tale
Told by an idiot, full of sound and fury,
Signifying nothing.
Macbeth (1606) act 5, sc. 5, l. 16

23 I 'gin to be aweary of the sun,
And wish the estate o' the world were now
undone.
Ring the alarum-bell! Blow, wind! come, wrack!
At least we'll die with harness on our back.
Macbeth (1606) act 5, sc. 5, l. 49

24 I bear a charmèd life, which must not yield
To one of woman born.
Macbeth (1606) act 5, sc. 7, l. 41; some editions prefer act 5,
sc. 10

25   Macduff was from his mother's
womb
Untimely ripped.
Macbeth (1606) act 5, sc. 7, l. 44; some editions prefer act 5,
sc. 10

26   Lay on, Macduff;
And damned be him that first cries, 'Hold,
enough!'
Macbeth (1606) act 5, sc. 7, l. 62; some editions prefer act 5,
sc. 10

MEASURE FOR MEASURE

27   Now, as fond fathers,
Having bound up the threat'ning twigs of birch,

Only to stick it in their children's sight
For terror, not to use, in time the rod
Becomes more mocked than feared; so our
decrees,
Dead to infliction, to themselves are dead,
And liberty plucks justice by the nose;
The baby beats the nurse, and quite athwart
Goes all decorum.
Measure for Measure (1604) act 1, sc. 3, l. 23

1 I hold you as a thing enskyed and sainted;
By your renouncement an immortal spirit,
And to be talked with in sincerity,
As with a saint.
Measure for Measure (1604) act 1, sc. 4, l. 34

2   A man whose blood
Is very snow-broth; one who never feels
The wanton stings and motions of the sense.
Measure for Measure (1604) act 1, sc. 4, l. 57

3 We must not make a scarecrow of the law,
Setting it up to fear the birds of prey,
And let it keep one shape, till custom make it
Their perch and not their terror.
Measure for Measure (1604) act 2, sc. 1, l. 1

4 'Tis one thing to be tempted, Escalus,
Another thing to fall.
Measure for Measure (1604) act 2, sc. 1, l. 17

5 This will last out a night in Russia,
When nights are longest there.
Measure for Measure (1604) act 2, sc. 1, l. [144]

6 No ceremony that to great ones 'longs,
Not the king's crown, nor the deputed sword,
The marshal's truncheon, nor the judge's robe,
Become them with one half so good a grace
As mercy does.
Measure for Measure (1604) act 2, sc. 2, l. 59

7   O! it is excellent
To have a giant's strength, but it is tyrannous
To use it like a giant.
Measure for Measure (1604) act 2, sc. 2, l. 107

8   Man, proud man,
Drest in a little brief authority,
Most ignorant of what he's most assured,
His glassy essence, like an angry ape,
Plays such fantastic tricks before high heaven,
As make the angels weep.
Measure for Measure (1604) act 2, sc. 2, l. 117

9 That in the captain's but a choleric word,
Which in the soldier is flat blasphemy.
Measure for Measure (1604) act 2, sc. 2, l. 130

10   Ever till now
When men were fond, I smiled and wondered
how.
Measure for Measure (1604) act 2, sc. 2, l. 192

11 The miserable have no other medicine
But only hope.
Measure for Measure (1604) act 3, sc. 1, l. 2

12 Be absolute for death; either death or life
Shall thereby be the sweeter. Reason thus with
life:

If I do lose thee, I do lose a thing
That none but fools would keep: a breath thou
art.
Measure for Measure (1604) act 3, sc. 1, l. 5

13   If I must die,
I will encounter darkness as a bride,
And hug it in mine arms.
Measure for Measure (1604) act 3, sc. 1, l. 81

14 CLAUDIO: Death is a fearful thing.
ISABELLA: And shamed life a hateful.
CLAUDIO: Ay, but to die, and go we know not
where;
To lie in cold obstruction and to rot;
This sensible warm motion to become
A kneaded clod; and the delighted spirit
To bathe in fiery floods or to reside
In thrilling region of thick-ribbèd ice.
Measure for Measure (1604) act 3, sc. 1, l. 114; some editions
prefer 'dilated spirit'

15 There, at the moated grange, resides this
dejected Mariana.
Measure for Measure (1604) act 3, sc. 1, l. [279]; see **TENNYSON**
797:17

16 When he makes water his urine is congealed ice.
Measure for Measure (1604) act 3, sc. 2, l. [119]; some editions
prefer act 3, sc. 1

17 Take, O take those lips away,
That so sweetly were forsworn;
And those eyes, the break of day,
Lights that do mislead the morn.
Measure for Measure (1604) act 4, sc. 1, l. 1

18   Music oft hath such a charm
To make bad good, and good provoke to harm.
Measure for Measure (1604) act 4, sc. 1, l. 16

19 The old fantastical Duke of dark corners.
Measure for Measure (1604) act 4, sc. 3, l. 156

20 Haste still pays haste, and leisure answers
leisure;
Like doth quit like, and Measure still for
Measure.
Measure for Measure (1604) act 5, sc. 1, l. [411]

21 They say best men are moulded out of faults,
And, for the most, become much more the
better
For being a little bad: so may my husband.
Measure for Measure (1604) act 5, sc. 1, l. [440]

THE MERCHANT OF VENICE

22 In sooth I know not why I am so sad:
It wearies me; you say it wearies you.
The Merchant of Venice (1596–8) act 1, sc. 1, l. 1

23 I hold the world but as the world, Gratiano;
A stage where every man must play a part,
And mine a sad one.
The Merchant of Venice (1596–8) act 1, sc. 1, l. 77

24   I am Sir Oracle,
And when I ope my lips let no dog bark!
The Merchant of Venice (1596–8) act 1, sc. 1, l. 93

25 In Belmont is a lady richly left,
And she is fair, and fairer than the word,

Of wondrous virtues.
The Merchant of Venice (1596–8) act 1, sc. 1, l. [162]

1 They are as sick that surfeit with too much, as they that starve with nothing.
The Merchant of Venice (1596–8) act 1, sc. 2, l. [5]

2 If to do were as easy as to know what were good to do, chapels had been churches, and poor men's cottages princes' palaces. It is a good divine that follows his own instructions; I can easier teach twenty what were good to be done, than be one of the twenty to follow mine own teaching.
The Merchant of Venice (1596–8) act 1, sc. 2, l. [13]

3 God made him, and therefore let him pass for a man.
The Merchant of Venice (1596–8) act 1, sc. 2, l. [59]

4 I think he bought his doublet in Italy, his round hose in France, his bonnet in Germany, and his behaviour everywhere.
The Merchant of Venice (1596–8) act 1, sc. 2, l. [78]

5 Ships are but boards, sailors but men; there be land-rats and water-rats, land-thieves and water-thieves.
The Merchant of Venice (1596–8) act 1, sc. 3, l. [22]

6 I will buy with you, sell with you, talk with you, walk with you, and so following; but I will not eat with you, drink with you, nor pray with you. What news on the Rialto?
The Merchant of Venice (1596–8) act 1, sc. 3, l. [36]

7 He hates our sacred nation, and he rails,
Even there where merchants most do
    congregate,
On me, my bargains, and my well-won thrift,
Which he calls interest.
The Merchant of Venice (1596–8) act 1, sc. 3, l. [49]

8 The devil can cite Scripture for his purpose.
The Merchant of Venice (1596–8) act 1, sc. 3, l. [99]

9 Still have I borne it with a patient shrug,
For sufferance is the badge of all our tribe.
You call me misbeliever, cut-throat dog,
And spit upon my Jewish gaberdine,
And all for use of that which is mine own.
The Merchant of Venice (1596–8) act 1, sc. 3, l. [110]

10 Mislike me not for my complexion,
The shadowed livery of the burnished sun,
To whom I am a neighbour and near bred.
The Merchant of Venice (1596–8) act 2, sc. 1, l. 1

11 My conscience says, 'Launcelot, budge not.'
'Budge,' says the fiend. 'Budge not,' says my conscience. 'Conscience,' say I, 'you counsel well;' 'fiend,' say I, 'you counsel well.'
The Merchant of Venice (1596–8) act 2, sc. 2, l. [19]

12 It is a wise father that knows his own child.
The Merchant of Venice (1596–8) act 2, sc. 2, l. [83]; see
PROVERBS 636:8

13 Truth will come to light; murder cannot be hid long.
The Merchant of Venice (1596–8) act 2, sc. 2, l. [86]

14 My daughter! O my ducats! O my daughter!
The Merchant of Venice (1596–8) act 2, sc. 8, l. 15

15 The portrait of a blinking idiot.
The Merchant of Venice (1596–8) act 2, sc. 9, l. 54

16 The Goodwins, I think they call the place; a very dangerous flat, and fatal, where the carcasses of many a tall ship lie buried, as they say, if my gossip Report be an honest woman of her word.
The Merchant of Venice (1596–8) act 3, sc. 1, l. [4]

17 Let him look to his bond.
The Merchant of Venice (1596–8) act 3, sc. 1, l. [51]

18 Hath not a Jew eyes? hath not a Jew hands, organs, dimensions, senses, affections, passions?
The Merchant of Venice (1596–8) act 3, sc. 1, l. [63]

19 If you prick us, do we not bleed? if you tickle us, do we not laugh? if you poison us, do we not die? and if you wrong us, shall we not revenge?
The Merchant of Venice (1596–8) act 3, sc. 1, l. [69]

20 The villainy you teach me I will execute, and it shall go hard but I will better the instruction.
The Merchant of Venice (1596–8) act 3, sc. 1, l. [76]

21   He makes a swan-like end,
Fading in music.
The Merchant of Venice (1596–8) act 3, sc. 2, l. 44

22 Tell me where is fancy bred.
Or in the heart or in the head?
The Merchant of Venice (1596–8) act 3, sc. 2, l. 63

23 So may the outward shows be least themselves:
The world is still deceived with ornament.
The Merchant of Venice (1596–8) act 3, sc. 2, l. 73

24 ... An unlessoned girl, unschooled, unpractised;
Happy in this, she is not yet so old
But she may learn; happier than this,
She is not bred so dull but she can learn.
The Merchant of Venice (1596–8) act 3, sc. 2, l. 160

25 I will have my bond.
The Merchant of Venice (1596–8) act 3, sc. 3, l. 17

26 I am not bound to please thee with my answer.
The Merchant of Venice (1596–8) act 4, sc. 1, l. 65

27 I am a tainted wether of the flock,
Meetest for death: the weakest kind of fruit
Drops earliest to the ground.
The Merchant of Venice (1596–8) act 4, sc. 1, l. 114

28 I never knew so young a body with so old a head.
The Merchant of Venice (1596–8) act 4, sc. 1, l. [163]

29 The quality of mercy is not strained,
It droppeth as the gentle rain from heaven
Upon the place beneath: it is twice blessed;
It blesseth him that gives and him that takes:
'Tis mightiest in the mightiest: it becomes
The thronèd monarch better than his crown.
The Merchant of Venice (1596–8) act 4, sc. 1, l. [182]

30 Though justice be thy plea, consider this,
That in the course of justice none of us
Should see salvation: we do pray for mercy,

And that same prayer doth teach us all to render
The deeds of mercy.
The Merchant of Venice (1596–8) act 4, sc. 1, l. [197]

1 My deeds upon my head! I crave the law.
The Merchant of Venice (1596–8) act 4, sc. 1, l. [206]

2 Wrest once the law to your authority:
To do a great right, do a little wrong.
The Merchant of Venice (1596–8) act 4, sc. 1, l. [215]

3 A Daniel come to judgement! yea, a Daniel!
The Merchant of Venice (1596–8) act 4, sc. 1, l. [223]

4 Now, infidel, I have you on the hip.
The Merchant of Venice (1596–8) act 4, sc. 1, l. [229]

5 The court awards it, and the law doth give it.
The Merchant of Venice (1596–8) act 4, sc. 1, l. [301]

6 Nay, take my life and all; pardon not that:
You take my house when you do take the prop
That doth sustain my house; you take my life
When you do take the means whereby I live.
The Merchant of Venice (1596–8) act 4, sc. 1, l. [375]

7 He is well paid that is well satisfied.
The Merchant of Venice (1596–8) act 4, sc. 1, l. [416]

8 The moon shines bright: in such a night as this

. . .

Troilus methinks mounted the Troyan walls,
And sighed his soul toward the Grecian tents,
Where Cressid lay that night.
The Merchant of Venice (1596–8) act 5, sc. 1, l. 1

9   In such a night
Stood Dido with a willow in her hand
Upon the wild sea-banks, and waft her love
To come again to Carthage.
The Merchant of Venice (1596–8) act 5, sc. 1, l. 9

10 How sweet the moonlight sleeps upon this bank!
Here will we sit, and let the sounds of music
Creep in our ears; soft stillness and the night
Become the touches of sweet harmony.
The Merchant of Venice (1596–8) act 5, sc. 1, l. 54

11   Look, how the floor of heaven
Is thick inlaid with patines of bright gold.
The Merchant of Venice (1596–8) act 5, sc. 1, l. 58; some
editions prefer 'inlaid with patens'

12 I am never merry when I hear sweet music.
The Merchant of Venice (1596–8) act 5, sc. 1, l. 69

13 The man that hath no music in himself,
Nor is not moved with concord of sweet sounds,
Is fit for treasons, stratagems, and spoils.
The Merchant of Venice (1596–8) act 5, sc. 1, l. 79

14 How far that little candle throws his beams!
So shines a good deed in a naughty world.
The Merchant of Venice (1596–8) act 5, sc. 1, l. 90

15 These blessed candles of the night.
The Merchant of Venice (1596–8) act 5, sc. 1, l. 220

THE MERRY WIVES OF WINDSOR

16 I will make a Star-Chamber matter of it.
The Merry Wives of Windsor (1597) act 1, sc. 1, l. 1

17 Here will be an old abusing of God's patience,
and the king's English.
The Merry Wives of Windsor (1597) act 1, sc. 4, l. [5]

18 We burn daylight.
The Merry Wives of Windsor (1597) act 2, sc. 1, l. [54]

19 Why, then the world's mine oyster,
Which I with sword will open.
The Merry Wives of Windsor (1597) act 2, sc. 2, l. 2

20 There is divinity in odd numbers, either in
nativity, chance or death.
The Merry Wives of Windsor (1597) act 5, sc. 1, l. 3

A MIDSUMMER NIGHT'S DREAM

21 To live a barren sister all your life,
Chanting faint hymns to the cold fruitless moon.
A Midsummer Night's Dream (1595–6) act 1, sc. 1, l. 72

22 But earthlier happy is the rose distilled,
Than that which withering on the virgin thorn
Grows, lives, and dies, in single blessedness.
A Midsummer Night's Dream (1595–6) act 1, sc. 1, l. 76

23 The course of true love never did run smooth.
A Midsummer Night's Dream (1595–6) act 1, sc. 1, l. 134

24 So quick bright things come to confusion.
A Midsummer Night's Dream (1595–6) act 1, sc. 1, l. 149

25 Love looks not with the eyes, but with the
mind,
And therefore is winged Cupid painted blind.
A Midsummer Night's Dream (1595–6) act 1, sc. 1, l. 234

26 The most lamentable comedy, and most cruel
death of Pyramus and Thisby.
A Midsummer Night's Dream (1595–6) act 1, sc. 2, l. [11]

27 I could play Ercles rarely, or a part to tear a cat
in, to make all split.
A Midsummer Night's Dream (1595–6) act 1, sc. 2, l. [31]

28 This is Ercles' vein, a tyrant's vein.
A Midsummer Night's Dream (1595–6) act 1, sc. 2, l. [43]

29 Nay, faith, let me not play a woman; I have a
beard coming.
A Midsummer Night's Dream (1595–6) act 1, sc. 2, l. [50]

30 I will roar you as gently as any sucking dove; I
will roar you as 'twere any nightingale.
A Midsummer Night's Dream (1595–6) act 1, sc. 2, l. [85]

31 Pyramus is a sweet-faced man; a proper man, as
one shall see in a summer's day.
A Midsummer Night's Dream (1595–6) act 1, sc. 2, l. [89]

32 Hold, or cut bow-strings.
A Midsummer Night's Dream (1595–6) act 1, sc. 2, l. [115]

33 PUCK: How now, spirit! whither wander you?
FAIRY: Over hill, over dale,
Thorough bush, thorough brier,
Over park, over pale,
Thorough flood, thorough fire,
I do wander everywhere,
Swifter than the moone's sphere;
And I serve the fairy queen.
A Midsummer Night's Dream (1595–6) act 2, sc. 1, l. 1

34 The cowslips tall her pensioners be;
In their gold coats spots you see;
Those be rubies, fairy favours,
In those freckles live their savours:
I must go seek some dew-drops here,

And hang a pearl in every cowslip's ear.
A Midsummer Night's Dream (1595–6) act 2, sc. 1, l. 10

1 The wisest aunt, telling the saddest tale.
A Midsummer Night's Dream (1595–6) act 2, sc. 1, l. 51

2 Ill met by moonlight, proud Titania.
A Midsummer Night's Dream (1595–6) act 2, sc. 1, l. 60

3 The fold stands empty in the drownèd field,
And crows are fatted with the murrain flock;
The nine men's morris is filled up with mud.
A Midsummer Night's Dream (1595–6) act 2, sc. 1, l. 96

4 Therefore the moon, the governess of floods,
Pale in her anger, washes all the air,
That rheumatic diseases do abound:
And thorough this distemperature we see
The seasons alter: hoary-headed frosts
Fall in the fresh lap of the crimson rose.
A Midsummer Night's Dream (1595–6) act 2, sc. 1, l. 103

5 Since once I sat upon a promontory,
And heard a mermaid on a dolphin's back
Uttering such dulcet and harmonious breath,
That the rude sea grew civil at her song,
And certain stars shot madly from their spheres,
To hear the sea-maid's music.
A Midsummer Night's Dream (1595–6) act 2, sc. 1, l. 149

6 And the imperial votaress passed on,
In maiden meditation, fancy-free.
Yet marked I where the bolt of Cupid fell:
It fell upon a little western flower,
Before milk-white, now purple with love's
wound,
And maidens call it, Love-in-idleness.
A Midsummer Night's Dream (1595–6) act 2, sc. 1, l. 163

7 I'll put a girdle round about the earth
In forty minutes.
A Midsummer Night's Dream (1595–6) act 2, sc. 1, l. 175

8 I know a bank whereon the wild thyme blows,
Where oxlips and the nodding violet grows
Quite over-canopied with luscious woodbine,
With sweet musk-roses, and with eglantine.
A Midsummer Night's Dream (1595–6) act 2, sc. 1, l. 249

9 And there the snake throws her enamelled skin,
Weed wide enough to wrap a fairy in.
A Midsummer Night's Dream (1595–6) act 2, sc. 1, l. 255

10 You spotted snakes with double tongue,
Thorny hedge-hogs, be not seen;
Newts, and blind-worms, do no wrong;
Come not near our fairy queen.
A Midsummer Night's Dream (1595–6) act 2, sc. 2, l. 9

11 Weaving spiders come not here;
Hence you long-legged spinners, hence!
Beetles black, approach not near;
Worm nor snail, do no offence.
A Midsummer Night's Dream (1595–6) act 2, sc. 2, l. 20

12 God shield us!—a lion among ladies, is a most
dreadful thing; for there is not a more fearful
wild-fowl than your lion living.
A Midsummer Night's Dream (1595–6) act 3, sc. 1, l. [32]

13 Look in the almanack; find out moonshine, find
out moonshine.
A Midsummer Night's Dream (1595–6) act 3, sc. 1, l. [55]

14 What hempen home-spuns have we swaggering
here,
So near the cradle of the fairy queen?
A Midsummer Night's Dream (1595–6) act 3, sc. 1, l. [82]

15 Bless thee, Bottom! bless thee! thou art
translated.
A Midsummer Night's Dream (1595–6) act 3, sc. 1, l. [124]

16 What angel wakes me from my flowery bed?
A Midsummer Night's Dream (1595–6) act 3, sc. 1, l. [135]

17 Out of this wood do not desire to go.
A Midsummer Night's Dream (1595–6) act 3, sc. 1, l. [159]

18 Lord, what fools these mortals be!
A Midsummer Night's Dream (1595–6) act 3, sc. 2, l. 115

19 Two lovely berries moulded on one stem;
So, with two seeming bodies, but one heart.
A Midsummer Night's Dream (1595–6) act 3, sc. 2, l. 211

20 O! when she's angry she is keen and shrewd.
She was a vixen when she went to school:
And though she be but little, she is fierce.
A Midsummer Night's Dream (1595–6) act 3, sc. 2, l. 323

21 . . . Night's swift dragons cut the clouds full fast,
And yonder shines Aurora's harbinger;
At whose approach, ghosts, wandering here and
there,
Troop home to churchyards.
A Midsummer Night's Dream (1595–6) act 3, sc. 2, l. 379

22 Cupid is a knavish lad,
Thus to make poor females mad.
A Midsummer Night's Dream (1595–6) act 3, sc. 2, l. 440;
some editions prefer act 3, sc. 3

23 Jack shall have Jill;
Nought shall go ill;
The man shall have his mare again,
And all shall be well.
A Midsummer Night's Dream (1595–6) act 3, sc. 2, l. 461; some
editions prefer act 3, sc. 3

24 Let us have the tongs and the bones.
A Midsummer Night's Dream (1595–6) act 4, sc. 1, l. [33]

25 Methinks I have a great desire to a bottle of
hay: good hay, sweet hay, hath no fellow.
A Midsummer Night's Dream (1595–6) act 4, sc. 1, l. [37]

26 I have an exposition of sleep come upon me.
A Midsummer Night's Dream (1595–6) act 4, sc. 1, l. [43]

27 My Oberon! what visions have I seen!
Methought I was enamoured of an ass.
A Midsummer Night's Dream (1595–6) act 4, sc. 1, l. [82]

28 I was with Hercules and Cadmus once,
When in a wood of Crete they bayed the bear
With hounds of Sparta: never did I hear . . .
So musical a discord, such sweet thunder.
A Midsummer Night's Dream (1595–6) act 4, sc. 1, l. [118]

29 I have had a dream, past the wit of man to say
what dream it was.
A Midsummer Night's Dream (1595–6) act 4, sc. 1, l. [211]

1 The eye of man hath not heard, the ear of man hath not seen, man's hand is not able to taste, his tongue to conceive, nor his heart to report, what my dream was.
A Midsummer Night's Dream (1595–6) act 4, sc. 1, l. [218]

2 The lunatic, the lover, and the poet,
Are of imagination all compact.
A Midsummer Night's Dream (1595–6) act 5, sc. 1, l. 7

3   The lover, all as frantic,
Sees Helen's beauty in a brow of Egypt:
The poet's eye, in a fine frenzy rolling,
Doth glance from heaven to earth, from earth to heaven;
And, as imagination bodies forth
The forms of things unknown, the poet's pen
Turns them to shapes, and gives to airy nothing
A local habitation and a name.
A Midsummer Night's Dream (1595–6) act 5, sc. 1, l. 10

4 Or in the night, imagining some fear,
How easy is a bush supposed a bear!
A Midsummer Night's Dream (1595–6) act 5, sc. 1, l. 21

5 Merry and tragical! tedious and brief!
That is, hot ice and wondrous strange snow.
A Midsummer Night's Dream (1595–6) act 5, sc. 1, l. 58

6   To show our simple skill,
That is the true beginning of our end.
A Midsummer Night's Dream (1595–6) act 5, sc. 1, l. [110]

7 I see a voice: now will I to the chink,
To spy an I can hear my Thisby's face.
A Midsummer Night's Dream (1595–6) act 5, sc. 1, l. [195]

8 The best in this kind are but shadows, and the worst are no worse, if imagination amend them.
A Midsummer Night's Dream (1595–6) act 5, sc. 1, l. [215]

9 The iron tongue of midnight hath told twelve;
Lovers, to bed; 'tis almost fairy time.
A Midsummer Night's Dream (1595–6) act 5, sc. 1, l. [372]

10 Now the hungry lion roars,
And the wolf behowls the moon;
Whilst the heavy ploughman snores,
All with weary task fordone.
A Midsummer Night's Dream (1595–6) act 5, sc. 2, l. 1

11   Not a mouse
Shall disturb this hallowed house:
I am sent with broom before,
To sweep the dust behind the door.
A Midsummer Night's Dream (1595–6) act 5, sc. 2, l. 17

12 If we shadows have offended,
Think but this, and all is mended,
That you have but slumbered here
While these visions did appear.
A Midsummer Night's Dream (1595–6) act 5, sc. 2, l. 54

MUCH ADO ABOUT NOTHING

13 He hath indeed better bettered expectation than you must expect of me to tell you how.
Much Ado About Nothing (1598–9) act 1, sc. 1, l. [15]

14 He is a very valiant trencher-man.
Much Ado About Nothing (1598–9) act 1, sc. 1, l. [52]

15 BEATRICE: I wonder that you will still be talking, Signior Benedick: nobody marks you.

BENEDICK: What! my dear Lady Disdain, are you yet living?
Much Ado About Nothing (1598–9) act 1, sc. 1, l. [121]

16 Lord! I could not endure a husband with a beard on his face: I had rather lie in the woollen.
Much Ado About Nothing (1598–9) act 2, sc. 1, l. [31]

17 Speak low, if you speak love.
Much Ado About Nothing (1598–9) act 2, sc. 1, l. [104]

18 Friendship is constant in all other things
Save in the office and affairs of love.
Much Ado About Nothing (1598–9) act 2, sc. 1, l. [184]

19 There was a star danced, and under that was I born.
Much Ado About Nothing (1598–9) act 2, sc. 1, l. [351]

20 Is it not strange, that sheeps' guts should hale souls out of men's bodies?
Much Ado About Nothing (1598–9) act 2, sc. 3, l. [62]

21 Sigh no more, ladies, sigh no more,
Men were deceivers ever;
One foot in sea, and one on shore,
To one thing constant never.
Much Ado About Nothing (1598–9) act 2, sc. 3, l. [65]

22 Sits the wind in that corner?
Much Ado About Nothing (1598–9) act 2, sc. 3, l. [108]

23 For look where Beatrice, like a lapwing, runs
Close by the ground, to hear our counsel.
Much Ado About Nothing (1598–9) act 3, sc. 1, l. 24

24 Disdain and scorn ride sparkling in her eyes.
Much Ado About Nothing (1598–9) act 3, sc. 1, l. 51

25 Contempt, farewell! and maiden pride, adieu!
No glory lives behind the back of such.
And, Benedick, love on; I will requite thee,
Taming my wild heart to thy loving hand.
Much Ado About Nothing (1598–9) act 3, sc. 1, l. 109

26 He hath a heart as sound as a bell, and his tongue is the clapper; for what his heart thinks his tongue speaks.
Much Ado About Nothing (1598–9) act 3, sc. 2, l. [12]

27 Well, every one can master a grief but he that has it.
Much Ado About Nothing (1598–9) act 3, sc. 2, l. [28]

28 Comparisons are odorous.
Much Ado About Nothing (1598–9) act 3, sc. 5, l. [18]; see PROVERBS 629:16

29 O! what men dare do! what men may do! what men daily do, not knowing what they do!
Much Ado About Nothing (1598–9) act 4, sc. 1, l. [19]

30 O God, that I were a man! I would eat his heart in the market-place.
Much Ado About Nothing (1598–9) act 4, sc. 1, l. [311]

31 Patch grief with proverbs.
Much Ado About Nothing (1598–9) act 5, sc. 1, l. 17

32   There was never yet philosopher
That could endure the toothache patiently.
Much Ado About Nothing (1598–9) act 5, sc. 1, l. 35

33 What though care killed a cat, thou hast mettle enough in thee to kill care.
Much Ado About Nothing (1598–9) act 5, sc. 1, l. [135]; see PROVERBS 628:33

1 No, I was not born under a rhyming planet.
Much Ado About Nothing (1598–9) act 5, sc. 2, l. [40]

OTHELLO

2 But I will wear my heart upon my sleeve
For daws to peck at: I am not what I am.
Othello (1602–4) act 1, sc. 1, l. 64

3 Even now, now, very now, an old black ram
Is tupping your white ewe.
Othello (1602–4) act 1, sc. 1, l. 88

4 Your daughter and the Moor are now making
the beast with two backs.
Othello (1602–4) act 1, sc. 1, l. [117]

5 Keep up your bright swords, for the dew will
rust them.
Othello (1602–4) act 1, sc. 2, l. 59

6 The wealthy curlèd darlings of our nation.
Othello (1602–4) act 1, sc. 2, l. 67

7   Rude am I in my speech,
And little blessed with the soft phrase of peace.
Othello (1602–4) act 1, sc. 3, l. 81

8 I will a round unvarnished tale deliver
Of my whole course of love; what drugs, what
charms,
What conjuration, and what mighty magic,
For such proceeding I am charged withal,
I won his daughter.
Othello (1602–4) act 1, sc. 3, l. 90

9 Wherein I spake of most disastrous chances,
Of moving accidents by flood and field.
Othello (1602–4) act 1, sc. 3, l. 134

10 And of the Cannibals that each other eat,
The Anthropophagi, and men whose heads
Do grow beneath their shoulders.
Othello (1602–4) act 1, sc. 3, l. 143

11   My story being done,
She gave me for my pains a world of sighs:
She swore, in faith, 'twas strange, 'twas passing
strange;
'Twas pitiful, 'twas wondrous pitiful.
Othello (1602–4) act 1, sc. 3, l. 158; some editions prefer
'world of kisses'

12 She loved me for the dangers I had passed,
And I loved her that she did pity them.
Othello (1602–4) act 1, sc. 3, l. 167

13 I do perceive here a divided duty.
Othello (1602–4) act 1, sc. 3, l. 181

14 The robbed that smiles steals something from
the thief.
Othello (1602–4) act 1, sc. 3, l. 208

15   Hell and night
Must bring this monstrous birth to the world's
light.
Othello (1602–4) act 1, sc. 3, l. [409]

16 Our great captain's captain.
Othello (1602–4) act 2, sc. 1, l. 74

17 To suckle fools and chronicle small beer.
Othello (1602–4) act 2, sc. 1, l. 163

18   If it were now to die,
'Twere now to be most happy.
Othello (1602–4) act 2, sc. 1, l. [192]

19 Silence that dreadful bell! it frights the isle
From her propriety.
Othello (1602–4) act 2, sc. 3, l. [177]

20 O! I have lost my reputation. I have lost the
immortal part of myself, and what remains is
bestial.
Othello (1602–4) act 2, sc. 3, l. [264]

21 O! thereby hangs a tail.
Othello (1602–4) act 3, sc. 1, l. [8]

22 Excellent wretch! Perdition catch my soul
But I do love thee! and when I love thee not,
Chaos is come again.
Othello (1602–4) act 3, sc. 3, l. 90

23 Who steals my purse steals trash; 'tis something,
nothing;
'Twas mine, 'tis his, and has been slave to
thousands;
But he that filches from me my good name
Robs me of that which not enriches him,
And makes me poor indeed.
Othello (1602–4) act 3, sc. 3, l. 157

24   O! beware, my lord, of jealousy;
It is the green-eyed monster which doth mock
The meat it feeds on.
Othello (1602–4) act 3, sc. 3, l. 165

25   If I do prove her haggard,
Though that her jesses were my dear heart-
strings,
I'd whistle her off and let her down the wind,
To prey at fortune.
Othello (1602–4) act 3, sc. 3, l. 260

26   I had rather be a toad,
And live upon the vapour of a dungeon,
Than keep a corner in the thing I love
For others' uses.
Othello (1602–4) act 3, sc. 3, l. 270

27 If she be false, O! then heaven mocks itself.
I'll not believe it.
Othello (1602–4) act 3, sc. 3, l. 278

28   Trifles light as air
Are to the jealous confirmations strong
As proofs of holy writ.
Othello (1602–4) act 3, sc. 3, l. 323

29   Not poppy, nor mandragora,
Nor all the drowsy syrups of the world,
Shall ever medicine thee to that sweet sleep
Which thou owedst yesterday.
Othello (1602–4) act 3, sc. 3, l. 331

30 Farewell the tranquil mind; farewell content!
Farewell the plumèd troop and the big wars
That make ambition virtue!
Othello (1602–4) act 3, sc. 3, l. 349

31 Pride, pomp, and circumstance of glorious war!
Othello (1602–4) act 3, sc. 3, l. 355

32 Othello's occupation's gone!
Othello (1602–4) act 3, sc. 3, l. 358

1 This denoted a foregone conclusion.
   Othello (1602–4) act 3, sc. 3, l. 429

2   Like to the Pontick sea,
   Whose icy current and compulsive course
   Ne'er feels retiring ebb, but keeps due on
   To the Propontic and the Hellespont,
   Even so my bloody thoughts, with violent pace,
   Shall ne'er look back.
   Othello (1602–4) act 3, sc. 3, l. 454

3 That handkerchief
   Did an Egyptian to my mother give.
   Othello (1602–4) act 3, sc. 4, l. 56

4 A sibyl, that had numbered in the world
   The sun to course two hundred compasses,
   In her prophetic fury sewed the work;
   The worms were hallowed that did breed the
      silk,
   And it was dyed in mummy which the skilful
   Conserved of maidens' hearts.
   Othello (1602–4) act 3, sc. 4, l. 71

5 But yet the pity of it, Iago! O! Iago, the pity of
   it, Iago!
   Othello (1602–4) act 4, sc. 1, l. [205]

6   Is this the noble nature
   Whom passion could not shake?
   Othello (1602–4) act 4, sc. 1, l. [277]; some editions prefer 'Is
   this the nature'

7 Those that do teach young babes
   Do it with gentle means and easy tasks;
   He might have chid me so; for, in good faith,
   I am a child to chiding.
   Othello (1602–4) act 4, sc. 2, l. 111

8   Unkindness may do much;
   And his unkindness may defeat my life,
   But never taint my love.
   Othello (1602–4) act 4, sc. 2, l. 159

9 The poor soul sat sighing by a sycamore tree,
   Sing all a green willow;
   Her hand on her bosom, her head on her knee,
   Sing willow, willow, willow.
   Othello (1602–4) act 4, sc. 3, l. [41]

10 Sing all a green willow must be my garland.
   Othello (1602–4) act 4, sc. 3, l. [49]; see **HEYWOOD** 398:2

11   This is the night
   That either makes me or fordoes me quite.
   Othello (1602–4) act 5, sc. 1, l. 128

12 It is the cause, it is the cause, my soul;
   Let me not name it to you, you chaste stars!
   It is the cause.
   Othello (1602–4) act 5, sc. 2, l. 1

13 Put out the light, and then put out the light.
   Othello (1602–4) act 5, sc. 2, l. 7

14 Kill me to-morrow; let me live to-night!
   Othello (1602–4) act 5, sc. 2, l. 80

15 It is the very error of the moon;
   She comes more near the earth than she was
      wont,
   And makes men mad.
   Othello (1602–4) act 5, sc. 2, l. 107

16   Murder's out of tune,
   And sweet revenge grows harsh.
   Othello (1602–4) act 5, sc. 2, l. 113

17 OTHELLO: She's like a liar gone to burning hell;
   'Twas I that killed her.
   EMILIA: O! the more angel she,
   And you the blacker devil.
   Othello (1602–4) act 5, sc. 2, l. 127

18   I will play the swan,
   And die in music.
   Othello (1602–4) act 5, sc. 2, l. 245

19 Here is my journey's end, here is my butt,
   And very sea-mark of my utmost sail.
   Othello (1602–4) act 5, sc. 2, l. 266

20   O ill-starred wench!
   Pale as thy smock! when we shall meet at
      compt,
   This look of thine will hurl my soul from
      heaven,
   And fiends will snatch at it. Cold, cold, my girl!
   Even like thy chastity.
   Othello (1602–4) act 5, sc. 2, l. 271; some editions prefer
   'meet at count'

21 Blow me about in winds! roast me in sulphur!
   Wash me in steep-down gulfs of liquid fire!
   O Desdemona! Desdemona! dead!
   Othello (1602–4) act 5, sc. 2, l. 278

22 An honourable murderer, if you will;
   For nought did I in hate, but all in honour.
   Othello (1602–4) act 5, sc. 2, l. 293

23 I have done the state some service, and they
      know 't;
   No more of that. I pray you, in your letters,
   When you shall these unlucky deeds relate,
   Speak of me as I am; nothing extenuate,
   Nor set down aught in malice: then, must you
      speak
   Of one that loved not wisely but too well;
   Of one not easily jealous, but, being wrought,
   Perplexed in the extreme; of one whose hand,
   Like the base Indian, threw a pearl away
   Richer than all his tribe.
   Othello (1602–4) act 5, sc. 2, l. 338

24 And say besides, that in Aleppo once,
   Where a malignant and a turbaned Turk
   Beat a Venetian and traduced the state,
   I took by the throat the circumcised dog,
   And smote him thus.
   Othello (1602–4) act 5, sc. 2, l. 351

25 I kissed thee ere I killed thee, no way but this,
   Killing myself to die upon a kiss.
   Othello (1602–4) act 5, sc. 2, l. 357

PERICLES

26 THIRD FISHERMAN: Master, I marvel how the
   fishes live in the sea.
   FIRST FISHERMAN: Why, as men do a-land: the
   great ones eat up the little ones.
   Pericles (1606–8) act 2, sc. 1, l. 26; some editions prefer sc. 5;
   see **SIDNEY** 750:9

RICHARD II

1 Old John of Gaunt, time-honoured Lancaster.
Richard II (1595) act 1, sc. 1, l. 1

2 The purest treasure mortal times afford
Is spotless reputation; that away,
Men are but gilded loam or painted clay.
Richard II (1595) act 1, sc. 1, l. 177

3 We were not born to sue, but to command.
Richard II (1595) act 1, sc. 1, l. 196; see **SCOTT** 688:8

4 The language I have learned these forty years,
My native English, now I must forego;
And now my tongue's use is to me no more
Than an unstringèd viol or a harp.
Richard II (1595) act 1, sc. 3, l. 159

5 How long a time lies in one little word!
Four lagging winters and four wanton springs
End in a word; such is the breath of kings.
Richard II (1595) act 1, sc. 3, l. 213

6 Things sweet to taste prove in digestion sour.
Richard II (1595) act 1, sc. 3, l. 236

7 All places that the eye of heaven visits
Are to a wise man ports and happy havens.
Teach thy necessity to reason thus;
There is no virtue like necessity.
Richard II (1595) act 1, sc. 3, l. 275

8 O! who can hold a fire in his hand
By thinking on the frosty Caucasus?
Or cloy the hungry edge of appetite,
By bare imagination of a feast?
Or wallow naked in December snow
By thinking on fantastic summer's heat?
Richard II (1595) act 1, sc. 3, l. 294

9 More are men's ends marked than their lives
before:
The setting sun, and music at the close,
As the last taste of sweets, is sweetest last,
Writ in remembrance more than things long
past.
Richard II (1595) act 2, sc. 1, l. 11

10 This royal throne of kings, this sceptred isle,
This earth of majesty, this seat of Mars,
This other Eden, demi-paradise,
This fortress built by Nature for herself
Against infection and the hand of war,
This happy breed of men, this little world,
This precious stone set in the silver sea.
Richard II (1595) act 2, sc. 1, l. 40; see **ORWELL** 587:6

11 This blessèd plot, this earth, this realm, this
England,
This nurse, this teeming womb of royal kings,
Feared by their breed and famous by their birth,
Renownèd for their deeds as far from home,—
For Christian service and true chivalry,—
As is the sepulchre in stubborn Jewry
Of the world's ransom, blessèd Mary's Son.
Richard II (1595) act 2, sc. 1, l. 50

12 Grace me no grace, nor uncle me no uncle.
Richard II (1595) act 2, sc. 3, l. 87

13 The caterpillars of the commonwealth.
Richard II (1595) act 2, sc. 3, l. 166

14 Things past redress are now with me past care.
Richard II (1595) act 2, sc. 3, l. 171

15 Eating the bitter bread of banishment.
Richard II (1595) act 3, sc. 1, l. 21

16 Not all the water in the rough rude sea
Can wash the balm from an anointed king;
The breath of worldly men cannot depose
The deputy elected by the Lord.
For every man that Bolingbroke hath pressed
To lift shrewd steel against our golden crown,
God for his Richard hath in heavenly pay
A glorious angel; then, if angels fight,
Weak men must fall, for heaven still guards the
right.
Richard II (1595) act 3, sc. 2, l. 54

17 O! call back yesterday, bid time return.
Richard II (1595) act 3, sc. 2, l. 69

18 Let's talk of graves, of worms, and epitaphs;
Make dust our paper, and with rainy eyes
Write sorrow on the bosom of the earth.
Let's choose executors, and talk of wills.
Richard II (1595) act 3, sc. 2, l. 145

19 For God's sake, let us sit upon the ground
And tell sad stories of the death of kings:
How some have been deposed, some slain in
war,
Some haunted by the ghosts they have deposed,
Some poisoned by their wives, some sleeping
killed;
All murdered.
Richard II (1595) act 3, sc. 2, l. 155

20 Within the hollow crown
That rounds the mortal temples of a king
Keeps Death his court, and there the antick sits,
Scoffing his state and grinning at his pomp;
Richard II (1595) act 3, sc. 2, l. 160

21 Comes at the last, and with a little pin
Bores through his castle wall, and farewell king!
Richard II (1595) act 3, sc. 2, l. 169

22 I'll give my jewels for a set of beads,
My gorgeous palace for a hermitage,
My gay apparel for an almsman's gown.
Richard II (1595) act 3, sc. 3, l. 147

23 And my large kingdom for a little grave,
A little little grave, an obscure grave.
Richard II (1595) act 3, sc. 3, l. 153

24 Go, bind thou up yon dangling apricocks.
Richard II (1595) act 3, sc. 4, l. 29; some editions prefer
'young dangling apricots'

25 Old Adam's likeness, set to dress this garden.
Richard II (1595) act 3, sc. 4, l. 73

26 Here did she fall a tear; here, in this place,
I'll set a bank of rue, sour herb of grace;
Rue, even for ruth, here shortly shall be seen,
In the remembrance of a weeping queen.
Richard II (1595) act 3, sc. 4, l. 104

1 Disorder, horror, fear and mutiny
Shall here inhabit, and this land be called
The field of Golgotha and dead men's skulls.
Richard II (1595) act 4, sc. 1, l. 142

2 God save the king! Will no man say, amen?
Am I both priest and clerk? Well then, amen.
Richard II (1595) act 4, sc. 1, l. 172

3 You may my glories and my state depose,
But not my griefs; still am I king of those.
Richard II (1595) act 4, sc. 1, l. 192

4 With mine own tears I wash away my balm,
With mine own hands I give away my crown.
Richard II (1595) act 4, sc. 1, l. 207

5   This is the way
To Julius Caesar's ill-erected tower.
Richard II (1595) act 5, sc. 1, l. 1

6   Who are the violets now
That strew the green lap of the new come
   spring?
Richard II (1595) act 5, sc. 2, l. 46

7 I wasted time, and now doth time waste me.
Richard II (1595) act 5, sc. 5, l. 49

8 Mount, mount, my soul! thy seat is up on high,
Whilst my gross flesh sinks downwards here to
   die.
Richard II (1595) act 5, sc. 5, l. 112

RICHARD III

9 Now is the winter of our discontent
Made glorious summer by this sun of York.
Richard III (1591) act 1, sc. 1, l. 1; some editions prefer 'son of
York'; see **NEWSPAPER HEADLINES AND LEADERS** 573:25

10 Grim-visaged war hath smoothed his wrinkled
   front;
And now, instead of mounting barbèd steeds,
To fright the souls of fearful adversaries,—
He capers nimbly in a lady's chamber
To the lascivious pleasing of a lute.
Richard III (1591) act 1, sc. 1, l. 9

11 But I, that am not shaped for sportive tricks,
Nor made to court an amorous looking-glass;
I, that am rudely stamped, and want love's
   majesty
To strut before a wanton ambling nymph;
I, that am curtailed of this fair proportion,
Cheated of feature by dissembling nature,
Deformed, unfinished, sent before my time
Into this breathing world, scarce half made up,
And that so lamely and unfashionable
That dogs bark at me, as I halt by them.
Richard III (1591) act 1, sc. 1, l. 14

12 This weak piping time of peace.
Richard III (1591) act 1, sc. 1, l. 24

13 And therefore, since I cannot prove a lover,
To entertain these fair well-spoken days,
I am determinèd to prove a villain,
And hate the idle pleasures of these days.
Richard III (1591) act 1, sc. 1, l. 28

14 No beast so fierce but knows some touch of
   pity.
Richard III (1591) act 1, sc. 2, l. 71

15 Was ever woman in this humour wooed?
Was ever woman in this humour won?
I'll have her, but I will not keep her long.
Richard III (1591) act 1, sc. 2, l. 229

16 Since every Jack became a gentleman
There's many a gentle person made a Jack.
Richard III (1591) act 1, sc. 3, l. 72

17 And thus I clothe my naked villainy
With odd old ends stol'n forth of holy writ,
And seem a saint when most I play the devil.
Richard III (1591) act 1, sc. 3, l. 336

18 Clarence is come,—false, fleeting, perjured
   Clarence.
Richard III (1591) act 1, sc. 4, l. 55

19 Woe to the land that's governed by a child!
Richard III (1591) act 2, sc. 3, l. 11; see **BIBLE** 90:13

20 So wise so young, they say, do never live long.
Richard III (1591) act 3, sc. 1, l. 79

21 Talk'st thou to me of 'ifs'? Thou art a traitor:
Off with his head!
Richard III (1591) act 3, sc. 4, l. 74; see **CIBBER** 231:11

22 I am not in the giving vein to-day.
Richard III (1591) act 4, sc. 2, l. 115

23 The sons of Edward sleep in Abraham's bosom.
Richard III (1591) act 4, sc. 3, l. 38

24 Harp not on that string.
Richard III (1591) act 4, sc. 4, l. 365

25 True hope is swift, and flies with swallow's
   wings;
Kings it makes gods, and meaner creatures
   kings.
Richard III (1591) act 5, sc. 2, l. 23

26 The king's name is a tower of strength.
Richard III (1591) act 5, sc. 3, l. 12

27 Give me another horse! bind up my wounds!
Have mercy, Jesu! Soft! I did but dream.
O coward conscience, how dost thou afflict me!
Richard III (1591) act 5, sc. 3, l. 178; some editions prefer act 5,
sc. 5

28 I shall despair. There is no creature loves me;
And if I die, no soul will pity me:
Nay, wherefore should they, since that I myself
Find in myself no pity to myself?
Richard III (1591) act 5, sc. 3, l. 201; some editions prefer act
5, sc. 5

29 By the apostle Paul, shadows to-night
Have struck more terror to the soul of Richard
Than can the substance of ten thousand soldiers.
Richard III (1591) act 5, sc. 3, l. 217; some editions prefer act 5,
sc. 5

30 Conscience is but a word that cowards use,
Devised at first to keep the strong in awe.
Richard III (1591) act 5, sc. 3, l. 310; some editions prefer act
5, sc. 6

31 A horse! a horse! my kingdom for a horse!
Richard III (1591) act 5, sc. 4, l. 7; some editions prefer act 5,
sc. 7

1 Slave! I have set my life upon a cast,
And I will stand the hazard of the die.
Richard III (1591) act 5, sc. 4, l. 9; some editions prefer act 5, sc. 7

ROMEO AND JULIET

2 A pair of star-crossed lovers.
Romeo and Juliet (1595) prologue

3 The two hours' traffick of our stage.
Romeo and Juliet (1595) prologue

4 Younger than she are happy mothers made.
Romeo and Juliet (1595) act 1, sc. 2, l. 12

5 O! then, I see, Queen Mab hath been with you
. . .
She is the fairies' midwife, and she comes
In shape no bigger than an agate-stone.
Romeo and Juliet (1595) act 1, sc. 4, l. 53

6 You and I are past our dancing days.
Romeo and Juliet (1595) act 1, sc. 5, l. [35]

7 O! she doth teach the torches to burn bright.
It seems she hangs upon the cheek of night
Like a rich jewel in an Ethiop's ear;
Beauty too rich for use, for earth too dear.
Romeo and Juliet (1595) act 1, sc. 5, l. [48]; some editions prefer 'As a rich jewel'

8 My only love sprung from my only hate!
Too early seen unknown, and known too late!
Romeo and Juliet (1595) act 1, sc. 5, l. [142]

9 He jests at scars, that never felt a wound.
But, soft! what light through yonder window
breaks?
It is the east, and Juliet is the sun.
Romeo and Juliet (1595) act 2, sc. 2, l. 1; some editions prefer act 2, sc. 1

10 See! how she leans her cheek upon her hand:
O! that I were a glove upon that hand,
That I might touch that cheek.
Romeo and Juliet (1595) act 2, sc. 2, l. 23; some editions prefer act 2, sc. 1

11 O Romeo, Romeo! wherefore art thou Romeo?
Romeo and Juliet (1595) act 2, sc. 2, l. 33; some editions prefer act 2, sc. 1

12 What's in a name? that which we call a rose
By any other name would smell as sweet.
Romeo and Juliet (1595) act 2, sc. 2, l. 43; some editions prefer 'By any other word' and act 2, sc. 1

13 For stony limits cannot hold love out,
And what love can do that dares love attempt.
Romeo and Juliet (1595) act 2, sc. 2, l. 67; some editions prefer act 2, sc. 1

14 O! swear not by the moon, the inconstant
moon,
That monthly changes in her circled orb,
Lest that thy love prove likewise variable.
Romeo and Juliet (1595) act 2, sc. 2, l. 109; some editions prefer act 2, sc. 1

15 It is too rash, too unadvised, too sudden.
Romeo and Juliet (1595) act 2, sc. 2, l. 118; some editions prefer act 2, sc. 1

16 Love goes toward love, as schoolboys from their
books;

But love from love, toward school with heavy
looks.
Romeo and Juliet (1595) act 2, sc. 2, l. 156; some editions prefer act 2, sc. 1

17 O! for a falconer's voice,
To lure this tassel-gentle back again.
Romeo and Juliet (1595) act 2, sc. 2, l. 158; some editions prefer act 2, sc. 1

18 How silver-sweet sound lovers' tongues by night,
Like softest music to attending ears!
Romeo and Juliet (1595) act 2, sc. 2, l. 165; some editions prefer act 2, sc. 1

19 Good-night, good-night! parting is such sweet
sorrow
That I shall say good-night till it be morrow.
Romeo and Juliet (1595) act 2, sc. 2, l. 184; some editions prefer act 2, sc. 1

20 O flesh, flesh, how art thou fishified!
Romeo and Juliet (1595) act 2, sc. 4, l. [41]; some editions prefer act 2, sc. 3

21 I am the very pink of courtesy.
Romeo and Juliet (1595) act 2, sc. 4, l. [63]; some editions prefer act 2, sc. 3

22 No, 'tis not so deep as a well, nor so wide as a
church door; but 'tis enough, 'twill serve.
Romeo and Juliet (1595) act 3, sc. 1, l. [100]

23 A plague o' both your houses!
Romeo and Juliet (1595) act 3, sc. 1, l. [112]

24 O! I am Fortune's fool.
Romeo and Juliet (1595) act 3, sc. 1, l. [142]

25 Gallop apace, you fiery-footed steeds,
Towards Phoebus' lodging.
Romeo and Juliet (1595) act 3, sc. 2, l. 1

26   Come, civil night,
Thou sober-suited matron, all in black.
Romeo and Juliet (1595) act 3, sc. 2, l. 10

27 Give me my Romeo: and, when he shall die,
Take him and cut him out in little stars,
And he will make the face of heaven so fine
That all the world will be in love with night,
And pay no worship to the garish sun.
Romeo and Juliet (1595) act 3, sc. 2, l. 21; some editions prefer 'when I shall die'

28 Adversity's sweet milk, philosophy.
Romeo and Juliet (1595) act 3, sc. 3, l. 54

29 Wilt thou be gone? it is not yet near day:
It was the nightingale, and not the lark,
That pierced the fearful hollow of thine ear.
Romeo and Juliet (1595) act 3, sc. 5, l. 1

30 Night's candles are burnt out, and jocund day
Stands tiptoe on the misty mountain tops.
Romeo and Juliet (1595) act 3, sc. 5, l. 9

31 I have more care to stay than will to go.
Romeo and Juliet (1595) act 3, sc. 5, l. 23

32 Thank me no thankings, nor proud me no
prouds.
Romeo and Juliet (1595) act 3, sc. 5, l. 153

33 Romeo's a dishclout to him.
Romeo and Juliet (1595) act 3, sc. 5, l. 221

1 Death lies on her like an untimely frost
Upon the sweetest flower of all the field.
Romeo and Juliet (1595) act 4, sc. 5, l. 28; some editions
prefer act 4, sc. 4

2 Tempt not a desperate man.
Romeo and Juliet (1595) act 5, sc. 3, l. 59

3 How oft when men are at the point of death
Have they been merry! which their keepers call
A lightning before death.
Romeo and Juliet (1595) act 5, sc. 3, l. 88

4   Seal with a righteous kiss
A dateless bargain to engrossing death!
Romeo and Juliet (1595) act 5, sc. 3, l. 114

THE TAMING OF THE SHREW

5 I must dance bare-foot on her wedding day,
And, for your love to her, lead apes in hell.
The Taming of the Shrew (1592) act 2, sc. 1, l. 33

6   You are called plain Kate,
And bonny Kate, and sometimes Kate the curst;
But, Kate, the prettiest Kate in Christendom;
Kate of Kate-Hall, my super-dainty Kate,
For dainties are all cates: and therefore, Kate,
Take this of me, Kate of my consolation.
The Taming of the Shrew (1592) act 2, sc. 1, l. 186

7 Kiss me Kate, we will be married o' Sunday.
The Taming of the Shrew (1592) act 2, sc. 1, l. 318

8 This is the way to kill a wife with kindness.
The Taming of the Shrew (1592) act 4, sc. 1, l. [211]

9 A woman moved is like a fountain troubled,
Muddy, ill-seeming, thick, bereft of beauty.
The Taming of the Shrew (1592) act 5, sc. 2, l. 143

10 Such duty as the subject owes the prince,
Even such a woman oweth to her husband.
The Taming of the Shrew (1592) act 5, sc. 2, l. 156

11 I am ashamed that women are so simple
To offer war where they should kneel for peace.
The Taming of the Shrew (1592) act 5, sc. 2, l. 162

THE TEMPEST

12 He hath no drowning mark upon him; his
complexion is perfect gallows.
The Tempest (1611) act 1, sc. 1, l. [33]; see **PROVERBS** 635:32

13 Now would I give a thousand furlongs of sea for
an acre of barren ground.
The Tempest (1611) act 1, sc. 1, l. [70]

14   What seest thou else
In the dark backward and abysm of time?
The Tempest (1611) act 1, sc. 2, l. 49; some editions prefer
'abyss of time'

15   My library
Was dukedom large enough.
The Tempest (1611) act 1, sc. 2, l. 109

16 The still-vexed Bermoothes.
The Tempest (1611) act 1, sc. 2, l. 229

17 As wicked dew as e'er my mother brushed
With raven's feather from unwholesome fen
Drop on you both! A southwest blow on ye,
And blister you all o'er!
The Tempest (1611) act 1, sc. 2, l. 321

18 You taught me language; and my profit on't
Is, I know how to curse: the red plague rid you,
For learning me your language!
The Tempest (1611) act 1, sc. 2, l. 363

19 I must obey; his art is of such power,
It would control my dam's god, Setebos,
And make a vassal of him.
The Tempest (1611) act 1, sc. 2, l. 372

20 Come unto these yellow sands,
And then take hands.
The Tempest (1611) act 1, sc. 2, l. 375

21 Full fathom five thy father lies;
Of his bones are coral made:
Those are pearls that were his eyes:
Nothing of him that doth fade,
But doth suffer a sea-change
Into something rich and strange.
The Tempest (1611) act 1, sc. 2, l. 394

22 He receives comfort like cold porridge.
The Tempest (1611) act 2, sc. 1, l. 10

23 What's past is prologue.
The Tempest (1611) act 2, sc. 1, l. [261]

24 A very ancient and fish-like smell.
The Tempest (1611) act 2, sc. 2, l. [27]

25 Misery acquaints a man with strange bedfellows.
The Tempest (1611) act 2, sc. 2, l. [42]

26 'Ban, 'Ban, Ca-Caliban,
Has a new master—Get a new man.
The Tempest (1611) act 2, sc. 2, l. [197]

27 Thou deboshed fish thou.
The Tempest (1611) act 3, sc. 2, l. [30]; some editions prefer
'debauched fish'

28 Flout 'em, and scout 'em; and scout 'em, and
flout 'em;
Thought is free.
The Tempest (1611) act 3, sc. 2, l. [133]

29 He that dies pays all debts.
The Tempest (1611) act 3, sc. 2, l. [143]; see **PROVERBS** 629:38

30 Be not afeard: the isle is full of noises,
Sounds and sweet airs, that give delight, and
hurt not.
The Tempest (1611) act 3, sc. 2, l. [147]

31 Our revels now are ended. These our actors,
As I foretold you, were all spirits and
Are melted into air, into thin air:
And, like the baseless fabric of this vision,
The cloud-capped towers, the gorgeous palaces,
The solemn temples, the great globe itself,
Yea, all which it inherit, shall dissolve
And, like this insubstantial pageant faded,
Leave not a rack behind. We are such stuff
As dreams are made on, and our little life
Is rounded with a sleep.
The Tempest (1611) act 4, sc. 1, l. 148

32 I do begin to have bloody thoughts.
The Tempest (1611) act 4, sc. 1, l. [221]

33   To the dread rattling thunder
Have I given fire, and rifted Jove's stout oak

With his own bolt.
The Tempest (1611) act 5, sc. 1, l. 44

1   Graves at my command
Have waked their sleepers, oped, and let 'em
   forth
By my so potent art. But this rough magic
I here abjure.
The Tempest (1611) act 5, sc. 1, l. 48

2   I'll break my staff,
Bury it certain fathoms in the earth,
And, deeper than did ever plummet sound,
I'll drown my book.
The Tempest (1611) act 5, sc. 1, l. 54

3 Where the bee sucks, there suck I
In a cowslip's bell I lie;
There I couch when owls do cry.
On the bat's back I do fly
After summer merrily:
Merrily, merrily shall I live now
Under the blossom that hangs on the bough.
The Tempest (1611) act 5, sc. 1, l. 88

4 How beauteous mankind is! O brave new world,
That has such people in't.
The Tempest (1611) act 5, sc. 1, l. 183

TIMON OF ATHENS

5 'Tis not enough to help the feeble up,
But to support him after.
Timon of Athens (c.1607) act 1, sc. 1, l. 108

6 Men shut their doors against a setting sun.
Timon of Athens (c.1607) act 1, sc. 2, l. [152]

7 We have seen better days.
Timon of Athens (c.1607) act 4, sc. 2, l. 27

8   The moon's an arrant thief,
And her pale fire she snatches from the sun.
Timon of Athens (c.1607) act 4, sc. 3, l. 437

9 Timon hath made his everlasting mansion
Upon the beachèd verge of the salt flood;
Who once a day with his embossèd froth
The turbulent surge shall cover.
Timon of Athens (c.1607) act 5, sc. 1, l. [220]; some editions
prefer act 5, sc. 2

TITUS ANDRONICUS

10 She is a woman, therefore may be wooed;
She is a woman, therefore may be won;
She is Lavinia, therefore must be loved.
Titus Andronicus (1590) act 2, sc. 1, l. 82; see **SHAKESPEARE**
709:20

11 Come, and take choice of all my library,
And so beguile thy sorrow.
Titus Andronicus (1590) act 4, sc. 1, l. 34

12   Both bakèd in this pie
Whereof their mother daintily hath fed,
Eating the flesh that she herself hath bred.
Titus Andronicus (1590) act 5, sc. 3, l. 59

TROILUS AND CRESSIDA

13 Things won are done; joy's soul lies in the
   doing.
Troilus and Cressida (1602) act 1, sc. 2, l. [311]

14 Take but degree away, untune that string,
And, hark! what discord follows.
Troilus and Cressida (1602) act 1, sc. 3, l. 109

15 I am giddy, expectation whirls me round.
The imaginary relish is so sweet
That it enchants my sense.
Troilus and Cressida (1602) act 3, sc. 2, l. [17]

16   To be wise, and love,
Exceeds man's might.
Troilus and Cressida (1602) act 3, sc. 2, l. [163]

17 Time hath, my lord, a wallet at his back,
Wherein he puts alms for oblivion,
A great-sized monster of ingratitudes:
Those scraps are good deeds past; which are
   devoured
As fast as they are made, forgot as soon
As done.
Troilus and Cressida (1602) act 3, sc. 3, l. 145

18   Perseverance, dear my lord,
Keeps honour bright.
Troilus and Cressida (1602) act 3, sc. 3, l. 150

19 One touch of nature makes the whole world
   kin.
Troilus and Cressida (1602) act 3, sc. 3, l. 175

20   Fie, fie upon her!
There's language in her eye, her cheek, her lip,
Nay, her foot speaks; her wanton spirits look out
At every joint and motive of her body.
Troilus and Cressida (1602) act 4, sc. 5, l. 54; some editions
prefer act 4, sc. 6

21   The end crowns all,
And that old common arbitrator, Time,
Will one day end it.
Troilus and Cressida (1602) act 4, sc. 5, l. 223; some editions
prefer act 4, sc. 7

22 Lechery, lechery; still, wars and lechery: nothing
else holds fashion.
Troilus and Cressida (1602) act 5, sc. 2, l. 192

23 Words, words, mere words, no matter from the
   heart.
Troilus and Cressida (1602) act 5, sc. 3, l. [109]

24 Hector is dead; there is no more to say.
Troilus and Cressida (1602) act 5, sc. 10, l. 22; some editions
prefer act 5, sc. 11

TWELFTH NIGHT

25 If music be the food of love, play on.
Twelfth Night (1601) act 1, sc. 1, l. 1

26 That strain again! it had a dying fall.
Twelfth Night (1601) act 1, sc. 1, l. 4

27   Enough! no more:
'Tis not so sweet now as it was before.
Twelfth Night (1601) act 1, sc. 1, l. 7

28 O! when mine eyes did see Olivia first,
Methought she purged the air of pestilence.
Twelfth Night (1601) act 1, sc. 1, l. 19

29 And what should I do in Illyria?
My brother he is in Elysium.
Twelfth Night (1601) act 1, sc. 2, l. 2

1 I am a great eater of beef, and I believe that does harm to my wit.
Twelfth Night (1601) act 1, sc. 3, l. [92]

2 I would I had bestowed that time in the tongues that I have in fencing, dancing, and bear-baiting. O! had I but followed the arts!
Twelfth Night (1601) act 1, sc. 3, l. [99]

3 Many a good hanging prevents a bad marriage.
Twelfth Night (1601) act 1, sc. 5, l. [20]

4 A plague o' these pickle herring!
Twelfth Night (1601) act 1, sc. 5, l. [127]

5 He is very well-favoured, and he speaks very shrewishly: one would think his mother's milk were scarce out of him.
Twelfth Night (1601) act 1, sc. 5, l. [170]

6 Make me a willow cabin at your gate,
And call upon my soul within the house;
Write loyal cantons of contemnèd love,
And sing them loud even in the dead of night;
Halloo your name to the reverberate hills,
And make the babbling gossip of the air
Cry out, 'Olivia!'
Twelfth Night (1601) act 1, sc. 5, l. [289]

7 Not to be a-bed after midnight is to be up betimes.
Twelfth Night (1601) act 2, sc. 3, l. 1

8 O mistress mine! where are you roaming?
O! stay and hear; your true love's coming,
That can sing both high and low.
Trip no further, pretty sweeting;
Journeys end in lovers meeting,
Every wise man's son doth know.
Twelfth Night (1601) act 2, sc. 3, l. [42]

9 What is love? 'tis not hereafter;
Present mirth hath present laughter;
What's to come is still unsure:
In delay there lies no plenty;
Then come kiss me, sweet and twenty,
Youth's a stuff will not endure.
Twelfth Night (1601) act 2, sc. 3, l. [50]

10 Am not I consanguineous? am I not of her blood?
Twelfth Night (1601) act 2, sc. 3, l. [85]

11 He does it with a better grace, but I do it more natural.
Twelfth Night (1601) act 2, sc. 3, l. [91]

12 Dost thou think, because thou art virtuous, there shall be no more cakes and ale?
Twelfth Night (1601) act 2, sc. 3, l. [124]

13 My purpose is, indeed, a horse of that colour.
Twelfth Night (1601) act 2, sc. 3, l. [184]

14 I was adored once too.
Twelfth Night (1601) act 2, sc. 3, l. [200]

15 Now, good Cesario, but that piece of song,
That old and antique song we heard last night.
Twelfth Night (1601) act 2, sc. 4, l. 2; some editions prefer 'antic song'

16 Let still the woman take
An elder than herself, so wears she to him,
So sways she level in her husband's heart.
Twelfth Night (1601) act 2, sc. 4, l. 29

17 The spinsters and the knitters in the sun.
Twelfth Night (1601) act 2, sc. 4, l. 44

18 Come away, come away, death,
And in sad cypress let me be laid;
Fly away, fly away, breath:
I am slain by a fair cruel maid.
Twelfth Night (1601) act 2, sc. 4, l. 51; some editions prefer 'Fie away'

19 Now, the melancholy god protect thee, and the tailor make thy doublet of changeable taffeta, for thy mind is a very opal.
Twelfth Night (1601) act 2, sc. 4, l. [74]

20 My father had a daughter loved a man,
As it might be, perhaps, were I a woman,
I should your lordship.
Twelfth Night (1601) act 2, sc. 4, l. [108]

21 DUKE: And what's her history?
VIOLA: A blank, my lord. She never told her love,
But let concealment, like a worm i' the bud,
Feed on her damask cheek: she pined in thought;
And with a green and yellow melancholy,
She sat like patience on a monument,
Smiling at grief. Was not this love indeed?
Twelfth Night (1601) act 2, sc. 4, l. [111]

22 I am all the daughters of my father's house,
And all the brothers too.
Twelfth Night (1601) act 2, sc. 4, l. [122]

23 Now is the woodcock near the gin.
Twelfth Night (1601) act 2, sc. 5, l. [93]

24 But be not afraid of greatness: some men are born great, some achieve greatness, and some have greatness thrust upon them.
Twelfth Night (1601) act 2, sc. 5, l. [158]; see **HELLER** 390:4

25 Remember who commended thy yellow stockings, and wished to see thee ever cross-gartered.
Twelfth Night (1601) act 2, sc. 5, l. [168]

26 Jove and my stars be praised! Here is yet a postscript.
Twelfth Night (1601) act 2, sc. 5, l. [190]

27 O! what a deal of scorn looks beautiful
In the contempt and anger of his lip.
Twelfth Night (1601) act 3, sc. 1, l. [159]

28 Love sought is good, but giv'n unsought is better.
Twelfth Night (1601) act 3, sc. 1, l. [170]

29 You are now sailed into the north of my lady's opinion; where you will hang like an icicle on a Dutchman's beard.
Twelfth Night (1601) act 3, sc. 2, l. [29]

30 As many lies as will lie in thy sheet of paper, although the sheet were big enough for the bed of Ware in England, set 'em down.
Twelfth Night (1601) act 3, sc. 2, l. [51]

31 Look, where the youngest wren of nine comes.
Twelfth Night (1601) act 3, sc. 2, l. [73]

1 He does smile his face into more lines than are in the new map with the augmentation of the Indies.
Twelfth Night (1601) act 3, sc. 2, l. [85]

2 In the south suburbs, at the Elephant, Is best to lodge.
Twelfth Night (1601) act 3, sc. 3, l. 39

3 I think we do know the sweet Roman hand.
Twelfth Night (1601) act 3, sc. 4, l. [31]

4 Why, this is very midsummer madness.
Twelfth Night (1601) act 3, sc. 4, l. [62]

5 If this were played upon a stage now, I could condemn it as an improbable fiction.
Twelfth Night (1601) act 3, sc. 4, l. [142]

6 More matter for a May morning.
Twelfth Night (1601) act 3, sc. 4, l. [158]

7 Still you keep o' the windy side of the law.
Twelfth Night (1601) act 3, sc. 4, l. [183]

8 In nature there's no blemish but the mind; None can be called deformed but the unkind.
Twelfth Night (1601) act 3, sc. 4, l. [403]

9 Thus the whirligig of time brings in his revenges.
Twelfth Night (1601) act 5, sc. 1, l. [388]

10 I'll be revenged on the whole pack of you.
Twelfth Night (1601) act 5, sc. 1, l. [390]

11 When that I was and a little tiny boy, With hey, ho, the wind and the rain; A foolish thing was but a toy, For the rain it raineth every day.
Twelfth Night (1601) act 5, sc. 1, l. [401]

THE TWO GENTLEMEN OF VERONA

12 I have no other but a woman's reason: I think him so, because I think him so.
The Two Gentlemen of Verona (1592–3) act 1, sc. 2, l. 23

13 Fie, fie! how wayward is this foolish love That, like a testy babe, will scratch the nurse And presently all humbled kiss the rod!
The Two Gentlemen of Verona (1592–3) act 1, sc. 2, l. 55

14 O! how this spring of love resembleth The uncertain glory of an April day.
The Two Gentlemen of Verona (1592–3) act 1, sc. 3, l. 84

15 Who is Silvia? what is she, That all our swains commend her? Holy, fair, and wise is she; The heaven such grace did lend her.
The Two Gentlemen of Verona (1592–3) act 4, sc. 2, l. 40

16 Is she kind as she is fair? For beauty lives with kindness.
The Two Gentlemen of Verona (1592–3) act 4, sc. 2, l. 45

THE WINTER'S TALE

17 Two lads that thought there was no more behind But such a day to-morrow as to-day, And to be boy eternal.
The Winter's Tale (1610–11) act 1, sc. 2, l. 63

18 But to be paddling palms and pinching fingers, As now they are, and making practised smiles, As in a looking-glass.
The Winter's Tale (1610–11) act 1, sc. 2, l. 116

19 A sad tale's best for winter. I have one of sprites and goblins.
The Winter's Tale (1610–11) act 2, sc. 1, l. 24

20 There may be in the cup A spider steeped, and one may drink, depart, And yet partake no venom, for his knowledge Is not infected; but if one present Th' abhorred ingredient to his eye, make known How he hath drunk, he cracks his gorge, his sides, With violent hefts. I have drunk, and seen the spider.
The Winter's Tale (1610–11) act 2, sc. 1, l. 39

21 It is a heretic that makes the fire, Not she which burns in 't.
The Winter's Tale (1610–11) act 2, sc. 3, l. 114

22 I am a feather for each wind that blows.
The Winter's Tale (1610–11) act 2, sc. 3, l. 153

23 What's gone and what's past help Should be past grief.
The Winter's Tale (1610–11) act 3, sc. 2, l. [223]

24 Exit, pursued by a bear.
stage direction
The Winter's Tale (1610–11) act 3, sc. 3

25 When daffodils begin to peer, With heigh! the doxy, over the dale, Why, then comes in the sweet o' the year.
The Winter's Tale (1610–11) act 4, sc. 2, l. 1; some editions prefer act 4, sc. 3

26 While we lie tumbling in the hay.
The Winter's Tale (1610–11) act 4, sc. 2, l. 12; some editions prefer act 4, sc. 3

27 My father named me Autolycus; who being, as I am, littered under Mercury, was likewise a snapper-up of unconsidered trifles.
The Winter's Tale (1610–11) act 4, sc. 2, l. [24]; some editions prefer act 4, sc. 3

28 Jog on, jog on the foot-path way, And merrily hent the stile-a: A merry heart goes all the day, Your sad tires in a mile-a.
The Winter's Tale (1610–11) act 4, sc. 2, l. [133]; some editions prefer act 4, sc. 3

29 For you there's rosemary and rue; these keep Seeming and savour all the winter long.
The Winter's Tale (1610–11) act 4, sc. 3, l. 74; some editions prefer act 4, sc. 4

30 The fairest flowers o' the season Are our carnations and streaked gillyvors, Which some call nature's bastards.
The Winter's Tale (1610–11) act 4, sc. 3, l. 81; some editions prefer act 4, sc. 4

31 Here's flowers for you; Hot lavender, mints, savory, marjoram; The marigold, that goes to bed wi' the sun, And with him rises weeping.
The Winter's Tale (1610–11) act 4, sc. 3, l. 103; some editions prefer act 4, sc. 4

1　　　　　O Proserpina!
For the flowers now that frighted thou let'st fall
From Dis's waggon! daffodils,
That come before the swallow dares, and take
The winds of March with beauty.
The Winter's Tale (1610–11) act 4, sc. 3, l. 118; some editions
prefer act 4, sc. 4

2　　　　　Pale prime-roses,
That die unmarried, ere they can behold
Bright Phoebus in his strength,—a malady
Most incident to maids; bold oxlips and
The crown imperial; lilies of all kinds,
The flower-de-luce being one.
The Winter's Tale (1610–11) act 4, sc. 3, l. 122; some editions
prefer act 4, sc. 4

3　　　　　Each your doing,
So singular in each particular,
Crowns what you are doing in the present deed,
That all your acts are queens.
The Winter's Tale (1610–11) act 4, sc. 3, l. 144; some editions
prefer act 4, sc. 4

4 The queen of curds and cream.
The Winter's Tale (1610–11) act 4, sc. 3, l. 161; some editions
prefer act 4, sc. 4

5 I love a ballad in print, a-life, for then we are
sure they are true.
The Winter's Tale (1610–11) act 4, sc. 3, l. [262]

6 Being now awake, I'll queen it no inch further,
But milk my ewes and weep.
The Winter's Tale (1610–11) act 4, sc. 3, l. [463]; some editions
prefer act 4, sc. 4

7 Though I am not naturally honest, I am so
sometimes by chance.
The Winter's Tale (1610–11) act 4, sc. 3, l. [734]; some editions
prefer act 4, sc. 4

8　　　　　Stars, stars!
And all eyes else dead coals.
The Winter's Tale (1610–11) act 5, sc. 1, l. 67

9　　　　　O! she's warm.
If this be magic, let it be an art
Lawful as eating.
The Winter's Tale (1610–11) act 5, sc. 3, l. 109

THE PASSIONATE PILGRIM (ATTRIBUTION DOUBTFUL)

10 Crabbed age and youth cannot live together:
Youth is full of pleasance, age is full of care.
The Passionate Pilgrim (1599) no. 12

11 Age, I do abhor thee, youth, I do adore thee.
The Passionate Pilgrim (1599) no. 12

THE RAPE OF LUCRECE

12 Beauty itself doth of itself persuade
The eyes of men without an orator.
The Rape of Lucrece (1594) l. 29

13 Time's glory is to calm contending kings,
To unmask falsehood, and bring truth to light.
The Rape of Lucrece (1594) l. 939

SONNETS

14 To the onlie begetter of these insuing sonnets,
Mr. W. H.
also attributed to Thomas Thorpe, the publisher
Sonnets (1609) dedication

15 From fairest creatures we desire increase,
That thereby beauty's rose might never die.
Sonnet 1

16 When forty winters shall besiege thy brow,
And dig deep trenches in thy beauty's field.
Sonnet 2

17 Thou art thy mother's glass, and she in thee
Calls back the lovely April of her prime.
Sonnet 3

18 Shall I compare thee to a summer's day?
Thou art more lovely and more temperate:
Rough winds do shake the darling buds of May,
And summer's lease hath all too short a date.
Sonnet 18

19 But thy eternal summer shall not fade,
Nor lose possession of that fair thou ow'st,
Nor shall death brag thou wander'st in his
shade,
When in eternal lines to time thou grow'st;
So long as men can breathe, or eyes can see,
So long lives this, and this gives life to thee.
Sonnet 18

20 As an unperfect actor on the stage,
Who with his fear is put beside his part,
Or some fierce thing replete with too much
rage,
Whose strength's abundance weakens his own
heart.
Sonnet 23

21 When in disgrace with fortune and men's eyes
I all alone beweep my outcast state.
Sonnet 29

22 Desiring this man's art, and that man's scope,
With what I most enjoy contented least.
Sonnet 29

23 Haply I think on thee,—and then my state,
Like to the lark at break of day arising
From sullen earth, sings hymns at heaven's gate.
Sonnet 29

24 When to the sessions of sweet silent thought
I summon up remembrance of things past.
Sonnet 30; see **PROUST** 625:4

25 Full many a glorious morning have I seen
Flatter the mountain-tops with sovereign eye,
Kissing with golden face the meadows green,
Gilding pale streams with heavenly alchemy.
Sonnet 33

26 Roses have thorns, and silver fountains mud;
Clouds and eclipses stain both moon and sun,
And loathsome canker lives in sweetest bud.
Sonnet 35

27 What is your substance, whereof are you made,
That millions of strange shadows on you tend?
Sonnet 53

28 Not marble, nor the gilded monuments
Of princes, shall outlive this powerful rhyme.
Sonnet 55

29 Like as the waves make towards the pebbled
shore,

So do our minutes hasten to their end.
Sonnet 60

1 When I have seen the hungry ocean gain
Advantage on the kingdom of the shore.
Sonnet 64

2 Since brass, nor stone, nor earth, nor boundless
sea,
But sad mortality o'ersways their power,
How with this rage shall beauty hold a plea,
Whose action is no stronger than a flower?
Sonnet 65

3 No longer mourn for me when I am dead
Than you shall hear the surly sullen bell
Give warning to the world that I am fled
From this vile world, with vilest worms to
dwell.
Sonnet 71

4 Bare ruined choirs, where late the sweet birds
sang.
Sonnet 73

5 So all my best is dressing old words new,
Spending again what is already spent.
Sonnet 76

6 Time's thievish progress to eternity.
Sonnet 77

7 Farewell! thou art too dear for my possessing.
Sonnet 87

8 Thus have I had thee, as a dream doth flatter,
In sleep a king, but, waking, no such matter.
Sonnet 87

9 For sweetest things turn sourest by their deeds;
Lilies that fester smell far worse than weeds.
Sonnet 94

10 When in the chronicle of wasted time
I see descriptions of the fairest wights,
And beauty making beautiful old rime,
In praise of ladies dead and lovely knights.
Sonnet 106

11 For we, which now behold these present days,
Have eyes to wonder, but lack tongues to praise.
Sonnet 106

12 Not mine own fears, nor the prophetic soul
Of the wide world dreaming on things to come.
Sonnet 107

13 Alas! 'tis true I have gone here and there,
And made myself a motley to the view.
Sonnet 110

14   My nature is subdued
To what it works in, like the dyer's hand.
Sonnet 111

15 Let me not to the marriage of true minds
Admit impediments. Love is not love
Which alters when it alteration finds,
Or bends with the remover to remove:
O, no! it is an ever-fixèd mark,
That looks on tempests and is never shaken.
Sonnet 116

16 Love's not Time's fool.
Sonnet 116

17 Love alters not with his brief hours and weeks,
But bears it out even to the edge of doom.
If this be error, and upon me proved,
I never writ, nor no man ever loved.
Sonnet 116

18 The expense of spirit in a waste of shame
Is lust in action; and till action, lust
Is perjured, murderous, bloody, full of blame,
Savage, extreme, rude, cruel, not to trust;
Enjoyed no sooner but despisèd straight.
Sonnet 129

19 My mistress' eyes are nothing like the sun;
Coral is far more red than her lips' red:
If snow be white, why then her breasts are dun;
If hairs be wires, black wires grow on her head.
Sonnet 130

20 And yet, by heaven, I think my love as rare
As any she belied with false compare.
Sonnet 130

21 Whoever hath her wish, thou hast thy *Will*,
And *Will* to boot, and *Will* in over-plus.
Sonnet 135

22 When my love swears that she is made of truth,
I do believe her, though I know she lies.
Sonnet 138

23 Two loves I have of comfort and despair,
Which like two spirits do suggest me still:
The better angel is a man right fair,
The worser spirit a woman, coloured ill.
Sonnet 144

24 So shalt thou feed on Death, that feeds on men,
And Death once dead, there's no more dying
then.
Sonnet 146

25 For I have sworn thee fair, and thought thee
bright,
Who art as black as hell, as dark as night.
Sonnet 147

VENUS AND ADONIS

26 If the first heir of my invention prove deformed,
I shall be sorry it had so noble a godfather.
Venus and Adonis (1593) dedication

27 Love is a spirit all compact of fire,
Not gross to sink, but light, and will aspire.
Venus and Adonis (1593) l. 145

28 Love comforteth like sunshine after rain.
Venus and Adonis (1593) l. 799

29 Item, I give unto my wife my second best bed,
with the furniture.
will, 1616; E. K. Chambers *William Shakespeare* (1930) vol. 2

Shammai *c.*1st century BC–*c.*AD 1st century
Jewish scholar and teacher

30 Say little and do much. Receive all men with a
cheerful countenance.
in *Talmud* Mishnah 'Pirqei Avot' 1:15

Bill Shankly 1913–81

Scottish footballer and football manager

1 Some people think football is a matter of life and death . . . I can assure them it is much more serious than that.

in *Guardian* 24 December 1973

Shantideva c.685–763

Indian scholar, monk, and poet

2 May I allay all the suffering of every living being.
I am the medicine for the sick. May I be both the doctor and their nurse, until the sickness does not recur.

Bodhicaryāvatāra ch. 3, v. 6

3 Whoever longs to rescue quickly both himself and others should practise the supreme mystery: exchange of self and other.

Bodhicaryāvatāra ch. 8, v. 120

4 All those who suffer in the world do so because of their desire for their own happiness. All those happy in the world are so because of their desire for the happiness of others.

Bodhicaryāvatāra ch. 8, v. 129

5 Whatever suffering is in store for the world, may it all ripen in me. May the world find happiness through all the pure deeds of the Bodhisattvas.

Bodhicaryāvatāra ch. 10, v. 56

Ariel Sharon 1928–

Israeli Likud statesman, Prime Minister 2001–6

6 I'm not going to make any compromise whatsoever.

on relations with the Palestinians
in *Sunday Times* 12 August 2001

George Bernard Shaw 1856–1950

Irish dramatist. On Shaw: see AGATE 9:7, LENIN 488:20, WILDE 856:12; see also MISQUOTATIONS 547:12

7 All great truths begin as blasphemies.

Annajanska (1919)

8 One man that has a mind and knows it can always beat ten men who haven't and don't.

The Apple Cart (1930) act 1

9 You can always tell an old soldier by the inside of his holsters and cartridge boxes. The young ones carry pistols and cartridges; the old ones, grub.

Arms and the Man (1898) act 1

10 Oh, you are a very poor soldier—a chocolate cream soldier!

Arms and the Man (1898) act 1

11 You see things; and you say 'Why?' But I dream things that never were; and I say 'Why not?'

Back to Methuselah (1921) pt. 1, act 1

12 I enjoy convalescence. It is the part that makes illness worth while.

Back to Methuselah (1921) pt. 2

13 Life is not meant to be easy, my child; but take courage: it can be delightful.

Back to Methuselah (rev. ed., 1930); see also **FRASER** 341:18

14 He [the Briton] is a barbarian, and thinks that the customs of his tribe and island are the laws of nature.

Caesar and Cleopatra (1901) act 2

15 When a stupid man is doing something he is ashamed of, he always declares that it is his duty.

Caesar and Cleopatra (1901) act 3

16 We have no more right to consume happiness without producing it than to consume wealth without producing it.

Candida (1898) act 1

17 It is easy—terribly easy— to shake a man's faith in himself. To take advantage of that to break a man's spirit is devil's work.

Candida (1898) act 1

18 I'm only a beer teetotaller, not a champagne teetotaller.

Candida (1898) act 3

19 The worst sin towards our fellow creatures is not to hate them, but to be indifferent to them: that's the essence of inhumanity.

The Devil's Disciple (1901) act 2

20 Martyrdom . . . the only way in which a man can become famous without ability.

The Devil's Disciple (1901) act 3

21 SWINDON: What will history say?
BURGOYNE: History, sir, will tell lies as usual.

The Devil's Disciple (1901) act 3

22 The British soldier can stand up to anything except the British War Office.

The Devil's Disciple (1901) act 3

23 There is at bottom only one genuinely scientific treatment for all diseases, and that is to stimulate the phagocytes.

The Doctor's Dilemma (1911) act 1

24 All professions are conspiracies against the laity.

The Doctor's Dilemma (1911) act 1

25 A government which robs Peter to pay Paul can always depend on the support of Paul.

Everybody's Political What's What? (1944) ch. 30

26 It's all that the young can do for the old, to shock them and keep them up to date.

Fanny's First Play (1914) 'Induction'

27 Home life as we understand it is no more natural to us than a cage is natural to a cockatoo.

Getting Married (1911) preface 'Hearth and Home'

28 The one point on which all women are in furious secret rebellion against the existing law is the saddling of the right to a child with the obligation to become the servant of a man.

Getting Married (1911) preface 'The Right to Motherhood'

29 Physically there is nothing to distinguish human society from the farm-yard except that children

are more troublesome and costly than chickens and calves, and that men and women are not so completely enslaved as farm stock.

Getting Married (1911) preface 'The Personal Sentimental Basis of Monogamy'

1 What God hath joined together no man ever shall put asunder: God will take care of that.

Getting Married (1911) p. 216; see BOOK OF COMMON PRAYER 139:3

2 I am a woman of the world, Hector; and I can assure you that if you will only take the trouble always to do the perfectly correct thing, and to say the perfectly correct thing, you can do just what you like.

Heartbreak House (1919) act 1

3 Go anywhere in England where there are natural, wholesome, contented, and really nice English people; and what do you always find? That the stables are the real centre of the household.

Heartbreak House (1919) act 3

4 The captain is in his bunk, drinking bottled ditch-water; and the crew is gambling in the forecastle. She will strike and sink and split. Do you think the laws of God will be suspended in favour of England because you were born in it?

Heartbreak House (1919) act 3

5 You have to choose (as a voter) between trusting to the natural stability of gold and the natural stability of the honesty and intelligence of the members of the Government. And, with due respect for these gentlemen, I advise you, as long as the Capitalist system lasts, to vote for gold.

The Intelligent Woman's Guide to Socialism and Capitalism (1928) ch. 55

6 Money is indeed the most important thing in the world; and all sound and successful personal and national morality should have this fact for its basis.

The Irrational Knot (1905) preface

7 A man who has no office to go to—I don't care who he is—is a trial of which you can have no conception.

The Irrational Knot (1905) ch. 18

8 John Bull's other island.

title of play (1907)

9 An Irishman's heart is nothing but his imagination.

John Bull's Other Island (1907) act 1

10 What really flatters a man is that you think him worth flattering.

John Bull's Other Island (1907) act 4

11 There are only two qualities in the world: efficiency and inefficiency, and only two sorts of people: the efficient and the inefficient.

John Bull's Other Island (1907) act 4

12 The greatest of evils and the worst of crimes is poverty . . . our first duty—a duty to which

every other consideration should be sacrificed—is not to be poor.

Major Barbara (1907) preface

13 Nobody can say a word against Greek: it stamps a man at once as an educated gentleman.

Major Barbara (1907) act 1

14 I am a Millionaire. That is my religion.

Major Barbara (1907) act 2

15 I can't talk religion to a man with bodily hunger in his eyes.

Major Barbara (1907) act 2

16 Wot prawce Selvytion nah?

Major Barbara (1907) act 2

17 Alcohol is a very necessary article . . . It enables Parliament to do things at eleven at night that no sane person would do at eleven in the morning.

Major Barbara (1907) act 2

18 He knows nothing; and he thinks he knows everything. That points clearly to a political career.

Major Barbara (1907) act 3

19 Nothing is ever done in this world until men are prepared to kill one another if it is not done.

Major Barbara (1907) act 3

20 Like all young men, you greatly exaggerate the difference between one young woman and another.

Major Barbara (1907) act 3; see MENCKEN 531:18

21 But a lifetime of happiness! No man alive could bear it: it would be hell on earth.

Man and Superman (1903) act 1

22 The more things a man is ashamed of, the more respectable he is.

Man and Superman (1903) act 1

23 Vitality in a woman is a blind fury of creation.

Man and Superman (1903) act 1

24 Of all human struggles there is none so treacherous and remorseless as the struggle between the artist man and the mother woman.

Man and Superman (1903) act 1

25 You think that you are Ann's suitor; that you are the pursuer and she the pursued . . . Fool: it is you who are the pursued, the marked down quarry, the destined prey.

Man and Superman (1903) act 2

26 MENDOZA: I am a brigand: I live by robbing the rich.

TANNER: I am a gentleman: I live by robbing the poor.

Man and Superman (1903) act 3

27 Hell is full of musical amateurs: music is the brandy of the damned.

Man and Superman (1903) act 3

28 Englishmen never will be slaves: they are free to do whatever the Government and public opinion allow them to do.

Man and Superman (1903) act 3

1 An Englishman thinks he is moral when he is only uncomfortable.
   Man and Superman (1903) act 3

2 In the arts of life man invents nothing; but in the arts of death he outdoes Nature herself, and produces by chemistry and machinery all the slaughter of plague, pestilence and famine.
   Man and Superman (1903) act 3

3 In the arts of peace Man is a bungler.
   Man and Superman (1903) act 3

4 As an old soldier I admit the cowardice: it's as universal as sea sickness, and matters just as little.
   Man and Superman (1903) act 3

5 When the military man approaches, the world locks up its spoons and packs off its womankind.
   Man and Superman (1903) act 3; see **EMERSON** 314:21

6 What is virtue but the Trade Unionism of the married?
   Man and Superman (1903) act 3

7 Those who talk most about the blessings of marriage and the constancy of its vows are the very people who declare that if the chain were broken and the prisoners were left free to choose, the whole social fabric would fly asunder. You can't have the argument both ways. If the prisoner is happy, why lock him in? If he is not, why pretend that he is?
   Man and Superman (1903) act 3

8 Beauty is all very well at first sight; but who ever looks at it when it has been in the house three days?
   Man and Superman (1903) act 4

9 Revolutions have never lightened the burden of tyranny: they have only shifted it to another shoulder.
   Man and Superman (1903) 'The Revolutionist's Handbook' foreword

10 The art of government is the organization of idolatry.
   Man and Superman (1903) 'Maxims: Idolatry'

11 Democracy substitutes election by the incompetent many for appointment by the corrupt few.
   Man and Superman (1903) 'Maxims: Democracy'

12 Liberty means responsibility. That is why most men dread it.
   Man and Superman (1903) 'Maxims: Liberty and Equality'

13 He who can, does. He who cannot, teaches.
   Man and Superman (1903) 'Maxims: Education'

14 Marriage is popular because it combines the maximum of temptation with the maximum of opportunity.
   Man and Superman (1903) 'Maxims: Marriage'

15 Titles distinguish the mediocre, embarrass the superior, and are disgraced by the inferior.
   Man and Superman (1903) 'Maxims: Titles'

16 If you strike a child take care that you strike it in anger, even at the risk of maiming it for life. A blow in cold blood neither can nor should be forgiven.
   Man and Superman (1903) 'Maxims: How to Beat Children'

17 Beware of the man whose god is in the skies.
   Man and Superman (1903) 'Maxims: Religion'

18 Self-denial is not a virtue: it is only the effect of prudence on rascality.
   Man and Superman (1903) 'Maxims: Virtues and Vice'

19 The reasonable man adapts himself to the world: the unreasonable one persists in trying to adapt the world to himself. Therefore all progress depends on the unreasonable man.
   Man and Superman (1903) 'Maxims: Reason'

20 The man who listens to Reason is lost: Reason enslaves all whose minds are not strong enough to master her.
   Man and Superman (1903) 'Maxims: Reason'

21 Decency is Indecency's conspiracy of silence.
   Man and Superman (1903) 'Maxims: Decency'

22 Life levels all men: death reveals the eminent.
   Man and Superman (1903) 'Maxims: Fame'

23 Home is the girl's prison and the woman's workhouse.
   Man and Superman (1903) 'Maxims: Women in the Home'

24 Every man over forty is a scoundrel.
   Man and Superman (1903) 'Maxims: Stray Sayings'

25 Youth, which is forgiven everything, forgives itself nothing: age, which forgives itself everything, is forgiven nothing.
   Man and Superman (1903) 'Maxims: Stray Sayings'

26 Take care to get what you like or you will be forced to like what you get.
   Man and Superman (1903) 'Maxims: Stray Sayings'

27 Beware of the man who does not return your blow: he neither forgives you nor allows you to forgive yourself.
   Man and Superman (1903) 'Maxims: Stray Sayings'

28 Self-sacrifice enables us to sacrifice other people without blushing.
   Man and Superman (1903) 'Maxims: Self-Sacrifice'

29 There is nothing so bad or so good that you will not find Englishmen doing it; but you will never find an Englishman in the wrong. He does everything on principle. He fights you on patriotic principles; he robs you on business principles; he enslaves you on imperial principles; he bullies you on manly principles; he supports his king on loyal principles and cuts off his king's head on republican principles.
   The Man of Destiny (1898)

30 Anarchism is a game at which the police can beat you.
   Misalliance (1914)

31 The only way for a woman to provide for herself decently is for her to be good to some man that can afford to be good to her.
   Mrs Warren's Profession (1898) act 2

1 A great devotee of the Gospel of Getting On.
Mrs Warren's Profession (1898) act 4

2 You'll never have a quiet world till you knock the patriotism out of the human race.
O'Flaherty V.C. (1919)

3 The secret of being miserable is to have leisure to bother about whether you are happy or not. The cure for it is occupation.
Parents and Children (1914) 'Children's Happiness'

4 A perpetual holiday is a good working definition of hell.
Parents and Children (1914) 'Children's Happiness'

5 There is only one religion, though there are a hundred versions of it.
Plays Pleasant and Unpleasant (1898) vol. 2, preface

6 It is impossible for an Englishman to open his mouth without making some other Englishman hate or despise him.
Pygmalion (1916) preface

7 I don't want to talk grammar, I want to talk like a lady.
Pygmalion (1916) act 2

8 PICKERING: Have you no morals, man?
DOOLITTLE: Can't afford them, Governor.
Pygmalion (1916) act 2

9 I'm one of the undeserving poor . . . up agen middle-class morality all the time . . . What is middle-class morality? Just an excuse for never giving me anything.
Pygmalion (1916) act 2

10 Gin was mother's milk to her.
Pygmalion (1916) act 3

11 Walk! Not bloody likely.
Pygmalion (1916) act 3

12 No Englishman is ever fairly beaten.
Saint Joan (1924) sc. 4

13 How can what an Englishman believes be heresy? It is a contradiction in terms.
Saint Joan (1924) sc. 4

14 Must then a Christ perish in torment in every age to save those that have no imagination?
Saint Joan (1924) epilogue

15 Assassination is the extreme form of censorship.
The Showing-Up of Blanco Posnet (1911) 'Limits to Toleration'

16 'Do you know what a pessimist is?' 'A man who thinks everybody is as nasty as himself, and hates them for it.'
An Unsocial Socialist (1887) ch. 5

17 You never can tell.
title of play (1898)

18 The great advantage of a hotel is that it's a refuge from home life.
You Never Can Tell (1898) act 2

19 The younger generation is knocking at the door, and as I open it there steps spritely in the incomparable Max.
on handing over the theatre review column to Max
BEERBOHM
in *Saturday Review* 21 May 1898 'Valedictory'

20 The photographer is like the cod which produces a million eggs in order that one may reach maturity.
introduction to the catalogue for Alvin Langdon Coburn's exhibition at the Royal Photographic Society, 1906; Bill Jay and Margaret Moore Bernard Shaw and Photography (1989)

21 You always hide just in the middle of the limelight.
to T. E. Lawrence, who had complained of Press attention; see **BERNERS** 74:9
Charles Kessler *The Diaries of a Cosmopolitan 1918–1937* (1971) 14 November 1929

22 The trouble, Mr Goldwyn, is that you are only interested in art and I am only interested in money.
telegraphed version of the outcome of a conversation between Shaw and Sam **GOLDWYN**
Alva Johnson *The Great Goldwyn* (1937) ch. 3

23 [Dancing is] a perpendicular expression of a horizontal desire.
in *New Statesman* 23 March 1962

Hartley Shawcross 1902–2003
British Labour politician

24 'But,' said Alice, 'the question is whether you can make a word mean different things.' 'Not so,' said Humpty-Dumpty, 'the question is which is to be the master. That's all.' We are the masters at the moment, and not only at the moment, but for a very long time to come.
speech in the House of Commons, 2 April 1946; see **CARROLL** 203:12, **MISQUOTATIONS** 548:23

Charles Shaw-Lefevre, Lord Eversley 1794–1888
British Whig politician

25 What is that fat gentleman in such a passion about?
as a child, on hearing Charles James **FOX** *speak in Parliament*
G. W. E. Russell *Collections and Recollections* (1898) ch. 11

Patrick Shaw-Stewart 1888–1917
British soldier and poet

26 I saw a man this morning
Who did not wish to die;
I ask and cannot answer
If otherwise wish I.
poem (1916); M. Baring *Have You Anything to Declare?* (1936)

27 Stand in the trench, Achilles,
Flame-capped, and shout for me.
poem (1916); M. Baring *Have You Anything to Declare?* (1936)

Lord Shelburne 1737–1805
British Whig politician; Prime Minister

28 The sun of Great Britain will set whenever she acknowledges the independence of America . . . the independence of America would end in the ruin of England.
in the House of Lords, October 1782

Mary Shelley (née Godwin) 1797–1851

English novelist; daughter of William **GODWIN** and Mary
WOLLSTONECRAFT, wife of Percy Bysshe **SHELLEY**

1 'We will each write a ghost story,' said Lord
Byron; and his proposition was acceded to.
There were four of us ... *Have you thought of a
story?* I was asked each morning, and each
morning I was forced to reply with a mortifying
negative ... On the morrow I announced that I
had *thought of a story* ... At first I thought but
of a few pages—of a short tale; but Shelley
urged me to develop the idea at greater length.
on beginning Frankenstein
   introduction to *Frankenstein* (ed. 3, 1831)

2 You seek for knowledge and wisdom as I once
did; and I ardently hope that the gratification of
your wishes may not be a serpent to sting you,
as mine has been.
   Frankenstein (1818) Letter 4

3 I beheld the wretch—the miserable monster
whom I had created.
   Frankenstein (1818) ch. 5

4 All men hate the wretched; how, then, must I be
hated, who am miserable beyond all living
things! Yet you, my creator, detest and spurn
me, thy creature, to whom thou art bound by
ties only dissoluble by the annihilation of one of
us.
   Frankenstein (1818) ch. 10

5 Everywhere I see bliss, from which I alone am
irrevocably excluded.
   Frankenstein (1818) ch. 10

6 Teach him to think for himself? Oh, my God,
teach him rather to think like other people!
   on her son's education
   Matthew Arnold *Essays in Criticism* Second Series (1888)
   'Shelley'

Percy Bysshe Shelley 1792–1822

English poet; husband of Mary **SHELLEY**. On Shelley: see
ARNOLD 31:22, **BROWNING** 166:18

7 The cemetery is an open space among the ruins,
covered in winter with violets and daisies. It
might make one in love with death, to think
that one should be buried in so sweet a place.
   Adonais (1821) preface

8 I weep for Adonais—he is dead!
O, weep for Adonais! though our tears
Thaw not the frost which binds so dear a head!
   Adonais (1821) st. 1; see **BION** 121:17

9   He died,
Who was the Sire of an immortal strain,
Blind, old and lonely.
   Adonais (1821) st. 4

10   The quick Dreams,
The passion-wingèd Ministers of thought.
   Adonais (1821) st. 9

11 She faded, like a cloud which had outwept its
rain.
   Adonais (1821) st. 10

12   Winter is come and gone,
But grief returns with the revolving year.
   Adonais (1821) st. 18

13 From the great morning of the world when first
God dawned on Chaos.
   Adonais (1821) st. 19

14 Alas! that all we loved of him should be,
But for our grief, as if it had not been,
And grief itself be mortal!
   Adonais (1821) st. 21

15 A pardlike Spirit, beautiful and swift—
A Love in desolation masked.
   Adonais (1821) st. 32

16 He wakes or sleeps with the enduring dead;
Thou canst not soar where he is sitting now—
Dust to the dust! but the pure spirit shall flow
Back to the burning fountain whence it came,
A portion of the Eternal.
   Adonais (1821) st. 38

17 He hath awakened from the dream of life.
   Adonais (1821) st. 39

18 He has out-soared the shadow of our night;
Envy and calumny and hate and pain,
And that unrest which men miscall delight,
Can touch him not and torture not again;
From the contagion of the world's slow stain
He is secure, and now can never mourn
A heart grown cold, a head grown grey in vain.
   Adonais (1821) st. 40

19 He lives, he wakes,—'tis Death is dead, not he.
   Adonais (1821) st. 41

20 He is a portion of the loveliness
Which once he made more lovely.
   Adonais (1821) st. 43

21 The One remains, the many change and pass;
Heaven's light forever shines, Earth's shadows
fly;
Life, like a dome of many-coloured glass,
Stains the white radiance of Eternity.
   Adonais (1821) st. 52

22 A widow bird sat mourning for her love
Upon a wintry bough.
   Charles the First (1822) sc. 5, l. 9

23 I bring fresh showers for the thirsting flowers.
   'The Cloud' (1819)

24 That orbèd maiden, with white fire laden,
Whom mortals call the Moon.
   'The Cloud' (1819)

25 I am the daughter of Earth and Water,
And the nursling of the Sky.
I pass through the pores of the ocean and
shores;
I change, but I cannot die.
   'The Cloud' (1819)

26 I silently laugh at my own cenotaph,
And out of the caverns of rain,

Like a child from the womb, like a ghost from
   the tomb,
I arise and unbuild it again.
   'The Cloud' (1819)

1 I never was attached to that great sect,
Whose doctrine is that each one should select
Out of the crowd a mistress or a friend,
And all the rest, though fair and wise, commend
To cold oblivion.
   'Epipsychidion' (1821) l. 149

2   The beaten road
Which those poor slaves with weary footsteps
   tread,
Who travel to their home among the dead
By the broad highway of the world, and so
With one chained friend, perhaps a jealous foe,
The dreariest and the longest journey go.
   'Epipsychidion' (1821) l. 154

3 Chameleons feed on light and air:
Poets' food is love and fame.
   'An Exhortation' (1820)

4 Let there be light! said Liberty,
And like sunrise from the sea,
Athens arose!
   Hellas (1822) l. 682

5 The world's great age begins anew,
The golden years return,
The earth doth like a snake renew
Her winter weeds outworn.
   Hellas (1822) l. 1060

6 O cease! must hate and death return?
Cease! must men kill and die?
   Hellas (1822) l. 1096

7 I pursued a maiden and clasped a reed.
Gods and men, we are all deluded thus!
It breaks in our bosom and then we bleed.
   'Hymn of Pan' (1824)

8 The awful shadow of some unseen Power
Floats though unseen among us,—visiting
This various world with as inconstant wing
As summer winds that creep from flower to
   flower.
   'Hymn to Intellectual Beauty' (1816)

9 The day becomes more solemn and serene
When noon is past—there is a harmony
In autumn, and a lustre in its sky,
Which through the summer is not heard or
   seen,
As if it could not be, as if it had not been!
   'Hymn to Intellectual Beauty' (1816)

10 Thou Paradise of exiles, Italy!
   'Julian and Maddalo' (1818) l. 57

11 *Me*—who am as a nerve o'er which do creep
The else unfelt oppressions of this earth.
   'Julian and Maddalo' (1818) l. 449

12   Most wretched men
Are cradled into poetry by wrong:
They learn in suffering what they teach in song.
   'Julian and Maddalo' (1818) l. 544

13 . . . London, that great sea, whose ebb and flow
At once is deaf and loud, and on the shore
Vomits its wrecks, and still howls on for more.
   'Letter to Maria Gisborne' (1820) l. 193

14 You will see Coleridge—he who sits obscure
In the exceeding lustre and the pure
Intense irradiation of a mind,
Which, with its own internal lightning blind,
Flags wearily through darkness and despair—
A cloud-encircled meteor of the air,
A hooded eagle among blinking owls.
   of Samuel Taylor **COLERIDGE**
   'Letter to Maria Gisborne' (1820) l. 202

15 You will see Hunt—one of those happy souls
Which are the salt of the earth, and without
   whom
This world would smell like what it is—a tomb.
   of Leigh **HUNT**
   'Letter to Maria Gisborne' (1820) l. 209

16   Have you not heard
When a man marries, dies, or turns Hindoo,
His best friends hear no more of him?
   'Letter to Maria Gisborne' (1820) l. 235

17   His fine wit
Makes such a wound, the knife is lost in it.
   of Thomas Love **PEACOCK**
   'Letter to Maria Gisborne' (1820) l. 240

18 When the lamp is shattered
The light in the dust lies dead—
When the cloud is scattered
The rainbow's glory is shed.
When the lute is broken,
Sweet tones are remembered not;
When the lips have spoken,
Loved accents are soon forgot.
   'Lines: When the lamp' (1824)

19 Beneath is spread like a green sea
The waveless plain of Lombardy.
   'Lines written amongst the Euganean Hills' (1818) l. 90

20 Underneath Day's azure eyes
Ocean's nursling, Venice lies,
A peopled labyrinth of walls,
Amphitrite's destined halls.
   'Lines written amongst the Euganean Hills' (1818) l. 94

21 Sun-girt city, thou hast been
Ocean's child, and then his queen;
Now is come a darker day,
And thou soon must be his prey.
   of Venice
   'Lines written amongst the Euganean Hills' (1818) l. 115

22 The fountains mingle with the river,
And the rivers with the ocean;
The winds of heaven mix for ever
With a sweet emotion;
Nothing in the world is single;
All things, by a law divine,
In one spirit meet and mingle.
Why not I with thine?
   'Love's Philosophy' (written 1819)

1 Whene'er he found those globes of deep red
gold
Which in the woods the strawberry-tree doth
bear,
Suspended in their emerald atmosphere.
'Marenghi'

2 I met Murder on the way—
He had a mask like Castlereagh—
Very smooth he looked, yet grim,
Seven bloodhounds followed him.
'The Mask of Anarchy' (1819) st. 2

3 His big tears, for he wept well,
Turned to mill-stones as they fell.

And the little children, who
Round his feet played to and fro,
Thinking every tear a gem,
Had their brains knocked out by them.
of 'Fraud' [*Lord Eldon*]
'The Mask of Anarchy' (1819) st. 4

4 Nought may endure but Mutability.
'Mutability' (1816)

5 I stood within the City disinterred;
And heard the autumnal leaves like light footfalls
Of spirits passing through the streets; and heard
The Mountain's slumberous voice at intervals
Thrill through those roofless halls.
'Ode to Naples' (1820) l. 1

6 O wild West Wind, thou breath of Autumn's
being,
Thou, from whose unseen presence the leaves
dead
Are driven, like ghosts from an enchanter
fleeing,
Yellow, and black, and pale, and hectic red,
Pestilence-stricken multitudes: O thou,
Who chariotest to their dark wintry bed
The wingèd seeds, where they lie cold and low,
Each like a corpse within its grave, until
Thine azure sister of the spring shall blow
Her clarion o'er the dreaming earth, and fill
(Driving sweet buds like flocks to feed in air)
With living hues and odours plain and hill:
Wild Spirit, which art moving everywhere;
Destroyer and preserver; hear, oh, hear!
'Ode to the West Wind' (1819) l. 1

7 There are spread
On the blue surface of thine aëry surge,
Like the bright hair uplifted from the head
Of some fierce Maenad.
'Ode to the West Wind' (1819) l. 18

8 Thou who didst waken from his summer dreams
The blue Mediterranean, where he lay,
Lulled by the coil of his crystàlline streams

Beside a pumice isle in Baiae's bay,
And saw in sleep old palaces and towers
Quivering within the wave's intenser day.
'Ode to the West Wind' (1819) l. 29

9 The sea-blooms and the oozy woods which wear
The sapless foliage of the ocean.
'Ode to the West Wind' (1819) l. 39

10 Oh, lift me as a wave, a leaf, a cloud!
I fall upon the thorns of life! I bleed!
'Ode to the West Wind' (1819) l. 53

11 Make me thy lyre, even as the forest is:
What if my leaves are falling like its own!
'Ode to the West Wind' (1819) l. 57

12 And, by the incantation of this verse,
Scatter, as from an unextinguished hearth
Ashes and sparks, my words among mankind!
'Ode to the West Wind' (1819) l. 65

13 O, Wind,
If Winter comes, can Spring be far behind?
'Ode to the West Wind' (1819) l. 69

14 Its horror and its beauty are divine.
'On the Medusa of Leonardo da Vinci' (1824)

15 I met a traveller from an antique land
Who said: Two vast and trunkless legs of stone
Stand in the desert.
'Ozymandias' (1819)

16 The hand that mocked them and the heart that
fed.
'Ozymandias' (1819)

17 'My name is Ozymandias, king of kings:
Look on my works, ye Mighty, and despair!'
Nothing beside remains. Round the decay
Of that colossal wreck, boundless and bare
The lone and level sands stretch far away.
'Ozymandias' (1819)

18 Hell is a city much like London—
A populous and smoky city.
'Peter Bell the Third' (1819) pt. 3, st. 1

19 Ere Babylon was dust,
The Magus Zoroaster, my dead child,
Met his own image walking in the garden,
That apparition, sole of men, he saw.
Prometheus Unbound (1819) act 1, l. 191

20 The good want power, but to weep barren tears.
The powerful goodness want: worse need for
them.
The wise want love; and those who love want
wisdom.
Prometheus Unbound (1820) act 1, l. 625

21 Peace is in the grave.
The grave hides all things beautiful and good:
I am a God and cannot find it there.
Prometheus Unbound (1820) act 1, l. 638

22 The dust of creeds outworn.
Prometheus Unbound (1820) act 1, l. 697

23 To be
Omnipotent but friendless is to reign.
Prometheus Unbound (1820) act 2, sc. 4, l. 47

24 He gave man speech, and speech created
thought,
Which is the measure of the universe.
Prometheus Unbound (1820) act 2, sc. 4, l. 72

1 My soul is an enchanted boat,
Which, like a sleeping swan, doth float
Upon the silver waves of thy sweet singing.
   Prometheus Unbound (1820) act 2, sc. 5, l. 72

2 The loathsome mask has fallen, the man remains
Sceptreless, free, uncircumscribed, but man
Equal, unclassed, tribeless, and nationless,
Exempt from awe, worship, degree, the king
Over himself; just, gentle, wise: but man
Passionless?—no, yet free from guilt or pain,
Which were, for his will made or suffered them,
Nor yet exempt, though ruling them like slaves,
From chance, and death, and mutability,
The clogs of that which else might oversoar
The loftiest star of unascended heaven,
Pinnacled dim in the intense inane.
   Prometheus Unbound (1820) act 3, sc. 4, l. 193

3 A traveller from the cradle to the grave
Through the dim night of this immortal day.
   Prometheus Unbound (1820) act 4, l. 551

4 To suffer woes which Hope thinks infinite;
To forgive wrongs darker than death or night;
To defy Power, which seems omnipotent;
To love, and bear; to hope till Hope creates
From its own wreck the thing it contemplates;
Neither to change, nor falter, nor repent;
This, like thy glory, Titan, is to be
Good, great and joyous, beautiful and free;
This is alone Life, Joy, Empire and Victory.
   Prometheus Unbound (1820) act 4, l. 570

5 How wonderful is Death,
Death and his brother Sleep!
   Queen Mab (1813) canto 1, l. 1; see **DANIEL** 264:6, **FLETCHER**
   335:12

6 I dreamed that, as I wandered by the way,
Bare Winter suddenly was changed to Spring.
   'The Question' (1822)

7 Daisies, those pearled Arcturi of the earth,
The constellated flower that never sets.
   'The Question' (1822)

8 A Sensitive Plant in a garden grew.
   'The Sensitive Plant' (1820) pt. 1, l. 1

9 And the jessamine faint, and the sweet tuberose,
The sweetest flower for scent that blows.
   'The Sensitive Plant' (1820) pt. 1, l. 37

10 Rarely, rarely, comest thou,
Spirit of Delight!
   'Song' (1824); epigraph to **ELGAR**'s Second Symphony

11 Men of England, wherefore plough
For the lords who lay ye low?
   'Song to the Men of England' (written 1819)

12 The seed ye sow, another reaps;
The wealth ye find, another keeps;
The robes ye weave, another wears;
The arms ye forge, another bears.
   'Song to the Men of England' (written 1819)

13 Lift not the painted veil which those who live
Call Life.
   'Sonnet' (1824)

14 An old, mad, blind, despised, and dying king.
of **GEORGE III**
   'Sonnet: England in 1819' (written 1819)

15 I see the waves upon the shore,
Like light dissolved in star-showers, thrown.
   'Stanzas Written in Dejection, near Naples' (1818)

16 Alas! I have nor hope nor health,
Nor peace within nor calm around,
Nor that content surpassing wealth
The sage in meditation found.
   'Stanzas Written in Dejection, near Naples' (1818)

17 Music, when soft voices die,
Vibrates in the memory—
Odours, when sweet violets sicken,
Live within the sense they quicken.
   'To—: Music, when soft voices die' (1824)

18 The desire of the moth for the star,
Of the night for the morrow,
The devotion to something afar
From the sphere of our sorrow.
   'To—: One word is too often profaned' (1824)

19 Hail to thee, blithe Spirit!
Bird thou never wert,
That from Heaven, or near it,
Pourest thy full heart
In profuse strains of unpremeditated art.
   'To a Skylark' (1819)

20 And singing still dost soar, and soaring ever
singest.
   'To a Skylark' (1819)

21 Thou art unseen, but yet I hear thy shrill
delight.
   'To a Skylark' (1819)

22 Like a Poet hidden
In the light of thought,
Singing hymns unbidden,
Till the world is wrought
To sympathy with hopes and fears it heeded not.
   'To a Skylark' (1819)

23 We look before and after,
And pine for what is not:
Our sincerest laughter
With some pain is fraught;
Our sweetest songs are those that tell of saddest
thought.
   'To a Skylark' (1819)

24 Teach me half the gladness
That thy brain must know,
Such harmonious madness
From my lips would flow
The world should listen then—as I am listening
now.
   'To a Skylark' (1819)

25 Less oft is peace in Shelley's mind,
Than calm in waters, seen.
   'To Jane: The Recollection' (written 1822)

26 Swiftly walk o'er the western wave,
Spirit of Night!
   'To Night' (1824)

1 Death will come when thou art dead,
Soon, too soon.
    'To Night' (1824)

2 Art thou pale for weariness
Of climbing heaven, and gazing on the earth,
Wandering companionless
Among the stars that have a different birth,—
And ever changing, like a joyless eye
That finds no object worth its constancy?
    'To the Moon' (1824)

3 In honoured poverty thy voice did weave
Songs consecrate to truth and liberty,—
Deserting these, thou leavest me to grieve,
Thus having been, that thou shouldst cease to
be.
    'To Wordsworth' (1816)

4 All but the sacred few who could not tame
Their spirits to the conquerors—but as soon
As they had touched the world with living
flame,
Fled back like eagles to their native noon.
    'The Triumph of Life' (written 1822)

5 And like a dying lady, lean and pale,
Who totters forth, wrapped in a gauzy veil.
    'The Waning Moon' (1824)

6 A lovely lady, garmented in light
From her own beauty.
    'The Witch of Atlas' (written 1820) st. 5

7 The discussion of any subject is a right that you
have brought into the world with your heart and
tongue. Resign your heart's blood before you
part with this inestimable privilege of man.
    An Address to the Irish People (1812)

8 The accident of her birth neither made her life
more virtuous nor her death more worthy of
grief.
    An Address to the People on the Death of the Princess Charlotte
    (1817)

9 Titles are tinsel, power a corrupter, glory a
bubble, and excessive wealth a libel on its
possessor.
    Declaration of Rights (1812) article 27

10 The vanity of translation; it were as wise to cast
a violet into a crucible that you might discover
the formal principle of its colour and odour, as
seek to transfuse from one language to another
the creations of a poet. The plant must spring
again from its seed, or it will bear no flower.
    A Defence of Poetry (written 1821)

11 The great instrument of moral good is the
imagination; and poetry administers to the effect
by acting on the cause.
    A Defence of Poetry (written 1821)

12 A single word even may be a spark of
inextinguishable thought.
    A Defence of Poetry (written 1821)

13 Poetry is the record of the best and happiest
moments of the happiest and best minds.
    A Defence of Poetry (written 1821)

14 Poets are the hierophants of an unapprehended
inspiration; the mirrors of the gigantic shadows
which futurity casts upon the present; the words
which express what they understand not; the
trumpets which sing to battle, and feel not what
they inspire; the influence which is moved not,
but moves. Poets are the unacknowledged
legislators of the world.
    A Defence of Poetry (written 1821); see **JOHNSON** 437:15

15 What is Love? It is that powerful attraction
towards all that we conceive, or fear, or hope
beyond ourselves.
    'On Love' (notebook essay, c.1815), in D. L. Clark (ed.) Shelley's
    Prose (1966)

16 Monarchy is only the string that ties the robber's
bundle.
    A Philosophical View of Reform (written 1819–20) ch. 2

17 Thought can with difficulty visit the intricate
and winding chambers which it inhabits. It is
like a river whose rapid and perpetual stream
flows outwards—like one in dread who speeds
through the recesses of some haunted pile and
dares not look behind.
    'Speculations on Metaphysics [On the Science of Mind]'
    (written 1815), in D. L. Clark (ed.) Shelley's Prose (1966)

William Shenstone 1714–63

English poet and essayist

18 The charm dissolves; th' aerial music's past;
The banquet ceases, and the vision flies.
    'Elegy 11. He complains how soon the pleasing novelty of life
    is over' (1764)

19 Whoe'er has travelled life's dull round,
Where'er his stages may have been,
May sigh to think he still has found
The warmest welcome, at an inn.
    'Written at an Inn at Henley' (1758); see **JOHNSON** 441:25

20 Laws are generally found to be nets of such a
texture, as the little creep through, the great
break through, and the middle-sized are alone
entangled in.
    Works in Verse and Prose (1764) vol. 2 'On Politics'; see
    ANACHARSIS 15:2

21 The world may be divided into people that read,
people that write, people that think, and fox-
hunters.
    Works . . . (1764) vol. 2 'On Writing and Books'

22 Every good poet includes a critic; the reverse
will not hold.
    Works . . . (1764) vol. 2 'On Writing and Books'

Philip Henry Sheridan 1831–88

American Union cavalry commander in the Civil War

23 The only good Indians I ever saw were dead.
    *in response to the Comanche chief Toch-a-way, who
    described himself as a 'good Indian'*
        at Fort Cobb, January 1869; attributed but denied by
        Sheridan; a similar remark had been made by J. M.
        Cavanaugh in Congress on 28 May 1868; see **PROVERBS**
        640:34

Richard Brinsley Sheridan 1751–1816

Irish dramatist and Whig politician. On Sheridan: see
ANONYMOUS 17:10, **BYRON** 192:7, **WALPOLE** 838:2

1 The newspapers! Sir, they are the most
villainous—licentious—abominable—infernal—
Not that I ever read them—No—I make it a rule
never to look into a newspaper.
The Critic (1779) act 1, sc. 1

2 If it is abuse,—why one is always sure to hear of
it from one damned goodnatured friend or
another!
The Critic (1779) act 1, sc. 1

3 Egad I think the interpreter is the hardest to be
understood of the two!
The Critic (1779) act 1, sc. 2

4 I wish sir, you would practise this without me. I
can't stay dying here all night.
The Critic (1779) act 3, sc. 1

5 O Lord, Sir—when a heroine goes mad she
always goes into white satin.
The Critic (1779) act 3, sc. 1

6 Enter Tilburina stark mad in white satin, and
her confidante stark mad in white linen.
The Critic (1779) act 3, sc. 1

7 An oyster may be crossed in love!
The Critic (1779) act 3, sc. 1

8 Conscience has no more to do with gallantry
than it has with politics.
The Duenna (1775) act 2, sc. 4

9 Illiterate him, I say, quite from your memory.
The Rivals (1775) act 1, sc. 2

10 'Tis safest in matrimony to begin with a little
aversion.
The Rivals (1775) act 1, sc. 2

11 Madam, a circulating library in a town is as an
evergreen tree of diabolical knowledge; it
blossoms throughout the year. And depend on it
. . . that they who are so fond of handling the
leaves, will long for the fruit at last.
The Rivals (1775) act 1, sc. 2

12 He is the very pineapple of politeness!
The Rivals (1775) act 3, sc. 3

13 An aspersion upon my parts of speech!
The Rivals (1775) act 3, sc. 3

14 If I reprehend any thing in this world, it is the
use of my oracular tongue, and a nice
derangement of epitaphs!
The Rivals (1775) act 3, sc. 3

15 She's as headstrong as an allegory on the banks
of the Nile.
The Rivals (1775) act 3, sc. 3

16 Our ancestors are very good kind of folks; but
they are the last people I should choose to have
a visiting acquaintance with.
The Rivals (1775) act 4, sc. 1

17 No caparisons, Miss, if you please!—Caparisons
don't become a young woman.
The Rivals (1775) act 4, sc. 2

18 You are not like Cerberus, three gentlemen at
once, are you?
The Rivals (1775) act 4, sc. 2

19 The quarrel is a very pretty quarrel as it
stands—we should only spoil it by trying to
explain it.
The Rivals (1775) act 4, sc. 3

20 My valour is certainly going!—it is sneaking
off!—I feel it oozing out as it were at the palms
of my hands!
The Rivals (1775) act 5, sc. 3

21 I own the soft impeachment—pardon my
blushes.
The Rivals (1775) act 5, sc. 3

22 You shall see them on a beautiful quarto page
where a neat rivulet of text shall meander
through a meadow of margin.
The School for Scandal (1777) act 1, sc. 1

23 You had no taste when you married me.
The School for Scandal (1777) act 2, sc. 1

24 MRS CANDOUR: I'll swear her colour is natural—I
have seen it come and go—
LADY TEAZLE: I dare swear you have, ma'am; it
goes of a night and comes again in the
morning.
The School for Scandal (1777) act 2, sc. 2

25 Here is the whole set! a character dead at every
word.
The School for Scandal (1777) act 2, sc. 2; see **POPE** 618:11

26 I'm called away by particular business—but I
leave my character behind me.
The School for Scandal (1777) act 2, sc. 2

27 Here's to the maiden of bashful fifteen
Here's to the widow of fifty
Here's to the flaunting, extravagant quean;
And here's to the housewife that's thrifty.
Let the toast pass—
Drink to the lass—
I'll warrant she'll prove an excuse for the glass!
The School for Scandal (1777) act 3, sc. 3

28 An unforgiving eye, and a damned disinheriting
countenance!
The School for Scandal (1777) act 4, sc. 1

29 ROWLEY: I believe there is no sentiment he has
more faith in as that 'Charity begins at home'.
SIR OLIVER SURFACE: And his I presume is of that
domestic sort which never stirs abroad at all.
The School for Scandal (1777) act 5, sc. 1; see **PROVERBS**
628:42

30 There is no trusting appearances.
The School for Scandal (1777) act 5, sc. 2

31 You write with ease, to show your breeding,
But easy writing's vile hard reading.
'Clio's Protest' (written 1771, published 1819)

32 A man may surely be allowed to take a glass of
wine by his own fireside.
*on being encountered drinking a glass of wine in the street,
while watching his theatre, the Drury Lane, burn down*
T. Moore *Life of Sheridan* (1825) vol. 2

1 The Right Honourable gentleman is indebted to his memory for his jests, and to his imagination for his facts.
  speech in reply to Mr Dundas, in T. Moore *Life of Sheridan* (1825) vol. 2

2 They talk of avarice, lust, ambition, as great passions. It is a mistake; they are little passions. Vanity is the great commanding passion of all.
  to Lord **HOLLAND**, Thomas Moore *Journal* (1984) 5 August 1824

3 To her! To that magnificent and appalling creature! I should as soon have thought of making love to the Archbishop of Canterbury!
  responding to Samuel Rogers's suggestion that Sheridan might 'make open love' to Mrs Siddons
  Henry Colborn (ed.) *Sheridaniana* (1826)

4 Won't you come into the garden? I would like my roses to see you.
  to a young lady; attributed

Hugh Sherlock 1905–

5 Lord, thy church on earth is seeking
  Thy renewal from above;
  Teach us all the art of speaking
  With the accent of thy love.
  'Lord, thy church on earth is seeking' (hymn)

Sidney Sherman 1805–73
American soldier

6 Remember the Alamo!
  battle cry at San Jacinto, 21 April 1836, traditionally attributed to Sherman

William Tecumseh Sherman 1820–91
American Union general

7 *Vox populi, vox humbug.*
  letter to his wife Jane, 2 June 1863; see **ALCUIN** 11:10, **PROVERBS** 646:4

8 Hold out. Relief is coming.
  usually quoted as 'Hold the fort! I am coming!'
  flag signal from Kennesaw Mountain to General John Murray Corse at Allatoona Pass, 5 October 1864; see **BLISS** 129:1

9 [Grant] stood by me when I was crazy, and I stood by him when he was drunk; and now we stand by each other always.
  of his relationship with his fellow Union commander, Ulysses S. GRANT
  in 1864; Geoffrey C. Ward *The Civil War* (1991)

10 War is the remedy our *enemies* have chosen, and I say let us give them all they want.
  in 1864; Geoffrey C. Ward *The Civil War* (1991)

11 There is many a boy here to-day who looks on war as all glory, but, boys, it is all hell.
  speech at Columbus, Ohio, 11 August 1880, in Lloyd Lewis *Sherman, Fighting Prophet* (1932)

12 I will not accept if nominated, and will not serve if elected.
  telegram to General Henderson, on being urged to stand as Republican candidate in the 1884 US presidential election
  Memoirs (4th ed., 1891) ch. 27

Carol Shields 1935–2003
American-born Canadian novelist and poet

13 To be like everyone else. Isn't that what we all want in the end?
  Larry's Party (1997) ch. 9

14 Canada is . . . a country always dressed in its Sunday go-to-meeting clothes. A country you wouldn't ask to dance a second waltz. Clean. Christian. Dull. Quiescent. But growing.
  The Stone Diaries (1993)

Arthur Shipley 1861–1927
English zoologist

15 When we were a soft amoeba, in ages past and gone,
  Ere you were Queen of Sheba, or I King Solomon,
  Alone and undivided, we lived a life of sloth,
  Whatever you did, I did; one dinner served for both.
  Anon came separation, by fission and divorce,
  A lonely pseudopodium I wandered on my course.
  Life (1923) ch. 13 'Ere you were Queen of Sheba'

William Shippen 1673–1743
English Jacobite politician

16 Robin and I are two honest men: he is for King George and I for King James, but those men in long cravats [Sandys, Rushout, Pulteney, and their following] only desire places under one or the other.
  view of his relationship with his political opponent Robert **WALPOLE**
  in *Dictionary of National Biography* (1917–)

James Shirley 1596–1666
English dramatist

17 The glories of our blood and state
  Are shadows, not substantial things;
  There is no armour against fate;
  Death lays his icy hand on kings.
  The Contention of Ajax and Ulysses (1659) act 1, sc. 3

18 Only the actions of the just
  Smell sweet, and blossom in their dust.
  The Contention of Ajax and Ulysses (1659) act 1, sc. 3

19 I presume you're mortal, and may err.
  The Lady of Pleasure (1637) act 2, sc. 2

20   How little room
  Do we take up in death, that, living know
  No bounds?
  The Wedding (1629) act 4, sc. 4

Mikhail Sholokhov 1905–84
Russian novelist

21 And quiet flows the Don.
  title of novel (1934)

Clare Short 1946–

British Labour politician

1 Reckless with our government; reckless with his own future, position and place in history. It's extraordinarily reckless.

when asked if she thought that Tony BLAIR was acting recklessly on Iraq

in an interview on *Westminster Hour* (BBC Radio 4), 9 March 2003

The Shorter Catechism (1647)

2 'What is the chief end of man?'
'To glorify God and to enjoy him for ever'.

Nevil Shute 1899–1960

English novelist

3 It has been said that an engineer is a man who can do for ten shillings what any fool can do for a pound.

Slide Rule (1954) ch. 3

Walter Sickert 1860–1942

English painter

4 Nothing knits man to man, the Manchester School wisely taught, like the frequent passage from hand to hand of cash.

'The Language of Art' in *New Age* 28 July 1910

The Siddur

Jewish prayer book

5 Hear, O Israel: the Lord our God, the Lord is One.

The Shema; see **BIBLE** 82:13

6 Blessed are you, O Lord our God and God of our fathers, God of Abraham, God of Isaac, God of Jacob, the great, mighty, and revered God, God most high, generous and kind, owner of all things. You remember the pious deeds of the patriarchs, and in love will bring a redeemer to their children's children, for your name's sake, O King, Helper, Saviour and Shield. Blessed are you, O Lord, the Shield of Abraham.

The Amidah Benediction 1

7 Blessed are you, O Lord our God, King of the universe, who has made a distinction between the holy and the profane, between light and darkness, between Israel and the nations, between the seventh day and the six working days.

The Havdalah

Algernon Sidney 1622–83

English conspirator, executed for his alleged part in the Rye House Plot, 1683

8 Liars ought to have good memories.

Discourses concerning Government (1698) ch. 2, sect. 15

9 Men lived like fishes; the great ones devoured the small.

Discourses concerning Government (1698) ch. 2, sect. 18; see **SHAKESPEARE** 729:26

10 'Tis not necessary to light a candle to the sun.

Discourses concerning Government (1698) ch. 2, sect. 23; see **BURTON** 181:19, **YOUNG** 876:15

11 The law is established, which no passion can disturb. 'Tis void of desire and fear, lust and anger . . . 'Tis deaf, inexorable, inflexible.

Discourses concerning Government (1698) ch. 3, sect. 15

Philip Sidney 1554–86

English soldier, poet, and courtier. On Sidney: see BROWNING 167:20, CAREW 198:5, COKAYNE 238:9, DYER 301:4, ROYDON 671:18

12 Shallow brooks murmur most, deep silent slide away.

Arcadia ('Old Arcadia', completed 1581) bk. 1 'First Eclogues: Lalus and Dorus'

13 Who shoots at the mid-day sun, though he be sure he shall never hit the mark; yet as sure he is he shall shoot higher than who aims but at a bush.

Arcadia ('New Arcadia', 1590) bk. 2

14 My true love hath my heart and I have his,
By just exchange one for the other giv'n.

Arcadia ('Old Arcadia', completed 1581) bk. 3

15 Biting my truant pen, beating myself for spite,
'Fool,' said my Muse to me; 'look in thy heart and write.'

Astrophil and Stella (1591) sonnet 1

16 With how sad steps, O Moon, thou climb'st the skies;
How silently, and with how wan a face.
What, may it be that even in heavenly place
That busy archer his sharp arrows tries?

Astrophil and Stella (1591) sonnet 31

17   O moon, tell me,
Is constant love deemed there but want of wit?
Are beauties there as proud as here they be?
Do they above love to be loved, and yet
These lovers scorn whom that love doth possess?
Do they call virtue there ungratefulness?

Astrophil and Stella (1591) sonnet 31

18 That sweet enemy, France.

Astrophil and Stella (1591) sonnet 41

19 Dumb swans, not chattering pies, do lovers prove;
They love indeed who quake to say they love.

Astrophil and Stella (1591) sonnet 54

20 I never drank of Aganippe well,
Nor ever did in shade of Tempe sit.

Astrophil and Stella (1591) sonnet 74

21 I am no pick-purse of another's wit.

Astrophil and Stella (1591) sonnet 74

22 Highway, since you my chief Parnassus be.

Astrophil and Stella (1591) sonnet 84

1 Stella, think not that I by verse seek fame;
Who seek, who hope, who love, who live, but
   thee:
Thine eyes my pride, thy lips my history;
If thou praise not, all other praise is shame.
  Astrophil and Stella (1591) sonnet 90

2 Leave me, O Love which reachest but to dust,
And thou, my mind, aspire to higher things;
Grow rich in that which never taketh rust;
Whatever fades, but fading pleasure brings.
  Certain Sonnets (written 1577–81) no. 32

3 O fair! O sweet! When I do look on thee,
In whom all joys so well agree,
Heart and soul do sing in me,
Just accord all music makes.
  'To the Tune of a Spanish Song' (written c.1581)

4 Nature never set forth the earth in so rich
tapestry as diverse poets have done . . . her
world is brazen, the poets only deliver a golden.
  The Defence of Poetry (1595)

5 Poetry therefore, is an art of *imitation* . . . that is
to say, a representing, counterfeiting, or figuring
forth to speak metaphorically. A speaking
picture, with this end: to teach and delight.
  The Defence of Poetry (1595)

6 With a tale forsooth he [the poet] cometh unto
you, with a tale which holdeth children from
play, and old men from the chimney corner.
  The Defence of Poetry (1595)

7 Comedy is an imitation of the common errors
of our life.
  The Defence of Poetry (1595)

8 Certainly I must confess mine own
barbarousness, I never heard the old song of
Percy and Douglas, that I found not my heart
moved more than with a trumpet.
  The Defence of Poetry (1595)

9 Laughter almost ever cometh of things most
disproportioned to our selves, and nature.
Delight hath a joy in it either permanent or
present. Laughter hath only a scornful tickling.
  The Defence of Poetry (1595)

10 Thy necessity is yet greater than mine.
  *on giving his water-bottle to a dying soldier on the battle-
field of Zutphen, 1586; commonly quoted as 'thy need is
greater than mine'*
  Fulke Greville *Life of Sir Philip Sidney* (1652) ch. 12

Emmanuel Joseph Sieyès 1748–1836
French abbot and statesman

11 *La mort, sans phrases.*
Death, without rhetoric.
  *on voting in the French Convention for the death of Louis
XVI, 16 January 1793*
  attributed to Sieyès, but afterwards repudiated by him; *Le
Moniteur* 20 January 1793 records his vote as 'La mort'

12 *J'ai vécu.*
I survived.
  when asked what he had done during the French Revolution
  F. A. M. Mignet *Notice historique sur la vie et les travaux de M.
le Comte de Sieyès* (1836)

Maurice Sigler 1901–61 *and* Al Hoffman
1902–60
American songwriters

13 Little man, you've had a busy day.
  title of song (1934)

Simone Signoret 1921–85
French actress

14 Chains do not hold a marriage together. It is
threads, hundreds of tiny threads which sew
people together through the years. That is what
makes a marriage last—more than passion or
even sex!
  in *Daily Mail* 4 July 1978

Sikh Scriptures
**a monotheistic religion founded in the Punjab in the 15th
century by Guru Nanak**
translated by W. H. McLeod, 1984

15 There is one Supreme Being, the Eternal Reality.
He is the Creator, without fear and devoid of
enmity. He is immortal, never incarnated, self-
existent, known by grace through the Guru.
  Adi Granth: Guru Nanak Japji mul mantra

16 If as the lord of powerful armies, if as a king
  enthroned,
Though my commands bring prompt obedience,
  yet would my strength be vain.
Grant that your name remain, O Master, in my
  thoughts and in my heart.
  Adi Granth: Guru Nanak Siri Raga I

17 When the Guru comes, O mother, joyous bliss is
  mine;
Boundless blessing, mystic rapture, rise within
  my soul.
Surging music, strains of glory, fill my heart
  with joy;
Breaking forth in songs of gladness, praise to
  God within.
Comes the Guru, I have found him; joyous bliss
  is mine.
  Adi Granth: Guru Amar Das Ramkali Anand

18 The Name of God is sweet ambrosia, source of
  all inner peace and joy.
The Name of God brings blissful peace to the
  hearts of the truly devout.
  Adi Granth: Guru Arjan Sukhmani

19 Better by far than any other way is the act of
  repeating the perfect Name of God.
Better by far than any other rite is the cleansing
  of one's heart in the company of the devout.
Better by far than any other skill is endlessly to
  utter the wondrous Name of God.

Better by far than any sacred text is hearing and repeating the praises of the Lord.
Better by far than any other place is the heart wherein abides that most precious Name of God.
Adi Granth: Guru Arjan *Sukhmani*

1 Grant me protection, merciful Lord, prostrate here at your door;
Guard me and keep me, Friend of the humble, weary from wandering far.
You love the devout and recover the sinful; to you alone I address this prayer:
Take me and hold me, merciful Lord, carry me safely to joy.
Adi Granth: Guru Arjan *Var Jaitasari*

2 Strengthen me, O Lord, that I shrink not from righteous deeds,
That freed from the fear of my enemies I may fight with faith and win.
The wisdom which I crave is the grace to sing your praises.
When this life's allotted course has run may I meet my death in battle.
Dasam Granth: Guru Gobind Singh *Chandi Charitra*

3 Around us lies God's dwelling place, his joyous presence on every side.
Self-existent and supremely beautiful, he dwells as a presence immanent in all creation.
Birth and death are abolished by his power, by the grace made manifest in his being.
Eternally present within all humanity he reigns in glory for ever.
Dasam Granth: Guru Gobind Singh *Jap*

4 Some worship stones, borne on their heads; some hang lingams from their necks.
Some claim that God dwells in the south, whilst others bow to the West.
Some worship idols, foolishly ignorant; others put trust in the tombs of the dead.
All are astray, seduced by false ritual; none knows the secret of God.
Dasam Granth: Guru Gobind Singh *Ten Savayyas*

5 A Sikh should rise as night draws near to dawn and begin each day with an early-morning bathe.
Devoutly reading the Guru's words he goes to the dharamsala to hear eternal truth.
Joining the sangat there assembled he hears with deepest reverence the Guru's sacred songs.
Bhai Gurdas (d. 1633) var 40, v. 11

6 The light which shone from each of the ten Masters shines now from the sacred pages of the Guru Granth Sahib. Turn your thoughts to its message and call on God, saying, *Vahiguru!*
Ardas

7 Grant to your Sikhs a true knowledge of their faith, the blessing of uncut hair, guidance in conduct, spiritual perception, patient trust,

abiding faith, and the supreme gift of the divine Name.
Ardas

8 You must always wear the Five Ks. These are uncut hair [*kes*], a sword or dagger [*kirpan*], a pair of shorts [*kachh*], a comb [*kangha*], and a steel bangle [*kara*].
Sikh Rahit Maryada

9 After three days and three nights had passed he [Guru Nanak] emerged from the stream, and having done so he declared: 'There is neither Hindu nor Muslim.'
Mahima Prakas Varatak

10 The Guru [Ram Das] then pronounced his blessing on the sacred pool [Amritsar]. 'He who bathes here with a heart filled with devotion to God shall thereby receive the deliverance which I confer. This will assuredly happen. Even a bird which flies over this pool shall attain to the same sure deliverance without any effort on its part. They who obtain this salvation will find blissful peace in mystical union with God.'
Mahima Prakas Kavita

Alan Sillitoe 1928–
English writer

11 The loneliness of the long-distance runner.
title of novel (1959)

Georges Simenon 1903–89
Belgian novelist

12 Writing is not a profession but a vocation of unhappiness.
interview in *Paris Review* Summer 1955

Paul Simon 1942–
American singer and songwriter

13 Like a bridge over troubled water
I will lay me down.
'Bridge over Troubled Water' (1970 song)

14 And here's to you, Mrs Robinson
Jesus loves you more than you will know.
'Mrs Robinson' (1967 song, from the film *The Graduate*)

15 People talking without speaking
People hearing without listening . . .
'Fools,' said I, 'You do not know
Silence like a cancer grows.'
'Sound of Silence' (1964 song)

16 Still crazy after all these years.
title of song (1975)

Simonides *c.*556–468 BC
Greek poet. See also EPITAPHS 317:13

17 Painting is silent poetry, poetry is eloquent painting.
Plutarch *Moralia* 'De Gloria Atheniensium' sect. 3

Konstantin Simonov 1915–79

Russian poet

1 Wait for me and I'll return . . .
Only you and I know how I survived.
It's because you waited as no one else did.
'Wait for Me' (1942)

Harold Simpson

2 Down in the forest something stirred:
It was only the note of a bird.
'Down in the Forest' (1906 song)

Kirke Simpson 1881–1972

American journalist

3 [Warren] Harding of Ohio was chosen by a
group of men in a smoke-filled room early
today as Republican candidate for President.
*often attributed to Harry Daugherty, one of Harding's
supporters, who appears merely to have concurred with this
version of events, when pressed for comment by Simpson*
news report, filed 12 June 1920; William Safire *New Language
of Politics* (1968)

Tom Simpson 1937–67

English cyclist

4 On, on, on.
*last words, after collapsing on Mont Ventoux in the Tour de
France; see* **MISQUOTATIONS** 548:16
William Fotheringham *Put Me Back on My Bike* (2002) ch. 2

George R. Sims 1847–1922

English journalist and dramatist

5 It is Christmas Day in the Workhouse.
'In the Workhouse—Christmas Day' (1879)

Upton Sinclair 1878–1968

American novelist and social reformer

6 It is difficult to get a man to understand
something when his salary depends on his not
understanding it.
I, Candidate for Governor (1935)

C. H. Sisson 1914–2003

English poet

7 Here lies a civil servant. He was civil
To everyone, and servant to the devil.
The London Zoo (1961)

Sitting Bull (Tatanka Iyotake) *c.*1831–90

Sioux chief

8 What law have I broken? Is it wrong for me to
love my own? Is it wicked for me because my
skin is red, because I am Sioux, because I was
born where my fathers lived, because I would
die for my people and my country?
*to Major Brotherton, recorded July 1881; Gary C. Anderson
Sitting Bull* (1996)

9 The Black Hills belong to me. If the whites try
to take them, I will fight.
Dee Brown *Bury My Heart at Wounded Knee* (1970) ch. 12

Edith Sitwell 1887–1964

English poet and critic. On Sitwell: see **BOWEN** 153:13

10 Jane, Jane,
Tall as a crane,
The morning light creaks down again.
Façade (1923) 'Aubade'

11 The fire was furry as a bear.
Façade (1923) 'Dark Song'

12 Still falls the Rain—
Dark as the world of man, black as our loss—
Blind as the nineteen hundred and forty nails
Upon the Cross.
'Still Falls the Rain' (1942)

13 I feel as if all my blood had been sucked, and
my brains eaten by clothes moths. What I
would give to be able to work uninterrupted!
letter to Allen Tanner, 15 August 1933, in Richard Green (ed.)
Selected Letters of Edith Sitwell (1997)

14 Calling a spade a spade never made the spade
interesting yet. Take my advice, leave spades
alone.
letter to Charles Henri Ford, 23 August 1933, in Richard Green
(ed.) *Selected Letters of Edith Sitwell* (1997)

15 I enjoyed talking to her, but thought *nothing* of
her writing. I considered her 'a beautiful little
knitter'.
of Virginia **WOOLF**
letter to Geoffrey Singleton, 11 July 1955, in John Lehmann
and Derek Palmer (eds.) *Selected Letters* (1970)

Osbert Sitwell 1892–1969

English writer

16 In reality, killing time
Is only the name for another of the multifarious
ways
By which Time kills us.
'Milordo Inglese' (1958); see **BOUCICAULT** 152:12

17 On the coast of Coromandel
Dance they to the tunes of Handel.
'On the Coast of Coromandel' (1943); see **LEAR** 485:15

Antonio Skarmeta 1940–

Chilean novelist

18 All men who first touch with words go much
further afterwards with their hands.
Burning Patience (1985) translated by Katherine Silver

19 Poetry belongs to those who use it, not those
who write it!
Burning Patience (1985) translated by Katherine Silver

John Skelton *c.*1460–1529

English poet

20 The sovereign'st thing that any man may have
Is little to say, and much to hear and see.
The Bouge of Court (1499) l. 211

1 Far may be sought
Erst that ye can find
So courteous, so kind,
As Merry Margaret,
This midsummer flower,
Gentle as falcon
Or hawk of the tower.
The Garland of Laurel (1523) 'To Mistress Margaret Hussey'

2 With margerain gentle,
The flower of goodlihead,
Embroidered the mantle
Is of your maidenhead.
The Garland of Laurel (1523) 'To Mistress Margery Wentworth'

3 So many vagabonds, so many beggars bold;
So much decay of monasteries and of religious
places;
So hot hatred against the Church, and charity so
cold;
So much of 'my Lord's Grace,' and in him no
grace is;
So much hollow hearts, and so double faces;
So much sanctuary-breaking, and privilege-
barred—
Since Deucalion's flood was never seen nor
lered.
'Speak, Parrot' (written c.1520) l. 498

Noel Skelton 1880–1935

British Conservative politician

4 To state as clearly as may be what means lie
ready to develop a property-owning democracy,
to bring the industrial and economic status of
the wage-earner abreast of his political and
educational, to make democracy stable and four-
square.
in *The Spectator* 19 May 1923

B. F. Skinner 1904–90

American psychologist

5 The real question is not whether machines think
but whether men do.
Contingencies of Reinforcement (1969) ch. 9

6 Education is what survives when what has been
learned has been forgotten.
New Scientist 21 May 1964

□ **Slogans** *see* **box opposite**

Joseph Roberts Smallwood 1900–91

**Canadian journalist and politician, Premier of
Newfoundland 1949–70**

7 I am king of my own little island, and that's all
I've ever wanted to be.
Richard Gwyn *Smallwood: The Unlikely Revolutionary* (1968)

Christopher Smart 1722–71

English poet. On Smart: see JOHNSON 439:16

8 Nature's decorations glisten
Far above their usual trim;

Birds on box and laurels listen,
As so near the cherubs hymn.
Hymns and Spiritual Songs (1765) 'The Nativity of Our Lord
and Saviour Jesus Christ'

9 God all-bounteous, all-creative,
Whom no ills from good dissuade,
Is incarnate, and a native
Of the very world he made.
Hymns and Spiritual Songs (1765) 'The Nativity of Our Lord
and Saviour Jesus Christ'

10 For in my nature I quested for beauty, but God,
God hath sent me to sea for pearls.
Jubilate Agno (c.1758–63) Fragment B, l. 30

11 For Charity is cold in the multitude of
possessions, and the rich are covetous of their
crumbs.
Jubilate Agno (c.1758–63) Fragment B, l. 154

12 For I will consider my Cat Jeoffrey.
For he is the servant of the Living God duly and
daily serving him.
For at the first glance of the glory of God in the
East he worships in his way.
For this is done by wreathing his body seven
times round with elegant quickness.
Jubilate Agno (c.1758–63) Fragment B, l. 695

13 For when his day's work is done his business
more properly begins.
For he keeps the Lord's watch in the night
against the adversary.
For he counteracts the powers of darkness by
his electrical skin and glaring eyes.
For he counteracts the Devil, who is death, by
brisking about the life.
Jubilate Agno (c.1758–63) Fragment B, l. 719

14 Ye beauties! O how great the sum
Of sweetness that ye bring;
On what a charity ye come
To bless the latter spring!
How kind the visit that ye pay,
Like strangers on a rainy day.
'On a Bed of Guernsey Lilies' (1764)

15 Strong is the lion—like a coal
His eye-ball—like a bastion's mole
His chest against his foes.
Strong, the gier-eagle on his sail,
Strong against tide, th' enormous whale
Emerges as he goes.
A Song to David (1763) st. 76

16 But stronger still, in earth and air,
And in the sea, the man of pray'r;
And far beneath the tide;
And in the seat to faith assigned,
Where ask is have, where seek is find,
Where knock is open wide.
A Song to David (1763) st. 77

17 Beauteous the garden's umbrage mild,
Walk, water, meditated wild,
And all the bloomy beds.
A Song to David (1763) st. 78

continued

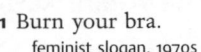 # Slogans

1 Burn your bra.
feminist slogan, 1970s

2 A dog is for life, not just for Christmas.
slogan of the National Canine Defence League, from 1978

3 Don't be evil.
informal corporate motto of the search engine Google

4 Guns don't kill people; people kill people.
National Rifle Association slogan

5 I'm backing Britain.
slogan coined by workers at the Colt factory, Surbiton, Surrey and subsequently used in a national campaign, in *The Times* 1 January 1968

6 It takes 40 dumb animals to make a fur coat, but only one to wear it.
slogan of an anti-fur campaign poster, 1980s; sometimes attributed to David **BAILEY**

7 *Je suis Marxiste—tendance Groucho.*
I am a Marxist—of the Groucho tendency.
slogan used at Nanterre in Paris, 1968

8 Just say no.
slogan of the Nancy **REAGAN** Drug Abuse Fund, founded 1985

9 Lousy but loyal.
London East End slogan at George V's Jubilee (1935)

10 Make love not war.
student slogan, 1960s

11 Pile it high, sell it cheap.
slogan coined by John Cohen (1898–1979), founder of Tesco

12 Save the whale.
environmental slogan associated with alarm over the rapidly declining whale population which led in 1985 to a moratorium on commercial whaling

13 Think globally, act locally.
Friends of the Earth slogan, c.1985

Christopher Smart *continued*

14 Glorious the northern lights astream;
Glorious the song, when God's the theme;
Glorious the thunder's roar:
Glorious hosanna from the den;
Glorious the catholic amen;
Glorious the martyr's gore.

Glorious—more glorious is the crown
Of Him that brought salvation down
By meekness, called thy Son;
Thou that stupendous truth believed,
And now the matchless deed's achieved,
Determined, dared, and done.
A Song to David (1763) st. 85

15 Ah! Posthumus, the years, the years
Glide swiftly on, nor can our tears
Or piety the wrinkled age forefend,
Or for one hour retard th' inevitable end.
translation of Horace *Odes* bk. 2, no. 14; see **HORACE** 412:10

Elizabeth Smart 1913–86
Canadian writer

16 By Grand Central Station I sat down and wept.
title of book (1945); see **BOOK OF COMMON PRAYER** 149:13

Samuel Smiles 1812–1904
English writer

17 We each day dig our graves with our teeth.
Duty (1880) ch. 16; see **DEFOE** 270:6

18 This extraordinary metal, the soul of every manufacture, and the mainspring perhaps of civilised society.
of iron
Men of Invention and Industry (1884) ch. 4

19 The spirit of self-help is the root of all genuine growth in the individual.
Self-Help (1859) ch. 1

20 The shortest way to do many things is to do only one thing at once.
Self-Help (1859) ch. 9

21 Middle class people are apt to live up to their incomes, if not beyond them.
Self-Help (1859) ch. 9

22 Cheerfulness gives elasticity to the spirit. Spectres fly before it.
Self-Help (1859) ch. 12

Adam Smith 1723–90
Scottish philosopher and economist

23 Wonder . . . and not any expectation of advantage from its discoveries, is the first principle which prompts mankind to the study of Philosophy, of that science which pretends to lay open the concealed connections that unite the various appearances of nature.
Essays on Philosophical Subjects (1795) 'The History of Astronomy' sect. 3, para. 3

24 And thus, *Place*, that great object which divides the wives of aldermen, is the end of half the labours of human life; and is the cause of all the tumult and bustle, all the rapine and injustice, which avarice and ambition have introduced into this world.
Theory of Moral Sentiments (1759) pt. 1, sect. 3, ch. 2

25 Though our brother is on the rack, as long as we ourselves are at our ease, our senses will never inform us of what he suffers . . . It is by imagination that we can form any conception of what are his sensations.
Theory of Moral Sentiments (2nd ed., 1762) p. 2

1 It is not from the benevolence of the butcher, the brewer, or the baker, that we expect our dinner, but from their regard to their own interest. We address ourselves not to their humanity but their self love.
Wealth of Nations (1776) bk. 1, ch. 2

2 People of the same trade seldom meet together, even for merriment and diversion, but the conversation ends in a conspiracy against the public, or in some contrivance to raise prices.
Wealth of Nations (1776) bk. 1, ch. 10, pt. 2

3 The chief enjoyment of riches consists in the parade of riches.
Wealth of Nations (1776) bk. 1, ch. 11

4 Every individual necessarily labours to render the annual revenue of society as great as he can. He generally neither intends to promote the public interest, nor knows how much he is promoting it. He intends only his own gain, and he is, in this, as in many other cases, led by an invisible hand to promote an end which was no part of his intention.
Wealth of Nations (1776) bk. 4, ch. 3

5 To found a great empire for the sole purpose of raising up a people of customers, may at first sight appear a project fit only for a nation of shopkeepers. It is, however, a project altogether unfit for a nation of shopkeepers; but extremely fit for a nation whose government is influenced by shopkeepers.
Wealth of Nations (1776) bk. 4, ch. 7, pt. 3; see **ADAMS** 4:1, **NAPOLEON I** 568:9

6 Consumption is the sole end and purpose of production; and the interest of the producer ought to be attended to only so far as it may be necessary for promoting that of the consumer.
Wealth of Nations (1776) bk. 4, ch. 8

7 The discipline of colleges and universities is in general contrived, not for the benefit of the students, but for the interest, or more properly speaking, for the ease of the masters.
Wealth of Nations (1776) bk. 5, ch. 1, pt. 3

8 There is no art which one government sooner learns of another than that of draining money from the pockets of the people.
Wealth of Nations (1776) bk. 5, ch. 2

9 If any of the provinces of the British empire cannot be made to contribute towards the support of the whole empire, it is surely time that Great Britain should free herself from the expense of defending those provinces in time of war, and of supporting any part of their civil or military establishments in time of peace, and endeavour to accommodate her future views and designs to the real mediocrity of her circumstances.
Wealth of Nations (1776) bk. 5, ch. 3

Alfred Emanuel Smith 1873–1944

American politician

10 All the ills of democracy can be cured by more democracy.
speech in Albany, 27 June 1933, in *New York Times* 28 June 1933; see **ADDAMS** 4:6

Delia Smith

English cook

11 A hen's egg is, quite simply, a work of art, a masterpiece of design and construction with, it has to be said, brilliant packaging.
How To Cook (1998)

Dodie Smith 1896–1990

English novelist and dramatist

12 The family—that dear octopus from whose tentacles we never quite escape.
Dear Octopus (1938)

13 I write this sitting in the kitchen sink.
I Capture the Castle (1948), opening words

14 Must talk, want to talk, got to talk, going to talk.
said as a very small child
Valerie Grove *Dear Dodie* (1996) ch. 1

Edgar Smith 1857–1938

American songwriter

15 You may tempt the upper classes
With your villainous demi-tasses,
But; Heaven will protect a working-girl!
'Heaven Will Protect the Working-Girl' (1909 song)

F. E. Smith, Lord Birkenhead

1872–1930

British Conservative politician and lawyer. On Smith: see **ASQUITH** 34:9, **CHESTERTON** 223:23

16 The world continues to offer glittering prizes to those who have stout hearts and sharp swords.
rectorial address, Glasgow University, 7 November 1923, in *The Times* 8 November 1923; 'The glittering prizes' was the title of a novel (1976) by Frederick **RAPHAEL**

17 We have the highest authority for believing that the meek shall inherit the earth; though I have never found any particular corroboration of this aphorism in the records of Somerset House.
Contemporary Personalities (1924) 'Marquess Curzon'; see **BIBLE** 98:25

18 JUDGE DARLING: And who is George Robey?
SMITH: Mr George Robey is the Darling of the music halls, m'lud.
A. E. Wilson *The Prime Minister of Mirth* (1956) ch. 1

19 JUDGE: What do you suppose I am on the Bench for, Mr Smith?
SMITH: It is not for me, Your Honour, to attempt to fathom the inscrutable workings of Providence.
2nd Earl of Birkenhead *F. E.* (1959 ed.) ch. 9

1 JUDGE: You are extremely offensive, young man.
SMITH: As a matter of fact, we both are, and the
only difference between us is that I am trying to
be, and you can't help it.
2nd Earl of Birkenhead *Earl of Birkenhead* (1933) vol. 1, ch. 9

Godfrey Smith 1926–

English journalist and columnist

2 In a world full of audio visual marvels, may
words matter to you and be full of magic.
letter to a new grandchild, in *Sunday Times* 5 July 1987

Iain Duncan Smith 1954–

British Conservative politician, Leader of the Conservative
Party 2001-3. On Smith: see **PORTILLO 620:2**

3 Do not underestimate the determination of a
quiet man.
speech to the Conservative Party Conference, 10 October
2002

Ian Smith 1919–2007

Rhodesian statesman, Prime Minister of Rhodesia (now
Zimbabwe) 1964-79

4 I don't believe in black majority rule in
Rhodesia—not in a thousand years.
broadcast speech, 20 March 1976, in *Sunday Times* 21 March
1976

John Smith 1938–94

Scottish-born Labour politician, Leader of the Labour Party
from 1992

5 The settled will of the Scottish people.
of the creation of a Scottish parliament
speech at the Scottish Labour Conference, 11 March 1994

Langdon Smith 1858–1908

6 When you were a tadpole, and I was a fish,
In the Palaeozoic time,
And side by side in the ebbing tide
We sprawled through the ooze and slime.
'A Toast to a Lady' in *The Scrap-Book* April 1906

Logan Pearsall Smith 1865–1946

American-born man of letters

7 There is more felicity on the far side of baldness
than young men can possibly imagine.
Afterthoughts (1931) 'Age and Death'

8 The test of a vocation is the love of the
drudgery it involves.
Afterthoughts (1931) 'Art and Letters'

9 A best-seller is the gilded tomb of a mediocre
talent.
Afterthoughts (1931) 'Art and Letters'

10 People say that life is the thing, but I prefer
reading.
Afterthoughts (1931) 'Myself'

11 Thank heavens, the sun has gone in, and I don't
have to go out and enjoy it.
Afterthoughts (1931) 'Myself'

12 What I like in a good author is not what he
says, but what he whispers.
All Trivia (1933) 'Afterthoughts' pt. 5

Samuel Francis Smith 1808–95

American poet and divine. On Smith: see **HOLMES 403:12**

13 My country, 'tis of thee,
Sweet land of liberty,
Of thee I sing:
Land where my fathers died,
Land of the pilgrims' pride,
From every mountain-side
Let freedom ring.
'America' (1831)

Stevie Smith (Florence Margaret Smith)
1902–71

English poet and novelist

14 Oh I am a cat that likes to
Gallop about doing good.
'The Galloping Cat' (1972)

15 A good time was had by all.
title of book (1937)

16 Why does my Muse only speak when she is
unhappy?
She does not, I only listen when I am unhappy.
'My Muse' (1964)

17 I was much too far out all my life
And not waving but drowning.
'Not Waving but Drowning' (1957)

18 People who are always praising the past
And especially the times of faith as best
Ought to go and live in the Middle Ages
And be burnt at the stake as witches and sages.
'The Past' (1957)

19 Private Means is dead
God rest his soul, officers and fellow-rankers
said.
'Private Means is Dead' (1962)

20 This Englishwoman is so refined
She has no bosom and no behind.
'This Englishwoman' (1937)

21 I long for the Person from Porlock
To bring my thoughts to an end,
I am growing impatient to see him
I think of him as a friend.
'Thoughts about the "Person from Porlock" ' (1962); see
COLERIDGE 240:3

22 If you cannot have your dear husband for a
comfort and a delight, for a breadwinner and a
crosspatch, for a sofa, chair or a hot-water
bottle, one can use him as a Cross to be Borne.
Novel on Yellow Paper (1936) p. 24

23 If there wasn't death, I think you couldn't go
on.
in *Observer* 9 November 1969

Sydney Smith 1771–1845
English clergyman and essayist

1 The moment the very name of Ireland is mentioned, the English seem to bid adieu to common feeling, common prudence, and common sense, and to act with the barbarity of tyrants, and the fatuity of idiots.
Letters of Peter Plymley (1807) letter 2

2 A Curate—there is something which excites compassion in the very name of a Curate!!!
'Persecuting Bishops' in *Edinburgh Review* (1822)

3 Bishop Berkeley destroyed this world in one volume octavo; and nothing remained, after his time, but mind; which experienced a similar fate from the hand of Mr Hume in 1739.
Sketches of Moral Philosophy (1849) introduction

4 We shall generally find that the triangular person has got into the square hole, the oblong into the triangular, and a square person has squeezed himself into the round hole. The officer and the office, the doer and the thing done, seldom fit so exactly that we can say they were almost made for each other.
Sketches of Moral Philosophy (1849) Lecture 9

5 I look upon Switzerland as an inferior sort of Scotland.
letter to Lord Holland, 1815, in N. C. Smith (ed.) *Letters of Sydney Smith* (1953)

6 Tory and Whig in turns shall be my host,
I taste no politics in boiled and roast.
letter to John Murray, November 1834, in *Letters of Sidney Smith* (1953)

7 I have no relish for the country; it is a kind of healthy grave.
letter to Miss G. Harcourt, 1838, in *Letters of Sidney Smith* (1953)

8 If there is a pure and elevated pleasure in this world it is a roast pheasant with bread sauce. Barn-door fowls for dissenters, but for the real Churchman, the thiry-nine-times articled clerk—the pheasant, the pheasant.
letter to R. H. Barham, 15 November 1841, in *Letters of Sidney Smith* (1953)

9 I have seen nobody since I saw you, but persons in orders. My only varieties are vicars, rectors, curates, and every now and then (by way of turbot) an archdeacon.
letter to Miss Berry, 28 January 1843, in *Letters of Sidney Smith* (1953)

10 It requires a surgical operation to get a joke well into a Scotch understanding. Their only idea of wit . . . is laughing immoderately at stated intervals.
Lady Holland *Memoir* (1855) vol. 1, ch. 2

11 That knuckle-end of England—that land of Calvin, oat-cakes, and sulphur.
of Scotland
Lady Holland *Memoir* (1855) vol. 1, ch. 2

12 Take short views, hope for the best, and trust in God.
Lady Holland *Memoir* (1855) vol. 1, ch. 6

13 No furniture so charming as books.
Lady Holland *Memoir* (1855) vol. 1, ch. 9; see **POWELL** 621:18

14 How can a bishop marry? How can he flirt? The most he can say is, 'I will see you in the vestry after service.'
Lady Holland *Memoir* (1855) vol. 1, ch. 9

15 As the French say, there are three sexes—men, women, and clergymen.
Lady Holland *Memoir* (1855) vol. 1, ch. 9

16 Daniel Webster struck me much like a steam-engine in trousers.
Lady Holland *Memoir* (1855) vol. 1, ch. 9

17 My definition of marriage . . . it resembles a pair of shears, so joined that they cannot be separated; often moving in opposite directions, yet always punishing anyone who comes between them.
Lady Holland *Memoir* (1855) vol. 1, ch. 11

18 He has occasional flashes of silence, that make his conversation perfectly delightful.
of **MACAULAY**
Lady Holland *Memoir* (1855) vol. 1, ch. 11

19 Let onion atoms lurk within the bowl,
And, scarce-suspected, animate the whole.
Lady Holland *Memoir* (1855) vol. 1, ch. 11 'Receipt for a Salad'

20 Serenely full, the epicure would say,
Fate cannot harm me, I have dined to-day.
Lady Holland *Memoir* (1855) vol. 1, ch. 11 'Receipt for a Salad'; see **DRYDEN** 297:6

21 Deserves to be preached to death by wild curates.
Lady Holland *Memoir* (1855) vol. 1, ch. 11

22 Brighton Pavilion looks as if St Paul's had slipped down to Brighton and pupped.
attributed; Alan Bell (ed.) *The Sayings of Sydney Smith* (1993)

23 Death must be distinguished from dying, with which it is often confused.
H. Pearson *The Smith of Smiths* (1934) ch. 11

24 I am just going to pray for you at St Paul's, but with no very lively hope of success.
H. Pearson *The Smith of Smiths* (1934) ch. 13

25 I never read a book before reviewing it; it prejudices a man so.
H. Pearson *The Smith of Smiths* (1934) ch. 3

26 Minorities . . . are almost always in the right.
H. Pearson *The Smith of Smiths* (1934) ch. 9

27 My idea of heaven is, eating *pâté de foie gras* to the sound of trumpets.
view ascribed by Smith to his friend Henry Luttrell
H. Pearson *The Smith of Smiths* (1934) ch. 10; see **DISRAELI** 286:16

28 Science is his forte, and omniscience his foible.
on **WHEWELL**
Isaac Todhunter *William Whewell* (1876) vol. 1

1 What a pity it is that we have no amusements in England but vice and religion!
 H. Pearson *The Smith of Smiths* (1934) ch. 10

2 What two ideas are more inseparable than Beer and Britannia?
 H. Pearson *The Smith of Smiths* (1934) ch. 11

Walter Chalmers Smith 1824–1908
Scottish clergyman

3 Immortal, invisible, God only wise.
 'God, All in All' (1867 hymn)

4 Unresting, unhasting, and silent as light,
 Nor wanting, nor wasting, thou rulest in might.
 'God, All in All' (1867 hymn)

5 We blossom and flourish as leaves on the tree,
 And wither and perish; but naught changeth thee.
 'God, All in All' (1867 hymn)

Tobias Smollett 1721–71
Scottish novelist

6 I think for my part one half of the nation is mad—and the other not very sound.
 The Adventures of Sir Launcelot Greaves (1762) ch. 6

7 The capital [London] is become an overgrown monster; which, like a dropsical head, will in time leave the body and extremities without nourishment and support.
 Humphry Clinker (1771) vol. 1 (letter from Matthew Bramble, 29 May)

8 'Begging your honour's pardon, (replied Clinker) may not the new light of God's grace shine upon the poor and the ignorant in their humility, as well as upon the wealthy, and the philosopher in all his pride of human learning?' What you imagine to be the new light of grace, (said his master) I take to be a deceitful vapour, glimmering through a crack in your upper storey.
 Humphry Clinker (1771) vol. 2 (letter from Jery Melford, 10 June)

9 Mourn, hapless Caledonia, mourn
 Thy banished peace, thy laurels torn.
 'The Tears of Scotland' (1746)

10 That great Cham of literature, Samuel Johnson.
 letter to John Wilkes, 16 March 1759, in James Boswell *Life of Samuel Johnson* (1934 ed.) vol. 1

Jan Christiaan Smuts 1870–1950
South African soldier and statesman, Prime Minister 1919–24 and 1939–48

11 Mankind is once more on the move. The very foundations have been shaken and loosened, and things are again fluid. The tents have been struck, and the great caravan of humanity is once more on the march.
 on the setting up of the League of Nations, in the wake of the First World War
 W. K. Hancock *Smuts* (1968)

C. P. Snow 1905–80
English novelist and scientist

12 The official world, the corridors of power.
 Homecomings (1956) ch. 22

13 The two cultures and the scientific revolution.
 title of The Rede Lecture (1959)

Socrates 469–399 BC
Greek philosopher. On Socrates: see **PLATO** 608:18; see also **BURTON** 181:13

14 How many things I can do without!
 on looking at a multitude of goods exposed for sale
 Diogenes Laertius *Lives of the Philosophers* bk. 2, ch. 25

15 I know nothing except the fact of my ignorance.
 Diogenes Laertius *Lives of the Philosophers* bk. 2, sect. 32; see **DAVIES** 267:18, **MILTON** 544:27

16 The rest of the world lives to eat, while I eat to live.
 Diogenes Laertius *Lives of the Philosophers* bk. 2, sect. 34; see **PROVERBS** 630:48

17 To fear death, my friends, is only to think ourselves wise, without being wise: for it is to think that we know what we do not know.
 Plato *Apology* 29a

18 If you were prepared to let me go on those terms [to give up practising philosophy], I should reply to you as follows: 'I have the greatest fondness and affection for you, fellow Athenians, but I will obey my god rather than you'.
 Plato *Apology* 29d

19 Most excellent man, are you who are a citizen of Athens, the greatest of cities and the most famous for wisdom and power, not ashamed to care for the acquisition of wealth and for reputation and honour, when you neither care nor take thought for wisdom and truth and the perfection of your soul?
 Plato *Apology* 29d

20 Virtue does not come from money, but from virtue comes money and all other good things to man, both to the individual and to the state.
 Plato *Apology* 30b

21 Then I, however, showed again, by action, not in word only, that I did not care a whit for death . . . but that I did care with all my might not to do anything unjust or unholy.
 on being ordered by the Thirty Commissioners to take part in the liquidation of Leon of Salamis
 Plato *Apology* 32d

22 The unexamined life is not worth living.
 Plato *Apology* 38a

23 It [death] is, you see, one or other of two things: either to be dead is to be non-existent, as it were, and a dead person has no awareness of anything at all; or else, as we are told, the soul undergoes some sort of transformation, or exchanging of this present world for another.
 Plato *Apology* 41c (translated by David Gallop)

1 But already it is time to depart, for me to die, for you to go on living; which of us takes the better course, is not known to anyone except God.
  Plato *Apology* 42a

2 It is never right to do wrong or to requite wrong with wrong, or when we suffer evil to defend ourselves by doing evil in return.
  Plato *Crito* 49d

3 It is perfectly certain that the soul is immortal and imperishable, and our souls will actually exist in another world.
  Plato *Phaedo* 107a

4 A man should feel confident concerning his soul, who has renounced those pleasures and fineries that go with the body, as being alien to him, and considering them to result more in harm than in good, but has pursued the pleasures that go with learning and made the soul fine with no alien but rather its own proper refinements, moderation and justice and courage and freedom and truth; thus he is ready for the journey to the world below, ready to go when Fate calls him.
  Plato *Phaedo* 114d

5 'What do you say about pouring a libation to some god from this cup? Is it allowed or not?' 'We only prepare just the right amount to drink, Socrates,' he [the jailer] said. 'I understand,' he went on; 'but it is allowed and necessary to pray to the gods, that my moving from hence to there may be blessed; thus I pray, and so be it.'
  Plato *Phaedo* 117b

6 But, my dearest Agathon, it is truth which you cannot contradict; you can without any difficulty contradict Socrates.
  Plato *Symposium* 201d

7 I am not Athenian or Greek but a citizen of the world.
  Plutarch *Moralia* bk. 7 'On Exile'

8 Crito, we owe a cock to Aesculapius; please pay it and don't forget it.
  last words; Plato *Phaedo* 118

Solon c.640–after 556 BC
Greek poet and Athenian statesman

9 I grow old ever learning many things.
  Theodor Bergk (ed.) *Poetae Lyrici Graeci* (1843) no. 18

10 Call no man happy before he dies, he is at best but fortunate.
  Herodotus *Histories* bk. 1, ch. 32; see **BIBLE** 97:17, **PROVERBS** 628:31

Alexander Solzhenitsyn 1918–2008
Russian novelist

11 You only have power over people as long as you don't take *everything* away from them. But when you've robbed a man of *everything* he's no longer in your power — he's free again.
  The First Circle (1968) ch. 17

12 The Gulag archipelago.
  title of book (1973–5)

13 How can you expect a man who's warm to understand one who's cold?
  One Day in the Life of Ivan Denisovich (1962) p. 22 (translated by Ralph Parker)

14 The thoughts of a prisoner—they're not free either. They keep returning to the same things.
  One Day in the Life of Ivan Denisovich (1962) p. 34 (translated by Ralph Parker)

15 After the suffering of decades of violence and oppression, the human soul longs for higher things, warmer and purer than those offered by today's mass living habits, introduced as by a calling card by the revolting invasion of commercial advertising, by TV stupor and by intolerable music.
  speech in Cambridge, Massachusetts, 8 June 1978

16 The clock of communism has stopped striking. But its concrete building has not yet come crashing down. For that reason, instead of freeing ourselves, we must try to save ourselves being crushed by the rubble.
  in *Komsomolskaya Pravda* 18 September 1990

17 The Iron Curtain did not reach the ground and under it flowed liquid manure from the West.
  speaking at Far Eastern Technical University, Vladivostok, 30 May 1994; see **CHURCHILL** 230:6

William Somerville 1675–1742
English country gentleman

18   My hoarse-sounding horn
  Invites thee to the chase, the sport of kings;
  Image of war, without its guilt.
  The Chase (1735) bk. 1, l. 13; see **D'AVENANT** 267:9, **SURTEES** 781:6

19 Hail, happy Britain! highly favoured isle,
  And Heaven's peculiar care!
  The Chase (1735) bk. 1, l. 84

Anastasio Somoza 1925–80
Nicaraguan dictator. On Somoza: see CARDENAL 198:3

20 You won the elections, but I won the count.
  replying to an accusation of ballot-rigging
  in *Guardian* 17 June 1977; see **STOPPARD** 777:13

Stephen Sondheim 1930–
American songwriter

21 I like to be in America!
  O.K. by me in America!
  Ev'rything free in America
  For a small fee in America!
  'America' (1957 song) in *West Side Story*

22 Every day a little death
  title of song (1973) in *A Little Night Music*

1 Ev'ry day a little death
   On the lips and in the eyes,
   In the murmurs, in the pauses,
   In the gestures, in the sighs.
   Ev'ry day a little dies.
   'Every Day a Little Death' (1973 song) in *A Little Night Music*

2 Everything's coming up roses.
   title of song (1959) in *Gypsy*

3 Isn't it rich?
   Are we a pair?
   Me here at last on the ground, you in mid-air.
   'Send in the Clowns' (1973 song) in *A Little Night Music*

4 Where are the clowns?
   Send in the clowns.
   'Send in the Clowns' (1973 song) in *A Little Night Music*

□ Songs, spirituals, and shanties *see*
box overleaf. *See also* **BALLADS**, **POLITICAL**
SLOGANS AND SONGS

Susan Sontag 1933–2004
American writer

5 Societies need to have one illness which becomes
   identified with evil, and attaches blame to its
   'victims'.
   AIDS and its Metaphors (1989)

6 What pornography is really about, ultimately,
   isn't sex but death.
   in *Partisan Review* Spring 1967

7 The white race *is* the cancer of human history,
   it is the white race, and it alone—its ideologies
   and inventions—which eradicates autonomous
   civilizations wherever it spreads, which has upset
   the ecological balance of the planet, which now
   threatens the very existence of life itself.
   in *Partisan Review* Winter 1967

Donald Soper 1903–98
English Methodist minister

8 It is, I think, good evidence of life after death.
   on the quality of debate in the House of Lords
   in *Listener* 17 August 1978

Sophocles *c.*496–406 BC
Greek dramatist. On Sophocles: see ARISTOPHANES 26:16,
ARISTOTLE 27:23, ARNOLD 31:1; see also ANONYMOUS 23:1,
HEANEY 387:8

9 My son, may you be happier than your father.
   Ajax l. 550

10 The happiest life is lived while one understands
   nothing, before one learns delight or pain.
   Ajax l. 554

11 Enemies' gifts are no gifts and do no good.
   Ajax l. 665

12 His death concerns the gods, not those men, no!
   of Ajax's enemies, the Greek leaders
   Ajax l. 970

13 There's nothing in the world so demoralizing as
   money.
   Antigone l. 295

14 There are many wonderful things, and nothing
   is more wonderful than man.
   Antigone l. 333

15 Nor could I think that a decree of yours—
   A man—could override the laws of Heaven
   Unwritten and unchanging. Not of today
   Or yesterday is their authority;
   They are eternal; no man saw their birth.
   Antigone l. 454

16 White Colonus, where the nightingale, a
   constant guest, trills her clear note.
   Oedipus Coloneus l. 670 (translation by R. C. Jebb)

17 Not to be born is, past all prizing, best.
   Oedipus Coloneus l. 1225 (translation by R. C. Jebb); see **AUDEN**
   36:28, **YEATS** 873:12

18 You are blind in your ears and mind, as well as
   your eyes.
   Oedipus to Tiresias
   Oedipus Tyrannus l. 370

19 I think I heard you say that Laius
   Was murdered at a place where three ways
   meet?
   Oedipus Tyrannus l. 729 (translated by H. D. F. Kitto)

20 So do not fear this marriage with your mother;
   Many a man has suffered this before—
   But only in his dreams.
   Oedipus Tyrannus l. 977 (translated by H. D. F. Kitto)

21 But it is a pleasant thing to get the prize of
   victory; be daring—in time we shall be shown to
   have been in the right.
   Philoctetes l. 81

22 Someone asked Sophocles, 'How is your sex-life
   now? Are you still able to have a woman?' He
   replied, 'Hush, man; most gladly indeed am I rid
   of it all, as though I had escaped from a mad
   and savage master.'
   Plato *Republic* bk. 1, 329b

Charles Hamilton Sorley 1895–1915
English poet

23 We swing ungirded hips,
   And lightened are our eyes,
   The rain is on our lips,
   We do not run for prize.
   'Song of the Ungirt Runners' (1916)

24 When you see millions of the mouthless dead
   Across your dreams in pale battalions go,
   Say not soft things as other men have said,
   That you'll remember. For you need not so.
   Give them not praise. For, deaf, how should they
   know
   It is not curses heaped on each gashed head?
   'A Sonnet' (1916)

continued

Songs, spirituals, and shanties

1 And Charlie he's my darling,
My darling, my darling,
And Charlie he's my darling,
The young Chevalier.
traditional song with many versions, including ones by
BURNS *and* **HOGG**

2 A-roving! A-roving!
Since roving's been my ru-i-n
I'll go no more a-roving
With you fair maid.
'A-roving' (traditional song)

3 *Auprès de ma blonde,*
Qu'il fait bon, fait bon, fait bon,
Auprès de ma blonde,
Qu'il fait bon dormir.
Next to my blonde girl, it's so good, so good,
so good, next to my blonde girl, it's so good
to sleep.
'Auprès de ma blonde' (traditional French song, 17th
century)

4 Come, landlord, fill the flowing bowl
Until it doth run over . . .
For to-night we'll merry be,
To-morrow we'll be sober.
'Come, Landlord, Fill the Flowing Bowl' (traditional song)

5 Come lasses and lads, get leave of your dads,
And away to the Maypole hie,
For every he has got him a she,
And the fiddler's standing by.
For Willie shall dance with Jane,
And Johnny has got his Joan,
To trip it, trip it, trip it, trip it, trip it up and
down.
'Come Lasses and Lads' (traditional song, c.1670)

6 Early one morning, just as the sun was rising,
I heard a maid sing in the valley below:
'Oh, don't deceive me; Oh, never leave me!
How could you use a poor maiden so?'
'Early One Morning' (traditional song)

7 Frankie and Albert were lovers, O Lordy, how
they could love.
Swore to be true to each other, true as the
stars above;
He was her man, but he done her wrong.
'Frankie and Albert', in John Huston Frankie and Johnny
(1930) (St Louis ballad later better known as 'Frankie and
Johnny')

8 God gave Noah the rainbow sign,
No more water, the fire next time.
Home in that Rock (Negro spiritual)

9 God save our gracious king!
Long live our noble king!
God save the king!
Send him victorious,
Happy, and glorious,
Long to reign over us:

God save the king!
'God save the King', attributed to various authors of the
mid eighteenth century, including Henry **CAREY**; *Jacobite*
variants, such as James Hogg 'The King's Anthem' in
Jacobite Relics of Scotland Second Series (1821) also exist

10 Confound their politics,
Frustrate their knavish tricks.
'God save the King'

11 Greensleeves was all my joy,
Greensleeves was my delight,
Greensleeves was my heart of gold,
And who but Lady Greensleeves?
'A new Courtly Sonnet of the Lady Greensleeves, to the
new tune of "Greensleeves" ', in A Handful of Pleasant
Delights (1584)

12 The holly and the ivy,
When they are both full grown,
Of all the trees that are in the wood,
The holly bears the crown:
The rising of the sun
And the running of the deer,
The playing of the merry organ,
Sweet singing in the choir.
'The Holly and the Ivy' (traditional carol)

13 I'll sing you twelve O.
Green grow the rushes O.
What is your twelve O?
Twelve for the twelve apostles,
Eleven for the eleven who went to heaven,
Ten for the ten commandments,
Nine for the nine bright shiners,
Eight for the eight bold rangers,
Seven for the seven stars in the sky,
Six for the six proud walkers,
Five for the symbol at your door,
Four for the Gospel makers,
Three for the rivals,
Two, two, the lily-white boys,
Clothed all in green O,
One is one and all alone
And ever more shall be so.
'The Dilly Song', in G. Grigson (ed.) The Faber Book of
Popular Verse (1971); see **BURNS** *178:9*

14 In good King Charles's golden days,
When loyalty no harm meant;
A furious High-Churchman I was,
And so I gained preferment.
Unto my flock I daily preached,
Kings are by God appointed,
And damned are those who dare resist,
Or touch the Lord's Anointed.
And this is law, I will maintain,
Unto my dying day, Sir,
That whatsoever King shall reign,
I will be the Vicar of Bray, sir!
'The Vicar of Bray' in British Musical Miscellany (1734) vol. 1

continued

Songs, spirituals, and shanties *continued*

1 John Brown's body lies a mould'ring in the grave,
His soul is marching on.
inspired by the execution of the abolitionist John **BROWN**, *after the raid on Harper's Ferry, on 2 December 1859*
　song (1861), variously attributed to Charles Sprague Hall, Henry Howard Brownell, and Thomas Brigham Bishop

2 We'll hang old Jeff Davis from a sour apple tree.
　early version of 'John Brown's Body' (1861)

3 Like a fine old English gentleman,
All of the olden time.
　'The Fine Old English Gentleman' (traditional song)

4 Maxwelton braes are bonnie
Where early fa's the dew.
　William Douglas of Fingland (fl. 1700) 'Annie Laurie'

5 And for bonnie Annie Laurie
I'd lay me doun and dee.
　William Douglas of Fingland (fl. 1700) 'Annie Laurie'

6 One Friday morn when we set sail,
And our ship not far from land,
We there did espy a fair pretty maid,
With a comb and a glass in her hand.
While the raging seas did roar,
And the stormy winds did blow,
And we jolly sailor-boys were all up aloft
And the land-lubbers lying down below.
　'The Mermaid' (traditional song)

7 On the first day of Christmas my true love sent to me
A partridge in a pear tree.
　'The Twelve Days of Christmas', traditional song listing gifts sent on each day of the Christmas season

8 Our fair-haired Donough, and he after being condemned;
There was a little white cap on him in place of a hat,
And a hempen rope in the place of a neckcloth.
　'Some Connachtman that was hanged in Galway' (Irish ballad, c. 1820)

9 O ye'll tak' the high road, and I'll tak' the low road,
And I'll be in Scotland afore ye,
But me and my true love will never meet again,
On the bonnie, bonnie banks o' Loch Lomon'.
　'The Bonnie Banks of Loch Lomon'' (traditional song)

10 A ship I have got in the North Country
And she goes by the name of the *Golden Vanity*,
O I fear she will be taken by a Spanish Ga-la-lee,
As she sails by the Low-lands low.
　'The Golden Vanity' (traditional song)

11 Some talk of Alexander, and some of Hercules;
Of Hector and Lysander, and such great names as these;
But of all the world's brave heroes, there's none that can compare
With a tow, row, row, row, row, row, for the British Grenadier.
　'The British Grenadiers' (traditional song)

12 Swing low, sweet chariot—
Comin' for to carry me home;
I looked over Jordan and what did I see?
A band of angels comin' after me—
Comin' for to carry me home.
　Negro spiritual (c.1850)

13 There is a tavern in the town,
And there my dear love sits him down,
And drinks his wine 'mid laughter free,
And never, never thinks of me.
Fare thee well, for I must leave thee,
Do not let this parting grieve thee,
And remember that the best of friends must part.
Adieu, adieu, kind friends, adieu, adieu, adieu,
I can no longer stay with you,
I'll hang my harp on a weeping willow-tree,
And may the world go well with thee.
　'There is a Tavern in the Town' (traditional song)

14 This lass so neat, with smiles so sweet,
Has won my right good-will,
I'd crowns resign to call thee mine,
Sweet lass of Richmond Hill.
　Leonard MacNally (1752–1820) 'The Lass of Richmond Hill'; also attributed to W. Upton in *The Oxford Song Book* (1916), and to W. Hudson in S. Baring-Gould *English Minstrelsie* (1895) vol. 3

15 Were you there when they crucified my Lord?
　title of Negro spiritual (1865)

16 When Israel was in Egypt land,
Let my people go,
Oppressed so hard they could not stand,
Let my people go.
Go down, Moses,
Way-down in Egypt land,
Tell old Pharaoh
To let my people go.
　'Go Down, Moses' (Negro spiritual); see **BIBLE** 81:4

17 Yankee Doodle came to town
Riding on a pony;
Stuck a feather in his cap
And called it Macaroni.
　'Yankee Doodle' (song, 1755 or earlier); Nicholas Smith *Stories of Great National Songs* (1899) ch. 2; see **COHAN** 238:4

18 Yes, Ireland shall be free,
From the centre to the sea;
Then hurrah for Liberty!
Says the Shan Van Vogh.
　'The Shan Van Vogh' (song, 1796)

Charles Hamilton Sorley *continued*

1 If Goethe really died saying 'more light', it was very silly of him: what *he* wanted was more warmth.
  letter, July 1914; *The Letters of Charles Sorley* (1919); see **GOETHE** 363:6

2 I do wish people would not deceive themselves by talk of a just war. There is no such thing as a just war. What we are doing is casting out Satan by Satan.
  letter to his mother from Aldershot, March 1915; *The Letters of Charles Sorley* (1919); see **BIBLE** 103:27

Robert South 1634–1716

English court preacher

3 An Aristotle was but the rubbish of an Adam, and Athens but the rudiments of Paradise.
  Twelve Sermons . . . (1692) vol. 1, no. 2

Thomas Southerne 1660–1746

Irish dramatist

4   When we're worn,
  Hacked hewn with constant service, thrown aside
  To rust in peace, or rot in hospitals.
  The Loyal Brother (1682) act 1

5 For love is but discovery:
  When that is made, the pleasure's done.
  Sir Anthony Love (1690) act 2 'Song'

Robert Southey 1774–1843

English poet and writer

6 It was a summer evening,
  Old Kaspar's work was done,
  And he before his cottage door
  Was sitting in the sun,
  And by him sported on the green
  His little grandchild Wilhelmine.
  'The Battle of Blenheim' (1800)

7 Now tell us all about the war,
  And what they fought each other for.
  'The Battle of Blenheim' (1800)

8 'And everybody praised the Duke,
  Who this great fight did win.'
  'But what good came of it at last?'
  Quoth little Peterkin.
  'Why that I cannot tell,' said he,
  'But 'twas a famous victory.'
  'The Battle of Blenheim' (1800)

9 No stir in the air, no stir in the sea,
  The ship was still as she could be.
  'The Inchcape Rock' (1802)

10 And then they knew the perilous rock,
  And blessed the Abbot of Aberbrothock.
  'The Inchcape Rock' (1802)

11 Oh Christ! It is the Inchcape Rock!
  'The Inchcape Rock' (1802)

12 My name is Death: the last best friend am I.
  'The Lay of the Laureate' (1816) st. 87

13 Blue, darkly, deeply, beautifully blue.
  Madoc (1805) pt. 1, canto 5 'Lincoya' l. 102

14 You are old, Father William, the young man cried,
  The few locks which are left you are grey;
  You are hale, Father William, a hearty old man,
  Now tell me the reason, I pray.
  'The Old Man's Comforts' (1799); see **CARROLL** 201:17

15   O ye who at your ease
  Sip the blood-sweetened beverage.
  of sugar-sweetened tea
  'Poems Concerning the Slave Trade' (1794) sonnet 3

16 The arts babblative and scribblative.
  Colloquies on the Progress and Prospects of Society (1829) no. 10, pt. 2

17 The march of intellect.
  Colloquies on the Progress and Prospects of Society (1829) no. 14

18 Your true lover of literature is never fastidious.
  The Doctor (1812) ch. 17

19 Show me a man who cares no more for one place than another, and I will show you in that same person one who loves nothing but himself. Beware of those who are homeless by choice.
  The Doctor (1812) ch. 34

20 Live as long as you may, the first twenty years are the longest half of your life.
  The Doctor (1812) ch. 130

21 Somebody has been sitting in my chair!
  The Doctor vol. 4 (1837) 'The Story of the Three Bears'

22 Men started at the intelligence, and turned pale, as if they had heard of the loss of a dear friend.
  on the death of **NELSON**
  The Life of Nelson (1813) ch. 9

23 She has made me in love with a cold climate, and frost and snow, with a northern moonlight.
  on Mary **WOLLSTONECRAFT**'s *letters from Sweden and Norway*
  letter to his brother Thomas, 28 April 1797, in Charles Southey *Life and Correspondence of Robert Southey* vol. 1 (1849); see **MITFORD** 551:7

24 Literature cannot be the business of a woman's life: and it ought not to be.
  letter to Charlotte Brontë, 12 March 1837, in Margaret Smith (ed.) *The Letters of Charlotte Brontë* (1995)

Robert Southwell *c*.1561–95

English poet and Roman Catholic martyr

25 As I in hoary winter night stood shivering in the snow,
  Surprised was I with sudden heat which made my heart to glow;
  And lifting up a fearful eye to view what fire was near
  A pretty Babe all burning bright did in the air appear.
  'The Burning Babe' (*c*.1590)

1 My faultless breast the furnace is,
The fuel wounding thorns;
Love is the fire, and sighs the smoke,
The ashes, shame and scorns;

The fuel Justice layeth on,
And Mercy blows the coals;
The metal in this furnace wrought
Are men's defiled souls.
'The Burning Babe' (c.1590)

2 To rise by other's fall
I deem a losing gain;
All states with others' ruins built
To ruin run amain.
'Content and Rich' (1595)

3 Times go by turns, and chances change by
course,
From foul to fair, from better hap to worse.
'Times go by Turns' (1595)

Wole Soyinka 1934–
Nigerian writer

4 Is it not a tax on
The habit of talking with paper?
of the stamp on a letter
The Lion and the Jewel (1963)

5 History is too full of failed Prometheans bathing
their wounded spirits in the tragic stream.
The Man Died (1972) ch. 12

6 Does a tiger feel its tigritude?
on the use of the word 'negritude'; often quoted in the
form 'A tiger does not proclaim his tigritude—he pounces'
in Time magazine 17 November 1967

Muriel Spark 1918–2006
Scottish novelist

7 I am a hoarder of two things: documents and
trusted friends.
Curriculum Vitae (1992)

8 Long ago in 1945 all the nice people in England
were poor, allowing for exceptions.
The Girls of Slender Means (1963), opening words

9 I am putting old heads on your young shoulders
. . . all my pupils are the crème de la crème.
The Prime of Miss Jean Brodie (1961) ch. 1

10 Give me a girl at an impressionable age, and she
is mine for life.
The Prime of Miss Jean Brodie (1961) ch. 1; see **SAYINGS** 684:21

11 One's prime is elusive. You little girls, when you
grow up, must be on the alert to recognise your
prime at whatever time of your life it may
occur.
The Prime of Miss Jean Brodie (1961) ch. 1

12 To me education is a leading out of what is
already there in the pupil's soul. To Miss Mackay
it is a putting in of something that is not there,
and that is not what I call education, I call it
intrusion.
The Prime of Miss Jean Brodie (1961) ch. 2

13 If you're going to do a thing, you should do it
thoroughly. If you're going to be a Christian,
you may as well be a Catholic.
in Independent 2 August 1989

14 Scottish by formation.
phrase coined as a criterion for entrants to the
Macallan/Scotland on Sunday short story competition in
1991
in Scotland on Sunday 6 June 1993

John Sparrow 1906–92
English academic, Warden of All Souls College, Oxford,
1952–77. See also **EPITAPHS** 320:4

15 That indefatigable and unsavoury engine of
pollution, the dog.
letter to The Times 30 September 1975

Edward Spears 1886–1974
British soldier and diplomat

16 Of all the crosses I have had to bear during this
war, the heaviest has been the Cross of
Lorraine.
in the Second World War the Cross of Lorraine was the
symbol of the Free French forces, led by General **DE GAULLE**
attributed in *Times* 1 June 2006, and often attributed to
Winston **CHURCHILL** who subsequently used it; Martin Gilbert
Churchill: A Life (1991)

Rachel Speght fl. 1621
English poet

17 God's image man doth bear
Without it he is but a human shape,
Worse than the Devil.
'Mortality's Memorandum' (1621)

Herbert Spencer 1820–1903
English philosopher

18 Science is organized knowledge.
Education (1861) ch. 2

19 People are beginning to see that the first
requisite to success in life is to be a good
animal.
Education (1861) ch. 2

20 Absolute morality is the regulation of conduct in
such a way that pain shall not be inflicted.
Essays (1891) vol. 3 'Prison Ethics'

21 Evolution . . . is—a change from an indefinite,
incoherent homogeneity, to a definite coherent
heterogeneity.
First Principles (1862) ch. 16

22 This survival of the fittest which I have here
sought to express in mechanical terms, is that
which Mr Darwin has called 'natural selection,
or the preservation of favoured races in the
struggle for life'.
Principles of Biology (1865) pt. 3, ch. 12; see **DARWIN** 266:15

23 How often misused words generate misleading
thoughts.
Principles of Ethics (1879) bk. 1, pt. 2, ch. 8, sect. 152

1 Progress, therefore, is not an accident, but a
necessity . . . It is a part of nature.
Social Statics (1850) pt. 1, ch. 2, sect. 4

2 A clever theft was praiseworthy amongst the
Spartans; and it is equally so amongst Christians,
provided it be on a sufficiently large scale.
Social Statics (1850) pt. 2, ch. 16, sect. 3

3 Hero-worship is strongest where there is least
regard for human freedom.
Social Statics (1850) pt. 4, ch. 30, sect. 6

4 No one can be perfectly free till all are free; no
one can be perfectly moral till all are moral; no
one can be perfectly happy till all are happy.
Social Statics (1850) pt. 4, ch. 30, sect. 16

Lord Spencer 1964–

English peer

5 She needed no royal title to continue to
generate her particular brand of magic.
tribute at the funeral of his sister, **DIANA**, *Princess of Wales,*
7 September 1997
in *Guardian* 8 September 1997

6 We, your blood family, will do all we can to
continue the imaginative way in which you were
steering these two exceptional young men so
that their souls are not simply immersed by duty
and tradition but can sing openly as you
planned.
referring to his nephews, Prince William and Prince Harry;
funeral tribute, 7 September 1997
in *Guardian* 8 September 1997

Raine, Countess Spencer 1929–

7 Alas, for our towns and cities. Monstrous
carbuncles of concrete have erupted in gentle
Georgian Squares.
The Spencers on Spas (1983) p. 14; see **CHARLES** 217:14

Stanley Spencer 1891–1959

English painter. On Spencer: see LEWIS 492:17

8 Painting is saying 'Ta' to God.
letter from Spencer's daughter Shirin, in Observer *7 February*
1988

Stephen Spender 1909–95

English poet. On Spender: see WAUGH 843:3

9 After the first powerful plain manifesto
The black statement of pistons, without more
fuss
But gliding like a queen, she leaves the station.
'The Express' (1933)

10 I think continually of those who were truly
great.
title of poem (1933)

11 Born of the sun they travelled a short while
towards the sun,
And left the vivid air signed with their honour.
'I think continually of those who were truly great' (1933)

12 Their collected
Hearts wound up with love, like little watch
springs.
'The Past Values' (1939)

13 Pylons, those pillars
Bare like nude, giant girls that have no secret.
'The Pylons' (1933)

14 What I had not foreseen
Was the gradual day
Weakening the will
Leaking the brightness away.
'What I expected, was' (1933)

15 Who live under the shadow of a war,
What can I do that matters?
'Who live under the shadow of a war' (1933)

Edmund Spenser *c.*1552–99

English poet. On Spenser: see CECIL 212:8

16 The merry cuckoo, messenger of Spring,
His trumpet shrill hath thrice already sounded.
Amoretti (1595) sonnet 19

17 Most glorious Lord of life, that on this day
Didst make thy triumph over death and sin:
And, having harrowed hell, didst bring away
Captivity thence captive, us to win.
Amoretti (1595) sonnet 68

18 One day I wrote her name upon the strand,
But came the waves and washèd it away:
Again I wrote it with a second hand,
But came the tide, and made my pains his prey.
Vain man, said she, that dost in vain assay,
A mortal thing so to immortalize.
Amoretti (1595) sonnet 75

19 So you great Lord, that with your counsel sway
The burden of this kingdom mightily,
With like delights sometimes may eke delay,
The rugged brow of careful Policy.
'Dedicatory Sonnet to Sir Christopher Hatton' (1590)

20 Hark how the cheerful birds do chant their lays
And carol of love's praise.
The merry lark her matins sings aloft,
The thrush replies, the mavis descant plays,
The ouzel shrills, the ruddock warbles soft,
So goodly all agree with sweet consent,
To this day's merriment.
'Epithalamion' (1595) l. 74

21 Open the temple gates unto my love,
Open them wide that she may enter in.
'Epithalamion' (1595) l. 204

22 Ah! when will this long weary day have end,
And lend me leave to come unto my love?
How slowly do the hours their numbers spend!
How slowly does sad Time his feathers move!
'Epithalamion' (1595) l. 278

23 Song made in lieu of many ornaments,
With which my love should duly have been
decked.
'Epithalamion' (1595) l. 427

1 The general end therefore of all the book is to fashion a gentleman or noble person in virtuous and gentle discipline.
The Faerie Queene (1596) preface

2 A gentle knight was pricking on the plain.
The Faerie Queene (1596) bk. 1, canto 1, st. 1

3 But on his breast a bloody cross he bore,
The dear remembrance of his dying Lord.
The Faerie Queene (1596) bk. 1, canto 1, st. 2

4 A bold bad man, that dared to call by name
Great Gorgon, Prince of darkness and dead night.
The Faerie Queene (1596) bk. 1, canto 1, st. 37; see **SHAKESPEARE** 710:15

5   Her angel's face
As the great eye of heaven shinèd bright,
And made a sunshine in the shady place;
Did never mortal eye behold such heavenly grace.
The Faerie Queene (1596) bk. 1, canto 3, st. 4

6 And all the hinder parts, that few could spy,
Were ruinous and old, but painted cunningly.
The Faerie Queene (1596) bk. 1, canto 4, st. 5

7 The noble heart, that harbours virtuous thought,
And is with child of glorious great intent,
Can never rest, until it forth have brought
Th' eternal brood of glory excellent.
The Faerie Queene (1596) bk. 1, canto 5, st. 1

8   A cruel crafty crocodile,
Which in false grief hiding his harmful guile,
Doth weep full sore, and sheddeth tender tears.
The Faerie Queene (1596) bk. 1, canto 5, st. 18

9 That darksome cave they enter, where they find
That cursèd man, low sitting on the ground,
Musing full sadly in his sullen mind.
The Faerie Queene (1596) bk. 1, canto 9, st. 35

10 Sleep after toil, port after stormy seas,
Ease after war, death after life does greatly please.
written on Joseph **CONRAD**'s *gravestone*
The Faerie Queene (1596) bk. 1, canto 9, st. 40

11 Upon her eyelids many Graces sate,
Under the shadow of her even brows.
The Faerie Queene (1596) bk. 2, canto 3, st. 25

12 And with rich metal loaded every rift.
The Faerie Queene (1596) bk. 2, canto 7, st. 28; see **KEATS** 458:16

13 And all for love, and nothing for reward.
The Faerie Queene (1596) bk. 2, canto 8, st. 2

14 So passeth, in the passing of a day,
Of mortal life the leaf, the bud, the flower,
No more doth flourish after first decay,
That erst was sought to deck both bed and bower.
The Faerie Queene (1596) bk. 2, canto 12, st. 75

15 Gather therefore the rose, whilst yet is prime,
For soon comes age, that will her pride deflower:

Gather the rose of love, whilst yet is time,
Whilst loving thou mayst lovèd be with equal crime.
The Faerie Queene (1596) bk. 2, canto 12, st. 75

16   The dunghill kind
Delights in filth and foul incontinence:
Let Grill be Grill, and have his hoggish mind.
The Faerie Queene (1596) bk. 2, canto 12, st. 87

17   Whether it divine tobacco were,
Or panachaea, or polygony.
The Faerie Queene (1596) bk. 3, canto 5, st. 32

18 And painful pleasure turns to pleasing pain.
The Faerie Queene (1596) bk. 3, canto 10, st. 60

19 And as she looked about, she did behold,
How over that same door was likewise writ,
Be bold, be bold, and everywhere Be bold . . .
At last she spied at that room's upper end
Another iron door, on which was writ
Be not too bold.
The Faerie Queene (1596) bk. 3, canto 11, st. 54

20 Dan Chaucer, well of English undefiled,
On Fame's eternal beadroll worthy to be filed.
The Faerie Queene (1596) bk. 4, canto 2, st. 32

21 For all that nature by her mother wit
Could frame in earth.
The Faerie Queene (1596) bk. 4, canto 10, st. 21

22 Ill can he rule the great, that cannot reach the small.
The Faerie Queene (1596) bk. 5, canto 2, st. 43

23 O sacred hunger of ambitious minds.
The Faerie Queene (1596) bk. 5, canto 12, st. 1

24 A monster, which the Blatant beast men call,
A dreadful fiend of gods and men ydrad.
The Faerie Queene (1596) bk. 5, canto 12, st. 37

25 The gentle mind by gentle deeds is known.
For a man by nothing is so well bewrayed,
As by his manners.
The Faerie Queene (1596) bk. 6, canto 3, st. 1

26 What man that sees the ever-whirling wheel
Of Change, the which all mortal things doth sway,
But that thereby doth find, and plainly feel,
How Mutability in them doth play
Her cruel sports, to many men's decay?
The Faerie Queene (1596) bk. 7, canto 6, st. 1

27 For all that moveth doth in Change delight:
But thenceforth all shall rest eternally
With Him that is the God of Sabbaoth hight:
O that great Sabbaoth God, grant me that Sabbaoth's sight.
The Faerie Queene (1596) bk. 7, canto 8, st. 2

28 That beauty is not, as fond men misdeem,
An outward show of things, that only seem.
'An Hymn in Honour of Beauty' (1596) l. 90

29 For of the soul the body form doth take;
For soul is form, and doth the body make.
'An Hymn in Honour of Beauty' (1596) l. 132

1 What more felicity can fall to creature,
Than to enjoy delight with liberty.
'Muiopotmos' (1591) l. 209

2 Calm was the day, and through the trembling air,
Sweet breathing Zephyrus did softly play.
Prothalamion (1596) l. 1

3 With that, I saw two swans of goodly hue,
Come softly swimming down along the Lee.
Prothalamion (1596) l. 37

4 So purely white they were,
That even the gentle stream, the which them bare,
Seemed foul to them, and bade his billows spare
To wet their silken feathers, lest they might
Soil their fair plumes with water not so fair
And mar their beauties bright,
That shone as Heaven's light,
Against their bridal day, which was not long:
Sweet Thames, run softly, till I end my song.
Prothalamion (1596) l. 46

5 Bring hither the pink and purple columbine,
With gillyflowers:
Bring coronation, and sops in wine,
Worn of paramours.
Strew me the ground with daffadowndillies,
And cowslips, and kingcups, and loved lilies.
The Shepherd's Calendar (1579) 'April' l. 136

6 And he that strives to touch the stars,
Oft stumbles at a straw.
The Shepherd's Calendar (1579) 'July' l. 99

7 Uncouth unkist, said the old famous poet Chaucer.
The Shepherd's Calendar (1579) 'Letter to Gabriel Harvey'; see **CHAUCER** 220:25

8 So now they have made our English tongue a gallimaufry or hodgepodge of all other speeches.
The Shepherd's Calendar (1579) 'Letter to Gabriel Harvey'

9 Out of every corner of the woods and glens they came creeping forth upon their hands, for their legs could not bear them; they looked like anatomies of death, they spake like ghosts crying out of their graves; they did eat the dead carrions . . . insomuch as the very carcases they spared not to scrape out of their graves; and, if they found a plot of watercresses or shamrocks, there they flocked as to a feast.
A View of the Present State of Ireland (1596)

Baruch Spinoza 1632–77
Dutch philosopher. On Spinoza: see **NOVALIS** 577:12

10 *Deus, sive Natura.*
God, or in other words, Nature.
Ethics (1677) pt. 1, para. 6

11 There is no hope without fear, and no fear without hope.
Ethics (1677) pt. 2, para. 178

12 I have striven not to laugh at human actions, not to weep at them, nor to hate them, but to understand them.
Tractatus Politicus (1677) ch. 1, sect. 4

Benjamin Spock 1903–98
American paediatrician

13 You know more than you think you do.
Common Sense Book of Baby and Child Care (1946) [later *Baby and Child Care*], opening words

14 To win in Vietnam, we will have to exterminate a nation.
Dr Spock on Vietnam (1968) ch. 7

William Archibald Spooner 1844–1930
English clergyman; Warden of New College, Oxford, 1903–24

15 You will find as you grow older that the weight of rages will press harder and harder upon the employer.
William Hayter *Spooner* (1977) ch. 6

16 Her late husband, you know, a very sad death—eaten by missionaries—poor soul!
William Hayter *Spooner* (1977) ch. 6

Thomas Sprat 1635–1713
English clergyman and writer

17 A most venomous thing in the making of sciences; for whoever has fixed on his cause, before he has experimented, can hardly avoid fitting his experiment to his own cause . . . rather than the cause to the truth of the experiment itself.
on 'Aristotelian experiments, intended to illustrate a preconceived truth and convince people of its validity'
History of the Royal Society (1667)

Cecil Spring-Rice 1859–1918
English diplomat; Ambassador to Washington from 1912

18 I vow to thee, my country—all earthly things above—
Entire and whole and perfect, the service of my love,
The love that asks no question: the love that stands the test,
That lays upon the altar the dearest and the best:
The love that never falters, the love that pays the price,
The love that makes undaunted the final sacrifice.
'I Vow to Thee, My Country' (written on the eve of his departure from Washington, 12 January 1918)

19 And there's another country, I've heard of long ago—
Most dear to them that love her, most great to them that know.
'I Vow to Thee, My Country' (written 1918)

1 Her ways are ways of gentleness and all her
paths are Peace.
'I Vow to Thee, My Country' (written 1918); see **BIBLE** 87:23

2 I am the Dean of Christ Church, Sir:
There's my wife; look well at her.
She's the Broad and I'm the High;
We are the University.
*the first couplet was unofficially altered to: 'I am the Dean,
and this is Mrs Liddell; / She the first, and I the second
fiddle'*
The Masque of Balliol (composed by and current among
members of Balliol College, Oxford, in the 1870s) in W. G.
Hiscock (ed.) *The Balliol Rhymes* (1939) see **ANONYMOUS** 19:3,
BEECHING 65:16

Bruce Springsteen 1949–
American rock singer and songwriter

3 Born in the USA.
title of song (1984)

4 Born down in a dead man's town
The first kick I took was when I hit the ground.
'Born in the USA' (1984 song)

5 We gotta get out while we're young,
'Cause tramps like us, baby, we were born to
run.
'Born to Run' (1974 song)

6 Is a dream a lie if it don't come true,
Or is it something worse?
'The River' (1980 song)

C. H. Spurgeon 1834–92
English nonconformist preacher

7 If you want truth to go round the world you
must hire an express train to pull it; but if you
want a lie to go round the world, it will fly: it is
as light as a feather, and a breath will carry it. It
is well said in the old proverb, 'a lie will go
round the world while truth is pulling its boots
on'.
Gems from Spurgeon (1859)

J. C. Squire 1884–1958
English man of letters

8 But I'm not so think as you drunk I am.
'Ballade of Soporific Absorption' (1931)

9 It did not last: the Devil howling 'Ho!
Let Einstein be!' restored the status quo.
'In continuation of Pope on Newton' (1926); see **POPE** 615:22

Mme de Staël (Anne-Louise-Germaine
Necker) 1766–1817
French writer

10 *Tout comprendre rend très indulgent.*
To be totally understanding makes one very
indulgent.
Corinne (1807) bk. 18, ch. 5; see **PROVERBS** 645:26

11 *Un homme peut braver l'opinion; une femme doit s'y
soumettre.*

A man can brave opinion, a woman must submit
to it.
Delphine (1802) epigraph

12 Speech happens not to be his language.
*on being asked what she found to talk about with her new
lover, a hussar*
attributed

Lord Stair 1648–1707
Scottish politician

13 It's a great work of charity to be exact in
rooting out that damnable sept, the worst in all
the Highlands.
*on hearing that Alasdair Maclan, chief of the Glencoe
MacDonalds, had been too late in taking the required oath
of loyalty to* **WILLIAM III**
letter to Thomas Livingston, 11 January 1692

Joseph Stalin (Iosif Vissarionovich
Dzhugashvili) 1879–1953
Soviet dictator

14 The State is an instrument in the hands of the
ruling class, used to break the resistance of the
adversaries of that class.
Foundations of Leninism (1924) section 4/6

15 There are various forms of production: artillery,
automobiles, lorries. You also produce
'commodities', 'works', 'products'. Such things
are highly necessary. Engineering things. For
people's souls. 'Products' are highly necessary
too. 'Products' are very important for people's
souls. You are engineers of human souls.
speech to writers at **GORKY**'s house, 26 October 1932; A.
Kemp-Welch *Stalin and the Literary Intelligentsia, 1928–39*
(1991); see **GORKY** 366:9

16 The Pope! How many divisions has *he* got?
*on being asked to encourage Catholicism in Russia by way
of conciliating the Pope, 13 May 1935*
W. S. Churchill *The Gathering Storm* (1948) ch. 8; see
NAPOLEON I 568:7

17 There is one eternally true legend—that of
Judas.
at the trial of Radek in 1937
Robert Payne *The Rise and Fall of Stalin* (1966)

18 One death is a tragedy, a million deaths a
statistic.
attributed

Bessie Anderson Stanley fl. 1905
American writer

19 He has achieved success who has lived well,
laughed often, and loved much; who has enjoyed
the trust of pure women, the respect of
intelligent men, and the love of little children;
. . . whose life was an inspiration, whose
memory a benediction.
'What Constitutes Success', in *Modern Women* December
1905, and often wrongly attributed to Ralph Waldo **EMERSON**

or Robert Louis **STEVENSON**; in *Notes and Queries* July 1976

Henry Morton Stanley 1841–1904
Welsh explorer and journalist

1 Dr Livingstone, I presume?
How I found Livingstone (1872) ch. 11

Charles E. Stanton 1859–1933
American soldier

2 *Lafayette, nous voilà!*

Lafayette, we are here.
at the tomb of Lafayette in Paris, 4 July 1917; in *New York Tribune* 6 September 1917

Edwin Mcmasters Stanton 1814–69
American lawyer

3 Now he belongs to the ages.
of Abraham **LINCOLN**, *following his assassination, 15 April 1865*
I. M. Tarbell *Life of Abraham Lincoln* (1900) vol. 2

Elizabeth Cady Stanton 1815–1902
American suffragist

4 It is impossible for one class to appreciate the wrongs of another.
History of Woman Suffrage (1881–1922) vol. 2, ch. 19

5 The Bible teaches that woman brought sin and death into the world, that she precipitated the fall of the race . . . marriage for her was to be a condition of bondage, maternity a period of suffering and anguish, and in silence and subjection, she was to play the role of a dependant on man's bounty for all her material wants.
The Woman's Bible (1895) pt. 1, introduction

6 Woman's degradation is in man's idea of his sexual rights. Our religion, laws, customs, are all founded on the belief that woman was made for man.
letter to Susan B. Anthony, 14 June 1860, in T. Stanton and H. Stanton Blatch (eds.) *Elizabeth Cady Stanton* (1922) vol. 2

Frank L. Stanton 1857–1927
American journalist and poet

7 Sweetes' li'l' feller,
Everybody knows;
Dunno what to call him,
But he's mighty lak' a rose!
'Mighty Lak' a Rose' (1901 song)

John Stark 1728–1822
American Revolutionary officer

8 We beat them to-day or Molly Stark's a widow.
before the Battle of Bennington, 16 August 1777, in *Cyclopaedia of American Biography* vol. 5

Statius (Publius Papinius Statius) *c.*AD 45–*c.*96
Roman poet

9 Fear first made gods in the world.
Thebaid (*c.*AD 90) bk. 3, l. 661

Christina Stead 1902–83
Australian novelist

10 A self-made man is one who believes in luck and sends his son to Oxford.
House of All Nations (1938) 'Credo'

David Steel 1938–
British Liberal politician; Leader of the Liberal Party 1976–88

11 I have the good fortune to be the first Liberal leader for over half a century who is able to say to you at the end of our annual assembly: go back to your constituencies and prepare for government.
speech to the Liberal Party Assembly, 18 September 1981

12 It is the settled will of the majority of people in Scotland that they want not just the symbol, but the substance of the return of democratic control over internal affairs.
on the announcement that the Stone of Destiny would be returned to Scotland
in *Scotsman* 4 July 1996

Richard Steele 1672–1729
Irish-born essayist and dramatist

13 The insupportable labour of doing nothing.
in *The Spectator* no. 54 (2 May 1711)

14 A woman seldom writes her mind but in her postscript.
in *The Spectator* no. 79 (31 May 1711); see **BACON** 46:18

15 There are so few who can grow old with a good grace.
in *The Spectator* no. 263 (1 January 1712)

16 It is to be noted that when any part of this paper appears dull there is a design in it.
in *The Tatler* no. 38 (7 July 1709)

17 To love her is a liberal education.
of Lady Elizabeth Hastings
in *The Tatler* no. 49 (2 August 1709)

18 Reading is to the mind what exercise is to the body.
in *The Tatler* no. 147 (18 March 1710)

19 It was very prettily said, that we may learn the little value of fortune by the persons on whom heaven is pleased to bestow it.
in *The Tatler* no. 203 (27 July 1710); see **LUTHER** 505:11, **SWIFT** 782:19

Lincoln Steffens 1866–1936
American journalist

20 I have seen the future; and it works.
following a visit to the Soviet Union in 1919
letter to Marie Howe, 3 April 1919, in *Letters* (1938) vol. 1; in

J. M. Thompson *Russia, Bolshevism and the Versailles Treaty* (1954) it is recalled that Steffens had composed the expression before he had even arrived in Russia

Edward Steichen 1879–1973

Luxembourg-born American photographer

1 The mission of photography is to explain man to man and each man to himself.

Cornell Capa (ed.) *The Concerned Photographer* (1972)

Gertrude Stein 1874–1946

American writer. On Stein: see **ANONYMOUS** 18:1, **FADIMAN** 322:13, **LEWIS** 492:16

2 Remarks are not literature.

Autobiography of Alice B. Toklas (1933) ch. 7

3 Pigeons on the grass alas.

Four Saints in Three Acts (1934) act 3, sc. 2

4 In the United States there is more space where nobody is than where anybody is. That is what makes America what it is.

The Geographical History of America (1936)

5 Rose is a rose is a rose is a rose, is a rose.

Sacred Emily (1913)

6 You are all a lost generation.

of the young who served in the First World War

the phrase having been borrowed (in translation) from a French garage mechanic, whom Stein heard address it disparagingly to an incompetent apprentice; Ernest **HEMINGWAY** subsequently took it as his epigraph to *The Sun Also Rises* (1926)

7 'What *is* the answer?' No answer came. She laughed and said, 'In that case what is the question?'

last words; Donald Sutherland *Gertrude Stein, A Biography of her Work* (1951)

John Steinbeck 1902–68

American novelist. See also **HOWE** 417:3

8 Man, unlike any other thing organic or inorganic in the universe, grows beyond his work, walks up the stairs of his concepts, emerges ahead of his accomplishments.

The Grapes of Wrath (1939) ch. 14

9 Okie use' ta mean you was from Oklahoma. Now it means you're a dirty son-of-a-bitch. Okie means you're scum. Don't mean nothing itself, it's the way they say it.

The Grapes of Wrath (1939) ch. 18

Gloria Steinem 1934–

American journalist. See also **SAYINGS** 685:21

10 We are becoming the men we wanted to marry.

in *Ms* July/August 1982

11 Outrageous acts and everyday rebellions.

title of book (1983)

Peter Steiner *see* Cartoon captions 205:14

Stendhal (Henri Beyle) 1783–1842

French novelist. On Stendhal: see **GIDE** 356:6

12 *La beauté n'est que la promesse du bonheur.*

Beauty is only a promise of happiness.

L'Amour (1822) ch. 17

13 *D'après le système actuel de l'éducation des jeunes filles, tous les génes qui naissent femmes sont perdus pour le bonheur du public.*

With the present system of education for girls any genius who happens to be born a *woman* can make no contribution to public happiness.

L'Amour (1822) ch. 56

14 *L'unique passion survivante à toutes les autres est l'argent.*

The only passion that has outlived all the rest is love of money.

La Chartreuse de Parme (1839) vol. 1, ch. 6

15 *La vérité, l'âpre vérité.*

Truth, bitter truth.

Le Rouge et le noir (1830) bk. 1 epigraph; attributed by Stendhal to **DANTON**, but amost certainly invented by Stendhal

16 *Le feu sacré avec lequel on se fait un nom.*

The sacred fire with which one makes one's name.

Le Rouge et le noir (1830) bk. 1, ch. 12

17 *Il est impossible d'être plus malheureuse . . . J'espère que je vais mourir . . . Je sens mon coeur se glacer.*

It would be impossible for a woman to be more wretched . . . I hope I am going to die . . . I feel my heart freezing.

Le Rouge et le noir (1830) bk. 1, ch. 23

18 *Un roman est un miroir qui se promène sur une grande route. Tantôt il reflète à vos yeux l'azur des cieux, tantôt la fange des bourbiers de la route.*

A novel is a mirror which passes over a highway. Sometimes it reflects to your eyes the blue of the skies, at others the churned-up mud of the road.

Le Rouge et le noir (1830) bk. 2, ch. 19

19 *La politique au milieu des intérêts d'imagination, c'est un coup de pistolet au milieu d'un concert.*

Politics in the middle of things that concern the imagination are like a pistol-shot in the middle of a concert.

Le Rouge et le noir (1830) bk. 2, ch. 22

20 *Pour qui a goûté de la profonde occupation d'écrire, lire n'est plus qu'un plaisir secondaire.*

For those who have tasted the profound activity of writing, reading is no more than a secondary pleasure.

Souvenirs d'égotisme (1892) ch. 9

21 *J'aimais, et j'aime encore, les mathématiques pour elles-mêmes comme n'admettant pas l'hypocrisie et le vague, mes deux bêtes d'aversion.*

I used to love mathematics for its own sake, and I still do, because it allows for no hypocrisy and no vagueness, my two *bêtes noires*.

La Vie d'Henri Brulard (1890) ch. 10

1 I know of only one rule: style cannot be too *clear*, too *simple*.

letter to Balzac, 30 October 1840

J. K. Stephen 1859–92

English journalist and writer of light verse

2 Ah! Matt.: old age has brought to me
Thy wisdom, less thy certainty:
The world's a jest, and joy's a trinket:
I knew that once: but now—I think it.

'Senex to Matt. Prior' (1891); see **EPITAPHS** 318:15

3 Two voices are there: one is of the deep;
It learns the storm-cloud's thunderous melody,
Now roars, now murmurs with the changing sea,
Now bird-like pipes, now closes soft in sleep:
And one is of an old half-witted sheep
Which bleats articulate monotony,
And indicates that two and one are three,
That grass is green, lakes damp, and mountains steep
And, Wordsworth, both are thine.

'A Sonnet' (1891); see **WORDSWORTH** 869:16

4 When the Rudyards cease from kipling
And the Haggards ride no more.

'To R.K.' (1891)

Leslie Stephen 1832–1904

English scholar and philosopher, first editor of the *Dictionary of National Biography*

5 The editor of such a work must, by the necessity of the case, be autocratic. He will do his best to be a considerate autocrat.

of the compilation of a dictionary of national biography
in *Athenaeum* 23 December 1882

James Stephens 1882–1950

Irish poet and nationalist

6 Finality is death. Perfection is finality. Nothing is perfect. There are lumps in it.

The Crock of Gold (1912) bk. 1, ch. 4

7 I hear a sudden cry of pain!
There is a rabbit in a snare:
Now I hear the cry again,
But I cannot tell from where . . .
Little one! Oh, little one!
I am searching everywhere.

'The Snare' (1915)

8 In my definition they were good men—men, that is, who willed no evil. No person living is the worse off for having known Thomas MacDonagh.

The Insurrection in Dublin (1916)

Laurence Sterne 1713–68

English novelist. On Sterne: see **JOHNSON** 443:7; see also **WALPOLE** 837:12

9 They order, said I, this matter better in France.

A Sentimental Journey (1768) opening words

10 I pity the man who can travel from Dan to Beersheba, and cry, 'tis all barren.

A Sentimental Journey (1768) 'In the Street. Calais'

11 If ever I do a mean action, it must be in some interval betwixt one passion and another.

A Sentimental Journey (1768) 'Montriul'

12 There are worse occupations in this world than feeling a woman's pulse.

A Sentimental Journey (1768) 'The Pulse. Paris'

13 God tempers the wind, said Maria, to the shorn lamb.

derived from a French proverb, but familiar in this form of words
A Sentimental Journey (1768) 'Maria'

14 Dear sensibility! source inexhausted of all that's precious in our joys, or costly in our sorrows!

A Sentimental Journey (1768) 'The Bourbonnois'

15 I wish either my father or my mother, or indeed both of them, as they were in duty both equally bound to it, had minded what they were about when they begot me.

Tristram Shandy (1759–67) bk. 1, ch. 1

16 'Pray, my dear,' quoth my mother, 'have you not forgot to wind up the clock?'—'Good G—!' cried my father, making an exclamation, but taking care to moderate his voice at the same time,—'Did ever woman, since the creation of the world, interrupt a man with such a silly question?'

Tristram Shandy (1759–67) bk. 1, ch. 1

17 As we jog on, either laugh with me, or at me, or in short do anything,—only keep your temper.

Tristram Shandy (1759–67) bk. 1, ch. 6

18 So long as a man rides his Hobby-Horse peaceably and quietly along the King's highway, and neither compels you or me to get up behind him,—pray, Sir, what have either you or I to do with it?

Tristram Shandy (1759–67) bk. 1, ch. 7

19 He was in a few hours of giving his enemies the slip for ever.

Tristram Shandy (1759–67) bk. 1, ch. 12

20 'Tis known by the name of perseverance in a good cause,—and of obstinacy in a bad one.

Tristram Shandy (1759–67) bk. 1, ch. 17

21 My uncle Toby would never offer to answer this by any other kind of argument, than that of whistling half a dozen bars of Lillabullero.

Tristram Shandy (1759–67) bk. 1, ch. 21; see **WHARTON** 849:12

22 Digressions, incontestably, are the sunshine;—they are the life, the soul of reading;—take them out of this book for instance,—you might as well take the book along with them.

Tristram Shandy (1759–67) bk. 1, ch. 22

1 I should have no objection to this method, but that I think it must smell too strong of the lamp.

Tristram Shandy (1759–67) bk. 1, ch. 23

2 Writing, when properly managed (as you may be sure I think mine is) is but a different name for conversation.

Tristram Shandy (1759–67) bk. 2, ch. 11

3 'I'll not hurt thee,' says my uncle Toby, rising from his chair, and going across the room, with the fly in his hand,—'I'll not hurt a hair of thy head:—Go,' says he, lifting up the sash, and opening his hand as he spoke, to let it escape;—'go, poor devil, get thee gone, why should I hurt thee?—This world surely is wide enough to hold both thee and me.'

Tristram Shandy (1759–67) bk. 2, ch. 12

4 Whenever a man talks loudly against religion,—always suspect that it is not his reason, but his passions which have got the better of his creed.

Tristram Shandy (1759–67) bk. 2, ch. 17

5 It is the nature of an hypothesis, when once a man has conceived it, that it assimilates every thing to itself, as proper nourishment; and, from the first moment of your begetting it, it generally grows the stronger by every thing you see, hear, read, or understand.

Tristram Shandy (1759–67) bk. 2, ch. 19

6 'Our armies swore terribly in Flanders,' cried my uncle Toby,—'but nothing to this.'

Tristram Shandy (1759–67) bk. 3, ch. 11

7 The corregiescity of Corregio.

Tristram Shandy (1759–67) bk. 3, ch. 12

8 Of all the cants which are canted in this canting world,—though the cant of hypocrites may be the worst,—the cant of criticism is the most tormenting!

Tristram Shandy (1759–67) bk. 3, ch. 12

9 True *Shandeism*, think what you will against it, opens the heart and lungs, and like all those affections which partake of its nature, it forces the blood and other vital fluids of the body to run freely through its channels, and makes the wheel of life run long and cheerfully round.

Tristram Shandy (1759–67) bk. 4, ch. 32

10 'There is no terror, brother Toby, in its [death's] looks, but what it borrows from groans and convulsions—and the blowing of noses, and the wiping away of tears with the bottoms of curtains, in a dying man's room—Strip it of these, what is it?'—''Tis better in battle than in bed', said my uncle Toby.

Tristram Shandy (1759–67) bk. 5, ch. 3

11 There is a North-west passage to the intellectual World.

Tristram Shandy (1759–67) bk. 5, ch. 42

12 'The poor soul will die:—' 'He shall not die, by G—', cried my uncle Toby.—The Accusing Spirit, which flew up to heaven's chancery with the oath, blushed as he gave it in;—and the Recording Angel, as he wrote it down, dropped a tear upon the word, and blotted it out for ever.

Tristram Shandy (1759–67) bk. 6, ch. 8

13 To say a man is fallen in love,—or that he is deeply in love,—or up to the ears in love,—and sometimes even over head and ears in it,—carries an idiomatical kind of implication, that love is a thing below a man:—this is recurring again to Plato's opinion, which, with all his divinityship,—I hold to be damnable and heretical:—and so much for that.

Let love therefore be what it will,—my uncle Toby fell into it.

Tristram Shandy (1759–67) bk. 6, ch. 37

14 My brother Toby, quoth she, is going to be married to Mrs Wadman.

Then he will never, quoth my father, lie *diagonally* in his bed again as long as he lives.

Tristram Shandy (1759–67) bk. 6, ch. 39

15 Now hang it! quoth I, as I look'd towards the French coast—A man should know something of his own country too, before he goes abroad.

Tristram Shandy (1759–67) bk. 7, ch. 2

16 And who are you? said he.—Don't puzzle me, said I.

Tristram Shandy (1759–67) bk. 7, ch. 33

17 Nothing is so perfectly amusement as a total change of ideas.

Tristram Shandy (1759–67) bk. 9 'A Dedication to a Great Man'

18 Everything presses on—whilst thou art twisting that lock,—see! it grows grey; and every time I kiss thy hand to bid adieu, and every absence which follows it, are preludes to that eternal separation which we are shortly to make.

Tristram Shandy (1759–67) bk. 9, ch. 10

19 L—d! said my mother, what is all this story about?— A Cock and a Bull, said Yorick.

Tristram Shandy (1759–67) bk. 9, ch. 33

20 This sad vicissitude of things.

Sermons (1767) no. 16 'The character of Shimei'

Brooks Stevens 1911–95

American industrial designer

21 Our whole economy is based on planned obsolescence.

Vance Packard *The Waste Makers* (1960) ch. 6

Wallace Stevens 1879–1955

American poet

22 The poet is the priest of the invisible.

'Adagia' (1957)

1 Chieftain Iffucan of Azcan in caftan
Of tan with henna hackles, halt!
'Bantams in Pine Woods' (1923)

2 Call the roller of big cigars,
The muscular one, and bid him whip
In kitchen cups concupiscent curds.
'The Emperor of Ice-Cream' (1923)

3 Let be be finale of seem.
The only emperor is the emperor of ice-cream.
'The Emperor of Ice-Cream' (1923)

4 Frogs Eat Butterflies. Snakes Eat Frogs. Hogs Eat
Snakes. Men Eat Hogs.
title of poem (1923)

5 Poetry is the supreme fiction, madame.
'A High-Toned old Christian Woman' (1923)

6 They said, 'You have a blue guitar,
You do not play things as they are.'

The man replied, 'Things as they are
Are changed upon the blue guitar.'
'The Man with the Blue Guitar' (1937)

7 They will get it straight one day at the
Sorbonne.
We shall return at twilight from the lecture
Pleased that the irrational is rational.
Notes Toward a Supreme Fiction (1947) 'It Must Give Pleasure'
no. 10

8 The palm at the end of the mind,
Beyond the last thought, rises . . .
A gold-feathered bird
Sings in the palm.
'Of Mere Being' (1957)

9 Music is feeling, then, not sound.
'Peter Quince at the Clavier' (1923) pt. 1

10 Beauty is momentary in the mind—
The fitful tracing of a portal;
But in the flesh it is immortal.
The body dies; the body's beauty lives.
'Peter Quince at the Clavier' (1923) pt. 4

11 Susanna's music touched the bawdy strings
Of those white elders.
'Peter Quince at the Clavier' (1923) pt. 4

12 One must have a mind of winter
To regard the frost and the boughs
Of the pine trees crusted with snow;
And have been cold a long time
To behold the junipers shagged with ice,
The spruces rough in the distant glitter
Of the January sun; and not to think
Of any misery in the sound of the wind.
'The Snow Man' (1921)

13 For the listener, who listens in the snow,
And, nothing himself, beholds
Nothing that is not there and the nothing that
is.
'The Snow Man' (1921)

14 Complacencies of the peignoir, and late
Coffee and oranges in a sunny chair,
And the green freedom of a cockatoo

Upon a rug mingle to dissipate
The holy hush of ancient sacrifice.
'Sunday Morning' (1923) st. 1

15 Deer walk upon our mountains, and the quail
Whistle about us their spontaneous cries;
Sweet berries ripen in the wilderness;
And, in the isolation of the sky,
At evening, casual flocks of pigeons make
Ambiguous undulations as they sink,
Downward to darkness, on extended wings.
'Sunday Morning' (1923) st. 8

16 I do not know which to prefer,
The beauty of inflections
Or the beauty of innuendoes,
The blackbird whistling
Or just after.
'Thirteen Ways of Looking at a Blackbird' (1923)

17 Style is not something applied. It is something
inherent, something that permeates.
lecture, Mount Holyoake College, 28 April 1951, *Two or Three
Ideas* (1957)

Adlai Stevenson 1900–65

American Democratic politician. See also **ANONYMOUS** 16:3

18 I suppose flattery hurts no one, that is, if he
doesn't inhale.
television broadcast, 30 March 1952, in N. F. Busch *Adlai E.
Stevenson* (1952) ch. 5

19 If they [the Republicans] will stop telling lies
about the Democrats, we will stop telling the
truth about them.
speech during 1952 Presidential campaign; in J. B. Martin
Adlai Stevenson and Illinois (1976) ch. 8

20 Let's talk sense to the American people. Let's
tell them the truth, that there are no gains
without pains.
speech of acceptance at the Democratic National Convention,
Chicago, Illinois, 26 July 1952; in *Speeches* (1952)

21 In America any boy may become President and I
suppose it's just one of the risks he takes!
speech in Indianapolis, 26 September 1952; in *Major Campaign
Speeches . . . 1952* (1953)

22 A free society is a society where it is safe to be
unpopular.
speech in Detroit, 7 October 1952; in *Major Campaign
Speeches . . . 1952* (1953)

23 The young man who asks you to set him one
heart-beat from the Presidency of the United
States.
of Richard NIXON as Vice-Presidential nominee
speech at Cleveland, Ohio, 23 October 1952, in *New York
Times* 24 October 1952

24 We hear the Secretary of State boasting of his
brinkmanship—the art of bringing us to the
edge of the abyss.
speech in Hartford, Connecticut, 25 February 1956; in *New
York Times* 26 February 1956; see **DULLES** 299:2

1 She would rather light a candle than curse the darkness, and her glow has warmed the world.
of Eleanor **ROOSEVELT**
in *New York Times* 8 November 1962; see **PROVERBS** 627:38

Anne Stevenson 1933–

English poet

2 Blackbirds are the cellos of the deep farms.
'Green Mountain, Black Mountain' (1982)

Robert Louis Stevenson 1850–94

Scottish novelist and writer

3 Every one lives by selling something.
Across the Plains (1892) 'Beggars' pt. 3

4 The harmless art of knucklebones has seen the fall of the Roman empire and the rise of the United States.
Across the Plains (1892) 'The Lantern-Bearers' pt. 1

5 The bright face of danger.
Across the Plains (1892) 'The Lantern-Bearers' pt. 4

6 Here lies one who meant well, tried a little, failed much:—surely that may be his epitaph, of which he need not be ashamed.
Across the Plains (1892) 'A Christmas Sermon' pt. 4

7 The web, then, or the pattern; a web at once sensuous and logical, an elegant and pregnant texture: that is style, that is the foundation of the art of literature.
The Art of Writing (1905) 'On some technical Elements of Style in Literature' (written 1885)

8 Politics is perhaps the only profession for which no preparation is thought necessary.
Familiar Studies of Men and Books (1882) 'Yoshida-Torajiro'

9 Am I no a bonny fighter?
Kidnapped (1886) ch. 10

10 I've a grand memory for forgetting, David.
Kidnapped (1886) ch. 18

11 I kept always two books in my pocket, one to read, one to write in.
Memories and Portraits (1887) ch. 4 'A College Magazine'

12 I have thus played the sedulous ape to Hazlitt, to Lamb, to Wordsworth, to Sir Thomas Browne, to Defoe, to Hawthorne, to Montaigne, to Baudelaire and to Obermann.
Memories and Portraits (1887) ch. 4 'A College Magazine'

13 These are my politics: to change what we can; to better what we can; but still to bear in mind that man is but a devil weakly fettered by some generous beliefs and impositions; and for no word however sounding, and no cause however just and pious, to relax the stricture of these bonds.
More New Arabian Nights: The Dynamiter (1885) 'Epilogue of the Cigar Divan'

14 I regard you with an indifference closely bordering on aversion.
New Arabian Nights (1882) 'The Rajah's Diamond: Story of the Bandbox'

15 The strange case of Dr Jekyll and Mr Hyde.
title of novel, 1886

16 With every day, and from both sides of my intelligence, the moral and the intellectual, I thus drew steadily nearer to that truth, by whose partial discovery I have been doomed to such a dreadful shipwreck: that man is not truly one, but truly two.
The Strange Case of Dr Jekyll and Mr Hyde (1886)

17 A faddling hedonist.
Travels with a Donkey (1879) 'The Boarders'

18 For my part, I travel not to go anywhere, but to go. I travel for travel's sake. The great affair is to move.
Travels with a Donkey (1879) 'Cheylard and Luc'

19 I own I like definite form in what my eyes are to rest upon; and if landscapes were sold, like the sheets of characters of my boyhood, one penny plain and twopence coloured, I should go the length of twopence every day of my life.
Travels with a Donkey (1879) 'Father Apollinaris'

20 Fifteen men on the dead man's chest
Yo-ho-ho, and a bottle of rum!
Drink and the devil had done for the rest—
Yo-ho-ho, and a bottle of rum!
Treasure Island (1883) ch. 1

21 Tip me the black spot.
Treasure Island (1883) ch. 3

22 Pieces of eight, pieces of eight, pieces of eight!
Treasure Island (1883) ch. 10

23 Many's the long night I've dreamed of cheese—toasted, mostly.
Treasure Island (1883) ch. 15

24 Even if the doctor does not give you a year, even if he hesitates about a month, make one brave push and see what can be accomplished in a week.
Virginibus Puerisque (1881) 'Aes Triplex'

25 There is no duty we so much underrate as the duty of being happy.
Virginibus Puerisque (1881) 'An Apology for Idlers'

26 Old and young, we are all on our last cruise.
Virginibus Puerisque (1881) 'Crabbed Age and Youth'

27 To travel hopefully is a better thing than to arrive, and the true success is to labour.
Virginibus Puerisque (1881) 'El Dorado'; see **PROVERBS** 636:13

28 In marriage, a man becomes slack and selfish, and undergoes a fatty degeneration of his moral being.
Virginibus Puerisque (1881) title essay, pt. 1

29 Even if we take matrimony at its lowest, even if we regard it as no more than a sort of friendship recognised by the police.
Virginibus Puerisque (1881) title essay, pt. 1

30 Marriage is like life in this—that it is a field of battle, and not a bed of roses.
Virginibus Puerisque (1881) title essay, pt. 1

1 To marry is to domesticate the Recording Angel. Once you are married, there is nothing left for you, not even suicide, but to be good.
Virginibus Puerisque (1881) title essay, pt. 2

2 Man is a creature who lives not upon bread alone, but principally by catchwords.
Virginibus Puerisque (1881) title essay, pt. 2; see **BIBLE** 98:20

3 The cruellest lies are often told in silence.
Virginibus Puerisque (1881) title essay, pt. 4

4 Though we are mighty fine fellows nowadays, we cannot write like Hazlitt.
Virginibus Puerisque (1881) 'Walking Tours'

5 On he went up the great, bare staircase of his duty, uncheered and undepressed.
Weir of Hermiston (1911) ch. 2

6 What hangs people . . . is the unfortunate circumstance of guilt.
The Wrong Box (with Lloyd Osbourne, 1889) ch. 7

7 Nothing like a little judicious levity.
The Wrong Box (with Lloyd Osbourne, 1889) ch. 7

8 Between the possibility of being hanged in all innocence, and the certainty of a public and merited disgrace, no gentleman of spirit could long hesitate.
The Wrong Box (with Lloyd Osbourne, 1889) ch. 10

9 If you are going to make a book end badly, it must end badly from the beginning.
letter to J. M. Barrie, November 1892, in Sidney Colvin (ed.) *Letters of Robert Louis Stevenson* (1911) vol. 4

10 I am an Epick writer with a k to it, but without the necessary genius.
letter to Henry James, 5 December 1892, in Sidney Colvin (ed.) *Letters of Robert Louis Stevenson* (1911) vol. 4

11 I believe in an ultimate decency of things.
letter to Sidney Colvin, 23 August 1893, in Sidney Colvin (ed.) *Letters of Robert Louis Stevenson* (1911) vol. 4

12 In winter I get up at night
And dress by yellow candle-light.
In summer, quite the other way,—
I have to go to bed by day.
A Child's Garden of Verses (1885) 'Bed in Summer'

13 The world is so full of a number of things,
I'm sure we should all be as happy as kings.
A Child's Garden of Verses (1885) 'Happy Thought'

14 I was the giant great and still
That sits upon the pillow-hill,
And sees before him, dale and plain,
The pleasant land of counterpane.
A Child's Garden of Verses (1885) 'The Land of Counterpane'

15 I have a little shadow that goes in and out with me,
And what can be the use of him is more than I can see.
He is very, very like me from the heels up to the head;
And I see him jump before me, when I jump into my bed.
A Child's Garden of Verses (1885) 'My Shadow'

16 Let us arise and go like men,
And face with an undaunted tread
The long black passage up to bed.
A Child's Garden of Verses (1885) 'North-West Passage. Good-Night'

17 A child should always say what's true,
And speak when he is spoken to,
And behave mannerly at table:
At least as far as he is able.
A Child's Garden of Verses (1885) 'Whole Duty of Children'

18 Whenever the moon and stars are set,
Whenever the wind is high,
All night long in the dark and wet,
A man goes riding by.
Late in the night when the fires are out,
Why does he gallop and gallop about?
A Child's Garden of Verses (1885) 'Windy Nights'

19 But all that I could think of, in the darkness and the cold,
Was that I was leaving home and my folks were growing old.
'Christmas at Sea' (1890)

20 In the highlands, in the country places,
Where the old plain men have rosy faces,
And the young fair maidens
Quiet eyes.
Songs of Travel (1896) 'In the highlands, in the country places'

21 I will make you brooches and toys for your delight
Of bird-song at morning and star-shine at night.
Songs of Travel (1896) 'I will make you brooches and toys for your delight'

22 I will make my kitchen, and you shall keep your room,
Where white flows the river and bright blows the broom,
And you shall wash your linen and keep your body white
In rainfall at morning and dewfall at night.
Songs of Travel (1896) 'I will make you brooches and toys for your delight'

23 Trusty, dusky, vivid, true,
With eyes of gold and bramble-dew,
Steel-true and blade-straight,
The great artificer
Made my mate.
Songs of Travel (1896) 'My Wife'

24 Sing me a song of a lad that is gone,
Say, could that lad be I?
Merry of soul he sailed on a day
Over the sea to Skye.
Songs of Travel (1896) 'Sing me a song of a lad that is gone'

25 Be it granted to me to behold you again in dying,
Hills of home! and to hear again the call;
Hear about the graves of the martyrs the peewees crying,
And hear no more at all.
Songs of Travel (1896) 'To S. R. Crockett'

1 Give to me the life I love,
Let the lave go by me,
Give the jolly heaven above
And the byway nigh me.
Bed in the bush with stars to see,
Bread I dip in the river—
There's the life for a man like me,
There's the life for ever.
   Songs of Travel (1896) 'The Vagabond'

2 Let the blow fall soon or late,
Let what will be o'er me;
Give the face of earth around
And the road before me.
Wealth I seek not, hope nor love,
Nor a friend to know me;
All I seek, the heaven above
And the road below me.
   Songs of Travel (1896) 'The Vagabond'

3 Of all my verse, like not a single line;
But like my title, for it is not mine.
That title from a better man I stole;
Ah, how much better, had I stol'n the whole!
   Underwoods (1887) foreword; see **JONSON** 447:6

4 Go, little book, and wish to all
Flowers in the garden, meat in the hall,
A bin of wine, a spice of wit,
A house with lawns enclosing it,
A living river by the door,
A nightingale in the sycamore!
   Underwoods (1887) 'Envoy'; see **CHAUCER** 221:11

5 Under the wide and starry sky
Dig the grave and let me lie.
Glad did I live and gladly die,
And I laid me down with a will.
This be the verse you grave for me:
'Here he lies where he longed to be;
Home is the sailor, home from sea,
And the hunter home from the hill.'
   Underwoods (1887) 'Requiem'

6 And what should Master Gauger play
But 'Over the hills and far away'?
   Underwoods (1887) 'A Song of the Road'; see **GAY** 351:4,
   NURSERY RHYMES 582:6

Ian Stewart 1945–
English mathematician

7 Genes are not like engineering blueprints; they
are more like recipes in a cookbook. They tell us
what ingredients to use, in what quantities, and
in what order—but they do not provide a
complete, accurate plan of the final result.
   Life's Other Secret (1998) preface

Sting (Gordon Sumner) 1951–
English rock singer, songwriter, and actor

8 If I were a Brazilian without land or money or
the means to feed my children, I would be
burning the rain forest too.
   in *International Herald Tribune* 14 April 1989

Caskie Stinnett 1911–
American writer

9 A diplomat . . . is a person who can tell you to
go to hell in such a way that you actually look
forward to the trip.
   Out of the Red (1960) ch. 4

Samuel John Stone 1839–1900
English clergyman

10 The Church's one foundation
Is Jesus Christ, her Lord;
She is his new creation
By water and the word:
From heaven he came and sought her
To be his holy bride,
With his own blood he bought her,
And for her life he died.
   Lyra Fidelium (1866) 'The Church's one foundation'

Winifred Sackville Stoner 1902–83
American poet

11 In fourteen hundred ninety-two, Columbus
sailed the ocean blue.
   'The History of The U.S.' (1919); versions of this line are on
   record from earlier in the 20th century

Marie Stopes 1880–1958
Scottish pioneer of birth-control clinics

12 An impersonal and scientific knowledge of the
structure of our bodies is the surest safeguard
against prurient curiosity and lascivious gloating.
   Married Love (1918) ch. 5

Tom Stoppard 1937–
Czechoslovakian-born British dramatist

13 It's not the voting that's democracy, it's the
counting.
   Jumpers (1972) act 1; see **SOMOZA** 760:20

14 The House of Lords, an illusion to which I have
never been able to subscribe—responsibility
without power, the prerogative of the eunuch
throughout the ages.
   Lord Malquist and Mr Moon (1966) pt. 6; see **DORFMAN**
   290:15, **KIPLING** 468:26

15 The media. It sounds like a convention of
spiritualists.
   Night and Day (1978) act 1

16 I'm with you on the free press. It's the
newspapers I can't stand.
   Night and Day (1978) act 1

17 Comment is free but facts are on expenses.
   Night and Day (1978) act 2; see **SCOTT** 687:18

18 You're familiar with the tragedies of antiquity,
are you? The great homicidal classics?
   Rosencrantz and Guildenstern are Dead (1967) act 1

19 I can do you blood and love without the
rhetoric, and I can do you blood and rhetoric

without the love, and I can do you all three concurrent or consecutive, but I can't do you love and rhetoric without the blood. Blood is compulsory—they're all blood, you see.
Rosencrantz and Guildenstern are Dead (1967) act 1

1 Eternity's a terrible thought. I mean, where's it all going to end?
Rosencrantz and Guildenstern are Dead (1967) act 2

2 The bad end unhappily, the good unluckily. That is what tragedy means.
Rosencrantz and Guildenstern are Dead (1967) act 2; see **WILDE** 854:22

3 Life is a gamble at terrible odds—if it was a bet, you wouldn't take it.
Rosencrantz and Guildenstern are Dead (1967) act 3

4 War is capitalism with the gloves off and many who go to war know it but they go to war because they don't want to be a hero.
Travesties (1975) act 1

William Stoughton 1631–1701
American clergyman

5 God hath sifted a nation that he might send choice grain into this wilderness.
sermon in Boston, 29 April 1669

Harriet Beecher Stowe 1811–96
American novelist. On Stowe: see **LINCOLN** 494:10

6 The bitterest tears shed over graves are for words left unsaid and deeds left undone.
Little Foxes (1871)

7 I s'pect I growed. Don't think nobody never made me.
Topsy
Uncle Tom's Cabin (1852) ch. 20

William Scott, Lord Stowell 1745–1836
English jurist

8 The elegant simplicity of the three per cents.
Lord Campbell *Lives of the Lord Chancellors* (1857) vol. 10, ch. 212; see **DISRAELI** 285:29

9 A precedent embalms a principle.
an opinion, while Advocate-General, 1788, quoted by Disraeli in House of Commons, 22 February 1848

Lytton Strachey 1880–1932
English biographer

10 Francis Bacon has been described more than once with the crude vigour of antithesis . . . He was no striped frieze; he was shot silk.
Elizabeth and Essex (1928) ch. 5

11 The time was out of joint, and he was only too delighted to have been born to set it right.
of Hurrell Froude
Eminent Victorians (1918) 'Cardinal Manning' pt. 2; see **SHAKESPEARE** 700:30

12 Her conception of God was certainly not orthodox. She felt towards Him as she might have felt towards a glorified sanitary engineer; and in some of her speculations she seems hardly to distinguish between the Deity and the Drains.
Eminent Victorians (1918) 'Florence Nightingale' pt. 4

13 CHAIRMAN OF MILITARY TRIBUNAL: What would you do if you saw a German soldier trying to violate your sister?
STRACHEY: I would try to get between them.
otherwise rendered as, 'I should interpose my body'
Robert Graves *Good-bye to All That* (1929) ch. 23

14 Discretion is not the better part of biography.
Michael Holroyd *Lytton Strachey* vol. 1 (1967) preface

15 If this is dying, then I don't think much of it.
on his deathbed, Michael Holroyd *Lytton Strachey* vol. 2 (1968) pt. 2, ch. 6

Thomas Wentworth, Lord Strafford
1593–1641
English statesman

16 The authority of a King is the keystone which closeth up the arch of order and government which, once shaken, all the frame falls together in a confused heap of foundation and battlement.
Hugh Trevor-Roper *Historical Essays* (1952) 'The Outbreak of the Great Rebellion'

William L. Strauss *and* A. J. E. Cave

17 Notwithstanding, if he could be reincarnated and placed in a New York subway—provided that he were bathed, shaved, and dressed in modern clothing—it is doubtful whether he would attract any more attention than some of its other denizens.
of Neanderthal man
in *Quarterly Review of Biology* Winter 1957

Igor Stravinsky 1882–1971
Russian composer

18 Tradition is entirely different from habit, even from an excellent habit, since habit is by definition an unconscious acquisition and tends to become mechanical, whereas tradition results from a conscious and deliberate acceptance . . . Tradition presupposes the reality of what endures.
Poetics of Music (1947) ch. 3 (translated by A. Knodel and I. Dahl)

19 Conductors' careers are made for the most part with 'romantic' music. 'Classic' music eliminates the conductor; we do not remember him in it.
Robert Craft *Conversations with Stravinsky* (1958) ch. 4

20 My music is best understood by children and animals.
in *Observer* 8 October 1961

21 Academism results when the reasons for the rule change, but not the rule.
attributed

John Whitaker ('Jack') Straw 1946–
British Labour politician

1 The divide in the modern world is not the so-called 'clash of civilizations' between Islam and the West. The divide is between order and chaos.
   in *Newsweek* 20 January 2003

2 There is no list, and Syria isn't on it.
   on the US description of Syria as a rogue state
   speech, Qatar; in *Guardian* 15 April 2003 (online edition)

August Strindberg 1849–1912
Swedish dramatist and novelist

3 I detest dogs, those protectors of cowards who have not the courage to bite the assailant themselves.
   popularly quoted as 'People who keep dogs are cowards who haven't got the guts to bite people themselves'
   A Madman's Manifesto (1895)

4 Family! . . . the home of all social evil, a charitable institution for comfortable women, an anchorage for house-fathers, and a hell for children.
   The Son of a Servant (1886)

Jan Struther (Joyce Anstruther) 1901–53
English-born novelist and poet

5 Lord of all hopefulness, Lord of all joy,
   Whose trust, ever childlike, no cares could destroy,
   Be there at our waking, and give us, we pray,
   Your bliss in our hearts, Lord, at the break of the day.
   'All Day Hymn' (1931 hymn)

6 When a knight won his spurs, in the stories of old,
   He was gentle and brave, he was gallant and bold.
   'When a Knight Won His Spurs' (1936)

7 Giving a party is very like having a baby: its conception is more fun than its completion, and once you have begun it is almost impossible to stop.
   Ysenda Maxtone Graham *The Real Mrs Miniver* (2001) ch. 3

William Stubbs 1825–1901
English historian and prelate. On Stubbs: see ROGERS 666:1

8 Froude informs the Scottish youth
   That parsons do not care for truth.
   The Reverend Canon Kingsley cries
   History is a pack of lies.
   What cause for judgements so malign?
   A brief reflection solves the mystery—
   Froude believes Kingsley a divine,
   And Kingsley goes to Froude for history.
   letter to J. R. Green, 17 December 1871, in *Letters* (1904)

G. A. Studdert Kennedy 1883–1929
English poet

9 Waste of Blood, and waste of Tears,
   Waste of youth's most precious years,
   Waste of ways the saints have trod,
   Waste of Glory, waste of God,
   War!
   More Rough Rhymes of a Padre by 'Woodbine Willie' (1919) 'Waste'

10 When Jesus came to Birmingham they simply passed Him by,
   They never hurt a hair of Him, they only let Him die.
   Peace Rhymes of a Padre (1921) 'Indifference'

John Suckling 1609–42
English poet and dramatist

11 Women enjoyed (whatsoe'er before they've been)
   Are like romances read, or sights once seen.
   'Against Fruition' (1646)

12 Why so pale and wan, fond lover?
   Prithee, why so pale?
   Will, when looking well can't move her,
   Looking ill prevail?
   Prithee, why so pale?
   Aglaura (1637) act 4, sc. 1 'Song'

13 Her feet beneath her petticoat,
   Like little mice, stole in and out.
   'A Ballad upon a Wedding' (1646) st. 8

14 Love is the fart
   Of every heart:
   It pains a man when 'tis kept close,
   And others doth offend, when 'tis let loose.
   'Love's Offence' (1646)

15 Out upon it, I have loved
   Three whole days together;
   And am like to love three more,
   If it prove fair weather.
   'A Poem with the Answer' (1659)

Sudraka
Indian dramatist, fl. at a period between 2nd century BC and 5th century AD

16 Ah! The lack of money is all evil's root!
   The Little Clay Cart act 1, sc. 14, translated by Arthur Ryder; see BIBLE 115:23, PROVERBS 639:2

Suger 1081–1151
French monk and statesman, abbot of Saint-Denis, and regent of France during the Second Crusade

17 Thus, when—out of my delight in the beauty of the house of God—the loveliness of the many-coloured gems has called me away from external cares, and worthy meditation has induced me to reflect, transferring that which is material to that which is immaterial, on the diversity of the sacred virtues; then it seems to me that I see

myself dwelling, as it were, in some strange region of the universe which neither exists entirely in the slime of the earth nor entirely in the purity of Heaven; and that, by the grace of God, I can be transported from this inferior to that higher world in an anagogical manner.
De Consecratione

1 No one among the countless thousands of people because of their very density could move a foot; that no one, because of their very congestion could do anything but stand like a marble statue, stay benumbed or, as a last resort, scream.
description of the church of St-Denis on a feast day
De Consecratione

Annie Sullivan 1866–1936
American educator; tutor of Helen **KELLER**

2 Language grows out of life, out of its needs and experiences . . . *Language* and *knowledge* are indissolubly connected; they are interdependent. Good work in language presupposes and depends on a real knowledge of things.
speech to the American Association to Promote the Teaching of Speech to the Deaf, July 1894; Helen Keller *The Story of My Life* (1902)

Louis Henri Sullivan 1856–1924
American architect

3 Form follows function.
The Tall Office Building Artistically Considered (1896)

Terry Sullivan *See also* **BEDFORD AND SULLIVAN**

4 She sells sea-shells on the sea-shore,
The shells she sells are sea-shells, I'm sure,
For if she sells sea-shells on the sea-shore,
Then I'm sure she sells sea-shore shells.
'She Sells Sea-Shells' (1908 song)

Timothy Daniel Sullivan 1827–1914
Irish writer and politician

5 'God save Ireland!' said the heroes;
'God save Ireland', say they all:
Whether on the scaffold high
Or the battlefield we die,
Oh, what matter when for Erin dear we fall.
'God Save Ireland' (1867); see **ALLEN, LARKIN, AND O'BRIEN** 13:7

Maximilien de Béthune, Duc de Sully 1559–1641
French statesman. See also **HENRI IV** 391:20

6 Tilling and grazing are the two breasts by which France is fed.
Mémoires (1638) pt. 1, ch. 15

7 The English take their pleasures sadly after the fashion of their country.
attributed

Arthur Hays Sulzberger 1891–1968
American newspaper proprietor

8 We tell the public which way the cat is jumping. The public will take care of the cat.
on journalism
in *Time* 8 May 1950

Edith Summerskill 1901–80
British Labour politician

9 Nagging is the repetition of unpalatable truths.
speech to the Married Women's Association, House of Commons, 14 July 1960; in *The Times* 15 July 1960

Charles Sumner 1811–74
American politician and orator

10 Where Slavery is, there Liberty cannot be; and where Liberty is, there Slavery cannot be.
'Slavery and the Rebellion'; speech at Cooper Institute 5 November 1864

11 There is the national flag. He must be cold, indeed, who can look upon its folds rippling in the breeze without pride of country.
Are We a Nation? 19 November 1867

Sun Tzu fl. *c*.400–320 BC
Chinese general and military theorist

12 Know the enemy and know yourself; in a hundred battles you will never be defeated.
The Art of War ch. 3

Henry Howard, Earl of Surrey
c.1517–47
English poet

13 Martial, the things for to attain
The happy life be these, I find:
The riches left, not got with pain;
The fruitful ground, the quiet mind.
'The Happy Life' (1547); translation of Martial *Epigrams* bk. 10, no. 47; see **MARTIAL** 524:10

14 Love, that doth reign and live within my thought,
And built his seat within my captive breast,
Clad in the arms wherein with me he fought,
Oft in my face he doth his banner rest.
'Love, that doth reign' (1557)

15 Set me whereas the sun doth parch the green,
Or where his beams may not dissolve the ice,
In temperate heat, where he is felt and seen,
With proud people, in presence sad and wise;
Set me in base, or yet in high degree,
In the long night, or in the shortest day,
In clear weather, or where mists thickest be,
In lusty youth, or when my hairs be grey . . .
Yours will I be, and with that only thought
Comfort myself when that my hap is nought.
'Set me whereas the sun doth parch the green' (1557)

16 So cruel prison how could betide, alas,
As proud Windsor? Where I in lust and joy

With a king's son my childish years did pass
In greater feast than Priam's sons of Troy.
'So cruel prison' (1557)

1 The soote season, that bud and bloom forth
brings.
soote = *sweet*
'A Spring Lament' (1557)

2 Each care decays, and yet my sorrow springs.
'A Spring Lament' (1557)

3 Wyatt resteth here, that quick could never rest;
Whose heavenly gifts increased by disdain,
And virtue sank the deeper in his breast;
Such profit he of envy could obtain.
'Wyatt resteth here' (1557)

R. S. Surtees 1805–64
English sporting journalist and novelist

4 More people are flattered into virtue than
bullied out of vice.
The Analysis of the Hunting Field (1846) ch. 1

5 The only infallible rule we know is, that the
man who is always talking about being a
gentleman never is one.
Ask Mamma (1858) ch. 1

6 'Unting is all that's worth living for—all time is
lost wot is not spent in 'unting—it is like the
hair we breathe—if we have it not we die—it's
the sport of kings, the image of war without its
guilt, and only five-and-twenty per cent of its
danger.
Handley Cross (1843) ch. 7; see **D'AVENANT** 267:9, **SOMERVILLE**
760:18

7 Many a good run I have in my sleep. Many a dig
in the ribs I gives Mrs J when I think they're
running into the warmint . . . No man is fit to
be called a sportsman wot doesn't kick his wife
out of bed on a haverage once in three weeks!
Handley Cross (1843) ch. 11

8 I'll fill hup the chinks wi' cheese.
Handley Cross (1843) ch. 15

9 It ar'n't that I loves the fox less, but that I loves
the 'ound more.
Handley Cross (1843) ch. 16

10 'Ounds choppin' foxes in cover is more a proof
of their wice.
Handley Cross (1843) ch. 34

11 Take not out your 'ounds on a werry windy day.
Handley Cross (1843) ch. 38

12 Three things I never lends—my 'oss, my wife,
and my name.
Hillingdon Hall (1845) ch. 33

13 Champagne certainly gives one werry
gentlemanly ideas, but for a continuance, I don't
know but I should prefer mild hale.
Jorrocks's Jaunts and Jollities (1838) 'Mr Jorrocks in Paris'

14 Better be killed than frightened to death.
Mr Facey Romford's Hounds (1865) ch. 32

15 Life would be very pleasant if it were not for its
enjoyments.
Mr Facey Romford's Hounds (1865) ch. 32; see **LEWIS** 492:6

16 Everyone knows that the real business of a ball
is either to look out for a wife, to look after a
wife, or to look after somebody else's wife.
Mr Facey Romford's Hounds (1865) ch. 56

17 The young ladies entered the drawing-room in
the full fervour of sisterly animosity.
Mr Sponge's Sporting Tour (1853) ch. 17

18 Women never look so well as when one comes
in wet and dirty from hunting.
Mr Sponge's Sporting Tour (1853) ch. 21

19 He was a gentleman who was generally spoken
of as having nothing a-year, paid quarterly.
Mr Sponge's Sporting Tour (1853) ch. 24

20 There is no secret so close as that between a
rider and his horse.
Mr Sponge's Sporting Tour (1853) ch. 31

David Sutton 1944–
English poet

21 Sorrow in all lands, and grievous omens.
Great anger in the dragon of the hills,
And silent now the earth's green oracles
That will not speak again of innocence.
'Geomancies' (1991)

Italo Svevo 1861–1928
Italian novelist and businessman

22 Last cigarette!!
Zeno's Conscience (1923) ch. 1 and elsewhere

23 That would really have been the last cigarette.
*last words, when refused a cigarette as he lay dying after a
car accident*
Livia Veneziani Svevo *Memoir of Italo Svevo* (1950)

Hannen Swaffer 1879–1962
English journalist

24 Freedom of the press in Britain means freedom
to print such of the proprietor's prejudices as
the advertisers don't object to.
Tom Driberg *Swaff* (1974) ch. 2

Annie S. Swan 1859–1953
Scottish-born popular novelist

25 O God, give me work till the end of my life
And life till the end of my work.
'A Worker's Prayer' in *We Travel Home* (1935); chosen by
Winifred **HOLTBY**'s mother as her daughter's epitaph: see
EPITAPHS 317:11

Jonathan Swift 1667–1745
Irish poet and satirist. On Swift: see **COLERIDGE** 242:6,
DRYDEN 297:26, **JOHNSON** 436:28; see also **EPITAPHS** 319:14

26 I conceive some scattered notions about a
superior power to be of singular use for the

common people, as furnishing excellent materials to keep children quiet when they grow peevish, and providing topics of amusement in a tedious winter-night.

An Argument Against Abolishing Christianity (1708)

1 Satire is a sort of glass, wherein beholders do generally discover everybody's face but their own.

The Battle of the Books (1704) preface

2 Instead of dirt and poison we have rather chosen to fill our hives with honey and wax; thus furnishing mankind with the two noblest of things, which are sweetness and light.

The Battle of the Books (1704); see **ARNOLD** 31:9, **FORSTER** 337:19

3 It is the folly of too many, to mistake the echo of a London coffee-house for the voice of the kingdom.

The Conduct of the Allies (1711)

4 I have heard of a man who had a mind to sell his house, and therefore carried a piece of brick in his pocket, which he shewed as a pattern to encourage purchasers.

The Drapier's Letters (1724) no. 2; see **JOHNSON** 437:2

5 He [the emperor] is taller by almost the breadth of my nail than any of his court, which alone is enough to strike an awe into the beholders.

Gulliver's Travels (1726) 'A Voyage to Lilliput' ch. 2

6 He put this engine to our ears, which made an incessant noise like that of a water-mill; and we conjecture it is either some unknown animal, or the god that he worships; but we are more inclined to the latter opinion.

a watch

Gulliver's Travels (1726) 'A Voyage to Lilliput' ch. 2

7 It is alleged indeed, that the high heels are most agreeable to our ancient constitution: but however this be, his Majesty hath determined to make use of only low heels in the administration of the government.

Gulliver's Travels (1726) 'A Voyage to Lilliput' ch. 4

8 It is computed, that eleven thousand persons have, at several times, suffered death, rather than submit to break their eggs at the smaller end. Many large volumes have been published upon this controversy: but the books of the Big-Endians have been long forbidden, and the whole party rendered incapable by law of holding employments.

Gulliver's Travels (1726) 'A Voyage to Lilliput' ch. 4

9 And he gave it for his opinion, that whoever could make two ears of corn or two blades of grass to grow upon a spot of ground where only one grew before, would deserve better of mankind, and do more essential service to his country than the whole race of politicians put together.

Gulliver's Travels (1726) 'A Voyage to Brobdingnag' ch. 7

10 He had been eight years upon a project for extracting sun-beams out of cucumbers, which were to be put into vials hermetically sealed, and let out to warm the air in raw inclement summers.

Gulliver's Travels (1726) 'A Voyage to Laputa, etc.' ch. 5

11 These unhappy people were proposing schemes for persuading monarchs to choose favourites upon the score of their wisdom, capacity and virtue; of teaching ministers to consult the public good; of rewarding merit, great abilities and eminent services; of instructing princes to know their true interest by placing it on the same foundation with that of their people: of choosing for employment persons qualified to exercise them; with many other wild impossible chimeras, that never entered before into the heart of man to conceive, and confirmed in me the old observation, that there is nothing so extravagant and irrational which some philosophers have not maintained for truth.

Gulliver's Travels (1726) 'A Voyage to Laputa, etc.' ch. 6; see **CICERO** 231:16

12 He replied that I must needs be mistaken, or that I *said the thing which was not.* (For they have no word in their language to express lying or falsehood.)

Gulliver's Travels (1726) 'A Voyage to the Houyhnhnms' ch. 3

13 I told him . . . that we ate when we were not hungry, and drank without the provocation of thirst.

Gulliver's Travels (1726) 'A Voyage to the Houyhnhnms' ch. 6

14 We are so fond of one another, because our ailments are the same.

Journal to Stella (in *Works*, 1768) 1 February 1711

15 Will she pass in a crowd? Will she make a figure in a country church?

Journal to Stella (in *Works*, 1768) 9 February 1711

16 I value not your bill of fare, give me your bill of company.

Journal to Stella (in *Works*, 1768) 2 September 1711

17 We were to do more business after dinner; but after dinner is after dinner—an old saying and a true, 'much drinking, little thinking'.

Journal to Stella (in *Works*, 1768) 26 February 1712

18 Proper words in proper places, make the true definition of a style.

Letter to a Young Gentleman lately entered into Holy Orders (9 January 1720)

19 If Heaven had looked upon riches to be a valuable thing, it would not have given them to such a scoundrel.

letter to Miss Vanhomrigh, 12–13 August 1720, in H. Williams (ed.) Correspondence of Jonathan Swift (1963) vol. 2; see **STEELE** 770:19

20 I have ever hated all nations, professions and communities, and all my love is towards individuals . . . But principally I hate and detest that animal called man; although I heartily love John, Peter, Thomas, and so forth.

letter to Pope, 29 September 1725, in H. Williams (ed.) Correspondence of Jonathan Swift (1963) vol. 3

1 Not die here in a rage, like a poisoned rat in a hole.
> letter to Bolingbroke, 21 March 1730, in H. Williams (ed.) *Correspondence of Jonathan Swift* (1963) vol. 3

2 I have been assured by a very knowing American of my acquaintance in London, that a young healthy child well nursed is at a year old a most delicious, nourishing, and wholesome food, whether stewed, roasted, baked, or boiled, and I make no doubt that it will equally serve in a fricassee, or a ragout.
> *A Modest Proposal for Preventing the Children of Ireland from being a Burden to their Parents or Country* (1729)

3 I mean, you lie—under a mistake.
> *Polite Conversation* (1738) Dialogue 1

4 She wears her clothes, as if they were thrown on her with a pitchfork.
> *Polite Conversation* (1738) Dialogue 1

5 He was a bold man that first eat an oyster.
> *Polite Conversation* (1738) Dialogue 2

6 Faith, that's as well said, as if I had said it myself.
> *Polite Conversation* (1738) Dialogue 2

7 I always love to begin a journey on Sundays, because I shall have the prayers of the church, to preserve all that travel by land, or by water.
> *Polite Conversation* (1738) Dialogue 2; see **BOOK OF COMMON PRAYER** 134:24

8 Books, like men their authors, have no more than one way of coming into the world, but there are ten thousand to go out of it, and return no more.
> *A Tale of a Tub* (1704) 'Epistle Dedicatory'; see **SENECA** 692:20

9 Satire, being levelled at all, is never resented for an offence by any.
> *A Tale of a Tub* (1704) 'Author's Preface'

10 What though his head be empty, provided his commonplace book be full.
> *A Tale of a Tub* (1704) ch. 7 'Digression in Praise of Digressions'

11 Last week I saw a woman flayed, and you will hardly believe, how much it altered her person for the worse.
> *A Tale of a Tub* (1704) ch. 9

12 I never saw, heard, nor read, that the clergy were beloved in any nation where Christianity was the religion of the country. Nothing can render them popular, but some degree of persecution.
> *Thoughts on Religion* (1765)

13 We have just enough religion to make us hate, but not enough to make us love one another.
> *Thoughts on Various Subjects* (1711)

14 When a true genius appears in the world, you may know him by this sign, that the dunces are all in confederacy against him.
> *Thoughts on Various Subjects* (1711)

15 What they do in heaven we are ignorant of; what they do *not* we are told expressly, that they neither marry, nor are given in marriage.
> *Thoughts on Various Subjects* (1711); see **BIBLE** 102:16

16 The stoical scheme of supplying our wants, by lopping off our desires, is like cutting off our feet when we want shoes.
> *Thoughts on Various Subjects* (1711)

17 The reasons why so few marriages are happy, is, because young ladies spend their time in making nets, not in making cages.
> *Thoughts on Various Subjects* (1711)

18 Few are qualified to shine in company; but it is in most men's power to be agreeable.
> *Thoughts on Various Subjects* (1727 ed.)

19 Every man desires to live long; but no man would be old.
> *Thoughts on Various Subjects* (1727 ed.)

20 Old men and comets have been reverenced for the same reason; their long beards, and pretences to foretell events.
> *Thoughts on Various Subjects* (1727 ed.)

21 Laws are like cobwebs, which may catch small flies, but let wasps and hornets break through.
> *A Tritical Essay upon the Faculties of the Mind* (1709); see **ANACHARSIS** 15:2

22 There is nothing in this world constant, but inconstancy.
> *A Tritical Essay upon the Faculties of the Mind* (1709)

23 A coming shower your shooting corns presage.
> 'A Description of a City Shower' (1710) l. 9

24 I often wished that I had clear,
For life, six hundred pounds a-year,
A handsome house to lodge a friend,
A river at my garden's end,
A terrace walk, and half a rood
Of land, set out to plant a wood.
> 'Imitation of Horace' (written 1714); see **HORACE** 414:20

25 How haughtily he lifts his nose,
To tell what every schoolboy knows.
> 'The Journal' (1727) l. 81

26 Nor do they trust their tongue alone,
But speak a language of their own;
Can read a nod, a shrug, a look,
Far better than a printed book;
Convey a libel in a frown,
And wink a reputation down.
> 'The Journal of a Modern Lady' (1729) l. 188

27 Hail, fellow, well met,
All dirty and wet:
Find out, if you can,
Who's master, who's man.
> 'My Lady's Lamentation' (written 1728) l. 165

28 Th' artillery of words.
> 'Ode to Dr William Sancroft' (written 1692)

29 Then, rising with Aurora's light,
The Muse invoked, sit down to write;
Blot out, correct, insert, refine,

Enlarge, diminish, interline.
'On Poetry' (1733) l. 85

1 As learned commentators view
In Homer more than Homer knew.
'On Poetry' (1733) l. 103

2 So geographers, in Afric-maps,
With savage-pictures fill their gaps;
And o'er unhabitable downs
Place elephants for want of towns.
'On Poetry' (1733) l. 177

3 Hobbes clearly proves, that every creature
Lives in a state of war by nature.
'On Poetry' (1733) l. 319

4 So, naturalists observe, a flea
Hath smaller fleas that on him prey;
And these have smaller fleas to bite 'em,
And so proceed *ad infinitum.*
Thus every poet, in his kind,
Is bit by him that comes behind.
'On Poetry' (1733) l. 337; see **PROVERBS** 628:3

5 Walls have tongues, and hedges ears.
'A Pastoral Dialogue between Richmond Lodge and Marble
Hill' (written 1727) l. 8; see **PROVERBS** 632:10

6 Humour is odd, grotesque, and wild,
Only by affectation spoiled;
'Tis never by invention got,
Men have it when they know it not.
'To Mr Delany' (written 1718) l. 25

7 Hated by fools, and fools to hate,
Be that my motto and my fate.
'To Mr Delany' (written 1718) l. 171

8 In all distresses of our friends,
We first consult our private ends;
While nature, kindly bent to ease us,
Points out some circumstance to please us.
'Verses on the Death of Dr Swift' (1731) l. 7

9 Poor Pope will grieve a month, and Gay
A week, and Arbuthnot a day.
St John himself will scarce forbear
To bite his pen, and drop a tear.
The rest will give a shrug, and cry,
'I'm sorry—but we all must die!'
'Verses on the Death of Dr Swift' (1731) l. 207

10 Yet malice never was his aim;
He lashed the vice, but spared the name;
No individual could resent,
Where thousands equally were meant.
'Verses on the Death of Dr Swift' (1731) l. 512

11 He gave the little wealth he had
To build a house for fools and mad;
And showed, by one satiric touch,
No nation wanted it so much.
'Verses on the Death of Dr Swift' (1731) l. 538

12 In Church your grandsire cut his throat;
To do the job too long he tarried,
He should have had my hearty vote,
To cut his throat before he married.
'Verses on the Upright Judge' (written 1724)

13 'Libertas et natale solum':
Fine words! I wonder where you stole 'em.
Libertas . . . = *Freedom and my native skies*
'Whitshed's Motto on his Coach' (written 1724)

14 Good God! what a genius I had when I wrote
that book.
of A Tale of a Tub
Sir Walter Scott (ed.) *Works of Swift* (1814) vol. 1

15 I shall be like that tree, I shall die at the top.
Sir Walter Scott (ed.) *Works of Swift* (1814) vol. 1

16 A stick and a string, with a fly at one end and a
fool at the other.
*description of angling; the remark has also been attributed
to Samuel* **JOHNSON***, in the form 'Fly fishing may be a very
pleasant amusement; but angling or float fishing I can only
compare to a stick and a string, with a worm at one end
and a fool at the other'*
in *The Indicator* 27 October 1819

17 It is useless to attempt to reason a man out of
what he was never reasoned into.
*attributed, but not traced in Swift's works, probably
apocryphal*

Algernon Charles Swinburne
1837–1909
English poet

18 Maiden, and mistress of the months and stars
Now folded in the flowerless fields of heaven.
Atalanta in Calydon (1865) l. 1

19 When the hounds of spring are on winter's
traces,
The mother of months in meadow or plain
Fills the shadows and windy places
With lisp of leaves and ripple of rain;
And the brown bright nightingale amorous
Is half assuaged for Itylus,
For the Thracian ships and the foreign faces,
The tongueless vigil and all the pain.
Atalanta in Calydon (1865) chorus 'When the hounds of
spring'

20 For winter's rains and ruins are over,
And all the season of snows and sins;
The days dividing lover and lover,
The light that loses, the night that wins;
And time remembered is grief forgotten,
And frosts are slain and flowers begotten,
And in green underwood and cover
Blossom by blossom the spring begins.
Atalanta in Calydon (1865) chorus 'When the hounds of
spring'

21 And soft as lips that laugh and hide
The laughing leaves of the tree divide,
And screen from seeing and leave in sight
The god pursuing, the maiden hid.
Atalanta in Calydon (1865) chorus 'When the hounds of
spring'

22 Before the beginning of years
There came to the making of man
Time with a gift of tears,

Grief with a glass that ran.
Atalanta in Calydon (1865) chorus 'Before the beginning of years'

1 Strength without hands to smite,
Love that endures for a breath;
Night, the shadow of light,
And Life, the shadow of death.
Atalanta in Calydon (1865) chorus 'Before the beginning of years'

2 For words divide and rend;
But silence is most noble till the end.
Atalanta in Calydon (1865) chorus 'Who hath given man speech'

3 Sleep; and if life was bitter to thee, pardon,
If sweet, give thanks; thou hast no more to live;
And to give thanks is good, and to forgive.
'Ave atque Vale' (1878) st. 17

4 Villon, our sad bad glad mad brother's name.
'Ballad of François Villon' (1878)

5 O slain and spent and sacrificed
People, the grey-grown speechless Christ.
'Before a Crucifix' (1871)

6 We shift and bedeck and bedrape us,
Thou art noble and nude and antique.
'Dolores' (1866) st. 7

7 Change in a trice
The lilies and languors of virtue
For the raptures and roses of vice.
'Dolores' (1866) st. 9

8 O splendid and sterile Dolores,
Our Lady of Pain.
'Dolores' (1866) st. 9

9 No thorns go as deep as a rose's,
And love is more cruel than lust.
'Dolores' (1866) st. 20

10 In a coign of the cliff between lowland and highland,
At the sea-down's edge between windward and lee,
Walled round with rocks as an inland island,
The ghost of a garden fronts the sea.
'A Forsaken Garden' (1878)

11 As a god self-slain on his own strange altar,
Death lies dead.
'A Forsaken Garden' (1878)

12 Pale, beyond porch and portal,
Crowned with calm leaves, she stands
Who gathers all things mortal
With cold immortal hands.
'The Garden of Proserpine' (1866)

13 We are not sure of sorrow,
And joy was never sure.
'The Garden of Proserpine' (1866)

14 From too much love of living,
From hope and fear set free,
We thank with brief thanksgiving
Whatever gods may be
That no man lives forever,

That dead men rise up never;
That even the weariest river
Winds somewhere safe to sea.
'The Garden of Proserpine' (1866)

15 Fiddle, we know, is diddle: and diddle, we take it, is dee.
The Heptalogia (1880) 'The Higher Pantheism in a Nutshell'; see **TENNYSON** 793:23

16 Even love, the beloved Republic, that feeds upon freedom lives.
'Hertha' (1871); see **FORSTER** 338:13

17 Glory to Man in the highest! for Man is the master of things.
'Hymn of Man' (1871); see **BIBLE** 104:14

18 Yea, is not even Apollo, with hair and harpstring of gold,
A bitter God to follow, a beautiful God to behold?
'Hymn to Proserpine' (1866)

19 Thou hast conquered, O pale Galilean; the world has grown grey from Thy breath;
We have drunken of things Lethean, and fed on the fullness of death.
'Hymn to Proserpine' (1866); see **JULIAN** 449:9

20 Though these that were Gods are dead, and thou being dead art a God,
Though before thee the throned Cytherean be fallen, and hidden her head,
Yet thy kingdom shall pass, Galilean, thy dead shall go down to thee dead.
'Hymn to Proserpine' (1866)

21 And the best and the worst of this is
That neither is most to blame,
If you have forgotten my kisses
And I have forgotten your name.
'An Interlude' (1866)

22 Swallow, my sister, O sister swallow,
How can thine heart be full of the spring?
A thousand summers are over and dead.
What hast thou found in the spring to follow?
What hast thou found in thine heart to sing?
What wilt thou do when the summer is shed?
'Itylus' (1864)

23 The small slain body, the flowerlike face,
Can I remember if thou forget?
O sister, sister, thy first-begotten!
The hands that cling and the feet that follow,
The voice of the child's blood crying yet
Who hath remembered me? Who hath forgotten?
Thou hast forgotten, O summer swallow,
But the world shall end when I forget.
'Itylus' (1864)

24 Apples of gold for the king's daughter.
'The King's Daughter'

25 Ah, yet would God this flesh of mine might be
Where air might wash and long leaves cover me;
Where tides of grass break into foam of flowers,
Or where the wind's feet shine along the sea.
'Laus Veneris' (1866)

1 I am the queen Aholibah
My lips kissed dumb the word of *Ah*.
'The Masque of Queen Bersabe' (1866)

2 If love were what the rose is,
And I were like the leaf,
Our lives would grow together
In sad or singing weather,
Blown fields or flowerful closes,
Green pleasure or grey grief.
'A Match' (1866)

3 There was a poor poet named Clough,
Whom his friends all united to puff,
But the public, though dull,
Had not such a skull
As belonged to believers in Clough.
'Matthew Arnold' (1875)

4 I will go back to the great sweet mother,
Mother and lover of men, the sea.
I will go down to her, I and no other,
Close with her, kiss her and mix her with me.
'The Triumph of Time' (1866)

5 I shall sleep, and move with the moving ships,
Change as the winds change, veer in the tide.
'The Triumph of Time' (1866)

Thomas Sydenham 1624–89
English physician

6 Almighty God hath not bestowed on mankind a
remedy of so universal an extent and so
efficacious in curing divers maladies as opiates.
manuscript version of published text, *Observationes Medicae*
(1676, G. G. Meynell (ed.) 1991)

John Millington Synge 1871–1909
Irish dramatist

7 'A man who is not afraid of the sea will soon be
drownded,' he said 'for he will be going out on
a day he shouldn't. But we do be afraid of the
sea, and we do only be drownded now and
again.'
The Aran Islands (1907) pt. 2

8 'A translation is no translation,' he said, 'unless it
will give you the music of a poem along with
the words of it.'
The Aran Islands (1907) pt. 3

9 All art is collaboration.
The Playboy of the Western World (1907) preface

10 Oh my grief, I've lost him surely. I've lost the
only Playboy of the Western World.
The Playboy of the Western World (1907) act 3, closing words

Thomas Szasz 1920–
Hungarian-born psychiatrist

11 A teacher should have maximal authority and
minimal power.
The Second Sin (1973) 'Education'

12 Happiness is an imaginary condition, formerly
often attributed by the living to the dead, now

usually attributed by adults to children, and by
children to adults.
The Second Sin (1973) 'Emotions'

13 The stupid neither forgive nor forget; the naïve
forgive and forget; the wise forgive but do not
forget.
The Second Sin (1973) 'Personal Conduct'

14 If you talk to God, you are praying; if God talks
to you, you have schizophrenia. If the dead talk
to you, you are a spiritualist; if God talks to
you, you are a schizophrenic.
The Second Sin (1973) 'Schizophrenia'

15 Formerly, when religion was strong and science
weak, men mistook magic for medicine; now,
when science is strong and religion weak, men
mistake medicine for magic.
The Second Sin (1973) 'Science and Scientism'

16 Two wrongs don't make a right, but they make
a good excuse.
The Second Sin (1973) 'Social Relations'; see **PROVERBS** 645:47

Albert von Szent-Györgyi 1893–1986
Hungarian-born biochemist

17 Discovery consists of seeing what everybody has
seen and thinking what nobody has thought.
Irving Good (ed.) *The Scientist Speculates* (1962)

Tacitus (Cornelius Tacitus)
*c.*AD 56–after 117
Roman senator and historian

18 *Res olim dissociabiles miscuerit, principatum ac
libertatem.*
He [Nerva] has united things long incompatible,
the principate and liberty.
Agricola ch. 3; see **DISRAELI** 285:10

19 *Haud semper errat fama.*
Rumour is not always wrong.
Agricola ch. 9

20 *Nunc terminus Britanniae patet, atque omne ignotum
pro magnifico est.*
Now the boundary of Britain is revealed, and
everything unknown is held to be glorious.
reporting the speech of a British leader, Calgacus
Agricola ch. 30

21 *Auferre trucidare rapere falsis niminibus imperium,
atque ubi solitudinem faciunt pacem appellant.*
To robbery, slaughter, plunder, they give the
lying name of empire, they make a wilderness
and call it peace.
Agricola ch. 30

22 *Proinde, ituri in aciem, et majores vestros et posteros
cogitate.*

Think, therefore, as you advance to battle, at once of your ancestors and your posterity.

Agricola ch. 32; see **ADAMS** 3:15

1 *Pessimum inimicorum genus, laudantes.*

The worst kind of enemies, those who praise you.

Agricola ch. 41

2 *Proprium humani ingenii est odisse quem laeseris.*

It is part of human nature to hate the man you have hurt.

Agricola ch. 42

3 *Sciant, quibus moris est inlicita mirari, posse etiam sub malis principibus magnos viros esse, obsequiumque ac modestiam, si industria ac vigor adsint, eo laudis excedere, quo plerique per abrupta, sed in nullum rei publicae usum, ambitiosa morte inclaruerunt.*

Those whose habit it is to admire what is forbidden ought to know that there can be great men even under bad emperors, and that duty and discretion, if coupled with energy and a career of action, will bring a man to no less glorious summits than are attained by perilous paths and ostentatious deaths that do not benefit the Commonwealth.

Agricola ch. 42 (translated by A. R. Birling)

4 *Praecipua sub Domitiano miseriarum pars erat videre et aspici.*

Under Domitian not the smallest part of one's misery was to see and be seen.

Agricola ch. 45

5 *Tu vero felix, Agricola, non vitae tantum claritate, sed etiam opportunitate mortis.*

You were indeed fortunate, Agricola, not only in the distinction of your life, but also in the lucky timing of your death.

Agricola ch. 45

6 *Sine ira et studio.*

With neither anger nor partiality.

Annals bk. 1, ch. 1

7 *Corruptissima re publica plurimae leges.*

The more corrupt the state, the more numerous the laws.

Annals bk. 3, ch. 27

8 *Elegantiae arbiter.*

The arbiter of taste.

of **PETRONIUS**

Annals bk. 16, ch. 18

9 *Rara temporum felicitate ubi sentire quae velis et quae sentias dicere licet.*

These times having the rare good fortune that you may think what you like and say what you think.

Histories bk. 1, ch. 1

10 *Maior privato visus dum privatus fuit, et omnium consensu capax imperii nisi imperasset.*

He seemed much greater than a private citizen while he still was a private citizen, and by

everyone's consent capable of reigning if only he had not reigned.

of the Emperor Galba

Histories bk. 1, ch. 49

11 *Cupido gloriae novissima exuitur.*

Love of fame is the last thing to be given up.

Histories bk. 4, ch. 6

12 *Deos fortioribus adesse.*

The gods are on the side of the stronger.

Histories bk. 4, ch. 17; see **BUSSY-RABUTIN** 182:16, **PROVERBS** 642:10

13 *Experientia docuit.*

Experience has taught.

commonly quoted as 'Experientia docet [experience teaches]'

The Histories bk. 5, ch. 6; see **DICKENS** 277:8, **PROVERBS** 631:40

William Howard Taft 1857–1930

American Republican statesman, 27th President of the US 1909–13

14 Next to the right of liberty, the right of property is the most important individual right guaranteed by the Constitution and the one which, united with that of personal liberty, has contributed more to the growth of civilization than any other institution established by the human race.

Popular Government (1913) ch. 3

☐ Taglines for films *see* box overleaf

Rabindranath Tagore 1861–1941

Bengali poet and philosopher

15 Bigotry tries to keep truth safe in its hand
With a grip that kills it.

Fireflies (1928)

16 The butterfly counts not months but moments,
And has time enough.

Fireflies (1928)

17 The same stream of life that runs through my veins night and day runs through the world and dances in rhythmic measures.

It is the same life that shoots in joy through the dust of the earth into numberless blades of grass and breaks into tumultuous waves of leaves and flowers.

Gitanjali (1912)

18 Touch my life with the magic of thy fire.

sung at the funeral of Mother **TERESA** *in Calcutta, 13 September 1997*

'The Magic of thy Fire'

19 Man goes into the noisy crowd to drown his own clamour of silence.

'Stray Birds' (1916)

Nellie Talbot

20 Jesus wants me for a sunbeam.

title of hymn (1921) *in CSSM Choruses* No. 1

Taglines for films

1 Be afraid. Be very afraid.
   The Fly (1986 film)

2 Being the adventures of a young man whose principal interests are rape, ultra-violence and Beethoven.
   A Clockwork Orange (1972 film)

3 Garbo talks.
   Anna Christie (1930 film), her first talkie

4 He said 'I'll be back!' . . . and he meant it!
   Terminator 2: Judgment Day (1991 film); see **FILM LINES** 328:17

5 In space no one can hear you scream.
   Alien (1979 film)

6 Just when you thought it was safe to go back in the water.
   Jaws 2 (1978 film)

7 A long time ago in a galaxy far, far away . . .
   Star Wars (1977 film)

8 Love means never having to say you're sorry.
   Love Story (1970 film); from the novel (1970) by Erich Segal (1937–)

9 Mean, Moody and Magnificent!
   The Outlaw (1946 film) starring Jane Russell

10 Please don't tell the ending. It's the only one we have.
   Psycho (1960 film)

11 Somewhere in the universe, there must be something better than Man.
   Planet of the Apes (1968 film)

12 They're young . . . they're in love . . . and they kill people.
   Bonnie and Clyde (1967 film)

13 We are not alone.
   Close Encounters of the Third Kind (1977 film)

14 Where were you in '62?
   American Graffiti (1973 film)

Charles-Maurice de Talleyrand

1754–1838

French statesman. On Talleyrand: see LOUIS PHILIPPE 501:13

15 *Voilà le commencement de la fin.*

This is the beginning of the end.
   on the announcement of Napoleon's Pyrrhic victory at Borodino, 1812
   attributed; Sainte-Beuve *M. de Talleyrand* (1870) ch. 3

16 It is not an event, it is an item of news.
   *on hearing of the death of **NAPOLEON I** in 1821*
   Philip Henry Stanhope *Notes of Conversations with the Duke of Wellington* (1888) 1 November 1831

17 *Surtout, Messieurs, point de zèle.*

Above all, gentlemen, not the slightest zeal.
   to young diplomats; P. Chasles *Voyages d'un critique à travers la vie et les livres* (1868) vol. 2; see **LAMBERT** 477:15

18 *Qui n'a pas vécu dans les années voisines de 1789 ne sait pas ce que c'est que le plaisir de vivre.*

He who has not lived during the years around 1789 can not know what is meant by the pleasure of life.
   M. Guizot *Mémoires pour servir à l'histoire de mon temps* (1858) vol. 1, ch. 6

19 *Ils n'ont rien appris, ni rien oublié.*

They have learnt nothing, and forgotten nothing.
   of the Bourbons in exile
   oral tradition, attributed to Talleyrand by the Chevalier de Panat in the form: '*Personne n'est corrigé, personne n'a su ni rien oublier ni rien apprendre* [Nobody has improved, nobody has known how to forget or to learn]'; letter to Mallet du Pan, January 1796; A. Sayons (ed.) *Mémoires et correspondance de Mallet du Pan* (1851) vol. 2; see **DUMOURIEZ** 299:7

20 That, Sire, is a question of dates.
   often quoted as, 'treason is a matter of dates'; replying to the Tsar's criticism of those who 'betrayed the cause of Europe'
   Duff Cooper *Talleyrand* (1932)

21 *Quelle triste vieillesse vous vous préparez.*

What a sad old age you are preparing for yourself.
   to a young diplomat who boasted of his ignorance of whist
   J. Amédée Pichot *Souvenirs Intimes sur M. de Talleyrand* (1870) 'Le Pour et le Contre'

The Talmud

compilation of Jewish civil and ceremonial law and legend, dating from the 5th century AD, and comprising the Mishnah and the Gemara. There are two versions of the Talmud, the Babylonian Talmud and the earlier Palestinian or Jerusalem Talmud. See also HILLEL, SHAMMAI

MISHNAH

22 A single man was created in the world, to teach that if any man caused a single soul to perish from Israel, Scripture imputes it to him as though he had caused a whole world to perish; and if any man saves alive a single soul from Israel Scripture imputes it to him as though he had saved alive a whole world.
   Mishnah Sanhedrin 4:5

23 Moses received the Law from Sinai and committed it to Joshua, and Joshua to the elders, and the elders to the Prophets; and the Prophets committed it to the men of the Great Synagogue. They said three things: Be deliberate in judgement, raise up many disciples, and make a fence around the Law.
   Mishnah Pirqei Avot 1:1

24 By three things is the world sustained: by the Law, by the [Temple-]service, and by deeds of loving-kindness.
   Mishnah Pirqei Avot 1:2

1 Love labour and hate mastery and seek not acquaintance with the ruling power.
Mishnah Pirqei Avot 1:10

2 By three things is the world sustained: by truth, by judgement, and by peace.
Mishnah Pirqei Avot 1:18

3 Let the property of thy fellow be dear to thee as thine own.
Mishnah Pirqei Avot 2:12

4 The day is short and the task is great and the labourers are idle and the wage is abundant and the master of the house is urgent.
Mishnah Pirqei Avot 2:15

5 The tradition is a fence around the Law.
Mishnah Pirqei Avot 3:14

6 Beloved is man, for he was created in the image [of God]; still greater was the love in that it was made known to him that he was created in the image of God.
Mishnah Pirqei Avot 3:15

7 All is foreseen, but freedom of choice is given; and the world is judged by grace, yet all is according to the excess of works [that be good or evil].
Mishnah Pirqei Avot 3:16

8 He that neglects the Law in wealth shall in the end neglect it in poverty.
Mishnah Pirqei Avot 4:9

9 He that performs one precept gets for himself one advocate . . . Repentance and good works are as a shield against retribution.
Mishnah Pirqei Avot 4:11

10 Turn it [Torah] and turn it again, for everything is in it.
Mishnah Pirqei Avot 5:22

GEMARA

11 Let thy tongue acquire the habit of saying, 'I know not', lest thou be led to falsehoods.
Babylonian Talmud Berakhot 4a

12 The seal of the Holy One, blessed be He, is *emeth* [truth].
Babylonian Talmud Shabbat 55a

13 If circumcision . . . supersedes the Sabbath, the saving of life, *a minori*, must supersede the Sabbath.
Babylonian Talmud Shabbat 132a

14 As to every man who becomes angry, if he is a sage, his wisdom departs from him; if he is a prophet, his prophecy departs from him.
Babylonian Talmud Pesahim 66b

15 Even an iron partition cannot interpose between Israel and their Father in Heaven.
Babylonian Talmud Pesahim 85b

16 *He shall live by them* [the laws of the Torah], but he shall not die because of them.
Babylonian Talmud Yoma 85b; see **BIBLE** 81:28

17 Repentance is so great that premeditated sins are accounted as though they were merits.
Babylonian Talmud Yoma 86b

18 The talk of the child in the market-place is either that of his father or of his mother.
Babylonian Talmud Sukkah 56b

19 A man's prayer is only answered if he takes his heart into his hand.
Babylonian Talmud Taanit 8a

20 A man . . . loves his wife as himself . . . honours her more than himself.
Babylonian Talmud Yevamot 62b

21 This nation [Israel] is distinguished by three characteristics; They are merciful, bashful, and benevolent.
Babylonian Talmud Yevamot 79a

22 Great is labour, for it honours the worker.
Babylonian Talmud Nedarim 49b

23 Whoever eats bread without previously washing the hands is as though he had intercourse with a harlot.
Babylonian Talmud Sotah 1.46

24 Unfaithfulness in the house is like a worm in a sesame plant.
Babylonian Talmud Sotah 3b

25 As to someone who started to do something which someone else came along and finished, Scripture regards the one who completed the task as if he had done [the whole of it].
Babylonian Talmud Sotah 13b

26 The father loves the son, and the son loves his sons.
Babylonian Talmud Sotah 49a

27 If a man divorces his first wife, even the altar sheds tears.
Babylonian Talmud Gittin 90b

28 He who does not teach his son a craft, teaches him brigandage.
Babylonian Talmud Qiddushin 29a

29 A man who gives charity in secret is greater than Moses.
Babylonian Talmud Bava Bathra 9b

30 It is the penalty of a liar, that should he even tell the truth, he is not listened to.
Babylonian Talmud Sanhedrin 89b

31 One is allowed to follow the road he wishes to pursue.
Babylonian Talmud Makkot 10b

32 If the soft [water] can wear away the hard [stone], how much more can the words of the Torah, which are hard like iron, carve a way into my heart which is of flesh and blood!
Babylonian Talmud Avot de Rabbi Nathan 20b

33 All that the Holy One, blessed be He, created in the world, He also created in man.
Babylonian Talmud Avot de Rabbi Nathan 29a

34 No man bruises his finger here on earth unless it was so decreed against him in heaven.
Babylonian Talmud Hullin 7b

35 Why [does Yohanan say that one may pray all day long]? Because prayer never loses its value.
Jerusalem Talmud Berakhot 1:1

1 One should not [recite one's prayers] as if he were reading a letter.
Jerusalem Talmud Berakhot 4:4

2 The Holy Spirit rests only on someone whose heart is happy.
Jerusalem Talmud Sukkah 5:1

3 [If] a man keeps himself from transgression one time, then a second and a third time, the Holy One, blessed be He, keeps him from transgressing further.
Jerusalem Talmud Qiddushin 1:9

Tantric Buddhist texts

ritualist form of Buddhism, dating from the 7th century or earlier

4 Just as water that has entered the ear may be removed by water and just as a thorn may be removed by a thorn, so those who know how, remove passion by means of passion itself.
Just as a washerman removes the grime from a garment by means of grime, so the wise man renders himself free of impurity by means of impurity itself.
Citta Vishuddhiprakarana v. 37

5 By the enjoyment of all desires, to which one devotes oneself just as one pleases, it is by such practice as this that one may speedily gain Buddhahood.
With the enjoyment of all desires, to which one devotes oneself just as one pleases, in union with one's chosen divinity, one worships oneself, the Supreme One.
Guhyasamāja Tantra v. 7

6 Mantras and tantras, meditation and concentration
They are all a cause of self-deception.
Do not defile in contemplation thought that is pure in its own nature,
But abide in the bliss of yourself and cease those torments.
Saraha *Dohākosha* (c.9th century) v. 23

7 Enjoying the world of sense, one is undefiled by the world of sense,
One plucks the lotus without touching the water.
So the yogi who has gone to the root of things, Is not enslaved by the senses although he enjoys them.
Saraha *Dohākosha* (c.9th century) v. 64

Booth Tarkington 1869–1946

American novelist

8 There are two things that will be believed of any man whatsoever, and one of them is that he has taken to drink.
Penrod (1914) ch. 10

Donna Tartt 1963–

American novelist

9 The snow in the mountains was melting and Bunny had been dead for several weeks before we came to understand the gravity of our situation.
The Secret History (1992), prologue (opening words)

Torquato Tasso 1544–95

Italian poet and writer

10 *Brama assai, poco spera, e nulla chiede.*
Much wished, hoped little, and demanded nought.
Jerusalem Delivered (1580) bk. 2, stanza 16; see **ELGAR** 306:16

Allen Tate 1899–1979

American poet

11 Alice grown lazy, mammoth but not fat,
Declines upon her lost and twilight age;
Above in the dozing leaves the grinning cat
Quivers forever with his abstract rage.
'Last Days of Alice' (1932)

12 Row after row with strict impunity
The headstones yield their names to the element,
The wind whirrs without recollection;
In the riven troughs the splayed leaves
Pile up, of nature the casual sacrament
To the seasonal eternity of death.
'Ode to the Confederate Dead' (1928)

13 The shut gate and the decomposing wall:
The gentle serpent, green in the mulberry bush,
Riots with his tongue through the hush—
Sentinel of the grave who counts us all!
'Ode to the Confederate Dead' (1928)

Catherine Tate *see* **Catchphrases** 207:2

Nahum Tate 1652–1715

English dramatist

14 As pants the hart for cooling streams
When heated in the chase.
New Version of the Psalms (1696) Psalm 42 (with Nicholas Brady); see **BOOK OF COMMON PRAYER** 142:4

15 Through all the changing scenes of life,
In trouble and in joy,
The praises of my God shall still
My heart and tongue employ.
New Version of the Psalms (1696) Psalm 34 (with Nicholas Brady)

16 While shepherds watched their flocks by night,
All seated on the ground,
The angel of the Lord came down,
And glory shone around.
Supplement to the New Version of the Psalms (1700) 'While Shepherds Watched'

R. H. Tawney 1880–1962
British economic historian

1 That seductive border region where politics grease the wheels of business and polite society smiles hopefully on both.
Business and Politics under James I (1958)

2 Those who dread a dead-level of income or wealth . . . do not dread, it seems, a dead-level of law and order, and of security for life and property.
Equality (4th ed., 1931) ch. 3, sect. 3

3 Freedom for the pike is death for the minnows.
Equality (ed. 4, rev. ed., 1938) ch. 5, sect. 2

4 Private property is a necessary institution, at least in a fallen world; men work more and dispute less when goods are private than when they are common. But it is to be tolerated as a concession to human frailty, not applauded as desirable in itself.
Religion and the Rise of Capitalism (1926) ch. 1, sect. 1

5 To take usury is contrary to Scripture; it is contrary to Aristotle; it is contrary to nature, for it is to live without labour; it is to sell time, which belongs to God, for the advantage of wicked men; it is to rob those who use the money lent, and to whom, since they make it profitable, the profits should belong.
Religion and the Rise of Capitalism (1926) ch. 1, sect. 2

6 Both the existing economic order, and too many of the projects advanced for reconstructing it, break down through their neglect of the truism that, since even quite common men have souls, no increase in material wealth will compensate them for arrangements which insult their self-respect and impair their freedom . . . unless industry is to be paralysed by recurrent revolts on the part of outraged human nature, it must satisfy criteria which are not purely economic.
Religion and the Rise of Capitalism (1926) conclusion

7 What harm have I ever done to the Labour Party?
declining the offer of a peerage
in *Evening Standard* 18 January 1962

A. J. P. Taylor 1906–90
English historian

8 German history reached its turning-point and failed to turn. This was the fateful essence of 1848.
The Course of German History (1945) ch. 4

9 He aroused every feeling except trust.
*of **LLOYD GEORGE***
English History 1914–1945 (1965) ch. 5

10 History gets thicker as it approaches recent times.
English History 1914–45 (1965); bibliography

11 Human blunders, usually, do more to shape history than human wickedness.
The Origins of the Second World War (1961) ch. 10

12 Crimea: The war that would not boil.
Rumours of Wars (1952) ch. 6; originally the title of an essay in *History Today* 2 February 1951

13 Bismarck was a political genius of the highest rank, but he lacked one essential quality of the constructive statesman: he had no faith in the future.
in *Encyclopedia Britannica* (1954)

Ann Taylor 1782–1866 *and* Jane Taylor
1783–1824
English writers of books for children

14 I thank the goodness and the grace
Which on my birth have smiled,
And made me, in these Christian days,
A happy English child.
Hymns for Infant Minds (1810) 'A Child's Hymn of Praise'

15 Who ran to help me when I fell,
And would some pretty story tell,
Or kiss the place to make it well?
My Mother.
Original Poems for Infant Minds (1804) 'My Mother'

16 Twinkle, twinkle, little star,
How I wonder what you are!
Up above the world so high,
Like a diamond in the sky!
Rhymes for the Nursery (1806) 'The Star'; see **CARROLL** 202:6

17 How pleasant it is, at the end of the day,
No follies to have to repent;
But reflect on the past, and be able to say,
That my time has been properly spent.
Rhymes for the Nursery (1806) 'The Way to be Happy'

Bayard Taylor 1825–78
American traveller and writer

18 Till the sun grows cold,
And the stars are old,
And the leaves of the Judgement Book unfold.
'Bedouin Song'

Edward Taylor ?1645–1729
American puritan divine and poet

19 Who laced and filleted the earth so fine
With rivers like green ribbons smaragdine?
Who made the seas its selvage, and its locks
Like a quilt ball within a silver box?
Who spread its canopy? Or curtains spun?
Who in this bowling alley bowled the sun?
'God's Determination Touching His Elect'; Perry Miller *The American Puritans* (1956)

Henry Taylor 1800–86
English poet and public servant

20 From such a sharp and waspish word as 'no'
To pluck the sting.
Philip Van Artvelde (1834) pt. 1, act 1, sc. 2

1 A secret may be sometimes best kept by keeping the secret of its being a secret.
The Statesman (1836) ch. 18

2 Good nature and kindness towards those with whom they come in personal contact, at the expense of public interests, that is of those whom they never see, is the besetting sin of public men.
The Statesman (1836)

Jeremy Taylor 1613–67
English divine

3 This thing . . . that can be understood and not expressed, may take a neuter gender;—and every schoolboy knows it.
The Real Presence . . . (1654) sect. 5, subsect. 1; see **MACAULAY** 507:13

4 As our life is very short, so it is very miserable, and therefore it is well it is short.
The Rule and Exercise of Holy Dying (1651) ch. 1, sect. 4

5 How many people there are that weep with want, or are mad with oppression, or are desperate by too quick a sense of a constant infelicity.
The Rule and Exercise of Holy Dying (1651) ch. 1, sect. 5; see **WORDSWORTH** 865:16

6 The union of hands and hearts.
XXV Sermons Preached at Golden Grove (1653) 'The Marriage Ring' pt. 1

7 But I shall say no more of this at this time; for this is to be felt and not to be talked of; and they that never touched it with their finger may secretly perhaps laugh at it in their heart and be never the wiser.
Via Intelligentiae (1662)

Tom Taylor 1817–80
English dramatist; editor of Punch from 1874

8 Hawkshaw, the detective.
usually quoted as 'I am Hawkshaw, the detective'
The Ticket-of-leave Man (1863) act 4, sc. 1

Norman Tebbit 1931–
British Conservative politician. On Tebbit: see **FOOT** 336:9

9 I grew up in the Thirties with our unemployed father. He did not riot, he got on his bike and looked for work.
speech at Conservative Party Conference, 15 October 1981, in *Daily Telegraph* 16 October 1981

10 The cricket test—which side do they cheer for? . . . Are you still looking back to where you came from or where you are?
on the loyalties of Britain's immigrant population
interview in *Los Angeles Times*, reported in *Daily Telegraph* 20 April 1990

Tecumseh 1768–1813
Shawnee chief

11 Where today are the Pequot? Where are the Narragansett, the Mohican, the Pokanoket, and many other once powerful tribes of our people? They have vanished before the avarice and oppression of the white man, as snow before the summer sun.
Dee Brown *Bury My Heart at Wounded Knee* (1970) ch. 1; see **CREWE** 259:19

Pierre Teilhard de Chardin 1881–1955
French Jesuit philosopher and palaeontologist. On Teilhard de Chardin: see **PIUS XII** 608:1

12 The history of the living world can be summarised as the elaboration of ever more perfect eyes within a cosmos in which there is always something more to be seen.
The Phenomenon of Man (1959)

William Temple 1628–99
English diplomat and essayist, husband of Dorothy **OSBORNE**

13 When all is done, human life is, at the greatest and the best, but like a froward child, that must be played with and humoured a little to keep it quiet till it falls asleep, and then the care is over.
Miscellanea. The Second Part (1690) 'Of Poetry'

William Temple 1881–1944
English theologian; Archbishop of Canterbury from 1942

14 Human status ought not to depend upon the changing demands of the economic process.
in *The Life of the Church and the Order of Society* (Malvern, 1941) p. 221

15 It is a mistake to suppose that God is only, or even chiefly, concerned with religion.
R. V. C. Bodley *In Search of Serenity* (1955) ch. 12

16 Personally, I have always looked on cricket as organized loafing.
attributed

John Tenniel 1820–1914
English draughtsman

17 Dropping the pilot.
on BISMARCK's departure from office
cartoon caption, and title of poem, in *Punch* 29 March 1890

Alfred, Lord Tennyson 1809–92
English poet. On Tennyson: see **BAGEHOT** 51:20, **BULWER-LYTTON** 170:12, **CHESTERTON** 225:20

18 Cleave ever to the sunnier side of doubt.
'The Ancient Sage' (1885) l. 68

19 Break, break, break,
On thy cold grey stones, O Sea!
And I would that my tongue could utter
The thoughts that arise in me.
'Break, Break, Break' (1842)

20 And the stately ships go on
To their haven under the hill;
But O for the touch of a vanished hand,

And the sound of a voice that is still!
'Break, Break, Break' (1842)

1 I come from haunts of coot and hern,
I make a sudden sally
And sparkle out among the fern,
To bicker down a valley.
'The Brook' (1855) l. 23

2 For men may come and men may go,
But I go on for ever.
'The Brook' (1855) l. 33

3 Half a league, half a league,
Half a league onward,
All in the valley of Death
Rode the six hundred.
'The Charge of the Light Brigade' (1854)

4 'Forward, the Light Brigade!'
Was there a man dismayed?
Not though the soldier knew
Some one had blundered:
Their's not to make reply,
Their's not to reason why,
Their's but to do and die:
Into the valley of Death
Rode the six hundred.

Cannon to right of them,
Cannon to left of them,
Cannon in front of them
Volleyed and thundered.
'The Charge of the Light Brigade' (1854)

5 Into the jaws of Death,
Into the mouth of Hell.
'The Charge of the Light Brigade' (1854)

6 Sunset and evening star,
And one clear call for me!
And may there be no moaning of the bar,
When I put out to sea.
'Crossing the Bar' (1889)

7 For though from out our bourne of time and
place
The flood may bear me far,
I hope to see my pilot face to face
When I have crossed the bar.
'Crossing the Bar' (1889)

8 A dream of fair women.
title of poem (1832)

9 A daughter of the gods, divinely tall,
And most divinely fair.
'A Dream of Fair Women' (1832) l. 87

10 He clasps the crag with crookèd hands;
Close to the sun in lonely lands,
Ringed with the azure world, he stands.

The wrinkled sea beneath him crawls;
He watches from his mountain walls,
And like a thunderbolt he falls.
'The Eagle' (1851)

11 And when they buried him the little port
Had seldom seen a costlier funeral.
'Enoch Arden' (1864)

12 The mellow lin-lan-lone of evening bells.
'Far–Far–Away' (1889)

13 O Love, O fire! once he drew
With one long kiss my whole soul through
My lips, as sunlight drinketh dew.
'Fatima' (1832) st. 3

14 There beneath the Roman ruin where the purple
flowers grow,
Came that 'Ave atque Vale' of the Poet's
hopeless woe,
Tenderest of Roman poets nineteen-hundred
years ago,
'Frater Ave atque Vale'—as we wander'd to and
fro
Gazing at the Lydian laughter of the Garda Lake
below
Sweet Catullus's all-but-island, olive-silvery
Sirmio!
'Frater Ave atque Vale' (1885); see CATULLUS 210:9, CATULLUS
211:6

15 More black than ashbuds in the front of March.
'The Gardener's Daughter' (1842) l. 28

16 A sight to make an old man young.
'The Gardener's Daughter' (1842) l. 140

17 I waited for the train at Coventry.
'Godiva' (1842) l. 1

18 Then she rode forth, clothed on with chastity.
'Godiva' (1842) l. 53

19 With twelve great shocks of sound, the
shameless noon
Was clashed and hammered from a hundred
towers.
'Godiva' (1842) l. 74

20   Ah! when shall all men's good
Be each man's rule, and universal peace
Lie like a shaft of light across the land?
'The Golden Year' (1846) l. 47

21 Through all the circle of the golden year.
'The Golden Year' (1846) l. 51

22 That a lie which is all a lie may be met and
fought with outright,
But a lie which is part a truth is a harder matter
to fight.
'The Grandmother' (1859) st. 8

23 Speak to Him thou for He hears, and Spirit with
Spirit can meet—
Closer is He than breathing, and nearer than
hands and feet.
'The Higher Pantheism' (1869); see SWINBURNE 785:15

24 Wearing the white flower of a blameless life,
Before a thousand peering littlenesses,
In that fierce light which beats upon a throne,
And blackens every blot.
of Prince ALBERT
Idylls of the King (1862 ed.) dedication l. 24

25 Man's word is God in man.
Idylls of the King 'The Coming of Arthur' (1869) l. 132

1 Clothed in white samite, mystic, wonderful.
   Idylls of the King 'The Coming of Arthur' (1869) l. 284; 'The
   Passing of Arthur' (1869) l. 199

2 From the great deep to the great deep he goes.
   Idylls of the King 'The Coming of Arthur' (1869) l. 410

3 Blow trumpet, for the world is white with May.
   Idylls of the King 'The Coming of Arthur' (1869) l. 481

4 Live pure, speak true, right wrong, follow the
   King—
   Else, wherefore born?
   Idylls of the King 'Gareth and Lynette' (1872) l. 117

5   The city is built
   To music, therefore never built at all,
   And therefore built for ever.
   Idylls of the King 'Gareth and Lynette' (1872) l. 272

6 To reverence the King, as if he were
   Their conscience, and their conscience as their
   King,
   To break the heathen and uphold the Christ,
   To ride abroad redressing human wrongs,
   To speak no slander, no, nor listen to it,
   To honour his own word as if his God's.
   Idylls of the King 'Guinevere' (1859) l. 465

7 To love one maiden only, cleave to her,
   And worship her by years of noble deeds,
   Until they won her; for indeed I knew
   Of no more subtle master under heaven
   Than is the maiden passion for a maid.
   Idylls of the King 'Guinevere' (1859) l. 472

8 I thought I could not breathe in that fine air
   That pure severity of perfect light—
   I yearned for warmth and colour which I found
   In Lancelot.
   Idylls of the King 'Guinevere' (1859) l. 640

9 We needs must love the highest when we see it.
   Idylls of the King 'Guinevere' (1859) l. 655

10 Elaine the fair, Elaine the loveable,
   Elaine, the lily maid of Astolat.
   Idylls of the King 'Lancelot and Elaine' (1859) l. 1

11 He is all fault who hath no fault at all:
   For who loves me must have a touch of earth.
   Idylls of the King 'Lancelot and Elaine' (1859) l. 132

12   In me there dwells
   No greatness, save it be some far-off touch
   Of greatness to know well I am not great.
   Idylls of the King 'Lancelot and Elaine' (1859) l. 447

13 His honour rooted in dishonour stood,
   And faith unfaithful kept him falsely true.
   Idylls of the King 'Lancelot and Elaine' (1859) l. 871

14 He makes no friend who never made a foe.
   Idylls of the King 'Lancelot and Elaine' (1859) l. 1082

15 The greater man, the greater courtesy.
   Idylls of the King 'The Last Tournament' (1871) l. 628

16 For man is man and master of his fate.
   Idylls of the King 'The Marriage of Geraint' (1859) l. 355

17 It is the little rift within the lute,
   That by and by will make the music mute,
   And ever widening slowly silence all.
   Idylls of the King 'Merlin and Vivien' (1859) l. 388

18 And trust me not at all or all in all.
   Idylls of the King 'Merlin and Vivien' (1859) l. 396

19 Man dreams of fame while woman wakes to
   love.
   Idylls of the King 'Merlin and Vivien' (1859) l. 458

20 I found Him in the shining of the stars,
   I marked Him in the flowering of His fields,
   But in His ways with men I find Him not.
   Idylls of the King 'The Passing of Arthur' (1869) l. 9

21 So all day long the noise of battle rolled
   Among the mountains by the winter sea.
   Idylls of the King 'The Passing of Arthur' (1869) l. 170

22 On one side lay the Ocean, and on one
   Lay a great water, and the moon was full.
   Idylls of the King 'The Passing of Arthur' (1869) l. 179

23 Authority forgets a dying king.
   Idylls of the King 'The Passing of Arthur' (1869) l. 289

24 And the days darken round me, and the years,
   Among new men, strange faces, other minds.
   Idylls of the King 'The Passing of Arthur' (1869) l. 405

25 The old order changeth, yielding place to new,
   And God fulfils himself in many ways,
   Lest one good custom should corrupt the world.
   Idylls of the King 'The Passing of Arthur' (1869) l. 408

26 If thou shouldst never see my face again,
   Pray for my soul. More things are wrought by
   prayer
   Than this world dreams of.
   Idylls of the King 'The Passing of Arthur' (1869) l. 414

27   I am going a long way . . .
   To the island-valley of Avilion;
   Where falls not hail, or rain, or any snow,
   Nor ever wind blows loudly; but it lies
   Deep-meadowed, happy, fair with orchard lawns
   And bowery hollows crowned with summer sea,
   Where I will heal me of my grievous wound.
   Idylls of the King 'The Passing of Arthur' (1869) l. 424

28   Like some full-breasted swan
   That, fluting a wild carol ere her death,
   Ruffles her pure cold plume, and takes the flood
   With swarthy webs.
   Idylls of the King 'The Passing of Arthur' (1869) l. 434

29 Our little systems have their day;
   They have their day and cease to be:
   They are but broken lights of thee,
   And thou, O Lord, art more than they.
   In Memoriam A. H. H. (1850) Prologue

30 Let knowledge grow from more to more,
   But more of reverence in us dwell;
   That mind and soul, according well,
   May make one music as before.
   In Memoriam A. H. H. (1850) Prologue

31 I held it truth, with him who sings
   To one clear harp in divers tones,
   That men may rise on stepping-stones
   Of their dead selves to higher things.
   In Memoriam A. H. H. (1850) canto 1

1 For words, like Nature, half reveal
And half conceal the Soul within.
In Memoriam A. H. H. (1850) canto 5

2 But, for the unquiet heart and brain,
A use in measured language lies;
The sad mechanic exercise,
Like dull narcotics, numbing pain.
In Memoriam A. H. H. (1850) canto 5

3   Never morning wore
To evening, but some heart did break.
In Memoriam A. H. H. (1850) canto 6

4 And ghastly through the drizzling rain
On the bald street breaks the blank day.
In Memoriam A. H. H. (1850) canto 7

5 The last red leaf is whirled away,
The rooks are blown about the skies.
In Memoriam A. H. H. (1850) canto 15

6 There twice a day the Severn fills;
The salt sea-water passes by,
And hushes half the babbling Wye,
And makes a silence in the hills.
In Memoriam A. H. H. (1850) canto 19

7 The Shadow cloaked from head to foot,
Who keeps the keys of all the creeds.
In Memoriam A. H. H. (1850) canto 23

8 I envy not in any moods
The captive void of noble rage,
The linnet born within the cage,
That never knew the summer woods.
In Memoriam A. H. H. (1850) canto 27

9 'Tis better to have loved and lost
Than never to have loved at all.
In Memoriam A. H. H. (1850) canto 27; see **BUTLER** 184:6,
CLOUGH 237:4, **CONGREVE** 247:20, **PROVERBS** 645:23

10 Short swallow-flights of song, that dip
Their wings in tears, and skim away.
In Memoriam A. H. H. (1850) canto 48

11 Be near me when my light is low,
When the blood creeps, and the nerves prick
And tingle; and the heart is sick,
And all the wheels of Being slow.

Be near me when the sensuous frame
Is racked with pains that conquer trust;
And Time, a maniac scattering dust,
And Life, a Fury slinging flame.
In Memoriam A. H. H. (1850) canto 50

12 Oh yet we trust that somehow good
Will be the final goal of ill.
In Memoriam A. H. H. (1850) canto 54

13 That nothing walks with aimless feet;
That not one life shall be destroyed,
Or cast as rubbish to the void,
When God hath made the pile complete.
In Memoriam A. H. H. (1850) canto 54

14   But what am I?
An infant crying in the night:
An infant crying for the light:
And with no language but a cry.
In Memoriam A. H. H. (1850) canto 54

15 So careful of the type she seems,
So careless of the single life.
of Nature
In Memoriam A. H. H. (1850) canto 55

16   The great world's altar-stairs
That slope through darkness up to God.
In Memoriam A. H. H. (1850) canto 55

17 Man . . .
Who trusted God was love indeed
And love Creation's final law—
Though Nature, red in tooth and claw
With ravine, shrieked against his creed.
In Memoriam A. H. H. (1850) canto 56

18 So many worlds, so much to do,
So little done, such things to be.
In Memoriam A. H. H. (1850) canto 73; see **RHODES** 659:12

19 Death has made
His darkness beautiful with thee.
In Memoriam A. H. H. (1850) canto 74

20 And round thee with the breeze of song
To stir a little dust of praise.
In Memoriam A. H. H. (1850) canto 75

21 O last regret, regret can die!
In Memoriam A. H. H. (1850) canto 78

22 Then fancy shapes, as fancy can.
In Memoriam A. H. H. (1850) canto 80

23 Laburnums, dropping-wells of fire.
In Memoriam A. H. H. (1850) canto 83

24 God's finger touched him, and he slept.
In Memoriam A. H. H. (1850) canto 85

25   Fresh from brawling courts
And dusty purlieus of the law.
In Memoriam A. H. H. (1850) canto 89; see **ETHEREGE** 320:13

26 You tell me, doubt is Devil-born.
In Memoriam A. H. H. (1850) canto 96

27 There lives more faith in honest doubt,
Believe me, than in half the creeds.
In Memoriam A. H. H. (1850) canto 96

28 Their meetings made December June,
Their every parting was to die.
In Memoriam A. H. H. (1850) canto 97

29 He seems so near and yet so far.
In Memoriam A. H. H. (1850) canto 97

30 Ring out, wild bells, to the wild sky,
The flying cloud, the frosty light:
The year is dying in the night;
Ring out, wild bells, and let him die.

Ring out the old, ring in the new,
Ring, happy bells, across the snow:
The year is going, let him go;
Ring out the false, ring in the true.
In Memoriam A. H. H. (1850) canto 106

31 Ring out the want, the care, the sin,
The faithless coldness of the times;
Ring out, ring out my mournful rhymes,
But ring the fuller minstrel in.
In Memoriam A. H. H. (1850) canto 106

1 Ring out the thousand wars of old,
Ring in the thousand years of peace.
Ring in the valiant man and free,
The larger heart, the kindlier hand;
Ring out the darkness of the land;
Ring in the Christ that is to be.
In Memoriam A. H. H. (1850) canto 106

2   Not the schoolboy heat,
The blind hysterics of the Celt.
In Memoriam A. H. H. (1850) canto 109

3 Now fades the last long streak of snow,
Now burgeons every maze of quick
About the flowering squares, and thick
By ashen roots the violets blow.
In Memoriam A. H. H. (1850) canto 115

4 And drowned in yonder living blue
The lark becomes a sightless song.
In Memoriam A. H. H. (1850) canto 115

5 There, where the long street roars, hath been
The stillness of the central sea.
In Memoriam A. H. H. (1850) canto 123

6   Wearing all that weight
Of learning lightly like a flower.
In Memoriam A. H. H. (1850) canto 131

7 One God, one law, one element,
And one far-off divine event,
To which the whole creation moves.
In Memoriam A. H. H. (1850) canto 131

8 The voice of the dead was a living voice to me.
'In the Valley of Cauteretz' (1864)

9 Below the thunders of the upper deep;
Far, far beneath in the abysmal sea,
His ancient, dreamless, uninvaded sleep
The Kraken sleepeth.
'The Kraken' (1830)

10 There hath he lain for ages and will lie
Battening upon huge seaworms in his sleep,
Until the latter fire shall heat the deep.
'The Kraken' (1830)

11 The daughter of a hundred Earls,
You are not one to be desired.
'Lady Clara Vere de Vere' (1842) st. 1

12 Kind hearts are more than coronets,
And simple faith than Norman blood.
'Lady Clara Vere de Vere' (1842) st. 7

13 On either side the river lie
Long fields of barley and of rye,
That clothe the wold and meet the sky;
And through the field the road runs by
To many-towered Camelot.
'The Lady of Shalott' (1832, revised 1842) pt. 1

14 Willows whiten, aspens quiver,
Little breezes dusk and shiver.
'The Lady of Shalott' (1832, revised 1842) pt. 1

15 Only reapers, reaping early
In among the bearded barley,
Hear a song that echoes cheerly
From the river winding clearly,
Down to towered Camelot.
'The Lady of Shalott' (1832, revised 1842) pt. 1

16 Or when the moon was overhead,
Came two young lovers lately wed;
'I am half sick of shadows,' said
The Lady of Shalott.
'The Lady of Shalott' (1832, revised 1842) pt. 2

17 A bow-shot from her bower-eaves,
He rode between the barley-sheaves,
The sun came dazzling through the leaves,
And flamed upon the brazen greaves
Of bold Sir Lancelot.
A red-cross knight for ever kneeled
To a lady in his shield,
That sparkled on the yellow field,
Beside remote Shalott.
'The Lady of Shalott' (1832, revised 1842) pt. 3

18 'Tirra lirra,' by the river
Sang Sir Lancelot.
'The Lady of Shalott' (1832, revised 1842) pt. 3

19 She left the web, she left the loom,
She made three paces through the room,
She saw the water-lily bloom,
She saw the helmet and the plume,
She looked down to Camelot.
Out flew the web and floated wide;
The mirror cracked from side to side;
'The curse is come upon me,' cried
The Lady of Shalott.
'The Lady of Shalott' (1832, revised 1842) pt. 3

20 But Lancelot mused a little space;
He said 'She has a lovely face;
God in his mercy lend her grace,
The Lady of Shalott.'
'The Lady of Shalott' (1832, revised 1842) pt. 4

21 Airy, fairy Lilian.
'Lilian' (1830)

22 In the spring a livelier iris changes on the
burnished dove;
In the spring a young man's fancy lightly turns
to thoughts of love.
'Locksley Hall' (1842) l. 19

23 He will hold thee, when his passion shall have
spent its novel force,
Something better than his dog, a little dearer
than his horse.
'Locksley Hall' (1842) l. 49

24   This is truth the poet sings,
That a sorrow's crown of sorrow is
remembering happier things.
'Locksley Hall' (1842) l. 75; see **BOETHIUS** 130:11, **DANTE** 264:18

25 But the jingling of the guinea helps the hurt
that Honour feels.
'Locksley Hall' (1842) l. 105

26 Men, my brothers, men the workers, ever
reaping something new:

That which they have done but earnest of the
things that they shall do:
'Locksley Hall' (1842) l. 117

1 For I dipped into the future, far as human eye
could see,
Saw the vision of the world, and all the wonder
that would be;
Saw the heavens fill with commerce, argosies of
magic sails,
Pilots of the purple twilight, dropping down
with costly bales;
Heard the heavens fill with shouting, and there
rained a ghastly dew
From the nations' airy navies grappling in the
central blue;
Far along the world-wide whisper of the south-
wind rushing warm,
With the standards of the peoples plunging
through the thunder-storm;
Till the war-drum throbbed no longer, and the
battle-flags were furled
In the Parliament of man, the Federation of the
world.
'Locksley Hall' (1842) l. 119

2 Science moves, but slowly slowly, creeping on
from point to point.
'Locksley Hall' (1842) l. 134

3 Yet I doubt not through the ages one increasing
purpose runs,
And the thoughts of men are widened with the
process of the suns.
'Locksley Hall' (1842) l. 137

4 Knowledge comes, but wisdom lingers.
'Locksley Hall' (1842) l. 141

5 I will take some savage woman, she shall rear
my dusky race.
'Locksley Hall' (1842) l. 168

6 I the heir of all the ages, in the foremost files of
time.
'Locksley Hall' (1842) l. 178

7   Forward, forward let us range,
Let the great world spin for ever down the
ringing grooves of change.
'Locksley Hall' (1842) l. 181

8 Better fifty years of Europe than a cycle of
Cathay.
'Locksley Hall' (1842) l. 184

9 Music that gentlier on the spirit lies,
Than tired eyelids upon tired eyes.
'The Lotos-Eaters' (1832) Choric Song, st. 1

10 There is no joy but calm!
'The Lotos-Eaters' (1832) Choric Song, st. 2

11 Death is the end of life; ah, why
Should life all labour be?
'The Lotos-Eaters' (1832) Choric Song, st. 4

12   Live and lie reclined
On the hills like Gods together, careless of
mankind.

For they lie beside their nectar, and the bolts are
hurled
Far below them in the valleys, and the clouds
are lightly curled
Round their golden houses, girdled with the
gleaming world.
'The Lotos-Eaters' (1832) Choric Song, st. 8 (1842 revision)

13 Surely, surely, slumber is more sweet than toil,
the shore
Than labour in the deep mid-ocean, wind and
wave and oar;
Oh rest ye, brother mariners, we will not
wander more.
'The Lotos-Eaters' (1832) Choric Song, st. 8

14   I saw the flaring atom-streams
And torrents of her myriad universe,
Ruining along the illimitable inane.
'Lucretius' (1868) l. 38

15   Nor at all can tell
Whether I mean this day to end myself,
Or lend an ear to Plato where he says,
That men like soldiers may not quit the post
Allotted by the Gods.
'Lucretius' (1868) l. 145

16 Passionless bride, divine Tranquillity,
Yearned after by the wisest of the wise,
Who fail to find thee, being as thou art
Without one pleasure and without one pain.
'Lucretius' (1868) l. 265

17 Weeded and worn the ancient thatch
Upon the lonely moated grange.
She only said, 'My life is dreary,
He cometh not,' she said;
She said, 'I am aweary, aweary,
I would that I were dead!'
'Mariana' (1830) st. 1; see SHAKESPEARE 723:15

18 I hate that dreadful hollow behind the little
wood.
Maud (1855) pt. 1, sect. 1

19 Faultily faultless, icily regular, splendidly null,
Dead perfection, no more.
Maud (1855) pt. 1, sect. 2

20 And most of all would I flee from the cruel
madness of love,
The honey of poison-flowers and all the
measureless ill.
Maud (1855) pt. 1, sect. 4, st. 10

21 That jewelled mass of millinery,
That oiled and curled Assyrian Bull.
Maud (1855) pt. 1, sect. 6, st. 6

22 She came to the village church,
And sat by a pillar alone;
An angel watching an urn
Wept over her, carved in stone.
Maud (1855) pt. 1, sect. 8

23 I kissed her slender hand,
She took the kiss sedately;
Maud is not seventeen,
But she is tall and stately.
Maud (1855) pt. 1, sect. 12, st. 4

1 Gorgonised me from head to foot
    With a stony British stare.
      Maud (1855) pt. 1, sect. 13, st. 2

2 A livelier emerald twinkles in the grass,
    A purer sapphire melts into the sea.
      Maud (1855) pt. 1, sect. 18, st. 6

3 Come into the garden, Maud,
    For the black bat, night, has flown,
    Come into the garden, Maud,
    I am here at the gate alone.
    And the woodbine spices are wafted abroad,
    And the musk of the rose is blown.

    For a breeze of morning moves,
    And the planet of Love is on high,
    Beginning to faint in the light that she loves
    On a bed of daffodil sky.
      Maud (1855) pt. 1, sect. 22, st. 1

4 All night has the casement jessamine stirred
    To the dancers dancing in tune;
    Till a silence fell with the waking bird,
    And a hush with the setting moon.
      Maud (1855) pt. 1, sect. 22, st. 3

5 Queen rose of the rosebud garden of girls.
      Maud (1855) pt. 1, sect. 22, st. 9

6 There has fallen a splendid tear
    From the passion-flower at the gate.
    She is coming, my dove, my dear;
    She is coming, my life, my fate;
    The red rose cries, 'She is near, she is near;'
    And the white rose weeps, 'She is late.'
    The larkspur listens, 'I hear, I hear;'
    And the lily whispers, 'I wait.'
      Maud (1855) pt. 1, sect. 22, st. 10

7 She is coming, my own, my sweet;
    Were it ever so airy a tread,
    My heart would hear her and beat,
    Were it earth in an earthy bed;
    My dust would hear her and beat,
    Had I lain for a century dead;
    Would start and tremble under her feet,
    And blossom in purple and red.
      Maud (1855) pt. 1, sect. 22, st. 11

8 O that 'twere possible
    After long grief and pain
    To find the arms of my true love
    Round me once again!
      Maud (1855) pt. 2, sect. 4, st. 1

9 But the churchmen fain would kill their church,
    As the churches have killed their Christ.
      Maud (1855) pt. 2, sect. 5, st. 2

10 O me, why have they not buried me deep
    enough?
    Is it kind to have made me a grave so rough,
    Me, that was never a quiet sleeper?
      Maud (1855) pt. 2, sect. 5, st. 11

11 My life has crept so long on a broken wing
    Through cells of madness, haunts of horror and
    fear,

That I come to be grateful at last for a little
    thing.
      Maud (1855) pt. 3, sect. 6, st. 1

12 The blood-red blossom of war with a heart of
    fire.
      Maud (1855) pt. 3, sect. 6, st. 4

13 It is better to fight for the good, than to rail at
    the ill;
    I have felt with my native land, I am one with
    my kind,
    I embrace the purpose of God, and the doom
    assigned.
      Maud (1855) pt. 3, sect. 6, st. 5

14 You must wake and call me early, call me early,
    mother dear;
    Tomorrow 'ill be the happiest time of all the
    glad New-year;
    Of all the glad New-year, mother, the maddest
    merriest day;
    For I'm to be Queen o' the May, mother, I'm to
    be Queen o' the May.
      'The May Queen' (1832)

15 *I* am Merlin
    Who follow the Gleam
      'Merlin and The Gleam' (1889) st. 1

16 O mighty-mouthed inventor of harmonies,
    O skilled to sing of time or eternity,
    God-gifted organ-voice of England,
    Milton, a name to resound for ages.
      'Milton: Alcaics' (1863)

17   All that bowery loneliness,
    The brooks of Eden mazily murmuring.
      'Milton: Alcaics' (1863)

18 O you chorus of indolent reviewers.
      'Milton: Hendecasyllabics' (1863)

19 Doänt thou marry for munny, but goä wheer
    munny is!
      'Northern Farmer. New Style' (1869) st. 5; see **PROVERBS**
      639:39

20 The last great Englishman is low.
      'Ode on the Death of the Duke of Wellington' (1852) st. 3

21 O good grey head which all men knew!
      'Ode on the Death of the Duke of Wellington' (1852) st. 4

22 O fall'n at length that tower of strength
    Which stood four-square to all the winds that
    blew!
      'Ode on the Death of the Duke of Wellington' (1852) st. 4

23 That world-earthquake, Waterloo!
      'Ode on the Death of the Duke of Wellington' (1852) st. 6

24 Who never sold the truth to serve the hour,
    Nor paltered with Eternal God for power.
      'Ode on the Death of the Duke of Wellington' (1852) st. 7

25 The path of duty was the way to glory.
      'Ode on the Death of the Duke of Wellington' (1852) st. 8

26 And at their feet the crocus brake like fire,
    Violet, amaracus, and asphodel,
    Lotos and lilies.
      'Oenone' (1832, revised 1842) l. 94

1 Still as, while Saturn whirls, his steadfast shade
Sleeps on his luminous ring.
'The Palace of Art' (1832) st. 4

2 An English home—grey twilight poured
On dewy pasture, dewy trees,
Softer than sleep—all things in order stored,
A haunt of ancient Peace.
'The Palace of Art' (1832) st. 22

3 With prudes for proctors, dowagers for deans,
And sweet girl-graduates in their golden hair.
The Princess (1847) 'Prologue' l. 141

4 And blessings on the falling out
That all the more endears,
When we fall out with those we love
And kiss again with tears!
The Princess (1847) pt. 2, song (added 1850)

5 And quoted odes, and jewels five-words-long,
That on the stretched forefinger of all Time
Sparkle for ever.
The Princess (1847) pt. 2, l. 355

6 Sweet and low, sweet and low,
Wind of the western sea,
Low, low, breathe and blow,
Wind of the western sea!
Over the rolling waters go,
Come from the dying moon, and blow,
Blow him again to me;
While my little one, while my pretty one, sleeps.
The Princess (1847) pt. 3, song (added 1850)

7 The splendour falls on castle walls
And snowy summits old in story:
The long light shakes across the lakes,
And the wild cataract leaps in glory.
Blow, bugle, blow, set the wild echoes flying,
Blow, bugle; answer, echoes, dying, dying, dying.
The Princess (1847) pt. 4, song (added 1850)

8 O sweet and far from cliff and scar
The horns of Elfland faintly blowing!
The Princess (1847) pt. 4, song (added 1850)

9 O love, they die in yon rich sky,
They faint on hill or field or river:
Our echoes roll from soul to soul,
And grow for ever and for ever.
The Princess (1847) pt. 4, song (added 1850)

10 Tears, idle tears, I know not what they mean,
Tears from the depth of some divine despair
Rise in the heart, and gather to the eyes,
In looking on the happy autumn-fields,
And thinking of the days that are no more.
The Princess (1847) pt. 4, l. 21, song (added 1850)

11 So sad, so fresh, the days that are no more.
The Princess (1847) pt. 4, l. 30, song (added 1850)

12 Ah, sad and strange as in dark summer dawns
The earliest pipe of half-awakened birds
To dying ears, when unto dying eyes
The casement slowly grows a glimmering
square;
So sad, so strange, the days that are no more.
Dear as remembered kisses after death,

And sweet as those by hopeless fancy feigned
On lips that are for others; deep as love,
Deep as first love, and wild with all regret;
O Death in Life, the days that are no more.
The Princess (1847) pt. 4, l. 31, song (added 1850)

13 O Swallow, Swallow, flying, flying South,
Fly to her, and fall upon her gilded eaves,
And tell her, tell her, what I tell to thee.

O tell her, Swallow, thou that knowest each,
That bright and fierce and fickle is the South,
And dark and true and tender is the North.
The Princess (1847) pt. 4, l. 75, song (added 1850)

14 Man is the hunter; woman is his game:
The sleek and shining creatures of the chase,
We hunt them for the beauty of their skins;
They love us for it, and we ride them down.
The Princess (1847) pt. 5, l. 147

15 Home they brought her warrior dead.
She nor swooned, nor uttered cry:
All her maidens, watching, said,
'She must weep or she will die.'
The Princess (1847) pt. 6, song (added 1850)

16 Rose a nurse of ninety years,
Set his child upon her knee—
Like summer tempest came her tears—
'Sweet my child, I live for thee.'
The Princess (1847) pt. 6, song (added 1850)

17 Now sleeps the crimson petal, now the white;
Nor waves the cypress in the palace walk;
Nor winks the gold fin in the porphyry font:
The fire-fly wakens: waken thou with me.
The Princess (1847) pt. 7, l. 161, song (added 1850)

18 Now lies the Earth all Danaë to the stars,
And all thy heart lies open unto me.
The Princess (1847) pt. 7, l. 167, song (added 1850)

19 Now folds the lily all her sweetness up,
And slips into the bosom of the lake:
So fold thyself, my dearest, thou, and slip
Into my bosom and be lost in me.
The Princess (1847) pt. 7, l. 171, song (added 1850)

20 Come down, O maid, from yonder mountain
height:
What pleasure lives in height?
The Princess (1847) pt. 7, l. 177, song (added 1850)

21 For Love is of the valley, come thou down
And find him; by the happy threshold, he,
Or hand in hand with Plenty in the maize,
Or red with spirted purple of the vats,
Or foxlike in the vine.
The Princess (1847) pt. 7, l. 184, song (added 1850)

22   Sweet is every sound,
Sweeter thy voice, but every sound is sweet;
Myriads of rivulets hurrying through the lawn,
The moan of doves in immemorial elms,
And murmuring of innumerable bees.
The Princess (1847) pt. 7, l. 203, song (added 1850)

23 No little lily-handed baronet he,
A great broad-shouldered genial Englishman.
The Princess (1847) 'Conclusion' l. 84

1 At Flores in the Azores Sir Richard Grenville lay,
And a pinnace, like a fluttered bird, came flying
from far away:
'Spanish ships of war at sea! we have sighted
fifty-three!'
Then sware Lord Thomas Howard: ''Fore God I
am no coward;
But I cannot meet them here, for my ships are
out of gear,
And the half my men are sick. I must fly, but
follow quick.
We are six ships of the line; can we fight with
fifty-three?'
Then spake Sir Richard Grenville: 'I know you
are no coward;
You fly them for a moment to fight with them
again.
But I've ninety men and more that are lying sick
ashore.
I should count myself the coward if I left them,
my Lord Howard,
To these Inquisition dogs and the devildoms of
Spain.'
'The Revenge' (1878) st. 1

2 And the sun went down, and the stars came out
far over the summer sea,
But never a moment ceased the fight of the one
and the fifty-three.
'The Revenge' (1878) st. 9

3 Sink me the ship, Master Gunner—sink her, split
her in twain!
Fall into the hands of God, not into the hands
of Spain!
'The Revenge' (1878) st. 11

4 And they praised him to his face with their
courtly foreign grace;
But he rose upon their decks, and he cried:
'I have fought for Queen and Faith like a valiant
man and true;
I have only done my duty as a man is bound to
do:
With a joyful spirit I Sir Richard Grenville die!'
And he fell upon their decks, and he died.
'The Revenge' (1878) st. 13

5 And the little Revenge herself went down by the
island crags
To be lost evermore in the main.
'The Revenge' (1878) st. 14

6 My strength is as the strength of ten,
Because my heart is pure.
'Sir Galahad' (1842)

7 Alone and warming his five wits,
The white owl in the belfry sits.
'Song—The Owl' (1830)

8 The woods decay, the woods decay and fall,
The vapours weep their burthen to the ground,
Man comes and tills the field and lies beneath,
And after many a summer dies the swan.
Me only cruel immortality

Consumes: I wither slowly in thine arms,
Here at the quiet limit of the world.
'Tithonus' (1860, revised 1864) l. 1

9 The gods themselves cannot recall their gifts.
'Tithonus' (1860, revised 1864) l. 52

10 Of happy men that have the power to die,
And grassy barrows of the happier dead.
'Tithonus' (1860, revised 1864) l. 70

11 All the charm of all the Muses
often flowering in a lonely word.
'To Virgil' (1882) st. 3

12 I salute thee, Mantovano,
I that loved thee since my day began,
Wielder of the stateliest measure
Ever moulded by the lips of man.
'To Virgil' (1882) st. 10

13 No life that breathes with human breath
Has ever truly longed for death.
'The Two Voices' (1842) st. 132

14 It little profits that an idle king,
By this still hearth, among these barren crags,
Matched with an agèd wife, I mete and dole
Unequal laws unto a savage race.
'Ulysses' (1842) l. 1

15   I am become a name;
For always roaming with a hungry heart
Much have I seen and known; cities of men
And manners, climates, councils, governments,
Myself not least, but honoured of them all;
And drunk delight of battle with my peers,
Far on the ringing plains of windy Troy.
'Ulysses' (1842) l. 16

16 I am a part of all that I have met;
Yet all experience is an arch wherethrough
Gleams that untravelled world, whose margin
fades
For ever and for ever when I move.
How dull it is to pause, to make an end,
To rust unburnished, not to shine in use!
As though to breathe were life.
'Ulysses' (1842) l. 23; see **ADAMS** 2:12

17   This grey spirit yearning in desire
To follow knowledge like a sinking star,
Beyond the utmost bound of human thought.
'Ulysses' (1842) l. 30

18 This is my son, mine own Telemachus.
'Ulysses' (1842) l. 33

19 Old age hath yet his honour and his toil;
Death closes all: but something ere the end,
Some work of noble note, may yet be done,
Not unbecoming men that strove with gods.
'Ulysses' (1842) l. 51

20   For my purpose holds
To sail beyond the sunset, and the baths
Of all the western stars, until I die.
It may be that the gulfs will wash us down:
It may be we shall touch the Happy Isles,
And see the great Achilles, whom we knew.
Though much is taken, much abides.
'Ulysses' (1842) l. 66

1   That which we are, we are;
One equal temper of heroic hearts,
Made weak by time and fate, but strong in will
To strive, to seek, to find, and not to yield.
'Ulysses' (1842) l. 74

2 Every moment dies a man,
Every moment one is born.
'The Vision of Sin' (1842) pt. 4, st. 9; see **BABBAGE** 44:12

3 Saxon and Norman and Dane are we
But all of us Danes in our welcome to thee,
Alexandra!
'A Welcome to Alexandra, March 7, 1863'; see **DEFOE** 270:24

4 I grow in worth, and wit, and sense,
Unboding critic-pen,
Or that eternal want of pence,
Which vexes public men.
'Will Waterproof's Lyrical Monologue' (1842) st. 6

5 A land of settled government,
A land of just and old renown,
Where Freedom slowly broadens down
From precedent to precedent.
'You ask me, why, though ill at ease' (1842) st. 3

6 In the end I accepted the honour, because
during dinner Venables told me, that, if I
became Poet Laureate, I should always when I
dined out be offered the liver-wing of a fowl.
on being made Poet Laureate in 1850
in *Alfred Lord Tennyson: A Memoir by his Son* (1897) vol. 1

7 I see land! Mr Kendal is just going to be
confirmed.
in Charlotte Yonge's novel The Young Stepmother, *the
happiness of the Kendal family depends on their being full
members of the Anglican church*
Alethea Hayter *Charlotte Yonge* (1996)

8 It is the height of luxury to sit in a hot bath and
read about little birds.
*having had running hot water installed in his new house at
Aldworth*
Hallam Tennyson *Tennyson and his Friends* (1911)

9 A louse in the locks of literature.
of Churton Collins
Evan Charteris *Life and Letters of Sir Edmund Gosse* (1931)
ch. 14

Terence (Publius Terentius Afer) *c*.190–159 BC
Roman comic dramatist

10 *Qui quom hunc accusant, Naevium Plautum Ennium
Accusant quos hic noster auctores habet,
Quorum aemulari exoptat neglegentiam
Potius quam istorum obscuram diligentiam.*

In attacking the present author they are really
attacking Naevius, Plautus and Ennius, whom he
takes for his models and whose 'carelessness' he
would far rather imitate than his critics' dreary
pedantry.
Andria prologue l. 18, translated by Betty Radice

11 *Hinc illae lacrimae.*
Hence those tears.
Andria l. 126

12 *Nullumst iam dictum quod non dictum sit prius.*
Nothing has yet been said that's not been said
before.
Eunuchus prologue l. 41

13 *Homo sum; humani nil a me alienum puto.*
I am a man, I count nothing human foreign to
me.
Heauton Timorumenos l. 77

14 *Nam deteriores omnes sumus licentiae.*
We all degenerate in the absence of control.
Heauton Timorumenos l. 483

15 *Fortis fortuna adiuvat.*
Fortune assists the brave.
Phormio l. 203; see **PROVERBS** 632:37, **VIRGIL** 831:8

16 *Quot homines tot sententiae: suus cuique mos.*
There are as many opinions as there are people:
each has his own correct way.
Phormio l. 454; see **PROVERBS** 643:20

Terentianus Maurus
Roman writer of the late 2nd century AD

17 *Pro captu lectoris habent sua fata libelli.*
The reader's fancy makes the fate of books.
De Syllabis et Metris

Mother Teresa 1910–97
**Roman Catholic nun and missionary, born in what is now
Macedonia of Albanian parentage**

18 We ourselves feel that what we are doing is just
a drop in the ocean. But if that drop was not in
the ocean, I think the ocean would be less
because of that missing drop. I do not agree
with the big way of doing things.
A Gift for God (1975)

19 Now let us do something beautiful for God.
letter to Malcolm Muggeridge before making a BBC TV
programme about the Missionaries of Charity, 1971; see
MUGGERIDGE 564:4

20 The biggest disease today is not leprosy or
tuberculosis, but rather the feeling of being
unwanted, uncared for and deserted by
everybody.
in *The Observer* 3 October 1971

21 I see God in every human being. When I wash
the leper's wounds I feel I am nursing the Lord
himself.
in 1977; in obituary, *Guardian* 6 September 1997

22 By blood and origin I am Albanian. My
citizenship is Indian. I am a Catholic nun. As to
my calling, I belong to the whole world. As to
my heart, I belong entirely to the heart of Jesus.
in *Independent* 6 September 1997; obituary

St Teresa of Ávila 1512–82

Spanish Carmelite nun and mystic. See also **JOHN** 434:3, **SAYINGS** 684:6

1 Our goodness derives not from our capacity to think but to love.
Book of the Foundations (1610)

2 The important thing is not to think much but to love much.
The Interior Castle (1588) Mansion 4, ch. 1, para. 7

3 Alas, O Lord, to what a state dost Thou bring those who love Thee!
Interior Castle Mansion 6, ch. 11, para. 6 (translated by the Benedictines of Stanbrook, 1921)

4 Let nothing trouble you, nothing frighten you. All things are passing; God never changes. Patient endurance attains all things. Whoever possesses God lacks nothing: God alone suffices.
'St Teresa's Bookmark'; found in her breviary after her death

St Teresa of Lisieux 1873–97

French Carmelite nun

5 I will spend my heaven doing good on earth.
T. N. Taylor (ed.) *Soeur Thérèse of Lisieux* (1912) epilogue

6 After my death I will let fall a shower of roses.
T. N. Taylor (ed.) *Soeur Thérèse of Lisieux* (1912) epilogue

Ellen Terry 1847–1928

English actress

7 Conceit is an insuperable obstacle to all progress.
The Story of My Life (1907) ch. 5

Tertullian (Quintus Septimius Florens Tertullianus) *c.*AD 160–*c.*225

Roman theologian and Church Father from Carthage

8 *O testimonium animae naturaliter Christianae.*
O evidence of a naturally Christian soul!
Apologeticus ch. 17, sect. 6

9 *'Vide', inquiunt, 'ut invicem se diligant'—ipsi enim invicem oderunt—'et ut pro alteruto mori sint parati'; ipsi enim od occidendum alterutrum paratiores erunt.*
'Look,' they say, 'how they [Christians] love one another' (for they themselves hate one another); 'and how they are ready to die for each other' (for they themselves are readier to kill each other).
usually quoted as, 'See how these Christians love one another'
Apologeticus ch. 39, sect. 7

10 *Si Tiberis ascendit in moenia, si Nilus non ascendit in arva, si caelum stetit, si terra movit, si fames, si lues, statim Christianos ad leonem. Tantos ad unum?*
If the Tiber rises, if the Nile does not rise, if the heavens give no rain, if there is an earthquake, famine, or pestilence, straightway the cry is 'The Christians to the lion!' So many to one?
Apologeticus ch. 40; see **ANONYMOUS** 16:16

11 *Plures efficimus quoties metimur a vobis, semen est sanguis Christianorum.*
As often as we are mown down by you, the more we grow in numbers; the blood of Christians is the seed.
traditionally 'The blood of the martyrs is the seed of the Church'
Apologeticus ch. 50, sect. 13; see **PROVERBS** 628:15

12 *Certum est quia impossibile est.*
It is certain because it is impossible.
often quoted as 'Credo quia impossibile [*I believe because it is impossible*]'
De Carne Christi ch. 5

13 *Quid ergo Athenis et Hierosolymnis?*
What has Athens to do with Jerusalem?
De Proescriptione Haereticorum bk. 7, ch. 9; see **ALCUIN** 11:9

A. S. J. Tessimond 1902–62

English poet

14 Cats, no less liquid than their shadows,
Offer no angles to the wind.
They slip, diminished, neat, through loopholes
Less than themselves.
Cats (1934) p. 20

William Makepeace Thackeray
1811–63

English novelist. On Thackeray: see **RUSKIN** 673:5

15 He who meanly admires mean things is a Snob.
The Book of Snobs (1848) ch. 2

16 'Tis not the dying for a faith that's so hard, Master Harry—every man of every nation has done that—'tis the living up to it that is difficult.
The History of Henry Esmond (1852) bk. 1, ch. 6

17 'Tis strange what a man may do, and a woman yet think him an angel.
The History of Henry Esmond (1852) bk. 1, ch. 7

18 Alas! We are the sport of destiny.
The Memoirs of Barry Lyndon (1856) ch. 3

19 For a slashing article, sir, there's nobody like the Capting.
Mr Bungay
Pendennis (1848–50) ch. 32

20 The *Pall Mall Gazette* is written by gentlemen for gentlemen.
Pendennis (1848–50) ch. 32

21 Business first; pleasure afterwards.
The Rose and the Ring (1855) ch. 1

22 She had the dismal precocity of poverty.
of Becky Sharp
Vanity Fair (1847–8) ch. 2

23 A woman with fair opportunities and without a positive hump, may marry whom she likes.
Vanity Fair (1847–8) ch. 4

1 If a man's character is to be abused, say what you will, there's nobody like a relation to do the business.
Vanity Fair (1847–8) ch. 19

2 Them's my sentiments!
Fred Bullock
Vanity Fair (1847–8) ch. 21

3 Darkness came down on the field and city: and Amelia was praying for George, who was lying on his face, dead, with a bullet through his heart.
Vanity Fair (1847–8) ch. 32

4 How to live well on nothing a year.
Vanity Fair (1847–8) ch. 36 (title)

5 I think I could be a good woman if I had five thousand a year.
Vanity Fair (1847–8) ch. 36

6 As she had never thought or done anything mortally guilty herself, she had not that abhorrence for wickedness which distinguishes moralists much more knowing.
Vanity Fair (1847–8) ch. 65

7 Ah! *Vanitas Vanitatum!* Which of us is happy in this world? Which of us has his desire? or, having it, is satisfied?—Come, children, let us shut up the box and the puppets, for our play is played out.
Vanity Fair (1847–8) ch. 67

8 Werther had a love for Charlotte
Such as words could never utter;
Would you know how first he met her?
She was cutting bread and butter.
'Sorrows of Werther' (1855)

9 Charlotte, having seen his body
Borne before her on a shutter,
Like a well-conducted person
Went on cutting bread and butter.
'Sorrows of Werther' (1855)

10 Mind, no biography!
injunction to his daughters
John Sutherland *Is Heathcliff a Murderer?* (1996)

Margaret Thatcher 1925–

British Conservative stateswoman, Prime Minister 1979–90.
On Thatcher: see **CALLAGHAN** 193:14, **HEALEY** 387:2,
KINNOCK 465:1, **MITTERRAND** 551:10

11 No woman in my time will be Prime Minister or Chancellor or Foreign Secretary—not the top jobs. Anyway I wouldn't want to be Prime Minister. You have to give yourself 100%.
on her appointment as Shadow Education Spokesman
in *Sunday Telegraph* 26 October 1969

12 In politics if you want anything said, ask a man. If you want anything done, ask a woman.
in *People* (New York) 15 September 1975

13 I stand before you tonight in my red chiffon evening gown, my face softly made up, my fair hair gently waved . . . the Iron Lady of the Western World! Me? A cold war warrior? Well, yes—if that is how they wish to interpret my defence of values and freedoms fundamental to our way of life.
speech at Finchley, 31 January 1976; 'the iron lady' was a name given to Thatcher by the Soviet defence ministry newspaper Red Star, which accused her of trying to revive the cold war, in Sunday Times 25 January 1976

14 Pennies don't fall from heaven. They have to be earned on earth.
in *Observer* 18 November 1979 'Sayings of the Week'; see **BURKE** 176:11

15 No one would remember the Good Samaritan if he'd only had good intentions. He had money as well.
television interview, 6 January 1980, in The Times 12 January 1980

16 To those waiting with bated breath for that favourite media catchphrase, the U-turn, I have only this to say. 'You turn if you want; the lady's not for turning.'
*speech at Conservative Party Conference in Brighton, 10 October 1980; see **FRY** 345:15*

17 Just rejoice at that news and congratulate our armed forces and the Marines. Rejoice!
on the recapture of South Georgia, usually quoted as, 'Rejoice, rejoice!'
to newsmen outside 10 Downing Street, 25 April 1982

18 It is exciting to have a real crisis on your hands, when you have spent half your political life dealing with humdrum issues like the environment.
on the Falklands campaign, 1982
speech to Scottish Conservative Party conference, 14 May 1982, in Hugo Young *One of Us* (1990) ch. 13

19 We have to see that the spirit of the South Atlantic—the real spirit of Britain—is kindled not only by war but can now be fired by peace. We have the first prerequisite. We know that we can do it—we haven't lost the ability. That is the Falklands Factor.
speech in Cheltenham, 3 July 1982

20 I was asked whether I was trying to restore Victorian values. I said straight out I was. And I am.
speech to the British Jewish Community, 21 July 1983, referring to an interview with Brian Walden on 17 January 1983

21 Now it must be business as usual.
on the steps of Brighton police station a few hours after the bombing of the Grand Hotel, Brighton; often quoted as 'We shall carry on as usual'
in *The Times* 13 October 1984

22 We can do business together.
of Mikhail **GORBACHEV**
in *The Times* 18 December 1984

23 We must try to find ways to starve the terrorist and the hijacker of the oxygen of publicity on which they depend.
speech to American Bar Association in London, 15 July 1985, in The Times 16 July 1985

1 There is no such thing as Society. There are individual men and women, and there are families.
   in *Woman's Own* 31 October 1987

2 We have become a grandmother.
   in *The Times* 4 March 1989

3 I am naturally very sorry to see you go, but understand . . . your wish to be able to spend more time with your family.
   reply to Norman **FOWLER***'s resignation letter*
      in *Guardian* 4 January 1990; see **FOWLER** 339:7

4 No! No! No!
   making clear her opposition to a single European currency, and more centralized controls from Brussels
      in the House of Commons, 30 October 1990

5 I fight on, I fight to win.
   having failed to win outright in the first ballot for party leader
      comment, 21 November 1990

6 It's a funny old world.
   on withdrawing from the contest for leadership of the Conservative party
      comment, 22 November 1990; see **FILM LINES** 328:22

7 Home is where you come to when you have nothing better to do.
   in *Vanity Fair* May 1991

Bob Thaves 1924–2006
American cartoonist

8 Sure he was great, but don't forget that Ginger Rogers did everything he did backwards . . . and in high heels!
   caption to 'Frank and Ernest' cartoon, c. 1982, showing a Fred Astaire film festival; often wrongly attributed to the American actress and dancer Ginger Rogers (1911–95) herself
      Ginger Rogers *Ginger: My Story* (1991) ch. 16

William Roscoe Thayer 1859–1923
American biographer and historian

9 Log-cabin to White House.
   title of biography (1910) of James **GARFIELD**

Themistocles *c.*528–*c.*462 BC
Greek historian and Athenian statesman

10 The wooden wall is your ships.
   interpreting the words of the Delphic oracle to the Athenians, before the battle of Salamis in 480 BC
      Plutarch *Parallel Lives* 'Themistocles' bk. 2, ch. 1; according to Herodotus *Histories* bk. 7, sect. 141, the words of the prophetess at Delphi were: 'Yet Zeus the all-seeing grants to Athene's prayer / That the wooden wall only shall not fall, but help you and your children'

Theocritus *c.*300–260 BC
Greek poet, born in Sicily

11 Something sweet is the whisper of the pine, O goatherd, that makes her music by yonder springs.
   Idylls no. 1

Louis Adolphe Thiers 1797–1877
French statesman and historian

12 [*Le roi*] règne et le peuple se gouverne.
   The king reigns, and the people govern themselves.
      unsigned article in *Le National*, 20 January 1830; in a signed article in *Le National*, 4 February 1830 Thiers wrote: '*Le roi n'administre pas, ne gouverne pas, il règne* [The king neither administers nor governs, he reigns]'

Thomas à Kempis *c.*1380–1471
German ascetical writer

13 I would far rather feel remorse than know how to define it.
   De Imitatione Christi bk. 1, ch. 1, sect. 3

14 O quam cito transit gloria mundi.
   Oh how quickly the glory of the world passes away!
      De Imitatione Christi bk. 1, ch. 3, sect. 6; see **ANONYMOUS** 23:12

15 Seek not to know who said this or that, but take note of what has been said.
   De Imitatione Christi bk. 1, ch. 5, sect. 1

16 It is much safer to be in a subordinate position than in authority.
   De Imitatione Christi bk. 1, ch. 9, sect. 1

17 Nam homo proponit, sed Deus disponit.
   For man proposes, but God disposes.
      De Imitatione Christi bk. 1, ch. 19, sect. 2; see **PROVERBS** 638:20

18 Never be completely idle, but either reading, or writing, or praying, or meditating, or at some useful work for the common good.
   De Imitatione Christi bk. 1, ch. 19, sect. 4

19 Nobody rules safely but he who has learned well how to obey.
   De Imitatione Christi bk. 1, ch. 20, sect. 2

20 Today the man is here; tomorrow he is gone. And when he is 'out of sight', quickly also is he out of mind.
   De Imitatione Christi bk. 1, ch. 23, sect. 1; see **PROVERBS** 641:25

21 Would that we had spent one whole day well in this world!
   De Imitatione Christi bk. 1, ch. 23, sect. 2

22 Many count the years since their conversion, but their lives often show little sign of improvement. If it is dreadful to die, it is perhaps more dangerous to live long. Happy is the man who keeps the hour of death always in mind, and daily prepares himself to die.
   De Imitatione Christi bk. 1, ch. 23, sect. 2

23 We are sometimes stirred by emotion and take it for zeal.
   De Imitatione Christi bk. 2, ch. 5, sect. 1

24 What you are, that you are: neither can you by words be made greater than what you are in the sight of God.
   De Imitatione Christi bk. 2, ch. 6, sect. 3

1 Man considers the actions, but God weighs the intentions.
  De Imitatione Christi bk. 2, ch. 6, sect. 3

2 If you bear the cross gladly, it will bear you.
  De Imitatione Christi bk. 2, ch. 12, sect. 5

3 Of the two evils the lesser is always to be chosen.
  De Imitatione Christi bk. 3, ch. 12, sect. 2

St Thomas Aquinas *c.*1225–74
Italian Dominican friar and Doctor of the Church

4 *Pange, lingua, gloriosi*
  Corporis mysterium,
  Sanguinisque pretiosi,
  Quem in mundi pretium
  Fructus ventris generosi
  Rex effudit gentium.

  Now, my tongue, the mystery telling
  Of the glorious Body sing,
  And the Blood, all price excelling,
  Which the Gentiles' Lord and King,
  In a Virgin's womb once dwelling,
  Shed for this world's ransoming.
  'Pange Lingua Gloriosi' (Corpus Christi hymn, translated by J. M. Neale, E. Caswall, and others); see **FORTUNATUS** 338:14

5 *Tantum ergo sacramentum*
  Veneremur cernui;
  Et antiquum documentum
  Novo cedat ritui.

  Therefore we, before him bending,
  This great Sacrament revere;
  Types and shadows have their ending,
  For the newer rite is here.
  'Pange Lingua Gloriosi' (Corpus Christi hymn, translated by J. M. Neale, E. Caswall, and others)

6 Moral science is better occupied when treating of friendship than of justice.
  Exposition of Aristotle's Ethics (c.1271) bk. 8, lecture 1

7 Now, the end of our desires is God; hence, the act whereby we are primarily joined to Him is basically and substantially our happiness. But we are primarily united with God by an act of understanding; and therefore, the very seeing of God, which is an act of the intellect, is substantially and basically our happiness.
  Quodlibetal Questions (c.1256) vol. 8, bk. 9, pt. 19 (translated by Bourke)

8 Therefore it is necessary to arrive at a prime mover, put in motion by no other; and this everyone understands to be God.
  Summa Theologicae (c.1265) pt. 1, qu. 2, art. 3 (translated by English Dominican Fathers)

9 If all evil were prevented, much good would be absent from the universe. A lion would cease to live, if there were no slaying of animals; and there would be no patience of martyrs if there were no tyrannical persecution.
  Summa Theologicae (c.1265) pt. 1, qu. 22, art. 2 (translated by English Dominican Fathers)

10 As Aristotle also points out, the slenderest acquaintance we can form with heavenly things is more desirable than a thorough grasp of mundane matters.
  Summa Theologiae (c.1265) pt. 1a, qu. 1, art. 5; see **ARISTOTLE** 27:16

11 Whatever the mind distinguishes in thought is distinct in reality.
  Summa Theologicae (c.1265) pt. 1a, qu. 50, art. 2

12 Everything I have written seems like straw by comparison with what I have seen and what has been revealed to me.
  following a mystical experience, after which he did no more teaching or writing
  on 6 December 1273

Brandon Thomas 1856–1914
English dramatist

13 I'm Charley's aunt from Brazil—where the nuts come from.
  Charley's Aunt (1892) act 1

Dylan Thomas 1914–53
Welsh poet

14 Though lovers be lost love shall not;
  And death shall have no dominion.
  'And death shall have no dominion' (1936); see **BIBLE** 110:34

15 Do not go gentle into that good night,
  Old age should burn and rave at close of day;
  Rage, rage against the dying of the light.
  'Do Not Go Gentle into that Good Night' (1952)

16 Oh as I was young and easy in the mercy of his means,
  Time held me green and dying
  Though I sang in my chains like the sea.
  'Fern Hill' (1946)

17 The force that through the green fuse drives the flower
  Drives my green age; that blasts the roots of trees
  Is my destroyer.
  And I am dumb to tell the crooked rose
  My youth is bent by the same wintry fever.
  'The force that through the green fuse drives the flower' (1934)

18 And I am dumb to tell the lover's tomb
  How at my sheet goes the same crooked worm.
  'The force that through the green fuse drives the flower' (1934)

19 The hand that signed the paper felled a city;
  Five sovereign fingers taxed the breath,
  Doubled the globe of dead and halved a country;
  These five kings did a king to death.
  'The hand that signed the paper felled a city' (1936)

20 The hand that signed the treaty bred a fever,
  And famine grew, and locusts came;
  Great is the hand that holds dominion over

Man by a scribbled name.
'The hand that signed the paper felled a city' (1936)

1 Light breaks where no sun shines;
Where no sea runs, the waters of the heart
Push in their tides.
'Light breaks where no sun shines' (1934)

2 It was my thirtieth year to heaven
Woke to my hearing from harbour and
neighbour wood
And the mussel pooled and the heron
Priested shore
The morning beckon.
'Poem in October' (1946)

3 Pale rain over the dwindling harbour
And over the sea wet church the size of a snail
With its horns through mist and the castle
Brown as owls
But all the gardens
Of spring and summer were blooming in the tall
vales
Beyond the border and under the lark full cloud.
There could I marvel
My birthday
Away but the weather turned around.
'Poem in October' (1946)

4 Deep with the first dead lies London's daughter,
Robed in the long friends,
The grains beyond age, the dark veins of her
mother,
Secret by the unmourning water
Of the riding Thames.
After the first death, there is no other.
'A Refusal to Mourn the Death, by Fire, of a Child in London'
(1946)

5 I can never remember whether it snowed for six
days and six nights when I was twelve or
whether it snowed for twelve days and twelve
nights when I was six.
A Child's Christmas in Wales (1954)

6 Books that told me everything about the wasp,
except why.
A Child's Christmas in Wales (1954)

7 There is only one position for an artist
anywhere: and that is, upright.
on the position of the artists of Wales
Quite Early One Morning (1954) pt. 2 'Wales and the Artist'

8 To begin at the beginning: It is spring, moonless
night in the small town, starless and bible-black.
Under Milk Wood (1954), opening words

9 Chasing the naughty couples down the
grassgreen gooseberried double bed of the
wood.
Under Milk Wood (1954)

10 Before you let the sun in, mind it wipes its
shoes.
Under Milk Wood (1954)

11 Oh, isn't life a terrible thing, thank God?
Under Milk Wood (1954)

12 I want, above all, to work like a fiend, a *good*
fiend.
letter to Edith **SITWELL**, 11 April 1947; *Collected Letters* (1987)

13 The land of my fathers. My fathers can have it.
of Wales
in *Adam* December 1953; see **JAMES** 429:6

14 A man you don't like who drinks as much as
you do.
definition of an alcoholic
Constantine Fitzgibbon *Life of Dylan Thomas* (1965) ch. 6

15 Poetry is not the most important thing in life
. . . I'd much rather lie in a hot bath reading
Agatha Christie and sucking sweets.
Joan Wyndham *Love is Blue* (1986) 6 July 1943

Edward Thomas 1878–1917
English poet

16 Yes; I remember Adlestrop—
The name, because one afternoon
Of heat the express-train drew up there
Unwontedly. It was late June.
'Adlestrop' (1917)

17 The past is the only dead thing that smells
sweet.
'Early one morning in May I set out' (1917)

18 If I should ever by chance grow rich
I'll buy Codham, Cockridden, and Childerditch,
Roses, Pyrgo, and Lapwater,
And let them all to my elder daughter.
'Household Poems: Bronwen' (1917)

19 I have come to the borders of sleep,
The unfathomable deep
Forest where all must lose
Their way.
'Lights Out' (1917)

20 I see and hear nothing;
Yet seem, too, to be listening, lying in wait
For what I should, yet never can, remember.
'Old Man' (1917)

21 Out in the dark over the snow
The fallow fawns invisible go
With the fallow doe;
And the winds blow
Fast as the stars are slow.
'Out in the dark' (1917)

22 As well as any bloom upon a flower
I like the dust on the nettles, never lost
Except to prove the sweetness of a shower.
'Tall Nettles' (1917)

Elizabeth Thomas 1675–1731
English poet

23 From marrying in haste, and repenting at
leisure;
Not liking the person, yet liking his treasure:
Libera nos.
'A New Litany, occasioned by an invitation to a wedding'
(1722); see **PROVERBS** 638:33

Gwyn Thomas 1913–81
Welsh novelist and dramatist

1 I wanted a play that would paint the full face of sensuality, rebellion and revivalism. In South Wales these three phenomena have played second fiddle only to Rugby Union which is a distillation of all three.
introduction to *Jackie the Jumper* (1962)

2 There are still parts of Wales where the only concession to gaiety is a striped shroud.
in *Punch* 18 June 1958

Irene Thomas 1919–2001
English writer and broadcaster

3 Protestant women may take the pill. Roman Catholic women must keep taking The Tablet.
in *Guardian* 28 December 1990

R. S. Thomas 1913–2000
Welsh poet and clergyman

4 The ousel singing in the woods of Cilgwri,
Tirelessly as a stream over the mossed stones,
Is not so old as the toad of Cors Fochno
Who feels the cold skin sagging round his
bones.
'The Ancients of the World' (1952)

5 Or the dry whisper of unseen wings,
Bats not angels, in the high roof.
'In a Country Church' (1955)

6   Doctors in verse
Being scarce now, most poets
Are their own patients, compelled to treat
Themselves first, their complaint being
Peculiar always.
'The Cure' (1958)

7 There is no love
For such, only a willed
gentleness.
'They' (1968)

8 Hate takes a long time
To grow in, and mine
Has increased from birth;
Not for the brute earth . . .
. . . I find
This hate's for my own kind . . .
'Those Others' (1961)

9   God is that great absence
In our lives, the empty silence
Within, the place where we go
Seeking, not in hope to
Arrive or find.
'Via Negativa' (1972)

10 There is no present in Wales,
And no future;
There is only the past,
Brittle with relics . . .
And an impotent people,

Sick with inbreeding,
Worrying the carcase of an old song.
'Welsh Landscape' (1955)

Francis Thompson 1859–1907
English poet

11 As the run-stealers flicker to and fro,
To and fro:—
O my Hornby and my Barlow long ago!
'At Lord's' (1913)

12 The fairest things have fleetest end,
Their scent survives their close:
But the rose's scent is bitterness
To him that loved the rose!
'Daisy' (1913)

13 Nothing begins, and nothing ends,
That is not paid with moan;
For we are born in other's pain,
And perish in our own.
'Daisy' (1913)

14 I fled Him, down the nights and down the days;
I fled Him, down the arches of the years;
I fled Him, down the labyrinthine ways
Of my own mind; and in the mist of tears
I hid from Him, and under running laughter.
'The Hound of Heaven' (1913) pt. 1

15 But with unhurrying chase,
And unperturbèd pace,
Deliberate speed, majestic instancy,
They beat—and a Voice beat
More instant than the Feet—
All things betray thee, who betrayest Me.
'The Hound of Heaven' (1913) pt. 1

16 I said to Dawn: Be sudden—to Eve:
Be soon.
'The Hound of Heaven' (1913) pt. 2

17 Such is: what is to be?
The pulp so bitter, how shall taste the rind?
'The Hound of Heaven' (1913) pt. 4

18 Yet ever and anon a trumpet sounds
From the hid battlements of Eternity;
Those shaken mists a space unsettle, then
Round the half-glimpsèd turrets slowly wash
again.
'The Hound of Heaven' (1913) pt. 4

19 Lo, all things fly thee, for thou fliest Me!
'The Hound of Heaven' (1913) pt. 5

20 There is no expeditious road
To pack and label men for God,
And save them by the barrel-load.
Some may perchance, with strange surprise,
Have blundered into Paradise.
'A Judgement in Heaven' (1913) epilogue

21 O world invisible, we view thee,
O world intangible, we touch thee,
O world unknowable, we know thee,
Inapprehensible, we clutch thee!
'The Kingdom of God' (1913)

1 The angels keep their ancient places;—
Turn but a stone, and start a wing!
'Tis ye, 'tis your estrangèd faces,
That miss the many-splendoured thing.
'The Kingdom of God' (1913)

2   Upon thy so sore loss
Shall shine the traffic of Jacob's ladder
Pitched betwixt Heaven and Charing Cross.
'The Kingdom of God' (1913)

3 And lo, Christ walking on the water
Not of Gennesareth, but Thames!
'The Kingdom of God' (1913)

4 Look for me in the nurseries of heaven.
'To My Godchild Francis M.W.M.' (1913)

Julian Thompson 1934–

British soldier, second-in-command of the land forces
during the Falklands campaign.

5 You don't mind dying for Queen and country,
but you certainly don't want to die for
politicians.
'The Falklands War—the Untold Story' (Yorkshire Television) 1
April 1987; see **FRANCE** 340:13, **GRAHAM** 367:11

Robert Norman Thompson 1914–97

American-born Canadian mission worker, politician and
academic

6 The Americans are our best friends whether we
like it or not.
Peter C. Newman *Home Country: People, Places, and Power
Politics* (1973)

William Hepworth Thompson
1810–86

English classicist; Master of Trinity College, Cambridge,
from 1866

7 What time he can spare from the adornment of
his person he devotes to the neglect of his
duties.
*of Sir Richard Jebb, later Professor of Greek at Cambridge
University*
M. R. Bobbit *With Dearest Love to All* (1960) ch. 7

James Thomson 1700–48

Scottish poet

8 When Britain first, at heaven's command,
Arose from out the azure main,
This was the charter of the land,
And guardian angels sung this strain:
'Rule, Britannia, rule the waves;
Britons never will be slaves.'
*when Thomas Arne set this to music the last two lines
became 'Rule, Britannia! Britannia rule the waves! Britons
never never never shall be slaves'*
Alfred: a Masque (1740) act 2;

9 A bard here dwelt, more fat than bard beseems.
The Castle of Indolence (1748) canto 1, st. 68 (of himself)

10 A little round, fat, oily man of God,
Was one I chiefly marked among the fry:
He had a roguish twinkle in his eye.
The Castle of Indolence (1748) canto 1, st. 69

11 The daisy, primrose, violet, darkly blue,
And polyanthus of unnumbered dyes;
The yellow wall-flower, stained with iron brown;
And lavish stock that scents the garden round.
The Seasons (1746) 'Spring' l. 531

12 Delightful task! to rear the tender thought,
To teach the young idea how to shoot.
The Seasons (1746) 'Spring' l. 1152

13 An elegant sufficiency, content,
Retirement, rural quiet, friendship, books.
The Seasons (1746) 'Spring' l. 1161

14 Ships, dim-discovered, dropping from the clouds.
The Seasons (1746) 'Summer' l. 946

15 Sighed and looked unutterable things.
The Seasons (1746) 'Summer' l. 1188

16 Or where the Northern Ocean, in vast whirls,
Boils round the naked melancholy isles
Of farthest Thule, and the Atlantic surge
Pours in among the stormy Hebrides.
The Seasons (1746) 'Autumn' l. 860

17 Find other lands beneath another sun.
The Seasons (1746) 'Autumn' l. 1286

18 See, Winter comes to rule the varied year,
Sullen and sad.
The Seasons (1746) 'Winter' l. 1

19 Welcome, kindred glooms!
Congenial horrors, hail!
The Seasons (1746) 'Winter' l. 5

20 Oh! Sophonisba! Sophonisba! oh!
Sophonisba (1730) act 3, sc. 2

21 Even Light itself, which every thing displays,
Shone undiscovered, till his brighter mind
Untwisted all the shining robe of day.
*on **NEWTON**'s Opticks*
'To the Memory of Sir Isaac Newton' (1727) l. 96

22 Did ever poet image aught so fair,
Dreaming in whispering groves, by the hoarse
brook!
Or prophet, to whose rapture heaven descends!
*on **NEWTON**'s explanation of the rainbow in terms of
refraction*
'To the Memory of Sir Isaac Newton' (1727) l. 119

James Thomson 1834–82

Scottish poet

23 The city of dreadful night.
title of poem, written 1870–3

24 As we rush, as we rush in the train,
The trees and the houses go wheeling back,
But the starry heavens above that plain
Come flying on our track.
'Sunday at Hampstead' (written 1863–5) st. 10

25 Give a man a horse he can ride,
Give a man a boat he can sail.
'Sunday up the River' (written 1865) st. 15

Roy Thomson 1894–1976

Canadian-born British newspaper proprietor

1 Like having a licence to print your own money.
on the profitability of commercial television in Britain
R. Braddon *Roy Thomson* (1965) ch. 32

Henry David Thoreau 1817–62

American writer. On Thoreau: see JAMES 429:16

2 There are more consequences to a shipwreck than the underwriters notice.
Cape Cod (1865) 'The Highland Light'

3 I heartily accept the motto, 'That government is best which governs least' . . . Carried out, it finally amounts to this, which I also believe,— 'That government is best which governs not at all.'
Civil Disobedience (1849); see O'SULLIVAN 589:6

4 Under a government which imprisons any unjustly, the true place for a just man is also a prison.
Civil Disobedience (1849)

5 What does education often do? It makes a straight-cut ditch of a free, meandering brook.
Journal c.November 1850

6 Some circumstantial evidence is very strong, as when you find a trout in the milk.
Journal 11 November 1850

7 How vain it is to sit down to write when you have not stood up to live.
Journal 19 August 1851

8 Not that the story need be long, but it will take a long while to make it short.
letter to Harrison Blake, 16 November 1857, in Writings *(1906 ed.) vol. 6; see* PASCAL 597:12

9 By avarice and selfishness, and a grovelling habit, from which none of us is free, of regarding the soil as property . . . the landscape is deformed.
Walden (1854) 'The Bean Field'

10 I have travelled a good deal in Concord.
Walden (1854) 'Economy'

11 As if you could kill time without injuring eternity.
Walden (1854) 'Economy'

12 The mass of men lead lives of quiet desperation.
Walden (1854) 'Economy'; *in* Histoire de ma vie *vol. 4 (1854), George Sand described Chopin as being in a state of 'désespérance tranquille'*

13 In any weather, at any hour of the day or night, I have been anxious to improve the nick of time, and notch it on my stick too; to stand on the meeting of two eternities, the past and the future, which is precisely the present moment; to toe that line.
Walden (1854) 'Economy'

14 Beware of all enterprises that require new clothes.
Walden (1854) 'Economy'

15 For more than five years I maintained myself thus solely by the labour of my hands, and I found, that by working about six weeks in a year, I could meet all the expenses of living.
Walden (1854) 'Economy'

16 As for Doing-good, that is one of the professions which are full.
Walden (1854) 'Economy'

17 There are a thousand hacking at the branches of evil to one who is striking at the root.
Walden (1854) 'Economy'

18 The three-o'-clock in the morning courage, which Bonaparte thought was the rarest.
Walden (1854) 'Sounds'; see NAPOLEON I 568:4

19 We can never have enough of nature . . . We need to witness our own limits transgressed, and some life pasturing freely where we never wander.
Walden (1854) 'Spring'

20 Wherever a man goes, men will pursue him and paw him with their dirty institutions, and, if they can, constrain him to belong to their desperate oddfellow society.
Walden (1854) 'The Village'

21 I had three chairs in my house; one for solitude, two for friendship, three for society.
Walden (1854) 'Visitors'

22 I wanted to live deep and suck out all the marrow of life . . . to drive life into a corner, and reduce it to its lowest terms, and, if it proved to be mean, why then to get the whole and genuine meanness of it, and publish its meanness to the world; or if it were sublime, to know it by experience.
Walden (1854) 'Where I lived, and what I lived for'

23 Our life is frittered away by detail . . . Simplify, simplify.
Walden (1854) 'Where I lived, and what I lived for'

24 I once had a sparrow alight upon my shoulder for a moment while I was hoeing in a village garden, and I felt that I was more distinguished by that circumstance than I should have been by any epaulette I could have worn.
Walden (1854) 'Winter Animals'

25 It is not worthwhile to go around the world to count the cats in Zanzibar.
Walden (1854) 'Conclusion'

26 If a man does not keep pace with his companions, perhaps it is because he hears a different drummer. Let him step to the music which he hears, however measured or far away.
Walden (1854) 'Conclusion'

27 Rather than love, than money, than fame, give me truth.
Walden (1854) 'Conclusion'

28 The government of the world I live in was not framed, like that of Britain, in after-dinner conversations over the wine.
Walden (1854) 'Conclusion'

1 In wildness is the preservation of the world.
Walking (1862)

2 It takes two to speak the truth,—one to speak, and another to hear.
A Week on the Concord and Merrimack Rivers (1849) 'Wednesday'

3 It were treason to our love
And a sin to God above
One iota to abate
Of a pure impartial hate.
'Indeed, Indeed I Cannot Tell' (1852)

Robert Thorne d. 1527
English merchant and geographical writer

4 There is no land unhabitable nor sea innavigable.
Richard Hakluyt *The Principal Navigations, Voyages, and Discoveries of the English Nation* (1589)

Jeremy Thorpe 1929–
British Liberal politician

5 Greater love hath no man than this, that he lay down his friends for his life.
on Harold **MACMILLAN***'s sacking seven of his Cabinet on 13 July 1962*
D. E. Butler and Anthony King *The General Election of 1964* (1965) ch. 1; see **BIBLE** 108:18

Thucydides *c.*455–*c.*400 BC
Greek historian

6 If [my history] should be judged useful by those enquirers who desire an exact knowledge of the past as an aid to the interpretation of the future . . . I shall be content.
History of the Peloponnesian War bk. 1, ch. 22 (translated by Richard Crawley, 1874)

7 I have written my work, not as an essay which is to win the applause of the moment, but as a possession for all time.
History of the Peloponnesian War bk. 1, ch. 22, sect. 18 (translated by Richard Crawley, 1874)

8 Of the gods we believe, and of men we know, that by a necessary law of their nature they rule wherever they can.
History of the Peloponnesian War bk. 5, ch. 105

James Thurber 1894–1961
American humorist. See also **CARTOON CAPTIONS** 205:9, **CARTOON CAPTIONS** 205:11, **CARTOON CAPTIONS** 205:18

9 Her own mother lived the latter years of her life in the horrible suspicion that electricity was dripping invisibly all over the house.
My Life and Hard Times (1933) ch. 2

10 You might as well fall flat on your face as lean over too far backward.
'The Bear Who Let It Alone' in *New Yorker* 29 April 1939

11 The war between men and women.
cartoon series title in *New Yorker* 20 January–28 April 1934

12 Early to rise and early to bed makes a male healthy and wealthy and dead.
'The Shrike and the Chipmunks' in *New Yorker* 18 February 1939; see **PROVERBS** 630:42

13 Humour is emotional chaos remembered in tranquillity.
in *New York Post* 29 February 1960; see **WORDSWORTH** 870:3

Edward, Lord Thurlow 1731–1806
English jurist; Lord Chancellor, 1778–83, 1783–92

14 Corporations have neither bodies to be punished, nor souls to be condemned, they therefore do as they like.
usually quoted as 'Did you ever expect a corporation to have a conscience, when it has no soul to be damned, and no body to be kicked?'
John Poynder *Literary Extracts* (1844) vol. 1; see **COKE** 238:16, **PROVERBS** 629:21

Edward, Lord Thurlow 1781–1829
English poet

15 Nature is always wise in every part.
'To a Bird, that haunted the Waters of Lacken, in the Winter'

Tiberius 42 BC–AD 37
Roman emperor from AD 14

16 It is the part of the good shepherd to shear his flock, not skin it.
to governors who recommended burdensome taxes
Suetonius *Lives of the Caesars* 'Tiberius'

The Tibetan Book of the Dead
A Tibetan Buddhist text recited during funerary rites, dating from the 8th century AD

17 When the consciousness-principle getteth outside [the body it sayeth to itself] 'Am I dead or am I not dead?' It cannot determine. It seeth its relatives and connections as it had been used to seeing them before. It even heareth the wailings.
bk. 1, pt. 1

Tibullus (Albius Tibullus) *c.*50–19 BC
Roman poet

18 *Te spectem, suprema mihi cum venerit hora,*
Et teneam moriens deficiente manu.
May I be looking at you when my last hour has come, and dying may I hold you with my weakening hand.
Elegies bk. 1, no. 1, l. 59

19 *Te propter nullos tellus tua postulat imbres,*
Arida nec pluvio supplicat herba Iovi.
Because of you your land never pleads for showers, nor does its parched grass pray to Jupiter the Rain-giver.
of the River Nile in Egypt
Elegies bk. 1, no. 7, l. 25

1 *Periuria ridet amantum Iuppiter.*

Jupiter laughs at lovers' perjuries.
Elegies bk. 3, no. 6, l. 49; see **PROVERBS** 636:47

Chidiock Tichborne *c.*1558–86

English Roman Catholic conspirator

2 My prime of youth is but a frost of cares;
My feast of joy is but a dish of pain;
My crop of corn is but a field of tares;
And all my good is but vain hope of gain.
The day is past, and yet I saw no sun;
And now I live, and now my life is done.
'Elegy' (composed in the Tower of London prior to his execution)

Thomas Tickell 1686–1740

English poet

3 There taught us how to live; and (oh! too high
The price for knowledge) taught us how to die.
'To the Earl of Warwick. On the Death of Mr Addison' (1721)
l. 76

Lionel Tiger 1937–

American anthropologist

4 Male bonding.
Men in Groups (1969)

Tiglath-pileser I *c.*1115–*c.*1077 BC

Assyrian king

5 Their fighting men I cast down in the midst of
the hills, like a gust of wind. I cut off their
heads like lambs . . . and the whole of the city I
laid waste.
announcing his destruction of the city of Hunusa
Richard Holmes (ed.) *Battlefield: Decisive Conflicts in History* (2006)

Paul Tillich 1886–1965

German-born Protestant theologian

6 Neurosis is the way of avoiding non-being by
avoiding being.
The Courage To Be (1952) pt. 2, ch. 3

7 Faith is the state of being ultimately concerned.
Dynamics of Faith (1957) ch. 1

Kahn Tineta-Horn 1940–

American-born Canadian political activist, fashion model and civil servant

8 Why don't you all go back to where you came
from? We own this land; we're your landlords.
And the rent is due.
on white Canadians occupying land belonging to Native Canadians
Myrna Kostash *Long Way From Home* (1980)

Tipu Sultan *c.*1750–99

9 In this world I would rather live two days like a
tiger, than two hundred years like a sheep.
Alexander Beatson *A View of the Origin and Conduct of the War with Tippoo Sultan* (1800) ch. 10; see **PROVERBS** 627:39

Titus (Titus Flavius Vespasianus) AD 39–81

Roman emperor from AD 79

10 *Amici, diem perdidi.*

Friends, I have lost a day.
on reflecting that he had done nothing to help anybody all day
Suetonius *Lives of the Caesars* 'Titus' ch. 8, sect. 1

□ **Toasts** *see* **box overleaf.** *See also* **BOSSIDY**
151:17, **DECATUR** 270:4, **JACKSON** 426:9

Alexis de Tocqueville 1805–59

French historian and politician

11 Freedom alone substitutes from time to time for
the love of material comfort more powerful and
more lofty passions; it alone supplies ambition
with greater objectives than the acquisition of
riches, and creates the light that makes it
possible to see and to judge the vices and
virtues of mankind.
L'Ancien régime (1856, ed. J. P. Mayer, 1951; translated by M. W. Patterson, 1933)

12 Where is the man of soul so base that he would
prefer to depend on the caprices of one of his
fellow men rather than obey the laws which he
has himself contributed to establish?
L'Ancien régime (1856)

13 Despots themselves do not deny that freedom is
excellent; only they desire it for themselves
alone, and they maintain that everyone else is
altogether unworthy of it.
L'Ancien régime (1856)

14 The French Revolution operated in reference to
this world in exactly the same manner as
religious revolutions acted in view of the other
world. It considered the citizen as an abstract
proposition apart from any particular society, in
the same way as religions considered man as
man, independent of country and time.
L'Ancien régime (1856)

15 History is a gallery of pictures in which there
are few originals and many copies.
L'Ancien régime (1856)

16 He who desires in liberty anything other than
itself is born to be a servant.
L'Ancien régime (1856)

17 It is not always by going from bad to worse that
a society falls into revolution . . . The social
order destroyed by a revolution is almost always
better than that which immediately preceded it,
and experience shows that the most dangerous
moment for a bad government is generally that
in which it sets about reform.
L'Ancien régime (1856)

continued

❧ Toasts ❧

1 A bloody war and a sickly season.
naval toast in the time of **NELSON**
  W. N. T. Beckett *A Few Naval Customs, Expressions,
  Traditions, and Superstitions* (1931) 'Customs'

2 George Washington, Commander of the
American Armies, who, like Joshua of old,
commanded the sun and the moon to stand
still, and they obeyed him.
proposed by Benjamin **FRANKLIN** (1706–90) *at a dinner at
Versailles, supposedly after the British minister had
proposed a toast to* **GEORGE III**, *likening him to the sun,
and the French minister had likened* **LOUIS XVI** *to the
moon*
  attributed, perhaps apocryphal

3 Here's tae us; wha's like us?
Gey few, and they're a' deid.
  Scottish toast, probably of 19th-century origin; the first line
  appears in T. W. H. Crosland *The Unspeakable Scot* (1902),
  and various versions of the second line are current

4 If I am obliged to bring religion into after-
dinner toasts (which indeed does not seem

quite the thing) I shall drink—to the Pope, if
you please—still, to Conscience first, and to
the Pope afterwards.
  John Henry Newman *A Letter Addressed to the Duke of
  Norfolk . . .* (1875) sect. 5

5 The King over the Water.
  Jacobite toast (18th-century)

6 PRINCE OF WALES: True blue and Mrs Crewe.
MRS CREWE: Buff and blue and all of you.
  toast proposed by **GEORGE IV** *when Prince of Wales to Mrs
  Crewe, in honour of her support for the Whigs and
  Charles James* **FOX** *in the Westminster election of 1784
  (buff and blue were the Whig colours)*
    at a dinner at Carlton House, May 1784; Amanda Foreman
    Georgiana Duchess of Devonshire (1998)

7 A willing foe and sea room.
naval toast in the time of **NELSON**
  W. N. T. Beckett *A Few Naval Customs, Expressions,
  Traditions, and Superstitions* (1931) 'Customs'

Alexis de Tocqueville *continued*

8 Providence has not created mankind entirely
independent or entirely free. It is true that
around every man a fatal circle is traced, beyond
which he cannot pass; but within the wide verge
of that circle he is powerful and free.
  De la Démocratie en Amérique (1835–40, translated by H.
  Reeve, 1841, ed. J. P. Mayer, 1951) vol. 1

9 Of all nations, those submit to civilization with
the most difficulty which habitually live by the
chase.
  De la Démocratie en Amérique (1835–40) vol. 1

10 It is impossible to destroy men with more
respect for the laws of humanity.
  of the treatment of the American Indians
  De la Démocratie en Amérique (1835–40) vol. 1

11 What is understood by republican government
in the United States is the slow and quiet action
of society upon itself.
  De la Démocratie en Amérique (1835–40) vol. 1

12 There are, at the present time, two great nations
in the world, which seem to tend towards the
same end, although they started from different
points; I allude to the Russians and the
Americans . . . Their starting point is different,
and their courses are not the same; yet each of
them seems to be marked out by the will of
Heaven to sway the destinies of half the globe.
  De la Démocratie en Amérique (1835–40) vol. 1

13 It is impossible to conceive a more troublesome
or more garrulous patriotism; it wearies even
those who are disposed to respect it.
  De la Démocratie en Amérique (1835–40) vol. 2

14 Unable to judge at once of the social position of
those he meets, an Englishman prudently avoids

all contact with them. Men are afraid lest some
slight service rendered should draw them into an
unsuitable acquaintance; they dread civilities, and
they avoid the obtrusive gratitude of a stranger
quite as much as his hatred.
  De la Démocratie en Amérique (1835–40)

15 The French want no-one to be their *superior*.
The English want *inferiors*. The Frenchman
constantly raises his eyes above him with anxiety.
The Englishman lowers his beneath him with
satisfaction. On either side it is pride, but
understood in a different way.
  Voyage en Angleterre et en Irlande de 1835 (ed. J. P. Mayer,
  1958) 8 May 1835

16 It is from the midst of this putrid sewer that the
greatest river of human industry springs up and
carries fertility to the whole world. From this
foul drain pure gold flows forth. Here it is that
humanity achieves for itself both perfection and
brutalization, that civilization produces its
wonders, and that civilized man becomes again
almost a savage.
  of Manchester
  Voyage en Angleterre et en Irlande de 1835 (ed. J. P. Mayer,
  1958) 2 July 1835

17 That disease called work which has afflicted man
since the beginning of his existence.
  note written November 1850, in J. P. Mayer et al. *Recollections:
  the French Revolution of 1848* (1970), p. 74

Alvin Toffler 1928–
American writer

18 Culture shock is relatively mild in comparison
with a much more serious malady that might be
called 'future shock'. Future shock is the

dizzying disorientation brought on by the premature arrival of the future.

in *Horizon* Summer 1965; the book *Future Shock* was published 1970

J. R. R. Tolkien 1892–1973

British philologist and writer. On Tolkien: see PRATCHETT 622:10

1 There and back again.

subtitle of *The Hobbit* (1937)

2 In a hole in the ground there lived a hobbit.

The Hobbit (1937) ch. 1, opening words

3 What has it got in its pocketses?

Gollum trying to solve Bilbo's riddle

The Hobbit (1937) ch. 5

4 Never laugh at live dragons.

The Hobbit (1937) ch. 12

5 One Ring to rule them all, One Ring to find them
One Ring to bring them all and in the darkness bind them.

The Fellowship of the Ring (1954) epigraph

6 Do not meddle in the affairs of Wizards, for they are subtle and quick to anger.

The Lord of the Rings pt. 1 *The Fellowship of the Ring* (1954) bk. 1, ch. 3

7 Precious . . . My Precious!

Gollum, referring to the Ring

The Lord of the Rings pt. 3 *The Return of the King* (1955) bk. 6, ch. 3

Leo Tolstoy 1828–1910

Russian novelist

8 All happy families resemble one another, but each unhappy family is unhappy in its own way.

Anna Karenina (1875–7) pt. 1, ch. 1 (translated by A. and L. Maude)

9 There are no conditions of life to which a man cannot get accustomed, especially if he sees them accepted by everyone about him.

Anna Karenina (1875–7) pt. 7, ch. 13 (translated by Rosemary Edmonds)

10 The candle by which she had been reading the book filled with trouble and deceit, sorrow and evil, flared up with a brighter light, illuminating for her everything that before had been enshrouded in darkness, flickered, grew dim, and went out for ever.

Anna Karenina (1875–7) pt. 7, ch. 31 (translated by Rosemary Edmonds)

11 What an immense mass of evil must result from allowing men to assume the right of anticipating what may happen.

The Kingdom of God is Within You (1894) ch.2

12 The hero of my tale—whom I love with all the power of my soul, whom I have tried to portray in all his beauty, who has been, is, and will be beautiful—is Truth.

Sevastopol in May (1855) ch. 16 (translated by A. and L. Maude)

13 In historical events great men—so-called—are but labels serving to give a name to the event, and like labels they have the least possible connexion with the event itself.

War and Peace (1868–9) bk. 3, pt. 1, ch. 1 (translated by Rosemary Edmonds)

14 The cudgel of the people's war was lifted with all its menacing and majestic might, and caring nothing for good taste and procedure, with dull-witted simplicity but sound judgement it rose and fell, making no distinctions.

War and Peace (1868–9) bk. 4, pt. 3, ch. 1 (translated by Rosemary Edmonds)

15 The strongest of all warriors are these two—time and patience.

War and Peace (1865–9) bk. 10, ch. 16

16 Our body is a machine for living. It is organized for that, it is its nature. Let life go on in it unhindered and let it defend itself, it will do more than if you paralyse it by encumbering it with remedies.

War and Peace (1865–9) bk. 10, ch. 29 (translated by A. and L. Maude); see LE CORBUSIER 487:2

17 By loving people without cause he discovered indubitable causes for loving them.

War and Peace (1865–9) bk. 15, ch. 19 (translated by A. and L. Maude)

18 I sit on a man's back, choking him and making him carry me, and yet assure myself and others that I am very sorry for him and wish to ease his lot by all possible means—except by getting off his back.

What Then Must We Do? (1886) ch. 16 (translated by A. Maude)

19 All newspaper and journalistic activity is an intellectual brothel from which there is no retreat.

letter to Prince V. P. Meshchersky, 22 August 1871, in *Letters* (ed. R. F. Christian, 1978) vol. 1

Wolfe Tone 1763–98

Irish nationalist and political writer

20 I find, then, I am but a bad anatomist.

in trying to cut his throat in prison he severed his windpipe instead of his jugular, and lingered for several days

last words; Oliver Knox *Rebels and Informers* (1998)

Augustus Montague Toplady 1740–78

English clergyman

21 Rock of Ages, cleft for me,
Let me hide myself in Thee.
Let the water and the blood,
From Thy riven side which flowed,
Be of sin the double cure,
Cleanse me from its guilt and power.

'Rock of Ages, cleft for me' (1776 hymn)

Michael Torke 1961–

American composer

1 Why waste money on psychotherapy when you can listen to the B Minor Mass?

in *Observer* 23 September 1990 'Sayings of the Week'

Robert Torrens 1780–1864

British economist

2 In the first stone which he [the savage] flings at the wild animals he pursues, in the first stick that he seizes to strike down the fruit which hangs above his reach, we see the appropriation of one article for the purpose of aiding in the acquisition of another, and thus discover the origin of capital.

An Essay on the Production of Wealth (1821) ch. 2

Cyril Tourneur *see* **Middleton** 534:9

A. Toussenel 1803–85

French writer

3 *Plus on apprend à connaître l'homme, plus on apprend à estimer le chien.*

The more one gets to know of men, the more one values dogs.

L'Esprit des bêtes (1847) ch. 3; see **ROLAND** 666:8

Pete Townshend 1945–

English rock musician and songwriter

4 Hope I die before I get old.

'My Generation' (1965 song)

Arnold Toynbee 1889–1975

English historian

5 Civilization is a movement and not a condition, a voyage and not a harbour.

in *Readers Digest* October 1958

Polly Toynbee 1946–

English journalist

6 Feminism is the most revolutionary idea there has ever been. Equality for women demands a change in the human psyche more profound than anything Marx dreamed of. It means valuing parenthood as much as we value banking.

in *Guardian* 19 January 1987

Thomas Traherne c.1637–74

English mystic

7 An empty book is like an infant's soul, in which anything may be written. It is capable of all things, but containeth nothing.

Centuries of Meditations 'First Century' opening line

8 You never enjoy the world aright, till the sea itself floweth in your veins, till you are clothed with the heavens, and crowned with the stars: and perceive yourself to be the sole heir of the whole world.

Centuries of Meditations 'First Century' sect. 29

9 All appeared new, and strange at first, inexpressibly rare and delightful and beautiful. I was a little stranger, which at my entrance into the world was saluted and surrounded with innumerable joys. My knowledge was divine.

Centuries of Meditations 'Third Century' sect. 3

10 All things were spotless and pure and glorious . . . I knew not that there were any sins or complaints or laws. I dreamed not of poverties, contentions or vices. All tears and quarrels were hidden from my eyes. Everything was at rest, free and immortal.

Centuries of Meditations 'Third Century' sect. 2

11 The corn was orient and immortal wheat, which never should be reaped, nor was ever sown. I thought it had stood from everlasting to everlasting.

Centuries of Meditations 'Third Century' sect. 3

12 The green trees when I saw them first . . . transported and ravished me, their sweetness and unusual beauty made my heart to leap and almost mad with ecstasy, they were such strange and wonderful things.

Centuries of Meditations 'Third Century' sect. 3

13 O what venerable creatures did the aged seem! Immortal cherubims! And young men glittering and sparkling angels, and maids strange seraphic pieces of life and beauty! Boys and girls tumbling in the street, and playing, were moving jewels. I knew not that they were born or should die; but all things abided eternally.

Centuries of Meditations 'Third Century' sect. 3

14 Contentment is a sleepy thing
If it in death alone must die;
A quiet mind is worse than poverty,
Unless it from enjoyment spring!
That's blessedness alone that makes a King!

'Of Contentment'

15 I within did flow
With seas of life, like wine.
I nothing in this world did know,
But 'twas divine!

'Wonder'

Henry Duff Traill 1842–1900

English journalist

16 Look in my face. My name is Used-to-was;
I am also called Played-out and Done-to-death,
And It-will-wash-no-more.

'After Dilettante Concetti' (i.e. Dante Gabriel Rossetti) st. 8; see **ROSSETTI** 669:20

Joseph Trapp 1679–1747

English poet and pamphleteer

17 The King, observing with judicious eyes
The state of both his universities,

To Oxford sent a troop of horse, and why?
That learned body wanted loyalty;
To Cambridge books, as very well discerning
How much that loyal body wanted learning.

lines written on **GEORGE I***'s donation of the Bishop of Ely's Library to Cambridge University*

John Nichols *Literary Anecdotes* (1812–16) vol. 3; see **BROWNE** 163:20

Merle Travis 1917–83
American country singer

1 Sixteen tons, what do you get?
Another day older and deeper in debt.
Say brother, don't you call me 'cause I can't go
I owe my soul to the company store.

'Sixteen Tons' (1947 song)

Herbert Beerbohm Tree 1852–1917
English actor-manager

2 He is an old bore. Even the grave yawns for him.
of Israel **ZANGWILL**
Max Beerbohm *Herbert Beerbohm Tree* (1920) appendix 4

3 Ladies, just a little more virginity, if you don't mind.
to a motley collection of females, assembled to play ladies-in-waiting to a queen
Alexander Woollcott *Shouts and Murmurs* (1923) 'Capsule Criticism'

4 My poor fellow, why not carry a watch?
to a man in the street, carrying a grandfather clock
Hesketh Pearson *Beerbohm Tree* (1956) ch. 12

5 Sirs, I have tested your machine. It adds a new terror to life and makes death a long-felt want.
when pressed by a gramophone company for a written testimonial
Hesketh Pearson *Beerbohm Tree* (1956) ch. 19; see **WETHERELL** 849:6

G. M. Trevelyan 1876–1962
English historian

6 Disinterested intellectual curiosity is the life-blood of real civilization.
English Social History (1942) introduction

7 If the French noblesse had been capable of playing cricket with their peasants, their chateaux would never have been burnt.
English Social History (1942) ch. 8

8 [Education] has produced a vast population able to read but unable to distinguish what is worth reading, an easy prey to sensations and cheap appeals.
English Social History (1942) ch. 18

9 In a world of voluble hates, he plotted to make men like, or at least tolerate one another.
of Stanley **BALDWIN**
in *Dictionary of National Biography 1941–50* (1959)

George Otto Trevelyan 1838–1928
British politician and writer

10 It may be doubted whether so small a number of men ever employed so short a space of time with greater and more lasting effects upon the history of the world.
of the American victory at Trenton, 1776, in the American War of Independence
George III and Charles Fox: the concluding part of The American Revolution (1912–14) vol. 1; see **CHURCHILL** 229:17

William Trevor (William Trevor Cox)
1928–
Irish novelist and short story writer

11 Marriage was all defeat and victory, and worked better when women were the defeated ones since men apparently could not bear to be and had no philosophy for that condition.
The Children of Dynmouth (1976) ch. 3

12 When you looked at the map Ireland and England seemed like lovers . . . 'Does the map remind you curiously of an embrace? A most extraordinary embrace to throw up all this.'
Fools of Fortune (1983)

Calvin Trillin 1935–
American journalist and writer

13 The shelf life of the modern hardback writer is somewhere between the milk and the yoghurt.
in *Sunday Times* 9 June 1991; attributed

David Trimble 1944–
Northern Irish politician, leader of the Ulster Unionist Party 1995–2005, and first First Minister of Northern Ireland

14 The fundamental Act of Union is there, intact.
of the Northern Ireland settlement
in *Daily Telegraph* 11 April 1998

Tommy Trinder 1909–89
English comedian

15 Overpaid, overfed, oversexed, and over here.
of American troops in Britain during the Second World War
associated with Trinder, but probably not his invention

Anthony Trollope 1815–82
English novelist, son of Frances **TROLLOPE**

16 He must have known me had he seen me as he was wont to see me, for he was in the habit of flogging me constantly. Perhaps he did not recognize me by my face.
Autobiography (1883) ch. 1

17 Take away from English authors their copyrights, and you would very soon take away from England her authors.
Autobiography (1883) ch. 6

18 A novel can hardly be made interesting or successful without love . . . It is necessary

because the passion is one which interests or has
interested all. Everyone feels it, has felt it, or
expects to feel it.
Autobiography (1883) ch. 12

1 Three hours a day will produce as much as a
man ought to write.
Autobiography (1883) ch. 15

2 A man who entertains in his mind any political
doctrine, except as a means of improving the
condition of his fellows, I regard as a political
intriguer, a charlatan, and a conjuror.
Autobiography (1883) ch. 16

3 I think that Plantagenet Palliser, Duke of
Omnium, is a perfect gentleman. If he be not,
then I am unable to describe a gentleman.
Autobiography (1883) ch. 20

4 A man's mind will very generally refuse to make
itself up until it be driven and compelled by
emergency.
Ayala's Angel (1881) ch. 41

5 She was rich in apparel, but not bedizened with
finery . . . she well knew the great architectural
secret of decorating her constructions, and never
descended to construct a decoration.
Barchester Towers (1857) ch. 9

6 The end of a novel, like the end of a children's
dinner-party, must be made up of sweetmeats
and sugar-plums.
Barchester Towers (1857) ch. 53

7 When taken in the refreshing waters of office
any . . . pill can be swallowed.
The Bertrams (1859) ch. 16

8 Those who have courage to love should have
courage to suffer.
The Bertrams (1859) ch. 27

9 A desire for wealth is the source of all progress.
Civilization comes from what men call greed.
Let your mercenary tendencies be combined
with honesty and they cannot take you astray.
Plantagenet Palliser
Can You Forgive Her? (1864) ch. 25

10 There is no road to wealth so easy and
respectable as that of matrimony.
Doctor Thorne (1858) ch. 16

11 Let no man boast himself that he has got
through the perils of winter till at least the
seventh of May.
Doctor Thorne (1858) ch. 47

12 'It's in Tipperary—not at all a desirable country
to live in.'
'Oh, dear, no! Don't they murder the people?'
The Eustace Diamonds (1872) ch. 8; see **KOHL** 470:14

13 They who do not understand that a man may be
brought to hope that which of all things is the
most grievous to him, have not observed with
sufficient closeness the perversity of the human
mind.
He Knew He Was Right (1869) ch. 38

14 It's dogged as does it. It ain't thinking about it.
Giles Hoggett
The Last Chronicle of Barset (1867) ch. 61

15 I have sometimes thought that there is no being
so venomous, so bloodthirsty as a professed
philanthropist.
North America (1862) vol. 1, ch. 16

16 We cannot bring ourselves to believe it possible
that a foreigner should in any respect be wiser
than ourselves. If any such point out to us our
follies, we at once claim those follies as the
special evidences of our wisdom.
Orley Farm (1862) ch. 18

17 It is because we put up with bad things that
hotel-keepers continue to give them to us.
Orley Farm (1862) ch. 18

18 Mr Turnbull had predicted evil consequences . . .
and was now doing the best in his power to
bring about the verification of his own
prophecies.
Phineas Finn (1869) ch. 25

19 A man destined to sit conspicuously on our
Treasury Bench, or on the seat opposite to it,
should ask the Gods for a thick skin as a first
gift.
Phineas Finn (1869) ch. 33; see **ADENAUER** 6:6

20 She knew how to allure by denying, and to
make the gift rich by delaying it.
Phineas Finn (1869) ch. 57

21 Newspaper editors sport daily with the names of
men of whom they do not hesitate to publish
almost the severest words that can be uttered;
but let an editor be himself attacked, even
without his name, and he thinks that the
thunderbolt of heaven should fall upon the
offender.
Phineas Redux (1874) ch. 27

22 Equality would be a heaven, if we could attain
it.
The Prime Minister (1876) ch. 68

23 Why is it that girls so constantly do this,—so
frequently ask men who have loved them to be
present at their marriages with other men?
There is no triumph in it. It is done in sheer
kindness and affection. They intend to offer
something which shall soften and not aggravate
the sorrow that they have caused . . . I fully
appreciate the intention, but in honest truth, I
doubt the eligibility of the proffered
entertainment.
The Small House at Allington (1864) ch. 9

24 Never think that you're not good enough
yourself. A man should never think that. My
belief is that in life people will take you very
much at your own reckoning.
The Small House at Allington (1864) ch. 32

25 The tenth Muse, who now governs the
periodical press.
The Warden (1855) ch. 14

1 Is it not singular how some men continue to obtain the reputation of popular authorship without adding a word to the literature of their country worthy of note? . . . To puff and to get one's self puffed have become different branches of a new profession.
The Way We Live Now (1875) ch. 1

2 Love is like any other luxury. You have no right to it unless you can afford it.
The Way We Live Now (1875) ch. 84

Frances Trollope 1780–1863

English writer, mother of Anthony **TROLLOPE**

3 I draw from life—but I always pulp my acquaintance before serving them up. You would never recognize a pig in a sausage.
remark, c.1848; S. Baring-Gould *Early Reminiscences 1834-1864* (1923)

Leon Trotsky (Lev Davidovich Bronstein)
1879–1940

Russian revolutionary

4 Old age is the most unexpected of all things that happen to a man.
Diary in Exile (1959) 8 May 1935

5 Civilization has made the peasantry its pack animal. The bourgeoisie in the long run only changed the form of the pack.
History of the Russian Revolution (1933) vol. 3, ch. 1

6 You [the Mensheviks] are pitiful isolated individuals; you are bankrupts; your role is played out. Go where you belong from now on — into the dustbin of history!
History of the Russian Revolution (1933) vol. 3, ch. 10; see **BIRRELL** 122:3

7 It was the supreme expression of the mediocrity of the apparatus that Stalin himself rose to his position.
My Life (1930) ch. 40

8 Where force is necessary, there it must be applied boldly, decisively and completely. But one must know the limitations of force; one must know when to blend force with a manoeuvre, a blow with an agreement.
What Next? (1932) ch. 14

9 Not believing in force is the same thing as not believing in gravitation.
G. Maximov *The Guillotine at Work* (1940)

Pierre Trudeau 1919–2000

Canadian Liberal statesman, Prime Minister 1968–79 and 1980–4

10 The state has no place in the nation's bedrooms.
interview, Ottawa, 22 December 1967

11 The twentieth century really belongs to those who will build it. The future can be promised to no one.
in 1968; see **LAURIER** 483:4

12 Living next to you is in some ways like sleeping with an elephant. No matter how friendly and even-tempered the beast, one is affected by every twitch and grunt.
on relations between Canada and the US
speech at National Press Club, Washington D. C., 25 March 1969

François Truffaut 1932–84

French film director

13 Airing one's dirty linen never makes for a masterpiece.
Bed and Board (1972)

14 I've always had the impression that real militants are like cleaning women, doing a thankless, daily but necessary job.
letter to Jean-Luc Godard, May-June 1973

Harry S. Truman 1884–1972

American Democratic statesman, 33rd President of the US 1945–53. On Truman: see **ROOSEVELT** 666:17; see also **NEWSPAPER HEADLINES AND LEADERS** 573:5

15 *to reporters the day after his accession to the Presidency on the death of Franklin D. ROOSEVELT:*
When they told me yesterday what had happened, I felt like the moon, the stars and all the planets had fallen on me.
on 13 April 1945

16 All the President is, is a glorified public relations man who spends his time flattering, kissing and kicking people to get them to do what they are supposed to do anyway.
letter to his sister, 14 November 1947, in *Off the Record* (1980)

17 What we are doing in Korea is this: we are trying to prevent a third world war.
after the recall of MACARTHUR
address to the nation, 16 April 1951

18 If you can't stand the heat, get out of the kitchen.
associated with Truman, but attributed by him to Harry Vaughan, his 'military jester'; in *Time* 28 April 1952; see **PROVERBS** 635:24

19 I never give them [the public] hell. I just tell the truth, and they think it is hell.
in *Look* 3 April 1956

20 A politician is a man who understands government, and it takes a politician to run a government. A statesman is a politician who's been dead 10 or 15 years.
in *New York World Telegram and Sun* 12 April 1958

21 It's a recession when your neighbour loses his job; it's a depression when you lose yours.
in *Observer* 13 April 1958

22 Wherever you have an efficient government you have a dictatorship.
lecture at Columbia University, 28 April 1959, in *Truman Speaks* (1960)

23 I didn't fire him [General MacArthur] because he was a dumb son of a bitch, although he was,

but that's not against the law for generals. If it was, half to three-quarters of them would be in jail.

Merle Miller *Plain Speaking* (1974) ch. 24

1 Always be sincere, even if you don't mean it.
attributed

2 The buck stops here.
unattributed motto on Truman's desk

Donald Trump 1946–
American businessman

3 Deals are my art form. Other people paint beautifully on canvas or write wonderful poetry. I like making deals, preferably big deals. That's how I get my kicks.

Donald Trump and Tony Schwartz *The Art of the Deal* (1987)

Sojourner Truth c.1797–1883
American evangelist and reformer

4 That man . . . says that women need to be helped into carriages, and lifted over ditches, and to have the best place everywhere. Nobody ever helps me into carriages, or over mud puddles, or gives me any best place, and aren't I a woman? . . . I have ploughed, and planted, and gathered into barns, and no man could head me—and aren't I a woman? I could work as much and eat as much as a man (when I could get it), and bear the lash as well—and aren't I a woman? I have borne thirteen children and seen them most all sold off into slavery, and when I cried out with a mother's grief, none but Jesus heard—and aren't I a woman?

speech at Women's Rights Convention, Akron, Ohio, 1851

5 That little man . . . he says women can't have as much rights as men, cause Christ wasn't a woman. Where did your Christ come from? From God and a woman. Man had nothing to do with Him.

speech at Women's Rights Convention, Akron, Ohio, 1851

6 There is a great stir about coloured men getting their rights, but not a word about the coloured women; and if coloured men get their rights, and not coloured women theirs, you see the coloured men will be masters over the women, and it will be just as bad as it was before. So I am for keeping the thing going while things are stirring; because if we wait till it is still, it will take a great while to get it going again.

speech, Equal Rights Convention, New York, 9 May 1867

Morgan Tsvangirai 1952–
Zimbabwean politician

7 Democracy is an orphan in Zimbabwe.
in *Guardian* 7 April 2008

Harriet Tubman c.1820–1913
American abolitionist

8 I had reasoned this out in my mind. There were two things I had a right to, liberty and death. If I could not have one, I would have the other, for no man should take me alive.

Sarah H. Bradford *Harriet, the Moses of Her People* (1869)

9 Children, if you are tired, keep going; if you are scared, keep going; if you are hungry, keep going; if you want to taste freedom, keep going.

attributed, but apparently a modern paraphrase of her views

Barbara W. Tuchman 1912–89
American writer

10 Dead battles, like dead generals, hold the military mind in their dead grip and Germans, no less than other peoples, prepare for the last war.

August 1914 (1962) ch. 2

11 For one August in its history Paris was French—and silent.

August 1914 (1962) ch. 20

Sophie Tucker (Sophia Abuza) 1884–1966
Russian-born American vaudeville artiste

12 From birth to 18 a girl needs good parents. From 18 to 35, she needs good looks. From 35 to 55, good personality. From 55 on, she needs good cash.

Michael Freedland *Sophie* (1978)

Martin Tupper 1810–89
English writer

13 A good book is the best of friends, the same to-day and for ever.

Proverbial Philosophy Series I (1838) 'Of Reading'

Ivan Turgenev 1818–83
Russian novelist

14 Superfluous, superfluous . . . A supernumerary—that's all. Nature, obviously, hadn't counted on my showing up and consequently treated me as an unexpected and uninvited guest.

Diary of a Superfluous Man (1850) 23 March (translated by Franklin Reeve)

15 Nature is not a temple, but a workshop, and man's the workman in it.

Fathers and Sons (1862) ch. 9 (translated by Rosemary Edmonds)

16 I share no one's ideas. I have my own.

Fathers and Sons (1862) ch. 13 (translated by Rosemary Edmonds)

17 Your sort, the gentry, can never go farther than well-bred resignation or well-bred indignation.

Fathers and Sons (1862) ch. 26 (translated by Rosemary Edmonds)

1 Just try and set death aside. It sets you aside, and that's the end of it!
>   *Fathers and Sons* (1862) ch. 27 (translated by Rosemary Edmonds)

2 The heart of another is a dark forest.
>   *A Month in the Country* (1850); see CATHER 209:16

3 No matter how often you knock at nature's door, she won't answer in words you can understand—for Nature is dumb. She'll vibrate and moan like a violin, but you mustn't expect a song.
>   *On the Eve* (1860) ch. 1 (translated by Gilbert Gardiner)

4 Death is like a fisherman, who, having caught a fish in his net, leaves it in the water for a time; the fish continues to swim about, but all the while the net is round it, and the fisherman will snatch it out in his own good time.
>   *On the Eve* (1860) ch. 35 (translated by Gilbert Gardiner)

5 Whatever a man prays for, he prays for a miracle. Every prayer reduces itself to this: Great God, grant that twice two be not four.
>   *Poems in Prose* (1881) 'Prayer'

6 The only people who remain misunderstood are those who either do not know what they want or are not worth understanding.
>   *Rudin* (1856) ch. 5 (translated by Richard Freeborn)

A. R. J. Turgot 1727–81
French economist and statesman

7 *Eripuit coelo fulmen, sceptrumque tyrannis.*
  He snatched the lightning shaft from heaven, and the sceptre from tyrants.
>   inscription for a bust of Benjamin FRANKLIN, inventor of the lightning conductor; see MANILIUS 519:7

Alan Turing 1912–54
English mathematician and codebreaker

8 We are not interested in the fact that the brain has the consistency of cold porridge.
>   A. P. Hodges *Alan Turing: the Enigma* (1983)

Charles Tennyson Turner 1808–79
English poet

9 Bright over Europe fell her golden hair.
>   'Letty's Globe' (1880)

J. M. W. Turner 1775–1851
English landscape painter. On Turner: see SCOTT 689:26

10 He *sees* more in my pictures than I ever painted!
>   *of John* RUSKIN
>   Mary Lloyd *Sunny Memories* (1879) vol. 1

11 I know of no genius but the genius of hard work.
>   John Ruskin *Notes by Mr Ruskin on His Collection of Drawings by the late J. M. W. Turner* (1878)

12 If I could find anything blacker than black, I'd use it.
>   *when a friend complained of the blackness of the sails in 'Peace—Burial at Sea' (1844)*
>   in *Dictionary of National Biography* (1917–)

13 I did not expect to escape, but I felt bound to record it if I did.
>   *of watching a storm at sea, while on board a Margate steamer*
>   in *Dictionary of National Biography* (1917–)

Thomas Turner 1729–93
English diarist

14 Our diversion was dancing (or jumping about) without a violin or any music, singing of foolish and bawdy healths and more such-like stupidity, and drinking all the time as fast as could be poured down; and the parson of the parish was one amongst the mixed multitude, all the time.
>   *Diary* (ed. D. Vaisey, 1984) 22 February 1758

Walter James Redfern Turner 1889–1946
Australian-born writer and critic

15 When I was but thirteen or so
  I went into a golden land,
  Chimborazo, Cotopaxi
  Took me by the hand.
>   'Romance' (1916)

John Tusa 1936–
British broadcaster and radio journalist

16 Management that wants to change an institution must first show it loves that institution.
>   in *Observer* 27 February 1994 'Sayings of the Week'; see ARNOLD 32:17

Desmond Tutu 1931–
South African Anglican clergyman, Archbishop of Cape Town

17 I have struggled against tyranny. I didn't do that in order to substitute one tyranny with another.
>   *on the attempt by the African National Congress to prevent publication of the Truth Commission report*
>   in *Irish Times* 31 October 1998 'This Week They Said'

Mark Twain (Samuel Langhorne Clemens) 1835–1910
American writer. See also ANONYMOUS 16:25

18 There was things which he stretched, but mainly he told the truth.
>   *The Adventures of Huckleberry Finn* (1884) ch. 1

19 'Pilgrim's Progress', about a man that left his family it didn't say why . . . The statements was interesting, but tough.
>   *The Adventures of Huckleberry Finn* (1884) ch. 17

20 All kings is mostly rapscallions.
>   *The Adventures of Huckleberry Finn* (1884) ch. 23

1 Hain't we got all the fools in town on our side? and ain't that a big enough majority in any town?
The Adventures of Huckleberry Finn (1884) ch. 26

2 Soap and education are not as sudden as a massacre, but they are more deadly in the long run.
A Curious Dream (1872) 'Facts concerning the Recent Resignation'

3 I find that principles have no real force except when one is well fed.
Extracts from Adam's Diary (1893)

4 Truth is the most valuable thing we have. Let us economize it.
Following the Equator (1897) ch. 7; see **ARMSTRONG** 28:21

5 It is by the goodness of God that in our country we have those three unspeakably precious things: freedom of speech, freedom of conscience, and the prudence never to practise either of them.
Following the Equator (1897) ch. 20

6 Man is the Only Animal that Blushes. Or needs to.
Following the Equator (1897) ch. 27

7 There are several good protections against temptations, but the surest is cowardice.
Following the Equator (1897) ch. 36

8 It takes your enemy and your friend, working together, to hurt you to the heart: the one to slander you and the other to get the news to you.
Following the Equator (1897) ch. 45

9 I can stand any society. All that I care to know is that a man is a human being—that is enough for me; he can't be any worse.
How To Tell a Story and other essays (1900) 'Concerning the Jews'

10 The innocents abroad.
title of book (1869)

11 They spell it Vinci and pronounce it Vinchy; foreigners always spell better than they pronounce.
The Innocents Abroad (1869) ch. 19

12 Lump the whole thing! say that the Creator made Italy from designs by Michael Angelo!
The Innocents Abroad (1869) ch. 27

13 There are laws to protect the freedom of the press's speech, but none that are worth anything to protect the people from the press.
'License of the Press' (1873)

14 What a good thing Adam had. When he said a good thing he knew nobody had said it before.
Notebooks (1935)

15 Familiarity breeds contempt—and children.
Notebooks (1935)

16 Good breeding consists in concealing how much we think of ourselves and how little we think of the other person.
Notebooks (1935)

17 Adam was but human—this explains it all. He did not want the apple for the apple's sake; he wanted it only because it was forbidden.
Pudd'nhead Wilson (1894) ch. 2

18 Whoever has lived long enough to find out what life is, knows how deep a debt of gratitude we owe to Adam, the first great benefactor of our race. He brought death into the world.
Pudd'nhead Wilson (1894) ch. 3

19 Cauliflower is nothing but cabbage with a college education.
Pudd'nhead Wilson (1894) ch. 5

20 All say, 'How hard it is to die'—a strange complaint to come from the mouths of people who have had to live.
Pudd'nhead Wilson (1894) ch. 10

21 When angry, count four; when very angry, swear.
Pudd'nhead Wilson (1894) ch. 10

22 As to the Adjective: when in doubt, strike it out.
Pudd'nhead Wilson (1894) ch. 11

23 Few things are harder to put up with than the annoyance of a good example.
Pudd'nhead Wilson (1894) ch. 19

24 There is a sumptuous variety about the New England weather that compels the stranger's admiration—and regret. The weather is always doing something there; always attending strictly to business; always getting up new designs and trying them on the people to see how they will go.
speech to New England Society, 22 December 1876, in *Speeches* (1910)

25 All you need in this life is ignorance and confidence; then success is sure.
letter to Mrs Foote, 2 December 1887, in B. DeCasseres *When Huck Finn Went Highbrow* (1934)

26 The report of my death was an exaggeration.
usually quoted as 'Reports of my death have been greatly exaggerated'
in *New York Journal* 2 June 1897

27 At bottom he was probably fond of them [Americans], but he was always able to conceal it.
of Thomas **CARLYLE**
in *New York World* 10 December 1899 'Mark Twain's Christmas Book'

28 Get your facts first, and then you can distort them as much as you please.
Rudyard Kipling *From Sea to Sea* (1899) letter 37

Kenneth Tynan 1927–80
English theatre critic

29 A good drama critic is one who perceives what is happening in the theatre of his time. A great drama critic also perceives what is *not* happening.
Tynan Right and Left (1967)

1 Oh, I think so, certainly. I doubt if there are very many rational people in this world to whom the word 'fuck' is particularly diabolical or revolting or totally forbidden.
on 13 November 1965 on a late-night programme called BBC-3
  Kathleen Tynan (ed.) *Kenneth Tynan: Letters* (1994)

2 A critic is a man who knows the way but can't drive the car.
  in *New York Times Magazine* 9 January 1966

3 A neurosis is a secret you don't know you're keeping.
  Kathleen Tynan *Life of Kenneth Tynan* (1987) ch. 19

William Tyndale *c.*1494–1536
English translator of the **BIBLE** and Protestant martyr

4 Saint Jerome also translated the Bible into his mother tongue. Why may not we also?
  The Obedience of a Christian Man (1528)

5 For the Greek tongue agreeth more with the English than with the Latin. And the properties of the Hebrew tongue agreeth a thousand times more with the English than with the Latin.
  The Obedience of a Christian Man (1528)

6 If God spare my life, ere many years I will cause a boy that driveth the plough shall know more of the scripture than thou doest!
to an opponent
  in *Dictionary of National Biography* (1917–)

7 Lord, open the King of England's eyes!
  last words, at the stake; John Foxe *Actes and Monuments* (1570)

Dudley Atkins Tyng 1825–58
American evangelist

8 Tell them to stand up for Jesus.
  *last words, to George **DUFFIELD**, inspiring him to write the hymn; see **DUFFIELD** 298:13*
  Ian Bradley (ed.) *The Penguin Book of Hymns* (1989)

Harlan K. Ullman *and* James P. Wade
American strategic analysts

9 The basis for rapid dominance rests in the ability to affect the will, perception, and understanding of the adversary through imposing sufficient Shock and Awe to achieve the necessary political, strategic, and operational goals of the conflict or crisis that led to the use of force.
  Shock and Awe: Achieving Rapid Dominance (1996) ch. 2

Ulpian (Domitius Ulpianus) d. 228
Roman jurist

10 *Nulla iniuria est, quae in volentem fiat.*
  No injustice is done to someone who wants that thing done.
  usually quoted as 'Volenti non fit iniuria'
  Corpus Iuris Civilis Digests bk. 47, ch. 10, sect. 1, subsect. 5

Umar ibn Abd al-Aziz *c.*682–720
Arab caliph

11 Prayer carries us half way to God, fasting brings us to the door of his palace, and alms procure us admission.
  George Sale *The Koran* (1734) 'Preliminary Discourse' sect. 4

Miguel de Unamuno 1864–1937
Spanish philosopher and writer

12 *La vida es duda,*
  y la fe sin la duda es sólo muerte.
  Life is doubt,
  And faith without doubt is nothing but death.
  Poesías (1907) 'Salmo II'

13 An idea does not pass from one language to another without change.
  The Tragic Sense of Life (1913)

14 Science is a cemetery of dead ideas.
  The Tragic Sense of Life (1913)

15 Cure yourself of the condition of bothering about how you look to other people. Concern yourself only with how you appear to God, with the idea that God has of you.
  Vida de Don Quixote y Sancho (1905) pt. 1

The Upanishads
Hindu sacred treatises written in Sanskrit *c.*800–200 BC

16 From delusion lead me to Truth.
  From darkness lead me to Light.
  from death lead me to immortality.
  Brihadāranyaka Upanishad ch. 1, pt. 3, v. 28; see **KUMAR** 474:3

17 Even as airy threads come from a spider, or small sparks come from a fire, so from Atman, the Spirit in man, come all the powers of life, all the worlds, all the gods: all beings. To know the Atman is to know the mystery of the *Upanishads*: the Truth of truth.
  Brihadāranyaka Upanishad ch. 2, pt. 1, v. 20

18 Then spoke Yajñavalkya:
  In truth it is not for the love of a husband that a husband is dear; but for the love of Soul in the husband that a husband is dear.
  It is not for love of a wife that a wife is dear; but for the love of the Soul in the wife that a wife is dear.
  to his wife Maitreyi
  Brihadāranyaka Upanishad ch. 2, pt. 4, v. 5

19 How can the Knower be known?
  Brihadāranyaka Upanishad ch. 2, pt. 4, v. 14

1 He who, dwelling in all things, yet is other than all things, whom all things do not know, whose body all things are, who controls all things from within—He is your Soul, the Inner Controller, the Immortal.
   Brihadāranyaka Upanishad ch. 3, pt. 7, v. 15

2 Even as a caterpillar, when coming to the end of a blade of grass, reaches out to another blade of grass and draws itself over to it, in the same way the Soul, leaving the body and unwisdom behind, reaches out to another body and draws itself over to it.
   Brihadāranyaka Upanishad ch. 4, pt. 4, v. 3

3 That Soul [*Atman*] is not this, it is not that [*neti, neti*]. It is unseizable, for it cannot be seized; it is indestructible, for it cannot be destroyed; unattached, for it does not attach itself; is unbound, does not tremble, is not injured.
   Brihadāranyaka Upanishad ch. 4, pt. 5, v. 15

4 This same thing does the divine voice hear, thunder, repeat: *Da! Da! Da!* that is, restrain yourselves, give, be compassionate. One should practise this same triad: self-restraint, giving, compassion.
   Brihadāranyaka Upanishad ch. 5, pt. 2, v. 3

5 We should consider that in the inner world Brahman is consciousness; and we should consider that in the outer world Brahman is space. These are the two meditations.
   Chāndogya Upanishad ch. 3, pt. 18, v. 1

6 This invisible and subtle essence is the Spirit of the whole universe. That is Reality. That is Truth. THOU ART THAT.
   Chāndogya Upanishad ch. 6, pt. 14

7 *Shantih, shantih, shantih.*
   Peace! Peace! Peace!
   Taittirīya Upanishad ch. 1, pt. 1, mantra; see **ELIOT** 311:19

8 Abiding in the midst of ignorance, thinking themselves wise and learned, fools go aimlessly hither and thither, like blind led by the blind.
   Katha Upanishad ch. 2, v. 5; see **BIBLE** 101:22

9 If any man thinks he slays, and if another thinks he is slain, neither knows the ways of truth. The Eternal in man cannot kill: the Eternal in man cannot die.
   Katha Upanishad ch. 2, v. 19; see **BHAGAVADGITA** 77:17, **EMERSON** 314:11

10 Concealed in the hearts of all beings is the Atman, the Spirit, the Self; smaller than the smallest atom, greater than the vast spaces.
   Katha Upanishad ch. 2, v. 20

11 Know the Atman as Lord of a chariot; and the body as the chariot itself. Know that reason is the charioteer; and the mind indeed is the reins. The horses they say are the senses; and their paths are the objects of sense.
   Katha Upanishad ch. 3, v. 3

12 Sages say the path is narrow and difficult to tread, narrow as the edge of a razor.
   Katha Upanishad ch. 3, v. 15

13 The Tree of Eternity has its roots in heaven above and its branches reach down to earth. It is Brahman, pure Spirit, who in truth is called the Immortal.
   Katha Upanishad ch. 6, v. 1

14 There is ONE in whose hands is the net of Maya, who rules with his power, who rules all the worlds with his power. He is the same at the time of creation and at the time of dissolution.
   Shvetāshvatara Upanishad ch. 3, v. 1

15 Two birds, close-linked companions,
   Cling to the selfsame tree:
   Of these the one eats of the sweet fruit,
   The other, eating nothing, looks on intent.
   Mundaka Upanishad ch. 3, pt. 2, v. 1

16 Whoever really knows that all-highest Brahman, really becomes Brahman.
   Mundaka Upanishad ch. 3, pt. 2, v. 9

17 Let the spirit of life surrender itself into what is called *turya*, the fourth condition of consciousness. For it has been said:
   There is something beyond our mind which abides in silence within our mind. It is the supreme mystery beyond thought.
   Maitri Upanishad ch. 6, v. 19

18 The sound of Brahman is OM. At the end of OM is silence. It is a silence of joy.
   Maitri Upanishad ch. 6, v. 23

John Updike 1932–2009
American novelist and short-story writer

19 A soggy little island huffing and puffing to keep up with Western Europe.
   of England
   Picked Up Pieces (1976) 'London Life' (written 1969)

20 America is a vast conspiracy to make you happy.
   Problems (1980) 'How to love America and Leave it at the Same Time'; see **DICKENS** 276:20

21 Without the cold war, what's the point of being an American?
   Rabbit at Rest (1990) pt. 3

22 Celebrity is a mask that eats into the face.
   Self-Consciousness: Memoirs (1989) ch. 1

23 Dreams come true; without that possibility nature would not incite us to have them.
   Self-Consciousness: Memoirs (1989) ch. 3

24 Neutrinos, they are very small
   They have no charge and have no mass
   And do not interact at all.
   'Cosmic Gall ' (1964)

25 I want to read only what will help me unpack my own bag.
   in *Paris Review* Winter 1968

26 The artist brings something into the world that didn't exist before, and . . . he does it without destroying something else.
   George Plimpton (ed.) *Writers at Work* (4th series, 1977) ch. 16

1 Some sense of religious mission is part of being American.
interview in New York Review of Books 29 February 1996

Urban II (Odo of Lagery) *c.*1035–99
French cleric, Pope from 1088

2 Let such as are going to fight for Christianity put the form of the cross upon their garments, that they might outwardly demonstrate their devotion to their inward faith.
launching the First Crusade
> at the Council of Clermont in 1095; William of Malmesbury *De Gestis Regum Anglorum*

3 Let no attachment to your native soil be an impediment, because . . . all the world is exile to the Christian, and all the world his country: thus exile is his country, and his country exile.
launching the First Crusade
> at the Council of Clermont in 1095; William of Malmesbury *De Gestis Regum Anglorum*

James Ussher 1581–1656
Irish prelate and scholar

4 Which beginning of time according to our Chronology, fell upon the entrance of the night preceding the twenty third day of *Octob.* in the year of the Julian Calendar, 710.
giving the date of the Creation as 4004 BC
> *The Annals of the World* (1658)

Peter Ustinov 1921–2004
British actor, director, and writer

5 Laughter . . . the most civilized music in the world.
> *Dear Me* (1977) ch. 3

6 I do not believe that friends are necessarily the people you like best, they are merely the people who got there first.
> *Dear Me* (1977) ch. 5; see ADAMS 2:11

7 At the age of four with paper hats and wooden swords we're all Generals. Only some of us never grow out of it.
> *Romanoff and Juliet* (1956) act 1

8 Laughter would be bereaved if snobbery died.
> *in Observer* 13 March 1955

Valerius Flaccus fl. *c.*AD 90
Roman poet

9 *Viridantem floribus hastas.*
Making spears green with flowers.
> *Argonautica* bk. 6, l. 136

Paul Valéry 1871–1945
French poet, critic, and man of letters

10 *Un poème n'est jamais achevé—c'est toujours un accident qui le termine, c'est-à-dire qui le donne au public.*
A poem is never finished; it's always an accident that puts a stop to it—i.e. gives it to the public.
often quoted in W. H. AUDEN' s paraphrase, 'A poem is never finished, only abandoned'
> *Littérature* (1930)

11 *Le rire est un refus de penser.*
Laughter is a refusal to think.
> *Mon Faust* (1946) 'Lust' act 1, sc. 1

12 Science means simply the aggregate of all the recipes that are always successful. The rest is literature.
> *Moralités* (1932) p. 41; see VERLAINE 826:8

13 God created man and, finding him not sufficiently alone, gave him a companion to make him feel his solitude more keenly.
> *Tel Quel 1* (1941) 'Moralités'

14 Politics is the art of preventing people from taking part in affairs which properly concern them.
> *Tel Quel 2* (1943) 'Rhumbs'

15 *Il faut entrer en soi-même armé jusqu'aux dents.*
To enter into your own mind you need to be armed to the teeth.
> *Oeuvres* (1960) vol. 2 'Quelques pensées de Monsieur Teste'

John Vanbrugh 1664–1726
English architect and dramatist. On Vanbrugh: see EPITAPHS 319:16

16 Much of a muchness.
> *The Provoked Husband* (1728) act 1, sc. 1

17 BELINDA: Ay, but you know we must return good for evil.
LADY BRUTE: That may be a mistake in the translation.
> *The Provoked Wife* (1697) act 1, sc. 1

18 LADY BRUTE: 'Tis a hard fate I should not be believed.
SIR JOHN: 'Tis a damned atheistical age, wife.
> *The Provoked Wife* (1697) act 5, sc. 2

19 So, now I am in for Hobbes's voyage, a great leap in the dark.
'Heartfree' on marriage
> *The Provoked Wife* (1697) act 5, sc. 5; see HOBBES 401:11

20 When once a woman has given you her heart, you can never get rid of the rest of her body.
> *The Relapse* (1696) act 3, sc. 1

Vivian van Damm *c.*1889–1960

English theatre manager

1 We never closed.
of the Windmill Theatre, London, during the Second World War
  Tonight and Every Night (1952) ch. 18

William Henry Vanderbilt 1821–85

American railway magnate

2 The public be damned!
on whether the public should be consulted about luxury trains
  letter from A. W. Cole to *New York Times* 25 August 1918

Laurens van der Post 1906–96

South African explorer and writer

3 Human beings are perhaps never more frightening than when they are convinced beyond doubt that they are right.
  Lost World of the Kalahari (1958)

Henry Van Dyke 1852–1933

American Presbyterian minister and writer

4 Time is
Too slow for those who wait,
Too swift for those who fear,
Too long for those who grieve,
Too short for those who rejoice;
But for those who love,
Time is eternity.
  'Time is too slow for those who wait' (1905), read at the funeral of **DIANA**, Princess of Wales; Nigel Rees in 'Quote . . . Unquote' October 1997 notes that the original form of the last line is 'Time is not'

Henry Vane 1613–62

English politician and writer, executed for treason at the Restoration

5 It is a bad cause which cannot bear the words of a dying man.
last words, as drums and trumpets were ordered to sound at his execution to drown anything he might say
  Charles Dickens *A Child's History of England* (1853) ch. 35

Raoul Vaneigem 1934–

Belgian philosopher

6 Work to survive, survive by consuming, survive to consume: the hellish cycle is complete.
  The Revolution of Everyday Life (1967)

Vincent Van Gogh 1853–90

Dutch painter

7 I cannot help it that my pictures do not sell. Nevertheless the time will come when people will see that they are worth more than the price of the paint.
  letter to his brother Theo, 20 October 1888; *Further Letters of Vincent Van Gogh to his Brother* (1929)

William Cornelius Van Horne 1843–1915

American-born Canadian railway official, general manager and president of the Canadian Pacific Railway

8 Building that railroad would have made a Canadian out of the German Emperor.
on the construction of the Canadian Pacific Railway across Canada
  in *Canadian Encyclopedia* (1988) vol. 1

Bartolomeo Vanzetti 1888–1927

American anarchist, born in Italy

9 Sacco's name will live in the hearts of the people and in their gratitude when Katzmann's and yours bones will be dispersed by time, when your name, his name, your laws, institutions, and your false god are but a deem rememoring of a cursed past in which man was wolf to the man.
statement disallowed at his trial, with Nicola Sacco, for murder and robbery; both were sentenced to death on 9 April 1927, and executed on 23 August 1927
  M. D. Frankfurter and G. Jackson *Letters of Sacco and Vanzetti* (1928); see **PLAUTUS** 609:8

10 If it had not been for these thing, I might have live out my life talking at street corners to scorning men. I might have die, unmarked, unknown, a failure. Now we are not a failure. This is our career and our triumph. Never in our full life could we hope to do such work for tolerance, for joostice, for man's onderstanding of man as now we do by accident.
  statement after being sentenced to death, in M. D. Frankfurter and G. Jackson *Letters of Sacco and Vanzetti* (1928) preface

Marcus Terentius Varro 116–27 BC

Roman scholar and satirist

11 And the grass springs up, called forth by the early rains.
  De Re Rustica bk. 2, ch. 2

Michel Vaucaire

French songwriter

12 *Non! rien de rien,*
Non! je ne regrette rien,
Ni le bien, qu'on m'a fait,
Ni le mal—tout ça m'est bien égal!
No, no regrets,
No, we will have no regrets,
As you leave, I can say—
Love was king, tho' for only a day.
  'Non, je ne regrette rien' (1960 song); sung by Edith Piaf

Henry Vaughan 1622–95

English poet

13 Man is the shuttle, to whose winding quest
And passage through these looms

God ordered motion, but ordained no rest.
Silex Scintillans (1650–5) 'Man'

1 Wise Nicodemus saw such light
As made him know his God by night.
Silex Scintillans (1650–5) 'The Night'

2 Most blest believer he!
Who in that land of darkness and blind eyes
Thy long expected healing wings could see
When Thou didst rise!
Silex Scintillans (1650–5) 'The Night'

3 Dear Night! this world's defeat;
The stop to busy fools; care's check and curb.
Silex Scintillans (1650–5) 'The Night'

4 My soul, there is a country
Far beyond the stars,
Where stands a wingèd sentry
All skilful in the wars.
Silex Scintillans (1650–5) 'Peace'

5 Happy those early days, when I
Shined in my angel-infancy.
Before I understood this place
Appointed for my second race,
Or taught my soul to fancy aught
But a white, celestial thought.
Silex Scintillans (1650–5) 'The Retreat'

6 And in those weaker glories spy
Some shadows of eternity.
Silex Scintillans (1650–5) 'The Retreat'

7 But felt through all this fleshly dress
Bright shoots of everlastingness.
Silex Scintillans (1650–5) 'The Retreat'

8 Some men a forward motion love,
But I by backward steps would move,
And when this dust falls to the urn,
In that state I came, return.
Silex Scintillans (1650–5) 'The Retreat'

9 They are all gone into the world of light,
And I alone sit lingering here.
Silex Scintillans (1650–5) 'They are all gone'

10 I see them walking in an air of glory,
Whose light doth trample on my days:
My days, which are at best but dull and hoary,
Mere glimmering and decays.
Silex Scintillans (1650–5) 'They are all gone'

11 Dear, beauteous death! the jewel of the just,
Shining nowhere but in the dark.
Silex Scintillans (1650–5) 'They are all gone'

12 And yet, as angels in some brighter dreams
Call to the soul when man doth sleep,
So some strange thoughts transcend our wonted
themes,
And into glory peep.
Silex Scintillans (1650–5) 'They are all gone'

13 If a star were confined into a tomb
Her captive flames must needs burn there;
But when the hand that locked her up gives
room,
She'll shine through all the sphere.
Silex Scintillans (1650–5) 'They are all gone'

14 I saw Eternity the other night,
Like a great ring of pure and endless light,
All calm, as it was bright;
And round beneath it, Time in hours, days,
years,
Driv'n by the spheres.
Silex Scintillans (1650–5) 'The World'

Janet-Maria Vaughan 1899–1993
English scientist

15 I am here—trying to do science in hell.
working as a doctor in Belsen at the end of the war
letter to a friend, 12 May 1945; P. A. Adams (ed.) *Janet-Maria Vaughan* (1993)

Luc de Clapiers, Marquis de Vauvenargues 1715–47
French moralist

16 We scorn many things in order not to scorn
ourselves.
The Reflections and Maxims of Luc de Clapiers Marquis of Vauvenargues (1940, ed. and tr. F. G. Stevens))

Thomas, Lord Vaux 1510–56
English writer and courtier

17 For age with stealing steps
Hath clawed me with his clutch,
And lusty life away she leaps,
As there had been none such.
'The Aged Lover Renounceth Love' (1557); a garbled version is sung by the gravedigger in *Hamlet*; see **SHAKESPEARE** 704:12

18 When all is done and said, in the end thus shall
you find,
He most of all doth bathe in bliss that hath a
quiet mind;
And, clear from worldly cares, to deem can be
content
The sweetest time in all his life in thinking to be
spent.
'The Pleasures of Thinking' (1576)

Thorstein Veblen 1857–1929
American economist and social scientist

19 Conspicuous consumption of valuable goods is a
means of reputability to the gentleman of
leisure.
Theory of the Leisure Class (1899) ch. 4

20 From the foregoing survey of conspicuous
leisure and consumption, it appears that the
utility of both alike for the purposes of
reputability lies in the element of waste that is
common to both. In the one case it is a waste of
time and effort, in the other it is a waste of
goods.
Theory of the Leisure Class (1899) ch. 4

Lope de Vega 1562–1635
Spanish dramatist and poet

1 Four trestles, four boards, two actors, a passion.
all he needed to create a play
> attributed; James Fitzmaurice-Kelly *Lope de Vega and the Spanish Drama* (1902)

Vegetius (Flavius Vegetius Renatus) fl. AD 379–95
Roman military writer

2 *Qui desiderat pacem, praeparet bellum.*
Let him who desires peace, prepare for war.
usually quoted as 'Si vis pacem, para bellum [If you want peace, prepare for war]'
> *Epitoma Rei Militaris* bk. 3, prologue; see **ARISTOTLE** 27:14, **PROVERBS** 635:35

Robert Venturi 1925–
American architect

3 Less is a bore.
> *Complexity and Contradiction in Architecture* (1966) ch. 2; see **PROVERBS** 637:19

Giovanni Verga 1840–1922
Italian novelist, dramatist, and short-story writer

4 *Le vicine avevano fatto come le lumache quando piove, e lungo la straduccio non si udiva che un continuo chiacchierio da un uscio all' altro.*
The neighbours had come out like snails after a rainstorm, and all down the road you heard the continuous murmur of people talking from doorway to doorway.
> *I Malavoglia* (The House by the Medlar Tree, 1881) ch. 2, translated by Raymond Rosenthal

5 *Il cuore si stanca anche lui, vedi; e se ne va a pezzo a pezzo, come le robe vecchie si disfanno nel bucato.*
The heart gets tired too; and it falls apart bit by bit, like an old cloth wears out in the wash.
> *I Malavoglia* (The House by the Medlar Tree, 1881) ch. 11, translated by Raymond Rosenthal

6 *Il peggio . . . è spatriare dal proprio paese, dove fino i sassi vi conoscono, e dev' essere una cosa da rompere il cuore il lasciarseli dietro per la strada.*
The worst thing . . . is to leave your own town, where even the stones know you, and it must break your heart to leave them behind on the road.
> *I Malavoglia* (The House by the Medlar Tree, 1881) ch. 11, translated by Raymond Rosenthal

Pierre Vergniaud 1753–93
French revolutionary; executed with other Girondists

7 There was reason to fear that the Revolution, like Saturn, might devour in turn each one of her children.
> Alphonse de Lamartine *Histoire des Girondins* (1847) bk. 38, ch. 20

Paul Verlaine 1844–96
French poet

8 *Et tout le reste est littérature.*
All the rest is mere fine writing.
> 'Art poétique' (1882); see **VALÉRY** 823:12

9 *Les sanglots longs*
Des violons
De l'automne
Blessent mon cœur
D'une langueur
Monotone.
The drawn-out sobs of autumn's violins wound my heart with a monotonous languor.
> 'Chanson d'Automne' (1866)

10 *Que vont charmant masques et bergamasques*
Jouant de luth et dansant et quasi
Tristes sous leurs déguisements fantasques.
Where masks and bergamasks go charming, playing the lute and dancing and almost sad beneath their fanciful disguises.
> 'Clair de Lune' (1869)

11 *Prends l'éloquence et tords-lui le cou.*
Take eloquence and break its neck.
> *Jadis et naguère* (1884)

12 *Et, Ô ces voix d'enfants chantants dans la coupole!*
And oh those children's voices, singing beneath the dome!
> 'Parsifal' A Jules Tellier (1886)

13 *Il pleure dans mon coeur*
Comme il pleut sur la ville.
Tears are shed in my heart like the rain on the town.
> *Romances sans paroles* (1874) 'Ariettes oubliées' no. 3

Jules Verne 1828–1905
French novelist

14 If there be green in paradise, it cannot but be of this shade, which most surely is the true green of hope!
> *The Green Ray* (1882) ch. 3

René Aubert, Abbé de Vertot 1655–1735
French historian

15 *Mon siège est fait.*
My siege is over.
on receiving long-awaited documents for his history of the siege of Rhodes when it had already been completed
> J. Le Rond d'Alembert *Œuvres* (1821 ed.) vol. 2, pt. 1

Hendrik Frensch Verwoerd 1901–66
South African statesman, Prime Minister from 1958

16 Up till now he [the Bantu] has been subjected to a school system which drew him away from his own community and practically misled him by showing him the green pastures of the European but still did not allow him to graze there . . . It is abundantly clear that unplanned education creates many problems, disrupts the communal life of the Bantu and endangers the communal life of the European.

speech in South African Senate, 7 June 1954

Vespasian (Titus Flavius Vespasianus) AD 9–79
Roman emperor from AD 69

1 *Pecunia non olet.*

Money has no smell.

upon **TITUS***'s objecting to his tax on public lavatories, Vespasian held a coin to Titus's nose; on being told it didn't smell, he replied, 'Atque e lotio est [Yes, that's made from urine]'*

traditional summary of Suetonius *Lives of the Caesars* 'Vespasian' sect. 23, subsect. 3; see **PROVERBS** 638:46

2 *Vae, puto deus fio.*

Woe is me, I think I am becoming a god.

when fatally ill

Suetonius *Lives of the Caesars* 'Vespasian' sect. 23, subsect. 4

3 An emperor ought to die standing.

last words; Suetonius *Lives of the Caesars* 'Vespasian' sect. 24

Giambattista Vico 1668–1744
Italian philosopher

4 Uniform ideas originating among entire peoples unknown to each other must have a common ground of truth.

The New Science (3rd ed., 1730) bk. 1, sect. 2, para. 13, no. 144

5 The nature of peoples is first crude, then severe, then benign, then delicate, finally dissolute.

The New Science (3rd ed., 1730) bk. 1, sect. 2, para. 67, no. 242

Queen Victoria 1819–1901
British monarch, Queen of the United Kingdom from 1837. On Victoria: see **DISRAELI** 285:13

6 I will be good.

on being shown a chart of the line of succession, 11 March 1830

Theodore Martin *The Prince Consort* (1875) vol. 1, ch. 2

7 It was with some emotion . . . that I beheld Albert—who is beautiful.

of her first meeting with the adult Prince **ALBERT***, c.1838*

attributed; Stanley Weintraub *Albert: Uncrowned King* (1997)

8 What you say of the pride of giving life to an immortal soul is very fine, dear, but I own I can not enter into that; I think much more of our being like a cow or a dog at such moments; when our poor nature becomes so very animal and unecstatic.

letter to the Princess Royal, 15 June 1858; Roger Fulford *Dearest Child* (1964)

9 Dirty, dark, and undevotional.

of St Paul's Cathedral, where a service of Thanksgiving had been held, following the recovery of the Prince of Wales from typhoid fever

attributed in this form, but recorded in her Journal, 27 February 1872, as 'so cold, dreary and dingy. It so badly lacks decoration and colour.'; G. E. Buckle (ed.) *Letters of Queen Victoria: 2nd Series* vol. 2 (1870–78)

10 The danger to the country, to Europe, to her vast Empire, which is involved in having all these great interests entrusted to the shaking hand of an old, wild, and incomprehensible man of 82, is very great!

on **GLADSTONE***'s last appointment as Prime Minister*

letter to Lord Lansdowne, 12 August 1892, in T. Wodehouse Legh *Lord Lansdowne* (1929)

11 The future Vice Roy must . . . not be guided by the *snobbish* and vulgar, over-bearing and offensive behaviour of our Civil and Political Agents, if we are to go on peaceably and happily in India . . . not trying to trample on the people and continuously reminding them and making them feel they are a conquered people.

letter to Lord Salisbury, 27 May 1898, in Kenneth Rose *Superior Person* (1969) ch. 23

12 He speaks to Me as if I was a public meeting.

of **GLADSTONE**

G. W. E. Russell *Collections and Recollections* (1898) ch. 14

13 We are not interested in the possibilities of defeat; they do not exist.

on the Boer War during 'Black Week', December 1899

Lady Gwendolen Cecil *Life of Robert, Marquis of Salisbury* (1931) vol. 3, ch. 6

14 We are not amused.

attributed, in Caroline Holland *Notebooks of a Spinster Lady* (1919) ch. 21, 2 January 1900

Gore Vidal 1925–
American novelist and critic

15 Whenever a friend succeeds, a little something in me dies.

in *Sunday Times Magazine* 16 September 1973

16 *of Truman* **CAPOTE***'s death:*

Good career move.

attributed, 1984

17 He will lie even when it is inconvenient: the sign of the true artist.

attributed

José Antonio Viera Gallo 1943–
Chilean politician

18 Socialism can only arrive by bicycle.

Ivan Illich *Energy and Equity* (1974) epigraph

Gilles Vigneault 1928–
Canadian singer, songwriter, and poet

19 *Mon pays ce n'est pas un pays, c'est l'hiver.*

My country is not a country, it is winter.

'Mon Pays' (1964)

Alfred de Vigny 1797–1863

French poet

1 *J'aime le son du cor, le soir, au fond des bois.*

I love the sound of the horn, at night, in the depth of the woods.
'Le Cor' (1826)

2 *J'aime la majesté des souffrances humaines.*

I love the majesty of human suffering.
La Maison du Berger (1844)

3 *Seul le silence est grand; tout le reste est faiblesse . . .*
Puis, après, comme moi, souffre et meurs sans parler.

Silence alone is great; all else is feebleness . . .
then as do I, say naught, but suffer and die.
'La mort du loup' (1843) pt. 3

Matteo Villani d. *c.*1363

Italian chronicler, of Florence

4 My mind is stupefied as it approaches the task of recording the sentence that divine justice mercifully delivered upon men, who deserve, because they have been corrupted by sin, a last judgement.
of the outbreak of the Black Death in the mid 14th century
Chronicle of Matteo Villani bk 1; M. Meiss *Painting in Florence and Siena after the Black Death* (1951)

Philippe-Auguste Villiers de L'Isle-Adam 1838–89

French writer

5 *Vivre? les serviteurs feront cela pour nous.*

Living? The servants will do that for us.
Axël (1890) pt. 4, sect. 2

François Villon *c.*1431– after 1463

French poet. On Villon: see **SWINBURNE** 785:4

6 *Frères humains qui après nous vivez,*
N'ayez les cœurs contre nous endurcis,
Car, si pitié de nous pauvres avez,
Dieu en aura plus tôt de vous mercis . . .
Mais priez Dieu que tous nous veuille absoudre!

Brothers in humanity who live after us, let not your hearts be hardened against us, for, if you take pity on us poor ones, God will be more likely to have mercy on you. But pray God that he may be willing to absolve us all.
'Ballade des pendus'

7 *Mais où sont les neiges d'antan?*

But where are the snows of yesteryear?
Le Grand Testament (1461) 'Ballade des dames du temps jadis' (translated by D. G. Rossetti)

8 *En cette foi je veux vivre et mourir.*

In this faith I wish to live and to die.
Le Grand Testament (1461) 'Ballade pour prier Nostre Dame'

St Vincent of Lerins d. *c.*AD 450

9 *Quod ubique, quod semper, quod ab omnibus creditum est.*

What is everywhere, what is always, what is by all people believed.
Commonitorium Primum sect. 2

Virgil (Publius Vergilius Maro) 70–19 BC

Roman poet. On Virgil: see **ARNOLD** 32:7, **DANTE** 264:16, **HORACE** 411:5, **PROPERTIUS** 625:1, **TENNYSON** 800:12; see also **ANONYMOUS** 23:10, **FRAZER** 341:19

10 *Arma virumque cano, Troiae qui primus ab oris*
Italiam fato profugus Laviniaque venit
Litora, multum ille et terris iactatus et alto
Vi superum, saevae memorem Iunonis ob iram.

I sing of arms and the man who first from the shores of Troy came destined an exile to Italy and the Lavinian beaches, a man much buffeted on land and on the deep by force of the gods because of fierce Juno's never-forgetting anger.
Aeneid bk. 1, l. 1; see **DRYDEN** 297:10

11 *Tantaene animis caelestibus irae?*

Why such great anger in those heavenly minds?
Aeneid bk. 1, l. 11

12 *Tantae molis erat Romanam condere gentem.*

So massive was the effort to found the Roman nation.
Aeneid bk. 1, l. 33

13 *Apparent rari nantes in gurgite vasto.*

A few figures swimming were glimpsed in the waste of waters.
Aeneid bk. 1, l. 118

14 *Furor arma ministrat.*

Anger supplies the arms.
Aeneid bk. 1, l. 150

15 *Constitit hic arcumque manu celerisque sagittas*
Corripuit fidus quae tela gerebat Achates.

Hereupon he stopped and snatched up in his hand a bow and swift arrows, the weapons that trusty Achates carried.
Aeneid bk. 1, l. 187

16 *O passi graviora, dabit deus his quoque finem.*

O you who have borne even heavier things, God will grant an end to these too.
Aeneid bk. 1, l. 199

17 *Forsan et haec olim meminisse iuvabit.*

Maybe one day it will be cheering to remember even these things.
Aeneid bk. 1, l. 203

18 *Dux femina facti.*

The leader of the enterprise a woman.
Aeneid bk. 1, l. 364

19 *Dixit et avertens rosea cervice refulsit,*
Ambrosiaeque comae divinum vertice odorem
Spiravere; pedes vestis defluxit ad imos,
Et vera incessu patuit dea.

Thus she spoke and turned away with a flash of her rosy neck, and her ambrosial hair exhaled a divine fragrance; her dress flowed right down to

her feet and her true godhead was evident from her walk.
Aeneid bk. 1, l. 405

1 *Sunt lacrimae rerum et mentem mortalia tangunt.*

There are tears shed for things even here and mortality touches the heart.
Aeneid bk. 1, l. 462

2 *Di tibi, si qua pios respectant numina, si quid*
Usquam iustitia est et mens sibi conscia recti,
Praemia digna ferant.

If the divine powers take note of the dutiful in any way, if there is any justice anywhere and a mind recognizing in itself what is right, may the gods bring you your earned rewards.
Aeneid bk. 1, l. 603

3 *Non ignara mali miseris succurrere disco.*

No stranger to trouble myself I am learning to care for the unhappy.
Aeneid bk. 1, l. 630

4 *Infandum, regina, iubes renovare dolorem.*

A grief too much to be told, O queen, you bid me renew.
Aeneid bk. 2, l. 3

5 *Quaeque ipse miserrima vidi*
Et quorum pars magna fui.

And the most miserable things which I myself saw and of which I was a major part.
Aeneid bk. 2, l. 5

6 *Equo ne credite, Teucri.*
Quidquid id est, timeo Danaos et dona ferentes.

Do not trust the horse, Trojans. Whatever it is, I fear the Greeks even when they bring gifts.
Aeneid bk. 2, l. 48; see **PROVERBS** 632:6

7 *. . . Crimine ab uno*
Disce omnis.

From the one crime recognize them all as culprits.
Aeneid bk. 2, l. 65

8 *Horresco referens.*

I shudder as I recall it.
Aeneid bk. 2, l. 204

9 *Tacitae per amica silentia lunae.*

Through the friendly silence of the soundless moonlight.
Aeneid bk. 2, l. 255

10 *Tempus erat quo prima quies mortalibus aegris*
Incipit et dono divum gratissima serpit.

It was the time when first sleep begins for weary mortals and by the gift of the gods creeps over them most welcomely.
Aeneid bk. 2, l. 268

11 *Quantum mutatus ab illo*
Hectore qui redit exuvias indutus Achilli.

How greatly changed from that Hector who came back arrayed in the armour of Achilles!
Aeneid bk. 2, l. 274

12 *Iam proximus ardet*
Ucalegon.

Ucalegon burns very near.
Aeneid bk. 2, l. 311

13 *Fuimus Troes, fuit Ilium et ingens*
Gloria Teucrorum.

We Trojans are at an end, Ilium has ended and the vast glory of the Trojans.
Aeneid bk. 2, l. 325

14 *Moriamur et in media arma ruamus.*
Una salus victis nullam sperare salutem.

Let us die even as we rush into the midst of the battle. The only safe course for the defeated is to expect no safety.
Aeneid bk. 2, l. 354

15 *Dis aliter visum.*

The gods thought otherwise.
Aeneid bk. 2, l. 428

16 *Non tali auxilio nec defensoribus istis*
Tempus eget.

Neither the hour requires such help, nor those defenders.
Aeneid bk. 2, l. 521

17 *Quid non mortalia pectora cogis,*
Auri sacra fames!

To what do you not drive human hearts, cursed craving for gold!
Aeneid bk. 3, l. 56

18 *Cum procul obscuros collis humileque videmus*
Italiam. Italiam primus conclamat Achates,
Italiam laeto socii clamore salutant.

We sighted, far away, dim hills and a low coast-line,
Italy. Achates was the first to hail, 'Italy!'
'Italy!' my comrades echoed in cheerful greeting.
Aeneid bk. 3, l. 522 (translated by C. Day Lewis)

19 *Monstrum horrendum, informe, ingens, cui lumen*
ademptum.

A monster horrendous, hideous and vast, deprived of sight.
Aeneid bk. 3, l. 658

20 *Agnosco veteris vestigia flammae.*

I feel again a spark of that ancient flame.
Aeneid bk. 4, l. 23; see **DANTE** 265:13

21 *Quis fallere possit amantem?*

Who could deceive a lover?
Aeneid bk. 4, l. 296

22 *Nec me meminisse pigebit Elissae*
Dum memor ipse mei, dum spiritus hos regit artus.

Nor will it ever upset me to remember Elissa so long as I can remember who I am, so long as the breath of life controls these limbs.
Aeneid bk. 4, l. 335

23 *Italiam non sponte sequor.*

Not of my own free will do I pursue Italy.
Aeneid bk. 4, l. 361

1   *Varium et mutabile semper*
Femina.

A fickle and changeable thing always is woman.

Aeneid bk. 4, l. 569; 'A windfane changabil huf puffe / Always is a woomman' in Richard Stanyhurst's translation, 1582

2 *Exoriare aliquis nostris ex ossibus ultor.*

Rise up from my dead bones, avenger!

Aeneid bk. 4, l. 625 (translated by C. Day-Lewis)

3 *Hos successus alit: possunt, quia posse videntur.*

These success encourages: they can because they think they can.

Aeneid bk. 5, l. 231

4   *Bella, horrida bella,*
Et Thybrim multo spumantem sanguine cerno.

I see wars, horrible wars, and the Tiber foaming with much blood.

Aeneid bk. 6, l. 86; see **POWELL** 622:2

5   *Facilis descensus Averno:*
Noctes atque dies patet atri ianua Ditis;
Sed revocare gradum superasque evadere ad auras,
Hoc opus, hic labor est.

Easy is the way down to the Underworld: by night and by day dark Hades' door stands open; but to retrace one's steps and to make a way out to the upper air, that's the task, that is the labour.

Aeneid bk. 6, l. 126

6 *Primo avulso non deficit alter.*

On the removal of one, another is not wanting.

Aeneid bk. 6, l. 143

7 *Procul, o procul este, profani.*

Far off, Oh keep far off, you uninitiated ones.

Aeneid bk. 6, l. 258

8 *Ibant obscuri sola sub nocte per umbram*
Perque domos Ditis vacuas et inania regna.

Darkling they went under the lonely night through the shadow and through the empty dwellings and unsubstantial realms of Hades.

Aeneid bk. 6, l. 268

9 *Vestibulum ante ipsum primisque in faucibus Orci*
Luctus et ultrices posuere cubilia Curae,
Pallentesque habitant Morbi tristisque Senectus,
Et Metus et malesuada Fames ac turpis Egestas,
Terribiles visu formae, Letumque Labosque.

Before the very forecourt and in the opening of the jaws of hell Grief and avenging Cares have placed their beds, and wan Diseases and sad Old Age live there, and Fear and Hunger that urges to wrongdoing, and shaming Destitution, figures terrible to see, and Death and Toil.

Aeneid bk. 6, l. 273

10 *Stabant orantes primi transmittere cursum*
Tendebantque manus ripae ulterioris amore.

They stood begging to be the first to make the voyage over and they reached out their hands in longing for the further shore.

Aeneid bk. 6, l. 313

11 *Non, mihi si linguae centum sint oraque centum,*
Ferrea vox, omnes scelerum comprendere formas,
Omnia poenarum percurrere nomina possim.

Nay, had I a hundred tongues, a hundred mouths, and voice of iron, I could not sum up all the forms of crime, or rehearse all the tales of torments.

Aeneid bk. 6, l. 625

12 *Spiritus intus alit, totamque infusa per artus*
Mens agitat molem et magno se corpore miscet.

The spirit within nourishes, and mind instilled throughout the living parts activates the whole mass and mingles with the vast frame.

Aeneid bk. 6, l. 726

13 *Extra anni solisque vias.*

Beyond the course of the years and the sun.

Aeneid bk. 6, l. 796

14 *Excudent alii spirantia mollius aera*
(Credo equidem), vivos ducent de marmore vultus,
Orabunt causas melius, caelique meatus
Describent radio et surgentia sidera dicent:
Tu regere imperio populos, Romane, memento
(Hae tibi erunt artes), pacique imponere morem,
Parcere subiectis et debellare superbos.

Others shall shape bronzes more smoothly so that they seem alive (yes, I believe it), shall mould from marble living faces, shall better plead their cases in court, and shall demonstrate with a pointer the motions of the heavenly bodies and tell the stars as they rise: you, Roman, make your task to rule nations by your government (these shall be your skills), to impose ordered ways upon a state of peace, to spare those who have submitted and to subdue the arrogant.

Aeneid bk. 6, l. 847

15 *Heu, miserande puer, si qua fata aspera rumpas,*
Tu Marcellus eris. Manibus date lilia plenis.

Alas, pitiable boy—if only you might break your cruel fate!—you are to be Marcellus. [People,] give me lilies in armfuls.

Aeneid bk. 6, l. 883

16 *Sunt geminae Somni portae, quarum altera fertur*
Cornea, qua veris facilis datur exitus umbris,
Altera candenti perfecta nitens elephanto,
Sed falsa ad caelum mittunt insomnia Manes.

There are two gates of Sleep, one of which it is held is made of horn and by it easy egress is given to real ghosts; the other shining, fashioned of gleaming white ivory, but the shades send deceptive visions that way to the light.

Aeneid bk. 6, l. 893

17   *Geniumque loci primamque deorum*
Tellurem Nymphasque et adhuc ignota precatur
Flumina.

He prays to the spirit of the place and to Earth, the first of the gods, and to the Nymphs and as yet unknown rivers.

Aeneid bk. 7, l. 136; see **POPE** 615:7

1 *Flectere si nequeo superos, Acheronta movebo.*

If I am unable to make the gods above relent, I shall move Hell.
   Aeneid bk. 7, l. 312

2 *Pedibus timor addidit alas.*

Fear gave wings to his feet.
   Aeneid bk. 8, l. 224

3 *Nox ruit et fuscit tellurem amplectitur alis.*

Night came down, and enfolded the earth in her dusky wings.
   Aeneid bk. 8, l. 369

4 *O mihi praeteritos referat si Iuppiter annos.*

Oh if only Jupiter would give me back my past years.
   Aeneid bk. 8, l. 560

5 *Quadripedante putrem sonitu quatit ungula campum.*

The hoof with a galloping sound is shaking the powdery plain.
   Aeneid bk. 8, l. 596

6 *Me, me, adsumqui feci, in me convertite ferrum.*

Here I am! Here I am! I am the one who did it! Aim your weapons at me!
   Aeneid bk. 9, l. 427 (translated by David West)

7 *Macte nova virtute, puer, sic itur ad astra.*

Blessings on your young courage, boy; that's the way to the stars.
   Aeneid bk. 9, l. 641

8 *Audentis Fortuna iuvat.*

Fortune assists the bold.
   often quoted as 'Fortune favours the brave'
   Aeneid bk. 10, l. 284; see **PROVERBS** 632:37, **TERENCE** 801:15

9 *Et dulcis moriens reminiscitur Argos.*

And dying remembers his sweet Argos.
   Aeneid bk. 10, l. 782

10 *Experto credite.*

Trust one who has gone through it.
   Aeneid bk. 11, l. 283

11 *Ac velut in somnis, oculos ubi languida pressit*
Nocte Quies, nequiquam avidos extendere cursus
Velle videmur et in mediis conatibus aegri
Succidimus; non lingua valet, non corpore notae
Sufficiunt vires nec vox aut verba sequuntur:
Sic Turno.

But, as it is in a nightmare, when sleep's narcotic hand
Is leaden on our eyes, we seem to be desperately trying
To run and run, but we cannot—for all our efforts, we sink down
Nerveless, our usual strength is just not there, and our tongue
Won't work at all—we can't utter a word or produce one sound:
So with Turnus.
   Aeneid bk. 12, l. 908 (translated by C. Day Lewis)

12 *Tityre, tu patulae recubans sub tegmine fagi*
Silvestrem tenui Musam meditaris avena.

Tityrus, you who lie under cover of the spreading beech-tree, you are practising your pastoral music on a thin stalk.
   Eclogues no. 1, l. 1

13 *O Meliboee, deus nobis haec otia fecit.*

O Meliboeus, it is a god that has made this peaceful life for us.
   Eclogues no. 1, l. 6

14 *Non equidem invideo, miror magis.*

Indeed I am not envious, rather I am amazed.
   Eclogues no. 1, l. 11

15 *At nos hinc alii sitientis ibimus Afros,*
Pars Scythiam et rapidum cretae veniemus Oaxen
Et penitus toto divisos orbe Britannos.

But we from here are to go some to the parched Africans, another group to Scythia and others of us shall come to the Oaxes swirling with clay, and amongst the Britons who are kept far away from the whole world.
   Eclogues no. 1, l. 64

16 *Et iam summa procul villarum culmina fumant,*
Maioresque cadunt altis de montibus umbrae.

Look over there—smoke rises already from the rooftops
And longer fall the shadows cast by the mountain heights.
   Eclogues no. 1, l. 82 (translated by C. Day Lewis)

17 *Formosum pastor Corydon ardebat Alexin,*
Delicias domini, nec quid speraret habebat.

The Shepherd, Corydon, burned with love for handsome Alexis, his master's favourite, but he was not getting what he hoped for.
   Eclogues no. 2, l. 1

18 *O formose puer, nimium ne crede colori.*

Don't bank too much on your complexion, lovely boy.
   Eclogues no. 2, l. 17

19 *Quem fugis, a! demens? Habitarunt di quoque silvas.*

Who are you running from, you crazy man? . . . Even gods have lived in the woods like me.
   Eclogues no. 2, l. 60

20 *Trahit sua quemque voluptas.*

Everyone is dragged on by their favourite pleasure.
   Eclogues no. 2, l. 65

21 *Malo me Galatea petit, lasciva puella,*
Et fugit ad salices et se cupit ante videri.

Galatea aims at me with an apple, sexy girl, and runs away into the willows and wants to have been spotted.
   Eclogues no. 3, l. 64

22 *Latet anguis in herba.*

There's a snake hidden in the grass.
   Eclogues no. 3, l. 93

23 *Non nostrum inter vos tantas componere lites.*

It's not in my power to decide such a great dispute between you.
   Eclogues no. 3, l. 108

1 *Claudite iam rivos, pueri; sat prata biberunt.*

Close the sluices now, lads; the fields have drunk enough.
> *Eclogues* no. 3, l. 111

2 *Sicelides Musae, paulo maiora canamus!*
Non omnis arbusta iuvant humilesque myricae;
Si canimus silvas, silvae sint consule dignae.
Ultima Cumaei venit iam carminis aetas;
Magnus ab integro saeclorum nascitur ordo.
Iam redit et virgo, redeunt Saturnia regna,
Iam nova progenies caelo demittitur alto.

Sicilian Muses, let us sing of rather greater things. Bushes and low tamarisks do not please everyone; if we sing of the woods, let them be woods of consular dignity. Now has come the last age according to the oracle at Cumae; the great series of lifetimes starts anew. Now too the virgin goddess returns, the golden days of Saturn's reign return, now a new race is sent down from high heaven.
> *Eclogues* no. 4, l. 1

3 *Incipe, parve puer, risu cognoscere matrem.*

Begin, baby boy, to recognize your mother with a smile.
> *Eclogues* no. 4, l. 60

4 *Incipe, parve puer: qui non risere parenti,*
Nec deus hunc mensa, dea nec dignata cubili est.

Begin, baby boy: if you haven't had a smile for your parent, then neither will a god think you worth inviting to dinner, nor a goddess to bed.
> *Eclogues* no. 4, l. 62

5 *Ambo florentes aetatibus, Arcades ambo,*
Et cantare pares et respondere parati.

Both in the flower of their youth, Arcadians both, and matched and ready alike to start a song and to respond.
> *Eclogues* no. 7, l. 4

6 *Saepibus in nostris parvam te roscida mala*
(Dux ego vester eram) vidi cum matre legentem.
Alter ab undecimo tum me iam acceperat annus,
Iam fragilis poteram a terra contingere ramos:
Ut vidi, ut perii, ut me malus abstulit error!

In our orchard I saw you as a child picking dewy apples with your mother (I was showing you the way). I had just turned twelve years old, I could reach the brittle branches even from the ground: as I saw you, how I perished [for love of you]! how an awful madness swept me away!
> *Eclogues* no. 8, l. 37

7 *Nunc scio quid sit Amor.*

Now I know what Love is.
> *Eclogues* no. 8, l. 43

8 *Non omnia possumus omnes.*

We can't all do everything.
> *Eclogues* no. 8, l. 63; see **LUCILIUS** 504:2

9   *Et me fecere poetam*
Pierides, sunt et mihi carmina, me quoque dicunt
Vatem pastores; sed non ego credulus illis.

Nam neque adhuc Vario videor nec dicere Cinna
Digna, sed argutos inter strepere anser olores.

Me too the Muses made write verse. I have songs of my own, the shepherds call me also a poet; but I'm not inclined to trust them. For I don't seem yet to write things as good either as Varius or as Cinna, but to be a goose honking amongst tuneful swans.
> *Eclogues* no. 9, l. 32

10 *Omnia vincit Amor: et nos cedamus Amori.*

Love conquers all things: let us too give in to Love.
> *Eclogues* no. 10, l. 69; see **CHAUCER** 218:11

11 *Ite domum saturae, venit Hesperus, ite capellae.*

Go on home, you have fed full, the evening star is coming, go on, my she-goats.
> *Eclogues* no. 10, l. 77

12 *Ultima Thule.*

Farthest Thule.
> *Georgics* no. 1, l. 30

13   *Pater ipse colendi*
Haud facilem esse viam voluit.

The great Father himself has willed that the path of husbandry should not run smooth.
> *Georgics* no. 1, l. 121

14   *Labor omnia vincit*
Improbus et duris urgens in rebus egestas.

        Unremitting labour
And harsh necessity's hand will master anything.
> *Georgics* no. 1, l. 145 (translated by C. Day Lewis)

15 *Nosque ubi primus equis Oriens adflavit anhelis*
Illic sera rubens accendit lumina Vesper.

And when the rising sun has first breathed on us with his panting horses, over there the red evening-star is lighting his late lamps.
> *Georgics* no. 1, l. 250

16 *Ter sunt conati imponere Pelio Ossam*
Scilicet atque Ossae frondosum involvere Olympum;
Ter pater exstructos disiecit fulmine montis.

Three times they endeavoured to pile Ossa on Pelion, no less, and to roll leafy Olympus on top of Ossa; three times our Father broke up the towering mountains with a thunderbolt.
> *Georgics* no. 1, l. 281

17 *O fortunatos nimium, sua si bona norint,*
Agricolas!

O farmers excessively fortunate if only they recognized their blessings!
> *Georgics* no. 2, l. 458

18 *Felix qui potuit rerum cognoscere causas.*

Lucky is he who has been able to understand the causes of things.
> *of **LUCRETIUS***
> *Georgics* no. 2, l. 490

19 *Fortunatus et ille deos qui novit agrestis.*

Fortunate too is the man who has come to know the gods of the countryside.
> *Georgics* no. 2, l. 493

1 *Optima quaeque dies miseris mortalibus aevi*
Prima fugit; subeunt morbi tristisque senectus
Et labor, et durae rapit inclementia mortis.

All the best days of life slip away from us poor
mortals first; illnesses and dreary old age and
pain sneak up, and the fierceness of harsh death
snatches away.
  Georgics no. 3, l. 66

2 *Sed fugit interea, fugit inreparabile tempus.*

But meanwhile it is flying, irretrievable time is
flying.
  usually quoted as 'tempus fugit [*time flies*]'
  Georgics no. 3, l. 284; see **PROVERBS** 645:17

3 *Litoraque alcyonen resonant, acalanthida dumi.*

And the shore echoes the song of the kingfisher,
and the woods echo the song of the goldfinch.
  Georgics bk. 3, l. 338

4 *Hi motus animorum atque haec certamina tanta*
Pulveris exigui iactu compressa quiescent.

These movements of souls and these contests,
however great, having been contained by the
throwing of a little dust, will be quiet.
  Georgics no. 4, l. 86 (of the battle of the bees)

5 *Non aliter, si parva licet componere magnis,*
Cecropias innatus apes amor urget habendi
Munere quamque suo.

Just so, if one may compare small things with
great, an innate love of getting drives these Attic
bees each with his own function.
  Georgics no. 4, l. 176

6 *At genus immortale manet, multosque per annos*
Stat fortuna domus, et avi numerantur avorum.

But the race remains immortal, the fortune of
the house stands firm for many years, and the
grandfathers' grandfathers are numbered in the
roll.
  of a community of bees
  Georgics no. 4, l. 208

7 *Septem illum totos perhibent ex ordine menses*
Rupe sub aëria deserti ad Strymonis undam
Flesse sibi et gelidis haec evolvisse sub antris
Mulcentem tigres et agentem carmine quercus;
Qualis populea maerens philomela sub umbra
Amissos queritur fetus.

Month after month, they say, for seven months
  alone
He wept beneath a crag high up by the lonely
  waters
Of Strymon, and under the ice-cold stars poured
  out his dirge
That charmed the tigers and made the oak-trees
  follow him.
As a nightingale he sang that sorrowing under a
  poplar's
Shade laments the young she has lost.
  Georgics no. 4, l. 507, translated by C. Day Lewis

8 *Sic vos non vobis mellificatis apes.*
Sic vos non vobis nidificatis aves.

Sic vos non vobis vellera fertis oves.

Thus you bees make honey not for yourselves.
Thus you birds build nests not for yourselves.
Thus you sheep bear fleeces not for yourselves.
  on Bathyllus claiming authorship of certain lines by Virgil
  attributed

Vitruvius fl. 1st century BC
Roman architect and military engineer

9 *Haec autem ita fieri debent, ut habeatur ratio*
firmitatis, utilitatis, venustatis.

Now these should be so carried out that account
is taken of strength, utility, grace.
  On Architecture bk. 1, ch. 3, sect. 2; see **WOTTON** 870:11

Voltaire (François-Marie Arouet) 1694–1778
French writer and philosopher. On Voltaire: see BLAKE
126:25, HUGO 419:8, WORDSWORTH 865:14; see also
MISQUOTATIONS 547:20

10 *Dans ce meilleur des mondes possibles . . . tout est*
au mieux.

In this best of possible worlds . . . all is for the
best.
  usually quoted as 'All is for the best in the best of all
  possible worlds'
  Candide (1759) ch. 1; see **PROVERBS** 626:18

11 *Si nous ne trouvons pas des choses agréables, nous*
trouverons du moins des choses nouvelles.

If we do not find anything pleasant, at least we
shall find something new.
  Candide (1759) ch. 17

12 *Vous savez que ces deux nations sont en guerre pour*
quelques arpens de neiges vers le Canada, et qu'elles
dépensent pour cette belle guerre beaucoup plus que
tout le Canada ne vaut.

These two nations have been at war over a few
acres of snow near Canada, and . . . they are
spending on this fine struggle more than Canada
itself is worth.
  of the struggle between the French and the British for the
  control of colonial north Canada
  Candide (1759) ch. 23

13 *Dans ce pays-ci il est bon de tuer de temps en temps*
un amiral pour encourager les autres.

In this country [England] it is thought well to
kill an admiral from time to time to encourage
the others.
  referring to the contentious execution of Admiral Byng
  (1704–57) for neglect of duty in failing to relieve Minorca
  Candide (1759) ch. 23; see **WALPOLE** 838:7

14 *Le travail éloigne de nous trois grands maux: l'ennui,*
le vice, et le besoin.

Work saves us from three great evils: boredom,
vice, and need.
  Candide (1759) ch. 30

15 *Il faut cultiver notre jardin.*

We must cultivate our garden.
  Candide (1759) ch. 30

1 *Ils ne se servent de la pensée que pour autoriser leurs injustices, et n'emploient les paroles que pour déguiser leurs pensées.*

[Men] use thought only to justify their injustices, and speech only to conceal their thoughts.
Dialogues (1763) 'Le Chapon et la poularde'

2 *Le mieux est l'ennemi du bien.*

The best is the enemy of the good.
Contes (1772) 'La Begueule' l. 2; though often attributed to Voltaire, the notion in fact derives from an Italian proverb quoted in his *Dictionnaire philosophique* (1770 ed.) 'Art Dramatique': '*Le meglio è l'inimico del bene*'; see **PROVERBS** 627:20

3 *On a déclamé contre le luxe depuis deux mille ans, en vers et en prose, et on l'a toujours aimé.*

Luxury has been railed at for two thousand years, in verse and in prose, and it has always been loved.
Dictionnaire philosophique (1764) 'Le Luxe' sect. 2

4 *Le sens commun est fort rare.*

Common sense is not so common.
Dictionnaire philosophique (1765) 'Sens Commun'

5 *La superstition met le monde entier en flammes; la philosophie les éteint.*

Superstition sets the whole world in flames; philosophy quenches them.
Dictionnaire philosophique (1764) 'Superstition'

6 *Le secret d'ennuyer est . . . de tout dire.*

The secret of being a bore . . . is to tell everything.
Discours en vers sur l'homme (1737) 'De la nature de l'homme' l. 172

7 *Tous les genres sont bons hors le genre ennuyeux.*

All styles are good except the tiresome kind.
L'Enfant prodigue (1736) preface

8 *Si Dieu n'existait pas, il faudrait l'inventer.*

If God did not exist, it would be necessary to invent him.
Épîtres no. 96 'A l'Auteur du livre des trois imposteurs'; see **OVID** 589:22

9 *Ce corps qui s'appelait et qui s'appelle encore le saint empire romain n'était en aucune manière ni saint, ni romain, ni empire.*

This agglomeration which was called and which still calls itself the Holy Roman Empire was neither holy, nor Roman, nor an empire.
Essai sur l'histoire générale et sur les moeurs et l'esprit des nations (1756) ch. 70

10 *En effet, l'histoire n'est que le tableau des crimes et des malheurs.*

Indeed, history is nothing more than a tableau of crimes and misfortunes.
L'Ingénu (1767) ch. 10; see **GIBBON** 354:6

11 *C'est une des superstitions de l'esprit humain d'avoir imaginé que la virginité pouvait être une vertu.*

It is one of the superstitions of the human mind to have imagined that virginity could be a virtue.
'The Leningrad Notebooks' (c.1735–50) in T. Besterman (ed.) *Voltaire's Notebooks* (2nd ed., 1968) vol. 2, p. 455

12 *Oh, le bon temps, que ce siecle de fer!*

Oh what a good time it was, that age of iron!
Le Mondain (1736) l. 21

13 *Le superflu, chose très nécessaire.*

The superfluous, a very necessary thing.
Le Mondain (1736) l. 22

14 *Il faut qu'il y ait des moments tranquilles dans les grands ouvrages, comme dans la vie après les instants de passions, mais non pas des moments de dégoût.*

There ought to be moments of tranquillity in great works, as in life after the experience of passions, but not moments of disgust.
'The Piccini Notebooks' (c.1735–50) in T. Besterman (ed.) *Voltaire's Notebooks* (2nd ed., 1968) vol. 2

15 *Il faut, dans le gouvernement, des bergers et des bouchers.*

Governments need both shepherds and butchers.
'The Piccini Notebooks' (c.1735–50) in T. Besterman (ed.) *Voltaire's Notebooks* (2nd ed., 1968) vol. 2

16 *Dieu n'est pas pour les gros bataillons, mais pour ceux qui tirent le mieux.*

God is on the side not of the heavy battalions, but of the best shots.
'The Piccini Notebooks' (c.1735–50) in T. Besterman (ed.) *Voltaire's Notebooks* (2nd ed., 1968) vol. 2; see **ANOUILH** 24:7, **BUSSY-RABUTIN** 182:16, **PROVERBS** 642:10

17 *On doit des égards aux vivants; on ne doit aux morts que la vérité.*

We owe respect to the living; to the dead we owe only truth.
'Première Lettre sur Oedipe' in *Oeuvres* (1785) vol. 1

18 *Usez, n'abusez point . . . L'abstinence ou l'excès ne fit jamais d'heureux.*

Use, do not abuse . . . Neither abstinence nor excess ever renders man happy.
Sept Discours en Vers sur l'Homme (1738) 'Cinquième discours: sur la nature de plaisir'

19 *Quoi que vous fassiez, écrasez l'infâme, et aimez qui vous aime.*

Whatever you do, stamp out abuses [superstition], and love those who love you.
letter to M. d'Alembert, 28 November 1762, in Voltaire Foundation (ed.) *Complete Works* vol. 25 (1973)

20 *Il est plaisant qu'on fait une vertu du vice de chasteté; et voilà encore une drôle de chasteté que celle qui mène tout droit les hommes au péché d'Onan, et les filles aux pâles couleurs!*

It is amusing that a virtue is made of the vice of chastity; and it's a pretty odd sort of chastity at that, which leads men straight into the sin of Onan, and girls to the waning of their colour.
letter to M. Mariott, 28 March 1766, in Voltaire Foundation (ed.) *Complete Works* vol. 30 (1973)

21 *Quand la populace se mêle de raisonner, tout est perdu.*

When the masses get involved in reasoning, everything is lost.
letter to Etienne Noël Darnilaville, 1 April 1766; Theodore Besterman et al. (eds.) *The Complete Works of Voltaire* (1973) vol. 114

1 *Je ne suis pas comme une dame de la cour de Versailles, qui disait: c'est bien dommage que l'aventure de la tour de Babel ait produit la confusion des langues; sans cela tout le monde aurait toujours parlé français.*

I am not like a lady at the court of Versailles, who said: 'What a dreadful pity that the bother at the tower of Babel should have got language all mixed up; but for that, everyone would always have spoken French.'
> letter to Catherine the Great, 26 May 1767, in Voltaire Foundation (ed.) *Complete Works* vol. 32 (1974)

2 *Le doute n'est pas un état bien agréable, mais l'assurance est un état ridicule.*

Doubt is not a pleasant condition. But certainty is an absurd one.
> letter to Frederick the Great, 28 November 1770

3 The art of government is to make two-thirds of a nation pay all it possibly can pay for the benefit of the other third.
> attributed; Walter Bagehot *The English Constitution* (1867) ch. 5

4 The composition of a tragedy requires *testicles*.
> *on being asked why no woman had ever written 'a tolerable tragedy'*
> letter from Byron to John Murray, 2 April 1817, in L. A. Marchand (ed.) *Byron's Letters and Journals* vol. 5 (1976)

5 The English plays are like their English puddings: nobody has any taste for them but themselves.
> Joseph Spence *Anecdotes* (ed. J. M. Osborn, 1966) no. 1033

6 *L'étymologie est une science où les voyelles ne font rien, et les consonnes font peu de chose*

Etymology is a science where vowels count for nothing and consonants for very little.
> attributed; Max Müller *Lectures on the Science of Language* (2nd series, 1864) 'On the Principles of Etymology'

7 *Habacuc était capable de tout.*

Habakkuk was capable of anything.
> attributed; in *Notes and Queries* 26 July 1941

8 Repose is a good thing, but boredom is its brother.
> attributed, 1921

9 What a fuss about an omelette!
> *what Voltaire apparently said on the burning of* De l'esprit
> James Parton *Life of Voltaire* (1881) vol. 2, ch. 25; see **MISQUOTATIONS** 547:20

10 This is no time for making new enemies.
> *on being asked to renounce the Devil, on his deathbed*
> attributed

Andrei Voznesensky 1933–
Russian poet

11 I am Goya
of the bare field, by the enemy's beak gouged
till the craters of my eyes gape,
I am grief,
I am the tongue

of war, the embers of cities
on the snows of the year 1941
I am hunger.
> 'Goya' (published 1960) (translated by Stanley Kunitz)

Peter Vyazemsky 1792–1878
Russian poet

12 God of frostbite, God of famine,
beggars, cripples by the yard,
farms with no crops to examine—
that's him, that's your Russian God.
> 'The Russian God' (1828) (translated by Alan Myers)

Richard Wagner 1813–83
German composer

13 *Frisch weht der Wind*
der Heimat zu:—
mein irisch Kind,
wo weilest du?

Freshly blows the wind homewards: my Irish child, where are you dwelling?
> *Tristan und Isolde* (1865) act 1, sc. 1

Derek Walcott 1930–
West Indian poet and dramatist

14 I who have cursed
The drunken officer of British rule, how choose
Between this Africa and the English tongue I
love?
> 'A Far Cry From Africa' (1962)

15 Famine sighs like scythe
across the field of statistics and the desert
is a moving mouth.
> 'The Fortunate Traveller' (1981)

16 Poetry, which is perfection's sweat but which must seem as fresh as the raindrops on a statue's brow, combines the natural and the marmoreal.
> *The Antilles: Fragments of Epic Memory* (1992) Nobel lecture

17 I come from a backward place: your duty is supplied by life around you. One guy plants bananas; another plants cocoa; I'm a writer, I plant lines. There's the same clarity of occupation, and the sense of devotion.
> in *Guardian* 12 July 1997

Lech Wałęsa 1943–
Polish trade unionist and statesman, President 1990–5

18 You have riches and freedom here but I feel no sense of faith or direction. You have so many computers, why don't you use them in the search for love?
> in Paris, on his first journey outside the Soviet area, in *Daily Telegraph* 14 December 1988

Alice Walker 1944–

American poet

1 Did this happen to your mother? Did your sister throw up a lot?
 title of poem (1979)

2 I thought love would adapt itself
 to my needs.
 But needs grow too fast;
 they come up like weeds.
 Through cracks in the conversation.
 Through silences in the dark.
 Through everything you thought was concrete.
 'Did This Happen to Your Mother? Did Your Sister Throw Up a Lot?' (1979)

3 Expect nothing. Live frugally
 on surprise.
 'Expect nothing' (1973)

4 The quietly pacifist peaceful
 always die
 to make room for men
 who shout. Who tell lies to
 children, and crush the corners
 off of old men's dreams.
 'The QPP' (1973)

5 We have a beautiful
 mother
 Her green lap
 immense
 Her brown embrace
 eternal
 Her blue body
 everything
 we know.
 'We Have a Beautiful Mother' (1991)

6 I think it pisses God off if you walk by the colour purple in a field somewhere and don't notice it.
 The Colour Purple (1982)

7 In search of our mothers' gardens.
 title of book, 1983

8 Writing saved me from the sin and *inconvenience* of violence.
 'One Child of One's Own' in Janet Sternburg *The Writer on her Work* (1980)

Felix Walker fl. 1820

American politician

9 I'm talking to Buncombe ['bunkum'].
 excusing a long, dull, irrelevant speech in the House of Representatives, c.1820 (Buncombe being his constituency)
 W. Safire *New Language of Politics* (2nd ed., 1972); see **CARLYLE** 200:12

Edgar Wallace 1875–1932

English thriller writer

10 Dreamin' of thee! Dreamin' of thee!
 'T. A. in Love' (1900); popularized by Cyril Fletcher in 1930s radio shows

George Wallace 1919–98

American Democratic politician

11 Segregation now, segregation tomorrow and segregation forever!
 inaugural speech as Governor of Alabama, January 1963, in *Birmingham World* 19 January 1963

Henry Wallace 1888–1965

American Democratic politician

12 The century on which we are entering—the century which will come out of this war—can be and must be the century of the common man.
 speech, 8 May 1942, in *Vital Speeches* (1942) vol. 8

William Wallace c.1270–1305

Scottish national hero, leader of Scottish resistance to Edward I

13 I hae brocht ye to the ring, now see gif ye can dance.
 before the battle of Falkirk, 1298; attributed in varying forms, including ' . . . hop if ye can'; James MacKay *William Wallace: Brave Heart* (1996)

William Ross Wallace 1819–81

American poet

14 For the hand that rocks the cradle
 Is the hand that rules the world.
 'What rules the world' (1865); see **PROVERBS** 633:39, **ROBINSON** 664:7

Graham Wallas 1858–1932

English politicial scientist

15 The little girl had the making of a poet in her who, being told to be sure of her meaning before she spoke, said, 'How can I know what I think till I see what I say?'
 The Art of Thought (1926) ch. 4

Edmund Waller 1606–87

English poet

16 So was the huntsman by the bear oppressed,
 Whose hide he sold—before he caught the beast!
 'The Battle of the Summer Islands' (1645) canto 2; see **PROVERBS** 630:27

17 Go, lovely rose!
 Tell her, that wastes her time and me,
 That now she knows,
 When I resemble her to thee,
 How sweet and fair she seems to be.
 'Go, lovely rose!' (1645)

18 Others may use the ocean as their road,
 Only the English make it their abode.
 'Of a War with Spain' (1658) l. 25

19 Poets that lasting marble seek
 Must carve in Latin or in Greek.
 'Of English Verse' (1645)

1 The soul's dark cottage, battered and decayed
Lets in new light through chinks that time has
made.
'Of the Last Verses in the Book' (1685) l. 18

2 Illustrious acts high raptures do infuse,
And every conqueror creates a Muse.
'Panegyric to My Lord Protector' (1655) st. 46

3 It is not that I love you less
Than when before your feet I lay:
But, to prevent the sad increase
Of hopeless love, I keep away.

In vain, alas! for every thing
Which I have known belong to you,
Your form does to my fancy bring
And makes my old wounds bleed anew.
'The Self-Banished' (1645)

4 Why came I so untimely forth
Into a world which, wanting thee,
Could entertain us with no worth,
Or shadow of felicity?
'To My Young Lady Lucy Sidney' (1645)

5 Under the tropic is our language spoke,
And part of Flanders hath received our yoke.
'Upon the Late Storm, and of the Death of His Highness
Ensuing the Same' (1659) l. 21

William Waller 1598–1668
English Parliamentary general

6 With what a perfect hatred I detest this war
without an enemy.
letter to the Royalist Ralph Hopton, 16 June 1643; Samuel R.
Gardiner *History of the Great Civil War* (1894)

Horace Walpole, Lord Orford 1717–97
English writer and connoisseur. On Walpole: see **MACAULAY**
507:12

7 Our supreme governors, the mob.
letter to Horace Mann, 7 September 1743, in *Correspondence*
(Yale ed. 1937–83) vol. 18

8 [Lovat] was beheaded yesterday, and died
extremely well, without passion, affectation,
buffoonery or timidity: his behaviour was
natural and intrepid.
letter to Horace Mann, 10 April 1747, in *Correspondence* (Yale
ed.) vol. 19

9 [Strawberry Hill] is a little plaything-house that I
got out of Mrs Chenevix's shop, and is the
prettiest bauble you ever saw. It is set in
enamelled meadows, with filigree hedges.
letter to Hon. Henry Conway, 8 June 1747, in *Correspondence*
(Yale ed.) vol. 37

10 But, thank God! the Thames is between me and
the Duchess of Queensberry.
letter to Hon. Henry Conway, 8 June 1747, in *Correspondence*
(Yale ed.) vol. 37

11 Every drop of ink in my pen ran cold.
letter to George Montagu, 30 July 1752, in *Correspondence*
(Yale ed.) vol. 9

12 At present, nothing is talked of, nothing
admired, but what I cannot help calling a very

insipid and tedious performance: it is a kind of
novel, called *The Life and Opinions of Tristram
Shandy*; the great humour of which consists in
the whole narration always going backwards.
letter to David Dalrymple, 4 April 1760, in *Correspondence*
(Yale ed.) vol. 15

13 One of the greatest geniuses that ever existed,
Shakespeare, undoubtedly wanted taste.
letter to Christopher Wren, 9 August 1764, in *Correspondence*
(Yale ed.) vol. 40

14 It is charming to totter into vogue.
letter to George Selwyn, 2 December 1765, in *Correspondence*
(Yale ed.) vol. 30

15 The best sun we have is made of Newcastle
coal.
letter to George Montagu, 15 June 1768, in *Correspondence*
(Yale ed.) vol. 10

16 Everybody talks of the constitution, but all sides
forget that the constitution is extremely well,
and would do very well, if they would but let it
alone.
letter to Horace Mann, 18–19 January 1770, in *Correspondence*
(Yale ed.) vol. 23

17 It was easier to conquer it [the East] than to
know what to do with it.
letter to Horace Mann, 27 March 1772, in *Correspondence* (Yale
ed.) vol. 23

18 The way to ensure summer in England is to
have it framed and glazed in a comfortable
room.
letter to Revd William Cole, 28 May 1774, in *Correspondence*
(Yale ed.) vol. 1

19 The next Augustan age will dawn on the other
side of the Atlantic. There will, perhaps, be a
Thucydides at Boston, a Xenophon at New York,
and, in time, a Virgil at Mexico, and a Newton
at Peru. At last, some curious traveller from
Lima will visit England and give a description of
the ruins of St Paul's, like the editions of Balbec
and Palmyra.
letter to Horace Mann, 24 November 1774, in *Correspondence*
(Yale ed.) vol. 24; see **MACAULAY** 507:16

20 By the waters of Babylon we sit down and
weep, when we think of thee, O America!
letter to Revd William Mason, 12 June 1775, in *Correspondence*
(Yale ed.) vol. 28; see **BOOK OF COMMON PRAYER** 149:13

21 This world is a comedy to those that think, a
tragedy to those that feel.
letter to Anne, Countess of Upper Ossory, 16 August 1776, in
Correspondence (Yale ed.) vol. 32

22 When will the world know that peace and
propagation are the two most delightful things
in it?
letter to Horace Mann, 7 July 1778, in *Correspondence* (Yale
ed.) vol. 24

23 It is the story of a mountebank and his zany.
of **BOSWELL**'s Tour of the Hebrides
letter to Hon. Henry Conway, 6 October 1785, in
Correspondence (Yale ed.) vol. 39

1 All his own geese are swans, as the swans of others are geese.
of Joshua REYNOLDS
letter to Anne, Countess of Upper Ossory, 1 December 1786, in *Correspondence* (Yale ed.) vol. 33

2 How should such a fellow as Sheridan, who has no diamonds to bestow, fascinate all the world?—yet witchcraft, no doubt there has been, for when did simple eloquence ever convince a majority?
letter to Lady Ossory, 9 February 1787, in *Correspondence* (Yale ed.) vol. 33

3 That hyena in petticoats, Mrs Wollstonecraft.
letter to Hannah More, 26 January 1795, in *Correspondence* (Yale ed.) vol. 31

4 His speeches were fine, but as much laboured as his extempore sayings.
of Lord CHESTERFIELD
Memoirs of the Reign of King George II (ed. Lord Holland, 1846) vol. 1, 1751

5 Whoever knows the interior of affairs, must be sensible to how many more events the faults of statesmen give birth, than are produced by their good intentions.
Memoirs of the Reign of King George II (ed. Lord Holland, 1846) vol. 1, 1754

6 The keenness of his sabre was blunted by the difficulty with which he drew it from the scabbard; I mean, the hesitation and ungracefulness of his delivery took off from the force of his arguments.
of Henry Fox, Lord HOLLAND
Memoirs of the Reign of King George II (ed. Lord Holland, 1846) vol. 2, 1755

7 While he felt like a victim, he acted like a hero.
of Admiral Byng, on the day of his execution
Memoirs of the Reign of King George II (ed. Lord Holland, 1846) vol. 2, 1757; see VOLTAIRE 833:13

8 All his passions were expressed by one livid smile.
of George GRENVILLE
Memoirs of the Reign of King George III (ed. D. Le Marchant, 1845) vol. 1, 1763

9 He lost his dominions in America, his authority over Ireland, and all influence in Europe, by aiming at despotism in England; and exposed himself to more mortifications and humiliations than can happen to a quiet Doge of Venice.
of King GEORGE III
Memoirs of the Reign of King George III (ed. D. Le Marchant, 1845) vol. 4, 1770

10 Pieces of land and sea so natural that one steps back for fear of being splashed.
of two landscapes by Thomas GAINSBOROUGH, *exhibited in 1781*
in *Dictionary of National Biography* (1917–)

11 Virtue knows to a farthing what it has lost by not having been vice.
L. Kronenberger *The Extraordinary Mr Wilkes* (1974) pt. 3, ch. 2

Robert Walpole, Lord Orford
1676–1745
English Whig statesman, first British Prime Minister 1721–42.
On Walpole: see SHIPPEN 749:16

12 They now *ring* the bells, but they will soon *wring* their hands.
on the declaration of war with Spain, 1739
W. Coxe *Memoirs of Sir Robert Walpole* (1798) vol. 1

13 All those men have their price.
of fellow parliamentarians
W. Coxe *Memoirs of Sir Robert Walpole* (1798) vol. 1; see PROVERBS 631:27

14 Madam, there are fifty thousand men slain this year in Europe, and not one Englishman.
to Queen CAROLINE, *1734, on the war of the Polish succession, in which the English had refused to participate*
John Hervey *Memoirs* (written 1734–43, published 1848) vol. 1

15 We must muzzle this terrible young cornet of horse.
of the elder William PITT, *who had held a cornetcy before his election to Parliament, c.1736*
in *Dictionary of National Biography* (1917–)

16 [Gratitude of place-expectants] is a lively sense of future favours.
W. Hazlitt *Lectures on the English Comic Writers* (1819) 'On Wit and Humour'; see LA ROCHEFOUCAULD 482:5

17 You can read. It is a great happiness. I totally neglected it while I was in business, which has been the whole of my life, and to such a degree that I cannot now read a page—a warning to all Ministers.
on seeing Henry Fox (Lord HOLLAND*) reading in the library at Houghton*
Edmund Fitzmaurice *Life of Shelburne* (1875) vol. 1

William Walsh 1663–1708
English poet

18 A lover forsaken
A new love may get,
But a neck when once broken
Can never be set.
'The Despairing Lover' l. 17

19 I can endure my own despair,
But not another's hope.
'Song: Of All the Torments'

Izaak Walton 1593–1683
English writer

20 Angling may be said to be so like the mathematics, that it can never be fully learnt.
The Compleat Angler (1653) 'Epistle to the Reader'

21 And for winter fly-fishing it is as useful as an almanac out of date.
The Compleat Angler (1653) 'Epistle to the Reader'

22 As no man is born an artist, so no man is born an angler.
The Compleat Angler (1653) 'Epistle to the Reader'

1 I shall stay him no longer than to wish him a rainy evening to read this following discourse; and that if he be an honest angler, the east wind may never blow when he goes a-fishing.

The Compleat Angler (1653) 'Epistle to the Reader'

2 I am, Sir, a Brother of the Angle.

The Compleat Angler (1653) pt. 1, ch. 1

3 Sir Henry Wotton . . . was also a most dear lover, and a frequent practiser of the art of angling; of which he would say, 'it was an employment for his idle time, which was then not idly spent . . . a rest to his mind, a cheerer of his spirits, a diverter of sadness, a calmer of unquiet thoughts, a moderator of passions, a procurer of contentedness; and that it begat habits of peace and patience in those that professed and practised it.'

The Compleat Angler (1653) pt. 1, ch. 1

4 Good company and good discourse are the very sinews of virtue.

The Compleat Angler (1653) pt. 1, ch. 2

5 An excellent angler, and now with God.

The Compleat Angler (1653) pt. 1, ch. 4

6 I love such mirth as does not make friends ashamed to look upon one another next morning.

The Compleat Angler (1653) pt. 1, ch. 5

7 A good, honest, wholesome, hungry breakfast.

The Compleat Angler (1653) pt. 1, ch. 5

8 No man can lose what he never had.

The Compleat Angler (1653) pt. 1, ch. 5

9 In so doing, use him as though you loved him.

on baiting a hook with a live frog

The Compleat Angler (1653) pt. 1, ch. 8

10 This dish of meat is too good for any but anglers, or very honest men.

The Compleat Angler (1653) pt. 1, ch. 8

11 I love any discourse of rivers, and fish and fishing.

The Compleat Angler (1653) pt. 1, ch. 18

12 Look to your health; and if you have it, praise God, and value it next to a good conscience; for health is the second blessing that we mortals are capable of; a blessing that money cannot buy.

The Compleat Angler (1653) pt. 1, ch. 21

13 Let the blessing of St Peter's Master be . . . upon all that are lovers of virtue; and dare trust in His providence; and be quiet; and go a-Angling.

The Compleat Angler (1653) pt. 1, ch. 21

14 But God, who is able to prevail, wrestled with him, as the Angel did with Jacob, and marked him; marked him for his own.

Life of Donne (1670 ed.)

15 The great Secretary of Nature and all learning, Sir Francis Bacon.

Life of Herbert (1670 ed.)

16 Of this blest man, let his just praise be given, Heaven was in him, before he was in heaven.

written in a copy of Dr Richard Sibbes's *The Returning Backslider*, now preserved in Salisbury Cathedral Library.

Sam Walton 1919–92

American businessman

17 There is only one boss. The customer. And he can fire everybody in the company from the chairman on down, simply by spending his money somewhere else.

Sam Walton: Made in America, My Story, with J. Huey (1990)

William Warburton 1698–1779

English theologian; Bishop of Gloucester from 1759

18 Orthodoxy is my doxy; heterodoxy is another man's doxy.

to Lord Sandwich, in Joseph Priestley *Memoirs* (1807) vol. 1; see **CARLYLE** 200:1

Artemus Ward (Charles Farrar Browne) 1834–67

American humorist

19 It is a pity that Chawcer, who had geneyus, was so unedicated. He's the wuss speller I know of.

Artemus Ward in London (1867) ch. 4

20 Let us all be happy, and live within our means, even if we have to borrer the money to do it with.

Artemus Ward in London (1867) ch. 7

21 I am happiest when I am idle. I could live for months without performing any kind of labour, and at the expiration of that time I should feel fresh and vigorous enough to go right on in the same way for numerous more months.

Artemus Ward in London (1867) ch. 9

22 He is dreadfully married. He's the most married man I ever saw in my life.

Artemus Ward's Lecture (1869) 'Brigham Young's Palace'

23 Why is this thus? What is the reason of this thusness?

Artemus Ward's Lecture (1869) 'Heber C. Kimball's Harem'

Barbara Ward 1914–81

English writer and educator

24 We cannot cheat on DNA. We cannot get round photosynthesis. We cannot say I am not going to give a damn about phytoplankton. All these tiny mechanisms provide the preconditions of our planetary life. To say we do not care is to say in the most literal sense that 'we choose death'.

Only One Earth (1972)

Nathaniel Ward 1578–1652

English clergyman

25 The world is full of care, much like unto a bubble;

Woman and care, and care and women, and
women and care and trouble.

epigram, attributed by Ward to a lady at the Court of the
Queen of Bohemia, in *The Simple Cobbler of Aggawam in
America* (1647)

Andy Warhol 1927–87

American artist and filmmaker

1 In the future everybody will be world famous
for fifteen minutes.

Andy Warhol (1968) (volume released to mark his exhibition
in Stockholm, February–March, 1968)

2 Being good in business is the most fascinating
kind of art.

Philosophy of Andy Warhol (*From A to B and Back Again*) (1975)

3 An artist is someone who produces things that
people don't need to have but that he—for *some
reason*—thinks it would be a good idea to give
them.

Philosophy of Andy Warhol (*From A to B and Back Again*) (1975)

4 The things I want to show are mechanical.
Machines have less problems.

Mike Wrenn *Andy Warhol: In His Own Words* (1991)

Sylvia Townsend Warner 1893–1978

English writer

5 One need not write in a diary what one is to
remember for ever.

diary, 22 October 1930

6 One cannot overestimate the power of a good
rancorous hatred on the part of the *stupid*. The
stupid have so much more industry and energy
to expend on hating. They build it up like coral
insects.

diary, 26 September 1954

7 Total grief is like a minefield. No knowing when
one will touch the tripwire.

diary, 11 December 1969

Earl Warren 1891–1974

**American lawyer and politician, Chief Justice of the US
Supreme Court**

8 In civilized life, law floats in a sea of ethics.

in *New York Times* 12 November 1962

Robert Penn Warren 1905–89

American poet, novelist, and critic

9 Long ago in Kentucky, I, a boy, stood
By a dirt road, in first dark, and heard
The great geese hoot northward.

Audubon (1969) 'Tell Me a Story'

10 Ages to our construction went,
Dim architecture, hour by hour:
And violence, forgot now, lent
The present stillness all its power.

'Bearded Oaks' (1942)

11 They were human, they suffered, wore long
black coat and gold watch chain.

They stare from daguerrotype with severe
reprehension,
Or from genuine oil, and you'd never guess any
pain
In those merciless eyes that now remark our
own time's sad declension.

'Promises' (1957)

Booker T. Washington 1856–1915

American educationist and emancipated slave

12 No race can prosper till it learns that there is as
much dignity in tilling a field as in writing a
poem.

Up from Slavery (1901)

13 You can't hold a man down without staying
down with him.

attributed

George Washington 1732–99

**American statesman, 1st President of the US 1789–97. On
Washington: see BYRON 190:19, LEE 487:9**

14 The time is now near at hand which must
probably determine whether Americans are to
be freemen or slaves; whether they are to have
any property they can call their own . . . The
fate of unborn millions will now depend, under
God, on the courage and conduct of this army.
Our cruel and unrelenting enemy leaves us only
the choice of brave resistance, or the most
abject submission. We have, therefore, to resolve
to conquer or die.

General orders, 2 July 1776, in J. C. Fitzpatrick (ed.) *Writings of
George Washington* vol. 5 (1932)

15 Few men have virtue to withstand the highest
bidder.

letter, 17 August 1779

16 'Tis our true policy to steer clear of permanent
alliances, with any portion of the foreign world.

President's Address . . . retiring from Public Life 17 September
1796

17 Let me . . . warn you in the most solemn
manner against the baneful effects of the spirit
of party.

President's Address . . . 17 September 1796

18 The nation which indulges toward another an
habitual hatred or an habitual fondness is in
some degree a slave. It is a slave to its animosity
or to its affection, either of which is sufficient to
lead it astray from its duty and its interest.

President's Address . . . 17 September 1796

19 I can't tell a lie, Pa; you know I can't tell a lie. I
did cut it with my hatchet.

M. L. Weems *Life of George Washington* (10th ed., 1810) ch. 2

20 Liberty, when it begins to take root, is a plant of
rapid growth.

attributed

Ned Washington 1901–76

American songwriter

1 Hi diddle dee dee (an actor's life for me).
  title of song (1940) from the film *Pinocchio*

2 The night is like a lovely tune,
  Beware my foolish heart!
  How white the ever-constant moon,
  Take care, my foolish heart!
  'My Foolish Heart' (1949 song)

Edward Waterfield

3 Two men wrote a lexicon, Liddell and Scott;
  Some parts were clever, but some parts were
     not.
  Hear, all ye learned, and read me this riddle,
  How the wrong part wrote Scott, and the right
     part wrote Liddell.
  *of Henry Liddell (1811–98) and Robert Scott (1811–87)
  co-authors of the Greek Lexicon (1843), Liddell being in the
  habit of ascribing to his co-author usages which he
  criticised in his pupils, and which they said that they had
  culled from the* Lexicon
  L. E. Tanner *Westminster School: A History* (1934) ch. 9

Rowland Watkyns *c.*1616–64

4 I love him not, but show no reason can
  Wherefore, but this, *I do not love* the man.
  'Antipathy'; see **BROWN** 161:14, **MARTIAL** 524:4

5 For every marriage then is best in tune,
  When that the wife is May, the husband June.
  'To the most Courteous and Fair Gentlewoman, Mrs Elinor
  Williams'

James Dewey Watson 1928–

American biologist. On Watson: see **MEDAWAR** 530:2; see
also **CRICK AND WATSON** 260:3

6 No *good* model ever accounted for *all* the facts,
  since some data was bound to be misleading if
  not plain wrong.
  Francis Crick *Some Mad Pursuit* (1988)

Thomas Watson Snr. 1874–1956

American businessman; Chairman of IBM 1914–52. See also
MISQUOTATIONS 548:3

7 You cannot be a success in any business without
  believing that it is the greatest business in the
  world . . . You have to put your heart in the
  business and the business in your heart.
  Robert Sobel *IBM: Colossus in Transition* (1981)

William Watson *c.*1559–1603

English Roman Catholic conspirator

8 *Fiat justitia et ruant coeli.*
  Let justice be done though the heavens fall.
  *A Decacordon of Ten Quodlibeticall Questions Concerning
  Religion and State* (1602), being the first citation in an English
  work of a famous maxim; see **MANSFIELD** 520:10, **MOTTOES**
  563:9

William Watson 1858–1936

English poet

9 April, April,
  Laugh thy girlish laughter.
  Then, the moment after,
  Weep thy girlish tears!
  'April'

10 His friends he loved. His direst earthly foes—
   Cats—I believe he did but feign to hate.
   My hand will miss the insinuated nose,
   Mine eyes the tail that wagged contempt at Fate.
   'An Epitaph'

Isaac Watts 1674–1748

English hymn-writer

11 How doth the little busy bee
   Improve each shining hour,
   And gather honey all the day
   From every opening flower!
   Divine Songs for Children (1715) 'Against Idleness and Mischief';
   see **CARROLL** 201:13

12 For Satan finds some mischief still
   For idle hands to do.
   Divine Songs for Children (1715) 'Against Idleness and Mischief';
   see **PROVERBS** 629:42

13 Let me be dressed fine as I will,
   Flies, worms, and flowers, exceed me still.
   Divine Songs for Children (1715) 'Against Pride in Clothes'

14 Let dogs delight to bark and bite,
   For God hath made them so.
   Divine Songs for Children (1715) 'Against Quarrelling'

15 But, children, you should never let
   Such angry passions rise;
   Your little hands were never made
   To tear each other's eyes.
   Divine Songs for Children (1715) 'Against Quarrelling'

16 Birds in their little nests agree
   And 'tis a shameful sight,
   When children of one family
   Fall out, and chide, and fight.
   Divine Songs for Children (1715) 'Love between Brothers and
   Sisters'; see **PROVERBS** 628:7

17 'Tis the voice of the sluggard; I heard him
      complain,
   'You have waked me too soon, I must slumber
      again'.
   As the door on its hinges, so he on his bed,
   Turns his sides and his shoulders and his heavy
      head.
   Divine Songs for Children (1715) 'The Sluggard'; see **CARROLL**
   202:15

18 Come, let us join our cheerful songs
   With angels round the throne;
   Ten thousand thousand are their tongues,
   But all their joys are one.
   'Worthy the Lamb that died,' they cry,
   'To be exalted thus;'
   'Worthy the Lamb,' our lips reply,

'For he was slain for us.'

Hymns and Spiritual Songs (1707) 'Come, let us join our cheerful songs'

1 We are a garden walled around,
Chosen and made peculiar ground;
A little spot enclosed by grace,
Out of the world's wide wilderness.

Hymns and Spiritual Songs (1707) 'The Church the Garden of Christ'

2 When I survey the wondrous cross
On which the prince of glory died,
My richest gain I count but loss,
And pour contempt on all my pride.

Hymns and Spiritual Songs (1707) 'Crucifixion to the World, by the Cross of Christ'

3 Hark! from the tombs a doleful sound.

Hymns and Spiritual Songs (1707) 'Hark! from the Tombs'

4 There is a land of pure delight,
Where saints immortal reign.

Hymns and Spiritual Songs (1707) 'A Prospect of Heaven makes Death easy'

5 Death like a narrow sea divides
This heavenly land from ours.

Hymns and Spiritual Songs (1707) 'A Prospect of Heaven makes Death easy'

6 Jesus shall reign where'er the sun
Does his successive journeys run;
His kingdom stretch from shore to shore,
Till moons shall wax and wane no more.

The Psalms of David Imitated (1719) Psalm 72

7 Our God, our help in ages past
Our hope for years to come,
Our shelter from the stormy blast,
And our eternal home.

Beneath the shadow of Thy Throne
Thy saints have dwelt secure;
Sufficient is Thine Arm alone,
And our defence is sure.

Before the hills in order stood,
Or earth received her frame,
From everlasting Thou art God,
To endless years the same.

A thousand ages in Thy sight
Are like an evening gone;
Short as the watch that ends the night
Before the rising sun.

Time, like an ever-rolling stream,
Bears all its sons away;
They fly forgotten, as a dream
Dies at the opening day.

'Our God' altered to 'O God' by John **WESLEY**, 1738

The Psalms of David Imitated (1719) Psalm 90

8 Alexander the Great . . . when he had conquered what was called the Eastern World . . . wept for want of more Worlds to conquer.

The Improvement of the Mind (1741); see **ALEXANDER** 12:3

Evelyn Waugh 1903–66

English novelist

9 I am not I: thou art not he or she: they are not they.

Brideshead Revisited (1945) 'Author's Note'

10 Charm is the great English blight. It does not exist outside these damp islands. It spots and kills anything it touches. It kills love, it kills art.

Brideshead Revisited (1945) bk. 3, ch. 2

11 Any who have heard that sound will shrink at the recollection of it; it is the sound of English county families baying for broken glass.

Decline and Fall (1928) 'Prelude'; see **BELLOC** 68:17

12 I expect you'll be becoming a schoolmaster, sir. That's what most of the gentlemen does, sir, that gets sent down for indecent behaviour.

Decline and Fall (1928) 'Prelude'

13 Any one who has been to an English public school will always feel comparatively at home in prison. It is the people brought up in the gay intimacy of the slums, Paul learned, who find prison so soul-destroying.

Decline and Fall (1928) pt. 3, ch. 4

14 Only when one has lost all curiosity about the future has one reached the age to write an autobiography.

A Little Learning (1964)

15 It is by crawling on the face of it that one learns a country.

Ninety-two Days (1934) ch. 8

16 His strongest tastes were negative. He abhorred plastics, Picasso, sunbathing and jazz—everything in fact that had happened in his own lifetime.

The Ordeal of Gilbert Pinfold (1957) ch. 1

17 *The Beast* stands for strong mutually antagonistic governments everywhere . . . Self-sufficiency at home, self-assertion abroad.

Scoop (1938) bk. 1, ch. 1

18 Up to a point, Lord Copper.

Scoop (1938) bk. 1, ch. 1

19 'Feather-footed through the plashy fen passes the questing vole' . . . 'Yes,' said the Managing Editor. 'That must be good style.'

Scoop (1938) bk. 1, ch. 1

20 Remember that the Patriots are in the right and are going to win . . . But they must win quickly. The British public has no interest in a war that drags on indecisively. A few sharp victories, some conspicuous acts of personal bravery on the Patriot side and a colourful entry into the capital. That is *The Beast* Policy for the war.

Scoop (1938) bk. 1, ch. 3

21 News is what a chap who doesn't care much about anything wants to read. And it's only news until he's read it. After that it's dead.

Scoop (1938) bk. 1, ch. 5

1 Other nations use 'force'; we Britons alone use 'Might'.
   Scoop (1938) bk. 2, ch. 5

2 All this fuss about sleeping together. For physical pleasure I'd sooner go to my dentist any day.
   Vile Bodies (1930) ch. 6

3 To see him fumbling with our rich and delicate language is to experience all the horror of seeing a Sèvres vase in the hands of a chimpanzee.
   of Stephen **SPENDER**
   in *The Tablet* 5 May 1951

4 Punctuality is the virtue of the bored.
   Michael Davie (ed.) *Diaries of Evelyn Waugh* (1976) 'Irregular Notes 1960–65', 26 March 1962

5 A typical triumph of modern science to find the only part of Randolph that was not malignant and remove it.
   on hearing that Randolph Churchill's lung, when removed, proved non-malignant
   Michael Davie (ed.) *Diaries of Evelyn Waugh* (1976) 'Irregular Notes 1960–65', March 1964

6 I drink for it.
   when asked, while at Oxford, what he did for his college
   attributed

Frederick Weatherly 1848–1929
English songwriter

7 Where are the boys of the old Brigade,
   Who fought with us side by side?
   'The Old Brigade' (1886 song)

8 Roses are flowering in Picardy,
   But there's never a rose like you.
   'Roses of Picardy' (1916 song)

Beatrice Webb 1858–1943
English socialist, wife of Sidney **WEBB**

9 I never visualised labour as separate men and women of different sorts and kinds . . . labour was an abstraction, which seemed to denote an arithmetically calculable mass of human beings, each individual a repetition of the other.
   My Apprenticeship (1926) ch. 1

Sidney Webb 1859–1947
English socialist, husband of Beatrice **WEBB**

10 The inevitability of gradualness.
   Presidential address to the annual conference of the Labour Party, 26 June 1923, in *The Labour Party on the Threshold* (Fabian Tract no. 207, 1923)

11 Marriage is the waste-paper basket of the emotions.
   Bertrand Russell *Autobiography* (1967) vol. 1, ch. 4

Byron Webber b. 1838
British poet

12 Hands across the sea,
   Feet on English ground,

The old blood is bold blood, the wide world round.
   'Hands across the Sea' (1860), in Burton Stevenson *The Home Book of Quotations* (1967 ed.); see **ROOSEVELT** 668:5

Max Weber 1864–1920
German sociologist

13 The protestant ethic and the spirit of capitalism.
   Archiv für Sozialwissenschaft u. Sozialpolitik vol. 20 (1904–5) (title of article)

14 In Baxter's view the care for external goods should only lie on the shoulders of the saint like 'a light cloak, which can be thrown aside at any moment.' But fate decreed that the cloak should become an iron cage.
   Gesammelte Aufsätze zur Religionssoziologie (1920) vol. 1 (translated by T. Parsons, 1930)

15 The State is a relation of men dominating men, a relation supported by means of legitimate (i.e. considered to be legitimate) violence.
   'Politik als Beruf' (1919) (translated by H. Gerth and C. Wright Mills, 1948)

16 The authority of the 'eternal yesterday'.
   'Politik als Beruf' (1919)

17 The experience of the irrationality of the world has been the driving force of all religious revolution.
   'Politik als Beruf' (1919)

18 The concept of the 'official secret' is its [bureaucracy's] specific invention.
   'Politik als Beruf' (1919)

Daniel Webster 1782–1852
American politician. On Webster: see **SMITH** 758:16

19 It is, Sir, as I have said, a small college. And yet *there are those who love it!*
   argument in the case of the Trustees of Dartmouth College v. Woodward, 10 March 1818

20 The past, at least, is secure.
   second speech in the Senate on Foote's Resolution, 26 January 1830; *Writings and Speeches* (1903) vol. 6

21 The people's government, made for the people, made by the people, and answerable to the people.
   second speech in the Senate on Foote's Resolution, 26 January 1830; *Writings and Speeches* (1903) vol. 6; see **LINCOLN** 494:1

22 Liberty *and* Union, now and forever, one and inseparable!
   second speech in the Senate on Foote's Resolution, 26 January 1830; *Writings and Speeches* (1903) vol. 6

23 On this question of principle, while actual suffering was yet afar off, they [the Colonies] raised their flag against a power, to which, for purposes of foreign conquest and subjugation, Rome, in the height of her glory, is not to be compared; a power which has dotted over the surface of the whole globe with her possessions and military posts, whose morning drum-beat,

following the sun, and keeping company with the hours, circles the earth with one continuous and unbroken strain of the martial airs of England.
speech in the Senate on the President's Protest, 7 May 1834; Writings and Speeches (1903) vol. 7

1 Whatever government is not a government of laws, is a despotism, let it be called what it may.
at a reception in Bangor, Maine, 25 August 1835; Writings and Speeches (1903) vol. 2

2 Thank God, I—I also—am an American!
speech on the completion of Bunker Hill Monument, 17 June 1843; Writings and Speeches (1903) vol. 1

3 The Law: It has honoured us, may we honour it.
speech at the Charleston Bar Dinner, 10 May 1847; Writings and Speeches (1903) vol. 4

4 I was born an American; I will live an American; I shall die an American.
speech in the Senate on 'The Compromise Bill', 17 July 1850; Writings and Speeches (1903) vol. 10

5 There is always room at the top.
on being advised against joining the overcrowded legal profession
attributed; see **PROVERBS** 644:21

John Webster *c.1580–c.1625*

English dramatist. On Webster: see ELIOT 311:20

6 Vain the ambition of kings
Who seek by trophies and dead things,
To leave a living name behind,
And weave but nets to catch the wind.
The Devil's Law-Case (1623) act 5, sc. 4

7   Why should only I . . .
Be cased up, like a holy relic? I have youth
And a little beauty.
The Duchess of Malfi (1623) act 3, sc. 2

8   O, that it were possible,
We might but hold some two days' conference
With the dead!
The Duchess of Malfi (1623) act 4, sc. 2

9 I am Duchess of Malfi still.
The Duchess of Malfi (1623) act 4, sc. 2

10 Glories, like glow-worms, afar off shine bright,
But looked to near, have neither heat nor light.
The Duchess of Malfi (1623) act 4, sc. 2

11 I know death hath ten thousand several doors
For men to take their exits.
The Duchess of Malfi (1623) act 4, sc. 2; see FLETCHER 335:8, MASSINGER 527:12, SENECA 692:20

12 Cover her face; mine eyes dazzle: she died young.
The Duchess of Malfi (1623) act 4, sc. 2

13 Physicians are like kings,—they brook no contradiction.
The Duchess of Malfi (1623) act 5, sc. 2

14 Strangling is a very quiet death.
The Duchess of Malfi (1623) act 5, sc. 4

15 We are merely the stars' tennis-balls, struck and bandied

Which way please them.
The Duchess of Malfi (1623) act 5, sc. 4

16 Is not old wine wholesomest, old pippins toothsomest, old wood burn brightest, old linen wash whitest? Old soldiers, sweethearts, are surest, and old lovers are soundest.
Westward Hoe (1607) act 2, sc. 2

17   Fortune's a right whore:
If she give aught, she deals it in small parcels,
That she may take away all at one swoop.
The White Devil (1612) act 1, sc. 1

18 'Tis just like a summer birdcage in a garden; the birds that are without despair to get in, and the birds that are within despair, and are in a consumption, for fear they shall never get out.
The White Devil (1612) act 1, sc. 2

19 A mere tale of a tub, my words are idle.
The White Devil (1612) act 2, sc. 1

20 Call for the robin-red-breast and the wren,
Since o'er shady groves they hover,
And with leaves and flowers do cover
The friendless bodies of unburied men.
The White Devil (1612) act 5, sc. 4

21 But keep the wolf far thence that's foe to men,
For with his nails he'll dig them up again.
The White Devil (1612) act 5, sc. 4

22 We think caged birds sing, when indeed they cry.
The White Devil (1612) act 5, sc. 4; see DUNBAR 299:8, SHAKESPEARE 716:26

23 And of all axioms this shall win the prize,—
'Tis better to be fortunate than wise.
The White Devil (1612) act 5, sc. 6

24 There's nothing of so infinite vexation
As man's own thoughts.
The White Devil (1612) act 5, sc. 6

25 My soul, like to a ship in a black storm,
Is driven, I know not whither.
The White Devil (1612) act 5, sc. 6

26 Prosperity doth bewitch men, seeming clear;
But seas do laugh, show white, when rocks are near.
The White Devil (1612) act 5, sc. 6

27   I have caught
An everlasting cold; I have lost my voice
Most irrecoverably.
The White Devil (1612) act 5, sc. 6

Josiah Wedgwood *1730–95*
English potter

28 Am I not a man and a brother.
legend on Wedgwood cameo, depicting a kneeling Negro slave in chains
reproduced in facsimile in E. Darwin *The Botanic Garden* pt. 1 (1791)

Simone Weil *1909–43*
French essayist and philosopher

29 I would suggest that barbarism be considered as a permanent and universal human characteristic

which becomes more or less pronounced according to the play of circumstances.

Écrits Historiques et politiques (1960) 'Réflexions sur la barbarie' (written c.1939)

1 An obligation which goes unrecognized by anybody loses none of the full force of its existence. A right which goes unrecognized by anybody is not worth very much.

L'Enracinement (1949) 'Les Besoins de l'âme' (translated by A. F. Wills)

2 Grace fills empty spaces, but it can only enter where there is a void to receive it, and it is grace itself which makes this void.

Gravity and Grace (1948)

3 All sins are attempts to fill voids.

Gravity and Grace (1948)

4 The authentic and pure values—truth, beauty, and goodness—in the activity of a human being are the result of one and the same act, a certain application of the full attention to the object.

Gravity and Grace (1948)

5 An intelligent man who is proud of his intelligence is like a condemned man who is proud of his cell.

'The Human Personality: the Just and the Unjust' in *La Table ronde* November 1950

6 That superb indifference which the powerful have for the weak.

Intimations of Christianity Among the Ancient Greeks (1957) 'The Iliad, Poem of Might'

7 What a country calls its vital economic interests are not the things which enable its citizens to live, but the things which enable it to make war.

W. H. Auden *A Certain World* (1971)

Max Weinreich 1894–1969

American Yiddish scholar

8 A language is a dialect with an army and a navy.

in *Yivo Bleter* January–February 1945

Arabella Weir *see* Catchphrases 207:12

Robert Stanley Weir 1856–1926

Canadian lawyer

9 O Canada! Terre de nos aïeux,
Ton front est ceint de fleurons glorieux!
Car ton bras sait porter l'épée,
Il sait porter la croix!

O Canada! Our home and native land!
True patriot love in all thy sons command.
With glowing hearts we see thee rise,
The True North strong and free!

'O Canada' (1908 song); French words written in 1880 by Adolphe-Basile Routhier (1839–1920)

Victor Weisskopf 1908–2002

American physicist

10 It was absolutely marvellous working for Pauli. You could ask him anything. There was no worry that he would think a particular question was stupid, since he thought *all* questions were stupid.

in *American Journal of Physics* 1977

Johnny Weissmuller *see* Misquotations

548:9

Chaim Weizmann 1874–1952

Russian-born Israeli statesman, President 1949–52

11 Something had been done for us which, after two thousand years of hope and yearning, would at last give us a resting-place in this terrible world.

of the Balfour declaration
speech in Jerusalem, 25 November 1936; see **BALFOUR** 53:13

Thomas Earle Welby 1881–1933

British writer

12 'Turbot, Sir,' said the waiter, placing before me two fishbones, two eyeballs, and a bit of black mackintosh.

The Dinner Knell (1932) 'Birmingham or Crewe?'

Joseph Welch 1890–1960

American lawyer

13 Until this moment, Senator, I think I never really gauged your cruelty or your recklessness . . . Have you no sense of decency, sir? At long last, have you left no sense of decency?

to Joseph MCCARTHY, 9 June 1954, defending the US Army against allegations of harbouring subversive activities; the televised confrontation was deeply damaging to McCarthy
in *American National Biography* (online edition) 'Joseph McCarthy'

Fay Weldon 1931–

British novelist and scriptwriter. See also **ADVERTISING SLOGANS** 7:26

14 There seems to be a general overall pattern in most lives, that nothing happens, and nothing happens, and then all of a sudden everything happens.

Auto da Fay (2002)

15 She was the kind of wife who looks out of her front door in the morning and, if it's raining, apologizes.

Heart of the Country (1987)

16 The life and loves of a she-devil.

title of novel (1984)

17 Guilt is to motherhood as grapes are to wine.

She May Not Leave (2005)

18 Every time you open your wardrobe, you look at your clothes and you wonder what you are going to wear. What you are really saying is 'Who am I going to be today?'

in *New Yorker* 26 June 1995

Orson Welles 1915–85

American actor and film director. See also **FILM LINES** 328:20, **FILM LINES** 329:10

1 This is the biggest electric train a boy ever had!
  of the RKO studios
    Roy Fowler *Orson Welles* (1946) ch. 6

2 I hate television. I hate it as much as peanuts. But I can't stop eating peanuts.
    in *New York Herald Tribune* 12 October 1956

3 There are only two emotions in a plane: boredom and terror.
    interview to celebrate his 70th birthday, in *The Times* 6 May 1985

Duke of Wellington 1769–1852

British soldier and Tory statesman, Prime Minister 1828–30 and 1834. On Wellington: see **BAGEHOT** 50:14, **BYRON** 185:5, **TENNYSON** 798:20

4 As Lord Chesterfield said of the generals of his day, 'I only hope that when the enemy reads the list of their names, he trembles as I do.'
  usually quoted as, 'I don't know what effect these men will have upon the enemy, but, by God, they frighten me'
    letter, 29 August 1810, in *Supplementary Despatches . . .* (1860) vol. 6

5 Up Guards and at them!
    letter from an officer in the Guards, 22 June 1815, in *The Battle of Waterloo* by a Near Observer [J. Booth] (1815); later denied by Wellington

6 Hard pounding this, gentlemen; let's see who will pound longest.
  at the Battle of Waterloo, 1815
    Sir Walter Scott *Paul's Letters* (1816) Letter 8

7 Next to a battle lost, the greatest misery is a battle gained.
    in *Diary of Frances, Lady Shelley 1787–1817* (ed. R. Edgcumbe, 1912) vol. 1, ch. 9; Wellington made a similar remark many times

8 Publish and be damned.
  replying to a blackmail threat prior to the publication of Harriette Wilson's Memoirs (1825); see WILSON 859:11
    attributed; Elizabeth Longford *Wellington: The Years of the Sword* (1969) ch. 10

9 I used to say of him that his presence on the field made the difference of forty thousand men.
  of NAPOLEON I
    Philip Henry Stanhope *Notes of Conversations with the Duke of Wellington* (1888) 2 November 1831

10 Ours is composed of the scum of the earth—the mere scum of the earth.
  of the army
    Philip Henry Stanhope *Notes of Conversations with the Duke of Wellington* (1888) 4 November 1831

11 I never saw so many shocking bad hats in my life.
  on seeing the first Reformed Parliament, 1832
    William Fraser *Words on Wellington* (1889)

12 All the business of war, and indeed all the business of life, is to endeavour to find out what you don't know by what you do; that's what I called 'guessing what was at the other side of the hill'.
    in *The Croker Papers* (1885) vol. 3 ch. 28

13 The battle of Waterloo was won on the playing fields of Eton.
    oral tradition, but probably apocryphal; the earliest reference is a remark said to have been made when revisiting Eton, 'It is here that the battle of Waterloo was won!' C. F. R. Montalembert *De l'avenir politique de l'Angleterre* (1856) ch. 10; see **ORWELL** 587:8

14 A conquerer, like a cannonball, must go on; if he rebounds, his career is over.
    attributed; Alistair Horne *How Far from Austerlitz?* (1996)

15 An extraordinary affair. I gave them their orders and they wanted to stay and discuss them.
  of his first Cabinet meeting as Prime Minister
    attributed; Peter Hennessy *Whitehall* (1990)

16 If you believe that, you'll believe anything.
  to a gentleman who had accosted him in the street saying, 'Mr Jones, I believe?'; George Jones RA (1786–1869), painter of military subjects, bore a striking resemblance to Wellington
    Elizabeth Longford *Pillar of State* (1972) ch. 10

17 You must build your House of Parliament upon the river . . . the populace cannot exact their demands by sitting down round you.
    William Fraser *Words on Wellington* (1889)

H. G. Wells 1866–1946

English novelist. See also **EPITAPHS** 317:10

18 It is leviathan retrieving pebbles. It is a magnificent but painful hippopotamus resolved at any cost, even at the cost of its dignity, upon picking up a pea which has got into a corner of its den.
  of Henry JAMES
    Boon (1915) ch. 4

19 He had read Shakespeare and found him weak in chemistry.
    Complete Short Stories (1927) 'Lord of the Dynamos'

20 'Sesquippledan,' he would say. 'Sesquippledan verboojuice.'
    The History of Mr Polly (1909) ch. 1, pt. 5; see **HORACE** 409:3

21 I was thinking jest what a Rum Go everything is.
    Kipps (1905) bk. 3, ch. 3, pt. 8

22 The Social Contract is nothing more or less than a vast conspiracy of human beings to lie to and humbug themselves and one another for the general Good. Lies are the mortar that bind the savage individual man into the social masonry.
    Love and Mr Lewisham (1900) ch. 23

23 Human history becomes more and more a race between education and catastrophe.
    The Outline of History (1920) vol. 2, ch. 41, pt. 4

24 The shape of things to come.
    title of book (1933)

25 The war that will end war.
    title of book (1914); see **LLOYD GEORGE** 496:15

1 We fight not to destroy a nation, but a nest of evil ideas . . . Our business is to kill ideas. The ultimate purpose of this war is propaganda, the destruction of certain beliefs, and the creation of others.
  The War That Will End War (1914) ch. 11

2 Moral indignation is jealousy with a halo.
  The Wife of Sir Isaac Harman (1914) ch. 9, sect. 2

3 The whole human memory can be, and probably in a short time will be, made accessible to every individual.
  The World Brain (1938) 'The Idea of a Permanent World Encyclopaedia'

Arnold Wesker 1932–

English dramatist

4 Chips with every damn thing. You breed babies and you eat chips with everything.
  Chips with Everything (1962) act 1, sc. 2

5 The Khomeini cry for the execution of Rushdie is an infantile cry. From the beginning of time we have seen that. To murder the thinker does not murder the thought.
  in *Weekend Guardian* 3 June 1989; see **KHOMEINI** 462:7

Charles Wesley 1707–88

English Methodist preacher and hymn-writer

6 Amazing love! How can it be
  That thou, my God, shouldst die for me?
  'And can it be' (1738 hymn)

7 My chains fell off, my heart was free,
  I rose, went forth, and followed thee.
  'And can it be' (1738 hymn)

8 Hark! how all the welkin rings,
  Glory to the King of kings.
  Peace on earth and mercy mild,
  God and sinners reconciled.
  Hymns and Sacred Poems (1739) 'Hymn for Christmas'; the first two lines were altered to: 'Hark! the herald-angels sing / Glory to the new born king' in George Whitefield *Hymns for Social Worship* (1753)

9 Hail, the heaven-born Prince of Peace!
  Hail, the Sun of Righteousness!
  Hymns and Sacred Poems (1739) 'Hymn for Christmas'; see **BIBLE** 96:19

10 O for a thousand tongues to sing.
  Hymns and Sacred Poems (1740) 'For the Anniversary Day of one's Conversion'

11 Jesu, lover of my soul,
  Let me to thy bosom fly.
  Hymns and Sacred Poems (1740) 'In Temptation'

12 Gentle Jesus, meek and mild,
  Look upon a little child;
  Pity my simplicity,
  Suffer me to come to thee.
  Hymns and Sacred Poems (1742) 'Gentle Jesus, Meek and Mild'

13 Wrestling, I will not let thee go,
  Till I thy name, thy nature know.
  Hymns and Sacred Poems (1742) 'Wrestling Jacob'

14 Forth in thy name, O Lord, I go,
  My daily labour to pursue;
  Thee, only thee, resolved to know,
  In all I think or speak or do.
  Hymns and Sacred Poems (1749) 'Forth in thy name, O Lord, I go'

15 Soldiers of Christ, arise,
  And put your armour on.
  Hymns and Sacred Poems (1749) 'The Whole Armour of God'

16 Rejoice, the Lord is King!
  Your Lord and King adore;
  Mortals, give thanks and sing,
  And triumph evermore:
  Lift up your heart, lift up your voice;
  Rejoice, again, I say rejoice.
  Hymns for our Lord's Resurrection (1746) 'Rejoice, the Lord is King!'

17 Love divine, all loves excelling,
  Joy of heav'n, to earth come down,
  Fix in us thy humble dwelling,
  All thy faithful mercies crown.
  Jesu, thou art all compassion,
  Pure unbounded love thou art;
  Visit us with thy salvation,
  Enter every trembling heart.
  Hymns for those that seek . . . Redemption (1747) 'Love divine', based on Dryden; see **DRYDEN** 296:7

18 Lo! He comes with clouds descending,
  Once for favoured sinners slain;
  Thousand thousand Saints attending
  Swell the triumph of His train.
  Hymns of Intercession for all Mankind (1758) 'Lo! He comes'

John Wesley 1703–91

English preacher; founder of Methodism. On Wesley: see JOHNSON 442:12

19 Thou hidden love of God, whose height,
  Whose depth unfathomed no man knows,
  I see from far thy beauteous light,
  Inly I sigh for thy repose.
  A Collection of Psalms and Hymns (1738) 'Divine Love' (a translation of G. Tersteegen's 'Verborgen Gottesliebe du', 1729)

20 The Gospel of Christ knows of no religion but social; no holiness but social holiness.
  Hymns and Sacred Poems (1739) Preface

21 I design plain truth for plain people.
  Sermons on Several Occasions (1746)

22 Slovenliness is no part of religion; that neither this, nor any text of Scripture, condemns neatness of apparel. Certainly this is a duty, not a sin. 'Cleanliness is, indeed, next to godliness.'
  Sermons on Several Occasions (1788) Sermon 88; see **PROVERBS** 629:7

23 No circumstances can make it necessary for a man to burst in sunder all the ties of humanity.
  Thoughts upon Slavery (1774) in *Works* (Centenary ed.) vol. 11, p. 72

24 I went to America to convert the Indians; but oh, who shall convert me?
  Journal (ed. N. Curnock) 24 January 1738

1 I felt my heart strangely warmed. I felt I did trust in Christ, Christ alone for salvation; and an assurance was given me that He had taken away *my* sins, even *mine*, and saved *me* from the law of sin and death.
on his conversion
Journal (ed. N. Curnock) 24 May 1738

2 I look upon all the world as my parish.
Journal (ed. N. Curnock) 11 June 1739

3 Either I or you mistake the whole meaning of Christianity from the beginning to the end.
letter to John Taylor, who rejected the accepted orthodoxy on the subject of original sin
Journal (ed. N. Curnock) 3 July 1759

4 I let you loose, George, on the great continent of America. Publish your message in the open face of the sun, and do all the good you can.
letter to a preacher, George Shadford, March 1773 in Letters (ed. J. Telford, 1931) vol. 6

5 Though I am always in haste, I am never in a hurry.
letter to Miss March, 10 December 1777, in Letters (ed. J. Telford, 1931) vol. 6

6 I have this day lived fourscore years . . . God grant that I may never live to be useless!
Journal (ed. N. Curnock) 28 June 1783

7 Time has shaken me by the hand and death is not far behind.
letter to Ezekiel Cooper, 1 February 1791, in Letters (ed. J. Telford, 1931) vol. 8; see **FORD** 337:8

8 Men may call me a knave or a fool, a rascal, a scoundrel, and I am content; but they shall never by my consent call me a Bishop!
Betty M. Jarboe *Wesley Quotations* (1990)

Mary Wesley 1912–2002
English novelist

9 When people discussed tonics, pick-me-ups after a severe illness, she kept to herself the prescription of a quick dip in bed with someone you liked but were not in love with. A shock of sexual astonishment which could make you feel astonishingly well and high spirited.
Not That Sort of Girl (1987)

Samuel Wesley 1662–1735
English clergyman and poet

10 Style is the dress of thought; a modest dress, Neat, but not gaudy, will true critics please.
'An Epistle to a Friend concerning Poetry' (1700); see **JOHNSON** 436:19, **POPE** 616:3, **SHAKESPEARE** 700:4

Mae West 1892–1980
American film actress. See also FILM LINES 328:24

11 I always say, keep a diary and some day it'll keep you.
Every Day's a Holiday (1937 film)

12 Beulah, peel me a grape.
I'm No Angel (1933 film)

13 It's not the men in my life that counts—it's the life in my men.
I'm No Angel (1933 film)

14 'Goodness, what beautiful diamonds!'
'Goodness had nothing to do with it.'
Night After Night (1932 film)

15 Why don't you come up sometime, and see me?
She Done Him Wrong (1933 film); see **MISQUOTATIONS** 549:6

16 Is that a gun in your pocket, or are you just glad to see me?
usually quoted as 'Is that a pistol in your pocket . . . '
Joseph Weintraub *Peel Me a Grape* (1975)

17 I used to be Snow White . . . but I drifted.
Joseph Weintraub *Peel Me a Grape* (1975)

Rebecca West (Cicily Isabel Fairfield)
1892–1983
English novelist and journalist

18 Were I to . . . take a [Yugoslav] peasant by the shoulders and whisper to him, 'In your lifetime, have you known peace?' wait for his answer, shake his shoulders and transform him into his father, and ask him the same question, and transform him in turn into his father, I would never hear the word 'yes' if I carried my questioning of the dead back for a thousand years.
Black Lamb and Grey Falcon (1940)

19 It is as if a fountain of negativism plays in the centre of Europe, killing all living things within the reach of its spray.
Black Lamb and Grey Falcon (1940) epilogue

20 Having watched the form of our traitors for a number of years, I cannot think that espionage can be recommended as a technique for building an impressive civilization. It's a lout's game.
The Meaning of Treason (1982 ed.), introduction

21 The point is that nobody likes having salt rubbed into their wounds, even if it is the salt of the earth.
The Salt of the Earth (1935) ch. 2

22 There is no such thing as conversation. It is an illusion. There are intersecting monologues, that is all.
There is No Conversation (1935) 'The Harsh Voice' sect. 1

23 I myself have never been able to find out precisely what feminism is: I only know that people call me a feminist whenever I express sentiments that differentiate me from a doormat or a prostitute.
in *The Clarion* 14 November 1913

24 Journalism—an ability to meet the challenge of filling the space.
in *New York Herald Tribune* 22 April 1956

1 Whatever happens, never forget that people would rather be led to *perdition* by a man, than to *victory* by a woman.

in conversation in 1979, just before Margaret THATCHER's *first election victory*

in *Sunday Telegraph* 17 January 1988

2 Every other inch a gentleman.

of Michael Arlen; the phrase is also attributed to Arlen himself

Victoria Glendinning *Rebecca West* (1987) pt. 3, ch. 5

William C. Westmoreland 1914–

American general

3 Vietnam was the first war ever fought without censorship. Without censorship, things can get terribly confused in the public mind.

attributed, 1982

John Fane, Lord Westmorland

1759–1841

4 *Merit*, indeed! . . . We are come to a pretty pass if they talk of *merit* for a bishopric.

noted in Lady Salisbury's diary, 9 December 1835; C. Oman *The Gascoyne Heiress* (1968) pt. 5

R. P. Weston 1878–1936 *and* Bert Lee

1880–1947

English songwriters

5 Good-bye-ee!—Good-bye-ee!
Wipe the tear, baby dear, from your eye-ee.
Tho' it's hard to part, I know,
I'll be tickled to death to go.
Don't cry-ee—don't sigh-ee!
There's a silver lining in the sky-ee!
Bonsoir, old thing! cheerio! chin-chin!
Nahpoo! Toodle-oo! Good-bye-ee!

'Good-bye-ee!' (c.1915 song)

Charles Wetherell 1770–1846

English lawyer and politician

6 Then there is my noble and biographical friend who has added a new terror to death.

of Lord Campbell

Lord St Leonards *Misrepresentations in Campbell's Lives of Lyndhurst and Brougham* (1869); see ARBUTHNOT 25:18, LYNDHURST 506:1

Adelheid Wette 1858–1916

German librettist; sister of Engelbert Humperdinck

7 When at night I go to sleep,
Fourteen angels watch do keep.
Two stand here beside me,
Two stand there to guide me . . .
Two more light the path to heaven!

Hansel and Gretel (1893); music by Engelbert Humperdinck

Edith Wharton 1862–1937

American novelist

8 An unalterable and unquestioned law of the musical world required that the German text of French operas sung by Swedish artists should be translated into Italian for the clearer understanding of English-speaking audiences.

The Age of Innocence (1920) bk. 1, ch. 1

9 My last page is always latent in my first; but the intervening windings of the way become clear only as I write.

A Backward Glance (1934)

10 There's only one way of being comfortable, and that is to stop running round after happiness. If you make up your mind not to be happy there's no reason why you shouldn't have a fairly good time.

often quoted as 'If only we'd stop trying to be happy we could have a pretty good time'

The Hermit and the Wild Woman and Other Stories (1908) 'The Last Asset'

11 Mrs Ballinger is one of the ladies who pursue Culture in bands, as though it were dangerous to meet it alone.

Xingu and Other Stories (1916) 'Xingu'

Thomas, Lord Wharton 1648–1715

English politician

12 Ara! but why does King James stay behind?
Lilli burlero bullen a la
Ho! by my shoul 'tis a Protestant wind.

'A New Song' (written 1687)

13 I sang a king out of three kingdoms.

said to have been Wharton's boast after 'A New Song' became a propaganda weapon against James II

in *Dictionary of National Biography* (1917–)

Richard Whately 1787–1863

English philosopher and theologian; Archbishop of Dublin from 1831

14 Preach not because you have to say something, but because you have something to say.

Apophthegms (1854)

15 Happiness is no laughing matter.

Apophthegms (1854)

16 It is a folly to expect men to do all that they may reasonably be expected to do.

Apophthegms (1854)

17 Honesty is the best policy; but he who is governed by that maxim is not an honest man.

Apophthegms (1854)

18 It is not that pearls fetch a high price *because* men have dived for them; but on the contrary, men dive for them because they fetch a high price.

Introductory Lectures on Political Economy (1832) p. 253

19 'Never forget, gentlemen,' he [Whately] said, to his astonished hearers, as he held up a copy of

the 'Authorized Version' of the Bible, 'never forget that this is *not* the Bible,' then, after a moment's pause, he continued, 'This, gentlemen, is only a *translation* of the Bible.'
> to a meeting of his diocesan clergy, in H. Solly *These Eighty Years* (1893) vol. 2, ch. 2

Phillis Wheatley *c.*1753–84
American poet

1 'Twas mercy brought me from my pagan land,
   Taught my benighted soul to understand
   That there's a God, that there's a Saviour too:
   Once I redemption neither sought nor knew.
   Some view our sable race with scornful eye,
   'Their colour is a diabolic dye.'
   Remember, Christians, Negroes black as Cain
   May be refined, and join th' angelic train.
   'On Being Brought from Africa to America' (1773)

William Whewell 1794–1866
English philosopher and scientist. On Whewell: see **SMITH** 758:28

2 Nature, so far as it is the object of scientific research, is a collection of facts governed by *laws*: our knowledge of nature is our knowledge of laws.
   Astronomy and General Physics considered with reference to Natural Theology (1834) ch. 1

3 Hence no force however great can stretch a cord however fine into an horizontal line which is accurately straight: there will always be a bending downwards.
   often cited as an example of accidental metre and rhyme, and changed in later editions
   Elementary Treatise on Mechanics (1819) ch. 4, problem 2

4 Man is the interpreter of nature, science the right interpretation.
   Philosophy of the Inductive Sciences (1840) Aphorism 17; see **BACON** 48:29

James McNeill Whistler 1834–1903
American-born painter. On Whistler: see **RUSKIN** 673:6

5 I am not arguing with you—I am telling you.
   The Gentle Art of Making Enemies (1890)

6 Art is upon the Town!
   Mr Whistler's 'Ten O'Clock' (1885) p. 7

7 Listen! There never was an artistic period. There never was an Art-loving nation.
   Mr Whistler's 'Ten O'Clock' (1885)

8 Nature is usually wrong.
   Mr Whistler's 'Ten O'Clock' (1885)

9 I maintain that two and two would continue to make four, in spite of the whine of the amateur for three, or the cry of the critic for five.
   Whistler v. Ruskin. Art and Art Critics (1878)

10 No, I ask it for the knowledge of a lifetime.
   in his case against **RUSKIN**, *replying to the question: 'For two days' labour, you ask two hundred guineas?'*
   D. C. Seitz *Whistler Stories* (1913)

11 OSCAR WILDE: How I wish I had said that.
   WHISTLER: You will, Oscar, you will.
   R. Ellman *Oscar Wilde* (1987) pt. 2, ch. 5

12 Yes madam, Nature is creeping up.
   to a lady who had been reminded of his work by an 'exquisite haze in the atmosphere'
   D. C. Seitz *Whistler Stories* (1913)

E. B. White 1899–1985
American humorist. See also **CARTOON CAPTIONS** 205:10

13 Commuter—one who spends his life
   In riding to and from his wife;
   A man who shaves and takes a train,
   And then rides back to shave again.
   'The Commuter' (1982)

14 Democracy is the recurrent suspicion that more than half of the people are right more than half of the time.
   in *New Yorker* 3 July 1944

Gilbert White 1720–93
English clergyman and naturalist

15 When I hear now and then of an abandoned mother that destroys her offspring, I am not so much amazed; since reason perverted, and the bad passions let loose, are capable of any enormity.
   The Natural History and Antiquities of Selborne (1789) letter 26 March 1773

H. Kirke White 1785–1806
English poet

16 Oft in danger, oft in woe,
   Onward, Christians, onward go.
   'Oft in danger, oft in woe' (1812 hymn)

Patrick White 1912–90
Australian novelist

17 Words are not what make you see.
   The Solid Mandala (1966) ch. 2

18 Conversation is imperative if gaps are to be filled, and old age, it is the last gap but one.
   The Tree of Man (1955) ch. 22

19 So that, in the end, there was no end.
   The Tree of Man (1955), closing words

20 In all directions stretched the great Australian Emptiness, in which the mind is the least of possessions.
   The Vital Decade (1968) 'The Prodigal Son'

21 The mystery of life is not solved by success, which is an end in itself, but in failure, in perpetual struggle, in becoming.
   Voss (1957) ch. 10

T. H. White 1906–64
English novelist

22 Everything not forbidden is compulsory.
   The Sword in the Stone (1938) ch. 13

Theodore H. White 1915–86
American writer and journalist

1 America is a nation created by all the hopeful wanderers of Europe, not out of geography and genetics, but out of purpose.
The Making of the President (1960)

2 The flood of money that gushes into politics today is a pollution of democracy.
in *Time* 19 November 1984

Alfred North Whitehead 1861–1947
English philosopher and mathematician

3 Life is an offensive, directed against the repetitious mechanism of the Universe.
Adventures of Ideas (1933) pt. 1, ch. 5

4 It is more important that a proposition be interesting than that it be true. This statement is almost a tautology. For the energy of operation of a proposition in an occasion of experience is its interest, and is its importance. But of course a true proposition is more apt to be interesting than a false one.
Adventures of Ideas (1933) pt. 4, ch. 16

5 The guiding motto in the life of every natural philosopher should be, Seek simplicity and distrust it.
The Concept of Nature (1920) ch. 7

6 There are no whole truths; all truths are half-truths. It is trying to treat them as whole truths that plays the devil.
Dialogues (1954) prologue

7 *Ideas won't keep.* Something must be done about them.
Dialogues (1954) 28 April 1938

8 Intelligence is quickness to apprehend as distinct from ability, which is capacity to act wisely on the thing apprehended.
Dialogues (1954) 15 December 1939

9 What is morality in any given time or place? It is what the majority then and there happen to like, and immorality is what they dislike.
Dialogues (1954) 30 August 1941

10 Art is the imposing of a pattern on experience, and our aesthetic enjoyment is recognition of the pattern.
Dialogues (1954) 10 June 1943

11 Civilization advances by extending the number of important operations which we can perform without thinking about them.
Introduction to Mathematics (1911) ch. 5

12 The safest general characterization of the European philosophical tradition is that it consists of a series of footnotes to Plato.
Process and Reality (1929) pt. 2, ch. 1

13 Since a babe was born in a manger, it may be doubted whether so great a thing has happened with so little stir.
on the scientific revolution in the sixteenth century
Science and the Modern World (1925) ch. 1

14 The symbolic elements in life have a tendency to run wild, like the vegetation in a tropical forest . . . A continuous process of pruning, and of adaptation to a future ever requiring new forms of expression, is a necessary function in every society.
Symbolism: Its Meaning and Effect (1928) ch. 3

Katharine Whitehorn 1928–
English journalist

15 An office party is not, as is sometimes supposed, the Managing Director's chance to kiss the tea-girl. It is the tea-girl's chance to kiss the Managing Director.
Roundabout (1962) 'The Office Party'

George Whiting
American songwriter

16 My blue heaven.
title of song (1927)

17 When you're all dressed up and have no place to go.
title of song (1912)

William Whiting 1825–78
English teacher; master of the Quiristers of Winchester College from 1842

18 Eternal Father, strong to save,
Whose arm doth bind the restless wave,
Who bidd'st the mighty ocean deep
Its own appointed limits keep:
O hear us when we cry to thee,
For those in peril on the sea.
'Eternal Father, Strong to Save' (1869 hymn)

Gough Whitlam 1916–
Australian Labor statesman, Prime Minister 1972–5

19 *the Governor-General, Sir John Kerr, had dismissed the Labor government headed by Gough Whitlam in November 1975:*
Well may he say 'God Save the Queen'. But after this nothing will save the Governor-General . . . Maintain your rage and your enthusiasm through the campaign for the election now to be held and until polling day.
speech in Canberra, 11 November 1975

Walt Whitman 1819–92
American poet. On Whitman: see **GINSBERG** 359:2

20 I dreamed in a dream I saw a city invincible to the attacks of the whole of the rest of the earth,
I dreamed that was the new city of Friends.
'I dreamed in a dream' (1867)

1 I sing the body electric.
  title of poem (1855)

2 O Captain! my Captain! our fearful trip is done,
  The ship has weathered every rack, the prize we
    sought is won,
  The port is near, the bells I hear, the people all
    exulting.
  'O Captain! My Captain!' (1871)

3 The ship is anchored safe and sound, its voyage
    closed and done.
  From fearful trip the victor ship comes in with
    object won;
  Exult O shores, and ring O bells! But I with
    mournful tread
  Walk the deck my Captain lies, Fallen cold and
    dead.
  'O Captain! My Captain!' (1871)

4 Out of the cradle endlessly rocking,
  Out of the mocking-bird's throat, the musical
    shuttle . . .
  A reminiscence sing.
  'Out of the cradle endlessly rocking' (1881)

5 Have you your pistols? have you your sharp-
    edged axes?
  Pioneers! O pioneers!
  'Pioneers! O Pioneers!' (1881)

6 Camerado, this is no book,
  Who touches this touches a man.
  'So Long!' (1881)

7 I celebrate myself, and sing myself.
  'Song of Myself' (written 1855) pt. 1

8 Urge and urge and urge,
  Always the procreant urge of the world.
  'Song of Myself' (written 1855) pt. 3

9 Has any one supposed it lucky to be born?
  I hasten to inform him or her, it is just as lucky
    to die and I know it.
  'Song of Myself' (written 1855) pt. 7

10 I believe a leaf of grass is no less than the
    journey-work of the stars,
  And the pismire is equally perfect, and a grain of
    sand, and the egg of the wren,
  And the tree toad is a chef-d'oeuvre for the
    highest,
  And the running blackberry would adorn the
    parlours of heaven.
  'Song of Myself' (written 1855) pt. 31

11 I think I could turn and live with animals, they
    are so placid and self-contained,
  I stand and look at them long and long.
  They do not sweat and whine about their
    condition,
  They do not lie awake in the dark and weep for
    their sins,
  They do not make me sick discussing their duty
    to God,
  Not one is dissatisfied, not one is demented with
    the mania of owning things,
  Not one kneels to another, nor to his kind that
    lived thousands of years ago,

Not one is respectable or unhappy over the
  whole earth.
  'Song of Myself' (written 1855) pt. 32

12 Behold, I do not give lectures or a little charity,
  When I give I give myself.
  'Song of Myself' (written 1855) pt. 40

13 My rendezvous is appointed, it is certain,
  The Lord will be there and wait till I come on
    perfect terms.
  'Song of Myself' (written 1855) pt. 45

14 Do I contradict myself?
  Very well then I contradict myself,
  (I am large, I contain multitudes.)
  'Song of Myself' (written 1855) pt. 51

15 I sound my barbaric yawp over the roofs of the
    world.
  'Song of Myself' (written 1855) pt. 52

16 Where the populace rise at once against the
    never-ending audacity of elected persons.
  'Song of the Broad Axe' (1881) pt. 5, l. 12

17 Afoot and light-hearted I take to the open road,
  Healthy, free, the world before me,
  The long brown path before me leading
    wherever I choose.
  'Song of the Open Road' (1871) pt. 1, l. 1

18 The earth does not argue,
  Is not pathetic, has no arrangements.
  'A Song of the Rolling Earth' (1881) pt. 1

19 This dust was once the man,
  Gentle, plain, just and resolute, under whose
    cautious hand,
  Against the foulest crime in history known in
    any land or age,
  Was saved the Union of these States.
  'This dust was once the man' (1881)

20 When lilacs last in the dooryard bloomed,
  And the great star early drooped in the western
    sky in the night,
  I mourned, and yet shall mourn with ever-
    returning spring.
  'When lilacs last in the dooryard bloomed' (1881) st. 1

21 The United States themselves are essentially the
  greatest poem.
  Leaves of Grass (1855) preface

Isabella Whitney fl. 1573
English poet

22 Had I a husband or a house, and all that longs
    thereto
  Myself could frame about to rouse as other
    women do,
  But til some household cares me tie
  My books and pen I will apply.
  A Sweet Nosegay (1573)

John Greenleaf Whittier 1807–92

American poet

1 'Shoot, if you must, this old grey head,
But spare your country's flag,' she said.
'Barbara Frietchie' (1863)

2 Dear Lord and Father of mankind,
Forgive our foolish ways!
Re-clothe us in our rightful mind,
In purer lives thy service find,
In deeper reverence praise.
'The Brewing of Soma' (1872)

3 For of all sad words of tongue or pen,
The saddest are these: 'It might have been!'
'Maud Muller' (1854); see **HARTE** 383:16

4 O brother man! fold to thy heart thy brother.
'Worship' (1848)

Robert Whittington c.1480–1553?

English grammarian

5 As time requireth, a man of marvellous mirth
and pastimes, and sometime of as sad gravity, as
who say: a man for all seasons.
of Sir Thomas **MORE**; see **ERASMUS** 316:19
Vulgaria (1521) pt. 2 'De constructione nominum'

Charlotte Whitton 1896–1975

Canadian writer and politician

6 Whatever women do they must do twice as well
as men to be thought half as good.
in Canada Month June 1963

Cornelius Whur

7 On firmer ties his joys depend
Who has a polished female friend . . .
While lasting joys the man attend
Who has a faithful female friend.
'The Female Friend' (1837)

William H. Whyte 1917–99

American writer

8 This book is about the organization man . . . I
can think of no other way to describe the
people I am talking about. They are not the
workers, nor are they the white-collar people in
the usual, clerk sense of the word. These people
only work for the Organization. The ones I am
talking about *belong* to it as well.
The Organization Man (1956) ch. 1

George John Whyte-Melville 1821–78

Scottish-born novelist, killed in the hunting-field

9 But I freely admit that the best of my fun
I owe it to horse and hound.
'The Good Grey Mare' (1933)

Ann Widdecombe 1947–

British Conservative politician

10 He has something of the night in him.
of the Conservative politician Michael Howard as a
contender for the Party leadership in 1997
in Sunday Times 11 May 1997 (electronic edition)

Elie Wiesel 1928–

Romanian-born American writer and Nobel Prize winner;
Auschwitz survivor

11 The opposite of love is not hate, it's indifference.
The opposite of art is not ugliness, it's
indifference. The opposite of faith is not heresy,
it's indifference. And the opposite of life is not
death, it's indifference.
in U.S. News and World Report 27 October 1986

12 Take sides. Neutrality helps the oppressor, never
the victim. Silence encourages the tormentor,
never the tormented.
accepting the Nobel Peace Prize
in New York Times 11 December 1986

13 God of forgiveness, do not forgive those
murderers of Jewish children here.
at Auschwitz
in The Times 27 January 1995

Michael Wigglesworth 1631–1705

English-born American puritan preacher and writer

14 By the power of eloquence old truth receives a
new habit; though its essence be the same, yet
its visage is so altered that it may currently pass
and be accepted as a novelty.
oration, 1650; Perry Miller The American Puritans (1956)

Samuel Wilberforce 1805–73

English prelate. On Wilberforce: see **HUXLEY** 423:16

15 If I were a cassowary
On the plains of Timbuctoo,
I would eat a missionary,
Cassock, band, and hymn-book too.
impromptu verse (attributed)

16 Was it through his grandfather or his
grandmother that he claimed his descent from a
monkey?
addressed to T. H. Huxley at a meeting of the British
Association for the Advancement of Science, Oxford, June
1860; in Macmillan's Magazine vol. 78 (October 1898); see
HUXLEY 423:16

William Wilberforce 1759–1833

British politician, philanthropist, and abolitionist

17 As soon as ever I had arrived thus far in my
investigation of the slave trade, I confess to you,
so enormous, so dreadful, so irremediable did its
wickedness appear that my own mind was
completely made up for the abolition.
speech, 12 May 1789; in W. Cobbett et al. (eds.) The
Parliamentary History of England (1806–20) vol. 28

Richard Wilbur 1921–

American poet

1 Spare us all word of the weapons, their force
    and range,
  The long numbers that rocket the mind.
  'Advice to a Prophet' (1961)

2 There is a poignancy in all things clear,
  In the stare of the deer, in the ring of a
    hammer in the morning.
  'Clearness' (1950)

3 We milk the cow of the world, and as we do
  We whisper in her ear, 'You are not true.'
  'Epistemology' (1950)

4 Mind in its purest play is like some bat
  That beats about in caverns all alone,
  Contriving by a kind of senseless wit
  Not to conclude against a wall of stone.
  'Mind' (1956)

5 The good grey guardians of art
  Patrol the halls on spongy shoes,
  Impartially protective, though
  Perhaps suspicious of Toulouse.
  'Museum Piece' (1950)

6 Love is the greatest mercy,
  A volley of the sun
  That lashes all with shade,
  That the first day be mended.
  'Someone Talking to Himself' (1961)

7 The suburbs deepen in their sleep of death.
  'To an American Poet Just Dead' (1950)

8 Limitation makes for power: the strength of the
  genie comes of his being confined in a bottle.
  'The Genie in the Bottle' in John Ciardi (ed.) *Mid-Century
  American Poets* (1950)

Ella Wheeler Wilcox 1855–1919

American poet

9 Laugh and the world laughs with you;
  Weep, and you weep alone;
  For the sad old earth must borrow its mirth,
  But has trouble enough of its own.
  'Solitude'

10 The two kinds of people on earth I mean
   Are the people who lift, and the people who
     lean.
   'Which Are You?' (1904)

11 So many gods, so many creeds,
   So many paths that wind and wind,
   While just the art of being kind
   Is all the sad world needs.
   'The World's Need'

Robert Wild 1615–79

English nonconformist minister and poet

12 For sudden joys, like griefs, confound at first.
   'Dr Wild's Humble Thanks for His Majesty's Gracious
   Declaration' (1672)

Oscar Wilde 1854–1900

Irish dramatist and poet. On Wilde: see BETJEMAN 75:9,
HOUSMAN 415:4, LEVERSON 491:3, PARKER 596:6, WHISTLER
850:11

13 We have really everything in common with
   America nowadays except, of course, language.
   The Canterville Ghost (1887); see MISQUOTATIONS 547:12

14 Really, if the lower orders don't set us a good
   example, what on earth is the use of them?
   The Importance of Being Earnest (1895) act 1

15 The truth is rarely pure, and never simple.
   The Importance of Being Earnest (1895) act 1

16 I have invented an invaluable permanent invalid
   called Bunbury, in order that I may be able to go
   down into the country whenever I choose.
   The Importance of Being Earnest (1899) act 1

17 In married life three is company and two none.
   The Importance of Being Earnest (1895) act 1

18 Ignorance is like a delicate exotic fruit; touch it
   and the bloom is gone. The whole theory of
   modern education is radically unsound.
   Fortunately, in England, at any rate, education
   produces no effect whatsoever.
   The Importance of Being Earnest (1895) act 1

19 To lose one parent, Mr Worthing, may be
   regarded as a misfortune; to lose both looks like
   carelessness.
   The Importance of Being Earnest (1895) act 1

20 LADY BRACKNELL: A handbag?
   The Importance of Being Earnest (1895) act 1

21 All women become like their mothers. That is
   their tragedy. No man does. That's his.
   The Importance of Being Earnest (1895) act 1; the same words
   occur in dialogue form in *A Woman of No Importance* (1893)
   act 2

22 The good ended happily, and the bad unhappily.
   That is what fiction means.
   The Importance of Being Earnest (1895) act 2; see STOPPARD
   778:2

23 I hope you have not been leading a double life,
   pretending to be wicked and being really good
   all the time. That would be hypocrisy.
   The Importance of Being Earnest (1895) act 2

24 Charity, dear Miss Prism, charity! None of us are
   perfect. I myself am peculiarly susceptible to
   draughts.
   The Importance of Being Earnest (1895) act 2

25 I never travel without my diary. One should
   always have something sensational to read in the
   train.
   The Importance of Being Earnest (1895) act 2

26 CECILY: When I see a spade I call it a spade.
   GWENDOLEN: I am glad to say that I have never
   seen a spade.
   The Importance of Being Earnest (1895) act 2

27 Thirty-five is a very attractive age. London
   society is full of women of the very highest

birth who have, of their own free choice, remained thirty-five for years.

The Importance of Being Earnest (1895) act 3

1 Every great man nowadays has his disciples, and it is always Judas who writes the biography.

Intentions (1891) 'The Critic as Artist' pt. 1

2 Meredith's a prose Browning, and so is Browning.

Intentions (1891) 'The Critic as Artist' pt. 1

3 The one duty we owe to history is to rewrite it.

Intentions (1891) 'The Critic as Artist' pt. 1

4 It is through Art, and through Art only, that we can realise our perfection; through Art, and through Art only, that we can shield ourselves from the sordid perils of actual existence.

Intentions (1891) 'The Critic as Artist' pt. 2

5 All art is immoral.

Intentions (1891) 'The Critic as Artist' pt. 2

6 A little sincerity is a dangerous thing, and a great deal of it is absolutely fatal.

Intentions (1891) 'The Critic as Artist' pt. 2

7 Life imitates Art far more than Art imitates Life.

Intentions (1891) 'The Decay of Lying'

8 Meredith! Who can define him? His style is chaos illuminated by flashes of lightning.

Intentions (1891) 'The Decay of Lying'; Ada Leverson *Letters to the Sphinx* (1930) attributes to Wilde a similar remark about **BROWNING**

9 I can resist everything except temptation.

Lady Windermere's Fan (1892) act 1; see **GRAHAM**

10 Many a woman has a past, but I am told that she has at least a dozen, and that they all fit.

Lady Windermere's Fan (1892) act 1

11 We are all in the gutter, but some of us are looking at the stars.

Lady Windermere's Fan (1892) act 3

12 A man who knows the price of everything and the value of nothing.

definition of a cynic

Lady Windermere's Fan (1892) act 3

13 Experience is the name every one gives to their mistakes.

Lady Windermere's Fan (1892) act 3

14 There is no such thing as a moral or an immoral book. Books are well written, or badly written.

The Picture of Dorian Gray (1891) preface

15 The nineteenth century dislike of Realism is the rage of Caliban seeing his own face in the glass.

The Picture of Dorian Gray (1891) preface

16 The moral life of man forms part of the subject matter of the artist, but the morality of art consists in the perfect use of an imperfect medium.

The Picture of Dorian Gray (1891) preface

17 There is only one thing in the world worse than being talked about, and that is not being talked about.

The Picture of Dorian Gray (1891) ch. 1

18 A man cannot be too careful in the choice of his enemies.

The Picture of Dorian Gray (1891) ch. 1

19 A cigarette is the perfect type of a perfect pleasure. It is exquisite, and it leaves one unsatisfied.

The Picture of Dorian Gray (1891) ch. 6

20 Anybody can be good in the country.

The Picture of Dorian Gray (1891) ch. 19

21 It is better to be beautiful than to be good. But . . . it is better to be good than to be ugly.

The Picture of Dorian Gray (1891) ch. 17

22 A thing is not necessarily true because a man dies for it.

The Portrait of Mr W. H. (1901)

23 MRS ALLONBY: They say, Lady Hunstanton, that when good Americans die they go to Paris.

LADY HUNSTANTON: Indeed? And when bad Americans die, where do they go to?

LORD ILLINGWORTH: Oh, they go to America.

A Woman of No Importance (1893) act 1; see **APPLETON** 25:8

24 The English country gentleman galloping after a fox—the unspeakable in full pursuit of the uneatable.

A Woman of No Importance (1893) act 1

25 One should never trust a woman who tells one her real age. A woman who would tell one that, would tell one anything.

A Woman of No Importance (1893) act 1

26 LORD ILLINGWORTH: The Book of Life begins with a man and a woman in a garden.

MRS ALLONBY: It ends with Revelations.

A Woman of No Importance (1893) act 1

27 Children begin by loving their parents; after a time they judge them; rarely, if ever, do they forgive them.

A Woman of No Importance (1893) act 2

28 GERALD: I suppose society is wonderfully delightful!

LORD ILLINGWORTH: To be in it is merely a bore. But to be out of it simply a tragedy.

A Woman of No Importance (1893) act 3

29 You should study the Peerage, Gerald . . . It is the best thing in fiction the English have ever done.

A Woman of No Importance (1893) act 3

30 He did not wear his scarlet coat,
For blood and wine are red,
And blood and wine were on his hands
When they found him with the dead.

The Ballad of Reading Gaol (1898) pt. 1, st. 1

31 I never saw a man who looked
With such a wistful eye
Upon that little tent of blue
Which prisoners call the sky.

The Ballad of Reading Gaol (1898) pt. 1, st. 3

32 Yet each man kills the thing he loves,
By each let this be heard,

Some do it with a bitter look,
Some with a flattering word.
The coward does it with a kiss,
The brave man with a sword!
The Ballad of Reading Gaol (1898) pt. 1, st. 7

1 The Governor was strong upon
The Regulations Act:
The Doctor said that Death was but
A scientific fact:
And twice a day the Chaplain called,
And left a little tract.
The Ballad of Reading Gaol (1898) pt. 3, st. 3

2 Something was dead in each of us,
And what was dead was Hope.
The Ballad of Reading Gaol (1898) pt. 3, st. 31

3 And the wild regrets, and the bloody sweats,
None knew so well as I:
For he who lives more lives than one
More deaths than one must die.
The Ballad of Reading Gaol (1898) pt. 3, st. 37

4 And alien tears will fill for him
Pity's long-broken urn,
For his mourners will be outcast men,
And outcasts always mourn.
inscribed on Wilde's tomb in Père Lachaise cemetery
The Ballad of Reading Gaol (1898) pt. 4, st. 23

5 How else but through a broken heart
May Lord Christ enter in?
The Ballad of Reading Gaol (1898) pt. 5, st. 14

6 All her bright golden hair
Tarnished with rust,
She that was young and fair
Fallen to dust.
'Requiescat' (1881)

7 Democracy means simply the bludgeoning of
the people by the people for the people.
in *Fortnightly Review* February 1891 'The Soul of Man under
Socialism'; see **LINCOLN** 494:1

8 When I ask for a watercress sandwich, I do not
mean a loaf with a field in the middle of it.
to a waiter
Max Beerbohm, letter to Reggie Turner, 15 April 1893

9 Ah, well, then, I suppose that I shall have to die
beyond my means.
at the mention of a huge fee for a surgical operation
R. H. Sherard *Life of Oscar Wilde* (1906) ch. 18

10 Do you want to know the great drama of my
life? It's that I have put my genius into my life;
all I've put into my works is my talent.
André Gide *Oscar Wilde* (1910) 'In Memoriam'

11 He has fought a good fight and has had to face
every difficulty except popularity.
*of W. E. **HENLEY***
unpublished character sketch, written for Rothenstein's
English Portraits; W. Rothenstein *Men and Memories* vol. 1
(1931) ch. 25

12 Shaw has not an enemy in the world; and none
of his friends like him.
letter from Bernard Shaw to Archibald Henderson, 22
February 1911; Bernard Shaw *Collected Letters, 1911–1925* (1985)

13 I have nothing to declare except my genius.
at the New York Custom House
Frank Harris *Oscar Wilde* (1918)

14 Work is the curse of the drinking classes.
H. Pearson *Life of Oscar Wilde* (1946) ch. 12

15 One of us must go.
of the wallpaper in the room where he was dying
attributed last words, probably apocryphal

Billy Wilder (Samuel Wilder) 1906–2002
American screenwriter and director. See also: **FILM LINES**
329:21, FILM LINES 330:2, FILM LINES 330:6

16 Hindsight is always twenty-twenty.
J. R. Columbo *Wit and Wisdom of the Moviemakers* (1979)
ch. 7

Thornton Wilder 1897–1975
American novelist and dramatist

17 Even memory is not necessary for love. There is
a land of the living and a land of the dead and
the bridge is love, the only survival, the only
meaning.
The Bridge of San Luis Rey (1927), closing words

18 Marriage is a bribe to make a housekeeper think
she's a householder.
The Merchant of Yonkers (1939) act 1

19 Literature is the orchestration of platitudes.
in *Time* 12 January 1953

Robert Wilensky 1951–
American academic

20 We've all heard that a million monkeys banging
on a million typewriters will eventually
reproduce the entire works of Shakespeare.
Now, thanks to the Internet, we know this is not
true.
in *Mail on Sunday* 16 February 1997 'Quotes of the Week'; see
EDDINGTON 302:15

Wilhelm II ('Kaiser Bill') 1859–1941
German monarch, emperor 1888–1918

21 We have . . . fought for our place in the sun and
have won it. It will be my business to see that
we retain this place in the sun unchallenged, so
that the rays of that sun may exert a fructifying
influence upon our foreign trade and traffic.
speech in Hamburg, 18 June 1901; in *The Times* 20 June 1901;
see **BÜLOW** 170:9

John Wilkes 1727–97
English parliamentary reformer

22 EARL OF SANDWICH: 'Pon my soul, Wilkes, I don't
know whether you'll die upon the gallows or of
the pox.
WILKES: That depends, my Lord, whether I first
embrace your Lordship's principles, or your
Lordship's mistresses.
Charles Petrie *The Four Georges* (1935); probably apocryphal

Emma Hart Willard 1787–1870

American pioneer of women's education

1 Rocked in the cradle of the deep.

title of song (1840), inspired by a prospect of the Bristol Channel

William I (William the Conqueror) 1027–87

Norman-born English monarch, Duke of Normandy and from 1066 King of England

2 If the Normans are disciplined under a just and firm rule they are men of great valour, who . . . fight resolutely to overcome all enemies. But without such rule they tear each other to pieces and destroy themselves, for they hanker after rebellion, cherish sedition, and are ready for any treachery.

attributed deathbed speech

Orderic Vitalis *Ecclesiastical History*

William III (William of Orange) 1650–1702

British monarch, King of Great Britain and Ireland from 1688

3 'Do you not see your country is lost?' asked the Duke of Buckingham. 'There is one way never to see it lost' replied William, 'and that is to die in the last ditch.'

Bishop Gilbert Burnet *History of My Own Time* (1838 ed.)

4 Every bullet has its billet.

John Wesley *Journal* (1827) 6 June 1765; see **PROVERBS** 631:14

William of Malmesbury *c.*1090–*c.*1143

English monastic chronicler

5 The English at that time wore short garments, reaching to the mid-knee; they had their hair cropped, their beards shaven, their arms laden with golden bracelets, their skin adorned with punctured designs; they were accustomed to eat until they became surfeited, and to drink till they were sick. These latter qualities they imparted to their conquerors.

De Gestis Regum Anglorum (A History of the Norman Kings)

6 The Normans are a race inured to war, and can hardly live without it, fierce in rushing against the enemy, and, where force fails of success, ready to use stratagem, or corrupt by bribery.

De Gestis Regum Anglorum (A History of the Norman Kings)

Heathcote Williams 1941–

English dramatist and poet

7 Whales play, in an amniotic paradise.
  Their light minds shaped by buoyancy,
    unrestricted by gravity,
  Somersaulting.
  Like angels, or birds;
  Like our own lives, in the womb.
  Whale Nation (1988)

Isaac Williams 1802–65

English clergyman

8 Be thou my Guardian and my Guide.

title of hymn (1842)

Peter Williams

9 Guide me, O thou great Jehovah,
  Pilgrim through this barren land;
  I am weak, but thou art mighty;
  Hold me with thy powerful hand;
  Bread of heaven, bread of heaven,
  Feed me till I want no more.
  first line frequently in the form 'O thou great Redeemer'
    'Praying for Strength' (1771); translation of 'Arglwydd, arwain trwy'r anialwch' (1745) by William Williams (1717–91)

10 When I tread the verge of Jordan,
  Bid my anxious fears subside.
  'Praying for Strength' (1771)

R. J. P. Williams 1926–

English chemist

11 Biology is the search for the chemistry that works.

lecture in Oxford, June 1996

Rowan Williams 1950–

Welsh Anglican clergyman, Archbishop of Canterbury from 2002

12 I can only ask your prayers as, like Augustine shivering in his shoes on the French coast at the prospect of dealing with the savage English, I stand on the shore wondering what lies ahead.

in *The Times* 28 September 2002

13 We have to learn to be human alongside all sorts of others, the ones whose company we don't greatly like.

in *Independent* 1 March 2003

Sarah Williams 1837–68

British writer

14 Though my soul may set in darkness, it will rise in perfect light;
  I have loved the stars too truly to be fearful of the night.
  'The Old Astronomer to His Pupil'

Shirley Williams 1930–

British Labour and Social Democrat politician

15 No test tube can breed love and affection. No frozen packet of semen ever read a story to a sleepy child.

in *Daily Mirror* 2 March 1978

16 The Catholic Church has never really come to terms with women. What I object to is being treated either as Madonnas or Mary Magdalenes.

in *Observer* 22 March 1981

Tennessee Williams (Thomas Lanier Williams) 1911–83
American dramatist

1 We have to distrust each other. It's our only defence against betrayal.
Camino Real (1953) block 10

2 We're all of us guinea pigs in the laboratory of God. Humanity is just a work in progress.
Camino Real (1953) block 12

3 What is the victory of a cat on a hot tin roof?—I wish I knew . . . Just staying on it, I guess, as long as she can.
Cat on a Hot Tin Roof (1955) act 1

4 BRICK: Well, they say nature hates a vacuum, Big Daddy.
BIG DADDY: That's what they say, but sometimes I think that a vacuum is a hell of a lot better than some of the stuff that nature replaces it with.
Cat on a Hot Tin Roof (1955) act 2

5 I didn't go to the moon, I went much further—for time is the longest distance between two places.
The Glass Menagerie (1945)

6 We're all of us sentenced to solitary confinement inside our own skins, for life!
Orpheus Descending (1958) act 2, sc. 1

7 Turn that off! I won't be looked at in this merciless glare!
A Streetcar Named Desire (1947) sc. 1

8 BLANCHE: I don't want realism.
MITCH: Naw, I guess not.
BLANCHE: I'll tell you what I want. Magic!
A Streetcar Named Desire (1947) sc. 9

9 I have always depended on the kindness of strangers.
A Streetcar Named Desire (1947) sc. 11

William Carlos Williams 1883–1963
American poet

10 Minds like beds always made up,
(more stony than a shore)
unwilling or unable.
Paterson (1946) bk. 1, preface

11 so much depends
upon

a red wheel
barrow

glazed with rain
water

beside the white
chickens.
'The Red Wheelbarrow' (1923)

12 Is it any better in Heaven, my friend Ford,
Than you found it in Provence?
'To Ford Madox Ford in Heaven' (1944)

13 No ideas but in things.
Autobiography (1967) ch. 58

Marianne Williamson 1953–
American writer and philanthropist

14 Our deepest fear is not that we are inadequate. Our deepest fear is that we are powerful beyond measure. It is our light, not our darkness, that most frightens us.
A Return to Love (1992) ch. 7

Roy Williamson 1936–90
Scottish folksinger and musician

15 O flower of Scotland, when will we see your like again,
that fought and died for your wee bit hill and glen
and stood against him, proud Edward's army,
and sent him homeward tae think again.
unofficial Scottish Nationalist anthem
'O Flower of Scotland' (1968)

Love Maria Willis (née Whitcomb) 1824–1908
American doctor's wife

16 Father, hear the prayer we offer:
Not for ease that prayer shall be,
But for strength that we may ever
Live our lives courageously.

Not for ever in green pastures
Do we ask our way to be,
But the steep and rugged pathway
May we tread rejoicingly.
'Father, hear the prayer we offer' (1864 hymn)

Wendell Willkie 1892–1944
American lawyer and politician

17 The constitution does not provide for first and second class citizens.
An American Programme (1944) ch. 2

18 Freedom is an indivisible word. If we want to enjoy it, and fight for it, we must be prepared to extend it to everyone, whether they are rich or poor, whether they agree with us or not, no matter what their race or the colour of their skin.
One World (1943) ch. 13

Angus Wilson 1913–91
English novelist and short-story writer

19 Once a Catholic always a Catholic.
The Wrong Set (1949) p. 168

Charles E. Wilson 1890–1961
American industrialist; President of General Motors, 1941–53. See also POLITICAL SLOGANS AND SONGS 612:8

20 For years I thought what was good for our country was good for General Motors and vice versa. The difference did not exist. Our company is too big. It goes with the welfare of the country.

testimony to the Senate Armed Services Committee on his proposed nomination for Secretary of Defence, 15 January 1953, in *New York Times* 24 February 1953

Edward O. Wilson 1929–

American sociobiologist

1 Every human brain is born not as a blank tablet (a *tabula rasa*) waiting to be filled in by experience but as 'an exposed negative waiting to be slipped into developer fluid'.

on the nature v. nurture debate

attributed; Tom Wolfe in *Independent on Sunday* 2 February 1997

Harold Wilson 1916–95

British Labour statesman, Prime Minister 1964–70, 1974–6. On Wilson: see **HOME** 404:5, **JUNOR** 450:5

2 All these financiers, all the little gnomes in Zurich.

speech in the House of Commons 12 November 1956

3 This party is a moral crusade or it is nothing.

speech at the Labour Party Conference, 1 October 1962; in *The Times* 2 October 1962

4 The university of the air.

an early term for the Open University

in *Glasgow Herald* 9 September 1963

5 The Britain that is going to be forged in the white heat of this revolution will be no place for restrictive practices or for outdated methods on either side of industry.

speech at the Labour Party Conference, 1 October 1963; see **MISQUOTATIONS** 549:5

6 A week is a long time in politics.

probably first said at the time of the 1964 sterling crisis

Nigel Rees *Sayings of the Century* (1984); see **CHAMBERLAIN** 214:1

7 From now the pound abroad is worth 14 per cent or so less in terms of other currencies. It does not mean, of course, that the pound here in Britain, in your pocket or purse or in your bank, has been devalued.

often quoted as 'the pound in your pocket'

ministerial broadcast, 19 November 1967, in *The Times* 20 November 1967

8 Get your tanks off my lawn, Hughie.

to the trade union leader Hugh Scanlon, at Chequers in June 1969

Peter Jenkins *The Battle of Downing Street* (1970)

9 If I had the choice between smoked salmon and tinned salmon, I'd have it tinned. With vinegar.

in *Observer* 11 November 1962

10 The Monarchy is a labour-intensive industry.

in *Observer* 13 February 1977

Harriette Wilson 1789–1846

English courtesan

11 I shall not say why and how I became, at the age of fifteen, the mistress of the Earl of Craven.

Memoirs (1825), opening words

John Wilson *see* **Christopher North**

Sandy Wilson 1924–

English songwriter

12 We've got to have
We plot to have
For it's so dreary not to have
That certain thing called the Boy Friend.

The Boyfriend (1954) title song

Woodrow Wilson 1856–1924

American Democratic statesman, 28th President of the US 1913–21. On Wilson: see **CLEMENCEAU** 235:9, **KEYNES** 462:1

13 The United States must be neutral in fact as well as in name.

message to the senate, 19 August 1914

14 It is like writing history with lightning. And my only regret is that it is all so terribly true.

on seeing D. W. Griffith's film The Birth of a Nation

at the White House, 18 February 1915

15 No nation is fit to sit in judgement upon any other nation.

speech in New York, 20 April 1915; in *Selected Addresses* (1918)

16 There is such a thing as a man being too proud to fight.

speech in Philadelphia, 10 May 1915; in *Selected Addresses* (1918) p. 88

17 We have stood apart, studiously neutral.

speech to Congress, 7 December 1915, in *New York Times* 8 December 1915

18 It must be a peace without victory . . . Only a peace between equals can last.

speech to US Senate, 22 January 1917, in *Messages and Papers* (1924) vol. 1

19 The world must be made safe for democracy.

speech to Congress, 2 April 1917, in *Selected Addresses* (1918); see **WOLFE** 862:21

20 Once lead this people into war and they will forget there ever was such a thing as tolerance.

John Dos Passos *Mr Wilson's War* (1917) pt. 3, ch. 12

21 Open covenants of peace, openly arrived at.

the first of the 'Fourteen Points'

speech to Congress, 8 January 1918, in *Selected Addresses* (1918)

22 Hunger does not breed reform; it breeds madness and all the ugly distempers that make an ordered life impossible.

speech to Congress, 11 November 1918, announcing the Armistice

1 America is the only idealistic nation in the world.
  speech at Sioux Falls, South Dakota, 8 September 1919; in *Messages and Papers* (1924) vol. 2

Walter Winchell 1897–1972
American journalist

2 Good evening, Mr and Mrs North America and all the ships at sea. Let's go to press! Flash!
  habitual introduction to network radio spot, 1931–56

Anne Finch, Lady Winchilsea
1661–1720

English poet

3 Thirst of wealth no quiet knows,
  But near the death-bed fiercer grows.
  'Enquiry after Peace' (1713) l. 30

4 Poetry's the feverish fit,
  Th' o'erflowing of unbounded wit.
  'Enquiry after Peace' (1713) l. 40

5 Alas! a woman that attempts the pen
  Such an intruder on the rights of men,
  Such presumptuous creature is esteemed
  The fault can by no virtue be redeemed.
  'The Introduction' (1713) l. 9

6 How are we fallen! Fallen by mistaken rules,
  And education's, more than nature's, fools;
  Debarred from all improvements of the mind,
  And to be dull, expected and designed.
  'The Introduction' (1713) l. 51

7 To some few friends, and to thy sorrows sing.
  For groves of laurel thou wert never meant;
  Be dark enough thy shades, and be thou there content.
  'The Introduction' (1713) l. 62

8 Give me yet before I die
  A sweet, yet absolute retreat,
  'Mongst paths so lost and trees so high
  That the world may ne'er invade
  Through such windings and such shade.
  'The Petition for an Absolute Retreat' (1713) l. 2

9 Now the jonquil o'ercomes the feeble brain;
  We faint beneath the aromatic pain.
  'The Spleen' (1701); see **POPE** 616:24

10 My hand delights to trace unusual things,
   And deviates from the known and common way;
   Nor will in fading silks compose
   Faintly the inimitable rose.
   'The Spleen' (1701) l. 82

Duchess of Windsor (Wallis Simpson)
1896–1986

American-born wife of the former **EDWARD VIII**. On Windsor: see **NEWSPAPER HEADLINES AND LEADERS** 573:17

11 You can never be too rich or too thin.
   attributed

Duke of Windsor *see* Edward VIII

Catherine Winkworth 1827–78
English translator of German hymns

12 Now thank we all our God,
   With heart and hands and voices,
   Who wondrous things hath done,
   In whom his world rejoices;
   Who from our mother's arms
   Hath blessed us on our way
   With countless gifts of love,
   And still is ours to-day.
   Lyra Germanica (1858) 'Now thank we all our God' (translation of Martin Rinkart's 'Nun danket alle Gott', c.1636)

13 Praise to the Lord! the Almighty, the King of creation!
   title of hymn (1863); translated from the German of Joachim Neander (1650–80)

14 Hast thou not seen?
   All that is needful hath been
   Granted in what he ordaineth.
   'Praise to the Lord! the Almighty . . . ' (1863 hymn)

15 *Peccavi*—I have Sindh.
   of Sir Charles Napier's conquest of Sindh, 1843, supposedly sent by Napier to Lord Ellenborough; peccavi = I have sinned
   in *Punch* 18 May 1844; attributed in *Notes and Queries* May 1954

Yvor Winters 1900–68
American poet and critic

16 The young are quick of speech.
   Grown middle-aged, I teach
   Corrosion and distrust,
   Exacting what I must.
   'On Teaching the Young' (1934)

John Winthrop 1588–1649
American settler

17 We must bear one another's burdens, we must not look only on our own things but also on the things of our brethren.
   Christian Charity, A Model Hereof (sermon, 1630) in Massachusetts Historical Society *Winthrop Papers* (1929–47) vol. 2; see **BIBLE** 113:24

18 We must consider that we shall be a city upon a hill, the eyes of all people are on us; so that if we shall deal falsely with our God in this work we have undertaken, and so cause Him to withdraw His present help from us, we shall be made a story and a byword through the world.
   Christian Charity, A Model Hereof (sermon, 1630) in Massachusetts Historical Society *Winthrop Papers* (1929–47) vol. 2

19 Whereas the way of God hath always been to gather his churches out of the world, now the world or civil state must be raised out of the churches.
   Reply to an Answer made to a Declaration . . . (1637)

Robert Charles Winthrop 1809–94

American politician

1 A Star for every State, and a State for every Star.
speech on Boston Common, 27 August 1862, in Addresses and Speeches vol. 2 (1867)

Nicholas Wiseman 1802–65

English Catholic priest, Cardinal-archbishop of Westminster

2 Full in the panting heart of Rome,
Beneath the apostle's crowning dome,
From pilgrims' lips that kiss the ground,
Breathes in all tongues one only sound:
God bless our Pope, the great, the good.
'Full in the panting heart of Rome'

Owen Wister 1860–1938

American novelist

3 When you call me that, *smile*!
'that' being 'you son-of-a—'
The Virginian (1902) ch. 2

George Wither 1588–1667

English poet and pamphleteer

4 When I behold the havoc and the spoil
Which, even within the compass of my days,
Is made through every quarter of this isle,
In woods and groves, which were this kingdom's praise.
A Collection of Emblems (1635) bk. 1, no. 35

5 We seek the present gain in everything,
Not caring (so our lust we may possess)
What damage to posterity we bring . . .
What our forefathers planted, we destroy:
A Collection of Emblems (1635) bk. 1, no. 35

6 I loved a lass, a fair one,
As fair as e'er was seen;
She was indeed a rare one,
Another Sheba queen.
A Description of Love (1620) 'I loved a lass, a fair one'

Ludwig Wittgenstein 1889–1951

Austrian-born philosopher

7 You get tragedy where the tree, instead of bending, breaks.
Culture and Value (1929)

8 Philosophy is a battle against the bewitchment of our intelligence by means of language.
Philosophische Untersuchungen (1953) pt. 1, sect. 109

9 The philosopher's treatment of a question is like the treatment of an illness.
Philosophische Untersuchungen (1953) pt. 1, sect. 255

10 What is your aim in philosophy?—To show the fly the way out of the fly-bottle.
Philosophische Untersuchungen (1953) pt. 1, sect. 309

11 One observes in order to see what one would not see if one did not observe.
Remarks on Colour (1977)

12 What can be said at all can be said clearly; and whereof one cannot speak thereof one must be silent.
Tractatus Logico-Philosophicus (1922) preface

13 The world is everything that is the case.
Tractatus Logico-Philosophicus (1922)

14 Death is not an event in life: we do not live to experience death.
Tractatus Logico-Philosophicus (1922)

15 The limits of my language mean the limits of my world.
Tractatus Logico-Philosophicus (1922)

16 The world of the happy is quite different from that of the unhappy.
Tractatus Logico-Philosophicus (1922)

17 For is what is linguistic not an experience? (Words are deeds.)
written before 1935, in Philosophical Grammar (1974, tr. Anthony Kenny)

18 Tell them I've had a wonderful life.
last words to his doctor's wife, before losing consciousness, 28 April 1951
Ray Monk Ludwig Wittgenstein (1990)

P. G. Wodehouse 1881–1975

English humorous writer; an American citizen from 1955. On Wodehouse: see O'CASEY 583:9; see also MISQUOTATIONS 547:11

19 Chumps always make the best husbands . . . All the unhappy marriages come from the husbands having brains.
The Adventures of Sally (1920) ch. 10

20 It is never difficult to distinguish between a Scotsman with a grievance and a ray of sunshine.
Blandings Castle and Elsewhere (1935) 'The Custody of the Pumpkin'

21 He spoke with a certain what-is-it in his voice, and I could see that, if not actually disgruntled, he was far from being gruntled.
The Code of the Woosters (1938) ch. 1

22 Slice him where you like, a hellhound is always a hellhound.
The Code of the Woosters (1938) ch. 1

23 It is no use telling me that there are bad aunts and good aunts. At the core, they are all alike. Sooner or later, out pops the cloven hoof.
The Code of the Woosters (1938) ch. 2

24 Roderick Spode? Big chap with a small moustache and the sort of eye that can open an oyster at sixty paces?
The Code of the Woosters (1938) ch. 2

25 To my daughter Leonora without whose never-failing sympathy and encouragement this book would have been finished in half the time.
The Heart of a Goof (1926) dedication

26 I turned to Aunt Agatha, whose demeanour was now rather like that of one who, picking daisies

on the railway, has just caught the down express in the small of the back.

The Inimitable Jeeves (1923) ch. 4

1 Sir Roderick Glossop . . . is always called a nerve specialist, because it sounds better, but everybody knows that he's really a sort of janitor to the looney-bin.

The Inimitable Jeeves (1923) ch. 7

2 When Aunt is calling to Aunt like mastodons bellowing across primeval swamps.

The Inimitable Jeeves (1923) ch. 16

3 It was my Uncle George who discovered that alcohol was a food well in advance of medical thought.

The Inimitable Jeeves (1923) ch. 16

4 It is a good rule in life never to apologize. The right sort of people do not want apologies, and the wrong sort take a mean advantage of them.

The Man Upstairs (1914) title story; see **HUBBARD** 417:13

5 In this life it is not aunts that matter but the courage which one brings to them.

The Mating Season (1949)

6 She fitted into my biggest armchair as if it had been built round her by someone who knew they were wearing armchairs tight about the hips that season.

My Man Jeeves (1919) 'Jeeves and the Unbidden Guest'

7 What with excellent browsing and sluicing and cheery conversation and what-not, the afternoon passed quite happily.

My Man Jeeves (1919) 'Jeeves and the Unbidden Guest'

8 Ice formed on the butler's upper slopes.

Pigs Have Wings (1952) ch. 5

9 The Right Hon. was a tubby little chap who looked as if he had been poured into his clothes and had forgotten to say 'When!'

Very Good, Jeeves (1930) 'Jeeves and the Impending Doom'

Terry Wogan 1938–

Irish broadcaster

10 Television contracts the imagination and radio expands it.

in *Observer* 30 December 1984 'Sayings of the Year'

Christa Wolf 1929–

German writer

11 It is this ability to bear what is unbearable and to go on living, to go on doing what one is used to doing—it is this uncanny ability that the existence of the human species is based on.

Medea (1996) ch. 10, translated by John Cullen

Naomi Wolf 1962–

American writer

12 To ask women to become unnaturally thin is to ask them to relinquish their sexuality.

The Beauty Myth (1990)

Charles Wolfe 1791–1823

Irish poet

13 Not a drum was heard, not a funeral note,
As his corse to the rampart we hurried.

'The Burial of Sir John Moore at Corunna' (1817)

14 We buried him darkly at dead of night,
The sods with our bayonets turning.

'The Burial of Sir John Moore at Corunna' (1817)

15 We carved not a line, and we raised not a stone—
But we left him alone with his glory.

'The Burial of Sir John Moore at Corunna' (1817)

Humbert Wolfe 1886–1940

British poet

16 You cannot hope
to bribe or twist,
thank God! the
British journalist.

But, seeing what
the man will do
unbribed, there's
no occasion to.

'Over the Fire' (1930)

James Wolfe 1727–59

British general; captor of Quebec. On Wolfe: see **GEORGE II** 352:10

17 The General . . . repeated nearly the whole of Gray's Elegy . . . adding, as he concluded, that he would prefer being the author of that poem to the glory of beating the French to-morrow.

J. Playfair *Biographical Account of J. Robinson* in *Transactions of the Royal Society of Edinburgh* vol. 7 (1815)

18 Now God be praised, I will die in peace.

last words; J. Knox *Historical Journal of the Campaigns in North America* (ed. A. G. Doughty, 1914) vol. 2

Thomas Wolfe 1900–38

American novelist

19 Which of us has not remained forever prison-pent? Which of us is not forever a stranger and alone?

foreword to *Look Homeward, Angel* (1929)

20 Most of the time we think we're sick, it's all in the mind.

Look Homeward, Angel (1929) pt. 1, ch. 1

21 'Where they got you stationed now, Luke?' said Harry Tugman peering up snoutily from a mug of coffee. 'At the p-p-p-present time in Norfolk at the Navy base,' Luke answered, 'm-m-making the world safe for hypocrisy.'

Look Homeward, Angel (1929) pt. 3, ch. 36; see **WILSON** 859:19

22 You can't go home again.

title of book, 1940

Tom Wolfe 1931–

American writer

1 The bonfire of the vanities.
title of novel (1987); deriving from Savonarola's 'burning of the vanities' in Florence, 1497

2 A liberal is a conservative who has been arrested.
The Bonfire of the Vanities (1987) ch. 24

3 Electric Kool-Aid Acid test.
title of novel on hippy culture (1968)

4 We are now in the Me Decade.
Mauve Gloves and Madmen (1976) 'The Me Decade'

5 Radical Chic . . . is only radical in Style; in its heart it is part of Society and its tradition—Politics, like Rock, Pop, and Camp, has its uses.
in *New York* 8 June 1970

Mary Wollstonecraft 1759–97

English feminist; mother of Mary **SHELLEY**. On Wollstonecraft: see **SOUTHEY** 764:23, **WALPOLE** 838:3

6 To give a sex to mind was not very consistent with the principles of a man [Rousseau] who argued so warmly, and so well, for the immortality of the soul.
A Vindication of the Rights of Woman (1792) ch. 3; see **MISQUOTATIONS** 548:10

7 The mind will ever be unstable that has only prejudices to rest on, and the current will run with destructive fury when there are no barriers to break its force.
A Vindication of the Rights of Woman (1792) ch. 4

8 She [woman] was created to be the toy of man, his rattle, and it must jingle in his ears whenever, dismissing reason, he chooses to be amused.
A Vindication of the Rights of Woman (1792) ch. 4

9 Confined, then, in cages like the feathered race, they have nothing to do but to plume themselves, and stalk with mock majesty from perch to perch.
A Vindication of the Rights of Woman (1792) ch. 4

10 I do not wish them [women] to have power over men; but over themselves.
A Vindication of the Rights of Woman (1792) ch. 4

11 When a man seduces a woman, it should, I think, be termed a *left-handed* marriage.
A Vindication of the Rights of Woman (1792) ch. 4

12 It is justice, not charity, that is wanting in the world.
A Vindication of the Rights of Woman (1792) ch. 5

13 Taught from infancy that beauty is woman's sceptre, the mind shapes itself to the body, and roaming round its gilt cage, only seeks to adorn its prison.
A Vindication of the Rights of Woman (1792) ch. 5

14 The pure animal spirits which make both mind and body shoot out, and unfold the tender blossoms of hope, are turned sour and vented in vain wishes, or pert repinings, that contract the faculties and spoil the temper; else they mount to the brain, and sharpening the understanding before it gains proportional strength, produce that pitiful cunning which disgracefully characterizes the female mind and I fear will characterize it whilst women remain the slaves of power.
A Vindication of the Rights of Woman (1792) ch. 9

15 A slavish bondage to parents cramps every faculty of the mind.
A Vindication of the Rights of Woman (1792) ch. 11

16 Was not the world a vast prison, and women born slaves?
The Wrongs of Woman: or, Maria (1798)

17 Minute attention to propriety stops the growth of virtue.
Collected Letters (ed. R. Wardle, 1979) p. 141

Thomas Wolsey *c.*1475–1530

English cardinal; Lord Chancellor, 1515–29

18 Father Abbot, I am come to lay my bones amongst you.
George Cavendish *Negotiations of Thomas Wolsey* (1641); see **SHAKESPEARE** 711:2

19 Had I but served God as diligently as I have served the King, he would not have given me over in my grey hairs.
George Cavendish *Negotiations of Thomas Wolsey* (1641); see **SHAKESPEARE** 711:1

Kenneth Wolstenholme 1920–2002

English sports commentator

20 They think it's all over—it is now.
television commentary in closing moments of the World Cup Final, 30 July 1966

Mrs Henry Wood (née Ellen Price)

1814–87

English novelist

21 Dead! and . . . never called me mother.
East Lynne (dramatized by T. A. Palmer, 1874, the words do not occur in the novel of 1861)

Woodbine Willie *see* G. A. Studdert

Kennedy

George Woodcock 1912–95

Canadian writer

22 Canadians do not like heroes, and so they do not have them.
Canada and the Canadians (1970)

Marion Woodman 1928–

Canadian Jungian analyst and writer

23 It takes great courage to break with one's past history and stand alone.
Addiction to Perfection: The Still Unravished Bride (1982)

Thomas Woodrooffe 1899–1978

British naval officer

1 At the present moment, the whole Fleet's lit up. When I say 'lit up', I mean lit up by fairy lamps.
live outside broadcast, Spithead Review, 20 May 1937
Asa Briggs *History of Broadcasting in the UK* (1965) vol. 2

Harry Woods

2 Oh we ain't got a barrel of money,
Maybe we're ragged and funny,
But we'll travel along
Singin' a song,
Side by side.
'Side by Side' (1927 song)

Virginia Woolf 1882–1941

English novelist. On Woolf: see **SITWELL** 753:15

3 Trivial personalities decomposing in the eternity of print.
The Common Reader (1925) 'The Modern Essay'

4 Examine for a moment an ordinary mind on an ordinary day.
The Common Reader (1925) 'Modern Fiction'

5 Life is not a series of gig lamps symmetrically arranged; life is a luminous halo, a semi-transparent envelope surrounding us from the beginning of consciousness to the end.
The Common Reader (1925) 'Modern Fiction'

6 Let us record the atoms as they fall upon the mind in the order in which they fall, let us trace the pattern, however disconnected and incoherent in appearance, which each sight or incident scores upon the consciousness. Let us not take it for granted that life exists more fully in what is commonly thought big than in what is commonly thought small.
The Common Reader (1925) 'Modern Fiction'

7 On or about December 1910 human nature changed . . . All human relations have shifted—those between masters and servants, husbands and wives, parents and children. And when human relations change there is at the same time a change in religion, conduct, politics, and literature.
'Mr Bennett and Mrs Brown' (1924)

8 A woman must have money and a room of her own if she is to write fiction.
A Room of One's Own (1929) ch. 1

9 Women have served all these centuries as looking-glasses possessing the magic and delicious power of reflecting the figure of a man at twice its natural size.
A Room of One's Own (1929) ch. 2

10 This is an important book, the critic assumes, because it deals with war. This is an insignificant book because it deals with the feelings of women in a drawing-room.
A Room of One's Own (1929) ch. 4

11 So that is marriage, Lily thought, a man and a woman looking at a girl throwing a ball.
To the Lighthouse (1927) pt. 1, ch. 13

12 Things have dropped from me. I have outlived certain desires; I have lost friends, some by death . . . others through sheer inability to cross the street.
The Waves (1931)

13 The scratching of pimples on the body of the bootboy at Claridges.
of James **JOYCE**'s Ulysses
letter to Lytton Strachey, 24 April 1922, in *Letters* (ed. N. Nicolson and J. Trautmann, 1976) vol. 2

14 I read the book of Job last night. I don't think God comes well out of it.
letter to Lady Robert Cecil, 12 November 1922, in *Letters* (ed. N. Nicolson and J. Trautmann, 1976) vol. 2

15 As an experience, madness is terrific . . . and in its lava I still find most of the things I write about.
letter to Ethel Smyth, 22 June 1930, in *Letters* (ed. N. Nicolson and J. Trautmann, 1976) vol. 2

Alexander Woollcott 1887–1943

American writer

16 She was like a sinking ship firing on the rescuers.
of Mrs Patrick **CAMPBELL**
While Rome Burns (1944) 'The First Mrs Tanqueray'

17 She is so odd a blend of Little Nell and Lady Macbeth. It is not so much the familiar phenomenon of a hand of steel in a velvet glove as a lacy sleeve with a bottle of vitriol concealed in its folds.
of Dorothy **PARKER**
While Rome Burns (1934) 'Our Mrs Parker'

18 All the things I really like to do are either illegal, immoral, or fattening.
R. E. Drennan *Wit's End* (1973)

Dorothy Wordsworth 1771–1855

English writer; sister of William **WORDSWORTH**

19 One only leaf upon the top of a tree—the sole remaining leaf—danced round and round like a rag blown by the wind.
'Alfoxden Journal' 7 March 1798, in *Journals* (ed. E. de Selincourt, 1941)

20 Coleridge dined with us. He brought his ballad [*The Ancient Mariner*] finished. A beautiful evening, very starry, the horned moon.
'Alfoxden Journal' 23 March 1798, in *Journals* (ed. E. de Selincourt, 1941); see **COLERIDGE** 240:24

21 We saw a raven very high above us. It called out, and the dome of the sky seemed to echo the sound. It called again and again as it flew onwards, and the mountains gave back the sound, seeming as if from their centre; a musical bell-like answering to the bird's hoarse voice.
'Grasmere Journal' 27 July 1800, in *Journals* (ed. E. de Selincourt, 1941)

1 I never saw daffodils so beautiful. They grew among the mossy stones about and about them; some rested their heads upon these stones as on a pillow for weariness; and the rest tossed and reeled and danced, and seemed as if they verily laughed with the wind that blew upon them over the lake.

'Grasmere Journal' 15 April 1802, in *Journals* (ed. E. de Selincourt, 1941); see **WORDSWORTH** 866:7

2 We walked up to the house and stood some minutes watching the swallows that flew about restlessly, and flung their shadows upon the sunbright walls of the old building; the shadows glanced and twinkled, interchanged and crossed each other, expanded and shrunk up, appeared and disappeared every instant.

'Recollections of a Tour made in Scotland' 16 August 1803, in *Journals* (ed. E. de Selincourt, 1941)

Elizabeth Wordsworth 1840–1932

English educationist; first Principal of Lady Margaret Hall, Oxford

3 If all the good people were clever,
And all clever people were good,
The world would be nicer than ever
We thought that it possibly could.
But somehow, 'tis seldom or never
The two hit it off as they should;
The good are so harsh to the clever,
The clever so rude to the good!

'Good and Clever'

William Wordsworth 1770–1850

English poet; brother of Dorothy **WORDSWORTH**. On Wordsworth: see **ARNOLD** 29:17, **ARNOLD** 31:26, **BAGEHOT** 51:20, **BROWNING** 166:12, **BULWER-LYTTON** 170:12, **BYRON** 188:26, **BYRON** 188:27, **BYRON** 190:2, **BYRON** 190:7, **BYRON** 192:4, **HAZLITT** 386:19, **JEFFREY** 432:17, **KEATS** 457:17, **SHELLEY** 747:3, **STEPHEN** 772:3; see also **ARNOLD** 32:7

4 My apprehensions come in crowds;
I dread the rustling of the grass;
The very shadows of the clouds
Have power to shake me as they pass.

'The Affliction of Margaret —' (1807)

5 And five times did I say to him
'Why, Edward, tell me why?'

'Anecdote for Fathers' (1798)

6 Who is the happy Warrior? Who is he
Whom every man in arms should wish to be?

'Character of the Happy Warrior' (1807); see **READ** 656:6

7 Earth has not anything to show more fair:
Dull would he be of soul who could pass by
A sight so touching in its majesty:
This City now doth like a garment wear
The beauty of the morning; silent, bare,
Ships, towers, domes, theatres, and temples lie
Open unto the fields, and to the sky;
All bright and glittering in the smokeless air.

'Composed upon Westminster Bridge' (1807)

8 Dear God! the very houses seem asleep;
And all that mighty heart is lying still!

'Composed upon Westminster Bridge' (1807)

9 The light that never was, on sea or land,
The consecration, and the Poet's dream.

on a picture of Peele Castle in a storm
'Elegiac Stanzas' (1807)

10 　　　　The Mind of Man—
My haunt, and the main region of my song.

The Excursion (1814) Preface, l. 40

11 Oh! many are the Poets that are sown
By Nature; men endowed with highest gifts,
The vision and the faculty divine;
Yet wanting the accomplishment of verse.

The Excursion (1814) bk. 1, l. 77

12 What soul was his, when from the naked top
Of some bold headland, he beheld the sun
Rise up, and bathe the world in light!

The Excursion (1827 ed.) bk. 1, l. 198

13 　　　　The good die first,
And they whose hearts are dry as summer dust
Burn to the socket.

The Excursion (1814) bk. 1, l. 500

14 This dull product of a scoffer's pen.

of **VOLTAIRE**'s Candide
The Excursion (1814) bk. 2, l. 484

15 　　　　'Tis a thing impossible, to frame
Conceptions equal to the soul's desires;
And the most difficult of tasks to keep
Heights which the soul is competent to gain.

The Excursion (1814) bk. 4, l. 136

16 　　　　Those among our fellow-men,
Who, offering no obeisance to the world,
Are yet made desperate by 'too quick a sense
Of constant infelicity'.

The Excursion (1814) bk. 6, l. 532; see **TAYLOR** 792:5

17 'To every Form of being is assigned,'
Thus calmly spoke the venerable Sage,
'An *active* Principle.'

The Excursion (1814) bk. 9, l. 1

18 How fast has brother followed brother,
From sunshine to the sunless land!

'Extempore Effusion upon the Death of James Hogg' (1835)

19 Bliss was it in that dawn to be alive,
But to be young was very heaven!

'The French Revolution, as it Appeared to Enthusiasts' (1809); also *The Prelude* (1850) bk. 9, l. 108

20 A genial hearth, a hospitable board,
And a refined rusticity.

'A genial hearth, a hospitable board' (1822)

21 　　　　Not choice
But habit rules the unreflecting herd.

'Grant that by this unsparing hurricane' (1822)

22 The moving accident is not my trade;
To freeze the blood I have no ready arts:
'Tis my delight, alone in summer shade,
To pipe a simple song for thinking hearts.

'Hart-Leap Well' (1800) pt. 2, l. 1

1   All shod with steel
We hissed along the polished ice, in games
Confederate.
'Influence of Natural Objects' (1809); also *The Prelude* (1850)
bk. 1, l. 414

2   Leaving the tumultuous throng,
To cut across the reflex of a star;
Image, that, flying still before me, gleamed
Upon the glassy plain.
'Influence of Natural Objects' (1809)

3   Yet still the solitary cliffs
Wheeled by me—even as if the earth had rolled
With visible motion her diurnal round!
'Influence of Natural Objects' (1809); also *The Prelude* (1850)
bk. 1, l. 458

4 It is a beauteous evening, calm and free;
The holy time is quiet as a nun
Breathless with adoration.
'It is a beauteous evening, calm and free' (1807)

5 We must be free or die, who speak the tongue
That Shakespeare spake; the faith and morals
hold
Which Milton held.
'It is not to be thought of that the Flood' (1807)

6 I travelled among unknown men,
In lands beyond the sea;
Nor England! did I know till then
What love I bore to thee.
'I travelled among unknown men' (1807)

7 I wandered lonely as a cloud
That floats on high o'er vales and hills,
When all at once I saw a crowd,
A host, of golden daffodils;
Beside the lake, beneath the trees,
Fluttering and dancing in the breeze.
'I wandered lonely as a cloud' (1815 ed.); see **WORDSWORTH**
865:1

8 For oft, when on my couch I lie
In vacant or in pensive mood,
They flash upon that inward eye
Which is the bliss of solitude;
And then my heart with pleasure fills,
And dances with the daffodils.
'I wandered lonely as a cloud' (1815 ed.)

9   I have owed to them
In hours of weariness, sensations sweet,
Felt in the blood, and felt along the heart;
And passing even into my purer mind,
With tranquil restoration:—feelings too
Of unremembered pleasure: such, perhaps,
As may have had no trivial influence
On that best portion of a good man's life,
His little, nameless, unremembered, acts
Of kindness and of love.
'Lines composed a few miles above Tintern Abbey' (1798)
l. 33

10   That blessed mood
In which the burthen of the mystery,
In which the heavy and the weary weight
Of all this unintelligible world,

Is lightened.
'Lines composed . . . above Tintern Abbey' (1798) l. 37

11   The sounding cataract
Haunted me like a passion: the tall rock,
The mountain, and the deep and gloomy wood,
Their colours and their forms, were then to me
An appetite.
'Lines composed . . . above Tintern Abbey' (1798) l. 72

12   I have learned
To look on nature, not as in the hour
Of thoughtless youth; but hearing oftentimes
The still, sad music of humanity.
'Lines composed . . . above Tintern Abbey' (1798) l. 88

13   And I have felt
A presence that disturbs me with the joy
Of elevated thoughts; a sense sublime
Of something far more deeply interfused,
Whose dwelling is the light of setting suns,
And the round ocean and the living air,
And the blue sky, and in the mind of man.
'Lines composed . . . above Tintern Abbey' (1798) l. 93

14   All the mighty world
Of eye and ear, both what they half-create,
And what perceive.
'Lines composed . . . above Tintern Abbey' (1798) l. 106; see
YOUNG 876:24

15 And much it grieved my heart to think
What man has made of man.
'Lines Written in Early Spring' (1798)

16 Milton! thou shouldst be living at this hour:
England hath need of thee: she is a fen
Of stagnant waters: altar, sword, and pen,
Fireside, the heroic wealth of hall and bower,
Have forfeited their ancient English dower
Of inward happiness.
'Milton! thou shouldst be living at this hour' (1807)

17   Some happy tone
Of meditation, slipping in between
The beauty coming and the beauty gone.
'Most sweet it is' (1835)

18 My heart leaps up when I behold
A rainbow in the sky:
So was it when my life began;
So is it now I am a man;
So be it when I shall grow old,
Or let me die!
The Child is father of the Man;
And I could wish my days to be
Bound each to each by natural piety.
'My heart leaps up when I behold' (1807); see **MILTON**
544:24, **PROVERBS** 628:46

19 Nuns fret not at their convent's narrow room;
And hermits are contented with their cells.
'Nuns fret not at their convent's narrow room' (1807)

20   Bound
Within the Sonnet's scanty plot of ground.
'Nuns fret not at their convent's narrow room' (1807)

21   With gentle hand
Touch—for there is a spirit in the woods.
'Nutting' (1800)

1 But Thy most dreaded instrument,
  In working out a pure intent,
  Is man—arrayed for mutual slaughter,
  —Yea, Carnage is thy daughter!
      'Ode 1815' (1845); substituted for the original 1816 version
      where a reference to 'the wicked in their dazzling mail' in
      relation to Waterloo had caused offence among
      Wordsworth's circle

2 There was a time when meadow, grove, and
      stream,
  The earth, and every common sight,
  To me did seem
  Apparelled in celestial light,
  The glory and the freshness of a dream.
      'Ode. Intimations of Immortality' (1807) st. 1

3 The rainbow comes and goes,
  And lovely is the rose,
  The moon doth with delight
  Look round her when the heavens are bare;
  Waters on a starry night
  Are beautiful and fair;
  The sunshine is a glorious birth;
  But yet I know, where'er I go,
  That there hath passed away a glory from the
      earth.
      'Ode. Intimations of Immortality' (1807) st. 2

4 A timely utterance gave that thought relief,
  And I again am strong.
      'Ode. Intimations of Immortality' (1807) st. 3

5 The winds come to me from the fields of sleep.
      'Ode. Intimations of Immortality' (1807) st. 3

6 Shout round me, let me hear thy shouts, thou
      happy Shepherd Boy!
      'Ode. Intimations of Immortality' (1807) st. 3

7 Both of them speak of something that is gone:
  The pansy at my feet
  Doth the same tale repeat:
  Whither is fled the visionary gleam?
  Where is it now, the glory and the dream?
      'Ode. Intimations of Immortality' (1807) st. 4

8 Our birth is but a sleep and a forgetting:
  The Soul that rises with us, our life's Star,
  Hath had elsewhere its setting,
  And cometh from afar:
  Not in entire forgetfulness,
  And not in utter nakedness,
  But trailing clouds of glory do we come
  From God, who is our home:
  Heaven lies about us in our infancy!
  Shades of the prison-house begin to close
  Upon the growing boy.
      'Ode. Intimations of Immortality' (1807) st. 5

9 And by the vision splendid
  Is on his way attended;
  At length the man perceives it die away,
  And fade into the light of common day.
      'Ode. Intimations of Immortality' (1807) st. 5

10 As if his whole vocation
   Were endless imitation.
      'Ode. Intimations of Immortality' (1807) st. 7

11   Thou Eye among the blind,
  That, deaf and silent, read'st the eternal deep,
  Haunted for ever by the eternal mind.
      'Ode. Intimations of Immortality' (1807) st. 8

12 Full soon thy Soul shall have her earthly freight,
   And custom lie upon thee with a weight,
   Heavy as frost, and deep almost as life!
      'Ode. Intimations of Immortality' (1807) st. 8

13 O joy! that in our embers
   Is something that doth live,
   That nature yet remembers
   What was so fugitive!
   The thought of our past years in me doth breed
   Perpetual benediction.
      'Ode. Intimations of Immortality' (1832 ed.) st. 9

14 Not for these I raise
   The song of thanks and praise;
   But for those obstinate questionings
   Of sense and outward things,
   Fallings from us, vanishings;
   Blank misgivings of a creature
   Moving about in worlds not realised,
   High instincts before which our mortal nature
   Did tremble like a guilty thing surprised.
      'Ode. Intimations of Immortality' (1807) st. 9; see
      SHAKESPEARE 699:5

15 Our noisy years seem moments in the being
   Of the eternal Silence: truths that wake,
   To perish never.
      'Ode. Intimations of Immortality' (1807) st. 9

16 Hence, in a season of calm weather,
   Though inland far we be,
   Our souls have sight of that immortal sea
   Which brought us hither,
   Can in a moment travel thither,
   And see the children sport upon the shore,
   And hear the mighty waters rolling evermore.
      'Ode. Intimations of Immortality' (1807) st. 9

17 Though nothing can bring back the hour
   Of splendour in the grass, of glory in the
       flower;
   We will grieve not, rather find
   Strength in what remains behind . . .
   In the faith that looks through death,
   In years that bring the philosophic mind.
      'Ode. Intimations of Immortality' (1807) st. 10

18 Another race hath been, and other palms are
       won.
   Thanks to the human heart by which we live,
   Thanks to its tenderness, its joys, and fears,
   To me the meanest flower that blows can give
   Thoughts that do often lie too deep for tears.
      'Ode. Intimations of Immortality' (1807) st. 11

19 Stern daughter of the voice of God!
   O Duty! if that name thou love
   Who art a light to guide, a rod
   To check the erring, and reprove.
      'Ode to Duty' (1807)

20 Plain living and high thinking are no more:
   The homely beauty of the good old cause

Is gone.

'O friend! I know not which way I must look' (1807); see **MILTON** 546:8

1 Once did she hold the gorgeous East in fee,
And was the safeguard of the West.

'On the Extinction of the Venetian Republic' (1807)

2 There's something in a flying horse,
There's something in a huge balloon;
But through the clouds I'll never float
Until I have a little Boat,
Shaped like the crescent-moon.

Peter Bell (1819) prologue, l. 1

3 Is it some party in a parlour,
Crammed just as they on earth were crammed—
Some sipping punch, some sipping tea,
But as you by their faces see
All silent, and all damned?

Peter Bell pt. 1, l. 541 in 1819 MS (subsequently deleted so as 'not to offend the pious')

4 Physician art thou?—one, all eyes,
Philosopher!—a fingering slave,
One that would peep and botanize
Upon his mother's grave?

'A Poet's Epitaph' (1800)

5 A reasoning, self-sufficing thing,
An intellectual All-in-all!

'A Poet's Epitaph' (1800)

6 In common things that round us lie
Some random truths he can impart,—
The harvest of a quiet eye
That broods and sleeps on his own heart.

'A Poet's Epitaph' (1800)

7 Escaped
From the vast city, where I long had pined
A discontented sojourner.

The Prelude (1850) bk. 1, l. 6

8 Made one long bathing of a summer's day.

The Prelude (1850) bk. 1, l. 290

9 Fair seed-time had my soul, and I grew up
Fostered alike by beauty and by fear.

The Prelude (1850) bk. 1, l. 301

10 Dust as we are, the immortal spirit grows
Like harmony in music; there is a dark
Inscrutable workmanship that reconciles
Discordant elements, makes them cling together
In one society.

The Prelude (1850) bk. 1, l. 340

11 And I was taught to feel, perhaps too much,
The self-sufficing power of Solitude.

The Prelude (1850) bk. 2, l. 76

12 To thee
Science appears but what in truth she is,
Not as our glory and our absolute boast,
But as a succedaneum, and a prop
To our infirmity.

The Prelude (1850) bk. 2, l. 211

13 The statue stood
Of Newton, with his prism, and silent face:

The marble index of a mind for ever
Voyaging through strange seas of Thought,
alone.

The Prelude (1850) bk. 3, l. 60

14 Spirits overwrought
Were making night do penance for a day
Spent in a round of strenuous idleness.

The Prelude (1850) bk. 4, l. 376

15 And, through the turnings intricate of verse,
Present themselves as objects recognised,
In flashes, and with glory not their own.

The Prelude (1850) bk. 5, l. 605

16 We were brothers all
In honour, as in one community,
Scholars and gentlemen.

The Prelude (1850) bk. 9, l. 227

17 All things have second birth;
The earthquake is not satisfied at once.

The Prelude (1850) bk. 10, l. 83

18 Not in Utopia,—subterranean fields,—
Or some secreted island, Heaven knows where!
But in the very world, which is the world
Of all of us,—the place where in the end
We find our happiness, or not at all!

The Prelude (1850) bk. 11, l. 140

19 There is
One great society alone on earth,
The noble Living, and the noble Dead.

The Prelude (1850) bk. 11, l. 393

20 I shook the habit off
Entirely and for ever, and again
In Nature's presence stood, as now I stand,
A sensitive being, a *creative* soul.

The Prelude (1850) bk. 12, l. 204

21 Imagination, which in truth,
Is but another name for absolute power
And clearest insight, amplitude of mind,
And Reason, in her most exalted mood.

The Prelude (1850) bk. 14, l. 190

22 I thought of Chatterton, the marvellous boy,
The sleepless soul that perished in its pride.

'Resolution and Independence' (1807) st. 7; see also **KEATS** 457:5

23 We poets in our youth begin in gladness;
But thereof comes in the end despondency and
madness.

'Resolution and Independence' (1807) st. 7

24 Cold, pain, and labour, and all fleshly ills;
And mighty Poets in their misery dead.

'Resolution and Independence' (1820 ed.) st. 17

25 Still glides the Stream, and shall for ever glide;
The Form remains, the Function never dies.

'The River Duddon' (1820) no. 34 'After-Thought'

26 Enough, if something from our hands have
power
To live, and act, and serve the future hour;
And if, as toward the silent tomb we go,
Through love, through hope, and faith's
transcendent dower,

We feel that we are greater than we know.
'The River Duddon' (1820) no. 34 'After-Thought'

1   The good old rule
Sufficeth them, the simple plan,
That they should take who have the power,
And they should keep who can.
'Rob Roy's Grave' (1807) l. 37

2 Scorn not the Sonnet; Critic, you have frowned,
Mindless of its just honours; with this key
Shakespeare unlocked his heart.
'Scorn not the Sonnet' (1827); see **BROWNING** 166:2

3 She dwelt among the untrodden ways
Beside the springs of Dove,
A maid whom there were none to praise
And very few to love.
'She dwelt among the untrodden ways' (1800)

4 A violet by a mossy stone
Half hidden from the eye!
'She dwelt among the untrodden ways' (1800)

5 She lived unknown, and few could know
When Lucy ceased to be;
But she is in her grave, and, oh,
The difference to me!
'She dwelt among the untrodden ways' (1800)

6 She was a phantom of delight.
title of poem (1807)

7 And now I see with eye serene
The very pulse of the machine;
A being breathing thoughtful breath;
A traveller betwixt life and death.
'She was a phantom of delight' (1807)

8 A perfect woman; nobly planned,
To warn, to comfort, and command.
'She was a phantom of delight' (1807)

9 A slumber did my spirit seal;
I had no human fears:
She seemed a thing that could not feel
The touch of earthly years.
'A slumber did my spirit seal' (1800)

10 Behold her, single in the field,
Yon solitary Highland lass!
'The Solitary Reaper' (1807)

11 Will no one tell me what she sings?
Perhaps the plaintive numbers flow
For old, unhappy, far-off things,
And battles long ago.
'The Solitary Reaper' (1807)

12 What, you are stepping westward?
'Stepping Westward' (1807)

13 Surprised by joy—impatient as the wind
I wished to share the transport—Oh! with
whom
But thee, long buried in the silent tomb.
'Surprised by joy—impatient as the wind' (1815)

14 One impulse from a vernal wood
May teach you more of man,
Of moral evil and of good,
Than all the sages can.
'The Tables Turned' (1798); see **BERNARD** 73:18

15 Our meddling intellect
Mis-shapes the beauteous forms of things:—
We murder to dissect.

Enough of science and of art;
Close up these barren leaves.
'The Tables Turned' (1798)

16 Two Voices are there; one is of the sea,
One of the mountains; each a mighty Voice:
In both from age to age thou didst rejoice,
They were thy chosen music, Liberty!
'Thought of a Briton on the Subjugation of Switzerland'
(1807); see **STEPHEN** 772:3

17 She shall be sportive as the fawn
That wild with glee across the lawn
Or up the mountain springs.
'Three years she grew in sun and shower' (1799)

18 Type of the wise who soar, but never roam;
True to the kindred points of heaven and home!
'To a Skylark' ('Ethereal minstrel! pilgrim of the sky', 1827)

19 O blithe new-comer! I have heard,
I hear thee and rejoice:
O Cuckoo! Shall I call thee bird,
Or but a wandering voice?
'To the Cuckoo' (1807)

20 Oft on the dappled turf at ease
I sit, and play with similes,
Loose types of things through all degrees.
'To the Daisy' ('With little here to do or see', 1820 ed.)

21 Though fallen thyself, never to rise again,
Live, and take comfort. Thou hast left behind
Powers that will work for thee; air, earth, and
skies;
There's not a breathing of the common wind
That will forget thee; thou hast great allies;
Thy friends are exultations, agonies,
And love, and man's unconquerable mind.
'To Toussaint L'Ouverture' (1807)

22 We are seven.
title of poem (1798)

23 A simple child, dear brother Jim,
That lightly draws its breath,
And feels its life in every limb,
What should it know of death?
'We are Seven' (1798)

24 The world is too much with us; late and soon,
Getting and spending, we lay waste our powers.
'The world is too much with us' (1807)

25   Great God! I'd rather be
A Pagan suckled in a creed outworn;
So might I, standing on this pleasant lea,
Have glimpses that would make me less forlorn;
Have sight of Proteus rising from the sea;
Or hear old Triton blow his wreathèd horn.
'The world is too much with us' (1807)

26 I propose to myself to imitate, and as far as
possible, to adopt the very language of men . . .
I wish to keep my reader in the company of
flesh and blood.
Lyrical Ballads (1800) preface

1 It may be safely affirmed, that there neither is, nor can be, any *essential* difference between the language of prose and metrical composition.
Lyrical Ballads (1800) preface

2 The Poet writes under one restriction only, namely, the necessity of giving immediate pleasure to a human Being possessed of that information which may be expected from him, not as a lawyer, a physician, a mariner, an astronomer or a natural philosopher, but as a Man.
Lyrical Ballads (2nd ed., 1802) preface

3 Poetry is the spontaneous overflow of powerful feelings: it takes its origin from emotion recollected in tranquillity.
Lyrical Ballads (2nd ed., 1802) preface; see **PARKER** 596:10, **THURBER** 810:13

4 Poetry is the breath and finer spirit of all knowledge; it is the impassioned expression which is in the countenance of all science.
Lyrical Ballads (2nd ed., 1802) Preface

5 Never forget what I believe was observed to you by Coleridge, that every great and original writer, in proportion as he is great and original, must himself create the taste by which he is to be relished.
letter to Lady Beaumont, 21 May 1807, in E. de Selincourt (ed.) *Letters of William and Dorothy Wordsworth* vol. 2 (revised by M. Moorman, 1969)

Terry Worrall fl. 1991
British spokesman for British Rail

6 We are having particular problems on this occasion with the type of snow, which is very dry and powdery and is actually penetrating all the protection we had on some of our locomotives.
explaining disruption on British Rail; popularly summarized as 'the wrong sort of snow'; see **NEWSPAPER HEADLINES AND LEADERS** 573:2
in *Evening Standard* 11 February 1991

Henry Wotton 1568–1639
English poet and diplomat. See also WALTON 839:3

7 This man is freed from servile bands,
Of hope to rise, or fear to fall:—
Lord of himself, though not of lands,
And having nothing, yet hath all.
'The Character of a Happy Life' (1614)

8 You meaner beauties of the night,
That poorly satisfy our eyes,
More by your number, than your light;
You common people of the skies,
What are you when the moon shall rise?
'On His Mistress, the Queen of Bohemia' (1624)

9 He first deceased; she for a little tried
To live without him: liked it not, and died.
'Upon the Death of Sir Albertus Moreton's Wife' (1651)

10 Dazzled thus with height of place,
Whilst our hopes our wits beguile,

No man marks the narrow space
'Twixt a prison and a smile.
'Upon the sudden restraint of the Earl of Somerset' (1651)

11 In architecture as in all other operative arts, the end must direct the operation. The end is to build well. Well building hath three conditions. Commodity, firmness, and delight.
Elements of Architecture (1624) pt. 1; see **VITRUVIUS** 833:9

12 An ambassador is an honest man sent to lie abroad for the good of his country.
written in the album of Christopher Fleckmore in 1604; Izaak Walton *Reliquiae Wottonianae* (1651) 'The Life of Sir Henry Wotton'

13 Critics are like brushers of noblemen's clothes.
Francis Bacon *Apophthegms New and Old* (1625) no. 64

14 Take heed of thinking, *The farther you go from the church of Rome, the nearer you are to God.*
Izaak Walton *Reliquiae Wottonianae* (1651) 'The Life of Sir Henry Wotton'

Frank Lloyd Wright 1867–1959
American architect

15 The necessities were going by default to save the luxuries until I hardly knew which were necessities and which luxuries.
Autobiography (1945) bk. 2

16 The physician can bury his mistakes, but the architect can only advise his client to plant vines—so they should go as far as possible from home to build their first buildings.
in *New York Times* 4 October 1953, sect. 6; see **QUARLES** 651:14

17 The modern city is a place for banking and prostitution and very little else.
Robert C. Twombly *Frank Lloyd Wright* (1973) ch. 9

James Wright 1927–80
American poet

18 Suddenly I realize
That if I stepped out of my body I would break
Into blossom.
'A Blessing' (1963)

19 Between two cold white shadows,
But I dreamed they would rise
Together,
My black Ohioan swan.
'Three Sentences for a Dead Swan' (1968)

Mehetabel ('Hetty') Wright (née Wesley) 1697–1750
English poet

20 Transient lustre, beauteous clay,
Smiling wonder of a day.
'To an Infant Expiring the Second Day of its Birth' (1733)

21 Thou tyrant whom I will not name,
Whom heaven and hell alike disclaim;
Abhorred and shunned, for different ends,
By angels, Jesuits, beasts and fiends!

What terms to curse thee shall I find,
Thou plague peculiar to mankind? . . .
That wretch, if such a wretch there be,
Who hopes for happiness from thee,
May search successfully as well
For truth in whores and ease in hell.
'Wedlock' (c.1730)

Lady Mary Wroth c.1586–c.1652

English poet

1 Love, a child, is ever crying:
Please him and he straight is flying,
Give him, he the more is craving,
Never satisfied with having.
'Love, a child, is ever crying' (1621)

St Wulfstan c.1009–95

English monk and prelate, bishop of Worcester from 1062

2 We miserable people have destroyed the work of
saints, that we may provide praise for ourselves.
The age of that most happy man did not know
how to build pompous buildings, but knew how
to offer themselves to God under any sort of
roof, and to attract to their example
subordinates. We on the contrary strive that,
neglecting our souls, we may pile up stones.
*on the demolition of St Oswald's Anglo-Saxon cathedral at
Worcester, the new Romanesque choir having been recently
completed*
William of Malmesbury *Gesta Pontificum* (Rolls series (1870)
vol. 52)

Thomas Wyatt c.1503–42

English poet

3 For hitherto though I have lost all my time,
Me lusteth no longer rotten boughs to climb.
'Farewell, Love' (1557)

4 They flee from me, that sometime did me seek
With naked foot, stalking in my chamber.
'They flee from me' (1557)

5 When her loose gown from her shoulders did
fall,
And she me caught in her arms long and small;
Therewith all sweetly did me kiss,
And softly said, 'Dear heart, how like you this?'
'They flee from me' (1557)

6 It was no dream: I lay broad waking.
'They flee from me' (1557)

7   I leave off therefore
Since in a net I seek to hold the wind.
'Whoso list to hunt, I know where is an hind' (1557)

8 There is written her fair neck round about:
'Noli me tangere for Caesar's I am,
And wild for to hold though I seem tame.'
'Whoso list to hunt, I know where is an hind' (1557)

9 With serving still
This have I won:
For my good will

To be undone.
And for redress
Of all my pain
Disdainfulness
I have again.
'With serving still'

William Wycherley c.1640–1716

English dramatist

10 A mistress should be like a little country retreat
near the town, not to dwell in constantly, but
only for a night and away.
The Country Wife (1675) act 1, sc. 1

11 Go to your business, I say, pleasure, whilst I go
to my pleasure, business.
The Country Wife (1675) act 2

12 Women and fortune are truest still to those that
trust 'em.
The Country Wife (1675) act 5, sc. 4

13 Nay, you had both felt his desperate deadly
daunting dagger:—there are your d's for you!
The Gentleman Dancing-Master (1672) act 5

14 You who scribble, yet hate all who write . . .
And with faint praises one another damn.
of drama critics
The Plain Dealer (1677) prologue; see **POPE** 614:22

15 A man without money needs no more fear a
crowd of lawyers than a crowd of pickpockets.
The Plain Dealer (1677) act 3, sc. 1

Tammy Wynette 1942–98 *and* Billy Sherrill c.1938–

16 Stand by your man.
title of song (1968)

Andrew of Wyntoun c.1350–c.1420

Scottish churchman

17 Quhen Alysander oure kyng wes dede,
That Scotland led in luve and le,
Away wes sons of ale and brede,
Of wyne and wax, of gamyn and gle;
Oure gold wes changyd into lede,
Cryst, borne into virgynyte,
Succour Scotland, and remede,
That stad is in perplexyte.
The Orygynale Cronykil (1795 ed.) vol. 1, bk. 7, ch. 10, l. 527

Xenophon c.428–c.354 BC

Greek historian

18 *Thalassa thalassa.*
The sea! the sea!
Anabasis bk. 4, ch. 7, sect. 24

Xerxes I *c.*519–465 BC

Persian monarch, King from 486 BC

1 My men have turned into women and my women into men.
on the exploits of Artemisia at Salamis, 480 BC
Herodotus *Histories* bk. 8, sect. 88

Augustin, Marquis de Ximénèz

1726–1817

French poet

2 *Attaquons dans ses eaux*
La perfide Albion!

Let us attack in her own waters perfidious Albion!
'L'Ère des Français' (October 1793) in *Poésies Révolutionnaires et contre-révolutionnaires* (1821) vol. 1; see **BOSSUET** 152:1

Isoroku Yamamoto 1884–1943

Japanese admiral, Commander-in-Chief responsible for planning the Japanese attack on Pearl Harbor

3 A military man can scarcely pride himself on having 'smitten a sleeping enemy'; in fact, to have it pointed out is more a matter of shame.
letter, 9 January 1942; Hirosuki Asawa *The Reluctant Admiral* (1979, tr. John Bester); see **FILM LINES** 328:13

Minoru Yamasaki 1912–88

American architect, designer of the World Trade Center (1973; destroyed by terrorist attack in September 2001)

4 The World Trade Center should, because of its importance, become a living representation of man's belief in humanity, his need for individual dignity, his belief in the cooperation of men, and through this cooperation his ability to find greatness.
Paul Heyer *Architects on Architecture* (1967)

William Yancey 1814–63

American Confederate politician

5 The man and the hour have met.
of Jefferson **DAVIS**, *President-elect of the Confederacy, in 1861*
Shelby Foote *The Civil War: Fort Sumter to Perryville* (1991)

Thomas Russell Ybarra b. 1880

6 A Christian is a man who feels
Repentance on a Sunday
For what he did on Saturday
And is going to do on Monday.
'The Christian' (1909)

W. F. Yeames 1835–1918

British painter

7 And when did you last see your father?
a Roundhead officer addressing the child of a Cavalier family
title of painting (1878), now in the Walker Art Gallery, Liverpool

W. B. Yeats 1865–1939

Irish poet. On Yeats: see **AUDEN** 37:8, **AUDEN** 37:10

8 O body swayed to music, O brightening glance,
How can we know the dancer from the dance?
'Among School Children' (1928)

9 A young man when the old men are done talking
Will say to an old man, 'Tell me of that lady
The poet stubborn with his passion sang us
When age might well have chilled his blood.'
'Broken Dreams' (1914)

10 The unpurged images of day recede;
The Emperor's drunken soldiery are abed.
'Byzantium' (1933)

11 A starlit or a moonlit dome disdains
All that man is,
All mere complexities,
The fury and the mire of human veins.
'Byzantium' (1933)

12 Those images that yet
Fresh images beget,
That dolphin-torn, that gong-tormented sea.
'Byzantium' (1933)

13 The intellect of man is forced to choose
Perfection of the life, or of the work,
And if it take the second must refuse
A heavenly mansion, raging in the dark.
'The Choice' (1933)

14 Now that my ladder's gone
I must lie down where all the ladders start,
In the foul rag-and-bone shop of the heart.
'The Circus Animals' Desertion' (1939) pt. 3

15 I made my song a coat
Covered with embroideries
Out of old mythologies
From heel to throat;
But the fools caught it,
Wore it in the world's eye
As though they'd wrought it.
Song, let them take it,
For there's more enterprise
In walking naked.
'A Coat' (1914)

16 We were the last romantics — chose for theme
Traditional sanctity and loveliness.
'Coole Park and Ballylee, 1931' (1933)

17 The years like great black oxen tread the world,
And God the herdsman goads them on behind,
And I am broken by their passing feet.
The Countess Cathleen (1895) act 4

1 A woman can be proud and stiff
When on love intent;
But Love has pitched his mansion in
The place of excrement;
For nothing can be sole or whole
That has not been rent.
'Crazy Jane Talks with the Bishop' (1932)

2 Nor dread nor hope attend
A dying animal;
A man awaits his end
Dreading and hoping all.
'Death' (1933)

3 He knows death to the bone—
Man has created death.
'Death' (1933)

4 Down by the salley gardens my love and I did meet;
She passed the salley gardens with little snow-white feet.
She bid me take love easy, as the leaves grow on the tree;
But I, being young and foolish, with her would not agree.
'Down by the Salley Gardens' (1889)

5 She bid me take life easy, as the grass grows on the weirs;
But I was young and foolish, and now am full of tears.
'Down by the Salley Gardens' (1889)

6 I have met them at close of day
Coming with vivid faces
From counter or desk among grey
Eighteenth-century houses.
I have passed with a nod of the head
Or polite meaningless words.
'Easter, 1916' (1921)

7 All changed, changed utterly:
A terrible beauty is born.
'Easter, 1916' (1921)

8 Too long a sacrifice
Can make a stone of the heart.
O when may it suffice?
'Easter, 1916' (1921)

9 I write it out in a verse—
MacDonagh and MacBride
And Connolly and Pearse
Now and in time to be,
Wherever green is worn,
Are changed, changed utterly:
A terrible beauty is born.
'Easter, 1916' (1921)

10 I see a schoolboy when I think of him
With face and nose pressed to a sweet-shop window.
of **KEATS**
'Ego Dominus Tuus' (1917)

11 The fascination of what's difficult
Has dried the sap of my veins, and rent
Spontaneous joy and natural content

Out of my heart.
'The Fascination of What's Difficult' (1910)

12 Never to have lived is best, ancient writers say;
Never to have drawn the breath of life, never to have looked into the eye of day;
The second best's a gay goodnight and quickly turn away.
'From *Oedipus at Colonus*' (1928); see **SOPHOCLES** 761:17

13 The ghost of Roger Casement
Is beating on the door.
'The Ghost of Roger Casement' (1939)

14 Had I the heavens' embroidered cloths,
Enwrought with golden and silver light,
The blue and the dim and the dark cloths
Of night and light and the half-light,
I would spread the cloths under your feet:
But I, being poor, have only my dreams;
I have spread my dreams under your feet;
Tread softly because you tread on my dreams.
'He Wishes for the Cloths of Heaven' (1899)

15 The light of evening, Lissadell,
Great windows open to the south,
Two girls in silk kimonos, both
Beautiful, one a gazelle.
'In Memory of Eva Gore Booth and Con Markiewicz' (1933)

16 The innocent and the beautiful
Have no enemy but time.
'In Memory of Eva Gore Booth and Con Markiewicz' (1933)

17 Soldier, scholar, horseman, he,
As 'twere all life's epitome.
What made us dream that he could comb grey hair?
'In Memory of Major Robert Gregory' (1919)

18 My country is Kiltartan Cross;
My countrymen Kiltartan's poor.
'An Irish Airman Foresees his Death' (1919)

19 Nor law, nor duty bade me fight,
Nor public men, nor cheering crowds,
A lonely impulse of delight
Drove to this tumult in the clouds;
I balanced all, brought all to mind,
The years to come seemed waste of breath,
A waste of breath the years behind
In balance with this life, this death.
'An Irish Airman Foresees his Death' (1919)

20 I will arise and go now, and go to Innisfree,
And a small cabin build there, of clay and wattles made;
Nine bean rows will I have there, a hive for the honey-bee,
And live alone in the bee-loud glade.
'The Lake Isle of Innisfree' (1893)

21 I hear lake water lapping with low sounds by the shore . . .
I hear it in the deep heart's core.
'The Lake Isle of Innisfree' (1893)

22 Land of Heart's Desire,
Where beauty has no ebb, decay no flood,
But joy is wisdom, Time an endless song.
The Land of Heart's Desire (1894) p. 36

1 A sudden blow: the great wings beating still
Above the staggering girl, her thighs caressed
By the dark webs, her nape caught in his bill,
He holds her helpless breast upon his breast.
How can those terrified vague fingers push
The feathered glory from her loosening thighs?
'Leda and the Swan' (1928)

2 A shudder in the loins engenders there
The broken wall, the burning roof and tower
And Agamemnon dead.
'Leda and the Swan' (1928)

3 Like a long-legged fly upon the stream
His mind moves upon silence.
'Long-Legged Fly' (1939)

4 Did that play of mine send out
Certain men the English shot?
'The Man and the Echo' (1939)

5 We had fed the heart on fantasies,
The heart's grown brutal from the fare;
More substance in our enmities
Than in our love; O, honey-bees
Come build in the empty house of the stare.
'Meditations in Time of Civil War' no. 6 'The Stare's Nest by
my Window' (1928)

6 Think where man's glory most begins and ends,
And say my glory was I had such friends.
'The Municipal Gallery Re-visited' (1939)

7 Why, what could she have done, being what she
is?
Was there another Troy for her to burn?
'No Second Troy' (1910)

8 I think it better that at times like these
A poet's mouth be silent, for in truth
We have no gift to set a statesman right;
He has had enough of meddling who can please
A young girl in the indolence of her youth
Or an old man upon a winter's night.
'On being asked for a War Poem' (1919)

9 Where, where but here have Pride and Truth,
That long to give themselves for wage,
To shake their wicked sides at youth
Restraining reckless middle-age?
'On hearing that the Students of our New University have
joined the Agitation against Immoral Literature' (1910)

10 A pity beyond all telling,
Is hid in the heart of love.
'The Pity of Love' (1893)

11 How but in custom and in ceremony
Are innocence and beauty born?
Ceremony's a name for the rich horn,
And custom for the spreading laurel tree.
'A Prayer for My Daughter' (1921)

12 Out of Ireland have we come.
Great hatred, little room,
Maimed us at the start.
I carry from my mother's womb
A fanatic heart.
'Remorse for Intemperate Speech' (1933)

13 That is no country for old men. The young
In one another's arms, birds in the trees

—Those dying generations—at their song,
The salmon-falls, the mackerel-crowded seas.
'Sailing to Byzantium' (1928)

14 An aged man is but a paltry thing,
A tattered coat upon a stick, unless
Soul clap its hands and sing, and louder sing
For every tatter in its mortal dress.
'Sailing to Byzantium' (1928)

15 And therefore I have sailed the seas and come
To the holy city of Byzantium.
'Sailing to Byzantium' (1928)

16 All shuffle there; all cough in ink;
All wear the carpet with their shoes;
All think what other people think;
All know the man their neighbour knows.
Lord, what would they say
Did their Catullus walk that way?
'The Scholars' (1919)

17 Turning and turning in the widening gyre
The falcon cannot hear the falconer;
Things fall apart; the centre cannot hold;
Mere anarchy is loosed upon the world,
The blood-dimmed tide is loosed, and
everywhere
The ceremony of innocence is drowned;
The best lack all conviction, while the worst
Are full of passionate intensity.
'The Second Coming' (1921)

18 The darkness drops again; but now I know
That twenty centuries of stony sleep
Were vexed to nightmare by a rocking cradle,
And what rough beast, its hour come round at
last,
Slouches towards Bethlehem to be born?
'The Second Coming' (1921)

19 Far-off, most secret and inviolate Rose.
'The Secret Rose' (1899)

20 A woman of so shining loveliness
That men threshed corn at midnight by a tress,
A little stolen tress.
'The Secret Rose' (1899)

21 Romantic Ireland's dead and gone,
It's with O'Leary in the grave.
'September, 1913' (1914)

22 O, who could have foretold
That the heart grows old?
'A Song' (1919)

23 The woods of Arcady are dead,
And over is their antique joy;
Of old the world on dreaming fed;
Grey Truth is now her painted toy.
'The Song of the Happy Shepherd' (1889)

24 And pluck till time and times are done
The silver apples of the moon,
The golden apples of the sun.
'Song of Wandering Aengus' (1899)

25 You think it horrible that lust and rage
Should dance attendance upon my old age;

They were not such a plague when I was young;
What else have I to spur me into song?
'The Spur' (1939)

1 We Irish, born into that ancient sect
But thrown upon this filthy modern tide
And by its formless spawning fury wrecked,
Climb to our proper dark, that we may trace
The lineaments of a plummet-measured face.
'The Statues' (1939)

2 Swift has sailed into his rest;
Savage indignation there
Cannot lacerate his breast.
Imitate him if you dare,
World-besotted traveller; he
Served human liberty.
'Swift's Epitaph' (1933); see **EPITAPHS** 319:14

3 But was there ever dog that praised his fleas?
'To a Poet, Who would have Me Praise certain bad Poets,
Imitators of His and of Mine' (1910)

4 Red Rose, proud Rose, sad Rose of all my days!
Come near me, while I sing the ancient ways.
'To the Rose upon the Rood of Time' (1893)

5 What shall I do with this absurdity—
O heart, O troubled heart—this caricature,
Decrepit age that has been tied to me
As to a dog's tail?
'The Tower' (1928) pt. 1

6 Michael Angelo left a proof
On the Sistine Chapel roof,
Where but half-awakened Adam
Can disturb globe-trotting Madam.
'Under Ben Bulben' (1939) pt. 4

7 Irish poets, learn your trade,
Sing whatever is well made.
'Under Ben Bulben' (1939) pt. 5

8 Cast your mind on other days
That we in coming days may be
Still the indomitable Irishry.
'Under Ben Bulben' (1939) pt. 5

9 On limestone quarried near the spot
By his command these words are cut:
Cast a cold eye
On life, on death.
Horseman, pass by!
'Under Ben Bulben' (1939) pt. 6

10 When you are old and grey and full of sleep,
And nodding by the fire, take down this book,
And slowly read, and dream of the soft look
Your eyes had once, and of their shadows deep.
'When You Are Old' (1893)

11 Unwearied still, lover by lover,
They paddle in the cold
Companionable streams or climb the air;
Their hearts have not grown old.
'The Wild Swans at Coole' (1919)

12 We make out of the quarrel with others,
rhetoric, but of the quarrel with ourselves,
poetry.
Essays (1924) 'Anima Hominis' sect. 5

13 Even when the poet seems most himself . . . he
is never the bundle of accident and incoherence
that sits down to breakfast; he has been reborn
as an idea, something intended, complete.
Essays and Introductions (1961) 'A General Introduction for my
Work'

14 In dreams begins responsibility.
Responsibilities (1914) epigraph

15 *of the Anglo-Irish:*
We . . . are no petty people. We are one of the
great stocks of Europe. We are the people of
Burke; we are the people of Swift, the people of
Emmet, the people of Parnell. We have created
most of the modern literature of this country.
We have created the best of its political
intelligence.
speech in the Irish Senate, 11 June 1925

16 Think like a wise man but express yourself like
the common people.
Letters on Poetry from W. B. Yeats to Dorothy Wellesley (1940)
21 December 1935; see **ASCHAM** 33:10

Boris Yeltsin 1931–2007
**Russian statesman, President of the Russian Federation
1991–9**

17 You can make a throne of bayonets, but you
can't sit on it for long.
*from the top of a tank, during the attempted military coup
against* **GORBACHEV**
in *Independent* 24 August 1991; see **INGE** 425:5

18 Today is the last day of an era past.
at a Berlin ceremony to end the Soviet military presence
in *Guardian* 1 September 1994

19 Europe is in danger of plunging into a cold
peace.
*at the summit meeting of the Conference on Security and
Co-operation in Europe*
in *Newsweek* 19 December 1994; see **BARUCH** 60:10

Sergei Yesenin 1895–1925
Russian poet

20 The poet's gift is to soothe and harass,
He bears the stamp of fate.
On earth I wanted to marry
A white rose to a pitch-black toad.
'I Have One Remaining Pastime' (1923) (translated by Gordon
McVay)

21 It's always the good feel rotten.
Pleasure's for those who are bad.
'Pleasure's for the Bad' (1923) (translated by Gordon McVay)

22 In this life there's nothing new in dying,
But nor, of course, is living any newer.
*his final poem, written in his own blood the day before he
hanged himself in his Leningrad hotel room, 28 December
1925*
'Goodbye, my Friend, Goodbye' (translated by Gordon
McVay)

Yevgeny Yevtushenko 1933–
Russian poet

1 Over Babiy Yar
There are no memorials.
The steep hillside like a rough inscription.
'Babiy Yar' (1961) (translated by Robin Milner-Gulland)

2 So on and on
we walked without thinking of rest
passing craters, passing fire,
under the rocking sky of '41
tottering crazy on its smoking columns.
'The Companion' (1954) (translated by Robin Milner-Gulland)

3 Who never knew
the price of happiness
will not be happy.
'Lies' (1952) (translated by Robin Milner-Gulland)

4 No people are uninteresting.
Their fate is like the chronicle of planets.
Nothing in them is not particular,
and planet is dissimilar from planet.
'No People are Uninteresting' (1961) (translated by Robin Milner-Gulland)

5 Life is a rainbow which also includes black.
in *Guardian* 11 August 1987

Shoichi Yokoi 1915–97
Japanese soldier

6 It is a terrible shame for me—I came back, still
alive, without having won the war.
on returning to Japan after surviving for 28 years in the jungles of Guam before surrendering to the Americans in 1972
in *Independent* 26 September 1997

Andrew Young 1932–
American clergyman and diplomat

7 Nothing is illegal if one hundred well-placed
business men decide to do it.
Morris K. Udall *Too Funny to be President* (1988)

Arthur Young 1741–1820
English agricultural reformer and writer

8 Give a man the secure possession of bleak rock,
and he will turn it into a garden; give him nine
years lease of a garden, and he will convert it
into a desert.
Travels, during the years 1787, 1788, and 1789 (1792)

9 The magic of property turns sand to gold.
Travels, during the years 1787, 1788, and 1789 (1792)

Edward Young 1683–1765
English poet and dramatist

10 Some for renown on scraps of learning dote,
And think they grow immortal as they quote.
The Love of Fame (1725–8) Satire 1, l. 89

11 None think the great unhappy, but the great.
The Love of Fame (1725–8) Satire 1, l. 238

12 Be wise with speed;
A fool at forty is a fool indeed.
The Love of Fame (1725–8) Satire 2, l. 282; see **PROVERBS** 632:27

13 Hot, envious, noisy, proud, the scribbling fry
Burn, hiss, and bounce, waste paper, stink, and
die.
The Love of Fame (1725–8) Satire 3, l. 65

14 One to destroy, is murder by the law;
And gibbets keep the lifted hand in awe;
To murder thousands, takes a specious name,
'War's glorious art', and gives immortal fame.
The Love of Fame (1725–8) Satire 7, l. 55; see **PORTEUS** 619:22, **ROSTAND** 670:7

15 How science dwindles, and how volumes swell,
How commentators each dark passage shun,
And hold their farthing candle to the sun.
The Love of Fame (1725–8) Satire 7, l. 96; see **BURTON** 181:19, **JOHNSON** 440:6, **SIDNEY** 750:10

16 Tired Nature's sweet restorer, balmy sleep!
Night Thoughts (1742–5) 'Night 1' l. 1

17 We take no note of Time
But from its loss.
Night Thoughts (1742–5) 'Night 1' l. 55

18 Death! Great proprietor of all! 'Tis thine
To tread out empire, and to quench the stars.
Night Thoughts (1742–5) 'Night 1' l. 204

19 Be wise to-day; 'tis madness to defer.
Night Thoughts (1742–5) 'Night 1' l. 390

20 Procrastination is the thief of time.
Night Thoughts (1742–5) 'Night 1' l. 393; see **PROVERBS** 642:6

21 At thirty a man suspects himself a fool;
Knows it at forty, and reforms his plan;
At fifty chides his infamous delay,
Pushes his prudent purpose to resolve;
In all the magnanimity of thought
Resolves; and re-resolves; then dies the same.
Night Thoughts (1742–5) 'Night 1' l. 417

22 All men think all men mortal, but themselves.
Night Thoughts (1742–5) 'Night 1' l. 424

23 By night an atheist half believes a God.
Night Thoughts (1742–5) 'Night 5' l. 176

24 [The senses] Take in at once the landscape of
the world,
At a small inlet, which a grain might close,
And half create the wondrous world they see.
Night Thoughts (1742–5) 'Night 6' l. 425; see **WORDSWORTH** 866:14

25 To know the world, not love her, is thy point,
She gives but little, nor that little, long.
Night Thoughts (1742–5) 'Night 8' l. 1276; see **GOLDSMITH** 364:14

26 Satan, thy master, I dare call a dunce.
Night Thoughts (1742–5) 'Night 8' l. 1417; see **BLAKE** 125:9

27 To know ourselves diseased, is half our cure.
Night Thoughts (1742–5) 'Night 9' l. 38

28 Devotion! daughter of astronomy!
An undevout astronomer is mad.
Night Thoughts (1742–5) 'Night 9' l. 769

1 The course of Nature is the art of God.
  Night Thoughts (1742–5) 'Night 9' l. 1267

2 Great let me call him; for he conquered me.
  The Revenge (1721) act 1, sc. 1

3 Life is the desert, life the solitude;
  Death joins us to the great majority.
  The Revenge (1721) act 4; see **PETRONIUS** 605:6

George W. Young 1846–1919

4 The lips that touch liquor must never touch
  mine.
  title of poem (*c*.1870); also attributed, in a different form, to
  Harriet A. Glazebrook, 1874

Neil Young 1945– *and* Jeff Blackburn

Canadian singer and songwriter

5 It's better to burn out
  Than to fade away.
  quoted by Kurt **COBAIN** *in his suicide note, 8 April 1994*
  'My My, Hey Hey (Out of the Blue)' (1978 song)

Marguerite Yourcenar 1903–87

French writer

6 Our merchants are sometimes our best
  geographers, our best astronomers, and our
  most learned naturalists.
  Memoirs of Hadrian (1951)

Yevgeny Zamyatin 1884–1937

Russian writer

7 Heretics are the only bitter remedy against the
  entropy of human thought.
  'Literature, Revolution and Entropy' quoted in *The Dragon and
  other Stories* (1967, translated by M. Ginsberg) introduction

8 Yesterday there was a tsar and there were slaves;
  today there is no tsar, but the slaves remain;
  tomorrow there will be only tsars . . . We have
  lived through the epoch of suppression of the
  masses; we are living in an epoch of suppression
  of the individual in the name of the masses;
  tomorrow will bring the liberation of the
  individual—in the name of man.
  'Tomorrow' (1919) in *A Soviet Heretic* (1970)

Israel Zangwill 1864–1926

Jewish spokesman and writer

9 Scratch the Christian and you find the
  pagan—spoiled.
  Children of the Ghetto (1892) bk. 2, ch. 6; see **PROVERBS**
  642:35

10 America is God's Crucible, the great Melting-Pot
  where all the races of Europe are melting and
  re-forming!
  The Melting Pot (1908) act 1

Emiliano Zapata 1879–1919

Mexican revolutionary. See also IBARRURI 424:2

11 Many of them, so as to curry favour with
  tyrants, for a fistful of coins, or through bribery
  or corruption, are shedding the blood of their
  brothers.
  *on the maderistas who, in Zapata's view, had betrayed the
  revolutionary cause*
  Plan de Ayala 28 November 1911, para. 10

Frank Zappa 1940–93

American rock musician and songwriter

12 A drug is neither moral or immoral—it's a
  chemical compound. The compound itself is not
  a menace to society until a human being treats
  it as if consumption bestowed a temporary
  licence to act like an asshole.
  The Real Frank Zappa Book (1989)

13 Rock journalism is people who can't write
  interviewing people who can't talk for people
  who can't read.
  Linda Botts *Loose Talk* (1980); see **CAPP** 197:13

Zeno of Citium *c*.335–*c*.263 BC

Greek philosopher, founder of Stoicism

14 The reason why we have two ears and only one
  mouth is that we may listen the more and talk
  the less.
  to a youth who was talking nonsense
  Diogenes Laertius *Lives of the Philosophers* 'Zeno' ch. 7

Ed Zern 1910–94

American humorous writer

15 This fictional account of the day-by-day life of
  an English gamekeeper is still of considerable
  interest to outdoor-minded readers, as it contains
  many passages on pheasant raising, the
  apprehending of poachers, ways to control
  vermin, and other chores and duties of the
  professional gamekeeper. Unfortunately one is
  obliged to wade through many pages of
  extraneous material in order to discover and
  savour these sidelights on the management of a
  Midlands shooting estate, and in this reviewer's
  opinion this book cannot take the place of J. R.
  Miller's *Practical Gamekeeping*.
  review of reissue of D. H. Lawrence Lady Chatterley's Lover
  in *Field and Stream* November 1959

Zhuangzi *see* Chuang Tzu

Mikhail Zhvanetsky 1934–

Russian writer

16 We enjoyed . . . his slyness. He mastered the art
  of walking backward into the future. He would
  say 'After me'. And some people went ahead,

and some went behind, and he would go backward.

of Mikhail **GORBACHEV**

in *Time* 12 September 1994; attributed

Philip Ziegler 1929–

British historian

1 Remember. In Spite of Everything, He Was A Great Man.

notice kept on his desk while working on his biography of **MOUNTBATTEN** (*published 1985*)

Andrew Roberts *Eminent Churchillians* (1994)

Ronald L. Ziegler 1939–2003

American government spokesman

2 [Mr Nixon's latest statement] is the Operative White House Position . . . and all previous statements are inoperative.

in *Boston Globe* 18 April 1973

Grigori Zinoviev 1883–1936

Soviet politician

3 Armed warfare must be preceded by a struggle against the inclinations to compromise which are embedded among the majority of British workmen, against the ideas of evolution and peaceful extermination of capitalism. Only then will it be possible to count upon complete success of an armed insurrection.

letter to the British Communist Party, 15 September 1924, in *The Times* 25 October 1924; the 'Zinoviev Letter', said by some to be a forgery

Hiller B. Zobel 1932–

American judge

4 Asking the ignorant to use the incomprehensible to decide the unknowable.

'The Jury on Trial' in *American Heritage* July–August 1995

5 Judges must follow their oaths and do their duty, heedless of editorials, letters, telegrams, threats, petitions, panellists and talk shows.

judicial ruling reducing the conviction of Louise Woodward from murder to manslaughter, 10 November 1997

Zohar

chief text of the Jewish Kabbalah, dating from the 13th century, presented as an allegorical or mystical interpretation of the Pentateuch

6 The Holy One, blessed be He, said to the world, when he had made it, and created man: O world, world, you and your laws can be sustained only through the Torah. That is why I created man [to live] in you, so that he might study it. But if he does not do so, I will return you to chaos.

bk. 1, 134b

7 Come and see . . . whatever is in the earth has its parallel in the world above. There is not a single thing, however small, in the world that does not depend on something that is higher . . . for everything is interdependent.

bk. 1, 156b

8 He made this world to match the world above, and whatever exists above has its counterpart below . . . and all is one.

bk. 2, 20a

9 We have taught that every man who talks of the Exodus from Egypt and rejoices fully in its narration will eventually rejoice in the *Shekinah* in the world to come, and this is the greatest joy of all.

bk. 2, 40b

10 After he had fashioned the image of the Chariot of Supernal Man, he descended into it and was known under the image of YHVH, so that man might apprehend him through his attributes, through each of them severally, and he was called El, Elohim, Shaddai, Zeva'ot, and YHVH, so that man might apprehend him through each of his attributes and perceive how the world is governed by kindness and by justice in accordance with men's deeds.

bk. 2, 42b

11 The narratives of the Torah are the garments of the Torah. If a man thinks that the garment is the actual Torah itself, and not something quite other, may his spirit depart, and may he have no portion in the world to come.

bk. 3, 152a

Émile Zola 1840–1902

French novelist

12 Don't go on looking at me like that, because you'll wear your eyes out.

La Bête humaine (1889–90) ch. 5

13 One forges one's style on the terrible anvil of daily deadlines.

Le Figaro 1881

14 Smut detected in it by moral men is theirs rather than mine. Scientific truth was my touchstone for every scene, even the most febrile.

Thérèse Raquin, preface to 2nd edition (1868)

15 *La vérité est en marche, et rien ne l'arrêtera.*

Truth is on the march, and nothing will stop it.

on the Dreyfus affair

in *Le Figaro* 25 November 1897

16 *J'accuse.*

I accuse.

title of an open letter to the President of the French Republic, in connection with the Dreyfus affair

in *L'Aurore* 13 January 1898

Zoroastrian Scriptures

a religion of ancient Persia founded by Zoroaster in the 6th century BC; texts compiled in the 4th century

translations by M. Boyce, 1984

1 We worship Mithra of wide pastures, possessing a thousand ears, possessing ten thousand eyes, the divinity worshipped with spoken name.

The Yashts yasht 10: Avestan Hymn to Mithra, v. 1

2 Never break a covenant, whether you make it with a false man or a just man of good conscience. The covenant holds for both, the false and the just.

The Yashts yasht 10: Avestan Hymn to Mithra, v. 2

3 O Green One [Haoma], I call down your intoxication, your strength, victory, health, healing, furtherance, increase, power for the whole body, ecstasy of all kinds.

The Gathas yasna 9, v. 17

4 I profess myself a Mazda-worshipper, a follower of Zarathustra, opposing the Daevas, accepting the Ahuric doctrine; one who praises the Amesha Spentas, who worships the Amesha Spentas.

The Gathas The Creed (Fravarane) yasna 12, v. 1

5 This one, Zarathustra Spitama, has been found here by me, who alone has hearkened to our teachings. He wishes, O Mazda, to chant hymns of praise for Us and for Truth. So let us give him sweetness of utterance.

The Gathas yasna 29, v. 8

6 Truly there are two primal Spirits, twins renowned to be in conflict. In thought and word, in act they are two: the better and the bad. And those who act well have chosen rightly between these two, not so the evildoers.

The Gathas yasna 30, v. 3

7 I am Zarathustra, Were I able, I should be a true foe to the Deceiver, but a strong support to the Just One.

The Gathas yasna 43, v. 8

8 May truth be embodied, strong with life.

The Gathas yasna 43, v. 16

9 This I ask Thee, tell me truly, Lord. Who in the beginning, at creation, was Father of Order [Asha]? Who established the course of sun and stars? Through whom does the moon wax, then wane? This and yet more, O Mazda, I seek to know.

The Gathas yasna 44, v. 3

10 Him shall I seek to glorify for us with sacrifices of devotion, Him who is known in the soul as Lord Mazda; for he has promised by his truth and good purpose that there shall be wholeness and immortality within His kingdom, strength and perpetuity within His house.

The Gathas yasna 45, v. 10

11 They truly shall be 'saoshyants' [saviours] of the lands who follow knowledge of Thy teaching, Mazda, with good purpose, with acts inspired by truth. They indeed have been appointed opponents of Fury.

The Gathas yasna 48, v. 12

12 But the wicked, of bad power, bad act, bad word, bad Inner Self, bad purpose . . . they shall be rightful guests in the House of the Lie.

The Gathas yasna 49, v. 11

13 As the Master, so is the Judge to be chosen in accord with truth. Establish the power of acts arising from a life lived with good purpose, for Mazda and for the lord whom they made pastor for the poor.

The Gathas 'Ahuna Vairyo'

14 It is thus revealed in the Good Religion that Ohrmazd was on high in omniscience and goodness. For boundless time He was ever in the light. That light is the space and place of Ohrmazd. Some call it Endless Light . . . Ahriman was abased in slowness of knowledge and the lust to smite. The lust to smite was his sheath and darkness his place. Some call it Endless Darkness. And between them was emptiness.

Greater Bundahishn ch. 1

15 For the sake of freedom in the end from the enmity of the Adversary, and restoration, whole and immortal, in the future body for ever and ever, they [the *fravahrs* or souls of men] agreed to go into the world.

Greater Bundahishn ch. 3

16 He [the Evil Spirit] defiled the whole creation . . . So the things of the material world appeared in duality, turning, opposites, fights, up and down, and mixture.

Greater Bundahishn ch. 4

Index

accident (*cont.*):
moving a. is not my trade — WORD 865:22
never the bundle of a. — YEAT 875:13
There's been an a. — GRAH 367:14
accidents A. will happen — PROV 626:4
A. will occur — DICK 277:18
chapter of a. — CHES 223:17
Of moving a. — SHAK 728:9
Omissions are not a. — MOOR 558:1
accommodating a. sort of virtue — MOLI 552:13
accompany a. me with a pure heart — BOOK 133:3
accomplice a. of liars — PÉGU 602:3
accomplices we are all his a. — MURR 566:5
accomplished a. in a week — STEV 775:24
a. man — HORA 414:14
desire a. — BIBL 88:8
accomplishments a. give lustre — CHES 223:16
emerges ahead of his a. — STEI 771:8
accord a. all music makes — SIDN 751:3
with one a. — BOOK 134:8
according a. to his abilities — MARX 526:5
a. to his strength — MORE 559:18
account give a. thereof — BIBL 101:7
sent to my a. — SHAK 700:22
accountable To whom are you a. — BENN 70:3
accounting a. for the moral sense — CARL 199:19
accounts make up my a. — MIDR 534:20
accumulate you can't a. — PROV 635:26
accuracy a. must be sacrificed — JOHN 435:15
accurately not thinking a. — HOLM 403:20
accursed think themselves a. — SHAK 709:8
accuse J'a. — ZOLA 878:16
less eloquence than to a. — HOBB 401:4
To a. is my duty — SCHI 685:23
To a. requires less eloquence — HOBB 401:4
accused a. of child death — RICH 660:6
before you be a. — CHAR 216:15
accuser conscience needs no a. — PROV 633:34
accuses excuses, a. himself — PROV 634:19
accusing a. the rest of the human race — CAMU 196:6
accustomed A. to her face — LERN 490:10
cannot get a. — TOLS 813:9
ace about to play the a. — FIEL 326:5
a. caff with a nice museum — ADVE 7:2
a. down his sleeve — LABO 474:4
Achaeans sufferings for the A. — HOME 404:6
well-greaved A. have suffered — HOME 404:11
Achates *fidus quae tela gerebat A.* — VIRG 828:15
ache ark of the a. — LEVE 491:5
Acheronta *A. movebo* — VIRG 831:1
achieve a. of, the mastery of — HOPK 408:5
I shall a. in time — GILB 357:11
some a. greatness — SHAK 735:24
achieved a. without enthusiasm — EMER 314:24
achievement Great a. is assured — HEGE 389:3
achieving Still a. — LONG 499:18
Achilles A.' cursed anger sing — HOME 404:4
A. his armour — BROW 162:4
A.' wrath — POPE 617:14
armour of A. — VIRG 829:11
in the trench, A. — SHAW 742:27
I've stood upon A.' tomb — BYRO 189:3
name A. assumed — BROW 162:14
see the great A. — TENN 800:20
aching A., shaking, crazy — ROCH 664:20
Achitophel false A. was first — DRYD 294:11
Achivi *plectuntur A.* — HORA 410:3
acid Electric Kool-Aid A. test — WOLF 863:3
acknowledge a. my faults — BOOK 143:4
a. thee to be the Lord — BOOK 133:9
acknowledgement a. passes for current payment — BURN 176:20
acorns oaks from little a. — PROV 633:31
acquaintance A. I would have — COWL 254:13
apology for dropping the a. — SCOT 689:17
auld a. be forgot — BURN 177:11
make a new a. — JOHN 444:8
make new a. — JOHN 439:11
visiting a. — SHER 748:16
acquainted a. with grief — BIBL 94:3
a. with the night — FROS 344:5

what I am not a. with — FLEM 334:21
acquiesce a. in the opinions — PEEL 601:12
acquisition not a personal a. — JUNG 449:10
acquitted guilty party is a. — PUBL 648:31
acre a. in Middlesex — MACA 507:7
a. of barren ground — SHAK 733:13
acres a. o' charms — BURN 178:11
few a. of snow — VOLT 833:12
few paternal a. — POPE 617:32
Three a. and a cow — POLI 613:11
Two wise a. and a cow — COWA 254:7
acrimonious a. and surly republican — JOHN 436:25
acrostic province in A. Land — DRYD 296:11
act a. but not to compete — LAO 480:14
a. of dying — JOHN 440:20
A. of Union is there — TRIM 815:14
A. well your part — POPE 617:6
Between the motion And the a. — ELIO 309:28
both a. and know — MARV 525:7
character of the fifth a. — LERM 490:3
easier to a. than to think — AREN 26:9
every a. of your life — AURE 40:7
If in the first a. — CHEK 222:14
in any A. of Parliament — HERB 393:16
in itself almost an a. — ROSS 669:22
sleep an a. or two — SHAK 711:10
swelling a. — SHAK 718:15
To see him a. — COLE 242:2
wants to get inta the a. — CATC 207:18
within the meaning of the A. — ANON 19:17
acted I a. so tragic — HARG 382:11
lofty scene be a. o'er — SHAK 712:19
acting A. a masochistic form — OLIV 585:4
a. of a dreadful thing — SHAK 712:4
when he was off he was a. — GOLD 364:20
action a. Is a most dangerous thing — CLOU 236:13
A. is consolatory — CONR 249:6
A. is the proper fruit — FULL 346:14
a. of the tiger — SHAK 708:16
a.'s dizzying eddy — ARNO 30:4
A. this day — MILI 535:1
a. to the word — SHAK 702:14
affairs without a. — LAO 479:7
again third, 'a.' — DEMO 273:1
end of man is an a. — CARL 200:22
honourable a. — AGES 9:12
in a. how like an angel — SHAK 701:11
lose the name of a. — SHAK 702:3
lust in a. — SHAK 738:18
Makes that and th' a. fine — HERB 394:7
man of a. — GALS 348:4
not knowledge but a. — ARIS 27:7
Place, and A. — DRYD 297:13
point of taking no a. — LAO 480:7
single completed a. — BOIL 131:4
talents of a. — BYRO 192:1
Thought is the child of A. — DISR 286:14
world only grasped by a. — BRON 157:19
actions a. are what they are — BUTL 182:20
a. of all men — MACH 511:11
a. of the just — SHIR 749:18
a. of two bodies — NEWT 574:5
A. receive their tincture — DEFO 270:19
a. speak louder than words — PROV 626:5
Great a. are not always — BUTL 183:17
laugh at human a. — SPIN 768:12
Man considers the a. — THOM 805:1
my a. are my ministers' — CHAR 217:9
Words without a. — HOOV 406:15
active a. line on a walk — KLEE 469:7
a. Principle — WORD 865:17
to seem a. — BONA 132:4
actor a.'s life for me — WASH 841:1
Like a dull a. — SHAK 698:13
unperfect a. on the stage — SHAK 737:20
actors A. are cattle — HITC 400:2
best a. in the world — SHAK 701:15
four boards, two a. — VEGA 826:1
actress a. to be a success — BARR 60:5
acts a. being seven ages — SHAK 696:27
all your a. are queens — SHAK 737:3

by a. and not by ideas — FRAN 340:11
desires but a. not — BLAK 126:6
first four a. — BERK 72:18
no second a. in American lives — FITZ 332:16
Our a. our angels are — FLET 335:9
actual for the a. object — BOCC 130:7
shackles of the a. — RUSS 675:12
What is rational is a. — HEGE 389:1
actualité economical with the *a.* — CLAR 233:12
actum *Nil a. credens* — LUCA 503:18
ad great a. campaign — BERN 74:6
reminded of that a. — MOND 553:8
adage poor cat i' the a. — SHAK 719:13
Adam A. from his fair spouse — MILT 543:13
A. Had 'em — ANON 16:4
A., the goodliest man — MILT 543:7
A. was a gardener — SHAK 710:2
A. was born hungry — BRIL 157:10
A. was but human — TWAI 820:17
good thing A. had — TWAI 820:16
gratitude we owe to A. — TWAI 820:18
half-awakened A. — YEAT 875:6
hold up A.'s profession — SHAK 704:9
in A. all die — BIBL 112:21
old A. in this Child — BOOK 138:6
Old A.'s likeness — SHAK 730:25
penalty of A. — SHAK 696:14
riverrun, past Eve and A.'s — JOYC 448:1
rubbish of an A. — SOUT 764:3
sleep to fall upon A. — BIBL 79:1
When A. dalfe — ROLL 666:12
When A. delved and Eve span — PROV 646:36
Whilst A. slept — ANON 21:11
whipped the offending A. — SHAK 708:9
adamant a. for drift — CHUR 229:8
frame of a. — JOHN 438:7
adapting right of a. my conduct — PEEL 601:10
adazzle sweet, sour; a., dim — HOPK 407:17
add a. a sentence — BABE 45:1
apt to a. three pages — RICH 660:16
added all these things shall be a. — BIBL 99:19
adder a. is breathing in time with it — MAND 519:3
A.'s fork — SHAK 721:16
brings forth the a. — SHAK 712:3
deaf as an a. — ADAM 2:20
like the deaf a. — BOOK 143:18
lion and a. — BOOK 146:2
stingeth like an a. — BIBL 88:33
addeth that a. more — MARV 525:15
addicted a. to prayers — ASHF 33:14
addiction a. is bad — JUNG 449:13
prisoners of a. — ILLI 424:18
addictive sin tends to be a. — AUDE 38:17
Addison Cato did, and A. approved — EPIT 320:1
addled a. delusion — ELIO 307:13
address non-existent a. — LEWI 492:1
adeste *A., fideles* — ANON 23:2
adieu A., she cries — GAY 351:26
Bidding a. — KEAT 456:1
to which we bid a. — ELLI 313:18
ad infinitum proceed *a.* — SWIF 784:4
adire *a. Corinthum* — HORA 410:13
adjective As to the A. — TWAI 820:22
Adlestrop Yes; I remember A. — THOM 806:16
administered Whate'er is best a. — POPE 617:3
administration a. of the government — SWIF 782:7
criticism of a. — BAGE 50:10
administrative a. won't — LYNN 506:2
admiral kill an a. from time to time — VOLT 833:13
mast Of some great a. — MILT 541:20
admirals A. extolled — COWP 256:3
admiralty price of a. — KIPL 467:12
admirari *Nil a.* — HORA 410:8
admiration disease of a. — MACA 507:10
exciting a. — PASC 597:17
great in a. — SHAK 711:9
admire a., we should not understand — CONG 247:5
Not to a., is all the art — POPE 617:18
scarce begun to a. the one — DRYD 297:18

alien a. people clutching their gods　ELIO 310:4
a. tears will fill for him　WILD 856:4
amid the a. corn　KEAT 456:10
blame the a.　AESC 8:33
damned if I'm an a.　GEOR 353:2
fringe of a. populations　NEWS 573:12
alienated any measure which a.　GRIF 373:3
alienation day of mental a.　RIEL 661:12
alieni A. appetens　SALL 679:6
alienum humani nil a me a.　TERE 801:13
alike all places were a. to him　KIPL 468:8
By nature men are a.　CONF 246:19
aliter Dis a. visum　VIRG 829:15
alive a. and well　ANON 18:9
a. I shall be delighted　HOLL 403:6
all be made a.　BIBL 112:21
came back, still a.　YOKO 876:6
gets out a.　MORR 561:4
gets out of it a.　FILM 328:22
Half dead and half a.　BETJ 75:11
hallelujah! I'm a.　OSBO 588:17
I am a. for evermore　BIBL 117:28
If he were still a.　NAPO 567:13
If we can't stay here a.　MONT 556:8
main thing, to be a.　BYAT 184:23
noise and tumult when a.　EDWA 304:8
no longer a.　BENT 71:15
not just being a.　MART 524:9
Not while I'm a.　BEVI 77:14
Officiously to keep a.　CLOU 236:22
show that one's a.　BURN 176:24
still a. at twenty-two　KING 464:17
was dead, and is a.　BIBL 106:2
ways of being a.　DAWK 269:2
what keeps you a.　CAST 206:10
all 1066 and a. that　SELL 691:22
A. by my own-alone　HARR 383:3
a. for love　SPEN 767:13
A. for one, one for all　DUMA 299:4
a. gone out of the way　BOOK 139:29
a. hell broke loose　MILT 543:16
a. in respect of nothing　PASC 597:15
a. men are evil　MACH 511:4
A.-merciful　KORA 470:18
a. must have prizes　CARR 201:15
A. my pretty ones　SHAK 679:6
a. our yesterdays　SHAK 722:22
a. shall be well　ELIO 309:22
a. shall be well　JULI 449:6
A. that a man hath　BIBL 86:12
A. that I am I give　BOOK 139:2
a. the silent manliness　GOLD 364:11
a. the world is young　KING 464:14
A. things are lawful for me　BIBL 112:10
a. things to all men　ANON 18:13
A. things to all men　BIBL 112:7
A. things were made by him　BIBL 106:35
a. this for a song　CECI 212:8
a. to Heaven　JONE 445:12
Christ is a.　BIBL 115:9
Evening, a.　CATC 207:17
Fair shares for a.　POLI 612:15
given Her a. on earth　BYRO 187:11
have a. in all　CARE 198:5
have his a. neglected　JOHN 439:5
Hear a., see all　PROV 634:29
Jack — I'm a. right　BONE 132:8
Lord upholdeth a.　BOOK 150:1
man for a. seasons　WHIT 853:5
or a. in all　TENN 794:18
we should at a. times　BOOK 137:14
you were a. to me　BROW 168:5
allegiance a. to the flag　BELL 67:15
religious a.　BAGE 50:5
to which you have pledged a.　BALD 52:16
allegory headstrong as an a.　SHER 748:15
things are an a.　BIBL 113:21
Alleluia A.! sing to Jesus　DIX 286:32
Allen love of Barbara A.　BALL 54:2
alley lives in our a.　CARE 199:2
rats' a.　ELIO 311:8
alleys vilest a. in London　DOYL 292:7
alleyways in the a.　CATU 210:14

alliance A., n. In international politics　BIER 121:2
In sad a.　CRAB 257:12
morganatic a.　HARD 380:3
alliances clear of permanent a.　WASH 840:16
entangling a. with none　JEFF 431:16
allies no a. to be polite to　GEOR 353:6
no eternal a.　PALM 595:2
alliteration A.'s artful aid　CHUR 228:15
allons A., enfants de la patrie　ROUG 670:11
allow Government and public opinion a.　SHAW 740:28
Allsopp Guinness, A., Bass　CALV 194:3
allure a. by denying　TROL 816:20
alluring more a. than a levee　CONG 247:25
Almack go to Carlisle's, and to A.'s too　ANST 24:15
almanac as an a. out of date　WALT 838:21
pious fraud of the a.　LOWE 503:1
almanack Look in the a.　SHAK 726:13
almighty a. dollar　IRVI 425:23
A. had placed it there　LABO 474:14
A.'s orders to perform　ADDI 4:11
A., the King of Creation　WINK 860:13
almond a. tree shall flourish　BIBL 90:20
almost A. thou persuadest me　BIBL 110:17
Englishman born and bred, a.　KURE 474:8
alms a. and oblations　BOOK 137:5
a. may be in secret　BIBL 99:10
a. procure us admission　UMAR 821:11
puts a. for oblivion　SHAK 734:17
alone adult is to be a.　ROST 670:6
all a. went she　KING 464:10
a. against smiling enemies　BOWE 153:11
A., alone, all, all alone　COLE 241:1
A. and palely loitering　KEAT 455:4
A. I did it　SHAK 698:16
A., poor maid　MEW 533:14
a. upon the house-top　BOOK 146:16
be a. on earth　BYRO 185:24
Being a. and liking it　HASK 384:2
being a. together　LA B 474:17
dangerous to meet it a.　WHAR 849:11
dreams a.　HARR 383:7
go home a.　JOPL 447:8
I'm all a.　NURS 578:20
I want to be a.　GARB 349:2
Let me a.　BIBL 86:24
Let well a.　PROV 637:25
live a. and smash his mirror　ANON 22:6
live, as we dream — a.　CONR 248:20
Lives not a.　BLAK 124:22
more a. while living　CARR 201:8
never a. with a Strand　ADVE 8:31
never less a.　ROGE 665:13
never walk a.　HAMM 379:4
not sufficiently a.　VALÉ 823:13
One is always a.　ELIO 308:23
One is one and all a.　SONG 762:13
One wants to be a.　PORT 619:21
past history and stand a.　WOOD 863:23
plough my furrow a.　ROSE 668:12
stranger and a.　WOLF 862:19
that the man should be a.　BIBL 78:22
travels a.　PROV 634:17
We are not a.　TAGL 788:13
We were a.　JAME 430:5
when wholly a.　SCIP 687:15
who travels a.　KIPL 466:13
would but let it a.　WALP 837:16
along All a., down along　BALL 56:8
aloof a. from the congregation　HILL 399:8
aloud Angels cry a.　BOOK 133:9
Prayed a.　AUBR 36:5
alp a. of unforgiveness　PLOM 610:3
many a fiery a.　MILT 542:14
Alpes saevas curre per A.　JUVE 451:15
Alph A., the sacred river, ran　COLE 240:4
Alpha A. and Omega　BIBL 117:23
alpine through an A. village　LONG 499:5
alps a. and archipelagoes　ALDR 11:14
A. of green ice　PHIL 606:3
A. on Alps arise　POPE 615:29

O'er the white A.　DONN 288:4
passages through the A.　COLM 244:5
altar a. of God　BOOK 142:9
a. with this inscription　BIBL 110:3
even the a. sheds tears　TALM 789:27
great world's a.-stairs　TENN 795:16
high a. on the move　BOWE 153:13
lays upon the a.　SPRI 768:18
on his own strange a.　SWIN 785:11
so will I go to thine a.　BOOK 141:7
To what green a.　KEAT 455:22
altars a. to the ground　JORD 447:9
thy a., O Lord　BOOK 145:13
alter tastes greatly a.　JOHN 440:13
alteram Audi partem a.　AUGU 39:16
alteration A. though it be　HOOK 406:9
alters when it a. finds　SHAK 738:15
altered a. her person for the worse　SWIF 783:11
alternative Considering the a.　CHEV 225:27
alternatives a. that are not their own　BONH 132:12
exhausted all other a.　EBAN 302:10
ignorance of a.　ANGE 15:17
altitudo to an O a.　BROW 162:26
altogether righteous a.　BOOK 140:11
altruism conscientiousness and a.　CONF 246:1
vigorously exercises a.　MENG 532:4
alway I am with you a.　BIBL 103:25
always a. be an England　PARK 596:22
a. get their man　MOTT 563:21
a. in the majority　KNOX 470:2
are a.　SALL 679:12
not a. be chiding　BOOK 147:1
Once a—, a a—　PROV 640:37
sometimes a.　RICH 661:4
Alzheimer about his A.'s disease　JUTR 450:9
he had A.'s disease　REAG 656:20
on A.'s disease　MURD 565:21
am a.—yet what I am　CLAR 233:1
I A. THAT I AM　BIBL 80:37
I think, therefore I a.　DESC 274:9
Ama A. et fac quod vis　AUGU 39:18
amantem Quis fallere possit a.　VIRG 829:21
amaranth no fields of a.　LAND 478:7
amare amans a.　AUGU 39:3
amari Surgit a.　LUCK 504:15
Amaryllis sport with A.　MILT 540:6
amateur a. is a man who can't　AGAT 9:9
whine of the a. for three　WHIS 850:9
amateurs Hell full of musical a.　SHAW 740:27
nation of a.　ROSE 668:11
amavi Sero te a.　AUGU 39:10
amaze vainly men themselves a.　MARV 525:2
amazed rather I am a.　VIRG 831:14
amazement explores his own a.　FRY 345:20
amazing A. grace　NEWT 574:12
A. love　WESL 847:6
ambassador a. is an honest man　WOTT 870:12
As your a. can see　QIAN 651:4
amber gold and a.　JONS 446:13
in a. to observe the forms　POPE 614:20
lutes of a.　HERR 396:20
ambergris a. on shore　MARV 524:16
ambiguity a. of words　REID 657:15
Seven types of a.　EMPS 315:29
ambition A. can creep　BURK 174:27
A. first sprung　POPE 614:5
A., in a private man a vice　MASS 527:9
A. leads me not only farther　COOK 250:10
A.'s debt is paid　SHAK 712:18
A. should be made　SHAK 713:4
a. with greater objectives　TOCQ 811:11
Art not without a.　SHAK 718:19
by a. hewn　DRAY 293:16
fling away a.　SHAK 710:22
Let not a. mock　GRAY 370:4
make a. virtue　SHAK 728:30
never yet exerted a.　BOSW 152:6
Vain the a. of kings　WEBS 844:6
Vaulting a.　SHAK 719:10
Who doth a. shun　SHAK 696:23
ambitious as he was a., I slew him　SHAK 712:26

ambitious (*cont.*):
Brutus says he was a.   SHAK 713:3
Caesar was a.   SHAK 713:1
of a. minds   SPEN 767:23
ambles who Time a. withal   SHAK 697:13
ambo *Arcades a.*   VIRG 832:5
Amboss *A. oder Hammer sein*   GOET 362:8
Ambree Mary A.   BALL 55:5
ambrosia God is sweet a.   SIKH 751:18
ambrosial a. hair   VIRG 828:19
Phallic and a.   POUN 621:4
âme *ô. est sans défauts*   RIMB 662:17
amemus *atque a.*   CATU 210:6
amen 'A.' Stuck in my throat   SHAK 720:5
Glorious the catholic a.   SMAR 755:14
Will no man say, a.   SHAK 731:2
amens few mumbled a.   HUNT 421:14
America America! A.   BATE 61:7
A. is a country   EMER 315:15
A. is a nation   WHIT 851:1
A. is a vast conspiracy   UPDI 822:21
A. is God's Crucible   ZANG 877:10
A. is just ourselves   ARNO 31:8
A. is now given over   HAWT 385:9
A. is the only idealistic   WILS 860:1
A. is the proof   MCCA 509:6
A.'s present need   HARD 380:6
A., thou half-brother   BAIL 52:7
a. thus top nation   SELL 692:8
Australia looks to A.   CURT 263:7
born in A.   MALC 517:9
cannot conquer A.   PITT 607:13
come back to A.   JAME 430:7
continent of A.   WESL 848:4
debated in A.   ADAM 3:5
Don't sell A. short   POLI 612:13
England and A. divided   MISQ 547:12
every man's love affair with A.   MAIL 516:8
glorious morning for A.   ADAM 3:20
God bless A.   BERL 73:1
huntsmen are up in A.   BROW 162:8
I like to be in A.   SOND 760:21
impresses me most about A.   EDWA 304:6
in common with A.   WILD 854:13
independence of A.   SHEL 742:28
in the living rooms of A.   MCLU 512:11
I, too, sing A.   HUGH 418:1
loss of A.   FREE 342:7
lost his dominions in A.   WALP 838:9
makes A. what it is   STEI 771:4
morning again in A.   POLI 612:25
next to god a.   CUMM 262:4
O my A.   DONN 288:6
think of thee, O A.   WALP 837:20
to A. to convert the Indians   WESL 847:24
United States of A.   PAGE 591:16
vacant lands in A.   JEFF 431:12
what A. did you have   GINS 359:2
whole A.   BURK 173:13
American A. as cherry pie   BROW 161:4
A. beauty rose   ROCK 665:1
A. continents   MONR 553:15
A. culture   COLO 244:8
A. Express   ADVE 7:5
A. families more like   BUSH 182:7
A. friends   BLAI 124:2
A.-outward-bound   HOPK 408:7
A. people have spoken   CLIN 236:9
A., this new man   CEÈV 259:18
A. women shoot   FORS 337:15
changed in A. life   LAHR 476:4
chief business of the A. people   COOL 250:15
free man, an A.   JOHN 435:3
Greeks in this A. empire   MACM 512:15
I also—am an A.   WEBS 844:2
I am A. bred   MILL 537:4
I'm an A.   GOLD 363:14
in love with A. names   BENÉ 69:13
I shall die an A.   WEBS 844:4
Miss A. Pie   MCLE 512:3
no A. infidels   SAHH 677:10
no second acts in A. lives   FITZ 332:16
not a Virginian, but an A.   HENR 392:13

oil controlling A. soil   DYLA 302:3
part of being A.   UPDI 823:1
point of being an A.   UPDI 822:21
send A. boys   JOHN 435:7
tenth A. muse   BRON 158:3
texture of A. life   JAME 429:15
truth, justice and the A. way   ANON 17:4
weakness of A. civilization   PRIE 623:14
welfare of the A. people   HEAR 388:2
Americanism A. with its sleeves rolled   MCCA 509:5
hyphenated A.   ROOS 668:4
Americans A. are our best friends   THOM 808:6
A. are to be freemen   WASH 840:14
A. when they die   PROV 633:16
Good A., when they die   APPL 25:7
ignorant A.   MASS 527:10
my fellow A.   KENN 460:10
passed to new generation of A.   KENN 460:5
Russians and the A.   TOCQ 812:12
when bad A. die   WILD 855:23
Americas off for the A.   BARR 60:4
amiable a. are thy dwellings   BOOK 145:13
amicus *A. Plato*   ARIS 28:8
Amis cocoa for Kingsley A.   COPE 251:6
amiss all is a.   BARN 59:10
mark what is done a.   BOOK 149:7
amitti *non a. sed praemitti*   CYPR 263:15
ammunition pass the a.   FORG 337:13
amniotic a. in an a. paradise   WILL 857:7
amo A., amas   O'KE 584:19
Non a. te   MART 524:4
Odi et a.   CATU 211:5
amoeba When we were a soft a.   SHIP 749:15
amok patriotism run a.   RATH 655:13
among A. them, but not of them   BYRO 186:16
amongst be a. you   BOOK 138:1
amor *a. che muove il sole*   DANT 265:17
A. vincit omnia   CHAU 218:11
Nunc scio quid sit A.   VIRG 832:7
Omnia vincit A.   VIRG 832:10
Suprema citius solvet a. die   HORA 411:17
amorem *subito deponere a.*   CATU 211:2
Amorites king of the A.   BOOK 149:11
amorous a. ditties   MILT 541:24
a. of their strokes   SHAK 694:22
be a., but be chaste   BYRO 190:3
from a. causes springs   POPE 618:4
my a. propensities   JOHN 438:26
reluctant a. delay   MILT 543:6
amour beginning of an A.   BEHN 66:19
c'est l'a.   BOUS 153:5
amphibi rational a. go   MARV 525:17
ample cabined a. Spirit   ARNO 30:1
ampullas *Proicit a.*   HORA 409:3
Amurath Not A. an Amurath succeeds   SHAK 708:1
amuse talent to a.   COWA 253:12
amused a. by its presumption   CART 205:9
We are not a.   VICT 827:14
amusement Nothing is so perfectly a.   STER 773:17
amusements but for its a.   LEWI 492:5
Anabaptists certain A.   BOOK 150:23
anagram mild a.   DRYD 296:11
analogies A. decide nothing   FREU 342:18
analytical A. Engine weaves   LOVE 501:14
anarch Thy hand, great A.   POPE 613:29
anarchism A. is a game   SHAW 741:30
A. stands for the liberation   GOLD 363:17
anarchist small a. community   BENN 70:11
anarchy a. and competition   RUSK 674:8
democracy, call it a.   HOBB 401:3
Mere a. is loosed   YEAT 874:17
anatomies a. of death   SPEN 768:9
anatomist am but a bad a.   TONE 813:20
anatomy A. is destiny   FREU 342:15
not in books of a.   GALE 347:17
ancestor If there were an a.   HUXL 423:16
ancestors a. are very good   SHER 748:16
a. lost no time in abandoning   LANC 477:23
half-civilized a. were hunting   BENJ 69:18
look backward to their a.   BURK 174:2

your a. and your posterity   TACI 786:22
ancestral A. voices prophesying war   COLE 240:7
ancestry pride of a.   POWE 622:8
trace my a.   GILB 357:2
anchor a. to let fall   ASKE 34:1
become our a.   HARR 383:8
anchored a. safe and sound   WHIT 852:3
ancient a. and fish-like smell   SHAK 733:24
a. nobility   BACO 47:20
A. of days   BIBL 95:27
A. of Days   GRAN 368:11
A. person of my heart   ROCH 664:20
A. times   BACO 45:22
Beauty so a.   AUGU 39:10
feet in a. time   BLAK 126:24
It is an A. Mariner   COLE 240:12
most a. profession   KIPL 468:4
rivers a. as the world   HUGH 418:2
signals of the a. flame   DANT 265:13
sing the a. ways   YEAT 875:4
spark of that a. flame   VIRG 829:20
With the a. is wisdom   BIBL 86:28
ancients a. dreaded death   HARE 382:8
a. without idolatry   CHES 223:7
architecture, the a.   CHAM 214:11
counsel of the a.   FULL 346:20
love the a.   CONF 246:6
and including 'a.'   MCCA 509:8
Andromache kissed his sad A.   CORN 252:1
anecdotage fell into his a.   DISR 286:4
anecdote a. dehumanizing   EPHR 316:8
anfractuosities a. of the human mind   JOHN 442:27
angel a. from your door   BLAK 127:10
a. in the house   PATM 599:11
A. o'er a new inn door   BYRO 185:12
a. of death   BRIG 157:1
A. of Death   BYRO 187:17
a. of the Lord came down   TATE 790:16
a. of the Lord came upon them   BIBL 104:12
a. rides in the whirlwind   PAGE 591:15
a. should write   MOOR 558:5
a. watching an urn   TENN 797:22
ape or an a.   DISR 284:20
as the A. did with Jacob   WALT 839:14
beautiful and ineffectual a.   ARNO 31:22
better a. is a man   SHAK 738:23
clip an A.'s wings   KEAT 455:14
Death's bright a.   PROC 624:18
domesticate the Recording A.   STEV 776:1
for an a. to pass   FIRB 327:14
Her a.'s face   SPEN 767:5
in action how like an a.   SHAK 701:11
Like a.-visits, few   CAMP 195:15
Look homeward a.   MILT 540:13
mighty a. took up a stone   BIBL 119:9
ministering a.   SHAK 704:18
ministering a. thou   SCOT 689:4
O! the more a. she   SHAK 729:17
Recording A., as he wrote it down   STER 773:12
say to the A. of Death   MIDR 534:20
Shined in my a.-infancy   VAUG 825:5
What a. wakes me   SHAK 726:16
White as an a.   BLAK 127:12
woman think him an a.   THAC 802:17
wrote like an a.   GARR 349:11
angelheaded a. hipsters burning   GINS 358:22
angeli *Non Angli sed A.*   GREG 372:6
angels Air and a.   DONN 288:23
all the a. stood   BIBL 118:13
a. all were singing   BYRO 191:11
A. and Archangels   BOOK 137:11
A. and ministers of grace   SHAK 700:11
A. are painted fair   OTWA 589:11
A. bending near the earth   SEAR 690:13
A. came and ministered   BIBL 98:23
A. cry aloud   BOOK 133:9
a. fear to tread   POPE 616:14
a. fear to tread   PROV 632:33
A. in jumpers   LEWI 492:17
a. in some brighter dreams   VAUG 825:12
a. keep their ancient places   THOM 808:1

a., nor principalities   BIBL 111:7
a. on the walls   MARL 523:8
a. would be gods   POPE 616:22
band of a. comin' after me   SONG 763:12
behold the a. of God   BIBL 80:9
better a. of our nature   LINC 493:14
By that sin fell the a.   SHAK 710:22
entertained a. unawares   BIBL 116:11
flights of a.   SHAK 705:4
Four a. round my head   PRAY 623:5
Fourteen a. watch   WETT 849:7
give his a. charge over thee   BOOK 146:2
glorious fault of a.   POPE 614:5
God and a.   BACO 45:16
Hear all ye a.   MILT 543:22
if a. fight   SHAK 730:16
If men were a.   MADI 514:7
lower than the a.   BOOK 139:23
make the a. weep   SHAK 723:8
maketh his a. spirits   BOOK 147:4
man did eat a.' food   BOOK 145:8
Michael and his a.   BIBL 118:24
neglect God and his A.   DONN 290:10
Not Angles but A.   GREG 372:6
Our acts our a. are   FLET 335:9
plead like a.   SHAK 719:8
saw a treefull of a.   BENÉ 69:17
sparkling a.   TRAH 814:13
tongues of men and of a.   BIBL 112:14
tree filled with a.   BLAK 128:13
'twixt air and a.' purity   DONN 288:24
what the a. know   NEWM 572:11
Where a. tremble   GRAY 370:20
With a. round the throne   WATT 841:18
women are a.   BYRO 191:9
Ye holy a. bright   GURN 374:19
anger Achilles' cursed a. sing   HOME 404:6
A. always thinks it has   PUBL 648:33
A. and jealousy   ELIO 308:4
A. is a short madness   HORA 410:6
A. is never without an argument   HALI 377:10
a. is not turned away   BIBL 92:5
A. is one of the sinews   FULL 346:10
A. makes dull men   BACO 49:8
a. of his lip   SHAK 735:27
a. of men who have no opinions   CHES 225:7
a. of the sovereign   MORE 559:10
A. supplies the arms   VIRG 828:14
Frozen a.   FREU 343:3
Great a. in the dragon   SUTT 781:21
Juno's never-forgetting a.   VIRG 828:10
lamb That carries a.   SHAK 713:26
life of telegrams and a.   FORS 338:2
Look back in a.   OSBO 588:16
monstrous a. of the guns   OWEN 591:3
more in sorrow than in a.   SHAK 699:29
neither a. nor partiality   TACI 787:6
neither keepeth he his a.   BOOK 147:1
slow to a.   BIBL 88:18
strike it in a.   SHAW 741:16
such great a.   VIRG 828:11
sun go down on your a.   PROV 639:37
angle Brother of the A.   WALT 839:2
Give me mine a.   SHAK 695:5
in every a. greet   MARV 524:19
angler excellent a.   WALT 839:5
if he be an honest a.   WALT 839:1
no man is born an a.   WALT 838:22
anglers too good for any but a.   WALT 839:10
angles Bats not a.   THOM 807:5
Not A. but Angels   GREG 372:6
Offer no a.   TESS 802:14
Angli Non A. sed Angeli   GREG 372:6
angling A. may be said to be   WALT 838:20
be quiet and go a-A.   WALT 839:13
Anglo-Irishman He was an A.   BEHA 66:14
Anglo-Saxon A. attitudes   CARR 203:16
idol of the A.   BAGE 50:16
angry a. and unsocial feelings   PEEL 601:13
a. look on the face   AURE 40:18
a. nearly every day   ALCO 11:8
a. with my friend   BLAK 127:22
A. young man   PAUL 600:1

Be ye a.   BIBL 114:7
hungry man is an a. man   PROV 634:49
man who becomes a.   TALM 789:14
O! when she's a.   SHAK 726:20
When he was a.   BECK 64:29
when very a., swear   TWAI 820:21
anguis Latet a. in herba   VIRG 831:22
anguish howls of a.   HEAL 386:28
With a. moist   KEAT 455:5
angusta Res a. domi   JUVE 450:21
anima Swift was a. Rabelaisii   COLE 242:6
animae A. dimidium meae   HORA 411:5
animal a. needing something   DEMO 272:17
attend a dying a.   YEAT 873:2
Be a good a.   LAWR 483:15
be a good a.   SPEN 765:19
every a. is sad   SAYI 685:9
Man is a noble a.   BROW 162:20
Man is the Only A.   TWAI 820:6
only a. in the world to fear   LAWR 483:19
political a.   ARIS 27:24
pure a. spirits   WOLL 863:14
religious a.   BURK 174:14
so very a. and unecstatic   VICT 827:8
vegetable, a., and mineral   GILB 358:6
Was he an a.   KAFK 452:4
animalculous beings a.   GILB 358:6
animals All a. are equal   ORWE 586:18
a. are divided   BORG 151:8
A., whom we have   DARW 266:20
at its mercy: a.   KUND 474:7
distinguishes us from mere a.   LEIB 488:6
distinguish us from other a.   BEAU 63:3
find the a. amusing   NIET 575:9
man from a.   OSLE 589:5
mind of the lower a.   DARW 266:22
minutely small a.   JAIN 428:12
not over-fond of a.   ATTE 35:6
production of the higher a.   DARW 266:16
takes 40 dumb a.   SLOG 755:6
turn and live with a.   WHIT 852:11
animam Liberavi a. meam   BERN 73:20
animate a. the whole   SMIT 758:19
animated all a. nature   COLE 239:13
animation too old for a.   DISN 284:1
animi natura a.   LUCR 504:11
vivida vis a.   LUCR 504:4
animosity sisterly a.   SURT 781:17
animula A. vagula blandula   HADR 375:7
animum Caelum non a. mutant   HORA 410:10
Anjou sweetness of A.   DU B 298:4
Ann that's little A.   NURS 579:13
Anna Here thou, great A.   POPE 618:10
Annabel Lee I and my A.   POE 610:14
annals a. are blank   MONT 556:7
a. of the poor   GRAY 370:4
War's a. will cloud   HARD 381:20
Anne of A. of Cleves   HENR 392:3
sister A., do you see nothing   PERR 604:2
Annie bonnie A. Laurie   SONG 763:5
annihilate a. but space and time   POPE 617:31
annihilated illimitable was a.   DISR 284:16
annihilating a. all civilization   SAKH 677:16
A. all that's made   MARV 525:5
annihilation a. of one of us   SHEL 743:4
my own a.   GUNN 374:14
anniversaries secret a.   LONG 499:8
Anno Domini only a.   HILT 399:10
annoy a. with what you write   AMIS 15:1
only does it to a.   CARR 202:3
annoyance a. of a good example   TWAI 820:23
source of a.   BAED 49:18
annuity a. is a very serious business   AUST 42:21
annus a. horribilis   ELIZ 313:3
motet a. et almum   HORA 413:18
anointed a. my head with oil   BOOK 140:21
balm from an a. king   SHAK 730:16
anointing Thou the a. Spirit art   BOOK 150:16
another always a. one walking   ELIO 311:17
a. fine mess   LAUR 483:1
a. shall gird thee   BIBL 109:8
in a. country   MARL 522:19

members one of a.   BIBL 114:6
not a. thing   BUTL 182:19
when comes such a.   SHAK 713:15
anser inter strepere a. olores   VIRG 832:9
answer A. a fool   BIBL 88:40
a. came there none   CARR 203:5
a. came there none   SCOT 688:6
a. is blowin' in the wind   DYLA 301:12
a. is 'himself'   IBSE 424:10
a. made it none   SHAK 699:28
a. the phone   CART 205:18
a. to 'Hi!'   CARR 203:27
a. to the Irish Question   SELL 692:7
nothing that does not a.   AUST 41:8
on the way to a pertinent a.   BRON 158:1
please thee with my a.   SHAK 724:26
sent an a. back to me   CARR 203:15
soft a.   BIBL 88:13
soft a. turneth   PROV 643:18
stay for an a.   BACO 48:10
what a dusty a.   MERE 532:22
What is the a.   STEI 771:7
wise men cannot a.   PROV 632:30
wisest man can a.   COLT 244:10
answerable a. for what we choose   NEWM 572:18
answerably a. to your Christian calling   BOOK 138:7
answered hath Caesar a. it   SHAK 713:1
no one a.   DE L 272:7
prayer is only a.   TALM 789:19
answering a. that of God   FOX 339:16
bell-like a.   WORD 864:21
answers Kind are her a.   CAMP 196:2
ant a. Appears a monstrous elephant   COTT 252:15
a.'s a centaur   POUN 621:9
a. which has foreseen   BART 60:7
good husband, little a.   LOVE 502:2
Go to the a.   BIBL 87:27
antagonist Our a. is our helper   BURK 174:19
antediluvian a. families   CONG 247:6
anthology a. is like all   RALE 654:17
Anthropophagi A., and men   SHAK 728:10
anti savage a.-everythings   HOLM 403:13
antic a. disposition   SHAK 700:28
dance an a. hay   MARL 522:13
old and a. song   SHAK 735:15
Antichrist against the a. of Communism   BUCH 169:10
anticipating right of a.   TOLS 813:11
anticipation only in the a. of it   HITC 400:5
antick old father a., the law   SHAK 705:10
anti-destin L'art est un a.   MALR 518:10
anti-Fascist premature a.   ANON 21:18
antipathy a. of good to bad   POPE 617:29
antipodes act our A.   BROW 162:8
like A. in shoes   MARV 525:17
sheer opposite, a.   KEAT 454:17
antique group that's quite a.   BYRO 188:12
noble and nude and a.   SWIN 785:6
old and a. song   SHAK 735:15
over is their a. joy   YEAT 874:23
traveller from an a. land   SHEL 745:15
antiquities A. are history defaced   BACO 45:10
antiquity I seek a.   PUGI 649:3
write for A.   LAMB 477:11
antiwar ecology and a.   HUNT 422:2
Antony A., Enthroned   SHAK 694:23
A. Shall be brought   SHAK 695:25
A. Would ruffle up   SHAK 713:13
catch a second A.   SHAK 696:7
O! my oblivion is a very A.   SHAK 694:16
anvil a. of daily deadlines   ZOLA 878:13
a. on which many a hammer   BEZA 77:15
be the a. or the hammer   GOET 362:8
Church is an a.   MACL 512:1
church is an a.   PROV 629:2
England's on the a.   KIPL 465:6
My sledge and a.   EPIT 319:3
anxiety A. love's greatest killer   NIN 576:9
taboo'd by a.   GILB 356:22
any A. old iron   COLL 243:2

anybody Is there a. there — DE L 272:6
no one's a. — GILB 356:14
anything A. for a quiet life — MIDD 534:7
A. goes — PORT 619:9
believe in a. — CHES 225:26
capable of a. — MAUP 528:15
If a. can go wrong — PROV 635:5
anywhere get a. in a marriage — MURD 565:16
apart have stood a. — WILS 859:17
of man's life a thing a. — BYRO 188:3
ape a. for his grandfather — HUXL 423:16
a.'s an ape — PROV 626:28
gorgeous buttocks of the a. — HUXL 423:2
Is man an a. — DISR 284:20
naked a. — MORR 560:9
played the sedulous a. — STEV 775:12
apes and peacocks — MASE 527:3
a. are apes — JONS 446:7
dogs and a. — BROW 165:24
ivory, and a. — BIBL 84:29
lead a. in hell — SHAK 733:5
people his a. — CHAU 218:27
aphorism a. should be like a burr — LAYT 485:1
aphorists A. can be wrong — FENT 325:2
aphrodisiac Power is the great a. — KISS 469:2
apocalypse write a new a. — HEIN 389:5
Apollo A. from his shrine — MILT 540:29
A. hunted Daphne — MARV 525:3
songs of A. — SHAK 717:26
swear by A. the physician — HIPP 399:16
Yea, is not even A. — SWIN 785:18
young A., golden-haired — CORN 252:3
Apollos A. watered — BIBL 111:26
Apollyon his name is A. — BUNY 171:8
apologies do not want a. — WODE 862:4
apologize good rule never to a. — WODE 862:4
Never a. — FISH 330:9
apologizes if it's raining, a. — WELD 845:15
apology a. for the Devil — BUTL 184:10
defence or a. — CHAR 216:15
God's a. for relations — KING 464:20
apostle great a. of the Philistines — ARNO 31:20
apostles a. of equality — ARNO 31:10
A.: praise thee — BOOK 133:9
A. would have done — BYRO 187:24
He gave some, a. — BIBL 114:5
I am the least of the a. — BIBL 112:18
Twelve for the twelve a. — SONG 762:13
apostolic Catholick and A. Church — BOOK 137:3
apothecary starved a. — LOCK 498:2
apparatus haunted a. sleeps — RAIN 653:11
mediocrity of the a. — TROT 817:7
Persicos odi, puer, a. — HORA 412:4
apparel a. oft proclaims the man — SHAK 700:4
put on glorious a. — BOOK 146:4
rich in a. — TROL 816:5
apparition Anno 1670, was an a. — AUBR 36:8
appeal a. against something — CAMU 196:6
a. from tyranny to God — BYRO 191:3
a. open from criticism — JOHN 437:4
a. unto Caesar — BIBL 110:13
appear a. considerable — JOHN 440:26
how you a. to God — UNAM 821:15
appearance a. always stately — EINH 305:4
a. of Your Majesty — BIBL 78:10
outward a. — BIBL 83:37
reality than in a. — HUME 420:10
appearances a. are deceptive — PROV 626:29
Keep up a. — CHUR 228:11
no trusting a. — SHER 748:30
appearing Television is for a. on — COWA 254:6
appetite A. comes with eating — PROV 626:30
a. grows by eating — RABE 652:7
good digestion wait on a. — SHAK 721:8
hungry edge of a. — SHAK 730:8
voracious a. — FIEL 326:19
were then to me An a. — WORD 866:11
appetites carnal lusts and a. — BOOK 138:21
Our a. as apt to change — DRYD 295:10
Subdue your a. — DICK 279:9
wrecched worldes a. — CHAU 221:14
applause A., n. The echo — BIER 121:3
in the sunshine and with a. — BUNY 171:12

to gain a., one must write — MOZA 563:25
apple aims at me with an a. — VIRG 831:21
a. a day — PROV 626:31
a. falling towards England — AUDE 37:21
a. never falls far — PROV 626:32
a. of his eye — BIBL 82:18
a. on its bough — CRAN 258:15
a. on the tree — DICK 281:16
a. pie and cheese — FIEL 326:3
a. which reddens — ROSS 669:11
astonish Paris with an a. — CÉZA 213:17
A was an a.-pie — NURS 577:18
cabbage-leaf to make an a.-pie — FOOT 336:13
for an a. damn'd mankind — OTWA 589:10
heart is like an a. tree — ROSS 668:18
make an a. pie from scratch — SAGA 677:7
rotten a. injures — PROV 642:31
sweet-a. reddens — SAPP 681:1
vor me the a. tree — BARN 59:7
want the a. for the apple's sake — TWAI 820:17
apples a., cherries, hops — DICK 280:15
a. of gold — BIBL 88:35
A. of gold — SWIN 785:24
a. on the Dead Sea's shore — BYRO 186:8
choice in rotten a. — PROV 643:17
flesh of tart a. — RIMB 662:9
golden a. of the sun — YEAT 874:24
moon-washed a. of wonder — DRIN 294:1
picking dewy a. — VIRG 832:6
Ripe a. drop — MARV 525:4
stolen, be your a. — HUNT 421:8
applications a. for situations — AUDE 37:20
applied no such things as a. sciences — PAST 599:2
Style is not something a. — STEV 774:17
apply a. our hearts unto wisdom — BOOK 145:22
appointed a. for all living — BIBL 87:4
even in the time a. — BOOK 145:11
to th'a. place we tend — DRYD 296:21
appointment a. at the end of the world — DINE 283:11
a. by the corrupt few — SHAW 741:11
A. in Samarra — O'HA 583:15
a. with him in Samarra — MAUG 528:12
create an a. — LOUI 501:5
have kept our a. — BECK 64:22
apprehensions a. come in crowds — WORD 865:4
apprenticeship a. for freedom — BARA 57:16
approbation A. from Sir Hubert — MORT 562:8
appropriate to each what is a. — AUCT 36:14
approve I do not a. — MILL 536:20
après A. nous le déluge — POMP 611:12
apricocks dangling a. — SHAK 730:24
apricot blushing a. — JONS 447:1
April A., April, Laugh — WATS 841:9
A. is the cruellest month — ELIO 311:1
A. of her prime — SHAK 737:17
A. of your youth — HERB 393:9
A. showers bring forth — PROV 626:33
A. shroud — KEAT 455:28
bright cold day in A. — ORWE 587:9
from one A. to another — LONG 500:10
glory of an A. day — SHAK 736:14
Men are A. when they woo — SHAK 697:20
Now that A.'s there — BROW 165:27
Whan that A. — CHAU 218:2
aprons made themselves a. — BIBL 79:6
apt A. Alliteration — CHUR 228:15
a. to die — SHAK 712:21
A. words have power — MILT 545:4
aquae scribuntur a. potoribus — HORA 410:17
Aquarius dawning of the age of A. — RADO 653:8
Aquitaine prince of A. — NERV 571:1
Arab A. world together — ARAF 25:14
Arabia gold of A. — BOOK 144:20
kings of A. and Saba — BOOK 144:19
perfumes of A. — SHAK 722:10
spell of A. — DE L 272:1
Arabian alone the A. bird — SHAK 698:17
in the A. woods — MILT 545:8
Arabians Cretes and A. — BIBL 109:13
Arabic as an A. Koran — KORA 472:8
Hebrew and A. mingling — RUME 672:4

Arabs hundred thousand A. — BALF 53:15
like the A. — LONG 499:1
Araby burns in glorious A. — DARL 266:3
Aram Eugene A. walked between — HOOD 405:14
Arbeit A. macht frei — ANON 22:13
arbiter a. of others' fate — BYRO 190:18
Elegantiae a. — TACI 787:8
high a. Chance governs all — MILT 542:17
arbitrary given way to an a. way — CHAR 216:20
supreme power must be a. — HALI 377:12
arbitrate a. the even — MILT 539:4
arbitrator old common a., Time — SHAK 734:21
arboreal a. in its habits — DARW 266:11
arbours His private a. — SHAK 713:14
arc a. is a long one — PARK 596:23
a. of a moral universe — KING 463:14
a. of history is long — OBAM 583:1
Arcades A. ambo — VIRG 832:5
Arcadia Et in A. ego — EPIT 317:4
Arcadians A. both — VIRG 832:5
Arcady woods of A. are dead — YEAT 874:23
arceo profanum vulgus et a. — HORA 412:14
arch all experience is an a. — TENN 800:16
a.-flatterer is a man's self — BACO 47:14
a. of order — STRA 778:16
a. Of the ranged empire — SHAK 694:9
experience is an a. — ADAM 2:12
like a triumphal a. — DUNN 300:3
triumphant a. — COMM 244:17
archangel A. a little damaged — LAMB 477:8
archangels Angels and A. — BOOK 137:14
archbishop a. had come to see me — BURG 172:7
black A. of York — RAMS 654:20
love to the A. — SHER 749:3
My Lord A. — BULL 170:8
archdeacon (by way of turbot) an a. — SMIT 758:9
archer a. his sharp arrows — SIDN 750:16
mark the a. little meant — SCOT 688:17
arches down the a. of the years — THOM 807:14
Underneath the A. — FLAN 332:21
archetypes known as a. — JUNG 449:10
archipelago Gulag a. — SOLZ 760:12
archipelagoes alps and a. — ALDR 11:14
architect a. can only advise — WRIG 870:6
a. of own fortune — PROV 631:28
A. of the Universe — JEAN 431:4
artist or an a. — GEHR 351:30
can be an a. — RUSK 673:7
consent to be the a. — DOST 291:1
architects great a. — LUTY 505:13
So a. do square and hew — MARV 524:20
architectural a. books — PUGI 649:6
a. man-milliner — RUSK 673:4
great a. secret — TROL 816:5
architecture A. acts the most slowly — DIMN 283:9
A. at the head — BLOM 129:7
A. in general — SCHE 683:6
A. is the art — JOHN 435:14
a., the ancients — CHAM 214:11
Christian A. — PUGI 649:4
Dim a. — WARR 840:10
frolic a. of the snow — EMER 314:16
Gothic a. — RUSK 674:12
great a. — LUTY 505:13
In a. as in all other — WOTT 870:11
rise and fall of English a. — BETJ 76:10
archwives Ye a., stondeth — CHAU 219:1
Arcturi Daisies, those pearled A. — SHEL 746:7
Arden Ay, now am I in A. — SHAK 696:19
ardet paries cum proximus a. — HORA 410:15
ardeur a. dans mes veines — RACI 652:17
ardua a. ad astra — MOTT 563:16
arduis rebus in a. — HORA 412:6
are a. what we repeatedly — ARIS 27:9
A. you now — POLI 612:3
be as they a. — CLEM 235:10
we know what we a. — SHAK 703:32
What you a., that you are — THOM 804:24
arena actually in the a. — ROOS 668:2
Argentinian young A. soldiers — RUNC 672:7
Argos remembers his sweet A. — VIRG 831:9

argosies a. of magic sails — TENN 797:1
argue absurd to a. men — NEWM 572:10
  a. freely — MILT 546:5
  cannot a. with — AUCT 36:10
  earth does not a. — WHIT 852:18
  those who a. — EBNE 302:12
arguing no good in a. — LOWE 503:2
  not a. with you — WHIS 850:5
  Waste no more time a. — AURE 40:23
  will be much a. — MILT 546:4
argument All a. is against it — JOHN 442:11
  a. for a week — SHAK 705:21
  a. of the broken window — PANK 595:15
  a. of tyrants — PITT 607:18
  exact and priggish a. — SAND 679:21
  height of this great a. — MILT 541:10
  I have found you an a. — JOHN 444:3
  impression, not an a. — HARD 381:1
  never without an a. — HALI 377:10
  nice knock-down a. — CARR 203:11
  no a. but force — BROW 163:20
  no force but a. — BROW 163:20
  rotten a. — ANON 20:20
  stir without great a. — SHAK 703:29
argumentative then talky, then a. — BYRO 192:3
arguments attract the worst a. — FISH 330:13
  force of his a. — WALP 838:6
argutos a. inter strepere — VIRG 832:9
Ariel Caliban casts out A. — POUN 621:4
  deal of A. — HENL 391:11
aright sought the Lord a. — BURN 177:23
arise a. and go like men — STEV 776:16
  a. and unbuild it again — SHEL 743:26
  A., shine — BIBL 94:18
  My lady sweet, a. — SHAK 698:19
  will a. and go now — YEAT 873:20
arising from the a. of this — PALI 594:5
aristocracy a. means government by — CHES 225:25
  a. of Great Britain — BRIG 157:2
  A. of the moneybag — CARL 200:4
  displeased with a. — HOBB 401:3
  natural a. among men — JEFF 432:6
aristocratic a. class — ARNO 31:11
Aristotle A. and his philosophie — CHAU 218:15
  A. was but the rubbish — SOUT 764:3
  God of A. — HA-L 377:5
arithmetic theology as in a. — MILT 546:1
arithmetical a. ratio — MALT 518:11
ark a. of bulrushes — BIBL 80:30
  entered into the a. — BIBL 102:27
  into the A. — BIBL 79:22
  two by two in the a. — LEVE 491:5
arm a. of an elm tree — EMER 315:19
  a. of the Lord — BIBL 94:2
  auld moon in her a. — BALL 55:15
  by a stretched out a. — BIBL 82:12
  did not put your a. around it — BLAC 123:7
  down the left a. — BARR 59:15
  long a. of coincidence — CHAM 214:9
  pearls upon an Ethiop's a. — DYER 301:9
  strength with his a. — BIBL 104:9
  Stretch your a. no further — PROV 643:44
  with his holy a. — BOOK 146:11
arma A. virumque cano — VIRG 828:10
  Cedant a. togae — CICE 231:23
  leges inter a. — CICE 232:8
  Moriamur et in media a. ruamus — VIRG 829:14
armadas till the great A. come — NEWB 571:9
Armageddon called in the Hebrew tongue A. — BIBL 119:6
  Lincoln County Road or A. — DYLA 302:2
  We stand at A. — ROOS 668:3
armchair like a good a. — MATI 528:1
armchairs a. tight about the hips — WODE 862:6
armed a. conflict — EDEN 303:3
  a. so strong in honesty — SHAK 713:23
  A. warfare must be preceded — ZINO 878:3
  a. with more than complete steel — ANON 18:4
  own mind you need to be a. — VALÉ 823:15
Armenteers Mademoiselle from A. — MILI 535:14
armes Aux a., citoyens — ROUG 670:11
armful very nearly an a. — GALT 348:6

armies a. clash by night — ARNO 29:6
  a. swore terribly — STER 773:6
  commander of three a. — CONF 246:10
  disbanding hired a. — CARL 200:18
  Kings with their a. — BOOK 144:8
  money and large a. — ANOU 24:7
  more dangerous than standing a. — JEFF 432:9
  stronger than all the a. — SAYI 685:12
Arminian A. clergy — PITT 607:12
armistice It is an a. for twenty years — FOCH 336:3
armour Achilles his a. — BROW 162:4
  a. of Achilles — VIRG 829:11
  a. of God — BIBL 114:14
  a. of light — BIBL 111:16
  a. of light — BOOK 135:10
  put your a. on — WESL 847:15
armoured a. cars of dreams — BISH 122:9
arms Anger supplies the a. — VIRG 828:14
  a. against a sea of troubles — SHAK 701:26
  a. and the man — VIRG 828:10
  a., and the man I sing — DRYD 297:10
  a. do flourish — BACO 48:16
  a. of a chambermaid — JOHN 442:21
  a. were made the Warrior — RIG 661:15
  a. ye forge — SHEL 746:12
  caught in her a. — WYAT 871:5
  Emparadised in one another's a. — MILT 543:8
  everlasting a. — BIBL 82:21
  he laid down his a. — HOOD 405:15
  if my love were in my a. — ANON 21:8
  in my a. — BALL 54:16
  it hath very long a. — HALI 377:15
  keep and bear a. — CONS 250:5
  Kings have long a. — PROV 637:6
  man's outspread a. — LEON 489:21
  mightier than they in a. — MILT 543:25
  proud in a. — MILT 538:21
  This world in a. — EISE 306:6
  To war and a. — LOVE 502:6
  world in a. — SHAK 714:15
army a. marches on its stomach — NAPO 568:6
  a. marches on its stomach — PROV 626:34
  a. of Martyrs — BOOK 133:9
  a. of unalterable law — MERE 532:2
  a. would be a base rabble — BURK 173:23
  contemptible little a. — ANON 17:3
  dialect with an a. — WEIN 845:8
  Forgotten A. — MOUN 562:16
  formation of an Irish a. — GRIF 373:4
  invasion by an a. — HUGO 419:3
  little ships brought the A. home — GUED 374:6
  terrible as an a. — BIBL 91:11
  Your poor a. — CROM 260:18
aroint A. thee, witch — SHAK 718:6
aroma a. of performing seals — HART 383:11
aromatic beneath the a. pain — WINC 860:9
  rose in a. pain — POPE 616:24
arose a. and followed him — BIBL 100:13
around goes a. comes around — SAYI 685:16
  Money makes the world go a. — EBB 302:11
aroused a. every feeling — TAYL 791:9
a-roving go no more a. — SONG 762:2
arrange French a. — CATH 209:10
arrangements has no a. — WHIT 852:18
arrears pay glad life's a. — BROW 167:8
arrest a. all beauty — CAME 194:13
  swift in his a. — SHAK 704:26
arrested a. one fine morning — KAFK 452:5
  conservative been a. — WOLF 863:2
arrival a. was most welcome — NELS 570:1
arrive A. or find — THOM 807:9
  a. where I am — BUNY 171:27
  a. where we started — ELIO 309:19
  barbarians are to a. — CAVA 211:13
  better thing than to a. — STEV 775:27
arrived a. and to prove it — CATC 208:11
arrogant subdue the a. — VIRG 830:14
arrow a. from the Almighty's bow — BLAK 125:14
  a.-head of grieving — PALI 594:22
  a. that flieth by day — BOOK 146:1
  Every a. that flies — LONG 499:2
  shot an a. — LONG 498:14

  time's a. — EDDI 302:14
arrows archer his sharp a. — SIDN 750:16
  a. of desire — BLAK 126:24
  Like as the a. — BOOK 149:3
  mine a. upon them — BIBL 82:20
  slings and a. — SHAK 701:26
  swift a. in my quiver — PIND 606:17
ars A. longa, vita brevis — HIPP 399:13
arse politician is an a. upon — CUMM 262:7
arsenal a. of old Europe — HEGE 388:16
  great a. of democracy — ROOS 667:11
arsenic like a. — FIEL 326:21
art Advertising is the greatest a. form — MCLU 512:12
  All a. is collaboration — SYNG 786:9
  all the rules of a. — ADDI 5:23
  almost lost in A. — COLL 243:16
  A. alone Enduring stays — DOBS 287:2
  A. always serves beauty — PAST 598:17
  A., and the summer lightning — HERZ 396:24
  A. a revolt against fate — MALR 518:10
  a. can wash her guilt away — GOLD 365:14
  A. constantly aspires — PATE 599:7
  A. does not reproduce the visible — KLEE 469:6
  A. for art's sake — CONS 249:21
  A. for art's sake — COUS 253:6
  A. for art's sake — DIET 283:3
  a. for the sake — SAND 680:1
  a. has no other end — FLAU 334:6
  A. has something to do — BELL 69:4
  A. has to move you — HOCK 401:15
  A. in its perfection — REYN 659:5
  a. is a comparable vocation — FRIN 343:14
  A. is a jealous mistress — EMER 314:20
  A. is an abstraction — GAUG 350:12
  a. is immoral — WILD 855:5
  A. is long — LONG 499:15
  A. is long — PROV 626:35
  A. is long and critics — JARR 430:23
  A. is meant to disturb — BRAQ 155:6
  A. is not a brassière — BARN 59:2
  a. is not a weapon — KENN 460:14
  A. is not truth — PICA 606:15
  A. is only Nature — HOLB 402:21
  A. is pattern informed by sensibility — READ 656:4
  A. is significant deformity — FRY 345:23
  A. is the imposing of a pattern — WHIT 851:10
  A. is the objectification — LANG 478:13
  A. is upon the Town — WHIS 850:6
  A. is vice — DEGA 271:6
  A. most cherishes — BROW 166:22
  a. must not be too much — MURD 565:18
  a. of balance — MATI 528:1
  a. of being wise — JAME 430:15
  a. of getting drunk — JOHN 442:24
  a. of the possible — BISM 122:16
  a. of the possible — GALB 347:15
  a. of the soluble — MEDA 530:1
  a.'s hid causes — JONS 446:4
  a. which one government sooner — SMIT 756:8
  A., whose honesty must work — RIDI 661:8
  beyond the reach of a. — POPE 615:27
  book of their a. — RUSK 673:16
  clever, but is it A. — KIPL 465:12
  dead a. Of poetry — POUN 621:2
  Deals are my a. form — TRUM 818:3
  Desiring this man's a. — SHAK 737:22
  Dying is an a. — PLAT 608:9
  E in A-level a. — HIRS 400:1
  end and test of a. — POPE 615:26
  enemy of good a. — CONN 248:8
  example of modern a. — CHUR 231:5
  fascinating kind of a. — WARH 840:2
  Fine a. is that — RUSK 674:2
  first taught A. — ROSS 669:19
  from a., not chance — POPE 616:6
  genius and a. — HAZL 386:13
  glib and oily a. — SHAK 714:19
  good grey guardians of a. — WILB 854:5
  great design of a. — DENN 273:13
  great religious a. of the world — CLAR 233:13

art (*cont.*):
have learned their a.   PIND 606:17
Here the great a. lies   MILT 545:25
history of a.   BUTL 184:9
If a. does not enlarge   ELIO 308:16
In a. the best is good enough   GOET 362:9
industry without a.   RUSK 673:8
in Jonson, A.   DENH 273:7
is the a. of God   YOUN 877:1
it is not a.   SCHO 686:10
last and greatest a.   GOET 363:3
last and greatest a.   POPE 617:24
Life imitates A.   WILD 855:7
Life is short, the a. long   HIPP 399:13
madness of a.   JAME 429:19
Minister that meddles with a.   MELB 530:14
morality of a.   WILD 855:16
More matter with less a.   SHAK 701:4
my job and my a.   MONT 555:11
nature is the a. of God   BROW 163:2
nature's handmaid a.   DRYD 295:11
Nature that is above all a.   DANI 264:5
necessary a.   DULL 299:2
never was an A.-loving nation   WHIS 850:7
next to Nature, A.   LAND 478:3
noblest point of a.   EPIT 317:7
offered you Conflict and A.   PRIE 623:11
only obliterated in a.   SHAW 742:22
people start on all this A.   HERB 393:12
perfect of all works of a.   SCHI 685:27
practical form of a.   COOP 251:4
probité de l'a.   INGR 425:14
purpose of a.   GOUL 366:14
rank of every a.   REYN 659:2
responsibility is to his a.   FAUL 324:18
Robust a. alone is eternal   GAUT 350:14
Shakespeare wanted a.   JONS 447:2
stick to murder and leave a.   EPST 316:13
Story the spoiled child of a.   JAME 429:9
supreme master of a.   CONR 249:9
symbol of Irish a.   JOYC 448:15
through A., and through Art only   WILD 855:4
true test of a.   INGR 425:14
War's glorious a.   YOUN 876:14
what a. means to me   O'KE 584:18
what great a. removes   BOLA 131:7
when A. is too precise   HERR 396:1
where the a. resides   SCHN 686:8
work of a.   SMIT 756:11
work of a. is good   RILK 662:3
works of a.   ALBE 11:4
Works of a.   RILK 662:4
artful a. Dodger   DICK 280:2
Arthur in A.'s bosom   SHAK 708:14
talks of A.'s death   SHAK 714:12
article excellent a.   BAGE 51:18
first a. of my faith   GAND 348:13
snuffed out by an a.   BYRO 189:14
articles These a. subscribed   CONG 247:27
articulate made a. all that I saw   BROW 160:16
artifact Death's a.   ABSE 1:5
artificer great a. Made my mate   STEV 776:23
lean unwashed a.   SHAK 714:12
artificial All things are a.   BROW 163:2
but an a. man   HOBB 400:14
said it was a. respiration   BURG 172:8
sort of a. inlet   FOST 338:20
artillery a. of words   SWIF 783:28
love's great a.   CRAS 259:7
terrible a.   FLAT 333:1
artisan employment to the a.   BELL 68:16
artist a. a receptacle   PICA 606:10
a. brings something into   UPDI 822:26
a. has no need to express   PROU 625:12
a. is his own fault   O'HA 583:16
a. is someone who   WARH 840:3
a. man and the mother woman   SHAW 740:24
a. must be in his work   FLAU 334:4
a. never dies   LONG 499:12
a. or an architect   GEHR 351:30
a. remains within or behind   JOYC 448:10
a. will be judged   CONN 248:13
become a good a. by copying   INGR 425:15

enemies to a real a.   GAIN 347:1
God only another a.   PICA 606:13
hard bargain with an a.   BEET 66:11
Industry, Which dignifies the a.   DYER 301:7
Never trust the a.   LAWR 483:14
no man is born an a.   WALT 838:22
one position for an a.   THOM 806:7
portrait of the a.   JOYC 448:5
sign of a true a.   VIDA 827:17
task of the a.   BECK 64:13
What an a. dies   NERO 570:9
artistic a. verisimilitude   GILB 357:14
never was an a. period   WHIS 850:7
artists A. not engineers of the soul
  KENN 460:14
arts a. at first from Nature came   LANI 479:4
a. babblative and scribblative   SOUT 764:16
cry both a. and learning   QUAR 651:15
Dear nurse of a.   SHAK 709:11
even the a. should take advantage
  MONT 555:22
fine a. had ever produced   PEEL 601:13
followed the a.   SHAK 735:2
France, famed in all great a.   ARNO 31:2
France, mother of a.   DU B 298:2
head of the a.   BLOM 129:2
interested in the a.   AYCK 43:14
In the a. of life   SHAW 741:2
mother of a.   MILT 544:25
No a.; no letters   HOBB 400:24
one of the fine a.   DE Q 273:21
recreation in the a.   CONF 246:7
studied the liberal a.   OVID 590:2
virtues were his a.   BURK 176:9
you 'a.' people   MCEW 510:13
artus *totamque infusa per a.*   VIRG 830:12
Aryan your A. eye   PLAT 608:5
ascendancy a. of the Whig party   MACA 507:11
ascended a. into heaven   BOOK 133:19
ascendeth a. up for ever and ever   BIBL 119:2
ascending angels of God a.   BIBL 80:9
lark a.   MERE 532:17
ascribe A. unto the Lord   BOOK 146:9
ash a. on an old man's sleeve   ELIO 309:16
avoid an a.   PROV 627:44
empty a. can   CRAN 258:14
Oak, and A., and Thorn   KIPL 467:18
oak is before the a.   PROV 647:1
Out of the a.   PLAT 608:10
ashamed a. and confounded   BOOK 144:15
a. thereof   BROW 163:6
a. to look upon one another   WALT 839:6
feel a. of home   DICK 278:9
more things a man is a. of   SHAW 740:22
something he is a. of   SHAW 739:15
ashbuds a. in the front of March   TENN 793:15
ashen in oure a. olde   CHAU 220:2
Your a. hair Shulamith   CELA 212:9
ashes a. for thirty   LAMP 477:21
a. new-create   SHAK 711:9
a. of an Oak   DONN 290:8
a. of his fathers   MACA 508:13
a. on the lips   MOOR 558:15
a. taken to Australia   ANON 18:5
a. to ashes   BOOK 139:10
a. to the taste   BYRO 186:8
a. under Uricon   HOUS 416:2
beauty for a.   BIBL 94:20
burnt to a.   GRAH 367:15
dust and a.   BIBL 87:3
Dust and a.   BROW 168:2
I am a.   BYRO 191:8
into a. all my lust   MARV 525:13
past is a bucket of a.   SAND 680:6
sour grapes and a.   ASHF 33:17
universe to a.   MISS 550:5
until they be a.   CHAP 216:13
Asia churches which are in A.   BIBL 117:22
churches which are in A.   BIBL 117:25
not in A.   ARDR 26:5
pampered jades of A.   MARL 523:10
Will end up in A.   BLY 129:15
Asian A. boys ought to be   JOHN 435:7

Asians A. could still smile   HEAD 386:26
aside set death a.   TURG 819:1
ask all that we do a.   BIBL 114:3
a. and cannot answer   SHAW 742:26
A., and it shall be given   BIBL 99:24
a. faithfully   BOOK 136:12
a. if you are enjoying   NESB 571:3
a. is have   SMAR 754:16
A. me no more   CARE 198:13
a. nothing   ELGA 306:16
a. not what your country   KENN 460:10
could a. him anything   WEIS 845:10
Don't a., don't tell   NUNN 577:17
Don't a. me, ask the horse   FREU 342:20
Don't let's a. for the moon   FILM 328:3
for our blindness we cannot a.   BOOK 138:4
if you gotta a.   ARMS 28:17
if you gotta a.   MISQ 548:8
To a. the hard question   AUDE 38:14
Would this man a. why   AUDE 37:2
askance looking a., other nations   GOGO 363:12
asked Nobody a. you   NURS 582:11
You've a. for it   MOLI 552:11
asketh Every one that a. receiveth   BIBL 99:25
asking a. too much   CANN 196:25
mere a. of a question   FORS 338:7
time of a.   BOOK 138:19
aslant grows a. a brook   SHAK 704:5
asleep Fall a., or hearing die   SHAK 710:17
Half a. as they stalk   HARD 381:19
men were all a.   BRID 156:19
mother was glad to get a.   EMER 315:17
sucks the nurse a.   SHAK 696:5
till it falls a.   TEMP 792:13
very houses seem a.   WORD 865:8
asp hole of the a.   BIBL 92:18
aspens Willows whiten, a. quiver   TENN 796:14
asperges *A. me, Domine*   MISS 546:15
A. me hyssopo   BIBL 119:27
aspersion a. upon my parts of speech
  SHER 748:13
aspersions Casting a. on those   FLAU 333:7
aspes as an a. leef   CHAU 221:3
asphalt only monument the a. road
  ELIO 310:24
aspidistra biggest a. in the world   HARP 382:17
Keep the a. flying   ORWE 587:4
aspiration a., to do nought   ROSS 669:22
aspire by due steps a.   MILT 538:20
gaze, and there a.   ARNO 30:20
light, and will a.   SHAK 738:27
aspirin a. for a brain tumour   CHAN 215:10
aspiring great a. spirits   DANI 264:10
ass a. may bray a good while   ELIO 308:9
call great Caesar a.   SHAK 696:4
crowned a.   HENR 391:21
dull a. will not mend   SHAK 704:11
enamoured of an a.   SHAK 726:27
firstborn the greatest a.   CARO 201:6
kiss my a. in Macy's window   JOHN 435:9
law is a a.   DICK 280:6
law is such an a.   CHAP 216:8
not covet his a.   BIBL 81:20
on his unwashed a.   PARS 597:11
with the jaw of an a.   BIBL 83:15
You're an a.   ROCH 664:19
assailed A., fight, taken   DONN 288:4
assassin copperheads and the a.   SAND 680:3
you are an a.   ROST 670:7
assassination absolutism moderated by a.
  ANON 16:27
a. Could trammel up   SHAK 719:6
A. has never changed   DISR 284:21
A. is the extreme form   SHAW 742:15
A. is the quickest   MOLI 552:20
assassins a. of idealism   HOOV 406:15
assault a. and hurt the soul   BOOK 135:16
assaults a. of our enemies   BOOK 134:2
a. of the devil   BOOK 134:16
assay a. so hard   CHAU 220:21
asserted boldly a.   BURR 180:13
asses go seek the a.   BIBL 83:30
seeking a. found   MILT 544:23

to those great a. | LUTH 505:11
assigned doom a. | TENN 798:13
assistance give me a little a. | COLU 244:14
assume A. a virtue | SHAK 703:19
assurance a. given by looks | ROYD 671:17
a. of incorruption | BIBL 97:5
low on whom a. sits | ELIO 311:14
make a. double sure | SHAK 721:21
Assyrian A. came down | BYRO 187:16
curled A. Bull | TENN 797:21
Astarte A., queen of heaven | MILT 541:23
Astolat lily maid of A. | TENN 794:10
astonish A. me | DIAG 275:11
a. Paris with an apple | CÉZA 213:17
a. the bourgeois | BAUD 62:4
astonished A. at eclipse | ORCH 586:2
a. at my own moderation | CLIV 236:10
rightly a. by events | BART 60:7
astonishment read every day, with a. | CHES 223:11
Your a.'s odd | KNOX 470:4
astounded a. by them | ATTE 35:6
astra ardua ad a. | MOTT 563:16
sic itur ad a. | VIRG 831:7
astray as sheep going a. | BIBL 111:7
like sheep have gone a. | BIBL 94:4
not send their works a. | KORA 472:19
astrologer a. came the astronomer | DOYL 292:26
astrologers A. or three wise men | LONG 500:11
astronomers and a. | QUIN 652:3
Christian must avoid a. | AUGU 39:17
astrology A. is a disease | MAIM 516:16
astronomer astrologer came the the a. | DOYL 292:26
undevout a. is mad | YOUN 876:28
astronomers A. and astrologers | QUIN 652:3
astronomy daughter of a. | YOUN 876:28
Astur cry is A. | MACA 508:16
asunder bones are smitten a. | BOOK 142:7
let no man put a. | BOOK 139:3
let not man put a. | BIBL 102:5
asylum lunatic a. run by lunatics | LLOY 496:18
taken charge of the a. | ROWL 671:12
was in an a. | PALM 595:8
ate a. when we were not hungry | SWIF 782:13
Freddie Starr a. my hamster | NEWS 573:9
With A. by his side | SHAK 712:23
atheism inclineth man's mind to a. | BACO 46:6
owlet A. | COLE 239:16
atheist a. half believes a God | YOUN 876:23
a. if the king were | LA B 475:2
a. is a man | BUCH 169:9
a.-laugh's a poor exchange | BURN 178:4
denial of Him by the a. | PROU 625:12
female a. | JOHN 438:1
from being an a. | SART 681:21
I am still an a. | BUÑU 171:2
remain a sound a. | LEWI 491:19
sort of a. | ORWE 587:2
superstitious a. | BROW 164:26
village a. brooding | CHES 225:19
was no a. | CHAR 217:3
atheistical damned a. age | VANB 823:18
atheists far from a. | CUDW 261:15
no a. in the foxholes | CUMM 262:14
Athenian not A. or Greek | SOCR 760:7
Athenians A. and strangers | BIBL 110:2
Athens A. arose | SHEL 744:4
A., the eye of Greece | MILT 544:25
A. to do with Jerumsalem | TERT 802:13
citizen of A. | SOCR 759:19
Ye men of A. | BIBL 110:3
A Theory A. of the Origins | MAYR 529:10
athirst give unto him that is a. | BIBL 119:17
athletes All pro a. are bilingual | HOWE 417:1
Atlanta A. is gone | CHES 222:17
Atlantic A. surge | THOM 808:16
steep A. stream | MILT 538:22
stormy North A. Ocean | LARD 480:15
atlas blank a. of your body | NERU 570:13
atman A., the Spirit in man | UPAN 821:17
A., the Spirit, the Self | UPAN 822:10

That [A.] is not this | UPAN 822:3
atmosphere shove against an a. | EDDI 302:17
atom a. has changed everything | EINS 305:13
carbon a. | JEAN 431:3
defence against the a. bomb | ANON 16:13
flaring a.-streams | TENN 797:14
grasped the mystery of the a. | BRAD 154:6
leads through the a. | EDDI 302:18
atomic primordial a. globule | GILB 357:2
win an a. war | BRAD 154:5
atoms a. and space | DEMO 272:16
a. of Democritus | BLAK 126:26
A. or systems | POPE 616:18
concurrence of a. | PALM 595:4
motions of a. in my brain | HALD 376:12
record the a. | WOOL 864:6
atone a. for our past | CHEK 221:20
atrocities a. however horrible | NAMI 567:7
attach wish to a. | AUST 41:21
attachment free from a. | BHAG 78:5
attack A. is best form of defence | PROV 627:2
by his plan of a. | SASS 682:11
lead such dire a. | MACA 508:17
Problems worthy of a. | HEIN 389:6
attacked when a. it defends itself | ANON 21:20
attacking I am a. | FOCH 336:2
attain I cannot a. unto it | BOOK 149:16
attainable We look at the a. | GLAD 360:6
attempt a. and not the deed | SHAK 720:3
that dares love a. | SHAK 732:13
attempted Something a. | LONG 500:5
attendant a. lord, one that will do | ELIO 310:11
attention a. must be paid | MILL 537:8
a. to the object | WEIL 845:4
memory is the art of a. | JOHN 436:11
attentive a. and favourable hearers | HOOK 406:7
attic A. grace | POUN 621:3
Beauty crieth in an a. | BUTL 184:19
brain a. stocked | DOYL 292:8
furniture in Tolkien's a. | PRAT 622:10
glory of the A. stage | ARNO 31:1
O A. shape | KEAT 455:21
sleeps up in the a. there | MEW 533:14
Where the A. bird | MILT 544:26
attire bride forget her a. | BIBL 94:24
Her rich a. | KEAT 454:10
attitude Fair a. | KEAT 455:23
attitudes Anglo-Saxon a. | CARR 203:16
attorney gentleman was an a. | JOHN 440:24
attraction A. and repulsion | BLAK 126:1
feels the a. of earth | LONG 499:2
put a. on | BEHN 66:22
that powerful a. | SHEL 747:15
attractions Costs register competing a. | KNIG 469:13
attractive make a. with his touch | HORA 409:9
attributes through each of his a. | ZOHA 878:10
Auber down by the dank tarn of a. | POE 611:6
auburn Sweet A., loveliest village | GOLD 364:1
audace toujours de l'a. | DANT 265:18
audacity Arm me, a. | SHAK 698:17
a. of elected persons | WHIT 852:16
tactful in a. | COCT 237:22
aude sapere a. | HORA 410:5
audendi a. semper fuit aequa potestas | HORA 408:15
audi A. partem alteram | AUGU 39:16
audience fit a. find | MILT 543:26
whisks his a. | HORA 409:8
audiences English-speaking a. | WHAR 849:8
two kinds of a. | SCHN 686:7
audio-visual full of a. marvels | SMIT 757:2
audit how his a. stands | SHAK 703:7
auditorem notas a. rapit | HORA 409:8
augmentation a. of the Indies | SHAK 736:1
augury we defy a. | SHAK 704:23
august A. for the people | AUDE 36:27
A. is a wicked month | O'BR 583:4
corny as Kansas in A. | HAMM 379:3
recommence in A. | BYRO 189:19
Augustan next A. age | WALP 837:19
Augustus A. was a chubby lad | HOFF 402:4

auld do wi' an a. man | BURN 180:9
For a. lang syne | BURN 177:12
aunt A. is calling to Aunt | WODE 862:2
Charley's a. from Brazil | THOM 805:13
aunts bad a. and good aunts | WODE 861:23
dull a., and croaking rooks | POPE 615:20
his cousins and his a. | GILB 357:27
not a. that matter | WODE 862:5
auprès A. de ma blonde | SONG 762:3
aurea A. prima sata | OVID 590:6
auream A. quisquis mediocritatem | HORA 412:8
auri A. sacra fames | VIRG 829:17
Auschwitz saved one Jew from A. | AUDE 38:23
write a poem after A. | ADOR 6:10
year spent in A. | LEVI 491:7
austere beauty cold and a. | RUSS 675:1
austerities monk destroys by a. | JAIN 428:9
Austerlitz A. and Waterloo | SAND 680:5
field of A. | KIPL 467:9
Australia Advance A. fair | MCCO 509:14
A. has a marvellous sky | LAWR 484:3
A. looks to America | CURT 263:7
convert it into A. | FLIN 335:20
emigrate to A. | MULD 564:15
history of A. | SEDD 690:14
take A. right back | KEAT 453:18
Australian A. selfhood | HUGH 418:6
great A. Emptiness | WHIT 850:20
Australians A. will stand beside | FISH 327:18
A. wouldn't give | ADVE 7:7
Austria Don John of A. is going | CHES 224:10
author amended By its A. | EPIT 317:1
a. and finisher of our faith | BIBL 116:7
a. and giver | BOOK 136:7
a. of his own disgrace | COWP 255:6
a. of peace | BOOK 134:2
a. ought to write | FITZ 332:17
a. who speaks | DISR 285:2
Choose an a. | DILL 283:6
expected to see an a. | PASC 597:14
go to the a. | RUSK 673:18
half an a.'s graces | MORE 558:19
in search of an a. | PIRA 607:4
like in a good a. | SMIT 757:12
majesty of the A. of things | LEIB 488:9
more than wit to become an a. | LA B 475:4
No a. ever spared a brother | GAY 351:13
rather have been the a. | ADDI 5:5
shrimp of an a. | GRAY 371:3
store Of the first a. | MARV 525:15
to be an a. | HAZL 386:18
authoress dared to be an a. | AUST 43:3
authorities imposed by the a. | PLAT 608:17
authority adduces a. | LEON 489:16
A. forgets a dying king | TENN 794:23
a. of the eternal yesterday | WEBE 843:16
A. without wisdom | BRAD 154:14
Experience, though noon a. | CHAU 220:8
in a. under her | BOOK 137:6
Lawful and settled a. | JOHN 437:9
little brief a. | SHAK 723:8
make your peace with a. | MORR 561:8
man under a. | BIBL 100:7
maximal a. and minimal power | SZAS 786:11
no a. from God to do mischief | MAYH 529:8
solely on a. | AYER 43:15
taught them as one having a. | BIBL 100:5
than in a. | THOM 804:16
authorized copy of the A. Version | WHAT 849:19
authors a. their copyrights | TROL 815:17
damn those a. | CHUR 228:1
great a. have their due | BACO 45:7
invades a. like a monarch | DRYD 297:16
praise of ancient a. | HOBB 401:9
women-a. | COOP 251:3
authorship popular a. | TROL 817:1
autobiography age to write an a. | WAUG 842:14
a. is an obituary | CRIS 260:5
A. is now as common | GRIG 373:7
pearl is the oyster's a. | FELL 324:23
autocrat a.: that's my trade | CATH 209:18

Nothing so b. but · PROV 640:21
put up with b. things · TROL 816:17
sad b. glad mad · SWIN 785:4
shocking b. hats · WELL 846:11
This bold b. man · SHAK 710:15
When b. men combine · BURK 175:4
when she was b. · LONG 500:7
badge b. of all our tribe · SHAK 724:9
red b. of courage · CRAN 258:20
badgers When b. fight · CLAR 232:18
badly end b. · STEV 776:9
man who has planned b. · HERO 395:11
worth doing b. · CHES 225:22
bag b. and baggage · GLAD 360:2
b. with holes · BIBL 96:18
Lays eggs inside a paper b. · ISHE 426:2
out of a tattered b. · PROV 644:39
unpack my own b. · UPDI 822:25
with b. and baggage · SHAK 697:8
baggage bag and b. · GLAD 360:2
b. loves me · CONG 247:10
Baghdad B. is determined · HUSS 422:8
B. is safe · SAHH 677:10
bagman Cobden is an inspired b. · CARL 200:30
bags carry other people's b. · FILM 330:2
bah 'B.,' said Scrooge · DICK 277:1
Bailey come home Bill B. · CANN 197:8
bailiff b.'s daughter · BALL 54:1
Bainters hate all Boets and B. · GEOR 352:7
bairns Fools and b. · PROV 632:29
baits b. do fleetest fish entice · GASC 350:5
bake b. so shall you brew · PROV 626:40
brew, so shall you b. · PROV 626:41
baked b. cookies and had teas · CLIN 236:2
b. in this pie · SHAK 734:12
baker b.'s man · NURS 580:16
butcher, the b. · NURS 581:5
bakers b. and breweries · LANG 478:17
Baker Street B. irregulars · DOYL 292:22
Bakewell B. in half-an-hour · RUSK 673:15
balance art of b. · MATI 528:1
b. and weight that equalizes · CERV 213:11
b. of power · NICO 575:1
b. of the Old · CANN 197:6
small dust of the b. · BIBL 93:18
uncertain b. of proud time · GREE 371:24
words in a b. · BIBL 97:26
balances weighed in the b. · BIBL 95:25
bald b., and short of breath · SASS 682:4
b. and unconvincing · GILB 357:14
b. as the bare mountain · ARNO 31:26
fight between two b. men · BORG 151:10
found him b. too · BROW 165:23
Go up, thou b. head · BIBL 85:24
baldness far side of b. · SMIT 757:7
Balfour of the B. declaration · WEIZ 845:11
Balkans damned silly thing in the B. · BISM 123:4
trouble in the B. in the spring · KIPL 468:17
ball b. no question makes · FITZ 331:22
girl throwing a b. · WOOL 864:11
real business of a b. · SURT 781:16
that portion of the b. · POPE 611:18
wind it into a b. · BLAK 125:16
yawning at a b. · LERM 490:4
ballad favourite b. · ADDI 5:5
love a b. in print · SHAK 737:5
metre b.-mongers · SHAK 706:10
met with a b. · CALV 194:2
ballads b., songs and snatches · GILB 357:1
permitted to make all the b. · FLET 335:1
Ballinderry B. in the springtime · FERG 325:6
Balliol God be with you, B. men · BELL 68:26
balloon b. of experience · JAME 429:11
something in a huge b. · WORD 868:2
balloons Of air-b. · BYRO 187:25
ballot b. is stronger than · MISQ 547:3
nuisances of the b. · SALI 678:16
rap at the b. box · CHIL 226:3
ballots peaceful b. · LINC 493:9
ball-point brandishes is a b. · FANT 323:5
balls B. will be lost always · BERR 75:1
rackets to these b. · SHAK 708:11

With two pitch b. · SHAK 717:14
Ballyjamesduff to B. · FREN 342:11
balm B. of hurt minds · SHAK 720:6
b. upon the world · KEAT 454:17
general b. · DONN 289:12
no b. in Gilead · BIBL 95:2
wash the b. · SHAK 730:16
balmy Ginger, you're b. · MURR 565:23
Baltimore then you're in B. · GORD 366:6
ban B. the bomb · POLI 612:5
banal b. Eldorado · BAUD 61:13
banality b. of evil · AREN 26:6
manufacture of b. · SARR 681:5
Banbury to B. Cross · NURS 581:2
band heaven-born b. · HOPK 408:12
of this ruined b. · SHAK 708:19
we b. of brothers · SHAK 709:8
bandage wound, not the b. · POTT 620:9
bandaged death b. my eyes · BROW 167:8
Bandar-log What the B. think · KIPL 468:5
bandied struck and b. · WEBS 844:15
bands b. of love · BIBL 96:5
b. of Orion · BIBL 87:12
b. of wickedness · BIBL 94:15
Bandusia spring of B. · HORA 413:4
bandy b. civilities · JOHN 440:14
bane Deserve the precious b. · MILT 541:30
baneful b. effects · WASH 840:17
bang B.! Now the animal Is dead · DE L 272:4
b.—went saxpence · PUNC 649:21
bigger b. for a buck · POLI 612:8
If the big b. does come · OSBO 588:19
Kiss Kiss B. Bang · KAEL 452:1
no terror in a b. · HITC 400:5
Not with a b. but a whimper · ELIO 310:1
bangs b. one about · ELIZ 313:7
banish b. not him · SHAK 706:6
b. them to their couches · KORA 471:15
I b. you · SHAK 698:8
banished Alone, a b. man · BALL 55:7
art b. hence · MILT 544:18
banishment bitter bread of b. · SHAK 730:15
bank b. and shoal of time · SHAK 719:6
b. will lend you money · HOPE 407:1
cry all the way to the b. · LIBE 492:20
deposit at a Swiss b. · ALLE 13:15
I know a b. · SHAK 726:8
pregnant b. swelled up · DONN 289:4
robbing a b. · BREC 156:1
sleeps upon this b. · SHAK 725:10
waly, up the b. · BALL 56:5
banker as a Scotch b. · DAVI 268:3
banking as much as we value b. · TOYN 814:6
b. and prostitution · WRIG 870:17
B. establishments are more · JEFF 432:9
bankrupt B. of life · DRYD 294:14
bankruptcy intellectual b. · HOLM 403:15
banks b. unscalable · SHAK 698:21
bonnie, bonnie b. · SONG 763:9
Letters from b. · AUDE 37:20
Ye b. and braes · BURN 177:16
banner b. with the strange device · LONG 499:5
Freedom's b. · DRAK 293:11
star-spangled b. · KEY 461:13
banners army with b. · BIBL 91:11
b. of the king advance · FORT 338:15
Confusion on thy b. wait · GRAY 369:19
royal b. forward go · FORT 338:15
banquet b. ceases · SHEN 747:18
Church's b. · HERB 394:18
banqueter b. fed full · LUCR 504:14
banqueting b. upon borrowing · BIBL 97:22
banter how does fortune b. us · BOLI 131:15
Bantu [B.] has been subjected · VERW 826:16
banyan like the great b. tree · PATI 599:10
baptism b., and the Supper · BOOK 138:15
b., a regeneration · ELIO 307:1
B. be administered · BOOK 138:5
in my B. · BOOK 138:5
baptize I b. with water · BIBL 107:4
bar no moaning of the b. · TENN 793:6
treat if met where any b. is · HARD 381:21
When I have crossed the b. · TENN 793:7

Barabbas B. was a publisher · CAMP 195:20
B. was a robber · BIBL 108:27
crowd will always save B. · COCT 237:23
Barbara love of B. Allen · BALL 54:2
barbarian as a b. boxes · DEMO 272:20
He is a b. · SHAW 739:14
barbarians b. are to arrive · CAVA 211:13
B., Philistines, and Populace · ARNO 31:8
Greeks, and to the B. · BIBL 110:20
in my own mind the B. · ARNO 31:11
without the b. · CAVA 211:14
young b. all at play · BYRO 186:24
barbaric sound my b. yawp · WHIT 852:15
barbarism b. be considered · WEIL 844:29
Everyone calls b. · MONT 555:2
barbarisms colloquial b. · JOHN 437:12
barbarity b. of tyrants · SMIT 758:1
barbarous b. dissonance · MILT 539:8
b., savage · DIDE 282:11
b. to write a poem · ADOR 6:10
invention of a b. age · MILT 541:6
barbarousness confess mine own b. · SIDN 751:8
barber like a b.'s chair · SHAK 694:4
bard goat-footed b. · KEYN 462:4
more fat than b. beseems · THOM 808:9
voice of the B. · BLAK 127:15
bards as b. will not · CRAB 258:7
worst of b. confessed · CATU 210:12
bare Back and side go b. · ANON 16:11
B. like nude, giant girls · SPEN 766:13
b. mountain tops · ARNO 31:26
B. ruined choirs · SHAK 738:4
barefoot always goes b. · PROV 643:4
b. friars · GIBB 355:4
bargain dateless b. · SHAK 733:4
hard b. with an artist · BEET 66:4
made a good b. · FRAN 341:5
two to make a b. · PROV 636:40
bargains rule for b. · DICK 278:20
barge b. she sat in · SHAK 694:22
Baring Rothschild and B. · GILB 356:24
bark come out, and b. · JOHN 443:11
dogs b. at me · SHAK 731:11
He began to b. · NURS 578:19
his b. cannot be lost · SHAK 718:7
keep a dog and b. yourself · PROV 647:23
see, they b. at me · SHAK 716:6
barking b. dog never bites · PROV 627:9
Barkis B. is willin' · DICK 277:7
barley among the bearded b. · TENN 796:15
Corn rigs, an' b. rigs · BURN 178:17
fields of b. and of rye · TENN 796:13
barleycorn bold John B. · BURN 179:17
Barlow Hornby and my B. · THOM 807:11
barn b. and the forge · HOUS 415:17
b.-cocks say Night is growing · HARD 381:22
Barnaby B. bright · PROV 627:10
like B. Rudge · LOWE 502:11
Barney Give him the money, B. · CATC 207:21
barns nor gather into b. · BIBL 99:16
baronet No little lily-handed b. · TENN 799:23
baronetage any book but the B. · AUST 41:24
barrel ain't got a b. of money · WOOD 864:2
drowned in a b. of Malmesey · FABY 322:11
grows out of the b. of a gun · MAO 521:3
meal in a b. · BIBL 85:7
barrel-organ played on a b. · MOZA 563:25
barren b. and dry land · BOOK 143:24
b. strand · JOHN 438:8
b. superfluity of words · GART 350:3
b. woman to keep house · BOOK 148:2
cry, 'tis all b. · STER 772:10
I am but a b. stock · ELIZ 312:1
live a b. sister · SHAK 725:21
none is b. · BIBL 91:4
barricade some disputed b. · SEEG 691:1
barrier b. of your teeth · HOME 404:12
barriers b. of our prison · EDGE 303:11
b. of the heavens · EPIT 317:3
there are no b. · WOLL 863:7
barrow there in your long b. · MULD 564:13

barrows grassy b. of the happier dead
TENN 800:10
Basan fat bulls of B. BOOK 140:17
Og the king of B. BOOK 149:11
base Labour without joy is b. RUSK 673:26
man of soul so b. TOCQ 811:12
people as b. as itself PULI 649:9
To what b. uses may we SHAK 704:16
Why bastard? wherefore b. SHAK 714:22
baseless b. fabric SHAK 733:31
baseness b.' varlet JONS 446:7
baser fellows of the b. sort BIBL 109:33
bashfulness particular b. ADDI 5:16
basia Da mi b. mille CATU 210:7
basics time to get back to b. MAJO 517:5
basil Hung over her sweet B. KEAT 454:28
steal my B.-pot KEAT 455:1
Basingstoke hidden meaning—like B.
GILB 358:11
basket come from the same b. CONR 249:8
eggs in one b. PROV 630:25
Basle At B. I founded HERZ 397:1
Basques say of the B. CHAM 215:2
Bass Guinness, Allsopp, B. CALV 194:3
bassoon heard the loud b. COLE 240:15
bastard all my eggs in one b. PARK 596:18
God . . . the b. BECK 64:7
more b. children SHAK 698:11
we knocked the b. off HILL 399:2
Why b.? wherefore base SHAK 714:22
bastardizing twinkled on my b. SHAK 715:1
bastards Don't let the b. SAYI 685:4
some call nature's b. SHAK 736:30
stand up for b. SHAK 714:23
Bastille Voltaire in the B. DE G 271:19
bat b. that beats about in caverns WILB 854:4
beetle and the b. JOHN 440:18
black b., night, has flown TENN 798:3
couldn't b. for the time COMP 245:1
Ere the b. hath flown SHAK 721:4
On the b.'s back SHAK 734:3
Twinkle, twinkle, little b. CARR 202:6
weak-eyed b. COLL 243:11
Wool of b. SHAK 721:16
bath rather lie in a hot b. THOM 806:15
sit in a hot b. TENN 801:8
sore labour's b. SHAK 720:6
test my b. before I sit NASH 568:21
tired of B. AUST 41:20
bathe b. in his tears DONN 290:1
b. those beauteous feet FLET 335:15
early-morning b. SIKH 752:5
bathes He who b. here SIKH 752:10
bathing caught the Whigs b. DISR 284:7
large b. machine GILB 356:23
one long b. of a summer's day WORD 868:8
bathroom can't feel revolutionary in a b.
LINK 495:4
baths Two walking b. CRAS 259:9
bathwater baby out with the b. PROV 630:30
baton marshal's b. LOUI 501:10
bâton dans sa giberne le b. LOUI 501:10
bats b. amongst birds BACO 48:5
b. have been broken HOWE 416:17
B. not angels THOM 807:5
b. will squeak and wheel NICO 575:1
batsman I am the b. LANG 478:10
batsmen opening b. to the crease
HOWE 416:17
battalions big b. PROV 642:10
in pale b. go SORL 761:24
not of the heavy b. VOLT 834:16
battening B. upon huge seaworms
TENN 796:10
batter B. my heart DONN 288:12
battle at Sheriffmuir A b. MCLE 512:7
b. and murder BOOK 134:19
b. done POTT 620:3
b. flags were furled TENN 797:1
b. fought of late HARI 382:12
b., n. A method BIER 121:4
b.'s lost and won SHAK 718:1
b. to the strong BIBL 90:11
b. to the strong DAVI 267:15
b. to the strong PROV 642:17
b. will be in the shade HERO 395:12
better in b. than in bed STER 773:10
defeated in a great b. LIVY 496:7
die in a b. SHAK 708:25
die in the b. CLOU 236:14
forefront of the hottest b. BIBL 84:15
foremost in b. BALL 55:5
France has lost a b. DE G 271:7
glorious b. FORT 338:14
half the b. GOLD 365:8
into the midst of the b. VIRG 829:14
Ireland's b. CONN 248:15
it is a field of b. STEV 775:30
Lord mighty in b. BOOK 141:2
make them ready to b. BOOK 148:16
meet my death in b. SIKH 752:2
Next to a b. lost WELL 846:7
noise of b. rolled TENN 794:21
out of b. I escaped OWEN 591:8
prepare himself to the b. BIBL 112:15
See the front o' b. BURN 179:9
smelleth the b. afar off BIBL 87:13
stand three times in the b. EURI 321:11
This b. fares SHAK 710:6
we b. for the Lord ROOS 668:3
battledore B. and shuttlecock DICK 280:18
battlefield b. is the heart DOST 290:17
battlements down from the white b.
HEAT 388:6
his head upon our b. SHAK 718:4
PERCHED ON B. BEER 66:4
battles b. long ago WORD 869:11
Dead b., like dead generals TUCH 818:10
forced marches, b. and death GARI 349:7
mother of all b. HUSS 422:7
O God of b. SHAK 709:4
opening b. of subsequent wars ORWE 587:8
baubles Take away these b. MISQ 548:20
Baum Lebens goldner B. GOET 362:1
bawcock king's a b. SHAK 708:21
bawdy Bloody, b. villain SHAK 701:23
touched the b. strings STEV 774:11
bay b. the moon SHAK 713:21
flourishing like a green b.-tree BOOK 141:26
bayonet b. is a weapon POLI 612:6
bayonets throne of b. INGE 425:5
throne of b. YELT 875:17
with our b. turning WOLF 862:14
Bayonne hams, B. POPE 613:27
bays oak, or b. MARV 525:2
be b.-all and the end-all SHAK 719:6
b. as they are CLEM 235:10
b. the change GAND 349:1
better to b. AUCT 36:13
B. what you would seem PROV 628:1
How less what we may b. BYRO 189:26
Let b. be finale of seem STEV 774:3
poem should not mean but b. MACL 512:6
that which shall b. BIBL 89:19
To b., or not to be SHAK 701:26
beach On the b. CHES 225:8
beachèd Upon the b. verge SHAK 734:9
beaches fight on the b. CHUR 229:15
beacon b.-light is quenched SCOT 688:19
beacons b. of wise men HUXL 423:15
beaded With b. bubbles KEAT 456:4
beadsman be your b. PEEL 602:2
beak b. from out my heart POE 611:3
in his b. Food enough MERR 533:3
beaker O for a b. full KEAT 456:4
Beale Miss Buss and Miss B. ANON 18:23
beam B. me up, Scotty MISQ 547:4
b. that is in thine own eye BIBL 99:22
beamish But oh, b. nephew CARR 204:2
my b. boy CARR 202:22
beams b. of his chambers BOOK 147:4
bean b. and the cod BOSS 151:17
Nine b. rows YEAT 873:20
not too French French b. GILB 357:20
beans B. meanz Heinz ADVE 7:8
put b. in the clay PROV 628:32

bear any of us can b. GIUL 359:11
B. and forbear PROV 627:11
B. of Very Little Brain MILN 538:1
b. thee in their hands BOOK 146:2
b. the yoke in his youth BIBL 95:11
B. up—trust to time FORS 338:5
b. very much reality ELIO 309:5
B. ye one another's burdens BIBL 113:24
bush supposed a b. SHAK 727:4
cannot b. them BIBL 108:21
Exit, pursued by a b. SHAK 736:24
fire was furry as a b. SITW 753:11
fitted by nature to b. AURE 40:13
Grizzly B. is huge and wild HOUS 415:5
heavy b. who goes with me SCHW 687:11
How a b. likes honey MILN 538:9
huntsman by the b. oppressed WALL 836:16
Puritan hated b.-baiting MACA 507:20
rugged Russian b. SHAK 721:10
so b. ourselves that CHUR 229:16
still less the b. FRER 342:13
till you have caught the b. PROV 630:27
who can b. BIBL 88:22
beard By thy long grey b. COLE 240:12
husband with a b. SHAK 727:16
I have a b. coming SHAK 725:29
King of Spain's B. DRAK 293:8
Loose his b. GRAY 369:20
Old Man with a b. LEAR 485:14
on a Dutchman's b. SHAK 735:29
womman hath no b. CHAU 219:19
bearded all scroungy and b. CORS 252:10
b. like the pard SHAK 697:1
beards long b., and pretences SWIF 783:20
when b. wag all PROV 636:21
beareth B. all things BIBL 112:14
b. up things light BACO 47:23
bears b. might come with buns ISHE 426:2
b. the marks of the last person HAIG 376:5
bigger b. try to pretend MILN 538:6
dancing dogs and b. HODG 401:18
rhythms for b. to dance FLAU 333:4
Teddy B. have their Picnic BRAT 155:9
beast above a b. BIBL 89:24
b. hath devoured him BIBL 80:19
b. or a fool KILV 463:1
b. or a god ARIS 27:25
b., or a god BACO 46:32
b. who is always spoiling MACA 509:1
B. With many heads SHAK 698:10
b. with two backs SHAK 728:4
Beauty killed the B. FILM 329:14
before he caught the b. WALL 836:16
Blatant b. men call SPEN 767:24
blond b. NIET 575:23
but a just b. ANON 16:12
fit night out for man or b. FIEL 327:8
life of his b. BIBL 88:4
Man's life is cheap as b.'s SHAK 715:12
mark, or the name of the b. BIBL 118:26
marks of the b. HARD 380:15
more subtil than any b. BIBL 79:4
No b. so fierce SHAK 731:14
number of the b. BIBL 118:27
questing b. MALO 517:19
serpent subtlest b. MILT 544:3
whan a b. is deed CHAU 219:8
What rough b. YEAT 874:18
Who is like unto the b. BIBL 118:25
who worship the b. BIBL 119:2
beastie cow'rin', tim'rous b. BURN 179:24
beasties long-leggety b. PRAY 623:3
beastly b. the bourgeois is LAWR 483:18
b. to the Germans COWA 253:10
beasts b. at Ephesus BIBL 112:23
b. of the earth BIBL 109:25
b. of the field BOOK 147:5
b. of the forest BOOK 143:2
b. of the forest BOOK 147:8
compared unto the b. BOOK 143:1
elders and the four b. BIBL 118:13
four b. BIBL 118:8
four b. full of eyes BIBL 118:4

invent new b.   HEIN 389:11
kin to the b.   BACO 46:7
like brute b.   BOOK 138:21
wild b. of the desert   BIBL 93:7
beat b. down Satan   BOOK 134:23
b. generation   KERO 461:5
b. him when he sneezes   CARR 202:3
b. their swords   BIBL 91:21
can't b. them, join them   PROV 635:21
dread b.   JOHN 435:1
he b. them all   BYRO 192:7
We b. them today   STAR 770:8
beaten b. path to his door   EMER 315:22
b. road   SHEL 744:2
No Englishman is ever fairly b.   SHAW 742:12
Thrice was I b.   BIBL 113:15
beateth one that b. the air   BIBL 112:9
beating b. Russia is for your country   ESPO 320:10
Charity and b.   FLET 335:14
driven by b.   ASCH 33:2
glory of b. the French   WOLF 862:17
Greeks take the b.   HORA 410:3
hearts b.   BROW 166:17
mend his pace with b.   SHAK 704:11
beatings dread of b.   BETJ 76:8
Beatles B.' first LP   LARK 480:18
beats b. as it sweeps   ADVE 7:36
Beattock Pulling up B.   AUDE 37:19
beatum ab omni Parte b.   HORA 412:11
vocaveris Recte b.   HORA 414:4
beatus B. ille, qui procul negotiis   HORA 411:3
B. vir qui timet Dominum   BIBL 120:2
beaut it's a b.   LA G 476:2
beauteous b. and sublime   AKEN 10:1
B. the garden's umbrage   SMAR 754:17
How b. mankind is   SHAK 734:4
It is a b. evening   WORD 866:4
beauties b.! O how great the sum   SMAR 754:14
many b. grace a poem   HORA 409:13
meaner b. of the night   WOTT 870:8
pale, unripened b.   ADDI 4:15
saved by b. not his own   POPE 611:15
beautified b. with his presence   BOOK 138:21
beautiful Albert is b.   VICT 827:7
All things bright and b.   ALEX 12:6
b. and damned   FITZ 332:4
b. and death-struck year   HOUS 416:5
b. and ineffectual angel   ARNO 31:22
b. and noble is the result   BAUD 61:15
b. and simple   HENR 392:9
b. and the clever   GREE 371:12
b. are thy feet   BIBL 91:13
b. cannot be the way   COUS 253:6
b. catastrophe   LE C 487:3
b. country   BROW 161:9
B. dreamer   FOST 338:21
b. face is a mute   PUBL 648:29
b. game   PELÉ 602:6
b. God to behold   SWIN 785:18
b. upon the mountains   BIBL 93:27
believe to be b.   MORR 560:18
better to be b.   WILD 855:21
Black is b.   POLI 612:10
comes up more b.   HORA 413:15
endless forms most b.   DARW 266:18
how b. they are   COLE 239:8
hunger to be b.   RHYS 659:14
in a b. way   O'KE 584:18
innocent and the b.   YEAT 873:16
Love is b. image   MICH 533:16
love of what is b.   PERI 603:23
most b. thing   SAPP 680:20
most b. things   RUSK 673:25
Names Most B.   KORA 473:7
scorn looks b.   SHAK 735:27
She's b.   SHAK 709:20
singing:—'Oh, how b.!'   KIPL 466:1
slaying of a b. hypothesis   HUXL 423:5
Small is b.   SCHU 687:1
Something b. for God   MUGG 564:4
something b. for God   TERE 801:19
When a woman isn't b.   CHEK 222:6

beauty all that b., all that wealth   GRAY 370:4
American b. rose   ROCK 665:1
arrest all b.   CAME 194:13
b. all very well at first sight   SHAW 741:8
b. being only skin-deep   KERR 461:8
b. coming and the beauty gone   WORD 866:17
B. crieth in an attic   BUTL 184:19
b. draws us   POPE 618:8
b. draws with single   PROV 627:12
B. endures only   SAPP 680:19
b. faded   PHIL 606:2
b. for ashes   BIBL 94:20
B. for some provides escape   HUXL 423:2
b. in music   IVES 426:6
b. in one's equations   DIRA 283:20
B. is but a flower   NASH 569:1
b. is in the eye   PROV 627:13
B. is momentary in the mind   STEV 774:10
B. is mysterious   DOST 290:17
b. is no quality   HUME 420:11
b. is not, as fond men misdeem   SPEN 767:28
B. is only a promise   STEN 771:12
b. is only sin deep   SAKI 678:5
b. is past change   HOPK 407:17
B. is power   ADVE 7:9
B. is the first test   HARD 380:9
B. is the lover's gift   CONG 247:23
B. is truth   KEAT 455:25
b. is woman's sceptre   WOLL 863:13
B. itself doth of itself   SHAK 737:12
B. killed the Beast   FILM 329:14
b. lives with kindness   SHAK 736:16
b. making beautiful old rime   SHAK 738:10
b. of holiness   BOOK 146:9
b. of holiness   MONS 554:2
b. of inflections   STEV 774:16
b. of Israel   BIBL 84:11
b. of the house of God   SUGE 779:17
b. only skin deep   PROV 627:14
B. so ancient   AUGU 39:10
b.'s rose   SHAK 737:15
b.'s self she is   ANON 19:6
b.'s Silent music   CAMP 196:1
B. that must die   KEAT 456:1
b. the joy of possessing form   PAST 598:17
b., though injurious   MILT 545:7
B. too rich for use   SHAK 732:7
b. unadorned   BEHN 67:7
B. vanishes   DE L 272:2
b. will be soon resolved   MARL 523:2
b. will save the world   DOST 291:6
b. without vanity   BYRO 191:20
befriended us with b.   CAVE 211:19
body's b. lives   STEV 774:10
dreamed that life was b.   HOOP 406:11
England, home and b.   ARNO 32:12
Exuberance is b.   BLAK 126:17
fatal gift of b.   BYRO 186:18
Fostered alike by b.   WORD 868:9
ghosts of B. glide   POPE 614:29
Helen's b.   SHAK 727:3
horror and its b.   SHEL 745:14
If you get simple b.   BROW 165:20
image of true b.   ROUS 670:16
imagination seizes as b.   KEAT 457:12
infant b. could beget   SEDL 690:16
innocence and b. born   YEAT 874:11
in thy b.'s field   SHAK 737:16
in true b.   CONG 247:14
I quested for b.   SMAR 754:10
issuing forth into b.   HUNT 421:12
looked on B. bare   MILL 536:22
Love built on b.   DONN 287:15
many kinds of b.   BAUD 62:3
no excellent b.   BACO 46:9
Of its own b.   BYRO 186:21
Only through b.'s gate   SCHI 683:16
only through B. that man   SCHI 685:26
order and b.   BAUD 61:12
principal b. in building   FULL 346:11
She walks in b.   BYRO 190:25
some b. lies   MILT 539:28
stone to b. grew   EMER 314:15

supreme b.   RUSS 675:1
terrible b. is born   YEAT 873:7
thick, bereft of b.   SHAK 733:9
thing of b.   KEAT 454:3
thing of b.   ROWL 671:10
we just b. see   JONS 446:21
Where B. was   GALS 348:3
winds of March with b.   SHAK 737:1
your b.'s orient deep   CARE 198:13
beaver Cock up your b.   HOGG 402:17
Harry, with his b. on   SHAK 706:16
because B. I do not hope to turn   ELIO 308:20
b. I think him so   SHAK 736:12
B. it's there   MALL 517:17
B. it was he   MONT 555:1
B. We're here   MILI 535:17
cannot do it, Sir, b.   CARR 203:15
beck upon the peple I b.   CHAU 219:27
beckoning What b. ghost   POPE 614:2
becks Nods, and b.   MILT 539:23
become all that may b. a man   SHAK 719:14
unborn, not b.   PALI 594:20
becomes nothing so b. a man   SHAK 708:16
becometh holiness b. thine house   BOOK 146:5
bed And so to b.   PEPY 603:1
as little as my b.   KEN 459:16
b. be blest that I lie on   PRAY 623:5
b. is the cold grave   BALL 54:9
better in battle than in b.   STER 773:10
blue b. to the brown   GOLD 365:12
boys go first to b.   HERB 394:17
By night on my b.   BIBL 91:3
corner of the b.   ROBB 663:3
deck both b. and bower   SPEN 767:14
Early to b.   PROV 630:42
for the b. of Ware   SHAK 735:30
found out thy b.   BLAK 128:2
four bare legs in a b.   PROV 644:16
gooseberried double b.   THOM 806:9
go to b. by day   STEV 776:12
go to b. early   PROU 625:5
go to b. in another world   HENS 392:16
go to b. with me   ALLE 13:13
home to b.   BARH 58:7
in b. with my catamite   BURG 172:7
in my b. again   ANON 21:8
kick his wife out of b.   SURT 781:7
Lying in b. would be   CHES 225:17
make your b., so you must lie   PROV 626:42
mind is not a b.   AGAT 9:8
mother, make my b.   BALL 54:3
mother, make my b.   BALL 55:1
(my Love!) in thy cold b.   KING 463:4
my second best b.   SHAK 738:29
never made my own b.   PU Y 648:27
newly gone to b.   MILT 541:5
no need to get out of b.   AMIS 14:17
nor a goddess to b.   VIRG 832:4
not having more than one man in b.   RAPH 655:10
on the lawn I lie in b.   AUDE 38:1
out of b. two hours sooner   JOHN 440:21
passage up to b.   STEV 776:16
prescription of a quick dip in b.   WESL 848:9
Rode their horses Up to b.   DE L 272:5
should of stood in b.   JACO 427:6
sweat of an enseamèd b.   SHAK 703:14
take up thy b., and walk   BIBL 107:17
This b. thy centre is   DONN 289:18
wore in b.   MONR 553:18
bedclothes b. a-heaving   DICK 281:8
bedfellows Adversity makes strange b.   PROV 626:7
strange b.   PROV 641:40
strange b.   SHAK 733:25
bedlam B. vision   BYRO 192:10
sigh like Tom o' B.   SHAK 715:2
bedroom French widow in every b.   HOFF 402:13
unless with b. eyes   AUDE 38:3
what you do in the b.   CAMP 195:2
bedrooms in the nation's b.   TRUD 817:10
beds Minds like b. always made up   WILL 858:10

beds (cont.):
not only the b. you lay on — CAVA 211:10
rejoice in their b. — BOOK 150:11
bedytime I would it were b., Hal — SHAK 706:22
bee b.-loud glade — YEAT 873:20
b. of sorrow — BABE 44:16
b. produces honey — GOLD 363:16
brisk as a b. — JOHN 438:25
How doth the little busy b. — WATT 841:11
I am the b. — FITZ 330:15
in my bosom like a b. — LODG 498:6
neither the honey nor the b. — SAPP 680:21
sting like a b. — ALI 13:2
Where the b. sucks — SHAK 734:3
while the b.-mouth sips — KEAT 456:1
beech spreading b.-tree — VIRG 831:12
beef B. and a sea-coal fire — OTWA 589:13
great eater of b. — SHAK 735:1
great meals of b. — SHAK 708:18
Roast B., Medium — FERB 325:4
roast b. of England — FIEL 326:10
roast b. of old England — BURK 175:3
Where's the b. — ADVE 8:28
Where's the b. — MOND 553:8
beefsteak as English as a b. — HAWT 385:7
been as if it had not b. — SHEL 743:14
B. there, done that — SAYI 684:2
beer B. and Britannia — SMIT 759:2
b. and skittles — PROV 637:28
b. of a man in Klondike — CHES 224:20
chronicle small b. — SHAK 728:17
desire small b. — SHAK 707:13
drinks b., thinks beer — PROV 634:6
here for the b. — ADVE 7:35
heresy, hops, and b. — PROV 645:40
muddy ecstasies of b. — CRAB 257:16
O B.! O Hodgson — CALV 194:3
only a b. teetotaller — SHAW 739:18
thine inspirer, B. — POPE 611:20
warm b., invincible suburbs — MAJO 517:4
beers other b. cannot reach — ADVE 7:30
Beersheba Dan even to B. — BIBL 83:21
from Dan to B. — STER 772:10
bees b. do it — PORT 619:15
b. make honey — VIRG 833:8
B. ransack flowers — MONT 554:26
from these Attic b. — VIRG 833:5
half a number of b. — LONG 500:8
industrious b. do hourly — COLL 242:21
innumerable b. — TENN 799:22
of b. or beavers — COND 245:11
rob the Hybla b. — SHAK 713:29
so work the honey-b. — SHAK 708:10
was it his b.-winged eyes — BETJ 75:9
Where b. are — PROV 647:6
Beethoven rape, ultra-violence and B. — TAGL 788:2
beetle b. and the bat — JOHN 440:18
b., nor the death-moth — KEAT 455:27
b. wheels his droning flight — GRAY 370:1
black water b. — BLY 130:1
shard-borne b. — SHAK 721:4
beetles B. black, approach not — SHAK 726:11
special preference for b. — HALD 376:13
befalleth b. the sons of men — BIBL 89:24
before B. we were her people — FROS 344:14
Christ is gone b. — BOOK 136:1
days b. the flood — BIBL 102:27
my thoughts long b. — BOOK 149:15
Not lost but gone b. — NORT 577:8
not lost but sent b. — CYPR 263:15
sent b. my time — SHAK 731:11
things which are b. — BIBL 115:1
beforehand Pay b. — PROV 641:30
beg b. in the streets — FRAN 340:8
began b. in order — BROW 162:6
when my life b. — WORD 866:18
beget get and b. — OSLE 589:4
never to b. — HOPK 408:11
begetter To the onlie b. — SHAK 737:14
beggar absent-minded b. — KIPL 465:5
b. amidst great riches — HORA 413:5
b. on horseback — PROV 643:1

b. would enfold himself — KIPL 468:19
b. would recognise guilt — PARS 597:11
Be not made a b. — BIBL 97:22
Sue a b. — PROV 643:48
whiles I am a b. — SHAK 714:6
beggared b. all description — SHAK 694:22
beggarman B., Thief — NURS 582:4
beggars b. are coming to town — NURS 578:18
B. can't be choosers — PROV 627:15
b. freezing — ROBI 664:6
b. would ride — PROV 635:20
Our basest b. — SHAK 715:12
so many b. bold — SKEL 754:3
When b. die — SHAK 712:12
beggary no vice, but b. — SHAK 714:6
There's b. in the love — SHAK 694:8
begged living HOMER b. his bread — ANON 20:9
begging his seed b. their bread — BOOK 141:25
begin B. at the beginning — CARR 202:17
b. at the beginning — THOM 806:8
b. the Beguine — PORT 619:10
b. with certainties — BACO 45:8
b. with the beginning — BYRO 187:20
But let us b. — KENN 460:9
Then I'll b. — CATC 207:5
warily to b. charges — BACO 46:28
beginning As it was in the b. — BOOK 133:8
badly from the b. — STEV 776:9
begin at the b. — THOM 806:8
b., a middle — ARIS 27:20
b., a muddle — LARK 481:14
b. is often the end — ELIO 309:20
b. of an Amour — BEHN 66:19
b. of any great matter — DRAK 293:7
b. of science — LEIB 488:5
b. of the end — TALL 788:15
b. of time — USSH 823:4
b. of wisdom — BOOK 147:21
b. of years — SWIN 784:22
b. thereof — BIBL 90:2
end of the b. — CHUR 230:1
good b. makes — PROV 633:17
In my b. is my end — ELIO 309:8
In my end is my b. — MARY 527:2
In the b. — BIBL 78:12
In the b. was the Word — BIBL 106:34
lovely at the b. — PALI 594:9
Movies should have a b. — GODA 360:21
new b., a raid on the inarticulate — ELIO 309:13
no b. to practice — DOGE 287:9
no difficulty in b. — JAME 430:6
pictures didn't have b. — POLL 611:9
Thou, Lord, in the b. — BOOK 146:17
told you from the b. — BIBL 93:19
true b. — SHAK 727:6
unnatural b. — AUST 42:1
beginnings B. are always troublesome — ELIO 308:17
ends by our b. know — DENH 273:6
from small b. grow — DRYD 295:11
begins glory most b. and ends — YEAT 874:6
tower of nine storeys b. — LAO 480:11
begot thing b. — KYD 474:10
when they b. me — STER 772:15
begotten b. by Despair — MARV 524:18
B., not made — BOOK 137:2
only b. of the Father — BIBL 107:2
beguile b. thy sorrow — SHAK 734:11
beguiled serpent b. me — BIBL 79:9
Beguine begin the B. — PORT 619:10
begun b., continued, and ended — BOOK 138:3
b. to fight — JONE 445:8
sooner b. — PROV 643:23
To have b. is half the job — HORA 410:5
Well b. is half done — PROV 646:13
behave all b. quite differently — COWA 253:21
b. in a proper fashion — MOLI 552:18
better we b. — BENT 71:5
difficult to b. like gentlemen — MACK 511:17
behaving language and ways of b. — JUVE 450:18
behaviour basis of all good human b. — ROOS 666:16
refines b. — OVID 590:2

studies human b. — ROBB 663:4
beheaded b. priests — HENR 392:4
[Lovat] was b. — WALP 837:8
behemoth Behold now b. — BIBL 87:14
behind b. the throne — PITT 607:11
b. your scenes — JOHN 438:26
Get thee b. me, Satan — BIBL 101:27
it will be b. me — REGE 657:12
let them go, B., before — DONN 288:6
no bosom and no b. — SMIT 757:20
one must ride b. — PROV 635:19
things which are b. — BIBL 115:1
those b. cried 'Forward!' — MACA 508:17
turn thee b. me — BIBL 85:32
with a light b. her — GILB 358:14
behold B. an Israelite — BIBL 107:7
B. my mother — BIBL 101:12
B. the man — BIBL 120:15
beholder eye of the b. — PROV 627:13
being avoiding b. — TILL 811:6
b. comes from non-being — LAO 480:4
darkness of mere b. — JUNG 449:12
have our b. — BIBL 110:5
may not be worried into b. — FROS 345:8
misery of b. — DRAB 293:6
Nothingness haunts b. — SART 681:8
not the same thing as b. — PLAT 609:15
one Supreme B. — SIKH 751:15
unbearable lightness of b. — KUND 474:5
way of b. — SART 681:11
beings beginning of b. — LEIB 488:5
belabour We b. each other — HORA 410:23
Belbroughton B. Road is bonny — BETJ 75:18
Belfast be kind to B. — CRAI 258:11
belfry while owl in the b. — TENN 800:7
Belgians idlers and B. — BAUD 62:2
Belgium B. put the kibosh on the Kaiser — ELLE 313:9
B. recovers — ASQU 34:4
B.'s capital had gathered — BYRO 186:5
Belgrave Square May beat in B. — GILB 356:17
Belial B., in act more graceful — MILT 542:3
B. with words — MILT 542:5
sons of B., flown with insolence — MILT 541:25
thou man of B. — BIBL 84:20
belied b. with false compare — SHAK 738:20
belief all b. is for it — JOHN 442:11
b. of truth — BACO 48:13
It is my b., Watson — DOYL 292:7
loved each other beyond b. — HEIN 389:12
that is b. — SART 681:18
beliefs dust of exploded b. — MADA 514:2
my b. are true — HALD 376:12
some generous b. — STEV 775:13
believe being born to b. — DISR 284:19
b. in life — DU B 298:8
b. in miracles — FOX 340:2
b. in the life to come — BECK 64:6
b. is not necessarily true — BELL 67:12
B. it or not — NEWS 573:1
B. me, you who come after — HORA 412:13
B. nothing of what you hear — PROV 627:17
b. that God loves them — HUME 419:13
b. things without evidence — HUXL 424:1
b. what isn't happening — COLE 239:1
b. what they wish — CAES 192:17
b. what we choose — NEWM 572:18
Corrected I b. — KNOX 470:3
determination to b. — HUME 420:1
don't b. in fairies — BARR 59:17
fight for what I b. in — CAST 206:10
Firmly I b. — NEWM 572:14
he couldn't b. it — CUMM 262:8
I b. in God the Father — BOOK 133:19
I do b. her — SHAK 738:22
I don't b. it — CATC 208:21
If you b., clap your hands — BARR 59:20
I will not b. — BIBL 108:39
Lord, I b. — BIBL 104:1
must b. *something* — RUSS 675:9
not the will to b. — RUSS 674:20
professing to b. — PAIN 592:5
recompense those who b. — KORA 472:5

save them that b.	BIBL 111:21
that they should b.	NAPO 567:17
Though ye b. not me	BIBL 108:5
We b. in God	KORA 471:11
ye will not b.	BIBL 107:16
you'll b. anything	WELL 846:16
believed all that b. were together	BIBL 109:14
b. in hope	BIBL 110:29
b. of any man	TARK 790:8
b. our report	BIBL 94:2
by all people b.	VINC 828:9
if b. during three days	MEDI 530:3
I should not be b.	VANB 823:18
Nothing can now be b.	JEFF 432:3
not seen, and yet have b.	BIBL 109:3
so firmly b.	MONT 555:5
believer In a b.'s ear	NEWT 574:14
Most blest b.	VAUG 825:2
believers all b.	BOOK 133:10
b. in Clough	SWIN 786:3
Light half-b. in our casual creeds	ARNO 30:11
protector of the b.	KORA 471:6
believes more readily b.	BACO 49:1
politician never b. what he says	DE G 271:14
believeth b. all things	BIBL 112:14
He that b. on me	BIBL 107:25
whosoever b. in him	BIBL 107:13
believing b. something	LICH 493:3
but b.	BIBL 109:1
Not b. in force	TROT 817:9
Seeing is b.	PROV 642:39
stop b. in God	CHES 225:26
torture them, into b.	NEWM 572:10
Belinda B. smiled	POPE 618:9
bell B., book, and candle	SHAK 714:8
b. invites me	SHAK 719:21
Cuckoo-echoing, b.-swarmèd	HOPK 407:6
Ding, dong, b.	NURS 578:12
dinner b.	BYRO 189:6
for whom the b. tolls	DONN 290:4
heart as sound as a b.	SHAK 727:26
hear the little b. tinkle	HEIN 389:15
Let's mock the midnight b.	SHAK 695:11
sexton tolled the b.	HOOD 405:17
Silence that dreadful b.	SHAK 728:19
surly sullen b.	SHAK 738:3
word is like a b.	KEAT 456:11
bella B., horrida bella	VIRG 830:4
Bellamy B.'s veal pies	PITT 607:22
belle b. chose que de savoir	MOLI 552:1
b. dame sans mercy	KEAT 454:14
b. folie	BANV 57:14
j'étais b.	RONS 666:15
bellies their b. empty	LOGU 498:11
bellman B. and True	GRAV 369:9
B., perplexed and distressed	CARR 204:1
fatal b.	SHAK 720:2
Bellona B.'s bridegroom	SHAK 718:5
bellowing b. cow soon forgets	PROV 627:18
bellows b. too have lost their wind	EPIT 319:3
bells b. are gonna chime	LERN 490:7
b. I hear	WHIT 852:2
b. of Hell	MILI 535:15
b. on her toes	NURS 581:2
b. ringeth to evensong	HAWE 384:10
daze with little b.	HUGO 419:6
floating many b. down	CUMM 262:3
From the b., bells, bells	POE 610:16
into a mist with b.	BROW 166:28
Like sweet b. jangled	SHAK 702:10
lin-lan-lone of evening b.	TENN 793:12
now ring the b.	WALP 838:12
Ring out, wild b.	TENN 795:30
ring the b. of Ecstasy	GINS 358:21
ring the b. of Heaven	HODG 401:18
Say the b.	NURS 580:15
silver b. and cockle shells	NURS 580:5
with a tower and b.	CRAB 257:8
belly accursed b.	HOME 405:5
b. God send thee	ANON 16:11
b. is as bright ivory	BIBL 91:10
b. like an heap of wheat	BIBL 91:14
filled his b.	BIBL 105:30

God is their b.	BIBL 115:2
in Jonadge's b.	DICK 278:26
my b. was bitter	BIBL 118:22
O wombe! O b.	CHAU 219:28
bellyful Rumble thy b.	SHAK 715:17
Belmont In B. is a lady	SHAK 723:25
belong b. not to you	GIBR 355:14
b. to it as well	WHYT 853:8
don't want to b. to any club	MARX 526:1
man doesn't b. out there	BRAU 155:10
To betray, you must first b.	PHIL 605:12
where we really b.	GREE 371:16
belongs Who b.	PHIL 606:6
beloved B. is man	TALM 789:6
Cry, the b. country	PATO 599:15
Dearly b.	BOOK 138:20
how far to be b.	SHAK 694:8
Let my b. come	BIBL 91:7
man greatly b.	BIBL 96:1
My b. is mine	BIBL 91:2
never be b.	BLAK 124:12
This is my b.	BIBL 91:10
This is my b. Son	BIBL 98:19
voice of my b.	BIBL 91:8
below above, between, b.	DONN 288:6
its counterpart b.	ZOHA 878:8
journey to the world b.	SOCR 760:4
love is a thing b. a man	STER 773:13
belt b. without hitting below it	ASQU 34:10
belted b. you and flayed you	KIPL 466:3
Ben Bolt remember sweet Alice, B.	ENGL 316:2
bend b. and I break not	LA F 475:13
b. to favour ev'ry client	GAY 351:17
B. what is stiff	LANG 479:3
right on round the b.	LAUD 482:18
sidelong would she b.	KEAT 455:8
bending always be a b. downwards	WHEW 850:3
instead of b., breaks	WITT 861:7
beneath B. is all the fiends'	SHAK 716:18
married b. me	ASTO 35:2
benedicite B., omnia opera Domini	BIBL 120:9
benediction breed Perpetual b.	WORD 867:13
memory a b.	STAN 769:19
benedictus B. qui venit	MISS 549:16
benefacta recordanti b. priora	CATU 211:1
benefactor become the b. of someone	DOST 291:4
b. of our race	TWAI 820:10
benefit Every human b.	BURK 173:18
benefits forget not all his b.	BOOK 146:18
obligated b. they confer	MACH 511:9
benevolence b. of mankind	BAGE 51:14
b. of the butcher	SMIT 756:1
enticed by b.	BAGE 50:4
benevolent bashful, and b.	TALM 789:21
B. Knowledge	BORG 151:8
benighted poor b. 'eathen	KIPL 465:19
benison For a b. to fall	HERR 395:14
Benjamin of the tribe of B.	BIBL 114:21
bent top of my b.	SHAK 703:2
bereaved b. if snobbery died	USTI 823:8
bereft b. Of wet	HOPK 407:12
bergamasques masques et b.	VERL 826:10
Berliner Ich bin ein B.	KENN 460:13
Bermoothes still-vexed B.	SHAK 733:16
Bermudas remote B. ride	MARV 524:14
berries Sweet b. ripen	STEV 774:15
Two lovely b.	SHAK 726:19
berry made a better b.	BUTL 184:20
Bertie Burlington B.	HARG 382:10
beryl rings set with the b.	BIBL 91:10
beseech pray and b. you	BOOK 133:3
beside b. thyself	BIBL 110:15
Christ b. me	PATR 599:18
fall b. me	BOOK 146:1
besiege b. thy brow	SHAK 737:16
best All's for the b.	PROV 626:18
all the great b.-sellers	PRIT 624:14
Always to be b.	HOME 404:14
ancients, what is b.	FULL 346:20
any other person's b.	HAZL 386:17
bad in the b. of us	ANON 20:18

being b. man is	MURR 566:2
b. and the worst of this	SWIN 785:21
b. chosen language	AUST 41:19
b. days of life	VIRG 833:1
b. in this kind	SHAK 727:8
b. is enemy of good	PROV 627:20
b. is like the worst	KIPL 466:16
b. is the best	QUIL 651:17
b. is the enemy of the good	VOLT 834:2
b. is yet to be	BROW 167:9
b. lack all conviction	YEAT 874:17
b.-laid schemes	PROV 627:25
b. men are dead	PUNC 650:9
b. of all possible worlds	BRAD 154:3
b. of all possible worlds	CABE 192:13
b. of all possible worlds	PROV 626:18
b. of all possible worlds	VOLT 833:10
b. of men	PROV 627:22
b. Prime Minister we have	BUTL 183:3
b.-seller is the gilded tomb	SMIT 757:9
b. thing God invents	BROW 165:20
b. things in life	PROV 627:24
b. things in life are free	DE S 274:16
b. years are gone	BECK 64:8
Corruption of the b.	SAYI 684:9
discreetest, b.	MILT 544:1
enemy of the b.	PROV 633:21
get what's b. for us	RICE 659:19
In art the b. is good enough	GOET 362:9
It was the b. of times	DICK 281:3
justest and b.	PLAT 608:18
leader is b.	LAO 479:10
past all prizing, b.	SOPH 761:17
poetry = the b. words	COLE 242:3
propagate the b. that is known	ARNO 31:18
pursuing of the b. ends	HUTC 422:9
record of the b.	SHEL 747:13
Send forth the b.	KIPL 468:2
that is the b.	AUST 42:3
we two, one another's b.	DONN 289:4
Whate'er is b. administered	POPE 617:3
Beste das B. gut genug	GOET 362:9
bestow b. on every airth a limb	MONT 556:14
bestride b. the narrow world	SHAK 711:19
bet You b. your sweet bippy	CATC 209:3
betake b. myself to that course	PEPY 603:18
Bethel O God of B.	DODD 287:7
Bethlehem But thou, B.	BIBL 96:13
little town of B.	BROO 160:5
Slouches towards B.	YEAT 874:18
betray All things b. thee	THOM 807:15
b. me to a lingering book	HERB 393:20
b. me to your mirth or hate	FORD 337:10
guts to b. my country	FORS 338:12
those who b. their friends	GAY 351:8
To b., you must first belong	PHIL 605:12
betrayal any act of b.	RENO 658:8
ecstasy of b.	GENE 352:5
only defence against b.	WILL 858:1
betrayed betrayer, and b.	SCOT 689:9
by ourselves, b.	CONG 247:11
If she's fair, b.	LEAP 485:12
night that he was b.	BOOK 137:16
one of them b.	BEAV 63:19
betrayer b., and betrayed	SCOT 689:9
betrayeth he that b. thee	BIBL 109:9
betrothed B., betrayer	SCOT 689:9
of my b. lady	MIDD 534:9
better All the b. to hear you with	PERR 604:3
appear the b. reason	MILT 542:3
b. angels of our nature	LINC 493:14
B. by far than any	SIKH 751:19
B. by far you should forget	ROSS 669:5
b. day, the worse deed	HENR 392:6
b. hap to worse	SOUT 765:3
B. is the end	BIBL 90:2
b. man than I am	KIPL 466:3
B. red than dead	POLI 612:7
better spared a b. man	SHAK 706:29
B. than a play	CHAR 217:2
b. than a thousand	BOOK 145:15
b. than it sounds	NYE 582:13
b. than Man	TAGL 788:11

better (cont.):
b. than ourselves — CAMU 196:7
b. than their ordinary life — PRIE 623:10
b. the day — PROV 627:36
b. the instruction — SHAK 724:20
b. to be — AUCT 36:13
b. to have fought and lost — CLOU 237:4
b. to have loved and lost — TENN 795:9
b. what we can — STEV 775:13
can only get b. — PETR 605:4
can only get b. — POLI 613:9
desires what is b. — AUCT 36:15
Every day, I am getting b. — COUÉ 253:4
Fail b. — BECK 64:26
far, far b. thing — DICK 281:7
for b. for worse — BOOK 139:1
from worse to b. — HOOK 406:9
from worse to b. — JOHN 435:16
Gad! she'd b. — CARL 200:28
give place to b. — SHAK 713:27
go b. with Coke — ADVE 8:21
go the b. things — CATH 209:12
He is not b. — ANON 16:7
Hereafter, in a b. world — SHAK 696:11
If way to the B. there be — HARD 381:16
I took thee for thy b. — SHAK 703:12
It would not be b. — HERA 392:21
I was in a b. place — SHAK 696:19
made b. by their presence — ELIO 308:13
make a b. mouse-trap — EMER 315:22
much b. than likely — BRON 158:22
nae b. than he shou'd be — BURN 177:28
nothing b. — CARR 203:18
nothing b. to do — THAT 804:7
reach anything b. — NIGH 576:1
see b. days — BEHN 67:3
seemed a little b. — IBSE 424:12
see the b. things — OVID 590:13
takes the b. course — SOCR 760:1
We have seen b. days — SHAK 734:7
bettered b. expectation — SHAK 727:13
between B. the idea And the reality — ELIO 309:28
'ouses in b. — BATE 61:6
try to get b. them — STRA 778:13
betwixt B. the stirrup and the ground — EPIT 319:2
beverage blood-sweetened b. — SOUT 764:15
bewailed b. at their birth — MONT 556:2
beware B., lest in the worm — BARB 57:20
B., madam — GRAV 369:10
B. my foolish heart — WASH 841:2
B. of desperate steps — COWP 255:11
B. of rudely crossing it — AUDE 38:3
B. of the dog — PETR 605:5
B. the ides of March — SHAK 711:13
bid you b. — KIPL 467:4
cry, B.! Beware — COLE 240:9
beweep b. my outcast state — SHAK 737:21
bewildered Bewitched, bothered, and b. — HART 383:10
to the utterly b. — CAPP 197:13
bewitch Do more b. me — HERR 396:1
bewitched B., bothered, and bewildered — HART 383:10
bewrapt B. past knowing — HARD 381:23
bewrayeth speech b. thee — BIBL 103:20
beyond already got b. — NIET 575:22
loved each other b. belief — HEIN 389:12
things which are b. it — PASC 598:4
bias impartiality is b. — REIT 658:3
mind's wrong b. — GREE 371:7
biases critic is a bundle of b. — BALL 56:11
bibendum Nunc est b. — HORA 412:3
bibisti edisti satis atque b. — HORA 411:2
Bible B. and the Bible only — CHIL 226:6
B.-Society . . . is found — CARL 199:21
B. teaches that woman — STAN 770:5
big ha'-B. — BURN 177:25
Both read the B. — BLAK 125:1
cadence of the B. verses — RUSK 674:11
English B. — MACA 507:21
have used the B. — KING 464:15

knows even his B. — ARNO 31:14
read in de B. — HEYW 397:18
starless and b.-black — THOM 806:8
that book is the B. — ARNO 32:9
translation of the B. — WHAT 849:19
bible read my B. very well — HAND 379:8
translated the B. into — TYND 821:4
Bibles B. laid open — HERB 394:25
bibles they had the b. — GEOR 353:9
bicker b. down a valley — TENN 793:1
bicycle arrive by b. — VIER 827:18
b.-pump the human heart — AMIS 14:14
fish without a b. — SAYI 685:21
so is a b. repair kit — CONN 248:5
bicycling old maids b. — MAJO 517:4
bicyclists illuminated trouser-clip for b. — MORT 562:5
bid b. the Devil good morrow — PROV 639:32
bidder withstand the highest b. — WASH 840:15
bien mieux est l'ennemi du b. — VOLT 834:2
bier upon his watery b. — MILT 540:4
big b. enough to take away everything — FORD 336:16
B. fish eat little fish — PROV 628:2
B. fleas have little fleas — PROV 628:3
b. squadrons against the small — BUSS 182:16
b. tent — POLI 612:9
b. way of doing things — TERE 801:18
b. words for little matters — JOHN 440:9
books of the B.-Endians — SWIF 782:8
commonly thought b. — WOOL 864:6
Does my bum look b. — CATC 207:12
fall victim to a b. lie — HITL 400:6
I am b. — FILM 330:6
shining B.-Sea-Water — LONG 499:22
What b. ears you have — PERR 604:3
bigamy B. is having — ANON 16:14
bigger b. bang for a buck — POLI 612:8
b. they are — FITZ 332:20
b. they are — PROV 628:4
biggest b. aspidistra in the world — HARP 382:17
b. electric train — WELL 846:1
bigness b. of Avogadro's number — BENT 71:1
bigoted more superstitious, more b. — NEWM 572:2
bigotry B. the anger of men who — CHES 225:7
B. tries to keep truth — TAGO 787:15
bike got on his b. — TEBB 792:9
Mind my b. — CATC 208:18
Put me back on my b. — MISQ 548:16
Bilbo B.'s the word — CONG 247:12
bilingual All pro athletes are b. — HOWE 417:1
bill called upon to pay the b. — HARD 380:3
give me your b. of company — SWIF 782:16
nape caught in his b. — YEAT 874:1
billabong swagman camped by a b. — PATE 599:9
billboard b. lovely as a tree — NASH 568:22
billet bullet has its b. — PROV 631:14
bullet has its b. — WILL 857:4
billets-doux bibles, b. — POPE 618:7
billiards play b. well — ROUP 670:12
billion b. dollar country — FOST 338:18
billow Fierce was the wild b. — ANAT 15:3
billows b. of enormous size — PHIL 606:3
bills By children and tradesmen's b. — MACN 513:10
inflammation of his weekly b. — BYRO 188:18
Receipted b. — AUDE 37:20
billy B., in one of his sashes — GRAH 367:15
That's the way for B. — HOGG 402:16
till his 'B.' boiled — PATE 599:9
bind B. me, or set me free — GODO 361:2
b. my hair — HUNT 422:1
b. their kings in chains — BOOK 150:11
b. the sweet influences — BIBL 87:12
b. unto myself today — ALEX 12:9
b. your sons to exile — KIPL 468:2
Obadiah B.-their-kings — MACA 508:3
Safe b., safe find — PROV 642:32
binds b. to himself a joy — BLAK 127:2
Blest be the tie that b. — FAWC 324:20
bin Laden having one b. — MUBA 564:1

Binnorie B., O Binnorie — BALL 54:5
binomial b. theorem — GILB 358:7
biographers B., translators — MACA 507:10
Grubstreet b. — ADDI 4:26
muck-raking b. — BENN 70:13
picklocks of b. — BENÉ 69:15
biographical noble and b. friend — WETH 849:6
biographies essence of innumerable b. — CARL 199:13
biography better part of b. — STRA 778:14
B. is about Chaps — BENT 71:14
Judas who writes the b. — WILD 855:1
no b. — THAC 803:10
no history; only b. — EMER 315:3
nothing but b. — DISR 285:23
biologist b. passes — ROST 670:5
biology B. is the search for — WILL 857:11
more to b. than rats — MAYR 529:10
bippy You bet your sweet b. — CATC 209:3
bird addled egg as an idle b. — PROV 626:37
b.-haunted English lawn — ARNO 29:20
b. in the hand — PROV 628:5
b. never flew on one — PROV 628:6
b. not gets — OXFO 591:13
b. of dawning — SHAK 699:6
b. of night — SHAK 712:1
b. of Paradise — HERB 394:19
B. of the wilderness — HOGG 402:19
b. of wonder dies — SHAK 711:9
b. on the wing — BOUL 152:15
b.'s battling in its own home — AESC 6:18
b. that cuts the airy way — BLAK 126:20
B. thou never wert — SHEL 746:19
Both man and b. — COLE 241:10
cannot catch the b. of paradise — KHRU 462:10
catch a b. — RICH 660:12
divine of Zeus — PIND 606:17
early b. catches worm — PROV 630:40
escaped even as a b. — BOOK 148:22
forgets the dying b. — PAIN 592:19
gold-feathered b. — STEV 774:8
immortal b. — KEAT 456:10
It's a b. — ANON 17:4
like a singing b. — ROSS 668:17
No b. soars too high — BLAK 126:10
obscure b. clamoured — SHAK 720:15
only the note of a b. — SIMP 753:2
rare b. on this earth — JUVE 451:2
self-begotten b. — MILT 545:8
Shall I call thee b. — WORD 869:19
sight of any b. — BIBL 87:20
sight of the b. — PROV 636:3
silence fell with the waking b. — TENN 798:4
some b. would trust — HERB 393:21
Stirred for a b. — HOPK 408:5
sweet b.'s throat — SHAK 696:21
Sweet b. that shunn'st — MILT 539:15
What b. so sings — LYLY 505:21
why the caged b. sings — DUNB 299:8
birdcage And a b., sir — DICK 280:24
like a summer b. — WEBS 844:18
birds All the b. of the air — NURS 582:12
As the flight of b. — MACL 512:5
b., and Prime Ministers — BALD 53:4
b. are faint — KEAT 456:17
b. are flown — CHAR 216:16
B. build — HOPK 408:3
b. build nests — VIRG 833:8
b. do chant their lays — SPEN 766:20
b. fly through it — HEIS 390:2
b. got to fly — HAMM 378:14
B. in their little nests — PROV 628:7
B. in their little nests agree — WATT 841:16
B. of a feather — PROV 628:8
b. of the air — BIBL 101:15
b. of the air have nests — BIBL 100:10
B. on box and laurels — SMAR 754:8
b. sing madrigals — MARL 523:1
b. that are without despair — WEBS 844:18
B. to her secret operations — D'AV 267:8
catch old b. with chaff — PROV 648:5
conference of the b. — ATTA 35:5
half-awakened b. — TENN 799:12

bleeding (*cont.*):

b., beating fire	JOHN 435:2
b. piece of earth	SHAK 712:22
instead of b., he sings	GARD 349:5
pageant of his b. heart	ARNO 30:22

bleeds 'til it b. daylight — COCK 237:17

blemish lamb shall be without b. — BIBL 81:6

no b. but the mind	SHAK 736:8

blend too short to b. — HILT 399:11

Blenheim still fighting B. — BEVA 76:15

bless B. 'em all — HUGH 417:18

b. me, With apple pie	FIEL 326:3
B. relaxes	BLAK 126:16
B. the Lord	BIBL 120:9
b. ye the Lord	BOOK 133:12
dying, b. the hand	DRYD 296:32
except thou b. me	BIBL 80:14
God b. us every one	DICK 277:3
holy priests B. her	SHAK 695:1
load and b. With fruit	KEAT 456:22

blessed B. are the dead — BIBL 119:3

B. are the eyes	BIBL 105:3
B. are the poor	BIBL 98:25
B. are the pure in heart	KEBL 458:20
B. are you, O Lord	SIDD 750:6
b. art thou among women	BIBL 104:7
B. art thou among women	PRAY 623:1
B. be he that cometh	BOOK 148:12
b. be the name of the Lord	BIBL 86:11
b. damozel	ROSS 669:12
B. is the man	BOOK 141:19
B. is the man	BOOK 145:14
b. them unaware	COLE 241:3
b. word Mesopotamia	ANON 20:16
blessest is b.	BIBL 82:6
from hence to there may be b.	SOCR 760:5
generations shall call me b.	BIBL 104:8
Judge none b.	BIBL 97:17
Lord b. the latter end	BIBL 87:19
more b. to give	BIBL 110:9
That b. mood	WORD 866:10
This b. plot	SHAK 730:11
thou hast b. them	BIBL 82:9
you should call b.	HORA 414:4

blessedness b. alone that makes a King

	TRAH 814:14
dies, in single b.	SHAK 725:22

blesses B. his stars — ADDI 4:13

blesseth b. him that gives — SHAK 724:29

blessing b. of a rainbow — ABSE 1:5

b. of God Almighty	BOOK 138:1
b. that money cannot buy	WALT 839:12
b. to the country	BISM 122:14
boon and a b.	ADVE 8:20
boon and a b.	PRIN 624:2
continual dew of thy b.	BOOK 134:7
contrariwise b.	BIBL 117:10
give us his b.	BOOK 144:5
national b.	HAMI 378:11
Prosperity is the b.	BACO 46:2
taken away thy b.	BIBL 80:8
unmixed b.	HORA 412:11
When thou dost ask me b.	SHAK 716:26
Yet possessing every b.	EDME 303:17

blessings B. brighten — PROV 628:12

b. of the light	KEN 459:15
b. on the falling out	TENN 799:4
glass of b.	HERB 394:20

blest always to be b. — ARMS 28:15

always To be b.	POPE 616:19
B. be the tie that binds	FAWC 324:20
B. pair of Sirens	MILT 538:17
b. that I lie on	PRAY 623:5
Kings may be b.	BURN 179:14
make us b. at last	ROCH 664:13
Of this b. man	WALT 839:16
O Mother b.	ALPH 13:20
promotion to the b.	DRYD 297:3

blew You b. it up — FILM 330:3

blight b. man was born for — HOPK 407:21

great English b.	WAUG 842:10

Blighty back to dear old B. — MILL 537:16

blimp Colonel B. — LOW 502:12

blind accompany my being b. — PEPY 603:18

b., but now I see	NEWT 574:17
b. guides	BIBL 102:19
b. in your ears and mind	SOPH 761:18
b. lead the blind	BIBL 101:22
b. led by the blind	UPAN 822:8
b. man in a dark room	BOWE 153:15
b. man's wife needs	PROV 628:13
B., old and lonely	SHEL 743:9
b. side of the heart	CHES 224:1
b. watchmaker	DAWK 269:1
b. wife	PROV 629:36
bold as a b. mare	PROV 640:22
Booth died b.	LIND 495:2
country of the b.	ERAS 316:17
country of the b.	PROV 636:2
Cupid painted b.	SHAK 725:25
darkness and b. eyes	VAUG 825:2
Eye among the b.	WORD 867:11
eyes to the b.	BIBL 87:2
giveth sight to the b.	BOOK 150:4
halt, and the b.	BIBL 105:23
I was b., now I see	BIBL 107:34
Justice, though she's painted b.	BUTL 183:27
knowledge e'er accompany the b.	
	SANA 679:18
Love is b.	ANON 22:5
Love is b.	PROV 638:6
none so b. as those	PROV 644:44
O b. entencioun	CHAU 220:23
old, mad, b.	SHEL 746:14
religion without science is b.	EINS 305:5
right to be b. sometimes	NELS 569:20
splendid work for the b.	SASS 682:6
though she be b.	BACO 46:31
Three b. mice	NURS 582:1
When the b. lead the blind	PROV 646:44
whole world b.	SAYI 684:17

blindness 'eathen in 'is b. — KIPL 465:14

for our b. we cannot ask	BOOK 138:4
heathen in his b.	HEBE 388:9
Love comes from b.	BUSS 182:14
reproach them for their b.	MILT 545:20
triple sight in b.	KEAT 457:6

blinds drawing-down of b. — OWEN 591:5

Self-interest, which b.	LA R 481:19
Truth, like the light, b.	CAMU 196:19

blindworm b.'s sting — SHAK 721:16

blindworms Newts, and b. — SHAK 726:10

blinked other fellow just b. — RUSK 673:3

blinking portrait of a b. idiot — SHAK 724:15

bliss appreciate domestic b. — SANT 680:15

B. goes but to a certain bound	GREV 372:14
b. in ale	CRAB 257:16
B. in our brows bent	SHAK 694:15
b. or woe	MILT 544:8
B. was it in that dawn	WORD 865:19
doth bathe in b.	VAUX 825:18
Everywhere I see b.	SHEL 743:5
joyous b. is mine	SIKH 751:17
men call domestic b.	PATM 599:13
Of b. on bliss	MILT 543:8
soul in b.	SHAK 716:23
source of all my b.	GOLD 364:13
Where ignorance is b.	GRAY 370:13
wingèd hours of b.	CAMP 195:15

blissful b. old times — BLAM 128:15

blister b. you all o'er — SHAK 733:17

blithe b. Spirit — SHEL 746:19

buxom, b., and debonair	MILT 539:22

blithesome B. and cumberless — HOGG 402:19

blitz b. of a boy is Timothy Winters — CAUS 211:9

blizzard walked to his death in a b. — EPIT 317:14

block each b. cut smooth — POUN 620:16

hew the b. off	POPE 613:24
old b. itself	BURK 175:20

blockhead b.'s insult — JOHN 438:2

bookful b.	POPE 616:13
diversion in a talking b.	FARQ 324:5
No man but a b.	JOHN 442:4
very great b.	CHAR 217:5

blocks You b., you stones — SHAK 711:12

blond b. beast — NIET 575:23

B. comme un soleil	BANV 57:14

blonde *Auprès de ma b.* — SONG 762:3

Being b. is definitely	MADO 514:12
b. to make a bishop kick	CHAN 215:8

blondes Gentlemen prefer b. — LOOS 500:13

blood am I not of her b. — SHAK 735:10

ancient troughs of b.	HILL 398:13
b. and ashes	PAIN 592:10
b. and iron	BISM 123:3
b. and love without	STOP 777:19
b. and wine	WILD 855:30
b. be the price	KIPL 467:12
b. come gargling	OWEN 591:6
b.-dimmed tide is loosed	YEAT 874:17
b. drawn with the lash	LINC 494:5
b. his blood	YEAT 872:9
b. is their argument	SHAK 708:25
b. Is very snow-broth	SHAK 723:2
b. more stirs	SHAK 705:14
b. of all the Howards	POPE 617:7
b. of an Englishman	ANON 17:6
b. of Christians is the seed	TERT 802:11
b. Of human sacrifice	MILT 541:22
b. of patriots	JEFF 431:11
b. of the martyrs	PROV 628:15
b.-red flag	BLOK 129:6
b.'s a rover	HOUS 415:13
B., sweat, and tear-wrung	BYRO 185:7
b.-sweetened beverage	SOUT 764:15
B. thicker than water	PROV 628:14
b., toil, tears and sweat	CHUR 229:12
B. will have blood	PROV 628:16
b. will have blood	SHAK 721:12
B. will tell	PROV 628:17
but with b.	BROW 161:8
by b. Albanian	TERE 801:22
cheeks as rosy as the b.	GRIM 373:9
Christ's b. streams	MARL 522:11
Come and see the b.	NERU 570:14
conjure up the b.	SHAK 708:16
coughed-up b.	RIMB 662:18
created Man of a b.-clot	KORA 473:9
Deliver me from b.-guiltiness	BOOK 143:8
Dread Beat an B.	JOHN 435:1
drink the b. of goats	BOOK 143:3
drop of Negro b.	HUGH 418:4
effusion of Christian b.	LAUD 482:17
enough of b. and tears	RABI 652:13
flesh and b.	BIBL 114:15
flesh and b. so cheap	HOOD 406:2
flow of human b.	HUGH 418:2
foaming with much b.	POWE 622:2
for cooling the b.	FLAN 332:23
fountain filled with b.	COWP 255:15
get b. from a stone	PROV 648:7
glories of our b. and state	SHIR 749:17
guiltless of his country's b.	GRAY 370:6
hawser of his b.-tie	HARR 383:8
heart within b.-tinctured	BROW 164:9
heavens suddenly turned to b.	MUNC 565:10
Here lies b.	EPIT 318:8
His b. be on us	BIBL 103:22
in b. Stepped in	SHAK 721:13
innocent of the b.	BIBL 103:21
I smell the b.	NASH 568:24
I smell the b.	SHAK 716:5
is this b., then, formed	BYRO 189:5
Let there be b.	BYRO 189:10
make thick my b.	SHAK 718:20
Man of B. was there	MACA 508:5
mingle my b.	BROW 161:7
my b. will invigorate India	GAND 348:10
my God feels as b.	HERB 393:24
near in b.	SHAK 720:20
of b. and soap	MITC 550:14
old b. is bold blood	WEBB 843:12
one glorious b.-red	BROW 165:29
on the b. of my men	LEE 487:18
pay the b. price	BLAI 124:4
Propinquity and property of b.	SHAK 714:17
pure and eloquent b.	DONN 288:19

raised to shed his b. POPE 616:17
rather have b. on my hands GREE 371:10
redeemed us by his b. DIX 286:32
rivers of b. JEFF 432:12
seas of b. COBB 237:11
shall his b. be shed BIBL 79:27
shedde oure b. LANG 478:21
shed innocent b. BIBL 94:17
sheds his b. with me SHAK 709:8
show business with b. BRUN 168:19
so much b. in him SHAK 722:8
stain of b. CURN 263:3
summon up the b. SHAK 708:16
thicks man's b. with cold COLE 240:22
this is my B. BOOK 137:16
Thy b. was shed for me ELLI 313:14
Tiber foaming with much b. VIRG 830:4
tincture in the b. DEFO 270:18
to take our b. NIET 575:15
voice of the child's b. SWIN 785:23
voice of thy brother's b. BIBL 79:15
waded thro' red b. BALL 55:22
washed in the b. of the Lamb LIND 495:1
wash this b. Clean SHAK 720:9
We be of one b. KIPL 468:6
We, your b. family SPEN 766:6
When b. is nipped SHAK 717:25
When the b. creeps TENN 795:11
white in the b. of the Lamb BIBL 118:15
With his own b. he bought her STON 777:10
Without shedding of b. BIBL 116:1
worked with my b. KOLL 470:16
Young b. must have its course KING 464:14
bloodhounds Seven b. followed SHEL 745:2
bloodless b. lay the untrodden snow
 CAMP 195:9
bloodshed war without b. MAO 521:2
bloodthirsty so venomous, so b. TROL 816:15
bloody Abroad is b. GEOR 353:1
b., bold, and resolute SHAK 721:20
b., but unbowed HENL 391:12
b. cross he bore SPEN 767:3
b. experience of Vietnam CRON 261:2
B., pale, and wan CLAU 234:7
b. principles and practices FOX 339:18
b. war and a sickly season TOAS 812:1
come out, thou b. man BIBL 84:20
dark and b. ground O'HA 584:17
have b. thoughts SHAK 733:32
last act is b. PASC 598:2
my b. thoughts SHAK 729:2
no right in the b. circus MAXT 528:17
Not b. likely SHAW 742:11
sang within the b. wood ELIO 310:27
Sunday, b. Sunday FILM 331:11
teach B. instructions SHAK 719:7
What b. man SHAK 718:3
wipe a b. nose GAY 351:15
Woe to the b. city BIBL 96:15
bloom b. in the spring GILB 357:15
b. is gone WILD 854:18
bud and b. forth SURR 781:1
How can ye b. sae fresh BURN 177:16
hung with b. HOUS 415:11
Leopold B. ate with relish JOYC 448:18
lilac is in b. BROO 159:6
look at things in b. HOUS 415:12
sort of b. on a woman BARR 59:22
with the b. go I ARNO 30:26
blooming grand to be b. well dead SARO 681:4
bloomy all the b. beds SMAR 754:17
blossom blood-red b. of war TENN 798:12
b. about me BOSW 152:2
b. and flourish SMIT 759:5
b. as the rose BIBL 93:8
B. by blossom SWIN 784:20
b. in purple and red TENN 798:7
b. in the dust SHIR 749:18
b. into a Duchess AILE 9:16
b. on the tomb CRAB 257:9
b. soup BASH 60:20
b. that hangs on the bough SHAK 734:3
break Into b. WRIG 870:18

frothiest, blossomiest b. POTT 620:8
hundred flowers b. MAO 521:5
wild cherry b. MOTO 562:15
blossoms beauteous b. to proceed D'AV 267:8
b., birds, and bowers HERR 395:15
to-morrow b. SHAK 710:19
blot art to b. POPE 617:24
b. on the escutcheon GRAY 369:17
B. out, correct SWIF 783:29
b. out his name BIBL 117:31
scarce received from him a b. HEMI 390:17
This world's no b. BROW 165:21
blotted b. a thousand JONS 447:3
b. from life's page BYRO 185:24
b. it out for ever STER 773:12
blow Blow, b., thou winter wind SHAK 697:4
B., bugle, blow TENN 799:7
b. fall soon or late STEV 777:2
B. him again to me TENN 799:6
B. out, you bugles BROO 159:4
B., thou wind of God KING 464:9
b. upon my garden BIBL 91:7
B. up the trumpet BOOK 145:11
B., winds, and crack SHAK 715:16
b. with an agreement TROT 817:8
first b. is half GOLD 365:8
great winds shorewards b. ARNO 29:12
hand that gave the b. DRYD 296:32
knock-down b. HUNT 421:15
not return your b. SHAW 741:27
strike the b. BYRO 185:23
sudden b.: the great wings YEAT 874:1
when will thou b. ANON 21:8
bloweth wind b. where it listeth BIBL 107:12
blowing answer is b. in the wind DYLA 301:12
I'm forever b. bubbles KENB 459:17
blown flower that once hath b. FITZ 331:19
no sooner b. but blasted MILT 540:19
pipe B. by surmises SHAK 707:3
rooks are b. TENN 795:5
blows b. so red The rose FITZ 331:17
It b. so hard HOUS 416:2
blubbering b. Cabinet GLAD 360:10
bludgeoning b. of the people WILD 856:7
bludgeonings b. of chance HENL 391:12
blue across the b. threshold ROST 670:3
b. above the trees KEAT 454:28
B. are the hills PROV 628:18
b. bed to the brown GOLD 365:12
B. Bonnets are bound SCOT 689:18
b.-eyed devil white man FARD 323:11
b. guitar STEV 774:6
b. is all in a rush HOPK 407:18
b. of the night CROS 261:3
b. remembered hills HOUS 416:4
B., silver-white KEAT 456:13
b. unfriendliness of space HOPE 406:18
cherish the pale b. dot SAGA 677:8
deeply, beautifully b. SOUT 764:13
Eyes of most unholy b. MOOR 558:7
Her b. body WALK 836:5
Lavender's b. NURS 579:14
Little Boy B. NURS 579:17
little tent of b. WILD 855:31
My b. heaven WHIT 851:16
sailed the ocean b. STON 777:11
Space is b. HEIS 390:2
True b. and Mrs Crewe TOAS 812:6
yonder living b. TENN 796:4
bluebell Mary, ma Scotch B. LAUD 482:19
bluebirds b. over the white cliffs BURT 180:20
blueprints Genes not like b. STEW 777:7
blues got the Weary B. HUGH 418:5
blunder frae mony a b. free us BURN 179:23
God's first b. NIET 575:9
it is a b. BOUL 152:13
so grotesque a b. BENT 71:19
Youth is a b. DISR 285:18
blundered Some one had b. TENN 793:4
blunders Human b. TAYL 791:11
Nature's agreeable b. COWL 254:23
blunt plain, b. man SHAK 713:11
blush b. into the cheek DICK 280:10

born to b. unseen GRAY 370:6
Truth makes the Devil b. PROV 645:38
blushed saw its God, and b. CRAS 258:23
blushes Bright burning b. LAND 478:2
Only Animal that B. TWAI 820:6
pardon my b. SHER 748:21
blushful b. Hippocrene KEAT 456:4
blushing bears his b. honours SHAK 710:19
b. apricot JONS 447:1
b. either for a sign CONG 247:19
other people without b. SHAW 741:28
boar tidy Bartholomew b.-pig SHAK 707:15
board back to the old drawing b. CART 205:17
carried on b. HUME 420:7
hospitable b. WORD 865:20
I struck the b. HERB 393:28
There wasn't any B. HERB 393:13
boards four b., two actors VEGA 826:1
Ships are but b. SHAK 724:5
boast B. not thyself of to morrow BIBL 89:3
b. of heraldry GRAY 370:4
do falsely b. BOOK 150:23
For frantic b. KIPL 467:8
Such is the patriot's b. GOLD 364:24
boasteth then he b. BIBL 88:28
boat Architecture and a b. PUGI 649:4
b. he can sail THOM 808:25
first launched his frail b. HORA 411:6
if men are together in a b. HALI 377:7
love b. has crashed MAYA 529:6
sank my b. KENN 460:15
sewer in a glass-bottomed b. MIZN 551:13
soul is an enchanted b. SHEL 746:1
Speed, bonnie b. BOUL 152:15
Until I have a little b. WORD 868:2
When the b. comes in NURS 578:9
boathook diplomatic b. SALI 678:13
boating Jolly b. weather CORY 252:11
boatman B., do not tarry CAMP 195:10
boats leathern b. MARV 525:17
messing about in b. GRAH 368:1
passengers off in small b. ANON 21:4
seek happiness in b. HORA 410:10
bobtail money on de b. nag FOST 338:22
Boche well-killed B. READ 656:6
bodes b. some strange eruption SHAK 699:3
Bodhidharma [B.] come to China MUMO 565:8
Bodhisattva B. who is full of pity MAHĀ 515:7
Bodhisattvas pure deeds of the B. SHAN 739:5
bodice lace my b. blue HUNT 422:1
bodies b. are buried in peace BIBL 98:5
b. but not their souls GIBR 355:14
b. into light NEWT 574:2
B. never lie DE M 272:15
b. of a stony nature RALE 653:17
b. of those EDWA 304:8
b. of unburied men WEBS 844:20
contact of two b. CHAM 215:1
men's poor b. JUVE 451:16
One soul inhabiting two b. ARIS 28:10
our dead b. SCOT 688:4
outwardly in our b. BOOK 135:16
Pile the b. high SAND 680:5
present your b. BIBL 111:9
scorn their b. BAST 61:5
souls out of men's b. SHAK 727:20
structure of our b. STOP 777:12
with two seeming b. SHAK 726:19
bodkin With a bare b. SHAK 702:1
body Absent in b. BIBL 111:29
Africa than my own b. ORTO 586:12
b. and the soul know ROET 665:9
b. as the chariot UPAN 822:11
b. between your knees CORY 252:11
b. Borne before her THAC 803:9
b. continues in its state of rest NEWT 574:3
b. cries, even in GRAH 367:17
b. form doth take SPEN 767:29
b. is a machine TOLS 813:16
b. is the temple BIBL 112:1
b., Nature is POPE 616:26
b. of a weak and feeble woman ELIZ 312:6
b. of Benjamin Franklin EPIT 317:1

body (cont.):
b. of this death — BIBL 110:38
b., of thought — CARL 200:21
B., remember not only — CAVA 211:10
b.'s beauty lives — STEV 774:10
b. still perseveres — AURE 40:15
b. swayed to music — YEAT 872:8
b. than raiment — BIBL 99:16
change our vile b. — BOOK 139:10
commit his b. to the deep — BOOK 150:15
commit his b. to the ground — BOOK 139:10
draw what I feel in my b. — HEPW 392:17
every interstice of my b. — EDDI 302:17
exercise is to the b. — STEE 770:18
Fretted the pigmy b. — DRYD 294:11
future b. for ever — ZORO 879:15
getteth outside [the b.] — TIBE 810:17
gigantic b. — MACA 506:17
Gin a body meet a b. — BURN 177:20
give my b. to be burned — BIBL 112:14
good-will of the b. — RIDI 661:7
her b. thought — DONN 288:19
huge distempered b. — MONT 556:1
I keep under my b. — BIBL 112:9
i like my b. — CUMM 262:12
in a sound b. — JUVE 451:17
in mind, b., or estate — BOOK 135:7
interpose my b. — STRA 778:13
in the midst of my b. — BOOK 140:18
John Brown's b. — SONG 763:1
keep your b. white — STEV 776:22
liberation of the human b. — GOLD 363:17
looking for a b. in the coach — HITC 400:3
Marry my b. to that dust — KING 463:4
my useless b. — BROW 160:16
no b. now on earth — SAYI 684:6
no b. to be kicked — THUR 810:14
Of the glorious B. sing — THOM 805:4
out of my b. — HAND 379:9
out of the b. — BIBL 113:17
renouncing his b. — JAIN 428:8
Resurrection of the b. — BOOK 133:19
rid of the rest of her b. — VANB 823:20
salutary to the b. — PROU 626:2
shapes itself to the b. — WOLL 863:13
sing the b. electric — WHIT 852:1
Soul, leaving the b. — UPAN 822:2
so young a b. — SHAK 724:28
spirit leaves his mortal b. — BHAG 77:18
stepped out of my b. — WRIG 870:18
strong of b. — PYTH 651:3
this is my b. — BIBL 103:12
use of this b. — BECK 64:10
wanders on to a new b. — BHAG 77:16
with my b. I thee worship — BOOK 139:2
woman watches her b. uneasily — COHE 238:7
wreathing his b. — SMAR 754:12
Boets hate all B. and Bainters — GEOR 352:7
bog Serbonian b. — MILT 542:13
Bognor Bugger B. — GEOR 353:4
bogs from b. and precipices — LOCK 497:13
bogus than a b. god — MACN 513:7
boil b. at different degrees — EMER 315:14
war that would not b. — TAYL 791:12
boiled in b. and roast — SMIT 758:6
boilers b. and vats — JOHN 443:5
boils watched pot never b. — PROV 646:9
bois au fond des b. — VIGN 828:1
Nous n'irons plus aux b. — ANON 22:8
bold Be b., be bold — SPEN 767:19
b. as a blind mare — PROV 640:22
b. as a hawk — CART 205:11
b. as a hawk — LOVE 502:11
b. as a lion — BIBL 89:7
b. bad man — SPEN 767:4
b. man that first — SWIF 783:5
Fortune assists the b. — VIRG 831:8
let our minds be b. — BRAN 154:18
made me b. — SHAK 720:1
This b. bad man — SHAK 710:15
boldly to b. go — RODD 665:2
boldness B., and again boldness — DANT 265:18
b. at least will deserve — PROP 624:21

B. be my friend — SHAK 698:17
B. is an ill keeper — BACO 46:12
what first? b. — BACO 46:11
Bolingbroke this canker, B. — SHAK 705:13
bolt b., and the breech — REED 657:5
b. is shot back somewhere — ARNO 29:3
bolts b. are hurled — TENN 797:12
bomb atom b. is a paper tiger — MAO 521:4
Ban the b. — POLI 612:5
b. them back into the Stone Age — LEMA 488:13
defence against the atom b. — ANON 16:13
ones we intended to b. — BLY 129:15
bombed glad we've been b. — ELIZ 313:5
protect him from being b. — BALD 53:5
bomber b. will always get through — BALD 53:5
bombers b. named for girls — JARR 430:22
bombinans chimera in vacuo b. — RABE 652:10
bombs b. redoubled on the hills — MOTI 562:11
Come, friendly b. — BETJ 76:5
bond b. between two people — RILK 662:7
B. James Bond. — FILM 329:9
b. nor free — BIBL 115:9
break that sole b. — BURK 173:22
great b. — SHAK 721:5
I will have my b. — SHAK 724:25
look to his b. — SHAK 724:17
take a b. of fate — SHAK 721:21
word is his b. — PROV 631:8
bondage b. of fear — PATO 599:16
b. of rhyming — MILT 541:7
b. to parents — WOLL 863:15
Cassius from b. will deliver — SHAK 712:2
condition of b. — STAN 770:5
house of b. — BIBL 81:15
spirit of b. — BIBL 111:2
bonding male b. — TIGE 811:4
bondman b.'s two hundred and fifty years — LINC 494:5
so base that would be a b. — SHAK 712:27
bonds b. of civil society — LOCK 497:16
except these b. — BIBL 110:18
surly b. of earth — MAGE 514:15
surly b. of earth — REAG 656:17
bondsmen Hereditary b. — BYRO 185:23
bondwoman of the b. — BIBL 113:21
bone B. of my bone — MILT 544:8
b. of my bones — BIBL 79:2
commend the b. — DICK 282:4
dog that will fetch a b. — PROV 630:13
fighting for a b. — PROV 647:15
hair about the b. — DONN 289:13
knows death to the b. — YEAT 873:3
nearer the b. — PROV 639:23
poor dog a b. — NURS 580:10
rag and a b. — KIPL 467:19
What's bred in the b. — PROV 646:26
boneless b. wonder — CHUR 229:7
bones b. are out of joint — BOOK 140:18
b. are smitten asunder — BOOK 142:7
b. of a single Pomeranian — BISM 122:19
b. of one British Grenadier — HARR 383:1
b. which thou hast broken — BOOK 143:6
Can these b. live — BIBL 95:20
come to lay his weary b. — SHAK 711:2
conjuring trick with b. — JENK 432:18
dead men lost their b. — ELIO 311:8
dead men's b. — BIBL 102:20
England keep my b. — SHAK 714:14
even have my b. — SCIP 687:16
for his honoured b. — MILT 540:18
from my dead b., avenger — VIRG 830:2
grind his b. — ANON 17:6
hadde pigges b. — CHAU 218:27
Hard words break no b. — PROV 633:46
he that moves my b. — EPIT 317:12
his b. are coral — SHAK 733:21
I may tell all my b. — BOOK 140:19
lay my b. amongst you — WOLS 863:18
little ones picked the b. O! — NURS 580:11
my b. consumed away — BOOK 141:16
O ye dry b. — BIBL 95:21
Rattle his b. — NOEL 576:19
subsist in b. — BROW 162:15

tongs and the b. — SHAK 726:24
turf that covers her soft b. — MART 524:7
valley full of b. — BIBL 95:19
you buy meat, you buy b. — PROV 647:39
bonfire b. of the vanities — WOLF 863:1
match lighting a b. — LIND 494:12
to the everlasting b. — SHAK 720:12
Bong-tree where the B. grows — LEAR 486:6
bonheur b. seul est salutaire — PROU 626:2
bonhomie natural b. — BENT 71:17
bonjour B. tristesse — ÉLUA 314:8
bon-mots b. from their places — MORE 558:19
bonnets Blue B. are bound — SCOT 689:18
b. of Bonny Dundee — SCOT 688:7
bonnie b. Annie Laurie — SONG 763:5
Maxwelton braes are b. — SONG 763:4
bonny Am I no a b. fighter — STEV 775:9
Belbroughton Road is b. — BETJ 75:18
bonnets of B. Dundee — SCOT 688:7
b., bonnie banks — SONG 763:9
longer in B. Dundee — SCOT 689:23
saw ye b. Lesley — BURN 177:19
bono Cui b. — CICE 232:9
bonum Summum b. — CICE 231:21
bonus b. homo — AUCT 36:16
videri b. malebat — SALL 679:9
Boojum Snark was a B. — CARR 204:4
book agree with the b. of God — OMAR 585:5
any b. but the Baronetage — AUST 41:24
Bell, b., and candle — SHAK 714:8
b. a devil's chaplain — DARW 266:19
B., and the Prophets — KORA 471:2
b. cannot take the place — ZERN 877:15
b. is the precious life-blood — MILT 545:23
b. is the purest essence — CARL 200:27
b. must be the axe — KAFK 452:9
b. of life — BIBL 117:31
B. of Life begins — WILD 855:26
b. of nature — GALI 347:16
b. of their art — RUSK 673:16
b. of the living — BOOK 144:14
b. of verse—and Thou — FITZ 331:15
b. that ever took him out of bed — JOHN 440:21
B. wherein is no doubt — KORA 470:20
b., who runs may read — KEBL 459:2
b. would have been finished — WODE 861:25
bred in a b. — SHAK 717:15
but his b. — JONS 446:18
Camerado, this is no b. — WHIT 852:6
damned, thick, square b. — GLOU 360:18
destroys a good b. — MILT 545:22
doth best commend a b. — HEMI 390:16
Each country B.-club — BYRO 190:1
empty b. is like an infant's — TRAH 814:7
Farewell my b. — CHAU 220:17
Galeotto was the b. — DANT 265:1
Go, litel b. — CHAU 221:11
Go, little b. — STEV 777:4
good b. is the best of friends — TUPP 818:13
great b. — CALL 193:17
great b. is a great evil — PROV 633:27
had been reading the b. — TOLS 813:10
I'll drown my b. — SHAK 734:2
insignificant b. because — WOOL 864:10
In the volume of the b. — BOOK 141:31
Kiss the b.'s outside — COWP 255:1
knows this out of the b. — DICK 279:10
leaves of the Judgement B. unfold — TAYL 791:18
little volume, but large b. — CRAS 259:6
look at the best b. — RUSK 673:20
make one b. — JOHN 441:17
Making a b. is a craft — LA B 475:4
my little b. — JUVE 450:14
nice new little b. — CATU 210:1
noble grand b. — GASK 350:10
no b. so bad that — PLIN 609:19
no Frigate like a B. — DICK 281:13
non-reading a b. — BYRO 192:9
noted in thy b. — BOOK 143:13
oldest rule in the b. — CARR 202:18
pain to pen the b. — OXFO 591:11
peruses a b. — ADDI 5:3
print My b. — HERR 396:16

bosom (*cont.*):
take fire in his b.   BIBL 87:29
bosoms Quiet to quick b.   BYRO 186:9
white b.   JOHN 438:26
boss only one b.   WALT 839:17
bossy by the b. for the bully   SELD 691:20
Boston B. man is the east wind   APPL 25:8
good old B.   BOSS 151:17
Boswelliana *Lues B.*   MACA 507:10
botanist I am not a b.   JOHN 439:13
I'd be a b.   FERM 325:11
botanize b. Upon his mother's grave   WORD 868:4
Botany Bay New colonies seek for at B.   FREE 342:7
botch make a b.   BELL 68:19
both long as ye b. shall live   BOOK 138:24
bother 'B. it' I may   GILB 357:26
Sufficient conscience to b. him   LLOY 496:21
Why do you b. the poor   SCOT 690:8
young whom I hope to b.   AUDE 38:9
bothered Bewitched, b., and bewildered   HART 383:10
Botticelli B.'s a cheese   PUNC 650:10
bottle being confined in a b.   WILB 854:8
bothers to buy a b.   DWOR 301:3
b. has just been opened   HESI 397:8
b. of hay   SHAK 726:25
b. on the chimley-piece   DICK 278:21
b. to give him   DICK 278:1
little for the b.   DIBD 276:2
tears into thy b.   BOOK 143:13
way out of the b.-bottle   WITT 861:10
bottles narrow-necked b.   POPE 618:22
new wine into b.   PROV 647:45
new wine into old b.   BIBL 100:17
bottom Bless thee, B.   SHAK 726:15
fairies at the b. of our garden   FYLE 346:22
forgotten man at the b.   ROOS 667:2
reach the b. first   GRAH 367:13
bottomless Law is a b. pit   ARBU 25:17
pit that is b.   JAME 428:21
boue *nostalgie de la b.*   AUGI 38:24
bough bloom along the b.   HOUS 415:11
blossom that hangs on the b.   SHAK 734:3
bread beneath the b.   FITZ 331:15
golden b.   FRAZ 341:19
Petals on a wet, black b.   POUN 621:7
boughs I got me b. off many a tree   HERB 394:4
rotten b. the company   WYAT 871:3
bought b. the company   ADVE 7:34
Gold be b. too dear   PROV 633:14
one has those she b.   MART 524:8
bound b. for the same bourn   HOUS 416:5
b. him a thousand years   BIBL 119:12
b. in misery and iron   BOOK 147:15
b. in the spirit   BIBL 110:8
tied and b.   BOOK 135:4
to another b.   GREV 372:16
boundary b. of Britain   TACI 786:20
right to fix the b.   PARN 597:9
bounded b. in a nut-shell   SHAK 701:10
bounden b. duty   BOOK 137:14
b. duty and service   BOOK 137:17
boundless b., endless, and sublime   BYRO 187:4
bounds shall thy b. be set   BENS 70:22
bounties morning b.   COWP 255:21
bountiful My Lady b.   FARQ 324:3
bouquet b. is better than the taste   POTT 620:12
bouquets broken Anne of gathering b.   FROS 345:2
bourgeois astonish the b.   BAUD 62:4
beastly the b. is   LAWR 483:18
b., *ce sont les autres*   RENA 658:6
b. climb up on them   FLAU 334:5
b. prefers comfort   HESS 397:11
Humour has always something b.   HESS 397:12
bourgeoisie b. in the long run   TROT 817:5
discreet charm of the b.   FILM 331:3
bourn bound for the same b.   HOUS 416:5
country from whose b.   SHAK 702:2
set a b. how far   SHAK 694:8

bourne b. of time and place   TENN 793:7
Bovary *Madame B., c'est moi*   FLAU 334:8
Bovril B. prevents   ADVE 7:11
bovvered Am I b.   CATC 207:2
bow B. down before him   MONS 554:2
b. myself   BIBL 85:21
b. of burning gold   BLAK 126:24
b. to no man   BRAN 155:5
b. was made in England   DOYL 293:3
b., ye tradesmen   GILB 356:15
breaketh the b.   BOOK 142:19
drew a b. at a venture   BIBL 85:21
every knee should b.   BIBL 114:19
from the Almighty's b.   BLAK 125:14
I b. my knees   BIBL 114:1
Lord of the unerring b.   BYRO 186:27
not always stretch his b.   HORA 412:9
set my b. in the cloud   BIBL 79:28
bowed At her feet he b.   BIBL 83:3
bowels b. of compassion   BIBL 117:17
b. of the earth   DRAY 293:16
in the b. of Christ   CROM 260:12
bower b. we shrined to Tennyson   HARD 381:9
deck both bed and b.   SPEN 767:14
lime-tree b. my prison   COLE 241:13
St Johnston's b.   BALL 54:17
bowers green and pleasant b.   BLAK 125:18
bowl B. fast, bowl faster   BRAD 154:8
b. we call The Sky   FITZ 331:24
fill the flowing b.   SONG 762:4
golden b. be broken   BIBL 90:20
lurk within the b.   SMIT 758:19
Morning in the b. of night   FITZ 330:17
bowled b. the sun   TAYL 791:19
bowler wild b. thinks he bowls   LANG 478:10
bowling lies poor Tom B.   DIBD 276:6
recommend the b.-green   GREE 371:7
bowls play at b. must look out   PROV 645:8
bows B. down to wood and stone   HEBE 388:9
bowstrings Hold, or cut b.   SHAK 725:32
bow windows putting b. to the house   DICK 277:9
bow-wow Big B. strain   SCOT 689:28
his b. way   PEMB 602:11
bow-wows to the demnition b.   DICK 279:22
box B. about   AUBR 36:6
b. where sweets lie   HERB 395:2
life like a b. of chocolates   FILM 329:11
Pandora's b.   BURG 172:5
twelve good men into a b.   BROU 169:10
Worth a guinea a b.   ADVE 8:29
boxes as a barbarian b.   DEMO 272:20
Little b. on the hillside   REYN 659:10
boxing B.'s just showbusiness   BRUN 168:19
boy Alas, pitiable b.   VIRG 830:15
and a b. forever   ROWL 671:10
any b. may become President   STEV 774:21
Being read to by a b.   ELIO 309:23
b. brought in the white sheet   LORC 500:17
b. eternal   SHAK 736:17
b. my greatness   SHAK 695:25
b. on the sea-shore   NEWT 574:9
b. out of the country   PROV 648:4
b. stood on the burning deck   HEMA 390:14
b.'s will is the wind's   LONG 499:11
b. to do a man's job   PROV 639:42
b. will ruin himself   GEOR 353:1
Chatterton, the marvellous b.   WORD 868:22
Let the b. win   EDWA 304:4
Little B. Blue   NURS 579:17
little tiny b.   SHAK 736:11
Mad about the b.   COWA 253:14
Minstrel B. to the war   MOOR 558:11
remain a fifteen-year-old b.   ROTH 670:9
sat the journeying b.   HARD 381:23
schoolrooms for 'the b.'   COOK 250:9
silly twisted b.   CATC 209:8
soaring human b.   DICK 276:16
Two boys are half a b.   PROV 645:43
Upon the growing b.   WORD 867:8
When I was a little b.   ANON 21:9
whining, purblind, wayward b.   SHAK 717:13
your little b.   CARR 202:3

boyfriend best way to obtain b.   FIEL 326:7
certain thing called the B.   WILS 859:12
boyhood b. of Judas   Æ 6:11
boys As flies to wanton b.   SHAK 716:11
B. and girls   NURS 578:3
b. get at one end   JOHN 441:23
b. go first to bed   HERB 394:17
b. in the back room   LOES 498:8
b. in the back rooms   BEAV 63:15
b. late at their play   ARNO 30:5
b. not going to be sent   ROOS 667:10
b. of the old Brigade   WEAT 843:7
B. will be boys   PROV 628:19
b. with breeches   BARB 58:1
Christian b.   ARNO 32:13
Deceive b. with toys   LYSA 506:3
for office b.   SALI 679:3
if the b. are still there   BARU 60:13
lightfoot b. are laid   HOUS 416:9
Like little wanton b.   SHAK 710:19
little b. made of   NURS 582:10
loaded guns with b.   CRAB 258:4
men that were b. when   BELL 68:2
send American b.   JOHN 435:7
slower than b.   FRAS 341:17
three merry b. are we   FLET 335:7
Till the b. come home   FORD 337:12
two sorts of b.   DICK 280:4
virgin girls and b.   HORA 412:14
bra Burn your b.   SLOG 755:1
I want a b.   BLUM 129:9
bracelet b. of bright hair   DONN 289:13
braces Damn b.   BLAK 126:16
bracing B. brain and sinew   KING 464:9
Bradford silk hat on a B. millionaire   ELIO 311:14
Bradshaw vocabulary of 'B.'   DOYL 293:1
brae stout heart to stey b.   PROV 642:13
braes among thy green b.   BURN 177:10
Ye banks and b.   BURN 177:16
brag B. is a good dog   PROV 628:20
Brahman B. is consciousness   UPAN 822:5
knows that all-highest B.   UPAN 822:16
braid b., braid road   BALL 55:21
braided b. her yellow hair   BALL 55:18
braids b. of lilies knitting   MILT 539:11
brain Bear of Very Little B.   MILN 538:1
b. attic stocked   DOYL 292:8
b. has the consistency   TURI 819:8
b.? my second favourite organ   ALLE 13:12
b. of feathers   POPE 611:17
b. to think again   BRON 158:16
dry b. in a dry season   ELIO 309:26
dull b. perplexes   KEAT 456:7
fibre from the b. does tear   BLAK 124:11
gleaned my teeming b.   KEAT 457:8
great regions of the b.   BROC 157:14
harmful to the b.   JAME 428:21
hasn't exactly got B.   MILN 538:13
heat-oppressed b.   SHAK 719:19
idle b. is devil's workshop   PROV 635:2
if the b. has oozed out   KRAU 473:14
instrumental to the b.   SHAK 699:10
leave that b. outside   GILB 356:19
losing your b.   FOX 340:1
motions of atoms in my b.   HALD 376:12
petrifactions of a plodding b.   BYRO 190:4
possess a poet's b.   DRAY 293:17
schoolmasters puzzle their b.   GOLD 365:3
tares of mine own b.   BROW 163:5
thus concern His b.   BYRO 187:27
brained large-b. woman   BROW 164:15
brains blow out your b.   KIPL 468:3
b. eaten by moths   SITW 753:13
b. go to his head   ASQU 34:9
b. of a Minerva   BARR 60:5
busy b. must beat on tickle toys   GASC 350:5
Cudgel thy b. no more   SHAK 704:11
dash'd the b. out   SHAK 719:15
girl with b. ought to   LOOS 500:14
Had their b. knocked out   SHEL 745:3
mix them with my b.   OPIE 585:13
brake invented the b.   NEME 570:8

brambles b. in the fortresses — BIBL 93:6
  b. like tall cedars show — COTT 252:15
branch b. shall grow — BIBL 92:16
  Cut is the b. — MARL 522:12
  on the high b. — SAPP 681:1
branches b. of evil — THOR 809:17
  b. of secret water — NERU 570:12
  lodge in the b. — BIBL 101:15
  rise through the b. — DANT 265:10
branchy b. between towers — HOPK 407:6
brandy B. for the parson — KIPL 467:10
  b. of the damned — SHAW 740:27
  drink b. — JOHN 442:23
  fou o' b. — BURN 178:13
  get me a glass of b. — GEOR 352:13
brass b., nor stone, nor earth — SHAK 738:2
  evil manners live in b. — SHAK 711:5
  I am become as sounding b. — BIBL 112:14
  muck there's b. — PROV 647:12
brassière Art is not a b. — BARN 59:2
brat rambling b. (in print) — BRAD 154:10
  spurious b., Tom Jones — RICH 660:17
brave b. bad man — CLAR 233:9
  b. deserve the fair — PROV 640:15
  b. man with a sword — WILD 855:32
  B. men lived before — PROV 628:21
  B. new world — HUXL 422:13
  b. world, Sir — BEHN 67:3
  cry, 'you are b.!' — GRAH 367:18
  Fears of the b. — JOHN 438:10
  Fortune assists the b. — TERE 801:15
  Fortune favours the b. — PROV 632:37
  Fortune favours the b. — VIRG 831:8
  home of the b. — KEY 461:13
  How sleep the b. — COLL 243:12
  Many b. men lived — HORA 414:3
  None but the b. — DRYD 295:4
  O b. new world — SHAK 734:4
  Oh, the b. music — FITZ 331:16
  one b. push — STEV 775:24
  one half of mankind b. — JOHN 442:20
  souls of the b. — CLOU 236:14
  Toll for the b. — COWP 255:18
  to-morrow to be b. — ARMS 28:16
  What's b., what's noble — SHAK 695:22
braver done one b. thing — DONN 289:20
bravery acts of personal b. — WAUG 842:20
  natural b. of your isle — SHAK 698:21
braw b. bricht moonlicht — MORR 561:9
  b. gallant — BALL 54:7
brawler not a b. — BIBL 115:19
brawling b. woman — BIBL 88:29
bray ass may b. a good while — ELIO 308:9
  Vicar of B. — SONG 762:14
brazen her world is b. — SIDN 751:4
Brazil Charley's aunt from B. — THOM 805:13
Brazilian If I were a B. — STIN 777:8
breach godwe to the b. of order — GODW 361:6
  More honoured in the b. — SHAK 700:10
  Once more unto the b. — SHAK 708:16
bread ate his b. in sorrow — GOET 362:17
  better than no b. — PROV 633:35
  bitter b. of banishment — SHAK 730:15
  bones to make my b. — ANON 17:6
  b. and circuses — JUVE 451:13
  b. beneath the bough — FITZ 331:15
  b. eaten in secret — BIBL 87:33
  b. eaten up — CERV 213:4
  b. is black — BARC 58:5
  b. never falls but — PROV 628:22
  b. of adversity — BIBL 93:3
  b. of affliction — BIBL 85:20
  b. of God — BIBL 107:22
  B. of heaven — WILL 857:9
  b. of poverty — HAGG 375:10
  b.-sauce of the happy ending — JAME 430:3
  b. should be so dear — HOOD 406:2
  b. to strengthen man's heart — BOOK 147:6
  b. with joy — BIBL 90:9
  breaking of b. — BIBL 106:32
  Cast thy b. upon the waters — BIBL 90:15
  crammed with distressful b. — SHAK 709:3
  cutting b. and butter — THAC 803:8

eat dusty b. — BOGA 130:12
I am the b. of life — BIBL 107:23
if his son ask b. — BIBL 99:26
live by b. alone — BIBL 98:20
live by b. alone — PROV 638:15
looked to government for b. — BURK 174:28
loud for b. — KING 464:1
made, like b. — LE G 488:1
not upon b. alone — STEV 776:2
one half-pennyworth of b. — SHAK 706:7
our daily b. — BIBL 99:12
ravens brought him b. — BIBL 85:6
Royal slice of b. — MILN 538:5
shalt thou eat b. — BIBL 79:12
taste of another man's b. — DANT 265:16
that which is not b. — BIBL 94:7
took B. — BOOK 137:16
took b., and blessed it — BIBL 103:12
took the b. and brake it — ELIZ 312:20
unleavened b. — BIBL 81:7
unleavened b. of sincerity — BIBL 111:31
we did eat b. — BIBL 81:14
Whoever eats b. without — TALM 789:23
breadth length and b. — BALL 54:12
break at the b. of the day — STRU 779:5
  bend and I b. not — LA F 475:13
  b. a man's spirit — SHAW 739:17
  B., break, break — TENN 792:19
  b. every yoke — BIBL 94:15
  b. Into blossom — WRIG 870:18
  b. them at pleasure — EDGE 303:12
  But b., my heart — SHAK 699:23
  Have a b. — ADVE 7:29
  if you b. the bloody glass — MACN 513:9
  I'll b. my staff — SHAK 734:2
  lark at b. of day — SHAK 737:23
  Never give a sucker an even b. — FIEL 327:6
  shall he not b. — BIBL 93:21
  sucker an even b. — PROV 639:35
  thyself must b. at last — ARNO 29:15
breakdown approaching nervous b. — RUSS 674:15
breaketh Madness need not be all b. — LAIN 476:6
  b. the bow — BOOK 142:19
  b. the cedar-trees — BOOK 141:12
breakfast committed b. with it — LEWI 492:3
  critical period is b.-time — HERB 393:17
  Hope is a good b. — BACO 49:7
  Hope is a good b. — PROV 634:43
  impossible things before b. — CARR 203:8
  One doth but b. here — HENS 392:16
  our b. take — BALL 56:1
  Sing before b. — PROV 643:12
  that sits down to b. — YEAT 875:13
  wholesome, hungry b. — WALT 839:7
breakfasted b. with you — BRUC 168:15
breaking b. of bread — BIBL 106:32
  b. of windows — MORE 558:18
  take pleasure in b. — NURS 578:5
  without b. eggs — PROV 648:10
breast b. high amid the corn — HOOD 405:25
  broods with warm b. — HOPK 407:8
  dwell, alas! in my b. — GOET 361:16
  faultless b. the furnace is — SOUT 765:1
  leaned on his b. at supper — BIBL 109:9
  Oak was round his b. — HORA 411:6
  parts of the b. — BYRD 184:26
  sooth a savage b. — CONG 247:8
  weariness May toss him to My b. — HERB 394:22
  with dauntless b. — GRAY 370:6
breastie panic's in thy b. — BURN 179:24
breastplate b. of faith — BIBL 115:14
  b. of judgement — BIBL 81:22
  b. of righteousness — BIBL 114:15
breasts betwixt my b. — BIBL 90:25
  b. are like two young roes — BIBL 91:4
  b. by which France is fed — SULL 780:6
  her b. are dun — SHAK 738:19
breath b. can make them — GOLD 364:1
  Breathe on me, B. of God — HATC 384:4
  breathes with human b. — TENN 800:13
  breathing thoughtful b. — WORD 869:7
  b. of life — BIBL 78:19

b. of worldly men — SHAK 730:16
B.'s a ware — HOUS 415:13
b. thou art — SHAK 723:12
call the fleeting b. — GRAY 370:5
down and out of b. — SHAK 706:31
drawn the b. of life — YEAT 873:12
draw thy b. in pain — SHAK 705:2
every thing that hath b. — BOOK 150:12
feather on the b. of God — HILD 398:7
fly away, b. — SHAK 735:18
having lost her b., she spoke — SHAK 694:24
healthy b. of morn — KEAT 454:20
last b. of Julius Caesar — JEAN 431:2
lighter than b. — BERR 74:17
lightly draws its b. — WORD 869:23
love thee with the b. — BROW 164:14
sweeter woman ne'er drew b. — INGE 425:8
taxed the b. — THOM 805:19
thou no b. at all — SHAK 717:8
toil of b. — COLE 239:15
waste of b. — YEAT 873:19
while you have it use your b. — FLET 335:5
breathe As though to b. were life — TENN 800:16
  b. by a sort of artificial inlet — FOST 338:20
  b. in that fine air — TENN 794:8
  b. in the faces — PEPY 603:14
  b. is not his name — MOOR 558:12
  B. on me, Breath of God — HATC 384:4
  b. when I expire — BYRO 186:23
  privilege to b. — ELEA 306:14
  So long as men can b. — SHAK 737:19
  summer's morn to b. — MILT 544:4
  yearning to be free — LAZA 485:3
breathes B. there the man — SCOT 688:14
breathing Closer is He than b. — TENN 793:23
breathless b. hush in the Close — NEWB 571:12
  b. on thy fate — LONG 498:15
  B. with adoration — WORD 866:4
bred B. en bawn in a brier-patch — HARR 383:4
  What's b. in the bone — PROV 646:26
Bredon In summertime on B. — HOUS 415:16
bree little abune her b. — BALL 55:18
breeches boys with b. — BARB 58:1
breed Border, nor B. — KIPL 465:8
  b. of their horses — PENN 602:16
  b. one work that wakes — HOPK 408:3
  Feared by their b. — SHAK 730:11
  happy b. of men — SHAK 730:10
  wife for b. — GAY 351:27
breeding b. consists in concealing — TWAI 820:16
  show your b. — SHER 748:31
  without any b. — CART 205:9
breeks b. aff a wild Highlandman — SCOT 689:13
breeze b. from foggy mount — BYRO 187:15
  b. is on the sea — SCOT 689:20
  b. of morning moves — TENN 798:3
  dancing in the b. — WORD 866:7
  wander like a b. — COLE 239:20
  with the b. of song — TENN 795:20
breezes b. dusk and shiver — TENN 796:14
breezy B., Sneezy, Freezy — ELLI 314:2
Breffny little waves of B. — GORE 366:8
Breguet B. had ever made — BALZ 57:1
brekekekex B. koax koax — ARIS 26:17
brethren b., to dwell together — BOOK 149:10
  Dearly beloved b. — BOOK 133:2
  least of these my b. — BIBL 103:7
  my mother and my b. — BIBL 101:12
  we be b. — BIBL 79:30
brevis Ars longa, vita b. — HIPP 399:13
  B. esse laboro — HORA 408:17
  Vitae summa b. — HORA 411:8
brevity B. is the sister — CHEK 222:9
  B. is the soul of wit — PROV 628:23
  B. is the soul of wit — SHAK 701:2
  Its body b. — COLE 239:14
brew bake so shall you b. — PROV 626:40
  b., so shall you bake — PROV 626:41
  b. that is true — FILM 329:15
brewers bakeres and b. — LANG 478:17
brewery take me to a b. — ANON 18:2
bribe b. or gratuity — PENN 602:18
  cannot hope to b. or twist — WOLF 862:16

bribe (cont.):
done without a b. — CENT 213:1
Marriage is a b. — WILD 856:18
Too poor for a b. — GRAY 370:23
bribery corrupt by b. — WILL 857:6
bribes open to b. — GREE 371:13
bricht braw b. moonlicht — MORR 561:9
brick b. in his pocket — JOHN 437:2
carried a piece of b. — SWIF 782:4
'Eave arf a b. at 'im — PUNC 649:18
Follow the yellow b. road — HARB 380:1
Goodbye yellow b. road — JOHN 434:9
hardly throw a b. — ORWE 587:20
inherited it b. — AUGU 40:4
paved with yellow b. — BAUM 62:7
threw it a b. at a time — HARG 382:11
bricks b. to Lewley — BETJ 76:4
make b. without straw — PROV 648:11
bridal Against their b. day — SPEN 768:4
b. of the earth and sky — HERB 395:2
dance at our b. — SCOT 689:1
bride as a b. adorned for her husband — BIBL 119:15
barren b. — POPE 614:28
b. forget her attire — BIBL 94:24
b. of a ducal coronet — DICK 279:4
b. that sun shines on — PROV 633:42
encounter darkness as a b. — SHAK 723:13
jealousy to the b. — BARR 59:21
my life and my b. — POE 610:15
never a b. — PROV 626:24
Never the blushing b. — LEIG 488:11
Passionless b. — TENN 797:16
ser' him for a b. — MACD 510:3
To be his holy b. — STON 777:10
unravished b. of quietness — KEAT 455:16
virgin, yet a b. — CARE 198:11
young b. was the idol — MANZ 521:1
bridegroom Bellona's b. — SHAK 718:5
cometh forth as a b. — BOOK 140:9
Like a b. — AYTO 44:6
bridegrooms Of b., brides — HERR 395:15
brides B. of Enderby — INGE 425:6
Of bride-grooms, b. — HERR 395:15
bridesmaid Always a b. — PROV 626:24
always the b. — LEIG 488:11
bridge Beautiful Railway B. — MCGO 510:15
b. is love — WILD 856:17
b. of gold — PROV 636:18
b. over troubled water — SIMO 752:13
cross the b. — PROV 630:20
going a b. too far — BROW 164:16
Horatius kept the b. — MACA 508:20
keep the b. with me — MACA 508:14
London B. is broken down — NURS 580:2
man on the b. — BALD 53:9
On the B. of Toome — CARB 197:17
speaks well of the b. — PROV 631:31
Women, and Champagne, and B. — BELL 68:18
brief Give b. orders — ABU 1:6
little b. authority — SHAK 723:8
strive to be b. — HORA 408:17
tedious and b. — SHAK 727:5
brier bawn in a b.-patch — HARR 383:4
instead of the b. — BIBL 94:10
Thorough bush, thorough b. — SHAK 725:33
briers O, how full of b. — SHAK 696:12
brig From B. o' Dread — BALL 55:3
brigade boys of the old B. — WEAT 843:7
brigand I am a b. — SHAW 740:26
brigandage teaches him b. — TALM 789:28
bright All things b. and beautiful — ALEX 12:6
b. and fierce and fickle — TENN 799:13
B. as the day — GRAN 368:18
b. day is done — SHAK 695:24
b. day that brings forth — SHAK 712:3
b. face of danger — STEV 775:5
b. northern star — LOVE 502:1
b. particular star — SHAK 694:2
B. the vision — MANT 520:12
dark and b. — BYRO 190:25
Death's b. angel — PROC 624:18
excessive b. — MILT 542:23

eyes are b. — KEAT 458:6
future's b. — ADVE 7:25
Goddess, excellently b. — JONS 446:3
Keep up your b. swords — SHAK 728:5
look, the land is b. — CLOU 237:7
makes the whole world b. — MUIR 564:8
obscurely b. — BYRO 187:13
quick b. things — SHAK 725:24
thought thee b. — SHAK 738:25
torches to burn b. — SHAK 732:7
Tyger, burning b. — BLAK 128:3
young lady named B. — BULL 170:7
brighten Blessings b. — PROV 628:12
brightest B. and best — HEBE 388:7
brightness Amazing b. — OTWA 589:11
B. falls from the air — NASH 569:2
b. of his presence — BOOK 140:6
his Darkness and his B. — BYRO 191:15
leaking the b. away — SPEN 766:14
Brighton B. Pavilion looks as if — SMIT 758:22
Brignal B. banks are wild — SCOT 689:7
brilliance Renew your b. — GRAC 367:8
brilliant dullard's envy of b. men — BEER 66:3
brillig 'Twas b. — CARR 202:21
brim sparkles near the b. — BYRO 186:2
winking at the b. — KEAT 456:4
brimstone fire and b. — BOOK 139:26
smouldering b. — ALAB 10:9
bring b. home knowledge — JOHN 442:16
B. me my arrows of desire — BLAK 126:24
B. out number — BLAK 126:9
day may b. forth — BIBL 89:3
what it will b. — PROV 647:36
bringer b. of unwelcome news — SHAK 707:4
bringing b. me up by hand — DICK 278:8
brink walked to the b. — DULL 299:2
brinkmanship boasting of his b. — STEV 774:24
brioche mangent de la b. — MARI 521:14
brisk b. as a bee — JOHN 438:25
b. little somebody — BROW 164:23
brisking b. about the life — SMAR 754:13
Britain boundary of B. — TACI 786:20
B. a fit country — LLOY 496:16
B.'s stand alone — DE V 275:2
B. will be honoured by historians — HARL 382:15
B. will still be — MAJO 517:4
dangerous man in B. — NEWS 573:13
government of B.'s isle — SHAK 709:21
hail, happy B. — SOME 760:19
Hath B. all the sun — SHAK 698:23
I'm backing B. — SLOG 755:5
should belong to B. — OFFI 584:9
speak for B. — GIRA 359:7
When B. first — BOOT 151:5
Without B., Europe — THOM 808:8
Britannia Beer and B. — ERHA 320:7
Rule, B. — SMIT 759:2
shouted 'Rule B.' — THOM 808:8
British as the B. public — KIPL 465:4
B-b-b. object — MACA 507:4
blood of a B. man — MALO 518:6
bones of one B. Grenadier — SHAK 716:5
B. Grenadier — HARR 383:1
B. Museum had lost its charm — SONG 763:11
B. Nation — GERS 353:12
B. subject I was born — ADDI 5:13
Come you back, you B. soldier — MACD 510:9
destinies of the B. Empire — KIPL 466:14
drunken officer of B. rule — DISR 284:17
I'm a B. object — WALC 835:14
removed By B. hands — MORR 560:6
so also a B. subject — BYRO 185:19
stony B. stare — PALM 595:3
thank God! the B. journalist — TENN 798:1
Briton glory in the name of B. — WOLF 862:16
No good man is a B. — GEOR 352:11
Britons B. alone use 'Might' — AUSO 41:1
B. never will be slaves — WAUG 843:1
B. who are kept far away — THOM 808:8
broad b. is the way — VIRG 831:15
B. of Church — BIBL 99:28
how b. and far — BETJ 76:9
— JOHN 445:2

She's the B. — SPRI 769:2
too b. for leaping — HOUS 416:9
broadens travel b. the mind; but — CHES 225:16
broadminded superior man is b. — CONF 245:17
Broadway sinners on this part of B. — RUNY 672:12
broccoli b., dear — CART 205:10
eat any more b. — BUSH 182:5
brogues not fit to tie his b. — SCOT 690:1
broke If it ain't b. — SAYI 684:24
broken bats have been b. — HOWE 416:17
bones which thou hast b. — BOOK 143:6
b. and contrite heart — BOOK 143:9
b. Anne of gathering bouquets — FROS 345:2
b. by their passing feet — YEAT 872:17
b.-hearted woman — HAYE 385:16
Can it be b. — JENK 432:19
healeth those that are b. — BOOK 150:6
house has been b. open — PEAC 600:12
London Bridge is b. down — NURS 580:2
made to be b. — NORT 577:4
made to be b. — PROV 642:7
Morning has b. — FARJ 323:12
neck once b. — WALS 838:18
not quickly b. — BIBL 89:26
old man, b. — SHAK 711:2
taken up the b. blade — DE G 271:9
through a b. heart — WILD 856:5
brokenhearted bind up the b. — BIBL 94:19
broker honest b. — BISM 123:2
bronze b. and stone — RUNY 672:14
B. is a mirror — AESC 8:34
monument more lasting than b. — HORA 413:9
noontide was b. — CHUR 230:16
bronzes Others shall shape b. — VIRG 830:14
brooches b. and toys — STEV 776:21
brood b. of folly — MILT 539:13
b. of glory — SPEN 767:7
broods b. with warm breast — HOPK 407:8
brook b. and river meet — LONG 499:10
dwelt by the b. Cherith — BIBL 85:6
free, meandering b. — THOR 809:5
grows aslant a b. — SHAK 704:5
noise like a hidden b. — COLE 241:6
salad from the b. — COWP 256:29
willows of the b. — BIBL 87:16
brooks b. of Eden — TENN 798:17
By b. too broad — HOUS 416:9
broom sent with b. before — SHAK 727:11
brooms New b. sweep clean — PROV 639:47
broth spoil the b. — PROV 645:30
brothel intellectual b. — TOLS 813:19
metaphysical b. for the emotions — KOES 470:10
brothels b. with bricks of religion — BLAK 126:12
Keep thy foot out of b. — SHAK 715:26
brother Be my b. — CHAM 215:5
BIG B. IS WATCHING YOU — ORWE 587:10
boredom is its b. — VOLT 835:8
b. came with subtilty — BIBL 80:8
B. can you spare a dime — HARB 379:16
b. followed brother — WORD 865:18
b., hail, and farewell — CATU 211:6
b. he is in Elysium — SHAK 734:29
b. in God — BELL 68:10
b. is born for adversity — BIBL 88:20
b. is on the rack — SMIT 755:25
B. of the Angle — WALT 839:2
b. sin against me — BIBL 102:4
b.'s soul — BARB 57:20
B. to Death — DANI 264:6
b. to dragons — BIBL 87:5
closer than a b. — BIBL 88:23
dear b. here departed — BOOK 139:10
Death and his b. — SHEL 746:5
especially Sir B. Sun — FRAN 340:16
every man's b. — BIBL 79:26
fold to thy heart thy b. — WHIT 853:4
glad mad b.'s name — SWIN 785:4
Had it been his b. — EPIT 318:3
hateth his b. — BIBL 117:20
he's my b. — RUSS 675:15
lo'ed him like a vera b. — BURN 179:13
man and a b. — WEDG 844:28

910 CANDLE · CARICATURE

candle Bell, book, and c. SHAK 714:8
better to light a c. BENE 69:12
Better to light one c. PROV 627:38
blew out the c. ALAI 10:11
called him 'C.-ends' CARR 203:28
c. burns at both ends MILL 536:21
c. by which she TOLS 813:10
c. in that great turnip CHUR 230:10
c. in the wind JOHN 434:5
c. in the wind JOHN 434:8
c. of understanding BIBL 96:24
c. to the sun SIDN 750:10
c. to the sun YOUN 876:15
farthing c. at Dover JOHN 440:6
Fire and fleet and c.-lighte BALL 55:2
lighted a c. BIBL 105:11
light such a c. LATI 482:16
little c. throws his beams SHAK 725:14
Out, out, brief c. SHAK 722:22
rather light a c. STEV 775:1
scarcely fit to hold a c. BYRO 185:3
set a c. in the sun BURT 181:19
candlelight Colours seen by c. BROW 164:10
dress by yellow c. STEV 776:12
get there by c. NURS 579:3
linen by c. PROV 639:33
Candlemas C. day be sunny and bright PROV 635:8
C. day, put beans PROV 628:32
candles c. are all out SHAK 719:18
c. burn their sockets HOUS 415:7
c. in the wind MERE 532:12
carry c. and set chairs HERV 396:23
Night's c. SHAK 732:30
These blessed c. SHAK 725:15
wind extinguishes c. LA R 482:3
candlestick baker, The c.-maker NURS 581:5
wrote over against the c. BIBL 95:24
candlesticks seven golden c. BIBL 117:26
candour combines force with c. CHUR 231:5
candy C. is dandy NASH 568:20
canem *Cave c.* PETR 605:5
canker loathsome c. lives SHAK 737:26
this c., Bolingbroke SHAK 705:13
cankerworm c., and the caterpillar BIBL 96:7
cannibal c. uses knife and fork LEC 486:22
cannibals Caesars, and with C. SHAK 707:14
C. that each other eat SHAK 728:10
cannon C. to right of them TENN 793:4
in the c.'s mouth SHAK 697:1
pulse like a c. EMER 314:23
shaking scythes at c. HEAN 387:15
cannonball c. took off his legs HOOD 405:15
like a c. WELL 846:14
cano *Arma virumque c.* VIRG 828:10
canoe coffin clapt in a c. BYRO 185:8
make love in a c. BERT 75:6
canoes heads in their c. MARV 525:17
canonization sort of natural c. HAZL 386:15
canopy excellent c., the air SHAK 701:11
rich embroidered c. SHAK 710:7
Canossa not go to C. BISM 122:18
cant c. about DECORUM BURN 178:22
can't c. go on BECK 64:14
cant c. of criticism STER 773:8
c. of *Not men* BURK 175:5
Clear your mind of c. JOHN 443:18
cantate *C. Domino canticum novum* BIBL 119:29
Canterbury to the Archbishop of C. SHER 749:3
canting in this c. world STER 773:8
cantons Write loyal c. SHAK 735:6
cantos c. of unvanquished space CRAN 258:12
Cantuar how full of C. BULL 170:8
canvasses c. and factions BACO 46:17
cap If the c. fits, wear it PROV 635:14
capability Negative C. KEAT 457:15
capable *c. de tout* VOLT 835:7
c. of all things TRAH 814:7
c. of anything MAUP 528:15
c. of reigning TACI 787:10
capacity almost infinite c. HUXL 422:20
caparisons No c., Miss SHER 748:17
cape Nobly, nobly C. Saint Vincent BROW 165:29
Round the c. BROW 166:26
capers He c. nimbly SHAK 731:10
capital C. must be propelled BAGE 50:4
Does c. punishment tend FRY 345:21
high c. Of Satan MILT 542:1
origin of c. TORR 814:2
capitalism C. is using its money CAST 206:13
c. with the gloves off STOP 778:4
extermination of c. ZINO 878:3
monopoly stage of c. LENI 488:15
spirit of c. WEBE 843:13
unacceptable face of c. HEAT 388:4
What is c. but buying CARD 198:1
capitalist slave of the c. society CONN 248:14
capitalists c. will sell us MISQ 547:6
Capitol strangers in the C. HEWI 397:15
capitulate I will not c. JOHN 444:9
capons cannot feed c. so SHAK 702:18
Capri letter came from C. JUVE 451:12
caprices depend on the c. TOCQ 811:12
caps C. tilted BLOK 129:5
captain broken by the team c. HOWE 416:17
c. is in his bunk SHAW 740:4
c. of my soul HENL 391:13
c. of the Hampshire grenadiers GIBB 355:3
c. of twenty-four soldiers ANON 22:3
Fighting in the c.'s tower DYLA 301:14
my C. lies, Fallen WHIT 852:3
nobody like the C. THAC 802:19
O C.! my Captain WHIT 852:2
Our great captain's c. SHAK 728:16
plain russet-coated c. CROM 260:9
royal c. of this ruined SHAK 708:19
ship's c. complaining POWE 622:5
tall and dandy c. ARCH 25:19
That in the c. SHAK 723:9
train-band c. eke was he COWP 255:8
captains All my sad c. SHAK 695:11
c. and the kings KIPL 467:5
c. courageous BALL 55:5
C. of industry CARL 200:17
Star c. glow FLEC 334:9
thunder of the c. BIBL 87:13
captive led captivity c. BOOK 144:10
within my c. breast SURR 780:14
captives all prisoners and c. BOOK 134:24
proclaim liberty to the c. BIBL 94:19
captivity c. of Sion BOOK 148:24
prisoners out of c. BOOK 144:7
Turn our c., O Lord BOOK 149:1
car Business is like a c. SAYI 684:4
buy a used c. POLI 613:18
can't drive the c. TYNA 821:2
c. could go straight upwards HOYL 417:11
c. crash as a sexual event BALL 56:9
c. in every garage HOOV 406:14
commodious c. JAME 429:11
gilded c. of day MILT 538:22
motor c. was poetry and tragedy LEWI 492:13
owl of Minerva in a hired c. PAUL 600:4
Carabas my lord the Marquis of C. PERR 604:4
caravan c. goes on PROV 630:12
great c. of humanity SMUT 759:11
Put up your c. HODG 402:1
carbon c. atom JEAN 431:3
carborundum *Nil c.* SAYI 685:4
carbuncle monstrous c. CHAR 217:14
carbuncles Monstrous c. SPEN 766:7
carcase c. of an old song THOM 807:10
Wheresoever the c. is BIBL 102:25
Where the c. is PROV 647:10
carcases c. of unburied men SHAK 698:8
carcass hew him as a c. SHAK 712:6
card c. up his sleeve LABO 474:14
memories are c.-indexes CONN 248:11
Orange c. CHUR 228:21
stood like a playing c. MAIL 516:10
cardboard C. Iron. Their hardships BOLA 131:6
over a c. sea HARB 379:17
cardinal on the C.'s chair BARH 58:8
cards buy a pack of c. COLE 242:15
c. with a man called Doc ALGR 12:15
learned to play at c. JOHN 438:20
Lucky at c. PROV 638:12
old age of c. POPE 614:29
pack the c. BACO 46:17
played At c. for kisses LYLY 505:20
shuffle the c. CERV 213:8
wicked pack of c. ELIO 311:4
care age is full of c. SHAK 737:10
better c. of myself BLAK 124:7
Black C. sits behind HORA 412:16
c. for nobody BICK 120:22
c. for the unhappy VIRG 829:3
C. killed the cat PROV 628:33
c. of all the churches BIBL 113:15
c.'s check and curb VAUG 825:3
c. whether Mr John Keats KEAT 457:25
closed our anxious c. EPIT 318:16
disclaim all my paternal c. SHAK 714:17
don't c. too much for money LENN 489:6
Don't c. was made to care PROV 630:17
Each c. decays SURR 781:2
feeling her c. HOOK 406:8
Heaven's peculiar c. SOME 760:19
Hippocleides doesn't c. HIPP 399:12
if, full of c. DAVI 268:8
kill c. SHAK 727:33
Killing c. SHAK 710:17
more c. to stay SHAK 732:31
much c. and valour SHAK 708:23
Nor c. beyond to-day GRAY 370:11
ravelled sleave of c. SHAK 720:6
she don't c. LENN 489:11
Sorrow and C. BURN 177:21
take c. of minutes CHES 223:4
Teach us to c. ELIO 308:21
Took great C. of his Mother MILN 538:3
To say we do not c. WARD 839:24
wish I could c. what you do MITC 551:4
with artful c. Affecting CONG 247:29
with me past c. SHAK 730:14
women and c. and trouble WARD 839:25
wrinkled C. derides MILT 539:24
career beginning of the c. NAPO 567:9
c. in tatters MAND 519:2
c. is over WELL 846:14
C. open to the talents CARL 199:17
c. open to the talents NAPO 568:8
East is a c. DISR 286:12
Good c. move VIDA 827:16
loyal to his own c. DALT 264:1
nothing in his long c. NEWS 573:22
our c. and our triumph VANZ 824:10
careful be c. out there CATC 208:16
cannot be too c. WILD 855:18
can't be good, be c. PROV 635:22
c. felicity PETR 605:8
c. of the type TENN 795:15
carefully got to be c. taught HAMM 379:5
You come most c. SHAK 698:27
careless c. of the single life TENN 795:15
C. she is with artful care CONG 247:29
C. talk costs lives OFFI 584:1
c. trifle SHAK 718:18
first fine c. rapture BROW 165:28
impudently c. CENT 212:13
They were c. people FITZ 332:13
carelessness both looks like c. WILD 854:19
carefullest c. BETJ 76:7
'c.' he would far rather TERE 801:10
cares anxious c., when past ROCH 664:13
c. can make the sweetest love GREE 371:25
c. that infest the day LONG 499:1
Children are certain c. PROV 628:48
Grief and avenging C. VIRG 830:9
Nobody c. MORT 562:4
none c. or knows CLAR 233:1
one c. for none of them AUST 42:27
when nobody c. SAUN 682:13
Carew grave of Mad C. HAYE 385:16
carf c. biforn his fader CHAU 218:7
caricature c. as far as I can SCAR 683:4
c., Decrepit age YEAT 875:5

cattle (*cont.*):
gangplank of a c. truck HEAN 387:12
grass for the c. BOOK 146:6
Hurry no man's c. PROV 634:50
thousands of great c. BURK 174:13
Catullus Did their C. walk that way YEAT 874:16
Poor C. CATU 210:8
caught man who shoots him gets c.
MAIL 516:11
cauldron Fire burn and c. bubble SHAK 721:15
cauliflower C. is nothing but cabbage
TWAI 820:19
causality law of c. RUSS 674:24
causas *rerum cognoscere c.* VIRG 832:18
vitam vivende perdere c. JUVE 451:10
cause already in the c. BERG 72:8
always has some c. ARIS 27:4
bad c. which cannot bear VANE 824:5
between c. and effect LA B 475:1
c. may be inconvenient BENN 70:17
c. of dullness in others FOOT 336:12
c. of the human nose COLE 242:1
c. of the widows BOOK 144:7
c., or just impediment BOOK 138:19
c. that perishes with them CLOU 236:14
c. that wit is SHAK 707:5
defend my c. BOOK 142:8
experiment to his own c. SPRA 768:17
full c. of weeping SHAK 715:14
good old C. MILT 546:8
good old c. WORD 867:20
great c. of cheering BENN 70:15
his c. being good MORE 559:8
it is the c., my soul SHAK 729:12
judge in his own c. PROV 640:11
judge thou my c. BIBL 95:13
little c. for carollings HARD 381:15
loving people without c. TOLS 813:17
Our c. is just DICK 282:6
penalty suffered, but by the c. AUGU 39:20
perseverance in a good c. STER 772:20
Rebel without a c. FILM 331:10
Report me and my c. SHAK 704:27
shew any just c. BOOK 138:23
Whose c. is God COWP 256:28
winning c. pleased the gods LUCA 503:16
causes aren't any good, brave c. OSBO 588:19
best c. tend to attract FISH 330:13
declare the c. JEFF 431:5
Home of lost c. ARNO 31:16
in its c. just DRYD 296:16
knowledge of c. BACO 48:28
malice, to breed c. JONS 446:16
thread of c. AURE 40:22
Tough on the c. of crime BLAI 123:17
caution c. in love RUSS 674:18
cautiously do c., and look to the end
ANON 23:11
cavaliero perfect c. BYRO 185:9
cavaliers C. (Wrong but Wromantic)
SELL 692:3
will not do with the c. LAMB 477:16
cavalry Some say an army of c. SAPP 680:20
cave burst stomach like a c. DOUG 291:13
C. canem PETR 605:5
darksome c. they enter SPEN 767:9
political C. of Adullam BRIG 157:5
vacant interlunar c. MILT 545:2
wall of the c. PLAT 609:2
cavern c. sparkling BYRO 190:9
caverns bat that beats about in c. WILB 854:4
c. measureless to man COLE 240:4
Sand-strewn c. ARNO 29:13
caves c. in which we hide FITZ 332:5
c. of ice COLE 240:6
dark unfathomed c. of ocean GRAY 370:6
there will be c. NIET 575:12
caviare c. to the general SHAK 701:16
Cawdor Glamis thou art, and C. SHAK 718:19
cease c. from exploration ELIO 309:19
c. from mental fight BLAK 126:24
C.! must men kill SHEL 744:6
c. to live ARNO 31:6

c. upon the midnight KEAT 456:9
Fall and c. SHAK 717:6
fears that I may c. to be KEAT 457:8
maketh wars to c. BOOK 142:19
that thou shouldst c. SHEL 747:3
Wonders will never c. PROV 647:33
ceased c. to be with Sarah BIBL 79:34
ceasing Remembering without c. BIBL 115:12
Ceaușescus C.' execution O'DO 583:12
Cecilia Blessed C., appear AUDE 36:23
cedar breaketh the c.-trees BOOK 141:12
moonlit C. ARNO 29:21
cedars c. of Lebanon BIBL 83:10
c. of Libanus BOOK 147:6
excellent as the c. BIBL 91:10
cedite *C. Romani scriptores* PROP 625:1
ceiling draw on the c. CHES 225:17
highest, hardest glass c. CLIN 236:4
lines of the c. ÉLUA 314:8
celebrity C. is a mask UPDI 822:22
of mathematical c. DOYL 292:16
celestial Apparelled in c. light WORD 867:2
C. Emporium BORG 151:8
lighten with c. fire BOOK 150:16
Celia Come, my C. JONS 446:14
celibacy c. has no pleasures JOHN 437:17
c. is almost always PEAC 600:16
cell Each in his narrow c. GRAY 370:3
hot c. of their hearts BOGA 130:12
proud of his c. WEIL 845:5
cellar born in a c. CONG 247:2
Born in a c. FOOT 336:10
cellos c. of the deep farms STEV 775:2
cells c. and gibbets COOK 250:9
little grey c. CHRI 227:2
vast assembly of nerve c. CRIC 260:1
Celt hysterics of the C. TENN 796:2
Celtic woods of C. antiquity KEYN 462:4
cement Palestine is the c. ARAF 25:14
With the same c. POPE 613:24
cemetery c. is an open space SHEL 743:7
c. of dead ideas UNAM 821:14
Help me down C. Road LARK 481:12
cenotaph laugh at my own c. SHEL 743:26
censor c. of the young HORA 409:10
censorship extreme form of c. SHAW 742:15
fought without c. WEST 849:3
results from a c. BENT 71:11
censure c. of a man's self JOHN 442:18
c. this mysterious writ DRYD 295:27
read, and c. HEMI 390:16
centaur ant's a c. POUN 621:9
moral c., man and wife BYRO 189:7
centre c. cannot hold YEAT 874:17
c. is everywhere ANON 19:4
My c. is giving way FOCH 336:2
This bed thy c. is DONN 289:18
cents simplicity of the three per c. DISR 285:29
centuries All c. but this GILB 357:4
forty c. look down NAPO 567:10
lie through c. BROW 165:5
Through what wild c. DE L 271:24
century c. of light BAHA 51:21
c. of the common man WALL 836:12
c.'s cool nursery AKHM 10:7
last for more than a c. CATU 210:3
sad, glittering c. BURC 172:4
So the 20th C. CRAN 258:17
when a new c. begins MANN 519:12
Cerberus C., and blackest Midnight
MILT 539:21
You are not like C. SHER 748:18
cerebellum If they've a brain and c.
GILB 356:19
ceremonies dreams, and c. SHAK 712:7
ceremony C. is an invention LAMB 476:12
c. of innocence is drowned YEAT 874:17
c. that to great ones 'longs SHAK 723:6
general c. SHAK 709:2
in custom and in c. YEAT 874:11
thrice-gorgeous c. SHAK 709:3
Ceres C. re-assume the land POPE 615:9
certain c. because it is impossible TERT 802:12

c. of nothing KEAT 457:12
c. thing called the Boy Friend WILS 859:12
four things c. KIPL 466:2
France in a c. way DE G 271:17
lady of a 'c. age' BYRO 189:9
nothing is c. PLIN 609:12
Nothing is c. but PROV 640:18
Nothing is c. but PROV 640:19
sure and c. hope BOOK 139:10
certainties begin with c. BACO 45:8
hot for c. MERE 532:22
most people's c. HARD 380:8
certainty C. Feeling PASC 598:13
c. is an absurd one VOLT 835:2
not the test of c. HOLM 403:18
only c. is that PLIN 609:12
certamina *atque haec c. tanta* VIRG 833:4
certezza *Di doman non ci è c.* MEDI 530:5
certified that I may be c. BOOK 141:28
cesspool London, that great c. DOYL 292:23
cetacean generous C. KIPL 468:14
Ceylon soft o'er C.'s isle HEBE 388:9
chaff catch old birds with c. PROV 648:5
king's c. is worth PROV 637:5
tastes like c. KEAT 458:15
wheat from the c. HUBB 417:15
chaffinch While the c. sings BROW 165:27
chagrin *c'est le c. qui développe* PROU 626:2
C. d'amour FLOR 335:23
chain c. is no stronger PROV 628:39
c. of our sins BOOK 135:4
flesh to feel the c. BRON 158:16
hangs a golden c. PUSH 650:21
sever The c. CORY 252:12
winds th'exhausted c. BURN 179:12
chained With one c. friend SHEL 744:2
chainless spirit of the c. mind BYRO 191:1
chains better to be in c. KAFK 452:7
bind their kings in c. BOOK 150:11
c. and darkness MONT 554:7
C. and slaverie BURN 179:9
C. do not hold a marriage SIGN 751:14
c. Of heart-debasing slavery GRAI 368:6
deliverance from c. DOUG 291:19
everywhere he is in c. ROUS 670:14
lose but their c. MARX 526:14
My c. fell off WESL 847:7
sang in my c. THOM 805:16
slightest c. EDGE 303:12
woman must wear c. FARQ 324:5
chainsaw imagination and a c. HIRS 400:1
chair *c. est triste* MALL 517:12
C. she sat in ELIO 311:6
Give Dayrolles a c. CHES 223:22
like a barber's c. SHAK 694:4
on the Cardinal's c. BARH 58:8
Seated in thy silver c. JONS 446:3
should not paint the c. MUNC 565:9
sitting in my c. SOUT 764:21
speaks of a c. BISH 122:11
With one enormous c. LERN 490:14
chairs carry candles and set c. HERV 396:23
empty c. in my drawing-room BURN 176:18
next suggested elbow-c. COWP 256:6
three c. in my house THOR 809:21
chaise longue hurly-burly of the c. CAMP 195:1
chalice c. from the palace FILM 329:15
chalices golden c. JEWE 433:18
challenge if you wish to c. Jupiter SENE 692:13
Cham great C. of literature SMOL 759:10
chamber bridegroom out of his c. BOOK 140:9
in my lady's c. NURS 578:16
in your c. BOOK 139:15
stalking in my c. WYAT 871:4
chambermaid arms of a c. JOHN 442:21
chamberpot fortune empties her c.
MACD 510:8
chambers beams of his c. BOOK 147:4
intricate and winding c. SHEL 747:17
chameleon add colours to the c. SHAK 710:9
c.'s dish SHAK 702:18
chameleons C. feed on light and air
SHEL 744:3

champagne c. and a chicken MONT 554:5
C. certainly gives one SURT 781:13
C. for my real friends BACO 49:14
c. or high heels BENN 70:17
get no kick from c. PORT 619:13
not a c. teetotaller SHAW 739:18
since I've had c. CHEK 222:15
Women, and C. BELL 68:18
chance All c., direction POPE 616:27
bastard child of c. KLEI 469:10
bludgeonings of c. HENL 391:12
c. and accident BACO 49:15
c., and death SHEL 746:2
c. favours only the prepared PAST 599:1
C. governs all MILT 542:17
C. has appointed her BUNT 170:18
C. herself DAVI 268:1
erring men call c. MILT 539:9
Give peace a c. LENN 489:8
I missed my c. LAWR 483:23
in the last c. saloon MELL 531:5
it was by c. BRAD 154:11
law, c., hath slain DONN 288:9
never eliminate c. MALL 517:14
no gifts from c. ARNO 30:3
Chancellor C. of the Exchequer LOWE 502:13
chances c. change SOUT 765:3
changes and c. BOOK 138:2
Chanel C. No. 5 MONR 553:18
change be the c. GAND 349:1
can c. the world MEAD 529:14
C. and decay LYTE 506:5
C. as the winds change SWIN 786:5
c., but I cannot die SHEL 743:25
c. from Jane to Elizabeth AUST 42:11
c. his spots PROV 637:18
C. horses in mid stream PROV 630:18
c. is as good as a rest PROV 628:40
C. is constant DISR 284:23
'C.' is scientific RUSS 675:11
c. our vile body BOOK 139:10
c. partners BERL 72:19
C. the name HORA 414:8
c. the name PROV 628:41
c. the past AGAT 9:10
c. the people who teach BYAT 184:24
c. we think we see FROS 344:8
c. what we can STEV 775:13
C. without inconvenience JOHN 435:16
c. your mind AURE 40:20
compelled to c. that state NEWT 574:3
doth in C. delight SPEN 767:27
glory's small c. HUGO 419:7
in all c. BAUD 62:1
it's bound to c. HART 383:18
lamentable c. SHAK 716:9
life can c. on a dime LAHR 476:4
Management that wants to c. TUSA 819:16
means of some c. BURK 173:30
more things c. KARR 453:8
most stupid do not c. CONF 246:20
necessary not to c. FALK 322:16
Neither to c., nor falter SHEL 746:4
point is to c. it MARX 526:9
relief in c. IRVI 425:22
religion, knavery, and c. BEHN 67:3
respond to c. QUIN 652:4
see c. in the things ARIS 27:11
shalt thou c. them BOOK 146:17
subject to c. PALI 593:10
things will have to c. LAMP 477:20
Times c. PROV 645:22
To live is to c. NEWM 572:7
torrent of c. CHES 225:14
total c. of ideas STER 773:17
try to c. things BOLD 131:10
wheel Of C. SPEN 767:26
wind of c. is blowing MACM 512:19
wish to c. in the child JUNG 449:17
without c. UNAM 821:13
changeable fickle and c. thing VIRG 830:1
changed all things are c. BACO 45:21
changed, c. utterly YEAT 873:7

changed, c. utterly YEAT 873:9
c. from that Hector VIRG 829:11
c. upon the blue guitar STEV 774:6
human nature c. WOOL 864:7
If voting c. anything LIVI 496:4
its name c. DANT 265:12
not how he c. MORR 561:11
perfect is to have c. NEWM 572:7
we shall all be c. BIBL 113:5
world c. while I slept EIRE 306:5
changes All things are c. AURE 40:24
c. and chances BOOK 138:2
c. we fear be thus irresistible JOHN 435:20
sundry and manifold c. BOOK 135:19
changing c. countries BREC 156:5
c. scenes of life TATE 790:15
ever c., like a joyless eye SHEL 747:2
everything within them was c. DIDE 282:13
fixed point in a c. age DOYL 292:13
stress on not c. one's mind MAUG 528:9
times they are a-c. DYLA 302:4
Chankly Hills of the C. Bore LEAR 485:18
channel C. forbids union GRAT 369:6
[C.] is a mere ditch NAPO 567:11
crossing the C. GILB 356:23
Fog in C. CART 205:8
in a different c. AKHM 10:4
masters of the C. NAPO 567:12
chanting C. faint hymns SHAK 725:21
chaos C. and darkness MARR 523:19
C. and old Night MILT 541:27
c. illuminated by lightning WILD 855:8
c. inside oneself NIET 575:20
C. is come again SHAK 728:22
c. often breeds life ADAM 2:15
C., rough and unordered mass OVID 590:5
C. umpire sits MILT 542:17
dread empire, C. POPE 613:29
God dawned on C. SHEL 743:13
Humour is emotional c. THUR 810:13
means of overcoming c. RICH 660:10
Not c.-like together crushed POPE 618:18
return you to c. ZOHA 878:6
stillness in the midst of c. BELL 69:4
chapel also build a c. LUTH 505:7
c. I was painting MICH 534:1
Devil will build a c. PROV 647:7
chapels nice in c. HUNT 421:8
chaplain twice a day the C. called WILD 856:1
chaps Biography is about C. BENT 71:14
nave to the c. SHAK 718:4
chapter c. of accidents CHES 223:17
repeat a complete c. JOHN 442:14
character about a fellow's c. REAG 656:14
by the content of their c. KING 463:11
c. dead at every word SHER 748:25
c. in the full current GOET 362:12
c. is destiny ELIO 308:8
c. is his fate HERA 393:1
c. is to be abused THAC 803:1
c. of the fifth act LERM 490:3
confession of c. EMER 314:22
discover their real c. EDGE 303:9
elucidation of c. CREI 259:16
Fate and c. NOVA 577:10
incrustations of national c. BULW 170:10
leave my c. behind me SHER 748:26
reap a c. READ 656:8
reveal more of a man's c. PLUT 610:10
Sports do not build c. BROU 160:15
turns on personal c. NAPO 567:18
What is c. JAME 429:21
wise about his c. ELIO 306:19
characteristics c. of the human species
GODW 361:3
characters c. and conduct of their rulers
ADAM 3:10
c. to lose BURN 178:22
high c. are drawn POPE 615:23
Six c. in search PIRA 607:4
charge c. of the clattering train BEAV 64:1
give his angels c. over thee BOOK 146:2
I'm in c. CATC 208:6

Take thou in c. MACA 508:18
charged c. the troops BROW 162:23
thought c. with emotion GIDE 356:6
charges c. cannot be brought MACH 511:11
die to save c. BURT 181:10
warily to begin c. BACO 46:28
charging marching, c. feet JAGG 427:11
Charing Cross existence is at C. JOHN 441:14
Heaven and C. THOM 808:2
chariot axle-tree of the c.-wheel BACO 48:15
body as the c. UPAN 822:11
c. of fire BLAK 126:24
C. of Supernal Man ZOHA 878:10
clouds his c. BOOK 147:4
Swing low, sweet c. SONG 763:12
Time's wingèd c. MARV 525:12
charioted c. by Bacchus KEAT 456:7
chariots burneth the c. BOOK 142:19
trust in c. BOOK 140:13
wheels of his c. BIBL 83:4
charitably c. dispose of any thing SHAK 708:25
charities cold c. CRAB 258:9
Defer not c. BACO 47:27
charity C. and beating FLET 335:14
C. and Mercy DICK 278:19
C. begins at home PROV 628:42
C. begins at home SHER 748:29
C. covers a multitude PROV 628:43
C., dear Miss Prism WILD 854:24
c. edifieth BIBL 112:5
c. for all LINC 494:6
c. is cold SMAR 754:11
C. never faileth BIBL 112:14
C. shall cover BIBL 117:12
c. so cold SKEL 754:3
C. suffereth long BIBL 112:14
c. will hardly water BACO 47:16
expect c. towards others BROW 163:11
gives c. in secret TALM 789:29
give with c. a stone BLAK 125:3
have not c. BIBL 112:14
He is all c. JULI 449:8
in love and c. BOOK 137:9
justice, not c. WOLL 863:12
Keeping books on c. PERÓ 604:1
lectures or a little c. WHIT 852:12
Let holy c. LITT 495:13
little earth for c. SHAK 711:2
living need c. ARNO 29:1
love and dear c. MORE 559:13
On what a c. ye come SMAR 754:14
charlatan a c., and a conjuror TROL 816:2
Charles C. II was always very merry SELL 692:4
gentle-hearted C. COLE 241:14
keep King C. the First out DICK 277:11
King C.'s golden days SONG 762:14
King C.'s head DICK 277:12
Charley C.'s aunt from Brazil THOM 805:13
Charlie C. he's my darling SONG 762:1
o'er the water to C. HOGG 402:18
Charlotte C. has been writing BRON 158:22
charm British Museum had lost its c.
GERS 353:12
By what sweet c. OVID 590:1
C. a sort of bloom on a woman BARR 59:22
c. dissolves SHEN 747:18
c. he never so wisely BOOK 143:18
c. in melancholy ROGE 665:15
c. of all the Muses TENN 800:11
c. of powerful trouble SHAK 721:16
C. the great English blight WAUG 842:10
Completing the c. ELIO 309:2
discreet c. of the bourgeoisie FILM 331:3
double c. DYER 301:9
hard words like a c. OSBO 588:10
Oozing c. from every pore LERN 490:15
What c. can soothe GOLD 365:14
what c. is CAMU 196:5
charmed c. it with smiles CARR 204:3
I bear a c. life SHAK 722:24
charmer voice of the c. BOOK 143:18
Were t'other dear c. away GAY 351:9
charms acres o' c. BURN 178:11

charms (*cont.*):
Do not all c. fly — KEAT 455:13
endearing young c. — MOOR 558:6
fields and flocks have c. — CRAB 258:6
hath a thousand c. — COWP 256:4
mere external c. — MORE 559:2
Music has c. — CONG 247:8
nameless c. unmarked — BYRO 185:14
Charon C. quit poling — GINS 359:2
charter c. of the land — THOM 808:8
chase have to c. after it — KLEE 469:8
live by the c. — TOCQ 812:9
stern c. a long chase — PROV 643:34
with unhurrying c. — THOM 807:15
chases your picture c. me — RACI 653:1
chassis worl's in a state o' c. — O'CA 583:8
chaste as c. as ice — SHAK 702:6
c. and fair — JONS 446:3
C. as the icicle — SHAK 698:15
c. as unsunned snow — SHAK 698:20
c. polygamy — CARE 198:11
C. to her husband — POPE 614:28
Married, charming, c. — BYRO 187:22
My English text is c. — GIBB 355:6
Nor ever c. — DONN 288:13
Was Jesus c. — BLAK 125:5
chasteneth he c. — BIBL 116:8
chastised c. you with whips — BIBL 85:3
chastisement c. of our peace — BIBL 94:4
chastity c. and continency — AUGU 39:6
C.—the most unnatural — HUXL 422:18
clothed on with c. — TENN 793:18
Even like thy c. — SHAK 729:20
'Tis c., my brother — MILT 539:5
vice of c. — VOLT 834:20
chat agreement kills a c. — CLEA 235:3
chateaux ô c. — RIMB 662:17
Chatham Great C. — ANON 17:11
chats spoiled the women's c. — BROW 167:1
Chattanooga C. Choo-choo — GORD 366:6
chatter only idle c. — GILB 357:19
chattering not c. pies — SIDN 750:19
Chatterley Between the end of the C. ban — LARK 480:18
Chatterton C., the marvellous boy — WORD 868:22
cheap c. but wholesome salad — COWP 256:29
c. sitting as standing — PROV 636:7
done as c. as other men — PEPY 603:6
flesh and blood so c. — HOOD 406:2
hold their manhoods c. — SHAK 709:8
how potent c. music is — COWA 254:2
maketh himself c. — BACO 46:15
Man's life is c. as beast's — SHAK 715:12
milk is so c. — PROV 647:22
sell it c. — SLOG 755:11
Talk is c. — PROV 644:5
Words are c. — CHAP 215:19
cheaper c. than a prawn sandwich — RATN 655:14
c. to do this — BUTL 184:13
in the c. seats — LENN 489:3
cheapest Buy in the c. market — PROV 628:29
c. and most common quality — GIBB 354:12
cheat cannot c. on DNA — WARD 839:24
c. at cards genteelly — BOSW 152:8
detecting what I think a c. — JOHN 441:10
so lucrative to c. — CLOU 237:2
cheated be exceedingly c. — EVEL 321:19
c. than not to trust — JOHN 437:10
Of being c. — BUTL 183:24
Old men who never c. — BETJ 75:13
cheating c. of our friends — CHUR 228:7
period of c. — BIER 121:8
cheats C. never prosper — PROV 628:44
c. with an oath — PLUT 610:13
cheek blush into the c. — DICK 280:10
c. of night — SHAK 732:7
dancing c.-to-cheek — BERL 72:20
Feed on her damask c. — SHAK 735:21
giveth his c. — BIBL 95:12
give this c. a little red — POPE 615:17
how she leans her c. — SHAK 732:10
iron tears down C.'s cheek — MILT 539:17

iron tears down Pluto's c. — MILT 539:17
loves a rosy c. — CARE 198:6
smite thee on thy right c. — BIBL 99:5
cheeks blood Spoke in her c. — DONN 288:19
crack your c.! rage! blow — SHAK 715:16
on thy c. — KEAT 455:5
ruddy c. Augustus had — HOFF 402:4
cheer Be ay of c. — CHAU 219:2
Be of good c. — BIBL 101:19
be of good c. — BIBL 108:23
c. but not inebriate — BERK 72:12
c. but not inebriate — COWP 256:19
Don't c., men — PHIL 606:1
let thy heart c. thee — BIBL 90:19
scarce forbear to c. — MACA 508:19
So c. up, my lads — HUGH 417:18
which side do they c. for — TEBB 792:10
with a c. — BROW 164:22
cheerer c. of his spirits — WALT 839:3
cheerful as c. as any man could — PEPY 603:2
c. countenance — BIBL 88:14
c. countenance — BOOK 147:6
c. giver — BIBL 113:12
It's being so c. — CATC 208:10
join our c. songs — WATT 841:18
make a c. noise — BOOK 145:11
with a c. countenance — SHAM 738:30
cheerfully evil so fully and c. — PASC 598:12
cheerfulness C. gives elasticity — SMIL 755:22
c. keeps up — ADDI 5:12
c. was always breaking in — EDWA 304:9
cheeriness Chintzy, Chintzy c. — BETJ 75:11
cheering c. us all up — BENN 70:15
cheerio c. my deario — MARQ 523:13
cheers Two c. for Democracy — FORS 338:13
cheese apple pie and c. — FIEL 326:3
Botticelli's a c. — PUNC 650:10
chinks wi' c. — SURT 781:8
I've dreamed of c. — STEV 775:23
like some valley c. — AUDE 38:10
of c. — FADI 322:12
pound of c. — CALV 194:2
second mouse that gets the c. — SAYI 684:31
varieties of c. — DE G 271:13
chemical made up of c. elements — MULL 564:16
two c. substances — JUNG 449:14
chemically They may be sound c. — HALD 376:12
chemist as objective as a c. — CHEK 222:7
c., fiddler, statesman — DRYD 294:20
chemistry captured for life by c. — HODG 401:17
c. that works — WILL 857:11
found him weak in c. — WELL 846:19
produces by c. — SHAW 741:2
cheque political blank c. — GOSC 366:11
chequerboard c. of nights and days — FITZ 331:21
cheques Blank c. — HOLM 403:15
cherchez C. la femme — DUMA 299:3
cherish c. those hearts — SHAK 710:23
love, c., and to obey — BOOK 139:1
cherished lay aside long-c. love — CATU 211:2
Chernobyl cultural C. — MNOU 551:14
cherries apples, c., hops — DICK 280:15
Life is just a bowl of c. — BROW 161:11
cherry American as c. pie — BROW 161:4
carve heads upon c.-stones — JOHN 444:1
c. hung with snow — HOUS 415:12
c. now — HOUS 415:11
C. ripe — CAMP 195:24
C.-ripe, ripe, ripe — HERR 395:17
c. year, a merry year — PROV 628:45
Under the c. — BASH 60:20
wild c. blossom — MOTO 562:15
cherubim C. and Seraphim — HEBE 388:10
c. does cease to sing — BLAK 124:11
helmèd c. — MILT 540:24
cherubims Immortal c. — TRAH 814:13
rode upon the c. — BOOK 140:5
sitteth between the c. — BOOK 146:14
cherubin C., and Seraphin — BOOK 133:9
cherubs so near the c. hymn — SMAR 754:8
Cheshire cosmic C. cat — HUXL 423:3
chess First of the c. — CHAU 218:1

chessboard c. is the world — HUXL 423:10
chest on the dead man's c. — STEV 775:20
Chesterton dared attack my C. — BELL 68:11
chestnut spreading c. tree — LONG 500:4
chestnuts pop like c. — FLAU 333:13
chevalier c. sans peur et sans reproche — ANON 22:1
young C. — SONG 762:1
Chevy Drove my C. to the levee — MCLE 512:3
Chevy Chase old song of C. — ADDI 5:5
chew can't fart and c. gum — JOHN 435:11
chewed c., are cast up — HOBB 401:7
cheweth c. not the cud — BIBL 81:26
chewing gum c. for the eyes — ANON 20:13
chews Pleasure c. and grinds — MONT 555:19
Chianti bottles of C. — SHAF 693:15
chic Radical C. . . . only radical in Style — WOLF 863:5
chicken champagne and a c. — MONT 554:5
c. in every pot — HOOV 406:14
c. in his pot — HENR 391:17
fed the c. every day — RUSS 675:2
Some c.! Some neck — CHUR 229:20
chickens all my pretty c. — SHAK 722:7
as a hen gathereth her c. — BIBL 102:21
beside the white c. — WILL 858:11
costly than c. — SHAW 739:29
count your c. — PROV 630:19
Curses, like c. — PROV 629:30
May c. come cheeping — PROV 638:35
chiding c. of the winter's wind — SHAK 696:14
I am a child to c. — SHAK 729:7
not alway be c. — BOOK 147:1
chief c. end of man — SHOR 750:2
C. Justice was rich — MACA 507:14
c. of the ways — BIBL 87:15
Cromwell, our c. of men — MILT 545:17
Sinners; of whom I am c. — BIBL 115:18
chieftain C. Iffucan of Azcan — STEV 774:1
c. o' the puddin'-race — BURN 179:22
child accused of c. death — RICH 660:6
As yet a c. — POPE 614:17
battle line than bear one c. — EURI 321:11
cherished c. — ELIO 307:3
C.! do not throw — BELL 67:17
c. for the first seven — SAYI 684:21
c. imposes on the man — DRYD 295:29
c. in a forest — BART 60:7
C. is father — WORD 866:18
c. is father of the man — PROV 628:46
c. is known by his doings — BIBL 88:26
c. is not a vase — RABE 652:11
c. is owed the greatest — JUVE 451:21
c. looks at a cake — GASK 350:11
c. of God — BOOK 138:8
c. of law — BENT 71:2
c. of Time — HALL 378:3
c. ought to be of the party — AUST 42:22
c.'s a plaything — LAMB 477:1
c. shall lead them — BIBL 92:17
c. should always know what's true — STEV 776:17
c.'s rattle — JOHN 440:13
devoured the infant c. — HOUS 415:5
disagreeable-looking c. — BURN 176:13
English c. — BLAK 127:12
every c. born therein — RUSK 674:1
every c. may reach — JONS 447:1
Get with c. a mandrake — DONN 289:14
God bless the c. — HOLI 403:4
governed by a c. — SHAK 731:19
happy English c. — TAYL 791:14
hare's own c. — HOFF 402:11
have a thankless c. — SHAK 715:6
healthy c. well nursed — SWIF 783:2
I am a c. to chiding — SHAK 729:7
I am to have his c. — BURG 172:8
If you strike a c. — SHAW 741:16
I heard one calling, 'C.' — HERB 394:2
Is it well with the c. — BIBL 85:25
I was a c. — POE 610:14
knows his own c. — SHAK 724:12
leave a c. alone — BROW 167:14
like a froward c. — TEMP 792:13

Weave a c. round him — COLE 240:9
wheel is come full c. — SHAK 717:4
circling sharks are c. — ANON 18:11
circumcised c. dog — SHAK 729:24
circumcision c. nor uncircumcision — BIBL 115:9
circumference c. is nowhere — ANON 19:4
circumlocution C. Office — DICK 278:13
circumnavigation c. of our globe — DISR 284:16
circumspectly walk c. — BIBL 114:10
circumspice *Si monumentum requiris, c.* — EPIT 319:10
circumstance fell clutch of c. — HENL 391:12
force of c. — DIDE 282:12
lie with c. — SHAK 697:26
Pride, pomp, and c. — SHAK 728:31
circumstances C. alter cases — PROV 629:3
C. beyond my control — DICK 277:22
play of c. — WEIL 844:29
circumstantial c. evidence — THOR 809:6
lie c. — SHAK 697:26
circumvent c. God — SHAK 704:13
circus no right in the c. — MAXT 528:17
shouldn't be in the c. — PROV 635:23
circuses bread and c. — JUVE 451:13
citadel his own airy c. — KEAT 457:19
cities C. and their civilities — PATM 599:14
c. we had learned about — JARR 430:22
flower of c. — ANON 18:18
hell to c. — AESC 6:15
hum Of human c. — BYRO 186:11
lousy skin scabbed by c. — BUNT 170:18
not look in great c. — AUST 41:14
Seven c. warred — HEYW 398:4
splendid C. — RIMB 662:16
streets of a hundred c. — HOOV 406:16
Towered c. please us — MILT 539:30
citizen c. as an abstract proposition — TOCQ 811:14
c., first in war — LEE 487:9
c. in this world — AURE 40:25
c. of no mean city — BIBL 110:10
c. of the world — BACO 47:4
c. of the world — BOSW 152:3
c. of the world — SOCR 760:7
c. or the police — AUDE 38:7
c.'s first duty — GRAS 369:1
Every c. will make — MORE 559:18
good man and a good c. — AUCT 36:16
greater than a private c. — TACI 787:10
I am a Roman c. — CICE 232:4
John Gilpin was a c. — COWP 255:8
zealous c. — BURK 174:22
citizens c. of death's grey land — SASS 682:7
committed c. — MEAD 529:14
first and second class c. — WILL 858:17
citizenship c. Indian — TERE 801:22
cito *Bis dat qui c. dat* — PUBL 648:30
città C. DOLENTE — DANT 264:13
city as of a c. — BROW 162:24
big hard-boiled c. — CHAN 215:9
bring us forth from this c. — KORA 471:17
buildings of a c. — KEAT 458:6
citizen of no mean c. — BIBL 110:10
c. consists in men — NICI 574:18
c. for everyone — FUEN 345:26
c. is built — TENN 794:5
c. is not a concrete jungle — MORR 560:8
C. now doth like a garment wear — WORD 865:7
c. of dreadful night — THOM 808:23
c. of God — AURE 40:9
c. of God — BOOK 145:18
c. of God — JOHN 445:2
c. of perspiring dreams — RAPH 655:11
c. of refuge — MILT 546:3
C. of the Big Shoulders — SAND 680:2
c. that is set on an hill — BIBL 98:27
c. upon a hill — WINT 860:18
c., where I long had pined — WORD 868:7
c. which hath foundations — BIBL 116:4
c. will follow you — CAVA 211:15
Despising, For you, the c. — SHAK 698:9
down the C. Road — MAND 518:15

evil in a c. — BIBL 96:11
feel, amid the c.'s jar — ARNO 29:16
first c. Cain — COWL 254:10
Hell is a c. — SHEL 745:18
holy c., new Jerusalem — BIBL 119:15
How doth the c. sit solitary — BIBL 95:8
in populous c. pent — MILT 544:4
In the great c., pent — COLE 239:20
Jerusalem is built as a c. — BOOK 148:19
live in a c. — COLT 244:11
long in c. pent — KEAT 457:7
Lord keep the c. — BOOK 149:2
modern c. is a place — WRIG 870:17
nation, not a c. — DISR 286:2
new c. of Friends — WHIT 851:20
no continuing c. — BIBL 116:13
oppressing c. — BIBL 96:17
paper felled a c. — THOM 805:19
people in the c. do — PLAT 608:19
people went up into the c. — BIBL 82:27
rose-red c. — BURG 172:12
set all the c. on an uproar — BIBL 109:33
stood within the C. disinterred — SHEL 745:5
street of the c. was gold — BIBL 119:18
streets and lanes of the c. — BIBL 105:23
Sun-girt c. — SHEL 744:21
that great c. — BIBL 119:1
this great hive, the c. — COWL 254:17
What is the c. but the people — SHAK 698:7
whole c. is paid — HESI 397:5
Without a c. wall — ALEX 12:10
Woe to the bloody c. — BIBL 96:15
civet Give me an ounce of c. — SHAK 716:18
civil Always be c. to the girls — MITF 551:8
c. discord — ADDI 4:24
c. question deserves — PROV 629:5
c. to everyone — SISS 753:7
In c. business — BACO 46:11
never lost our c. war — BIRN 122:2
nothing but a c. contract — SELD 691:13
Pray, good people, be c. — GWYN 375:3
rude sea grew c. — SHAK 726:5
utmost bound of c. liberty — MILT 545:21
world or c. state — WINT 860:19
civilian mushroom rich c. — BYRO 191:16
civilities bandy c. — JOHN 440:14
dread c. — TOCQ 812:14
civility C. costs nothing — MONT 554:10
C. costs nothing — PROV 629:4
c. of my knee — BROW 162:22
I see a wild c. — HERR 396:1
nothing lost by c. — PROV 644:33
civilization annihilating all c. — SAKH 677:16
can't say c. don't advance — ROGE 666:6
c. advances — MACA 507:1
c. advances by extending — WHIT 851:11
C. a movement — TOYN 814:5
C. and its discontents — RIVI 663:2
C. and profits — COOL 250:14
C. comes from what — TROL 816:9
c. has from time to time — ELLI 314:4
c. has made the peasantry — TROT 817:5
C. nothing more than — ORTE 586:10
c. of the Fabians — INGE 425:2
C. the progress — RAND 655:1
elements of modern c. — CARL 199:22
For a botched c. — POUN 621:6
in a state of c. — JEFF 432:7
items of high c. — JAME 429:15
last product of c. — RUSS 674:19
life-blood of real c. — TREV 815:6
rottenness of our c. — READ 656:2
Speech is c. itself — MANN 519:14
submit to c. — TOCQ 812:9
sweetness of present c. — HUGO 419:8
thought of modern c. — GAND 348:15
weight of a c. — FANO 322:17
civilized C. people must get off — FINK 327:11
c. suffice — CASS 206:9
of c. society — SMIL 755:18
that are called c. — PAIN 593:3
civilizers two c. of man — DISR 284:27
civilizes Cricket c. people — MUGA 564:2

civil servant c. doesn't make jokes — IONE 425:18
Here lies a c. — SISS 753:7
civil servants of c. — BRID 156:17
Civil Service c. has finished — REIT 658:2
C. is deferential — CROS 261:11
civis C. *Romanus sum* — CICE 232:4
C. *Romanus sum* — PALM 595:3
claes some upo' their c. — BURN 178:12
claim last territorial c. — HITL 400:9
claims c. are not false — RIEL 661:10
Extraordinary c. require — SAGA 677:6
clair *n'est pas c.* — RIVA 663:1
clairvoyante famous c. — ELIO 311:4
clamorous c. whispering sea — HOME 404:8
clamour c. of silence — TAGO 787:19
c. of the crowded street — LONG 499:13
clap C. her broad wings — FRER 342:14
Don't c. too hard — OSBO 588:14
If you believe, c. your hands — BARR 59:20
in the cheaper seats c. your hands — LENN 489:3
O c. your hands together — BOOK 142:20
Clapham man on the C. omnibus — BOWE 153:14
clapped-out c., post-imperial — DRAB 293:5
claps If someone c. his hand — HAKU 376:10
Clarence perjured C. — SHAK 731:18
claret c. is the liquor for boys — JOHN 442:23
Claridges body of the bootboy at C. — WOOL 864:13
clarion c. o'er the dreaming earth — SHEL 745:6
Clarissa C. lives — RICH 660:14
clash c. of civilizations — STRA 779:1
clasped C. by the golden light — HOOD 405:25
clasps C. the crag — TENN 793:10
class c. struggle — MARX 526:10
first and second c. citizens — WILL 858:17
hands of the ruling c. — STAL 769:14
history of c. struggles — MARX 526:13
I could have had c. — FILM 328:12
In education no c. distinction — CONF 246:18
one c. to appreciate the wrongs — STAN 770:4
whatever his c. — CHEK 222:2
While there is a lower c. — DEBS 270:3
classes But the two c. — FOST 338:19
lower c. had such white — CURZ 263:11
masses against the c. — GLAD 360:9
two c. of travel — BENC 69:8
While c. exist no one is free — CARD 198:1
classic c. is a book that — CALV 194:8
'c.' music eliminates — STRA 778:19
tread on c. ground — ADDI 4:27
classical c. mind at work — PIRS 607:6
C. quotation — JOHN 443:6
tragedy of the c. languages — MADA 514:1
classicism C. is health — GOET 363:4
classics bellyful of the c. — MILL 537:13
classify Germans c. — CATH 209:10
clattering charge of the c. train — BEAV 64:1
c. train — ANON 21:12
Claudel pardon Paul C. — AUDE 37:12
claudite C. *iam rivos* — VIRG 832:1
Claus ain't no Sanity C. — FILM 328:23
claw red in tooth and c. — TENN 795:17
clawed c. me with his clutch — VAUX 825:17
claws neatly spreads his c. — CARR 201:14
pair of ragged c. — ELIO 310:9
clay associate of this c. — HADR 375:7
ay, into the c. — O'Ra 585:17
beauteous c. — WRIG 870:20
C. is moulded — LAO 479:9
C. is the word — KAVA 453:14
C. lies still — HOUS 415:13
for this the c. grew tall — OWEN 591:7
grey stone and grassy c. — EPIT 318:16
had been a lump of c. — POPE 618:27
Kingdoms are c. — SHAK 694:9
mire and c. — BOOK 141:30
potter and c. endure — BROW 167:11
potter power over the c. — BIBL 111:8
Shall the c. say — BIBL 93:22
clean All c. and comfortable — KEAT 458:11
c. American backyards — MAIL 516:8
c. place to die — KAVA 453:15

Clunton C. and Clunbury HOUS 416:8
clutch clawed me with his c. VAUX 825:17
fell c. of circumstance HENL 391:12
clutching alien people c. their gods ELIO 310:4
c. the inviolable shade ARNO 30:13
Clyde poems should be C.-built DUNN 299:17
CMG C. (Call Me God) SAYI 685:3
coach c. and six horses RICE 660:1
indifference and a c. and six COLM 244:1
looking for a body in the c. HITC 400:3
rattling of a c. DONN 290:10
coaches Nine c. waiting MIDD 534:10
coal island made mainly of c. BEVA 76:12
like a c. His eye-ball SMAR 754:15
live c. in his hand BIBL 92:8
made of Newcastle c. WALP 837:15
coalition rainbow c. JACK 426:11
coalitions England does not love c. DISR 284:14
coals all eyes else dead c. SHAK 737:8
c. of fire BIBL 88:38
c. of fire BOOK 140:6
My c. are spent EPIT 319:3
coarse one of them is rather c. ROYD 671:16
coast c. of Coromandel SITW 753:17
dim hills and a low c.-line VIRG 829:18
On the c. of Coromandel LEAR 485:15
coaster Dirty British c. MASE 527:4
coat c. is so warm NURS 579:8
c. of many colours BIBL 80:16
Cut your c. PROV 629:32
eternal Footman hold my c. ELIO 310:10
long black c. WARR 840:11
made my song a c. YEAT 872:15
stick in his c. BROW 166:12
tattered c. upon a stick YEAT 874:14
cobble On c.-stones I lay FLAN 332:21
Cobbleigh Uncle Tom C. BALL 56:8
cobbler c. stick to his last PROV 637:22
c. to his last PROV 629:10
Cobden C. is an inspired bagman CARL 200:30
cobweb c. of the brain BUTL 183:19
cobwebs Laws are like c. SWIF 783:21
tickles with the c. FROS 344:6
cocaine C. habit-forming BANK 57:8
cock before the c. crow BIBL 103:13
C. a doodle doo! NURS 578:6
C. and a Bull STER 773:19
c. crowing on its own dunghill ALDI 11:11
C. had in his governaunce CHAU 219:23
C. up your beaver HOGG 402:17
c. who thought the sun ELIO 306:20
crowing of the c. SHAK 699:6
Every c. will crow PROV 631:16
good c. come out of PROV 644:39
immediately the c. crew BIBL 103:20
Lion and the C. GOGA 363:9
Our c. won't fight BEAV 64:8
owe a c. to Aesculapius SOCR 760:8
Ride a c.-horse NURS 581:2
walks till the first c. SHAK 716:1
Who killed C. Robin NURS 582:12
cockatoo cage is natural to a c. SHAW 739:27
green freedom of a c. STEV 774:14
cockatrice hand on the c.' den BIBL 92:18
cockle c. hat and staff SHAK 703:30
cockles c. boiled in silver shells JONS 445:15
cockleshells silver bells and c. NURS 580:5
Cockney C. impudence RUSK 673:6
cockpit Can this c. hold SHAK 708:8
c. of Christendom HOWE 417:6
cocks drowned the c. SHAK 715:16
cocksure c. of anything MELB 530:16
c. of many things HOLM 403:18
cocktail weasel under the c. cabinet PINT 607:3
cocoa c. for Kingsley Amis COPE 251:6
C. is a cad and coward CHES 224:19
cod bean and the c. BOSS 151:17
O stynkyng c. CHAU 219:28
photographer is like the c. SHAW 742:20
code trail has its own stern c. SERV 692:24
Codlin C.'s the friend DICK 279:23
coeli Rorate, c. BIBL 120:8

coelorum C. perrupit EPIT 317:3
coercion effect of c. JEFF 432:13
coeur Il pleure dans mon c. VERL 826:13
Coeur-de-Lion reputed son of C. SHAK 714:4
coffee C. and oranges STEV 774:14
c.-house SWIF 782:3
C. house babble DISR 285:6
C., (which makes the politician wise) POPE 618:14
if this is c. PUNC 650:12
measured out my life with c. spoons ELIO 310:8
o'er cold c. POPE 615:21
put poison in your c. CHUR 231:4
to some c.-house I stray GREE 371:8
coffin c. clapt in a canoe BYRO 185:8
in a Y-shaped c. ORTO 586:15
silver plate on a c. CURR 263:5
cogimur Omnes eodem c. HORA 412:7
cogito C., ergo sum DESC 274:9
cognoscere rerum c. causas VIRG 832:18
cohorts his c. were gleaming BYRO 187:16
coign c. of the cliff SWIN 785:10
coil Lulled by the c. SHEL 745:8
coin C., Tiberius DOBS 287:2
coincidence long arm of c. CHAM 214:9
coins for a fistful of c. ZAPA 877:11
coition way of c. BROW 163:12
coitu Foeda est in c. PETR 605:9
coitum Post c. SAYI 685:2
coke go better with C. ADVE 8:21
cold can be eaten c. PROV 642:21
Cast a c. eye YEAT 875:9
caught An everlasting c. WEBS 844:27
chilling c. had pierced SACK 676:13
c. a long time STEV 774:12
c. charities CRAB 258:9
Cold, c., my girl SHAK 729:20
c. coming they had of it ANDR 15:15
c. coming we had of it ELIO 310:2
c. grave BALL 56:4
C. hands, warm heart PROV 629:11
c. in blood SHAK 694:20
C. in the earth BRON 158:17
C. lights hurting JOHN 435:2
c. metal of economic theory SCHU 687:6
C. Pastoral KEAT 455:24
c. relation BURK 174:22
c. war BARU 60:10
c. war warrior THAT 803:13
come with your c. music BROW 168:1
Fallen c. and dead WHIT 852:3
Feed a c. PROV 632:8
fingers of c. are corpse fingers LAWR 484:5
ink in my pen ran c. WALP 837:11
in love with a c. climate SOUT 764:23
in the darkness and the c. STEV 776:19
i' the c. o' the moon BROW 165:10
lie in c. obstruction SHAK 723:14
like c. porridge SHAK 733:22
like rivers grow c. MONT 554:6
Love in a c. climate MITF 551:7
morn and c. indifference ROWE 671:5
neither c. nor hot BIBL 118:1
offspring of c. hearts BURK 174:9
O ye Frost and C. BOOK 133:15
past the common c. AYRE 44:4
plunging into a c. peace YELT 875:19
Poor Tom's a-c. SHAK 716:4
so the c. strengthens PROV 626:38
spy who came in from the c. LE C 487:1
straight is c. again SHAK 713:26
till I shrink with c. SHAK 696:14
'tis bitter c. SHAK 698:28
To c. oblivion SHEL 744:1
too c. for hell SHAK 720:12
understand one who's c. SOLZ 760:11
waxeth c. BIBL 56:6
Without the c. war UPDI 822:21
colder c. and dumber than a fish MULD 564:13
coldly C., sadly descends ARNO 30:5
Cole Old King C. NURS 580:9
Coliseum While stands the C. BYRO 186:26

You're the C. PORT 619:20
collaboration All art is c. SYNG 786:9
collapse c. in deepest humiliation EDDI 302:16
C. of Stout Party ANON 16:18
collar braw brass c. BURN 180:5
collateral c. security CHES 223:14
collect together and c. things HORA 409:17
collected if they were c. JONS 446:5
collections mutilators of c. LAMB 476:15
collective c. unconscious JUNG 449:10
collects beautiful c. MACA 507:19
college cabbage with a c. education TWAI 820:19
endow a c. POPE 615:4
Master of this c. BEEC 65:16
small c. WEBS 843:19
colleges discipline of c. SMIT 756:7
Collins marry Mr C. AUST 42:13
collision avoid foreign c. CLAY 234:12
colonel C. Blimp LOW 502:12
C.'s Lady KIPL 466:11
colonial tales of castaways, c. museums GENE 352:4
colonies commerce with our c. BURK 173:11
New c. seek FREE 342:7
colonization future c. MONR 553:15
colonnade sound of the cool c. COWP 255:24
Colonus Singer of sweet C. ARNO 31:1
colori nimium ne crede c. VIRG 831:18
colossus C. from a rock JOHN 444:1
Like a c. SHAK 711:19
colour any c. that he wants FORD 337:2
By convention there is c. DEMO 272:16
by the c. of their skin KING 463:11
cannot be of a bad c. PROV 633:20
cast thy nighted c. off SHAK 699:13
c., culture or ethnic origin MACP 513:18
C. has taken hold of me KLEE 469:8
c. is a diabolic dye WHEA 850:1
c. of his hair HOUS 415:4
c. purple WALK 836:6
C. seems to radiate CLIF 235:16
Her c. comes and goes DOBS 287:4
her c. is natural SHER 748:24
horse of that c. SHAK 735:13
I know the c. rose ABSE 1:4
Life is C. GREN 372:10
or the c. of their skin WILL 858:18
perceptible through c. MOND 553:9
problem of the c. line DU B 298:6
sense of c. BLUN 129:14
waning of their c. VOLT 834:20
yearned for warmth and c. TENN 794:8
coloured about the c. women TRUT 818:6
makes a man c. HUGH 418:4
no 'white' or 'c.' signs KENN 460:10
penny plain and twopence c. STEV 775:19
see the c. counties HOUS 415:16
colourless C. green ideas CHOM 226:14
colours add c. to the chameleon SHAK 710:9
coat of many c. BIBL 80:16
c. and their forms WORD 866:11
C. seen by candle-light BROW 164:10
c. will agree BACO 48:14
lines and c. POUS 621:17
map-makers' c. BISH 122:8
nailing his c. FIEL 326:6
Who put the c. BOOT 151:2
Columbia Hail, C.! happy land HOPK 408:12
columbine pink and purple c. SPEN 768:5
Columbus C. sailed the ocean STON 777:11
laughed at C. GERS 353:18
column Fifth c. MOLA 551:15
stately c. broke SCOT 688:19
columnae non concessere c. HORA 409:16
columns crazy on its smoking c. YEVT 876:2
coma state of resentful c. LASK 482:14
comae Arboribusque c. HORA 413:17
comb c. and a glass in her hand SONG 763:6
c. was redder than the fyn coral CHAU 219:23
siller c. BALL 54:19
two bald men over a c. BORG 151:10
combination call it c. PALM 595:4

combinations irregular c. JOHN 437:12
metrical c. FLAU 333:14
combine When bad men c. BURK 175:4
combining c. committee BAGE 50:9
come All things c. to those who wait
PROV 626:22
behold, I c. quickly BIBL 119:22
believe in the life to c. BECK 64:6
better not c. at all KEAT 457:20
But will they c. SHAK 706:9
cannot c. again HOUS 416:4
c. all the way for this MORR 560:15
C., and he cometh BIBL 100:7
C. away, come away, death SHAK 735:18
C., come, dear Night CHAP 216:6
C., dear children ARNO 29:11
C. down, O Love divine LITT 495:12
c. for your good GEOR 352:8
C., Holy Spirit LANG 479:2
C. in the speaking silence ROSS 668:19
C. into the garden TENN 798:3
C., let us join our cheerful songs WATT 841:18
c., let us sing BOOK 146:7
c., Lord Jesus BIBL 119:24
C. mothers and fathers DYLA 302:5
C., my Celia JONS 446:14
C. not between the dragon SHAK 714:18
C. on CATC 207:9
c. out, thou bloody man BIBL 84:20
c. over into Macedonia BIBL 109:31
C. to me in my dreams ARNO 29:10
c. to my father AUBR 36:6
c. to my heart ELLI 313:12
C. to the edge LOGU 498:10
C. unto me BIBL 101:2
c. unto my love SPEN 766:22
C. unto these yellow sands SHAK 733:20
C. what come may SHAK 718:17
c. without warning DAVI 268:14
don't want to c. out BERR 74:12
dreaming on things to c. SHAK 738:12
Easy c., easy go PROV 630:45
First c. PROV 632:19
he that should c. BIBL 100:32
I go—I c. back CATC 208:3
it needn't c. to that CARR 203:14
jump the life to c. SHAK 719:6
King of glory shall c. in BOOK 141:2
let him c. out JOHN 443:11
Light c., light go PROV 637:29
men may c. TENN 793:2
mine hour is not yet c. BIBL 107:8
Mr Watson, c. here BELL 67:10
nobody will c. SAND 680:7
O c., all ye faithful ANON 23:2
One to c., and one to go CARR 203:17
Quickly c., quickly go PROV 642:16
shape of things to c. WELL 846:24
Sumer is c. in ANON 20:14
That it should c. to this SHAK 699:19
therefore I cannot c. BIBL 105:22
'tis not to c. SHAK 704:23
What's to c. is still unsure SHAK 735:9
wheel is c. full circle SHAK 717:4
when death is c., we are not EPIC 316:11
where do they all c. from LENN 489:7
wherefore art thou c. BIBL 103:18
which is to c. BIBL 117:22
whistle, an' I'll c. BURN 179:7
Why don't you c. up WEST 848:15
comeback c. kid CLIN 236:6
comedies All c. are ended BYRO 188:17
comedy All I need to make a c. CHAP 215:4
C. is an imitation SIDN 751:7
C. is tragedy that happens CART 204:12
c. to those that think WALP 837:21
C. wears itself out HAZL 386:9
most lamentable c. SHAK 725:26
tragedy, c., history SHAK 701:15
comely black, but c. BIBL 90:24
comes c. again in the morning SHER 748:24
conquering hero c. MORE 559:17
Look, where it c. again SHAK 699:2

nobody c. BECK 64:19
Tomorrow never c. PROV 645:28
comest c. into thy kingdom BIBL 106:24
O Death, thou c. ANON 19:10
cometh Blessed be he that c. BOOK 148:12
c. unto the Father BIBL 108:14
c. with clouds BIBL 117:23
He c. not TENN 797:17
Him that c. to me BIBL 107:24
master of the house c. BIBL 104:5
comets country c. MARV 525:8
no c. seen SHAK 712:12
Old men and c. SWIF 783:20
comfort a' the c. we're to get BURN 180:4
bourgeois prefers c. HESS 397:11
carrion c., Despair HOPK 407:5
c. all that mourn BIBL 94:19
c. and despair SHAK 738:23
c. and help the weak-hearted BOOK 134:23
c. and relieve them BOOK 135:7
c. cruel men CHES 224:6
c. in my people's happiness ELIZ 312:9
c. of feeling safe ANON 19:12
c. of thy help BOOK 143:7
C.'s a cripple DRAY 293:12
c. ye my people BIBL 93:14
found I any to c. me BOOK 144:12
good c., Master Ridley LATI 482:16
great source of c. NIET 575:17
love her, c. her BOOK 138:24
love of material c. TOCQ 811:11
naught for your c. CHES 223:26
our c. flows PRIO 624:11
receives c. SHAK 733:22
Sacrament to your c. BOOK 137:9
take c. a little BIBL 86:24
to c., and command WORD 869:8
waters of c. BOOK 140:20
What a c. CARR 202:20
comfortable All clean and c. KEAT 458:11
c. and the accepted GALB 347:10
c. estate of widowhood GAY 351:3
c. words BOOK 137:11
comfortably lived c. so long together
GAY 350:19
sitting c. CATC 207:5
Speak ye c. BIBL 93:14
comforted c. his people BIBL 94:1
they shall be c. BIBL 98:25
would not be c. BIBL 98:13
comforter C. will not come BIBL 108:20
Guide, a C. AUBE 35:14
O C., draw near LITT 495:12
comforters Miserable c. BIBL 86:31
comforting cloud of c. convictions RUSS 675:5
where is your c. HOPK 407:13
comfortless leave us not c. BOOK 136:1
comforts recapture the c. BRYS 169:3
uncertain c. PROV 628:48
comic business of a c. poet CONG 246:24
comical Beautiful c. things HARV 384:1
I often think it's c. GILB 356:18
coming cold c. we had of it ELIO 310:2
c. as fast as I can LAUD 482:17
C. events cast PROV 629:13
c. for us that night BALD 53:1
C. in on a wing and a pray'r ADAM 4:4
c. of the King of Heaven ANON 21:16
c. of the Son of Man BIBL 102:27
C. thro' the rye BURN 177:20
c. to that holy room DONN 288:17
Everything's c. up roses SOND 761:2
good time c. SCOT 689:24
He is c. AYTO 44:6
my c. down MORE 559:14
She is c., my dove TENN 798:6
their c. hither SHAK 716:25
Yanks are c. COHA 238:3
comma c.-hunting CORN 252:5
kiss can be a c. MIST 550:11
command cannot obey cannot c. PROV 634:3
c. of any kind as an exceptional MILL 536:15
c. success ADDI 4:12

c. the rain PEPY 603:5
give what you c. AUGU 39:11
left that c. MILT 544:5
not born to sue, but to c. SHAK 730:3
sue than to c. SCOT 688:8
to comfort, and c. WORD 869:8
to the c. of another OSBO 588:13
commander c. of three armies CONF 246:10
commandest thing which thou c. BOOK 135:19
commandment c. of the Lord BOOK 140:10
first and great c. BIBL 102:17
commandments gave the ten c. to the
world BAUE 62:6
hearkened to my c. BIBL 93:24
keep his c. BIBL 90:22
learn by these C. BOOK 138:10
Ten for the ten c. SONG 762:13
commands Whosoever c. the sea RALE 654:8
commencement c. de la fin TALL 788:15
commend c. my spirit BIBL 106:26
c. my spirit BOOK 141:15
c. the bone DICK 282:4
virtue to c. CONG 248:1
commendatio Formosa facies muta c.
PUBL 648:29
commendeth obliquely c. himself BROW 162:1
comment C. is free SCOT 687:18
C. is free STOP 777:17
couldn't possibly c. CATC 209:4
commentaries a-swarm with c. MONT 555:26
commentators c. each dark passage
YOUN 876:15
learned c. view SWIF 784:1
commerce c. between equals GOLD 364:30
c. with our colonies BURK 173:11
effected without c. LIVI 496:3
In matters of c. CANN 196:25
Peace, c. JEFF 431:16
where c. long prevails GOLD 364:25
commercial put to c. use EDIS 303:16
commit c. his body to the deep BOOK 150:15
c. his body to the ground BOOK 139:10
committed c. breakfast with it LEWI 492:3
c. citizens MEAD 529:14
committee combining c. BAGE 50:9
C.—a group of men ALLE 13:5
c. a group of unwilling SAYI 684:8
c. is a group of the unwilling ANON 16:19
horse designed by a c. ISSI 426:5
commodious c. car JAME 429:11
commodities Demand for c. MILL 536:10
commodity C., firmness, and delight
WOTT 870:11
common according to the c. weal JAME 429:2
all things held in c. CALL 193:16
Ay, madam, it is c. SHAK 699:14
call not thou c. BIBL 109:26
century of the c. man WALL 836:12
c. as the air GRAN 368:18
c. chord again BROW 164:18
C. fame is seldom PROV 629:14
c. law itself COKE 238:11
C. Law of England HERB 393:19
c. man BEVI 77:10
c. pursuit LEAV 486:16
c. reader JOHN 436:22
c. things that round us WORD 868:6
had all things c. BIBL 109:14
light of c. day WORD 867:9
like the c. people YEAT 875:16
make it too c. SHAK 707:9
nor lose the c. touch KIPL 466:6
not already c. LOCK 497:2
not c. BOOK 150:23
nothing c. did or mean MARV 525:6
prefers c.-looking people LINC 494:2
speak as the c. people do ASCH 33:10
steals a c. ANON 17:5
steals the c. POLI 613:13
trivial round, the c. task KEBL 459:1
utter c. notions HORA 409:5
what we all have in c. BERR 74:18
with whom one has nothing in c. PYM 650:26

controversy c. is either superfluous
    NEWM 572:12
  important c. GIBB 354:10
  man of c. GALB 347:10
contumely proud man's c. SHAK 702:1
convalescence enjoy c. SHAW 739:12
convenience prefers c. to liberty HESS 397:11
  'Twixt treason and c. EPIT 318:8
convenient c. that there be gods OVID 589:22
  food c. for me BIBL 89:11
convent C. of the Sacred Heart ELIO 310:27
  c.'s narrow room WORD 866:19
convention By c. there is colour DEMO 272:16
  Lords of C. SCOT 688:7
conventional c. truth NAGA 567:2
  merely c. signs CARR 203:29
conventionality C. is not morality BRON 158:4
conversation always spoiling c. MACA 509:1
  bee in c. JOHN 438:25
  careless c. EDGE 303:9
  c. among gentlemen JOHN 442:1
  C. is imperative WHIT 850:18
  c. perfectly delightful SMIT 758:18
  c.-scraps, Kitchen-cabals CRAB 257:10
  c. with the best men DESC 274:6
  different name for c. STER 773:2
  no such thing as c. WEST 848:22
  rhymed c. GERS 353:19
  subject of c. CHES 222:21
  third-rate c. PLOM 610:4
  use metaphors in c. ARIS 27:2
  Wit is the salt of c. HAZL 386:1
conversations after-dinner c. THOR 809:28
  without pictures or c. CARR 201:11
converse c.with my equals, my vegetables
    CHES 223:18
conversing With thee c. MILT 543:11
conversion c. of the Jews MARV 525:11
convert to c. England PUGI 649:5
  who shall c. me WESL 847:24
converted Except ye be c. BIBL 101:29
  have not c. a man MORL 560:4
converts can true c. make FARQ 324:10
convict c. stain HUGH 418:6
conviction best lack all c. YEAT 874:17
  what is called c. HUNT 421:15
convictions cloud of comforting c. RUSS 675:5
  c. are hills FITZ 332:5
convince we c. ourselves JUNI 450:3
convinces man who c. the world DARW 267:4
convincing less c. than one HUXL 422:19
  Oh! too c. BYRO 187:10
conviva plenus vitae c. LUCR 504:14
convoy crowns for c. SHAK 709:6
convulsions gall'ry in c. POPE 614:16
cook than the c. ARIS 28:2
cookery c. do MERE 532:15
cookies baked c. and had teas CLIN 236:2
cooking C. is the most ancient BRIL 157:10
  c. of the Mediterranean DAVI 267:12
  'plain' c. cannot be entrusted MORP 560:5
cooks as c. go SAKI 678:3
  Devil sends c. GARR 349:13
  Devil sends c. PROV 633:11
  literary c. MORE 558:19
  praise it, not the c. HARI 382:13
  Synod of C. JOHN 440:8
  Too many c. PROV 645:30
cool Be still and c. FOX 339:17
  c. as a mountain stream ADVE 7:14
  c. web of language GRAV 369:11
  in the c. of the day BIBL 79:6
  rather be dead than c. COBA 237:10
  remain always c. JEFF 432:8
  Sweet day, so c. HERB 395:2
cooled C. a long age KEAT 456:3
cooling for c. the blood FLAN 332:23
cools Time c. MANN 520:4
cooperation belief in c. YAMA 872:4
  Government and c. RUSK 674:8
  partnership and c. ANON 16:20
coot haunts of c. and hern TENN 793:1
cope use a c. like that PUGI 649:5

copied c. the old authors PLIN 609:11
copier mere c. of nature REYN 658:19
copies few originals and many c. TOCQ 811:15
  Make c. INGR 425:15
copperheads c. and the assassin SAND 680:3
coppers like the old time 'c.' COLL 243:3
cops C. are like a doctor CHAN 215:10
copulating skeletons c. BEEC 65:11
copulation Birth, and c., and death
    ELIO 310:25
  Let c. thrive SHAK 716:17
copy take it and c. it FRAN 340:14
  to every book its c. COLU 244:13
copyrights authors their c. TROL 815:17
coque *pénétra ma c.* RIMB 662:9
coquetry tiresome as c. LERM 490:1
coquette Gay c. SANS 680:12
cor C. *ad cor loquitur* MOTT 563:6
  C. meum eructavit BIBL 119:26
  J'aime le son du c. VIGN 828:1
coral C. is far more red SHAK 738:19
  c. lip admires CARE 198:6
  his bones are c. SHAK 733:21
  India's c. strand HEBE 388:8
  like c. insects WARN 840:6
  redder than the fyn c. CHAU 219:23
corbies twa c. BALL 56:3
cord silver c. be loosed BIBL 90:20
  stretch a c. however fine WHEW 850:3
  threefold c. BIBL 89:26
  triple c. BURK 172:18
corda *Sursum c.* MISS 549:14
Cordelia such sacrifices, my C. SHAK 717:2
cordial Love . . . That c. drop ROCH 664:11
cords scourge of small c. BIBL 107:10
core c. of a world's culture BOLD 131:8
  c. of power CANE 196:23
  deep heart's c. YEAT 873:21
Corinth lucky enough to get to C. HORA 410:13
Corinthian C. capital BURK 174:17
Corinthum *adire C.* HORA 410:13
cork c. out of my lunch FIEL 327:7
corkscrew tumbler, and a c. DICK 279:19
corkscrews crooked as c. AUDE 36:28
cormorant common c. (or shag) ISHE 426:2
  C. devouring Time SHAK 717:11
  Sat like a c. MILT 543:1
corn amid the alien c. KEAT 456:10
  breast high amid the c. HOOD 405:25
  c. as high as an elephant's eye HAMM 378:19
  C. King beckoning JARR 430:21
  C. rigs, an' barley rigs BURN 178:17
  c. was orient TRAH 814:11
  lower the price of c. MELB 530:17
  My crop of c. TICH 811:2
  our sustaining c. SHAK 716:14
  raise the price of c. BYRO 185:6
  stop raising c. LEAS 486:15
  there was c. in Egypt BIBL 80:23
  thick with c. BOOK 144:3
  threshed c. at midnight YEAT 874:20
  two ears of c. SWIF 782:9
  yellow like ripe c. ROSS 669:13
cornea C., *qua veris facilis* VIRG 830:16
corner At every c., I meet my Father
    LOWE 503:6
  came round the c. MILN 538:6
  c. in the thing I love SHAK 728:26
  c. of a foreign field BROO 159:13
  drive life into a c. THOR 809:22
  head-stone in the c. BOOK 148:11
  in a c., some untidy spot AUDE 37:17
  just around the c. COWA 253:20
  not done in a c. BIBL 110:16
  round the c. of nonsense COLE 242:9
  Sat in the c. NURS 579:18
  wind in that c. SHAK 727:22
corners age in c. thrown SHAK 696:16
  clearing up the obscure c. HUXL 423:11
  c. of the earth BOOK 146:8
  Duke of dark c. SHAK 723:19
  polished c. of the temple BOOK 149:24
  round earth's imagined c. DONN 288:8

sheet knit at the four c. BIBL 109:25
  three c. of the world SHAK 714:15
cornet young c. of horse WALP 838:15
cornfield o'er the green c. SHAK 697:24
Cornish twenty thousand C. men HAWK 384:11
corns shooting c. presage SWIF 783:23
corny c. as Kansas in August HAMM 379:3
Coromandel coast of C. SITW 753:17
  On the coast of C. LEAR 485:15
coronation c., and sops in wine SPEN 768:5
coronet bride of a ducal c. DICK 279:4
coronets more than c. TENN 796:12
corporate c. welfare bums LEWI 492:4
corporation c. to have a conscience
    THUR 810:14
corporations [c.] cannot commit treason
    COKE 238:16
  C. have neither bodies PROV 629:21
corpore *Mens sana in c. sano* JUVE 451:17
corpse carry one's father's c. APOL 25:5
  c. in a coffin PEPY 603:11
  c. in the case BARH 58:12
  good wishes to the c. BARR 59:21
  make a lovely c. DICK 278:24
corpses laid the c. BOCC 130:6
  mock the riddled c. SASS 682:5
corpulent c. man of fifty HUNT 421:17
corpus *Ave verum c.* ANON 23:4
corpuscula *hominum c.* JUVE 451:16
correct All present and c. MILI 535:2
  Blot out, c. SWIF 783:29
  can't c. what one *does* GIDE 356:5
  c. with those men CICE 232:11
  do the perfectly c. thing SHAW 740:2
corrected C. and amended EPIT 317:1
correcteth he c. BIBL 87:21
Correggios Raphaels, C., and stuff
    GOLD 364:22
corregiescity c. of Corregio STER 773:7
Corregio corregiescity of C. STER 773:7
correlative objective c. ELIO 311:21
correspondent c. for posterity BAGE 51:19
corridors c. of power SNOW 759:12
corriger *c. le monde* MOLI 552:14
corroborative c. detail GILB 357:14
corrupt Among a people generally c.
    BURK 173:3
  c. good manners BIBL 113:1
  c. my air SHAK 698:8
  c. the heart BYRO 190:5
  more c. the state TACI 787:7
  moth and rust doth c. BIBL 99:13
  Peace to c. MILT 544:15
  power is apt to c. PITT 607:10
  should c. the world TENN 794:25
  society can c. a man CHAM 214:13
  visitor is going to c. you HERO 395:10
corrupted c. by sentiment GREE 371:13
  C. honest men SHAK 695:12
  c. the youth SHAK 710:3
  hath not been c. BOOK 133:1
corruptible c. crown BIBL 112:9
  c. to an incorruptible crown CHAR 216:22
  this c. must put on BIBL 113:5
corruptio C. *optimi pessima* SAYI 684:9
corruption C. of the best SAYI 684:9
  C., the most infallible symptom GIBB 354:11
  C. wins not more SHAK 710:23
  danger of great c. KNOX 470:7
  dong and of c. CHAU 219:28
  see c. BOOK 140:4
  sown in c. BIBL 113:3
  Stewed in c. SHAK 703:14
  to be turned into c. BOOK 150:15
corrupts absolute power c. ACTO 1:16
  Power c. PROV 641:46
corse c. to the rampart WOLF 862:13
  thou, dead c. SHAK 700:12
Cortez like stout C. KEAT 456:15
Corydon *pastor C. ardebat Alexin* VIRG 831:17
cosiness c. and irritation PYM 650:26
cosmetics tired of the c. SEXT 693:5
  we make c. REVS 658:15

cost at what c.	BECK 64:4
c. of setting him up in poverty	NAID 567:3
counteth the c.	BIBL 105:25
count the c.	IGNA 424:14
independence may c.	DOST 291:8
costly c. in our sorrows	STER 772:14
C. thy habit	SHAK 700:4
costs C. register competing attractions	
	KNIG 469:13
c. them nothing	BURT 181:15
cot c. beside the hill	ROGE 665:16
paint the c.	CRAB 258:7
Cotopaxi Chimborazo, C.	TURN 819:15
Cotswold As of C.: war told me	GURN 374:18
cottage c. is not happy	DISR 286:24
Love and a c.	COLM 244:1
poorest man may in his c.	PITT 607:9
soul's dark c.	WALL 837:1
straw c. to a palace turns	DYER 301:7
cottages poets talk of c.	COWP 257:7
cotton c. is high	HEYW 397:19
C. is King	CHRI 227:5
c. is king	HUGO 419:5
cou tords-lui le c.	VERL 826:11
couch c. when owls do cry	SHAK 734:3
water my c. with my tears	BOOK 139:20
when on my c. I lie	WORD 866:8
couché Longtemps, je me suis c.	PROU 625:5
couches banish them to their c.	KORA 471:15
cough all c. in ink	YEAT 874:16
c. by them ready made	CHUR 228:5
Love and a c. cannot	PROV 638:4
coughing one c., and one not	SCHN 686:7
coughs C. and sneezes	OFFI 584:3
could It c. be you	ADVE 7:37
councils C. of war never fight	PROV 629:22
still vex your c.	OTWA 589:14
counsel c. and might	BIBL 92:16
c. of the ungodly	BOOK 139:11
c. that I once heard	EMER 315:2
c. that you think best	ELIZ 311:27
darkeneth c.	BIBL 87:7
evil c. is most evil	HESI 397:6
give good c.	BURT 181:15
intention to keep my c.	GLAD 360:7
Night brings c.	PROV 639:49
princely c. in his face	MILT 542:7
sometimes c. take	POPE 618:10
took sweet c.	BOOK 143:11
you c. well	SHAK 724:11
counsellor Wonderful, C.	BIBL 92:14
counsellors kings and c.	BIBL 86:16
when c. blanch	BACO 46:16
wisest of all c.	PERI 603:28
counsels all good c.	BOOK 134:9
count c. everything	CORN 251:17
c. the cost	IGNA 424:14
c. your chickens	PROV 630:19
Don't c. on me	RICH 660:5
if you can c. your money	GETT 354:2
I won the c.	SOMO 760:20
Let me c. the ways	BROW 164:13
let us c. our spoons	JOHN 439:22
some did c. him mad	BUNY 171:23
When angry, c. four	TWAI 820:21
counted c. as the small dust	BIBL 93:18
c. loss for Christ	BIBL 114:22
c. our spoons	EMER 314:21
c. them all out	HANR 379:11
countenance cheerful c.	BIBL 88:14
cheerful c.	BOOK 147:6
c. cannot lie	ROYD 671:17
C. Divine	BLAK 126:24
c. is as Lebanon	BIBL 91:10
c. of truth	MILT 546:11
c. was as the sun	BIBL 117:27
disinheriting c.	SHER 748:28
grim grew his c.	BALL 54:10
help of my c.	BOOK 142:10
Knight of the Doleful C.	CERV 213:3
light of his c.	BOOK 144:4
light of thy c.	BOOK 139:16
light of thy c.	BOOK 145:10

Lord lift up his c.	BIBL 82:2
of a beautiful c.	BIBL 84:1
originality of your c.	CLAI 232:17
counter All things c.	HOPK 407:17
countercheck c. quarrelsome	SHAK 697:26
counterfeit c. a gloom	MILT 539:16
sleep, death's c.	SHAK 720:17
counterfeited laughed with c. glee	
	GOLD 364:7
counterpane land of c.	STEV 776:14
counterpoint Too much c.	BEEC 65:14
counterpoints c. to hack post-horses	
	MOZA 563:26
counters Words are wise men's c.	HOBB 400:17
counties coloured c.	HOUS 415:16
Forget six c.	MORR 560:14
counting it's the c.	STOP 777:13
countries all c. before his own	OVER 589:15
changing c.	BREC 156:5
country all their c.'s wishes	COLL 243:12
Anyone who loves his c.	GARI 349:7
ask not what your c.	KENN 460:10
beating Russia is for your c.	ESPO 320:10
beautiful c.	BROW 161:9
be good in the c.	WILD 855:20
betraying my c.	FORS 338:12
billion dollar c.	FOST 338:18
boy out of the c.	PROV 648:4
Britain a fit c.	LLOY 496:16
Canada is not a real c.	BOUC 152:11
c. be always successful	ADAM 3:16
c. governed by a despot	JOHN 442:15
c. habit has me	SACK 677:1
c. has the government	MAIS 517:1
C. in the town	MART 524:12
c. is lost	WILL 857:3
c. is the world	PAIN 593:4
c. needs good farmers	NIXO 576:13
c. of young men	EMER 315:15
c. takes her place	EMME 315:23
c. town is my detestation	BURN 177:3
c. which has no history	PROV 633:43
c. will be called upon	HARD 380:3
Cry, the beloved c.	PATO 599:15
departed into their own c.	BIBL 98:12
died to save their c.	CHES 224:4
die for one's c.	HORA 412:17
dying for your c.	FRAN 340:13
every c. but his own	GILB 357:4
everyday story of c. folk	CATC 207:19
exile is his c.	URBA 823:3
fate of this c.	DISR 285:3
fight for its King and C.	GRAH 367:11
first, best c.	GOLD 364:24
for his c.'s sake	FITZ 330:16
for our c.'s good	CART 204:14
friend of every c.	CANN 197:1
friends of every c.	DISR 285:7
from c. to country	GOLD 365:9
From yon far c.	HOUS 416:4
God made the c.	COWP 256:8
God made the c.	PROV 633:7
go down into the c.	WILD 854:16
good news from a far c.	BIBL 88:39
good of his c.	WOTT 870:12
good of one's c.	FARQ 324:7
green c. town	PENN 602:20
grow up with the c.	GREE 371:5
hame to my ain c.	CUNN 262:16
How can you govern a c.	DE G 271:13
how I leave my c.	PITT 607:22
I love thee still— My c.	COWP 256:10
impossible to live in a c.	KEAT 457:22
in a c. village	AUST 43:2
in another c.	MARL 522:19
in defence of one's c.	HOME 404:18
in the c. places	STEV 776:20
In this frozen whited c.	HUGH 418:13
I pray for the c.	HALE 376:16
journey into a far c.	BIBL 105:29
King and c. need you	MILI 535:20
know something of his own c.	STER 773:15
learns a c.	WAUG 842:15

leave his c. as good	COBB 237:12
like a little c. retreat	WYCH 871:10
likes the c.	COWP 256:1
lose for my c.	HALE 377:2
love his c.	SHAK 712:27
Love of our c.	GODW 361:4
Love thy c.	DODI 287:8
love to serve my c.	GIBR 355:12
make unto me one c.	BROW 163:9
My c. is Kiltartan Cross	YEAT 873:18
My c. is not a country	VIGN 827:19
My c., right or wrong	SCHU 687:9
my c. 'tis of centuries	CUMM 262:4
My c., 'tis of thee	SMIT 757:13
My soul, there is a c.	VAUG 825:4
never despises his own c.	GOLD 363:18
no c. for old men	YEAT 874:13
no relish for the c.	SMIT 758:7
Our c. is the world	GARR 349:18
our c., right or wrong	DECA 270:4
own c. as a foreign land	CHES 225:18
past is a foreign c.	HART 383:20
quarrel in a far away c.	CHAM 214:5
Queen and c.	THOM 808:5
right part of the c.	FROS 345:10
Science knows no c.	PAST 599:4
serve our c.	ADDI 4:18
service of their c.	PAIN 592:13
she is my c. still	CHUR 228:3
sucked on c. pleasures	DONN 289:7
there's another c.	SPRI 768:19
This was my c.	BLUN 129:13
to all the c. dear	GOLD 364:5
to be had in the c.	HAZL 386:8
too long in c. towns	CATH 209:14
tremble for my c.	JEFF 432:14
understand the c.	LESS 490:17
undone his c.	ADDI 4:17
Ungrateful c.	SCIP 687:16
unmapped c.	ELIO 307:8
vow to thee, my c.	SPRI 768:18
we can do for our c.	HOLM 403:16
what was good for our c.	WILS 858:20
While there's a c. lane	PARK 596:22
win our c. back	FABE 322:5
you are my c. and my friends	CLEA 235:2
Your c. needs you	MILI 535:19
your King and your c.	RUBE 672:1
You've never seen this c.	PURD 650:14
countryman c. must have praise	BLYT 130:3
countrymen advice to my c.	O'CO 583:11
c. are all mankind	GARR 349:18
Friends, Romans, c.	SHAK 712:28
hearts of his c.	LEE 487:9
rebels are our c.	GRAN 368:14
countryside gods of the c.	VIRG 832:19
smiling and beautiful c.	DOYL 292:7
county C. Guy, the hour is nigh	SCOT 689:20
English c. families	WAUG 842:11
countymen fellow-c. won't kill me	COLL 243:7
coup c. de dés	MALL 517:14
couple young c. between the wars	PLOM 610:4
courage Be strong and of a good c.	BIBL 82:24
c. and skill	BUNY 171:27
C. in your own	GORD 366:5
C. is the knowledge	NICI 574:17
C. is the price that Life	EARH 302:7
C., mon ami	READ 656:7
c. never to submit	MILT 541:13
C. not simply one of the virtues	LEWI 492:2
c. of a soldier	GIBB 354:12
c. the greater	ANON 23:14
c. to be the secret	BRAN 154:19
c. to suffer	TROL 816:8
c. which one brings	WODE 862:5
c. without ferocity	BYRO 191:20
endurance and c.	SCOT 688:4
enough c.—or money	MITC 551:2
have the c. to dare	DOST 291:3
in the morning c.	THOR 809:18
Moral c. is a rarer commodity	KENN 460:20
Pathos, piety, c.	FORS 338:8
red badge of c.	CRAN 258:20

courage (*cont.*):
screw your c. — SHAK 719:15
test of c. — HAZL 386:5
two o'clock in the morning c. — NAPO 568:4
warm c. — BUSH 182:9
warm c. — ROOS 667:6
with a good c. — BOOK 141:18
courageous captains c. — BALL 55:5
freedom depends on being c. — PERI 603:26
couriers Vaunt-c. — SHAK 715:16
cours *Suspendez votre c.* — LAMA 476:9
course c. of human events — JEFF 431:5
c. of true love — SHAK 725:23
finished my c. — BIBL 115:28
I must stand the c. — SHAK 716:7
myself to that c. — PEPY 603:18
Of c., of course — JAME 430:9
run his c. — BOOK 140:9
what c. thou wilt — SHAK 713:16
courses Horses for c. — PROV 634:45
court bright lustre of a c. — CECI 212:7
case that comes to c. — JUVE 451:4
c. awards it — SHAK 725:5
c. for owls — BIBL 93:6
C. of Session — PROV 634:35
c. others in verse — PRIO 624:3
envious c. — SHAK 696:14
four ways in c. — ASCH 33:5
not having a C. — BAGE 51:3
Say to the c., it glows — RALE 653:15
she will c. you — JONS 446:19
Talk of c. news — SHAK 717:1
courteous C. he was, lowely — CHAU 218:7
c. to strangers — BACO 47:4
courtesy candy deal of c. — SHAK 705:16
Grace of God is in C. — BELL 68:6
greater man, the greater c. — TENN 794:15
mirour of alle c. — CHAU 219:14
very pink of c. — SHAK 732:21
women with perfect c. — KITC 469:4
courtier heel of the c. — SHAK 704:14
Here lies a noble c. — EPIT 318:2
courtmartialled c. in my absence — BEHA 66:15
courts applying to the c. — BLAC 123:12
Approach with joy his c. — KETH 461:10
case is still before the c. — HORA 409:2
C. and camps — CHES 223:1
C. for cowards were erected — BURN 178:21
c. of the Lord — BOOK 145:13
c. of the sun — CHES 224:7
Fresh from brawling c. — TENN 795:25
one day in thy c. — BOOK 145:15
courtship C. to marriage — CONG 247:17
cousins his c. and his aunts — GILB 357:27
covenant c. with death — BIBL 93:2
c. with death — GARR 350:1
Never break a c. — ZORO 879:2
token of a c. — BIBL 79:28
covenanted c. with him — BIBL 103:10
covenants Open c. of peace — WILS 859:21
Coventry for the train at C. — TENN 793:17
cover C. her face — WEBS 844:12
c. of a jest — HORA 414:7
Duck and c. — OFFI 584:7
I c. all — SAND 680:5
tell a book by its c. — PROV 648:1
covered c. his face — BIBL 92:6
coverlet length of his c. — PROV 631:32
covers c. a multitude of sins — PROV 628:43
covet Thou shalt not c. — BIBL 81:20
Thou shalt not c. — CLOU 237:3
covetous not c. — BIBL 115:19
covetousness inclined to c. — KORA 471:22
uncleanness, or c. — BIBL 114:8
cow bellowing c. soon forgets — PROV 627:18
Better a good c. — PROV 627:28
c. is of the bovine ilk — NASH 568:14
c. jumped over — NURS 578:21
c.'s horn — PROV 645:13
c.'s in the corn — NURS 579:17
c. with the crumpled horn — NURS 581:16
grass to graze a c. — BETJ 76:5
keep a c. — BUTL 184:13

like a c. or a dog — VICT 827:8
milk the c. of the world — WILB 854:3
never saw a Purple C. — BURG 172:10
swallow the c. — PROV 636:19
three acres and a c. — POLI 613:11
To every c. her calf — COLU 244:13
Truth, Sir, is a c. — JOHN 440:2
Two wise acres and a c. — COWA 254:7
Was the c. crossed — HERB 393:18
Why buy a c. when — PROV 647:22
coward bully is always a c. — PROV 628:24
c. does it with a kiss — WILD 855:32
c. on instinct — SHAK 706:2
c. shame — BURN 178:25
No c. soul is mine — BRON 158:15
sea hates a c. — O'NE 585:11
cowardice c. keeps us in peace — JOHN 442:20
I admit the c. — SHAW 741:4
surest is c. — TWAI 820:7
cowardly murderous, c. pack — MCKA 511:16
cowards all men would be c. — ROCH 664:17
being all c. — JOHN 442:20
Conscience makes c. — PROV 629:19
C. die many times — SHAK 712:13
c. in reasoning — SHAF 693:18
C. in scarlet — GRAN 368:19
C. may die many times — PROV 629:24
keep dogs are c. — STRI 779:3
make c. of us all — SHAK 702:3
many other mannish c. — SHAK 696:13
not because men are c. — LEWI 492:18
word that c. use — SHAK 731:30
cowl c. does not make monk — PROV 629:25
cows contented—that's for the c. — CHAN 215:15
C. are my passion — DICK 278:3
cowslip C. and shad-blow — CRAN 258:13
In a c.'s bell — SHAK 734:3
I' the bottom of a c. — SHAK 698:18
O'er the c.'s velvet head — MILT 539:12
cowslips c. on the cliff — BLAI 123:16
c. tall her pensioners be — SHAK 725:34
coxcombs some made c. — POPE 615:24
coy sometimes c. — SEDL 690:19
Then be not c. — HERR 396:18
coyness This c., lady — MARV 525:10
cozenage greatest c. — CROM 260:17
crab make a c. walk straight — ARIS 26:19
crabbed C. age and youth — SHAK 737:10
crabs like wet c. in a basket — DURR 300:16
sidelong c. had scrawled — CRAB 257:13
crack C. and sometimes break — ELIO 309:7
c. in the tea-cup opens — AUDE 36:25
c. in your upper storey — SMOL 759:8
heaven's vaults should c. — SHAK 717:5
cracked c. from side to side — TENN 796:19
crackling c. of thorns — BIBL 90:1
cracks c. in the conversation — WALK 836:2
Now c. a noble heart — SHAK 705:4
cradle c. and the grave — DYER 301:8
c. endlessly rocking — WHIT 852:4
c. of an infant — BURK 173:2
c. of the deep — WILL 857:1
c. of the fairy queen — SHAK 726:14
c. rocks above an abyss — NABO 566:19
c. to the grave — SHEL 746:3
from the c. to the grave — CHUR 230:3
hand that rocks the c. — PROV 633:39
hand that rocks the c. — WALL 836:14
rocking the c. — ROBI 664:7
cradles babies in the c. — BROW 167:1
cradling evil c. — KORA 471:8
craft c. and credulity — BURK 172:20
c. so long to lerne — CHAU 220:21
not teach his son a c. — TALM 789:28
craftier c. to pley she was — CHAU 218:1
crafts c. and assaults — BOOK 134:16
crag c. with crookèd hands — TENN 793:10
craggy c. paths of study — JONS 446:10
cramped won't lie too c. — CELA 212:9
cranberry And a C. Tart — LEAR 485:20
crane tall as a c. — SITW 753:10
cranks into sages and c. — QUIN 652:3
cras *C. ingens iterabimus aequor* — HORA 411:12

Hodie mihi, c. tibi — EPIT 318:12
crash car c. as a sexual event — BALL 56:9
whether it would c. — BERN 74:10
crastina *Pereat, qui c. curat* — ANON 23:10
Sera nimis vita est c. — MART 524:3
craters passing c., passing fire — YEVT 876:2
crave my mind forbids to c. — DYER 301:5
craving full as c. too — DRYD 295:10
getting rid of c. — PALI 594:3
he the more is c. — WROT 871:1
crawling c. on the face of it — WAUG 842:15
crawls sea-worm c.—grotesque — HARD 381:12
crazed c. with the love of light — MONT 555:27
c. with the spell of far Arabia — DE L 272:1
crazy C. like a fox — PERE 603:20
c. to fly more missions — HELL 390:3
he's football c. — MCGR 511:2
Still c. after all — SIMO 752:16
stood by me when I was c. — SHER 749:9
two c. people together — HART 383:13
creaking c. door hangs longest — PROV 629:26
c. to the barn — LOWE 503:7
creaks morning light c. down again — SITW 753:10
cream choking it with c. — PROV 644:10
c.-faced loon — SHAK 722:15
queen of curds and c. — SHAK 737:4
crease with not a c. — ROST 670:3
create c. the taste — WORD 870:5
c. the wondrous world — YOUN 876:24
genuinely c. Europe — MONN 553:12
must c. a system — BLAK 125:11
new-c. another heir — SHAK 711:9
to c. more worlds — MILT 542:18
transmit but do not c. — CONF 246:6
What I cannot c. — FEYN 326:2
what they half-c. — WORD 866:14
created all men are c. equal — ANON 21:6
c. all things — BIBL 118:6
c. him in his own image — DOST 290:18
c. in the image — TALM 789:6
c. Man of a blood-clot — KORA 473:9
C. sick — GREV 372:16
He also c. in man — TALM 789:33
just c. like mistakes — EMEC 314:10
men are c. equal — JEFF 431:6
monster whom I had c. — SHEL 743:3
Nothing can be c. — LUCR 504:7
why I c. man — ZOHA 878:6
creation bless thee for our c. — BOOK 135:8
blind fury of c. — SHAW 740:23
C. has become so broad — BÜCH 169:14
c. rises again — MISS 550:6
eternal act of c. — COLE 241:20
finds c. so perfect — PROU 625:12
from the first c. — LLOY 496:11
I hold C. in my foot — HUGH 418:8
immanent in all c. — SIKH 752:3
love c.'s final law — TENN 795:17
originates c. — KORA 472:5
present at the C. — ALFO 12:12
this c. has arisen — RIG 661:14
whole c. groaneth — BIBL 111:4
whole c. moves — TENN 796:7
your niche in c. — HALL 378:5
creative c. hate — CATH 209:17
c. soul — WORD 868:20
c. urge — BAKU 52:10
Deception is not as c. — SAUN 682:14
man's c. powers — SCHU 687:4
creator abide with my C. God — CLAR 233:2
can dispense with a c. — PROU 625:12
C., if He exists — HALD 376:13
C. made Italy — TWAI 820:12
C., without fear — SIKH 751:15
creature more than the C. — BIBL 110:22
existence of the C. — MAIM 516:12
glory of the C. — BACO 45:9
great c. from his work — MILT 543:28
image of the C. — BONA 132:6
myself and my C. — NEWM 571:16
Of the C. — MERW 533:6
Remember now thy C. — BIBL 90:20

creature c. hath a purpose — KEAT 458:6
c. more than the Creator — BIBL 110:22
God's first C. — BACO 48:27
lone lorn c. — DICK 277:5
no lyves c. Withouten love — CHAU 220:30
one tiny c. — DOST 291:1
creatures c. great and small — ALEX 12:6
c. set upon tables — JOHN 441:21
living, sentient c. — JAIN 428:1
credat C. Iudaeus Apella — HORA 414:15
credence no c. to his word — BOOK 147:13
credit citizen Of c. and renown — COWP 255:8
c. where credit is due — PROV 633:2
greatly to his c. — GILB 358:3
In science the c. goes — DARW 267:4
let the c. go — FITZ 331:16
my c. in this world — FITZ 331:27
people who get the c. — MORR 561:13
To c. marvels — HEAN 387:10
credite Experto c. — VIRG 831:10
credo C. in unum Deum — MISS 549:11
C. quia impossibile — TERT 802:12
credulity craft and c. — BURK 172:20
soften into a c. — BURK 175:2
credulous are the most c. — POPE 618:24
Man is a c. animal — RUSS 675:9
sceptical are the most c. — PASC 598:6
creed Calvinistic c. — PITT 607:12
c. of slaves — PITT 607:18
got the better of his c. — STER 773:4
last article of my c. — GAND 348:13
my political c. — ADAM 3:9
Sapping a solemn c. — BYRO 186:13
suckled in a c. outworn — WORD 869:25
This c. of the Nirgranthas — JAIN 428:14
creeds dust of c. outworn — SHEL 745:22
keys of all the c. — TENN 795:27
Light half-believers in our casual c. — ARNO 30:11
live their c. — GUES 374:9
so many c. — WILC 854:11
than in half the c. — TENN 795:27
creep Ambition can c. — BURK 174:27
bade me c. past — BROW 167:8
c. again, leap again — DE L 272:4
c. into thy narrow bed — ARNO 29:15
make your flesh c. — DICK 280:16
music C. in our ears — SHAK 725:10
creeping c. things — BIBL 109:25
every c. thing — BIBL 78:16
creeps C. in this petty pace — SHAK 722:22
c. rustling to her knees — KEAT 454:10
crème c. de la crème — SPAR 765:9
crescent with c. horns — MILT 541:23
Crete people of C. — SAKI 678:2
Cretes C. and Arabians — BIBL 109:13
crevasse like a scream from a c. — GREE 371:17
crew We were a ghastly c. — COLE 241:5
Crewe True blue and Mrs C. — TOAS 812:6
crib shadow of the c. — BISH 122:10
cribbed cabined, c., confined — SHAK 721:7
cricket C.—a game which the English — MANC 518:14
c. as organized loafing — TEMP 792:16
C. civilizes people — MUGA 564:2
c. on the hearth — MILT 539:16
c. test — TEBB 792:10
c. with their peasants — TREV 815:7
everything lost but c. — CARD 198:4
When you play Test c. — BRAD 154:8
cried little children c. — MOTL 562:13
pig c., Wee-wee-wee — NURS 581:18
poor have c. — SHAK 713:4
when he c. — AUDE 37:3
cries on me she c. — BALL 54:16
crieth c. in the wilderness — BIBL 93:15
Crillon Hang yourself, brave C. — HENR 391:18
crime catalogue of human c. — CHUR 229:13
commonplace a c. — DOYL 292:6
C. doesn't pay — PROV 629:27
c. of being a young man — PITT 607:8
c. so shameful as poverty — FARQ 324:4
c. to love too well — POPE 614:3
c. you haven't committed — POWE 621:21

foulest c. in history — WHIT 852:19
From the one c. — VIRG 829:7
lovèd be with equal c. — SPEN 767:15
mother of folly and of c. — DISR 285:31
my wilful c. — MILT 544:18
Napoleon of c. — DOYL 292:16
never a c. — CORN 251:15
No c.'s so great — CHUR 228:2
Poverty is not a c. — PROV 641:45
punishment fit the c. — GILB 357:11
Tough on c. — BLAI 123:17
was thought a c. — BLAK 127:21
worse than a c. — BOUL 152:13
worse than a c. — BRAD 153:21
crimes all his c. broad blown — SHAK 703:7
c. are committed in thy name — ROLA 666:9
c., follies, and misfortunes — GIBB 354:6
c. of this guilty land — BROW 161:8
one virtue, and a thousand c. — BYRO 187:12
Successful c. alone — DRYD 296:15
virtues made or c. — DEFO 270:19
with reiterated c. — MILT 541:17
worst of c. — SHAW 740:12
criminal crime and the c. — AREN 26:7
ends I think c. — KEYN 461:14
severity of the c. law — PEEL 601:9
while there is a c. element — DEBS 270:3
criminals if there were no c. — SALI 679:4
Looney Tunes, and squalid c. — REAG 656:16
crimine C. ab uno — VIRG 829:7
crimson Cat with c. whiskers — LEAR 486:10
c. thread of kinship — PARK 597:3
Now sleeps the c. petal — TENN 799:17
cringe Australian Cultural C. — PHIL 606:5
to the cultural c. — KEAT 453:18
cripples If c., then no matter — PAST 598:21
crisis C.? What Crisis? — MISQ 547:8
C.? What crisis — NEWS 573:4
drama out of a c. — ADVE 8:27
Moments of c. produce in man — CHAT 217:19
real c. on your hands — THAT 803:18
crisp Deep and c. and even — NEAL 569:7
Crispian feast of C. — SHAK 709:6
Crispin C. Crispian shall ne'er go by — SHAK 709:8
crisps like eating c. — BOY 153:20
criterion infallible c. of wisdom — BURK 172:14
critic average English c. — LAMB 477:15
C. and whippersnapper — BROW 164:23
c. is a bundle of biases — BALL 56:11
c. is a man who knows the way — TYNA 821:2
c. spits on what is done — HOOD 406:3
C., you have frowned — WORD 869:2
cry of the c. for five — WHIS 850:9
function of the c. — BELL 67:11
good c. is he who relates — FRAN 340:10
great drama c. — TYNA 820:29
important book, the c. assumes — WOOL 864:10
knew the c.'s part — COLL 243:16
not the c. who counts — ROOS 668:2
poet includes a c. — SHEN 747:22
true c. ought — ADDI 5:10
Unboding c.-pen — TENN 801:4
criticism cant of c. — STER 773:8
C. is a life without risk — LAHR 476:3
c. of life — ARNO 31:25
father of English c. — JOHN 436:20
from c. to nature — JOHN 437:4
my own definition of c. — ARNO 31:18
near to them than c. — RILK 662:4
no c. of the president — ROOS 668:7
People ask you for c. — MAUG 528:10
wreathed the rod of c. — D'IS 286:31
criticize c. What you can't understand — DYLA 302:5
criticized to be c. is not always — EDEN 303:4
critics c. all are ready made — BYRO 189:30
C. are like brushers — WOTT 870:13
c. are the insects of a day — JARR 430:23
c. of the next — FITZ 332:17
c.' own dreary pedantry — TERE 801:14
c.; they want, not to hurt — NIET 575:15
know who the c. are — DISR 286:5
therefore they turn c. — COLE 241:26

Turned c. next — POPE 615:25
croaks c. the fatal entrance — SHAK 718:20
crocodile cruel crafty c. — SPEN 767:8
How doth the little c. — CARR 201:13
manner o' thing is your c. — SHAK 695:7
these c.'s tears — BURT 181:21
crocodiles wisdom of the c. — BACO 48:19
crocus c. brake like fire — TENN 798:26
Cromwell C., I charge thee — SHAK 710:22
ruin that C. knocked about — BEDF 65:9
Some C. guiltless — GRAY 370:6
Cronkite lost Walter C. — JOHN 435:8
crony rusty, drouthy c. — BURN 179:13
crook President is a c. — NIXO 576:12
crookbacked C. he was — SACK 676:14
crooked crag with c. hands — TENN 793:10
c. as corkscrews — AUDE 36:28
c. be made straight — ELIO 309:2
c. shall be made straight — BIBL 93:15
C. things may be as stiff — LOCK 497:10
c. timber of humanity — KANT 453:4
set the c. straight — MORR 560:13
There was a c. man — NURS 581:12
croon Wanna cry, wanna c. — HARB 379:18
crop c.-headed Parliament — BROW 166:15
fruitful c. should bring — IRWI 425:24
Good seed makes good c. — PROV 633:24
croppy Hoppy, C., Droppy — ELLI 314:2
crops c. the flowery food — POPE 616:17
cross bear the c. gladly — THOM 805:2
bloody c. he bore — SPEN 767:3
by the C. and Passion — BOOK 134:20
c. him in nothing — SHAK 694:13
c. of gold — BRYA 169:1
c. of Jesus — BARI 58:16
c. of Lorraine — SPEA 765:16
c. the bridge — PROV 630:20
c. upon their garments — URBA 823:2
death upon the c. — BOOK 137:15
first at Cradle and the C. — SAYE 683:3
hangs upon the C. — DONN 290:1
mystery of the c. — FORT 338:15
no c., no crown — PENN 602:14
No c., no crown — PROV 640:1
old rugged c. — BENN 70:6
orgasm has replaced the C. — MUGG 564:5
see thee ever c.-gartered — SHAK 735:25
survey the wondrous c. — WATT 842:2
There for you to c. — PAUL 600:5
use him as a C. — SMIT 757:22
crossbow With my c. I shot — COLE 240:17
crossed may be c. in love — SHER 748:7
Was the cow c. — HERB 393:18
crosses Between the c., row on row — MCCR 509:16
clinging to their c. — CHES 223:23
C. are ladders — PROV 629:28
tumbled down the c. — JORD 447:9
with c. of fire — NERU 570:13
crossing double c. of a pair of heels — HART 383:11
crossness make c. and dirt succeed — FORS 337:19
crosspatch C., Draw the latch — NURS 578:7
crossways understands everything c. — SALI 678:17
crow before the cock c. — BIBL 103:13
carrion c., that loathsome beast — GASC 350:4
c. Makes wing — SHAK 721:5
c. upon his own dunghill — PROV 631:10
jump Jim C. — NURS 582:8
one for the c. — PROV 640:45
risen to hear him c. — ELIO 306:20
thenk upon the c. — CHAU 219:16
upstart c. — GREE 372:1
crowd c. flowed over London Bridge — ELIO 311:5
c. is not company — BACO 46:33
c. will always save Barabbas — COCT 237:23
Far from the madding c.'s — GRAY 370:8
madding c. — HARD 380:12
not feel the c. — COWP 256:20
pass in a c. — SWIF 782:15
try to c. out real life — FORS 338:10

CURANTUR · **DAME** 929

curantur *Similia similibus c.* MOTT 563:20
curate c. faced the laurels GRAH 367:18
like a shabby c. AUDE 38:19
name of a C. SMIT 758:2
pale young c. GILB 358:13
curates abundant shower of c. BRON 158:9
Bishops, and C. BOOK 134:7
Bishops and C. BOOK 137:7
C., long dust BROO 159:8
preached to death by wild c. SMIT 758:21
curb rusty c. SHAK 705:10
use the snaffle and the c. CAMP 195:4
curds queen of c. and cream SHAK 737:4
cure better than c. PROV 642:3
c. for admiring BAGE 50:19
c. for the ills of Democracy ADDA 4:6
c. of all diseases BROW 163:14
c. of a romantic first flame BURN 176:19
C. the disease BACO 47:1
c. thine heart BEDD 65:4
half our c. YOUN 876:27
malady without a c. DRYD 296:17
no c. for birth and death SANT 680:18
no C. for this Disease BELL 67:21
No c., no pay PROV 640:2
palliate what we cannot c. JOHN 435:20
cured can't be c. must be endured PROV 646:17
c. by hanging from a string KING 464:18
c. by more democracy SMIT 756:10
C. yesterday of my disease PRIO 624:8
cures c. are suggested CHEK 221:18
Like c. like MOTT 563:20
curfew begins at c. SHAK 716:1
c. tolls the knell GRAY 370:1
curiosa *c. felicitas* PETR 605:8
curiosities c. would be quite forgot AUBR 35:16
curiosity c. about the future WAUG 842:14
c., freckles, and doubt PARK 596:3
C. killed the cat PROV 629:29
c. of individuals ARTS 32:20
Disinterested intellectual c. TREV 815:6
curious c. in unnecessary matters BIBL 97:9
curiouser C. and curiouser CARR 201:12
curl had a little c. LONG 500:7
curlèd wealthy c. darlings SHAK 728:6
curls Frocks and C. DICK 282:3
curly C. locks, Wilt thou NURS 578:8
currency c. that buys all CERV 213:11
Debasing the moral c. ELIO 307:16
debauch the c. KEYN 462:2
one c. NAPO 567:16
current c. to the whole HOPK 408:8
c. will run with fury WOLL 863:7
icy c. SHAK 729:2
what a strong c. ideas are FLAU 333:12
currents their c. turn awry SHAK 702:3
curried short horse soon c. PROV 643:5
curs You common cry of c. SHAK 698:8
curse c. be ended ELIO 309:2
C. God, and die BIBL 86:14
c. is come upon me TENN 796:19
c. mine enemies BIBL 82:9
c. of the drinking classes WILD 856:14
C. on his virtues ADDI 4:17
C. the blasted, jelly-boned swines LAWR 484:1
c. thine own inconstancy CARE 198:16
c. with their heart BOOK 143:21
I know how to c. SHAK 733:18
open foe may prove a c. GAY 351:16
real c. of Eve RHYS 659:14
terrible c. BARH 58:10
than to c. the darkness PROV 627:38
What terms to c. thee WRIG 870:21
cursed C. be the heart BALL 54:16
c. him in sleeping BARH 58:9
cursest is c. BIBL 82:6
That c. man SPEN 767:9
curses c. from pole to pole BLAK 125:6
C., like chickens PROV 629:30
not c. heaped SORL 761:24
cursing blessing and c. BIBL 82:17
curst c. be he that moves my bones EPIT 317:12
to all succeeding ages c. DRYD 294:11
curtain Bring down the c. RABE 652:12
c. of the night PUSH 650:22
iron c. CHUR 230:6
Iron C. did not reach SOLZ 760:17
kept behind a c. PAIN 593:1
lets the c. fall POPE 613:29
putteth aside the c. BIBL 78:11
stage c. of his heart RILK 661:16
Up with the c. BROW 165:23
curtained C. with cloudy red MILT 541:1
curtains spider weaves the c. MEHM 530:6
curtiosity full of 'satiable c. KIPL 468:10
curtsey C. while you're thinking CARR 202:23
curveship of the c. lend a myth CRAN 258:18
Cusha Cusha! Cusha! C. INGE 425:7
cushion c. and soft Dean POPE 615:8
custodes *quis custodiet ipsos C.* JUVE 451:5
custodiet *quis c. ipsos Custodes* JUVE 451:5
custody *Wragg is in c.* ARNO 31:17
custom c. and experience HUME 420:1
C. is the great guide HUME 419:14
c. lie upon thee WORD 867:12
c. loathsome to the eye JAME 428:21
c. must give way to truth LIBO 493:1
C. reconciles us BURK 173:27
c. stale Her infinite variety SHAK 695:1
C. that is before all law DANI 264:5
C., that unwritten law D'AV 267:5
follow the c. AMBR 14:4
in c. and in ceremony YEAT 874:11
Lest one good c. TENN 794:25
receipt of c. BIBL 100:13
That monster, c. SHAK 703:19
unwritten c. supported CATT 209:23
customary what is not c. to him MONT 555:2
customer c. is always right PROV 629:31
c. is never wrong RITZ 662:19
only one boss. The c. WALT 839:17
customers people of c. SMIT 756:5
customs ancient c. and its manhood ENNI 316:4
choose its own c. HERO 395:9
c. of his tribe SHAW 739:14
cut c. from the reedbed JALA 428:17
c. him out in little stars SHAK 732:27
c. his ear off MEDA 529:17
c. his throat before SWIF 784:12
c. my conscience to fit HELL 390:7
c. off BIBL 94:5
c. off my head CHAR 216:17
C. your coat PROV 629:32
etiquette to c. any one CARR 203:24
guardsman's c. and thrust HUXL 423:6
in the evening it is c. down BOOK 145:20
Look at the c. LOES 498:9
man who c. his country's BYRO 190:11
most unkindest c. of all SHAK 713:9
shall not be c. off BIBL 94:11
we are going to c. it off POWE 621:22
will I c. off Israel BIBL 84:26
cute Dress c. HILT 399:11
cutpurse c. of the empire SHAK 703:15
cuts c. from Homer AESC 8:35
cutting hand the c. edge of the mind BRON 157:19
cuttlefish like a c. ORWE 587:24
Cutty-sark Weel done, C. BURN 179:19
cycle c. of Cathay TENN 797:8
cyclone crest of the South Bend c. RICE 659:22
Cyclops c. with one eye COLE 241:25
cylinder in terms of the c. CÉZA 213:16
cymbal talk but a tinkling c. BACO 46:33
tinkling c. BIBL 112:14
cymbals well-tuned c. BOOK 150:12
Cynara faithful to thee, C. DOWS 292:3
cynic definition of a c. WILD 855:12
cynicism C. is intellectual dandyism MERE 532:14
cynosure c. of neighbouring eyes MILT 539:28
Cynthia C. first, with her eyes PROP 624:19
cypress in sad c. SHAK 735:18
outside the c. groves LAWR 483:17
Cyprus rings black C. FLEC 334:13
Cyrene Libya about C. BIBL 109:13
Cyril Nice one, C. ADVE 8:9
Cythera C., so they say BAUD 61:13
Cytherean throned C. be fallen SWIN 785:20
Czechoslovak C. government NEWS 573:12

D never use a big, big D. GILB 357:26
there are your d.'s for you WYCH 871:13
da *D.! Da! Da* UPAN 822:4
dad girls in slacks remember D. BETJ 75:10
if the d. is present ORTO 586:13
They fuck you up, your mum and d. LARK 481:9
To meet their D. BURN 177:22
dada mama of d. FADI 322:13
daddy D.'s gone a-hunting NURS 578:4
D., what did you do SAYI 684:10
Dance to your d. NURS 578:9
heart belongs to d. PORT 619:17
Oh, yo' d.'s rich HEYW 397:19
daemon D. was with me KIPL 468:22
daemonum call poesy *vinum d.* BACO 45:17
daffadowndillies d., And cowslips SPEN 768:5
daffodil bed of d. sky TENN 798:3
daffodils d., That come before SHAK 737:1
dances with the d. WORD 866:8
Fair d., we weep HERR 396:14
host, of golden d. WORD 866:7
never saw d. so beautiful WORD 865:1
what d. were for Wordsworth LARK 481:15
When d. begin to peer SHAK 736:25
daffy D.-down-dilly NURS 578:10
daft thinks the tither d. SCOT 689:21
dagger d. of the mind SHAK 719:19
deadly daunting d. WYCH 871:13
Is this a d. SHAK 719:19
daggers d. in a hogshead SCOT 690:5
d. in men's smiles SHAK 720:20
Give me the d. SHAK 720:8
speak d. to her SHAK 703:4
daguerrotype stare from d. WARR 840:11
daily d. complaining BOOK 141:16
d. increase in thy holy Spirit BOOK 138:18
d. Labour to pursue WESL 847:14
our d. bread BIBL 99:12
dainties d. are all cates SHAK 733:6
fed of the d. SHAK 717:15
spiced d. KEAT 454:13
daintily I must have things d. served BETJ 75:14
dainty d. rogue in porcelain MERE 532:13
d. that is in that hous CHAU 219:15
dairymaid Queen asked the D. MILN 538:5
daisies Buttercups and d. HOWI 417:8
d. growing over me KEAT 458:17
d. pied and violets blue SHAK 717:24
D., those pearled Arcturi SHEL 746:7
foot upon twelve d. PROV 636:25
Meadows trim with d. pied MILT 539:27
Swiche as men callen d. CHAU 220:18
daisy 'd.,' or elles the 'ye of day' CHAU 220:19
d., primrose, violet THOM 808:11
Dakotas D., I am for war RED 657:1
dalliance d. in the wardrobe lies SHAK 708:12
primrose path of d. SHAK 700:2
dam pretty chickens and their d. SHAK 722:7
damage d. to the earth COUS 253:7
I can pay for the d. CLOU 236:18
MORAL OR INTELLECTUAL D. KRUG 473:20
seriously d. your health OFFI 584:12
damaged Archangel a little d. LAMB 477:8
D. people are dangerous HART 383:9
damages d. his mind ANON 23:1
Damascus rivers of D. BIBL 85:28
damasked deep-d. wings KEAT 454:9
dame belle d. sans merci KEAT 455:9
belle d. sans mercy KEAT 454:14
My d. has lost her shoe NURS 578:6
nothin' like a d. HAMM 379:2

dammed saved by being d.   HOOD 406:6
damn D. braces   BLAK 126:16
D. the age   LAMB 477:11
d. the consequences   MILN 538:15
D. the torpedoes   FARR 324:13
d. those authors   CHUR 228:1
D. with faint praise   POPE 614:22
D. you all to hell   FILM 330:3
d. you England   OSBO 588:21
don't give a d.   MITC 551:4
give a singel d.   FLEM 334:18
I care not a d.   CLOU 236:18
I don't give a d.   FILM 328:8
man who said, 'D.'   HARE 382:9
one another d.   WYCH 871:14
with a spot I d. him   SHAK 713:18
damnation d. of his taking-off   SHAK 719:8
everlasting d.   BOOK 134:16
From sleep and from d.   CHES 224:6
Heap on himself d.   MILT 541:17
damnations Twenty-nine distinct d.
  BROW 167:19
damned All silent, and all d.   WORD 868:3
beautiful and d.   FITZ 332:4
brandy of the d.   SHAW 740:27
D. below Judas   COWP 255:3
D. from here to Eternity   KIPL 465:20
d. if you don't   DOW 292:2
d. (looking dismally)   JOHN 443:23
d. to everlasting fame   POPE 617:10
d. to Fame   POPE 611:19
d. would make no noise   HERR 396:20
Faustus must be d.   MARL 522:11
for an apple d. mankind   OTWA 589:10
lies, d. lies and statistics   DISR 286:28
public be d.   VAND 824:2
Publish and be d.   WELL 846:8
souls to be d.   PROV 629:21
written a d. play   REYN 658:16
damnedest doing one's d. with one's mind
  BRID 156:16
damning d. those they have no mind to
  BUTL 183:14
damnosa D. hereditas   GAIU 347:8
D. quid non imminuit dies   HORA 413:2
damozel blessed d.   ROSS 669:12
damp d. souls of housemaids   ELIO 310:14
damsel d. with a dulcimer   COLE 240:8
Dan D. even to Beer-sheba   BIBL 83:21
Dangerous D. McGrew   SERV 692:28
Danaë all D. to the stars   TENN 799:18
Danaos timeo D. et dona ferentes   VIRG 829:6
dance ae best d. e'er cam   BURN 178:1
at least before they d.   POPE 617:16
d. at our bridal   SCOT 689:1
D., dance, dance, little lady   COWA 253:9
d. is a measured pace   BACO 45:15
D. is the hidden language   GRAH 367:16
d. it but to bust   GREN 372:9
d. round in a ring   FROS 345:1
D. tiptoe, bull   BUNT 171:1
d. to the music of time   POWE 621:19
D. to your daddy   NURS 578:9
d. with me   BERL 72:19
d. wyt me, in irlaunde   ANON 17:19
know the dancer from the d.   YEAT 872:8
Let's face the music and d.   BERL 73:2
Lord of the D.   CART 205:2
Love makes them d.   DAVI 267:21
Mystical d.   MILT 543:23
On with the d.   BYRO 186:6
princes and monarchs d.   HALL 378:1
see gif ye can d.   WALL 836:13
see me d. the Polka   GROS 373:14
They that d. must pay   PROV 644:48
too far from the d.   POUN 621:13
will you join the d.   CARR 202:14
danced d. by the light of the moon   LEAR 486:8
d. his did   CUMM 262:3
d. in the morning   CART 205:2
d. with the Prince of Wales   FARJ 323:11
David d. before the Lord   BIBL 84:14
reeled and d.   WORD 865:1

remaining leaf—d.   WORD 864:19
There was a star d.   SHAK 727:19
ye have not d.   BIBL 100:34
dancer know the d. from the dance   YEAT 872:8
dancers Breaks time, as d.   CAMP 196:2
d. are all gone under the hill   ELIO 309:10
d. dancing in tune   TENN 798:4
nation of d.   EQUI 316:14
dances d. to an ill tune   PROV 634:10
d. were procession   CORB 251:11
d. with the daffodils   WORD 866:8
it d.   LIGN 493:6
truest expression in its d.   DE M 272:15
danceth d. without music   HERB 395:5
dancing birth to a d. star   NIET 575:20
[D.] a perpendicular expression   SHAW 742:23
D. appears glamorous   GRAH 367:17
d. cheek-to-cheek   BERL 72:20
d. dogs and bears   HODG 401:18
D., double-talking   CAUS 211:8
d. is love's proper exercise   DAVI 267:20
d. not on a volcano   FLAU 333:11
diversion was d.   TURN 819:14
Fluttering and d.   WORD 866:7
like a Mask d.   ACHE 1:11
manners of a d. master   JOHN 439:4
mature women, d.   FRIE 343:13
more like wrestling than d.   AURE 40:19
past our d. days   SHAK 732:6
dandy Yankee Doodle D.   COHA 238:4
dandyism intellectual d.   MERE 532:14
Dane paying the D.-geld   KIPL 467:21
Roman than a D.   SHAK 705:1
Danes all of us D.   TENN 801:3
danger big with d. and mischief   GIBB 354:5
bright face of d.   STEV 775:5
clear and present d.   HOLM 403:19
d. from all men   ADAM 3:1
d. from those that work   HALI 377:8
D. is a good teacher   HAZL 386:21
d. of her former tooth   SHAK 721:2
d. of the past   FROM 344:3
D., the spur   CHAP 216:11
d. to the country   VICT 827:10
everything is in d.   NIET 575:11
in d. of hell fire   BIBL 99:2
less d. from the wiles   NASH 568:15
life free from d.   EURI 321:11
New Labour, new d.   POLI 613:3
no d. to a man   CHAP 216:5
Oft in d.   WHIT 850:16
only when in d.   OWEN 590:22
out of d.   PROV 641:24
out of d. sit   ASTE 34:12
Out of this nettle, d.   SHAK 705:23
post of d.   PROV 641:43
run into any kind of d.   BOOK 134:3
so much as to be out of d.   HUXL 423:8
What d. threatens   FRIS 343:17
dangerous Damaged people are d.   HART 383:9
d. deceits   BOOK 150:20
d. edge of things   BROW 164:26
d. to know   LAMB 476:10
d. to meet it alone   WHAR 849:11
delays are d. in war   DRYD 297:5
generalizations d.   DUMA 299:5
knowledge is d.   HUXL 423:8
left out he would be d.   MELB 530:15
little knowledge is d.   PROV 637:40
many a d. thing   BISH 122:9
more d. and more numerous   CICE 232:12
more d. than an idea   ALAI 10:10
more d. than failure   GREE 371:22
more d. than justice   PICA 606:8
more d. than standing armies   JEFF 432:9
most d. man   NEWS 573:13
most d. moment   TOCQ 811:17
such men are d.   SHAK 711:22
dangers D. by being despised   BURK 176:4
d. of the seas   PARK 596:20
d. of this night   BOOK 134:14
d. thou canst make us scorn   BURN 179:17
No d. fright him   JOHN 438:7

She loved me for the d.   SHAK 728:12
so many great d.   BOOK 135:14
tomorrow's d.   DONN 290:11
dangling d. apricocks   SHAK 730:24
Daniel D. come to judgement   SHAK 725:3
Danish fame of D. kings   ANON 23:15
Danny hangin' D. Deever   KIPL 465:13
dapper You look d.   COLL 243:2
dapple d.-dawn-drawn Falcon   HOPK 408:4
dappled d. things   HOPK 407:16
dare to know   HORA 410:5
for our unworthiness we d. not   BOOK 138:4
have the courage to d.   DOST 291:3
I d. not.   SHAK 719:13
licence to d. anything   HORA 408:15
none d. call it treason   HARI 382:14
O! what men d. do   SHAK 727:29
Take me if you d.   PANK 595:14
What man d., I dare   SHAK 721:10
You who d.   MERE 532:23
dared d., and done   SMAR 755:14
dares that d. love attempt   SHAK 732:13
Who d. do more is none   SHAK 719:14
Who d. wins   MOTT 563:23
Darien Silent, upon a peak in D.   KEAT 456:15
daring be d.   SOPH 761:21
d. is gone   SCHI 683:8
d. pilot in extremity   DRYD 294:12
d. young man   LEYB 492:19
Life is either a d. adventure   KELL 459:5
dark agree in the d.   BACO 48:14
All cats are grey in the d.   PROV 626:12
another is a d. forest   CATH 209:16
another is a d. forest   TURG 819:2
as good i' th' d.   HERR 396:4
blanket of the d.   SHAK 719:2
blind man in a d. room   BOWE 153:15
come out of the d.   MANN 520:1
comes the d.   COLE 240:23
d. and bloody ground   O'HA 584:17
d. and bright   BYRO 190:25
d. and evil days   INGR 425:12
d. and stormy night   BULW 170:13
d. and true and tender   TENN 799:13
d. as night   SHAK 738:25
D. as the world of man   SITW 753:12
D. behind it rose the forest   LONG 499:23
d. cold day   AUDE 37:7
d., dark, dark   MILT 545:1
D. forces   MISQ 547:9
d. into the life   BERR 74:17
d. is light enough   FRY 345:13
d. materials to create   MILT 542:18
d. night of the soul   FITZ 332:14
d. night of the soul   MISQ 547:13
d. Satanic mills   BLAK 126:24
d. summer dawns   TENN 799:12
D. the sky   PUSH 650:16
D. with excessive bright   MILT 542:23
d. world of sin   BICK 120:23
d. world where gods   ROET 665:9
days must be d. and dreary   LONG 499:19
Duke of d. corners   SHAK 723:19
fear to go in the d.   BACO 46:20
feeling in the d.   JALA 428:16
go home in the d.   HENR 392:11
great leap in the d.   VANB 823:19
His d. materials   PULL 649:11
I knew you in the d.   OWEN 591:10
In a d. wood I saw   ROET 665:8
In the d. backward   SHAK 733:14
In the nightmare of the d.   AUDE 37:11
in thy d. streets   BROO 160:5
leap in the d.   HOBB 401:11
leap into the d.   BROW 161:13
O d. dark dark   ELIO 309:11
Out in the d.   THOM 806:21
raging in the d.   YEAT 872:13
Tired of his d. dominion   MERE 532:20
we are for the d.   SHAK 695:24
We work in the d.   JAME 429:19
What in me is d.   MILT 541:10
within a d. wood   DANT 264:12

darken Never d. my Dior again LILL 493:7
darkeneth d. counsel BIBL 87:7
darker I am the d. brother HUGH 418:1
darkest d. day COWP 255:11
d. hour PROV 629:33
darkies Oh! d., how my heart FOST 339:3
darkling D. I listen KEAT 456:9
d. plain ARNO 29:6
darkly thinks more d. BARR 59:15
through a glass, d. BIBL 112:14
darkness cast off the works of d. BIBL 111:16
chains and d. MONT 554:7
Chaos and d. MARR 523:19
counteracts the powers of d. SMAR 754:13
curse the d. STEV 775:1
d. and silence LEAR 485:17
d. a swaddlingband BIBL 87:10
d. brings not sleep PUSH 650:22
d. comprehended it not BIBL 106:36
d. falls at Thy behest ELLE 313:10
d. had no beginning MACD 510:7
d. of mere being JUNG 449:12
d. of the land TENN 796:1
d. visible MILT 541:12
d. was upon the face BIBL 78:12
d. which may be felt BIBL 81:5
Dawn on our d. HEBE 388:7
Downward to d. STEV 774:5
encounter d. as a bride SHAK 723:13
even d. and silence KELL 459:7
Go out into the d. HASK 384:3
Gorgon, Prince of d. SPEN 767:4
Got to kick at the d. COCK 237:17
heart of an immense d. CONR 248:18
his D. and his Brightness BYRO 191:15
horror of great d. BIBL 79:31
In me d. BONH 132:11
in the d. and the cold STEV 776:19
in the d. bind them TOLK 813:5
into outer d. BIBL 100:9
land of d. BIBL 86:24
leaves the world to d. GRAY 370:1
Lighten our d. BOOK 134:10
light excelleth d. BIBL 89:22
light is as d. BIBL 86:25
light to them that sit in d. BIBL 104:10
little d. LAUD 482:17
long in d. pined SCOT 690:12
lump bred up in d. KYD 474:10
made His d. beautiful TENN 795:19
make d. more visible EDGE 303:11
Men loved d. BIBL 107:14
ocean of d. FOX 339:13
on the shores of d. KEAT 457:6
people that walked in d. BIBL 92:13
pestilence that walketh in d. BOOK 146:1
prince of d. SHAK 716:3
rulers of the d. BIBL 114:15
sit in d. BOOK 147:15
sit in d. here MILT 542:8
soul may set in d. WILL 857:14
struggling with the d. COLE 240:2
Swaddled with d. ELIO 309:24
than curse the d. BENE 69:12
than to curse the d. PROV 627:38
there is d. everywhere NEHR 569:10
Thou makest d. BOOK 147:8
through d. up to God TENN 795:16
time of d. BREC 156:4
two eternities of d. NABO 566:19
universal d. buries all POPE 613:29
works of d. BOOK 135:10
darksome d. road CATU 210:5
spent the d. hours GOET 362:17
darling call you d. after sex BARN 59:5
Charlie he's my d. SONG 762:1
d. buds of May SHAK 737:18
d. in an urn CARE 198:12
d. man, a daarlin' man O'CA 583:7
D. of the music halls SMIT 756:18
my d. from the lions BOOK 141:23
Nature's d. GRAY 370:19
Of my d., my darling POE 610:15

old man's d. PROV 627:30
darlings wealthy curlèd d. SHAK 728:6
dart shook a dreadful d. MILT 542:15
Time shall throw a d. EPIT 319:15
darts fiery d. of the wicked BIBL 114:15
dastard d. in war SCOT 688:23
data some d. was bound to be WATS 841:6
date d. which will live in infamy ROOS 667:13
doubles your chances for a d. ALLE 13:16
keep them up to d. SHAW 739:26
Standards are always out of d. BENN 70:9
dateless d. bargain SHAK 733:4
dates Manna and d. KEAT 454:13
matter of d. TALL 788:20
daubed d. it with slime BIBL 80:30
daughter bailiff's d. BALL 54:1
Carnage is thy d. WORD 867:1
Cato's d. SHAK 712:11
D. am I in my mother's house KIPL 467:2
D. lovelier than HORA 411:18
d. of a hundred earls TENN 796:11
d. of debate ELIZ 312:7
d. of Earth and Water SHEL 743:25
d. of the gods TENN 793:9
d. of Zion BIBL 91:19
d.'s my daughter PROV 639:21
d. went through the river BUNY 171:26
Don't put your d. on the stage COWA 253:16
ever rear a d. GAY 350:18
farmer's d. CALV 194:2
father had a d. SHAK 735:20
for the d.'s daughter SWIN 785:24
King's d. BOOK 142:1
lies London's d. THOM 806:4
Like mother, like d. PROV 637:34
Lord Ullin's d. CAMP 195:1
O my ducats! O my d. SHAK 724:14
so is her d. BIBL 95:14
Sole of his voice MILT 544:5
taken his little d. LONG 500:6
to my elder d. THOM 806:18
virgin-d. of the skies DRYD 297:3
wish his d. to see ANON 17:7
daughterly d. love MORE 559:13
daughters d. of men BIBL 79:21
d. of my father's house SHAK 735:22
d. of the Philistines BIBL 84:11
Kings' d. BOOK 142:14
that our d. may be BOOK 149:24
thunder, fire, are my d. SHAK 715:17
Words are men's d. MADD 514:3
words are the d. JOHN 435:17
dauntless D. the slug-horn BROW 165:12
so d. in war SCOT 688:22
with d. breast GRAY 370:6
dauphin kingdom of daylight's d. HOPK 408:4
David D. his ten thousands BIBL 84:7
D. wrote the Psalms NAYL 569:5
royal D.'s city ALEX 12:8
Davis Thomas D., is thy toil FERG 325:6
Davy Sir Humphrey D. BENT 71:16
daw no wiser than a d. SHAK 709:16
See-saw, Margery D. NURS 581:6
Dawley Webb from D. BETJ 76:4
dawn Between dusk and d. MÜLL 564:18
d. comes up like thunder KIPL 466:15
D. on our darkness HEBE 388:7
first d. of life EGER 304:12
grey d. is breaking CRAW 259:13
in that d. to be alive WORD 865:19
just before d. PROV 629:33
redemption's happy d. CASW 206:16
reflect the d. MACA 507:8
rosy-fingered d. HOME 405:3
see by the d.'s early CUMM 262:4
when that d. will come PATO 599:16
dawning bird of d. SHAK 699:6
d. of the age of Aquarius RADO 653:8
dawns dark summer d. TENN 799:12
day Action this D. MILI 535:1
all in one d. BOIL 131:4
Another d., another dollar PROV 626:25
arrow that flieth by d. BOOK 146:1

at the latter d. BIBL 86:34
be the d. long PROV 627:26
better the d. PROV 627:36
breaks the blank d. TENN 795:4
bright d. is done SHAK 695:24
built in a d. PROV 642:30
burn thee by d. BOOK 148:17
Clear shafts of d. LUCR 504:6
d. becomes more solemn SHEL 744:9
D. by day BOOK 133:11
D. her sultry fires CAMP 195:17
d. is at hand BIBL 111:16
d. is past TICH 811:2
d. is short TALM 789:4
d. joins the past eternity BYRO 186:17
d. may bring forth BIBL 89:3
d. most surely wasted CHAM 214:12
d. of his death AUDE 37:7
d. of his wrath is come BIBL 118:11
d. of small nations CHAM 214:3
d. of the Lord is near BIBL 96:9
d. of vengeance BIBL 94:19
d. of wrath MISS 550:5
d. or a brief period ARIS 27:8
d.'s at the morn BROW 167:3
D.'s azure eyes SHEL 744:20
d.'s garish eye MILT 539:19
d. star arise BIBL 117:14
d. that I die MCLE 512:3
d. the music died MCLE 512:2
d. Thou gavest, Lord ELLE 313:10
d.-to-day business LAFO 475:22
d. war broke out CATC 207:10
d. which the Lord hath made BOOK 148:11
death of each d.'s life SHAK 720:6
dwell in realms of d. BLAK 124:20
each d. dies with sleep HOPK 407:15
each d. that has dawned HORA 410:7
end of a perfect d. BOND 132:7
Every d. dawned clear RACI 653:2
every d. that Fate allows HORA 411:13
every d. to be lost JOHN 444:8
Every d. we die JERO 433:6
Every dog has his d. PROV 631:17
Ev'ry d. a little dies SOND 761:1
first d. BIBL 78:13
first, last, everlasting d. DONN 288:25
gold of the d. CROS 261:3
Good things of d. SHAK 721:5
heat of the d. BIBL 102:11
I have lost a d. TITU 811:10
Joy ruled the d. DRYD 296:24
knell of parting d. GRAY 370:1
lark at break of d. SHAK 737:23
Let the d. perish BIBL 86:15
long d.'s journey O'NE 585:9
Lord went before them by d. BIBL 81:12
make my d. FILM 328:9
Mars a d. ADVE 8:3
met them at close of d. YEAT 873:6
murmur of a summer's d. ARNO 30:7
night and d., brother BORR 151:11
night succeeds thy little d. EPIT 318:16
Not a d. without a line APEL 25:1
not a second on the d. COOK 250:8
not the purchase of a d. PAIN 592:15
not yet near d. SHAK 732:29
now is the d. of salvation BIBL 113:10
Now's the d. BURN 179:9
of this immortal d. SHEL 746:3
on an ordinary d. WOOL 864:4
one d. as a tiger PROV 627:39
one d. in thy courts BOOK 145:15
on the Lord's d. BIBL 117:24
penance for a d. WORD 868:14
perfect d. nor night SHAK 710:6
robs us of the fair d. HORA 413:18
rule the d. BIBL 78:15
seize the d. HORA 411:16
sinks the d.-star MILT 540:14
So foul and fair a d. SHAK 718:9
spent one whole d. THOM 804:21
Sufficient unto the d. BIBL 99:20

day (*cont.*):

Sufficient unto the d.	PROV 643:49
They have their d.	TENN 794:29
think each d. your own	EURI 321:4
this d. as if thy last	KEN 459:14
through her busy d.	JAGG 427:9
to a summer's d.	SHAK 737:18
tomorrow is another d.	MITC 551:5
Tomorrow is another d.	PROV 645:27
Until the d. break	BIBL 91:2
unto the perfect d.	BIBL 87:25
wave's intenser d.	SHEL 745:8
weary d. have end	SPEN 766:22
welcome d.	BUNY 171:26
who can see each d.	HORA 413:8
Without all hope of d.	MILT 545:1
write every other d.	DOUG 291:17

daylight d. in upon magic — BAGE 51:5

kind of d.	ADDI 5:12
kingdom of d.'s dauphin	HOPK 408:4
'til it bleeds d.	COCK 237:17
We burn d.	SHAK 725:18

Dayrolles Give D. a chair — CHES 223:22

days all the d. of my life — BOOK 140:21

behold these present d.	SHAK 738:11
best d. of life	VIRG 833:1
brave d. of old	MACA 508:15
burnt-out ends of smoky d.	ELIO 310:21
Cast your mind on other d.	YEAT 875:8
chequerboard of nights and d.	FITZ 331:21
D. and months are travellers	BASH 61:1
d. are evil	BIBL 114:10
d. are in the yellow leaf	BYRO 190:21
d. are swifter	BIBL 86:22
D. are where we live	LARK 481:1
d. darken round me	TENN 794:24
d. grow short	ANDE 15:10
d. of Methuselah	BIBL 79:20
d. of wine and roses	DOWS 292:5
d. on the earth are as a shadow	BIBL 86:1
d. that are no more	TENN 799:10
E'er half my d.	MILT 545:14
fair well-spoken d.	SHAK 731:13
first 1,000 d.	KENN 460:9
former d. were better	BIBL 90:3
forty d. it will remain	PROV 642:33
good d. speed and depart	MART 524:6
in length of d.	BIBL 86:28
in the house three d.	SHAW 741:8
in the midst of his d.	BIBL 95:6
Length of d.	BIBL 87:22
multitude of d.	JOHN 438:9
number of my d.	BOOK 141:28
number our d.	BOOK 145:22
of few d.	BIBL 86:30
only three d. old	JEAN 431:1
our eleven d.	POLI 612:18
O ye Nights, and D.	BOOK 133:15
see better d.	BEHN 67:3
seemed but a few d.	BIBL 80:12
Six d. shalt thou labour	BIBL 81:18
six working d.	SIDD 750:7
Ten d. that shook the world	REED 657:10
that thy d. may be long	BIBL 81:20
Three whole d. together	SUCK 779:15
two d. like a tiger	TIPU 811:9
We have seen better d.	SHAK 734:7

daytime cry in the d. — BOOK 140:15

daze d. with little bells — HUGO 419:6

dazzle d. for an hour — MORE 559:1

mine eyes d. — WEBS 844:12

dazzled D. thus with height — WOTT 870:10

Eyes still d. — LIND 495:2

dea *vera incessu patuit d.* — VIRG 828:19

dead act as if we were d. — POUN 621:8

already three parts d.	RUSS 674:22
Am I d. or am I not dead	TIBE 810:17
among the d.	BIBL 106:28
and Guildenstern are d.	SHAK 705:5
and the noble D.	WORD 868:19
Ay, d.	BROW 168:11
barrows of the happier d.	TENN 800:10
being d.	BENT 71:15

best men are d.	PUNC 650:9
Better red than d.	POLI 612:7
better than a d. lion	PROV 637:49
bivouac of the d.	O'HA 584:16
Blessed are the d.	BIBL 119:3
buried is not d.	SCHR 686:16
character d. at every word	SHER 748:25
cold and pure and very d.	LEWI 492:1
completely consistent are the d.	HUXL 422:15
composer is to be d.	HONE 405:9
conference With the d.	WEBS 844:8
cut in half; he's d.	GRAH 367:14
D.! and never called me	WOOD 863:21
D. battles, like d. generals	TUCH 818:10
d. Body wears	PLAT 608:7
d.-born from the press.	HUME 420:15
d. bury the dead	PROV 637:23
d. bury their dead	BIBL 100:11
d., but in the Elysian fields	DISR 286:20
d. by fate	BEAU 63:9
d. donkey	DICK 281:1
d. don't die	LAWR 484:4
D., for a ducat	SHAK 703:10
D. from the waist down	BROW 165:26
D. he is not	LONG 499:12
d. he would like to see me	HOLL 403:6
d. is to be non-existent	SOCR 759:23
d. level	ELIO 308:6
d. lion	BIBL 90:8
d. man's town	SPRI 769:4
D. men don't bite	PROV 629:34
d. men lost their bones	ELIO 311:8
d. men's shoes	PROV 636:36
D. men tell no tales	PROV 629:35
dead Past bury its d.	LONG 499:16
d. rest well	CLAR 232:23
D., Right Reverends	DICK 276:22
d. shall be raised incorruptible	BIBL 113:5
d. shall go down to thee	SWIN 785:20
d. shall live	DRYD 296:30
d. shall not have died in vain	LINC 494:1
d. sinner	BIER 121:10
d. that the rain rains on	PROV 628:10
d. there is no rivalry	MACA 507:6
d. these two years	CHES 223:20
dead which are already d.	BIBL 89:25
d. which he slew at his death	BIBL 83:19
d. woman bites not	GRAY 369:18
d. writers are remote	ELIO 311:23
democracy of the d.	CHES 225:12
doors of the d.	RILK 662:2
Down among the d.	DYER 301:11
dread a d.-level of income	TAWN 791:2
Either he's d.	FILM 328:4
ere I am laid out d.	HERR 395:16
Evelyn Hope is d.	BROW 165:19
face of the d.	BEER 66:7
Fair Adonis is d.	BION 121:17
famous calm and d.	BROW 165:22
fell at his feet as d.	BIBL 117:27
food that d. men eat	DOBS 287:3
fortnight d.	ELIO 311:16
found, when she was d.	GOLD 364:15
God is d.	FROM 344:3
grand to be blooming well d.	SARO 681:4
had already been d. a year	LEHR 488:4
Harrow the house of the d.	AUDE 38:11
healthy and wealthy and d.	THUR 810:12
Hector is d.	SHAK 734:24
He is d. and gone, lady	SHAK 703:31
he is d., who will not fight	GREN 372:10
home among the d.	SHEL 744:2
HOMER d.	ANON 20:9
if the d. rise not	BIBL 112:23
If the d. talk to you	SZAS 786:14
if two of them are d.	PROV 645:11
immortal d. who live again	ELIO 308:13
In praise of ladies d.	SHAK 738:10
I see d. people	FILM 328:21
judge the quick and the d.	BOOK 133:19
King of all these the d.	HOME 405:6
know that thou wert d.	CONS 249:15
lain for a century d.	TENN 798:7

land of the d.	WILD 856:17
lang time d.	MOTT 563:4
Lilacs out of the d. land	ELIO 311:1
Lycidas is d.	MILT 540:3
mansions of the d.	CRAB 257:17
millions of the mouthless d.	SORL 761:24
Mistah Kurtz—he d.	CONR 249:2
more than the d.	ARNO 29:1
more to say when I am d.	ROBI 663:18
My d. king	JOYC 448:7
No one wept for the d.	AGNO 9:15
not d.—but gone	ROGE 665:13
not d., but sleepeth	BIBL 100:19
Not many d.	COCK 237:18
Of their d. selves	TENN 794:31
one rose from the d.	BIBL 106:8
only the d. smiled	AKHM 10:5
on the d. man's chest	STEV 775:20
oure kyng wes d.	WYNT 871:17
our English d.	SHAK 708:16
past is the only d. thing	THOM 806:17
past never d.	FAUL 324:14
pay for my d. people	JOSE 447:12
quick, and the d.	DEWA 275:9
rather be d. than cool	COBA 237:10
remind me of the d.	SASS 682:8
resurrection of the d.	BIBL 113:3
saying 'Lord Jones D.'	CHES 225:24
sculptured d.	KEAT 454:5
sea gave up the d.	BIBL 119:14
Sea shall give up her d.	BOOK 150:15
sheeted d. Did squeak	SHAK 699:4
She, she is d.	DONN 287:14
simplify me when I'm d.	DOUG 291:12
sleeping and the d.	SHAK 720:8
speak ill of the d.	PROV 639:43
Stone-d. hath no fellow	PROV 643:41
talks you d.	JOHN 438:1
Tallis is d.	BYRD 184:27
There are no d.	MAET 514:14
they're a' d.	TOAS 812:3
thirteen men lay d.	HEAN 387:14
those who are d.	BURK 174:16
told me you were d.	CORY 252:13
to the d. we owe only truth	VOLT 834:17
very d. of Winter	ANDR 15:15
very d. of winter	ELIO 310:2
voice of the d.	TENN 796:8
was alive and is d.	EPIT 318:3
was d., and is alive	BIBL 106:2
water—fire live—and we d.	BYRO 189:5
ways of being d.	DAWK 269:2
we are all d.	KEYN 462:5
Weep me not d.	DONN 289:22
wench is d.	MARL 522:19
we, that are d. to sin	BIBL 110:32
what was d. was Hope	WILD 856:2
When I am d.	MCGO 511:1
When I am d.	ROSS 669:9
Where d. men meet	BUTL 184:18
where there was not one d.	BIBL 81:10
wife, or himself must be d.	AUST 42:26
without works is d.	BIBL 116:22
with the enduring d.	SHEL 743:16
would that I were d.	TENN 797:17
you're ten years d.	HAYE 385:15

deaded told you I'd be d. — CATC 209:6

deadener Habit is a great d. — BECK 64:25

deadline stimulated by a d. — KRAU 473:13

deadlines daily d. — ZOLA 878:13

deadlock Holy d. — HERB 393:15

deadly more d. in the long run — TWAI 820:2

more d. than the male	KIPL 465:18
more d. than the male	PROV 632:9

Dead Sea apples on the D.'s shore — BYRO 186:8

Like D. fruits — MOOR 558:15

deaf d. as an adder — ADAM 2:20

d., how should they know	SORL 761:24
d. husband	PROV 629:36
d., inexorable	SIDN 750:11
none so d. as those	PROV 644:45
prove me d. and blind	BROW 167:25

D. as first love	TENN 799:12	In defeat; d.	CHUR 230:21	Studies serve for d.	BACO 47:32

D. as first love — TENN 799:12
D. in the shady sadness — KEAT 454:20
d. silent slide away — SIDN 750:12
d. sleep of England — ORWE 587:3
D.-versed in books — MILT 544:28
face of the d. — BIBL 78:12
From the great d. — TENN 794:2
I am not d. — BALZ 57:6
Not d. the Poet sees — ARNO 30:2
One d. calleth another — BOOK 142:6
one is of the d. — STEP 772:3
Out of the d. — BOOK 149:7
Plunge it into d. water — HORA 413:15
spirits from the vasty d. — SHAK 706:9
Still waters run d. — PROV 643:37
thunders of the upper d. — TENN 796:9
too d. for tears — WORD 867:18
wonders in the d. — BOOK 147:17
deepens d. like a coastal shelf — LARK 481:10
deeper d. than did ever plummet — SHAK 734:2
d. than the sea — BALL 55:10
In d. reverence praise — WHIT 853:2
deer a-chasing the d. — BURN 179:3
D. walk upon our mountains — STEV 774:15
dying d. — AYTO 44:7
I was a stricken d. — COWP 256:13
running of the d. — SONG 762:12
stare of the d. — WILB 854:2
stricken d. — SHAK 702:25
Deever hangin' Danny D. — KIPL 465:13
défauts âme est sans d. — RIMB 662:17
defeat d. is an orphan — CIAN 231:9
In d.; defiance — CHUR 230:21
In d. unbeatable — CHUR 230:14
possibilities of d. — VICT 827:13
this world's d. — VAUG 825:3
triumph and d. — LONG 499:13
defeated d. in a great battle — LIVY 496:7
Down with the d. — LIVY 496:5
history to the d. — AUDE 38:13
Love is never d. — JOHN 434:10
safe course for the d. — VIRG 829:14
when women were the d. — TREV 815:11
defeats d. more triumphant than victories — MONT 555:4
Dewey d. Truman — NEWS 573:5
defect fair d. of nature — MILT 544:12
she did make d. perfection — SHAK 694:24
defects d. become them — LA R 481:25
defence at one gate to make d. — MILT 545:6
best d. is a good offence — SAYI 684:3
best form of d. — PROV 627:2
d. against the atom bomb — ANON 16:13
D., not defiance — MOTT 563:7
d. of the country — ARIS 26:21
d. of the indefensible — ORWE 588:1
house of d. — BOOK 146:2
in d. of one's country — HOME 404:18
Lord is thy d. — BOOK 148:17
Never make a d. — CHAR 216:15
only d. against betrayal — WILL 858:1
only d. is in offence — BALD 53:5
our d. is sure — WATT 842:7
think of the d. of England — BALD 53:6
defend d. as a man — AYES 44:3
d. my cause — BOOK 142:8
D., O Lord — BOOK 138:18
d. ourselves with guns — GOEB 361:7
d. to the death your right — MISQ 547:20
d. us from all perils — BOOK 134:10
D. us thy humble servants — BOOK 134:2
defendants whole number of the d. — CROM 260:11
defended God abandoned, these d. — HOUS 415:8
defending d. those provinces — SMIT 756:9
means by d. freedom — NIEM 575:7
defends when attacked it d. itself — ANON 21:20
defensoribus tali auxilio nec d. — VIRG 829:16
defer madness to d. — YOUN 876:19
deferred Hope d. — PROV 634:41
defiance Defence, not d. — MOTT 563:7
d. in their eye — GOLD 364:26

deficiencies sense enough to perceive his d. — HAZL 385:18
defied Age will not be d. — BACO 47:24
defiled shall be d. — BIBL 97:18
touches pitch shall be d. — PROV 634:11
defileth d. a man — BIBL 101:21
define d. true madness — SHAK 701:3
know how to d. it — THOM 804:13
definition d. is the enclosing — BUTL 184:11
d. of the best government — HALI 377:14
working d. of hell — SHAW 742:4
definitions words; which . . . they call D. — HOBB 400:16
deflower will her pride d. — SPEN 767:15
deformed D., unfinished — SHAK 731:11
None can be called d. — SHAK 736:8
prove d. — SHAK 738:26
deformity Art is significant d. — FRY 345:23
defrauding d. of the State — PENN 602:18
defy d. the foul fiend — SHAK 715:26
degenerate d. in the absence — TERE 801:14
degeneration d. of his moral being — STEV 775:28
degradation breath of d. — BYRO 190:13
degraded each d. mind — CRAB 257:12
degree exalted them of low d. — BIBL 104:9
degrees through all d. — WORD 869:20
dehumanizing anecdote d. — EPHR 316:8
dei D. gloriam — MOTT 563:1
vox D. — ALCU 11:10
deities some other new d. — PLAT 608:13
deity D. and the Drains — STRA 778:12
D. disowns me — COWP 255:4
D. offended — BURN 178:4
Half dust, half d. — BYRO 190:13
déjà d. vu all over again — BERR 74:14
delay deny, or d. — MAGN 515:2
In d. there lies no plenty — SHAK 735:9
In me is no d. — MILT 544:18
Nothing lost by d. — GREE 371:11
reluctant amorous d. — MILT 543:6
delayed d. till I am indifferent — JOHN 439:7
Justice d. — SAYI 684:32
delaying One man by d. — ENNI 316:5
rich by d. — TROL 816:20
delays D. are dangerous — PROV 629:39
d. are dangerous in war — DRYD 297:5
most fatiguing d. — BURK 176:10
delectable D. Mountains — BUNY 171:15
delectando d. pariterque monendo — HORA 409:12
delegate When in trouble, d. — BORE 151:6
delenda D. est Carthago — CATO 209:19
deleted Expletive d. — ANON 17:2
Delia While D. is away — JAGO 427:14
deliberate Where both d. — MARL 522:15
deliberates woman who d. — ADDI 4:16
deliberation D. sat and public care — MILT 542:7
delicias D. domini — VIRG 831:17
delicious Afloat. We move: D. — CLOU 236:17
delight begins in d. — FROS 345:5
born to sweet d. — BLAK 124:19
D. hath a joy — SIDN 751:9
d. in conceiving — KEAT 458:3
D. in lust — PETR 605:9
d. is in lies — BOOK 143:21
d. with liberty — SPEN 768:1
do ill our sole d. — MILT 541:14
Energy is Eternal D. — BLAK 126:2
ever new d. — MILT 543:17
firmness, and d. — WOTT 870:11
give d., and hurt not — SHAK 733:30
hear thy shrill d. — SHEL 746:21
immense world of d. — BLAK 126:9
labour we d. in — SHAK 720:14
land of pure d. — WATT 842:4
Let dogs d. — WATT 841:14
men miscall d. — SHEL 743:18
phantom of d. — WORD 869:6
Spirit of D. — SHEL 746:10
still my d. — BURN 178:19

temple of D. — KEAT 456:1
thing that conceives d. — MILT 544:4
turn d. into a sacrifice — HERB 393:26
delighteth king d. to honour — BIBL 86:7
neither d. he — BOOK 150:7
delightful it can be d. — SHAW 739:13
no d. ones — LA R 481:23
delighting d. the reader — HORA 409:12
delights king of intimate d. — COWP 256:21
man d. not me — SHAK 701:11
some d. condemn — MOLI 552:23
delinquencies indulge in a few d. — ELIO 308:12
delinquent condemns a less d. — BUTL 184:1
delirant Quidquid d. reges — HORA 410:3
delitabill Storys to rede ar d. — BARB 58:3
deliver D. Israel, O God — BOOK 141:5
d. us from evil — BIBL 99:12
d. us from evil — MISS 549:17
d. us, good Lord — CHES 224:6
let him d. him — BOOK 140:16
Lord, d. us — BOOK 134:16
O d. me from the deceitful — BOOK 142:8
O d. my soul — BOOK 141:23
who shall d. me — BIBL 110:38
deliverance d. from chains — DOUG 291:19
delivered d. my soul — BOOK 148:7
d. them — BIBL 82:31
God hath d. him — BIBL 84:9
delivereth he d. them — BOOK 147:18
delivery ungracefulness of his d. — WALP 838:6
delphiniums d. (blue) and geraniums (red) — MILN 538:4
Delphos steep of D. leaving — MILT 540:29
deluding dear d. woman — BURN 180:2
deluge Après nous le d. — POMP 611:12
move on to the D. — RACI 653:5
déluge Passons au d. — RACI 653:5
delusion d., a mockery — DENM 273:9
under some d. — BURK 175:23
delusive d. seduction — BURN 177:2
demand goodness is not in d. — BREC 155:14
not d. for labour — MILL 536:10
demanded d. nought — TASS 790:10
demands cannot exact their d. — WELL 846:17
demens Quem fugis, a! d. — VIRG 831:19
demi-paradise other Eden, d. — SHAK 730:10
demitasses villainous d. — SMIT 756:15
democracies d. against despots — DEMO 272:22
in d. it is the only sacred — FRAN 340:5
democracy conception of D. — ADDA 4:5
cured by more d. — SMIT 756:10
cure for the ills of D. — ADDA 4:6
D. and socialism are means — NEHR 569:12
D. is an orphan — TSVA 818:7
D. is the current suspicion — WHIT 850:14
D. is the name we give — FLER 334:23
D. is the theory — MENC 531:20
D. is the worst form — CHUR 230:7
d. means government — ATTL 35:10
D. means government by — CHES 225:25
D. means simply — WILD 856:7
d. of the dead — CHES 225:12
d. or absolute oligarchy — ARIS 28:4
D. resumed her reign — BELL 68:13
D. substitutes election — SHAW 741:11
d. unbearable — PERE 603:21
five hundred years of d. — FILM 328:20
great arsenal of d. — ROOS 667:11
grieved under a d. — HOBB 401:3
justice makes d. possible — NIEB 575:5
less d. to save — ATKI 35:4
made safe for d. — WILS 859:19
modern d. is a tyranny — MAIL 516:9
no d. can afford — BEVE 77:5
no d. in physics — ALVA 14:2
not the voting that's d. — STOP 777:13
perfect d. — BURK 174:15
pollution of d. — WHIT 851:2
property-owning d. — SKEL 754:4
risk more d. — BRAN 155:3
Russia an empire or d. — BRZE 169:4
Two cheers for D. — FORS 338:13

democrat Senator, and a D.   JOHN 435:3
democratic basis of a d. state   ARIS 28:6
democrats D. object to men being
    disqualified   CHES 225:13
Democritus D. would laugh   HORA 410:21
demolish can't really d. it   RANK 655:4
demolition d. of a man   LEVI 491:7
demon d.'s that is dreaming   POE 611:4
    wailing for her d.-lover   COLE 240:5
demonstrandum Quod erat d.   EUCL 320:17
den d. of thieves   BIBL 102:13
denial d. of Him by the atheist   PROU 625:12
denied comes to be d.   MONT 554:4
    Justice d.   MILL 537:1
    justice d.   SAYI 684:32
denies spirit that always d.   GOET 361:17
deniges Who d. of it   DICK 279:1
denizen spider is sole d.   HARD 381:9
Denmark in the state of D.   SHAK 700:15
    it may be so in D.   SHAK 700:24
    throne of D.   SHAK 699:10
denomination d. does not interfere
    FRED 341:22
dens d. o' Yarrow   BALL 54:13
    hid themselves in the d.   BIBL 118:11
dentist sooner go to my d.   WAUG 843:2
deny d. a God   BACO 46:7
    d. me thrice   BIBL 103:13
    d., or delay   MAGN 515:2
    d. the being of a devil   MATH 527:15
    He teaches to d.   QUAR 651:12
    I never d.   DISR 286:22
    will I not d. thee   BIBL 103:14
    You must d. yourself   GOET 361:19
denying allure by d.   TROL 816:20
    they were d.   FREE 342:5
Deo D. gratias   MISS 549:10
    Jubilate D., omnis terra   BIBL 120:1
deoch-an-doris Just a wee d.   MORR 561:9
deorum Parcus d. cultor   HORA 412:2
depart already time to d.   SOCR 760:1
    desire to d.   BIBL 114:17
    servant d. in peace   BIBL 104:16
    will not d.   BIBL 88:31
departed Dead he is not, but d.   LONG 499:12
    dear brother here d.   BOOK 139:10
    d., he withdrew   CICE 232:3
    d. into their own country   BIBL 98:12
    D., never to return   BURN 177:18
    d. this life   BOOK 137:8
    glory is d.   BIBL 83:29
    glory is d.   BROW 168:8
    Lord was d.   BIBL 83:17
departing and at my d.   PRAY 623:4
departure point of d.   METT 533:9
dépêches Une de ces d.   PROU 625:16
dependant d. on man's bounty   STAN 770:5
depends d. on the tip   FILM 330:2
    d. upon a red wheel barrow   WILL 858:11
    d. what you mean by   CATC 208:8
dépeuplé tout est d.   LAMA 476:8
deportment adapt her methods and d.
    CRAN 258:16
    for his D.   DICK 276:15
depose my state d.   SHAK 731:3
deposit greater the d.   LAYT 485:2
depraved suddenly became d.   JUVE 450:17
depravity sense of innate d.   MELV 531:6
    stupidity than d.   JOHN 440:22
depression d. when you lose yours
    TRUM 817:21
depressions terrible d.   SEI 691:7
deprivation D. is for me   LARK 481:15
depth d. and breadth and height   BROW 164:13
    d. of every acre   GURN 384:18
    far beyond my d.   SHAK 710:19
    love knows not its own d.   GIBR 355:13
deputy d. elected by the Lord   SHAK 730:16
derangement nice d. of epitaphs   SHER 748:14
Derry oak would sprout in D.   HEAN 387:16
descansada Que d. vida   LUIS 504:16
descending comes with clouds d.   WESL 847:18
descensus Facilis d. Averno   VIRG 830:5

descent d. from a monkey   WILB 853:16
description beggared all d.   SHAK 694:22
descriptions d. of the fairest wights
    SHAK 738:10
Desdemona D.! dead   SHAK 729:21
desert convert it into a d.   YOUN 876:8
    d. is a moving mouth   WALC 835:15
    d. shall rejoice   BIBL 93:8
    d. sighs in the bed   AUDE 36:25
    d. were my dwelling-place   BYRO 186:28
    in a d. land   BIBL 82:18
    Life is the d.   YOUN 877:3
    make straight in the d.   BIBL 93:15
    Nothing went unrewarded, but d.   DRYD 294:21
    on the d. air   GRAY 370:6
    out into the d.   CLOU 238:8
    owl that is in the d.   BOOK 146:16
    scare myself with my own d.   FROS 344:12
    Stand in the d.   SHEL 745:15
    Use every man after his d.   SHAK 701:18
    water but the d.   BYRO 186:20
deserted towns are d.   BERN 74:1
deserts d. of the heart   AUDE 37:13
    D. of vast eternity   MARV 525:12
    his d. are small   MONT 556:15
    she d. the night   MILT 545:2
deserve and d. to get it   MENC 531:20
    d. any thanks   CATU 210:17
    d. success   ADDI 4:12
    I d. it   PRIE 623:15
    only d. it   CHUR 229:18
    you somehow haven't to d.   FROS 344:11
deserves Everyone gets what he d.   BOLD 131:8
    gets what he d.   ANON 22:14
    Stonehenge than d.   HAWK 384:12
desiccated d. calculating machine   BEVA 76:20
desiccation preserves the soul from d.
    LYTT 506:9
design good d. for a bus   HOCK 401:15
    integrity in d.   KARA 453:6
    there is a d. in it   STEE 770:16
    two rules for d.   PUGI 649:1
designs at large to his own dark d.   MILT 541:17
    d. were strictly honourable   FIEL 326:22
    instruments of their crooked d.   GODW 361:4
    Official d.   BETJ 76:2
desinat D. in piscem   HORA 408:14
desipere Dulce est d.   HORA 414:5
desire by nature d. knowledge   ARIS 27:3
    d. accomplished   BIBL 88:8
    d. and longing   BOOK 145:13
    d. for their own happiness   SHAN 739:4
    d. is great   GOET 362:3
    d. of power   HOBB 400:20
    d. of the moth   SHEL 746:18
    d. other men's goods   BOOK 138:14
    d. shall fail   BIBL 90:20
    d. should so many years   SHAK 707:16
    few things to d.   BACO 46:26
    few things to d.   BLAK 128:9
    fond d.   ADDI 4:20
    gratified d.   BLAK 127:3
    her d.,— Shining suspension   CRAN 258:15
    land of d.   HEGE 388:16
    Land of Heart's D.   YEAT 873:22
    man's d. is for the woman   COLE 242:4
    nothing like d.   PROU 625:11
    provokes the d.   SHAK 720:13
    weariness treads on d.   PETR 605:9
    what I've tasted of d.   FROS 344:13
    when the d. cometh   BIBL 88:6
    Which of us has his d.   THAC 803:7
    without any quiver of d.   PALI 594:24
desired chiefly to be d.   CICE 232:10
    I have d. to go   HOPK 407:11
    More to be d.   BOOK 140:11
    not one to be d.   TENN 796:11
    You who d. so much—   CRAN 258:19
desires all d. known   BOOK 136:19
    all holy d.   BOOK 134:9
    answer back to d.   HORA 415:2
    d. and petitions   BOOK 134:8
    d. but acts not   BLAK 126:5

    d. of our own hearts   BOOK 133:4
    d. of the heart   AUDE 36:28
    d. of the mind   BACO 45:11
    d. that seem big   RICE 659:19
    d. which thereof did ensue   DONN 288:3
    doing what one d.   MILL 536:8
    end of our d.   THOM 805:7
    enjoyment of all d.   TANT 790:5
    fondly flatter our d.   DRAY 293:13
    lopping off our d.   SWIF 783:16
    nurse unacted d.   BLAK 126:18
    proportion to our d.   MANN 519:11
desirest d. no sacrifice   BOOK 143:9
desireth as the hart d.   BOOK 142:4
desiring D. this man's art   SHAK 737:22
desirous ought else on earth d.   GAY 351:5
desk d. to write upon   BUTL 183:20
    modern man's subservience to the d.
    FRAN 341:14
    Turn upward from the d.   ELIO 311:12
desks Stick close to your d.   GILB 358:2
desolate d. and oppressed   BOOK 135:1
    d. places   BIBL 86:16
    sold in the d. market   BLAK 125:10
    vast d. night   BYRO 185:15
desolated province they have d.   GLAD 360:2
desolation abomination of d.   BIBL 102:24
    D. in immaculate public places   ROET 665:6
    Love in D.   SHEL 743:15
    Magnificent d.   ALDR 12:1
    years of d.   JEFF 432:12
despair begotten by D.   MARV 524:18
    better than d.   PITT 607:15
    Bid me d.   HERR 396:13
    carrion comfort, D.   HOPK 407:5
    comfort and d.   SHAK 738:23
    D. a smilingness assume   BYRO 186:4
    D. had a wife   BUNY 171:14
    D. yawns   HUGO 419:4
    Do not d.   PUDN 648:34
    Don't d., not even   KAFK 452:11
    endure my own d.   WALS 838:19
    far side of d.   SART 681:13
    Giant D.   BUNY 171:13
    Heaven in Hell's d.   BLAK 127:17
    In d. there are   DOST 291:7
    in our own d.   AESC 6:13
    I shall d.   SHAK 731:28
    needst not then d.   ARNO 29:9
    perpetual d.   CARL 200:16
    some divine d.   TENN 799:10
    unyielding d.   RUSS 674:25
    what resolution from d.   MILT 541:16
    ye Mighty, and d.   SHEL 745:17
despairer Too quick d.   ARNO 30:27
desperandum Nil d.   HORA 411:11
desperate Beware of d. steps   COWP 255:11
    D. diseases   PROV 629:40
    Diseases d. grown   SHAK 703:23
    Tempt not a d. man   SHAK 733:2
desperation lives of quiet d.   THOR 809:12
despise and d. him   DICK 279:14
    capacity to d. himself   SANT 680:17
    ere you d. the other   DRYD 297:18
    shalt thou not d.   BOOK 143:9
    work for a Government I d.   KEYN 461:14
despised Dangers by being d.   BURK 176:4
    d. and rejected   BIBL 94:3
    d. the world   HAZL 386:6
despises wise traveller never d.   GOLD 363:18
despising By d. all that   HAZL 386:4
despite Hell in Heaven's d.   BLAK 127:18
despond slough was D.   BUNY 171:5
despondency d. and madness   WORD 868:23
    last words of Mr D.   BUNY 171:26
    SPREAD ALARM AND D.   PENI 602:12
    unnecessary alarm and d.   MILI 535:7
despot country governed by a d.   JOHN 442:15
despotism D. accomplishes great things
    BALZ 57:4
    d. in England   WALP 838:9
    d., let it be called   WEBS 844:1
    d., or unlimited sovereignty   ADAM 3:9

d. tempered by epigrams   CARL 200:3
d. will come   ARIS 28:4
root of d.   ROBE 663:12
despots against d.—suspicion   DEMO 272:22
D. themselves do not deny   TOCQ 811:13
dessin d. est la probité   INGR 425:14
destinies d. of half the globe   TOCQ 812:12
destiny Anatomy is d.   FREU 342:15
character is d.   ELIO 308:8
d. obscure   GRAY 370:4
d. of man   MANN 520:5
D. with Men for pieces   FITZ 331:21
fabric of human d.   DOST 291:1
gods ordained the d. of men   HOME 405:1
manifest d.   O'SU 589:7
sport of d.   THAC 802:18
tide of d.   PAST 598:20
wiving go by d.   PROV 633:41
destitution shaming D.   VIRG 830:9
sumptuous d.   DICK 281:18
destroy against us to d. us   HAGG 375:11
d. the town to save it   ANON 18:7
gods wish to d.   CONN 248:7
impossible to d. men   TOCQ 812:10
in search of monsters to d.   ADAM 3:17
man determined to d. himself   CUMM 262:11
not to d., but to fulfil   BIBL 98:29
One to d.   YOUN 876:14
planted, we d.   WITH 861:5
power to d.   MARS 523:24
shall be able to d.   OVID 590:15
shall not hurt nor d.   BIBL 92:18
Whom the gods would d.   PROV 647:18
Whom the mad would d.   LEVI 491:8
winged life d.   BLAK 127:2
worms d. this body   BIBL 86:31
destroyed Carthage must be d.   CATO 209:19
enemy that shall be d.   BIBL 112:22
name d.   HILL 399:6
not one life shall be d.   TENN 795:13
ought to be d.   OMAR 585:5
treated generously or d.   MACH 511:6
destroyer D. and preserver   SHEL 745:6
d. of worlds   OPPE 585:14
destroyeth d. in the noon-day   BOOK 146:1
destroying without d. something   UPDI 822:26
destroys d. a good book   MILT 545:22
Time which d. all things   BHAG 78:4
destruction d. of the poor   BIBL 87:35
d. of the whole world   HUME 420:19
for d. ice Is also great   FROS 344:13
leadeth to d.   BIBL 99:28
means of total d.   SAKH 677:16
Pride goeth before d.   BIBL 88:17
to his own d.   FRAM 340:3
to their d. draw   DONN 288:25
urge for d.   BAKU 52:10
whether the mad d. is wrought   GAND 348:11
destructive smiling, d. man   LEE 487:14
To the d. element   CONR 249:4
would be simply d.   MELB 530:15
detached except he be d.   BAHA 52:1
detail corroborative d.   GILB 357:14
frittered away by d.   THOR 809:23
occupied in trivial d.   BAGE 50:14
details Devil is in the d.   SAYI 684:12
God is in the d.   MIES 534:22
mind which reveres d.   LEWI 492:14
detect lose it in the moment you d.   POPE 615:12
detection D. is an exact science   DOYL 292:19
detective d. story is about   JAME 430:12
Hawkshaw, the d.   TAYL 792:8
deteriora D. sequor   OVID 590:13
determination d. of a quiet man   SMIT 757:3
d. of incident   JAME 429:21
determine we d. our deeds   ELIO 306:19
determined D., dared, and done   SMAR 755:14
determinèd d. to prove a villain   SHAK 731:13
deterrent punishment of jail is not d.   NIGH 576:6
detest d. at leisure   BYRO 189:17
I hate and d.   SWIF 782:20

detraction D. is but baseness' varlet   JONS 446:7
Deum D. de Deo   MISS 549:12
deus d. nobis haec otia fecit   VIRG 831:13
puto d. fio   VESP 827:2
Deutschland D. über alles   HOFF 402:3
devastating d. or redeeming fires   GONC 365:23
developer slipped into d.   WILS 859:1
development what is called d.   NAIR 567:6
De Vere name and dignity of D.   CREW 259:19
deviates d. into sense   DRYD 296:10
deviation Without hesitation, d.   CATC 208:35
device imagined such a d.   BOOK 140:14
with the strange d.   LONG 499:5
devices d. and desires   BOOK 133:4
man of many d.   HOME 405:2
devil act like a d.   MALC 517:11
apology for the D.   BUTL 184:10
assaults of the d.   BOOK 134:16
Better the d. you know   PROV 627:37
bid the D. good morrow   PROV 639:32
blue-eyed d. white man   FARD 323:11
can the d. speak true   SHAK 718:14
cleft the D.'s foot   DONN 289:14
counteracts the D.   SMAR 754:13
covenant with the D.   MISQ 547:16
D. always builds a chapel   DEFO 270:21
d. and all his works   BOOK 138:9
d. can cite Scripture   SHAK 724:8
d. can quote Scripture   PROV 629:41
d. damn thee black   SHAK 722:15
d. doesn't exist   DOST 290:18
d. finds work   PROV 629:42
d. have all the best tunes   PROV 647:24
D. howling 'Ho'   SQUI 769:9
d. is an egotist   GOET 361:18
D. is dead   READ 656:7
D. is in the details   SAYI 684:12
d. is not so black   PROV 629:43
D. knows Latin   KNOX 470:5
d. looks after his own   PROV 629:44
d. makes his Christmas pies   PROV 629:45
D. Moon in your eyes   HARB 379:18
d. more wicked   BALL 55:10
d.-porter it no further   SHAK 720:12
D. said when he found himself   PROV 634:35
d.'s awa wi' th'Exciseman   BURN 178:1
D. sends cooks   GARR 349:13
D. sends cooks   PROV 633:11
d. should have all   HILL 399:1
D. should have right   MORE 559:8
d.'s leavings   POPE 618:23
d.'s luck   PROV 629:46
d.'s madness—War   SERV 692:27
d.'s most devilish   BROW 164:3
d., so far as I'm aware   KLEI 469:9
d.'s walking parody   CHES 224:2
D. take the hindmost   PROV 629:47
D. take the hindmost   PROV 631:26
d. taketh him up   BIBL 98:22
d., taking him up   BIBL 104:20
d. understands Welsh   SHAK 706:11
d. was sick   PROV 629:48
d. weakly fettered   STEV 775:13
D. whoops   KIPL 465:12
D. will build a chapel   PROV 647:7
d. will come   MARL 522:11
d. would also build   LUTH 505:7
doubt is D.-born   TENN 795:26
dreamed of the d.   ANST 24:14
dream of the d.   BARH 58:9
Drink and the d.   STEV 775:20
easier to raise the D.   PROV 636:15
envy of the d.   BIBL 96:27
face the d.   BURN 179:17
fears a painted d.   SHAK 720:8
first Whig was the D.   JOHN 442:19
flesh, and the d.   BOOK 134:18
given the d. a foul fall   MORE 559:9
Give the d. his due   PROV 633:3
God and d.   DOST 290:17
go to the d.   JOHN 438:14

go to the d.   NORF 577:1
got over the D.'s back   PROV 646:22
Haste is from the D.   PROV 633:47
idle brain is d.'s workshop   PROV 635:2
laughing d.   BYRO 187:7
of the D.'s party   BLAK 126:3
of the witty d.   GRAV 369:10
of your father the d.   BIBL 107:31
Poetry is d.'s wine   AUGU 39:12
puzzle the d.   BURN 179:11
reference to the d.   CHUR 230:23
serpent, which is the D.   BIBL 119:12
shame the D.   PROV 644:8
sups with the D.   PROV 634:27
synonym for the D.   MACA 506:18
Talk of the D.   PROV 644:6
there is a D.   MATH 527:15
Truth makes the D. blush   PROV 645:38
wedlock's the d.   BYRO 191:9
What the d. was he doing   MOLI 552:10
when most I play the d.   SHAK 731:17
when the d. drives   PROV 639:30
white man was *created* a d.   MALC 517:8
Young saint, old d.   PROV 648:22
your adversary the d.   BIBL 117:13
you the blacker d.   SHAK 729:17
devilish most d. thing   FLEM 334:19
Tough, and d. sly   DICK 277:24
devils casteth out d.   BIBL 100:20
d. in life and condition   ASCH 33:8
d. must print   MOOR 558:5
d. would set on me   LUTH 505:5
fight like d.   SHAK 708:18
devised so well d.   BOOK 133:1
devolution D. Day   SALM 679:13
d. takes longer   CART 205:13
Devon glorious D.   BOUL 152:14
If the Dons sight D.   NEWB 571:8
devote d. themselves to what men do   FITZ 332:1
devotion D.! daughter of astronomy   YOUN 876:28
my bok and my d.   CHAU 220:17
Tell zeal it wants d.   RALE 653:16
devour d. in turn each one   VERG 826:7
seeking whom he may d.   BIBL 117:13
when they would d.   BACO 48:19
devoured beast hath d. him   BIBL 80:19
devourer Time the d.   OVID 590:14
devourers become so great d.   MORE 559:3
devout for being d.   MOLI 552:21
dew as sunlight drinketh d.   TENN 793:13
begotten the d.   BIBL 87:11
continual d. of thy blessing   BOOK 134:7
d. bespangling herb   HERR 395:18
d. shall weep thy fall   HERB 395:2
d. will rust them   SHAK 728:5
drenched with d.   DE L 272:10
Drop down d., heavens   BIBL 120:8
early fa's the d.   SONG 763:4
fades awa' like morning d.   BALL 56:6
let there be no d.   BIBL 84:11
morning d.   ARNO 30:28
On whom the d. of heaven drops   FORD 337:6
resolve itself into a d.   SHAK 699:17
Showers, and D.   BOOK 133:14
smell the d. and rain   HERB 394:10
soft falls the d.   BEER 66:7
Walks o'er the d.   SHAK 699:7
wicked d.   SHAK 733:17
dewdrop Starlight and d.   FOST 338:21
dewdrops seek some d. here   SHAK 725:34
dewfall d. at night   STEV 776:22
dews early d. were falling   INGE 425:7
dewy d. pasture, dewy trees   TENN 799:2
shakes his d. wings   D'AV 267:10
dhamma D. has been taught   PALI 593:14
sees D. sees me   PALI 594:7
teach you D.   PALI 593:9
dharamsala goes to the d.   SIKH 752:5
dharma discourse on d. as a raft   MAHĀ 515:11
rain of d.   MAHĀ 515:16
di d. omen avertant   CICE 232:6

diable *d. est mort* READ 656:7
diabolical tree of d. knowledge SHER 748:11
diadem d. of frost BLOK 129:6
precious d. stole SHAK 703:15
diagnostician makes a good d. OSLE 589:2
diagonally lie d. in his bed STER 773:14
dial d. spoke not DRYD 296:33
dialect Babylonish d. BUTL 183:9
d. I understand very little PEPY 603:8
d. with an army WEIN 845:8
D. words HARD 380:15
purify the d. of the tribe ELIO 309:18
dial-plate looking on the d. JOHN 440:15
diamond d. and safire bracelet LOOS 500:15
D. cuts diamond PROV 630:1
d. in the sky TAYL 791:16
d. is forever ADVE 7:15
matchwood, immortal d. HOPK 408:1
O D.! Diamond NEWT 574:10
polished d. CHES 223:12
diamonds d. a girl's best friend ROBI 663:15
has no d. WALP 838:2
what beautiful d. WEST 848:14
Dian hangs on D.'s temple SHAK 698:15
Diana D., breathless, hunted MOTI 562:12
D.'s foresters SHAK 705:7
Great is D. BIBL 110:7
diapason d. closing full DRYD 296:27
diarist To be a good d. NICO 575:3
diary discreet d. CHAN 215:17
keep a d. and some day WEST 848:11
never travel without my d. WILD 854:25
write a d. every day POWE 622:4
write in a d. WARN 840:5
diaspora for the new d. DUNN 300:4
dic *sed tantum d. verbo* MISS 549:20
dice God does not play d. EINS 305:8
throw of the d. MALL 517:14
Dick D. the shepherd SHAK 717:25
Mr. D. had been for upwards of ten years DICK 277:11
dicky D.-bird, why do you sit GILB 357:16
dictate *suggest*, never to d. BRON 158:14
dictates still d. to us ALLI 13:18
woman d. ELIO 307:20
dictation told at d. speed AMIS 14:11
dictator d. of Nicaragua CARD 198:3
Every d. uses religion BHUT 78:8
dictators D. ride to and fro upon tigers CHUR 229:9
weed d. may cultivate BEVE 77:5
dictatorship d. impossible PERE 603:21
d. of the proletariat MARX 526:10
elective d. HAIL 376:8
establish a d. ORWE 587:18
have a d. TRUM 817:22
dictionaries D. are like watches JOHN 444:7
d. is dull work JOHN 435:21
Lexicographer. A writer of d. JOHN 436:1
dictionary but a walking d. CHAP 216:12
D. is CARR 202:20
dictum D. *sapienti* PLAU 609:9
non d. sit prius TERE 801:12
did danced his d. CUMM 262:3
d. for them both SASS 682:11
I d. it my way ANKA 16:1
diddle D., diddle, dumpling NURS 578:11
d., we take it, is dee SWIN 785:15
Hey d. diddle NURS 578:11
Dido Stood D. with a willow SHAK 725:9
die Americans when they d. PROV 633:16
and gladly d. STEV 777:5
And shall Trelawny d. HAWK 384:11
apt to d. SHAK 712:21
as if you were to d. tomorrow EDMU 304:1
Ay, but to d., and go SHAK 723:14
being born, to d. BACO 49:11
better to d. on your feet IBAR 424:2
bid me d. HERR 396:13
bleed, fall, and d. DONN 288:4
bravely d. POPE 614:4
Christian can d. ADDI 6:2
clean place to d. KAVA 453:15

conquer or d. WASH 840:14
Cowards d. many times SHAK 712:13
Cowards may d. many times PROV 629:24
Curse God, and d. BIBL 86:14
day that I d. MCLE 512:3
Death thou shalt d. DONN 288:11
determine to d. here BEE 65:10
did not wish to d. SHAW 742:26
d. a Christian CHAR 216:21
d. all, die merrily SHAK 706:17
D., and endow a college POPE 615:4
d. before I wake PRAY 623:6
d. beyond my means WILD 856:9
d. but do not surrender CAMB 194:10
d.—but never to live JAME 430:7
d. but once ADDI 4:18
die, dear, d. BEDD 65:4
d. eating ortolans DISR 286:16
d. for adultery SHAK 716:17
d. for him to-morrow BALL 54:3
d. for one's country HORA 412:17
d. for politicians THOM 808:5
d. for the industrialists FRAN 340:13
d. for the people BIBL 108:8
D. he or justice must MILT 542:22
d. here in a rage SWIF 783:1
d. in music SHAK 729:18
d. in my week JOPL 447:7
d. in peace WOLF 862:16
d. in that man's company SHAK 709:6
d. in the flower of their age BIBL 83:24
d. in the last ditch WILL 857:3
d. is cast CAES 193:1
d. like a true-blue rebel HILL 398:15
d. like men BOOK 145:12
D., my dear Doctor PALM 595:11
d. of that roar ELIO 307:26
d. to save charges BURT 181:10
d. to vex me MELB 530:13
d. upon a kiss SHAK 729:25
d. when the body dies BHAG 77:17
d. when the trees were green CLAR 232:19
d. with harness SHAK 722:23
d. with thee BIBL 103:14
Don't d. of ignorance OFFI 584:6
do we not d. SHAK 724:19
Easy live and quiet d. SCOT 689:10
easy ways to d. SHAK 696:8
envious may d. MOLI 553:1
Every day we d. JERO 433:6
faith is something you d. for BENN 70:2
Fall asleep, or hearing d. SHAK 710:17
Few d. and none resign MISQ 547:14
few d. well SHAK 708:25
for me to d. SOCR 760:1
for tomorrow we d. PROV 630:47
frogs don't d. for 'fun' BION 121:18
Gods love d. young PROV 647:17
Good Americans, when they d. APPL 25:7
good d. early DEFO 270:16
good d. young PROV 633:18
have the power to d. TENN 800:10
hazard of the d. SHAK 732:1
he can d. who complains BROW 163:8
he must d. NICH 574:15
He shall not d. STER 773:12
Hope I d. before TOWN 814:4
how can man d. better MACA 508:13
How hard it is to d. TWAI 820:20
how to d. PORT 620:1
I did not d. FRYE 345:25
I die because I do not d. JOHN 434:3
I d. happy FOX 339:12
I d., if he die not ANDR 15:13
if he d., I die too ANDR 15:13
If I should d. BROO 159:13
If I should d. KEAT 458:14
If it were now to d. SHAK 728:18
If we must d. MCKA 511:15
I'll d. young BRUC 168:14
in Adam all d. BIBL 112:21
I shall d. at the top SWIF 784:15
I shall d. today MORE 559:10

I shall not altogether d. HORA 413:10
I Sir Richard Grenville d. TENN 800:4
it was sure to d. MOOR 558:14
I who am about to d. JOHN 444:18
I will d. with them NELS 569:21
I would d. ROSS 669:24
just as lucky to d. WHIT 852:9
last Jews to d. MEIR 530:7
lay me doun and d. SONG 763:5
Let me d. a youngman's death MCGO 510:17
Let us d. VIRG 829:14
Let us do—or d. BURN 179:10
let us do or d. CAMP 195:7
like Douglas d. HOME 404:4
longed to d. PROU 625:8
love her till I d. ANON 20:17
love one another or d. AUDE 38:7
make a malefactor d. sweetly DRYD 297:25
man can d. but once SHAK 707:22
marked to d. SHAK 709:5
Muse forbids to d. HORA 414:2
natural to d. BACO 46:22
not d. because of them TALM 789:16
not so difficult to d. BYRO 190:15
not that I'm afraid to d. ALLE 13:14
often are we to d. POPE 618:20
Old soldiers never d. FOLE 336:4
Old soldiers never d. PROV 640:33
O love, they d. TENN 799:9
only let Him d. STUD 779:10
Only we d. in earnest RALE 653:18
or dare to d. POPE 617:5
ought to d. standing VESP 827:3
People can't d. DICK 277:19
prepare myself to d. RIEL 661:12
seemed to d. BIBL 96:28
seems it rich to d. KEAT 456:9
shall Harry d. SHAK 707:31
she dared to d. CRAB 257:15
something he will d. for KING 463:10
sooner d. than think RUSS 675:14
taught us how to d. TICK 811:3
Their's but to do and d. TENN 793:4
these who d. as cattle OWEN 591:3
They that d. by famine HENR 392:8
those who are about to d. ANON 23:3
thou must d. HERB 395:2
thou shalt surely d. BIBL 78:21
time to d. BIBL 89:23
To d. and know it LOWE 503:8
To d. in wisdom CERV 213:12
to d. is gain BIBL 114:16
To d. will be an awfully big BARR 59:18
To go away is to d. HARA 379:14
to live and to d. VILL 828:8
tomorrow we d. BIBL 112:23
to morrow we shall d. BIBL 92:22
unlamented let me d. POPE 617:33
we all must d. SWIF 784:9
weep or she will d. TENN 799:15
we needs must d. BIBL 84:19
went abroad to d. LETT 491:1
We shall d. alone PASC 598:3
What 'tis to d. BEAU 63:11
When beggars d. SHAK 712:12
when they come to d. MATH 527:16
when you d. HILL 398:14
when you have to d. MOLI 552:16
where myths Go when they d. FENT 325:1
Who saw him d. NURS 582:12
who would wish to d. BORR 151:11
will d. of strangeness MURR 566:4
wisdom shall d. with you BIBL 86:27
wretch that dares not d. BURN 178:25
You and I ought not to d. ADAM 3:8
You can only d. once PROV 647:42
Young men may d. PROV 648:21
Dieb *er war ein D.* HEIN 389:12
died could have d. contented DICK 277:27
d. an hour before SHAK 720:19
d. extremely well WALP 837:8
D., has he LOUI 501:13
d. hereafter SHAK 722:22

d. in a good old age BIBL 86:2
d. in faith BIBL 116:5
d. last night of my physician PRIO 624:8
d. of grieving KEAT 454:26
D. some, pro patria POUN 621:5
d. to save their country CHES 224:4
d. unto sin once BIBL 110:34
dog it was that d. GOLD 364:16
He that d. o' Wednesday SHAK 706:25
'I never d.,' says he HAYE 385:15
liked it not, and d. WOTT 870:9
made the books and he d. FAUL 324:16
Mithridates, he d. old HOUS 416:11
Mother d. today CAMU 196:17
question why we d. KIPL 465:11
she d. young WEBS 844:12
think of the ones who d. CARD 198:2
What millions d. CAMP 195:14
would God I had d. for thee BIBL 84:21
Would to God we had d. BIBL 81:14
diem carpe d. HORA 411:16
d. perdidi TITU 811:10
d. tibi diluxisse supremum HORA 410:7
dienen d. und verlieren GOET 362:8
dies because a man d. for it WILD 855:22
before he d. SOLO 760:10
d. from lack of sex ATWO 35:13
D. irae MISS 550:5
d. only once MOLI 552:4
d., or turns Hindoo SHEL 744:16
d. to himself unknown SENE 692:21
d. young MENA 531:16
Every moment d. a man BABB 44:12
He that d. SHAK 733:29
He that d. this year SHAK 707:23
kingdom where nobody d. MILL 536:19
king never d. BLAC 123:10
love seldom d. of hunger LENC 488:14
man who d. . . . . rich CARN 201:3
matters not how a man d. JOHN 440:20
moment d. a man TENN 801:2
no man happy till he d. PROV 628:31
once hath blown for ever d. FITZ 331:19
Optima quaeque d. miseris VIRG 833:1
something in me d. VIDA 827:15
then d. the same YOUN 876:21
diest Where thou d., will I die BIBL 83:23
diet best doctors are Dr D. PROV 627:19
d. unparalleled DICK 279:6
dietetics first law of d. ASIM 33:20
diets feel about d. KERR 461:7
Dieu *D. est mort* NERV 570:17
Si D. n'existait pas VOLT 834:8
differ all things d. POPE 618:18
d. from others BAGE 51:16
difference d. of forty thousand WELL 846:9
exaggerate the d. SHAW 740:20
made all the d. FROS 344:22
oh, The d. to me WORD 869:5
wear your rue with a d. SHAK 704:3
What d. does it make GAND 348:11
differences against small d. FREU 342:17
in language there are only d. SAUS 682:16
different boil at d. degrees EMER 315:14
convictions d. from your own EMPS 315:28
D. strokes SAYI 684:13
follow d. paths HORA 414:6
hears a d. drummer THOR 809:26
How d. from us ANON 18:23
how very d. ANON 17:18
other naturs thinks d. DICK 278:22
rich are d. from you and me FITZ 332:3
something completely d. CATC 207:3
Think d. ADVE 8:22
thought they were d. ELIO 310:3
differential integral and d. calculus GILB 358:6
differently do things d. there HART 383:20
freedom for the one who thinks d.
LUXE 505:14
difficile *D. est* JUVE 450:11
D. est longum CATU 211:2
difficult d.; and left untried CHES 225:21
D. do you call it, Sir JOHN 444:14

d. is done at once PROV 630:2
d. takes a little time NANS 567:8
d. to be a father BUSC 181:26
d. to speak BURK 176:1
d. we do immediately MILI 535:6
fascination of what's d. YEAT 873:11
first step that is d. DU D 298:11
first step that is d. PROV 636:27
not so d. to die BYRO 190:15
Poets must be *d.* ELIO 311:25
such a d. problem DÜRR 301:1
too d. for artists SCHN 686:9
difficulties d. do not make one doubt
NEWM 572:5
d. for several generations NAPO 568:5
little local d. MACM 512:18
Man needs d. JUNG 449:16
somebody is in d. LUCR 504:9
difficulty d. in saying things MOOR 558:2
England's d. PROV 631:5
every d. except popularity WILD 856:11
no d. in beginning JAME 430:6
solving every d. PEEL 601:14
with d. and labour MILT 542:21
with great d. I am got hither BUNY 171:27
diffidence her name was D. BUNY 171:14
diffugere *D. nives* HORA 413:17
diffusion d. of knowledge MADI 514:11
dig D. for victory OFFI 584:4
d. our graves DEFO 270:6
he'll d. them up again WEBS 844:21
I could not d. KIPL 465:16
I'll d. with it HEAN 387:9
digest learn, and inwardly d. BOOK 135:11
digestion good d. wait on appetite SHAK 721:8
in d. sour SHAK 730:6
diggeth He that d. a pit BIBL 90:12
dignified d. parts BAGE 50:6
dignitate *Cum d. otium* CICE 232:10
dignities by indignities men come to d.
BACO 47:8
dignity conciliate with d. GREN 372:11
d. in tilling a field WASH 840:12
d. of history BOLI 131:12
d. of this high calling BURK 173:25
d. which His Majesty BALD 53:8
individual d. YAMA 872:4
only true d. of man SANT 680:17
with silent d. GROS 374:2
dignum *D. et justum* MISS 549:15
D. laude virum Musa vetat mori HORA 414:2
dignus *non sum d.* MISS 549:20
digression began a lang d. BURN 180:6
not a d. from it PLIN 610:2
digressions D. are the sunshine STER 772:22
eloquent d. HUXL 423:16
Dijon young man of D. ANON 22:2
dilettante d. in fur GAUT 350:15
dilige *D. et quod vis fac* AUGU 39:18
diligence D. is the mother CERV 213:9
D. is the mother PROV 630:3
diligentiam *obscuram d.* TERE 801:10
dillied But I d. and dallied COLL 243:3
dilly-dally Don't d. on the way COLL 243:3
dim d. religious light MILT 539:20
flickered, grew d. TOLS 813:10
Nor d. nor red COLE 240:18
dime Brother can you spare a d. HARB 379:16
life can change on a d. LAHR 476:4
dimension fourth d. RUSS 675:12
dimensions my d. are as well compact
SHAK 714:22
Time has three d. HOPK 408:8
dimidium *Animae d. meae* HORA 411:5
diminished ought to be d. DUNN 300:5
dimittis *Nunc d.* BIBL 120:12
dimming d. of the lights NICO 575:2
dine d. exact at noon POPE 615:21
gang and d. BALL 56:3
dined I have d. today SMIT 758:20
more d. against BOWR 153:19
ding D., dong, bell NURS 578:12

dining-room d. will be well-lighted
LAND 478:8
dinner after d. is after dinner SWIF 782:17
After d. rest awhile PROV 626:9
ask him to d. CARL 200:31
best number for a d. party GULB 374:12
d. bell BYRO 189:6
D. in the diner GORD 366:6
d. of herbs BIBL 88:15
d. of herbs PROV 627:27
good d. and feasting PEPY 603:12
good d. upon his table JOHN 444:22
have had a better d. JOHN 440:8
hungry for d. at eight HART 383:12
refrain from asking it to d. HALS 378:9
three hours' march to d. HAZL 386:24
we expect our d. SMIT 756:1
with broken d.-knives KIPL 466:1
worth inviting to d. VIRG 832:4
dinners Homer's mighty d. AESC 8:35
dinosaurs D. are a touchstone RUSS 675:16
diocese All the air is thy D. DONN 288:7
Diogenes would be D. ALEX 12:2
Dior Never darken my D. again LILL 493:7
diplomacy D. is to do and say GOLD 363:13
diplomat d. . . . . is a person STIN 777:9
diplomatic d. boathook SALI 678:13
diplomats D. tell lies KRAU 473:11
direct d. and rule our hearts BOOK 136:9
lie d. SHAK 697:26
directed all d. your way HORA 410:2
direction d., which thou canst not see
POPE 616:27
move in a given d. HOUS 416:15
pitch or d. HOPK 408:8
some particular d. JOHN 436:18
directions By indirections find d. out
SHAK 701:1
rode madly off in all d. LEAC 485:9
directors way with these d. GOLD 365:19
direful d. death indeed FLEM 334:18
d. in the sound AUST 41:9
to Greece the d. spring POPE 617:14
dirge their d. is sung COLL 243:13
dirt d. doesn't get any worse CRIS 260:4
D. is only matter GRAY 369:17
eat a peck of d. PROV 646:14
in d. the reasoning engine ROCH 664:16
In poverty, hunger, and d. HOOD 406:1
in the d. lay justice HEAN 387:16
make crossness and d. succeed FORS 337:19
painted child of d. POPE 614:24
thicker will be the d. GALB 347:11
Throw d. enough PROV 645:15
dirty Airing one's d. linen TRUF 817:13
Dear, d. Dublin JOYC 447:18
D., dark, and undevotional VICT 827:9
d. old town MACC 509:12
D. water will quench PROV 630:4
hard and d. work RUSK 673:19
Is sex d. ALLE 13:10
journalistic d.-mindedness LAWR 484:6
'Jug Jug' to d. ears ELIO 311:7
throw out your d. water PROV 630:29
too d. for the light CLAR 232:22
wash one's d. linen PROV 640:42
You d. rat MISQ 549:7
dis *D. aliter visum* VIRG 829:15
disability My d. is that I cannot HANS 379:13
disagree if they d. OMAR 585:5
when doctors d. POPE 615:3
disagreeable d.-looking child BURN 176:13
disappear d. from within JUTR 450:9
only d. FLAT 333:2
disappointed d. by that stroke JOHN 436:27
never be d. PROV 628:11
you have d. us BELL 68:2
disappointeth d. him not BOOK 140:2
disappointing least d. BARU 60:12
disappointment D. all I endeavour end
HOPK 408:2
disappointments most mortifying d.
BURK 176:10

disapproval moral d.	AYER 43:17
disapprove d. of what you say	MISQ 547:20
disapproves condemns whatever he d.	BURN 177:1
disarm d. a military capacity	COOK 250:12
disaster 'Gainst all d.	DEAR 269:14
triumph and d.	KIPL 466:5
disasters d. in his morning face	GOLD 364:7
guilty of our own d.	SHAK 714:24
disastrous d. and the unpalatable	GALB 347:15
win a war is as d.	CHRI 227:1
disbelief willing suspension of d.	COLE 241:21
discandy d., melt their sweets	SHAK 695:14
disce D. omnis	VIRG 829:7
discern do we d.	ARNO 29:19
discerning genius a better d.	GOLD 365:3
discharge d. for loving one	MATL 528:4
no d. in that war	BIBL 90:6
disciple d. did outrun Peter	BIBL 108:35
d. is not above his master	BIBL 100:26
d. whom Jesus loved	BIBL 109:9
in the name of a d.	BIBL 100:31
disciples great man has his d.	WILD 855:1
discipline D. must be maintained	DICK 276:19
d. of colleges	SMIT 756:7
gentle d.	SPEN 767:1
of Dhamma, of D.	PALI 593:17
one thing to praise d.	CERV 213:13
order and military d.	MILI 535:5
wholesome d. impossible	JAIN 428:5
disciplines by category-d.	RYLE 676:8
disclaim d. her for a mother	GIBB 354:19
disclose wise to d.	SCHI 683:15
disco *mali miseris succurrere d.*	VIRG 829:3
Discobbolos Darling Mr D.	LEAR 486:2
discomfort great d. of my soul	BOOK 141:22
discommendeth He who d. others	BROW 162:1
discontent in common—d.	ARNO 31:7
winter of d.	CALL 193:12
Winter of d.	NEWS 573:25
winter of our d.	SHAK 731:9
discontented every one that was d.	BIBL 84:8
none who were d.	NIGH 576:1
discontents Civilization and its d.	RIVI 663:2
source of all our d.	LEAC 485:4
discord civil d.	ADDI 4:24
d. doth sow	ELIZ 312:7
hark! what d. follows	SHAK 734:14
discordant D. elements	WORD 868:10
still-d. wavering multitude	SHAK 707:3
discors Concordia d.	HORA 410:11
discouragement strife and the d.	LONG 498:17
There's no d.	BUNY 171:25
discourse company and good d.	WALT 839:4
d. of rivers	WALT 839:11
Miss not the d.	BIBL 97:13
pleasures of d.	PLAT 608:20
discover another can d.	DOYL 292:18
d. new lands	GIDE 356:1
discovered once they are d.	GALI 347:19
discoverers ill d.	BACO 45:13
discovery D. consists of seeing	SZEN 786:17
d. of a new dish	BRIL 157:9
d. of truth	LAVA 483:6
love is but d.	SOUT 764:5
Medicinal d.	AYRE 44:4
discreet d. charm of the bourgeoisie	FILM 331:3
d. diary	CHAN 215:17
discretion d. end	AUST 42:15
D. is better part	PROV 630:5
D. is not the better part	STRA 778:14
fair woman without d.	BIBL 88:2
guide his words with d.	BOOK 148:1
inform their d.	JEFF 432:11
part of valour is d.	SHAK 706:30
surety to subsequent d.	BURN 176:19
their happiness in thy d.	ELIZ 312:9
discunt *dum docent d.*	SENE 692:14
discuss stay and d. them	WELL 846:15
discussing d. if it existed	GUNN 374:15
discussion compliance with my wishes after reasonable d.	CHUR 230:24
d. of any subject	SHEL 747:7
government by d.	ATTL 35:10
disdain D. and scorn	SHAK 727:24
little d. is not amiss	CONG 247:24
my dear Lady D.	SHAK 727:15
disdained If now I be d.	ANON 20:10
disdainfulness D. I have again	WYAT 871:9
disdains d. all things	OVER 589:15
disease afflictive d.	MOOR 557:18
age, D., or sorrows	CLOU 236:20
Astrology is a d.	MAIM 516:15
biggest d. today	TERE 801:20
cannot ascertain a d.	KEAT 458:18
Cured yesterday of my d.	PRIO 624:8
Cure the d.	BACO 47:1
desperate d.	FAWK 324:21
d. at its onset	PERS 604:10
d. called work	TOCQ 812:17
d. has grown strong	OVID 590:16
D., Ignorance, and Idleness	BEVE 77:6
D. is an experience	EDDY 303:2
d. is incurable	CHEK 221:18
d. is incurable	SHAK 707:11
d. of admiration	MACA 507:10
d. of modern life	ARNO 30:12
d. of not listening	SHAK 707:6
incurable d. of writing	JUVE 451:6
Life is an incurable d.	COWL 254:20
Love's a d.	MACA 506:12
no Cure for this D.	BELL 67:21
Progress is a comfortable d.	CUMM 262:9
remedy is worse than the d.	BACO 47:31
sexually transmitted d.	SAYI 685:1
suffering from the particular d.	JERO 433:12
this long d., my life	POPE 614:18
twenty drugs for each d.	OSLE 589:3
diseased mind d.	BYRO 186:21
minister to a mind d.	SHAK 722:17
To know ourselves d.	YOUN 876:27
diseases cure of all d.	BROW 163:14
Desperate d.	PROV 629:40
D. and sad Old Age	VIRG 830:9
D. desperate grown	SHAK 703:23
D. of the soul	CICE 232:12
extreme d.	HIPP 399:14
spread d.	OFFI 584:3
disenchantment mistook d. for truth	SART 681:17
disentangle cannot d.	ANON 20:10
disestablishment sense of d.	KING 463:18
disgrace author of his own d.	COWP 255:6
Even to a full d.	SHAK 698:13
in d. with fortune	SHAK 737:21
Intellectual d. Stares	AUDE 37:11
no d. t'be poor	HUBB 417:16
passing d.	DIDE 282:12
Poverty is no d.	PROV 641:44
private life is a d.	ANON 20:3
public and merited d.	STEV 776:8
disgraced dies . . . rich dies d.	CARN 201:3
disgraceful something d. in mind	JUVE 451:21
disgruntled if not actually d.	WODE 861:21
disguise better go in d.	BRAT 155:9
D. fair nature	SHAK 708:16
d. which can hide love	LA R 481:20
men in d.	ABSE 1:3
naked is the best d.	CONG 246:29
this identical d.	BROO 160:1
disguised England is a d. republic	BAGE 50:21
disgust capacity for d.	MANN 519:11
not moments of d.	VOLT 834:14
play began to d.	EVEL 321:21
dish discovery of a new d.	BRIL 157:9
d. fit for the gods	SHAK 712:6
d. ran away	NURS 578:21
in a lordly d.	BIBL 83:2
than an empty d.	PROV 627:29
dishclout Romeo's a d.	SHAK 732:33
dishcover d. the riddle	CARR 203:25
dishes these the choice d.	GARR 349:13
these were the d.	AUGU 39:4
washing of d.	EPIT 318:1
who does the d.	FREN 342:10
dishonour another unto d.	BIBL 111:8
rooted in d.	TENN 794:13
dishonourable d. graves	SHAK 711:19
disiecti *Etiam d. membra poetae*	HORA 414:13
disinfectants best of d.	BRAN 155:2
disinheriting d. countenance	SHER 748:28
disintegration d. and dismemberment	GLAD 360:4
out of its own d.	FUEN 345:26
disinterested d. endeavour	ARNO 31:18
D. intellectual curiosity	TREV 815:6
D. love for all living	DARW 266:8
dislike d. every thing	CENT 213:2
d. the matter	SHAK 694:21
hesitate d.	POPE 614:22
I, too, d. it	MOOR 557:14
like and d. the same	SALL 679:7
dismal beset him round With d. stories	BUNY 171:25
d. precocity of poverty	THAC 802:22
D. Science	CARL 200:13
dismayed neither be thou d.	BIBL 82:24
Was there a man d.	TENN 793:4
dismemberment d. of the Empire	GLAD 360:4
dismiss d. such a good master	BEAU 63:4
Lord, d. us	BUCK 170:2
Disney Mouse over at D.	MAYE 529:7
of Euro D.	BALL 56:10
of Euro D.	MNOU 551:14
Disneyfication D. of Christianity	CUPI 262:19
disobedience children of d.	BIBL 114:9
crown d. with laurels	KLEI 469:10
man's first d.	MILT 541:8
disorder D., horror, fear	SHAK 731:1
d. in its geometry	DE B 269:19
sweet d. in the dress	HERR 396:1
with brave d. part	POPE 615:27
dispatch in business than d.	ADDI 4:25
displeasing not d. to us	LA R 482:11
displeasure away in his d.	CULP 262:1
dispoged when I am so d.	DICK 278:21
disposable everything has to be d.	MILL 537:10
disposal d. of the King	CHRI 227:4
dispose d. of all things	ANON 23:9
d. the way of thy servants	BOOK 138:2
disposes God d.	THOM 804:17
disposition antic d.	SHAK 700:28
truant d.	SHAK 699:24
dispossessed imprisoned or d.	MAGN 515:1
dispraised Of whom to be d.	MILT 544:21
disprove able to d. my assertion	RUSS 675:13
disputants d. put me in mind	ADDI 5:20
disputations Doubtful is.	BIBL 111:18
dispute great d. between you	VIRG 831:23
disqualified d. for holding any office	MORE 559:5
disquieted d. within me	BOOK 142:5
disquieteth d. himself in vain	BOOK 141:29
disregard Atones for later d.	FROS 344:21
dissatisfied human being d.	MILL 536:16
I'm d.	MOOR 557:19
Not one is d.	WHIT 852:11
dissect creatures you d.	POPE 615:12
murder to d.	WORD 869:15
dissent dissidence of d.	BURK 173:14
dissenters Barn-door fowls for d.	SMIT 758:8
dissentious you d. rogues	SHAK 698:3
dissimulation one word—d.	DISR 285:24
dissipation d. without pleasure	GIBB 355:2
dissolute then delicate, finally d.	VICO 827:5
dissolution lingering d.	BECK 64:3
dissolve d., and quite forget	KEAT 456:5
d. the people	BREC 156:3
dissolved d. into something	CATH 209:13
tabernacle were d.	BIBL 113:9
dissonance barbarous d.	MILT 539:8
distaff mind the d.	LEWI 492:5
distance at such a d. from them	HEIN 389:14
d. is nothing	DU D 298:11
d. lends enchantment	CAMP 195:12
D. lends enchantment	PROV 630:6

longest d. between two places WILL 858:5
scale of the d. SALI 678:14
distant d. from Heaven BURT 181:17
music of a d. drum FITZ 331:16
prospect of a d. good DRYD 295:28
relation of d. misery GIBB 354:14
distempered questions the d. part ELIO 309:12
distempers all the ugly d. WILS 859:22
distillation d. of rumour CARL 199:25
distinction D. is what we all seek REYN 659:8
make no d. BUSH 182:8
think that there is no d. JOHN 439:22
distinctive man's d. mark BROW 165:15
distinguish style which will d. MATH 527:14
distinguished d. above the rest HOME 404:14
d. by that circumstance THOR 809:24
d. thing JAME 430:11
distinguishes mind d. in thought THOM 805:11
distort then you can d. them TWAI 820:28
distracted this d. globe SHAK 700:23
distraction thrown Into a fine d. HERR 396:1
distress d. of another RICH 660:15
every one that was in d. BIBL 84:8
Far as d. GREV 372:14
out of their d. BOOK 147:18
pray in their d. BLAK 127:8
distressed afflicted, or d. BOOK 135:7
I am d. for thee BIBL 84:13
distresses d. of our friends SWIF 784:8
distressful most d. country POLI 612:24
distribute d. as fairly as he can LOWE 502:13
distrust d. of the people ROMI 666:13
have to d. each other WILL 858:1
simplicity and d. it WHIT 851:5
ditch [Channel] is a mere d. NAPO 567:11
die in the last d. WILL 857:3
D.-delivered. by a drab SHAK 721:17
dull as d. water DICK 280:12
environed with a great d. CROM 260:19
fall into the d. BIBL 101:22
makes a straight-cut d. THOR 809:5
ditchers gardeners, d. SHAK 704:9
ditties amorous d. MILT 541:24
ditty played an ancient d. KEAT 454:14
diurnal her d. round WORD 866:3
dive must d. below DRYD 295:8
diver Don't forget the d. CATC 207:13
diversa laudet d. sequentis HORA 414:6
diverse d., and like the waves MONT 554:17
diversity d. of human events MONT 555:18
some d. BARC 58:5
universal quality is d. MONT 555:20
divide D. and rule PROV 630:7
d. the spoil BIBL 92:13
though he d. the hoof BIBL 81:26
divided All that is d. HÖLD 403:3
d. aims ARNO 30:12
d. by a common language MISQ 547:12
D. by the morning tea MACN 513:10
d. duty SHAK 728:13
d. into three parts CAES 192:16
d. self LAIN 476:5
d. the spoil BOOK 144:8
d. we fall PROV 646:1
has harshly d. SCHI 683:10
He d. the sea BOOK 145:7
house d. cannot stand PROV 634:46
If a house be d. BIBL 103:28
in their death not d. BIBL 84:12
dividend no d. from time's tomorrow
SASS 682:7
divides what d. men KING 464:19
dividing by d. we fall DICK 282:7
divination d. too will perish MAND 519:5
divine believes Kingsley a d. STUB 779:8
Come down, O Love d. LITT 495:12
d. Majority DICK 281:20
d. plain face LAMB 477:9
d. powers take note VIRG 829:2
faculty d. WORD 865:11
good d. that follows his own SHAK 724:2
hand that made us is d. ADDI 5:18
heavy, but no less d. BYRO 188:25

horror and its beauty are d. SHEL 745:14
human form d. BLAK 127:9
knowledge was d. TRAH 814:9
More needs she the d. SHAK 722:12
one far-off d. event TENN 796:7
possess d. legislation MEND 531:24
Right D. of Kings POPE 613:23
say that D. providence JOHN 434:11
some d. despair TENN 799:10
To forgive, d. POPE 616:10
to forgive d. PROV 645:25
what the form d. LAND 478:5
divinely most d. fair TENN 793:9
divineness participation of d. BACO 45:11
divinest two d. things HUNT 421:9
diving-bell religious d. FOST 338:20
divinity d. doth hedge a king SHAK 704:1
d. in odd numbers SHAK 725:20
d. that shapes our ends SHAK 704:21
d. that stirs ADDI 4:21
mysteries in d. BROW 162:25
piece of d. in us BROW 163:16
division D. is as bad ANON 19:2
we make no d. between any KORA 471:11
divisions growing factions and d. OTWA 589:14
How many d. has he got STAL 769:16
divisos penitus toto d. orbe VIRG 831:15
divorce long d. of steel SHAK 710:14
divorces d. his first wife TALM 789:27
dixeris D. egregie notum HORA 408:18
dixit Ipse d. CICE 231:20
dizzy d. 'tis to cast one's eyes SHAK 716:15
DNA cannot cheat on D. WARD 839:24
do All one has to d. is I-HS 424:15
Can I d. you now, sir CATC 207:7
can't all d. everything VIRG 832:8
damned if you d. DOW 292:2
did not d. things themselves RAVE 656:1
D. as I say PROV 630:8
D. as I say SELD 691:19
D. as you would be done by CHES 223:3
D. as you would be done by PROV 630:9
D. IT YOURSELF BARH 58:15
Do not d. to others what CONF 246:16
d. not to your neighbour HILL 399:4
don't d. it at all BISH 122:12
d. only one thing SMIL 755:20
D. other men DICK 278:20
D. unto others as you would PROV 630:33
d. what I please FRED 342:4
d. what is right HUXL 423:7
D. what thou wilt CROW 261:14
d. what thou wouldst do HATC 384:4
d. ye even so to them BIBL 99:27
fine pleasure is not to d. HOPK 408:11
George—don't d. that CATC 207:20
HOW NOT TO D. IT DICK 278:13
I can d. no other LUTH 505:4
If to d. were as easy SHAK 724:2
I'll do, I'll do, and I'll d. SHAK 718:6
I'll d.'t before I speak SHAK 714:19
know not what they d. BIBL 106:23
Let's d. it PORT 619:15
Let us d.—or die BURN 179:10
let us d. or die CAMP 195:7
Love and d. what you will AUGU 39:18
never know what you can d. PROV 648:17
not knowing what they d. SHAK 727:29
people who d. things MORR 561:13
Say little and d. much SHAM 738:30
so much to d. RHOD 659:12
supposed to d. anyway TRUM 817:16
thousand things to d. BEVE 77:7
to my servant, D. this BIBL 100:7
We cannot d. it, Sir CARR 203:15
what I d. in any thing HERB 394:5
What must I d. to be saved BIBL 109:32
what we repeatedly d. ARIS 27:9
what you are afraid to d. EMER 315:2
would they should d. unto me BOOK 138:11
you not able to d. AUGU 39:7
doc cards with a man called D. ALGR 12:15
What's up, D. CATC 208:33

docent dum d. discunt SENE 692:14
doctor any other d. whatsoever HOBB 400:17
d. does not give you a year STEV 775:24
d. found, when she was dead GOLD 364:15
d. full of phrase ARNO 31:6
fee the d. DRYD 295:20
God and the d. OWEN 590:22
keeps the d. away PROV 626:31
doctors believe the d. SALI 678:15
best d. are Dr Diet PROV 627:19
budge d. of the stoic fur MILT 539:10
D. in verse THOM 807:6
d. know a hopeless case CUMM 262:10
More d. smoke Camels ADVE 8:5
when d. disagree POPE 615:3
when the d. try LUCR 504:8
doctrinal On the d. side QUIN 652:1
doctrine all the winds of d. MILT 546:6
blast of vain d. BOOK 136:14
d. of ignoble ease ROOS 667:17
d. of the enclitic De BROW 165:26
d. something you kill for BENN 70:2
every wind of d. BIBL 114:5
life and d. BOOK 137:7
loved the d. DEFO 270:17
Much d. lies under FANS 323:3
not for the d. POPE 616:4
doctrines d. without words LAO 479:7
makes all d. plain BUTL 183:25
documents d. and friends SPAR 765:7
dodge those who d. EBNE 302:12
dodger artful D. DICK 280:2
dodgy d. dossier NEWS 573:6
doers be ye d. of the word BIBL 116:19
Evil d. evil dreaders PROV 631:37
does D. she or doesn't she ADVE 7:16
He who can d. PROV 634:18
doest That thou d., do quickly BIBL 108:11
dog Am I a d. BIBL 84:6
barking d. never bites PROV 627:9
beaten d. beneath the hail POUN 621:10
better than his d. TENN 796:23
Beware of the d. PETR 605:5
black d. JOHN 443:19
call a d. Hervey JOHN 438:23
cut-throat d. SHAK 724:9
D. does not eat dog PROV 630:10
d. in the night-time DOYL 292:17
d. is allowed one bite PROV 631:18
d. is for life SLOG 755:2
d. is turned to his own vomit BIBL 117:15
d. it was that died GOLD 364:16
d. returneth to his vomit BIBL 88:41
D. returns to his Vomit KIPL 466:2
d. returns to its vomit PROV 630:11
d. shall bear him company POPE 616:21
d.-star rages POPE 614:15
d. starved at his master's gate BLAK 124:11
d.'s tooth PROV 645:13
d.'s walking on his hinder legs JOHN 440:7
d. that will fetch a bone PROV 630:13
D., the Meat and the Reflection AESO 8:37
d. with eyes as big as ANDE 15:9
engine of pollution, the d. SPAR 765:15
Every d. has his day PROV 631:17
every d. his day KING 464:14
face of a d. GARC 349:3
Give a d. a bad name PROV 632:46
good d. goes to church PROV 633:52
Has a the Buddha-Nature MUMO 565:4
heart to a d. to tear KIPL 467:4
I had rather be a d. SHAK 713:21
I never heard thy d. HEYW 398:3
Is thy servant a d. BIBL 85:31
keep a d. and bark yourself PROV 647:23
lame d. over a stile CHIL 226:7
let no d. bark SHAK 723:24
limps the hungry d. BLOK 129:6
live d. is better PROV 637:49
living d. BIBL 90:8
lost d. somewhere ANOU 24:13
Lovell our d. COLL 242:23
Love me, love my d. PROV 638:10

dog (*cont.*):
man bites a d. — DANA 264:3
more ridiculous than a d. — NERV 571:2
My d.! what remedy remains — COWP 255:17
nobody knows you're a d. — CART 205:14
over the lazy d. — ANON 20:2
poor d. had none — NURS 580:10
poor d. that's not worth — PROV 636:5
poor d. Tray — CAMP 195:8
stick to beat a d. — PROV 636:17
teach an old d. new tricks — PROV 647:46
to a d.'s tail — YEAT 875:5
tongue of d. — SHAK 721:16
very d. to the commonalty — SHAK 698:2
was there ever d. — YEAT 875:3
ways of killing a d. — PROV 644:11
ways of killing a d. — PROV 644:12
whose d. are you — POPE 614:13
woman, d., and walnut tree — PROV 647:29
working like a d. — LENN 489:9
Doge quiet D. of Venice — WALP 838:9
dogged d. as does it — PROV 636:34
d. as does it — TROL 816:14
doggie How much is that d. — MERR 532:25
dogma Any stigma to beat a d. — GUED 374:5
d. has been the fundamental principle — NEWM 572:3
no d., no Dean — DISR 286:26
dogmatize d. and am contradicted — JOHN 444:17
dogs all things as straw d. — LAO 479:8
cruel as d. one to another — PEPY 603:11
d. and apes — BROW 165:24
D. are Shakespearean — SCHW 687:10
d. bark at me — SHAK 731:11
D. bark, but the caravan — PROV 630:12
d. do bark — NURS 578:18
d. eat of the crumbs — BIBL 101:23
d. go on with their doggy life — AUDE 37:17
d., horses — JENY 433:2
d. licked his sores — BIBL 106:6
D. look up to us — CHUR 231:3
d. of Europe bark — AUDE 37:11
fought the d. — BROW 167:1
gaze of d. — CALV 194:6
go to the d. tonight — HERB 393:10
hates d. and babies — ROST 670:8
Lame d. over stiles — KING 464:5
Let d. delight — WATT 841:14
Let sleeping d. lie — PROV 637:20
let slip the d. of war — SHAK 712:23
lie down with d. — PROV 635:29
like dancing d. — JOHN 441:21
little d. and all — SHAK 716:6
little d., with golden hair — LUTH 505:6
mad and hungry d. — MCKA 511:15
Mad d. and Englishmen — COWA 253:15
more I like d. — ROLA 666:8
more one values d. — TOUS 814:3
na men, but d. — BURN 180:7
People who keep d. — STRI 779:3
Throw physic to the d. — SHAK 722:18
two d. are fighting — PROV 647:15
without are d. — BIBL 119:23
doing As for D.-good — THOR 809:16
continuance in well d. — BIBL 110:23
d. in that galley — MOLI 552:10
joy's soul lies in the d. — SHAK 734:13
learn by d. — ARIS 27:10
not be weary in well d. — BIBL 113:26
one way of d. — RUSK 674:3
put me to d. — METH 533:8
see what she's d. — PUNC 650:1
still be d. — BUTL 183:13
This is the Lord's d. — BOOK 148:11
doings child is known by his d. — BIBL 88:26
doleful Knight of the D. Countenance — CERV 213:3
dolendum d. est Primum ipsi tibi — HORA 409:4
dolente CITTÀ D. — DANT 264:13
doll d. in the doll's house — DICK 284:7
living d., everywhere you look — PLAT 608:3
dollar almighty d. — IRVI 425:23

Another day, another d. — PROV 626:25
billion d. country — FOST 338:18
costs only a d. — ARDE 26:4
dolmens d. round my childhood — MONT 554:16
dolore Nessun maggior d. — DANT 264:18
dolorem iubes renovare d. — VIRG 829:4
Dolores splendid and sterile D. — SWIN 785:8
dolorous d. mansions — MILT 540:27
dolour d. of pad and paper-weight — ROET 665:6
d. that they made — MALO 518:3
dolphin d.-torn, that gong-tormented — YEAT 872:12
mermaid on a d.'s back — SHAK 726:5
dolphins butter made of d.' milk — JONS 445:15
gentler d. — MOOR 558:3
dome d. of many-coloured glass — SHEL 743:21
d. of the sky — WORD 864:21
singing beneath the d. — VERL 826:12
starlit or a moonlit d. — YEAT 872:11
domestic appreciate d. bliss — SANT 680:15
d. business — MONT 555:6
d. sort which never stirs — SHER 748:29
Malice d. — SHAK 721:3
men call d. bliss — PATM 599:13
respectable d. establishment — BENN 70:7
tranquil current of d. happiness — BRUN 168:22
domesticate d. the Recording Angel — STEV 776:1
domi Res angusta d. — JUVE 450:21
dominant Hark, the d.'s persistence — BROW 167:26
domination against white d. — MAND 518:16
dominations Thrones, d. — MILT 543:22
domine D., defende nos — GODL 361:1
dominion death hath no more d. — BIBL 110:34
death shall have no d. — THOM 805:14
d. from sea to sea — BIBL 119:28
d. of kings changed — PRIC 622:15
d. of the English — ANON 20:12
d. of the master — HUME 420:7
hand that holds d. — THOM 805:20
His d. shall be also — BOOK 144:19
let them have d. — BIBL 78:16
Man's d. — BURN 179:25
dominions His Majesty's d. — NORT 577:3
not set in my d. — SCHI 683:13
domino 'falling d.' principle — EISE 306:8
dominus D. illuminatio mea — BIBL 119:25
D. illuminatio mea — MOTT 563:8
D. vobiscum — MISS 546:16
Nisi D. — BIBL 120:5
domum Ite d. saturae — VIRG 832:11
domus Stat fortuna d. — VIRG 833:6
don D. John of Austria is going — CHES 224:10
d. manqué — LAMB 477:15
quiet flows the D. — SHOL 749:21
Remote and ineffectual D. — BELL 68:11
dona d. nobis pacem — MISS 549:19
Requiem aeternam d. eis — MISS 550:4
timeo Danaos et d. ferentes — VIRG 829:6
done Been there, d. that — SAYI 684:2
decide that nothing can be d. — ALLE 13:5
Do as you would be d. by — CHES 223:3
Do as you would be d. by — PROV 630:9
D. because we are too menny — HARD 380:14
d. so far is nothing — NAPO 567:9
d. the state some service — SHAK 729:23
d. very well out of the war — BALD 53:2
d. when 'tis done — SHAK 719:6
ever d. for us — FILM 329:23
he d. her wrong — SONG 762:7
If you want anything d. — THAT 803:12
Inasmuch as ye have d. — BIBL 103:7
it will be d. — ORWE 588:4
men and women have d. — AUGU 39:7
My work is d. — EAST 302:9
My work is d. — MILL 536:18
Nay, I have d. — DRAY 293:14
not a genius, I'm d. for — BALZ 57:5
not d. in a corner — BIBL 110:16
Nothing to be d. — BECK 64:15
remained to be d. — LUCA 503:18
something d. — LONG 500:5

Something must be d. — WHIT 851:7
surprised to find it d. — JOHN 440:7
that which is d. — BIBL 89:19
Things won are d. — SHAK 734:13
this that thou hast d. — BIBL 79:8
thou hast not d. — DONN 288:18
want a thing d. well — PROV 635:34
we have d. those things — BOOK 133:5
What could she have d. — YEAT 874:7
Whatever man has d. — PROV 646:19
What is to be d. — LENI 488:1
What's d. cannot be undone — PROV 646:27
What's d. cannot be undone — SHAK 722:11
what's d. is done — SHAK 721:2
what should be d. — MELB 531:4
dong D. with a luminous nose — LEAR 485:16
donkey dead d. — DICK 281:1
donkeys Lions led by d. — MILI 535:12
Donne another Newton, a new D. — HUXL 423:1
John D., Anne Donne — DONN 290:14
donné Si le Roi m'avait d. — ANON 22:10
Donough Our fair-haired D. — SONG 763:8
Don Quixote D., Robinson Crusoe — JOHN 444:25
dons If the D. sight Devon — NEWB 571:8
don't about to marry.—'d.' — PUNC 649:14
damned if you d. — DOW 292:2
D. ask me, ask the horse — FREU 342:20
doodle Cock a d. doo! — NURS 578:6
Yankee D. — SONG 763:17
doom changed his d. — CLEV 235:15
d. assigned — TENN 798:13
great d.'s image — SHAK 720:17
Master of the Day of D. — KORA 470:18
national d. is sealed — HEAR 388:2
regardless of their d. — GRAY 370:11
scaffold and the d. — AYTO 44:6
to the edge of d. — SHAK 738:17
doomed D. for a certain term — SHAK 700:16
Doomsday D. is near — SHAK 706:17
Doon braes o' bonny D. — BURN 177:16
door angel from your d. — BLAK 127:10
beating on the d. — YEAT 873:13
coming in at one d. — BEDE 65:8
creaking d. hangs longest — PROV 629:26
Death's shadow at the d. — BLUN 129:10
d. flew open — HOFF 402:7
d. must be either shut — PROV 630:31
d. we never opened — ELIO 309:4
handle of the big front d. — GILB 357:28
hard at death's d. — BOOK 147:16
I am the d. — BIBL 108:1
knock at the d. — LAMB 476:16
knocking at Preferment's d. — ARNO 30:8
knocking at the d. — SHAW 742:19
make a d. and bar — BIBL 97:26
my d. stayed shut — RACI 653:3
Never open the d. — GRAC 367:7
prejudices through the d. — FRED 342:2
rapping at my chamber d. — POE 610:19
stand at the d., and knock — BIBL 118:2
Then—shuts the D. — DICK 281:20
through the d. with a gun — CHAN 215:14
When one d. shuts — PROV 646:42
when the d. opens — GREE 371:18
whining of a d. — DONN 290:10
wide as a church d. — SHAK 732:22
wrong side of the d. — CHES 224:1
doorkeeper d. in the house of my God — BOOK 145:15
doormat d. in a world of boots — RHYS 659:17
d. or a prostitute — WEST 848:23
doors close softly the d. — JUST 450:6
Death has a thousand d. — MASS 527:12
Death hath so many d. — FLET 335:8
d. of perception — BLAK 126:22
Men shut their d. — SHAK 734:6
ten thousand several d. — WEBS 844:11
thousand d. open on to it — SENE 692:20
with both d. open — HUGH 417:17
ye everlasting d. — BOOK 141:2
your living d. — MILT 543:28
doorstep do this on the d. — JUNO 450:5
sweep his own d. — PROV 635:9

doorway from d. to doorway — VERG 826:4
dooryard last in the d. bloomed — WHIT 852:20
Dorcas D.: this woman — BIBL 109:24
dormitat bonus d. Homerus — HORA 409:14
Dorset FUNERAL MONDAY D. — BEER 66:5
dossier dodgy d. — NEWS 573:6
  draft d. produced — GILL 358:17
dot cherish the pale blue d. — SAGA 677:8
dotage streams of d. flow — JOHN 438:10
dote D. on his imperfections — EPHE 316:7
Dotheboys D. Hall — DICK 279:6
dots damned d. meant — CHUR 229:1
double Double, d. toil and trouble — SHAK 721:15
  Labour's d. whammy — POLI 612:30
  leading a d. life — WILD 854:23
  peace of the d.-bed — CAMP 195:1
doubles d. your chances for a date — ALLE 13:16
doublet bought his d. in Italy — SHAK 724:4
  tailor make thy d. — SHAK 735:19
doublethink D. means the power — ORWE 587:17
doubt Book wherein is no d. — KORA 470:20
  curiosity, freckles, and d. — PARK 596:3
  do not make one d. — NEWM 572:5
  d. and sorrow — BARI 58:17
  d. is Devil-born — TENN 795:26
  D. is not a pleasant — VOLT 835:2
  Humility is the only d. — BLAK 125:4
  in d., strike it out — TWAI 820:22
  in d. what should be done — MELB 531:4
  let us never, never d. — BELL 68:15
  Life is d. — UNAM 821:12
  more faith in honest d. — TENN 795:27
  No possible d. whatever — GILB 356:11
  Our d. is our passion — JAME 429:19
  philosophy calls all in d. — DONN 287:13
  shameful to d. one's friends — LA R 481:21
  sunnier side of d. — TENN 792:18
  time will d. of Rome — BYRO 189:3
  When in d., do nowt — PROV 646:40
  wherefore didst thou d. — BIBL 101:20
doubter d. and the doubt — EMER 314:12
doubtful D. disputations — BIBL 111:18
  I die d. — ARIS 28:12
doubting D. Castle — BUNY 171:13
doubtless d. come again with joy — BOOK 149:1
doubts Ah whiles hae ma d. — PUNC 650:7
  end in d. — BACO 45:8
  His d. are better — HARD 380:8
  Kind jealous d. — ROCH 664:13
  saucy d. and fears — SHAK 721:7
Douglas doughty D. — BALL 54:4
  Like D. conquer — HOME 404:4
dove all the d. — CRAS 259:2
  at eagles with a d. — HERB 394:23
  d. found no rest — BIBL 79:23
  on the burnished d. — TENN 796:22
  sweet d. died — KEAT 454:26
  wings like a d. — BOOK 143:10
  wings of a d. — BOOK 144:8
dovecote eagle in a d. — SHAK 698:16
Dover farthing candle at D. — JOHN 440:6
  milestones on the D. Road — DICK 278:14
  white cliffs of D. — BURT 180:20
doves condemns the d. — JUVE 450:16
  d.' eyes — BIBL 91:4
  harmless as d. — BIBL 100:25
  moan of d. — TENN 799:22
dovetailedness universal d. — DICK 279:17
dowagers d. for deans — TENN 799:3
dower faith's transcendent d. — WORD 868:26
  truth then be thy d. — SHAK 714:17
dowie d. dens — BALL 54:13
down born with D.'s syndrome — DE G 271:18
  D. among the dead — DYER 301:11
  d. and out in Paris — ORWE 587:1
  d. and out of breath — SHAK 706:31
  d. express in the small of the back — WODE 861:26
  D. in the forest — SIMP 753:2
  D. into the darkness — MILL 536:20
  D. to Gehenna — KIPL 466:13
  Easy is the way d. — VIRG 830:5
  fled Him, d. the nights — THOM 807:14

go d. to the sea — BOOK 147:17
Had me low and had me d. — GERS 353:12
He that is d. — BUNY 171:21
kicked d. stairs — HALI 377:24
knowest my d.-sitting — BOOK 149:15
little, lost, D. churches — KIPL 467:13
meet 'em on your way d. — MIZN 551:11
quite, quite, d. — SHAK 702:9
soft young d. of her — MEW 533:14
staying d. with him — WASH 840:13
What goes up must come d. — PROV 646:21
downfall regress is either a d. — BACO 47:8
downhearted Are we d. — KNIG 469:12
  Are we d. — MILI 535:4
downhill run by itself except d. — SAYI 684:4
downs in the D. the fleet was moored — GAY 351:24
downstairs kick me d. — BICK 120:20
downwards gross flesh sinks d. — SHAK 731:8
  look no way but d. — BUNY 171:19
doxy Heterodoxy or Thy-d. — CARL 200:1
dozens Whom he reckons up by d. — GILB 357:27
drab Ditch-delivered by a d. — SHAK 721:17
dragging naked, d. themselves — GINS 358:22
dragnet swept like a d. — DRYD 297:22
dragon d. and his wrath — SHAK 714:18
  d.-green, the luminous — FLEC 334:10
  d. of the hills — SUTT 781:21
  d. of the sea — MELV 531:11
  fought against the d. — BIBL 118:24
  laid hold on the d. — BIBL 119:12
  lion and the d. — BOOK 146:2
  O to be a d. — MOOR 557:13
  under the d.'s tail — SHAK 715:1
dragonish cloud that's d. — SHAK 695:16
dragons Bores have succeeded to d. — DISR 286:17
  brother to d. — BIBL 87:5
  d., and all deeps — BOOK 150:9
  d. in their pleasant palaces — BIBL 92:19
  habitation of d. — BIBL 93:6
  laugh at live d. — TOLK 813:4
drain From this foul d. pure gold — TOCQ 812:16
drains Deity and the D. — STRA 778:12
  opiate to the d. — KEAT 456:2
drake D. he's in his hammock — NEWB 571:9
drama d. onto the moral plane — GIDE 355:20
  d. out of a crisis — ADVE 8:27
  d.'s laws — JOHN 438:3
  great d. critic — TYNA 820:29
dramas other people's d. — LERM 490:3
dramatist d. want more liberties — JAME 429:12
dramatize D. it, dramatize it — JAME 429:8
Drang Sturm und D. — KAUF 453:12
drank d. my ale — FARQ 324:2
  d. of Aganippe well — SIDN 750:20
  d. without the provocation — SWIF 782:13
drastic D. measures — ANST 24:16
draughts susceptible to d. — WILD 854:24
draw be able to d. upon — HORA 409:17
  d. like these children — PICA 606:11
  D. near with faith — BOOK 137:9
  D. not up seas — DONN 289:22
  d. to our end — BIBL 97:3
  d. you to her — DRYD 297:9
  rarely d. what I see — HEPW 392:17
drawers d. of water — BIBL 82:28
drawing back to the old d. board — CART 205:17
  D. is the true test — INGR 425:14
  d. on the level of an untaught child — BLUN 129:14
  no d. back — BRON 159:1
drawing-room feelings of women in a d. — WOOL 864:10
  same men in the d. — HALI 377:11
  through my d. — EDEN 303:5
dread d. beat — JOHN 435:1
  d. of beatings — BETJ 76:8
  From Brig o' D. — BALL 55:3
  let him be your d. — BIBL 92:12
  Nor d. nor hope attend — YEAT 873:2
  secret d. — ADDI 4:20
  What d. hand — BLAK 128:4

dreaded most d. instrument — WORD 867:1
dreadful acting of a d. thing — SHAK 712:4
  city of d. night — THOM 808:23
  deed of d. note — SHAK 721:4
dreading D. and hoping all — YEAT 873:2
dreadnoughts as much to keep up as two D. — LLOY 496:13
dream as a d. Dies — WATT 842:7
  as a d. doth flatter — SHAK 738:8
  behold it was a d. — BUNY 171:18
  but a brief d. — PETR 604:18
  children d. not — BROW 163:19
  d., a lightning flash — MAHĀ 515:13
  d. But of a shadow — CHAP 216:2
  d. I am dreaming — COWA 253:18
  d. my dreams away — FLAN 332:21
  D. of a funeral — PROV 630:34
  d. of fair women — TENN 793:8
  d. of our own imagination — BACO 48:21
  d. of peace — HUNT 421:4
  d. of reason — GOYA 367:6
  d. of the devil — BARH 58:9
  d. that is dying — O'SH 588:23
  D. the impossible — DARI 266:2
  d. things that never were — SHAW 739:11
  d. within a dream — POE 610:17
  d. you are crossing — GILB 356:23
  falls into a d. — CONR 249:3
  freshness of a d. — WORD 867:2
  from the d. of life — SHEL 743:17
  glory and the d. — WORD 867:7
  hideous d. — SHAK 712:4
  if I d. I have you — DONN 289:3
  I have a d. — KING 463:11
  In a d. you are never eighty — SEXT 693:8
  Is a d. a lie — SPRI 769:6
  It was no d. — WYAT 871:6
  life to a d. — MONT 555:17
  like unto them that d. — BOOK 148:24
  love's young d. — MOOR 558:10
  No one can d. any more — SCHI 683:8
  not d. them — KING 464:4
  old men's d. — DRYD 294:16
  Paradise in a d. — COLE 241:18
  peace is a d. — MOLT 553:7
  salesman is got to d. — MILL 537:9
  say what d. it was — SHAK 726:29
  sight to d. of — COLE 239:6
  silence of a d. — ROSS 668:19
  so d. all night — KEAT 454:23
  Soft! I did but d. — SHAK 731:27
  thou must not d. — ARNO 29:9
  till you find your d. — HAMM 378:15
  To sleep: perchance to d. — SHAK 701:26
  vanished like a d. — CARL 200:7
  waking d. — KEAT 456:12
  We live, as we d. — CONR 248:20
  what my d. was — SHAK 727:1
  without my d. — ROST 670:4
dreamed d. in a dream — WHIT 851:20
  d. I saw Joe Hill — HAYE 385:15
  d. of, in any philosophy — HALD 376:11
  d. of the devil — ANST 24:14
  d. out in words — MURR 566:3
  d. that I dwelt — BUNN 170:17
  d. that life was beauty — HOOP 406:11
  he d., and behold — BIBL 80:9
  I've d. of cheese — STEV 775:23
dreamer Beautiful d. — FOST 338:21
  Behold, this d. cometh — BIBL 80:18
  d. of dreams — BIBL 82:14
  D. of dreams — MORR 560:13
  not a d. — FOX 340:2
  poet and the d. — KEAT 454:17
dreamers d. of another existence — BYRO 192:1
  We are the d. of dreams — O'SH 588:22
dreaming butterfly d. that — CHUA 227:11
  demon's that is d. — POE 611:4
  d. of a white Christmas — BERL 73:6
  D.' of thee — WALL 836:10
  d. on the verge of strife — CORN 252:3
  d. spires — ARNO 30:25
  world on d. fed — YEAT 874:23

every D. in London MACD 510:11
I am D. of Malfi still WEBS 844:9
That's my last D. BROW 166:19
duck D. and cover OFFI 584:7
just forgot to d. DEMP 273:2
walks like a d. CARE 199:3
duckling when I was the ugly d. ANDE 15:7
ducks d., produce bad parents MORS 561:17
I turn to d. HARV 384:1
stealing d. ARAB 25:12
dude d. with a pencil DIDD 282:9
due Give the Devil his d. PROV 633:3
in d. time BOOK 135:2
to every one his d. JUST 450:7
without d. process of law CONS 250:6
dues Render to all their d. BIBL 111:15
dugs old man with wrinkled d. ELIO 311:13
duke D. of Plaza Toro GILB 356:10
everybody praised the D. SOUT 764:8
fully-equipped d. LLOY 496:13
knows enough who knows a d. COWP 256:31
dukedom d. large enough SHAK 733:15
dukes drawing room full of d. AUDE 38:19
dulce D. est desipere HORA 414:5
D. et decorum est HORA 412:17
D. et decorum est OWEN 591:6
D. ridentem HORA 412:1
dulcet d. and harmonious breath SHAK 726:5
dulci qui miscuit utile d. HORA 409:12
dulcimer damsel with a d. COLE 240:8
psaltery, d. BIBL 95:22
dull at best but d. and hoary VAUG 825:10
Clean. Christian. D. SHIE 749:14
dictionaries is d. work JOHN 435:21
d. and deep potations GIBB 354:20
d. as ditch water DICK 280:12
d. in a new way JOHN 441:12
d. in himself FOOT 336:12
d. it is to pause TENN 800:16
D. 'mongst the dullest CHUR 228:17
d. product of a scoffer's pen WORD 865:14
D. would he be of soul WORD 865:7
makes Jack a d. boy PROV 626:23
not bred so d. SHAK 724:24
paper appears d. STEE 770:16
Sherry is d. JOHN 440:5
smoothly d. POPE 611:20
some d. opiate KEAT 456:2
very d., dreary affair MAUG 528:13
What's this d. town to me KEPP 461:4
who can be d. in Fleet Street LAMB 477:4
dullard d.'s envy of brilliant men BEER 66:3
dullness cause of d. in others FOOT 336:12
d. and stupidity ASTE 34:13
Gentle D. POPE 611:16
his serene d. FLAU 333:3
dumb as a sheep is d. BIBL 94:4
d. son of a bitch TRUM 817:23
d. to tell THOM 805:18
My lips kissed d. SWIN 786:1
Nature is d. TURG 819:3
otherwise I shall be d. KEAT 458:5
So d. he can't fart JOHN 435:11
takes 40 d. animals SLOG 755:6
tongue of the d. BIBL 93:10
dump What a d. FILM 329:22
dumpling Diddle, diddle, d. NURS 578:11
dun her breasts are d. SHAK 738:19
Duncan fatal entrance of D. SHAK 718:20
dunce dare call a d. YOUN 876:26
dearest, you're a d. JOHN 443:7
d. that has been sent COWP 255:27
d. with wits POPE 611:21
Satan, thou art but a d. BLAK 125:9
duncery tyrannical d. MILT 546:10
dunces d. are all in confederacy SWIF 783:14
Dundee bonnets of Bonny D. SCOT 688:7
longer in bonny D. SCOT 689:23
Dunfermline D. town BALL 55:13
dung die in their own d. KIPL 466:17
d.-heaps CHEK 222:7
Fulfilled of d. CHAU 219:28
dungeons Brightest in d., Liberty BYRO 191:1

dungfork man with a d. HOPK 408:9
dunghill cock crowing on its own d. ALDI 11:11
crow upon his own d. PROV 631:16
d. kind Delights in filth SPEN 767:16
Dunkirk D. to Belgrade DAVI 268:12
dunnest d. smoke of hell SHAK 719:2
Dunsinane high D. hill SHAK 722:1
remove to D. SHAK 722:14
duodecimos humbler band of d. CRAB 257:18
dupe d. of friendship HAZL 386:6
duped be d. by them LA R 481:21
dupes If hopes were d. CLOU 237:6
duplicity sign of d. BALZ 57:2
durable true love is a d. fire RALE 654:4
duration fallacy in d. BROW 162:15
dure Pourvu que ça d. BONA 132:2
dusk Between d. and dawn MÜLL 564:18
each slow d. OWEN 591:5
falling of the d. HEGE 389:2
forty-three In the d. GILB 358:14
dusky D. like night BYRO 190:9
rear my d. race TENN 797:5
dust blossom in the d. SHIR 749:18
by our mother's d. FORD 337:10
chimney-sweepers, come to d. SHAK 698:24
d. and ashes BIBL 87:3
D. and ashes BROW 168:2
D. as we are WORD 868:10
d. falls to the urn VAUG 825:8
D. hath closed Helen's eye NASH 569:2
d. of creeds outworn SHEL 745:22
d. of exploded beliefs MADA 514:2
d. of the Churchyard DONN 290:9
d. on the nettles THOM 806:22
d. return to the earth BIBL 90:20
d. thou art BIBL 79:13
D. thou art LONG 499:14
d. to dust BOOK 139:10
D. to the dust SHEL 743:16
d. upon the paper eye DOUG 291:13
d. was once the man WHIT 852:19
d. would hear her and beat TENN 798:7
enemies shall lick the d. BOOK 144:19
Excuse my d. EPIT 317:5
Fallen to d. WILD 856:6
fear in a handful of d. ELIO 311:3
forbear To dig the d. EPIT 317:12
give d. a tongue HERB 394:3
Grind them into the d. BRAD 154:8
Half d., half deity BYRO 190:13
handful of d. CONR 249:12
honour turn to d. MARV 525:13
Hope raises no d. ÉLUA 314:7
in the d., in the cool tombs SAND 680:3
in the d. my vice is laid EPIT 319:3
Less than the d. HOPE 407:4
little d. of praise TENN 795:20
lovers o'er the d. BYRO 185:19
Marry my body to that d. KING 463:4
much learned d. COWP 256:14
not without d. and heat MILT 545:24
not worth the d. SHAK 716:12
O'er English d. MACA 508:6
of the d. of the ground BIBL 78:19
peck of March d. PROV 641:31
provoke the silent d. GRAY 370:5
quintessence of d. SHAK 701:11
raised a d. BERK 72:16
rich earth a richer d. BROO 159:13
shake off the d. BIBL 100:24
small d. of the balance BIBL 93:18
sweep the d. SHAK 727:11
Tell flesh it is but d. RALE 653:16
This quiet D. DICK 282:3
throwing of a little d. VIRG 833:4
To d. and ashes LITT 495:12
we are d. and shadow HORA 414:1
what a d. do I raise BACO 48:15
Where can the d. alight HUI- 419:9
with age and d. RALE 654:6
without the d. of racing HORA 409:20
writes in d. BACO 49:10
dustbin d. of history TROT 817:6

dustheap d. called 'history' BIRR 122:3
dusty what a d. answer MERE 532:22
Dutch fault of the D. CANN 196:25
Dutchman on a D.'s beard SHAK 735:29
duties All virtues and d. BAHY 52:4
d. as well as its rights DRUM 294:4
d. of the heart BAHY 52:2
d. will be determined MORE 559:18
If I had no d. JOHN 442:8
neglect of his d. THOM 808:7
spiritual d. HOBY 401:14
dutiful take note of the d. VIRG 829:2
duty act of d. and religion OSBO 588:13
as much a d. as cooperation GAND 348:14
bare staircase of his d. STEV 776:5
bounden d. and service BOOK 137:17
citizen's first d. GRAS 369:1
daily stage of d. KEN 459:13
dare to do our d. LINC 493:12
declares it is his d. SHAW 739:15
die in one's d. is life BHAG 78:3
divided d. SHAK 728:13
do our d. as such SALI 678:18
Do your d. CORN 251:14
d. is to obey orders JACK 427:2
D. is what no-one else will do FITZ 332:19
d. of an Opposition DERB 274:2
d. of government PAIN 592:12
d. of the four classes LAWS 484:19
d. towards God BOOK 138:10
d. we owe to history WILD 855:3
d. we so much underrate STEV 775:25
every man's d. COBB 237:12
every man will do his d. NELS 570:4
Every subject's d. SHAK 708:26
first d. of a State RUSK 674:1
forgot that he had a d. GIBB 354:21
God, Immortality, D. ELIO 308:19
I have done my d. NELS 570:7
I've done my d. FIEL 327:3
life was d. HOOP 406:11
little d. and less love SHAK 709:19
Love is then our d. GAY 351:7
Moor has done his d. SCHI 685:22
no lasting teacher of d. CICE 232:5
Nor law, nor d. YEAT 873:19
of the voice of God! O D. WORD 867:19
only done my d. TENN 800:4
owe a d. BEHN 67:1
path of d. TENN 798:25
performing a public d. GRAN 368:17
picket's off d. forever BEER 66:7
sense of d. useful RUSS 674:17
Such d. as the subject owes SHAK 733:10
supreme d. of a man LAWS 484:17
terrible notions of d. CLOU 236:13
To accuse is my d. SCHI 685:23
When D. whispers low EMER 314:17
whole d. of man BIBL 90:22
dux D. femina facti VIRG 828:18
dwarf d. sees farther COLE 241:23
my d. shall dance JONS 446:13
dwarfish d. whole COLE 239:14
dwarfs d. on the shoulders BERN 73:17
State which d. its men MILL 536:9
dwell all that d. in it BOOK 139:5
constrained to d. with Mesech BOOK 148:15
d. in a corner BIBL 88:29
d. in realms of day BLAK 124:20
d. in the house of the Lord BOOK 140:21
d. in their tents BOOK 144:13
d. in the land BIBL 92:13
d. in thy tabernacle BOOK 140:1
d. with sothfastnesse CHAU 221:16
people that on earth do d. KETH 461:9
dwelleth d. not in temples BIBL 110:4
dwelling desert were my d.-place BYRO 186:28
d. in all things UPAN 822:1
d. is the light WORD 866:13
God's d. place SIKH 752:3
lovely is thy d.-place SCOT 690:10
dwellings amiable are thy d. BOOK 145:13
dwells She d. with Beauty KEAT 456:1

dwelt d. among the untrodden ways

	WORD 869:3
d. among us	BIBL 107:2
d. by the brook Cherith	BIBL 85:6
dwindle d. into a wife	CONG 247:27
dyer like the d.'s hand	SHAK 738:14
dyes stains and splendid d.	KEAT 454:9
dying achieve it through not d.	ALLE 13:17
attend a d. animal	YEAT 873:2
Autumn sunsets exquisitely d.	HUXL 423:2
behold you again in d.	STEV 776:25
bliss of d.	POPE 614:1
can't stay d. here all night	SHER 748:4
Christian can only fear d.	HARE 382:8
continually d.	PETR 605:3
distinguished from d.	SMIT 758:23
D. and living	BOOK 137:18
D. a very dull, dreary	MAUG 528:13
d., bless the hand	DRYD 296:32
d. breath of Socrates	JEAN 431:2
d., but fighting back	MCKA 511:16
d. deer	AYTO 44:7
d. for a faith	THAC 802:16
d., has made us gifts	BROO 159:4
d. in the last dyke	BURK 176:2
D. is an art	PLAT 608:9
d. is nothing	ANOU 24:12
d. man's room	STER 773:10
d. may I hold you	TIBU 810:18
d. of a hundred good symptoms	POPE 618:26
d. of the light	THOM 805:15
d. remembers	VIRG 831:9
d. with help	ALEX 12:4
d. without having laughed	LA B 474:16
feel that he is d.	CALI 193:9
groans of love to those of the d.	LOWR 503:14
he hung, the d. Lord	JACO 427:7
I am d., Egypt	SHAK 695:19
If this is d.	STRA 778:15
indisposeth us for d.	BROW 162:13
like a d. lady	SHEL 747:5
lips of d. men	ARNO 30:17
man's d. is more the survivors' affair	
	MANN 520:2
man spend d.	NERU 570:10
mouth of the d. day	AUDE 37:7
My d. sight	BLOK 129:3
no more d. then	SHAK 738:24
not death, but d.	FIEL 326:8
nothing new in d.	YESE 875:22
poor devils are d.	PHIL 606:1
sacraments to a d. god	HEIN 389:15
Those d. generations	YEAT 874:13
To d. ears	TENN 799:12
Turkey is a d. man	NICH 574:15
unconscionable time d.	CHAR 217:10
words of a d. man	VANE 824:5
dyke auld fail d.	BALL 56:3
February fill d.	PROV 632:7
last d. of prevarication	BURK 176:2
dynamite barrel of d.	MAYA 529:2
dynamo starry d.	GINS 358:22

E E. = mc²

each beating each to e.	BROW 166:17
eager rule are least e.	PLAT 609:3
eagle all the e. in thee	CRAS 259:2
e. among blinking owls	SHEL 744:14
E. has landed	ARMS 28:19
e. in a dove-cote	SHAK 698:16
e. in the air	BIBL 89:12
e. know what is in the pit	BLAK 124:21
Fate is not an e.	BOWE 153:10
In and out the E.	MAND 518:15
with e. eyes	KEAT 456:15
eagles e. be gathered	BIBL 102:25
e. be gathered together	PROV 647:10
E. don't catch flies	PROV 630:39
Fled back like e.	SHEL 747:4
hawk at e.	HERB 394:23
swifter than e.	BIBL 84:12
with wings as e.	BIBL 93:20

ear cleave the general e.	SHAK 701:21
close at the e. of Eve	MILT 543:15
cut his e. off	MEDA 529:17
dull cold e. of death	GRAY 370:5
e. begins to hear	BRON 158:16
e., did hear that tongue	ROYD 671:18
e. of jealousy	BIBL 96:25
e. of man hath not seen	SHAK 727:1
God's own e. Listens	MILT 543:23
hath the sow by the right e.	HENR 392:2
hearing e.	BIBL 88:27
hearing of the e.	BIBL 87:18
He that planted the e.	BOOK 146:6
nor e. filled	BIBL 89:18
nor e. heard	BIBL 111:25
Oon e. it herde	CHAU 221:6
out of your wife's e.	MORT 562:3
Reason's e.	ADDI 5:18
silk purse out of sow's e.	PROV 647:43
than meets the e.	MILT 539:18
upon my whorlèd e.	HOPK 407:9
Vexing the dull e.	SHAK 714:10
earl As far as the fourteenth e.	HOME 404:5
e. and a knight of the garter	ATTL 35:8
E. of Fitzdotterel's eldest	BROU 160:7
earlier Here's one I made e.	CATC 207:29
earls daughter of a hundred e.	TENN 796:1
early awake right e.	BOOK 143:17
e. bird catches worm	PROV 630:40
E. Christian that gets the fattest	SAKI 678:4
E. in the morning	HEBE 388:10
e. man never borrows	PROV 630:41
E. one morning	SONG 762:6
E. to bed	PROV 630:42
E. to rise	THUR 810:12
get up e.	LOWE 502:16
go to bed e.	PROU 625:5
had it been e.	JOHN 439:7
I was up e.	BALZ 57:1
rise e.	JOHN 438:15
Vote e. and vote often	MILE 534:25
earn little to e.	KING 464:13
earned e. on earth	THAT 803:14
penny e.	PROV 641:33
earnest I am in e.	GARR 349:17
Life is e.	LONG 499:14
time to be in e.	JOHN 436:13
earnestly truly and e. repent	BOOK 137:9
earrings e. for under £1	RATN 655:14
ears and hedges e.	SWIF 784:5
blind in your e. and mind	SOPH 761:18
don thyn e. glowe	CHAU 220:29
e., and hear not	BOOK 148:5
e. of every one	BIBL 83:27
Enemy e. are listening	OFFI 584:14
Eyes and e.	HERA 393:6
hath e. to hear	BIBL 103:29
heard with our e.	BOOK 142:11
hungry stomach has no e.	LA F 475:19
lend me your e.	SHAK 712:28
lets the e. lie back	IVES 426:6
let thine e. consider	BOOK 149:7
Little pitchers have large e.	PROV 637:42
Look with thine e.	SHAK 716:19
music Creep in our e.	SHAK 725:10
seven good e.	BIBL 80:22
stoppeth her e.	BOOK 143:18
That man's e.	HUGH 417:17
Walls have e.	PROV 646:5
we have two e.	ZENO 877:14
What big e. you have	PERR 604:3
woods have e.	PROV 632:10
earth all the e. were paper	LYLY 505:23
anywhere else on e.	GURN 374:16
as if the e. had rolled	WORD 866:3
bleeding piece of e.	SHAK 712:22
call this planet E.	CLAR 233:16
cold e. upon me	KEAT 458:17
Cold in the e.	BRON 158:17
conquest of the e.	CONR 248:19
corners of the e.	BOOK 146:8
creepeth upon the e.	BIBL 78:16
damage to the e.	COUS 253:7

daughter of E. and Water	SHEL 743:25
deep-delvèd e.	KEAT 456:3
done to the e.	MORR 561:6
dust return to the e.	BIBL 90:20
earned on e.	THAT 803:14
E. all Danaë to the stars	TENN 799:18
e. be moved	BOOK 142:17
e. breaks up	BROW 165:8
e. covereth	QUAR 651:14
e. does not argue	WHIT 852:18
e. doth like a snake renew	SHEL 744:5
E. felt the wound	MILT 544:6
E. has not anything to show	WORD 865:7
e. in an earthy bed	TENN 798:7
e. in fast thick pants	COLE 240:5
e. is all the home I have	AYTO 44:9
e. is flat	INGE 425:11
e. is full of his glory	BIBL 92:6
e. is the Lord's	BIBL 112:11
e. is the Lord's	BOOK 141:1
e. is what we all have	BERR 74:18
E., lie heavily	ROSS 669:6
e. of majesty	SHAK 730:10
E., receive an honoured guest	AUDE 37:10
e. received her frame	WATT 842:7
e. remaineth	BIBL 79:25
E.'s crammed with heaven	BROW 164:4
e. shall be filled	AING 9:18
e. shall be full	BIBL 92:18
e. shall melt away	BOOK 142:18
e. shook	BOOK 144:7
e. soaks up the rain	COWL 254:8
E.'s the right place for love	FROS 344:7
e. stood hard as iron	ROSS 669:2
E., the first of the gods	VIRG 830:17
e. to earth	BOOK 139:10
end of e.	ADAM 3:18
ends of the e.	BOOK 144:2
Everything on e.	GOGO 363:12
face of e. around	STEV 777:2
famous men have the whole e.	PERI 603:25
feel the e. move	HEMI 391:2
filleted the e. so fine	TAYL 791:19
flowery lap of e.	ARNO 29:17
food out of the e.	BOOK 147:6
foundation of the e.	BOOK 146:17
foundation of the e.	SHAK 706:8
foundations of the e.	BIBL 87:8
frame in the e.	SPEN 767:21
from e. to heaven	PLAT 609:6
get away from e. awhile	FROS 344:7
giants in the e.	BIBL 79:21
girdle round about the e.	SHAK 726:7
given Her all on e.	BYRO 187:11
glory from the e.	WORD 867:3
going to and fro in the e.	BIBL 86:9
goodly frame, the e.	SHAK 701:11
heaven and the e.	BIBL 78:12
he craves the e.	SEXT 693:6
hydroptic e. hath drunk	DONN 289:12
if e. Be but the shadow	MILT 543:21
inhabitants o' the e.	SHAK 718:10
inherit the e.	BIBL 98:25
in the water under the e.	BIBL 81:15
It fell to e.	LONG 498:14
lap of E.	GRAY 370:9
Lay her i' the e.	SHAK 704:18
let the E. bless the Lord	BOOK 133:16
Lie heavy on him, E.	EPIT 319:16
little e. for charity	SHAK 711:2
low as where this e.	ROSS 669:14
made heaven and e.	BOOK 138:16
made heaven and e.	BOOK 148:22
more near the e.	SHAK 729:15
more things in heaven and e.	HALD 376:11
move the e.	ARCH 26:3
must have a touch of e.	TENN 794:11
new heaven and a new e.	BIBL 119:15
new heaven, new e.	SHAK 694:8
new heavens and a new e.	BIBL 94:23
Nor by the e.	BIBL 99:4
not for the brute e.	THOM 807:8
not heavy upon her, e.	MART 524:7

EARTHEN · **EDITOR** 947

of the e., earthy BIBL 113:4
on e. peace BIBL 104:14
On e. there is nothing great HAMI 378:13
One does not sell the e. CRAZ 259:15
pilgrims on the e. BIBL 116:5
pilgrims on this e. RYDE 676:6
poetry of e. KEAT 456:17
rich e. a richer dust BROO 159:13
round e.'s imagined corners DONN 288:8
round e.'s shore ARNO 29:4
sad old e. must borrow WILC 854:9
salt of the e. BIBL 98:26
shadow of the E. MISQ 547:21
shall inherit the e. SMIT 756:17
sleepers in that quiet e. BRON 158:21
slime of the e. SUGE 779:17
surly bonds of e. MAGE 514:15
surly bonds of e. REAG 656:17
terms with the e. ALAI 11:1
this e., this realm SHAK 730:11
tread on E. unguessed at ARNO 30:16
way of all the e. BIBL 82:30
Which men call e. MILT 538:19
whole e. would henceforth BYRO 190:23
work i' the e. SHAK 700:26
Yours is the E. KIPL 466:6
earthen e. voider BARN 59:11
earthquake against an e. ADDI 6:1
e. is not satisfied WORD 868:17
Lord was not in the e. BIBL 85:14
Small e. in Chile COCK 237:18
world-e., Waterloo TENN 798:23
earthy of the earth, e. BIBL 113:4
ease age of e. GOLD 364:3
at e. in a room PASC 597:18
at e. with himself CHUA 227:7
Counselled ignoble e. MILT 542:5
done with so much e. DRYD 294:9
e. in hell WRIG 870:21
e. of the masters SMIT 756:7
e. thine heart BEDD 65:3
elegance and e. GAY 351:18
for another gives its e. BLAK 127:17
ignoble e. ROOS 667:17
kindly bent to e. us SWIF 784:8
never at heart's e. SHAK 711:25
Not for e. that prayer WILL 858:16
prodigal of e. DRYD 294:14
Studious of laborious e. COWP 256:18
take their e. And sleep SHAK 711:10
take thine e. BIBL 105:14
True e. in writing POPE 616:6
Virtue shuns e. MONT 555:12
we ourselves are at our e. SMIT 755:25
easeful e. Death KEAT 456:9
easer e. of all woes FLET 335:12
easier will be e. for you CHIL 226:5
easiness e. doth make them hard HOOK 406:10
easing e. the Spring REED 657:5
east brims over in the E. GIRA 359:6
Britain calls the Far E. MENZ 532:5
E. is a career DISR 286:12
E. is East KIPL 465:8
E. is east PROV 630:43
E. of Suez KIPL 466:16
E., west, home's best PROV 630:44
e. wind made flesh APPL 25:8
e. wind may never blow WALT 839:1
face neither E. nor West NKRU 576:17
gorgeous E. in fee WORD 868:1
how wide also the e. is BOOK 147:2
I' the e. my pleasure lies SHAK 695:3
It is the e. SHAK 732:9
look the E. End in the face ELIZ 313:5
neither from the e. BOOK 145:2
neither of the E. KORA 472:12
on the e. of Eden BIBL 79:18
politics in the E. DISR 285:24
through the e.-wind BOOK 142:24
tried to hustle the E. KIPL 467:1
wind is in the e. PROV 647:2
wind's in the e. DICK 276:13
wise men from the e. BIBL 98:10
Easter E. energy about it HEAN 387:19
eastern against the e. gate MILT 539:25
E. promise ADVE 7:24
Eastertide Wearing white for E. HOUS 415:11
eastward garden e. in Eden BIBL 78:19
easy E. come, easy go PROV 630:45
E. does it PROV 630:46
E. is the way down VIRG 830:5
E. live and quiet die SCOT 689:10
e. to take refuge in IBSE 424:9
e. ways to die SHAK 696:8
e. writing's vile hard reading SHER 748:31
If to do were as e. SHAK 724:2
Life is not meant to be e. FRAS 341:18
Life is not meant to be e. SHAW 739:13
no e. way of becoming REYN 659:9
normal and e. JAME 430:1
not that e. being green RAPO 655:12
rack of a too e. chair POPE 613:26
should be free and e. OSBO 588:10
Summer time an' the livin' is e. HEYW 397:19
Too e. for children SCHN 686:9
woman of e. virtue HAIL 376:7
Words e. to be understood BUNY 171:3
eat Big fish e. little fish PROV 628:2
Dog does not e. dog PROV 630:10
don't work shan't e. PROV 635:27
e. and drunk and lived JOHN 441:2
e. anything with a face MCCA 509:9
e. a peck of dirt PROV 646:14
e. at a place called Mom's ALGR 12:15
e. bulls' flesh BOOK 143:3
e., drink, and be merry BIBL 105:14
E., drink and be merry PROV 630:47
E. my shorts CATC 207:15
e. one of Bellamy's veal pies PITT 607:22
e. the fat of the land BIBL 80:26
e. to live MOLI 551:17
E. to live PROV 630:48
e. up and swallow down MORE 559:3
great ones e. up SHAK 729:26
have meat and cannot e. BURN 178:23
have your cake and e. it PROV 648:8
I did e. BIBL 79:7
I would e. his heart SHAK 727:30
Let them e. cake MARI 521:14
Let us e. and drink BIBL 92:22
let us e. and drink BIBL 112:23
lives to e. SOCR 759:16
neither should he e. BIBL 115:17
see what I e. CARR 202:5
shalt thou e. bread BIBL 79:12
Take, e. BIBL 103:12
Take, e., this is my Body BOOK 137:16
Tell me what you e. BRIL 157:8
thou shalt not e. of it BIBL 78:21
to e., and to drink BIBL 90:7
ye e. but ye have not enough BIBL 96:18
Ye shall e. it in haste BIBL 81:8
You are what you e. PROV 647:38
eaten e. and drunk enough HORA 411:2
e. by missionaries SPOO 768:16
e. by the bear HOUS 415:5
e. of worms BIBL 109:28
e. to death with rust SHAK 707:10
God made and e. BROW 165:5
They'd e. every one CARR 203:5
we've already e. BENN 69:20
eater great e. of beef SHAK 735:1
Out of the e. BIBL 83:12
eateth e. grass as an ox BIBL 87:14
Why e. your Master BIBL 100:14
eating Appetite comes with e. PROV 626:30
appetite grows by e. RABE 652:7
E. people is wrong FLAN 332:24
e. the sea ROBE 663:5
eats e. of the sweet fruit UPAN 822:15
Man is what he e. FEUE 325:15
eau *L'e. verte pénétra* RIMB 662:9
eave e.-drops fall COLE 240:1
Ebenezer Pale E. thought it wrong BELL 68:21
ebony hair as black as e. GRIM 373:9
his image, cut in e. FULL 346:8
ecce *E. homo* BIBL 120:15
eccentric E. intervolved MILT 543:23
ecclesia *Ubi Petrus, ibi ergo e.* AMBR 14:3
ecclesiam *Salus extra e.* AUGU 39:14
Ecclesiastes *Vanitas vanitatum, dixit E.* BIBL 120:7
ecclesiastic E. tyranny DEFO 271:3
ecclesiologist keen e. BETJ 76:9
echo E. beyond the Mexique Bay MARV 524:17
e. of a noble mind LONG 500:9
e. of a pistol-shot DURR 300:17
e. of a platitude BIER 121:3
E., sweetest nymph MILT 539:2
Footfalls e. in the memory ELIO 309:4
sound must seem an e. POPE 616:6
waiting for the e. MARQ 523:17
echoes Our e. roll TENN 799:9
stage but e. back JOHN 438:3
wild e. flying TENN 799:7
echoing e. straits between us ARNO 31:3
eclipse astonished at e. ORCH 586:2
at least an e. BACO 47:8
E. first O'KE 584:21
In the moons' e. SAVA 682:18
in the moon's e. SHAK 721:17
merciful e. GILB 356:13
total e. MILT 545:1
eclipsed e. the gaiety JOHN 436:27
eclipses Clouds and e. SHAK 737:26
ecology e. and antiwar HUNT 422:2
economic because of the e. position ADDA 4:8
cold metal of e. theory SCHU 687:6
demands of the e. process TEMP 792:14
e. law of motion MARX 526:6
not purely e. TAWN 791:6
vital e. interests WEIL 845:7
economical e. with the *actualité* CLAR 233:12
e. with the truth ARMS 28:21
economics E. is the science ROBB 663:4
it is bad e. ROOS 667:9
study of e. SCHU 687:1
economist political e. BAGE 51:10
economists e., and calculators BURK 174:7
economize Let us e. it TWAI 820:4
economy E. is going without HOPE 406:19
e. of truth BURK 175:10
E. was always 'elegant' GASK 350:7
fear of Political E. SELL 692:5
It's the e., stupid POLI 612:27
Principles of Political E. BENT 71:17
There can be no e. DISR 284:24
ecstasy e. of being ever BROW 162:21
e. of betrayal GENE 352:5
mad with e. TRAH 814:12
ring the bells of E. GINS 358:21
seraph-wings of e. GRAY 370:20
What wild e. KEAT 455:17
ecstatic such e. sound HARD 381:15
eddy dizzying e. ARNO 30:4
Eden brooks of E. TENN 798:17
E.'s dread probationary tree COWP 255:28
garden eastward in E. BIBL 78:19
happier E. MILT 543:8
In E. the only wealth FUEN 346:1
loss of E. MILT 541:8
on the east of E. BIBL 79:18
other E. SHAK 730:10
Through E. took MILT 544:20
voice that breathed o'er E. KEBL 459:3
walls of E. BYRO 185:15
edge Come to the e. LOGU 498:10
dangerous e. of things BROW 164:26
hungry e. of appetite SHAK 730:8
teeth are set on e. BIBL 95:15
edged Science is an e. tool PEAC 600:13
edifice found that e. DOST 291:1
edifieth charity e. BIBL 112:5
Edinburgh travels north to E. BEAV 63:13
edisti *e. satis atque bibisti* HORA 411:2
edition new And more beautiful e. EPIT 317:1
editions e. of Balbec and Palmyra WALP 837:19
editor E.: a person employed HUBB 417:15
e. himself be attacked TROL 816:21

editor (cont.):
e. of such a work STEP 772:5
Edom over E. will I cast out BOOK 143:20
wisdom in E. MIDR 534:18
educate e. our masters MISQ 548:24
e. our party DISR 284:22
educated as an e. gentleman SHAW 740:13
clothed, fed, and e. RUSK 674:1
e. and the uneducated FOST 338:19
government by the badly e. CHES 225:25
Wit is e. insolence ARIS 27:1
women are not e. CAVE 211:20
education ask of e. NAPO 567:17
between e. and catastrophe WELL 846:23
By e. most have been misled DRYD 295:29
cabbage with a college e. TWAI 820:19
difference of e. ADAM 1:19
discretion by e. JEFF 432:11
e., education, and education BLAI 123:18
e. forms the common mind POPE 615:14
E. has been theirs AUST 42:4
[E.] has produced TREV 815:8
e. is a little too CONG 247:7
e. is to a human soul ADDI 5:8
E. is what survives SKIN 754:6
E. is when you read SEEG 691:3
E. made us what we are HELV 390:12
E. makes a people BROU 160:10
e. of the heart SCOT 690:4
e. of the people DISR 285:3
e. produces no effect WILD 854:18
e. serves as a rattle ARIS 28:7
e.'s, more than nature's WINC 860:6
e. to Greece PERI 603:24
fertilised by e. BRON 158:6
first part of politics? E. MICH 534:3
I do not call it e. SPAR 765:12
In e. no class distinction CONF 246:18
in their own e. SCOT 690:7
is a liberal e. STEE 770:17
liberal e. BANK 57:10
part of e. BACO 48:9
poor e. I have received BOTT 152:10
Real e. ultimately limited POUN 621:15
roots of e. are bitter ARIS 28:9
Soap and e. TWAI 820:2
substance of female e. MART 524:1
thank your e. JONS 446:16
that is e. ROGE 666:2
unfit of any to be used in e. LOCK 497:18
unplanned e. creates VERW 826:16
What does e. often do THOR 809:5
eels e. boil'd in broo BALL 55:1
effect found in the e. BERG 72:8
little e. after much labour AUST 43:4
name for an e. COWP 256:28
produce any e. at all HAZL 386:12
effects more lasting e. TREV 815:10
effectually obtain e. BOOK 136:12
efficiency where there is no e. DISR 284:24
efficient e. and the inefficient SHAW 740:11
e. parts BAGE 50:6
have an e. government TRUM 817:22
effort e. be too great ANON 19:1
make one e. PITT 607:15
no e. is necessary I-HS 424:15
not the e. nor the failure tires EMPS 315:27
redoubling your e. SANT 680:13
Superhuman e. isn't worth SHAC 693:11
when you're making some e. AESO 9:3
written without e. JOHN 445:1
effugere Soles e. atque abire sentit MART 524:6
effugies non e. CATU 211:7
Égalité É.! Fraternité POLI 613:1
egg added e. as an idle bird PROV 626:37
eating a demnition e. DICK 279:15
e. boiled very soft AUST 41:3
e. by pleasure laid COWP 255:26
e. is, quite simply SMIT 756:11
e. of the wren WHIT 852:10
e. on our face BROK 157:6
From the e. HORA 414:11
got a bad e. PUNC 650:11

Go to work on an e. ADVE 7:26
hairless as an e. HERR 396:7
hatched from a swan's e. ANDE 15:6
lays an e. NEWS 573:21
little e., a nucleus EUGÉ 321:1
looks like a poached e. NUFF 577:16
one addled e. ELIO 307:13
radish and an e. COWP 256:22
See this e. DIDE 282:16
shell of a snowbird's e. KENO 461:2
egghead E. weds hourglass NEWS 573:7
eggs all my e. in one bastard PARK 596:18
as a weasel sucks e. SHAK 696:22
e. at the smaller end SWIF 782:8
e. for gentlemen NURS 579:1
e. in one basket PROV 630:25
grandmother to suck e. PROV 630:28
Lays e. inside a paper bag ISHE 426:2
partridge sitteth on e. BIBL 95:6
roasting of e. PROV 644:36
roast their e. BACO 48:18
ways to dress e. MOOR 558:4
eglantine with e. SHAK 726:8
ego Et in Arcadia e. EPIT 317:4
fulfils a man's e. ROOT 668:8
egotism e., selfishness, evil GREE 371:15
egotist devil is an e. GOET 361:18
whims of an e. KEAT 457:17
egotistical e. sublime KEAT 458:3
Egypt brow of E. SHAK 727:3
E.'s might COLE 239:4
firstborn in the land of E. BIBL 81:9
great cry in E. BIBL 81:10
Israel came out of E. BOOK 148:3
out of the land of E. BIBL 81:15
there was corn in E. BIBL 80:23
We do not want E. PALM 595:5
wonders in the land of E. BIBL 81:2
Egyptian E. to my mother SHAK 729:3
Egyptians spoiled the E. BIBL 81:11
eheu E. fugaces Labuntur anni HORA 412:10
eight Pieces of e. STEV 775:22
We want e. ANON 21:7
eighteen before you reach e. EINS 305:15
e.-forty-eight TAYL 791:8
eightfold E. Path PALI 594:12
eighty In a dream you are never e. SEXT 693:8
rottenness of e. years BYRO 191:12
Einstein Let E. be SQUI 769:9
either e. to other BOOK 139:4
happy could I be with e. GAY 351:9
Elaine E., the lily maid TENN 794:10
élan é. vital BERG 72:9
elasticity Cheerfulness gives e. SMIL 755:22
elbow e. has a fascination GILB 357:12
elder but five days e. BROW 162:27
e. man not at all BACO 47:18
take An e. than herself SHAK 735:16
elderly e. man of 42 ASHF 33:12
elders discourse of the e. BIBL 97:13
e. and the four beasts BIBL 118:13
four and twenty e. BIBL 118:8
Of those white e. STEV 774:11
Eldorado E. of all the old fools BAUD 61:13
elect dissolve the people and e. BREC 156:3
I was e., I was born fit GURN 374:18
knit together like e. BOOK 136:15
elected audacity of e. persons WHIT 852:16
e. by the manhood ELLI 314:5
will not serve if e. SHER 749:12
election e. by the incompetent many SHAW 741:11
e. is coming ELIO 307:12
When you have won the e. CARD 198:2
elections e. are won ADAM 2:9
You won the e. SOMO 760:20
elective E. affinities GOET 362:13
e. dictatorship HAIL 376:8
Electra Mourning becomes E. O'NE 585:10
electric biggest e. train WELL 846:1
E. Kool-Aid Acid test WOLF 863:3
sing the body e. WHIT 852:1
tried to mend the E. Light BELL 68:16

electrical e. skin and glaring eyes SMAR 754:13
electricity e. was dripping THUR 810:9
usefulness of e. FARA 323:10
electrification e. of the whole country LENI 488:18
electronic new e. interdependence MCLU 512:9
elegance e. and ease GAY 351:18
elegant Economy was always 'e.' GASK 350:7
e. and pregnant texture STEV 775:7
e. but not ostentatious JOHN 436:16
e. simplicity STOW 778:8
e. sufficiency THOM 808:13
Most intelligent, very e. BUCK 169:15
so e. ELIO 311:9
with e. quickness SMAR 754:12
You e. fowl LEAR 486:6
elegy character of his e. JOHN 436:22
whole of Gray's E. WOLF 862:17
eleison Kyrie e. MISS 546:21
element Thy e.'s below SHAK 715:10
To the destructive e. CONR 249:4
elementary E., my dear Watson MISQ 547:11
'E.,' said he DOYL 292:15
elements Become our e. MILT 542:6
conflict of its e. BYRO 190:13
element our e. mar BYRO 189:5
e. So mixed in him SHAK 714:3
formation of heavier e. EDDI 302:13
I tax not you, you e. SHAK 715:17
made cunningly Of e. DONN 288:14
with the fretful e. SHAK 715:15
elephant Appears a monstrous e. COTT 252:15
at the E. SHAK 736:2
can say is 'e.' CHAP 215:19
corn as high as an e.'s eye HAMM 378:19
couldn't hit an e. SEDG 690:15
E.'s Child KIPL 468:10
fit the profile of an e. GAMO 348:8
herd of e. pacing DINE 283:11
masterpiece, an e. DONN 288:21
reality of the e. JALA 428:16
sleeping with an e. TRUD 817:12
thought he saw an E. CARR 204:6
elephanto candenti perfecta nitens e.
VIRG 830:16
elephants e. for want of towns SWIF 784:2
elevated generous and e. mind JOHN 437:24
elevates e. above the vulgar herd GAIS 347:5
elevation No permanent e. of a people LIVI 496:3
eleven fine before e. PROV 642:18
our e. days POLI 612:18
elf deceiving e. KEAT 456:11
little child, a limber e. COLE 239:7
elfland horns of E. TENN 799:8
Elginbrodde Martin E. EPIT 317:15
Eli Eli, E., lama sabachthani BIBL 103:24
Elijah as E. did Elisha BURN 180:11
E. passed by him BIBL 85:15
E. went up by a whirlwind BIBL 85:22
spirit of E. BIBL 85:23
eliminated e. the impossible DOYL 292:20
Elisha rest on E. BIBL 85:23
Elizabeth my sonne's wife, E. INGE 425:8
elk hunted as an e. RIEL 661:11
Ellen fair E. of brave Lochinvar SCOT 688:23
elm arm of an e. tree EMER 315:19
Every e. has its man PROV 631:19
Round the e.-tree bole BROW 165:27
signal-e. ARNO 30:24
vine about the e. DAVI 267:21
elms Behind the e. last night PRIO 624:12
Beneath those rugged e. GRAY 370:3
e., Fade into dimness ARNO 30:5
in immemorial e. TENN 799:22
elopement love-story or an e. DOYL 292:19
eloquence e. is tedious PASC 598:9
e. the soul MILT 542:11
ornate e. in our English CAXT 212:2
parliamentary e. CARL 200:14
power of e. WIGG 853:14

simple e. ever convince	WALP 838:2	Canadian out of the German E.	VAN 824:8	**enchantments** e. of the Middle Age	
Take E. and break	VERL 826:11	dey makes you E.	O'NE 585:7		ARNO 31:16
Talking and e.	JONS 447:5	E. has nothing on	ANDE 15:5	e. of the Middle Age	BEER 66:2
To accuse requires less e.	HOBB 401:4	e. holds the key	CUST 263:13	**enchants** e. my sense	SHAK 734:15
eloquent e. in a more sublime language		E. is everything	METT 533:12	**encircling** amid the e. gloom	NEWM 572:16
	MACA 507:3	e. of ice-cream	STEV 774:3	**encompassed** e. but one man	SHAK 711:21
else happening to Somebody E.	ROGE 666:4	E.'s drunken soldiery	YEAT 872:10	**encompasses** God e. everything	KORA 471:21
elsewhere Real life is e.	RIMB 662:15	e. to die standing	VESP 827:3	**encounter** beyond the first e.	MOLT 553:5
There is a world e.	SHAK 698:9	sacred E.	BRAM 154:16	e. darkness as a bride	SHAK 723:13
Elsinore stormy steep, E.	CAMP 195:5	**emperors** E. can do nothing	BREC 155:20	**encounters** Close e.	FILM 331:2
elves criticizing e.	CHUR 228:18	great men even under bad e.	TACI 787:3	**encourage** e. those who betray	GAY 351:8
e. also, Whose little eyes glow	HERR 396:3	**empire** All e. is no more	DRYD 294:17	right to e.	BAGE 51:6
Elysian in the E. fields	DISR 286:20	arch Of the ranged e.	SHAK 694:9	to e. the others	VOLT 833:13
Elysium brother he is in E.	SHAK 734:29	course of e.	BERK 72:18	**encourager** e. les autres	VOLT 833:13
Keep alive our lost E.	BETJ 76:1	cut-purse of the e.	SHAK 703:15	**encroachments** silent e.	MADI 514:8
What E. have ye known	KEAT 455:15	destinies of the British E.	DISR 284:17	**end** ane e. of ane old song	OGIL 583:14
embalming For my E. (Sweetest)	HERR 396:11	dismemberment of the E.	GLAD 360:4	any beginning or any e.	POLL 611:9
embarras e. des richesses	ALLA 13:4	E. splendidly isolated	NEWS 573:18	appointment at the e. of the world	
embarrassment annoyance and e.	BAED 49:18	E. strikes back	FILM 331:4		DINE 283:11
e. of riches	ALLA 13:4	e., vast as it is	CUST 263:13	at the e. of the day	TAYL 791:17
embers glowing e. through the room		e. walking very slowly	FITZ 332:15	be-all and the e.-all	SHAK 719:6
	MILT 539:16	e. writes back	RUSH 673:1	beginning of the e.	TALL 788:15
joy! that in our e.	WORD 867:13	evil e.	REAG 656:15	Better is the e.	BIBL 90:2
emblem e. of mortality	DISR 285:12	found a great e.	SMIT 756:5	came to an e. all wars	LLOY 496:15
My legs, the e.	BUCK 170:1	glorious e.	BURK 173:25	commit adultery at one e.	CARY 206:2
embrace do there e.	MARV 525:13	great e. and little minds	BURK 173:24	continuing unto the e.	DRAK 293:7
e. your Lordship's principles	WILK 856:22	Greeks in this American e.	MACM 512:15	draw to our e.	BIBL 97:3
most extraordinary e.	TREV 815:12	How's the E.	GEOR 353:5	eggs at the smaller e.	SWIF 782:8
pity, then e.	POPE 616:32	ideological e.	NAIP 567:4	e. badly	STEV 776:9
embraces age in her e.	ROCH 664:12	idlers of the E.	DOYL 292:23	e. cannot justify the means	HUXL 422:16
embraceth mercy e. him	BOOK 141:17	Life, Joy, E.	SHEL 746:4	e. crowns all	SHAK 734:21
embracing e. knowledge	POLA 611:8	lost an e.	ACHE 1:13	e. crowns the work	PROV 631:2
embroidered heavens' e. cloths	YEAT 873:14	lying name of e.	TACI 786:21	e. in doubts	BACO 45:8
embroideries Covered with e.	YEAT 872:15	meaning of E. Day	CHES 224:20	e. is bitter as wormwood	BIBL 87:26
embuggerance e.	PRAT 622:11	metropolis of the e.	COBB 237:14	e. is not yet	BIBL 102:22
Emelye up roos E.	CHAU 219:12	nor Roman, nor an e.	VOLT 834:9	e. is where we start from	ELIO 309:20
emendation e. wrong	JOHN 437:7	provinces of the British e.	SMIT 756:9	e. justifies the means	BUSE 182:1
emerald e. atmosphere	SHEL 745:1	Russia an e. or democracy	BRZE 169:4	e. justifies the means	PROV 631:3
green as e.	COLE 240:16	sea is the only e.	FLET 335:2	e., never as means	KANT 453:3
like unto an e.	BIBL 118:3	tread out e.	YOUN 876:18	e. of all things	BIBL 117:11
livelier e. twinkles	TENN 798:2	unity of the e.	BURK 173:22	e. of a novel	TROL 816:6
men, of the E. Isle	DREN 293:20	way she disposed of an e.	HARL 382:15	e. of a thousand years of history	GAIT 347:7
emergency compelled by e.	TROL 816:4	**empires** day of E.	CHAM 214:3	e. of earth	ADAM 3:18
one e. following upon another	FISH 327:19	e. of the future	CHUR 230:5	e. of history	FUKU 346:3
emeritus called a *professor e.*	LEAC 485:7	Hatching vain e.	MILT 542:8	e. of man is an action	CARL 200:22
emigration doubt but that our e.	CART 204:14	Vaster than e.	MARV 525:11	e. of Solomon Grundy	NURS 581:9
emigravit *E.* is the inscription	LONG 499:12	**empirical** e. *scientific system*	POPP 619:1	e. of the beginning	CHUR 230:1
Emily E., hear	CRAN 258:19	**empiricist** e. view	CHOM 226:15	e. of these men	BOOK 144:21
eminence raised To that bad e.	MILT 542:2	**employed** innocently e.	JOHN 441:11	e. of the way inescapable	PAST 598:19
eminency some e. in ourselves	HOBB 400:13	**employee** In a hierarchy every e.	PETE 604:16	e. the gods may bestow	HORA 411:15
eminent death reveals the e.	SHAW 741:22	**employer** harder upon the e.	SPOO 768:15	e. to be without honour	BIBL 97:2
Emmanuel from E.'s veins	COWP 255:15	**employment** e. for his idle time	WALT 839:3	e. to enlightenment	DOGE 287:9
emolument positions of considerable e.		e. may be reckoned dishonest	GAY 351:8	e. to the beginnings of all wars	ROOS 667:16
	GAIS 347:5	e. to the artisan	BELL 68:16	e. to the old Britain	BROW 161:1
emotion degree of my aesthetic e.	BELL 67:11	seek gainful e.	ACHE 1:12	e. where I began	DONN 289:21
dependable international e.	ALSO 13:21	**emporium** Celestial E.	BORG 151:8	Everything has an e.	PROV 631:34
e. recollected in tranquillity	WORD 870:3	**emprisoned** E. in black	KEAT 454:5	flood unto the world's e.	BOOK 144:19
masses conveying an e.	HEPW 392:18	**emptiness** Form is e.	MAHĀ 515:9	God be at my e.	PRAY 623:4
morality touched by e.	ARNO 32:3	great Australian E.	WHIT 850:20	God will grant an e.	VIRG 828:16
stirred by e.	THOM 804:23	**empty** Bring on the e. horses	CURT 263:8	good things must come to an e.	PROV 626:13
thought charged with e.	GIDE 356:6	E. sacks will never	PROV 630:49	happiness, which is an e.	ARIS 27:13
tranquillity remembered in e.	PARK 596:10	e. spaces Between stars	FROS 344:12	highest political e.	ACTO 1:15
emotional e. agitation	ADLE 6:8	e., swept, and garnished	BIBL 101:10	In my beginning is my e.	ELIO 309:8
Gluttony an e. escape	DE V 275:4	E. vessels make	PROV 631:1	In my e. is my beginning	MARY 527:2
emotions all the human e.	GOGO 363:10	fold stands e.	SHAK 726:3	Is this the promised e.	SHAK 717:6
e. were riveted	FOOT 336:7	Grace fills e. spaces	WEIL 845:2	let me know mine e.	BOOK 141:28
for the noble e.	RUSK 673:9	house would e. be	BOOT 151:4	look to the e.	ANON 23:11
gamut of the e.	PARK 596:12	let me be e.	METH 533:8	Lord blessed the latter e.	BIBL 87:19
metaphysical brothel for the e.	KOES 470:10	rich he hath sent e. away	BIBL 104:9	made a good e.	SHAK 704:3
only two e. in a plane	WELL 846:3	singer of an e. day	MORR 560:12	make an e.	JONS 447:4
realm of the e.	GIDE 355:19	turn down an e. glass	FITZ 331:29	make an e. the sooner	BACO 46:24
receptacle for e.	PICA 606:10	very e. heads	BACO 49:6	middle, and an e.	ARIS 27:20
refusal to admit our e.	RATT 655:16	world is e.	PALI 594:8	muddle, and an e.	LARK 481:14
waste-paper basket of the e.	WEBB 843:11	**enamelled** e. meadows	WALP 837:9	must not be an e.	FLAU 334:7
world of the e.	COLE 242:13	throws her e. skin	SHAK 726:9	on to the e. of the road	LAUD 482:18
emparadised E. in one another's arms		**enamoured** So e. on peace	CLAR 233:8	Our e. is Life	MACN 513:15
	MILT 543:8	**enchanted** e. isles	MILT 539:7	reserved for some e.	CLIV 236:11
		Enter these e. woods	MERE 532:23	retard th'inevitable e.	SMAR 755:15
emperice e. and flour	CHAU 220:19	holy and e.	COLE 240:5	right true e. of love	DONN 288:2
		Some e. evening	HAMM 378:21	sans singer, and—sans E.	FITZ 331:18
emperor belong to the E.	BORG 151:8	**enchantment** distance lends e.	CAMP 195:12	she had a good e.	MALO 518:2
		Distance lends e.	PROV 630:6	terror without e.	SCHI 683:9
				there's an e. on't	ANON 21:10

end (*cont.*):
there's an e. on't — JOHN 440:17
there was no e. — WHIT 850:19
this day to e. myself — TENN 797:15
This was the e. — PLAT 608:18
till you come to the e. — CARR 202:17
unto the e. of the world — BIBL 103:25
Waiting for the e. — EMPS 315:25
war that will e. war — WELL 846:25
where's it all going to e. — STOP 778:1
Whoever wills the e. — KANT 453:1
wills the e. — PROV 634:28
work till my life shall e. — EPIT 317:11
work till the e. of my life — SWAN 781:25
world may e. tonight — BROW 166:9
world will e. in fire — FROS 344:13
world without e. — BOOK 133:8
endearing e. young charms — MOOR 558:6
ended continued, and e. in thee — BOOK 138:3
Georges e. — LAND 478:6
Ilium has e. — VIRG 829:13
Mass is e. — MISS 550:1
Enderby Brides of E. — INGE 425:6
ending bread-sauce of the happy e. — JAME 430:3
Don't tell the e. — TAGL 788:10
makes a good e. — PROV 633:17
so quick, so clean an e. — HOUS 416:6
way of e. a war — ORWE 588:7
endless born to e. night — BLAK 124:19
e. forms most beautiful — DARW 266:18
E. Light — ZORO 879:14
in e. night — GRAY 370:20
is e. nothing — LARK 481:4
endogenous neoclassical e. growth — BROW 160:17
endow I thee e. — BOOK 139:2
ends All's well that e. well — PROV 626:19
between e. and scarce means — ROBB 663:4
divinity that shapes our e. — SHAK 704:21
e. by our beginnings know — DENH 273:6
e. of the earth — BOOK 144:2
e. of the world — BOOK 140:9
More are men's e. marked — SHAK 730:9
pursuing of the best e. — HUTC 422:9
tell where it e. — BENT 71:11
endue E. her plenteously — BOOK 134:5
endurance e. and courage — SCOT 688:4
e. is godlike — LONG 499:4
e. of toil — OVID 590:7
e. rather than of truth — MONT 555:10
limits of e. — MATI 528:3
endure Children's talent to e. — ANGE 15:17
e. for a night — BOOK 141:14
e. my own despair — WALS 838:19
e. Their going hence — SHAK 716:25
e. them — AURE 40:21
e., then pity — POPE 616:32
e. the toothache — SHAK 727:32
E. the winter's cold — SHAK 711:16
human hearts e. — JOHN 438:4
man will not merely e. — FAUL 324:17
nature itselfe cant e. — FLEM 334:19
potter and clay e. — BROW 167:11
stuff will not e. — SHAK 735:9
thou shalt e. — BOOK 146:17
endured can't be cured must be e. — PROV 646:17
e. with patient resignation — RUSS 674:17
Once you e. worse — HOME 405:8
state to be e. — JOHN 437:16
endureth e. all things — BIBL 112:14
e. for ever — BOOK 147:21
mercy e. for ever — BOOK 149:12
Endymion In E., I leaped — KEAT 458:2
enemies alone against smiling e. — BOWE 153:11
assaults of our e. — BOOK 134:2
choice of his e. — WILD 855:18
conquering one's e. — GENG 352:6
curse mine e. — BIBL 82:9
e. be scattered — BOOK 144:6
E.' gifts are no gifts — SOPH 761:11
e. of Freedom do not argue — INGE 425:1

e. of liberty — HUME 420:8
e. of truth — BROW 162:23
e. shall lick the dust — BOOK 144:19
e. to a real artist — GAIN 347:1
e. to laws — BURK 175:16
e. will not believe — HUBB 417:13
forgive an e. — BLAK 126:27
giving his e. — STER 772:19
guard even our e. — MISQ 549:1
left me naked to mine e. — SHAK 711:1
Love your e. — BIBL 104:25
making new e. — VOLT 835:10
no perpetual e. — PALM 595:2
not e. when we acquire them — SENE 692:15
number of his e. — FLAU 334:1
speak with their e. — BOOK 149:3
thine e. thy footstool — BOOK 147:19
we make our e. — CHES 225:6
wish their e. dead — MONT 554:13
worst kind of e. — TACI 787:1
enemy afraid of his e. — PLUT 610:13
better class of e. — MILL 537:15
bridge to a flying e. — PROV 636:18
E. ears are listening — OFFI 584:14
e. of good art — CONN 248:8
e. of my enemy — SAYI 684:16
e. of the best — PROV 633:21
e. oppresseth me — BOOK 142:7
e. see your spirit — MUSA 566:8
e.'s main force — MOLT 553:5
e. that shall be destroyed — BIBL 112:22
e. that will run me through — BURN 176:16
e. to the human race — MILL 537:13
every man your e. — NELS 569:18
first contact with the e. — MISQ 548:12
forgive an e. — BLAK 125:19
greatest e. is inclination — BAHY 52:3
guard even his e. from oppression — PAIN 592:17
help a friend or hurt an e. — CLEA 235:2
high speed toward the e. — HALS 378:10
Hush! Here comes the e. — COND 245:10
I am the e. you killed — OWEN 591:10
If thine e. be hungry — BIBL 88:38
Know the e. — SUN 780:12
large one, an e. — SENE 692:10
last e. — BIBL 112:22
life, its e. — ANOU 24:10
met the e. — CART 205:16
met the e. — PERR 604:7
near'st and dearest e. — SHAK 706:13
no e. but time — YEAT 873:16
no little e. — PROV 644:30
not an e. in the world — WILD 856:12
O mine e. — BIBL 85:18
one e. — ALI 12:16
Our friends, the e. — BÉRA 72:5
outwit an e. — PLUT 610:9
potter is potter's e. — HESI 397:2
see No e. But winter — SHAK 696:21
smitten a sleeping e. — YAMA 872:3
sometimes his own worst e. — BEVI 77:14
spoils of the e. — MARC 521:10
sweet e., France — SIDN 750:18
taught by the e. — OVID 590:12
vision's greatest e. — BLAK 124:23
war without an e. — WALL 837:6
will have upon the e. — WELL 846:4
your e. and your friend — TWAI 820:8
energy E. is Eternal Delight — BLAK 126:2
important source of e. — EINS 305:12
Symbol or e. — ADAM 2:18
enfants e. de la patrie — ROUG 670:11
Les e. terribles — GAVA 350:16
enfin E. Malherbe vint — BOIL 131:2
enfolded e. the earth — VIRG 831:3
engine be a Really Useful E. — AWDR 43:11
e. of pollution, the dog — SPAR 765:15
He put this e. to our ears — SWIF 782:6
human e. waits — ELIO 311:12
I am An e. — HARE 382:9
in dirt reasoning e. — ROCH 664:16
two-handed e. — MILT 540:11
engineer e. is a man who can do — SHUT 750:3

engineering E. with fabric — MUIR 564:12
engineers age of the e. — HOGB 402:15
e. of human souls — STAL 769:15
e. of the soul — GORK 366:9
not e. of the soul — KENN 460:14
enginer have the e. Hoist — SHAK 703:21
engines e. to play a little — BURK 173:29
England ah, faithless E. — BOSS 152:1
always be an E. — PARK 596:22
apple falling towards E. — AUDE 37:21
Be E. what she will — CHUR 228:3
between France and E. — JERR 433:16
bored for E. — MUGG 564:6
children in E. — NURS 578:5
Church of E. — CHAR 216:21
damn you E. — OSBO 588:21
deep sleep of E. — ORWE 587:3
end in the ruin of E. — SHEL 742:28
E. and America divided — MISQ 547:12
E. and Ireland — BOWE 153:7
E. and Saint George — SHAK 708:17
E.! awake — BLAK 125:17
E. expects — NELS 570:4
E. has changed — PHIL 606:6
E. has saved herself — PITT 607:20
E. hath need of thee — WORD 866:16
E., home and beauty — ARNO 32:12
E. invented the phrase — BAGE 50:10
E. is a disguised republic — BAGE 50:21
E. is a garden — KIPL 466:1
E. is a nation of shopkeepers — NAPO 568:9
E. is an empire — MICH 534:4
E. is the paradise of women — PROV 631:4
E. keep my bones — SHAK 714:14
E., my England — HENL 391:14
E. not the jewelled isle — ORWE 587:6
E.'s difficulty — PROV 631:5
E.'s green and pleasant — BLAK 125:18
E.'s green and pleasant land — BLAK 126:24
E. shall perish — ELIZ 312:15
E. should be free — MAGE 514:17
E.'s not a bad country — DRAB 293:5
E.'s on the anvil — KIPL 465:6
E.'s the one land — BROO 159:9
E.'s winding sheet — BLAK 124:18
E., their England — MACD 510:12
E. then indeed be free — FABE 322:5
E. to be the workshop — DISR 284:4
E. was too pure an Air — ANON 19:14
E. will have her neck wrung — CHUR 229:20
E., with all thy faults — COWP 256:10
ensure summer in E. — WALP 837:18
gentlemen of E. — PARK 596:20
gives E. her soldiers — MERE 532:11
God punish E. — FUNK 346:21
Goodbye, E.'s rose — JOHN 434:7
Gott strafe E. — FUNK 346:21
Gott strafe E. — POLI 612:19
Heart of E. — DRAY 293:15
here did E. help me — BROW 166:1
History is now and E. — ELIO 309:21
history of E. — MACA 507:9
in E. a particular bashfulness — ADDI 5:16
in E. people have — MIKE 534:23
in E.'s song for ever — NEWB 571:10
in regard to this aged E. — EMER 314:23
Ireland and E. seemed like lovers — TREV 815:12
keep your E. — MUGA 564:3
landscape of E. — AUST 41:11
leads him to E. — JOHN 439:20
Let not E. forget — MILT 546:7
lot that make up E. today — LAWR 484:1
no amusements in E. — SMIT 759:1
Nor E.! did I know till then — WORD 866:10
Oh, to be in E. — BROW 165:27
roast beef of old E. — BURK 175:3
Rule all E. — COLL 242:23
Slaves cannot breathe in E. — COWP 256:9
Speak for E. — AMER 14:6
stately homes of E. — HEMA 390:15
strong arm of E. — PALM 595:3
Such is E. herself — CANN 197:7
suspended in favour of E. — SHAW 740:4

That is for ever E.	BROO 159:13
that will be E. gone	LARK 481:3
think of E.	SAYI 684:7
think of the defence of E.	BALD 53:6
This E. never did	SHAK 714:15
this Realm of E.	BOOK 150:21
this realm, this E.	SHAK 730:11
to convert E.	PUGI 649:5
Wake up, for	GEOR 352:14
we are the people of E.	CHES 224:15
who only E. know	KIPL 465:15
world where E. is finished	MILL 537:4
Ye Mariners of E.	CAMP 195:18
youth of E.	SHAK 708:12
Englanders Little E.	ANON 18:14
English as E. as a beefsteak	HAWT 385:7
attain an E. style	JOHN 436:16
baby doesn't understand E.	KNOX 470:5
bird-haunted E. lawn	ARNO 29:20
can't think of the E.	CARR 202:25
Certain men the E. shot	YEAT 874:4
Cricket—a game which the E.	MANC 518:14
diversity In E.	CHAU 221:11
dominion of the E.	ANON 20:12
E. a nation of	PROV 631:6
E. are busy	MONT 556:6
E. are foul-mouthed	HAZL 386:22
E. are very little indeed inferior	NORT 577:2
E. at that time	WILL 857:5
E. Bible	MACA 507:21
E. child	BLAK 127:12
E. Church shall be free	MAGN 514:18
E. have forgot	BORR 151:15
E. home	TENN 799:2
E. in taste	MACA 508:23
E. is the language	BAGE 51:17
E. kept history in mind	BOWE 153:12
E. know-how	COLO 244:8
E. make it their abode	WALL 836:18
E. never smash in a face	HALS 378:9
E., not the Turkish court	SHAK 708:1
E. plays are like	VOLT 835:5
E. subject's sole prerogative	DRYD 297:1
E. sweete upon his tonge	CHAU 218:13
E. take their pleasures	SULL 780:7
E. than with the Latin	TYND 821:5
E. tongue I love	WALC 835:14
E. unofficial rose	BROO 159:7
E. up with which I will not put	CHUR 230:8
E. want *inferiors*	TOCQ 812:15
expression in E.	ARNO 31:19
fine old E. gentleman	SONG 763:3
flower of E. nobility	ORDE 586:5
fragments of the E. scene	ORWE 587:7
God does not love the E.	CARD 198:3
great E. blight	WAUG 842:10
happy E. child	TAYL 791:14
hard E. men	KING 464:8
in E. the undergrowth	EMPS 315:30
in the E. language	JAME 430:10
king's E.	SHAK 725:17
made our E. tongue	SPEN 768:8
mobilized the E. language	MURR 566:6
Most E. talk	JAME 429:13
My native E.	SHAK 730:4
our sweet E. tongue	FLEC 334:14
raped and speaks E.	ANON 16:9
really nice E. people	SHAW 740:3
rolling E. road	CHES 224:12
Saxon-Danish-Norman E.	DEFO 270:24
scarcely known in E. provinces	ORDE 586:6
second E. satirist	HALL 378:2
seven feet of E. ground	HARO 382:16
shed one E. tear	MACA 508:6
talent of our E. nation	DRYD 296:22
to the E. that of the sea	RICH 661:5
trick of our E. nation	SHAK 707:9
we E. will long maintain	CARL 200:6
We French, we E.	BIRN 122:2
well of E. undefiled	SPEN 767:20
writing in E.	JOYC 448:25
Englishman blood of an E.	ANON 17:6
blood of an E.	NASH 568:24
broad-shouldered genial E.	TENN 799:23
E. born and bred, almost	KURE 474:8
E. can't feel	FORS 337:16
E., even if he is alone	MIKE 534:24
E. in the wrong	SHAW 741:29
E. of the strongest type	DAVI 268:18
E. prudently avoids	TOCQ 812:14
E.'s consitution	AUST 41:16
E.'s home	PROV 631:9
E.'s word	PROV 631:8
E. thinks he is moral	SHAW 741:1
E. to open his mouth	SHAW 742:6
E. to rule in India	NEHR 569:15
Every E. is an island	NOVA 577:11
for E. or Jew	BLAK 125:7
Give but an E.	OTWA 589:13
He is an E.	GILB 358:3
He remains an E.	GILB 358:4
last great E.	TENN 798:20
No E. is ever fairly beaten	SHAW 742:12
not one E.	WALP 838:14
One E. can beat	PROV 640:43
one E. could beat	ADDI 5:13
right of every E.	BLAC 123:12
rights of an E.	JUNI 450:2
There is in the E.	DICK 280:10
thing, an E.	DEFO 270:23
truth-telling E.	HUGH 418:14
what an E. believes	SHAW 742:13
Englishmen don't give E. an inch	BRAD 154:8
E. never will be slaves	SHAW 740:28
first to his E.	MILT 546:2
Mad dogs and E.	COWA 253:15
prefer to be E.	RHOD 659:11
very name as E.	PITT 607:19
When two E. meet	JOHN 436:7
Englishness all the eternal E.	CARD 198:4
Englishwoman E. is so refined	SMIT 757:20
Princess leave the E.	BISM 122:14
engrafted e. word	BIBL 116:18
enigma e. of the fever chart	ELIO 309:12
mystery inside an e.	CHUR 229:11
enjoy business of life is to e.	BUTL 184:3
e. both operations at once	CARY 206:2
e. convalescence	SHAW 739:12
e. him for ever	SHOR 750:2
e. Paradise	BECK 65:1
E. yourself	BÜCH 169:7
have to go out and e. it	SMIT 757:11
inherent will to e.	HARD 381:3
time you're wasting	MISQ 548:21
we may e. them	BOOK 135:2
what I most e.	SHAK 737:22
who can alone	MILT 543:29
enjoyed little to be e.	JOHN 437:16
something you e.	BLAN 128:19
still to be e.	KEAT 455:21
enjoying from e. themselves	RUSS 675:8
if you are e.	NESB 571:3
oh think, it worth e.	DRYD 295:6
enjoyment chief e. of riches	SMIT 756:3
complete e.	HUME 420:6
e. of all desires	TANT 790:5
from e. spring	TRAH 814:14
not for worldly e.	SADI 677:5
stock of intellectual e.	ADDA 4:8
was it done with e.	RUSK 673:22
enjoyments Fire-side e.	COWP 256:21
if it were not for its e.	SURT 781:15
insufficiency of human e.	JOHN 437:19
most intense e.	DOST 291:7
enlarge could e. the world	CURN 263:2
E., diminish	SWIF 783:29
enlargement stability or e.	JOHN 435:18
enlightened knows himself is e.	LAO 480:2
enlightenment end to e.	DOGE 287:9
leads to e.	PALI 594:10
motto of the E.	KANT 453:5
supreme e.	MAHĀ 516:1
winning full e.	MAHĀ 515:8
enmities e. of twenty generations	MACA 507:15
enmity no e. among seekers	AUCT 36:18
there was e.	KORA 472:16
ennoble What can e. sots	POPE 617:7
ennuie *L'éloquence continue e.*	PASC 598:9
ennuyer *secret d'e.*	VOLT 834:6
ennuyeux *hors le genre e.*	VOLT 834:7
Enoch E. walked with God	BIBL 79:19
enough eaten and drunk e.	HORA 411:2
E. as good as a feast	PROV 631:9
e. for everyone's need	BUCH 169:11
E. is enough	PROV 631:10
E.! no more	SHAK 734:27
e. of blood and tears	RABI 652:13
E. that he heard it	BROW 164:17
Give a man rope e.	PROV 632:47
Hold, e.	SHAK 722:26
know is e.	PERS 604:11
never know what is e.	BLAK 126:15
not to go far e.	CONF 246:12
Patriotism is not e.	CAVE 211:16
'tis e., 'twill serve	SHAK 732:22
too much is not e.	BEAU 63:5
two thousand years is e.	PIUS 608:1
Whatever you are is never e.	ACHE 1:9
When thou hast e.	BIBL 97:21
ye eat but ye have not e.	BIBL 96:18
ense *quam sit calamus saevior e.*	BURT 181:12
ensign imperial e.	MILT 541:26
enskyed thing e. and sainted	SHAK 723:1
enslave impossible to e.	BROU 160:10
enslaved should have been more e.	CAVE 211:19
ensue seek peace, and e. it	BOOK 141:21
entangled middle-sized are alone e.	SHEN 747:20
Entbehren *E. sollst Du*	GOET 361:19
enter about to e. a room	EDDI 302:17
e. into the kingdom of heaven	BIBL 99:1
E. not into judgement	BOOK 149:23
King of England cannot e.	PITT 607:9
Let no one e.	ANON 22:16
rich man to e.	BIBL 102:8
shall not e.	BIBL 101:29
she may e. in	SPEN 766:21
you who e.	DANT 264:13
entered iron e. into his soul	BOOK 147:11
enterprise more e. In walking naked	YEAT 872:15
voyages of the starship E.	RODD 665:2
enterprised not by any to be e.	BOOK 138:21
enterprises e. of great pith and moment	SHAK 702:3
entertain e. divine Zenocrate	MARL 523:8
e. the lag-end of my life	SHAK 706:20
e. this starry stranger	CRAS 259:4
E., when they might instruct	MORE 559:1
entertained e. angels unawares	BIBL 116:11
entertainment irrational e.	JOHN 436:23
mere gossiping e.	HUNT 421:14
proffered e.	TROL 816:23
enthral Except you e. me	DONN 288:13
enthralled but not e.	MILT 539:9
enthusiasm achieved without e.	EMER 314:24
do them with e.	COLE 242:19
no e.	LAMB 477:15
ordinary human e.	OSBO 588:17
with a holy e.	ROUS 670:16
enthusiasts few e. can be trusted	BALF 53:11
how to deal with e.	MACA 507:17
entia *E. non sunt multiplicanda*	OCCA 583:10
entice e. thee secretly	BIBL 82:15
enticing with her e. parts	ANON 18:6
entire E. and whole and perfect	SPRI 768:18
e. form of the human condition	MONT 555:21
e. surrender	BELH 67:9
entrails golden e.	DRAY 293:16
swords In our own proper e.	SHAK 714:1
entrance give back my e. ticket	DOST 290:19
entrances exits and their e.	SHAK 696:21
entreat e. heaven daily	ELIZ 312:9
entropy e. of human thought	ZAMY 877:7
envelope e. of its technical forms	MAIN 516:19
semi-transparent e.	WOOL 864:5
envelopes backs of tattered e.	HOPE 407:2

envied Better e. than pitied   PROV 627:31
envious e. may die   MOLI 553:1
   e. sliver broke   SHAK 704:7
   Hot, e., noisy   YOUN 876:13
   I am not e.   VIRG 831:14
environed e. with a great ditch   CROM 260:19
environment humdrum issues like the e.
    THAT 803:18
environmental e. history   SEDD 690:14
envy competition, and mutual e.   HOBB 401:9
   E. and wrath   BIBL 97:27
   E. can scarcely hold back   OVID 590:10
   e., hatred, and malice   BOOK 134:17
   e., never   MOLI 553:1
   e. not in any moods   TENN 795:8
   e. of the devil   BIBL 96:27
   E.'s a sharper spur   GAY 351:13
   E.'s greener   BALL 55:10
   e. the pair of phoenixes   HO 400:12
   extinguisheth e.   BACO 46:23
   in e. of great Caesar   SHAK 714:3
   inspires us with so much e.   LA R 482:4
   moved with e.   BIBL 109:33
   prisoners of e.   ILLI 424:18
   reduce the force of e.   RETZ 658:13
   Toil, e., want   JOHN 438:6
   Too low for e.   COWL 254:12
   with e. and revenge   MILT 541:11
épater é. le bourgeois   BAUD 62:4
epaulette been by any e.   THOR 809:24
Ephesians Diana of the E.   BIBL 110:7
Ephesus beasts at E.   BIBL 112:23
Ephraim grapes of E.   BIBL 83:8
epic E. writer with a k   STEV 776:10
   name of E.'s no misnomer   BYRO 188:4
epicure Serenely full, the e.   SMIT 758:20
Epicurus E.' herd of pigs   HORA 410:7
   E. owene sone   CHAU 218:18
epigram Impelled to try an e.   PARK 596:6
   purrs like an e.   MARQ 523:18
   What is an E.   COLE 239:14
epigrams despotism tempered by e.
    CARL 200:3
epilogue good play needs no e.   SHAK 698:1
epiphany e. a sudden spiritual   JOYC 448:12
episcopal e. hat   AUBR 35:15
episode but the occasional e.   HARD 380:16
epistula Verbosa et grandis e.   JUVE 451:12
epitaph better have a bad e.   SHAK 701:17
   carve my e.   BROW 165:4
   e. to be my story   FROS 344:16
   no man write my e.   EMME 315:23
   that may be his e.   STEV 775:6
epitaphs nice derangement of e.   SHER 748:14
   of worms, and e.   SHAK 730:18
epitome all life's e.   YEAT 873:17
   all mankind's e.   DRYD 294:20
eppur E. si muove   GALI 348:1
equal all men are created e.   LINC 494:1
   consider our e.   DARW 266:20
   e. division of unequal earnings   ELLI 313:16
   e. in dignity and rights   ANON 16:5
   E. Pay   ANTH 24:18
   e. to any other person   PRIE 624:1
   e. with God   BIBL 114:18
   faith shines e.   BRON 158:15
   law has made him e.   DARR 266:6
   men are created e.   JEFF 431:6
   more e. than others   ORWE 586:18
   one e. eternity   DONN 290:13
   separate and e. station   JEFF 431:5
   to that e. sky   POPE 616:21
   we'll be e.   PAST 598:21
   Woman is the e. of man   LOY 503:15
equality apostles of e.   ARNO 31:10
   E. for women demands   TOYN 814:6
   e. in the servants' hall   BARR 59:14
   E. may perhaps be   BALZ 56:15
   E. would be heaven   TROL 816:22
   liberty and e.   ARIS 28:3
   majestic e. of the law   FRAN 340:8
   not e. or fairness   BERL 73:10
   we value e.   ADAM 3:19

equalization natural e.   CHUA 227:8
equalize never e.   BURK 174:3
equally [Death] comes e.   DONN 290:8
equals commerce between e.   GOLD 364:30
   converse with my e., my vegetables
    CHES 223:18
   least of all between e.   BACO 46:29
   live together as e.   MILL 536:15
   peace between e.   WILS 859:18
   Pigs treat us as e.   CHUR 231:3
equanimity face with e.   GILB 356:20
equation each e. would halve the sales
    HAWK 385:1
   e. for me has no meaning   RAMA 654:19
equations beauty in one's e.   DIRA 283:20
   fire into the e.   HAWK 385:3
   in disagreement with Maxwell's e.   EDDI 302:16
   politics and e.   EINS 306:3
equators North Poles and E.   CARR 203:29
equi currite noctis e.   MARL 522:11
   currite noctis e.   OVID 589:17
equinox when was the e.   BROW 162:19
equity people with e.   BOOK 146:13
equivocate I will not e.   GARR 349:17
equo E. ne credite   VIRG 829:6
eradicate e. from the heart   BRON 158:6
eradication e. of conferences   MAYA 529:3
erected least e. spirit   MILT 541:29
Erin for E. dear we fall   SULL 780:5
   fresh-stirred hearts in E.   FERG 325:6
eripuit E. coelo fulmen   TURG 819:7
eripuitque E. Jovi   MANI 519:7
err e. is human   SAYI 685:15
   Man will e.   GOET 361:13
   mortal, and may e.   SHIR 749:19
   most may e.   DRYD 295:1
   prefer To e.   ANON 21:15
   To e. is human   POPE 616:10
   To e. is human   PROV 645:25
errand thy joyous e.   FITZ 331:29
errands Meet to be sent on e.   SHAK 713:19
   run on little e.   GILB 356:12
erred e., and strayed from thy ways
    BOOK 133:4
   e. exceedingly   BIBL 84:10
erreur L'e. n'a jamais approché   METT 533:13
erroneous conscience, may be e.   HOBB 401:6
error E. has never approached   METT 533:13
   e. is immense   BOLI 131:14
   he is in e.   LOCK 497:7
   Hence into deadly e.   SANA 679:18
   leading his soul into e.   AUGU 39:17
   limit to infinite e.   BREC 155:15
   made the e. double   CLAR 232:21
   men are liable to e.   LOCK 497:11
   positive in e. as in truth   LOCK 497:10
   Reject that vulgar e.   BUCK 169:16
   stalking-horse to e.   BOLI 131:11
   troops of e.   BROW 162:23
   ut me malus abstulit e.   VIRG 832:6
   very e. of the moon   SHAK 729:15
errors common e. of our life   SIDN 751:7
   e. and absurdities   BURN 176:17
   E., like straws   DRYD 295:8
   E. look so very ugly   ELIO 308:12
   e. of a wise man   BLAK 126:28
   reasoned e.   HUXL 423:14
eructavit Cor meum e.   BIBL 119:26
erupit evasit, e.   CICE 232:3
eruption bodes some strange e.   SHAK 699:3
Esau E. my brother   BIBL 80:6
   E. selleth his birthright   BIBL 80:3
   E. was a cunning hunter   BIBL 80:4
   hands are the hands of E.   BIBL 80:7
escalier esprit de l'e.   DIDE 282:14
escape Beauty for some provides e.   HUXL 423:2
   can be no e. from it   CHUA 227:12
   did not expect to e.   TURN 819:13
   e. can be shown   PALI 594:20
   e. kitsch completely   KUND 474:6
   e. my iambics   CATU 211:7
   Gluttony an emotional e.   DE V 275:4
   great ones e.   PROV 637:45

   let me ever e.   BOOK 149:22
   Let no guilty man e.   GRAN 368:17
   many deaths do they e.   BYRO 189:2
   nothing to e. to   ELIO 308:23
   not to e. others   PORT 619:21
   What struggle to e.   KEAT 455:17
escaped e. with the skin of my teeth   BIBL 86:33
   Our soul is e.   BOOK 148:22
   through language and e.   BROW 167:10
eschew E. evil   BOOK 141:21
   If we cannot e. hatred   SETH 693:1
escutcheon blot on the e.   GRAY 369:17
Eskdale E. and Liddesdale   SCOT 689:18
Eskimo E. forgets his language   OKPI 584:22
esperance Now, E.! Percy   SHAK 706:26
   stands still in e.   SHAK 716:9
espionage e. can be recommended
    WEST 848:20
espoused My fairest, my e.   MILT 543:17
   my late e. saint   MILT 545:16
esprit e. de l'escalier   DIDE 282:14
   n'a jamais approché de mon e.   METT 533:13
essay ends in e.   MACA 508:1
   e. much   ELGA 306:16
esse E. quam videri bonus   SALL 679:9
essence e. is very real   LAO 479:12
   e. of a human soul   CARL 200:27
   e. of human life   MACD 510:4
   e. of innumerable biographies   CARL 199:13
   e. of the true sublime   BYRO 190:2
   precedes and rules e.   SART 681:9
essenced long e. hair   MACA 508:5
essential e. ingredient   PHIL 605:15
   what is e.   SAIN 677:14
established so sure e.   BOOK 133:1
estate e. of the Catholick Church   BOOK 135:6
   e. o' the world   SHAK 722:23
   fourth e. of the realm   MACA 506:15
   holy e.   BOOK 138:21
   in mind, body, or e.   BOOK 135:7
   low e. of his handmaiden   BIBL 104:8
   ordered their e.   ALEX 12:7
esteemed e. him not   BIBL 94:3
estranging unplumbed, salt, e. sea   ARNO 31:5
esuriens Graeculus e.   JUVE 450:19
esurientes E. implevit bonis   BIBL 120:11
état L'É. c'est moi   LOUI 501:3
éteint qui ne s'é.   RENO 658:9
eternal authority of the e. yesterday
    WEBE 843:16
   boy e.   SHAK 736:17
   by the e. mind   WORD 867:11
   contact with e. beings   ARIS 27:16
   E. Father, strong to save   WHIT 851:18
   e. Footman hold my coat   ELIO 310:10
   E. in man cannot kill   BHAG 77:17
   E. in man cannot kill   UPAN 822:9
   E. Passion   ARNO 29:22
   e. rocks beneath   BRON 158:19
   e. silence   PASC 598:1
   E. sunshine of the spotless mind   POPE 614:11
   e. triangle   ANON 16:26
   Grant them e. rest   MISS 550:4
   Hope springs e.   POPE 616:19
   Hope springs e.   PROV 634:44
   lose not the things e.   BOOK 136:4
   our e. home   WATT 842:7
   ourselves to be e.   JERO 433:6
   portion of the E.   SHEL 743:16
   Promised from e. years   CASW 206:16
   Robust art alone is e.   GAUT 350:14
   thy e. summer   SHAK 737:19
   way to e. suffering   DANT 264:13
   whose e. Word   MARR 523:19
eternally things abided e.   TRAH 814:13
eternities between two e.   CARL 200:9
   meeting of two e.   THOR 809:13
eternity battlements of E.   THOM 807:18
   candidates for e.   MORE 559:1
   day joins the past e.   BYRO 186:17
   Deserts of vast e.   MARV 525:12
   e. hath triumphed   RALE 654:9
   e. in an hour   BLAK 124:9

E. is in love	BLAK 126:8
e. of print	WOOL 864:3
E.'s a terrible thought	STOP 778:1
E. shut in a span	CRAS 259:5
E.'s sunrise	BLAK 127:2
E.'s too short	ADDI 5:15
E.! thou pleasing, dreadful thought	ADDI 4:22
E. was in our lips and eyes	SHAK 694:15
E. was in that moment	CONG 247:15
Heads Were toward E.	DICK 281:12
image of e.	BYRO 187:4
mansions in e.	BLAK 128:12
one equal e.	DONN 290:13
palace of e.	MILT 538:20
pinprick of e.	AURE 40:16
progress to e.	SHAK 738:6
same sweet e.	HERR 396:2
saw E. the other night	VAUG 825:14
shadows of e.	VAUG 825:6
Silence is deep as E.	CARL 199:16
some conception of e.	MANC 518:14
speak of e.	BROW 162:27
speculations of e.	ADDI 5:14
teacher affects e.	ADAM 2:16
through nature to e.	SHAK 699:14
travellers of e.	BASH 61:1
Tree of E.	UPAN 822:13
white radiance of E.	SHEL 743:21
who love, time is e.	VAN 824:4
without injuring e.	THOR 809:11
etherized patient e. upon a table	ELIO 310:5
patient e. upon a table	LEWI 491:20
ethic protestant e.	WEBE 843:13
ethical e. dimension	COOK 250:11
nuclear giants and e. infants	BRAD 154:7
ethics law floats in a sea of e.	WARR 840:8
Ethiop E.'s ear	SHAK 732:7
Ethiopian E. change his skin	BIBL 95:3
ethnological in the e. section	EMPS 315:24
etiquette It isn't e.	CARR 203:24
Eton playing-fields of E.	ORWE 587:8
playing fields of E.	WELL 846:13
étonne É.-moi	DIAG 275:11
étrange é. entreprise	MOLI 552:2
Etrurian where the E. shades	MILT 541:21
Etruscans long-nosed E.	LAWR 483:17
etymology E. is a science	VOLT 835:6
Euclid E. alone has looked	MILL 536:22
fifth proposition of E.	DOYL 292:19
Eugene Aram E., though a thief	CALV 194:5
eunuch female e.	GREE 372:4
intellectual e. Castlereàgh	BYRO 187:19
kills me to be time's e.	HOPK 408:11
prerogative of the e.	STOP 777:14
strain, Time's e.	HOPK 408:3
eunuchs seraglio of e.	FOOT 336:8
euphoric In an e. dream	AUDE 38:6
Euphrates bathed in the E.	HUGH 418:3
Eureka E.! [I've got it!]	ARCH 26:2
Euripides chorus-ending from E.	BROW 164:24
Europe another war in E.	BISM 123:4
arsenal of old E.	HEGE 388:16
Bright over E.	TURN 819:9
corrupt as in E.	JEFF 431:12
create a nation E.	MONN 553:13
depravations of E.	MATH 527:13
dogs of E. bark	AUDE 37:11
E. a continent of energetic mongrels	
	FISH 327:20
E. by her example	PITT 607:20
E. has never existed	MONN 553:12
E. in danger of plunging	YELT 875:19
E. made his woe her own	ARNO 30:22
E. of nations	DE G 271:12
E. the unfinished negative	MCCA 509:6
E. took their gold	CHUR 228:9
fifty years of E.	TENN 797:8
glory of E.	BURK 174:7
great stocks of E.	YEAT 875:15
in the centre of E.	WEST 848:19
I pine for E.	RIMB 662:12
keep up with Western E.	UPDI 822:19
lamps are going out all over E.	GREY 373:1

last gentleman in E.	LEVE 491:3
Leave this E.	FANO 323:1
map of E. has been changed	CHUR 229:5
nationalities of E.	ASQU 34:4
part of the community of E.	SALI 678:18
poor are E.'s blacks	CHAM 215:4
security of E.	MITC 550:15
spectre is haunting E.	MARX 526:12
sunk in E.	BANK 57:13
take over the whole of E.	RIDL 661:9
that's old E.	RUMS 672:6
Whoever speaks of E.	BISM 123:1
whole of E.	NAPO 567:16
Without Britain, E.	ERHA 320:7
European by any E. powers	MONR 553:15
E. war might do it	REDM 657:2
great E. race	DAVI 268:16
green pastures of the E.	VERW 826:16
I'm E.	HEWI 397:16
not a characteristic of a E.	CHAN 215:15
on E. Monetary Union	CHIR 226:8
policy of E. integration	KOHL 470:13
Europeans You are learned E.	MASS 527:10
Euston in E. waiting-room	CORN 252:1
evasit e., erupit	CICE 232:3
eve and E. spane	ROLL 666:12
E. from his side arose	ANON 21:11
fairest of her daughters E.	MILT 543:7
From far, from e.	HOUS 416:3
nor E. the rites	MILT 543:13
real curse of E.	RHYS 659:14
riverrun, past E. and Adam's	JOYC 448:1
When Adam delved and E. span	PROV 646:36
Evelyn E. Hope is dead	BROW 165:19
even Don't get mad, get e.	SAYI 684:15
E. as you and I	KIPL 467:19
E. less am I	HOPE 407:4
evening along the road of e.	DE L 272:10
autumn e.	ARNO 30:5
came still e. on	MILT 543:9
E., all	CATC 207:17
e. and the morning	BIBL 78:13
e.—any evening—	LEWI 491:20
e. is spread out against the sky	ELIO 310:5
e. of life	GIBB 355:7
e. sacrifice	BOOK 149:21
e. star	MILT 544:14
e. star is coming	VIRG 832:11
exhalation in the e.	SHAK 710:18
in the e. it is cut down	BOOK 145:20
It is a beauteous e.	WORD 866:4
light of e., Lissadell	YEAT 873:15
like an e. gone	WATT 842:7
red e.-star is lighting	VIRG 832:15
Some enchanted e.	HAMM 378:21
welcome peaceful e. in	COWP 256:19
When e.'s come	COLL 242:20
When it is e.	BIBL 101:24
winter e. settles down	ELIO 310:21
evensong bells ringeth to e.	HAWE 384:10
ringeth to e.	PROV 627:26
event as the e. decides	AUST 42:6
greatest e. it is	FOX 339:11
hurries to the main as in e.	HORA 409:8
not an e.	TALL 788:16
wise after the e.	PROV 636:16
eventide fast falls the e.	LYTE 506:4
events Coming e. cast	PROV 629:13
diversity of human e.	MONT 555:18
E., dear boy	MACM 513:3
e. have controlled me	LINC 494:3
e. overlapping each other	DURR 300:16
opposition of e.	MACM 513:3
train of e.	AMER 14:5
We cannot make e.	ADAM 4:2
ever e.-fixèd mark	SHAK 738:15
For e. panting	KEAT 455:21
Hardly e.	GILB 357:25
have you e. been	POLI 612:3
Nothing is for e.	SAYI 685:6
WELL, DID YOU E.	PORT 619:19
Everest climbed Mount E.	JOHN 434:15
evergreen e. tree	SHER 748:11

everlasting caught An e. cold	WEBS 844:27
e. arms	BIBL 82:21
e. Father	BIBL 92:14
e. life	BIBL 107:13
e. life	BIBL 107:25
e. mansion	SHAK 734:9
e. No	CARL 200:23
from e. thou art God	WATT 842:7
from e. time	AURE 40:17
from e. to everlasting	TRAH 814:11
give them an e. name	BIBL 94:11
life e.	BOOK 133:19
thy e. kingdom	BOOK 138:18
everlastingness shoots of e.	VAUG 825:7
evermore e. shalt be	HEBE 388:10
for e.	BOOK 148:18
name liveth for e.	BIBL 98:5
name liveth for e.	EPIT 319:12
every E. day a little death	SOND 760:22
E. day, I am getting better	COUÉ 253:4
E. which way	FILM 331:5
To e. thing	BIBL 89:23
everybody E. has won	CARR 201:15
E.'s business	PROV 631:13
E. wants to get inta	CATC 207:18
What e. says	PROV 646:20
where is e.	FERM 325:13
everyday against the e.	MAYA 529:6
e. story of country folk	CATC 207:19
science and e. life	FRAN 341:13
Everyman Death would summon E.	
	HEAN 387:6
E., I will go with thee	ANON 17:1
everyone can't please e.	PROV 647:44
E. burst out singing	SASS 682:9
like e. else	DE G 271:18
To be like e. else	SHIE 749:13
When e. is wrong	LA C 475:5
everything against e.	KENN 460:18
cannot all do e.	LUCI 504:2
can't all do e.	VIRG 832:8
chips with e.	WESK 847:4
E. has an end	PROV 631:34
E. has been said	LA B 475:3
e. in its place	BEVA 77:4
E. is fitting	AURE 40:9
e. is in it	TALM 789:10
E. is not itself	RILK 661:17
E. passes	ANON 22:12
e. that is the case	WITT 861:13
E. what it is	BUTL 182:19
God encompasses e.	KORA 471:21
Greek can do e.	JUVE 450:19
knowledge of e.	HERO 395:13
Life, the Universe and E.	ADAM 2:5
Macaulay is of e.	MELB 530:16
Money isn't e.	PROV 638:47
place for e.	PROV 641:38
robbed a man of e.	SOLZ 760:11
sans taste, sans e.	SHAK 697:3
smattering of e.	DICK 281:2
terrain is e.	PAST 599:5
time for e.	PROV 644:19
too much of e.	FERB 325:3
everywhere behaviour e.	SHAK 724:4
centre is e.	ANON 19:4
children . . . e.	CATC 207:25
Functioning e. means	LAO 479:13
Out of the e.	MACD 510:6
Water, water, e.	COLE 240:21
evidence before you have all the e.	
	DOYL 292:24
believe things without e.	HUXL 424:1
circumstantial e.	THOR 809:6
clearer e. than this	ARAB 25:11
e. of things not seen	BIBL 116:3
it's not e.	DICK 280:22
only e. of life	NEWM 572:1
require extraordinary e.	SAGA 677:6
soldier said isn't e.	PROV 646:30
wordy e. of the fact	ELIO 307:17
evidences E. of Christianity	COLE 241:17
evil all e.'s root	SUDR 779:16

evil (*cont*.):
all men are e. — MACH 511:4
All partial e. — POPE 616:27
all the e. he does — LA R 482:2
axis of e. — BUSH 182:11
banality of e. — AREN 26:6
becoming a principle of e. — CAMU 196:15
branches of e. — THOR 809:17
call e. good — BIBL 92:4
dark and e. days — INGR 425:12
days are e. — BIBL 114:10
deeds were e. — BIBL 107:14
deliver us from e. — BIBL 99:12
deliver us from e. — MISS 549:17
Do e. in return — AUDE 38:5
do e., that good may come — BIBL 110:26
do e. that good may come — PROV 639:34
doing e. in return — SOCR 760:2
done e. to his neighbour — BOOK 140:1
Don't be e. — SLOG 755:3
don't think that he's e. — ALLE 13:11
Eschew e. — BOOK 141:21
e. and adulterous generation — BIBL 101:8
E., be thou my good — MILT 542:30
E. be to him who evil thinks — MOTT 563:10
E. communications — BIBL 113:1
E. communications — PROV 631:36
e. counsel is most evil — HESI 397:6
e. cradling — KORA 471:8
E. doers evil dreaders — PROV 631:37
e. empire — REAG 656:15
e. from his youth — BIBL 79:24
e. in a city — BIBL 96:11
e. in thy sight — BOOK 143:4
e. in young minds — ARNO 32:16
e. is wrought — HOOD 405:19
e. manners live in brass — SHAK 711:5
e. that men do lives — SHAK 712:28
e. thereof — BIBL 99:20
e. thereof — PROV 643:49
e. turn to good — MILT 544:16
e. which I would not — BIBL 110:37
expect e. of those — ABEL 1:2
face of 'e.' — BURR 180:15
far deeper than the e. — FORS 338:4
fear nae e. — BURN 179:17
Few and e. — BIBL 80:28
find means of e. — MILT 541:15
for e. to triumph — MISQ 548:4
God by curse Created e. — MILT 542:14
God prepares e. — ANON 23:1
Good and e. shall not be held — KORA 472:16
great book is a great e. — PROV 633:27
he that doeth e. — BIBL 117:21
Hypocrisy, the only e. — MILT 542:26
idleness being the root of e. — KIER 462:12
Idleness is root of all e. — PROV 635:4
If all e. were prevented — THOM 805:9
illness identified with e. — SONT 761:5
immense mass of e. — TOLS 813:11
knowing good and e. — BIBL 79:5
like great e. — CALL 193:17
man produces e. — GOLD 363:16
means to fight an e. — DAWS 269:5
meet e.-willers — ELIZ 312:4
my tongue from e.-speaking — BOOK 138:13
necessary e. — BRAD 154:3
necessary e. — PAIN 592:8
never do e. so fully — PASC 598:12
no e. happen unto thee — BOOK 146:2
non-cooperation with e. — GAND 348:14
not wholly e. — BARR 59:19
on the e. and on the good — BIBL 99:7
open and notorious e. liver — BOOK 136:16
overcome e. with good — BIBL 111:13
perplexity of radical e. — AREN 26:7
presuppose that all men are e. — RALE 654:7
prevention from e. — MANN 519:9
punishment in itself is e. — BENT 71:7
rash hand in e. hour — MILT 544:6
refuse the e. — BIBL 92:11
rendering evil for e. — BIBL 117:10
represent poverty as no e. — JOHN 440:1

Resist not e. — BIBL 99:5
return good for e. — VANB 823:17
rewarded me e. for good — BOOK 141:22
root of all e. — BIBL 115:23
root of all e. — PROV 639:2
See no e. — PROV 642:41
supernatural source of e. — CONR 249:11
unruly e. — BIBL 116:24
what constitutes e. — DURA 300:7
whatever e. visits thee — KORA 471:18
What we call e. — FORD 337:4
willed no e. — STEP 772:8
wish me e. — BOOK 144:15
withstand in the e. day — BIBL 114:15
evils enamoured of existing e. — BIER 121:6
E., Theodorus, can never pass — PLAT 609:6
expect new e. — BACO 47:12
fighting e. — BERL 73:8
greatest of e. — SHAW 740:12
least of e. — GRAC 367:7
make imaginary e. — GOLD 365:1
necessary e. — JOHN 437:8
Of the two e. — THOM 805:3
Of two e. choose — PROV 640:28
Two e., monstrous either one — RANS 655:7
War being the greatest of e. — MELV 531:14
evolution E. . . . is—a change — SPEN 765:21
e. is more like pushing — HEAN 387:19
interested in e. — JONE 445:10
Some call it e. — CARR 204:8
ewe one little e. lamb — BIBL 84:16
tupping your white e. — SHAK 728:3
ewes milk my e. and weep — SHAK 737:6
my e. breed not — BARN 59:10
Ewig-Weibliche E. zieht uns hinan — GOET 362:7
exact Detection is an e. science — DOYL 292:19
not to be e. — BURK 173:6
writing an e. man — BACO 48:2
exactitude L'e. est la politesse — LOUI 501:11
exaggerate e. the difference — SHAW 740:20
exaggerated have been greatly e. — TWAI 820:26
exaggeration E. is a truth — GIBR 355:17
exalt e. us unto the same place — BOOK 136:1
exalted e. among the heathen — BOOK 142:19
e. them of low degree — BIBL 104:9
highly e. him — BIBL 114:19
Reason, in her most e. mood — WORD 868:21
Sorrow proud to be e. — ANON 18:6
valley shall be e. — BIBL 93:15
exalteth whosoever e. himself — BIBL 105:20
exam have an e. at 11 — NEIL 569:16
examinations E. are formidable — COLT 244:10
In e., those who do not wish — RALE 654:15
examine E. for a moment — WOOL 864:4
E. me, O Lord — BOOK 141:6
e. my thoughts — BOOK 149:20
example annoyance of a good e. — TWAI 820:23
Europe by her e. — PITT 607:20
E. better than precept — PROV 631:38
E. is always more efficacious — JOHN 437:18
E. is the school — BURK 175:12
set us a good e. — WILD 854:14
examples infinite e. — MONT 555:18
philosophy from e. — DION 283:18
exceed e. his grasp — BROW 164:19
exceedingly E. good cakes — ADVE 7:23
excel daring to e. — CHUR 228:2
thou shalt not e. — BIBL 80:29
excelled could have e. — QUIN 652:6
excellence Between us and e. — HESI 397:7
in conformity with e. — ARIS 27:8
ne'er will reach an e. — DRYD 297:4
excellencies rather upon e. — ADDI 5:10
excellent e. thing in woman — SHAK 717:7
e. things for mean — LOCK 497:5
his Name only is e. — BOOK 150:10
too wonderful and e. — BOOK 149:16
Very e. things — BOOK 145:18
excellently Goddess, e. bright — JONS 446:3
see them all so e. fair — COLE 239:8
excelling all loves e. — WESL 847:17
Excelsior strange device E. — LONG 499:5
excelsis Gloria in e. — MISS 549:8

except E. the Lord build — BOOK 149:2
exception allowing for e. — SPAR 765:8
e. proves the rule — PROV 631:39
e. to every rule — PROV 644:22
e. to the ordinary rules — HAZL 385:19
glad to make an e. — MARX 526:2
excess abstinence nor e. — VOLT 834:18
e. of light — GRAY 370:20
e. of stupidity — JOHN 440:5
Nothing in e. — ANON 22:17
poverty and e. — PENN 602:15
ridiculous e. — SHAK 714:11
road of e. — BLAK 126:4
excessit Abiit, e. — CICE 232:3
excessive e. bright — MILT 542:23
right of an e. wrong — BROW 167:15
exchange By just e. one for the other — SIDN 750:14
e. of self and other — SHAN 739:3
fair e. no robbery — PROV 631:50
excise E.. A hateful tax — JOHN 435:22
exciseman deil's awa wi' th'E. — BURN 178:1
excite e. my amorous propensities — JOHN 438:26
excitement it engendered e. — PAGE 592:1
exciting films are too e. — BERR 75:4
excluded castes who are e. — LAWS 484:18
E. from honours — ADAM 2:3
irrevocably e. — SHEL 743:5
excommunicate thou, poor e. — CARE 198:16
excrement in the place of e. — YEAT 873:1
excursion called the 'E.' — BYRO 188:26
made an e. to hell — PRIE 623:13
excuse bad e. better than none — PROV 627:3
began to make e. — BIBL 105:21
cruelty with an e. — COMP 245:3
e. every man will plead — SELD 691:11
E. my dust — EPIT 317:5
I will not e. — GARR 349:17
make a good e. — SZAS 786:16
no e. for breaking it — PROV 635:39
excuses e., accuses himself — PROV 634:19
e. for our failures — FULB 346:4
Several e. — HUXL 422:19
excusing too much e. — ACTO 1:17
execute people who e. them — MILL 536:14
zealous Muslims to e. — KHOM 462:7
executing thought-e. fires — SHAK 715:16
execution Ceaușescus' e. — O'DO 583:12
fascination of a public e. — FOOT 336:7
stringent e. — GRAN 368:16
executioner I am mine own E. — DONN 290:3
executioners victims who respect their e. — SART 681:15
executive e. expression — BRIT 157:13
salary of the chief e. — GALB 347:12
executives e. Would never want — AUDE 37:9
executors Let's choose e. — SHAK 730:18
exercise all, e. — GREE 371:7
e. is to the body — STEE 770:18
e. myself in great matters — BOOK 149:9
e. of his soul's faculties — ARIS 27:8
for cure, on e. depend — DRYD 295:20
love's proper e. — DAVI 267:20
sad mechanic e. — TENN 795:2
with oneself is a good e. — FREU 342:19
exertion e. is too much for me — PEAC 600:18
exertions saved herself by her e. — PITT 607:20
exhalation Like a bright e. — SHAK 710:18
exhaust e. the little moment — BROO 160:1
exhibited publicly e. — ALBE 11:4
exigency to the e. of the moment — PEEL 601:10
exile destined as an e. — VIRG 828:10
die in e. — GREG 372:7
e. is his country — URBA 823:3
silence, e., and cunning — JOYC 448:11
exiled Marcellus e. — POPE 617:9
outlawed or e. — MAGN 515:1
exiles none save e. feel — AYTO 44:8
Paradise of e. — SHEL 744:10
exist could not possibly e. — DESC 274:10
didn't e. before — UPDI 822:26
e. in order to save us — DE V 275:5
He doesn't e. — BECK 64:7

eye (cont.):
My tiny watching e. — DE L 272:12
neither e. to see — LENT 489:15
obscured that e. — KEAT 457:5
Of e. and ear — WORD 866:14
one e. is weeping — FROS 344:6
On it may stay his e. — HERB 394:6
Please your e. — PROV 641:39
see e. to eye — BIBL 94:1
seeing — BIBL 88:27
soft black e. — MOOR 558:14
still-soliciting e. — SHAK 714:20
through the e. — EPIT 317:7
to the e. of God — OLIV 585:3
unforgiving e. — SHER 748:28
untrusting e. on all they do — GELL 352:2
What the e. doesn't see — PROV 646:29
'with his e. on the object' — ARNO 32:7
with his glittering e. — COLE 240:13
With my little e. — NURS 582:12
with, not through, the e. — BLAK 125:4
eyeball e. to eyeball — RUSK 673:3
like a coal His e. — SMAR 754:15
eyebrows e. made of platinum — FORS 337:15
eyed one e. man is king — PROV 636:2
eyeless E. in Gaza — MILT 544:31
work of an e. computer — BETJ 76:2
eyelids e. heavy and red — HOOD 406:1
tired e. upon tired eyes — TENN 797:9
Upon her e. many Graces — SPEN 767:11
eyes all e. else dead coals — SHAK 737:8
And her e. were wild — KEAT 455:6
bodily hunger in his e. — SHAW 740:15
buyer needs hundred e. — PROV 628:28
chewing gum for the e. — ANON 20:13
Closed his e. — GRAY 370:20
Close your e. — SAYI 684:7
close your e. before — AYCK 43:13
close your e. with holy dread — COLE 240:9
cold commemorative e. — ROSS 669:21
constitutional e. — LINC 494:7
cynosure of neighbouring e. — MILT 539:28
Cynthia first, with her e. — PROP 624:19
dark e. darting light — BYRO 188:11
death bandaged my e. — BROW 167:8
Donna Julia's e. — BYRO 187:25
doves' e. — BIBL 91:4
drew his e. along — AUGU 39:5
electrical skin and glaring e. — SMAR 754:13
Eternity was in our lips and e. — SHAK 694:15
ever more perfect e. — TEIL 792:12
E. and ears — HERA 393:6
e. are bright — KEAT 458:6
e. are oddly made — HAMM 379:5
e. are window of soul — PROV 631:45
e. as big as millstones — ANDE 15:9
e. as wide as a football-pool — CAUS 211:9
e. became so terrible — BECK 64:29
e. did see Olivia — SHAK 734:28
e. have all the seeming — POE 611:4
e. have seen — LOWE 503:3
e. have they, and see not — BOOK 148:5
e. like lead — BROW 165:23
e. like the fishpools — BIBL 91:15
e. of Caligula — MITT 551:10
E. of most unholy blue — MOOR 558:7
E. still dazzled — LIND 495:2
e. that looked so mild — BALL 54:18
e. to behold the sun — BIBL 90:18
e. to the blind — BIBL 87:2
e. to wonder — SHAK 738:11
e. upon his graces — JOHN 437:6
e. were as a flame — BIBL 117:27
e. were blacker than the sloe — CARB 197:15
e. which see — BIBL 105:3
Fields have e. — PROV 632:10
Foolish e. — SANS 680:12
four beasts full of e. — BIBL 118:4
Four e. see more — PROV 632:38
friendship closes its e. — ANON 22:5
From women's e. — SHAK 717:17
From women's e. — SHAK 717:19
full of e. within — BIBL 118:5

Get thee glass e. — SHAK 716:21
God be in my e. — PRAY 623:4
Hath not a Jew e. — SHAK 724:18
her e., her hair — MEW 533:14
Her e. the glow-worm lend — HERR 396:3
hid from thine e. — BIBL 106:16
King of England's e. — TYND 821:7
lightened are our e. — SORL 761:23
Looking into his e. — PURD 650:15
Love in thine e. — LODG 498:7
Love looks not with the e. — SHAK 725:25
maidens Quiet e. — STEV 776:20
marvellous in our e. — BOOK 148:11
Mine e. have seen — HOWE 417:3
mock our e. with air — SHAK 695:16
My mistress' e. — SHAK 738:19
night has a thousand e. — BOUR 153:2
Night hath a thousand e. — LYLY 505:22
one, all e. — WORD 868:4
open The king's e. — SHAK 710:15
optics of these e. — BROW 163:7
pearls that were his e. — SHAK 733:21
pick out hawks' e. — PROV 633:50
Pure e. and Christian hearts — KEBL 459:2
put out the people's e. — MILT 545:20
Seal her sweet e. — ROSS 669:6
Smoke gets in your e. — HARB 379:15
soft look Your e. had once — YEAT 875:10
Stars scribble on our e. — CRAN 258:12
stuck in her face for e. — SHAK 717:14
Take a pair of sparkling e. — GILB 356:13
tempts your wand'ring e. — GRAY 370:17
Thine e. my pride — SIDN 751:1
those e., the break of day — SHAK 723:17
through another man's e. — SHAK 697:22
turn'st mine e. — SHAK 703:13
unto dying e. — TENN 799:12
was it his bees-winged e. — BETJ 75:9
why the good Lord made your e. — LEHR 488:2
will lift mine e. — SCOT 690:11
with fortune and men's e. — SHAK 737:21
with his half-shut e. — POPE 618:14
Within my e. — LODG 498:6
with no e. — SHAK 716:19
with thine e. — JONS 446:20
You have lovely e. — CHEK 222:6
you'll see your e. out — ZOLA 878:12
eyeservice Not with e. — BIBL 114:13

faber F. est suae — CLAU 234:5
Fabians civilization of the F. — INGE 425:2
good man fallen among F. — LENI 488:20
fabill nocht bot f. — BARB 58:3
fable f. will not do — BYRO 189:25
life's sweet f. — CRAS 259:11
fables blasphemous f. — BOOK 150:20
f. in the legend — BACO 46:5
Hesperian f. — MILT 543:2
profane and old wives' f. — BIBL 115:20
fabric Engineering with f. — MUIR 564:12
f. of this vision — SHAK 733:31
fabula F. narratur — HORA 414:8
fac Dilige et quod vis f. — AUGU 39:18
face Accustomed to her f. — LERN 490:10
angry look on the f. — AURE 40:18
beautiful f. is a mute — PUBL 648:29
born with a different f. — BLAK 125:22
bright f. of danger — STEV 775:5
construction in the f. — SHAK 718:18
covered his f. — BIBL 92:6
Cover her f. — WEBS 844:12
darkness was upon the f. — BIBL 78:12
disasters in his morning f. — GOLD 364:7
divine plain f. — LAMB 477:9
draw a full f. — DRYD 297:24
eat anything with a f. — MCCA 509:9
English never smash in a f. — HALS 378:9
f. in a glass — BIBL 116:18
f. is my fortune — NURS 582:11
f. looks like a wedding-cake — AUDE 38:22
f. neither East nor West — NKRU 576:17
f. of a dog — GARC 349:3

f. of Agamemnon — SCHL 686:6
f. of a Venus — BARR 60:5
f. of 'evil' — BURR 180:15
f. of the dead — BEER 66:7
f. of the waters — BIBL 78:12
f. of this congregation — BOOK 138:20
f. so pleased my mind — ANON 20:17
f. the index — CRAB 258:3
fall flat on your f. — THUR 810:10
False f. must hide — SHAK 719:17
first I saw your f. — ANON 20:10
garden in her f. — CAMP 195:24
garden of your f. — HERB 393:9
glorifies your f. — BROW 168:11
God hath given you one f. — SHAK 702:7
God's f. is above — MIDR 534:21
had a lonely f. — HARD 380:18
harsh, distorted f. — BOWE 153:7
has the f. he deserves — ORWE 588:8
hear my Thisby's f. — SHAK 727:7
hides a smiling f. — COWP 255:13
hide thy f. from me — BOOK 139:27
hide us from the f. — BIBL 118:11
his prism, and silent f. — WORD 868:13
honest, sonsie f. — BURN 179:22
I am the family f. — HARD 381:18
in the public's f. — RUSK 673:6
keep your f. — CART 205:7
like truth, had one f. — MONT 554:18
Look in my f. — ROSS 669:20
Look in my f. — TRAI 814:16
Lord make his f. shine — BIBL 82:2
lying on his f., dead — THAC 803:3
mask that eats into the f. — UPDI 822:22
men stand f. to face — KIPL 465:8
mist in my f. — BROW 167:7
Moses hid his f. — BIBL 80:35
never forget a f. — MARX 526:2
never see my f. again — TENN 794:26
night's starred f. — KEAT 457:9
not recognize me by my f. — TROL 815:16
Once the bright f. — MIDD 534:9
original f. — HUI- 419:10
painted her f. — BIBL 85:34
Pity a human f. — BLAK 127:9
plain before my f. — BOOK 139:18
rabbit has a charming f. — ANON 20:3
rogue's f. — CONG 247:1
seen God f. to face — BIBL 80:15
shining morning f. — SHAK 696:28
sing in the robber's f. — JUVE 451:11
smile on the f. of the tiger — ANON 20:1
socialism would not lose its human f. — DUBČ 298:1
spirit passed before my f. — BIBL 86:19
spite your f. — PROV 630:22
stamping on a human f. — ORWE 587:19
then f. to face — BIBL 112:14
touched the f. of God — MAGE 514:16
unacceptable f. of capitalism — HEAT 388:4
View but her f. — FORD 337:11
Visit her f. too roughly — SHAK 699:20
Was this the f. — MARL 522:9
whole life shows in your f. — BACA 45:3
your f. burns and tickles — FROS 344:6
your f. in your hands — ANON 18:2
Your f., my thane — SHAK 719:3
faces breathe in the f. — PEPY 603:14
Coming with vivid f. — YEAT 873:6
f. are but a gallery — BACO 46:33
f. in the crowd — POUN 621:7
God knows the f. I shall see — ROSS 669:18
grace-proud f. — BURN 180:3
grind the f. of the poor — BIBL 91:22
hid as it were our f. — BIBL 94:3
not having any f. — PRIE 623:12
old familiar f. — LAMB 476:22
Private f. in public places — AUDE 37:22
red f., and loose hair — EQUI 316:15
slope of f. — COWP 256:23
wears almost everywhere two f. — DRYD 297:18
facets iceberg cuts its f. — BISH 122:7
facilis F. descensus Averno — VIRG 830:5

f. of fat things　BIBL 92:23
f. of languages　SHAK 717:20
f. of reason　POPE 617:26
going to a f.　JONS 446:4
Paris is a movable f.　HEMI 391:3
upon our solemn f.-day　BOOK 145:11
When I make a f.　HARI 382:13
feasting dinner and f.　PEPY 603:12
feasts nights and f. divine　HORA 419:1
feather Birds of a f.　PROV 628:8
　f.-footed through the plashy fen　WAUG 842:19
　f. for each wind　SHAK 736:22
　f. in his cap　SONG 763:17
　f. on the breath of God　HILD 398:7
　f. to tickle　LAMB 476:19
　go to heaven in f.-beds　MORE 559:7
　my each f.　HUGH 418:8
feathered f. glory　YEAT 874:1
　f. race　FRER 342:13
　like the f. race　WOLL 863:9
featherless two-footed f. animal　DIOG 283:15
feathers f. like gold　BOOK 144:8
　Fine f.　PROV 632:14
　largest possible amount of f.　COLB 238:19
feats What f. he did that day　SHAK 709:7
feature not a bug, it's a f.　SAYI 684:29
February f. fill dyke　PROV 632:7
　F. there be no rain　PROV 635:11
　not Puritanism but F.　KRUT 474:1
fed both have f. as well　SHAK 731:18
　clothed, f., and educated　RUSK 674:1
　except when one is well f.　TWAI 820:3
　f. of the dainties　SHAK 717:11
　f. the chicken every day　RUSS 675:2
　insolent, and will be f.　POPE 618:1
　you have f. full　VIRG 832:11
federal Our F. Union　JACK 426:9
federation F. of the world　TENN 797:1
fee For a small f.　SOND 760:21
　gorgeous East in f.　WORD 868:1
feeble confirm the f. knees　BIBL 93:9
　f. can seldom persuade　GIBB 354:16
　help the f. up　SHAK 734:5
　man of such a f. temper　SHAK 711:18
　Most forcible F.　SHAK 707:20
　o'ercomes the f. brain　WINC 860:9
　unjust as a f. government　BURK 174:24
feebleness all else is f.　VIGN 828:3
feed doth this our Caesar f.　SHAK 711:20
　F. a cold　PROV 632:8
　f. his flock　BIBL 93:17
　f. me in a green pasture　BOOK 140:20
　F. my lambs　BIBL 109:5
　F. my sheep　BIBL 109:6
　f. on Death　SHAK 738:24
　F. the brute　PUNC 650:8
　f. with the rich　JOHN 440:16
　will you still f. me　LENN 489:12
　you f. him for a day　SAYI 684:20
feeding Love is mutually f.　HEAD 386:27
feel be, f., live　HERD 395:6
　draw what I f. in my body　HEPW 392:17
　Englishman can't f.　FORS 337:16
　f. it happen　CATU 211:5
　f. that he is dying　CALI 193:7
　f. that you could　HOPK 408:11
　f. the heart-break　GIBS 355:18
　f. what wretches feel　SHAK 715:24
　I f. you all feel　RIDD 661:6
　learn not to f. it　ALCO 11:8
　making people f. good　CHRÉ 226:18
　more to do than f.　LAMB 477:2
　see and hear and f.　JOYC 448:21
　to One does f.　KNOX 470:3
　tragedy to those that f.　WALP 837:21
　would make us f.　CHUR 228:18
feeling Certainty. F.　PASC 598:13
　depth of f.　BYRO 189:27
　f. is bad form　FORS 337:16
　f. of Sunday is the same　RHYS 659:16
　f. which I feel　RIDD 661:6
　formal f. comes　DICK 281:10
　generous and honest f.　BURK 175:6

lost pulse of f.　ARNO 29:3
mess of imprecision of f.　ELIO 309:13
more true f.　JOWE 447:15
Music is f., then　STEV 774:9
objectification of f.　LANG 478:13
other person is f.　BURR 180:16
sensible To f.　SHAK 719:19
without f. gay　CHUR 228:13
feelings follow their f.　MENG 532:2
　governed more by their f.　ADAM 4:2
　He nursed the f.　CRAB 257:14
　overflow of powerful f.　WORD 870:3
　very f. which ought　AUST 42:2
　Without them [f.]　CHUA 227:6
　woman to define her f.　HARD 380:13
feeling-toned f. complexes　JUNG 449:10
feels Everyone f. it　TROL 815:18
　happiness he f.　LACL 475:10
　man is as old as he f.　PROV 638:16
fees answered, as they took their F.　BELL 67:21
　school f. are heavy　CARL 199:11
　smirks accompanied by a few f.　HUNT 421:14
feet aching hands and bleeding f.　ARNO 29:19
　at a young man's f.　BIBL 109:18
　At her f. he bowed　BIBL 83:3
　bathe those beauteous f.　FLET 335:15
　beautiful are thy f.　BIBL 91:13
　before your f. I lay　WALL 837:3
　better to die on your f.　IBAR 424:2
　cutting off our f.　SWIF 783:16
　dust of your f.　BIBL 100:24
　faults of his f.　BECK 64:16
　Fear gave wings to his f.　VIRG 831:2
　f. are always in the water　AMES 14:8
　f. beneath her petticoat　SUCK 779:13
　f. go down to death　BIBL 87:26
　f. have they, and walk not　BOOK 148:5
　f. in ancient time　BLAK 126:24
　f. of him that bringeth　BIBL 93:27
　f. shall stand　BOOK 148:19
　f. was I to the lame　BIBL 87:2
　F., why do I need them　KAHL 452:13
　fell at his f. as dead　BIBL 117:27
　fog comes on little cat f.　SAND 680:4
　from his f. the Servants　RIG 661:15
　guide our f.　BIBL 104:10
　Its f. were tied　KEAT 454:26
　lantern unto my f.　BOOK 148:14
　Lord, dost thou wash my f.　BIBL 108:10
　man who had no f.　SADI 677:4
　man with no f.　SAYI 684:23
　marching, charging f.　JAGG 427:11
　moon under her f.　BIBL 118:23
　more care of their f.　CAVE 211:20
　my f. from falling　BOOK 148:7
　nations under our f.　BOOK 142:21
　palms before my f.　CHES 224:3
　pierced my hands and my f.　BOOK 140:19
　praise the tender f.　SAMB 679:15
　Scots lords at his f.　BALL 55:17
　set my f. upon the rock　BOOK 141:30
　set my printless f.　MILT 539:12
　seven f. of English ground　HARO 382:16
　shoes from off thy f.　BIBL 80:34
　skull, and the f.　BIBL 85:37
　slipping underneath our f.　FITZ 331:20
　stablish their f.　BIBL 96:22
　stranger's f. may find　HOUS 415:9
　Til crowes f. be growe　CHAU 220:28
　Time's iron f.　MONT 556:11
　two white f.　PROV 641:18
　under our f.　BOOK 134:23
　what dread f.　BLAK 128:4
　Whose f. they hurt　BOOK 147:11
　with reluctant f.　LONG 499:10
　would not wet her f.　PROV 628:38
feign it will not f.　DE P 273:15
felices F. ter et amplius　HORA 411:17
felicities of Solomon　BACO 46:3
felicity Absent thee from f.　SHAK 705:2
　behold f.　BROW 163:7
　careful f.　PETR 605:8
　Our own f. we make　JOHN 438:4

shadow of f.　WALL 837:4
What more f.　SPEN 768:1
felix F. qui potuit rerum　VIRG 832:18
　O f. culpa　MISS 550:10
fell f. among thieves　BIBL 105:4
　f. at his feet as dead　BIBL 117:27
　f. before the throne　BIBL 118:13
　From morn to noon he f.　MILT 541:31
　help me when I f.　TAYL 791:15
　It f. by itself　JOHN 434:11
　touch the rosebud, and it f.　PHIL 606:4
feller Sweetes' li'l' f.　STAN 770:7
fellow Damn the f.　GAIN 347:3
　loves his f.-men　HUNT 421:5
　property of thy f.　TALM 789:3
　testy, pleasant f.　ADDI 5:4
fellow-feeling f. makes one wond'rous kind　GARR 349:12
fellows f. of infinite tongue　SHAK 709:12
　f. whom it hurts　HOUS 416:10
　shoes that were not f.　DEFO 270:12
fellowship F. is heaven　MORR 560:17
　one communion and f.　BOOK 136:15
　right hands of f.　BIBL 113:20
felt darkness which may be f.　BIBL 81:5
　has f. about it　MUNC 565:9
female cast on f. wits　BRAD 154:11
　characterizes the f. mind　WOLL 863:14
　created you male and f.　KORA 473:3
　f. atheist　JOHN 438:1
　f. eunuch　GREE 372:4
　f. heart can gold despise　GRAY 370:15
　f. mind　IRWI 425:24
　f. of the species　KIPL 465:18
　f. of the species　PROV 632:9
　f. overcomes the male　LAO 480:10
　f. pen　ALCO 11:6
　f. worker slave of that slave　CONN 248:14
　in the f. sex　ADAM 2:3
　involved with the f. principle　CLAR 233:13
　know a f. reign　EGER 304:13
　Male and f.　BIBL 78:17
　male and the f.　BIBL 79:22
　no f. mind　GILM 358:19
　no f. Mozart　PAGL 592:2
　polished f. friend　WHUR 853:7
　substance of f. education　MART 524:13
　uninformed f.　AUST 43:3
femina Dux f. facti　VIRG 828:18
feminine beautiful f. tissue　HARD 381:2
　'f.' principles　RODD 665:3
　Taste is the f.　FITZ 332:2
feminism discussions of f.　FREN 342:10
feminist call me a f.　WEST 848:23
　Fat is a f. issue　ORBA 585:18
femme Cherchez la f.　DUMA 299:3
fen f. Of stagnant waters　WORD 866:16
　through the plashy f.　WAUG 842:19
fence colours to the f.　FIEL 326:6
　Don't f. me in　PORT 619:11
　f. is just too high　MAUG 528:5
　f. leaps Sunny Jim　ADVE 7:31
　make a f. around the Law　TALM 788:23
　other side of the f.　PROV 633:26
　Please f. me in baby　BOGA 130:13
　tradition is a f.　TALM 789:5
fences barbed wire f.　JOHN 445:3
　f. make good neighbours　PROV 633:19
　Good f. make good neighbours　FROS 344:18
　tied her with f.　MORR 561:6
Fenian grave of a dead F.　COLL 243:4
　left us our F. dead　PEAR 601:2
fens reek o' the rotten f.　SHAK 698:8
fercula erant f.　AUGU 39:4
feriam Sublimi f. sidera vertice　HORA 411:4
Fermanagh dreary steeples of F.　CHUR 229:5
Fermat F.'s last theorem　FERM 325:10
ferments like generous wine f.　BUTL 183:29
fern receipt of f.-seed　SHAK 705:18
ferocious f. in battle　COLL 243:8
　most f. murderer　DOST 291:5
feros nec sinit esse f.　OVID 590:2
ferry row us o'er the f.　CAMP 195:10

fertile f. soil — BACO 49:12
In such a fix to be so f. — NASH 568:12
fertilizer use him as a f. — MULL 564:16
festal line of f. light — ARNO 30:10
fester Lilies that f. — SHAK 738:9
limbs that f. — ABSE 1:4
festina F. lente — AUGU 40:3
fetishist f. who yearns — KRAU 473:12
fettered devil weakly f. — STEV 775:13
fetters F. of gold — ASTE 34:14
f. rent in twain — DAVI 268:13
in love with his f. — BACO 45:26
Milton wrote in f. — BLAK 126:3
fever enigma of the f. chart — ELIO 309:12
f. called 'Living' — POE 610:18
f. of life is over — NEWM 572:13
f. when he was in Spain — SHAK 711:17
her f. might be it — DONN 289:6
life's fitful f. — SHAK 721:3
Of chills and f. — RANS 655:6
starve a f. — PROV 632:8
treaty bred a f. — THOM 805:20
weariness, the f. — KEAT 456:5
Février Janvier and F. — NICH 574:16
few All but the sacred f. — SHEL 747:4
as grossly as the f. — DRYD 295:1
Far and f. — LEAR 485:19
F. and evil — BIBL 80:28
f. and far between — CAMP 195:15
f. are chosen — BIBL 102:14
f. child's squalls — HUNT 421:14
f. things to desire — BLAK 128:9
fit audience find, though f. — MILT 543:26
Gey f. — TOAS 812:3
governed by the f. — HUME 420:5
hated the ruling f. — BENT 71:12
let thy words be f. — BIBL 89:27
Many worse, better f. — LOCK 498:3
so much owed by so many to so f.
— CHUR 229:17
very f. things matter — BALF 53:16
We few, we happy f. — SHAK 709:8
fewer one man f. — METT 533:11
fiancée wish his f. to see — ANON 17:7
fiat F. in my soul — BEDD 65:5
f. justitia — MANS 520:10
F. justitia — MOTT 563:9
F. justitia — WATS 841:8
f. voluntas — MISS 549:17
fickle F. is the South — TENN 799:13
Whatever is f., freckled — HOPK 407:17
fico F. [I'm staying] — PEDR 601:8
fiction best thing in f. — WILD 855:29
continuous f. — BEVA 77:2
f. is a necessity — CHES 225:3
f. lags after truth — BURK 173:11
house of f. — JAME 429:22
if she is to write f. — WOOL 864:8
I hate things all *f.* — BYRO 192:6
improbable f. — SHAK 736:5
narrative is no f. — JACO 427:4
Poetry is the supreme f. — STEV 774:5
sometimes f. — MACA 507:23
Stranger than f. — BYRO 189:22
stranger than f. — PROV 631:46
stranger than f. — PROV 645:36
That is what f. means — WILD 854:22
fictions f. only and false hair — HERB 394:12
truth to their f. — HUME 420:17
fiddle cat and the f. — NURS 578:21
F.-de-dee — NURS 578:13
f., sir, and spade — SCOT 689:11
F., we know, is diddle — SWIN 785:15
important beyond all this f. — MOOR 557:14
I the second f. — SPRI 769:2
played on an old f. — PROV 644:40
fiddler must pay the f. — PROV 644:48
fiddlers his f. three — NURS 580:9
fide *f. et gaude in Christo
Punica f.* — SALL 679:11
Fidele fair F.'s grassy tomb — COLL 243:10
fideles *Adeste, f.* — ANON 23:2
fidelity stone f. they hardly meant — LARK 480:19

thinks he is worth my f. — LACL 475:9
Your idea of f. — RAPH 655:10
fidgety f. Phil — HOFF 402:5
fidus *f. quae tela gerebat Achates* — VIRG 828:15
field comes and tills the f. — TENN 800:8
corner of a foreign f. — BROO 159:13
fair f. full of folk — LANG 478:16
f. is won — MORE 559:11
f. of Golgotha — SHAK 731:1
F. Strewn — ARNO 30:5
lay f. to field — BIBL 92:3
lilies of the f. — BIBL 99:18
man of the f. — BIBL 80:4
not as simple as to cross a f. — PAST 598:19
Not that fair f. Of Enna — MILT 543:4
only inhabitants of the f. — BURK 174:13
presence on the f. — WELL 846:9
single in the f. — WORD 869:10
What though the f. be lost — MILT 541:13
fields babbled of green f. — SHAK 708:15
f. and flocks have charms — CRAB 258:6
f. from Islington — BLAK 125:13
f. have eyes — PROV 632:10
f., painted with various — MICK 534:5
f. where roses fade — HOUS 416:9
flowerless f. of heaven — SWIN 784:18
from the f. of sleep — WORD 867:5
I go among the f. — KEAT 458:6
In Flanders f. — MCCR 509:17
Open unto the f. — WORD 865:7
plough the f. — CAMP 194:15
tills his ancestral f. — HORA 411:3
fiend defy the foul f. — SHAK 715:26
dreadful f. — SPEN 767:24
f. Flibbertigibbet — SHAK 716:1
f. hid in a cloud — BLAK 127:20
f. Walked up and down — MILT 542:24
foul F. — BUNY 171:8
frightful f. — COLE 241:7
swung the f. — MERE 532:20
thou f. to me — BYRO 190:24
work like a f. — THOM 806:12
fiends Beneath is all the f.' — SHAK 716:18
fierce as I raved and grew more f. — HERB 394:2
but little, she is f. — SHAK 726:20
F. as ten Furies — MILT 542:15
f. light which beats — TENN 793:24
F. was the wild billow — ANAT 15:3
fiery burning f. furnace — BIBL 95:22
f. darts of the wicked — BIBL 114:15
full of f. shapes — SHAK 706:8
throne was like the f. flame — BIBL 95:27
fife practised on a f. — CARR 204:6
Thane of F. had a wife — SHAK 722:9
fifteen At the age of f. — JUNG 450:1
at the age of f. — WILS 859:11
famous for f. minutes — WARH 840:1
F. men on the dead man's chest — STEV 775:20
f. wild Decembers — BRON 158:17
old age always f. years older — BARU 60:11
fifth came f. and lost — JOYC 448:20
F. column — MOLA 551:16
fifths three f. of all other persons — CONS 250:2
fifty At f. chides his infamous delay — YOUN 876:21
At f., everyone — ORWE 588:8
corpulent man of f. — HUNT 421:17
F.-four forty — POLI 612:16
until he's f. — FAUL 324:19
until I was nearly f. — HEAN 387:10
fig f. for those by law protected — BURN 178:21
sewed f. leaves together — BIBL 79:6
figements *f. violets* — RIMB 662:11
fight begun to f. — JONE 445:8
better to f. for the good — TENN 798:10
Councils of war never f. — PROV 629:22
don't want to f. — HUNT 421:3
end of the f. is a tombstone — KIPL 467:1
Fifty-four forty, or f. — POLI 612:16
f. against the future — GLAD 359:17
f. and fight again — GAIT 347:6
f. and no be slain — BURN 179:21
f. and not to heed the wounds — IGNA 424:14

F. fire with fire — PROV 632:11
f. for freedom — PANK 595:13
f. for freedom and truth — IBSE 424:6
f. for its King and Country — GRAH 367:11
f. for their law — HERA 393:8
f. for the living — JONE 445:9
f. for what I believe in — CAST 206:10
f. in defence — HOME 404:18
f. in the way of God — KORA 471:4
f. in the way of God — KORA 471:16
f. in the way of God — KORA 471:17
f. it out on this line — GRAN 368:13
f. no more — JOSE 447:11
F. on, my men — BALL 55:12
F. on, my merry men — BALL 54:8
f. on the beaches — CHUR 229:15
f. on to the end — HAIG 376:6
f. our country's battles — MILI 535:9
F. the good fight — BIBL 115:24
F. the good fight — MONS 554:1
f. with faith and win — SIKH 752:2
f. with them again — TENN 800:1
fought a good f. — BIBL 115:28
fought a good f. — WILD 856:11
fought The better f. — MILT 543:25
give the f. up — BROW 166:25
go f. tomorrow — BALL 54:13
Good at a f. — ANON 17:10
he is dead, who will not f. — GREN 372:10
I f. on — THAT 804:5
I will f. — SITT 753:9
like men, and f. — BIBL 83:28
never a moment ceased the f. — TENN 800:2
Never give up the f. — MARL 522:4
nor duty bade me f. — YEAT 873:19
no stomach to this f. — SHAK 709:6
refuse to f. — POLI 613:15
rise and f. againe — BALL 55:12
those who bade me f. — EWER 322:1
thought it wrong to f. — BELL 68:21
too proud to f. — WILS 859:16
Ulster will f. — CHUR 228:22
When badgers f. — CLAR 232:18
fighter Am I no a bonny f. — STEV 775:9
f. not a quitter — MAND 519:2
I was ever a f. — BROW 167:8
fighting dying, but f. back — MCKA 511:16
f. for this woman's honour — FILM 329:16
F. in the captain's tower — DYLA 301:14
F. still — DRYD 295:6
f. with daggers — SCOT 690:5
first-class f. man — KIPL 465:19
foremost f., fell — BYRO 186:7
not fifty ways of f. — MALR 518:8
still f. Blenheim — BEVA 76:15
street f. man — JAGG 427:11
Their f. men I cast down — TIGL 811:5
two dogs are f. — PROV 647:15
What are we f. for — SERV 692:27
who dies f. has increase — GREN 372:10
fights f. and runs away — PROV 634:20
figs f. of thistles — BIBL 100:1
love long life better than f. — SHAK 694:10
figurative f., a metaphorical God — DONN 290:2
figure a poem makes — FROS 345:5
f. in the carpet — JAME 429:14
f. that thou here seest — JONS 446:18
losing her f. or her face — CART 205:7
make a f. — SWIF 782:15
figures f. in words only — MURR 566:3
prove anything by f. — CARL 199:5
fihi F. ma fihi — JALA 428:15
filches f. from me my good name — SHAK 728:23
files foremost f. of time — TENN 797:6
filia *f. pulchrior* — HORA 411:18
filial may be called f. — CONF 245:13
filigree f. hedges — WALP 837:9
fill Ah, f. the cup — FITZ 331:20
F. me with life anew — HATC 384:4
f. the hour — EMER 315:8
O f. me — MACN 513:12
space you f. — COOP 251:5
take our f. of love — BIBL 87:30

first (cont.):
f. of human qualities — CHUR 230:17
f. step that is difficult — DU D 298:11
f. that ever burst — COLE 240:19
F. things first — PROV 632:22
F. thoughts are best — PROV 632:23
f. with the most men — MISQ 547:15
for the f. time — ELIO 309:19
if they speak f. — CONG 246:30
last shall be f. — BIBL 102:10
latent in my f. — WHAR 849:9
no last nor f. — BROW 167:4
nothing should be done for the f. time
  — CORN 252:4
no truck with f. impulses — MONT 556:12
not to take the f. step — CLAU 234:10
people who got there f. — USTI 823:6
romantic f. flame — BURN 176:19
what to put f. — PASC 597:13
firstborn brought forth her f. son — BIBL 104:12
f. the greatest ass — CARO 201:6
smite all the f. — BIBL 81:9
fish All f. that comes to net — PROV 626:14
as good f. in the sea — PROV 644:9
Better are small f. — PROV 627:29
Big f. eat little fish — PROV 628:2
black and ugly f. — HORA 408:14
broiled f. — BIBL 106:33
colder and dumber than a f. — MULD 564:13
f. always stinks — PROV 632:24
f. and fishing — WALT 839:11
F. and guests stink — PROV 632:25
F. are jumpin' — HEYW 397:19
F. fiddle-de-dee — LEAR 486:9
F. fuck in it — FIEL 327:9
F. got to swim — HAMM 378:14
f. of the sea — BIBL 78:16
f. that *talks* — DE L 271:23
f. the last Food — BASS 61:3
f. without a bicycle — SAYI 685:21
f. with the worm — SHAK 703:25
Give a man a f. — SAYI 684:20
I was a f. — SMIT 757:6
Keep your own f.-guts — PROV 637:1
Little f. are sweet — PROV 637:39
no f. ye're buying — SCOT 689:8
Phone for the f.-knives — BETJ 75:14
small 'Stute F. — KIPL 468:14
surrounded by f. — BEVA 76:12
Thou deboshed f. — SHAK 733:27
to torture f. — COLM 244:6
Un-dish-cover the f. — CARR 203:25
What cat's averse to f. — GRAY 370:15
fishbone monument sticks like a f. — LOWE 503:5
fishbones two f., two eyeballs — WELB 845:12
fisher gallant f.'s life — CHAL 213:19
fisherman Death is like a f. — TURG 819:4
fishermen f. hold flowers — DYLA 301:14
fishers Blest f. — BASS 61:3
f. of men — BIBL 98:24
f. went sailing away — KING 464:12
fishes f. flew and forests walked — CHES 224:2
f. in our habit — EMER 315:19
F., that tipple — LOVE 502:4
how the f. live in the sea — SHAK 729:26
little f. of the sea — CARR 203:15
Men lived like f. — SIDN 750:9
Tawny-finned f. — SHAK 695:5
two small f. — BIBL 107:20
welcomes little f. in — CARR 201:14
fishified how art thou f. — SHAK 732:20
fishing I go a f. — BIBL 109:4
when he goes a-f. — WALT 839:1
fishlike ancient and f. smell — SHAK 733:24
fishpond great f. (the sea) — DEKK 271:20
fishpools eyes like the f. — BIBL 91:15
fishy You shall have a f. — NURS 578:9
fist closed f. of a teacher — PALI 593:14
clunking f. — BLAI 124:6
of f. most valiant — SHAK 708:21
fistful for a f. of coins — ZAPA 877:11
fists F. clenched — LOGU 498:11
groan and shake their f. — HOUS 415:4

fit f. audience find — MILT 543:26
f. for this world — KEAT 457:14
I am f. for nothing — HERV 396:23
only the F. survive — SERV 692:26
fitful life's f. fever — SHAK 721:3
fitly word f. spoken — BIBL 88:35
fits If the cap f., wear it — PROV 635:14
If the shoe f. — PROV 635:16
fittest Survival of the F. — DARW 266:15
survival of the f. — SPEN 765:22
fitting right and f. — MISS 549:15
five At f. in the afternoon — LORC 500:17
f. minutes too late — COWL 254:21
f. per cent — MACA 507:5
F. to one — MORR 561:4
Full fathom f. — SHAK 733:21
had f. thousand a year — THAC 803:5
I have wedded f. — CHAU 220:9
in a f.-pound note — LEAR 486:5
market for maybe f. computers — MISQ 548:3
she hadde f. — CHAU 218:19
warming his f. wits — TENN 800:7
fix don't f. it — SAYI 684:24
f. up his automobile — CLAR 233:19
looking for an angry f. — GINS 358:22
fixed f. point in a changing age — DOYL 292:13
great gulf f. — BIBL 106:7
flag allegiance to the f. — BELL 67:15
blood-red f. — BLOK 129:6
brought back the f. — GRIF 373:4
f. of the future — PEAR 601:7
f. to which you have pledged — BALD 52:16
High as a f. — HAMM 379:3
Jelly-bellied F.-flapper — KIPL 468:24
keep the red f. flying — CONN 248:4
national f. — SUMN 780:11
people's f. is deepest red — CONN 248:3
raised their f. — WEBS 843:23
shall not f. or fail — CHUR 229:15
spare your country's f. — WHIT 853:1
Trade follows the f. — PROV 645:32
flagellation Not f., not pederasty — RATT 655:16
flagitium f. timet — HORA 414:4
flagpole run it up the f. — SAYI 684:34
flame all in one f. — EVEL 321:22
Both moth and f. — ROET 665:10
Chloe is my real f. — PRIO 624:6
eyes were as a f. — BIBL 117:21
feed his sacred f. — COLE 240:10
F.-capped, and shout — SHAW 742:27
f. I still deplore — GARR 349:15
f. out like shining — HOPK 407:7
full of subtil f. — BEAU 63:8
hard, gemlike f. — PATE 599:8
plays about the f. — GAY 350:17
romantic first f. — BURN 176:19
signals of the ancient f. — DANT 265:13
spark of that ancient f. — VIRG 829:20
that little f. — RENO 658:9
thin blue f. — COLE 239:19
throne was like the fiery f. — BIBL 95:27
thy holy f. bestowing — LITT 495:12
tongues of f. are in-folded — ELIO 309:22
tongues of living f. — AUBE 35:14
When a lovely f. dies — HARB 379:15
flames bursting into f. — MORR 561:2
by her like thin f. — ROSS 669:15
Commit it then to the f. — HUME 419:16
f. in the forehead — MILT 540:14
f. must waste away — CARE 198:6
love. F. for a year — LAMP 477:21
rich f. and hired tears — BROW 162:10
flaming f. bounds of place and time
  — GRAY 370:20
ministers a f. fire — BOOK 147:4
flammae veteris vestigia f. — VIRG 829:20
flamme cette petite f. — RENO 658:9
Flanders brought him a F. mare — HENR 392:3
In F. fields the poppies blow — MCCR 509:16
part of F. — WALL 837:5
flash frozen f. of history — ANON 17:6
flashes f. of silence — SMIT 758:18
In f., and with glory — WORD 868:15

flashing His f. eyes — COLE 240:9
flask f. of wine — FITZ 331:15
flat F. and flexible truths — BROW 162:4
half so f. as Walter Scott — ANON 19:15
never surprises, it is f. — FORS 337:18
very dangerous f. — SHAK 724:16
Very f., Norfolk — COWA 254:1
flats sharps and f. — BROW 167:1
flatten hide is sure to f. 'em — BELL 67:18
flatter before you f. a man — JOHN 442:22
F. the mountain-tops — SHAK 737:25
fondly f. our desires — DRAY 293:13
lie, to f. — ASCH 33:5
flattered being then most f. — SHAK 712:8
f. always takes your word — GAY 351:19
f. into virtue — SURT 781:4
f. its rank breath — BYRO 186:14
neither feared nor f. — DOUG 291:11
flatterer foremost and greatest f. — PLUT 610:8
hypocrite and f. — BLAK 125:15
flatterers petty f. — BACO 47:14
sycophants and f. — HARD 380:3
tell him he hates f. — SHAK 712:8
within a week the same f. — HALI 377:11
flatteries against f. — MACH 511:14
flattering f., kissing and kicking — TRUM 817:16
f. unction — SHAK 703:17
think him worth f. — SHAW 740:10
flattery Everyone likes f. — DISR 286:19
f. hurts no one — STEV 774:18
f. is worth his having — JOHN 442:22
f. lost on poet's ear — SCOT 688:12
f. never seems absurd — GAY 351:19
f. of one's peers — LODG 498:5
f. soothe the dull cold ear — GRAY 370:5
paid with f. — JOHN 436:4
refer to it is 'f.' — PLAT 608:15
sincerest form of f. — PROV 635:42
This is no f. — SHAK 696:14
flaunting f., extravagant quean — SHER 748:27
flavour high celestial f. — BYRO 188:15
flaw no kind of fault or f. — GILB 356:16
flaws hundred thousand f. — SHAK 715:14
Psychological f. — ANON 19:22
flax smoking f. — BIBL 93:21
Three pounds of f. — MUMO 565:6
flayed saw a woman f. — SWIF 783:11
flea gripping the f. — PROV 640:20
literature's performing f. — O'CA 583:9
louse and a f. — JOHN 443:16
naturalists observe, a f. — SWIF 784:4
fleas Big f. have little fleas — PROV 628:3
educated f. do it — PORT 619:15
f. that tease in the High Pyrenees — BELL 68:25
get up with f. — PROV 635:29
praised his f. — YEAT 875:3
flectere F. si nequeo superos — VIRG 831:1
fled f. far, far away — COCK 237:15
f. From this vile world — SHAK 738:3
F. is that music — KEAT 456:12
I f. Him — THOM 807:14
sea saw that, and f. — BOOK 148:3
flee death shall f. from them — BIBL 118:20
f., and were discomfited — BOOK 144:8
f. away, and be at rest — BOOK 143:10
f. from the wrath to come — BIBL 98:17
F. fro the press — CHAU 221:16
f. when no man pursueth — BIBL 89:7
They f. from me — WYAT 871:4
fleece f. was white as snow — HALE 377:3
His forest f. — HOUS 416:1
won the F. and then came home — DU B 298:3
fleeces sheep bear f. — VIRG 833:8
fleet care of our f. — ADDI 5:13
Fire and f. — BALL 55:2
F. in which we serve — BOOK 150:13
F. the time carelessly — SHAK 696:9
in the Downs the f. was moored — GAY 351:24
whole F.'s lit up — WOOD 864:1
fleetest have f. end — THOM 807:12
fleeth My soul f. — BOOK 149:8
fleets Ten thousand f. — BYRO 187:2
Fleet Street F. to our poets — BROW 164:1

who can be dull in F.	LAMB 477:4
flere Si vis me f.	HORA 409:4
flesh All f. is grass	BIBL 93:16
all f. shall see it	BIBL 93:15
born after the f.	BIBL 113:21
bread and f.	BIBL 85:6
delicate white human f.	FIEL 326:19
east wind made f.	APPL 25:8
eat bulls' f.	BOOK 143:3
Eating the f.	SHAK 734:12
fair and unpolluted f.	SHAK 704:18
flattered any f.	DOUG 291:11
f., alas, is wearied	MALL 517:12
f. and blood	BIBL 114:15
f. and blood so cheap	HOOD 406:2
f., and the devil	BOOK 134:18
f. is as grass	BIBL 117:1
f. is weak	BIBL 103:17
F. of flesh	MILT 544:8
f. of my flesh	BIBL 79:2
f. of them shall not reach	KORA 472:10
F. perishes. I live on	HARD 381:18
f. to feel the chain	BRON 158:16
f. was sacramental	ROBI 664:5
gross f. sinks downwards	SHAK 731:8
heart o' f.	BALL 55:19
human f. subsisting	BOOK 134:14
in my f. shall I see God	BIBL 86:34
lusts of the f.	BOOK 138:9
makes man and wife one f.	CONG 246:27
make your f. creep	DICK 280:16
more f. than another man	SHAK 706:15
my heart and my f.	BOOK 145:13
My Lord should take Frail f.	CROS 261:12
O flesh,	SHAK 732:20
outlive all f.	BYRO 189:28
provision for the f.	BIBL 111:17
shall all f. come	BOOK 144:1
Tell f. it is but dust	RALE 653:16
these our f. upright	DONN 288:5
they shall be one f.	BIBL 79:3
things of the f.	BIBL 111:1
this too too solid f.	SHAK 699:17
thorn in the f.	BIBL 113:18
trust in the f.	BIBL 114:21
we are one, One f.	MILT 544:9
Word was made f.	BIBL 107:2
WORD WAS MADE F.	MISS 550:3
world and its shadow, The f.	RIDI 661:7
would God this f.	SWIN 785:25
fleshly all this f. dress	VAUG 825:7
flesh pots we sat by the f.	BIBL 81:14
flew and they f.	LOGU 498:10
f. between me and the sun	BLUN 129:13
f. over the cuckoo's nest	NURS 580:13
flexible Flat and f. truths	BROW 162:4
your f. friend	ADVE 7:1
Flibbertigibbet fiend F.	SHAK 716:1
flicker moment of my greatness f.	ELIO 310:10
flies As f. to wanton boys	SHAK 716:11
catch small f.	SWIF 783:21
Eagles don't catch f.	PROV 630:39
F., worms, and flowers	WATT 841:13
full fast he f.	BLAI 123:15
Honey catches more f.	PROV 634:40
joy as it f.	BLAK 127:2
murmurous haunt of f.	KEAT 456:8
shut mouth catches no f.	PROV 643:8
swart f. move	DOUG 291:13
Time f.	PROV 645:17
fliest for thou f. Me	THOM 807:19
flight His cloistered f.	SHAK 721:4
His f. was madness	SHAK 722:2
not attained by sudden f.	LONG 499:9
puts the stars to f.	FITZ 330:17
flights f. upon the banks	JONS 446:26
flinders Little Polly F.	NURS 579:20
fling the ringleaders	ARNO 32:15
flint as the f. bears fire	SHAK 713:26
flirtation innocent f.	BYRO 189:16
flittings tellest my f.	BOOK 143:13
float f. lazily downstream	SALI 678:13
F. like a butterfly	ALI 13:2

f. upon his watery bier	MILT 540:4
floating f. bulwark of the island	BLAC 123:11
his f. hair	COLE 240:9
floats She f., she hesitates	RACI 652:16
flock feed his f.	BIBL 93:17
keeping watch over their f.	BIBL 104:12
tainted wether of the f.	SHAK 724:27
flocks My father feeds his f.	HOME 404:3
My f. feed not	BARN 59:10
shepherds watched their f.	TATE 790:16
sweet buds like f.	SHEL 745:6
flog f. the rank and file	ARNO 32:15
flogging in the habit of f. me	TROL 815:16
less f. in our great schools	JOHN 441:23
flood days before the f.	BIBL 102:27
f. could not wash away	CONG 247:6
f. unto the world's end	BOOK 144:19
just cause reaches its f.-tide	CATT 209:24
return it as a f.	GLAD 360:13
Since Deucalion's f.	SKEL 754:3
swam the brackish f.	DRAY 293:16
taken at the f.	SHAK 713:28
ten years before the f.	MARV 525:11
Thorough f., thorough fire	SHAK 725:33
Thunder like a mighty f.	DIX 286:32
verge of the salt f.	SHAK 734:9
flooded STREETS F.	BENC 69:10
floodgate F. of the deeper heart	FLEC 334:15
floods f. are risen	BOOK 146:5
f. drown it	BIBL 91:17
haystack in the f.	MORR 560:15
most like to f.	RALE 654:1
quells the f. below	CAMP 195:19
floor fell upon the sanded f.	PAYN 600:9
f. of heaven	SHAK 725:11
floors Scuttling across the f. of silent seas	ELIO 310:9
flopping go f. yourself down	DICK 281:5
flopshus F. Cad	KIPL 468:24
Flora Tasting of F.	KEAT 456:3
floraisons mois des f.	ARAG 25:15
Florence lily of F.	LONG 499:6
Rode past fair F.	KEAT 454:27
Flores F. in the Azores	TENN 800:1
flos Ut f. in saeptis	CATU 210:15
flourish f. after first decay	SPEN 767:14
f. and complain	CRAB 257:23
Princes and lords may f.	GOLD 364:2
things f. where you turn	POPE 618:2
Truth shall f.	BOOK 145:17
flourisheth f. as a flower	BOOK 147:3
flourishing f. like a green bay-tree	BOOK 141:26
flout scout 'em, and f. 'em	SHAK 733:28
flow blood must yet f.	JEFF 432:12
F. gently, sweet Afton	BURN 177:10
f. of words	BALZ 52:3
I within did f.	TRAH 814:15
What need you f. so fast	ANON 21:5
flower as the f. of the field	BIBL 93:16
[Buddha] held up a f.	MUMO 565:5
Chaucer, of makaris f.	DUNB 299:11
cometh forth like a f.	BIBL 86:30
constellated f.	SHEL 746:7
cracks into furious f.	BROO 160:3
die in the f. of their age	BIBL 83:24
drives the f.	THOM 805:17
every leaf is a f.	CAMU 196:18
every opening f.	WATT 841:11
fairest f., no sooner blown	MILT 540:19
flourisheth as a f.	BOOK 147:3
f. fadeth	BIBL 93:16
f. grows concealed	CATU 210:15
f. in his hand	COLE 241:18
f. of all the field	SHAK 733:1
f. of any kind of experience	HUNT 421:12
f. of English nobility	ORDE 586:5
f. of floures alle	CHAU 220:19
f. of goodlihead	SKEL 754:2
f. of roses	BIBL 98:6
f. of Scotland	WILL 858:5
f. that once hath blown	FITZ 331:19
f. thereof falleth	BIBL 117:1

Full many a f. is born	GRAY 370:6
heaven in a wild f.	BLAK 124:9
Herself a fairer f.	MILT 543:4
it will bear no f.	SHEL 747:10
leaf, the bud, the f.	SPEN 767:14
lightly like a f.	TENN 796:6
like the innocent f.	SHAK 719:3
little western f.	SHAK 726:6
London, thou art the f.	ANON 18:18
meanest f. that blows	WORD 867:18
no stronger than a f.	SHAK 738:2
pluck this f., safety	SHAK 705:23
seize the f.	BURN 179:15
short-lived f.	LEAP 485:12
sweetest f. for scent	SHEL 746:9
this same f. that smiles	HERR 396:17
white f. of a blameless	TENN 793:24
flowering About the f. squares	TENN 796:3
f. of His fields	TENN 794:20
flowerlike f. face	SWIN 785:23
flowerpots your damned f.	BROW 167:18
flowers among the f.	LUCR 504:15
beckon to the f.	HERB 394:13
Bees ransack f.	MONT 554:26
bring forth May f.	PROV 626:33
cool-rooted f.	KEAT 456:13
droop-headed f.	KEAT 455:28
Ensnared with f.	MARV 525:4
fairest f. o' the season	SHAK 736:30
fishermen hold f.	DYLA 301:14
Flies, worms, and f.	WATT 841:13
f. and fruits of love	BYRO 190:21
f. appear on the earth	BIBL 90:27
F. in the garden	STEV 777:4
f. in the mede	CHAU 220:18
F. of all hue	MILT 543:3
f. of the forest	COCK 237:16
f. of the forest	ELLI 313:13
f. that bloom in the spring	GILB 357:15
f. the tenderness of patient minds	OWEN 591:5
foam of f.	SWIN 785:25
hundred f. blossom	MAO 521:5
I got me f. to strew	HERB 394:4
No f., by request	AING 9:17
No path of f. leads	LA F 475:20
other men's f.	MONT 555:25
path is strewed with f.	FARA 323:7
Say it with f.	ADVE 8:14
souls do couch on f.	SHAK 695:18
spears green with f.	VALE 823:9
speckled gigantic f.	DINE 283:12
thirsting f.	SHEL 743:23
Too many f.	SCOT 690:3
Where have all the f. gone	SEEG 691:2
wild f., and Prime Ministers	BALD 53:4
won't be f.	AUDE 38:16
flowery crops the f. food	POPE 616:17
f. lap of earth	ARNO 29:17
f. plains of honour	JONS 446:10
f. way	SHAK 694:6
flowing f. sea	CUNN 262:15
f. with milk and honey	BIBL 80:36
flown birds are f.	CHAR 216:16
flows Everything f.	HERA 393:3
fluidity solid for f.	CHUR 229:8
flummery f. of a birth place	KEAT 457:24
flung f. himself from the room	LEAC 485:9
flush for the f. of youth	ROSS 669:3
flute f. and hautboys	COLM 244:5
f., harp, sackbut	BIBL 95:22
soft complaining f.	DRYD 296:29
flutter F. and bear him up	BETJ 75:12
fluttering F. and dancing	WORD 866:7
fly all things F. thee	THOM 807:19
f. at one end	SWIF 784:16
F. at your Lord's command	GURN 374:19
F. away home	NURS 579:13
F. envious Time	MILT 541:4
f. from	BYRO 186:10
F. hence, our contact fear	ARNO 30:12
f. in his hand	STER 773:3
f. like thee	BLAK 127:19
f. sat upon the axletree	BACO 48:15

never said a f. thing — EPIT 317:16
No man was more f. — JOHN 443:1
pound f. — PROV 641:34
say a f. thing but oft — BROW 164:2
These f. things — MARV 525:18
young and f. — YEAT 873:4
foolishest f. act a wise man commits
— BROW 163:12
foolishness Mix a little f. — HORA 414:5
unto the Greeks f. — BIBL 111:23
fools all the f. in town — TWAI 820:1
Children and f. tell — PROV 628:47
flannelled f. at the wicket — KIPL 466:9
F. and bairns — PROV 632:29
f. and knaves — BUCK 169:18
F. are my theme — BYRO 189:29
F. ask questions — PROV 632:30
F. build houses — PROV 632:31
f. by heavenly compulsion — SHAK 714:24
F.! For I also had my hour — CHES 224:3
F. for luck — PROV 632:32
f. go aimlessly — UPAN 822:8
F. here below for minor pleasures — GRES 372:12
F. out of favour — DEFO 270:20
f. rush in — POPE 616:14
F. rush in — PROV 632:33
f. said would happen — MELB 531:1
f., the fools, the fools — PEAR 601:2
f., who came to scoff — GOLD 364:6
For f. to sing — BURN 180:8
Fortune favours f. — PROV 632:36
Hated by f. — SWIF 784:1
heart of f. — BIBL 89:29
house for f. and mad — SWIF 784:11
I am two f. — DONN 289:19
kept from children and from f. — DRYD 296:26
leaves 'em still two f. — CONG 246:27
let f. contest — POPE 617:3
lighted f. The way — SHAK 722:22
millions mostly f. — CARL 200:12
money of f. — HOBB 400:17
Nature meant but f. — POPE 615:24
not with f. exclusively — BROW 164:2
one half the world f. — JEFF 432:13
Paradise of F. — MILT 542:25
perish together as f. — KING 463:12
plain f. at last — POPE 615:25
poor f. decoyed — PEPY 603:13
scarecrows of f. — HUXL 423:15
shoal of f. — CONG 247:21
suffer f. gladly — BIBL 113:13
term Invented to awe f. — JONS 446:15
this great stage of f. — SHAK 716:22
utmost industry bred f. — CHUD 227:17
virtue of f. — BACO 45:24
what f. these mortals be — SHAK 726:18
world is full of f. — ANON 22:6
foot accent of a coming F. — DICK 281:15
caught my f. in the mat — GROS 374:2
f. already in the stirrup — CERV 213:15
f. feel, being shod — HOPK 407:7
foot—f.—sloggin' — KIPL 465:10
f. for foot — BIBL 81:21
F.-in-the-grave young man — GILB 357:23
f. less prompt — ARNO 30:28
f. standeth right — BOOK 141:8
Forty-second F. — HOOD 405:16
her f. was light — KEAT 455:6
hurt not thy f. — BOOK 146:2
I hold Creation in my f. — HUGH 418:8
Nay, her f. speaks — SHAK 734:20
No f., no horse — PROV 640:4
One f. in sea — SHAK 727:21
One white f. — PROV 641:18
print of a man's naked f. — DEFO 270:13
sets f. upon a worm — COWP 256:30
silver f. in his mouth — RICH 660:8
sole of her f. — BIBL 79:23
squeeze a right-hand f. — CARR 203:22
suffer thy f. to be moved — BOOK 148:17
Withdraw thy f. — BIBL 88:37
with shining f. shall pass — FITZ 331:29
football fighting Army f. team — RICE 659:22

f. a matter of life and death — SHAN 739:1
F.? the beautiful game — PELÉ 602:6
he's f. crazy — MCGR 511:2
owe to f. — CAMU 196:20
footfalls demurest of f. — BROW 168:9
F. echo in the memory — ELIO 309:4
leaves like light f. — SHEL 745:5
footman eternal F. hold my coat — ELIO 310:10
footnotes series of f. to Plato — WHIT 851:12
footpath jog on the f. — SHAK 736:28
footprints F. on the sands — LONG 499:17
those f. scare me — HORA 410:2
footsteps our f. guideth — BAKE 52:8
plants his f. in the sea — COWP 255:12
footstool it is God's f. — BIBL 99:4
thine enemies thy f. — BOOK 147:19
foppery f. of the world — SHAK 714:24
for F. ever panting — KEAT 455:21
not f. anything — CONF 245:18
who is f. me — HILL 399:7
forasmuch f. as without thee — BOOK 136:9
forbear Bear and f. — PROV 627:11
forbearance f. ceases to be a virtue
— BURK 173:4
forbid f. them not — BIBL 104:2
God f. — BIBL 106:17
God f. — BIBL 110:32
He shall live a man f. — SHAK 718:7
forbidden because it was f. — TWAI 820:17
Everything not f. — WHIT 850:22
Of that f. tree — MILT 541:8
totally f. — TYNA 821:1
force By verray f. — CHAU 220:14
combines f. with candour — CHUR 231:5
driving f. of all — WEBE 843:17
every living f. — DOST 290:16
F., and fraud — HOBB 401:1
F. is not a remedy — BRIG 157:6
F. is the food — ADVE 7:31
f. that through the green — THOM 805:17
F., unaided by judgement — HORA 412:22
f. with a manoeuvre — TROT 817:8
may the f. be with you — FILM 329:6
more than our f. — BURK 174:20
motive f. impressed — NEWT 574:4
no argument but f. — BROW 163:20
no f. however great — WHEW 850:3
Not believing in f. — TROT 817:9
oppressive f. — BARB 57:19
Other nations use 'f.' — WAUG 843:1
principles have no real f. — TWAI 820:3
reduce the use of f. to — ORTE 586:10
spent its novel f. — TENN 796:23
Surprised by unjust f. — MILT 539:9
use of f. alone — BURK 173:12
Who overcomes By f. — MILT 541:28
forces Dark f. — MISQ 547:9
f. impressed upon it — NEWT 574:2
two f. were at work — HARD 381:3
forcible Most f. Feeble — SHAK 707:20
forcibly f. if we must — CLAY 234:13
ford I am a F., not a Lincoln — FORD 336:17
my friend F. — WILL 858:12
forearmed Forewarned is f. — PROV 632:35
forefathers be as their f. — BOOK 145:6
cannot reform our f. — ELIO 307:4
f. of the hamlet sleep — GRAY 370:3
Think of your f. — ADAM 3:15
forefinger f. of all Time — TENN 799:5
forefront f. of the hottest battle — BIBL 84:15
foregone denoted a f. conclusion — SHAK 729:1
forehead Flames in the f. — MILT 540:14
f. was prodigious — HUNT 421:11
foreign avoid f. collision — CLAY 234:12
corner of a f. field — BROO 159:13
courtly f. grace — TENN 800:4
does not know f. languages — GOET 362:11
enriched with f. matter — REYN 659:4
far, f. fields — DAVI 268:12
f. country — DURA 300:8
f. policy — COOK 250:11
f. policy: I wage war — CLEM 235:7
from a f. yoke — MAZZ 529:11

into any f. wars — ROOS 667:10
Life is a f. language — MORL 560:2
nothing human f. to me — TERE 801:13
past is a f. country — HART 383:20
portion of the f. world — WASH 840:16
remote countries and f. nations — GIBB 354:15
set foot on f. land — CHES 225:18
shape its f. policy — HEAR 388:2
third-rate f. conductors — BEEC 65:15
foreigner possible that a f. — TROL 816:16
foreigners f. always spell better — TWAI 820:11
f. are fiends — MITF 551:9
more f. I saw — BELL 69:5
Foreign Secretary attacking the F. — BEVA 76:18
F. naked into the conference — BEVA 76:19
Foreland Dawn off the F. — KIPL 466:18
forelock occasion's f. watchful — MILT 544:22
foremost f. in battle — BALL 55:5
none who would be f. — MACA 508:17
foreseen All is f. — TALM 789:7
What I had not f. — SPEN 766:14
foresight aftersight and f. — ELIO 309:18
forest another is a dark f. — CATH 209:16
another is a dark f. — TURG 819:2
beasts of the f. — BOOK 143:2
beasts of the f. — BOOK 147:8
behind it rose the f. — LONG 499:23
burning the rain f. — STIN 777:8
carry timber to the f. — HORA 414:17
Cutting through the f. — LIND 494:15
Deep in the f. — RACI 653:1
Down in the f. — SIMP 753:2
flowers of the f. — COCK 237:16
flowers of the f. — ELLI 313:13
fool i' the f. — SHAK 696:24
f. laments — CHUR 228:20
f. primeval — LONG 499:3
f.'s ferny floor — DE L 272:6
hedge is to a f. — JOHN 444:13
In the f. — CHES 225:8
lost to the f. — SCOT 688:9
through an untrodden f. — MURR 566:1
To the f. edge — DURC 300:10
unfathomable deep f. — THOM 806:19
forests fishes flew and f. walked — CHES 224:2
F. keep disappearing — CHEK 222:5
f. of the night — BLAK 128:3
vast f., immense fields — CHEK 221:19
foretaste f. of death — SCHO 686:14
foretell ability to f. — CHUR 231:2
pretences to f. — SWIF 783:20
foretold Long f., long last — PROV 638:1
who could have f. — YEAT 874:22
forever continue thine f. — BOOK 138:18
diamond is f. — ADVE 7:15
F., and forever, farewell — SHAK 713:30
f. hold his peace — BOOK 138:23
joy f. — KEAT 454:3
Man has F. — BROW 165:24
mercy endureth f. — BOOK 149:12
not be destroyed f. — PRAY 623:9
picket's off duty f. — BEER 66:7
forewarned F. is forearmed — PROV 632:35
forfended music of f. spheres — PATM 599:14
forgave f. the offence — DRYD 295:19
forge barn and the f. — HOUS 415:17
f. and working-house — SHAK 709:9
my f. decayed — EPIT 319:3
forgers liars and f. — PÉGU 602:3
forget Better by far you should f. — ROSS 669:5
cannot learn to f. — REED 657:6
do not quite f. — CHES 224:15
do not thou f. me — ASTL 34:18
Don't f. the diver — CATC 207:13
Don't f. the fruit gums — ADVE 7:18
f. because we must — ARNO 29:2
f. not all his benefits — BOOK 146:18
F. six counties — MORR 560:14
f. so much — DAVI 267:17
f. thee, O Jerusalem — BOOK 149:14
f. there ever was such a thing — WILS 859:20
f. we are gentlemen — BURK 175:7
f. you first — ADAM 3:4

forget (cont.):
forgive but do not f.   SZAS 786:13
How long wilt thou f. me   BOOK 139:27
if thou wilt, f.   ROSS 669:9
I sometimes f.   DISR 286:22
Lest we f.   KIPL 467:5
never f. a face   MARX 526:2
nor allows them to f. her   OVID 590:1
nor worms f.   DICK 279:3
not f. the suspenders   KIPL 468:13
Old men f.   SHAK 709:7
Sun himself cannot f.   ANON 20:15
to communicate f. not   BIBL 116:14
to f. the self   DOGE 287:10
will I not f. thee   BIBL 93:26
forgets bellowing cow soon f.   PROV 627:18
forgetting consist in merely f.   MAND 519:1
f. is so long   NERU 570:16
F. those things   BIBL 115:1
grand memory for f.   STEV 775:10
memory against f.   KUND 474:4
sleep and a f.   WORD 867:8
world f.   POPE 614:10
forgive allows you to f. yourself   SHAW 741:27
do not f. those murderers   WIES 853:13
do they f. them   WILD 855:27
easier to f.   BLAK 125:9
Father, f. them   BIBL 106:23
f. enemies   BLAK 126:27
f. him   BIBL 102:4
F., O Lord, my little jokes   FROS 344:9
F. our foolish ways   WHIT 853:2
f. our friends   MEDI 530:4
f. them as a Christian   AUST 42:18
f. those who bore us   LA R 482:6
f. us our debts   BIBL 99:12
f. us our trespasses   BOOK 133:7
f. wrongs darker than death   SHEL 746:4
lambs could not f.   DICK 279:3
Lord will f. me   CATH 209:18
mercy to f.   DRYD 295:25
seldom f. twice   LAVA 483:8
to f. a wrong   ELEA 306:13
To f., divine   POPE 616:10
to f. divine   PROV 645:25
To know all is to f. all   PROV 645:26
Wilt thou f. that sin   DONN 288:18
wise f. but do not forget   SZAS 786:13
woman can f. a man   MAUG 528:8
Women can't f. failure   CHEK 221:23
would f. you   ALAI 10:12
forgiven f. everything   SHAW 741:25
Her sins are f.   BIBL 104:27
restored, f.   LYTE 506:6
Wrongs are often f.   CHES 223:9
forgiveness After such knowledge, what f.   ELIO 309:25
ask of thee f.   SHAK 716:21
f. is a lovely idea   LEWI 491:16
F. of each vice   BLAK 125:8
F. of sins   BOOK 133:19
F. to the injured   DRYD 295:16
forgiveth f. sins   BIBL 97:4
forgot auld acquaintance be f.   BURN 177:11
by the world f.   POPE 614:10
curiosities would be quite f.   AUBR 35:16
English have f.   BORR 151:15
F. it not   ROSS 669:11
f. the fart   ELIZ 312:19
f. the taste of fears   SHAK 722:20
I have f. my part   SHAK 698:13
just f. to duck   DEMP 273:2
names ignoble, born to be f.   COWP 255:20
Napoleon f. Blücher   CHUR 228:24
proposed as things f.   POPE 616:12
she f. the stars   KEAT 454:28
forgotten always a f. thing   CHES 224:1
been learned has been f.   SKIN 754:6
books undeservedly f.   AUDE 38:20
F. Army   MOUN 562:16
f. as a nameless number   PAST 598:18
f. even by God   BROW 166:25
f. man at the bottom   ROOS 667:2

f. nothing and learnt nothing   DUMO 299:7
he himself had f. it   PALM 595:8
I am all f.   SHAK 694:16
injury is much sooner f.   CHES 222:24
learnt nothing and f. nothing   TALL 788:19
likely to be f.   ABU 1:6
not one of them is f.   BIBL 105:13
ruins of f. times   BROW 162:9
things one has f.   CANE 196:24
Thou hast f.   SWIN 785:23
fork pick up mercury with a f.   LLOY 496:20
forked poor, bare, f. animal   SHAK 715:27
forks made before f.   PROV 632:16
pursued it with f.   CARR 204:3
forlorn faery lands f.   KEAT 456:10
F.! the very word   KEAT 456:11
maiden all f.   NURS 581:16
wait f.   ARNO 30:21
form earth was without f.   BIBL 78:12
find a f.   BECK 64:13
F. follows function   SULL 780:3
f. from off my door   POE 611:3
F. is emptiness   MAHĀ 515:9
f. of a servant   BIBL 114:18
f. of sound words   BIBL 115:26
F. remains   WORD 868:25
f. the key to organic life   PAST 598:17
human f. divine   BLAK 128:6
lick it into f.   BURT 181:6
mould of f.   SHAK 702:9
no action or physical f.   CHUA 227:13
Thou, silent f.   KEAT 455:24
To every F. of being   WORD 865:17
formal every f. visit   AUST 42:22
f. feeling comes   DICK 281:10
formalistic more f. than conservatives   CALV 194:7
formation Scottish by f.   SPAR 765:14
formed him that f. it   BIBL 111:8
perhaps it f. itself   RIG 661:14
small, but perfectly f.   COOP 251:2
former f. and the latter   BOOK 135:9
f. days were better   BIBL 90:3
f. things are passed away   BIBL 119:16
formerly not what we were f. told   BLUN 129:12
formosa F. facies muta commendatio   PUBL 648:29
forms By f. unseen   COLL 243:13
endless f. most beautiful   DARW 266:18
f. of government   POPE 617:3
f. of things unknown   SHAK 727:3
give A breath to f.   BYRO 189:28
I like definite f.   STEV 775:19
manifests itself in many f.   EURI 321:7
fornication F., and all uncleanness   BIBL 114:8
fors F. dierum cumque dabit   HORA 411:13
forsake f. me not   BOOK 144:17
F. not an old friend   BIBL 97:15
nor f. thee   BIBL 82:23
forsaken never the righteous f.   BOOK 141:25
O, father f.   JOYC 448:24
primrose that f. dies   MILT 540:12
utterly f.   BETT 76:11
why hast thou f. me   BIBL 103:24
why hast thou f. me   BOOK 140:15
forsaking f. all other   BOOK 138:24
forsworn so sweetly were f.   SHAK 723:17
fort Hold the f.   BLIS 129:1
Hold the f.   SHER 749:8
fortes Vixere f.   HORA 414:3
forth F. in thy name   WESL 847:14
F., pilgrim   CHAU 221:17
fortifications f. called castles   ORDE 586:6
fortissimo F. at last   MAHL 516:4
fortiter pecca f.   LUTH 505:3
fortitude f. the Soul contains   DICK 281:15
fortnight beyond the next f.   CHAM 214:1
f. dead   ELIO 311:16
fortress f. built by Nature   SHAK 730:10
f. rising above the horizon   LOUI 501:8
petty f.   JOHN 438:8
fortresses brambles in the f.   BIBL 93:6
fortuna Audentis F. iuvat   VIRG 831:8

Stat f. domus   VIRG 833:6
fortunate at best but f.   SOLO 760:10
better to be f.   WEBS 844:23
farmers excessively f.   VIRG 832:17
fortunatus F. et ille deos qui novit   VIRG 832:19
fortune architect of own f.   PROV 631:28
Blind F. still Bestows   JONS 446:6
Caesar and his f.   CAES 192:20
face is my f.   NURS 582:11
F. assists the brave   TERE 801:15
F. empties her chamberpot   MACD 510:8
F. favours fools   PROV 632:36
F. favours the brave   PROV 632:37
F. list to flee   CHAU 219:20
F.'s a right whore   WEBS 844:17
f.s sharpe adversitee   CHAU 221:5
good f. of men   MACH 511:5
good f. than a good husband   OSBO 588:11
good f. to others   BIER 121:5
good housewife F.   SHAK 696:10
great, ere f. made him so   DRYD 295:22
he shall see F.   BACO 46:31
hostages to f.   BACO 47:15
how does f. banter us   BOLI 131:15
I am F.'s fool   SHAK 732:24
leads on to f.   SHAK 713:28
leave the rest to f.   EURI 321:4
little value of f.   STEE 770:19
method of making a f.   GRAY 370:23
mother of good f.   CERV 213:9
mould of a man's f.   BACO 46:30
outrageous f.   SHAK 701:26
people of f.   ELIO 308:12
possession of a good f.   AUST 42:8
rob a lady of her f.   FIEL 326:22
secret parts of F.   SHAK 701:8
sick in f.   SHAK 714:24
smiling of F.   COCK 237:15
smith of his own f.   CLAU 234:5
take good f.   MOLI 553:3
to f. and to fame unknown   GRAY 370:9
upon a plentiful f.   JOHN 440:1
vicissitudes of f.   SADI 677:4
with f. and men's eyes   SHAK 737:21
Women and f.   WYCH 871:12
fortunes content with his f. fit   SHAK 715:21
my f. have   SHAK 695:12
forty at f., the judgement   FRAN 341:6
Every man over f.   SHAW 741:24
fairy when she's f.   HENL 391:10
Fat, fair and f.   O'KE 584:20
fool at f.   PROV 632:27
fool at f.   YOUN 876:12
f. days it will remain   PROV 642:33
f. stripes save one   BIBL 113:15
F. years long   BOOK 146:8
F. years on   BOWE 153:6
In f. minutes   SHAK 726:7
Knows it at f.   YOUN 876:21
Life begins at f.   PITK 607:7
Life begins at f.   PROV 637:27
look young till f.   DRYD 296:12
Men at f.   JUST 450:6
miner, F.-niner   MONT 556:17
When f. winters shall besiege   SHAK 737:16
forty-five At f., what next   LOWE 503:6
forty-three pass for f.   GILB 358:14
forward F., forward let us range   TENN 797:7
f. motion love   VAUG 825:8
from this day f.   BOOK 139:1
look f. to posterity   BURK 174:2
looking f. to the past   OSBO 588:18
marched breast f.   BROW 164:21
nothing to look f. to   FROS 344:10
those behind cried 'F.!'   MACA 508:17
Foss F. is the name of his cat   LEAR 486:4
fossil Language is f. poetry   EMER 315:10
fossils God hid the f.   GOSS 366:12
foster f.-child of silence   KEAT 455:16
fostered F. alike by beauty   WORD 868:9
fou f. for weeks thegither   BURN 179:13
f. o' brandy   BURN 178:13
I wasna f.   BURN 177:27

fought better to have f. and lost — CLOU 237:4
f. against me — BOOK 149:5
f. against Sisera — BIBL 83:1
f. a good fight — BIBL 115:28
f. a long hour — SHAK 706:31
f. each other for — SOUT 764:7
f. the dogs — BROW 167:1
to have f. well — COUB 253:3
we f. at Arques — HENR 391:18
foul F. as their soil — BYRO 187:15
F. deeds will rise — SHAK 700:1
f. Fiend — BUNY 171:8
f. is fair — SHAK 718:2
f.-mouthed nation — HAZL 386:22
however f. within — CHUR 228:11
Murder most f. — SHAK 700:20
really f. things up — SAYI 685:15
So f. and fair a day — SHAK 718:9
some f. play — SHAK 699:30
soon be made so f. — BERN 73:21
thank the gods I am f. — SHAK 697:14
ways be f. — SHAK 717:25
foulest commonly the f. — BACO 45:19
foully play'dst most f. for't — SHAK 720:22
fouls it's own nest — PROV 636:33
found awoke and f. me here — KEAT 455:10
f. a kingdom — MILT 544:23
F. him in the shining — TENN 794:20
f. my sheep which was lost — BIBL 105:27
f. no more of her — BIBL 85:37
f. the Roman nation — VIRG 828:12
Hast thou f. me — BIBL 85:18
man who has f. himself out — BARR 60:2
was lost, and is f. — BIBL 106:2
When f., make a note — DICK 278:1
foundation Church's one f. — STON 777:10
f. of all good things — BURK 174:23
f. of his own ruin — FIEL 327:1
f. of most governments — ADAM 3:13
f. of the earth — BOOK 146:17
f. of unyielding despair — RUSS 674:25
foundations city which hath f. — BIBL 116:4
earth's f. fled — HOUS 415:8
f. of the earth — BIBL 87:8
f. of the earth — BOOK 147:4
founded f. the Jewish state — HERZ 391:1
founder f. and embellisher — CAXT 212:2
founding f. a bank — BREC 156:1
inspiration of the f. fathers — HARD 380:7
fount f. whence honour springs — MARL 523:7
fountain Back to the burning f. — SHEL 743:16
Doth a f. send forth — BIBL 116:25
f. filled with blood — COWP 255:15
f. in a waste — MUIR 564:8
f. momently was forced — COLE 244:2
f. of all goodness — BOOK 134:6
f. of delights — LUCR 504:15
f. of good sense — DRYD 297:21
f. of honour — BACO 46:1
f. of negativism — WEST 848:19
f. of the water of life — BIBL 119:17
f. sealed — BIBL 91:6
healing f. — AUDE 37:13
It is that f. — RALE 653:14
like a f. troubled — SHAK 733:9
Like a summer-dried f. — SCOT 688:9
fountains Afric's sunny f. — HEBE 388:8
f. mingle with the river — SHEL 744:22
living f. — AKEN 10:1
sad f. — ANON 21:5
silver f. mud — SHAK 737:26
founts White f. falling — CHES 224:7
four all f.-footed things — CHES 224:2
At the age of f. — USTI 823:7
fiery f.-in-hand — COLE 242:9
f. beasts full of eyes — BIBL 118:4
F. eyes see more — PROV 632:38
f.-footed beasts — BIBL 109:25
f. for a birth — PROV 640:44
F. lagging winters — SHAK 730:5
f.-legged friend — BROO 160:4
F. legs good — ORWE 586:17
f.-year-old child could — FILM 330:1

say that two plus two make f. — ORWE 587:14
twice two be not f. — TURG 819:5
fourscore come to f. years — BOOK 145:21
fourteenth f. Mr Wilson — HOME 404:5
fourth f. estate of the realm — MACA 506:15
This is the F. — JEFF 432:16
fous C'étaient des f. — RENO 658:9
fowl f. of the air — BIBL 78:16
liver-wing of a f. — TENN 801:6
fowler snare of the f. — BOOK 148:22
fowls all small f. singis — DOUG 291:10
Barn-door f. for dissenters — SMIT 758:8
f. of the air — BIBL 99:16
f. of the air — BIBL 109:25
f. of the air — BOOK 147:5
smale f. maken melodye — CHAU 218:3
fox beset the historical f. — HUXL 423:4
certain f. wanted — LA F 475:21
Crazy like a f. — PERE 603:20
f. is off to his den — NURS 580:11
f. knows many things — ARCH 26:1
F. who was my friend — READ 656:5
galloping after a f. — WILD 855:24
loves the f. less — SURT 781:9
people that think, and f.-hunters — SHEN 747:21
prince must be a f. — MACH 511:10
quick brown f. — ANON 20:2
sharp hot stink of f. — HUGH 418:11
They've shot our f. — BIRC 122:1
what the wary f. said — HORA 410:2
foxed If ever I was f. — PEPY 603:4
foxes choppin' f. — SURT 781:10
f. have a sincere interest — ELIO 307:12
f. have holes — BIBL 100:10
f., that spoil the vines — BIBL 91:1
portion for f. — BOOK 143:25
second to the f. — BERL 73:9
foxholes no atheists in the f. — CUMM 262:14
signs on the f. — KENN 460:12
foxlike f. in the vine — TENN 799:21
frabjous O f. day — CARR 202:22
fraction wretched f. — CARL 199:5
fragment not a geographical f. — PARN 597:8
fragments f. that remain — BIBL 107:21
These f. I have shored — ELIO 311:18
fragrance Isles of f. — POPE 613:25
frail F. crowds — MOOR 558:3
frailty concession to human f. — TAWN 791:4
f. of our nature — BOOK 135:14
f. of the mind — SHAD 693:13
F., thy name is woman — SHAK 699:21
love's the noblest f. — DRYD 296:2
therefore more f. — SHAK 706:15
frame f. in the earth — SPEN 767:21
f. of adamant — JOHN 438:7
f. of nature — ADDI 5:2
f. of the world — BERK 72:17
my f. perish — BYRO 186:23
universal f. — BACO 46:5
framed f. and glazed — WALP 837:18
français n'est pas f. — RIVA 663:1
France better in F. — STER 772:9
between F. and England — JERR 433:16
by which F. is fed — SULL 780:6
F., famed in all great arts — ARNO 31:2
F. has lost a battle — DE G 271:7
F. has more need of me — NAPO 568:3
F. in a certain way — DE G 271:17
F. is a person — MICH 534:4
F., mother of arts — DU B 298:2
F. wants you to take part — CHIR 226:8
F. was long a despotism — CARL 200:3
F. will say that I am a German — EINS 305:9
Gentlemen of F. — HAY 385:10
I now speak for F. — DE G 271:8
not love the English in F. — CARD 198:3
Political thought, in F. — ARON 32:18
round hose in F. — SHAK 724:4
stood the wind for F. — DRAY 293:19
sweet enemy, F. — SIDN 750:18
vasty fields of F. — SHAK 708:8
wield the sword of F. — DE G 271:9

Francesca di Rimini F., miminy — GILB 357:22
Frankie F. and Albert — SONG 762:7
frankincense f., and myrrh — BIBL 98:11
frankly F., my dear — FILM 328:8
frantic fascination f. — GILB 357:17
frater f., ave atque vale — CATU 211:6
Fraternité Égalité F. — POLI 613:1
fraternize beckon you to f. — AUDE 38:3
fratrum Par nobile f. — HORA 414:19
fraud Force, and f. — HOBB 401:1
May is a pious f. — LOWE 503:1
frauds all great men are f. — BONA 132:5
freak grotesque composite f. — HENN 391:16
freckled f. like a pard — KEAT 455:11
Whatever is fickle, f. — HOPK 407:17
freckles curiosity, f., and doubt — PARK 596:3
In those f. — SHAK 725:34
Fred Here lies F. — EPIT 318:3
free as any spirit f. — CHAU 219:3
as soon write f. verse — FROS 345:11
be perfectly f. — SPEN 766:4
best things are f. — PROV 627:24
best things in life are f. — DE S 274:16
Bind me, or set me f. — GODO 361:2
bond nor f. — BIBL 115:9
born f. — ANON 16:5
born f. as Caesar — SHAK 711:16
but it's f. — KRIS 473:18
Church shall be f. — MAGN 514:18
Comment is f. — SCOT 687:18
condemned to be f. — SART 681:10
England should be f. — MAGE 514:17
Ev'rything f. in America — SOND 760:21
favours f. speech — BROU 160:13
f. again — SOLZ 760:11
f. agent — AURE 40:20
f. and immortal — TRAH 814:10
f. as nature first made man — DRYD 295:15
F. at last — EPIT 317:8
F. by '93 — POLI 612:17
f. church — CAVO 212:1
freedom to the f. — LINC 493:18
f. man, an American — JOHN 435:3
f. society is a society where — STEV 774:22
F. women are not women — COLE 242:16
Greece might still be f. — BYRO 188:22
half f. — LINC 493:10
I am a f. man — MCGO 510:16
I am not f. — DEBS 270:3
ignorant and f. — JEFF 432:7
in a f. country — BURK 173:20
in chains than to be f. — KAFK 452:7
Ireland shall be f. — SONG 763:18
I was f. born — BIBL 110:11
know our will is f. — JOHN 440:17
land of the f. — KEY 461:13
let him go f. — BOOK 147:12
Man was born f. — ROUS 670:14
men everywhere could be f. — LINC 493:17
Mother of the F. — BENS 70:22
naturally were born f. — MILT 546:13
No f. man shall be taken — MAGN 515:1
no such thing as a f. lunch — SAYI 685:13
not a f. press but a managed — RADC 653:6
not f. either — SOLZ 760:14
Not of my own f. will — VIRG 829:23
not only to be f. — PANK 595:13
protection of f. speech — HOLM 403:19
set f. in our remembering — BERR 74:17
should themselves be f. — BROO 159:3
so far kept us f. — JEFF 431:15
Teach the f. man — AUDE 37:13
that moment they are f. — COWP 256:9
Thou art f. — ARNO 30:15
Thought is f. — PROV 645:9
Thought is f. — SHAK 733:28
tongues too should be f. — ERAS 316:18
truth makes men f. — AGAR 9:6
truth shall make you f. — BIBL 107:30
Was he f. — AUDE 38:15
We must be f. or die — WORD 866:5
wholly slaves or wholly f. — DRYD 295:26

free (*cont.*):
Who would be f. — BYRO 185:23
free-born f. mouse — BARB 57:19
freed f. my soul — BERN 73:20
freedom abridgement of f. — MADI 514:8
  abridging the f. of speech — CONS 250:4
  apprenticeship for f. — BARA 57:16
  better organised than f. — PÉGU 602:4
  But what is F. — COLE 239:2
  can often picture f. — MURD 565:15
  cause of F. — BOWL 153:18
  conditioned to a f. — KENY 461:3
  depends on f. of the press — JEFF 431:7
  destroy the f. — ADAM 3:11
  enemies of f. do not argue — INGE 425:1
  fight for f. and truth — IBSE 424:6
  first is f. of speech — ROOS 667:12
  for human f. — SPEN 766:3
  For the sake of f. — ZORO 879:15
  F. alone he earns — GOET 362:5
  F. alone substitutes — TOCQ 811:11
  f. alone that we fight — ANON 20:12
  F. and not servitude — BURK 173:17
  F. and slavery are mental states — GAND 348:12
  F. and Whisky — BURN 177:14
  F. an English subject's — DRYD 297:1
  F. cannot exist — METT 533:9
  f. depends on being courageous — PERI 603:26
  f. for the one who thinks differently — LUXE 505:14
  f. for the pike — TAWN 791:3
  f. from fear — AUNG 40:6
  F. has a thousand charms — COWP 256:4
  F. hunted — PAIN 592:11
  F. is an indivisible word — WILL 858:16
  f. is a noble thing — BARB 58:4
  f. is but a light — GUMI 374:13
  f. is excellent — TOCQ 811:13
  F. is not a gift — NKRU 576:16
  F. is slavery — ORWE 587:11
  f. is something — BALD 52:14
  F. is the freedom to say — ORWE 587:14
  f. of person — JEFF 431:17
  f. of speech — TWAI 820:5
  F. of the press guaranteed — LIEB 493:4
  F. of the press in Britain — SWAF 781:24
  f. of the press's speech — TWAI 820:13
  F.'s banner — DRAK 293:11
  F. shrieked—as Kosciuszko fell — CAMP 195:13
  F.'s just another word — KRIS 473:18
  F. slowly broadens down — TENN 801:5
  f. to offend — RUSH 673:2
  f. to the slave — LINC 493:18
  from slavery to f. — HAGG 376:1
  gave my life for f. — EWER 322:1
  give to man F. — GRAI 368:6
  green f. of a cockatoo — STEV 774:14
  If we choose f. — POPP 618:28
  Let f. ring — SMIT 757:13
  love not f., but licence — MILT 546:12
  man makes his way to F. — SCHI 685:26
  means by defending f. — NIEM 575:7
  no easy walk-over to f. — NEHR 569:13
  obtained I this f. — BIBL 110:11
  O F., what liberties are taken — GEOR 353:10
  only f. which deserves — MILL 536:3
  own true f. — MONT 555:7
  participation of f. — BURK 173:22
  peace from f. — MALC 517:10
  Perfect f. is reserved — COLL 243:1
  plan for f. — POPP 619:4
  preserve and enlarge f. — LOCK 497:13
  preserve its f. — MADI 514:10
  riches and f. — WAŁĘ 835:18
  road toward f. — MORR 561:7
  sell your f. — PUBL 648:28
  service is perfect f. — BOOK 134:2
  taste of F. — PALI 594:14
  there can be no f. — LENI 488:16
  they treasure f. — ADAM 3:19
  true political f. — SCHI 685:27
  unless f. is universal — HILL 398:10
freedoms four essential human f. — ROOS 667:12

F. you'll not to me allow — BEHN 67:2
freehold given to none f. — LUCR 504:12
freeing f. some — LINC 493:17
freely F. ye have received — BIBL 100:23
  life pasturing f. — THOR 809:19
Freeman F. butters Stubbs — ROGE 666:1
freemen Americans are to be f. — WASH 840:14
  rule o'er f. — BROO 159:3
freewoman he of the f. — BIBL 113:21
freeze f. my humanity — MACN 513:12
  f. thy young blood — SHAK 700:18
freezes Yours till Hell f. — FISH 330:10
freezing feel my heart f. — STEN 771:17
frei *Arbeit macht f.* — ANON 22:13
freight shall have her earthly f. — WORD 867:12
Freiheit F. *is immer nur* — LUXE 505:14
freits follows f. — PROV 634:7
French always have spoken F. — VOLT 835:1
  Before F. culture — RENA 658:5
  drawn out of F. — MALO 518:1
  F. are with equal advantage — CANN 196:25
  F. arrange — CATH 209:10
  F. government — COLO 244:8
  F. is the *patois* — BAGE 51:17
  F. of Parys — CHAU 218:9
  F., or Turk — GILB 358:4
  F. Revolution operated — TOCQ 811:14
  F. want no-one to be — TOCQ 812:15
  F. widow in every bedroom — HOFF 402:13
  glory of beating the F. — WOLF 862:17
  how it's improved her F. — GRAH 367:12
  If the F. noblesse — TREV 815:7
  Learning F. is some trouble — EMPS 315:30
  new F. books — BROW 164:26
  no more F. — ANON 19:8
  not clear is not F. — RIVA 663:1
  not too French F. bean — GILB 357:20
  Paris was F.—and silent — TUCH 818:11
  professor of F. letters — JOYC 448:22
  Speak in F. — CARR 202:25
  to men F. — CHAR 217:12
  to the F. the empire of the land — RICH 661:5
  We F., we English — BIRN 122:2
Frenchman must hate a F. — NELS 569:18
Frenchmen beat three F. — ADDI 5:13
  beat three F. — PROV 640:43
  Fifty million F. — MILI 535:8
frenzy Demoniac f. — MILT 544:13
  poet's eye, in a fine f. — SHAK 727:3
  What is life? a f. — CALD 193:7
frequency very fact of f. — ELIO 307:27
frequent f. hearses — POPE 614:6
frère *Sois mon f.* — CHAM 215:5
frères *f. humains après nous* — VILL 833:6
fresh ancient and so f. — AUGU 39:10
  f. air and fun — EDGA 303:6
  f. as is the month of May — CHAU 219:6
  F. as the Angel — BYRO 185:12
  f. lap of the crimson rose — SHAK 726:4
  It's tingling — ADVE 7:40
  O yonge, f. folkes — CHAU 221:13
  So sad, so f. — TENN 799:11
  What f. hell is this — PARK 596:19
fret fever, and the f. — KEAT 456:5
  f. a passage through — FULL 346:12
  F. not thyself — BOOK 141:24
frets struts and f. his hour — SHAK 722:22
fretted F. the pigmy body — DRYD 294:11
Freud trouble with F. — DODD 287:6
Freude F., *schöner Götterfunken* — SCHI 683:10
Freudian still had her F. papa — LOWE 503:4
friars cannot all be f. — CERV 213:5
  f. were singing vespers — GIBB 355:4
fricassee f., or a ragout — SWIF 783:2
friction f. which no man can imagine — CLAU 234:8
Friday F.'s child — NURS 580:6
  My man F. — DEFO 270:14
  on a F. fil al this meschaunce — CHAU 219:26

one F. morn — SONG 763:6
friend angry with my f. — BLAK 127:22
  as you choose a f. — DILL 283:6
  betraying my f. — FORS 338:12
  Boldness be my f. — SHAK 698:17
  candid f. — CANN 197:3
  Codlin's the f. — DICK 279:23
  countervail a f. — GRIM 373:8
  damned goodnatured f. — SHER 748:2
  deceive a f. — PLUT 610:9
  diamonds a girl's best f. — ROBI 663:15
  ease some f. — POPE 614:18
  enemy is my f. — SAYI 684:16
  faithful f. — BIBL 97:11
  familiar f. — BOOK 142:3
  fat f. — BRUM 168:16
  favourite has no f. — GRAY 370:16
  forgave a f. — BLAK 126:27
  forgive a f. — BLAK 125:19
  Forsake not an old f. — BIBL 97:15
  four-legged f. — BROO 160:4
  F. and associate of this clay — HADR 375:7
  f. and helper — EURI 321:14
  f.-and-relation — MILN 537:20
  F., go up higher — BIBL 105:19
  f. in need — PROV 632:39
  f. in power — ADAM 2:13
  f. loveth at all times — BIBL 88:20
  f. of every country — CANN 197:1
  F. of my better days — HALL 378:7
  F. of the humble — SIKH 752:1
  f. should bear — SHAK 713:24
  f. sincere enough — BULW 170:16
  f. that sticketh closer — BIBL 88:23
  f. that will go to jail — BURN 176:16
  F., wherefore — BIBL 103:18
  guide, philosopher, and f. — POPE 617:12
  help a f. or hurt an enemy — CLEA 235:2
  He was my f. — SHAK 713:3
  homes without a f. — CLAR 232:24
  house to lodge a f. — SWIF 783:24
  I finds a f. — DIBD 276:4
  I lose a f. — SARG 681:3
  In every f. we lose a part — POPE 618:20
  Is such a f. — COWP 255:2
  last best F. am I — SOUT 764:12
  lay down his wife for his f. — JOYC 448:22
  Little F. of all the World — KIPL 468:16
  look like a f. — SHAK 699:13
  lose your f. — PROV 637:16
  loss of a dear f. — SOUT 764:22
  lost no f. — POPE 615:19
  Lover for a f. — ETHE 320:16
  makes not f. — TENN 794:14
  man, That love my f. — SHAK 713:11
  mine own familiar f. — BOOK 143:11
  mistress or a f. — SHEL 744:1
  no f. like a sister — ROSS 669:1
  Nor a f. to know me — STEV 777:2
  O f. unseen — FLEC 334:14
  only way to have a f. — EMER 314:25
  Phone a f. — CATC 208:24
  polished female f. — WHUR 853:7
  poor man's dearest f. — BURN 179:1
  pretended f. is worse — GAY 351:16
  'Strange f.,' I said — OWEN 591:9
  think of him as a f. — SMIT 757:21
  To find a f. — DOUG 291:15
  want a f. in need — DICK 278:1
  Whatever you think of your f. — MIDR 534:16
  What is a f. — ARIS 28:10
  Whenever a f. succeeds — VIDA 827:15
  wounds of a f. — BIBL 89:5
  your enemy and your f. — TWAI 820:8
  your f. that loves you — SHAK 711:14
friendless f. bodies of unburied men — WEBS 844:20
friendliness friendship and f. — SHEL 745:23
friendliness friendship and f. — MALA 517:7
friends All her family and her f. — CORS 252:10
  Americans are our best f. — THOM 808:6
  best f. hear no more — SHEL 744:16
  best of f. — TUPP 818:13

best of f. must part	SONG 763:13
Champagne for my real f.	BACO 49:14
choice of f.	COWL 254:13
closest f. won't tell you	ADVE 7:21
comes to meet one's f.	BURN 176:24
distresses of our f.	SWIF 784:8
documents and f.	SPAR 765:7
doubt one's f.	LA R 481:21
Fair face show f.	GOOG 366:1
falling out of faithful f.	EDWA 304:11
fewer f. than we imagine	HOFM 402:14
forgive our f.	MEDI 530:4
f. are necessarily	USTI 823:6
f. do not need it	HUBB 417:13
f.' houses	JOHN 443:13
f. in the garrison	HALI 377:6
f. must part	PROV 627:21
f. of every country	DISR 285:7
F. part forever	BASH 60:16
F., Romans, countrymen	SHAK 712:28
f. thou hast	SHAK 700:3
f. were not unearthly beautiful	RICH 660:7
His f. he loved	WATS 841:10
his only f.	CAMP 195:23
I had such f.	YEAT 874:6
I have lost f.	WOOL 864:12
in the house of God as f.	BOOK 143:11
I wish thee f.	CORB 251:12
lay down his f. for his life	THOR 810:5
life for his f.	BIBL 108:18
love of f.	BELL 68:27
Make to yourselves f.	BIBL 106:4
misfortune of our best f.	LA R 482:11
Money couldn't buy f.	MILL 537:15
my f. pictured within	ELGA 306:15
my list of f.	COWP 256:30
nearly deceiving your f.	CORN 252:6
new city of F.	WHIT 851:20
newspapers should have no f.	PULI 649:10
none of his f. like him	WILD 856:12
no true f. in politics	CLAR 233:11
Old f. are best	SELD 691:9
old f. to trust	BACO 45:20
Our f., the enemy	BÉRA 72:5
Save us from our f.	PROV 642:34
separateth very f.	BIBL 88:19
Some of my best f. are white	DURE 300:11
tavern for his f.	DOUG 291:16
tell it to your f.	MONT 556:13
thousand f.	ALI 12:16
to all thy f.	BIBL 95:7
To some few f.	WINC 860:7
treat my f.	MALL 517:16
two close f.	LERM 490:2
want of f.	BRET 156:12
we are f.	BREC 155:19
We make our f.	CHES 225:6
win f. and influence people	CARN 201:4
with a little help from my f.	LENN 489:13
friendship cultivate your f.	JOHN 443:9
dupe of f.	HAZL 386:6
Every long f.	LAMB 476:11
f. closes its eyes	ANON 22:5
f. ever ends in love	GAY 351:11
F. from knowledge	BUSS 182:14
f. in constant repair	JOHN 439:11
F. is a disinterested commerce	GOLD 364:30
F. is constant	SHAK 727:18
F. is Love	BYRO 190:10
F. not always the sequel	JOHN 436:29
f. recognised by the police	STEV 775:29
f. with all nations	JEFF 431:16
In f. false	DRYD 294:15
Levin wanted f.	MALA 517:7
little f. in the world	BACO 46:29
mechanism of f.	COLE 242:18
Most f. is feigning	SHAK 697:5
most important is f.	EPIC 316:12
spoke of f.	EMER 315:19
that is true f.	SALL 679:7
to f. clear	CARE 198:10
treating of f.	THOM 805:6
two for f.	THOR 809:21

friendships F. begin with liking	ELIO 307:9
frieze no striped f.	STRA 778:10
frigate no F. like a Book	DICK 281:13
fright f. and a hiss	DEAN 269:13
wake in a f.	BARH 58:9
frighten by God, they f. me	WELL 846:4
f. the horses	CAMP 195:2
f. those who might hate her	AUST 41:2
frightened children are f. of me	GEOR 353:3
than f. to death	SURT 781:14
frightening never more f.	VAN 824:3
frightful f.'s when one's dead	POPE 615:17
frigid f. as their snows	BYRO 187:15
frippery what you call f.	ADAM 2:2
frisch F. weht der Wind	WAGN 835:13
fritter 'Fry me!' or 'F.-my-wig!'	CARR 203:27
Friuli blue F.'s mountains	BYRO 186:17
frocks F. and Curls	DICK 282:3
frog f. he would a-wooing go	NURS 578:14
f. remains	ROST 670:5
leap-splash—a f.	BASH 60:18
toe of f.	SHAK 721:16
frogs F. and snails	NURS 582:10
f. are slightly better	MITF 551:9
f. don't die for 'fun'	BION 121:18
F. eat Butterflies	STEV 774:4
from F. far, from eve	HOUS 416:3
front F. and back follow	LAO 479:7
present your f. to the world	MOLI 551:16
frontier f.-grave is far away	NEWB 571:11
f. of my Person	AUDE 38:3
new f.	KENN 460:4
frontiers old f. are gone	BALD 53:6
frost abide his f.	BOOK 150:8
but a f. of cares	TICH 811:2
diadem of f.	BLOK 129:6
f. performs its secret ministry	COLE 239:17
Heavy as f.	WORD 867:12
like an untimely f.	SHAK 733:1
secret ministry of f.	COLE 240:1
Thaw not the f.	SHEL 743:8
third day comes a f.	SHAK 710:9
frostbite God of f.	VYAZ 835:12
frosts Caledonian f.	CLAU 234:3
Dews, and F.	BOOK 133:15
f. are slain	SWIN 784:20
hoary-headed f.	SHAK 726:4
so many f. in May	PROV 643:21
frosty F., but kindly	SHAK 696:17
f. starlight	ARNO 30:18
froth mostly f. and bubble	GORD 366:5
Froude goes to F. for history	STUB 779:8
froward f. generation	BIBL 82:19
like a f. child	TEMP 792:13
frown fear at your f.	ENGL 316:2
libel in a f.	SWIF 783:26
make the sweetest love to f.	GREE 371:25
without f. or smile	SEDL 690:18
frowning Behind a f. providence	COWP 255:13
frozen F. anger	FREU 343:3
f. flash of history	ANON 17:8
f. in an out-of-date mould	JENK 432:19
f. music	SCHE 683:6
f. sea within us	KAFK 452:9
indifference or f. stare	ELIO 307:24
locked and f. in each eye	AUDE 37:11
milk comes f. home	SHAK 717:25
sends the f.-ground-swell	FROS 344:17
through the f. grass	KEAT 454:4
Your tiny hand is f.	GIAC 354:3
fructify [Money should] f.	GLAD 360:15
frugal She had a f. mind	COWP 255:10
fruges f. consumere nati	HORA 410:4
fruit bent with thickset f.	ROSS 668:18
bore thy f. and mine	KYD 474:11
bring forth f.	BOOK 135:9
brought forth f.	BIBL 101:13
delicate exotic f.	WILD 854:18
eateth not of the f.	BIBL 112:6
eats of the sweet f.	UPAN 822:15
everything is f.	AURE 40:9
f. fails, welcome haws	PROV 646:37
f. is sweet	ARIS 28:9

f. of good works	BOOK 136:13
f. of knowledge	FULL 346:14
f. Of that forbidden tree	MILT 541:8
f. of the Spirit	BIBL 113:23
f. of thy womb	PRAY 623:1
f., she plucked	MILT 544:6
f.'s in the loft	PROV 642:44
f. that can fall	MONT 554:3
Hang there like f.	SHAK 698:26
Man stole the f.	HERB 394:24
she f. designs	D'AV 267:8
Some f. for him	HERB 394:8
Stolen f. is sweet	PROV 643:39
too little f.	SCOT 690:3
tree is known by his f.	BIBL 101:5
tree is known by its f.	PROV 645:34
trees bear strange f.	ALLE 13:6
weakest kind of f.	SHAK 724:27
would eat the f.	PROV 634:15
fruitful as the f. vine	BOOK 149:4
Be f., and multiply	BIBL 78:18
f. ground	SURR 780:13
f. hill	BIBL 91:23
fruitfulness mellow f.	KEAT 456:22
fruition f. of an earthly crown	MARL 523:6
fruits By their f.	BIBL 100:2
eat his pleasant f.	BIBL 91:7
first f. of them that slept	BIBL 112:21
flowers and f. of love	BYRO 190:21
f., and foliage, not my own	COLE 239:10
kindly f. of the earth	BOOK 135:2
Like Dead Sea f.	MOOR 558:15
mercy bears richer f.	LINC 494:8
frustra Nisi Dominus f.	MOTT 563:13
frustrate each f. ghost	BROW 167:24
F. their knavish tricks	SONG 762:10
fry scribbling f.	YOUN 876:13
Such as 'F. me!'	CARR 203:27
frying-pan frizzled in my f.	ENGE 316:1
f. of your words	FLAU 333:13
talks In the f.	DE L 271:23
fuck Fish f. in it	FIEL 327:9
They f. you up, your mum and dad	LARK 481:9
word 'f.' is particularly	TYNA 821:1
zipless f.	JONG 445:13
fudge two-fifths sheer f.	LOWE 502:17
fugaces Eheu f. Labuntur anni	HORA 412:10
fugit f. inreparabile tempus	VIRG 833:2
fugitive f. and cloistered virtue	MILT 545:24
f. from th' law of averages	MAUL 528:14
Führer ein F.	POLI 612:14
fuimus F. Troes	VIRG 829:13
Fuji F. through mist	BASH 60:17
fulfil F. now, O Lord	BOOK 134:8
not to destroy, but to f.	BIBL 98:29
fulfilled almost never f.	LA R 482:10
f. a long time	BIBL 97:1
fulfilling f. his word	BOOK 150:9
full commonplace book be f.	SWIF 783:10
F. cup, steady hand	PROV 632:44
f. fathom five	SHAK 733:21
f. man and a fasting	PROV 636:35
F. speed ahead	FARR 324:13
f. tide of human existence	JOHN 441:14
let me be f.	METH 533:8
Serenely f., the epicure	SMIT 758:20
fuller f.'s earth for reputations	GAY 351:2
fullness f. of the heart	PROV 641:26
fulmen Eripuit coelo f.	TURG 819:7
fulmina Bruta f.	PLIN 609:13
fulness f. thereof	BIBL 112:11
f. thereof	BOOK 141:1
fum Fy, fa, f.	NASH 568:24
fume black, stinking f.	JAME 428:21
fumitor Crowned with rank f.	SHAK 716:14
fumo ex f. dare lucem	HORA 409:7
fumum F. et opes	HORA 413:7
fun Ain't we got f.	KAHN 452:15
desire to have all the f.	SAYE 682:20
frogs don't die for 'f.'	BION 121:18
f. you think they had	JONG 445:14
Gladstone read Homer for f.	CHUR 230:19
I rhyme for f.	BURN 180:1

fun (cont.):
more f. to be with — NASH 568:15
most f. I ever had — ALLE 13:8
no reference to f. — HERB 393:16
noted for fresh air and f. — EDGA 303:6
Oh, what f. — DE L 272:4
people have f. — MONT 556:5
taken my f. where I've found it — KIPL 466:10
two is f. — SAYI 684:5
wish I thought *What Jolly F.* — RALE 654:16
function each with his own f. — VIRG 833:5
Form follows f. — SULL 780:3
frightful word [f.] — LE C 487:4
f. Is smothered — SHAK 718:16
F. never dies — WORD 868:25
fundament frigid on the f. — NASH 568:21
fundamental f. things apply — HUPF 422:4
funeral costlier f. — TENN 793:16
Dream of a f. — PROV 630:34
f. baked meats — SHAK 699:25
F. marches to the grave — LONG 499:15
f. of the past — CLAR 233:3
not a f. note — WOLF 862:13
One f. makes many — PROV 640:46
PREPARE VAULT FOR F. — BEER 66:5
funk in a blue f. — CRAN 258:16
funny Everything is f. — ROGE 666:4
f. old world — FILM 328:22
f. old world — THAT 804:6
F.-peculiar or funny ha-ha — HAY 385:12
Isn't it f. — MILN 538:9
Whatever is f. is subversive — ORWE 588:5
fur dilettante in f. — GAUT 350:15
On some other f. — ANON 21:15
to make a f. coat — SLOG 755:6
furca *Naturam expelles f.* — HORA 410:9
furies Fierce as ten F. — MILT 542:15
furious f. in religion — PENN 602:19
grew fast and f. — BURN 179:18
time cracks into f. flower — BROO 160:3
furiously driveth f. — BIBL 85:33
green ideas sleep f. — CHOM 226:14
heathen so f. rage — BOOK 139:12
furled bright girdle f. — ARNO 29:4
furnace as a greet f. — CHAU 218:23
burning fiery f. — BIBL 95:22
faultless breast the f. is — SOUT 765:1
f. of affliction — BIBL 93:23
Heat not a f. — SHAK 710:13
truth from inspiration's f. — LEWI 492:7
furnish Books do f. a room — POWE 621:18
f. all we ought to ask — KEBL 459:1
f. the war — HEAR 388:3
furnished Cambridge ladies in f. souls — CUMM 262:13
F. and burnish'd — BETJ 76:6
how poorly f. you are — PERS 604:12
furniture don't trip over the f. — COWA 254:5
f. on the deck of the Titanic — MORT 562:7
No f. so charming — SMIT 758:13
rearranges the f. — PRAT 622:10
stocked with all the f. — DOYL 292:8
furor *Ira f. brevis est* — HORA 410:6
furrow on a half-reaped f. — KEAT 457:1
plough my f. alone — ROSE 668:12
furrows made long f. — BOOK 149:6
furry fire was f. as a bear — SITW 753:11
further Always a little f. — FLEC 334:11
but no f. — PIUS 607:23
f. one goes — LAO 480:6
f. they have to fall — FITZ 332:20
f. us — BOOK 138:3
Go f. and fare worse — PROV 633:5
fury blind f. of creation — SHAW 740:23
Comes the blind F. — MILT 540:7
filth and the f. — NEWS 573:8
f. and the mire of human veins — YEAT 872:11
f., like a woman scorned — CONG 247:9
f. of a patient man — DRYD 295:3
Hell hath no f. — PROV 634:31
In her prophetic f. — SHAK 729:4
opponents of F. — ZORO 879:11
sound and f. — SHAK 722:22

War hath no f. — MONT 554:14
furze When the f. is in bloom — PROV 646:46
fuse line is a f. — MAYA 529:2
through the green f. — THOM 805:17
fuss f. about an omelette — VOLT 835:9
fustest f. with the mostest — MISQ 547:15
fustian f.'s so sublimely bad — POPE 614:21
futility fatal f. of fact — JAME 430:2
future Back to the f. — FILM 331:1
Children of the f. age — BLAK 127:21
controls the f. — ORWE 587:12
curiosity about the f. — WAUG 842:14
danger of the f. — FROM 344:3
dedication to Canada's f. — DIEF 283:2
dipped into the f. — TENN 797:1
empires of the f. — CHUR 230:5
fight against the f. — GLAD 359:17
flag of the f. — PEAR 601:7
f. ain't what it used to be — BERR 74:11
f. and the past — BOLA 131:7
F. as a promised land — LEWI 491:17
f. can be promised to no one — TRUD 817:11
f. of the human race — JEAN 431:1
f.'s bright — ADVE 7:25
F. shock — TOFF 812:18
f. states of both — BYRO 188:17
hopes of the f. — BURK 174:29
interpretation of the f. — THUC 810:6
lets the f. in — GREE 371:18
never think of the f. — EINS 305:10
no faith in the f. — TAYL 791:13
no trust in the f. — HORA 411:16
once and f. king — MALO 518:5
past, present and f. — EINS 306:1
perhaps present in time f. — ELIO 309:3
picture of the f. — ORWE 587:19
plan the f. by the past — BURK 172:17
predict the f. — KAY 453:17
scaffold sways the f. — LOWE 502:20
seen the f. and it works — STEF 770:20
sense of f. favours — WALP 838:16
serve the f. hour — WORD 868:26
Trust no F. — LONG 499:16
walking backward into f. — ZHVA 877:16
futurum *Quid sit f.* — HORA 411:13
fuzzy-wuzzy 'ere's *to* you, F. — KIPL 465:19
Fyfe David Patrick Maxwell F. — ANON 19:5
fyr is f. yreke — CHAU 220:2

gabardine my Jewish g. — SHAK 724:9
gable Skimming our g. — HEAN 387:5
gadget g.-filled paradise — NIEB 575:6
gadgets One servant worth a thousand g. — SCHU 687:8
Gael hearthstone of the G. — JOHN 445:3
hearthstone of the G. — ROSS 668:16
Gaels great G. of Ireland — CHES 223:27
gag tight g. of place — HEAN 387:18
Gaia G. is a tough bitch — MARG 521:13
gaiety eclipsed the g. — JOHN 436:27
only concession to g. — THOM 807:2
Our own g. — BLY 129:15
gaily G. into Ruislip gardens — BETJ 76:1
gain another man's g. — PROV 641:7
deem a losing g. — SOUT 765:2
g., not glory — POPE 617:20
g., not pain — OXFO 591:12
g. of a few — POPE 618:19
g. the whole world — BIBL 103:34
g. to me — BIBL 114:22
loss without some g. — PROV 644:43
No pain, no g. — PROV 640:12
So might I g. — BROW 166:10
to die is g. — BIBL 114:16
gained misery is a battle f. — WELL 846:7
gainful seek g. employment — ACHE 1:12
gains Light g. make heavy purses — BACO 46:14
no g. without pains — STEV 774:20
gait as much as his g. — MATH 527:14
gaiters gas and g. — DICK 279:20
Galatea *Malo me G. petit* — VIRG 831:21
Galatians great text in G. — BROW 167:19

galaxy g. far, far away — TAGL 788:7
gale g., it plies the saplings — HOUS 416:2
Galen as G. says — GOGA 363:9
Galeotto G. was the book — DANT 265:1
galère *dans cette g.* — MOLI 552:10
gales cool g. shall fan — POPE 618:16
cool g. shall fan the glade — POPE 618:2
Galilean O pale G. — SWIN 785:19
pilot of the G. lake — MILT 540:9
You have won, G. — JULI 449:9
Galilee nightly on deep G. — BYRO 187:16
Galileo G. in two thousand years — PIUS 608:1
status of G. — GOUL 367:1
gall gave me g. to eat — BOOK 144:12
take my milk for g. — SHAK 719:1
wormwood and the g. — BIBL 95:10
gallant braw g. — BALL 54:7
died a very g. gentleman — EPIT 317:14
gallantry no more to do with g. — SHER 748:8
What men call g. — BYRO 187:23
galleon Stately as a g. — GREN 372:9
gallery g. of pictures — BACO 46:33
galley doing in that g. — MOLI 552:10
Gallia *G. est omnis divisa* — CAES 192:16
gallimaufry g. or hodgepodge — SPEN 768:8
gallop G. about doing good — SMIT 757:14
G. apace — SHAK 732:25
Why does he g. — STEV 776:18
galloped we g. all three — BROW 166:4
galloping hoof with a g. sound — VIRG 831:5
gallops who Time g. withal — SHAK 697:13
gallow grew a g. — KYD 474:11
gallows die upon the g. — WILK 856:22
g. in every one — CARL 200:26
g. in my garden — CHES 223:25
g.-maker; for that frame — SHAK 704:10
g. that he had prepared — BIBL 86:6
Jack on the g.-tree — SCOT 689:14
nothing but the g. — BURK 174:10
perfect g. — SHAK 733:12
Under the G.-Tree — FLET 335:7
galumphing went g. back — CARR 202:22
gamble Life is a g. — STOP 778:3
gambler whore and the g. — BLAK 124:18
game Anarchism is a g. — SHAW 741:30
beautiful g. — PELÉ 602:6
don't like this g. — CATC 208:1
g. is about glory — BLAN 128:18
g. of the few — BERK 72:13
g. on these lone heaths — HAZL 386:24
g.'s afoot — SHAK 708:17
giving over of a g. — BEAU 63:11
how you played the G. — RICE 659:20
nature of my g. — JAGG 427:13
not being a g. — LEAC 485:10
play the g. — NEWB 571:12
see most of the g. — PROV 638:3
'The g.,' said he — CRAB 258:2
time to win this g. — DRAK 293:10
war's a g. — COWP 256:25
woman is his g. — TENN 799:14
gamecocks Wits are g. — GAY 351:13
gamekeeper life of an English g. — ZERN 877:15
makes the best g. — PROV 640:31
games better than g. — SCOT 688:3
dread of g. — BETJ 76:8
G. people play — BERN 74:7
g. should be seen — MONT 554:25
gamesmanship theory and practice of g. — POTT 620:13
gammon world of g. and spinnage — DICK 277:16
gamut g. of the emotions — PARK 596:12
gander goosey g. — NURS 578:16
Grey goose and g. — NURS 578:17
sauce for the g. — PROV 646:28
gangrenous G. limbs cannot be — HEGE 388:12
gangsters great nations acted like g. — KUBR 474:2
gaol world's thy g. — DONN 289:24
gap last g. but one — WHIT 850:18
made a g. in nature — SHAK 694:23
this great g. of time — SHAK 694:17
gaps God lived in g. — DRUM 294:3

garage to the full g.	HOOV 406:14
garbage G. in, garbage out	SAYI 684:19
Garbo G. talks	TAGL 788:3
Garcia Lorca —and you, G.	GINS 359:1
Garde La G. meurt	CAMB 194:10
garden all your life plant a g.	PROV 635:37
as a lodge in a g.	BIBL 91:19
Back to the g.	MITC 551:1
blow upon my g.	BIBL 91:7
Come into the g.	TENN 798:3
enclosed g.	CATU 210:15
England is a g.	KIPL 466:1
fairies at the bottom of our g.	FYLE 346:22
gallows in my g.	CHES 223:25
g. eastward in Eden	BIBL 78:19
g. inclosed	BIBL 91:6
g. in her face	CAMP 195:24
g. is a lovesome thing	BROW 161:12
g. of bright images	BRAM 154:15
g. of the world	MARV 525:16
g. of your face	HERB 393:9
g.'s umbrage mild	SMAR 754:17
g. with pedantic weeds	CARE 198:7
ghost of a g.	SWIN 785:10
God the first g. made	COWL 254:10
imperfections of my g.	MONT 554:22
in a lofty G.	KORA 473:8
Lord God walking in the g.	BIBL 79:6
man and a woman in a g.	WILD 855:26
nearer God's Heart in a g.	GURN 374:16
planted a g.	BACO 47:2
rosebud g. of girls	TENN 798:5
Round and round the g.	NURS 581:4
set to dress this g.	SHAK 730:25
sunlight on the g.	MACN 513:14
too much time in the g.	HOBY 401:14
turn it into a g.	YOUN 876:8
We are a g. walled around	WATT 842:1
where a g. should be	HORA 414:20
Gārdena Hwæt! wē G.	ANON 23:15
gardener Adam was a g.	SHAK 710:2
I am but a young g.	JEFF 432:4
supposing him to be the g.	BIBL 108:37
gardeners g., ditchers	SHAK 704:9
gardening g. is but landscape-painting	POPE 618:25
gardens search of our mothers' g.	WALK 836:7
Sowe Carrets in your G.	GARD 349:4
sweetest delight of g.	BROW 162:7
garish day's g. eye	MILT 539:19
loved the g. day	NEWM 572:17
no worship to the g. sun	SHAK 732:27
garland green willow is my g.	HEYW 398:2
O! withered is the g.	SHAK 695:21
willow must be my g.	SHAK 729:10
garlands may gather g.	SCOT 689:7
Posterity weaves no g.	SCHI 685:24
they are g.	BENN 70:8
garlic clove of g. round my neck	O'BR 583:3
Wel loved he g.	CHAU 218:25
garment g. of harmony	FORK 337:14
g. of thought	CARL 200:21
g. was white as snow	BIBL 95:27
leaves an old g.	BHAG 77:18
left his g. in her hand	BIBL 80:20
like as with a g.	BOOK 147:4
not know the g. from the man	BLAK 125:9
wax old as doth a g.	BOOK 146:17
garmented g. in light	SHEL 747:6
garments cross upon their g.	URBA 823:2
g. of the Torah	ZOHA 878:11
part my g.	BOOK 140:19
Reasons are not like g.	ESSE 320:11
Stuffs out his vacant g.	SHAK 714:9
garnished empty, swept, and g.	BIBL 101:10
garret Born in the g.	BYRO 190:27
Genius in a g.	ROBI 664:6
living in a g.	FOOT 336:10
garrison friends in the g.	HALI 377:6
garrulous g. patriotism	TOCQ 812:13
Garsington Hey for G.	KETT 461:11
garter knight of the g.	ATTL 35:8
like about the Order of the G.	MELB 531:2
garters own heir-apparent g.	SHAK 705:19
gas g. and gaiters	DICK 279:20
G. smells awful	PARK 596:7
g. was on	BETJ 76:4
got as far as poison-g.	HARD 381:10
gash be it g. or gold	BROO 160:1
gasp last g.	BIBL 98:9
gate at one g. to make defence	MILT 545:6
cabin at your g.	SHAK 735:6
Death . . . openeth the g.	BACO 46:23
drops on g.-bars hang	HARD 382:3
enemies in the g.	BOOK 149:3
g. hangs well that hinders none	ELLI 314:1
g. of glory	BOOK 137:18
g. of heaven	BIBL 80:11
how strait the g.	HENL 391:13
laid at his g.	BIBL 106:6
leads to the broad g.	SHAK 694:6
lead you to Heaven's g.	BLAK 125:16
man at the g. of the year	HASK 384:3
November at the g.	PUSH 650:19
Only through beauty's g.	SCHI 683:16
out of the ivory g.	BROW 163:9
Wide is the g.	BIBL 99:28
gates besiege your g.	POPE 614:6
enter then his g.	KETH 461:10
g. are mind to open	KIPL 467:2
g. of hell	BIBL 101:26
g. of it shall not be shut	BIBL 119:19
g. of perception	MAIM 516:14
g. to the glorious and unknown	FORS 337:21
Open the temple g.	SPEN 766:21
O ye g.	BOOK 141:2
Sprouting despondently at area g.	ELIO 310:14
stand in thy g.	BOOK 148:19
suicide at its g.	HUSS 422:8
to the g. of Hell	PIUS 607:23
two g. of Sleep	VIRG 830:16
Gath Tell it not in G.	BIBL 84:11
gather G. ye rosebuds	HERR 396:17
He will surely g. you	KORA 471:20
who shall g. them	BOOK 141:29
gathered cannot be g. up again	BIBL 84:19
eagles be g. together	PROV 647:10
g. together in my name	BIBL 102:3
two or three are g.	BOOK 134:8
gathering g. where thou hast not strawed	BIBL 103:3
gat-toothed G. I was	CHAU 220:13
gaude g. in Christo	LUTH 505:3
gaudeamus G. igitur, Juvenes dum sumus	ANON 23:7
gaudia ira voluptas G.	JUVE 450:14
gaudy g., blabbing, and remorseful day	SHAK 709:23
Neat, but not g.	WESL 848:10
one other g. night	SHAK 695:11
rich, not g.	SHAK 700:4
gauger what should Master G. play	STEV 771:6
Gaul G. as a whole is divided	CAES 192:16
Gaunt G.'s embattled pile	MACA 508:2
Old John of G.	SHAK 730:1
gauntlet g. is the head	DANT 265:19
gauze shoot her through g.	BANK 57:11
gauzy wrapped in a g. veil	SHEL 747:5
gave Lord g., and the Lord	BIBL 86:11
she g. me of the tree	BIBL 79:7
What wee g., wee have	EPIT 320:2
gay g. deceiver	COLM 244:3
g. Lothario	ROWE 671:6
good and g.	PROV 638:44
heart was warm and g.	HAMM 378:18
if I could, be g.	ROGE 665:15
impiously g.	CRAB 257:20
making Gay rich, and Rich g.	JOHN 436:21
oddly g.	PARN 597:10
second best's a g. goodnight	YEAT 873:12
So g. the band	GREN 372:9
without feeling g.	CHUR 228:13
Gaza Eyeless in G.	MILT 544:31
gaze bade me g.	ARNO 30:20
gazelle never loved a dear G.	CARR 204:5
nursed a dear G.	DICK 279:24
nursed a dear g.	MOOR 558:14
one a g.	YEAT 873:15
gazelles g. appear	MOOR 558:3
gazer g. wipe his eye	HERB 395:2
gazette Pall Mall G. is written	THAC 802:20
gazing at each other	SAIN 677:15
g. up into heaven	BIBL 109:11
géant ailes de g.	BAUD 61:9
geese G. are swans	ARNO 29:15
g., like a snow cloud	RANS 655:5
great g. honk northward	WARR 840:9
kill all turkeys, g.	PROV 640:35
Like g. about the sky	AUDE 36:24
swans of others are g.	WALP 838:1
wild g. are flighting	KIPL 466:8
wild G. lost	BASH 60:16
Gehazi Whence comest thou, G.	BIBL 85:30
Gehenna Down to G.	KIPL 466:13
Geist Ich bin der G.	GOET 361:17
gem g. of purest ray serene	GRAY 370:6
precious g. was hidden	MITF 551:6
Thinking every tear a g.	SHEL 745:3
geminae g. Somni portae	VIRG 830:16
gemlike hard, g. flame	PATE 599:8
gender of the feminine g.	O'KE 584:19
tired of the g.	SEXT 693:5
general caviare to the g.	SHAK 701:16
feet of the great g.	OVID 590:19
find in that great g.	JUVE 451:14
G. notions	MONT 554:8
good g. because he has	CHAM 215:3
know man in g.	LA R 482:9
generalities glittering and sounding g.	CHOA 226:12
Glittering g.	EMER 315:21
generalizations g. dangerous	DUMA 299:5
generally g. necessary to salvation	BOOK 138:15
talk of g. held ideas	BAUD 61:16
General Motors good for G.	WILS 858:20
generals against the law for g.	TRUM 817:23
bite some of my other g.	GEOR 352:10
Dead battles, like dead g.	TUCH 818:10
g. than in particulars	HUME 420:10
Russia has two g.	NICH 574:16
we're all G.	USTI 823:7
generation beat g.	KERO 461:5
best minds of my g.	GINS 358:22
chosen g.	BIBL 117:3
Every g. revolts	MUMF 565:2
evil and adulterous g.	BIBL 101:8
faithless and stubborn g.	BOOK 145:6
flourishing of a g.	ORTE 586:11
froward g.	BIBL 82:19
g. passeth away	BIBL 89:16
g. was stolen	FREE 342:5
G. X	COUP 253:5
grieved with this g.	BOOK 146:8
Had it been the whole g.	EPIT 318:3
in their g. wiser	BIBL 106:3
lost g.	STEI 771:6
O g. of vipers	BIBL 98:17
one g. from extinction	CARE 198:17
third and fourth g.	BIBL 81:16
generations g. have trod	HOPK 407:7
g. of men	HOME 404:13
G. pass	BROW 162:16
g. shall call me blessed	BIBL 104:8
hungry g.	KEAT 456:10
in three g.	PROV 632:41
manners of future g.	JOHN 437:15
only three g.	PROV 632:40
Those dying g.	YEAT 874:13
three g. to make	PROV 636:39
generosity exercise our g.	SART 681:20
generous always g. ones	MONT 556:12
g. and elevated mind	JOHN 437:24
g. and honest feeling	BURK 175:6
just before you're g.	PROV 632:6
more g. sentiments	JOHN 440:3
My mind as g.	SHAK 714:22
generously treated g. or destroyed	
	MACH 511:6

genes G. not like blueprints — STEW 777:7
go by the name of g. — DAWK 269:4
true of the g. — JONE 445:10
what males do to g. — JONE 445:11
Genesis Conditioned G. — PALI 594:2
genetic mechanism for g. material — CRIC 260:3
genetics geography and g. — WHIT 851:1
Geneva grim G. ministers — AYTO 44:7
genie strength of the g. — WILB 854:8
genitals make my g. to quiver — JOHN 438:26
geniumque G. loci — VIRG 830:17
genius except my g. — WILD 856:13
feminine of g. — FITZ 332:2
g. a better discerning — GOLD 365:3
g. and art — HAZL 386:13
g. and regularity — GAIN 347:2
g. and virtue — HAZL 386:15
g. born a *woman* — STEN 771:13
G. capacity for taking pains — PROV 632:45
G. does what it must — MERE 532:24
G. from the throne — BYRO 190:1
G. in a garret — ROBI 664:6
g. in religion — ARNO 32:6
g. into my life — WILD 856:10
G. is one per cent inspiration — EDIS 303:15
g. is only a greater aptitude — BUFF 170:5
G. is the child — REYN 659:3
g. of Einstein leads to Hiroshima — PICA 606:14
g. of hard work — TURN 819:11
g. of its scientists — EISE 306:6
g. of the Constitution — PITT 607:14
g. of the place — POPE 615:7
g. overlooks individual — SCHO 686:12
'G.' which means — CARL 199:23
g. would wish to live — ADAM 2:1
gentlemen—a g. — SCHU 687:5
great g. — BEAU 63:6
If I'm not a g. — BALZ 57:5
kind of universal g. — DRYD 297:12
lively g. — GERV 354:1
Milton, Madam, was a g. — JOHN 444:1
Mr Wordsworth's g. — HAZL 386:19
Poetic G. of my country — BURN 180:11
singular g. — DIDE 282:17
stupendous g.! damned fool — BYRO 192:4
talent instantly recognizes g. — DOYL 293:2
taste or g. — REYN 659:1
Three-fifths of him g. — LOWE 502:17
true g. — JOHN 436:18
true g. appears — SWIF 783:14
what a g. I had — SWIF 784:14
Whence to g. wildly flashed — KEAT 457:5
works of a great g. — ADDI 5:23
geniuses One of the greatest g. — WALP 837:13
genres Tous les g. sont bons — VOLT 834:7
gent indeed a valiant G. — EVEL 321:18
genteel g. when he gets drunk — BOSW 152:8
to the truly g. — HARD 380:15
gentes Laudate Dominum, omnes g. — BIBL 120:4
gentil verray, parfit g. knyght — CHAU 218:5
Gentiles boasting as the G. use — KIPL 467:7
light to lighten the G. — BIBL 104:17
preach among the G. — BIBL 113:29
gentility marks of g. — BLAK 125:2
gentle Do not go g. — THOM 805:15
G. as falcon — SKEL 754:1
G. Child of gentle Mother — DEAR 269:15
g.-hearted Charles — COLE 241:14
g. his condition — SHAK 709:8
G. Jesus — WESL 847:12
g. mind by gentle deeds — SPEN 767:5
g. rain from heaven — SHAK 724:29
His life was g. — SHAK 714:3
gentleman as an educated g. — SHAW 740:13
cannot make a g. — BURK 176:8
definition of a g. — NEWM 572:8
describe a g. — TROL 816:3
died a very gallant g. — EPIT 317:14
Every other inch a g. — WEST 849:2
fashion a g. — SPEN 767:1
fine old English g. — SONG 763:3
first true g. — DEKK 271:21
g. and scholar — BURN 180:5

g. in Whitehall — JAY 430:25
g. should never go beyond — ETHE 320:15
g.'s park — CONS 249:18
g. who was generally spoken — SURT 781:19
God send every g. — BALL 56:2
I am a g. — SHAW 740:26
in linen like a g. — JOHN 436:12
Jack became a g. — SHAK 731:16
last g. in Europe — LEVE 491:3
make a g. — PROV 636:39
mariner with the g. — DRAK 293:9
not quite a g. — ASHF 33:13
officer and a g. — MILI 535:3
Once a g. — DICK 278:17
prince of darkness is a g. — SHAK 716:3
talking about being a g. — SURT 781:5
too pedantic for a g. — CONG 247:7
what a g. should be — DEFO 270:5
who was then the g. — PROV 646:36
gentlemanly g. conduct — ARNO 32:14
werry g. ideas — SURT 781:13
gentlemen Damn g. — GAIN 347:1
difficult to behave like g. — MACK 511:17
eggs for g. — NURS 579:1
forget we are g. — BURK 175:7
G. and Ladies — DICK 282:3
g. both — CARL 200:25
G. do not take soup at luncheon — CURZ 263:12
G. go by — KIPL 467:10
g. in England — SHAK 709:8
g. of England — PARK 596:20
G. of France — HAY 385:10
G. prefer blondes — LOOS 500:13
G.-rankers — KIPL 465:20
Great-hearted g. — BROW 166:16
nation of g. — MUGA 564:2
religion for g. — CHAR 217:4
Scholars and g. — WORD 868:16
since g. came up — SHAK 709:24
Three jolly g. — DE L 272:5
written by gentlemen for g. — THAC 802:20
gentleness g. And show of love — SHAK 711:14
only a willed g. — THOM 807:7
ways are ways of g. — SPRI 769:1
gently his faults lie g. — SHAK 711:3
roar you as g. — SHAK 725:30
genuflexion never grudge a g. — OLIV 585:1
genuine g. poetry is conceived — ARNO 31:24
place for the g. — MOOR 557:14
genus Hoc g. omne — HORA 414:10
geographers g., in Afric-maps — SWIF 784:2
our best g. — YOUR 877:6
geographical g. concept — BISM 123:1
g. expression — METT 533:10
g. precision — FLIN 335:19
not a g. fragment — PARN 597:8
geography g. and genetics — WHIT 851:1
G. is about Maps — BENT 71:14
too much g. — KING 464:2
geologists g. into infidelity — GOSS 366:12
g. would let me alone — RUSK 674:11
geometrical g. ratio — MALT 518:11
geometricians g. only by chance — JOHN 436:24
geometry always doing g. — PLAT 609:7
as precise as g. — FLAU 334:2
demonstration in g. — REYN 659:6
disorder in its g. — DE B 269:19
does not know g. — ANON 22:16
g. of fear — READ 656:3
G. (which is the only science — HOBB 400:16
'royal road' to g. — EUCL 320:19
George accession of G. the Third — MACA 507:11
England and Saint G. — SHAK 708:17
G.—don't do that — CATC 207:20
Georges G. ended — LAND 478:6
Georgia G. on my mind — GORR 366:10
red hills of G. — KING 463:11
Georgie G. Porgie, pudding and pie — NURS 578:15
geranium madman shakes a dead g. — ELIO 310:22
geraniums delphiniums (blue) and g. (red) — MILN 538:4

germ G. of Buddhahood — MAHĀ 515:15
German all a G. racket — RIDL 661:9
G. history reached — TAYL 791:8
language of poems is G. — CELA 212:12
to my horse—G. — CHAR 217:12
Germans beastly to the G. — COWA 253:10
G. . . . are going to be squeezed — GEDD 351:29
G. classify — CATH 209:10
G. that of—the air — RICH 661:5
Germany at war with G. — CHAM 214:7
bonnet in G. — SHAK 724:4
Christian life in G. — BONH 132:10
contemporary taste in G. — FRED 342:3
Death is a master from G. — CELA 212:11
G. above all — HOFF 402:3
G. calling — JOYC 448:26
G. in the saddle — BISM 122:17
G. is a nation — MICH 534:4
G. will declare that I am a Jew — EINS 305:9
offering G. too little — NEVI 571:7
rebellious G. — OVID 590:19
remaining cities of G. — HARR 383:1
germs Kills all known g. — ADVE 7:43
Gershwin G. songs — FISH 330:11
Gesang Das ist der ewige G. — GOET 361:19
Weib und G. — LUTH 505:12
Gestern G. liebt' ich — LESS 490:19
gestures In the g. — SOND 761:1
get G. me to the church — LERN 490:7
G. out as early as you can — LARK 481:10
g. out of these wet clothes — FILM 328:24
G. thee behind me, Satan — BIBL 101:27
g. up airily — LOWE 502:16
g. what you like — SHAW 741:26
g. where I am today without — CATC 207:31
What you see is what you g. — SAYI 685:18
getting G. and spending — WORD 869:24
Gospel of G. On — SHAW 742:1
gewgaw This g. world — DRYD 295:9
ghastly G. good taste — BETJ 76:10
G., grim and ancient — POE 611:2
g. through the drizzling rain — TENN 795:4
We were a g. crew — COLE 241:5
ghost but a kind of g. — DONN 288:27
each frustrate g. — BROW 167:24
each write a g. story — SHEL 743:1
gave up the g. — BIBL 109:28
g. asked them to do — O'BR 583:2
G. in the Machine — RYLE 676:9
g. of a garden — SWIN 785:10
g. of a great name — LUCA 503:17
g. of a rose — BROW 162:7
g. of Roger Casement — YEAT 873:13
g. of the deceased — HOBB 401:8
G. unlaid forbear thee — SHAK 698:25
I am the g. — PLAT 608:8
If the g. cries — RAIN 653:11
I'll make a g. of him — SHAK 700:14
Moves like a g. — SHAK 719:20
some old lover's g. — DONN 289:10
Vex not his g. — SHAK 717:9
What beck'ning g. — POPE 614:2
ghosties ghoulies and g. — PRAY 623:3
ghosts allowed to us moderns, are g. — FIEL 326:21
egress is given to real g. — VIRG 830:16
g. from an enchanter — SHEL 745:6
g. of a nation — PEAR 601:3
g. of Beauty glide — POPE 614:29
g. of departed quantities — BERK 72:11
g. of the slaughtered — CLAU 234:7
g. outnumber us — DUNN 299:16
G., wandering here and there — SHAK 726:21
lack of g. — BIRN 122:2
make the g. gaze — SHAK 695:18
ghoul dug them up like a G. — DICK 277:26
g.-haunted woodland of Weir — POE 611:6
living on another like a g. — HEAD 386:27
ghoulies g. and ghosties — PRAY 623:3
giant awakened a sleeping g. — FILM 328:13
G. Despair — BUNY 171:13
G. Despair — BUNY 171:14
g. great and still — STEV 776:14

G. on the mountain stands	BYRO 185:17
g.'s strength	SHAK 723:7
g.'s wings	BAUD 61:9
hand of the g.	BOOK 149:3
like a g.	BOOK 145:9
like a g.'s robe	SHAK 722:13
rejoiceth as a g.	BOOK 140:9
sees farther than the g.	COLE 241:23
giants for war like precocious g.	PEAR 601:6
G. can be surprised	RATT 655:15
g. in the earth	BIBL 79:21
nuclear g. and ethical infants	BRAD 154:7
on the shoulders of g.	NEWT 574:7
shoulders of g.	BERN 73:17
there we saw the g.	BIBL 82:4
Want one only of five g.	BEVE 77:6
we ought to be g.	CHEK 221:19
gibber squeak and g.	SHAK 699:4
gibbets cells and g.	COOK 250:9
g. keep the lifted hand in awe	YOUN 876:14
Gibbon Eh! Mr G.	GLOU 360:18
Gibeon stand thou still upon G.	BIBL 82:29
giberne dans sa g. le bâton	LOUI 501:10
gibes great master of g.	DISR 285:4
giblet liked thick g. soup	JOYC 448:18
Gibraltar G. may tumble	GERS 353:15
giddy I am g.	SHAK 734:15
So g. the sight	GREN 372:9
Gideon Lord came upon G.	BIBL 83:6
gift Beauty is the lover's g.	CONG 247:23
every perfect g.	BIBL 116:17
Freedom is not a g.	NKRU 576:16
g. horse in the mouth	PROV 639:38
g. of God	BIBL 109:20
g. of the divine Name	SIKH 752:7
gods' most lovely g.	EURI 321:13
last best g.	MILT 543:17
love is the g. of oneself	ANOU 24:11
make the g. rich	TROL 816:20
what a personal g. is	HEIN 389:5
You have a g.	JONS 446:16
your g. survived it all	AUDE 37:8
gifted vividly g. in love	DUFF 298:14
young, g. and black	HANS 379:12
Young, g. and black	IRVI 425:20
giftie g. gie us	BURN 179:23
gifts Bestows her g.	JONS 446:6
bring g.	BOOK 144:19
buy g. at Jim Gibson's	LONG 500:11
cannot recall their g.	TENN 800:9
countless of love	WINK 860:12
diversities of g.	BIBL 112:13
Enemies' g. are no gifts	SOPH 761:11
even when they bring g.	VIRG 824:9
g. of God are strown	HEBE 388:9
Greeks bearing g.	PROV 632:6
He would adore my g.	HERB 394:21
no g. from chance	ARNO 30:3
Of all the heavenly g.	GRIM 373:8
presented unto him g.	BIBL 98:11
received g. for men	BOOK 144:10
gigantic g. body	MACA 506:17
gild g. refinèd gold	BYRO 188:20
g. refinèd gold	SHAK 714:11
I'll g. it	SHAK 707:1
gilded g. car of day	MILT 538:22
g. loam	SHAK 730:2
gilding amusement is the g.	RICH 660:18
G. pale streams	SHAK 737:25
Gilead G. is mine	BOOK 143:19
no balm in G.	BIBL 95:2
gill hang by its own g.	PROV 631:20
Gilpin John G. was a citizen	COWP 255:8
gilt g. comes off in our hands	FLAU 333:7
gin get out the g.	REED 657:7
g. and vermouth	DE V 275:3
G. was mother's milk	SHAW 742:10
Of all the g. joints	FILM 329:13
woodcock near the g.	SHAK 735:23
ginger G., you're balmy	MURR 565:23
ginless wicked as a g. tonic	COPE 251:7
Gioconda one isn't the real G.	CRAN 258:16
Giotto G. has the palm	DANT 265:11

G.'s tower	LONG 499:6
giovinezza Quanto è bella g.	MEDI 530:5
Gipfeln Über allen G. Ist Ruh'	GOET 362:15
Gipper Win just one for the G.	GIPP 359:5
gipsy Time, you old g. man	HODG 402:1
giraffe g., in their gracefulness	DINE 283:12
giraffes G.!—a People Who live	CAMP 195:3
girded g. himself with strength	BOOK 146:4
g. up his loins	BIBL 85:12
g. with praise	GRAN 368:11
girdle bright g. furled	ARNO 29:4
g. round about the earth	SHAK 726:7
to the g.	SHAK 716:18
girdled g. with the gleaming world	TENN 797:12
girl Above the staggering g.	YEAT 874:1
can't get no g. reaction	JAGG 427:10
danced with a g.	FARJ 323:13
diamonds a g.'s best friend	ROBI 663:15
g. at an impressionable age	SPAR 765:10
g. in the indolence of youth	YEAT 874:8
g. needs good parents	TUCK 818:12
g. throwing a ball	WOOL 864:11
g. with brains ought to	LOOS 500:14
Poor little rich g.	COWA 253:17
pretty g. is like a melody	BERL 73:3
speak like a green g.	SHAK 700:7
sweetest g. I know	JUDG 449:4
unlessoned g.	SHAK 724:24
was a little g.	LONG 500:7
girlish g. glee	GILB 357:5
Laugh thy g. laughter	WATS 841:9
girls Always be civil to the g.	MITF 551:8
assumption that g.	FRAS 341:17
bombers named for g.	JARR 430:22
Boys and g.	NURS 578:3
G. aren't like that	AMIS 14:14
g. in slacks remember Dad	BETJ 75:10
g. that are so smart	CARE 199:2
g. who wear glasses	PARK 596:4
lads for the g.	HOUS 415:17
little g. made of	NURS 582:10
not that g. should think	NAPO 567:17
nude, giant g.	SPEN 766:13
rosebud garden of g.	TENN 798:5
rose-lipt g. are sleeping	HOUS 416:9
Secrets with g.	CRAB 258:4
Thank heaven for little g.	LERN 490:13
Treaties like g. and roses	DE G 271:15
white feet of laughing g.	MACA 508:11
without complaints from g.	HORA 413:6
Gitche Gumee By the shore of G.	LONG 499:22
give All that I am I g.	BOOK 139:2
better to g. than to receive	PROV 636:12
freely g.	BIBL 100:23
G., and it shall be given	BIBL 104:26
g. and not to count	IGNA 424:14
G. and take fair play	PROV 633:1
g. a singel dam	FLEM 334:18
G. a thing	PROV 632:48
G. crowns and pounds	HOUS 415:15
g. me back my legions	AUGU 40:2
G. me my Romeo	SHAK 732:27
G. me yet before I die	WINC 860:8
G. to me the life I love	STEV 777:1
g. to the poor	BIBL 102:6
G. us back	POLI 612:18
g. what you command	AUGU 39:11
more blessed to g.	BIBL 110:9
not as the world giveth, g. I	BIBL 108:17
peace which the world cannot g.	BOOK 134:9
receive but what we g.	COLE 239:9
such as I have g. I thee	BIBL 109:15
given g. away by a novel	KEAT 458:8
I would have g. gladly	JOHN 435:4
much is g.	BIBL 105:17
shall be g.	BIBL 103:4
taking what is not g.	PALI 593:12
To whom nothing is g.	FIEL 326:12
giver author and g.	BOOK 136:7
cheerful g.	BIBL 113:12
Lord and g. of life	BOOK 137:3
gives g. twice who gives quickly	PROV 633:51

happiness she g.	LACL 475:10
who g. soon	PUBL 648:30
giving g. and receiving of a Ring	BOOK 139:4
Godlike in g.	ANON 17:10
not in the g. vein	SHAK 731:22
glacier g. knocks in the cupboard	AUDE 36:25
glad g. confident morning	BROW 166:14
G. did I live	STEV 777:5
g. father	BIBL 87:34
g. when they said unto me	BOOK 148:19
just g. to see me	WEST 848:16
maketh g. the heart	BOOK 147:6
rejoice and be g.	BOOK 148:11
shew ourselves g. in him	BOOK 146:7
too soon made g.	BROW 166:20
glade bee-loud g.	YEAT 873:20
crown the wat'ry g.	GRAY 370:10
fan the g.	POPE 618:16
gladiators g. of Rome	BORR 151:12
gladly bear the cross g.	THOM 805:2
g. wolde he lerne	CHAU 218:16
I would have given g.	JOHN 435:4
gladness As with g. men of old	DIX 287:1
obtain joy and g.	BIBL 93:11
oil of g.	BOOK 142:13
serve the Lord with g.	BOOK 146:5
Teach me half the g.	SHEL 746:24
gladsome g. light	COKE 238:13
Let us with a g. mind	MILT 540:1
Glamis G. hath murdered sleep	SHAK 720:7
G. thou art, and Cawdor	SHAK 718:19
glance g. from heaven to earth	SHAK 727:3
O brightening g.	YEAT 872:8
glare looked at in this merciless g.	WILL 858:7
red g. on Skiddaw	MACA 508:2
Glasgow G. Empire on a Saturday night	DODD 287:6
glass baying for broken g.	WAUG 842:11
brighter than g.	HORA 413:4
comb and a g. in her hand	SONG 763:6
dome of many-coloured g.	SHEL 743:21
excuse for the g.	SHER 748:27
face in a g.	BIBL 116:18
Get thee g. eyes	SHAK 716:21
g. I drink from	MUSS 566:9
g. of blessings	HERB 394:20
g. the opulent	HARD 381:12
Grief with a g.	SWIN 784:22
highest, hardest g. ceiling	CLIN 236:4
if you break the bloody g.	MACN 513:9
liked the Sound of Broken G.	BELL 68:17
live in g. houses	PROV 645:7
made mouths in a g.	SHAK 715:18
man that looks on g.	HERB 394:6
No g. of ours was raised	HEAN 387:13
own face in the g.	WILD 855:15
Satire is a sort of g.	SWIF 782:1
sea of g.	BIBL 118:4
sea of g.	BIBL 119:4
set you up a g.	SHAK 703:9
sun-comprehending g.	LARK 481:4
take a g. of wine	SHER 748:32
through a g., darkly	BIBL 112:14
turn down an empty g.	FITZ 331:29
glasses broke our painted g.	JORD 447:9
Fill all the g. there	COWL 254:9
girls who wear g.	PARK 596:4
ladder and some g.	BATE 61:6
Such cruel g.	HOWE 417:7
glassy around the g. sea	HEBE 388:10
g., cool, translucent	MILT 539:11
in the g. stream	SHAK 704:5
Upon the g. plain	WORD 866:2
gleam follow the G.	TENN 798:15
g. of time	CARL 200:9
gleaning g. of the grapes	BIBL 83:8
glee girlish g.	GILB 357:5
wild with g.	WORD 869:17
glen Down the rushy g.	ALLI 13:19
glib g. and oily art	SHAK 714:19
gliding like a queen	SPEN 766:9
glimmering fades the g. landscape	GRAY 370:1
Mere g. and decays	VAUG 825:10

glimpses g. of the moon — SHAK 700:12
g. that would make me — WORD 869:25
glittering g. and sounding generalities — CHOA 226:12
g. in the smokeless air — WORD 865:7
g. prizes — SMIT 756:16
how that g. taketh me — HERR 396:19
with his g. eye — COLE 240:13
glitters All that g. is not gold — PROV 626:20
medal g. — CHUR 229:21
gloaming In the g. — ORRE 586:7
Roamin' in the g. — LAUD 482:20
gloat I g. — KIPL 468:23
global g. thinking — LUCE 504:1
image of a g. village — MCLU 512:9
globally Think g. — SLOG 755:13
globaloney still g. — LUCE 504:1
globe g.-trotting Madam — YEAT 875:6
great g. itself — SHAK 733:31
hunted round the g. — PAIN 592:11
rattle of a g. — DRYD 295:9
this distracted g. — SHAK 700:23
globèd wealth of g. peonies — KEAT 455:28
globes g. of deep red gold — SHEL 745:1
globule primordial atomic g. — GILB 357:2
Glöckchen das G. klingeln — HEIN 389:15
gloom counterfeit a g. — MILT 539:16
inspissated g. — JOHN 440:18
glooms kindred g. — THOM 808:19
gloomy by g. Dis Was gathered — MILT 543:4
gloria G. in excelsis — MISS 549:8
G. Patri — MISS 546:19
Sic transit g. mundi — ANON 23:12
gloriam Dei g. — MOTT 563:1
glories G., like glow-worms — WEBS 844:10
g. of our blood and state — SHIR 749:17
in those weaker g. spy — VAUG 825:6
my g. and my state — SHAK 731:3
glorified g. not in one — BRUN 168:21
glorious all-g. above — GRAN 368:11
all g. within — BOOK 142:15
By the g. Koran — KORA 473:4
g. by my pen — MONT 556:16
g. Devon — BOUL 152:14
G. things of thee — NEWT 574:13
more g. to them — ELIZ 312:11
Mud! G. mud — FLAN 332:23
nothing g. left undone — FLAT 333:2
Tam was g. — BURN 179:14
What a g. morning — ADAM 3:20
glory all things give him g. — HOPK 408:9
alone with his g. — WOLF 862:15
brood of g. — SPEN 767:7
crowned with g. now — KELL 459:11
day of g. has arrived — ROUG 670:11
days of our g. — BYRO 191:6
declare the g. of God — BOOK 140:8
deed is all, the g. nothing — GOET 362:6
drowned my g. — FITZ 331:27
earth is full of his g. — BIBL 92:6
flowers leads to g. — LA F 475:20
from another star in g. — BIBL 113:2
full of thy g. — BOOK 137:14
game is about g. — BLAN 128:18
g. a bubble — SHEL 747:9
g. and shame — MILT 542:12
g. and the dream — WORD 867:7
g. and the freshness — WORD 867:2
g. and the nothing — BYRO 187:5
g. as of the only begotten — BIBL 107:2
G. be to God — HOPK 407:16
G. be to the Father — BOOK 133:8
g. from the earth — WORD 867:3
g. in the church — BIBL 114:3
g. in the name of Briton — GEOR 352:11
g. is departed — BIBL 83:29
g. is departed — BROW 168:8
g. is in their shame — BIBL 115:2
g., laud, and honour — NEAL 569:6
g., like the phoenix — BYRO 190:8
g. never dies — ANON 24:4
g. not their own — WORD 868:15
g. of Europe — BURK 174:7

g. of God — BLAK 126:13
g. of Gothic — RUSK 674:12
g. of great men — LA R 481:26
g. of man as the flower — BIBL 117:1
g. of my crown — ELIZ 312:10
g. of the Attic stage — ARNO 31:1
g. of the coming — HOWE 417:3
g. of the Creator — BACO 45:9
g. of the Lord — BIBL 93:15
g. of the Lord — BIBL 94:18
g. of the Lord shone — BIBL 104:12
g. of them — BIBL 98:22
g. of the Trojans — VIRG 829:13
g. of the winning — MERE 532:18
g. of the world — ANON 23:12
g. of this world passes — THOM 804:14
g. shone around — TATE 790:16
g.'s small change — HUGO 419:7
g. that was Greece — POE 611:5
G. to God in the highest — BIBL 104:14
g. to her — BIBL 112:12
G. to Man in the highest — SWIN 785:17
greater g. of God — MOTT 563:1
greatest g. of a woman — PERI 603:27
hope of g. — BOOK 135:8
I felt it was g. — BYRO 191:7
I go to g. — DUNC 299:13
joy and g. — ABEL 1:1
King of g. — BOOK 141:2
Land of Hope and G. — BENS 70:22
living man is the g. — IREN 425:19
looks on war as all g. — SHER 749:11
Majesty: of thy G. — BOOK 133:9
name thee Old G. — DRIV 294:2
Not as our g. — WORD 868:12
paths of g. — GRAY 370:4
power, and the g. — BIBL 99:12
question of your g. — COLB 238:18
say my g. was — YEAT 874:6
scandal and g. — RAMS 654:20
sea Of g. streams along — BYRO 186:17
short of the g. of God — BIBL 110:27
Solomon in all his g. — BIBL 99:18
some desperate g. — OWEN 591:6
There's g. for you — CARR 203:11
Thy g. is upon my tongue — JUDA 449:3
trailing clouds of g. — WORD 867:8
triumph without g. — CORN 251:13
uncertain g. — SHAK 736:14
walking in an air of g. — VAUG 825:10
way to g. — TENN 798:25
what g. is it — BIBL 117:6
What price g. — ANDE 15:11
yields the true g. — DRAK 293:7
gloss all we do is g. each other — MONT 555:26
gain is g. — CUNN 262:17
Glossop Roderick G. — WODE 862:1
Gloucester tailor in G. — POTT 620:4
glove O! that I were a g. — SHAK 732:10
played at the g. — BALL 54:7
white g. pulpit — REAG 656:10
gloves brandy and summer g. — JOSE 447:13
capitalism with the g. off — STOP 778:4
cat in g. — PROV 628:36
people in g. and such — CHES 224:5
through the fields in g. — CORN 252:2
with my g. on my hand — HARG 382:10
glow don thyn eris g. — CHAU 220:29
g. has warmed the world — STEV 775:1
made my heart to g. — SOUT 764:25
glowers sits there and g. — BARH 58:13
glowing g. kiss had won — HOOD 405:25
glow-worm g., or some other — MAHĀ 515:8
g. that shines — HAGG 376:3
Her eyes the g. lend — HERR 396:3
glow-worms Glories, like g. — WEBS 844:10
glut g. thy sorrow — KEAT 455:28
glutton Of praise a mere g. — GOLD 364:21
gluttony G. an emotional escape — DE V 275:4
Glyn With Elinor G. — ANON 21:15
gnashing g. of teeth — BIBL 100:9
gnat strain at a g. — BIBL 102:19
gnats small g. mourn — KEAT 457:3

gnomes g. in Zurich — WILS 859:2
go can't g. on — BECK 64:14
G. ahead, make my day — FILM 328:9
G., and catch — DONN 289:14
G., and do thou likewise — BIBL 105:7
G., and sin no more — BIBL 107:29
G., and the Lord be with thee — BIBL 84:4
g. anywhere I damn well please — BEVI 77:11
g. away at any rate — ANON 19:1
G. down, Moses — SONG 763:16
G., for they call you — ARNO 30:6
G. further and fare worse — PROV 633:5
g. into the house — BOOK 148:19
G., litel bok — CHAU 221:11
G., little book — STEV 777:4
G., lovely rose — WALL 836:17
g. no more a-roving — BYRO 191:4
G. to jail — SAYI 684:22
G. to the ant — BIBL 87:27
g. to the devil — JOHN 438:14
g. unto the altar of God — BOOK 142:9
g. we know not where — SHAK 723:14
G. West, young man — GREE 371:5
g. with all your heart — CONF 246:23
G. ye into all the world — BIBL 104:6
I g.—I come back — CATC 208:3
I g. on for ever — TENN 793:2
I g. to the Father — BIBL 108:22
I have a g. — OSBO 588:15
In the name of God, g. — AMER 14:7
In the name of God, g. — CROM 260:14
I say to this man, G. — BIBL 100:7
I shall g. to him — BIBL 84:18
I will not let thee g. — WESL 847:13
Let my people g. — BIBL 81:4
neither g. nor hang — BIGO 121:11
never g. back again — MORE 559:9
no place to g. — BURT 180:19
no place to g. — WHIT 851:17
not fail to g. — MORE 559:6
not g. to Canossa — BISM 122:18
not let thee g. — BIBL 80:14
Nowhere to g. but out — KING 463:3
One of us must g. — WILD 856:15
One to come, and one to g. — CARR 203:17
Quickly come, quickly g. — PROV 642:16
Rain, rain, g. away — NURS 581:1
that I g. away — BIBL 108:20
There you g. again — REAG 656:13
thus far shalt thou g. — PARN 597:9
to boldly g. — RODD 665:2
To g. away is to die — HARA 379:14
to hell I will g. — MILL 535:24
unto Caesar shalt thou g. — BIBL 110:14
wherever he wants to g. — BRAU 155:10
with thee to g. — MILT 544:18
goal final g. of ill — TENN 795:12
moving freely, without a g. — KLEE 469:7
goals muddied oafs at the g. — KIPL 466:9
positive g. — BERL 73:8
goat fleecy hairy g. — BELL 68:13
Gall of g. — SHAK 721:17
lust of the g. — BLAK 126:13
with their g. feet — MARL 522:13
goats Cadwallader and all his g. — SHAK 709:10
drink the blood of g. — BOOK 143:3
from the g. — MISS 550:8
g. on the left — BIBL 103:5
go on, my she-g. — VIRG 832:11
hair is as a flock of g. — BIBL 91:4
refuge for the wild g. — BOOK 147:7
gobbledygoo your g. — PLAT 608:5
goblet navel like a round g. — BIBL 91:14
goblin or g. damned — SHAK 700:11
goblins sprites and g. — SHAK 736:19
God acceptable unto G. — BIBL 111:9
afraid to look upon G. — BIBL 80:35
All things are possible with G. — PROV 626:21
and now with G. — WALT 839:5
appeal from tyranny to G. — BYRO 191:3
armour of G. — BIBL 114:14
As a g. self-slain — SWIN 785:11
beast or a g. — ARIS 27:25

they first make g. — LEVI 491:8
Thou shalt have no other g. — BIBL 81:15
use the g.' gifts wisely — HORA 414:4
utterance of the early g. — KEAT 454:22
Whatever g. may be — SWIN 785:14
What men or g. — KEAT 455:17
Whom the g. love — MENA 531:16
Whom the G. love — PROV 647:17
Whom the g. would destroy — PROV 647:16
Ye shall be as g. — BIBL 79:5
you g., Give to your boy — DRYD 295:9
goes g. around comes around — SAYI 685:16
g. of a night — SHER 748:24
goest whithersoever thou g. — BIBL 82:24
whither thou g., I will go — BIBL 83:23
Goethe every Rasputin has his G. — GRAS 369:4
going At the g. down of the sun — BINY 121:15
country wears their g. — DUNN 300:4
endure Their g. hence — SHAK 716:25
g. gets tough — KENN 460:17
g. the way of all the earth — BIBL 82:30
g. to a feast — JONS 446:4
g. to and fro in the earth — BIBL 86:9
Keep g. — TUBM 818:9
not know where he is g. — LIN 495:7
order of your g. — SHAK 721:11
puck is g. to be — GRET 372:13
to what he was g. — HARD 381:23
we are g. — JOHN 441:27
When the g. gets tough — PROV 646:47
goings numberless g.-on of life — COLE 239:18
ordered my g. — BOOK 141:30
gold all done up in g. — ASHF 33:15
All that glitters is not g. — PROV 626:20
apples of g. — BIBL 88:35
Apples of g. — SWIN 785:24
as much g. as they desire — COLU 244:14
be it gash or g. — BROO 160:1
bridge of g. — PROV 636:18
bringing g., and silver — BIBL 84:29
building roofs of g. — SHAK 708:10
candelabrum of g. — BERN 74:2
clothing is of wrought g. — BOOK 142:15
cross of g. — BRYA 169:1
cursed craving for g. — VIRG 829:17
eighty years in g. — BYRO 191:12
feathers like g. — BOOK 144:8
fetch the age of g. — MILT 540:26
fetters, though of g. — BACO 45:26
get much g. — BIBL 98:7
gild refinèd g. — SHAK 714:11
globes of deep red g. — SHEL 745:1
g. and amber — JONS 446:13
g., and frankincense — BIBL 98:11
g. and silver becks me — SHAK 714:8
G.? a transient, shining trouble — GRAI 368:5
G. be bought too dear — PROV 633:14
g. filling in a mouthful of decay — OSBO 588:20
g. of Arabia — BOOK 144:20
g. of the day — CROS 261:3
g. shines like fire — PIND 606:16
g. wes changyd into lede — WYNT 871:17
g., yea, than much fine gold — BOOK 140:11
harpstring of g. — SWIN 785:18
If g. ruste, what shall iren do — CHAU 218:21
in purple and g. — BYRO 187:16
Love is mor than g. — LYDG 505:18
natural stability of g. — SHAW 740:5
Nor all, that glisters, g. — GRAY 370:17
pale—is yet of g. — CRAB 257:24
path of g. — BROW 166:26
patines of bright g. — SHAK 725:11
poop was beaten g. — SHAK 694:22
pure g. flows forth — TOCQ 812:16
queen in a vesture of g. — BOOK 142:14
rarer gifts than g. — BROO 159:4
realms of g. — KEAT 456:14
religion of g. — BAGE 50:16
street of the city was g. — BIBL 119:18
streets are paved with g. — COLM 244:2
streets being paved with g. — LOUI 501:8
stuffed their mouths with g. — BEVA 77:3
This g., my dearest — LEAP 485:11

thousands of g. and silver — BOOK 148:13
to India for g. — MARL 522:6
trodden g. — MILT 541:29
turns sand to g. — YOUN 876:9
what's become of all the g. — BROW 168:4
Within its net of g. — MACN 513:14
your glistering g. — BRAD 154:13
golden beside the g. door — LAZA 485:3
burnished with g. rind — MILT 543:2
Casting down their g. crowns — HEBE 388:10
circle of the g. year — TENN 793:21
Clasped by the g. light — HOOD 405:25
end of a g. string — BLAK 125:16
fell her g. hair — TURN 819:9
g. bough — FRAZ 341:19
g. bowl be broken — BIBL 90:20
G. Calf of Self-love — CARL 199:10
g. days of Saturn's reign — VIRG 832:2
g. entrails — DRAY 293:16
g. key can open — PROV 633:15
G. lads and girls — SHAK 698:24
g. lamps in a green night — MARV 524:15
g. moments of our history — GLAD 360:8
G. opinions — SHAK 719:11
g. priests — JEWE 433:18
G. Road to Samarkand — FLEC 334:12
G. slumbers kiss your eyes — DEKK 271:22
G. stockings — GOGA 363:8
G. was that first age — OVID 590:6
g. years return — SHEL 744:5
hand that lays the g. egg — GOLD 365:19
hangs a g. chain — PUSH 650:21
His g. locks — PEEL 601:17
in the g. world — SHAK 696:9
in their g. hair — TENN 799:3
Jerusalem the g. — NEAL 569:8
King Charles's g. days — SONG 762:14
little dogs, with g. hair — LUTH 505:6
love in a g. bowl — BLAK 124:21
loves the g. mean — HORA 412:8
morning had been g. — CHUR 230:16
name of the G. Vanity — SONG 763:10
poets only deliver a g. — SIDN 751:4
Roll down their g. sand — HEBE 388:8
seven g. candlesticks — BIBL 117:26
Silence is g. — PROV 643:10
We are g. — MITC 551:1
went into a g. land — TURN 819:15
your g. hair Margareta — CELA 212:9
Goldengrove G. unleaving — HOPK 407:19
goldfinch song of the g. — VIRG 833:3
goldsmith To Oliver G., A Poet — EPIT 319:4
golf g. may be played on Sunday — LEAC 485:10
made more Liars than G. — ROGE 666:3
thousand lost g. balls — ELIO 310:24
too young to take up g. — ADAM 2:8
Golgotha field of G. — SHAK 731:1
in the Hebrew G. — BIBL 108:28
gondola Did'st ever see a g. — BYRO 185:8
g. of London — DISR 286:3
What else is like the g. — CLOU 236:17
gone All, all are g. — LAMB 476:24
And they are g. — KEAT 454:15
g. altogether beyond — MAHĀ 515:10
G. before — LAMB 476:21
g. from original righteousness — BOOK 150:18
g. into the world of light — VAUG 825:9
g. with the wind — DOWS 292:3
He is g. — JOHN 441:27
not dead—but g. — ROGE 665:13
She's g. for ever — SHAK 717:5
Ship and stores have g. — SHAC 693:10
something that is g. — WORD 867:7
they are g. forever — MANN 519:10
welcomest when they are g. — SHAK 709:15
what haste I can to be g. — CROM 261:1
What's g. — SHAK 736:23
when I am g. — ROSS 669:4
Wilt thou be g. — SHAK 732:29
gong that g.-tormented sea — YEAT 872:12
gongs Strong g. groaning — CHES 224:10
struck regularly like g. — COWA 254:3
good Address to the unco g. — BURN 177:7

and doth no g. — RALE 653:15
And now g. morrow — DONN 289:8
annoyance of g. example — TWAI 820:23
antipathy of g. to bad — POPE 617:29
Any g. of George the Third — LAND 478:6
any g. thing — BIBL 107:6
anything g. to say — LONG 500:12
As for Doing-g. — THOR 809:16
as g. as he found it — COBB 237:12
be a g. animal — SPEN 765:19
be g. for long — BREC 155:14
be g. in the country — WILD 855:20
Be g., sweet maid — KING 464:4
be g. to some man — SHAW 741:31
being really g. — WILD 854:23
Beneath the g. how far — GRAY 370:22
best is enemy of g. — PROV 627:20
best is the enemy of the g. — VOLT 834:2
Better a g. cow — PROV 627:28
better than the G. Old Days — BINC 121:14
better to be g. — WILD 855:21
better to fight for the g. — TENN 798:13
call a man a g. man — JOHN 443:20
call g. evil — BIBL 92:4
call no being g. — MILL 535:24
can't be g., be careful — PROV 635:22
choose the g. — BIBL 92:11
common g. to all — SHAK 714:3
could be a g. woman — THAC 803:5
does most g. or harm — BAGE 51:14
does what does him g. — BÜCH 169:13
do evil, that g. may come — BIBL 110:26
do evil that g. may come — PROV 639:34
do g. and to communicate — BIBL 116:14
Do g. by stealth — POPE 617:28
do g. to them — BIBL 104:25
either g. or bad — SHAK 701:9
Evil, be thou my g. — MILT 542:30
evil turn to g. — MILT 544:16
Exceedingly g. cakes — ADVE 7:23
few Know their own g. — DRYD 297:8
for our country's g. — CART 204:14
for your g., for all your goods — GEOR 352:8
For your own g. — FRAM 340:3
future apparent g. — HOBB 400:19
Gallop about doing g. — SMIT 757:14
giver of all g. things — BOOK 136:7
go about doing g. — CREI 259:17
God saw that it was g. — BIBL 78:14
g. action by stealth — LAMB 477:12
G. and evil shall not be held — KORA 472:16
g. and faithful servant — BIBL 103:2
g. and immoral — CHUR 229:4
g. as he may be — MONT 555:24
G. at which all things aim — ARIS 27:5
g. becomes indistinguishable — DAWS 269:5
g. beginning makes — PROV 633:17
G., but not religious-good — HARD 381:5
g. Compensate bad — BROW 167:17
g. day to bury bad news — MISQ 547:17
g. die early — DEFO 270:16
g. die first — WORD 865:13
g. die young — PROV 633:18
g. ended happily — WILD 854:22
g. fences make good neighbours — FROS 344:18
g. for inside of a man — PROV 644:35
g. for the people of England — GLAD 360:6
g. in the worst of us — ANON 20:18
g. is oft interrèd — SHAK 712:28
g. is the enemy — PROV 633:21
g. Jack makes a good Jill — PROV 633:22
g. man and a good citizen — AUCT 36:16
g. man, and a just — BIBL 106:27
g. man is merciful — BOOK 148:1
g. man to do nothing — MISQ 548:4
G. men are scarce — PROV 633:23
g. men should look on — MILL 536:1
g. minute goes — BROW 168:6
g. name — BIBL 88:30
g. news from Ghent to Aix — BROW 166:3
G. night and good luck — CATC 207:24
g. of human nature — BACO 48:13
g. of man — ARIS 27:6

good (cont.):

G. of man	ARIS 27:8
g. of one's country	FARQ 324:7
g. of subjects	DEFO 271:4
g. of the people	CICE 231:18
g. *old Cause*	MILT 546:8
g. old cause	WORD 867:20
g. people were clever	WORD 865:3
g. provoke to harm	SHAK 723:18
G. seed makes good crop	PROV 633:24
g. sense and good taste	LA B 475:1
g. that I would I do not	BIBL 110:37
g., the bad, and the ugly	FILM 331:6
g. things must come to an end	PROV 626:13
G. things of day	SHAK 721:5
g. time coming	SCOT 689:24
g. time it was	VOLT 834:12
g. time was had by all	SMIT 757:15
g. to feel rotten	YESE 875:21
g. to talk	ADVE 7:39
g. unluckily	STOP 778:2
g. want power	SHEL 745:20
g. Will be the final goal	TENN 795:12
g. will never be our task	MILT 541:14
g. will toward men	BIBL 104:14
G. wine needs no bush	PROV 633:25
g. without qualification	KANT 452:18
G. women always think	BROO 159:15
G. words do not last long	JOSE 447:12
g. works are not wasted	CALD 193:6
Greed is g.	FILM 328:10
Guinness is g. for you	ADVE 7:27
had been g. for that man	BIBL 103:11
Hanging is too g. for him	BUNY 171:10
have a g. thing	SHAK 707:9
heaven doing g. on earth	TERE 802:5
He wos wery g. to me	DICK 276:14
highest g.	CICE 231:21
His own g.	MILL 536:2
hold fast that which is g.	BIBL 115:16
human nature is g.	MENG 532:2
impulsive to g.	MANN 519:9
In art the best is g. enough	GOET 362:9
it cannot come to g.	SHAK 699:23
It's a g. thing	CATC 208:9
I will be g.	VICT 827:6
kept the g. wine	BIBL 107:9
knowing g. and evil	BIBL 79:5
learn the luxury of doing g.	GOLD 364:23
leave assurèd g.	DRAY 293:16
like a g. fiend	THOM 806:12
looked like a g. thing	HENR 392:10
loves what he is g. at	SHAD 693:14
luxury of doing g.	CRAB 258:1
luxury was doing g.	GART 350:2
making people feel g.	CHRÉ 226:18
Men have never been g.	BART 60:6
much g. would be absent	THOM 805:9
neither g. nor bad	BALZ 56:14
never had it so g.	MACM 512:17
never so g. or so bad	MACK 511:18
No g. man is a Briton	AUSO 41:1
no ills from g. dissuade	SMAR 754:9
none that doeth g.	BOOK 139:28
not enough to have a g. mind	DESC 274:8
not g. company	AUST 42:3
nothing to be had	HAZL 386:8
obscurely g.	ADDI 4:19
Of g. and evil much they argued	MILT 542:12
of g. report	BIBL 115:5
One g. turn deserves	PROV 640:47
only g. Indian	PROV 640:34
only g. Indians	SHER 747:23
only g. thing left	MUSS 566:11
on the evil and on the g.	BIBL 99:7
or be thought half as g.	WHIT 853:6
our own g. in our own way	MILL 536:3
out of g. still to find	MILT 541:15
overcome evil with g.	BIBL 111:13
policy of the g. neighbour	ROOS 667:5
prospect of a distant g.	DRYD 295:28
records g. things of good men	BEDE 65:7
rejected what was g.	AESO 9:4

return g. for evil	VANB 823:17
rewarded me evil for g.	BOOK 141:22
Roman Conquest was a *G. Thing*	SELL 691:24
said a g. thing	TWAI 820:14
Seek to be g.	LYTT 506:8
So shines a g. deed	SHAK 725:14
temptation to be g.	BREC 155:12
than to seem g.	SALL 679:9
that you're not g. enough	TROL 816:24
they were g. men	STEP 772:8
thy g. with brotherhood	BATE 61:7
too much of a g. thing	PROV 647:41
truly great who are truly g.	CHAP 216:9
universal licence to be g.	COLE 239:2
Universally G.	MAHĀ 516:3
utter as g. things	JONS 446:5
very g. day	MOOR 557:11
what a g. man should be	AURE 40:23
Whatever g. visits thee	KORA 471:18
what g. came of it	SOUT 764:8
what was g. for our country	WILS 858:20
when shall all men's g.	TENN 793:20
When she was g.	LONG 500:7
woman was full of g. works	BIBL 104:14
work together for g.	BIBL 111:5
would be a g. idea	GAND 348:15
would do g. to another	BLAK 125:15
your g. works	BIBL 98:28
goodbye Every time we say g.	PORT 619:12
G.!—Good-bye-ee	WEST 849:5
G., moralitee	HERB 393:12
G., Piccadilly	JUDG 449:4
G. to all that	GRAV 369:14
goodlihead flower of g.	SKEL 754:2
goodly g. to look to	BIBL 84:1
I have a g. heritage	BOOK 140:3
goodman our g.'s awa	MICK 534:6
goodness fountain of all g.	BOOK 134:6
G., beautiful today	SAPP 680:19
g. derives not from	TERE 802:1
g. entirely human	ELIO 308:18
g. faileth never	BAKE 52:9
G. had nothing to do with it	WEST 848:14
g. infinite	MILT 544:16
g. is not in demand	BREC 155:14
G. is not the same thing	PLAT 609:1
g. of the Lord	BOOK 141:11
If g. lead him not	HERB 394:22
inclination to g.	BACO 47:5
long-suffering, and of great g.	BOOK 147:1
My G., My Guinness	ADVE 8:6
goodnight gives the stern'st g.	SHAK 720:2
G., children	CATC 207:25
g., sweet ladies	SHAK 703:33
G., sweet prince	SHAK 705:4
I shall say g.	SHAK 732:19
John Thomas says g.	LAWR 483:12
My last G.	KING 463:4
second best's a gay g.	YEAT 873:12
goods all my worldly g.	BOOK 133:2
care for external g.	WEBE 843:14
desire other men's g.	BOOK 138:14
for your good, for all your g.	GEOR 352:8
g. are in peace	BIBL 105:10
g. the gods provide	PROV 644:3
Ill gotten g. never thrive	PROV 635:40
Riches and G.	BOOK 150:23
when g. are private	TAWN 791:4
goodwill In peace; g.	CHUR 230:21
name was Great G.	HARI 382:12
goose cried in g., alas	RANS 655:5
every g. a swan	KING 464:14
g. honking amongst tuneful swans	VIRG 832:9
G., if I had you	SHAK 715:9
Grey g. and gander	NURS 578:17
grey g. is gone	NURS 580:11
on the ground at G. Green	KINN 464:22
sauce for the g.	PROV 646:28
steal a g.	POLI 613:13
steals a g.	ANON 17:5
that g. look	SHAK 722:15
gooseberried g. double bed	THOM 806:9
goosey G., goosey gander	NURS 578:16

gordian She was a g. shape	KEAT 455:11
gore hope it mayn't be human g.	DICK 276:8
gored you tossed and g.	BOSW 152:7
gorgeous g. East in fee	WORD 868:1
g. East with richest hand	MILT 542:2
gorgon G., Prince of darkness	SPEN 767:4
gorgonized G. me from head to foot	TENN 798:1
gormed I'm G.—and I can't say	DICK 277:23
gorse G. fires are smoking	LONG 500:10
g. is out of bloom	PROV 646:48
gory never shake Thy g. locks	SHAK 721:9
Welcome to your g. bed	BURN 179:9
Goschen forgot G.	CHUR 228:24
gosh by gee by g. by gum	CUMM 262:4
goshawk gay g.	BALL 54:14
gospel Four for the G. makers	SONG 762:13
G. of Christ	WESL 847:20
G. of Getting On	SHAW 742:1
likeness in the G.	KORA 473:2
preach the g.	BIBL 104:6
truth of thy holy G.	BOOK 136:14
gossip babbling g. of the air	SHAK 735:6
g. from all the nations	AUDE 37:20
G. is a sort of smoke	ELIO 307:6
Like all g.	FORS 338:10
my g. Report	SHAK 724:16
got If not, have you g. him	SELL 692:1
I g. rhythm	GERS 353:14
in our case we have not g.	REED 657:5
gotcha G.	NEWS 573:10
Gotham Three wise men of G.	NURS 582:3
Gothic cars the great G. cathedrals	BART 60:9
glory of G.	RUSK 674:12
modern G. room	PUGI 649:2
more than G. ignorance	FIEL 326:20
Gott G. strafe England	POLI 612:19
ist unser G.	LUTH 505:8
gotta g. use words when I talk to you	ELIO 310:26
Gotte *einem sterbenden G.*	HEIN 389:15
gotten g. himself the victory	BOOK 146:11
gout give them the g.	MONT 554:13
gouverner *G. c'est choisir*	LÉVI 491:10
govern cannot g. itself	MCNA 513:6
easy to g.	BROU 160:10
g. according to the common	JAME 429:2
g. in prose	CUOM 262:18
g. New South Wales	BELL 68:2
g. our conditions	SHAK 716:13
Let the people think they g.	PENN 602:17
of Kings to g. wrong	POPE 613:23
people g. themselves	THIE 804:12
to g. is to choose	LÉVI 491:10
With words we g. men	DISR 285:22
governance by thy g.	BOOK 136:5
governed best g.	PLAT 609:3
faith in The People g.	DICK 281:9
g. by the few	HUME 420:5
g. by thy good Spirit	BOOK 135:6
nation is not g.	BURK 173:12
not so well g.	HOOK 406:7
objected to being g. at all	CHES 225:11
governer G. was strong upon	WILD 856:1
governess Be a g.	BRON 158:10
governing incapable of g.	CHES 223:19
right of g.	FOX 339:10
government abandon a g.	JEFF 431:15
administration of the g.	SWIF 782:7
art of g.	VOLT 835:3
art of g. is	SHAW 741:10
at g. expense	ARTS 32:20
best g. is that which	O'SU 589:6
definition of the best g.	HALI 377:14
duty of g.	PAIN 592:12
end of g.	ADAM 3:12
every form of g.	JOHN 441:3
for a bad g.	TOCQ 811:17
forms of g.	POPE 617:3
frame any state or g.	RALE 654:7
g. above the law	SCAR 683:5
G. and co-operation	RUSK 674:8
G. and public opinion	SHAW 740:28

G. at Washington lives GARF 349:6
g. by discussion ATTL 35:10
g. by the uneducated CHES 225:25
G., even in its best state PAIN 592:8
G. is a contrivance BURK 174:5
g. is best THOR 809:3
g. is influenced by SMIT 756:5
g. it deserves MAIS 517:1
g. of Britain's isle SHAK 709:21
g. of laws ADAM 3:2
g. of laws MARS 523:23
G. of laws and not of men FORD 337:1
g. of statesmen DISR 285:16
G. of the busy SELD 691:20
g. of the people LINC 494:1
g. of the people PAGE 591:16
g. of the world THOR 809:28
g. shall be upon his shoulder BIBL 92:14
g. which imprisons THOR 809:4
g. which robs Peter SHAW 739:25
g. without a king BANC 57:7
great service to a g. MEDI 530:3
greedy hand of g. PAIN 592:23
have an efficient g. TRUM 817:22
If the G. is big enough FORD 336:16
in a disorderly g. HALI 377:13
increase of his g. BIBL 92:14
land of settled g. TENN 801:5
members of the G. SHAW 740:5
No G. can be long secure DISR 285:15
no g. would be necessary MADI 514:7
not a g. of laws WEBS 844:1
not depend on g. MISQ 547:5
not get all of the g. FRIE 343:11
one g. sooner learns SMIT 756:8
only instrument of g. LOCK 497:18
Parliamentary g. is impossible DISR 284:25
Peace, order, and good g. ANON 19:16
people's g. WEBS 843:21
pillars of g. BACO 47:28
prepare for g. STEE 770:11
representative g. DISR 286:10
restraints of g. GOLD 363:17
rule nations by your g. VIRG 830:14
signifies the want of g. HOBB 401:3
sister is given to g. DICK 278:5
structure of g. HAVE 384:8
support their g. CLEV 235:13
system of G. GLAD 359:14
to run a g. TRUM 817:20
understood by republican g. TOCQ 812:11
unjust as a feeble g. BURK 174:24
virtue of paper g. BURK 173:9
vulgar arts of g. PEEL 601:14
wee pretendy g. CONN 248:6
well-ordered g. HALI 377:9
work for a G. I despise KEYN 461:14
worst form of G. CHUR 230:7
governments foundation of most g.
ADAM 3:13
G. always want RADC 653:6
g. had better get out of the way EISE 306:9
g. need both shepherds VOLT 834:15
g. of Europe JEFF 431:8
Never believe g. GELL 352:2
governor save the G.-General WHIT 851:19
governors g., teachers BOOK 138:12
supreme g., the mob WALP 837:7
governs g. his state by virtue CONF 245:14
g. the passions HUME 420:6
that which g. least O'SU 589:6
which g. not at all THOR 809:3
gowd man's the g. BURN 178:7
Gower O moral G. CHAU 221:15
gown wrap me in a g. HERB 393:20
Goya I am G. VOZN 835:11
grab G. this land MORR 561:10
Gracchos Quis tulerit G. JUVE 450:15
grace Amazing G. NEWT 574:12
Angels and ministers of g. SHAK 700:11
attractive kind of g. ROYD 671:17
But for the g. of God BRAD 154:1
by special g. BOOK 135:17

by the g. of God BIBL 112:18
courtly foreign g. TENN 800:4
fallen from g. BIBL 113:22
full of g. PRAY 623:1
full of g. PROV 638:44
G. be unto you BIBL 117:22
g. did much more abound BIBL 110:31
G. fills empty spaces WEIL 845:2
G. is given of God CLOU 236:16
G. me no grace SHAK 730:12
g., new birth ARNO 32:2
g. of a boy BETJ 76:7
G. of God is in Courtesy BELL 68:6
g. of God which was with me BIBL 112:19
g.-proud faces BURN 180:3
G. under pressure HEMI 391:6
grow old with a good g. STEE 770:15
inward and spiritual g. BOOK 138:15
lend her g. TENN 796:20
means of g. BOOK 135:8
new light of g. SMOL 759:8
REGRET INFORM YOUR G. BEER 66:4
snatch a g. POPE 615:27
speech be alway with g. BIBL 115:11
strength, utility, g. VITR 833:9
strong toil of g. SHAK 696:7
such g. did lend her SHAK 736:15
such heavenly g. SPEN 767:5
sweet attractive g. MILT 543:5
that g. may abound BIBL 110:32
throne of the heavenly g. BOOK 133:3
unbought g. of life BURK 174:8
with a better g. SHAK 735:11
wordy o' a g. BURN 179:22
world is judged by g. TALM 789:7
graceful g. air and heavenly mug FLEM 334:22
Such a g. exit JUNO 450:5
graces G. do not seem to be natives
CHES 223:12
g. slighted CRAB 257:9
sacrifice to the g. BURK 174:25
Upon her eyelids many G. SPEN 767:11
gracing either other Sweetly g. CAMP 196:1
gracious all his g. parts SHAK 714:9
he is g. BOOK 149:12
how g. the Lord is BOOK 141:19
Lord is g. BIBL 117:2
O be favourable and g. BOOK 143:9
So hallowed and so g. SHAK 699:6
gradient g.'s against her AUDE 37:19
gradual g. day weakening SPEN 766:14
gradualness inevitability of g. WEBB 843:10
graduates sweet girl-g. TENN 799:3
Graeculus G. esuriens JUVE 450:19
graft G. in our hearts BOOK 136:7
grail g. of laughter CRAN 258:14
grain choice g. STOU 778:5
g. of salt PLIN 609:18
painted with various g. MICK 534:5
rain is destroying his g. HERB 393:11
world in a g. of sand BLAK 124:9
gramina g. campis HORA 413:17
grammar attention to g. CHAM 213:20
destroy every g. school CROS 261:5
don't want to talk g. SHAW 742:7
erecting a g. school SHAK 710:3
g., and nonsense GOLD 365:3
G., the ground of al LANG 478:20
Heedless of g. BARH 58:11
talking bad g. DISR 285:14
grammatical g. purity JOHN 437:12
grammatici G. certant HORA 409:2
grammaticus G., rhetor, geometres JUVE 450:19
gramophone g. company TREE 815:5
puts a record on the g. ELIO 311:15
granary on a g. floor KEAT 457:1
grand down the G. Canyon MARQ 523:17
G. Duchesses are doing NAPO 568:1
g. Perhaps BROW 164:25
g. style ARNO 32:10
g. to be blooming well dead SARO 681:4
grandeur certain spiritual g. ELIO 307:18
charged with the g. HOPK 407:7

g. hear with a disdainful smile GRAY 370:4
g. in this view DARW 266:17
g. that was Rome POE 611:5
g. underlying the sorriest things HARD 381:7
old Scotia's g. BURN 177:26
grandfather ape for his g. HUXL 423:16
carrying a g. clock TREE 815:4
g. or his grandmother WILB 853:16
grandfathers g.'s grandfathers VIRG 833:6
makes friends with its g. MUMF 565:2
grandmother grandfather or his g.
WILB 853:16
teach your g. PROV 630:28
We have become a g. THAT 804:2
grandsire g. cut his throat SWIF 784:12
grange at the moated g. SHAK 723:15
lonely moated g. TENN 797:17
granites Through g. which titanic wars
OWEN 591:8
grant g. me this in return CATU 211:4
half g. what I wish FROS 344:7
OLD CARY G. FINE GRAN 368:9
granted taking things for g. HUXL 422:20
Granth Guru G. Sahib SIKH 752:6
grape burst Joy's g. KEAT 456:1
G. is my mulatto mother HUGH 418:13
peel me a g. WEST 848:12
unripe g. AURE 40:24
grapes brought forth wild g. BIBL 92:1
gleaning of the g. BIBL 83:8
g. of thorns BIBL 100:1
g. of wrath HOWE 417:3
need any sour g. AESO 8:38
sour g. BIBL 95:15
sour g. and ashes ASHF 33:17
grapeshot whiff of g. CARL 199:24
grapple G. them to thy soul SHAK 700:3
grasp exceed his g. BROW 164:19
G. it like a man of mettle HILL 398:9
grasped haven't g. the situation KERR 461:6
grass All flesh is g. BIBL 93:16
bringeth forth g. BOOK 147:6
but as g. BOOK 147:3
eateth g. as an ox BIBL 87:14
everywhere nibble g. FAGU 322:14
flesh is as g. BIBL 117:1
g. below CLAR 233:2
g. beyond the door ROSS 669:23
g. cannot dissolve BLY 129:15
g. grows on the weirs YEAT 873:5
g. is always greener PROV 633:26
g. looking green PERR 604:2
g. returns to the fields HORA 413:17
g. springs up VARR 824:11
g. to graze a cow BETJ 76:5
g. will grow in the streets HOOV 406:16
greener than the g. BALL 55:10
green g. growing over me BALL 56:7
green g. shorn BACO 47:3
hearing the g. grow ELIO 307:26
I am the g. SAND 680:5
I fall on g. MARV 525:4
leaf of g. is no less WHIT 852:10
like the g. BOOK 145:20
parched g. pray TIBU 810:19
people is like g. CONF 246:14
Pigeons on the g. STEI 771:3
snake hidden in the g. VIRG 831:22
splendour in the g. WORD 867:17
star-scattered on the g. FITZ 331:29
tides of g. SWIN 785:25
twinkles in the g. TENN 798:2
two blades of g. SWIF 782:9
While the g. grows PROV 647:13
grasses by short g. PORT 620:2
grasshopper g. shall be a burden BIBL 90:20
grasshoppers half a dozen g. BURK 174:13
we were as g. BIBL 82:4
grassy fair Fidele's g. tomb COLL 243:10
grate fire is dying in the g. MERE 532:21
fluttered on the g. COLE 239:19
grateful anybody can be g. CATU 210:17
single g. thought LESS 490:20

gratefully O g. sing — GRAN 368:11
gratias Deo g. — MISS 549:10
gratified g. desire — BLAK 127:3
Love g. — RICH 660:13
gratissima g. serpit — VIRG 829:10
gratitude g. is merely a secret hope — LA R 482:5
G., like love — ALSO 13:21
g. of a stranger — TOCQ 812:14
g. we owe to Adam — TWAI 820:18
liking or g. — ELIO 307:9
gratuity bribe or g. — PENN 602:18
grau G. ist alle Theorie — GOET 362:1
grave And on that g. — HART 383:15
at her g. — BALL 56:4
bed is the cold g. — BALL 54:9
cold g. — BALL 56:4
come to seek a g. — DONN 289:26
cradle and the g. — DYER 301:8
cradle to the g. — SHEL 746:3
Dig the g. and let me lie — STEV 777:5
ditchers and g.-makers — SHAK 704:9
dread The g. as little — KEN 459:16
Even the g. yawns — TREE 815:2
from the cradle to the g. — CHUR 230:3
frontier-g. is far away — NEWB 571:11
Funeral marches to the g. — LONG 499:15
give birth astride of a g. — BECK 64:24
go into my g. — PEPY 603:18
gone wild into his g. — SHAK 708:2
g., and not taunting — BACO 47:9
g. hides all things — SHEL 745:21
g. is not its goal — LONG 499:14
g. of a dead Fenian — COLL 243:4
g. of Mad Carew — HAYE 385:16
g.'s a fine and private — MARV 525:13
g., where is thy victory — BIBL 113:6
g., whither thou goest — BIBL 90:10
G. without thought — CHUR 228:13
In every g. make room — D'AV 267:6
in peace in his g. — DONN 290:1
into the darkness of the g. — MILL 536:20
Is that ayont the g. — BURN 180:4
jealousy is cruel as the g. — BIBL 91:16
kind of healthy g. — SMIT 758:7
kingdom for a little g. — SHAK 730:23
lead but to the g. — GRAY 370:4
letters in the g. — JOHN 444:11
made me a g. so rough — TENN 798:10
Marriage is the g. — CAVE 211:18
now in his colde g. — CHAU 219:13
pompous in the g. — BROW 162:20
renowned be thy g. — SHAK 698:25
requires g. statesmen — DISR 285:26
root is ever in its g. — HERB 395:2
send you to the g. — ORTO 586:15
Sentinel of the g. — TATE 790:13
she is in her g. — WORD 869:5
shovel a g. in the air — CELA 212:9
shown Longfellow's g. — MOOR 557:16
sitting crowned upon the g. — HOBB 401:8
stand at my g. and cry — FRYE 345:25
thank God for the quiet g. — KEAT 458:17
this side of the g. — LAND 478:7
When my g. is broke up — DONN 289:11
Without a g. — BYRO 187:3
with sorrow to the g. — BIBL 80:25
years and honour to the g. — KIPL 466:17
graved G. inside of it — BROW 165:16
gravelled g. for lack of matter — SHAK 697:19
graven g. image — BIBL 81:15
graves dig our g. with our teeth — SMIL 755:17
dishonourable g. — SHAK 711:19
g. of deceased languages — DICK 277:26
g. of little magazines — PRES 622:12
g. of their neighbours — EDWA 304:8
g. of the martyrs — STEV 776:25
g. stood tenantless — SHAK 699:4
Let's talk of g. — SHAK 730:18
our g. with our teeth — DEFO 270:6
voluntary g. — HERB 394:17
watch from their g. — BROW 166:13
with us in our g. — DONN 290:7
graveyard for each g. — BOCC 130:6

gravitation not believing in g. — TROT 817:9
gravy Abominated g. — BENT 71:16
grazing Tilling and g. — SULL 780:6
grease gets the g. — PROV 643:33
greasy grey-green, g., Limpopo — KIPL 468:11
top of the g. pole — DISR 286:21
great aim not to be g. — LYTT 506:8
all g. men are frauds — BONA 132:5
between the small and g. — COWP 257:1
both g. and small — COLE 241:10
desireth g. matters — QUAR 651:7
far above the g. — GRAY 370:22
From the g. deep — TENN 794:2
g. and lofty things — MONT 554:19
g. book — CALL 193:17
g. book is a great evil — PROV 633:27
g. break through — SHEN 747:20
g., ere fortune made him so — DRYD 295:22
g. gulf fixed — BIBL 106:7
g. have kindness — POPE 614:23
g. have no heart — LA B 474:18
G.-hearted gentlemen — BROW 166:16
g. illusion — ANGE 15:16
G. is Diana — BIBL 110:7
G. is the hand — THOM 805:20
g. is truth — BROO 160:6
G. let me call him — YOUN 877:2
g. life if you don't weaken — BUCH 169:7
g. man has his disciples — WILD 855:1
g. man helped the poor — MACA 508:15
G. men — BIBL 87:6
g. men even under bad emperors — TACI 787:3
g. men make mistakes — CHUR 228:24
g. men—so-called — TOLS 813:13
G. minds think alike — PROV 633:30
g. ones devoured the small — SIDN 750:9
g. regions of the mind — BROC 157:14
g. seemed to him little — MACA 507:12
G. Society — JOHN 435:5
g.—the major novelists — LEAV 486:17
g. things from the valley — CHES 225:9
g. to them that know — SPRI 768:19
g. was the fall — BIBL 100:4
grown so g. — SHAK 711:20
he is always g. — DRYD 297:15
He Was A G. Man — ZIEG 878:1
How g. a matter — BIBL 116:23
Ill can he rule the g. — SPEN 767:22
know well I am not g. — TENN 794:12
lay g. and greatly fallen — HOME 404:19
Lives of g. men — LONG 499:17
make the Way g. — CONF 246:17
many people think him g. — JOHN 441:12
name made g. — HILL 399:6
no small steps in g. affairs — RETZ 658:11
nothing g. but man — HAMI 378:13
Nothing g. was ever achieved — EMER 314:24
only truly g. — DISR 285:21
Rightly to be g. — SHAK 703:29
small things with g. — VIRG 833:5
so g. a thing happened — WHIT 851:13
some men are born g. — SHAK 735:24
think the g. unhappy — YOUN 876:11
those who were truly g. — SPEN 766:10
though fallen, g. — BYRO 185:22
thou wouldst be g. — SHAK 718:19
To be g. is to be misunderstood — EMER 315:7
truly g. man — RUSK 673:12
truly g. who are truly good — CHAP 216:9
with small men no g. thing — MILL 536:9
Great Britain G. has lost an empire — ACHE 1:13
G. should free herself — SMIT 756:9
natives of G. — CHES 223:12
greater G. love hath no man — BIBL 108:18
g. man, the greater courtesy — TENN 794:15
g. prey upon the less — GREE 371:6
g. than a private citizen — TACI 787:10
g. than Solomon — BIBL 101:9
g. than the whole — HESI 397:3
g. than vast spaces — UPAN 822:10
g. than we know — WORD 868:26
g. the sinner — PROV 633:28
he is g. than they — RUSK 674:4

they behold a g. — SHAK 711:25
thy need is g. — SIDN 751:10
greatest firstborn the g. ass — CARO 201:6
foremost and g. flatterer — PLUT 610:8
g. event it is — FOX 339:11
g. happiness — HUTC 422:10
g. thing in the world — MONT 555:8
happiness of the g. number — BENT 71:4
I'm the g. — ALI 13:1
life to live as the g. he — RAIN 653:10
greatly g. to his credit — GILB 358:3
would g. win — BYRO 190:16
greatness dispense with g. — GUIZ 374:11
farewell, to all my g. — SHAK 710:19
g. going off — SHAK 695:15
G. knows itself — SHAK 706:19
g. of the Lord — BIBL 104:8
g., save it be some far-off — TENN 794:12
g. thrust upon them — SHAK 735:24
intended g. for men — ELIO 308:2
moment of my g. flicker — ELIO 310:10
nature of all g. — BURK 173:6
Greece Athens, the eye of G. — MILT 544:25
Cold is the heart, fair G. — BYRO 185:19
education to G. — PERI 603:24
Fair G.! sad relic — BYRO 185:22
for G. a tear — BYRO 188:23
glory that was G. — POE 611:5
G. is fallen and Troy — COLE 239:4
G. might still be free — BYRO 188:22
isles of G. — BYRO 188:21
To Gaul, to G. — COWP 256:2
greed G. is all right — BOES 130:10
G. is good — FILM 328:10
g. of speculators — LAUR 483:3
infectious g. — GREE 372:3
not enough for everyone's g. — BUCH 169:11
greedy G. for the property — SALL 679:6
g. hand of government — PAIN 592:23
I am g. — PUNC 650:5
mind g. for praise — HORA 410:20
Greek adapting G. temples — PUGI 649:7
G. can do everything — JUVE 450:19
G. in its origin — MAIN 516:21
G. particles — HUGH 418:14
G. tongue agreeth more — TYND 821:5
half G., half Latin — SCOT 688:1
in Latin or in G. — WALL 836:19
it was G. to me — SHAK 711:27
loving, natural, and G. — BYRO 188:12
neither G. nor Jew — BIBL 115:9
pages of your G. models — HORA 409:11
pay at the G. Kalends — AUGU 40:5
say a word against G. — SHAW 740:13
small Latin, and less G. — JONS 446:24
study of G. literature — GAIS 347:5
When G. meets Greek — PROV 646:38
wife talks G. — JOHN 444:22
Greeks For G. a blush — BYRO 188:23
G., and to the Barbarians — BIBL 110:20
G. bearing gifts — PROV 632:6
G. had a word — AKIN 10:8
G. in this American empire — MACM 512:15
G. joined Greeks — LEE 487:12
G. seek after wisdom — BIBL 111:22
G. take the beating — HORA 410:3
I fear the G. — VIRG 829:6
Let G. be Greeks — BRAD 154:12
make way, G. — PROP 625:1
unto the G. foolishness — BIBL 111:23
writings of the G. — OMAR 585:5
green and a g. gown — NURS 578:10
bordered by its gardens g. — MORR 560:14
Colourless g. ideas — CHOM 226:14
die when the trees were g. — CLAR 232:19
drives my g. age — THOM 805:17
feed me in a g. pasture — BOOK 140:20
Flora and the country g. — KEAT 456:3
g. and pleasant bowers — BLAK 125:18
g. and pleasant land — BLAK 126:24
g. as emerald — COLE 240:16
g. banks of Shannon — CAMP 195:8
g. country town — PENN 602:20

G. Eye — HAYE 385:16
g.-eyed monster — SHAK 728:24
g. grass shorn — BACO 47:3
G. grow the rashes, O — BURN 178:9
G. grow the rushes O — SONG 762:13
g. herb — BOOK 147:6
g. hill far away — ALEX 12:10
G. how I want you — LORC 500:18
g. in judgment — SHAK 694:20
g. pastures of the European — VERW 826:16
G. pleasure or grey grief — SWIN 786:2
g. shoots of recovery — MISQ 547:18
g. thing that stands in — BLAK 128:11
g. trees when I saw them — TRAH 814:12
g. Yule makes — PROV 633:32
heard on the g. — BLAK 127:13
Her g. lap — WALK 836:5
How g. was my valley — LLEW 496:9
in a g. tree — BIBL 106:22
in g. pastures — WILL 858:16
In the morning it is g. — BOOK 145:20
In thy g. lap — GRAY 370:19
laid him on the g. — BALL 54:6
lamps in a g. night — MARV 524:15
laughs to see the g. man — HOFF 402:9
life springs ever g. — GOET 362:1
Make it a *g.* peace — DARN 266:4
Making spears g. — VALE 823:9
Making the g. one red — SHAK 720:9
memory be g. — SHAK 699:8
My passport's g. — HEAN 387:13
not that easy being g. — RAPO 655:12
O all ye G. Things — BOOK 133:17
O G. One [Haoma] — ZORO 879:3
one g. — BASH 60:15
Places of nestling g. — HUNT 421:10
Praise the g. earth — BUNT 170:18
shoot the sleepy, g.-coat man — HOFF 402:10
strew the g. lap — SHAK 731:6
sun doth parch the g. — SURR 780:15
To a g. thought — MARV 525:5
true g. of hope — VERN 826:14
wearin' o' the G. — POLI 612:22
Wherever g. is worn — YEAT 873:9
greener grass is always g. — PROV 633:26
g. than the grass — BALL 55:10
greenery g. of the trees — DANT 265:11
In a mountain g. — HART 383:13
greenery-yallery g., Grosvenor Gallery
— GILB 357:23
greenhouse g. gases — MARG 521:13
greening g. of America — REIC 657:13
Greenland From G.'s icy mountains — HEBE 388:8
greenness recovered g. — HERB 394:9
Greenpeace G. had a ring to it — HUNT 422:2
greens healing g. — ABSE 1:4
Greensleeves G. was all my joy — SONG 762:11
greenwood to the g. go — BALL 55:7
Under the g. tree — SHAK 696:21
greet G. the unseen — BROW 164:2
How should I g. thee — BYRO 191:19
Greise *Kopf zum G.* — MÜLL 564:18
grenadier British G. — SONG 763:11
Pomeranian g. — BISM 122:19
Grenville Richard G. lay — TENN 800:1
grey All cats are g. in the dark — PROV 626:12
bring down my g. hairs — BIBL 80:25
could comb g. hair — YEAT 873:17
good g. head — TENN 798:21
Green pleasure or g. grief — SWIN 786:2
g.-green, greasy, Limpopo — KIPL 468:11
G. silent fragments — HUGH 418:10
hair is g. — BYRO 190:22
in my g. hairs — WOLS 863:19
lend me your g. mare — BALL 56:8
little g. cells — CHRI 227:2
philosophy paints its g. — HEGE 389:2
this old g. head — WHIT 853:1
world has grown g. — SWIN 785:19
you are old and g. — YEAT 875:10
greyhound This fawning g. — SHAK 705:16
greyhounds g. in the slips — SHAK 708:17
grief acquainted with g. — BIBL 94:3

between g. and nothing — FAUL 324:15
But g. returns — SHEL 743:12
excessive g. — SHAK 694:1
feed on g. — FRY 345:14
first feel g. yourself — HORA 409:4
forethought of g. — BERR 74:15
Green pleasure or grey g. — SWIN 786:2
G. and avenging Cares — VIRG 830:9
g. felt so like fear — LEWI 491:15
G. fills the room up — SHAK 714:9
g. flieth to it — BACO 46:21
g. forgotten — SWIN 784:20
G. has no wings — QUIL 651:18
g. I did sustain — CONS 249:15
G. is a species of idleness — JOHN 441:5
G. is itself a med'cine — COWP 254:25
g. is like a minefield — WARN 840:7
G. is the price — PARK 597:2
g. itself be mortal — SHEL 743:14
g. of heart — SHAK 710:17
g. that does not speak — SHAK 722:6
g. too much to be told — VIRG 829:4
G. with a glass — SWIN 784:22
hopeless g. is passionless — BROW 164:8
I am g. — VOZN 835:11
in false g. hiding — SPEN 767:8
long g. and pain — TENN 798:8
master a g. — SHAK 727:27
more worthy of g. — SHEL 747:8
Of g. I died — ROET 665:10
pain and g. — BOOK 141:27
Patch g. with proverbs — SHAK 727:31
pitch of g. — HOPK 407:13
see another's g. — BLAK 127:14
Should be past g. — SHAK 736:23
shows of g. — SHAK 699:15
Silence augmenteth g. — DYER 301:4
silent manliness of g. — GOLD 364:11
Smiling at g. — SHAK 735:21
Thine be the g. — AYTO 44:5
thirsty g. in wine we steep — LOVE 502:4
griefs borne our g. — BIBL 94:3
But not my g. — SHAK 731:3
cutteth g. in halves — BACO 46:34
g. and fears — BACO 47:21
g. that harrass — JOHN 438:2
like g. confound — WILD 854:12
soothed the g. — MACA 507:19
grievance doon offte gret g. — LYDG 505:16
Scotsman with a g. — WODE 861:20
grieve g. or triumph — GOET 362:8
heart doesn't g. over — PROV 646:29
Pope will g. a day — SWIF 784:9
what could it g. for — KEAT 454:26
grieved g. my heart to think — WORD 866:15
g. with this generation — BOOK 146:8
grieves thing that g. not — MARK 521:15
grieving áre you g. — HOPK 407:19
grievous most g. fault — MISS 546:20
most g. to him — TROL 816:13
remembrance of them is g. — BOOK 137:10
grill Let G. be Grill — SPEN 767:16
grim g. grew his countenance — BALL 54:10
grimace accelerated g. — POUN 621:3
grin cheerfully he seems to g. — CARR 201:14
ending with the g. — CARR 202:4
one universal g. — FIEL 327:2
Relaxed into a universal g. — COWP 256:23
grind bastards g. you down — SAYI 685:4
g. in the prison house — BIBL 83:18
g. the faces of the poor — BIBL 91:22
Laws g. the poor — GOLD 364:27
mill cannot g. with — PROV 638:38
mills of God g. slowly — LONG 499:20
mills of God g. slowly — PROV 638:39
one demd horrid g. — DICK 279:21
grinders g. cease — BIBL 90:20
incisors and g. — BAGE 51:11
grinds Pleasure chews and g. — MONT 555:19
Grisilde G. is deed — CHAU 218:29
grist g. that comes to the mill — PROV 626:15
groan Condemned alike to g. — GRAY 370:12
g. and shake their fists — HOUS 415:4

groaneth whole creation g. — BIBL 111:4
groaning g. under walls — MARL 522:18
weary of my g. — BOOK 139:20
groans g. of love to those of the dying
— LOWR 503:14
grocer made the wicked G. — CHES 224:17
groined titanic wars had g. — OWEN 591:8
Gromboolian G. plain — LEAR 485:17
grooves moves In predestinate g. — HARE 382:9
ringing g. of time — TENN 797:7
groping g. for words — LEWI 492:9
gross g. as a mountain — SHAK 705:28
Not g. to sink — SHAK 738:27
Things rank and g. — SHAK 699:19
grosser g. name — SHAK 704:6
Grosvenor Gallery greenery-yallery, G.
— GILB 357:23
grotesque g. situation — HAUG 384:6
ornate, and g. — BAGE 51:20
Groucho of the G. tendency — SLOG 755:7
ground acre of barren g. — SHAK 733:13
as water spilt on the g. — BIBL 84:19
Chosen and made peculiar g. — WATT 842:1
commit his body to the g. — BOOK 139:10
crieth from the g. — BIBL 79:15
fell into good g. — BIBL 101:13
gain a little patch of g. — SHAK 703:26
Grammar, the g. of al — LANG 478:20
G. control to Major Tom — BOWI 153:17
g. of my heart — BOOK 149:20
g. won to-day — ARNO 30:11
here at last on the g. — SOND 761:3
holy g. — BIBL 80:34
in a fair g. — BOOK 140:3
In his own g. — POPE 617:32
let us sit upon the g. — SHAK 730:19
see me cover the g. — GROS 373:14
seven feet of English g. — HARO 382:16
stirrup and the g. — EPIT 319:2
They are the g. — SHAK 717:17
tread on classic g. — ADDI 4:27
upon the g. I se thee stare — CHAU 220:5
when I hit the g. — SPRI 769:4
grounds laying out of g. — PEAC 600:15
group let us eschew g. hatred — SETH 693:1
grouse Ould G. in the gun-room — GOLD 365:6
grove g. of chimneys — MORR 560:7
olive g. of Academe — MILT 544:26
windings of the g. — BEAT 62:13
groves g. of Academe — HORA 410:22
g. of *their* academy — BURK 174:10
G. whose rich trees — MILT 543:2
whispering g. — THOM 808:22
grow g. in worth — TENN 801:4
g. To fruit or shade — HERB 393:21
g. up with the country — GREE 371:5
one to go — PROV 640:45
Please help me g. God — BLUM 129:9
They shall g. not old — BINY 121:15
growed I s'pect I g. — STOW 778:7
growl sit and g. — JOHN 443:11
growth children of a larger g. — CHES 223:10
children of a larger g. — DRYD 295:10
G. [is] the only evidence — NEWM 572:1
neoclassical endogenous g. — BROW 160:17
root of all genuine g. — SMIL 755:19
grub old ones, g. — SHAW 739:9
Grubstreet G. biographers — ADDI 4:26
grudge ancient g. I bear him — SHAK 724:7
gruel g. thick and slab — SHAK 721:17
grumbling rhythmical g. — ELIO 311:26
Grundy more of Mrs G. — LOCK 498:1
Solomon G. — NURS 581:9
What will Mrs G. think — MORT 562:9
grunt expect from a pig but a g. — PROV 646:18
gruntled far from being g. — WODE 861:21
guarantees g. all others — CHUR 230:17
guard Be on your g. — OFFI 584:14
g. even our enemies — MISQ 549:1
G. us, guide us — EDME 303:17
g. you while you sleep — KIPL 467:16
guarded requires to be ever g. — GOLD 365:13
well-g. mind — PALI 594:17

guardian G. and my Guide	WILL 857:8
only safe g.	MILL 535:22
guardians good grey g. of art	WILB 854:5
guards Brigade of G.	MACM 513:1
G. die	CAMB 194:10
Up G. and at them	WELL 846:5
who is to guard the g.	JUVE 451:5
guardsman g.'s cut and thrust	HUXL 423:6
gubu acronym G.	HAUG 384:6
gude g. time coming	SCOT 689:24
gué au g.	ANON 22:10
guenille ma g. m'est chère	MOLI 552:7
guerre ce n'est pas la g.	BOSQ 151:16
guerrilla by means of g. bands	MAZZ 529:11
g. wins if he does not	KISS 469:1
guess Medical Men g.	KEAT 458:18
guessing G. so much and so much	CHES 224:5
g. what was at the other side	WELL 846:12
mind which is good at g.	PLAT 608:15
guest be your g. tomorrow night	ANON 21:16
Earth, receive an honoured g.	AUDE 37:10
g. that tarrieth but a day	BIBL 97:4
g. will judge better	ARIS 28:2
nightingale, a constant g.	SOPH 761:16
second g. to entertain	DONN 289:13
speed the going g.	POPE 617:27
Speed the parting g.	POPE 617:27
uninvited g.	TURG 818:14
Wedding-G. here beat	COLE 240:15
guests Fish and g. stink	PROV 632:25
G. can be delightful	ELIZ 313:8
g. should praise it	HARI 382:13
g. star-scattered	FITZ 331:29
hosts and g.	BEER 65:17
Unbidden g.	SHAK 709:15
guidance Messenger with the g.	KORA 472:20
sent down to be a g.	KORA 471:3
guide better g. in ourselves	AUST 41:17
God to be his g.	BUNY 171:21
Guardian and my G.	WILL 857:8
G., a Comforter	AUBE 35:14
g. by the light of reason	BRAN 154:18
G. me, O thou great Jehovah	WILL 857:9
g. our feet	BIBL 104:10
g., philosopher, and friend	POPE 617:12
g. what goes off the road	LANG 479:3
G. where our infant Redeemer	HEBE 388:7
ruler and g.	BOOK 136:4
very g. of life	BUTL 182:18
guided g. missiles	KING 463:16
guides blind g.	BIBL 102:19
guiding g.-star of a whole brave nation	MOTL 562:13
thy g. hand	MILT 544:30
Guildenstern Rosencrantz and G.	SHAK 705:5
guile hiding his harmful g.	SPEN 767:8
in whom is no g.	BIBL 107:7
lips, that they speak no g.	BOOK 141:21
there is no g.	BOOK 141:16
urban, squat, and packed with g.	BROO 159:10
guilt assumption of g.	CROS 261:7
beggar would recognise g.	PARS 597:11
dwell on g.	AUST 41:18
for a sign of g.	CONG 247:19
free from g. or pain	SHEL 746:2
G. in his heart	CHUR 228:17
G. is to motherhood	WELD 845:17
g. of Stalin	GORB 366:3
Let g. or fear	ADDI 4:23
Life without industry is g.	RUSK 673:8
no wish to carry the g.	CLAU 234:6
unfortunate circumstance of g.	STEV 776:6
war without its g.	SURT 781:6
wash her g. away	GOLD 365:14
without its g.	SOME 760:18
guilty crimes of this g. land	BROW 161:8
g. conscience needs	PROV 633:34
g. man is acquitted	JUVE 451:19
G. of dust and sin	HERB 394:14
g. of our own disasters	SHAK 714:24
g. of some offence	FRIS 343:6
g. party is acquitted	PUBL 648:31
g. thing surprised	WORD 867:14

haunts the g. mind	SHAK 710:12
Let no g. man escape	GRAN 368:17
Make mad the g.	SHAK 701:21
Saints should be judged g.	ORWE 588:3
started like a g. thing	SHAK 699:5
ten g. persons escape	BLAC 123:14
guinea but the g.'s stamp	BURN 178:7
disc of fire like a g.	BLAK 128:8
g. pigs in the laboratory of God	WILL 858:2
g. you have in your pocket	RUSK 674:6
jingling of the g.	TENN 796:25
to one g.	JOHN 444:15
Worth a g. a box	ADVE 8:29
guinea pig skin of a g.	LIST 495:11
Guinness G., Allsopp, Bass	CALV 194:3
G. is good for you	ADVE 7:27
My Goodness, My G.	ADVE 8:6
guitar blue g.	STEV 774:6
sang to a small g.	LEAR 486:5
gulag G. archipelago	SOLZ 760:12
gulf great g. fixed	BIBL 106:7
g. profound	MILT 542:13
redwood forest to the G. Stream	GUTH 375:2
gulfs g. of liquid fire	SHAK 729:21
g. will wash us down	TENN 800:20
whelmed in deeper g.	COWP 254:24
gullet g. of New York	MILL 537:11
gullible g. interpret as a sign	FLAU 333:8
gulls cry of g.	ELIO 311:16
gum can't fart and chew g.	JOHN 435:11
gums Don't forget the fruit g.	ADVE 7:18
wept odorous g.	MILT 543:2
gun cat with a machine g.	DIDD 282:9
Fire your little g.	DE L 272:4
grows out of the barrel of a g.	MAO 521:3
had a little g.	NURS 581:14
Happiness is a warm g.	LENN 489:1
Maxim G.	BELL 68:12
no g., but I can spit	AUDE 38:3
through the door with a g.	CHAN 215:14
gunboat send a g.	BEVA 76:15
gunfire towards the sound of g.	GRIM 373:12
Gunga Din than I am, G.	KIPL 466:3
gunner g. to his linstock	PROV 629:10
Sink me the ship, Master G.	TENN 800:3
gunpowder G., Printing	CARL 199:22
g. ran out	FOOT 336:13
G. Treason and Plot	ANON 19:20
Printing, g.	BACO 49:3
gun-room Ould Grouse in the g.	GOLD 365:6
guns g. and sharp swords	DYLA 301:15
G. aren't lawful	PARK 596:7
G. don't kill people	SLOG 755:4
hundred men with g.	PUZO 650:25
loaded g. with boys	CRAB 258:4
monstrous anger of the g.	OWEN 591:3
not found any smoking g.	BLIX 129:2
rather have butter or g.	GOER 361:9
They got the g.	MORR 561:4
with g. not with butter	GOEB 361:7
gunslinger Hip young g.	ANON 17:17
gurgite rari nantes in g. vasto	VIRG 828:13
gurly g. grew the sea	BALL 54:10
guru by grace through the G.	SIKH 751:15
G. Granth Sahib	SIKH 752:6
known as his g.	LAWS 484:12
reading the G.'s words	SIKH 752:5
When the G. comes	SIKH 751:17
gusts our g. and storms	ELIO 307:8
gut Truth taht comes from the g.	COLB 238:20
Gutenberg G. made everybody	MCLU 512:13
gutless sort of g. Kipling	ORWE 587:21
guts full of g.	ARCH 25:19
g. of the last priest	DIDE 282:10
lug the g.	SHAK 703:22
Mrs Thatcher 'showed g.'	KINN 464:22
sheeps' g.	SHAK 727:20
Spill your g. at Wimbledon	CONN 248:16
strangled with the g.	MESL 533:7
gutta G. cavat lapidem	OVID 590:4
gutter in the g. with that guy	EISE 306:7
Journalists belong in g.	PRIE 622:17
We are all in the g.	WILD 855:11

guys G. and dolls	RUNY 672:9
Nice g. finish last	DURO 300:15
gwir Creu g. fel gwydr	LEWI 492:7
gypsies play with the g.	NURS 580:7
gyre Did g. and gimble	CARR 202:21
gyves With g. upon his wrist	HOOD 405:14

ha H., ha	BIBL 87:13
habeas corpus protection of h.	JEFF 431:17
habit Cocaine h.-forming	BANK 57:8
entirely different from h.	STRA 778:18
Growing old a bad h.	MAUR 528:16
H. is a great deadener	BECK 64:25
H. is second nature	AUCT 36:9
h. of talking with paper	SOYI 765:4
H. with him was all	CRAB 257:11
long h. of living	BROW 162:13
Not choice But h.	WORD 865:21
order breeds h.	ADAM 2:15
shook the h. off	WORD 868:20
Sow a h.	READ 656:8
habitarunt H. di quoque silvas	VIRG 831:19
habitation God in his holy h.	BOOK 144:7
h. among the tents of Kedar	BOOK 148:15
h. be void	BOOK 144:13
h. of dragons	BIBL 93:6
local h. and a name	SHAK 727:3
soul's h. henceforth	RUSS 674:25
habitations everlasting h.	BIBL 106:4
habits Old h. die hard	PROV 640:30
prejudices and h.	GIBB 354:18
habitual h. hatred	WASH 840:18
nothing is h. but indecision	JAME 430:14
hack Do not h. me	MONM 553:11
hacked H. with constant service	SOUT 764:4
Hackney Marshes You could see to H.	BATE 61:6
had What I ne'er h.	ASTE 34:12
Hades dark H.' door	VIRG 830:5
gates of H.	HOME 404:17
unsubstantial realms of H.	VIRG 830:8
haedis ab h. me sequestra	MISS 550:8
hag h. obscene	BEAT 62:13
haggard prove her h.	SHAK 728:25
Haggards H. ride no more	STEP 772:4
hags black, and midnight h.	SHAK 721:19
Haig ask for H.	ADVE 7:17
hail beaten dog beneath the h.	POUN 621:10
Fire and h.	BOOK 150:9
h., and farewell	CATU 211:6
H., fellow, well met	SWIF 783:27
H. holy queen	PRAY 623:7
H. Mary	PRAY 623:1
h. the power	PERR 604:5
H., thou that art highly favoured	BIBL 104:7
H. to thee, blithe Spirit	SHEL 746:19
sharp and sided h.	HOPK 407:11
hair All her h.	BROW 167:6
amber-dropping h.	MILT 539:11
bind my h.	HUNT 422:1
bracelet of bright h.	DONN 289:13
braided her yellow h.	BALL 55:18
bright golden h.	WILD 856:6
colour of his h.	HOUS 415:4
draws with a single h.	PROV 627:12
fell her golden h.	TURN 819:9
h. has become very white	CARR 201:17
h. is as a flock of goats	BIBL 91:4
h. is grey	BYRO 190:22
h. of a woman	HOWE 417:5
h. of his head	BIBL 95:27
h. of my flesh stood up	BIBL 86:19
h. that lay upon her back	ROSS 669:13
h. to stand on end	SHAK 700:18
h. turns white	BERR 74:16
her eyes, her h.	MEW 533:14
Her h. was long	KEAT 455:6
if a woman have long h.	BIBL 112:12
Like the bright h. uplifted	SHEL 745:7
little bugs, with golden h.	LUTH 505:6
long essenced h.	MACA 508:5
part my h. behind	ELIO 310:13

hands (cont.):
terrible, man-slaying h. HOME 404:22
think with my h. HODG 401:16
union of h. and hearts TAYL 792:6
washed his h. BIBL 103:21
wash my h. in innocency BOOK 141:7
With mine own h. SHAK 731:4
with one of his h. BIBL 86:3
world's great h. HUNT 421:6
your face in your h. ANON 18:8
handsaw know a hawk from a h. SHAK 701:14
handsome H. is as handsome does
PROV 633:38
handwriting legibility in his h. HAY 385:13
hang all h. together FRAN 341:8
Go h. thyself SHAK 705:19
h. a man first MOLI 552:17
h. a pearl SHAK 725:34
H. a thief when he's young PROV 633:40
H. it all, Robert Browning POUN 620:18
h. my hat JERO 433:14
h. old Jeff Davis SONG 763:2
h. the man over again BARH 58:7
h. upon him DONN 290:1
H. yourself, brave Crillon HENR 391:18
in them which will h. him RICH 661:1
let him h. there EHRL 305:1
neither go nor h. BIGO 121:11
will not h. myself today CHES 223:25
with which to h. them MISQ 547:6
wretches h. POPE 618:12
you would h. yourself JOHN 441:4
hanged born to be h. PROV 635:32
Confess and be h. PROV 629:17
farmer that h. himself SHAK 720:11
h., drawn, and quartered PEPY 603:2
h. for a sheep PROV 641:9
h. for stealing horses HALI 377:19
h. in a fortnight JOHN 442:9
h. in all innocence STEV 776:8
ill name is half h. PROV 634:9
Little thieves are h. PROV 637:45
man who has been h. PROV 639:40
must they all be h. SHAK 722:4
my poor fool is h. SHAK 717:8
our harps, we h. them up BOOK 149:13
see him h. BELL 68:7
So they h. Haman BIBL 86:6
hanging bare h. DRYD 297:25
Catching's before h. PROV 628:35
cured by h. from a string KING 464:18
deserve h. MONT 555:24
dog than h. it PROV 644:12
H. and wiving PROV 633:41
h. Danny Deever KIPL 465:13
H. is too good for him BUNY 171:10
h.-look to me CONG 247:1
h. men an' women POLI 612:22
H. of his cat BRAT 155:8
Many a good h. SHAK 735:3
postcards of the h. DYLA 301:13
hangman h.'s thrusting The final nail
BLOK 129:3
naked to the h.'s noose HOUS 415:14
hangs H. in the uncertain balance GREE 371:24
thereby h. a tale SHAK 696:25
What h. people STEV 776:6
hank bone and a h. of hair KIPL 467:19
Hannibal em Expende H. JUVE 451:14
hante h. la tempête BAUD 61:9
Haoma O Green One [H.] ZORO 879:3
happen can't h. here LEWI 492:15
fools said would h. MELB 531:1
h. to your mother WALK 836:1
no evil h. unto thee BOOK 146:2
poetry makes nothing h. AUDE 37:9
happened after they have h. IONE 425:17
never h. SALL 679:12
things h. to men HERA 392:21
happening believe what isn't h. COLE 239:1
what is *not* h. TYNA 820:29
happens be there when it h. ALLE 13:14
Nothing h. BECK 64:19

nothing h. WELD 845:14
Nothing, like something, h. anywhere
LARK 481:5
what h. to her ELIO 307:14
happier h. than your father SOPH 761:9
make life h. MART 524:10
remembering h. things TENN 796:24
seek No h. state MILT 543:14
happiest h. and best minds SHEL 747:13
h. life is lived SOPH 761:10
h. people in the world OSBO 588:9
h. women ELIO 308:7
happily h. ever after ANON 16:8
happiness another person's h. MOOR 557:12
basically our h. THOM 805:7
brief period of h. ARIS 27:8
consume h. without producing SHAW 739:16
contribution to public h. STEN 771:13
desire for their own h. SHAN 739:4
enemy to human h. JOHN 443:12
ensure h. throughout EPIC 316:12
fatal to true h. RUSS 674:18
greatest h. HUTC 422:10
h. alone is salutary PROU 626:2
h. and final misery MILT 542:12
H. depends on being free PERI 603:26
H., for you MONT 555:28
h. he feels LACL 475:10
H. is a cigar ADVE 7:28
H. is a how HESS 397:13
H. is a mystery CHES 225:5
H. is an imaginary SZAS 786:12
H. is a warm gun LENN 489:1
H. is no laughing matter WHAT 849:15
H. is not an ideal KANT 453:2
h. is produced JOHN 441:25
h. lies in conquering GENG 352:6
h. makes up in height FROS 344:15
h. mankind can gain DRYD 296:4
h. nor annihilation HOLT 404:1
h. of society ADAM 3:12
h. of the greatest number BENT 71:4
h. of the human race BURK 173:25
h. of the next world BROW 162:12
H.! our being's end POPE 617:5
h. she herself brought FLAU 333:3
h. that went on CHEK 222:10
h. was but the occasional HARD 380:16
H. washes away many things BÖLL 131:18
h., which is an end ARIS 27:13
home-born h. COWP 256:21
hopes for h. from thee WRIG 870:21
In solitude What h. MILT 543:29
let me forget this h. NERU 570:12
lifetime of h. SHAW 740:21
lightning of individual h. HERZ 396:24
look into h. SHAK 697:22
Money can't buy h. PROV 638:45
more for human h. BRIL 157:9
my people's h. ELIZ 312:9
no greatest h. principle CARL 199:19
one's true h. LACL 475:11
only one h. in life SAND 679:20
or justice or human h. BERL 73:10
politics of h. HUMP 421:2
prayer to h. ALAI 11:2
price of h. YEVT 876:3
promise of h. STEN 771:12
pursuit of h. ANON 21:6
pursuit of h. JEFF 431:6
recipe for h. AUST 41:15
result h. DICK 277:10
ruin of all h. BURN 176:22
searching for his own h. PALI 594:22
secret of h. MORE 558:21
seek h. in boats HORA 410:10
short-lived h. BEHN 66:22
suited to human h. DEFO 270:11
take away his h. IBSE 424:11
that is h. CATH 209:13
that is h. EMER 315:8
that we call h. GIDE 356:3
two combined make H. BUCH 169:6

ways of seeking h. BAUD 62:3
We find our h. WORD 868:18
happy all be as h. as kings STEV 776:13
all who are h. JOHN 440:12
ask if they were h. CHAN 215:15
attain The h. life SURR 780:13
aware that you are h. KRIS 473:17
bread-sauce of the h. ending JAME 430:3
Call no man h. SOLO 760:10
conspiracy to make me h. DICK 276:20
conspiracy to make you h. UPDI 822:20
duty of being h. STEV 775:25
earthlier h. SHAK 725:22
had a h. life HAZL 386:25
h. as one hopes LA R 482:12
H. birthday to you HILL 398:16
h. breed of men SHAK 730:10
h. could I be with either GAY 351:9
h. families resemble TOLS 813:8
H. field or mossy cavern KEAT 455:15
h. for a week PROV 635:37
h. he who crowns in shades GOLD 364:3
H. he who like Ulysses DU B 298:3
h. highways where I went HOUS 416:4
H. in this SHAK 724:24
h. issue BOOK 135:7
H. is the country PROV 633:43
H. is the man BOOK 149:3
H. is the man who fears BIBL 120:2
H. Land MAHĀ 515:19
h. men that have the power TENN 800:10
h. noise to hear HOUS 415:16
h. Rome, born when I CICE 232:13
H. the hare at morning AUDE 37:1
H. the man DRYD 297:6
H. the man HORA 411:3
H. the man POPE 617:32
H. the people MONT 556:7
h. those early days VAUG 825:5
h. while y'er leevin MOTT 563:4
hope for a h. exit KAHL 452:14
I die h. FOX 339:12
independent and h. MADI 514:9
in general be as h. JOHN 441:26
make a man h. HORA 410:8
make men h. POPE 617:18
man would be as h. JOHN 442:21
must laugh before we are h. LA B 474:16
no man h. till he dies PROV 628:31
object of making men h. DOST 291:1
one of those h. souls SHEL 744:15
one thing to make me h. HAZL 386:3
one who has been h. BOET 130:11
Point me out the h. man GREE 371:15
policeman's lot is not a h. one GILB 358:8
prevent from being h. ANOU 24:13
remember a h. time DANT 264:18
remembers the h. things LOVE 502:8
so late their h. seat MILT 544:19
someone, somewhere, may be h. MENC 531:19
soul that loves is h. GOET 361:12
splendid and a h. land GOLD 364:10
stop trying to be h. WHAR 849:10
This is the h. warrior READ 656:6
till all are h. SPEN 766:4
touch the H. Isles TENN 800:20
'Twere now to be most h. SHAK 728:18
Was he h. AUDE 38:15
was the carver h. RUSK 673:22
whether you are h. SHAW 742:3
Whoever wants to be h. MEDI 530:5
Who is the h. Warrior WORD 865:6
whose heart is h. TALM 790:2
world of the h. WITT 861:16
harbinger Love's h. MILT 544:14
harbour h. bar be moaning KING 464:13
those who h. them BUSH 182:8
voyage not a h. TOYN 814:5
hard h. awakening HAFI 375:9
h. day's night LENN 489:9
h. English men KING 464:8
h.-faced men BALD 53:2
h. rain's a gonna fall DYLA 301:15

herbs (cont.):
dinner of h. — BIBL 88:15
for a garden of h. — BIBL 85:17
Hercules is not love a H. — SHAK 717:18
I to H. — SHAK 699:22
some of H. — SONG 763:11
herd elevates above the vulgar h. — GAIS 347:5
h. wind slowly o'er the lea — GRAY 370:1
Morality is the h.-instinct — NIET 575:13
unreflecting h. — WORD 865:21
herdsman God the h. goads — YEAT 872:17
here Are *you* h. — DANT 265:2
can't happen h. — LEWI 492:15
he answered, H. am I — BIBL 83:25
H. am I — BIBL 92:9
h. because we're queer — BEHA 66:16
h. for the beer — ADVE 7:35
H. I am — MACM 512:14
H.'s a how-de-doo — GILB 357:9
H.'s looking at you — FILM 328:11
H.'s tae us — TOAS 812:3
H.'s to thee, Corbet — AUBR 35:15
h.'s to you, Mrs Robinson — SIMO 752:14
H. today—in next week tomorrow — GRAH 368:2
H. were decent godless people — ELIO 310:24
If we can't stay h. alive — MONT 556:8
I have been h. before — ROSS 669:23
Mr Watson, come h. — BELL 67:10
Well h. I am — SENT 692:22
We're h. — MILI 535:17
we should not be h. — NAPO 567:13
What you seek is h. — HORA 410:10
hereafter died h. — SHAK 722:22
h. for ever — BOOK 138:23
points out our h. — ADDI 4:21
world may talk of h. — COLL 242:24
hereditary H. bondsmen — BYRO 185:23
h. monarch was insane — BAGE 50:13
idea of h. legislators — PAIN 592:21
hereditas *Damnosa h.* — GAIU 348:8
Hereford H., and Hampshire — LERN 490:12
heresies begin as h. — HUXL 423:13
heresy believes be h. — SHAW 742:13
h. signifies no more — HOBB 400:21
Turkey, h., hops — PROV 645:40
heretic h. which makes the fire — SHAK 736:21
oppressor or a h. — CAMU 196:14
heretics H. the only bitter remedy — ZAMY 877:7
heritage h. unto Israel — BOOK 149:11
I have a goodly h. — BOOK 140:3
Hermes H. in the wax — ARIS 28:11
hermit h.'s fast — KEAT 455:12
hermitage for an h. — LOVE 502:5
palace for a h. — SHAK 730:22
hermits h. are contented — WORD 866:19
hern haunts of coot and h. — TENN 793:1
hero acted like a h. — WALP 838:7
aspires to be a h. — JOHN 442:23
conquering h. comes — MORE 559:17
don't want to be a h. — STOP 778:4
h. becomes a bore — EMER 315:12
h. from his prison — AYTO 44:6
h. is one who does — ROLL 666:11
h. of my tale — TOLS 813:12
h. perish — POPE 616:18
h. to his valet — CORN 252:7
h. to his valet — PROV 640:6
H.-worship strongest — SPEN 766:3
Millions a h. — PORT 619:22
seemed a h. — BYRO 185:9
Show me a h. — FITZ 332:8
Herod for an hour of H. — HOPE 406:21
H. is his name — CAUS 211:8
out-herods H. — SHAK 702:13
heroes Canadians do not like h. — WOOD 863:22
feats worked by those h. — ANON 23:15
fit country for h. — LLOY 496:16
go after the h. — O'Ra 585:17
greatest h. — COLL 242:22
h. of old — BROW 167:8
of all the worlds brave h. — SONG 763:11
speed glum h. — SASS 682:4
Thin red line of h. — KIPL 467:17

Unhappy the land that needs h. — BREC 155:16
heroic finished A life h. — MILT 545:9
h. for earth too hard — BROW 164:17
h. poem of its sort — CARL 199:15
H. womanhood — LONG 499:21
heroics not h., but healing — HARD 380:6
heroine take a h. — AUST 43:7
when a h. goes mad — SHER 748:5
heroines h. of novels — FLAU 333:5
herring Every h. must hang — PROV 631:20
plague o' these pickle h. — SHAK 735:4
roast thee like a h. — BURN 179:20
shoals of h. — MACC 509:13
herrings As many red h. — NURS 580:4
herrschen *h. und gewinnen* — GOET 362:8
Hertford H., Hereford, and Hampshire — LERN 490:12
Hervey call a dog H. — JOHN 438:23
Herveys men, women, and H. — MONT 554:12
Herz *Mein H. ist schwer* — GOET 362:4
hesitate could long h. — STEV 776:8
hesitates h. is lost — PROV 634:21
She floats, she h. — RACI 652:16
hesitating H. doesn't matter — BREC 155:13
hesitation H. increases — HEMI 391:8
Without h., deviation — CATC 208:35
Hesperides climbing trees in the H. — SHAK 717:18
Hesperus H. entreats thy light — JONS 446:3
It was the schooner H. — LONG 500:6
venit H. — VIRG 832:11
heterodoxy h. is another man's doxy — WARB 839:18
H. or Thy-doxy — CARL 200:1
heterogeneity coherent h. — SPEN 765:21
heu *H., miserande puer* — VIRG 830:15
heures *h. propices* — LAMA 476:9
Heute *H. leid' ich* — LESS 490:19
hew h. him as a carcass — SHAK 712:6
hewers h. of wood — BIBL 82:28
hewn h. out her seven pillars — BIBL 87:32
hey h. for boot and horse — KING 464:14
H. for God Almighty — KETT 461:11
'H.-ho!' says Rowley — NURS 578:14
hi answer to 'H.!' — CARR 203:27
hic *H. jacet* — RALE 654:11
Quod petis h. est — HORA 410:10
hick Sticks nix h. pix — NEWS 573:19
hickety H., pickety — NURS 579:1
hickory H., dickory, dock — NURS 579:2
hid cannot be h. — BIBL 98:27
h. as it were our faces — BIBL 94:3
h. from thine eyes — BIBL 106:16
h. themselves in the dens — BIBL 118:11
I h. from Him — THOM 807:14
Which is, to keep that h. — DONN 289:20
hidden follows the h. path — LUIS 504:16
h. connection is stronger — HERA 393:2
h. from the eye — WORD 869:4
h. love of God — WESL 847:6
h. persuaders — PACK 591:14
teems with h. meaning — GILB 358:11
hide chose from man to h. — CRAB 257:13
disguise which can h. love — LA R 481:20
he can't h. — LOUI 501:12
h. in cooling trees — KEAT 456:17
h. is sure to flatten 'em — BELL 67:18
h. just in the middle — SHAW 742:21
h. of a rhinoceros — BARR 60:5
h. our own hurts — ELIO 307:19
h. thy face from me — BOOK 139:27
h. us from the face — BIBL 118:11
in a woman's h. — SHAK 710:5
Let me h. myself — TOPL 813:21
nothing more to h. — QUIN 651:19
Those who h. can find — PROV 645:6
Whose h. he sold — WALL 836:16
wise man h. a pebble — CHES 225:8
wrapped in a player's h. — GREE 372:1
hideous Making night h. — SHAK 700:12
hides H. from himself his state — JOHN 438:9
h. one thing in his heart — HOME 404:17

hiding bloody good h. — GRAN 368:8
girl in her h.-place — HORA 411:14
My heart in h. — HOPK 408:5
Hieronimo H. is mad again — KYD 474:13
Hierusalem H., my happy home — ANON 17:16
high Be ye never so h. — DENN 273:10
Be you never so h. — FULL 346:15
cannot rate me very h. — LACL 475:9
corn as h. as an elephant's eye — HAMM 378:19
from h. life — POPE 615:13
get h. with a little help — LENN 489:13
h. heels are most agreeable — SWIF 782:7
h.-minded. descendants — CATU 210:14
h. road — JOHN 439:20
h. that proved too high — BROW 164:17
h.-water mark of Socialist literature — ORWE 587:21
house of defence very h. — BOOK 146:2
how h. the heaven is — BOOK 147:2
I'm the H. — SPRI 769:2
Lord, I am not h.-minded — BOOK 149:9
Lord most H. — BOOK 137:14
No bird soars too h. — BLAK 126:10
Pile it h. — SLOG 755:11
slain upon thy h. places — BIBL 84:11
This h. man — BROW 165:25
too h. for me — BOOK 149:9
upon the h. horse — BROW 161:6
wickedness in h. places — BIBL 114:15
ye'll tak' the h. road — SONG 763:9
higher Friend, go up h. — BIBL 105:19
he shall shoot h. — SIDN 750:13
h. one goes — DANT 265:8
h. the monkey climbs — PROV 634:33
production of the h. animals — DARW 266:16
Stuart or Nassau go h. — PRIO 624:5
subject unto the h. powers — BIBL 111:14
highest children of the most H. — BOOK 145:12
h. good — CICE 231:21
h., hardest glass ceiling — CLIN 236:4
in the h. room — BIBL 105:18
needs must love the h. — TENN 794:9
Highland heart is H. — GALT 348:5
solitary H. lass! — WORD 869:10
Highlandman breeks aff a wild H. — SCOT 689:13
highlands H. and ye Lawlands — BALL 54:6
In the h. — STEV 776:20
My heart's in the H. — BURN 179:3
worst in all the H. — STAI 769:13
highly what thou wouldst h. — SHAK 718:19
highness his H.' dog at Kew — POPE 614:13
highway broad h. of the world — SHEL 744:2
each and ev'ry h. — ANKA 16:1
h. for our God — BIBL 93:15
H., since you my chief — SIDN 750:22
passes over a h. — STEN 771:18
highwayman h. came riding — NOYE 577:14
highways happy h. where I went — HOUS 416:4
into the h. and hedges — BIBL 105:24
hilarity h. like a scream — GREE 371:17
hill city that is set on an h. — BIBL 98:27
city upon a h. — WINT 860:18
cot beside the h. — ROGE 665:16
dancers are all gone under the h. — ELIO 309:10
green h. far away — ALEX 12:10
haven under the h. — TENN 792:20
heard on the h. — BLAK 127:13
hides the green h. — KEAT 455:28
h. that holds his peace — BERR 74:17
hunter home from h. — STEV 777:5
light on the h. — CHIF 226:1
mountain and h. — BIBL 93:15
On a huge h. — DONN 288:22
On the cold h.'s side — KEAT 455:10
rest upon thy holy h. — BOOK 140:1
self-same h. — MILT 540:5
unto thy holy h. — BOOK 142:9
hills and the little h. — BOOK 144:18
Black H. belong to me — SITT 753:9
Blue are the h. — PROV 628:18
blue remembered h. — HOUS 416:4
cattle upon a thousand h. — BOOK 143:2

holiday Butchered to make a Roman h.
BYRO 186:24
I am in a h. humour SHAK 697:18
Is this a h. SHAK 711:11
perpetual h. SHAW 742:4
to take a h. RUSS 674:15
holidays holiest of all h. LONG 499:8
playing h. SHAK 705:12
holier h. than thou BIBL 94:22
holiest Praise to the H. NEWM 572:15
holiness beauty of h. BOOK 146:9
beauty of h. MONS 554:2
h. becometh thine house BOOK 146:5
holiness but social h. WESL 847:20
h. of the heart's affections KEAT 457:12
put off h. BLAK 125:20
Holland children in H. NURS 578:5
H. . . . lies so low HOOD 406:6
hollow Down to the h. FLAN 332:23
hate the dreadful h. TENN 797:18
regiment's in h. square KIPL 465:13
We are the h. men ELIO 309:27
Within the h. crown SHAK 730:20
holly English oak and h. HART 383:15
heigh-ho! the h. SHAK 697:5
h. and the ivy SONG 762:12
Hollywood H. money isn't money PARK 596:16
not have been invited to H. CHAN 215:12
holocaust erewhile a h. MILT 545:8
holy coming to that h. room DONN 288:17
from the h. land RALE 654:3
h. and the profane SIDD 750:7
h. city, new Jerusalem BIBL 119:15
H. deadlock HERB 393:15
H., fair, and wise SHAK 736:15
h. ground BIBL 80:34
H., Holy, Holy HEBE 388:10
H., holy, holy, Lord BIBL 118:5
H., holy, holy, Lord BOOK 137:14
Holy, H., Holy: Lord God BOOK 133:9
h., is the Lord of hosts BIBL 92:6
h. kiss BIBL 111:20
h. nation BIBL 117:3
h. simplicity JERO 433:4
H. Spirit rests only TALM 790:2
h.-water death MCGO 510:17
h. white birds flying after MASE 527:5
h. writ SHAK 731:17
in h. wedlock BOOK 139:4
light of thy H. Spirit BOOK 136:2
neither h., nor Roman VOLT 834:9
nothing is h. BOOK 136:4
prison is a h. place BYRO 191:2
sabbath day, keep it h. BIBL 81:18
stand in the h. place BIBL 102:24
suffer thy H. One BOOK 140:4
that which is h. PLAT 608:14
unto thy h. hill BOOK 142:9
Holy Ghost and to the H. BOOK 133:8
be any H. BIBL 110:6
blasphemy against the h. BIBL 101:4
Come, H. BOOK 150:16
gifts of the H. BUTL 183:1
H. moveth ne'er JULI 449:8
H. over the bent World HOPK 407:8
H. which is given BIBL 110:30
pencil of the h. BACO 46:3
temple of the h. BIBL 112:1
homage do her h. HOOK 406:8
h. of a tear BYRO 185:20
home all the comforts of h. BRYS 169:3
all the h. I have AYTO 44:9
at h. while they fight wars EURI 321:11
battling in its own h. AESC 6:18
beating begins at h. FLET 335:14
by staying at h. LIN 495:8
can't find your way h. COLL 243:3
can't go h. again WOLF 862:22
Charity begins at h. PROV 628:42
come h. Bill Bailey CANN 197:8
comes safe h. SHAK 709:6
comfortably at h. AUST 41:5

drive one from h. HOOD 405:20
East, west, h.'s best PROV 630:44
England, h. and beauty ARNO 32:12
Englishman's h. PROV 631:7
E.T. phone h. FILM 328:5
feel ashamed of h. DICK 278:9
for to carry me h. SONG 763:12
go h. in the dark HENR 392:11
goodman is not at h. BIBL 87:30
Go on h. VIRG 832:11
hear news of h. PROV 633:4
hearth-fire and the h.-acre KIPL 466:4
Hierusalem, my happy h. ANON 17:16
H. again, home again NURS 582:5
H. art gone SHAK 698:24
H. is home PROV 634:36
H. is home, as the Devil said PROV 634:35
H. is the girl's prison SHAW 741:23
H. is the place FROS 344:11
H. is the sailor STEV 777:5
h. is the Sule Skerry BALL 54:15
H. is where the heart is PROV 634:37
H. is where you come to THAT 804:7
H. James HILL 399:3
H. life as we understand it SHAW 739:27
h. life of our own dear Queen ANON 17:16
H. of lost causes ARNO 31:16
h. of the brave KEY 461:13
h., rejoicing, brought me BAKE 52:9
h. sweet home JERO 433:14
H., sweet home PAYN 600:10
H. they brought her warrior TENN 799:15
h., you idle creatures SHAK 711:11
house is not a h. ADLE 6:9
hunter h. from hill STEV 777:5
in h. cosmography HABI 375:5
I was leaving h. STEV 776:19
Keep the H.-fires burning FORD 337:12
kept at h. COWP 255:27
leaves h. to mend himself GOLD 365:9
Look as much like h. FRY 345:18
man goeth to his long h. BIBL 90:20
murder into the h. HITC 400:4
never h. came she KING 464:11
never is at h. COWP 254:30
no place like h. PAYN 600:11
no place like h. PROV 644:46
O, h., hame CUNN 262:16
points of heaven and h. WORD 869:18
princes are come h. again SHAK 714:15
refuge from h. life SHAW 742:18
shortest way h. PROV 637:51
so now we'll go h. SHAC 693:10
Sweet Stay-at-h. DAVI 268:9
there's nobody at h. POPE 614:12
thinks to found a h. DOUG 291:16
Till the boys come h. FORD 337:12
unto God all things come h. KORA 472:18
what is it to be at h. BECK 64:3
What's the good of a h. GROS 373:15
whole world looks like h. HESS 397:10
woman's place in the h. PROV 647:31
won't go h. till morning BUCK 170:3
won the Fleece and then came h. DU B 298:3
homeland loved my h. BELL 69:5
homeless by choice SOUT 764:19
h., tempest-tossed LAZA 485:3
homely h. was their food GART 350:2
never so h. PROV 634:36
home-made H. dishes HOOD 405:20
Homer excellent H. nods HORA 409:14
Gladstone read H. for fun CHUR 230:19
H. dead ANON 20:9
H.'s mighty dinners AESC 8:35
H. smote 'is bloomin' lyre KIPL 468:1
H. sometimes nods PROV 634:38
H. sometimes sleeps BYRO 188:27
more than H. knew SWIF 784:1
must not call it H. BENT 72:2
warred for H., being dead HEYW 398:4
Home Rule morning H. passes CARS 204:9
homes h. without a friend CLAR 232:24
In h., a haunted apparatus RAIN 653:11

Stately H. of England COWA 253:19
stately h. of England HEMA 390:15
homespuns What hempen h. SHAK 726:14
homeward h. take your way COLL 242:20
Look h. angel MILT 540:13
ploughman h. plods GRAY 370:1
homicidal h. classics STOP 777:18
homo Ecce h. BIBL 120:15
ET H. FACTUS EST MISS 549:13
homogeneity incoherent h. SPEN 765:21
homogeneous more h. State NEWS 573:12
homosexual composer and not h. DIAG 275:12
h. sex you know exactly BURR 180:16
honest anything that's h. and good MUIR 564:8
beat the h. men SHAK 722:4
Being totally h. with oneself FREU 342:19
buy it like an h. man NORT 577:7
Corrupted h. men SHAK 695:12
few h. men CROM 260:8
general h. thought SHAK 714:3
h. broker BISM 123:2
h. God INGE 425:9
h. madam's issue SHAK 714:22
h. man is laughed at HALI 377:20
h. man's the noblest work BURN 177:26
h. man's the noblest work POPE 617:8
h. men come by their own PROV 647:4
h., sonsie face BURN 179:22
H. to God ROBI 664:4
h. woman of her word SHAK 724:16
I am not naturally h. SHAK 737:7
is not an h. man WHAT 849:17
least h. with themselves AUST 41:13
looking for an h. man DIOG 283:16
most h. of men RICH 661:1
poor but she was h. MILI 535:16
Robin and I are two h. men SHIP 749:16
third h. wealth ANON 22:18
whatsoever things are h. BIBL 115:5
while the nation is h. DOUG 292:1
honestly If possible h. HORA 410:1
honesty armed so strong in h. SHAK 713:23
h. is not to be based RUSK 673:27
H. is praised JUVE 450:12
H. is the best policy PROV 634:39
H. is the best policy WHAT 849:17
h. must work through artifice RIDI 661:8
saving of thine h. MORE 559:15
honey bee produces h. GOLD 363:16
bees make h. VIRG 833:8
Eating bread and h. NURS 581:8
flowing with milk and h. BIBL 80:36
gather h. all the day WATT 841:11
hive for the h.-bee YEAT 873:20
hives with h. and wax SWIF 782:2
H. catches more flies PROV 634:40
h. of Hybla SHAK 705:8
h. of poison-flowers TENN 797:20
H. of roses HERB 394:11
h. on the goblet's rim LUCR 504:8
H., quoth she NURS 581:13
h. shall he eat BIBL 92:11
h. still for tea BROO 159:11
h. to smear his face SCHW 687:11
H., your silk stocking SELL 691:25
How a bear likes h. MILN 538:9
I did but taste a little h. BIBL 83:34
in my mouth sweet as h. BIBL 118:22
locusts and wild h. BIBL 98:16
neither the h. nor the bee SAPP 680:21
sweeter also than h. BOOK 140:11
there is h. PROV 647:6
they make h. MONT 554:26
took some h. LEAR 486:5
With milk and h. blessed NEAL 569:8
honeycomb drop as an h. BIBL 87:26
honey, and the h. BOOK 140:11
of an h. BIBL 106:33
honeydew he on h. hath fed COLE 240:9
honeyed h. middle of the night KEAT 454:7
honeysuckle You are my honey, h. FITZ 330:15
honi H. soie qui mal y pense SELL 691:25

H. soit qui mal y pense MOTT 563:10
honking goose h. amongst tuneful swans
VIRG 832:9

honores *contemnere h.* HORA 415:2
honour abide in h. BOOK 143:1
all in h. SHAK 729:22
All is lost save h. MISQ 547:1
As he was valiant, I h. him SHAK 712:26
cannot be maintained with h. RUSS 675:19
everything, indeed, except his h. ROBE 663:6
existence to h. JUVE 451:10
Fear God. H. the King KITC 469:4
flowery plains of h. JONS 446:10
for this woman's h. FILM 329:16
fountain of h. BACO 46:1
greater share of h. SHAK 709:5
great peaks of h. LLOY 496:14
H. all men BIBL 117:5
h. among thieves PROV 644:24
h., and keep her BOOK 138:24
h. and life FRAN 340:15
h. and renown ye ANON 20:10
H. a physician BIBL 97:31
h. aspireth to it BACO 46:21
H. but an empty bubble DRYD 295:6
h. due unto his Name BOOK 144:9
H. is like a match PAGN 592:3
H. pricks me on SHAK 706:24
h. rooted in dishonour TENN 794:13
h. sinks where commerce GOLD 364:25
h.'s voice GRAY 370:5
H. the greatest poet DANT 264:16
h. therof EDWA 304:2
h. those whom they have slain DOST 291:2
h. thy father and thy mother BIBL 81:20
h. turn to dust MARV 525:13
H.! tut, a breath JONS 446:15
h. unto Luke Evangelist ROSS 669:19
h. unto the wife BIBL 117:9
H., without money RACI 653:4
hurt that H. feels TENN 796:25
in h. clear POPE 615:19
In h. I gained them NELS 569:21
Keeps h. bright SHAK 734:18
king delighteth to h. BIBL 86:7
Leisure with h. CICE 232:10
loss of h. was a wrench GRAH 367:12
louder he talked of his h. EMER 314:21
Loved I not h. more LOVE 502:7
may we h. it WEBS 844:3
one vessel unto h. BIBL 111:8
peace I hope with h. DISR 285:8
peace with h. CHAM 214:6
pluck bright h. SHAK 705:15
pluck up drownèd h. SHAK 705:15
post of h. ADDI 4:19
post of h. PROV 641:43
property or h. MACH 511:13
prophet is not without h. BIBL 101:17
prophet not without h. PROV 642:9
ready her to h. BEST 75:7
reputation and h. SOCR 759:19
riches and h. BIBL 87:22
Riches, knowledge and h. HOBB 400:18
right of h. GURN 374:17
roll of h. CLEV 235:12
safety, h., and welfare CHAR 217:8
signed with their h. SPEN 766:11
some smatch of h. SHAK 714:2
stain in thine h. BIBL 97:30
take mine h. from me KIPL 466:12
there all the h. lies POPE 617:6
Trouthe and h. CHAU 218:4
What is h. SHAK 706:25
whence h. springs MARL 523:7
When h.'s at the stake SHAK 703:29
where their h. died POPE 614:29
without h. BIBL 97:2
years and h. to the grave KIPL 466:17
honourable Brutus is an h. man SHAK 713:2
designs were strictly h. FIEL 326:22
h. alike in what we give LINC 493:18
h. among all men BOOK 138:21

h. by being necessary HALE 377:1
humble as h. CHUA 227:10
make an h. retreat SHAK 697:8
more h. man BIBL 105:18
only h. provision AUST 42:14
thy h. women BOOK 142:14
honoured h. me of late SHAK 719:11
More h. in the breach SHAK 700:10
honours bears his blushing h. SHAK 710:19
despise h. HORA 415:2
good card to play for H. BENN 70:20
h. her more than himself TALM 789:20
h. the worker TALM 789:22
neither h. nor wages GARI 349:7
hood bold Robin H. BALL 54:12
hoodie hug a h. COAK 237:9
Hug a h. MISQ 547:19
hoodies see h. as aggressive CAME 194:12
hoof No h., no horse PROV 640:4
though he divide the h. BIBL 81:26
hoof-marks many h. going in AESO 9:2
hoofs h. of a swinish multitude BURK 174:12
plunging h. were gone DE L 272:8
hook bended h. shall pierce SHAK 695:5
h.-nosed fellow of Rome SHAK 707:25
That nose, the h. BYRO 185:5
thy h. Spares the next swath KEAT 457:1
with an h. BIBL 87:17
hooter because the h. hoots CHES 224:11
hooting H. and shrieking SHAK 712:1
h. at the glorious sun COLE 239:16
hop for what were h.-yards meant HOUS 416:10
H. forty paces SHAK 694:24
h. if ye can WALL 836:13
Why h. ye so BOOK 144:9
hope Abandon all h. DANT 264:13
All my h. on God BRID 156:18
All our h. is fallen HORA 413:16
believed in h. BIBL 110:29
Can something, h. HOPK 407:5
Evelyn H. is dead BROW 165:19
failure of h. GIBB 355:7
From h. and fear set free SWIN 785:14
God is our h. BOOK 142:17
have not h. nor health SHEL 746:16
He has no h. COWP 257:2
heirs through h. BOOK 137:18
He that lives in h. HERB 395:5
He that lives upon h. FRAN 341:7
h. and agitation BARA 57:18
h. and history rhyme HEAN 387:8
h. beyond ourselves SHEL 747:15
H. deferred BIBL 88:6
H. deferred PROV 634:41
h., fear, rage, pleasure JUVE 450:14
H., for a season CAMP 195:13
h. for the best PROV 634:42
h. for the best SMIT 758:12
h. for years to come WATT 842:7
h. grew ground me COLE 239:10
h. in Christ BIBL 112:20
H. is a good breakfast BACO 49:7
H. is a good breakfast PROV 634:43
h. is gone AUST 42:5
h. is perished BIBL 95:10
Hopeless h. hopes on CLAR 232:24
h. little ELGA 306:16
H. maketh not ashamed BIBL 110:30
h. of all the ends BOOK 142:2
h. of glory BOOK 135:8
h. of the ungodly BIBL 97:4
h. once crushed ARNO 30:28
H. raises no dust ÉLUA 314:7
H. springs eternal POPE 616:19
H. springs eternal PROV 634:44
h. till Hope creates SHEL 746:4
I can give you no h. EDDI 302:16
I fear and h. PETR 605:1
in the store we sell h. REVS 658:15
Land of H. and Glory BENS 70:22
last best h. LINC 493:18
life there's h. PROV 647:14
lives in h. PROV 634:10

look forward to with h. FROS 344:10
more h. of a fool BIBL 89:1
Never to h. again SHAK 710:20
no h. without fear SPIN 768:11
Nor dread nor h. attend YEAT 873:2
not another's h. WALS 838:19
not for h., heart would break PROV 635:12
nursing the unconquerable h. ARNO 30:13
only h. that keeps up GAY 351:3
phantoms of h. JOHN 437:13
pleasing h. ADDI 4:20
poise of h. and fear MILT 539:4
propensity to h. and joy HUME 420:13
Some blessed H. HARD 381:15
sure and certain h. BOOK 139:10
tender leaves of h. SHAK 710:19
there is h. CROS 261:10
There is no h. CHES 222:17
Through love, through h. WORD 868:26
tiny ripple of h. KENN 460:19
triumph of h. over experience JOHN 440:25
true green of h. VERN 826:14
True h. is swift SHAK 731:25
two thousand years of h. WEIZ 845:11
warns us not to h. HORA 413:18
Was the h. drunk SHAK 719:12
we may gain from h. MILT 541:16
Whatever h. is yours OWEN 591:9
What is h. BYRO 192:2
what was dead was H. WILD 856:2
Where there is despair, h. FRAN 340:17
Work without h. COLE 241:15
Youth and H. COLE 242:11
hoped Much wished, h. little TASS 790:10
things h. for BIBL 116:3
hoped-for become the h. heaven EPIT 319:18
hopeful droopingly, but with a h. heart
LAWR 483:12
hopefully travel h. PROV 636:13
travel h. is a better thing STEV 775:27
hopefulness Lord of all h. STRU 779:5
hopeless doctors know a h. case CUMM 262:10
h. are starkly sincere RHYS 659:15
h. grief is passionless BROW 164:8
H. hope hopes on CLAR 232:24
perennially h. DICK 276:10
hopelessness h. and calm BARA 57:18
h. of one's position DOST 291:7
hopes enter on far-reaching h. HORA 411:8
happy as one h. LA R 482:12
h. and fears BROO 160:5
h. and fears it heeded not SHEL 746:22
h. of its children EISE 306:6
h. our wits beguile WOTT 870:10
If h. were dupes CLOU 237:6
no great h. from Birmingham AUST 41:9
no h. but from power BURK 175:16
scribbled lines like fallen h. HOPE 407:2
set my h. in thee PRAY 623:9
vanity of human h. JOHN 437:11
wholly h. to be BROW 165:15
hopeth h. all things BIBL 112:14
hoping Dreading and h. all YEAT 873:2
hops apples, cherries, h. DICK 280:15
heresy, h., and beer PROV 645:40
Horatius H. kept the bridge MACA 508:20
horizon always somebody else's h. GRAH 368:2
Death is only an h. PRAY 623:9
fortress rising above the h. LOUI 501:8
h. adorning HEBE 388:7
In research the h. recedes PATT 599:19
horizons immense fields, wide h. CHEK 221:19
In these stones h. sing LEWI 492:8
horizontal h. desire SHAW 742:23
Life is a h. fall COCT 237:20
vertical to the eternal h. GRAS 369:3
horn blow his wreathèd h. WORD 869:25
h. of the hunter CRAW 259:13
horn, the lusty h. SHAK 697:21
one of which is made of h. VIRG 830:16
sound of the h. VIGN 828:1
through the mellow h. COLL 243:14
won't come out of your h. PARK 596:1

iced three parts i. over ARNO 32:1
Iceland Natural History of I. JOHN 442:14
iceman i. cometh O'NE 585:8
Ichabod I., Ichabod BROW 168:8
named the child I. BIBL 83:29
icicle Chaste as the i. SHAK 698:15
hang like an i. SHAK 735:29
icicles hang them up in silent i. COLE 240:1
When i. hang by the wall SHAK 717:25
icy lays his i. hand on kings SHIR 749:17
id PUT THE I. BACK IN YID ROTH 670:10
idea Between the i. And the reality ELIO 309:28
does get an i. MARQ 523:16
endowed with the i. of God DESC 274:10
forgiveness is a lovely i. LEWI 491:16
good i.—son CATC 207:22
i. does not pass UNAM 821:13
i. first occurs DARW 267:4
i. whose time has come SAYI 685:12
invasion by an i. HUGO 419:3
landed with an i. BIRT 122:4
more dangerous than an i. ALAI 10:10
no grand i. was ever born FITZ 332:7
only one i. DISR 286:7
pain of a new i. BAGE 51:13
poet as an i. SCHI 686:3
possess but one i. JOHN 440:23
stretched by a new i. HOLM 403:10
teach the young i. THOM 808:12
wilderness of i. BUTL 184:11
would be a good i. GAND 348:15
ideal i. for which I am prepared MAND 518:16
i. of reason KANT 453:2
i. reader suffering from JOYC 448:2
stands up for an i. KENN 460:19
idealism assassins of i. HOOV 406:15
morphine or i. JUNG 449:13
idealistic only i. nation WILS 860:1
ideals do for his i. is to lie SCHU 687:7
i. of a nation DOUG 291:14
men without i. CAMU 196:4
ideas because he has plenty of i. CHAM 215:3
business is to kill i. WELL 847:1
by acts and not by i. FRAN 340:11
cemetery of dead i. UNAM 821:14
Colourless green i. CHOM 226:14
express your i. GRAC 367:9
From it our i. are born GENE 352:3
genuine i., Bright Ideas BENT 71:20
i. to literature BOUR 153:4
i. which least belong to us BERG 72:10
I. won't keep WHIT 851:7
No i. but in things WILL 858:13
share no one's i. TURG 818:16
signs of i. JOHN 435:17
talk of generally held i. BAUD 61:16
total change of i. STER 773:17
two opposed i. FITZ 332:6
Uniform i. originating VICO 827:4
identical they exist, but are i. FORS 338:8
Two things are i. LEIB 488:8
ideological i. empire NAIP 567:4
ides Beware the i. of March SHAK 711:13
i. of March are come SHAK 712:15
proud I., when the squadron rides MACA 508:7
idioms i. appropriate to another RYLE 676:7
licentious i. JOHN 437:12
idiot i. who praises GILB 357:4
portrait of a blinking i. SHAK 724:15
tale Told by an i. SHAK 722:22
idiots fatuity of i. SMIT 758:1
idle addled egg as an i. bird PROV 626:37
be not i. BURT 181:24
employment for his i. time WALT 839:3
Every i. word BIBL 101:7
For i. hands to do WATT 841:12
happiest when I am i. WARD 839:21
home, you i. creatures SHAK 711:11
i. as a painted ship COLE 240:20
i. brain is devil's workshop PROV 635:2
i. have the least leisure PROV 635:3
i., shivering creatures AUST 41:5
i. singer of an empty day MORR 560:12

i. smoke of praise DANI 264:7
i. tales BIBL 106:29
little profits that an i. king TENN 800:14
most i. and unprofitable GIBB 354:19
Never be completely i. THOM 804:18
occupation for an i. hour AUST 41:24
only i. chatter GILB 357:19
solitary, be not i. JOHN 442:26
Tears, i. tears TENN 799:10
We would all be i. JOHN 442:3
when wholly i. SCIP 687:15
work for i. hands PROV 629:42
idleness Grief is a species of i. JOHN 441:5
i. being the root of evil KIER 462:12
I. cannot degrade a man MARA 521:7
I. is only the refuge CHES 223:13
I. is root of all evil PROV 635:4
i. keeps ignorant JOHN 436:10
in I. alone CARL 200:16
penalties of i. POPE 613:26
round of strenuous i. WORD 868:14
idlers i. and Belgians BAUD 62:2
i. of the Empire DOYL 292:23
idling impossible to enjoy i. JERO 433:9
idol God and an i. LUTH 505:9
i. of its own BYRO 190:1
i. of the Anglo-Saxon BAGE 50:16
i. that is nothing PARA 595:16
one-eyed yellow i. HAYE 385:16
young bride was the i. MANZ 521:1
idolaters murderers, and i. BIBL 119:23
never of the i. KORA 471:10
idolatries bowed To its i. BYRO 186:14
idolatry ancients without i. CHES 223:7
god of our i. COWP 255:28
organization of i. SHAW 741:10
idols i. I have loved FITZ 331:27
maltreat our i. FLAU 333:7
if I. it moves, salute it MILI 535:10
i. you can keep your head KERR 461:6
I. you can keep your head KIPL 466:5
much virtue in 'i.' SHAK 697:27
ifs If i. and ands were pots and pans PROV 635:10
Talk'st thou to me of 'i.' SHAK 731:21
ignara Non i. mali VIRG 829:3
ignis fatuus Reason, an i. ROCH 664:15
ignoble i. ease ROOS 667:17
names i., born to be forgot COWP 255:20
ignorance Disease, I., and Idleness BEVE 77:6
Don't die of i. OFFI 584:6
else an absolute i. GREE 371:15
evil is simply i. FORD 337:4
fact of my i. SOCR 759:15
From i. our comfort flows PRIO 624:11
from i. the Western World JOHN 437:25
hindrance of i. PALI 594:21
i. and confidence TWAI 820:25
i. and simple-heartedness LERM 490:1
I. excuses from sin AUCT 36:12
I. is an evil weed BEVE 77:5
I. is bliss PROV 647:8
I. is like a delicate WILD 854:18
i. is never better FERM 325:12
I. is not innocence BROW 166:7
I. is strength ORWE 587:11
i. of nature HOLB 403:1
I. of the law PROV 635:39
I. of the law SELD 691:11
i. or profaneness MATH 527:15
in i. sedate JOHN 438:11
more than Gothic i. FIEL 326:20
no sin but i. MARL 522:16
Only i. SEWE 693:3
pity his i. DICK 279:14
pure i. JOHN 439:9
smallest allowance for i. HUXL 423:10
some i. or other BALZ 56:16
understand a writer's i. COLE 241:19
Where i. is bliss GRAY 370:13
With a knowing i. JOHN 434:4
women in a state of i. KNOX 470:8
ignorant always be i. AUST 41:21

Asking the i. ZOBE 878:4
Be not i. of any thing BIBL 97:10
Confound the i. SHAK 701:21
idleness keeps i. JOHN 436:10
i. and free JEFF 432:7
i. armies clash ARNO 29:6
i. of these magnificent things MCEW 510:13
In language, the i. DUPP 300:6
judgements of the i. BURK 176:10
many i. men are sure DARR 266:5
right of the i. man CARL 199:6
To be i. CICE 231:24
ignorantly i. worship BIBL 110:3
ignores most poetry i. most people MITC 550:12
Ignotus I. moritur sibi SENE 692:21
Ike I like I. POLI 612:21
Iliad greater than the I. PROP 625:1
Ilium fuit I. VIRG 829:13
topless towers of I. MARL 522:9
ill do bravely i. LEE 487:13
ever to do i. MILT 541:14
final goal of i. TENN 795:12
For certain i. DRAY 293:16
i. and the stopping of ill PALI 594:1
ill-clad, i.-nourished ROOS 667:8
I. fares the land GOLD 364:2
i.-favoured thing, sir SHAK 697:25
i.-fed, ill-killed JOHN 443:22
I. gotten goods never thrive PROV 635:40
i. he cannot cure ARNO 31:6
I. met by moonlight SHAK 726:2
I. news hath wings DRAY 293:12
i. wind that blows PROV 636:31
Looking i. prevail SUCK 779:12
means to do i. deeds SHAK 714:13
Nothing i. come near thee SHAK 698:25
one-third of a nation i.-housed ROOS 667:8
or of i. breeding CONG 247:19
she's not really i. JAGG 427:9
so illiberal and so i.-bred CHES 223:8
Some think him i.-tempered LEAR 486:3
speak i. of the dead PROV 639:43
suppressed i.-feeling BAGE 51:9
vain, i.-natured DEFO 270:23
warn you not to fall i. KINN 465:1
illacrimabiles omnes i. HORA 414:3
illegal i., immoral, or fattening WOOL 864:18
means that it is not i. NIXO 576:14
Nothing is i. if YOUN 876:7
illegally accomplishes great things i. BALZ 57:4
illegitimate i. child of Karl Marx ATTL 35:9
no i. children GLAD 359:12
illegitimi Nil carborundum i. SAYI 685:4
illiberal so i. and so ill-bred CHES 223:8
illimitable i. was annihilated DISR 284:16
illiterate i. bulk of mankind BERK 72:15
I. him, I say SHER 748:9
i. king HENR 391:21
illness i. identified with evil SONT 761:5
I. is the doctor PROU 625:13
i. should attend it SHAK 718:19
Living is an i. CHAM 214:14
makes i. worthwhile SHAW 739:12
treatment of an i. WITT 861:9
illnesses i. and dreary old age VIRG 833:1
ills climax of all human i. BYRO 188:18
cure for the i. of Democracy ADDA 4:6
i. of democracy SMIT 756:10
i. to come GRAY 370:11
mark what i. JOHN 438:6
O'er a' the i. o' life BURN 179:14
illuminated i. his kingdom JOIN 445:5
i. trouser-clip for bicyclists MORT 562:5
illuminating i. for her everything TOLS 813:10
illuminatio Dominus i. mea BIBL 119:25
Dominus i. mea MOTT 563:8
illumine What in me is dark, I. MILT 541:10
illusion great i. ANGE 15:16
only an i. EINS 306:1
sophistry and i. HUME 419:16
illusions friend of flattering i. CONR 249:6
life's i. I recall MITC 550:17

illusions (*cont.*):
specious i. GODW 361:4
illustration i. of character JAME 429:21
illustrious I. acts high raptures WALL 837:2
Illyria what should I do in I. SHAK 734:29
image age demanded an i. POUN 621:3
Best i. of myself MILT 543:18
created him in his own i. DOST 290:18
God's i. man doth bear SPEG 765:17
graven i. BIBL 81:15
his i., cut in ebony FULL 346:8
his Maker's i. DRYD 294:8
i. of death ELIO 308:10
i. of eternity BYRO 187:4
i. of God TALM 789:6
i. of his God GRAI 368:6
i. of his person BIBL 115:30
i. of passion BART 60:8
i. of the Creator BONA 132:6
I., that, flying WORD 866:2
just an i. GODA 360:20
kills the i. of God MILT 545:22
kindly paternal i. DANT 265:3
make man in our i. BIBL 78:16
Met his own i. SHEL 745:19
votre i. me suit RACI 653:1
worship the golden i. BIBL 95:22
imagery for their i. MCEW 510:13
images Bygone i. COLE 242:11
Fresh i. beget YEAT 872:12
garden of bright i. BRAM 154:15
I. split the truth LEVE 491:4
reflects i. ADAM 2:14
unpurged i. of day YEAT 872:10
imaginary i. relish SHAK 734:15
i. rights BENT 71:2
indistinguishable from the i. GIDE 355:19
make i. evils GOLD 365:1
imagination ages of i. BLAK 126:21
blow [dealt] to all i. DISR 284:16
car of the i. JAME 429:11
dream of our own i. BACO 48:21
exercising the i. GIRA 359:9
f—gg—g his i. BYRO 192:10
force of i. DRYD 296:5
hunting-grounds for the poetic i. ELIO 307:21
ideal of i. KANT 453:2
i. amend them SHAK 727:8
i. bodies forth SHAK 727:3
i. cold and barren BURK 173:11
i. droops her pinion BYRO 188:29
i. for his facts SHER 749:1
i. is not required JOHN 439:19
I. is the highest kite BACA 45:2
I., not invention CONR 249:9
i. of a boy KEAT 454:2
i. of man's heart BIBL 79:24
i. of their hearts BIBL 104:9
i. resembled MACA 507:22
i. sleeps CAMU 196:16
i. the rudder KEAT 457:11
i. to the proper pitch LACK 475:6
I., which in truth WORD 868:21
It is by i. SMIT 755:25
lava of the i. BYRO 191:25
nothing but his i. SHAW 740:9
of i. all compact SHAK 727:2
of moral good is the i. SHEL 747:11
primary i. COLE 241:20
save those that have no i. SHAW 742:14
shaping spirit of i. COLE 239:11
stimulate the i. RUSS 675:12
sweeten my i. SHAK 716:18
takes a lot of i. BAIL 52:5
Television contracts i. WOGA 862:10
truth of i. KEAT 457:12
Vision or i. BLAK 128:7
Where there is no i. DOYL 292:25
imaginations their own i. BOOK 139:19
imaginative function of i. literature EMPS 315:28
imagine *buona i. paterna* DANT 265:3
fewer friends than we i. HOFM 402:14

I. there's no heaven LENN 489:2
people i. a vain thing BOOK 139:12
imagined i. such a device BOOK 140:14
imaginibus *Ex umbris et i.* EPIT 317:6
imagining i. as one's own GIDE 356:4
imaginings horrible i. SHAK 718:16
imitate i. the action SHAK 708:16
i. what is before him BAGE 51:15
Immature poets i. ELIO 311:22
never failed to i. BALD 52:12
imitated can be i. by none CHAT 217:18
i. humanity SHAK 702:16
imitation art of I. LLOY 496:11
art of i. SIDN 751:5
child of i. REYN 659:3
i. in lines and colours POUS 621:17
I. is the sincerest form PROV 635:42
Were endless i. WORD 867:10
imitative most i. of creatures ARIS 27:18
imitatores *O i., servum pecus* HORA 410:18
imitators no garlands for i. SCHI 685:24
immanent I. Will HARD 381:13
Immanuel call his name I. BIBL 92:11
immaturity expression of human i.
BRIT 157:13
immemorial in i. elms TENN 799:22
immense error is i. BOLI 131:14
immolation i. so belied SASS 682:12
immoral art is i. WILD 855:5
good and i. CHUR 229:4
illegal, i., or fattening WOOL 864:18
moral or an i. book WILD 855:14
immorality i. is what they dislike WHIT 851:9
immortal death that is i. LUCR 504:13
do not seek i. life PIND 606:18
free and i. TRAH 814:10
I have I. longings SHAK 696:2
i. as they quote YOUN 876:10
i. hand or eye BLAK 128:3
i. in his own despite POPE 617:20
I., invisible SMIT 759:3
i. part of myself SHAK 728:20
i. spirit grows WORD 868:10
i. with a kiss MARL 522:9
race remains i. VIRG 833:6
sight of that i. sea WORD 867:16
Sire of an i. strain SHEL 743:9
soul is i. PLAT 609:5
soul is i. SOCR 760:3
With cold i. hands SWIN 785:12
immortalia *I. ne speres* HORA 413:18
immortality belief in i. DOST 290:16
cruel i. Consumes TENN 800:8
God, I., Duty ELIO 308:19
i. through my work ALLE 13:17
i. within His kingdom ZORO 879:10
just Ourselves— And I. DICK 281:11
lead me to i. UPAN 821:16
load of i. KEAT 458:1
Milk's leap toward i. FADI 322:12
Millions long for i. ERTZ 320:8
nothing for my i. SCHI 683:14
put on i. BIBL 113:5
they gave, their i. BROO 159:4
Imogen Iago as an I. KEAT 458:3
imp i. of fame SHAK 708:21
impact understand their true i. HEGE 388:14
impaling I. worms COLM 244:6
impartial i. administration PEEL 601:9
neutrality of an i. judge BURK 176:6
pure i. hate THOR 810:3
impartiality i. is bias REIT 658:3
impatience i. would be so much fretted
JOHN 441:4
one cardinal sin: i. KAFK 452:2
impatient growing i. to see him SMIT 757:21
never so i. BOOK 146:14
impavidum *I. ferient ruinae* HORA 412:19
impeachment soft i. SHER 748:21
impediment cause, or just i. BOOK 138:19
impelled i. the steel BYRO 190:6
impenetrable dark i. wood SCOT 689:5
imperative i. is Categorical KANT 452:20

imperatur *non i.* BACO 49:4
imperfect i. man JEFF 431:18
use of an i. medium WILD 855:16
yet being i. BOOK 149:19
imperfections Dote on his i. EPHE 316:7
i. on my head SHAK 700:22
than i. ADDI 5:10
imperial act Of the i. theme SHAK 718:15
our great I. family ELIZ 313:1
imperialism I. is the monopoly stage
LENI 488:15
I.'s face AUDE 38:6
imperialisms prey of rival i. KENY 461:3
imperium *I. et Libertas* DISR 285:10
impermanent consider what is i. PALI 593:10
impertinent ask an i. question BRON 158:1
ask i. questions DARW 267:2
impious lift an i. hand BRON 158:4
implacable i. in hate DRYD 294:15
importance i. of a work of art FLAU 334:1
no greater i. to the universe HUME 420:12
taking decisions of i. PARK 597:7
important being less i. MONT 555:6
i. book, the critic assumes WOOL 864:10
i. to be clever *about* MEDA 530:2
same as i. PRAT 622:9
trivial and the i. POTT 620:8
imports i. and exports ARIS 26:21
importunate no less i. MONT 555:6
importunity ever-haunting i. LAMB 477:10
impossibilities i. enough in religion
BROW 162:25
Probable i. ARIS 27:22
impossibility Upon I. MARV 524:18
impossible certain because it is i. TERT 802:12
Dream the i. DARI 266:2
eliminated the i. DOYL 292:20
i. shore ARNO 30:23
i. takes a little longer MILI 535:6
i. takes a little longer NANS 567:8
i. takes a little longer PROV 630:2
i.? that will be done CALO 194:1
i. to be silent BURK 176:1
i. to carry the heavy burden EDWA 304:5
i. to enjoy idling JERO 433:9
nothing is i. BISH 122:5
six i. things CARR 203:8
something is i. CLAR 233:14
That not i. she CRAS 259:12
'Tis a thing i. WORD 865:15
wish it were i. JOHN 444:14
impostors invented by i. GODW 361:4
treat those two i. KIPL 466:5
impotent i. people, sick THOM 807:10
imprecision Decay with i. ELIO 309:7
mess of i. of feeling ELIO 309:13
impresses i. me most about America
EDWA 304:6
impression novel is an i. HARD 381:1
impressionable at an i. age SPAR 765:10
impressions First i. PROV 632:21
first i. of his youth GOET 362:16
unweaving of false i. ELIO 308:14
imprint set it in i. CAXT 212:4
imprison Take me to you, i. me DONN 288:13
imprisoned taken or i. MAGN 515:1
imprisonment protracted i. of the accused
HUME 421:1
improbability high degree of i. FISH 330:14
life is statistical i. DAWK 269:3
improbable i. possibilities ARIS 27:22
whatever remains, *however i.* DOYL 292:20
improper noun, proper or i. FULL 346:6
impropriety It is an i. BRAD 153:21
without i. GILB 356:22
improve I. each shining hour WATT 841:11
i. the nick of time THOR 809:13
we i. them as far as GOET 362:21
improved i. by death SAKI 678:1
improvement Each thing called i. BLAM 128:15
lives show little i. THOM 804:22
schemes of political i. JOHN 440:19

improvements new i. had superseded BABB 44:10
no great i. MILL 535:21
improves one i. *oneself* GIDE 356:5
improvident i., indecent hearts BROW 163:23
impudence starve for want of i. DRYD 295:18
impudent called John a I. Bitch FLEM 334:20
impulse first i. CORN 251:15
i. from a vernal wood WORD 869:14
i. of the moment AUST 42:10
impulses no truck with first i. MONT 556:12
impune *Nemo me i. lacessit* MOTT 563:12
impunity provokes me with i. MOTT 563:12
impure to the Puritan all things are i. LAWR 483:11
imputantur *pereunt et i.* MART 524:6
imputeth Lord i. no sin BOOK 141:16
in going out, and thy coming i. BOOK 148:18
I. it is what is in it JALA 428:15
KNEW YOU HAD IT I. YOU PARK 596:14
who's i., who's out SHAK 717:1
inability i. to cross the street WOOL 864:12
i. to live GONC 365:24
inaccuracy i. sometimes saves SAKI 678:7
inaction i. sap the vigour LEON 489:18
inactivity genius for i. LIPP 495:9
masterly i. MACK 511:19
inadequate not that we are i. WILL 858:14
so much as an i. life BREC 155:17
inadvertence by chance or i. HAIL 376:9
inane in the intense i. SHEL 746:2
inapprehensible I., we clutch THOM 807:21
inarticulate raid on the i. ELIO 309:13
inaudible I. as dreams COLE 239:18
inborn is is i. JUNG 449:10
inbreeding sick with i. THOM 807:10
incantation i. of this verse SHEL 745:12
incapable i. of governing CHES 223:19
incapacity courted by I. BLAK 126:5
sanctuary of i. CHES 222:22
incarnadine multitudinous seas i. SHAK 720:9
incarnate Is i. SMAR 754:9
incarnatus *i. est* MISS 549:13
incense gods themselves throw i. SHAK 717:2
stupefying i.-smoke BROW 165:5
unfabled I. Tree DARL 266:3
incensed I. with indignation MILT 542:16
incest i. and folk-dancing ANON 21:17
inch every i. a king SHAK 716:16
Every other i. a gentleman WEST 849:2
Inchcape It is the I. Rock SOUT 764:11
inches die by i. HENR 392:8
thirty i. from my nose AUDE 38:3
incident curious i. of the dog DOYL 292:17
determination of i. JAME 429:21
incipe *I., parve puer* VIRG 832:3
incisors i. and grinders BAGE 51:11
incite nature would not i. UPDI 822:23
incivility i. and procrastination DE Q 273:22
inclementia *durae rapit i. mortis* VIRG 833:1
inclination door of i. DEFO 270:9
greatest enemy is i. BAHY 52:3
i. to goodness BACO 47:5
just as i. leads him JOHN 439:21
incline I. our hearts BOOK 136:21
i. your ears BOOK 145:5
inclined he i. unto me BOOK 141:30
sins, they are i. to BUTL 183:14
include i. me out GOLD 365:18
incognito preserving my I. ELIO 308:15
income Annual i. twenty pounds DICK 277:10
certain level of i. FRIS 343:16
dread a dead-level of i. TAWN 791:2
Expenditure rises to meet i. PARK 597:4
however great the i. CATO 209:20
large i. the best recipe AUST 41:15
live beyond its i. BUTL 184:8
moderate i. DURH 300:13
incomes apt to live up to their i. SMIL 755:21
income tax I. made more liars ROGE 666:3
incommunicable burden of the i. DE Q 273:16
distrust the i. SART 682:2
incomparable i. Max SHAW 742:19

incompatible Thought i. by men LEWI 492:5
united things long i. TACI 786:18
incompetence rise to his level of i. PETE 604:16
incompleteness afraid of i. MURD 565:18
incomprehensible most i. fact EINS 305:11
use the i. ZOBE 878:4
incomprehensibles three i. BOOK 134:13
inconceivable i. that I should be the age MERW 533:4
something i. GILB 357:2
inconnu *Au fond de l'i.* BAUD 61:14
inconsiderable Pain is an i. thing SENE 692:12
inconsistency found in it much i. KORA 471:19
inconstancy constant, but i. SWIF 783:22
Constant, in Nature were i. COWL 254:15
thine own i. CARE 198:16
this i. is such LOVE 502:7
inconstant i. toads MONT 554:9
i. woman GAY 351:23
incontinence filth and foul i. SPEN 767:16
inconvenience Change without i. JOHN 435:16
great i. PROV 641:44
i. is often considerable AUST 41:7
i. is only an adventure CHES 225:1
i. of violence WALK 836:8
inconveniences i., and those weighty HOOK 406:9
i. there must be HALI 377:14
inconvenient cause may be i. BENN 70:17
even when it is i. VIDA 827:17
i. to be poor COWP 254:26
incorporate very members i. BOOK 137:18
incorporeal there is a Being i. NEWT 574:1
incorruptible dead shall be raised i. BIBL 113:5
seagreen I. CARL 200:2
to an i. crown CHAR 216:22
incorruption assurance of i. BIBL 97:5
put on i. BIBL 113:5
raised in i. BIBL 113:3
increase bring forth her i. BOOK 144:5
God gave the i. BIBL 111:26
I. and multiply BOOK 136:4
i. in thy holy Spirit BOOK 138:18
i. of his government BIBL 92:14
Some races i. LUCR 504:10
we desire i. SHAK 737:15
who dies fighting has i. GREN 372:10
increased i. by one penny CART 205:15
increasing has increased, is i. DUNN 300:5
incredible i. as if you fired RUTH 676:4
incrédules *I. les plus crédules* PASC 598:6
incurable Life is an i. disease COWL 254:20
indecency I.'s conspiracy of silence SHAW 741:21
indecent sent down for i. behaviour WAUG 842:12
indecision nothing is habitual but i. JAME 430:14
indefensible defence of the i. ORWE 588:1
indemnity BILL OF I. . . . . FOR RAID KRUG 473:20
independence i. of America SHEL 742:28
i. of judges DENN 273:11
right to i. NAMI 567:7
independent easy to be i. JACK 426:13
entirely i. TOCQ 812:8
most truly i. MADI 514:9
simply i. choice DOST 291:8
indestructible i. Union CHAS 217:17
it is i. UPAN 822:3
index i. of a feeling mind CRAB 258:3
wasn't even in the i. CURR 263:6
indexes memories are card-i. CONN 248:11
India beautiful in I. NEHR 569:14
driven out of I. BURK 175:21
Englishman to rule in I. NEHR 569:15
final message of I. FORS 338:11
I.'s coral strand HEBE 388:8
I. will awake to life NEHR 569:9
key of I. DISR 285:11
my blood will invigorate I. GAND 348:10
Nothing in I. is identifiable FORS 338:7
peaceably and happily in I. VICT 827:11
Indian be an I. and not be proud GAND 348:9

Every step the I. takes RIEL 661:10
I. boy, how exotic KURE 474:9
I. Crown ROSS 669:10
I. in blood and colour MACA 508:23
I. wilderness MATH 527:13
Like the base I. SHAK 729:23
Lo! the poor I. POPE 616:20
only good I. PROV 640:34
Indians excluding I. not taxed CONS 250:2
I. are you BALD 52:16
only good I. SHER 747:23
to convert the I. WESL 847:24
indictment i. against an whole people BURK 173:15
Indies augmentation of the I. SHAK 736:1
indifference ill at ease under i. ELIO 307:5
i. and a coach and six COLM 244:1
i. begun RICH 660:13
i. closely bordering on STEV 775:14
i. or frozen stare ELIO 307:24
it's i. WIES 853:11
morn and cold i. ROWE 671:5
superb i. WEIL 845:6
indifferent delayed till I am i. JOHN 439:7
I. in his choice ADDI 4:23
It is simply i. HOLM 403:9
to be i. to them SHAW 739:19
indifferently i. minister justice BOOK 137:6
indigenous i. variety FINK 327:11
indigestion moral i. ANTR 24:20
indignant this i. page BLAK 127:21
indignatio *facit i. versum* JUVE 450:13
I. principis mors est MORE 559:10
indignation fierce i. EPIT 319:14
i. makes me write verse JUVE 450:13
Moral i. is jealousy WELL 847:2
Savage i. there YEAT 875:2
well-bred i. TURG 818:17
indignities by i. men come to dignities BACO 47:8
indirections By i. find directions out SHAK 701:1
indiscretion cliché and an i. MACM 512:16
inditing i. of a good matter BOOK 142:12
individual accessible to every i. WELL 847:3
each separate i. ROBE 663:9
genius overlooks i. SCHO 686:12
in an i. way HORA 409:5
i. men and women THAT 804:1
liberty of the i. MILL 536:7
No i. could resent SWIF 784:10
not an i. FIEL 326:13
not the i., but the species JOHN 437:14
individualism system of rugged i. HOOV 406:13
individuals I. pass like shadows BURK 175:18
love is towards i. SWIF 782:20
shortcomings of i. HEGE 388:14
indivisible Freedom is an i. word WILL 858:18
Peace is i. LITV 495:15
indolence girl in the i. of youth YEAT 874:8
indolent i. expression BELL 68:13
indomitable i. Irishry YEAT 875:8
indulgent makes one very i. STAË 769:10
industrial i. worker would sooner BLYT 130:3
industrialists die for the i. FRAN 340:13
industry Captains of i. CARL 200:17
i., and vigilance BEET 66:13
i. applies ANON 20:7
i. is to be paralysed TAWN 791:6
i. seems inefficient SCHU 687:3
I., Which dignifies the artist DYER 301:7
i. will improve them REYN 658:18
i. without art RUSK 673:8
national i. of Prussia MIRA 546:14
not his i. only BURK 175:15
river of human i. TOCQ 812:16
spur of i. HUME 420:2
that of a major i. SARR 681:5
indutus *redit exuvias i. Achilli* VIRG 829:11
inebriate cheer but not i. BERK 72:12
cheer but not i. COWP 256:19
ineffectual beautiful and i. angel ARNO 31:22

ineffectual (cont.):
Remote and i. Don — BELL 68:11
inefficient efficient and the i. — SHAW 740:11
industry seems i. — SCHU 687:3
inertia *Strenua nos exercet i.* — HORA 410:10
inessential save five *sous* on i. things — COLB 238:18
inestimable thine i. love — BOOK 135:8
inevitability i. of gradualness — WEBB 843:10
inevitable arguing with the i. — LOWE 503:2
inexactitude terminological i. — CHUR 229:2
inexcusable done something i. — ALAI 10:12
inexorable deaf, i. — SIDN 750:11
inexperienced i. house — JERO 433:11
inextinguishable i. thought — SHEL 747:12
infallible only i. rule — SURT 781:5
infâme *écrasez l'i.* — VOLT 834:19
infamous rich, quiet, and i. — MACA 507:14
infamy date which will live in i. — ROOS 667:13
infancy about us in our i. — WORD 867:8
like men, have their i. — BOLI 131:13
infandum *I., regina* — VIRG 829:4
infant i. beauty could beget — SEDL 690:16
i. crying in the night — TENN 795:14
i., Mewling and puking — SHAK 696:28
i. phenomenon — DICK 279:16
Sooner murder an i. — BLAK 126:18
infantile second i. — ARIS 26:15
infected All seems i. — POPE 616:11
infection Against i. — SHAK 730:10
infectious i. greed — GREE 372:3
infects bad news i. — SHAK 694:12
i. the world — ARNO 30:4
infelicity Of constant i. — WORD 865:16
sense of a constant i. — TAYL 792:5
inferior disgraced by the i. — SHAW 741:15
i. man is partisan — CONF 245:17
i. to the gods — HORA 413:1
intoxication which i. men — BALZ 56:13
make you feel i. — ROOS 667:1
myself i. to myself — MILT 546:9
inferiority conscious of an i. — JOHN 442:5
feeling of i. — ADLE 6:8
inferiors English want i. — TOCQ 812:15
inferno i. of his passions — JUNG 449:11
infidel Now, i., I have you — SHAK 725:4
infidelity absence of i. — LAWS 484:17
geologists into i. — GOSS 366:12
I. does not consist — PAIN 592:5
infidels no American i. — SAHH 677:10
infini *l'i. me tourmente* — MUSS 566:10
infinite advance into the i. — GOET 363:2
door to i. wisdom — BREC 155:15
i. in faculty — SHAK 701:11
i. in his desires — LAMA 476:7
i.-resource-and-sagacity — KIPL 468:15
I. riches — MARL 522:17
i. spaces — PASC 598:1
i. torments — MUSS 566:10
i. Void — PALI 594:18
I. wrath — MILT 542:29
in the i. I AM — COLE 241:20
number of worlds is i. — ALEX 12:3
realize the i. — CHUA 227:15
Though i. — MARV 524:19
infinities numberless i. — DONN 288:8
infinitive care what a split i. — FOWL 339:5
when I split an i. — CHAN 215:13
infinity Hold i. — BLAK 124:9
i. of things — PASC 598:4
i. of worlds — BRUN 168:21
To i. and beyond — FILM 329:19
infirmi *i. est animi* — JUVE 451:20
infirmities bear his friend's i. — SHAK 713:24
i. were not noxious — JOHN 439:16
infirmity feblit with i. — DUNB 299:10
i. of his age — SHAK 714:21
i. of noble mind — MILT 540:6
i. of others — HOBB 400:13
prop To our i. — WORD 868:12
inflammation i. of his weekly bills — BYRO 188:18
inflation I. one form of taxation — FRIE 343:10
pay to get i. down — LAMO 477:18

inflections beauty of i. — STEV 774:16
inflicted pain shall not be i. — SPEN 765:20
influence i. in society — LACL 475:7
i. of the Crown — DUNN 300:5
i. on human life — MULL 564:17
no trivial i. — WORD 866:9
planetary i. — SHAK 714:24
under the name of I. — BURK 175:1
where his i. stops — ADAM 2:16
win friends and i. people — CARN 201:4
influences bind the sweet i. — BIBL 87:12
in-folded tongues of flame are i. — ELIO 309:22
inform i. his princes — BOOK 147:12
not to i. the reader — ACHE 1:14
occasions do i. against me — SHAK 703:27
information Didactic rushes of i. — BYAT 184:22
find i. upon it — JOHN 441:19
I only ask for i. — DICK 277:14
knowledge we have lost in i. — ELIO 310:23
little i. — AUST 42:9
more i. than I needed — FILM 329:18
informed i. by the light of nature — BACO 45:12
infrequens *cultor et i.* — HORA 412:2
Ingeld I. to do with Christ — ALCU 11:9
ingeminate i. the word *Peace* — CLAR 233:7
ingenious harmonical and i. soul — AUBR 36:1
Inglese *I. Italianato* — ASCH 33:8
ingots don't take i. to market — CHAM 214:15
ingratitude I. is the blackest — JUDA 449:2
I., thou marble-hearted fiend — SHAK 715:5
so unkind As man's i. — SHAK 697:4
inhabitants i. o' the earth — SHAK 718:10
inhale didn't i. — CLIN 236:5
if he doesn't i. — STEV 774:18
inherit i. the earth — BIBL 98:25
inheritance Ruinous i. — GAIU 347:8
inherited I have i. nothing — MIDR 534:19
i. from your fathers — GOET 361:15
i. it brick — AUGU 40:4
inheritor i. of the kingdom of heaven — BOOK 138:8
inhibitions cultivate a few i. — LOOS 500:16
inhumanity essence of i. — SHAW 739:19
i. meant cruelty — FROM 344:3
Man's i. to man — BURN 178:27
inimitable i. rose — WINC 860:10
iniquities bruised for our i. — BIBL 94:4
iniquity grey i. — SHAK 706:5
hated i. — BOOK 142:13
hated i. — GREG 372:7
i. of oblivion — BROW 162:18
right hand of i. — BOOK 149:24
initiation i. into a new state — ELIO 307:1
injured Forgiveness to the i. — DRYD 295:16
i. lover's hell — MILT 543:20
i. Woman — BARB 57:21
injuries i. and attempts of other men — LOCK 497:14
insult to i. — MOOR 557:4
redress of i. — BLAC 123:12
revenge for slight i. — MACH 511:6
injury i. is much sooner forgotten — CHES 222:24
[i.] to be the bondage — JAIN 427:16
tone of i. — HELV 390:11
injustice enemies against i. — MISQ 549:1
I. anywhere a threat — KING 463:8
i. makes democracy necessary — NIEB 575:5
justice or i. — JOHN 438:13
No i. is done — ULPI 821:10
protect him against i. — PALM 595:3
so finely felt, as i. — DICK 278:7
That's social i. — FILM 330:2
injustices justify their i. — VOLT 834:1
ink all cough in i. — YEAT 874:16
all the sea were i. — LYLY 505:23
all the sea were i. — NURS 579:5
he hath not drunk i. — SHAK 717:15
i. in my pen ran cold — WALP 837:11
inky not alone my i. cloak — SHAK 699:15
inlaid thick i. with patines — SHAK 725:11
inland i. far we be — WORD 867:16
inlet At a small i. — YOUN 876:24
inmost i. part of you — SHAK 703:9

inn chamber in the i. — ANON 21:16
Do you remember an I., Miranda — BELL 68:24
earth his sober i. — CAMP 195:23
gain the timely i. — SHAK 721:6
i.'s worst room — POPE 615:6
no room for them in the i. — BIBL 104:12
not an i., but an hospital — BROW 163:15
tavern or i. — JOHN 441:25
this soul's second i. — DONN 288:20
warmest welcome, at an i. — SHEN 747:19
world's an i. — DRYD 296:21
innavigable nor sea i. — THOR 810:4
inner have no I. Resources — BERR 75:3
in the i. man — BIBL 114:1
innings get me this i. — JOYC 448:21
Innisfree go to I. — YEAT 873:20
innocence assumption of i. easy — CROS 261:7
badge of lost i. — PAIN 592:8
ceremony of i. is drowned — YEAT 874:17
hanged in all i. — STEV 776:8
Ignorance is not i. — BROW 166:7
i. and beauty born — YEAT 874:11
i. is like a dumb leper — GREE 371:19
I. is next God — LANG 478:21
I. no earthly weapon — HILL 398:13
insists on his i. — CAMU 196:6
loss of i. — HOWA 416:16
moral security of i. — RICH 660:15
Never such i. again — LARK 481:6
not in i. — ARDR 26:5
not to know we sin is i. — D'AV 267:7
speak again of i. — SUTT 781:21
start from an i. — HEMI 391:4
innocency wash my hands in i. — BOOK 141:7
innocent heart whose love is i. — BYRO 190:26
i. and the beautiful — YEAT 873:16
i. are so few — BOWE 153:8
i. men, women, and children — JEFF 432:13
i. of the blood — BIBL 103:21
one i. suffer — BLAC 123:14
shall not be i. — BIBL 89:8
shed i. blood — BIBL 94:17
taken reward against the i. — BOOK 140:2
We are i. — ROSE 668:14
innocents i. abroad — TWAI 820:10
innovation i. in religion — MAEC 514:13
innovations ill-shapen, so are all i. — BACO 47:11
innovator time is the greatest i. — BACO 47:12
inns go to i. to dine — CHES 224:17
I. are not residences — MOOR 557:17
i. should be well kept — PALM 595:5
innuendoes beauty of i. — STEV 774:16
innuendos i. Will serve him no longer — PULT 649:13
inopem *I. me copia fecit* — OVID 590:11
inoperative all previous statements i. — ZIEG 878:2
inquiry subject of i. — BUTL 182:17
inquisition Spanish I. — MONT 557:2
To these I. dogs — TENN 800:1
insane eaten on the i. root — SHAK 718:13
hereditary monarch was i. — BAGE 50:13
Man is quite i. — MONT 555:16
insanius *ligna feras i.* — HORA 414:17
inscription altar with this i. — BIBL 110:3
like a rough i. — YEVT 876:1
inscriptions In lapidary i. — JOHN 441:22
inscrutable I. workmanship — WORD 868:10
insect one is but an i. — JOHN 439:2
'Tortis' is a i. — PUNC 649:22
transformed into a gigantic i. — KAFK 452:3
insects critics are the i. of a day — JARR 430:23
I. sting, not out of malice — NIET 575:15
insecurity international i. — NIEB 575:6
insensibility stark i. — JOHN 438:21
inseparable one and i. — WEBS 843:22
inside i. the tent pissing out — JOHN 435:10
insight i. and the stretch — BROW 164:20
insignificance of the utmost i. — CURZ 263:10
sterling i. — AUST 42:23
insignificant i. and is aware of it — BECK 64:2
i. office — ADAM 3:7

insincerity enemy of clear language i.
　　　　　　　　　　　　　ORWE 587:24
　mark of i. of purpose　　　　BRAM 154:16
insolence flown with i. and wine　MILT 541:25
　i. is not invective　　　　　DISR 284:13
　i. of wealth　　　　　　　JOHN 442:17
　supports with i.　　　　　JOHN 436:4
　Wit is educated i.　　　　　ARIS 27:1
insolent Hunger is i.　　　　POPE 618:1
insomnia *mittunt i. Manes*　VIRG 830:16
　suffering from ideal i.　　　JOYC 448:2
inspiration Genius is one per cent i.
　　　　　　　　　　　　　EDIS 303:15
　i. of the founding fathers　　HARD 380:7
　life was an i.　　　　　　STAN 769:19
　truth from i.'s furnace　　　LEWI 492:7
inspire our souls i.　　　　BOOK 150:16
inspired i. by divine revelation　BACO 45:12
inspissated i. gloom　　　　JOHN 440:18
instability mark of i.　　　　GALB 347:10
instant in season　　　　　BIBL 115:27
instantaneous i. courage　　NAPO 568:4
instinct believe upon i.　　　BRAD 154:2
　coward on i.　　　　　　SHAK 706:2
　do work by i.　　　　　　MATI 528:2
　healthy i. for it　　　　　BUTL 184:12
　intimate with by i.　　　　AUST 41:16
instincts i. and abilities　　　BALZ 56:14
　panders to i.　　　　　　BENN 70:7
　true to your i.　　　　　LAWR 483:15
institute on in the I.　　　　BETJ 76:4
institution change an i.　　　TUSA 819:16
　i. which does not suppose　ROBE 663:11
　It's an i.　　　　　　　HUGH 418:16
　place, person, or i.　　　ARNO 32:17
　transformed into an i.　　SART 682:3
institutional i. racism　　　MACP 513:18
institutions acquiring their i. by chance
　　　　　　　　　　　　　HAIL 376:9
　amending her own i.　　　GODW 361:6
　with their dirty i.　　　　THOR 809:20
instruct i. them　　　　　AURE 40:21
　when they might i.　　　　MORE 559:1
instructing same time as i. him　HORA 409:12
instruction benefits of i.　　DEFO 270:7
　better the i.　　　　　　SHAK 724:20
　horses of i.　　　　　　BLAK 126:14
　i. in the Law　　　　　JAIN 428:3
　I. is the pill　　　　　RICH 660:18
　needs no i.　　　　　　JAIN 427:17
　no i. book came with it　FULL 346:7
instructions AWAITING I.　　BEER 66:4
instrument i. of science　　JOHN 435:17
　i. of Your peace　　　　FRAN 340:17
　I tune the i.　　　　　DONN 288:17
　State is an i.　　　　　STAL 769:14
instrumental i. to the brain　SHAK 699:10
　original or i.　　　　　HOBB 400:19
instruments i. of their crooked designs
　　　　　　　　　　　　　GODW 361:4
　with the aid of the i.　　HOLB 402:21
insubstantial this i. pageant　SHAK 733:31
insufferable Oxford has made me i.
　　　　　　　　　　　　　BEER 65:18
insular i. country, subject to fogs　DISR 285:26
insularum *Paene i.*　　　CATU 210:9
insult blockhead's i.　　　JOHN 438:2
　i. to injuries　　　　　MOOR 557:4
　sooner forgotten than an i.　CHES 222:24
　threatened her with i.　　BURK 174:6
insulted never *hope* to get i.　DAVI 268:11
insulting i. Christmas card　GROS 374:3
insupportable i. labour　　STEE 770:13
insuppressible i. island　　KETT 461:12
insurance form of moral i.　BROD 157:15
　National compulsory i.　　CHUR 230:3
intact is there, i.　　　　TRIM 815:14
intangible world i., we touch　THOM 807:21
integer *I. vitae*　　　　HORA 411:19
integers God made the i.　　KRON 473:15
integral i. and differential calculus　GILB 358:6
integration policy of European i.　KOHL 470:13
integrity I. has no need of rules　CAMU 196:10

i. of my intellect　　　　FARA 323:9
i. without knowledge　　　JOHN 437:20
intellect highest i.　　　MACA 507:8
　integrity of my i.　　　　FARA 323:9
　i. of man is forced to choose　YEAT 872:13
　march of i.　　　　　　SOUT 764:17
　not i. but rather memory　LEON 489:16
　Our meddling i.　　　　WORD 869:15
　put on i.　　　　　　BLAK 125:20
　restless and versatile i.　HUXL 423:16
　scepticism of the i.　　NEWM 572:6
　strengthening one's i.　KEAT 458:12
　tickle the i.　　　　　LAMB 476:19
intellects hearts and i.　　EPIT 319:18
intellectual i. ability　　　ARNO 32:14
　i. All-in-all　　　　　WORD 868:5
　i., amongst the noblest　CALV 194:5
　i. bankruptcy　　　　HOLM 403:15
　i. degradation　　　　MORE 559:2
　I. disgrace Stares　　AUDE 37:11
　i. eunuch Castlereagh　BYRO 187:19
　i. improvement　　　JOHN 441:7
　i. is someone whose mind　CAMU 196:3
　i. nature　　　　　JOHN 436:24
　'I.' suggests　　　　AUDE 37:18
　ladies i.　　　　　BYRO 187:21
　no i. superiority　　　AUST 41:2
　tear is an i. thing　　BLAK 125:14
　to the i. world　　　STER 773:11
intellectuals treachery of the i.　BEND 69:11
intelligence arresting human i.　LEAC 485:6
　bewitchment of our i.　WITT 861:8
　first-rate i.　　　　FITZ 332:6
　I. is quickness to apprehend　WHIT 851:8
　people have little i.　LA B 474:18
　proud of his i.　　　WEIL 845:5
　started at the i.　　SOUT 764:22
　you pawn your i.　　CUMM 262:5
intelligent Every i. voter　ADAM 2:7
　most i. and most stupid　CONF 246:20
　Most i., very elegant　BUCK 169:15
　not necessarily i.　CHAM 215:3
　pleasing one i. man　MAIM 516:13
　rule of i. tinkering　EHRL 304:14
　so i.　　　　　ELIO 311:9
intemperance brisk i. of youth　GIBB 354:20
intend what I well i.　SHAK 714:19
intensity full of passionate i.　YEAT 874:17
intent first avowed i.　BUNY 171:25
　glorious great i.　SPEN 767:7
　hospitable thoughts i.　MILT 543:19
　i. is al　　　　　CHAU 221:10
　sides of my i.　　SHAK 719:10
　told with bad i.　BLAK 124:14
intention i. to keep my counsel　GLAD 360:7
intentions devour second i.　RABE 652:10
　God weighs the i.　THOM 805:1
　i. make blackguards　LACL 475:8
　only had good i.　THAT 803:15
　paved with good i.　PROV 642:26
　produced by their good i.　WALP 838:5
interact do not i. at all　UPDI 822:24
intercession made i.　BIBL 94:6
interdependence closely knit i.　HARD 381:6
interdependent everything is i.　ZOHA 878:7
interest i.'s on the dangerous edge
　　　　　　　　　　　　　BROW 164:26
　i. that keeps peace　CROM 260:16
　its duty and its i.　WASH 840:18
　language of i.　HELV 390:11
　natural i. of money　MACA 507:5
　passion or i.　LOCK 497:11
　regard to their own i.　SMIT 756:1
　unbound by any i.　HORA 411:3
interested i. him no more　HART 383:17
　i. in life　　　CHAM 214:10
　i. in the arts　AYCK 43:14
　i. in things　CURI 262:20
　only i. in art　SHAW 742:22
interesting i. actions　BAGE 51:1
　i., but tough　TWAI 819:19
　live in i. times　KENN 460:21
　live in i. times　SAYI 685:2

proposition be i.　　　WHIT 851:4
things and characters i.　SCOT 689:28
Very i. . . . but　　　CATC 208:30
interests Our i. are eternal　PALM 595:2
　own rights and i.　MILL 535:22
interfere denomination does not i.
　　　　　　　　　　　　　FRED 341:22
interjection is but an I.　BYRO 189:23
interline diminish, i.　SWIF 783:29
intermission i. of pain　SELD 691:17
internal i. attrition　AURE 40:14
international dependable i. emotion
　　　　　　　　　　　　　ALSO 13:21
　i. wrong　　　　AUDE 38:6
Internationale *L'I.*　POTT 620:14
Internet I. is an élite　CHOM 226:17
　I., nobody knows you're a dog
　　　　　　　　　　　　　CART 205:14
　thanks to the I.　WILE 856:20
interpose i. my body　STRA 778:13
interpretation i. of the future　THUC 810:6
　lost in i.　　　FROS 345:12
interpretations interpreting i.　MONT 555:26
interpret i.　　　DERR 274:5
interpreted i. the world　MARX 526:9
interpreter i. is the hardest　SHER 748:3
　i. of nature　WHEW 850:4
　Nature's agent and i.　BACO 48:29
interpreters i. between us and the millions
　　　　　　　　　　　　　MACA 508:23
interrèd good is oft i.　SHAK 712:28
intersecting i. monologues　WEST 848:22
interstellar vacant i. spaces　ELIO 309:11
interstice every i. of my body　EDDI 302:17
interstices i. between the intersections
　　　　　　　　　　　　　JOHN 436:2
intervals lucid i.　BACO 48:22
intervening i. windings　WHAR 849:9
interview strange and fatal i.　DONN 288:3
interviewer i. allows you to say　BENN 70:5
intimacy avoid any i.　KITC 469:4
　determine i.　AUST 42:24
　every old i.　LAMB 476:11
intimate i. with by instinct　AUST 41:16
intimidation without i.　ROBE 663:14
intolerable burden of them is i.　BOOK 137:10
　Suffering is only i.　SAUN 682:13
intolerance I. of groups　FREU 342:17
intolerant not to tolerate the i.　POPP 619:3
intoxicated God-i. man　NOVA 577:12
　i. with power　BURK 172:15
　when he is i.　JOHN 442:24
intoxication best of life is but i.　BYRO 188:10
　i. which inferior men　BALZ 56:13
intreat I. me not to leave thee　BIBL 83:23
intrepid natural and i.　WALP 837:8
intricated Poor i. soul　DONN 290:12
intrigues I. half-gathered　CRAB 257:10
intrinsicate knot i. Of life　SHAK 696:4
introduce allow me to i. myself　JAGG 427:12
introduced been i. to　CARR 203:24
introduction i. to any literary work　JOHN 439:8
　pages of I.　ELIO 308:17
introibo *I. at altare Dei*　MISS 546:18
intruding rash, i. fool　SHAK 703:12
intrusion I call it i.　SPAR 765:12
intuition I. of truth　BLAK 128:10
invades first i. the ear　DRYD 295:12
　i. authors like a monarch　DRYD 297:16
invalid i. called Bunbury　WILD 854:16
invasion i. by an idea　HUGO 419:3
invective insolence is not i.　DISR 284:13
invent first i. the universe　SAGA 677:7
　fitter to i.　BACO 48:20
　necessary to i. him　VOLT 834:8
　one man can i.　DOYL 292:18
　to i. it　KAY 453:17
invented England i. the phrase　BAGE 50:10
　i. the brake　NEME 570:8
　Truth exists, lies are i.　BRAQ 155:7
invention brightest heaven of i.　SHAK 708:7
　[bureaucracy's] specific i.　WEBE 843:18
　by i. got　SWIF 784:6
　heir of my i.　SHAK 738:26

made I. from designs — TWAI 820:12
Oh, my own I. — PETR 604:19
Paradise of exiles, I. — SHEL 744:10
itch i. of literature — LOVE 502:10
poor i. of your opinion — SHAK 698:3
itching have an i. palm — SHAK 713:20
ite *I. domum saturae* — VIRG 832:11
I. missa est — MISS 550:1
iteration damnable i. — SHAK 705:11
i. of the nuptials — CONG 247:28
itself Everything is not i. — RILK 661:17
Forever be I. again — GINS 358:21
itur *sic i. ad astra* — VIRG 831:7
Itylus half assuaged for I. — SWIN 784:19
iubeo *sic i.* — JUVE 451:3
iubes *i. renovare dolorem* — VIRG 829:4
Iudaeus *Credit I. Apella* — HORA 414:15
iudice *se I.* — JUVE 451:19
sub i. lis est — HORA 409:2
iunctura *Reddiderit i. novum* — HORA 408:18
iurare *i. in verba magistri* — HORA 409:18
ivory as if done in i. — FULL 346:8
belly is as bright i. — BIBL 91:10
cargo of i. — MASE 527:3
gleaming white i. — VIRG 830:16
in his i. tower — SAIN 677:12
i., and apes — BIBL 84:29
i. on which I work — AUST 43:4
neck is as a tower of i. — BIBL 91:15
out of the i. gate — BROW 163:19
upon an i. sled — MARL 523:2
ivy holly and the i. — SONG 762:12
it was agony, I. — CATC 207:16
pluck an i. branch for me — ROSS 669:3
yonder i.-mantled tow'r — GRAY 370:2

Jabberwock Beware the J., my son — CARR 202:21
jack about J. a Nory — NURS 579:7
Damn you, J. — BONE 132:8
Every J. has his Jill — PROV 631:21
good J. makes a good Jill — PROV 633:22
house that J. built — NURS 581:16
J. and Jill — NURS 579:10
J. as good as his master — PROV 636:43
J. became a gentleman — SHAK 731:16
J. be nimble — NURS 579:11
J. of all trades — PROV 636:44
J. shall have Jill — SHAK 726:23
J. Sprat could eat no fat — NURS 579:12
Little J. Horner — NURS 579:18
makes J. a dull boy — PROV 626:23
news of my boy J. — KIPL 466:19
This J., joke — HOPK 408:1
jackals J. piss at their foot — FLAU 334:5
jackdaw J. sat on the Cardinal's chair — BARH 58:8
jacket *short* j. — EDWA 304:3
thresh his old j. — COWP 257:5
jackknife j. has Macheath — BREC 155:24
jacks calls the knaves, J. — DICK 278:6
Jackson J. with his Virginians — BEE 65:10
Jacob as the Angel did with J. — WALT 839:14
God of J. — BIBL 80:38
God of J. — BOOK 142:18
house of J. — BOOK 148:3
J. served seven years — BIBL 80:12
J. was a plain man — BIBL 80:4
sold his birthright unto J. — BIBL 80:5
traffic of J.'s ladder — THOM 808:2
voice is J.'s voice — BIBL 80:7
jade Go spin, you j. — SCOT 689:27
Let the galled j. wince — SHAK 702:24
jades pampered j. — MARL 523:10
pampered j. of Asia — SHAK 707:14
Jael J. Heber's wife — BIBL 82:32
JAH his name J. — BOOK 144:7
jail being in a j. — JOHN 439:12
dey gits you in j. — O'NE 585:7
Go to j. — SAYI 684:22
patron, and the j. — JOHN 438:6
jailbird looks like a j. — BLOK 129:5

jails emptied the British j. — DAY- 269:9
jam j. to-morrow — CARR 203:6
J. tomorrow — PROV 636:45
j. we thought was for — BENN 69:20
jamais j. triste archy — MARQ 523:15
James Bond. J. Bond — FILM 329:9
Home J. — HILL 399:3
J. I, James II, and the Old Pretender — GUED 374:8
J. James Morrison Morrison — MILN 538:3
King J. stay behind — WHAR 849:12
Jameson RAID BY DR J. — KRUG 473:20
Jane J., Jane, tall as a crane — SITW 753:10
you J. — MISQ 548:9
Janus very J. of poets — DRYD 297:18
Janvier J. and Février — NICH 574:16
Japan J.'s advantage — HIRO 399:22
Japanese spirit of a true J. — MOTO 562:15
jar does so J. — GASK 350:10
jargon from J. born to rescue Law — LLOY 496:10
j. of languages — DEFO 270:5
jargons clear of the j. — NIGH 576:3
Jarndyce J. and Jarndyce — DICK 276:10
Wards in J. — DICK 276:23
Jason J. hath received — BIBL 109:34
jasper j. and a sardine stone — BIBL 118:3
jaundiced yellow to the j. eye — POPE 616:11
jaw j.-jaw is always better — CHUR 230:11
let the j. go by — PROV 636:46
with the j. of an ass — BIBL 83:15
jaws gently smiling j. — CARR 201:14
Into the j. of Death — TENN 793:5
j. of hell — VIRG 830:9
j. of power — ADAM 3:11
keep quiet, j. clenched — PAVE 600:6
through the j. of death — LAUD 482:17
jazz J. music is to be played — MORT 562:6
sunbathing and j. — WAUG 842:16
jealous am a j. God — BIBL 81:16
Art is a j. mistress — EMER 314:20
J. in honour — SHAK 697:1
one not easily j. — SHAK 729:23
to the j. — SHAK 728:28
tramp is j. of tramp — HESI 397:2
jealousy Anger and j. — ELIO 308:4
beware, my lord, of j. — SHAK 728:24
ear of j. — BIBL 96:25
J. a human face — BLAK 128:6
j. extinguishes love — MARG 521:12
j. is all the fun — JONG 445:14
j. is cruel as the grave — BIBL 91:16
j. is feeling alone — BOWE 153:11
j. of rivals — ADAM 1:19
j. to the bride — BARR 59:21
j. with a halo — WELL 847:2
No j. Was understood — MILT 543:20
resting from all j. — BEAU 63:11
To j. nothing is more frighful — SAGA 677:9
Jeanie J. with the light brown hair — FOST 339:1
jeepers J. Creepers — MERC 532:8
jeers flouts and j. — DISR 285:4
Jefferson J.—still surv— — ADAM 3:14
Jehovah O thou great J. — WILL 857:9
Jehu J., the son of Nimshi — BIBL 85:33
Jekyll Dr J. and Mr Hyde — STEV 775:15
Jellicoe J. was the only man on either side — CHUR 231:1
jellies With j. soother — KEAT 454:13
jelly blasted, j.-boned swines — LAWR 484:1
J.-bellied Flag-flapper — KIPL 468:24
Meaty j., too — DICK 280:9
nail currant j. — ROOS 667:21
Out, vile j. — SHAK 716:8
jellybeans way of eating j. — REAG 656:14
je-ne-sais-quoi J. young man — GILB 357:22
Jenny J. kissed me — HUNT 421:7
jeopardy in j. of their lives — BIBL 84:24
twice be put in j. — CONS 250:6
jerks bring me up by j. — DICK 278:8
Jerusalem Athens to do with J. — TERT 802:13
hills stand about J. — BOOK 148:23
holy city, new J. — BIBL 119:15
In that J. — SHAK 707:31

J. is built as a city — BOOK 148:19
J. the golden — NEAL 569:8
J. thy sister calls — BLAK 125:17
Next year in J. — HAGG 376:2
O Jerusalem, J. — BIBL 102:21
peace of J. — BOOK 148:20
performed in J. — BOOK 144:1
Till we have built J. — BLAK 126:24
unto J. — BIBL 110:8
waste places of J. — BIBL 94:1
jessamine casement j. stirred — TENN 798:4
j. faint — SHEL 746:9
pale j. — MILT 540:12
Jesse stem of J. — BIBL 92:16
jesses j. were my dear heart-strings — SHAK 728:25
jest bitter is a scornful j. — JOHN 438:2
cover of a j. — HORA 414:7
fellow of infinite j. — SHAK 704:15
good j. for ever — SHAK 705:21
j.'s prosperity — SHAK 717:23
laughing at some j. — KIPL 465:17
Life is a j. — EPIT 318:15
poison in j. — SHAK 702:23
that's no j. — RALE 653:18
true word spoken in j. — PROV 638:27
world's a j. — STEP 772:2
jesting talking, nor j. — BIBL 114:8
jests He j. at scars — SHAK 732:9
to his memory for his j. — SHER 749:1
Jesu J., good above all other — DEAR 269:15
J., lover of my soul — WESL 847:11
J., the very thought — CASW 206:14
Jesuit thing, a tool, a J. — KING 464:16
Jesus another king, one J. — BIBL 109:34
at the name of J. — BIBL 114:19
At the name of J. — NOEL 576:18
blame J. for what was done — BENN 70:1
bon Sansculotte J. — DESM 274:13
come, Lord J. — BIBL 119:24
cross of J. — BARI 58:16
disciple whom J. loved — BIBL 109:9
Gentle J. — WESL 847:12
If J. Christ were to come — CARL 200:31
J. Christ — BIBL 116:12
J. Christ, her Lord — STON 777:10
J. Christ his only Son — BOOK 133:19
J. is there only for others — BONH 132:13
J. loves you more — SIMO 752:14
J. OF NAZARETH — BIBL 108:29
J. shall reign — WATT 842:6
J. the author — BIBL 116:7
J. the most scientific — EDDY 303:1
j. told him; he wouldn't — CUMM 262:8
J. wants me for a sunbeam — TALB 787:20
J. wept — BIBL 108:7
J. wept — HUGO 419:8
J.! with all thy faults — BUTL 184:16
Messiah, J. son of Mary — KORA 472:1
more popular than J. now — LENN 489:4
O J., I have promised — BODE 130:8
power of J.' Name — PERR 604:5
Socrates, and J., and Luther — EMER 315:7
stand up for J. — DUFF 298:13
stand up for J. — TYNG 821:8
sweet the name of J. — NEWT 574:14
thinks he is J. Christ — CLEM 235:9
this J. will not do — BLAK 125:7
to the heart of J. — TERE 801:22
Was J. chaste — BLAK 125:5
Was J. gentle — BLAK 125:2
Was J. humble — BLAK 125:3
When J. came to Birmingham — STUD 779:10
jeunesse *Si j. savait* — ESTI 320:12
Jew especially a J. — MALA 517:6
for Englishman or J. — BLAK 125:7
Germany will declare that I am a J. — EINS 305:9
Hath not a J. eyes — SHAK 724:18
J. and the language — CELA 212:12
J. can never allow himself — MEIR 530:8
Just J.-*ish* — MILL 537:14
Let Apella the J. believe it — HORA 414:15
Liver of blaspheming J. — SHAK 721:17

Keats K.'s vulgarity LEAV 486:18
Kedar habitation among the tents of K.
BOOK 148:15
keel Joan doth k. the pot SHAK 717:25
keener edged tool that grows k. IRVI 425:21
with his k. eye MARV 525:6
keep honour, and k. her BOOK 138:24
Ideas won't k. WHIT 851:7
If you can k. your head KIPL 466:5
I k. away WALL 837:3
intention to k. my counsel GLAD 360:7
K. a thing seven years PROV 636:49
k. me, King of Kings KEN 459:15
k. the bridge with me MACA 508:14
k. thee in all thy ways BOOK 146:2
k. who can WORD 869:1
k. your England MUGA 564:3
many to k. KING 464:13
shop will k. you PROV 637:2
some day it'll k. you WEST 848:11
ware that will not k. HOUS 415:13
will not k. her long SHAK 731:15
keeper Lord himself is thy k. BOOK 148:17
my brother's k. BIBL 79:14
keepers Finders k. PROV 632:12
k. of the walls BIBL 91:9
keepeth he that k. thee BOOK 148:17
keepings Findings k. PROV 632:13
keeps gave it us for k. AYRE 44:4
Kelly K. from the Isle of Man MURP 565:22
Kempenfeld When K. went down COWP 255:19
ken D'ye k. John Peel GRAV 369:8
Kendal Mr K. is going to be confirmed
TENN 801:7
kenne k. mich auch nicht GOET 363:5
Kennedy you're no Jack K. BENT 72:4
kennst K. du das Land GOET 362:18
Kensal Green Paradise by way of K.
CHES 224:14
Kent everybody knows K. DICK 280:15
Kentish K. Sir Byng BROW 166:15
Kentucky Long ago in K. WARR 840:9
kept k. the faith BIBL 115:28
k. them in thy name BIBL 108:24
What wee k., wee lost EPIT 320:2
kersey honest k. noes SHAK 717:22
Ketch as Jack K.'s wife said DRYD 297:25
kettle back to the tea-k. DISR 284:10
filled with the k.'s breath HILL 398:12
k. and the earthen pot BIBL 97:19
Polly put the k. NURS 580:19
speech is like a cracked k. FLAU 333:4
Kew Go down to K. NOYE 577:13
his Highness' dog at K. POPE 614:23
key golden k. can open PROV 633:15
I keep the k. MONT 554:7
just hands on that golden k. MILT 538:20
k. of India DISR 285:11
k. of knowledge BIBL 105:12
k. of the Union CLAY 234:16
out of k. with his time POUN 621:2
possession of the k. PAIN 592:9
Turn the k. KEAT 456:21
With this k. Shakespeare WORD 869:2
keyboards people want k. JOBS 433:19
keys half that's got my k. GRAH 367:14
k. of all the creeds TENN 795:7
k. of hell and of death BIBL 117:28
k. of my prison DONN 289:25
massy k. he bore MILT 540:9
pattered with his k. BYRO 191:14
keystone k. which closeth STRA 778:16
Khatmandu to the north of K. HAYE 385:16
kibosh put the k. on the Kaiser ELLE 313:9
kick first k. I took SPRI 769:4
get no k. from champagne PORT 619:13
Got to k. at the darkness COCK 237:17
great k. at misery LAWR 484:2
k. against the pricks BIBL 109:22
k. his wife out of bed SURT 781:7
k. me downstairs BICK 120:20
k. to come to the top KEAT 457:23
k. you downstairs CARR 202:1

kicked k. up stairs HALI 377:24
no body to be k. THUR 810:14
kicking flattering, kissing and k. TRUM 817:16
K. you seems the common lot BROW 168:11
kid comeback k. CLIN 236:6
Here's looking at you, k. FILM 328:11
lie down with the k. BIBL 92:17
kiddies k. have crumpled the serviettes
BETJ 75:14
kidding k., Mister Hitler PERR 604:6
kidneys liked grilled mutton k. JOYC 448:18
kids don't have any k. yourself LARK 481:10
how many k. did you kill POLI 612:20
just a couple of k. HOLI 403:5
kill as k. a good book MILT 545:22
get out and k. something LEAC 485:8
Guns don't k. people SLOG 755:4
how many kids did you k. POLI 612:20
in every war they k. you in a new way
ROGE 666:6
Just how many did we k. LEWI 492:9
k. a king SHAK 703:11
k. all the lawyers SHAK 709:25
k. a mockingbird LEE 487:8
k. animals and stick in stamps NICO 575:4
k. a wife with kindness SHAK 733:8
k. care SHAK 727:33
k. me to-morrow SHAK 729:14
K. millions of men ROST 670:7
K. not the moth BLAK 124:13
k. sick people MARL 522:18
K. them all ARNA 28:22
k. the patient BACO 47:1
k. us for their sport SHAK 716:11
k. you if you quote it BURG 172:11
K. your parents or relatives I-HS 424:16
licence to k. FLEM 334:17
licensed to k. FILM 328:16
Licensed to k. MISQ 548:7
licenses to k. LEE 487:13
not to k. anything JAIN 428:11
or I k. you CHAM 215:5
Otherwise k. me MACN 513:13
prepared to k. one another SHAW 740:19
something you k. for BENN 70:2
they k. people TAGL 788:12
Thou shalt not k. BIBL 81:20
Thou shalt not k. CLOU 236:22
time to k. BIBL 89:23
we are going to k. it POWE 621:22
won't k. me COLL 243:7
would k. their church TENN 798:9
killed Better be k. SURT 781:14
Care k. the cat PROV 628:33
Curiosity k. the cat PROV 629:29
don't mind your being k. KITC 469:5
I am the enemy you k. OWEN 591:10
If hate k. men BROW 167:18
I'm k., Sire BROW 166:6
I was k. ANON 18:10
k. with my own treachery SHAK 704:25
King Harold was k. ANON 24:1
kissed thee ere I k. thee SHAK 729:25
so many people k. AUST 42:27
(who k. him) thought BELL 68:21
killer lover and k. are mingled DOUG 291:13
killeth letter k. BIBL 113:7
killing K. myself SHAK 729:25
K. no murder PROV 637:3
K. no murder SEXB 693:4
k. time Is only the name SITW 753:16
medal for k. two men MATL 528:4
talk of k. time BOUC 152:12
ways of k. a cat PROV 644:10
ways of k. a dog PROV 644:11
ways of k. a dog PROV 644:12
kills grip that k. it TAGO 787:15
k. all its pupils BERL 73:13
K.. all known germs ADVE 7:43
k. the thing he loves WILD 855:32
pace that k. PROV 636:29
pity k. BALZ 57:3
suicide k. two people MILL 537:5

that which k. DE B 269:16
waking that k. us BROW 163:17
Kiltartan My country is K. Cross YEAT 873:18
kilted k. her green kirtle BALL 55:18
kimonos girls in silk k. YEAT 873:15
kin little more than k. SHAK 699:11
makes the whole world k. SHAK 734:19
one's own k. and kith NASH 568:15
kind cruel only to be k. SHAK 703:20
cruel to be k. COMP 245:3
fordon the lawe of k. CHAU 220:24
for my own k. THOM 807:8
had been k. JOHN 439:7
if ye be k. towards women KORA 471:22
K. are her answers CAMP 196:2
k. as she is fair SHAK 736:16
K. hearts are more than coronets TENN 796:12
k. parent to man PLIN 609:14
less than k. SHAK 699:11
makes one wond'rous k. GARR 349:12
People will always be k. SASS 682:6
Too k., too kind NIGH 576:7
kindergarten kind of k. ROBI 664:1
kindest k. and the best BURN 179:1
k. man MALO 518:4
kindle And k. it LITT 495:12
kindled K. he was, and blasted BYRO 186:12
kindliness cool k. of sheets BROO 159:5
kindling it only requires k. PLUT 610:7
kindly k. fruits of the earth BOOK 135:2
kindness breath of k. ANON 19:12
generates k. JOHN 438:20
good human behaviour is k. ROOS 666:16
kill a wife with k. SHAK 733:8
k. and lies are worth GREE 371:14
K. in another's trouble GORD 366:5
k. in reserve POPE 614:23
k. to his Majesty HALL 378:6
milk of human k. GUED 374:7
milk of human k. SHAK 718:19
Of k. and of love WORD 866:9
on the k. of strangers WILL 858:9
spontaneous k. JOHN 443:9
tak a cup o' k. yet BURN 177:12
True k. presupposes GIDE 356:4
kindnesses thought of k. done CATU 211:1
kine seven fat k. BIBL 80:21
king a' for our rightfu' K. BURN 178:16
Agamemnon, K. of Men HOME 404:7
all the k.'s men NURS 579:4
another k., one Jesus BIBL 109:34
As to the K. CHAR 216:19
atheist if the k. were LA B 475:2
authority forgets a dying k. TENN 794:23
authority of a k. STRA 778:16
banners of the k. advance FORT 338:15
blessedness alone that makes a K.
TRAH 814:14
born K. of the Jews BIBL 98:10
but yesterday a k. BYRO 190:17
cat may look at a k. PROV 628:37
coming of the K. of Heaven ANON 21:16
Conscience as their K. TENN 794:6
constitutional k. BAGE 51:7
Cotton is K. CHRI 227:5
cotton is k. HUGO 419:5
cuts off his k.'s head SHAW 741:29
despised and dying k. SHEL 746:14
disposal of the K. CHRI 227:4
divinity doth hedge a k. SHAK 704:1
duty is the k.'s SHAK 708:26
every inch a k. SHAK 716:16
fight for its K. and Country GRAH 367:11
five kings did a k. to death THOM 805:19
follow the K. TENN 794:4
God bless the K. BYRO 185:4
God for K. Charles BROW 166:16
God save k. Solomon BIBL 84:25
God save our gracious k. SONG 762:9
God save the k. BIBL 83:32
God save the k. SHAK 731:2
God save the k. SONG 762:9
government without a k. BANC 57:7

kissed (cont.):
My lips k. dumb — SWIN 786:1
never k. an ugly girl — EPIT 318:4
wist, before I k. — BALL 56:7
kisses fine romance with no k. — FIEL 327:4
forgotten my k. — SWIN 785:21
Give me a thousand k. — CATU 210:7
k. are his daily feast — LODG 498:6
k. of his mouth — BIBL 90:23
Love's mart of k. — CHAP 216:6
more than k. — DONN 289:23
played At cards for k. — LYLY 505:20
Stolen k. — HUNT 421:8
sweet k., pigeon-wise — DIAN 275:15
kissing I wasn't k. her — MARX 525:19
K. don't last — MERE 532:15
K. goes by favour — PROV 646:7
k. had to stop — BROW 168:3
k.'s out of fashion — PROV 646:48
K. with golden face — SHAK 437:4
k. your hand — LOOS 500:15
like k. God — BRUC 168:14
wonder who's k. her — ADAM 2:6
kit have a K.-Kat — ADVE 7:29
old k.-bag — MILI 535:18
kitchen better mind the k. — FITZ 332:1
brocades of the k. — DAVI 267:13
get out of the k. — PROV 635:24
get out of the k. — TRUM 817:18
ghastly k. — BERN 74:4
in the k. bred — BYRO 190:27
K.-cabals, and nursery-mishaps — CRAB 257:10
send me to eat in the k. — HUGH 418:1
sitting in the k. sink — SMIT 756:13
whip in k. cups — STEV 774:2
kite Imagination is the highest k. — BACA 45:2
not sufficient for a k.'s dinner — QUAR 651:7
kitsch escape k. completely — KUND 474:6
kitten I had rather be a k. — SHAK 706:10
kittens Three little k. — NURS 582:2
Wanton k. make sober — PROV 646:7
kitty K., a fair, but frozen maid — GARR 349:15
Kjartan killed K. — ANON 24:5
kleine eine k. Pause — FERR 325:14
Klondike beer of a man in K. — CHES 224:20
knappeth k. the spear in sunder — BOOK 142:19
knave epithet for a k. — MACA 506:18
k. is not punished — HALI 377:20
K. of Hearts he stole — NURS 580:21
man must be supposed a k. — HUME 420:16
To feed the titled k. — BURN 180:4
knaves calls the k., Jacks — DICK 278:6
fools and k. — BUCK 169:18
k. in place — DEFO 270:20
knee blude to the k. — BALL 55:22
civility of my k. — BROW 162:22
Every k. shall bow — NOEL 576:18
every k. should bow — BIBL 114:19
head on his k. — BARH 58:13
in the heart, not in the k. — JERR 433:15
little abune her k. — BALL 55:18
kneel k. and adore him — MONS 554:2
k. before him — BOOK 144:19
k. before the Lord our Maker — BOOK 146:8
k. for peace — SHAK 733:11
kneeling meekly k. — BOOK 137:9
knees body between your k. — CORY 252:11
clasped in his hands his k. — HOME 404:22
confirm the feeble k. — BIBL 93:9
creeps rustling to her k. — KEAT 454:10
I bow my k. — BIBL 114:1
live on your k. — IBAR 424:2
knell it is a k. — SHAK 719:21
k. of parting day — GRAY 370:1
like a rising k. — BYRO 186:5
their k. is rung — COLL 243:13
knew If you looked away, you k. — SERE 692:23
I k. almost as much — JOHN 440:4
I k. that once — STEP 772:2
Johnny, I hardly k. ye — BALL 54:18
k. it best — BACO 46:10
K. YOU HAD IT IN YOU — PARK 596:14
told what he k. — AMIS 14:11

world k. him not — BIBL 107:1
knife cannibal uses k. and fork — LEC 486:22
deadly k. Long aimed — FANS 323:3
k. is lost in it — SHEL 744:17
k. see not the wound — SHAK 719:2
k. that probes far deeper — FORS 338:4
my oyster k. — HURS 422:5
smylere with the k. — CHAU 219:11
walk on a k. edge — MONT 555:28
War to the k. — PALA 593:7
will not use the k. — HIPP 399:18
knight as the armèd k. — ASKE 34:1
courteoust k. — MALO 518:4
Fearless, blameless k. — ANON 22:1
gentle k. was pricking — SPEN 767:2
k. at arms — KEAT 455:4
k.-errantry is religion — CERV 213:5
k. like the young Lochinvar — SCOT 688:22
K. of the Doleful Countenance — CERV 213:3
k. was indeed a valiant Gent — EVEL 321:18
monk and a k. — HENR 392:5
new-slain k. — BALL 56:3
red-cross k. for ever kneeled — TENN 796:17
that was your k. — PEEL 602:2
verray, parfit gentil k. — CHAU 218:5
When a k. won his spurs — STRU 779:6
knighthoods MBEs and your k. — KEAT 453:18
knights ladies dead and lovely k. — SHAK 738:10
lances of ancient k. — ROOT 668:8
knit k. together thine elect — BOOK 136:15
life to k. me — HOUS 416:3
knits k. man to man — SICK 750:4
Sleep that k. up — SHAK 720:6
knitter beautiful little k. — SITW 753:15
knitters k. in the sun — SHAK 735:17
knives night of the long k. — HITL 400:7
knock k., and it shall be opened — BIBL 99:24
K. as you please — POPE 614:12
K. at a star — HERR 395:16
k. at the door — LAMB 476:16
k., breathe, shine — DONN 288:12
k. him down first — JOHN 442:2
k. is open wide — SMAR 754:16
nice k.-down argument — CARR 203:11
right to k. him down — JOHN 442:28
stand at the door, and k. — BIBL 118:2
when you k. — COWP 254:30
knocked ruin that Cromwell k. about — BEDF 65:9
we k. the bastard off — HILL 399:2
what they k. down — FENT 324:24
knocker Tie up the k. — POPE 614:15
knocking Here's a k., indeed — SHAK 720:11
k. at Preferment's door — ARNO 30:8
K. on the moonlit door — DE L 272:6
knocks k. you down with the butt — GOLD 365:15
never k. twice — PROV 641:21
knot crowned k. of fire — ELIO 309:22
cuts the k. of serious — HORA 414:16
k. intrinsicate Of life — SHAK 696:4
political k. — BIER 121:4
So the k. be unknotted — ELIO 309:2
knots pokers into true-love k. — COLE 240:11
knotted Sat and k. — SEDL 690:18
knotty moorish, and wild, and k. — BRON 158:11
know all I k. is what I read — ROGE 666:5
all ye need to k. — KEAT 455:25
Better the devil you k. — PROV 627:37
dare to k. — HORA 410:5
Dare to k. — KANT 453:5
does not k. himself — LA F 475:17
do not pretend to k. — DARR 266:5
don't k. can't hurt you — PROV 646:31
don't k. what I'm doing — BRAU 155:11
fear, To be we k. not what — DRYD 295:13
find out what you don't k. — WELL 846:12
go we k. not where — SHAK 723:14
hate any one that we k. — HAZL 386:23
He must k. sumpin' — HAMM 378:20
his place k. him — BIBL 86:23
How do they k. — PARK 596:15
How little do we k. — BYRO 189:26
I do not k. myself — GOET 363:5

I k. nothing — SOCR 759:15
I k. not the Lord — BIBL 81:1
I k. not the man — BIBL 103:20
I k. thee not, old man — SHAK 708:4
It's not what you k. — SAYI 684:30
k. a man seven years — PROV 648:24
k. a man who can — ADVE 7:12
k., and not be known — COLT 244:11
k. a thing or two — MOLI 552:1
k. better what is good for people — JAY 430:25
k. enough of hate — FROS 344:13
k. everything — MOLI 552:19
k. Him, love him — CATE 209:9
k. man in general — LA R 482:9
k. more of mankind — JOHN 443:20
k. not what they do — BIBL 106:23
k. our will is free — JOHN 440:17
k. that I am God — BOOK 142:19
k. that my redeemer liveth — BIBL 86:34
K. the enemy — SUN 780:12
K. then thyself — POPE 616:29
K. the place — ELIO 309:19
K. the world — YOUN 876:25
K. this to be thus — JAIN 428:13
K. thyself — PROV 637:8
k. to know no more — MILT 543:14
k. what I mean, Harry — BRUN 168:20
k. what I think — WALL 836:15
k. what we are talking about — RUSS 674:23
k. you're . . . God — BARN 59:6
K. you the land — GOET 362:18
let me k. mine end — BOOK 141:28
master of those who k. — DANT 264:17
men naturally desire to k. — AUCT 36:17
More people k. Tom Fool — PROV 639:11
more than we k. — HOFM 402:14
never k. what is enough — BLAK 126:15
never k. what you can do — PROV 648:17
no one to k. — ANON 16:21
not as we k. it — MISQ 548:5
not k. where he is going — LIN 495:7
nought did k. — DAVI 267:18
say, 'I k. not' — TALM 789:11
Tell me what you k. — EMER 315:20
that kan hymselven k. — CHAU 219:21
things they didn't k. — POUN 621:1
those who do not wish to k. — RALE 654:15
thought so once; but now I k. it — EPIT 318:15
To k. all is to forgive all — PROV 645:26
to k. little — BACO 48:6
To k. this only — MILT 544:27
to think that we k. — SOCR 759:17
We must k. — EPIT 319:17
What do I k. — MONT 555:15
What I k. — PERS 604:11
what should they k. of England — KIPL 465:15
what we would, we k. — ARNO 29:3
which we least k. — MONT 555:5
You k. more than you think — SPOC 768:13
you k. who — ADVE 8:15
you'll never k. — ARMS 28:17
you'll never k. — MISQ 548:8
you may k. one another — KORA 473:3
you yourselves do k. — SHAK 713:12
knowed all that there is to be k. — GRAH 368:4
Knower How can the K. be known — UPAN 821:19
knowest k. all things — BIBL 109:7
k. my down-sitting — BOOK 149:15
thou k. not — BIBL 89:3
knoweth k. not God — BIBL 117:18
knowing Bewrapt past k. — HARD 381:23
lust of k. — FLEC 334:12
misfortune of k. anything — AUST 41:21
one who INSISTS on k. — POUN 621:15
With a k. ignorance — JOHN 434:4
knowingly Never k. undersold — ADVE 8:8
knowledge After such k., what forgiveness — ELIO 309:25
all k. — BIBL 112:14
all k. to be my province — BACO 48:24
All our k. is — POPE 617:13
bars To perfect k. — BYRO 187:25

Benevolent K.   BORG 151:8
bring home k.   JOHN 442:16
by nature desire k.   ARIS 27:3
communicate k.   DE Q 273:20
Courage is the k.   NICI 574:17
Debarred from k.   CHUD 227:17
desire more love and k.   SHAK 696:11
diffusion of k.   MADI 514:11
envied kind of k.   ADAM 3:10
exact k. of the past   THUC 810:6
five ports of k.   BROW 162:5
follow k. like a sinking star   TENN 800:17
follow virtue and k.   DANT 265:4
Friendship from k.   BUSS 182:14
fruit of k.   FULL 346:14
identical with his k.   MAIM 516:15
impediment to the advancement of k.
   REID 657:15
increaseth k.   BIBL 89:21
in the way of k.   LOCK 497:3
key of k.   BIBL 105:12
k. and wonder   BACO 45:5
k. belongs to humanity   PAST 599:4
K. comes   TENN 797:4
K. denied from senses   SA'A 676:11
K. dwells In heads   COWP 256:26
K. enormous   KEAT 454:25
k. in mathematics   BACO 49:16
k. in the making   MILT 546:4
k. is a greater pleasure   ARIS 27:16
k. is bought   CLOU 236:16
k. is dangerous   HUXL 423:8
K. is of two kinds   JOHN 441:19
K. is power   PROV 637:9
K. is proud   COWP 256:27
k. is transmitted   BLAK 126:23
k. itself is power   BACO 48:25
k., it shall vanish away   BIBL 112:14
K. may give weight   CHES 223:16
k. of a lifetime   WHIS 850:10
k. of causes   BACO 48:28
k. of God   LEIB 488:5
k. of good and evil   BIBL 78:20
K. of good and evil   COWP 255:28
k. of human nature   AUST 41:19
k. of man is as the waters   BACO 45:12
k. of nature   HOLB 403:1
k. of nature   WHEW 850:2
k. of nothing   DICK 281:2
k. of the extinction   PALI 593:13
k. of the Lord   BIBL 92:18
k. of the world   CHES 222:23
k. of truth   BACO 48:13
k. puffeth up   BIBL 112:5
k. shall be increased   BIBL 96:2
k. that they are so   OSBO 588:9
k. was divine   TRAH 814:9
k. we have lost in information   ELIO 310:23
k. when the day was done   KEAT 454:28
k. which they cannot lose   OPPE 585:15
k. without integrity   JOHN 437:20
Language and k.   SULL 780:2
Let k. grow   TENN 794:30
literature of k.   DE Q 274:1
little k. is dangerous   PROV 637:40
make k. available   BLAC 123:7
never better than k.   FERM 325:12
no k. but I know it   BEEC 65:16
No man's k.   LOCK 497:6
not k. but action   ARIS 27:7
objects of k.   PLAT 609:1
organized k.   SPEN 765:18
Out-topping k.   ARNO 30:15
passeth k.   BIBL 114:2
penetrate the land of k.   SCHI 683:16
price for k.   TICK 811:3
province of k. to speak   HOLM 403:1
raising us to k.   LEIB 488:6
Riches. k. and honour   HOBB 400:18
show of k.   DOUG 291:18
Sorrow is k.   BYRO 190:12
spirit of k.   BIBL 92:16
struggling for k.   HALI 377:22

Such k. is too wonderful   BOOK 149:16
touchstone of k.   AUCT 36:20
tree of diabolical k.   SHER 748:11
tree of the k.   BIBL 78:21
Unto this k.   DONN 289:6
What is all k.   CARL 199:12
words without k.   BIBL 87:7
You seek for k.   SHEL 743:2
known all that is k.   NEWM 572:11
child is k. by his doings   BIBL 88:26
devil where he is k.   JOHN 438:14
don't choose to have it k.   CHES 223:20
even as also I am k.   BIBL 112:14
hast thou not k. me   BIBL 108:15
Have ye not k.   BIBL 93:19
heard and k.   BOOK 145:5
How can the Knower be k.   UPAN 821:19
If you would be k.   COLT 244:11
k. and the unknown   PINT 607:2
k. by company he keeps   PROV 638:17
k. luminously   NEWM 572:19
k. no more than other men   AUBR 35:17
k. too late   SHAK 732:8
k. unto God   EPIT 319:11
safer than a k. way   HASK 384:3
thy way may be k.   BOOK 144:4
till I am k.   JOHN 439:7
tree is k. by its fruit   PROV 645:34
knows Every schoolboy k.   MACA 507:13
has a mind and k. it   SHAW 739:8
He k. nothing   SHAW 740:18
He who k. others is wise   LAO 480:2
if you k. of a better 'ole   CART 205:19
knows about it all—HE k.   FITZ 331:22
k. even his Bible   ARNO 31:14
k. how much it needs   DEMO 272:17
k. nothing of his own   GOET 362:11
k. that all-highest Brahman   UPAN 822:16
K. Things   MILN 538:13
k. what he fights for   CROM 260:9
less one k.   LAO 480:6
sits in the middle and k.   FROS 345:1
who k. does not speak   LAO 480:8
knuckle k.-end of England   SMIT 758:11
knucklebones harmless art of k.   STEV 775:4
Kopf K. zum Greise   MÜLL 564:18
Koran By the glorious K.   KORA 473:4
K. was sent down   KORA 471:3
not ponder the K.   KORA 471:19
Korea doing in K.   TRUM 817:17
Kosciuszko Freedom shrieked—as K. fell
   CAMP 195:13
Kraken K. sleepeth   TENN 796:9
Kremlin Over the K.'s pavement   BROW 168:9
Krorluppia Nasticreechia K.   LEAR 485:21
Kruger killing K. with your mouth   KIPL 465:4
Kubla In Xanadu did K. Khan   COLE 240:4
Kunst In der K.   GOET 362:9
Kurtz Mistah K.—he dead   CONR 249:2
Kyrie K. eleison   MISS 546:21

label without a rag of a l.   HUXL 423:4
labels l. serving to give a name   TOLS 813:13
labor hic l. est   VIRG 830:5
laborare L. est orare   MOTT 563:11
laboratory guinea pigs in the l. of God
   WILL 858:2
laborem spectare l.   LUCR 504:9
laborious Studious of l. ease   COWP 256:18
labour all his l.   BIBL 89:16
all ye that l.   BIBL 101:2
brow of l.   BRYA 169:1
daily L. to pursue   WESL 847:14
done to the L. Party   TAWN 791:7
Don't let L. ruin it   POLI 613:2
from one kind of l.   FRAN 340:4
full of l.   BIBL 89:18
Great is l.   TALM 789:22
l l. for peace   BOOK 148:16
incessant l.   CONS 249:16
In l. there is profit   BIBL 88:11
insupportable l.   STEE 770:13

l. against our own cure   BROW 163:14
l. and not to ask   IGNA 424:14
l. and sorrow   BOOK 145:21
l.-intensive industry   WILS 859:10
L. isn't working   POLI 612:29
l. of love   BIBL 115:12
l. of my hands   THOR 809:15
l. of women in the house   GILM 358:18
l. of your life   MONT 554:23
L. Party owes more to Methodism   PHIL 606:7
L.'s call   POLI 612:15
L.'s double whammy   POLI 612:30
L. spin doctors   CAMP 194:14
l. we delight in   SHAK 720:14
L. without joy is base   RUSK 673:26
life all l. be   TENN 797:11
Love l. and hate mastery   TALM 789:1
many still must l.   BYRO 187:6
mental l. employed   REYN 659:2
never visualised l.   WEBB 843:9
New L., new danger   POLI 613:3
not demand for l.   MILL 536:10
reward of l. is life   MORR 560:19
right leader for the L. Party   BEVA 76:20
Six days shalt thou l.   BIBL 81:18
sore l.'s bath   SHAK 720:6
spend your l.   BIBL 94:7
their l. is but lost   BOOK 149:2
to live without l.   TAWN 791:5
true success is to l.   STEV 775:27
Unremitting l.   VIRG 832:14
We l. soon   BURN 180:4
with difficulty and l.   MILT 542:21
youth of l.   GOLD 364:3
laboured fine, but as much l.   WALP 838:4
l. more abundantly   BIBL 112:19
labourer l. is worthy of his hire   BIBL 105:1
l. to take his pension   RUSK 674:5
l. worthy of hire   PROV 637:10
labourers l. are few   BIBL 100:21
l. are idle   TALM 789:4
labouring l. man, that tills   OXFO 591:12
sleep of a l. man   BIBL 89:28
to the l. man   BUNY 171:16
women l. of child   BOOK 134:24
labours Children sweeten l.   BACO 47:22
completed l. are pleasant   CICE 231:17
line too l.   POPE 616:7
no l. tire   JOHN 438:7
rest from their l.   BIBL 119:3
laburnums L., dropping-wells of fire
   TENN 795:23
labyrinth peopled l. of walls   SHEL 744:20
labyrinthical perplexed, l. soul   DONN 290:12
labyrinthine down the l. ways   THOM 807:14
l. buds the rose   BROW 167:21
lac sine dolo l. concupiscite   BIBL 120:18
lace l. my bodice blue   HUNT 422:1
Nottingham l. of the curtains   BETJ 75:9
lacessit Nemo me impune l.   MOTT 563:12
lack can I l. nothing   BOOK 140:20
lions do l.   BOOK 141:20
lacked questioning, If I l. any thing
   HERB 394:14
lacking nothing is l.   LEON 489:19
lacrimae Hinc illae l.   TERE 801:11
Sunt l. rerum   VIRG 829:1
lacy l. sleeve with vitriol   WOOL 864:17
lad l. does not care   JOHN 440:13
l. that is gone   STEV 776:24
ladder behold a l.   BIBL 80:9
dropping down the l.   KIPL 465:21
l. of our vices   AUGU 39:23
l. of predictable progress   GOUL 367:2
path of the celestial l.   HEIK 389:4
traffic of Jacob's l.   THOM 808:2
Wiv a l.   BATE 61:6
ladders Crosses are l.   PROV 629:28
Holy One makes l.   MIDR 534:14
where all the l. start   YEAT 872:14
laden heavy l.   BIBL 101:2
ladies from a l.' seminary   GILB 357:6
Gentlemen and L.   DICK 282:3

ladies (*cont.*):
good for l.   PROV 632:4
In praise of l. dead   SHAK 738:10
l. declare war on me   LOUI 501:7
l.' favours   SHAK 709:12
l., God bless them   SAYE 683:3
l. intellectual   BYRO 187:21
L., just a little   TREE 815:3
l. of St James's   DOBS 287:4
l. should ever sit down   MORE 559:1
Ladies were l.   RAVE 656:1
lion among l.   SHAK 726:12
made the carlines l.   JAME 429:4
may the l. sit   BALL 55:16
remember the l.   ADAM 1:18
seminaries of young l.   KNOX 470:7
way the l. ride   NURS 581:17
worth any number of old l.   FAUL 324:18
young l. entered   SURT 781:17
ladies from the cooks' own l.   BROW 167:1
lads Come lasses and l.   SONG 762:5
Golden l. and girls   SHAK 698:24
l. in their hundreds   HOUS 415:17
l. that will never be old   HOUS 415:17
lady bird than a l.   RICH 660:12
called her his l. fair   KIPL 467:19
Here lies a l.   RANS 655:6
I met a l.   KEAT 455:6
Joan as my L.   HERR 396:4
l. doth protest too much   SHAK 702:22
l. fair   BALL 56:3
l. in a cage   CHES 224:18
L. Look owre   BALL 54:7
l. loved a swine   NURS 581:13
l. loves Milk Tray   ADVE 7:6
l. of a 'certain age'   BYRO 189:9
l. of Christ's College   AUBR 36:2
L. of Shalott   TENN 796:16
L. of Spain   REAV 656:21
l.'s in the case   GAY 351:14
l.-smocks all silver-white   SHAK 717:24
l.'s not for burning   FRY 345:15
l.'s not for turning   THAT 803:16
l. sweet and kind   ANON 20:17
l. that's known as Lou   SERV 692:28
L. with a Lamp   LONG 499:21
little l. comes by   GAY 351:28
lovely l., garmented   SHEL 747:6
My L. Bountiful   FARQ 324:3
ne'er wan A l.   BURN 179:27
Our L. of Pain   SWIN 785:8
our L. of the Snows   KIPL 467:2
saw my l. weep   ANON 18:6
talk like a l.   SHAW 742:7
To see a fine l.   NURS 581:2
why the l. is a tramp   HART 383:12
ladybird L., ladybird   NURS 579:13
Lafayette L., *nous voilà*   STAN 770:2
lag l.-end of my life   SHAK 706:20
laggard l. in love   SCOT 688:23
laid when I'm l. by thee   HERR 396:11
where they have l. him   BIBL 108:36
laily l. worm   BALL 54:19
lain There hath he l. for ages   TENN 796:10
laisser-faire de l.   QUES 651:16
L.   ARGE 26:11
laissez-faire L.   ANON 22:4
laity conspiracies against the l.   SHAW 739:24
lake l. water lapping   YEAT 873:21
slips into the bosom of the l.   TENN 799:19
with a l. of fire   FLEC 334:13
lama Eli, Eli, l. sabachthani   BIBL 103:24
lamb Behold the L. of God   BIBL 107:5
fell down before the L.   BIBL 118:8
for a sheep as a l.   PROV 641:9
goes out like a l.   PROV 638:30
he who made the L.   BLAK 128:5
holy L. of God   BLAK 126:24
l. shall be without blemish   BIBL 81:6
l. to the slaughter   BIBL 94:4
leads me to the L.   COWP 255:16
Little L. who made Thee   BLAK 127:11
Mary had a little l.   HALE 377:3

O L. of God, I come   ELLI 313:14
one little ewe l.   BIBL 84:16
Pipe a song about a L.   BLAK 127:6
provide himself a l.   BIBL 80:1
skin of an innocent l.   SHAK 710:1
tempers wind to shorn l.   PROV 633:13
to the shorn l.   STER 772:13
white in the blood of the L.   BIBL 118:15
wolf shall dwell with the l.   BIBL 92:17
Worthy the L. that died   WATT 841:18
wrath of the L.   BIBL 118:11
yokèd with a l.   SHAK 713:26
lambs Feed my l.   BIBL 109:5
gather the l.   BIBL 93:17
l. who've lost our way   KIPL 465:20
lame feet was I to the l.   BIBL 87:2
L. dogs over stiles   KING 464:5
l. man   BIBL 93:10
Science without religion is l.   EINS 305:5
lamentation l., and weeping   BIBL 98:13
Moderate l.   SHAK 694:1
must be no l.   SAPP 681:2
lamentations Strange l. assailed   DANT 265:5
lamented ye have not l.   BIBL 100:34
laments forest l.   CHUR 228:20
Lammastide fell about the L.   BALL 54:4
lamp Lady with a L.   LONG 499:21
l. is shattered   SHEL 744:18
l. of day   DOUG 291:10
lift my l.   LAZA 485:3
Slaves of the L.   ARNO 28:23
too strong of the l.   STER 773:1
unlit l.   BROW 167:24
lampada *vitai l.*   LUCR 504:10
lamp post leaning on a l.   GAY 351:28
lamp posts drunken man uses l.   LANG 478:12
lamprey surfeit by eating of a l.   FABY 322:10
lamps Heav'n's great l.   CAMP 195:21
l. are going out all over Europe   GREY 373:1
Life not a series of gig l.   WOOL 864:5
[monks] should live as l.   PALI 593:15
old l. for new   ARAB 25:9
women . . . who are the l.   LAWS 484:16
Lancashire L. merchants   CHES 224:20
Lancaster time-honoured L.   SHAK 730:1
land by sea as by l.   GILB 356:8
Ceres re-assume the l.   POPE 615:9
empire of the l.   RICH 661:5
Every l. has its own law   PROV 631:22
fat of the l.   BIBL 80:26
from l. to land   COLE 241:9
Grab this l.   MORR 561:10
heavenly l. from ours   WATT 842:5
house and l. are gone   PROV 646:39
if by l., one   REVE 658:14
Ill fares the l.   GOLD 364:2
I see l.   TENN 801:7
l. flowing with milk   BIBL 80:36
l. God gave to Cain   CART 205:4
l. of counterpane   STEV 776:14
l. of darkness   BIBL 86:24
L. of Heart's Desire   YEAT 873:22
L. of Hope and Glory   BENS 70:22
l. of lost content   HOUS 416:4
l. of my fathers   JAME 429:6
l. of my fathers   THOM 806:13
l. of pure delight   WATT 842:4
l. of the free   KEY 461:13
l. of the living   BIBL 94:5
l. of Uz   BIBL 86:8
l. of vainglory   BUNY 171:6
L. that I love   BERL 73:1
l. was ours before   FROS 344:14
L. where my fathers died   SMIT 757:13
l. . . . where the light   BIBL 86:25
lane to the l. of the dead   AUDE 36:25
more precious than l.   SADA 677:2
nakedness of the l.   BIBL 80:24
no l. unhabitable   THOR 810:4
no yard of l.   ANON 24:2
one if by l.   LONG 500:1
Ours is the l.   MAYA 529:5
piece of l.   HORA 414:20

possessed his l.   BIBL 82:5
prepared the dry l.   BOOK 146:8
ready by water as by l.   ELST 314:6
seems a moving l.   MILT 543:27
seen the promised l.   KING 463:15
splendid and a happy l.   GOLD 364:10
spy out the l.   BIBL 82:3
that pleasant l.   BOOK 147:13
There's the l., or cherry-isle   HERR 395:17
They love their l.   HALL 378:6
think there is no l.   BACO 45:13
This l. is your land   GUTH 375:2
to enjoy thy l.   SHAK 714:4
travel by l. or by water   BOOK 134:24
Unhappy the l. that needs heroes   BREC 155:16
we had the l.   GEOR 353:9
windy sea of l.   MILT 542:24
Woe to the l.   SHAK 731:19
landed Eagle has l.   ARMS 28:19
l. with an idea   BIRT 122:4
landing fight on the l. grounds   CHUR 229:15
successful l. in France   LIND 494:12
landlord l., fill the flowing bowl   SONG 762:4
paid to the l.   RICA 659:18
Sir Roger is l.   ADDI 5:6
landlords we're your l.   TINE 811:8
landlubbers l. lying down below   SONG 763:6
landmark Remove not the ancient l.   BIBL 88:32
lands discover new l.   GIDE 356:1
Find other l.   THOM 808:17
sound is gone out into all l.   BOOK 140:9
take us l. away   DICK 281:13
though not of l.   WOTT 870:7
landscape gardening is but l.-painting   POPE 618:25
In Claude's l.   CONS 249:19
l. is deformed   THOR 809:9
l. of England   AUST 41:11
l. of the world   YOUN 876:24
part in a l.   CHEK 222:7
sculpture put in a l.   MOOR 557:9
Who owns this l.   MCCA 509:3
landslide pay for a l.   KENN 460:3
lane l. to the land of the dead   AUDE 36:25
long l. that has no turning   PROV 636:4
lanes streets and l. of the city   BIBL 105:23
lang For auld l. syne   BURN 177:12
How l., O Lord   BULL 170:8
language any l. you choose   GILB 356:22
as much the l. of heaven   FANT 323:6
best chosen l.   AUST 41:19
broke through l.   BROW 167:10
by means of l.   WITT 861:8
clear and beautiful l.   EMPS 315:30
cool web of l.   GRAV 369:11
dear l. that I spake   MACA 508:6
divided by a common l.   MISQ 547:12
enemy of clear l.   ORWE 587:24
enlargement of the l.   JOHN 435:18
entrance into the l.   BACO 48:9
everything else in our l.   MACA 507:21
except, of course, l.   WILD 854:13
from one l. to another   SHEL 747:10
from one l. to another   UNAM 821:13
hidden l. of the soul   GRAH 367:16
In l., the ignorant   DUPP 300:6
in l. there are only differences   SAUS 682:16
In such lovely l.   LAWR 483:25
l. all nations understand   BEHN 67:6
l. and ways of behaving   JUVE 450:18
l. an opera is sung in   APPL 25:6
l. becomes clear   BABE 45:1
l., by your skill made pliant   GAY 351:17
l. can be compared   SAUS 682:17
l. chiefly made by men   HARD 380:13
l. grows out of life   SULL 780:2
l. I have learned   SHAK 730:4
l. in her eye   SHAK 734:20
l. is a dialect with   WEIN 845:8
L. is a form of human reason   LÉVI 491:11
L. is called the garment   CARL 200:21
L. is fossil poetry   EMER 315:10
L. is only the instrument   JOHN 435:17

own l. has a fool PROV 638:23
to a corporate l. COMM 244:17
lawyers crowd of l. WYCH 871:15
kill all the l. SHAK 709:25
l. can, with ease GAY 351:17
L. may revere FERG 325:9
l.' tongues PROV 629:45
two l. the battledores DICK 280:18
Woe unto you, l. BIBL 105:12
lay Cleric before, and L. behind BUTL 183:18
I l. me down to sleep PRAY 623:6
l. down his life BIBL 108:18
L. her i' the earth SHAK 704:18
l. me down in peace BOOK 139:17
l. mee downe BALL 55:12
L. on, Macduff SHAK 722:26
L.-overs for meddlers PROV 637:13
L. your sleeping head AUDE 37:15
layman neither cleric nor l. BERN 73:19
lays constructing tribal l. KIPL 466:7
Lazarus certain beggar named L. BIBL 106:6
Come forth, L. JOYC 448:20
L. mystified HILL 398:11
laziness differs from l. MARA 521:7
some from l. EURI 321:8
lazy l. leaden-stepping hours MILT 541:4
l., long, lascivious DEFO 271:1
Long and l. PROV 637:50
LBJ All the way with L. POLI 612:2
Hey, L., how many kids POLI 612:20
lead blind l. the blind BIBL 101:22
child shall l. them BIBL 92:17
easy to l. BROU 160:10
evening l. CHUR 230:16
gold wes changyd into l. WYNT 871:17
l. a horticulture PARK 596:17
L., kindly Light NEWM 572:16
l. me in the right way BOOK 141:10
l. those that are with young BIBL 93:17
L. us, Heavenly Father EDME 303:17
l. us not into temptation BIBL 99:12
think we l. BYRO 191:10
When the blind l. the blind PROV 646:44
wherever it may l. DOST 291:8
leaden voice revives the l. strings CAMP 195:22
With l. foot JAGO 427:14
leader fanatic is a great l. BROU 160:14
I am their l. LEDR 487:5
l. is best LAO 479:10
l. of the enterprise VIRG 828:18
one people, one l. POLI 612:14
Take me to your l. CATC 208:28
test of a l. LIPP 495:10
leaders l. of a revolution CONR 249:10
leadership L. means making CHRÉ 226:18
leaf And I were like the l. SWIN 786:2
as an aspes l. CHAU 221:3
days are in the yellow l. BYRO 190:27
every l. is a flower CAMU 196:18
fade as a l. BIBL 94:21
Falls with the l. FLET 335:6
in tiny l. BROW 165:27
last red l. TENN 795:5
l., the bud, the flower SPEN 767:14
light as l. on lynde CHAU 219:2
Now every l. DENH 273:5
sole remaining l. WORD 864:19
where the dead l. fell KEAT 454:21
wise man hide a l. CHES 225:8
yellow l. SHAK 722:16
league hadna sailed a l. BALL 54:10
Half a l. onward TENN 793:3
leak One l. will sink BUNY 171:20
leaks Little l. sink the ship PROV 637:41
lean could eat no l. NURS 579:12
if a man l. BIBL 85:38
l. and hungry look SHAK 711:22
l. as much to the contrary HALI 377:7
l. on one another BURK 175:8
l. over too far backward THUR 810:10
people who l. WILC 854:10
leaning l. all awry FITZ 331:25
leap giant l. for mankind ARMS 28:20

great l. in the dark VANB 823:19
l. as an hart BIBL 93:10
l. in the dark HOBB 401:11
l. into the dark BROW 161:13
l. into the ocean HUME 420:7
l. over the wall BOOK 140:7
Look before you l. PROV 638:2
methinks it were an easy l. SHAK 705:15
leaped have I l. over a wall BIBL 84:22
leaping l. from place to place HARD 381:18
too broad for l. HOUS 416:9
Walking, and l. BIBL 109:16
learn but she can l. SHAK 724:24
cannot l. to forget REED 657:6
craft so long to l. CHAU 220:21
don't want to l. SELL 691:21
l. about the pine BASH 61:2
l., and inwardly digest BOOK 135:11
l. by doing ARIS 27:10
l. how to be aged BLYT 130:4
l. in suffering SHEL 744:12
l. men from books DISR 286:14
l. the world CHES 223:1
L. to write well BUCK 169:17
live and l. POMF 611:11
Live and l. PROV 637:47
much desire to l. MILT 546:4
never too late to l. PROV 636:22
Never too old to l. PROV 639:45
People must l. to hate MAND 518:18
pleasure to l. CONF 245:12
We l. so little DAVI 267:17
while they teach, men l. SENE 692:14
learned been l. has been forgotten SKIN 754:6
l. anything from history HEGE 388:13
l. well how to obey THOM 804:19
loads of l. lumber POPE 616:13
much l. dust COWP 256:14
obscurity of a l. language GIBB 355:6
opinion with the l. CONG 246:30
prescribed laws to the l. DUPP 300:6
Things l. on earth BROW 166:22
this l. man MARL 522:12
learning and in l. rules CRAB 257:19
a' the l. I desire BURN 178:5
attain good l. ASCH 33:2
commonwealth of l. LOCK 497:3
cry both arts and l. QUAR 651:15
desire of l. in women BUTT 184:21
enough of l. to misquote BYRO 189:30
Get l. BIBL 98:7
l. is a process of remembering PLAT 608:16
L. is better than house PROV 637:14
l. is most excellent PROV 646:39
l. lightly like a flower TENN 796:6
l. many things SOLO 760:9
l.'s crumbs BROW 165:18
L. teacheth more ASCH 33:6
L., that cobweb BUTL 183:19
L. will be cast BURK 174:12
little l. is a dangerous thing POPE 615:28
loyal body wanted l. TRAP 814:17
man of polite l. DEFO 270:5
much l. doth make thee mad BIBL 110:15
nonsense, and l. GOLD 365:3
of a state, l. BACO 48:16
of liberty, and of l. DISR 285:1
pleasures that go with l. SOCR 760:4
pursuit of l. LAO 480:7
rights in l.'s world EGER 304:13
royal road to l. PROV 644:31
scraps of l. YOUN 876:10
traitor to l. JOHN 434:2
twins of l. SHAK 711:7
Wear your l. CHES 223:6
Whence is thy l. GAY 351:12
will to l. ASCH 33:3
written for our l. BOOK 135:11
learns fool l. by suffering HESI 397:4
l. a country WAUG 842:15
l. delight or pain SOPH 761:10
learnt forgotten nothing and l. nothing DUMO 299:7

They have l. nothing TALL 788:19
lease summer's l. SHAK 737:18
leasehold l. for all LUCR 504:12
least faithful in that which is l. BIBL 106:5
l. of all seeds BIBL 101:15
l. of these my brethren BIBL 103:7
leather nothing like l. PROV 644:32
leave for ever taking l. RILK 661:18
If you can't l. in a taxi FILM 328:15
Intreat me not to l. thee BIBL 83:23
L. all things behind BHAG 78:7
L. me, O Love SIDN 751:2
L. not a rack behind SHAK 733:31
L. not a stain BIBL 97:30
L. off first BIBL 97:28
l. spades alone SITW 753:14
l. the outcome CORN 251:14
l. the word of God BIBL 109:17
l. things alone you leave them CHES 225:14
l. without the King ELIZ 313:6
moment during l.-taking FLAU 333:10
Once I leave, I l. BALD 53:9
ready to l. MONT 554:21
shall a man l. his father BIBL 79:3
leaven l. leaveneth the whole lump BIBL 111:30
l. of malice BOOK 135:18
l. of malice and wickedness BIBL 111:31
leaves burning of the l. BINY 121:16
Crowned with calm l. SWIN 785:12
flaps its glad green l. HARD 381:8
laughing l. of the tree SWIN 784:21
l. are falling SHEL 745:11
l. behind a part of oneself HARA 379:14
l. cover me SWIN 785:25
l. dead Are driven SHEL 745:6
l. fall early POUN 621:11
l. like light footfalls SHEL 745:5
l. of the tree BIBL 119:21
l. to a tree KEAT 457:20
l. to the trees HORA 413:17
noise among the l. KEAT 455:2
stipple l. with sun SACK 677:1
tender l. of hope SHAK 710:19
Thick as autumnal l. MILT 541:21
thou among the l. KEAT 456:5
Very like l. HOME 404:13
withered l. ARNO 30:5
Words are like l. DILL 283:4
leaving L. his country FITZ 330:16
like the l. it SHAK 718:18
Lebanon cedared L. KEAT 454:13
cedars of L. BIBL 83:10
Lebens L. goldner Baum GOET 362:1
lecher small gilded fly Does l. SHAK 716:17
lecherous L. as a sparwe CHAU 218:24
rough and l. SHAK 715:1
lechery L., sir, it provokes SHAK 720:13
wars and l. SHAK 734:22
lectorem L. delectando HORA 409:12
lecture l., love, in love's philosophy DONN 289:9
lecturer requisite to a l. FARA 323:7
lectures l. or a little charity WHIT 852:12
led we are most l. BYRO 191:10
lees wine on the l. BIBL 92:23
left better to be l. CONG 247:20
but of my l. hand MILT 546:9
down the l. arm BARR 59:15
everything is l. out JAME 429:15
goats on the l. BIBL 103:5
l. a lot o' little things KIPL 465:5
L. hand down a bit CATC 208:15
l.-handed marriage WOLL 863:11
l. thy first love BIBL 117:29
let not thy l. hand know BIBL 99:10
O let them be l. HOPK 407:12
other l. BIBL 102:28
something l. to treat MALL 517:16
leg does not resemble a l. APOL 25:4
here I leave my second l. HOOD 405:16
lift a lawless l. BURN 178:14
my Julia's dainty l. HERR 396:7
legally accomplishing small things l. BALZ 57:4

lege Tolle l. — AUGU 39:8
legend before your l. ever did — JOHN 434:5
  before your l. will — JOHN 434:8
  fables in the l. — BACO 46:5
  true l. — STAL 769:17
  When the l. becomes fact — FILM 329:24
legends Men must have l. — MURR 566:4
Leger come back on St L. day — SAYI 685:10
leges l. inter arma — CICE 232:8
legibility dawn of l. — HAY 385:13
Legion My name is L. — BIBL 103:31
legions give me back my l. — AUGU 40:2
legislation imports and exports, l. — ARIS 26:21
  possess divine l. — MEND 531:24
  true basis of English l. — GLAD 360:6
legislator l. of mankind — JOHN 437:15
  people is the true l. — BURK 175:9
legislators idea of hereditary l. — PAIN 592:21
  unacknowledged l. — SHEL 747:14
legislature work for a L. — ELLI 314:5
legitimate l. warfare — NEWM 571:15
legs any man's l. — BOOK 150:7
  born with your l. apart — ORTO 586:15
  cannon-ball took off his l. — HOOD 405:15
  dog's walking on his hinder l. — JOHN 440:7
  four bare l. in a bed — PROV 644:16
  Four l. good — ORWE 586:17
  If you could see my l. — DICK 278:4
  l. are as pillars of marble — BIBL 91:10
  loves to fold his l. — JOHN 442:12
  My l., the emblem — BUCK 170:1
  not for your bad l. — ELIZ 312:8
  strength, not of l. — MONT 555:3
  stretches his l. — PROV 631:32
  use of his l. — DICK 279:13
  vast and trunkless l. — SHEL 745:15
  Walk under his huge l. — SHAK 711:19
legunt sed ista l. — MART 524:5
Leicester Farewell, L. Square — JUDG 449:4
  Here lies the Earl of L. — EPIT 318:2
Leicestershire finest run in L. — PAGE 592:1
leiden L. oder triumphieren — GOET 362:8
leisure At l. married — CONG 247:16
  busiest have most l. — PROV 628:26
  conspicuous l. — VEBL 825:20
  detest at l. — BYRO 189:17
  fill l. intelligently — RUSS 674:19
  have l. to bother — SHAW 742:3
  Idle have the least l. — PROV 635:3
  improvement arises from l. — JOHN 441:7
  increased l. — DISR 284:27
  l. answers leisure — SHAK 723:20
  L. with honour — CICE 232:10
  life of l. — MORE 558:21
  luck in l. — PROV 644:25
  never at l. — JOHN 442:12
  opportunity of l. — BIBL 97:33
  polish it at l. — DRYD 297:11
  Politicians also have no l. — ARIS 27:15
  repent at l. — PROV 638:33
  When I have l. — HILL 399:9
leman such l. — BALL 56:2
lemon in the squeezing of a l. — GOLD 365:5
  l.-trees bloom — GOET 362:18
lemonade make l. — SAYI 684:25
lemons If life hands you l. — SAYI 684:25
  Oranges and l. — NURS 580:15
lend l. me your ears — SHAK 712:28
  L. you money and lose — PROV 637:16
  men who l. — LAMB 476:14
lender borrower, nor a l. be — SHAK 700:5
lenders pen from l.' books — SHAK 715:26
lendeth merciful, and l. — BOOK 148:1
lendings Off, off, you l. — SHAK 715:27
lends Three things I never l. — SURT 781:12
length drags its dreary l. — DICK 276:10
  drags its slow l. — POPE 616:5
  in l. of days — BIBL 86:28
  l. and breadth — BALL 54:12
  L. begets loathing — PROV 637:17
  L. of days — BIBL 87:22
  what it lacks in l. — FROS 344:15
lengthens As the day l. — PROV 626:38

lengths go to the l. of God — FRY 345:19
lengthy meaning of l. speech — SCHI 683:18
Lenore angels name L. — POE 611:1
lente Festina l. — AUGU 40:3
  L. currite noctis equi — OVID 589:17
  l., lente, currite — MARL 522:11
leoni vulpes aegroto cauta l. — HORA 410:2
Léonie Weep not for little L. — GRAH 367:12
leopard l. change his spots — BIBL 95:3
  l. does not change — COMP 245:6
  l. does not change — PROV 637:18
  l. shall lie down — BIBL 92:17
leopards three white l. sat — ELIO 308:22
leper innocence is like a dumb l. — GREE 371:19
  wash the l.'s wounds — TERE 801:21
leprosy skin was white as l. — COLE 240:22
lerne gladly wolde he l. — CHAU 218:16
Lesbia L. whom Catullus once loved — CATU 210:14
  L. with her sparrow — MILL 537:3
  Let us live, my L. — CATU 210:6
  My sweetest L. — CAMP 195:21
Lesley bonnie L. — BURN 177:19
less for nothing l. than thee — DONN 289:2
  had he pleased us l. — ADDI 4:9
  How l. what we may be — BYRO 189:26
  L. is a bore — VENT 826:3
  L. is more — PROV 637:19
  L. than the dust — HOPE 407:4
  l. we love her — PUSH 650:18
  little l. — BROW 165:9
  more and more about l. and less — BUTL 183:2
  small Latin, and l. Greek — JONS 446:24
  you can't take l. — CARR 202:7
lessen l. from day to day — CARR 202:12
lesser l. breeds — KIPL 467:7
  l. to be chosen — THOM 805:3
lessons l. to be drawn — ELIZ 313:4
  reason they're called l. — CARR 202:12
lest L. we forget — KIPL 467:5
let l. and hindered — BOOK 135:12
  L. my people go — BIBL 81:4
  L. my people go — SONG 763:16
  L.'s go to work — FILM 329:1
  l. them all to my elder — THOM 806:18
  l. the sounds of music — SHAK 725:10
  L. us with a gladsome mind — MILT 540:1
Lethe go not to L. — KEAT 455:26
  waters of L. — GINS 359:2
Lethean drunken of things L. — SWIN 785:19
letter by speech than by l. — BACO 47:19
  how large a l. — BIBL 113:27
  huge wordy l. — JUVE 451:12
  l. by strange letter — HEAN 387:5
  l. from his wife — CARR 204:6
  l. killeth — BIBL 113:7
  l. to my love — BALL 54:14
  made this [l.] longer — PASC 597:12
  my l. to the world — DICK 282:2
  name and not the l. — PROV 628:41
  scarlet l. — HAWT 385:8
  Someone wants a l. — ADVE 8:16
  thou unnecessary l. — SHAK 715:8
  uncertain process of l.-writing — ELIO 308:14
  used to start a l. — PLIN 610:1
  very touch of the l. — NIN 576:8
  were reading a l. — TALM 790:15
  when he wrote a l. — BACO 46:18
letters burn your l. — ADAM 3:4
  can't write l. — BISH 122:13
  L. for the rich — AUDE 37:19
  l. get in the wrong places — MILN 538:12
  l. in the grave — JOHN 444:11
  l., methinks, should be free — OSBO 588:10
  l. mingle souls — DONN 289:23
  L. of thanks — AUDE 37:20
  l. to a non-existent — LEWI 492:1
  like women's l. — HAZL 385:20
  nat the l. space — CHAU 221:10
  No arts; no l. — HOBB 400:24
  professor of French l. — JOYC 448:22
  twenty-two fundamental l. — SEFE 691:5
letting l. each other go — RILK 662:1

proved in the l. go — DAY- 269:10
lettuce eating too much l. — POTT 620:6
letumque L. Labosque — VIRG 830:9
levee Drove my Chevy to the l. — MCLE 512:3
  more alluring than a l. — CONG 247:25
level l. of provincial existence — ELIO 308:6
  Those who attempt to l. — BURK 174:3
  to one dead l. ev'ry mind — POPE 613:24
leveller Death is the great l. — PROV 629:37
leviathan draw out l. — BIBL 87:17
  L., called a commonwealth — HOBB 400:14
  L. Hugest of living creatures — MILT 543:27
  l. retrieving pebbles — WELL 846:18
  there is that L. — BOOK 147:9
levity little judicious l. — STEV 776:7
lewd certain l. fellows — BIBL 109:33
Lewley bricks to L. — BETJ 76:4
lex Salus populi suprema l. — SELD 691:16
  suprema est l. — CICE 231:18
lexicographer L. A writer of dictionaries — JOHN 436:1
  wake a l. — JOHN 435:19
lexicon Two men wrote a l. — WATE 841:3
lexicons We are walking l. — LIVE 496:2
liar answered 'Little L.' — BELL 68:4
  best l. — BUTL 184:5
  every man a l. — BIBL 110:25
  he is a l. — BIBL 107:31
  l. should be outlawed — HALI 377:9
  l. to have good memory — PROV 637:26
  opposite of what the l. — MONT 554:18
  penalty of a l. — TALM 789:30
  proved l. — HAIL 376:7
  She's like a l. — SHAK 729:17
liars All men are l. — BOOK 148:8
  fears may be l. — CLOU 237:6
  Income Tax made more L. — ROGE 666:3
  l. and swearers — SHAK 722:4
  L. ought to have good memories — SIDN 750:8
  Poets . . . though l. — HUME 420:17
  prove the greatest l. — DRAY 293:13
libation pouring a l. — SOCR 760:5
libel excessive wealth a l. — SHEL 747:9
  greater the l. — PROV 633:29
  l. in a frown — SWIF 783:26
libellum novum l. — CATU 210:1
liber L. scriptus — MISS 550:6
liberal as distinguished from the L. — BIER 121:6
  damned l. majority — IBSE 424:4
  either a little L. — GILB 356:18
  first L. leader — STEE 770:11
  is a l. education — STEE 770:17
  l. education — BANK 57:10
  l. is a conservative who — WOLF 863:2
  l. of another man's — BACO 47:27
  panted for a l. profession — COLM 244:4
liberality l. becomes a source — BAED 49:18
liberals l. can understand — BRUC 168:13
liberation l. of the human mind — GOLD 363:17
liberavi L. animam meam — BERN 73:20
libertas Imperium et L. — DISR 285:10
  L. et natale solum — SWIF 784:13
Liberté L.! Égalité — POLI 613:1
liberties give up their l. — BURK 175:23
  l. are taken in thy name — GEOR 353:10
  L. . . . depend on the silence — HOBB 401:2
  not to have l. — PYM 651:1
libertine puffed and reckless l. — SHAK 700:2
liberty ardour for l. — PRIC 622:15
  be light! said L. — SHEL 744:4
  Brightest in dungeons, L. — BYRO 191:1
  certainly destroys l. — JOHN 443:12
  chosen music, L. — WORD 869:16
  conceived in all l. — LINC 494:1
  contend for their l. — HALI 377:17
  contrary to l. — BENT 71:9
  cost of l. — DU B 298:5
  dangers to l. lurk — BRAN 155:1
  delight with l. — SPEN 768:1
  democratic state is l. — ARIS 28:6
  desires in l. — TOCQ 811:16
  divests himself of natural l. — LOCK 497:16
  endanger the public l. — ADAM 3:1

Such is l. — KELL 459:10
suicide wills l. — SCHO 686:15
take my l. — FARQ 324:8
take my l. and all — SHAK 725:6
taken over one's mortal l. — LUCR 504:13
taking l. by the throat — FROS 345:9
That l. so short — CHAU 220:21
That which we call l. — DONN 289:27
There's the l. for ever — STEV 777:1
they which he slew in his l. — BIBL 83:19
this gives l. to thee — SHAK 737:19
This l. is most jolly — SHAK 697:5
this long disease, my l. — POPE 614:18
Thou art my l. — HERR 396:13
Thou art my l. — QUAR 651:11
three-fourths of our l. — ARNO 32:4
Time to taste l. — BROW 165:23
tired of l. — JOHN 442:10
took a man's l. with him — CARL 199:18
torch of l. — LUCR 504:10
Touch my l. — TAGO 787:18
tree of l. — BIBL 78:20
tree of l. — BIBL 88:6
try to crowd out real l. — FORS 338:10
understand just one l. — RUSH 672:16
upon the thorns of l. — SHEL 745:10
value of l. — MONT 554:24
view of l. — DARW 266:17
voyage of their l. — SHAK 713:28
walk in newness of l. — BIBL 110:33
warm full blooded l. — JOYC 448:21
Was my l. also — OWEN 591:9
way, the truth, and the l. — BIBL 108:14
well-written L. — CARL 199:14
We should show l. — CHEK 221:22
What a relaxed l. — LUIS 504:16
What is l. — ROST 670:4
What is l.? a frenzy — CALD 193:7
What is this l. — DAVI 268:8
what is your l. — BIBL 116:26
What l. and death is — CHAP 216:5
what l. is then to a man — BIBL 97:29
what matters in your l. — RUSH 672:15
wheel of l. run long — STER 773:9
which tells of l. — COLE 241:14
While there's l. — PROV 647:14
whole l. shows in your face — BACA 45:3
Wholesome of l. — HORA 411:19
Who saw l. steadily — ARNO 31:1
wine should l. employ — GAY 351:5
With long l. — BOOK 146:3
Without work, l. goes rotten — CAMU 196:21
work till the end of my l. — SWAN 781:25
write the l. of a man — JOHN 441:2
years of my l. — BIBL 80:28
you lived your l. — JOHN 434:5
your longer l. — ELIZ 312:9
life-blood l. of a master spirit — MILT 545:23
lifeless virtue is l. — PAST 598:16
life-lie Take the l. away — IBSE 424:11
lifetime knowledge of a l. — WHIS 850:10
l. of happiness — SHAW 740:21
lift L. her with care — HOOD 405:10
l. me as a wave — SHEL 745:10
l. up mine eyes — BOOK 148:17
L. up your heads — BOOK 141:2
L. up your heart — WESL 847:16
L. up your hearts — BOOK 137:12
Lord, l. thou up — BOOK 139:16
Lord l. up his countenance — BIBL 82:2
people who l. — WILC 854:10
lifting l. up of my hands — BOOK 149:21
light armour of l. — BIBL 111:16
armour of l. — BOOK 135:10
as the shining l. — BIBL 87:25
bathe the world in l. — WORD 865:12
bear witness of that L. — BIBL 106:38
between l. and darkness — SIDD 750:7
blaze of living l. — BYRO 187:13
brief crack of l. — NABO 566:19
brings l. to others — LA R 481:19
Buddha of Infinite L. — MAHÀ 515:19
burning and a shining l. — BIBL 107:18

certain Slant of l. — DICK 281:22
children of l. — BIBL 106:3
children of l. — BOOK 138:7
crazed with the love of l. — MONT 555:27
Creature, which was L. — BACO 48:27
crying for the l. — TENN 795:14
dark is l. enough — FRY 345:13
darkness rather than l. — BIBL 107:14
day-labour, l. denied — MILT 545:15
dim religious l. — MILT 539:20
dying of the l. — THOM 805:15
Endless L. — ZORO 879:14
Even L. itself — THOM 808:21
excess of l. — GRAY 370:20
fierce l. which beats — TENN 793:24
fire, to give them l. — BIBL 81:12
freedom is but a l. — GUMI 374:13
From darkness lead me to L. — UPAN 821:16
from the serene L. — HILD 398:8
garmented in l. — SHEL 747:6
Give me a l. — HASK 384:3
gives a lovely l. — MILL 536:21
giveth l. unto the eyes — BOOK 140:10
God is L. — BLAK 124:20
growing l. — SHAK 710:6
hath the l. shined — BIBL 92:13
how my l. is spent — MILT 545:14
infinite ocean of l. — FOX 339:13
into the world of l. — VAUG 825:9
Jeanie with the l. brown hair — FOST 339:1
know what l. is — JOHN 442:6
Lead, kindly L. — NEWM 572:16
Let's in new l. — WALL 837:1
Let there be l. — BIBL 78:12
Let there be l. — BYRO 189:10
Let there be l. — MARR 523:19
Let there be l. — SHEL 744:4
Let your l. so shine — BIBL 98:28
l. after smoke — HORA 409:7
l., and will aspire — SHAK 738:27
l. at the end of the tunnel — DICK 282:8
l. at the end of the tunnel — LOWE 503:10
l. break forth — BIBL 94:16
L. breaks where no sun — THOM 806:1
l. but the shadow — BROW 162:3
L. come, light go — PROV 637:29
l. dissolved in star-showers — SHEL 746:15
l. excelleth darkness — BIBL 89:22
l. fantastic round — MILT 538:24
l. fantastic toe — MILT 539:24
l. gleams an instant — BECK 64:24
L. (God's eldest daughter) — FULL 346:11
l. has gone out of our lives — NEHR 569:10
l. in the darkness of mere being — JUNG 449:12
l. in the dust — SHEL 744:18
l. into bodies — NEWT 574:2
l. is as darkness — BIBL 86:25
l. is come — BIBL 94:18
l. is sweet — BIBL 90:18
l. is to painting — BOUR 153:4
l. my fire — MORR 561:5
l. of common day — WORD 867:9
l. of evening, Lissadell — YEAT 873:15
l. of his countenance — BOOK 144:4
l. of Jurisprudence — COKE 238:13
L. of Light — BOOK 137:2
l. of Terewth — DICK 276:18
l. of the heavens — KORA 472:12
l. of the world — BIBL 98:27
l. of thy countenance — BOOK 139:10
l. of thy countenance — BOOK 145:10
l. of thy Holy Spirit — BOOK 136:2
l. on the hill — CHIF 226:1
l., shade, and perspective — CONS 249:20
l. shineth in darkness — BIBL 106:36
l. that never was — WORD 865:9
l. to lighten the Gentiles — BIBL 104:17
l. to shine upon the road — COWP 255:16
l. to them that sit in darkness — BIBL 104:10
l. unto my paths — BOOK 148:14
line of festal l. — ARNO 30:10
Lonely and lost to l. — BYRO 187:8
long l. shakes — TENN 799:7

meditate on the lovely l. — RIG 661:13
More l. — GOET 363:6
more l. — SORL 761:24
my l., and my salvation — BOOK 141:9
neither heat nor l. — WEBS 844:10
new l. of grace — SMOL 759:8
noose of l. — FITZ 330:17
once our brief l. has set — CATU 210:6
once we lose this l. — JONS 446:12
particles of l. — BLAK 126:26
perpetual l. — MISS 550:4
place of l. — DISR 285:1
progeny of l. — MILT 543:22
pure and endless l. — VAUG 825:14
pure severity of perfect l. — TENN 794:8
Put out the l. — SHAK 729:13
reft the sonne his l. — CHAU 219:5
seen a glorious l. — SCOT 690:12
seen a great l. — BIBL 92:13
set is our little l. — CAMP 195:21
shew l. at Calais — JOHN 440:6
silent as l. — SMIT 759:4
soft! what l. — SHAK 732:9
speed far faster than l. — BULL 170:7
sudden gust of l. — MOTI 562:11
sweetness and l. — ARNO 31:9
sweetness and l. — SWIF 782:2
Teach l. to counterfeit a gloom — MILT 539:16
Thou art my l. — QUAR 651:11
through the realms of l. — GURN 374:19
thy l. and thy truth — BOOK 142:9
tried to mend the Electric L. — BELL 68:16
universal l. — POPE 615:26
upon the steps of the l. — MACD 510:7
waited for the l. — ROBI 663:20
Warmth and L. — GREN 372:10
when my l. is low — TENN 795:11
Wherefore is l. given — BIBL 86:18
where sweetness and l. failed — FORS 337:19
while the l. fails — ELIO 309:21
Will l. only shine — BERN 74:2
with a l. behind her — GILB 358:14
with Thee l. — BONH 132:11
Light Brigade Forward, the L. — TENN 793:4
lighten let thy mercy l. upon us — BOOK 133:11
L. our darkness — BOOK 134:10
l. with celestial fire — BOOK 150:16
lighter l. than vanity — BUNY 171:9
lightest l. things swim at the top — HALI 377:13
lighthouse Keeping a l. with his eyes — CAMP 195:3
sitivation at the l. — DICK 280:26
lightly l. as it comth — CHAU 220:1
unadvisedly, l., or wantonly — BOOK 138:21
lightness unbearable l. of being — KUND 474:5
lightning Art, and the summer l. — HERZ 396:24
bottled l. — DICK 279:19
chaos illuminated by l. — WILD 855:8
from Jove the l. — MANI 519:7
known the l.'s hour — DAY- 269:8
l. and lashed rod — HOPK 408:6
l. fall from heaven — BIBL 105:2
L. never strikes — PROV 637:30
loosed the fateful l. — HOWE 417:3
postillion struck by l. — DESP 274:14
Shakespeare by flashes of l. — COLE 242:2
snatched the l. — TURG 819:7
to keep the l. out — ISHE 426:2
writing history with l. — WILS 859:14
lights dimming of the l. — NICO 575:2
Father of l. — BIBL 116:17
Followed false l. — DRYD 295:24
glare of l. — CHRÉ 226:19
God made two great l. — BIBL 78:15
l. are dim and low — ORRE 586:7
l. around the shore — ROSS 669:23
may bear all l. — SHAF 693:19
northern l. astream — SMAR 755:14
Turn up the l. — HENR 392:11
watching the tail l. — CRAN 258:17
your l. burning — BIBL 105:16
ligno Regnavit a l. Deus — FORT 338:16
like but you'll l. it — CATC 209:5

wanteth not l. — BIBL 91:14
lirra Tirra l. — TENN 796:18
lisped l l. in numbers — POPE 614:17
Somwhat he l. — CHAU 218:13
list I've got a little l. — GILB 357:3
List, list, O, l. — SHAK 700:17
snatched up the l. — AKHM 10:6
There is no l. — STRA 779:2
listen Darkling l l. — KEAT 456:9
l. all day — CARR 202:1
L., my children — LONG 499:25
l. the more — ZENO 877:14
only l. when I am unhappy — SMIT 757:16
privilege of wisdom to l. — HOLM 403:11
Stop-look-and-l. — OFFI 584:13
world should l. then — SHEL 746:24
listened he is not l. to — TALM 789:30
listener always be a mere l. — JUVE 450:10
l., who listens in the snow — STEV 774:13
listeners L. never hear any good — PROV 637:37
listening disease of not l. — SHAK 707:6
l., lying in wait — THOM 806:20
People hearing without l. — SIMO 752:15
listeth wind bloweth where it l. — BIBL 107:12
lit whole Fleet's l. up — WOOD 864:1
literal say a l. God — DONN 290:2
literary If I had to do l. work — SALI 679:2
l. and scientific — ARNO 31:21
l. cooks — MORE 558:19
l. man — DICK 280:7
l. prejudices — JOHN 436:22
l. productions — GIBB 354:7
Never l. attempt — HUME 420:15
Of all the l. scenes — PRES 622:12
parole of l. men — JOHN 443:6
unsuccessful l. man — BELL 68:13
with St Paul are l. — ARNO 32:2
literature function of imaginative l. — EMPS 315:28
great Cham of l. — SMOL 759:10
ideas to l. — BOUR 153:4
in l., the oldest — BULW 170:15
in the locks of l. — TENN 803:6
itch of l. — LOVE 502:10
life ruined by l. — BROO 159:18
like their l. clear and cold — LEWI 492:12
l. can and should do — BYAT 184:24
L. cannot be the business — SOUT 764:24
l. is a drug — BORR 151:13
L. is a luxury — CHES 225:3
l. is more dependable — BROD 157:15
l. is my mistress — CHEK 222:8
L. is news — POUN 621:14
L. mostly about having sex — LODG 498:4
l. of *power* — DE Q 274:1
L.'s always a good card — BENN 70:20
l. seeks to communicate — DE Q 273:20
l.'s performing flea — O'CA 583:9
L. the orchestration of platitudes — WILD 856:19
lover of l. — SOUT 764:18
Philistine of genius in l. — ARNO 32:6
profession of l. — JOHN 437:21
province of l. — MACA 507:23
Remarks are not l. — STEI 771:2
rest is l. — COLE 242:17
rest is l. — VALÉ 823:12
superior man studies l. — CONF 246:5
wash l. off — ARTA 32:19
lites *inter vos tantas componere l.* — VIRG 831:23
litigious l. lady — NEWT 574:8
littérature *tout le reste est l.* — VERL 826:8
little as bad as too l. — FERB 325:3
big words for l. matters — JOHN 440:9
by l. and little — BIBL 97:23
cry of the L. Peoples — LE G 487:20
eat up the l. ones — SHAK 729:26
Every l. helps — PROV 631:23
Ev'ry day a l. death — SOND 761:1
Go, l. bok — CHAU 221:11
had a l. gun — NURS 581:14
here a l., and there a little — BIBL 93:1
hobgoblin of l. minds — EMER 315:6
how l. the mind — JOHN 441:16

how l. we think of the other — TWAI 820:16
l. and loud — PROV 637:50
L. boxes on the hillside — REYN 659:10
l. creep through — SHEN 747:20
L. drops of water — CARN 201:5
L. Englanders — ANON 18:14
l. fire kindleth — BIBL 116:23
L. fish are sweet — PROV 637:39
l. grey cells — CHRI 227:2
l. learning is a dangerous thing — POPE 615:28
little l. grave — SHAK 730:23
Little man, l. man — ELIZ 312:13
L. man, you've had a busy day — SIGL 751:13
L. Miss Muffet — NURS 579:19
l. more — BROW 165:9
L. one! Oh, little one — STEP 772:7
l. people pay taxes — HELM 390:8
l. pot is soon hot — PROV 637:40
l. saint — HERR 396:10
l. seemed to him great — MACA 507:12
l. ships of England — GUED 374:6
L. strokes fell great oaks — PROV 637:44
L. subject, little wit — CARE 198:18
L. things please — PROV 637:46
l. to say — SKEL 753:20
l. volume, but large book — CRAS 259:6
l. while — BIBL 108:22
l. woman who wrote — LINC 494:10
Love me l. — PROV 638:9
Man wants but l. — GOLD 364:14
Many a l. — PROV 638:24
no l. enemy — PROV 644:30
offering Germany too l. — NEVI 571:7
one of these l. ones — BIBL 100:31
our l. life — SHAK 733:31
Say l. and do much — SHAM 738:30
She gives but l. — YOUN 876:25
So l. done — RHOD 659:12
so l. done — TENN 795:18
Thank heaven for l. girls — LERN 490:13
this l. world — SHAK 730:10
though she be but l. — SHAK 726:20
too l. or too much — BARR 59:13
very l. one — MARR 523:20
wants that l. strong — HOLM 403:14
with so l. stir — WHIT 851:13
littleness For the long l. of life — CORN 252:3
liturgy Popish l. — PITT 607:12
Publick L. — BOOK 132:15
live as if you were to l. for ever — EDMU 304:1
be, feel, l. — HERD 395:6
better l. as we think — BOUR 153:3
Bid me to l. — HERR 396:12
cannot l. with you — MART 524:11
Can these bones l. — BIBL 95:20
cease to l. — ARNO 31:6
Come l. with me — DONN 288:26
Come l. with me — MARL 522:20
Come l. with me — PROV 629:12
Could she not l. — BYRO 185:21
dangerous to l. long — THOM 804:22
Days are where we l. — LARK 481:1
desires to l. long — SWIF 783:19
Easy l. and quiet die — SCOT 689:10
Eat to l. — PROV 630:48
enable its citizens to l. — WEIL 845:7
find out why we l. — CHEK 222:4
forgets to l. — LA B 474:19
Glad did l l. — STEV 777:5
hast no more to l. — SWIN 785:3
he isn't fit to l. — KING 463:10
He shall l. — BOOK 144:20
He shall l. by them — TALM 789:16
he shall l. in them — BIBL 81:28
He shall not l. — SHAK 713:18
how long I have to l. — BOOK 141:28
If you don't l. it — PARK 596:1
I joy to see My self now l. — HERR 396:8
I l. not in myself — BYRO 186:11
in him we l., and move — BIBL 110:5
in order to l. — DIDI 283:1
just shall l. by faith — BIBL 110:21
know how to l. right — HORA 411:2

let me l. to-night — SHAK 729:14
Let us l., my Lesbia — CATU 210:6
like the times they l. in — ALI 12:17
l. a dignified human life — AUNG 40:6
L. all you can — JAME 429:10
l. and last — CATU 210:3
l. and learn — POMF 611:11
L. and learn — PROV 637:47
L. and let live — PROV 637:49
l. and lie reclined — TENN 797:12
l. and take comfort — WORD 869:21
l. a novel — HARD 380:17
L. any longer in sin — BIBL 110:32
l. a thousand years — SHAK 712:21
l. beyond its income — BUTL 184:8
l. by bread alone — PROV 638:15
l. by sight — BUNY 172:2
l. dog is better — PROV 637:49
l. in a fantasy world — MURD 565:20
L. in despite of murder — CHAP 216:4
l. in interesting times — KENN 460:21
l. in interesting times — SAYI 685:2
l. in peace — ARIS 27:14
l. in society — ARIS 27:25
l. longest, see most — PROV 644:49
l., not as we wish — MENA 531:17
l. on this Crumpetty Tree — LEAR 486:11
l. on your knees — IBAR 424:2
l. or die wi' Charlie — HOGG 402:18
l. their creeds — GUES 374:9
l. this long — BLAK 124:7
l. through someone else — FRIE 343:7
l. till tomorrow — COWP 255:11
l. to do that — MART 524:3
l. together as brothers — KING 463:12
l. too long — DANI 264:9
l. to please — JOHN 438:3
l. to study — BACO 48:26
l. under the shadow of a war — SPEN 766:15
l., unseen, unknown — POPE 617:33
l. until you die — SAUN 682:15
l. well on nothing a year — THAC 803:4
L. with yourself — PERS 604:12
l. your life not as simple — PAST 598:19
long as ye both shall l. — BOOK 138:24
long to l. — BOOK 134:5
Man is born to l. — PAST 598:14
martyrdom to l. — BROW 162:12
means whereby I l. — SHAK 725:6
might as well l. — PARK 596:7
mortal millions l. *alone* — ARNO 31:3
must l. — ARGE 26:10
nations how to l. — MILT 546:7
never l. to be useless — WESL 848:6
no man see me and l. — BIBL 81:25
nothing to do but l. — COET 238:2
not l. to eat — MOLI 551:17
not stood up to l. — THOR 809:7
people who have had to l. — TWAI 820:20
Sacco's name will l. — VANZ 824:9
see so much, nor l. so long — SHAK 717:10
short time to l. — BOOK 139:8
should a man l. — PLAT 608:20
taught us how to l. — TICK 811:3
Teach me to l. — KEN 459:16
that people l. — FRAN 340:11
to l. dangerously — NIET 575:14
to l. is Christ — BIBL 114:16
To l. is like to love — BUTL 184:12
to l. is not — POMP 611:13
To l. is to change — NEWM 572:7
To l. without him — WOTT 870:9
to l. without labour — TAWN 791:5
To l. with thee — RALE 653:13
Too small to l. in — ANON 21:2
turn and l. with animals — WHIT 852:11
wanted to l. deep — THOR 809:22
way they have to l. — CATH 209:15
we bear to l. — POPE 617:5
We l., as we dream — CONR 248:20
We l. our lives — RILK 661:18
wouldn't l. under Niagara — CARL 200:29
would you l. for ever — FRED 342:1

lived Had we l. — SCOT 688:4
I have l. long enough — SHAK 722:16
l. during the years around 1789 — TALL 788:18
l. in social intercourse — JOHN 441:2
l. light in the spring — ARNO 29:8
never loved, has never l. — GAY 351:10
Never to have l. is best — YEAT 873:12
say 'I have l.' — HORA 413:8
lively l. Oracles of God — CORO 252:8
true and l. Word — BOOK 137:7
liver l. is on the right — MOLI 552:12
L. of blaspheming Jew — SHAK 721:17
l.-wing of a fowl — TENN 801:6
open and notorious evil l. — BOOK 136:16
livered But I am pigeon-l. — SHAK 701:22
liveries summer l. — LANI 479:5
Liverpool folk that live in L. — CHES 224:11
livery in her sober l. all things clad — MILT 543:9
shadowed l. — SHAK 724:10
lives Careless talk costs l. — OFFI 584:1
Clarissa l. — RICH 660:14
Everything that l. — BLAK 124:22
evil that men do l. — SHAK 712:28
He l., he wakes — SHEL 743:19
He that l. upon hope — FRAN 341:7
he who l. more lives than one — WILD 856:3
how he l. — JOHN 440:20
how the other half l. — PROV 641:1
in jeopardy of their l. — BIBL 84:24
it's men's l. — SCOT 689:8
light wind l. or dies — KEAT 457:3
l. along the line — POPE 616:25
l. by the sword — PROV 634:24
l. long who lives well — PROV 634:2
l. of quiet desperation — THOR 809:12
l. to eat — SOCR 759:16
l. would grow together — SWIN 786:2
make our l. sublime — LONG 499:17
ninety l. have been taken — MCGO 510:15
not where it l. — FULL 346:18
passing their l. together — HUME 420:4
pleasant in their l. — BIBL 84:12
their l. before — SHAK 730:9
way to conduct our l. — PLAT 608:22
woman who l. for others — LEWI 491:18
liveth he that l. longest — HENS 392:16
know that my redeemer l. — BIBL 86:34
l. unto God — BIBL 110:34
name l. for evermore — BIBL 98:5
name l. for evermore — EPIT 319:12
that l., and was dead — BIBL 117:28
livid one l. smile — WALP 838:8
living affords a rule of l. — ADDA 4:5
appointed for all l. — BIBL 87:4
are you yet l. — SHAK 727:15
book of the l. — BOOK 144:14
Earned a precarious l. — ANON 16:25
enemy to the l. — SHAK 694:1
envy of the l. — HOBB 401:9
even for the l. God — BOOK 142:4
fever called 'l.' — POE 610:18
fight for the l. — JONE 445:9
fillest all things l. — BOOK 150:2
for you to go on l. — SOCR 760:1
get mine own l. — BOOK 138:14
go on l. even after death — FRAN 341:1
hands of the l. God — BIBL 116:2
house is a machine for l. in — LE C 487:2
land of the l. — BIBL 94:5
land of the l. — WILD 856:17
language of the l. — ELIO 309:15
life is not worth l. — SOCR 759:22
l. according to nature — MORE 559:4
L. and partly living — ELIO 310:16
l. at this hour — WORD 866:16
l. death — MILT 545:3
l. dog — BIBL 90:8
l. doll, everywhere you look — PLAT 608:3
l. in a time — BREC 156:4
l. in Philadelphia — EPIT 318:7
L. is abnormal — IONE 425:16
L. is an illness — CHAM 214:14
L. is my job — MONT 555:11

l. know No bounds — SHIR 749:20
l. man is the glory — IREN 425:19
l. need charity — ARNO 29:1
l. sacrifice — BIBL 111:9
L.? The servants will do that — VILL 828:5
l. to some purpose — PAIN 593:6
l. up to it that is difficult — THAC 802:16
long habit of l. — BROW 162:13
machine for l. — TOLS 813:16
more alone while l. — CARR 201:8
more than the l. — BIBL 89:25
nets to catch the l. — WEBS 844:6
noble L. — WORD 868:19
no l. of its own — JENN 432:20
no l. people in it — CHEK 221:22
no l. with thee — ADDI 5:4
no man l. — BOOK 149:23
Plain l. and high thinking — WORD 867:20
reasons for l. — JUVE 451:10
respect to the l. — VOLT 834:17
riotous l. — BIBL 105:29
start by l. — ANOU 24:12
Summer time an' the l. is easy — HEYW 397:19
those who are l. — BURK 174:16
to go on l. — WOLF 862:11
too much love of l. — SWIN 785:14
well and l. in Paris — ANON 18:9
Who, l., had no roof — HEYW 398:4
Why seek ye the l. — BIBL 106:28
world does not owe us a l. — PHIL 605:13
you'll learn the art of l. — GOET 362:2
Livingstone Dr L., I presume — STAN 770:1
livres l. cadrent mal — MOLI 552:9
lizard L.'s leg — SHAK 721:16
llama L. is a sort of fleecy goat — BELL 68:13
Lloyd George L. knew my father — ANON 18:16
lo L.! He comes — WESL 847:18
L.! the poor Indian — POPE 616:20
load l. and bless With fruit — KEAT 456:22
L. every rift — KEAT 458:16
loaf Half a l. is better — PROV 633:35
l. with a field in the middle — WILD 856:8
slice off a cut l. — PROV 643:14
with a l. of bread — FITZ 331:15
loafing cricket as organized l. — TEMP 792:16
loan l. oft loses — SHAK 700:5
loathe l. all things held — CALL 193:16
loathing Length begets l. — PROV 637:17
loaves five barley l. — BIBL 107:20
lobster l. be any more ridiculous — NERV 571:2
seen the mailed l. rise — FRER 342:14
voice of the L. — CARR 202:15
local little l. difficulties — MACM 512:18
l., but prized elsewhere — AUDE 38:10
l. habitation and a name — SHAK 727:3
l. thing called Christianity — HARD 380:10
locally act l. — SLOG 755:13
Lochinvar young L. is come — SCOT 688:21
loci Geniumque l. — VIRG 830:17
lock l. o' his gowden hair — BALL 56:3
why l. him in — SHAW 741:7
locked hand that l. her up — VAUG 825:13
locket Lucy l. lost — NURS 580:3
locks in the l. of literature — TENN 801:9
knotted and combinèd l. — SHAK 700:18
l. were like the raven — BURN 178:18
l. which are left you — SOUT 764:14
never shake Thy gory l. — SHAK 721:9
locksmiths Love laughs at l. — PROV 638:7
loco parentis Esse l. — JUVE 451:8
locust hath the l. eaten — BIBL 96:6
years that the l. hath eaten — BIBL 96:7
locusts l. and wild honey — BIBL 98:16
locuta Roma l. est — AUGU 39:22
lodestar he was the l. — LYDG 505:15
lodestone l. to the north — DAVI 267:21
lodge as a l. in a garden — BIBL 91:19
best to l. — SHAK 736:2
l. Him in the manger — ANON 21:16
lodged L. with me useless — MILT 545:14
lodging Hard was their l. — GART 350:2
lodgings l. in a head — BUTL 183:12
loft windy, untidy l. — CANN 197:9

lofty great and l. things — MONT 554:19
L. and sour — SHAK 711:6
log King L. — AESO 9:4
L.-cabin to White House — THAY 804:9
logic Good, too, L., of course — CLOU 236:15
l. and rhetoric — BACO 48:3
l. of our times — DAY- 269:11
Second L. then — ARIS 26:14
That's l. — CARR 203:2
logical L. consequences — HUXL 423:15
logically does not make them sound l. — HALD 376:12
must act l. — FRED 341:20
logs Tom bears l. — SHAK 717:25
loin ungirt l. — BROW 167:24
loins girded up his l. — BIBL 85:12
Let your l. be girded — BIBL 105:16
shudder in the l. engenders — YEAT 874:2
thicker than my father's l. — BIBL 85:2
Loire L. more than the Latin Tiber — DU B 298:4
loitered l. my life away — HAZL 386:3
loitering Alone and palely l. — KEAT 455:4
Lolita L., light of my life — NABO 566:16
Lombardy waveless plain of L. — SHEL 744:19
London 1938 in L. — MIDL 534:13
arch of L. Bridge — MACA 507:16
best club in L. — DICK 280:11
city much like L. — SHEL 745:18
crowd flowed over L. Bridge — ELIO 311:5
describes L. — BAGE 51:19
foggy day in L. Town — GERS 353:12
gazed at the L. skies — BETJ 75:9
going to L. — ELIO 308:3
gondola of L. — DISR 286:3
in L. only is a trade — DRYD 296:23
I've been to L. — NURS 580:20
key of India is L. — DISR 285:11
lies L.'s daughter — THOM 806:4
L.: a nation — DISR 286:2
L. Bridge is broken down — NURS 580:2
L. doth pour out — SHAK 709:9
L. is a fine town — COLM 244:2
L. is a modern Babylon — DISR 286:13
[L.] is become an overgrown — SMOL 759:7
L. is to Paddington — CANN 197:4
L. particular . . . A fog — DICK 276:11
L., small and white and clean — MORR 560:14
L. spread out in the sun — LARK 481:13
L.'s towers — BLAK 125:18
L., that great cesspool — DOYL 292:23
L., that great sea — SHEL 744:13
L., thou art of townes — ANON 18:17
L., thou art the flower — ANON 18:18
lungs of L. — PITT 607:17
rainy Sunday in L. — DE Q 273:18
tired of L. — JOHN 442:10
vilest alleys in L. — DOYL 292:7
Yankee Doodle came to L. — COHA 238:4
lone From the l. shieling — GALT 348:5
l. lorn creetur — DICK 277:5
l. unhaunted place — DONN 288:20
walking by his wild l. — KIPL 468:9
loneliness bowery l. — TENN 798:17
l. of the long-distance — SILL 752:11
well of l. — HALL 378:4
lonely All the l. people — LENN 489:7
heart is a l. hunter — MCCU 509:18
mirrors are l. — AUDE 38:4
None but the l. heart — GOET 362:20
Only the l. — ORBI 585:19
troubled with her l. life — PEPY 603:7
lonesome on a l. road — COLE 241:7
lonesomeness starlight lit my l. — HARD 382:4
long be the day l. — PROV 627:26
dangerous to live l. — THOM 804:22
foot and a half l. — HORA 409:3
For a l. time — PROU 625:5
for such a l. time — MOLI 552:4
fulfilled a l. time — BIBL 97:1
How l. a time — SHAK 730:5
How l. does a man — NERU 570:10
how l. I have to live — BOOK 141:28
how l. it takes to succeed — MONT 556:4

lord (*cont.*):
way of the L.	BIBL 93:15
we battle for the L.	ROOS 668:3
Welcum the l. of lycht	DOUG 291:10
what hour your L. doth come	BIBL 103:1
when they crucified my L.	SONG 763:15
Whom the L. loveth	BIBL 116:8

lords admiring the House of L.
	BAGE 50:19
from the House of L.	NORF 577:1
I made the carles l.	JAME 429:4
l. have their pleasures	MONT 556:5
L. in ermine	ROBI 664:6
l. of human kind	GOLD 364:26
l. o' the creation	BURN 180:6
l. who lay ye low	SHEL 746:11
l. whose parents were	DEFO 271:2
I will alway	BARC 58:5
New l., new laws	PROV 639:48
one of the l. of life	LAWR 483:23
Scots l. at his feet	BALL 55:17
wit among L.	JOHN 439:3
with those L. I had gone so far	MORE 559:9

lordships good enough for their l. ANON 20:20

lore l. its scholars need KEBL 459:2
volume of forgotten l.	POE 610:19

Lorraine cross of L. SPEA 765:16

lose cannot fear to l. ASTE 34:12
if you l., you lose nothing	PASC 598:5
is to l. it	ORWE 588:7
l. his own soul	BIBL 103:34
l. one parent	WILD 854:19
l. the name of action	SHAK 702:3
l. the war in an afternoon	CHUR 231:1
l. to-morrow	ARNO 30:11
l. what he never had	WALT 839:8
l. what you never had	PROV 648:9
nothing much to l.	HOUS 415:10
nothing to l.	MARX 526:14
nothing to l. but our aitches	ORWE 587:22
shall l. it	BIBL 100:30
to l. thee were to lose	MILT 544:9
way to l. him	SHAK 694:13
we don't want to l. you	RUBE 672:1
What you l. on the swings	PROV 646:33
win or l. it all	MONT 556:15
you l. a few	PROV 648:26

losers both should l. be HERB 394:21
he shall be among the l.	KORA 471:12
l. weepers	PROV 632:12
no winners, but all are l.	CHAM 214:4

loses l. his misery ARNO 30:14
Who l., and who wins	SHAK 717:1

losing conduct of a l. party BURK 172:14
deem a l. gain	SOUT 765:2
Hath but a l. office	SHAK 707:4
l. everything Except	DURC 300:9
l. one pleased Cato	LUCA 503:16
l. trade	BORR 151:13
l. your brain	FOX 340:1
l. your sight	SASS 682:6

loss but from its l. YOUN 876:17
counted l. for Christ	BIBL 114:22
do our country l.	SHAK 709:5
l. of innocence	HOWA 416:16
no great l. without	PROV 644:43
One man's l.	PROV 641:7
profit and l.	ELIO 311:16
text was l.	CUNN 262:17

lost All is l. save honour MISQ 547:1
All is not l.	MILT 541:13
All love is l.	DUNB 299:12
all was l.	MILT 544:6
and we are l.	PYRR 651:2
Are you l. daddy	LARD 480:16
Balls will be l. always	BERR 75:1
better to have fought and l.	CLOU 237:4
better to have loved and l.	PROV 646:3
better to have loved and l.	TENN 795:9
country is l.	WILL 857:3
Die in the l., lost fight	CLOU 236:14
every day to be l.	JOHN 444:8
everything is l.	VOLT 834:21

found my sheep which was l.	BIBL 105:27
France has not l. the war	DE G 271:7
hesitates is l.	PROV 634:21
Home of l. causes	ARNO 31:16
I have l. a day	TITU 811:10
I once was l.	NEWT 574:12
land of l. content	HOUS 416:4
let it be l.	CATU 210:8
l. all the names	JOHN 443:8
l. an empire	ACHE 1:13
l. boyhood of Judas	Æ 6:11
l. chord	PROC 624:16
l. dog somewhere	ANOU 24:13
l. evermore in the main	TENN 800:5
l., except a little life	BYRO 190:20
l. generation	STEI 771:6
l. me in your liking	SHAK 714:20
l. sheep	BIBL 100:22
l., that is unsought	CHAU 220:25
l. their mittens	NURS 582:2
l. the only Playboy	SYNG 786:10
l. the world for love	DRYD 296:19
l. traveller's dream	BLAK 125:9
l. Walter Cronkite	JOHN 435:8
L., yesterday	MANN 519:10
never l. till won	CRAB 258:2
never to have l. at all	BUTL 184:6
Next to a battle l.	WELL 846:7
none of them is l.	BIBL 108:24
nothing be l.	BIBL 107:21
Not l. but gone before	NORT 577:8
not l. but sent before	CYPR 263:15
not that you won or l.	RICE 659:20
paradises we have l.	PROU 626:1
they're l. to us	MART 524:6
Vietnam was l. in	MCLU 512:11
was l., and is found	BIBL 106:2
what is l. in translation	FROS 345:12
wherever we're l.	FRY 345:18
who deliberates is l.	ADDI 4:16

lot l. is fallen unto me BOOK 140:3
not a l. . . . . but you'll like	CATC 209:5
policeman's l. is not a happy one	GILB 358:8
Remember L.'s wife	BIBL 106:10

Lothario gay L. ROWE 671:6
Lothian West L. DALY 264:2
lotos L. and lilies TENN 798:26
lots cast l. upon my vesture BOOK 140:19
lottery judgement is a mere l. DRYD 297:17
l. is a taxation	FIEL 326:15
L., with weekly pay-out	ORWE 587:15
Marriage is a l.	PROV 638:31

lotus jewelled l. throne MAHĀ 516:3
plucks the l. without	TANT 790:7

Lou lady that's known as L. SERV 692:28
loud upon the l. cymbals BOOK 150:12
louder l. he talked of his honour EMER 314:21
loungers l. and idlers DOYL 292:23
lounging L. 'roun' en suffer'n' HARR 383:5
louse l. and a flea JOHN 443:16
l. in the locks of literature	TENN 801:9

lousy *House Beautiful* is play l. PARK 596:11
L. but loyal	SLOG 755:9
l. skin scabbed by cities	BUNT 170:18

lout l.'s game WEST 848:20
Louvre You're the L. PORT 619:20
love Absence is to l. BUSS 182:15
acquainted with L.	JOHN 439:6
Ah, l., let us be true	ARNO 29:5
Ah! what is l.	GREE 371:25
Alas! the l. of women	BYRO 188:25
all did l. him once	SHAK 713:6
all for l.	SPEN 767:3
All l. at first	BUTL 183:29
All l. is lost	DUNB 299:12
All's fair in l. and war	PROV 626:17
All that matters is l. and work	FREU 343:2
Amazing l.	WESL 847:6
and be my l.	MARL 522:20
and be thy l.	RALE 653:13
and L. the night	DRYD 296:24
And yet I l. this false	EPHE 316:7
Anxiety l.'s greatest killer	NIN 576:9

Any kiddie in school can l.	NASH 568:19
arms of my true l.	TENN 798:8
as she did l.	KEAT 455:7
bands of l.	BIBL 96:5
be wise, and l.	SHAK 734:16
bid me take l. easy	YEAT 873:4
bridge is l.	WILD 856:17
bring those who l. Thee	TERE 802:3
brotherly l. continue	BIBL 116:10
burned with l.	VIRG 831:17
but one true l.	BALL 56:4
but to l. much	TERE 802:2
came I to l. thee	AUGU 39:10
cannot l. a woman so well	ELIO 308:2
cantons of contemnèd l.	SHAK 735:6
caution in l.	RUSS 674:18
Christ's particular l.'s sake	BROW 167:14
come unto my l.	SPEN 766:22
commonly called l.	FIEL 326:19
constant l. deemed there	SIDN 750:17
corner in the thing I l.	SHAK 728:26
courage to l.	TROL 816:8
course of true l.	PROV 629:23
crime to l. too well	POPE 614:3
cruel madness of l.	TENN 797:20
dark secret l.	BLAK 128:2
daughterly l.	MORE 559:13
dearest l. in all the world	RODG 665:4
Dear l., for nothing less	DONN 289:2
Deep as first l.	TENN 799:12
desire more l. and knowledge	SHAK 696:11
disguise which can hide l.	LA R 481:20
Disinterested l. for all living	DARW 266:8
doesn't l. a wall	FROS 344:17
done a great deal for l.	FRAN 340:6
do not l. thee, Dr Fell	BROW 161:14
earth could never living l.	EPIT 318:2
Earth's the right place for l.	FROS 344:7
every man's l. affair with America	MAIL 516:8
experienced my greatest l.	PROU 625:8
failures in l.	MURD 565:14
faith and l.	BIBL 115:14
fall in l. today	GERS 353:13
fall in l. with me	SHAK 697:16
fate of l. is	BARR 59:13
fear casteth out l.	CONN 248:12
fear l. is to fear life	RUSS 674:22
first virtues aroused by l.	BALZ 56:17
flowers and fruits of l.	BYRO 190:21
food is l. and fame	SHEL 744:3
fool of l.	HAZL 386:6
For ever wilt thou l.	KEAT 455:19
for the l. he had to her	BIBL 80:12
for us, it's l.	BOUS 153:5
fou o' l. divine	BURN 178:13
Friendship is L.	BYRO 190:10
from the l. of God	BIBL 111:7
gates unto my l.	SPEN 766:21
Gather the rose of l.	SPEN 767:15
gentleness And show of l.	SHAK 711:14
gin l. be bonnie	BALL 56:6
God is l., but	LEE 487:7
God of l.	HERB 395:1
God si L.	FORS 338:11
good man's l.	SHAK 697:15
got l. well weighed up	AMIS 14:15
Greater l. hath no man	BIBL 108:18
greater l. hath no man	THOR 810:5
Greater l. than this	JOYC 448:22
groans of l. to those of the dying	LOWR 503:14
had a l. for Charlotte	THAC 803:8
half in l.	KEAT 456:9
hate is conquered by l.	PALI 594:16
Hearts wound up with l.	SPEN 766:12
heart whose l. is innocent	BYRO 190:26
Hell is to l. no more	BERN 73:16
He was all for l.	DIBD 276:2
He would l.	BRET 156:13
hidden l. of God	WESL 847:19
hid in the heart of l.	YEAT 874:10
hold l. out	SHAK 732:13
hold so fast, as l. can do	BURT 181:20
honeying and making l.	SHAK 703:14

love (cont.):

L. to the loveless shown	CROS 261:12
l. toward thee	BOOK 136:6
l. up groweth	CHAU 221:13
l. was passion's essence	BYRO 186:12
l. were what the rose is	SWIN 786:2
l. . . . whatever that may	CHAR 217:13
l. what thou dost love	HATC 384:4
L. will find a way	PROV 638:11
l. will steer the stars	RADO 653:8
l. will yield to business	OVID 590:17
l. without the rhetoric	STOP 777:19
L. with unconfinèd wings	LOVE 502:3
L. wol nat been constreyned	CHAU 219:3
l. you because I need you	FROM 344:2
l. you just the same	KIER 462:14
l. your enemies	BIBL 104:25
L. you ten years before	MARV 525:11
loving to l.	AUGU 39:3
make l. in a canoe	BERT 75:6
Make l. not war	SLOG 755:10
making l. all year round	BEAU 63:3
making l. to the Archbishop	SHER 749:3
Man's l. is of man's life	AMIS 14:14
Man's l. is of man's life	BYRO 188:3
Man's l. of God	MAIM 516:15
man, That l. my friend	SHAK 713:11
man you l. to hate	ADVE 8:2
man you l. to hate	FILM 329:5
marry them for l.	OSBO 588:12
may be crossed in l.	SHER 748:7
Men l. in haste	BYRO 189:17
met the L.-Talker	CARB 197:15
ministers of L.	COLE 240:10
money can't buy me l.	LENN 489:6
Most people l. love	PAST 598:15
music be the food of l.	SHAK 734:25
my l. and I did meet	YEAT 873:4
My l. and I would lie	HOUS 415:16
My l. for Heathcliff	BRON 158:19
my l.'s in tune	PROV 646:46
My only l.	SHAK 732:8
My song is l. unknown	CROS 261:12
needs must l. the highest	TENN 794:9
never l. a stranger	BENS 70:23
never taint my l.	SHAK 729:8
new l. may get	WALS 838:18
no l. for such	THOM 807:7
no lyves creature Withouten l.	CHAU 220:30
not enough to make us l.	SWIF 783:13
nothing but in l.	BACO 47:13
not that I l. you less	WALL 837:3
Now I know what L. is	VIRG 832:7
Now with his l.	CHAU 219:13
object of l.	LAMB 476:12
of connubial l.	MILT 543:13
office and affairs of l.	SHAK 727:18
off with the old l.	PROV 636:9
Of kindness and of l.	WORD 866:9
O L., O fire	TENN 793:13
O lyric L.	BROW 167:12
O my l. is slain	DONN 288:4
one jot of former l.	DRAY 293:14
ones we choose to l.	HARR 383:8
Only by l. can men see me	BHAG 78:5
Only l. can apprehend	RILK 662:4
onset and waning of l.	LA B 474:17
Onstage I make l.	JOPL 447:8
opposite of l.	WIES 853:11
our l. hath no decay	DONN 288:25
over hir housbond as hir l.	CHAU 220:15
pangs of disprized l.	SHAK 702:1
passing the l. of women	BIBL 84:13
path of true l.	EWAR 321:23
perfect l. casteth out fear	BIBL 117:19
philosopher of l.	DRYD 296:8
Pity is akin to l.	PROV 641:37
pluck the rose And l. it	BROW 168:6
power and effect of l.	BURT 181:19
presume too much upon my l.	SHAK 713:22
price we pay for l.	PARK 597:2
putting L. away	DICK 281:14
Queen's l.	BALL 54:7

quick-eyed L., observing	HERB 394:14
Rather than l., than money	THOR 809:27
renewing is of l.	EDWA 304:11
right true end of l.	DONN 288:2
same as for l.	FROS 345:5
search for l.	WALE 835:18
secret l.	BIBL 89:4
serves to resist l.	LA R 482:10
Service and l. above all other	DUNB 299:9
She never told her l.	SHAK 735:21
shows of l. to other men	SHAK 711:15
sports of l.	JONS 446:14
still their l. comes home to me	LAWL 483:9
successful without l.	TROL 815:18
support of the woman I l.	EDWA 304:5
survive of us is l.	LARK 480:19
sweet l.! was thought a crime	BLAK 127:21
take our fill of l.	BIBL 87:30
Tell l. it is but lust	RALE 653:16
them that l. God	BIBL 111:5
them that l. him	BIBL 111:25
them which l. you	BIBL 99:8
there are those who l. it	WEBS 843:19
There is l. of course	ANOU 24:10
There is only l.	MCEW 510:14
They l. indeed	SIDN 750:19
They l. their land	HALL 378:6
They l. us for it	TENN 799:14
they're in l.	TAGL 788:12
think my l. as rare	SHAK 738:20
this spring of l.	SHAK 736:14
those who l. the Lord	HUNT 421:4
thought l. would adapt itself	WALK 836:2
thought that l. would last	AUDE 37:5
Through l., through hope	WORD 868:26
time to l.	BIBL 89:23
tired of L.	BELL 68:9
'tis the hour of l.	BYRO 188:28
To live is like to l.	BUTL 184:12
to l. and be loved	SAND 679:20
to l. and rapture's due	ROCH 664:10
To manage l.	BUTL 183:28
tomb of l.	CASA 206:3
To see her is to l. her	BURN 177:19
to think but to l.	TERE 802:1
treason to our l.	THOR 810:3
true l. hath my heart	SIDN 750:14
true l. is a durable fire	RALE 654:4
true l. is, it showeth	DE P 273:15
'Twixt women's l., and men's	DONN 288:24
unity, and godly l.	BOOK 137:5
unlucky in l.	PROV 638:12
vegetable l. should grow	MARV 525:11
very few to l.	WORD 869:3
vividly gifted in l.	DUFF 298:14
War's like l.	HARE 382:7
was the song of l.	ROSS 669:17
waters cannot quench l.	BIBL 91:17
wayward is this foolish l.	SHAK 736:13
well-nourished l.	COLE 242:17
what is l.	RALE 653:14
What is l.	SHAK 735:9
What is L.	SHEL 747:15
What l. I bore to thee	WORD 866:6
When l. congeals	HART 383:11
When my l. swears	SHAK 738:22
where I cannot l.	BEHN 67:1
where l. is	BIBL 88:15
where the l. of God goes	LIGH 493:5
Where there is great l.	CATH 209:11
where there is no l.	BACO 46:33
who l., time is eternity	VAN 824:4
who l. want wisdom	SHEL 745:20
Whom the gods l.	MENA 531:16
Whom the Gods l.	PROV 647:17
Whom the gods l. die young	BYRO 189:2
whom we l. most	ABEL 1:2
wilder shores of l.	BLAN 128:17
wi' L. o'ercome	BURN 178:20
winds were l.-sick	SHAK 694:22
wish I were in l. again	HART 383:11
With l., even too much	BEAU 63:5
with my true l.	RALE 654:3

withstand L.'s shock	GOGA 363:9
woman's l. for us increases	PUSH 650:18
woman wakes to l.	TENN 794:19
Work first—l. next	GILM 358:20
Work is l. made visible	GIBR 355:16
world and l. were young	RALE 653:13
You can only l. one war	GELL 352:1
You may give them your l.	GIBR 355:14
'You must sit down,' says L.	HERB 394:15
your true l.'s coming	SHAK 735:8
loved all we l. of him	SHEL 743:14
always been l.	VOLT 834:3
And the l. one	BROW 166:21
better to have l. and lost	BUTL 184:6
better to have l. and lost	PROV 645:23
better to have l. and lost	TENN 795:9
Dante, who l. well	BROW 166:23
disciple whom Jesus l.	BIBL 109:9
feared than l.	MACH 511:7
God so l. the world	BIBL 107:13
him I l. the most	ANON 24:6
how much you were l.	CAVA 211:10
idols I have l.	FITZ 331:27
I have l.	SUCK 779:15
I l. a lass	WITH 861:6
I l. Ophelia	SHAK 704:20
I l. thee once	AYTO 44:5
I saw and l.	GIBB 354:23
Lavinia, therefore must be l.	SHAK 734:10
l. by the gods	PLAT 608:14
l. Caesar less	SHAK 712:25
l. each other beyond belief	HEIN 389:12
l. him so	BROW 166:13
l. him too much	RACI 652:14
L. I not honour more	LOVE 502:7
l. not at first sight	MARL 522:15
l. not at first sight	SHAK 697:17
l. the doctrine	DEFO 270:17
l. you, so I drew these tides	LAWR 484:9
men who have l. them	TROL 816:23
Might she have l. me	BROW 166:10
never be by woman l.	BLAK 124:12
never to have been l.	CONG 247:20
she l. much	BIBL 104:27
She who has never l.	GAY 351:10
Solomon l. many strange women	BIBL 85:1
thirst to be l.	RHYS 659:14
till we l.	DONN 289:7
To be l. as to love	FRAN 340:17
use him as though you l. him	WALT 839:9
We l., sir	BROW 165:13
who never l. before	ANON 23:6
wish I l. the Human Race	RALE 654:16
loveless Love to the l. shown	CROS 261:12
lovelier l. than your lovely mother	HORA 411:18
loveliness l. and perfection	MILT 545:27
l. I never knew	COLE 239:3
miracle of l.	GILB 357:12
portion of the l.	SHEL 743:20
weak from your l.	BETJ 76:7
woman of shining l.	YEAT 874:20
your l.	KEAT 458:9
lovely altogether l.	BIBL 91:10
Look thy last on all things l.	DE L 272:3
l. and pleasant	BIBL 84:12
l. at the beginning	PALI 594:9
l. boy	VIRG 831:18
L. enchanting language	HERB 394:11
l. is the rose	WORD 867:3
l. is thy dwelling-place	SCOT 690:10
l. woman stoops to folly	ELIO 311:15
l. woman stoops to folly	GOLD 365:14
more l. and more temperate	SHAK 737:18
once he made more l.	SHEL 743:20
She has a l. face	TENN 796:20
That they might l. be	CROS 261:12
what a l. war	LITT 495:14
whatsoever things are l.	BIBL 115:5
woods are l.	FROS 345:3
wouldn't it be l.	LERN 490:14
You have l. eyes	CHEK 222:6
lover affliction taught a l.	POPE 614:8

as true a l. — SHAK 696:20
Beauty is the l.'s gift — CONG 247:23
binds the l. — SANS 680:12
dividing l. and lover — SWIN 784:20
injured l.'s hell — MILT 543:20
l. and his lass — SHAK 697:24
l. and killer are mingled — DOUG 291:13
l., and the poet — SHAK 727:2
l. by lover — YEAT 875:11
l. of my soul — WESL 847:11
l.'s quarrel with the world — FROS 344:16
l. stole my rose — BURN 177:17
prove a l. — SHAK 731:13
roaming l. — CALL 193:16
she was a true l. — MALO 518:2
sighed as a l. — GIBB 355:1
some old l.'s ghost — DONN 289:10
truest l. — MALO 518:4
what is left of a l. — ROWL 671:9
Who could deceive a l. — VIRG 829:21
woman loves her l. — BYRO 188:14
woman says to her lusting l. — CATU 210:16
lovers Journeys end in l. meeting — SHAK 735:8
laughs at l.' perjuries — OVID 589:21
laughs at l.' perjuries — TIBU 811:1
laughs at l.' perjury — PROV 636:47
l.' declarations — AUDE 37:20
l.' perjury — DRYD 296:18
L., to bed — SHAK 727:9
l. were all untrue — DRYD 296:25
make two l. happy — POPE 617:31
old l. are soundest — WEBS 844:16
quarrel of l. — PROV 642:15
sleepless l. — POPE 618:5
star-crossed l. — SHAK 732:2
These l. fled away — KEAT 454:15
wonder if it's l. — MULD 564:14
loves all her l. around her — BYRO 190:9
all she l. is love — BYRO 188:14
baggage l. me — CONG 247:10
because God l. it — JULI 449:5
believe that God l. them — HUME 419:13
die to that which one l. — HARA 379:11
fooled by that which one l. — MOLI 552:22
For who l. that — MILT 545:13
He l. us not — SHAK 722:3
kills the thing he l. — WILD 855:32
lady l. Milk Tray — ADVE 7:6
life and l. of a she-devil — WELD 845:16
lines (so l.) oblique — MARV 524:19
l. his wife as himself — TALM 789:20
l. nothing but himself — SOUT 764:19
l. the fox less — SURT 781:9
l. what he is good at — SHAD 693:14
l. which follow — LA B 474:15
no creature l. me — SHAK 731:28
our l., must I remember them — APOL 25:3
reigned with your l. — ELIZ 312:10
son l. his sons — TALM 789:26
soul that l. is happy — GOET 361:12
where it l. — FULL 346:18
who l. me must have — TENN 794:11
Who l. ya, baby — CATC 208:34
woman whom nobody l. — CORN 252:2
lovesome garden is a l. thing — BROW 161:12
lovest l. thou me more — BIBL 109:5
poor sinner, l. thou me — COWP 255:14
loveth he that l. another — BIBL 111:15
He that l. not — BIBL 117:18
him whom my soul l. — BIBL 91:3
prayeth well, who l. well — COLE 241:10
whom the Lord l. — BIBL 87:21
Whom the Lord l. — BIBL 116:8
loving Can't help l. dat man — HAMM 378:14
discharge for l. one — MATL 528:4
For l., and for saying so — DONN 289:19
heart be still as l. — BYRO 191:4
I ain't had no l. — NORW 577:9
l. and giving — PROV 638:44
l. himself better than all — COLE 241:16
l.-kindness and mercy — BOOK 140:21
l. longest — AUST 42:5
l. people without cause — TOLS 813:17

l. the land that has taught — MOOR 558:4
l. to love — AUGU 39:3
most l. mere folly — SHAK 697:5
wickedness that hinders l. — BROW 166:23
loving-kindness deeds of l. — TALM 788:24
low dost thou lie so l. — SHAK 712:20
exalted them of l. degree — BIBL 104:9
Had me l. and had me down — GERS 353:12
l. as where this earth — ROSS 669:14
l. estate of his handmaiden — BIBL 104:8
l. on whom assurance sits — ELIO 311:14
Malice is of a l. stature — HALI 377:15
Sweet and l. — TENN 799:6
That l. man — BROW 165:25
Too l. for envy — COWL 254:12
upper station of l. life — DEFO 270:11
lowbrow first militant l. — BERL 73:12
Lowells L. talk to the Cabots — BOSS 151:17
lower l. classes had such white — CURZ 263:11
l. orders don't set us a good — WILD 854:14
l. than the angels — BOOK 139:23
l. than vermin — BEVA 76:13
While there is a l. class — DEBS 270:3
lowest l. and most dejected — SHAK 716:9
take the l. room — BIBL 105:18
lowlands Highlands and ye L. — BALL 54:6
sails by the L. — SONG 763:10
lowliness l. become mine inner clothing — LITT 495:13
lowly l. air Of Seven Dials — GILB 356:17
meek and l. in heart — BIBL 101:2
loyal Lousy but l. — SLOG 755:9
l. to his own career — DALT 264:1
loyalties l. which centre upon number one — CHUR 230:22
tragic conflict of l. — HOWE 416:18
loyalty constitute l. — BOSW 152:4
I want l. — JOHN 435:9
learned body wanted l. — TRAP 814:17
L. the Tory's secret weapon — KILM 462:17
l. we feel to unhappiness — GREE 371:16
LSD PC is the L. of the '90s — LEAR 486:13
Lucasta L., that bright northern star — LOVE 502:1
lucem ex fumo dare l. — HORA 409:7
lucid freqent l. intervals — CERV 213:6
l. intervals — BACO 48:22
Lucifer falls like L. — SHAK 710:20
L. arose — MERE 532:20
L., son of the morning — BIBL 92:20
luck believes in l. — STEA 770:10
devil's l. — PROV 629:46
Fools for l. — PROV 632:32
Good night and good l. — CATC 207:24
have had a stroke of l. — HERO 395:11
know about it [l.] — HART 383:18
l. in leisure — PROV 644:25
l. in odd numbers — PROV 644:26
l. of our name lost — HORA 413:16
mother of good l. — PROV 630:3
nae l. about the house — MICK 534:6
watching his l. — SERV 692:28
wished you good l. — BOOK 148:12
luckless What l. apple — MARV 525:16
lucky born l. than rich — PROV 636:11
L. at cards — PROV 638:12
l. if he gets out of it — FILM 328:22
l. to be born — WHIT 852:9
Third time l. — PROV 645:4
lucrative so l. to cheat — CLOU 237:2
lucre greedy of filthy l. — BIBL 115:19
lucro Fors dierum cumque dabit l. — HORA 411:13
Lucy L. ceased to be — WORD 869:5
L. Locket lost — NURS 580:3
Ludlow to L. come in — HOUS 415:17
Luftwaffe With your L. — PLAT 608:5
lug l. the guts — SHAK 703:22
lugete L., O Veneres — CATU 210:4
lugger Once aboard the l. — MISQ 548:13
Luke honour unto L. Evangelist — ROSS 669:19
lukewarm thou art l. — BIBL 118:1
lukewarmness L. I account a sin — COWL 254:16
lullaby dreamy l. — GILB 357:1

I will sing a l. — DEKK 271:22
Once in a l. — HARB 379:19
lumber loads of learned l. — POPE 616:13
lumen l. de lumine — MISS 549:12
luminous beating his l. wings — ARNO 31:22
l. home of waters — ARNO 30:19
with a l. nose — LEAR 485:16
luminously known l. — NEWM 572:19
lump leaven leaveneth the whole l. — BIBL 111:30
l. bred up in darkness — KYD 474:10
L. the whole thing — TWAI 820:12
lumps l. in it — STEP 772:6
luna great Lord of L. — MACA 508:16
in the vats of L. — MACA 508:11
sol et l. — AUGU 39:4
lunae Tacitae per amica silentia l. — VIRG 829:9
lunatic l., the lover — SHAK 727:2
lunatics lunatic asylum run by l. — LLOY 496:18
l. have taken charge — ROWL 671:12
lunch cork out of my l. — FIEL 327:7
for life, not for l. — SAYI 684:28
L. is for wimps — FILM 329:2
no such thing as a free l. — SAYI 685:13
unable to l. today — PORT 619:16
luncheon Breakfast, supper, dinner, l. — BROW 167:2
take soup at l. — CURZ 263:12
lungs dangerous to the l. — JAME 428:21
from froth-corrupted l. — OWEN 591:6
l. of London — PITT 607:17
Lupercal on the L. I thrice — SHAK 713:5
lupus L. est homo homini — PLAU 609:8
lurcher half l. and half cur — COWP 256:24
lurching L. to rag-time tunes — SASS 682:5
lure l. it back — FITZ 331:23
l. this tassel-gentle — SHAK 732:17
lurk dangers to liberty l. — BRAN 155:1
l. outside — GRAC 367:7
lurks l. a politician — ARIS 26:20
luscious l. woodbine — SHAK 726:8
lusisti l. satis — HORA 411:2
lust Delight in l. — PETR 605:9
fash'd wi' fleshly l. — BURN 178:14
generous in mere l. — ROCH 664:14
horrible that l. and rage — YEAT 874:25
hutch of tasty l. — HOPK 407:10
into ashes all my l. — MARV 525:13
love is more cruel than l. — SWIN 785:9
l. in action — SHAK 738:18
l. of knowing — FLEC 334:12
Tell love it is but l. — RALE 653:16
to l. after it — LEWI 492:3
lustily sing praises l. unto him — BOOK 141:18
lustre bright l. of a court — CECI 212:7
Where is thy l. now — SHAK 716:8
lusts Abstain from fleshly l. — BIBL 117:4
fulfil the l. thereof — BIBL 111:17
l. of the flesh — BOOK 138:9
l. of your father — BIBL 107:31
lust'st Thou hotly l. — SHAK 716:20
lusty seye Of l. folk — CHAU 220:12
lute Apollo's l. — MILT 539:6
harp with the l. — BOOK 145:11
l. and harp — BOOK 143:17
l. is broken — SHEL 744:18
Orpheus with his l. — SHAK 710:16
playing the l. — VERL 826:10
pleasing of a l. — SHAK 731:10
rift within the l. — TENN 794:17
to her l. Corinna sings — CAMP 195:22
lutes l. of amber — HERR 396:20
Luther beyond what L. saw — ROBI 664:3
lux l. perpetua — MISS 550:4
luxuries and which l. — WRIG 870:15
l. of life — MOTL 562:14
luxury calls it l. — ADDI 4:13
height of l. — TENN 801:8
learn the l.of doing good — GOLD 364:23
like any other l. — TROL 817:2
Literature is a l. — CHES 225:3
L. has been railed at — VOLT 834:3
l., not a necessity — ANTH 24:19
l. of doing good — CRAB 258:1

luxury (cont.):
l., peace — BAUD 61:12
l. was doing good — GART 350:2
mainly a l. — BRIG 157:7
Morality is a costly l. — ADAM 2:17
Pessimism is a l. — MEIR 530:8
swinish l. of the rich — MORR 560:20
trust people is a l. — FORS 338:1
Lycidas L. is dead — MILT 540:3
lying branch of the art of l. — CORN 252:6
express l. or falsehood — SWIF 782:12
listening, l. in wait — THOM 806:20
l., and slandering — BOOK 138:13
l. into a universal principle — KAFK 452:8
L. lips are abomination — BIBL 88:5
L., on the other hand — CAMU 196:19
l. till noon — JOHN 438:15
One of you is l. — PARK 596:9
smallest amount of l. — BUTL 184:5
world is given to l. — SHAK 706:31
Lyonnesse When I set out for L. — HARD 382:4
lyre armour and my l. — HORA 413:6
Make me thy l. — SHEL 745:11
'Omer smote 'is bloomin' l. — KIPL 468:1
lyric among the l. poets — HORA 411:4
good l. should be — GERS 353:19
lyricis me l. vatibus inseres — HORA 411:4

Mab Queen M. hath been with — SHAK 732:5
macaroni called it M. — SONG 763:17
Macaulay as Tom M. — MELB 530:16
M.'s few pages — ELIO 308:17
Macavity M. WASN'T THERE — ELIO 310:20
Macbeth had Lady M. — KNIG 469:14
harm M. — SHAK 721:20
Little Nell and Lady M. — WOOL 864:17
M. does murder sleep — SHAK 720:6
M. shall never vanquished be — SHAK 722:1
M. shall sleep no more — SHAK 720:7
night I appeared as M. — HARG 382:11
MacCorley Rody M. goes to die — CARB 197:17
Macduff Lay on, M. — SHAK 722:26
M. was from his mother's womb — SHAK 722:25
mace fool's bauble, the m. — CROM 260:15
Macedonia Come over into M. — BIBL 109:31
MacGregor Where M. sits — PROV 647:9
Macheath jack-knife has M. — BREC 155:24
Machiavel murderous M. — SHAK 710:9
machine body is a m. — TOLS 813:16
desiccated calculating m. — BEVA 76:20
Ghost in the M. — RYLE 676:9
house is a m. for living in — LE C 487:2
m. for converting — CARL 199:21
m. for peeling a potato — BABB 44:11
m. for turning the red wine — DINE 283:13
pulse of the m. — WORD 869:7
sausage m. — CHRI 227:3
machinery Age of M. — CARL 199:20
m. of the night — GINS 358:22
machines M. have less problems — WARH 840:4
m. which had never been finished — BABB 44:10
their survival m. — DAWK 269:4
whether m. think — SKIN 754:5
macht Arbeit m. frei — ANON 22:13
mackerel like rotten m. — RAND 655:3
m. of the sea — BALL 54:19
Not so the m. — FRER 342:13
mackintosh bit of black m. — WELB 845:12
mad All poets are m. — BURT 181:8
bad and m. it was — BROW 165:13
believed him m. — BEAT 62:11
called me m. — LEE 487:15
Don't get m., get even — SAYI 684:15
glad m. brother's name — SWIN 785:4
half of the nation is m. — SMOL 759:6
Hieronimo is m. again — KYD 474:13
house for fools and m. — SWIF 784:11
M. about the boy — COWA 253:14
m. all my life — JOHN 438:16
m. and savage master — SOPH 761:22
M., bad, and dangerous — LAMB 476:10
M. dogs and Englishmen — COWA 253:15

m. north-north-west — SHAK 701:14
M. world! mad kings — SHAK 714:5
Make m. the guilty — SHAK 701:21
make poor females m. — SHAK 726:22
makes men m. — SHAK 729:15
man is m. — BYRO 191:21
men that God made m. — CHES 223:27
much learning doth make thee m. — BIBL 110:15
nobly wild, not m. — HERR 396:5
O fool! I shall go m. — SHAK 715:14
old, m., blind — SHEL 746:14
O! let me not be m. — SHAK 715:7
pleasure sure, In being m. — DRYD 296:31
saint run m. — POPE 617:19
some did count him m. — BUNY 171:23
they first make m. — PROV 647:18
We all are born m. — BECK 64:23
when a heroine goes m. — SHER 748:5
Whom the m. would destroy — LEVI 491:8
world was m. — SABA 676:12
madam globe-trotting M. — YEAT 875:4
M. I may not call you — ELIZ 312:18
madame Ah, m.! truly it's not right — CRAN 258:16
madding Far from the m. crowd's — GRAY 370:8
m. crowd — HARD 380:12
made All things were m. by him — BIBL 106:35
almost m. for each other — SMIT 758:4
Begotten, not m. — BOOK 137:2
day which the Lord hath m. — BOOK 148:11
earth and the world were m. — BOOK 145:19
fearfully and wonderfully m. — BOOK 149:18
God m. and eaten — BROW 165:5
Here's one I m. earlier — CATC 207:29
he that hath m. us — BOOK 146:15
he who m. the Lamb — BLAK 128:5
I m. it — FILM 328:1
Little Lamb who m. thee — BLAK 127:11
m. heaven and earth — BOOK 138:16
m., like bread — LE G 488:1
m. me thus — BIBL 111:8
man was m. to mourn — BURN 178:26
not born but m. — JERO 433:7
nothing that thou hast m. — BOOK 135:15
Who m. you — CATE 209:9
Madeira M., m'dear — FLAN 332:22
madeleine little piece of m. — PROU 625:6
Madelon Ce n'est que M. — BOUS 153:5
mademoiselle M. from Armenteers — MILI 535:14
madhouse don't want m. — EMPS 315:26
m. there exists no law — CLAR 232:22
madhouses M., prisons — CLAR 232:20
madly m. wild — PARN 597:10
madman If a m. were to come — JOHN 442:2
m. shakes a dead geranium — ELIO 310:22
m. who thought he was — COCT 237:21
madmen none but m. know — DRYD 296:31
They were m. — RENO 658:9
worst of m. — POPE 617:19
madness accounted his life m. — BIBL 97:2
cells of m. — TENN 798:11
cruel m. of love — TENN 797:20
define true m. — SHAK 701:3
despondency and m. — WORD 868:23
destroyed through m. — GINS 358:22
devil's m.—War — SERV 692:27
For that fine m. — DRAY 293:17
harmonious m. — SHEL 746:24
His flight was m. — SHAK 722:2
it is m. — CONG 247:13
m. is terrific — WOOL 864:15
M.! Madness — FILM 329:3
M. need not be all breakdown — LAIN 476:6
m. of art — JAME 429:19
m. of many — POPE 618:19
m. their kings commit — HORA 410:3
moon-struck m. — MILT 544:13
O! that way m. lies — SHAK 715:22
some seductive m. — HORA 412:20
Though this be m. — SHAK 701:16
to m. near allied — DRYD 294:13
very midsummer m. — SHAK 736:4

Madonnas M. or Mary Magdalenes — WILL 857:16
madrigal woeful stuff this m. would be — POPE 616:8
madrigals birds sing m. — MARL 523:1
maenad Of some fierce M. — SHEL 745:7
maestro m. di color che sanno — DANT 264:17
magazines graves of little m. — PRES 622:12
Magdalen fourteen months at M. College — GIBB 354:19
maggot create a m. — MONT 555:16
magic daylight in upon m. — BAGE 51:5
house rose like m. — HARG 382:11
If this be m. — SHAK 737:9
indistinguishable from m. — CLAR 233:15
m. casements — KEAT 456:10
m. of your fire — TAGO 787:18
mistake medicine for m. — SZAS 786:15
Ms. Rowling's m. world — BYAT 184:25
old black m. — MERC 532:10
Parents can plant m. — MACN 513:17
rough m. I here abjure — SHAK 734:1
secret m. of numbers — BROW 162:28
tell you what I want. M. — WILL 858:8
tightness of the m. circle — MACL 512:8
magical it is a m. event — PRIE 622:18
Maginn bright, broken M. — LOCK 498:3
magistrate m. corruptible — ROBE 663:11
shocks the m. — RUSS 675:7
magistri iurare in verba m. — HORA 409:18
magna M. Charta is such a fellow — COKE 238:17
M. est veritas, et praevalet — BIBL 120:19
magnanimity M. in politics — BURK 173:24
magnanimous m. in victory — COLL 243:8
magnificat M. anima mea Dominum — BIBL 120:10
magnificent M. desolation — ALDR 12:1
Mean, Moody and M. — TAGL 788:9
mild and m. eye — BROW 166:13
Mute and m. — DRYD 296:34
magnifique C'est m. — BOSQ 151:16
magnify m. thy holy Name — BOOK 136:19
praise him, and m. him — BOOK 133:14
soul doth m. the Lord — BIBL 104:8
we m. thee — BOOK 133:11
magnis parva licet componere m. — VIRG 833:5
magpie swollen m. in a fitful sun — POUN 621:10
magpies pair of m. fly — HO 400:12
Maguire M. and his men — KAVA 453:14
magus M. Zoroaster, my dead child — SHEL 745:19
Mahomet mountain will not come to M. — PROV 635:15
maid Being an old m. — FERB 325:5
Can a m. forget her ornaments — BIBL 94:24
espy a fair pretty m. — SONG 763:6
fair, but frozen m. — GARR 349:15
heard a m. sing — SONG 762:6
I once was a m. — BURN 178:19
m. and her wight — HARD 381:20
m. is mine — MISQ 548:13
m. is not dead — BIBL 100:19
m. was in the garden — NURS 581:8
m. whom there were none to praise — WORD 869:3
man with a m. — BIBL 89:12
my pretty m. — NURS 582:11
neglected m. — LEAP 485:12
She could not live a m. — PEEL 601:16
maiden god pursuing, the m. hid — SWIN 784:21
love one m. only — TENN 794:7
m. all forlorn — NURS 581:16
m. meditation, fancy-free — SHAK 726:6
m. of bashful fifteen — SHER 748:27
pursued a m. — SHEL 744:7
rare and radiant m. — POE 611:1
maidenhead he rafte hire m. — CHAU 220:14
maidens all the m. pretty — COLM 244:2
laughter of comely m. — DE V 275:1
m.' hearts — SHAK 729:4
What m. loth — KEAT 455:17
Young men and m. — BOOK 150:10
maids m. are May — SHAK 697:20

man (cont.):
M. is born unto trouble — BIBL 86:21
m. is but a devil — STEV 775:13
m. is dead — FROM 344:3
m. is man — TENN 794:16
M. is man's A.B.C. — QUAR 651:13
M. is Nature's sole mistake — GILB 358:9
m. is of kin to the beasts — BACO 46:7
M. is quite insane — MONT 555:16
m. . . . is so in the way — GASK 350:6
M. is something to be surpassed — NIET 575:19
M. is the hunter — TENN 799:14
M. is the interpreter of naure — WHEW 850:4
M. is the master — SWIN 785:17
M. is the measure — PROT 625:2
M. is the measure — PROV 638:18
m. is the only animal — JEFF 431:8
M. is the Only Animal — TWAI 820:6
M. is the only creature — ORWE 586:16
M. is the shuttle — VAUG 824:13
M. is to be held — EDGE 303:12
m. made the town — COWP 256:8
M. may not marry his Mother — BOOK 150:24
m. not truly one — STEV 775:16
m. of all hours — ERAS 316:19
m. of restless intellect — HUXL 423:16
M. owes his entire existence — HEGE 388:15
M. partly is — BROW 165:15
M. plays only when — SCHI 686:2
M. proposes — PROV 638:20
m. proposes — THOM 804:17
M., proud man — SHAK 723:8
m. recovered of the bite — GOLD 364:16
M. remains Sceptreless — SHEL 746:2
m.'s a man for a' that — BURN 178:8
m.'s desire is for the woman — COLE 242:4
M.'s dominion — BURN 179:25
m. sent from God — BIBL 106:31
m.'s first disobedience — MILT 541:8
m. shall have his mare — SHAK 726:23
M. shall not live — BIBL 98:20
m. shouldn't fool — FAUL 324:19
M.'s inhumanity to man — BURN 178:27
m.'s the gowd — BURN 178:7
M. stole the fruit — HERB 394:24
M.'s word is God in man — TENN 793:25
m. that hath no music — SHAK 725:13
M. that is born — BIBL 86:30
m. that is born of a woman — BOOK 139:8
m. that looks on glass — HERB 394:6
m. that trusteth in him — BOOK 141:19
M. wants but little — GOLD 364:14
M. was by Nature — CONG 247:11
M. was formed for society — BLAC 123:9
M. was made for joy and woe — BLAK 124:15
m. was made to mourn — BURN 178:26
m. who has found himself out — BARR 60:2
M. who has no office — SHAW 740:7
m. who should loose me — LOWE 502:14
m. who used to notice — HARD 381:8
m. who would be king — KIPL 468:18
M. will err — GOET 361:13
m. will not merely endure — FAUL 324:17
M. with all his noble qualities — DARW 266:12
m. with a maid — BIBL 89:12
m. write a better book — EMER 315:22
m. you love to hate — ADVE 8:2
m. you love to hate — FILM 329:5
met a m. who wasn't there — MEAR 529:16
moral centaur, m. and wife — BYRO 189:7
more like a m. — LERN 490:8
more wonderful than m. — SOPH 761:14
mortal m. — BIBL 86:20
My m. Friday — DEFO 270:14
never done talking of M. — FANO 323:1
new m. may be raised up — BOOK 138:6
no m. ever shall put asunder — SHAW 740:1
No m. hath seen God — BIBL 107:3
m. not wanted much — EMER 315:9
no m. see me and live — BIBL 81:25
No moon, no m. — PROV 640:8
nor no m. ever loved — SHAK 738:17
not m. for the sabbath — BIBL 103:26

One m. in a thousand — KIPL 467:14
one small step for a m. — ARMS 28:20
only m. is vile — HEBE 388:9
perfect M. — BOOK 134:14
piece of work is a m. — SHAK 701:11
plain, blunt m. — SHAK 713:11
Reasonable M. — HERB 393:19
right m. in the right place — JEFF 432:15
said, ask a m. — THAT 803:12
saw a m. this morning — SHAW 742:26
shares m.'s smell — HOPK 407:7
she was taken out of M. — BIBL 79:2
So much resemble m. — COWP 255:17
Stand by your m. — WYNE 871:16
standing by my m. — CLIN 236:1
state of m. — SHAK 710:19
strange what a m. may do — THAC 802:17
study of m. is man — CHAR 217:16
Style is the m. — BUFF 170:4
That is the m. — BISM 123:6
that the m. should be alone — BIBL 78:22
the m. who — CART 205:12
There was a little m. — NURS 581:14
This bold bad m. — SHAK 710:15
This is Plato's m. — DIOG 283:15
this M. and this Woman — BOOK 138:20
This was a m. — SHAK 714:3
Thou art the m. — BIBL 84:17
To the m.-in-the-street — AUDE 37:18
What bloody m. — SHAK 718:3
Whatever m. has done — PROV 646:19
what is a m. — PIND 606:19
What is m. — BOOK 139:23
what is m. — LENO 489:14
What m. has made of man — WORD 866:15
what manner of m. he was — BIBL 116:18
What ought a m. to be — IBSE 424:10
when a m. should marry — BACO 47:18
When God at first made m. — HERB 394:20
when I became a m. — BIBL 112:14
who kills a m. — MILT 545:22
Who's master, who's m. — SWIF 783:27
Whoso would be a m. — EMER 315:5
woman was made for m. — STAN 770:6
woman without a m. — SAYI 685:21
You'll be a M., my son — KIPL 466:6
manage m. without butter — GOEB 361:7
managed disgracefully m. — FIRB 327:15
not a free press but a m. — RADC 653:6
management M. that wants to change — TUSA 819:16
manager No m. ever got fired — ADVE 8:10
managers m. of affairs of women — KORA 471:14
managing kiss the M. Director — WHIT 851:15
Manchester school of M. — DISR 286:27
What M. says today — PROV 646:24
mancipio Vitaque m. — LUCR 504:12
Mandalay come you back to M. — KIPL 466:14
road to M. — KIPL 466:15
mandarin M. style — CONN 248:9
mandate M. of Heaven — CONF 245:15
royal m. ran — BURN 178:6
Manderley went to M. again — DU M 299:6
mandragora Give me to drink m. — SHAK 694:17
mandrake frightful as a M. — BYRO 191:21
Get with child a m. — DONN 289:14
this quiet m. — DONN 288:20
manes With draped m. — HUGH 418:10
manger babe was born in a m. — WHIT 851:14
in the rude m. lies — MILT 540:23
laid him in a m. — BIBL 104:12
lodge Him in the m. — ANON 21:16
m. for his bed — ALEX 12:8
mangrove held together by m. roots — BISH 122:6
manhood ancient customs and its m. — ENNI 316:4
harsh and embittered m. — GOGO 363:10
M. a struggle — DISR 285:18
M. taken by the Son — NEWM 572:11
My m., long misled — DRYD 295:24
touching his M. — BOOK 134:14
manhoods hold their m. cheap — SHAK 709:8

manibus M. date lilia plenis — VIRG 830:15
manifesto first powerful plain m. — SPEN 766:9
manifold m. sins and wickedness — BOOK 133:2
sundry and m. changes — BOOK 135:19
manilla misery of m. folders — ROET 665:6
mankind all m. — BALL 55:6
countrymen are all m. — GARR 349:18
crucify m. — BRYA 169:1
Everything m. does — JUVE 450:14
giant leap for m. — ARMS 28:20
has not created m. — TOCQ 812:8
hate, m. — BYRO 186:10
How beauteous m. is — SHAK 734:4
legislator of m. — JOHN 437:15
M. always sets itself — MARX 526:4
m. and womankind — BAHA 51:21
M. has done more damage — COUS 253:7
M. is a dream — PIND 606:19
M. is on the move — SMUT 759:11
M. must put an end to war — KENN 460:11
M.'s moral test — KUND 474:7
no history of m. — POPP 619:5
not in Asia, was m. born — ARDR 26:5
proper study of m. — POPE 616:29
proper study of m. is books — HUXL 422:14
ride m. — EMER 314:14
school of m. — BURK 175:12
slain m. altogether — KORA 472:3
manliness silent m. of grief — GOLD 364:11
manly than m. wise — MARL 523:9
manna Exalted m. — HERB 394:19
his tongue Dropped m. — MILT 542:3
loathe our m. — DRYD 296:14
m. of a day — GREE 371:8
rained down m. — BOOK 145:8
manned safeliest when with one man m. — DONN 288:6
manner after the m. of men — BIBL 112:23
all m. of thing — JULI 449:6
All m. of thing shall be well — ELIO 309:22
m. of his speech — SHAK 694:21
to the m. born — SHAK 700:10
manners As by his m. — SPEN 767:25
corrupt good m. — BIBL 113:1
corrupt good m. — PROV 631:36
droppings of the well of m. — BULW 170:10
evil m. live in brass — SHAK 711:5
for m.' sake — BIBL 97:28
gentleness of your m. — CLAI 232:17
good table m. — MIKE 534:23
had very good m. — SELL 691:25
lack of m. — HATH 384:5
M. maketh man — PROV 638:19
m. of a dancing master — JOHN 439:4
m. of a Marquis — GILB 358:10
Morals and m. — CHAM 213:20
not men, but m. — FIEL 326:13
Of m. gentle — POPE 615:23
Oh, the m. — CICE 232:2
Other times, other m. — PROV 641:22
polished m. — COWP 256:30
rectify m. — MILT 545:26
soften m., but corrupt — BYRO 190:5
thoughts and m. — JOHN 437:15
Manningtree roasted M. ox — SHAK 706:5
manoeuvre force with a m. — TROT 817:8
manque Un seul être vous m. — LAMA 476:8
mansion Back to its m. — GRAY 370:5
everlasting — SHAK 734:9
heavenly m., raging in the dark — YEAT 872:13
Love has pitched his m. — YEAT 873:1
m.-house of liberty — MILT 546:3
mansions dolorous m. — MILT 540:27
m. in eternity — BLAK 128:12
m. of the dead — CRAB 257:17
many m. — BIBL 108:13
man-slaying terrible, m. hands — HOME 404:22
mantle cast his m. upon him — BIBL 85:15
green m. — SHAK 716:2
her silver m. threw — MILT 543:10
in russet m. clad — SHAK 699:7
m. that covers all — CERV 213:11
purple m. to the light — RONS 666:14

twitched his m. blue	MILT 540:17
Mantovano salute thee, M.	TENN 800:12
mantras M. and tantras	TANT 790:6
Mantuan old M.! Who understandeth thee	
	SHAK 717:16
manufacture content to m. life	BERN 73:14
soul of every m.	SMIL 755:18
manufactures no use for your country's m.	
	QIAN 651:4
manunkind this busy monster, m.	CUMM 262:9
manure liquid m. from the West	SOLZ 760:17
Money, like m.	PROV 639:4
natural m.	JEFF 431:11
manuscript youth's sweet-scented m.	
	FITZ 331:28
many How m. things	SOCR 759:14
Just how m. did we kill	LEWI 492:9
makes so m. of them	LINC 494:2
m. are called	BIBL 102:14
m. are called	PROV 638:26
m. are governed	HUME 420:5
M. hands make light work	PROV 638:29
m.-headed monster	POPE 617:25
m.-splendoured thing	THOM 808:1
m. still must labour	BYRO 187:6
m. ways out	SENE 692:16
shed for you and for m.	BOOK 139:2
So m. worlds	TENN 795:18
so much owed by so m. to so few	CHUR 229:17
we are m.	BIBL 103:31
what are they among so m.	BIBL 107:20
map Does the m. remind you	TREV 815:12
in the new m.	SHAK 736:1
make a m. of it	JONE 445:10
m.-makers' colours	BISH 122:8
m. me no maps	FIEL 326:17
Roll up that m.	PITT 607:21
use a larger m.	SALI 678:14
mapmakers m. should place the Mississippi	
	BELL 69:3
maps Geography is about M.	BENT 71:14
in Afric-m.	SWIF 784:2
m. on a small scale	SALI 678:14
mar cannot m.	ARNO 29:16
marathon M. looks on the sea	BYRO 188:22
trivial skirmish fought near M.	GRAV 369:12
marble cutting m. slabs	HORA 412:12
dreary m. halls	CALV 194:4
dwelt in m. halls	BUNN 170:17
Glowed on the m.	ELIO 311:6
I am m.-constant	SHAK 695:26
lasting m. seek	WALL 836:19
left it m.	AUGU 40:4
legs are as pillars of m.	BIBL 91:10
m. index of a mind	WORD 868:13
m., nor the gilded monuments	SHAK 737:28
m. not yet carved	MICH 533:15
m. to retain	BYRO 185:10
more than hard m.	DU B 298:4
mould from m. living faces	VIRG 830:14
placid m.	HUNT 421:11
What sculpture is to a block of m.	ADDI 5:8
marbly great smooth m. limbs	BROW 165:4
Marcellus M. exiled	POPE 617:9
Tu M. eris	VIRG 830:15
march Beware the ides of M.	SHAK 711:13
boundary of the M. of a nation	PARN 596:2
do not m. on Moscow	MONT 556:9
droghte of M.	CHAU 218:2
ides of M. are come	SHAK 712:15
in the front of M.	TENN 793:15
mad M. days	MASE 527:4
M. comes in like a lion	PROV 638:30
M., march, Ettrick	SCOT 689:18
m. my troops towards	GRIM 373:12
m. of intellect	SOUT 764:17
m. of mind	PEAC 600:12
m. on their stomachs	SELL 692:6
m. through rapine	GLAD 360:4
m. towards it	CALL 193:11
M., whan God first maked man	CHAU 219:25
m. with sovereign tread	BLOK 129:6
Men who m. away	HARD 381:22

On the first of M.	PROV 640:36
peck of M. dust	PROV 641:31
So many mists in M.	PROV 643:21
take The winds of M.	SHAK 737:1
three hours' m. to dinner	HAZL 386:24
Truth is on the m.	ZOLA 878:15
marche congrès ne m. pas	LIGN 493:6
marched m. breast forward	BROW 164:21
M. them along	BROW 166:16
marches forced m., battles and death	
	GARI 349:7
Funeral m. to the grave	LONG 499:15
marching M. as to war	BARI 58:16
m., charging feet	JAGG 427:11
M. to the Promised Land	BARI 58:17
M. where it likes	ARNO 31:12
people m. on	MORR 560:11
soul is m. on	SONG 763:1
truth is m. on	HOWE 417:3
mare brought him a Flanders m.	HENR 392:3
grey m. is the better	PROV 633:33
lend me your grey m.	BALL 56:8
man shall have his m.	SHAK 726:23
Money makes the m. to go	PROV 639:7
qui trans m. currunt	HORA 410:10
Margaret It's me, M.	BLUM 129:9
M. you mourn for	HOPK 407:21
Merry M.	SKEL 754:1
margerain With m. gentle	SKEL 754:2
Margery See-saw, M. Daw	NURS 581:6
margin m. too narrow	FERM 325:10
mari a m. usque ad mare	BIBL 119:28
m. usque ad mare	MOTT 563:2
Maria Aunt M. flung herself	GRAH 367:18
Ave M.	PRAY 623:1
Ave M.! 'tis the hour	BYRO 188:28
ex M. Virgine	MISS 549:13
Mariana this dejected M.	SHAK 723:15
Marie I am M. of Roumania	PARK 596:2
Maries Queen had four M.	BALL 55:9
marigold m., that goes to bed	SHAK 736:31
marijuana experimented with m.	CLIN 236:5
mariner It is an ancient M.	COLE 240:12
m. with the gentleman	DRAK 293:9
mariners rest ye, brother m.	TENN 797:13
Ye M. of England	CAMP 195:18
marjoram no longer thyme or m.	MONT 554:26
savory, m.	SHAK 736:31
mark man's distinctive m.	BROW 165:15
m., or the name of the beast	BIBL 118:26
m. upon Cain	BIBL 79:17
M. well her bulwarks	BOOK 142:25
m. what is done amiss	BOOK 149:7
no drowning m.	SHAK 733:12
not a m.	ROST 670:3
often hit the m.	BUNY 171:3
press toward the m.	BIBL 115:1
read, m., learn	BOOK 135:11
would hit the m.	LONG 499:2
market bought in the m.	CLOU 236:16
enterprise of the m.	ANON 16:20
Enthroned i' the m.-place	SHAK 694:23
fast through the m.	PROV 639:3
gathered in the m.-place	CAVA 211:13
heart in the m.-place	SHAK 727:30
m. for maybe five computers	MISQ 548:3
marry a m.-gardener	DICK 279:24
pig went to m.	NURS 581:18
salutations in the m.	BIBL 104:3
sold in the desolate m.	BLAK 125:10
To m., to market	NURS 582:5
Market Harborough AM IN M.	CHES 225:2
marking malady of not m.	SHAK 707:6
marks m. and scars I carry	BUNY 171:27
m. of the beast	HARD 380:15
marl Over the burning m.	MILT 541:20
Marlborough Duke of M.	MARL 522:3
From M.'s eyes	JOHN 438:10
M.'s mighty soul	ADDI 4:10
marmasyte Tullia's ape a m.	ANON 17:15
marquis Abducted by a French M.	GRAH 367:12
manners of a M.	GILB 358:10

my lord the M. of Carabas	PERR 604:4
marred man that's m.	SHAK 694:5
young man m.	PROV 648:20
marriage blessings of m.	SHAW 741:7
by way of m.	FIEL 326:22
Chains do not hold a m.	SIGN 751:14
Christian m.	MARG 521:11
Courtship to m.	CONG 247:17
definition of m.	SMIT 758:17
dictates before m.	ELIO 307:20
drags the m. chain	CENT 212:13
ended by a m.	BYRO 188:17
every m. then is best in tune	WATK 841:5
furnish forth the m. tables	SHAK 699:25
get anywhere in a m.	MURD 565:16
giving in m.	BIBL 102:27
hear of a m.	PROV 630:34
heart of m. is memories	COSB 252:14
in companionship as in m.	ADAM 2:11
In m., a man becomes slack	STEV 775:28
joys of m.	FORD 337:7
left-handed m.	WOLL 863:11
live in a state of m.	JOHN 441:1
Love and m.	BYRO 188:15
m. as the sole object	MART 524:13
M. a wonderful invention	CONN 248:5
m. brings more joy	EURI 321:3
m. for her was to be	STAN 770:5
m. had always been her object	AUST 42:14
M. has many pains	JOHN 437:17
M. is a bribe	WILD 856:18
M. is a lottery	PROV 638:31
M. is a sacrament which	CASA 206:3
m. is holy and sacred	MOLI 552:18
M. is like life	STEV 775:30
M. is nothing but	SELD 691:13
M. isn't a word	FILM 329:7
M. is one long fit	KING 464:21
M. is popular because	SHAW 741:14
M. is the grave	CAVE 211:18
M. is the waste-paper basket	WEBB 843:11
m. makes man and wife	CONG 246:27
M. may often be a stormy lake	PEAC 600:16
m. of true minds	SHAK 738:15
m. on the rocks	MERR 533:2
m. than a ministry	BAGE 50:23
M., to women	ANTH 24:19
M. was all defeat	TREV 815:11
m. with your mother	SOPH 761:20
more to m. than four	PROV 644:16
nor are given in m.	SWIF 783:15
prevents a bad m.	SHAK 735:3
primal m. blessing	KEBL 459:3
Reading and m.	MOLI 552:9
retrieve his fortunes by m.	DICK 278:15
so bent on m.	AUST 42:25
So that is m.	WOOL 864:11
three of us in this m.	DIAN 275:14
value of m.	DE V 275:6
wo that is in m.	CHAU 220:8
marriages All the unhappy m.	WODE 861:19
few happy m.	ASTE 34:16
few m. are happy	SWIF 783:17
happiest m. on earth	DE V 275:3
have no more m.	SHAK 702:8
M. are made in heaven	PROV 638:32
M. would in general	JOHN 441:26
present at their m.	TROL 816:23
There are good m.	LA R 481:23
thousands of m.	LARK 481:6
married At leisure m.	CONG 247:16
before he m.	SWIF 784:12
can't get m. at all	FILM 329:21
delight we m. people have	PEPY 603:13
Each thirteenth year he m.	MERR 533:1
getting m. in the morning	LERN 490:7
going to be m.	STER 773:14
honest man who m.	GOLD 365:10
if ever we had been m.	GAY 350:19
If m. life were all that	MILL 536:14
imprudently m. the barber	FOOT 336:13
In m. life three is company	WILD 854:17
let us be m.	LEAR 486:6

married (cont.):
m. beneath me — ASTO 35:2
M., charming, chaste — BYRO 187:22
m. me with a ring — RAIN 653:12
m. past redemption — DRYD 296:13
m. to a poem — KEAT 458:8
m. to a single life — CRAS 259:8
m.—to be the more together — MACN 513:10
Miss will soon be m. — HAYW 385:17
Mocks m. men — SHAK 717:24
most m. man I ever saw — WARD 839:22
One was never m. — BURT 181:14
Reader, I m. him — BRON 158:8
Trade Unionism of the m. — SHAW 741:6
well-bred as if we were not m. — CONG 247:26
when they got m. — HOLI 403:5
when you m. me — SHER 748:23
young man m. — PROV 648:20
young man m. — SHAK 694:5
marries in love when he m. — BURN 176:21
m. without any consideration — OSBO 588:11
signify whom one m. — ROGE 665:17
when a man m. — PROV 639:29
When a man m. — SHEL 744:16
marrow suck out all the m. — THOR 809:22
marry advise no man to m. — JOHN 444:24
better to m. than to burn — BIBL 112:2
Better to m. than to burn — PROV 627:40
Can't get away to m. you — LEIG 488:10
Doänt thou m. for munny — TENN 798:19
How can a bishop m. — SMIT 758:14
m. a man who hates his mother — BENN 70:21
m. a market-gardener — DICK 279:24
M. in haste — PROV 638:33
M. in May — PROV 638:34
m. Mr Collins — AUST 42:13
M. my body to that dust — KING 463:4
m. one another — BUTL 184:7
m. whom she likes — THAC 802:23
m. with his brother — SHAK 703:11
m. your mistress — GOLD 363:19
may not m. his Mother — BOOK 150:24
men we wanted to m. — STEI 771:10
neither m., nor are given — BIBL 102:16
never know who they may m. — MITF 551:8
Never m. for money — PROV 639:39
persons about to m. — PUNC 649:14
taken in when they m. — AUST 41:13
they neither m. — SWIF 783:15
To m. is to domesticate — STEV 776:1
when a man should m. — BACO 47:18
while ye may, go m. — HERR 396:18
women m. off in haste — ASTE 34:17
marrying m. in haste — THOM 806:23
Mars Men are from M. — GRAY 369:16
marshal m.'s baton — LOUI 501:10
Martha M. was cumbered — BIBL 105:8
martial m. airs of England — WEBS 843:23
swashing and a m. outside — SHAK 696:13
valiant and m. — BACO 48:8
Martin Saint M.'s summer — SHAK 709:14
Martini into a dry M. — FILM 328:24
medium Vodka dry M. — FLEM 334:16
Martinis Those dry M. — ADE 6:4
martlet temple-haunting m. — SHAK 719:5
martyr Glorious the m.'s gore — SMAR 755:14
groan of the m.'s woe — BLAK 125:14
if thow deye a m. — CHAU 221:7
m. of the people — CHAR 216:20
regarded as a m. — KHOM 462:7
soul of a m. — BAGE 50:3
martyrdom M. is the test — JOHN 442:28
m. must run its course — AUDE 37:17
M. only way in which a man can — SHAW 739:20
m. to live — BROW 162:12
True m. is not determined — AUGU 39:20
martyred shrouded oft our m. dead — CONN 248:3
martyrs army of M. — BOOK 133:9
blood of the m. — PROV 628:15
graves of the m. — STEV 776:3
love their m. — DOST 291:2
no patience of m. — THOM 805:9

stones and clouts make m. — BROW 162:11
marvel m. at nothing — HORA 410:8
m. my birthday away — THOM 806:3
marvelled m. to see such things — BOOK 142:23
marvellous Chatterton, the m. boy — WORD 868:22
hath done m. things — BOOK 146:11
m. demonstration — FERM 325:10
m. in our eyes — BOOK 148:11
towards the m. — HUME 419:17
marvels to credit m. — HEAN 387:10
workest great m. — BOOK 134:7
Marx blame M. for what was done — BENN 70:1
illegitimate child of Karl M. — ATTL 35:9
in M.'s pages — SCHU 687:6
Marxism more to Methodism than to M. — PHIL 606:7
Marxist I am a M. — SLOG 755:7
I am not a M. — MARX 526:11
Marxiste Je suis M. — SLOG 755:7
Mary Hail M. — PRAY 623:1
M. Ambree — BALL 55:5
M. had a little lamb — HALE 377:3
M. hath chosen — BIBL 105:9
M., quite contrary — NURS 580:5
M.'s prayers — FABE 322:5
M. was found in adulterous bed — BLAK 125:5
Where the lady M. is — ROSS 669:16
winking M.-buds — SHAK 698:19
Mary Jane What is the matter with M. — MILN 538:7
Mary Magdalene cometh M. early — BIBL 108:34
Mary Magdalenes Madonnas or M. — WILL 857:16
mascot best m. is a good mechanic — EARH 302:8
masculine m. part, the poet in me — BEHN 66:21
mask had a m. like Castlereagh — SHEL 745:2
like a M. dancing — ACHE 1:11
loathsome m. has fallen — SHEL 746:2
m. that eats into the face — UPDI 822:22
No m. like open truth — CONG 246:29
masks m. and bergamasks — VERL 826:10
masochistic m. form of exhibitionism — OLIV 585:4
masons singing m. building — SHAK 708:10
Where did the m. go — BREC 156:2
masquerade m., a murdered peer — ALCO 11:6
truth in m. — BYRO 189:13
mass activates the whole m. — VIRG 830:12
blessed mutter of the m. — BROW 165:5
listen to the B Minor M. — TORK 814:1
M. is ended — MISS 550:1
Meat and m. never hindered — PROV 638:36
methods of m.-production — LANC 477:23
Paris is well worth a m. — HENR 391:19
rough and unordered m. — OVID 590:5
two thousand years of m. — HARD 381:10
Massachusetts denied in M. — MILL 537:1
massacre not as sudden as a m. — TWAI 820:2
masses bow, ye m. — GILB 356:15
calling 'em the m. — PRIE 623:12
huddled m. yearning — LAZA 485:3
If it is for the m. — SCHO 686:10
m. against the classes — GLAD 360:9
m. conveying an emotion — HEPW 392:18
m. get involved — VOLT 834:21
sacrifices of M. — BOOK 150:20
massy huge m. face — MACA 506:17
mast m. Of some great admiral — MILT 541:20
master allegiance to any m. — HORA 409:18
be m. and win — GOET 362:8
Caliban, Has a new m. — SHAK 733:26
choice and m. spirits — SHAK 712:21
Death is a m. from Germany — CELA 212:11
disciple is not above his m. — BIBL 100:26
dismiss such a good m. — BEAU 63:4
dominion of the m. — HUME 420:7
eye of a m. — PROV 631:44
Jack as good as his m. — PROV 636:43
Like m., like man — PROV 637:33
love is m. — GOWE 367:4
mad and savage m. — SOPH 761:22

Man is the m. — SWIN 785:17
m. a grief — SHAK 727:27
M.-morality — NIET 575:18
m. of his fate — TENN 794:16
m. of my fate — HENL 391:13
m. of none — PROV 636:44
m. of the house cometh — BIBL 104:5
m. of the Party — HEAL 387:3
m. of those who know — DANT 264:17
M., we have toiled — BIBL 104:22
only the M. shall praise — KIPL 467:22
Satan, thy m. — YOUN 876:26
slew his m. — BIBL 85:35
This is our m. — BROW 165:22
which is to be m. — CARR 203:12
Who's m., who's man — SWIF 783:27
Why eateth your M. — BIBL 100:14
without m.-builders — LOCK 497:3
masterly m. inactivity — MACK 511:19
masterpiece Nature's great m. — DONN 288:21
never makes for a m. — TRUF 817:13
masterpieces in the midst of m. — FRAN 340:10
masters anything but new m. — HALI 377:17
ease of the m. — SMIT 756:7
educate our m. — MISQ 548:24
had two m. — BEAV 63:19
m. of the Channel — NAPO 567:12
m. of their fates — SHAK 711:19
never wrong, the Old M. — AUDE 37:16
people are the m. — BURK 175:19
serve two m. — BIBL 99:15
serve two m. — PROV 640:5
spiritual pastors and m. — BOOK 138:12
We are not the m. — BLAI 123:19
We are the m. — SHAW 742:24
We are the m. now — MISQ 548:23
mastery m. of the thing — HOPK 408:5
mastiff m.? the right hon. Gentleman's poodle — LLOY 496:12
mastodons like m. bellowing — WODE 862:2
masturbation Don't knock m. — ALLE 13:9
m. of war — RAE 653:9
sort of mental m. — BYRO 192:10
match Honour is like a m. — PAGN 592:3
lighted m. — BROW 166:17
m. the world above — ZOHA 878:8
matched m. us with His hour — BROO 159:12
Thou wert never m. — MALO 518:4
matches with that stick of m. — MADI 514:4
matchless m. deed's achieved — SMAR 755:14
matchwood m., immortal diamond — HOPK 408:1
mate great artificer Made my m. — STEV 776:23
mater Stabat M. dolorosa — JACO 427:7
material bound by m. things — CHUA 227:14
surpasses the m. — OVID 590:8
materialism deteriorate into m. — MOLT 553:7
materials dark m. to create — MILT 542:18
His dark m. — PULL 649:11
I use simple m. — LOWR 503:13
maternity m. a period of suffering — STAN 770:5
mathematical advantage of the m. sciences — HUME 419:15
m. heads — ASCH 33:4
m. language — GALI 347:18
of m. celebrity — DOYL 292:16
mathematician appear as a pure m. — JEAN 431:4
mathematicians beware of m. — MISQ 547:16
mathematics avoid pregnancy by resort to m. — MENC 531:22
In m. you don't — NEUM 571:5
knowledge in m. — BACO 49:16
M. may be defined — RUSS 674:23
M., rightly viewed — RUSS 675:1
m., subtile — BACO 48:3
mystical m. — BROW 162:6
no place for ugly m. — HARD 380:9
so like the m. — WALT 838:20
study m. intensively — HALD 376:14
used to love m. — STEN 771:21
Matilda M. told such Dreadful Lies — BELL 68:3
matrimony as that of m. — TROL 816:10

critical period in m.	HERB 393:17
in favour of m.	AUST 43:5
joined together in holy M.	BOOK 138:19
m. at its lowest	STEV 775:29
religion and m.	CHES 222:20
safest in m.	SHER 748:10
matron sober-suited m.	SHAK 732:26
matter altering the position of m.	RUSS 674:21
away from the world of m.	BAHA 51:22
between spirit and m.	HEIN 389:13
dislike the m.	SHAK 694:21
Does it m.	SASS 682:6
if it is it doesn't m.	GILB 358:12
inditing of a good m.	BOOK 142:12
m. because you are you	SAUN 682:15
m. enough to save	BROW 166:11
m. out of place	GRAY 369:17
M., the wickedest offspring	ROCH 664:22
More m. with less art	SHAK 701:4
root of the m.	BIBL 86:35
speculations upon m.	JOHN 436:24
sum of m.	BACO 45:21
take away the m.	BACO 47:29
this m. better in France	STER 772:9
'twas no m. what he said	BYRO 189:12
what does that m.	GOET 362:19
What is M.	PUNC 649:19
What is the m. with Mary Jane	MILN 538:7
wretched m. and lame metre	MILT 541:6
matters big words for little m.	JOHN 440:9
exercise myself in great m.	BOOK 149:9
Most of what m.	RUSH 672:15
Nobody that m.	MILL 536:19
Nothing m. very much	BALF 53:16
that's what m. most	BROW 161:2
What can I do that m.	SPEN 766:15
What m. is what works	SAYI 685:17
Matthew M. Mark, Luke, and John	PRAY 623:5
mattress crack it open on a m.	MILL 537:7
mattresses through twenty m.	ANDE 15:8
mature M. love says	FROM 344:2
m. women, *dancing*	FRIE 343:13
maturing mind is m. late	NASH 568:17
Maud into the garden, M.	TENN 798:3
mausoleum as its m.	AMIS 14:10
mawkish sweetly m.	POPE 611:20
mawkishness thence proceeds m.	KEAT 454:2
Max happened to M. and Moritz	BUSC 181:25
incomparable M.	SHAW 742:19
maxim just political m.	HUME 420:16
M. Gun	BELL 68:12
will that my m.	KANT 452:19
maxima *mea m. culpa*	MISS 546:20
Maxwelton M. braes are bonnie	SONG 763:4
may bring forth M. flowers	PROV 626:33
darling buds of M.	SHAK 737:18
fressh as is the month of M.	CHAU 218:6
I'm to be Queen o' the M.	TENN 798:14
maids are M.	SHAK 697:20
Marry in M.	PROV 638:34
matter for a M. morning	SHAK 736:6
M. chickens come cheeping	PROV 638:35
M. is a pious fraud	LOWE 503:1
M. month flaps its leaves	HARD 381:8
M.'s new-fangled mirth	SHAK 717:12
M. to December	ANDE 15:10
meadow in M.	BABE 44:17
merry month of M.	BALL 54:2
merry month of M.	BALL 55:11
month of M.	MALO 518:2
month of M. Is comen	CHAU 220:17
on a M. morning	LANG 478:15
rose in M.	CHAU 220:20
Sell in M. and go away	SAYI 685:10
seventh of M.	TROL 816:11
so many frosts in M.	PROV 643:21
swarm in M.	PROV 644:1
till M. be out	PROV 639:31
what we m. be	SHAK 703:32
will not when he m.	PROV 634:12
world is white with M.	TENN 794:3
Maya net of M.	UPAN 822:14

maying let's go a-M.	HERR 395:19
mayor tart who has married the M.	BAXT 62:8
maypole away to the M. hie	SONG 762:5
M. in the Strand	BRAM 154:17
organ and the m.	JORD 447:9
maypoles I sing of M.	HERR 395:15
Mazda in the soul as Lord M.	ZORO 879:10
M.-worshipper	ZORO 879:4
mazes m. intricate	MILT 543:23
MBEs M. and your knighthoods	KEAT 453:18
McCarthyism M. is Americanism with	MCCA 509:5
McGregor Mr M.'s garden	POTT 620:7
McNamara M.'s War	MCNA 513:4
me Aim your weapons at m.	VIRG 831:6
For you but not for m.	MILI 535:15
M. Tarzan	MISQ 548:9
now in the M. Decade	WOLF 863:4
save thee and m.	OWEN 590:23
meadow m. in May	BABE 44:17
painted m.	ADDI 4:28
meadows M. trim with daisies pied	MILT 539:27
paint the m.	SHAK 717:24
meal gives a m. man-appeal	ADVE 8:11
handful of m.	BIBL 85:7
mean admires m. things	THAC 802:15
citizen of no m. city	BIBL 110:10
depends what you m. by	CATC 208:8
do a m. action	STER 772:11
Down these m. streets	CHAN 215:11
even if you don't m. it	TRUM 818:1
for m. or no uses	LOCK 497:5
having a m. Court	BAGE 51:3
Know what I m., Harry	BRUN 168:20
loves the golden m.	HORA 412:8
M., Moody and Magnificent	TAGL 788:9
no m. of death	SHAK 712:21
nothing common did or m.	MARV 525:6
poem should not m. but be	MACL 512:6
say what you m.	CARR 202:5
They may not m. to	LARK 481:6
They m. well	DISR 285:33
whatever that may m.	CHAR 217:13
what we m., we say	ARNO 29:3
Meander M.'s margent green	MILT 539:2
meaner m. beauties of the night	WOTT 870:8
only m. things	ELIO 307:14
meanest m. thing	ELLI 313:18
meaning emptied of m.	CAMU 196:16
get at his m.	RUSK 673:18
Is there a m. to music	COPL 251:8
Love is our Lord's m.	JULI 449:7
m. doesn't matter	GILB 357:19
m. to afford	CARY 206:1
mistake the m.	WESL 848:3
richest without m.	RUSK 673:23
take your m.	BROW 167:25
teems with hidden m.	GILB 358:11
To find its m.	BROW 165:21
to some faint m. make pretence	DRYD 296:10
What is the brief m.	SCHI 683:18
within the m. of the Act	ANON 19:17
meaningless almost m.	ANON 20:11
meanings m. in political terms	MANN 520:5
two m. packed up	CARR 203:13
wrestle With words and m.	ELIO 309:9
meanly all m. wrapped	MILT 540:23
m. lose	LINC 493:18
meanness land of m., sophistry	BYRO 187:14
Loses its m.	ELLI 313:18
m. of opportunity	ELIO 307:18
publish its m.	THOR 809:22
means all m. are permitted	DAWS 269:5
between ends and scarce m.	ROBB 663:4
beyond our m. to pay	DOST 290:19
by the best m.	HUTC 422:9
die beyond my m.	WILD 856:9
end cannot justify the m.	HUXL 422:16
end justifies the m.	BUSE 182:1
end justifies the m.	PROV 631:3

end, never as m.	KANT 453:3
Increased m.	DISR 284:27
live within our m.	WARD 839:20
m. all he says	ADAM 2:19
m. just what I choose	CARR 203:11
m. of grace	BOOK 135:8
m. of rising	JOHN 441:20
m. they used to acquire	LA R 481:26
m. to do ill deeds	SHAK 714:13
m. whereby I live	SHAK 725:6
my m. may lie	COWL 254:12
never know what it m.	SALI 678:16
persons of small m.	ELIO 308:12
politics by other m.	CLAU 234:11
Private M. is dead	SMIT 757:19
Whatever 'in love' m.	DUFF 298:14
wills also the m.	KANT 453:1
wills the m.	PROV 634:28
Without m.	BYRO 192:7
meant damned dots m.	CHUR 229:1
dare not say I ever m.	ELIZ 312:3
knew what it m.	BROW 168:12
knew what it m.	KLOP 469:11
more is m.	MILT 539:18
'w-a-t-e-r' m. the wonderful	KELL 459:6
what he m. by that	LOUI 501:13
measles m. of the human race	EINS 306:2
measure good m., pressed down	BIBL 104:26
If you cannot m. it	KELV 459:12
impossible to m. it	BENT 71:11
lead but one m.	SCOT 689:2
leave to heaven the m.	JOHN 438:12
Man is the m.	PROV 638:18
m. in all things	PROV 644:27
m. of all things	PROT 625:2
m. of movement	AUCT 36:22
m. of the universe	SHEL 745:24
M. still for Measure	SHAK 723:20
M. your mind's height	BROW 166:24
serves to grace my m.	PRIO 624:8
Shrunk to this little m.	SHAK 712:20
strength beyond due m.	EURI 321:12
With what m. ye mete	BIBL 103:30
measured dance is a m. pace	BACO 45:15
m. against the means	LA R 481:26
m. language lies	TENN 795:2
m. out my life with coffee spoons	ELIO 310:8
measureless caverns m. to man	COLE 240:4
over the m. whole	LUCR 504:4
measures in short m.	JONS 446:21
M. not men	CANN 197:5
M. not men	GOLD 365:12
Not men, but m.	BURK 175:5
meat all manner of m.	BOOK 147:16
appointed to buy the m.	SELD 691:14
but He sends m.	PROV 639:3
came forth m.	BIBL 83:12
dish of m. is too good	WALT 839:10
gavest m. or drink	BALL 55:4
get m. without violence	LAWS 484:14
givest them their m.	BOOK 150:2
God sends m.	PROV 633:11
have m. and cannot eat	BURN 178:23
Heaven sends us good m.	GARR 349:13
hungred, and ye gave me m.	BIBL 103:6
life more than m.	BIBL 99:16
M. and mass never hindered	PROV 638:36
m. in the hall	STEV 777:4
One man's m.	PROV 641:8
On our m., and on us all	HERR 395:14
Out-did the m.	HERR 396:6
seek their m. from God	BOOK 147:8
sent them m. enough	BOOK 145:8
solid m. for men	DRYD 297:22
taste my m.	HERB 394:15
Upon what m.	SHAK 711:20
meats funeral baked m.	SHAK 699:25
Meaulnes call le grand M.	ALAI 10:11
meazles Love iz like the m.	BILL 121:13
mechanic best mascot is a good m.	EARH 302:8
m. part of wit	ETHE 320:15

M. are vile — MONT 554:9
m. as trees, walking — BIBL 103:33
M. at forty — JUST 450:6
m. confused with life — FRID 343:5
m. don most harm — LANG 478:17
M. drawn by worth — PEMB 602:7
M. eat Hogs — STEV 774:4
m. from the barn — HOUS 415:17
m. have got love — AMIS 14:15
m. have had every advantage — AUST 42:4
M. have precedency — BRAD 154:12
m. have turned into women — XERX 872:1
m. hurrying back — MULD 564:14
m. in disguise — ABSE 1:3
m. in shape and fashion — ASCH 33:8
m. in women do require — BLAK 127:3
men know so little of m. — DU B 298:7
m., like satyrs — MARL 522:13
M. lived like fishes — SIDN 750:9
m. may come — TENN 793:2
m. must work — KING 464:13
M., my brothers — TENN 796:26
m. naturally desire to know — AUCT 36:17
m. naturally were born free — MILT 546:13
m. of like passions — BIBL 109:30
M. seldom make passes — PARK 596:4
m.'s lack of manners — HATH 384:5
m. that were boys when — BELL 68:22
M.! the only animal to fear — LAWR 483:19
M. were deceivers ever — SHAK 727:21
m. we wanted to marry — STEI 771:10
m. who are just like women — LA F 475:18
m. who have loved them — TROL 816:13
M. who march away — HARD 381:22
m. who will support me — MELB 531:3
m. with the muck-rakes — ROOS 664:22
m., women, and Herveys — MONT 554:12
M. would be angels — POPE 616:22
m. would be false — LYLY 505:19
m. would be tyrants — ADAM 1:18
Mocks married m. — SHAK 717:24
more I see of m. — ROLA 666:8
need of a world of m. — BROW 166:26
not m., but manners — FIEL 326:13
Not m., but measures — BURK 175:5
not the m. in my life that counts — WEST 848:13
power over m. — WOLL 863:10
proper young m. — BURN 178:19
Rejoiced they were na m. — BURN 180:7
schemes o' mice an' m. — BURN 179:26
State is a relation of m. — WEBE 843:15
studied books than m. — BACO 48:23
think all m. mortal — YOUN 876:22
to m. French — CHAR 217:12
transform M. into monsters — FORD 337:9
two strong m. — KIPL 465:8
very language of m. — WORD 869:26
wealth accumulates, and m. decay — GOLD 364:2
We are the hollow m. — ELIO 309:27
What m. or gods — KEAT 455:17
Women nicer than m. — AMIS 14:16
menace m. to be defeated — SCAR 683:5
mend Make do and m. — OFFI 584:10
never too late to m. — PROV 636:23
out of our power to m. — LA R 481:24
shine, and seek to m. — DONN 288:12
mendax *Splendide m.* — HORA 413:3
mended all is m. — SHAK 727:12
Least said, soonest m. — PROV 637:15
nothing else but to be m. — BUTL 183:13
mendicus *M. es* — PLAU 609:10
mending ever want m. — PROV 637:30
mene M., TEKEL, UPHARSIN — BIBL 95:25
meningitis M. It was a word — DEAN 269:13
menpleasers with eyeservice, as m. — BIBL 114:13
mens *M. agitat molem* — VIRG 830:12
M. sana in corpore sano — JUVE 451:17
mensonge *m. suit* — PROU 625:16
mental cease from m. fight — BLAK 126:24
day of m. alienation — RIEL 661:12
Freedom and slavery are m. states — GAND 348:12

m. cages — MURD 565:15
m. decay — NICO 575:2
m. pleasure produced — REYN 659:2
m. processes — HALD 376:12
mentality m. of children — RUSS 675:16
mention make m. of you always — BIBL 110:19
m. of you in our prayers — BIBL 115:12
never m. her — BAYL 62:9
mentioned names to be m. — AUST 42:18
mer *Poème De la M.* — RIMB 662:10
Mercator M.'s North Poles — CARR 203:29
mercenary m. and the prudent — AUST 42:15
m. calling — HOUS 415:8
merchandise mechanical arts and m. — BACO 48:16
merchant like unto a m. man — BIBL 101:16
m. shall hardly keep himself — BIBL 97:24
m., to secure his treasure — PRIO 624:6
merchantman monarchy is a m. — AMES 14:8
merchants Our m. are sometimes — YOUR 877:6
mercies For his m. ay endure — MILT 540:1
new m. I see — CHIS 226:11
tender m. of the wicked — BIBL 88:4
Thanks for m. past — BUCK 170:2
merciful Blessed are the m. — BIBL 98:25
God be m. — ANON 23:8
God be m. — BIBL 106:13
God be m. unto us — BOOK 144:2
m., bashful — TALM 789:21
m. eclipse — GILB 356:13
m. one to another — KORA 473:1
Name of God, the M. — KORA 470:17
these were m. men — BIBL 98:5
merciless black and m. things — JAME 429:17
looked at in this m. glare — WILL 858:7
mercury like feathered M. — SHAK 706:16
m. sank — AUDE 37:7
pick up m. with a fork — LLOY 496:20
words of M. — SHAK 717:26
mercy belle dame sans m. — KEAT 454:14
Charity and M. — DICK 278:19
compassion and m. — BIBL 97:7
crowning m. — CROM 260:13
folks over to God's m. — ELIO 307:2
God's gracious m. — BOOK 139:6
Hae m. o' my soul — EPIT 317:15
have m. and to forgive — BOOK 135:4
have m. on you — VILL 828:6
Have m. upon us — BOOK 134:15
Justice with m. — MILT 544:10
leaving to m. to heaven — FIEL 326:18
Lord, have m. upon us — BOOK 133:11
Love is the greatest m. — WILB 854:6
love m. — BIBL 96:14
M. and truth — BOOK 145:17
m. bears richer fruits — LINC 494:8
m. brought me — WHEA 850:1
m. embraceth him — BOOK 141:17
m. endureth for ever — BOOK 149:12
M. has a human heart — BLAK 127:9
M. I asked, mercy I found — EPIT 319:2
m. I to others show — POPE 618:17
M. . . . laboured much — BUNY 171:24
m. on my poor country — FLET 335:4
m. to forgive — DRYD 295:25
quality of m. — SHAK 724:29
render The deeds of m. — SHAK 724:30
shut the gates of m. — GRAY 370:7
so good a grace As m. — SHAK 723:6
so great is his m. — BOOK 147:2
so is his m. — BIBL 97:8
they shall obtain m. — BIBL 98:25
Thy m. on Thy People — KIPL 467:8
wideness in God's m. — FABE 322:7
merde *M.* — CAMB 194:10
Meredith M., we're in — CATC 208:17
merit how he esteems your m. — COWP 255:2
m. a thing absolute — MELV 531:7
m. for a bishopric — WEST 849:4
m.'s all his own — CHUR 228:19
no damned m. about it — MELB 531:2
not their m. but our folly — OSBO 588:12
What is m. — PALM 595:9

merits not weighing our m. — BOOK 137:17
mermaid Done at the M. — BEAU 63:8
m. on a dolphin's back — SHAK 726:5
M. Tavern — KEAT 455:15
mermaids heard the m. singing — ELIO 310:13
hear m. singing — DONN 289:14
merrier more the m. — PROV 639:12
merrily die all, die m. — SHAK 706:17
m. hent the stile-a — SHAK 736:28
m. meet in heaven — MORE 559:13
Merrily, m. shall I live — SHAK 734:3
Sing we m. — BOOK 145:11
merriment m. of parsons — JOHN 443:4
merry all their wars are m. — CHES 223:27
always very m. — SELL 692:4
be m. — BIBL 90:7
eat, drink, and be m. — BIBL 105:14
eat, drink and be m. — PROV 630:47
Fight on, my m. men — BALL 54:8
Have they been m. — SHAK 733:3
I am never m. — SHAK 725:12
M. and tragical — SHAK 727:5
m. heart — BIBL 88:14
m. heart doeth good — BIBL 88:21
m. heart goes all the day — SHAK 736:28
m. in hall — PROV 636:21
m. monarch — ROCH 664:18
m. month of May — BALL 54:2
m. month of May — BALL 55:11
m. old soul — NURS 580:9
m. someris day — CHAU 221:2
never a m. world — SELD 691:15
never m. world in England — SHAK 709:24
to-night we'll m. be — SONG 762:4
with a m. noise — BOOK 142:22
merrygoround It's no go the m. — MACN 513:8
merses *M. profundo* — HORA 413:15
Mesech constrained to dwell with M. — BOOK 148:15
Meshach Shadrach, M., and Abed-nego — BIBL 95:23
meshes Though its m. are wide — LAO 480:12
Mesopotamia blessed word M. — ANON 20:16
word 'M.' — GARR 349:16
mess accommodates the m. — BECK 64:13
Another fine m. — LAUR 483:1
In every m. I finds — DIBD 276:4
m. of pottage — BIBL 80:3
m. of pottage — BIBL 88:15
m. we have made of things — ELIO 309:1
message medium is the m. — MCLU 512:10
m. of your play — BEHA 66:17
m. to Albert — DISR 285:13
Publish your m. — WESL 848:4
messager bisy larke, m. of day — CHAU 219:9
messages m. should be delivered — GOLD 365:22
messenger m.-boy Presidency — SCHL 686:4
m. of Death — SACK 676:14
M. of God — KORA 472:13
M. of God — KORA 473:1
M. with the guidance — KORA 472:20
only the M. of God — KORA 472:1
messengers staying m. — RILK 662:2
messing m. about in boats — GRAH 368:1
met Hail, fellow, well m. — SWIF 783:2
Ill m. by moonlight — SHAK 726:2
m. the enemy — CART 205:16
m. the enemy — PERR 604:7
m. together — BOOK 145:17
m. us in your Son — BOOK 137:18
M. you not with my true love — RALE 654:3
We m. at nine — LERN 490:9
metal Here's m. more attractive — SHAK 702:19
with rich m. loaded — SPEN 767:12
metamorphoses month of m. — ARAG 25:15
metaphorical m. God — DONN 290:2
metaphors use m. in conversation — ARIS 27:2
metaphysic high As m. wit can fly — BUTL 183:11
metaphysical m. brothel for the emotions — KOES 470:10
metaphysicians say of m. — CHAM 215:2
metaphysics Explaining m. — BYRO 187:18
M. is the finding — BRAD 154:2

1036 METAPHYSICS · MILTON

metaphysics (*cont.*):
more towards m. DARW 266:21
mete With what measure ye m. BIBL 103:30
meteor cloud-encircled m. SHEL 744:14
hair Streamed, like a m. GRAY 369:20
Shone like a m. MILT 541:26
method know my m. DOYL 292:14
yet there is m. in't SHAK 701:6
Methodism more to M. than to Marxism PHIL 606:7
Methodist morals of a M. GILB 358:10
methods You know my m. DOYL 292:21
methought M. I saw MILT 545:16
Methuselah days of M. BIBL 79:20
métier *c'est son m.* HEIN 389:17
Mon m. et mon art MONT 555:11
metope o to be a m. CUMM 262:6
metre laws of God and man and m. EPIT 318:6
m. ballad-mongers SHAK 706:10
wretched m. and lame m. MILT 541:6
metrical m. composition WORD 870:1
metropolis m. of the empire COBB 237:14
mettle thy undaunted m. SHAK 719:16
metuant *Oderint, dum m.* ACCI 1:7
metus *M. et malesuada Fames* VIRG 830:9
meum *M. est propositum* ANON 23:8
meurt *La Garde m.* CAMB 194:10
mew be a kitten and cry m. SHAK 706:10
mewling infant, M. and puking SHAK 696:28
Mexico M., so far from God DIAZ 276:1
Mexique beyond the M. Bay MARV 524:17
mezzo *Nel m. del cammin* DANT 264:12
mice as long as it catches m. DENG 273:3
catches no m. PROV 628:36
Like little m. SUCK 779:13
m. will play PROV 646:45
schemes o' m. an' men BURN 179:26
than will catch m. PROV 636:50
Three blind m. NURS 582:1
Michael M. and his angels BIBL 118:24
Michelangelo designs by M. TWAI 820:12
M. left a proof YEAT 875:6
name of—M. REYN 659:7
Talking of M. ELIO 310:6
miching m. mallecho SHAK 702:21
Mickey Mouse You're M. PORT 619:20
mickle makes a m. PROV 638:24
Many a m. PROV 638:25
microbe inoculation of some m. LIST 495:11
m. is nothing PAST 599:5
M. is so very small BELL 68:14
microbes *on the antiquity of m.* ANON 16:4
microphone paid for this m. REAG 656:12
microscopic man a m. eye POPE 616:23
mid you in m.-air SOND 761:3
middenpit workshop, larder, m. BUNT 170:18
middle beginning, a m. ARIS 27:20
Heaven, a m. state MALL 517:16
life's m. state COWP 257:1
m. of the journey of our life DANT 264:12
m. of the limelight SHAW 742:21
M. Path PALI 594:10
m.-sized are alone entangled SHEN 747:20
m. way is none at all ADAM 3:3
mine was the m. state DEFO 270:11
people in the m. of the road BEVA 76:16
safely by the m. way OVID 590:9
Secret sits in the m. FROS 345:1
middle age dead centre of m. ADAM 2:8
enchantments of the M. BEER 66:2
last enchantments of the M. ARNO 31:16
reckless m. YEAT 874:9
middle-aged Grown m. WINT 860:16
Middle Ages go and live in the M. SMIT 757:18
middle class great English m. ARNO 31:15
m. morality SHAW 742:9
M. people are apt SMIL 755:21
M. was quite prepared BELL 68:2
Philistines proper, or m. ARNO 31:11
sinking m. ORWE 587:22
middle classes bow, ye lower m. GILB 356:15
Middlesex acre in M. MACA 507:7
Rural M. again BETJ 76:1
midge like a fretful m. ROSS 669:14
no bigger than a m.'s wing PROV 639:16
Midian host of M. BIBL 83:7
Midlands living in the M. BELL 68:23
midnight a-bed after m. SHAK 735:7
black, and m. hags SHAK 721:19
budding morrow in m. KEAT 457:6
came upon a m. clear SEAR 690:13
cease upon the m. KEAT 456:9
Cerberus, and blackest M. MILT 539:21
chimes at m. SHAK 707:21
consumed the m. oil GAY 351:12
fire-bell at m. BURK 175:14
Holding hands at m. GERS 353:16
hour's sleep before m. PROV 641:4
iron tongue of m. SHAK 727:9
Let's mock the m. bell SHAK 695:11
m. never come MARL 522:10
m. ride of Paul Revere LONG 499:25
M. shakes the memory ELIO 310:22
M. Without Pity JOHN 434:14
our m. oil QUAR 651:9
stroke of the m. hour NEHR 569:9
'Tis the year's m. DONN 289:11
upon a m. dreary POE 610:19
upon a m. pillow SHAK 696:20
woes at m. rise LYLY 505:21
midst go up in the m. of thee BIBL 81:24
In the m. of life BOOK 139:9
there am I in the m. BIBL 102:3
midsummer high M. pomps ARNO 30:27
very m. madness SHAK 736:4
midwife fairies' m. SHAK 732:5
midwinter In the bleak m. ROSS 669:2
mie *J'aime mieux ma m.* ANON 22:10
mieux *m. est l'ennemi du bien* VOLT 834:2
tout est au m. VOLT 833:10
might as our m. lessens ANON 23:14
Britons alone use 'M.' WAUG 843:1
counsel and m. BIBL 92:16
do it with thy m. BIBL 90:10
Exceeds man's m. SHAK 734:16
It m. have been HART 383:16
It m. have been WHIT 853:3
M. is right PROV 638:37
my name is M.-have-been ROSS 669:20
right makes m. LINC 493:12
Through the dear m. MILT 540:15
mightier make thee m. yet BENS 70:22
pen m. than the sword BULW 170:14
mightiest m. in the mightiest SHAK 724:29
mighty all that m. heart WORD 865:8
bringeth m. things to pass BOOK 148:10
how are the m. fallen BIBL 84:11
Lord m. in battle BOOK 141:2
Marlowe's m. line JONS 446:23
m. God BIBL 92:14
M. lak' a rose STAN 770:7
m. man is he LONG 500:4
m. man of valour BIBL 83:5
m. Poets in their misery WORD 868:24
m. working BOOK 139:10
Nimrod the m. hunter BIBL 79:29
put down the m. BIBL 104:9
rushing m. wind BIBL 109:12
things which are m. BIBL 111:24
thou art m. yet SHAK 714:1
through a m. hand BIBL 82:12
To produce a m. book MELV 531:12
mignonne *M., allons voir* RONS 666:14
migraine Love is a universal m. GRAV 369:13
migrations all our m. GOLD 365:12
mild draw'd m. DICK 278:23
m. and magnificent eye BROW 166:13
prefer m. hale SURT 781:13
milder Not m. ARNO 30:4
mildest m. mannered man BYRO 188:19
mile compel thee to go a m. BIBL 99:6
miss is as good as a m. PROV 638:42
walked a crooked m. NURS 581:12
miles How many m. NURS 579:3
m. to go before I sleep FROS 345:3
milestones m. on the Dover Road DICK 278:14
militant Christ's Church m. BOOK 137:4
first m. lowbrow BERL 73:12
militants m. like cleaning women TRUF 817:14
military disarm a m. capacity COOK 250:12
entrust to m. men CLEM 235:6
m. divisions HAVE 384:8
M. force MCNA 513:6
m. man approaches SHAW 741:5
M. Two-step GREN 372:9
order and m. discipline MILI 535:5
milk Adversity's sweet m. SHAK 732:28
buy wine and m. BIBL 94:7
crying over spilt m. PROV 636:24
drunk the m. of Paradise COLE 240:9
end is moo, the other, m. NASH 568:14
flowing with m. and honey BIBL 80:36
Gin was mother's m. SHAW 742:10
his mother's m. SHAK 735:5
lady loves M. Tray ADVE 7:6
m. and the yoghurt TRIL 815:13
m. comes frozen home SHAK 717:25
m. is more likely BUTL 184:13
m. is so cheap PROV 647:22
m. my ewes and weep SHAK 737:6
m. of human kindness GUED 374:7
m. of human kindness SHAK 718:19
m. of the word BIBL 117:2
m. of the word BIBL 120:18
M.'s leap toward immortality FADI 322:12
M.-soup men call domestic PATM 599:13
m. the bull JOHN 440:2
m. the cow of the world WILB 854:3
m.-white steed BALL 55:20
putting m. into babies CHUR 230:4
she gave him m. BIBL 83:2
take my m. for gall SHAK 719:1
trout in the m. THOR 809:6
weyveth m. and flessh CHAU 219:15
With m. and honey blessed NEAL 569:8
milka Drinka Pinta M. Day ADVE 7:19
milkmaid m. singeth blithe MILT 539:26
milky M. Way, the bird of Paradise HERB 394:19
steeped in stars, and m. RIMB 662:10
mill at the m. with slaves MILT 544:31
clappeth as a m. CHAU 219:1
forge and the m. HOUS 415:17
grist that comes to the m. PROV 626:15
m. cannot grind with PROV 638:38
neither a m. HUNT 422:3
old m. by the stream ARMS 28:14
mille *Da mi basia m.* CATU 210:7
millennium after the m. RAOU 655:9
calico m. CARL 200:30
miller hackneyed jokes from M. BYRO 189:30
jolly m. BICK 120:21
milliner jewelled mass of m. TENN 797:21
million aiming at a m. BROW 165:25
Fifty m. Frenchmen MILI 535:8
m. deaths a statistic STAL 769:18
m. million spermatozoa HUXL 423:1
want to make a m. ANON 18:3
millionaire And an old-fashioned m. FISH 330:12
I am a M. SHAW 740:14
m. who bought it MCCA 509:3
silk hat on a Bradford m. ELIO 311:14
millions I will be m. EPIT 318:13
M. long for immortality ERTZ 320:8
m. of strange shadows SHAK 737:27
m. of the mouthless dead SORL 761:24
mortal m. live *alone* ARNO 31:3
multiplying m. O'SU 589:7
pour out m. COLB 238:18
What m. died CAMP 195:14
mills dark Satanic m. BLAK 126:24
m. of God grind slowly LONG 499:20
m. of God grind slowly PROV 638:39
millstone m. were hanged about his neck BIBL 102:1
millstones eyes as big as m. ANDE 15:9
Turned to m. SHEL 745:3
Milton malt does more than M. HOUS 416:10
M.! thou shouldst be living WORD 866:16

minutes (cont.):
have the seven m. — COLL 243:6
m. hasten to their end — SHAK 737:29
rate of sixty m. an hour — LEWI 491:17
sixty diamond m. — MANN 519:10
take care of m. — CHES 223:4
Three m.' thought — HOUS 416:12
when the waves turn the m. — LIGH 493:5
Mirabeau Under M. Bridge — APOL 25:3
miracle m. in his own person — HUME 420:1
m. of a youth — EVEL 321:20
m. of our age — CARE 198:5
m. of rare device — COLE 240:6
miracles age of m. — PROV 626:11
age of m. hadn't passed — GERS 353:12
believe in m. — FOX 340:2
there are always m. — CATH 209:11
miraculous most m. organ — SHAK 701:24
Miranda Do you remember an Inn, M. — BELL 68:24
mire cast into the m. — BURK 174:12
m. and clay — BOOK 141:30
Sow returns to her M. — KIPL 466:2
mirk m., mirk night — BALL 55:22
mirror live alone and smash his m. — ANON 22:6
mind is like a m. — CHUA 227:16
m. cracked from side to side — TENN 796:19
M., mirror on the wall — GRIM 373:10
m. of alle curteisye — CHAU 219:14
m. of the face — AESC 8:34
m. the image we cast there — GIDE 356:2
m. up to nature — SHAK 702:15
novel is like a m. — STEN 771:18
stand of m. bright — HUI- 419:9
sunlit m. — ABSE 1:5
mirrors m. are lonely — AUDE 38:4
m. meant To glass the opulent — HARD 381:12
m. of the gigantic shadows — SHEL 747:14
mirth betray me to your m. or hate — FORD 337:10
house of m. — BIBL 89:29
I love such m. — WALT 839:6
M. is like a flash — ADDI 5:12
m.-subdual — GISS 359:10
must borrow its m. — WILC 854:9
Present m. — SHAK 735:9
song of the birds for m. — GURN 374:16
Than M. can do — ANON 18:6
misbeliever You call me m. — SHAK 724:9
misce M. stultitiam consiliis — HORA 414:5
mischance fil all this m. — CHAU 219:26
mischief evil and m. — BOOK 134:16
execute any m. — CLAR 233:6
if m. befall him — BIBL 80:25
In every deed of m. — GIBB 354:13
intended m. against thee — BOOK 140:14
it means m. — SHAK 702:21
m. then into the world — DRAY 293:16
m., thou art afoot — SHAK 713:16
m. thou hast done — NEWT 574:10
mother of m. — PROV 639:16
no authority from God to do m. — MAYH 529:8
punishment is m. — BENT 71:7
sown the world with m. — BUCH 169:8
Spectatress of the m. — ROWE 671:7
what m. is in hand — BYRO 189:4
mischiefs heap m. upon them — BIBL 82:20
misconceive hardly m. you — BROW 167:25
misconduct no m. in anyone — NELS 570:3
miscuit qui m. utile dulci — HORA 409:12
misdoings these our m. — BOOK 137:10
miserable make a man m. — CHAR 217:3
Me m.! which way shall I fly — MILT 542:29
M. comforters — BIBL 86:31
m. have no other medicine — SHAK 723:11
m. human being — JAME 430:14
m. sinners — BOOK 134:15
m. state of mind — BACO 46:26
most m. things — VIRG 829:5
of all men most m. — BIBL 112:20
secret of being m. — SHAW 742:3
so is it very m. — TAYL 792:4
two people m. — BUTL 184:7

miserande Heu, m. puer — VIRG 830:15
miserere m. nobis — MISS 549:19
miseria Nella m. — DANT 264:18
miseries in shallows and in m. — SHAK 713:28
miserrima Quaeque ipse m. vidi — VIRG 829:5
miserum Nec m. fieri — LUCR 504:13
misery bound in m. and iron — BOOK 147:15
coined our m. — DRAY 293:16
full of m. — BOOK 139:8
great kick at m. — LAWR 484:2
guilt and m. — AUST 41:18
happiness and final m. — MILT 542:12
loses his m. — ARNO 30:14
Man hands on m. to man — LARK 481:10
mighty Poets in their m. — WORD 868:24
mine affliction and my m. — BIBL 95:10
M. acquaints a man — SHAK 733:25
m. is a battle gained — WELL 846:7
M. loves company — PROV 638:40
m. of being — DRAB 293:6
m. of manilla folders — ROET 665:6
m. which it is his duty — LOWE 502:13
nothing but pure m. — JOHN 443:2
Oppressed the m. — CRAB 257:14
part of one's m. — TACI 787:4
relation of distant m. — GIBB 354:14
result m. — DICK 277:10
splendid m. — ROSS 669:10
to him that is in m. — BIBL 86:18
vale of m. — BOOK 145:14
when one is in m. — DANT 264:18
misfits m., Looney Tunes, and criminals — REAG 656:16
misfortune after a recent m. — MANZ 520:13
m. of our best friends — LA R 482:11
m. to ourselves — BIER 121:5
What a m. it is — EDGE 303:11
misfortunes All the m. of men — PASC 597:18
crimes and m. — VOLT 834:10
crimes, follies, and m. — GIBB 354:6
make m. more bitter — BACO 47:22
M. never come singly — PROV 638:41
m. of others — LA R 481:18
talks of his m. — JOHN 443:2
misguided m. men — KING 463:16
mislaid afterwards m. — PAST 598:18
mislead mystify, m., and surprise — JACK 427:1
one to m. the public — ASQU 34:7
misleading bound to be m. — WATS 841:6
m. thoughts — SPEN 765:23
misled most have been m. — DRYD 295:29
mislike M. me not for my complexion — SHAK 724:10
misnomer name of Epic's no m. — BYRO 188:4
misquotation M. the privilege of the learned — PEAR 601:4
misquote enough of learning to m. — BYRO 189:30
misrepresentation some degree of m. — ELIO 308:14
misrule Thirteen years of Tory m. — POLI 613:10
miss calls her 'M.' — CHES 224:18
little m. — HUME 420:6
m. but a tree — BLAM 128:15
m. for pleasure — GAY 351:27
m. is as good as a mile — PROV 638:42
M. not the discourse — BIBL 97:13
M. respectably unmarried — CART 204:13
never had you never m. — PROV 646:35
never m. the water — PROV 648:18
so might I m. — BROW 166:10
missa Ite m. est — MISS 550:1
missed m. a good opportunity — CHIR 226:10
m. the bus — CHAM 214:8
never would be m. — GILB 357:3
No one would have m. her — EPIT 318:3
Woman much m. — HARD 382:1
misses m. family and friends — EPIT 318:14
missing M. so much and so much — CORN 252:2
mission m. workers came out too early — RUNY 672:12
my duty and my m. — SCHI 685:23
My m. is to pacify — GLAD 360:1

sense of religious m. — UPDI 823:1
missionaries eaten by m. — SPOO 768:16
missionary I would eat a m. — WILB 853:15
Mississippi place the m. — BELL 69:3
singing of the M. — HUGH 418:3
Missouri admit M. to the Union — COBB 237:11
misspent thy m. time — KEN 459:14
missus M., my Lord — PUNC 650:6
mist air broke into a m. — BROW 166:28
drizzling m. — ASKE 34:1
Fuji through m. — BASH 60:17
meanness, sophistry, and m. — BYRO 187:14
m. and hum — ARNO 30:18
m. in my face — BROW 167:7
m. is dispelled — GAY 351:6
mistake Among all forms of m. — ELIO 307:22
have made a great m. — MORS 561:16
made any such m. — DICK 279:11
make a m. — LA G 476:2
m. in the translation — VANB 823:17
m. shall not be repeated — EPIT 319:8
m. the meaning — WESL 848:3
Nature's sole m. — GILB 358:9
overlooks a m. — HUXL 423:10
Shome m., shurely — CATC 208:26
song and a m. — OVID 590:18
under a m. — SWIF 783:3
mistaken possible you may be m. — CROM 260:12
mistakes gives to their m. — WILD 855:13
great men make m. — CHUR 228:24
If he makes m. they must be covered — CHUR 230:22
If you don't make m. — PROV 635:25
just created like m. — EMEC 314:10
knows some of the worst m. — HEIS 390:1
make no m. — CONR 249:7
man who makes no m. — PHEL 605:11
search for our m. — POPP 619:7
mistress Art is a jealous m. — EMER 314:20
court a m. — JONS 446:19
deck her m.' head — BYRO 190:27
In ev'ry port a m. — GAY 351:25
literature is my m. — CHEK 222:8
marry your m. — GOLD 363:19
m. I am ashamed to call you — ELIZ 312:18
m. in my own — KIPL 467:2
m. of herself — POPE 615:1
m. of the Earl — WILS 859:11
m. of the months — SWIN 784:18
m. of the Party — HEAL 387:3
m. or a friend — SHEL 744:1
m. should be like — WYCH 871:10
new m. now I chase — LOVE 502:6
O m. mine — SHAK 735:8
teeming m. — POPE 614:28
worst m. — BACO 45:23
mistresses I shall have m. — GEOR 352:9
like all his other m. — FLAU 333:6
m. with great smooth — BROW 165:4
or your Lordship's m. — WILK 856:22
Wives are young men's m. — BACO 47:17
mists Season of m. — KEAT 456:22
So many m. in March — PROV 643:21
misty ful m. morwe — CHAU 221:2
misunderstood people who remain m. — TURG 819:6
To be great is to be m. — EMER 315:7
truth m. — JAME 430:16
misuse m., then cast their toys away — COWP 255:5
misused m. words generate — SPEN 765:23
mites threw in two m. — BIBL 104:4
with m. of stars — MAYA 529:1
Mithra M. of wide pastures — ZORO 879:1
Mithridates M., he died old — HOUS 416:11
mittens lost their m. — NURS 582:2
mix M. a little foolishness — HORA 414:5
m. her with me — SWIN 786:4
m. them with my brains — OPIE 585:13
mixen Better wed over the m. — PROV 627:42
mixture m. of a lie — BACO 48:11
strange m. of blood — CEÈV 259:18

m. Piglet wasn't there — MILN 537:19
m. than all — NEWM 572:11
m. than Homer knew — SWIF 784:1
m. than somewhat — RUNY 672:11
m. the merrier — PROV 639:12
m. things in heaven — SHAK 700:27
M. will mean worse — AMIS 14:18
m. you get — PROV 639:13
Much would have m. — PROV 639:19
no m. to say — SHAK 734:24
O m. than moon — DONN 289:22
take m. than nothing — CARR 202:7
you get no m. of me — DRAY 293:14
mores Emollit m. — OVID 590:2
Et linguam et m. — JUVE 450:18
O tempora, O m. — CICE 232:2
morganatic m. alliance — HARD 380:8
Morgen M. sterb' ich — LESS 490:19
mori In taberna m. — ANON 23:8
pro patria m. — HORA 412:17
moriamur M. et in media arma ruamus
— VIRG 829:14
moriar Non omnis m. — HORA 413:10
moribus M. antiquis res — ENNI 316:4
morituri Ave Caesar, m. te salutant
— ANON 23:3
Moritz happened to Max and M. — BUSC 181:25
morn But, look, the m. — SHAK 699:7
Each m. a thousand roses — FITZ 331:14
From m. to noon he fell — MILT 541:31
m. and cold indifference — ROWE 671:5
m. Of bright carnations — DRUM 294:6
new m. she saw not — KEAT 454:28
Salute the happy m. — BYRO 185:2
still m. went out — MILT 540:16
this the happy m. — MILT 540:21
morning arrested one fine m. — KAFK 452:5
before the m. watch — BOOK 149:8
danced in the m. — CART 205:2
disasters in his m. face — GOLD 364:7
Early in the m. — HEBE 388:10
Early one m. — SONG 762:6
evening and the m. — BIBL 78:13
glad confident m. — BROW 166:14
Good m., sir — CATC 207:23
have the m. well-aired — BRUM 168:17
In the m. it is green — BOOK 145:20
joy cometh in the m. — BOOK 141:14
Lucifer, son of the m. — BIBL 92:20
many a glorious m. — SHAK 737:25
m. after — ADE 6:4
m. again in America — POLI 612:25
m. cometh — BIBL 92:21
M. dreams come true — PROV 639:15
m. gilds the skies — CASW 206:17
m. had been golden — CHUR 230:16
M. has broken — FARJ 323:12
M. in the bowl of night — FITZ 330:9
m. light creaks down again — SITW 753:10
m. of the world — SHEL 743:13
m. rose — KEAT 455:28
M.'s at seven — BROW 167:3
m.'s minion — HOPK 408:4
m.'s war — SHAK 710:6
Never m. wore — TENN 795:3
New every m. — KEBL 458:21
pay thy m. sacrifice — KEN 459:13
shining m. face — SHAK 696:28
take you in the m. — BALD 53:1
viewed the m. with alarm — GERS 353:12
What a glorious m. — ADAM 3:20
wings of the m. — BOOK 149:17
won't go home till m. — BUCK 170:3
Mornington present of M. Crescent
— HARG 382:11
Morocco we're M. bound — BURK 176:12
moron consumer isn't a m. — OGIL 583:13
See the happy m. — ANON 20:8
morphine m. or idealism — JUNG 449:13
Morris M. Minor prototype — NUFF 577:16
nine men's m. — SHAK 726:3
morrow bid the Devil good m. — PROV 639:32
Eagerly I wished the m. — POE 611:1
no thought for the m. — BIBL 99:20

mors Illi m. gravis incubat — SENE 692:21
Indignatio principis m. est — MORE 559:10
M. aurem vellens — ANON 23:10
M. stupebit — MISS 550:6
Mortalem vitam m. — LUCR 504:13
Nil igitur m. — LUCR 504:11
Pallida M. — HORA 411:7
morsel I found you as a m. — SHAK 695:10
morsels ice like m. — BOOK 150:8
mort La m. ne surprend — LA F 475:16
La m., sans phrases — SIEY 751:11
mortal gathers all things m. — SWIN 785:12
Her last disorder m. — GOLD 364:15
laugh at any m. thing — BYRO 189:1
m., and may err — SHIR 749:19
m. men, mortal men — SHAK 706:18
m. tongue — GURN 374:19
shuffled off this m. coil — SHAK 701:26
something m. — LUCR 504:11
think all men m. — YOUN 876:22
this m. life — BOOK 135:10
this m. life — BOOK 138:2
this m. must put on — BIBL 113:5
mortality emblem of m. — DISR 285:12
frail m. — BACO 49:10
m. touches the heart — VIRG 829:1
M. Weighs heavily on me — KEAT 456:16
Old m. — BROW 162:9
sad m. o'ersways — SHAK 738:2
sepulchres of m. — CREW 259:19
smells of m. — SHAK 716:18
mortals good that m. know — ADDI 5:1
not for m. — ARMS 28:15
not in m. — ADDI 4:12
startle Composing m. — AUDE 36:23
what fools these m. be — SHAK 726:18
mortar Lies are the m. — WELL 846:22
mortifications m. and humiliations
— WALP 838:9
mortifying m. reflections — CONG 248:1
Mortimer Are you Edmund M. — SELL 692:1
mortis Timor m. conturbat me — DUNB 299:10
morts Il n'y a pas de m. — MAET 514:14
mortuus Passer m. est — CATU 210:4
Moscow do not march on M. — MONT 556:9
If I lived in M. — CHEK 222:3
M.: those syllables — PUSH 650:20
who in M. — BROW 168:9
Moses From M. to Moses — EPIT 317:9
Go down, M. — SONG 763:16
greater than M. — TALM 789:29
M. hid his face — BIBL 80:35
sitting in M.' chair — BLAK 125:6
Mosque from the Holy M. — KORA 472:6
mosques build m. and temples — FRED 341:21
mosquito just another m. — OKPI 584:22
moss gathers no m. — PROV 642:29
mossy Happy field or m. cavern — KEAT 455:15
violet by a m. stone — WORD 869:4
most first with the m. men — MISQ 547:15
mostest fustest with the m. — MISQ 547:15
mote m. that is in thy brother's eye — BIBL 99:22
moth beetle, nor the death-m. — KEAT 455:27
Both m. and flame — ROET 665:10
Kill not the m. — BLAK 124:13
like a m., the simple maid — GAY 350:17
m. and rust doth corrupt — BIBL 99:13
m. for the star — SHEL 746:18
mother all thy m.'s graces — CORB 251:12
artist man and the m. woman — SHAW 740:24
art thy m.'s glass — SHAK 737:17
As is the m. — BIBL 95:14
Behold thy m. — BIBL 108:31
by our m.'s dust — FORD 337:10
Can you hear me, m. — CATC 207:8
Christ and his m. — HOPK 407:22
church for his m. — CYPR 263:14
expediency itself is the m. — HORA 414:12
father was frightened of his m. — GEOR 353:3
for the m.'s sake — COLE 241:12
France, m. of arts — DU B 298:2
From whence his m. rose — SEDL 690:17
gave her m. forty whacks — ANON 18:15

Gentle Child of gentle M. — DEAR 269:15
great sweet m. — SWIN 786:4
happen to your m. — WALK 836:1
have a beautiful m. — WALK 836:5
heaviness of his m. — BIBL 87:34
her m. tends her — MERE 532:19
Honour thy father and thy m. — BIBL 81:20
I arose a m. — BIBL 82:33
joyful m. — BOOK 148:2
leave his father and his m. — BIBL 79:3
Like m., like daughter — PROV 637:34
lovelier than your lovely m. — HORA 411:18
make love to the m. — PROV 642:1
marriage with your m. — SOPH 761:20
marry a man who hates his m. — BENN 70:21
may not marry his M. — BOOK 150:24
m. bids me bind — HUNT 422:1
m. bore me in the southern wild — BLAK 127:12
M. died today — CAMU 196:17
m., do not cry — FARM 323:15
M., give me the sun — IBSE 424:7
m. laid her baby — ALEX 12:8
m., make my bed — BALL 54:3
M. needs something today — JAGG 427:9
M. of Aeneas' race — LUCR 504:3
m. of all battles — HUSS 422:7
M. OF HARLOTS — BIBL 119:8
m. of invention — PROV 639:27
m. of mankind — MILT 541:11
m. of Parliaments — BRIG 157:4
m. of sciences — BACO 49:2
M. of the Free — BENS 70:22
m. said I never should — NURS 580:7
m.'s grief — BRET 156:14
m.'s little helper — JAGG 427:9
m.'s safeguard — NAPO 567:17
m.'s yearning — ELIO 307:3
m. told me as a boy — BERR 75:3
m. was glad to get asleep — EMER 315:17
m. who talks about her own — DISR 285:2
m. will be there — HERB 393:10
my father or my m. — STER 772:15
my m. and my brethren — BIBL 101:12
My m. groaned — BLAK 127:20
my m. I see in myself — FRID 343:4
never called me m. — WOOD 863:21
O M. blest — ALPH 13:20
plans to resemble: her m. — BROO 159:16
recognize your m. — VIRG 832:3
rob him the m. — FAUL 324:18
their Dacian m. — BYRO 186:24
to make it well? My M. — TAYL 791:15
Took great care of his M. — MILN 538:3
Upon his m.'s grave — WORD 868:4
motherhood Guilt is to m. — WELD 845:17
mothers Come m. and fathers — DYLA 302:5
happy m. made — SHAK 732:4
m.-in-law and Wigan Pier — BRID 156:17
m. of large families — BELL 67:19
m. who sent their sons — ATAT 35:3
search of our m.' gardens — WALK 836:7
sorrows of the m. — FREN 342:8
women become like their m. — WILD 854:21
moths eaten by m. — SITW 753:13
motion alteration of m. — NEWT 574:4
Between the m. And the act — ELIO 309:28
Devoid of sense and m. — MILT 542:4
economic law of m. — MARX 526:6
God ordered m. — VAUG 824:13
m. of the wheels — HUME 420:3
perpetual m. — DICK 280:25
poetry in m. — KAUF 453:11
poetry of m. — GRAH 368:2
so many concepts of m. — RILK 662:6
uniform m. in a right line — NEWT 574:3
motions secret m. — BACO 48:28
motive m.-hunting of motiveless — COLE 241:24
motives better m. for all the trouble
— GREE 371:20
m. they act by — ASTE 34:16
motley made myself a m. — SHAK 738:13
M.'s the only wear — SHAK 696:26
motor heart's stalled m. — MAYA 529:4

mulatto Grape is my m. mother — HUGH 418:13
mule m. of politics — DISR 285:19
Sicilian m. was to me — GLAD 360:11
mules m. of politics — POWE 622:8
mulier m. formosa superne — HORA 408:14
mullets We will eat our m. — JONS 445:15
Mulligan plump Buck M. — JOYC 448:13
multiplication M. is vexation — ANON 19:2
multiplicity m. of agreeable — JOHN 440:12
multiply Be fruitful, and m. — BIBL 78:18
Increase and m. — BOOK 136:4
m. my signs and my wonders — BIBL 81:2
multitude hoofs of a swinish m. — BURK 174:12
m. is in the wrong — DILL 283:8
m. of days — JOHN 438:9
m. of sins — BIBL 117:12
m. of the isles — BOOK 146:10
m. of tongues — HAND 379:6
m., that numerous piece — BROW 163:10
m. the blind instruments — GODW 361:4
m., the *hoi polloi* — DRYD 297:17
m., which no man could number — BIBL 118:12
multitudes I contain m. — WHIT 852:14
m. in the valley of decision — BIBL 96:9
Pestilence-stricken m. — SHEL 745:6
mum oafish louts remember M. — BETJ 75:10
They fuck you up, your m. and dad — LARK 481:9
mumble When in doubt, m. — BORE 151:6
mumbled few m. cakes — HUNT 421:14
mummy dyed in m. — SHAK 729:4
munch m. on, crunch on — BROW 167:2
mundane grasp of m. matters — THOM 805:10
in this m. life — MURA 565:11
mundi *peccata m.* — MISS 549:19
Sic transit gloria m. — ANON 23:12
mundus *pereat m.* — MOTT 563:9
muneribus *deorum M. sapiente uti* — HORA 414:4
muove *amor che m. il sole* — DANT 265:17
Eppur si m. — GALI 348:1
murder about a m. — ORWE 586:22
battle and m. — BOOK 134:19
decided to m. his wife — ILES 424:17
do no m. — BOOK 137:1
Don't they m. the people — TROL 816:12
I met M. on the way — SHEL 745:2
indulges himself in m. — DE Q 273:22
I wanted to m. — DOST 291:4
Killing no m. — PROV 637:3
Killing no m. — SEXB 693:4
Live in despite of m. — CHAP 216:4
love and m. will out — CONG 246:28
Macbeth does m. sleep — SHAK 720:6
Most sacrilegious m. — SHAK 720:16
most unnatural m. — SHAK 700:19
m. by the law — YOUN 876:14
m. by the throat — LLOY 496:17
m. cannot be hid long — SHAK 724:13
M. considered — DE Q 273:21
m. into the home — HITC 400:4
m., like talent — LEWE 491:13
m. men everywhere — FANO 323:1
M. most foul — SHAK 700:20
m. respectable — ORWE 588:2
M.'s out of tune — SHAK 729:16
m. the thinker — WESK 847:5
m., though it have no tongue — SHAK 701:24
m. to dissect — WORD 869:15
m. whiles I smile — SHAK 710:8
M. will out — PROV 639:20
M. wol out — CHAU 219:24
m. yet is but fantastical — SHAK 718:12
One m. made a villain — PORT 619:22
Sooner m. an infant — BLAK 126:18
stick to m. and leave art — EPST 316:13
story is about not m. — JAME 430:12
stroke of m. — DRYD 296:33
to m., for the truth — ADLE 6:7
Vanity, like m., will out — COWL 254:22
We hear war called m. — MACD 510:10
withered m. — SHAK 719:20
murdered Each one a m. self — ROSS 669:18
m. peer — ALCO 11:6
m. reputations — CONG 247:18

Our royal master's m. — SHAK 720:18
their m. man — KEAT 454:27
murderer honourable m. — SHAK 729:22
m. for fancy prose style — NABO 566:17
m. from the beginning — BIBL 107:31
tender m. — BROW 164:26
murderers m., and idolaters — BIBL 119:23
m. of Jewish children — WIES 853:13
m. take the first step — KARR 453:7
murderous m. hand a drowsy bench — CRAB 258:10
murders m. and assaults — KOHL 470:14
murmur m. at his case — COWP 255:6
m. of a summer's day — ARNO 30:7
murmured m. in their tents — BOOK 147:13
murmuring mazily m. — TENN 798:17
m. of innumerable bees — TENN 799:22
murmurs hollow m. died away — COLL 243:15
In the m. — SOND 761:1
m. of self-will — BODE 130:9
Murphy M.'s Law — PROV 635:5
Murray slain the Earl of M. — BALL 54:6
mus *nascetur ridiculus m.* — HORA 409:6
muscle take the m. from bone — ELIO 310:18
muscles M. better and nerves more — CUMM 262:12
muscular His Christianity was m. — DISR 285:25
muse every conqueror creates a M. — WALL 837:2
grace my barren m. — LANI 479:4
like a tenth m. — ANON 17:14
Livelier liquor than the M. — HOUS 416:10
M. but served to ease — POPE 614:18
M. forbids to die — HORA 414:2
M. invoked — SWIF 783:29
m. on dromedary trots — COLE 240:11
O! for a M. of fire — SHAK 708:7
tenth American m. — BRON 158:3
tenth M. — TROL 816:25
Tragic M. first trod the stage — POPE 618:3
Why does my M. only speak — SMIT 757:16
mused m. a little space — TENN 796:20
muses charm of all the M. — TENN 800:11
house that serves the M. — SAPP 681:2
M.' garden with pedantic weeds — CARE 198:7
M. made write verse — VIRG 832:9
M. sing of happy swains — CRAB 258:5
museum ace caff with a nice M. — ADVE 7:2
m. inside our heads — LIVE 496:2
mushroom I am . . . a m. — FORD 337:6
Life too short to stuff a m. — CONR 249:14
m. rich civilian — BYRO 191:16
supramundane m. — LAUR 483:2
music accord all m. makes — SIDN 751:3
aerial m.'s past — SHEN 747:18
alive with the sound of m. — HAMM 379:1
all kinds of m. — BIBL 95:22
all m. is folk music — ARMS 28:18
all m. jars — CERV 213:10
Beauty in m. — IVES 426:6
beauty's Silent m. — CAMP 196:1
body swayed to m. — YEAT 872:8
built to m. — TENN 794:5
but the m. there — POPE 616:4
chosen m., liberty — WORD 869:16
'classic' m. eliminates — STRA 778:19
come with your cold m. — BROW 168:1
compulsion doth in m. lie — MILT 538:16
condition of m. — PATE 599:7
danceth without m. — HERB 395:5
dance to the m. of time — POWE 621:19
Darling of the m. halls — SMIT 756:18
day the m. died — MCLE 512:2
die in m. — SHAK 729:18
essence of m. — MOZA 563:26
Fading in m. — SHAK 724:21
finds its food in m. — LILL 493:8
Fled is that m. — KEAT 456:12
From their own m. — CAMP 196:2
frozen m. — SCHE 683:6
Give me some m. — SHAK 695:4
honey-sweet m. from our lips — HOME 405:7
how potent cheap m. is — COWA 254:2
In sweet m. — SHAK 710:17

I shall be made thy m. — DONN 288:17
Is there a meaning to m. — COPL 251:8
Let's face the m. and dance — BERL 73:2
let the sounds of m. — SHAK 725:10
Like softest m. — SHAK 732:18
make the m. mute — TENN 794:17
man that hath no m. — SHAK 725:13
May make one m. — TENN 794:30
most civilized m. — USTI 823:5
M. alone with sudden charms — CONG 247:30
M. and women — PEPY 603:15
m. at the close — SHAK 730:9
M. begins to atrophy — POUN 621:13
m. be the food of love — SHAK 734:25
M. breathing from her face — BYRO 185:14
m. business is not — MORR 561:12
m. by yonder springs — THEO 804:11
m. could capture him so completely — KAFK 452:4
m. dies — BYRD 184:27
M. has charms — CONG 247:8
m. in the air — ELGA 306:18
M. is essentially useless — SANT 680:16
M. is feeling, then — STEV 774:9
M. is not written in — MELB 530:10
M. is your own experience — PARK 596:1
m. of a *distant* drum — FITZ 331:16
m. of a poem — SYNG 786:8
m. of forfended spheres — PATM 599:14
M. oft hath such a charm — SHAK 723:18
m. of the spheres — BROW 163:13
m. sent up to God — BROW 164:17
M. shall untune the sky — DRYD 296:30
m. that excels — FISH 330:11
M. that gentlier on the spirit — TENN 797:9
m. that I care to hear — HOPK 407:9
m. the brandy of the damned — SHAW 740:27
M., the greatest good — ADDI 5:1
M., when soft voices die — SHEL 746:17
My m. is best understood — STRA 778:20
Of m. Dr Johnson used to say — JOHN 444:23
passion cannot M. raise — DRYD 296:28
perfected by m. — CONF 246:8
practising your pastoral m. — VIRG 831:12
seduction of martial m. — BURN 177:2
silence sank Like m. — COLE 241:8
sound of soft m. — DISR 286:16
still, sad m. — WORD 866:12
Susanna's m. — STEV 774:11
thou hast thy m. too — KEAT 457:2
trees are singing in my m. — ELGA 306:17
uproar's your only m. — KEAT 457:16
We are the m. makers — O'SH 588:22
What then is m. — HEIN 389:13
when I hear sweet m. — SHAK 725:12
worth expressing in m. — DELI 272:14
musical found out m. tunes — BIBL 98:3
Most m., most melancholy — MILT 539:15
m. as is Apollo's lute — MILT 539:6
Silence more m. — ROSS 669:7
So m. a discord — SHAK 726:28
musician far below the m. — LEON 489:23
musing M. full sadly — SPEN 767:9
peace, and lonely m. — COLL 243:15
musk coming m.-rose — KEAT 456:8
sweet m.-roses — SHAK 726:8
musket Sam, pick up tha' m. — HOLL 403:8
shouldered a m. — LAUR 483:3
Muslim go into the M. mosque — JALA 428:18
neither Hindu nor M. — SIKH 752:9
Muslims named you M. — KORA 472:11
zealous M. to execute — KHOM 462:7
Muss M. es sein — BEET 66:8
mussels gaping m., left — CRAB 257:13
must do wrong when he m. — MACH 511:12
forget because we m. — ARNO 29:2
It m. be — BEET 66:8
Must! Is m. a word — ELIZ 312:13
Needs m. — PROV 639:30
This year, the m. shall foam — MACA 508:11
We m. know — EPIT 319:17
What m. be, must be — PROV 646:25
whispers low, *Thou m.* — EMER 314:17

must (cont.):
you m. go on BECK 64:14
mustard faith as a grain of m. seed BIBL 101:28
grain of m. seed BIBL 101:15
Pass the m. GILB 358:15
mutabile Varium et m. semper Femina VIRG 830:1
mutability death, and m. SHEL 746:2
M. in them doth play SPEN 767:26
Nought may endure but M. SHEL 745:4
mutant Caelum non animum m. HORA 410:10
mutantur spatio m. LUCR 504:10
mutato M. nomine de te HORA 414:8
mutatus Quantum m. ab illo VIRG 829:11
mute M. and magnificent DRYD 296:34
m. recommendation PUBL 648:29
seem stark m. ELIZ 312:3
mutilate fold, spindle or m. SAYI 684:14
spindle or m. ANON 16:24
mutiny fear and m. SHAK 731:1
rise and m. SHAK 713:13
mutter blessed m. of the mass BROW 165:5
mutton make them into m.-pies CARR 203:21
object to eating a m. chop LIST 495:11
mutual M. cowardice JOHN 442:20
my Orthodoxy or M.-doxy CARL 200:1
sitting in m. chair SOUT 764:21
myriad Our m.-minded Shakespeare COLE 241:22
There died a m. POUN 621:6
myrrh bundle of m. BIBL 90:25
frankincense, and m. BIBL 98:11
myrtle m. and turkey AUST 41:15
m. tree BIBL 94:10
myrtles Ye m. brown MILT 540:2
myself I celebrate m. WHIT 852:7
I do not know m. GOET 363:5
If I am not for m. HILL 399:7
I have searched m. HERA 393:7
love him as m. BOOK 138:11
Madame Bovary is m. FLAU 334:8
my mother I see in m. FRID 343:4
M. alone I seek to please GAY 351:18
talking to m. BARN 59:6
thinking for m. GILB 358:1
When I give I give m. WHIT 852:12
mysteries most holy m. DION 283:19
m. in divinity BROW 162:25
m. of Hecate SHAK 714:17
m. of our religion HOBB 401:7
m. that are hidden HEIK 389:4
Stewards of the m. BIBL 111:27
mysterious moves in a m. way COWP 255:12
nothing m. or supernatural HUME 419:17
mystery burthen of the m. WORD 866:10
grasped the m. of the atom BRAD 154:6
Happiness is a m. CHES 225:5
heart of my m. SHAK 702:26
I shew you a m. BIBL 113:5
lose myself in a m. BROW 162:26
M., BABYLON THE GREAT BIBL 119:8
m. of the cross FORT 338:15
my tongue, the, the m. telling THOM 805:4
penetralium of m. KEAT 457:15
riddle wrapped in a m. CHUR 229:11
mystic m., wonderful TENN 794:1
mystical m. body of thy Son BOOK 137:18
m. mathematics BROW 162:6
m. way of Pythagoras BROW 162:28
mystify m., mislead, and surprise JACK 427:1
myth m. not a fairy story RYLE 676:7
print the m. JOHN 434:16
purpose of m. LÉVI 491:12
thing itself and not the m. RICH 660:4
mythologies Out of old m. YEAT 872:15
myths Science must begin with m. POPP 619:6
where m. Go when they die FENT 325:1

nabobs nattering n. AGNE 9:14
Naboth Ahab spake unto N. BIBL 85:17
nagging N. is the repetition SUMM 780:9
nail blows his n. SHAK 717:25

I n. my pictures together SCHW 687:14
looks like a n. SAYI 685:19
n. currant jelly ROOS 667:21
n. into his temples BIBL 82:32
One n. drives out PROV 641:10
thrusting The final n. BLOK 129:3
want of a n. PROV 632:34
nailing n. his colours FIEL 326:6
nails blowing of his n. SHAK 710:6
My n. are drove EPIT 319:3
n. bitten and pared MACA 506:17
nineteen hundred and forty n. SITW 753:12
print of the n. BIBL 108:39
three cloves like n. HEAT 388:6
with his n. he'll dig WEBS 844:21
naive n. domestic Burgundy CART 205:9
n. forgive and forget SZAS 786:13
naked Half n., loving BYRO 188:12
left me n. to mine enemies SHAK 711:1
Love is a child and n. OVID 589:16
more enterprise In walking n. YEAT 872:15
my n. villainy SHAK 731:17
N., and ye clothed me BIBL 103:6
n. ape MORR 560:9
n. into the conference chamber BEVA 76:19
n. is the best disguise CONG 246:29
n. shingles of the world ARNO 29:4
n. to the hangman's noose HOUS 415:14
stark n. truth CLEL 235:5
starving hysterical n. GINS 358:22
When a' was n. SHAK 707:24
With n. foot WYAT 871:4
nakedness n. of the land BIBL 80:24
n. of woman BLAK 126:13
not in utter n. WORD 867:8
only wealth is n. FUEN 346:1
namby-pamby N.'s little rhymes CARE 199:1
name above every n. BIBL 114:19
at the n. of Jesus BIBL 114:19
At the n. of Jesus NOEL 576:18
blot out his n. BIBL 117:31
Change the n. HORA 414:8
change the n. PROV 628:41
dare not speak its n. DOUG 291:9
deed without a n. SHAK 721:19
distain his n. BURN 178:25
fear my n. BIBL 96:19
filches from me my good n. SHAK 728:23
forgotten your n. SWIN 785:21
former n. Is heard no more MILT 543:24
freedom which deserves the n. MILL 536:3
gathered together in my n. BIBL 102:3
general n. applicable FLIN 335:19
ghost of a great n. LUCA 503:17
gift of the divine N. SIKH 752:7
Give a dog a bad n. PROV 632:46
give them an everlasting n. BIBL 94:11
glory as an unsullied n. ELEA 306:12
glory in the n. of Briton GEOR 352:11
good n. BIBL 88:30
Grant that your n. remain SIKH 751:16
Halloo your n. SHAK 735:6
Hallowed be thy n. BIBL 99:12
his N. is great BOOK 145:3
his N. only is excellent BOOK 150:10
honour due unto his N. BOOK 146:9
I am become a n. TENN 800:15
I do not like her n. SHAK 697:12
ill n. is half hanged PROV 634:9
in a borrowed n. PRIO 624:6
In the n. of God, go AMER 14:7
In the n. of God, go CROM 260:14
In the N. of the Father MISS 546:17
In the n. of thy Lord KORA 473:9
its n. changed DANT 265:12
kept them in thy n. BIBL 108:24
king's n. SHAK 731:26
left a Corsair's n. BYRO 187:12
left a n. behind them BIBL 98:4
left the n. JOHN 438:8
Let me not n. it SHAK 729:12
liberties are taken in thy n. GEOR 353:10
local habitation and a n. SHAK 727:3

mark, or the n. of the beast BIBL 118:26
my n. and memory BACO 49:13
my n. is Jowett BEEC 65:16
My n. is Legion BIBL 103:31
My n. is Ozymandias SHEL 745:17
My n. is Used-to-was TRAI 814:16
My n. too will be linked OVID 589:24
my n. with a sign PARI 595:17
my new n. BIBL 117:32
my wife, and my n. SURT 781:12
n. Achilles assumed BROW 162:14
n. great in story BYRO 191:6
n. had been Edmund KEAT 458:13
n. is never heard BAYL 62:9
n. like yours CARR 203:9
n. liveth for ever SASS 682:12
n. liveth for evermore BIBL 98:5
n. liveth for evermore EPIT 319:12
n. made great HILL 399:6
n. of God in vain BIBL 81:17
N. of God is sweet SIKH 751:18
N. of God, the Merciful KORA 470:17
n. of—Michael Angelo REYN 659:7
n. of the Lord BOOK 138:16
N. of the Lord BOOK 148:12
N. of the Lord BOOK 148:22
N. of the Lord our God BOOK 140:13
n. shall be called BIBL 92:14
n. the names AKHM 10:6
n. to all succeeding ages curst DRYD 294:11
n. upon the strand SPEN 766:18
n. we give the people FLER 334:23
n. were not so terrible SHAK 707:10
no profit but the n. SHAK 703:26
nothing of a n. BYRO 187:5
Not in my n. POLI 613:5
one makes one's n. STEN 771:16
one whose n. was writ EPIT 318:5
only differ in the n. CHUD 227:18
People you know, yet can't quite n. LARK 481:8
perfect N. of God SIKH 751:19
power of Jesus' N. PERR 604:5
prefer a self-made n. HAND 379:7
problem that has no n. FRIE 343:6
problem that has no n. FRIE 343:8
provides us with n. and nation BUNT 170:18
spared the n. SWIF 784:10
spell my n. right COHA 238:5
state with the prettiest n. BISH 122:6
thy n., thy nature know WESL 847:13
unto thy N. give the praise BOOK 148:4
What's in a n. SHAK 732:12
what was done in his n. BENN 70:1
whispering its n. COCT 238:1
Who gave you this N. BOOK 138:8
worshipped with spoken n. ZORO 879:1
worth an age without a n. MORD 558:17
writing our n. there HEAN 387:5
named N. is the mother LAO 479:6
n. you Muslims KORA 472:11
nameless intolerably n. names SASS 682:12
N. here for evermore POE 611:1
n. in worthy deeds BROW 162:17
N. is the origin LAO 479:6
n., unremembered, acts WORD 866:9
names All n. are shaken HORA 412:15
Called him soft n. KEAT 456:9
called them by wrong n. BROW 165:2
calleth them all by their n. BOOK 150:6
confused things with their n. SART 681:18
in love with American n. BENÉ 69:13
lost all the n. JOHN 443:8
n. ignoble, born to be forgot COWP 255:20
N. Most Beautiful KORA 473:7
n. of all these particles FERM 325:11
n. of men TROL 816:21
n. of those who love HUNT 421:4
N. that should be CALV 194:3
n. to be mentioned AUST 42:18
No n., no pack-drill PROV 640:9
Not unholy n. DICK 278:19
syllable men's n. MILT 539:1

naming N. of Cats — ELIO 310:19
n. of parts — REED 657:4
nap short n. at sermon — ADDI 5:6
napalm smell of n. in the morning — FILM 328:19
nape n. caught in his bill — YEAT 874:1
Napoleon N. of crime — DOYL 292:16
N.'s armies — SELL 692:6
thinks he is N. — CLEM 235:9
Napoleons Caesars and N. — HUXL 422:17
narcotic n. be alcohol — JUNG 449:13
narcotics Like dull n. — TENN 795:2
Narragansett Where are the N. — TECU 792:11
narration medium of n. — MANN 520:3
n. always going backwards — WALP 837:12
narrative descriptive n. — EPHR 316:8
n. is no fiction — JACO 427:4
no materials for n. — BRUN 168:22
unconvincing n. — GILB 357:14
narrow find the road n. — MAIM 516:13
mind is too n. — AUGU 39:9
n. is the way — BIBL 99:29
n.-souled people — POPE 618:22
n. souls cannot dare — CONG 247:14
path is n. and difficult — UPAN 822:12
saft and n. — BALL 54:3
narrower n. by going farther — HOOD 405:24
Nassau Stuart or N. — PRIO 624:5
Nasticreechia N. Krorluppia — LEAR 485:21
nastiest n. thing in the nicest way — GOLD 363:13
nasty as n. as himself — SHAW 742:16
is a n. creature — MOLI 553:2
n., brutish, and short — HOBB 400:24
n. party — MAY 528:19
Something n. in the woodshed — GIBB 355:10
natale Libertas et n. solum — SWIF 784:13
nation AMERICA thus top n. — SELL 692:8
boundary of the march of a n. — PARN 597:9
broad mass of n. — HITL 400:6
can deprive a n. — NAMI 567:7
create a n. Europe — MONN 553:13
every man and n. — LOWE 502:19
existence as a n. — PITT 607:19
exterminate a n. — SPOC 768:14
fate of a n. — LONG 500:2
ghosts of a n. — PEAR 601:3
holy n. — BIBL 117:3
n. a le gouvernment — MAIS 517:1
n. expects to be ignorant — JEFF 432:7
n. grieve — DRYD 294:18
n. is not governed — BURK 173:12
n. is the universality — MAZZ 529:12
n., not a city — DISR 286:2
n. of amateurs — ROSE 668:11
n. of dancers — EQUI 316:14
n. of shop-keepers — ADAM 4:1
n. of shopkeepers — NAPO 568:9
n. of shop-keepers — PROV 631:6
n. of shopkeepers — SMIT 756:5
N. once again — DAVI 268:13
n. shall not lift up sword — BIBL 91:21
n. shall rise — BIBL 102:23
N. shall speak peace — REND 658:7
N. spoke to a Nation — KIPL 467:2
n. talking to itself — MILL 537:12
n. that had lion's heart — CHUR 230:12
n. which indulges toward another — WASH 840:18
new n. — LINC 494:1
No n. could preserve — MADI 514:10
No n. is fit — WILS 859:15
No n. wanted it so much — SWIF 784:11
not to destroy a n. — WELL 847:1
of the n.'s care — PRIO 624:7
old and haughty n. — MILT 538:21
one-third of a n. ill-housed — ROOS 667:8
provides us with name and n. — BUNT 170:18
rich and lazy n. — KIPL 467:21
Righteousness exalteth a n. — BIBL 88:12
single n. of brothers — SCHI 685:25
small n. that stood alone — DE V 275:2
so goes the n. — POLI 612:4
Still better for the n. — EPIT 318:3
terrorize a whole n. — MURR 566:5

voice of a n. — RUSS 675:18
what our N. stands for — BETJ 75:16
while the n. is honest — DOUG 292:1
national above n. prejudices — NORT 577:2
Art is not n. — MELB 530:10
incrustations of n. character — BULW 170:10
n. debt — HAMI 378:11
N. Debt is a very Good Thing — SELL 692:5
n. flag — SUMN 780:11
n. home for the Jewish people — BALF 53:13
n. morality should have this — SHAW 740:6
nationalism N. is an infantile sickness — EINS 306:2
n. is a silly cock — ALDI 11:11
nationalities n. of Europe — ASQU 34:4
nationality n., language, religion — JOYC 448:8
what n. he would prefer — RHOD 659:11
nations belong to other n. — GILB 358:4
belong to two different n. — FOST 338:19
day of small n. — CHAM 214:3
enrich unknowing n. — DANI 264:8
Europe of n. — DE G 271:12
father of many n. — BIBL 110:29
fierce contending n. — ADDI 4:24
formed Two N. — DISR 286:8
friendship with all n. — JEFF 431:16
gossip from all the n. — AUDE 37:20
great n. acted like gangsters — KUBR 474:2
hating all other n. — GASK 350:9
healing of the n. — BIBL 119:21
Let n. rage — BISH 122:10
lion of the n. — BIBL 95:18
n. are as a drop — BIBL 93:18
n. how to live — MILT 546:7
N., like men — BOLI 131:13
n. shall do him service — BOOK 144:19
N. touch at their summits — BAGE 50:20
n. under our feet — BOOK 142:21
other n. and states draw aside — GOGO 363:12
Other n. use 'force' — WAUG 843:1
pedigree of n. — JOHN 438:17
place among the n. — EMME 315:23
Praise the Lord, all n. — BIBL 120:4
rule n. by your government — VIRG 830:14
smote divers n. — BOOK 149:11
two great n. in the world — TOCQ 812:12
Two n. — DISR 286:6
two n. have been at war — VOLT 833:12
two n. warring — DURH 300:14
waits for the n. — MIDR 534:15
wealth of n. — DEFO 271:5
native adieu! my n. shore — BYRO 185:16
breathe his n. air — POPE 617:32
by their n. shore — COWP 255:18
in his n. place — JOHN 440:26
more n. to the heart — SHAK 699:10
my n. land — SCOT 688:14
n. land draws all men — OVID 590:1
n. of the rocks — JOHN 439:6
n. Of the very world — SMAR 754:9
n. stands on the edge — RIEL 661:10
n. wood-notes wild — MILT 539:31
our ideas about the n. — LESS 490:17
rooms of thy n. country — FULL 346:9
with his n. land — EDGE 303:8
nativity At my n. — SHAK 706:8
n. was under *ursa major* — SHAK 715:1
nattering n. nabobs — AGNE 9:14
natura N. enim non imperatur — BACO 49:4
natural her colour is n. — SHER 748:24
I do it more n. — SHAK 735:11
interested in n. history — SCOT 688:3
more than n. — SHAK 701:13
n. and intrepid — WALP 837:8
n. man has only two — OSLE 589:4
N. rights — BENT 71:3
N. Selection — DARW 266:13
N. selection a mechanism — FISH 330:14
n., simple, affecting — GOLD 364:20
n. to die — BACO 46:22
so far from being n. — JOHN 441:1
twice as n. — CARR 203:19
wants the n. touch — SHAK 722:3

naturalists n. observe, a flea — SWIF 784:4
naturalness N. and ease of manner — FLAU 333:8
nature accordant with man's n. — HARD 380:18
acts according to his n. — BÜCH 169:13
all animated n. — COLE 239:13
Allow not n. more — SHAK 715:12
Art is only N. — HOLB 402:21
Arts at first from N. came — LANI 479:4
arts of death outdoes N. — SHAW 741:2
Auld n. swears — BURN 178:10
better angels of our n. — LINC 493:14
body, N. is — POPE 616:26
book of n. — GALI 347:18
by n. desire knowledge — ARIS 27:3
By n. men are alike — CONF 246:19
can drive out n. — PROV 647:40
can't be N. — CHUR 228:4
conquered human n. — DICK 279:9
Constant, in N. were inconstancy — COWL 254:15
course of N. — YOUN 877:1
cruel works of n. — DARW 266:19
[Death is] n.'s way — ANON 16:23
dictates of n. — BERK 72:15
does N. live — COLE 239:9
do violence to own n. — MENG 531:26
drive out n. — HORA 410:9
education's, more than n.'s — WINC 860:6
experiencing n. — BAGE 51:12
Eye N.'s walks — POPE 616:15
fair defect of n. — MILT 544:12
fire of my n. — BRON 158:7
frame of n. — ADDI 5:2
from criticism to n. — JOHN 437:4
fulfils great N.'s plan — BURN 178:6
God and n. — AUCT 36:11
Good painters imitate n. — CERV 213:14
great n.'s second course — SHAK 720:6
great wonders of N. — ORCH 586:2
have enough of n. — THOR 809:19
heartless, witless n. — HOUS 415:9
Holy Scripture and n. — GALI 348:2
How N. always does contrive — GILB 356:18
huge scream course through n. — MUNC 565:10
human n. is finer — KEAT 457:17
ignorance of n. — HOLB 403:1
informed by the light of n. — BACO 45:12
In n. there are neither — INGE 425:16
in other words, N. — SPIN 768:10
intellectual n. — JOHN 436:24
interpreted n. as freely — GIRA 359:9
interpreter of n. — JOHN 437:15
interpreter of n. — WHEW 850:4
It is a part of n. — SPEN 766:1
Kind n. first doth cause — DAVI 267:21
knowledge of n. — WHEW 850:2
law of n. — BURK 176:5
law of their n. — THUC 810:8
like N. to go no further — LEIB 488:9
linger yet with n. — BYRO 190:14
living according to n. — MORE 559:4
look on n., not as in the hour — WORD 866:12
looks thro' N. — POPE 617:30
made a gap in n. — SHAK 694:23
man the less, but n. more — BYRO 187:1
mere copier of n. — REYN 658:19
mirror up to n. — SHAK 702:15
more direct than does N. — LEON 489:19
My n. is subdued — SHAK 738:14
N. abhors a vacuum — PROV 639:22
N. abhors a vacuum — RABE 652:8
N. always desires — AUCT 36:15
N., and Nature's laws — POPE 615:22
n. began gradually — SCHI 686:3
n. by her mother wit — SPEN 767:21
n. cannot be fooled — FEYN 326:1
N. cannot be ordered — BACO 49:4
N. does nothing in vain — NEWT 574:1
N. does nothing uselessly — ARIS 28:1
N. from her seat — MILT 544:6
N. gives to each — AUCT 36:14
N. had not befriended us — CAVE 211:19
n. her custom holds — SHAK 704:8
n. I actually have — DESC 274:10

nature (cont.):
N. in awe to him — MILT 540:23
N. in him was almost lost — COLL 243:16
N. in you stands — SHAK 715:11
N. is always wise — THUR 810:15
N. is a temple — BAUD 61:11
N. is but a name — COWP 256:28
n. is but art — POPE 616:27
N. is creeping up — WHIS 850:12
N. is dumb — TURG 819:3
N. is not a temple — TURG 818:15
n. is the art of God — BROW 163:2
n. is tugging — EMER 314:19
N. is usually wrong — WHIS 850:8
n. itselfe cant endure — FLEM 334:19
n., kindly bent to ease us — SWIF 784:8
N. made her what she is — BURN 177:19
n. made him — ARIO 26:12
N., Mr Allnutt — FILM 329:12
N. never makes — LOCK 497:5
N. never set forth — SIDN 751:4
N., obviously, hadn't — TURG 818:14
n. of my game — JAGG 427:13
n. of war — HOBB 400:23
N., red in tooth and claw — TENN 795:17
N.'s agent and interpreter — BACO 48:29
N.'s agreeable blunders — COWL 254:23
N. say one thing — BURK 174:26
N.'s decorations — SMAR 754:8
N.'s great masterpiece — DONN 288:21
n.'s handmaid art — DRYD 295:11
n.'s journeymen — SHAK 702:16
N.'s law — BURN 178:26
N.'s social union — BURN 179:25
N.'s sole mistake — GILB 358:9
N.'s sweet restorer — YOUN 876:16
n.'s way of telling you — SAYI 684:11
N. that is above all art — DANI 264:5
n. to act upon him — NIGH 576:4
N. to advantage dressed — POPE 616:2
n. to explore — POPE 617:1
N. was degraded — BLAK 124:8
N. wears one universal grin — FIEL 327:2
n. would not incite — UPDI 822:23
n. yet remembers — WORD 867:13
next to N. — LAND 478:3
not n. — CONS 249:18
observe n. — OSLE 589:1
observe the works of n. — GALE 347:17
Of slower N. got the start — DENH 273:7
One touch of n. — SHAK 734:19
paint too much direct from n. — GAUG 350:12
priketh hem n. — CHAU 218:3
read N. — DRYD 297:15
rest in N., not the God — HERB 394:21
rest on N. fix — COKE 238:15
Secretary of N. — WALT 839:15
spark o' N.'s fire — BURN 178:5
state of war by n. — SWIF 784:3
state that n. hath provided — LOCK 497:12
stuff that n. replaces it with — WILL 858:4
subtlety of n. — BACO 48:30
through n. to eternity — SHAK 699:14
thy name, thy n. know — WESL 847:13
Treat n. in terms — CÉZA 213:16
Unerring N. — POPE 615:26
various appearances of n. — SMIT 755:23
war of n. — DARW 266:16
weakness of our mortal n. — BOOK 136:3
whatever N. has in store — FERM 325:12
wholly against n. — AURE 40:18
Wise n. did never put — BACO 49:6
naught it is n. — BIBL 88:28
n. for your comfort — CHES 223:26
naughtiness n. of thine heart — BIBL 84:2
naughty former n. life — BOOK 136:17
in a n. world — SHAK 725:14
N. but nice — ADVE 8:7
N. but nice — FILM 331:8
nauseous n. draught of life — ROCH 664:11
naval N. tradition — CHUR 230:9
nave n. to the chaps — SHAK 718:4
navel n. like a round goblet — BIBL 91:14

navibus n. atque Quadrigis — HORA 410:10
navies nations' airy n. — TENN 797:1
our n. melt away — KIPL 467:6
navigare N. necesse est — POMP 611:13
navita N. de ventis — PROP 624:20
navy N. is the arm — MONR 553:16
n. nothing but rotten timber — BURK 173:23
Ruler of the Queen's N. — GILB 357:28
upon the n. — CHAR 217:8
nay royal n. of England — BLAC 123:11
your n., nay — BIBL 116:28
Nazareth come out of N. — BIBL 107:6
Neaera tangles of N.'s hair — MILT 540:6
Neanderthal N. skeleton — HAWK 384:13
of N. man — STRA 779:1
near come not n. to me — BIBL 94:22
more n. the earth — SHAK 729:15
n. in blood — SHAK 720:20
N. is my kirtle — PROV 639:25
N. is my shirt — PROV 639:26
so n. and yet so far — TENN 795:29
while he is n. — BIBL 94:8
nearer little n. Spenser — BASS 61:4
n. God's Heart in a garden — GURN 374:16
N., my God, to thee — ADAM 4:3
n. one Yet, than all other — HOOD 405:11
n. than hands and feet — TENN 793:23
n. the bone — PROV 639:23
n. to him than the jugular — KORA 473:5
n. you are to God — WOTT 870:14
nearest n. and dearest enemy — SHAK 706:13
nearly n. kept waiting — LOUI 501:4
neat N., but not gaudy — WESL 848:10
Still to be n. — JONS 446:4
neatness Plain in thy n. — HORA 411:10
Nebuchadnezzar N. the king — BIBL 95:22
necessarily ain't n. so — HEYW 397:18
Not n. conscription — KING 464:3
necessary absolutely n. — OCCA 583:10
for whom it is n. — LIVY 496:6
honourable by being n. — HALE 377:1
if it is deemed n. — BROW 161:7
journey really n. — OFFI 584:8
little visible delight, but n. — BRON 158:19
Make yourself n. — EMER 314:18
n. evil — BRAD 154:3
n. evil — PAIN 592:8
n. evils — JOHN 437:8
n. not to change — FALK 322:16
n. to salvation — BOOK 150:17
To sail in n. — POMP 611:13
very n. thing — VOLT 834:13
necessities dispense with its n. — MOTL 562:14
n. call out virtues — ADAM 2:1
which were n. — WRIG 870:15
necessity Cruel n. — CROM 260:10
do not see the n. — ARGE 26:10
door of n. — DEFO 270:9
exceptional n. — MILL 536:15
fiction is n. — CHES 225:3
grown out of n. — RILK 662:3
harsh n.'s hand — VIRG 832:14
N. has no law — PUBL 648:32
N. has the face — GARC 349:3
N. hath no law — CROM 260:17
N. is the mother — PROV 639:27
N. is the plea — PITT 607:18
N. knows no law — PROV 639:28
N. never made — FRAN 341:5
n. of God — FRY 345:14
N. with her impartial law — HORA 412:15
no virtue like n. — SHAK 730:7
pragmatic n. — DIDI 282:19
stronger than N. — EURI 321:5
villains by n. — SHAK 714:24
neck at last wrings its n. — RUSS 675:2
break its n. — VERL 826:11
had but one n. — CALI 193:8
hanged about his n. — BIBL 102:1
my n. is very short — MORE 559:15
n. God made for other use — HOUS 415:14
n. is as a tower of ivory — BIBL 91:15
n. is like the tower — BIBL 91:4

n. once broken — WALS 838:18
Some chicken! Some n. — CHUR 229:20
strecche forth the n. — CHAU 219:27
neckcurls remember the n. — ROET 665:7
necklace with our n. — MADI 514:4
necks bowing our n. — JERO 433:5
nectar comprehend a n. — DICK 281:21
draws n. in a sieve — COLE 241:15
lie beside their n. — TENN 797:12
nectarine n., and curious peach — MARV 525:4
need all ye n. to know — KEAT 455:25
boredom, vice, and n. — VOLT 833:14
face of total n. — BURR 180:15
France has more n. of me — NAPO 568:3
friend in n. — PROV 632:39
love you because I n. you — FROM 344:2
n. in this life is ignorance — TWAI 820:25
n. of a world of men — BROW 166:26
not enough for everyone's n. — BUCH 169:11
O reason not the n. — SHAK 715:12
People who n. people — MERR 532:26
Requires sorest n. — DICK 281:21
things that people don't n. — WARH 840:3
thy n. is greater — SIDN 751:10
We n. spring — GZOW 375:4
What can I want or n. — HERB 395:1
Will you still n. me — LENN 489:12
needed All I have n. — CHIS 226:11
needful All that is n. — WINK 860:14
needle eye of a n. — BIBL 102:8
n. and the pen — LEWI 492:5
n. better fits — BRAD 154:11
Plying her n. and thread — HOOD 406:1
upon a n.'s point — CUDW 261:15
needles N. and pins — PROV 639:29
needs according to his n. — MARX 526:5
knows how much it n. — DEMO 272:17
my n. grow too fast — WALK 836:3
N. must — PROV 639:30
Your country n. you — MILI 535:19
needy poor and n. — BOOK 142:2
nefas scire n. — HORA 411:15
negation n. of God — GLAD 359:14
negative Europe the unfinished n. — MCCA 509:6
N. Capability — KEAT 457:15
n. waiting to be slipped — WILS 859:1
prefers a n. peace — KING 463:9
your n. perception — HANS 379:13
negativism fountain of n. — WEST 848:19
neglect n. of governments — LAUR 483:3
n. of his duties — THOM 808:7
tender mercy is n. — CRAB 258:10
this n. arises — ADAM 1:19
neglected have his all n. — JOHN 439:5
neglects He that n. the Law — TALM 789:8
negotiate n. out of fear — KENN 460:8
negotiating N. with de Valera — LLOY 496:20
negotiis procul n. — HORA 411:3
Negro drop of N. blood — HUGH 418:4
life of the N. race — DARR 266:6
N.'s great stumbling block — KING 463:9
places where the average N. — DAVI 268:11
Negroes drivers of n. — JOHN 437:23
neiges où sont les n. d'antan — VILL 828:7
neighbour done evil to his n. — BOOK 140:1
do not to your n. — HILL 399:4
duty to my N. — BOOK 138:10
duty towards my N. — BOOK 138:11
God makes our next-door n. — CHES 225:6
guts into the n. room — SHAK 703:22
love thy n. — BIBL 82:1
love thy n. as thyself — BIBL 102:17
make war upon a n. nation — FAIR 322:15
n.'s house is on fire — BURK 173:29
next-door n. for so many years — SCOT 689:17
policy of the good n. — ROOS 667:5
rob a n. — MACA 506:14
thy n.'s house — BIBL 81:20
thy n.'s house — BIBL 88:37
To whom I am a n. — SHAK 724:1
What a n. gets — PROV 646:16
neighbourhood n. of voluntary spies — AUST 41:23

n. Living WORD 868:19
n. mind DOYL 292:12
n. savage ran DRYD 295:15
O! what a n. mind SHAK 702:9
silence is most n. SWIN 785:2
than a n. death EURI 321:10
What's brave, what's n. SHAK 695:22
nobleman king may make a n. BURK 176:8
Underrated N. GILB 356:10
nobleness allied with perfect n. ARNO 32:9
nobler Whether 'tis n. in the mind SHAK 701:26
nobles n. by the right MACA 507:3
n. with links of iron BOOK 150:11
noblesse N. oblige LÉVI 491:9
noblest honest man's the n. work BURN 177:26
n. of mankind CALV 194:5
n. prospect JOHN 439:20
n. Roman of them all SHAK 714:3
n. work of God POPE 617:8
n. work of man INGE 425:9
ruins of the n. man SHAK 712:22
nobly N., nobly Cape Saint Vincent
BROW 165:29
n. save LINC 493:18
nobody care for n. BICK 120:22
n. came FILM 331:12
N. came GINS 358:21
n. comes BECK 64:19
n.'s going to stop 'em BERR 74:12
n.'s perfect FILM 329:21
n. will come SAND 680:7
noctes O n. cenaeque deum HORA 415:1
noctis currite n. equi MARL 522:11
currite n. equi OVID 589:17
nod dwelt in the land of N. BIBL 79:18
n.'s as good as a wink PROV 640:3
Old N., the shepherd DE L 272:10
nodded n. with his darkish brows HOME 404:10
nods excellent Homer n. HORA 409:14
Homer sometimes n. PROV 634:38
N., and becks MILT 539:23
noes honest kersey n. SHAK 717:22
nohow for nothing. N. CARR 203:1
noire triste et n. BAUD 61:13
noise Go placidly amid the n. EHRM 305:2
happy n. to hear HOUS 415:16
little noiseless n. KEAT 455:2
loud n. at one end KNOX 470:6
make a cheerful n. BOOK 145:11
more n. they make POPE 618:22
n. is an effective means GOEB 361:8
n. like that of a water-mill SWIF 782:6
n., my dear ANON 19:7
n. of battle rolled TENN 794:21
Nursed amid her n. LAMB 477:5
so little n. LAWR 483:17
such n. that beast made MALO 517:19
those who make the n. BURK 174:13
till they make a n. CRAB 258:4
wi' flichterin' n. BURN 177:22
with a merry n. BOOK 142:22
noiseless little n. noise KEAT 455:2
n. tenor of their way GRAY 370:8
noises isle is full of n. SHAK 733:30
noisy into the n. crowd TAGO 787:19
n. years seem moments WORD 867:15
Nokomis wigwam of N. LONG 499:22
noli N. me tangere BIBL 120:17
N. me tangere WYAT 871:8
nom de plume n. secures all ELIO 308:15
nomen Omne capax movet urna n. HORA 412:15
nominated will not accept if n. SHER 749:12
nomination When you have got the n.
CARD 198:2
nominative her n. case O'KE 584:19
nomine In N. Patris MISS 546:17
nominis magni n. umbra LUCA 503:17
non avoiding n.-being TILL 811:6
comes from n.-being LAO 480:4
no fury like a n.-combatant MONT 554:14
n.-being into utility LAO 479:9
n.-cooperation with evil GAND 348:14
N.-violence is the first article GAND 348:13

organization of n.-violence BAEZ 50:1
saturam n. scribere JUVE 450:11
nonconformist man must be a n. EMER 315:5
none answer came there n. CARR 203:5
answer came there n. SCOT 688:6
answer made it n. SHAK 699:28
malice toward n. LINC 494:6
n. that doeth good BOOK 139:28
This is n. of I NURS 578:19
nonexistent obsolescent and n. BREN 156:9
non-existent dead is to be n. SOCR 759:23
nonsense His n. suits their nonsense
CHAR 217:5
lump of clotted n. DRYD 297:23
n., and learning GOLD 365:3
n. upon stilts BENT 71:3
round the corner of n. COLE 242:9
your damned n. RICH 661:4
nook obscure n. for me BROW 166:25
noon amid the blaze of n. MILT 545:1
athwart the n. COLE 239:16
Far from the fiery n. KEAT 454:20
lying till n. JOHN 438:15
returned before n. SAIN 677:12
to their native n. SHEL 747:4
When n. is past SHEL 744:9
noonday destroyeth in the n. BOOK 146:1
no-one Duty is what n. else will do FITZ 332:19
noose naked to the hangman's n. HOUS 415:14
n. of light FITZ 330:17
Norfolk bear him up the N. sky BETJ 75:12
Very flat, N. COWA 254:1
normal n. and easy JAME 430:1
normalcy not nostrums but n. HARD 380:6
Norman like our N. King KIPL 465:6
Saxon and N. TENN 801:3
simple faith than N. blood TENN 796:12
Normans If N. are disciplined WILL 857:2
N. are a race WILL 857:6
Noroway To N. o'er the faem BALL 55:14
north against the people of the N. LEE 487:17
Awake, O n. wind BIBL 91:7
beauties of the n. ADDI 4:15
heart of the N. is dead LAWR 484:5
He was my N., my South AUDE 37:5
mad n.-north-west SHAK 701:14
n. of my lady's opinion SHAK 735:29
N.-west passage STER 773:11
n. wind doth blow NURS 580:8
tender is the N. TENN 799:13
to us the near n. MENZ 532:5
triumph from the n. MACA 508:4
True N. strong and free WEIR 845:9
wild N.-easter KING 464:7
North America Mr and Mrs N. WINC 860:2
Northcliffe N. has sent for the King
ANON 17:12
northern bright n. star LOVE 502:1
constant as the n. star SHAK 712:16
n. lights astream SMAR 755:14
N. reticence, the tight gag HEAN 387:18
Norval My name is N. HOME 404:3
nose at the end of his n. LEAR 486:6
cause of the human n. COLE 242:1
Cleopatra's n. been shorter PASC 597:19
cut off your n. PROV 630:22
great hook n. BLAK 124:23
hadde a semely n. CHAU 220:6
hateful to the n. JAME 428:21
insinuated n. WATS 841:10
jolly red n. BEAU 63:7
large n. is in fact the sign ROST 670:2
lifts his n. SWIF 783:25
n. and cheeks stand out DRYD 297:24
n. May ravage with impunity BROW 167:22
N. of Turk SHAK 721:17
n.-painting, sleep SHAK 720:13
n. was as sharp as a pen SHAK 708:15
plucks justice by the n. SHAK 722:27
run up your n. dead against BALD 53:10
That n., the hook BYRO 185:5
thirty inches from my n. AUDE 38:3
very shiny n. MARK 521:16

wipe a bloody n. GAY 351:15
with a luminous n. LEAR 485:16
noses assaulting n. MITC 550:14
n. cast is of the roman FLEM 334:22
n. have they, and smell not BOOK 148:5
slightly flatter n. CONR 248:19
Where do the n. go HEMI 391:1
nosethirles n. blake were CHAU 218:23
nostalgia N. isn't what SAYI 685:5
nostalgie n. de la boue AUGI 38:24
noster Pater n. MISS 549:17
nostrils breathed into his n. BIBL 78:19
nostrums not n. but normalcy HARD 380:6
not find out what you are n. LOY 503:15
if this is n. PALI 594:5
n. I, but the wind LAWR 483:24
n.-incurious in God's handiwork BROW 165:18
N. so much a programme ANON 19:9
N. unto us, O Lord BOOK 148:4
n. wisely but too well SHAK 729:23
Thou shalt n. kill BIBL 81:20
notable meet a n. GERS 353:17
note living had no n. GIBB 355:8
longest suicide n. KAUF 453:10
n. I wanted JAME 430:1
only the n. of a bird SIMP 753:2
When found, make a n. DICK 278:1
noted n. in thy book BOOK 143:13
notes N. are often necessary JOHN 437:8
n. I handle no better SCHN 686:8
quality of his n. SCHN 686:9
right n. at the right time BACH 45:4
These rough n. SCOT 688:4
thick-warbled n. MILT 544:26
thinks two n. a song DAVI 268:5
too many n. JOSE 447:10
nothing better than n. PROV 643:22
between grief and n. FAUL 324:15
brought n. into this world BIBL 115:22
but n. came BYRO 185:15
Caesar or n. MOTT 563:3
Death is n. to us EPIC 316:11
desired to know n. JOHN 441:15
doing n. COWP 256:3
do n. MELB 531:4
do n. for ever and ever EPIT 318:1
do n. without it BUTL 184:14
don't believe in n. CHES 225:26
do with seeing n. AUST 41:8
drawing n. up COWP 256:15
Emperor has n. on ANDE 15:5
Emperors can do n. BREC 155:20
forgotten nothing and learnt n. DUMO 299:7
get something for n. PROV 648:16
gives to airy n. SHAK 727:3
good man to do n. MISQ 548:4
Goodness had n. to do with it WEST 848:14
hatest n. that thou BOOK 135:15
have not charity, I am n. BIBL 112:14
having n. BIBL 113:11
having n. to say ELIO 307:17
having n., yet hath all WOTT 870:7
I have done n. yet BRON 158:13
individually can do n. ALLE 13:5
I will say n. SHAK 715:19
labour of doing n. STEE 770:13
let me have n. METH 533:8
live well on n. a year THAC 803:4
look on and do n. MILL 536:1
marvel at n. HORA 410:8
men who are n. NAIP 567:5
N. LOUI 501:9
N. ain't worth nothin' KRIS 473:18
N., and is nowhere LARK 481:4
n. a-year, paid quarterly SURT 781:19
N. begins THOM 807:13
N. beside remains SHEL 745:17
n. better CARR 203:18
N. can be created LUCR 504:7
N. can be required FIEL 326:12
n. can be sole or whole YEAT 873:1
N. comes of nothing PROV 640:16
n. extenuate SHAK 729:23

nothing (*cont.*):
N. for nothing — PROV 640:17
N. for nothink — PUNC 649:23
n. happens — AURE 40:13
N. happens — BECK 64:19
n. happens — WELD 845:14
N. in excess — ANON 22:17
n. in his long career — NEWS 573:22
n. in respect of infinite — PASC 597:15
n. is But what is not — SHAK 718:16
n. is certain — PLIN 609:12
N. is ever done in this world — SHAW 740:19
N. is for ever — SAYI 685:6
N. is here for tears — MILT 545:10
n. is known luminously — NEWM 572:19
N. is law — POWE 622:7
N. is more dangerous — ALAI 10:10
n. left remarkable — SHAK 695:21
n. like leather — PROV 644:32
N., like something, happens anywhere — LARK 481:5
N. matters very much — BALF 53:16
n. more to hide — QUIN 651:19
n. of a name — BYRO 187:5
n. should be done for the first time — CORN 252:4
N. to be done — BECK 64:15
N. to do but work — KING 463:2
n. to do with the case — GILB 357:15
n. to look backward to — FROS 344:10
n. to say — CAGE 193:4
n. to say — COLT 244:9
n. to what I could say — CARR 202:11
n. to write about — PLIN 610:1
n. to you — BIBL 95:9
N. venture — PROV 640:24
N. venture — PROV 640:25
N. will come of nothing — SHAK 714:16
not there and the n. that is — STEV 774:13
on the n. new — BECK 64:11
power over n. — HERO 395:13
say n. — HEAN 387:18
say n. — PROV 634:29
Signifying n. — SHAK 722:22
something cannot become n. — BÜCH 169:14
take *more* than n. — CARR 202:7
Tar-baby ain't sayin' n. — HARR 383:6
that he knows — MILT 544:27
their rights, and n. less — ANTH 24:17
Thinking n. done — LUCA 503:18
Think n. done — ROGE 665:12
those who do n. — CONR 249:7
We strain at achieving n. — HORA 410:10
who does n. — LINC 493:16
without whom n. is strong — BOOK 136:4
You ain't heard n. yet — JOLS 445:6
nothingness N. haunts being — SART 681:8
to n. do sink — KEAT 457:10
notice escaped our n. — CRIC 260:3
man who used to n. — HARD 381:8
n. of my labours — JOHN 439:7
notions General n. — MONT 554:8
terrible n. of duty — CLOU 236:13
notorious open and n. evil liver — BOOK 136:16
nought n. did I in hate — SHAK 729:22
n. shall make us rue — SHAK 714:15
thing of n. — CRAS 258:22
noun n., proper or improper — FULL 346:6
nouns N. of number — COBB 237:13
nourish n. all the world — SHAK 717:19
N. thy children — BIBL 96:22
n. us with all goodness — BOOK 136:7
nourisher Chief n. in life's feast — SHAK 720:6
nourishes n. them, incites them — MONT 555:13
nouveau *trouver du n.* — BAUD 61:14
nouvelles *moins des choses n.* — VOLT 833:11
Nova Scotia N. shall have the blessing — HOWE 417:2
novel end of a n. — TROL 816:6
given away by a n. — KEAT 458:8
History begins in n. — MACA 508:1
live a n. — HARD 380:17
no more n.-writing — HARD 382:5

n. can hardly be made interesting — TROL 815:18
n. is an impression — HARD 381:1
n. is like a mirror — STEN 771:18
n. tells a story — FORS 337:17
only a n. — AUST 41:19
reading a n. — ELIO 307:25
read in many a n. — CALV 194:4
subject of a n. — MURA 565:11
want to read a n. — DISR 286:30
novelist only the n. can — BREN 156:7
novelists great—the major n. — LEAV 486:17
novels heroines of n. — FLAU 333:5
novelty antiquity not n. — PUGI 649:3
n., novelty, novelty — HOOD 406:4
This n. on earth — MILT 544:12
November no leaves, no birds,— N. — HOOD 405:22
N. at the gate — PUSH 650:19
remember the Fifth of N. — ANON 19:20
novo *N. cedat ritui* — THOM 805:5
novum *Reddiderit iunctura n.* — HORA 408:18
now If it be n. — SHAK 704:23
If not n. when — HILL 399:7
Leave N. for dogs — BROW 165:24
Let those love n. — ANON 23:6
N. fades the landscape — GRAY 370:1
N. I lay me down to sleep — PRAY 623:6
n. is the accepted time — BIBL 113:10
N. more than ever — KEAT 456:9
Right N. is better — BINC 121:14
sees what is n. — AURE 40:17
We are the masters n. — MISQ 548:23
what I am n. — EPIT 319:7
nowhere circumference is n. — ANON 19:4
Eclipse first, the rest n. — O'KE 584:21
not with you it is n. — HÉLO 390:10
nowness n. of everything — POTT 620:8
nowt say n. — PROV 634:29
When in doubt, do n. — PROV 646:40
noxious Of all n. animals — KILV 462:18
nubbly Nice but n. — KIPL 468:14
nuclear n. giants and ethical infants — BRAD 154:7
nucleus n. of more wars — EUGÉ 321:1
nude keep one from going n. — KING 463:2
noble and n. and antique — SWIN 785:6
nudge nudge n., snap snap — MONT 556:18
nugas *aliquid putare n.* — CATU 210:2
nuisance not make himself a n. — MILL 536:7
one n. for another nuisance — ELLI 314:3
nuisances small n. of peace-time — HAY 385:11
null splendidly n. — TENN 797:19
nullius *N. addictus iurare* — HORA 409:18
N. in verba — MOTT 563:14
NUM against the Pope or the N. — BALD 53:10
number best n. for a dinner party — GULB 374:12
bigness of Avogadro's n. — BENT 71:1
called the wrong n. — CART 205:18
forgotten as a nameless n. — PAST 598:18
full of a n. of things — STEV 776:13
half a n. of bees — LONG 500:8
happiness of the greatest n. — BENT 71:4
I am not a n. — MCGO 510:16
multitude, which no man could n. — BIBL 118:12
Not on the n. — COWL 254:13
Nouns of n. — COBB 237:13
n. of my days — BOOK 141:28
n. of perfection — AUGU 39:1
n. of the beast — BIBL 118:27
n. of your years — MONT 554:24
n. our days — BOOK 145:22
n. weight and measure — BLAK 126:9
very interesting n. — RAMA 654:18
numbered all n. — BIBL 100:27
God hath n. thy kingdom — BIBL 95:25
n. with the transgressors — BIBL 94:6
numberless n. goings-on of life — COLE 239:18
n. infinities — DONN 288:8
numbers better than n. — CROM 260:8
divinity in odd n. — SHAK 725:20
greatest n. — HUTC 422:10
I lisped in n. — POPE 614:17
luck in odd n. — PROV 644:26

n. that rocket the mind — WILB 854:1
safety in n. — PROV 644:37
secret magic of n. — BROW 162:28
ten primordial n. — SEFE 691:5
we got the n. — MORR 561:4
numbness drowsy n. pains — KEAT 456:2
numerous more n. the laws — TACI 787:7
n. piece of monstrosity — BROW 163:10
numerus *Nos n. sumus* — HORA 410:4
numinous no place for the n. — BYAT 184:25
nun Come, pensive n. — MILT 539:14
quiet as a n. — WORD 866:4
nunc *et n., et semper* — MISS 546:19
N. dimittis — BIBL 120:12
N. est bibendum — HORA 412:3
nunnery Get thee to a n. — SHAK 702:5
n. Of thy chaste breast — LOVE 502:6
nuns N. fret not at their convent's — WORD 866:19
nuptials day set apart for her n. — KELL 459:8
iteration of the n. — CONG 247:28
Nuremberg prosecution at N. — JACK 426:15
nurse always keep a-hold of N. — BELL 68:1
baby beats the n. — SHAK 722:27
Dear n. of arts — SHAK 709:11
lull the babe at n. — BYRO 190:7
n. of ninety years — TENN 799:16
n. sleeps sweetly — COWP 256:7
scratch the n. — SHAK 736:13
sucks the n. asleep — SHAK 696:5
what a n. should be — NIGH 576:5
what the n. began — DRYD 295:29
nursed n. a dear gazelle — MOOR 558:14
n. the pinion — BYRO 190:6
n. the self-same hill — MILT 540:5
nurseries n. of all vice — FIEL 326:14
n. of heaven — THOM 808:4
nursery century's cool n. — AKHM 10:7
Kitchen-cabals, and n.-mishaps — CRAB 257:10
nurses old men's n. — BACO 47:17
nursing n. the unconquerable hope — ARNO 30:13
What n. has to do — NIGH 576:4
nurture n. of the Lord — BOOK 138:22
nut had a little n. tree — NURS 579:8
spicy n.-brown ale — MILT 539:29
nutmeg But a silver n. — NURS 579:6
nuts gods send n. — PROV 633:12
N. — MCAU 509:2
where the n. come from — THOM 805:13
nutshell bounded in a n. — SHAK 701:10
nymph Not as a n. — MARV 525:3
N., in thy orisons — SHAK 702:4
nymphs to the N. — VIRG 830:17

O Within this wooden O. — SHAK 708:8
oafish o. louts remember Mum — BETJ 75:10
oafs muddied o. at the goals — KIPL 466:9
oak ashes of an O. — DONN 290:8
Beware of an o. — PROV 627:44
English o. and holly — HART 383:15
Heart of o. — GARR 349:10
Jove's stout o. — SHAK 733:33
juniper talks to the o. — PAUL 600:3
O., and Ash, and Thorn — KIPL 467:18
o.-cleaving. thunderbolts — SHAK 715:16
o. is before the ash — PROV 647:1
O. was round his breast — HORA 411:6
o. would sprout in Derry — HEAN 387:16
round that o. hangs — PUSH 650:21
thunders from her native o. — CAMP 195:19
oaks families last not three o. — BROW 162:16
hews down o. with rushes — SHAK 698:4
Little strokes fell great o. — PROV 637:44
o. from little acorns — PROV 633:31
Tall o., branch-charmèd — KEAT 454:18
oak-trees made the o. follow him — VIRG 833:7
oar heavy o. the pen is — FLAU 333:12
oatcakes o., and sulphur — SMIT 758:11
oath cheats with an o. — PLUT 610:13
Hire gretteste o. — CHAU 218:8
man is not upon o. — JOHN 441:22

oaths Judges must follow their o. ZOBE 878:5
o. are but words BUTL 183:22
soldier, Full of strange o. SHAK 697:1
oats feeds the horse enough o. GALB 347:13
O. A grain JOHN 436:3
Oaxen *rapidum cretae veniemus O.* VIRG 831:15
Obadiah O. Bind-their-kings MACA 508:3
obedience hold in o. remote GIBB 354:15
o. of planetary influence SHAK 714:24
o. to God BRAD 154:9
soldier is o. PROV 632:20
obedient o. to their laws we lie EPIT 317:13
penitent, and o. heart BOOK 133:2
Righteous women are o. KORA 471:15
obeisance made o. to my sheaf BIBL 80:17
obey cannot o. cannot command PROV 634:3
duty is to o. orders JACK 427:2
learned well how to o. THOM 804:19
love, cherish, and to o. BOOK 139:1
o. my god rather than you SOCR 759:18
O. orders PROV 640:27
o. them HORS 415:3
pain we o. PROU 625:13
To o. is better BIBL 83:35
woman to o. PEMB 602:7
obeyed o. as a son GIBB 355:1
right to be o. JOHN 433:20
She who must be o. HAGG 376:4
obeying except by o. BACO 49:4
obituary o. in serial form CRIS 260:5
your own o. BEHA 66:18
object B-b-british o. MALO 518:6
I'm a British o. MORR 560:6
My o. all sublime GILB 357:11
no o. worth its constancy SHEL 747:2
see the o. ARNO 32:8
with his eye on the o. ARNO 32:7
objected o. to being governed at all
CHES 225:11
objectification o. of feeling LANG 478:13
objectionable doubtless o. ANON 20:11
objective have a great o. CHIF 226:1
o. correlative ELIO 311:21
oblation o. of himself BOOK 137:15
oblations alms and o. BOOK 137:5
obligated feel as much o. MACH 511:9
obligation not always the sequel of o.
JOHN 436:29
o. which goes unrecognized WEIL 845:1
obligations Nobility has o. LÉVI 491:9
oblige *Noblesse o.* LÉVI 491:9
obliteration policy is o. BELL 67:13
oblivion compose an o. REED 657:6
from place to place over o. HARD 381:18
iniquity of o. BROW 162:18
journey towards o. LAWR 483:21
love, and then o. MCEW 510:14
mere o. SHAK 697:3
O! my o. is a very Antony SHAK 694:16
puts alms for o. SHAK 734:17
sank unwept into o. ELIO 307:18
stepmother to memory, o. JOHN 434:2
To cold o. SHEL 744:1
obnoxious I am o. BRAD 154:11
obscene Sailing on o. wings COLE 239:16
obscenity 'o.' not capable of exact definition
RUSS 675:7
obscure become o. HORA 408:17
Deep and o. LAO 479:12
o. nook for me BROW 166:25
through the palpable o. MILT 542:9
obscurely o. bright BYRO 187:13
obscuri *Ibant o. sola sub nocte* VIRG 830:8
obscurity man from o. REYN 658:16
o. of a learned language GIBB 355:6
rise out of o. JUVE 450:21
obscurus O. *fio* HORA 408:17
obsequies solemnized their o. BROW 162:10
observation common sense, and o.
BROW 163:5
O. is a passive science BERN 74:3
o. is concerned PAST 599:1
o. of facts COND 245:11

o. of trifles DOYL 292:14
o. with extensive view JOHN 438:5
observe o. the works of nature GALE 347:11
You see, but you do not o. DOYL 292:10
observed o. of all observers SHAK 702:9
observer for th'o.'s sake POPE 615:11
He is a great o. SHAK 711:23
keen o. of life AUDE 37:18
observes o. in order to see WITT 861:11
observeth o. the wind BIBL 90:17
obsolescence adolescence and o. LINK 495:5
planned o. STEV 773:21
obsolescent o. and nonexistent BREN 156:9
obsolete Either war is o. or men are
FULL 346:5
obstacle Conceit is an insuperable o.
TERR 802:7
obstinacy O. in a bad cause BROW 163:3
o. in a bad one STER 772:20
obstruct circumstances o. JUVE 450:21
obstruction consecrated o. BAGE 51:2
obtain o. effectually BOOK 136:12
obvious in o. distress BALF 53:14
Occam O.'s Razor OCCA 583:10
occasion o. of all wars FOX 339:14
o.'s forelock watchful MILT 544:22
occasions o. do inform against me
SHAK 703:27
their lawful o. BOOK 150:14
occidit *Occidit, o. Spes omnis* HORA 413:16
occupation cure for it is o. SHAW 742:3
diligent o. MORE 558:21
o. for an idle hour AUST 41:24
Othello's o.'s gone SHAK 728:32
Waiting is still an o. PAVE 600:7
occupations let us love our o. DICK 276:24
occupy o. their business BOOK 147:11
occurred never to have o. BENT 71:19
ocean abandon the o. CLAY 234:12
all great Neptune's o. SHAK 720:9
all the O.'s sons DENH 273:4
cause the O. to attend BEST 75:7
day-star in the o. bed MILT 540:14
deep and dark blue O. BYRO 187:2
drop in the o. TERE 801:18
Earth when it is clearly O. CLAR 233:16
foliage of the o. SHEL 745:9
great o. of truth NEWT 574:9
In the o.'s bosom MARV 524:14
leap into the o. HUME 420:7
love you till the o. AUDE 36:24
mighty o. deep WHIT 851:18
o. as their road WALL 836:18
o. forbids separation GRAT 369:6
o. has but one taste PALI 594:14
o. of darkness FOX 339:13
o. on a western beach LANG 478:11
O.'s child SHEL 744:21
o. sea BARN 59:9
O.'s nursling, Venice SHEL 744:20
On one side lay the O. TENN 794:22
on the vast o. HORA 411:12
Ransack the o. MARL 522:6
rivers with the o. SHEL 744:22
rolled the o. BYRO 186:3
rolling on of o. MORR 560:11
round o., and the living air WORD 866:13
sailed the o. blue STON 777:11
seen the hungry o. SHAK 738:1
ship Upon a painted o. COLE 240:20
thou, vast o. MONT 556:11
oceanic his own o. mind COLE 242:10
oceans compendious CRAS 259:9
To the o. white with foam BERL 73:1
octavos o. fill a spacious plain CRAB 257:18
October O.'s strife GURN 374:17
O., that ambiguous month LESS 490:18
octopus dear o. SMIT 756:12
odd But not so o. BROW 161:15
divinity in o. numbers SHAK 725:20
God must think it exceedingly o. KNOX 470:4
How o. Of God EWER 322:2
It's an o. job MOLI 552:2

Nothing o. will do JOHN 441:24
oddfellow desperate o. society THOR 809:20
oddly eyes are o. made HAMM 379:5
o.gay PARN 597:10
odds facing fearful o. MACA 508:13
how am I to face the o. HOUS 415:6
what o. CRAS 259:10
oderint O., *dum metuant* ACCI 1:7
odi O. *et amo* CATU 211:5
O. *profanum vulgus* HORA 412:14
odious Comparisons are o. PROV 629:16
O.! in woollen POPE 615:16
odium lived in the o. BENT 71:16
odorous Comparisons are o. SHAK 727:28
odours golden vials full of o. BIBL 118:8
haste with o. sweet MILT 540:22
o. tangle DICK 282:5
Odysseus Like O., the President KEYN 462:1
Odyssey thunder of the O. LANG 478:11
oferēode *þæs o.* ANON 23:16
off O. with her head CARR 202:8
O. with his head CIBB 231:11
O. with his head SHAK 731:21
offence best defence is a good o. SAYI 684:3
conscience void of o. BIBL 110:12
detest th'o. POPE 614:9
for a rock of o. BIBL 92:12
forgave the o. DRYD 295:19
I was like to give o. FROS 344:19
o. at a few faults HORA 409:13
o. inspires less horror GIBB 354:9
O! my o. is rank SHAK 703:5
only defence is in o. BALD 53:5
resented for an o. SWIF 783:9
What dire o. POPE 618:4
where the o. is SHAK 704:4
offences o. of my youth BOOK 141:4
offend doth o., when 'tis let loose SUCK 779:14
freedom to o. RUSH 673:2
offendar *non ego paucis O. maculis*
HORA 409:13
offended him have I o. SHAK 712:27
not o. the king MORE 559:16
shadows have o. SHAK 727:12
offender hugged the o. DRYD 295:19
love th'o. POPE 614:9
offenders O. never pardon PROV 640:29
society o. GILB 357:3
offensive extremely o. SMIT 757:1
Life is an o. WHIT 851:3
offer close with the o. HUXL 423:7
o. he can't refuse PUZO 650:24
would refuse this o. SCOT 690:2
offering o. too little CANN 196:25
office campaigns for public o. MORE 559:5
for o. boys SALI 679:3
holding public o. ACHE 1:12
in o. but not in power LAMO 477:19
insignificant o. ADAM 3:7
insolence of o. SHAK 702:1
man unfit for o. FABI 322:9
no o. to go to SHAW 740:7
o. party is not WHIT 851:15
receives the seals of o. ROSE 668:13
waters of o. TROL 816:7
officer fear each bush an o. SHAK 710:12
o. and a gentleman MILI 535:3
official concept of the o. secret WEBE 843:18
This high o., all allow HERB 393:13
officialism Where there is o. FORS 338:9
offspring Time's noblest o. BERK 72:18
wickedest o. of thy race ROCH 664:22
oft as o. as ye shall drink it BOOK 137:16
by o. falling LATI 482:15
O. in danger WHIT 850:16
o. was thought POPE 616:2
often Vote early and vote o. MILE 534:25
Og O. the king of Basan BOOK 149:11
oh o.! Sophonisba THOM 808:20
Ohioan black O. swan WRIG 870:19
Ohrmazd O. was on high ZORO 879:14
oil anointed my head with o. BOOK 140:21
consumed the midnight o. GAY 351:12

oil (*cont.*):

mix like o. and vinegar	GAIN 347:2
o. controlling American soil	DYLA 302:3
o. in a cruse	BIBL 85:7
o. of gladness	BOOK 142:13
o. of joy for mourning	BIBL 94:20
o. of refined politeness	COLE 242:18
o. to make him	BOOK 147:6
O., vinegar, sugar	GOLD 364:17
o. which renders	HUME 420:3
Scotland's o.	POLI 612:26
smoother than o.	BIBL 87:26
smoother than o.	BOOK 143:12
sound of the o. wells	FISH 330:11
whose o. wellnigh would shine	KORA 472:12
with boiling o. in it	GILB 357:13

oiled in the o. wards — KEAT 456:21
O. his way around the floor — LERN 490:15

oily glib and o. art — SHAK 714:19

ointment o. might have been sold — BIBL 103:9
very precious o. — BIBL 103:8

Okie O. means you're scum — STEI 771:9

old adherence to the o. — LINC 493:11

Any o. iron	COLL 243:2
As with gladness men of o.	DIX 287:1
attendance on my o. age	YEAT 874:25
balance of the O.	CANN 197:6
Being an o. maid	FERB 325:5
being o. is having lighted rooms	LARK 481:8
better than the Good O. Days	BINC 121:14
blessing of the O.	BACO 46:2
boys of the o. Brigade	WEAT 843:7
catch o. birds with chaff	PROV 648:5
chilly and grown o.	BROW 168:4
considered the days of o.	BOOK 145:4
die before I get o.	TOWN 814:4
died in a good o. age	BIBL 86:2
Diseases and sad O. Age	VIRG 830:9
dreary o. age	VIRG 833:1
dressing o. words new	SHAK 738:5
ere thou grow o.	ROCH 664:20
foolish, fond o. man	SHAK 716:24
getting too o.	DISN 284:1
good o. age	BIBL 79:32
good o. Cause	MILT 546:8
Growing o. a bad habit	MAUR 528:16
Growing o. is like	POWE 621:21
Grow o. along with me	BROW 167:9
grow o. with a good grace	STEE 770:15
hard sentences of o.	BOOK 145:5
heart grows o.	YEAT 874:22
HOW O. CARY GRANT	GRAN 368:9
I grow o.	SOLO 760:9
I grow o. . . . I grow old	ELIO 310:12
I'm growing o.	LOUI 501:7
in abundance in o. age	GOET 361:11
instead of o. ones	PEEL 601:11
into a world too o.	MUSS 566:12
lads that will never be o.	HOUS 415:17
make an o. man young	TENN 793:16
make me conservative when o.	FROS 344:20
man is as o. as he feels	PROV 638:16
man who reviews the o.	CONF 245:16
Mithridates, he died o.	HOUS 416:11
my folks were growing o.	STEV 776:19
name thee O. Glory	DRIV 294:2
Never too o. to learn	PROV 639:45
no country for o. men	YEAT 874:13
no fool like an o. fool	PROV 644:42
no man would be o.	SWIF 783:19
not yet so o.	SHAK 724:24
now am not too o.	BLUN 129:12
now am o.	BOOK 141:25
off with the o. love	PROV 636:9
o. Adam in this Child	BOOK 138:6
o. age always fifteen years older	BARU 60:11
O. Age, and Experience	ROCH 664:16
O. Age a regret	DISR 285:18
O.-age, a second child	CHUR 228:10
o. age has brought to me	STEP 772:2
O. age hath yet his honour	TENN 800:19
O. age is the most unexpected	TROT 817:4
o. age of cards	POPE 614:29

O. age should burn	THOM 805:15
o. age, the last gap but one	WHIT 850:18
o. and faded	MARL 522:3
O. and young	STEV 775:26
o. before my time	ROSS 669:3
o. black magic	MERC 532:10
o. familiar faces	LAMB 476:22
O. friends are best	SELD 691:9
o. head on young shoulders	PROV 648:12
o. heads on your young shoulders	SPAR 765:9
o. in a second childhood	ARIS 26:15
o. is better	BIBL 104:23
O. King Cole	NURS 580:9
o. lamps for new	ARAB 25:9
o. Lie: Dulce et decorum	OWEN 591:6
o., mad, blind	SHEL 746:14
o. man does not care	JOHN 440:13
o. man in a dry month	ELIO 309:23
o. man in a hurry	CHUR 228:23
o. man of Thermopylae	LEAR 486:1
O. man river	HAMM 378:20
o. man's darling	PROV 627:30
o. man upon a winter's night	YEAT 874:8
o. men and children	BOOK 150:10
O. men and comets	SWIF 783:20
o. men from the chimney corner	SIDN 751:6
o. men must die	PROV 648:21
o. men shall dream dreams	BIBL 96:8
O. Mother Hubbard	NURS 580:10
O. order changeth	TENN 794:25
O. soldiers never die	FOLE 336:4
o. truth receives a new	WIGG 853:14
o., unhappy, far-off things	WORD 869:11
o., wild, and incomprehensible man	
	VICT 827:10
o. wine wholesomest	WEBS 844:16
o. wood best to burn	BACO 45:20
O, sir! you are o.	SHAK 715:11
planned by o. men	RICE 659:21
problem of growing o.	MORR 561:11
ruinous and o.	SPEN 767:6
sad o. age	TALL 788:21
Say I'm growing o.	HUNT 421:7
shift an o. tree	PROV 648:15
sing the o. songs	CLAR 233:10
so o. a head	SHAK 724:28
so o. a story	HEIN 389:10
story always o.	BROW 167:13
suppose an o. man decayed	JOHN 443:14
teach an o. dog new tricks	PROV 647:46
Tell me the o., old story	HANK 379:10
that horror—the o. woman	COLE 242:15
that's o. Europe	RUMS 672:6
They shall grow not o.	BINY 121:15
thinking of the o. 'un	DICK 277:6
though an o. man	JEFF 432:4
times begin to wax o.	BIBL 96:23
too o. to rush up to the net	ADAM 2:8
want an o.-fashioned house	FISH 330:12
warn you not to grow o.	KINN 465:1
wax o. as doth a garment	BOOK 146:17
well an o. age is out	DRYD 296:25
what an o. courtier is like	CHAM 214:13
When I am an o. woman	JOSE 447:13
when thou shalt be o.	BIBL 109:8
when 'tis o.	BALL 56:6
When you are very o.	RONS 666:15
you are o. and grey	YEAT 875:10
You are o., Father William	CARR 201:17
You are o., Father William	SOUT 764:14
young can do for the o.	SHAW 739:26
Young folks think o. folks	PROV 648:19

older Another day o. — TRAV 815:1

As we get o.	REED 657:3
O. men declare war	HOOV 406:17
o. than the rocks	PATE 599:6
so much o. then	DYLA 302:1

oldest o. hath borne most — SHAK 717:10
o. rule in the book — CARR 202:18
o. sins — SHAK 707:30

olet *Pecunia non o.* — VESP 827:1

oligarchy *aristocracy*, call it o. — HOBB 401:3

olive children like the o.-branches — BOOK 149:4

Olivia Cry out, 'O.!'	SHAK 735:6
eyes did see O.	SHAK 734:28

olla putrida what a clumsy o. — LAWR 484:6

ologies instructed in the 'o.' — CARL 200:15

olores *inter strepere anser o.* — VIRG 832:9

Olympian O. bolts — DISR 284:12

Olympus made great O. tremble — HOME 404:10
O. on top of Ossa — VIRG 832:16
Pelion on top of shady O. — HORA 412:21

om end of o. is silence — UPAN 822:18

Omega Alpha and O. — BIBL 117:23

omelette fuss about an o. — VOLT 835:9
make an o. without — PROV 648:10
o. all over our suits — BROK 157:16

omen gods avert this o. — CICE 232:6
Procul o. abesto — OVID 589:10
This is the one best o. — HOME 404:18

omens grievous o. — SUTT 781:21

omissions O. are not accidents — MOOR 558:1

omitted O., all the voyage — SHAK 713:28

omne *o. immensum peragravit* — LUCR 504:4

omnes *Laudate Dominum, o. gentes* — BIBL 120:4

omnia *Amor vincit o.* — CHAU 218:11
non o. possumus omnes — LUCI 504:2
Non o. possumus omnes — VIRG 832:8
O. vincit Amor — VIRG 832:10

omnibus man on the Clapham o. — BOWE 153:14

omnipotence proof of God's o. — DE V 275:5

omnipotent land of the o. No — BOLD 131:9
O. but friendless — SHEL 745:23

omnis *Non o. moriar* — HORA 413:10

omniscience o. his foible — SMIT 758:28
their o. — MARA 521:8

omnium Duke of O. — TROL 816:3

on O., on, on — SIMP 753:4

Onan into the sin of O. — VOLT 834:20

once I was adored o. — SHAK 735:14

oblation of himself o. offered	BOOK 137:15
O. a—, always a—	PROV 640:37
o. and future king	MALO 518:5
O. in royal David's city	ALEX 12:8
O. more unto the breach	SHAK 708:16
O. to every man	LOWE 502:19
O. upon a time	ANON 19:13
O. upon a time	PULL 649:12
through this world but o.	GREL 372:8
You can only die o.	PROV 647:42

one All for o., one for all — DUMA 299:4

all is o.	ZOHA 878:8
all things and I are o.	CHUA 227:9
At o. fell swoop	SHAK 722:7
But the O. was Me	HUXL 423:1
doeth good, no not o.	BOOK 139:28
encompassed but o. man	SHAK 711:21
How to be o. up	POTT 620:10
Long-expected o.-and-twenty	JOHN 444:10
Lord is O.	SIDD 750:5
loyalties which centre upon number o.	
	CHUR 230:22
man not truly o.	STEV 775:16
o. being is wanting	LAMA 476:8
o. by one back	FITZ 331:21
o. day in thy courts	BOOK 145:15
o.-eyed man is king	ERAS 316:17
o.-eyed yellow idol	HAYE 385:16
O. flew east	NURS 580:13
o. for my baby	MERC 532:9
O. for sorrow	PROV 640:44
O. for the mouse	PROV 640:45
o. if by land	LONG 500:1
O. in Three	ALEX 12:9
o. man fewer	METT 533:11
O. man shall have one vote	CART 205:20
O. remains, the many change	SHEL 743:21
o. thing at once	SMIL 755:20
O., two, buckle	NURS 580:14
ought to be Number O.	CARR 202:18
square root of minus o.	BECK 64:28
Tao produced the O.	LAO 480:5
When I was o.-and-twenty	HOUS 415:15

oneself carefully at o. — MOLI 552:15
Hell is o. — ELIO 308:23
how to be o. — MONT 555:8

palaces (*cont.*):
saw in sleep old p.   SHEL 745:8
paladin starry p.   BROW 167:20
Palaeozoic In the P. time   SMIT 757:6
palate P., the hutch of tasty lust   HOPK 407:10
steps down the p.   NABO 566:16
pale behold a p. horse   BIBL 118:10
bond Which keeps me p.   SHAK 721:5
P. as thy smock   SHAK 729:20
P., beyond porch and portal   SWIN 785:12
p. fire she snatches   SHAK 734:8
P. grew thy cheek   BYRO 191:18
P. hands I loved   HOPE 407:3
p.—is yet of gold   CRAB 257:24
P. prime-roses   SHAK 737:2
p., unripened beauties   ADDI 4:15
p. young curate   GILB 358:13
pink pills for p. people   ADVE 7:20
turned p.   SOUT 764:22
whiter shade of p.   REID 657:14
Why so p. and wan   SUCK 779:12
world grew p.   JOHN 438:8
palely Alone and p. loitering   KEAT 455:4
Palestine establishment in P.   BALF 53:13
P. is the cement   ARAF 25:14
To sweeten P.   RUME 672:4
paletot Mon p. aussi   RIMB 662:13
paling piece-bright p.   HOPK 407:22
Palladium P. of all the civil   JUNI 450:2
pallida P. Mors   HORA 411:7
Palliser Plantagenet P.   TROL 816:3
pallor p. of girls' brows   OWEN 591:5
palls everything p.   ANON 22:12
palm bear the p. alone   SHAK 711:18
has won it bear the p.   MOTT 563:15
have an itching p.   SHAK 713:20
No pain, no p.   PENN 602:14
p. at the end   STEV 774:8
Turner's p. as itchy   SCOT 689:26
winning the p.   HORA 409:20
win the p.   MARV 525:2
palmae sine pulvere p.   HORA 409:20
palmerworm p. hath left   BIBL 96:6
palms other p. are won   WORD 867:18
p. before my feet   CHES 224:3
p. of her hands   BIBL 85:37
palmy most high and p. state   SHAK 699:4
palpable poem should be p.   MACL 512:4
very p. hit   SHAK 704:24
paltry aged man is but a p. thing   YEAT 874:14
Pam P., I adore you   BETJ 76:3
pampered p. jades   MARL 523:10
pan great god P.   BROW 164:11
P. did after Syrinx speed   MARV 525:3
panachaea p., or polygony   SPEN 767:17
panache Mon p.   ROST 670:3
pancreas adorable p.   KERR 461:8
pandemonium P., the high capital   MILT 542:1
Pandora open that P.'s Box   BEVI 77:12
P.'s box   BURG 172:5
panem P. et circenses   JUVE 451:13
pange P., lingua   FORT 338:14
P., lingua   THOM 805:4
pangs free of any p.   CURT 263:7
panic p.'s in thy breastie   BURN 179:24
wonderful p.   HECH 388:11
Panjandrum grand P. himself   FOOT 336:13
panoramic p. view of hell   BYRO 188:4
pans If ifs and ands were pots and p.
   PROV 635:10
pansies p., that's for thoughts   SHAK 704:2
pansy p. at my feet   WORD 867:7
pantaloon lean and slippered p.   SHAK 697:2
panteth As the hart p.   BOOK 142:4
panther Black P. Party   NEWT 572:20
panting For ever p.   KEAT 455:21
p. heart of Rome   WISE 861:2
pants As p. the hart   TATE 790:14
deck your lower limbs in p.   NASH 568:23
in fast thick p.   COLE 240:5
Panzer P.-man, panzer-man   PLAT 608:5
papa word P., besides   DICK 278:16
papacy p. is not other   HOBB 401:8

paper All reactionaries are p. tigers   MAO 521:4
all the earth were p.   LYLY 505:23
at a piece of tissue p.   RUTH 676:4
built a p.-mill   SHAK 710:3
By the evening p.   MACN 513:10
habit of talking with p.   SOYI 765:4
he hath not eat p.   SHAK 717:15
If all the world were p.   NURS 579:5
keep the p. work down   ORTO 586:14
no more personality than a p. cup   CHAN 215:9
only a p. moon   HARB 379:17
p. appears dull   STEE 770:16
p. from the outside world   KENO 461:2
p. hats and wooden swords   USTI 823:7
plays with on unastonishing p.   FANT 323:5
ran the p. for propaganda   BEAV 63:16
scrap of p.   BETH 75:8
sheet of p.   SAUS 682:17
virtue of p. government   BURK 173:9
worth the p. it is written on   GOLD 365:20
papers He's got my p.   PINT 607:1
reads p.   FRIS 343:17
turns over your p.   LAVA 483:7
what I read in the p.   ROGE 666:5
Papist P., yet a Calvinist   EPIT 318:8
parable open my mouth in a p.   BOOK 145:5
parachutes Minds are like p.   DEWA 275:8
parade life might be put on p.   EULA 321:2
p. of riches   SMIT 756:3
parades produce victory p.   HOBS 401:13
paradise admit them to P.   KORA 472:19
blundered into P.   THOM 807:20
cannot catch the bird of P.   KHRU 462:10
driven out of P.   KAFK 452:2
drunk the milk of P.   COLE 240:9
eastern side beheld Of P.   MILT 544:19
enjoy P.   BECK 65:1
gadget-filled p.   NIEB 575:6
Gates of P.   BLAK 125:8
green in p.   VERN 826:14
keys of p.   DE Q 273:19
moment spent in P.   SCHI 683:12
P. by way of Kensal Green   CHES 224:14
P. of exiles   SHEL 744:10
P. of Fools   MILT 542:25
P. of four seas   MARV 525:16
p. of women   PROV 631:4
p. on earth   KHUS 462:11
p. within thee   MILT 544:17
pass through P.   COLE 241:18
paved p.   MITC 550:16
rudiments of P.   SOUT 764:3
weave A p.   KEAT 454:16
wilderness is p. enow   FITZ 331:15
with me in p.   BIBL 106:25
paradises true p. are   PROU 626:1
paradox Man is an embodied p.   COLT 244:12
paragon p. of animals   SHAK 701:11
parallel North of the 49th p.   ADAM 3:19
p. in the world above   ZOHA 878:7
so truly p.   MARV 524:19
parallelograms Princess of P.   BYRO 191:22
parameters five free p.   GAMO 348:8
paranoid Only the p. survive   GROV 374:4
parapets of the ancient p.   RIMB 662:12
parcelled hardships p. within them   BOLA 131:6
parcere P. subiectis et debellare   VIRG 830:14
parch sun doth p. the green   SURR 780:15
parchment should be made p.   SHAK 710:1
parcus P. deorum cultor   HORA 412:2
pardlike p. Spirit   SHEL 743:15
pardon Alas but cannot p.   AUDE 38:13
Bretful of p.   CHAU 218:26
God may p. you   ELIZ 312:12
God will p. me   HEIN 389:17
kiss of the sun for p.   GURN 374:16
Offenders never p.   PROV 640:29
P. all   BUCK 170:2
p. and peace   BOOK 136:10
P. me boy   GORD 366:6
p., who have done the wrong   DRYD 295:16
With a thousand Ta's and P.'s   BETJ 76:1
pardoned praised than to be p.   JONS 447:3

pardoning p. our offences   BOOK 137:17
pardons P. him   AUDE 37:12
parens king is truly p. patriae   JAME 429:1
parent kind p. to man   PLIN 609:14
lose one p.   WILD 854:19
one child makes you a p.   FROS 344:4
p. of settlement   BURK 174:1
p. who could see his boy   LEAC 485:5
put any p. mad   FLEM 334:18
role of a revered p.   JUVE 451:8
smile for your p.   VIRG 832:4
parenthood means valuing p.   TOYN 814:6
parents begin by loving their p.   WILD 855:27
bondage to p.   WOLL 863:15
girl needs good p.   TUCK 818:12
Jewish man with p. alive   ROTH 670:9
joys of p.   BACO 47:21
Of p. good   SHAK 708:21
only illegitimate p.   GLAD 359:12
Our p.' age   HORA 413:2
P. can plant magic   MACN 513:17
P. love their children   AUCT 36:19
p. obey their children   EDWA 304:6
p. take more care   CAVE 211:20
p. were the Lord knows who   DEFO 271:2
produce bad p.   MORS 561:17
sacrifice and p.' tears   MILT 541:22
sharp and severe p.   GREY 373:2
stranger to one of your p.   AUST 42:13
parentum Aetas p.   HORA 413:2
parfit verray, p. gentil knyght   CHAU 218:5
paries p. cum proximus ardet   HORA 410:15
Paris after they've seen P.   LEWI 492:10
astonish P. with an apple   CÉZA 213:17
Down and out in P.   ORWE 587:1
go to P.   APPL 25:7
Is P. burning   HITL 400:11
king must have given me P.   ANON 22:10
last time I saw P.   HAMM 378:18
P. is a movable feast   HEMI 391:3
P. vaut bien une messe   HENR 391:19
P. was French—and silent   TUCH 818:11
poverty and P.   SCHI 683:7
they go to P.   WILD 855:23
when they die go to P.   PROV 633:16
without me P. would be taken   ANON 22:3
parish all the world as my p.   WESL 848:2
p. of rich women   AUDE 37:8
pension from his p.   RUSK 674:5
park come out to the ball p.   BERR 74:12
gentleman's p.   CONS 249:18
p., a policeman   CHAP 215:18
Poisoning pigeons in the p.   LEHR 488:3
wandering round a stately p.   MAUG 528:5
within the new p. wall   DUFF 298:12
parking put up a p. lot   MITC 550:16
parks p. are the lungs of London   PITT 607:17
parles their treasonous p.   BROW 166:16
parley-voo Hinky, dinky, p.   MILI 535:14
parliament build your House of P.   WELL 846:11
crop-headed P.   BROW 166:15
enables P. to do things   SHAW 740:17
Mob, P., Rabble   COBB 237:13
[p.] a lot of hard-faced men   BALD 53:2
p. can do any thing   PEMB 602:10
P. of man   TENN 797:1
P. speaking through reporters   CARL 200:12
Scottish P.   EWIN 322:3
Scottish P.   SALM 679:14
shall be a Scottish p.   ANON 20:19
shall be a Scottish p.   DEWA 275:7
united P.   FLET 335:3
parliamentarian safe pleasure for a p.
   CRIT 260:6
parliamentary old P. hand   GLAD 360:7
p. eloquence   CARL 200:14
parliaments mother of P.   BRIG 157:4
parlour party in a p.   WORD 868:3
walk into my p.   HOWI 417:9
Parnassus my chief P. be   SIDN 750:22
Parnell Poor P.   JOYC 448:7
parochial he was p.   JAME 429:16
parody devil's walking p.   CHES 224:2

past (*cont.*):
give me back my p. VIRG 831:4
God cannot alter the p. BUTL 184:2
knowledge of its p. DIEF 283:2
lament the p. BURK 174:29
last day of an era p. YELT 875:18
looking forward to the p. OSBO 588:18
Many a woman has a p. WILD 855:10
neither repeat his p. AUDE 38:18
nothing but the p. KEYN 462:3
nothing more than the p. BERG 72:8
p. as a watch BOOK 145:20
p., brittle with relics THOM 807:10
p. is a bucket of ashes SAND 680:6
p. is a foreign country HART 383:20
p. is lost CHAP 216:14
p. is secure WEBS 843:20
p. is the only dead thing THOM 806:17
p. never dead FAUL 324:14
p. our dancing days SHAK 732:6
p., present and future EINS 306:1
p. was a sleep BROW 167:23
plan the future by the p. BURK 172:17
Remembrance of things p. PROU 625:4
remembrance of things p. SHAK 737:24
soul of the whole P. CARL 200:7
things long p. SHAK 730:9
Things p. cannot be recalled PROV 645:2
Things p. redress SHAK 730:14
Think only of the p. AUST 42:20
Time present and time p. ELIO 309:3
upon the p. has power DRYD 297:7
What's p. is prologue SHAK 733:23
Who controls the p. ORWE 587:12
years that are p. BOOK 145:4
pastime take his p. therein BOOK 147:9
pastoral Cold P. KEAT 455:24
practising your p. music VIRG 831:12
pastors p. and teachers BIBL 114:5
P. she sends to help CHUR 228:9
some ungracious p. SHAK 700:2
spiritual p. and masters BOOK 138:12
pasture feed me in a green p. BOOK 140:20
people of his p. BOOK 146:8
sheep of his p. BOOK 146:15
pastures fresh woods, and p. new MILT 540:17
In p. green SCOT 690:9
Pipe me to p. HOPK 407:9
pat Now might I do it p. SHAK 703:6
P.-a-cake NURS 580:16
patch P. grief with proverbs SHAK 727:31
poor potsherd, p. HOPK 408:1
patches king of shreds and p. SHAK 703:16
thing of shreds and p. GILB 357:1
pate beat your p. POPE 614:12
p. of a politician SHAK 704:13
pâté de foie gras eating *p.* SMIT 758:27
pater *P. noster* MISS 549:17
paterna *buona imagine p.* DANT 265:3
P. rura HORA 411:3
paternal disclaim all my p. care SHAK 714:17
kindly p. image DANT 265:3
paternalism lessons of p. CLEV 235:13
paternoster No penny, no p. PROV 640:13
path beaten p. to his door EMER 315:22
Eightfold P. PALI 594:12
in the straight p. KORA 470:19
invisible p. PALI 594:18
long brown p. before me WHIT 852:17
Middle P. PALI 594:10
No p. of flowers leads LA F 475:20
p. is narrow and difficult UPAN 822:12
p. of duty TENN 798:25
p. of gold BROW 166:26
p. of the just BIBL 87:25
p. of the passions ROUS 670:15
p. of true love EWAR 321:23
P. of Wickedness BALL 55:21
rough and thorny p. MONT 555:12
pathetic Is not p. WHIT 852:18
P. Fallacy RUSK 673:10
That's what it is. P. MILN 538:10
too p. for the feelings AUST 41:12
pathless pleasure in the p. woods BYRO 187:1
too much like a p. wood FROS 344:6
Truth is a p. land KRIS 473:16
pathos P., piety, courage FORS 338:8
paths all her p. are peace BIBL 87:23
all her p. are Peace SPRI 769:1
craggy p. of study JONS 446:10
light unto my p. BOOK 148:14
p. of glory GRAY 370:4
So many p. WILC 854:11
Thirty-two wondrous p. SEFE 691:5
wherever friendly p. intersect HESS 397:10
pathway p. of a life unnoticed HORA 410:16
patience abuse our p. CICE 232:1
abusing of God's p. SHAK 725:17
aptitude for p. BUFF 170:5
burning p. RIMB 662:16
childhood had taught her p. COLE 242:14
deed, and eek hire p. CHAU 218:29
habits of peace and p. WALT 839:3
Have p., heart HOME 405:8
laughed him into p. SHAK 695:6
my p. is now at an end HITL 400:10
p., and shuffle the cards CERV 213:8
P. and tenacity of purpose HUXL 423:9
p. have her perfect work BIBL 116:15
P. is a virtue PROV 641:29
p. of Job BIBL 116:27
p. on a monument SHAK 735:21
p. to appreciate SANT 680:15
p. under their sufferings BOOK 135:7
p. will achieve BURK 174:20
pattern of all p. SHAK 715:19
preached up p. PRIO 624:7
preacheth p. HERB 393:27
time and p. TOLS 813:15
patient fury of a p. man DRYD 295:3
kill the p. BACO 47:1
not so p. SHAK 707:7
P. continuance BIBL 110:23
P. endurance attains all TERE 802:4
p. etherized upon a table ELIO 310:5
p. etherized upon a table LEWI 491:20
p. in the best condion NIGH 576:4
patiently take it p. BIBL 117:6
waited p. for the Lord BOOK 141:30
patients hurry his p. along MOLI 552:16
poets are their own p. THOM 807:6
patines p. of bright gold SHAK 725:11
patria Died some, pro p. POUN 621:5
pro p. mori HORA 412:17
sed pro p. NEWB 571:11
patriarchal wi' p. grace BURN 177:25
patrician This is the P. DONN 290:9
patrie *enfants de la p.* ROUG 670:11
patries *Europe des p.* DE G 271:12
patrimony all his p. SABA 676:12
patriot honest p., in the full tide JEFF 431:15
p. of the world CANN 197:1
p. yet, but was a fool DRYD 295:2
Such is the p.'s boast GOLD 364:24
patriotism garrulous p. TOCQ 812:13
knock the p. out of the human race SHAW 742:2
no Canadian p. BOUR 153:1
P. in the female sex ADAM 2:3
P. is a lively sense ALDI 11:11
P. is not enough CAVE 211:16
P. is the last refuge JOHN 441:18
p. run amok RATH 655:13
That kind of p. GASK 350:9
patriots all these country p. BYRO 185:6
blood of p. JEFF 431:11
P. are in the right WAUG 842:20
So to be p. BURK 175:7
True p. we CART 204:14
patron not a P., my Lord JOHN 439:7
p., and the jail JOHN 438:6
P. Commonly a wretch JOHN 436:4
patronage private p. ALBE 11:4
patrons great p. LUTY 505:13
patter pagan p. FANT 323:6
rapid, unintelligible p. GILB 358:12
pattern Art is the imposing of a p. WHIT 851:10
Made him our p. BROW 166:13
p. informed by sensibility READ 656:4
p. in most lives WELD 845:14
p. of all patience SHAK 715:19
p. of the world BACO 48:21
shewed as a p. SWIF 782:4
trace the p. WOOL 864:6
web, then, or the p. STEV 775:7
patterns if one follows p. SENE 692:9
weaves algebraic p. LOVE 501:14
What are p. for LOWE 502:14
paucity p. of human pleasures JOHN 444:20
Paul If Saint P.'s day be fair PROV 635:13
with St P. are literary ARNO 32:2
Pauli P. [exclusion] principle GAMO 348:7
pauper He's only a p. NOEL 576:19
pauperiem *Duramque callet p.* HORA 414:4
paupertas *infelix p.* JUVE 450:20
pause dull it is to p. TENN 800:16
eine kleine P. FERR 325:14
I p. for a reply SHAK 712:27
p. in the day's occupations LONG 498:16
pauses happy p. BACO 48:22
p. between the notes SCHN 686:8
paved p. paradise MITC 550:16
streets are p. with gold COLM 244:2
pavement P. slippery ROBI 664:6
riches of heaven's p. MILT 541:29
pavilioned P. in splendour GRAN 368:11
paving lawned areas with p. OFFI 584:15
paw ear on its p. MAYA 529:1
pawn you p. your intelligence CUMM 262:5
pax *in terra p.* MISS 549:8
P. Domini MISS 549:18
P. Vobis BIBL 120:13
pay cannot p., let him pray PROV 634:4
Can't p., won't pay POLI 612:12
Crime doesn't p. PROV 629:27
devil to p. ANON 17:10
Equal P. ANTH 24:18
I can p. for the damage CLOU 236:18
No cure, no p. PROV 640:2
Not a penny off the p. COOK 250:8
p. any price KENN 460:6
p. at the Greek Kalends AUGU 40:5
P. beforehand PROV 641:30
p. for by one and one KIPL 467:15
P. given to a state hireling JOHN 436:5
p. glad life's arrears BROW 167:8
P., pack, and follow BURT 181:1
p. the blood price BLAI 124:4
p. us, pass us CHES 224:15
saved the sum of things for p. HOUS 415:8
sharper spur than p. GAY 351:13
two-thirds of a nation p. VOLT 835:3
unless you mean to p. them PROV 643:31
we are made to p. for FRIE 343:11
We won't p. FO 336:1
wonders what's to p. HOUS 415:7
paycock mornin' til night like a p. O'CA 583:6
paying P. the Dane-geld KIPL 467:21
price well worth p. LAMO 477:18
payment passes for current p. BURN 176:20
pays *Mon p. ce n'est pas un pays* VIGN 827:19
p. the piper PROV 634:25
third time p. for all PROV 645:5
You p. your money PROV 648:23
You p. your money PUNC 649:15
PC P. is the LSD of the '90s LEAR 486:13
pea beautiful p.-green. boat LEAR 486:5
picking up a p. WELL 846:18
she had felt the p. ANDE 15:8
peace all her paths are p. BIBL 87:23
all her paths are P. SPRI 769:1
arch of p. morticed NICO 575:1
author of p. BOOK 134:2
banished p. SMOL 759:9
belong unto thy p. BIBL 106:16
blessing of p. BOOK 141:13
by judgement, and by p. TALM 789:2
call it p. TACI 786:21
came not to send p. BIBL 100:28

chastisement of our p. — BIBL 94:4
[Christ] came and preached p. — BIBL 113:28
cowardice keeps us in p. — JOHN 442:20
exacts for granting p. — EARH 302:7
for ever hold his p. — BOOK 138:23
for p. like retarded pygmies — PEAR 601:6
Give p. a chance — LENN 489:8
goods are in p. — BIBL 105:10
good war, or a bad p. — FRAN 341:9
Had Zimri p. — BIBL 85:35
hard and bitter p. — KENN 460:5
haunt of ancient P. — TENN 799:2
have you known p. — WEST 848:18
I find to p. — PETR 605:1
If you want p. — VEGE 826:2
I labour for p. — BOOK 148:16
ingeminate the word P. — CLAR 233:7
In His will is our p. — DANT 265:15
In p.; goodwill — CHUR 230:21
In p. there's nothing — SHAK 708:16
instrument of Your p. — FRAN 340:17
interest that keeps p. — CROM 260:16
In the arts of p. — SHAW 741:3
into the way of p. — BIBL 104:10
in what p. a Christian can die — ADDI 6:2
Joy. P. — PASC 598:13
just and lasting p. — LINC 494:6
kneel for p. — SHAK 733:11
lay me down in p. — BOOK 139:17
Let p. fill our heart — KUMA 474:3
Let us have p. — GRAN 368:15
Let war yield to p. — CICE 231:23
Love of p. — COLL 243:15
loving p. and pursuing peace — HILL 399:5
luxury, p. — BAUD 61:12
Make it a green p. — DARN 266:4
makes a good p. — HERB 395:4
make your p. with authority — MORR 561:8
may not be a just p. — IZET 426:7
mountains also shall bring p. — BOOK 144:18
my child may have p. — PAIN 592:14
My p. is gone — GOET 362:4
never stable p. — COTT 253:2
news and Prince of P. — FLET 335:15
no p. unto the wicked — BIBL 93:25
Nor p. within — SHEL 746:16
Nor shall this p. sleep — SHAK 711:9
no such thing as inner p. — LEBO 486:20
not a p. treaty — FOCH 336:3
no way to p. — MUST 566:15
on earth p. — BIBL 104:14
Open covenants of p. — WILS 859:21
ordered ways upon a state of p. — VIRG 830:14
Over all the mountain tops is p. — GOET 362:15
pardon and p. — BOOK 136:10
p. above all earthly dignities — SHAK 710:21
p. and propagation — WALP 837:22
p. at the last — NEWM 572:13
p. been as a river — BIBL 93:24
P. be to this house — BOOK 139:5
p. between equals — WILS 859:18
P. be unto you — BIBL 120:13
p. Built on complacency — GAUN 350:13
P., commerce — JEFF 431:16
p. for our time — CHAM 214:6
p. from freedom — MALC 517:10
peaceful sloth, Not p. — MILT 542:5
P. hath her victories — MILT 545:18
p. I hope with honour — DISR 285:8
P. I leave with you — BIBL 108:17
p. in our time — BOOK 134:1
p. in Shelley's mind — SHEL 746:25
p. is a dream — MOLT 553:7
p. is a modern invention — MAIN 516:20
p. is a very apoplexy — SHAK 698:11
P. is indivisible — LITV 495:15
P. is in the grave — SHEL 745:21
p. is much more precious — SADA 677:2
P. is poor reading — HARD 380:11
'P.! it is I.' — ANAT 15:3
P. its ten thousands — PORT 619:23
P., n. In international affairs — BIER 121:8

P. nothing but slovenliness — BREC 155:18
p. of God — BIBL 115:4
p. of God — JAME 429:3
p. of Jerusalem — BOOK 148:20
p. of the double-bed — CAMP 195:1
p. of thine — ARNO 29:16
p. of wild things — BERR 74:15
P. on earth — WESL 847:8
p. on the earth — SEAR 690:13
P., order, and good government — ANON 19:16
P.! Peace! Peace — UPAN 822:7
P., perfect peace — BICK 120:23
P., retrenchment, and reform — BRIG 157:3
P., the human dress — BLAK 127:9
p. there may be in silence — EHRM 305:2
P. to corrupt — MILT 544:15
p. to him that is far off — BIBL 94:14
'P. upon earth!' was said — HARD 381:10
p. which the world cannot give — BOOK 134:9
p. will guide the planets — RADO 653:8
p. with honour — CHAM 214:6
P. without Joy — BUCH 169:6
people want p. so much — EISE 306:9
plunging into a cold p. — YELT 875:19
poor, and manglèd P. — SHAK 709:11
potent advocates of p. — GEOR 352:15
prefers a negative p. — KING 463:9
Prince of P. — WESL 847:9
publisheth p. — BIBL 93:27
righteousness and p. — BOOK 145:17
rust in p. — SOUT 764:4
seek p., and ensue it — BOOK 141:21
servant depart in p. — BIBL 104:16
sing The merry songs of p. — SHAK 711:8
So enamoured on p. — CLAR 233:8
soft phrase of p. — SHAK 728:7
speak p. unto nation — REND 658:7
tell me p. has broken out — BREC 155:22
than to make p. — CLEM 235:8
that we may live in p. — ARIS 27:14
there is no p. — BIBL 94:27
thousand years of p. — TENN 796:1
time of p. — BIBL 89:23
time of p. — SHAK 731:12
universal p. — TENN 793:20
want p., prepare for war — PROV 635:35
war and p. in 21st century — KOHL 470:13
War is p. — ORWE 587:11
we cannot speak of p. — BRAN 155:4
What hast thou to do with p. — BIBL 85:32
peaceably living p. — BIBL 98:3
p. if we can — CLAY 234:13
so p. ordered — BOOK 136:5
peaceful made this p. life for us — VIRG 831:13
quietly pacifist p. — WALK 836:4
peacefully p. towards its close — DAWS 269:6
peacemakers Blessed are the p. — BIBL 98:25
peach dare to eat a p. — ELIO 310:13
Last-supper-carved-on-a-p.-stone — LANC 477:22
nectarine, and curious p. — MARV 525:4
woolly p. — JONS 447:1
peaches What p. — GINS 359:1
peacock Eyed like a p. — KEAT 455:11
mornin' til night like a p. — O'CA 583:6
pride of the p. — BLAK 126:13
peacocks apes, and p. — BIBL 84:29
p. and lilies — RUSK 673:25
peak small things from the p. — CHES 225:9
peal night's yawning p. — SHAK 721:4
peanuts hate it as much as p. — WELL 846:2
pay p., get monkeys — PROV 635:30
pear And a golden p. — NURS 579:6
Here we go round the prickly p. — ELIO 309:28
partridge in ap. tree — SONG 763:7
pearl barbaric p. and gold — MILT 542:2
orient p. — MARL 522:6
p. in every cowslip's ear — SHAK 725:34
p. is the oyster's autobiography — FELL 324:23
p. of great price — BIBL 101:16
splendid p. — SEXT 693:7
threw a p. away — SHAK 729:23
Too rich a p. — BUTL 183:23
pearls Give p. away — HOUS 415:15

He who would search for p. — DRYD 295:8
p. before swine — BIBL 99:23
p. fetch a high price — WHAT 849:18
p. roll in all directions — ORCH 586:1
p. that were his eyes — SHAK 733:21
p. upon an Ethiop's arm — DYER 301:9
p. were strung — JAME 429:14
throw p. to swine — PROV 630:16
to sea for p. — SMAR 754:10
pears Walnuts and p. — PROV 646:6
Pearse Tom P. — BALL 56:8
Pearsean P. ghost in the eye — O'BR 583:2
peartree p. leaves and blooms — HOPK 407:18
peasan toe of the p. — SHAK 704:14
peasant p. and a philosopher — JOHN 440:12
rogue and p. slave — SHAK 701:19
peasantry p. its pack animal — TROT 817:5
p., their country's pride — GOLD 364:2
peasants cricket with their p. — TREV 815:7
p. now Resign their pipes — CRAB 258:5
pease P. porridge hot — NURS 580:17
pebble smoother p. — NEWT 574:9
wise man hide a p. — CHES 225:8
pebbles leviathan retrieving p. — WELL 846:18
peccata p. mundi — MISS 549:19
peccator Esto p. — LUTH 505:3
peccavi P.—I have Sindh — WINK 860:15
p. nimis cogitatione — MISS 546:20
pecker p. in my pocket — JOHN 435:9
pectora non mortalia p. cogis — VIRG 829:17
peculiar Chosen and made p. ground — WATT 842:1
Funny-p. or funny ha-ha — HAY 385:12
p. people — BIBL 117:3
pecunia P. non olet — VESP 827:1
pedant apothegmatical P. — NASH 568:24
pedantic garden with p. weeds — CARE 198:7
too p. for a gentleman — CONG 247:7
pedantry critics' own dreary p. — TERE 801:10
pedants learned p. much affect — BUTL 183:9
peddle no shoddier than what they p. — BECK 64:9
pede nunc p. libero — HORA 412:3
pederasty Not flagellation, not p. — RATT 655:16
pedestrians two classes of p. — DEWA 275:9
pedigree languages are the p. — JOHN 438:17
peel orange p. picked out — RALE 654:17
p. me a grape — WEST 848:12
peep Nevermore to p. again — DE L 272:4
p. at such a world — COWP 256:20
peepers where you get them p. — MERC 532:8
peeping sun Came p. in at morn — HOOD 405:18
peepshow ticket for the p. — MACN 513:8
peer hath not left his p. — MILT 540:3
many a p. of England — HOUS 416:10
murdered p. — ALCO 11:6
reluctant p. — BENN 69:19
peerage p., or Westminster Abbey — NELS 569:19
should study the P. — WILD 855:29
When I want a p. — NORT 577:7
peerless Buddha, p. among men — PALI 594:4
Here lies that p. paper peer — EPIT 318:6
unveiled her p. light — MILT 543:10
peers flattery of one's p. — LODG 498:5
House of P. — GILB 356:21
judgement of his p. — MAGN 515:1
Lord in the P. — BROU 160:7
peewees p. crying — STEV 776:25
Pegasus thought it P. — KEAT 456:19
peignoir Complacencies of the p. — STEV 774:14
peine joie venait toujours après la p. — APOL 25:3
pelago p. ratem — HORA 411:6
pelican bird is the p. — MERR 533:3
p. in the wilderness — BOOK 146:16
Pelion P. imposuisse Olympo — HORA 412:21
pile Ossa on P. — VIRG 832:16
pellet p. with the poison — FILM 329:15
Pemberley shades of P. — AUST 42:17
pen Before my p. has gleaned — KEAT 457:8
bite his p. — SWIF 784:9
Biting my truant p. — SIDN 750:15
books and p. I will apply — WHIT 852:22
female p. — ALCO 11:6

pen (cont.):
fingers held the p.   COWP 255:19
glorious by my p.   MONT 556:16
heavy oar the p. is   FLAU 333:12
holding a p.   DICK 279:13
mightier than the p.   HOGB 402:15
My tongue is the p.   BOOK 142:12
needle and the p.   LEWI 492:5
nose was as sharp as a p.   SHAK 708:15
pain to the book   OXFO 591:13
p. has been in their hands   AUST 42:4
p. in his hand   JOHN 438:25
p. in his hand   JOHN 443:1
p., in our age   LEWE 491:14
p. is mightier   PROV 641:32
p. is worse than the sword   BURT 181:12
p. mightier than the sword   BULW 170:14
scratching of a p.   LOVE 502:10
squat p. rests   HEAN 387:9
victorious p.   PRIN 624:2
Waverley p.   ADVE 8:20
woman's p.   BOOT 151:4
woman that attempts the p.   WINC 860:5
penalty p. of Adam   SHAK 696:14
penance making night do p.   WORD 868:14
pence eternal want of p.   TENN 801:4
Take care of the p.   LOWN 503:12
Take care of the p.   PROV 644:2
pencil coloured p. long enough CHES 225:17
dude with a p.   DIDD 282:9
p. of the Holy Ghost   BACO 46:3
pencils feel for their blue p. ESHE 320:9
p. and what-not   MILN 538:14
sadness of p.   ROET 665:6
penetralium p. of mystery   KEAT 457:15
peninsulas bright eye of p.   CATU 210:9
penitent p., and obedient heart BOOK 133:2
p. drunkennesses   RIMB 662:18
Restore thou them that are p.   BOOK 133:6
penitus p. toto divisos orbe   VIRG 831:15
pennant wind or the p.   HUI- 419:11
pennies P. don't fall from heaven THAT 803:14
p. from heaven   BURK 176:11
Pennsylvania leave the P. station GORD 366:6
penny bad p. always turns up   PROV 627:6
In for a p.   PROV 636:1
No p., no paternoster   PROV 640:13
Not a p. off the pay   COOK 250:8
One a p.   NURS 580:12
one p. the worse   BARH 58:10
p. plain and twopence coloured   STEV 775:19
p. saved   PROV 641:33
P. wise   PROV 641:34
pens Let other p. dwell   AUST 41:18
Penshurst Thou art not, P.   JONS 446:27
pension made his p. jingle   COWP 257:5
p. from his parish   RUSK 674:5
p. list of the republic   CLEV 235:12
P. Pay given   JOHN 436:5
spend my p. on brandy   JOSE 447:13
pensive Come, p. nun   MILT 539:14
her p. soul   COLL 243:14
vacant or in p. mood   WORD 866:8
pent In the great city, p.   COLE 239:20
pentagon P., that immense monument
                                   FRAN 341:14
penthouse his p. lid   SHAK 718:7
Pentridge P. by the river   BARN 59:8
peonies wealth of globèd p.   KEAT 455:28
people afraid Of p.   HAMM 379:5
All p. that on earth do dwell   KETH 464:9
American p. have spoken   CLIN 236:9
And the p.   ANON 19:7
as if p. mattered   SCHU 687:1
as many opinions as p.   TERE 801:16
August for the p.   AUDE 36:27
Before we were her p.   FROS 344:14
bludgeoning of the p.   WILD 856:7
builds on the p.   MACH 511:8
by the p.   PAGE 591:16
confidence of the p.   CONF 246:13
debauch her p.   JENY 433:1
die for the p.   BIBL 108:8

dissolve the p.   BREC 156:3
distrust of the p.   ROMI 666:13
faces of p. going by   PEPY 603:14
faith in the p.   DICK 281:9
fiery, impulsive p.   HOUS 416:15
fool all the p.   LINC 494:11
full of p.   BIBL 95:8
good of the p.   CICE 231:18
Guns don't kill p.   SLOG 755:4
I am myself the p.   ROBE 663:7
indictment against an whole p.   BURK 173:15
in favour of the p.   BURK 174:30
I would be of the p.   LA B 474:18
Let my p. go   BIBL 81:4
Let my p. go   SONG 763:16
Like p., like priest   BIBL 96:3
Like p., like priest   PROV 637:35
look after our p.   SCOT 688:5
love of the p.   BURK 173:23
made for the p.   WEBS 843:21
martyr of the p.   CHAR 216:20
more than half the p. are right   WHIT 850:14
Most p. ignore most poetry   MITC 550:12
my p.'s happiness   ELIZ 312:9
new p. takes the land   CHES 224:16
No permanent elevation of a p.   LIVI 496:3
no petty p.   YEAT 875:15
Now, Sir, there are p.   JOHN 443:3
one p., one leader   POLI 612:14
opium of the p.   MARX 526:3
p. are only human   COMP 245:4
p. are the masters   BLAI 123:19
p. are the masters   BURK 175:19
p. arose as one   BIBL 83:22
p. as base as itself   PULI 649:9
P. die, but books never die   ROOS 667:14
p. don't do such things   IBSE 424:8
p. govern themselves   THIE 804:12
p. imagine a vain thing   BOOK 139:12
p. is grass   BIBL 93:16
p. is the true legislator   BURK 175:9
p. made the Constitution   MARS 523:25
p. marching on   MORR 560:11
p. of his pasture   BOOK 146:8
p. overlaid with taxes   BACO 48:8
p.'s prayer   DRYD 294:16
P.'s Princess   BLAI 123:20
p.'s voice is odd   POPE 617:22
p. that read   SHEN 747:21
p. that walked in darkness   BIBL 92:13
p. went up into the city   BIBL 82:27
p. who got there first   USTI 823:6
People who need p.   MERR 532:26
P. you know, yet can't quite name LARK 481:8
Power to the p.   POLI 613:7
Privileged and the P.   DISR 286:8
same as if they was p.   DURE 300:11
save the p.   ELLI 313:17
strength unto his p.   BOOK 141:13
support of the p.   CLEV 235:13
suppose the p. good   ROBE 663:11
thy p. shall be my people   BIBL 83:23
thy p. which call upon thee   BOOK 135:13
understanded of the p.   BOOK 150:19
voice of the p.   ALCU 11:10
voice of the p.   PROV 646:4
we are the p. of England   CHES 224:15
What is the city but the p.   SHAK 698:7
world is bereft of p.   LAMA 476:8
ye are the p.   BIBL 86:27
peopled conquered and p.   SEEL 691:4
peoples cry of the Little P.   LE G 487:20
scripture of p.   JERO 433:8
Peoria play in P.   POLI 612:24
pepper peck of pickled p.   NURS 580:18
per P. ME SI VA   DANT 264:13
perceive p. and know   BOOK 135:13
percentage reasonable p.   BECK 64:17
perception Agent of all human P. COLE 241:20
doors of p.   BLAK 126:22
gates of p.   MAIM 516:14
no p., appellation   MAHĀ 515:6
perchance To sleep: p. to dream SHAK 701:26

Percy Lord P. sees my fall   BALL 54:8
perdition led to p. by a man   WEST 849:1
P. catch my soul   SHAK 728:22
son of p.   BIBL 108:24
perdrix Toujours p.   ANON 22:11
pereat p. mundus   MOTT 563:9
P., qui crastina curat   ANON 23:10
perenne maneat p. saeclo   CATU 210:3
perennial Falsehood has a p. spring
                                   BURK 173:7
perennius Exegi monumentum aere p.
                                   HORA 413:9
perestroika restructuring [p.] GORB 366:4
pereunt Qui nobis p.   MART 524:6
perfect being made p.   BIBL 97:1
Be ye therefore p.   BIBL 99:9
end of a p. day   BOND 132:7
Entire and whole and p.   SPRI 768:18
ever more p. eyes   TEIL 792:12
Homage to thee, P. Wisdom   MAHĀ 515:4
If thou wilt be p.   BIBL 102:6
life may p. be   JONS 446:21
made p.   BIBL 116:9
made p. in weakness   BIBL 113:19
making p. characters   BUCK 169:16
nobody's p.   FILM 329:21
None of us are p.   WILD 854:24
Nothing is p.   STEP 772:6
One p. rose   PARK 596:5
patience have her p. work   BIBL 116:15
p. democracy   BURK 174:15
P. fear casteth out   CONN 248:12
P. God   BOOK 134:14
p. in this world   DONN 290:11
p. is to have changed   NEWM 572:7
p. Name of God   SIKH 751:19
p. use of an imperfect medium   WILD 855:16
p. woman; nobly planned   WORD 869:8
Practice makes p.   PROV 641:47
service is p. freedom   BOOK 134:2
that which is p. is come   BIBL 112:14
this one is p.   PALI 594:23
unto the p. day   BIBL 87:25
perfected p. by music   CONF 246:8
p. your religion   KORA 472:2
woman a p.   PLAT 608:7
perfectibility P. most unequivocal
                                   GODW 361:3
perfection Dead p., no more   TENN 797:19
ever approaches p.   HAZL 386:14
loveliness and p.   MILT 545:27
number of p.   AUGU 39:1
p. is not the true basis   GLAD 360:6
P. is the child   HALL 378:3
p. of reason   COKE 238:12
P. of the life   YEAT 872:13
p. of wisdom   MAHĀ 515:5
p.'s sweat   WALC 835:16
pictures of p.   AUST 43:6
pursuit of p.   ARNO 31:9
realise our p.   WILD 855:4
road to p.   JAIN 428:14
she did make defect p.   SHAK 694:24
think of p.   BURN 176:17
Trifles make p.   MICH 534:2
very pink of p.   GOLD 365:4
What's come to p.   BROW 166:22
perfections where all p. keep ANON 18:6
with his sweet p. caught   ROYD 671:18
perfectly p. love thee   BOOK 136:19
P. pure and good   BROW 167:5
small, but p. formed   COOP 251:2
perfide ah, la p. Angleterre   BOSS 152:1
perfidious p. Albion   XIMÉ 872:2
p. friends   MEDI 530:4
perform Almighty's orders to p. ADDI 4:11
not able to p.   BOOK 140:14
p. without thinking   WHIT 851:11
zeal will p. this   BIBL 92:15
performance all words And no p. MASS 527:11
insipid and tedious p.   WALP 837:12
p., as he is now   SHAK 711:4
p. every thing   HUNT 421:13

spray of Western p. HART 383:15
whisper of the p. THEO 804:11
pineapple not slice a p. BABB 44:11
p. of politeness SHER 748:12
pines lofty p. DRAY 293:16
pinguem p. et nitidum bene HORA 410:7
pinion imagination droops her p. BYRO 188:29
nursed the p. BYRO 190:6
pinions with p. skim the air FRER 342:13
pink p. pills for pale people ADVE 7:20
very p. of courtesy SHAK 732:21
very p. of perfection GOLD 365:4
pinkly p. bursts the spray BETJ 75:18
pinko really p.-grey FORS 335:18
pinnace p. like a fluttered bird TENN 800:1
pinnacled p. dim SHEL 746:2
pinprick p. of eternity AURE 40:16
pins files of p. extend POPE 618:7
pinstripe come in a p. suit FEIN 324:22
pint p. of plain O'BR 583:5
p.—that's very nearly GALT 348:6
quart into a p. pot PROV 648:6
pinta Drinka P. Milka Day ADVE 7:19
pioneers are simply p. MURR 566:1
P.! O pioneers WHIT 852:5
pios si qua p. respectant numina VIRG 829:2
pious p. Aeneas HORA 414:1
p. man is one who LA B 475:2
rarther p. ASHF 33:14
pipe p. a simple song WORD 865:22
p. Blown by surmises SHAK 707:3
P. me to pastures HOPK 407:9
p. might fall out FORS 337:16
p. of half-awakened birds TENN 799:12
p. with solemn interposing puff COWP 254:28
piped We have p. unto you BIBL 100:34
piper pays the p. PROV 634:25
Peter P. picked a peck NURS 580:18
Tom he was a p.'s son NURS 582:6
Tom, Tom, the p.'s son NURS 582:7
pipes on their scrannel p. MILT 540:10
open the b. BYRD 184:26
What p. and timbrels KEAT 455:17
piping For ever p. songs KEAT 455:20
Helpless, naked, p. loud BLAK 127:20
P. songs of pleasant glee BLAK 127:6
weak p. time SHAK 731:12
Pippa P. passes BEER 66:1
pips until the p. squeak GEDD 351:29
pirate To be a P. King GILB 358:5
piscem Desinat in p. HORA 408:14
pismire p. is equally perfect WHIT 852:10
piss pitcher of warm p. GARN 349:8
pissing inside the tent p. out JOHN 435:10
pistol echo of a p.-shot DURR 300:17
I reach for my p. JOHS 445:4
p. in your pocket WEST 848:16
p. on the wall CHEK 222:14
p.-shot in the middle STEN 771:19
pun is a p. LAMB 476:19
when his p. misses fire GOLD 365:15
pistols Have you your p. WHIT 852:9
young ones carry p. SHAW 739:9
piston steam and p. stroke MORR 560:14
pistons black statement of p. SPEN 766:9
pit digged a p. before me BOOK 143:16
eagle know what is in the p. BLAK 124:21
He that diggeth a p. BIBL 90:12
Law is a bottomless p. ARBU 25:17
monster of the p. POPE 617:25
out of the horrible p. BOOK 141:30
sulphurous p. SHAK 716:18
pitbull hockey mom and a p. PALI 595:1
pitch He that toucheth p. BIBL 97:18
imagination to the proper p. LACK 475:6
p. of grief HOPK 407:13
p. or direction HOPK 408:8
touches p. shall be defiled PROV 634:11
pitcher p. be broken at the fountain BIBL 90:20

p. will go to the well PROV 641:36
pitchers Little p. have large ears PROV 637:42
pitchfork drive out nature with a p. HORA 410:9
nature with a p. PROV 647:40
thrown on her with a p. SWIF 783:4
use my wit as a p. LARK 481:11
pith p. is in the postscript HAZL 385:20
pitied Any one is to be p. HAZL 385:18
Better envied than p. PROV 627:31
pitieth p. his own children BOOK 147:2
pitiful God be p. BROW 164:7
long-suffering, and very p. BIBL 97:7
'twas wondrous p. SHAK 728:11
pitifulness p. of thy great mercy BOOK 135:4
pity by means of p. and fear ARIS 27:9
cherish p. BLAK 127:10
endure, then p. POPE 616:32
full of p. and concerned MAHÁ 515:7
Midnight Without P. JOHN 434:14
no p. to myself SHAK 731:28
O source of p. MISS 550:7
P. a human face BLAK 127:9
p. beyond all telling YEAT 874:10
p. him afterwards JOHN 442:2
p. his ignorance DICK 279:14
P. is akin to love PROV 641:37
p. kills BALZ 57:3
p., like a naked new-born SHAK 719:9
p. never ceases to be shown DRYD 294:22
p. renneth soone CHAU 219:10
P. the reapers DUCK 298:9
p. this busy monster CUMM 262:9
P. was always a waste PAVE 600:6
Poetry is in the p. OWEN 591:1
saint took p. on COLE 241:1
Scots deserve no p. FLET 335:3
seas of p. lie AUDE 37:11
shafts barbed with p. DANT 265:5
she did p. them SHAK 728:12
some to have p. on me BOOK 144:12
some touch of p. SHAK 731:14
yet the p. of it, Iago SHAK 729:5
pix Sticks nix hick p. NEWS 573:19
place all in one p. BOIL 131:4
all other things give p. GAY 351:14
and the p. thereof BOOK 147:3
bourne of time and p. TENN 793:7
could have no p. BIBL 97:20
Ere time and p. were ROCH 664:21
exalt us unto the same p. BOOK 136:1
for one p. than another SOUT 764:19
gathered to the same p. HORA 412:7
genius of the p. POPE 615:7
Get p. and wealth POPE 617:17
Gratitude of p.-expectants WALP 838:16
have no p. in it NAIP 567:5
his p. know him BIBL 86:23
In p. of strife CAST 206:11
keep in the same p. CARR 202:24
know the p. ELIO 309:19
lone unhaunted p. DONN 288:20
Lord is in this p. BIBL 80:10
love of p. and precedency DONN 290:7
Men in great p. BACO 47:6
no p. to go WHIT 851:17
not in the same p. HIPP 399:15
p. for everything PROV 641:38
p. in the sun BÜLO 170:9
p. in the sun WILH 856:21
P., that great object SMIT 755:24
p. within the meaning ANON 19:17
p. without reproof ROSE 668:10
prepare a p. for you BIBL 108:13
right man in the right p. JEFF 432:15
rising to great p. BACO 47:10
rising unto p. BACO 47:8
spirit of the p. VIRG 830:17
stand in the holy p. BIBL 92:3
thus with height of p. WOTT 870:10
till there be no p. BIBL 92:3
time and p. JOHN 437:15
time and p. for PROV 644:23

time and the p. BROW 166:21
Time, P. DRYD 297:13
woman's p. in the home PROV 647:31
placem ut p. genus irritabile vatum HORA 411:1
placeo Quod spiro et p. HORA 413:14
placere Nulla p. diu carmina possunt
HORA 410:17
places All p., all airs BROW 163:9
all p. thou MILT 544:18
all p. were alike to him KIPL 468:8
father's fortunes, and his p. CORB 251:12
longest distance between two p. WILL 858:5
New p. you will not find CAVA 211:15
p. that the eye of heaven SHAK 730:7
P. where they sing BOOK 134:4
Proper words in proper p. SWIF 782:18
quietest p. HOUS 416:8
placidly Go p. amid the noise EHRM 305:2
plackets hand out of p. SHAK 715:26
placuisse Principibus p. viris HORA 410:13
plafond lignes du p. ÉLUA 314:8
plagiaire l'état de p. MUSS 566:9
plagiarism from one author, it's p.
MIZN 551:12
plagiarist situation of the p. MUSS 566:9
plagiarize P.! Let no one else's work
LEHR 488:2
plague foulest p. of all AESC 8:32
instruments to p. us SHAK 717:3
p. and pestilence NASH 569:3
p. come nigh thy dwelling BOOK 146:2
p. making us cruel PEPY 603:11
p. o' both your houses SHAK 732:23
p. the inventor SHAK 719:7
that's his p. BURT 181:14
plagues Great p. remain BOOK 141:17
of all p. DEFO 271:3
omit those two main p. BURT 181:11
plain best p. set BACO 46:8
Books will speak p. BACO 46:16
darkling p. ARNO 29:6
divine p. face LAMB 477:9
Gromboolian p. LEAR 485:17
make it p. upon tables BIBL 96:16
Make thy way p. BOOK 139:18
making things p. HUXL 423:11
no p. women on television FORD 336:15
penny p. and twopence coloured STEV 775:19
pint of p. O'BR 583:5
p., blunt man SHAK 713:11
'p.' cooking cannot be entrusted MORP 560:5
P. in thy neatness HORA 411:10
p. Kate SHAK 733:6
P. living and high thinking WORD 867:20
p. Michael Faraday FARA 323:9
P. women he regarded ELIO 307:23
pricking on the p. SPEN 767:2
rough places p. BIBL 93:15
truth for p. people WESL 847:21
plainness Manifest p. LAO 479:11
perfect p. of speech ARNO 32:9
plains flowery p. of honour JONS 446:10
ringing p. of windy Troy TENN 800:15
plaintive p. treble DISR 284:12
plaire n'est pas de p. MOLI 552:3
plaisir P. d'amour FLOR 335:23
plaister p. of the wall BIBL 95:24
plan by his p. of attack SASS 682:11
coherent p. to the universe HOYL 417:12
cunning p. CATC 208:4
no p. of operations reaches MOLT 553:5
no p. survives first contact MISQ 548:12
p. the future by the past BURK 172:17
rest on its original p. BURK 173:2
wagon of his 'P.' PAST 598:21
plane It's a p. ANON 17:4
only two emotions in a p. WELL 846:3
planet born under a rhyming p. SHAK 728:1
hanging from a round p. EDDI 302:17
Jove's p. BROW 166:1
new p. swims into his ken KEAT 456:15

planetary p. influence — SHAK 714:24
planets chronicle of the p. — YEVT 876:4
people p. of its own — BYRO 189:28
p. circle other suns — POPE 616:16
p. in their stations — MILT 543:28
stars and all the p. — TRUM 817:15
plank landing on a p. — EDDI 302:17
planned man who has p. badly — HERO 395:11
order of the acts is p. — PAST 598:19
p. obsolescence — STEV 773:21
planning Failure of p. — HARE 382:6
p. is indispensable — EISE 306:10
plans no fixed p. — LAO 480:1
p. are useless — EISE 306:10
plant Fame is no p. — MILT 540:8
I p. lines — WALC 835:17
p. for your heirs — PROV 646:6
p. of rapid growth — WASH 840:20
Sensitive P. — SHEL 746:8
That busy p. — HERB 394:8
time to p. — BIBL 89:23
What is a weed? A p. — EMER 315:11
Plantagenet where is P. — CREW 259:19
planted I have p. — BIBL 111:26
What our forefathers p. — WITH 861:5
planter house of the p. — CLAR 233:17
Ulsterman, of p. stock — HEWI 397:16
planting p. my cabbages — MONT 554:22
plants as the young p. — BOOK 149:24
forced p. — JOHN 442:29
He that p. trees — FULL 346:16
p. suck in the earth — COWL 254:8
talk to the p. — CHAR 217:15
plasterer agog at the p. — HEAN 387:5
plasters p., pills, and ointment — LOCK 498:2
plastics p., Picasso, sunbathing — WAUG 842:16
platinum bullets made of p. — BELL 67:18
eyebrows made of p. — FORS 337:15
platitude echo of a p. — BIER 121:3
longitude with no p. — FRY 345:17
p. is simply a truth repeated — BALD 53:3
stroke a p. until it purrs — MARQ 523:18
platitudes orchestration of p. — WILD 856:19
Plato attachment à la P. — GILB 357:20
be wrong with P. — CICE 232:11
P. is dear to me — ARIS 28:8
P.'s retirement — MILT 544:26
P., thou reason'st well — ADDI 4:20
p. told him: he couldn't — CUMM 262:8
series of footnotes to P. — WHIT 851:12
This is P.'s man — DIOG 283:15
plaudits p. of the throng — LONG 499:13
plausible neat, p., and wrong — MENC 531:23
plausibly p. maintained — BURR 180:13
play all the p., the insight — BROW 164:20
All work and no p. — PROV 626:23
better at a p. — ANON 17:10
Better than a p. — CHAR 217:2
boys late at their p. — ARNO 30:5
cannot p. well — BACO 46:17
children at p. — MONT 554:25
come out to p. — NURS 578:3
Did that p. of mine send out — YEAT 874:4
Fair p.'s a jewel — PROV 632:1
Games people p. — BERN 74:7
good p. needs no epilogue — SHAK 698:1
holdeth children from p. — SIDN 751:6
I could p. Ercles rarely — SHAK 725:27
If you p. with fire — PROV 635:31
Judge not the p. — QUAR 651:8
Kings would not p. at — COWP 256:25
let me not p. a woman — SHAK 725:29
little victims p. — GRAY 370:11
may now sit and p. — ASTL 35:1
only to p. fair — LABO 474:14
our p. is played out — THAC 803:7
p. began to disgust — EVEL 321:21
p. in Peoria — POLI 612:24
P. it again, Sam — FILM 328:14
P. it again, Sam — MISQ 548:14
p. it over again — LAMB 477:14

p.'s the thing — SHAK 701:25
p. the game — NEWB 571:12
p. things as they are — STEV 774:6
p. with my cat — MONT 555:14
p. without a woman — KYD 474:12
p. with souls — BROW 166:11
p. with the gypsies — NURS 580:7
presents you with a p. — BOOT 151:4
rest of the p. — PASC 598:2
some foul p. — SHAK 699:30
than see a p. — BURT 181:18
very dull p. — CONG 247:17
work, rest and p. — ADVE 8:3
wouldst not p. false — SHAK 718:19
written a damned p. — REYN 658:16
y is p. — EINS 305:14
Your p.'s hard to act — CHEK 221:22
You would p. upon me — SHAK 702:26
playbills time to read p. — BURN 176:24
playboy lost the only P. — SYNG 786:10
played He p. the King — FIEL 326:5
p. the fool — BIBL 84:10
playedst p. most foully for't — SHAK 720:22
player as strikes the p. — FITZ 331:22
p. on the other side — HUXL 423:10
poor p., That struts — SHAK 722:22
wrapped in a p.'s hide — GREE 372:1
players men and women merely p. — SHAK 696:27
P., Sir! I look — JOHN 441:21
see the p. well bestowed — SHAK 701:17
playing stood like a p. card — MAIL 516:10
won on the p. fields — WELL 846:13
work terribly hard at p. — MORT 562:1
plays English p. are like — VOLT 835:5
He that p. the king — SHAK 701:12
loves no p. — SHAK 711:24
Man p. only when — SCHI 686:2
Shaw's p. — AGAT 9:7
plaything child's a p. — LAMB 477:1
little p.-house — WALP 837:9
Plaza Toro Duke of P. — GILB 356:10
plea Though justice be thy p. — SHAK 724:30
without one p. — ELLI 313:14
pleasance Youth is full of p. — SHAK 737:10
pleasant abridgement of all that was p. — GOLD 364:19
completed labours are p. — CICE 231:17
do not find anything p. — VOLT 833:11
green and p. bowers — BLAK 125:18
green and p. land — BLAK 126:24
in p. places — BOOK 140:3
joyful and p. thing — BOOK 150:6
Life would be very p. — SURT 781:15
p. and clean work — RUSK 673:19
p. it is to have money — CLOU 236:19
P. to know Mr Lear — LEAR 486:3
p. to them that — ELIZ 312:11
something p. happens — MONT 556:13
that p. land — BOOK 147:13
pleasantness ways are ways of p. — BIBL 87:23
please can't p. everyone — PROV 647:44
circumstance to p. us — SWIF 784:8
do what I p. — FRED 342:4
Little things p. — PROV 637:46
live to p. — JOHN 438:3
Myself alone I seek to p. — GAY 351:18
never fails to p. — SEDL 690:19
Nothing can p. many — JOHN 437:1
only Self to p. — BLAK 127:18
p. thee with my answer — SHAK 724:26
p. the touchy breed of poets — HORA 411:1
P. your eye — PROV 641:39
those whom I wished to p. — JOHN 439:10
To tax and to p. — BURK 173:8
'twas natural to p. — DRYD 294:9
pleased consists in being p. — HAZL 386:10
have p. leading men — HORA 410:13
in whom I am well p. — BIBL 98:19
more had p. us — ADDI 4:9
p. not the million — SHAK 701:16
p. with what he gets — SHAK 696:23

pleases every prospect p. — HEBE 388:9
pleaseth this age best p. me — HERR 396:8
pleasing art of p. — HAZL 386:10
method that I know of p. — CHES 223:3
nothing more p. — CICE 231:22
p. one intelligent man — MAIM 516:13
turns to p. pain — SPEN 767:18
pleasure aching P. nigh — KEAT 456:1
aspires not to p. — ARIS 27:12
Business before p. — PROV 628:27
by their favourite p. — VIRG 831:20
cabinet of p. — HERB 394:16
doth ever add p. — BACO 48:11
egg by p. laid — COWP 255:26
fading p. — SIDN 751:2
fine p. is not to do — HOPK 408:11
fool bolts p. — ANTR 24:20
For physical p. — WAUG 843:2
for thy p. — BIBL 118:6
full of p. — CHAL 213:19
give p. — MOLI 552:3
giving immediate p. — WORD 870:2
go to my p., business — WYCH 871:11
go to sea for p. — PROV 634:16
greatest p. I know — LAMB 477:12
great source of p. — JOHN 436:17
Green p. or grey grief — SWIN 786:2
harmless p. — JOHN 436:27
heart with p. fills — WORD 866:8
If they have p. — BARC 58:5
if this is p. — COWA 253:11
impression of p. — BACO 45:5
I' the east my p. lies — SHAK 695:3
left you for their p. — BROW 167:27
little p. in the house — MICK 534:6
Love ceases to be a p. — BEHN 66:20
make poetry and give p. — HORA 413:14
meant by the p. of life — TALL 788:18
miss for p. — GAY 351:27
mixed profit with p. — HORA 409:12
no p. in the strength — BOOK 150:7
No p., nor no pain — SEDL 690:16
not in p. — DRYD 296:4
on p. she was bent — COWP 255:10
painful p. — SPEN 767:18
pay a debt to p. — ROCH 664:10
p. after pain — DRYD 295:5
p. afterwards — THAC 802:21
p. and repentance — RALE 653:14
P. at the helm — GRAY 369:22
P. chews and grinds — MONT 555:19
p. in poetic pains — COWP 256:11
p. in recalling — CATU 211:1
p. in the pathless woods — BYRO 187:1
p. is momentary — CHES 223:21
p. is not enhanced — AUST 41:7
P. is nothing else — SELD 691:17
p. lives in height — TENN 799:20
p. me in his top-boots — MARL 522:2
P. never is at home — KEAT 454:18
p. of gods and mortals — LUCR 504:3
P.'s a sin — BYRO 188:2
p.'s done — SOUT 764:5
P.'s for those who are bad — YESE 875:21
p. so exquisite — HUNT 421:18
p. sure, In being mad — DRYD 296:31
p. to learn — CONF 245:12
p. to the spectators — MACA 507:20
p. was his business — EDGE 303:10
privilege and p. — GILB 356:12
read without p. — JOHN 445:1
secondary p. — STEN 771:20
Short p. — SCOT 687:17
soul of p. — BEHN 67:4
stately p.-dome decree — COLE 240:4
suburbs Of your good p. — SHAK 712:10
sum total of p. — BRIL 157:11
taking a p. — CHAR 217:3
to p. all they find — GREE 371:9
type of a perfect p. — WILD 855:19
Without one p. — TENN 797:16
Youth and P. meet — BYRO 186:6
pleasures all the p. prove — MARL 522:20

celibacy has no p. JOHN 437:17
childish p. ALAI 10:11
deprive us of all the p. HAYW 385:17
English take their p. SULL 780:7
fool who delights in p. JAIN 427:17
hate the idle p. SHAK 731:13
here below for minor p. GRES 372:12
hypocrite in his p. JOHN 444:4
less we indulge our p. JUVE 451:18
lords have their p. MONT 556:5
owes its p. COWP 256:17
paucity of human p. JOHN 444:20
p. and palaces PAYN 600:11
p. are like poppies BURN 179:15
p. of discourse PLAT 608:20
p. of sense BHAG 78:2
purest of human p. BACO 47:2
renounced those p. SOCR 760:4
some new p. prove DONN 288:26
Summers p. they are gone CLAR 233:4
tear our p. MARV 525:14
two supreme p. ROSE 668:13
understand the p. AUST 41:4
yesterday's p. DONN 290:11
plebeian this the P. bran DONN 290:9
plectuntur p. Achivi HORA 410:3
pledge I will p. with mine JONS 446:20
p. allegiance BELL 67:15
pledged p. their troth BOOK 139:4
Pleiades influences of P. BIBL 87:12
pleni P. sunt coeli MISS 549:16
plenteously p. bringing forth BOOK 136:13
plenteousness all things living with p.
BOOK 150:2
p. with thy palaces BOOK 148:20
plenty but just had p. BURN 177:27
expectation of p. SHAK 720:11
here is God's p. DRYD 297:20
In delay there lies no p. SHAK 735:9
P. has made me poor OVID 590:11
P. in the maize TENN 799:21
Where P. smiles CRAB 258:8
pleuré quelquefois p. MUSS 566:11
pleut il p. sa ville VERL 826:13
pli sans un p. ROST 670:3
plie Je p. et ne romps pas LA F 475:13
taking their p. BURG 172:13
plight p. thee my troth BOOK 139:1
plods ploughman homeward p. GRAY 370:1
plot discerned in history a p. FISH 327:19
Gunpowder Treason and P. ANON 19:20
now the p. thickens BUCK 169:20
p. for a short story CHEK 222:1
Sonnet's scanty p. WORD 866:20
This blessèd p. SHAK 730:11
What is the p. good for BUCK 169:19
plots All my plays' p. CAVE 211:17
P., true or false DRYD 294:10
plough boy that driveth the p. TYND 821:6
plod behind the p. CRAB 258:5
p. my furrow alone ROSE 668:12
p. the fields CAMP 194:15
put his hand to the p. BIBL 104:28
wherefore p. SHEL 746:11
ploughed p. with my heifer BIBL 83:13
ploughman heavy p. snores SHAK 727:10
p. and professor JEFF 430:14
p. homeward plods GRAY 370:1
wrong even the poorest p. CHAR 216:18
ploughs p., ladies, bears CANN 197:9
ploughshare Soldiers of the p. RUSK 674:7
ploughshares swords into p. BIBL 91:21
plowers p. plowed upon my back BOOK 149:6
pluck I'll p. it down SHAK 710:9
p. it out BIBL 102:2
p. till time and times are done YEAT 874:24
plucked p. my nipple SHAK 719:15
plum biscuit, or confectionary p. COWP 255:21
buy a p. bun NURS 582:5
p. year, a dumb year PROV 628:45
pulled out a p. NURS 579:18
Some gave them p. cake NURS 579:15
plumage pities the p. PAIN 592:19

plumber choose to be a p. EINS 305:17
plumbers good p. NIXO 576:13
plume blast-beruffled p. HARD 381:14
p. themselves WOLL 863:9
Ruffles her pure cold p. TENN 794:28
plummet did ever p. sound SHAK 734:2
plums p. and orange peel RALE 654:17
plunder no man stop to p. MACA 508:9
What a place to p. MISQ 549:3
plures Abiit ad p. PETR 605:6
plus Il n'y a p. de Pyrénées LOUI 501:6
P. ça change KARR 453:8
Plutonian Night's P. shore POE 611:2
Plymouth dreamin' arl the time o' P. Hoe
NEWB 571:9
poacher old p. makes the best PROV 640:31
p. staggering MCCA 509:3
Pobble P. who has no toes LEAR 486:9
pocket guinea you have in your p. RUSK 674:6
gun in your p. WEST 848:16
hand in its breeches p. KEAT 457:18
in Britain, in your p. WILS 859:7
in each other's p. BIER 121:2
lost her p. NURS 580:3
not scruple to pick a p. DENN 273:12
pecker in my p. JOHN 435:9
put it in his p. SHAK 703:15
two books in my p. STEV 775:11
pockets hands in holey p. RIMB 662:13
in the p. of the people GLAD 360:15
jingle in his p. COWP 257:5
no p. in which to store it OVID 589:16
Shrouds have no p. PROV 643:7
young man feels his p. HOUS 415:7
pocketses got in its p. TOLK 813:3
poem begin a p. MCGO 511:1
being the author of that p. WOLF 862:17
drowsy frowzy p. BYRO 188:26
essentially the greatest p. WHIT 852:21
Even the simplest p. MITC 550:13
figure a p. makes FROS 345:5
heroic p. of its sort CARL 199:15
himself to be a true p. MILT 545:19
long p. is a test KEAT 457:11
many beauties grace a p. HORA 409:13
married to a p. KEAT 458:8
music of a p. SYNG 786:8
p. is like a painting HORA 409:15
p. is never finished VALÉ 823:10
p. lovely as a tree KILM 462:15
p. must ride on its own melting FROS 345:8
P. of the Sea RIMB 662:6
p. should be palpable MACL 512:4
p. should not mean but be MACL 512:6
p., whose subject CHAP 216:10
pretty p., Mr Pope BENT 72:2
write a p. after Auschwitz ADOR 6:10
poemata Scribimus indocti doctique p.
HORA 410:19
poems lesser p., of later growth JONS 447:6
no p. than bad poems LARK 481:16
P. are made by fools like me KILM 462:16
p. should be Clyde-built DUNN 299:17
we all scribble p. HORA 410:19
Poesie P. des Lebens GOET 362:10
poesis Ut pictura p. HORA 409:15
poesy call p. vinum daemonum BACO 45:17
overwhelm Myself in p. KEAT 456:18
P. was ever thought BACO 45:11
viewless wings of P. KEAT 456:7
poet All a p. can do is warn OWEN 591:2
and the P.'s dream WORD 865:9
ask a p. to sing BOLD 131:10
business of a comic p. CONG 246:24
business of a p. JOHN 437:14
dreams of a p. JOHN 435:19
every fool is not a p. POPE 614:14
every p., in his kind SWIF 784:4
Fat-head p. that nobody reads CHES 224:5
flattery lost on p.'s ear SCOT 688:12
found no sacred p. ELIO 307:18
grete p. of Ytaille CHAU 219:22
hate what every p. hates KAVA 453:16

have a p. able-bodied MACN 513:16
Honour the greatest p. DANT 264:16
Is this the great p. GARR 349:13
I was a p., I was young FLEC 334:14
lack their sacred p. HORA 414:3
Like a P. hidden SHEL 746:22
limbs of a p. HORA 414:13
Love made me p. EPIT 319:1
lover, and the p. SHAK 727:2
masculine part, the p. in me BEHN 66:21
modern p.'s fate HOOD 406:3
never be a p. DRYD 297:26
No p. ever interpreted GIRA 359:9
Not deep the P. sees ARNO 30:2
Now, children, the p. FANT 323:5
P. and Saint COWL 254:19
p. and the dreamer KEAT 454:17
p. and the theme COWP 257:3
p. as an idea SCHI 686:3
p. image aught so fair THOM 808:22
p. includes a critic SHEN 747:22
p. is like the prince BAUD 61:9
p. is the priest STEV 773:22
p. kings KEAT 456:20
p. ranks far below the painter LEON 489:23
p. seems most himself YEAT 875:13
p.'s eye, in a fine frenzy SHAK 727:3
p.'s gift is to soothe YESE 875:20
p.'s hope: to be AUDE 38:10
p.'s inward pride DAY- 269:8
p.'s mouth be shut YEAT 874:8
p.'s pen, all scorn BRAD 154:11
p. spewed up a good lump DRYD 297:23
p. stubborn with his passion YEAT 872:9
p. will give up writing CELA 212:12
P. writes under one restriction WORD 870:2
poor p. named Clough SWIN 786:3
possess a p.'s brain DRAY 293:17
skilled p. PIND 606:17
starved p. LOCK 498:2
there is a p. indulging MAHO 516:7
war p. whose right of honour GURN 374:17
was a true P. BLAK 126:3
what is left the p. here BYRO 188:23
poetae Etiam disiecti membra p. HORA 414:13
poète p. est semblable BAUD 61:9
poetic constitutes p. faith COLE 241:21
nurse for a p. child SCOT 688:16
P. Genius of my country BURN 180:11
P. Justice POPE 611:14
P. LICENCE BANV 57:15
poetical As to the p. character KEAT 458:3
claim to p. honours JOHN 436:22
poetis Mediocribus esse p. HORA 409:16
Pictoribus atque p. HORA 408:15
poetry best piece of p. JONS 446:17
bother about p. COCT 238:1
by no means rank p. BYRO 191:25
campaign in p. CUOM 262:18
car was p. and tragedy LEWI 492:13
cradled into p. by wrong SHEL 744:12
dead art Of p. POUN 621:2
drops into p. DICK 280:8
Emptied of its p. AUDE 37:10
give p. a proper flow BOIL 131:2
grand style arises in p. ARNO 32:10
I can repeat p. CARR 203:14
If p. comes not KEAT 457:20
Ireland hurt you into p. AUDE 37:8
It is not p. POPE 614:21
Language is fossil p. EMER 315:10
language of p. GRAY 371:1
misfortune of p. AUST 42:2
most p. ignores most people MITC 550:12
neither p. nor any thing else BYRO 192:10
no more define p. HOUS 416:13
p. administers to the effect SHEL 747:11
p. almost necessarily declines MACA 507:1
p. begins to atrophy POUN 621:13
P. belongs to those who use SKAR 753:19
p. in money GRAV 369:15
p. in motion KAUF 453:11
P., in the most comprehensive HUNT 421:12

poetry (cont.):
P. is a subject as precise — FLAU 334:2
P. is at bottom — ARNO 31:25
P. is a way — FROS 345:9
[P.] is capable of saving us — RICH 660:10
P. is certainly something more — COLE 242:5
P. is devil's wine — AUGU 39:12
p. is eloquent painting — SIMO 752:17
P. is in the pity — OWEN 591:1
p. is more philosophical — ARIS 27:21
P. is not most important — THOM 806:15
P. is pre-eminently the medium — FLAU 333:14
P. is the achievement — SAND 680:8
P. is the breath — WORD 870:4
P. is the language — FRY 345:20
P. is the record of the best — SHEL 747:13
P. is the spontaneous overflow — WORD 870:3
P. is the supreme fiction — STEV 774:5
P. is what is lost — FROS 345:12
P. is when some of them — BENT 71:13
p. makes nothing happen — AUDE 37:9
P. must be *as well written* — POUN 621:16
p. of earth — KEAT 456:17
p. of life — GOET 362:10
p. of motion — GRAH 368:2
p., prophecy, and religion — RUSK 673:13
P.'s a mere drug — FARQ 324:12
P.'s another word — DURC 300:9
P. shall tune her sacred voice — JOHN 437:25
P. should be great — KEAT 457:18
P.'s the feverish fit — WINC 860:4
p. = the *best* words — COLE 242:3
P. there, is an art — SIDN 751:5
P. Unearths from among the dead — HILL 398:11
P. wants something — DIDE 282:11
p., which is in Oxford — DRYD 296:23
P., which is perfection's — WALC 835:16
polar star of p. — KEAT 457:11
quarrel with ourselves, p. — YEAT 875:12
saying it and that is p. — CAGE 193:4
saying so In whining p. — DONN 289:19
She that with p. is won — BUTL 183:20
Sir, what is p. — JOHN 442:6
stimulated by p. — CONF 246:8
That I make p. — HORA 413:14
their p. is conceived — ARNO 31:24
trying to say was p. — OVID 590:20
turn to p. — ARNO 31:23
We hate p. that has — KEAT 457:18
What is p. — RUSK 673:9
Writing a book of p. — MARQ 523:17

poets All p. are mad — BURT 181:8
amatory p. sing — BYRO 189:4
for p. made — HUNT 421:10
for wits, then p. passed — POPE 615:25
Greek, Latin p. — CAVE 211:17
if there's room for p. — BROW 163:24
impossible to hold the p. back — GIRA 359:8
Irish p., learn your trade — YEAT 875:7
mature p. steal — ELIO 311:22
mighty P. in their misery — WORD 868:24
No death has hurt p. more — HEAN 388:1
only p. know — COWP 256:11
Painters and p. — HORA 408:15
p. and wine at home — MANI 519:6
P. are the hierophants — SHEL 747:14
p. are their own patients — THOM 807:6
p. being second-rate — HORA 409:16
p. bicycle-pump the human heart — AMIS 14:14
P.' food is love — SHEL 744:3
P. must be *difficult* — ELIO 311:25
p. only deliver a golden — SIDN 751:4
p. talk of cottages — COWP 257:7
P. that are sown — WORD 865:11
P. that lasting marble seek — WALL 836:19
P. . . . though liars — HUME 420:17
p. witty — BACO 48:3
powerful p. of the century — ELIO 311:24
prince of p. — BYRO 188:25
romantic p. — LEAP 485:11
Souls of p. dead — KEAT 455:15
Tenderest of Roman p. — TENN 793:14
theft in other p. — DRYD 297:16

think all p. were Byronic — COPE 251:7
touchy breed of p. — HORA 411:1
We p. in our youth — WORD 868:23
who wants p. at all — HÖLD 403:2
worst of p. ranks — CATU 210:12
youthful p. dream — MILT 539:31
point different p. of view — NAPO 567:15
from p. to point — TENN 797:2
p. a moral — JOHN 438:8
still p. of the turning world — ELIO 309:6
upon a needle's p. — CUDW 261:15
Up to a p., Lord Copper — WAUG 842:18
You've hit the p. — PLAU 609:10
points P. have no parts — LIND 494:13
poising p. every weight — MARV 525:1
poison administer a p. to anybody — HIPP 399:17
another man's p. — PROV 641:8
food only a cover for p. — BURK 175:3
got as far as p.-gas — HARD 381:10
honey of p.-flowers — TENN 797:20
if you p. us — SHAK 724:19
p. in jest — SHAK 702:23
p. the wells — NEWM 571:15
p. the whole blood stream fills — EMPS 315:27
p. wells — MARL 522:18
put p. in your coffee — CHUR 231:4
strongest p. ever known — BLAK 124:16
tell them to drink the p. — PLAT 608:17
Turning to p. — KEAT 456:1
poisoned p. rat in a hole — SWIF 783:1
poisoning P. pigeons — LEHR 488:3
poisonous for its p. wine — KEAT 455:26
p. reptiles to live in it — GIRA 359:7
poisons well of p. — GIRA 359:6
poke p. poor Billy — GRAH 367:15
poker p. of whom every one is afraid — MITF 551:6
pokers p. into true-love knots — COLE 240:11
polar p. star of poetry — KEAT 457:11
pole curses from p. to pole — BLAK 125:6
from pole to p. — COLE 241:4
top of the greasy p. — DISR 286:21
polecat semi-house-trained p. — FOOT 336:9
poles explored the P. — JOHN 434:15
police among p. officers — ORTO 586:14
citizen or the p. — AUDE 38:7
friendship recognised by the p. — STEV 775:29
p. can beat you — SHAW 741:30
p. were to blame — GRAN 368:3
policeman p. and a pretty girl — CHAP 215:18
p.'s lot — GILB 358:8
terrorist and the p. — CONR 249:8
than a p. — SALI 679:4
would not do for a p. — NIGH 576:5
policy English p. is to float — SALI 678:13
foreign p. — COOK 250:11
home p.: I wage war — CLEM 235:7
Honesty is the best p. — PROV 634:39
Honesty is the best p. — WHAT 849:17
If the p. isn't hurting — MAJO 517:3
My [foreign] p. — BEVI 77:11
national p. — BRIA 156:15
p. of the good neighbour — ROOS 667:5
religion or p. — RUSK 673:27
rugged brow of careful P. — SPEN 766:19
tyrants from p. — BURK 174:11
polish contented to p. — MORE 559:1
p. it at leisure — DRYD 297:11
polished I p. up the handle — GILB 357:28
O p. perturbation — SHAK 707:27
p. corners of the temple — BOOK 149:24
p. dry with pumice — CATU 210:1
p. female friend — WHUR 853:7
polite no allies to be p. to — GEOR 353:6
p. meaningless words — YEAT 873:6
time to be p. — MONT 556:6
politeness glance of great p. — BYRO 191:15
oil of refined p. — COLE 242:18
pineapple of p. — SHER 748:12
p. of kings — LOUI 501:11
p. of princes — PROV 642:11
suave p. — KNOX 470:3
political fear of P. Economy — SELL 692:5

half your p. life — THAT 803:18
healthy state of p. life — MILL 536:6
highest p. end — ACTO 1:15
meanings in p. terms — MANN 520:5
my p. creed — ADAM 3:9
personal is p. — POLI 613:6
points to a p. career — SHAW 740:18
p. animal — ARIS 27:24
p. Cave of Adullam — BRIG 157:5
p. consequences — MANS 520:10
p. economist — BAGE 51:10
p. genius — TAYL 791:13
p. intriguer — TROL 816:2
P. language . . . is designed — ORWE 588:2
p. lives end in failure — POWE 622:6
p. power of another — LOCK 497:15
p. speech and writing — ORWE 588:1
P. thought, in France — ARON 32:18
p. will — LYNN 506:2
Principles of P. Economy — BENT 71:17
schemes of p. improvement — JOHN 440:19
true p. freedom — SCHI 685:27
politician like a scurvy p. — SHAK 716:21
lurks a p. — ARIS 26:20
makes the p. wise — POPE 618:14
pate of a p. — SHAK 704:13
p. is a man — TRUM 817:20
p. is an arse upon — CUMM 262:7
p. never believes what he says — DE G 271:14
p. ought to sacrifice — BURK 174:25
P.'s corpse — BELL 68:7
p. to complain about — POWE 622:5
p. tops his part — GAY 351:20
p. urges them to rebel — PERU 604:14
p. was a person — LLOY 496:19
popular p. — ARIS 26:18
when a p. does get an idea — MARQ 523:16
wise p. — OLIV 585:1
politicians die for p. — THOM 808:5
Old p. chew — POPE 615:18
P. also have no leisure — ARIS 27:15
p. hear the word 'culture' — ESHE 320:9
too serious to be left to p. — DE G 271:11
whole race of p. — SWIF 782:9
politics Confound their p. — SONG 762:10
continuation of p. — CLAU 234:11
first part of p. — MICH 534:3
From p., it was an easy step — AUST 41:22
In p., if you want anything — THAT 803:12
in p. the middle way — ADAM 3:3
In p., there is no use — CHAM 214:1
In p., what begins in fear — COLE 242:7
invisible hand in p. — FRIE 343:9
I taste no p. — SMIT 758:6
language of p. — DISR 284:15
Magnanimity in p. — BURK 173:24
mule of p. — DISR 285:19
no true friends in p. — CLAR 233:11
Philistine of genius in p. — ARNO 32:6
playful moderation in p. — HUNT 421:14
p. and equations — EINS 306:3
P. and the fate — CAMU 196:4
P. are now nothing more — JOHN 441:20
P., as a practice — ADAM 2:10
P., executive expression — BRIT 157:13
p. grease — TAWN 791:1
P. in the middle — STEN 771:19
P. is not the art — GALB 347:15
p. is present history — FREE 342:6
P. is the art of preventing — VALÉ 823:14
P. is the Art of the Possible — BUTL 183:5
P. is the only profession — STEV 775:8
p. is war without bloodshed — MAO 521:2
p. like ours profess — GREE 371:6
P. makes strange — PROV 641:40
p. of happiness — HUMP 421:2
p. of the left — JENK 432:19
P. supposed to be — REAG 656:11
P. too serious a matter — DE G 271:11
practice of p. — DISR 285:24
science of p. — ARIS 27:6
secret of p. — BISM 122:15
solve that problem of p. — SCHI 685:26

p. doth reign — MACA 508:8
P. for ever — BOOK 147:20
p. of the invisible — STEV 773:22
p. of the Muses — HORA 412:14
p. persuades humble people — PERU 604:14
religion from the p. — GOLD 365:16
rid me of this turbulent p. — HENR 392:1
'twixt the P. and Clerk — HERR 396:4
priesthood royal p. — BIBL 117:3
priests beheaded p. — HENR 392:4
dominion of p. — PRIC 622:15
P., and Deacons — BOOK 134:22
p. by the imposition — MACA 507:3
p. have been enemies — HUME 420:8
p. on their way to bury — BOCC 130:5
treen p. — JEWE 433:18
with the guts of p. — MESL 533:7
priggish p. schoolgirl — GRIG 373:6
prigs p. and pedants — DISR 284:17
prime arrive at a p. mover — THOM 805:8
having lost but once your p. — HERR 396:18
My p. of youth — TICH 811:2
One's p. is elusive — SPAR 765:11
spent my youthfu' p. — BURN 180:8
Prime Minister best P. we have — BUTL 183:3
buried the Unknown P. — ASQU 34:6
HOW DARE YOU BECOME P. — BONH 132:9
model of a modern P. — HENN 391:16
next P. but three — BELL 68:2
No woman will be P. — THAT 803:11
P. has resigned — ANON 17:12
P. has to be a butcher — BUTL 183:4
P. is like the banyan — PATI 599:10
Prime Ministers P. have never yet been — CHUR 230:18
wild flowers, and P. — BALD 53:4
primerole She was a p. — CHAU 219:18
primeval forest p. — LONG 499:3
primitive p. nothing — ROCH 664:21
primrose go the p. way — SHAK 720:12
P. first born child — FLET 335:11
p. path of dalliance — SHAK 700:2
p. that forsaken dies — MILT 540:12
soft silken p. — MILT 540:19
withered p. — BOLT 131:22
Primrose Hill P. and Saint John's Wood — BLAK 125:13
primroses Pale p. — SHAK 737:2
prince Advise the p. — ELIO 310:11
bless the P. of Wales — LINL 495:6
danced with the P. of Wales — FARJ 323:13
dominion of a p. — HUME 420:7
draws sword against p. — PROV 647:20
Good-night, sweet p. — SHAK 705:4
Gorgon, P. of darkness — SPEN 767:4
great p. in prison lies — DONN 289:5
Hamlet without the P. — SCOT 689:25
in a p. the virtue — MASS 527:9
news and P. of Peace — FLET 335:15
p. among my own people — BRAN 155:5
P. calls in the good old money — LAMB 476:11
p. must be a fox — MACH 511:10
p. of Aquitaine — NERV 571:1
p. of darkness — SHAK 716:3
p. of glory died — WATT 842:2
P. of Peace — BIBL 92:14
P. of Wales not a position — BENN 70:12
p. sets himself up above the law — MAYH 529:9
p. who begins early — BAGE 51:7
p. who gets a reputation — NAPO 567:14
safer for a p. — MACH 511:7
send the companion a better p. — SHAK 707:8
Who made thee a p. — BIBL 80:31
princedoms p., virtues — MILT 543:22
princes death of p. — SHAK 712:12
inform his p. — BOOK 147:12
like one of the p. — BOOK 145:12
mine were p. of the earth — BENJ 69:18
P. and lords may flourish — GOLD 364:2
p. and monarchs dance — HALL 378:1
p. are come home again — SHAK 714:15
p. in all lands — BOOK 142:16
teachers of p. — FRED 341:20

trust in p. — BOOK 150:3
princess People's P. — BLAI 123:20
P. leave the Englishwoman — BISM 122:14
P. of Parallelograms — BYRO 191:22
P. of Wales — AUST 43:1
see she was a real p. — ANDE 15:8
principalities against p. — BIBL 114:15
angels, nor p. — BIBL 111:7
p., or powers — BIBL 115:7
principate p. and liberty — TACI 786:18
principibus P. placuisse viris — HORA 410:13
principiis P. obsta — OVID 590:16
principio In p. erat Verbum — MISS 550:2
principis Indignatio p. mors est — MORE 559:10
principle active P. — WORD 865:17
does everything on p. — SHAW 741:29
feel the p. of God — FOX 339:17
little of the p. left — REIT 658:2
precedent embalms a p. — STOW 778:9
p. of all social progress — FOUR 339:4
p. of the English law — DICK 276:21
Protection is not a p. — DISR 284:8
rebels from p. — BURK 174:11
useful thing about a p. — MAUG 528:6
principles bloody p. and practices — FOX 339:18
Damn your p. — DISR 286:18
denies the first p. — AUCT 36:10
either morals or p. — GLAD 360:5
embrace your Lordship's p. — WILK 856:22
fundamental p. are thirteen — MAIM 516:12
he has good p. — JOHN 439:18
p. are the same — JOHN 443:10
p. have no real force — TWAI 820:3
print devils must p. — MOOR 558:5
eternity of p. — WOOL 864:3
fit to p. — ADVE 7:4
licence to p. money — THOM 809:1
love a ballad in p. — SHAK 737:5
p. My book — HERR 396:16
p. of a man's naked foot — DEFO 270:13
p. the legend — FILM 329:24
p. the myth — JOHN 434:16
rambling brat (in p.) — BRAD 154:10
say in p. — ROBI 663:17
when you read the fine p. — SEEG 691:3
printing caused p. to be used — SHAK 710:3
Gunpowder, P. — CARL 199:22
invented the art of p. — CARL 200:18
p., gunpowder — BACO 49:3
p. house in Hell — BLAK 126:23
regulate p. — MILT 545:26
printless clerical, p. toe — BROO 159:8
set my p. feet — MILT 539:12
priorities language of p. — BEVA 76:14
p. have gone all wrong — BEVA 77:1
prisca Ut p. gens mortalium — HORA 411:3
prism his p., and silent face — WORD 868:13
prunes and p. — DICK 278:16
prison at home in p. — WAUG 842:13
born in p. — MALC 517:9
Come, let's away to p. — SHAK 716:26
do not a p. make — LOVE 502:5
forever p.-pent — WOLF 862:19
great prince in p. lies — DONN 289:5
grind in the p. house — BIBL 83:18
hero from p. — AYTO 44:6
Home is the girl's p. — SHAW 741:23
in p., and ye came unto me — BIBL 103:6
is also a p. — THOR 809:4
lime-tree bower my p. — COLE 241:13
looseth men out of p. — BOOK 150:4
mourn in p. — MONT 554:7
only a p. — CUST 263:13
opening of the p. — BIBL 94:19
palace and a p. on each hand — BYRO 186:15
p. and a smile — WOTT 870:10
prison in a p. — DICK 280:24
p. is a holy place — BYRO 191:2
p. of his days — AUDE 37:13
seeks to adorn its p. — WOLL 863:13
Shades of the p.-house — WORD 867:8
ship but a p. — BURT 181:16
So cruel p. — SURR 780:16

while there is a soul in p. — DEBS 270:3
wider p. unto me — BYRO 190:23
world a vast p. — WOLL 863:16
world not a 'p. house' — ROBI 664:1
prisoner if the p. is happy — SHAW 741:7
object to your being taken p. — KITC 469:5
p. of the Lord — BIBL 114:4
takes the reason p. — SHAK 718:13
thoughts of a p. — SOLZ 760:14
prisoners all p. and captives — BOOK 134:24
p. call the sky — WILD 855:31
p. of addiction — ILLI 424:18
p. out of captivity — BOOK 144:7
weapons of all p. — COLE 242:14
prisons Madhouses, p. — CLAR 232:20
P. are built with stones — BLAK 126:12
privacy society of p. — RAND 655:1
private at a p. view — EDWA 304:3
consult our p. ends — SWIF 784:8
fine and p. place — MARV 525:13
Give me a p. station — GAY 351:21
his p. parts — BUTL 184:15
know nothing of their p. life — HEIN 389:14
my p. will — ELIZ 311:27
no p. life — ELIO 307:11
P. faces in public places — AUDE 37:22
p. life is a disgrace — ANON 20:3
P. Means is dead — SMIT 757:19
P. property is a necessary — TAWN 791:4
p. station — ADDI 4:19
p. will governs — ROBE 663:9
sphere of p. life — MELB 530:18
privates Faith, her p. — SHAK 701:8
privilege inestimable p. of man — SHEL 747:7
only extended p. — HILL 398:10
power which stands on P. — BELL 68:18
p. and pleasure — GILB 356:12
p. I claim — AUST 42:5
p. of seeing one another — JENY 433:2
p. to breathe — ELEA 306:14
p. to see so much — MOOR 557:20
privileged P. and the People — DISR 286:8
They were p. children — BROO 159:17
privileges p. you were born with — BROW 161:1
you will stand for your p. — HEMI 390:16
prize do not run for p. — SORL 761:23
lawful p. — GRAY 370:17
one receiveth the p. — BIBL 112:8
prized local, but p. elsewhere — AUDE 38:10
prizes all must have p. — CARR 201:15
glittering p. — SMIT 756:16
winners of the big p. — ORWE 587:15
probabilities Human p. are not sufficient — FAIR 322:15
probability p. is the very guide — BUTL 182:18
probable many sensations are p. — CICE 231:19
P. impossibilities — ARIS 27:22
that are not p. — AGAT 9:11
probationary Eden's dread p. tree — COWP 255:28
Probitas P. laudatur et alget — JUVE 450:12
problem All in all he's a p. — BURN 179:11
can't see the p. — CHES 225:15
Houston, we've had a p. — LOVE 502:9
part of the p. — SAYI 684:26
p. of the colour line — DU B 298:6
p.-solving minds — KAUN 453:13
p. that has no name — FRIE 343:6
p. that has no name — FRIE 343:8
refused to work at any p. — EDIS 303:16
such a difficult p. — DÜRR 301:1
three-pipe p. — DOYL 292:9
you're part of the p. — CLEA 235:4
problems Machines have less p. — WARH 840:4
p. as it can solve — MARX 526:4
P. worthy of attack — HEIN 389:6
procedure interstices of p. — MAIN 516:19
proceed just works do p. — BOOK 134:9
proceedeth p. from the Father — BOOK 137:3
proceedings subsequent p. — HART 383:17
process without p. of law — CONS 250:6
procession torchlight p. — O'SU 589:8
proclaims apparel oft p. the man — SHAK 700:4

prose All that is not p. MOLI 551:18
as well written as p. POUN 621:16
but p. run mad POPE 614:21
differs in nothing from p. GRAY 371:1
for p. and verse CARE 198:5
Good p. like a window-pane ORWE 586:20
govern in p. CUOM 262:18
harmony of p. DRYD 297:19
in p. or rhyme MILT 541:9
language of p. WORD 870:1
love others in p. PRIO 624:3
Meredith's a p. Browning WILD 855:2
Not verse now, only p. BROW 165:7
pin up my hair with p. CONG 247:22
p. and the passion FORS 338:3
p. is verse BYRO 190:2
P. is when all the lines BENT 71:13
P. was born yesterday FLAU 333:14
P. = words in their best order COLE 242:3
shut me up in p. DICK 282:1
speaking p. without knowing it MOLI 551:19
Stein's p.-song LEWI 492:16
Proserpine P. gathering flowers MILT 543:4
prospect every p. pleases HEBE 388:9
noblest p. JOHN 439:20
prospects undetermined p. ADDI 5:14
prosper I grow, I p. SHAK 714:23
sinners' ways p. HOPK 408:2
Treason doth never p. HARI 382:14
prospering puzzled and p. JEFF 432:5
prosperity day of p. BIBL 90:4
jest's p. SHAK 717:23
liberty and p. JENY 433:1
man to han ben in p. CHAU 221:5
man who can stand p. CARL 200:10
P. brings with it BALZ 56:13
P. doth best BACO 46:4
P. doth bewitch men WEBS 844:26
P. is the blessing BACO 46:2
wisdom in p. ERAS 320:6
prosperous make a nation p. BACO 49:12
prostitute doormat of p. WEST 848:23
prostitutes small nations like p. KUBR 474:2
prostitution banking and p. WRIG 870:17
prostrating bowing, p. KORA 473:2
protect p. a working-girl SMIT 756:15
p. the writer ACHE 1:14
two solitudes p. RILK 662:5
protection calls mutely for p. GREE 371:19
Grant me p. SIKH 752:1
mercy and p. BOOK 139:6
p. against war BEVI 77:10
P. is not a principle DISR 284:8
protector appoint to us a p. KORA 471:17
Friend and P. BARB 58:2
God, the p. BOOK 136:4
p. of the believers KORA 471:6
protest lady doth p. too much SHAK 702:22
Protestant Hitler attacked the P. church NIEM 575:8
I am the P. whore GWYN 375:3
live Thy P. to be HERR 396:12
P. counterpoint BEEC 65:14
p. ethic WEBE 843:13
P. Province of Ulster CARS 204:9
P. Religion CARL 199:22
P. with a horse BEHA 66:14
'tis a P. wind WHAR 849:12
Protestantism P., even the most cold BURK 173:14
Protestants in the hands of P. PUGI 649:6
religion of P. CHIL 226:6
Proteus sight of P. rising WORD 869:25
protoplasmal p. primordial globule GILB 357:2
protracted p. imprisonment of the accused HUME 421:1
p. my work JOHN 439:10
p. woe JOHN 438:9
proud all the p. and mighty have DYER 301:8
be an Indian and not be p. GAND 348:9
Death be not p. DONN 288:10
I have no p. looks BOOK 149:9
make death p. SHAK 695:22

mote ye lyve, and alle p. CHAU 220:28
p. and yet a wretched thing DAVI 267:19
proudest of the p. CHUR 228:17
p. if you'll be wise CHUD 227:19
p. in arms MILT 538:21
p. me no prouds SHAK 732:32
p. of his intelligence WEIL 845:5
p. of the fact RUSS 674:13
P. people breed sad sorrows BRON 158:18
scattered the p. BIBL 104:9
too p. for a wit GOLD 364:18
too p. to fight WILS 859:16
too p. to importune GRAY 370:23
prove chance to p. it MURR 566:2
I could p. everything PINT 607:1
O Lord, and p. me BOOK 141:6
P. all things BIBL 115:16
p. a lover SHAK 731:13
p. anything by figures CARL 199:5
p. me, and examine BOOK 149:20
p. our chance DRAY 293:19
to p. it I'm here CATC 208:11
proved God p. them BIBL 96:28
mighty soul was p. ADDI 4:10
p. me, and saw my works BOOK 146:8
p. most royally SHAK 705:6
you have p. to be HARD 381:17
Provence found it in P. WILL 858:12
proverb Israel shall be a p. BIBL 84:26
p. is one man's wit RUSS 675:21
proverbs Patch grief with p. SHAK 727:31
Solomon wrote the P. NAYL 569:5
proves exception p. the rule PROV 631:39
provide God will p. BIBL 80:1
goods the gods p. PROV 644:3
providence assert eternal p. MILT 541:10
Behind a frowning p. COWP 255:13
inscrutable workings of P. SMIT 756:19
P. had sent a few men RUMB 672:3
P. has not created TOCQ 812:8
P. on the side PROV 642:10
p. so ordereth MATH 527:16
P. their guide MILT 544:20
way that P. dictates HITL 400:8
provident They are p. instead BOGA 130:12
province all knowledge to be my p. BACO 48:24
Ireland should be a p. GOOL 366:2
p. they have desolated GLAD 360:2
provinces defending those p. SMIT 756:9
provincial He was worse than p. JAME 429:16
level of p. existence ELIO 308:6
provincialism taken in p. HUXL 422:12
proving pleasure in p. their falseness DARW 266:10
provision p. for the flesh BIBL 111:17
provocation as in the p. BOOK 146:8
p. I have had POPE 617:29
provoke fathers, p. not BIBL 114:12
provoker Drink, sir, is a great p. SHAK 720:13
provokes No one p. me MOTT 563:12
proximus *paries cum p. ardet* HORA 410:15
prudence effect of p. on rascality SHAW 741:18
forced into p. AUST 42:1
P. bring thee back CHUR 228:12
P. is a rich, ugly BLAK 126:5
P. is the other woman ANON 19:21
prudent every p. act BURK 173:18
mercenary and the p. AUST 42:15
p. man aspires not to pleasure ARIS 27:12
prudes p. for proctors TENN 799:3
pruner sorry p. RICH 660:16
prunes p. and prism DICK 278:16
pruninghooks spears into p. BIBL 91:21
prurient p. curiosity STOP 777:2
Prussia military domination of P. ASQU 34:4
national industry of P. MIRA 546:14
Prussian P., Or perhaps Ital-ian GILB 358:4
psalm practising the hundredth p. BYRO 191:17
p. of thanksgiving BOOK 146:12
Take the p. BOOK 145:11
psalmist sweet p. of Israel BIBL 84:23
psalms David wrote the P. NAYL 569:5

with p. BOOK 146:7
psaltery p., dulcimer BIBL 95:22
pseudopodium lonely p. SHIP 749:15
Psyche Your mournful P. KEAT 455:27
psychiatrist man who goes to a p. GOLD 365:21
psychic manifests all p. powers MAHĀ 516:3
psychological P. flaws ANON 19:22
psychotherapy waste money on p. TORK 814:1
puberty p. assisted BYRO 187:27
public as if I was a p. meeting VICT 827:12
assumes a p. trust JEFF 432:2
carry on great p. schemes BURK 176:10
complainers for the p. BURK 173:5
consult the p. good SWIF 782:11
Desolation in immaculate p. places ROET 665:6
English p. school WAUG 842:13
excites the p. odium CLAY 234:14
expense of p. interests TAYL 792:2
glorified p. relations man TRUM 817:16
hand into the p. purse PEEL 601:14
I and the p. know AUDE 38:5
Nor p. men YEAT 873:19
one p. which follows another CHAM 215:6
one to mislead the p. ASQU 34:7
precedence over p. relations FEYN 326:1
Private faces in p. places AUDE 37:22
p. and merited disgrace STEV 776:8
p. be damned VAND 824:2
P. Prayer in the Church BOOK 150:19
p. rallies around an idea ASIM 33:19
p. scandal that constitutes MOLI 552:24
p. school accent LEAV 486:18
P. schools are the nurseries FIEL 326:14
p. seldom forgive LAVA 483:8
p. thinks long JOHN 436:15
respect p. opinion RUSS 674:16
sound Of p. scorn MILT 544:11
tell the p. which way SULZ 780:8
vexes p. men TENN 801:4
what he thinks the p. wants REIT 658:1
wider p. life ELIO 307:11
publicans even the p. BIBL 99:8
p. and sinners BIBL 100:14
publications previous p. HILB 398:6
publicity Any p. is good publicity PROV 626:27
bad p. BEHA 66:18
channels of modern p. BUCH 169:8
eternal p. BENN 70:16
oxygen of p. THAT 803:23
p. is justly commended BRAN 155:2
P. is the very soul BENT 71:10
publish P. and be damned WELL 846:8
p. it not BIBL 84:11
p., right or wrong BYRO 189:29
P. your message WESL 848:4
publisher Barabbas was a p. CAMP 195:20
makes everybody a p. MCLU 512:13
publishers numerous p. ADE 6:3
p. are not women ROBI 663:17
publishing p. faster than think PAUL 600:2
Puck streak of P. HENL 391:11
puck p. is going to be GRET 372:13
pudding chieftain o' the p.-race BURN 179:22
Mrs Carter, could make a p. JOHN 438:24
proof of the p. PROV 642:8
p. and pie NURS 578:15
p. in his belly SHAK 706:5
solid p. POPE 611:14
Take away that p. CHUR 231:8
puddings like their English p. VOLT 835:5
puddle shining into a p. PROV 643:50
puellis *Vixi p.* HORA 413:6
puerisque *Virginibus p. canto* HORA 412:14
puero *p. reverentia* JUVE 451:21
puff friends all united to p. SWIN 786:3
p. and get oneself puffed TROL 817:1
p.—and speak COWP 254:28
p. of a dunce GOLD 364:21
puffs P., powders, patches POPE 618:7
pug O most charming p. FLEM 334:22
pugna *P. magna victi sumus* LIVY 496:7
puking infant, Mewling and p. SHAK 696:28

racked searched out and r.   ORCH 586:3
racket all a German r.   RIDL 661:9
rackets r. to these balls   SHAK 708:11
rackrent pleased with Castle R.   EDGE 303:13
radar This is the writer's r.   HEMI 391:7
radiance Stains the white r.   SHEL 743:21
radiances R. know him   BERR 74:17
radical never dared be r. when young
  FROS 344:20
R. Chic . . . only radical in Style   WOLF 863:5
radio had the r. on   MONR 553:17
R. and television   SARR 681:5
r. expands it   WOGA 862:10
radish like a forked r.   SHAK 707:24
r. and an egg   COWP 256:22
raft discourse on dharma as a r.   MAHĀ 515:11
Parable of the R.   PALI 593:18
republic is a r.   AMES 14:8
rag foul r.-and-bone shop   YEAT 872:14
r. and a bone   KIPL 467:19
r. blown by the wind   WORD 864:19
Shakespeherian R.   ELIO 311:9
rage die here in a r.   SWIF 783:1
hard-favoured r.   SHAK 708:16
heathen so furiously r.   BOOK 139:12
Heaven has no r.   CONG 247:9
Heaven in a r.   BLAK 124:10
horrible that lust and r.   YEAT 874:25
r. against the dying of the light   THOM 805:15
r. of Caliban   WILD 855:15
replete with too much r.   SHAK 737:20
temp'ring virtuous r.   POPE 615:23
wretched r. for order   MAHO 516:7
writing increaseth r.   DYER 301:4
rages weight of r.   SPOO 768:15
ragged pair of r. claws   ELIO 310:9
raggedness windowed r.   SHAK 715:23
raging r. in the dark   YEAT 872:13
r. of the sea   BOOK 144:2
strong drink is r.   BIBL 88:24
ragout fricassee, or a r.   SWIF 783:2
rags are as filthy r.   BIBL 94:21
r. and contempt   BUNY 171:12
r. and tatters   MOLI 552:7
r. of time   DONN 289:17
raid R. BY DR JAMESON   KRUG 473:20
r. on the inarticulate   ELIO 309:13
rail r. at me   CONG 247:10
six young on the r.   BROW 166:8
railing R. at life   CHUR 228:10
railing for r.   BIBL 117:10
railroad Building that r.   VAN 824:8
enterprised a r.   RUSK 673:15
railway R. termini   FORS 337:21
with a r.-share   CARR 204:3
raiment body than r.   BIBL 99:16
man clothed in soft r.   BIBL 100:33
rain abundance of r.   BIBL 85:10
buried in the r.   MILL 537:2
clouds and wind without r.   BIBL 88:36
clouds return after the r.   BIBL 90:20
command the r.   PEPY 603:5
credit for the r.   MORR 561:14
cries against the r.   GASC 350:4
dead that the r. rains on   PROV 628:10
drop of r. maketh a hole   LATI 482:15
earth soaks up the r.   COWL 254:8
fall like r.   AUDE 38:16
February there be no r.   PROV 635:11
gentle r. from heaven   SHAK 724:29
glazed with r. water   WILL 858:11
had outwept its r.   SHEL 743:11
hard r.'s a gonna fall   DYLA 301:15
Hath the r. a father   BIBL 87:11
Jupiter the R.-giver   TIBU 810:19
latter r.   BOOK 135:9
like sunshine after r.   SHAK 738:28
out of the caverns of r.   SHEL 743:26
R. before seven   PROV 642:18
r. in Spain   LERN 490:11
r. is destroying his grain   HERB 393:11
r. is on our lips   SORL 761:23
r. is over and gone   BIBL 90:27

r. it raineth every day   SHAK 715:21
r. it raineth every day   SHAK 736:11
r., it raineth on the just   BOWE 153:16
r. of Dharma   MAHĀ 515:16
R., rain, go away   NURS 581:1
R.! Rain! Rain   KEAT 457:22
real sad r.   CASH 206:7
sendeth r.   BIBL 99:7
send my roots r.   HOPK 408:3
small drops of r.   BALL 56:4
small r. down can rain   ANON 21:8
smell the dew and r.   HERB 394:10
soft refreshing r.   CAMP 194:15
some r. must fall   LONG 499:19
Still falls the r.   SITW 753:12
through the drizzling r.   TENN 795:4
wailing of the r.   LEDW 487:6
waiting for it to r.   COHE 238:8
waiting for r.   ELIO 309:23
wedding-cake in the r.   AUDE 38:22
rainbow another hue Unto the r.   SHAK 714:11
blessing of a r.   ABSE 1:5
colours in r.   BOOT 151:2
gave Noah the r.   SONG 762:8
Lord survives the r.   LOWE 503:9
melting r.   AKEN 10:2
r. and a cuckoo's song   DAVI 268:6
r. coalition   JACK 426:11
r. comes and goes   WORD 867:3
R. gave thee birth   DAVI 268:7
r. of the salt sand-wave   KEAT 455:28
r. round about the throne   BIBL 118:3
r.'s glory is shed   SHEL 744:18
r. which includes black   YEVT 876:5
Somewhere over the r.   HARB 379:19
Unweave a r.   KEAT 455:14
when I behold A r.   WORD 866:18
rained r. down manna   BOOK 145:8
raineth R. drop and staineth slop   POUN 620:15
rainfall r. at morning   STEV 776:22
raining if it's r., apologizes   WELD 845:15
rains called forth by the early r.   VARR 824:11
never r. but it pours   PROV 636:30
r. pennies from heaven   BURK 176:11
rainy r. day   BIBL 89:6
R. days   BASH 60:19
r. Sunday in London   DE Q 273:18
strangers on a r. day   SMAR 754:14
wish him a r. evening   WALT 839:1
raise easier to r. the Devil   PROV 636:15
Lord shall r. me up   RALE 654:6
raised It is easily r.   FIEL 326:15
r. not a stone   WOLF 862:15
raising stop r. corn   LEAS 486:15
raison r. tonne en son cratère   POTT 620:14
rake r. in reading   MONT 554:11
ram r. caught in a thicket   BIBL 80:2
Rama In R. was there a voice   BIBL 98:13
Ramadan month of R.   KORA 471:3
ramas Verdes r.   LORC 500:18
rambling r. brat (in print)   BRAD 154:10
rampage On the R., Pip   DICK 278:10
rampart corse to the r.   WOLF 862:13
rams mountains skipped like r.   BOOK 148:3
than the fat of r.   BIBL 83:35
Ramsbottom Mr and Mrs R.   EDGA 303:6
ran both r. together   BIBL 108:35
r. before Ahab   BIBL 85:12
they r. awa'   MCLE 512:7
They r., one fleeing   HOME 404:21
Who r. to help me   TAYL 791:15
Randal Lord R.   BALL 55:1
random word, at r. spoken   SCOT 688:17
rangers Eight for the eight bold r.   SONG 762:13
rank O! my offence is r.   SHAK 703:5
r. is but the guinea's stamp   BURN 178:7
r. me with whom you will   METH 533:8
Things r. and gross   SHAK 699:19
rankers Gentlemen-r.   KIPL 465:20
ranks glittering r.   MILT 540:24
In the r. of death   MOOR 558:11
r. of Tuscany   MACA 508:19

ransom world's r., blessèd Mary's Son
  SHAK 730:11
ransomed R., healed   LYTE 506:6
rap r. at the ballot box   CHIL 226:3
rape procrastinated r.   PRIT 624:14
r., ultra-violence and Beethoven   TAGL 788:2
you r. it   DEGA 271:6
raped r. and speaks English   ANON 16:9
Raphael draw like R.   PICA 606:11
Raphaels talked of their R.   GOLD 364:22
rapid r., unintelligible patter   GILB 358:12
rapine march through r.   GLAD 360:4
rapist r. bothers to buy a bottle   DWOR 301:3
rapists all men are r.   FREN 342:9
rapping r. at my chamber door   POE 610:19
rapscallions kings mostly r.   TWAI 819:20
rapture first fine careless r.   BROW 165:28
Modified r.   GILB 357:7
raptures high r. do infuse   WALL 837:2
r. and roses   SWIN 785:7
Rapunzel R., let down your hair   GRIM 373:11
rara R. avis   JUVE 451:2
rare man of culture r.   GILB 357:18
O r. Ben Jonson   EPIT 319:5
was indeed a r. one   WITH 861:6
rarely R., rarely, comest thou   SHEL 746:10
rarer r. than the unicorn   JONG 445:13
rari r. nantes in gurgite vasto   VIRG 828:13
rascal you dirty r.   NURS 579:9
rascality effect of prudence on r.   SHAW 741:18
rascals R., would you live   FRED 342:1
rash Her r. hand   MILT 544:6
He was not r.   GRAH 367:18
too r., too unadvised   SHAK 732:15
Rasputin every R. has his Goethe   GRAS 369:4
Rast Ohne Hast, aber ohne R.   GOET 363:1
rat Anyone can r.   CHUR 229:6
Cat, the R., and Lovell   COLL 242:23
creeps like a r.   BOWE 153:10
giant r. of Sumatra   DOYL 292:11
How now! a r.   SHAK 703:10
poisoned r. in a hole   SWIF 783:1
r. swimming towards   CHUR 231:6
r. without a tail   SHAK 718:6
smell a r.   ROCH 664:9
terrier can define a r.   HOUS 416:13
You dirty r.   MISQ 549:7
rate cannot r. me very high   LACL 475:9
ratem pelago r.   HORA 411:6
rathe r. primrose that forsaken dies
  MILT 540:12
ratio geometrical r.   MALT 518:11
ratiocination pay with r.   BUTL 183:7
rationabile Sicut modo geniti infantes, r.
  BIBL 120:18
rational call the r. soul   LEIB 488:6
irrational is r.   STEV 774:7
What is r. is actual   HEGE 389:1
rationalized never be r.   CHES 225:5
rationed so precious it must be r.   LENI 488:21
rats r.' alley   ELIO 311:8
R.! They fought the dogs   BROW 167:1
r. under 'em   DICK 281:8
rattle education serves as a r.   ARIS 28:1
hearing 'em r. a little   FARQ 324:5
Pleased with a r.   POPE 617:2
R. his bones   NOEL 576:19
toy of man, his r.   WOLL 863:8
raucle has a r. tongue   BURN 177:13
ravage nose May r. with impunity   BROW 167:22
ravaged R. and plundered   MORR 561:6
raved as I r. and grew more fierce   HERB 394:7
ravelling worn to a r.   POTT 620:5
raven grim and ancient r.   POE 611:2
Poe with this r.   LOWE 502:17
r. himself is hoarse   SHAK 718:20
r., you do have a voice   AESO 9:1
saw a r. very high   WORD 864:21
With r.'s feather   SHAK 733:17
ravening r. wolves   BIBL 99:30
ravens acquitting the r.   JUVE 450:16
r. brought him bread   BIBL 85:6
seen the r. flock   AYTO 44:7

three r. | BALL 56:1
turbulently, like r. | PIND 606:17
ravish except you r. me | DONN 288:13
ravished transported and r. | TRAH 814:12
would have r. her | FIEL 326:11
ravishing dear r. thing | BEHN 66:19
raw I was r. | JALA 428:19
ray r. of rays | DICK 276:18
r. of sunshine | WODE 861:20
razor mirror and a r. | JOYC 448:13
Occam's R. | OCCA 583:10
r. rusting | PLAT 608:8
reach could not r. it | SAPP 681:1
flesh of them shall not r. | KORA 472:10
I r. for my pistol | JOHS 445:4
man's r. should exceed | BROW 164:19
My soul can r. | BROW 164:13
other beers cannot r. | ADVE 7:30
r. the brittle branches | VIRG 832:6
r. the promised land | CALL 193:11
things above his r. | OVER 589:15
reaching r. forth | BIBL 115:1
reaction can't get no girl r. | JAGG 427:10
if there is any r. | JUNG 449:14
opposed an equal r. | NEWT 574:5
reactionaries All r. are paper tigers | MAO 521:4
read be able to r. a building | ROGE 665:11
Being r. to by a boy | ELIO 309:23
bokes for to r. I me delyte | CHAU 220:17
but r. these | MART 524:5
cannot now r. a page | WALP 838:17
did not r. any more | DANT 265:1
even to r. his books | ISID 426:4
fast as they can r. | HAZL 386:17
has r. too widely | PEAR 601:4
his books were r. | BELL 68:20
In science, r. | BULW 170:15
I r., and sigh | HERB 393:21
I r. very hard | JOHN 440:4
man ought to r. | JOHN 439:21
not r. Eliot, Auden | RICH 660:11
not that I ever r. them | SHER 748:1
only news until he's r. it | WAUG 842:21
others who can't r. | CHUR 228:9
people that r. | SHEN 747:21
people who can't r. | ZAPP 877:13
Pray, r., and work | MOTT 563:11
r. a book before reviewing it | SMIT 758:25
r., and censure | HEMI 390:16
r. a nod, a shrug | SWIF 783:26
r. any good books lately | CATC 207:26
r. as much as other men | AUBR 35:17
r. books *through* | JOHN 441:8
r. every day, with astonishment | CHES 223:11
r. in the train | WILD 854:25
r., mark, learn | BOOK 135:11
r., much of the night | ELIO 311:2
R. my lips | BUSH 182:4
R. not to contradict | BACO 47:34
R. out my words | FLEC 334:14
R. somewhat seldomer | BROW 165:1
r. strange matters | SHAK 719:3
r. The Hunter's thoughts | AUDE 37:1
r. without pleasure | JOHN 445:1
superfluous to r. | HILB 398:6
Take up and r. | AUGU 39:8
want to r. a novel | DISR 286:30
want to r. only | UPDI 822:25
What do you r. | SHAK 701:5
what I r. in the papers | ROGE 666:5
who don't r. the books | BYAT 184:24
whom they never r. | CHUR 228:1
reader common r. | JOHN 436:22
delighting the r. | HORA 409:12
Hypocrite r. | BAUD 61:10
ideal r. suffering from | JOYC 448:2
no tears in the r. | FROS 345:7
one r. in a hundred years | KOES 470:12
R., I married him | BRON 158:8
r. of the works of God | COWP 256:16
r. seldom peruses | ADDI 5:3
r.'s fancy makes the fate | TERE 801:17
readers on fire all his r. | NASH 569:4

r. better to enjoy | JOHN 436:6
readeth he may run that r. it | BIBL 96:16
readiness r. is all | SHAK 704:23
reading careful of his r. | LEWI 491:19
English r. public | JOYC 448:25
health through r. | RILK 662:8
he was r. | AUGU 39:5
in the R.-room | GISS 359:10
lie in a hot bath r. | THOM 806:15
Much r.is an oppression | PENN 602:13
not worth r. | AUST 41:10
Peace is poor r. | HARD 380:11
pleasure in the r. | QUAR 651:6
prefer r. | SMIT 757:10
rake in r. | MONT 554:11
R. and marriage | MOLI 552:9
r., in order to write | JOHN 441:17
r. is no more than | STEN 771:20
R. isn't an occupation | ORTO 586:14
r. is right | JOHN 437:7
R. is to the mind | STEE 770:18
R. maketh a full man | BACO 48:2
r. of good books | DESC 274:6
r. of such a book | ASCH 33:9
r. or non-reading | BYRO 192:9
r., or writing | THOM 804:18
r. *Robinson Crusoe* | FLIN 335:22
r. the book of himself | MALL 517:15
soul of r. | STER 772:22
vile hard r. | SHER 748:31
were r. a letter | TALM 790:1
what is worth r. | TREV 815:8
reads He r. much | SHAK 711:23
ready always r. to go | LA F 475:16
conference a r. man | BACO 48:2
fire when you are r. | DEWE 275:10
gracious and r. help | BOOK 138:2
necessity of being r. | LINC 493:15
of a r. writer | BOOK 142:12
R. to be any thing | BROW 162:21
real Canada is not a r. country | BOUC 152:11
Life is r. | LONG 499:14
r. is indistinguishable | GIDE 355:19
r. Simon Pure | CENT 212:14
r. slow walk | CASH 206:7
speechless r. | BARZ 60:14
your r. nature | HUI- 419:10
realism dislike of R. | WILD 855:15
I don't want r. | WILL 858:8
realistic make a 'r. decision' | MCCA 509:7
reality bear very much r. | ELIO 309:5
Between the idea And the r. | ELIO 309:28
comes out into r. | KIER 462:13
distinct in r. | THOM 805:11
employs r. as little | MOND 553:10
find r. | MURD 565:20
in r. there are atoms | DEMO 272:16
less in r. | HUME 420:10
Love is the discovery of r. | MURD 565:17
makes r. more bearable | BYRO 189:25
paint my own r. | KAHL 452:12
r. and lies | COCT 237:19
r. is incomplete | MURD 565:18
r. take precedence | FEYN 326:1
separate itself from r. | CAMU 196:15
suffer r. to *suggest* | BRON 158:14
they are a r. | DEWA 275:7
too far from r. | SAHH 677:11
to the r. | EPIT 317:6
worth and spiritual r. | HEGE 388:15
really as in itself it r. is | ARNO 32:8
be a R. Useful Engine | AWDR 43:11
what I r. really want | ROWB 671:3
realm One r., one people | POLI 612:14
this earth, this r. | SHAK 730:11
realms r. of gold | KEAT 456:14
through the r. of light | GURN 374:19
whom three r. obey | POPE 618:10
reap As you sow, so you r. | PROV 626:43
neither do they r. | BIBL 99:16
r. a character | READ 656:8
r., if we faint not | BIBL 113:26
r. in joy | BOOK 149:1

r. the whirlwind | BIBL 96:4
r. the whirlwind | PROV 645:1
that shall he also r. | BIBL 113:25
reaped should never be r. | TRAH 814:11
reapers Pity the r. | DUCK 298:9
r., reaping early | TENN 796:15
reaping ever r. something new | TENN 796:26
No, r. | BOTT 152:9
r. where thou hast not sown | BIBL 103:3
reaps another r. | SHEL 746:12
rear r. the tender thought | THOM 808:12
reason appear the better r. | MILT 542:3
Blotting out r. | GRAV 369:13
by their feelings than by r. | ADAM 4:2
Can they r. | BENT 71:8
conquers r. still | POPE 615:9
courage to use your own r. | KANT 453:5
discourse of r. | SHAK 699:21
erring R.'s spite | POPE 616:28
feast of r. | POPE 617:26
form of human r. | LÉVI 491:11
Give you a r. | SHAK 705:29
guide by the light of r. | BRAN 154:18
ideal of r. | KANT 453:2
if it be against r. | COKE 238:10
kills r. itself | MILT 545:22
last proceeding of r. | PASC 598:4
man who listens to R. | SHAW 741:20
most sovereign r. | SHAK 702:10
noble in r. | SHAK 701:11
Nothing without a r. | LEIB 488:7
not his r., but his passions | STER 773:4
not r. and compare | BLAK 125:11
O r. not the need | SHAK 715:12
perfection of r. | COKE 238:12
pursue my r. | BROW 162:26
R. always means | GASK 350:8
r. and conscience | PRIC 622:15
r., and justice | BURK 173:16
R. and the sciences | LEIB 488:6
R., an *ignis fatuus* | ROCH 664:15
r. does buckle | BACO 45:11
R. herself will respect | GIBB 354:18
R., in her most exalted mood | WORD 868:21
r. in the roasting | PROV 644:36
r. is against it | BUTL 184:12
R. is, and ought to be | HUME 420:18
r. is insufficient | HUME 420:1
R. is natural revelation | LOCK 497:9
r. is our law | MILT 544:5
r. is silent | HELV 390:13
r. is stifled | BURK 172:20
R. is the life of the law | COKE 238:11
r. knows nothing of | PASC 598:7
r. perverted | WHIT 850:15
r. produces monsters | GOYA 367:6
R.'s ear | ADDI 5:18
r. shall my heart direct | ETHE 320:16
r. themselves out again | SHAK 709:12
R. the natural image | BONA 132:6
R. to rule | DRYD 295:25
r. why I cannot tell | BROW 161:14
render a r. | BIBL 89:2
result of r.and calculation | BAUD 61:15
right deed for the wrong r. | ELIO 310:17
show no r. can | WATK 841:4
takes the r. prisoner | SHAK 718:13
that is not r. | POWE 622:7
Their's not to r. why | TENN 793:4
triumph of human r. | HAWK 385:4
ultimate r. of things | LEIB 488:5
woman's r. | SHAK 736:12
words clothed in r.'s garb | MILT 542:5
reasonable of a r. soul | BOOK 134:14
R. Man | HERB 393:19
r. man adapts | SHAW 741:19
will must be r. | JEFF 431:14
reasonableness sweet r. of Jesus | ARNO 32:5
reasonably r. be expected to do | WHAT 849:16
reasoned never r. into | SWIF 784:17
reasoning abstract r. | HUME 419:16
cowards in r. | SHAF 693:18

reasoning (*cont.*):
in dirt the r. engine ROCH 664:16
involved in r. VOLT 834:21
r., self-sufficing thing WORD 868:5
reasons finding of bad r. BRAD 154:2
five r. ALDR 11:13
Good r. must, of force SHAK 713:27
heart has its r. PASC 598:7
Poor men's r. FULL 346:17
R. are not like garments ESSE 320:11
r. for living JUVE 451:10
r. for the rule change STRA 778:21
r. will certainly MANS 520:11
We want better r. RUSS 675:17
rebel die like a true-blue r. HILL 398:15
experienced r., Time FLAT 333:1
I am *still* a r. BROW 161:10
R. without a cause FILM 331:10
starve or r. DUND 299:14
still an Irish r. DUFF 298:15
What is a r. CAMU 196:12
rebellion little r. now and then JEFF 431:9
r. and revivalism THOM 807:1
r. is as the sin BIBL 83:36
R. lay in his way SHAK 706:21
R. to tyrants BRAD 154:9
R. to tyrants MOTT 563:17
r. was the certain consequence MANS 520:10
rum, Romanism, and r. BURC 172:3
rebellions everyday r. STEI 771:11
rebellious r. heart BIBL 94:25
rebels r. are our countrymen GRAN 368:14
subjects are r. BURK 174:11
reborn being r. therein MAHĀ 516:2
youth would not be r. ROUS 671:1
rebounds unless it r. JOHN 441:13
rebuke Open r. BIBL 89:4
r. hath broken my heart BOOK 144:12
r. the people BOOK 150:11
recall cannot r. their gifts TENN 800:9
takes wing beyond r. HORA 410:14
recalled once spoke can never be r. DILL 283:5
Things past cannot be r. PROV 645:2
recapitulates ontogeny r. HAEC 375:8
receipt r. of custom BIBL 100:13
receive better to give than to r. PROV 636:12
r. but what we give COLE 239:9
r. one such little child BIBL 102:1
than to r. BIBL 110:9
received Freely ye have r. BIBL 100:23
his own r. him not BIBL 107:1
receiver have left the r. off the hook
KOES 470:11
r. is always thought CHES 222:19
receivers no r., no thieves PROV 635:18
receiveth Every one that asketh r. BIBL 99:25
receiving giving and r. of a Ring BOOK 139:4
receptacle r. for emotions PICA 606:10
recesses r. in my mind BRON 158:7
recession r. when your neighbour TRUM 817:21
spend way out of a r. CALL 193:10
recipes like r. in a cookbook STEW 777:7
r. that are always successful VALÉ 823:12
recirculation commodious vicus of r.
JOYC 448:1
recited r. verses in writing BIBL 98:3
reckless r. with our government SHOR 750:1
reckoned love that can be r. SHAK 694:8
reckoning at your own r. TROL 816:24
comes the r. PROV 626:10
encounter my r. KORA 473:8
No r. made SHAK 700:22
sense of r. SHAK 709:4
reckonings Short r. PROV 643:6
recks r. not his own rede SHAK 700:2
recognize not r. me by my face TROL 815:16
only a trial if I r. it KAFK 452:6
recognized objects r. WORD 868:15
recommend tries to r. him JOHN 437:2

recompense r. those who believe KORA 472:5
reconciles feasting r. everybody PEPY 603:12
reconciliation bridge of r. RUNC 672:7
silence and r. MACA 507:15
True r. does not MAND 519:1
reconstruct r. it there NEUR 571:6
reconstruction r. of Christian life BONH 132:10
reconvened hereby r. EWIN 322:3
record bound to r. it TURN 819:13
put down in his r. ANON 24:2
r. of blissful old times BLAM 128:15
recordanti r. benefacta priora CATU 211:1
recording domesticate the R. Angel
STEV 776:1
R. Angel, as he wrote it down STER 773:12
recover r. the use of his legs DICK 279:13
recovered may nought r. be CHAU 221:8
recrudescence r. of Puritanism RUSS 675:4
rectangular proceedings are quite r.
BYRO 191:22
recte *Si possis r.* HORA 410:1
Vivere si r. nescis HORA 411:2
rectum one in the r. OSLE 589:2
recurret *usque r.* HORA 410:9
red As many r. herrings NURS 580:4
Better r. than dead POLI 612:7
blows so r. The rose FITZ 331:17
feel the r. in my mind DICK 282:5
gentlemen, In coats of r. DE L 272:5
give this cheek a little r. POPE 615:17
her lips' r. SHAK 738:19
jolly r. nose BEAU 63:7
keep the r. flag flying CONN 248:4
Luve's like a r., red rose BURN 179:8
Making the green one r. SHAK 720:9
my skin is r. SITT 753:8
Nor dim nor r. COLE 240:18
people's flag is deepest r. CONN 248:3
Pluck a r. rose SHAK 709:18
raiment all r. MACA 508:4
r. in tooth and claw TENN 795:17
r. men scalped each other MACA 506:14
R. sky at night PROV 642:19
r. wheel barrow WILL 858:11
rise with my r. hair PLAT 608:10
thin r. line RUSS 676:1
Thin r. line of 'eroes KIPL 467:17
wine when it is r. BIBL 88:33
wrists and fingers r. MACA 508:21
redbreast r. whistles KEAT 457:4
reddens sweet-apple r. SAPP 681:1
redder r. than the fyn coral CHAU 219:23
rede recks not his own r. SHAK 700:2
redeem R. thy mis-spent time KEN 459:14
redeemed r. Jerusalem BIBL 94:1
redeemer infant R. is laid HEBE 388:7
know that my r. liveth BIBL 86:34
O thou great R. WILL 857:9
Our blest R. AUBE 35:14
strength, and my r. BOOK 140:12
such a mighty R. MISS 550:10
To thee, R. NEAL 569:6
redeeming devastating or r. fires GONC 365:23
R. the time BIBL 114:10
redemption great r. from above MILT 540:21
married past r. DRYD 296:13
r.'s happy dawn CASW 206:16
redemptorem *meruit habere* R. MISS 550:10
redoubling r. of life CHAT 217:19
redress r. Of all my pain WYAT 871:9
Things past r. SHAK 730:14
reds honour the indomitable R. DUNN 299:17
redtape r. talking-machine CARL 200:14
redwood r. forest to the Gulf Stream
GUTH 375:2
reed bruised r. BIBL 85:38
bruised r. BIBL 93:21
but for a r. MARV 525:3
clasped a r. SHEL 744:7

he is a thinking r. PASC 598:8
r. before the wind PROV 642:20
r. shaken with the wind BIBL 100:33
story told by the r. JALA 428:17
reeds floods over the r. PAST 598:20
in the r. by the river BROW 164:11
r. in the river BROW 164:12
reeking r. into Cadiz Bay BROW 165:29
reel R. in a drunkard CHUR 228:12
They r. to and fro BOOK 147:18
reeled Until r. the mind GIBB 355:11
reels There's threesome r. BURN 178:1
referee having two you are a r. FROS 344:4
reference sensitive to frames of r. QUIN 652:3
within my terms of r. HUTT 422:11
references verify your r. ROUT 671:2
refine insert, r. SWIF 783:29
r. our language JOHN 437:12
refined disgust this r. age EVEL 321:21
Englishwoman is so r. SMIT 757:20
people of r. sentiments KELL 459:9
R. himself to soul DRYD 295:14
reflex r. of a star WORD 866:2
reform able to r. MORE 559:1
cannot r. our forefathers ELIO 307:4
desire to r. ARNO 32:17
Hunger does not breed r. WILS 859:22
party of progress or r. MILL 536:6
Peace, retrenchment, and r. BRIG 157:3
r. or revolution BERL 73:8
r. the criminal FRY 345:22
sets about r. TOCQ 811:17
thunder for r. NEWS 573:20
Universities never r. themselves MELB 530:12
reformation plotting some new r.
DRYD 296:22
reforming of R. MILT 546:2
reformer r. is a guy who rides MIZN 551:13
refraining R. from taking life PALI 593:12
refresh R., and pay ELLI 314:1
r. it when it was dry BOOK 135:9
refreshed r. with wine BOOK 145:9
refreshes r. the parts ADVE 7:30
refuge Dhamma as your r. PALI 593:15
easy to take r. in IBSE 424:9
God is thy r. BIBL 82:21
God of Jacob is our r. BOOK 142:18
gone to him as a r. PALI 593:11
hills are a r. BOOK 147:7
Patriotism is the last r. JOHN 441:18
r. from home life SHAW 742:18
thou hast been our r. BOOK 145:19
refusal great r. DANT 264:15
Laughter is a r. VALÉ 823:11
refuse offer he can't r. PUZO 650:24
r. of your teeming tents LAZA 485:3
r. to fight POLI 613:15
Which he did thrice r. SHAK 713:5
refused practice in being r. DIOG 283:17
stone which the builders r. BOOK 148:11
refuses sea r. no river PROV 642:36
refute I r. it *thus* JOHN 440:10
r. anyone who argues SA'A 676:10
r. a sneer PALE 593:9
regard least r. for SPEN 766:3
regarder *se r. soi-même* MOLI 552:15
regardless r. of their doom GRAY 370:11
regeneration baptism, a r. ELIO 307:1
reges *Quidquid delirant r.* HORA 410:3
regiment head of one r. LINC 493:16
r. of women KNOX 470:1
regina *Salve, r.* PRAY 623:7
region r. of my song WORD 865:10
regions r. in your mind HABI 375:5
register r. of the crimes, follies GIBB 354:6
règle *grande* r. MOLI 552:3
regnavit R. *a ligno Deus* FORT 338:16
regnum *adveniat r. tuum* MISS 549:17
regret Old Age a r. DISR 285:18

r. can die	TENN 795:21	system of outdoor r.	BRIG 157:2
wild with all r.	TENN 799:12	**relieve** comfort and r. them	BOOK 135:7
regrets Miss Otis r.	PORT 619:16	**relieved** By desperate appliances are r.	
no r.	VAUC 824:12		SHAK 703:23
wild r., and the bloody sweats	WILD 856:3	**religio** Tantum r. potuit	LUCR 504:5
regrette je ne r. rien	VAUC 824:12	**religion** act of duty and r.	OSBO 588:13
Je r. l'Europe	RIMB 662:12	affront her r.	JENY 433:1
regular Brought r.	DICK 278:23	all of the same r.	DISR 285:28
icily r.	TENN 797:19	another r. than Islam	KORA 471:12
regularity genius and r.	GAIN 347:2	As if R. were intended	BUTL 183:13
R. and Decorum	COOP 251:3	As to r.	PAIN 592:12
regulate r. printing	MILT 545:26	become a popular r.	INGE 425:3
regulated R. hatred	HARD 380:5	born for the sake of r.	LAWS 484:11
regulations strong upon the R. Act	WILD 856:1	brothels with bricks of r.	BLAK 126:12
regumque R. turris	HORA 411:7	but of one r.	SHAF 693:17
reheat cannot r. a soufflé	MCCA 509:10	can't talk r. to	SHAW 740:15
Reich Ein R.	POLI 612:14	Christianity was the r.	SWIF 783:12
reign begins early to r.	BAGE 51:7	concerned with r.	TEMP 792:15
Better to r. in hell	MILT 541:19	cultivation of r.	SADI 677:5
friendless is to r.	SHEL 745:23	dominion of r.	GOLD 363:17
Long to r. over us	SONG 762:9	establishment of r.	CONS 250:4
Love, that doth r.	SURR 780:14	Every dictator uses r.	BHUT 78:8
r. of Chaos and old Night	MILT 541:27	feature of any r.	PAIN 592:22
reigned if he had not r.	TACI 787:10	Freedom of r.	JEFF 431:17
r. with your loves	ELIZ 312:10	furious in r.	PENN 602:19
reigning answered 'r.'	BENT 71:6	had only a little r.	ANON 22:2
reigns king r.	THIE 804:12	handmaid to r.	BACO 45:18
Reilly Come back, Paddy R.	FREN 342:11	impossibilities enough in r.	BROW 162:25
reindeer Red-Nosed R.	MARK 521:16	increase in us true r.	BOOK 136:7
reinforcement What r. we may gain		in love as in r.	COWL 254:16
	MILT 541:16	innovation in r.	MAEC 514:13
		In their r. they are so uneven	DEFO 270:22
reins try out my r.	BOOK 141:6	just enough r.	SWIF 783:13
rejected despised and r.	BIBL 94:3	Knight-errantry is r.	CERV 213:5
rejoice as men r.	BIBL 92:13	matters of r.	CHES 222:20
desert shall r.	BIBL 93:8	men's minds to r.	BACO 46:6
hills shall r.	BOOK 144:3	more fierce in its r.	NEWM 572:2
let us heartily r.	BOOK 146:7	much wrong could r. induce	LUCR 504:5
Let us then r.	ANON 23:7	mysteries of our r.	HOBB 401:7
may r.	BOOK 143:6	No compulsion in r.	KORA 471:5
Philistines r.	BIBL 84:11	no part of r.	WESL 847:22
r. and be glad	BOOK 148:11	no r. but social	WESL 847:20
r. at that news	THAT 803:17	One r. is as true	BURT 181:23
R. evermore	BIBL 115:15	only one r.	SHAW 742:5
r. in Christ	LUTH 505:3	perfected your r.	KORA 472:2
R. in the Lord	BIBL 115:3	Philistine of genius in r.	ARNO 32:4
r., rejoice	HEAT 388:5	poetry, prophecy, and r.	RUSK 673:13
r. the heart	BOOK 140:10	politics as well as in r.	JUNI 450:3
R., the Lord is King	WESL 847:16	Pure r. and undefiled	BIBL 116:21
R. with them	BIBL 111:10	r., and not atheism	BURK 173:17
rejoiced R. they were na men	BURN 180:7	r. and philosophy	ARNO 31:23
spirit hath r.	BIBL 104:8	r., as a mere sentiment	NEWM 572:3
rejoices poor heart that never r.	PROV 636:6	r. at the lowest	CHES 223:14
rejoiceth r. as a giant	BOOK 140:9	R. blushing	POPE 613:28
rejoicing home, r., brought me	BAKE 52:9	r. but a childish toy	MARL 522:16
relation cold r.	BURK 174:22	r. for gentlemen	CHAR 217:4
nobody like a r.	THAC 803:1	r. for religion's sake	COUS 253:6
State is a r. of men	WEBE 843:15	r. from the priest	GOLD 365:16
relations God's apology for r.	KING 464:20	r. has always been to me	POTT 620:9
in personal r.	RUSS 674:17	r. into after-dinner toasts	TOAS 812:4
not have sexual r.	CLIN 236:7	r. is allowed to invade	MELB 530:18
Personal r.	FORS 338:2	R. is an all-important matter	NAPO 567:17
relationship every human r. suffers	FORS 338:9	R. is by no means	CHES 222:21
Their r. consisted	GUNN 374:15	r. is made	MONT 555:13
relative set out one day in a r. way	BULL 170:7	r. is not circumambient	FOST 338:20
Success is r.	ELIO 309:1	r. is powerless to bestow	FORB 336:14
relaxation can only find r.	FRAN 340:4	R. is the sigh	MARX 526:3
relaxes Bless r.	BLAK 126:16	r. is to do good	PAIN 593:4
release called r. from bondage	CHUA 227:14	r., justice, counsel	BACO 47:28
relent make him once r.	BUNY 171:25	r., knavery, and change	BEHN 67:3
make the gods above r.	VIRG 831:1	r. most prevalent	BURK 173:14
relic Fair Greece! sad r.	BYRO 185:22	r. of feeble minds	BURK 174:18
like a holy r.	WEBS 844:7	r. of humanity	PAIN 592:16
relics his r. are laid	MOOR 558:12	r. of Socialism	BEVA 76:14
with thise r.	CHAU 218:27	r. or policy	RUSK 673:27
relief death is rather a r.	FITZ 332:1	R.'s in the heart	JERR 433:15
For this r. much thanks	SHAK 698:28	R. the frozen thought of men	KRIS 473:15
gave that thought r.	WORD 867:4	r. weak	SZAS 786:15
r. of man's estate	BACO 45:9	r. without a prelate	BANC 57:7
seek for kind r.	BLAK 127:14	r. without science is blind	EINS 305:5
		R.? Yes; but which	BYRO 189:25
		reproach to r.	PENN 602:15
		rum and true r.	BYRO 188:7

some of r.	EDGE 303:7		
start your own r.	ANON 18:3		
system of r.	PAIN 592:6		
talks loudly against r.	STER 773:4		
That is my r.	SHAW 740:14		
that regards r.	ADDI 5:16		
They are for r.	BUNY 171:12		
tourism is their r.	RUNC 672:8		
true meaning of r.	ARNO 32:3		
true r. is Islam	KORA 471:9		
vice and r.	SMIT 759:1		
way to plant r.	BROW 163:4		
religions All r. are just as good	FRED 341:21		
All r. must be tolerated	FRED 341:22		
r. considered man as man	TOCQ 811:14		
sixty different r.	CARA 197:14		
they alone who found r.	PROU 625:10		
religiose r. And mystic	DUNN 300:2		
religious all r. revolution	WEBE 843:17		
but not r.-good	HARD 381:5		
dim r. light	MILT 539:20		
great r. art of the world	CLAR 233:13		
his r. opinions	BUTL 184:15		
Old r. factions	BURK 176:3		
r. and moral principles	ARNO 32:14		
r. animal	BURK 174:14		
r. enquiries	NEWM 572:6		
R. persecution	BURK 175:24		
r. prejudice	HUXL 423:16		
seemeth to be r.	BIBL 116:20		
sense of r. mission	UPDI 823:1		
suspended my r. inquiries	GIBB 354:22		
relish one begins to have a r.	HAYW 385:17		
relished by which he is to be r.	WORD 870:5		
reluctance superstitious r. to sit	JOHN 442:27		
reluctant r. peer	BENN 69:19		
with r. feet	LONG 499:10		
rem quocumque modo r.	HORA 410:1		
R. tene	CATO 209:22		
remain fragments that r.	BIBL 107:21		
r. with you always	BOOK 138:1		
things have been, things r.	CLOU 237:5		
remains aught r. to do	ROGE 665:12		
remarkable anything r. about it	PAST 598:15		
nothing left r.	SHAK 695:21		
remarks R. are not literature	STEI 771:2		
said our r. before us	DONA 287:11		
remedies by violent r.	MONT 556:1		
desperate r.	PROV 629:40		
Extreme r.	HIPP 399:14		
r. oft in ourselves do lie	SHAK 694:3		
will not apply new r.	BACO 47:12		
remedy bestowed on mankind a r.	SYDE 786:6		
dangerous r.	FAWK 324:21		
Force is not a r.	BRIG 157:6		
My dog! what r. remains	COWP 255:17		
no r. presents itself so soon	DONN 289:25		
r. for everything except	PROV 644:18		
r. is death	CHAM 214:14		
r. is worse than the disease	BACO 47:31		
r. our enemies have chosen	SHER 749:10		
Things without all r.	SHAK 721:2		
'Tis a sharp r.	RALE 654:12		
remember Body, r. not only	CAVA 211:10		
cannot r. the past	SANT 680:14		
Do you r. an Inn, Miranda	BELL 68:24		
if thou wilt, r.	ROSS 669:9		
I r., I remember	HOOD 405:18		
I r. it well	LERN 490:9		
Lord, r. me	BIBL 106:24		
man to r. me	RUNY 672:14		
R.	CHAR 217:1		
r. a happy time	DANT 264:18		
r. and be sad	ROSS 669:5		
r. even these things	VIRG 828:17		
r. for ever	WARN 840:5		
R. me	ROSS 669:4		
R. me when I am dead	DOUG 291:12		
r. more than seven	BELL 67:16		
r. not past years	NEWM 572:17		
R. now thy Creator	BIBL 90:20		
r. sweet Alice	ENGL 316:2		
R. the Alamo	SHER 749:6		

wind, Which I r. not — SHAK 713:23
respectability r. and airconditioning — BARA 57:17
save a shred of r. — READ 656:2
respectable more r. he is — SHAW 740:22
most devilish when r. — BROW 164:3
Not one is r. or unhappy — WHIT 852:11
respecter no r. of persons — BIBL 109:27
respice r. *finem* — ANON 23:11
respiration said it was artificial r. — BURG 172:8
responsare R. *cupidinibus* — HORA 415:2
responsibility In dreams begins r. — YEAT 875:14
Liberty means r. — SHAW 741:12
no sense of r. — KNOX 470:6
Power without r. — KIPL 468:26
R. without power — DORF 290:15
r. without power — STOP 777:14
there was a r. — BROW 161:3
responsible know who are r. — PLAT 608:17
r. for such an absurd world — DUHA 299:1
rest After dinner r. awhile — PROV 626:9
all shall r. eternally — SPEN 767:27
change is as good as a r. — PROV 628:40
choose Their place of r. — MILT 544:20
dove found no r. — BIBL 79:23
Everything was at r. — TRAH 814:10
far, far better r. — DICK 281:7
flee away, and be at r. — BOOK 143:10
give yourself r. — AURE 40:7
Grant them eternal r. — MISS 550:4
holy r. — NEWM 572:13
I will give you r. — BIBL 101:2
no r. day or night — BIBL 119:2
not to seek for r. — IGNA 424:14
ordained no r. — VAUG 824:13
peace and r. at last — DOST 291:1
r. from their labours — BIBL 119:3
R. in soft peace — JONS 446:17
r. is literature — COLE 242:17
r. is mere fine writing — VERL 826:8
r. is silence — SHAK 705:3
r. not day and night — BIBL 118:5
R., rest, perturbèd spirit — SHAK 700:29
r. upon thy holy hill — BOOK 140:1
r. were little ones — ELIZ 312:17
robs me of my r. — LODG 498:6
Swift has sailed into his r. — YEAT 875:2
take my r. — BOOK 139:17
take no r. — BOOK 140:15
talk about the r. of us — ANON 20:18
weary be at r. — BIBL 86:17
Without haste, but without r. — GOET 363:1
work, r. and play — ADVE 8:3
restaurant table at a good r. — LEBO 486:21
rested r. the seventh day — BIBL 81:19
resteth Wyatt r. here — SURR 781:3
resting give us a r.-place — WEIZ 845:11
restituit *cunctando r. rem* — ENNI 316:5
restless heart is r. — AUGU 39:2
rolls back the r. stone — DUCK 298:10
restoration Church's R. — BETJ 75:15
not revolution, but r. — HARD 380:6
restore R. thou them that are penitent — BOOK 133:6
restored r., forgiven — LYTE 506:6
R. to life, and power — KEBL 458:21
restorer Nature's sweet r. — YOUN 876:16
restrain r. yourselves — UPAN 822:4
restraint population, moral r. — MALT 518:12
r. with which they write — CAMP 195:4
restructuring r. [perestroika] — GORB 366:4
rests until it r. in you — AUGU 39:2
result looks at their r. — MACH 511:1
r. happiness — DICK 277:10
results quick and effective r. — BULL 170:6
than for r. — BAGE 51:8
unless it achieves r. — SHAC 693:11
resurrection by thy glorious R. — BOOK 134:20
foretaste of the r. — SCHO 686:14
in the r. — BIBL 102:16
on the Day of R. — KORA 471:13
r., and the life — BIBL 108:6
R. of the body — BOOK 133:19

r. of the dead — BIBL 112:21
r. of the dead — BIBL 113:3
R. to eternal life — BOOK 139:10
retained Him, they r. — GERV 354:1
retaliate r. for a soul slain — KORA 472:3
retard r. what we cannot repel — JOHN 435:20
reticence Northern r., the tight gag — HEAN 387:18
R., in three volumes — GLAD 360:14
reticulated *Network*. Anything r. — JOHN 436:2
retire r. from this station — JEFF 431:18
retirement there must be no r. — HAIG 376:6
retort r. courteous — SHAK 697:26
retreat absolute r. — WINC 860:8
make an honourable r. — SHAK 697:8
more untroubled r. — AURE 40:8
noblest station is r. — LYTT 506:8
not r. a single inch — GARR 349:17
This r., so sweet — HORA 410:12
retreating Have you seen yourself r. — NASH 568:23
my right is r. — FOCH 336:2
retrenchment Peace, r., and reform — BRIG 157:3
retrograde r. if it does not advance — GIBB 354:17
retrorsum *nulla r.* — HORA 410:2
return he shall not r. to me — BIBL 84:18
I shall r. — MACA 506:10
I will r. — EPIT 318:13
not r. your blow — SHAW 741:27
r. no more to his house — BIBL 86:23
r. of democratic control — STEE 770:12
r., O Shulamite — BIBL 91:12
r. unto God — BIBL 90:20
Should I never r. — MANS 520:9
state I came, r. — VAUG 825:8
They shall not r. to us — KIPL 466:17
unto dust shalt thou r. — BIBL 79:13
whence I shall not r. — BIBL 86:24
returned r. on the previous night — BULL 170:7
returning R. were as tedious — SHAK 721:13
returns r. to the sore tooth — PROV 645:29
they say no one r. — CATU 210:5
reveal like Nature, half r. — TENN 795:1
r. Himself — MILT 546:2
r. whatsoever He will — KORA 472:17
revealed careless, when r. — CENT 212:13
Lord shall be r. — BIBL 93:15
nothing of r. religion — MEND 531:24
what has been r. — THOM 805:12
revelation except by r. — KORA 472:17
first hole is a r. — MOOR 557:8
inspired by divine r. — BACO 45:12
Reason is natural r. — LOCK 497:9
revelations ends with R. — WILD 855:26
extraordinary r. — BUTL 183:1
offers stupendous r. — HOFF 402:13
revelry r. by night — BYRO 186:5
revels Our r. now are ended — SHAK 733:31
r. long o' nights — SHAK 712:14
revenge deaths become r. by morning — MOTI 562:11
God's r. — FOOT 336:11
man that studieth r. — BACO 47:26
Punishment is not for r. — FRY 345:22
ranging for r. — SHAK 712:23
r. for slight injuries — MACH 511:6
R. herself went down — TENN 800:5
R. his foul — SHAK 700:19
R. is a dish — PROV 642:21
r. is a kind of wild justice — BACO 47:25
r. is always the pleasure — JUVE 451:20
R. is sweet — PROV 642:22
r.! Timotheus cries — DRYD 295:7
R. triumphs over death — BACO 46:21
shall we not r. — SHAK 724:19
spur my dull r. — SHAK 703:27
study of r. — MILT 541:13
Sweet is r. — BYRO 188:1
sweet r. grows harsh — SHAK 729:16
tribal, intimate r. — HEAN 387:14
with envy and r. — MILT 541:11

wrought in r. — CRAB 257:15
revenged I'll be r. — SHAK 736:10
revenges brings in his r. — SHAK 736:9
revenons R. *à ces moutons* — ANON 22:9
revenue standing r. — BURK 173:19
Thrift is a great r. — PROV 645:14
reverence In deeper r. praise — WHIT 853:2
mystic r. — BAGE 50:5
R. for Life — SCHW 687:12
r. the King — TENN 794:6
so poor to do him r. — SHAK 713:7
reverends Wrong R. of every Order — DICK 276:22
reveries r. so airy — COWP 256:15
reversion r. in the sky — POPE 614:4
review your r. before me — REGE 657:12
reviewers indolent r. — TENN 798:18
R. are usually people who — COLE 241:26
reviewing read a book before r. it — SMIT 758:25
revising power of r. — GIDE 356:5
revisited r. ideas — OLDF 584:23
revivalism rebellion and r. — THOM 807:1
revivals history of r. — BUTL 184:9
revive r. in New South Wales — BANK 57:13
strive to r. — PUGI 649:3
reviving r. the *castrati* — REED 657:8
revolt It is a big r. — LA R 482:13
r., disorder — MORR 561:7
revolting r. and a rebellious heart — BIBL 94:25
revolution After a r. — HALI 377:11
after the r. — AREN 26:8
age of r. — JEFF 431:17
crust over a volcano of r. — ELLI 314:4
destroyed by a r. — TOCQ 811:17
entered into this R. — BROW 161:10
explain the French R. — BAUD 62:1
French R. operated — TOCQ 811:14
it is a big r. — LA R 482:13
leaders of a r. — CONR 249:10
not r., but restoration — HARD 380:6
reform or r. — BERL 73:8
R. a parent — BURK 174:1
r. does not last more — ORTE 586:11
r. is the kicking down — HEAN 387:19
R., like Saturn — VERG 826:7
r. of rising expectations — CLEV 235:14
r. without revolution — ROBE 663:8
safeguard a r. — ORWE 587:18
revolutionaries R. are more formalistic — CALV 194:7
revolutionary can't feel r. in a bathroom — LINK 495:4
Clemency also a r. measure — DESM 274:12
Every r. ends — CAMU 196:14
forge his r. spirit — GUEV 374:10
revolutionists age fatal to R. — DESM 274:13
revolutions All modern r. — CAMU 196:13
main cause of r. — INGE 425:2
R. are not made — PROV 642:23
R. have never lightened — SHAW 741:9
r. never go backward — SEWA 693:2
r. with rosewater — HEAL 387:4
share in two r. — PAIN 593:6
revolver resembles a r. — FANO 323:2
revolving with the r. year — SHEL 743:12
reward in no wise lose his r. — BIBL 100:31
nothing for r. — SPEN 767:13
not to ask for any r. — IGNA 424:14
only r. of virtue — EMER 314:25
r. is when we die — RYDE 676:6
taken r. against the innocent — BOOK 140:2
Virtue is its own r. — PROV 646:3
what r. have ye — BIBL 99:8
Work not for a r. — BHAG 78:1
rewarded of thee be plenteously r. — BOOK 136:13
r. me evil for good — BOOK 141:22
rewardest r. every man — BOOK 143:23
rewards r. and Fairies — CORB 251:9
rewrite is to r. it — WILD 855:3
rex r. *quondam* — MALO 518:5
R. *tremendae maiestatis* — MISS 550:7
Reynolds R. died — BLAK 124:8

r. to tell people ORWE 588:6
r. which goes unrecognized WEIL 845:1
r. wrong TENN 794:4
scientists are probably r. ASIM 33:19
Self-government is our r. CASE 206:5
setting people r. MOOR 557:18
sheep on his r. hand BIBL 103:5
Sit thou on my r. hand BOOK 147:19
that which was r. BIBL 83:20
thing which is r. BOOK 140:1
to be decorative and to do r. FIRB 327:13
To do a great r. SHAK 725:2
Two wrongs don't make a r. PROV 645:47
Two wrongs don't make a r. SZAS 786:16
united by a sense of r. CICE 231:10
vast r.-wing conspiracy CLIN 236:3
Want to do r. RICH 660:5
Whatever IS, is R. POPE 616:28
what is r. when he can MACH 511:12
what's r. and fair HUGH 418:15
righteous godly, r., and sober life BOOK 150:3
have seen the r. forsaken BLUN 129:12
never the r. forsaken BOOK 141:25
not come to call the r. BIBL 100:16
prayer of a r. man BIBL 116:29
r. are bold BIBL 89:7
r. man BIBL 88:4
r. perisheth BIBL 94:13
r. shall be had BOOK 148:1
souls of the r. BIBL 96:19
righteousness breastplate of r. BIBL 114:15
clouds rain down r. BIBL 120:8
looked for r. BIBL 92:2
loved r., and hated iniquity BOOK 142:13
paths of r. SCOT 690:9
pursue r. PLAT 609:5
r. and peace BOOK 145:17
r. as the waves of the sea BIBL 93:24
R. exalteth a nation BIBL 88:12
r. hath not been forgotten BIBL 98:5
r. of the scribes BIBL 99:1
Sun of r. BIBL 96:19
Sun of R. WESL 847:9
superior understands r. CONF 246:2
thirst after r. BIBL 98:25
what r. really is ARNO 32:5
With r. shall he judge BOOK 146:13
righteousnesses r. are as filthy rags BIBL 94:21
rightful will to be r. JEFF 431:14
rights all your r. become CASE 206:6
as much r. as men TRUT 818:5
Bill of R. COMM 244:17
coloured men getting r. TRUT 818:6
duties as well as its r. DRUM 294:4
equal in dignity and r. ANON 16:5
extension of women's r. FOUR 339:4
from the South its dearest r. LEE 487:17
inalienable r. ROBE 663:10
intruder on r. of men WINC 860:5
Natural r. BENT 71:3
of his natural r. PRIE 624:1
own r. and interests MILL 535:22
r. are disregarded BROW 161:7
r. inherent and inalienable JEFF 431:6
r. in learning's world EGER 304:13
r. of an Englishman JUNI 450:2
r. of the smaller nationalities ASQU 34:4
'r.' of women NIGH 576:3
Stand up for your r. MARL 522:4
support of our neutral r. MONR 553:15
their r., and nothing less ANTH 24:17
unalienable r. ANON 21:6
rigol from this golden r. SHAK 707:28
rigour r. for desert FOWL 339:8
rigs Corn r., an' barley rigs BURN 178:17
rime making beautiful old r. SHAK 738:10
r. sparse PETR 604:17
r. was on the spray HARD 382:4
Rimmon in the house of R. BIBL 85:29
rind how shall taste the r. THOM 807:17
ring brocht ye to the r. WALL 836:13
dance with us in the same r. HALL 378:1
giving and receiving of a R. BOOK 139:4

Like a great r. VAUG 825:14
not get the r. without the finger MIDD 534:8
now r. the bells WALP 838:12
One R. to rule them all TOLK 813:5
on his luminous r. TENN 799:1
only pretty r. time SHAK 697:24
R.-a-ring o'roses NURS 581:3
r. at the end of his nose LEAR 486:6
r. is worn away OVID 590:4
r. of bright water RAIN 653:12
R. out, wild bells TENN 795:30
R. out, ye crystal spheres MILT 540:25
r. the bells of Heaven HODG 401:18
sell for one shilling Your r. LEAR 486:7
small circle of a wedding-r. CIBB 231:10
wear the devil's gold r. PROV 632:48
What shall we do for a r. LEAR 486:6
With this R. I thee wed BOOK 139:2
Ring-Bo-Ree bottles of R. LEAR 485:20
ringleaders fling the r. ARNO 32:15
rings hands are as gold r. BIBL 91:10
postman always r. twice CAIN 193:5
riot r. is at bottom KING 463:17
riotous r. living BIBL 105:29
ripe Cherry r. CAMP 195:24
I became r. JALA 428:19
Soon r., soon rotten PROV 643:24
we r. and ripe SHAK 696:25
ripeness R. is all SHAK 716:25
ripening greatness is a-r. SHAK 710:19
white with our r. BERR 74:16
ripper no female Jack the R. PAGL 592:2
ripple tiny r. of hope KENN 460:19
rise Created half to r. POPE 616:30
early to r. PROV 630:42
Early to r. THUR 810:12
fall to r. BROW 164:21
if the dead r. not BIBL 112:23
into this world to r. above FILM 329:12
Must r. at five CLAR 234:2
power to drink or r. PEAC 600:17
resistible r. of Arturo Ui BREC 155:23
r. against nation BIBL 102:23
r. and fight againe BALL 55:12
r. at ten thirty HARG 382:10
r. by other's fall SOUT 765:2
r. early JOHN 438:15
r. on stepping-stones TENN 794:31
r. out of obscurity JUVE 450:21
r. throught the branches DANT 265:10
R. up, my love BIBL 90:27
r. with the lark BRET 156:11
still, like air, I'll r. ANGE 15:18
stream cannot r. above PROV 643:43
risen floods are r. BOOK 146:5
rises sun also r. HEMI 391:5
rising means of r. JOHN 441:20
revolution of r. expectations CLEV 235:14
r. tide lifts all boats PROV 642:25
r. to great place BACO 47:10
r. up against us HAGG 375:11
risk conquer without r. CORN 251:13
increases in relation to r. HEMI 391:8
life without r. LAHR 476:1
r. more democracy BRAN 155:3
risks just one of the r. he takes STEV 774:21
risu r. cognoscere matrem VIRG 832:3
Solventur r. tabulae HORA 414:18
rites payens corsed olde r. CHAU 221:14
ritui Novo cedat r. THOM 805:15
Ritz open to all—like the R. MATH 527:18
rival craftsman's r. HESI 397:2
rivalry dead there is no r. MACA 507:6
rivals jealousy of r. ADAM 1:19
Three for the r. SONG 762:13
rive soul and body r. not more SHAK 695:15
river Across the r. JACK 427:3
Among the r. sallows KEAT 457:3
as in a r. HALI 377:13
black flowing r. HOOD 405:12
brook and r. meet LONG 499:10
Ceaselessly the r. flows KAMO 452:16
daughter went through the r. BUNY 171:26

either side the r. lie TENN 796:13
even the weariest r. SWIN 785:14
Fame is like a r. BACO 47:23
House of Parliament upon the r. WELL 846:17
if I were a r. AKHM 10:4
in the reeds by the r. BROW 164:11
Let us cross over the r. JACK 427:3
majestic r. ARNO 30:18
mingle with the r. SHEL 744:22
Ol' man r. HAMM 378:20
Over the one-strand r. NURS 578:17
peace been as a r. BIBL 93:24
Pentridge by the r. BARN 59:8
reeds in the r. BROW 164:12
r. at my garden's end SWIF 783:24
r. by the door STEV 777:4
r. in the tree DICK 282:5
r. Is a strong brown god ELIO 309:14
r. jumps over the mountains AUDE 36:24
r. of crystal light FIEL 326:4
r. of human industry TOCQ 812:16
r. of water of life BIBL 119:20
rook-racked, r.-rounded HOPK 407:6
see upon the r.'s reaches BLOK 129:3
Sleepless as the r. CRAN 258:18
twice into the same r. HERA 393:4
riverrun r., past Eve and Adam's JOYC 448:1
rivers as yet unknown r. VIRG 830:17
discourse of r. WALT 839:11
I've known r. HUGH 418:2
like r. grow cold MONT 554:6
R. and mountain-spring OAKL 582:15
r. cannot quench SHAK 710:11
r. dry up CHEK 222:5
r. in the south BOOK 149:1
r. like green ribbons TAYL 791:19
r. of blood JEFF 432:12
r. of Damascus BIBL 85:28
r. of water BIBL 93:5
r. run into the sea BIBL 89:17
rivulet neat r. of text SHER 748:22
road along the 'ard 'igh r. PUNC 649:20
And the r. below me STEV 777:2
braid, braid r. BALL 55:21
darksome r. CATU 210:5
Don't leave them on the r. GOGO 363:10
Follow the yellow brick r. HARB 380:1
Golden R. to Samarkand FLEC 334:12
Goodbye yellow brick r. JOHN 434:9
high r. JOHN 439:20
light to shine upon the r. COWP 255:16
on a lonesome r. COLE 241:7
one more for the r. MERC 532:9
on to the end of the r. LAUD 482:18
people in the middle of the r. BEVA 76:16
r. a thorny way CARB 197:16
r. he wishes to pursue TALM 789:31
r. of excess BLAK 126:4
R. to Heaven BALL 55:21
r. to hell is paved PROV 642:26
r. to the City of Emeralds BAUM 62:7
r. toward freedom MORR 561:7
r. to wealth TROL 816:10
r. up and the road down HERA 393:5
r. was a ribbon of moonlight NOYE 577:14
r. wind up-hill ROSS 669:8
rolling English r. CHES 224:12
royal r. to learning PROV 644:31
shut the r. through the woods KIPL 467:20
up the white r. ELIO 311:17
watched the ads and not the r. NASH 568:16
winding r. before me HAZL 386:24
ye'll tak' the high r. SONG 763:9
roads All r. lead to Rome PROV 626:16
How many r. DYLA 301:12
Two r. diverged FROS 344:22
without fear the lawless r. MUIR 564:9
roam don't know where to r. COLL 243:3
Everywhere I r. FOST 339:3
power to r. BYRO 186:3
sent to r. COWP 255:27
soar, but never r. WORD 869:18
roaming R. in the gloamin' LAUD 482:20

roaming (*cont.*):
r. with a hungry heart — TENN 800:15
where are you r. — SHAK 735:8
roar called upon to give the r. — CHUR 230:12
die of that r. — ELIO 307:26
long, withdrawing r. — ARNO 29:4
r. of London's traffic — CATC 208:22
r. their ribs out — GILB 358:15
r. you as gently — SHAK 725:30
roareth What is this that r. thus — GODL 361:1
roaring r. after their prey — BOOK 147:8
r. of the wind — KEAT 458:4
roast in boiled and r. — SMIT 758:6
In hell they'll r. thee — BURN 179:20
R. beef and Yorkshire — ORWE 586:22
R. Beef, Medium — FERB 325:4
r. me in sulphur — SHAK 729:21
r. their eggs — BACO 48:18
roasting r. of eggs — PROV 644:36
rob r. a lady of her fortune — FIEL 326:22
r. his mother — FAUL 324:18
robbed We was r. — JACO 427:5
robber Barabbas was a r. — BIBL 108:27
r.'s bundle — SHEL 747:16
robbers in perils of r. — BIBL 113:16
robbery In scandal, as in r. — CHES 222:19
wrong and r. — BOOK 143:22
robbing from r. he comes next — DE Q 273:22
r. a bank — BREC 156:1
r. of a foe — CHUR 228:7
r. the human race — MILL 536:5
robe Give me my r. — SHAK 696:2
judge's r. — SHAK 722:6
like a giant's r. — SHAK 722:13
shining r. of day — THOM 808:21
white r. of churches — RAOU 655:9
robes arrayed in white r. — BIBL 118:14
r. ye weave — SHEL 746:12
washed their r. — BIBL 118:15
When all her r. are gone — ANON 19:6
Robey R. the Darling of the music halls — SMIT 756:18
robin bold R. Hood — BALL 54:12
bonny sweet R. — SHAK 704:3
Call for the r.-red-breast — WEBS 844:20
R. and I are two honest men — SHIP 749:16
r. and the wren — PROV 642:27
R. Hood could brave — PROV 642:28
r. red breast — BLAK 124:10
R.'s not near — KEPP 461:4
Sweet R. is in the bush — SCOT 689:16
what will poor r. do — NURS 580:8
Who killed Cock R. — NURS 582:12
Robinson here's to you, Mrs R. — SIMO 752:14
Robinson Crusoe *Don Quixote, R.* — JOHN 444:25
robot r. may not injure a human — ASIM 33:18
robotics Rules of R. — ASIM 33:18
robots men may become r. — FROM 344:3
robs government which r. Peter — SHAW 739:25
robur *r. et aes triplex* — HORA 411:6
robust r. exchange of ideas — BREN 156:8
rock for a r. of offence — BIBL 92:12
founded upon a r. — BIBL 100:3
from the Tarpeian r. — ARNO 32:15
It is the Inchcape R. — SOUT 764:11
I've gotten a r. — BLAM 128:14
knew the perilous r. — SOUT 764:10
like the R. of Gibraltar — GAMO 348:7
R. journalism is people — ZAPP 877:13
R. of Ages — TOPL 813:21
Rock them, r. them, lullaby — DEKK 271:22
ruled by the r. — PROV 647:21
secure possession of a bleak r. — YOUN 876:8
serpent upon a r. — BIBL 89:12
set my feet upon the r. — BOOK 141:30
Sex and drugs and r. and roll — DURY 301:2
shadow of a great r. — BIBL 93:5
tall r., The mountain — WORD 866:11
upon this r. — BIBL 101:26
rocked R. in the cradle of the deep — WILL 857:1
r. the system — ROBI 664:7
rocket numbers that r. the mind — WILB 854:1
rose like a r. — PAIN 592:18

Rockies R. may crumble — GERS 353:15
rocking Brothers and sisters r. — JOHN 435:1
cradle endlessly r. — WHIT 852:4
r. a grown man — BURK 173:2
rocking horse upon a r. — KEAT 456:19
rocks eternal r. beneath — BRON 158:19
fossils in the r. — GOSS 366:12
hand that r. the cradle — WALL 836:14
marriage on the r. — MERR 533:2
native of the r. — JOHN 439:6
older than the r. — PATE 599:6
R., caves, lakes, fens — MILT 542:14
r. for the conies — BOOK 147:7
r. of the mountains — BIBL 118:11
R., torrents, gulfs — BEAT 62:12
r. unscalable — SHAK 698:21
seas roll over but the r. remain — HERB 393:14
when r. are near — WEBS 844:26
rod Aaron's r. — BIBL 81:3
bruise them with a r. of iron — BOOK 139:13
kiss the r. — SHAK 736:13
lightning and lashed r. — HOPK 408:6
r., which is the only instrument — LOCK 497:18
shall come forth a r. — BIBL 92:16
Spare the r. — PROV 643:28
spare the r., and spoil the child — BUTL 183:21
spareth his r. — BIBL 88:9
thy r. and staff — SCOT 690:9
thy r. and thy staff — BOOK 140:21
rode r. madly off — LEAC 485:9
r. upon the cherubims — BOOK 140:5
roe like to a r. — BIBL 91:18
roes breasts are like two young r. — BIBL 91:4
rogue call r. and villain — DRYD 297:24
dainty r. in porcelain — MERE 532:13
r. and peasant slave — SHAK 701:19
r.'s face — CONG 247:1
rogues Four r. in buckram — SHAK 705:27
roi *que le r.* — SAYI 684:27
r. d'Yvetot — BÉRA 72:6
Si le R. m'avait donné — ANON 22:10
Roland *Childe R. to the Dark Tower* — BROW 165:12
Child R. to the dark tower — SHAK 716:5
roll drugs and rock and r. — DURY 301:2
Let's r. — BEAM 62:10
r. all our strength — MARV 525:14
R. on, thou deep — BYRO 187:2
R. up that map — PITT 607:21
rolled bottoms of my trousers r. — ELIO 310:12
rolling jus' keeps r. along — HAMM 378:20
Like a r. stone — DYLA 301:18
r. English road — CHES 224:12
r. stone gathers — PROV 642:29
rolls r. back the restless stone — DUCK 298:10
r. it under his tongue — HENR 392:7
Roman Before the R. came to Rye — CHES 224:12
by a R. Valiantly vanquished — SHAK 695:20
deceased R. Empire — HOBB 401:8
fall of the R. empire — STEV 775:4
found the R. nation — VIRG 828:12
high R. fashion — SHAK 695:22
I am a R. citizen — CICE 232:4
make a R. holiday — BYRO 186:24
more an antique R. — SHAK 705:1
neither holy, nor R. — VOLT 834:9
noblest R. of them all — SHAK 714:3
noses cast is of the r. — FLEM 334:22
R. and his trouble — HOUS 416:2
R. for that — FARQ 324:7
R., make your task to rule — VIRG 830:14
R. meal . . . . . . a radish — COWP 256:22
R. people — CALI 193:8
R.-Saxon-Danish-Norman — DEFO 270:24
R.'s life — MACA 508:18
R. thought hath struck him — SHAK 694:11
R. world is falling — JERO 433:5
such a R. — SHAK 713:21
sweet R. hand — SHAK 736:3
Tenderest of R. poets — TENN 793:14
would not be a R. — SHAK 712:27
you R. writers — PROP 625:1
Romana *stat R. virisque* — ENNI 316:4
Roman Catholic R. Church — MACA 507:16

romance any historical r. — CLAR 234:1
fine r. with no kisses — FIEL 327:4
learned r. — AUST 42:1
music and love and r. — BERL 73:2
not a little given to r. — EVEL 321:18
symbols of a high r. — KEAT 457:9
romances like r. read — SUCK 779:11
Romanism rum, R., and rebellion — BURC 172:3
Romans do as the R. do — PROV 646:41
Friends, R., countrymen — SHAK 712:28
R. call it stoicism — ADDI 4:14
R. ever done — FILM 329:23
R. were like brothers — MACA 508:15
romantic airline ticket to r. places — MARV 525:18
once r. to burlesque — BYRO 188:29
R. Ireland's dead and gone — YEAT 874:21
'r.' music — STRA 778:19
r. poets — LEAP 485:11
ruin that's r. — GILB 357:17
Wrong but R. — SELL 692:3
romanticism r. is disease — GOET 363:4
romantics We were the last r. — YEAT 872:16
Romanus *Civis R. sum* — CICE 232:4
Civis R. sum — PALM 595:3
Rome All roads lead to R. — PROV 626:16
Bishop of R. — BOOK 150:21
comen from R. al hoot — CHAU 218:26
cruel men of R. — SHAK 711:12
Everything in R. — JUVE 451:1
from the Church of R. — WOTT 870:14
grandeur that was R. — POE 611:5
Half-Way House to R. — PUNC 649:16
happy R., born when I — CICE 232:13
hook-nosed fellow of R. — SHAK 707:25
Let R. in Tiber melt — SHAK 694:9
loved R. more — SHAK 712:25
Men, I'm getting out of R. — GARI 349:7
Now is it R. indeed — SHAK 711:21
Oh R.! my country — BYRO 186:19
palmy state of R. — SHAK 699:4
panting heart of R. — WISE 861:2
R., believe me — CLOU 236:12
R. has spoken — AUGU 39:22
R. hath lost her crown — COLE 239:4
R. immortal — GURN 374:17
R., in the height of her glory — WEBS 843:23
R. shall stand — BYRO 186:26
R.'s whitest day — MACA 508:7
R. was not built — PROV 642:30
second at R. — CAES 192:19
sitting at R. — PROV 636:20
strangers of R. — BIBL 109:13
time will doubt of R. — BYRO 189:3
voice of R. — JONS 446:2
wealth and din of R. — HORA 413:7
When I go to R. — AMBR 14:4
When in R., do as — PROV 646:41
Romeo wherefore art thou R. — SHAK 732:11
romping r. of sturdy children — DE V 275:1
Romulus dregs of R. — CICE 231:15
Ronsard *R. me célébrait* — RONS 666:15
rood half a r. Of land — SWIF 783:24
roof cat on a hot tin r. — WILL 858:3
come under my r. — BIBL 100:6
enter under my r. — MISS 549:20
heavens my wide r.-tree — AYTO 44:9
r. whirl around — JONS 446:13
r.-wrecked; damps there drip — HARD 381:9
this majestical r. — SHAK 701:11
Who, living, had no r. — HEYW 398:4
roofless through these r. halls — SHEL 745:5
roofs tiles on the r. — LUTH 505:5
rook r.-racked, river-rounded — HOPK 407:6
rooks r. are blown — TENN 795:5
r. in families homeward go — HARD 382:3
room about to enter a r. — EDDI 302:17
All I want is a r. — LERN 490:14
always r. at the top — PROV 644:21
always r. at the top — WEBS 844:5
at ease in a r. — PASC 597:18
Books do furnish a r. — POWE 621:18
boys in the back r. — LOES 498:8
cut out to make a r. — LAO 479:9

Great hatred, little r.	YEAT 874:12	Luve's like a red, red r.	BURN 179:8	one to r.	PROV 640:45
How little r. Do we take up	SHIR 749:20	Mighty lak' a r.	STAN 770:7	r. in hospitals	SOUT 764:4
In every grave make r.	D'AV 267:6	morning r.	KEAT 455:28	we r. and rot	SHAK 696:25
into the next r.	HOLL 403:7	no more desire a r.	SHAK 717:12	**Rothschild** R. and Baring	GILB 356:24
just entering the r.	BROU 160:14	No thorns go as deep as a r.'s	SWIN 785:9	**rots** Winter never r.	PROV 647:27
large upper r.	BIBL 106:18	One perfect r.	PARK 596:5	**rotted** simply r. early	NASH 568:17
little r.	HOUS 415:12	one r. from the dead	BIBL 106:8	**rotten** choice in r. apples	PROV 643:17
make more r.	BASS 61:4	Pluck a red r.	SHAK 709:18	good to feel r.	YESE 875:21
money and a r. of her own	WOOL 864:8	pluck a white r.	SHAK 709:17	hypocrite is really r.	AREN 26:7
no r. for them in the inn	BIBL 104:12	pluck the r.	BROW 168:6	like r. mackerel	RAND 655:3
riches in a little r.	MARL 522:17	Queen r. of the rosebud garden	TENN 798:5	r. apple injures	PROV 642:31
r. at your head	BALL 54:9	ravage with impunity a r.	BROW 167:22	r. boughs to climb	WYAT 871:3
r. grows chilly	GRAH 367:15	r. again from the dead	BOOK 133:19	shines like r. wood	RALE 653:15
r. in my heart for thee	ELLI 313:12	r. By any other name	SHAK 732:12	Something is r.	SHAK 700:15
smallest r. of my house	REGE 657:12	R.-cheeked Laura	CAMP 196:1	Soon ripe, soon r.	PROV 643:24
smoke-filled r.	SIMP 753:3	r. distilled	SHAK 725:22	tree was already r.	JOHN 434:12
struggle for r.	MALT 518:13	r. in aromatic pain	POPE 616:24	You r. swines	CATC 209:6
sufficient r.	BARN 59:9	r. in dark and evil days	INGR 425:12	**rottenness** r. begins in his conduct	JEFF 431:13
wasn't r. to swing a cat	DICK 277:20	R. is a rose	STEI 771:5	r. of eighty years	BYRO 191:12
rooms boys in the back r.	BEAV 63:15	R. of all my days	YEAT 875:4	r. of our civilization	READ 656:2
colder r.	AUST 41:5	r. of Sharon	BIBL 90:26	**rotundity** r. o' the world	SHAK 715:16
lighted r. inside your head	LARK 481:8	r. of yesterday	FITZ 331:14	**rotundus** teres, atque r.	HORA 415:2
Other voices, other r.	CAPO 197:12	r. Of youth	SHAK 695:9	**rough** al r. and long yherd	CHAU 219:19
R. don't change	GREE 371:21	r.-red city	BURG 172:12	r. and lecherous	SHAK 715:1
r. of thy native country	FULL 346:9	r.-red sissy	PLOM 610:6	r. and ready man	BROW 165:1
Rooshans people . . . may be R.	DICK 278:22	r. should shut	KEAT 454:12	R.-hew them how we will	SHAK 704:21
roost come home to r.	PROV 629:30	r.'s scent is bitterness	THOM 807:12	r. magic I here abjure	SHAK 734:1
root all evil's r.	SUDR 779:16	R., thou art sick	BLAK 128:2	r. places plain	BIBL 93:15
axe is laid unto the r.	BIBL 98:18	r. to a pitch-black toad	YESE 875:20	R. winds do shake	SHAK 737:18
axe to the r.	PAIN 592:20	R., were you not	PRIO 624:12	**roughness** r. breedeth hate	BACO 47:9
begins to take r.	WASH 840:20	r. with all its sweetest leaves	BYRO 189:24	**roughs** among his fellow r.	DOYL 293:4
eaten on the insane r.	SHAK 718:13	r. without the thorn	HERR 396:9	**round** earth's r. shadow	SAVA 682:18
idleness being the r. of evil	KIER 462:12	Roves back the r.	DE L 271:24	flat pretending to be r.	FORS 337:18
Idleness is r. of all evil	PROV 635:4	secret and inviolate R.	YEAT 874:19	in that little r.	FORD 337:11
nips his r.	SHAK 710:19	sweet lovely r.	SHAK 705:13	into the r. hole	SMIT 758:4
perced to the r.	CHAU 218:2	Sweet r., whose hue	HERB 395:2	Love makes the world go r.	PROV 638:8
r. is ever in its grave	HERB 395:2	vanish with the r.	FITZ 331:28	made the r. world so sure	BOOK 146:4
r. of all evil	BIBL 115:23	wavers to a r.	DOBS 287:4	R. and round the circle	ELIO 309:2
r. of all evil	PROV 639:2	white r. of Scotland	MACD 510:5	Round and r. the garden	NURS 581:4
r. of heath	BRON 158:11	white r. weeps	TENN 798:6	r. as a ball	JULI 449:5
r. of the matter	BIBL 86:35	without thorn the r.	MILT 543:3	R. both the shires	HOUS 415:16
square r. of half a number	LONG 500:8	yet a r. full-blown	HERR 396:21	r. earth's imagined corners	DONN 288:8
striking at the r.	THOR 809:17	**rosea** avertens r. cervice	VIRG 828:19	r., fat, oily man	THOM 808:10
roots drought is destroying his r.	HERB 393:11	**rosebud** I did but touch the r.	PHIL 606:4	R. the world	ARNO 29:14
out of his r.	BIBL 92:16	R. is just a piece	FILM 329:10	r. unvarnished tale	SHAK 728:8
r. of education are bitter	ARIS 28:9	**rosebuds** crown ourselves with r.	BIBL 96:26	R. up the usual suspects	FILM 329:4
r. that can be pulled up	ELIO 307:9	Gather ye r.	HERR 396:17	said the world was r.	GERS 353:18
send my r. rain	HOPK 408:3	**rosemary** r. and rue	SHAK 736:29	**roundabouts** gain on the r.	PROV 646:33
rope by the r. we know	JAME 429:11	r., that's for remembrance	SHAK 704:2	**rounded** polished and well-r.	HORA 415:2
fourfold r. of nerves	HEAT 388:6	**Rosencrantz** R. and Guildenstern	SHAK 705:5	r. with a sleep	SHAK 733:31
Give a man r. enough	PROV 632:47	**roses** ash the burnt r. leave	ELIO 309:16	**Roundheads** R. (Right but Repulsive)	
hempen r. in the place	SONG 763:8	criticism with r.	D'IS 286:31		SELL 692:3
Never mention r.	PROV 639:40	days of wine and r.	DOWS 292:5	**Rousseau** ask Jean Jacques R.	COWP 255:23
refuse to set his hand to a r.	DRAK 293:9	Each morn a thousand r.	FITZ 331:14	**routine** care more for r.	BAGE 51:8
sell us the r.	MISQ 547:6	Everything's coming up r.	SOND 761:2	**rove** r. as well as you	BEHN 67:2
rorate R., coeli	BIBL 120:8	fields where r. fade	HOUS 416:9	**rover** blood's a r.	HOUS 415:13
rosa r. Sera moretur	HORA 412:5	flower of r.	BIBL 98:6	**roving** go no more a-r.	BYRO 191:4
Rosalind No jewel is like R.	SHAK 697:7	Flung r., roses	DOWS 292:3	**row** R. after row with strict impunity	
rose allons voir si la r.	RONS 666:14	Honey of r.	HERB 394:11		TATE 790:12
American beauty r.	ROCK 665:1	let fall a shower of r.	TERE 802:6	r. Of polished pillars	JONS 446:27
beauty's r.	SHAK 737:15	like my r. to see you	SHER 749:4	r. one way and look another	BURT 181:7
blossom as the r.	BIBL 93:8	lilac and the r.	ARAG 25:15	**rowan** r. leaves are dank	BLOK 129:3
blows so red The r.	FITZ 331:17	not a bed of r.	STEV 775:30	**rowed** All r. fast	MISQ 547:2
English unofficial r.	BROO 159:7	on a bed of r.	HORA 411:9	**rowing** looking one way, and r.	BUNY 171:11
expectancy and r.	SHAK 702:9	Plant thou no r.	ROSS 669:9	**Rowley** 'Heigh-ho!' says R.	NURS 578:14
fading r.	CARE 198:13	raptures and r.	SWIN 785:7	**royal** needed no r. title	SPEN 766:5
fayr as is the r.	CHAU 220:20	Ring-a-ring o'r.	NURS 581:3	r. banners forward go	FORT 338:15
fire and the r. are one	ELIO 309:22	R. are flowering in Picardy	WEAT 843:8	r. captain of this ruined	SHAK 708:19
fresh lap of the crimson r.	SHAK 726:4	r. for the flush	ROSS 669:3	r. priesthood	BIBL 117:3
Gather therefore the r.	SPEN 767:15	R. have thorns	SHAK 737:26	'r. road' to geometry	EUCL 320:19
ghost of a r.	BROW 162:7	r. of thy lips	LODG 498:7	r. road to learning	PROV 644:31
Go, lovely r.	WALL 836:17	roses, r., all the way	BROW 166:27	r. road to the unconscious	MISQ 547:10
Goodbye, England's r.	JOHN 434:7	r. within	MARV 525:9	R. Society desires to confer	FARA 323:9
I know the colour r.	ABSE 1:4	scent of the r.	MOOR 558:8	r. throne of kings	SHAK 730:10
inimitable r.	WINC 860:10	smells like r.	JOHN 435:9	this is the r. Law	CORO 252:8
Into the r.-garden	ELIO 309:4	soft as the r.	BYRO 185:13	**royalist** more of a r.	SAYI 684:27
I r., went forth	WESL 847:7	Treaties like girls and r.	DE G 271:15	**royaliste** plus r.	SAYI 684:27
labyrinthine buds the r.	BROW 167:21	Two red r.	MORR 560:16	**royally** proved most r.	SHAK 705:6
last r. of summer	MOOR 558:13	**rosewater** made with r.	PROV 642:23	**Royal Society** proposed to the R.	ARTS 33:1
late r. may yet linger	HORA 412:5	revolutions with r.	HEAL 387:4	**royalty** R. is a government	BAGE 51:1
lovely is the r.	WORD 867:3	**rosy** plain men have r. faces	STEV 776:20	r. is to be reverenced	BAGE 51:5
love were what the r. is	SWIN 786:2	r.-fingered dawn	HOME 405:3	r. of Albion's king	SHAK 709:21
luver stole my r.	BURN 177:17	**rot** in cold obstruction and to r.	SHAK 723:14	R. the gold filling	OSBO 588:20

royalty (cont.):
R. will be strong — BAGE 51:1
when you come to R. — DISR 286:19
rub ay, there's the r. — SHAK 701:26
r. up against money — RUNY 672:10
rubbers look out for r. — PROV 645:8
rubbish cast as r. to the void — TENN 795:13
r. of an Adam — SOUT 764:3
some of the r. — LOCK 497:3
What r. — BLÜC 129:8
rubble crushed by the r. — SOLZ 760:16
rubies above r. — BIBL 87:1
pearls away and r. — HOUS 415:15
price is far above r. — BIBL 89:14
rubs fog that r. its back — ELIO 310:7
rudder heart was to thy r. tied — SHAK 695:8
rhyme the r. is — BUTL 183:16
r. of painting — LEON 489:20
ruled by the r. — PROV 647:21
ruddy r., and beautiful — BIBL 84:1
rude R. am I in my speech — SHAK 728:7
r. and wild — BELL 68:5
so r. to the good — WORD 865:3
You have been very r. — CHIR 226:9
rudest r. work that tells a story — RUSK 673:23
Rudolph R., the Red-Nosed — MARK 521:16
rue nought shall make us r. — SHAK 714:15
rosemary and r. — SHAK 736:29
R., even for ruth — SHAK 730:26
There's r. for you — SHAK 704:3
ruffian father r. — SHAK 706:5
menaces of a r. — JOHN 441:10
ruffle r. up your spirits — SHAK 713:13
ruffled r. feathers sex can — EWAR 321:23
rugby R. Union which is — THOM 807:1
rugged harsh cadence of a r. line — DRYD 297:2
old r. cross — BENN 70:6
steep and r. pathway — WILL 858:16
system of r. individualism — HOOV 406:13
rugs like a million bloody r. — FITZ 332:15
Ruh *Meine R.' ist hin* — GOET 362:4
Über allen Gipfeln Ist R.' — GOET 362:15
Ruhm *Tat ist alles, nichts der R.* — GOET 362:6
ruin foundation of his own r. — FIEL 327:1
God to r. has designed — DRYD 296:1
its r. didst not share — DODI 287:8
Majestic though in r. — MILT 542:7
Resolved to r. — DRYD 294:15
roving's been my r. — SONG 762:2
r. himself in twelve months — GEOR 353:1
r. of all happiness — BURN 176:22
R. seize thee — GRAY 369:19
r. that Cromwell knocked about — BEDF 65:9
r. that's romantic — GILB 357:17
r. upon ruin — MILT 542:20
ruin—yet what r. — BYRO 186:25
ruinae *Impavidum ferient r.* — HORA 412:19
ruined home of r. reputations — ELIO 307:15
O r. piece of nature — SHAK 716:18
r. at our own request — MORE 558:20
r. on the side — BURK 175:11
r. sides of kings — BEAU 63:9
They r. us — DUNN 300:1
ruinous r. and old — SPEN 767:6
R. inheritance — GAIU 347:8
ruins human mind in r. — DAVI 268:4
Of all r. — DOYL 292:12
others' r. built — SOUT 765:2
r. of the noblest man — SHAK 712:22
r. of time — BLAK 128:12
r. would strike him unafraid — HORA 412:19
shored against my r. — ELIO 311:18
Ruislip Gaily into R. gardens — BETJ 76:1
rule all be done by the r. — SHAK 695:2
bear r. in their kingdoms — BIBL 98:2
Be each man's r. — TENN 793:20
Divide and r. — PROV 630:7
exception proves the r. — PROV 631:39
exception to every r. — PROV 644:22
first r. of life — MELB 530:9
good old r. — WORD 869:1
greatest r. of all — MOLI 552:3
Ill can he r. the great — SPEN 767:22

little r., a little sway — DYER 301:8
make your r. — BLAK 126:28
oldest r. in the book — CARR 202:18
One Ring to r. them all — TOLK 813:5
only infallible r. — SURT 781:5
reasons for the r. change — STRA 778:21
Reason to r. — DRYD 295:25
rich men r. the law — GOLD 364:27
R. 1, on page 1 — MONT 556:9
r. are least eager — PLAT 609:3
r. because you hold yourself — HORA 413:1
R., Britannia — THOM 808:8
r. o'er freemen — BROO 159:3
r. of speech — HORA 409:1
r. the day — BIBL 78:15
r. the state — DRYD 294:15
r. wherever they can — THUC 810:8
You work, we r. — DUNN 300:1
ruled r. by the rudder — PROV 647:21
ruler choose a r. — BAGE 50:17
r. and guide — BOOK 136:4
r. in Israel — BIBL 96:13
r. is like wind — CONF 246:5
r. of all his substance — BOOK 147:12
R. of the Queen's Navee — GILB 357:28
rulers conduct of their r. — ADAM 3:10
R. have no authority — MAYH 529:8
r., mostly knaves — BIER 121:7
r. of the darkness — BIBL 114:15
rules all the r. of art — ADDI 5:23
break known r. — CROM 260:17
by any hypercritical r. — LINC 493:13
disregard of all the r. — ORWE 587:23
exception to the ordinary r. — HAZL 385:19
Fallen by mistaken r. — WINC 860:6
hand that r. the world — WALL 836:14
Integrity has no need of r. — CAMU 196:10
keep making up these sex r. — SALI 678:9
Nobody r. safely — THOM 804:19
r. all the worlds — UPAN 822:14
R. and models — HAZL 386:13
R. of Robotics — ASIM 33:18
r. of the game — HUXL 423:10
r. the world — PROV 633:39
taste or genius by r. — REYN 659:1
two r. for design — PUGI 649:1
wouldn't obey the r. — BENN 70:11
ruleth r. his spirit — BIBL 88:18
ruling r. passion conquers — POPE 615:5
Search then the R. Passion — POPE 615:15
rum r. and true religion — BYRO 188:7
r., Romanism, and rebellion — BURC 172:3
r., sodomy, prayers, and the lash — CHUR 230:9
what a R. Go everything is — WELL 846:21
rumble r. of a distant drum — FITZ 331:16
R. thy bellyful — SHAK 715:17
rumour distillation of r. — CARL 199:25
Enter R., painted — SHAK 707:2
R. is a pipe — SHAK 707:3
R. not always wrong — TACI 786:19
sound and r. — MORR 560:11
rumours wars and r. of wars — BIBL 102:22
rump r.-fed runnion — SHAK 718:6
run born to r. — SPRI 769:5
enabled him to r. — MACA 507:22
finest r. in Leicestershire — PAGE 592:1
He can r. — LOUI 501:12
he may r. that readeth it — BIBL 96:16
In the long r. — KEYN 462:5
makes the cup r. over — PROV 637:11
Many a good r. — SURT 781:7
never did r. smooth — SHAK 725:23
Now Teddy must r. — KENN 461:1
r. after two hares — PROV 635:33
R. and find out — KIPL 468:7
r. from me and the child — BALL 54:18
r. over a cad — CLOU 236:18
R., run, Orlando — SHAK 697:6
r.-stealers flicker — THOM 807:11
r. the race with Death — JOHN 444:6
r. to and fro — BIBL 96:2
r. with patience — BIBL 116:7
r. with the hare — PROV 648:13

shine, and r. to and fro — BIBL 96:29
They get r. down — BEVA 76:16
they which r. in a race — BIBL 112:8
trying To r. and run — VIRG 831:11
walk before we can r. — PROV 646:15
we will make him r. — MARV 525:14
What makes Sammy r. — SCHU 686:18
runagates r. continue in scarceness — BOOK 144:7
runaway curb a r. young star — BYRO 191:11
r. Presidency — SCHL 686:4
runcible ate with a r. spoon — LEAR 486:8
R. Cat with crimson whiskers — LEAR 486:10
weareth a r. hat — LEAR 486:4
runic sort of R. rhyme — POE 610:16
runnable r. stag — DAVI 267:14
runner long-distance r. — SILL 752:11
running all the r. *you can do* — CARR 202:24
r. over — BIBL 104:26
r. over with knowledge — KEAT 458:5
r. with the pack — BUTL 183:6
runnion rump-fed r. — SHAK 718:6
runs book, who r. may read — KEBL 459:2
fights and r. away — PROV 634:20
r. against Time — JOHN 436:26
Rupert Prince R. — DISR 284:6
R. of Debate — BULW 170:11
R. of the Rhine — MACA 508:5
rura *Paterna r.* — HORA 411:3
rural Retirement, r. quiet — THOM 808:13
r. spot — HUNT 421:9
r. virtues leave — GOLD 364:12
rus *R. in urbe* — MART 524:12
rush fools r. in — POPE 616:14
Fools r. in — PROV 632:33
rushed r. into the field — BYRO 186:7
rushes Green grow the r., O — BURN 178:9
Green grow the r. O — SONG 762:13
rushing r. mighty wind — BIBL 109:12
russet plain r.-coated captain — CROM 260:9
r. yeas — SHAK 717:22
Russia forecast the action of R. — CHUR 229:11
last out a night in R. — SHAK 723:5
power of R. — MITC 550:15
R. and British India — SALI 678:14
R. an empire or democracy — BRZE 169:4
R. has two generals — NICH 574:16
Russian he might have been a R. — GILB 358:4
R. knows only — CHEK 222:11
Scratch a R. — PROV 642:35
tumult in the R. heart — PUSH 650:20
with a R. soul — LERM 490:5
Russians R. and the Americans — TOCQ 812:12
rust moth and r. doth corrupt — BIBL 99:13
r. in peace — SOUT 764:4
r. unburnished, not to shine — TENN 800:16
Tarnished with r. — WILD 856:6
wear out than to r. out — CUMB 262:2
wear out than to r. out — PROV 627:41
which never taketh r. — SIDN 751:2
rusticity refined r. — WORD 865:20
rustle r. in your dying throat — FILM 330:5
rustling r. of the grass — WORD 865:4
rusty grown r. — BUTL 183:15
Ruth sad heart of R. — KEAT 456:10
Rutherford R. was a disaster — BULL 170:6
ruthless Ruin seize thee, r. King! — GRAY 369:19
rye Before the Roman came to R. — CHES 224:12
catcher in the r. — SALI 678:8
catcher in the r. — SALI 678:11
Comin thro' the r. — BURN 177:20
fields of barley and of r. — TENN 796:13
pocket full of r. — NURS 581:8
r. reach to the chin — PEEL 601:16

Saba kings of Arabia and S. — BOOK 144:19
sabachthani Eli, Eli, lama s. — BIBL 103:24
Sabaoth grant me that S.'s sight — SPEN 767:27
Lord God of S. — BOOK 133:9
sabbata *sunt illa s.* — ABEL 1:1
sabbath born on the S. day — NURS 580:6
Lord blest the s. day — BIBL 81:19

saltness sugar, and s. — GOLD 364:17
salus S. extra ecclesiam — AUGU 39:14
S. populi — CICE 231:18
S. populi suprema lex — SELD 691:16
salutant Ave Caesar, morituri te s. — ANON 23:3
salutations s. in the market — BIBL 104:3
salute If it moves, s. it — MILI 535:10
S. one another — BIBL 111:20
s. thee, Mantovano — TENN 800:12
S. the happy morn — BYRO 185:2
those about to die s. you — ANON 23:3
salutes see if anyone s. it — SAYI 684:34
salva S. me — MISS 550:7
salvaged ships have been s. — HALS 378:10
salvation bottle of s. — RALE 653:19
cannot be s. — CYPR 263:16
can seek s. — FRED 341:22
generally necessary to s. — BOOK 138:15
hope of s. — BIBL 115:14
my light, and my s. — BOOK 141:9
necessary to s. — BOOK 150:17
none of us Should see s. — SHAK 724:30
no s. outside the church — AUGU 39:14
Now is our s. nearer — BIBL 111:16
now is the day of s. — BIBL 113:10
publisheth s. — BIBL 93:27
shew him my s. — BOOK 146:3
strength of our s. — BOOK 146:7
Visit us with thy s. — WESL 847:17
Work out your own s. — BIBL 114:20
Wot prawce s. nah — SHAW 740:16
salve S., regina — PRAY 623:7
Sam nephew of my Uncle S.'s — COHA 238:4
Play it again, S. — FILM 328:14
Play it again, S. — MISQ 548:14
S., pick up tha' musket — HOLL 403:8
Samaritan remember the Good S. — THAT 803:15
Samarkand Golden Road to S. — FLEC 334:12
silken S. — KEAT 454:13
Samarra Appointment in S. — O'HA 583:15
appointment with him in S. — MAUG 528:12
same all say the s. — MELB 530:17
but thou art the s. — BOOK 146:17
Ever the s. — MOTT 563:18
more they are the s. — KARR 453:8
much the s. — ANON 16:7
s. yesterday, and to day — BIBL 116:12
would be all the s. — DICK 279:11
you are the s. — MART 524:11
samite Clothed in white s. — TENN 794:1
Sammy What makes S. run — SCHU 686:18
Samnites like S. — HORA 410:23
Samson S. hath quit himself — MILT 545:9
Samuel Lord called S. — BIBL 83:25
sancta S. simplicitas — JERO 433:4
sanctified s. by the wife — BIBL 112:3
sanctify S. the Lord of hosts — BIBL 92:12
sanctions Baldwin denouncing s. — BEAV 63:13
sanctuary classes which need s. — BALD 53:4
Cunning is the dark s. — CHES 222:22
So much s.-breaking — SKEL 754:3
sanctus S., sanctus, sanctus — MISS 549:16
sand and a grain of s. — WHIT 852:10
house upon the s. — BIBL 100:4
Little grains of s. — CARN 201:5
on the edge of the s. — LEAR 486:8
quantities of s. — CARR 203:3
s. against the wind — BLAK 126:25
s. in the porridge — COWA 253:11
s.-strewn caverns — ARNO 29:13
turns s. to gold — YOUN 876:9
world in a grain of s. — BLAK 124:9
sandal s. shoon — SHAK 703:30
sandals with s. grey — MILT 540:16
sandbank no s., thrown up — DAVI 268:16
sands Across the s. of Dee — KING 464:10
Come unto these yellow s. — SHAK 733:20
Footprints on the s. — LONG 499:17
lone and level s. — SHEL 745:17
riddle of the s. — CHIL 226:4
s., ignoble things — BEAU 63:9
s. upon the Red sea shore — BLAK 126:26
sandwich ask for a watercress s. — WILD 856:8

cheaper than a prawn s. — RATN 655:14
taste again that raw-onion s. — BARN 59:4
sane if he was s. he had to fly — HELL 390:3
remain s. — HALD 376:14
San Francisco left my heart in S. — CROS 261:8
sang morning stars s. — BIBL 87:9
Perhaps it may turn out a s. — BURN 178:2
s. a king out of three kingdoms — WHAR 849:13
s. his didn't he — CUMM 262:3
s. in my chains — THOM 805:16
s. within the bloody wood — ELIO 310:27
sanglots Les s. longs — VERL 826:9
Sangreal story of the S. — MALO 518:1
sanitary glorified s. engineer — STRA 778:12
sanitas S. sanitatum — MÉNA 531:15
sanitatum Sanitas s. — MÉNA 531:15
sanity ain't no S. Claus — FILM 328:23
sank s. my boat — KENN 460:15
Sighted sub, s. same — MASO 527:8
sano Mens sana in corpore s. — JUVE 451:17
sans sans singer, and—s. End — FITZ 331:18
S. teeth, sans eyes — SHAK 697:3
sansculotte bon S. Jésus — DESM 274:13
Santa Claus death or S. — BERN 74:8
there is a S. — NEWS 573:26
saoshyants truly shall be 's.' — ZORO 879:11
sap dried the s. of my veins — YEAT 873:11
world's whole s. is sunk — DONN 289:12
sapere s. aude — HORA 410:5
sapient s. head — ARNO 31:6
s. sutlers — ELIO 310:15
sapless s. foliage of the ocean — SHEL 745:9
saplings wind it plies the s. — HOUS 416:1
sapphire purer s. melts — TENN 798:2
sapphires ivory overlaid with s. — BIBL 91:10
Sappho Where burning S. loved — BYRO 188:21
Sarah ceased to be with S. — BIBL 79:34
sardine jasper and a s. stone — BIBL 118:3
sardines s. will be thrown — CANT 197:10
Sarum had you upon S. plain — SHAK 715:9
sash s. my father wore — POLI 613:8
sashes one of his nice new s. — GRAH 367:15
Saskatchewan on the banks of the S. — LAUR 483:3
sat everyone has s. except a man — CUMM 262:7
I s. down and wept — SMAR 755:16
S. and knotted — SEDL 690:18
s. down under a juniper tree — BIBL 85:13
s. too long here — CROM 260:14
s. upon a promontory — SHAK 726:5
She s. down — JACK 426:12
we s. down and wept — BOOK 149:13
Satan Auld Hornie, S. — BURN 177:6
beat down S. — BOOK 134:23
beheld S. — BIBL 105:2
casting out S. by Satan — SORL 764:2
Get thee behind me, S. — BIBL 101:27
high capital Of S. — MILT 542:1
Lord said unto S. — BIBL 86:9
S. cast out Satan — BIBL 103:27
S. exalted sat — MILT 542:2
S. finds some mischief still — WATT 841:12
S. met his ancient friend — BYRO 191:16
S., so call him now — MILT 543:24
S. stood Unterrified — MILT 542:16
S., thou art but a dunce — BLAK 125:9
S., thy master — YOUN 876:26
Satanic dark S. mills — BLAK 126:24
satellite With s. TV — O'DO 583:12
satiable full of s. curtiosity — KIPL 468:10
satiety occasion of s. — BACO 46:15
satin ease a heart like a s. gown — PARK 596:8
mad in white s. — SHER 748:6
satire hard not to write s. — JUVE 450:11
let s. be my song — BYRO 189:29
S., being levelled at all — SWIF 783:9
S. indeed is entirely our own — QUIN 652:5
S. is a sort of glass — SWIF 782:1
S. is what closes Saturday — KAUF 453:9
S. or sense — POPE 614:24
s. out of time — CHUR 228:14
satiric one s. touch — SWIF 784:11

satirical sign of a s. wit — AUBR 36:3
satirist s. may laugh — GIBB 354:18
second English S. — HALL 378:2
satis s. est sapio — PERS 604:11
satisfaction can't get no s. — JAGG 427:10
murder, for my own s. — DOST 291:4
satisfied can't be s. — HUGH 418:5
fool s. — MILL 536:16
love s. — RICH 660:13
Never s. with having — WROT 871:1
well paid that is well s. — SHAK 725:7
satisfies Where most she s. — SHAK 695:1
satisfieth that which s. not — BIBL 94:7
satisfy poorly s. our eyes — WOTT 870:8
will I s. him — BOOK 146:3
satisfying s. a voracious appetite — FIEL 326:19
satura S. quidem tota nostra est — QUIN 652:5
saturam s. non scribere — JUVE 450:11
Saturday closes S. night — KAUF 453:9
Glasgow Empire on a S. night — DODD 287:6
S.'s child — NURS 580:6
what he did on S. — YBAR 872:6
Saturn grey-haired S. — KEAT 454:20
Revolution, like S. — VERG 826:7
while S. whirls — TENN 799:1
Saturnia redeunt S. regna — VIRG 832:2
Saturnus S., with his frosty face — SACK 676:13
satyr Hyperion to a s. — SHAK 699:20
s. shall cry — BIBL 93:7
satyrs men, like s. — MARL 522:13
sauce Hunger is the best s. — PROV 634:48
only one s. — CARA 197:14
s. for the goose — PROV 646:28
Saul Is S. also among the prophets — BIBL 83:31
name was S. — BIBL 109:18
S. and Jonathan — BIBL 84:12
S. hath slain his thousands — BIBL 84:7
S. was consenting — BIBL 109:19
S., why persecutest thou me — BIBL 109:21
weep over S. — BIBL 84:12
sausage pig in a s. — TROL 817:3
s. machine — CHRI 227:3
sausages Laws are like s. — MISQ 548:6
savage days of the Noble S. — BIKO 121:12
dealing with the s. English — WILL 857:12
laws unto a s. race — TENN 800:14
mad and s. master — SOPH 761:22
noble s. ran — DRYD 295:15
not allow it to be s. — OVID 590:2
now the s. race — CHUR 228:9
s. wields his club — HUXL 423:6
sooth a s. breast — CONG 247:8
take some s. woman — TENN 797:5
savaged s. by a dead sheep — HEAL 387:1
savages love of s. — LERM 490:1
save Beauty will s. the world — DOST 291:6
destroy the town to s. it — ANON 18:7
exist in order to s. us — DE V 275:5
God s. king Solomon — BIBL 84:25
God s. the king — SONG 762:9
himself he cannot s. — BIBL 103:23
rushed through life trying to s. — ROGE 666:7
s. five sous on unessential things — COLB 238:14
s. his soul — BIBL 95:16
s. me — MISS 550:7
Save me, oh, s. me — CANN 197:3
s. one's own — BROW 166:11
s. the Governor-General — WHIT 851:19
s. the people — ELLI 313:17
s. the Union — LINC 493:17
s. those that have no imagination — SHAW 742:14
s. time — BACO 46:25
S. us from our friends — PROV 642:34
To s. your world — AUDE 37:2
saved be s. in this World — HALI 377:23
could have s. sixpence — BECK 64:4
He s. others — BIBL 103:23
only s. the world — CHES 224:4
penny s. — PROV 641:33
s. alive a whole world — TALM 788:22
we are not s. — BIBL 95:1
What must I do to be s. — BIBL 109:32

Whosoever will be s. BOOK 134:11
youthful hose well s. SHAK 697:2
saving capable of s. us RICH 660:10
s. of life must supersede TALM 789:13
thy s. health BOOK 144:4
saviour because I am the S. JAIN 428:13
our S. dear BASS 61:3
S.'s birth is celebrated SHAK 699:6
s. spring to life BIBL 120:8
savoir belle chose que de s. MOLI 552:1
savory s., marjoram SHAK 736:31
savour keep Seeming and s. SHAK 736:29
salt have lost his s. BIBL 98:26
saw do not s. the air SHAK 702:12
I came, I s., I conquered CAES 193:2
I came, s., and overcame SHAK 707:25
I s. and loved GIBB 354:23
Saxon ancient S. phrase LONG 499:7
S. and Norman TENN 801:3
say all s. *the same* MELB 530:17
anything good to s. LONG 500:12
could s. if I chose CARR 202:11
Do as I s. PROV 630:8
Do as I s. SELD 691:19
don't s. nothin' HAMM 378:20
find anything to s. FLAU 333:10
Have something to s. ARNO 32:11
I s., before the morning BOOK 149:8
Lat thame s. MOTT 563:22
many things to s. unto you BIBL 108:21
more to s. when I am dead ROBI 663:18
no more to s. SHAK 734:24
nothing to s. CAGE 193:4
nothing to s. COLT 244:9
not much to s. COMP 245:8
not s. what one thinks EURI 321:16
S. I'm weary, say I'm sad HUNT 421:7
S. it ain't so ANON 20:5
S. it with flowers ADVE 8:14
S. little and do much SHAM 738:30
s. nowt PROV 634:29
s. only the word MISS 549:20
s. something GOOD 365:26
s. *something* about me COHA 238:5
s. the perfectly correct thing SHAW 740:2
s. what they please FRED 342:4
s. what you mean CARR 202:5
s. what you think TACI 787:9
see what I s. WALL 836:15
shall not s. much MATH 527:16
someone else has got to s. GASK 350:8
some s. that we wan MCLE 512:7
something to s. WHAT 849:14
what circumstances we s. it HAVE 384:7
whatever you s. HEAN 387:18
wink wink, s. no more MONT 556:18
saying For loving, and for s. so DONN 289:19
never finished s. CALV 194:8
not worth s. BEAU 63:1
were s. yesterday LUIS 505:1
sayings s. are like women's letters HAZL 385:20
says not what he s. SMIT 757:12
What everybody s. PROV 646:20
What Manchester s. today PROV 646:24
Who s. A must say B PROV 647:19
scabbard threw away the s. CLAR 233:5
throw the s. away PROV 647:20
scabs Make yourselves s. SHAK 698:3
scaffold forever on the s. LOWE 502:20
s. and the doom AYTO 44:6
to a s. from a throne FANS 323:3
scale best s. for an experiment FISH 330:7
sufficiently large s. SPEN 766:2
with her lifted s. POPE 611:14
scallop s.-shell of quiet RALE 653:19
scaly s. horror of his folded tail MILT 540:28
scan gently s. your brother man BURN 177:8
scandal In s., as in robbery CHES 222:19
Love and s. FIEL 326:16
no s. like rags FARQ 324:4
s. and glory RAMS 654:20
s. by a woman of easy virtue HAIL 376:7
s. that constitutes offence MOLI 552:24

tea and s. CONG 246:25
scandalous s. and poor ROCH 664:18
scapegoat Let him go for a s. BIBL 81:27
scar s. on the conscience BLAI 124:3
wears their going like a s. DUNN 300:4
scarce Good men are s. PROV 633:23
scarceness runagates continue in s.
BOOK 144:7
scare s. myself with my own desert
FROS 344:12
those footprints s. me HORA 410:2
scarecrow make a s. of the law SHAK 723:3
scarecrows mechanized s. KAVA 453:14
s. of fools HUXL 423:15
scared always been s. of *you* PLAT 608:5
scarf S. up the tender eye SHAK 721:5
scarlet apes, though clothed in s. JONS 446:7
clad in silk or s. PROV 626:28
Cowards in s. GRAN 368:19
His sins were s. BELL 68:20
line of s. thread BIBL 82:25
lips like a thread of s. BIBL 91:4
raise the s. standard CONN 248:4
s. letter HAWT 385:8
s. soldiers AUDE 38:2
sins be as s. BIBL 91:20
wear his s. coat WILD 855:30
scars He jests at s. SHAK 732:9
marks and s. I carry BUNY 171:27
show his s. SHAK 709:7
scattered enemies be s. BOOK 144:6
s. the proud BIBL 104:9
s. verses PETR 604:17
scatterest thou s. them BOOK 145:20
scelerisque s. *purus* HORA 411:19
scene life's last s. JOHN 438:10
lofty s. be acted o'er SHAK 712:19
Speaks a new s. QUAR 651:8
scenery among savage s. HOFF 402:13
end of all natural s. RUSK 673:14
God paints the s. HART 383:13
S. is fine KEAT 457:21
scenes behind your s. JOHN 438:26
s. where man hath never CLAR 233:2
scent s. of the roses MOOR 558:8
s. survives their close THOM 807:12
s. the fair annoys COWP 254:29
sweetest flower for s. SHEL 746:9
sceptic s. could inquire for BUTL 183:10
too much of a s. HUXL 423:17
sceptical s. are the most credulous PASC 598:6
scepticism lead to s. BERK 72:14
s. kept her SART 681:21
s. of the intellect NEWM 572:6
sceptre His the s. DIX 286:32
s. and the ball SHAK 709:3
sceptred avails the s. race LAND 478:5
s. isle SHAK 730:10
sceptreless S., free SHEL 746:2
schemes best-laid s. PROV 627:25
s. of political improvement JOHN 440:19
s. o' mice an' men BURN 179:26
scherzando S.! ma non troppo GILB 356:9
schizoid S. self-alienation FROM 344:3
schizophrenic you are a s. SZAS 786:14
Schleswig-Holstein S. question PALM 595:8
scholar before a great s. LOCK 497:19
gentleman and s. BURN 180:5
He was a s. SHAK 711:6
mere s. DEFO 270:5
s. all Earth's volumes carry CHAP 216:12
s.'s life assail JOHN 438:6
Soldier, s., horseman YEAT 873:17
scholars philosophers and s. PASC 598:13
S. and gentlemen WORD 868:16
S. dispute HORA 409:2
school At s. I never minded MORT 562:1
been to a good s. SAKI 678:6
destroy every grammar s. CROS 261:5
erecting a grammar s. SHAK 710:3
every s. knows it TAYL 792:3
Experience keeps dear s. PROV 631:42
goeth to s. BACO 48:9

learned about in s. JARR 430:22
s. of Manchester DISR 286:27
s. of mankind BURK 175:12
s. of Stratford atte Bowe CHAU 218:9
sent to s. HUGH 418:14
tell tales out of s. PROV 639:44
Unwillingly to s. SHAK 696:28
vixen when she went to s. SHAK 726:20
schoolboy Every s. knows MACA 507:13
I see a s. YEAT 873:10
method that of a s. BLUN 129:14
Not the s. heat TENN 796:2
s. with a satchel BLAI 123:15
tell what every s. knows SWIF 783:25
whining s., with his satchel SHAK 696:28
schoolboys duly to delight s. JUVE 451:15
s. from their books SHAK 732:16
s. playing in the stream PEEL 601:16
schoolchildren What all s. learn AUDE 38:5
schoolgirl Pert as a s. GILB 357:5
priggish s. GRIG 373:6
s. complexion ADVE 7:42
schoolman no s.'s subtle art POPE 614:25
schoolmaster becoming a s. WAUG 842:12
s. is abroad BROU 160:9
so gentle a s. GREY 373:2
schoolmasters best of s. CARL 199:11
s. puzzle their brain GOLD 365:3
schoolrooms s. for 'the boy' COOK 250:9
schools banished from the s. CHUD 227:17
hundred s. of thought contend MAO 521:5
in our great s. JOHN 441:23
in the maze of s. POPE 615:24
Oh wrangling s. DONN 289:6
schooner It was the s. Hesperus LONG 500:6
sciatica S.: he cured it AUBR 36:4
science after learning s. FEYN 325:17
aim of s. BREC 155:15
All s. physics or stamp collecting RUTH 676:2
applications of s. PAST 599:2
beams of s. fall POPE 611:18
beginning of s. LEIB 488:5
countenance of all s. WORD 870:4
disease, not a s. MAIM 516:16
Dismal S. CARL 200:13
do in hell VAUG 825:15
essence of s. BRON 158:1
experimentation an active s. BERN 74:3
Fair S. frowned not GRAY 370:9
fear s. POLA 611:8
Geometry (which is the only s. HOBB 400:16
grand aim of all s. EINS 305:16
hand of s. AKEN 10:2
How s. dwindles YOUN 876:15
In s., read BULW 170:15
In s. the credit goes DARW 267:4
In s., we must be CURI 262:20
instrument of s. JOHN 435:17
investigated by s. ELIO 307:23
it is not s. KELV 459:12
opinion and s. HUME 420:10
plundered this new s. MCEW 510:13
redefined the task of s. HAWK 385:2
s. and everyday life FRAN 341:13
s. and nature will have charms FARA 323:7
S. appears WORD 868:12
S. finds ANON 20:7
s., in humbling our pride BERN 74:5
S. is a cemetery UNAM 821:14
S. is an edged tool PEAC 600:13
s. is at a loss CHOM 226:16
S. is built up of facts POIN 611:7
S. is for the cultivation SADI 677:5
S. is his forte SMIT 758:28
S. is nothing but trained HUXL 423:6
S. is organized knowledge SPEN 765:18
S. is part of culture GOUL 367:3
S. is satisfying the curiosity ARTS 32:20
s. is strong SZAS 786:15
s. is the right interpretation WHEW 850:4
S. knows no country PAST 599:4
S. moves, but slowly TENN 797:2
S. must begin with myths POPP 619:6

science (cont.):
s. of life · BERN 74:4
s. of the tender passion · PUSH 650:17
s. reassures · BRAQ 155:6
S. the aggregate of all · VALÉ 823:12
s. which pretends to lay open · SMIT 755:23
s. will appear incomplete · ARNO 31:23
S. without religion is lame · EINS 305:5
separation of state and s. · FEYE 325:16
tragedy of S. · HUXL 423:5
triumph of modern s. · WAUG 843:5
true s. and study · CHAR 217:16
ultimate destiny of s. · PEAC 600:14
sciences advancing the s. · LOCK 497:3
bent on these s. · ASCH 33:4
Books must follow s. · BACO 49:5
mother of s. · BACO 49:2
Reason and the s. · LEIB 488:6
scientific as if they were s. terms · ARNO 32:2
Death was but a s. fact · WILD 856:1
empirical s. system · POPP 619:1
importance of s. work · HILB 398:6
Jesus the most s. · EDDY 303:1
know the s. names · GILB 358:6
new s. truth · PLAN 608:2
on the most s. principles · PEAC 600:12
plunges into s. questions · HUXL 423:16
s. and geographical · CHER 222:16
s. faith's absurd · BROW 165:17
s. method doing one's damnedest · BRID 156:16
s. opinion · ARNO 31:21
s. power has outrun · KING 463:16
S. truth · MAXW 528:18
scientis Signum s. · AUCT 36:20
scientist elderly s. states · CLAR 233:14
exercise for a research s. · LORE 501:2
not try to become a s. · EINS 305:17
s.'s laws · QUIN 652:2
s. thinks of a method · PERU 604:14
s. were to cut his ear · MEDA 529:17
scientists company of s. · AUDE 38:19
s. are probably right · ASIM 33:19
than most young s. · MEDA 530:2
scire s. nefas · HORA 411:15
scissor long, red-legged s.-man · HOFF 402:7
scoff fools, who came to s. · GOLD 364:6
scoffer product of a s.'s pen · WORD 865:14
scoffing S. his state · SHAK 730:20
scold what a s. you are · BULL 170:8
scope that man's s. · SHAK 737:22
score time required to s. 500 · COMP 245:1
scorer One Great S. · RICE 659:20
scores He shoots! He s. · CATC 207:30
scorn Disdain and s. · SHAK 727:24
Laugh no man to s. · BIBL 97:12
s. is alluring · CONG 247:24
S. not the Sonnet · WORD 869:2
s. their bodies · BAST 61:5
s. which mocked the smart · ARNO 30:22
sound Of public s. · MILT 544:11
surmounted by s. · CAMU 196:9
think foul s. · ELIZ 312:6
thought s. · BOOK 147:13
very s. of men · BOOK 140:16
We s. many things · VAUV 825:16
what a deal of s. · SHAK 735:27
scorned fury, like a woman s. · CONG 247:9
scornful only a s. tickling · SIDN 751:9
seat of the s. · BOOK 139:11
scorpions chastise you with s. · BIBL 85:3
Scot Had Cain been S. · CLEV 235:15
Scotch as a S. banker · DAVI 268:3
inferior to a S. · NORT 577:2
into a S. understanding · SMIT 758:10
Mary, ma S. Bluebell · LAUD 482:19
scotched s. the snake · SHAK 721:2
Scotchman S. ever sees · JOHN 439:20
Scotia chief of S.'s food · BURN 177:24
old S.'s grandeur · BURN 177:26
Scotland fair S.'s spear · SCOT 689:6
fair S.'s strand · BURN 178:16
flower of S. · WILL 858:15
I do indeed come from S. · JOHN 439:14

inferior sort of S. · SMIT 758:5
in S. afore ye · SONG 763:9
in S. supports the people · JOHN 436:3
In S. we live between · CRAW 259:14
of S. · BYRO 187:14
our infinite S. · MACD 510:1
S. has a raucle tongue · BURN 177:13
S., land of the omnipotent No · BOLD 131:9
S.'s oil · POLI 612:26
Stands S. · SHAK 722:5
white rose of S. · MACD 510:5
Scots S. deserve no pity · FLET 335:3
S. lords at his feet · BALL 55:17
S., wha hae wi' Wallace bled · BURN 179:9
six or seven dozen of S. · SHAK 705:24
Scotsman S. on the make · BARR 60:1
S. with a grievance · WODE 861:20
Scott half so flat as Walter S. · ANON 19:15
wrong part wrote S. · WATE 841:3
Scottish auld S. sang · BURN 177:21
S. by formation · SPAR 765:14
S. Parliament · EWIN 322:3
S. parliament · SALM 679:14
shall be a S. parliament · ANON 20:19
shall be a S. parliament · DEWA 275:7
will of the S. people · SMIT 757:5
Scotty Beam me up, S. · MISQ 547:4
scoundrel over forty is a s. · SHAW 741:24
plea of the s. · BLAK 125:15
refuge of a s. · JOHN 441:18
to such a s. · SWIF 782:19
scoured s. to nothing · SHAK 707:10
scourge s. of small cords · BIBL 107:10
scout s. 'em, and flout 'em · SHAK 733:28
scrabble s. with all the vowels · ELLI 313:11
scrannel on their s. pipes · MILT 540:10
scrap s. of paper · BETH 75:8
scrape s. himself withal · BIBL 86:13
s. your strings darker · CELA 212:10
scraps stolen the s. · SHAK 717:20
scratch quick sharp s. · BROW 166:17
S. a Russian · PROV 642:35
S. the Christian · ZANG 877:9
s. the nurse · SHAK 736:13
scratching s. of a pen · LOVE 502:10
s. of my finger · HUME 420:19
s. of pimples on the body · WOOL 864:13
scream as a last resort, s. · SUGE 780:1
hilarity like a s. · GREE 371:17
huge s. course through nature · MUNC 565:10
no one can hear you s. · TAGL 788:5
s. in a low voice · BYRO 191:23
screw s. your courage · SHAK 719:15
to seek the right s. · HOLU 404:2
turn of the s. · JAME 430:4
scribblative babblative and s. · SOUT 764:16
scribble Always s., scribble, scribble · GLOU 360:18
scrawl, and s. · POPE 617:23
You who s. · WYCH 871:4
scribbled by a s. name · THOM 805:20
s. lines like fallen hopes · HOPE 407:2
scribbling mob of s. women · HAWT 385:9
s. fry · YOUN 876:13
scribendi S. cacoethes · JUVE 451:6
scribere rapida s. · CATU 210:16
saturam non s. · JUVE 450:11
scribes Beware of the s. · BIBL 104:3
s. and Pharisees · BIBL 99:1
s. and Pharisees, hypocrites · BIBL 102:18
scribimus S. indocti doctique poemata · HORA 410:19
scrip My s. of joy · RALE 653:19
with s. and scrippage · SHAK 697:8
scriptores Cedite Romani s. · PROP 625:1
scripture devil can cite S. · SHAK 724:8
devil can quote S. · PROV 629:41
Holy S. and nature · GALI 348:2
Holy S. containeth · BOOK 135:9
know more of the s. · TYND 821:6
S. moveth us · BOOK 133:2
s. of peoples · JERO 433:8
scriptures all holy S. · BOOK 135:11

Let us look at the s. · SELD 691:8
S. in the hands · PUGI 649:6
Search the s. · BIBL 107:19
scroll charged with punishments the s. · HENL 391:13
scrotumtightening s. sea · JOYC 448:14
scroungy all s. and bearded · CORS 252:10
scruple have no s. · FRAN 340:14
s. Of thinking too precisely · SHAK 703:28
scrupulosity oriental s. · JOHN 436:28
scrutamini s. scripturas · SELD 691:8
scullion Away, you s. · SHAK 707:12
sculptor great s. or painter · RUSK 673:7
sculpture like that of s. · RUSS 675:1
S. in stone · MOOR 557:7
s. put in a landscape · MOOR 557:9
What s. is to a block of marble · ADDI 5:8
sculptured s. dead · KEAT 454:5
scum Okie means you're s. · STEI 771:9
rich are the s. of the earth · CHES 225:4
s. of the earth · WELL 846:10
scuttling S. across the floors of silent seas · ELIO 310:9
Scylla S. and Charybdis · NEWM 572:4
scythe mower whets his s. · MILT 539:26
sighs like s. · WALC 835:15
scythes shaking s. at cannon · HEAN 387:15
Scythia another group to S. · VIRG 831:15
se s. ludice · JUVE 451:19
sea all the s. were ink · LYLY 505:23
Alone on a wide wide s. · COLE 241:1
around the glassy s. · HEBE 388:10
as good fish in the s. · PROV 644:9
As is the ribbed s.-sand · COLE 240:25
as the waters cover the s. · BIBL 92:18
beneath a rougher s. · COWP 254:24
best thing is—the s. · JERR 433:16
black s.-brute bulling · MERW 533:5
boat on the rough s. · HORA 411:6
burst Into that silent s. · COLE 240:19
clamorous whispering s. · HOME 404:8
cloud out of the s. · BIBL 85:11
cold grey stones, O S. · TENN 792:19
complaining about the s. · POWE 622:5
Death like a narrow s. · WATT 842:5
deep, deep s. · CONR 249:4
deeper than the s. · BALL 55:10
dominion from s. to sea · BIBL 119:28
dominion of the s. · COVE 253:8
Down to a sunless s. · COLE 240:4
dragon of the s. · MELV 531:11
eating the s. · ROBE 663:5
find another s. · CAVA 211:15
flowing s. · CUNN 262:15
forbear To teach the s. · DONN 289:22
From s. unto sea · MOTT 563:2
garden front the s. · SWIN 785:10
go to s. for pleasure · PROV 634:16
gurly grew the s. · BALL 54:10
hands across the s. · ROOS 668:5
Hands across the s. · WEBB 843:12
having been at s. · JOHN 442:13
headlong into the s. · KEAT 458:2
He divided the s. · BOOK 145:7
home from s. · STEV 777:5
houses are all gone under the s. · ELIO 309:10
if we gang to s. · BALL 55:15
if Ye take away the s. · KIPL 466:12
in a s. of glory · SHAK 710:19
In a solitude of the s. · HARD 381:11
induced to go to s. · FLIN 335:22
in earth and air, And in the s. · SMAR 754:16
in my chains like the s. · THOM 805:16
in our s. of confusion · GAMO 348:7
in perils in the s. · BIBL 113:16
in the abysmal s. · TENN 796:9
in the s. of life · ARNO 31:3
Into a s. of dew · FIEL 326:4
into the midst of the s. · BOOK 142:17
like bathing in the s. · LEIG 488:12
London, that great s. · SHEL 744:13
looks s.-ward · BROW 166:8
lover of men, the s. · SWIN 786:4

security (*cont.*):
watchword is s. — PITT 607:16
securus S. iudicat — AUGU 39:13
sedentary s. humour — MONT 554:11
sedge s. has withered — KEAT 455:4
seditione de s. querentes — JUVE 450:15
seditions way to prevent s. — BACO 47:29
seducer strong s., opportunity — DRYD 295:17
seduction delusive s. — BURN 177:2
In s., the rapist — DWOR 301:3
seductive some s. madness — HORA 412:20
sedulous played the s. ape — STEV 775:12
see All that we s. — POE 610:17
And for to s. — CHAU 220:12
by my form did s. me — MAHÂ 515:12
complain we cannot s. — BERK 72:16
eyes which s. — BIBL 105:3
I'll s. you again — COWA 253:13
In all things Thee to s. — HERB 394:5
into the wilderness to s. — BIBL 100:33
I s. a voice — SHAK 727:7
I s. dead people — FILM 328:21
I s., not feel — COLE 239:8
I shall never s. — KILM 462:15
I was blind, now I s. — BIBL 107:34
last s. your father — YEAM 872:7
like my roses to s. you — SHER 749:4
live longest, s. most — PROV 644:49
make you s. — CONR 249:5
more people s. than weigh — CHES 223:16
never s. him — FLAU 334:4
never s. so much — SHAK 717:10
Nice to s. you — CATC 208:19
no man s. me and live — BIBL 81:25
no man s. me more — SHAK 710:18
not worth going to s. — JOHN 442:25
observes in order to s. — WITT 861:11
one can s. rightly — SAIN 677:14
Plenty to s. and hear — JOYC 448:21
rather s. than be one — BURG 172:10
s. and hear nothing — THOM 806:20
s. another's woe — BLAK 127:14
s. better days — BEHN 67:3
s. every day without surprise — CHES 223:11
s. it no better — RUSK 673:11
s. me dance the Polka — GROS 373:14
s. me sometime — MISQ 549:6
S. no evil — PROV 642:41
S. one promontory — BURT 181:13
s. oursels as others see us — BURN 179:23
S.-saw, Margery Daw — NURS 581:6
s. the coloured counties — HOUS 415:16
s. the goodness — BOOK 141:11
s. the hours pass — CIOR 232:16
s. the object — ARNO 32:8
s. the things thou dost not — SHAK 716:21
s. things; and you say 'Why' — SHAW 739:11
s. what I eat — CARR 202:5
s. what I say — WALL 836:15
s. with, not through, the eye — BLAK 125:4
shall not s. me — BIBL 108:22
taste and s. — BOOK 141:19
they shall s. God — BIBL 98:25
they shall s. our God — KEBL 458:20
those who will not s. — PROV 644:44
to s. and be seen — TACI 787:4
To s. her is to love her — BURN 177:19
wait and s. — ASQU 34:3
whatever you s. — LUCA 503:20
what make you s. — WHIT 850:17
What the eye doesn't s. — PROV 646:29
What you s. is what you get — SAYI 685:18
wish to s. — GAND 349:1
yet I s. thee still — SHAK 719:19
You s., but you do not observe — DOYL 292:10
seed beareth forth good s. — BOOK 149:1
blood of Christians is the s. — TERT 802:11
Good s. makes good crop — PROV 633:24
good s. on the land — CAMP 194:15
lord will have the s. — OXFO 591:12
No s. is sown — IRWI 425:24
not one light s. — KEAT 454:21
Parsley s. goes nine — PROV 641:28

s. of knowledge — BACO 45:5
s. of what we know — BERR 74:16
s.-time had my soul — WORD 868:9
s. ye sow — SHEL 746:12
spring again from its s. — SHEL 747:10
seeding One year's s. — PROV 641:19
seeds into the s. of time — SHAK 718:11
least of all s. — BIBL 101:15
s. fell by the wayside — BIBL 101:13
wingèd s. — SHEL 745:6
seedtime s. and harvest — BIBL 79:25
seeing do with s. nothing — AUST 41:8
one way of s. — RUSK 674:3
S. is believing — PROV 642:39
s. what everybody has seen — SZEN 786:17
very s. of God — THOM 805:7
seek All I s., the heaven above — STEV 777:2
Distinction is what we all s. — REYN 659:8
go s. the asses — BIBL 83:30
If you s. a monument — EPIT 319:10
Myself alone I s. to please — GAY 351:18
s., and ye shall find — BIBL 99:24
S. and ye shall find — PROV 642:40
s. is find — SMAR 754:16
S. not to know — THOM 804:15
S. simplicity and distrust — WHIT 851:5
S. thou this soul of mine — LITT 495:12
S. ye first the kingdom — BIBL 99:19
S. ye the Lord — BIBL 94:8
shall men s. death — BIBL 118:20
sometime did me s. — WYAT 871:4
strive, to s., to find — TENN 801:1
We s. him here — ORCZ 586:4
Who s., who hope, who love — SIDN 751:1
Why s. ye the living — BIBL 106:28
you would not s. me — PASC 598:11
seeketh he that s. findeth — BIBL 99:25
seeking S. asses found — MILT 544:23
S., not in hope to — THOM 807:9
Seelen Zwei S. wohnen — GOET 361:16
seem Be what you would s. — PROV 628:1
Let be be finale of s. — STEV 774:3
that only s. — SPEN 767:28
to s. active — BONA 132:4
seeming keep S. and savour — SHAK 736:29
seemly it is s. so to do — KETH 461:10
seems I know not 's.' — SHAK 699:15
s. too little or — BARR 59:13
seen anybody here s. Kelly — MURP 565:22
as long as it can be s. — SAPP 680:19
being s. for what one is — DRAB 293:6
evidence of things not s. — BIBL 116:3
God whom he hath not s. — BIBL 117:20
Hast thou not s. — WINK 860:14
having not s., ye love — BIBL 116:30
I have s. God — BIBL 80:15
I have s. war — ROOS 667:7
needs only to be s. — DRYD 295:23
No man hath s. God — BIBL 107:3
not s., and yet have believed — BIBL 109:3
s. and not heard — PROV 629:1
s. is merely their own mind — MAHÂ 515:14
s. one city slum — AGNE 9:13
seen what I have s. — SHAK 702:11
should be s. to be done — HEWA 397:14
things have we s. — BEAU 63:8
things that I have s. — MARC 521:9
Too early s. unknown — SHAK 732:8
what I have s. — THOM 805:12
Who hath not s. thee — KEAT 457:1
You've never s. this country — PURD 650:14
sees s. and hears all we do — PUNC 650:6
s. Dhamma sees me — PALI 594:7
s. more in my pictures — TURN 819:10
s. what is now — AURE 40:17
seeth Lord s. not as man — BIBL 83:37
segregation S. now — WALL 836:11
walls of s. — JACK 426:12
Seine flows the S. — APOL 25:3
Seinte Loy ooth was but by S. — CHAU 218:8
seize s. the day — HORA 411:16
s. the flow'r — BURN 179:15
select each one should s. — SHEL 744:1

guests few and s. — LAND 478:8
Not a s. party — KEAT 458:12
selection Natural S. — DARW 266:13
Natural s. a mechanism — FISH 330:14
self contrary to His own s. — JULI 449:8
divided s. — LAIN 476:5
exchange of s. and other — SHAN 739:3
nature of s. — PALI 594:6
only S. to please — BLAK 127:18
s. is hateful — PASC 598:10
S.-praise no recommendation — PROV 642:42
S.-preservation is first law — PROV 642:43
spirit is the true s. — CICE 231:25
To study the s. — DOGE 287:10
to thine own s. be true — SHAK 700:6
versions of s. — PORT 619:21
self-assertion s. abroad — WAUG 842:17
self-consumer s. of my woes — CLAR 233:1
self-contempt S., well-grounded — LEAV 486:19
self-control energy in s. — JAIN 428:3
self-deceit Nothing is easier than s. — DEMO 272:18
self-defence it was in s. — MARL 522:5
self-denial S. is not a virtue — SHAW 741:18
self-esteem s., grounded on just — MILT 544:2
s. has not diminished — FONT 336:6
self-evident s. beings — NEWM 571:16
truths to be s. — ANON 21:6
self-government S. is our right — CASE 206:5
self-help spirit of s. — SMIL 755:19
selfhood s. begins with — DAY- 269:10
self-interest heedless s. — ROOS 667:9
propelled by s. — BAGE 50:4
S., which blinds — LA R 481:19
selfish All sensible people are s. — EMER 314:19
How small and s. is sorrow — ELIZ 313:7
selfishness Reduce s. — LAO 479:11
self-love but their s. — SMIT 756:1
Golden Calf of S. — CARL 199:10
s. and social — POPE 617:4
self-lovers nature of extreme s. — BACO 48:18
self-made s. man is one who believes — STEA 770:10
s. man may prefer — HAND 379:7
self-preservation s. in the other — JEFF 432:10
self-respect insult their s. — TAWN 791:6
self-righteousness S. is not religion — BRON 158:4
self-sacrifice S. enables us — SHAW 741:28
self-schooled S., self-scanned — ARNO 30:16
self-slain As a god s. — SWIN 785:11
self-slaughter fixed His canon 'gainst s. — SHAK 699:17
self-sufficiency S. at home — WAUG 842:17
self-sufficing reasoning, s. thing — WORD 868:5
s. power of Solitude — WORD 868:11
Selima pensive S. reclined — GRAY 370:14
selkie s. in the sea — BALL 54:15
Selkirk S. knew the plight — KAVA 453:16
sell Don't s. America short — POLI 612:13
Don't s. the skin — PROV 630:27
dreams to s. — BEDD 65:6
I'll s. him — LEAC 485:5
I s. here, Sir — BOUL 152:16
mind to s. his house — SWIF 782:4
no man might buy or s. — BIBL 118:26
One does not s. the earth — CRAZ 259:15
S. in May and go away — SAYI 685:10
s. in the dearest — PROV 628:29
s. it cheap — SLOG 755:11
s. Jack like soapflakes — KENN 460:16
s., or deny, or delay — MAGN 515:2
s. that thou hast — BIBL 102:6
s. the present life — KORA 471:16
s. your freedom — PUBL 648:28
to s. time — TAWN 791:5
selling lives by s. something — STEV 775:3
S. off the family silver — MISQ 548:17
s. postcards — DYLA 301:13
seltzer weak hock and s. — BETJ 75:9
semblable Hypocrite lecteur,—mon s. — BAUD 61:10

semblances outface it with their s.
SHAK 696:13
semen no frozen s. ever read a story
WILL 857:15
semi s.-house-trained polecat
FOOT 336:9
seminaries s. of young ladies
KNOX 470:7
seminary from a ladies'
GILB 357:6
semita *Fallentis s. vitae*
HORA 410:16
semper *et nunc, et s.*
MISS 546:19
Quod ubique, quod s.
VINC 828:9
S. aliquid novi
PLIN 609:16
S. eadem
MOTT 563:18
Sic s. tyrannis
MOTT 563:19
senator S., and a Democrat
JOHN 435:3
senators I look at the s.
HALE 376:16
s. burst with laughter
AUDE 37:3
s. of mighty woods
KEAT 454:23
teach his s. wisdom
BOOK 147:12
send S. in the clowns
SOND 761:4
s. me
BIBL 92:9
sending s. down of the Book
KORA 472:15
sends He s. out into
EICH 305:3
senectus *Morbi tristisque S.*
VIRG 830:9
sennights Weary s.
SHAK 718:7
sensational s. to read in the train
WILD 854:25
sensations easy prey to s.
TREV 815:8
O for a life of s.
KEAT 457:13
sense bind The wand'ring s.
CONG 247:30
borrows all her rays from s.
POPE 615:10
Common s. is not
VOLT 834:4
curb the s.
DRYD 295:14
deviates into s.
DRYD 296:10
Devoid of s. and motion
MILT 542:4
echo to the s.
POPE 616:6
fountain of good s.
DRYD 297:21
good s. and good taste
LA B 475:1
Have you no s. of decency
WELC 845:13
it is not s.
CHUR 228:4
just s. enough to perceive
HAZL 385:18
light of nature, s.
ROCH 664:15
men of s. never tell
SHAF 693:17
Money is like a sixth s.
MAUG 528:11
motions of the s.
SHAK 723:2
one grain of s.
DRYD 295:18
pleasures of s.
BHAG 78:2
Satire or s.
POPE 614:24
s. for sense
ALFR 12:13
servilely creeps after s.
DRYD 297:4
Short gleams of s.
CHUR 228:14
something more than good s.
COLE 242:5
Take care of the s.
CARR 202:10
talk s. to the American people
STEV 774:20
to his own s. doth smell
MONT 555:23
want of s.
DILL 283:7
senseless kind of s. wit
WILB 854:4
so many s. scholars
PENN 602:13
worse than s. things
SHAK 711:12
senses by your s. five
BLAK 126:20
horses are the s.
UPAN 822:11
If Parson lost his s.
HODG 401:18
knowledge denied from s.
SA'A 676:11
not enslaved by the s.
TANT 790:7
s. will never inform us
SMIT 755:25
snatches away all the s.
CATU 210:13
subtlety of the s.
BACO 48:30
Unto our gentle s.
SHAK 719:4
sensibilité equivalent to s.
PALM 595:10
sensibility Dear s.
STER 772:14
dissociation of s.
ELIO 311:24
it is an immense s.
JAME 429:20
pattern informed by s.
READ 656:4
sensible All s. people are selfish
EMER 314:19
S. men
DISR 285:28
s. of his natural rights
PRIE 624:1
This s. warm motion
SHAK 723:14
sensitive s. being
WORD 868:20
S. Plant
SHEL 746:8
try to be s.
MURA 565:12
sensual s. pleasure without vice
JOHN 444:23
sensuality s. and strength
FRIN 343:15
s., rebellion
THOM 807:1
sent man s. from God
BIBL 106:37
s. before my time
SHAK 731:11

sentence add a s.
BABE 45:1
Give s. with me, O God
BOOK 142:8
isn't a word . . . it's a s.
FILM 329:7
life s. goes on
CONL 248:2
Makes half a s.
COWP 254:28
No! No! S. first
CARR 202:19
recording the s.
VILL 828:4
s. is enough
PLAU 609:9
s. is factually significant
AYER 43:16
sentenced s. to death in my absence
BEHA 66:15
sentences Backward ran s.
GIBB 355:11
half-finished s.
EDGE 303:9
hard s. of old
BOOK 145:5
sentiment corrupted by s.
GREE 371:13
S. is what I am not
FLEM 334:21
sentiments his words and his s.
DEMO 272:19
my own s.
BAGE 51:18
not have opinions, only s.
LAUR 483:5
people of refined s.
KELL 459:9
resign their own s.
HUME 420:5
Them's my s.
THAC 803:2
sentinel scarce worth the s.
GOLD 365:13
S. of the grave
TATE 790:13
sentinels s. to warn
MARL 523:8
sentry quadrille in a s.-box
JAME 429:13
stands a wingèd s.
VAUG 825:4
separate able to s. us
BIBL 111:7
can't s. peace
MALC 517:10
s. and equal station
JEFF 431:5
separated they cannot be s.
SMIT 758:17
separately all hang s.
FRAN 341:8
separateth s. very friends
BIBL 88:19
separation impel them to the s.
JEFF 431:5
prospect of an easy s.
HUME 420:4
real s. of powers
DENN 273:11
s., but fission and divorce
SHIP 749:15
s. gives a foretaste
SCHO 686:14
s. of state and science
FEYE 325:16
that eternal s.
STER 773:18
until the hour of s.
GIBR 355:13
sept that damnable s.
STAI 769:13
September days hath S.
SAYI 685:14
S. blow soft
PROV 642:44
When you reach S.
ANDE 15:10
sepulchre first to the s.
BIBL 108:35
living s. of life
CLAR 233:3
No man knoweth of his s.
BIBL 82:22
s. there by the sea
POE 610:15
taken away from the s.
BIBL 108:34
sepulchres s. of mortality
CREW 259:19
whited s.
BIBL 102:20
sepulcra *Per s. regionum*
MISS 550:6
sequel natural s.
AUST 42:1
sequestered one of those s. spots
HARD 381:6
sera *rosa S. moretur*
HORA 412:5
seraglio s. of eunuchs
FOOT 336:8
seraphim bright s. in burning row
MILT 538:18
sworded s.
MILT 540:24
seraphims Above it stood the s.
BIBL 92:6
one of the s.
BIBL 92:8
seraphin Cherubin, and S.
BOOK 133:9
Serbonian S. bog
MILT 542:8
sere Now my s. fancy
BYRO 188:29
serene from the s. Light
HILD 398:8
s., That men call age
BROO 159:4
serf another man's s.
HOME 405:6
serfdom abolish s.
ALEX 12:5
sergeant This fell s., death
SHAK 704:26
serial obituary in s. form
CRIS 260:5
serious disputed of in s. manner
HOOK 406:10
joke's a s. thing
CHUR 228:8
Murder is a s. business
ILES 424:17
s. and the smirk
DICK 279:12
s.-minded activity
MONT 554:25
War is too s.
CLEM 235:6
seriously S., though
CATC 208:25
sermon honest and painful s.
PEPY 603:3
Perhaps, turn out a s.
BURN 178:2
rejected the S. on the Mount
BRAD 154:6
who a s. flies
HERB 393:26
sermons S. and soda-water
BYRO 188:9
S. in stones
SHAK 696:9

sero *S. te amavi*
AUGU 39:10
serpent be the s. under't
SHAK 719:3
biteth like a s.
BIBL 88:33
infernal s.
MILT 541:11
my s. of old Nile
SHAK 694:19
Now the s. was more subtil
BIBL 79:4
s. beguiled me
BIBL 79:9
s., green in the mulberry bush
TATE 790:13
s.-haunted sea
FLEC 334:10
s. subtlest beast
MILT 544:3
s. upon a rock
BIBL 89:12
s., which is the Devil
BIBL 119:12
sharper than a s.'s tooth
DICK 280:12
sharper than a s.'s tooth
SHAK 715:6
serpents wise as s.
BIBL 100:25
servant as a humble s.
MAND 518:17
become the s. of a man
SHAW 739:28
born to be a s.
TOCQ 811:16
carried His s. by night
KORA 472:6
cracked lookingglass of a s.
JOYC 448:15
Fire is a servant
PROV 632:17
form of a s.
BIBL 114:18
good and faithful s.
BIBL 103:2
Is thy s. a dog
BIBL 85:31
judgement with thy s.
BOOK 149:23
keep a good s.
BEAU 63:4
life of a s. of God
NEWM 572:11
nor the s. above his lord
BIBL 100:26
One s. worth a thousand gadgets
SCHU 687:8
sent down on Our s.
KORA 471:1
s. depart in peace
BIBL 104:16
S. of God, well done
MILT 543:25
s. of the Living God
SMAR 754:12
s. shall have small
BARC 58:5
s. to the devil
SISS 753:7
s. with this clause
HERB 394:7
thou wast a s.
BIBL 82:12
thy s. heareth
BIBL 83:26
well enough for a s.
CONG 247:7
Wife and S.
CHUD 227:18
Your s.'s cut in half
GRAH 367:14
servants Between them and s.
BARC 58:5
equality in the s.' hall
BARR 59:14
purgatory of s.
PROV 631:4
s. of the sovereign
BACO 47:6
s. will do that for us
VILL 828:5
wife or your s. to read
GRIF 373:5
Women and s. most difficult
CONF 246:22
serve Fleet in which we s.
BOOK 150:13
he must s. it too
EMER 315:16
left me to s. alone
BIBL 105:8
love to s. my country
GIBR 355:12
not yet able to s. man
CONF 246:11
s. and lose
GOET 362:8
s. Him in this world
CATE 209:9
s. in the wars
BOOK 150:22
s. thee with a quiet mind
BOOK 136:10
s. the Lord with gladness
BOOK 146:15
s. two masters
BIBL 99:15
s. two masters
PROV 640:5
s. until my last breath
GAND 348:10
s. your captives' need
KIPL 468:2
than s. in heaven
MILT 541:19
Thee only we s.
KORA 470:19
They also s.
MILT 545:15
will not s. if elected
SHER 749:12
served first s.
PROV 632:19
Had I but s. my God
SHAK 711:1
s. her, perhaps mistakenly
GLAD 360:12
s. to him course by course
CHUR 229:10
well s.
PROV 635:38
Worshipped and s.
BIBL 110:22
Youth must be s.
PROV 648:25
serveth as he that s.
BIBL 106:19
service All s. ranks the same
BROW 167:4
bounden duty and s.
BOOK 137:17
devoted to your s.
ELIZ 313:1
done the state some s.
SHAK 729:23
Every kind of s.
HALE 377:1
Hacked with constant s.
SOUT 764:4
No s.
RACI 653:3
Pressed into s.
FROS 345:2
S. and love above all other
DUNB 299:9

service (*cont.*):
s. is perfect freedom — BOOK 134:2
s. of my love — SPRI 768:18
s.? The rent we pay — CLAY 235:1
serviettes kiddies have crumpled the s. — BETJ 75:14
servile freed from s. bands — WOTT 870:7
servilely s. creeps after sense — DRYD 297:4
serving cumbered about much s. — BIBL 105:8
six honest s.-men — KIPL 468:12
With s. still — WYAT 871:9
servitude base laws of s. — DRYD 295:15
Freedom and not s. — BURK 173:17
servum O *imitatores, s. pecus* — HORA 410:18
sesame Open S. — ARAB 25:10
worm in a s. plant — TALM 789:24
sesquipedalia *s. verba* — HORA 409:3
sesquippedlan S. verboojuice — WELL 846:20
sessions s. of sweet silent thought — SHAK 737:24

set play a s. — SHAK 708:11
s. fair — BENN 70:14
s. himself doggedly to it — JOHN 439:1
S. me whereas the sun — SURR 780:15
s. our sins from us — BOOK 147:2
S. thine house in order — BIBL 93:12
would not have s. out — CAVA 211:12
Setebos my dam's god, S. — SHAK 733:19
S., Setebos — BROW 165:10
sets sun never s. — NORT 577:3
setter Proud s. up — SHAK 710:10
setting against a s. sun — SHAK 734:6
s. people right — MOOR 557:18
time is s. with me — BURN 179:6
settled s. will — SMIT 757:5
s. will — STEE 770:12
settlement parent of s. — BURK 174:1
through the Act of S. — RICE 660:1
seven acts being s. ages — SHAK 696:27
first s. years — SAYI 684:21
have the s. minutes — COLL 243:6
hewn out her s. pillars — BIBL 87:32
Jacob served s. years — BIBL 80:12
Keep a things s. years — PROV 636:49
lowly air Of S. Dials — GILB 356:17
man with s. wives — NURS 578:1
Rain before s. — PROV 642:18
remember more than s. — BELL 67:16
s. churches — BIBL 117:25
s. days are more than enough — AUST 42:24
s. fat kine — BIBL 80:21
s. feet of English ground — HARO 382:16
s. golden candlesticks — BIBL 117:26
s. maids with seven mops — CARR 203:3
s.-stone weakling — ADVE 7:41
S. types of ambiguity — EMPS 315:29
Until seventy times s. — BIBL 102:4
We are s. — WORD 869:22
sevenfold s. gifts impart — BOOK 150:16
seventeen Maud is not s. — TENN 797:23
seventh moon is in the s. house — RADO 653:8
opened the s. seal — BIBL 118:18
rested the s. day — BIBL 81:19
s. day is the sabbath — BIBL 81:18
seventy At s.-seven it is time — JOHN 436:13
Palmerston is now s. — DISR 286:25
s. years young — HOLM 403:17
Until s. times seven — BIBL 102:4
sever kiss, and then we s. — BURN 177:9
s. The chain — CORY 252:12
severae *procul este, s.* — OVID 589:19
several S. excuses — HUXL 422:19
severance their s. ruled — ARNO 31:4
severe first crude, then s. — VICO 827:5
man s. he was — GOLD 364:7
to nothing but herself s. — CARE 198:10
severity pure s. of perfect light — TENN 794:8
Severity breedeth s. — BACO 47:9
with its usual s. — COLE 242:12
Severn S.'s right of maker — GURN 374:18
thick on S. — HOUS 416:1
twice a day the S. fills — TENN 795:6
sew It can s., it can cook — PLAT 608:3

s., sew, prick our fingers — BROW 163:22
sewer midst of this putrid s. — TOCQ 812:16
s. in a glass-bottomed boat — MIZN 551:13
sewers houses thick and s. — MILT 544:4
sewing job of s. on a button — BROU 160:11
sex attempt to insult s. — LAWR 483:13
because of my s. — BEHN 66:21
call you darling after s. — BARN 59:5
dies from lack of s. — ATWO 35:13
feathers s. can soothe — EWAR 321:23
for my own s. — AUST 42:5
give a s. to mind — WOLL 863:6
if s. rears its ugly head — AYCK 43:13
isn't s. but death — SONT 761:6
Is s. dirty — ALLE 13:10
Mind has no s. — MISQ 548:10
Money was exactly like s. — BALD 52:15
mostly about having s. — LODG 498:4
no stronger than my s. — SHAK 712:11
of s. — ALLE 13:8
only unnatural s. act — KINS 465:3
portray this [s.] relation — ROBI 664:5
practically conceal its s. — NASH 568:12
S. and drugs and rock and roll — DURY 301:2
S. and taxes — JONE 445:11
s. business isn't worth — LAWR 484:10
S. never an obsession — BOY 153:20
s. object if you're pretty — GIOV 359:4
S. something I really don't understand — SALI 678:9
s. that brings forth — DE B 269:16
s. with someone I love — ALLE 13:9
soft, unhappy s. — BEHN 67:8
subordination of one s. — MILL 536:11
weaker s. — ALEX 12:11
When you have money, it's s. — DONL 287:12
sexes personalities of the two s. — MEAD 529:13
there are three s. — SMIT 758:15
sexier make it s. — GILL 358:17
sexton s. tolled the bell — HOOD 405:17
that bald s., Time — SHAK 714:7
sexual car crash as a s. event — BALL 56:9
draws so oddly with the s. — GUNN 374:14
man's idea of his s. rights — STAN 770:6
moral power strong as s. — CONF 246:9
not have s. relations — CLIN 236:7
of all the s. perversions — HUXL 422:18
s. intercourse — AURE 40:14
S. intercourse began — LARK 480:18
shock of s. astonishment — WESL 848:9
sexuality relinquish their s. — WOLF 862:12
when s. is repressed — AUGU 39:15
sexually s. transmitted disease — SAYI 685:1
shabby s. equipment always deteriorating — ELIO 309:13
shackles Memories are not s. — BENN 70:8
Shackleton give me S. — CHER 222:16
pray for S. — MISQ 549:4
shadblow Cowslip and s. — CRAN 258:13
shade battle will be in the s. — HERO 395:12
clutching the inviolable s. — ARNO 30:13
farewell to the s. — COWP 255:24
gentlemen of the s. — SHAK 705:7
his steadfast s. — TENN 799:1
in a green s. — MARV 525:5
in s. of Tempe sit — SIDN 750:20
let it sleep in the s. — MOOR 558:12
light, s., and perspective — CONS 249:20
sitting in the s. — KIPL 466:1
sly s. of a Rural Dean — BROO 159:8
sweeter s. To shepherds — SHAK 710:7
whiter s. of pale — REID 657:14
windings and such s. — WINC 860:8
shades S. of the prison-house — WORD 867:8
till the s. lengthen — NEWM 572:13
shadow also casts a s. — CHUR 229:21
but the s. of heaven — MILT 543:21
cast their s. before — PROV 629:13
days on the earth are as a s. — BIBL 86:1
dream But of a s. — CHAP 216:2
dream of a s. — PIND 606:19
earth's round s. — SAVA 682:18
Falls the S. — ELIO 309:28

fleeth also as a s. — BIBL 86:30
Follow a s. — JONS 446:19
in the s. of death — BIBL 104:10
in the s. of the earth — BROW 163:18
Life's but a walking s. — SHAK 722:22
little s. that goes — STEV 776:15
little s. that runs — CROW 261:13
little s. that runs — HAGG 376:3
live under the s. of a war — SPEN 766:15
mere s. of death — LAUD 482:17
S. cloaked from head to foot — TENN 795:7
s. of a great rock — BIBL 93:5
s. of death — BIBL 86:24
s. of death — BIBL 92:13
s. of death — BOOK 147:15
s. of felicity — WALL 837:4
s. of God — BROW 162:3
s. of her even brows — SPEN 767:11
s. of our night — SHEL 743:18
s. of some unseen Power — SHEL 744:8
s. of the Earth — MISQ 547:21
s. of the Valois — CHES 224:8
s. of thy Throne — WATT 842:7
s. of turning — BIBL 116:17
s. on the moon — INGE 425:11
s. stands over us — ALLI 13:18
s. will be shown — NIET 575:12
through the s. — VIRG 830:8
valley of the s. of death — BOOK 140:21
walketh in a vain s. — BOOK 141:29
shadowing employ any depth of s. — DRYD 297:24
shadowless s. like Silence — HOOD 405:23
shadows but s. — SHAK 727:8
cold white s. — WRIG 870:19
From s. and types — EPIT 317:6
half sick of s. — TENN 796:16
Individuals pass like s. — BURK 175:18
less liquid than their s. — TESS 802:14
longer fall the s. — VIRG 831:16
long s. on county grounds — MAJO 517:4
millions of strange s. — SHAK 737:27
Old sins cast long s. — PROV 640:32
Our fatal s. — FLET 335:9
puppets in a play of s. — BHAG 78:6
see only their own s. — PLAT 609:2
s. and twilights — Æ 6:11
s. flee away — BIBL 91:2
s. have offended — SHAK 727:12
s., not substantial things — SHIR 749:17
s. now so long do grow — COTT 252:15
s. of the clouds — WORD 865:4
s. of us men — JONS 446:19
s. to-night — SHAK 731:29
s. upon the sunbright walls — WORD 865:2
Types and s. — THOM 805:5
When the sun sets, s. — LEE 487:11
Shadrach S., Meshach, and Abed-nego — BIBL 95:23
shady s. trees — BIBL 87:16
shaft Lie like a s. of light — TENN 793:20
s., at random sent — SCOT 688:17
shafts Clear s. of day — LUCR 504:6
Its s. remain — ROET 665:5
s. barbed with pity — DANT 265:5
shag common cormorant (or s.) — ISHE 426:2
shaggy S., and lean — COWP 256:24
shake Earth must s. — HORA 412:3
give it a good s. — JOHN 434:12
only S.-scene in a country — GREE 372:1
s. hands with a king — HALL 378:6
s. off the dust — BIBL 100:24
s. their heads — BOOK 140:16
this god did s. — SHAK 711:17
shaken is never s. — SHAK 738:15
S. and not stirred — FLEM 334:16
s. me by the hand — WESL 848:7
to be well s. — COLM 244:7
shakers movers and s. — O'SH 588:22
shakes s. so my single state — SHAK 718:16
Shakespeare abominable plays of S. — FRED 342:3
less S. he — BROW 166:2

Our *myriad-minded* S.	COLE 241:22
Our sweetest S.	MILT 539:31
reproduce works of S.	WILE 856:20
S., another Newton	HUXL 423:1
S. by flashes of lightning	COLE 242:2
S. is like bathing	LEIG 488:12
S. is of no age	COLE 242:10
S. one gets	AUST 41:16
S.—the nearest thing	OLIV 585:3
S. unlocked his heart	WORD 869:2
S. was of us	BROW 166:13
S. would have grasped	MCEW 510:13
She had read S.	WELL 846:19
talk of my being like S.	SCOT 690:1
When I read S.	LAWR 483:25
Shakespearean Dogs are S.	SCHW 687:10
That S. rag	BUCK 169:15
Shakespeherian S. Rag	ELIO 311:9
shaking entrusted to the s. hand	VICT 827:10
fall without s.	MONT 554:3
s. fastens more	HERB 393:23
Shalimar loved beside the S.	HOPE 407:3
shall mark you His absolute 's.'	SHAK 698:6
picked the s. was of s.	CUMM 262:11
so s. thou be	EPIT 319:7
shallow S. brooks murmur	SIDN 750:12
s. in himself	MILT 544:28
s. murmur	RALE 654:1
shallows in s. and in miseries	SHAK 713:28
Shalott Lady of S.	TENN 796:16
shalt Thou s. have no other gods	BIBL 81:15
Thou s. not	PULL 649:12
sham real pain for my s. friends	BACO 49:14
shame Ain't it all a bleedin' s.	MILI 535:16
coward s.	BURN 178:25
fruit of my vanity is s.	PETR 604:18
glory is in their s.	BIBL 115:2
mourn with her in s.	EMEC 314:9
nightingale dies for s.	BURT 181:9
secret s. destroyed	RICH 660:11
S. on the soul	AURE 40:15
s. the devil	PROV 644:8
s. unto him	BIBL 112:12
terrible s. for me	YOKO 876:6
waste of s.	SHAK 738:18
worst kind of s.	LIVY 496:8
shameless most s. thing	BURK 174:15
nothing more s.	HOME 405:5
What . . . can be more s.	GODW 361:6
shamrocks watercresses or s.	SPEN 768:9
Shandeism True S.	STER 773:9
shank too wide For his shrunk s.	SHAK 697:2
Shannon green banks of S.	CAMP 195:8
shantih S., shantih	ELIO 311:19
Shan Van Vogh Says the S.	SONG 763:18
shape might be any s.	CARR 203:9
pressed out of s.	FROS 345:2
s. of things to come	WELL 846:24
Take any s. but that	SHAK 721:10
shaped s., sir, like itself	SHAK 695:7
shapen s. in wickedness	BOOK 143:5
shapes Change s. with Proteus	SHAK 710:9
fancy s.	TENN 795:22
shaping s. spirit of imagination	COLE 239:11
share all persons alike s.	ARIS 28:3
all that I have I s.	BOOK 139:2
greater s. of honour	SHAK 709:5
its ruin didst not s.	DODI 287:8
s. no one's ideas	TURG 818:16
s. the transport	WORD 869:13
shared trouble s.	PROV 645:35
shares Fair s. for all	POLI 612:15
s. are a penny	GILB 356:24
shark s. has pretty teeth	BREC 155:24
sharks s. are circling	ANON 18:11
s. circling, and waiting	CLAR 233:11
Sharon rose of S.	BIBL 90:26
sharp s. as a two-edged sword	BIBL 87:26
so s. the conquerynge	CHAU 220:21
'Tis a s. remedy	RALE 654:12
sharpening s. my oyster knife	HURS 422:5
sharper s. than a serpent's tooth	DICK 280:12
s. than a serpent's tooth	SHAK 715:6
s. the storm	PROV 643:3
sharpness s. of death	BOOK 133:10
sharps s. and flats	BROW 167:1
shatter s. the vase	MOOR 558:8
shaves s. and takes a train	WHIT 850:13
Shaw S.'s plays	AGAT 9:7
shawms trumpets also, and s.	BOOK 146:12
she And then again S. does	JAST 430:24
chaste, and unexpressive s.	SHAK 697:6
life and loves of a s.-devil	WELD 845:16
S. sells sea-shells	SULL 780:4
S., she is dead	DONN 287:14
S. who must be obeyed	HAGG 376:4
That not impossible s.	CRAS 259:12
sheaf made obeisance to my s.	BIBL 80:17
shear good shepherd to s. his flock	TIBE 810:16
shearers sheep before her s.	BIBL 94:4
shears resembles a pair of s.	SMIT 758:17
with th' abhorrèd s.	MILT 540:7
sheathe s. the sword	ASQU 34:4
sheaves bring his s. with him	BOOK 149:1
s. of sacred fire	CHAP 216:6
your s. stood	BIBL 80:17
Sheba Another S. queen	WITH 861:6
Ere you were Queen of S.	SHIP 749:15
queen of S.	BIBL 84:27
shed Burke under a s.	JOHN 443:21
prepare to s. them now	SHAK 713:8
shall his blood be s.	BIBL 79:27
s. for you and for many	BOOK 137:16
s. innocent blood	BIBL 94:17
shedding Without s. of blood	BIBL 116:1
sheen s. is the sonne	LANG 479:1
sheep Among the s.	MISS 550:8
as s. going astray	BIBL 117:7
bleating s. loses bite	PROV 628:9
care of s.	DYER 301:6
craved the life of a s.	LA F 475:21
ensample to his s.	CHAU 218:20
Feed my s.	BIBL 109:6
folds shall be full of s.	BOOK 144:3
found my s. which was lost	BIBL 105:27
get back to these s.	ANON 22:9
giveth his life for the s.	BIBL 108:2
hanged for a s.	PROV 641:9
has lost her s.	NURS 579:16
hills like young s.	BOOK 148:3
hungry s. look up	MILT 540:10
in s.'s clothing	BIBL 99:30
keep s. and cows	OSBO 588:9
like lost s.	BOOK 133:4
like s. have gone astray	BIBL 94:4
little black s.	KIPL 465:20
looking on their silly s.	SHAK 710:7
lost s.	BIBL 100:22
mere s.-herding	POUN 621:15
mountain s. are sweeter	PEAC 600:20
old half-witted s.	STEP 772:3
Other s. I have	BIBL 108:4
savaged by a dead s.	HEAL 387:1
s. bear fleeces	VIRG 833:8
s. before her shearers	BIBL 94:4
s. born carnivorous	FAGU 322:14
s. in sheep's clothing	CHUR 231:7
s. in sheep's clothing	GOSS 366:13
s. of his hand	BOOK 146:8
s. on his right hand	BIBL 103:5
s.'s in the meadow	NURS 579:17
s. that have not a shepherd	BIBL 85:19
s., that were wont to be	MORE 559:3
s. to pass resolutions	INGE 425:4
teeth are like a flock of s.	BIBL 91:4
thousand years as a s.	PROV 627:39
two hundred years like a s.	TIPU 811:9
wolf in s.'s clothing	AESO 9:5
sheeps s.' guts	SHAK 727:20
sheet brought in the white s.	LORC 500:17
England's winding s.	BLAK 124:18
How at my s.	THOM 805:18
s. knit at the four corners	BIBL 109:25
s. were big enough	SHAK 735:30
turn over the s.	SAND 680:11
waters were his winding s.	BARN 59:9
wet s.	CUNN 262:15
sheets cool kindliness of s.	BROO 159:5
s. with hay over	JOHN 436:12
Shekinah rejoice in the S.	ZOHA 878:9
shelf s. life of the modern	TRIL 815:13
shell fired a 15-inch s.	RUTH 676:4
gloomy s.	ANON 19:5
prettier s.	NEWT 574:9
thou s. of death	MIDD 534:9
Shelley Burns, S., were with us	BROW 166:13
did you once see S.	BROW 166:18
peace in S.'s mind	SHEL 746:25
shells choirs of wailing s.	OWEN 591:4
shelter s. from the stormy blast	WATT 842:7
shelves symmetry of s.	LAMB 476:15
shepherd call you, S.	ARNO 30:6
Dick the s.	SHAK 717:25
God of love my S. is	HERB 395:1
good s.	BIBL 108:2
good s. to shear his flock	TIBE 810:16
happy S. Boy	WORD 867:6
like a s.	BIBL 93:17
Lord is my s.	BOOK 140:20
Lord's my s.	SCOT 690:9
my s. is	BAKE 52:9
Old Nod, the s.	DE L 272:10
returned unto the S.	BIBL 117:7
sheep that have not a s.	BIBL 85:19
s., blowing of his nails	SHAK 710:6
S., Corydon, burned with love	VIRG 831:17
s. his sheep	PROP 624:20
s.'s delight	PROV 642:19
s. tells his tale	MILT 539:26
shepherds s. abiding in the field	BIBL 104:12
s. and butchers	VOLT 834:15
s. call me also a poet	VIRG 832:9
s. give a grosser name	SHAK 704:6
s. watched their flocks	TATE 790:16
sheriff I shot the s.	MARL 522:5
Sheriffmuir at S. A battle	MCLE 512:7
Sherman general (yes mam) s.	CUMM 262:8
sherry s. flowing into second-rate whores	PLOM 610:4
shibboleth Say now S.	BIBL 83:11
shield broken was her s.	SCOT 689:6
efforts to s. children	ADDA 4:7
faith shall be my s.	ASKE 34:1
lady in his s.	TENN 796:17
Our S. and Defender	GRAN 368:11
s. against retribution	TALM 789:9
s. and buckler	BOOK 145:23
S. of Abraham	SIDD 750:6
S. of British fair play	AITK 9:19
s. of faith	BIBL 114:15
trusty s.	LUTH 505:8
shieling From the lone s.	GALT 348:5
shift let me s. for myself	MORE 559:14
s. in what the public wants	CALL 193:14
shifted s. his trumpet	GOLD 364:22
shilling our last s.	FISH 327:18
sell for one s. Your ring	LEAR 486:7
s. life will give you	AUDE 38:8
shillings can do for ten s.	SHUT 750:3
shine Arise, s.	BIBL 94:18
Boy you can gimme a s.	GORD 366:6
Let your light so s.	BIBL 98:28
Lord make his face s.	BIBL 82:2
s. all through the sphere	VAUG 825:13
s., and run to and fro	BIBL 96:29
s. in company	SWIF 783:18
s. on, harvest moon	NORW 577:9
shiners Nine for the nine bright s.	SONG 762:13
shines s. and stinks	RAND 655:3
s. sae bright	BURN 180:10
shingles naked s. of the world	ARNO 29:4
shining I see it s. plain	HOUS 416:4
s. from shook foil	HOPK 407:7
s. into a puddle	PROV 643:50
s. morning face	SHAK 696:28
S. nowhere but in the dark	VAUG 825:11
S. suspension	CRAN 258:15
sun was s. everywhere	GERS 353:12
with s. foot shall pass	FITZ 331:29

shining (*cont.*):
woman of s. loveliness — YEAT 874:20
ship all I ask is a tall s. — MASE 527:6
being in a s. — JOHN 439:12
build your s. of death — LAWR 483:21
idle as a painted s. — COLE 240:20
infantry or a fleet of s. — SAPP 680:20
like a sinking s. — WOOL 864:16
must rebuild their s. — NEUR 571:6
one for the s. — PROV 641:2
O S. of State — LONG 498:15
S. and stores have gone — SHAC 693:10
s. appeared in the air — HEAN 387:11
s. has weathered every rack — WHIT 852:2
s. I have got — SONG 763:10
s. in a black storm — WEBS 844:25
s. in the midst of the sea — BIBL 89:12
s. me somewheres — KIPL 466:16
s. on the sea — LORC 500:18
s. substantial — ASKE 34:1
s. was as still — SOUT 764:9
s. would *not* travel — CARR 204:1
Sink me the s., Master Gunner — TENN 800:3
spoil the s. — PROV 630:15
towards a sinking s. — CHUR 231:6
What is a s. — BURT 181:16
will sink a s. — BUNY 171:20
woman and a s. ever want — PROV 647:30
ships all the s. at sea — WINC 860:2
Hell to s. — AESC 6:15
launched a thousand s. — MARL 522:9
little s. of England — GUED 374:6
Loose lips sink s. — MILI 535:13
move with the moving s. — SWIN 786:5
Of shoes—and s. — CARR 203:4
S. are but boards — SHAK 724:5
S., dim-discovered — THOM 808:14
s. empty of men — NICI 574:18
s. have been salvaged — HALS 378:10
s. of the sea — BOOK 142:24
s. sail like swans asleep — FLEC 334:13
S. that pass in the night — LONG 500:3
S., towers, domes — WORD 865:7
something wrong with our bloody s.
— BEAT 62:14
Spanish s. of war — TENN 800:1
stately s. go on — TENN 792:20
There go the s. — BOOK 147:9
to the sea in s. — BOOK 147:17
we've got the s. — HUNT 421:3
wooden wall is your s. — THEM 804:10
shipwreck more consequences to a s.
— THOR 809:2
s. of time — BACO 45:10
suffered s. — BIBL 113:15
shire That s. which we may call — DRAY 293:15
shires bugles calling from sad s. — OWEN 591:4
Round both the s. — HOUS 415:16
shirt Near is my s. — PROV 639:26
Song of the S. — HOOD 406:16
shirtsleeves From s. to — PROV 632:41
shit s. in a silk stocking — NAPO 568:11
s.-wiping stick — MUMO 565:7
shock-proof s. detector — HEMI 391:7
shiver praised and left to s. — JUVE 450:12
tremble and s. — HOOD 405:12
shivering like Augustine s. — WILL 857:12
shoal bank and s. of time — SHAK 719:6
s. of fools — CONG 247:21
shoals s. of herring — MACC 509:13
shock characterized by s. — FRAN 341:16
Future s. — TOFF 812:18
S. and Awe — ANON 19:18
S. and Awe — ULLM 821:9
S.-headed Peter — HOFF 402:12
s. of the new — DUNL 299:15
s. of your joy — HUGH 418:12
s. them and keep them up to date
— SHAW 739:26
short, sharp s. — GILB 357:8
we shall s. them — SHAK 714:15
shocked s. by this subject — BOHR 130:14

shocking looked on as something s.
— PORT 619:9
shocks s. the magistrate — RUSS 675:7
s. the mind of a child — PAIN 592:6
thousand natural s. — SHAK 701:26
twelve great s. of sound — TENN 793:19
shod All s. with steel — WORD 866:1
foot feel, being s. — HOPK 407:7
shoddier no s. than what they peddle
— BECK 64:9
shoe Buckle my s. — NURS 580:14
careless s.-string — HERR 396:1
cast out my s. — BOOK 143:20
embrace a woman's s. — KRAU 473:12
If the s. fits — PROV 635:16
I kiss his dirty s. — SHAK 708:21
Into a left-hand s. — CARR 203:22
lived in a s. — NURS 581:16
s.'s latchet — BIBL 107:4
want of a s. — PROV 632:34
shoemaker s.'s son always — PROV 643:4
shoes from the s. — GOLD 365:16
shoes call for his old s. — SELD 691:9
changing s. — BREC 156:5
dead men's s. — PROV 636:36
ere those s. were old — SHAK 699:21
I had no s. — SAYI 684:23
mind it wipes its s. — THOM 806:10
never tied my s. — PU Y 648:27
Of s.—and ships — CARR 203:4
Put off thy s. — BIBL 80:34
s. of his soldiers — BAGE 50:14
s. that were not fellows — DEFO 270:12
thy feet with s. — BIBL 91:13
want of s. — SADI 677:4
shoeshine riding on a smile and a s. — MILL 537:9
shook earth s. — BOOK 144:7
monk who s. the world — MONT 556:10
more it's s. it shines — HAMI 378:12
s. hands with time — FORD 337:8
Ten days that s. the world — REED 657:10
shoot Don't s., mates — MORR 560:6
he shall s. higher — SIDN 750:13
S., if you must — WHIT 853:1
s. me in my absence — BEHA 66:15
s. me through linoleum — BANK 57:11
s. out their lips — BOOK 140:16
s. the Hippopotamus — BELL 67:18
s. the hippopotamus — FORS 337:15
s. the pianist — ANON 19:19
s. the sleepy, green-coat man — HOFF 402:10
They s. horses don't they — MCCO 509:15
they shout and they s. — INGE 425:1
young idea how to s. — THOM 808:12
You s. a fellow down — HARD 381:21
shooting s.-stars attend thee — HERR 396:3
war minus the s. — ORWE 587:23
shoots green s. of recovery — MISQ 547:18
He s.! He scores — CATC 207:30
man who s. him gets caught — MAIL 516:11
shop back to the s. — LOCK 498:2
foul rag-and-bone s. — YEAT 872:14
little back s. — MONT 555:7
s. will keep you — PROV 637:2
shopkeepers nation of s. — ADAM 4:1
nation of s. — NAPO 568:9
nation of s. — PROV 631:6
nation of s. — SMIT 756:5
shopping main thing today is—s. — MILL 537:10
shore adieu! my native s. — BYRO 185:16
after-silence on the s. — BYRO 190:20
for the further s. — VIRG 830:10
high s. of this world — SHAK 709:3
impossible s. — ARNO 30:23
kingdom of the s. — SHAK 738:1
lights around the s. — ROSS 669:23
lose sight of the s. — GIDE 356:1
rapture on the lonely s. — BYRO 187:1
s. Of the wide world — KEAT 457:10
some naked s. — HABI 375:6
sounds by the s. — YEAT 873:21
stayed upon the green s. — KEAT 458:2
stretch from s. to shore — WATT 842:6

To the other s. — PAUL 600:5
unknown and silent s. — LAMB 476:21
shored s. against my ruins — ELIO 311:18
shoreless s. watery wild — ARNO 31:3
shores betwixt their s. — ARNO 31:5
on the s. of darkness — KEAT 457:6
recognize my s. — AKHM 10:4
wilder s. of love — BLAN 128:1?
shorewards great winds s. blow — ARNO 29:12
shorn come home s. — PROV 638:28
green grass s. — BACO 47:3
priest all shaven and s. — NURS 581:16
sheep that are even s. — BIBL 91:4
tempers wind to s. lamb — PROV 633:13
short Anger is a s. madness — HORA 410:6
by s. grasses — PORT 620:2
Don't sell America s. — POLI 612:13
in a s. time — BIBL 97:1
it is well it is s. — TAYL 792:4
Life's s. span — HORA 411:8
long and the s. and the tall — HUGH 417:18
nasty, brutish, and s. — HOBB 400:24
not S. — DICK 279:23
s. and bandy-legged — ARCH 25:19
s. horse soon curried — PROV 643:5
s. in the story — BIBL 98:8
s. notice, soon past — PROV 638:1
s. of the glory of God — BIBL 110:27
S. reckonings — PROV 643:6
s., sharp shock — GILB 357:8
s. time to live — BOOK 139:8
s. time to stay — HERR 396:15
s. way — ASCH 33:7
Take s. views — SMIT 758:12
That lyf so s. — CHAU 220:21
too s. to blend — HILT 399:11
while to make it s. — THOR 809:8
shortcomings easier to perceive the s.
— HEGE 388:14
o'er its own s. — LITT 495:13
shorter s. by the head — ELIZ 312:5
time to make it s. — PASC 597:12
shortest longest day and s. night — PROV 627:10
s. way — BACO 45:19
s. way home — PROV 637:51
shorts Eat my s. — CATC 207:15
shot be s. at — HARD 382:5
Certain men the English s. — YEAT 874:4
fired the s. — BALL 54:16
I s. the sheriff — MARL 522:5
s. at for sixpence a-day — DIBD 276:3
s. heard round the world — EMER 314:13
S.? so quick, so clean — HOUS 416:6
They've s. our fox — BIRC 122:1
shotgun blew his head off with a s. — BLY 129:15
shots of the best s. — VOLT 834:16
shoulder giant's s. to mount on — COLE 241:23
government shall be upon his s. — BIBL 92:14
keep looking over his s. — BARU 60:13
left s.-blade — GILB 357:12
shifted it to another s. — SHAW 741:9
stand s. to shoulder — BLAI 124:2
shoulders Borne on our s. — BROW 165:22
City of the Big S. — SAND 680:2
from her s. did fall — WYAT 871:5
grow beneath their s. — SHAK 728:10
lawn about the s. — HERR 396:1
old head on young s. — PROV 648:12
on the s. of giants — NEWT 574:7
on your young s. — SPAR 765:9
s. held the sky suspended — HOUS 415:8
s. of giants — BERN 73:17
shout hardly a s. — ARNO 30:5
shouted with a great s. — BIBL 82:27
S. round me, let me hear — WORD 867:6
s. that tore hell's concave — MILT 541:27
S. with the largest — DICK 280:17
they s. and they shoot — INGE 425:1
shouted sons of God s. — BIBL 87:9
shouting thunder and the s. — BIBL 87:13
tumult and the s. — KIPL 467:5
shovelled quatrains s. — LOWE 503:11
shovelling S. white steam — AUDE 37:19

show business like s. business	BERL 73:5	**Sicelides** S. Musae	VIRG 832:2	**sighs** on the Bridge of S.	BYRO 186:15
learned not to s. it	ALCO 11:8	**sick** And I am s. at heart	SHAK 698:28	sound of s.	PETR 604:17
make a s. themselves	OVID 589:20	Created s.	GREV 372:16	world of s.	SHAK 728:11
only a s.	GOET 361:14	devil was s.	PROV 629:48	**sight** all very well at first s.	SHAW 741:8
s. any just cause	BOOK 138:23	do not make me s.	WHIT 852:11	deprived of s.	VIRG 829:19
s. business with blood	BRUN 168:19	do the s. no harm	NIGH 576:2	evil in thy s.	BOOK 143:4
s. him my salvation	BOOK 146:3	extremely s.	PRIO 624:12	giveth s. to the blind	BOOK 150:4
s. our simple skill	SHAK 727:6	half s. of shadows	TENN 796:16	in the s. of God	BOOK 138:20
s. that you have one	CHES 223:6	hired to watch the s.	COWP 256:7	in the s. of God	THOM 804:24
s. the light	BOOK 145:10	I am s., I must die	NASH 569:2	in the s. of the Lord	BOOK 148:9
s. thy praise	BOOK 143:9	I am s. of both	JOHN 442:7	in thy s.	BOOK 149:23
shower abundant s. of curates	BRON 158:9	is Brutus s.	SHAK 712:9	lose s. of the shore	GIDE 356:1
coming s.	SWIF 783:23	make him s.	DONN 288:2	My dying s.	BLOK 129:3
have a summer s.	MACD 510:8	medicine for the s.	SHAN 739:2	neatly out of s.	CRAN 258:17
sweetness of a s.	THOM 806:22	most s. and most healthy	HA-L 377:4	Out of s.	PROV 641:25
showers After sharpest s.	LANG 479:1	Pass the s. bag, Alice	CATC 208:23	out of s.	THOM 804:20
April s. bring forth	PROV 626:33	Rose, thou art s.	BLAK 128:2	s. of means	SHAK 714:13
bring fresh s.	SHEL 743:23	s. and wicked	AUST 43:6	s. to dream of	COLE 239:6
land never pleads for s.	TIBU 810:19	s., and ye visited me	BIBL 103:6	s. to make an old man young	TENN 793:16
S., and Dew	BOOK 133:14	s. for home	KEAT 456:10	s. was often puzzled	BOCC 130:7
with his s. soote	CHAU 218:2	s. hurry	ARNO 30:12	thousand years in thy s.	BOOK 145:20
showery S., Flowery, Bowery	ELLI 314:2	s. in fortune	SHAK 714:24	To feeling as to s.	SHAK 719:19
showeth true love is, it s.	DE P 273:15	They are as s.	SHAK 724:1	triple s. in blindness	KEAT 457:6
showing worth s.	DANT 266:1	they that are s.	BIBL 100:15	**sights** few more impressive s.	BARR 60:1
shows outward s.	SHAK 724:23	think we're s.	WOLF 862:20	s. as youthful poets dream	MILT 539:31
shreds king of s. and patches	SHAK 703:16	treatment to help the s.	HIPP 399:17	**sign** If only God would give some s.	ALLE 13:15
thing of s. and patches	GILB 357:1	visits the s.	MAIM 516:11	In this s. shalt thou conquer	CONS 250:1
shrewd s. was that snatch	BROW 165:3	when he is s.	JOHN 443:13	Jews require a s.	BIBL 111:22
shrewishly speaks very s.	SHAK 735:5	**sickened** s. at all triumphs	CHUR 228:16	outward and visible s.	BOOK 138:15
Shrewsbury by S. clock	SHAK 706:31	**sickle** s. in the fruitful field	BLAK 127:4	Queen must s.	BAGE 51:4
shriek hollow s. the steep	MILT 540:29	**sickly** bloody war and a s. season	TOAS 812:1	seeketh after a s.	BIBL 101:8
short shrill s.	COLL 243:11	kind of s. smile	HART 383:17	**signal** do not see the s.	NELS 569:20
shrieking Hooting and s.	SHAK 712:1	**sickness** age, grief, or s.	KING 463:4	Only a s. shown	LONG 500:3
s. and squeaking	BROW 167:1	falling s.	SHAK 711:26	s.-elm	ARNO 30:24
shrieks Not louder s.	POPE 618:15	helper against s.	EURI 321:14	**signals** s. of the ancient flame	DANT 265:13
shrimp s. learns to whistle	KHRU 462:8	in s. and in health	BOOK 139:1	**signed** hand that s. the paper	THOM 805:19
s. of an author	GRAY 371:3	medicine to heal their s.	BOOK 150:6	I s. my death warrant	COLL 243:5
shrimps s. to swim again	JONS 445:15	s., or any other adversity	BOOK 137:8	**significance** s. of an event	CART 205:6
shrine Erects a s.	BYRO 190:1	s. that destroyeth	BOOK 146:1	s. of its own	JUNG 449:15
fits a little s.	HERR 396:10	**Sid** Tell S.	ADVE 8:19	**signo** In hoc s. vinces	CONS 250:1
shrined bower we s. to Tennyson	HARD 381:9	**Sidcup** get down to S.	PINT 607:1	**signposts** s. to socialist Utopia	CROS 261:4
shrines mouldering s. removed	BYRO 185:19	**side** bosom and half her s.	COLE 239:6	**signs** made shrewd s.	DRYD 296:33
shrink all the boards did s.	COLE 240:21	Hear the other s.	AUGU 39:16	merely conventional s.	CARR 203:29
never make thee s.	BALL 55:4	my hand into his s.	BIBL 108:39	multiply my s. and my wonders	BIBL 81:2
shroud April s.	KEAT 455:28	on every s.	BOOK 141:17	no 'white' or 'coloured' s.	KENN 460:12
stain the stiff dishonoured s.	ELIO 310:27	on our s. today	MACA 508:9	read s. of the times	CHOI 226:13
striped s.	THOM 807:2	on the other s.	BUNY 172:1	s. and wonders	BIBL 107:16
shrouds S. have no pockets	PROV 643:7	on the s. of the house	HOPP 408:13	S. are the natural language	SHAD 693:12
shrug read a nod, a s.	SWIF 783:26	on the s. of those	ANOU 24:7	s. of the times	BIBL 101:25
with a patient s.	SHAK 724:9	other s. of the hill	WELL 846:12	words are but the s.	JOHN 435:17
shrunk S. to this little measure	SHAK 712:20	passed by on the other s.	BIBL 105:5	**Sikhs** Grant to your S.	SIKH 752:7
shudder I s. as I recall	VIRG 829:8	S. by side	WOOD 864:2	**silence** after-s. on the shore	BYRO 190:20
s. at it beforehand	DOST 291:5	Which S. Are You On	DYLA 301:14	answered best with s.	JONS 446:11
s. in the loins engenders	YEAT 874:2	which s. do they cheer for	TEBB 792:10	but s. is golden	PROV 643:32
shuffle All s. there	YEAT 874:16	Who is on my s.	BIBL 85:36	chequered s.	AKHM 10:7
s. the cards	CERV 213:8	**sidelong** s. would she bend	KEAT 455:8	clamour of s.	TAGO 787:19
shuffled reduced to a s. pack	NERU 570:11	**sidera** Sublimi feriam s. vertice	HORA 411:4	conspiracy of s.	COMT 245:9
s. off this mortal coil	SHAK 701:26	**sides** looked at life from both s.	MITC 550:17	darkness again and a s.	LONG 500:3
Shulamite return, O S.	BIBL 91:12	said on both s.	ADDI 5:7	darkness and s.	LEAR 485:17
shun let me s. that	SHAK 715:22	two s. to every question	PROV 644:15	Deep is the s.	DRIN 294:1
s. that wretched state	CHUD 227:19	**sidestreets** down the s.	GINS 358:23	easy step to s.	AUST 41:22
shut either s. or open	PROV 630:31	**siege** My s. is over	VERT 826:15	end of OM is s.	UPAN 822:18
gates of it shall not be s.	BIBL 119:19	She kept the s.	HILL 398:12	eternal s.	PASC 598:1
Men s. their doors	SHAK 734:6	**Siegfried** washing on the S. Line	KENN 460:2	even darkness and s.	KELL 459:7
ought to be s. up	JOHN 439:16	**siesta** Englishmen detest a s.	COWA 253:15	flashes of s.	SMIT 758:18
s. mouth catches no flies	PROV 643:8	**sieve** draws nectar in a s.	COLE 241:15	foster-child of s.	KEAT 455:16
s. the door	POPE 614:15	in a s. I'll thither sail	SHAK 718:6	Gospel of S.	MORL 560:3
s. the stable-door	PROV 636:37	went to sea in a S.	LEAR 485:19	Go to where the s. is	GOOD 365:26
S. up he explained	LARD 480:16	**sifted** s. a nation	STOU 778:5	I kept s.	BOOK 141:27
shuts When one door s.	PROV 646:42	**siftings** let their liquid s. fall	ELIO 310:27	Indecency's conspiracy of s.	SHAW 741:21
shutter before her on a s.	THAC 803:9	**sigh** Born of the very s.	KEAT 455:2	in that s. we the tempest	DRYD 295:12
click the s.	EISE 306:11	s. for thy repose	WESL 847:19	I shall state s.	BECK 64:5
shutters close the s. fast	COWP 256:19	s. in thanking	BROW 163:21	lies are often told in s.	STEV 776:3
shuttle contingency for the space s.		s. is just a sigh	HUPF 422:4	Lo! all in s.	CRAB 257:18
	ANON 16:22	s. is the sword	BLAK 125:14	mind moves upon s.	YEAT 874:3
Man is the s.	VAUG 824:13	s. like Tom o' Bedlam	SHAK 715:2	My gracious s., hail	SHAK 698:5
musical s.	WHIT 852:4	s. no more, ladies	SHAK 727:21	Of the eternal S.	WORD 867:15
swifter than a weaver's s.	BIBL 86:22	**sighed** S. and looked	THOM 808:15	other side of s.	ELIO 307:26
shuttlecock Battledore and s.	DICK 280:18	s. as a lover	GIBB 355:1	rest is s.	SHAK 705:3
shy Once bitten, twice s.	PROV 640:40	s. his soul	SHAK 725:8	shadowless like S.	HOOD 405:23
si S. possis recte	HORA 410:1	**sighing** ability and S.	DICK 282:3	sigh that s. heaves	KEAT 455:2
Sibyl saw the S. at Cumae	ROSS 669:24	poor soul sat s.	SHAK 729:9	s. all the airs	MILT 545:26
Sibyllam Nam S. quidem Cumis	PETR 605:7	s. of a contrite heart	BOOK 135:3	S. alone is great	VIGN 828:3

silence (*cont.*):
s. also does not — ELIO 307:13
S. augmenteth grief — DYER 301:4
s., exile, and cunning — JOYC 448:11
s. fell with the waking bird — TENN 798:4
s. in heaven — BIBL 118:18
s. in the hills — TENN 795:6
S. is a woman's — AUCT 36:21
S. is a woman's best — PROV 643:9
S. is deep as Eternity — CARL 199:16
S. is golden — PROV 643:10
s. is most noble — SWIN 785:2
S. is the virtue — BACO 45:24
S. like a cancer grows — SIMO 752:15
S. means consent — PROV 643:11
S. more musical — ROSS 669:7
s. of a dream — ROSS 668:19
s. of the law — HOBB 401:2
s. sank Like music — COLE 241:8
S., sing to me — HOPK 407:9
s. surged softly backward — DE L 272:8
S. that dreadful bell — SHAK 728:19
S.! Voilà l'ennemi — COND 245:10
small change of s. — MERE 532:16
Sorrow and s. — LONG 499:4
speech is better than s. — ROSA 668:9
stain upon the s. — BECK 64:27
Still-born S. — FLEC 334:15
talent pour le s. — CARL 200:6
Through the friendly s. — VIRG 829:9
trembles into s. — BYRO 187:8
twofold s. — ROSS 669:17
With s. and tears — BYRO 191:19
world of s. — EPIT 317:2
silenced because you have s. him — MORL 560:4
silencing justified in s. — MILL 536:4
silent All s., and all damned — WORD 868:3
Be s. — ROSA 668:9
great ones are s. — SENE 692:18
Grey s. fragments — HUGH 418:10
impossible to be s. — BURK 176:1
into the s. land — ROSS 669:4
Laws are s. — CICE 232:8
mornings are strangely s. — CARS 204:11
one must be s. — WITT 861:12
Paris was French—and s. — TUCH 818:11
s. in seven languages — BAGE 50:14
s. majority — NIXO 576:10
s. manliness of grief — GOLD 364:11
s. over Africa — BROW 166:1
s. touches of time — BURK 176:7
S., upon a peak in Darien — KEAT 456:15
strong, s. man — MORL 560:3
t is s. — ASQU 34:8
unlocked her s. throat — GIBB 355:8
with the s. Virgin — HORA 413:11
silentia *Tacitae per amica s. lunae* — VIRG 829:9
silk breed the s. — SHAK 729:4
clad in s. or scarlet — PROV 626:28
he was shot s. — STRA 778:10
make a s. purse — MORT 562:3
make his couche of s. — CHAU 219:15
shit in a s. stocking — NAPO 568:11
s. hat on a Bradford millionaire — ELIO 311:14
s. makes the difference — FULL 346:19
s. purse out of sow's ear — PROV 647:43
s. stockings — JOHN 438:26
soft as s. remains — HILL 398:9
worn with a s. hat — EDWA 304:3
silken s. terms precise — SHAK 717:21
s. tie — SCOT 688:13
silks in fading s. compose — WINC 860:10
in s. my Julia goes — HERR 396:19
silkworm of s. size or immense — MOOR 557:13
s. expend her yellow labours — MIDD 534:11
silkworms s. droop — BASH 60:19
sillier s. than a silly laugh — CATU 210:10
silliest s. part of God's creation — ROCH 664:19
s. woman can manage a clever man — KIPL 468:20
silliness capacity for s. — LYTT 506:9
silly Ask a s. question — PROV 626:44
it's good to be s. — HORA 414:5

s. twisted boy — CATC 209:8
such a s. question — STER 772:16
such s. things — HOOK 406:10
'tis very s. — BYRO 188:20
You were s. like us — AUDE 37:8
silvae *paulum s. super his* — HORA 414:20
s. sint consule dignae — VIRG 832:2
silvam *In s. . . . ligna feras* — HORA 414:17
silvas *Habitarunt di quoque s.* — VIRG 831:19
inter s. Academi — HORA 410:22
silver About a s. lining — COWA 253:20
all the Georgian s. — MACM 513:2
bringing gold, and s. — BIBL 84:29
cloud has a s. lining — PROV 631:15
covered with s. wings — BOOK 144:8
for a handful of s. — BROW 166:12
gold and s. becks me — SHAK 714:8
in her s. shoon — DE L 272:11
pictures of s. — BIBL 88:35
Selling off the family s. — MISQ 548:17
S. and gold have I none — BIBL 109:15
s. apples of the moon — YEAT 874:24
s. cord be loosed — BIBL 90:20
s. foot in his mouth — RICH 660:8
s. link — SCOT 688:13
s. pin — BALL 56:7
s. plate on a coffin — CURR 263:5
s., snarling trumpets — KEAT 454:6
s.-sweet sound lovers' tongues — SHAK 732:18
Speech is s. — PROV 643:32
take s. or small change — CHAM 214:15
There's a s. lining — FORD 337:12
thirty pieces of s. — BEVA 76:17
thirty pieces of s. — BIBL 103:10
thousands of gold and s. — BOOK 148:13
time hath to s. turned — PEEL 601:17
tuneable s. sound — BANK 57:12
silvery so s. is thy voice — HERR 396:20
silvestrem *S. tenui Musam* — VIRG 831:12
Silvia Who is S. — SHAK 736:15
similes play with s. — WORD 869:20
similia *S. similibus curantur* — MOTT 563:20
Simon real S. Pure — CENT 212:14
Simple S. met a pieman — NURS 581:7
simple and never s. — WILD 854:15
ask the hard question is s. — AUDE 38:14
beautiful and s. — HENR 392:9
C'est tellement s. — PRÉV 622:13
Everything is very s. in war — CLAU 234:8
I'm a s. man — LOWR 503:13
S. Simon met a pieman — NURS 581:7
smile with the s. — GARR 349:9
too clear, too s. — STEN 772:1
women are so s. — SHAK 733:11
simplicitas *O sancta s.* — HUSS 422:6
simplicity Cultivate s. — LAMB 477:3
elegant s. — STOW 778:8
Embrace s. — LAO 479:11
holy s. — JERO 433:4
O holy s. — HUSS 422:6
Pity my s. — WESL 847:12
Seek s. and distrust — WHIT 851:5
s., a child — POPE 615:23
s. of the three per cents — DISR 285:29
simplify s. me when I'm dead — DOUG 291:12
S., simplify — THOR 809:23
Simpson I'm Bart S. — CATC 208:5
Simpsons less like the S. — BUSH 182:7
simulacrum dark s. — BROW 162:3
sin all the causes of s. — JAIN 427:15
And the s. I impute — BROW 167:24
bare the s. of many — BIBL 94:6
beauty is only s. deep — SAKI 678:5
brother s. against me — BIBL 102:4
brought s. and death — STAN 770:5
by making a s. of it — FRAN 340:6
By that s. fell the angels — SHAK 710:22
dark world of s. — BICK 120:23
died unto s. once — BIBL 110:34
dreadful record of s. — DOYL 292:7
Excepting Original S. — CAMP 195:16

fall into no s. — BOOK 134:3
go, and s. no more — BIBL 107:29
go away and s. no more — ANON 19:1
hate the s. — AUGU 39:21
He that is without s. — BIBL 107:28
Ignorance excuses from s. — AUCT 36:12
I had not known s. — BIBL 110:36
in secret's. — CHUR 228:11
in s. hath my mother — BOOK 143:5
keep us this day without s. — BOOK 133:11
Lord imputeth no s. — BOOK 141:16
lose the s. — POPE 614:9
Lukewarmness I account a s. — COWL 254:16
made almost a s. — DRYD 295:14
My s., my soul — NABO 566:16
no s. but ignorance — MARL 522:16
no s., but to be rich — SHAK 714:6
not innocence but s. — BROW 166:7
One s. will destroy — BUNY 171:20
only one real s. — LESS 490:16
original s. — MELV 531:6
physicists have known s. — OPPE 585:15
quantum o' the s. — BURN 178:3
rebellion is as the s. — BIBL 83:36
researches in original s. — PLOM 610:5
Shall we continue in s. — BIBL 110:32
s. against the human mind — HUXL 424:1
s., death, and Hell — BUNY 171:22
single venial s. — NEWM 572:9
s. in secret — MOLI 552:24
S. is behovely — JULI 449:6
s. is ever before me — BOOK 143:4
s. not — BIBL 114:7
s. of public men — TAYL 792:2
s.—passion can commit — SAYE 683:1
s.'s a pleasure — BYRO 188:2
s. tends to be addictive — AUDE 38:17
s. with caution — CENT 212:13
s. ye do by two and two — KIPL 467:15
Stand in awe, and s. not — BOOK 139:15
taketh away the s. — BIBL 107:5
triumph over death and s. — SPEN 766:17
wages of s. is death — BIBL 110:35
want of power to s. — DRYD 296:20
we have no s. — BIBL 117:16
what did he say about s. — COOL 250:17
Where s. abounded — BIBL 110:31
Which is my s. — DONN 288:18
worst s. towards our fellow — SHAW 739:19
Would you like to s. — ANON 21:15
your s. will find you out — BIBL 82:10
sincere Always be s. — TRUM 818:1
be as wholly s. — JUDA 449:1
be s. — MENG 532:4
friend s. enough — BULW 170:16
starkly s. — RHYS 659:15
sincerely s. want to be rich — CORN 251:18
sincerity be talked with in s. — SHAK 723:1
s. is a dangerous thing — WILD 855:6
unleavened bread of s. — BIBL 111:31
Sindh I have S. — WINK 860:15
sinecure no s. — BYRO 192:5
sinews Money is the s. of love — FARQ 324:11
money the s. of war — BACO 48:7
s. of the soul — FULL 346:10
s. of thy heart — BLAK 128:4
s. of war — CICE 232:7
Stiffen the s. — SHAK 708:16
very s. of virtue — WALT 839:4
sing Alleluia! s. to Jesus — DIX 286:32
bygynneth to s. — CHAU 221:4
can s. and won't sing — PROV 637:38
celebrate myself, and s. myself — WHIT 852:7
come, let us s. — BOOK 146:7
do what men may s. — PEMB 602:8
I came here to s. — NERU 570:15
I'll s. you twelve O — SONG 762:13
In these stones horizons s. — LEWI 492:8
in thine heart to s. — SWIN 785:22
I s. of brooks — HERR 395:15
I, too, s. America — HUGH 418:1
laugh and s. — BOOK 144:3
never heard no horse s. — ARMS 28:18

skill (cont.):
S. comes so slow — DAVI 267:17
skilled S. or unskilled — HORA 410:19
skimming S. our gable — HEAN 387:5
skin ask the Gods for a thick s. — TROL 816:19
beauty being only s.-deep — KERR 461:8
Beauty only s. deep — PROV 627:14
Can the Ethiopian change his s. — BIBL 95:3
castle of my s. — LAMM 477:17
cold s. sagging — THOM 807:4
Don't sell the s. — PROV 630:27
my s. is red — SITT 753:8
nearer is my s. — PROV 639:26
on his s. the swart flies — DOUG 291:13
shear his flock, not s. it — TIBE 810:16
s. from the arm — ELIO 310:18
s. is a different shade — HAMM 379:5
s. of an innocent lamb — SHAK 710:1
s. of my teeth — BIBL 86:33
skull beneath the s. — ELIO 311:20
thick s. a gift — ADEN 6:6
throws her enamelled s. — SHAK 726:9
way to s. a cat — PROV 644:28
skinny fear thy s. hand — COLE 240:25
skins beauty of their s. — TENN 799:14
sisters under their s. — KIPL 466:11
such white s. — CURZ 263:11
skip s. like a calf — BOOK 141:2
skipped mountains s. like rams — BOOK 148:3
skipper s. had taken his little daughter — LONG 500:6
skirmish trivial s. fought near Marathon — GRAV 369:12
skittles beer and s. — PROV 637:28
skivvies take a dozen s. — MCGR 511:2
Skugg Here S. Lies snug — EPIT 318:9
skull place of a s. — BIBL 108:28
s., and the feet — BIBL 85:37
s. beneath the skin — ELIO 311:20
skuttle fish in mind of the s. — ADDI 5:20
sky above, the vaulted s. — CLAR 233:2
And the blue s. — WORD 866:13
bowl we call The S. — FITZ 331:24
clean the s. — ELIO 310:18
clear blue s. over my head — HAZL 386:24
climbin' clear up to the s. — HAMM 378:19
diamond in the s. — TAYL 791:16
ethereal s. — ADDI 5:17
evening is spread out against the s. — ELIO 310:5
If the s. falls — PROV 635:17
Music shall untune the s. — DRYD 296:30
pie in the s. — HILL 398:14
prisoners call the s. — WILD 855:31
Red s. at night — PROV 642:19
rocking s. of '41 — YEVT 876:2
shoulders held the s. suspended — HOUS 415:8
s. changes — SHAK 697:20
s. is darkening — AUDE 38:16
s. is red — BIBL 101:24
soars to match the s. — PROC 624:15
to that equal s. — POPE 616:21
triple-towered s. — DAY- 269:7
wide and starry s. — STEV 777:5
yon twelve-winded s. — HOUS 416:3
Skye Over the sea to S. — BOUL 152:15
Over the sea to S. — STEV 776:24
skylark s. wounded in the wing — BLAK 124:11
slacks girls in s. remember Dad — BETJ 75:10
slag post-industrial s.-heap — DRAB 293:5
slain Death, ere thou hast s. another — EPIT 319:15
fifty thousand men s. — WALP 838:14
fight and no be s. — BURN 179:21
hurt but I am not s. — BALL 55:12
law, chance, hath s. — DONN 288:9
new-s. knight — BALL 56:3
s. a thousand men — BIBL 83:15
s. by a fair cruel maid — SHAK 735:18
s. his thousands — BIBL 84:7
s. in the way of God — KORA 472:19
s., nor treated with violence — JAIN 428:1

s. think he is slain — EMER 314:11
Small s. body — SWIN 785:23
slander one to s. you — TWAI 820:8
slandered s. his neighbour — BOOK 140:1
slandering lying, and s. — BOOK 138:13
slang S. is a language — SAND 680:9
slanged sneered and s. — BELL 68:7
slant certain S. of light — DICK 281:22
slap Slip, slop, s. — OFFI 584:11
slashing s. article — THAC 802:19
slate something off a s. — KIPL 465:5
thoughts upon a s. — HOOD 406:3
slaughter arrayed for mutual s. — WORD 867:1
lamb to the s. — BIBL 94:4
ox goeth to the s. — BIBL 87:31
s. of plague, pestilence — SHAW 741:2
s. will ensue — CONG 247:12
through s. to a throne — GRAY 370:7
Yet was the s. small — HARI 382:12
slaughtered ghosts of the s. — CLAU 234:7
slave always the s. of the other — LERM 490:2
Better be a s. — BRON 158:10
entered the world a s. — BROW 165:10
female worker slave of that s. — CONN 248:14
freedom to the s. — LINC 493:18
freeing any s. — LINC 493:17
half s. — LINC 493:10
has been s. to thousands — SHAK 728:23
investigation of s. trade — WILB 853:17
moment the s. resolves — GAND 348:12
No s. is a slave to the same lengths — MILL 536:13
passion's s. — SHAK 702:17
Philosopher! a lingering s. — WORD 868:4
s.-morality — NIET 575:18
s. of the passions — HUME 420:18
s.'s condition — EURI 321:16
s. to its animosity — WASH 840:18
S. to no sect — POPE 617:11
s. trade is contrary — HART 383:19
womankind's in every state a s. — EGER 304:12
wretched s. — SHAK 709:3
young man's s. — PROV 627:30
you were a Christian s. — HENL 391:15
slavery Chains and s. — BURN 179:9
chains Of heart-debasing s. — GRAI 368:6
liberty and s. — CAMD 194:11
S. is — SUMN 780:10
S. they can have — BURK 173:21
sold off into s. — TRUT 818:4
state of s. — GILL 358:16
testimony against s. — DOUG 291:19
wise and good in s. — MACA 507:2
slaves Air for S. to breathe — ANON 19:14
at the mill with s. — MILT 544:31
Britons never will be s. — THOM 808:8
creed of s. — PITT 607:18
Englishmen never will be s. — SHAW 740:28
freemen or s. — WASH 840:14
have made our s. — DARW 266:20
millions of royal s. — GENE 352:4
no tsar, but the s. remain — ZAMY 877:8
S. cannot breathe in England — COWP 256:9
s., howe'er contented — COWP 256:4
S. of the Lamp — ARNO 28:23
s. that dig the golden ore — CRAB 258:8
s. with weary footsteps — SHEL 744:2
sons of former s. — KING 463:11
tyrant grinds down his s. — BRON 158:20
wholly s. or wholly free — DRYD 295:26
women are born s. — ASTE 34:15
women born s. — WOLL 863:16
slavish O imitators, you s. herd — HORA 410:18
slay s. and slay and slay — MACA 508:9
Though he s. me — BIBL 86:29
slayer s. think he slays — EMER 314:11
slew the s. — MACA 508:8
slaying s. of a beautiful hypothesis — HUXL 423:5
slays If any man thinks he s. — UPAN 822:9
man thinks he s. — BHAG 77:17
slayer think he s. — EMER 314:11

Whoso s. a soul — KORA 472:3
sledge great s. drops in vain — ROET 665:5
My s. and anvil — EPIT 319:3
sleek S.-headed men — SHAK 711:22
sleekit Wee, s., cow'rin' — BURN 179:24
sleep arousing from s. — MANZ 520:13
as before, Love, —Only s. — BROW 168:10
balmy s. — YOUN 876:16
borders of s. — THOM 806:19
cannot s. at night — PEPY 603:16
Care-charmer S. — DANI 264:6
Care-charming S. — FLET 335:12
comfort in s. — BROW 162:7
darkness brings not s. — PUSH 650:22
Death and his brother S. — SHEL 746:5
deep and dreamless s. — BROO 160:5
deep s. of England — ORWE 587:3
do I wake or s. — KEAT 456:12
Do s. well — CATC 207:14
each day dies with s. — HOPK 407:15
even as a s. — BOOK 145:20
exposition of s. — SHAK 726:26
fain I would s. — BALL 54:9
first approach of s. — BYRO 190:9
first s. — ANON 21:11
from my mother's s. — JARR 430:20
From s. and from damnation — CHES 224:6
from the fields of s. — WORD 867:5
God caused a deep s. — BIBL 79:1
green ideas s. furiously — CHOM 226:14
grey and full of s. — YEAT 875:10
guard you while you s. — KIPL 467:16
have I had in my s. — SURT 781:9
have to go to s. — GINS 359:3
him who invented s. — CERV 213:11
hour's s. before midnight — PROV 641:4
How s. the brave — COLL 243:12
I lay me down to s. — PRAY 623:6
In s. a king — SHAK 738:8
in soot I s. — BLAK 127:7
in their s. of death — WILB 854:7
I shall s. — SWIN 786:5
I s., but my heart waketh — BIBL 91:8
lasting s. — BEAU 63:11
like unwilling s. — KEAT 456:16
little s. — BIBL 87:28
Macbeth does murder s. — SHAK 720:6
Macbeth shall s. no more — SHAK 720:7
Me biful for to s. — LANG 478:15
men who s. badly — RUSS 674:13
miles to go before I s. — FROS 345:3
Newton's s. — BLAK 125:21
night to do with s. — MILT 538:23
One short s. past — DONN 288:11
O s.'s enchantment — EURI 321:14
past was a s. — BROW 167:23
put the world to s. — MUIR 564:10
rounded with a s. — SHAK 733:31
season of all natures, s. — SHAK 721:14
Shake off this downy s. — SHAK 720:17
She looks like s. — SHAK 696:7
Six hours in s. — COKE 238:15
Six hours s. for a man — PROV 643:13
S. after toil — SPEN 767:10
s. and a forgetting — WORD 867:8
S.; and if life was bitter — SWIN 785:3
s., and urine — SHAK 720:13
sleep, dear, s. — BEDD 65:3
S. I can get nane — BURN 177:15
s. is sound indeed — SHAK 707:28
S. is sweet — BUNY 171:16
S.! it is a gentle thing — COLE 241:4
S. no more — SHAK 720:6
s. of a labouring man — BIBL 89:28
S. on Blest pair — MILT 543:14
s. one ever-during night — CAMP 195:21
S. on (my Love!) — KING 463:4
s. out this great gap of time — SHAK 694:17
s. provides relief — CHAM 214:14
S. shall neither night — SHAK 718:7
S. so soundly — SHAK 709:3
S. to wake — BROW 164:21
s. under bridges — FRAN 340:8

s. upon ale FARQ 324:2
slept an azure-lidded s. KEAT 454:13
Softer than s. TENN 799:2
some must s. SHAK 702:25
sons of Edward s. SHAK 731:23
such as s. o' nights SHAK 711:22
suffer nobody to s. ADDI 5:6
take their ease And s. SHAK 711:10
that sweet s. SHAK 728:29
Through s. and darkness KEBL 458:21
time enough to s. HOUS 415:13
time when first s. begins VIRG 829:10
To die: to s. SHAK 701:26
two gates of S. VIRG 830:16
uninvaded s. TENN 796:9
We shall not all s. BIBL 113:5
We shall not s. MCCR 509:17
We term s. a death BROW 163:17
when you s. you remind me SASS 682:8
will not s. BOOK 148:17
sleeper never a quiet s. TENN 798:10
sleepers seven s. den DONN 289:7
s. in that quiet earth BRON 158:21
sleepeth not dead, but s. BIBL 100:19
peradventure he s. BIBL 85:9
sleeping art thou s. there below NEWB 571:9
awakened a s. giant FILM 328:13
cursed him in s. BARH 58:9
fuss about s. together WAUG 843:2
Lay your s. head AUDE 37:15
Lest he find you s. BIBL 104:5
Let s. dogs lie PROV 637:20
like a s. Princess LAWR 484:3
s. and the dead SHAK 720:8
s., by a brother's hand SHAK 700:22
s. hound to wake CHAU 221:1
s. pill is white SEXT 693:7
s. with an elephant TRUD 817:12
smitten a s. enemy YAMA 872:3
waking s. MONT 555:17
sleepless S. as the river CRAN 258:18
s. soul that perished WORD 868:22
s. with cold commemorative ROSS 669:21
sleeps Homer sometimes s. BYRO 188:27
it s. obedience PAIN 593:2
Now s. the crimson petal TENN 799:17
wakes or s. SHEL 743:16
while the world's NEHR 569:9
sleepwalker assurance of a s. HITL 400:8
sleepy Contentment is a s. thing TRAH 814:14
I'm not s. DYLA 301:20
sleeve Ash on an old man's s. ELIO 309:16
heart upon my s. SHAK 728:2
lacy s. with vitriol WOOL 864:17
no further than your s. PROV 643:44
sleeves Americanism with its s. rolled
MCCA 509:5
language that rolls up its s. SAND 680:9
Tie up my s. HUNT 422:1
sleight perceive a juggler's s. BUTL 183:24
slenderly s. known himself SHAK 714:21
slepen s. al the nyght with open ye CHAU 218:3
slept first fruits of them that s. BIBL 112:21
he thought I s. PATM 599:12
His saints s. ANON 24:3
I should have s. BIBL 86:16
s. with his fathers BIBL 85:5
Whilst Adam s. ANON 21:11
world changed while I s. EIRE 306:5
slew as he was ambitious, I s. him SHAK 712:26
dead which he s. at his death BIBL 83:19
s. his master BIBL 85:35
s. mighty kings BOOK 149:11
s. the slayer MACA 508:8
slice not s. a pineapple BABB 44:11
S. him where you like WODE 861:22
s. off a cut loaf PROV 643:14
slime daubed it with s. BIBL 80:30
slimy hot s. channel CRAB 257:13
s. things did crawl COLE 240:21
thousand s. things COLE 241:2
slings s. and arrows SHAK 701:26
slip catch no s. by the way BUNY 171:7

enemies the s. for ever STER 772:19
gave us all the s. BROW 168:7
many a s. 'twixt cup PROV 644:41
s., slide, perish ELIO 309:7
S., slop, slap OFFI 584:11
slipper Old Mother S. Slopper NURS 580:11
slippered lean and s. pantaloon SHAK 697:2
slippers in his golden s. BUNY 171:12
pair of s., sir BROW 163:22
slippery standing is s. BACO 47:8
slipping tail lights s. CRAN 258:17
slit S. your girl's KING 464:17
slits s. the thin-spun life MILT 540:7
slitty all be s.-eyed PHIL 605:14
sliver envious s. broke SHAK 704:7
Sloane S. turned secular saint BURC 172:4
sloe blacker than the s. CARB 197:15
slogans instead of principles, s. BENT 71:20
slogged s. up to Arras SASS 682:11
slop Slip, s., slap OFFI 584:11
woman with a s.-pail HOPK 408:9
slopes butler's upper s. WODE 862:8
sloth my own amazing s. BISH 122:12
peaceful s., Not peace MILT 542:5
Shake off dull s. KEN 459:13
time in studies is s. BACO 47:33
slouches S. towards Bethlehem YEAT 874:18
slough friendly bombs, fall on S. BETJ 76:5
s. was Despond BUNY 171:5
slovenliness Peace nothing but s. BREC 155:18
S. is no part of religion WESL 847:22
slow come he s. SCOT 688:20
comes ever s. DRAY 293:12
S. and steady wins the race PROV 643:15
S. but sure PROV 643:16
s. of speech BIBL 80:39
s. to anger BIBL 88:18
s. to speak BIBL 116:18
telling you to s. down ANON 16:23
telling you to s. down SAYI 684:11
Time is too s. VAN 824:4
slower had to be s. FRAS 341:17
slowly angel to pass, flying s. FIRB 327:14
Architecture acts the most s. DIMN 283:9
Make haste s. AUGU 40:3
Make haste s. PROV 638:13
mills of God grind s. LONG 499:20
mills of God grind s. PROV 638:39
Run s. OVID 589:17
Science moves, but s. TENN 797:2
twist s. in the wind EHRL 305:1
slugabed Get up, sweet S. HERR 395:18
sluggard foul s.'s comfort CARL 199:8
s. is wiser BIBL 89:2
thou s. BIBL 87:27
voice of the s. WATT 841:17
slughorn Dauntless the s. BROW 165:12
sluices Close the s. VIRG 832:1
sluicing browsing and s. WODE 862:7
slum seen one city s. AGNE 9:13
slumber little s. BIBL 87:28
neither s. nor sleep BOOK 148:17
s. did my spirit steal WORD 869:9
s. is more sweet than toil TENN 797:13
S.'s chain has bound me MOOR 558:16
to soothing s. seven JONE 445:12
slumbered you have but s. here SHAK 727:12
slumbers Golden s. kiss your eyes DEKK 271:22
slums gay intimacy of the s. WAUG 842:13
slurp s. into the barrels FISH 330:11
slush pure as the driven s. BANK 57:9
slut I am not a s. SHAK 697:14
sluts foul s. in dairies CORB 251:9
sly s. shade of a Rural Dean BROO 159:8
small accept something however s. ACHE 1:9
Better are s. fish PROV 627:29
between the s. and great COWP 257:1
big squadrons against the s. BUSS 182:16
both great and s. COLE 241:10
commonly thought s. WOOL 864:6
day of s. nations CHAM 214:3
grind exceeding s. LONG 499:20
how s. is the thing HORA 410:20

how s. the world is GROS 374:1
In s. proportions JONS 446:21
Microbe is so very s. BELL 68:14
no s. steps in great affairs RETZ 658:11
pictures that got s. FILM 330:6
s., but perfectly formed COOP 251:2
s. college WEBS 843:19
S. is beautiful SCHU 687:1
s. Latin JONS 446:24
s. packages PROV 627:23
S. sorrows speak SENE 692:18
s.-talking world FRY 345:17
s. things with great VIRG 833:5
so s. a number of men TREV 815:10
so s. a thing ARNO 29:8
Speech is the s. change MERE 532:16
still s. voice BIBL 85:14
that cannot reach the s. SPEN 767:22
they are very s. UPDI 822:24
Too s. to live in ANON 21:2
Town s.-talk flows CRAB 257:10
with s. men no great thing MILL 536:9
smaller s. fleas to bite 'em SWIF 784:4
s. than smallest atom UPAN 822:10
smallest s. amount of lying BUTL 184:5
s. room of my house REGE 657:12
smaragdine green ribbons s. TAYL 791:19
smart girls that are so s. CARE 199:2
love and all its s. BEDD 65:3
scorn which mocked the s. ARNO 30:22
s. for it BIBL 88:1
smash English never s. in a face HALS 378:9
smashed s. it into because CUMM 262:11
s. up things and creatures FITZ 332:13
smatch some s. of honour SHAK 714:2
smattering s. of everything DICK 281:2
smell ancient and fish-like s. SHAK 733:24
I s. the blood SHAK 716:5
Money has no s. PROV 638:46
Money has no s. VESP 827:1
shares man's s. HOPK 407:7
s. and hideous hum GODL 361:12
s. a rat ROCH 664:9
s. of napalm in the morning FILM 328:19
s. too strong STER 773:1
sweet keen s. ROSS 669:23
Sweet s. of success FILM 331:13
to his own sweet sense doth s. MONT 555:23
smelleth s. the battle afar off BIBL 87:13
smells it s. to heaven SHAK 703:5
s. like roses JOHN 435:9
s. of mortality SHAK 716:18
smile Asians could still s. HEAD 386:26
call me that, s. WIST 861:3
Cambridge people rarely s. BROO 159:10
enchain him with a s. CARY 206:1
has a nice s. GROM 373:13
hear a s. CROS 261:9
Is it Colman's s. EWAR 321:24
kind of sickly s. HART 383:17
murder whiles I s. SHAK 710:8
my Julia's lips do s. HERR 395:1
one livid s. WALP 838:8
prison and a s. WOTT 870:10
riding on a s. and a shoeshine MILL 537:9
s., and be a villain SHAK 700:24
S. at us, pay us CHES 224:15
s. dwells a little longer CHAP 216:1
s. his face SHAK 736:1
s. his work to see BLAK 128:5
s. of accomplishment PLAT 608:7
s. of cosmic Cheshire cat HUXL 423:3
s. of fate DYER 301:8
s. on the face of the tiger ANON 20:1
s., smile, smile MILI 535:18
s. with the simple GARR 349:9
s. with the wise JOHN 440:16
vain tribute of a s. SCOT 688:12
why, we shall s. SHAK 713:30
your mother with a s. VIRG 832:3
smiled only the dead s. AKHM 10:5
S. like yon knot BLAI 123:16
Voltaire s. HUGO 419:8

smiler s. with the knyf — CHAU 219:11
smiles charmed it with s. — CARR 204:3
  daggers in men's s. — SHAK 720:20
  greeted with s. — BROO 159:17
  making practised s. — SHAK 736:18
  robbed that s. — SHAK 728:14
smilest Thou s. and art still — ARNO 30:15
smiling hides a s. face — COWP 255:13
  S. at grief — SHAK 735:21
  s., damnèd villain — SHAK 700:24
  s., destructive man — LEE 487:14
  s. of Fortune — COCK 237:15
  s. surface of the sea — PLUT 610:12
  S. through her tears — HOME 404:16
  S. wonder of a day — WRIG 870:20
smilingness Despair a s. assume — BYRO 186:4
smirk serious and the s. — DICK 279:12
smite ready to s. once — MILT 540:11
  s. all the firstborn — BIBL 81:9
  s. thee on thy right cheek — BIBL 99:5
  without hands to s. — SWIN 785:1
smiteth to him that s. him — BIBL 95:12
smith by naming him S. — HOLM 403:12
  Chuck it, S. — CHES 223:24
  s., a mighty man is he — LONG 500:4
  s. of his own fortune — CLAU 234:5
smithy village s. stands — LONG 500:4
smitten bones are s. asunder — BOOK 142:7
  s. a sleeping enemy — YAMA 872:3
smock nearer is my s. — PROV 639:25
smoke between clothes and s. — NERU 570:11
  Gossip is a sort of s. — ELIO 307:6
  her beloved s. — LAMB 477:5
  hills, they shall s. — BOOK 147:10
  idle s. of praise — DANI 264:7
  light after s. — HORA 409:7
  little s., in pallid moonshine — KEAT 454:8
  More doctors s. Camels — ADVE 8:5
  No s. without fire — PROV 640:14
  rise then as s. to the sky — CELA 212:10
  s. and stir of this dim spot — MILT 538:19
  s. and wealth — HORA 413:7
  s.-filled room — SIMP 753:3
  S. gets in your eyes — HARB 379:15
  s. of their torment — BIBL 119:2
  s. rises already — VIRG 831:16
  Stygian s. — JAME 428:21
smoked s. salmon and tinned — WILS 859:9
smokeless in the s. air — WORD 865:7
smoking not found any s. guns — BLIX 129:2
  S. can seriously damage — OFFI 584:12
  s. flax — BIBL 93:21
smoky burnt-out ends of s. days — ELIO 310:21
smooth husbandry should not run s.
  — VIRG 832:13
  I am a s. man — BIBL 80:6
  never did run s. — PROV 629:23
  never did run s. — SHAK 725:23
  s. the ice — SHAK 714:11
smoother s. than oil — BIBL 87:26
  s. than oil — BOOK 143:12
smote Israel s. him — BIBL 82:5
  s. divers nations — BOOK 149:11
  s. him thus — SHAK 729:24
  s. the king of Israel — BIBL 85:21
  s. them hip and thigh — BIBL 83:14
smudge wears man's s. — HOPK 407:7
smug s. minority — BERT 75:5
smut S. detected in it — ZOLA 878:14
snail creeping like s. — SHAK 696:28
  said a whiting to a s. — CARR 202:13
  seeing the s. — DONN 289:24
  s.'s on the thorn — BROW 167:3
snails like s. after a rainstorm — VERG 826:4
snake doth like a s. renew — SHEL 744:5
  like a wounded s. — POPE 616:5
  move about like a s. — HELL 390:6
  scotched the s. — SHAK 721:2
  s. came to my water-trough — LAWR 483:22
  s. hidden in the grass — VIRG 831:22
  s. throws her enamelled skin — SHAK 726:9
snakes no s. to be met with — JOHN 442:14
  S. eat Frogs — STEV 774:4

You spotted s. — SHAK 726:10
snakeskin s.-titles — BENÉ 69:13
snapper s.-up of unconsidered trifles
  — SHAK 736:27
snare mockery, and a s. — DENM 273:9
  rabbit in a s. — STEP 772:7
  s. of the fowler — BOOK 148:22
  s. of the hunter — BOOK 145:23
  world's great s. — SHAK 695:13
snares rain s. — BOOK 139:26
  s. of death — BOOK 148:6
snaring s. the poor world — CRAN 258:16
Snark S. was a Boojum — CARR 204:4
snatch Shrewd was that s. — BROW 165:3
  s. me away — FROS 344:7
snatched s. from Jove — MANI 519:7
  s. the lightning — TURG 819:7
snatching s. his victuals from the table
  — CHUR 229:10
sneaky snouty, s. mind — NICO 575:3
sneer devil in his s. — BYRO 187:7
  refute a s. — PALE 593:9
  teach the rest to s. — POPE 614:22
  They s. at me — FITZ 331:25
  with solemn s. — BYRO 186:13
sneering I was born s. — GILB 357:2
sneezed not to be s. at — SCOT 690:2
sneezes beat him when he s. — CARR 202:3
  Coughs and s. — OFFI 584:3
sneezing people s. — ROBI 664:6
snicker hold my coat, and s. — ELIO 310:10
  vorpal blade went s.-snack — CARR 202:22
snip S.! Snap! Snip — HOFF 402:8
snipe so wet you could shoot s. off him
  — POWE 621:20
snob admires mean things is a S. — THAC 802:15
snobbery bereaved if s. died — USTI 823:8
  S. with Violence — BENN 70:10
snobbish s. and vulgar — VICT 827:11
snobbishness S. is the desire — KING 464:19
snoring s., she disturbs — COWP 256:7
snorted not one s. — HUGH 418:10
  Or s. we — DONN 289:7
snotgreen s. sea — JOYC 448:14
snout had as wise as s. on — FERG 325:8
  in a swine's s. — BIBL 88:2
snouty s., sneaky mind — NICO 575:3
snow amid the winter's s. — CASW 206:16
  architecture of the s. — EMER 314:16
  as white as s. — BIBL 117:27
  bloodless lay the untrodden s. — CAMP 195:9
  chaste as unsunned s. — SHAK 698:20
  congealed s. — PARK 596:16
  dark over the s. — THOM 806:21
  few acres of s. — VOLT 833:12
  first fall of s. — PRIE 622:18
  geese, like a s. cloud — RANS 655:5
  giveth s. like wool — BOOK 150:8
  Ice and S. — BOOK 133:15
  I, this incessant s. — DE L 272:4
  last long streak of s. — TENN 796:3
  like the s. geese — OKPI 584:22
  listens in the s. — STEV 774:13
  little s.-white feet — YEAT 873:4
  naked in December s. — SHAK 730:8
  shivering in the s. — SOUT 764:25
  skin was as white as s. — GRIM 373:9
  s. and vapours — BOOK 150:9
  s. before the summer sun — TECU 792:11
  s. came flying — BRID 156:19
  s. falling faintly — JOYC 447:17
  s. flutters down — BLOK 129:4
  s. in the mountains — TART 790:9
  s. in winter — CAMP 194:15
  s. of ferne yere — CHAU 221:9
  S. on snow — ROSS 669:2
  s. the leaves — HOUS 416:1
  used to be S. White — WEST 848:17
  we shall have s. — NURS 580:8
  white as s. — BIBL 91:20
  whiter than s. — BOOK 143:6
  wish a s. — SHAK 717:12
  wondrous strange s. — SHAK 727:5

wrapped in wild s. — BLOK 129:6
wrong sort of s. — NEWS 573:2
wrong sort of s. — WORR 870:6
snowed s. for six days — THOM 806:5
snowflake crown of s. pearls — BLOK 129:6
snowflakes s. hurry — PUSH 650:16
snows our Lady of the S. — KIPL 467:2
  s. have fled — HORA 413:17
  s. of yesteryear — VILL 828:7
snowy S., Flowy, Blowy — ELLI 314:2
snuff only took s. — GOLD 364:22
  You abuse s. — COLE 242:1
snuffed s. out by an article — BYRO 189:14
snug s. As a bug In a rug — EPIT 318:9
  s. little Island — DIBD 276:7
so And s. do I — HARD 382:2
  if it was s., it might be — CARR 203:2
soak expect a s. — PROV 647:1
soaked s. to the skin — COHE 238:8
soap of blood and s. — MITC 550:14
  smiles and s. — CARR 204:3
  S. and education — TWAI 820:2
  What! no s. — FOOT 336:13
soapflakes sell Jack like s. — KENN 460:16
soar creep as well as s. — BURK 174:27
  not to s. — MACA 507:22
  Type of the wise who s. — WORD 869:18
soaring s. ever singest — SHEL 746:20
soars No bird s. too high — BLAK 126:10
  s. to match the sky — PROC 624:15
sobbing a-sighing and a-s. — NURS 582:12
sober at least not s. — JOHN 438:16
  Be s., be vigilant — BIBL 117:13
  compulsorily s. — MAGE 514:17
  godly, righteous, and s. life — BOOK 133:6
  go to bed s. — FLET 335:6
  s. me up — FITZ 332:10
  S., steadfast, and demure — MILT 539:14
  To-morrow we'll be s. — SONG 762:4
  to Philip s. — ANON 16:10
  Wordsworth drunk and Porson s. — HOUS 416:14
sobs drawn-out s. — VERL 826:9
social fluctuating waves of our s. life
  — HAWT 385:6
  judge at once of the s. position — TOCQ 812:14
  no religion but s. — WESL 847:20
  self-love and s. — POPE 617:4
  s. and economic experiment — HOOV 406:12
  s. contract — ROUS 670:13
  S. Contract is nothing more — WELL 846:22
socialism Democracy and s. are means
  — NEHR 569:12
  religion of S. — BEVA 76:14
  S. can only arrive — VIER 827:18
  s. would not lose its human face — DUBČ 298:1
socialist be a s. at twenty — SAYI 685:7
  high-water mark of S. literature — ORWE 587:21
  signposts to s. Utopia — CROS 261:4
socialists s. throw it away — CAST 206:13
  We are all s. now — HARC 380:2
society action of s. upon itself — TOCQ 812:11
  affluent s. — GALB 347:9
  bonds of civil s. — LOCK 497:16
  can stand any s. — TWAI 820:9
  capital of polished s. — BURK 174:17
  consolidates s. — JOHN 438:20
  desperate oddfellow s. — THOR 809:20
  Great S. — JOHN 435:5
  happiness of s. — ADAM 3:12
  have s. upon his own terms — EMER 315:16
  influence in s. — LACL 475:7
  in one s. — WORD 868:10
  live in s. — ARIS 27:25
  Man was formed for s. — BLAC 123:9
  moves about in s. — CHOI 226:13
  no letters; no s. — HOBB 400:24
  no such thing as S. — THAT 804:1
  One great s. — WORD 868:19
  selects her own S. — DICK 281:20
  so-called affluent s. — BEVA 77:1
  s. distributes itself — ARNO 31:8
  s. founded on trash — SAYE 682:19
  S. is indeed a contract — BURK 174:16

S. is now one polished horde	BYRO 189:20
s. is wonderfully delightful	WILD 855:28
S. needs to condemn	MAJO 517:3
s. of privacy	RAND 655:1
s. where it is safe to be	STEV 774:22
s., with all its combinations	BURK 174:4
s. would be a hell upon earth	MILL 536:14
three for s.	THOR 809:21
unfit a man for s.	CHAM 214:15
sock hole in a s.	EINS 306:4
Jonson's learnèd s.	MILT 539:31
socket Burn to the s.	WORD 865:13
sockets candles burn the s.	HOUS 415:7
s. of fine gold	BIBL 91:10
socks inability to put on your s.	GONC 365:24
Socrates contradict S.	SOCR 760:6
S., I shall not accuse you	PLAT 608:17
sod under my head a s.	BALL 54:12
withered in the s.	BRON 158:12
soda Sermons and s.-water	BYRO 188:9
wash their feet in s. water	ELIO 311:11
sodden s. and unkind	BELL 68:23
sodium discovered S.	BENT 71:16
Sodom S. and Gomorrah	BIBL 96:12
sodomy rum, s., prayers, and the lash	CHUR 230:9
sods s. with our bayonets turning	WOLF 862:14
sofa accomplished s. last	COWP 256:6
Alternately on a S.	AUST 41:12
sing the s.	COWP 256:5
s. upholstered in panther skin	PLOM 610:5
under the s.	HOLU 404:2
soft does not make us s.	PERI 603:23
her s. and chilly nest	KEAT 454:11
Ovid, the s. philosopher	DRYD 296:8
s. and narrow	BALL 54:3
s. answer	BIBL 88:13
s. answer turneth	PROV 643:18
s. as the dawn	CART 205:11
s. as the dawn	LOVE 502:11
s. can wear away the hard	TALM 789:32
s. impeachment	SHER 748:21
s. phrase of peace	SHAK 728:7
s. under-belly of Europe	MISQ 548:18
s., unhappy sex	BEHN 67:8
s. was the sun	LANG 478:14
turf that covers her s. bones	MART 524:7
softened s. by the effects	PEEL 601:13
softer s. than butter	BOOK 143:12
softly Fair and s.	PROV 631:49
go s. all my years	BIBL 93:13
S. along the road	DE L 272:10
s. and suddenly vanish	CARR 204:2
S. come and softly go	ORRE 586:7
Softly, s., catchee	PROV 643:19
s. tread, said Christabel	COLE 239:5
Tread s.	YEAT 873:14
softness For s. she	MILT 543:5
s. of my body will be guarded	LOWE 502:14
whisper s. in chambers	MILT 545:26
soggy s. little island	UPDI 822:19
soil fertile s.	BACO 49:12
Freedom's s. beneath our feet	DRAK 293:11
grows in every s.	BURK 173:21
powers of the s.	RICA 659:18
regarding the s. as property	THOR 809:9
s. Is bare now	HOPK 407:7
s. which is soon exhausted	REYN 659:4
tied to the s.	HOME 405:6
sojourner discontented s.	WORD 868:7
sojourners s., as were all our fathers	BIBL 86:1
sol s. et luna	AUGU 39:4
sold Never s. the truth	TENN 798:24
ointment might have been s.	BIBL 103:9
s. all that he had	BIBL 101:16
s. his birthright	BIBL 80:5
s. my reputation	FITZ 331:27
what cannot be s.—liberty	GRAT 369:5
soldier always tell an old s.	SHAW 739:9
Ben Battle was a s.	HOOD 405:15
British s. can stand up to	SHAW 739:22
chocolate cream s.	SHAW 739:10
courage of a s.	GIBB 354:12
death, who had the s. singled	DOUG 291:13
Drinking is the s.'s pleasure	DRYD 295:5
first duty of a s.	PROV 632:20
For a s. I listed	DIBD 276:3
German s. trying to violate	STRA 778:13
go to your Gawd like a s.	KIPL 468:3
great s.—of to-day	BAGE 50:14
having been a s.	JOHN 442:13
in the s.	SHAK 723:9
iron-armed s.	POLI 612:23
s. details his wounds	PROP 624:20
s., Full of strange oaths	SHAK 697:1
s. is better accommodated	SHAK 707:19
s. of the Great War	EPIT 319:11
s. said isn't evidence	PROV 646:30
S., Sailor	NURS 582:4
S., scholar, horseman	YEAT 873:17
s.'s life is terrible hard	MILN 538:2
s.'s pole is fall'n	SHAK 695:21
s.'s pride	BROW 166:6
what the s. said	DICK 280:22
soldiers believe the s.	SALI 678:15
gives England her s.	MERE 532:11
like s. may not quit	TENN 797:15
Old s. never die	FOLE 336:4
Old s. never die	PROV 640:33
Onward, Christian s.	BARI 58:16
our s. slighted	QUAR 651:5
scarlet s.	AUDE 38:2
s. and wool abroad	MANI 519:6
S. are citizens of death's grey land	SASS 682:7
s., mostly fools	BIER 121:7
S. of Christ, arise	WESL 847:15
S. of the ploughshare	RUSK 674:7
S., this solitude	DE L 272:9
s. under me	BIBL 100:7
steel my s.' hearts	SHAK 709:4
ten thousand s.	SHAK 731:29
With twenty-six lead s.	ANON 22:3
young Argentinian s.	RUNC 672:7
soldiery Emperor's drunken s.	YEAT 872:10
licentious s.	BURK 175:22
sole amor che muove il s.	DANT 265:17
nothing can be s. or whole	YEAT 873:1
s. of her foot	BIBL 79:23
solecism without a s.	BROW 162:27
soleil J'ai vu le s. bas	RIMB 662:11
s. d'Italie	BANV 57:14
solemn Sapping a s. creed	BYRO 186:13
upon our s. feast-day	BOOK 145:11
soles S. effugere atque abire sentit	MART 524:6
soliciting still-s. eye	SHAK 714:20
solid s. for fluidity	CHUR 229:8
solidity appearance of s. to pure wind	ORWE 588:2
solitariness s. of our work	FRIN 343:14
solitary Be not s.	BURT 181:24
ennui of a s. existence	BONA 132:1
How doth the city sit s.	BIBL 95:8
how s. they be	ASCH 33:4
s., be not idle	JOHN 442:26
s. confinement inside our own skins	WILL 858:6
s. Highland lass!	WORD 869:10
tedium of s. duties	GALB 347:14
Their s. way	MILT 544:20
till I am s.	JOHN 439:7
solitude bliss of s.	WORD 868:8
delighted in s.	BACO 46:32
each protects the s.	RILK 662:7
feel his s. more keenly	VALÉ 823:13
harmless s.	MOLL 553:4
In s. What happiness	MILT 543:29
one for s.	THOR 809:21
seclusion and s.	MONT 555:7
self-sufficing power of S.	WORD 868:11
s. of the sea	HARD 381:11
s. Through which we go	DE L 272:9
solitudes two s. protect	RILK 662:5
solitudinem S. faciunt pacem	TACI 786:21
Solomon all S.'s wisdom	BIBL 84:27
anointed S.	BIBL 84:25
felicities of S.	BACO 46:3
greater than S.	BIBL 101:9
S. Grundy	NURS 581:9
S., I have vanquished	JUST 450:8
S. in all his glory	BIBL 99:18
S. loved many strange women	BIBL 85:1
S. wrote the Proverbs	NAYL 569:5
soluble art of the s.	MEDA 530:1
solution always a well-known s.	MENC 531:23
can't see the s.	CHES 225:15
conditions for its s.	MARX 526:4
either part of the s.	CLEA 235:4
final s.	HEYD 397:17
kind of s.	CAVA 211:14
part of the s.	SAYI 684:26
total s.	GOER 361:10
solutus S. omni faenore	HORA 411:3
solve I did not come to s. anything	NERU 570:15
solventur S. risu tabulae	HORA 414:18
some fool s. of the people	LINC 494:11
S. mishtake, shurely	CATC 208:26
somebody brisk little s.	BROW 164:23
S. has been sitting in	SOUT 764:21
When every one is s.	GILB 356:14
someday S. I'll find you	COWA 253:18
someone it was s. else	ROGE 665:17
necessary to s.	EMER 314:18
s., somewhere, may be happy	MENC 531:19
S. wants a letter	ADVE 8:16
something get s. for nothing	PROV 648:16
is that s. itself	BECK 64:12
say s. about me	COHA 238:5
s. cannot become nothing	BÜCH 169:14
s. completely different	CATC 207:3
s. for Posterity	ADDI 5:22
S. is better than	PROV 643:22
S. must be done	MISQ 548:19
s. of the night	WIDD 853:10
S. should be done	EDWA 304:4
s. to forgive	LEWI 491:16
s. to say	WHAT 849:14
Time for a little s.	MILN 538:11
was there s.	CATC 207:23
who does s.	LINC 493:16
sometime see me s.	MISQ 549:6
woman is a s. thing	HEYW 398:1
sometimes s. always	RICH 661:4
somewhat more than s.	RUNY 672:11
s. against thee	BIBL 117:29
somewhere get s. else	CARR 202:24
S. over the rainbow	HARB 379:19
son bear a s.	BIBL 92:11
bear our s.	KYD 474:11
be called thy s.	BIBL 105:31
brought forth her firstborn s.	BIBL 104:12
coming of the S. of Man	BIBL 102:27
Epicurus owene s.	CHAU 218:18
Fitzdotterel's eldest s.	BROU 160:7
Forgive your s.	JOYC 448:24
good idea—s.	CATC 207:22
hateth his s.	BIBL 88:9
his only begotten S.	BIBL 107:13
if his s. ask bread	BIBL 99:26
leichter of a fair s.	ELIZ 312:1
Like father, like s.	PROV 637:32
my s. was dead	BIBL 106:2
O Absalom, my s., my son	BIBL 84:21
s. loves his sons	TALM 789:26
s. of Adam	PRIO 624:5
s. of his old age	BIBL 80:16
S. of man	BIBL 100:10
S. of Morn in weary Night's decline	BLAK 125:9
S. of Saint Louis	FIRM 327:16
S. of York	SHAK 731:9
s. shall hear	SCOT 689:6
s. till he gets him a wife	PROV 639:21
s. was killed	KIPL 465:17
Take now thy s.	BIBL 79:37
This is my beloved S.	BIBL 98:19
This is my s.	TENN 800:18
unto us a s. is given	BIBL 92:14
unto us by his S.	BIBL 115:30
what's a s.	KYD 474:10

son (cont.):
wise s.	BIBL 87:34
With a king's s.	SURR 780:16
Woman, behold thy s.	BIBL 108:31
younger s. gathered all together	BIBL 105:29
your s.'s tender years	JUVE 451:21

song all this for a s. | CECI 212:8
ane end of ane old s.	OGIL 583:14
Assist our s.	GURN 374:19
auld Scotish s.	BURN 177:21
becomes a sightless s.	TENN 796:4
before his presence with a s.	BOOK 146:15
beyond a s. or a billet	ETHE 320:15
burthen of his s.	BICK 120:22
carcase of an old s.	THOM 807:10
frame my s.	CHES 222:18
glorious s. of old	SEAR 690:13
hate a s. that has sold	BERL 73:7
let satire be my s.	BYRO 189:29
listen to our s.	HOME 405:7
low lone s.	CARP 201:7
made my s. a coat	YEAT 872:15
My s. is love unknown	CROS 261:12
my s. would come	OVID 590:20
old and antique s.	SHAK 735:15
old s. of Percy and Douglas	SIDN 751:8
On wings of s.	HEIN 389:8
play a s. for me	DYLA 301:20
region of the s.	WORD 865:10
Sans wine, sans s.	FITZ 331:18
sing the Lord's s.	BOOK 149:14
sold my reputation for a s.	FITZ 331:27
s. and a mistake	OVID 590:18
s. charms the sense	MILT 542:11
s. is ended	BERL 73:4
S. made in lieu	SPEN 766:23
s. my paddle sings	JOHN 435:12
s. of praise be sung	POTT 620:3
s. of songs	BIBL 90:23
s. of the birds for mirth	GURN 374:16
s. of the kingfisher	VIRG 833:3
S. of the Shirt	HOOD 406:1
s. that echoes cheerly	TENN 796:15
s. that found a path	KEAT 456:10
s. that never ends	GOET 361:19
s. the Syrens sang	BROW 162:14
s. was wordless	SASS 682:10
spur me into s.	YEAT 874:25
start a s.	VIRG 832:5
suck melancholy out of a s.	SHAK 696:22
sung as it were a new s.	BIBL 118:28
sung a s. of death	BLAK 127:4
swallow-flights of s.	TENN 795:10
thinks two notes a s.	DAVI 268:5
Thy speech, thy s.	JAME 429:7
till I end my s.	SPEN 768:4
Time is our tedious s.	MILT 541:2
trouble with a folk s.	LAMB 477:14
unto the Lord a new s.	BOOK 141:18
unto the Lord a new s.	BOOK 146:11
was the s. of love	ROSS 669:17
what they teach in s.	SHEL 744:12
wine and s.	LUTH 505:12
with the breeze of s.	TENN 795:20

songs all their s. are sad | CHES 223:27
For ever piping s.	KEAT 455:20
I have s. of my own	VIRG 832:9
lean and flashy s.	MILT 540:10
Sing no sad s.	ROSS 669:9
sing the old s.	CLAR 233:10
Sing thou the s. of love	GURN 375:1
S. consecrate to truth	SHEL 747:3
s. never heard	HORA 412:14
s. of Apollo	SHAK 717:26
s. of expectation	BARI 58:17
s. of gladness, praise	SIKH 751:17
s. of peaceful Zion	DIX 286:32
s. of pleasant glee	BLAK 127:6
s. of Spring	KEAT 457:2
s. were Ave Marys	CORB 251:11
sweetest s. are those	SHEL 746:23

sonitu putrem s. quatit ungula | VIRG 831:5
sonnet Scorn not the S. | WORD 869:2

S.'s scanty plot	WORD 866:20

sonneteer starved hackney s. | POPE 616:8
sonnets written s. all his life | BYRO 188:16
sons Bears all its s. away | WATT 842:7
Clergymen's s. always	PROV 629:8
cruel s. of Cain	LE G 487:20
God's s. are things	MADD 514:3
in war fathers bury their s.	HERO 395:8
My s. ought to study mathematics	ADAM 3:6
s. and daughters of Life	GIBR 355:14
s. and daughters shall prophesy	BIBL 96:8
s. Of Belial, flown with insolence	MILT 541:25
s. of God	BIBL 79:21
s. of God shouted	BIBL 87:9
S. of the dark and bloody ground	O'HA 584:17
s. of the morning	HEBE 388:7
That our s. may grow up	BOOK 149:24
they have become our s.	ATAT 35:3

soon short notice, s. past | PROV 638:1
S. can mean in one second	BÖLL 131:17
S., too soon	SHEL 747:1
to Eve: Be s.	THOM 807:16

sooner make an end the s. | BACO 46:24
s. begun	PROV 643:23
s. every party breaks up	AUST 41:6

soot in s. I sleep | BLAK 127:7
soote s. season | SURR 781:1
sophist neither saint nor s.-led | ARNO 29:7
sophistication product of s. | FLAU 333:8
sophistry s. and illusion | HUME 419:16
s. I can control	ASTE 34:11

Sophonisba Oh! S. | THOM 808:20
soporific lettuce is 's.' | POTT 620:6
sops s. in wine | SPEN 768:5
Sorbonne one day at the S. | STEV 774:7
sorcerers s., and whoremongers | BIBL 119:23
Sordello but the one 'S.' | POUN 620:18
sore we are s. let | BOOK 135:12
soreness leave a little s. | LAYT 485:1
sores dogs licked his s. | BIBL 106:6
sorriness s. underlying the grandest things
	HARD 381:7

sorrow and the s. thereof | MALO 517:20
any sorrow like unto my s.	BIBL 95:9
ate his bread in s.	GOET 362:17
bee of s.	BABE 44:16
beguile thy s.	SHAK 734:11
doubt and s.	BARI 58:17
forgather wi' S.	BURN 177:21
From my books surcease of s.	POE 611:1
from s. to joy	HAGG 376:1
Give s. words	SHAK 722:6
glut thy s.	KEAT 455:28
help you to s.	PROV 634:32
How small and selfish is s.	ELIZ 313:7
increaseth s.	BIBL 89:21
In s. thou shalt bring forth	BIBL 79:11
in trouble, s.	BOOK 137:8
labour and s.	BOOK 145:21
Labour without s.	RUSK 673:26
Love's s. lasts all through life	FLOR 335:23
more in s. than in anger	SHAK 699:29
not be in s. too	BLAK 127:14
not sure of s.	SWIN 785:13
One for s.	PROV 640:44
s. and sighing	BIBL 93:11
S. and silence	LONG 499:4
s. comes with years	BROW 164:6
S. in all lands	SUTT 781:21
S. is knowledge	BYRO 190:12
S. is tranquillity remembered	PARK 596:10
S. proud to be exalted	ANON 18:6
s.'s crown of sorrow	TENN 796:24
s. unforeseen	PHIL 606:4
sphere of our s.	SHEL 746:18
such sweet s.	SHAK 732:19
thou climbing s.	SHAK 715:10
whipping S. driveth	GREV 372:15
with s. to the grave	BIBL 80:25
Write s. on the bosom	SHAK 730:18
yet my s. springs	SURR 781:2

sorrowful heart is s. | BIBL 88:10
He went away s.	BIBL 102:7

way to the s. city	DANT 264:13

sorrowing borrowing, goes a s. | PROV 634:8
sorrows age, Disease, or s. | CLOU 236:20
carried our s.	BIBL 94:3
costly in our s.	STER 772:14
Half the s. of women	ELIO 307:10
man of s.	BIBL 94:3
Proud people breed sad s.	BRON 158:18
Small s. speak	SENE 692:18
soothes his s.	NEWT 574:14
s. of the mothers	FREN 342:8
to thy s. sing	WINC 860:7
When s. come	SHAK 703:34

sorry Better be safe than s. | PROV 627:33
having to say you're s.	TAGL 788:8
heartily s.	BOOK 137:10
I'm s., now, I wrote it	BURG 172:11
S. CAN'T COME	BERE 72:7
S. for itself	LAWR 483:20
s. pruner	RICH 660:16
that I shall be s. for	SHAK 713:22

sortem nemo, quam sibi s. | HORA 414:6
sortir l'en faire s. | LOUI 501:10
sorts all s. and conditions | BOOK 135:5
takes all s.	PROV 636:38

Sosostris Madame S. | ELIO 311:4
sot s. savant | MOLI 552:8
soufflé cannot reheat a s. | MCCA 509:10
sought Being, of all, least s. for | CRAN 258:19
Love s. is good	SHAK 735:28
never s. in vain	BURN 177:23
s. from Him	DANT 265:10
s. it with thimbles	CARR 204:3

soul adventures of his s. | FRAN 340:10
assault and hurt the s.	BOOK 135:16
believes in s.	JAIN 427:15
bitterness of his s.	BIBL 97:12
bitterness of my s.	BIBL 93:13
brother's s.	BARB 57:20
Call to the s.	VAUG 825:12
call upon my s.	SHAK 735:6
Calm s. of all things	ARNO 29:16
captain of my s.	HENL 391:13
casket of my s.	KEAT 456:21
city of the s.	BYRO 186:19
composed in the s.	ARNO 31:24
confident concerning his s.	SOCR 760:4
dark night of the s.	FITZ 332:14
dark night of the s.	MISQ 547:13
delivered my s.	BOOK 148:7
depth of your s.	ROUS 670:16
Diseases of the s.	CICE 232:12
eager s., biting for anger	FULL 346:12
engineers of the s.	GORK 366:9
equal to the s.'s desires	WORD 865:15
essence of a human s.	CARL 200:27
every subject's s.	SHAK 708:26
eyes are window of s.	PROV 631:45
FIAT in my s.	BEDD 65:5
fine point of his s.	KEAT 457:14
flow of s.	POPE 617:26
fortitude the S. contains	DICK 281:15
freed my s.	BERN 73:20
give his own s.	BOLT 131:21
God rest his s.	SMIT 757:19
good for the s.	PROV 629:18
half conceal the S. within	TENN 795:1
Half my own s.	HORA 411:5
Heart and s. do sing	SIDN 751:3
Heaven take my s.	SHAK 714:14
hidden language of the s.	GRAH 367:16
hurl my s. from heaven	SHAK 729:20
hurt of my s.	BOOK 143:25
if I have a s.	ANON 19:11
if your s. were	BIBL 86:32
into my very s.	SHAK 703:13
iron entered into his s.	BOOK 147:11
lean over the s. we love	GIDE 356:2
leave my s. in hell	BOOK 140:4
lie in the s.	JOWE 447:14
life unto the bitter in s.	BIBL 86:18
lift my s. to heaven	SHAK 710:14
like an infant's s.	TRAH 814:7

like s., my soul	SHAK 698:26
longeth my s. after thee	BOOK 142:4
lose his own s.	BIBL 103:34
love in another's s.	LAYT 485:2
love of S. in the husband	UPAN 821:18
lover of my s.	WESL 847:11
Marlbro's mighty s.	ADDI 4:10
Medicine for the s.	ANON 18:21
mind and s., according	TENN 794:30
My s., bear thou thy part	GURN 375:1
My s. can reach	BROW 164:13
My s. fleeth	BOOK 149:8
My s. in agony	COLE 241:1
my s. is white	BLAK 127:12
My s., like to a ship	WEBS 844:25
My s., there is a country	VAUG 825:4
my unconquerable s.	HENL 391:12
No coward s. is mine	BRON 158:15
no s. to be damned	THUR 810:14
not engineers of the s.	KENN 460:14
One s. inhabiting two bodies	ARIS 28:10
owe my s. to the company store	TRAV 815:1
Perdition catch my s.	SHAK 728:22
perfection of your s.	SOCR 759:19
Poor intricated s.	DONN 290:12
Pray for the repose of His s.	ROLF 666:10
pray the Lord my s. to take	PRAY 623:6
preserves the s. from desiccation	LYTT 506:9
prophetic s.	SHAK 738:12
purest s.	CARE 198:9
Refined himself to s.	DRYD 295:14
require his sheep's s.	RADE 653:7
retreat in his own s.	AURE 40:8
save his s.	BIBL 95:16
saves her s.	BROW 164:26
Shame on the s.	AURE 40:15
sighed his s.	SHAK 725:8
sinews of the s.	FULL 346:10
s. above buttons	COLM 244:4
S. and body part	CRAS 259:11
s., a spirit	FAUL 324:17
S. clap its hands and sing	YEAT 874:14
s. doth magnify the Lord	BIBL 104:8
s. has to itself decreed	KEAT 456:18
s. he doth restore	SCOT 690:9
s. in bliss	SHAK 716:23
s. is all existing	ARIS 27:17
s. is an enchanted boat	SHEL 746:1
s. is Christ's abode	KEBL 458:20
s. is form	SPEN 767:29
s. is immortal	PLAT 609:5
s. is immortal	SOCR 760:3
s. is marching on	SONG 763:1
s. is not where	FULL 346:18
S., leaving the body	UPAN 822:2
s. of a man is born	JOYC 448:8
s. of fire	JOHN 438:7
s. of justice	BENT 71:10
s. of our dear brother	BOOK 139:10
s. of pleasure	BEHN 67:4
s. of Rabelais	COLE 242:6
S. of the Age	JONS 446:22
s. of the same stature	MONT 554:19
s. of the whole Past	CARL 200:7
s.'s dark cottage	WALL 837:1
S. selects her own	DICK 281:20
s. shall be required of thee	BIBL 105:15
S. shall have her earthly freight	WORD 867:12
s., sit thou	QUAR 651:8
s.'s out of tune	CERV 213:10
s.'s reduced to a shuffled	NERU 570:11
s. swooned slowly	JOYC 447:17
S. that rises with us	WORD 867:8
s. that should not have been born	HOUS 416:7
S., the Inner Controller	UPAN 822:1
S., thou hast much goods	BIBL 105:14
s. to feel the flesh	BRON 158:16
s. undergoes some sort	SOCR 759:22
strong in s.	PYTH 651:3
sweet and virtuous S.	HERB 395:3
Tell out my s.	BIBL 104:8
than that one s.	NEWM 572:9
That S. is not this	UPAN 822:3

this s. of mine	LITT 495:12
this s.'s second inn	DONN 288:20
through thy own s.	BIBL 104:18
to an immortal s.	VICT 827:8
two to bear my s. away	PRAY 623:5
vale of s.-making	KEAT 458:7
wake the s. by tender strokes	POPE 618:3
war against the s.	BIBL 117:4
What s. was his	WORD 865:12
windows of the s.	BLAK 125:4
with all thy s.	BIBL 102:17
with a Russian s.	LERM 490:5
with s. so dead	SCOT 688:14
women have no s.	ASTE 34:11
worth of a s.	EQUI 316:16
soulless when work is s.	CAMU 196:21
souls Bishop of your s.	BIBL 117:7
bodies but not their s.	GIBR 355:14
common men have s.	TAWN 791:6
damp s. of housemaids	ELIO 310:14
engineers of human s.	STAL 769:15
letters mingle s.	DONN 289:23
movements of s.	VIRG 833:4
narrow s. cannot dare	CONG 247:14
neglecting our s.	WULF 871:2
open windows into men's s.	ELIZ 312:16
Our s. exult	BLAK 125:18
our waking s.	DONN 289:8
play with s.	BROW 166:11
pure lovers' s. descend	DONN 289:5
s. do couch on flowers	SHAK 695:18
s. mounting up to God	ROSS 669:15
S. of poets dead	KEAT 455:15
s. of the brave	CLOU 236:14
s. of the righteous	BIBL 96:28
s. out of men's bodies	SHAK 727:20
s. to each other draw	POPE 614:7
s. who dwell in night	BLAK 124:20
they have no s.	COKE 238:16
times that try men's s.	PAIN 592:13
Two s.	HALM 378:8
Two s. dwell	GOET 361:16
two virtuous s.	BYRO 189:7
sound alive with the s. of music	HAMM 379:1
all is not s.	JONS 446:4
commanded to be s.	GREV 372:16
deep s. strikes	BYRO 186:5
feeling, then, not s.	STEV 774:9
form of s. words	BIBL 115:26
from the tombs a doleful s.	WATT 842:3
in a s. body	JUVE 451:17
other half is not very s.	SMOL 759:6
s. and fury	SHAK 722:22
s. and rumour	MORR 560:11
s. is gone out into all lands	BOOK 140:9
s. me from my lowest note	SHAK 702:26
s. mind	BIBL 115:25
s. must seem an echo	POPE 616:6
s. of abundance	BIBL 85:10
s. of surprise	BALL 56:12
s. the back	SAUS 682:17
trumpet give an uncertain s.	BIBL 112:15
tuneable silver s.	BANK 57:12
what is that s.	AUDE 38:2
soundbite s. all an interviewer	BENN 70:5
soundbites not a time for s.	BLAI 124:1
soundest old lovers are s.	WEBS 844:16
sounding s. through the town	BALL 54:7
sounds better than it s.	NYE 582:13
concord of sweet s.	SHAK 725:13
let the s. of music	SHAK 725:10
S. and sweet airs	SHAK 733:30
s. will take care	CARR 202:10
sweetest s. I'll ever hear	RODG 665:4
soup blossom s.	BASH 60:20
cake of portable s.	BOSW 152:5
I won't have any s. today	HOFF 402:4
licked the s.	BROW 167:1
S. of the evening	CARR 202:16
take s. at luncheon	CURZ 263:12
soupe Je vis de bonne s.	MOLI 552:6
sour need any s. grapes	AESO 8:38
s. apple tree	SONG 763:2

s. grapes	BIBL 95:15
s. grapes and ashes	ASHF 33:17
s., sober beverage	BYRO 188:15
source rise above its s.	PROV 643:43
s. of little visible delight	BRON 158:19
sourest sweetest things turn s.	SHAK 738:9
south fickle is the S.	TENN 799:13
full of the warm S.	KEAT 456:4
go s. in the winter	ELIO 311:2
hills of the S. Country	BELL 68:22
hills of the S. Country	BELL 68:23
I want to go s.	LAWR 484:5
Lawn is full of s.	DICK 282:5
nor yet from the s.	BOOK 145:2
rivers in the s.	BOOK 149:1
S. is avenged	BOOT 150:25
s.-wind rushing warm	TENN 797:1
wrest from the S.	LEE 487:17
Yes, but not in the S.	POTT 620:11
southern bore me in the s. wild	BLAK 127:12
S. trees bear strange	ALLE 13:6
southward once went singing s.	CHES 224:9
souvenirs s. sont cors de chasse	APOL 25:2
sovereign change for a s.	NESB 571:4
civilities with my S.	JOHN 440:14
has sixpence is s.	CARL 200:20
Here lies my s. lord	EPIT 317:16
he will have no s.	COKE 238:17
S. has	BAGE 51:6
s. Nation	PAGE 591:16
s. oppresses his people	JOHN 441:3
s. or state	BACO 47:6
subject and a s.	CHAR 216:19
to be a S.	ELIZ 312:4
sovereignest s. that any man may have	SKEL 753:20
sovereigns name ourselves its s.	BYRO 190:13
what s. are doing	NAPO 568:1
sovereignties addition of s.	MONN 553:12
sovereignty s. is an artificial soul	HOBB 400:14
s. of nature	SHAK 698:12
sovereynetee Wommen desiren to have s.	CHAU 220:15
soviet Communism is S. power	LENI 488:18
S. Union has indeed	FULB 346:4
soviets All power to the S.	POLI 612:1
sow As you s., so you reap	PROV 626:43
hath the s. by the right ear	HENR 392:2
old s. that eats her farrow	JOYC 448:9
shall not s.	BIBL 90:17
silk purse out of s.'s ear	PROV 647:43
S. dry and set wet	PROV 643:25
s. in tears	BOOK 149:1
s. may whistle	PROV 643:26
S. returns to her Mire	KIPL 466:2
s. the wind	PROV 645:1
they's not	BIBL 99:16
went forth to s.	BIBL 101:13
sower s. went forth	BIBL 101:13
soweth whatsoever a man s.	BIBL 113:25
sown poets that are s.	WORD 865:11
s. the wind	BIBL 96:4
where thou hast not s.	BIBL 103:3
Ye have s. much	BIBL 96:18
space art of how to waste s.	JOHN 435:14
blue unfriendliness of s.	HOPE 406:18
Brahman is s.	UPAN 822:5
cantos of unvanquished s.	CRAN 258:12
contingency for the s. shuttle	ANON 16:22
Filling a s.	O'KE 584:18
filling the s.	WEST 848:24
head outward into s.	EDDI 302:17
Here is my s.	SHAK 694:9
In s., no one can hear you	TAGL 788:5
king of infinite s.	SHAK 701:10
more s. where nobody is	STEI 771:4
silent too as s.	BYRO 189:27
S. is blue	HEIS 390:2
S. isn't remote	HOYL 417:11
s. of life between	KEAT 454:2
s. you leave behind	COOP 251:5
time and s.	LAMB 477:6
untrespassed sanctity of s.	MAGE 514:16

spoons counted our s. — EMER 314:21
let us count our s. — JOHN 439:22
world locks up its s. — SHAW 741:5
sport Detested s. — COWP 256:17
ended his s. with Tess — HARD 381:4
kill us for their s. — SHAK 716:11
owe to s. — CAMU 196:20
real love of your s. — GREE 371:23
Serious s. — ORWE 587:23
s. for our neighbours — AUST 42:19
s. of destiny — THAC 802:18
s. of kings — D'AV 267:9
s. of kings — SOME 760:18
s. of kings — SURT 781:6
S. that wrinkled Care derides — MILT 539:24
s. with Amaryllis — MILT 540:6
s. would be as tedious — SHAK 705:12
sported s. on the green — SOUT 764:6
sportive s. as the fawn — WORD 869:17
sports mountaineous s. girl — BETJ 76:3
play Her cruel s. — SPEN 767:26
S. do not build character — BROU 160:15
s. of love — JONS 446:14
sportsman fit to be called a s. — SURT 781:7
s. is a man who — LEAC 485:8
spot no s. in thee — BIBL 91:5
Out, damned s. — SHAK 722:8
sumpshous s. — ASHF 33:15
Tip me the black s. — STEV 775:21
with a s. I damn him — SHAK 713:18
spotless All things were s. — TRAH 814:10
Eternal sunshine of the s. mind — POPE 614:11
spots change his s. — PROV 637:18
leopard change his s. — BIBL 95:3
s. rather a credit — COMP 245:6
spotted wants to have been s. — VIRG 831:21
You s. snakes — SHAK 726:10
spouse in s. occasion to complain — CENT 212:13
my sister, my s. — BIBL 91:6
President's s. — BUSH 182:2
shuts the s. Christ home — HOPK 407:22
spout cataracts and hurricanoes s. — SHAK 715:16
sprang s. to the stirrup — BROW 166:4
spray pinkly bursts the s. — BETJ 75:18
rime was on the s. — HARD 382:4
singis on the s. — DOUG 291:10
spread except it be s. — BACO 47:30
hatred to s. — SART 681:16
no good till it is s. — PROV 639:4
S. ALARM AND DESPONDENCY — PENI 602:12
s. my dreams under your feet — YEAT 873:14
spring accomplish all the s. — D'AV 267:8
Alas, that s. should vanish — FITZ 331:28
as short a S. — HERR 396:15
azure sister of the s. — SHEL 745:6
beckoning to his S. Queen — JARR 430:21
bloom in the s. — GILB 357:15
Blossom by blossom the s. — SWIN 784:20
can S. be far behind — SHEL 745:13
commonly called the s. — COWP 257:6
easing the S. — REED 657:5
Falsehood has a perennial s. — BURK 173:7
hounds of s. — SWIN 784:19
In the s. a young man's fancy — TENN 796:22
in the s. to follow — SWIN 785:22
less quick to s. — ARNO 30:28
lived light in the s. — ARNO 29:8
new come s. — SHAK 731:6
no second s. — PHIL 606:2
No s., nor summer beauty — DONN 288:1
not s. until you can plant — PROV 636:25
only the right to s. — FOND 336:5
Pierian s. — DRAY 293:18
rifle all the breathing s. — COLL 243:10
second s., where every leaf — CAMU 196:18
songs of S. — KEAT 457:2
s. breaks through again — COWA 253:13
S. Flow down the woods — SACK 677:1
s. has gone out of the year — PERI 603:22
s. has kept in its folds — ARAG 25:15
s. is wound up tight — ANOU 24:8
s. now comes unheralded — CARS 204:11
s. of business — BAGE 50:8

s. of endless lies — COWP 255:28
s. of light — COLE 239:3
s. of the year — BIBL 98:6
S. restores balmy warmth — CATU 210:11
s. shut up, a fountain sealed — BIBL 91:6
s. summer autumn winter — CUMM 262:3
suddenly was changed to S. — SHEL 746:6
Sweet lovers love the s. — SHAK 697:24
Sweet s., full of sweet days — HERB 395:2
this s. of love — SHAK 736:14
trouble in the Balkans in the s. — KIPL 468:17
We need s. — GZOW 375:4
with ever-returning s. — WHIT 852:20
year's at the s. — BROW 167:3
springe woodcock to mine own s. — SHAK 704:25
springes s. to catch woodcocks — SHAK 700:8
springlike limbs that fester are not s. — ABSE 1:4
springs Fifty s. — HOUS 415:12
s. into the rivers — BOOK 147:5
Wastes without s. — CLAR 232:24
Where s. not fail — HOPK 407:11
springtime Ballinderry in the s. — FERG 325:6
Merry S.'s Harbinger — FLET 335:11
sprite fleeting, wav'ring s. — HADR 375:7
sprites s. and goblins — SHAK 736:19
sprouting S. despondently at area gates — ELIO 310:14
spun s. twelve ells — ANON 24:5
spur Fame is the s. — MILT 540:6
I have no s. — SHAK 719:10
s. me into song — YEAT 874:25
s. of all great minds — CHAP 216:11
spurious s. brat, Tom Jones — RICH 660:17
spurs this day to wynne his s. — EDWA 304:2
When a knight won his s. — STRU 779:6
win his s. — EDWA 304:2
spy letters for a s. — KIPL 467:10
s. out the land — BIBL 82:3
s. who came in from the cold — LE C 487:1
squad awkward s. fire over me — BURN 180:12
squadrons big s. against the small — BUSS 182:16
wingèd s. of the sky — MILM 537:18
square architects do s. and hew — MARV 524:20
I have not kept the s. — SHAK 695:2
S. deal afterwards — ROOS 667:20
s. on the hypotenuse — GILB 358:7
s. person has squeezed himself — SMIT 758:4
s. root of half a number — LONG 500:8
squares on the lines or s. — MILN 538:6
squat s. like a toad — MILT 543:15
s. pen rests — HEAN 387:9
urban, s., and packed with guile — BROO 159:10
squats s. on the hearthstone — QUIL 651:18
squawking seven stars go s. — AUDE 36:24
squeak s. and gibber — SHAK 699:4
until the pips s. — GEDD 351:29
squeaking shrieking and s. — BROW 167:1
s. Cleopatra — SHAK 695:25
s. wheel gets — PROV 643:33
squeeze s. a right-hand foot — CARR 203:22
squeezing s. of a lemon — GOLD 365:5
squint banish s. suspicion — MILT 539:4
squire s. and his relations — DICK 276:24
squires last sad s. ride — CHES 224:16
stab do I s. at thee — MELV 531:13
No iron can s. the heart — BABE 44:14
saw him s. — READ 656:6
stabant S. orantes — VIRG 830:10
stabat S. Mater dolorosa — JACO 427:7
stability natural s. of gold — SHAW 740:5
party of order or s. — MILL 536:6
s. or enlargement — JOHN 435:18
stable born in a s. — PROV 638:22
nothing s. in the world — KEAT 457:16
stable-door shut the s. — PROV 636:37
stables S. are the centre — SHAW 740:3
stablish s. me with thy free Spirit — BOOK 143:7
staff cockle hat and s. — SHAK 703:30
I'll break my s. — SHAK 734:2
s. of faith to walk upon — RALE 653:19
thy rod and thy s. — BOOK 140:21
trustest upon the s. — BIBL 85:38

stag lean as a rutting S. — BYRO 191:21
runnable s. — DAVI 267:14
stage All the world's a s. — SHAK 696:27
Don't put your daughter on the s. — COWA 253:16
drown the s. with tears — SHAK 701:21
middle age of a s. — BACO 48:16
On the s. — GOLD 364:20
played upon a s. — SHAK 736:5
s. where every man must play — SHAK 723:23
this great s. of fools — SHAK 716:22
traffick of our s. — SHAK 732:3
wonder of our s. — JONS 446:22
stagecoach s. from London to Oxford — HAZL 386:20
stages four s. of man — LINK 495:5
stagger s. like a drunken man — BOOK 147:18
stagnant fen Of s. waters — WORD 866:16
stagnation keeps life from s. — BURN 176:15
stain bright s. on the vision — GRAV 369:13
convict s. — HUGH 418:6
darkening like a s. — AUDE 38:16
s. in thine honour — BIBL 97:30
s. of blood — CURN 263:3
s. the stiff dishonoured shroud — ELIO 310:27
s. upon the silence — BECK 64:27
world's slow s. — SHEL 743:18
stained kick a hole in a s. glass window — CHAN 215:8
s. with their own works — BOOK 147:14
stains Innumerable of s. — KEAT 454:9
s. the white radiance — SHEL 743:21
stair by a winding s. — BACO 47:10
staircase bare s. of his duty — STEV 776:5
stairs another man's s. — DANT 265:16
stake deep s. they have — BURK 173:23
I am tied to the s. — SHAK 716:7
s. driven through his heart — O'BR 583:3
what it is we have at s. — PITT 607:19
stale How weary, s., flat — SHAK 699:18
Tho' s., not ripe — POPE 611:20
staled S. are my thoughts — DYER 301:4
stalemate end in a s. — CRON 261:2
Stalin guilt of S. — GORB 366:3
S. himself rose — TROT 817:7
Stalingrad cultural S. — BALL 56:10
stalk Half asleep as they s. — HARD 381:19
s. with mock majesty — WOLL 863:9
stalking like a s.-horse — SHAK 697:28
s.-horse to error — BOLI 131:11
s. in my chamber — WYAT 871:4
stall Baby in an ox's s. — BETJ 75:10
stalled heart's s. motor — MAYA 529:4
S. OX — BIBL 88:15
stallions bared teeth of s. — CRAN 258:13
stamp but the guinea's s. — BURN 178:7
physics or s. collecting — RUTH 676:2
stamps kill animals and stick in s. — NICO 575:4
stand By uniting we s. — DICK 282:7
can't s. the heat — TRUM 817:18
firm spot on which to s. — ARCH 26:3
Get up, s. up — MARL 522:4
Here s. I — LUTH 505:4
house divided cannot s. — PROV 634:46
no time to s. and stare — DAVI 268:8
s. and look at them — WHIT 852:11
s. at the door, and knock — BIBL 118:2
s. at the latter day — BIBL 86:34
S. by thyself — BIBL 94:22
S. by your man — WYNE 871:16
s. in the holy place — BIBL 102:24
s. in thy gates — BOOK 148:19
s. on either hand — MACA 508:14
s. on its own bottom — PROV 631:35
s. out of my sun — DIOG 283:14
s. secure — ADDI 5:2
S. still — MARL 522:10
s. up for bastards — SHAK 714:23
s. up for Jesus — DUFF 298:13
s. up for Jesus — TYNG 821:8

s. up to anything except — SHAW 739:22
strengthen such as do s. — BOOK 134:23
we might all s. up — JACK 426:12
who only s. and wait — MILT 545:15
who shall be able to s. — BIBL 118:11
standard defending s. of living — NIEM 575:7
float that s. sheet — DRAK 293:11
raise the scarlet s. — CONN 248:4
standards fictitious demand for lower s.
— REIT 658:1
S. are always out of date — BENN 70:9
standeth help s. in the Name — BOOK 148:22
standing cheap sitting as s. — PROV 636:7
mantle of the s. pool — SHAK 716:2
ought to die s. — VESP 827:3
s. by my man — CLIN 236:1
St Andrews S. by the Northern sea — LANG 478:9
stands s. about the woodland ride
— HOUS 415:11
S. Scotland — SHAK 722:5
S. the Church clock — BROO 159:11
sun now s. — JOSE 447:11
stane heart o' s. — BALL 55:19
star Being a s. has made it possible — DAVI 268:11
birth to a dancing s. — NIET 575:20
bright northern s. — LOVE 502:1
bright Occidental s. — BIBL 78:9
bright particular s. — SHAK 694:2
Bright s. — KEAT 454:1
By a high s. our course — MACN 513:15
catch a falling s. — DONN 289:14
come back a s. — FILM 330:4
constant as the northern s. — SHAK 712:16
curb a runaway young s. — BYRO 191:11
day s. arise — BIBL 117:14
evening s. — MILT 544:14
eve's one s. — KEAT 454:20
great s. early drooped — WHIT 852:20
guests s.-scattered — FITZ 331:29
guiding s. — CARS 204:10
guiding s. behold — DIX 287:1
Hitch your wagon to a s. — EMER 315:13
Knock at a s. — HERR 395:16
light dissolved in s.-showers — SHEL 746:15
like a falling s. — MILT 541:31
loftiest s. — SHEL 746:2
maidenliest s. — SHAK 715:1
moth for the s. — SHEL 746:18
O eastern s. — SHAK 696:5
our life's s. — WORD 867:8
reflex of a s. — WORD 866:2
S. captains glow — FLEC 334:9
S.-Chamber matter — SHAK 725:16
s.-crossed lovers — SHAK 732:2
s. differeth from another — BIBL 113:2
S. for every State — WINT 861:1
s. is called Wormwood — BIBL 118:19
s.-led wizards — MILT 540:22
S. of the east — HEBE 388:7
s.-spangled banner — KEY 461:13
s. to steer her by — MASE 527:6
s. were confined — VAUG 825:13
Sunset and evening s. — TENN 793:6
sweet S. of the Sea — FABE 322:8
There was a s. danced — SHAK 727:19
twinkle, little s. — TAYL 791:16
we have seen his s. — BIBL 98:10
with one bright s. — COLE 240:24
stardust We are s. — MITC 551:1
stare indifference or frozen s. — ELIO 307:24
never to s. at people — BALF 53:14
no time to stand and s. — DAVI 268:8
s. of the deer — WILB 854:2
stony British s. — TENN 798:1
upon the ground I se thee s. — CHAU 220:5
starfighters see Black S. — BLY 129:15
stark Molly S.'s a widow — STAR 770:8
s. insensibility — JOHN 438:21
starless s. and bible-black — THOM 806:8
starlight frosty s. — ARNO 30:18
nae s. — BALL 55:22
S. and dewdrop — FOST 338:21

s. lit my lonesomeness — HARD 382:4
starlit s. or a moonlit dome — YEAT 872:11
starred No memory of having s. — FROS 344:21
On a s. night — MERE 532:20
starry beautiful evening, very s. — WORD 864:20
entertain this s. stranger — CRAS 259:4
in her s. shade — BYRO 190:14
s. dynamo — GINS 358:22
s. paladin — BROW 167:20
wide and s. sky — STEV 777:5
stars all Danaë to the s. — TENN 799:18
all the S. Hide — MILT 542:27
any kinship with the s. — MERE 532:21
As s., a fault of vision — MAHÃ 515:13
Blesses his s. — ADDI 4:13
certain s. shot madly — SHAK 726:5
climb half-way to the s. — CROS 261:8
crowned with the s. — TRAH 814:8
crown of twelve s. — BIBL 118:23
cut him out in little s. — SHAK 732:27
day-blind s. — BERR 74:15
didst the s. and sunbeams know — ARNO 30:16
earnest s. — KEAT 454:23
erratik s. — CHAU 221:12
every bough like s. — BLAK 128:13
Far beyond the s. — VAUG 825:4
heard it's in the s. — PORT 619:19
heaventree of s. — JOYC 448:23
in his right hand seven s. — BIBL 117:27
journey-work of the s. — WHIT 852:10
knowledge of the s. — EDDI 302:18
like s. on the sea — BYRO 187:16
looking at the s. — WILD 855:11
loved the s. too truly — WILL 857:14
melt the s. — FLAU 333:4
morning s. sang — BIBL 87:9
new-bathed s. Emerge — ARNO 30:19
not in our s. — SHAK 711:19
of the months and s. — SWIN 784:18
opposition of the s. — MARV 524:19
power about The s. — BUTL 183:28
puts the s. to flight — FITZ 330:17
quench the s. — YOUN 876:18
ready to mount to the s. — DANT 265:14
same bright, patient s. — KEAT 454:24
see the s. again — DANT 265:6
Seven for the seven s. — SONG 762:13
seven s. go squawking — AUDE 36:24
shakes the s. down — ELIO 308:9
shining of the s. — TENN 794:20
silent s. go by — BROO 160:5
s. above us — SHAK 716:13
s. are not hot enough — EDDI 302:13
s. are old — TAYL 791:18
s. begin to flicker — PARI 595:17
s. came out — TENN 800:2
s., garters, buttons — MOOR 557:12
s. in her hair — ROSS 669:12
s. in their courses — BIBL 83:1
s. keep not their motion — SHAK 706:27
s. move still — MARL 522:11
s. of heaven appear to us — HEIN 389:14
s. rush out — COLE 240:23
S. scribble on our eyes — CRAN 258:12
Stars, s. — SHAK 737:8
s.' tennis-balls — WEBS 844:15
s. threw down their spears — BLAK 128:5
s. through the window pane — KEAT 458:4
s. where no human race is — FROS 344:12
s., which are the brain of heaven — MERE 532:20
steeped in s. — RIMB 662:10
strike the s. — HORA 411:4
struggle to the s. — MOTT 563:16
sun and the other s. — DANT 265:17
telleth the number of the s. — BOOK 150:6
tell the s. as they rise — VIRG 830:14
Tempt not the s. — FORD 337:5
touch the s. — SPEN 768:6
troops of s. — COLE 240:2
useful s. — PEPY 603:19
way to the s. — VIRG 831:7
We have the s. — FILM 328:3
We've got more s. — MAYE 529:7

with mites of s. — MAYA 529:1
you chaste s. — SHAK 729:12
starshine s. at night — STEV 776:21
starship voyages of the s. *Enterprise*
— RODD 665:2
start 'Brutus' will s. a spirit — SHAK 711:20
end is where we s. from — ELIO 309:20
hard at the s. — DANT 265:8
s. from their spheres — SHAK 700:18
s. in the streets — KENN 460:1
s. out by getting married — MOLI 552:18
s. together and finish — BEEC 65:13
s. to the finish — HORA 414:11
Stop it at the s. — OVID 590:16
started arrive where we s. — ELIO 309:19
s. like a guilty thing — SHAK 699:5
s. so I'll finish — CATC 208:12
s. to do something — TALM 789:25
starter few thought he was a s. — ATTL 35:8
Your s. for ten — CATC 209:7
startle come down and s. — AUDE 36:23
does not s. it — KEAT 457:18
starts everything by s. — DRYD 294:20
s. from where one stands — LAO 480:11
starvation night s. — ADVE 7:32
S. Dundas — DUND 299:14
starve good men s. — DRYD 295:18
Let not poor Nelly s. — CHAR 217:11
let our people s. — NYER 582:14
s. a fever — PROV 632:8
s. or rebel — DUND 299:14
whom he helped to s. — POPE 614:23
starved many are s. — KING 464:1
s. poet — LOCK 498:2
starves steed s. — PROV 647:13
starving s. hysterical naked — GINS 358:22
you have a s. population — DISR 284:5
state all were for the s. — MACA 508:15
basis of a democratic s. — ARIS 28:6
bosom of a single s. — DURH 300:14
defrauding of the S. — PENN 602:18
done the s. some service — SHAK 729:23
faithful to the s. — ELIZ 311:27
first duty of a S. — RUSK 674:1
Founding a firm s. — MARV 525:1
glories of our blood and s. — SHIR 749:17
Here's a s. of things — GILB 357:10
I am the S. — LOUI 501:3
in a free s. — CAVO 212:1
In a free s. — ERAS 316:18
In that s. I came — VAUG 825:8
last s. of that man — BIBL 101:11
mine was the middle s. — DEFO 270:11
my glories and my s. — SHAK 731:3
no harm come to the s. — ANON 23:5
no such thing as the S. — AUDE 38:7
Only in the s. — HEGE 388:15
O Ship of S. — LONG 498:15
Our s. cannot be severed — MILT 544:9
put the s. to rights — ENNI 316:5
reinforcement of the S. — CAMU 196:13
ruin of the S. — BLAK 124:11
rule the s. — DRYD 294:15
sacrifice to the s. — ROBE 663:6
Scoffing his s. — SHAK 730:20
separation of s. and science — FEYE 325:16
sovereign or s. — BACO 47:6
S. business is a cruel trade — HALI 377:21
s. can exist — CONF 246:13
S. for every Star — WINT 861:1
s. has no place — TRUD 817:10
S. in wonted manner keep — JONS 446:3
s. is an instrument — STAL 769:14
S. is a relation of men — WEBE 843:15
S. is not 'abolished' — ENGE 315:31
s. of life — BOOK 138:14
s. of the Union — CONS 250:3
s. to be endured — JOHN 437:16
S. which dwarfs its men — MILL 536:9
s. without the means — BURK 173:30
s. with the prettiest name — BISH 122:6
storms of s. — SHAK 711:2
sun begins his s. — MILT 539:25

state (*cont.*):
to what a s. dost Thou bring | TERE 802:3
While the S. exists | LENI 488:16
stately She is tall and s. | TENN 797:23
S. as a galleon | GREN 372:9
S. Homes of England | COWA 253:19
s. homes of England | HEMA 390:15
S., plump Buck Mulligan | JOYC 448:13
with his s. stride | MACA 508:16
statement black s. of pistons | SPEN 766:9
s. that is quotable | GERS 353:17
statements all previous s. inoperative | ZIEG 878:2
states goodly s. and kingdoms | KEAT 456:14
independent S. | ADAM 3:5
indestructible S. | CHAS 217:17
many sovereign S. | PAGE 591:16
rights of s. | BROW 161:10
s. unborn | SHAK 712:19
Union of these S. | WHIT 852:19
which are called s. | CICE 231:26
statesman chemist, fiddler, s. | DRYD 294:20
constitutional s. | BAGE 50:2
he was a s. | LLOY 496:19
set a s. right | YEAT 874:8
s. is a politician | TRUM 817:20
S., yet friend to Truth | POPE 615:19
Too nice for a s. | GOLD 364:18
statesmen faults of s. | WALP 838:5
government of s. | DISR 285:16
like great S. | GAY 351:8
station antique s. | BEER 66:2
By Grand Central S. | SMAR 755:16
her s. keeping | JACO 427:7
private s. | ADDI 4:19
stations know our proper s. | DICK 276:24
statistic million deaths a s. | STAL 769:18
statistical life is s. improbability | DAWK 269:3
statistics experiment needs s. | RUTH 676:3
give plenty of s. | CARR 204:7
lies, damned lies and s. | DISR 286:28
uses s. as a drunken man | LANG 478:12
We are just s. | HORA 410:4
statuary form of s. | ANON 17:7
statue like a marble s. | SUGE 780:1
s. implicit in bronze | ARIS 28:11
statues Ep's s. are junk | ANON 18:1
stature cubit unto his s. | BIBL 99:17
Malice of a low s. | HALI 377:15
of lofty s. | EINH 305:4
status *from* S. | MAIN 512:14
Human s. ought not to depend | TEMP 792:14
status quo restored the s. | SQUI 769:9
statutes keep my s. | BIBL 81:28
s. of the Lord | BOOK 140:10
staves comest to me with s. | BIBL 84:6
stay here I s. | MACM 512:14
If we can't s. here alive | MONT 556:8
love is here to s. | GERS 353:15
more care to s. | SHAK 732:31
S. a little | BACO 46:24
S. for me there | KING 463:4
S. out all night | CHUR 228:12
s. up all night | BRYS 169:2
things to s. as they are | LAMP 477:20
without thee here to s. | MILT 544:18
staying s. messengers | RILK 662:2
Tell the people I'm s. | PEDR 601:8
stays never s. too long | MACA 507:6
nothing s. | HERA 393:3
s. together | SAYI 684:18
stead in my soul's s. | BIBL 86:32
steadfast s. as thou art | KEAT 454:1
steady Full cup, s. hand | PROV 632:44
Slow and s. wins the race | PROV 643:15
so s. a voice | CORN 251:16
S., boys, steady | GARR 349:10
steak he wanted s. | MALA 517:7
not the meat of the s. | PRIE 623:14
steaks smell of s. in passageways | ELIO 310:21
steal lest I s. | DEFO 270:10
One man may s. a horse | PROV 641:6
silently s. away | LONG 499:1

sin to s. a pin | PROV 636:32
s. a goose | POLI 613:13
s. bread | FRAN 340:8
s. from many, it's research | MIZN 551:12
S. from the world | POPE 617:33
s. more than a hundred men | PUZO 650:25
s. my Basil-pot | KEAT 455:1
s. my thunder | DENN 273:14
s. the very teeth | ARAB 25:13
thieves break through and s. | BIBL 99:13
Thou shalt not s. | BIBL 81:20
Thou shalt not s. | CLOU 237:2
stealing For de little s. | O'NE 585:7
hanged for s. horses | HALI 377:12
his s. steps | SHAK 704:12
picking and s. | BOOK 138:13
s. ducks | ARAB 25:12
S. money is wrong | AYER 43:17
steals s. my purse | SHAK 728:23
s. something | SHAK 728:14
stealth Do good by s. | POPE 617:28
except by s. | HAZL 386:14
good action by s. | LAMB 477:12
steam employ s. navigation | LARD 480:15
Shovelling white s. | AUDE 37:19
s.-engine in trousers | SMIT 758:16
traces the s.-engine | DISR 284:10
steamer s. from Harwich | GILB 356:23
steamers little holiday s. | PRIE 623:13
steaming wealth of s. phrases | SCHU 687:6
steamy Throws up a s. column | COWP 256:19
steed his s. was the best | SCOT 688:21
milk-white s. | BALL 55:20
set her on my pacing s. | KEAT 455:8
s. starves | PROV 647:13
s. That knows his rider | BYRO 185:25
steeds mounting barbèd s. | SHAK 731:10
steel All shod with s. | WORD 866:1
clad in complete s. | MILT 539:5
Give them the cold s. | ARMI 28:13
hoops of s. | SHAK 700:3
impelled the s. | BYRO 190:6
in complete s. | SHAK 700:12
long divorce of s. | SHAK 710:14
more than complete s. | ANON 18:4
S.-true and blade-straight | STEV 776:23
with a line of s. | RUSS 676:1
worthy of their s. | SCOT 688:10
wounded surgeon plies the s. | ELIO 309:12
steep s. and rugged pathway | WILL 858:16
steeple lone religious s. | CAMP 195:3
North Church s. | REVE 658:14
three s.-house spires | FOX 339:15
steeples dreary S. of Fermanagh | CHUR 229:5
drenched our s. | SHAK 715:16
s. far and near | HOUS 415:16
steer s. their courses | BUTL 183:16
Stein family S. | ANON 18:1
stelle *muove il sole e l'altre s.* | DANT 265:17
riveder le s. | DANT 265:6
stem s. of Jesse | BIBL 92:16
Stendhal great secret of S. | GIDE 356:6
step first s. that is difficult | DU D 298:11
first s. that is difficult | PROV 636:27
not to take the first s. | CLAU 234:10
One more s. along | CART 205:3
one small s. for a man | ARMS 28:20
One s. at a time | PROV 641:13
one s. enough for me | NEWM 572:16
To s. aside is human | BURN 177:8
stepmother s. to memory, oblivion | JOHN 434:2
stony-hearted s. | DE Q 273:17
step-mother harsh s. | PLIN 609:14
stepped in blood S. in | SHAK 721:13
stepping rise on s.-stones | TENN 794:31
s. westward | WORD 869:12
s. where his comrade stood | SCOT 689:5
steps five s. from the table | ROBB 663:3
no small s. in great affairs | RETZ 658:11
sad s., O Moon | SIDN 750:16
s. take hold on hell | BIBL 87:26
uneasy s. Over the burning marl | MILT 541:20

wandering s. and slow | MILT 544:20
sterbenden *einem s. Gotte* | HEIN 389:15
sterile s. promontory | SHAK 701:11
stern s. chase a long chase | PROV 643:34
S. daughter of the voice of God | WORD 867:19
sterner made of s. stuff | SHAK 713:4
sternest s. knight | MALO 518:4
steward commended the unjust s. | BIBL 106:3
stewards S. of the mysteries | BIBL 111:27
stewed S. in corruption | SHAK 703:14
stick carry a big s. | ROOS 667:19
fell like the s. | PAIN 592:18
rattling of a s. inside | ORWE 587:5
s. and a string | SWIF 784:16
S. close to your desks | GILB 358:2
s. more close than a brother | KIPL 467:14
s. that he seizes | TORR 814:2
s. to beat a dog | PROV 636:17
tattered coat upon a s. | YEAT 874:14
sticketh friend that s. closer | BIBL 88:23
sticks S. and stones | PROV 643:35
S. nix hick pix | NEWS 573:19
stiff woman can be proud and s. | YEAT 873:1
stiffnecked thou art a s. people | BIBL 81:24
stiffness too much s. in refusing | BOOK 132:15
stigma Any s. to beat a dogma | GUED 374:5
stile lame dog over a s. | CHIL 226:7
still Because they liked me 's.' | DICK 282:1
beside the s. waters | BOOK 140:20
best be s. | ARNO 29:15
be s. | BOOK 139:15
Be s. and cool | FOX 339:17
Be s. then, and know | BOOK 142:19
do them s. | DONN 288:18
heart is lying s. | WORD 865:8
monk is s. | PALI 594:24
ship was as s. | SOUT 764:9
S. crazy after all | SIMO 752:16
S. falls the rain | SITW 753:12
S. glides the Stream | WORD 868:25
s. it is not we | CHES 224:16
s., like air, I'll rise | ANGE 15:18
s. point of the turning world | ELIO 309:6
s., sad music | WORD 866:12
s. small voice | BIBL 85:14
s. they gazed | GOLD 364:9
s. tongue makes wise head | PROV 643:36
s.-vexed Bermoothes | SHAK 733:16
S. waters run deep | PROV 643:37
s. we see thee lie | BROO 160:5
'What gars ye rin sae s.?' | ANON 20:6
stillness air a solemn s. holds | GRAY 370:1
horrid s. first invades | DRYD 295:12
modest s. and humility | SHAK 708:16
present s. | WARR 840:10
s. in the midst of chaos | BELL 69:4
s. of the central sea | TENN 796:5
stilly Oft, in the s. night | MOOR 558:16
Stilton no end of S. Cheese | LEAR 485:20
stilts nonsense upon s. | BENT 71:3
stimulate s. the phagocytes | SHAW 739:23
stimulation unnatural s. | MILL 536:12
sting bite and s. you | KAFK 452:10
death, where is thy s. | BIBL 113:6
it is a s. | PEEL 601:15
pluck the s. | TAYL 791:20
s. like a bee | ALI 13:2
s. you for your pains | PROV 635:28
where is thy s.-a-ling-a-ling | MILI 535:15
stingeth s. like an adder | BIBL 88:33
stings s. in their tails | BIBL 118:21
s., The crowd, and buzz | COWL 254:17
s. you for your pains | HILL 398:9
wanton s. | SHAK 723:2
stink Fish and guests s. | PROV 632:25
stinker Outrageous S. | KIPL 468:24
stinks fish always s. | PROV 632:24
that s. and stings | POPE 614:24
worse it s. | PROV 639:14
stir before you s. his fire | PROV 648:24
more you s. it | PROV 639:14
No s. in the air | SOUT 764:9
No s. of air was there | KEAT 454:21

smoke and s. of this dim spot | MILT 538:19
s. men's blood | SHAK 713:12
s. up undisputed matters | SALL 679:8
S. up, we beseech thee | BOOK 136:13
s. without great argument | SHAK 703:29
stirbt er s. ab | ENGE 315:31
stirred Shaken and not s. | FLEM 334:16
something s. | SIMP 753:2
stirring s. the fire | AUST 42:11
stirrup foot already in the s. | CERV 213:15
sprang to the s. | BROW 166:4
s. and the ground | EPIT 319:2
stirs Will that s. and urges | HARD 381:13
stitch s. in time saves | PROV 643:38
S.! stitch! stitch | HOOD 406:1
St Ives going to S. | NURS 578:1
St James ladies of S.'s | DOBS 287:4
stock s. that scents the garden | THOM 808:11
Woman s. is rising | CHIL 226:3
stocking glimpse of s. | PORT 619:9
silk s.'s hanging down | SELL 691:25
stockings Golden s. | GOGA 363:8
s. were hung | MOOR 557:3
thy yellow s. | SHAK 735:25
stocks hurt in the s. | BOOK 147:11
stoic budge doctors of the S. fur | MILT 539:10
stoical s. scheme of supplying | SWIF 783:16
stoicism Romans call it s. | ADDI 4:14
stole I wonder where you s. 'em | SWIF 784:13
son of a bitch s. my watch | FILM 329:17
stolen generation was s. | FREE 342:5
had I s. the whole | STEV 777:3
s., be your apples | HUNT 421:8
S. fruit is sweet | PROV 643:39
s. his wits away | DE L 272:1
S. sweets are best | CIBB 231:14
s. the scraps | SHAK 717:20
S. waters are sweet | BIBL 87:33
S. waters are sweet | PROV 643:40
stolid S. and stunned | MARK 521:15
stomach army marches on its s. | NAPO 568:6
army marches on its s. | PROV 626:34
burst s. like a cave | DOUG 291:13
for thy s.'s sake | BIBL 115:21
hungry s. has no ears | LA F 475:19
nor a stew-pan—but a s. | HUNT 422:3
no s. to this fight | SHAK 709:6
s. of a king | ELIZ 312:6
s. of the country | GLAD 359:15
through his s. | PROV 646:10
stomachs march on their s. | SELL 692:6
stone against a s. | BOOK 146:2
At his heels a s. | SHAK 703:31
blossoming in s. | LONG 499:6
bomb them back into the S. Age | LEMA 488:13
brass, nor s., nor earth | SHAK 738:2
bronze and s. | RUNY 672:14
flung the s. | FITZ 330:17
for a s. of stumbling | BIBL 92:12
get blood from a s. | PROV 648:7
give him a s. | BIBL 99:26
give them the s. | MONT 554:13
hollows out a s. | OVID 590:4
jasper and a sardine s. | BIBL 118:3
let him first cast a s. | BIBL 107:28
Let them not make me a s. | MACN 513:13
Like a rolling s. | DYLA 301:18
like a s. wall | BEE 65:10
look honestly like s. | MOOR 557:7
make a s. of the heart | YEAT 873:8
mighty angel took up a s. | BIBL 119:9
nickname is the heaviest s. | HAZL 386:11
not a s. Tell where I lie | POPE 617:33
on sufferers from s. | HIPP 399:18
quiet as a s. | KEAT 454:20
Raise the s. | ANON 20:4
rolling s. gathers | PROV 642:29
rolls back the restless s. | DUCK 298:10
S.-dead hath no fellow | PROV 643:41
s. taken away | BIBL 108:34
s. the twenty-first | BROW 165:11
s. to beauty grew | EMER 314:15
S. walls do not a prison make | LOVE 502:5

s. which he flings | TORR 814:2
s. which the builders refused | BOOK 148:11
sword out of this s. | MALO 517:18
take the s. from stone | ELIO 310:18
This precious s. | SHAK 730:10
through a piece of s. | MOOR 557:8
Turn but a s. | THOM 808:1
Under every s. | ARIS 26:20
under this little s. | FANS 323:3
Virtue is like a rich s. | BACO 46:8
wears away a s. | PROV 629:20
Stonehenge S. it deserves | HAWK 384:12
stones chose him five smooth s. | BIBL 84:5
Drive gently over the s. | PROV 630:37
even the s. know you | VERG 826:6
in pilèd s. | MILT 540:18
In these s. horizons sing | LEWI 492:8
man that spares these s. | EPIT 317:12
move The s. of Rome | SHAK 713:13
pile up s. | WULF 871:2
scuttled under s. | ROET 665:8
Sermons in s. | SHAK 696:15
shouldn't throw s. | PROV 645:7
Sticks and s. | PROV 643:35
s. and clouts make martyrs | BROW 162:11
s. will teach you | BERN 73:18
s. would cry out | BIBL 106:15
You buy land, you buy s. | PROV 647:39
stony bodies of a s. nature | RALE 653:17
fell upon s. places | BIBL 101:13
morre s. than a shore | WILL 858:10
S. limits | SHAK 732:13
S. outcrop of the Burren | BETJ 75:17
stood not s. up to live | THOR 809:7
should of s. in bed | JACO 427:6
s. against the world | SHAK 713:7
s. by me when I was crazy | SHER 749:9
s. four-square to all the winds | TENN 798:22
stools Between two s. | PROV 627:43
necessity invented s. | COWP 256:6
stoop dares to s. and take it | DOST 291:3
stop come to the end: then s. | CARR 202:17
could not s. for Death | DICK 281:11
full s. at the right place | BABE 44:14
impossible to s. | STRU 779:7
kissing had to s. | BROW 168:3
Might s. a hole | SHAK 704:17
nobody's going to s. 'em | BERR 74:12
nothing will s. it | ZOLA 878:15
so plain a s. | SHAK 707:3
S. all the clocks | AUDE 37:4
S. it at the start | OVID 590:16
S.-look-and-listen | OFFI 584:13
S. me and buy one | ADVE 8:17
S. the world | NEWL 571:13
s. to busy fools | VAUG 825:3
s. trying to be happy | WHAR 849:10
stoppeth s. one of three | COLE 240:12
stops buck s. here | TRUM 818:2
know my s. | SHAK 702:26
storage thought in cold s. | SAMU 679:16
store amid thy s. | KEAT 457:1
in the s. we sell hope | REVS 658:15
storehouse rich s. | BACO 45:9
storey crack in your upper s. | SMOL 759:8
storied S. of old | MILT 539:7
stories beset him round With dismal s. | BUNY 171:25
S. to rede ar delitabill | BARB 58:3
tell ourselves s. | DIDI 283:1
tell sad s. | SHAK 730:19
stork S. from butter | ADVE 7:13
storm After a s. comes a calm | PROV 626:8
Any port in a s. | PROV 626:26
carry you through the s. | EWAR 321:24
coming s. | GLAD 359:13
directs the s. | ADDI 4:11
directs this s. | PAGE 591:15
fled away into the s. | KEAT 454:15
Head to the s. | KIPL 466:8
pelting of this pitiless s. | SHAK 715:23
pilot of the s. | BAGE 50:12
rides upon the s. | COWP 255:12

sharper the s. | PROV 643:3
ship in a black s. | WEBS 844:25
S. and stress | KAUF 453:12
s.-clouds gather | LEAR 485:18
S.-clouds whirl | PUSH 650:16
wind and s. | BOOK 150:9
storms He sought the s. | DRYD 294:12
waves and s. | BOOK 142:6
stormy dark and s. night | BULW 170:13
O s. peple | CHAU 218:28
S. weather | KOEH 470:9
to 'scape s. days | DONN 288:16
story about you, that s. | HORA 414:8
dreaming s. | JARR 430:21
Have you thought of a s. | SHEL 743:1
It's our own s. | CART 205:11
name great in s. | BYRO 191:6
novel tells a s. | FORS 337:17
One s. is good | PROV 641:14
picture tells a s. | ADVE 7:22
picture tells a s. | PROV 631:33
plot for a short s. | CHEK 222:1
read Richardson for the s. | JOHN 441:4
short in the s. | BIBL 98:8
so old a s. | HEIN 389:10
s. always old | BROW 167:13
s. and a byword | WINT 860:18
s. chronicled | MALO 518:1
s. need be long | THOR 809:8
s. of Ould Grouse | GOLD 365:6
s. of our days | RALE 654:6
S. the spoiled child of art | JAME 429:9
tell my s. | SHAK 705:2
tell you a s. | NURS 579:7
work that tells a s. | RUSK 673:23
stout Collapse of S. Party | ANON 16:18
s. heart to stey brae | PROV 642:13
St Pancras Towers of S. Station | BEEC 65:12
St Paul's ruins of S. | MACA 507:16
ruins of S. | WALP 837:19
Say I am designing S. | BENT 71:18
S. had slipped over | SMIT 758:22
Strachan Sir Richard S. | ANON 17:11
strafe Gott s. England | POLI 612:19
Strafford S., who was hurried hence | EPIT 318:8
straight crooked shall be made s. | BIBL 93:15
get it s. one day | STEV 774:7
line which is accurately s. | WHEW 850:3
make a crab walk s. | ARIS 26:19
make his paths s. | BIBL 98:15
makes a s.-cut ditch | THOR 809:5
no s. thing | KANT 453:4
nothing ever ran quite s. | GALS 348:3
street which is called S. | BIBL 109:23
unflexible as s. | LOCK 497:10
strain s. at a gnat | BIBL 102:19
s., Time's eunuch | HOPK 408:3
That s. again | SHAK 734:26
train take the s. | ADVE 7:44
Words s. | ELIO 309:7
strait S. is the gate | BIBL 99:29
straits echoing s. between us | ARNO 31:3
strand fair Scotland's s. | BURN 178:16
Maypole in the S. | BRAM 154:17
name upon the s. | SPEN 766:18
never alone with a S. | ADVE 8:31
sailing to the s. | BALL 55:16
walk down the S. | HARG 382:10
strands last s. of man | HOPK 407:5
strange among the s. people | BOOK 148:3
foul, s., and unnatural | SHAK 700:20
hand of s. children | BOOK 149:24
How s. it seems | BROW 166:18
in a s. land | BOOK 149:14
Let us be very s. | CONG 247:26
millions of s. shadows | SHAK 737:27
new and s. at first | TRAH 814:9
new men, s. faces | TENN 794:24
now wonder nyce and s. | CHAU 220:27
something rich and s. | SHAK 733:21
s. and sinister | JAME 430:1
'S. friend,' I said | OWEN 591:9
s. intelligence | SHAK 718:12

strange (*cont.*):

stranger in a s. land	BIBL 80:32
s. that one so young	BYRO 187:27
s. to see the humour	DANI 264:10
too s. a hand	SHAK 711:14
strangeness s. in the proportion	BACO 46:9
will die of s.	MURR 566:4
stranger by a complete s.	ANNE 16:2
entertain Him like a s.	ANON 21:16
entertain this starry s.	CRAS 259:4
gratitude of a s.	TOCQ 812:14
I am a s. grown	BURN 178:24
I, a s. and afraid	HOUS 415:6
I was a little s.	TRAH 814:9
Look, s.	AUDE 37:14
never love a s.	BENS 70:23
s. and alone	WOLF 862:19
s., and ye took me in	BIBL 103:6
s.? 'Eave 'arf a brick	PUNC 649:18
s. in a strange land	BIBL 80:32
S. than fiction	BYRO 189:22
s. than fiction	PROV 645:36
s. to my heart and me	SHAK 714:17
s. to one of your parents	AUST 42:13
S., unless with bedroom eyes	AUDE 38:3
surety for a s.	BIBL 88:1
who's a s.	PHIL 606:6
wiles of the s.	NASH 568:15
You may see a s.	HAMM 378:21
strangers careth for the s.	BOOK 150:5
courteous to s.	BACO 47:4
entertain s.	BIBL 116:11
on the kindness of s.	WILL 858:9
s. and pilgrims	BIBL 116:5
s. in the Capitol	HEWI 397:15
s. of Rome	BIBL 109:13
s. on a rainy day	SMAR 754:14
we are s. before thee	BIBL 86:1
we may be better s.	SHAK 697:11
strangled And s. her	BROW 167:6
s. with the guts	MESL 533:7
strangling s. in a string	HOUS 415:14
S. is a very quiet death	WEBS 844:14
strategy S. is a system of expedients	
	MOLT 553:6
Stratford atte Bowe scole of S.	CHAU 218:9
strathspeys hornpipes and s.	BURN 178:1
straw all things as s. dogs	LAO 479:8
clutch at a s.	PROV 630:38
Headpiece filled with s.	ELIO 309:27
He gets the s.	OXFO 591:12
last s. that breaks	PROV 636:28
lion shall eat s.	BIBL 92:18
make bricks without s.	PROV 648:11
seems like s.	THOM 805:12
stumbles at a s.	SPEN 768:6
Take a s. and throw it up	SELD 691:12
strawberries s. grow in the sea	NURS 580:4
S. swimming in the cream	PEEL 601:16
strawberry Like s. wives	ELIZ 312:17
of the s.	BUTL 184:20
S. fields forever	LENN 489:10
Strawberry Hill [S.] is	WALP 837:9
strawberry-tree s. doth bear	SHEL 745:1
strawed where thou hast not s.	BIBL 103:3
straws S. tell which way	PROV 643:42
stray If with me you'd fondly s.	GAY 351:4
strayed erred, and s. from thy ways	
	BOOK 133:4
streak thin red s.	RUSS 676:1
stream change horses in mid s.	PROV 630:18
cool as a mountain s.	ADVE 7:14
like an ever-rolling s.	WATT 842:7
long-legged fly upon the s.	YEAT 874:3
old mill by the s.	ARMS 28:14
purling s.	ADDI 4:28
purling s.	POPE 614:19
salt weed sways in the s.	ARNO 29:13
Still glides the S.	WORD 868:25
s. cannot rise above	PROV 643:43
streamers s. waving in the wind	GAY 351:24
streams cold Companionable s.	YEAT 875:11
Gilding pale s.	SHAK 737:25

hart for cooling s.	TATE 790:14
his crystàlline s.	SHEL 745:8
s. in the firmament	MARL 522:11
s. of dotage flow	JOHN 438:10
strebt so lang er s.	GOET 361:13
street almost a continued s.	BROO 159:2
don't do it in the s.	CAMP 195:2
inability to cross the s.	WOOL 864:12
jostling in the s.	BLAK 127:1
live in a s.	ELIO 308:3
On the bald s.	TENN 795:4
s. fighting man	JAGG 427:11
s. of the city was gold	BIBL 119:18
s. which is called Straight	BIBL 109:23
sunny side of the s.	FIEL 327:5
talking at s. corners	VANZ 824:10
where the long s. roars	TENN 796:5
streets blood In the s.	NERU 570:14
children died in the s.	AUDE 37:3
Down these mean s.	CHAN 215:11
grass will grow in the s.	HOOV 406:16
negro s. at dawn	GINS 358:22
start in the s.	KENN 460:1
s. and lanes of the city	BIBL 105:23
s. are paved with gold	COLM 244:2
s. being paved with gold	LOUI 501:8
S. FLOODED	BENC 69:10
s. that no longer exist	FENT 324:24
strength as the s. of ten	TENN 800:6
Ephraim also is the s.	BOOK 143:19
Even if s. fail	PROP 624:21
exhausting its s.	MONT 556:1
from s. to strength	BOOK 145:14
giant's s.	SHAK 723:7
girded himself with s.	BOOK 146:4
His s. the more is	BUNY 171:25
is their s. then	BOOK 145:21
My s. and my hope	BIBL 95:10
ordained s.	BOOK 139:22
our hope and s.	BOOK 142:17
renew their s.	BIBL 93:20
roll all our s.	MARV 525:14
sensuality and s.	FRIN 343:15
S. and honour are her clothing	BIBL 89:15
s. is lacking	OVID 590:3
s. is made perfect	BIBL 113:19
s. is weak	GOET 362:3
s., not of legs	MONT 555:3
s. of an horse	BOOK 150:7
s. of his spirit	LUCR 504:4
S. through joy	POLI 612:28
s. unto his people	BOOK 141:13
s., utility, grace	VITR 833:9
s. with his arm	BIBL 104:9
S. without hands to smite	SWIN 785:1
s. without insolence	BYRO 191:20
Sun in his s.	BIBL 78:10
that tower of s.	TENN 798:22
tower of s.	SHAK 731:26
Union is s.	PROV 645:49
yet would my s. be vain	SIKH 751:16
strengthen bread to s. man's heart	
	BOOK 147:6
S. me, O Lord	SIKH 752:2
s. such as do stand	BOOK 134:23
s. while one stands	ROSS 669:1
S. ye the weak hands	BIBL 93:9
strengtheneth Christ which s. me	BIBL 115:6
strengthens s. our nerves	BURK 174:19
strenua S. nos exercet inertia	HORA 410:10
strenuous s. life	ROOS 667:17
strepitumque opes s. Romae	HORA 413:7
stress Storm and s.	KAUF 453:12
stretch insight and the s.	BROW 164:20
not always s. his bow	HORA 412:9
S. him out longer	SHAK 717:9
s. the human frame	SCAR 683:4
S. your arm no further	PROV 643:44
stretched by a s. out arm	BIBL 82:12
hand is s. out	BIBL 92:5
man's mind is s.	HOLM 403:10
things he s.	TWAI 819:18
stretches s. his legs	PROV 631:32

stricken I was a s. deer	COWP 256:13
s. deer	SHAK 702:25
well s. in age	BIBL 79:34
strictly more s. we are watched	BENT 71:5
stride At one s. comes the dark	COLE 240:23
strides Tarquin's ravishing s.	SHAK 719:20
strife In place of s.	CAST 206:11
Let there be no s.	BIBL 79:30
man of s.	BIBL 95:4
none was worth my s.	LAND 478:3
Of that stern s.	SCOT 689:6
s. and the discouragement	LONG 498:17
s. is o'er	POTT 620:3
void of s.	CHAL 213:19
strike in doubt, s. it out	TWAI 820:22
s. against public safety	COOL 250:13
S. him	CALI 193:9
s. his father's crown	SHAK 708:11
s. it in anger	SHAW 741:16
s. it out	JOHN 441:9
s. not awry	MORE 559:15
S. the tent	LEE 487:19
S. while the iron	PROV 643:45
thunder, S. flat	SHAK 715:16
yet afraid to s.	POPE 614:22
striker no s.	BIBL 115:19
strikes as s. the player	FITZ 331:22
Empire s. back	FILM 331:4
s. the same place twice	PROV 637:30
string end of a golden s.	BLAK 125:16
one long yellow s.	BROW 167:6
strangling in a s.	HOUS 415:14
s. that ties	SHEL 747:16
s. that ties them	MONT 555:25
untune that s.	SHAK 734:14
stringent s. execution	GRAN 368:16
strings scrape your s. darker	CELA 212:10
s. . . . . in the human heart	DICK 276:9
strip s. his sleeve	SHAK 709:7
S. thine own back	SHAK 716:20
stripe s. for stripe	BIBL 81:21
striped s. like a zebra	KEAT 455:11
s. shroud	THOM 807:2
stripes forty s. save one	BIBL 113:15
with his s. we are healed	BIBL 94:4
stripling s. Thames	ARNO 30:9
strive need'st not s.	CLOU 236:22
s. on untiringly	PALI 593:16
s., to seek, to find	TENN 801:1
strives err while yet he s.	GOET 361:13
striving s. evermore for these	GREN 372:10
stroke greater s. astonisheth	CONS 249:15
none so fast as s.	MISQ 547:2
s. of murder	DRYD 296:33
s. people with words	FITZ 332:9
strokes amorous of their s.	SHAK 694:22
Different s.	SAYI 684:13
strong all s. enough	LA R 481:18
battle to the s.	BIBL 90:11
battle to the s.	DAVI 267:15
battle to the s.	PROV 642:17
Be s. and of a good courage	BIBL 82:24
conquers himself is s.	LAO 480:2
keep the s. in awe	SHAK 731:30
men be so s.	BOOK 145:21
nature of s. people	BONH 132:12
only the S. shall thrive	SERV 692:26
out of the s.	BIBL 83:12
realize how s. she is	REAG 656:9
river Is a s. brown god	ELIO 309:14
Sorrow and silence are s.	LONG 499:4
s. drink	BIBL 89:13
s. drink is raging	BIBL 88:24
s. in soul	PYTH 651:3
s. in the arm	PROV 647:37
S. is the lion	SMAR 754:15
s. man armed	BIBL 105:10
s. name of the Trinity	ALEX 12:9
s., silent man	MORL 560:3
wants that little s.	HOLM 403:14
weak overcomes the s.	LAO 480:13
without whom nothing is s.	BOOK 136:4
stronger grows the s.	STER 773:5

stand out of my s. DIOG 283:14
staring at the s. BELL 67:20
s. also rises HEMI 391:5
s. and moon AUGU 39:4
S. and Moon should doubt BLAK 124:17
s. and moon to stand TOAS 812:2
s. begins his state MILT 539:25
s. does not set SCHI 683:13
s. doth parch the green SURR 780:15
S.-girt city SHEL 744:21
s. go down on your anger PROV 639:37
s. go down upon your wrath BIBL 114:7
s. grows cold TAYL 791:18
s. has gone in SMIT 757:11
s. himself cannot forget ANON 20:15
S. in his strength BIBL 78:10
s. is always setting NAIP 567:4
s. is laid to sleep JONS 446:3
s. is lost DONN 287:13
s. loses nothing PROV 643:50
s. loste his hewe CHAU 219:5
s. never sets NORT 577:3
s. now stands JOSE 447:11
S. of righteousness BIBL 96:19
S. of Righteousness WESL 847:9
s. of York SHAK 731:9
s. reigns supreme LE C 487:4
s. shall not burn thee BOOK 148:17
s. shone BECK 64:11
s. showing up the dust PERR 604:2
S.'s rim dips COLE 240:23
S., stand thou still BIBL 82:29
s. to me is dark MILT 545:2
S.-treader, life and light BROW 166:29
s. was shining everywhere GERS 353:12
S. wot won it NEWS 573:16
teapot revolving about the s. RUSS 675:13
tired the s. with talking CORY 252:13
under the s. BIBL 89:16
Up roos the s. CHAU 219:12
when the s. in bed MILT 541:1
when the s. rise BLAK 128:8
where no s. shines THOM 806:1
while the s. shines PROV 638:14
woman clothed with the s. BIBL 118:23
yet I saw no s. TICH 811:2
sunbeam Jesus wants me for a s. TALB 787:20
s. in a winter's day DYER 301:8
sunbeams didst the stars and s. know
ARNO 30:16
s. out of cucumbers SWIF 782:10
sunbright upon the s. walls WORD 865:2
Sunday feeling of S. is the same RHYS 659:16
Here of a S. morning HOUS 415:16
killing of a mouse on S. BRAT 155:8
may be played on S. LEAC 485:10
Never on S. FILM 331:9
rainy S. afternoon ERTZ 320:8
rainy S. in London DE Q 273:18
She was the S. CLAR 233:18
S., bloody Sunday FILM 331:11
S. go-to-meeting clothes SHIE 749:14
working week and S. best AUDE 37:5
Sundays begin a journey on S. SWIF 783:7
sundial s., and I make a botch BELL 68:19
sundry s. and manifold changes BOOK 135:19
sunflower Bring me the s. MONT 555:27
S.! weary of time BLAK 127:16
sung s. as it were a new song BIBL 118:28
s. from noon to noon MORR 560:16
sunk s. beneath the wave COWP 255:18
sunless Down to a s. sea COLE 240:4
to the s. land WORD 865:18
sunlight paint s. HOPP 408:13
S. is said to be BRAN 155:2
s. on the garden MACN 513:14
sunnier s. side of doubt TENN 792:18
sunny Candlemas day be s. and bright
PROV 635:8
leaps S. Jim ADVE 7:31
lived in a warm, s. climate COWA 253:21
s. pleasure-dome COLE 240:6
s. side of the street FIEL 327:5

sunrise Eternity's s. BLAK 127:2
suns in countless s. BRUN 168:21
light of setting s. WORD 866:13
planets circle other s. POPE 616:16
process of the s. TENN 797:3
S. can set and come CATU 210:6
S., that set JONS 446:12
sunset make a fine s. MADA 514:2
sail beyond the s. TENN 800:20
S. and evening star TENN 793:6
s. breezes shiver NEWB 571:10
s. of my life REAG 656:20
S. ran BROW 165:29
s.-seas ALDR 11:14
there's a s.-touch BROW 164:24
sunsets Autumn s. exquisitely dying
HUXL 423:2
horror of s. PROU 625:14
sunshine Digressions are the s. STER 772:22
Eternal s. of the spotless mind POPE 614:11
in the s. and with applause BUNY 171:12
like s. after rain SHAK 738:28
ray of s. WODE 861:20
s. in the shady place SPEN 767:5
s. is a glorious birth WORD 867:3
s. of the heart CONS 249:19
s. to the sunless land WORD 865:18
sunt Sint ut s. CLEM 235:10
sup liveth longest doth but s. HENS 392:16
s. with my Lord Jesus Christ BRUC 168:15
superbos et debellare s. VIRG 830:14
superficial ridiculous and s. MURA 565:12
superfluity barren s. of words GART 350:3
superfluous in the poorest thing s.
SHAK 715:12
nothing is s. LEON 489:19
s., a very necessary thing VOLT 834:13
s. in me ADAM 2:4
S., superfluous TURG 818:14
superhuman S. effort isn't worth SHAC 693:11
superior being s. to time JOHN 437:15
embarrass the s. SHAW 741:15
most s. person ANON 19:3
no-one to be their s. TOCQ 812:15
notions about a s. power SWIF 781:26
s. man is broadminded CONF 245:17
S. people never make long visits MOOR 557:16
superman I teach you the s. NIET 575:19
It's S. ANON 17:4
supernatural nothing mysterious or s.
HUME 419:17
s. source of evil CONR 249:11
superstition character of a s. CHOM 226:15
main source of s. RUSS 675:10
species of s. HUME 420:14
s. in avoiding superstition BACO 48:4
S. is the poetry of life GOET 362:10
S. is the religion BURK 174:18
s. sets the whole world VOLT 834:5
s. to enslave a philosophy INGE 425:3
superstitions end as s. HUXL 423:13
s. of the human mind VOLT 834:11
superstitious he is s. grown SHAK 712:7
in all things ye are too s. BIBL 110:3
more s., more bigoted NEWM 572:3
s. reluctance to sit JOHN 442:27
supped Hobson has s. MILT 541:5
s. full with horrors SHAK 722:21
supper after s. walk a mile PROV 626:9
consider s. as a turnpike EDWA 304:10
good s. at night ANST 24:14
Last-s.-carved-on-a-peach-stone LANC 477:22
leaned on his breast at s. BIBL 109:9
Sings for his s. NURS 580:1
S. of the Lord BOOK 138:15
suppliant s. for his own BYRO 190:18
thus the s. prays JOHN 438:9
supplications make our common s.
BOOK 134:8
supplies just bought fresh s. BREC 155:22
support depend on the s. of Paul SHAW 739:25
help and s. of the woman EDWA 304:5
look for popular s. ROMI 666:13

no invisible means of s. BUCH 169:9
s. him after SHAK 734:5
s. me when I am in the wrong MELB 531:3
s. of the people CLEV 235:13
s. us all the day long NEWM 572:13
swears that he will s. it JACK 426:10
visible means of s. BIER 121:9
supports s. with insolence JOHN 436:4
suppose universe queerer than we s.
HALD 376:11
suppress power of s. NORT 577:6
supramundane s. mushroom LAUR 483:2
supreme in none s. ARNO 31:2
S. God EMPS 315:24
s. power must be arbitrary HALI 377:12
sups s. with the Devil PROV 634:27
surcease catch With his s. success SHAK 719:6
sure joy was never s. SWIN 785:13
made the round world so s. BOOK 146:4
Slow but s. PROV 643:16
What nobody is s. about BELL 68:15
surely Shome mishtake, s. CATC 208:26
surety s. for a stranger BIBL 88:1
surf s. floods over the reeds PAST 598:20
surface looks dingy on the s. PIRS 607:6
surfeit s. by eating of a lamprey FABY 322:10
s. of our own behaviour SHAK 714:24
s. with too much SHAK 724:1
surge s. and thunder LANG 478:11
thine aëry s. SHEL 745:7
turbulent s. shall cover SHAK 734:9
surgeon not call the s. DICK 282:4
There can be no s. PARA 595:16
wounded s. plies the steel ELIO 309:12
surges s. lash the sounding shore POPE 616:7
surmise smothered in s. SHAK 718:16
with a wild s. KEAT 456:15
surprise Life is a great s. NABO 566:18
Live frugally on s. WALK 836:3
mystify, mislead, and s. JACK 427:1
no little s. BARH 58:10
No s. for the writer FROS 345:7
Respect was mingled with s. SCOT 688:10
sound of s. BALL 56:12
wise man by s. LA F 475:16
surprised Giants can be s. RATT 655:15
guilty thing s. WORD 867:14
S. by joy WORD 869:13
S. by unjust force MILT 539:9
surprises millions of s. HERB 394:25
S. are foolish things AUST 41:7
surprising everything is s. BYAT 184:23
surquidry s. and foul presumpcioun
CHAU 220:23
surrender die but do not s. CAMB 194:10
entire s. BELH 67:9
I s. to you GERO 353:11
No s. POLI 613:4
to Him we s. KORA 471:11
unconditional and immediate s. GRAN 368:12
we shall never s. CHUR 229:15
surrendered never s. her soul DE V 275:2
surroundings I plus my s. ORTE 586:8
sursum S. corda MISS 549:14
survey monarch of all I s. COWP 257:4
s. of all the world SHAK 706:28
s. the wondrous cross WATT 842:2
survival s. game CHRÉ 226:19
S. of the Fittest DARW 266:15
s. of the fittest SPEN 765:22
their s. machines DAWK 269:4
without victory, there is no s. CHUR 229:14
survive Dare hope to s. HUXL 423:1
expect to s. JEAN 431:1
know they can s. HART 383:9
Only the paranoid s. GROV 374:4
s. of us is love LARK 480:19
s. to consume VANE 824:6
survived I s. SIEY 751:12
know how I s. SIMO 753:1
survivors more the s.' affair MANN 520:2
Susan black-eyed S. came aboard GAY 351:24
susceptible s. to draughts WILD 854:24

suspect Always s. everybody DICK 279:25
makes a man s. much BACO 48:6
s. the worst ERAS 320:6
suspected New opinions are always s.
LOCK 497:2
suspects Round up the usual s. FILM 329:4
suspended s. my religious inquiries
GIBB 354:22
suspenders *not* forget the s. KIPL 468:13
suspension Shining s. CRAN 258:15
willing s. of disbelief COLE 241:21
suspicion above s. CAES 192:18
above s. PROV 628:30
against despots—s. DEMO 272:22
banish squint s. MILT 539:4
S. always haunts SHAK 710:12
s. that more than half WHIT 850:14
suspicions S. amongst thoughts BACO 48:5
Sussex S. won't be druv PROV 643:51
sustaining our s. corn SHAK 716:14
sutlers sapient s. ELIO 310:15
swaddled S. with darkness ELIO 309:24
swaddling wrapped him in s. clothes
BIBL 104:12
swaddlingband darkness a s. BIBL 87:10
swagman Once a jolly s. PATE 599:9
swains all our s. commend her SHAK 736:15
swallow and the s. a nest BOOK 145:13
before the s. dares SHAK 737:1
O summer's SWIN 785:23
speed of a s. BETJ 76:7
s. a camel BIBL 102:19
s. does not make summer PROV 641:15
s.-flights of song TENN 795:10
S., flying, flying South TENN 799:13
s. has set her six young BROW 166:8
S., my sister SWIN 785:22
s. the cow PROV 636:19
s. the world RUSH 672:16
swallowed soon to be s. BLY 130:1
They had s. us up quick BOOK 148:21
swallows gathering s. twitter KEAT 457:4
watching the s. WORD 865:2
swamp botanize in the s. CHES 225:19
swamps across primeval s. WODE 862:2
swan black Ohioan s. WRIG 870:19
hatched from a s.'s egg ANDE 15:6
I will play the s. SHAK 729:18
Leda's goose a s. ANON 17:15
like a sleeping s. SHEL 746:1
silver s. GIBB 355:8
some full-breasted s. TENN 794:28
so much as a black s. JUVE 451:2
Sweet S. of Avon JONS 446:26
Swanee down upon the S. River FOST 339:2
swanlike He makes a s. end SHAK 724:21
Swann no more talk of S. PROU 625:7
swans amongst tuneful s. VIRG 832:9
Dumb s., not chattering pies SIDN 750:19
I saw two s. SPEN 768:3
ships sail like s. asleep FLEC 334:13
s. are geese ARNO 29:15
s. of others are geese WALP 838:1
swap s. horses when crossing LINC 494:4
swarm s. in May PROV 644:1
S. over, death BETJ 76:5
swarthy in its s. monotony HARD 380:18
swashing s. and a martial outside SHAK 696:13
swath thy hook Spares the next s. KEAT 457:1
sway little rule, a little s. DYER 301:8
sways So s. she level SHAK 735:16
swear And s. No where DONN 289:15
s. by Apollo the physician HIPP 399:16
s. not at all BIBL 99:4
s. not by the moon SHAK 732:14
when very angry, s. TWAI 820:21
swearers and s. swear BURN 178:14
liars and s. SHAK 722:4
sweareth s. unto his neighbour BOOK 140:2
swears Money doesn't talk, it s. DYLA 301:16
sweat Blood, s., and tear-wrung BYRO 185:7
blood, toil, tears and s. CHUR 229:12
die of a s. SHAK 708:6

In the s. of thy face BIBL 79:12
none will s. but for promotion SHAK 696:18
perfection's s. WALC 835:16
placed the s. of our brows HESI 397:7
spend our midday s. QUAR 651:9
s. of an enseamèd bed SHAK 703:14
s. of its labourers EISE 306:6
work by the s. of his brow CHEK 222:2
sweats Falstaff s. to death SHAK 705:22
wild regrets, and the bloody s. WILD 856:3
sweep he'd s. the country DISR 286:25
Mountains of Mourne s. down FREN 342:12
s. his own door-step PROV 635:9
s. the dust SHAK 727:11
your chimneys I s. BLAK 127:7
sweeping S. up the Heart DICK 281:14
sweeps beats as it s. ADVE 7:36
s. a room as for Thy laws HERB 394:7
sweet All is not s. HENR 392:7
as a s. morsel HENR 392:7
buried in so s. a place SHEL 743:7
dead thing that smells s. THOM 806:17
fruit is s. ARIS 28:9
Home, s. home PAYN 600:10
how it was s. BROW 165:13
How s. the moonlight sleeps SHAK 725:10
if TO-DAY be s. FITZ 331:20
in my mouth s. as honey BIBL 118:22
kiss me, s. and twenty SHAK 735:9
Life is very s. BORR 151:11
light is s. BIBL 90:18
Pyramus is a s.-faced man SHAK 725:31
seasons shall be s. COLE 239:21
Sleep is s. BUNY 171:16
Stolen waters are s. BIBL 87:33
such s. sorrow SHAK 732:19
such s. thunder SHAK 726:28
S. and low TENN 799:6
S. are the uses of adversity SHAK 696:15
s. as summer SHAK 711:6
S. day, so cool HERB 395:2
S. is revenge BYRO 188:1
s. is the whisper of the pine THEO 804:11
s. o' the year SHAK 736:25
s. peas, on tip-toe KEAT 455:3
s. reasonableness of Jesus ARNO 32:5
S. smell of success FILM 331:13
S., soft, plenty rhythm MORT 562:6
s. the name of Jesus NEWT 574:14
s. water and bitter BIBL 116:25
technically s. OPPE 585:16
Tell me not, s. LOVE 502:6
Things s. to taste SHAK 730:6
'Tis not so s. now SHAK 734:27
took s. counsel BOOK 143:11
wit enough to keep it s. JOHN 444:5
sweetened blood-s. beverage SOUT 764:15
sweeteners s. of tea FIEL 326:16
sweeter mountain sheep are s. PEAC 600:20
s. also than honey BOOK 140:11
those unheard Are s. KEAT 455:18
sweetest From the s. wine PROV 632:43
Success is counted s. DICK 281:21
s. girl I know JUDG 449:4
s. sounds I'll ever hear RODG 665:4
sweetheart Blanch, and S. SHAK 716:6
Like the s. of the sun HOOD 405:25
sweetly Lalage, who laughs so s. HORA 412:1
sweetmeats pyramids of s. DRYD 297:22
s. and sugar-plums TROL 816:6
sweetness came forth s. BIBL 83:12
O how great the sum Of s. SMAR 754:14
s. and light ARNO 31:9
s. and light SWIF 782:2
s. of Anjou DU B 298:4
s. of a shower THOM 806:22
waste its s. GRAY 370:6
where s. and light failed FORS 337:19
sweets bag of boiled s. CRIT 260:6
brought'st Thy s. HERB 394:4
discandy, melt their s. SHAK 695:14
last taste of s. SHAK 730:9
Stolen s. HUNT 421:8

Stolen s. are best CIBB 231:14
s. compacted lie HERB 395:2
S. into your list HUNT 421:7
s. of place with power ROSE 668:10
S. to the sweet SHAK 704:19
sweetshop pressed to a s. window
YEAT 873:10
swell deep sea s. ELIO 311:16
s. a progress ELIO 310:11
Thou s.! Thou witty HART 383:14
What a s. party PORT 619:19
swelling s. act SHAK 718:15
swept empty, s., and garnished BIBL 101:10
I s. the floor GILB 357:28
S. it for half a year CARR 203:3
swift Be s. to hear BIBL 116:18
Cousin S. DRYD 297:26
race is not to the s. BIBL 90:11
race is not to the s. PROV 642:17
race is to the s. DAVI 267:15
S. expires a driv'ler JOHN 438:10
swifter s. than a weaver's shuttle BIBL 86:22
s. than eagles BIBL 84:12
swiftness O s. never ceasing PEEL 601:17
prizes for s. of foot HOME 404:21
swim learn how to s. PROV 630:23
s., so hard of heart HORA 413:13
swimmer s. in his agony BYRO 188:8
swimmers s. into cleanness leaping
BROO 159:12
swimming Come softly s. SPEN 768:3
few figures s. VIRG 828:13
S. from tree to tree LOWE 503:7
s. in the air EDWA 304:7
s. *under water* FITZ 332:18
swindles all truly great s. HENR 392:9
swine husks that the s. did eat BIBL 105:30
in a s.'s snout BIBL 88:2
lady loved a s. NURS 581:13
Nor yet feed the s. NURS 578:8
pearls before s. BIBL 99:23
s. cheweth not the cud BIBL 81:26
throw pearls to s. PROV 630:16
turkeys, geese and s. PROV 640:35
whole herd of s. BIBL 100:12
swines You rotten s. CATC 209:6
swing ain't got that s. MILL 537:17
s. for it KING 464:17
S. low, sweet chariot SONG 763:12
s. our ungirded hips SORL 761:23
Swing, s. together CORY 252:11
want to s. a cat DICK 277:20
swings What you lose on the s. PROV 646:33
Swiss No money, no S. PROV 640:7
Swithun Saint S.'s day PROV 642:33
Switzerland I look upon S. SMIT 758:5
In S. they had FILM 328:20
swoop all at one s. WEBS 844:17
At one fell s. SHAK 722:7
sword brave man with a s. WILD 855:32
but a s. BIBL 100:28
draws s. against prince PROV 647:20
edge of the s. BOOK 143:25
fallen by the edge of the s. BIBL 97:25
famous by my s. MONT 556:16
first drew the s. CLAR 233:5
His father's s. he has MOOR 558:11
I gave them a s. NIXO 576:15
lives by the s. PROV 634:24
make his s. BIBL 87:15
mightier than the s. PROV 641:32
My s., I give BUNY 171:27
nation shall not lift up s. BIBL 91:21
pen is worse than the s. BURT 181:12
pen mightier than the s. BULW 170:14
perish with the s. BIBL 103:19
put to the s. CROM 260:11
Put up thy s. BIBL 108:25
sharp as a two-edged s. BIBL 87:26
sheathe the s. ASQU 34:4
sigh is the s. BLAK 125:14
s., a horse, a shield LOVE 502:6
s. of a Norman Baron LEWE 491:14

s. of truth AITK 9:19
s. out of this stone MALO 517:18
s. shall pierce BIBL 104:18
s. sleep in my hand BLAK 126:24
s. sung on the barren heath BLAK 127:4
s. was in the sheath COWP 255:19
terrible swift s. HOWE 417:3
two-edged s. BIBL 117:27
two-edged s. BOOK 150:11
watery if not flaming s. MARV 525:15
wield the s. of France DE G 271:9
with the edge of the s. BIBL 82:5
swords books are either dreams or s.
LOWE 502:15
Keep up your bright s. SHAK 728:5
s. In our own proper entrails SHAK 714:1
s. into plowshares BIBL 91:21
s. shall play the orators MARL 523:3
ten thousand s. leapt BURK 174:6
yet they be very s. BOOK 143:12
swore armies s. terribly STER 773:6
My tongue s. EURI 321:9
when the son s. BURT 181:22
sworn had I so s. as you SHAK 719:15
sycamore nightingale in the s. STEV 777:4
sycophants s. and flatterers HARD 380:3
syllable chase A panting s. COWP 256:2
s. men's names MILT 539:1
To the last s. SHAK 722:22
syllables light s. leaped ROET 665:7
S. govern the world SELD 691:18
sylph only s. I ever saw DICK 279:18
symbol Five for the s. at your door
SONG 762:13
S. or energy ADAM 2:18
symboles *forêts de s.* BAUD 61:11
symbolic s. elements in life WHIT 851:14
s. expression MAXW 528:18
symbolical works of women are s.
BROW 163:22
symbols forests of s. BAUD 61:11
s. of a high romance KEAT 457:9
symmetry fearful s. BLAK 128:3
S. is tedious HUGO 419:4
s. of his body EINH 305:4
sympathetic s. wife EURI 321:17
sympathies enlarge men's s. ELIO 308:16
sympathy give or take s. RHYS 659:15
messages of s. AYCK 43:14
secret s. SCOT 688:13
s. is cold GIBB 354:14
Tea and s. ANDE 15:12
symphony angelic s. MILT 540:25
Ninth S. will remain BAKU 52:11
s. like the world MAHL 516:5
symptoms hundred good s. POPE 618:26
synagogues chief seats in the s. BIBL 104:3
syne For auld lang s. BURN 177:12
synod S. of Cooks JOHN 440:8
Syrens song the S. sang BROW 162:14
Syria S. isn't on it STRA 779:2
Syrian S. damsels to lament his fate
MILT 541:24
S. Orontes JUVE 450:18
syrops lucent s. KEAT 454:13
system cannot be a true s. PAIN 592:6
must create a s. BLAK 125:11
rocked the s. ROBI 664:7
s. into system runs POPE 616:16
s. of Government GLAD 359:14
s. of outdoor relief BRIG 157:2
systems little s. have their day TENN 794:29
s. into ruin hurled POPE 616:18

T t. is silent ASQU 34:8
ta saying 'T.' to God SPEN 766:8
tabby Demurest of the t. kind GRAY 370:14
tabernacle dwell in thy t. BOOK 140:1
t. were dissolved BIBL 113:9
tabernacles t. of thy grace SCOT 690:10
tabernas *pauperum t.* HORA 411:7
table behave mannerly at t. STEV 776:17

biform his fader at the t. CHAU 218:7
cannot make a t. JOHN 439:17
fall from their masters' t. BIBL 101:23
fell from the rich man's t. BIBL 106:6
five steps from the t. ROBB 663:3
on a t.?—and under it BYRO 192:8
patient etherized upon a t. ELIO 310:5
prepare a t. before me BOOK 140:21
round about thy t. BOOK 149:4
T., at the Communion-time BOOK 136:18
takes the t. clean away BARN 59:11
tableau t. of crimes VOLT 834:10
tables make it plain upon t. BIBL 96:15
serve t. BIBL 109:17
tablet keep taking The T. THOM 807:3
tablets thy t., Memory ARNO 29:18
taboo t.'d by anxiety GILB 356:22
tabret bring hither the t. BOOK 145:11
tabulae *Solventur risu t.* HORA 414:18
tache *sans une t.* ROST 670:3
tactful t. in audacity COCT 237:22
tactics art of t. BAGE 50:14
tadpole When you were a t. SMIT 757:6
taffeta doublet of changeable t. SHAK 735:4
T. phrases SHAK 717:21
Taffy T. was a Welshman NURS 581:10
tail choke on the t. PROV 636:19
Improve his shining t. CARR 201:13
more he shows his t. PROV 634:33
O! thereby hangs a t. SHAK 728:21
rat without a t. SHAK 718:6
scaly horror of his folded t. MILT 540:28
sensations of its "t." DISR 284:9
t. that wagged WATS 841:10
treading on my t. CARR 202:13
tailor coat from the t. GOLD 365:16
ninth part even of a t. CARL 199:9
t. in Gloucester POTT 620:4
t. make thy doublet SHAK 735:19
Tinker, T. NURS 582:4
tailors eighteen t. CARL 200:25
Nine t. make a man PROV 639:50
tails bring their t. behind them NURS 579:16
stings in their t. BIBL 118:21
taint never t. my love SHAK 729:8
tainted t. wether of the flock SHAK 724:27
taisez-vous *T.! Méfiez-vous* OFFI 584:14
take begins to t. it away SENE 692:17
big enough to t. away everything FORD 336:16
Give and t. fair play PROV 633:1
O t. those lips away SHAK 723:17
something people t. BALD 52:14
T. a pair of sparkling eyes GILB 356:13
T., a thing PROV 632:48
T., eat BIBL 103:12
T., eat, this is my Body BOOK 137:16
T. me to your leader CATC 208:28
t. my life FARQ 324:8
t. my life and all SHAK 725:6
t. not thy holy Spirit BOOK 143:7
T. now thy son BIBL 79:37
t. the nasty soup away HOFF 402:4
T. up the White Man's Burden KIPL 468:2
t. who have the power WORD 869:1
t. you in the morning BALD 53:1
taken Lord hath t. away BIBL 86:11
much is t., much abides TENN 800:20
One shall be t. BIBL 102:28
shall be t. away BIBL 103:4
she was t. out of Man BIBL 79:2
t. away my Lord BIBL 108:36
t. in when they marry AUST 41:13
When t. COLM 244:7
takes if it t. all summer GRAN 368:13
t. just like a woman DYLA 301:17
that it t. away BYRO 191:5
taketh t. away the sin BIBL 107:5
taking t. life by the throat FROS 345:9
we're t. over MORR 561:4
tale adorn a t. JOHN 438:8
fortunate for t.-tellers SCOT 689:19
had a t. to tell SCOT 688:4
I could a t. unfold SHAK 700:18

mere t. of a tub WEBS 844:19
most tremendous t. of all BETJ 75:10
plain t. shall put you down SHAK 706:1
round unvarnished t. SHAK 728:8
sad t.'s best for winter SHAK 736:19
t. never loses in telling PROV 644:4
t. should be judicious COWP 254:27
t. Told by an idiot SHAK 722:22
t. which holdeth children SIDN 751:6
telling the saddest t. SHAK 726:1
Tell t. tit NURS 581:11
thereby hangs a t. SHAK 696:25
Trust the t. LAWR 483:14
twice-told t. SHAK 714:10
talent into my works is my t. WILD 856:10
Murder, like t. LEWE 491:13
no t. for writing BENC 69:9
sister of t. CHEK 222:9
T. develops in quiet places GOET 362:12
T. does what it can MERE 532:24
t. instantly recognizes genius DOYL 293:2
t., not an object HESS 397:13
t. of a liar BYRO 192:6
t. pour le silence CARL 200:6
t. to amuse COWA 253:12
t. which is death to hide MILT 545:14
tomb of a mediocre t. SMIT 757:9
talents career open to the t. NAPO 568:8
If you have great t. REYN 658:18
ministry of all the t. ANON 18:22
virtue and t. JEFF 432:6
What'er the t. POPE 613:22
tales Dead men tell no t. PROV 629:35
idle t. BIBL 106:29
increased with t. BACO 46:20
tell t. out of school PROV 639:44
tali *t. auxilio nec defensoribus* VIRG 829:16
talk Can they t. BENT 71:8
Careless t. costs lives OFFI 584:1
don't t. like one DIDE 282:15
good to t. ADVE 7:39
gotta use words when I t. to you ELIO 310:26
have out his t. JOHN 442:12
If you t. to God SZAS 786:14
I long to t. DONN 289:10
It can t., talk, talk PLAT 608:3
let the people t. DANT 265:9
Money doesn't t., it swears DYLA 301:16
Most English t. JAME 429:13
Must t. SMIT 756:14
no more t. of Swann PROU 625:7
No use to t. HOUS 415:15
people who can't t. ZAPP 877:13
ran the sun down with t. CALL 193:15
t. about the rest of us ANON 20:18
t. but a tinkling cymbal BACO 46:33
T. is cheap PROV 644:5
t. like a lady SHAW 742:7
t. of many things CARR 203:4
t. of the child TALM 789:18
T. of the Devil PROV 644:6
t. of wills SHAK 730:18
t. on for ever HAZL 386:2
t. six times BYRO 189:15
t. the less ZENO 877:14
t. too much DRYD 294:10
t. to the plants CHAR 217:15
They always t. PRIO 624:13
very easy to t. DICK 279:15
ways of making you t. CATC 208:32
we had a good t. BOSW 152:7
world may t. of hereafter COLL 242:24
talked I believe they t. of me FARQ 324:6
least t. about by men PERI 603:27
not being t. about WILD 855:17
not to be t. of TAYL 792:7
t. like poor Poll GARR 349:11
t. of their Raphaels GOLD 364:22
t. shop ANON 17:14
t. with us by the way BIBL 106:31
talkers present is an age of t. HAZL 386:16
ten thousand t. DYLA 301:15
talking foolish t. BIBL 114:8

talking (cont.):
habit of t. with paper — SOYI 765:4
He is t. — BIBL 85:9
know what we are t. about — RUSS 674:23
leaves off t. — BUTL 184:17
nation t. to itself — MILL 537:12
People t. without speaking — SIMO 752:15
redtape t.-machine — CARL 200:14
stop people t. — ATTL 35:10
T. and eloquence — JONS 447:5
t., Signior Benedick — SHAK 727:15
t. to myself — BARN 59:6
tired the sun with t. — CORY 252:13
talks Garbo t. — TAGL 788:3
Money t. — PROV 639:8
t. of Arthur's death — SHAK 714:12
t. of his misfortunes — JOHN 443:2
tall all I ask is a t. ship — MASE 527:6
divinely t. — TENN 793:9
don't look t. — PORT 620:2
exceeding t. men — BACO 49:6
for this the clay grew t. — OWEN 591:7
long and the short and the t. — HUGH 417:18
t. as a crane — SITW 753:10
'Tis a t. building — CRAB 257:8
taller t. by almost the breadth — SWIF 782:5
t. than other men — HARO 382:16
Tallis T. is dead — BYRD 184:27
Talmuds rotted T. of my childhood — BABE 44:15
Tam T. was glorious — BURN 179:14
tambourine Mr T. Man — DYLA 301:20
play the t. — DICK 279:18
tame tongue can no man t. — BIBL 116:24
taming T. my wild heart — SHAK 727:25
Tam Lin ken this night, T. — BALL 55:19
tamper never want to t. — AUDE 37:9
Tandy met wid Nappy T. — POLI 612:22
tangere Noli me t. — BIBL 120:17
tangle odors t. — DICK 282:5
tangled t. web we weave — SCOT 689:3
tangles t. of Neaera's hair — MILT 540:6
tango Takes two to t. — HOFF 402:2
takes two to t. — PROV 636:42
tank T. come down the stalls — SASS 682:5
tiger in your t. — ADVE 8:13
tanks Get your t. off my lawn — WILS 859:8
tanstaafl T. — SAYI 685:13
tantae T. molis erat — VIRG 828:12
tantras Mantras and t. — TANT 790:6
tantum T. ergo sacramentum — THOM 805:5
T. religio potuit — LUCR 504:5
Tao not the eternal T. — LAO 479:6
one is near T. — CHUA 227:7
T. has reality and evidence — CHUA 227:13
Therefore T. is great — LAO 479:13
tap t. being turned off — KIPL 468:22
taper Out went the t. — KEAT 456:3
with t. light To seek — SHAK 714:11
tapestry earth in so rich t. — SIDN 751:4
Turkey t. — HOWE 417:4
tapping suddenly there came a t. — POE 610:19
tar ha'porth of t. — PROV 630:15
T.-baby ain't sayin' nuthin' — HARR 383:6
T. water — BERK 72:12
Tara through T.'s halls — MOOR 558:9
when T. rose so high — LAND 478:4
taratantara t. dixit — ENNI 316:6
tarde cinco en punto de la t. — LORC 500:17
tares but a field of t. — TICH 811:2
t. of mine own brain — BROW 163:5
tarn down by the dank t. of Auber — POE 611:6
tarnished neither t. nor afraid — CHAN 215:11
Tarquin great house of T. — MACA 508:10
T.'s ravishing strides — SHAK 719:20
tarried too long he t. — SWIF 784:12
too long we have t. — LEAR 486:6
tarry Boatman, do not t. — CAMP 195:10
t. till I come — BIBL 109:10
why t. the wheels — BIBL 83:4
You may for ever t. — HERR 396:18
tarrying make no long t. — BOOK 142:1
tart t. cathartic virtue — EMER 315:1
t. who has married the Mayor — BAXT 62:8

tartar find a T. — PROV 642:35
T.'s lips — SHAK 721:17
tarts stole the t. — NURS 580:21
Tarzan Me T. — MISQ 548:9
task completed the t. — TALM 789:25
have a t. — MOOR 557:10
in love with its t. — AURE 40:10
long day's t. — SHAK 695:17
thy worldly t. hast done — SHAK 698:24
what he reads as a t. — JOHN 439:21
with weary t. fordone — SHAK 727:10
tasks have been my t. — KOLL 470:15
tassel lure this t.-gentle — SHAK 732:17
tassie fill it in a silver t. — BURN 179:2
taste arbiter of t. — TACI 787:8
bad t. — HOPK 408:10
bad t. of the smoker — ELIO 307:6
bouquet is better than the t. — POTT 620:12
create the t. — WORD 870:5
difference of t. in jokes — ELIO 307:7
Every man to his t. — PROV 631:29
forgot the t. of fears — SHAK 722:20
ghastly good t. — BETJ 76:10
good sense and good t. — LA B 475:1
Good t. and humour — MUGG 564:7
I did but t. a little honey — BIBL 83:34
last t. of sweets — SHAK 730:9
never t. who always drink — PRIO 624:13
nobody has any t. for them — VOLT 835:5
No! let me t. — BROW 167:8
no t. when you married — SHER 748:23
nothing for good t. — TOLS 813:14
nowhere worse t. — JOWE 447:15
ocean has but one t. — PALI 594:14
t. and see — BOOK 141:19
T. is the feminine — FITZ 332:2
t. it but sparingly — AUST 42:2
t. my meat — HERB 394:15
t. or genius — REYN 659:1
Things sweet to t. — SHAK 730:6
undoubtedly wanted t. — WALP 837:13
tasted books are to be t. — BACO 48:1
so be ye have t. — BIBL 117:2
tastes if it t. good, it's bad — ASIM 33:20
no accounting for t. — PROV 644:29
strongest t. were negative — WAUG 842:16
T. differ — PROV 644:7
t. greatly alter — JOHN 440:13
tasting T. of Flora — KEAT 456:3
Tat T. ist alles, nichts der Ruhm — GOET 362:6
Tathagata called T. — PALI 593:17
tattered t. coat upon a stick — YEAT 874:14
wars have t. his ears — HUGH 418:7
tatters rags and t. — MOLI 552:7
taught afterward he t. — CHAU 218:20
as if you t. them not — POPE 616:12
Cristes loore He t. — CHAU 218:22
got to be carefully t. — HAMM 379:5
t. anything — MOLI 552:19
t. by the enemy — OVID 590:12
t. them as one having authority — BIBL 100:5
t. to any purpose — REYN 658:17
what we have t. her — GAY 350:18
You t. me language — SHAK 733:18
taunting grave, and not t. — BACO 47:9
tavern hostess of the t. — SHAK 705:8
in a t. drinking — ANON 23:8
'So is the London T.' — ANON 17:9
t. for his friends — DOUG 291:16
t. in the town — SONG 763:13
t. or inn — JOHN 441:25
tax Excise. A hateful t. — JOHN 435:22
I t. not you, you elements — SHAK 715:17
power to t. — MARS 523:24
soon be able to t. it — FARA 323:10
To t. and to please — BURK 173:8
taxation art of t. consists — COLB 238:19
Inflation one form of t. — FRIE 343:10
lottery is a t. — FIEL 326:15
T. and representation — CAMD 194:11
T. without representation — OTIS 591:2
taxed world should be t. — BIBL 104:11
taxes as true . . . as t. — DICK 277:15

death and t. — DEFO 270:8
death and t. — FRAN 341:10
death and t. — PROV 640:18
Death and t. and childbirth — MITC 551:3
little people pay t. — HELM 390:8
no new t. — BUSH 182:4
overlaid with t. — BACO 48:8
Sex and t. — JONE 445:11
t. must fall upon agriculture — GIBB 354:8
taxi If you can't leave in a t. — FILM 328:15
t. throbbing waiting — ELIO 311:12
taxi-cab look like a t. — HUGH 417:17
taxing t. machine — LOWE 502:13
Tay Bridge of the Silv'ry T. — MCGO 510:15
tayl likerous t. — CHAU 220:10
te T. Deum laudamus — PRAY 623:8
tea and sometimes t. — POPE 618:10
honey still for t. — BROO 159:11
if this is t. — PUNC 650:12
Latin word for T. — BELL 69:1
low-class t.-shops — BRAM 154:16
shameless t.-drinker — JOHN 436:14
some sipping t. — WORD 868:3
sweeteners of t. — FIEL 326:16
Take some more t. — CARR 202:7
T., although an Oriental — CHES 224:19
t. and scandal — CONG 246:25
T. and sympathy — ANDE 15:12
t. for two — CAES 192:15
t.'s out of the way — REED 657:7
took t. and comfortable advice — KEAT 458:2
We'll all have t. — NURS 580:19
teabag woman is like a t. — REAG 656:9
teach ability to t. — AUCT 36:20
change the people who t. — BYAT 184:24
Even while they t. — SENE 692:14
gladly t. — CHAU 218:16
not t. his son a craft — TALM 789:28
qualified to t. others — CONF 245:16
t. Bloody instructions — SHAK 719:7
t., convince, subdue — AUBE 35:14
T. him how to live — PORT 620:1
t. him rather to think — SHEL 743:6
t. his senators wisdom — BOOK 147:12
T. me, my God and King — HERB 394:5
T. me thy way, O Lord — BOOK 141:10
T. me to feel — POPE 618:17
T. me to live — KEN 459:16
t. others to despise — HAZL 386:4
t. taste or genius — REYN 659:1
T. the free man — AUDE 37:13
T. the torches — SHAK 732:7
t. the young idea — THOM 808:12
T. us to care — ELIO 308:21
t. young babes — SHAK 729:7
t. your grandmother — PROV 630:28
to t. and delight — SIDN 751:5
tress won't t. me — PLAT 608:19
wants to t. — SELL 691:21
what they t. in song — SHEL 744:12
teacher closed fist of a t. — PALI 593:14
Danger is a good t. — HAZL 386:21
Experience is best t. — PROV 631:40
for the t.'s sake — DEFO 270:17
for the t.'s sake — FARQ 324:10
no lasting t. of duty — CICE 232:5
t. affects eternity — ADAM 2:16
t. should have maximal authority — SZAS 786:11
t. should have the role — JUVE 451:8
Time is a great t. — BERL 73:13
teachers been their own t. — REYN 658:17
governors, t. — BOOK 138:12
rigorous t. — ARNO 30:20
t. of the Art of Painting — DÜRE 300:12
t. of the world — FRED 341:20
wore out the wretched t. — JUVE 451:7
teaches experience t. — TACI 787:13
he who cannot, t. — PROV 634:18
He who cannot, t. — SHAW 741:13
teachest Thou t. like a fool — SHAK 694:13
teacheth t. more in one year — ASCH 33:6
teaching follow mine own t. — SHAK 724:2
t. nations how to live — MILT 546:7

Wheel of T.   PALI 594:23
teacup crack in the t. opens   AUDE 36:25
team Stanley Cup's for your t.   ESPO 320:10
teapot t. revolving about the sun   RUSS 675:13
   warming the t.   MANS 520:7
tear dropped a t. upon the word   STER 773:12
   homage of a t.   BYRO 185:20
   shed a bitter t.   CARR 203:3
   shed one English t.   MACA 508:6
   some melodious t.   MILT 540:4
   t. down this wall   REAG 656:18
   t. each other's eyes   WATT 841:15
   T. him for his bad verses   SHAK 713:17
   t. is an intellectual thing   BLAK 125:14
   t. trickling down my cheek   HORA 413:13
   that divine t.   HUGO 419:8
   unanswerable t.   BYRO 187:10
   Wipe the t., baby dear   WEST 849:5
   without a t.   DRYD 296:34
tears all thy t.   FITZ 331:23
   big t., for he wept   SHEL 745:3
   bitterest t. shed over graves   STOW 778:6
   bitter t. to shed   CORY 252:13
   blood, toil, t. and sweat   CHUR 229:12
   brought me t.   CALL 193:15
   came her t.   TENN 799:16
   Come back in t.   ROSS 668:19
   crocodiles, that shed t.   BACO 48:19
   Drop, drop, slow t.   FLET 335:15
   enough of blood and t.   RABI 652:13
   even the altar sheds t.   TALM 789:27
   God will wipe away t.   BIBL 92:24
   heaven with their t.   BLAK 128:5
   Hence those t.   TERE 801:11
   hold back her t.   OVID 590:10
   I forbid my t.   SHAK 704:8
   If you have t.   SHAK 713:8
   iron t. down Pluto's cheek   MILT 539:17
   keep your t.   PUDN 648:35
   Like Niobe, all t.   SHAK 699:21
   loosed our heart in t.   ARNO 29:17
   mine eyes from t.   BOOK 148:7
   moistened it with t.   KEAT 454:28
   No t. in the writer   FROS 345:7
   Nothing is here for t.   MILT 545:10
   now am full of t.   YEAT 873:5
   rich flames and hired t.   BROW 162:10
   sheddeth tender t.   SPEN 767:8
   Smiling through her t.   HOME 404:16
   sow in t.   BOOK 149:1
   t. I cannot hide   HARB 379:15
   T., idle tears   TENN 799:10
   t. into thy bottle   BOOK 143:13
   t. out the heart of it   KNOW 469:15
   t. shed for things   VIRG 829:1
   these crocodile's t.   BURT 181:21
   this vale of t.   PRAY 623:7
   through my t.   FLET 335:16
   Time with a gift of t.   SWIN 784:22
   too deep for t.   WORD 867:18
   water my couch with my t.   BOOK 139:20
   whence no t. can win us   HARD 381:22
   wipe away all t.   BIBL 118:17
   wipe away all t.   BIBL 119:16
   With mine own t.   SHAK 731:4
   With silence and t.   BYRO 191:19
   world is wet with t.   BAHA 51:22
tearsday moanday, t., wailsday   JOYC 448:3
tease fleas that t. in the High Pyrenees
   BELL 68:25
   t. us out of thought   KEAT 455:24
teases Because he knows it t.   CARR 202:3
tea tray t. in the sky   CARR 202:6
   t. painter   BLUN 129:14
technically t. sweet   OPPE 585:16
Technik Vorsprung durch T.   ADVE 8:24
technology advanced t. is   CLAR 233:15
   new t. imposed   SEDD 690:14
   Progress through t.   ADVE 8:24
   T. . . . the knack of so arranging   FRIS 343:18
   white heat of t.   MISQ 549:5
tecum Nec t. possum vivere   MART 524:11
   T. habita   PERS 604:12

Ted isn't it, T.   LINE 495:3
teddy Like a t. bear   NURS 581:4
   Now T. must run   KENN 461:1
   T. Bears have their Picnic   BRAT 155:9
tedious eloquence is t.   PASC 598:9
   t. and brief   SHAK 727:5
   t. as a twice-told tale   SHAK 714:10
tedium road to t.   FOWL 339:6
   t. is the very basis of mourning   HUGO 419:4
teeming gleaned my t. brain   KEAT 457:8
teems t. with hidden meaning   GILB 358:11
teeth barrier of your t.   HOME 404:12
   cast me in the t.   BOOK 142:7
   dig our graves with our t.   SMIL 755:17
   gnashing of t.   BIBL 100:9
   he's got iron t.   GROM 373:13
   old bitch gone in the t.   POUN 621:6
   our graves with our t.   DEFO 270:6
   shark has pretty t.   BREC 155:24
   skin of my t.   BIBL 86:33
   steal the very t.   ARAB 25:13
   t. are like a flock of sheep   BIBL 91:4
   t. are set on edge   BIBL 95:15
   t. are spears   BOOK 143:15
   t. like splinters   CAUS 211:9
   Thais' t. are black   MART 524:8
   those who have no t.   PROV 633:12
   untying with the t.   BIER 121:4
teetotaller only a beer t.   SHAW 739:18
Teflon T.-coated Presidency   SCHR 686:17
tehee 'T.!' quod she   CHAU 219:19
tekel MENE, T., UPHARSIN   BIBL 95:25
telegram visual t.   CASS 206:8
telegrams life of t. and anger   FORS 338:2
Telemachus mine own T.   TENN 800:18
telephones Tudor monarchy with t.
   BURG 172:9
telescopic T. philanthropy   DICK 276:12
television I hate t.   WELL 846:2
   no plain women on t.   FORD 336:15
   Radio and t.   SARR 681:5
   T. brought brutality   MCLU 512:11
   T. contracts imagination   WOGA 862:10
   T. has brought back murder   HITC 400:4
   T. has made dictatorship   PERE 603:21
   T. is for appearing on   COWA 254:6
   T.? word is half Greek   SCOT 688:1
tell closest friends won't t. you   ADVE 7:21
   Don't ask, don't t.   NUNN 577:17
   Don't t. the ending   TAGL 788:10
   Go, t. the Spartans   EPIT 317:13
   men of sense never t.   SHAF 693:17
   t. her she mustn't   PUNC 650:1
   T. it not in Gath   BIBL 84:11
   T. me not, Sweet   LOVE 502:6
   T. me the old, old story   HANK 379:10
   T. out my soul   BIBL 104:8
   t. sad stories   SHAK 730:19
   T. Sid   ADVE 8:19
   T. tale tit   NURS 581:11
   T. them I came   DE L 272:7
   t. them of us and say   EPIT 320:3
   t. the most heart-easing things   KEAT 456:20
   t. the towers thereof   BOOK 142:25
   wait till I t. you   HENR 392:10
telleth t. the number of the stars   BOOK 150:6
telling I am t. you   WHIS 850:5
   pity beyond all t.   YEAT 874:10
   tale never loses in t.   PROV 644:4
Téméraire Fighting T.   NEWB 571:10
temper enforce with t.   GREN 372:11
   including my t.   NEHR 569:11
   Keep me in t.   SHAK 715:7
   lose your t. with the Press   PANK 595:12
   only keep your t.   STER 772:17
   t. Justice with mercy   MILT 544:10
   truth that has lost its t.   GIBR 355:17
   uncertain t.   AUST 42:9
temperance May t. befriend me   EURI 321:13
   t. would be difficult   JOHN 444:12
temperate more lovely and more t.
   SHAK 737:18
temperature acquire a t.   SCHU 687:6

tempers God t. the wind   STER 772:13
tempest Like summer t.   TENN 799:16
   rides out the t.   BAUD 61:9
   we the t. know   DRYD 295:12
tempestas Quo me cumque rapit t.
   HORA 409:18
tempests looks on t.   SHAK 738:15
tempest-tost it shall be t.   SHAK 718:7
tempête hante la t.   BAUD 61:9
temple drove them all out of the t.   BIBL 107:10
   Lord's anointed t.   SHAK 720:16
   Nature is a t.   BAUD 61:11
   Open the t. gates   SPEN 766:21
   polished corners of the t.   BOOK 149:24
   t. of Delight   KEAT 456:1
   t. of silence   MACA 507:15
   t. of the Holy Ghost   BIBL 112:1
   train filled the t.   BIBL 92:6
temples adapting Greek t.   PUGI 649:7
   nail into his t.   BIBL 82:32
   out of which they build t.   KRIS 473:15
   solemn t.   SHAK 733:31
   t. like a piece of a pomegranate   BIBL 91:4
   t. made with hands   BIBL 110:4
   t. of his gods   MACA 508:13
tempora O t., O mores   CICE 232:2
temporal pass through things t.   BOOK 136:4
temporary force alone is but t.   BURK 173:12
temps O t.! suspend ton vol   LAMA 476:9
tempt T. me no more   DAY- 269:8
   T. not a desperate man   SHAK 733:2
   T. not the stars   FORD 337:5
   t. the Lord thy God   BIBL 98:21
temptation endureth t.   BIBL 116:16
   enter not into t.   BIBL 103:17
   everything except t.   WILD 855:9
   get the better of t.   GRAH 367:10
   last t. is the greatest treason   ELIO 310:17
   lead us not into t.   BIBL 99:12
   maximum of t.   SHAW 741:14
   resisting t.   BECK 65:2
   resisting t.   KNOX 470:8
   t. in the wilderness   BOOK 146:8
   t. to a rich and lazy nation   KIPL 467:21
   t. to be good   BREC 155:12
   under t. to it   LOCK 497:11
   yield to t.   HOPE 406:20
temptations in spite of all t.   GILB 358:4
   protections against t.   TWAI 820:7
   t. both in wine and women   KITC 469:4
   through all t.   BOOK 135:14
tempted One thing to be t.   SHAK 723:4
   your fathers t. me   BOOK 146:8
tempus fugit inreparabile t.   VIRG 833:2
   T. abire tibi est   HORA 411:2
   T. edax rerum   OVID 590:14
   T. erat quo prima quies   VIRG 829:10
ten aren't no T. Commandments   KIPL 466:16
   as the strength of t.   TENN 800:6
   beat t. men who haven't   SHAW 739:8
   T.-sixty-six and all that   SELL 691:22
   t. thousand   BIBL 95:27
   Your starter for t.   CATC 209:7
tenacity Patience and t. of purpose   HUXL 423:9
tenantless graves stood t.   SHAK 699:4
tenants T. of life's middle   COWP 257:1
   T. of the house   ELIO 309:26
tendebantque T. manus   VIRG 830:10
tender dark and true and t.   TENN 799:13
   I'll be irreproachably t.   MAYA 528:20
   praise the t. feet   SAMB 679:15
   t. for another's pain   GRAY 370:12
   t. is the night   KEAT 456:7
   t. mercies of the wicked   BIBL 88:4
   t. years of youth   GOGO 363:10
tenderly Take her up t.   HOOD 405:10
tenderness species of t.   BYRO 191:24
   Want of t.   JOHN 440:22
tends t. and spares us   LYTE 506:7
ténébreux Je suis le t.   NERV 571:1
tenebricosum iter t.   CATU 210:5
tenement Into a clayey t.   CARE 198:9
tennis Anyone for t.   CATC 207:4

tennis (cont.):
play t. with the net down — FROS 345:11
stars' t.-balls — WEBS 844:15
Tennyson bower we shrined to T. — HARD 381:9
tenor noiseless t. of their way — GRAY 370:8
tent big t. — POLI 612:9
inside the t. pissing out — JOHN 435:10
little t. of blue — WILD 855:31
Strike the t. — LEE 487:19
tenth like a t. muse — ANON 17:14
submerged t. — BOOT 151:3
t. Muse — TROL 816:25
tents dwelling in t. — BIBL 80:4
dwell in their t. — BOOK 144:13
fold their t. — LONG 499:1
habitation among the t. of Kedar — BOOK 148:15
Israel's t. do shine — BLAK 126:26
murmured in their t. — BOOK 147:13
t. have been struck — SMUT 759:11
t. of Kedar — BIBL 90:24
t. of ungodliness — BOOK 145:15
To your t., O Israel — BIBL 85:4
ter T. sunt conati imponere — VIRG 832:16
teres t., atque rotundus — HORA 415:2
Terewth light of T. — DICK 276:18
term Invented to awe fools — JONS 446:15
termagant o'erdoing T. — SHAK 702:13
terminological t. inexactitude — CHUR 229:2
termite thought of himself as a t. — COET 238:2
terms come on perfect t. — WHIT 852:13
come to t. with Him — MOLI 552:23
happiest t. I have — SHAK 707:1
have society upon his own t. — EMER 315:16
let me go on those t. — SOCR 759:18
terra in t. pax — MISS 549:8
terrace t. walk — SWIF 783:24
terrain t. is everything — PAST 599:5
terrible appear most long and t. — LEE 487:11
Better a t. end — SCHI 683:9
eyes became so t. — BECK 64:29
isn't life a t. thing — THOM 806:11
just the t. choice — BROW 167:17
lend the eye a t. aspect — SHAK 708:16
t. as an army — BIBL 91:11
t. as hell — MILT 542:15
t. beauty is born — YEAT 873:7
T. is the temptation — BREC 155:12
T. that old life of decency — LOWE 503:4
t. to the enemy — SHAK 707:10
would not be t. — JOHN 440:9
terrier t. can define a rat — HOUS 416:13
terrified t. vague fingers — YEAT 874:1
terrifying what made them t. — MARA 521:8
territorial last t. claim — HITL 400:9
terror another t. to death — LYND 506:1
boredom and t. — WELL 846:3
From all that t. teaches — CHES 224:6
new t. to death — WETH 849:6
new t. to life — TREE 815:5
no t., brother Toby — STER 773:10
no t., Cassius, in your threats — SHAK 713:23
no t. in a bang — HITC 400:5
T. arises from a sense — KING 463:18
t. by night — BOOK 146:1
T. the human form divine — BLAK 128:6
t. to the soul of Richard — SHAK 731:29
t. to thyself — BIBL 95:7
t. without end — SCHI 683:9
Thy t., O Christ, O God — HOPK 408:6
unity against t. — BUSH 182:9
victory in spite of all t. — CHUR 229:14
terrorism democratic world and t. — BLAI 124:2
this war on t. — BUSH 182:10
trying to suppress t. — SCHU 687:4
terrorist t. and the hijacker — THAT 803:23
t. and the policeman — CONR 249:8
terrorists t. who committed — BUSH 182:8
terrorize t. a whole nation — MURR 566:5
terrors great t. of fire — PEPY 603:16
little t. — GAVA 350:16
new t. of Death — ARBU 25:18
t. of the earth — SHAK 715:13
Tess ended his sport with T. — HARD 381:4

test Beauty is the first t. — HARD 380:9
cricket t. — TEBB 792:10
Fire is the t. of gold — SENE 692:19
No t. tube can breed love — WILL 857:15
testament ministers of the new t. — BIBL 113:7
testicles requires t. — VOLT 835:4
testify t. of me — BIBL 107:19
testimonies Thy t., O Lord — BOOK 146:5
testimony t. against slavery — DOUG 291:19
t. to the whole world — FOX 339:18
testing form of very virtue at the t. point — LEWI 492:2
tetigisti T. acu — PLAU 609:10
teutonophile exaggeratedly t. — LAMB 477:15
Tewkesbury Between T. and Stroudway — GURN 374:18
text God takes a t. — HERB 393:27
great t. in Galatians — BROW 167:19
neat rivulet of t. — SHER 748:22
of that t. a pulled hen — CHAU 218:12
outside of the t. — DERR 274:4
t. was loss — CUNN 262:17
Thames clear T. bordered — MORR 560:14
look, how T., enriched — DANI 264:4
not of Gennesareth, but T. — THOM 808:3
stripling T. — ARNO 30:9
Sweet T., run softly — SPEN 768:4
T. is between me and the Duchess — WALP 837:10
T. is liquid history — BURN 177:5
T., the most loved — DENH 273:4
upon the banks of T. — JONS 446:26
youthful T. — ARNO 30:24
thank God, I t. thee — BIBL 106:12
Now t. we all our God — WINK 860:12
terrible thing, t. God — THOM 806:11
t. heaven, fasting — SHAK 697:15
T. me no thankings — SHAK 732:32
t. the goodness and the grace — TAYL 791:14
t. you for a Valentine — LOCH 497:1
thanked When I'm not t. — FIEL 327:3
thankful to be t. — BOOK 150:6
thanking sigh in t. — BROW 163:21
thankit let the Lord be t. — BURN 178:23
thankless have a t. child — SHAK 715:6
thanks deserve any t. — CATU 210:17
gives you warmest t. — CATU 210:12
give t. to God — BIBL 115:12
give t. unto thee — BOOK 137:14
give t. unto thee — BOOK 149:18
give t. unto thee, O God — BOOK 142:9
give t. unto the Lord — BOOK 149:12
In everything give t. — BIBL 115:15
return your t. — BROW 168:11
T. for mercies past — BUCK 170:2
T. for the memory — ROBI 663:16
to give t. is good — SWIN 785:3
when he had given t. — BOOK 137:16
thanksgiving before his presence with t. — BOOK 146:7
shew the voice of t. — BOOK 141:7
Tharsis Kings of T. — BOOK 144:19
that man's a man for a' t. — BURN 178:8
THOU ART T. — UPAN 822:6
thatch round the t.-eaves run — KEAT 456:22
worn the ancient t. — TENN 797:17
thaw t. wind — PROV 642:28
thcream I'll t. and thcream — CROM 260:7
theatre I like the t. — HART 383:12
shouting fire in a t. — HOLM 403:19
t. of man's life — BACO 45:16
t. of the world — MARY 527:1
This House today is a t. — BALD 53:8
theatres domes, t., temples — WORD 865:7
theatrical t. writers — SCOT 689:19
thee Dreamin' of t. — WALL 836:10
save t. and me — OWEN 590:23
theek t. our nest — BALL 56:3
theft clever t. was praiseworthy — SPEN 766:2
Property is t. — PROU 625:3
shone conscious of the t. — ROWE 671:4
t. in other poets — DRYD 297:16
theist offer the t. — AYER 44:1

them Lat t. say — MOTT 563:22
theme choose a mighty t. — MELV 531:12
Fools are my t. — BYRO 189:29
it has no t. — CHUR 231:8
t. For reason — DONN 289:2
t. Too high doth seem — GURN 374:19
themselves did not do things t. — RAVE 656:1
laid violent hands upon t. — BOOK 139:7
law unto t. — BIBL 110:24
theologians believe the t. — SALI 678:15
t. have employed — ARNO 32:2
theology golden rule in t. — MILT 546:1
schools of t. — DIDE 282:16
theorem binomial t. — GILB 358:7
Theorie Grau ist alle T. — GOET 362:1
theories let our false t. die — POPP 619:7
T. pass — ROST 670:5
theorist t. could fit — GAMO 348:8
theorize capital mistake to t. — DOYL 292:24
theory All t., dear friend, is grey — GOET 362:1
Died of a T. — DAVI 268:10
life without t. — DISR 285:23
sometimes t. — MACA 507:23
t. against the second law — EDDI 302:16
therapy T., tenth American muse — BRON 158:3
there Because it's t. — MALL 517:17
be t. when it happens — ALLE 13:14
cry over me, T., there — BOOK 144:15
I am not t. — FRYE 345:25
MACAVITY WASN'T T. — ELIO 310:20
met a man who wasn't t. — MEAR 529:16
Over t. — COHA 238:3
T. and back again — TOLK 813:1
T. but for the grace of God — BRAD 154:1
T. you go again — REAG 656:13
thou art t. — BOOK 149:17
Were you t. — SONG 763:15
you were not t. — HENR 391:18
thereby O! t. hangs a tail — SHAK 728:21
therein all that t. is — BOOK 141:1
thereof and the place t. — BOOK 147:3
thermodynamics second law of t. — EDDI 302:16
Thermopylae make a new T. — BYRO 188:24
old man of T. — LEAR 486:1
thesaurus T. in his cabin — BARR 59:19
they t. are not they — WAUG 842:9
thick ask the Gods for a t. skin — TROL 816:19
lay it on so t. — BUTL 184:4
thcream till I'm t. — CROM 260:7
t. on Severn — HOUS 416:1
t. skin a gift — ADEN 6:6
t. with corn — BOOK 144:3
thickens now the plot t. — BUCK 169:20
thicker History gets t. — TAYL 791:10
little finger shall be t. — BIBL 85:2
thicket ram caught in a t. — BIBL 80:2
thief first cries stop t. — CONG 247:4
Hang a t. when he's young — PROV 633:40
he was a t. — HEIN 389:12
honest t. — BROW 164:26
I come as a t. — BIBL 119:5
Opportunity makes a t. — PROV 641:20
postern door makes a t. — PROV 641:42
Set a t. to catch — PROV 643:2
something from the t. — SHAK 728:14
subtle t. of youth — MILT 545:12
Taffy was a t. — NURS 581:10
t. doth fear — SHAK 710:12
t. of time — YOUN 876:20
thought as bad as the t. — CHES 222:19
which is the t. — SHAK 716:19
thieves den of t. — BIBL 102:13
fell among t. — BIBL 105:4
Her t. are never hung — FERG 325:9
honour among t. — PROV 644:24
Little t. are hanged — PROV 637:45
more laws, the more t. — PROV 639:10
more t. and bandits — LAO 480:9
no receivers, no t. — PROV 635:18
One of the t. — BECK 64:17
t. break through and steal — BIBL 99:13
T. respect property — CHES 225:10
When t. fall out — PROV 647:4

thought (cont.):
oft was t. POPE 616:2
one that was never t. of BIBL 97:16
pale cast of t. SHAK 702:3
Perish the t. CIBB 231:12
put t. in a concentration camp ROOS 667:14
rear the tender t. THOM 808:12
Religion the frozen t. of men KRIS 473:15
right t. PALI 594:12
Roman t. hath struck him SHAK 694:11
single grateful t. LESS 490:20
speech created t. SHEL 745:24
strange seas of t. WORD 868:13
sudden t. BROW 165:14
sweet silent t. SHAK 737:24
tease us out of t. KEAT 455:24
T. can with difficulty visit SHEL 747:17
t. charged with emotion GIDE 356:6
T. does not crush ROET 665:5
t.-executing fires SHAK 715:16
t. in cold storage SAMU 679:16
T. is free PROV 645:9
T. is free SHAK 733:28
T. is the child of Action DISR 286:14
t. is the front SAUS 682:17
t. is viscous ADAM 2:19
T. shall be the harder ANON 23:14
t. so once; but now I know it EPIT 318:15
t.'s the slave of life SHAK 706:28
thought the t. BALL 54:16
t., word, and deed MISS 546:20
Three minutes' t. HOUS 416:12
To a green t. MARV 525:5
very t. of Thee CASW 206:14
want of t. HOOD 405:19
what he t., he uttered HEMI 390:17
white, celestial t. VAUG 825:5
wish is father to the t. PROV 647:28
working-house of t. SHAK 709:9
years of human t. too late LAB 475:3

thoughtcrime t. literally impossible ORWE 587:13

thoughts all evil t. BOOK 135:16
As man's own t. WEBS 844:24
bring my t. to an end SMIT 757:21
Cleanse the t. of our hearts BOOK 136:19
conceal their t. VOLT 834:1
examine my t. BOOK 149:20
First t. are best PROV 632:23
Good t. CAMP 195:23
have bloody t. SHAK 733:32
hospitable t. intent MILT 543:19
Hunter's waking t. AUDE 37:1
in a shroud Of t. BYRO 186:16
in the t. of children LOCK 497:4
long, long t. LONG 499:11
misleading t. SPEN 765:23
my bloody t. SHAK 729:2
my t. are not your thoughts BIBL 94:9
ought to control our t. DARW 266:9
pansies, that's for t. SHAK 704:2
present t. build our life PALI 594:15
rather than of t. KEAT 457:13
Second t. are best PROV 642:37
secret t. ALBE 11:5
Staled are my t. DYER 301:4
thoroughfare for all t. KEAT 458:12
t. and manners JOHN 437:15
t. are legible in the eye ROYD 671:17
T., boundless, deep BYRO 189:27
t. of a prisoner SOLZ 760:14
t. of men are widened TENN 797:3
t. of other men COWP 256:26
t. that arise in me TENN 792:19
T., that breathe GRAY 370:21
T. that do often lie WORD 867:18
t. within the breasts KORA 472:14
Words without t. SHAK 703:8
your love but not your t. GIBR 355:14

thousand better than a t. BOOK 145:15
blotted a t. JONS 447:3
cattle upon a t. hills BOOK 143:2
Death has a t. doors MASS 527:12

Empire lasts for a t. years CHUR 229:16
first t. days KENN 460:9
Give me a t. kisses CATU 210:7
had five t. a year THAC 803:5
night has a t. eyes BOUR 153:2
Night hath a t. eyes LYLY 505:22
not in a t. years SMIT 757:4
possessing ten t. eyes ZORO 879:1
ten t. BIBL 95:27
ten t. things LAO 480:5
t. ages in Thy sight WATT 842:7
t. doors open on to it SENE 692:20
t. shall fall BOOK 146:1
t. things to do BEVE 77:7
t. thousand slimy things COLE 241:2
t. tongues to sing WESL 847:10
t. years in thy sight BOOK 145:20
t. years of history GAIT 347:7

thousands limp father of t. JOYC 448:19
t. equally were meant SWIF 784:10
t. of gold and silver BOOK 148:13

thrall Thee hath in t. KEAT 455:9

thread crimson t. of kinship PARK 597:3
line of scarlet t. BIBL 82:25
tied, With a silken t. KEAT 454:26
with a twined t. BURT 181:20

threads hundreds of tiny t. SIGN 751:14

threaten t. to overrule him PAXM 600:8

threatened t. its life CARR 204:3
t. men live long PROV 645:10

threats no terror, Cassius, in your t. SHAK 713:23

something of t. KORA 472:8
t. unexecuted JOHN 437:22

three at t. years old LEON 489:22
confessing the T. PATR 599:17
divided into t. parts CAES 192:16
give him t. sides MONT 556:3
grant but t. BYRO 188:24
strike out t. BOIL 131:5
tell you t. times CARR 203:26
Though he was only t. MILN 538:3
T. acres and a cow POLI 613:11
T. bags full NURS 578:2
T. blind mice NURS 582:1
t. corners of the world SHAK 714:15
t. events in his life LAB 474:19
t. for a wedding PROV 640:44
t.-fourths of our life ARNO 32:4
t. gentlemen at once SHER 748:18
T. hours a day TROL 816:1
T. in One ALEX 12:9
t. is a houseful SAYI 684:5
t. is company WILD 854:17
T. may keep a secret PROV 645:11
t. merry boys are we FLET 335:7
T. minutes' thought HOUS 416:12
t. o'clock in the morning FITZ 332:14
t.-o-clock in the morning THOR 809:18
t. of us in this marriage DIAN 275:14
t.-pipe problem DOYL 292:9
t. ravens BALL 56:1
T. whole days together SUCK 779:15
T. wise men of Gotham NURS 582:3
two or t. are gathered BOOK 134:8
When shall we t. meet SHAK 718:1
where t. ways meet SOPH 761:19
where two or t. BIBL 102:3

threefold t. cord BIBL 89:26
way of superior man is t. CONF 246:15

threes Bad things come in t. PROV 627:7

threescore t. years and ten BOOK 145:21

threshold goes over the t. FULL 346:9
t. of a new house ATWO 35:12

threw t. him to a scaffold FANS 323:3

thrice deny me t. BIBL 103:13
T. is he armed SHAK 709:22

thrift T. is a great revenue PROV 645:14
Thrift, t., Horatio SHAK 699:25

thriftily men who left them t. KIPL 466:17

thriftless t. and hopeless DAVI 268:17

thrills t. the ear AUDE 38:2

thrive Bold knaves t. DRYD 295:18

He that would t. CLAR 234:2
Ill gotten goods never t. PROV 635:40
t. must first ask his wife PROV 634:13

throat 'Amen' Stuck in my t. SHAK 720:5
cut his t. before SWIF 784:12
fog in my t. BROW 167:7
her little t. around BROW 167:6
if your t. 'tis hard to slit KING 464:17
in the city's t. LOWE 503:5
murder by the t. LLOY 496:17
rustle in your dying t. FILM 330:5
scuttled ship or cut a t. BYRO 188:19
seize fate by the t. BEET 66:10
So he has cut his t. BYRO 190:11
taking life by the t. FROS 345:9
unlocked her silent t. GIBB 355:8
your sweet t. dividing t. CARE 198:14

throne beats upon a t. TENN 793:24
behind the t. PITT 607:11
Bust outlasts the t. DOBS 287:2
fell before the t. BIBL 118:13
God's t. BIBL 99:4
High on a t. MILT 542:2
his the t. DIX 286:32
I saw a great white t. BIBL 119:13
like a burnished t. ELIO 311:6
like a burnished t. SHAK 694:22
living t. GRAY 370:20
Lord sitting upon a t. BIBL 92:6
rainbow round about the t. BIBL 118:3
round about the t. BIBL 118:4
royal t. of kings SHAK 730:10
shadow of thy T. WATT 842:7
stood before the t. BIBL 118:12
that sitteth upon the t. BIBL 118:11
t. he sits on SHAK 709:3
t. of bayonets INGE 425:5
t. of bayonets YELT 875:17
t. of Denmark SHAK 699:10
t. of the heavenly grace BOOK 133:3
T. sent word to a Throne KIPL 467:2
t. was like the fiery flame BIBL 95:27
through slaughter to a t. GRAY 370:7
to a scaffold from a t. FANS 323:3
up to the t. KIPL 466:13
vacancy of the t. GIBB 354:5
what is a t. FRAN 340:7

thrones Not t. and crowns, but men ELLI 313:17
T., dominations MILT 543:22
t., or dominions BIBL 115:7

throng Leaving the tumultuous t. WORD 866:2

through let them go t. BOOK 145:7
live t. someone else FRIE 343:7
one who has gone t. it VIRG 831:10
read books t. JOHN 441:8
t. you but not from you GIBR 355:14

throw sister t. up a lot WALK 836:1
t. away SHAK 718:18
T. dirt enough PROV 645:15
t. out your dirty water PROV 630:29
who t. themselves away MENG 531:26

thrown All this t. away MARY 526:16
t. out, as good for nothing JOHN 438:19

thrush aged t. HARD 381:14
That's the wise t. BROW 165:28
t. replies SPEN 766:20

thrust guardsman's cut and t. HUXL 423:6

Thule farthest T. THOM 808:16
Ultima T. VIRG 832:12

thumb t. each other's books RUSK 673:21

thumbs both his t. are off HOFF 402:8
By the pricking of my t. SHAK 721:18

Thummim Urim and the T. BIBL 81:22

thumps t. upon your back COWP 255:2

thunder as the voice of a great t. BIBL 118:28
dawn comes up like t. KIPL 466:15
dread rattling t. SHAK 733:33
falling houses t. JOHN 438:1
Glorious the t.'s roar SMAR 755:14
steal my t. DENN 273:14
such sweet t. SHAK 726:28
surge and t. LANG 478:11

time (cont.):

T. is that wherein	HIPP 399:20
t. is the greatest innovator	BACO 47:12
T. is the great physician	DISR 285:32
T. is the measure	AUCT 36:22
t. is the medium	MANN 520:3
T. is too slow	VAN 824:4
T., like an ever-rolling stream	WATT 842:7
T. makes these decay	CARE 198:6
t. of asking	BOOK 138:19
t. of darkness	BREC 156:4
t. of our tribulation	BOOK 134:21
T., Place	DRYD 297:13
T. present and time past	ELIO 309:3
t. remembered	SWIN 784:20
t. runs	MARL 522:11
t.'s arrow	EDDI 302:14
T.'s devouring hand	BRAM 154:17
T.'s glory is to calm	SHAK 737:13
t. shall throw a dart	EPIT 319:15
T.'s iron feet	MONT 556:11
T.'s noblest offspring	BERK 72:18
T. spent on any item	PARK 597:6
T. stays, *we* go	DOBS 287:5
T.'s thievish progress	SHAK 738:6
T.'s wheel runs back or stops	BROW 167:11
T.'s wingèd chariot	MARV 525:12
t. that shall surely be	AING 9:18
T. that's lost	BUCK 170:2
t., that takes survey	SHAK 706:28
T., the avenger	BYRO 186:22
T. the devourer	OVID 590:14
t. the longest distance	WILL 858:5
T. the subtle thief	MILT 545:12
t. to be in earnest	JOHN 436:13
t. to every purpose	BIBL 89:23
t. to read play-bills	BURN 176:24
t. to think before I speak	DARW 267:2
t. to win this game	DRAK 293:10
T. travels in divers paces	SHAK 697:13
T. was away and somewhere else	MACN 513:11
t. was out of joint	STRA 778:11
T. we may comprehend	BROW 162:27
T. which destroys all things	BHAG 78:4
t., which is the author	BACO 45:7
t. will come	DISR 284:3
t. will doubt of Rome	BYRO 189:3
t. will run back	MILT 540:26
t. will tell	PROV 645:20
T. with a gift of tears	SWIN 784:22
T. works wonders	PROV 645:21
t. ylost	CHAU 221:8
t. you enjoy wasting	MISQ 548:21
T., you old gipsy man	HODG 402:1
T., you thief	HUNT 421:7
to fill the t. available	PARK 597:5
To it comes T.	BARN 59:11
took t. to consider	ASTE 34:17
to sell t.	TAWN 791:5
to the church on t.	LERN 490:7
triumphed over t.	RALE 654:9
uncertain balance of proud t.	GREE 371:24
unconscionable t. dying	CHAR 217:10
use your t.	HERR 396:18
very good t. it was	JOYC 448:6
waste of t. and effort	VEBL 825:20
ways By which T. kills us	SITW 753:16
whips and scorns of t.	SHAK 702:1
whirligig of t.	SHAK 736:9
wisest of all counsellors, T.	PERI 603:28
womb of t.	HEIN 389:16
world enough, and t.	MARV 525:10

timely t. compliance — FIEL 326:11
t. utterance — WORD 867:4

timeo t. Danaos et dona ferentes — VIRG 829:6

times bad t. just around — COWA 253:20

blissful old t.	BLAM 128:15
coldness of the t.	TENN 795:31
five t. did I say	WORD 865:5
It was the best of t.	DICK 281:3
like the.they live in	ALI 12:17
live in interesting t.	KENN 460:21
live in interesting t.	SAYI 685:2
method of working fits the t.	MACH 511:5
nature of the t. deceased	SHAK 707:18
Oh, the t.	CICE 232:2
one year's experience 30 t.	CARR 201:10
Other t., other manners	PROV 641:22
praiser of past t.	HORA 409:10
signs of the t.	BIBL 101:25
t. begin to wax old	BIBL 96:23
T. change	PROV 645:22
T. go by turns	SOUT 765:3
T. has made many ministries	BAGE 50:11
t. in which a genius	ADAM 2:1
t. past	HERR 396:8
t. that try men's souls	PAIN 592:13
t. they are a-changin'	DYLA 302:4
t. will not mend	PARK 596:21
Top people take *The T.*	ADVE 8:23
wise at all t.	PLIN 609:15

timet *flagitium t.* — HORA 414:4

timing t. of your death — TACI 787:5

timor *T. mortis conturbat me* — DUNB 299:10

Timothy T. has passed — EPIT 319:13
T. Winters comes to school — CAUS 211:9

tin cat on a hot t. roof — WILL 858:3
cheap t. trays — MASE 527:4
corrugated t. roof — BEEC 65:11

tincture Actions receive their t. — DEFO 270:19
no t. of philosophy — RUSS 675:3
t. in the blood — DEFO 270:18

ting bells of Hell go t.-a-ling — MILI 535:15

tingle ears shall t. — BIBL 83:27

tingling It's t. fresh — ADVE 7:40

tinker T., Tailor — NURS 582:4

tinkering rule of intelligent t. — EHRL 304:14

tinkers no work for t.' hands — PROV 635:10

tinklings t. lull the distant folds — GRAY 370:1

tinned smoked salmon and t. — WILS 859:9

tintinnabulation To the t. — POE 610:16

tiny My t. watching eye — DE L 272:12
Your t. hand is frozen — GIAC 354:3

tip depends on the t. — FILM 330:2
Within the nether t. — COLE 240:24

Tippecanoe soldier of T. — POLI 612:23
T. and Tyler, too — POLI 613:12

Tipperary It's in T. — TROL 816:12
long way to T. — JUDG 449:4
notorious county of T. — KOHL 470:14

tipple Fishes, that t. — LOVE 502:4

tippled Have ye t. drink — KEAT 455:15

tiptoe Dance t., bull — BUNT 171:1
jocund day Stands t. — SHAK 730:30
stand a t. — SHAK 709:6
sweet peas, on t. — KEAT 455:3

tired Give me your t., your poor — LAZA 485:3
heart gets t. too — VERG 826:5
He was so t. — ROLF 666:10
I'm t. — GINS 359:3
Thou art t. — ARNO 29:15
t. her head — BIBL 85:34
t., keep going — TUBM 818:9
t. of Bath — AUST 41:20
t. of being a woman — SEXT 693:5
t. of London — JOHN 442:10
t. of Love — BELL 68:9
t. of the struggle — GOET 362:14
t. the sun with talking — CORY 252:13
woman who always was t. — EPIT 318:1

Tiresias T., old man with wrinkled dugs — ELIO 311:13

tiresome except the t. — VOLT 834:7

tiring T. thy wits — DANI 264:7

tirra T. lirra — TENN 796:18

tissue beautiful feminine t. — HARD 381:2

Titan like thy glory, T. — SHEL 746:4

titanic furniture on the deck of the T. — MORT 562:7
T. sails at dawn — DYLA 301:14
t. wars had groined — OWEN 591:8

Tite *O T. tute Tati* — ENNI 316:3

tithes t. of mint and cumin — BIBL 102:18

Titian at heart about T. — RUSK 674:4

title farcèd t. — SHAK 709:3
feel his t. Hang loose — SHAK 722:13

gained no t.	POPE 615:19
needed no royal t.	SPEN 766:5
right, t., and possession	BOOK 150:23
t. from a better man I stole	STEV 777:3
whatever t. suit thee	BURN 177:6

titles rich for t. — PEAR 601:5
their t. take — CHAN 215:7
T. are shadows — DEFO 271:4
T. are tinsel — SHEL 747:9
T. distinguish the mediocre — SHAW 741:15
t. thou hast given away — SHAK 715:3

tittle t. tattle. prittle prattle — BURN 177:3

titwillow Willow, t. — GILB 357:16

Tityre *T., tu patulae recubans* — VIRG 831:12

toad Give me your arm, old t. — LARK 481:12
let the t. work — LARK 481:11
like the t., ugly — SHAK 696:15
not so old as the t. — THOM 807:4
rather be a t. — SHAK 728:26
rose to a pitch-black t. — YESE 875:20
squat like a t. — MILT 543:15
t. beneath the harrow — KIPL 467:3

toads imaginary gardens with real t. — MOOR 557:15
inconstant t. — MONT 554:9

toast Let the t. pass — SHER 748:14
My t. would be — ADAM 3:16
never had a piece of t. — PAYN 600:9
t. that pleased the most — DIBD 276:5

toasted cheese—t., mostly — STEV 775:23
his enemies, 'T.-cheese' — CARR 203:28

tobacco divine t. were — SPEN 767:17
For thy sake, T. — LAMB 476:20
leave off t. — LAMB 477:7
lives without t. — MOLI 552:5
that tawney weed t. — JONS 446:1

tocsin t. of the soul — BYRO 189:6

today get where I am t. without — CATC 207:31
if T. be sweet — FITZ 331:20
I have lived t. — DRYD 297:6
let us do something t. — COLL 242:24
live t. — MART 524:3
my lot t., yours tomorrow — EPIT 318:12
never jam t. — CARR 203:6
Not of t. Or yesterday — SOPH 761:15
standing here t. — JOHN 435:4
these gave their t. — EDMO 303:18
t. I am fifty-five — REED 657:3
T. if ye will hear — BOOK 146:8
T. is the last day — YELT 875:18
T. I suffer — LESS 490:19
T. shalt thou be with me — BIBL 106:25
t. the struggle — AUDE 38:12
T. we have naming of parts — REED 657:4
T. you; tomorrow me — PROV 645:24
to-morrow as t. — SHAK 736:17
we gave our t. — EPIT 320:3
What Manchester says t. — PROV 646:24
what you can do t. — PROV 639:41
will not hang myself t. — CHES 223:25

toe big t. ends up making a hole — EINS 306:4
clerical, printless t. — BROO 159:8
light fantastic t. — MILT 539:24
t. of the peasant — SHAK 704:14

toes Pobble who has no t. — LEAR 486:9

toff Saunter along like a t. — HARG 382:10

together all that believed were t. — BIBL 109:14
keep them t. — JOHN 441:1
lived comfortably so long t. — GAY 350:19
Men work t. — FROS 345:4
persons acting t. — ARAB 25:11
t. and collect things — HORA 409:17

togetherness spaces in your t. — GIBR 355:15

toil bleared, smeared with t. — HOPK 407:7
blood, t., tears and sweat — CHUR 229:12
day in t. — QUAR 651:9
Death and T. — VIRG 830:9
Double, double t. and trouble — SHAK 721:15
Horny-handed sons of t. — SALI 679:1
horny hands of t. — LOWE 502:18
mock their useful t. — GRAY 370:4
slumber is more sweet than t. — TENN 797:13
strong t. of grace — SHAK 696:7

they t. not	BIBL 99:18	T. do thy worst	DRYD 297:6
t. after virtue	LAMB 477:13	T. for the young	AUDE 38:12
t. and not to seek for rest	IGNA 424:14	t. I die	LESS 490:19
T., envy, want	JOHN 438:6	t. is another day	MITC 551:5
unrequited t.	LINC 494:5	T. is another day	PROV 645:27
with t. of breath	COLE 239:15	T. never comes	PROV 645:28
toiled Master, we have t.	BIBL 104:22	t.'s life's too late	MART 524:3
toiling t. upward in the night	LONG 499:9	t. there's no knowing	MEDI 530:5
toils poorly recompense their t.	COLL 242:21	t. to be brave	ARMS 28:16
token t. of a covenant	BIBL 79:28	t. we shall die	BIBL 92:22
t. snatched from her arm	HORA 411:14	T. we shall sail again	HORA 411:12
tokens Words are the t.	BACO 45:14	Unborn T.	FITZ 331:20
told half was not t. me	BIBL 84:28	we thought was for t.	BENN 69:20
I t. you so	EPIT 317:10	what t. may bring	HORA 411:13
not t. even half	MARC 521:9	**tomorrows** For your t. these gave	
not what we were formerly t.	BLUN 129:12		EDMO 303:18
our fathers have t. us	BOOK 142:11	**tomtit** little t. Sang	GILB 357:16
phrase, 'I t. you so.'	BYRO 189:21	**tone** t. of the company	CHES 223:2
plato t. him: he couldn't	CUMM 262:8	**tones** t. are remembered not	SHEL 744:18
t. my wrath	BLAK 127:22	**tongs** taken with the t.	BIBL 92:8
t. you from the beginning	BIBL 93:19	t. and the bones	SHAK 726:24
Toledo T. trusty	BUTL 183:15	**tongue** Bite out the t.	ROBE 663:5
tolerable Life would be t.	LEWI 492:6	bridleth not his t.	BIBL 116:20
tolerance such a thing as t.	WILS 859:20	cannot resist a man's t.	COLL 243:9
T. the essential	PHIL 605:15	each carping t.	BRAD 154:11
tolerate like, or at least t.	TREV 815:9	Englissh sweete upon his t.	CHAU 218:13
not to t. the intolerant	POPP 619:3	eye, and such a t.	SHAK 714:20
toleration t. produced mutual indulgence		fallen by the t.	BIBL 97:25
	GIBB 354:4	fellows of infinite t.	SHAK 709:12
toll T. for the brave	COWP 255:18	give dust a t.	HERB 394:3
t. me back from thee	KEAT 456:11	grow a second t.	MONT 554:15
tolle T. lege	AUGU 39:8	has a raucle t.	BURN 177:13
tollis t. peccata mundi	MISS 549:19	him whose strenuous t.	KEAT 456:1
tolls for whom the bell t.	DONN 290:4	his t. Dropped manna	MILT 542:3
Tom Ground control to Major T.	BOWI 153:17	hold your t.	DONN 289:1
Poor T.'s a-cold	SHAK 716:4	I held my t.	BOOK 141:27
spurious brat, T. Jones	RICH 660:17	I must hold my t.	SHAK 699:23
T. he was a piper's son	NURS 582:6	in the vulgar t.	BOOK 138:5
T. Pearse	BALL 56:8	into his mother t.	TYND 821:4
T., Tom, the piper's son	NURS 582:7	iron t. of midnight	SHAK 727:9
Uncle T. Cobbleigh	BALL 56:8	I would feel my t.	HEAN 387:12
tomatoes babies in the t.	GINS 359:1	Keep thy t. from evil	BOOK 141:21
tomb blossom on the t.	CRAB 257:9	Kepe wel they t.	CHAU 219:16
confined into a t.	VAUG 825:13	Let thy t. acquire	TALM 789:11
empty in thy t.	KING 463:4	lies of t. and pen	CHES 224:6
fair Fidele's grassy t.	COLL 243:10	my t. could utter	TENN 792:19
in the silent t.	WORD 869:13	my t. from evil-speaking	BOOK 138:13
like what it is—a t.	SHEL 744:15	My t. is the pen	BOOK 142:12
mother to the t.	MACA 508:21	My t. swore	EURI 321:9
sea was made his t.	BARN 59:9	my t. the mystery telling	THOM 805:4
tell the lover's t.	THOM 805:18	nor t. to speak	LENT 489:15
this side the t.	BYRO 186:4	of a slow t.	BIBL 80:39
thought to your t.	HORA 412:12	our t. with joy	BOOK 148:24
threefold, fourfold t.	BASS 61:4	ox is treading on my t.	AESC 6:12
t. by the side of the sea	POE 610:15	rolls it under his t.	HENR 392:7
t. of a mediocre talent	SMIT 757:9	sharp t.	IRVI 425:21
t. of love	CASA 206:3	Sing, my t.	FORT 338:14
t. of wit	CAVE 211:18	speaking the same t.	MAZZ 529:12
tombs from the t. a doleful sound	WATT 842:3	still t. makes wise head	PROV 643:36
in the cool t.	SAND 680:3	tip of the t.	NABO 566:16
t. of all regions	MISS 550:6	t. always returns	PROV 645:29
tombstone end of the fight is at t.	KIPL 467:1	t. a sharp sword	BOOK 143:15
t. where he lies	LONG 499:12	t. can no man tame	BIBL 116:24
written on its t.	DAVI 268:10	t. freezes into silence	SAPP 680:22
tomcat t. lies stretched flat	HUGH 418:7	t. In every wound	SHAK 713:13
Tommy Little T. Tucker	NURS 580:1	t. is the clapper	SHAK 727:26
T. this, an' Tommy that	KIPL 467:17	t. not understood	BOOK 150:19
Tomnoddy my Lord T.	BARH 58:7	t. of the dumb	BIBL 93:10
tomorrow Boast not thyself of t.	BIBL 89:3	t. shall be slit	NURS 581:11
build our life of t.	PALI 594:15	t. That Shakespeare spake	WORD 866:5
for t. we die	PROV 630:47	t. to conceive	SHAK 727:1
For your t. we gave	EPIT 320:3	t. to persuade	CLAR 233:6
Here today—in next week t.	GRAH 368:2	t. Won't work at all	VIRG 831:11
jam t.	CARR 203:6	treasure of our t.	DANI 264:8
Jam t.	PROV 636:45	use of my oracular t.	SHER 748:14
Leave t. behind	COWA 253:9	voice and t.	AUGU 39:5
Never put off till t.	PROV 639:41	while I held my t.	BOOK 141:16
no dividend from time's t.	SASS 682:7	yield to the t.	BIER 121:4
put off till t.	PUNC 649:17	**tongued** t. with fire	ELIO 309:15
This, no t. hath	DÓNN 288:25	**tongueless** t. vigil	SWIN 784:19
Today you; t. me	PROV 645:24	**tongues** airy t.	MILT 539:1
T., and to-morrow	SHAK 722:22	Had I a hundred t.	VIRG 830:11
t. as to-day	SHAK 736:17	Hush your t.	HORA 412:14

lack t. to praise	SHAK 738:11		
multitude of t.	BREN 156:8		
multitude of t.	HAND 379:6		
nor spoke with t. of gold	RICH 660:7		
painted full of t.	SHAK 707:2		
speak in our t.	BIBL 109:13		
thousand t. to sing	WESL 847:10		
time in the t.	SHAK 735:2		
t. in trees	SHAK 696:15		
t. like as of fire	BIBL 109:12		
t. of living flame	AUBE 35:14		
t. of men and of angels	BIBL 112:14		
t., they shall cease	BIBL 112:14		
t. too should be free	ERAS 316:18		
t. were all broken	DYLA 301:15		
Walls have t.	SWIF 784:5		
tonic Hatred is a t.	BALZ 57:3		
tonight Not t., Josepehine	NAPO 568:10		
tons Sixteen t.	TRAV 815:1		
too T. kind, too kind	NIGH 576:7		
we are t. menny	HARD 380:14		
took 'E went an' t.	KIPL 468:1		
t. a man's life with him	CARL 199:18		
tool edged t. that grows keener	IRVI 425:21		
humble as a t.	FUGA 346:2		
Man is a t.-making animal	FRAN 341:11		
Man is a t.-using animal	CARL 200:19		
Science is an edged t.	PEAC 600:13		
tooled t. in a post-chaise	BYRO 192:8		
tools bad workman blames his t.	PROV 627:8		
Give us the t.	CHUR 229:19		
quarrel with their t.	BYRO 188:5		
secrets are edged t.	DRYD 296:26		
t. to him that can handle them	CARL 199:17		
Toome On the Bridge of T.	CARB 197:17		
tooth danger of her former t.	SHAK 721:2		
hadde alwey a coltes t.	CHAU 220:13		
red in t. and claw	TENN 795:17		
returns to the sore t.	PROV 645:29		
sharper than a serpent's t.	SHAK 715:6		
t. for tooth	BIBL 81:21		
where each t.-point goes	KIPL 467:3		
toothache endure the t.	SHAK 727:32		
Venerable Mother T.	HEAT 388:6		
toothpaste t. is out of the tube	HALD 376:15		
top always room at the t.	PROV 644:21		
always room at the t.	WEBS 844:5		
I shall die at the t.	SWIF 784:15		
Life is a t.	GREV 372:15		
t. of it reached to heaven	BIBL 80:9		
T. of the world	FILM 328:1		
T. people	ADVE 8:23		
t. thing in the world	KEAT 458:10		
You're the t.	PORT 619:20		
toper Lo! the poor t.	CRAB 257:16		
topics providing t. of amusement	SWIF 781:26		
two t., yourself and me	JOHN 442:7		
topless t. towers of Ilium	MARL 522:9		
topmost on the t. twig	ROSS 669:11		
topography T. displays no favourites			
	BISH 122:8		
Torah found in the T.	ELEA 306:13		
garments of the T.	ZOHA 878:11		
only through the T.	ZOHA 878:6		
T. are likened to fire	MIDR 534:17		
T., hard like iron	TALM 789:32		
T. in Edom	MIDR 534:18		
Turn it [T.]	TALM 789:10		
torch t. borne in the wind	CHAP 216:2		
t. of life	LUCR 504:10		
t. passed to a new generation	KENN 460:5		
Truth, like a t.	HAMI 378:12		
we throw The t.	MCCR 509:17		
torches Lighting our little t.	COKA 238:9		
teach the t.	SHAK 732:7		
t. of the tomb	LAND 478:2		
torchlight t. procession	O'SU 589:8		
Tories both T.	BOSW 152:4		
T. born wicked	ANON 18:20		
T. own no argument	BROW 163:20		
torment measure of our t.	KIPL 465:21		
More grievous t.	KEAT 455:12		
most hateful t. for men	HERO 395:13		

torment (*cont.*):
no t. touch them · BIBL 96:28
smoke of their t. · BIBL 119:2
tormenting t. the people · NAPO 568:5
torments many t. lie · CIBB 231:10
t. also may in length of time · MILT 542:6
T. not moved · ALAB 10:9
tornado set off a t. in Texas · LORE 501:1
torpedo becomes a t. · JOHN 438:25
torpedoes Damn the t. · FARR 324:13
torrent Time is a violent t. · AURE 40:11
t. of his fate · JOHN 438:11
torrents t. of her myriad universe · TENN 797:14
torso remain only a t. · ERHA 320:7
tortoise How t.-like · MARV 525:17
'T.' is a insect · PUNC 649:22
torture tire T. and Time · BYRO 186:23
t. one poor word · DRYD 296:11
t. them, into believing · NEWM 572:10
t. to death · DOST 291:1
tortured T. with the telephone generator · BLY 129:15
torturer t.'s horse scratches · AUDE 37:17
tortures T. are a dangerous invention · MONT 555:10
Tory deep burning hatred for the T. Party · BEVA 76:13
Loyalty the T.'s secret weapon · KILM 462:17
Thirteen years of T. misrule · POLI 613:10
to like T. MPs · CAMP 194:14
T. and Whig in turns · SMIT 758:6
T. Corps d'Armée · GLAD 360:3
T. men and Whig measures · DISR 285:17
wise T. · JOHN 443:10
tossed t. to and fro · BIBL 114:5
you t. and gored · BOSW 152:7
total t. solution · GOER 361:10
totalitarianism under the name of t. · GAND 348:11
totter t. into vogue · WALP 837:14
totters Who t. forth · SHEL 747:5
totus *et in se ipso* t. · HORA 415:2
touch exquisite t. · SCOT 689:28
gently t. a nettle · PROV 635:28
little t. of Harry · SHAK 708:20
make attractive with his t. · HORA 409:9
men who first t. with words · SKAR 753:18
Nelson t. · NELS 570:2
nothing, Can t. him further · SHAK 721:3
One t. of nature · SHAK 734:19
puts it not unto the t. · MONT 556:15
T.— for there is a spirit · WORD 866:21
T. me not · BIBL 108:38
T. not the cat · SCOT 689:12
t. of earthly years · WORD 869:9
t. of the unknown · CANE 196:22
t. the hills · BOOK 147:10
very t. of the letter · NIN 576:8
wants the natural t. · SHAK 722:3
touched t. none that he did not adorn · EPIT 319:4
t. thy lips · BIBL 92:8
Who t. my clothes · BIBL 103:32
touches Each of us t. one place · JALA 428:16
silent t. of time · BURK 176:7
t. of sweet harmony · SHAK 725:10
Who t. this touches a man · WHIT 852:6
toucheth He that t. pitch · BIBL 97:18
tough in t. joints · RUNY 672:11
T., and devilish sly · DICK 277:24
t. get going · KENN 460:17
T. on crime · BLAI 123:17
When the going gets t. · PROV 646:47
toughness T. doesn't have to come · FEIN 324:22
tourism t. is their religion · RUNC 672:8
What an odd thing t. is · BRYS 169:3
tourist loathsome is the British t. · KILV 462:18
whisper to the t. · BEER 66:2
tourmente *l'infini me* t. · MUSS 566:10
tout *capable de* t. · VOLT 835:7
T. passe · ANON 22:12
toves slithy t. · CARR 202:21

tower build a t. · BIBL 105:25
Child Roland to the dark t. · SHAK 716:5
fall'n at length that t. · TENN 798:22
Fighting in the captain's t. · DYLA 301:14
Giotto's t. · LONG 499:6
Julius Caesar's ill-erected t. · SHAK 731:5
prisoner in the T. · FABY 322:11
to the Dark T. came · BROW 165:12
t. of David · BIBL 91:4
t. of nine storeys begins · LAO 480:11
t. of strength · SHAK 731:26
watchman on the lonely t. · SCOT 688:18
with a t. and bells · CRAB 257:8
with the blasted t. · NERV 571:1
towered t. cities please us · MILT 539:30
towering own t. style · CHES 225:20
towers branchy between t. · HOPK 407:6
cloud-capped t. · SHAK 733:31
from a hundred t. · TENN 793:19
tell the t. thereof · BOOK 142:25
t. of Afrasiab · MEHM 530:6
Whispering from her t. · ARNO 31:16
ye antique t. · GRAY 370:10
towery T. city · HOPK 407:6
town Country in the t. · MART 524:12
country t. is my detestation · BURN 177:3
destroy the t. to save it · ANON 18:7
Dirty old t. · MACC 509:12
green country t. · PENN 602:20
haunted t. it is to me · LANG 478:9
leave your own t. · VERG 826:6
little t. of Bethlehem · BROO 160:5
lived in a pretty how t. · CUMM 262:3
man made the t. · COWP 256:8
man made the t. · PROV 633:7
never go down to the end of the t. · MILN 538:3
retreat near the t. · WYCH 871:10
sounding through the t. · BALL 54:7
spreading of the hideous t. · MORR 560:14
studies it in t. · COWP 256:1
tavern in the t. · SONG 763:13
t.-crier spoke my lines · SHAK 702:12
way that takes the t. · HERB 393:20
towns London, thou art of t. · ANON 18:17
Seven wealthy t. · ANON 20:9
too long in country t. · CATH 209:14
toy be the t. of man · WOLL 863:8
foolish thing was but a t. · SHAK 736:11
toys brooches and t. · STEV 776:21
Deceive boys with t. · LYSA 506:3
misuse, then cast their t. away · COWP 255:5
toyshop moving t. of the heart · POPE 618:6
trace t. unusual things · WINC 860:10
traces on winter's t. · SWIN 784:19
tracing fitful t. of a portal · STEV 774:10
track flying on our t. · THOM 808:24
leaves no t. · LAO 480:1
T. twenty nine · GORD 366:6
tracks hungry on the t. · CRAN 258:17
staring at its own t. · MAND 519:4
tract left a little t. · WILD 856:1
trade all is seared with t. · HOPK 407:7
articles of t. · ALBE 11:4
arts of t. · DYER 301:6
autocrat: that's my t. · CATH 209:18
commands the t. · RALE 654:8
Every man to his t. · PROV 631:30
from the vulgar t. · MARL 522:17
great t. · BURK 173:6
in London only is a t. · DRYD 296:23
Irish poets, learn your t. · YEAT 875:7
It is his t. · HEIN 389:17
People of the same t. · SMIT 756:2
There isn't any T. · HERB 393:13
T. follows the flag · PROV 645:32
t. to make tables · JOHN 439:17
tricks in every t. · PROV 644:14
Two of a t. never agree · PROV 645:46
us that t. in love · SHAK 695:4
War is the t. of kings · DRYD 296:6
wheels of t. · HUME 420:3
trades Jack of all t. · PROV 636:44
live by twa t. · SCOT 689:11

tradesmen bow, ye t. · GILB 356:15
trade unionism t. of the married · SHAW 741:6
trade unionist British T. · BEVI 77:8
trading t. on the blood · LEE 487:18
tradition revolting against their t. · GRAN 368:10
t. Approves · CLOU 237:3
t. is a fence · TALM 789:5
T. is entirely different · STRA 778:18
T. means giving votes to · CHES 225:12
t. objects to their being disqualified · CHES 225:13
traditions those barbarous t. · FINK 327:12
traduced t. Joseph K. · KAFK 452:5
traffic Hushing the latest t. · BRID 156:19
means of t. · MARL 522:17
roar of London's t. · CATC 208:22
trade and t. · PUSH 650:22
t. of Jacob's ladder · THOM 808:2
two hours' t. · SHAK 732:3
trafficking permitted t. · KORA 471:7
tragedies All t. are finished · BYRO 188:17
t. of antiquity · STOP 777:18
tragedy blustering about Imperial T. · BROW 161:6
comedy is t. that happens · CART 204:12
composition of a t. · VOLT 835:4
convenient in t. · ANOU 24:8
element of t. · ELIO 307:27
Fate wrote her a t. · BEER 66:6
first time as t. · BARN 59:4
first time as t. · MARX 526:8
get t. where the tree · WITT 861:7
go, litel myn t. · CHAU 221:11
it is a t. · AUST 41:10
I will write you a t. · FITZ 332:8
out of it simply a t. · WILD 855:28
That is their t. · WILD 854:21
t., comedy, history · SHAK 701:15
T. is clean · ANOU 24:9
t. is thus an imitation · ARIS 27:19
t. of a man · OLIV 585:2
t. of a man who has found · BARR 60:2
t. of Science · HUXL 423:5
t. of the age · DU B 298:7
t. of the classical languages · MADA 514:1
T. ought to be a great kick · LAWR 484:2
t. to those that feel · WALP 837:21
weak, washy way of true t. · KAVA 453:15
what t. means · STOP 778:2
You *may* abuse a t. · JOHN 439:17
tragic I acted so t. · HARG 382:11
spirits in the t. stream · SOYI 765:5
t. and passionate · FLAU 333:9
t. failure · ELIO 307:18
T. Muse first trod the stage · POPE 618:3
tragical Merry and t. · SHAK 727:5
trahison t. *des clercs* · BEND 69:11
trahit T. *sua quemque voluptas* · VIRG 831:20
trail long, long t. · KING 463:19
t. has its own stern code · SERV 692:24
trailing t. clouds of glory · WORD 867:8
train biggest electric t. · WELL 846:1
charge of the clattering t. · BEAV 64:1
clattering t. · ANON 21:12
express-t. drew up there · THOM 806:16
headlight of an oncoming t. · DICK 282:8
light of the oncoming t. · LOWE 503:10
like a runaway t. · CONL 248:2
pack, and take a t. · BROO 159:9
read in the t. · WILD 854:25
Runs the red electric t. · BETJ 76:1
rush in the t. · THOM 808:24
shaves and takes a t. · WHIT 850:13
Shaw is like a t. · LEIG 488:12
t. filled the temple · BIBL 92:6
t. is arriving on time · MUSS 566:13
t. of events · AMER 14:5
t. take the strain · ADVE 7:44
T. up a child · BIBL 88:31
waited for the t. · TENN 793:17
trained We t. hard · MISQ 549:2
traitor hate the t. · DANI 264:11
shot dead the household t. · HOUS 416:7

TRAITORS · **TREES** 1127

t. to learning JOHN 434:2
traitors fears do make us t. SHAK 722:2
form of our t. WEST 848:20
hate t. and the treason love DRYD 295:30
tram not even a bus, I'm a t. HARE 382:9
trammel t. up the consequence SHAK 719:6
tramp why the lady is a t. HART 383:12
trample t. the very values RATH 655:13
t. the vices AUGU 39:23
trampling right of t. on them CHIL 226:2
trance fell into a t. BIBL 109:25
tranced t. summer-night KEAT 454:23
trances t. of the blast COLE 240:1
tranquil Farewell the t. mind SHAK 728:30
man of humanity is t. CONF 246:4
t. current of domestic happiness BRUN 168:22
tranquillity chaos remembered in t. THUR 810:13
divine T. TENN 797:16
Fame and t. MONT 555:9
feeling of inward t. FORB 336:14
moments of t. VOLT 834:14
overcomes male by t. LAO 480:10
recollected in t. WORD 870:3
T. Base here ARMS 28:19
t. remembered in emotion PARK 596:10
transcendental of a t. kind GILB 357:19
T. moonshine CARL 200:15
transformed t. into a gigantic insect KAFK 452:3
transgression keeps himself from t. TALM 790:3
there is no t. BIBL 110:28
transgressions wounded for our t. BIBL 94:4
transgressors numbered with the t. BIBL 94:6
way of t. BIBL 88:7
transient t. is the smile DYER 301:8
T. lustre WRIG 870:20
transit *O quam cito t. gloria mundi* THOM 804:14
Sic t. gloria mundi ANON 23:12
transitory this t. life BOOK 137:8
translate such as cannot write, t. DENH 273:8
t. Epictetus JOHN 438:24
translated bless thee! thou art t. SHAK 726:15
T. Daughter, come AUDE 36:23
t. into another tongue BIBL 97:6
t. into Italian WHAR 849:8
t. the Bible into TYND 821:4
translation mistake in the t. VANB 823:17
t. is no translation SYNG 786:8
T. it is that openeth BIBL 78:11
t. of the Bible WHAT 849:19
t.'s thief MARV 525:15
unfaithful to the t. BORG 151:9
vanity of t. SHEL 747:10
what is lost in t. FROS 345:12
translations hold t. not unlike HOWE 417:4
performed in German t. FRED 342:3
transmigrates elements once out of it, it t. SHAK 695:7
transmit t. but do not create CONF 246:6
transmutations delighted with t. NEWT 574:2
transport share the t. WORD 869:13
transported t. and ravished TRAH 814:12
trapeze on the flying t. LEYB 492:19
trappings t. and the suits of woe SHAK 699:16
traps recognize the t. MACH 511:10
trash society founded on t. SAYE 682:19
steals t. SHAK 728:23
traurig *ich so t. bin* HEIN 389:9
travaileth t. in pain BIBL 111:4
travel books of t. ELIO 308:5
in a moment t. thither WORD 867:16
Men t. faster now CATH 209:12
obliged to t. again CHAR 217:7
preserve all that t. SWIF 783:7
real way to t. GRAH 368:2
Some minds improve by t. HOOD 405:24
T. broadens the mind PROV 645:33
t. broadens the mind; but CHES 225:16
t. by land or by water BOOK 134:24
t. for travel's sake STEV 775:18
t. from Dan to Beersheba STER 772:10
t. hopefully PROV 636:13
t. hopefully is a better thing STEV 775:27
t. I'm too late RICH 661:3
t. in the direction of our fear BERR 75:2
T., in the younger sort BACO 48:9
T. light JUVE 451:11
T. them HABI 375:5
two classes of t. BENC 69:8
whole object of t. CHES 225:18
travelled care which way he t. BEAV 63:14
took the one less t. FROS 344:22
t. a good deal in Concord THOR 809:10
t. among unknown men WORD 866:6
traveller fellow t. ANON 20:15
good t. has no LAO 480:1
good t. is one LIN 495:7
lost t.'s dream BLAK 125:9
No t. returns SHAK 702:2
said the T. DE L 272:6
spurs the lated t. SHAK 721:6
t. betwixt life and death WORD 869:7
t. from an antique land SHEL 745:15
t. need have no scruple BAED 49:18
wise t. never despises GOLD 363:18
travellers returning t. BYAT 184:22
t. must be content SHAK 696:19
t. of eternity BASH 61:1
travelling t. at twenty miles a second EDDI 302:17
T. is the ruin BURN 176:22
travels t. fastest PROV 634:17
t. the fastest KIPL 466:13
t. the world in search MOOR 557:6
trawler When seagulls follow a t. CANT 197:10
tray T., Blanch SHAK 716:6
treachery fear their subjects' t. SHAK 710:7
killed with my own t. SHAK 704:25
not an absolution for t. ASHC 33:11
ready for any t. WILL 857:2
t. cannot trust JUNI 450:4
t. of the intellectuals BEND 69:11
tread Doth close behind him t. COLE 241:7
face with an undaunted t. STEV 776:16
May we t. rejoicingly WILL 858:16
so airy a t. TENN 798:7
softly t., said Christabel COLE 239:5
t. on classic ground ADDI 4:27
T. softly YEAT 873:14
t. the verge of Jordan WILL 857:10
Where'er you t. POPE 618:2
treason bloody t. flourished SHAK 713:10
[corporations] cannot commit t. COKE 238:16
Gunpowder T. and Plot ANON 19:20
hate traitors and the t. love DRYD 295:30
In trust I have found t. MISQ 548:1
last temptation is the greatest t. ELIO 310:17
love the t. DANI 264:11
moderation is a sort of t. BURK 172:19
none dare call it t. HARI 382:14
popular humanity is t. ADDI 4:17
t. a matter TALL 788:20
t. can but peep SHAK 704:1
T. has done his worst SHAK 721:3
t. is not owned DRYD 296:15
t., make the most of it HENR 392:12
t. of all clerks AUDE 36:26
t. to his country JOHN 436:5
t. to our love THOR 810:3
'Twixt t. and convenience EPIT 318:8
treasonous their t. parles BROW 166:16
treasons fit for t., stratagems SHAK 725:13
treasure liking his t. THOM 806:23
our hearts' t. ROCH 664:13
purest t. mortal times afford SHAK 730:2
stolen the t. CONG 247:4
t. in earthen vessels BIBL 113:8
t. in heaven BIBL 102:6
t. of our tongue DANI 264:8
t. to dispose ASTE 34:12
t. without measure SCOT 687:17
What trusty t. GRIM 373:8
Where your t. is BIBL 99:14
your chiefest t. BELL 67:17
treasures t. upon earth BIBL 99:13
treasury on our T. Bench TROL 816:19
T. is the spring BAGE 50:8
treble of the T. Bench DISR 284:12
treat t. 'em just the same DURE 300:11
t. if met where any bar is HARD 381:21
t. them as if they were GOET 362:21
treaties T. like girls and roses DE G 271:15
treatise T. of Human Nature HUME 420:15
treatment suitable case for t. MERC 532:6
t. of a question WITT 861:9
treaty hand that signed the t. THOM 805:20
not a peace t. FOCH 336:3
T. emptied the British jails DAY- 269:9
t. with Russia BISM 122:15
tree apple on the t. DICK 281:16
billboard lovely as a t. NASH 568:22
falls far from t. PROV 626:32
finds that this t. KNOX 470:4
fool sees not the same t. BLAK 126:7
get tragedy where the t. WITT 861:7
golden t. of actual life GOET 362:1
I must climb the t. HERB 394:24
in a green t. BIBL 106:22
in a t. did end their race MARV 525:3
leaves of the t. BIBL 119:21
miss but a t. BLAM 128:15
must climb the t. PROV 634:15
Of that forbidden t. MILT 541:8
only God can make a t. KILM 462:16
on the t. of life MILT 543:1
on this Crumpetty T. LEAR 486:11
outstretched beneath the t. BLAK 128:1
partridge in a pear t. SONG 763:7
poem lovely as a t. KILM 462:15
revere that t. FERG 325:9
river in the t. DICK 282:5
shall be like that t. SWIF 784:15
she gave me of the t. BIBL 79:7
shift an old t. PROV 648:15
so is the t. inclined PROV 626:39
sour apple t. SONG 763:2
spare the beechen t. CAMP 195:6
Till the t. die SHAK 698:26
to my mind than a t. MORR 560:7
t. falls, so shall it lie PROV 626:36
t. filled with angels BLAK 128:13
t. in the front garden MUMO 565:8
t. is known by his fruit BIBL 101:5
t. is known by its fruit PROV 645:34
T. of Eternity UPAN 822:13
t. of knowledge BIBL 78:20
T. of Knowledge BYRO 190:12
t. of liberty JEFF 431:11
t. of life BIBL 78:20
t. of life BIBL 88:6
t. of the knowledge BIBL 78:21
t.'s inclined POPE 615:14
t. that moves some BLAK 128:11
t. was already rotten JOHN 434:12
Under the greenwood t. SHAK 696:21
unfabled Incense t. DARL 266:3
where the t. falleth BIBL 90:16
wish I were a t. HERB 393:21
Woodman, spare that t. MORR 560:10
treefull t. of angels BENÉ 69:17
treen t. priests JEWE 433:18
trees all the t. are green KING 464:14
apple t. will never get across FROS 344:18
climbing t. in the Hesperides SHAK 717:18
die when the t. were green CLAR 232:19
Green t. that in the forests MARV 524:20
harden like t. MONT 554:6
He that plants t. FULL 346:16
I like t. CATH 209:15
into the t. JACK 427:3
known by the t. CLAR 233:17
Loveliest of t. HOUS 415:11
men as t., walking BIBL 103:33
plants the t. to serve another CAEC 192:14
root of the t. BIBL 98:18
shade of the t. JACK 427:3

TWOPENCE · **UNDERSTAND** 1131

sweet t.-and-twenty BYRO 191:6
Takes t. to tango HOFF 402:2
takes t. to tango PROV 636:42
tea for t. CAES 192:15
There went in t. and two BIBL 79:22
twice t. be not four TURG 819:5
T. and two only NEWM 571:16
t. and two would continue to make WHIS 850:9
T. boys are half a boy PROV 645:43
t. by two in the ark LEVE 491:5
t. cultures SNOW 759:13
t. dogs are fighting PROV 647:15
t. ears of corn SWIF 782:9
t.-edged sword BIBL 117:27
t.-edged sword BOOK 150:11
t. for mirth PROV 640:44
t. glasses and two chairs MACN 513:11
t.-handed engine MILT 540:11
T. heads are better than one PROV 645:44
t. hours' traffick SHAK 732:3
t. hundred thousand men NAPO 568:7
T. is company PROV 645:45
t. is fun SAYI 684:5
T. nations DISR 286:6
t. o'clock in the morning NAPO 568:4
t. or three are gathered BOOK 134:8
t. people miserable BUTL 184:7
t. primal Spirits ZORO 879:6
t. ride on a horse PROV 635:19
t. things about the horse ROYD 671:16
t. things that will be believed TARK 790:8
t. to make a bargain PROV 636:40
t. to make a quarrel PROV 636:41
T. voices are there STEP 772:3
We're number t. ADVE 8:26
where t. or three BIBL 102:3
with t. seeming bodies SHAK 726:19
twopence penny plain and t. coloured STEV 775:19
Tyburn damned T.-face CONG 247:1
tyger T., Tyger BLAK 128:3
tygers t. of wrath BLAK 126:14
Tyler Tippecanoe and T., too POLI 613:12
type careful of the t. TENN 795:15
people couldn't t. JOBS 433:19
wasn't even my t. PROU 625:8
types device of *Movable T.* CARL 200:18
From shadows and t. EPIT 317:6
Seven t. of ambiguity EMPS 315:29
T. and shadows THOM 805:5
typewriter changing a t. ribbon BENC 69:6
typewriters banging on million t. WILE 856:20
monkeys strumming on t. EDDI 302:15
tyranne *tibi tanta t. tulisti* ENNI 316:3
tyrannical against a t. majority BALF 53:12
tyrannis *Sic semper t.* BOOT 150:25
Sic semper t. MOTT 563:19
tyrannous t. To use it like a giant SHAK 723:7
tyranny appeal from t. to God BYRO 191:3
burden of t. SHAW 741:9
call it *t.* HOBB 401:3
conditions of t. AREN 26:9
Death's unbounded t. FLAT 333:2
Ecclesiastic t. DEFO 271:3
remedy in human nature against t. JOHN 441:3
straining order into t. GODW 361:6
struggled against t. TUTU 819:17
t. be over-past BOOK 143:14
t. had supplanted the law DUFF 298:15
T. is always better organized PÉGU 602:4
t. whose borders MAIL 516:9
unnecessary t. RUSS 674:16
wage war against a monstrous t. CHUR 229:13
Wherever law ends, t. begins LOCK 497:20
without representation is t. OTIS 589:9
worst sort of t. BURK 175:17
tyrant loses the king in the t. MAYH 529:9
No t. need fear till ARIS 28:5
O t. Titus Tatius ENNI 316:3
spurned a t.'s chain BARB 57:19
T. and Hector BARB 58:2
t. grinds down his slaves BRON 158:20
t. of his fields withstood GRAY 370:6
t. staring him in the face HORA 412:18
t.'s vein SHAK 725:28
t. whom I will not name WRIG 870:21
tyrants all men would be t. DEFO 270:18
argument of t. PITT 607:18
barbarity of t. SMIT 758:1
between t. and slaves GOLD 364:30
Excessive dealings with t. DEMO 272:21
God gave t. in his wrath CULP 262:1
Kings will be t. BURK 174:11
men would be t. ADAM 1:18
patriots and t. JEFF 431:11
Rebellion to t. BRAD 154:9
Rebellion to t. MOTT 563:17
sceptre from t. TURG 819:7
T. seldom want pretexts BURK 172:16
Tyre men still call T. FLEC 334:13
Nineveh and T. KIPL 467:6
tyres concrete and t. LARK 481:3
Tyrian budded T. KEAT 456:13

ubi *U. Petrus, ibi ergo ecclesia* AMBR 14:3
ubique *Quod u., quod semper* VINC 828:9
ubiquities blazing u. EMER 315:21
Ucalegon U. burns very near VIRG 829:12
uffish in u. thought he stood CARR 202:22
ugly constancy to a bad, u. woman BYRO 191:13
Despised, if u. LEAP 485:12
good, the bad, and the u. FILM 331:6
never saw an u. thing CONS 249:20
no place for u. mathematics HARD 380:9
than to be u. WILD 855:21
u. fact HUXL 423:5
u., heavy and complex FLAU 334:6
when I was the u. duckling ANDE 15:7
Ullin Lord U.'s daughter CAMP 195:11
Ulster Protestant Province of U. CARS 204:9
to which U. will not go BONA 132:3
U. will fight CHUR 228:22
Ulsterman U., of planter stock HEWI 397:16
ulterioris *ripae u. amore* VIRG 830:10
ultima *U. Thule* VIRG 832:12
ultimate u. decency of things STEV 776:11
u. truth NAGA 567:2
ultio *voluptas U.* JUVE 451:20
ultrices *Luctus et u. posuere* VIRG 830:9
Ulva chief of U.'s isle CAMP 195:11
Ulysses Happy he who like U. DU B 298:3
umble so very 'u. DICK 277:13
umbra it is but *U. Mortis* LAUD 482:17
magni nominis u. LUCA 503:17
umbrage garden's u. mild SMAR 754:17
u. of the walls of Eden BYRO 185:15
umbrella shadow, an u. FLET 335:10
steals the just's u. BOWE 153:16
umbris *Ex u. et imaginibus* EPIT 317:6
umpire Chaos u. sits MILT 542:17
una *spinis de pluribus u.* HORA 411:2
unable unwilling or u. WILL 858:10
unacceptable u. face of capitalism HEAT 388:4
unacknowledged u. legislators SHEL 747:14
unadvisedly u., lightly, or wantonly BOOK 138:21
unaffected Affecting to seem u. CONG 247:29
unafraid ruins would strike him u. HORA 412:19
unanswered u. question BELL 67:14
unarm U., Eros SHAK 695:17
unattempted u. yet in prose or rhyme MILT 541:9
unattractive not against the u. GREE 371:12
unaware And I was u. HARD 381:15
Sees, some morning, u. BROW 165:27
unbearable bear what is u. WOLF 862:11
in victory u. CHUR 230:14
seems for a moment u. ELIO 306:21
u. lightness of being KUND 474:5
unbeatable In defeat u. CHUR 230:14
unbeautiful u. and have comfortable minds CUMM 262:13
unbecoming u. the character MILI 535:3
unbelief help thou mine u. BIBL 104:1
unbelievers Fire prepared for u. KORA 471:1
hard against the u. KORA 473:1
unbelieving u. husband BIBL 112:3
unbirthday u. present CARR 203:10
unborn u., not become PALI 594:20
unbought u. grace of life BURK 174:8
unbowed bloody, but u. HENL 391:12
unbroken part of u. stream HAWK 384:13
unbuild arise and u. it again SHEL 743:26
unburied bodies of u. men WEBS 844:20
unbutton Come; u. here SHAK 715:27
uncertain I lived u. ARIS 28:12
trumpet give an u. sound BIBL 112:15
U., coy, and hard to please SCOT 689:4
uncertainty limits set by the u. principle HAWK 385:2
uncharitable so u. to ourselves BROW 163:11
uncharitableness from all u. BOOK 134:17
uncheered u. and undepressed STEV 776:5
uncircumcised daughters of the u. BIBL 84:11
uncle My u. SHAK 700:21
u. me no uncle SHAK 730:12
U. Tom Cobbleigh BALL 56:8
unclean people of u. lips BIBL 92:7
u. spirit BIBL 101:10
uncleanness all u. BIBL 102:20
Fornication, and all u. BIBL 114:8
unclouded u. blaze BYRO 187:13
unclubbable very u. man JOHN 440:11
unco Address to the u. guid BURN 177:7
uncoffined u., and unknown BYRO 187:3
uncomfortable when he is only u. SHAW 741:1
unconditional u. and immediate surrender GRAN 368:12
unconfined with u. wings LOVE 502:3
unconquerable man's u. mind WORD 869:21
nursing the u. hope ARNO 30:13
u. will MILT 541:13
unconscionable u. time dying CHAR 217:10
unconscious knowledge of the u. FREU 342:16
personal u. JUNG 449:10
road to the u. MISQ 547:10
unconsidered u. trifles SHAK 736:27
unconvincing bald and u. GILB 357:14
uncorrupt leadeth an u. life BOOK 140:1
uncouth His u. way MILT 542:9
U. unkist SPEN 768:7
uncreated one u. BOOK 134:13
uncreating u. word POPE 613:29
unction flattering u. SHAK 703:17
uncultured u. souls HERA 393:6
undaunted my u. heart FOWL 339:8
undefiled my love, my dove, my u. BIBL 91:8
Pure religion and u. BIBL 116:21
well of English u. SPEN 767:20
undepressed uncheered and u. STEV 776:5
under employed as an u.-labourer LOCK 497:3
get out and get u. CLAR 233:19
go u. the earth BOOK 143:25
those that work u. them HALI 377:8
underachiever basically he's an u. ALLE 13:11
underbelly soft u. of Europe MISQ 548:18
u. of the Axis CHUR 230:2
underground Johnny u. PUDN 648:34
undergrowth u. is part of the language EMPS 315:30
underlings ourselves, that we are u. SHAK 711:19
underneath U. the Arches FLAN 332:21
undersold Never knowingly u. ADVE 8:8
understand can anyone u. Ein ANON 18:1
child could u. FILM 330:1
criticize What you can't u. DYLA 302:5
doesn't u. the situation MURR 566:7
dogs who don't u. CALV 194:6
don't u. things NEUM 571:5
easy to u. GALI 347:19
failed to u. BOHR 130:14
get a man to u. something SINC 753:6
Grown-ups never u. anything SAIN 677:13
I do not u. FEYN 326:2

understand (*cont.*):
liberals can u. — BRUC 168:13
little of what they u. — GRAC 367:9
none could u. what she said — BUNY 171:26
something I really don't u. — SALI 678:9
thought I to u. this — BOOK 144:21
to u. them — SPIN 768:12
u. a little less — MAJO 517:3
u. nothing — CORN 251:17
u. one another — CHAM 215:2
u. the country — LESS 490:17
we should not u. — CONG 247:5
understanded tongue not u. — BOOK 150:19
understandeth u. thee not — SHAK 717:16
understanding candle of u. — BIBL 96:24
declare, if thou hast u. — BIBL 87:8
find you an u. — JOHN 444:3
good u. — BOOK 147:21
ignorant of his u. — COLE 241:19
in length of days u. — BIBL 86:28
it is u. — HOLT 404:1
likely to propagate u. — JOHN 444:24
ocean of true u. — BAHA 52:1
pass all u. — JAME 429:3
passeth all u. — BIBL 115:4
pass man's u. — BOOK 136:6
sketchy u. of life — CRIC 260:2
To be totally u. — STAË 769:10
wisdom and u. — BIBL 92:16
with all thy getting get u. — BIBL 87:24
understandings muddy u. — BURK 174:9
understands as he u. it — JACK 426:10
he who u. baboon — DARW 266:21
while one u. nothing — SOPH 761:10
world u. my language — HAYD 385:14
understood hardest to be u. — SHER 748:3
I have u. you — DE G 271:10
music u. by children — STRA 778:20
to be u. — CURI 263:1
u., and not be believed — BLAK 126:19
u. by others — JACK 426:10
words easy to be u. — BIBL 112:16
Words easy to be u. — BUNY 171:3
undertakers As u.—walk before — GARR 349:14
like so many u. — ADDI 4:26
undertaking no such u. has been received — CHAM 214:7
underwood this of U. — JONS 447:6
underworld down to the U. — VIRG 830:5
underwriters than the u. notice — THOR 809:2
undeservedly books u. forgotten — AUDE 38:20
undeserving u. poor — SHAW 742:9
undevotional Dirty, dark, and u. — VICT 827:9
undiscovered u. country — SHAK 702:2
undivided Alone and u. — SHIP 749:15
undo For thee does she u. herself — MIDD 534:11
u. the folded lie — AUDE 38:7
u. this button — SHAK 717:8
undone death had u. so many — ELIO 311:5
deeds left u. — STOW 778:6
I am u. — BIBL 92:7
John Donne, Anne Donne, U. — DONN 290:14
'tis we must be u. — BEHN 66:22
We have left u. — BOOK 133:5
What's done cannot be u. — PROV 646:27
What's done cannot be u. — SHAK 722:11
undress when I u. me — FIEL 326:3
undulating u. throat — BELL 68:13
uneasiness u. when being explained — BALF 53:19
uneasy from u. dreams — KAFK 452:3
U. lies the head — SHAK 707:17
uneatable pursuit of the u. — WILD 855:24
uneconomic shown it to be 'u.' — SCHU 687:2
uneducated government by the u. — CHES 225:25
u. man to read books — CHUR 230:20
unemployed u. youth — BAGE 50:22
unemployment rising u. — LAMO 477:18
unendurable which are u. — LEWI 492:18
unequal equal division of u. earnings — ELLI 313:16

unespied In the ocean's bosom u. — MARV 524:14
unexamined u. life is not worth — SOCR 759:22
unexpected accomplish the u. — EURI 321:7
not find out the u. — HERA 392:19
Old age is the most u. — TROT 817:4
sudden and u. — AURE 40:19
u. always happens — PROV 645:48
unexpectedness I call u. — PEAC 600:15
unexplained you're u. as yet — HALL 378:5
unextinguishable u. laugh in heaven — BROW 162:2
unfabled u. Incense Tree — DARL 266:3
unfaithful faith u. — TENN 794:13
original is u. — BORG 151:9
unfaithfulness U. in the house — TALM 789:24
unfamiliar u. terms — GALE 347:16
unfathomable u. deep forest — THOM 806:19
unfathomed depth u. — WESL 847:19
unfed houseless heads and u. sides — SHAK 715:23
unfeeling u. for his own — GRAY 370:12
unfeignedly them that u. love thee — BOOK 136:15
unfinished Liberty is u. business — ANON 18:12
unfit chosen from the u. — ANON 16:19
chosen from the u. — SAYI 684:8
u. to be trusted — CHES 223:19
unforeseen certain but the u. — PROV 640:19
unforgiveness alp of u. — PLOM 610:3
unforgiving fill the u. minute — KIPL 466:6
u. eye — SHER 748:28
unfortunate u. man — BOET 130:11
unfriendliness blue u. of space — HOPE 406:18
unfruitful becometh u. — BIBL 101:14
unfurnished to be u. let u. — BUTL 183:12
ungodliness tents of u. — BOOK 145:15
ungodly because of the u. — BOOK 141:24
counsel of the u. — BOOK 139:11
hope of the u. — BIBL 97:4
plagues remain for the u. — BOOK 141:17
u. in great power — BOOK 141:26
Upon the u. — BOOK 139:26
ungraceful no more u. figure — CECI 212:6
ungrammatical be a little u. — FROS 345:10
ungrateful U. country — SCIP 687:16
ungratefulness call virtue there u. — SIDN 750:17
unguem Ad u. Factus homo — HORA 414:14
unguessed tread on Earth u. at — ARNO 30:16
ungula putrem sonitu quatit u. — VIRG 831:5
unhabitable no land u. — THOR 810:4
unhanged three good men u. — SHAK 705:25
unhappily bad end u. — STOP 778:2
unhappiness loyalty we feel to u. — GREE 371:16
prefer u. — SANT 680:15
putting-off of u. — GREE 371:11
u. develops the forces of the mind — PROU 626:2
vocation of u. — SIME 752:12
unhappy as u. as one thinks — LA R 482:12
cannot be made u. — LUCR 504:13
care for the u. — VIRG 829:3
each u. family — TOLS 813:8
I'm u. — CHEK 221:21
Men who are u. — RUSS 674:13
moral as soon as one is u. — PROU 625:9
Not one is respectable or u. — WHIT 852:11
only speak when she is u. — SMIT 757:16
soft, u. sex — BEHN 67:8
that of the u. — WITT 861:16
think the great u. — YOUN 876:11
u. can either give — RHYS 659:15
u., far-off things — WORD 869:11
U. the land that needs heroes — BREC 155:16
unhasting Unresting, u. — SMIT 759:4
unheard language of the u. — KING 463:17
those u. Are sweeter — KEAT 455:18
unholy sights u. — MILT 539:21
unjust or u. — SOCR 759:21
unhonoured Unwept, u. — SCOT 688:15
unhoused U., disappointed — SHAK 700:22
unicorn like a young u. — BOOK 141:12
lion and the u. — NURS 579:15
rarer than the u. — JONG 445:13

uniform good u. must work — DICK 280:23
U. ideas originating — VICO 827:4
uniformity preferred before u. — BACO 46:13
u. [of opinion] — JEFF 432:13
uniforms Makin' mock o' u. — KIPL 467:16
uninitiated keep far off, you u. — VIRG 830:7
uninspiring may be u. — GEOR 353:2
unintelligible all this u. world — WORD 866:10
rapid, u. patter — GILB 358:12
so u. that no rational being — MOZA 563:25
uninterrupted work u. — SITW 753:13
unintroduced u. neighbour — ELIO 307:24
union Act of U. is there — TRIM 815:14
Channel forbids u. — GRAT 369:6
determined to preserve this U. — HOUS 416:15
devotion to the u. — CARS 204:10
indestructible U. — CHAS 217:17
Join the u. — ANTH 24:18
key of the U. — CLAY 234:16
Liberty and U. — WEBS 843:22
O U., strong and great — LONG 498:15
Our Federal U. — JACK 426:9
our u. is perfect — DICK 282:6
save the U. — LINC 493:17
state of the U. — CONS 250:3
U. is strength — PROV 645:49
u. of hands and hearts — TAYL 792:6
U. of these States — WHIT 852:9
U. will be dissolved — COBB 237:11
unions when Hitler attacked the u. — NIEM 575:8
unit Misses an u. — BROW 165:25
unite Workers of the world, u. — MARX 526:14
united U. Colonies — ADAM 3:5
U. we stand — PROV 646:1
United States believe in the U. — PAGE 591:16
close to the U. — DIAZ 276:1
rise of the U. — STEV 775:4
U. must be neutral — WILS 859:13
U. themselves — WHIT 852:21
unites value what u. them — KING 464:19
unities Three U. — DRYD 297:13
u. are a completeness — DICK 279:17
u. of time and place — SCOT 689:19
uniting By u. we stand — DICK 282:7
unity at u. in itself — BOOK 148:19
dwell together in u. — BOOK 149:10
national u. — BUSH 182:9
national u. — ROOS 667:6
Trinity in U. — BOOK 134:12
truth, u., and concord — BOOK 137:5
u. of the empire — BURK 173:22
u. of the faith — BIBL 114:5
universal become a u. law — KANT 452:19
kind of u. genius — DRYD 297:12
lying into a u. principle — KAFK 452:8
one u. grin — FIEL 327:2
Relaxed into a u. grin — COWP 256:23
u. dovetailedness — DICK 279:17
u. frame — BACO 46:5
u. good — POPE 616:27
u. monarchy of wit — CARE 198:8
u. quality is diversity — MONT 555:20
universality Look abroad into u. — BACO 45:6
universe Architect of the U. — JEAN 431:4
coherent plan to the u. — HOYL 417:12
fact about the u. — EINS 305:11
first invent the u. — SAGA 677:7
hell of a good u. next door — CUMM 262:10
If the U. is hidden — CHUA 227:12
knows the u. — LA F 475:17
Life, the U. and Everything — ADAM 2:5
measure of the u. — SHEL 745:24
ordering of the u. — ALFO 12:12
pet theory of the u. — EDDI 302:16
Put back Thy u. — JONE 445:7
repetitious mechanism of the U. — WHIT 851:3
Somewhere in the u. — TAGL 788:11
torrents of her myriad u. — TENN 797:14
u. and I exist together — CHUA 227:9
u. go to all the bother — HAWK 385:3
u. is not hostile — HOLM 403:9
u. is truly in love — AURE 40:10
u. . . . others call the Library — BORG 151:7

u. queerer than we suppose HALD 376:11
u.'s existence is made known PENR 602:21
u. sleeps MAYA 529:1
we and the u. exist HAWK 385:4
universities colleges and u. SMIT 756:7
U. never reform themselves MELB 530:12
university able to get to a u. KINN 465:2
benefiting from u. AMIS 14:18
bred at an U. CONG 247:7
gained in the u. of life BOTT 152:10
God-sustaining U. GLAD 360:12
u. of Oxtail JOYC 448:22
u. of the air WILS 859:4
U. of these days CARL 200:8
U. should be DISR 285:1
We are the U. SPRI 769:2
unjoined u. system ANON 17:20
unjust commended the u. steward BIBL 106:3
on the just and on the u. BIBL 99:7
u. or unholy SOCR 759:21
u. steals BOWE 153:16
unjustly teach to talk u. ARIS 26:14
unkind I am u. LOVE 502:6
sodden and u. BELL 68:23
unkindest most u. cut of all SHAK 713:9
unkindness u. may defeat my life SHAK 729:8
unking u. himself MAYH 529:9
unkist Uncouth u. SPEN 768:7
Unknowe, u., and lost CHAU 220:25
unknowable decide on the u. ZOBE 878:4
world u., we know THOM 807:21
unknowe U., unkist, and lost CHAU 220:25
unknowing cloud of u. ANON 16:17
u. and unknown BURN 178:24
unknown buried the U. Prime Minister ASQU 34:6
dies to himself u. SENE 692:21
entire peoples u. to each other VICO 827:4
forms of things u. SHAK 722:3
gates to the glorious and u. FORS 337:21
known and the u. PINT 607:2
live, unseen, u. POPE 617:33
mind loves the u. MAGR 515:3
My song is love u. CROS 261:12
She lived u. WORD 869:5
things u. POPE 616:12
Through the u. BAUD 61:14
to the u. god BIBL 110:3
touch of u. CANE 196:22
travelled among u. men WORD 866:6
tread safely into the u. HASK 384:3
uncoffined, and u. BYRO 187:3
unknowing and u. BURN 178:24
u. and silent shore LAMB 476:21
u. is held to be glorious TACI 786:20
u. regions preserved ELIO 307:21
u. to himself HAZL 386:14
unmourned and u. HORA 414:3
unseen, unborn, u. FLEC 334:14
Woman is the great u. HARD 380:4
unlearned u. and uninformed AUST 43:3
unleavened u. bread BIBL 81:7
u. bread HAGG 375:12
u. bread of sincerity BIBL 111:31
unleaving Goldengrove u. HOPK 407:19
unlessoned u. girl SHAK 724:24
unlike through u. forms DION 283:19
unloose not worthy to u. BIBL 107:4
unluckily good u. STOP 778:2
unlucky u. in love PROV 638:12
unmaking things are in the u. KING 463:18
unmapped u. country ELIO 307:8
unmarried prime-roses, That die u. SHAK 737:2
unmask To u. falsehood SHAK 737:13
unmeritable slight u. man SHAK 713:19
unmixed u. blessing HORA 412:11
unmourned u. and unknown HORA 414:3
unmuzzled come among you 'u.' GLAD 359:16
unnatural cruel, not u. SHAK 703:4
most u. murder SHAK 700:19
only u. sex act KINS 465:3
unnecessary do the u. ANON 16:19

in u. matters BIBL 97:9
thou u. letter SHAK 715:8
to do the u. SAYI 684:8
unnoticed pathway of a life u. HORA 410:16
unofficial English u. rose BROO 159:7
unpack u. my own bag UPDI 822:25
unpalatable disastrous and the u. GALB 347:15
unparalleled lies A lass u. SHAK 696:6
unpatriotic u. and servile ROOS 668:7
unperson abolished, an u. ORWE 587:16
unplayable another u. work SCHO 686:11
unpleasantness put up with u. NAPO 567:15
unplumbed u., salt, estranging sea ARNO 31:5
unpolicied great Caesar ass U. SHAK 696:4
unpolitical no such thing as an u. man MALA 517:6
unpopular safe to be u. STEV 774:22
unpremeditated u. art SHEL 746:19
unprepared Magnificently u. CORN 252:3
unprincipled sold by the u. CAPP 197:13
unprofitable flat, and u. SHAK 699:18
most idle and u. GIBB 354:19
unprotected u. race CLAR 232:25
unquiet be the earth never so u. BOOK 146:14
u. heart and brain TENN 795:2
unreality atmosphere of u. BAGE 51:9
unreasonable progress depends on u. man SHAW 741:19
unrefined u. stuff of mine BRAD 154:13
unreflecting u. herd WORD 865:21
unregarded U. age SHAK 696:16
unreliable Even death is u. BECK 64:28
u. ally in the battle COHE 238:7
unremembered nameless, u., acts WORD 866:9
unrequited what u. affection is DICK 278:4
unrest u. which men miscall delight SHEL 743:18
unresting U., unhasting SMIT 759:4
unrewarded Nothing went u. DRYD 294:21
unrighteousness mammon of u. BIBL 106:4
unripe u. grape AURE 40:24
unruffled cool and u. JEFF 432:8
unruly old fool, u. sun DONN 289:16
u. evil BIBL 116:24
u. wills and affections BOOK 135:19
unsad U. and evere untrewe CHAU 218:28
unsafe at any speed KEAT 458:19
U. at any speed NADE 567:1
unsaid words left u. STOW 778:6
unsatisfied leaves one u. WILD 855:19
unseamed Till he u. him SHAK 718:4
unsearchable heart of kings is u. BIBL 88:34
u. riches of Christ BIBL 113:29
unseen born to blush u. GRAY 370:6
effect, itself u. REYN 659:5
God knows the U. KORA 472:14
Greet the u. BROW 164:22
O friend u. FLEC 334:14
Thou art u. SHEL 746:21
u. among us SHEL 744:8
u. things above HANK 379:10
walk the earth U. MILT 543:12
unsex U. me here SHAK 718:20
unshackled open and u. press HOWE 417:2
unshook u. amidst a bursting world POPE 614:16
unsifted like a green girl, U. SHAK 700:7
unsoiled delicately and u. CHUR 230:15
unsolicited u. advice COOL 250:16
unsought lost, that is u. CHAU 220:25
unspeakable come to those u. joys BOOK 136:15
joy u. BIBL 116:30
u. in full pursuit WILD 855:24
unspotted keep himself u. BIBL 116:21
unstable absolutely u. ARTS 33:1
U. as water BIBL 80:29
unsubstantial u. realms of Hades VIRG 830:8
unsung unhonoured, and u. SCOT 688:15
untalented product of the u. CAPP 197:13
untaught U. the noble end IRWI 426:1
untender So young, and so u. SHAK 714:17

unterrified Satan stood U. MILT 542:16
untilled land u. IRWI 425:24
untimely came I so u. forth WALL 837:4
U. ripped SHAK 722:25
unto give u. this last BIBL 102:12
u. us a child is born BIBL 92:14
untravelled Gleams that u. world TENN 800:16
untried difficult; and left u. CHES 225:21
new and u. LINC 493:11
untrodden among the u. ways WORD 869:3
through an u. forest MURR 566:1
untroubled u. where I lie CLAR 233:2
untrue man who's u. to his wife AUDE 37:18
Unsad and evere u. CHAU 218:28
untruth one wilful u. NEWM 572:9
truth and u. BACO 46:32
untune Music shall u. the sky DRYD 296:30
untwisted U. all the shining robe THOM 808:21
unusual cruel and u. punishment CONS 250:7
Harry Potter was an u. boy ROWL 671:13
moved by what is not u. ELIO 307:27
unutterable looked u. things THOM 808:15
unvarnished round u. tale SHAK 728:8
unwanted feeling of being u. TERE 801:20
unwary all u. GILB 357:6
unwashed lean u. artificer SHAK 714:12
unwearied U. still, lover by lover YEAT 875:11
unweave U. a rainbow KEAT 455:14
unwept U., unhonoured SCOT 688:15
Upon his watery bier U. MILT 540:4
unwholesome not u. AUST 41:3
unwilling committee is a group of the u. ANON 16:19
group of the u. SAYI 684:8
u. or unable WILL 858:10
unwillingly U. to school SHAK 696:28
unwise sight of the u. BIBL 96:28
to the wise, and to the u. BIBL 110:20
unworthiness for our u. we dare not BOOK 138:4
unworthy fear of being u. BALZ 56:17
unwritten Custom, that u. law D'AV 267:5
U. and unchanging SOPH 761:15
up be u. betimes SHAK 735:7
Is notwithstanding u. SHAK 712:14
nice to people on your way u. MIZN 551:11
U. and down MAND 518:15
u. go we QUAR 651:15
U. Guards and at them WELL 846:5
u.-hill all the way ROSS 669:8
U., lad HOUS 415:13
U., Lord BOOK 139:24
U. to a point, Lord Copper WAUG 842:18
U. with your damned nonsense RICH 661:4
What goes u. must come down PROV 646:21
upharsin MENE, TEKEL, U. BIBL 95:25
upper butler's u. slopes WODE 862:8
large u. room BIBL 106:18
Like many of the U. Class BELL 68:17
man have the u. hand BOOK 139:24
prove the u. classes COWA 253:19
tempt the u. classes SMIT 756:15
u. station of low life DEFO 270:11
upright God hath made man u. BIBL 90:5
stand u. in the winds BOLT 131:20
that is, u. THOM 806:7
uprightness born with u. CONF 246:3
uprising mine u. BOOK 149:15
Our wakening and u. KEBL 458:21
uproar set all the city on an u. BIBL 109:33
u.'s your only music KEAT 457:16
upsets trifle u. us PASC 597:16
upside turneth it u. down BOOK 150:5
world u. down BIBL 109:34
upstairs kicked u. HALI 377:24
u. into the world CONG 247:2
upstanding clean u. chap like you KING 464:17
upward Eternal Woman draws us u. GOET 362:7
upwards car could go straight u. HOYL 417:11
uranium element u. may be turned EINS 305:12

urban u., squat, and packed with guile
BROO 159:10

urbe *Rus in u.*
MART 524:12

urge Always the procreant u.
WHIT 852:8

u. for destruction
BAKU 52:10

urgent Why is it now so u.
COOK 250:12

urges Will that stirs and u.
HARD 381:13

Uriah Set ye U. in the forefront
BIBL 84:15

Uricon ashes under U.
HOUS 416:2

Urim U. and the Thummim
BIBL 81:22

urine red wine of Shiraz into u.
DINE 283:13

sleep, and u.
SHAK 720:13

tang of faintly scented u.
JOYC 448:18

u. is congealed ice
SHAK 723:16

urn darling in an u.
CARE 198:12

loud-hissing u.
COWP 256:19

Pity's long-broken u.
WILD 856:4

storied u.
GRAY 370:5

urna *Omne capax movet u. nomen*
HORA 412:15

urns u. and sepulchres
CREW 259:19

ursa major nativity was under u.
SHAK 715:1

us he is u.
CART 205:16

Not unto u., O Lord
BOOK 148:4

USA Born in the U.
SPRI 769:3

usage if u. so choose
HORA 409:1

use Beauty too rich for u.
SHAK 732:7

let u. be preferred
BACO 46:13

main thing is to u. it well
DESC 274:8

Poetry belongs to those who u.
SKAR 753:19

such as cannot u. them
JONS 446:6

true u. of speech
GOLD 364:29

u. alone that sanctifies
POPE 615:10

u. a poor maiden so
SONG 762:6

U. every man after his desert
SHAK 701:18

u. him as though you loved him
WALT 839:9

u. of a new-born child
FRAN 341:12

u. rather than ostentation
GIBB 354:7

worn away by u.
OVID 590:4

used buy a u. car
POLI 613:18

get u. to them
NEUM 571:5

My name is U.-to-was
TRAI 814:16

Things ain't what they u. to be
PERS 604:13

useful be a Really U. Engine
AWDR 43:11

know to be u.
MORR 560:18

magistrate, as equally u.
GIBB 354:4

some u. work
THOM 804:18

way to what is u.
COUS 253:6

useless absolutely, completely u.
DOST 291:5

are the most u.
RUSK 673:25

essentially u.
SANT 680:16

Lodged with me u.
MILT 545:14

never live to be u.
WESL 848:6

plans are u.
EISE 306:10

U.! useless
BOOT 151:1

usquebae Wi' u., we'll face
BURN 179:17

USSR Back in the U.
LENN 489:5

usual Business carried on as u.
CHUR 229:3

usura With u. hath no man a house
POUN 620:16

usurpations sudden u.
MADI 514:8

usury forbidden u.
KORA 471:7

given his money upon u.
BOOK 140:2

u. is contrary to Scripture
TAWN 791:5

usus *si volet u.*
HORA 409:1

uti *deorum Muneribus sapienter u.*
HORA 414:4

utile *qui miscuit u. dulci*
HORA 409:12

utility non-being into u.
LAO 479:9

strength, u., grace
VITR 833:9

u. to its conditions
SANT 680:16

Utopia Not in U.
WORD 868:18

possibly be attained in U.
GLAD 360:6

principality in U.
MACA 507:7

signposts to socialist U.
CROS 261:4

Utopias all the static U.
INGE 425:2

utterance timely u.
WORD 867:4

u. of the early gods
KEAT 454:22

utterly should u. have fainted
BOOK 141:11

uttermost u. parts of the sea
BOOK 149:17

U-turn media catchphrase, the U.
THAT 803:16

Uz land of U.
BIBL 86:8

V with a "V." or a "W"
DICK 280:21

vacancies v. to be obtained
JEFF 432:1

vacancy another v. soon
PRIE 623:15

create a job v.
GOLD 363:19

vacant spoke the v. mind
GOLD 364:4

Stuffs out his v. garments
SHAK 714:9

V. heart and hand
SCOT 689:10

v. interstellar spaces
ELIO 309:11

v. or in pensive mood
WORD 866:8

vacations No extras, no v.
DICK 279:6

vacuous be absolutely v.
CHUA 227:15

vacuum Nature abhors a v.
PROV 639:22

Nature abhors a v.
RABE 652:8

v. a hell of a lot better
WILL 858:4

v. or space
DESC 274:11

vadis *Quo v.*
BIBL 120:14

vae *V. victis*
LIVY 496:5

vagabond is a v.
GOLD 365:9

vagabonds So many v.
SKEL 754:3

vagrancy instructed v.
ELIO 308:5

vague don't be v.
ADVE 7:17

V. and eluding
LAO 479:12

vagueness no hypocrisy and no v.
STEN 771:21

vain deceive you with v. words
BIBL 114:9

disquieteth himself in v.
BOOK 141:29

knowledge that he lived in v.
BYRO 186:4

name of God in v.
BIBL 81:17

people imagine a v. thing
BOOK 139:12

this man's religion is v.
BIBL 116:20

v., ill-natured
DEFO 270:23

V. man, said she
SPEN 766:18

v. repetitions
BIBL 99:11

V. the ambition of kings
WEBS 844:6

V. wisdom all
MILT 542:12

watchman waketh but in v.
BOOK 149:2

vainglory land of v.
BUNY 171:6

vainly V. begot
GREV 372:16

v. men themselves amaze
MARV 525:2

vale *ave atque v.*
CATU 211:6

cool sequestered v. of life
GRAY 370:8

in that hollow v.
KING 463:4

shady sadness of a v.
KEAT 454:20

this v. of tears
PRAY 623:7

v. of misery
BOOK 145:14

v. of soul-making
KEAT 458:7

valentine Hail, Bishop V.
DONN 288:7

thank you for a V.
LOCH 497:1

valere *sed v. vita est*
MART 524:9

vales lily-silver'd v.
POPE 613:25

thy hills and v.
JAME 429:7

valet hero to his v.
CORN 252:7

hero to his v.
PROV 640:6

to his very v. seemed
BYRO 185:9

valiant As he was v., I honour him
SHAK 712:26

He who would v. be
DEAR 269:14

v. Jack Falstaff
SHAK 706:6

v. never taste of death
SHAK 712:13

valley great things from the v.
CHES 225:9

How green was my v.
LLEW 496:9

in the v. below
SONG 762:6

in the v. of Death
TENN 793:3

Love is of the v.
TENN 799:21

multitudes in the v. of decision
BIBL 96:9

V. and lowland, sing
OAKL 582:15

v. full of bones
BIBL 95:19

v. of Humiliation
BUNY 171:7

v. of the shadow of death
BOOK 140:21

v. shall be exalted
BIBL 93:15

valleys down the v. wild
BLAK 127:6

lily of the v.
BIBL 90:26

v. also shall stand
BOOK 144:3

v., groves, hills
MARL 522:20

Vallombrosa V., where the Etrurian shades
MILT 541:21

Valois shadow of the V.
CHES 224:8

valorous childish v.
MARL 523:9

valour better part of v.
PROV 630:5

better part of v.
SHAK 706:30

For contemplation he and v.
MILT 543:5

For v., is not love
SHAK 717:18

men of great v.
WILL 857:2

mighty man of v.
BIBL 83:5

much care and v.
SHAK 708:23

My v. is certainly going
SHER 748:20

true v. see
BUNY 171:25

valuable Truth is the most v. thing
TWAI 820:4

value Four things of paramount v.
JAIN 428:3

little v. of fortune
STEE 770:19

Nothing has v.
FORS 338:8

of more v. than many sparrows
BIBL 100:27

prayer never loses its v.
TALM 789:35

v. a virtuous
LOCK 497:19

v. of life
MONT 554:24

v. of nothing
WILD 855:12

V. yourselves
CHUD 227:19

world does set a v. on them
REYN 659:8

values authentic and pure v.
WEIL 845:4

leads to the extinction of v.
ORTE 586:9

moneys are for v.
BACO 45:14

Victorian v.
THAT 803:20

van Follow the v.
COLL 243:3

Vandyke V. is of the company
GAIN 347:4

vanish softly and suddenly v.
CARR 204:2

v. with the rose
FITZ 331:28

vanished This time it v.
CARR 202:4

this v. being
HAWK 384:13

touch of a v. hand
TENN 792:20

v. before the white man
TECU 792:11

v. like a dream
CARL 200:7

vanisheth and then v.
BIBL 116:26

vanishings Fallings from us, v.
WORD 867:14

vanitas Ah! *V. Vanitatum*
THAC 803:3

V. vanitatum
BIBL 120:7

vanities bonfire of the v.
WOLF 863:1

vanity all is v.
BIBL 89:16

forbidden v.
GREV 372:16

fruit of my v.
PETR 604:18

lighter than v.
BOOK 143:22

lions, or V.-Fair
BUNY 171:22

mouth talketh of v.
BOOK 149:24

name of the *Golden V.*
SONG 763:10

name of V.-Fair
BUNY 171:9

pomps and v.
BOOK 138:9

Pull down thy v.
POUN 621:10

revenge against v.
FOOT 336:11

v. and vexation of spirit
BIBL 89:20

v. in years
SHAK 706:5

V. is as ill at ease
ELIO 307:5

V., like murder, will out
COWL 254:22

v. of human hopes
JOHN 437:11

v. of others
AUST 41:21

V. of vanities
BIBL 89:16

v. the great passion
SHER 749:2

ye that work v.
BOOK 139:21

vanquished I have v. thee
JUST 450:8

Valiantly v.
SHAK 695:20

vapour deceitful v.
SMOL 759:8

I absorb the v.
GLAD 360:13

It is even a v.
BIBL 116:26

v. sometime like a bear
SHAK 695:16

vapours congregation of v.
SHAK 701:11

snow and v.
BOOK 150:9

v. weep their burthen
TENN 800:8

variable love prove likewise v.
SHAK 732:14

variableness with whom is no v.
BIBL 116:17

variation admitting any v.
BOOK 132:15

variety change and v.
QUIN 652:4

order in v. we see
POPE 618:18

source of pleasure is v.
JOHN 436:17

stale Her infinite v.
SHAK 695:1

V. is the soul
BEHN 67:4

V. is the spice of life
PROV 646:2

V.'s the very spice
COWP 256:12

variorum Life is all a v.
BURN 178:22

various how v. he is
GAIN 347:3

man so v.
DRYD 294:20

varium *V. et mutabile semper Femina*
VIRG 830:1

Varus V., give me back my legions
AUGU 40:2

vase not a v. to be filled
RABE 652:11

Sèvres v. in the hands
WAUG 843:3

shatter the v.
MOOR 558:8

vast v. right-wing conspiracy
CLIN 236:3

vasty v. hall of death
ARNO 30:1

vate *carent quia v. sacro*
HORA 414:3

vats boilers and v.
JOHN 443:5

purple in the v.
TENN 799:21

vatum *genus irritabile v.*
HORA 411:1

looking upon men as v. BOLI 131:16
men grow v. POPE 618:23
value a v. LOCK 497:19
v. woman BIBL 89:14
v. woman is a crown BIBL 88:3
virtute Macte nova v. VIRG 831:7
viruses computer v. should count as life
HAWK 385:5
vis V. consili expers mole HORA 412:22
visibilium v. omnium MISS 549:11
visible all things v. and invisible BOOK 137:2
darkness v. MILT 541:11
it makes v. KLEE 469:6
outward and v. sign BOOK 138:15
representation of v. things LEON 489:23
Work is love made v. GIBR 355:16
vision Bedlam v. BYRO 192:10
Bright the v. MANT 520:12
by the v. splendid WORD 867:9
fabric of this v. SHAK 733:31
In v. beatific MILT 541:1
Saw the v. of the world TENN 797:1
single central v. BERL 73:9
Single v. and Newton's sleep BLAK 125:21
v. and the faculty WORD 865:11
v. flies SHEN 747:18
V. of Christ BLAK 124:23
V. or Imagination BLAK 128:7
v. thing BUSH 182:3
Was it a v. KEAT 456:12
Where there is no v. BIBL 89:10
Write the v. BIBL 96:16
young men's v. DRYD 294:16
visionary Whither is fled the v. gleam
WORD 867:7
visioned V. One sees all PALI 594:4
visions Cecilia, appear in v. AUDE 36:23
shades send deceptive v. VIRG 830:16
these v. did appear SHAK 727:12
what v. have I seen SHAK 726:27
young men shall see v. BIBL 96:8
visit Christ came to v. us BOOK 135:10
v. the fatherless and widows BIBL 116:21
visitation time of their v. BIBL 96:29
visited sick, and ye v. me BIBL 103:6
visitest thou v. him BOOK 139:23
visiting ordinary v.-card BAED 49:19
v. acquaintance SHER 748:16
v. the iniquity BIBL 81:16
visitor travel as a v. HORA 409:18
visits Superior people never make long v.
MOOR 557:16
v. the sick MAIM 516:17
visual v. telegram CASS 206:8
vita Ars longa, v. brevis HIPP 399:13
cammin di nostra v. DANT 264:12
vitae Integer v. HORA 411:9
V. summa brevis HORA 411:8
vitai v. lampada LUCR 504:10
vital V. spark POPE 614:1
v. spirit BERG 72:9
vitality v. enough to preserve it JOHN 444:5
V. in a woman SHAW 740:23
vitam Si v. puriter egi CATU 211:3
vitriol sleeve with bottle of v. WOOL 864:17
vivam sapientis dicere 'V.' MART 524:3
vivamus V., mea Lesbia CATU 210:6
vivendi vitam v. perdere causas JUVE 451:10
vivere Nec tecum possum v. MART 524:11
Quadrigis petimus bene v. HORA 410:10
vivid left the v. air signed SPEN 766:11
v. rather than happy LOVE 502:8
vivite 'v.' ait ANON 23:10
vivre V.? les serviteurs feront cela VILL 828:5
vixen v. when she went to school SHAK 726:20
vixi Dixisse V. HORA 413:8
vobis Pax V. BIBL 120:13
vobiscum Dominus v. MISS 546:16
sit semper v. MISS 549:18
vocabula nunc sunt in honore v. HORA 409:1
vocabulary not a word in God's v. NIGH 576:6
v. of 'Bradshaw' DOYL 293:1
vocation art is a comparable v. FRIN 343:14

As if his whole v. WORD 867:10
test of a v. SMIT 757:8
v. of unhappiness SIME 752:12
worthy of the v. BIBL 114:4
vodka medium V. dry Martini FLEM 334:16
vogue totter into v. WALP 837:14
voi Siete v. qui DANT 265:2
voice All I have is a v. AUDE 38:7
daughter of the v. of God WORD 867:19
far-away tentative v. ALAI 11:2
followed me by my v. MAHĀ 515:12
great v. as of a trumpet BIBL 117:24
her v. the harmony HOOK 406:8
Her v. was ever soft SHAK 717:7
horrible v. ARIS 26:18
humble v. BOOK 133:3
I have lost my v. WEBS 844:27
inexhaustible v. FAUL 324:17
In Rama was there a v. BIBL 98:13
I see a v. SHAK 727:1
I've lost my v. MORR 561:3
lift up your v. WESL 847:16
Lord, hear my v. BOOK 149:7
No v.; but oh COLE 241:8
Only a look and a v. LONG 500:3
people's v. is odd POPE 617:22
raven, you do have a v. AESO 9:1
scream in a low v. BYRO 191:23
so silvery is thy v. HERR 396:20
so steady a v. CORN 251:16
sound of a v. that is still TENN 792:20
still small v. BIBL 85:14
supplicating v. JOHN 438:12
Thunder is the v. of God MATH 527:17
tune her sacred v. JOHN 437:25
v. and nothing more ANON 23:13
V., and Verse MILT 538:17
v. as the sound of many waters BIBL 117:27
v. from heaven BIBL 118:28
v. is full of money FITZ 332:12
v. is Jacob's voice BIBL 80:7
v. of a nation RUSS 675:18
v. of Doris Day FISH 330:11
v. of my beloved BIBL 91:8
v. of one crying BIBL 98:15
v. of Rome JONS 446:2
v. of the Bard BLAK 127:15
v. of the charmer BOOK 143:18
v. of the dead TENN 796:8
v. of the kingdom SWIF 782:3
v. of the Lobster CARR 202:15
v. of the Lord BOOK 141:12
v. of the Lord God BIBL 79:6
v. of the people ALCU 11:10
v. of the people PROV 646:4
v. of the sluggard WATT 841:17
v. of the turtle BIBL 90:27
v. of thy brother's blood BIBL 79:15
v. revives the leaden strings CAMP 195:22
v. that breathed o'er Eden KEBL 459:3
v. was that of Mr Churchill ATTL 35:7
v. will run KEAT 456:17
voices Ancestral v. prophesying war COLE 240:7
Other v., other rooms CAPO 197:12
Two v. are there STEP 772:3
Two V. are there WORD 869:16
v. of children BLAK 127:13
when soft v. die SHEL 746:17
void conscience v. of offence BIBL 110:12
habitation be v. BOOK 143:18
infinite V. PALI 594:18
v. to receive it WEIL 845:2
without form, and v. BIBL 78:12
voids attempts to fill v. WEIL 845:3
vol suspend ton v. LAMA 476:9
volat v. irrevocabile verbum HORA 410:14
volatile v. spirits SANT 680:15
volcano crust over a v. of revolution ELLI 314:4
dancing not the v. FLAU 333:11
volcanoes range of exhausted v. DISR 284:26
v. burnt out BURK 176:3
vole passes the questing v. WAUG 842:19
volenti V. non fit iniuria ULPI 821:10

Volk ein V. POLI 612:14
Volkswagen V. parked in the gap MULD 564:14
volley v. of the sun WILB 854:6
v. we have just heard COLL 243:4
volo Hoc v. JUVE 451:3
volontade E'n la sua v. DANT 265:15
Voltaire V. in the Bastille DE G 271:19
V.'s Candide had come off the press
GRAN 368:10
voluisse in magnis et v. sat est PROP 624:21
volume in one v. octavo SMIT 758:3
In the v. of the book BOOK 141:31
take in our hand any v. HUME 419:16
volumes all Earth's v. CHAP 216:12
creators of odd v. LAMB 476:15
thirty fine v. MORL 560:3
voluntary Composing's not v. BIRT 122:4
v. spies AUST 41:23
voluntas fiat v. MISS 549:17
sit pro ratione v. JUVE 451:3
tamen est laudanda v. OVID 590:3
volunteer One v. is worth PROV 641:16
voluptas Trahit sua quemque v. VIRG 831:20
voluptuous V. as the first BYRO 190:9
vomit dog is turned to his own v. BIBL 117:15
dog returneth to his v. BIBL 88:41
Dog returns to his V. KIPL 466:2
dog returns to its v. PROV 630:11
returning to one's own v. POWE 622:4
Vorsprung V. durch Technik ADVE 8:24
votaress imperial v. SHAK 726:6
vote always v. against FIEL 327:10
brute v. BAGE 50:15
Don't buy a single v. more KENN 460:3
One man shall have one v. CART 205:20
turkeys v. for Christmas CALL 193:13
v. against somebody ADAM 2:9
V. early and vote often MILE 534:25
V. for the man who promises least BARU 60:12
v. just as their leaders tell 'em GILB 356:19
voted only have v. for myself BAUD 61:16
v. at my party's call GILB 358:1
v. cent per cent BYRO 185:7
voter Every intelligent v. ADAM 2:7
votes V. for women POLI 613:14
v. to get the things done SAMU 679:17
voting If v. changed anything LIVI 496:4
not the v. that's democracy STOP 777:13
votis Hoc erat in v. HORA 414:20
vouchsafe V., O Lord: to keep us BOOK 133:11
voulu Vous l'avez v. MOLI 552:11
vow v. be performed BOOK 144:1
v. to thee, my country SPRI 768:18
vowels U green, O blue: v. RIMB 662:18
v. count for nothing VOLT 835:6
with all the v. missing ELLI 313:11
vows cancel all our v. DRAY 293:14
first v. sworn DIDE 282:13
pay my v. now BOOK 148:9
v. made in wine SHAK 697:16
vox V. et praeterea nihil ANON 23:13
v. humbug SHER 749:7
V. populi ALCU 11:10
voyage during this hurried v. COLU 244:14
in for Hobbes's v. VANB 823:19
make the v. over VIRG 830:10
take my last v. HOBB 401:11
v. not a harbour TOYN 814:5
v. of their life SHAK 713:28
v. to the moon LARD 480:15
voyages v. of the starship Enterprise
RODD 665:2
voyaging V. through strange seas
WORD 868:13
vulgar great v., and the small COWL 254:11
in the v. tongue BOOK 138:5
it's v. PUNC 650:3
let the v. stuff alone BELL 69:1
money-spending always 'v.' GASK 350:7
trivial and v. way BROW 163:12
v. expression CONG 246:26
vulpes v. aegroto cauta leoni HORA 410:2

W with a "V" or a "W." — DICK 280:21
wabe gimble in the w. — CARR 202:21
wade should I w. no more — SHAK 721:13
waded w. thro' red blude — BALL 55:22
Waffen Wehr und W. — LUTH 505:8
wag W. as it will — BYRO 185:1
Wood, the Weed, the W. — RALE 654:2
wage give themselves for w. — YEAT 874:9
home policy: I w. war — CLEM 235:7
wager lost the w. — SHAK 698:17
wagering w. that God is — PASC 598:5
wages earneth w. — BIBL 96:18
neither honours nor w. — GARI 349:7
paid in full your w. — KORA 471:13
ta'en thy w. — SHAK 698:24
took their w. — HOUS 415:8
w. of sin is death — BIBL 110:35
wagged tail that w. — WATS 841:10
Wagner W. has lovely moments — ROSS 670:1
W.'s music — NYE 582:13
wagon Hitch your w. to a star — EMER 315:13
w. of his 'Plan' — PAST 598:21
wail nothing to w. — MILT 545:10
wrynge, and w. — CHAU 219:2
wailing w. for her demon-lover — COLE 240:5
wains hangs heavy from the w. — GIBB 355:9
wainscot In w. tubs — DRAY 293:16
waist live about her w. — SHAK 701:8
waistcoat open your w. — HUNT 421:15
yolk runs down the w. — DICK 279:15
wait All things come to those who w. — PROV 626:22
having nothing to w. for — PAVE 600:7
laid great w. for me — BOOK 142:3
Time and tide w. — PROV 645:16
too slow for those who w. — VAN 824:4
w. and see — ASQU 34:3
w. a wee — BURN 180:10
w. for ever — MACA 507:2
W. for me — SIMO 753:1
w. for what will come — ROBI 663:19
w. upon the Lord — BIBL 93:20
we won't w. — ANON 21:7
who only stand and w. — MILT 545:15
Why w. — EAST 302:9
waited w. patiently for the Lord — BOOK 141:30
waiter myself and a dam' good head w. — GULB 374:12
waiting nearly kept w. — LOUI 501:4
w. for Godot — BECK 64:18
w. for the Earl of Chatham — ANON 17:11
W. for the end — EMPS 315:25
W. is still an occupation — PAVE 600:7
w. means hurrying on — MANN 519:13
w. seven hundred years — COLL 243:6
w. somewhere for me — RODG 665:4
What are we w. for — CAVA 211:13
wake do I w. or sleep — KEAT 456:12
slepyng hound to w. — CHAU 221:1
w. in a fright — BARH 58:9
w. the soul by tender strokes — POPE 618:3
W. up, England — GEOR 352:14
we w. eternally — DONN 288:11
waked You have w. me too soon — WATT 841:17
wakening Our w. and uprising — KEBL 458:21
wakes breed one work that w. — HOPK 408:3
Hock-carts, wassails, w. — HERR 395:15
w. or sleeps — SHEL 743:16
w. them himself — ADDI 5:6
What angel w. me — SHAK 726:16
Wordsworth sometimes w. — BYRO 188:27
waking I lay broad w. — WYAT 871:6
w., no such matter — SHAK 738:8
w. that kills us — BROW 163:17
Wales bless the Prince of W. — LINL 495:6
live ever in W. — JAME 429:7
no present in W. — THOM 807:10
Princess of W. — AUST 43:1
Side and W. Gate — GURN 374:18
still parts of W. — THOM 807:2
whole world . . . But for W. — BOLT 131:21
womanhood of W. — ELLI 314:5

walet His w., biforn him in his lappe — CHAU 218:26
walk after supper w. a mile — PROV 626:9
Can two w. together — BIBL 96:10
closer w. with God — COWP 255:16
machine that would w. — APOL 25:4
make a crab w. straight — ARIS 26:19
men must w. — POPE 617:16
never w. alone — HAMM 379:4
no easy w.-over to freedom — NEHR 569:13
not easy to w. on ways — JAIN 428:12
take up thy bed, and w. — BIBL 107:17
taking a w. that day — BRON 158:5
time to w. round me — BALZ 57:6
upon which the people w. — CRAZ 259:15
W. about Sion — BOOK 142:25
w. abroad o' nights — MARL 522:18
W. across my swimming pool — RICE 660:2
w. a little faster — CARR 202:13
w. before we can run — PROV 646:15
W. cheerfully over the world — FOX 339:16
w. circumspectly — BIBL 114:10
w. humbly with thy God — BIBL 96:14
w. in fear and dread — COLE 241:7
w. in newness of life — BIBL 110:33
w. o'er the western wave — SHEL 746:26
w. on the wild side — ALGR 12:14
w. the night — SHAK 700:16
W. under his huge legs — SHAK 711:19
W. upon England's mountains green — BLAK 126:24
w. within the purlieus — ETHE 320:13
w. ye — BIBL 93:4
Where'er you w. — POPE 618:2
Yea, though I w. — BOOK 140:21
walked He w. by himself — KIPL 468:8
people that w. in darkness — BIBL 92:13
slowly w. away — BURT 180:18
W. day and night — LOGU 498:11
w. they ever so slowly — RUSK 673:11
w. through the wilderness — BUNY 171:4
walkedst w. whither thou wouldest — BIBL 109:8
walkers Six for the six proud w. — SONG 762:13
walketh w. in a vain shadow — BOOK 141:29
w. upon the wings — BOOK 147:4
walking begins with a w. away — DAY- 269:10
craves wary w. — SHAK 712:3
empire w. very slowly — FITZ 332:15
fingers do the w. — ADVE 8:1
Lord God w. in the garden — BIBL 79:6
men as trees, w. — BIBL 103:33
W., and leaping — BIBL 109:16
w. by his wild lone — KIPL 468:9
w. in an air of glory — VAUG 825:10
w. on the sea — BIBL 101:18
w. up and down — BIBL 86:9
wings prevent him from w. — BAUD 61:9
walks Gibbon levelled w. — COLM 244:5
left you all his w. — SHAK 713:14
She w. in beauty — BYRO 190:25
w. always beside you — ELIO 311:17
w. like a duck — CARE 199:3
w. put on their summer liveries — LANI 479:5
wall against a w. of stone — WILB 854:4
as for their city w. — HERA 393:8
close the w. up — SHAK 708:16
doesn't love a w. — FROS 344:17
have I leaped over a w. — BIBL 84:22
leap over the w. — BOOK 140:7
like a stone w. — BEE 65:10
look like a w. — DUNN 300:3
plaister of the w. — BIBL 95:24
tear down this w. — REAG 656:18
w. fell down flat — BIBL 82:27
w. next door catches fire — HORA 410:15
W. Street lays an egg — NEWS 573:21
w. to a layman — COMM 244:17
Watch the w., my darling — KIPL 467:10
weakest go to the w. — PROV 646:11
With our backs to the w. — HAIG 376:6
Without a city w. — ALEX 12:10
wooden w. is your ships — THEM 804:10
Wallace hae wi' W. bled — BURN 179:9

wallet Time hath, my lord, a w. — SHAK 734:17
wallflower yellow w. — THOM 808:11
walling What I was w. in — FROS 344:19
wallow w. In glorious mud — FLAN 332:23
walls angels on the w. — MARL 523:8
not in w. — NICI 574:18
Stone w. do not a prison make — LOVE 502:5
these w. thy sphere — DONN 289:18
Thy w. defaced — BYRO 185:19
W. have ears — PROV 646:5
W. have tongues — SWIF 784:5
w. of Eden — BYRO 185:15
w. of stone or brass — COTT 253:1
within thy w. — BOOK 148:20
wooden w. are the best — COVE 253:8
walnut woman, dog, and w. tree — PROV 647:29
walnuts W. and pears — PROV 646:6
walrus W. and the Carpenter — CARR 203:3
Walsingham holy land Of W. — RALE 654:3
Waltons more like the W. — BUSH 182:7
waltz dance a second w. — SHIE 749:14
zest goes out of a beautiful w. — GREN 372:9
waltzing You'll come a-w., Matilda — PATE 599:9
waly w., waly — BALL 56:5
wan Why so pale and w. — SUCK 779:12
wander love to w. — CASS 206:9
Nor forced him w. — CLEV 235:15
w. in the ways of men — BURN 178:24
w. like a breeze — COLE 239:20
Whither shall I w. — NURS 578:16
will not w. more — TENN 797:13
wandered w. far and wide — HOME 405:2
w. lonely as a cloud — WORD 866:7
wanderer do not we, W., await it too — ARNO 30:11
wandering but a w. voice — WORD 869:19
by long w. — ASCH 33:7
I'm just w. — MURD 565:21
W. between two worlds — ARNO 30:21
w. minstrel I — GILB 357:1
w. outlaw — BYRO 186:1
Werchynge and w. — LANG 478:16
waning onset and w. of love — LA B 474:17
want don't w. him — MILN 537:20
feel the w. of it — COLE 241:17
get what you w. in life — LURI 505:2
in w. of a wife — AUST 42:8
I shall not w. — BOOK 140:20
I w. some more — DICK 280:1
more you w. — PROV 639:13
preservative from w. — AUST 42:14
probably won't w. — HOPE 406:19
Ring out the w. — TENN 795:31
that people know what they w. — MENC 531:20
third is freedom from w. — ROOS 667:12
Though much I w. — DYER 301:5
Toil, envy, w. — JOHN 438:6
w. it the most — CHES 223:5
w. no manner of thing — BOOK 141:20
w. of a nail — PROV 632:34
w. of decency — DILL 283:7
W. one only of five giants — BEVE 77:6
Waste not, w. not — PROV 646:8
weep with w. — TAYL 792:5
we w. it now — MORR 561:4
What can I w. or need — HERB 395:1
What does a woman w. — FREU 343:1
what I really really w. — ROWB 671:3
Wilful waste makes woeful w. — PROV 647:26
You must w. nothing — SENE 692:13
wanted no man is w. much — EMER 315:9
w. everything — HAZL 386:3
w. nothing but death — AUST 43:8
w. simply you — HÉLO 390:9
wanting another is not w. — VIRG 830:6
found w. — BIBL 95:25
wanton W. kittens make sober — PROV 646:7
w. stings — SHAK 723:2
wightly w. — SHAK 717:14
wantonly unadvisedly, lightly, or w. — BOOK 138:21
wantonness in clothes a w. — HERR 396:1
wants Man w. but little — GOLD 364:14

physical w. BAGE 50:7
provide for human *w.* BURK 174:5
scheme of supplying our w. SWIF 783:16
what he thinks the public w. REIT 658:1
who w. poets at all HÖLD 403:2
wanwood worlds of w. leafmeal HOPK 407:20
war able to make w. with him BIBL 118:25
After each w. ATKI 35:4
Alas, it is w. CLAU 234:6
All's fair in love and w. PROV 626:17
Ancestral voices prophesying w. COLE 240:7
another w. in Europe BISM 123:4
at w. with Germany CHAM 214:7
better than to w.-war CHUR 230:11
blast of w. SHAK 708:16
blood-red blossom of w. TENN 798:12
bloody w. and a sickly season TOAS 812:1
bungled, unwise w. PLOM 610:3
business of w. WELL 846:12
but it is not w. BOSQ 151:16
calamities of w. JOHN 436:8
cold w. BARU 60:10
cold w. warrior THAT 803:13
condition which is called w. HOBB 400:22
Councils of w. never fight PROV 629:22
cruellest and most terrible w. LLOY 496:15
cudgel of the people's w. TOLS 813:14
day w. broke out CATC 207:10
delays are dangerous in w. DRYD 297:5
desolation of w. GEOR 352:15
determined without w. HOBB 401:5
devil's madness—w. SERV 692:27
done very well out of the w. BALD 53:2
Don John of Austria is going to the w.
    CHES 224:10
easier to make w. CLEM 235:8
Either w. is obsolete or men are FULL 346:5
enable it to make w. WEIL 845:7
endless w. still breed MILT 540:20
essence of w. is violence MACA 506:16
European w. might do it REDM 657:2
Everything is very simple in w. CLAU 234:8
except the British W. Office SHAW 739:22
first invented w. MARL 523:4
first w. fought without WEST 849:3
fog of w. CLAU 234:9
France has not lost the w. DE G 271:7
furnish the w. HEAR 388:3
garland of the w. SHAK 695:21
gone wrong since the W. AMIS 14:9
Grim-visaged w. SHAK 731:10
guarantee success in w. CHUR 229:18
hand of w. SHAK 730:10
his father's great w. helm HOME 404:15
home policy: I wage w. CLEM 235:7
I am for w. RED 657:1
I am the tongue of w. VOZN 835:11
if someone gave a w. GINS 358:21
I hate w. ROOS 667:7
I have seen w. ROOS 667:7
Image of w. SOME 760:18
I must study politics and w. ADAM 3:6
in every w. they kill you in a new way
    ROGE 666:6
in w. fathers bury their sons HERO 395:8
In w. it is necessary BONA 132:4
In w., no winners CHAM 214:4
in w.; resolution CHUR 230:21
in w. the two cardinal virtues HOBB 401:1
In w., three-quarters turns NAPO 567:18
I renounce it FOSD 338:17
justifiable act of w. BELL 67:13
ladies declare w. on me LOUI 501:7
lead this people into w. WILS 859:20
Let me have w. SHAK 698:11
let slip the dogs of w. SHAK 712:23
Let w. stay abroad AESC 6:18
Let w. yield to peace CICE 231:23
liking for w. BENN 70:7
live under the shadow of a w. SPEN 766:15
looks on w. as all glory SHER 749:11
Lord is a man of w. BIBL 81:13
lose the w. in an afternoon CHUR 231:1

made this great w. LINC 494:10
Make love not w. SLOG 755:10
makes a good w. HERB 395:4
make w. that we may live ARIS 27:14
Mankind must put an end to w. KENN 460:11
McNamara's W. MCNA 513:4
money the sinews of w. BACO 48:7
morning's w. SHAK 710:6
nature of w. HOBB 400:23
neither shall they learn w. BIBL 91:21
never was a good w. FRAN 341:9
no declaration of w. EDEN 303:3
no discharge in that w. BIBL 90:6
Older men declare w. HOOV 406:17
Only in w. MAND 519:5
page 1 of the book of w. MONT 556:9
pattern a w. LOWE 502:14
pestilence and w. MILT 542:16
Power and W. KIPL 465:9
prepare for w. VEGE 826:2
protection against w. BEVI 77:10
provoke a new civil w. JUAN 448:27
quaint and curious w. is HARD 381:21
race inured to w. WILL 857:6
recourse to w. BRIA 156:15
rich wage w. SART 681:7
seek no wider w. JOHN 435:6
seven days w. MUIR 564:10
silent in time of w. CICE 232:8
sinews of w. CICE 232:7
soon as w. is declared GIRA 359:8
state of w. by nature SWIF 784:3
subject is W. OWEN 591:1
Suppose they gave a w. FILM 331:12
talk of a just w. SORL 764:2
tell us all about the w. SOUT 764:7
tempered by w. KENN 460:5
then comes the tug of w. PROV 646:38
they'll give a w. SAND 680:7
third world w. TRUM 817:17
this is w. ADAM 2:4
this w. on terrorism BUSH 182:10
time of w. BIBL 89:23
to the w. is gone MOOR 558:11
To w. and arms LOVE 502:6
two nations have been at w. VOLT 833:12
used to w.'s alarms HOOD 405:15
wage a pitiless w. GREE 371:12
wage w. against a monstrous tyranny
    CHUR 229:13
want peace, prepare for w. PROV 635:35
W. always finds a way BREC 155:21
w. and peace ARIS 26:21
w. and peace in 21st century KOHL 470:13
W. appears to be as old MAIN 516:20
W. being the greatest of evils MELV 531:14
w. between men THUR 810:11
w. creates order BREC 155:18
w., dearth, age, agues DONN 288:9
w. has its laws NEWM 571:15
w. has used up words JAME 430:8
W. hath no fury MONT 554:14
W., he sung, is toil DRYD 295:6
w. in heaven BIBL 118:24
w. in his heart BOOK 143:12
w. is a necessary part MOLT 553:7
W. is capitalism with STOP 778:4
W. is continuation of politics CLAU 234:11
W. is hell, and all that HAY 385:11
W. is just, Samnites LIVY 496:6
w. is over GRAN 368:14
W. is peace ORWE 587:11
w. is politics with bloodshed MAO 521:2
w. is so terrible LEE 487:16
W. is the father of all HERA 392:20
W. is the national industry MIRA 546:14
W. is the remedy SHER 749:10
W. is the trade of kings DRYD 296:6
W. is the universal perversion RAE 653:9
W. is too serious CLEM 235:6
W. its thousands slays PORT 619:23
W. makes good history HARD 380:11
w. minus the shooting ORWE 587:23

w. of nature DARW 266:16
w. poet whose right of honour GURN 374:17
w.'s a game COWP 256:25
W.'s annals will cloud HARD 381:20
W.'s glorious art YOUN 876:14
w. situation HIRO 399:22
w.'s like love HARE 382:7
w. that drags on WAUG 842:20
w. that will end war WELL 846:25
w. that would not boil TAYL 791:12
W. told me truth GURN 374:18
W. to the knife PALA 593:7
w. to waste MILT 544:15
W. which existed in order to HOBS 401:13
w. will cease POLI 613:15
w. without an enemy WALL 837:6
w. without its guilt SURT 781:6
waste of God, W. STUD 779:9
way of ending a w. ORWE 588:7
weapons of w. BIBL 84:13
We hear w. called murder MACD 510:10
we prepare for w. PEAR 601:6
what a lovely w. LITT 495:14
what did you do in the W. SAYI 684:10
When w. enters a country ANON 22:15
When w. is declared SAYI 685:20
win an atomic w. BRAD 154:5
win a w. is as disastrous CHRI 227:1
with himself at w. SHAK 711:15
without having won the w. YOKO 876:6
won the last w. ROOS 666:18
You can only love one w. GELL 352:1
warbler Attic w. pours GRAY 370:18
warder w. silent on the hill SCOT 688:19
wardrobe dalliance in the w. lies SHAK 708:12
open your w. WELD 845:18
wards W. in Jarndyce DICK 276:23
ware Breath's a w. HOUS 415:13
for the bed of W. SHAK 735:30
warfare Armed w. must be preceded
    ZINO 878:3
legitimate w. NEWM 571:15
midst of continual w. MADI 514:10
true method of w. MAZZ 529:11
w. is accomplished BIBL 93:14
Who goeth a w. BIBL 112:6
Waring What's become of W. BROW 168:7
warlord concubine of a w. JUNG 450:1
warm For ever w. KEAT 455:21
lived in a w., sunny climate COWA 253:21
man who's w. to understand SOLZ 760:13
O! she's w. SHAK 737:9
too w. work, Hardy NELS 570:5
W. beds JOYC 448:21
w., but pure BYRO 190:3
w. courage BUSH 182:9
w. courage ROOS 667:6
W., live, improvident BROW 163:23
W. what is cold LANG 479:3
winters and keeps w. CARE 198:14
warmed heart strangely w. WESL 848:1
warming w. the teapot MANS 520:7
warmth awful load of w. KEAT 458:1
more w. SORL 761:24
Spring restores balmy w. CATU 210:11
vigorous w. DRYD 294:8
W. and Light GREN 372:10
yearned for w. and colour TENN 794:8
warn All a poet can do is w. OWEN 591:2
right to w. BAGE 51:6
w., to comfort, and command WORD 869:8
w. you not to be ordinary KINN 465:1
warning carry a Government w. MITC 550:13
ruin in spite of w. JUDA 449:2
w. from another's wound JERO 433:3
w. to the world SHAK 738:3
With horrid w. KEAT 455:10
warp Weave the w. GRAY 369:21
warrant not a sufficient w. MILL 536:2
warring two nations w. DURH 300:14
W. in heaven MILT 542:28
warrior cold war w. THAT 803:13
Here lies a valiant w. EPIT 318:2

warrior (*cont.*):
Home they brought her w.   TENN 799:15
This is the happy w.   READ 656:6
Who is the happy W.   WORD 865:6
wars all their w. are merry   CHES 223:27
at home while they fight w.   EURI 321:11
came to an end all w.   LLOY 496:15
end to the beginnings of all w.   ROOS 667:16
History littered with the w.   POWE 622:1
how do w. start   KRAU 473:11
into any foreign w.   ROOS 667:10
its w. are over   HORA 413:6
maketh w. to cease   BOOK 142:19
nucleus of more w.   EUGÉ 321:1
occasion of all w.   FOX 339:14
serve in the w.   BOOK 150:22
thousand w. of old   TENN 796:1
w. and lechery   SHAK 734:22
w. and rumours of wars   BIBL 102:22
w. brought nothing about   DRYD 296:25
w., horrible wars   VIRG 830:4
w. planned by old men   RICE 659:21
Warsaw Order reigns in W.   ANON 22:7
wartime any w. President   BIDD 121:1
warts w. and all   MISQ 548:22
Warwick impudent and shameless W.   SHAK 710:10
wary craves w. walking   SHAK 712:3
was picked the w. of shall   CUMM 262:11
Thinks what ne'er w.   POPE 616:1
wash Lord, dost thou w. my feet   BIBL 108:10
Moab is my w.-pot   BOOK 143:20
thou shalt w. me   BOOK 143:6
w. literature off   ARTA 32:19
w. me throughly   BOOK 143:4
w. my hands in innocency   BOOK 141:7
w. one's dirty linen   PROV 640:42
w. out a word of it   FITZ 331:23
w. that man right outa   HAMM 378:16
w. the balm   SHAK 730:16
w. their feet in soda water   ELIO 311:11
w. the wind   ELIO 310:18
W. what is dirty   LANG 479:3
washed He w. himself   JOHN 436:28
never w. my own feet   PU Y 648:27
w. his hands   BIBL 103:21
w. in the blood of the Lamb   LIND 495:1
w. their robes   BIBL 118:15
washerman w. removes the grime   TANT 790:4
washes Happiness w. away many things   BÖLL 131:18
One hand w. the other   PROV 641:3
Persil w. whiter   ADVE 8:12
washing came up from the w.   BIBL 91:4
country w.   BRUM 168:18
previously w. the hands   TALM 789:23
taking in one another's w.   ANON 16:25
w. on the Siegfried Line   KENN 460:2
Where w. ain't done   EPIT 318:1
Washington come to W. to be loved   GRAM 368:7
Government at W. lives   GARF 349:6
wasp everything about the w.   THOM 806:6
waspish w. word   TAYL 791:20
wasps w. and hornets break through   SWIF 783:21
wassails Hock-carts, w., wakes   HERR 395:15
waste art of how to w. space   JOHN 435:14
Don't w. time in mourning   HILL 398:15
file your w.-paper basket   BENN 70:4
Haste makes w.   PROV 633:48
now doth time w. me   SHAK 731:7
To what purpose is this w.   BIBL 103:9
war to w.   MILT 544:15
w. howling wilderness   BIBL 82:18
W. not, want not   PROV 646:8
w. of breath   YEAT 873:19
w. of goods   VEBL 825:20
w. of shame   SHAK 738:18
w.-paper basket of the emotions   WEBB 843:11
w. places of Jerusalem   BIBL 94:1
w. remains and kills   EMPS 315:27
we lay w. our powers   WORD 869:24

whole of the city I laid w.   TIGL 811:5
Wilful w. makes woeful want   PROV 647:26
world's perplexing w.   BYRO 189:27
wasted day most surely w.   CHAM 214:12
spend on advertising is w.   LEVE 491:2
w. his substance   BIBL 105:29
wasteful clumsy, w., blundering   DARW 266:19
wastes tossed them to the howling w.   LAWL 483:9
W. without springs   CLAR 232:24
wasting time you enjoy w.   MISQ 548:21
watch before the morning w.   BOOK 149:8
could ye not w. with me   BIBL 103:16
delicious thin w.   BALZ 57:1
done much better by a w.   BELL 68:19
Fourteen angels w.   WETT 849:7
hang on a w.-chain   ANON 21:2
keeping w. above his own   LOWE 502:20
keeping w. over their flock   BIBL 104:12
knew how a w. was made   JOHN 440:15
learning, like your w.   CHES 223:6
like a fat gold w.   PLAT 608:11
like little w. springs   SPEN 766:12
my w. has stopped   FILM 328:4
old w. chain   COLL 243:2
Set a w., O Lord   BOOK 149:21
some must w.   SHAK 702:25
son of a bitch stole my w.   FILM 329:17
W. and pray   BIBL 103:17
W. and pray   ELLI 313:15
w. a sailing cloud   LIN 495:8
w. between me and thee   BIBL 80:13
w. in the night   BOOK 145:20
w. must have had a maker   PALE 593:8
w. not one another   DONN 289:8
W. therefore   BIBL 103:1
W. the wall, my darling   KIPL 467:10
W. ye therefore   BIBL 104:5
why not carry a w.   TREE 815:4
watched more strictly we are w.   BENT 71:5
w. pot never boils   PROV 646:9
watcher posted presence of the w.   JAME 429:22
w. of the skies   KEAT 456:15
watchful occasion's forelock w.   MILT 544:22
watching BIG BROTHER IS W. YOU   ORWE 587:10
My tiny w.   DE L 272:12
w. yourself do it   MATI 528:2
watchmaker blind w.   DAWK 269:1
watchman w. on the lonely tower   SCOT 688:18
w. waketh but in vain   BOOK 149:2
W., what of the night   BIBL 92:21
watchmen w. that went about the city   BIBL 91:9
watchword w. is security   PITT 607:16
water as w. spilt on the ground   BIBL 84:19
back in the w.   TAGL 788:6
blackens all the w.   ADDI 5:20
Blood thicker than w.   PROV 628:14
branches of secret w.   NERU 570:12
bridge over troubled w.   SIMO 752:13
Burned on the w.   SHAK 694:22
By w. and the word   STON 777:10
clear and sunny w.   LONG 499:23
conscious w. saw its God   CRAS 258:23
daughter of Earth and W.   SHEL 743:25
delights in w.   CONF 246:4
desireth the w.-brooks   BOOK 142:4
Dirty w. will quench   PROV 630:4
Don't go near the w.   PROV 630:23
drawers of w.   BIBL 82:28
drinkers of w.   HORA 410:17
feet are always in the w.   AMES 14:8
fountain of the w. of life   BIBL 119:17
glass of pure w.   MACD 510:4
go across salt w.   DICK 281:4
green w. penetrates   RIMB 662:9
hardly w. the ground   BACO 47:16
He asked w.   BIBL 83:2
I baptize with w.   BIBL 107:4
if I were water   KEAT 457:12
in the w. under the earth   BIBL 81:15
King over the W.   TOAS 812:5

Lay a great w.   TENN 794:22
limns the w.   BACO 49:10
Little drops of w.   CARN 201:5
little w. clears us   SHAK 720:10
Meditation and w.   MELV 531:9
Minnehaha, Laughing W.   LONG 499:24
name was writ in w.   EPIT 318:5
never miss the w.   PROV 648:18
noise of the w.-pipes   BOOK 142:6
No more w.   SONG 762:8
poured out like w.   BOOK 140:18
presence of still w.   BERR 74:15
reached the calm of w.   ADAM 2:14
ready by w. as by land   ELST 314:6
ring of bright w.   RAIN 653:12
river of w. of life   BIBL 119:20
spring of ever-flowing w.   HORA 414:20
sweet w. and bitter   BIBL 116:25
take a horse to the w.   PROV 648:3
Tar w.   BERK 72:12
That stretch of w.   PAUL 600:5
to cup w. in our hands   HOLU 404:2
Too much of w. hast thou   SHAK 704:8
travel by land or by w.   BOOK 134:24
Unstable as w.   BIBL 80:29
virtues We write in w.   SHAK 711:5
walking on the w.   THOM 808:3
w. and a crust   KEAT 455:12
w. but the desert   BYRO 186:20
w. hollows out   OVID 590:4
w. in the rough rude sea   SHAK 730:16
W. is best   PIND 606:16
w. is never the same   KAMO 452:16
w. like Pilate   GREE 371:10
'w.' meant the wonderful   KELL 459:6
w. my couch with my tears   BOOK 139:20
w. of affliction   BIBL 85:20
w. that is past   PROV 638:38
W., water, everywhere   COLE 240:21
w. what is dry   LANG 479:3
weaker than w.   LAO 480:13
We'll o'er the w.   HOGG 402:18
where no w. is   BOOK 143:24
where the w. goes   CHES 224:21
wind and swift-flowing w.   CATU 210:16
watercress ask for a w. sandwich   WILD 856:8
watered Apollos w.   BIBL 111:26
w. heaven with their tears   BLAK 128:5
w. our houses in Helicon   CHAP 216:7
waterfall From the w. he named her   LONG 499:24
watering w. mouth   GASK 350:11
Waterloo Austerlitz and W.   SAND 680:5
battle of W.   WELL 846:13
battle of W. won   ORWE 587:8
W.'s ensanguined plain   ANON 19:15
world-earthquake, W.   TENN 798:23
waterman great-grandfather was but a w.   BUNY 171:11
watermelons down by the w.   GINS 359:1
watermen w., that row one way   BURT 181:7
watermill noise like that of a w.   SWIF 782:6
waters all that move in the W.   BOOK 133:18
as the voice of many w.   BIBL 118:28
as the w. cover the sea   BIBL 92:18
beside the still w.   BOOK 140:20
By the w. of Babylon   BOOK 149:13
By the w. of Babylon   WALP 837:20
Cast thy bread upon the w.   BIBL 90:15
cold w. to a thirsty soul   BIBL 88:39
come ye to the w.   BIBL 94:7
face of the w.   BIBL 78:12
in great w.   BOOK 147:17
in perils of w.   BIBL 113:16
in the waste of w.   VIRG 828:13
in the w.   BOOK 147:4
knowledge of man is as the w.   BACO 45:12
lion of the w.   MELV 531:11
luminous home of w.   ARNO 30:19
mighty w. rolling evermore   WORD 867:16
Once more upon the w.   BYRO 185:25
pomp of w.   DANI 264:4
quiet w. by   SCOT 690:9

weary (cont.):
w. be at rest   BIBL 86:17
w. of my groaning   BOOK 139:20
w. warl goes round   BLAM 128:14
w. wi' hunting   BALL 55:1
with w. task fordone   SHAK 727:10
weasel as a w. sucks eggs   SHAK 696:22
Pop goes the w.   MAND 518:15
w. under the cocktail cabinet   PINT 607:3
w. word   ROOS 668:6
weather care what the w. was like   CHEK 252:3
first talk is of the w.   JOHN 436:7
hard grey w.   KING 464:8
Jolly boating w.   CORY 252:11
most extraordinary w.   GOGA 363:7
not in fine w.   CLOU 236:15
sad or singing w.   SWIN 786:2
Some are w.-wise   FRAN 341:4
Stormy w.   KOEH 470:9
w. gynneth clere   CHAU 220:6
w. is always doing something   TWAI 820:24
w. the cuckoo likes   HARD 382:2
w. turned around   THOM 806:3
will be fair w.   BIBL 101:24
winter and rough w.   SHAK 696:21
you won't hold up the w.   MACN 513:9
weave tangled web we w.   SCOT 689:3
W. the warp   GRAY 369:21
weaver swifter than a w.'s shuttle   BIBL 86:22
weaving my own hand's w.   KEAT 454:26
web cool w. of language   GRAV 369:11
She left the w.   TENN 796:19
tangled w. we weave   SCOT 689:3
weaving of the w.   HEIK 389:4
w., then, or the pattern   STEV 775:7
wove a w. in childhood   BRON 158:12
Webb W. from Dawley   BETJ 76:4
webs By the dark w.   YEAT 874:1
like spiders' w.   ANAC 15:2
Webster Like W.'s Dictionary   BURK 176:12
wed Better w. over the mixen   PROV 627:42
December when they w.   SHAK 697:20
for any good yeman to w.   CHAU 219:18
I w. again   CLAR 232:21
Som Cristen man shall w. me   CHAU 220:9
think to w. it   SHAK 694:2
w. the fair Ellen   SCOT 688:23
With this Ring I thee w.   BOOK 139:2
wedded I have w. fyve   CHAU 220:9
No w. man so hardy be   CHAU 218:29
w. wife   BOOK 138:24
were this wild thing w.   MERE 532:19
wedding as she did her w. gown   GOLD 365:1
earliest w.-day   KEBL 459:3
face looks like a w.-cake   AUDE 38:22
O God, and the w.   CORS 252:10
One w. brings another   PROV 641:17
small circle of a w.-ring   CIBB 231:10
to a w.   BIBL 105:18
w. clothes   ADDI 5:19
w. dresses ready   BYRO 189:15
W.-Guest here beat   COLE 240:15
wedlock in holy w.   BOOK 139:4
W., indeed, hath oft   DAVI 267:16
W. is a padlock   PROV 646:12
w.'s the devil   BYRO 191:9
Wednesday W.'s child   NURS 580:6
weds Egghead w. hourglass   NEWS 573:7
wee cried, W.-wee-wee   NURS 581:18
expectant w.-things   BURN 177:22
w. pretendy government   CONN 248:6
W., sleekit, cow'rin'   BURN 179:24
w. wifie waitin'   MORR 561:9
W. Willie Winkie   NURS 582:9
weed Ignorance is an evil w.   BEVE 77:5
law to w. it out   BACO 47:25
Pernicious w.   COWP 254:29
salt w. sways in the stream   ARNO 29:13
w. that grows   BURK 173:21
What is a w.? A plant   EMER 315:11
Wood, the W., the Wag   RALE 654:12
weeded W. and worn   TENN 797:17
weeding seven years w.   PROV 641:19

weeds all the idle w.   SHAK 716:14
bred among the w.   BROW 163:5
come up like w.   WALK 836:2
coronet w.   SHAK 704:7
grubbing w. from gravel paths   KIPL 466:1
Ill w. grow apace   PROV 635:41
Long live the w.   HOPK 407:12
smell far worse than w.   SHAK 738:9
w. spontaneous rise   IRWI 425:24
week accomplished in a w.   STEV 775:24
die in my w.   JOPL 447:7
Sunday In every w.   CLAR 233:18
w. after next   CARR 203:23
w. a long time in politics   WILS 859:6
w. of death   DONN 289:27
weekend long w.   FORS 337:20
w. starts here   CATC 208:31
weep Doth w. full sore   SPEN 767:8
Fair daffodils, we w.   HERR 396:14
fear of having to w.   BEAU 63:2
If you want me to w.   HORA 409:4
I may not w.   BYRO 189:1
I w. for Adonais   SHEL 743:8
make the angels w.   SHAK 723:8
milk my ewes and w.   SHAK 737:6
pale, and wan, and w.   CLAU 234:7
saw my lady w.   ANON 18:6
scarcely cry ''w.! 'weep!'   BLAK 127:7
She wolde w.   CHAU 218:10
sit down and w.   WALP 837:20
That he should w. for her   SHAK 701:20
time to w.   BIBL 89:23
w. and know why   HOPK 407:20
w., and wrynge   CHAU 219:2
w. and you weep alone   PROV 637:12
W., and you weep alone   WILC 854:9
w. as a woman   AYES 44:3
W., children   NERV 570:17
W. me not dead   DONN 289:22
W. not for little Léonie   GRAH 367:12
w. or she will die   TENN 799:15
w. over Saul   BIBL 84:12
weep with them that w.   BIBL 111:10
W. you no more   ANON 21:5
women must w.   KING 464:13
weepers losers w.   PROV 632:12
weepest Woman, why w. thou   BIBL 108:37
weeping full cause of w.   SHAK 715:14
goeth on his way w.   BOOK 149:1
hear the children w.   BROW 164:6
two w. motions   CRAS 259:9
w. and gnashing   BIBL 100:9
w. and the laughter   DOWS 292:4
W. and watching   GOET 362:17
w. and with laughter   MACA 508:20
w. for her children   BIBL 98:13
w. queen   SHAK 730:26
weeps w. with loathing   LITT 495:13
Weib W. und Gesang   LUTH 505:12
weigh more people see than w.   CHES 223:16
w. and consider   BACO 47:34
w. it down on one side   HALI 377:7
w. thy words   BIBL 97:26
weighed w. in the balances   BIBL 95:25
weighing not w. our merits   BOOK 137:17
weight bear the w. of Antony   SHAK 694:18
heavy and the weary w.   WORD 866:10
w. of rages   SPOO 768:15
w. of the whole world   SART 681:11
weights system of w. and measures   NAPO 568:5
weilest wo w. du   WAGN 835:13
Wein W., Weib und Gesang   LUTH 505:12
weird w. sisters   SHAK 718:8
w. women promised   SHAK 722:22
welcome Advice is seldom w.   CHES 223:5
be w. back again   BURN 179:21
good evening, and w.   CATC 207:27
Love bade me w.   HERB 394:14
warmest w., at an inn   SHEN 747:19
W., all wonders   CRAS 259:5
w. day   BUNY 171:26
W. the coming   POPE 617:27

W. the sixte   CHAU 220:9
W. to your gory bed   BURN 179:9
welcomes w. at once all the world   ANST 24:15
welcomest w. when they are gone   SHAK 709:15
welfare anxious for its w.   BURK 173:5
concerned with the w.   MAHĀ 515:7
corporate w. bums   LEWI 492:4
w. of this realm   CHAR 217:8
welkin all the w. rings   WESL 847:8
well alive and w.   ANON 18:9
all shall be w.   ELIO 309:22
all shall be w.   JULI 449:6
All's w. that ends well   PROV 626:19
at the bottom of a w.   PROV 645:37
being w.   MART 524:9
deep as a w.   SHAK 732:22
Didn't she do w.   CATC 207:11
does himself extremely w.   ANON 19:5
Do sleep w.   CATC 207:14
drink from every w.   CALL 193:16
foolish thing w. done   JOHN 441:6
handsome, w.-shaped. man   AUBR 36:7
have the morning w.-aired   BRUM 168:17
Is it w. with the child   BIBL 85:25
It is not done w.   JOHN 440:7
Let w. alone   PROV 637:25
Like a w.-conducted person   THAC 803:9
looking w. can't move her   SUCK 779:12
men shall speak w. of you   BIBL 104:24
never speaks w. of me   CONG 247:10
not feeling very w.   PUNC 650:9
not wisely but too w.   SHAK 729:23
one who meant w.   STEV 775:6
pitcher will go to the w.   PROV 641:36
Pussy's in the w.   NURS 578:12
rare as a w.-spent one   CARL 199:14
sense of being w.-dressed   FORB 336:14
shall be w. again   ARNO 29:10
spent one whole day w.   THOM 804:21
that's as w. said   SWIF 783:6
till the w. runs dry   PROV 648:18
use it for a w.   BOOK 145:14
want a thing done w.   PROV 635:34
want to do something w.   BISH 122:12
W. begun is half done   PROV 646:13
w.-beloved hath a vineyard   BIBL 91:23
w.-bred as if we were not married   CONG 247:26
w.-bred resignation   TURG 818:17
W. done   BIBL 103:2
w.-informed mind   AUST 41:21
w. of English undefiled   SPEN 767:20
w. of loneliness   HALL 378:4
w. of love   COLE 239:3
w. of poisons   GIRA 359:6
w.-tuned cymbals   BOOK 150:12
w.-written Life   CARL 199:14
when ye do w.   BIBL 117:6
would do very w.   WALP 837:16
wellbeloved my w. unto me   BIBL 90:25
Wellesley fat with W.'s glory   BYRO 189:11
wells poison the w.   NEWM 571:15
poison w.   MARL 522:18
Welsh conquered the W.   BORR 151:15
devil understands W.   SHAK 706:11
Welshman Taffy was a W.   NURS 581:10
valour in this W.   SHAK 708:23
Weltgeschichte W. ist das Weltgericht   SCHI 683:20
wen great w. of all   COBB 237:14
Wenceslas Good King W.   NEAL 569:7
wench O ill-starred w.   SHAK 729:20
w. is dead   MARL 522:19
wenches many young w.   OSBO 588:9
Wenlock On W. Edge   HOUS 416:1
went He w. forth conquering   BIBL 118:9
wept He w. beneath a crag   VIRG 833:7
I sat down and w.   SMAR 755:16
Jesus w.   BIBL 108:7
No one w. for the dead   AGNO 9:15
sometimes w.   MUSS 566:11
w. for want of more Worlds   WATT 842:8

who (*cont.*):
tell me w. I am — SHAK 715:4
W. am I going to be today — WELD 845:18
W. dares wins — MOTT 563:23
W. is in charge — ANON 21:12
W. is on my side — BIBL 85:36
W., or why, or which — LEAR 485:13
w. the hell are you — CATC 208:5
W.? Whom — LENI 488:19
whole better than the w. — PROV 633:36
faith hath made thee w. — BIBL 100:18
greater than the w. — HESI 397:3
had I stol'n the w. — STEV 777:3
nothing can be sole or w. — YEAT 873:1
seeing the w. — RUSK 674:3
They that be w. — BIBL 100:15
to make you w. — ACHE 1:9
we shall be w. — BOOK 145:10
w. is more than — ANON 21:13
w. is something over — ARIS 27:4
w. man in himself — HORA 415:2
wholesome out of his w. bed — SHAK 712:9
whom W. are you — ADE 6:5
Who? W. — LENI 488:19
whooping out of all w. — SHAK 697:9
whopping Latin for a w. — ANST 24:16
whore Fortune's a right w. — WEBS 844:17
I am the Protestant w. — GWYN 375:3
I' the posture of a w. — SHAK 695:25
judgement of the great w. — BIBL 119:7
lash that w. — SHAK 716:20
like a chaste w. — MUGG 564:7
morals of a w. — JOHN 439:4
Once a w. — PROV 640:39
prisons, w.-shops — CLAR 232:20
w. and the gambler — BLAK 124:18
young man's w. — JOHN 440:13
whoremongers sorcerers, and w. — BIBL 119:23
whores second-rate w. — PLOM 610:4
to work, ye w. — PEMB 602:9
truth in w. — WRIG 870:21
whoring went a w. — BOOK 147:14
whose W. finger — NEWS 573:24
whoso W. doeth these things — BOOK 140:2
whosoever W. will be saved — BOOK 134:11
why about the wasp, except w. — THOM 806:6
but also w., to whom — HAVE 384:7
can't tell you w. — MART 524:4
finding only w. — CUMM 262:11
For every w. he had a wherefore — BUTL 183:10
I say 'W. not' — SHAW 739:11
W., Edward, tell me why — WORD 865:5
W. not? Why not? Yeah — LEAR 486:14
Would this man ask w. — AUDE 37:2
wibrated better not be w. — DICK 276:9
wicked all the world w. — BURK 175:2
All things truly w. — HEMI 394:6
August is a w. month — O'BR 583:4
deceitful and w. man — BOOK 142:8
desperately w. — BIBL 95:5
fiery darts of the w. — BIBL 114:15
no peace unto the w. — BIBL 93:25
not that men are w. — DU B 298:7
pretending to be w. — WILD 854:23
sick and w. — AUST 43:6
Something w. this way comes — SHAK 721:18
tender mercies of the w. — BIBL 88:4
Tories born w. — ANON 18:20
what is more w. — BALL 55:10
w. and moral — CHUR 229:4
w. cease from troubling — BIBL 86:17
w. flee — BIBL 89:7
w. pack of cards — ELIO 311:4
worse than w. — PUNC 650:3
wickedness abhorrence for w. — THAC 803:6
bands of w. — BIBL 94:15
capable of every w. — CONR 249:11
Hated w. — BROW 166:23
malice and w. — BOOK 135:18
manifold sins and w. — BOOK 133:2
Path of W. — BALL 55:21
shapen in w. — BOOK 143:5
than human w. — TAYL 791:11

turneth away from his w. — BIBL 95:16
w. in high places — BIBL 114:15
[w.] is not punished — COMP 245:7
W. is the root — ROBE 663:12
wicket flannelled fools at the w. — KIPL 466:9
Widdicombe Fair want for to go to W.
— BALL 56:8
wide how w. also the east is — BOOK 147:2
I am very w. — BALZ 57:6
Poet sees, but w. — ARNO 30:2
w. as a church door — SHAK 732:22
W. is the gate — BIBL 99:28
wideness w. in God's mercy — FABE 322:7
wider seek no w. war — JOHN 435:6
w. prison unto me — BYRO 190:23
w. still and wider — BENS 70:22
widow certain poor w. — BIBL 104:4
fatherless and w. — BOOK 150:5
French w. in every bedroom — HOFF 402:13
Molly Stark's a w. — STAR 770:8
old grey W.-maker — KIPL 466:4
retired w. — BAGE 50:22
w. bird sat mourning — SHEL 743:22
w. of fifty — SHER 748:27
W. The word consumes itself — PLAT 608:12
widowhood comfortable estate of w.
— GAY 351:3
widows cause of the w. — BOOK 144:7
devour w.' houses — BIBL 104:3
fatherless children, and w. — BOOK 135:1
These w., Sir — ADDI 5:11
visit the fatherless and w. — BIBL 116:21
w. whose husbands are alive — BERN 74:1
wife as a w. is — MILL 536:13
as his w. — BRON 158:7
blind man's w. needs — PROV 628:13
blind w. — PROV 629:36
Brutus took to w. — SHAK 712:11
Caesar's w. — CAES 192:18
Caesar's w. — PROV 628:30
cleave unto his w. — BIBL 79:3
come in to win his w.'s side — LAMB 476:11
covet thy neighbour's w. — BIBL 81:20
decided to murder his w. — ILES 424:17
Despair had a w. — BUNY 171:14
divorces his first w. — TALM 789:27
dwindle into a w. — CONG 247:27
happy for a week take a w. — PROV 635:37
his [Lot's] w. looked back — BIBL 79:36
honour unto the w. — BIBL 117:9
husband and w. — FIEL 326:23
I'd have no w. — CRAS 259:8
If I were your w. — CHUR 231:4
I have a w. — LUCA 503:19
I have married a w. — BIBL 105:22
in want of a w. — AUST 42:8
keeps up a w.'s spirits — GAY 351:3
kick his w. out of bed — SURT 781:7
kill a w. with kindness — SHAK 733:8
lay down his w. for his friend — JOYC 448:22
Like Caesar's w. — ANON 18:13
look out for a w. — SURT 781:16
love his w. as himself — TALM 789:20
Man and W. — BOOK 139:4
man who's untrue to his w. — AUDE 37:18
Medicine is my lawful w. — CHEK 222:8
moral centaur, man and w. — BYRO 189:7
my sonne's w., Elizabeth — INGE 425:8
my w., and my name — SURT 781:12
My w., who, poor wretch — PEPY 603:7
My w. won't let me — LEIG 488:10
Petrarch's w. — BYRO 188:16
quarrelled with my w. — PEAC 600:19
Remember Lot's w. — BIBL 106:10
riding to and from his w. — WHIT 850:13
she is your w. — OGIL 583:13
some friend, not w. — POPE 614:18
sympathetic w. — EURI 321:17
Thane of Fife had a w. — SHAK 722:9
There's my w. — SPRI 769:2
thrive must first ask his w. — PROV 634:13
took from me my w. — CLAR 232:21
true and honourable w. — SHAK 712:10

wedded w. — BOOK 138:24
w. and children — BACO 47:15
W. and Servant — CHUD 227:18
w. for breed — GAY 351:27
w. has ever taken — SHAF 693:15
w. in bondage — LEAP 485:12
w. is May — WATK 841:5
w. or your servants to read — GRIF 373:5
w. shall be as the fruitful vine — BOOK 149:4
w. talks Greek — JOHN 444:22
w. who looks out of door — WELD 845:15
wind is my w. — KEAT 458:4
with a w. — SHAK 707:19
world and his w. — ANST 24:15
wifehood Meek w. is no part — BRIT 157:12
wig w. with the scorched foretop — MACA 506:17
Wigan mothers-in-law and W. Pier — BRID 156:17
wights descriptions of the fairest w.
— SHAK 738:10
wigwam w. of Nokomis — LONG 499:22
wild brought forth w. grapes — BIBL 92:1
call of the w. — LOND 498:12
gone w. into his grave — SHAK 708:2
grew more fierce and w. — HERB 394:2
madly w. — PARN 597:10
never saw a w. thing — LAWR 483:20
nobly w., not mad — HERR 396:5
not a more fearful w.-fowl — SHAK 726:12
O Caledonia! stern and w. — SCOT 688:16
peace of w. things — BERR 74:15
tendency to run w. — WHIT 851:14
three w. lads were we — SCOT 689:14
walk on the w. side — ALGR 12:14
waving his w. tail — KIPL 468:9
were this w. thing wedded — MERE 532:19
w. for to hold — WYAT 871:8
w. geese are flighting — KIPL 466:8
w. with all regret — TENN 799:12
wilder w. shores of love — BLAN 128:17
wilderness crieth in the w. — BIBL 93:15
crying in the w. — BIBL 98:15
day's journey into the w. — BIBL 85:13
dwellings of the w. — BOOK 144:3
grain into the w. — STOU 778:5
in perils in the w. — BIBL 113:16
in the w. — BIBL 105:26
into the w. — BIBL 81:27
into the w. to see — BIBL 100:33
savage w. — BURK 173:25
singing in the w. — FITZ 331:15
temptation in the w. — BOOK 146:8
They make a w. — TACI 786:21
To the w. I wander — ANON 21:14
walked through the w. — BUNY 171:4
weeds and the w. — HOPK 407:12
w. of idea — BUTL 184:11
Women have no w. — BOGA 130:12
world's wide w. — WATT 842:1
wildness In w. is the preservation — THOR 810:1
wet and w. — HOPK 407:12
wilful w. man must have his way — PROV 647:25
Wilhelmine little grandchild W. — SOUT 764:6
will according to the common w. — JAME 429:2
against the w. of God — BUTT 184:21
complies against his w. — BUTL 183:26
complies against his w. — PROV 634:5
death with one's w. — JAIN 428:4
except a *good* w. — KANT 452:18
general w. rules — ROBE 663:9
Immanent W. — HARD 381:13
In His w. is our peace — DANT 265:15
knowing that we do Thy w. — IGNA 424:14
know our w. is free — JOHN 440:17
let my w. replace — JUVE 451:3
not because we w. — ARNO 29:2
not my w., but thine, be done — BIBL 106:20
Not of my own free w. — VIRG 829:23
One single w. — ROBE 663:13
political w. — LYNN 506:2
resigning up one's w. — OSBO 588:13
settled w. — SMIT 757:5
settled w. — STEE 770:12
Thy w. be done — BIBL 99:12

years (*cont.*):
For him in after y. — PUDN 648:35
Forty y. on — BOWE 153:6
gave up the y. to be — BROO 159:4
go softly all my y. — BIBL 93:13
Jacob served seven y. — BIBL 80:12
love of finished y. — ROSS 668:19
more than a hundred y. — FROS 344:14
next thirty y. — FITZ 332:11
nor the y. condemn — BINY 121:15
of the y. and the sun — VIRG 830:13
thousand y. as a sheep — PROV 627:39
thousand y. in thy sight — BOOK 145:20
threescore y. and ten — BOOK 145:21
touch of earthly y. — WORD 869:9
two hundred y. like a sheep — TIPU 811:9
two thousand y. of hope — WEIZ 845:11
y. are slipping by — HORA 412:10
y. like great black oxen — YEAT 872:17
y. of desolation — JEFF 432:12
Y. steal Fire from the mind — BYRO 186:2
y. that the locust hath eaten — BIBL 96:7
y. to come — YEAT 873:19
yeas russet y. — SHAK 717:22
yell angry spirit's y. — BEAT 62:13
yellow by the y. Tiber — MACA 508:12
Come unto these y. sands — SHAK 733:20
expend her yellow y. — MIDD 534:11
falls into the y. Leaf — BYRO 188:9
Follow the y. brick road — HARB 380:1
Goodbye y. brick road — JOHN 434:9
one long y. string — BROW 167:6
paved with y. brick — BAUM 62:7
sparkled on the y. field — TENN 796:17
thy y. stockings — SHAK 735:25
With a y. petticoat — NURS 578:10
Y., and black, and pale — SHEL 745:6
Y. God forever gazes — HAYE 385:16
y. leaf — SHAK 722:16
y. like ripe corn — ROSS 669:13
yelps loudest y. for liberty — JOHN 437:23
yeoman did me y.'s service — SHAK 704:22
yes getting the answer y. — CAMU 196:5
I did say y. O at lightning — HOPK 408:6
never hear the word 'y.' — WEST 848:18
Y., but not in the South — POTT 620:11
'Y.,' I answered you — BROW 164:10
Y. it hurt — POLI 613:19
Y., Minister! No, Minister — CROS 261:11
Y., Virginia — NEWS 573:26
Y., we can — POLI 613:21
y. you don't mean — RUME 672:5
yesterday authority of the eternal y. — WEBE 843:16
but as y. — BOOK 145:20
but y. a King — BYRO 190:17
dead y. — FITZ 331:20
give me y. — JONE 445:7
keeping up with y. — MARQ 523:11
O! call back y. — SHAK 730:17
perhaps it was y. — CAMU 196:17
rose of y. — FITZ 331:14
same y., and to day — BIBL 116:12
thoughts of y. — PALI 594:15
were saying y. — LUIS 505:1
Y. I loved — LESS 490:19
Y.'s men — POLI 613:20
yesterdays all our y. — SHAK 722:22
yesteryear snows of y. — VILL 828:7
yet as y. there were none — BOOK 149:19
but not y. — AUGU 39:6
young man not y. — BACO 47:18
yew Of true wood, of y. wood — DOYL 293:3
slips of y. — SHAK 721:17
YHVH image of Y. — ZOHA 878:10
yid PUT THE ID BACK IN Y. — ROTH 670:10
yield and not to y. — TENN 801:1
just to y. to it — GRAH 367:10
yin carry the y. — LAO 480:5
yo Y., Blair — BUSH 182:13
Y.-ho-ho, and a bottle of rum — STEV 775:20
yoga Y. is evenness of mind — BHAG 78:1
yogi y. has gone to the root — TANT 790:7

yoke bear the y. in his youth — BIBL 95:11
break every y. — BIBL 94:15
hath received our y. — WALL 837:5
my y. is easy — BIBL 101:2
y. of prelaty — MILT 546:10
yoked y. with a lamb — SHAK 713:26
yolk y. runs down the waistcoat — DICK 279:15
Yonghy-Bonghy-Bó Lived the Y. — LEAR 485:15
Yorick Alas, poor Y. — SHAK 704:15
Yorkshire Y. born — PROV 647:37
you cannot live with y. — MART 524:11
For y. but not for me — MILI 535:15
It could be y. — ADVE 7:37
matter because y. are you — SAUN 682:15
wanted simply y. — HÉLO 390:9
Y.'ll never walk — HAMM 379:4
Your country needs y. — MILI 535:19
Y. too, Brutus — CAES 193:3
Y.'ve got to be carefully taught — HAMM 379:5
'Y.' your joys and sorrows — CRIC 260:1
young artist as a y. man — JOYC 448:5
censor of the y. — HORA 409:10
country of y. men — EMER 315:15
crime of being a y. man — PITT 607:8
defrauded y. — KIPL 465:16
dies y. — MENA 531:16
evil in y. minds — ARNO 32:16
for ever y. — KEAT 455:21
get out while we're y. — SPRI 769:5
Gods love die y. — PROV 647:17
good die y. — PROV 633:18
Hang a thief when he's y. — PROV 633:40
Hip y. gunslinger — ANON 17:17
If I were y. — MARL 522:3
I have been y. — BLUN 129:12
I have been y. — BOOK 141:25
I'll die y. — BRUC 168:14
in the will of a y. gentleman — ASCH 33:9
I was a poet, I was y. — FLEC 334:14
knew the worst too y. — KIPL 465:21
lead those that are with y. — BIBL 93:17
look y. till forty — DRYD 296:12
love's y. dream — MOOR 558:10
make an old man y. — TENN 793:16
Old and y. — STEV 775:26
on your y. shoulders — SPAR 765:9
O y., fresshe folkes — CHAU 221:13
proper y. men — BURN 178:19
resolute, the y. — KIPL 466:17
seventy years y. — HOLM 403:17
So wise so y. — SHAK 731:20
so y. a body — SHAK 724:28
So y., and so untender — SHAK 714:17
They're y. — TAGL 788:12
too y. to fall asleep for ever — SASS 682:8
too y. to take up golf — ADAM 2:8
What can a y. lassie do — BURN 180:9
what the world would call y. men — PEEL 601:11
When thou wast y. — BIBL 109:8
While we are y. — ANON 23:7
Whom the gods love die y. — BYRO 189:2
Women never have y. minds — DELA 272:13
y. and foolish — YEAT 873:4
y. are quick of speech — WINT 860:16
Y. blood must have its course — KING 464:14
y. can do for the old — SHAW 739:26
Y. folks think old folks — PROV 648:19
y., gifted and black — HANS 379:12
Y., gifted and black — IRVI 425:20
y. man married — PROV 648:20
y. man married — SHAK 694:5
y. man not yet — BACO 47:18
y. man's slave — PROV 627:30
Y. men and maidens — BOOK 150:10
Y. men are fitter — BACO 48:20
y. men glittering — TRAH 814:13
Y. men have more virtue — JOHN 440:3
Y. men may die — PROV 648:21
y. men shall see visions — BIBL 96:8
y. men's vision — DRYD 294:16
Y. men think it is — HOUS 415:10
Y. saint, old devil — PROV 648:22

y. was very heaven — WORD 865:19
y. whom I hope to bother — AUDE 38:9
younger y. race succeeds — DILL 283:4
y. son gathered all together — BIBL 105:29
Y. than she — SHAK 732:4
y. than that now — DYLA 302:1
youngster You're going out a y. — FILM 330:4
yours never y., Augustus — DICK 279:4
no hands but y. — SAYI 684:6
y. and yours — MARK 522:1
Y. till Hell freezes — FISH 330:10
yourself DO IT Y. — BARH 58:15
do it y. — PROV 635:34
know y. — SUN 780:12
see to everything y. — MELB 530:9
yourselves make honey not for y. — VIRG 833:8
youth April of your y. — HERB 393:9
bear the yoke in his y. — BIBL 95:11
Crabbed age and y. — SHAK 737:10
days of our y. — BYRO 191:6
days of thy y. — BIBL 90:20
evil from his y. — BIBL 79:24
first impressions of his y. — GOET 362:16
flattering y. defy — ROCH 664:20
flower of their y. — VIRG 832:5
from my y. up — BOOK 149:5
How beautiful is y. — MEDI 530:5
If y. knew — ESTI 320:12
I have y. — WEBS 844:7
In lusty y. — SURR 780:15
in the days of thy y. — BIBL 90:19
it is y. who must fight — HOOV 406:17
miracle of a y. — EVEL 321:20
My prime of y. — TICH 811:2
offences of my y. — BOOK 141:4
promises of y. — JOHN 437:13
red sweet wine of y. — BROO 159:4
remember my y. — CONR 249:12
remembreth me Upon my y. — CHAU 220:11
rose Of y. — SHAK 695:9
seized my y. — ARNO 30:20
shake their wicked sides at y. — YEAT 874:9
sign of an ill-spent y. — ROUP 670:12
spice-islands of Y. — COLE 242:11
subtle thief of y. — MILT 545:12
sweet period of my y. — ROUS 671:1
tender years of y. — GOGO 363:10
thoughts of y. are long — LONG 499:11
To y. and age in common — ARNO 31:7
unemployed y. — BAGE 50:22
Where y. grows pale — KEAT 456:6
wishes for in y. — GOET 361:11
world has lost his y. — BIBL 96:23
Y. and Pleasure meet — BYRO 186:6
y., I do adore thee — SHAK 737:11
Y. is a blunder — DISR 285:18
Y. is not an absolution — ASHC 33:11
Y. is something very new — CHAN 215:16
Y. is vivid — LOVE 502:8
Y. must be served — PROV 648:25
Y. of a Nation — DISR 286:9
y. of a state — BACO 48:16
y. of England — SHAK 708:12
y. of frolics — POPE 614:29
y. of his generation — FITZ 332:17
y. of labour — GOLD 364:3
y. of the realm — SHAK 710:3
y. of the world — BACO 45:22
Y. on the prow — GRAY 369:22
Y. pined away — BLAK 127:16
y. replies, *I can* — EMER 314:17
Y.'s a stuff — SHAK 735:9
y.'s sweet-scented manuscript — FITZ 331:28
Y.'s the season — GAY 351:7
y. to fortune — GRAY 370:9
y. to the gallows — PAIN 593:3
y. unkind — BAST 61:5
Y., what man's age is like — DENH 273:6
Y., which is forgiven — SHAW 741:25
Y. would be an ideal state — ASQU 34:5
Yule green Y. makes — PROV 633:32
Yvetot king of Y. — BÉRA 72:6